44

55

66

76

45

56

77

46

57

68

78

47

58

69

79

48

59

70

80

49

60

71

81

50

61

72

82

51

62

73

83

52

63

74

84

53

64

75

85

54

65

**Illustrations by Alain Baudouin show every
winning Grand Prix car since 1950
www.abmotoringart.com**

See page 4 for key to illustrations

GRAND PRIX
PRIX
DATA BOOK

'What the reviewers said:

The two authors have produced a stunning plethora of minutiae covering all the races, cars, drivers, and much more besides, in an easy to follow and ordered volume, which is an invaluable reference work for all F1 enthusiasts.
Ferrari World

Complete and comprehensive. Everything you wanted to know, and more. It's all here. Never again will you have to wonder why a particular driver retired from a specific race.
F1 News

It includes the sort of minutiae that has never, to our knowledge, been put together anywhere else. The ultimate F1 guide.
Performance Ford

All the things you wanted to know about Formula 1. Split into easy to use sections. A fascinating reference for every Grand Prix fan.
Auto Express

If you like starting sentences 'did you know?', then this is the book for you.
The Express

Superb stuff.
Ben Edwards, Eurosport

A great present for someone who just loves F1; or perhaps just buy it for yourself.
Retro Classics

The most staggering detail. It represents tremendous value.
Doug Nye, Superclassics

If you can manage to digest even a small bit of this, you'll be able to impress friends and amaze your family at the depth of your knowledge of F1.
Performance Car

A must for Formula 1 fanatics.
Manchester Evening News

An impressive feat of research and a useful reference work.
Race Car Engineering

Diligently compiled.
Rallye Racing, Germany

It is a lovely book for the fanatic.
Auto Visie, Netherlands

The heart of the real F1 enthusiast will beat undoubtedly faster.
GP Speciale, Belgium

The most complete data book on Formula 1.
Teknikens Värld, Sweden

If Grand Prix makes the earth move for you, then you must own a copy.
All Sport + Leisure Monthly

Should not be missing from any serious motorsport collector's library.
Motorsport Aktuell, Switzerland

This is the world's best F1 statistical book.
Autopluss, Estonia

Its soul will remain intact for anyone who cares to take a simple statistic and turn it into a fondly recalled moment of yesteryear.
Evening News, Worcester

The ultimate reference book on F1, the ultimate argument settler.
Pitstop bookshop, Australia

An invaluable book.
Total Sport

It is incredible.
Autosprint, Italy

The book is an essential reference manual for anyone with an interest in Formula 1.
Lynn News

A man could lose a lot of money betting on F1 statistics using any other book, but he could make a packet using yours.
Ayrton Senna Remembrance Society

Here's a good book in which to invest. Chock full of stats, facts and info. Hours of good reading.
The F/1 Newsletter, California, USA

GRAND PRIX
DATA BOOK

A complete statistical record of the Formula 1 World Championship since 1950

David Hayhoe & David Holland

FOREWORD BY STEVE RIDER

First edition published in 1989 by Haynes Publishing
Second edition published in 1995 by David Hayhoe
Third edition published in 1996 by Duke Marketing
This fourth edition published in 2006 by Haynes Publishing

ISBN 1 84425 223 X

Library of Congress catalogue card no. 2005935250

A catalogue record for this book is available from the British Library

Published by Haynes Publishing, Sparkford, Yeovil, Somerset BA22 7JJ, UK
Tel: 01963 442030 Fax: 01963 440001
Int.tel: +44 1963 442030 Int. fax: +44 1963 440001
E-mail: sales@haynes.co.uk
Website: www.haynes.co.uk

Haynes North America Inc., 861 Lawrence Drive, Newbury Park, California 91320, USA

Originally designed by David Hayhoe and David Holland
Fourth edition designed and page built by James Robertson
Printed and bound in Britain by J. H. Haynes & Co. Ltd, Sparkford

Key to endpaper illustrations

1 Alfa Romeo 158/159 1950-51 **2** Ferrari 375 1951 **3** Ferrari 500 1952-53 **4** Maserati A6GCM 1953 **5** Ferrari 553 Squalo 1954 **6** Mercedes-Benz W196 1954-55 **7** Mercedes-Benz W196 Streamliner 1954-55 **8** Ferrari 625 1954-55 **9** Maserati 250F 1954 & 1956-57 **10** Lancia-Ferrari D50 555 1956 **11** Vanwall 1957-58 **12** Cooper-Climax T43/T45 1958 **13** Ferrari Dino 246 1958-60 **14** BRM P25 1959 **15** Cooper-Climax T51 1959-60 **16** Cooper-Climax T53 1960 **17** Lotus-Climax 18/18-21 1960-61 **18** Ferrari 156 1961 **19** Lotus-Climax 21 1961 **20** Cooper-Climax T60 1962 **21** Porsche 804 1962 **22** BRM P57 1962-63 **23** Lotus-Climax 25 1962 & 1963-64 **24** Ferrari 156 1963-64 **25** Brabham-Climax BT7 1964 **26** Ferrari 158 1964 **27** Lotus-Climax 25/33 1964-65 **28** BRM P261 1964-66 **29** Honda RA272 1965 **30** Ferrari 312 1966 **31** Lotus-BRM 43 1966 **32** Brabham-Repco BT19/20 1966-67 **33** Cooper-Maserati T81 1966-67 **34** Honda RA300 1967 **35** Brabham-Repco BT24 1967 **36** Eagle-Weslake T1G 1967 **37** Lotus-Ford 49 1967-68 **38** Ferrari 312 1968 **39** Lotus-Ford 49B 1968-69 **40** Matra-Ford MS10 1968-69 **41** McLaren-Ford M7A 1968-69 **42** Lotus-Ford 49C 1970 **43** Matra-Ford MS80 1969 **44** Brabham-Ford BT26A/BT33 1969-70 **45** March-Ford 701 1970 **46** BRM P153 1970 **47** Lotus-Ford 72C 1970 **48** Ferrari 312B/312B2 1970-72 **49** BRM P160 1971 **50** Tyrrell-Ford 002/003 1971 **51** BRM P160B 1972 **52** McLaren-Ford M19A 1972 **53** Tyrrell-Ford 003/005/006 1972-73 **54** Lotus-Ford 72D/E 1972-74 **55** McLaren-Ford M23 1973 **56** Ferrari 312B3 1974 **57** Tyrrell-Ford 007 1974-75 **58** McLaren-Ford M23 1974-75 **59** Brabham-Ford BT44/44B 1974-75 **60** March-Ford 751 1975 **61** Hesketh-Ford 308 1975 **62** Ferrari 312T 1975-76 **63** McLaren-Ford M23 1976 **64** Tyrrell-Ford P34 1976 **65** Penske-Ford PC4 1976 **66** Lotus-Ford 77 1976 **67** March-Ford 761 1976 **68** Ferrari 312T2 1976-78 **69** McLaren- Ford M26 1977 **70** Shadow-Ford DN8 1977 **71** Ligier-Matra JS7 1977 **72** Wolf-Ford WR1 1977 **73** Lotus-Ford 78 1977-78 **74** Ferrari 312T3 1978 **75** Brabham-Alfa Romeo BT46/BT46B 1978 **76** Tyrrell-Ford 008 1978 **77** Lotus-Ford 79 1978 **78** Ferrari 312T4 1979 **79** Williams-Ford FW07 1979 **80** Renault RS10 1979 **81** Ligier-Ford JS11/JS11-15 1979-80 **82** Renault RE20 1980 **83** Williams-Ford FW07B/C 1980-81 **84** Brabham-Ford BT49/49C/49D 1980-82 **85** Talbot Ligier-Matra JS17 1981 **86** Renault RE30 1981 **87** Ferrari 126CK 1981 **88** McLaren-Ford MP4/MP4B 1981-82 **89** Tyrrell-Ford 011 1982 **90** Williams-Ford FW08 1982 **91** Brabham-B MW BT50 1982 **92** Lotus-Ford 91 1982 **93** Renault RE30B 1982 **94** Ferrari 126C2 1982 **95** Tyrrell-Ford 011 1983 **96** Williams-Ford FW08C 1983 **97** Brabham-BMW BT52/52B 1983 **98** Renault RE40 1983 **99** McLaren-Ford MP4/1C 1983 **100** Ferrari 126C2B/C3 1983 **101** Ferrari 126C4 1984 **102** McLaren-TAG Porsche MP4/2 1984 **103** Williams-Honda FW09 1984 **104** Brabham-BMW BT53 1984 **105** McLaren-TAG Porsche MP4/2B 1985 **106** Ferrari 156-85 1985 **107** Williams-Ford FW10 1985 **108** Brabham-BMW BT54 1985 **109** Lotus-Renault 97T/98T 1985-86 **110** Benetton-BMW B186 1986 **111** McLaren-TAG Porsche MP4/2C 1986 **112** Williams-Ford FW11 1986-87 **113** Williams-Ford FW11B 1987 **114** Lotus-Honda 99T 1987 **115** McLaren-TAG Porsche MP4/3 1987 **116** Ferrari F1-87/F1-87/88C 1987-88 **117** McLaren-Honda MP4/4 1988 **118** Ferrari 640 1989 **119** Williams-Renault FW12C 1989 **120** McLaren-Honda MP4/5 1989 **121** Benetton-Ford B189 1989 **122** Williams-Renault FW13 1989 **123** McLaren-Honda MP4/5B 1990 **124** Ferrari 641 & 641/2 1990 **125** Williams-Renault FW13B 1990 **126** Benetton-Ford B190 1990 **127** McLaren-Honda MP4/6 1991 **128** Benetton-Ford B191 1991 **129** Williams-Renault FW14 1991 **130** Williams-Renault FW14B 1992 **131** McLaren-Honda MP4/7A 1992 **132** Benetton-Ford B192 1992 **133** Williams-Renault FW15C 1993 **134** McLaren-Ford MP4/8 1993 **135** Benetton-Ford B193B 1993 **136** Benetton-Ford B194 1994 **137** Williams-Renault FW16/16B 1994 **138** Ferrari 412T1B 1994 **139** Benetton-Renault B195 1995 **140** Williams-Renault FW17/FW17B 1995 **141** Ferrari 412T2 1995 **142** Williams-Renault FW18 1996 **143** Ferrari F310 1996 **144** Ligier-Mugen-Honda JS43 1996 **145** Ferrari F310B 1997 **146** Williams-Renault FW19 1997 **147** McLaren-Mercedes MP4-12 1997 **148** Benetton-Renault B197 1997 **149** Ferrari F300 1998 **150** McLaren-Mercedes MP4-13 1998 **151** Jordan-Mugen Honda 198/199 1998-99 **152** Ferrari F399 1999 **153** McLaren-Mercedes MP4-14 1999 **154** Stewart-Ford SF-3 1999 **155** Ferrari F1 2000 2000 **156** McLaren-Mercedes MP4-15 2000 **157** Ferrari F2001 2001-02 **158** Williams-BMW FW23 & FW24 2001-02 **159** McLaren-Mercedes MP4-16/17 2001-02 **160** Ferrari F2002 2002 **161** Jordan-Ford EJ13 2003 **162** Williams FW25 2003 **163** McLaren-Mercedes MP4-17D 2003 **164** Ferrari F2003-GA 2003 **165** Renault R23B 2003 **166** Ferrari F2004 2004 **167** Renault R24 2004 **168** Williams FW26 2004 **169** McLaren-Mercedes MP4-19B 2004 **170** McLaren-Mercedes MP4-20 2005 **171** Renault R25 2005

Contents

Abbreviations

NATIONALITIES / COUNTRIES

A	- Austria *
AUS	- Australia *
B	- Belgium *
BR	- Brazil *
BRN	- Bahrain *
CDN	- Canada *
CH	- Switzerland *
CHN	- China *
CO	- Colombia
CZ	- Czech Republic
D	- Germany *
DK	- Denmark
E	- Spain *
F	- France *
FIN	- Finland
FL	- Liechtenstein
GB	- Britain *
H	- Hungary *
I	- Italy *
IL	- Israel
IND	- India
IRL	- Ireland
J	- Japan *
L	- Luxembourg
MA	- Morocco *
MAL	- Malaysia *
MC	- Monaco *
MEX	- Mexico *
NL	- Netherlands *
NZ	- New Zealand
P	- Portugal *
PL	- Poland
RA	- Argentina *
RCH	- Chile
ROU	- Uruguay
RSM	- San Marino *
RSR	- South Rhodesia (now Zimbabwe)
S	- Sweden *
T	- Thailand
TR	- Turkey *
USA	- United States of America *
YV	- Venezuela
ZA	- South Africa *

* Countries hosting a Championship race

Other races

DAL	- Dallas (USA)
DET	- Detroit (USA)
EUR	- Europe
INDY	- Indianapolis 500 (USA)
LV	- Caesars Palace, Las Vegas (USA)
PAC	- Pacific
PES	- Pescara (Italy)
USAE	- USA East
USAW	- USA West

European GP held in Britain (1983, 85 & 93),
Germany (1984, 95, 96, 99–2005)
and Spain (1994 & 97)
Luxembourg GP held in Germany
Pacific GP held in Japan
San Marino GP held in Italy
Swiss GP held in France (1982).

ENGINES

Climax	- Coventry Climax
Weslake	- Gurney Weslake

All Castellotti engines are rebadged Ferrari, while all Megatron engines are rebadged BMW.

ABBREVIATIONS & SYMBOLS

=	- shared
ap	- also practiced
dq	- disqualified
ew	- entry withdrawn
exc	- excluded
f	- fastest lap
nc	- not classified
npq	- non pre-qualified
nq	- qualified
ns	- non started
r	- retired
†	- driver died during that year

Foreword

by Steve Rider

Presenter of ITV's live coverage of Formula 1 from 2006. Host of BBC's Grandstand *since 1991 and, before that, host of* Sportsnight

The Olympic Games, the Six Nations Championship, the Masters and the Ryder Cup – sport has been good to me with BBC Television. But when the chance came to go back to ITV, where I started my career, to host their Formula 1 coverage it did not require a great deal of agonising to return to a sport that had been one of my great enthusiasms.

When the news was announced in 1995 that ITV had plucked Formula 1 from BBC Television's seemingly impregnable portfolio of sport, it was like someone had just cut off a limb. The *Grandstand* team were in Estoril at the time, putting the finishing touches to a documentary on Michael Schumacher, and we could not absorb the fact that in the cut-throat world of television rights it had suddenly become someone else's turn. I had been trackside when Andretti won with Lotus, when Nigel was the hero at Silverstone and that dreadful day when Ayrton perished at Imola. I'd taken my leave of Grand Prix motor racing with a definite sense of unfinished business.

Now, despite the outstanding job done by my good friend Jim Rosenthal, he had now moved and I was offered the opportunity to take over his role. But with the new job came a self doubt that just maybe the sport had moved on without me. In those situations it is a great reassurance that every sport has its bible. Cricket has *Wisden*, football and rugby have detailed yearbooks, and now, to my great relief, there is a fourth edition of the *Grand Prix Data Book*, which is rapidly becoming the publication of record in Formula 1.

What David Hayhoe and David Holland have done with some style is to turn a book of stats into something that actually hangs together as a very good read. Here the figures in columns are combined with well-placed information that allows you to bring every team, race and season alive in the memory.

I've got a few weeks of swotting up ahead of me

before the first race in Bahrain in March 2006. Reference books like this make the chore a pleasure. Not only will I be able to fill in the details of everything that has been happening over the past ten years, but I will greatly enjoy letting the mind and the memory wander back 30 years to the teams and the races that got me hooked on this wonderful sport.

So thanks to the authors and also to Haynes Publishing. So much is written about Grand Prix motor racing but rarely is it compiled with such detail and authority.

Steve Rider

Preface

by Christopher Hilton

Long-time user of the Grand Prix Data Book, *and best-selling author whose recent books for Haynes have included* Grand Prix Century *and* Memories of Ayrton

If you follow Grand Prix racing you need this book. That's a very easy thing to write and I'll be defending the truth of it in a moment but, here and now, I want to expand on it: if you *work* in Grand Prix racing, in whatever guise – team owner to driver to humblest mechanic; sponsor to press relations to the media, whatever – you need this book too.

Every sport lives by statistics because *measuring* what happens any other way is impossible. Some – like football – do this simply, counting each goal as 1. How else could you know which side won? Even the sports which rely on judges need their marks in numerals so they can be added up – to find who won and where all the others came.

Some – like cricket – become citadels of statistics, an unending immensity of them. You only have to gaze at a scorecard to see the possibilities and, in its most extreme form, the statistics become an entity of their own, almost divorced from the human beings who created them with bat and ball.

Motor racing, like all other forms of racing – horses, athletes, swimmers and so on – is subtly different because what matters is who crosses the line first and you need eyesight (or photo finishes), not pocket calculators, to tell you that. There is no escape from the statistics, however, in deciding the grid, compiling a lap chart, working out winning margins, the fastest laps and the record speeds, all an intrinsic part of the whole. Imagine motor racing without them.

Moreover, the timing devices are so sophisticated that, in an activity where everybody argues over everything else the whole time, they are never disputed. The qualifying sessions, those grid positions and the race results have been universally accepted for a generation. Across the shifting daily mosaic of controversies, disputes and protests, the fractions to three decimal places which the timing monitors record can be chiselled in stone; and in a sense are.

Hence the primary importance of the *Grand Prix Data Book*. The fractions are here and the fractions are what *really* happened, because that is the currency Grand Prix racing measures itself in, just as the Stock Exchange measures itself in £s and $s and the TV companies in viewing figures.

Around this primary importance, Hayhoe and Holland have achieved something invaluable by doing original research to the highest standard of accuracy, often correcting errors recycled by others down the years. They have agonised over the smallest details (like how and where to include a driver breaking down on the parade lap) and the result is far more than a complete record of every race in the World Championship from its beginning in 1950. This is so reliable that it, also, can be chiselled in stone.

How do I know? Because, writing about Grand Prix racing, I have used an earlier edition the whole time and I'll let you into a little secret. If you go round the offices of motoring magazines and photographic agencies you'll see editions of the *Grand Prix Data Book* bound by thick tape to hold them together because they have been worked to the point of destruction – thick brown tape in the case of my 1996 edition…

The beauty of the book is that you can use it at whatever level you want: to settle an argument about a race you watched on television, remind yourself of the first Grand Prix you went to, chart a driver's career race by race – Fangio, say, or Schumacher or Alonso. You can simply lose yourself in the fascinating facts (and factoids) at the back. You have a query about a particular circuit? There's a map of it, its alterations and when they were done. Who were the AGS team? It's here. How many races did Mark Blundell drive in and when? It's here.

And if you are an author writing captions for a book on the first 100 years of Grand Prix racing, as I did recently, and you have a photograph of five cars coming in a column at Monaco in 1982 and you want to know who was who, it's here. Peer at the (just visible) numbers on the cars and look up these numbers in the 470-page section detailing every statistic of every race since 1950 – so it was Prost behind Patrese, and Pironi behind Prost and … and now you know why my edition has the thick brown tape round it. There's every chance yours will one day when you've worked it to destruction too.

Introduction

As the review tributes on page 2 suggest, we have set out to compile a picture of Grand Prix racing since 1950 that is as comprehensive and accurate as possible – the complex calculations relished by statisticians, as well as straightforward records of every race, driver, team and circuit, plus lots of little gems you never knew you wanted to know until now. As new information becomes available, our database is updated and we are pleased to hear that the *Grand Prix Data Book* is today regarded as the premier reference work for anyone seriously interested in Formula 1.

Our very special thanks go to Steve Rider, for sparing valuable time and having sufficient confidence in us to write a foreword, to Christopher Hilton for his generous preface, and to Matthias Brunner, João Paulo Cunha, Donald Davidson, Germán Demartino, Peter Duke, Peter Higham, Richard Jenkins, Colin Lane, Wolfgang Leipert, Maureen Magee, Danny Marting, Aleš Norský, Doug Nye, John Ross, Claire Skerrett, Steve Small, Quentin Spurring, Christer Svensson, Dave Webb, Kevin Wood, John Wright, LAT and everybody else who has taken time to contribute.

Performance records in this book are taken up to the end of the 2005 season.

Throughout this book the distances and average speeds have been recalculated to remove any errors there may have been in previous editions. There may be apparent discrepancies, because of rounding.

Drivers are referred to by their most commonly used names or nicknames, although a table in Chapter 3 details drivers' proper names.

Happy reading...

DAVID HAYHOE and DAVID HOLLAND

DAVID HAYHOE

David Hayhoe, born in Beckenham, Kent, in 1954, spent 33 years working in the Departments of Environment and Transport until 2004, his last 12 years as an inspector of British airports. As a motorsport enthusiast since the 1980s, he researched heavily into the sport's history and statistics and compiled his own database. This formed the basis of his first *Grand Prix Data Book* in 1989. He has developed the database progressively and further editions of the book have been enthusiastically received around the world by the media, who use it as an essential reference tool, as do F1 fans. David has been Statistician for the *Autocourse* annual, covering Formula 1 and non-F1 events. He frequently attends race meetings in the USA and covers historical meetings within the UK.

With more time on his hands now that he is newly retired, he is working on a European football book and also, with a passion for music from the classics to recent rock and pop, he is learning to play the violin.

DAVID HOLLAND

David Holland, born in Peterborough in 1961, works as a salesman in the timber and building industry and his limited spare time is taken up with music, fishing and football. A childhood interest has developed into detailed research of Formula 1, its history, personalities and machinery, which led to his involvement in the *Grand Prix Data Book* project. In 2002 David contributed to Sky Sports Interactive coverage of that F1 season, concentrating on the history behind each Grand Prix.

1

RACES

Race Entrants and Results

Lap Leaders

Driver Points

Constructor Points
points in brackets are those scored but not counted
towards the final Championship total

Left: *Ferrari driver Mike Hawthorn (16) leads Fangio (Maserati A6GCM)
over the line at the 1953 French Grand Prix, one of the closest-fought
races in history.* (LAT)

Key to engine configurations:

4, 6, 8	straight / in-line
F4, F8, F12	flat or boxer
H16	double flat
V2, V6, V8,	
V10, V12, V16	V formation
W12	W formation
s	supercharged
t	turbocharged
tbne	turbine

the number denotes how many cylinders

PARADE LAPS

Drivers who did not complete the parade lap and take the official start are regarded as non-starters. Examples are the 14 Michelin runners at the 2005 USA Grand Prix and Alain Prost at San Marino in 1991.

Full listings of these instances are given in the RECORDS & TRIVIA chapter.

RESTARTED RACES

Races that have been restarted within the first two laps are regarded as a new race under current legislation, but this leads to confusion concerning drivers who then didn't take the restart.

In this book, these drivers are regarded as starters who have retired from the race. It would be wrong to claim Niki Lauda in Germany 1976 and Jacques Laffite in Britain 1986 were non-starters when considering their severe injuries at the start of these races.

RETIREMENTS

In the early years of the World Championship, classifications were somewhat haphazard. Drivers who retired were generally not classified unless they pushed their car over the line after the winner took the flag. For instance Graham Hill in Belgium 1960 completed enough laps to be classified 3rd, but retired in the pits as opposed to pushing the car over the line. Conversely, Harry Schell was classified 7th in Germany 1959 despite his car failing 11 laps from the end of the 60 lap race.

This anomaly was cleared up in 1966 with the advent of the rule requiring cars to complete 90% of the race distance to be classified.

FORMULA 2

Formula 2 cars have often raced in World Championship Grands Prix. In 1952 and 1953 the formula only permitted Formula 2 cars due to the lack of quality Formula 1 entrants. On occasion, F2 cars were included on equal terms with F1 entrants to simply make up the numbers, as in Italy 1960. However in six races (Germany 57, 58, 66, 67 & 69 and Morocco 58) Formula 2 cars raced simultaneously for separate honours and although not eligible for points were regarded as starters. Their results are shown with the prefix 'F2:'.

SHARED DRIVES

It was common practice in the 50s for drivers to share a car, either by taking over from a team-mate or by swapping cars. In most cases points were shared.

INDIANAPOLIS

From 1950 until 1960, the Indy 500 featured as part of the World Championship. Very few drivers crossed from one discipline to the other, which was the original intention. Although points were awarded in a similar manner, the final point was awarded for fastest 'leading' lap.

The time and speed given as 'Pole Position Speed' relates to the average of four laps.

These races were not regarded as Grands Prix, the first United States Grand Prix in the championship being held at Sebring in 1959.

Race Entrants and Results

The Fédération Internationale de l'Automobile decided to create a new World Championship for drivers, similar to the European championships of the 1930s and the motorcycle championship of 1949. Motor racing was getting back to normal after the turmoil of war and the new formula was made up of the cars that were available. This meant the basic pre-war designs of 1.5 litre supercharged or blown engines (voiturette cars) and the 4.5 litre unblown cars, formed a parallel and equivalent formula. Alfa Romeo had resumed racing after a year off and were firm favourites.

ALFA ROMEO
SA Alfa Romeo: Farina, Fangio, Fagioli, Parnell, Sanesi, Taruffi

FERRARI
Scuderia Ferrari: Ascari, Villoresi, Sommer, Serafini
Privateers: Whitehead, Biondetti

MASERATI
Officine Alfieri Maserati: Chiron, Rol
Scuderia Ambrosiana: Murray, Hampshire, Parnell
Enrico Platé: de Graffenried, Bira
Scuderia Achille Varzi: González, (Pián), Pagani, Branca
Scuderia Milano: Bonetto, Comotti
Privateers: Fry, Shawe-Taylor, Branca, Pietsch

SIMCA GORDINI
Equipe Gordini: Manzon, Trintignant

ALTA
Privateers: Kelly, Crossley

TALBOT LAGO
Automobiles Talbot-Darracq SA: Giraud-Cabantous, Martin, Rosier (CH,B,F), Étançelin (B), Sommer (F)
Ecurie Rosier: Rosier, Louveau
Ecurie Belge: Claes
Ecurie Bleue: Schell
Ecurie Lutetia: Chaboud
Privateers: Étançelin, Sommer, Levegh, Pozzi, Mairesse

ERA
ERA Ltd: Johnson
Privateers: Harrison, Gerard, Walker, Rolt

COOPER
Horschell Racing Corp: Schell

(Drivers whose names are in brackets, were non-starters. Race codes are shown, where a driver was with more than one entrant of the same constructor during the season)

13 May 1950		BRITAIN: Silverstone							(Round 1)	(Race 1)	
		70 laps x 4.649 km/2.889 miles = 325.458 km/202.230 miles									
Pos	No	Driver	Car	Model	Engine		Laps	Time/Reason for Retirement		Grid Pos	Row
1	2	G Farina	Alfa Romeo	158	Alfa Romeo	8s	70	2h 13m 23.600s		1	1
2	3	L Fagioli	Alfa Romeo	158	Alfa Romeo	8s	70	2h 13m 26.200s		2	1
3	4	R Parnell	Alfa Romeo	158	Alfa Romeo	8s	70	2h 14m 15.600s		4	1
4	14	Y Giraud-Cabantous	Talbot Lago	T26C-DA	Talbot	6	68			6	2
5	15	L Rosier	Talbot Lago	T26C	Talbot	6	68			9	3
6	12	B Gerard	ERA	B/C	ERA	6s	67			13	4
7	11	C Harrison	ERA	B	ERA	6s	67			15	5
8	16	P Étançelin	Talbot Lago	T26C	Talbot	6	65			14	4
9	6	D Hampshire	Maserati	4CLT/48	Maserati	4s	64			16	5
10=	10	J Fry	Maserati	4CL	Maserati	4s				20	6
10=	10	B Shawe-Taylor	Maserati	4CL	Maserati	4s	64			20	6
11	18	J Claes	Talbot Lago	T26C	Talbot	6	64			21	6
r	1	J M Fangio	Alfa Romeo	158	Alfa Romeo	8s	61	oil line / connecting rod		3	1
nc	23	J Kelly	Alta	GP	Alta	4s	57			19	6
r	21	B Bira	Maserati	4CLT/48	Maserati	4s	48	fuel injection		5	2
r	5	D Murray	Maserati	4CLT/48	Maserati	4s	43	engine		18	5
r	24	G Crossley	Alta	GP	Alta	4s	43	transmission		17	5
r	20	E de Graffenried	Maserati	4CLT/48	Maserati	4s	33	connecting rod		8	3
r	19	L Chiron	Maserati	4CLT/48	Maserati	4s	23	clutch		11	3
r	17	E Martin	Talbot Lago	T26C-DA	Talbot	6	9	oil pressure		7	2
r=	9	P Walker	ERA	E	ERA	6s				10	3
r=	9	T Rolt	ERA	E	ERA	6s	4	gearbox			
r	8	L Johnson	ERA	E	ERA	6s	1	supercharger		12	4

Winning speed 146.390 km/h, 90.963 mph
Pole Position speed 151.063 km/h, 93.866 mph (G Farina, 1 min:50.800 sec)
Fastest Lap speed 151.337 km/h, 94.036 mph (G Farina, 1 min:50.600 sec on lap 2)
Lap Leaders G Farina 1-9,16-37,39-70 (63); L Fagioli 10-14,38 (6); J M Fangio 15 (1).

Also the Grand Prix of Europe.

21 May 1950   MONACO: Monte-Carlo   (Round 2)   (Race 2)

100 laps x 3.180 km, 1.976 miles = 318.000 km, 197.596 miles

Pos	No	Driver	Car	Model	Engine		Laps	Time/Reason for Retirement	Grid Pos	Row
1	34	J M Fangio	Alfa Romeo	158	Alfa Romeo	8s	100	3h 13m 18.700s	1	1
2	40	A Ascari	Ferrari	125	Ferrari	V12s	99		7	3
3	48	L Chiron	Maserati	4CLT/48	Maserati	4s	98		8	3
4	42	R Sommer	Ferrari	125	Ferrari	V12s	97		9	4
5	50	B Bira	Maserati	4CLT/48	Maserati	4s	95		15	6
6	26	B Gerard	ERA	A	ERA	6s	94		16	7
7	6	J Claes	Talbot Lago	T26C	Talbot	6	94		19	8
r	38	L Villoresi	Ferrari	125	Ferrari	V12s	62	rear axle	6	3
r	14	P Étançelin	Talbot Lago	T26C	Talbot	6	35	oil line	4	2
r	2	F González	Maserati	4CLT/48	Maserati	4s	0	accident / fire	3	1
r	36	L Fagioli	Alfa Romeo	158	Alfa Romeo	8s	0	accident	5	2
r	32	G Farina	Alfa Romeo	158	Alfa Romeo	8s	0	accident	2	1
r	16	L Rosier	Talbot Lago	T26C	Talbot	6	0	accident	10	4
r	10	R Manzon	Simca Gordini	T15	Gordini	4s	0	accident	12	5
r	8	H Schell	Cooper	T12	JAP	V2	0	accident	20	8
r	52	E de Graffenried	Maserati	4CLT/48	Maserati	4s	0	accident	11	5
r	12	M Trintignant	Simca Gordini	T15	Gordini	4s	0	accident	13	5
r	24	C Harrison	ERA	B	ERA	6s	0	accident	14	6
r	44	F Rol	Maserati	4CLT/48	Maserati	4s	0	accident / injury	17	7
ns	4	A Pián	Maserati	4CLT/48	Maserati	4s		accident	18	7
ns	28	P Whitehead	Ferrari	125	Ferrari	V12s		engine		

Winning speed 98.701 km/h, 61.330 mph
Pole Position speed 103.884 km/h, 64.550 mph (J M Fangio, 1 min:50.200 sec)
Fastest Lap speed 103.135 km/h, 64.085 mph (J M Fangio, 1 min:51.000 sec)
Lap Leaders J M Fangio 1-100 (100).

First two rows of the grid determined by first day's practice.
Cars on row 5 lined up incorrectly.

30 May 1950   INDIANAPOLIS: 500   (Round 3)   (Race 3)

138 laps x 4.023 km, 2.500 miles = 555.224 km, 345.000 miles

Pos	No	Driver	Car	Model	Engine		Laps	Time/Reason for Retirement	Grid Pos	Row
1	1	J Parsons	Kurtis Kraft		Offenhauser	4	138	2h 46m 55.970s	5	2
2	3	B Holland	Deidt		Offenhauser	4	137	2h 48m 47.367s	10	4
3	31	M Rose	Deidt		Offenhauser	4	137		3	1
4	54	C Green	Kurtis Kraft	3000	Offenhauser	4	137		12	4
5=	17	J Chitwood	Kurtis Kraft	2000	Offenhauser	4			9	3
5=	17	T Bettenhausen	Kurtis Kraft	2000	Offenhauser	4	136			
6	8	L Wallard	Moore		Offenhauser	4	136		23	8
7	98	W Faulkner	Kurtis Kraft	2000	Offenhauser	4	135		1	1
8	5	G Connor	Lesovsky		Offenhauser	4	135		4	2
9	7	P Russo	Nichels		Offenhauser	4	135		19	7
10	59	P Flaherty	Kurtis Kraft	3000	Offenhauser	4	135		11	4
11	2	M Fohr	Marchese		Offenhauser	4	133		16	6
12	18	D Carter	Stevens		Offenhauser	4s	133		13	5
13	15	M Hellings	Silnes		Offenhauser	4	132		26	9
14r	49	J McGrath	Kurtis Kraft	3000	Offenhauser	4	131	spin	6	2
15	55	T Ruttman	Lesovsky		Offenhauser	4	130		24	8
16	75	G Hartley	Langley		Offenhauser	4	128		31	11
17	22	J Davies	Ewing		Offenhauser	4	128		27	9
18	62	J McDowell	Kurtis Kraft	2000	Offenhauser	4	128		33	11
19	4	W Brown	Silnes		Offenhauser	4	127		20	7
20	21	S Webb	Maserati	8CTF	Offenhauser	4	126		14	5
21	81	J Hoyt	Kurtis Kraft	2000	Offenhauser	4	125		15	5
22	27	W Ader	Rae		Offenhauser	4s	123		29	10
23r	77	J Holmes	Olson		Offenhauser	4	123	spin	30	10
24	76	J Rathmann	Wetteroth		Offenhauser	4	122		28	10
25=	12	H Banks	Maserati	8CTF	Offenhauser	4s			21	7
25=	12	F Agabashian	Maserati	8CTF	Offenhauser	4s	112			
26r	67	B Schindler	Rassey		Offenhauser	4	111	universal joint	22	8
27r=	24	B Levrett	Adams		Offenhauser	4			17	6
27r=	24	B Cantrell	Adams		Offenhauser	4	108	oil pressure		
28r	28	F Agabashian	Kurtis Kraft	3000	Offenhauser	4s	64	oil line	2	1
29r	61	J Jackson	Kurtis Kraft		Cummins	6s	52	supercharger	32	11
30r	23	S Hanks	Kurtis Kraft	2000	Offenhauser	4	42	oil pressure	25	9
31r	14	T Bettenhausen	Deidt		Offenhauser	4	30	wheel bearing	8	3
32r	45	D Rathmann	Watson		Offenhauser	4	25	stalled	18	6
33r	69	D Dinsmore	Kurtis Kraft	2000	Offenhauser	4	10	oil leak	7	3

Winning speed 199.562 km/h, 124.002 mph
Pole Position speed 216.206 km/h, 134.344 mph (W Faulkner, 1 min: 6.992 sec)
Fastest Lap speed not available (J Parsons)

Stopped early because of rain.

4 Jun 1950   SWITZERLAND: Bremgarten   (Round 4)   (Race 4)

42 laps x 7.280 km, 4.524 miles = 305.760 km, 189.990 miles

Pos	No	Driver	Car	Model	Engine		Laps	Time/Reason for Retirement	Grid Pos	Row
1	16	G Farina	Alfa Romeo	158	Alfa Romeo	8s	42	2h 02m 53.700s	2	1
2	12	L Fagioli	Alfa Romeo	158	Alfa Romeo	8s	42	2h 02m 54.100s	3	1
3	10	L Rosier	Talbot Lago	T26C-DA	Talbot	6	41		10	4
4	30	B Bira	Maserati	4CLT/48	Maserati	4s	40		8	3
5	34	F Bonetto	Maserati Milano	4CLT/50	Maserati Milano	4s	40		12	5
6	32	E de Graffenried	Maserati	4CLT/48	Maserati	4s	40		11	5
7	2	N Pagani	Maserati	4CLT/48	Maserati	4s	39		15	6
8	44	H Schell	Talbot Lago	T26C	Talbot	6	39		18	7
9	26	L Chiron	Maserati	4CLT/48	Maserati	4s	39		16	7
10	4	J Claes	Talbot Lago	T26C	Talbot	6	38		14	6
11	40	T Branca	Maserati	4CL	Maserati	4s	35		17	7
r	14	J M Fangio	Alfa Romeo	158	Alfa Romeo	8s	33	engine	1	1
r	42	P Étançelin	Talbot Lago	T26C	Talbot	6	25	gearbox	6	3
r	20	R Sommer	Ferrari	166	Ferrari	V12	19	suspension	13	5
r	8	E Martin	Talbot Lago	T26C-DA	Talbot	6	19	accident / injury	9	4
r	22	L Villoresi	Ferrari	125	Ferrari	V12s	9	transmission	4	2
r	18	A Ascari	Ferrari	125	Ferrari	V12s	4	oil pump	5	2
r	6	Y Giraud-Cabantous	Talbot Lago	T26C-DA	Talbot	6	0	accident	7	3

Winning speed 149.279 km/h, 92.757 mph
Pole Position speed 161.678 km/h, 100.462 mph (J M Fangio, 2 min:42.100 sec)
Fastest Lap speed 162.178 km/h, 100.773 mph (G Farina, 2 min:41.600 sec on lap 8)
Lap Leaders J M Fangio 1-6,21-22 (8); G Farina 7-20,24-42 (33); L Fagioli 23 (1).

18 Jun 1950   BELGIUM: Spa-Francorchamps   (Round 5)   (Race 5)

35 laps x 14.120 km, 8.774 miles = 494.200 km, 307.082 miles

Pos	No	Driver	Car	Model	Engine		Laps	Time/Reason for Retirement	Grid Pos	Row
1	10	J M Fangio	Alfa Romeo	158	Alfa Romeo	8s	35	2h 47m 26.000s	2	1
2	12	L Fagioli	Alfa Romeo	158	Alfa Romeo	8s	35	2h 47m 40.000s	3	1
3	14	L Rosier	Talbot Lago	T26C-DA	Talbot	6	35	2h 49m 45.000s	6	3
4	8	G Farina	Alfa Romeo	158	Alfa Romeo	8s	35	2h 51m 31.000s	1	1
5	4	A Ascari	Ferrari	275	Ferrari	V12	34		8	3
6	2	L Villoresi	Ferrari	125	Ferrari	V12s	33		4	2
7	22	P Levegh	Talbot Lago	T26C	Talbot	6	33		10	4
8	24	J Claes	Talbot Lago	T26C	Talbot	6	31		14	6
9	26	G Crossley	Alta	GP	Alta	4s	30		12	5
10	30	T Branca	Maserati	4CL	Maserati	4s	29		13	5
r	20	E Chaboud	Talbot Lago	T26C	Talbot	6	22	engine	11	5
r	6	R Sommer	Talbot Lago	T26C	Talbot	6	20	engine	5	2
r	16	P Étançelin	Talbot Lago	T26C-DA	Talbot	6	15	engine overheating	7	3
r	18	Y Giraud-Cabantous	Talbot Lago	T26C-DA	Talbot	6	2	engine	9	4

Winning speed 177.097 km/h, 110.043 mph
Pole Position speed 183.509 km/h, 114.027 mph (G Farina, 4 min:37.000 sec)
Fastest Lap speed 185.451 km/h, 115.234 mph (G Farina, 4 min:34.100 sec on lap 18)
Lap Leaders J M Fangio 1-6,20-35 (22); G Farina 7-11,18-19 (7); L Fagioli 12 (1); R Sommer 13-17 (5).
The line-up on rows 3 and 5 is uncertain.

2 Jul 1950   FRANCE: Reims-Gueux   (Round 6)   (Race 6)

64 laps x 7.816 km, 4.857 miles = 500.224 km, 310.825 miles

Pos	No	Driver	Car	Model	Engine		Laps	Time/Reason for Retirement	Grid Pos	Row
1	6	J M Fangio	Alfa Romeo	158	Alfa Romeo	8s	64	2h 57m 52.800s	1	1
2	4	L Fagioli	Alfa Romeo	158	Alfa Romeo	8s	64	2h 58m 18.500s	3	1
3	14	P Whitehead	Ferrari	125	Ferrari	V12s	61		19	8
4	44	R Manzon	Simca Gordini	T15	Gordini	4s	61		13	5
5=	16	P Étançelin	Talbot Lago	T26C-DA	Talbot	6			4	2
5=	16	E Chaboud	Talbot Lago	T26C-DA	Talbot	6	59			
6=	26	C Pozzi	Talbot Lago	T26C	Talbot	6			16	7
6=	26	L Rosier	Talbot Lago	T26C	Talbot	6	56			
7r	2	G Farina	Alfa Romeo	158	Alfa Romeo	8s	55	fuel pump	2	1
8	18	Y Giraud-Cabantous	Talbot Lago	T26C-DA	Talbot	6	52		5	2
r	22	P Levegh	Talbot Lago	T26C	Talbot	6	36	engine	9	4
r	40	F Bonetto	Maserati Milano	4CLT/50	Maserati Milano	4s	14	engine	11	5
r	42	J Claes	Talbot Lago	T26C	Talbot	6	11	engine overheating	15	6
r	20	L Rosier	Talbot Lago	T26C-DA	Talbot	6	10	engine overheating	6	3
r	32	R Parnell	Maserati	4CLT/48	Maserati	4s	9	engine	12	5
r	28	F Rol	Maserati	4CLT/48	Maserati	4s	6	engine	7	3
r	30	L Chiron	Maserati	4CLT/48	Maserati	4s	6	engine	14	6
r	34	D Hampshire	Maserati	4CLT/48	Maserati	4s	5	engine	18	7
r	12	R Sommer	Talbot Lago	T26C-GS	Talbot	6	4	engine overheating	17	7
r	36	F González	Maserati	4CLT/48	Maserati	4s	3	engine	8	3
ns	24	E Chaboud	Talbot Lago	T26C	Talbot	6		shared with Étançelin instead	10	4
ns	8	L Villoresi	Ferrari	125/275	Ferrari	V12		drove in different race		
ns	10	A Ascari	Ferrari	125/275	Ferrari	V12		drove in different race		

Winning speed 168.729 km/h, 104.843 mph
Pole Position speed 186.837 km/h, 116.095 mph (J M Fangio, 2 min:30.600 sec)
Fastest Lap speed 180.833 km/h, 112.364 mph (J M Fangio, 2 min:35.600 sec on lap 52)
Lap Leaders G Farina 1-16 (16); J M Fangio 17-64 (48).

Races

80 laps x 6.300 km, 3.915 miles = 504.000 km, 313.171 miles

Pos	No	Driver	Car	Model	Engine		Laps	Time/Reason for Retirement	Grid Pos	Row
1	10	G Farina	Alfa Romeo	158	Alfa Romeo	8s	80	2h 51m 17.400s	3	1
2=	48	D Serafini	Ferrari	375	Ferrari	V12				6	2
2=	48	A Ascari	Ferrari	375	Ferrari	V12	80	2h 52m 36.000s		
3	36	L Fagioli	Alfa Romeo	158	Alfa Romeo	8s	80	2h 52m 53.000s	5	2
4	58	L Rosier	Talbot Lago	T26C	Talbot	6	75		13	4
5	24	P Étançelin	Talbot Lago	T26C	Talbot	6	75		16	4
6	38	E de Graffenried	Maserati	4CLT/48	Maserati	4s	72		17	5
7	8	P Whitehead	Ferrari	125	Ferrari	V12s	72		18	5
r	50	D Murray	Maserati	4CLT/48	Maserati	4s	55	gearbox / valve	24	6
r	32	C Harrison	ERA	B	ERA	6s	51	radiator	21	6
r	12	R Sommer	Talbot Lago	T26C	Talbot	6	48	gearbox	8	2
r	40	G Mairesse	Talbot Lago	T26C	Talbot	6	41	oil pipe	11	3
r	4	F Rol	Maserati	4CLT/48	Maserati	4s	38	engine	9	3
r=	60	P Taruffi	Alfa Romeo	158	Alfa Romeo	8s			7	2
r=	60	J M Fangio	Alfa Romeo	158	Alfa Romeo	8s	34	valve		
r	56	P Levegh	Talbot Lago	T26C	Talbot	6	29	gearbox	20	5
r	18	J M Fangio	Alfa Romeo	158	Alfa Romeo	8s	23	gearbox	1	1
r	2	J Claes	Talbot Lago	T26C	Talbot	6	22	engine overheating	22	6
r	16	A Ascari	Ferrari	375	Ferrari	V12	21	engine	2	1
r	64	H Louveau	Talbot Lago	T26C-GS	Talbot	6	16	brakes	14	4
r	22	C Biondetti	Ferrari	166S	Jaguar	6	16	engine	25	7
r	62	F Comotti	Maserati Milano	4CLT/50	Maserati Milano	4s	15	engine	26	7
r	6	L Chiron	Maserati	4CLT/48	Maserati	4s	14	oil pressure	19	5
r	42	M Trintignant	Simca Gordini	T15	Gordini	4s	13	water pipe	12	3
r	46	C Sanesi	Alfa Romeo	158	Alfa Romeo	8s	11	engine	4	1
r	44	R Manzon	Simca Gordini	T15	Gordini	4s	8	transmission	10	3
r	30	B Bira	Maserati	4CLT/48	Maserati	4s	2	engine	15	4
r	28	P Pietsch	Maserati	4CLT/48	Maserati	4s	0	engine	27	7
ns	52	F Bonetto	Milano		Speluzzi	4s			23	6

Winning speed 176.543 km/h, 109.699 mph
Pole Position speed 191.231 km/h, 118.825 mph (J M Fangio, 1 min:58.600 sec)
Fastest Lap speed 189.000 km/h, 117.439 mph (J M Fangio, 2 min: 0.000 sec on lap 7)
Lap Leaders G Farina 1-13,16-80 (78); A Ascari 14-15 (2).

Lap Leaders 1950

Pos	Driver	Car-Engine	GPs	laps	km	miles
1	G Farina	Alfa Romeo	5	197	1,248.4	775.7
2	J M Fangio	Alfa Romeo	5	179	1,066.7	662.8
3	L Fagioli	Alfa Romeo	3	8	49.3	30.6
4	R Sommer	Talbot Lago	1	5	70.6	43.9
5	A Ascari	Ferrari	1	2	12.6	7.8
			6	**391**	**2,447.6**	**1,520.9**

Driver Points 1950

		GB	MC	INDY	CH	B	F	I	Total	
1	G Farina	9	-	-	9	4	-	8	30	
2	J M Fangio	-	9	-	-	8	9	1	27	
3	L Fagioli	6	-	-	6	6	6	(4)	24	(4)
4	L Rosier	2	-	-	4	4	-	3	13	
5	A Ascari	-	6	-	-	2	-	3	11	
6	J Parsons	-	-	9	-	-	-	-	9	
7	B Holland	-	-	6	-	-	-	-	6	
8	B Bira	-	2	-	3	-	-	-	5	
9	R Parnell	4	-	-	-	-	-	-	4	
	L Chiron	-	4	-	-	-	-	-	4	
	M Rose	-	-	4	-	-	-	-	4	
	P Whitehead	-	-	-	-	-	4	-	4	
13	Y Giraud-Cabantous	3	-	-	-	-	-	-	3	
	R Sommer	-	3	-	-	-	-	-	3	
	C Green	-	-	3	-	-	-	-	3	
	R Manzon	-	-	-	-	-	3	-	3	
	D Serafini	-	-	-	-	-	-	3	3	
	P Étançelin	-	-	-	-	-	1	2	3	
19	F Bonetto	-	-	-	2	-	-	-	2	
20	T Bettenhausen	-	-	1	-	-	-	-	1	
	J Chitwood	-	-	1	-	-	-	-	1	
	E Chaboud	-	-	-	-	-	1	-	1	

*8,6,4,3 and 2 points awarded to the first five finishers. The driver setting the
fastest lap scored a point also. Points shared for shared drives. Best 4 scores.*

Race Entrants and Results

The formula continued into its second year with the promise of stiffer competition from the 4.5-litre Ferrari and the long awaited V16 BRM. The Talbot entries were now in private hands and sadly missing from their number would be the popular Raymond Sommer, killed in a minor French race at the end of the previous season.

ALFA ROMEO
SA Alfa Romeo: Farina, Fangio, Sanesi, Bonetto, de Graffenried, Fagioli, Pietsch

FERRARI
Scuderia Ferrari: Ascari, Villoresi, Taruffi, González
G A Vandervell: Parnell, Shawe-Taylor, Whitehead (GB)
Ecurie Espadon: Fischer
Privateers: Whitehead, Landi

MASERATI
Enrico Platé: de Graffenried, Schell, Chiron
Scuderia Ambrosiana: Murray
Scuderia Milano: Marimón, Godia, (Jover)
Ecurie Siam: Bira
Privateers: Fotheringham-Parker, James, Branca

OSCA
OSCA Automobili: Rol

SIMCA GORDINI
Equipe Gordini: Manzon, Trintignant, Simon, Gordini

ERA
Privateers: Gerard, Shawe-Taylor

TALBOT LAGO
Ecurie Rosier: Rosier, Chiron, Louveau
Ecurie Belgique: Mairesse, Swaters, Pilette
Ecurie Belge: Claes
Privateers: Giraud-Cabantous, Étançelin, Levegh, Hamilton, González, Chaboud, Grignard

ALTA
Privateer: Kelly

HWM
HW Motors: Abecassis, Moss

BRM
BRM Ltd: Parnell, Walker, (Richardson, Stuck)

VERITAS
Ecurie Espadon: Hirt

27 May 1951		SWITZERLAND: Bremgarten						(Round 1)		(Race 8)	
		42 laps x 7.280 km, 4.524 miles = 305.760 km, 189.990 miles									
Pos	No	Driver	Car	Model	Engine		Laps	Time/Reason for Retirement	Grid Pos	Row	
1	24	J M Fangio	Alfa Romeo	159	Alfa Romeo	8s	42	2h 07m 53.640s	1	1	
2	44	P Taruffi	Ferrari	375	Ferrari	V12	42	2h 08m 48.880s	6	3	
3	22	G Farina	Alfa Romeo	159	Alfa Romeo	8s	42	2h 09m 12.950s	2	1	
4	28	C Sanesi	Alfa Romeo	159	Alfa Romeo	8s	41		4	2	
5	26	E de Graffenried	Alfa Romeo	159	Alfa Romeo	8s	40		5	2	
6	20	A Ascari	Ferrari	375	Ferrari	V12	40		7	3	
7	30	L Chiron	Maserati	4CLT/48	Maserati	4s	40		19	8	
8	14	S Moss	HWM	(51)	Alta	4	40		14	6	
9	8	L Rosier	Talbot Lago	T26C-DA	Talbot	6	39		8	3	
10	4	P Étançelin	Talbot Lago	T26C-DA	Talbot	6	39		12	5	
11	38	R Fischer	Ferrari	212	Ferrari	V12	39		10	4	
12	32	H Schell	Maserati	4CLT/48	Maserati	4s	38		17	7	
r	16	P Whitehead	Ferrari	125	Ferrari	V12s	36	accident	9	4	
13	2	J Claes	Talbot Lago	T26C-DA	Talbot	6	35		18	7	
14	40	G Mairesse	Talbot Lago	T26C	Talbot	6	31		21	9	
r	10	H Louveau	Talbot Lago	T26C	Talbot	6	30	accident / injury	11	5	
r	12	G Abecassis	HWM	(51)	Alta	4	23	magneto	20	8	
r	6	Y Giraud-Cabantous	Talbot Lago	T26C	Talbot	6	14	ignition	15	6	
r	18	L Villoresi	Ferrari	375	Ferrari	V12	12	accident	3	1	
r	42	F González	Talbot Lago	T26C-GS	Talbot	6	10	oil pump	13	5	
r	52	P Hirt	Veritas	Meteor	Veritas	6	0	fuel pump	16	7	

Winning speed 143.444 km/h, 89.132 mph
Pole Position speed 168.108 km/h, 104.457 mph (J M Fangio, 2 min:35.900 sec)
Fastest Lap speed 153.174 km/h, 95.178 mph (J M Fangio, 2 min:51.100 sec on lap 33)
Lap Leaders J M Fangio 1-23,29-42 (37); G Farina 24-28 (5).

30 May 1951 INDIANAPOLIS: 500 (Round 2) (Race 9)

200 laps x 4.023 km, 2.500 miles = 804.672 km, 500.000 miles

Pos	No	Driver	Car	Model	Engine		Laps	Time/Reason for Retirement	Grid Pos	Row
1	99	L Wallard	Kurtis Kraft		Offenhauser	4	200	3h 57m 38.050s	2	1
2	83	M Nazaruk	Kurtis Kraft		Offenhauser	4	200	3h 59m 25.293s	7	3
3=	9	J McGrath	Kurtis Kraft	3000	Offenhauser	4			3	1
3=	9	M Ayulo	Kurtis Kraft	3000	Offenhauser	4	200			
4	57	A Linden	Silnes-Sherman		Offenhauser	4	200		31	11
5	52	B Ball	Schroeder		Offenhauser	4	200		29	10
6	1	H Banks	Moore		Offenhauser	4	200		17	6
7	68	C Forberg	Kurtis Kraft	3000	Offenhauser	4	193		24	8
8	27	D Carter	Deidt		Offenhauser	4	180		4	2
9r	5	T Bettenhausen	Deidt		Offenhauser	4	178	spin	9	3
10r	18	D Nalon	Kurtis Kraft		Novi	8s	151	stalled	1	1
11r	69	G Force	Kurtis Kraft	2000	Offenhauser	4	142	oil pressure	22	8
12r	25	S Hanks	Kurtis Kraft	3000	Offenhauser	4	135	connecting rod / spin	12	4
13r	10	B Schindler	Kurtis Kraft	2000	Offenhauser	4	129	connecting rod	16	6
14r	16	M Rose	Deidt		Offenhauser	4	126	wheel / spin	5	2
15r	2	W Faulkner	Kuzma		Offenhauser	4	123	crankshaft	14	5
16r	76	J Davies	Silnes-Pawl		Offenhauser	4	110	rear end drive gears	27	9
17r	59	F Agabashian	Kurtis Kraft	3000	Offenhauser	4	109	clutch	11	4
18r	73	C Scarborough	Kurtis Kraft	2000	Offenhauser	4	100	front axle	15	5
19r	71	B Mackey	Stevens		Offenhauser	4	97	clutch shaft	33	11
20r	8	C Stevenson	Marchese		Offenhauser	4	93	fire	19	7
21r	3	J Parsons	Kurtis Kraft	3000	Offenhauser	4	87	magneto	8	3
22r	4	C Green	Kurtis Kraft	3000	Offenhauser	4	80	connecting rod	10	4
23r	98	T Ruttman	Kurtis Kraft	2000	Offenhauser	4	78	crankshaft	6	2
24r	6	D Dinsmore	Schroeder		Offenhauser	4	73	engine overheating	32	11
25r	32	C Miller	Kurtis Kraft		Novi	8s	56	ignition	28	10
26r	44	W Brown	Kurtis Kraft	3000	Offenhauser	4	55	magneto	13	5
27r	48	R Ward	Bromme		Offenhauser	4	34	oil line	25	9
28r	23	C Griffith	Kurtis Kraft	2000	Offenhauser	4	30	rear axle	18	6
29r	81	B Vukovich	Trevis		Offenhauser	4	29	oil tank	20	7
30r	22	G Connor	Lesovsky		Offenhauser	4	29	universal joint	21	7
31r	19	M Hellings	Deidt		Offenhauser	4	18	piston	23	8
32r	12	J McDowell	Maserati	8CTF	Offenhauser	4s	15	fuel tank	26	9
33r	26	J James	Watson		Offenhauser	4	8	driveshaft	30	10

Winning speed 203.171 km/h, 126.244 mph
Pole Position speed 219.672 km/h, 136.498 mph (D Nalon, 1 min: 5.935 sec)
Fastest Lap speed 215.345 km/h, 133.809 mph (L Wallard, 1 min: 7.260 sec on lap 23)
Fastest qualifier W Faulkner (220.274 km/h, 136.872 mph).

17 Jun 1951 BELGIUM: Spa-Francorchamps (Round 3) (Race 10)

36 laps x 14.120 km, 8.774 miles = 508.320 km, 315.855 miles

Pos	No	Driver	Car	Model	Engine		Laps	Time/Reason for Retirement	Grid Pos	Row
1	4	G Farina	Alfa Romeo	159	Alfa Romeo	8s	36	2h 45m 46.200s	2	1
2	8	A Ascari	Ferrari	375	Ferrari	V12	36	2h 48m 37.200s	4	2
3	10	L Villoresi	Ferrari	375	Ferrari	V12	36	2h 50m 08.100s	3	1
4	14	L Rosier	Talbot Lago	T26C-DA	Talbot	6	34		7	3
5	22	Y Giraud-Cabantous	Talbot Lago	T26C	Talbot	6	34		8	3
6	24	A Pilette	Talbot Lago	T26C	Talbot	6	33		12	5
7	16	J Claes	Talbot Lago	T26C-DA	Talbot	6	33		11	5
8	26	P Levegh	Talbot Lago	T26C	Talbot	6	32		13	5
9	2	J M Fangio	Alfa Romeo	159	Alfa Romeo	8s	32		1	1
r	18	L Chiron	Talbot Lago	T26C	Talbot	6	28	piston	9	4
r	6	C Sanesi	Alfa Romeo	159	Alfa Romeo	8s	11	radiator	6	3
r	12	P Taruffi	Ferrari	375	Ferrari	V12	8	rear axle	5	2
r	20	P Étançelin	Talbot Lago	T26C-DA	Talbot	6	0	transmission	10	4

Winning speed 183.985 km/h, 114.323 mph
Pole Position speed 191.819 km/h, 119.191 mph (J M Fangio, 4 min:25.000 sec)
Fastest Lap speed 193.941 km/h, 120.510 mph (J M Fangio, 4 min:22.100 sec on lap 10)
Lap Leaders L Villoresi 1-2 (2); G Farina 3-14,16-36 (33); J M Fangio 15 (1).

1 Jul 1951   FRANCE: Reims-Gueux   (Round 4)   (Race 11)

77 laps x 7.816 km, 4.857 miles = 601.832 km, 373.961 miles

Pos	No	Driver	Car	Model	Engine		Laps	Time/Reason for Retirement	Grid Pos	Row
1=	8	L Fagioli	Alfa Romeo	159	Alfa Romeo	8s			7	3
1=	8	J M Fangio	Alfa Romeo	159	Alfa Romeo	8s	77	3h 22m 11.000s		
2=	14	F González	Ferrari	375	Ferrari	V12			6	3
2=	14	A Ascari	Ferrari	375	Ferrari	V12	77	3h 23m 09.200s		
3	10	L Villoresi	Ferrari	375	Ferrari	V12	74		4	2
4	26	R Parnell	Thin Wall Ferrari	375 tw	Ferrari	V12	73		9	4
5	2	G Farina	Alfa Romeo	159	Alfa Romeo	8s	73		2	1
6	42	L Chiron	Talbot Lago	T26C	Talbot	6	71		8	3
7	46	Y Giraud-Cabantous	Talbot Lago	T26C	Talbot	6	71		11	5
8	44	E Chaboud	Talbot Lago	T26C-GS	Talbot	6	69		14	6
9	48	G Mairesse	Talbot Lago	T26C	Talbot	6	66		19	8
10	6	C Sanesi	Alfa Romeo	159	Alfa Romeo	8s	58		5	2
11=	4	J M Fangio	Alfa Romeo	159	Alfa Romeo	8s			1	1
11=	4	L Fagioli	Alfa Romeo	159	Alfa Romeo	8s	55			
r	28	J Claes	Talbot Lago	T26C-DA	Talbot	6	54	accident (hit a house)	12	5
r	40	L Rosier	Talbot Lago	T26C-DA	Talbot	6	43	rear axle	13	5
r	38	P Étançelin	Talbot Lago	T26C-DA	Talbot	6	37	inlet manifold	10	4
r	36	A Gordini	Simca Gordini	T11	Gordini	4s	27	valve gear	17	7
r	20	H Schell	Maserati	4CLT/48	Maserati	4s	24	steering	22	9
r	32	M Trintignant	Simca Gordini	T15	Gordini	4s	11	valves	18	7
r	12	A Ascari	Ferrari	375	Ferrari	V12	10	gearbox	3	1
r	34	A Simon	Simca Gordini	T15	Gordini	4s	7	engine	21	9
r	30	R Manzon	Simca Gordini	T15	Gordini	4s	3	engine	23	9
r	50	O Marimón	Maserati Milano	4CLT/50	Maserati Milano	4s	2	piston	15	6
r	18	E de Graffenried	Maserati	4CLT/48	Maserati	4s	1	transmission	16	7
r	24	P Whitehead	Ferrari	125	Ferrari	V12s	1	gasket	20	8
ns	26	B Shawe-Taylor	Thin Wall Ferrari	375 tw	Ferrari	V12		car raced by Parnell		

Winning speed 178.600 km/h, 110.977 mph
Pole Position speed 193.120 km/h, 119.999 mph (J M Fangio, 2 min:25.700 sec)
Fastest Lap speed 190.376 km/h, 118.294 mph (J M Fangio, 2 min:27.800 sec on lap 32)
Lap Leaders A Ascari 1-8,45-50 (14); J M Fangio 9,51-77 (28); G Farina 10-44 (35).

Also the Grand Prix of Europe.

14 Jul 1951   BRITAIN: Silverstone   (Round 5)   (Race 12)

90 laps x 4.649 km, 2.889 miles = 418.446 km, 260.010 miles

Pos	No	Driver	Car	Model	Engine		Laps	Time/Reason for Retirement	Grid Pos	Row
1	12	F González	Ferrari	375	Ferrari	V12	90	2h 42m 18.200s	1	1
2	2	J M Fangio	Alfa Romeo	159	Alfa Romeo	8s	90	2h 43m 09.200s	2	1
3	10	L Villoresi	Ferrari	375	Ferrari	V12	88		5	2
4	4	F Bonetto	Alfa Romeo	159	Alfa Romeo	8s	87		7	2
5	6	R Parnell	BRM	P15	BRM	V16s	85		20	6
6	3	C Sanesi	Alfa Romeo	159	Alfa Romeo	8s	84		6	2
7	7	P Walker	BRM	P15	BRM	V16s	84		19	6
8	9	B Shawe-Taylor	ERA	B	ERA	6s	84		12	4
9	14	P Whitehead	Thin Wall Ferrari	375 tw	Ferrari	V12	83		8	3
10	22	L Rosier	Talbot Lago	T26C-DA	Talbot	6	83		9	3
11	8	B Gerard	ERA	B/C	ERA	6s	82		10	3
12	18	D Hamilton	Talbot Lago	T26C	Talbot	6	81		11	3
13	25	J Claes	Talbot Lago	T26C-DA	Talbot	6	80		14	4
nc	5	J Kelly	Alta	GP	Alta	4s	75		18	5
r	1	G Farina	Alfa Romeo	159	Alfa Romeo	8s	75	clutch / fire	3	1
r	11	A Ascari	Ferrari	375	Ferrari	V12	56	gearbox	4	1
r	17	P Fotheringham-Parker	Maserati	4CL	Maserati	4s	46	oil pipe	16	5
r	15	D Murray	Maserati	4CLT/48	Maserati	4s	45	valve spring	15	5
r	23	L Chiron	Talbot Lago	T26C	Talbot	6	41	brakes	13	4
r	16	J James	Maserati	4CLT/48	Maserati	4s	23	radiator	17	5

Winning speed 154.690 km/h, 96.120 mph
Pole Position speed 161.874 km/h, 100.584 mph (F González, 1 min:43.400 sec)
Fastest Lap speed 160.941 km/h, 100.004 mph (G Farina, 1 min:44.000 sec on lap 38)
Lap Leaders F Bonetto 1 (1); F González 2-9,39-47,49-90 (59); J M Fangio 10-38,48 (30).

29 Jul 1951   GERMANY: Nürburgring   (Round 6)   (Race 13)

20 laps x 22.810 km, 14.173 miles = 456.200 km, 283.470 miles

Pos	No	Driver	Car	Model	Engine		Laps	Time/Reason for Retirement	Grid Pos	Row
1	71	A Ascari	Ferrari	375	Ferrari	V12	20	3h 23m 03.300s	1	1
2	75	J M Fangio	Alfa Romeo	159	Alfa Romeo	8s	20	3h 23m 33.800s	3	1
3	74	F González	Ferrari	375	Ferrari	V12	20	3h 27m 42.300s	2	1
4	72	L Villoresi	Ferrari	375	Ferrari	V12	20	3h 28m 53.500s	5	2
5	73	P Taruffi	Ferrari	375	Ferrari	V12	20	3h 30m 52.400s	6	2
6	91	R Fischer	Ferrari	212	Ferrari	V12	19		8	3
7	82	R Manzon	Simca Gordini	T15	Gordini	4s	19		9	3
8	84	L Rosier	Talbot Lago	T26C-DA	Talbot	6	19		15	5
9	90	P Levegh	Talbot Lago	T26C	Talbot	6	18		19	6
10	93	J Swaters	Talbot Lago	T26C	Talbot	6	18		22	7
11	94	J Claes	Talbot Lago	T26C-DA	Talbot	6	17		18	5
r	87	Y Giraud-Cabantous	Talbot Lago	T26C	Talbot	6	17	accident	11	3
r	81	M Trintignant	Simca Gordini	T15	Gordini	4s	13	engine	14	4
r	77	F Bonetto	Alfa Romeo	159	Alfa Romeo	8s	12	magneto	10	3
r	88	D Hamilton	Talbot Lago	T26C	Talbot	6	12	oil pressure	20	6
r	83	A Simon	Simca Gordini	T15	Gordini	4s	11	engine	12	4
r	78	P Pietsch	Alfa Romeo	159	Alfa Romeo	8s	11	accident	7	2
r	76	G Farina	Alfa Romeo	159	Alfa Romeo	8s	8	gearbox	4	1
r	86	P Étançelin	Talbot Lago	T26C-DA	Talbot	6	4	gearbox	21	6
r	92	T Branca	Maserati	4CLT/48	Maserati	4s	3	engine	17	5
r	85	L Chiron	Talbot Lago	T26C	Talbot	6	3	ignition	13	4
r	79	E de Graffenried	Maserati	4CLT/48	Maserati	4s	2	engine	16	5
ns	89	D Murray	Maserati	4CLT/48	Maserati	4s		accident		

Winning speed 134.801 km/h, 83.761 mph
Pole Position speed 137.825 km/h, 85.640 mph (A Ascari, 9 min:55.800 sec)
Fastest Lap speed 137.825 km/h, 85.640 mph (J M Fangio, 9 min:55.800 sec on lap 12)
Lap Leaders J M Fangio 1-4,11-14 (8); A Ascari 5-9,15-20 (11); F González 10 (1).

16 Sep 1951   ITALY: Monza   (Round 7)   (Race 14)

80 laps x 6.300 km, 3.915 miles = 504.000 km, 313.171 miles

Pos	No	Driver	Car	Model	Engine		Laps	Time/Reason for Retirement	Grid Pos	Row
1	2	A Ascari	Ferrari	375	Ferrari	V12	80	2h 42m 39.300s	3	1
2	6	F González	Ferrari	375	Ferrari	V12	80	2h 43m 23.900s	4	1
3=	40	F Bonetto	Alfa Romeo	159	Alfa Romeo	8s			7	2
3=	40	G Farina	Alfa Romeo	159	Alfa Romeo	8s	79			
4	4	L Villoresi	Ferrari	375	Ferrari	V12	79		5	2
5	8	P Taruffi	Ferrari	375	Ferrari	V12	78		6	2
6	48	A Simon	Simca Gordini	T15	Gordini	4s	74		11	3
7	18	L Rosier	Talbot Lago	T26C-DA	Talbot	6	73		15	4
8	24	Y Giraud-Cabantous	Talbot Lago	T26C	Talbot	6	72		14	4
9	44	F Rol	OSCA	4500G	OSCA	V12	67		18	5
r	38	J M Fangio	Alfa Romeo	159	Alfa Romeo	8s	39	piston	1	1
r	46	R Manzon	Simca Gordini	T15	Gordini	4s	29	engine	13	4
r	50	M Trintignant	Simca Gordini	T15	Gordini	4s	29	piston	12	3
r	20	L Chiron	Talbot Lago	T26C	Talbot	6	23	ignition	17	5
r	22	P Levegh	Talbot Lago	T26C	Talbot	6	9	engine	20	5
r	28	J Swaters	Talbot Lago	T26C	Talbot	6	7	engine overheating	22	6
r	34	G Farina	Alfa Romeo	159	Alfa Romeo	8s	6	lubrication	2	1
r	26	J Claes	Talbot Lago	T26C-DA	Talbot	6	4	oil scavenge pump	21	6
r	36	E de Graffenried	Alfa Romeo	159	Alfa Romeo	8s	1	supercharger	9	3
r	16	P Whitehead	Ferrari	125	Ferrari	V12s	1	magneto	19	5
r	12	C Landi	Ferrari	375	Ferrari	V12	0	transmission	16	4
ns	30	R Parnell	BRM	P15	BRM	V16s		engine / gearbox	8	2
ns	32	K Richardson	BRM	P15	BRM	V16s		incorrect licence	10	3
ns	32	H Stuck	BRM	P15	BRM	V16s		engine / gearbox		
ns	14	R Fischer	Ferrari	212	Ferrari	V12		accident		

Winning speed 185.915 km/h, 115.522 mph
Pole Position speed 200.353 km/h, 124.494 mph (J M Fangio, 1 min:53.200 sec)
Fastest Lap speed 194.678 km/h, 120.967 mph (G Farina, 1 min:56.500 sec on lap 64)
Lap Leaders J M Fangio 1-3,8-13 (9); A Ascari 4-7,14-80 (71).

28 Oct 1951   **SPAIN: Pedralbes**   **(Round 8)**   **(Race 15)**

70 laps x 6.316 km, 3.925 miles = 442.120 km, 274.721 miles

Pos	No	Driver	Car	Model	Engine		Laps	Time/Reason for Retirement	Grid Pos	Row
1	22	J M Fangio	Alfa Romeo	159	Alfa Romeo	8s	70	2h 46m 54.100s	2	1
2	6	F González	Ferrari	375	Ferrari	V12	70	2h 47m 48.380s	3	1
3	20	G Farina	Alfa Romeo	159	Alfa Romeo	8s	70	2h 48m 39.640s	4	1
4	2	A Ascari	Ferrari	375	Ferrari	V12	68		1	1
5	24	F Bonetto	Alfa Romeo	159	Alfa Romeo	8s	68		8	3
6	26	E de Graffenried	Alfa Romeo	159	Alfa Romeo	8s	66		6	2
7	28	L Rosier	Talbot Lago	T26C-DA	Talbot	6	64		20	6
8	34	P Étançelin	Talbot Lago	T26C-DA	Talbot	6	63		13	4
9	14	R Manzon	Simca Gordini	T15	Gordini	4s	63		9	3
10	44	C Godia	Maserati	4CLT/48	Maserati	4s	60		17	5
r	16	A Simon	Simca Gordini	T15	Gordini	4s	48	engine	10	3
r	4	L Villoresi	Ferrari	375	Ferrari	V12	48	ignition	5	2
r	36	J Claes	Talbot Lago	T26C-DA	Talbot	6	37	accident	15	5
r	8	P Taruffi	Ferrari	375	Ferrari	V12	30	suspension / wheel lost	7	2
r	12	M Trintignant	Simca Gordini	T15	Gordini	4s	25	engine	11	3
r	38	G Grignard	Talbot Lago	T26C-DA	Talbot	6	23	engine	16	5
r	32	Y Giraud-Cabantous	Talbot Lago	T26C	Talbot	6	7	engine overheating	14	4
r	30	L Chiron	Talbot Lago	T26C	Talbot	6	4	ignition	12	4
r	18	B Bira	Maserati	4CLT/48	OSCA	V12	1	engine	19	6
ns	46	J Jover	Maserati	4CLT/48	Maserati	4s		engine	18	5

Winning speed 158.939 km/h, 98.760 mph
Pole Position speed 174.114 km/h, 108.190 mph (A Ascari, 2 min:10.590 sec)
Fastest Lap speed 166.053 km/h, 103.180 mph (J M Fangio, 2 min:16.930 sec on lap 3)
Lap Leaders A Ascari 1-3 (3); J M Fangio 4-70 (67).

Revised fastest lap time as issued by race organisers.

Lap Leaders 1951

Pos	Driver	Car-Engine	GPs	laps	km	miles
1	J M Fangio	Alfa Romeo	7	180	1,304.2	810.4
2	A Ascari	Ferrari	4	99	826.6	513.6
3	G Farina	Alfa Romeo	3	73	775.9	482.1
4	F González	Ferrari	2	60	297.1	184.6
5	L Villoresi	Ferrari	1	2	28.2	17.5
6	F Bonetto	Alfa Romeo	1	1	4.6	2.9
			7	**415**	**3,236.6**	**2,011.2**

Driver Points 1951

		CH	INDY	B	F	GB	D	I	E	Total	
1	J M Fangio	9	-	(1)	(5)	6	7	-	9	31	(6)
2	A Ascari	-	-	6	3	-	8	8	(3)	25	(3)
3	F González	-	-	-	(3)	8	4	6	6	24	(3)
4	G Farina	4	-	8	(2)	(1)	-	3	4	19	(3)
5	L Villoresi	-	-	4	4	4	3	(3)	-	15	(3)
6	P Taruffi	6	-	-	-	-	2	2	-	10	
7	L Wallard	-	9	-	-	-	-	-	-	9	
8	F Bonetto	-	-	-	-	3	-	2	2	7	
9	M Nazaruk	-	6	-	-	-	-	-	-	6	
10	R Parnell	-	-	-	3	2	-	-	-	5	
11	L Fagioli	-	-	-	4	-	-	-	-	4	
12	C Sanesi	3	-	-	-	-	-	-	-	3	
	A Linden	-	3	-	-	-	-	-	-	3	
	L Rosier	-	-	3	-	-	-	-	-	3	
15	E de Graffenried	2	-	-	-	-	-	-	-	2	
	M Ayulo	-	2	-	-	-	-	-	-	2	
	B Ball	-	2	-	-	-	-	-	-	2	
	J McGrath	-	2	-	-	-	-	-	-	2	
	Y Giraud-Cabantous	-	-	2	-	-	-	-	-	2	

8,6,4,3 and 2 points awarded to the first five finishers. The driver setting the fastest lap scored a point also. Points shared for shared drives. Best 4 scores.

1952

Race Entrants and Results

With Alfa's withdrawal and BRM's unreliability, race organisers had little option but to turn to the existing F2 category for closer racing. The FIA agreed to move the World Championship to this formula, which at the time consisted of 2-litre unblown and 750 cc supercharged. This would provide larger entries and prepare teams for the forthcoming 2.5-litre formula. Ferrari remained favourites, especially as their main opponent, Maserati, was weakened by the absence of Fangio, seriously injured at Monza in June.

FERRARI
Scuderia Ferrari: Ascari, Farina, Taruffi, Villoresi, Simon
Ecurie Espadon: R Fischer, Hirt, Schoeller, (Stuck)
Scuderia Marzotto: Carini, Comotti
Ecurie Francorchamps: de Tornaco, Laurent
Ecurie Rosier: Rosier, (Trintignant)
G Caprara: Salvadori
Privateer: P Whitehead

MASERATI
Officine Alfieri Maserati: Bonetto, Rol, González
Enrico Platé: de Graffenried, Schell, (Crespo)
Escuderia Bandeirantes: Bianco, Cantoni, Landi, Etançelin, Flinterman

OSCA
Privateer: Bayol

CISITALIA
Privateer: (Dusio)

GORDINI
Equipe Gordini: Manzon, Behra, Trintignant, Bira, Claes (B)
Ecurie Belge: Claes, Frère
Alfred Dattner: de Terra
Privateer: O'Brien

ERA
ERA Ltd: Moss

ALTA
Privateers: G Whitehead, P Whitehead

COOPER
Ecurie Richmond: Brandon, Brown
L D Hawthorn: Hawthorn
A H M Bryde: Hawthorn (F), Parnell
Scuderia Franera: Wharton
Ecurie Ecosse: Murray

HWM
HW Motors: Collins, Macklin, Frère, Hamilton, Laurent, Abecassis, Moss, Giraud-Cabantous, Claes, van der Lof
Privateer: Gaze

FRASER NASH
Scuderia Franera: Wharton
Privateer: Crook

ASTON
W S Aston: Aston, Montgomerie-Charrington

CONNAUGHT
Connaught Engineering: McAlpine, Poore, Thompson, Downing, Moss
Privateer: Downing (NL)

VERITAS
Motor-Presse-Verlag: Pietsch
Privateers: Ulmen, Riess, Helfrich, Brudes, Klenk, Peters, Legat

AFM
AFM: Stuck
Privateers: Heeks, Niedermayr, (L Fischer, Krakau)

BMW
Privateers: Balsa, Nacke, Klodwig, Krause, (Merkel)

18 May 1952		SWITZERLAND: Bremgarten						(Round 1)		(Race 16)	
		62 laps x 7.280 km, 4.524 miles = 451.360 km, 280.462 miles									
Pos	**No**	**Driver**	**Car**	**Model**	**Engine**		**Laps**	**Time/Reason for Retirement**	**Grid Pos**	**Row**
1	30	P Taruffi	Ferrari	500	Ferrari	4	62	3h 01m 46.100s	2	1
2	42	R Fischer	Ferrari	500	Ferrari	4	62	3h 04m 23.300s	5	2
3	6	J Behra	Gordini	T16	Gordini	6	61		7	3
4	22	K Wharton	Frazer Nash	FN48	Bristol	6	60		13	5
5	26	A Brown	Cooper	T20	Bristol	6	59		15	6
6	38	E de Graffenried	Maserati Platé	4CLT	Maserati Platé	4	58		8	3
7	44	P Hirt	Ferrari	212	Ferrari	V12	56		19	8
8	24	E Brandon	Cooper	T20	Bristol	6	55		17	7
r	10	B Bira	Simca Gordini	T15	Gordini	4	52	engine	11	5
r=	32	A Simon	Ferrari	500	Ferrari	4			4	2
r=	32	G Farina	Ferrari	500	Ferrari	4	51	magneto		
r	40	H Schell	Maserati Platé	4CLT	Maserati Platé	4	31	engine	18	7
r	46	S Moss	HWM	(52)	Alta	4	24	withdrawn by team	9	4
r	20	L Macklin	HWM	(52)	Alta	4	24	withdrawn by team	12	5
r	8	R Manzon	Gordini	T16	Gordini	6	20	radiator	3	1
r	28	G Farina	Ferrari	500	Ferrari	4	16	magneto	1	1
r	18	P Collins	HWM	(52)	Alta	4	12	driveshaft / accident	6	3
r	16	G Abecassis	HWM	(52)	Alta	4	12	driveshaft / accident	10	4
r	4	T Ulmen	Veritas	Meteor	Veritas	6	4	fuel tank	16	7
r	2	H Stuck	AFM		Küchen	V8	4	piston	14	6
r	12	L Rosier	Ferrari	500	Ferrari	4	2	accident	20	8
r	50	M de Terra	Simca Gordini	T11	Gordini	4	1	engine	21	9
ns	14	M Trintignant	Ferrari	166	Ferrari	V12		engine		

Winning speed 148.990 km/h, 92.578 mph
Pole Position speed 156.466 km/h, 97.223 mph (G Farina, 2 min:47.500 sec)
Fastest Lap speed 154.985 km/h, 96.303 mph (P Taruffi, 2 min:49.100 sec on lap 46)
Lap Leaders G Farina 1-16 (16); P Taruffi 17-62 (46).

30 May 1952   **INDIANAPOLIS: 500**   (Round 2)   (Race 17)

200 laps x 4.023 km, 2.500 miles = 804.672 km, 500.000 miles

Pos	No	Driver	Car	Model	Engine		Laps	Time/Reason for Retirement	Grid Pos	Row
1	98	T Ruttman	Kuzma		Offenhauser	4	200	3h 52m 41.880s	7	3
2	59	J Rathmann	Kurtis Kraft	3000	Offenhauser	4	200	3h 56m 44.209s	10	4
3	18	S Hanks	Kurtis Kraft	3000	Offenhauser	4	200		5	2
4	1	D Carter	Lesovsky		Offenhauser	4	200		6	2
5	33	A Cross	Kurtis Kraft	4000	Offenhauser	4	200		20	7
6	77	J Bryan	Kurtis Kraft	3000	Offenhauser	4	200		21	7
7	37	J Reece	Kurtis Kraft	4000	Offenhauser	4	200		23	8
8	54	G Connor	Kurtis Kraft	3000	Offenhauser	4	200		14	5
9	22	C Griffith	Kurtis Kraft	2000	Offenhauser	4	200		9	3
10	5	J Parsons	Kurtis Kraft		Offenhauser	4	200		31	11
11	4	J McGrath	Kurtis Kraft	3000	Offenhauser	4	200		3	1
12	29	J Rigsby	Watson		Offenhauser	4	200		26	9
13	14	J James	Kurtis Kraft	4000	Offenhauser	4	200		16	6
14	7	B Schindler	Stevens		Offenhauser	4	200		15	5
15	65	G Fonder	Silnes-Sherman		Offenhauser	4	197		13	5
16	81	E Johnson	Trevis		Offenhauser	4	193		24	8
17r	26	B Vukovich	Kurtis Kraft	500A	Offenhauser	4	191	steering / accident	8	3
18	16	C Stevenson	Kurtis Kraft	4000	Offenhauser	4	187		11	4
19	2	H Banks	Lesovsky		Offenhauser	4	184		12	4
20	8	M Ayulo	Lesovsky		Offenhauser	4	184		28	10
21	31	J McDowell	Kurtis Kraft		Offenhauser	4	182		33	11
22r	48	S Webb	Bromme		Offenhauser	4	162	oil leak	29	10
23r	34	R Ward	Kurtis Kraft	4000	Offenhauser	4	130	oil pressure	22	8
24r	27	T Bettenhausen	Deidt		Offenhauser	4	93	starter	30	10
25r	36	D Nalon	Kurtis Kraft		Novi	8s	84	supercharger shaft	4	2
26r	73	B Sweikert	Kurtis Kraft	2000	Offenhauser	4	77	differential	32	11
27r	28	F Agabashian	Kurtis Kraft		Cummins	6s	71	supercharger	1	1
28r	67	G Hartley	Kurtis Kraft	4000	Offenhauser	4	65	exhaust pipe	18	6
29r	93	B Scott	Kurtis Kraft	2000	Offenhauser	4	49	driveshaft	25	9
30r	21	C Miller	Kurtis Kraft		Novi	8s	41	supercharger shaft	27	9
31r	12	A Ascari	Ferrari	375	Ferrari	V12	40	hub flange / spin	19	7
32r	55	B Ball	Stevens		Offenhauser	4	34	gear case	17	6
33r	9	A Linden	Kurtis Kraft	4000	Offenhauser	4s	20	oil leak	2	1

Winning speed 207.481 km/h, 128.922 mph
Pole Position speed 222.108 km/h, 138.011 mph (F Agabashian, 1 min: 5.212 sec)
Fastest Lap speed 217.479 km/h, 135.135 mph (B Vukovich, 1 min: 6.600 sec on lap 8)
Fastest qualifier C Miller (223.754 km/h, 139.034 mph).

---

22 Jun 1952   **BELGIUM: Spa-Francorchamps**   (Round 3)   (Race 18)

36 laps x 14.120 km, 8.774 miles = 508.320 km, 315.855 miles

Pos	No	Driver	Car	Model	Engine		Laps	Time/Reason for Retirement	Grid Pos	Row
1	4	A Ascari	Ferrari	500	Ferrari	4	36	3h 03m 46.300s	1	1
2	2	G Farina	Ferrari	500	Ferrari	4	36	3h 05m 41.500s	2	1
3	14	R Manzon	Gordini	T16	Gordini	6	36	3h 08m 14.700s	4	2
4	8	M Hawthorn	Cooper	T20	Bristol	6	35		6	3
5	28	P Frère	HWM	(52)	Alta	4	34		8	3
6	10	A Brown	Cooper	T20	Bristol	6	34		9	4
7	34	C de Tornaco	Ferrari	500	Ferrari	4	33		13	5
8	18	J Claes	Gordini	T16S	Gordini	6	33		19	8
9	12	E Brandon	Cooper	T20	Bristol	6	33		12	5
10	20	B Bira	Simca Gordini	T15	Gordini	4	32		18	7
11	24	L Macklin	HWM	(52)	Alta	4	32		14	6
12	30	R Laurent	HWM	(52)	Alta	4	32		20	8
13	38	A Legat	Veritas	Meteor	Veritas	6	31		21	9
14	44	R O'Brien	Simca Gordini	T15	Gordini	4	30		22	9
15	42	T Gaze	HWM	(51)	Alta	4	30		16	7
r	40	R Montgomerie-Charrington	Aston	NB	Butterworth	F4	17	misfire	15	6
r	16	J Behra	Gordini	T16	Gordini	6	13	accident	5	2
r	6	P Taruffi	Ferrari	500	Ferrari	4	13	accident	3	1
r	36	K Wharton	Frazer Nash	FN48	Bristol	6	10	accident	7	3
r	22	L Rosier	Ferrari	500	Ferrari	4	6	transmission	17	7
r	26	P Collins	HWM	(52)	Alta	4	3	driveshaft	11	5
r	32	S Moss	ERA	G	Bristol	6	0	gudgeon pin / accident	10	4

Winning speed 165.962 km/h, 103.124 mph
Pole Position speed 183.509 km/h, 114.027 mph (A Ascari, 4 min:37.000 sec)
Fastest Lap speed 172.312 km/h, 107.070 mph (A Ascari, 4 min:55.000 sec on lap 2 & 7)
Lap Leaders J Behra 1 (1); A Ascari 2-36 (35).

Also the Grand Prix of Europe.

Races

6 Jul 1952   FRANCE: Rouen-les-Essarts   (Round 4)   (Race 19)
76 laps x 5.100 km, 3.169 miles = 387.600 km, 240.843 miles

Pos	No	Driver	Car	Model	Engine		Laps	Time/Reason for Retirement	Grid Pos	Row
1	8	A Ascari	Ferrari	500	Ferrari	4	76	3h 00m 20.267s	1	1
2	10	G Farina	Ferrari	500	Ferrari	4	76	3h 01m 04.700s	2	1
3	12	P Taruffi	Ferrari	500	Ferrari	4	75		3	1
4	2	R Manzon	Gordini	T16	Gordini	6	74		5	2
5	44	M Trintignant	Simca Gordini	T15	Gordini	4	72		6	3
6	22	P Collins	HWM	(52)	Alta	4	70		8	3
7	4	J Behra	Gordini	T16	Gordini	6	70		4	2
8	28	P Étançelin	Maserati	A6GCM	Maserati	6	70		18	7
9	20	L Macklin	HWM	(52)	Alta	4	70		14	6
10	24	Y Giraud-Cabantous	HWM	(52)	Alta	4	68		10	4
11=	36	R Fischer	Ferrari	212	Ferrari	V12			17	7
11=	36	P Hirt	Ferrari	212	Ferrari	V12	66			
12	38	F Comotti	Ferrari	166	Ferrari	V12			16	7
r	6	B Bira	Gordini	T16	Gordini	6	56	rear axle	7	3
r	42	M Hawthorn	Cooper	T20	Bristol	6	51	ignition	15	6
r=	16	E de Graffenried	Maserati Platé	4CLT	Maserati Platé	4			12	5
r=	16	H Schell	Maserati Platé	4CLT	Maserati Platé	4	34	brakes		
r	26	P Whitehead	Alta	F2	Alta	4	26	clutch	13	5
r	14	L Rosier	Ferrari	500	Ferrari	4	17	engine	9	4
r	32	J Claes	Simca Gordini	T15	Gordini	4	15	connecting rod	20	8
r	18	H Schell	Maserati Platé	4CLT	Maserati Platé	4	7	gearbox	11	5
r	40	P Carini	Ferrari	166	Ferrari	V12	2	cylinder head gasket	19	8

Winning speed 128.958 km/h, 80.131 mph
Pole Position speed 136.202 km/h, 84.632 mph (A Ascari, 2 min:14.800 sec)
Fastest Lap speed 133.722 km/h, 83.091 mph (A Ascari, 2 min:17.300 sec on lap 28)
Lap Leaders A Ascari 1-76 (76).

Race stopped after 3 hours had elapsed. Cars on rows 3, 5 and 7 did not line up exactly according to their practice times, those affected being: B Bira (qualified 8), P Collins (7), H Schell (12), E de Graffenried (11), F Comotti (18), P Étançelin (16). R Fischer used car 34 during qualifying.

19 Jul 1952   BRITAIN: Silverstone   (Round 5)   (Race 20)
85 laps x 4.711 km, 2.927 miles = 400.397 km, 248.795 miles

Pos	No	Driver	Car	Model	Engine		Laps	Time/Reason for Retirement	Grid Pos	Row
1	15	A Ascari	Ferrari	500	Ferrari	4	85	2h 44m 11.000s	2	1
2	17	P Taruffi	Ferrari	500	Ferrari	4	84		3	1
3	9	M Hawthorn	Cooper	T20	Bristol	6	83		7	2
4	6	D Poore	Connaught	A	Lea Francis	4	83		8	3
5	5	E Thompson	Connaught	A	Lea Francis	4	82		9	3
6	16	G Farina	Ferrari	500	Ferrari	4	82		1	1
7	8	R Parnell	Cooper	T20	Bristol	6	82		6	2
8	14	R Salvadori	Ferrari	500	Ferrari	4	82		19	6
9	4	K Downing	Connaught	A	Lea Francis	4	82		5	2
10	21	P Whitehead	Ferrari	125	Ferrari	V12	81		20	6
11	26	B Bira	Gordini	T16	Gordini	6	81		10	3
12	1	G Whitehead	Alta	F2	Alta	4	80		12	4
13	19	R Fischer	Ferrari	500	Ferrari	4	80		15	5
14	27	J Claes	Simca Gordini	T15	Gordini	4	79		23	7
15	31	L Macklin	HWM	(52)	Alta	4	79		29	9
16	3	K McAlpine	Connaught	A	Lea Francis	4	79		17	5
17	33	H Schell	Maserati Platé	4CLT	Maserati Platé	4	78		32	9
18	34	G Bianco	Maserati	A6GCM	Maserati	6	77		28	8
19	32	E de Graffenried	Maserati Platé	4CLT	Maserati Platé	4	76		31	9
20	10	E Brandon	Cooper	T20	Bristol	6	76		18	5
21	23	T Crook	Frazer Nash	421	Bristol	6	75		25	7
r	29	P Collins	HWM	(52)	Alta	4	73	misfire	14	4
22	11	A Brown	Cooper	T20	Bristol	6	69		13	4
r	30	D Hamilton	HWM	(52)	Alta	4	44	engine	11	3
r	12	S Moss	ERA	G	Bristol	6	36	cylinder head	16	5
r	25	M Trintignant	Gordini	T16	Gordini	6	22	gearbox	21	6
r	28	T Gaze	HWM	(52)	Alta	4	20	cylinder head gasket	26	8
r	7	D Murray	Cooper	T20	Bristol	6	14	spark plugs	22	7
r	24	R Manzon	Gordini	T16	Gordini	6	9	clutch	4	1
r	20	P Hirt	Ferrari	212	Ferrari	V12	3	brakes	24	7
r	35	E Cantoni	Maserati	A6GCM	Maserati	6	1	brakes	27	8
ns	2	B Aston	Aston	NB	Butterworth	F4		withdrew	30	9

Winning speed 146.323 km/h, 90.921 mph
Pole Position speed 154.163 km/h, 95.793 mph (G Farina, 1 min:50.000 sec)
Fastest Lap speed 151.411 km/h, 94.082 mph (A Ascari, 1 min:52.000 sec on lap 9)
Lap Leaders A Ascari 1-85 (85).

3 Aug 1952 **GERMANY: Nürburgring** **(Round 6)** **(Race 21)**

18 laps x 22.810 km, 14.173 miles = 410.580 km, 255.123 miles

Pos	No	Driver	Car	Model	Engine		Laps	Time/Reason for Retirement	Grid Pos	Row
1	101	A Ascari	Ferrari	500	Ferrari	4	18	3h 06m 13.300s	1	1
2	102	G Farina	Ferrari	500	Ferrari	4	18	3h 06m 27.400s	2	1
3	117	R Fischer	Ferrari	500	Ferrari	4	18	3h 13m 23.400s	6	2
4	103	P Taruffi	Ferrari	500	Ferrari	4	17		5	2
5	108	J Behra	Gordini	T16	Gordini	6	17		11	3
6	119	R Laurent	Ferrari	500	Ferrari	4	16		17	5
7	121	F Riess	Veritas	RS	Veritas	6	16		12	4
8	125	T Ulmen	Veritas	RS	Veritas	6	16		15	5
9	124	H Niedermayr	AFM		BMW	6	15		22	7
10	113	J Claes	HWM	(52)	Alta	4	15		32	9
11	128	H Klenk	Veritas	Meteor	Veritas	6	14		8	3
12	135	E Klodwig	BMW	Heck	BMW	6	14		29	9
r	107	R Manzon	Gordini	T16	Gordini	6	8	wheel lost	4	1
r	123	W Heeks	AFM		BMW	6	7	engine	9	3
r	120	T Gaze	HWM	(52)	Alta	4	6	gearbox	14	4
r	110	M Balsa	BMW	Speciale	BMW	6	5	engine	25	7
r	126	A Brudes	Veritas	Meteor	Veritas	6	5	engine	19	6
r	130	B Nacke	BMW	Eigenbau	BMW	6	5	spark plugs	30	9
r	116	E Cantoni	Maserati	A6GCM	Maserati	6	4	rear axle	26	8
r	136	R Krause	BMW	Greifzu	BMW	6	3	engine	23	7
r	118	R Schoeller	Ferrari	212	Ferrari	V12	3	suspension	24	7
r	114	B Aston	Aston	NB	Butterworth	F4	2	oil pressure	21	6
r	104	P Carini	Ferrari	166	Ferrari	V12	1	brakes	27	8
r	127	P Pietsch	Veritas	Meteor	Veritas	6	1	gearbox	7	2
r	122	T Helfrich	Veritas	RS	Veritas	6	1	engine	18	5
r	112	P Frère	HWM	(52)	Alta	4	1	de Dion tube	13	4
r	129	J Peters	Veritas	RS	Veritas	6	1	engine	20	6
dq	105	F Bonetto	Maserati	A6GCM	Maserati	6	1	push start after spin	10	3
r	109	M Trintignant	Gordini	T16	Gordini	6	1	gearbox / accident	3	1
r	115	G Bianco	Maserati	A6GCM	Maserati	6	0	engine	16	5
ns	133	W Krakau	AFM		BMW	6			28	8
ns	131	L Fischer	AFM		BMW	6			31	9
ns	134	H Merkel	BMW	Eigenbau	BMW	6				
ns	111	P Collins	HWM	(52)	Alta	4		crankshaft		

Winning speed 132.288 km/h, 82.200 mph
Pole Position speed 135.864 km/h, 84.422 mph (A Ascari, 10 min: 4.400 sec)
Fastest Lap speed 135.706 km/h, 84.324 mph (A Ascari, 10 min: 5.100 sec on lap 5)
Lap Leaders A Ascari 1-18 (18).

17 Aug 1952 **NETHERLANDS: Zandvoort** **(Round 7)** **(Race 22)**

90 laps x 4.193 km, 2.605 miles = 377.370 km, 234.487 miles

Pos	No	Driver	Car	Model	Engine		Laps	Time/Reason for Retirement	Grid Pos	Row
1	2	A Ascari	Ferrari	500	Ferrari	4	90	2h 53m 28.500s	1	1
2	4	G Farina	Ferrari	500	Ferrari	4	90	2h 54m 08.600s	2	1
3	6	L Villoresi	Ferrari	500	Ferrari	4	90	2h 55m 02.900s	4	2
4	32	M Hawthorn	Cooper	T20	Bristol	6	88		3	1
5	10	R Manzon	Gordini	T16	Gordini	6	87		8	3
6	12	M Trintignant	Gordini	T16	Gordini	6	87		5	2
7	28	D Hamilton	HWM	(52)	Alta	4	85		10	4
8	26	L Macklin	HWM	(52)	Alta	4	84		9	4
9=	16	C Landi	Maserati	A6GCM	Maserati	6			16	7
9=	16	J Flinterman	Maserati	A6GCM	Maserati	6	83			
r	34	K Wharton	Frazer Nash	421	Bristol	6	76	rear axle	7	3
r	36	S Moss	ERA	G	Bristol	6	73	connecting rod	18	7
nc	30	D van der Lof	HWM	(52)	Alta	4	70		14	6
r	22	K Downing	Connaught	A	Lea Francis	4	27	oil pressure	13	5
r	24	C de Tornaco	Ferrari	500	Ferrari	4	19	valve	17	7
r	14	P Frère	Simca Gordini	T15	Gordini	4	15	gearbox / clutch	11	5
r	8	J Behra	Gordini	T16	Gordini	6	10	carburettor / magneto	6	3
r	20	J Flinterman	Maserati	A6GCM	Maserati	6	7	differential	15	6
r	18	G Bianco	Maserati	A6GCM	Maserati	6	4	rear axle	12	5

Winning speed 130.521 km/h, 81.102 mph
Pole Position speed 141.735 km/h, 88.070 mph (A Ascari, 1 min:46.500 sec)
Fastest Lap speed 137.475 km/h, 85.423 mph (A Ascari, 1 min:49.800 sec on lap 89)
Lap Leaders A Ascari 1-90 (90).

Races

80 laps x 6.300 km, 3.915 miles = 504.000 km, 313.171 miles

Pos	No	Driver	Car	Model	Engine		Laps	Time/Reason for Retirement	Grid Pos	Row
1	12	A Ascari	Ferrari	500	Ferrari	4	80	2h 50m 45.600s	1	1
2	26	F González	Maserati	A6GCM	Maserati	6	80	2h 51m 47.400s	5	2
3	16	L Villoresi	Ferrari	500	Ferrari	4	80	2h 52m 49.800s	2	1
4	10	G Farina	Ferrari	500	Ferrari	4	80	2h 52m 57.000s	3	1
5	22	F Bonetto	Maserati	A6GCM	Maserati	6	79		13	4
6	8	A Simon	Ferrari	500	Ferrari	4	79		8	2
7	14	P Taruffi	Ferrari	500	Ferrari	4	77		6	2
8	48	C Landi	Maserati	A6GCM	Maserati	6	76		18	5
9	40	K Wharton	Cooper	T20	Bristol	6	76		15	4
10	62	L Rosier	Ferrari	500	Ferrari	4	75		17	5
11	50	E Cantoni	Maserati	A6GCM	Maserati	6	75		23	6
12	30	D Poore	Connaught	A	Lea Francis	4	74		19	5
13	36	E Brandon	Cooper	T20	Bristol	6	73		20	5
14	2	R Manzon	Gordini	T16	Gordini	6	71		7	2
15	38	A Brown	Cooper	T20	Bristol	6	68		21	6
r	32	S Moss	Connaught	A	Lea Francis	4	60	push rod	9	3
r	46	G Bianco	Maserati	A6GCM	Maserati	6	46	engine	24	6
r	6	J Behra	Gordini	T16	Gordini	6	42	valve	11	3
nc	42	M Hawthorn	Cooper	T20	Bristol	6	38		12	3
r	24	F Rol	Maserati	A6GCM	Maserati	6	24	engine	16	4
r	4	M Trintignant	Gordini	T16	Gordini	6	5	valve gear	4	1
r	28	K McAlpine	Connaught	A	Lea Francis	4	4	rear suspension	22	6
r	18	R Fischer	Ferrari	500	Ferrari	4	3	engine	14	4
r	34	É Bayol	OSCA	20	OSCA	6	0	gearbox	10	3
nq	70	C de Tornaco	Ferrari	500	Ferrari	4				
nq	58	A Crespo	Maserati Platé	4CLT	Maserati Platé	4				
nq	60	E de Graffenried	Maserati Platé	4CLT	Maserati Platé	4				
nq	54	P Collins	HWM	(52)	Alta	4				
nq	68	P Whitehead	Ferrari	125	Ferrari	V12				
nq	56	T Gaze	HWM	(52)	Alta	4				
nq	64	B Aston	Aston	NB	Butterworth	F4				
nq	52	L Macklin	HWM	(52)	Alta	4				
nq	20	H Stuck	Ferrari	212	Ferrari	V12				
nq	66	J Claes	Simca Gordini	T15	Gordini	4				
nq	44	P Dusio	Cisitalia	D46	BPM					

Winning speed 177.091 km/h, 110.039 mph
Pole Position speed 180.430 km/h, 112.114 mph (A Ascari, 2 min: 5.700 sec)
Fastest Lap speed 179.857 km/h, 111.758 mph (A Ascari / F González, 2 min: 6.100 sec on lap 56 / 57 & 60)
Lap Leaders F González 1-36 (36); A Ascari 37-80 (44).

Lap Leaders 1952

Pos	Driver	Car-Engine	GPs	laps	km	miles
1	A Ascari	Ferrari	6	348	2,347.4	1,458.6
2	P Taruffi	Ferrari	1	46	334.9	208.1
3	F González	Maserati	1	36	226.8	140.9
4	G Farina	Ferrari	1	16	116.5	72.4
5	J Behra	Gordini	1	1	14.1	8.8
			7	447	3,039.7	1,888.8

Driver Points 1952

		CH	INDY	B	F	GB	D	NL	I	Total	
1	A Ascari	-	-	9	9	9	9	(9)	(8.5)	36	(17.5)
2	G Farina	-	-	6	6	-	6	6	(3)	24	(3)
3	P Taruffi	9	-	-	4	6	3	-	-	22	
4	R Fischer	6	-	-	-	-	4	-	-	10	
	M Hawthorn	-	-	3	-	4	-	3	-	10	
6	R Manzon	-	-	4	3	-	-	2	-	9	
7	T Ruttman	-	8	-	-	-	-	-	-	8	
	L Villoresi	-	-	-	-	-	-	4	4	8	
9	F González	-	-	-	-	-	-	-	6.5	6.5	
10	J Rathmann	-	6	-	-	-	-	-	-	6	
	J Behra	4	-	-	-	-	2	-	-	6	
12	S Hanks	-	4	-	-	-	-	-	-	4	
13	K Wharton	3	-	-	-	-	-	-	-	3	
	D Carter	-	3	-	-	-	-	-	-	3	
	D Poore	-	-	-	-	-	3	-	-	3	
16	A Brown	2	-	-	-	-	-	-	-	2	
	A Cross	-	2	-	-	-	-	-	-	2	
	P Frère	-	-	2	-	-	-	-	-	2	
	M Trintignant	-	-	-	2	-	-	-	-	2	
	E Thompson	-	-	-	-	2	-	-	-	2	
	F Bonetto	-	-	-	-	-	-	-	2	2	
20	B Vukovich	-	1	-	-	-	-	-	-	1	

8,6,4,3 and 2 points awarded to the first five finishers. The driver setting the fastest lap scored a point also. Points shared for shared drives. Best 4 scores.

Race Entrants and Results

The second year of the Formula 2 World Championship continued with Ferrari setting the pace, although Maserati produced a revised version of their car and Fangio was back as team leader. During the two year period of this stop-gap formula there wasn't a single World Championship entry based on the 750 cc supercharged category.

FERRARI
Scuderia Ferrari: Ascari, Farina, Villoresi, Hawthorn, Maglioli, Carini
Ecurie Espadon: Adolff, Hirt, de Terra
Ecurie Francorchamps: Swaters, (de Tornaco)
Ecurie Rosier: Rosier

OSCA
Privateers: Chiron, Bayol

MASERATI
Officine Alfieri Maserati: Fangio, Bonetto, González, Marimón, Gálvez, Claes, Lang, Mantovani, Musso
Scuderia Milano: Landi, Bira
Privateers: de Graffenried, Landi (CH)

GORDINI
Equipe Gordini: Behra, Trintignant, Schell, Manzon, Mières, Menditéguy, Birger, Wacker
Privateer: Berger

COOPER
Cooper Car Co: Moss, Wharton (GB), Brown (RA), Barber, Schwelm Cruz
Equipe Anglaise: Brown, (Glöckler)
R J Chase: Brown (GB)
Atlantic Stable: Whitehead
Ecurie Ecosse: J Stewart
Privateers: Wharton, Gerard, Crook, Nuckey

HWM
HW Motors: Macklin, Collins, Frère, Giraud-Cabantous, Hamilton, Fairman, Scherrer, Fitch

CONNAUGHT
Connaught Engineering: McAlpine, Salvadori, Bira, Moss, Fairman
Ecurie Belge: Claes, Pilette
R R C Walker Racing Team: Rolt
Ecurie Ecosse: I Stewart

VERITAS
H Klenk: Herrmann
Privateers: Seidel, Heeks, Helfrich, Karch, Loof, Bauer, Legat

AFM
H Niedermayr: Fitzau
Privateers: Stuck, Bechem

BMW
Dora Greifzu: Krause
Privateer: Klodwig

EMW
EMW Rennkollectiv: Barth

18 Jan 1953		ARGENTINA: Buenos Aires No.2						(Round 1)		(Race 24)	
		97 laps x 3.912 km, 2.431 miles = 379.464 km, 235.788 miles									
Pos	No	Driver	Car	Model	Engine		Laps	Time/Reason for Retirement	Grid Pos	Row	
1	10	A Ascari	Ferrari	500	Ferrari	4	97	3h 01m 04.600s		1	1
2	14	L Villoresi	Ferrari	500	Ferrari	4	96			3	1
3	4	F González	Maserati	A6GCM	Maserati	6	96			5	2
4	16	M Hawthorn	Ferrari	500	Ferrari	4	96			6	2
5	8	O Gálvez	Maserati	A6GCM	Maserati	6	96			9	3
6	30	J Behra	Gordini	T16	Gordini	6	94			11	3
7=	28	M Trintignant	Gordini	T16	Gordini	6				7	2
7=	28	H Schell	Gordini	T16	Gordini	6	91				
8	22	J Barber	Cooper	T23	Bristol	6	90			16	5
9	20	A Brown	Cooper	T20	Bristol	6	87			12	4
r	26	R Manzon	Gordini	T16	Gordini	6	67	rear wheel lost		8	3
r	2	J M Fangio	Maserati	A6GCM	Maserati	6	35	propeller shaft		2	1
r	6	F Bonetto	Maserati	A6GCM	Maserati	6	32	gearbox		15	5
r	12	G Farina	Ferrari	500	Ferrari	4	31	accident (spectator killed)		4	1
r	32	C Menditéguy	Gordini	T16	Gordini	6	24	gearbox		10	3
r	34	P Birger	Simca Gordini	T15	Gordini	4	21	crown wheel & pinion		14	4
r	24	A Schwelm Cruz	Cooper	T20	Bristol	6	20	wheel lost		13	4

Winning speed 125.736 km/h, 78.129 mph
Pole Position speed 122.038 km/h, 75.831 mph (A Ascari, 1 min:55.400 sec)
Fastest Lap speed 129.919 km/h, 80.728 mph (A Ascari, 1 min:48.400 sec)
Lap Leaders A Ascari 1-97 (97).

200 laps x 4.023 km, 2.500 miles = 804.672 km, 500.000 miles

Pos	No	Driver	Car	Model	Engine		Laps	Time/Reason for Retirement	Grid Pos	Row
1	14	B Vukovich	Kurtis Kraft	500A	Offenhauser	4	200	3h 53m 01.690s	1	1
2	16	A Cross	Kurtis Kraft	4000	Offenhauser	4	200	3h 56m 32.562s	12	4
3=	3	S Hanks	Kurtis Kraft	4000	Offenhauser	4			9	3
3=	3	D Carter	Kurtis Kraft	4000	Offenhauser	4	200			
4=	59	F Agabashian	Kurtis Kraft	500B	Offenhauser	4			2	1
4=	59	P Russo	Kurtis Kraft	500B	Offenhauser	4	200			
5	5	J McGrath	Kurtis Kraft	4000	Offenhauser	4	200		3	1
6	48	J Daywalt	Kurtis Kraft	3000	Offenhauser	4	200		21	7
7=	2	J Rathmann	Kurtis Kraft	500B	Offenhauser	4			25	9
7=	2	E Johnson	Kurtis Kraft	500B	Offenhauser	4	200			
8	12	E McCoy	Stevens		Offenhauser	4	200		20	7
9r=	98	T Bettenhausen	Kuzma		Offenhauser	4			6	2
9r=	98	C Stevenson	Kuzma		Offenhauser	4				
9r=	98	G Hartley	Kuzma		Offenhauser	4	196	axle / accident		
10	53	J Davies	Kurtis Kraft	500B	Offenhauser	4	193		32	11
11r	9	D Nalon	Kurtis Kraft		Novi	8s	191	spin avoiding Bettenhausen	26	9
								(died later of heat exhaustion)		
12=	73	C Scarborough	Kurtis Kraft	2000	Offenhauser	4			19	7
12=	73	B Scott	Kurtis Kraft	2000	Offenhauser	4	190			
13r	88	M Ayulo	Kuzma		Offenhauser	4	184	connecting rod	4	2
14	8	J Bryan	Schroeder		Offenhauser	4	183		31	11
15r=	49	B Holland	Kurtis Kraft	500B	Offenhauser	4			28	10
15r=	49	J Rathmann	Kurtis Kraft	500B	Offenhauser	4	177	cam gear		
16r=	92	R Ward	Kurtis Kraft		Offenhauser	4	177	rear axle	10	4
16r=	92	A Linden	Kurtis Kraft		Offenhauser	4				
16r=	92	D Dinsmore	Kurtis Kraft		Offenhauser	4				
17=	23	W Faulkner	Kurtis Kraft	500A	Offenhauser	4			14	5
17=	23	J Mantz	Kurtis Kraft	500A	Offenhauser	4	176			
18r	22	M Teague	Kurtis Kraft	4000	Offenhauser	4	169	oil leak	22	8
19r=	62	S Webb	Kurtis Kraft	3000	Offenhauser	4			18	6
19r=	62	J Thomson	Kurtis Kraft	3000	Offenhauser	4				
19r=	62	J Holmes	Kurtis Kraft	3000	Offenhauser	4	166	oil leak		
20r	51	B Sweikert	Kuzma		Offenhauser	4	151	suspension radius rod	29	10
21r	83	M Nazaruk	Turner		Offenhauser	4	146	stalled	23	8
22r	77	P Flaherty	Kurtis Kraft	3000	Offenhauser	4	115	accident	24	8
23r=	55	J Hoyt	Kurtis Kraft	4000	Offenhauser	4			7	3
23r=	55	C Stevenson	Kurtis Kraft	4000	Offenhauser	4				
23r=	55	A Linden	Kurtis Kraft	4000	Offenhauser	4	107	cockpit too hot		
24r	4	D Carter	Lesovsky		Offenhauser	4	94	ignition	27	9
25r	7	P Russo	Kurtis Kraft	3000	Offenhauser	4	89	magneto	17	6
26r	21	J Parsons	Kurtis Kraft	500B	Offenhauser	4	86	crankshaft	8	3
27r	38	D Freeland	Watson		Offenhauser	4	76	accident	15	5
28r	41	G Hartley	Kurtis Kraft	4000	Offenhauser	4	53	accident	13	5
29r	97	C Stevenson	Kuzma		Offenhauser	4	42	fuel leak	16	6
30r	99	C Niday	Kurtis Kraft		Offenhauser	4	30	magneto	30	10
31r	29	B Scott	Bromme		Offenhauser	4	14	oil leak	11	4
32r	56	J Thomson	Del Roy-Allen		Offenhauser	4	6	ignition	33	11
33r	32	A Linden	Stevens		Offenhauser	4	3	accident	5	2

Winning speed 207.187 km/h, 128.740 mph
Pole Position speed 222.723 km/h, 138.393 mph (B Vukovich, 1 min: 5.032 sec)
Fastest Lap speed 218.661 km/h, 135.870 mph (B Vukovich, 1 min: 6.240 sec on lap 27)

7 Jun 1953 NETHERLANDS: Zandvoort (Round 3) (Race 26)
90 laps x 4.193 km, 2.605 miles = 377.370 km, 234.487 miles

Pos	No	Driver	Car	Model	Engine		Laps	Time/Reason for Retirement	Grid Pos	Row
1	2	A Ascari	Ferrari	500	Ferrari	4	90	2h 53m 35.800s	1	1
2	6	G Farina	Ferrari	500	Ferrari	4	90	2h 53m 46.200s	3	1
3=	16	F Bonetto	Maserati	A6GCM	Maserati	6			13	5
3=	16	F González	Maserati	A6GCM	Maserati	6	89			
4	8	M Hawthorn	Ferrari	500	Ferrari	4	89		6	3
5	18	E de Graffenried	Maserati	A6GCM	Maserati	6	88		7	3
6	24	M Trintignant	Gordini	T16	Gordini	6	87		12	5
7	10	L Rosier	Ferrari	500	Ferrari	4	86		8	3
8	36	P Collins	HWM	(53)	Alta	4	84		16	7
9	34	S Moss	Connaught	A	Lea Francis	4	83		9	4
r	4	L Villoresi	Ferrari	500	Ferrari	4	67	throttle control	4	2
r	28	K McAlpine	Connaught	A	Lea Francis	4	63	engine	14	6
r	20	H Schell	Gordini	T16	Gordini	6	59	transmission	10	4
nc	30	J Claes	Connaught	A	Lea Francis	4	52		17	7
r	12	J M Fangio	Maserati	A6GCM	Maserati	6	36	rear axle	2	1
r	22	R Mières	Gordini	T16	Gordini	6	28	transmission	19	8
r	14	F González	Maserati	A6GCM	Maserati	6	22	rear axle	5	2
r	32	K Wharton	Cooper	T23	Bristol	6	19	rear suspension	18	7
r	26	R Salvadori	Connaught	A	Lea Francis	4	14	valves	11	5
r	38	L Macklin	HWM	(53)	Alta	4	7	throttle control	15	6
ns	40	F Wacker	Gordini	T16	Gordini	6		engine used by Schell		

Winning speed 130.430 km/h, 81.045 mph
Pole Position speed 135.867 km/h, 84.424 mph (A Ascari, 1 min:51.100 sec)
Fastest Lap speed 133.819 km/h, 83.151 mph (G Villoresi, 1 min:52.800 sec on lap 59)
Lap Leaders A Ascari 1-90 (90).

21 Jun 1953 BELGIUM: Spa-Francorchamps (Round 4) (Race 27)
36 laps x 14.120 km, 8.774 miles = 508.320 km, 315.855 miles

Pos	No	Driver	Car	Model	Engine		Laps	Time/Reason for Retirement	Grid Pos	Row
1	10	A Ascari	Ferrari	500	Ferrari	4	36	2h 48m 30.300s	2	1
2	8	L Villoresi	Ferrari	500	Ferrari	4	36	2h 51m 18.500s	5	2
r=	6	J Claes	Maserati	A6GCM	Maserati	6			10	4
r=	6	J M Fangio	Maserati	A6GCM	Maserati	6	35	steering / accident		
3	28	O Marimón	Maserati	A6GCM	Maserati	6	35		6	3
4	30	E de Graffenried	Maserati	A6GCM	Maserati	6	35		9	4
5	18	M Trintignant	Gordini	T16	Gordini	6	35		8	3
6	14	M Hawthorn	Ferrari	500	Ferrari	4	35		7	3
7	20	H Schell	Gordini	T16	Gordini	6	33		12	5
8	32	L Rosier	Ferrari	500	Ferrari	4	33		13	5
9	38	F Wacker	Gordini	T16	Gordini	6	32		15	6
10	24	P Frère	HWM	(53)	Alta	4	30		11	5
11	40	A Pilette	Connaught	A	Lea Francis	4	29		18	7
r	22	L Macklin	HWM	(53)	Alta	4	19	engine	17	7
r	12	G Farina	Ferrari	500	Ferrari	4	16	engine	4	2
r	4	J M Fangio	Maserati	A6GCM	Maserati	6	13	engine	1	1
r	2	F González	Maserati	A6GCM	Maserati	6	11	throttle	3	1
r	16	J Behra	Gordini	T16	Gordini	6	9	cylinder head gasket	14	6
r	26	P Collins	HWM	(53)	Alta	4	4	clutch	16	7
r	34	G Berger	Simca Gordini	T15	Gordini	4	3	engine	20	8
r	36	A Legat	Veritas	Meteor	Veritas	6	0	transmission	19	8
ns	42	J Swaters	Ferrari	500	Ferrari	4		withdrew		
ns	44	C de Tornaco	Ferrari	500	Ferrari	4		withdrew		

Winning speed 180.999 km/h, 112.467 mph
Pole Position speed 188.267 km/h, 116.983 mph (J M Fangio, 4 min:30.000 sec)
Fastest Lap speed 185.518 km/h, 115.276 mph (F González, 4 min:34.000 sec on lap 2, 3, 9 & 11)
Lap Leaders F González 1-11 (11); J M Fangio 12-13 (2); A Ascari 14-36 (23).

5 Jul 1953   FRANCE: Reims   (Round 5)   (Race 28)

60 laps x 8.347 km, 5.187 miles = 500.820 km, 311.195 miles

Pos	No	Driver	Car	Model	Engine		Laps	Time/Reason for Retirement	Grid Pos	Row
1	16	M Hawthorn	Ferrari	500	Ferrari	4	60	2h 44m 18.600s	7	3
2	18	J M Fangio	Maserati	A6GCM	Maserati	6	60	2h 44m 19.600s	4	2
3	20	F González	Maserati	A6GCM	Maserati	6	60	2h 44m 20.000s	5	2
4	10	A Ascari	Ferrari	500	Ferrari	4	60	2h 44m 23.200s	1	1
5	14	G Farina	Ferrari	500	Ferrari	4	60	2h 45m 26.200s	6	3
6	12	L Villoresi	Ferrari	500	Ferrari	4	60	2h 45m 34.500s	3	1
7	46	E de Graffenried	Maserati	A6GCM	Maserati	6	58		9	4
8	44	L Rosier	Ferrari	500	Ferrari	4	56		10	4
9	22	O Marimón	Maserati	A6GCM	Maserati	6	55		8	3
10	2	J Behra	Gordini	T16	Gordini	6	55		22	9
11	38	B Gerard	Cooper	T23	Bristol	6	55		12	5
12	48	J Claes	Connaught	A	Lea Francis	4	53		21	9
13	28	P Collins	HWM	(53)	Alta	4	52		17	7
14	30	Y Giraud-Cabantous	HWM	(53)	Alta	4	50		18	7
15	32	L Chiron	OSCA	20	OSCA	6	43		25	10
r	24	F Bonetto	Maserati	A6GCM	Maserati	6	42	engine	2	1
r	36	S Moss	Cooper	Spl.	Alta	4	38	clutch	13	5
r	42	B Bira	Connaught	A	Lea Francis	4	29	differential	11	5
r	34	É Bayol	OSCA	20	OSCA	6	18	engine	15	6
r	40	K Wharton	Cooper	T23	Bristol	6	17	bearings	14	6
r	4	M Trintignant	Gordini	T16	Gordini	6	14	transmission	23	9
r	26	L Macklin	HWM	(53)	Alta	4	9	clutch	16	7
r	8	R Mières	Gordini	T16	Gordini	6	4	rear axle	24	10
r	6	H Schell	Gordini	T16	Gordini	6	4	connecting rod	20	8
r	50	R Salvadori	Connaught	A	Lea Francis	4	2	ignition	19	8

Winning speed 182.881 km/h, 113.637 mph
Pole Position speed 186.409 km/h, 115.829 mph (A Ascari, 2 min:41.200 sec)
Fastest Lap speed 186.525 km/h, 115.901 mph (J M Fangio / A Ascari, 2 min:41.100 sec on lap 25 / 37)
Lap Leaders F González 1-29 (29); J M Fangio 30-31,35-36,39-41,45-47,49-53,55-56 (17); M Hawthorn 32-34,37-38,42-44,48,54,57-60 (14).

18 Jul 1953   BRITAIN: Silverstone   (Round 6)   (Race 29)

90 laps x 4.711 km, 2.927 miles = 423.949 km, 263.430 miles

Pos	No	Driver	Car	Model	Engine		Laps	Time/Reason for Retirement	Grid Pos	Row
1	5	A Ascari	Ferrari	500	Ferrari	4	90	2h 50m 00.000s	1	1
2	23	J M Fangio	Maserati	A6GCM	Maserati	6	90	2h 51m 00.000s	4	1
3	6	G Farina	Ferrari	500	Ferrari	4	88		5	2
4	24	F González	Maserati	A6GCM	Maserati	6	88		2	1
5	8	M Hawthorn	Ferrari	500	Ferrari	4	87		3	1
6	25	F Bonetto	Maserati	A6GCM	Maserati	6	82		16	5
7	10	B Bira	Connaught	A	Lea Francis	4	82		19	6
8	16	K Wharton	Cooper	T23	Bristol	6	80		11	3
r	18	J Stewart	Cooper	T20	Bristol	6	79	accident	15	5
9	20	P Whitehead	Cooper	T24	Alta	4	79		14	4
10	9	L Rosier	Ferrari	500	Ferrari	4	78		24	7
r	14	T Rolt	Connaught	A	Lea Francis	4	70	half shaft	10	3
r	7	L Villoresi	Ferrari	500	Ferrari	4	66	rear axle	6	2
r	26	O Marimón	Maserati	A6GCM	Maserati	6	66	engine	7	2
r	19	A Brown	Cooper	T23	Bristol	6	61	fan belt	21	6
r	2	P Collins	HWM	(53)	Alta	4	56	accident	23	7
r	4	J Fairman	HWM	(53)	Alta	4	54	clutch	27	8
r	12	R Salvadori	Connaught	A	Lea Francis	4	50	rear suspension radius rod	28	8
r	31	E de Graffenried	Maserati	A6GCM	Maserati	6	34	clutch	26	8
r	1	L Macklin	HWM	(53)	Alta	4	31	clutch	12	4
r	30	J Behra	Gordini	T16	Gordini	6	30	fuel pump	22	7
r	15	I Stewart	Connaught	A	Lea Francis	4	26	ignition	20	6
r	3	D Hamilton	HWM	(53)	Alta	4	15	clutch	17	5
r	29	M Trintignant	Gordini	T16	Gordini	6	14	rear axle	8	3
r	17	B Gerard	Cooper	T23	Bristol	6	8	front suspension	18	5
r	28	H Schell	Gordini	T16	Gordini	6	5	magneto	9	3
r	22	T Crook	Cooper	T20	Bristol	6	0	fuel injection	25	7
r	11	K McAlpine	Connaught	A	Lea Francis	4	0	split hose	13	4
ns	27	L Chiron	OSCA	20	OSCA	6				

Winning speed 149.629 km/h, 92.975 mph
Pole Position speed 157.018 km/h, 97.567 mph (A Ascari, 1 min:48.000 sec)
Fastest Lap speed 154.163 km/h, 95.793 mph (A Ascari / F González, 1 min:50.000 sec)
Lap Leaders A Ascari 1-90 (90).

2 Aug 1953		**GERMANY: Nürburgring**						**(Round 7)**		**(Race 30)**

18 laps x 22.810 km, 14.173 miles = 410.580 km, 255.123 miles

Pos	No	Driver	Car	Model	Engine		Laps	Time/Reason for Retirement	Grid Pos	Row
1	2	G Farina	Ferrari	500	Ferrari	4	18	3h 02m 25.000s	3	1
2	5	J M Fangio	Maserati	A6GCM	Maserati	6	18	3h 03m 29.000s	2	1
3	3	M Hawthorn	Ferrari	500	Ferrari	4	18	3h 04m 08.600s	4	1
4	7	F Bonetto	Maserati	A6GCM	Maserati	6	18	3h 11m 13.600s	7	2
5	17	E de Graffenried	Maserati	A6GCM	Maserati	6	17		11	3
6	19	S Moss	Cooper	T23	Alta	4	17		12	4
7	18	J Swaters	Ferrari	500	Ferrari	4	17		19	6
8=	1	A Ascari	Ferrari	500	Ferrari	4			1	1
8=	1	L Villoresi	Ferrari	500	Ferrari	4	17		1	1
9	31	H Herrmann	Veritas	Meteor	Veritas	6	17		14	4
10	20	L Rosier	Ferrari	500	Ferrari	4	17		22	7
11	40	R Nuckey	Cooper	T23	Bristol	6	16		20	6
12	24	T Helfrich	Veritas	RS	Veritas	6	16		28	8
13	16	K McAlpine	Connaught	A	Lea Francis	4	16		16	5
14	36	R Krause	BMW	Greifzu	BMW	6	16		26	8
r=	4	L Villoresi	Ferrari	500	Ferrari	4			6	2
r=	4	A Ascari	Ferrari	500	Ferrari	4	15	engine		
r	38	A Brown	Cooper	T23	Bristol	6	15	misfire / accident	17	5
15	37	E Klodwig	BMW	Heck	BMW	6	15		32	9
16	22	W Seidel	Veritas	RS	Veritas	6	14		29	9
r	8	O Marimón	Maserati	A6GCM	Maserati	6	13	suspension	8	3
r	12	J Claes	Connaught	A	Lea Francis	4	12	engine	25	7
r	35	E Barth	EMW		EMW	6	12	exhaust	24	7
r	26	O Karch	Veritas	RS	Veritas	6	10	engine	34	10
r	23	W Heeks	Veritas	Meteor	Veritas	6	8	transmission	18	5
r	9	J Behra	Gordini	T16	Gordini	6	7	gearbox	9	3
r	11	H Schell	Gordini	T16	Gordini	6	6	cylinder head gasket	10	3
r	14	B Bira	Connaught	A	Lea Francis	4	6	rocker	15	5
r	28	T Fitzau	AFM		BMW	6	3	engine	21	6
r	34	K Adolff	Ferrari	166	Ferrari	V12	3	transmission	27	8
r	41	G Bechem	AFM		BMW	6	2	engine	30	9
r	15	R Salvadori	Connaught	A	Lea Francis	4	1	rocker	13	4
r	32	E Bauer	Veritas	RS	Veritas	6	1	engine	33	10
r	10	M Trintignant	Gordini	T16	Gordini	6	1	differential	5	2
r	21	H Stuck	AFM		Bristol	6	0	engine	23	7
r	30	E Loof	Veritas	Meteor	Veritas	6	0	fuel pump	31	9
ns	39	H Glöckler	Cooper	T23	Bristol	6		engine		

Winning speed 135.047 km/h, 83.914 mph
Pole Position speed 136.906 km/h, 85.069 mph (A Ascari, 9 min:59.800 sec)
Fastest Lap speed 137.779 km/h, 85.612 mph (A Ascari, 9 min:56.000 sec on lap 12)
Lap Leaders A Ascari 1-4 (4); M Hawthorn 5-7 (3); G Farina 8-18 (11).

23 Aug 1953		**SWITZERLAND: Bremgarten**						**(Round 8)**		**(Race 31)**

65 laps x 7.280 km, 4.524 miles = 473.200 km, 294.033 miles

Pos	No	Driver	Car	Model	Engine		Laps	Time/Reason for Retirement	Grid Pos	Row
1	46	A Ascari	Ferrari	500	Ferrari	4	65	3h 01m 34.400s	2	1
2	24	G Farina	Ferrari	500	Ferrari	4	65	3h 02m 47.330s	3	1
3	26	M Hawthorn	Ferrari	500	Ferrari	4	65	3h 03m 10.360s	7	3
4=	32	J M Fangio	Maserati	A6GCM	Maserati	6			1	1
4=	32	F Bonetto	Maserati	A6GCM	Maserati	6	64		1	1
5	34	H Lang	Maserati	A6GCM	Maserati	6	62		11	5
6	28	L Villoresi	Ferrari	500	Ferrari	4	62		6	3
7	20	K Wharton	Cooper	T23	Bristol	6	62		9	4
r	4	C Landi	Maserati	A6GCM	Maserati	6	54	gearbox	20	8
8	40	M de Terra	Ferrari	166	Ferrari	V12	51		19	8
9	18	A Scherrer	HWM	(53)	Alta	4	49		18	7
r	42	E de Graffenried	Maserati	A6GCM	Maserati	6	48	camshaft drive	8	3
r	36	O Marimón	Maserati	A6GCM	Maserati	6	46	oil pipe	5	2
r	8	M Trintignant	Gordini	T16	Gordini	6	43	rear axle	4	2
r	6	J Behra	Gordini	T16	Gordini	6	37	oil pressure	12	5
r=	30	F Bonetto	Maserati	A6GCM	Maserati	6			10	4
r=	30	J M Fangio	Maserati	A6GCM	Maserati	6	29	valve		
r	16	L Macklin	HWM	(53)	Alta	4	29	valve	15	6
r	38	P Hirt	Ferrari	500	Ferrari	4	17	oil loss	17	7
r	14	P Frère	HWM	(53)	Alta	4	1	connecting rod	16	7
r	10	L Rosier	Ferrari	500	Ferrari	4	0	accident	14	6
r	2	J Swaters	Ferrari	500	Ferrari	4	0	accident	13	5
ns	12	L Chiron	OSCA	20	OSCA	6				
ns	22	É Bayol	OSCA	20	OSCA	6				
ns	44	F Wacker	Gordini	T16	Gordini	6		accident / injury		

Winning speed 156.367 km/h, 97.162 mph
Pole Position speed 163.698 km/h, 101.717 mph (J M Fangio, 2 min:40.100 sec)
Fastest Lap speed 162.480 km/h, 100.960 mph (A Ascari, 2 min:41.300 sec on lap 50)
Lap Leaders A Ascari 1-40,54-65 (52); G Farina 41-53 (13).

Pos	No	Driver	Car	Model	Engine		Laps	Time/Reason for Retirement	Grid Pos	Row
1	50	J M Fangio	Maserati	A6GCM	Maserati	6	80	2h 49m 45.900s	2	1
2	6	G Farina	Ferrari	500	Ferrari	4	80	2h 49m 47.300s	3	1
r	4	A Ascari	Ferrari	500	Ferrari	4	79	accident	1	1
3	2	L Villoresi	Ferrari	500	Ferrari	4	79		5	2
4	8	M Hawthorn	Ferrari	500	Ferrari	4	79		6	2
5	36	M Trintignant	Gordini	T16	Gordini	6	79		8	3
r	52	F Bonetto	Maserati	A6GCM	Maserati	6	77	out of fuel	7	3
6	40	R Mières	Gordini	T16	Gordini	6	77		16	6
7=	56	S Mantovani	Maserati	A6GCM	Maserati	6			12	4
7=	56	L Musso	Maserati	A6GCM	Maserati	6	76			
r	54	O Marimón	Maserati	A6GCM	Maserati	6	75	accident	4	2
8	10	U Maglioli	Ferrari	553	Ferrari	4	75		11	4
9	38	H Schell	Gordini	T16	Gordini	6	75		15	5
10	32	L Chiron	OSCA	20	OSCA	6	72		25	9
11	44	B Bira	Maserati	A6GCM	Maserati	6	72		23	8
r	58	E de Graffenried	Maserati	A6GCM	Maserati	6	70	engine	9	3
12	46	A Brown	Cooper	T23	Bristol	6	70		24	8
13	28	S Moss	Cooper	T23	Alta	4	70		10	4
14	48	H Stuck	AFM		Bristol	6	67		29	10
15	16	Y Giraud-Cabantous	HWM	(53)	Alta	4	67		28	10
16	64	L Rosier	Ferrari	500	Ferrari	4	65		17	6
nc	20	J Fairman	Connaught	A	Lea Francis	4	61		22	8
nc	30	K Wharton	Cooper	T23	Bristol	6	57		19	7
nc	24	K McAlpine	Connaught	A	Lea Francis	4	56		18	6
r	12	P Carini	Ferrari	553	Ferrari	4	40	engine	20	7
r	22	R Salvadori	Connaught	A	Lea Francis	4	33	throttle linkage	14	5
r	42	C Landi	Maserati	A6GCM	Maserati	6	18	piston	21	7
r	34	É Bayol	OSCA	20	OSCA	6	17	engine	13	5
r	18	J Fitch	HWM	(53)	Alta	4	14	engine	26	9
r	26	J Claes	Connaught	A	Lea Francis	4	7	fuel line	30	10
r	14	L Macklin	HWM	(53)	Alta	4	6	engine	27	9

Winning speed 178.129 km/h, 110.684 mph
Pole Position speed 184.841 km/h, 114.855 mph (A Ascari, 2 min: 2.700 sec)
Fastest Lap speed 182.169 km/h, 113.194 mph (J M Fangio, 2 min: 4.500 sec on lap 39)
Lap Leaders A Ascari 1-6,9,14-22,27-31,34-36,39-40,42,44-45,47-49,53-79 (59); J M Fangio 7-8,11,23,25-26,32-33,37,41,50-52,80 (14); G Farina 10,12-13,24,38,43,46 (7).

Lap Leaders 1953

Pos	Driver	Car-Engine	GPs	laps	km	miles
1	A Ascari	Ferrari	7	415	2,347.1	1,458.4
2	F González	Maserati	2	40	397.4	246.9
3	J M Fangio	Maserati	3	33	258.3	160.5
4	G Farina	Ferrari	3	31	389.7	242.1
5	M Hawthorn	Ferrari	2	17	185.3	115.1
			8	**536**	**3,577.7**	**2,223.1**

Driver Points 1953

		RA	INDY	NL	B	F	GB	D	CH	I	Total	
1	A Ascari	9	-	8	(8)	(3.5)	8.5	(1)	9	-	34.5	(12.5)
2	J M Fangio	-	-	-	-	6.5	6	6	(1.5)	9	27.5	(1.5)
3	G Farina	-	-	6	-	(2)	(4)	8	6	6	26	(6)
4	M Hawthorn	3	-	(3)	-	8	(2)	4	4	(3)	19	(8)
5	L Villoresi	6	-	1	6	-	-	-	-	4	17	
6	F González	4	-	2	(1)	4	3.5	-	-	-	13.5	(1)
7	B Vukovich	-	9	-	-	-	-	-	-	-	9	
8	E de Graffenried	-	-	2	3	-	-	2	-	-	7	
9	F Bonetto	-	-	2	-	-	-	3	1.5	-	6.5	
10	A Cross	-	6	-	-	-	-	-	-	-	6	
11	O Marimón	-	-	-	4	-	-	-	-	-	4	
	M Trintignant	-	-	-	2	-	-	-	-	2	4	
13	O Gálvez	2	-	-	-	-	-	-	-	-	2	
	S Hanks	-	2	-	-	-	-	-	-	-	2	
	D Carter	-	2	-	-	-	-	-	-	-	2	
	J McGrath	-	2	-	-	-	-	-	-	-	2	
	H Lang	-	-	-	-	-	-	-	2	-	2	
18	F Agabashian	-	1.5	-	-	-	-	-	-	-	1.5	
	P Russo	-	1.5	-	-	-	-	-	-	-	1.5	

8,6,4,3 and 2 points awarded to the first five finishers. The driver setting the fastest lap scored a point also. Points shared for shared drives. Best 4 scores.

Race Entrants and Results

The year saw the return of true Formula 1 cars with the introduction of the 2.5-litre formula. With this stability, major manufacturers committed themselves to racing at the top level, Mercedes and Lancia re-entered Grand Prix racing, signing the two big names, Fangio and Ascari, who were free to race for others until the cars were available.

FERRARI
Scuderia Ferrari: González, Hawthorn, Trintignant, Farina, Taruffi, Maglioli, Ascari, Manzon (CH)
Ecurie Rosier: Rosier, Manzon
Ecurie Francorchamps: Swaters
Scuderia Ambrosiana: Parnell

MASERATI
Officine Alfieri Maserati: Marimón, Fangio, Musso, Mantovani, Mières, Bira (RA), Moss (CH-E), Ascari, Villoresi, Schell (CH), Rosier (I), Godia
Prince Bira: Bira, Flockhart
Gilby Engineering Ltd: Salvadori
Owen Racing Organisation: Wharton
Baron de Graffenried: de Graffenried, Volonterio
Ecurie Rosier: Rosier
O Marimón: (Menditéguy),
Privateers: Moss, Mières (RA-D), Schell, Daponte, (de Riu)

LANCIA
Scuderia Lancia: Ascari, Villoresi

GORDINI
Equipe Gordini: Behra, Pilette, Bayol, Loyer, Frère, Pollet, Bucci, Wacker
Privateer: Berger

COOPER
Ecurie Richmond: Brandon, Nuckey
Gould's Garage (Bristol): Gould
R J Chase: (Brown)
Privateers: Gerard, Whitehead

HWM
HW Motors: Macklin

CONNAUGHT
R R C Walker Racing Team: Riseley-Prichard
Ecurie Ecosse: Thorne
Sir Jeremy Boles: Beauman
Privateers: Marr, Whitehouse

VANWALL
G A Vandervell: Collins

MERCEDES-BENZ
Daimler Benz AG: Fangio, Kling, Herrmann, Lang

KLENK
Hans Klenk: Helfrich

17 Jan 1954		**ARGENTINA: Buenos Aires No.2**						(Round 1)	(Race 33)	
		87 laps x 3.912 km, 2.431 miles = 340.344 km, 211.480 miles								
Pos	No	Driver	Car	Model	Engine		Laps	Time/Reason for Retirement	Grid Pos	Row
1	2	J M Fangio	Maserati	250F	Maserati	6	87	3h 00m 55.800s	3	1
2	10	G Farina	Ferrari	625	Ferrari	4	87	3h 02m 14.800s	1	1
3	12	F González	Ferrari	625	Ferrari	4	87	3h 02m 56.800s	2	1
4	26	M Trintignant	Ferrari	625	Ferrari	4	86		5	2
5	20	É Bayol	Gordini	T16	Gordini	6	85		14	4
6	28	H Schell	Maserati	A6GCM	Maserati	6	84		10	3
7	8	B Bira	Maserati	A6GCM	Maserati	6	83		9	3
8	30	E de Graffenried	Maserati	A6GCM	Maserati	6	83		12	4
9	16	U Maglioli	Ferrari	625	Ferrari	4	82		11	3
dq	18	J Behra	Gordini	T16	Gordini	6	61	push start after spin	16	5
dq	14	M Hawthorn	Ferrari	625	Ferrari	4	52	push start after spin	4	1
r	4	O Marimón	Maserati	250F	Maserati	6	48	engine	6	2
r	32	R Mières	Maserati	A6GCM	Maserati	6	37	oil leak	8	3
r	22	R Loyer	Gordini	T16	Gordini	6	19	oil pressure	15	5
r	34	J Daponte	Maserati	A6GCM	Maserati	6	19	gearbox	17	5
r	24	L Rosier	Ferrari	500	Ferrari	4	1	brakes / accident	13	4
ns	6	L Musso	Maserati	A6GCM	Maserati	6		engine	7	2
ns	36	C Menditéguy	Maserati	A6GCM	Maserati	6		engine		

Winning speed 112.865 km/h, 70.131 mph
Pole Position speed 134.382 km/h, 83.501 mph (G Farina, 1 min:44.800 sec)
Fastest Lap speed 130.159 km/h, 80.877 mph (F González, 1 min:48.200 sec)
Lap Leaders G Farina 1-14,63-64 (16)*; F González 15-32,47-58,61-62 (32)*; M Hawthorn 33-34 (2); J M Fangio 35-46,59-60,65-87 (37)*.
* estimated from contemporary text

Pos	No	Driver	Car	Model	Engine		Laps	Time/Reason for Retirement	Grid Pos	Row
1	14	B Vukovich	Kurtis Kraft	500A	Offenhauser	4	200	3h 49m 17.270s	19	7
2	9	J Bryan	Kuzma		Offenhauser	4	200	3h 50m 27.221s	3	1
3	2	J McGrath	Kurtis Kraft	500C	Offenhauser	4	200		1	1
4=	34	T Ruttman	Kurtis Kraft	500A	Offenhauser	4	200		11	4
4=	34	D Carter	Kurtis Kraft	500A	Offenhauser	4				
5	73	M Nazaruk	Kurtis Kraft	500C	Offenhauser	4	200		14	5
6	77	F Agabashian	Kurtis Kraft	500C	Offenhauser	4	200		24	8
7	7	D Freeland	Phillips		Offenhauser	4	200		6	2
8=	5	P Russo	Kurtis Kraft	500A	Offenhauser	4			32	11
8=	5	J Hoyt	Kurtis Kraft	500A	Offenhauser	4	200			
9	28	L Crockett	Kurtis Kraft	3000	Offenhauser	4	200		25	9
10	24	C Niday	Stevens		Offenhauser	4	200		13	5
11=	45	A Cross	Kurtis Kraft	4000	Offenhauser	4			27	9
11=	45	J Parsons	Kurtis Kraft	4000	Offenhauser	4				
11=	45	S Hanks	Kurtis Kraft	4000	Offenhauser	4				
11=	45	A Linden	Kurtis Kraft	4000	Offenhauser	4				
11=	45	J Davies	Kurtis Kraft	4000	Offenhauser	4	200			
12=	98	C Stevenson	Kuzma		Offenhauser	4			5	2
12=	98	W Faulkner	Kuzma		Offenhauser	4	199			
13	88	M Ayulo	Kurtis Kraft	500C	Offenhauser	4	197		22	8
14	17	B Sweikert	Kurtis Kraft	4000	Offenhauser	4	197		9	3
15=	16	D Carter	Kurtis Kraft	4000	Offenhauser	4			8	3
15=	16	J Jackson	Kurtis Kraft	4000	Offenhauser	4	196			
15=	16	T Bettenhausen	Kurtis Kraft	4000	Offenhauser	4				
15=	16	M Teague	Kurtis Kraft	4000	Offenhauser	4				
16	32	E McCoy	Kurtis Kraft	500B	Offenhauser	4	194		20	7
17	25	J Reece	Pankratz		Offenhauser	4	194		7	3
18r=	27	E Elisian	Stevens		Offenhauser	4			31	11
18r=	27	B Scott	Stevens		Offenhauser	4	193	engine overheating		
19=	71	F Armi	Silnes		Offenhauser	4	193		33	11
19=	71	G Fonder	Silnes		Offenhauser	4				
20r=	1	S Hanks	Kurtis Kraft	4000	Offenhauser	4			10	4
20r=	1	J Davies	Kurtis Kraft	4000	Offenhauser	4				
20r=	1	J Rathmann	Kurtis Kraft	4000	Offenhauser	4	191	crankshaft / spin		
21r	35	P O'Connor	Kurtis Kraft	500C	Offenhauser	4	181	spin	12	4
22r=	12	R Ward	Eddie Allen		Offenhauser	4	172	stalled	16	6
22r=	12	E Johnson	Eddie Allen		Offenhauser	4				
23r=	31	G Hartley	Kurtis Kraft	4000	Offenhauser	4			17	6
23r=	31	M Teague	Kurtis Kraft	4000	Offenhauser	4	168	engine		
24r=	43	J Thomson	Nichels		Offenhauser	4			4	2
24r=	43	A Linden	Nichels		Offenhauser	4				
24r=	43	B Homeier	Nichels		Offenhauser	4	165	stalled		
25r=	74	A Linden	Schroeder		Offenhauser	4			23	8
25r=	74	B Scott	Schroeder		Offenhauser	4	165	torsion bar		
26r	99	J Hoyt	Kurtis Kraft		Offenhauser	4	130	engine	30	10
27r	19	J Daywalt	Kurtis Kraft	500C	Offenhauser	4	111	spin / hit wall & Flaherty	2	1
28r=	38	J Rathmann	Kurtis Kraft	500C	Offenhauser	4			28	10
28r=	38	P Flaherty	Kurtis Kraft	500C	Offenhauser	4	110	accident		
29r	10	T Bettenhausen	Kurtis Kraft	500C	Offenhauser	4	105	connecting rod	21	7
30r=	65	S Webb	Bromme		Offenhauser	4			29	10
30r=	65	D Kladis	Bromme		Offenhauser	4	104	oil leak		
31r=	33	L Duncan	Schroeder		Offenhauser	4			26	9
31r=	33	G Fonder	Schroeder		Offenhauser	4	101	brake cylinder		
32r	15	J Parsons	Kurtis Kraft	500C	Offenhauser	4	79	stalled in pits	15	5
33r	51	B Homeier	Kurtis Kraft	500C	Offenhauser	4	74	hit wall leaving pits	18	6

Winning speed 210.566 km/h, 130.840 mph.
Pole Position speed 226.970 km/h, 141.033 mph (J McGrath, 1 min: 3.815 sec)
Fastest Lap speed 226.173 km/h, 140.537 mph (J McGrath, 1 min: 4.040 sec on lap 29)

20 Jun 1954   BELGIUM: Spa-Francorchamps   (Round 3)   (Race 35)

36 laps x 14.120 km, 8.774 miles = 508.320 km, 315.855 miles

Pos	No	Driver	Car	Model	Engine		Laps	Time/Reason for Retirement	Grid Pos	Row
1	26	J M Fangio	Maserati	250F	Maserati	6	36	2h 44m 42.400s	1	1
2	8	M Trintignant	Ferrari	625	Ferrari	4	36	2h 45m 06.600s	6	3
3	22	S Moss	Maserati	250F	Maserati	6	35		9	4
4=	10	M Hawthorn	Ferrari	625	Ferrari	4			5	2
4=	10	F González	Ferrari	625	Ferrari	4	35			
5	18	A Pilette	Gordini	T16	Gordini	6	35		8	3
6	20	B Bira	Maserati	250F	Maserati	6	35		13	5
7	30	S Mantovani	Maserati	250F	Maserati	6	34		11	5
r	16	P Frère	Gordini	T16	Gordini	6	14	rear axle	10	4
r	4	G Farina	Ferrari	553	Ferrari	4	14	engine	3	1
r	12	J Behra	Gordini	T16	Gordini	6	12	rear suspension	7	3
r	28	O Marimón	Maserati	250F	Maserati	6	3	valve	4	2
r	2	J Swaters	Ferrari	500	Ferrari	4	1	engine	14	6
r	6	F González	Ferrari	553	Ferrari	4	1	oil line	2	1
r	24	R Mières	Maserati	A6GCM	Maserati	6	0	fuel on exhaust pipe / fire	12	5

Winning speed 185.173 km/h, 115.061 mph
Pole Position speed 193.941 km/h, 120.510 mph (J M Fangio, 4 min:22.100 sec)
Fastest Lap speed 191.458 km/h, 118.966 mph (J M Fangio, 4 min:25.500 sec on lap 13)
Lap Leaders G Farina 1-2,11-13 (5); J M Fangio 3-10,14-36 (31).

E de Graffenried was present in a camera car – Maserati A6GCM-Maserati 6 (50).

4 Jul 1954   FRANCE: Reims   (Round 4)   (Race 36)

61 laps x 8.302 km, 5.159 miles = 506.422 km, 314.676 miles

Pos	No	Driver	Car	Model	Engine		Laps	Time/Reason for Retirement	Grid Pos	Row
1	18	J M Fangio	Mercedes-Benz	W196 str.	Mercedes-Benz	8	61	2h 42m 47.900s	1	1
2	20	K Kling	Mercedes-Benz	W196 str.	Mercedes-Benz	8	61	2h 42m 48.000s	2	1
3	34	R Manzon	Ferrari	625	Ferrari	4	60		12	5
4	46	B Bira	Maserati	250F	Maserati	6	60		6	3
5	14	L Villoresi	Maserati	250F	Maserati	6	58		14	6
6	24	J Behra	Gordini	T16	Gordini	6	56		17	7
r	28	P Frère	Gordini	T16	Gordini	6	50	rear axle	19	8
r	4	M Trintignant	Ferrari	625	Ferrari	4	36	piston	9	4
r	12	O Marimón	Maserati	250F	Maserati	6	27	gear selector	5	2
r	36	L Rosier	Ferrari	500	Ferrari	4	27	engine	13	5
r	16	R Mières	Maserati	A6GCM	Maserati	6	24	piston	11	5
r	48	H Schell	Maserati	A6GCM	Maserati	6	19	fuel pump	21	9
r	42	K Wharton	Maserati	250F	Maserati	6	19	propeller shaft	16	7
r	22	H Herrmann	Mercedes-Benz	W196 str.	Mercedes-Benz	8	16	piston	7	3
r	44	R Salvadori	Maserati	250F	Maserati	6	15	half shaft	10	4
r	2	F González	Ferrari	553	Ferrari	4	13	engine	4	2
r	32	L Macklin	HWM	(53)	Alta	4	10	engine	15	6
r	6	M Hawthorn	Ferrari	553	Ferrari	4	9	engine	8	3
r	30	G Berger	Gordini	T16	Gordini	6	9	valve	20	8
r	26	J Pollet	Gordini	T16	Gordini	6	8	engine	18	7
r	10	A Ascari	Maserati	250F	Maserati	6	1	transmission	3	1
ns	40	S Mantovani	Maserati	250F	Maserati	6				

Winning speed 186.644 km/h, 115.975 mph
Pole Position speed 200.048 km/h, 124.304 mph (J M Fangio, 2 min:29.400 sec)
Fastest Lap speed 195.469 km/h, 121.459 mph (H Herrmann, 2 min:32.900 sec on lap 3)
Lap Leaders K Kling 1-2,29-33,38,54-57,60 (13); J M Fangio 3-28,34-37,39-53,58-59,61 (48)

17 Jul 1954　　BRITAIN: Silverstone　　　　　　　　　　　　　　　　(Round 5)　(Race 37)
90 laps x 4.711 km, 2.927 miles = 423.949 km, 263.430 miles

Pos	No	Driver	Car	Model	Engine		Laps	Time/Reason for Retirement	Grid Pos	Row
1	9	F González	Ferrari	625	Ferrari	4	90	2h 56m 14.000s	2	1
2	11	M Hawthorn	Ferrari	625	Ferrari	4	90	2h 57m 24.000s	3	1
3	33	O Marimón	Maserati	250F	Maserati	6	89		28	8
4	1	J M Fangio	Mercedes-Benz	W196 str.	Mercedes-Benz	8	89		1	1
5	10	M Trintignant	Ferrari	625	Ferrari	4	87		8	3
6	4	R Mières	Maserati	A6GCM	Maserati	6	87		31	9
7	2	K Kling	Mercedes-Benz	W196 str.	Mercedes-Benz	8	87		6	2
8	8	K Wharton	Maserati	250F	Maserati	6	86		9	3
9	19	A Pilette	Gordini	T16	Gordini	6	86		12	4
10	29	B Gerard	Cooper	T23	Bristol	6	85		18	5
11	25	D Beauman	Connaught	A	Lea Francis	4	84		17	5
12	3	H Schell	Maserati	A6GCM	Maserati	6	83		16	5
13	23	L Marr	Connaught	A	Lea Francis	4	82		22	7
r	7	S Moss	Maserati	250F	Maserati	6	80	driveshaft	4	1
14	26	L Thorne	Connaught	A	Lea Francis	4	78		23	7
r	22	B Whitehouse	Connaught	A	Lea Francis	4	63	fuel system	19	6
r	17	J Behra	Gordini	T16	Gordini	6	54	rear suspension	5	2
r=	5	R Salvadori	Maserati	250F	Maserati	6	53	transmission	7	2
r=	6	B Bira	Maserati	250F	Maserati	6			10	3
r=	6	R Flockhart	Maserati	250F	Maserati	6	44	accident		
15	28	H Gould	Cooper	T23	Bristol	6	44		20	6
r=	32	L Villoresi	Maserati	250F	Maserati	6			27	8
r=	32	A Ascari	Maserati	250F	Maserati	6	40	connecting rod		
r	24	J Riseley-Prichard	Connaught	A	Lea Francis	4	40	accident	21	6
r	12	R Parnell	Ferrari	500	Ferrari	4	25	water jacket	14	4
r	31	A Ascari	Maserati	250F	Maserati	6	21	dropped valve	30	9
r	18	C Bucci	Gordini	T16	Gordini	6	18	accident	13	4
r	20	P Collins	Vanwall	Spl.	Vanwall	4	16	cylinder head gasket	11	3
r	14	R Manzon	Ferrari	625	Ferrari	4	15	cylinder head	15	5
r	21	P Whitehead	Cooper	T24	Alta	4	4	oil line	24	7
r	30	E Brandon	Cooper	T23	Bristol	6	2	engine	25	7
r	15	L Rosier	Ferrari	500	Ferrari	4	2	valve	29	9
ns	27	A Brown	Cooper	T23	Bristol	6			26	8
ns	30	R Nuckey	Cooper	T23	Bristol	6		car raced by Brandon		

Winning speed 144.337 km/h, 89.687 mph
Pole Position speed 161.505 km/h, 100.354 mph (J M Fangio, 1 min:45.000 sec)
Fastest Lap speed 154.163 km/h, 95.793 mph (Ascari/Behra/Fangio/González/Hawthorn/Marimón/Moss, 1 min:50.000 sec)
Lap Leaders F González 1-90 (90).

1 Aug 1954　　GERMANY: Nürburgring　　　　　　　　　　　　　　　(Round 6)　(Race 38)
22 laps x 22.810 km, 14.173 miles = 501.820 km, 311.816 miles

Pos	No	Driver	Car	Model	Engine		Laps	Time/Reason for Retirement	Grid Pos	Row
1	18	J M Fangio	Mercedes-Benz	W196	Mercedes-Benz	8	22	3h 45m 45.800s	1	1
2=	1	F González	Ferrari	625	Ferrari	4			5	2
2=	1	M Hawthorn	Ferrari	625	Ferrari	4	22	3h 47m 22.300s	7	3
3	2	M Trintignant	Ferrari	625	Ferrari	4	22	3h 50m 54.400s	7	3
4	19	K Kling	Mercedes-Benz	W196	Mercedes-Benz	8	22	3h 51m 52.300s	23	9
5	7	S Mantovani	Maserati	250F	Maserati	6	22	3h 54m 36.300s	15	6
6	4	P Taruffi	Ferrari	625	Ferrari	4	21		13	5
7	15	H Schell	Maserati	A6GCM	Maserati	6	21		14	6
8	25	L Rosier	Ferrari	500	Ferrari	4	21		18	7
9	24	R Manzon	Ferrari	625	Ferrari	4	20		12	5
10	9	J Behra	Gordini	T16	Gordini	6	20		9	4
r	14	B Bira	Maserati	250F	Maserati	6	18	steering	19	8
r	21	H Lang	Mercedes-Benz	W196	Mercedes-Benz	8	10	spin	11	5
r	11	C Bucci	Gordini	T16	Gordini	6	8	stub axle / wheel lost	16	7
r	22	T Helfrich	Klenk	Meteor	BMW	6	8	engine	21	9
r	20	H Herrmann	Mercedes-Benz	W196 str.	Mercedes-Benz	8	7	fuel injection pipe	4	2
r	10	P Frère	Gordini	T16	Gordini	6	4	stub axle / wheel lost	6	3
r	3	M Hawthorn	Ferrari	625	Ferrari	4	3	rear axle	2	1
r	8	R Mières	Maserati	250F	Maserati	6	3	fuel tank	17	7
r	16	S Moss	Maserati	250F	Maserati	6	1	big end bearing	3	1
r	12	A Pilette	Gordini	T16	Gordini	6	0	front suspension	20	8
ns	6	O Marimón	Maserati	250F	Maserati	6		fatal accident	8	3
ns	5	L Villoresi	Maserati	250F	Maserati	6		withdrew after Marimón accident	10	4
ns	17	K Wharton	Maserati	250F	Maserati	6		withdrew	22	9

Winning speed 133.366 km/h, 82.870 mph
Pole Position speed 139.156 km/h, 86.468 mph (J M Fangio, 9 min:50.100 sec)
Fastest Lap speed 137.987 km/h, 85.741 mph (K Kling, 9 min:55.100 sec on lap 16)
Lap Leaders J M Fangio 1-14,17-22 (20); K Kling 15-16 (2).

Also the Grand Prix of Europe.

22 Aug 1954		**SWITZERLAND: Bremgarten**						(Round 7)		(Race 39)

66 laps x 7.280 km, 4.524 miles = 480.480 km, 298.556 miles

Pos	No	Driver	Car	Model	Engine		Laps	Time/Reason for Retirement	Grid Pos	Row
1	4	J M Fangio	Mercedes-Benz	W196	Mercedes-Benz	8	66	3h 00m 34.500s	2	1
2	20	F González	Ferrari	625	Ferrari	4	66	3h 01m 32.300s	1	1
3	6	H Herrmann	Mercedes-Benz	W196	Mercedes-Benz	8	65		7	3
4	30	R Mières	Maserati	250F	Maserati	6	64		12	5
5	28	S Mantovani	Maserati	250F	Maserati	6	64		9	4
6	18	K Wharton	Maserati	250F	Maserati	6	64		8	3
7	24	U Maglioli	Ferrari	553	Ferrari	4	61		11	5
8	2	J Swaters	Ferrari	500	Ferrari	4	58		16	7
r	8	K Kling	Mercedes-Benz	W196	Mercedes-Benz	8	38	fuel injection pump	5	2
r	26	M Trintignant	Ferrari	625	Ferrari	4	33	engine	4	2
r	22	M Hawthorn	Ferrari	625	Ferrari	4	30	oil pump	6	3
r	34	H Schell	Maserati	250F	Maserati	6	23	oil pump	13	5
r	32	S Moss	Maserati	250F	Maserati	6	21	oil pump	3	1
r	14	F Wacker	Gordini	T16	Gordini	6	10	transmission	15	6
r	10	J Behra	Gordini	T16	Gordini	6	8	clutch	14	6
r	12	C Bucci	Gordini	T16	Gordini	6	0	fuel pump	10	4
ns	24	R Manzon	Ferrari	553	Ferrari	4		accident		

Winning speed 159.650 km/h, 99.202 mph
Pole Position speed 164.313 km/h, 102.100 mph (F González, 2 min:39.500 sec)
Fastest Lap speed 164.108 km/h, 101.972 mph (J M Fangio, 2 min:39.700 sec on lap 34)
Lap Leaders J M Fangio 1-66 (66).

5 Sep 1954		**ITALY: Monza**						(Round 8)		(Race 40)

80 laps x 6.300 km, 3.915 miles = 504.000 km, 313.171 miles

Pos	No	Driver	Car	Model	Engine		Laps	Time/Reason for Retirement	Grid Pos	Row
1	16	J M Fangio	Mercedes-Benz	W196 str.	Mercedes-Benz	8	80	2h 47m 47.900s	1	1
2	40	M Hawthorn	Ferrari	625	Ferrari	4	79		7	3
3=	38	U Maglioli	Ferrari	625	Ferrari	4			13	5
3=	38	F González	Ferrari	625	Ferrari	4	78			
4	12	H Herrmann	Mercedes-Benz	W196	Mercedes-Benz	8	77		8	3
5	30	M Trintignant	Ferrari	625	Ferrari	4	75		11	4
6	42	F Wacker	Gordini	T16	Gordini	6	75		18	6
7	10	P Collins	Vanwall	Spl.	Vanwall	4	75		16	6
8	26	L Rosier	Maserati	250F	Maserati	6	74		20	7
9	18	S Mantovani	Maserati	250F	Maserati	6	74		9	3
10	28	S Moss	Maserati	250F	Maserati	6	71		3	1
11	8	J Daponte	Maserati	A6GCM	Maserati	6	70		19	7
r	34	A Ascari	Ferrari	625	Ferrari	4	48	valves	2	1
r	22	L Villoresi	Maserati	250F	Maserati	6	42	clutch spring	6	2
r	14	K Kling	Mercedes-Benz	W196 str.	Mercedes-Benz	8	36	accident	4	2
r	24	R Mières	Maserati	250F	Maserati	6	34	suspension	10	4
r	20	L Musso	Maserati	250F	Maserati	6	32	transmission	14	5
r	32	F González	Ferrari	553	Ferrari	4	16	gearbox oil seal	5	2
r	6	R Manzon	Ferrari	625	Ferrari	4	16	engine	15	5
r	46	C Bucci	Gordini	T16	Gordini	6	13	transmission	17	6
r	44	J Behra	Gordini	T16	Gordini	6	2	engine	12	4
ns	2	G de Riu	Maserati	A6GCM	Maserati	6				

Winning speed 180.216 km/h, 111.981 mph
Pole Position speed 190.588 km/h, 118.426 mph (J M Fangio, 1 min:59.000 sec)
Fastest Lap speed 187.748 km/h, 116.661 mph (F González, 2 min: 0.800 sec on lap 2)
Lap Leaders K Kling 1-3 (3); J M Fangio 4-5,23,68-80 (16); A Ascari 6-22,24-44,46-48 (41); S Moss 45,49-67 (20).

24 Oct 1954   **SPAIN: Pedralbes**   **(Round 9)**   **(Race 41)**

80 laps x 6.316 km, 3.925 miles = 505.280 km, 313.966 miles

Pos	No	Driver	Car	Model	Engine		Laps	Time/Reason for Retirement	Grid Pos	Row
1	38	M Hawthorn	Ferrari	553	Ferrari	4	80	3h 13m 52.100s	3	1
2	14	L Musso	Maserati	250F	Maserati	6	80	3h 15m 05.300s	7	2
3	2	J M Fangio	Mercedes-Benz	W196	Mercedes-Benz	8	79		2	1
4	10	R Mières	Maserati	250F	Maserati	6	79		11	3
5	4	K Kling	Mercedes-Benz	W196	Mercedes-Benz	8	79		12	4
6	16	C Godia	Maserati	250F	Maserati	6	76		13	4
7	26	L Rosier	Maserati	250F	Maserati	6	74		20	6
8	28	K Wharton	Maserati	250F	Maserati	6	74		14	4
9	18	B Bira	Maserati	250F	Maserati	6	68		15	5
r	12	S Mantovani	Maserati	250F	Maserati	6	58	brakes / accident	10	3
r=	22	E de Graffenried	Maserati	A6GCM	Maserati	6			21	6
r=	22	O Volonterio	Maserati	A6GCM	Maserati	6	57	engine		
r	6	H Herrmann	Mercedes-Benz	W196	Mercedes-Benz	8	50	fuel injection pump	9	3
r	40	M Trintignant	Ferrari	625	Ferrari	4	47	gearbox	8	3
r	48	J Pollet	Gordini	T16	Gordini	6	37	engine	16	5
r	24	H Schell	Maserati	250F	Maserati	6	29	rear axle	4	1
r	8	S Moss	Maserati	250F	Maserati	6	20	oil scavenge pump	6	2
r	46	J Behra	Gordini	T16	Gordini	6	17	brakes	18	5
r	30	J Swaters	Ferrari	500	Ferrari	4	16	engine	19	6
r	34	A Ascari	Lancia	D50	Lancia	V8	10	oil seal / clutch	1	1
r	36	L Villoresi	Lancia	D50	Lancia	V8	2	brakes	5	2
r	20	R Manzon	Ferrari	625	Ferrari	4	2	engine	17	5
ns	42	P Collins	Vanwall	Spl.	Vanwall	4		accident		

Winning speed 156.378 km/h, 97.169 mph
Pole Position speed 164.646 km/h, 102.306 mph (A Ascari, 2 min:18.100 sec)
Fastest Lap speed 161.949 km/h, 100.630 mph (A Ascari, 2 min:20.400 sec on lap 3)
Lap Leaders H Schell 1-2,10,13,15-17,19,21,23 (10); A Ascari 3-9 (7); M Trintignant 11-12,14,18,20 (5); M Hawthorn 22,24-80 (58).

Lap Leaders 1954

Pos	Driver	Car-Engine	GPs	laps	km	miles
1	J M Fangio	Maserati	2	68*	582.5	361.9
		Mercedes-Benz	4	150	1,436.0	892.3
			6	218	2,018.5	1,254.2
2	F González	Ferrari	2	122*	549.2	341.2
3	M Hawthorn	Ferrari	2	60	374.2	232.5
4	A Ascari	Ferrari	1	41	258.3	160.5
		Lancia	1	7	44.2	27.5
			2	48	302.5	188.0
5	G Farina	Ferrari	2	21*	133.2	82.8
6	S Moss	Maserati	1	20	126.0	78.3
7	K Kling	Mercedes-Benz	3	18	172.4	107.2
8	H Schell	Maserati	1	10	63.2	39.2
9	M Trintignant	Ferrari	1	5	31.6	19.6
lap totals include estimates			8	522	3,770.7	2,343.0

Driver Points 1954

		RA	INDY	B	F	GB	D	CH	I	E	Total	
1	J M Fangio	8	-	9	8	(3*)	8	9	(8)	(4)	42	(15.14)
2	F González	5	-	(1.5)	-	8*	3	6	3	-	25.14	(1.5)
3	M Hawthorn	-	-	1.5	-	6*	3	-	6	8	24.64	
4	M Trintignant	3	-	6	-	2	4	-	2	-	17	
5	K Kling	-	-	-	6	-	4	-	-	2	12	
6	B Vukovich	-	8	-	-	-	-	-	-	-	8	
	H Herrmann	-	-	-	1	-	-	4	3	-	8	
8	G Farina	6	-	-	-	-	-	-	-	-	6	
	J Bryan	-	6	-	-	-	-	-	-	-	6	
	L Musso	-	-	-	-	-	-	-	-	6	6	
	R Mières	-	-	-	-	-	-	3	-	3	6	
12	J McGrath	-	5	-	-	-	-	-	-	-	5	
13	S Moss	-	-	4	-	*	-	-	-	-	4.14	
	O Marimón	-	-	-	-	4*	-	-	-	-	4.14	
15	R Manzon	-	-	-	4	-	-	-	-	-	4	
	S Mantovani	-	-	-	-	-	2	2	-	-	4	
17	B Bira	-	-	-	3	-	-	-	-	-	3	
18	E Bayol	2	-	-	-	-	-	-	-	-	2	
	M Nazaruk	-	2	-	-	-	-	-	-	-	2	
	A Pilette	-	-	2	-	-	-	-	-	-	2	
	L Villoresi	-	-	-	2	-	-	-	-	-	2	
	U Maglioli	-	-	-	-	-	-	-	2	-	2	
23	T Ruttman	-	1.5	-	-	-	-	-	-	-	1.5	
	D Carter	-	1.5	-	-	-	-	-	-	-	1.5	
25	A Ascari	-	-	-	-	*	-	-	-	1	1.14	
26	J Behra	-	-	-	-	*	-	-	-	-	0.14	

8,6,4,3 and 2 points awarded to the first five finishers. The driver setting the fastest lap scored a point also. Points shared for shared drives. Best 5 scores.
* Point for fastest lap shared by seven drivers.

Race Entrants and Results

Mercedes dominance continued into 1955, with Moss moving into the big time as Fangio's team-mate. Ascari was killed at Monza while trying out a Ferrari sports car, just days after surviving a ducking in the Monaco harbour. Worse was to come with the Le Mans tragedy that took the lives of more than 80 spectators and resulted in many cancelled World Championship races. This led to a temporary motorsport ban in France and a ban of all circuit racing in Switzerland (which still remains). In July, Lancia handed over their complete racing team to Ferrari.

FERRARI
Scuderia Ferrari: Trintignant, Farina, Castellotti, Taruffi, González, Frère, Maglioli, Hawthorn, Schell
Equipe Nationale Belge: Claes

LANCIA
Scuderia Lancia: Ascari, Villoresi, Castellotti, Chiron
Scderia Ferrari: (Farina, Villoresi (I))

MASERATI
Officine Alfieri Maserati: Behra, Musso, Mières, Perdisa, Menditéguy, Schell, Mantovani, Bucci, Simon, Collins (I), Gould (I)
Stirling Moss Ltd: Macklin, Walker, Fitch (Claes)
Ecurie Rosier: Rosier
Gould's Garage (Bristol): Gould
Gilby Engineering Ltd: Salvadori
Owen Racing Organisation: Collins
Privateer: Uría

ARZANI VOLPINI
Privateer: (Piotti)

GORDINI
Equipe Gordini: Manzon, Pollet, da Silva Ramos, Bayol, Sparken, Lucas, Birger, Iglesias

CONNAUGHT
Connaught Engineering: McAlpine, (Fairman)
R R C Walker Racing Team: Rolt, Walker
Privateer: Marr

COOPER
Cooper Car Co: Brabham

HWM
Privateer: (Whiteaway)

VANWALL
Vandervell Products Ltd: Hawthorn, Wharton, Schell

MERCEDES-BENZ
Daimler Benz AG: Fangio, Moss, Kling, Herrmann, Taruffi, Simon

16 Jan 1955		ARGENTINA: Buenos Aires No.2							(Round 1)	(Race 42)	
		96 laps x 3.912 km, 2.431 miles = 375.552 km, 233.357 miles									
Pos	No	Driver	Car	Model	Engine		Laps	Time/Reason for Retirement		Grid Pos	Row
1	2	J M Fangio	Mercedes-Benz	W196	Mercedes-Benz	8	96	3h 00m 38.600s		3	1
2=	12	F González	Ferrari	625	Ferrari	4				1	1
2=	12	G Farina	Ferrari	625	Ferrari	4	96	3h 02m 08.200s			
2=	12	M Trintignant	Ferrari	625	Ferrari	4					
3=	10	G Farina	Ferrari	625	Ferrari	4				5	2
3=	10	U Maglioli	Ferrari	625	Ferrari	4	94				
3=	10	M Trintignant	Ferrari	625	Ferrari	4					
4=	8	H Herrmann	Mercedes-Benz	W196	Mercedes-Benz	8				10	3
4=	8	K Kling	Mercedes-Benz	W196	Mercedes-Benz	8					
4=	8	S Moss	Mercedes-Benz	W196	Mercedes-Benz	8	94				
5	18	R Mières	Maserati	250F	Maserati	6	91			16	5
6=	28	H Schell	Maserati	250F	Maserati	6				7	2
6=	28	J Behra	Maserati	250F	Maserati	6	88				
7=	22	L Musso	Maserati	250F	Maserati	6				18	5
7=	22	S Mantovani	Maserati	250F	Maserati	6					
7=	22	H Schell	Maserati	250F	Maserati	6	83				
r=	20	S Mantovani	Maserati	250F	Maserati	6				19	6
r=	20	L Musso	Maserati	250F	Maserati	6					
r=	20	J Behra	Maserati	250F	Maserati	6	55	fuel pressure			
r=	26	C Bucci	Maserati	250F	Maserati	6				20	6
r=	26	H Schell	Maserati	250F	Maserati	6					
r=	26	C Menditéguy	Maserati	250F	Maserati	6	55	fuel pressure			
r	42	J Iglesias	Gordini	T16	Gordini	6	38	transmission		17	5
r	14	M Trintignant	Ferrari	625	Ferrari	4	36	valve		14	4
r=	36	E Castellotti	Lancia	D50	Lancia	V8				12	4
r=	36	L Villoresi	Lancia	D50	Lancia	V8	35	accident			
r	6	S Moss	Mercedes-Benz	W196	Mercedes-Benz	8	29	fuel vaporisation		8	3
r	30	A Uría	Maserati	A6GCM	Maserati	6	22	fuel pressure		21	6
r	32	A Ascari	Lancia	D50	Lancia	V8	21	accident		2	1
r	38	É Bayol	Gordini	T16	Gordini	6	7	transmission		15	5
r	4	K Kling	Mercedes-Benz	W196	Mercedes-Benz	8	1	accident		6	2
r	16	J Behra	Maserati	250F	Maserati	6	1	accident		4	1
r	24	C Menditéguy	Maserati	250F	Maserati	6	1	accident		13	4
r	40	P Birger	Gordini	T16	Gordini	6	1	accident		9	3
r	34	L Villoresi	Lancia	D50	Lancia	V8	1	fuel line		11	3

Winning speed 124.738 km/h, 77.509 mph
Pole Position speed 136.597 km/h, 84.878 mph (F González, 1 min:43.100 sec)
Fastest Lap speed 130.039 km/h, 80.802 mph (J M Fangio, 1 min:48.300 sec on lap 45)
Lap Leaders J M Fangio 1-2,27-35,43-96 (65); A Ascari 3-5,12-21 (13); F González 6-11,22-26 (11); H Schell 36-42 (7).

22 May 1955   **MONACO: Monte-Carlo**   **(Round 2)**   **(Race 43)**

100 laps x 3.145 km, 1.954 miles = 314.500 km, 195.421 miles

Pos	No	Driver	Car	Model	Engine		Laps	Time/Reason for Retirement	Grid Pos	Row
1	44	M Trintignant	Ferrari	625	Ferrari	4	100	2h 58m 09.700s	9	4
2	30	E Castellotti	Lancia	D50	Lancia	V8	100	2h 58m 30.000s	4	2
3=	34	J Behra	Maserati	250F	Maserati	6			5	2
3=	34	C Perdisa	Maserati	250F	Maserati	6	99			
4	42	G Farina	Ferrari	625	Ferrari	4	99		14	6
5	28	L Villoresi	Lancia	D50	Lancia	V8	99		7	3
6	32	L Chiron	Lancia	D50	Lancia	V8	95		19	8
7	10	J Pollet	Gordini	T16	Gordini	6	91		20	8
r=	40	C Perdisa	Maserati	250F	Maserati	6			11	5
r=	40	J Behra	Maserati	250F	Maserati	6	86	clutch / spin		
8=	48	P Taruffi	Ferrari	555	Ferrari	4			15	6
8=	48	P Frère	Ferrari	555	Ferrari	4	86			
9	6	S Moss	Mercedes-Benz	W196	Mercedes-Benz	8	81		3	1
r	26	A Ascari	Lancia	D50	Lancia	V8	80	accident	2	1
r	46	H Schell	Ferrari	555	Ferrari	4	68	engine	18	7
r	36	R Mières	Maserati	250F	Maserati	6	64	rear axle	6	3
r	12	É Bayol	Gordini	T16	Gordini	6	63	rear axle	16	7
r	2	J M Fangio	Mercedes-Benz	W196	Mercedes-Benz	8	49	transmission	1	1
r	8	R Manzon	Gordini	T16	Gordini	6	38	gearbox	13	5
r	4	A Simon	Mercedes-Benz	W196	Mercedes-Benz	8	24	oil pipe	10	4
r	18	M Hawthorn	Vanwall	VW (55)	Vanwall	4	22	throttle linkage	12	5
r	14	L Rosier	Maserati	250F	Maserati	6	8	spin / fuel tank	17	7
r	38	L Musso	Maserati	250F	Maserati	6	7	transmission	8	3
nq	22	L Macklin	Maserati	250F	Maserati	6				
nq	24	T Whiteaway	HWM	(53)	Alta	4				
ns	4	H Herrmann	Mercedes-Benz	W196	Mercedes-Benz	8		accident / injury		

Winning speed 105.915 km/h, 65.813 mph
Pole Position speed 111.988 km/h, 69.586 mph (J M Fangio, 1 min:41.100 sec)
Fastest Lap speed 110.566 km/h, 68.703 mph (J M Fangio, 1 min:42.400 sec on lap 27)
Lap Leaders J M Fangio 1-49 (49); S Moss 50-80 (31); M Trintignant 81-100 (20).

Also the Grand Prix of Europe.

30 May 1955   **INDIANAPOLIS: 500**   **(Round 3)**   **(Race 44)**

200 laps x 4.023 km, 2.500 miles = 804.672 km, 500.000 miles

Pos	No	Driver	Car	Model	Engine		Laps	Time/Reason for Retirement	Grid Pos	Row
1	6	B Sweikert	Kurtis Kraft	500D	Offenhauser	4	200	3h 53m 59.530s	14	5
2=	10	T Bettenhausen	Kurtis Kraft	500C	Offenhauser	4	200	3h 56m 43.088s	2	1
2=	10	P Russo	Kurtis Kraft	500C	Offenhauser	4				
3	15	J Davies	Kurtis Kraft	500B	Offenhauser	4	200		10	4
4	44	J Thomson	Kuzma		Offenhauser	4	200		33	11
5=	77	W Faulkner	Kurtis Kraft	500C	Offenhauser	4	200		7	3
5=	77	B Homeier	Kurtis Kraft	500C	Offenhauser	4				
6	19	A Linden	Kurtis Kraft	4000	Offenhauser	4	200		8	3
7	71	A Herman	Silnes		Offenhauser	4	200		16	6
8	29	P O'Connor	Kurtis Kraft	500D	Offenhauser	4	200		19	7
9	48	J Daywalt	Kurtis Kraft		Offenhauser	4	200		17	6
10	89	P Flaherty	Kurtis Kraft	500B	Offenhauser	4	200		12	4
11	98	D Carter	Kuzma		Offenhauser	4	197		18	6
12	41	C Weyant	Kurtis Kraft	3000	Offenhauser	4	196		25	9
13	83	E Johnson	Trevis		Offenhauser	4	196		32	11
14	33	J Rathmann	Epperly		Offenhauser	4	191		20	7
15r	12	D Freeland	Phillips		Offenhauser	4	178	transmission	21	7
16r	22	C Niday	Kurtis Kraft	500B	Offenhauser	4	170	accident / fire	9	3
17r	99	A Cross	Kurtis Kraft	500D	Offenhauser	4	168	connecting rod	24	8
18r	81	S Templeman	Trevis		Offenhauser	4	142	transmission	31	11
19r	8	S Hanks	Kurtis Kraft	500C	Offenhauser	4	134	transmission	6	2
20r	31	K Andrews	Schroeder		Offenhauser	4	120	ignition	28	10
21r	16	J Parsons	Kurtis Kraft	500D	Offenhauser	4	119	magneto	27	9
22r	37	E Russo	Eddie Allen		Offenhauser	4	112	ignition	13	5
23r	49	R Crawford	Kurtis Kraft	500B	Offenhauser	4	111	valve	23	8
24r	1	J Bryan	Kuzma		Offenhauser	4	90	fuel pump	11	4
25r	4	B Vukovich	Kurtis Kraft	500C	Offenhauser	4	56	fatal accident	5	2
26r	3	J McGrath	Kurtis Kraft	500C	Offenhauser	4	54	magneto	3	1
27r	42	A Keller	Kurtis Kraft	2000	Offenhauser	4	54	accident	22	8
28r	27	R Ward	Kuzma		Offenhauser	4	53	accident	30	10
29r	39	J Boyd	Kurtis Kraft	500C	Offenhauser	4	53	accident	26	9
30r	68	E Elisian	Kurtis Kraft	4000	Offenhauser	4	53	stopped to help Vukovich	29	10
31r	23	J Hoyt	Stevens		Offenhauser	4	40	oil leak	1	1
32r	14	F Agabashian	Kurtis Kraft	500D	Offenhauser	4	39	spin	4	2
33r	5	J Reece	Pankratz		Offenhauser	4	10	connecting rod / spin	15	5

Winning speed 206.333 km/h, 128.209 mph
Pole Position speed 225.381 km/h, 140.045 mph (J Hoyt, 1 min: 4.265 sec)
Fastest Lap speed 227.487 km/h, 141.354 mph (B Vukovich, 1 min: 3.670 sec on lap 27)
Fastest qualifier J McGrath (229.460 km/h, 142.580 mph).

5 Jun 1955		BELGIUM: Spa-Francorchamps							(Round 4)	(Race 45)

36 laps x 14.120 km, 8.774 miles = 508.320 km, 315.855 miles

Pos	No	Driver	Car	Model	Engine		Laps	Time/Reason for Retirement	Grid Pos	Row
1	10	J M Fangio	Mercedes-Benz	W196	Mercedes-Benz	8	36	2h 39m 29.000s	2	1
2	14	S Moss	Mercedes-Benz	W196	Mercedes-Benz	8	36	2h 39m 37.100s	3	1
3	2	G Farina	Ferrari	555	Ferrari	4	36	2h 41m 09.500s	4	2
4	6	P Frère	Ferrari	555	Ferrari	4	36	2h 42m 54.500s	8	3
5=	24	R Mières	Maserati	250F	Maserati	6			13	5
5=	24	J Behra	Maserati	250F	Maserati	6	35			
6	4	M Trintignant	Ferrari	555	Ferrari	4	35		10	4
7	22	L Musso	Maserati	250F	Maserati	6	34		7	3
8	26	C Perdisa	Maserati	250F	Maserati	6	33		11	5
9	28	L Rosier	Maserati	250F	Maserati	6	33		12	5
r	12	K Kling	Mercedes-Benz	W196	Mercedes-Benz	8	21	oil line	6	3
r	30	E Castellotti	Lancia	D50	Lancia	V8	16	gearbox	1	1
r	40	M Hawthorn	Vanwall	VW (55)	Vanwall	4	8	gearbox	9	4
r	20	J Behra	Maserati	250F	Maserati	6	3	accident	5	2
ns	38	J Claes	Maserati	250F	Maserati	6		engine		

Winning speed 191.238 km/h, 118.829 mph
Pole Position speed 196.947 km/h, 122.377 mph (E Castellotti, 4 min:18.100 sec)
Fastest Lap speed 195.058 km/h, 121.203 mph (J M Fangio, 4 min:20.600 sec on lap 18)
Lap Leaders J M Fangio 1-36 (36).

19 Jun 1955		NETHERLANDS: Zandvoort							(Round 5)	(Race 46)

100 laps x 4.193 km, 2.605 miles = 419.300 km, 260.541 miles

Pos	No	Driver	Car	Model	Engine		Laps	Time/Reason for Retirement	Grid Pos	Row
1	8	J M Fangio	Mercedes-Benz	W196	Mercedes-Benz	8	100	2h 54m 23.800s	1	1
2	10	S Moss	Mercedes-Benz	W196	Mercedes-Benz	8	100	2h 54m 24.100s	2	1
3	18	L Musso	Maserati	250F	Maserati	6	100	2h 55m 20.900s	4	2
4	16	R Mières	Maserati	250F	Maserati	6	99		7	3
5	6	E Castellotti	Ferrari	555	Ferrari	4	97		9	4
6	14	J Behra	Maserati	250F	Maserati	6	97		6	3
7	2	M Hawthorn	Ferrari	555	Ferrari	4	97		5	2
8	22	N da Silva Ramos	Gordini	T16	Gordini	6	92		14	6
9	28	L Rosier	Maserati	250F	Maserati	6	92		13	5
10	24	J Pollet	Gordini	T16	Gordini	6	90		12	5
11	30	J Claes	Ferrari	500	Ferrari	4	88		16	7
r	4	M Trintignant	Ferrari	555	Ferrari	4	64	gearbox	8	3
r	20	R Manzon	Gordini	T16	Gordini	6	43	rear axle	11	5
r	32	H Gould	Maserati	250F	Maserati	6	23	accident	15	6
r	12	K Kling	Mercedes-Benz	W196	Mercedes-Benz	8	21	spin	3	1
r	26	P Walker	Maserati	250F	Maserati	6	2	wheel bearing / spin	10	4

Winning speed 144.257 km/h, 89.637 mph
Pole Position speed 150.948 km/h, 93.795 mph (J M Fangio, 1 min:40.000 sec)
Fastest Lap speed 149.602 km/h, 92.958 mph (R Mières, 1 min:40.900 sec on lap 3)
Lap Leaders J M Fangio 1-100 (100).

90 laps x 4.828 km, 3.000 miles = 434.523 km, 270.000 miles

Pos	No	Driver	Car	Model	Engine		Laps	Time/Reason for Retirement	Grid Pos	Row
1	12	S Moss	Mercedes-Benz	W196	Mercedes-Benz	8	90	3h 07m 21.200s	1	1
2	10	J M Fangio	Mercedes-Benz	W196	Mercedes-Benz	8	90	3h 07m 21.400s	2	1
3	14	K Kling	Mercedes-Benz	W196	Mercedes-Benz	8	90	3h 08m 33.000s	4	2
4	50	P Taruffi	Mercedes-Benz	W196	Mercedes-Benz	8	89		5	2
5	4	L Musso	Maserati	250F	Maserati	6	89		9	4
6=	16	M Hawthorn	Ferrari	625	Ferrari	4			12	5
6=	16	E Castellotti	Ferrari	625	Ferrari	4	87			
7	26	M Sparken	Gordini	T16	Gordini	6	81		23	9
8	46	L Macklin	Maserati	250F	Maserati	6	79		16	7
9=	28	K Wharton	Vanwall	VW (55)	Vanwall	4			15	6
9=	28	H Schell	Vanwall	VW (55)	Vanwall	4	72			
r	18	M Trintignant	Ferrari	625	Ferrari	4	59	cylinder head	13	5
r	6	R Mières	Maserati	250F	Maserati	6	47	piston	6	3
r	40	J Brabham	Cooper	T40	Bristol	6	31	valve	25	10
r	32	K McAlpine	Connaught	B str.	Alta	4	30	oil line	17	7
r	42	P Collins	Maserati	250F	Maserati	6	29	clutch	24	10
r	24	N da Silva Ramos	Gordini	T16	Gordini	6	26	oil pressure / engine	18	7
r	44	R Salvadori	Maserati	250F	Maserati	6	23	gearbox	20	8
r	48	H Gould	Maserati	250F	Maserati	6	22	brakes	22	9
r	30	H Schell	Vanwall	VW (55)	Vanwall	4	20	throttle	7	3
r=	36	T Rolt	Connaught	B	Alta	4			14	6
r=	36	P Walker	Connaught	B	Alta	4	19	throttle control		
r	38	L Marr	Connaught	B str.	Alta	4	18	brakes / accident	19	8
r	20	E Castellotti	Ferrari	625	Ferrari	4	16	transmission	10	4
r	8	A Simon	Maserati	250F	Maserati	6	9	gearbox	8	3
r	2	J Behra	Maserati	250F	Maserati	6	9	oil line	3	1
r	22	R Manzon	Gordini	T16	Gordini	6	4	transmission	11	5
ns	34	J Fairman	Connaught	B	Alta	4		engine	21	9

Winning speed 139.156 km/h, 86.468 mph
Pole Position speed 144.360 km/h, 89.701 mph (S Moss, 2 min: 0.400 sec)
Fastest Lap speed 144.360 km/h, 89.701 mph (S Moss, 2 min: 0.400 sec on lap 88)
Lap Leaders J M Fangio 1-2,18-25 (10); S Moss 3-17,26-90 (80).

50 laps x 10.000 km, 6.214 miles = 500.000 km, 310.686 miles

Pos	No	Driver	Car	Model	Engine		Laps	Time/Reason for Retirement	Grid Pos	Row
1	18	J M Fangio	Mercedes-Benz	W196 str.	Mercedes-Benz	8	50	2h 25m 04.400s	1	1
2	14	P Taruffi	Mercedes-Benz	W196	Mercedes-Benz	8	50	2h 25m 05.100s	9	4
3	4	E Castellotti	Ferrari	555	Ferrari	4	50	2h 25m 50.600s	4	2
4	36	J Behra	Maserati	250F str.	Maserati	6	50	2h 29m 01.900s	6	3
5	34	C Menditéguy	Maserati	250F	Maserati	6	49		16	7
6	12	U Maglioli	Ferrari	555	Ferrari	4	49		12	5
7	28	R Mières	Maserati	250F	Maserati	6	48		7	3
8	8	M Trintignant	Ferrari	555	Ferrari	4	47		15	6
9	40	J Fitch	Maserati	250F	Maserati	6	46		20	8
r	6	M Hawthorn	Ferrari	555	Ferrari	4	38	gearbox mounting	14	6
r	20	K Kling	Mercedes-Benz	W196	Mercedes-Benz	8	32	gearbox	3	1
r	38	H Gould	Maserati	250F	Maserati	6	31	suspension	21	9
r	30	L Musso	Maserati	250F	Maserati	6	31	gearbox	10	4
r	16	S Moss	Mercedes-Benz	W196 str.	Mercedes-Benz	8	27	engine	2	1
r	26	J Pollet	Gordini	T16	Gordini	6	26	engine	19	8
r	22	N da Silva Ramos	Gordini	T16	Gordini	6	23	fuel pump	18	7
r	32	P Collins	Maserati	250F	Maserati	6	22	rear suspension	11	5
r	42	H Schell	Vanwall	VW (55)	Vanwall	4	7	de Dion tube	13	5
r	24	J Lucas	Gordini	T32	Gordini	8	7	engine	22	9
r	44	K Wharton	Vanwall	VW (55)	Vanwall	4	0	fuel injection pump	17	7
ns	2	G Farina	Lancia	D50	Lancia	V8		tyre safety concern	5	2
ns	10	L Villoresi	Lancia	D50	Lancia	V8		tyre safety concern	8	3
ns	46	L Piotti	Arzani Volpini		Maserati	4		engine		

Winning speed 206.792 km/h, 128.495 mph
Pole Position speed 216.216 km/h, 134.351 mph (J M Fangio, 2 min:46.500 sec)
Fastest Lap speed 215.698 km/h, 134.029 mph (S Moss, 2 min:46.900 sec on lap 21)
Lap Leaders J M Fangio 1-7,9-50 (49); S Moss 8 (1).

Lap Leaders 1955

Pos	Driver	Car-Engine	GPs	laps	km	miles
1	J M Fangio	Mercedes-Benz	6	309	1,874.3	1,164.6
2	S Moss	Mercedes-Benz	3	112	493.7	306.8
3	M Trintignant	Ferrari	1	20	62.9	39.1
4	A Ascari	Lancia	1	13	50.9	31.6
5	F González	Ferrari	1	11	43.0	26.7
6	H Schell	Maserati	1	7	27.4	17.0
			6	**472**	**2,552.2**	**1,585.9**

Driver Points 1955

		RA	MC	INDY	B	NL	GB	I	Total	
1	J M Fangio	9	(1)	-	9	8	6	8	40	(1)
2	S Moss	1	-	-	6	6	9	1	23	
3	E Castellotti	-	6	-	-	2	-	4	12	
4	M Trintignant	3.33	8	-	-	-	-	-	11.33	
5	G Farina	3.33	3	-	4	-	-	-	10.33	
6	P Taruffi	-	-	-	-	-	3	6	9	
7	B Sweikert	-	-	8	-	-	-	-	8	
8	R Mières	2	-	-	1	4	-	-	7	
9	L Musso	-	-	-	-	4	2	-	6	
	J Behra	-	2	-	1	-	-	3	6	
11	K Kling	1	-	-	-	-	4	-	5	
12	J Davies	-	-	4	-	-	-	-	4	
13	T Bettenhausen	-	-	3	-	-	-	-	3	
	P Russo	-	-	3	-	-	-	-	3	
	J Thomson	-	-	3	-	-	-	-	3	
	P Frère	-	-	-	3	-	-	-	3	
17	F González	2	-	-	-	-	-	-	2	
	C Perdisa	-	2	-	-	-	-	-	2	
	L Villoresi	-	2	-	-	-	-	-	2	
	C Menditéguy	-	-	-	-	-	-	2	2	
21	U Maglioli	1.33	-	-	-	-	-	-	1.33	
22	H Herrmann	1	-	-	-	-	-	-	1	
	W Faulkner	-	-	1	-	-	-	-	1	
	B Homeier	-	-	1	-	-	-	-	1	
	B Vukovich	-	-	1	-	-	-	-	1	

8,6,4,3 and 2 points awarded to the first five finishers. The driver setting the fastest lap scored a point also. Points shared for shared drives. Best 5 scores.

1956

Race Entrants and Results

Mercedes withdrew at the end of 1955 just as British cars were beginning to be more prominent with the reappearance of BRM and the success of Connaught in the non-championship Syracuse Grand Prix in October 1955. Fangio moved to the Ferrari team which continued to modify the Lancia cars. Disc brakes became more evident.

FERRARI
Scuderia Ferrari: Fangio, Collins, Castellotti, Musso, de Portago, Gendebien, Frère, Pilette, (von Trips)
Scuderia Centro Sud: Scarlatti

MASERATI
Officine Alfieri Maserati: Moss, Behra, Godia, Perdisa, Villoresi (I), Maglioli (D,I), Landi, Gerini (RA), F González, Menditéguy, Taruffi, Bonnier
Scuderia Centro Sud: Villoresi (B), Schell, de Graffenried, (Chiron)
Scuderia Guastella: Maglioli (GB), Gerini (I)
Owen Racing Organisation: Hawthorn
Gilby Engineering Ltd: Salvadori
Ecurie Rosier: Rosier
L Piotti: Piotti, Villoresi
A Uría: Uría, O González
Gould's Garage (Bristol): Gould
Privateers: Volonterio, Simon, Halford, Brabham

GORDINI
Equipe Gordini: Manzon, da Silva Ramos, Pilette, Bayol, Milhoux, Simon

BUGATTI
Automobiles Bugatti: Trintignant

BRM
Owen Racing Organisation: Hawthorn, Brooks, Flockhart

COOPER
Privateer: Gerard

CONNAUGHT
Connaught Engineering: Fairman, Flockhart, Scott Brown, Leston, Titterington
Privateer: Scotti

EMERYSON
Emeryson Cars: Emery

VANWALL
Vandervell Products Ltd: Schell, Trintignant, Hawthorn, F González, Taruffi, (Chapman)

22	Jan 1956		ARGENTINA: Buenos Aires No.2					(Round 1)	(Race 49)	
			98 laps x 3.912 km, 2.431 miles = 383.376 km, 238.219 miles							
Pos	No	Driver	Car	Model	Engine		Laps	Time/Reason for Retirement	Grid Pos	Row
1=	34	L Musso	Lancia Ferrari	D50	Lancia Ferrari	V8			3	1
1=	34	J M Fangio	Lancia Ferrari	D50	Lancia Ferrari	V8	98	3h 00m 03.700s		
2	4	J Behra	Maserati	250F	Maserati	6	98	3h 00m 28.100s	4	1
3	14	M Hawthorn	Maserati	250F	Maserati	6	96		8	3
4=	10	C Landi	Maserati	250F	Maserati	6			11	3
4=	10	G Gerini	Maserati	250F	Maserati	6	92			
5	38	O Gendebien	Ferrari	555	Lancia Ferrari	V8	91		10	3
6=	16	A Uría	Maserati	A6GCM	Maserati	6			13	4
6=	16	O González	Maserati	A6GCM	Maserati	6	88			
r	2	S Moss	Maserati	250F	Maserati	6	81	engine	7	2
r	36	P Collins	Ferrari	555	Ferrari	4	58	accident	9	3
r	8	L Piotti	Maserati	250F	Maserati	6	57	accident	12	4
r	6	C Menditéguy	Maserati	250F	Maserati	6	42	half shaft / spin	6	2
r	32	E Castellotti	Lancia Ferrari	D50	Lancia Ferrari	V8	40	gearbox	2	1
r	12	F González	Maserati	250F	Maserati	6	24	valve	5	2
r	30	J M Fangio	Lancia Ferrari	D50	Lancia Ferrari	V8	22	fuel pump	1	1

Winning speed 127.748 km/h, 79.379 mph
Pole Position speed 137.397 km/h, 85.375 mph (J M Fangio, 1 min:42.500 sec)
Fastest Lap speed 133.744 km/h, 83.104 mph (J M Fangio, 1 min:45.300 sec)
Lap Leaders F González 1-3 (3); C Menditéguy 4-42 (39); S Moss 43-66 (24); J M Fangio 67-98 (32).

MONACO: Monte-Carlo (Round 2) (Race 50)

100 laps x 3.145 km, 1.954 miles = 314.500 km, 195.421 miles

Pos	No	Driver	Car	Model	Engine		Laps	Time/Reason for Retirement	Grid Pos	Row
1	28	S Moss	Maserati	250F	Maserati	6	100	3h 00m 32.900s	2	1
2=	26	P Collins	Lancia Ferrari	D50	Lancia Ferrari	V8				9	4
2=	26	J M Fangio	Lancia Ferrari	D50	Lancia Ferrari	V8	100	3h 00m 39.000s		
3	30	J Behra	Maserati	250F	Maserati	6	99		4	2
4=	20	J M Fangio	Lancia Ferrari	D50	Lancia Ferrari	V8			1	1
4=	20	E Castellotti	Lancia Ferrari	D50	Lancia Ferrari	V8	94			
5	6	N da Silva Ramos	Gordini	T16	Gordini	8	93		10	4
r	2	R Manzon	Gordini	T16	Gordini	6	90	transmission / accident	12	5
6=	4	É Bayol	Gordini	T32	Gordini	8			11	5
6=	4	A Pilette	Gordini	T32	Gordini	8	88			
7	32	C Perdisa	Maserati	250F	Maserati	6	86		7	3
8	18	H Gould	Maserati	250F	Maserati	6	85		14	6
r	8	L Rosier	Maserati	250F	Maserati	6	72	engine	13	5
r	22	E Castellotti	Lancia Ferrari	D50	Lancia Ferrari	V8	14	gearbox	3	1
r	14	M Trintignant	Vanwall	VW (56)	Vanwall	4	13	engine overheating	6	3
r	16	H Schell	Vanwall	VW (56)	Vanwall	4	2	accident	5	2
r	24	L Musso	Lancia Ferrari	D50	Lancia Ferrari	V8	2	accident	8	3
ns	10	M Hawthorn	BRM	P25	BRM	4		engine		
ns	12	T Brooks	BRM	P25	BRM	4		valve		
ns	34	L Chiron	Maserati	250F	Maserati	6		engine		
nq	36	G Scarlatti	Ferrari	500	Ferrari	4				

Winning speed 104.515 km/h, 64.943 mph
Pole Position speed 108.865 km/h, 67.646 mph (J M Fangio, 1 min:44.000 sec)
Fastest Lap speed 108.448 km/h, 67.387 mph (J M Fangio, 1 min:44.400 sec on lap 100)
Lap Leaders S Moss 1-100 (100).

INDIANAPOLIS: 500 (Round 3) (Race 51)

200 laps x 4.023 km, 2.500 miles = 804.672 km, 500.000 miles

Pos	No	Driver	Car	Model	Engine		Laps	Time/Reason for Retirement	Grid Pos	Row
1	8	P Flaherty	Watson		Offenhauser	4	200	3h 53m 28.840s	1	1
2	4	S Hanks	Kurtis Kraft	500C	Offenhauser	4	200	3h 53m 49.290s	13	5
3	16	D Freeland	Phillips		Offenhauser	4	200		26	9
4	98	J Parsons	Kuzma		Offenhauser	4	200		6	2
5	73	D Rathmann	Kurtis Kraft	500C	Offenhauser	4	200		4	2
6	1	B Sweikert	Kuzma		Offenhauser	4	200		10	4
7	14	B Veith	Kurtis Kraft	500E	Offenhauser	4	200		23	8
8	19	R Ward	Kurtis Kraft	500C	Offenhauser	4	200		15	5
9	26	J Reece	Lesovsky		Offenhauser	4	200		21	7
10	27	C Griffith	Stevens		Offenhauser	4	199		30	10
11	82	G Hartley	Kurtis Kraft	500C	Offenhauser	4	196		22	8
12	42	F Agabashian	Kurtis Kraft	500D	Offenhauser	4	196		7	3
13	57	B Christie	Kurtis Kraft	500D	Offenhauser	4	196		25	9
14	55	A Keller	Kurtis Kraft	4000	Offenhauser	4	195		28	10
15	81	E Johnson	Kuzma		Offenhauser	4	195		32	11
16	41	B Garrett	Kuzma		Offenhauser	4	194		29	10
17	64	D Dinsmore	Kurtis Kraft	500A	Offenhauser	4	191		33	11
18	7	P O'Connor	Kurtis Kraft	500D	Offenhauser	4	187		3	1
19	2	J Bryan	Kuzma		Offenhauser	4	185		19	7
20r	24	J Rathmann	Kurtis Kraft	500C	Offenhauser	4	175	oil pressure	2	1
21r	34	J Tolan	Kurtis Kraft	500D	Offenhauser	4	173		31	11
22r	99	T Bettenhausen	Kurtis Kraft	500D	Offenhauser	4	160	tyre burst / accident	5	2
23r=	10	E Elisian	Kurtis Kraft	500C	Offenhauser	4			14	5
23r=	10	E Russo	Kurtis Kraft	500C	Offenhauser	4	160	stalled		
24r	48	J Daywalt	Kurtis Kraft	500C	Offenhauser	4	134	accident	16	6
25r	54	J Turner	Kurtis Kraft	500B	Offenhauser	4	131	engine	24	8
26r	89	K Andrews	Kurtis Kraft	500B	Offenhauser	4	94	spin	20	7
27r	5	A Linden	Kurtis Kraft	500C	Offenhauser	4	90	oil leak	9	3
28r	12	A Herman	Kurtis Kraft	500B	Offenhauser	4	74	tyre burst / accident	27	9
29r	49	R Crawford	Kurtis Kraft	500G	Offenhauser	4	49	accident	17	6
30r	15	J Boyd	Kurtis Kraft	500D	Offenhauser	4	35	engine	12	4
31r	53	T Ruttman	Kurtis Kraft	500C	Offenhauser	4	22	spin	11	4
32r	88	J Thomson	Kuzma		Offenhauser	4	22	spin in pits / struck mechanic	18	6
33r	29	P Russo	Kurtis Kraft		Novi	8s	21	tyre burst / accident	8	3

Winning speed 206.785 km/h, 128.490 mph
Pole Position speed 234.314 km/h, 145.596 mph (P Flaherty, 1 min: 1.815 sec)
Fastest Lap speed 232.415 km/h, 144.416 mph (P Russo, 1 min: 2.320 sec on lap 19)

3 Jun 1956   BELGIUM: Spa-Francorchamps   (Round 4)   (Race 52)

36 laps x 14.120 km, 8.774 miles = 508.320 km, 315.855 miles

Pos	No	Driver	Car	Model	Engine		Laps	Time/Reason for Retirement	Grid Pos	Row
1	8	P Collins	Lancia Ferrari	D50	Lancia Ferrari	V8	36	2h 40m 00.300s	3	1
2	6	P Frère	Lancia Ferrari	D50	Lancia Ferrari	V8	36	2h 41m 51.600s	8	3
3=	34	C Perdisa	Maserati	250F	Maserati	6			9	4
3=	34	S Moss	Maserati	250F	Maserati	6	36	2h 43m 16.900s		
4	10	H Schell	Vanwall	VW (56)	Vanwall	4	35		6	3
5	22	L Villoresi	Maserati	250F	Maserati	6	34		11	5
6	20	A Pilette	Lancia Ferrari	D50	Lancia Ferrari	V8	33		15	6
7	32	J Behra	Maserati	250F	Maserati	6	33		4	2
8	24	L Rosier	Maserati	250F	Maserati	6	33		10	4
r	2	J M Fangio	Lancia Ferrari	D50	Lancia Ferrari	V8	23	transmission	1	1
r	12	M Trintignant	Vanwall	VW (56)	Vanwall	4	11	valve	7	3
r	4	E Castellotti	Lancia Ferrari	D50	Lancia Ferrari	V8	10	transmission	5	2
r	30	S Moss	Maserati	250F	Maserati	6	10	rear wheel lost	2	1
r	28	P Scotti	Connaught	B	Alta	4	10	brakes	12	5
r	26	H Gould	Maserati	250F	Maserati	6	2	gearbox	14	6
r	36	C Godia	Maserati	250F	Maserati	6	0	accident	13	5
ns	38	M Hawthorn	Maserati	250F	Maserati	6		withdrew		

Winning speed 190.614 km/h, 118.442 mph
Pole Position speed 203.491 km/h, 126.443 mph (J M Fangio, 4 min: 9.800 sec)
Fastest Lap speed 199.576 km/h, 124.011 mph (S Moss, 4 min:14.700 sec on lap 30)
Lap Leaders S Moss 1-4 (4); J M Fangio 5-23 (19); P Collins 24-36 (13).

1 Jul 1956   FRANCE: Reims   (Round 5)   (Race 53)

61 laps x 8.302 km, 5.159 miles = 506.422 km, 314.676 miles

Pos	No	Driver	Car	Model	Engine		Laps	Time/Reason for Retirement	Grid Pos	Row
1	14	P Collins	Lancia Ferrari	D50	Lancia Ferrari	V8	61	2h 34m 23.400s	3	1
2	12	E Castellotti	Lancia Ferrari	D50	Lancia Ferrari	V8	61	2h 34m 23.700s	2	1
3	4	J Behra	Maserati	250F	Maserati	6	61	2h 35m 53.300s	7	3
4	10	J M Fangio	Lancia Ferrari	D50	Lancia Ferrari	V8	61	2h 35m 58.500s	1	1
5=	6	C Perdisa	Maserati	250F	Maserati	6			16	7
5=	6	S Moss	Maserati	250F	Maserati	6	59			
6	36	L Rosier	Maserati	250F	Maserati	6	58		13	5
7	40	C Godia	Maserati	250F	Maserati	6	57		17	7
8	32	N da Silva Ramos	Gordini	T32	Gordini	8	57		14	6
9	30	R Manzon	Gordini	T32	Gordini	8	56		15	6
10=	24	M Hawthorn	Vanwall	VW (56)	Vanwall	4			6	3
10=	24	H Schell	Vanwall	VW (56)	Vanwall	4	56			
11	34	A Pilette	Gordini	T16	Gordini	6	55		19	8
r	42	A Simon	Maserati	250F	Maserati	6	45	engine	20	8
r	8	P Taruffi	Maserati	250F	Maserati	6	39	engine	12	5
r	44	O Gendebien	Lancia Ferrari	D50	Lancia Ferrari	V8	38	engine	11	5
r	38	L Villoresi	Maserati	250F	Maserati	6	22	brakes	10	4
r	16	A de Portago	Lancia Ferrari	D50	Lancia Ferrari	V8	20	gearbox	9	4
r	28	M Trintignant	Bugatti	T251	Bugatti	8	18	throttle linkage	18	7
r	2	S Moss	Maserati	250F	Maserati	6	11	gear lever	8	3
r	22	H Schell	Vanwall	VW (56)	Vanwall	4	5	fuel injection	4	2
ns	26	C Chapman	Vanwall	VW (56)	Vanwall	4		accident	5	2

Winning speed 196.809 km/h, 122.291 mph
Pole Position speed 208.564 km/h, 129.596 mph (J M Fangio, 2 min:23.300 sec)
Fastest Lap speed 204.988 km/h, 127.373 mph (J M Fangio, 2 min:25.800 sec on lap 61)
Lap Leaders P Collins 1,47-48,50-61 (15); E Castellotti 2-3,39-46,49 (11); J M Fangio 4-38 (35).

C Chapman's qualifying time was set by H Schell.
The cars on the front row of the grid lined up in reverse, with P Collins in pole and J M Fangio in 3rd place.

14 Jul 1956 — BRITAIN: Silverstone — (Round 6) (Race 54)

101 laps x 4.711 km, 2.927 miles = 475.766 km, 295.627 miles

Pos	No	Driver	Car	Model	Engine		Laps	Time/Reason for Retirement	Grid Pos	Row
1	1	J M Fangio	Lancia Ferrari	D50	Lancia Ferrari	V8	101	2h 59m 47.000s	2	1
2=	4	A de Portago	Lancia Ferrari	D50	Lancia Ferrari	V8			12	4
2=	4	P Collins	Lancia Ferrari	D50	Lancia Ferrari	V8	100		12	4
3	8	J Behra	Maserati	250F	Maserati	6	99		13	4
4	21	J Fairman	Connaught	B	Alta	4	98		21	6
5	31	H Gould	Maserati	250F	Maserati	6	97		14	4
6	11	L Villoresi	Maserati	250F	Maserati	6	96		19	6
7	9	C Perdisa	Maserati	250F	Maserati	6	95		15	5
8	10	C Godia	Maserati	250F	Maserati	6	94		25	7
9	15	R Manzon	Gordini	T32	Gordini	8	94		18	5
r	7	S Moss	Maserati	250F	Maserati	6	94	rear axle	1	1
10=	3	E Castellotti	Lancia Ferrari	D50	Lancia Ferrari	V8			8	3
10=	3	A de Portago	Lancia Ferrari	D50	Lancia Ferrari	V8	92	pushed over line	8	3
11	26	B Gerard	Cooper	T23	Bristol	6	88		22	7
r	16	H Schell	Vanwall	VW (56)	Vanwall	4	86	fuel line	5	2
r	20	D Titterington	Connaught	B	Alta	4	74	connecting rod	11	3
r	14	N da Silva Ramos	Gordini	T32	Gordini	8	71	rear axle	26	8
r	17	M Trintignant	Vanwall	VW (56)	Vanwall	4	69	fuel line	16	5
r	2	P Collins	Lancia Ferrari	D50	Lancia Ferrari	V8	63	oil pressure	4	1
r	28	R Salvadori	Maserati	250F	Maserati	6	58	fuel pressure	7	2
r	24	T Brooks	BRM	P25	BRM	4	40	throttle / accident	9	3
r	27	L Rosier	Maserati	250F	Maserati	6	23	magneto	27	8
r	23	M Hawthorn	BRM	P25	BRM	4	23	universal joint	3	1
r	29	B Halford	Maserati	250F	Maserati	6	22	piston	20	6
r	12	U Maglioli	Maserati	250F	Maserati	6	21	gearbox	24	7
r	19	A Scott Brown	Connaught	B	Alta	4	16	rear stub axle / wheel lost	10	3
r	32	P Emery	Emeryson	(56)	Alta	4	12	ignition	23	7
r	30	J Brabham	Maserati	250F	Maserati	6	3	engine	28	8
r	25	R Flockhart	BRM	P25	BRM	4	1	engine	17	5
r	18	F González	Vanwall	VW (56)	Vanwall	4	0	driveshaft	6	2

Winning speed 158.780 km/h, 98.661 mph
Pole Position speed 167.901 km/h, 104.329 mph (S Moss, 1 min:41.000 sec)
Fastest Lap speed 164.322 km/h, 102.105 mph (S Moss, 1 min:43.200 sec on lap 71)
Lap Leaders M Hawthorn 1-15 (15); S Moss 16-68 (53); J M Fangio 69-101 (33).

5 Aug 1956 — GERMANY: Nürburgring — (Round 7) (Race 55)

22 laps x 22.810 km, 14.173 miles = 501.820 km, 311.816 miles

Pos	No	Driver	Car	Model	Engine		Laps	Time/Reason for Retirement	Grid Pos	Row
1	1	J M Fangio	Lancia Ferrari	D50	Lancia Ferrari	V8	22	3h 38m 43.700s	1	1
2	7	S Moss	Maserati	250F	Maserati	6	22	3h 39m 30.100s	4	1
3	6	J Behra	Maserati	250F	Maserati	6	22	3h 46m 22.000s	8	3
4	20	C Godia	Maserati	250F	Maserati	6	20		16	5
dq	21	B Halford	Maserati	250F	Maserati	6	20	push start after spin	11	3
5	15	L Rosier	Maserati	250F	Maserati	6	19		14	4
nc	22	O Volonterio	Maserati	A6GCM	Maserati	6	16		20	6
r	11	A Milhoux	Gordini	T32	Gordini	8	15	misfire	17	5
r=	5	A de Portago	Lancia Ferrari	D50	Lancia Ferrari	V8			10	3
r=	5	P Collins	Lancia Ferrari	D50	Lancia Ferrari	V8	14	accident	10	3
r	18	L Villoresi	Maserati	250F	Maserati	6	13	engine	19	6
r	12	H Schell	Maserati	250F	Maserati	6	12	engine overheating	12	4
r=	4	L Musso	Lancia Ferrari	D50	Lancia Ferrari	V8			5	2
r=	4	E Castellotti	Lancia Ferrari	D50	Lancia Ferrari	V8	12	accident	5	2
r	2	P Collins	Lancia Ferrari	D50	Lancia Ferrari	V8	8	fuel line / leak	2	1
r	3	E Castellotti	Lancia Ferrari	D50	Lancia Ferrari	V8	5	magneto	3	1
r	8	U Maglioli	Maserati	250F	Maserati	6	3	steering	7	2
r	19	H Gould	Maserati	250F	Maserati	6	3	oil pressure	13	4
r	16	R Salvadori	Maserati	250F	Maserati	6	2	rear suspension	9	3
r	10	R Manzon	Gordini	T32	Gordini	8	0	front suspension	15	5
r	14	G Scarlatti	Ferrari	500	Ferrari	4	0	engine	18	5
ns	8	C Perdisa	Maserati	250F	Maserati	6		accident / injury	6	2
ns	11	A Pilette	Gordini	T32	Gordini	8		accident / injury		
ns	18	L Piotti	Maserati	250F	Maserati	6		car raced by Villoresi		

Winning speed 137.656 km/h, 85.535 mph
Pole Position speed 138.897 km/h, 86.307 mph (J M Fangio, 9 min:51.200 sec)
Fastest Lap speed 141.190 km/h, 87.731 mph (J M Fangio, 9 min:41.600 sec on lap 14)
Lap Leaders J M Fangio 1-22 (22).

Pos	No	Driver	Car	Model	Engine		Laps	Time/Reason for Retirement	Grid Pos	Row
1	36	S Moss	Maserati	250F	Maserati	6	50	2h 23m 41.300s	6	2
2=	26	P Collins	Lancia Ferrari	D50	Lancia Ferrari	V8				7	3
2=	26	J M Fangio	Lancia Ferrari	D50	Lancia Ferrari	V8	50	2h 23m 47.000s		
3	4	R Flockhart	Connaught	B	Alta	4	49		23	8
4	38	C Godia	Maserati	250F	Maserati	6	49		17	6
r	28	L Musso	Lancia Ferrari	D50	Lancia Ferrari	V8	47	steering	3	1
5	6	J Fairman	Connaught	B	Alta	4	47		15	5
6	40	L Piotti	Maserati	250F	Maserati	6	47		14	5
7	14	E de Graffenried	Maserati	250F	Maserati	6	46		18	6
8=	22	J M Fangio	Lancia Ferrari	D50	Lancia Ferrari	V8			1	1
8=	22	E Castellotti	Lancia Ferrari	D50	Lancia Ferrari	V8	46			
9	12	A Simon	Gordini	T16	Gordini	6	45		24	8
r=	46	U Maglioli	Maserati	250F	Maserati	6			12	4
r=	46	J Behra	Maserati	250F	Maserati	6	42	steering		
10	42	G Gerini	Maserati	250F	Maserati	6	42		16	6
11	44	R Salvadori	Maserati	250F	Maserati	6	41		13	5
r	18	H Schell	Vanwall	VW (56)	Vanwall	4	32	transmission	10	4
r	32	J Behra	Maserati	250F	Maserati	6	23	magneto	5	2
r	48	B Halford	Maserati	250F	Maserati	6	16	engine	21	7
r	20	M Trintignant	Vanwall	VW (56)	Vanwall	4	13	rear suspension	11	4
r	16	P Taruffi	Vanwall	VW (56)	Vanwall	4	12	rear suspension	4	2
r	24	E Castellotti	Lancia Ferrari	D50	Lancia Ferrari	V8	9	tyre / accident	2	1
r=	34	L Villoresi	Maserati	250F	Maserati	6			8	3
r=	34	J Bonnier	Maserati	250F	Maserati	6	7	engine		
r	10	R Manzon	Gordini	T32	Gordini	8	7	gearbox	22	8
r	2	L Leston	Connaught	B	Alta	4	6	torsion bar	19	7
r	30	A de Portago	Lancia Ferrari	D50	Lancia Ferrari	V8	6	tyre / accident	9	3
r	8	N da Silva Ramos	Gordini	T32	Gordini	8	3	engine	20	7
ns	4	A Scott Brown	Connaught	B	Alta	4		refused race entry		
ns	50	W von Trips	Lancia Ferrari	D50	Lancia Ferrari	V8		accident		

Winning speed 208.785 km/h, 129.733 mph
Pole Position speed 221.402 km/h, 137.573 mph (J M Fangio, 2 min:42.600 sec)
Fastest Lap speed 217.523 km/h, 135.162 mph (S Moss, 2 min:45.500 sec on lap 47)
Lap Leaders E Castellotti 1-4 (4); S Moss 5-10,12-45,48-50 (43); H Schell 11 (1); L Musso 46-47 (2).

Also the Grand Prix of Europe.

Lap Leaders 1956

Pos	Driver	Car-Engine	GPs	laps	km	miles
1	S Moss	Maserati	5	224	1,144.6	711.2
2	J M Fangio	Ferrari	5	141	1,341.3	833.5
3	C Menditéguy	Maserati	1	39	152.6	94.8
4	P Collins	Ferrari	2	28	308.1	191.4
5	E Castellotti	Ferrari	2	15	131.3	81.6
	M Hawthorn	BRM	1	15	70.7	43.9
7	F González	Maserati	1	3	11.7	7.3
8	L Musso	Ferrari	1	2	20.0	12.4
9	H Schell	Vanwall	1	1	10.0	6.2
			7	**468**	**3,190.2**	**1,982.3**

Driver Points 1956

		RA	MC	INDY	B	F	GB	D	I	Total	
1	J M Fangio	5	4	-	-	4	8	9	(3)	30	(3)
2	S Moss	-	8	-	3	1	(1)	6	9	27	(1)
3	P Collins	-	3	-	8	8	3	-	3	25	
4	J Behra	6	4	-	-	4	4	4	-	22	
5	P Flaherty	-	-	8	-	-	-	-	-	8	
6	E Castellotti	-	1.5	-	-	6	-	-	-	7.5	
7	S Hanks	-	-	6	-	-	-	-	-	6	
	P Frère	-	-	-	6	-	-	-	-	6	
	C Godia	-	-	-	-	-	-	3	3	6	
10	J Fairman	-	-	-	-	-	3	-	2	5	
11	M Hawthorn	4	-	-	-	-	-	-	-	4	
	L Musso	4	-	-	-	-	-	-	-	4	
	D Freeland	-	-	4	-	-	-	-	-	4	
	R Flockhart	-	-	-	-	-	-	-	4	4	
15	J Parsons	-	-	3	-	-	-	-	-	3	
	H Schell	-	-	-	3	-	-	-	-	3	
	A de Portago	-	-	-	-	-	3	-	-	3	
	C Perdisa	-	-	-	2	1	-	-	-	3	
19	O Gendebien	2	-	-	-	-	-	-	-	2	
	N da Silva Ramos	-	2	-	-	-	-	-	-	2	
	D Rathmann	-	-	2	-	-	-	-	-	2	
	L Villoresi	-	-	-	2	-	-	-	-	2	
	H Gould	-	-	-	-	-	2	-	-	2	
	L Rosier	-	-	-	-	-	-	2	-	2	
25	G Gerini	1.5	-	-	-	-	-	-	-	1.5	
	C Landi	1.5	-	-	-	-	-	-	-	1.5	
27	P Russo	-	-	1	-	-	-	-	-	1	

8,6,4,3 and 2 points awarded to the first five finishers. The driver setting the fastest lap scored a point also. Points shared for shared drives. Best 5 scores.
J M Fangio was classified both 2nd and 4th in shared drives at Monaco. He only received points for his 2nd place.

1957

Race Entrants and Results

Gordini withdrew from racing and Connaught followed soon after the Monaco Grand Prix. Formula 2 re-emerged with rear engine Coopers showing the way forward. Ferrari, Maserati and Vanwall dominated the races; the highlight of which was Fangio's stunning performance at the Nürburgring, often regarded as the championship's finest race.

FERRARI
Scuderia Ferrari: Musso, Hawthorn, Collins, Trintignant, von Trips, Castellotti, Perdisa, González, de Portago
Scuderia Centro Sud: de Tomaso

MASERATI
Officine Alfieri Maserati: Fangio, Behra, Schell, Menditéguy, Scarlatti, Moss, (Herrmann)
Scuderia Centro Sud: Gregory, Bonnier, Schell (MC), Herrmann (D), (Simon)
Gilby Engineering Ltd: Bueb
Ottorino Volonterio: Volonterio, Simon (I)
Privateers: Godia, Gould, Halford, Piotti, Bonnier (GB)

BRM
Owen Racing Organisation: Flockhart, Leston, MacKay-Fraser, Fairman, (Salvadori)

COOPER
Cooper Car Co: Brabham, Salvadori, MacDowel, (Leston)
Privateer: Gerard

CONNAUGHT
Connaught Engineering: Lewis-Evans, Bueb

VANWALL
Vandervell Products Ltd: Moss, Brooks, Lewis-Evans, Salvadori
(Entries for the F2 section are not included)

13 Jan 1957		ARGENTINA: Buenos Aires No.2						(Round 1)	(Race 57)	
		100 laps x 3.912 km, 2.431 miles = 391.200 km, 243.080 miles								
Pos	No	Driver	Car	Model	Engine		Laps	Time/Reason for Retirement	Grid Pos	Row
1	2	J M Fangio	Maserati	250F	Maserati	6	100	3h 00m 55.900s	2	1
2	6	J Behra	Maserati	250F	Maserati	6	100	3h 01m 14.200s	3	1
3	8	C Menditéguy	Maserati	250F	Maserati	6	99		8	3
4	22	H Schell	Maserati	250F	Maserati	6	98		9	3
5=	20	F González	Lancia Ferrari	801	Lancia Ferrari	V8			10	3
5=	20	A de Portago	Lancia Ferrari	801	Lancia Ferrari	V8	98			
6=	18	C Perdisa	Lancia Ferrari	801	Lancia Ferrari	V8			11	3
6=	18	P Collins	Lancia Ferrari	801	Lancia Ferrari	V8				
6=	18	W von Trips	Lancia Ferrari	801	Lancia Ferrari	V8	98			
7	24	J Bonnier	Maserati	250F	Maserati	6	95		13	4
8	4	S Moss	Maserati	250F	Maserati	6	93		1	1
9	26	A de Tomaso	Ferrari	500	Ferrari	4	91		12	4
10	28	L Piotti	Maserati	250F	Maserati	6	90		14	4
r	14	E Castellotti	Lancia Ferrari	801	Lancia Ferrari	V8	75	hub shaft	4	1
r	16	M Hawthorn	Lancia Ferrari	801	Lancia Ferrari	V8	34	clutch	7	2
r	12	L Musso	Lancia Ferrari	801	Lancia Ferrari	V8	30	clutch	6	2
r	10	P Collins	Lancia Ferrari	801	Lancia Ferrari	V8	26	clutch	5	2

Winning speed 129.729 km/h, 80.610 mph
Pole Position speed 137.263 km/h, 85.291 mph (S Moss, 1 min:42.600 sec)
Fastest Lap speed 134.510 km/h, 83.581 mph (S Moss, 1 min:44.700 sec on lap 75)
Lap Leaders J Behra 1-2,9-12,81,84 (8); E Castellotti 3-8 (6); P Collins 13-25 (13); J M Fangio 26-80,82-83,85-100 (73).

19 May 1957 MONACO: Monte-Carlo (Round 2) (Race 58)

105 laps x 3.145 km, 1.954 miles = 330.225 km, 205.192 miles

Pos	No	Driver	Car	Model	Engine		Laps	Time/Reason for Retirement	Grid Pos	Row
1	32	J M Fangio	Maserati	250F	Maserati	6	105	3h 10m 12.800s	1	1
2	20	T Brooks	Vanwall	VW (57)	Vanwall	4	105	3h 10m 38.000s	4	2
3	2	M Gregory	Maserati	250F	Maserati	6	103		10	4
4	10	S Lewis-Evans	Connaught	B	Alta	4	102		13	5
5	30	M Trintignant	Lancia Ferrari	801	Lancia Ferrari	V8	100		6	3
6	14	J Brabham	Cooper	T43	Climax	4	100		15	6
7r=	24	W von Trips	Lancia Ferrari	801	Lancia Ferrari	V8			9	4
7r=	24	M Hawthorn	Lancia Ferrari	801	Lancia Ferrari	V8	95	engine / accident		
r=	34	G Scarlatti	Maserati	250F	Maserati	6			14	6
r=	34	H Schell	Maserati	250F	Maserati	6	64	oil leak		
r	6	R Flockhart	BRM	P25	BRM	4	59	timing gear	11	5
r	36	C Menditéguy	Maserati	250F	Maserati	6	50	accident	7	3
r	12	I Bueb	Connaught	B	Alta	4	46	fuel tank	16	6
r	38	H Schell	Maserati	250F	Maserati	6	22	front suspension	8	3
r	22	H Gould	Maserati	250F	Maserati	6	9	oil tank / engine	12	5
r	28	M Hawthorn	Lancia Ferrari	801	Lancia Ferrari	V8	3	accident	5	2
r	26	P Collins	Lancia Ferrari	801	Lancia Ferrari	V8	3	accident	2	1
r	18	S Moss	Vanwall	VW (57)	Vanwall	4	3	accident	3	1
nq	40	H Herrmann	Maserati	250F	Maserati	6				
nq	4	A Simon	Maserati	250F	Maserati	6				
nq	8	R Salvadori	BRM	P25	BRM	4				
nq	42	L Piotti	Maserati	250F	Maserati	6				
nq	16	L Leston	Cooper	T43	Climax	4				

Winning speed 104.165 km/h, 64.725 mph
Pole Position speed 110.243 km/h, 68.502 mph (J M Fangio, 1 min:42.700 sec)
Fastest Lap speed 107.216 km/h, 66.621 mph (J M Fangio, 1 min:45.600 sec)
Lap Leaders S Moss 1-4 (4); J M Fangio 5-105 (101).

30 May 1957 INDIANAPOLIS: 500 (Round 3) (Race 59)

200 laps x 4.023 km, 2.500 miles = 804.672 km, 500.000 miles

Pos	No	Driver	Car	Model	Engine		Laps	Time/Reason for Retirement	Grid Pos	Row
1	9	S Hanks	Epperly		Offenhauser	4	200	3h 41m 14.250s	13	5
2	26	J Rathmann	Epperly		Offenhauser	4	200	3h 41m 35.711s	32	11
3	1	J Bryan	Kuzma		Offenhauser	4	200		15	5
4	54	P Russo	Kurtis Kraft		Novi	8s	200		10	4
5	73	A Linden	Kurtis Kraft	500G	Offenhauser	4	200		12	4
6	6	J Boyd	Kurtis Kraft	500G	Offenhauser	4	200		5	2
7	48	M Teague	Kurtis Kraft	500C	Offenhauser	4	200		28	10
8	12	P O'Connor	Kurtis Kraft	500G	Offenhauser	4	200		1	1
9	7	B Veith	Phillips		Offenhauser	4	200		16	6
10	22	G Hartley	Lesovsky		Offenhauser	4	200		14	5
11	19	J Turner	Kurtis Kraft	500G	Offenhauser	4	200		19	7
12	10	J Thomson	Kuzma		Offenhauser	4	199		11	4
13	95	B Christie	Kurtis Kraft	500C	Offenhauser	4	197		33	11
14	82	C Weyant	Kurtis Kraft	500C	Offenhauser	4	196		25	9
15	27	T Bettenhausen	Kurtis Kraft		Novi	8s	195		22	8
16	18	J Parsons	Kurtis Kraft	500G	Offenhauser	4	195		17	6
17	3	D Freeland	Kurtis Kraft	500D	Offenhauser	4	192		21	7
18r	5	J Reece	Kurtis Kraft	500C	Offenhauser	4	182	throttle	6	2
19r	92	D Edmunds	Kurtis Kraft	500G	Offenhauser	4	170	spin	27	9
20r	28	J Tolan	Kuzma		Offenhauser	4	138	clutch	31	11
21r	89	A Herman	Dunn		Offenhauser	4	111	accident	30	10
22r	14	F Agabashian	Kurtis Kraft	500G	Offenhauser	4	107	fuel leak	4	2
23r	88	E Sachs	Kuzma		Offenhauser	4	105	piston	2	1
24r	77	M Magill	Kurtis Kraft	500G	Offenhauser	4	101	fuel leak	18	6
25r	43	E Johnson	Kurtis Kraft	500G	Offenhauser	4	93	front wheel bearing	20	7
26r	31	B Cheesbourg	Kurtis Kraft	500G	Offenhauser	4	81	fuel leak	23	8
27r	16	A Keller	Kurtis Kraft	500G	Offenhauser	4	75	accident	8	3
28r	57	J Daywalt	Kurtis Kraft	500C	Offenhauser	4	53	accident	29	10
29r	83	E Elisian	Kurtis Kraft	500C	Offenhauser	4	51	timing gear	7	3
30r	8	R Ward	Lesovsky		Offenhauser	4s	27	supercharger bearing	24	8
31r	52	T Ruttman	Watson		Offenhauser	4	13	engine overheating	3	1
32r	55	E Russo	Kurtis Kraft	500C	Offenhauser	4	0	accident	26	9
33r	23	E George	Kurtis Kraft	500B	Offenhauser	4	0	accident	9	3

Winning speed 218.228 km/h, 135.601 mph
Pole Position speed 231.664 km/h, 143.949 mph (P O'Connor, 1 min: 2.522 sec)
Fastest Lap speed 230.822 km/h, 143.426 mph (J Rathmann, 1 min: 2.750 sec on lap 127)
Fastest qualifier P Russo (233.060 km/h, 144.817 mph).

77 laps x 6.542 km, 4.065 miles = 503.734 km, 313.006 miles

Pos	No	Driver	Car	Model	Engine		Laps	Time/Reason for Retirement	Grid Pos	Row
1	2	J M Fangio	Maserati	250F	Maserati	6	77	3h 07m 46.400s	1	1
2	10	L Musso	Lancia Ferrari	801	Lancia Ferrari	V8	77	3h 08m 37.200s	3	1
3	12	P Collins	Lancia Ferrari	801	Lancia Ferrari	V8	77	3h 09m 52.400s	5	2
4	14	M Hawthorn	Lancia Ferrari	801	Lancia Ferrari	V8	76		7	3
5	6	H Schell	Maserati	250F	Maserati	6	70		4	2
6	4	J Behra	Maserati	250F	Maserati	6	69	pushed over line	2	1
7=	24	M MacDowel	Cooper	T43	Climax	4			15	6
7=	24	J Brabham	Cooper	T43	Climax	4	68			
r	8	C Menditéguy	Maserati	250F	Maserati	6	30	engine	9	4
r	18	S Lewis-Evans	Vanwall	VW (57)	Vanwall	4	30	steering	10	4
r	20	R Salvadori	Vanwall	VW (57)	Vanwall	4	25	valve spring	6	3
r	28	H MacKay-Fraser	BRM	P25	BRM	4	24	transmission	12	5
r	16	M Trintignant	Lancia Ferrari	801	Lancia Ferrari	V8	23	magneto	8	3
r	30	H Gould	Maserati	250F	Maserati	6	4	rear axle	14	6
r	22	J Brabham	Cooper	T43	Climax	4	4	accident	13	5
r	26	R Flockhart	BRM	P25	BRM	4	3	accident	11	5

Winning speed 160.960 km/h, 100.016 mph
Pole Position speed 166.440 km/h, 103.421 mph (J M Fangio, 2 min:21.500 sec)
Fastest Lap speed 165.388 km/h, 102.767 mph (L Musso, 2 min:22.400 sec on lap 65)
Lap Leaders L Musso 1-3 (3); J M Fangio 4-77 (74).

J Behra's final lap (70) was completed slower than the minimum time allowed, after he had pushed his car across the line. He was therefore considered as only completing 69 laps.

90 laps x 4.828 km, 3.000 miles = 434.523 km, 270.000 miles

Pos	No	Driver	Car	Model	Engine		Laps	Time/Reason for Retirement	Grid Pos	Row
1=	20	T Brooks	Vanwall	VW (57)	Vanwall	4			3	1
1=	20	S Moss	Vanwall	VW (57)	Vanwall	4	90	3h 06m 37.800s		
2	14	L Musso	Lancia Ferrari	801	Lancia Ferrari	V8	90	3h 07m 03.400s	10	4
3	10	M Hawthorn	Lancia Ferrari	801	Lancia Ferrari	V8	90	3h 07m 20.600s	5	2
4=	16	M Trintignant	Lancia Ferrari	801	Lancia Ferrari	V8			9	4
4=	16	P Collins	Lancia Ferrari	801	Lancia Ferrari	V8	88			
5	36	R Salvadori	Cooper	T43	Climax	4	85		15	6
6	38	B Gerard	Cooper	T44	Bristol	6	82		18	7
7	22	S Lewis-Evans	Vanwall	VW (57)	Vanwall	4	82		6	3
r	34	J Brabham	Cooper	T43	Climax	4	74	clutch	13	5
8	32	I Bueb	Maserati	250F	Maserati	6	71		19	8
r	4	J Behra	Maserati	250F	Maserati	6	69	clutch	2	1
r	12	P Collins	Lancia Ferrari	801	Lancia Ferrari	V8	53	radiator pipe	8	3
r=	18	S Moss	Vanwall	VW (57)	Vanwall	4			1	1
r=	18	T Brooks	Vanwall	VW (57)	Vanwall	4	51	engine		
r	2	J M Fangio	Maserati	250F	Maserati	6	49	engine	4	2
r	24	J Fairman	BRM	P25	BRM	4	46	engine	16	7
r	26	L Leston	BRM	P25	BRM	4	44	engine	12	5
r	6	H Schell	Maserati	250F	Maserati	6	39	water pump	7	3
r	8	C Menditéguy	Maserati	250F	Maserati	6	35	transmission	11	5
r	28	J Bonnier	Maserati	250F	Maserati	6	18	gearbox	17	7
ns	30	H Gould	Maserati	250F	Maserati	6		accident / injury	14	6

Winning speed 139.696 km/h, 86.803 mph
Pole Position speed 144.600 km/h, 89.850 mph (S Moss, 2 min: 0.200 sec)
Fastest Lap speed 145.813 km/h, 90.604 mph (S Moss, 1 min:59.200 sec)
Lap Leaders S Moss 1-22,70-90 (43); J Behra 23-69 (47).

Also the Grand Prix of Europe.

4 Aug 1957   GERMANY: Nürburgring   (Round 6)   (Race 62)

22 laps x 22.810 km, 14.173 miles = 501.820 km, 311.816 miles

Pos	No	Driver	Car	Model	Engine		Laps	Time/Reason for Retirement	Grid Pos	Row
1	1	J M Fangio	Maserati	250F	Maserati	6	22	3h 30m 38.300s	1	1
2	8	M Hawthorn	Lancia Ferrari	801	Lancia Ferrari	V8	22	3h 30m 41.900s	2	1
3	7	P Collins	Lancia Ferrari	801	Lancia Ferrari	V8	22	3h 31m 13.900s	4	1
4	6	L Musso	Lancia Ferrari	801	Lancia Ferrari	V8	22	3h 34m 15.900s	8	3
5	10	S Moss	Vanwall	VW (57)	Vanwall	4	22	3h 35m 15.800s	7	2
6	2	J Behra	Maserati	250F	Maserati	6	22	3h 35m 16.800s	3	1
7	3	H Schell	Maserati	250F	Maserati	6	22	3h 37m 25.800s	6	2
8	16	M Gregory	Maserati	250F	Maserati	6	21		10	3
9	11	T Brooks	Vanwall	VW (57)	Vanwall	4	21		5	2
10	4	G Scarlatti	Maserati	250F	Maserati	6	21		13	4
11	15	B Halford	Maserati	250F	Maserati	6	21		16	5
F2: 1	21	E Barth	Porsche	RS550	Porsche	F4	21		12	4
F2: 2	28	B Naylor	Cooper	T43	Climax	4	20		17	5
F2: 3	27	C G de Beaufort	Porsche	RS550	Porsche	F4	20		20	6
F2: 4	25	T Marsh	Cooper	T43	Climax	4	17		22	7
r	17	H Herrmann	Maserati	250F	Maserati	6	14	engine	11	3
F2: r	20	U Maglioli	Porsche	RS550	Porsche	F4	13	engine	15	5
r	18	C Godia	Maserati	250F	Maserati	6	11	steering	21	6
F2: r	23	R Salvadori	Cooper	T43	Climax	4	11	front suspension	14	4
r	12	S Lewis-Evans	Vanwall	VW (57)	Vanwall	4	10	gearbox	9	3
F2: r	24	J Brabham	Cooper	T43	Climax	4	6	transmission	18	5
F2: r	26	P England	Cooper	T41	Climax	4	4	distributor	23	7
F2: r	29	D Gibson	Cooper	T43	Climax	4	2	steering	24	7
r	19	H Gould	Maserati	250F	Maserati	6	2	rear axle	19	6

Winning speed 142.943 km/h, 88.820 mph
Pole Position speed 145.184 km/h, 90.213 mph (J M Fangio, 9 min:25.600 sec)
Fastest Lap speed 147.320 km/h, 91.540 mph (J M Fangio, 9 min:17.400 sec on lap 20)
Lap Leaders M Hawthorn 1-2,15-20 (8); J M Fangio 3-11,21-22 (11); P Collins 12-14 (3).

Formula 2 cars raced simultaneously with F1, and are shown in italics.

18 Aug 1957   PESCARA: Pescara   (Round 7)   (Race 63)

18 laps x 25.579 km, 15.894 miles = 460.422 km, 286.093 miles

Pos	No	Driver	Car	Model	Engine		Laps	Time/Reason for Retirement	Grid Pos	Row
1	26	S Moss	Vanwall	VW (57)	Vanwall	4	18	2h 59m 22.700s	2	1
2	2	J M Fangio	Maserati	250F	Maserati	6	18	3h 02m 36.600s	1	1
3	6	H Schell	Maserati	250F	Maserati	6	18	3h 06m 09.500s	5	2
4	14	M Gregory	Maserati	250F	Maserati	6	18	3h 07m 39.200s	7	3
5	30	S Lewis-Evans	Vanwall	VW (57)	Vanwall	4	17		8	3
6	8	G Scarlatti	Maserati	250F	Maserati	6	17		10	4
7	24	J Brabham	Cooper	T43	Climax	4	15		16	7
r	10	C Godia	Maserati	250F	Maserati	6	10	engine	12	5
r	20	B Halford	Maserati	250F	Maserati	6	9	differential	14	6
r	34	L Musso	Lancia Ferrari	801	Lancia Ferrari	V8	9	oil tank	3	1
r	16	J Bonnier	Maserati	250F	Maserati	6	7	engine overheating	9	4
r	4	J Behra	Maserati	250F	Maserati	6	4	oil line	4	2
r	22	R Salvadori	Cooper	T43	Climax	4	3	accident / rear suspension	15	6
r	18	H Gould	Maserati	250F	Maserati	6	1	accident	11	5
r	28	T Brooks	Vanwall	VW (57)	Vanwall	4	1	engine	6	3
r	12	L Piotti	Maserati	250F	Maserati	6	1	engine	13	5

Winning speed 154.006 km/h, 95.695 mph
Pole Position speed 157.517 km/h, 97.876 mph (J M Fangio, 9 min:44.600 sec)
Fastest Lap speed 157.517 km/h, 97.876 mph (S Moss, 9 min:44.600 sec on lap 9)
Lap Leaders L Musso 1 (1); S Moss 2-18 (17).

87 laps x 5.750 km, 3.573 miles = 500.250 km, 310.841 miles

Pos	No	Driver	Car	Model	Engine		Laps	Time/Reason for Retirement	Grid Pos	Row
1	18	S Moss	Vanwall	VW (57)	Vanwall	4	87	2h 35m 03.900s	2	1
2	2	J M Fangio	Maserati	250F	Maserati	6	87	2h 35m 45.100s	4	1
3	36	W von Trips	Lancia Ferrari	801	Lancia Ferrari	V8	85		8	3
4	26	M Gregory	Maserati	250F	Maserati	6	84		11	3
5=	8	G Scarlatti	Maserati	250F	Maserati	6			12	4
5=	8	H Schell	Maserati	250F	Maserati	6	84			
6	34	M Hawthorn	Lancia Ferrari	801	Lancia Ferrari	V8	83		10	3
7	22	T Brooks	Vanwall	VW (57)	Vanwall	4	82		3	1
8	32	L Musso	Lancia Ferrari	801	Lancia Ferrari	V8	82		9	3
9	10	C Godia	Maserati	250F	Maserati	6	81		15	5
10	14	H Gould	Maserati	250F	Maserati	6	78		18	5
11=	28	A Simon	Maserati	250F	Maserati	6			16	5
11=	28	O Volonterio	Maserati	250F	Maserati	6	72			
r	30	P Collins	Lancia Ferrari	801	Lancia Ferrari	V8	62	valve	7	2
r	6	J Behra	Maserati	250F	Maserati	V12	50	engine overheating	5	2
r	20	S Lewis-Evans	Vanwall	VW (57)	Vanwall	4	49	header tank	1	1
r	16	B Halford	Maserati	250F	Maserati	6	47	engine	14	4
r	4	H Schell	Maserati	250F	Maserati	6	34	oil line	6	2
r	24	J Bonnier	Maserati	250F	Maserati	6	31	engine overheating	13	4
r	12	L Piotti	Maserati	250F	Maserati	6	3	engine	17	5

Winning speed 193.564 km/h, 120.275 mph
Pole Position speed 202.148 km/h, 125.609 mph (S Lewis-Evans, 1 min:42.400 sec)
Fastest Lap speed 199.614 km/h, 124.035 mph (T Brooks, 1 min:43.700 sec on lap 74)
Lap Leaders S Moss 1-3,5,11,21-87 (72); J Behra 4,6 (2); J M Fangio 7-10 (4); T Brooks 12-15 (4); S Lewis-Evans 16-20 (5).

Lap Leaders 1957

Pos	Driver	Car-Engine	GPs	laps	km	miles
1	J M Fangio	Maserati	5	263	1,361.2	845.8
2	S Moss	Vanwall	4	136	1,069.0	664.3
3	J Behra	Maserati	3	57	269.7	167.6
4	P Collins	Ferrari	2	16	119.3	74.1
5	M Hawthorn	Ferrari	1	8	182.5	113.4
6	E Castellotti	Ferrari	1	6	23.5	14.6
7	S Lewis-Evans	Vanwall	1	5	28.7	17.9
8	L Musso	Ferrari	2	4	45.2	28.1
	T Brooks	Vanwall	1	4	23.0	14.3
			7	**499**	**3,122.2**	**1,940.0**

Driver Points 1957

		RA	MC	INDY	F	GB	D	PES	I	Total	
1	J M Fangio	8	9	-	8	-	9	6	(6)	40	(6)
2	S Moss	1	-	-	-	5	2	9	8	25	
3	L Musso	-	-	-	7	6	3	-	-	16	
4	M Hawthorn	-	-	-	3	4	6	-	-	13	
5	T Brooks	-	6	-	-	4	-	-	1	11	
6	M Gregory	-	4	-	-	-	-	3	3	10	
	H Schell	3	-	-	2	-	-	4	1	10	
8	S Hanks	-	-	8	-	-	-	-	-	8	
	P Collins	-	-	-	4	-	4	-	-	8	
10	J Rathmann	-	-	7	-	-	-	-	-	7	
11	J Behra	6	-	-	-	-	-	-	-	6	
12	S Lewis-Evans	-	3	-	-	-	-	2	-	5	
	M Trintignant	-	2	-	-	3	-	-	-	5	
14	C Menditéguy	4	-	-	-	-	-	-	-	4	
	J Bryan	-	-	4	-	-	-	-	-	4	
	W von Trips	-	-	-	-	-	-	-	4	4	
17	P Russo	-	-	3	-	-	-	-	-	3	
18	A Linden	-	-	2	-	-	-	-	-	2	
	R Salvadori	-	-	-	-	2	-	-	-	2	
20	F González	1	-	-	-	-	-	-	-	1	
	A de Portago	1	-	-	-	-	-	-	-	1	
	G Scarlatti	-	-	-	-	-	-	-	1	1	

8,6,4,3 and 2 points awarded to the first five finishers. The driver setting the fastest lap scored a point also. Points shared for shared drives. Best 5 scores.
P Collins received no points for a shared 4th place in Britain, because he covered insufficient distance (3 laps)(M Trintignant awarded all 3 points).

There was confusion in some contemporary sources, with J Behra and H Schell both being awarded 2 points at the French Grand Prix.

Race Entrants and Results

New fuel regulations were announced. Cars were to run on commercial petrol, which meant aviation fuel to 130 octane (Avgas). Race distances were reduced to 300 km or 2 hours and there would be no points awarded for shared drives. The Constructors' Championship was inaugurated. The factory Maserati team withdrew, as rear engined cars emerged the quickest.

FERRARI
Scuderia Ferrari: Hawthorn, Collins, Musso, von Trips, Gendebien, P Hill

MASERATI
Scuderia Centro Sud: Gerini, Shelby, Gregory, Ruttman, Seidel, Herrmann (D), Trintignant, Allison, Bonnier
Scuderia Sud Americana: Fangio (RA), Menditéguy
Temple Buell: Gregory (I,MA) Shelby (P)
Joakim Bonnier: Bonnier, Herrmann, P Hill, Cabianca, Schell
Ken Kavanagh: (Kavanagh, Taramazzo), Behra
Privateers: Gould, Godia, Fangio, Scarlatti, de Filippis, (Testut, Chiron)

OSCA
Automobili OSCA: (Piotti, Cabianca)

BRM
Owen Racing Organisation: Schell, Behra, Bonnier, Trintignant, Flockhart

LOTUS
Team Lotus: Allison, G Hill, Stacey

CONNAUGHT
B C Ecclestone: Bueb, Fairman, (Kessler, Emery, Ecclestone)

COOPER
Cooper Car Co: Salvadori, Brabham, Burgess, Fairman
R R C Walker Racing Team: Trintignant, Moss, (Flockhart)

VANWALL
Vandervell Products Ltd: Moss, Brooks, Lewis-Evans

PORSCHE
Ecurie Maarsbergen: de Beaufort

(Entries for the F2 section are not included)

19 Jan 1958		ARGENTINA: Buenos Aires No.2					(Round 1)	(Race 65)	
		80 laps x 3.912 km, 2.431 miles = 312.960 km, 194.464 miles							
Pos	**No**	**Driver**	**Car**	**Model**	**Engine**	**Laps**	**Time/Reason for Retirement**	**Grid Pos**	**Row**
1	14	S Moss	Cooper	T43	Climax	4	80	2h 19m 33.700s	7	2
2	16	L Musso	Ferrari	Dino 246	Ferrari	V6	80	2h 19m 36.400s	5	2
3	20	M Hawthorn	Ferrari	Dino 246	Ferrari	V6	80	2h 19m 46.300s	2	1
4	2	J M Fangio	Maserati	250F	Maserati	6	80	2h 20m 26.700s	1	1
5	4	J Behra	Maserati	250F	Maserati	6	78		4	1
6	8	H Schell	Maserati	250F	Maserati	6	77		8	3
7	6	C Menditéguy	Maserati	250F	Maserati	6	76		6	2
8	10	C Godia	Maserati	250F	Maserati	6	75		9	3
9	12	H Gould	Maserati	250F	Maserati	6	71		10	3
r	18	P Collins	Ferrari	Dino 246	Ferrari	V6	0	driveshaft	3	1

Winning speed 134.547 km/h, 83.604 mph
Pole Position speed 138.071 km/h, 85.793 mph (J M Fangio, 1 min:42.000 sec)
Fastest Lap speed 138.342 km/h, 85.962 mph (J M Fangio, 1 min:41.800 sec on lap 30)
Lap Leaders J Behra 1 (1); M Hawthorn 2-9 (8); J M Fangio 10-34 (25); S Moss 35-80 (46).

This was the first victory for a rear-engined car.

18 May 1958 **MONACO: Monte-Carlo** (Round 2) (Race 66)

100 laps x 3.145 km, 1.954 miles = 314.500 km, 195.421 miles

Pos	No	Driver	Car	Model	Engine		Laps	Time/Reason for Retirement	Grid Pos	Row
1	20	M Trintignant	Cooper	T45	Climax	4	100	2h 52m 27.900s	5	2
2	34	L Musso	Ferrari	Dino 246	Ferrari	V6	100	2h 52m 48.100s	10	4
3	36	P Collins	Ferrari	Dino 246	Ferrari	V6	100	2h 53m 06.700s	9	4
4	16	J Brabham	Cooper	T45	Climax	4	97		3	1
5	8	H Schell	BRM	P25	BRM	4	91		12	5
r	40	W von Trips	Ferrari	Dino 246	Ferrari	V6	91	engine	11	5
6	24	C Allison	Lotus	12	Climax	4	87		13	5
r	58	J Bonnier	Maserati	250F	Maserati	6	72	accident	16	7
r	26	G Hill	Lotus	12	Climax	4	70	half shaft	15	6
r	18	R Salvadori	Cooper	T45	Climax	4	56	gearbox	4	2
r	38	M Hawthorn	Ferrari	Dino 246	Ferrari	V6	47	fuel pump	6	3
r	28	S Moss	Vanwall	VW (57)	Vanwall	4	38	valve	8	3
r	6	J Behra	BRM	P25	BRM	4	30	brakes	2	1
r	46	G Scarlatti	Maserati	250F	Maserati	6	27	engine	14	6
r	30	T Brooks	Vanwall	VW (57)	Vanwall	4	22	spark plug	1	1
r	32	S Lewis-Evans	Vanwall	VW (57)	Vanwall	4	12	engine overheating	7	3
nq	22	R Flockhart	Cooper	T43	Climax	4				
nq	4	C Godia	Maserati	250F	Maserati	6				
nq	50	K Kavanagh	Maserati	250F	Maserati	6				
nq	50	L Taramazzo	Maserati	250F	Maserati	6				
nq	48	G Gerini	Maserati	250F	Maserati	6				
nq	12	B Kessler	Connaught	B	Alta	4				
nq	14	P Emery	Connaught	B	Alta	4				
nq	44	M T de Filippis	Maserati	250F	Maserati	6				
nq	56	A Testut	Maserati	250F	Maserati	6				
nq	56	L Chiron	Maserati	250F	Maserati	6				
nq	52	G Cabianca	OSCA	OSCA		4				
nq	54	L Piotti	OSCA	OSCA		4				
nq	42	H Gould	Maserati	250F	Maserati	6				
nq	12	B Ecclestone	Connaught	B	Alta	4				

Winning speed 109.414 km/h, 67.986 mph
Pole Position speed 113.447 km/h, 70.493 mph (T Brooks, 1 min:39.800 sec)
Fastest Lap speed 112.545 km/h, 69.932 mph (M Hawthorn, 1 min:40.600 sec on lap 36)
Lap Leaders J Behra 1-27 (27); M Hawthorn 28-32,39-47 (14); S Moss 33-38 (6); M Trintignant 48-100 (53).

---

26 May 1958 **NETHERLANDS: Zandvoort** (Round 3) (Race 67)

75 laps x 4.193 km, 2.605 miles = 314.475 km, 195.406 miles

Pos	No	Driver	Car	Model	Engine		Laps	Time/Reason for Retirement	Grid Pos	Row
1	1	S Moss	Vanwall	VW (57)	Vanwall	4	75	2h 04m 49.200s	2	1
2	15	H Schell	BRM	P25	BRM	4	75	2h 05m 37.100s	7	3
3	14	J Behra	BRM	P25	BRM	4	75	2h 06m 31.500s	4	2
4	7	R Salvadori	Cooper	T45	Climax	4	74		9	4
5	5	M Hawthorn	Ferrari	Dino 246	Ferrari	V6	74		6	3
6	17	C Allison	Lotus	12	Climax	4	73		11	5
7	6	L Musso	Ferrari	Dino 246	Ferrari	V6	73		12	5
8	8	J Brabham	Cooper	T45	Climax	4	73		5	2
9	9	M Trintignant	Cooper	T45	Climax	4	72		8	3
10	11	J Bonnier	Maserati	250F	Maserati	6	71		15	6
11	18	C G de Beaufort	Porsche	RSK	Porsche	F4	69		17	7
r	10	G Scarlatti	Maserati	250F	Maserati	6	50	rear axle	16	7
r	3	S Lewis-Evans	Vanwall	VW (57)	Vanwall	4	45	valve	1	1
r	16	G Hill	Lotus	12	Climax	4	41	gasket / engine overheating	13	5
r	4	P Collins	Ferrari	Dino 246	Ferrari	V6	32	gearbox / spin	10	4
r	12	M Gregory	Maserati	250F	Maserati	6	16	fuel pump	14	6
r	2	T Brooks	Vanwall	VW (57)	Vanwall	4	13	rear axle	3	1
ns	12	H Gould	Maserati	250F	Maserati	6		car raced by Gregory		

Winning speed 151.166 km/h, 93.930 mph
Pole Position speed 155.456 km/h, 96.596 mph (S Lewis-Evans, 1 min:37.100 sec)
Fastest Lap speed 154.660 km/h, 96.101 mph (S Moss, 1 min:37.600 sec)
Lap Leaders S Moss 1-75 (75).

30 May 1958 INDIANAPOLIS: 500 (Round 4) (Race 68)

200 laps x 4.023 km, 2.500 miles = 804.672 km, 500.000 miles

Pos	No	Driver	Car	Model	Engine		Laps	Time/Reason for Retirement	Grid Pos	Row
1	1	J Bryan	Epperly		Offenhauser	4	200	3h 44m 13.800s	7	3
2	99	G Amick	Epperly		Offenhauser	4	200	3h 44m 41.429s	25	9
3	9	J Boyd	Kurtis Kraft	500G	Offenhauser	4	200		8	3
4	33	T Bettenhausen	Epperly		Offenhauser	4	200		9	3
5	2	J Rathmann	Epperly		Offenhauser	4	200		20	7
6	16	J Reece	Watson		Offenhauser	4	200		3	1
7	26	D Freeland	Phillips		Offenhauser	4	200		13	5
8	44	J Larson	Watson		Offenhauser	4	200		19	7
9	61	E Johnson	Kurtis Kraft	500G	Offenhauser	4	200		26	9
10	54	B Cheesbourg	Kurtis Kraft		Novi	8s	200		33	11
11	52	A Keller	Kurtis Kraft	500G-2	Offenhauser	4	200		21	7
12	45	J Parsons	Kurtis Kraft	500G	Offenhauser	4	200		6	2
13	19	J Tolan	Kuzma		Offenhauser	4	200		30	10
14r	65	B Christie	Kurtis Kraft	500E	Offenhauser	4	189	spin	17	6
15r	59	D Wilson	Kuzma		Offenhauser	4	151	clutch / refuelling fire	32	11
16r	29	A J Foyt	Kuzma		Offenhauser	4	148	spin	12	4
17	77	M Magill	Kurtis Kraft	500G	Offenhauser	4	136		31	11
18r	15	P Russo	Kurtis Kraft		Novi	8s	122	radiator	14	5
19r	83	S Templeman	Kurtis Kraft	500C	Offenhauser	4	116	brakes	23	8
20r	8	R Ward	Lesovsky		Offenhauser	4	93	fuel pump	11	4
21r	43	B Garrett	Kurtis Kraft	500G	Offenhauser	4	80	cam gear	15	5
22r	88	E Sachs	Kuzma		Offenhauser	4	68	universal joint	18	6
23r	7	J Thomson	Kurtis Kraft		Offenhauser	4	52	steering	22	8
24r	89	C Weyant	Dunn		Offenhauser	4	38	brakes locked / accident	29	10
25r	25	J Turner	Lesovsky		Offenhauser	4	21	fuel pump	10	4
26r	14	B Veith	Kurtis Kraft	500G	Offenhauser	4	1	accident	4	2
27r	97	D Rathmann	Watson		Offenhauser	4	0	accident	1	1
28r	5	E Elisian	Watson		Offenhauser	4	0	accident	2	1
29r	4	P O'Connor	Kurtis Kraft	500G	Offenhauser	4	0	fatal accident	5	2
30r	31	P Goldsmith	Kurtis Kraft	500G	Offenhauser	4	0	accident	16	6
31r	92	J Unser	Kurtis Kraft	500G	Offenhauser	4	0	accident	24	8
32r	68	L Sutton	Kurtis Kraft	500G	Offenhauser	4	0	accident	27	9
33r	57	A Bisch	Kuzma		Offenhauser	4	0	accident	28	10

Winning speed 215.316 km/h, 133.791 mph
Pole Position speed 234.922 km/h, 145.974 mph (D Rathmann, 1 min: 1.655 sec)
Fastest Lap speed 232.229 km/h, 144.300 mph (T Bettenhausen, 1 min: 2.370 sec on lap 55)

15 Jun 1958 BELGIUM: Spa-Francorchamps (Round 5) (Race 69)

24 laps x 14.100 km, 8.761 miles = 338.400 km, 210.272 miles

Pos	No	Driver	Car	Model	Engine		Laps	Time/Reason for Retirement	Grid Pos	Row
1	4	T Brooks	Vanwall	VW (57)	Vanwall	4	24	1h 37m 06.300s	5	2
2	16	M Hawthorn	Ferrari	Dino 246	Ferrari	V6	24	1h 37m 27.000s	1	1
3	6	S Lewis-Evans	Vanwall	VW (57)	Vanwall	4	24	1h 40m 07.200s	11	5
4	40	C Allison	Lotus	12	Climax	4	24	1h 41m 21.800s	12	5
5	10	H Schell	BRM	P25	BRM	4	23		7	3
6	20	O Gendebien	Ferrari	Dino 246	Ferrari	V6	23		6	3
7	28	M Trintignant	Maserati	250F	Maserati	6	23		16	7
8	24	R Salvadori	Cooper	T45	Climax	4	23		13	5
9	36	J Bonnier	Maserati	250F	Maserati	6	22		14	6
10	26	M T de Filippis	Maserati	250F	Maserati	6	22		19	8
r	38	C Godia	Maserati	250F	Maserati	6	22	engine	18	7
r	22	J Brabham	Cooper	T45	Climax	4	16	gasket / engine overheating	8	3
r	42	G Hill	Lotus	12	Climax	4	12	engine	15	6
r	18	L Musso	Ferrari	Dino 246	Ferrari	V6	5	accident	2	1
r	14	P Collins	Ferrari	Dino 246	Ferrari	V6	5	engine overheating	4	2
r	8	J Behra	BRM	P25	BRM	4	5	oil pressure / engine	10	4
r	32	W Seidel	Maserati	250F	Maserati	6	4	rear axle / engine	17	7
r	2	S Moss	Vanwall	VW (57)	Vanwall	4	1	valves	3	1
r	30	M Gregory	Maserati	250F	Maserati	6	1	engine	9	4
ns	34	K Kavanagh	Maserati	250F	Maserati	6		engine		

Winning speed 209.093 km/h, 129.925 mph
Pole Position speed 214.087 km/h, 133.027 mph (M Hawthorn, 3 min:57.100 sec)
Fastest Lap speed 213.009 km/h, 132.358 mph (M Hawthorn, 3 min:58.300 sec on lap 24)
Lap Leaders T Brooks 1,3,5-24 (22); P Collins 2,4 (2).

Also the Grand Prix of Europe. Front row of the grid reversed by request of M Hawthorn (pole).
During practice, some cars had different numbers from those in the race.

50 laps x 8.302 km, 5.159 miles = 415.100 km, 257.931 miles

Pos	No	Driver	Car	Model	Engine		Laps	Time/Reason for Retirement	Grid Pos	Row
1	4	M Hawthorn	Ferrari	Dino 246	Ferrari	V6	50	2h 03m 21.300s	1	1
2	8	S Moss	Vanwall	VW (57)	Vanwall	4	50	2h 03m 45.900s	6	3
3	6	W von Trips	Ferrari	Dino 246	Ferrari	V6	50	2h 04m 21.000s	21	9
4	34	J M Fangio	Maserati	250F	Maserati	6	50	2h 05m 51.900s	8	3
5	42	P Collins	Ferrari	Dino 246	Ferrari	V6	50	2h 08m 46.200s	4	2
6	22	J Brabham	Cooper	T45	Climax	4	49		12	5
7	36	P Hill	Maserati	250F	Maserati	6	49		13	5
8	38	J Bonnier	Maserati	250F	Maserati	6	48		16	7
9	32	G Gerini	Maserati	250F	Maserati	6	47		15	6
10	30	T Ruttman	Maserati	250F	Maserati	6	45		18	7
r	16	H Schell	BRM	P25	BRM	4	40	engine overheating	3	1
r	14	J Behra	BRM	P25	BRM	4	40	fuel pump	9	4
11	20	R Salvadori	Cooper	T45	Climax	4	37		14	6
r=	12	S Lewis-Evans	Vanwall	VW (57)	Vanwall	4			10	4
r=	12	T Brooks	Vanwall	VW (57)	Vanwall	4	35	engine		
r	24	G Hill	Lotus	16	Climax	4	33	engine overheating	19	8
r	40	C Godia	Maserati	250F	Maserati	6	27	accident	11	5
r	18	M Trintignant	BRM	P25	BRM	4	23	oil line	7	3
r	10	T Brooks	Vanwall	VW (57)	Vanwall	4	15	gearbox	5	2
r	2	L Musso	Ferrari	Dino 246	Ferrari	V6	9	fatal accident	2	1
r	28	C Shelby	Maserati	250F	Maserati	6	9	engine	17	7
r	26	C Allison	Lotus	12	Climax	4	6	engine	20	8

Winning speed 201.905 km/h, 125.458 mph
Pole Position speed 210.919 km/h, 131.059 mph (M Hawthorn, 2 min:21.700 sec)
Fastest Lap speed 206.261 km/h, 128.165 mph (M Hawthorn, 2 min:24.900 sec on lap 45)
Lap Leaders M Hawthorn 1-50 (50).

C Godia's qualifying time was set by J M Fangio.

75 laps x 4.711 km, 2.927 miles = 353.291 km, 219.525 miles

Pos	No	Driver	Car	Model	Engine		Laps	Time/Reason for Retirement	Grid Pos	Row
1	1	P Collins	Ferrari	Dino 246	Ferrari	V6	75	2h 09m 04.200s	6	2
2	2	M Hawthorn	Ferrari	Dino 246	Ferrari	V6	75	2h 09m 28.400s	4	1
3	10	R Salvadori	Cooper	T45	Climax	4	75	2h 09m 54.800s	3	1
4	9	S Lewis-Evans	Vanwall	VW (57)	Vanwall	4	75	2h 09m 55.000s	7	2
5	20	H Schell	BRM	P25	BRM	4	75	2h 10m 19.000s	2	1
6	11	J Brabham	Cooper	T45	Climax	4	75	2h 10m 27.400s	10	3
7	8	T Brooks	Vanwall	VW (57)	Vanwall	4	74		9	3
8	4	M Trintignant	Cooper	T43	Climax	4	73		12	4
9	5	C Shelby	Maserati	250F	Maserati	6	72		15	5
r	3	W von Trips	Ferrari	Dino 246	Ferrari	V6	59	engine bearings	11	3
r	22	J Bonnier	Maserati	250F	Maserati	6	49	gearbox	13	4
r	6	G Gerini	Maserati	250F	Maserati	6	43	gearbox	18	5
r	12	I Burgess	Cooper	T45	Climax	4	40	clutch	16	5
r	7	S Moss	Vanwall	VW (57)	Vanwall	4	25	engine	1	1
r	17	C Allison	Lotus	12	Climax	4	21	oil pressure	5	2
r	15	I Bueb	Connaught	B	Alta	4	19	gearbox oil pump	17	5
r	18	A Stacey	Lotus	16	Climax	4	19	oil pressure / engine overheating	20	6
r	19	J Behra	BRM	P25	BRM	4	19	rear suspension / tyre	8	3
r	16	G Hill	Lotus	16	Climax	4	17	oil pressure / engine overheating	14	4
r	14	J Fairman	Connaught	B	Alta	4	7	ignition	19	6

Winning speed 164.232 km/h, 102.049 mph
Pole Position speed 170.603 km/h, 106.008 mph (S Moss, 1 min:39.400 sec)
Fastest Lap speed 168.234 km/h, 104.536 mph (M Hawthorn, 1 min:40.800 sec on lap 50)
Lap Leaders P Collins 1-75 (75).

3 Aug 1958   GERMANY: Nürburgring   (Round 8)   (Race 72)

15 laps x 22.810 km, 14.173 miles = 342.150 km, 212.602 miles

Pos	No	Driver	Car	Model	Engine		Laps	Time/Reason for Retirement	Grid Pos	Row
1	8	T Brooks	Vanwall	VW (57)	Vanwall	4	15	2h 21m 15.000s	2	1
2	10	R Salvadori	Cooper	T45	Climax	4	15	2h 24m 44.700s	6	2
3	11	M Trintignant	Cooper	T45	Climax	4	15	2h 26m 26.200s	7	2
4	4	W von Trips	Ferrari	Dino 246	Ferrari	V6	15	2h 27m 31.300s	5	2
F2: 1	20	*B McLaren*	*Cooper*	*T45*	*Climax*	*4*	*15*	*2h 27m 41.300s*	*12*	*4*
F2: 2	21	*E Barth*	*Porsche*	*RSK*	*Porsche*	*F4*	*15*	*2h 27m 47.400s*	*13*	*4*
F2: 3	26	*I Burgess*	*Cooper*	*T43*	*Climax*	*4*	*15*	*2h 28m 14.300s*	*11*	*3*
F2: 4	30	*T Marsh*	*Cooper*	*T45*	*Climax*	*4*	*15*	*2h 28m 24.900s*	*14*	*4*
F2: 5	23	*P Hill*	*Ferrari*	*Dino 156*	*Ferrari*	*V6*	*15*	*2h 29m 00.500s*	*10*	*3*
5	12	C Allison	Lotus	16	Climax	4	13		24	7
F2: r	28	*I Bueb*	*Lotus*	*12*	*Climax*	*4*	*12*	*oil line*	*16*	*5*
r	3	M Hawthorn	Ferrari	Dino 246	Ferrari	V6	11	clutch	1	1
r	2	P Collins	Ferrari	Dino 246	Ferrari	V6	10	fatal accident	4	1
F2: r	22	*W Seidel*	*Cooper*	*T43*	*Climax*	*4*	*8*	*suspension*	*17*	*5*
r	6	H Schell	BRM	P25	BRM	4	8	brakes	8	3
F2: r	25	*G Hill*	*Lotus*	*16*	*Climax*	*4*	*4*	*oil line*	*22*	*7*
F2: r	27	*C Goethals*	*Cooper*	*T43*	*Climax*	*4*	*3*	*fuel pump*	*23*	*7*
r	17	H Herrmann	Maserati	250F	Maserati	6	3	engine	20	6
r	5	J Behra	BRM	P25	BRM	4	3	suspension / handling	9	3
F2: r	18	*C G de Beaufort*	*Porsche*	*RS550*	*Porsche*	*F4*	*3*	*engine*	*15*	*5*
r	7	S Moss	Vanwall	VW (57)	Vanwall	4	3	magneto	3	1
F2: r	19	*D Gibson*	*Cooper*	*T43*	*Climax*	*4*	*2*	*engine*	*18*	*5*
r	16	J Bonnier	Maserati	250F	Maserati	6	1	engine	21	6
F2: r	29	*B Naylor*	*Cooper*	*T45*	*Climax*	*4*	*0*	*fuel pump*	*25*	*7*
F2: r	24	*J Brabham*	*Cooper*	*T45*	*Climax*	*4*	*0*	*accident*	*19*	*6*
ns	14	T Ruttman	Maserati	250F	Maserati	6		engine		

Winning speed 145.338 km/h, 90.309 mph
Pole Position speed 148.224 km/h, 92.102 mph (M Hawthorn, 9 min:14.000 sec)
Fastest Lap speed 149.519 km/h, 92.907 mph (S Moss, 9 min: 9.200 sec on lap 3)
Lap Leaders S Moss 1-3 (3); M Hawthorn 4 (1); P Collins 5-10 (6); T Brooks 11-15 (5).

Drivers on rows 6 and 7 were relegated to these positions due to infringements during practice. F2 cars raced simultaneously with F1, and are shown in italics.
B McLaren finished 5th 'on the road', but was not eligible for points due to being in the F2 section of the race. C Allison's 5th place was ineligible for points as he finished behind Formula 2 entrants.

24 Aug 1958   PORTUGAL: Porto   (Round 9)   (Race 73)

50 laps x 7.407 km, 4.602 miles = 370.350 km, 230.125 miles

Pos	No	Driver	Car	Model	Engine		Laps	Time/Reason for Retirement	Grid Pos	Row
1	2	S Moss	Vanwall	VW (57)	Vanwall	4	50	2h 11m 27.800s	1	1
2	22	M Hawthorn	Ferrari	Dino 246	Ferrari	V6	50	2h 16m 40.550s	2	1
3	6	S Lewis-Evans	Vanwall	VW (57)	Vanwall	4	49		3	1
4	8	J Behra	BRM	P25	BRM	4	49		4	2
5	24	W von Trips	Ferrari	Dino 246	Ferrari	V6	49		6	3
6	10	H Schell	BRM	P25	BRM	4	49		7	3
7	14	J Brabham	Cooper	T45	Climax	4	48		8	3
8	12	M Trintignant	Cooper	T43	Climax	4	48		9	4
r	28	C Shelby	Maserati	250F	Maserati	6	47	brakes / accident	10	4
9	16	R Salvadori	Cooper	T45	Climax	4	46		11	5
r	4	T Brooks	Vanwall	VW (57)	Vanwall	4	36	accident	5	2
r	20	G Hill	Lotus	16	Climax	4	25	accident	12	5
r	18	C Allison	Maserati	250F	Maserati	6	15	engine	13	5
r	32	J Bonnier	Maserati	250F	Maserati	6	9	driver ill	14	6
r	30	M T de Filippis	Maserati	250F	Maserati	6	6	engine	15	6

Winning speed 169.028 km/h, 105.029 mph
Pole Position speed 172.915 km/h, 107.444 mph (S Moss, 2 min:34.210 sec)
Fastest Lap speed 175.003 km/h, 108.742 mph (M Hawthorn, 2 min:32.370 sec on lap 36)
Lap Leaders S Moss 1,8-50 (44); M Hawthorn 2-7 (6).

70 laps x 5.750 km, 3.573 miles = 402.500 km, 250.102 miles

Pos	No	Driver	Car	Model	Engine		Laps	Time/Reason for Retirement	Grid Pos	Row
1	28	T Brooks	Vanwall	VW (57)	Vanwall	4	70	2h 03m 47.800s	2	1
2	14	M Hawthorn	Ferrari	Dino 246	Ferrari	V6	70	2h 04m 12.000s	3	1
3	18	P Hill	Ferrari	Dino 246	Ferrari	V6	70	2h 04m 16.100s	7	2
4=	32	M Gregory	Maserati	250F	Maserati	6			11	3
4=	32	C Shelby	Maserati	250F	Maserati	6	69			
5	6	R Salvadori	Cooper	T45	Climax	4	62		14	4
6	38	G Hill	Lotus	16	Climax	4	62		12	4
7	36	C Allison	Lotus	12	Climax	4	61		16	5
r	42	M T de Filippis	Maserati	250F	Maserati	6	57	connecting rod	21	6
r	22	G Cabianca	Maserati	250F	Maserati	6	51	fuel pipe	20	6
r	8	J Behra	BRM	P25	BRM	4	42	brakes / clutch	8	3
r	24	H Herrmann	Maserati	250F	Maserati	6	32	valves	18	5
r	30	S Lewis-Evans	Vanwall	VW (57)	Vanwall	4	30	engine overheating	4	1
r	2	M Trintignant	Cooper	T45	Climax	4	24	gearbox	13	4
r	26	S Moss	Vanwall	VW (57)	Vanwall	4	17	gearbox	1	1
r	12	J Bonnier	BRM	P25	BRM	4	14	transmission / fire	10	3
r	20	O Gendebien	Ferrari	Dino 246	Ferrari	V6	4	rear suspension	5	2
r	40	G Gerini	Maserati	250F	Maserati	6	2	accident	19	6
r	34	C Shelby	Maserati	250F	Maserati	6	1	front wheel	17	5
r	10	H Schell	BRM	P25	BRM	4	0	accident	9	3
r	16	W von Trips	Ferrari	Dino 246	Ferrari	V6	0	accident / injury	6	2
r	4	J Brabham	Cooper	T45	Climax	4	0	front suspension / accident	15	5

Winning speed 195.078 km/h, 121.216 mph
Pole Position speed 205.970 km/h, 127.984 mph (S Moss, 1 min:40.500 sec)
Fastest Lap speed 201.166 km/h, 124.999 mph (P Hill, 1 min:42.900 sec on lap 26)
Lap Leaders P Hill 1-4,35-37 (7); M Hawthorn 5-6,9,15-34,38-60 (46); S Moss 7-8,10-14 (7); T Brooks 61-70 (10).

M Gregory and C Shelby were originally disqualified for sharing a car but later reinstated, although they received no points.

53 laps x 7.618 km, 4.734 miles = 403.754 km, 250.881 miles

Pos	No	Driver	Car	Model	Engine		Laps	Time/Reason for Retirement	Grid Pos	Row
1	8	S Moss	Vanwall	VW (57)	Vanwall	4	53	2h 09m 15.100s	2	1
2	6	M Hawthorn	Ferrari	Dino 246	Ferrari	V6	53	2h 10m 39.800s	1	1
3	4	P Hill	Ferrari	Dino 246	Ferrari	V6	53	2h 10m 40.600s	5	2
4	18	J Bonnier	BRM	P25	BRM	4	53	2h 11m 01.800s	8	3
5	16	H Schell	BRM	P25	BRM	4	53	2h 11m 48.800s	10	4
6	22	M Gregory	Maserati	250F	Maserati	6	52		13	5
7	30	R Salvadori	Cooper	T45	Climax	4	51		14	6
8	32	J Fairman	Cooper	T45	Climax	4	50		11	5
9	24	H Herrmann	Maserati	250F	Maserati	6	50		18	7
10	34	C Allison	Lotus	12	Climax	4	49		16	7
F2: 1	*50*	*J Brabham*	*Cooper*	*T45*	*Climax*	*4*	*49*		*19*	*8*
11	28	G Gerini	Maserati	250F	Maserati	6	48		17	7
F2: 2	*52*	*B McLaren*	*Cooper*	*T45*	*Climax*	*4*	*48*		*21*	*9*
F2: 3	*58*	*R La Caze*	*Cooper*	*T45*	*Climax*	*4*	*48*		*23*	*9*
F2: 4	*48*	*A Guelfi*	*Cooper*	*T45*	*Climax*	*4*	*48*		*25*	*10*
12	36	G Hill	Lotus	16	Climax	4	45		12	5
r	12	S Lewis-Evans	Vanwall	VW (57)	Vanwall	4	41	engine / fatal accident	3	1
r	2	O Gendebien	Ferrari	Dino 246	Ferrari	V6	29	accident	6	3
r	10	T Brooks	Vanwall	VW (57)	Vanwall	4	29	connecting rod / accident	7	3
F2: r	*54*	*F Picard*	*Cooper*	*T43*	*Climax*	*4*	*28*	*accident*	*24*	*10*
F2: r	*56*	*T Bridger*	*Cooper*	*T45*	*Climax*	*4*	*28*	*accident*	*22*	*9*
r	14	J Behra	BRM	P25	BRM	4	26	engine	4	2
r	26	W Seidel	Maserati	250F	Maserati	6	15	accident	20	8
r	20	R Flockhart	BRM	P25	BRM	4	15	camshaft	15	6
r	38	M Trintignant	Cooper	T45	Climax	4	9	engine	9	4

Winning speed 187.427 km/h, 116.462 mph
Pole Position speed 191.648 km/h, 119.084 mph (M Hawthorn, 2 min:23.100 sec)
Fastest Lap speed 192.455 km/h, 119.586 mph (S Moss, 2 min:22.500 sec on lap 21)
Lap Leaders S Moss 1-53 (53).

Formula 2 cars raced simultaneously with F1, and are shown in italics.
During practice, some cars had different numbers from those in the race.
A Guelfi used car 60 during qualifying.

Lap Leaders 1958

Pos	Driver	Car-Engine	GPs	laps	km	miles
1	S Moss	Cooper-Climax	1	46	180.0	111.8
		Vanwall	6	188	1,171.7	728.1
			7	234	1,351.7	839.9
2	M Hawthorn	Ferrari	6	125	822.2	510.9
3	P Collins	Ferrari	3	83	518.4	322.1
4	M Trintignant	Cooper-Climax	1	53	166.7	103.6
5	T Brooks	Vanwall	3	37	481.8	299.3
6	J Behra	BRM	1	27	84.9	52.8
		Maserati	1	1	3.9	2.4
			2	28	88.8	55.2
7	J M Fangio	Maserati	1	25	97.8	60.8
8	P Hill	Ferrari	1	7	40.2	25.0
			10	592	3,567.5	2,216.8

Driver Points 1958

		RA	MC	NL	INDY	B	F	GB	D	P	I	MA	Total	
1	M Hawthorn	(4)	(1)	(2)	-	7	9	7	-	7	6	6	42	(7)
2	S Moss	8	-	9	-	-	6	-	1	8	-	9	41	
3	T Brooks	-	-	-	-	8	-	-	8	-	8	-	24	
4	R Salvadori	-	-	3	-	-	-	4	6	-	2	-	15	
5	P Collins	-	4	-	-	-	2	8	-	-	-	-	14	
	H Schell	-	2	6	-	2	-	2	-	-	-	2	14	
7	M Trintignant	-	8	-	-	-	-	-	4	-	-	-	12	
	L Musso	6	6	-	-	-	-	-	-	-	-	-	12	
9	S Lewis-Evans	-	-	-	-	4	-	3	-	4	-	-	11	
10	P Hill	-	-	-	-	-	-	-	-	-	5	4	9	
	J Behra	2	-	4	-	-	-	-	-	3	-	-	9	
	W von Trips	-	-	-	-	-	4	-	3	2	-	-	9	
13	J Bryan	-	-	-	8	-	-	-	-	-	-	-	8	
14	J M Fangio	4	-	-	-	-	3	-	-	-	-	-	7	
15	G Amick	-	-	-	6	-	-	-	-	-	-	-	6	
16	T Bettenhausen	-	-	-	4	-	-	-	-	-	-	-	4	
	J Boyd	-	-	-	4	-	-	-	-	-	-	-	4	
18	J Brabham	-	3	-	-	-	-	-	-	-	-	-	3	
	C Allison	-	-	-	-	3	-	-	-	-	-	-	3	
	J Bonnier	-	-	-	-	-	-	-	-	-	-	3	3	
21	J Rathmann	-	-	-	2	-	-	-	-	-	-	-	2	

8,6,4,3 and 2 points awarded to the first five finishers. The driver setting the fastest lap scored a point also.
Points only awarded to drivers who handled the car throughout the race.
Best 6 scores. M Gregory and C Shelby (Maserati) were ineligible for points in Italy, because of their shared drive.

Constructor Points 1958

		RA	MC	NL	INDY	B	F	GB	D	P	I	MA	Total	
1	Vanwall	-	-	8	-	8	(6)	(3)	8	8	8	8	48	(9)
2	Ferrari	6	6	(2)	-	6	8	8	(3)	6	(6)	(6)	40	(17)
3	Cooper-Climax	8	8	3	-	-	-	4	6	-	2	-	31	
4	BRM	-	2	6	-	2	-	2	-	3	-	3	18	
5	Maserati	3	-	-	-	-	3	-	-	-	-	-	6	
6	Lotus-Climax	-	-	-	-	3	-	-	-	-	-	-	3	

8,6,4,3 and 2 points awarded to the first five finishers. Indianapolis excluded.
Points only for highest placed car. Best 6 scores.

1959

Race Entrants and Results

The new World Champion Mike Hawthorn announced his retirement but was sadly killed when his Jaguar saloon left the road near Guildford in January. Vanwall withdrew from serious competition citing ill health, but the many racing fatalities of the previous season were regarded as the true reason. A new formula based on the existing Formula 2 was announced for the 1961 season.

FERRARI
Scuderia Ferrari: Brooks, P Hill, Allison, Gurney, Behra, Gendebien, von Trips

MASERATI
Scuderia Centro Sud: d'Orey (Bayardo)
Scuderia Ugolini: Scarlatti, de Beaufort
Ottorino Volonterio: Cabianca
Monte-Carlo Auto Sport: (Testut)
Privateer: (Cade)

BRM
Owen Racing Organisation: Bonnier, Schell, Flockhart
British Racing Partnership: S Moss, Herrmann

COOPER
Cooper Car Co: Brabham, McLaren, Gregory, Scarlatti
R R C Walker Racing Team: Trintignant, S Moss
Scuderia Centro Sud: Burgess, Davis, Cabral, Herrmann
High Efficiency Motors: Salvadori, Fairman
British Racing Partnership: Bueb, Bristow
Alan Brown Equipe: Ashdown, M Taylor
R H H Parnell: H Taylor, (Parnell)
Ecurie Bleue: Schell
Automobili OSCA: de Tomaso
Mike Taylor: Constantine
Privateer: (Lucienbonnet)
Gilby Engineering Co Ltd: (Greene)
Ace Garage (Rotherham): (T Taylor)
Equipe Nationale Belge: (Bianchi, de Changy)
United Racing Stable: (B Moss)

CONNAUGHT
Paul Emery Connaught Cars: Said

ASTON MARTIN
David Brown Corporation: Salvadori, Shelby

LOTUS
Team Lotus: G Hill, Ireland, Stacey, (Lovely)
Dorchester Service Station: Piper
John Fisher: Halford
Privateer: (D Taylor)

VANWALL
Vandervell Products Ltd: Brooks

JBW
J B Naylor: Naylor

FRY
David Fry: (Parkes)

PORSCHE
Dr Ing F Porsche KG: von Trips, (de Filippis)
Ecurie Maarsbergen: de Beaufort
Blanchard Automobile Co: Blanchard
Privateer: (Behra)

TEC MEC
Camoradi USA/Gordon Pennington Jr: d'Orey

KURTIS KRAFT
Leader Cards Inc.: Ward

10 May 1959		MONACO: Monte-Carlo						(Round 1)		(Race 76)
		100 laps x 3.145 km, 1.954 miles = 314.500 km, 195.421 miles								

Pos	No	Driver	Car	Model	Engine		Laps	Time/Reason for Retirement	Grid Pos	Row
1	24	J Brabham	Cooper	T51	Climax	4	100	2h 55m 51.300s	3	1
2	50	T Brooks	Ferrari	Dino 246	Ferrari	V6	100	2h 56m 11.700s	4	2
3	32	M Trintignant	Cooper	T51	Climax	4	98		6	3
4	48	P Hill	Ferrari	Dino 246	Ferrari	V6	97		5	2
5	22	B McLaren	Cooper	T51	Climax	4	96		13	5
6	38	R Salvadori	Cooper	T45	Maserati	4	83	transmission (pushed over line)	8	3
r	30	S Moss	Cooper	T51	Climax	4	81	transmission	1	1
r	20	R Flockhart	BRM	P25	BRM	4	64	brakes / spin	10	4
r	16	H Schell	BRM	P25	BRM	4	48	accident	9	4
r	18	J Bonnier	BRM	P25	BRM	4	44	brakes / accident	7	3
r	46	J Behra	Ferrari	Dino 246	Ferrari	V6	24	engine	2	1
r	40	G Hill	Lotus	16	Climax	4	21	oil fire	14	6
r	26	M Gregory	Cooper	T51	Climax	4	6	gearbox	11	5
r	44	B Halford	Lotus	16	Climax	4	1	accident	16	7
r	52	C Allison	Ferrari	Dino 156	Ferrari	V6	1	accident	15	6
r	6	W von Trips	Porsche	718	Porsche	F4	1	accident	12	5
nq	34	I Bueb	Cooper	T51	Climax	4				
nq	54	G Scarlatti	Maserati	250F	Maserati	6				
nq	10	L Bianchi	Cooper	T51	Climax	4				
nq	12	A de Changy	Cooper	T51	Climax	4				
nq	4	M T de Filippis	Behra Porsche		Porsche	F4				
nq	42	P Lovely	Lotus	16	Climax	4				
nq	14	J Lucienbonnet	Cooper	T45	Climax	4				
nq	56	A Testut	Maserati	250F	Maserati	6				

Winning speed 107.304 km/h, 66.676 mph
Pole Position speed 113.675 km/h, 70.634 mph (S Moss, 1 min:39.600 sec)
Fastest Lap speed 112.769 km/h, 70.071 mph (J Brabham, 1 min:40.400 sec on lap 83)
Lap Leaders J Behra 1-21 (21); S Moss 22-81 (60); J Brabham 82-100 (19).

30 May 1959 **INDIANAPOLIS: 500** (Round 2) (Race 77)

200 laps x 4.023 km, 2.500 miles = 804.672 km, 500.000 miles

Pos	No	Driver	Car	Model	Engine		Laps	Time/Reason for Retirement	Grid Pos	Row
1	5	R Ward	Watson		Offenhauser	4	200	3h 40m 49.200s	6	2
2	16	J Rathmann	Watson		Offenhauser	4	200	3h 41m 12.477s	3	1
3	3	J Thomson	Lesovsky		Offenhauser	4	200		1	1
4	1	T Bettenhausen	Epperly		Offenhauser	4	200		15	5
5	99	P Goldsmith	Epperly		Offenhauser	4	200		16	6
6	33	J Boyd	Epperly		Offenhauser	4	200		11	4
7	37	D Carter	Kurtis Kraft		Offenhauser	4	200		12	4
8	19	E Johnson	Kurtis Kraft	500G	Offenhauser	4	200		8	3
9	45	P Russo	Kurtis Kraft	500G	Offenhauser	4	200		27	9
10	10	A J Foyt	Kuzma		Offenhauser	4	200		17	6
11	88	G Hartley	Kuzma		Offenhauser	4	200		9	3
12	74	B Veith	Moore		Offenhauser	4	200		7	3
13	89	A Herman	Dunn		Offenhauser	4	200		23	8
14	66	J Daywalt	Kurtis Kraft	500E	Offenhauser	4	200		13	5
15	71	C Arnold	Kurtis Kraft		Offenhauser	4	200		21	7
16	58	J McWithey	Kurtis Kraft	500C	Offenhauser	4	200		33	11
17r	44	E Sachs	Kuzma		Offenhauser	4	182	gear tower bolt / spin	2	1
18r	57	A Keller	Kuzma		Offenhauser	4	163	pistons	28	10
19r	64	P Flaherty	Watson		Offenhauser	4	162	accident	18	6
20r	73	D Rathmann	Watson		Offenhauser	4	150	caught fire in pits	4	2
21r	53	B Cheesbourg	Kuzma		Offenhauser	4	147	magneto	30	10
22r	15	D Freeland	Kurtis Kraft	500G	Offenhauser	4	136	valve spring	25	9
23r	49	R Crawford	Elder		Offenhauser	4	115	accident	32	11
24r	9	D Branson	Phillips		Offenhauser	4	112	torsion bar	10	4
25r	65	B Christie	Kurtis Kraft	500D	Offenhauser	4	109	rod bolt	24	8
26r	48	B Grim	Kurtis Kraft	500G	Offenhauser	4	85	piston	5	2
27r	24	J Turner	Christensen		Offenhauser	4	47	fuel tank	14	5
28r	47	C Weyant	Kurtis Kraft	500J	Offenhauser	4	45	accident	29	10
29r	7	J Larson	Kurtis Kraft	500J	Offenhauser	4	45	accident	19	7
30r	77	M Magill	Kurtis Kraft	500G	Offenhauser	4	45	accident	31	11
31r	87	R Amick	Kurtis Kraft	500C	Offenhauser	4	45	accident	26	9
32r	8	L Sutton	Lesovsky		Offenhauser	4s	34	accident	22	8
33r	6	J Bryan	Epperly		Offenhauser	4	1	clutch / cam gear	20	7

Winning speed 218.641 km/h, 135.857 mph
Pole Position speed 234.815 km/h, 145.907 mph (J Thomson, 1 min: 1.683 sec)
Fastest Lap speed 234.030 km/h, 145.419 mph (J Thomson, 1 min: 1.890 sec on lap 64)

31 May 1959 **NETHERLANDS: Zandvoort** (Round 3) (Race 78)

75 laps x 4.193 km, 2.605 miles = 314.475 km, 195.406 miles

Pos	No	Driver	Car	Model	Engine		Laps	Time/Reason for Retirement	Grid Pos	Row
1	7	J Bonnier	BRM	P25	BRM	4	75	2h 05m 26.800s	1	1
2	8	J Brabham	Cooper	T51	Climax	4	75	2h 05m 41.000s	2	1
3	9	M Gregory	Cooper	T51	Climax	4	75	2h 06m 49.800s	7	3
4	12	I Ireland	Lotus	16	Climax	4	74		9	4
5	1	J Behra	Ferrari	Dino 246	Ferrari	V6	74		4	2
6	3	P Hill	Ferrari	Dino 246	Ferrari	V6	73		12	5
7	14	G Hill	Lotus	16	Climax	4	73		5	2
8	10	M Trintignant	Cooper	T51	Climax	4	73		11	5
9	16	C Allison	Ferrari	Dino 246	Ferrari	V6	71		15	6
10	15	C G de Beaufort	Porsche	RSK	Porsche	F4	68		14	6
r	11	S Moss	Cooper	T51	Climax	4	63	gearbox	3	1
r	6	H Schell	BRM	P25	BRM	4	46	gearbox	6	3
r	2	T Brooks	Ferrari	Dino 246	Ferrari	V6	43	oil leak	8	3
r	5	C Shelby	Aston Martin	DBR4	Aston Martin	6	25	engine	10	4
r	4	R Salvadori	Aston Martin	DBR4	Aston Martin	6	4	engine overheating	13	5

Winning speed 150.411 km/h, 93.461 mph
Pole Position speed 157.238 km/h, 97.703 mph (J Bonnier, 1 min:36.000 sec)
Fastest Lap speed 156.099 km/h, 96.996 mph (S Moss, 1 min:36.700 sec on lap 42)
Lap Leaders J Bonnier 1,12-29,34-59,63-75 (58); M Gregory 2-11 (10); J Brabham 30-33 (4); S Moss 60-62 (3).

FRANCE: Reims (Round 4) (Race 79)

50 laps x 8.302 km, 5.159 miles = 415.100 km, 257.931 miles

Pos	No	Driver	Car	Model	Engine		Laps	Time/Reason for Retirement	Grid Pos	Row
1	24	T Brooks	Ferrari	Dino 246	Ferrari	V6	50	2h 01m 26.500s	1	1
2	26	P Hill	Ferrari	Dino 246	Ferrari	V6	50	2h 01m 54.000s	3	1
3	8	J Brabham	Cooper	T51	Climax	4	50	2h 03m 04.200s	2	1
4	22	O Gendebien	Ferrari	Dino 246	Ferrari	V6	50	2h 03m 14.000s	11	5
5	12	B McLaren	Cooper	T51	Climax	4	50	2h 03m 14.200s	10	4
6	44	R Flockhart	BRM	P25	BRM	4	50	2h 03m 32.200s	13	5
7	6	H Schell	BRM	P25	BRM	4	47		9	4
dq	2	S Moss	BRM	P25	BRM	4	42	push start after spin	4	2
8	40	G Scarlatti	Maserati	250F	Maserati	6	41		21	9
9	42	C G de Beaufort	Maserati	250F	Maserati	6	40		20	8
10	38	F d'Orey	Maserati	250F	Maserati	6	40		18	7
11	14	M Trintignant	Cooper	T51	Climax	4	36		8	3
r	30	J Behra	Ferrari	Dino 246	Ferrari	V6	31	piston	5	2
r	16	R Salvadori	Cooper	T45	Maserati	4	20	piston	16	7
r	28	D Gurney	Ferrari	Dino 246	Ferrari	V6	19	radiator	12	5
r	18	I Burgess	Cooper	T51	Maserati	4	13	engine	19	8
r	34	I Ireland	Lotus	16	Climax	4	13	front wheel bearing	15	6
r	10	M Gregory	Cooper	T51	Climax	4	8	driver exhausted	7	3
r	32	G Hill	Lotus	16	Climax	4	7	radiator	14	6
r	20	C Davis	Cooper	T51	Maserati	4	7	oil line	17	7
r	4	J Bonnier	BRM	P25	BRM	4	6	cylinder head gasket	6	3
nq	36	A Bayardo	Maserati	250F	Maserati	6				

Winning speed 205.086 km/h, 127.435 mph
Pole Position speed 214.399 km/h, 133.221 mph (T Brooks, 2 min:19.400 sec)
Fastest Lap speed 209.294 km/h, 130.049 mph (S Moss, 2 min:22.800 sec on lap 40)
Lap Leaders T Brooks 1-50 (50).

Also the Grand Prix of Europe. S Moss's fastest lap was allowed to stand, despite being disqualified.

---

18 Jul 1959 **BRITAIN: Aintree** (Round 5) (Race 80)

75 laps x 4.828 km, 3.000 miles = 362.102 km, 225.000 miles

Pos	No	Driver	Car	Model	Engine		Laps	Time/Reason for Retirement	Grid Pos	Row
1	12	J Brabham	Cooper	T51	Climax	4	75	2h 30m 11.600s	1	1
2	6	S Moss	BRM	P25	BRM	4	75	2h 30m 33.800s	7	3
3	16	B McLaren	Cooper	T51	Climax	4	75	2h 30m 34.000s	8	3
4	8	H Schell	BRM	P25	BRM	4	74		3	1
5	18	M Trintignant	Cooper	T51	Climax	4	74		4	2
6	2	R Salvadori	Aston Martin	DBR4	Aston Martin	6	74		2	1
7	14	M Gregory	Cooper	T51	Climax	4	73		5	2
8	30	A Stacey	Lotus	16	Climax	4	71		12	5
9	28	G Hill	Lotus	16	Climax	4	70		9	4
10	48	C Bristow	Cooper	T51	Borgward	4	70		16	7
11	58	H Taylor	Cooper	T51	Climax	4	69		21	9
12	52	P Ashdown	Cooper	T45	Climax	4	69		23	9
13	46	I Bueb	Cooper	T51	Borgward	4	69		18	7
r	4	C Shelby	Aston Martin	DBR4	Aston Martin	6	68	ignition	6	3
r	40	F d'Orey	Maserati	250F	Maserati	6	56	accident	20	8
r	42	R Flockhart	BRM	P25	BRM	4	53	spin	11	5
r	10	J Bonnier	BRM	P25	BRM	4	37	brakes	10	4
r	38	J Fairman	Cooper	T45	Climax	4	37	gearbox	15	6
r	22	I Burgess	Cooper	T51	Maserati	4	31	gearbox	13	5
r	24	H Herrmann	Cooper	T51	Maserati	4	20	clutch	19	8
r	64	D Piper	Lotus	16	Climax	4	19	cylinder head gasket	22	9
r	36	B Naylor	JBW	(59)	Maserati	4	17	transmission	14	6
r	50	M Taylor	Cooper	T45	Climax	4	15	transmission	24	10
r	20	T Brooks	Vanwall	VW (59)	Vanwall	4	12	ignition	17	7
ns	30	I Ireland	Lotus	16	Climax	4		driver ill / car raced by Stacey		
nq	56	B Moss	Cooper	T51	Climax	4				
nq	60	M Parkes	Fry		Climax	4				
nq	44	T Taylor	Cooper	T51	Climax	4				
nq	54	K Greene	Cooper	T45	Climax	4				
nq	66	T Parnell	Cooper	T45	Climax	4				
nq	62	D Taylor	Lotus	12	Climax	4				

Winning speed 144.655 km/h, 89.884 mph
Pole Position speed 147.296 km/h, 91.525 mph (J Brabham, 1 min:58.000 sec)
Fastest Lap speed 148.555 km/h, 92.308 mph (S Moss / B McLaren, 1 min:57.000 sec on lap 69 / 75)
Lap Leaders J Brabham 1-75 (75).

A Stacey's qualifying time was set by I Ireland.

2 Aug 1959 **GERMANY: AVUS** (Round 6) (Race 81)

60 laps x 8.300 km, 5.157 miles = 498.000 km, 309.443 miles

Pos	No	Driver	Car	Model	Engine		Laps	Time/Reason for Retirement	Grid Pos	Row
1	4	T Brooks	Ferrari	Dino 246	Ferrari	V6	60	2h 09m 31.600s	1	1
2	6	D Gurney	Ferrari	Dino 246	Ferrari	V6	60	2h 09m 33.500s	3	1
3	5	P Hill	Ferrari	Dino 246	Ferrari	V6	60	2h 10m 36.400s	6	2
4	8	M Trintignant	Cooper	T51	Climax	4	59		12	4
5	9	J Bonnier	BRM	P25	BRM	4	58		7	2
6	18	I Burgess	Cooper	T51	Maserati	4	56		15	5
7	10	H Schell	BRM	P25	BRM	4	49	clutch (pushed over line)	8	3
r	2	B McLaren	Cooper	T51	Climax	4	35	clutch	9	3
r	11	H Herrmann	BRM	P25	BRM	4	35	accident	11	3
r	3	M Gregory	Cooper	T51	Climax	4	23	engine	5	2
r	1	J Brabham	Cooper	T51	Climax	4	15	clutch	4	1
r	16	G Hill	Lotus	16	Climax	4	10	oil radiator	10	3
r	15	I Ireland	Lotus	16	Climax	4	7	gear selectors	13	4
r	17	C Allison	Ferrari	Dino 246	Ferrari	V6	3	clutch	14	4
r	7	S Moss	Cooper	T51	Climax	4	1	gearbox	2	1
ns	12	J Behra	Behra Porsche		Porsche	F4		fatal accident in support race		
ns	14	W von Trips	Porsche	718	Porsche	F4		withdrew after Behra accident		

Winning speed 230.686 km/h, 143.342 mph
Pole Position speed 237.331 km/h, 147.471 mph (T Brooks, 2 min: 5.900 sec)
Fastest Lap speed 240.000 km/h, 149.129 mph (T Brooks, 2 min: 4.500 sec on lap 18)
Lap Leaders T Brooks 1-2,4-13,18,20-21,23-30,32-35,37-38,40,42,46-47,52-60 (42); M Gregory 3,15,19,22 (4); D Gurney 14,16-17,41,43-44,50-51 (8); P Hill 31,36,39,45,48-49 (6).

Race staged in 2 heats of 30 laps each, with results being on aggregate.
C Allison set a time quick enough for pole position, but being a reserve driver, had to start from the penultimate row of the grid.

23 Aug 1959 **PORTUGAL: Monsanto Park** (Round 7) (Race 82)

62 laps x 5.440 km, 3.380 miles = 337.280 km, 209.576 miles

Pos	No	Driver	Car	Model	Engine		Laps	Time/Reason for Retirement	Grid Pos	Row
1	4	S Moss	Cooper	T51	Climax	4	62	2h 11m 55.410s	1	1
2	2	M Gregory	Cooper	T51	Climax	4	61		3	1
3	16	D Gurney	Ferrari	Dino 246	Ferrari	V6	61		6	3
4	5	M Trintignant	Cooper	T51	Climax	4	60		4	2
5	6	H Schell	BRM	P25	BRM	4	59		9	4
6	10	R Salvadori	Aston Martin	DBR4	Aston Martin	6	59		12	5
7	8	R Flockhart	BRM	P25	BRM	4	59		11	5
8	9	C Shelby	Aston Martin	DBR4	Aston Martin	6	58		13	5
9	14	T Brooks	Ferrari	Dino 246	Ferrari	V6	57		10	4
10	18	M Cabral	Cooper	T51	Maserati	4	56		14	6
r	3	B McLaren	Cooper	T51	Climax	4	38	clutch	8	3
r	1	J Brabham	Cooper	T51	Climax	4	23	accident	2	1
r	7	J Bonnier	BRM	P25	BRM	4	10	fuel feed	5	2
r	15	P Hill	Ferrari	Dino 246	Ferrari	V6	5	accident	7	3
r	11	G Hill	Lotus	16	Climax	4	5	accident	15	6
r	12	I Ireland	Lotus	16	Climax	4	3	gearbox	16	7

Winning speed 153.398 km/h, 95.317 mph
Pole Position speed 159.362 km/h, 99.023 mph (S Moss, 2 min: 2.890 sec)
Fastest Lap speed 156.584 km/h, 97.297 mph (S Moss, 2 min: 5.070 sec on lap 28)
Lap Leaders S Moss 1-62 (62).

13 Sep 1959   **ITALY: Monza**   **(Round 8)**   **(Race 83)**

72 laps x 5.750 km, 3.573 miles = 414.000 km, 257.248 miles

Pos	No	Driver	Car	Model	Engine		Laps	Time/Reason for Retirement	Grid Pos	Row
1	14	S Moss	Cooper	T51	Climax	4	72	2h 04m 05.400s	1	1
2	32	P Hill	Ferrari	Dino 246	Ferrari	V6	72	2h 04m 52.100s	5	2
3	12	J Brabham	Cooper	T51	Climax	4	72	2h 05m 17.900s	3	1
4	36	D Gurney	Ferrari	Dino 246	Ferrari	V6	72	2h 05m 25.000s	4	2
5	34	C Allison	Ferrari	Dino 246	Ferrari	V6	71		8	3
6	38	O Gendebien	Ferrari	Dino 246	Ferrari	V6	71		6	3
7	2	H Schell	BRM	P25	BRM	4	70		7	3
8	6	J Bonnier	BRM	P25	BRM	4	70		11	5
9	16	M Trintignant	Cooper	T51	Climax	4	70		13	5
10	26	C Shelby	Aston Martin	DBR4	Aston Martin	6	70		19	8
11	40	C Davis	Cooper	T51	Maserati	4	68		18	7
12	10	G Scarlatti	Cooper	T51	Climax	4	68		12	5
13	4	R Flockhart	BRM	P25	BRM	4	67		15	6
14	42	I Burgess	Cooper	T51	Maserati	4	67		16	7
15	28	G Cabianca	Maserati	250F	Maserati	6	64		21	9
r	24	R Salvadori	Aston Martin	DBR4	Aston Martin	6	44	engine	17	7
r	8	B McLaren	Cooper	T51	Climax	4	22	engine	9	4
r	22	J Fairman	Cooper	T45	Maserati	4	18	piston	20	8
r	20	I Ireland	Lotus	16	Climax	4	14	brakes	14	6
r	18	G Hill	Lotus	16	Climax	4	1	engine	10	4
r	30	T Brooks	Ferrari	Dino 246	Ferrari	V6	0	clutch	2	1

Winning speed 200.177 km/h, 124.384 mph
Pole Position speed 207.623 km/h, 129.011 mph (S Moss, 1 min:39.700 sec)
Fastest Lap speed 206.175 km/h, 128.111 mph (P Hill, 1 min:40.400 sec on lap 32)
Lap Leaders S Moss 1,4,15,33-72 (43); P Hill 2-3,5-14,16-32 (29).

12 Dec 1959   **USA: Sebring**   **(Round 9)**   **(Race 84)**

42 laps x 8.369 km, 5.200 miles = 351.481 km, 218.400 miles

Pos	No	Driver	Car	Model	Engine		Laps	Time/Reason for Retirement	Grid Pos	Row
1	9	B McLaren	Cooper	T51	Climax	4	42	2h 12m 35.700s	10	4
2	6	M Trintignant	Cooper	T51	Climax	4	42	2h 12m 36.600s	5	2
3	2	T Brooks	Ferrari	Dino 246	Ferrari	V6	42	2h 15m 36.600s	4	2
4	8	J Brabham	Cooper	T51	Climax	4	42	2h 17m 33.000s (pushed over line)	2	1
5	10	I Ireland	Lotus	16	Climax	4	39		9	4
6	4	W von Trips	Ferrari	Dino 246	Ferrari	V6	38		6	3
7	17	H Blanchard	Porsche	RSK	Porsche	F4	38		16	7
r	12	R Salvadori	Cooper	T45	Maserati	4	23	transmission	11	5
r	3	C Allison	Ferrari	Dino 246	Ferrari	V6	22	clutch	7	3
r	1	R Ward	Kurtis Kraft	Midget	Offenhauser	4	20	clutch	19	8
r	14	A de Tomaso	Cooper	T43	OSCA	4	13	brakes	14	6
r	5	P Hill	Ferrari	Dino 246	Ferrari	V6	8	clutch	8	3
r	15	F d'Orey	Tec Mec	F415	Maserati	6	6	oil leak	17	7
r	19	H Schell	Cooper	T51	Climax	4	5	clutch	3	1
r	16	G Constantine	Cooper	T45	Climax	4	5	cylinder head gasket	15	6
r	7	S Moss	Cooper	T51	Climax	4	4	gearbox	1	1
r	11	A Stacey	Lotus	16	Climax	4	1	clutch	12	5
r	18	B Said	Connaught	C	Alta	4	0	engine / accident	13	5
ns	22	P Cade	Maserati	250F	Maserati	6		engine	18	7

Winning speed 159.047 km/h, 98.827 mph
Pole Position speed 167.372 km/h, 104.000 mph (S Moss, 3 min: 0.000 sec)
Fastest Lap speed 162.848 km/h, 101.189 mph (M Trintignant, 3 min: 5.000 sec on lap 39)
Lap Leaders S Moss 1-5 (5); J Brabham 6-41 (36); B McLaren 42 (1).

Lap Leaders 1959

Pos	Driver	Car-Engine	GPs	laps	km	miles
1	S Moss	Cooper-Climax	5	173	827.7	514.3
2	J Brabham	Cooper-Climax	4	134	739.9	459.8
3	T Brooks	Ferrari	2	92	763.7	474.5
4	J Bonnier	BRM	1	58	243.2	151.1
5	P Hill	Ferrari	2	35	216.6	134.6
6	J Behra	Ferrari	1	21	66.0	41.0
7	M Gregory	Cooper-Climax	2	14	75.1	46.7
8	D Gurney	Ferrari	1	8	66.4	41.3
9	B McLaren	Cooper-Climax	1	1	8.4	5.2
			8	536	3,007.0	1,868.4

Driver Points 1959

		MC	INDY	NL	F	GB	D	P	I	USA	Total	
1	J Brabham	9	-	6	4	8	-	-	4	(3)	31	(3)
2	T Brooks	6	-	-	8	-	9	-	-	4	27	
3	S Moss	-	-	1	1	6.5	-	9	8	-	25.5	
4	P Hill	3	-	-	6	-	4	-	7	-	20	
5	M Trintignant	4	-	-	-	2	3	3	-	7	19	
6	B McLaren	2	-	-	2	4.5	-	-	-	8	16.5	
7	D Gurney	-	-	-	-	-	6	4	3	-	13	
8	J Bonnier	-	-	8	-	-	2	-	-	-	10	
	M Gregory	-	-	4	-	-	-	6	-	-	10	
10	R Ward	-	8	-	-	-	-	-	-	-	8	
11	J Rathmann	-	6	-	-	-	-	-	-	-	6	
12	J Thomson	-	5	-	-	-	-	-	-	-	5	
	I Ireland	-	-	3	-	-	-	-	-	2	5	
	H Schell	-	-	-	-	3	-	2	-	-	5	
15	T Bettenhausen	-	3	-	-	-	-	-	-	-	3	
	O Gendebien	-	-	-	3	-	-	-	-	-	3	
17	P Goldsmith	-	2	-	-	-	-	-	-	-	2	
	J Behra	-	-	2	-	-	-	-	-	-	2	
	C Allison	-	-	-	-	-	-	-	2	-	2	

8,6,4,3 and 2 points awarded to the first five finishers. The driver setting the fastest lap scored a point also.
Points only awarded to drivers who handled the car throughout the race. Best 5 scores.

Constructor Points 1959

		MC	INDY	NL	F	GB	D	P	I	USA	Total	
1	Cooper-Climax	8	-	(6)	(4)	8	(3)	8	8	8	40	(13)
2	Ferrari	6	-	(2)	8	-	8	4	6	(4)	32	(6)
3	BRM	-	-	8	-	6	2	2	-	-	18	
4	Lotus-Climax	-	-	3	-	-	-	-	-	2	5	

8,6,4,3 and 2 points awarded to the first five finishers. Indianapolis excluded. Points only for highest placed car. Best 5 scores.

1960

Race Entrants and Results

The point for fastest lap was dropped and replaced by a point for sixth place. Lotus, BRM and even the traditionalist Ferrari turned to rear engined cars. This was the last year for a front engine victory and the new Scarab and Aston Martin were soon outdated. The Belgian Grand Prix meeting was a black weekend for racing with two drivers killed and two seriously injured.

FERRARI
Scuderia Ferrari: P Hill, von Trips, Ginther, Mairesse, Allison, González

MASERATI
Joe Lubin: Drake
Privateers: Chimeri, Creus, Estéfano, Munaron, Scarlatti, (Gould)

ASTON MARTIN
David Brown Corporation: Salvadori, Trintignant

BRM
Owen Racing Organisation: G Hill, Bonnier, Gurney

COOPER
Cooper Car Co: Brabham, McLaren, Flockhart, Daigh
R R C Walker Racing Team: Moss, Trintignant (RA), (Reventlow)
Yeoman Credit Racing Team: Brooks, Gendebien, H Taylor, Bristow, P Hill, Halford (F)
Scuderia Centro Sud: Gregory, Trintignant, Burgess, Bonomi, Cabral, Thiele, von Trips, Menditéguy
Scuderia Castellotti: Munaron, Scarlatti, Cabianca
High Efficiency Motors: Salvadori
C T Atkins: Fairman
Fred Tuck Cars: Bianchi, (Halford)
Equipe Nationale Belge: Bianchi (B)
Ecurie Maarsbergen: de Beaufort
Scuderia Colonia: Drogo
Gilby Engineering Co Ltd: Greene
Fred Armbruster: Lovely
Ecurie Bleue: Schell
Equipe Prideux/Dick Gibson: Wilson
Privateers: Owen, Seidel

JBW
J B Naylor: Naylor

LOTUS
Team Lotus: Ireland, Clark, Stacey, Surtees, Flockhart, Larreta
R R C Walker Racing Team: Moss
Robert Bodle Ltd: Piper
Taylor-Crawley Racing Team: (M Taylor)
Privateer: Hall

VANWALL
Vandervell Products Ltd: Brooks

PORSCHE
Dr Ing F Porsche KG: Barth
Porsche System Engineering: Herrmann
Camoradi International: Gregory, Gamble

SCARAB
Reventlow Automobiles Inc.: Reventlow, Daigh, (Ginther)

7 Feb 1960		**ARGENTINA: Buenos Aires No.2**							**(Round 1)**		**(Race 85)**
		80 laps x 3.912 km, 2.431 miles = 312.960 km, 194.464 miles									
Pos	No	Driver	Car	Model	Engine		Laps	Time/Reason for Retirement		Grid Pos	Row
1	16	B McLaren	Cooper	T51	Climax	4	80	2h 17m 49.500s		13	4
2	24	C Allison	Ferrari	Dino 246	Ferrari	V6	80	2h 18m 15.800s		7	2
3=	38	M Trintignant	Cooper	T51	Climax	4				8	3
3=	38	S Moss	Cooper	T51	Climax	4	80	2h 18m 26.400s			
4	6	C Menditéguy	Cooper	T51	Maserati	4	80	2h 18m 42.800s		12	4
5	30	W von Trips	Ferrari	Dino 246	Ferrari	V6	79			5	2
6	20	I Ireland	Lotus	18	Climax	4	79			2	1
7	40	J Bonnier	BRM	P25	BRM	4	79			4	1
8	26	P Hill	Ferrari	Dino 246	Ferrari	V6	77			6	2
9	46	R Larreta	Lotus	16	Climax	4	77			15	5
10	32	F González	Ferrari	Dino 246	Ferrari	V6	77			11	3
11	4	R Bonomi	Cooper	T51	Maserati	4	76			17	5
12	2	M Gregory	Behra Porsche		Porsche	F4	76			16	5
13	14	G Munaron	Maserati	250F	Maserati	6	72			19	6
14	10	N Estéfano	Maserati	250F	Maserati	6	70			20	6
r	34	H Schell	Cooper	T51	Climax	4	64	fuel pump		9	3
r	18	J Brabham	Cooper	T51	Climax	4	43	gearbox		10	3
r	36	S Moss	Cooper	T51	Climax	4	41	rear suspension		1	1
r	42	G Hill	BRM	P25	BRM	4	38	oil pressure / engine overheating		3	1
r	22	A Stacey	Lotus	16	Climax	4	24	driver exhausted		14	4
r	44	E Chimeri	Maserati	250F	Maserati	6	24	driver exhausted		21	6
r	12	A Creus	Maserati	250F	Maserati	6	17	driver exhausted		22	7
r	8	G Scarlatti	Maserati	250F	Maserati	6	11	engine overheating		18	5

Winning speed 136.242 km/h, 84.657 mph
Pole Position speed 145.337 km/h, 90.309 mph (S Moss, 1 min:36.900 sec)
Fastest Lap speed 142.398 km/h, 88.482 mph (S Moss, 1 min:38.900 sec on lap 37)
Lap Leaders I Ireland 1 (1); J Bonnier 2-15,21-36,41-67 (57); S Moss 16-20,37-40 (9); B McLaren 68-80 (13).

29 May 1960   MONACO: Monte-Carlo   (Round 2)   (Race 86)

100 laps x 3.145 km, 1.954 miles = 314.500 km, 195.421 miles

Pos	No	Driver	Car	Model	Engine		Laps	Time/Reason for Retirement	Grid Pos	Row
1	28	S Moss	Lotus	18	Climax	4	100	2h 53m 45.500s	1	1
2	10	B McLaren	Cooper	T53	Climax	4	100	2h 54m 37.600s	11	5
3	36	P Hill	Ferrari	Dino 246	Ferrari	V6	100	2h 54m 47.400s	10	4
4	18	T Brooks	Cooper	T51	Climax	4	99		3	1
5	2	J Bonnier	BRM	P48	BRM	4	82		5	2
6	34	R Ginther	Ferrari	Dino 246MP	Ferrari	V6	70	(pushed over line)	9	4
7r	6	G Hill	BRM	P48	BRM	4	66	accident	6	3
8r	38	W von Trips	Ferrari	Dino 246	Ferrari	V6	61	clutch	8	3
9	22	I Ireland	Lotus	18	Climax	4	55	(pushed over line)	7	3
r	4	D Gurney	BRM	P48	BRM	4	48	rear suspension	14	6
dq	8	J Brabham	Cooper	T53	Climax	4	44	push start after spin	2	1
r	14	R Salvadori	Cooper	T51	Climax	4	29	engine overheating	12	5
r	24	A Stacey	Lotus	18	Climax	4	23	engine mountings	13	5
r	26	J Surtees	Lotus	18	Climax	4	18	transmission	15	6
r	16	C Bristow	Cooper	T51	Climax	4	17	gearbox	4	2
r	44	M Trintignant	Cooper	T51	Maserati	4	4	gearbox	16	7
nq	12	B Halford	Cooper	T51	Climax	4				
nq	20	B Naylor	JBW	(59)	Maserati					
nq	30	G Scarlatti	Cooper	T51	Castellotti					
nq	32	C Allison	Ferrari	Dino 246	Ferrari	V6		accident / injury		
nq	40	M Gregory	Cooper	T51	Maserati					
nq	42	I Burgess	Cooper	T51	Maserati	4				
nq	46	C Daigh	Scarab		Scarab	4				
nq	48	L Reventlow	Scarab		Scarab	4				
nq	30	G Munaron	Cooper	T51	Castellotti					

Winning speed 108.599 km/h, 67.480 mph
Pole Position speed 117.570 km/h, 73.055 mph (S Moss, 1 min:36.300 sec)
Fastest Lap speed 117.692 km/h, 73.131 mph (B McLaren, 1 min:36.200 sec on lap 11)
Lap Leaders J Bonnier 1-16,61-67 (23); S Moss 17-33,41-60,68-100 (70); J Brabham 34-40 (7).

30 May 1960   INDIANAPOLIS: 500   (Round 3)   (Race 87)

200 laps x 4.023 km, 2.500 miles = 804.672 km, 500.000 miles

Pos	No	Driver	Car	Model	Engine		Laps	Time/Reason for Retirement	Grid Pos	Row
1	4	J Rathmann	Watson		Offenhauser	4	200	3h 36m 11.360s	2	1
2	1	R Ward	Watson		Offenhauser	4	200	3h 36m 24.109s	3	1
3	99	P Goldsmith	Epperly		Offenhauser	4	200		26	9
4	7	D Branson	Phillips		Offenhauser	4	200		8	3
5	3	J Thomson	Lesovsky		Offenhauser	4	200		17	6
6	22	E Johnson	Trevis		Offenhauser	4	200		7	3
7	98	L Ruby	Watson		Offenhauser	4	200		12	4
8	44	B Veith	Meskowski		Offenhauser	4	200		25	9
9	18	B Tingelstad	Trevis		Offenhauser	4	200		28	10
10	38	B Christie	Kurtis Kraft	500D	Offenhauser	4	200		14	5
11	27	R Amick	Epperly		Offenhauser	4	200		22	8
12	17	D Carter	Kuzma		Offenhauser	4	200		27	9
13	39	B Homeier	Kuzma		Offenhauser	4	200		31	11
14	48	G Hartley	Kurtis Kraft	500G	Offenhauser	4	196		24	8
15	65	C Stevenson	Watson		Offenhauser	4	196		9	3
16	14	B Grim	Meskowski		Offenhauser	4	194		21	7
17	26	S Templeman	Kurtis Kraft	500E	Offenhauser	4	191		19	7
18r	56	J Hurtubise	Christensen		Offenhauser	4	185	connecting rod	23	8
19r	10	J Bryan	Epperly		Offenhauser	4	152	fuel pump drive	10	4
20r	28	T Ruttman	Watson		Offenhauser	4	134	rear end gear	6	2
21r	6	E Sachs	Ewing		Offenhauser	4	132	magneto	1	1
22r	73	D Freeland	Kurtis Kraft		Offenhauser	4	129	magneto	11	4
23r	2	T Bettenhausen	Watson		Offenhauser	4	125	connecting rod	18	6
24r	32	W Weiler	Kuzma		Offenhauser	4	103	accident	15	5
25r	5	A J Foyt	Kurtis Kraft		Offenhauser	4	90	clutch	16	6
26r	46	E Russo	Kurtis Kraft	500J	Offenhauser	4	84	accident	29	10
27r	8	J Boyd	Epperly		Offenhauser	4	77	piston	13	5
28r	37	G Force	Kurtis Kraft	500G	Offenhauser	4	74	brakes	20	7
29r	16	J McWithey	Epperly		Offenhauser	4	60	brakes	32	11
30r	9	L Sutton	Watson		Offenhauser	4	47	engine	5	2
31r	97	D Rathmann	Watson		Offenhauser	4	42	brake line	4	2
32r	76	A Herman	Ewing		Offenhauser	4	34	clutch	30	10
33r	23	D Wilson	Kurtis Kraft	500G	Offenhauser	4	11	magneto point spring	33	11

Winning speed 223.324 km/h, 138.767 mph
Pole Position speed 235.917 km/h, 146.592 mph (E Sachs, 1 min: 1.395 sec)
Fastest Lap speed 235.170 km/h, 146.128 mph (J Rathmann, 1 min: 1.590 sec on lap 197)
Fastest qualifier J Hurtubise (239.882 km/h, 149.056 mph).

6 Jun 1960 **NETHERLANDS: Zandvoort** (Round 4) (Race 88)

75 laps x 4.193 km, 2.605 miles = 314.475 km, 195.406 miles

Pos	No	Driver	Car	Model	Engine		Laps	Time/Reason for Retirement	Grid Pos	Row
1	11	J Brabham	Cooper	T53	Climax	4	75	2h 01m 47.200s	2	1
2	4	I Ireland	Lotus	18	Climax	4	75	2h 02m 11.200s	3	1
3	16	G Hill	BRM	P48	BRM	4	75	2h 02m 43.800s	5	2
4	7	S Moss	Lotus	18	Climax	4	75	2h 02m 44.900s	1	1
5	2	W von Trips	Ferrari	Dino 246	Ferrari	V6	74		15	6
6	3	R Ginther	Ferrari	Dino 246	Ferrari	V6	74		12	5
7	10	H Taylor	Cooper	T51	Climax	4	70		14	6
8	20	C G de Beaufort	Cooper	T51	Climax	4	69		17	7
r	5	A Stacey	Lotus	18	Climax	4	58	transmission	8	3
r	1	P Hill	Ferrari	Dino 246	Ferrari	V6	55	engine	13	5
r	14	J Bonnier	BRM	P48	BRM	4	54	engine / accident	4	2
r	6	J Clark	Lotus	18	Climax	4	41	transmission	11	5
r	18	M Trintignant	Cooper	T51	Maserati	4	39	gearbox	16	7
r	15	D Gurney	BRM	P48	BRM	4	11	brakes / accident	6	3
r	8	C Bristow	Cooper	T51	Climax	4	9	engine	7	3
r	12	B McLaren	Cooper	T53	Climax	4	8	universal joint	9	4
r	9	T Brooks	Cooper	T51	Climax	4	4	gearbox	10	4
ns	22	C Daigh	Scarab		Scarab	4		starting money dispute		
ns	21	L Reventlow	Scarab		Scarab	4		starting money dispute		
ns	17	R Salvadori	Aston Martin	DBR4	Aston Martin	6		starting money dispute		
ns	19	M Gregory	Cooper	T51	Maserati	4		starting money dispute		

Winning speed 154.931 km/h, 96.270 mph
Pole Position speed 161.961 km/h, 100.638 mph (S Moss, 1 min:33.200 sec)
Fastest Lap speed 160.925 km/h, 99.994 mph (S Moss, 1 min:33.800 sec on lap 75)
Lap Leaders J Brabham 1-75 (75).

19 Jun 1960 **BELGIUM: Spa-Francorchamps** (Round 5) (Race 89)

36 laps x 14.100 km, 8.761 miles = 507.600 km, 315.408 miles

Pos	No	Driver	Car	Model	Engine		Laps	Time/Reason for Retirement	Grid Pos	Row
1	2	J Brabham	Cooper	T53	Climax	4	36	2h 21m 37.300s	1	1
2	4	B McLaren	Cooper	T53	Climax	4	36	2h 22m 40.600s	13	5
r	10	G Hill	BRM	P48	BRM	4	35	crankshaft	5	2
3	34	O Gendebien	Cooper	T51	Climax	4	35		4	2
4	24	P Hill	Ferrari	Dino 246	Ferrari	V6	35		3	1
5	18	J Clark	Lotus	18	Climax	4	34		9	4
6	32	L Bianchi	Cooper	T51	Climax	4	28		14	6
r	16	A Stacey	Lotus	18	Climax	4	24	fatal accident	16	7
r	22	W Mairesse	Ferrari	Dino 246	Ferrari	V6	24	transmission	12	5
r	26	W von Trips	Ferrari	Dino 246	Ferrari	V6	22	transmission	10	4
r	36	C Bristow	Cooper	T51	Climax	4	19	fatal accident	8	3
r	30	C Daigh	Scarab		Scarab	4	16	engine	17	7
r	6	J Bonnier	BRM	P48	BRM	4	14	engine	6	3
r	14	I Ireland	Lotus	18	Climax	4	13	spin	7	3
r	8	D Gurney	BRM	P48	BRM	4	4	engine	11	5
r	38	T Brooks	Cooper	T51	Climax	4	3	gearbox	2	1
r	28	L Reventlow	Scarab		Scarab	4	1	engine	15	6
ns	12	S Moss	Lotus	18	Climax	4		accident / injury		
ns	20	M Taylor	Lotus	18	Climax	4		accident / injury		

Winning speed 215.052 km/h, 133.627 mph
Pole Position speed 220.696 km/h, 137.134 mph (J Brabham, 3 min:50.000 sec)
Fastest Lap speed 218.887 km/h, 136.010 mph (P Hill / J Brabham / I Ireland, 3 min:51.900 sec)
Lap Leaders J Brabham 1-36 (36).

50 laps x 8.302 km, 5.159 miles = 415.100 km, 257.931 miles

Pos	No	Driver	Car	Model	Engine		Laps	Time/Reason for Retirement	Grid Pos	Row
1	16	J Brabham	Cooper	T53	Climax	4	50	1h 57m 24.900s	1	1
2	44	O Gendebien	Cooper	T53	Climax	4	50	1h 58m 13.200s	11	5
3	18	B McLaren	Cooper	T53	Climax	4	50	1h 58m 16.800s	9	4
4	46	H Taylor	Cooper	T51	Climax	4	49		13	5
5	24	J Clark	Lotus	18	Climax	4	49		12	5
6	22	R Flockhart	Lotus	18	Climax	4	49		8	3
7	20	I Ireland	Lotus	18	Climax	4	43		4	2
8r	48	B Halford	Cooper	T51	Climax	4	40	engine	16	7
9	40	M Gregory	Cooper	T51	Maserati	4	37		17	7
10	42	I Burgess	Cooper	T51	Maserati	4	36		20	8
11r	4	W von Trips	Ferrari	Dino 246	Ferrari	V6	31	transmission	6	3
12r	2	P Hill	Ferrari	Dino 246	Ferrari	V6	29	transmission	2	1
r	8	J Bonnier	BRM	P48	BRM	4	23	engine	10	4
r	36	L Bianchi	Cooper	T51	Climax	4	18	transmission	15	6
r	10	D Gurney	BRM	P48	BRM	4	18	valves	7	3
r	30	G Munaron	Cooper	T51	Castellotti	4	17	transmission	19	8
r	6	W Mairesse	Ferrari	Dino 246	Ferrari	V6	15	transmission	5	2
r	14	T Brooks	Vanwall	VW11	Vanwall	4	8	rear vibration	14	6
r	38	M Trintignant	Cooper	T51	Maserati	4	0	accident	18	7
r	12	G Hill	BRM	P48	BRM	4	0	accident	3	1
ns	28	R Ginther	Scarab		Scarab	4		engine		
ns	34	D Piper	Lotus	16	Climax	4		engine		
ns	26	C Daigh	Scarab		Scarab	4		engine		

Winning speed 212.119 km/h, 131.805 mph
Pole Position speed 218.474 km/h, 135.753 mph (J Brabham, 2 min:16.800 sec)
Fastest Lap speed 217.361 km/h, 135.062 mph (J Brabham, 2 min:17.500 sec on lap 25)
Lap Leaders J Brabham 1-3,5,7,9-10,12,14,18-50 (42); P Hill 4,6,8,11,13,15-17 (8).

77 laps x 4.711 km, 2.927 miles = 362.712 km, 225.379 miles

Pos	No	Driver	Car	Model	Engine		Laps	Time/Reason for Retirement	Grid Pos	Row
1	1	J Brabham	Cooper	T53	Climax	4	77	2h 04m 24.600s	1	1
2	9	J Surtees	Lotus	18	Climax	4	77	2h 05m 14.200s	11	3
3	7	I Ireland	Lotus	18	Climax	4	77	2h 05m 54.200s	5	2
4	2	B McLaren	Cooper	T53	Climax	4	76		3	1
5	12	T Brooks	Cooper	T51	Climax	4	76		9	3
6	11	W von Trips	Ferrari	Dino 246	Ferrari	V6	74		7	2
7	10	P Hill	Ferrari	Dino 246	Ferrari	V6	74		10	3
8	15	H Taylor	Cooper	T51	Climax	4	74		16	5
9	14	O Gendebien	Cooper	T51	Climax	4	74		12	4
10	5	D Gurney	BRM	P48	BRM	4	74		6	2
11	19	M Trintignant	Aston Martin	DBR5	Aston Martin	6	72		21	6
12	26	D Piper	Lotus	16	Climax	4	72		23	7
13	25	B Naylor	JBW	(59)	Maserati	4	72		18	5
r	4	G Hill	BRM	P48	BRM	4	71	accident	2	1
14	16	M Gregory	Cooper	T51	Maserati	4	71		14	4
15	21	G Munaron	Cooper	T51	Castellotti	4	70		24	7
16	8	J Clark	Lotus	18	Climax	4	70		8	3
r	24	L Bianchi	Cooper	T51	Climax	4	61	magneto	17	5
r	6	J Bonnier	BRM	P48	BRM	4	60	rear suspension	4	1
r	3	C Daigh	Cooper	T51	Climax	4	57	engine overheating	19	6
r	17	I Burgess	Cooper	T51	Maserati	4	57	valve spring	20	6
r	23	J Fairman	Cooper	T51	Climax	4	45	fuel pump	15	5
r	18	R Salvadori	Aston Martin	DBR5	Aston Martin	6	45	steering	13	4
r	22	K Greene	Cooper	T45	Maserati	4	12	engine overheating	22	7
ns	3	L Reventlow	Cooper	T51	Climax	4		car raced by Daigh		

Winning speed 174.928 km/h, 108.695 mph
Pole Position speed 179.260 km/h, 111.387 mph (J Brabham, 1 min:34.600 sec)
Fastest Lap speed 179.640 km/h, 111.623 mph (G Hill, 1 min:34.400 sec on lap 56)
Lap Leaders J Brabham 1-54,72-77 (60); G Hill 55-71 (17).

14 Aug 1960   **PORTUGAL: Porto**   **(Round 8)**   **(Race 92)**

55 laps x 7.407 km, 4.602 miles = 407.385 km, 253.137 miles

Pos	No	Driver	Car	Model	Engine		Laps	Time/Reason for Retirement	Grid Pos	Row
1	2	J Brabham	Cooper	T53	Climax	4	55	2h 19m 00.030s	3	1
2	4	B McLaren	Cooper	T53	Climax	4	55	2h 19m 58.000s	6	3
3	14	J Clark	Lotus	18	Climax	4	55	2h 20m 53.260s	8	3
4	28	W von Trips	Ferrari	Dino 246	Ferrari	V6	55	2h 20m 58.840s	9	4
dq	12	S Moss	Lotus	18	Climax	4	51	drove in wrong direction	4	2
5	6	T Brooks	Cooper	T51	Climax	4	49		12	5
6	16	I Ireland	Lotus	18	Climax	4	48		7	3
7	8	O Gendebien	Cooper	T51	Climax	4	46		14	6
r	32	M Cabral	Cooper	T51	Maserati	4	37	gearbox	15	6
r	18	J Surtees	Lotus	18	Climax	4	36	radiator	1	1
r	26	P Hill	Ferrari	Dino 246	Ferrari	V6	30	accident	10	4
r	24	D Gurney	BRM	P48	BRM	4	25	engine overheating	2	1
r	30	M Gregory	Cooper	T51	Maserati	4	21	gearbox	11	5
r	22	G Hill	BRM	P48	BRM	4	8	gearbox	5	2
r	20	J Bonnier	BRM	P48	BRM	4	6	cylinder head gasket	13	5
ns	10	H Taylor	Cooper	T51	Climax	4		accident / injury		

Winning speed 175.849 km/h, 109.268 mph
Pole Position speed 183.190 km/h, 113.829 mph (J Surtees, 2 min:25.560 sec)
Fastest Lap speed 180.744 km/h, 112.309 mph (J Surtees, 2 min:27.530 sec on lap 33)
Lap Leaders D Gurney 1-10 (10); J Surtees 11-35 (25); J Brabham 36-55 (20).

---

4 Sep 1960   **ITALY: Monza**   **(Round 9)**   **(Race 93)**

50 laps x 10.000 km, 6.214 miles = 500.000 km, 310.686 miles

Pos	No	Driver	Car	Model	Engine		Laps	Time/Reason for Retirement	Grid Pos	Row
1	20	P Hill	Ferrari	Dino 246	Ferrari	V6	50	2h 21m 09.200s	1	1
2	18	R Ginther	Ferrari	Dino 246	Ferrari	V6	50	2h 23m 36.800s	2	1
3	16	W Mairesse	Ferrari	Dino 246	Ferrari	V6	49		3	1
4	2	G Cabianca	Cooper	T51	Castellotti	4	48		4	2
5	22	W von Trips	Ferrari	Dino 246MP	Ferrari	V6	48		6	3
6	26	H Herrmann	Porsche	718	Porsche	F4	47		10	4
7	24	E Barth	Porsche	718	Porsche	F4	46		12	5
8	12	P Drogo	Cooper	T43	Climax	4	45		15	6
9	10	W Seidel	Cooper	T45	Climax	4	44		13	5
10	28	F Gamble	Behra Porsche		Porsche	F4	41		14	6
r	6	B Naylor	JBW	(59)	Maserati	4	41	gearbox	7	3
r	34	A Thiele	Cooper	T51	Maserati	4	32	gearbox	9	4
r	4	G Munaron	Cooper	T51	Castellotti	4	27	oil line	8	3
r	36	G Scarlatti	Cooper	T51	Maserati	4	26	throttle linkage	5	2
r	30	V Wilson	Cooper	T43	Climax	4	24	sump	16	7
r	8	A Owen	Cooper	T45	Climax	4	0	accident	11	5
ns	14	H Gould	Maserati	250F	Maserati	6		crossed fuel lines		

Winning speed 212.535 km/h, 132.063 mph
Pole Position speed 223.048 km/h, 138.596 mph (P Hill, 2 min:41.400 sec)
Fastest Lap speed 220.049 km/h, 136.732 mph (P Hill, 2 min:43.600 sec on lap 23)
Lap Leaders R Ginther 1-16,18-25 (24); P Hill 17,26-50 (26).

Also the Grand Prix of Europe.

20 Nov 1960　　**USA: Riverside**　　　　　　　　　　　　　　　　　　**(Round 10)**　　**(Race 94)**

75 laps x 5.271 km, 3.275 miles = 395.295 km, 245.625 miles

Pos	No	Driver	Car	Model	Engine		Laps	Time/Reason for Retirement	Grid Pos	Row
1	5	S Moss	Lotus	18	Climax	4	75	2h 28m 52.200s	1	1
2	10	I Ireland	Lotus	18	Climax	4	75	2h 29m 30.200s	7	3
3	3	B McLaren	Cooper	T53	Climax	4	75	2h 30m 14.200s	10	4
4	2	J Brabham	Cooper	T53	Climax	4	74		2	1
5	15	J Bonnier	BRM	P48	BRM	4	74		4	2
6	9	P Hill	Cooper	T51	Climax	4	74		13	5
7	24	J Hall	Lotus	18	Climax	4	74		12	5
8	14	R Salvadori	Cooper	T51	Climax	4	73		15	6
9	26	W von Trips	Cooper	T51	Maserati	4	72		16	7
10	23	C Daigh	Scarab		Scarab	4	70		18	7
11	25	P Lovely	Cooper	T45	Castellotti	4	69		20	8
12	7	O Gendebien	Cooper	T51	Climax	4	69		8	3
13	20	B Drake	Maserati	250F	Maserati	6	68		22	9
14	8	H Taylor	Cooper	T51	Climax	4	68		14	6
15	18	M Trintignant	Cooper	T51	Maserati	4	66		19	8
16	12	J Clark	Lotus	18	Climax	4	60		5	2
r	17	G Hill	BRM	P48	BRM	4	34	gearbox	11	5
r	19	I Burgess	Cooper	T51	Maserati	4	26	ignition	23	9
r	21	B Naylor	JBW	(59)	Maserati	4	20	engine	17	7
r	16	D Gurney	BRM	P48	BRM	4	18	engine overheating	3	1
r	4	R Flockhart	Cooper	T51	Climax	4	12	transmission	21	9
r	6	T Brooks	Cooper	T51	Climax	4	6	spin	9	4
r	11	J Surtees	Lotus	18	Climax	4	3	accident	6	3

Winning speed 159.318 km/h, 98.996 mph
Pole Position speed 165.858 km/h, 103.059 mph (S Moss, 1 min:54.400 sec)
Fastest Lap speed 163.148 km/h, 101.376 mph (J Brabham, 1 min:56.300 sec on lap 71)
Lap Leaders J Brabham 1-4 (4); S Moss 5-75 (71).

Lap Leaders 1960

Pos	Driver	Car-Engine	GPs	laps	km	miles
1	J Brabham	Cooper-Climax	7	244	1,644.7	1,021.9
2	S Moss	Cooper-Climax	1	9	35.2	21.9
		Lotus-Climax	2	141	594.4	369.3
			3	150	629.6	391.2
3	J Bonnier	BRM	2	80	295.3	183.5
4	P Hill	Ferrari	2	34	326.4	202.8
5	J Surtees	Lotus-Climax	1	25	185.2	115.1
6	R Ginther	Ferrari	1	24	240.0	149.1
7	G Hill	BRM	1	17	80.1	49.8
8	B McLaren	Cooper-Climax	1	13	50.9	31.6
9	D Gurney	BRM	1	10	74.1	46.0
10	I Ireland	Lotus-Climax	1	1	3.9	2.4
			9	**598**	**3,530.1**	**2,193.5**

Driver Points 1960

		RA	MC	INDY	NL	B	F	GB	P	I	USA	Total	
1	J Brabham	-	-	-	8	8	8	8	8	-	3	43	
2	B McLaren	8	6	-	-	6	4	(3)	6	-	4	34	(3)
3	S Moss	-	8	-	3	-	-	-	-	-	8	19	
4	I Ireland	1	-	-	6	-	-	4	1	-	6	18	
5	P Hill	-	4	-	-	3	-	-	-	8	1	16	
6	O Gendebien	-	-	-	-	4	6	-	-	-	-	10	
	W von Trips	2	-	-	2	-	-	1	3	2	-	10	
8	J Rathmann	-	-	8	-	-	-	-	-	-	-	8	
	R Ginther	-	1	-	1	-	-	-	-	6	-	8	
	J Clark	-	-	-	-	2	2	-	4	-	-	8	
11	T Brooks	-	3	-	-	-	-	2	2	-	-	7	
12	C Allison	6	-	-	-	-	-	-	-	-	-	6	
	R Ward	-	-	6	-	-	-	-	-	-	-	6	
	J Surtees	-	-	-	-	-	-	6	-	-	-	6	
15	P Goldsmith	-	-	4	-	-	-	-	-	-	-	4	
	G Hill	-	-	-	4	-	-	-	-	-	-	4	
	W Mairesse	-	-	-	-	-	-	-	-	4	-	4	
	J Bonnier	-	2	-	-	-	-	-	-	-	2	4	
19	C Menditéguy	3	-	-	-	-	-	-	-	-	-	3	
	D Branson	-	-	3	-	-	-	-	-	-	-	3	
	H Taylor	-	-	-	-	-	3	-	-	-	-	3	
	G Cabianca	-	-	-	-	-	-	-	-	3	-	3	
23	J Thomson	-	-	2	-	-	-	-	-	-	-	2	
24	E Johnson	-	-	1	-	-	-	-	-	-	-	1	
	L Bianchi	-	-	-	-	1	-	-	-	-	-	1	
	R Flockhart	-	-	-	-	-	1	-	-	-	-	1	
	H Herrmann	-	-	-	-	-	-	-	-	1	-	1	

8,6,4,3,2 and 1 point awarded to the first six finishers. Best 6 scores.
M Trintignant and S Moss (Cooper-Climax) were ineligible for points for their 3rd place in Argentina, because of the shared drive.

Constructor Points 1960

		RA	MC	INDY	NL	B	F	GB	P	I	USA	Total	
1	Cooper-Climax	8	(6)	-	8	8	8	8	8	-	(4)	48	(10)
2	Lotus-Climax	(1)	8	-	6	2	(2)	6	4	-	8	34	(3)
3	Ferrari	6	4	-	2	3	-	(1)	3	8	-	26	(1)
4	BRM	-	2	-	4	-	-	-	-	-	2	8	
5	Cooper-Maserati	3	-	-	-	-	-	-	-	-	-	3	
	Cooper-Castellotti	-	-	-	-	-	-	-	-	3	-	3	

8,6,4,3,2 and 1 point awarded to the first six finishers. Indianapolis excluded.
Points only for highest placed car. Best 6 scores. Porsche received no points for their 6th place in Italy, due to entering a Formula 2 car.

Race Entrants and Results

The new 1.5-litre formula, although announced some three years earlier, caught most of the British teams off guard. They hoped for a last-minute reprise of the existing rules, and had to rely on old four cylinder engines until the V8s were ready. Ferrari on the other hand developed their already successful F2 team and clearly had the early season advantage. Now there would be 9 points for a win.

FERRARI
Scuderia Ferrari SpA SEFAC: P Hill, von Trips, Ginther, Gendebien, Mairesse, Rodríguez
FISA: Baghetti (F)
Scuderia Sant Ambroeus: Baghetti

DE TOMASO
Scuderia Serenissima: Scarlatti, Vaccarella
Scuderia Settecolli: Lippi
Isobele de Tomaso: Bussinello

BRM
Owen Racing Organisation: G Hill, Brooks

COOPER
Cooper Car Co: Brabham, McLaren
Yeoman Credit Racing Team: Surtees, Salvadori
Camoradi International: Gregory, Burgess
Scuderia Centro Sud: Bandini, Natili
Scuderia Serenissima: Trintignant
Pescara Racing Club: Pirocchi
H & L Motors: Lewis
Fred Tuck: Fairman
Momo Corporation: Hansgen
John M Wyatt III: Penske
Privateers: Collomb, Sharp

EMERYSON
Equipe Nationale Belge: Bianchi, Gendebien, Pilette

FERGUSON
R R C Walker Racing Team: Fairman, Moss

GILBY
Gilby Engineering Co Ltd: Greene

JBW
JBW Cars: Naylor

LOTUS
Team Lotus: Clark, Ireland, T Taylor, Mairesse (F)
R R C Walker Racing Team: Moss
UDT Laystall Racing Team: H Taylor, Bianchi, Gregory, Allison, Gendebien, (Bordeu)
Scuderia Colonia: May, Seidel
Camoradi International: Burgess
Equipe Nationale Belge: Mairesse, Bianchi (B)
Louise Bryden-Brown: Maggs
J Wheeler Autosport: Ryan
J Frank Harrison: Ruby
Privateers: Parnell, Ashmore, Marsh, Starrabba, Hall

PORSCHE
Porsche System Engineering: Gurney, Bonnier, Herrmann
Ecurie Maarsbergen: de Beaufort, Herrmann (NL)

14 May 1961		MONACO: Monte-Carlo							(Round 1)	(Race 95)	
		100 laps x 3.145 km, 1.954 miles = 314.500 km, 195.421 miles									
Pos	No	Driver	Car	Model	Engine		Laps	Time/Reason for Retirement		Grid Pos	Row
1	20	S Moss	Lotus	18	Climax	4	100	2h 45m 50.100s		1	1
2	36	R Ginther	Ferrari	156	Ferrari	V6	100	2h 45m 53.700s		2	1
3	38	P Hill	Ferrari	156	Ferrari	V6	100	2h 46m 31.400s		5	2
4r	40	W von Trips	Ferrari	156	Ferrari	V6	98	engine / accident		6	3
5	4	D Gurney	Porsche	718	Porsche	F4	98			10	4
6	26	B McLaren	Cooper	T55	Climax	4	95			7	3
7	42	M Trintignant	Cooper	T51	Maserati	4	95			15	6
8	32	C Allison	Lotus	18	Climax	4	93			14	6
9	6	H Herrmann	Porsche	718	Porsche	F4	91			12	5
10	28	J Clark	Lotus	21	Climax	4	89			3	1
11r	22	J Surtees	Cooper	T53	Climax	4	68	fuel pump		11	5
12r	2	J Bonnier	Porsche	787	Porsche	F4	59	fuel pump drive		9	4
13r	16	T Brooks	BRM	P48/57	Climax	4	54	valve		8	3
r	8	M May	Lotus	18	Climax	4	42	gearbox		13	5
r	24	J Brabham	Cooper	T55	Climax	4	38	ignition / misfire		16	7
r	18	G Hill	BRM	P48/57	Climax	4	11	fuel pump drive		4	2
ns	30	I Ireland	Lotus	21	Climax	4		accident / injury			
nq	14	M Gregory	Cooper	T53	Climax	4					
nq	10	L Bianchi	Emeryson	(61)	Maserati	4					
nq	34	H Taylor	Lotus	18	Climax	4					
nq	12	O Gendebien	Emeryson	(61)	Maserati	4					

Winning speed 113.788 km/h, 70.704 mph
Pole Position speed 114.248 km/h, 70.991 mph (S Moss, 1 min:39.100 sec)
Fastest Lap speed 117.570 km/h, 73.055 mph (R Ginther / S Moss, 1 min:36.300 sec on lap 84 / 85)
Lap Leaders R Ginther 1-13 (13); S Moss 14-100 (87).

22 May 1961　　**NETHERLANDS: Zandvoort**　　　　　　　　**(Round 2)**　　**(Race 96)**

75 laps x 4.193 km, 2.605 miles = 314.475 km, 195.406 miles

Pos	No	Driver	Car	Model	Engine		Laps	Time/Reason for Retirement	Grid Pos	Row
1	3	W von Trips	Ferrari	156	Ferrari	V6	75	2h 01m 52.100s	2	1
2	1	P Hill	Ferrari	156	Ferrari	V6	75	2h 01m 53.000s	1	1
3	15	J Clark	Lotus	21	Climax	4	75	2h 02m 05.200s	10	4
4	14	S Moss	Lotus	18	Climax	4	75	2h 02m 14.300s	4	2
5	2	R Ginther	Ferrari	156	Ferrari	V6	75	2h 02m 14.400s	3	1
6	10	J Brabham	Cooper	T55	Climax	4	75	2h 03m 12.200s	7	3
7	12	J Surtees	Cooper	T53	Climax	4	75	2h 03m 18.800s	9	4
8	4	G Hill	BRM	P48/57	Climax	4	75	2h 03m 21.900s	5	2
9	5	T Brooks	BRM	P48/57	Climax	4	74		8	3
10	7	D Gurney	Porsche	787	Porsche	F4	74		6	3
11	6	J Bonnier	Porsche	787	Porsche	F4	73		11	5
12	11	B McLaren	Cooper	T55	Climax	4	73		13	5
13	16	T Taylor	Lotus	18	Climax	4	73		14	6
14	8	C G de Beaufort	Porsche	718	Porsche	F4	72		15	6
15	9	H Herrmann	Porsche	718	Porsche	F4	72		12	5
ns	17	M Gregory	Cooper	T53	Climax	4		reserve entry		
ns	18	I Burgess	Lotus	18	Climax	4		reserve entry		

Winning speed 154.827 km/h, 96.205 mph
Pole Position speed 157.730 km/h, 98.009 mph (P Hill, 1 min:35.700 sec)
Fastest Lap speed 158.061 km/h, 98.214 mph (J Clark, 1 min:35.500 sec on lap 7)
Lap Leaders W von Trips 1-75 (75).

---

18 Jun 1961　　**BELGIUM: Spa-Francorchamps**　　　　　　**(Round 3)**　　**(Race 97)**

30 laps x 14.100 km, 8.761 miles = 423.000 km, 262.840 miles

Pos	No	Driver	Car	Model	Engine		Laps	Time/Reason for Retirement	Grid Pos	Row
1	4	P Hill	Ferrari	156	Ferrari	V6	30	2h 03m 03.800s	1	1
2	2	W von Trips	Ferrari	156	Ferrari	V6	30	2h 03m 04.500s	2	1
3	6	R Ginther	Ferrari	156	Ferrari	V6	30	2h 03m 23.300s	5	2
4	8	O Gendebien	Ferrari	156	Ferrari	V6	30	2h 03m 49.400s	3	1
5	24	J Surtees	Cooper	T53	Climax	4	30	2h 04m 30.600s	4	2
6	20	D Gurney	Porsche	718	Porsche	F4	30	2h 04m 34.800s	10	4
7	18	J Bonnier	Porsche	718	Porsche	F4	30	2h 05m 50.900s	9	4
8	14	S Moss	Lotus	18/21	Climax	4	30	2h 06m 59.400s	8	3
9	40	J Lewis	Cooper	T53	Climax	4	29		13	5
10	44	M Gregory	Cooper	T53	Climax	4	29		12	5
11	22	C G de Beaufort	Porsche	718	Porsche	F4	28		14	6
12	34	J Clark	Lotus	21	Climax	4	24		16	7
13	38	T Brooks	BRM	P48/57	Climax	4	24		7	3
r	36	G Hill	BRM	P48/57	Climax	4	24	oil leak	6	3
r	26	M Trintignant	Cooper	T51	Maserati	4	23	transmission	20	8
r	46	L Bandini	Cooper	T53	Maserati	4	20	oil pressure	17	7
r	28	J Brabham	Cooper	T55	Climax	4	12	connecting rod	11	5
r	12	L Bianchi	Lotus	18	Climax	4	9	oil line	21	9
r	32	I Ireland	Lotus	21	Climax	4	9	engine	18	7
r	30	B McLaren	Cooper	T55	Climax	4	9	fuel system	15	6
r	10	W Mairesse	Lotus	18	Climax	4	7	engine	19	8
ns	42	T Marsh	Lotus	18	Climax	4		no starting money		
ns	48	W Seidel	Lotus	18	Climax	4		no starting money		
ns	50	I Burgess	Lotus	18	Climax	4		no starting money		
ns	16	C Allison	Lotus	18	Climax	4		accident / injury		

Winning speed 206.235 km/h, 128.149 mph
Pole Position speed 212.119 km/h, 131.804 mph (P Hill, 3 min:59.300 sec)
Fastest Lap speed 211.676 km/h, 131.530 mph (R Ginther, 3 min:59.800 sec on lap 20)
Lap Leaders P Hill 1,3-5,8,11-13,15,17-18,21-23,25-30 (20); O Gendebien 2,6-7 (3); W von Trips 9-10,14,16,19-20,24 (7).

J Clark and I Ireland lined up on the grid in reverse order.

2 Jul 1961   **FRANCE: Reims**   (Round 4)   (Race 98)

52 laps x 8.302 km, 5.159 miles = 431.704 km, 268.248 miles

Pos	No	Driver	Car	Model	Engine		Laps	Time/Reason for Retirement	Grid Pos	Row
1	50	G Baghetti	Ferrari	156	Ferrari	V6	52	2h 14m 17.500s	12	5
2	12	D Gurney	Porsche	718	Porsche	F4	52	2h 14m 17.600s	9	4
3	8	J Clark	Lotus	21	Climax	4	52	2h 15m 18.600s	5	2
4	6	I Ireland	Lotus	21	Climax	4	52	2h 15m 27.800s	10	4
5	4	B McLaren	Cooper	T55	Climax	4	52	2h 15m 59.300s	8	3
6	22	G Hill	BRM	P48/57	Climax	4	52	2h 15m 59.400s	6	3
7	10	J Bonnier	Porsche	718	Porsche	F4	52	2h 17m 32.900s	13	5
8	42	R Salvadori	Cooper	T53	Climax	4	51		15	6
9	16	P Hill	Ferrari	156	Ferrari	V6	50		1	1
10	30	H Taylor	Lotus	18/21	Climax	4	49		25	10
11	46	M May	Lotus	18	Climax	4	48		22	9
12	36	M Gregory	Cooper	T53	Climax	4	43		16	7
13	32	M Trintignant	Cooper	T51	Maserati	4	42		23	9
14	38	I Burgess	Lotus	18	Climax	4	42		24	10
15r	18	R Ginther	Ferrari	156	Ferrari	V6	40	oil pressure	3	1
r	26	S Moss	Lotus	18/21	Climax	4	31	accident / suspension	4	2
r	48	W Mairesse	Lotus	21	Climax	4	27	fuel system	20	8
r	14	C G de Beaufort	Porsche	718	Porsche	F4	23	engine	17	7
r	28	L Bianchi	Lotus	18/21	Climax	4	21	clutch	19	8
r	20	W von Trips	Ferrari	156	Ferrari	V6	18	cylinder head gasket	2	1
r	34	G Scarlatti	De Tomaso	F1	OSCA	4	15	engine	26	11
r	2	J Brabham	Cooper	T55	Climax	4	14	oil pressure	14	6
r	52	B Collomb	Cooper	T53	Climax	4	6	valve	21	9
r	44	J Lewis	Cooper	T53	Climax	4	4	engine overheating	18	7
r	40	J Surtees	Cooper	T53	Climax	4	4	accident	7	3
r	24	T Brooks	BRM	P48/57	Climax	4	4	engine overheating	11	5
ns	28	J M Bordeu	Lotus	18/21	Climax	4		car raced by Bianchi		

Winning speed 192.880 km/h, 119.850 mph
Pole Position speed 206.261 km/h, 128.165 mph (P Hill, 2 min:24.900 sec)
Fastest Lap speed 203.176 km/h, 126.248 mph (P Hill, 2 min:27.100 sec)
Lap Leaders P Hill 1-12,18-37 (32); W von Trips 13-17 (5); R Ginther 38-40 (3); G Baghetti 41-43,45,47,50,52 (7); J Bonnier 44 (1); D Gurney 46,48-49,51 (4).

15 Jul 1961   **BRITAIN: Aintree**   (Round 5)   (Race 99)

75 laps x 4.828 km, 3.000 miles = 362.102 km, 225.000 miles

Pos	No	Driver	Car	Model	Engine		Laps	Time/Reason for Retirement	Grid Pos	Row
1	4	W von Trips	Ferrari	156	Ferrari	V6	75	2h 40m 53.600s	4	2
2	2	P Hill	Ferrari	156	Ferrari	V6	75	2h 41m 39.600s	1	1
3	6	R Ginther	Ferrari	156	Ferrari	V6	75	2h 41m 40.400s	2	1
4	12	J Brabham	Cooper	T55	Climax	4	75	2h 42m 02.200s	9	4
5	8	J Bonnier	Porsche	718	Porsche	F4	75	2h 42m 09.800s	3	1
6	36	R Salvadori	Cooper	T53	Climax	4	75	2h 42m 19.800s	13	5
7	10	D Gurney	Porsche	718	Porsche	F4	74		12	5
8	14	B McLaren	Cooper	T55	Climax	4	74		14	6
9	22	T Brooks	BRM	P48/57	Climax	4	73		6	3
10	16	I Ireland	Lotus	21	Climax	4	72		7	3
11	42	M Gregory	Cooper	T53	Climax	4	71		16	7
12	60	L Bandini	Cooper	T53	Maserati	4	71		21	9
13	50	T Maggs	Lotus	18	Climax	4	70		24	10
14	44	I Burgess	Lotus	18	Climax	4	70		25	10
15	54	K Greene	Gilby	(61)	Climax	4	69		23	9
16	56	C G de Beaufort	Porsche	718	Porsche	F4	69		18	7
r	18	J Clark	Lotus	21	Climax	4	62	oil line	8	3
17	52	W Seidel	Lotus	18	Climax	4	58		22	9
dq=	26	J Fairman	Ferguson	P99	Climax	4			20	8
dq=	26	S Moss	Ferguson	P99	Climax	4	56	push start in pits (Fairman)		
r	32	L Bianchi	Lotus	18/21	Climax	4	45	gearbox	30	12
r	28	S Moss	Lotus	18/21	Climax	4	44	brake pipe	5	2
r	20	G Hill	BRM	P48/57	Climax	4	43	valve spring	11	5
r	58	G Baghetti	Ferrari	156	Ferrari	V6	27	spin	19	8
r	25	T Marsh	Lotus	18	Climax	4	25	ignition	27	11
r	34	J Surtees	Cooper	T53	Climax	4	23	differential	10	4
r	38	T Parnell	Lotus	18	Climax	4	12	clutch	29	12
r	46	J Lewis	Cooper	T53	Climax	4	7	handling	15	6
r	40	G Ashmore	Lotus	18	Climax	4	7	misfire	26	11
r	30	H Taylor	Lotus	18/21	Climax	4	5	accident	17	7
r	62	M Natili	Cooper	T51	Maserati	4	0	engine	28	11

Winning speed 135.034 km/h, 83.907 mph
Pole Position speed 146.304 km/h, 90.909 mph (P Hill, 1 min:58.800 sec)
Fastest Lap speed 147.546 km/h, 91.681 mph (T Brooks, 1 min:57.800 sec on lap 72)
Lap Leaders P Hill 1-6 (6); W von Trips 7-75 (69).

Races   77

15 laps x 22.810 km, 14.173 miles = 342.150 km, 212.602 miles

Pos	No	Driver	Car	Model	Engine		Laps	Time/Reason for Retirement	Grid Pos	Row
1	7	S Moss	Lotus	18/21	Climax	4	15	2h 18m 12.400s	3	1
2	3	W von Trips	Ferrari	156	Ferrari	V6	15	2h 18m 33.800s	5	2
3	4	P Hill	Ferrari	156	Ferrari	V6	15	2h 18m 34.900s	1	1
4	14	J Clark	Lotus	21	Climax	4	15	2h 19m 29.500s	8	3
5	18	J Surtees	Cooper	T53	Climax	4	15	2h 20m 05.500s	10	3
6	2	B McLaren	Cooper	T55	Climax	4	15	2h 20m 53.800s	12	4
7	9	D Gurney	Porsche	718	Porsche	F4	15	2h 21m 35.000s	7	2
8	5	R Ginther	Ferrari	156	Ferrari	V6	15	2h 23m 35.500s	14	4
9	28	J Lewis	Cooper	T53	Climax	4	15	2h 23m 36.100s	18	5
10	19	R Salvadori	Cooper	T53	Climax	4	15	2h 30m 23.900s	15	5
11	33	T Maggs	Lotus	18	Climax	4	14		22	7
12	30	I Burgess	Cooper	T53	Climax	4	14		24	7
13	11	H Herrmann	Porsche	718	Porsche	F4	14		11	3
14	31	C G de Beaufort	Porsche	718	Porsche	F4	14		17	5
r	6	W Mairesse	Ferrari	156	Ferrari	V6	13	accident	13	4
15	37	T Marsh	Lotus	18	Climax	4	13		20	6
16	27	G Ashmore	Lotus	18	Climax	4	13		25	7
17	20	M Trintignant	Cooper	T51	Maserati	4	12		21	6
r	38	B Collomb	Cooper	T53	Climax	4	11	engine	26	8
r	32	L Bandini	Cooper	T53	Maserati	4	10	engine	19	6
r	16	T Brooks	BRM	P48/57	Climax	4	6	valve spring	9	3
r	8	J Bonnier	Porsche	718	Porsche	F4	5	engine	4	1
r	26	W Seidel	Lotus	18	Climax	4	3	steering	23	7
r	15	I Ireland	Lotus	21	Climax	4	1	fire	16	5
r	17	G Hill	BRM	P48/57	Climax	4	1	accident	6	2
r	1	J Brabham	Cooper	T58	Climax	V8	0	throttle jammed / accident	2	1
ns	25	M May	Lotus	18	Climax	4		accident		

Winning speed 148.538 km/h, 92.297 mph
Pole Position speed 153.430 km/h, 95.337 mph (P Hill, 8 min:55.200 sec)
Fastest Lap speed 152.689 km/h, 94.876 mph (P Hill, 8 min:57.800 sec on lap 10)
Lap Leaders S Moss 1-15 (15).

Also the Grand Prix of Europe.

43 laps x 10.000 km, 6.214 miles = 430.000 km, 267.190 miles

Pos	No	Driver	Car	Model	Engine		Laps	Time/Reason for Retirement	Grid Pos	Row
1	2	P Hill	Ferrari	156	Ferrari	V6	43	2h 03m 13.000s	4	2
2	46	D Gurney	Porsche	718	Porsche	F4	43	2h 03m 44.200s	12	6
3	12	B McLaren	Cooper	T55	Climax	4	43	2h 05m 41.400s	14	7
4	60	J Lewis	Cooper	T53	Climax	4	43	2h 05m 53.400s	16	8
5	26	T Brooks	BRM	P48/57	Climax	4	43	2h 05m 53.500s	13	7
6	40	R Salvadori	Cooper	T53	Climax	V8	42		18	9
7	74	C G de Beaufort	Porsche	718	Porsche	F4	41		15	8
8	62	L Bandini	Cooper	T53	Maserati	4	41		21	11
9	48	M Trintignant	Cooper	T51	Maserati	4	41		22	11
10	16	T Parnell	Lotus	18	Climax	4	40		27	14
11	20	H Taylor	Lotus	18/21	Climax	4	39		23	12
12	58	R Pirocchi	Cooper	T51	Maserati	4	38		29	15
r	28	S Moss	Lotus	21	Climax	4	36	front wheel bearing	11	6
r	6	R Ginther	Ferrari	156	Ferrari	V6	23	engine	3	2
r	72	G Starrabba	Lotus	18	Maserati	4	19	engine	30	15
r	44	J Bonnier	Porsche	718	Porsche	F4	15	rear suspension	8	4
r	50	N Vaccarella	De Tomaso	F1	Conrero	4	13	engine	20	10
r	32	G Baghetti	Ferrari	156	Ferrari	V6	13	engine	6	3
r	8	R Rodríguez	Ferrari	156	Ferrari	V6	13	fuel pump	2	1
r	22	M Gregory	Lotus	18/21	Climax	4	11	rear suspension	17	9
r	24	G Hill	BRM	P48/57	Climax	4	10	engine	5	3
r	10	J Brabham	Cooper	T58	Climax	V8	8	engine overheating	10	5
r	14	B Naylor	JBW	(61)	Climax	4	6	engine	31	16
r	30	J Fairman	Cooper	T45	Climax	4	5	engine	26	13
r	38	I Ireland	Lotus	18/21	Climax	4	5	chassis	9	5
r	42	J Surtees	Cooper	T53	Climax	4	2	accident	19	10
r	56	W Seidel	Lotus	18	Climax	4	1	engine	28	14
r	54	R Bussinello	De Tomaso	F1	Conrero	4	1	engine	24	12
r	52	R Lippi	De Tomaso	F1	OSCA	4	1	engine	32	16
r	36	J Clark	Lotus	21	Climax	4	1	accident	7	4
r	4	W von Trips	Ferrari	156	Ferrari	V6	1	fatal accident	1	1
r	18	G Ashmore	Lotus	18	Climax	4	0	accident	25	13
nq	68	A Pilette	Emeryson	(61)	Climax	4				
ns	58	M Natili	Cooper	T51	Maserati	4		car raced by Pirocchi		

Winning speed 209.387 km/h, 130.107 mph
Pole Position speed 216.476 km/h, 134.512 mph (W von Trips, 2 min:46.300 sec)
Fastest Lap speed 213.777 km/h, 132.835 mph (G Baghetti, 2 min:48.400 sec on lap 2)
Lap Leaders P Hill 1-3,5,7,10,14-43 (36); R Ginther 4,6,8-9,11-13 (7).

8 Oct 1961   USA: Watkins Glen   (Round 8)   (Race 102)

100 laps x 3.701 km, 2.300 miles = 370.149 km, 230.000 miles

Pos	No	Driver	Car	Model	Engine		Laps	Time/Reason for Retirement	Grid Pos	Row
1	15	I Ireland	Lotus	21	Climax	4	100	2h 13m 45.800s	8	4
2	12	D Gurney	Porsche	718	Porsche	F4	100	2h 13m 50.100s	7	4
3	5	T Brooks	BRM	P48/57	Climax	4	100	2h 14m 34.800s	6	3
4	2	B McLaren	Cooper	T55	Climax	4	100	2h 14m 43.800s	4	2
5	4	G Hill	BRM	P48/57	Climax	4	99		2	1
6	11	J Bonnier	Porsche	718	Porsche	F4	98		10	5
r	19	R Salvadori	Cooper	T53	Climax	4	96	engine bearings	12	6
7	14	J Clark	Lotus	21	Climax	4	96		5	3
8	6	R Penske	Cooper	T53	Climax	4	96		16	8
9	16	P Ryan	Lotus	18/21	Climax	4	96		13	7
10	3	H Sharp	Cooper	T53	Climax	4	93		17	9
11=	21	O Gendebien	Lotus	18/21	Climax	4		15	8
11=	21	M Gregory	Lotus	18/21	Climax	4	92			
r	26	L Ruby	Lotus	18	Climax	4	76	magneto	19	10
r	17	J Hall	Lotus	18	Climax	4	76	fuel pipe	18	9
r	7	S Moss	Lotus	18/21	Climax	4	58	engine bearings	3	2
r	1	J Brabham	Cooper	T58	Climax	V8	57	engine overheating	1	1
r	22	M Gregory	Lotus	18/21	Climax	4	23	gear selector	11	6
r	60	W Hansgen	Cooper	T53	Climax	4	14	accident	14	7
r	18	J Surtees	Cooper	T53	Climax	4	0	connecting rod	9	5

Winning speed 166.032 km/h, 103.167 mph
Pole Position speed 173.057 km/h, 107.532 mph (J Brabham, 1 min:17.000 sec)
Fastest Lap speed 170.401 km/h, 105.882 mph (J Brabham, 1 min:18.200 sec on lap 28   & 30)
Lap Leaders S Moss 1-5,16,24-25,34-35,39-58 (30); J Brabham 6-15,17-23,26-33,36-38 (28); I Ireland 59-100 (42).

Lap Leaders 1961

Pos	Driver	Car-Engine	GPs	laps	km	miles
1	W von Trips	Ferrari	4	156	787.8	489.5
2	S Moss	Lotus-Climax	3	132	726.8	451.6
3	P Hill	Ferrari	4	94	936.6	582.0
4	I Ireland	Lotus-Climax	1	42	155.4	96.6
5	J Brabham	Cooper-Climax	1	28	103.6	64.4
6	R Ginther	Ferrari	3	23	135.8	84.4
7	G Baghetti	Ferrari	1	7	58.1	36.1
8	D Gurney	Porsche	1	4	33.2	20.6
9	O Gendebien	Ferrari	1	3	42.3	26.3
10	J Bonnier	Porsche	1	1	8.3	5.2
			8	**490**	**2,988.0**	**1,856.7**

Driver Points 1961

		MC	NL	B	F	GB	D	I	USA	Total	
1	P Hill	4	6	9	-	6	(4)	9	-	34	(4)
2	W von Trips	3	9	6	-	9	6	-	-	33	
3	S Moss	9	3	-	-	-	9	-	-	21	
	D Gurney	2	-	1	6	-	-	6	6	21	
5	R Ginther	6	2	4	-	4	-	-	-	16	
6	I Ireland	-	-	-	3	-	-	-	9	12	
7	J Clark	-	4	-	4	-	3	-	-	11	
	B McLaren	1	-	-	2	-	1	4	3	11	
9	G Baghetti	-	-	-	9	-	-	-	-	9	
10	T Brooks	-	-	-	-	-	-	2	4	6	
11	J Brabham	-	1	-	-	3	-	-	-	4	
	J Surtees	-	-	2	-	-	2	-	-	4	
13	O Gendebien	-	-	3	-	-	-	-	-	3	
	J Lewis	-	-	-	-	-	-	3	-	3	
	J Bonnier	-	-	-	-	2	-	-	1	3	
	G Hill	-	-	-	1	-	-	-	2	3	
17	R Salvadori	-	-	-	-	1	-	1	-	2	

9,6,4,3,2 and 1 point awarded to the first six finishers. Best 5 scores.

Constructor Points 1961

		RA	MC	INDY	F	GB	D	PES	I	Total	
1	Ferrari	(6)	8	8	8	8	(6)	8	-	40	(12)
2	Lotus-Climax	8	4	-	4	-	8	-	8	32	
3	Porsche	2	-	(1)	6	2	-	6	6	22	(1)
4	Cooper-Climax	(1)	(1)	2	2	3	(2)	4	3	14	(4)
5	BRM-Climax	-	-	-	1	-	-	2	4	7	

8,6,4,3,2 and 1 point awarded to the first six finishers. Points only for highest placed car. Best 5 scores.

1962

Race Entrants and Results 1962

Stirling Moss was seriously injured at Goodwood before the championship had begun, effectively ending his racing career. The British teams began to dominate as the V8 engines emerged. Lotus re-introduced the monocoque to top line racing with the Type 25 model. Ferrari suffered a mass walk-out when many of its leading engineers went on to form the ATS team, while the factory introduced its revised car at the German Grand Prix. The famous twin-nostril Ferrari was consigned to the scrap heap.

FERRARI
Scuderia Ferrari SpA SEFAC: P Hill, Rodríguez, Baghetti, Bandini, Mairesse

DE TOMASO
Scuderia de Tomaso: (Estéfano)
Scuderia Settecolli: Lippi

BRM
Owen Racing Organisation: G Hill, Ginther
Ecurie Galloise: (Lewis)
Privateer: Johnstone

BRABHAM
Brabham Racing Organisation: Brabham

COOPER
Cooper Car Co: McLaren, Maggs, Mayer
Ecurie Galloise: Lewis
Anglo-American Equipe: Burgess
Privateers: Collomb, Sharp, Love, Harris

EMERYSON
Emeryson Cars: Settember
Ecurie Maarsbergen: Seidel

GILBY
Gilby Engineering Co Ltd: Greene

LOLA
Bowmaker-Yeoman Racing Team: Surtees, Salvadori

LOTUS
Team Lotus: Clark, T Taylor
Rob Walker Racing Team: Trintignant

UDT Laystall Racing Team: Ireland, Gregory
Brabham Racing Organisation: Brabham
Scuderia SSS Republica di Venezia: Vaccarella
Ecurie Filipinetti: Schiller, Siffert
Emeryson Cars: Campbell-Jones
Equipe Nationale Belge: Bianchi
Autosport Team Wolfgang Seidel: Seidel, (Gurney, Seiffert)
Ecurie Excelsior: Chamberlain
John Dalton: Shelly, (Greene)
Dupont Team Zerex: Penske
John Mecom: Schroeder
Scuderia Jolly Club: (Prinoth)
Ecurie Nationale Suisse: (Siffert (MC))
Privateers: Pieterse, Lederle, Hall, (Ashmore)

PORSCHE
Porsche System Engineering: Bonnier, Gurney, (P Hill)
Ecurie Maarsbergen: de Beaufort, Pon
Ecurie Filipinetti: Walter
Scuderia SSS Republica di Venezia: Vaccarella

ENB
Equipe Nationale Belge: Bianchi

LDS
Otelle Nucci: Serrurier

20 May 1962		**NETHERLANDS: Zandvoort**							**(Round 1)**	**(Race 103)**	
		80 laps x 4.193 km, 2.605 miles = 335.440 km, 208.433 miles									
Pos	**No**	**Driver**	**Car**	**Model**	**Engine**		**Laps**	**Time/Reason for Retirement**		**Grid Pos**	**Row**
1	17	G Hill	BRM	P57	BRM	V8	80	2h 11m 02.100s		2	1
2	5	T Taylor	Lotus	24	Climax	V8	80	2h 11m 29.300s		10	4
3	1	P Hill	Ferrari	156	Ferrari	V6	80	2h 12m 23.200s		9	4
4	2	G Baghetti	Ferrari	156	Ferrari	V6	79			12	5
5	7	T Maggs	Cooper	T55	Climax	4	78			15	6
6	14	C G de Beaufort	Porsche	718	Porsche	F4	76			14	6
7	11	J Bonnier	Porsche	804	Porsche	F8	75			13	5
r	3	R Rodríguez	Ferrari	156	Ferrari	V6	73	spin		11	5
r	18	R Ginther	BRM	P48/57	BRM	V8	71	accident		7	3
8	21	J Lewis	Cooper	T53	Climax	4	70			19	8
9	4	J Clark	Lotus	25	Climax	V8	70			3	1
r	9	I Ireland	Lotus	24	Climax	V8	61	spin		6	3
r	10	M Gregory	Lotus	18/21	Climax	4	54	gearbox		16	7
nc	16	W Seidel	Emeryson	(61)	Climax	4	52			20	8
r	12	D Gurney	Porsche	804	Porsche	F8	47	gearbox		8	3
r	6	B McLaren	Cooper	T60	Climax	V8	21	gearbox		5	2
r	20	R Salvadori	Lola	Mk 4	Climax	V8	12	withdrew		17	7
r	19	J Surtees	Lola	Mk 4	Climax	V8	8	front suspension / accident		1	1
r	8	J Brabham	Lotus	24	Climax	V8	4	accident		4	2
r	15	B Pon	Porsche	787	Porsche	F4	2	accident		18	7

Winning speed 153.596 km/h, 95.440 mph
Pole Position speed 163.187 km/h, 101.400 mph (J Surtees, 1 min:32.500 sec)
Fastest Lap speed 159.903 km/h, 99.359 mph (B McLaren, 1 min:34.400 sec on lap 5)
Lap Leaders J Clark 1-11 (11); G Hill 12-80 (69).

Also the Grand Prix of Europe.

3 Jun 1962   MONACO: Monte-Carlo   (Round 2)   (Race 104)
100 laps x 3.145 km, 1.954 miles = 314.500 km, 195.421 miles

Pos	No	Driver	Car	Model	Engine		Laps	Time/Reason for Retirement	Grid Pos	Row
1	14	B McLaren	Cooper	T60	Climax	V8	100	2h 46m 29.700s	3	1
2	36	P Hill	Ferrari	156	Ferrari	V6	100	2h 46m 31.000s	9	4
3	38	L Bandini	Ferrari	156	Ferrari	V6	100	2h 47m 53.800s	10	4
4	28	J Surtees	Lola	Mk 4	Climax	V8	99		11	5
5	2	J Bonnier	Porsche	718	Porsche	F4	93		15	6
6r	10	G Hill	BRM	P57	BRM	V8	92	engine	2	1
7r	40	W Mairesse	Ferrari	156	Ferrari	V6	90	oil pressure	4	2
8r	22	J Brabham	Lotus	24	Climax	V8	77	front suspension / accident	6	3
r	34	I Ireland	Lotus	24	Climax	V8	64	fuel pump	8	3
r	18	J Clark	Lotus	25	Climax	V8	55	clutch	1	1
r	26	R Salvadori	Lola	Mk 4	Climax	V8	44	suspension	12	5
r	16	T Maggs	Cooper	T55	Climax	4	43	gearbox	16	7
r	20	T Taylor	Lotus	24	Climax	V8	24	oil leak	14	6
r	4	D Gurney	Porsche	804	Porsche	F8	0	accident	5	2
r	8	R Ginther	BRM	P48/57	BRM	V8	0	throttle jammed / accident	13	5
r	30	M Trintignant	Lotus	24	Climax	V8	0	accident	7	3
ns	40	R Rodríguez	Ferrari	156	Ferrari	V6		car raced by Mairesse		
nq	44	C G de Beaufort	Porsche	718	Porsche	F4				
nq	46	J Siffert	Lotus	21	Climax	4				
nq	24	J Lewis	BRM	P48/57	BRM	V8				
nq	32	M Gregory	Lotus	24	BRM	V8				
nq	42	N Vaccarella	Lotus	18/21	Climax	4				

Winning speed 113.337 km/h, 70.424 mph
Pole Position speed 118.679 km/h, 73.744 mph (J Clark, 1 min:35.400 sec)
Fastest Lap speed 118.555 km/h, 73.667 mph (J Clark, 1 min:35.500 sec on lap 42)
Lap Leaders B McLaren 1-6,93-100 (14); G Hill 7-92 (86).

17 Jun 1962   BELGIUM: Spa-Francorchamps   (Round 3)   (Race 105)
32 laps x 14.100 km, 8.761 miles = 451.200 km, 280.363 miles

Pos	No	Driver	Car	Model	Engine		Laps	Time/Reason for Retirement	Grid Pos	Row
1	16	J Clark	Lotus	25	Climax	V8	32	2h 07m 32.300s	12	5
2	1	G Hill	BRM	P57	BRM	V8	32	2h 08m 16.400s	1	1
3	9	P Hill	Ferrari	156	Ferrari	V6	32	2h 09m 38.800s	4	2
4	12	R Rodríguez	Ferrari	156	Ferrari	V6	32	2h 09m 38.900s	7	3
5	5	J Surtees	Lola	Mk 4	Climax	V8	31		11	5
6	15	J Brabham	Lotus	24	Climax	V8	30		15	6
7	7	C G de Beaufort	Porsche	718	Porsche	F4	30		13	5
8	18	M Trintignant	Lotus	24	Climax	V8	30		16	7
9	19	L Bianchi	Lotus	18/21	Climax	4	29		18	7
10	22	J Siffert	Lotus	21	Climax	4	29		17	7
r	17	T Taylor	Lotus	24	Climax	V8	25	accident	3	1
r	10	W Mairesse	Ferrari	156	Ferrari	V6	25	accident	6	3
r	2	R Ginther	BRM	P57	BRM	V8	22	transmission	9	4
r	26	T Maggs	Cooper	T60	Climax	V8	22	gearbox	10	4
r	25	B McLaren	Cooper	T60	Climax	V8	19	oil pressure	2	1
11	4	J Campbell-Jones	Lotus	18	Climax	4	16		19	8
r	21	M Gregory	Lotus	24	BRM	V8	13	withdrew	8	3
r	20	I Ireland	Lotus	24	Climax	V8	9	rear suspension	5	2
r	11	G Baghetti	Ferrari	156	Ferrari	V6	4	ignition wiring	14	6
ns	23	D Gurney	Lotus	24	BRM	V8		car unraceworthy		

Winning speed 212.266 km/h, 131.896 mph
Pole Position speed 214.177 km/h, 133.084 mph (G Hill, 3 min:57.000 sec)
Fastest Lap speed 215.450 km/h, 133.874 mph (J Clark, 3 min:55.600 sec on lap 15)
Lap Leaders G Hill 1 (1); T Taylor 2-3,5,7-8 (5); W Mairesse 4,6 (2); J Clark 9-32 (24).

8 Jul 1962   FRANCE: Rouen-les-Essarts   (Round 4)   (Race 106)
54 laps x 6.542 km, 4.065 miles = 353.268 km, 219.511 miles

Pos	No	Driver	Car	Model	Engine		Laps	Time/Reason for Retirement	Grid Pos	Row
1	30	D Gurney	Porsche	804	Porsche	F8	54	2h 07m 35.500s	6	3
2	24	T Maggs	Cooper	T60	Climax	V8	53		11	5
3	10	R Ginther	BRM	P57	BRM	V8	52		10	4
4	22	B McLaren	Cooper	T60	Climax	V8	51		3	1
5	18	J Surtees	Lola	Mk 4	Climax	V8	51		5	2
6	38	C G de Beaufort	Porsche	718	Porsche	F4	51		17	7
7	28	M Trintignant	Lotus	24	Climax	V8	50		13	5
8	14	T Taylor	Lotus	25	Climax	V8	48		12	5
9	8	G Hill	BRM	P57	BRM	V8	44		2	1
10r	32	J Bonnier	Porsche	804	Porsche	F8	42	gearbox	9	4
r	12	J Clark	Lotus	25	Climax	V8	33	front suspension	1	1
r	42	J Lewis	Cooper	T53	Climax	4	27	brakes / accident	16	7
r	20	R Salvadori	Lola	Mk 4	Climax	V8	20	oil pressure	14	6
r	34	M Gregory	Lotus	24	BRM	V8	14	ignition	7	3
r	26	J Brabham	Lotus	24	Climax	V8	10	rear suspension	4	2
r	40	J Siffert	Lotus	24	BRM	V8	5	clutch	15	6
r	36	I Ireland	Lotus	24	Climax	V8	1	spin / tyre / wheel buckled	8	3

Winning speed 166.124 km/h, 103.225 mph
Pole Position speed 174.712 km/h, 108.561 mph (J Clark, 2 min:14.800 sec)
Fastest Lap speed 172.032 km/h, 106.896 mph (G Hill, 2 min:16.900 sec on lap 32)
Lap Leaders G Hill 1-29,33-41 (38); J Clark 30-32 (3); D Gurney 42-54 (13).

21 Jul 1962   BRITAIN: Aintree   (Round 5)   (Race 107)
75 laps x 4.828 km, 3.000 miles = 362.102 km, 225.000 miles

Pos	No	Driver	Car	Model	Engine		Laps	Time/Reason for Retirement	Grid Pos	Row
1	20	J Clark	Lotus	25	Climax	V8	75	2h 26m 20.800s	1	1
2	24	J Surtees	Lola	Mk 4	Climax	V8	75	2h 27m 10.000s	2	1
3	16	B McLaren	Cooper	T60	Climax	V8	75	2h 28m 05.600s	4	2
4	12	G Hill	BRM	P57	BRM	V8	75	2h 28m 17.600s	5	2
5	30	J Brabham	Lotus	24	Climax	V8	74		9	4
6	18	T Maggs	Cooper	T60	Climax	V8	74		13	5
7	34	M Gregory	Lotus	24	Climax	V8	74		14	6
8	22	T Taylor	Lotus	24	Climax	V8	74		10	4
9	8	D Gurney	Porsche	804	Porsche	F8	73		6	3
10	42	J Lewis	Cooper	T53	Climax	4	72		15	6
11	40	T Settember	Emeryson	(61)	Climax	4	71		19	8
12	36	I Burgess	Cooper	T53	Climax	4	71		16	7
13	14	R Ginther	BRM	P57	BRM	V8	70		8	3
14	54	C G de Beaufort	Porsche	718	Porsche	F4	69		17	7
15	46	J Chamberlain	Lotus	18	Climax	4	64		20	8
16	32	I Ireland	Lotus	24	Climax	V8	61		3	1
r	2	P Hill	Ferrari	156	Ferrari	V6	46	distributor	12	5
r	26	R Salvadori	Lola	Mk 4	Climax	V8	34	ignition	11	5
r	10	J Bonnier	Porsche	804	Porsche	F8	26	crown wheel & pinion	7	3
r	44	W Seidel	Lotus	24	BRM	V8	10	brakes / engine overheating	21	9
r	48	T Shelly	Lotus	18/21	Climax	4	5	engine overheating	18	7
ns	48	K Greene	Lotus	18/21	Climax	4		car raced by Shelly		

Winning speed 148.457 km/h, 92.247 mph
Pole Position speed 153.001 km/h, 95.070 mph (J Clark, 1 min:53.600 sec)
Fastest Lap speed 151.138 km/h, 93.913 mph (J Clark, 1 min:55.000 sec on lap 36)
Lap Leaders J Clark 1-75 (75).

5 Aug 1962 GERMANY: Nürburgring (Round 6) (Race 108)

15 laps x 22.810 km, 14.173 miles = 342.150 km, 212.602 miles

Pos	No	Driver	Car	Model	Engine		Laps	Time/Reason for Retirement	Grid Pos	Row
1	11	G Hill	BRM	P57	BRM	V8	15	2h 38m 45.300s	2	1
2	14	J Surtees	Lola	Mk 4	Climax	V8	15	2h 38m 47.800s	4	1
3	7	D Gurney	Porsche	804	Porsche	F8	15	2h 38m 49.700s	1	1
4	5	J Clark	Lotus	25	Climax	V8	15	2h 39m 27.400s	3	1
5	9	B McLaren	Cooper	T60	Climax	V8	15	2h 40m 04.900s	5	2
6	3	R Rodríguez	Ferrari	156	Ferrari	V6	15	2h 40m 09.100s	10	3
7	8	J Bonnier	Porsche	804	Porsche	F8	15	2h 43m 22.600s	6	2
8	12	R Ginther	BRM	P57	BRM	V8	15	2h 43m 45.400s	7	2
9	10	T Maggs	Cooper	T55	Climax	4	15	2h 43m 52.100s	23	7
10	2	G Baghetti	Ferrari	156	Ferrari	V6	15	2h 47m 00.000s	13	4
11	25	I Burgess	Cooper	T53	Climax	4	15	2h 47m 00.600s	16	5
12	19	J Siffert	Lotus	21	Climax	4	15	2h 47m 03.800s	17	5
13	18	C G de Beaufort	Porsche	718	Porsche	F4	15	2h 47m 57.100s	8	3
14	32	H Walter	Porsche	718	Porsche	F4	14		14	4
15	26	N Vaccarella	Porsche	718	Porsche	F4	14		15	5
16	21	L Bianchi	ENB		Maserati	4	14		25	7
17r	20	J Lewis	Cooper	T53	Climax	4	10	engine	21	6
r	16	J Brabham	Brabham	BT3	Climax	V8	9	throttle linkage	24	7
r	1	P Hill	Ferrari	156	Ferrari	V6	9	rear suspension	12	4
r	27	K Greene	Gilby	(62)	BRM	V8	7	front suspension	19	6
r	17	M Trintignant	Lotus	24	Climax	V8	4	gear selection	11	3
r	4	L Bandini	Ferrari	156	Ferrari	V6	4	accident	18	5
r	15	R Salvadori	Lola	Mk 4	Climax	V8	4	gearbox	9	3
r	28	H Schiller	Lotus	24	BRM	V8	4	oil pressure	20	6
r	31	B Collomb	Cooper	T53	Climax	4	2	gearbox	22	7
r	6	T Taylor	Lotus	24	Climax	V8	0	accident	26	8
nq	29	T Shelly	Lotus	18/21	Climax	4				
nq	34	W Seidel	Lotus	24	BRM	V8				
nq	30	J Chamberlain	Lotus	18	Climax	4				
nq	34	G Seifert	Lotus	24	BRM	V8				

Winning speed 129.312 km/h, 80.351 mph
Pole Position speed 155.759 km/h, 96.784 mph (D Gurney, 8 min:47.200 sec)
Fastest Lap speed 134.133 km/h, 83.346 mph (G Hill, 10 min:12.200 sec on lap 3)
Lap Leaders D Gurney 1-2 (2); G Hill 3-15 (13).

T Taylor qualified 22nd, but was put on back row because he failed to complete 5 laps in practice.

16 Sep 1962 ITALY: Monza (Round 7) (Race 109)

86 laps x 5.750 km, 3.573 miles = 494.500 km, 307.268 miles

Pos	No	Driver	Car	Model	Engine		Laps	Time/Reason for Retirement	Grid Pos	Row
1	14	G Hill	BRM	P57	BRM	V8	86	2h 29m 08.400s	2	1
2	12	R Ginther	BRM	P57	BRM	V8	86	2h 29m 38.200s	3	2
3	28	B McLaren	Cooper	T60	Climax	V8	86	2h 30m 06.200s	4	2
4	8	W Mairesse	Ferrari	156	Ferrari	V6	86	2h 30m 06.600s	10	5
5	2	G Baghetti	Ferrari	156	Ferrari	V6	86	2h 30m 39.700s	18	9
6	18	J Bonnier	Porsche	804	Porsche	F8	85		9	5
7	30	T Maggs	Cooper	T60	Climax	V8	85		12	6
8	6	L Bandini	Ferrari	156	Ferrari	V6	84		17	9
9	24	N Vaccarella	Lotus	24	Climax	V8	84		14	7
10	32	C G de Beaufort	Porsche	718	Porsche	F4	81		20	10
11	10	P Hill	Ferrari	156	Ferrari	V6	81		15	8
12	38	M Gregory	Lotus	24	BRM	V8	77		6	3
13r	16	D Gurney	Porsche	804	Porsche	F8	66	crown wheel & pinion	7	4
14r	4	R Rodríguez	Ferrari	156	Ferrari	V6	63	ignition	11	6
r	40	I Ireland	Lotus	24	Climax	V8	45	front suspension	5	3
r	46	J Surtees	Lola	Mk 4A	Climax	V8	42	engine	8	4
r	44	R Salvadori	Lola	Mk 4	Climax	V8	41	engine	13	7
r	22	T Taylor	Lotus	25	Climax	V8	25	transmission	16	8
r	48	T Settember	Emeryson	(61)	Climax	4	18	cylinder head gasket	21	11
r	36	M Trintignant	Lotus	24	Climax	V8	17	electrics	19	10
r	20	J Clark	Lotus	25	Climax	V8	12	transmission	1	1
nq	60	T Shelly	Lotus	24	BRM	V8				
nq	56	K Greene	Gilby	(62)	BRM	V8				
nq	52	G Ashmore	Lotus	18/21	Climax	4				
nq	62	I Burgess	Cooper	T53	Climax	4				
nq	42	J Siffert	Lotus	24	BRM	V8				
nq	54	E Prinoth	Lotus	18	Climax	4				
nq	50	R Lippi	De Tomaso	F1	OSCA	4				
nq	26	J Chamberlain	Lotus	18	Climax	4				
nq	34	N Estéfano	De Tomaso	801	De Tomaso	F8				

Winning speed 198.941 km/h, 123.616 mph
Pole Position speed 206.278 km/h, 128.175 mph (J Clark, 1 min:40.350 sec)
Fastest Lap speed 202.346 km/h, 125.732 mph (G Hill, 1 min:42.300 sec on lap 3 & 4)
Lap Leaders G Hill 1-86 (86).

Races

7 Oct 1962　　　**USA: Watkins Glen**　　　　　　　　　　　　　**(Round 8)**　　**(Race 110)**

100 laps x 3.701 km, 2.300 miles = 370.149 km, 230.000 miles

Pos	No	Driver	Car	Model	Engine		Laps	Time/Reason for Retirement	Grid Pos	Row
1	8	J Clark	Lotus	25	Climax	V8	100	2h 07m 13.000s	1	1
2	4	G Hill	BRM	P57	BRM	V8	100	2h 07m 22.200s	3	2
3	21	B McLaren	Cooper	T60	Climax	V8	99		6	3
4	17	J Brabham	Brabham	BT3	Climax	V8	99		5	3
5	10	D Gurney	Porsche	804	Porsche	F8	99		4	2
6	16	M Gregory	Lotus	24	BRM	V8	99		7	4
7	22	T Maggs	Cooper	T60	Climax	V8	97		10	5
8	15	I Ireland	Lotus	24	Climax	V8	96		15	8
9	14	R Penske	Lotus	24	Climax	V8	96		12	6
10	26	R Schroeder	Lotus	24	Climax	V8	93		16	8
11	24	H Sharp	Cooper	T53	Climax	4	91		14	7
12	9	T Taylor	Lotus	25	Climax	V8	85		8	4
13	11	J Bonnier	Porsche	804	Porsche	F8	79		9	5
r	5	R Ginther	BRM	P57	BRM	V8	35	gearbox oil leak	2	1
r	6	M Trintignant	Lotus	24	Climax	V8	32	brake fluid leak	17	9
r	23	T Mayer	Cooper	T53	Climax	4	31	gear lever	11	6
r	18	J Surtees	Lola	Mk 4	Climax	V8	19	oil line	18	9
r	12	C G de Beaufort	Porsche	718	Porsche	F4	9	accident	13	7
ns	19	R Salvadori	Lola	Mk 4	Climax	V8		car raced by Surtees		
ns	25	J Hall	Lotus	21	Climax	4		dropped valve		
ns	11	P Hill	Porsche	804	Porsche	F8		not a serious attempt		

Winning speed 174.576 km/h, 108.476 mph
Pole Position speed 175.796 km/h, 109.235 mph (J Clark, 1 min:15.800 sec)
Fastest Lap speed 177.672 km/h, 110.400 mph (J Clark, 1 min:15.000 sec on lap 70)
Lap Leaders J Clark 1-11,19-100 (93); G Hill 12-18 (7).

---

29 Dec 1962　　　**SOUTH AFRICA: East London**　　　　　　　　　　**(Round 9)**　　**(Race 111)**

82 laps x 3.920 km, 2.436 miles = 321.470 km, 199.752 miles

Pos	No	Driver	Car	Model	Engine		Laps	Time/Reason for Retirement	Grid Pos	Row
1	3	G Hill	BRM	P57	BRM	V8	82	2h 08m 03.300s	2	1
2	8	B McLaren	Cooper	T60	Climax	V8	82	2h 08m 53.100s	8	4
3	9	T Maggs	Cooper	T60	Climax	V8	82	2h 08m 53.600s	6	3
4	10	J Brabham	Brabham	BT3	Climax	V8	82	2h 08m 57.100s	3	2
5	11	I Ireland	Lotus	24	Climax	V8	81		4	2
6	20	N Lederle	Lotus	21	Climax	4	78		10	5
7	4	R Ginther	BRM	P57	BRM	V8	78		7	4
8	18	J Love	Cooper	T55	Climax	4	78		12	6
9	5	B Johnstone	BRM	P48/57	BRM	V8	76		17	9
10	14	E Pieterse	Lotus	21	Climax	4	71		13	7
11r	15	C G de Beaufort	Porsche	718	Porsche	F4	70	fuel pump	16	8
r	21	D Serrurier	LDS	Mk 2	Alfa Romeo	4	62	radiator	14	7
r	1	J Clark	Lotus	25	Climax	V8	61	oil leak	1	1
r	7	R Salvadori	Lola	Mk 4	Climax	V8	56	fuel tank	11	6
r	22	M Harris	Cooper	T53	Alfa Romeo	4	31	big end bearings	15	8
r	6	J Surtees	Lola	Mk 4	Climax	V8	26	valve	5	3
r	2	T Taylor	Lotus	25	Climax	V8	11	gearbox	9	5

Winning speed 150.624 km/h, 93.594 mph
Pole Position speed 158.044 km/h, 98.204 mph (J Clark, 1 min:29.300 sec)
Fastest Lap speed 155.091 km/h, 96.369 mph (J Clark, 1 min:31.000 sec on lap 3)
Lap Leaders J Clark 1-61 (61); G Hill 62-82 (21).

Lap Leaders 1962

Pos	Driver	Car-Engine	GPs	laps	km	miles
1	G Hill	BRM	8	321	1,721.7	1,069.8
2	J Clark	Lotus-Climax	6	267	1,349.6	838.6
3	D Gurney	Porsche	2	15	130.7	81.2
4	B McLaren	Cooper-Climax	1	14	44.0	27.4
5	T Taylor	Lotus-Climax	1	5	70.5	43.8
6	W Mairesse	Ferrari	1	2	28.2	17.5
			9	624	3,344.7	2,078.3

Driver Points 1962

		NL	MC	B	F	GB	D	I	USA	ZA	Total	
1	G Hill	9	(1)	6	-	(3)	9	9	(6)	9	42	(10)
2	J Clark	-	-	9	-	9	3	-	9	-	30	
3	B McLaren	-	9	-	(3)	4	(2)	4	4	6	27	(5)
4	J Surtees	-	3	2	2	6	6	-	-	-	19	
5	D Gurney	-	-	-	9	-	4	-	2	-	15	
6	P Hill	4	6	4	-	-	-	-	-	-	14	
7	T Maggs	2	-	-	6	1	-	-	-	4	13	
8	R Ginther	-	-	-	4	-	-	6	-	-	10	
9	J Brabham	-	-	1	-	2	-	-	3	3	9	
10	T Taylor	6	-	-	-	-	-	-	-	-	6	
11	G Baghetti	3	-	-	-	-	-	2	-	-	5	
12	L Bandini	-	4	-	-	-	-	-	-	-	4	
	R Rodríguez	-	-	3	-	-	1	-	-	-	4	
14	W Mairesse	-	-	-	-	-	-	3	-	-	3	
	J Bonnier	-	2	-	-	-	-	1	-	-	3	
16	I Ireland	-	-	-	-	-	-	-	-	2	2	
	C G de Beaufort	1	-	-	1	-	-	-	-	-	2	
18	M Gregory	-	-	-	-	-	-	-	1	-	1	
	N Lederle	-	-	-	-	-	-	-	-	1	1	

9,6,4,3,2 and 1 point awarded to the first six finishers. Best 5 scores.

Constructor Points 1962

		NL	MC	B	F	GB	D	I	USA	ZA	Total	
1	BRM	9	(1)	6	(4)	(3)	9	9	(6)	9	42	(14)
2	Lotus-Climax	6	-	9	-	9	3	-	9	(2)	36	(2)
3	Cooper-Climax	(2)	9	-	6	4	(2)	4	(4)	6	29	(8)
4	Lola-Climax	-	3	2	2	6	6	-	-	-	19	
5	Porsche	1	2	-	9	-	4	(1)	2	-	18	(1)
	Ferrari	4	6	4	-	-	1	3	-	-	18	
7	Brabham-Climax	-	-	-	-	-	-	-	3	3	6	
8	Lotus-BRM	-	-	-	-	-	-	-	1	-	1	

9,6,4,3,2 and 1 point awarded to the first six finishers. Points only for highest placed car. Best 5 scores.

1963

Race Entrants and Results

Surtees joined Ferrari which, along with BRM, produced its first semi-monocoque. The factory Porsche effort closed with Gurney moving to the emerging Brabham team. Drivers now had to cover two-thirds race distance to be classified.

FERRARI
Scuderia Ferrari SpA SEFAC: Surtees, Bandini, Mairesse, Scarfiotti

ATS
Automobili Turismo e Sport: P Hill, Baghetti

DE TOMASO
Scuderia Settecolli: (Lippi)

BRABHAM
Brabham Racing Organisation: Brabham, Gurney
Privateer: Prophet

BRP
British Racing Partnership: Ireland

BRM
Owen Racing Organisation: G Hill, Ginther
Scuderia Centro Sud: Bandini, Trintignant, Solana

COOPER
Cooper Car Co: McLaren, Maggs
R R C Walker Racing Team: Bonnier
Scuderia Centro Sud: Cabral, (Brambilla)
Scuderia Lupini: Blokdyk
Privateers: Love, (Dochnal)

LOTUS
Team Lotus: Clark, Taylor, Rodríguez, Spence, (Arundell)
British Racing Partnership: Hall, Ireland
Reg Parnell (Racing): Sharp, Trintignant, Hailwood, Amon, Ward, Gregory (GB)
Tim Parnell: Gregory, (Pilette, Parnell)
Brabham Racing Organisation: Brabham
Ecurie Filipinetti: P Hill
Siffert Racing Team: Siffert
Ted Lanfear: Niemann
Selby Auto Spares: (Driver)
Privateers: Collomb, Pieterse, (Kuhnke, Pilette (I))

GILBY
Ian Raby (Racing): Raby

LOLA
Reg Parnell (Racing): Amon, Gregory, Trintignant, Bianchi, Hailwood
Tim Parnell: Campbell-Jones
DW Racing Enterprises: Anderson

SCIROCCO
Scirocco-Powell (Racing Cars): Settember, Burgess

STEBRO
Canadian Stebro Racing: Broeker

PORSCHE
Ecurie Maarsbergen: de Beaufort, Mitter

ALFA SPECIAL
Otelle Nucci: de Klerk

LDS
Otelle Nucci: Serrurier
Privateer: Tingle

26 May 1963		**MONACO: Monte-Carlo**							**(Round 1)**	**(Race 112)**	
		100 laps x 3.145 km, 1.954 miles = 314.500 km, 195.421 miles									
Pos	**No**	**Driver**	**Car**	**Model**	**Engine**		**Laps**	**Time/Reason for Retirement**		**Grid Pos**	**Row**
1	6	G Hill	BRM	P57	BRM	V8	100	2h 41m 49.700s		2	1
2	5	R Ginther	BRM	P57	BRM	V8	100	2h 41m 54.300s		4	2
3	7	B McLaren	Cooper	T66	Climax	V8	100	2h 42m 02.500s		8	4
4	21	J Surtees	Ferrari	156	Ferrari	V6	100	2h 42m 03.800s		3	2
5	8	T Maggs	Cooper	T66	Climax	V8	98			10	5
6	10	T Taylor	Lotus	25	Climax	V8	98			9	5
7	11	J Bonnier	Cooper	T60	Climax	V8	94			11	6
8r	9	J Clark	Lotus	25	Climax	V8	78	gear selection / accident		1	1
9	3	J Brabham	Lotus	25	Climax	V8	77			15	8
r	14	I Ireland	Lotus	24	BRM	V8	40	gearbox / accident		5	3
r	20	W Mairesse	Ferrari	156	Ferrari	V6	37	clutch		7	4
r	17	M Trintignant	Lola	Mk 4A	Climax	V8	34	oil loss / engine		14	7
r	4	D Gurney	Brabham	BT7	Climax	V8	25	crown wheel & pinion		6	3
r	12	J Hall	Lotus	24	BRM	V8	20	gearbox		13	7
r	25	J Siffert	Lotus	24	BRM	V8	3	engine		12	6
ns	15	C Amon	Lola	Mk 4A	Climax	V8		car raced by Trintignant			
nq	24	B Collomb	Lotus	24	Climax	V8		too slow			

Winning speed 116.605 km/h, 72.455 mph
Pole Position speed 120.064 km/h, 74.604 mph (J Clark, 1 min:34.300 sec)
Fastest Lap speed 119.810 km/h, 74.446 mph (J Surtees, 1 min:34.500 sec on lap 100)
Lap Leaders G Hill 1-17,79-100 (39); J Clark 18-78 (61).

Also the Grand Prix of Europe.

9 Jun 1963   BELGIUM: Spa-Francorchamps   (Round 2)   (Race 113)

32 laps x 14.100 km, 8.761 miles = 451.200 km, 280.363 miles

Pos	No	Driver	Car	Model	Engine		Laps	Time/Reason for Retirement	Grid Pos	Row
1	1	J Clark	Lotus	25	Climax	V8	32	2h 27m 47.600s	8	3
2	14	B McLaren	Cooper	T66	Climax	V8	32	2h 32m 41.600s	5	2
3	18	D Gurney	Brabham	BT7	Climax	V8	31		2	1
4	8	R Ginther	BRM	P57	BRM	V8	31		9	4
5	12	J Bonnier	Cooper	T60	Climax	V8	30		13	5
6	29	C G de Beaufort	Porsche	718	Porsche	F4	30		18	7
7r	15	T Maggs	Cooper	T66	Climax	V8	27	spin	4	2
8r	24	T Settember	Scirocco	SP	BRM	V8	25	spin	19	8
r	9	J Surtees	Ferrari	156	Ferrari	V6	19	fuel feed	10	4
r	7	G Hill	BRM	P57	BRM	V8	17	gearbox	1	1
r	22	L Bianchi	Lola	Mk 4	Climax	V8	17	accident	16	7
r	5	J Hall	Lotus	24	BRM	V8	16	accident	12	5
r	28	J Siffert	Lotus	24	BRM	V8	16	spin	14	6
r	26	P Hill	ATS	100	ATS	V8	13	gearbox	17	7
r	17	J Brabham	Brabham	BT3	Climax	V8	12	fuel injection pump	6	3
r	21	C Amon	Lola	Mk 4A	Climax	V8	10	oil leak	15	6
r	4	I Ireland	BRP	Mk 1	BRM	V8	9	gearbox	7	3
r	27	G Baghetti	ATS	100	ATS	V8	7	gearbox	20	8
r	10	W Mairesse	Ferrari	156	Ferrari	V6	7	dropped valve	3	1
r	2	T Taylor	Lotus	25	Climax	V8	5	oil pressure	11	5

Winning speed 183.175 km/h, 113.819 mph
Pole Position speed 216.830 km/h, 134.732 mph (G Hill, 3 min:54.100 sec)
Fastest Lap speed 213.188 km/h, 132.469 mph (J Clark, 3 min:58.100 sec on lap 16)
Lap Leaders J Clark 1-32 (32).

23 Jun 1963   NETHERLANDS: Zandvoort   (Round 3)   (Race 114)

80 laps x 4.193 km, 2.605 miles = 335.440 km, 208.433 miles

Pos	No	Driver	Car	Model	Engine		Laps	Time/Reason for Retirement	Grid Pos	Row
1	6	J Clark	Lotus	25	Climax	V8	80	2h 08m 13.700s	1	1
2	18	D Gurney	Brabham	BT7	Climax	V8	79		14	6
3	2	J Surtees	Ferrari	156	Ferrari	V6	79		5	2
4	30	I Ireland	BRP	Mk 1	BRM	V8	79		7	3
5	14	R Ginther	BRM	P57	BRM	V8	79		6	3
6	4	L Scarfiotti	Ferrari	156	Ferrari	V6	78		11	5
7	36	J Siffert	Lotus	24	BRM	V8	77		17	7
8	42	J Hall	Lotus	24	BRM	V8	77		18	7
9	32	C G de Beaufort	Porsche	718	Porsche	F4	75		19	8
r	12	G Hill	BRM	P57	BRM	V8	69	engine overheating	2	1
r	16	J Brabham	Brabham	BT7	Climax	V8	68	spin / chassis	4	2
10	8	T Taylor	Lotus	25	Climax	V8	66		10	4
11	28	J Bonnier	Cooper	T60	Climax	V8	56		8	3
r	10	C Amon	Lola	Mk 4A	Climax	V8	29	water pump	12	5
r	26	G Baghetti	ATS	100	ATS	V8	17	ignition	15	6
r	24	P Hill	ATS	100	ATS	V8	15	rear stub axle	13	5
r	22	T Maggs	Cooper	T66	Climax	V8	14	engine overheating	9	4
r	20	B McLaren	Cooper	T66	Climax	V8	7	gearbox	3	1
r	34	G Mitter	Porsche	718	Porsche	F4	2	clutch	16	7

Winning speed 156.958 km/h, 97.529 mph
Pole Position speed 164.790 km/h, 102.396 mph (J Clark, 1 min:31.600 sec)
Fastest Lap speed 161.097 km/h, 100.101 mph (J Clark, 1 min:33.700 sec on lap 56)
Lap Leaders J Clark 1-80 (80).

30 Jun 1963   FRANCE: Reims   (Round 4)   (Race 115)

53 laps x 8.302 km, 5.159 miles = 440.006 km, 273.407 miles

Pos	No	Driver	Car	Model	Engine		Laps	Time/Reason for Retirement	Grid Pos	Row
1	18	J Clark	Lotus	25	Climax	V8	53	2h 10m 54.300s	1	1
2	12	T Maggs	Cooper	T66	Climax	V8	53	2h 11m 59.200s	8	3
3	2	G Hill	BRM	P61	BRM	V8	53	2h 13m 08.200s*	2	1
4	6	J Brabham	Brabham	BT7	Climax	V8	53	2h 13m 09.500s	5	2
5	8	D Gurney	Brabham	BT7	Climax	V8	53	2h 13m 27.700s	3	1
6	36	J Siffert	Lotus	24	BRM	V8	52		10	4
7	30	C Amon	Lola	Mk 4A	Climax	V8	51		15	6
8	28	M Trintignant	Lotus	24	Climax	V8	50		14	6
9	32	I Ireland	BRP	Mk 1	BRM	V8	49		9	4
10	46	L Bandini	BRM	P57	BRM	V8	45		19	8
11	34	J Hall	Lotus	24	BRM	V8	45		16	7
12r	10	B McLaren	Cooper	T66	Climax	V8	42	ignition	6	3
13r	20	T Taylor	Lotus	25	Climax	V8	41	crown wheel & pinion	7	3
nc	42	P Hill	Lotus	24	BRM	V8	34		13	5
nc	44	J Bonnier	Cooper	T60	Climax	V8	32		11	5
r	48	M Gregory	Lotus	24	BRM	V8	30	gearbox	17	7
r	16	J Surtees	Ferrari	156	Ferrari	V6	12	fuel pump	4	2
r	38	T Settember	Scirocco	SP	BRM	V8	5	rear hub bearing	18	7
r	4	R Ginther	BRM	P57	BRM	V8	4	radiator	12	5
ns	14	L Scarfiotti	Ferrari	156	Ferrari	V6		accident / injury		
ns	22	P Arundell	Lotus	25	Climax	V8		drove in different race		

Winning speed 201.676 km/h, 125.315 mph
Pole Position speed 213.175 km/h, 132.461 mph (J Clark, 2 min:20.200 sec)
Fastest Lap speed 211.068 km/h, 131.151 mph (J Clark, 2 min:21.600 sec on lap 12)
Lap Leaders J Clark 1-53 (53).

* G. Hill's time includes a 1 minute penalty for receiving a push start.

20 Jul 1963   BRITAIN: Silverstone   (Round 5)   (Race 116)

82 laps x 4.711 km, 2.927 miles = 386.265 km, 240.014 miles

Pos	No	Driver	Car	Model	Engine		Laps	Time/Reason for Retirement	Grid Pos	Row
1	4	J Clark	Lotus	25	Climax	V8	82	2h 14m 09.600s	1	1
2	10	J Surtees	Ferrari	156	Ferrari	V6	82	2h 14m 35.400s	5	2
3	1	G Hill	BRM	P57	BRM	V8	82	2h 14m 47.200s	3	1
4	2	R Ginther	BRM	P57	BRM	V8	81		9	3
5	3	L Bandini	BRM	P57	BRM	V8	81		8	3
6	12	J Hall	Lotus	24	BRM	V8	80		13	4
7	19	C Amon	Lola	Mk 4A	Climax	V8	80		14	4
8	20	M Hailwood	Lotus	24	Climax	V8	78		17	5
9	7	T Maggs	Cooper	T66	Climax	V8	78		7	2
10	23	C G de Beaufort	Porsche	718	Porsche	F4	76		21	6
11	21	M Gregory	Lotus	24	BRM	V8	75		22	7
12	22	B Anderson	Lola	Mk 4	Climax	V8	75		16	5
13	24	J Campbell-Jones	Lola	Mk 4	Climax	V8	74		23	7
r	25	J Siffert	Lotus	24	BRM	V8	66	gearbox	15	5
r	14	J Bonnier	Cooper	T66	Climax	V8	65	oil pressure	12	4
r	26	I Raby	Gilby	(62)	BRM	V8	59	gearbox	19	6
r	9	D Gurney	Brabham	BT7	Climax	V8	59	engine	2	1
r	16	I Burgess	Scirocco	SP	BRM	V8	36	ignition	20	6
r	8	J Brabham	Brabham	BT7	Climax	V8	27	engine	4	1
dq	11	I Ireland	BRP	Mk 1	BRM	V8	26	push start in pits	11	3
dq	5	T Taylor	Lotus	25	Climax	V8	23	push start in pits	10	3
r	15	T Settember	Scirocco	SP	BRM	V8	20	ignition	18	5
r	6	B McLaren	Cooper	T66	Climax	V8	6	engine	6	2

Winning speed 172.748 km/h, 107.341 mph
Pole Position speed 179.640 km/h, 111.623 mph (J Clark, 1 min:34.400 sec)
Fastest Lap speed 176.646 km/h, 109.763 mph (J Surtees, 1 min:36.000 sec on lap 3)
Lap Leaders J Brabham 1-3 (3); J Clark 4-82 (79).

4 Aug 1963		**GERMANY: Nürburgring**								**(Round 6)**	**(Race 117)**
		15 laps x 22.810 km, 14.173 miles = 342.150 km, 212.602 miles									

Pos	No	Driver	Car	Model	Engine		Laps	Time/Reason for Retirement	Grid Pos	Row
1	7	J Surtees	Ferrari	156	Ferrari	V6	15	2h 13m 06.800s	2	1
2	3	J Clark	Lotus	25	Climax	V8	15	2h 14m 24.300s	1	1
3	2	R Ginther	BRM	P57	BRM	V8	15	2h 15m 51.700s	6	2
4	26	G Mitter	Porsche	718	Porsche	F4	15	2h 21m 18.300s	15	5
5	20	J Hall	Lotus	24	BRM	V8	14		16	5
6	16	J Bonnier	Cooper	T66	Climax	V8	14		12	4
7	9	J Brabham	Brabham	BT7	Climax	V8	14		8	3
8	4	T Taylor	Lotus	25	Climax	V8	14		18	5
9r	18	J Siffert	Lotus	24	BRM	V8	10	differential	9	3
10	28	B Collomb	Lotus	24	Climax	V8	10		21	6
r	17	C G de Beaufort	Porsche	718	Porsche	F4	9	rear wheel lost	17	5
r	6	T Maggs	Cooper	T66	Climax	V8	7	camshaft	10	3
r	10	D Gurney	Brabham	BT7	Climax	V8	6	gearbox	13	4
r	22	M Cabral	Cooper	T60	Climax	V8	6	gearbox	20	6
r	24	I Burgess	Scirocco	SP	BRM	V8	5	steering	19	6
r	23	T Settember	Scirocco	SP	BRM	V8	5	accident	22	7
r	5	B McLaren	Cooper	T66	Climax	V8	3	accident	5	2
r	21	C Amon	Lola	Mk 4A	Climax	V8	2	steering / accident	14	4
r	1	G Hill	BRM	P57	BRM	V8	2	gearbox	4	1
r	8	W Mairesse	Ferrari	156	Ferrari	V6	1	accident	7	2
r	14	I Ireland	Lotus	24	BRM	V8	1	accident	11	3
r	15	L Bandini	BRM	P57	BRM	V8	0	accident	3	1
nq	29	A Pilette	Lotus	18/21	Climax	4				
nq	25	I Raby	Gilby	(62)	BRM	V8				
nq	30	T Parnell	Lotus	18/21	Climax	4				
nq	27	K Kuhnke	Lotus	18	Borgward	4				

Winning speed 154.222 km/h, 95.829 mph
Pole Position speed 156.173 km/h, 97.042 mph (J Clark, 8 min:45.800 sec)
Fastest Lap speed 155.818 km/h, 96.821 mph (J Surtees, 8 min:47.000 sec on lap 9)
Lap Leaders R Ginther 1 (1); J Surtees 2-3,5-15 (13); J Clark 4 (1).

8 Sep 1963		**ITALY: Monza**								**(Round 7)**	**(Race 118)**
		86 laps x 5.750 km, 3.573 miles = 494.500 km, 307.268 miles									

Pos	No	Driver	Car	Model	Engine		Laps	Time/Reason for Retirement	Grid Pos	Row
1	8	J Clark	Lotus	25	Climax	V8	86	2h 24m 19.600s	3	2
2	10	R Ginther	BRM	P57	BRM	V8	86	2h 25m 54.600s	4	2
3	18	B McLaren	Cooper	T66	Climax	V8	85		8	4
4r	32	I Ireland	BRP	Mk 1	BRM	V8	84	engine	10	5
5	22	J Brabham	Brabham	BT3	Climax	V8	84		7	4
6	20	T Maggs	Cooper	T66	Climax	V8	84		13	7
7	58	J Bonnier	Cooper	T66	Climax	V8	84		11	6
8	30	J Hall	Lotus	24	BRM	V8	84		16	8
9	66	M Trintignant	BRM	P57	BRM	V8	83		19	10
10	40	M Hailwood	Lola	Mk 4	Climax	V8	82		17	9
11	16	P Hill	ATS	100	ATS	V8	79		14	7
12	48	B Anderson	Lola	Mk 4	Climax	V8	79		18	9
13r	6	M Spence	Lotus	25	Climax	V8	73	oil pressure	9	5
14r	24	D Gurney	Brabham	BT7	Climax	V8	64	fuel injection	5	3
15	14	G Baghetti	ATS	100	ATS	V8	63		20	10
16r	12	G Hill	BRM	P61	BRM	V8	59	clutch	2	1
r	54	J Siffert	Lotus	24	BRM	V8	40	oil pressure	15	8
r	2	L Bandini	Ferrari	156	Ferrari	V6	37	gearbox	6	3
r	42	M Gregory	Lotus	24	BRM	V8	26	cam follower	12	6
r	4	J Surtees	Ferrari	156	Ferrari	V6	16	engine	1	1
ns	38	C Amon	Lola	Mk 4A	Climax	V8		accident / injury		
nq	64	M Cabral	Cooper	T60	Climax	V8				
nq	50	I Raby	Gilby	(62)	BRM	V8				
nq	34	T Settember	Scirocco	SP	BRM	V8				
nq	28	C G de Beaufort	Porsche	718	Porsche	F4				
nq	62	T Brambilla	Cooper	T53	Maserati	4				
nq	46	A Pilette	Lotus	18/21	Climax	4				
nq	44	R Lippi	De Tomaso	F1	Ferrari	V6				

Winning speed 205.575 km/h, 127.739 mph
Pole Position speed 212.744 km/h, 132.193 mph (J Surtees, 1 min:37.300 sec)
Fastest Lap speed 209.302 km/h, 130.054 mph (J Clark, 1 min:38.900 sec on lap 60)
Lap Leaders G Hill 1-3,24-26,29-30,32,34-35,39,41 (13); J Surtees 4-16 (13); J Clark 17-22,28,36,40,42-43,45,47-51,53-54,56-86 (50);
D Gurney 23,27,31,33,37-38,44,46,52,55 (10).

6 Oct 1963   **USA: Watkins Glen**   **(Round 8)**   **(Race 119)**

110 laps x 3.701 km, 2.300 miles = 407.164 km, 253.000 miles

Pos	No	Driver	Car	Model	Engine		Laps	Time/Reason for Retirement	Grid Pos	Row
1	1	G Hill	BRM	P57	BRM	V8	110	2h 19m 22.100s	1	1
2	2	R Ginther	BRM	P57	BRM	V8	110	2h 19m 56.400s	4	2
3	8	J Clark	Lotus	25	Climax	V8	109		2	1
4	5	J Brabham	Brabham	BT7	Climax	V8	108		5	3
5	24	L Bandini	Ferrari	156	Ferrari	V6	106		9	5
6	12	C G de Beaufort	Porsche	718	Porsche	F4	99		19	10
7	21	P Broeker	Stebro	Mk IV	Ford	4	88		21	11
8	11	J Bonnier	Cooper	T66	Climax	V8	85		12	6
9r	23	J Surtees	Ferrari	156	Ferrari	V6	82	valve spring	3	2
10r	16	J Hall	Lotus	24	BRM	V8	76	gearbox	16	8
11r	3	B McLaren	Cooper	T66	Climax	V8	74	fuel pump	11	6
r	14	J Siffert	Lotus	24	BRM	V8	56	gearbox	14	7
r	18	R Ward	Lotus	24	BRM	V8	44	gearbox	17	9
r	4	T Maggs	Cooper	T66	Climax	V8	44	engine	10	5
r	6	D Gurney	Brabham	BT7	Climax	V8	42	chassis	6	3
r	10	P Rodríguez	Lotus	25	Climax	V8	36	camshaft / piston	13	7
r	9	T Taylor	Lotus	25	Climax	V8	24	ignition	7	4
r	17	M Gregory	Lola	Mk 4A	Climax	V8	14	oil pressure / engine overheating	8	4
r	22	H Sharp	Lotus	24	BRM	V8	6	tappet	18	9
r	25	P Hill	ATS	100	ATS	V8	4	oil pump	15	8
r	26	G Baghetti	ATS	100	ATS	V8	0	oil pump	20	10

Winning speed 175.290 km/h, 108.920 mph
Pole Position speed 181.545 km/h, 112.807 mph (G Hill, 1 min:13.400 sec)
Fastest Lap speed 178.864 km/h, 111.141 mph (J Clark, 1 min:14.500 sec on lap 50, 59 & 61)
Lap Leaders G Hill 1-6,32,35,83-110 (36); J Surtees 7-31,33-34,36-82 (74).

---

27 Oct 1963   **MEXICO: Mexico City**   **(Round 9)**   **(Race 120)**

65 laps x 5.000 km, 3.107 miles = 325.000 km, 201.946 miles

Pos	No	Driver	Car	Model	Engine		Laps	Time/Reason for Retirement	Grid Pos	Row
1	8	J Clark	Lotus	25	Climax	V8	65	2h 09m 52.100s	1	1
2	5	J Brabham	Brabham	BT7	Climax	V8	65	2h 11m 33.200s	10	5
3	2	R Ginther	BRM	P57	BRM	V8	65	2h 11m 46.800s	5	3
4	1	G Hill	BRM	P57	BRM	V8	64		3	2
5	11	J Bonnier	Cooper	T66	Climax	V8	62		8	4
6	6	D Gurney	Brabham	BT7	Climax	V8	62		4	2
7	22	H Sharp	Lotus	24	BRM	V8	61		16	8
8	16	J Hall	Lotus	24	BRM	V8	61		15	8
9	14	J Siffert	Lotus	24	BRM	V8	59		9	5
10	12	C G de Beaufort	Porsche	718	Porsche	F4	58		18	9
11r	13	M Solana	BRM	P57	BRM	V8	57	cam follower	11	6
r	25	P Hill	ATS	100	ATS	V8	40	rear suspension	17	9
r	24	L Bandini	Ferrari	156	Ferrari	V6	36	engine	7	4
r	3	B McLaren	Cooper	T66	Climax	V8	30	camshaft	6	3
r	10	P Rodríguez	Lotus	25	Climax	V8	26	rear suspension	20	10
r	17	M Gregory	Lola	Mk 4A	Climax	V8	23	rear suspension	14	7
r	9	T Taylor	Lotus	25	Climax	V8	19	cam follower	12	6
dq	23	J Surtees	Ferrari	156	Ferrari	V6	19	push start in pits	2	1
r	26	G Baghetti	ATS	100	ATS	V8	12	carburation	21	11
r	18	C Amon	Lotus	24	BRM	V8	9	gearbox	19	10
r	4	T Maggs	Cooper	T66	Climax	V8	7	engine	13	7
ns	20	F Dochnal	Cooper	T53	Climax	4		accident		

Winning speed 150.152 km/h, 93.300 mph
Pole Position speed 151.515 km/h, 94.147 mph (J Clark, 1 min:58.800 sec)
Fastest Lap speed 152.413 km/h, 94.705 mph (J Clark, 1 min:58.100 sec)
Lap Leaders J Clark 1-65 (65).

28 Dec 1963   **SOUTH AFRICA: East London**   **(Round 10)**   **(Race 121)**
85 laps x 3.920 km, 2.436 miles = 333.231 km, 207.060 miles

Pos	No	Driver	Car	Model	Engine		Laps	Time/Reason for Retirement	Grid Pos	Row
1	1	J Clark	Lotus	25	Climax	V8	85	2h 10m 36.900s	1	1
2	9	D Gurney	Brabham	BT7	Climax	V8	85	2h 11m 43.700s	3	1
3	5	G Hill	BRM	P57	BRM	V8	84		6	3
4	10	B McLaren	Cooper	T66	Climax	V8	84		9	4
5	4	L Bandini	Ferrari	156	Ferrari	V6	84		5	2
6	12	J Bonnier	Cooper	T66	Climax	V8	83		11	5
7	11	T Maggs	Cooper	T66	Climax	V8	82		10	4
8	2	T Taylor	Lotus	25	Climax	V8	81		8	3
9	19	J Love	Cooper	T55	Climax	4	80		13	5
10	14	C G de Beaufort	Porsche	718	Porsche	F4	79		20	8
11	16	D Serrurier	LDS	Mk 2	Alfa Romeo	4	78		18	7
12	23	T Blokdyk	Cooper	T51	Maserati	4	77		19	8
13r	8	J Brabham	Brabham	BT7	Climax	V8	70	accident	2	1
14	21	B Niemann	Lotus	22	Ford	4	66		15	6
r	18	P de Klerk	Alfa Special		Alfa Romeo	4	53	gearbox	16	7
r	22	D Prophet	Brabham	BT6	Ford	4	49	oil pressure	14	6
r	6	R Ginther	BRM	P57	BRM	V8	43	half shaft	7	3
r	3	J Surtees	Ferrari	156	Ferrari	V6	43	engine	4	2
r	7	E Pieterse	Lotus	21	Climax	4	3	engine	12	5
r	20	S Tingle	LDS	Mk 1	Alfa Romeo	4	2	half shaft	17	7
ns	15	P Driver	Lotus	24	BRM	V8		accident		

Winning speed 153.075 km/h, 95.116 mph
Pole Position speed 158.755 km/h, 98.646 mph (J Clark, 1 min:28.900 sec)
Fastest Lap speed 158.398 km/h, 98.424 mph (D Gurney, 1 min:29.100 sec on lap 33)
Lap Leaders J Clark 1-85 (85).

Lap Leaders 1963

Pos	Driver	Car-Engine	GPs	laps	km	miles
1	J Clark	Lotus-Climax	9	506	2,759.2	1,714.5
2	J Surtees	Ferrari	3	100	645.2	400.9
3	G Hill	BRM	3	88	330.6	205.5
4	D Gurney	Brabham-Climax	1	10	57.5	35.7
5	J Brabham	Brabham-Climax	1	3	14.1	8.8
6	R Ginther	BRM	1	1	22.8	14.2
			10	**708**	**3,829.4**	**2,379.5**

Driver Points 1963

		MC	B	NL	F	GB	D	I	USA	MEX	ZA	Total	
1	J Clark	-	9	9	9	9	(6)	9	(4)	9	(9)	54	(19)
2	G Hill	9	-	-	-	4	-	-	9	3	4	29	
	R Ginther	6	3	(2)	-	(3)	4	6	6	4	-	29	(5)
4	J Surtees	3	-	4	-	6	9	-	-	-	-	22	
5	D Gurney	-	4	6	2	-	-	-	-	1	6	19	
6	B McLaren	4	6	-	-	-	-	4	-	-	3	17	
7	J Brabham	-	-	-	3	-	-	2	3	6	-	14	
8	T Maggs	2	-	-	6	-	-	1	-	-	-	9	
9	I Ireland	-	-	3	-	-	-	3	-	-	-	6	
	L Bandini	-	-	-	-	2	-	-	2	-	2	6	
	J Bonnier	-	2	-	-	-	1	-	-	2	1	6	
12	G Mitter	-	-	-	-	-	3	-	-	-	-	3	
	J Hall	-	-	-	-	1	2	-	-	-	-	3	
14	C G de Beaufort	-	1	-	-	-	-	-	1	-	-	2	
15	T Taylor	1	-	-	-	-	-	-	-	-	-	1	
	L Scarfiotti	-	-	1	-	-	-	-	-	-	-	1	
	J Siffert	-	-	-	1	-	-	-	-	-	-	1	

9,6,4,3,2 and 1 point awarded to the first six finishers. Best 6 scores. G Hill (BRM)
was classified 3rd in France, but awarded no points because he was push-started on the grid.

Constructor Points 1963

		MC	B	NL	F	GB	D	I	USA	MEX	ZA	Total	
1	Lotus-Climax	(1)	9	9	9	9	(6)	9	(4)	9	(9)	54	(20)
2	BRM	9	(3)	(2)	-	4	4	6	9	4	(4)	36	(9)
3	Brabham-Climax	-	4	6	3	-	-	(2)	3	6	6	28	(2)
4	Ferrari	3	-	4	-	6	9	-	2	-	2	26	
5	Cooper-Climax	4	6	-	6	-	(1)	4	-	2	3	25	(1)
6	BRP-BRM	-	-	3	-	-	-	3	-	-	-	6	
7	Porsche	-	1	-	-	-	3	-	1	-	-	5	
8	Lotus-BRM	-	-	1	1	2	-	-	-	-	-	4	

9,6,4,3,2 and 1 point awarded to the first six finishers. Points only for highest placed car. Best 6 scores.

1964

Race Entrants and Results

New for this season was a full monocoque for BRM, with the P261 and the debut of Honda, with its transverse mounted V12 engine. John Surtees became the first man to win a world title on four as well as two wheels. A new 3-litre formula for 1966 was announced.

FERRARI
Scuderia Ferrari SpA SEFAC: Surtees, Bandini, Scarfiotti
North American Racing Team: Surtees, Bandini, Rodríguez (USA,MEX)

ATS
Derrington-Francis Racing Team: Cabral

BRABHAM
Brabham Racing Organisation: Brabham, Gurney
R R C Walker Racing Team: Bonnier, Siffert (USA,MEX), Sharp, Rindt, (Geki)
DW Racing Enterprises: Anderson
John Willment Automobiles: Gardner
Privateers: Siffert, Raby

BRM
Owen Racing Organisation: G Hill, Ginther, (Attwood)
Scuderia Centro Sud: Baghetti, Maggs
Privateer: Trintignant

COOPER
Cooper Car Co: McLaren, P Hill, (Love)
R R C Walker Racing Team: Bonnier, Barth
Bob Gerard Racing: J Taylor
Fabre Urbain: (Rudaz)

BRP
British Racing Partnership: Ireland, T Taylor

LOTUS
Team Lotus: Clark, Spence, Arundell, Mitter, Hansgen, Solana
Reg Parnell (Racing): Hailwood, Amon, Revson (B,F)
British Racing Partnership: T Taylor, (Ireland)
Privateers: Revson, Siffert, (Collomb)

PORSCHE
Ecurie Maarsbergen: de Beaufort

SCIROCCO
Equipe Scirocco Belge: Pilette

HONDA
Honda R & D Co: Bucknum

---

10 May 1964 **MONACO: Monte-Carlo** (Round 1) (Race 122)
100 laps x 3.145 km, 1.954 miles = 314.500 km, 195.421 miles

Pos	No	Driver	Car	Model	Engine		Laps	Time/Reason for Retirement	Grid Pos	Row
1	8	G Hill	BRM	P261	BRM	V8	100	2h 41m 19.500s	3	2
2	7	R Ginther	BRM	P261	BRM	V8	99		8	4
3	11	P Arundell	Lotus	25	Climax	V8	97		6	3
4r	12	J Clark	Lotus	25	Climax	V8	96	engine	1	1
5	19	J Bonnier	Cooper	T66	Climax	V8	96		11	6
6	18	M Hailwood	Lotus	25	BRM	V8	96		15	8
7r	16	B Anderson	Brabham	BT11	Climax	V8	86	gearbox mounting	12	6
8	24	J Siffert	Lotus	24	BRM	V8	78		16	8
9r	9	P Hill	Cooper	T73	Climax	V8	70	rear suspension	9	5
10r	20	L Bandini	Ferrari	156	Ferrari	V6	68	gearbox	7	4
r	6	D Gurney	Brabham	BT7	Climax	V8	62	gearbox	5	3
r	4	M Trintignant	BRM	P57	BRM	V8	53	driver exhausted	13	7
r	5	J Brabham	Brabham	BT7	Climax	V8	29	fuel injection	2	1
r	10	B McLaren	Cooper	T66	Climax	V8	17	oil leak	10	5
r	21	J Surtees	Ferrari	158	Ferrari	V8	15	gearbox	4	2
r	15	T Taylor	BRP	Mk 1	BRM	V8	8	fuel leak	14	7
ns	14	I Ireland	Lotus	24	BRM	V8		accident / injury		
nq	17	C Amon	Lotus	25	BRM	V8				
nq	2	P Revson	Lotus	24	BRM	V8				
nq	3	B Collomb	Lotus	24	Climax	V8				

Winning speed 116.969 km/h, 72.681 mph
Pole Position speed 120.447 km/h, 74.842 mph (J Clark, 1 min:34.000 sec)
Fastest Lap speed 120.575 km/h, 74.922 mph (G Hill, 1 min:33.900 sec on lap 53)
Lap Leaders J Clark 1-36 (36); D Gurney 37-52 (16); G Hill 53-100 (48).

24 May 1964　　**NETHERLANDS: Zandvoort**　　　　　　　　　　　　　　　　**(Round 2)**　　**(Race 123)**

80 laps x 4.193 km, 2.605 miles = 335.440 km, 208.433 miles

Pos	No	Driver	Car	Model	Engine		Laps	Time/Reason for Retirement	Grid Pos	Row
1	18	J Clark	Lotus	25	Climax	V8	80	2h 07m 35.400s	2	1
2	2	J Surtees	Ferrari	158	Ferrari	V8	80	2h 08m 29.000s	4	2
3	20	P Arundell	Lotus	25	Climax	V8	79		6	3
4	6	G Hill	BRM	P261	BRM	V8	79		3	1
5	10	C Amon	Lotus	25	BRM	V8	79		13	5
6	34	B Anderson	Brabham	BT11	Climax	V8	78		11	5
7	24	B McLaren	Cooper	T73	Climax	V8	78		5	2
8	22	P Hill	Cooper	T73	Climax	V8	76		9	4
9	26	J Bonnier	Brabham	BT11	BRM	V8	76		12	5
10	32	G Baghetti	BRM	P57	BRM	V8	74		16	7
11	8	R Ginther	BRM	P261	BRM	V8	64		8	3
12r	12	M Hailwood	Lotus	25	BRM	V8	57	crown wheel & pinion	14	6
13	36	J Siffert	Brabham	BT11	BRM	V8	55		18	7
r	14	J Brabham	Brabham	BT7	Climax	V8	44	ignition	7	3
r	16	D Gurney	Brabham	BT7	Climax	V8	23	steering wheel	1	1
r	4	L Bandini	Ferrari	158	Ferrari	V8	20	fuel injection pump	10	4
r	28	C G de Beaufort	Porsche	718	Porsche	F4	8	valve	17	7
ns	30	T Maggs	BRM	P57	BRM	V8		accident	15	6

Winning speed 157.743 km/h, 98.017 mph
Pole Position speed 165.513 km/h, 102.845 mph (D Gurney, 1 min:31.200 sec)
Fastest Lap speed 162.659 km/h, 101.072 mph (J Clark, 1 min:32.800 sec on lap 6)
Lap Leaders J Clark 1-80 (80).

---

14 Jun 1964　　**BELGIUM: Spa-Francorchamps**　　　　　　　　　　　　　　　　**(Round 3)**　　**(Race 124)**

32 laps x 14.100 km, 8.761 miles = 451.200 km, 280.363 miles

Pos	No	Driver	Car	Model	Engine		Laps	Time/Reason for Retirement	Grid Pos	Row
1	23	J Clark	Lotus	25	Climax	V8	32	2h 06m 40.500s	6	3
2	20	B McLaren	Cooper	T73	Climax	V8	32	2h 06m 43.900s	7	3
3	14	J Brabham	Brabham	BT7	Climax	V8	32	2h 07m 28.600s	3	1
4	2	R Ginther	BRM	P261	BRM	V8	32	2h 08m 39.100s	8	3
5r	1	G Hill	BRM	P261	BRM	V8	31	out of fuel	2	1
6r	15	D Gurney	Brabham	BT7	Climax	V8	31	out of fuel	1	1
7	4	T Taylor	BRP	Mk 2	BRM	V8	31		12	5
8	6	G Baghetti	BRM	P57	BRM	V8	31		17	7
9	24	P Arundell	Lotus	25	Climax	V8	28		4	2
10	3	I Ireland	BRP	Mk 1	BRM	V8	28		16	7
dq	29	P Revson	Lotus	24	BRM	V8	28	push start after engine cut	10	4
r	17	J Siffert	Brabham	BT11	BRM	V8	14	piston	13	5
r	21	P Hill	Cooper	T73	Climax	V8	13	connecting rod	15	6
r	11	L Bandini	Ferrari	158	Ferrari	V8	12	oil loss / engine	9	4
r	28	A Pilette	Scirocco	SP	Climax	V8	11	engine	18	7
r	16	J Bonnier	Brabham	BT11	BRM	V8	8	driver ill	14	6
r	27	C Amon	Lotus	25	BRM	V8	3	connecting rod	11	5
r	10	J Surtees	Ferrari	158	Ferrari	V8	3	piston	5	2
ns	7	T Maggs	BRM	P57	BRM	V8		engine		
ns	18	B Anderson	Brabham	BT11	Climax	V8		ignition		

Winning speed 213.712 km/h, 132.795 mph
Pole Position speed 219.835 km/h, 136.599 mph (D Gurney, 3 min:50.900 sec)
Fastest Lap speed 221.466 km/h, 137.613 mph (D Gurney, 3 min:49.200 sec on lap 27)
Lap Leaders D Gurney 1-2,4-29 (28); J Surtees 3 (1); G Hill 30-31 (2); J Clark 32 (1).

28 Jun 1964   FRANCE: Rouen-les-Essarts   (Round 4)   (Race 125)

57 laps x 6.542 km, 4.065 miles = 372.894 km, 231.706 miles

Pos	No	Driver	Car	Model	Engine		Laps	Time/Reason for Retirement	Grid Pos	Row
1	22	D Gurney	Brabham	BT7	Climax	V8	57	2h 07m 49.100s	2	1
2	8	G Hill	BRM	P261	BRM	V8	57	2h 08m 13.200s	6	3
3	20	J Brabham	Brabham	BT7	Climax	V8	57	2h 08m 14.000s	5	2
4	4	P Arundell	Lotus	25	Climax	V8	57	2h 08m 59.700s	4	2
5	10	R Ginther	BRM	P261	BRM	V8	57	2h 10m 01.200s	9	4
6	12	B McLaren	Cooper	T73	Climax	V8	56		7	3
7	14	P Hill	Cooper	T73	Climax	V8	56		10	4
8	6	M Hailwood	Lotus	25	BRM	V8	56		13	5
9	26	L Bandini	Ferrari	158	Ferrari	V8	55		8	3
10	34	C Amon	Lotus	25	BRM	V8	53		14	6
11	28	M Trintignant	BRM	P57	BRM	V8	52		16	7
12	19	B Anderson	Brabham	BT11	Climax	V8	50		15	6
r	16	I Ireland	BRP	Mk 1	BRM	V8	32	spin	11	5
r	2	J Clark	Lotus	25	Climax	V8	31	engine	1	1
r	24	J Surtees	Ferrari	158	Ferrari	V8	6	engine	3	1
r	18	T Taylor	BRP	Mk 2	BRM	V8	6	brakes / accident	12	5
r	30	J Siffert	Brabham	BT11	BRM	V8	4	clutch	17	7
ns	36	P Revson	Lotus	25	BRM	V8		car raced by Hailwood		

Winning speed 175.042 km/h, 108.766 mph
Pole Position speed 181.722 km/h, 112.917 mph (J Clark, 2 min: 9.600 sec)
Fastest Lap speed 179.233 km/h, 111.370 mph (J Brabham, 2 min:11.400 sec on lap 44)
Lap Leaders J Clark 1-30 (30); D Gurney 31-57 (27).

11 Jul 1964   BRITAIN: Brands Hatch   (Round 5)   (Race 126)

80 laps x 4.265 km, 2.650 miles = 341.181 km, 212.000 miles

Pos	No	Driver	Car	Model	Engine		Laps	Time/Reason for Retirement	Grid Pos	Row
1	1	J Clark	Lotus	25	Climax	V8	80	2h 15m 07.000s	1	1
2	3	G Hill	BRM	P261	BRM	V8	80	2h 15m 09.800s	2	1
3	7	J Surtees	Ferrari	158	Ferrari	V8	80	2h 16m 27.600s	5	2
4	5	J Brabham	Brabham	BT7	Climax	V8	79		4	2
5	8	L Bandini	Ferrari	156	Ferrari	V6	78		8	3
6	10	P Hill	Cooper	T73	Climax	V8	78		15	6
7	19	B Anderson	Brabham	BT11	Climax	V8	78		7	3
8	4	R Ginther	BRM	P261	BRM	V8	77		14	6
9	2	M Spence	Lotus	25	Climax	V8	77		13	5
10	11	I Ireland	BRP	Mk 2	BRM	V8	77		10	4
11	20	J Siffert	Brabham	BT11	BRM	V8	76		16	7
12	18	G Baghetti	BRM	P57	BRM	V8	76		21	9
13	6	D Gurney	Brabham	BT7	Climax	V8	75		3	1
14	22	J Taylor	Cooper	T73	Ford	4	56		20	8
r	16	J Bonnier	Brabham	BT11	BRM	V8	45	brake pipe	9	4
r	24	P Revson	Lotus	24	BRM	V8	43	engine	22	9
r	23	I Raby	Brabham	BT3	BRM	V8	37	rear hub	17	7
r	17	T Maggs	BRM	P57	BRM	V8	37	gearbox	23	9
r	12	T Taylor	Lotus	24	BRM	V8	23	driver unfit (practice accident)	18	7
r	14	M Hailwood	Lotus	25	BRM	V8	17	oil line	12	5
r	15	C Amon	Lotus	25	BRM	V8	9	clutch	11	5
r	9	B McLaren	Cooper	T73	Climax	V8	7	gearbox	6	3
r	26	F Gardner	Brabham	BT10	Ford	4	0	accident	19	8
ns	21	D Attwood	BRM	P67	BRM	V8		withdrew		
nq	25	M Trintignant	BRM	P57	BRM	V8				

Winning speed 151.505 km/h, 94.141 mph
Pole Position speed 156.505 km/h, 97.248 mph (J Clark, 1 min:38.100 sec)
Fastest Lap speed 155.396 km/h, 96.559 mph (J Clark, 1 min:38.800 sec on lap 73)
Lap Leaders J Clark 1-80 (80).

Also the Grand Prix of Europe.

2 Aug 1964		**GERMANY: Nürburgring**						**(Round 6)**	**(Race 127)**	

15 laps x 22.810 km, 14.173 miles = 342.150 km, 212.602 miles

Pos	No	Driver	Car	Model	Engine		Laps	Time/Reason for Retirement	Grid Pos	Row
1	7	J Surtees	Ferrari	158	Ferrari	V8	15	2h 12m 04.800s	1	1
2	3	G Hill	BRM	P261	BRM	V8	15	2h 13m 20.400s	5	2
3	8	L Bandini	Ferrari	156	Ferrari	V6	15	2h 16m 57.600s	4	1
4	19	J Siffert	Brabham	BT11	BRM	V8	15	2h 17m 27.900s	10	3
5r	22	M Trintignant	BRM	P57	BRM	V8	14	battery	14	4
6	26	T Maggs	BRM	P57	BRM	V8	14		16	5
7	4	R Ginther	BRM	P261	BRM	V8	14		11	3
8	2	M Spence	Lotus	33	Climax	V8	14		17	5
9	23	G Mitter	Lotus	25	Climax	V8	14		19	6
10	5	D Gurney	Brabham	BT7	Climax	V8	14		3	1
11r	14	C Amon	Lotus	25	BRM	V8	12	steeering / accident	9	3
12r	6	J Brabham	Brabham	BT11	Climax	V8	11	crown wheel & pinion	6	2
13r	20	R Bucknum	Honda	RA271	Honda	V12	11	spin	22	7
14r	27	P Revson	Lotus	24	BRM	V8	10	accident	18	5
r	1	J Clark	Lotus	33	Climax	V8	7	valve gear	2	1
r	9	B McLaren	Cooper	T73	Climax	V8	4	valve spring	7	2
r	16	B Anderson	Brabham	BT11	Climax	V8	4	suspension	15	5
r	12	E Barth	Cooper	T66	Climax	V8	3	clutch	20	6
r	18	G Baghetti	BRM	P57	BRM	V8	2	throttle control	21	6
r	10	P Hill	Cooper	T73	Climax	V8	1	engine	8	3
r	11	J Bonnier	Brabham	BT11	BRM	V8	0	ignition	12	4
r	15	M Hailwood	Lotus	25	BRM	V8	0	engine	13	4
ns	29	C G de Beaufort	Porsche	718	Porsche	F4		fatal accident		
nq	28	A Pilette	Scirocco	SP	Climax	V8				

Winning speed 155.429 km/h, 96.579 mph
Pole Position speed 158.403 km/h, 98.427 mph (J Surtees, 8 min:38.400 sec)
Fastest Lap speed 158.220 km/h, 98.313 mph (J Surtees, 8 min:39.000 sec on lap 11)
Lap Leaders J Clark 1 (1); J Surtees 2-3,5-15 (13); D Gurney 4 (1).

23 Aug 1964		**AUSTRIA: Zeltweg**						**(Round 7)**	**(Race 128)**	

105 laps x 3.200 km, 1.988 miles = 336.000 km, 208.781 miles

Pos	No	Driver	Car	Model	Engine		Laps	Time/Reason for Retirement	Grid Pos	Row
1	8	L Bandini	Ferrari	156	Ferrari	V6	105	2h 06m 18.230s	7	2
2	4	R Ginther	BRM	P261	BRM	V8	105	2h 06m 24.410s	5	2
3	22	B Anderson	Brabham	BT11	Climax	V8	102		14	4
4	19	T Maggs	BRM	P57	BRM	V8	102		19	6
5	14	I Ireland	BRP	Mk 2	BRM	V8	102		11	3
6	11	J Bonnier	Brabham	BT7	Climax	V8	101		10	3
7	18	G Baghetti	BRM	P57	BRM	V8	98		15	5
8	17	M Hailwood	Lotus	25	BRM	V8	95		18	5
9	6	J Brabham	Brabham	BT11	Climax	V8	73		6	2
r	12	J Rindt	Brabham	BT11	BRM	V8	58	steering	13	4
r	10	P Hill	Cooper	T66	Climax	V8	58	accident / fire	20	6
r	5	D Gurney	Brabham	BT7	Climax	V8	47	front suspension	4	1
r	9	B McLaren	Cooper	T73	Climax	V8	43	valve spring	9	3
r	2	M Spence	Lotus	33	Climax	V8	41	driveshaft	8	3
r	1	J Clark	Lotus	33	Climax	V8	40	driveshaft	3	1
r	15	T Taylor	BRP	Mk 1	BRM	V8	21	rear suspension	16	5
r	20	J Siffert	Brabham	BT11	BRM	V8	18	spin	12	4
r	7	J Surtees	Ferrari	158	Ferrari	V8	9	rear suspension	2	1
r	16	C Amon	Lotus	25	Climax	V8	7	engine	17	5
r	3	G Hill	BRM	P261	BRM	V8	5	distributor	1	1

Winning speed 159.615 km/h, 99.180 mph
Pole Position speed 164.948 km/h, 102.494 mph (G Hill, 1 min: 9.840 sec)
Fastest Lap speed 163.265 km/h, 101.448 mph (D Gurney, 1 min:10.560 sec on lap 32)
Lap Leaders D Gurney 1,8-46 (40); J Surtees 2-7 (6); L Bandini 47-105 (59).

6 Sep 1964 **ITALY: Monza** (Round 8) (Race 129)

78 laps x 5.750 km, 3.573 miles = 448.500 km, 278.685 miles

Pos	No	Driver	Car	Model	Engine		Laps	Time/Reason for Retirement	Grid Pos	Row
1	2	J Surtees	Ferrari	158	Ferrari	V8	78	2h 10m 51.800s	1	1
2	26	B McLaren	Cooper	T73	Climax	V8	78	2h 11m 57.800s	5	2
3	4	L Bandini	Ferrari	158	Ferrari	V8	77		7	3
4	20	R Ginther	BRM	P261	BRM	V8	77		9	4
5	46	I Ireland	BRP	Mk 2	BRM	V8	77		13	5
6	10	M Spence	Lotus	33	Climax	V8	77		8	3
7	12	J Siffert	Brabham	BT11	BRM	V8	77		6	3
8	30	G Baghetti	BRM	P57	BRM	V8	77		15	6
9	6	L Scarfiotti	Ferrari	156	Ferrari	V6	77		16	7
10	16	D Gurney	Brabham	BT7	Climax	V8	75		2	1
11	22	B Anderson	Brabham	BT11	Climax	V8	75		14	6
12	34	J Bonnier	Brabham	BT7	Climax	V8	74		12	5
13	38	P Revson	Lotus	24	BRM	V8	72		18	7
14r	14	J Brabham	Brabham	BT11	Climax	V8	59	connecting rod	11	5
r	8	J Clark	Lotus	25	Climax	V8	27	piston	4	2
r	50	M Cabral	Derrington Francis (D-F)		ATS	V8	24	ignition	19	8
r	48	M Trintignant	BRM	P57	BRM	V8	21	fuel injection	20	8
r	28	R Bucknum	Honda	RA271	Honda	V12	12	brakes / oil leak	10	4
r	40	M Hailwood	Lotus	25	BRM	V8	4	cam follower	17	7
r	18	G Hill	BRM	P261	BRM	V8	0	clutch	3	1
ns	60	J-C Rudaz	Cooper	T60	Climax	V8		piston		
nq	44	T Taylor	BRP	Mk 1	BRM	V8				
nq	36	Geki	Brabham	BT11	BRM	V8				
nq	24	J Love	Cooper	T73	Climax	V8				
nq	56	I Raby	Brabham	BT3	BRM	V8				

Winning speed 205.634 km/h, 127.775 mph
Pole Position speed 212.526 km/h, 132.057 mph (J Surtees, 1 min:37.400 sec)
Fastest Lap speed 209.514 km/h, 130.186 mph (J Surtees, 1 min:38.800 sec on lap 63 & 67)
Lap Leaders D Gurney 1,6-7,10,12-14,16,22,25-26,29,32,37-38,45,47-48,50-52,55 (22);
J Surtees 2-5,8-9,11,15,17-21,23-24,27-28,30-31,33-36,39-44,46,49,53-54,56-78 (56).

---

4 Oct 1964 **USA: Watkins Glen** (Round 9) (Race 130)

110 laps x 3.701 km, 2.300 miles = 407.164 km, 253.000 miles

Pos	No	Driver	Car	Model	Engine		Laps	Time/Reason for Retirement	Grid Pos	Row
1	3	G Hill	BRM	P261	BRM	V8	110	2h 16m 38.000s	4	2
2	7	J Surtees	Ferrari	158	Ferrari	V8	110	2h 17m 08.500s	2	1
3	22	J Siffert	Brabham	BT11	BRM	V8	109		12	6
4	4	R Ginther	BRM	P261	BRM	V8	107		13	7
5	17	W Hansgen	Lotus	33	Climax	V8	107		17	9
6	12	T Taylor	BRP	Mk 2	BRM	V8	106		15	8
7r=	2	M Spence	Lotus	33	Climax	V8			6	3
7r=	2	J Clark	Lotus	33	Climax	V8	102	fuel pump		
8r	14	M Hailwood	Lotus	25	BRM	V8	101	oil line	16	8
r	6	D Gurney	Brabham	BT7	Climax	V8	69	oil pressure	3	2
nc	23	H Sharp	Brabham	BT11	BRM	V8	65		18	9
r	8	L Bandini	Ferrari	1512	Ferrari	F12	58	engine	8	4
r=	1	J Clark	Lotus	25	Climax	V8			1	1
r=	1	M Spence	Lotus	25	Climax	V8	54	fuel injection		
r	28	R Bucknum	Honda	RA271	Honda	V12	50	cylinder head gasket	14	7
r	15	C Amon	Lotus	25	BRM	V8	47	starter motor	11	6
r	16	J Bonnier	Brabham	BT7	Climax	V8	37	stub axle	9	5
r	9	B McLaren	Cooper	T73	Climax	V8	27	valve	5	3
r	5	J Brabham	Brabham	BT11	Climax	V8	14	piston	7	4
r	10	P Hill	Cooper	T73	Climax	V8	4	ignition	19	10
r	11	I Ireland	BRP	Mk 2	BRM	V8	2	gear lever	10	5

Winning speed 178.799 km/h, 111.100 mph
Pole Position speed 183.419 km/h, 113.971 mph (J Clark, 1 min:12.650 sec)
Fastest Lap speed 183.293 km/h, 113.893 mph (J Clark, 1 min:12.700 sec)
Lap Leaders J Surtees 1-12,44 (13); J Clark 13-43 (31); G Hill 45-110 (66).

25 Oct 1964   **MEXICO: Mexico City**   **(Round 10)**   **(Race 131)**

65 laps x 5.000 km, 3.107 miles = 325.000 km, 201.946 miles

Pos	No	Driver	Car	Model	Engine		Laps	Time/Reason for Retirement	Grid Pos	Row
1	6	D Gurney	Brabham	BT7	Climax	V8	65	2h 09m 50.320s	2	1
2	7	J Surtees	Ferrari	158	Ferrari	V8	65	2h 10m 59.260s	4	2
3	8	L Bandini	Ferrari	1512	Ferrari	F12	65	2h 10m 59.950s	3	2
4	2	M Spence	Lotus	25	Climax	V8	65	2h 11m 12.180s	5	3
5r	1	J Clark	Lotus	33	Climax	V8	64	oil leak / engine	1	1
6	18	P Rodríguez	Ferrari	156	Ferrari	V6	64		9	5
7	9	B McLaren	Cooper	T73	Climax	V8	64		10	5
8	4	R Ginther	BRM	P261	BRM	V8	64		11	6
9r	10	P Hill	Cooper	T73	Climax	V8	63	piston	15	8
10	17	M Solana	Lotus	33	Climax	V8	63		14	7
11	3	G Hill	BRM	P261	BRM	V8	63		6	3
12	11	I Ireland	BRP	Mk 2	BRM	V8	61		16	8
13	23	H Sharp	Brabham	BT11	BRM	V8	60		19	10
r	15	C Amon	Lotus	25	BRM	V8	46	gearbox	12	6
r	5	J Brabham	Brabham	BT11	Climax	V8	44	electrics	7	4
r	14	M Hailwood	Lotus	25	BRM	V8	12	engine overheating	17	9
r	22	J Siffert	Brabham	BT11	BRM	V8	11	fuel pump	13	7
r	16	J Bonnier	Brabham	BT7	Climax	V8	9	front suspension	8	4
r	12	T Taylor	BRP	Mk 2	BRM	V8	5	engine overheating	18	9

Winning speed 150.186 km/h, 93.321 mph
Pole Position speed 153.531 km/h, 95.400 mph (J Clark, 1 min:57.240 sec)
Fastest Lap speed 152.066 km/h, 94.489 mph (J Clark, 1 min:58.370 sec)
Lap Leaders J Clark 1-63 (63); D Gurney 64-65 (2).

Lap Leaders 1964

Pos	Driver	Car-Engine	GPs	laps	km	miles
1	J Clark	Lotus-Climax	8	322	1,452.8	902.7
2	D Gurney	Brabham-Climax	7	136	909.1	564.9
3	G Hill	BRM	3	116	423.4	263.1
4	J Surtees	Ferrari	5	89	699.9	434.9
5	L Bandini	Ferrari	1	59	188.8	117.3
			10	**722**	**3,674.0**	**2,282.9**

Driver Points 1964

		MC	NL	B	F	GB	D	A	I	USA	MEX	Total	
1	J Surtees	-	6	-	-	4	9	-	9	6	6	40	
2	G Hill	9	3	(2)	6	6	6	-	-	9	-	39	(2)
3	J Clark	3	9	9	-	9	-	-	-	-	2	32	
4	L Bandini	-	-	-	-	2	4	9	4	-	4	23	
	R Ginther	6	-	3	2	-	-	6	3	3	-	23	
6	D Gurney	-	-	1	9	-	-	-	-	-	9	19	
7	B McLaren	-	-	6	1	-	-	-	6	-	-	13	
8	P Arundell	4	4	-	3	-	-	-	-	-	-	11	
	J Brabham	-	-	4	4	3	-	-	-	-	-	11	
10	J Siffert	-	-	-	-	-	3	-	-	4	-	7	
11	B Anderson	-	1	-	-	-	-	4	-	-	-	5	
12	T Maggs	-	-	-	-	-	1	3	-	-	-	4	
	M Spence	-	-	-	-	-	-	-	1	-	3	4	
	I Ireland	-	-	-	-	-	2	2	-	-	-	4	
15	J Bonnier	2	-	-	-	-	-	1	-	-	-	3	
16	C Amon	-	2	-	-	-	-	-	-	-	-	2	
	M Trintignant	-	-	-	-	-	2	-	-	-	-	2	
	W Hansgen	-	-	-	-	-	-	-	-	2	-	2	
19	M Hailwood	1	-	-	-	-	-	-	-	-	-	1	
	P Hill	-	-	-	-	1	-	-	-	-	-	1	
	T Taylor	-	-	-	-	-	-	-	-	1	-	1	
	P Rodríguez	-	-	-	-	-	-	-	-	-	1	1	

9,6,4,3,2 and 1 point awarded to the first six finishers. Best 6 scores.

Constructor Points 1964

		MC	NL	B	F	GB	D	A	I	USA	MEX	Total	
1	Ferrari	-	6	-	-	(4)	9	9	9	6	6	45	(4)
2	BRM	9	(3)	(3)	6	6	6	6	(3)	9	-	42	(9)
3	Lotus-Climax	4	9	9	3	9	-	-	(1)	(2)	3	37	(3)
4	Brabham-Climax	-	1	4	9	3	-	4	-	-	9	30	
5	Cooper-Climax	2	-	6	1	1	-	-	6	-	-	16	
6	Brabham-BRM	-	-	-	-	-	3	-	-	4	-	7	
7	BRP-BRM	-	-	-	-	-	-	2	2	1	-	5	
8	Lotus-BRM	1	2	-	-	-	-	-	-	-	-	3	

9,6,4,3,2 and 1 point awarded to the first six finishers. Points only for highest placed car. Best 6 scores.

1965

Race Entrants and Results

Tyre development increased dramatically, with treads becoming wider. Clark totally dominated, and also won the Indy 500 for good measure. Surtees was seriously injured at Mosport at the end of the season. Coventry Climax announced an end to its Formula 1 involvement with the final season of the 1.5-litre formula.

FERRARI
Scuderia Ferrari SpA SEFAC: Surtees, Bandini, Vaccarella, (Scarfiotti)
North American Racing Team: Rodríguez, Bondurant

BRABHAM
Brabham Racing Organisation: Brabham, Gurney, Hulme, Baghetti
R R C Walker Racing Team: Bonnier, Siffert
John Willment Automobiles: Gardner, Hawkins
DW Racing Enterprises: Anderson
Ian Raby (Racing): Raby, (Amon)
Privateer: Prophet

BRM
Owen Racing Organisation: Hill, Stewart
Scuderia Centro Sud: Gregory, Bussinello, Bassi, Bianchi, (Mairesse)

COOPER
Cooper Car Co: McLaren, Rindt
Gerard Racing: Rhodes, (Rollinson)
Privateers: Love, (Blokdyk)

LOTUS
Team Lotus: Clark, Spence, Solana, Mitter, Geki
Reg Parnell (Racing): Attwood, Ireland, Amon, Maggs, Hailwood, Bondurant
DW Racing Enterprises: Hawkins
Lawson Organisation: (Pieterse)
Scuderia Scribante: (Lederle)
Ted Lanfear: (Niemann)
Privateers: (Gubby, Puzey, Charlton)

HONDA
Honda R & D Co: Ginther, Bucknum

ALFA SPECIAL
Otelle Nucci: de Klerk

LDS
Otelle Nucci: (Serrurier)
Privateers: Tingle, (Pretorius)

1 Jan 1965		SOUTH AFRICA: East London						(Round 1)		(Race 132)	
		85 laps x 3.920 km, 2.436 miles = 333.231 km, 207.060 miles									
Pos	No	Driver	Car	Model	Engine		Laps	Time/Reason for Retirement		Grid Pos	Row
1	5	J Clark	Lotus	33	Climax	V8	85	2h 06m 46.000s		1	1
2	1	J Surtees	Ferrari	158	Ferrari	V8	85	2h 07m 15.000s		2	1
3	3	G Hill	BRM	P261	BRM	V8	85	2h 07m 17.800s		5	2
4	6	M Spence	Lotus	33	Climax	V8	85	2h 07m 40.400s		4	2
5	9	B McLaren	Cooper	T77	Climax	V8	84			8	3
6	4	J Stewart	BRM	P261	BRM	V8	83			11	5
7	12	J Siffert	Brabham	BT11	BRM	V8	83			14	6
8	7	J Brabham	Brabham	BT11	Climax	V8	81			3	1
9	18	P Hawkins	Brabham	BT10	Ford	4	81			16	7
10	20	P de Klerk	Alfa Special		Alfa Romeo	4	79			17	7
11	15	T Maggs	Lotus	25	BRM	V8	77			13	5
12	16	F Gardner	Brabham	BT11	BRM	V8	75			15	6
13	25	S Tingle	LDS	Mk 1	Alfa Romeo	4	73			20	8
14	19	D Prophet	Brabham	BT10	Ford	4	71			19	8
15r	2	L Bandini	Ferrari	1512	Ferrari	F12	66	ignition		6	3
nc	14	B Anderson	Brabham	BT11	Climax	V8	50			12	5
r	11	J Bonnier	Brabham	BT7	Climax	V8	42	clutch / gearbox		7	3
r	10	J Rindt	Cooper	T73	Climax	V8	39	electrics		10	4
r	17	J Love	Cooper	T55	Climax	4	20	half shaft		18	7
r	8	D Gurney	Brabham	BT11	Climax	V8	11	ignition		9	4
nq	28	T Blokdyk	Cooper	T59	Ford	4					
nq	23	N Lederle	Lotus	21	Climax	4					
nq	21	D Serrurier	LDS	Mk 2	Climax	4					
nq	27	B Niemann	Lotus	22	Ford	4					
nq	22	E Pieterse	Lotus	21	Climax	4					
npq	24	C Puzey	Lotus	18/21	Climax	4					
npq	29	J Pretorius	LDS	Mk 1	Alfa Romeo	4					
npq	32	D Charlton	Lotus	20	Ford	4					

Winning speed 157.722 km/h, 98.004 mph
Pole Position speed 161.850 km/h, 100.569 mph (J Clark, 1 min:27.200 sec)
Fastest Lap speed 161.111 km/h, 100.110 mph (J Clark, 1 min:27.600 sec on lap 80)
Lap Leaders J Clark 1-85 (85).

30 May 1965   MONACO: Monte-Carlo   (Round 2)   (Race 133)

100 laps x 3.145 km, 1.954 miles = 314.500 km, 195.421 miles

Pos	No	Driver	Car	Model	Engine		Laps	Time/Reason for Retirement	Grid Pos	Row
1	3	G Hill	BRM	P261	BRM	V8	100	2h 37m 39.600s	1	1
2	17	L Bandini	Ferrari	1512	Ferrari	F12	100	2h 38m 43.600s	4	2
3	4	J Stewart	BRM	P261	BRM	V8	100	2h 39m 21.500s	3	2
4r	18	J Surtees	Ferrari	158	Ferrari	V8	99	out of fuel	5	3
5	7	B McLaren	Cooper	T77	Climax	V8	98		7	4
6	14	J Siffert	Brabham	BT11	BRM	V8	98		10	5
7	12	J Bonnier	Brabham	BT7	Climax	V8	97		13	7
8	2	D Hulme	Brabham	BT7	Climax	V8	92		8	4
9	9	B Anderson	Brabham	BT11	Climax	V8	85		9	5
10r	10	P Hawkins	Lotus	33	Climax	V8	79	accident	14	7
r	15	D Attwood	Lotus	25	BRM	V8	43	accident	6	3
r	1	J Brabham	Brabham	BT11	Climax	V8	43	engine	2	1
r	19	R Bucknum	Honda	RA272	Honda	V12	33	gear linkage	15	8
r	11	F Gardner	Brabham	BT11	BRM	V8	29	engine mounting	11	6
r	16	M Hailwood	Lotus	25	BRM	V8	11	gearbox	12	6
r	20	R Ginther	Honda	RA272	Honda	V12	1	driveshaft	16	8
nq	8	J Rindt	Cooper	T77	Climax	V8				

Winning speed 119.688 km/h, 74.371 mph
Pole Position speed 122.400 km/h, 76.056 mph (G Hill, 1 min:32.500 sec)
Fastest Lap speed 123.468 km/h, 76.719 mph (G Hill, 1 min:31.700 sec on lap 82)
Lap Leaders G Hill 1-24,65-100 (60); J Stewart 25-29 (5); L Bandini 30-33,43-64 (26); J Brabham 34-42 (9).

13 Jun 1965   BELGIUM: Spa-Francorchamps   (Round 3)   (Race 134)

32 laps x 14.100 km, 8.761 miles = 451.200 km, 280.363 miles

Pos	No	Driver	Car	Model	Engine		Laps	Time/Reason for Retirement	Grid Pos	Row
1	17	J Clark	Lotus	33	Climax	V8	32	2h 23m 34.800s	2	1
2	8	J Stewart	BRM	P261	BRM	V8	32	2h 24m 19.600s	3	1
3	4	B McLaren	Cooper	T77	Climax	V8	31		9	4
4	14	J Brabham	Brabham	BT11	Climax	V8	31		10	4
5	7	G Hill	BRM	P261	BRM	V8	31		1	1
6	10	R Ginther	Honda	RA272	Honda	V12	31		4	2
7	18	M Spence	Lotus	33	Climax	V8	31		12	5
8	21	J Siffert	Brabham	BT11	BRM	V8	31		8	3
9	2	L Bandini	Ferrari	1512	Ferrari	F12	30		15	6
10	15	D Gurney	Brabham	BT11	Climax	V8	30		5	2
11	5	J Rindt	Cooper	T77	Climax	V8	29		14	6
12	27	L Bianchi	BRM	P57	BRM	V8	29		17	7
13	22	I Ireland	Lotus	25	BRM	V8	27		16	7
14r	23	D Attwood	Lotus	25	BRM	V8	26	accident / fire	13	5
r	29	M Gregory	BRM	P57	BRM	V8	12	fuel pump / rear suspension	20	8
r	11	R Bucknum	Honda	RA272	Honda	V12	9	gearbox	11	5
r	20	R Bonnier	Brabham	BT7	Climax	V8	9	ignition	7	3
r	1	J Surtees	Ferrari	158	Ferrari	V8	5	ignition	6	3
r	26	F Gardner	Brabham	BT11	BRM	V8	3	ignition	18	7
ns	24	B Anderson	Brabham	BT11	Climax	V8		withdrew	19	8
ns	28	W Mairesse	BRM	P57	BRM	V8				

Winning speed 188.550 km/h, 117.159 mph
Pole Position speed 225.200 km/h, 139.933 mph (G Hill, 3 min:45.400 sec)
Fastest Lap speed 200.712 km/h, 124.716 mph (J Clark, 4 min:12.900 sec on lap 23)
Lap Leaders J Clark 1-32 (32).

Also the Grand Prix of Europe.

27 Jun 1965   FRANCE: Clermont-Ferrand   (Round 4)   (Race 135)

40 laps x 8.055 km, 5.005 miles = 322.200 km, 200.206 miles

Pos	No	Driver	Car	Model	Engine		Laps	Time/Reason for Retirement	Grid Pos	Row
1	6	J Clark	Lotus	25	Climax	V8	40	2h 14m 38.400s	1	1
2	12	J Stewart	BRM	P261	BRM	V8	40	2h 15m 04.700s	2	1
3	2	J Surtees	Ferrari	158	Ferrari	V8	40	2h 17m 11.900s	4	2
4	16	D Hulme	Brabham	BT11	Climax	V8	40	2h 17m 31.500s	6	3
5	10	G Hill	BRM	P261	BRM	V8	39		13	5
6	36	J Siffert	Brabham	BT11	BRM	V8	39		14	6
7	8	M Spence	Lotus	33	Climax	V8	39		10	4
8r	4	L Bandini	Ferrari	1512	Ferrari	F12	36	rear wheel lost / accident	3	1
9r	30	B Anderson	Brabham	BT11	Climax	V8	34	electrics	15	6
r	18	B McLaren	Cooper	T77	Climax	V8	23	rear suspension / handling	9	4
r	34	J Bonnier	Brabham	BT7	Climax	V8	21	alternator drive	11	5
r	24	C Amon	Lotus	25	BRM	V8	20	fuel injection	8	3
r	22	I Ireland	Lotus	25	BRM	V8	18	gearbox	17	7
r	14	D Gurney	Brabham	BT11	Climax	V8	16	engine	5	2
r	26	R Ginther	Honda	RA272	Honda	V12	9	ignition	7	3
r	28	R Bucknum	Honda	RA272	Honda	V12	4	ignition	16	7
r	20	J Rindt	Cooper	T77	Climax	V8	3	accident	12	5

Winning speed 143.583 km/h, 89.218 mph
Pole Position speed 146.233 km/h, 90.865 mph (J Clark, 3 min:18.300 sec)
Fastest Lap speed 145.792 km/h, 90.591 mph (J Clark, 3 min:18.900 sec on lap 34)
Lap Leaders J Clark 1-40 (40).

10 Jul 1965 BRITAIN: Silverstone (Round 5) (Race 136)
80 laps x 4.711 km, 2.927 miles = 376.844 km, 234.160 miles

Pos	No	Driver	Car	Model	Engine		Laps	Time/Reason for Retirement	Grid Pos	Row
1	5	J Clark	Lotus	33	Climax	V8	80	2h 05m 25.400s	1	1
2	3	G Hill	BRM	P261	BRM	V8	80	2h 05m 28.600s	2	1
3	1	J Surtees	Ferrari	1512	Ferrari	F12	80	2h 05m 53.000s	5	2
4	6	M Spence	Lotus	33	Climax	V8	80	2h 06m 05.000s	6	2
5	4	J Stewart	BRM	P261	BRM	V8	80	2h 06m 40.000s	4	1
6	7	D Gurney	Brabham	BT11	Climax	V8	79		7	2
7	15	J Bonnier	Brabham	BT7	Climax	V8	79		14	4
8	17	F Gardner	Brabham	BT11	BRM	V8	78		13	4
9	16	J Siffert	Brabham	BT11	BRM	V8	78		18	5
10	9	B McLaren	Cooper	T77	Climax	V8	77		11	3
11	24	I Raby	Brabham	BT3	BRM	V8	73		20	6
12	12	M Gregory	BRM	P57	BRM	V8	70		19	6
13	22	D Attwood	Lotus	25	BRM	V8	63		16	5
14r	10	J Rindt	Cooper	T77	Climax	V8	62	engine	12	4
r	23	I Ireland	Lotus	25	BRM	V8	41	engine	15	5
r	20	J Rhodes	Cooper	T60	Climax	V8	38	ignition	21	6
r	18	B Anderson	Brabham	BT11	Climax	V8	33	gearbox	17	5
r	14	D Hulme	Brabham	BT7	Climax	V8	29	alternator belt	10	3
r	11	R Ginther	Honda	RA272	Honda	V12	26	ignition	3	1
r	2	L Bandini	Ferrari	158	Ferrari	V8	2	piston	9	3
ns	7	J Brabham	Brabham	BT11	Climax	V8		car raced by Gurney	8	3
ns	24	C Amon	Brabham	BT3	BRM	V8		car raced by Raby		
nq	25	A Rollinson	Cooper	T71/73	Ford	4				
nq	26	B Gubby	Lotus	24	Climax	V8				

Winning speed 180.275 km/h, 112.017 mph
Pole Position speed 186.762 km/h, 116.048 mph (J Clark, 1 min:30.800 sec)
Fastest Lap speed 183.926 km/h, 114.286 mph (G Hill, 1 min:32.200 sec on lap 80)
Lap Leaders J Clark 1-80 (80).

18 Jul 1965 NETHERLANDS: Zandvoort (Round 6) (Race 137)
80 laps x 4.193 km, 2.605 miles = 335.440 km, 208.433 miles

Pos	No	Driver	Car	Model	Engine		Laps	Time/Reason for Retirement	Grid Pos	Row
1	6	J Clark	Lotus	33	Climax	V8	80	2h 03m 59.100s	2	1
2	12	J Stewart	BRM	P261	BRM	V8	80	2h 04m 07.100s	6	3
3	16	D Gurney	Brabham	BT11	Climax	V8	80	2h 04m 12.100s	5	2
4	10	G Hill	BRM	P261	BRM	V8	80	2h 04m 44.200s	1	1
5	14	D Hulme	Brabham	BT11	Climax	V8	79		7	3
6	22	R Ginther	Honda	RA272	Honda	V12	79		3	1
7	2	J Surtees	Ferrari	1512	Ferrari	F12	79		4	2
8	8	M Spence	Lotus	25	Climax	V8	79		8	3
9	4	L Bandini	Ferrari	158	Ferrari	V8	79		12	5
10	38	I Ireland	Lotus	25	BRM	V8	78		13	5
11	30	F Gardner	Brabham	BT11	BRM	V8	77		11	5
12	34	D Attwood	Lotus	25	BRM	V8	77		17	7
13	28	J Siffert	Brabham	BT11	BRM	V8	55		10	4
r	20	J Rindt	Cooper	T77	Climax	V8	48	oil pressure	14	6
r	18	B McLaren	Cooper	T77	Climax	V8	36	crown wheel & pinion	9	4
r	26	J Bonnier	Brabham	BT7	Climax	V8	16	ignition / fuel system	15	6
r	36	B Anderson	Brabham	BT11	Climax	V8	11	cylinder head gasket	16	7

Winning speed 162.329 km/h, 100.867 mph
Pole Position speed 166.426 km/h, 103.412 mph (G Hill, 1 min:30.700 sec)
Fastest Lap speed 166.609 km/h, 103.526 mph (J Clark, 1 min:30.600 sec on lap 5)
Lap Leaders R Ginther 1-2 (2); G Hill 3-5 (3); J Clark 6-80 (75).

1 Aug 1965   **GERMANY: Nürburgring**   **(Round 7)**   **(Race 138)**

15 laps x 22.810 km, 14.173 miles = 342.150 km, 212.602 miles

Pos	No	Driver	Car	Model	Engine		Laps	Time/Reason for Retirement	Grid Pos	Row
1	1	J Clark	Lotus	33	Climax	V8	15	2h 07m 52.400s	1	1
2	9	G Hill	BRM	P261	BRM	V8	15	2h 08m 08.300s	3	1
3	5	D Gurney	Brabham	BT11	Climax	V8	15	2h 08m 13.800s	5	2
4	12	J Rindt	Cooper	T77	Climax	V8	15	2h 11m 22.000s	8	3
5	4	J Brabham	Brabham	BT11	Climax	V8	15	2h 12m 33.600s	14	4
6	8	L Bandini	Ferrari	158	Ferrari	V8	15	2h 13m 01.000s	7	2
7	16	J Bonnier	Brabham	BT7	Climax	V8	15	2h 13m 50.900s	9	3
8	24	M Gregory	BRM	P57	BRM	V8	14		18	5
r	7	J Surtees	Ferrari	1512	Ferrari	F12	11	gearbox	4	1
r	17	J Siffert	Brabham	BT11	BRM	V8	9	camshaft	11	3
r	3	G Mitter	Lotus	25	Climax	V8	8	water pipe	12	4
r	2	M Spence	Lotus	33	Climax	V8	8	driveshaft	6	2
r	20	D Attwood	Lotus	25	BRM	V8	7	water pipe	16	5
r	11	B McLaren	Cooper	T77	Climax	V8	7	gearbox	10	3
r	6	D Hulme	Brabham	BT7	Climax	V8	5	fuel leak	13	4
r	22	P Hawkins	Lotus	33	Climax	V8	4	oil leak	19	6
r	19	C Amon	Lotus	25	BRM	V8	3	ignition	15	5
r	10	J Stewart	BRM	P261	BRM	V8	2	front suspension	2	1
r	21	F Gardner	Brabham	BT11	BRM	V8	0	gearbox	17	5
ns	18	B Anderson	Brabham	BT11	Climax	V8		accident		
nq	25	R Bussinello	BRM	P57	BRM	V8				
nq	23	I Raby	Brabham	BT3	BRM	V8				

Winning speed 160.542 km/h, 99.756 mph
Pole Position speed 163.350 km/h, 101.501 mph (J Clark, 8 min:22.700 sec)
Fastest Lap speed 162.896 km/h, 101.219 mph (J Clark, 8 min:24.100 sec on lap 10)
Lap Leaders J Clark 1-15 (15).

12 Sep 1965   **ITALY: Monza**   **(Round 8)**   **(Race 139)**

76 laps x 5.750 km, 3.573 miles = 437.000 km, 271.539 miles

Pos	No	Driver	Car	Model	Engine		Laps	Time/Reason for Retirement	Grid Pos	Row
1	32	J Stewart	BRM	P261	BRM	V8	76	2h 04m 52.800s	3	1
2	30	G Hill	BRM	P261	BRM	V8	76	2h 04m 56.100s	4	2
3	12	D Gurney	Brabham	BT11	Climax	V8	76	2h 05m 09.300s	9	4
4	4	L Bandini	Ferrari	1512	Ferrari	F12	76	2h 06m 08.700s	5	2
5	16	B McLaren	Cooper	T77	Climax	V8	75		11	5
6	40	D Attwood	Lotus	25	BRM	V8	75		13	5
7	42	J Bonnier	Brabham	BT7	Climax	V8	74		14	6
8	18	J Rindt	Cooper	T77	Climax	V8	74		7	3
9	38	I Ireland	Lotus	25	BRM	V8	74		18	7
10r	24	J Clark	Lotus	33	Climax	V8	63	fuel pump	1	1
11r	26	M Spence	Lotus	33	Climax	V8	62	alternator	8	3
12r	6	N Vaccarella	Ferrari	158	Ferrari	V8	58	engine	15	6
13r	50	R Bussinello	BRM	P57	BRM	V8	58	oil pressure	21	9
14r	20	R Ginther	Honda	RA272	Honda	V12	56	ignition	17	7
r	14	D Hulme	Brabham	BT11	Climax	V8	46	front suspension	12	5
r	46	F Gardner	Brabham	BT11	BRM	V8	45	engine	16	7
r	44	J Siffert	Brabham	BT11	BRM	V8	43	gearbox	10	4
r	28	Geki	Lotus	25	Climax	V8	37	crown wheel & pinion	20	8
r	8	J Surtees	Ferrari	1512	Ferrari	F12	34	clutch	2	1
r	22	R Bucknum	Honda	RA272	Honda	V12	27	engine	6	3
r	48	M Gregory	BRM	P57	BRM	V8	22	gearbox	23	9
r	10	G Baghetti	Brabham	BT7	Climax	V8	12	connecting rod	19	8
r	52	G Bassi	BRM	P57	BRM	V8	8	engine	22	9

Winning speed 209.962 km/h, 130.464 mph
Pole Position speed 215.850 km/h, 134.123 mph (J Clark, 1 min:35.900 sec)
Fastest Lap speed 214.730 km/h, 133.427 mph (J Clark, 1 min:36.400 sec on lap 46)
Lap Leaders J Clark 1-2,4,7,10,18,21,27,33-36,38,44,46,51,53-54,57 (19); G Hill 3,5,25-26,28,40-41,43,45,50,55-56, 64,70-71,73,74 (17); J Stewart 6,8-9,11-17,19-20,22-24,29-32,37,39,42,47-49,52,58-63,65-69,72,75-76 (40).

110 laps x 3.701 km, 2.300 miles = 407.164 km, 253.000 miles

Pos	No	Driver	Car	Model	Engine		Laps	Time/Reason for Retirement	Grid Pos	Row
1	3	G Hill	BRM	P261	BRM	V8	110	2h 20m 36.100s	1	1
2	8	D Gurney	Brabham	BT11	Climax	V8	110	2h 20m 48.600s	8	4
3	7	J Brabham	Brabham	BT11	Climax	V8	110	2h 21m 33.600s	7	4
4	2	L Bandini	Ferrari	1512	Ferrari	F12	109		5	3
5	14	P Rodríguez	Ferrari	1512	Ferrari	F12	109		15	8
6	10	J Rindt	Cooper	T77	Climax	V8	108		13	7
7	11	R Ginther	Honda	RA272	Honda	V12	108		3	2
8	15	J Bonnier	Brabham	BT7	Climax	V8	107		10	5
9	24	B Bondurant	Ferrari	158	Ferrari	V8	106		14	7
10	21	D Attwood	Lotus	25	BRM	V8	101		16	8
11	16	J Siffert	Brabham	BT11	BRM	V8	99		11	6
12	18	M Solana	Lotus	25	Climax	V8	95		17	9
13	12	R Bucknum	Honda	RA272	Honda	V12	92		12	6
r	4	J Stewart	BRM	P261	BRM	V8	12	accident / front suspension	6	3
r	9	B McLaren	Cooper	T77	Climax	V8	11	oil pressure	9	5
r	5	J Clark	Lotus	33	Climax	V8	11	engine	2	1
r	22	I Ireland	Lotus	25	BRM	V8	9	driver ill (influenza)	18	9
r	6	M Spence	Lotus	33	Climax	V8	9	engine	4	2

Winning speed 173.752 km/h, 107.965 mph
Pole Position speed 187.023 km/h, 116.211 mph (G Hill, 1 min:11.250 sec)
Fastest Lap speed 185.332 km/h, 115.160 mph (G Hill, 1 min:11.900 sec on lap 105)
Lap Leaders G Hill 1,5-110 (107); J Clark 2-4 (3).

65 laps x 5.000 km, 3.107 miles = 325.000 km, 201.946 miles

Pos	No	Driver	Car	Model	Engine		Laps	Time/Reason for Retirement	Grid Pos	Row
1	11	R Ginther	Honda	RA272	Honda	V12	65	2h 08m 32.100s	3	2
2	8	D Gurney	Brabham	BT11	Climax	V8	65	2h 08m 34.990s	2	1
3	6	M Spence	Lotus	33	Climax	V8	65	2h 09m 32.250s	6	3
4	16	J Siffert	Brabham	BT11	BRM	V8	65	2h 10m 26.520s	11	6
5	12	R Bucknum	Honda	RA272	Honda	V12	64		10	5
6	21	D Attwood	Lotus	25	BRM	V8	64		16	8
7	14	P Rodríguez	Ferrari	1512	Ferrari	F12	62		13	7
8	2	L Bandini	Ferrari	1512	Ferrari	F12	62		7	4
r	3	G Hill	BRM	P261	BRM	V8	56	engine	5	3
r	18	M Solana	Lotus	25	Climax	V8	55	ignition	9	5
r	15	J Bonnier	Brabham	BT7	Climax	V8	43	front suspension	12	6
r	10	J Rindt	Cooper	T77	Climax	V8	39	ignition	15	8
r	7	J Brabham	Brabham	BT11	Climax	V8	38	oil leak	4	2
r	4	J Stewart	BRM	P261	BRM	V8	35	clutch	8	4
r	22	B Bondurant	Lotus	33	BRM	V8	29	rear suspension	17	9
r	9	B McLaren	Cooper	T77	Climax	V8	25	gear selector	14	7
r	5	J Clark	Lotus	33	Climax	V8	8	engine	1	1
ns	24	L Scarfiotti	Ferrari	1512	Ferrari	F12		car raced by Rodríguez		
ns	22	I Ireland	Lotus	25	BRM	V8		dismissed by team		

Winning speed 151.710 km/h, 94.268 mph
Pole Position speed 154.945 km/h, 96.279 mph (J Clark, 1 min:56.170 sec)
Fastest Lap speed 155.387 km/h, 96.553 mph (D Gurney, 1 min:55.840 sec on lap 57)
Lap Leaders R Ginther 1-65 (65).

Lap Leaders 1965

Pos	Driver	Car-Engine	GPs	laps	km	miles
1	J Clark	Lotus-Climax	8	349	2,260.5	1,404.6
2	G Hill	BRM	4	187	695.0	431.9
3	R Ginther	Honda	2	67	333.4	207.2
4	J Stewart	BRM	2	45	245.7	152.7
5	L Bandini	Ferrari	1	26	81.8	50.8
6	J Brabham	Brabham-Climax	1	9	28.3	17.6
			10	683	3,644.7	2,264.7

Driver Points 1965

		ZA	MC	B	F	GB	NL	D	I	USA	MEX	Total	
1	J Clark	9	-	9	9	9	9	9	-	-	-	54	
2	G Hill	4	9	(2)	(2)	6	(3)	6	6	9	-	40	(7)
3	J Stewart	(1)	4	6	6	2	6	-	9	-	-	33	(1)
4	D Gurney	-	-	-	-	1	4	4	4	6	6	25	
5	J Surtees	6	3	-	4	4	-	-	-	-	-	17	
6	L Bandini	-	6	-	-	-	-	1	3	3	-	13	
7	R Ginther	-	-	1	-	-	1	-	-	-	9	11	
8	M Spence	3	-	-	-	3	-	-	-	-	4	10	
	B McLaren	2	2	4	-	-	-	-	2	-	-	10	
10	J Brabham	-	-	3	-	-	-	2	-	4	-	9	
11	D Hulme	-	-	-	3	-	2	-	-	-	-	5	
	J Siffert	-	1	-	1	-	-	-	-	-	3	5	
13	J Rindt	-	-	-	-	-	-	3	-	1	-	4	
14	P Rodríguez	-	-	-	-	-	-	-	-	2	-	2	
	R Bucknum	-	-	-	-	-	-	-	-	-	2	2	
	D Attwood	-	-	-	-	-	-	-	1	-	1	2	

9,6,4,3,2 and 1 point awarded to the first six finishers. Best 6 scores.

Constructor Points 1965

		ZA	MC	B	F	GB	NL	D	I	USA	MEX	Total	
1	Lotus-Climax	9	-	9	9	9	9	9	-	-	(4)	54	(4)
2	BRM	(4)	9	6	6	6	(6)	(6)	9	9	-	45	(16)
3	Brabham-Climax	-	-	3	(3)	(1)	4	4	4	6	6	27	(4)
4	Ferrari	6	6	-	4	4	-	(1)	3	3	-	26	(1)
5	Cooper-Climax	2	2	4	-	-	-	3	2	1	-	14	
6	Honda	-	-	1	-	-	1	-	-	-	9	11	
7	Brabham-BRM	-	1	-	1	-	-	-	-	-	3	5	
8	Lotus-BRM	-	-	-	-	-	-	-	1	-	1	2	

9,6,4,3,2 and 1 point awarded to the first six finishers. Points only for highest placed car. Best 6 scores.

1966

Race Entrants and Results

The long awaited return to power started with a splutter, with many teams unable to field the new 3-litre engine. Yet again, most of the British teams were unprepared, while Ferrari race-readied their sports car engine. Their season was disrupted when Surtees walked out and joined Cooper. BRM introduced another complicated engine design with the unique H16, while Brabham went in the other direction with the simple and reliable Repco units. Firestone entered Grand Prix racing. Giuseppe Farina was killed in a road accident, en route to the French GP. A rule was introduced which required cars to complete 90% of the race distance (rounded down) to be classified.

FERRARI
Scuderia Ferrari SpA SEFAC: Bandini, Surtees, Parkes, Scarfiotti
Reg Parnell Racing Ltd: Baghetti

BRABHAM
Brabham Racing Organisation: Brabham, Hulme, Irwin
R R C Walker Racing Team: Siffert
DW Racing Enterprises: Anderson
David Bridges: J Taylor
Joakim Bonnier Racing Team: Bonnier
Privateer: (Amon)

BRM
Owen Racing Organisation: G Hill, Stewart
Team Chamaco-Collect: Bondurant, (Wilson)
Bernard White Racing: Ireland

LOTUS
Team Lotus: Clark, Arundell, Rodríguez, Geki
Reg Parnell Racing Ltd: Spence, (Baghetti)

COOPER
Cooper Car Co: Rindt, Surtees, Ginther, Amon, Solana
Joakim Bonnier Racing Team: Bonnier
R R C Walker Racing Team: Siffert
J A Pearce Engineering Ltd: Lawrence
Privateer: Ligier

McLAREN
Bruce McLaren Motor Racing: McLaren

SHANNON
Shannon Racing Cars: T Taylor

EAGLE
Anglo American Racers: Gurney, Bondurant, (P Hill)

HONDA
Honda R & D Co: Ginther, Bucknum

(Entries for the F2 section are not included)

22 May 1966		MONACO: Monte-Carlo					(Round 1)	(Race 142)	
		100 laps x 3.145 km, 1.954 miles = 314.500 km, 195.421 miles							
Pos	**No**	**Driver**	**Car**	**Model**	**Engine**		**Laps**	**Time/Reason for Retirement**	**Grid Pos**	**Row**
1	12	J Stewart	BRM	P261	BRM	V8	100	2h 33m 10.500s	3	2
2	16	L Bandini	Ferrari	246	Ferrari	V6	100	2h 33m 50.700s	5	3
3	11	G Hill	BRM	P261	BRM	V8	99		4	2
4	19	B Bondurant	BRM	P261	BRM	V8	95		16	8
r	9	R Ginther	Cooper	T81	Maserati	V12	80	driveshaft	9	5
nc	21	G Ligier	Cooper	T81	Maserati	V12	75		15	8
nc	18	J Bonnier	Cooper	T81	Maserati	V12	73		14	7
r	4	J Clark	Lotus	33	Climax	V8	60	rear suspension	1	1
r	10	J Rindt	Cooper	T81	Maserati	V12	56	engine	7	4
r	14	J Siffert	Brabham	BT11	BRM	V8	35	clutch	13	7
r	6	M Spence	Lotus	25	BRM	V8	34	rear suspension	12	6
r	7	J Brabham	Brabham	BT19	Repco	V8	17	gearbox	11	6
r	17	J Surtees	Ferrari	312	Ferrari	V12	16	rear axle	2	1
r	8	D Hulme	Brabham	BT22	Climax	4	15	driveshaft	6	3
r	2	B McLaren	McLaren	M2B	Ford	V8	9	oil leak	10	5
r	15	B Anderson	Brabham	BT11	Climax	4	3	engine	8	4

Winning speed 123.192 km/h, 76.548 mph
Pole Position speed 125.940 km/h, 78.255 mph (J Clark, 1 min:29.900 sec)
Fastest Lap speed 126.080 km/h, 78.343 mph (L Bandini, 1 min:29.800 sec on lap 90)
Lap Leaders J Surtees 1-14 (14); J Stewart 15-100 (86).

12 Jun 1966 **BELGIUM: Spa-Francorchamps** (Round 2) (Race 143)

28 laps x 14.100 km, 8.761 miles = 394.800 km, 245.317 miles

Pos	No	Driver	Car	Model	Engine		Laps	Time/Reason for Retirement	Grid Pos	Row
1	6	J Surtees	Ferrari	312	Ferrari	V12	28	2h 09m 11.300s	1	1
2	19	J Rindt	Cooper	T81	Maserati	V12	28	2h 09m 53.400s	2	1
3	7	L Bandini	Ferrari	246	Ferrari	V6	27		5	2
4	3	J Brabham	Brabham	BT19	Repco	V8	26		4	2
5	18	R Ginther	Cooper	T81	Maserati	V12	25		8	3
nc	22	G Ligier	Cooper	T81	Maserati	V12	24		12	5
nc	27	D Gurney	Eagle	T1G	Climax	4	23		15	6
r	4	D Hulme	Brabham	BT22	Climax	4	0	accident	13	5
r	21	J Siffert	Cooper	T81	Maserati	V12	0	accident	14	6
r	14	G Hill	BRM	P261	BRM	V8	0	accident	9	4
r	24	B Bondurant	BRM	P261	BRM	V8	0	accident	11	5
r	15	J Stewart	BRM	P261	BRM	V8	0	accident / injury	3	1
r	16	M Spence	Lotus	25	BRM	V8	0	accident	7	3
r	20	J Bonnier	Cooper	T81	Maserati	V12	0	accident	6	3
r	10	J Clark	Lotus	33	Climax	V8	0	engine	10	4
ns	24	B McLaren	McLaren	M2B	Serenissima	V8		bearings		
ns	8	V Wilson	BRM	P261	BRM	V8		car raced by Bondurant		
ns	11	P Arundell	Lotus	43	BRM	H16		engine		

Winning speed 183.360 km/h, 113.935 mph
Pole Position speed 232.844 km/h, 144.683 mph (J Surtees, 3 min:38.000 sec)
Fastest Lap speed 196.212 km/h, 121.920 mph (J Surtees, 4 min:18.700 sec on lap 18)
Lap Leaders J Surtees 1,3,24-28 (7); L Bandini 2 (1); J Rindt 4-23 (20).

P Hill was present in a camera car - McLaren-Ford V8 (28). B Bondurant changed his number on race day from number 8 due to the requirements of the MGM film 'Grand Prix'.

---

3 Jul 1966 **FRANCE: Reims** (Round 3) (Race 144)

48 laps x 8.302 km, 5.159 miles = 398.496 km, 247.614 miles

Pos	No	Driver	Car	Model	Engine		Laps	Time/Reason for Retirement	Grid Pos	Row
1	12	J Brabham	Brabham	BT19	Repco	V8	48	1h 48m 31.300s	4	2
2	22	M Parkes	Ferrari	312	Ferrari	V12	48	1h 48m 40.800s	3	1
3	14	D Hulme	Brabham	BT20	Repco	V8	46		9	4
4	6	J Rindt	Cooper	T81	Maserati	V12	46		5	2
5	26	D Gurney	Eagle	T1G	Climax	4	45		14	6
6	44	J Taylor	Brabham	BT11	BRM	V8	45		15	6
7	36	B Anderson	Brabham	BT11	Climax	4	44		13	5
8	8	C Amon	Cooper	T81	Maserati	V12	44		7	3
nc	42	G Ligier	Cooper	T81	Maserati	V12	42		11	5
r	2	P Rodríguez	Lotus	33	Climax	V8	40	oil line	12	5
nc	20	L Bandini	Ferrari	312	Ferrari	V12	37		1	1
nc	30	J Bonnier	Brabham	BT22	Climax	4	32		17	7
r	16	G Hill	BRM	P261	BRM	V8	13	camshaft	8	3
r	38	J Siffert	Cooper	T81	Maserati	V12	10	engine overheating	6	3
r	32	M Spence	Lotus	25	BRM	V8	8	clutch	10	4
r	10	J Surtees	Cooper	T81	Maserati	V12	5	engine overheating	2	1
r	4	P Arundell	Lotus	43	BRM	H16	3	gear selection	16	7
ns	2	J Clark	Lotus	33	Climax	V8		hit in face by bird		

Winning speed 220.322 km/h, 136.902 mph
Pole Position speed 233.859 km/h, 145.313 mph (L Bandini, 2 min: 7.800 sec)
Fastest Lap speed 227.625 km/h, 141.440 mph (L Bandini, 2 min:11.300 sec on lap 30)
Lap Leaders L Bandini 1-31 (31); J Brabham 32-48 (17).

Also the Grand Prix of Europe.
P Rodriguez recorded 14th fastest time in qualifying but took over J Clark's time.

16 Jul 1966   **BRITAIN: Brands Hatch**   **(Round 4)**   **(Race 145)**

80 laps x 4.265 km, 2.650 miles = 341.181 km, 212.000 miles

Pos	No	Driver	Car	Model	Engine		Laps	Time/Reason for Retirement	Grid Pos	Row
1	5	J Brabham	Brabham	BT19	Repco	V8	80	2h 13m 13.400s	1	1
2	6	D Hulme	Brabham	BT20	Repco	V8	80	2h 13m 23.000s	2	1
3	3	G Hill	BRM	P261	BRM	V8	79		4	2
4	1	J Clark	Lotus	33	Climax	V8	79		5	2
5	11	J Rindt	Cooper	T81	Maserati	V12	79		7	3
6	14	B McLaren	McLaren	M2B	Serenissima	V8	78		13	5
7	7	C Irwin	Brabham	BT22	Climax	4	78		12	5
8	22	J Taylor	Brabham	BT11	BRM	V8	76		16	7
9	25	B Bondurant	BRM	P261	BRM	V8	76		14	6
10	19	G Ligier	Cooper	T81	Maserati	V12	75		17	7
11	24	C Lawrence	Cooper	T73	Ferrari	V12	73		19	8
nc	20	J Siffert	Cooper	T81	Maserati	V12	70		11	5
nc	21	B Anderson	Brabham	BT11	Climax	4	70		10	4
r	12	J Surtees	Cooper	T81	Maserati	V12	67	rear axle	6	3
r	18	J Bonnier	Brabham	BT7	Climax	V8	42	clutch	15	6
r	2	P Arundell	Lotus	33	BRM	V8	32	gear selection	20	8
r	4	J Stewart	BRM	P261	BRM	V8	17	engine	8	3
r	17	M Spence	Lotus	25	BRM	V8	15	oil leak	9	4
r	16	D Gurney	Eagle	T1G	Climax	4	9	engine	3	1
r	23	T Taylor	Shannon	Mk 1	Climax	V8	0	fuel tank	18	7

Winning speed 153.658 km/h, 95.479 mph
Pole Position speed 162.467 km/h, 100.952 mph (J Brabham, 1 min:34.500 sec)
Fastest Lap speed 158.280 km/h, 98.351 mph (J Brabham, 1 min:37.000 sec on lap 60)
Lap Leaders J Brabham 1-80 (80).

---

24 Jul 1966   **NETHERLANDS: Zandvoort**   **(Round 5)**   **(Race 146)**

90 laps x 4.193 km, 2.605 miles = 377.370 km, 234.487 miles

Pos	No	Driver	Car	Model	Engine		Laps	Time/Reason for Retirement	Grid Pos	Row
1	16	J Brabham	Brabham	BT19	Repco	V8	90	2h 20m 32.500s	1	1
2	12	G Hill	BRM	P261	BRM	V8	89		7	3
3	6	J Clark	Lotus	33	Climax	V8	88		3	1
4	14	J Stewart	BRM	P261	BRM	V8	88		8	3
5	32	M Spence	Lotus	25	BRM	V8	87		12	5
6	2	L Bandini	Ferrari	312	Ferrari	V12	87		9	4
7	30	J Bonnier	Cooper	T81	Maserati	V12	84		13	5
8	38	J Taylor	Brabham	BT11	BRM	V8	84		17	7
9	36	G Ligier	Cooper	T81	Maserati	V12	84		16	7
r	28	J Siffert	Cooper	T81	Maserati	V12	79	engine	11	5
r	34	B Anderson	Brabham	BT11	Climax	4	73	rear suspension	14	6
r	24	J Surtees	Cooper	T81	Maserati	V12	44	electrics	10	4
r	18	D Hulme	Brabham	BT20	Repco	V8	37	ignition	2	1
r	8	P Arundell	Lotus	33	BRM	V8	28	ignition	15	6
r	10	D Gurney	Eagle	T1G	Climax	4	26	oil line	4	2
r	4	M Parkes	Ferrari	312	Ferrari	V12	10	accident	5	2
r	26	J Rindt	Cooper	T81	Maserati	V12	2	accident	6	3
ns	20	B McLaren	McLaren	M2B	Serenissima	V8		engine		

Winning speed 161.107 km/h, 100.107 mph
Pole Position speed 171.337 km/h, 106.464 mph (J Brabham, 1 min:28.100 sec)
Fastest Lap speed 166.609 km/h, 103.526 mph (D Hulme, 1 min:30.600 sec on lap 2)
Lap Leaders J Brabham 1-26,76-90 (41); J Clark 27-75 (49).

15 laps x 22.810 km, 14.173 miles = 342.150 km, 212.602 miles

Pos	No	Driver	Car	Model	Engine		Laps	Time/Reason for Retirement	Grid Pos	Row
1	3	J Brabham	Brabham	BT19	Repco	V8	15	2h 27m 03.000s	5	2
2	7	J Surtees	Cooper	T81	Maserati	V12	15	2h 27m 47.400s	2	1
3	8	J Rindt	Cooper	T81	Maserati	V12	15	2h 29m 35.600s	9	3
4	5	G Hill	BRM	P261	BRM	V8	15	2h 33m 44.400s	10	3
5	6	J Stewart	BRM	P261	BRM	V8	15	2h 35m 31.900s	3	1
6	9	L Bandini	Ferrari	312	Ferrari	V12	15	2h 37m 59.400s	6	2
7	12	D Gurney	Eagle	T1G	Climax	4	14		8	3
F2: 1	34	*J-P Beltoise*	*Matra*	*MS5*	*Ford Cosworth*	4	14		18	5
F2: 2	26	*H Hahne*	*Matra*	*MS5*	*BRM*	4	14		27	8
F2: 3	33	*J Schlesser*	*Matra*	*MS5*	*Ford Cosworth*	4	14		19	6
F2: 4	28	*H Herrmann*	*Brabham*	*BT18*	*Ford Cosworth*	4	14		22	7
8	2	P Arundell	Lotus	33	BRM	V8	14		17	5
r	15	M Spence	Lotus	25	BRM	V8	12	alternator	13	4
r	1	J Clark	Lotus	33	Climax	V8	11	accident	1	1
r	20	C Lawrence	Cooper	T73	Ferrari	V12	10	front suspension	26	8
r	11	L Scarfiotti	Ferrari	246	Ferrari	V6	9	electrics	4	1
r	10	M Parkes	Ferrari	312	Ferrari	V12	9	accident	7	2
r	4	D Hulme	Brabham	BT20	Repco	V8	8	ignition	15	5
F2: r	31	*P Rodriguez*	*Lotus*	*44*	*Ford Cosworth*	4	7	*engine*	20	6
r	17	J Bonnier	Cooper	T81	Maserati	V12	4	engine	12	4
F2: r	29	*A Rees*	*Brabham*	*BT18*	*Ford Cosworth*	4	4	*engine*	24	7
F2: r	32	*P Courage*	*Lotus*	*44*	*Ford Cosworth*	4	3	*accident*	23	7
r	14	B Bondurant	BRM	P261	BRM	V8	3	engine	11	3
F2: r	25	*K Ahrens*	*Brabham*	*BT18*	*Ford Cosworth*	4	3	*gearbox*	21	6
r	19	B Anderson	Brabham	BT11	Climax	4	2	transmission	14	4
F2: r	27	*J Ickx*	*Matra*	*MS5*	*Ford Cosworth*	4	1	*accident*	16	5
r	16	J Taylor	Brabham	BT11	BRM	V8	0	fatal accident	25	7
F2: ns	35	*S Moser*	*Brabham*	*BT16*	*Ford Cosworth*	4		*engine*		
F2: ns	30	*G Mitter*	*Lotus*	*44*	*Ford Cosworth*	4		*driver unfit (earlier accident)*		
ns	18	G Ligier	Cooper	T81	Maserati	V12		accident / injury		

Winning speed 139.606 km/h, 86.747 mph
Pole Position speed 165.390 km/h, 102.768 mph (J Clark, 8 min:16.500 sec)
Fastest Lap speed 155.229 km/h, 96.455 mph (J Surtees, 8 min:49.000 sec on lap 4)
Lap Leaders J Brabham 1-15 (15).

Formula 2 cars raced simultaneously with F1, and are shown in italics.

68 laps x 5.750 km, 3.573 miles = 391.000 km, 242.956 miles

Pos	No	Driver	Car	Model	Engine		Laps	Time/Reason for Retirement	Grid Pos	Row
1	6	L Scarfiotti	Ferrari	312	Ferrari	V12	68	1h 47m 14.800s	2	1
2	4	M Parkes	Ferrari	312	Ferrari	V12	68	1h 47m 20.600s	1	1
3	12	D Hulme	Brabham	BT20	Repco	V8	68	1h 47m 20.900s	10	4
4	16	J Rindt	Cooper	T81	Maserati	V12	67		8	3
5	32	M Spence	Lotus	25	BRM	V8	67		14	6
6	40	B Anderson	Brabham	BT11	Climax	4	66		15	6
7	48	B Bondurant	BRM	P261	BRM	V8	65		18	7
8r	24	P Arundell	Lotus	33	BRM	V8	63	engine	13	5
9	20	Geki	Lotus	33	Climax	V8	63		20	8
nc	44	G Baghetti	Ferrari	246	Ferrari	V6	59		16	7
r	22	J Clark	Lotus	43	BRM	H16	58	gearbox	3	1
r	36	J Siffert	Cooper	T81	Maserati	V12	46	engine	17	7
r	2	L Bandini	Ferrari	312	Ferrari	V12	33	ignition	5	2
r	14	J Surtees	Cooper	T81	Maserati	V12	31	fuel leak	4	2
r	18	R Ginther	Honda	RA273	Honda	V12	16	rear tyre / accident	7	3
r	30	D Gurney	Eagle	T1G	Weslake	V12	7	oil overheating	19	8
r	10	J Brabham	Brabham	BT19	Repco	V8	7	oil leak	6	3
r	28	J Stewart	BRM	P83	BRM	H16	5	fuel leak	9	4
r	38	J Bonnier	Cooper	T81	Maserati	V12	3	throttle linkage	12	5
r	26	G Hill	BRM	P83	BRM	H16	0	camshaft	11	5
nq	34	P Hill	Eagle	T1G	Climax	4				
nq	32	C Amon	Brabham	BT11	BRM	V8				

Winning speed 218.748 km/h, 135.924 mph
Pole Position speed 226.725 km/h, 140.880 mph (M Parkes, 1 min:31.300 sec)
Fastest Lap speed 224.026 km/h, 139.203 mph (L Scarfiotti, 1 min:32.400 sec on lap 49)
Lap Leaders L Bandini 1 (1); M Parkes 2,8-10,12,27 (6); J Surtees 3 (1); J Brabham 4-7 (4); D Hulme 11 (1); L Scarfiotti 13-26,28-68 (55).

G Baghetti also practised in a Lotus 25-BRM V8, but after an engine failure, was loaned a Ferrari for the race.
J Clark and Geki exchanged car numbers after practice. M Spence used 42 in practice and took his race number from C Amon.

2 Oct 1966　　　　**USA: Watkins Glen**　　　　　　　　　　　　　　　　　　　　**(Round 8)**　　**(Race 149)**

108 laps x 3.701 km, 2.300 miles = 399.761 km, 248.400 miles

Pos	No	Driver	Car	Model	Engine		Laps	Time/Reason for Retirement	Grid Pos	Row
1	1	J Clark	Lotus	43	BRM	H16	108	2h 09m 40.100s	2	1
2	8	J Rindt	Cooper	T81	Maserati	V12	107		9	5
3	7	J Surtees	Cooper	T81	Maserati	V12	107		4	2
4	19	J Siffert	Cooper	T81	Maserati	V12	105		13	7
5	17	B McLaren	McLaren	M2B	Ford	V8	105		11	6
6	2	P Arundell	Lotus	33	Climax	V8	101		19	10
r	10	I Ireland	BRM	P261	BRM	V8	96	alternator	17	9
nc	12	R Ginther	Honda	RA273	Honda	V12	81		8	4
r	18	M Spence	Lotus	25	BRM	V8	74	ignition	12	6
r	14	R Bucknum	Honda	RA273	Honda	V12	58	transmission	18	9
nc	22	J Bonnier	Cooper	T81	Maserati	V12	57		15	8
r	5	J Brabham	Brabham	BT20	Repco	V8	55	engine	1	1
r	4	J Stewart	BRM	P83	BRM	H16	53	engine	6	3
r	3	G Hill	BRM	P83	BRM	H16	52	crown wheel & pinion	5	3
r	9	L Bandini	Ferrari	312	Ferrari	V12	34	engine	3	2
r	6	D Hulme	Brabham	BT20	Repco	V8	18	oil pressure	7	4
r	15	D Gurney	Eagle	T1G	Weslake	V12	13	clutch	14	7
r	11	P Rodríguez	Lotus	33	BRM	V8	13	starter	10	5
dq	16	B Bondurant	Eagle	T1G	Climax	4	5	push start	16	8

Winning speed 184.977 km/h, 114.939 mph
Pole Position speed 194.758 km/h, 121.017 mph (J Brabham, 1 min: 8.420 sec)
Fastest Lap speed 191.264 km/h, 118.846 mph (J Surtees, 1 min: 9.670 sec on lap 31)
Lap Leaders L Bandini 1-9,20-34 (24); J Brabham 10-19,35-55 (31); J Clark 56-108 (53).

J Rindt completed 108 laps, but was only credited with 107, as his final lap exceeded twice the time of the winner's fastest lap.
J Clark practised in car no. 1 and no. 2.

23 Oct 1966　　　　**MEXICO: Mexico City**　　　　　　　　　　　　　　　　　　**(Round 9)**　　**(Race 150)**

65 laps x 5.000 km, 3.107 miles = 325.000 km, 201.946 miles

Pos	No	Driver	Car	Model	Engine		Laps	Time/Reason for Retirement	Grid Pos	Row
1	7	J Surtees	Cooper	T81	Maserati	V12	65	2h 06m 35.340s	1	1
2	5	J Brabham	Brabham	BT20	Repco	V8	65	2h 06m 43.220s	4	2
3	6	D Hulme	Brabham	BT20	Repco	V8	64		6	3
4	12	R Ginther	Honda	RA273	Honda	V12	64		3	2
5	15	D Gurney	Eagle	T1G	Climax	4	64		9	5
6	22	J Bonnier	Cooper	T81	Maserati	V12	63		12	6
7	2	P Arundell	Lotus	33	BRM	V8	61		17	9
8	14	R Bucknum	Honda	RA273	Honda	V12	60		13	7
r	11	P Rodríguez	Lotus	33	Climax	V8	49	crown wheel & pinion	8	4
r	17	B McLaren	McLaren	M2B	Ford	V8	40	engine	14	7
r	19	J Siffert	Cooper	T81	Maserati	V12	33	front suspension	11	6
r	8	J Rindt	Cooper	T81	Maserati	V12	32	front suspension	5	3
r	10	I Ireland	BRM	P261	BRM	V8	28	gearbox	16	8
r	4	J Stewart	BRM	P83	BRM	H16	26	oil leak	10	5
r	16	B Bondurant	Eagle	T1G	Weslake	V12	24	fuel injection	18	9
r	3	G Hill	BRM	P83	BRM	H16	18	engine	7	4
r	9	M Solana	Cooper	T81	Maserati	V12	9	engine overheating	15	8
r	1	J Clark	Lotus	43	BRM	H16	9	gearbox	2	1
ns	18	M Spence	Lotus	25	BRM	V8		accident		

Winning speed 154.042 km/h, 95.717 mph
Pole Position speed 159.039 km/h, 98.822 mph (J Surtees, 1 min:53.180 sec)
Fastest Lap speed 158.242 km/h, 98.327 mph (R Ginther, 1 min:53.750 sec on lap 58)
Lap Leaders R Ginther 1 (1); J Brabham 2-5 (4); J Surtees 6-65 (60).

Lap Leaders 1966

Pos	Driver	Car-Engine	GPs	laps	km	miles
1	J Brabham	Brabham-Repco	7	192	1,154.1	717.1
2	J Clark	Lotus-BRM	1	53	196.2	121.9
		Lotus-Climax	1	49	205.6	127.7
			2	102	401.6	249.5
3	J Stewart	BRM	1	86	270.5	168.1
4	J Surtees	Cooper-Maserati	2	61	305.7	190.0
		Ferrari	2	21	142.7	88.7
			4	82	448.4	278.7
5	L Bandini	Ferrari	4	57	366.0	227.4
6	L Scarfiotti	Ferrari	1	55	316.2	196.5
7	J Rindt	Cooper-Maserati	1	20	282.0	175.2
8	M Parkes	Ferrari	1	6	34.5	21.4
9	D Hulme	Brabham-Repco	1	1	5.7	3.6
	R Ginther	Honda	1	1	5.0	3.1
			9	602	3,284.2	2,040.7

Driver Points 1966

Pos	Driver	MC	B	F	GB	NL	D	I	USA	MEX	Total	
1	J Brabham	-	(3)	9	9	9	9	-	-	6	42	(3)
2	J Surtees	-	9	-	-	-	6	-	4	9	28	
3	J Rindt	-	6	3	(2)	-	4	3	6	-	22	(2)
4	D Hulme	-	-	4	6	-	-	4	-	4	18	
5	G Hill	4	-	-	4	6	3	-	-	-	17	
6	J Clark	-	-	-	3	4	-	-	9	-	16	
7	J Stewart	9	-	-	-	3	2	-	-	-	14	
8	M Parkes	-	-	6	-	-	-	6	-	-	12	
	L Bandini	6	4	-	-	1	1	-	-	-	12	
10	L Scarfiotti	-	-	-	-	-	-	9	-	-	9	
11	R Ginther	-	2	-	-	-	-	-	-	3	5	
12	D Gurney	-	-	2	-	-	-	-	-	2	4	
	M Spence	-	-	-	-	2	-	2	-	-	4	
14	B Bondurant	3	-	-	-	-	-	-	-	-	3	
	J Siffert	-	-	-	-	-	-	-	3	-	3	
	B McLaren	-	-	-	1	-	-	-	2	-	3	
17	J Taylor	-	-	1	-	-	-	-	-	-	1	
	B Anderson	-	-	-	-	-	-	1	-	-	1	
	P Arundell	-	-	-	-	-	-	-	1	-	1	
	J Bonnier	-	-	-	-	-	-	-	-	1	1	

9,6,4,3,2 and 1 point awarded to the first six finishers. Best 5 scores.

Constructor Points 1966

Pos		MC	B	F	GB	NL	D	I	USA	MEX	Total	
1	Brabham-Repco	-	(3)	9	9	9	9	(4)	-	6	42	(7)
2	Ferrari	6	9	6	-	1	(1)	9	-	-	31	(1)
3	Cooper-Maserati	-	6	3	(2)	-	6	(3)	6	9	30	(5)
4	BRM	9	-	-	4	6	3	-	-	-	22	
5	Lotus-BRM	-	-	-	-	2	-	2	9	-	13	
6	Lotus-Climax	-	-	-	3	4	-	-	1	-	8	
7	Eagle-Climax	-	-	2	-	-	-	-	-	2	4	
8	Honda	-	-	-	-	-	-	-	-	3	3	
9	McLaren-Ford	-	-	-	-	-	-	-	2	-	2	
10	Brabham-BRM	-	-	1	-	-	-	-	-	-	1	
	McLaren-Serenissima	-	-	-	1	-	-	-	-	-	1	
	Brabham-Climax	-	-	-	-	-	-	1	-	-	1	

9,6,4,3,2 and 1 point awarded to the first six finishers. Points only for highest placed car. Best 5 scores.

1967

Race Entrants and Results

Brabham produced a similar, smaller car, still based on the spaceframe chassis. The Ford Cosworth DFV (Double Four Valve) engine made a dramatic entry to Formula 1 in the Lotus 49, winning the Dutch Grand Prix. Hill returned to Lotus, making a very strong partnership with double champion Clark. Honda turned to Lola for help and won first time out with the new car.

FERRARI
Scuderia Ferrari SpA SEFAC: Bandini, Amon, Parkes, Scarfiotti, Williams

BRABHAM
Brabham Racing Organisation: Brabham, Hulme
DW Racing Enterprises: Anderson
Scuderia Scribante: Charlton
Privateers: Botha, Ligier

BRM
Owen Racing Organisation: Stewart, Spence
Reg Parnell Racing Ltd: Irwin, Courage
Bernard White Racing: Hobbs

COOPER
Cooper Car Co: Rindt, Rodríguez, Ickx, Rees, Attwood
Rob Walker/Jack Durlacher Racing Team: Siffert
Joakim Bonnier Racing Team: Bonnier, de Adamich
Charles Vögele: Moser
Privateers: Ligier, Love, (Jones)

LOTUS
Team Lotus: Clark, Hill, Solana, Wietzes, Baghetti
Reg Parnell Racing Ltd: Courage, Irwin
Privateer: Fisher

LOLA
Bayerische Motoren Werke AG: Hahne

McLAREN
Bruce McLaren Motor Racing: McLaren

MATRA
Matra Sports: Beltoise, Servoz-Gavin

EAGLE
Anglo American Racers: Gurney, McLaren, Scarfiotti, (Ginther)
Castrol Oils Ltd: Pease

HONDA
Honda Racing: Surtees

LDS
Privateer: Tingle

(Entries for the F2 section are not included)

2 Jan 1967				SOUTH AFRICA: Kyalami				(Round 1)		(Race 151)	
				80 laps x 4.094 km, 2.544 miles = 327.534 km, 203.520 miles							
Pos	No	Driver	Car	Model	Engine		Laps	Time/Reason for Retirement		Grid Pos	Row
1	4	P Rodríguez	Cooper	T81	Maserati	V12	80	2h 05m 45.900s		4	2
2	17	J Love	Cooper	T79	Climax	4	80	2h 06m 12.300s		5	3
3	11	J Surtees	Honda	RA273	Honda	V12	79			6	3
4	2	D Hulme	Brabham	BT20	Repco	V8	78			2	1
5	14	B Anderson	Brabham	BT11	Climax	4	78			10	5
6	1	J Brabham	Brabham	BT20	Repco	V8	76			1	1
nc	19	D Charlton	Brabham	BT11	Climax	4	63			8	4
nc	20	L Botha	Brabham	BT11	Climax	4	60			17	9
r	18	S Tingle	LDS	Mk 3B	Climax	4	56	accident		14	7
r	16	P Courage	Lotus	25	BRM	V8	51	engine		18	9
r	9	D Gurney	Eagle	T1G	Climax	4	44	rear suspension		11	6
r	12	J Siffert	Cooper	T81	Maserati	V12	41	engine overheating		16	8
r	3	J Rindt	Cooper	T81	Maserati	V12	38	engine		7	4
r	6	M Spence	BRM	P83	BRM	H16	31	oil line		13	7
r	15	J Bonnier	Cooper	T81	Maserati	V12	30	engine		12	6
r	7	J Clark	Lotus	43	BRM	H16	22	engine		3	2
r	8	G Hill	Lotus	43	BRM	H16	6	accident		15	8
r	5	J Stewart	BRM	P83	BRM	H16	2	engine		9	5

Winning speed 156.260 km/h, 97.095 mph
Pole Position speed 166.920 km/h, 103.719 mph (J Brabham, 1 min:28.300 sec)
Fastest Lap speed 163.949 km/h, 101.873 mph (D Hulme, 1 min:29.900 sec on lap 3)
Lap Leaders D Hulme 1-60 (60); J Love 61-73 (13); P Rodríguez 74-80 (7).

7 May 1967		**MONACO: Monte-Carlo**						**(Round 2)**		**(Race 152)**

100 laps x 3.145 km, 1.954 miles = 314.500 km, 195.421 miles

Pos	No	Driver	Car	Model	Engine		Laps	Time/Reason for Retirement	Grid Pos	Row
1	9	D Hulme	Brabham	BT20	Repco	V8	100	2h 34m 34.300s	4	2
2	14	G Hill	Lotus	33	BRM	V8	99		8	4
3	20	C Amon	Ferrari	312	Ferrari	V12	98		14	7
4	16	B McLaren	McLaren	M4B	BRM	V8	97		10	5
5	11	P Rodríguez	Cooper	T81	Maserati	V12	96		16	8
6	5	M Spence	BRM	P83	BRM	H16	96		12	6
r	18	L Bandini	Ferrari	312	Ferrari	V12	81	fatal accident	2	1
r	6	P Courage	BRM	P261	BRM	V8	64	spin	13	7
r	12	J Clark	Lotus	33	Climax	V8	42	rear suspension	5	3
r	7	J Surtees	Honda	RA273	Honda	V12	32	engine	3	2
r	17	J Siffert	Cooper	T81	Maserati	V12	31	engine	9	5
r	10	J Rindt	Cooper	T81	Maserati	V12	14	gearbox	15	8
r	4	J Stewart	BRM	P261	BRM	V8	14	crown wheel & pinion	6	3
r	23	D Gurney	Eagle	T1G	Weslake	V12	4	fuel pump drive	7	4
r	2	J Servoz-Gavin	Matra	MS7	Ford Cosworth	4	4	fuel injection	11	6
r	8	J Brabham	Brabham	BT19	Repco	V8	0	engine	1	1
nq	15	B Anderson	Brabham	BT11	Climax	4				
nq	1	J-P Beltoise	Matra	MS7	Ford Cosworth	4				
nq	22	R Ginther	Eagle	T1G	Weslake	V12				

Winning speed 122.079 km/h, 75.857 mph
Pole Position speed 129.247 km/h, 80.310 mph (J Brabham, 1 min:27.600 sec)
Fastest Lap speed 126.503 km/h, 78.605 mph (J Clark, 1 min:29.500 sec on lap 38)
Lap Leaders L Bandini 1 (1); D Hulme 2-5,15-100 (90); J Stewart 6-14 (9).

4 Jun 1967		**NETHERLANDS: Zandvoort**						**(Round 3)**		**(Race 153)**

90 laps x 4.193 km, 2.605 miles = 377.370 km, 234.487 miles

Pos	No	Driver	Car	Model	Engine		Laps	Time/Reason for Retirement	Grid Pos	Row
1	5	J Clark	Lotus	49	Ford Cosworth	V8	90	2h 14m 45.100s	8	3
2	1	J Brabham	Brabham	BT19	Repco	V8	90	2h 15m 08.700s	3	1
3	2	D Hulme	Brabham	BT20	Repco	V8	90	2h 15m 10.800s	7	3
4	3	C Amon	Ferrari	312	Ferrari	V12	90	2h 15m 12.400s	9	4
5	4	M Parkes	Ferrari	312	Ferrari	V12	89		10	4
6	22	L Scarfiotti	Ferrari	312	Ferrari	V12	89		15	6
7	18	C Irwin	Lotus	25	BRM	V8	88		13	5
8	10	M Spence	BRM	P83	BRM	H16	87		12	5
9	21	B Anderson	Brabham	BT11	Climax	4	86		17	7
10	20	J Siffert	Cooper	T81	Maserati	V12	83		16	7
r	7	J Surtees	Honda	RA273	Honda	V12	73	throttle slides	6	3
r	9	J Stewart	BRM	P83	BRM	H16	51	brakes	11	5
r	12	J Rindt	Cooper	T81B	Maserati	V12	41	front suspension / handling	4	2
r	14	P Rodríguez	Cooper	T81	Maserati	V12	39	gearbox	5	2
r	6	G Hill	Lotus	49	Ford Cosworth	V8	11	timing gears	1	1
r	15	D Gurney	Eagle	T1G	Weslake	V12	8	fuel injection	2	1
r	17	B McLaren	McLaren	M4B	BRM	V8	1	accident	14	6

Winning speed 168.029 km/h, 104.408 mph
Pole Position speed 178.426 km/h, 110.868 mph (G Hill, 1 min:24.600 sec)
Fastest Lap speed 171.376 km/h, 106.488 mph (J Clark, 1 min:28.080 sec on lap 67)
Lap Leaders G Hill 1-10 (10); J Brabham 11-15 (5); J Clark 16-90 (75).

Races   111

18 Jun 1967   **BELGIUM: Spa-Francorchamps**   (Round 4)   (Race 154)

28 laps x 14.100 km, 8.761 miles = 394.800 km, 245.317 miles

Pos	No	Driver	Car	Model	Engine		Laps	Time/Reason for Retirement	Grid Pos	Row
1	36	D Gurney	Eagle	T1G	Weslake	V12	28	1h 40m 49.400s	2	1
2	14	J Stewart	BRM	P83	BRM	H16	28	1h 41m 52.400s	6	3
3	1	C Amon	Ferrari	312	Ferrari	V12	28	1h 42m 29.400s	5	2
4	29	J Rindt	Cooper	T81B	Maserati	V12	28	1h 43m 03.300s	4	2
5	12	M Spence	BRM	P83	BRM	H16	27		11	5
6	21	J Clark	Lotus	49	Ford Cosworth	V8	27		1	1
7	34	J Siffert	Cooper	T81	Maserati	V12	27		16	7
8	19	B Anderson	Brabham	BT11	Climax	4	26		17	7
9r	30	P Rodríguez	Cooper	T81	Maserati	V12	25	engine	13	5
10	32	G Ligier	Cooper	T81	Maserati	V12	25		18	7
nc	2	L Scarfiotti	Ferrari	312	Ferrari	V12	24		9	4
r	25	J Brabham	Brabham	BT24	Repco	V8	15	engine	7	3
r	26	D Hulme	Brabham	BT19	Repco	V8	14	engine	14	6
r	39	J Bonnier	Cooper	T81	Maserati	V12	10	fuel feed	12	5
r	22	G Hill	Lotus	49	Ford Cosworth	V8	3	clutch	3	1
r	17	C Irwin	BRM	P261	BRM	V8	1	camshaft	15	6
r	7	J Surtees	Honda	RA273	Honda	V12	1	crankshaft	10	4
r	3	M Parkes	Ferrari	312	Ferrari	V12	0	accident / injury	8	3

Winning speed 234.946 km/h, 145.988 mph
Pole Position speed 243.921 km/h, 151.566 mph (J Clark, 3 min:28.100 sec)
Fastest Lap speed 239.547 km/h, 148.848 mph (D Gurney, 3 min:31.900 sec on lap 19)
Lap Leaders J Clark 1-12 (12); J Stewart 13-20 (8); D Gurney 21-28 (8).

2 Jul 1967   **FRANCE: Bugatti au Mans**   (Round 5)   (Race 155)

80 laps x 4.422 km, 2.748 miles = 353.760 km, 219.816 miles

Pos	No	Driver	Car	Model	Engine		Laps	Time/Reason for Retirement	Grid Pos	Row
1	3	J Brabham	Brabham	BT24	Repco	V8	80	2h 13m 21.300s	2	1
2	4	D Hulme	Brabham	BT24	Repco	V8	80	2h 14m 10.800s	6	3
3	10	J Stewart	BRM	P261	BRM	V8	79		10	4
4	18	J Siffert	Cooper	T81	Maserati	V12	77		11	5
5r	15	C Irwin	BRM	P83	BRM	H16	76	engine	9	4
6	14	P Rodríguez	Cooper	T81	Maserati	V12	76		13	5
nc	16	G Ligier	Cooper	T81	Maserati	V12	68		15	6
r	2	C Amon	Ferrari	312	Ferrari	V12	47	throttle linkage	7	3
r	9	D Gurney	Eagle	T1G	Weslake	V12	40	fuel line	3	1
r	12	J Rindt	Cooper	T81B	Maserati	V12	33	piston	8	3
r	8	B McLaren	Eagle	T1G	Weslake	V12	26	ignition	5	2
r	6	J Clark	Lotus	49	Ford Cosworth	V8	23	crown wheel & pinion	4	2
r	17	B Anderson	Brabham	BT11	Climax	4	16	ignition	14	6
r	7	G Hill	Lotus	49	Ford Cosworth	V8	13	crown wheel & pinion	1	1
r	11	M Spence	BRM	P83	BRM	H16	9	final drive output shaft	12	5

Winning speed 159.166 km/h, 98.901 mph
Pole Position speed 165.480 km/h, 102.825 mph (G Hill, 1 min:36.200 sec)
Fastest Lap speed 164.625 km/h, 102.293 mph (G Hill, 1 min:36.700 sec on lap 7)
Lap Leaders G Hill 1,11-13 (4); J Brabham 2-4,24-80 (60); J Clark 5-10,14-23 (16).

BRITAIN: Silverstone (Round 6) (Race 156)

80 laps x 4.711 km, 2.927 miles = 376.844 km, 234.160 miles

Pos	No	Driver	Car	Model	Engine		Laps	Time/Reason for Retirement	Grid Pos	Row
1	5	J Clark	Lotus	49	Ford Cosworth	V8	80	1h 59m 25.600s	1	1
2	2	D Hulme	Brabham	BT24	Repco	V8	80	1h 59m 38.400s	4	1
3	8	C Amon	Ferrari	312	Ferrari	V12	80	1h 59m 42.200s	6	2
4	1	J Brabham	Brabham	BT24	Repco	V8	80	1h 59m 47.400s	3	1
5	12	P Rodríguez	Cooper	T81	Maserati	V12	79		9	3
6	7	J Surtees	Honda	RA273	Honda	V12	78		7	2
7	15	C Irwin	BRM	P261	BRM	V8	77		13	4
8	20	D Hobbs	BRM	P261	BRM	V8	77		14	4
9	14	A Rees	Cooper	T81	Maserati	V12	76		15	5
10	18	G Ligier	Brabham	BT20	Repco	V8	76		21	6
r	19	B Anderson	Brabham	BT11	Climax	4	67	engine	17	5
r	6	G Hill	Lotus	49	Ford Cosworth	V8	64	engine	2	1
r	4	M Spence	BRM	P83	BRM	H16	44	ignition	11	3
r	9	D Gurney	Eagle	T1G	Weslake	V12	34	clutch	5	2
r	22	S Moser	Cooper	T77	ATS	V8	29	oil pressure	20	6
r	11	J Rindt	Cooper	T86	Maserati	V12	26	engine	8	3
r	3	J Stewart	BRM	P83	BRM	H16	20	transmission	12	4
r	10	B McLaren	Eagle	T1G	Weslake	V12	14	engine	10	3
r	17	J Siffert	Cooper	T81	Maserati	V12	10	engine	18	5
r	23	J Bonnier	Cooper	T81	Maserati	V12	0	engine	19	6
ns	16	P Courage	BRM	P261	BRM	V8		car raced by Irwin	16	5

Winning speed 189.327 km/h, 117.642 mph
Pole Position speed 198.804 km/h, 123.531 mph (J Clark, 1 min:25.300 sec)
Fastest Lap speed 194.919 km/h, 121.117 mph (D Hulme, 1 min:27.000 sec on lap 3)
Lap Leaders J Clark 1-25,55-80 (51); G Hill 26-54 (29).

GERMANY: Nürburgring (Round 7) (Race 157)

15 laps x 22.835 km, 14.189 miles = 342.525 km, 212.835 miles

Pos	No	Driver	Car	Model	Engine		Laps	Time/Reason for Retirement	Grid Pos	Row
1	2	D Hulme	Brabham	BT24	Repco	V8	15	2h 05m 55.700s	2	1
2	1	J Brabham	Brabham	BT24	Repco	V8	15	2h 06m 34.200s	7	2
3	8	C Amon	Ferrari	312	Ferrari	V12	15	2h 06m 34.700s	8	3
4	7	J Surtees	Honda	RA273	Honda	V12	15	2h 08m 21.400s	6	2
F2: 1	24	*J Oliver*	*Lotus*	*48*	*Ford Cosworth*	*4*	*15*	*2h 12m 04.900s*	*19*	*6*
5	16	J Bonnier	Cooper	T81	Maserati	V12	15	2h 14m 37.800s	16	5
F2: 2	22	*A Rees*	*Brabham*	*BT23*	*Ford Cosworth*	*4*	*15*	*2h 14m 43.600s*	*20*	*6*
6	15	G Ligier	Brabham	BT20	Repco	V8	14		17	5
7	18	C Irwin	BRM	P83	BRM	H16	13		15	5
F2: 3	27	*D Hobbs*	*Lola*	*T100*	*BMW*	*4*	*13*		*22*	*7*
8	6	P Rodríguez	Cooper	T81	Maserati	V12	13		10	3
r	9	D Gurney	Eagle	T1G	Weslake	V12	12	driveshaft	4	1
F2: r	29	*J Ickx*	*Matra*	*MS7*	*Ford Cosworth*	*4*	*12*	*front suspension*	*18*	*6*
F2: nc	25	*B Hart*	*Protos*		*Ford Cosworth*	*4*	*12*		*25*	*8*
nc	14	J Siffert	Cooper	T81	Maserati	V12	11		12	4
r	4	G Hill	Lotus	49	Ford Cosworth	V8	8	rear suspension	13	4
r	17	H Hahne	Lola	T100	BMW	4	6	front suspension	14	4
r	11	J Stewart	BRM	P115	BRM	H16	5	crown wheel & pinion	3	1
r	5	J Rindt	Cooper	T86	Maserati	V12	4	steering	9	3
r	3	J Clark	Lotus	49	Ford Cosworth	V8	4	front suspension / tyre	1	1
F2: r	26	*K Ahrens*	*Protos*		*Ford Cosworth*	*4*	*4*	*radiator*	*23*	*7*
r	10	B McLaren	Eagle	T1G	Weslake	V12	3	oil line	5	2
r	12	M Spence	BRM	P83	BRM	H16	3	crown wheel & pinion	11	3
F2: r	23	*J Schlesser*	*Matra*	*MS5*	*Ford Cosworth*	*4*	*2*	*clutch*	*21*	*6*
F2: r	20	*G Mitter*	*Brabham*	*BT23*	*Ford Cosworth*	*4*	*0*	*engine*	*24*	*7*
F2: ns	28	*B Redman*	*Lola*	*T100*	*Ford Cosworth*	*4*				

Winning speed 163.200 km/h, 101.408 mph
Pole Position speed 169.812 km/h, 105.516 mph (J Clark, 8 min: 4.100 sec)
Fastest Lap speed 166.039 km/h, 103.172 mph (D Gurney, 8 min:15.100 sec on lap 3)
Lap Leaders J Clark 1-3 (3); D Gurney 4-12 (9); D Hulme 13-15 (3).

Formula 2 cars raced simultaneously with F1, and are shown in italics.
J Oliver finished 5th, but was not eligible for points due to being in the F2 section of the race.

27 Aug 1967 **CANADA: Mosport Park** (Round 8) (Race 158)

90 laps x 3.957 km, 2.459 miles = 356.164 km, 221.310 miles

Pos	No	Driver	Car	Model	Engine		Laps	Time/Reason for Retirement	Grid Pos	Row
1	1	J Brabham	Brabham	BT24	Repco	V8	90	2h 40m 40.000s	7	3
2	2	D Hulme	Brabham	BT24	Repco	V8	90	2h 41m 41.900s	3	1
3	10	D Gurney	Eagle	T1G	Weslake	V12	89		5	2
4	4	G Hill	Lotus	49	Ford Cosworth	V8	88		2	1
5	16	M Spence	BRM	P83	BRM	H16	87		10	4
6	20	C Amon	Ferrari	312	Ferrari	V12	87		4	2
7	19	B McLaren	McLaren	M5A	BRM	V12	86		6	3
8	9	J Bonnier	Cooper	T81	Maserati	V12	85		14	6
9	12	D Hobbs	BRM	P261	BRM	V8	85		12	5
10	8	D Attwood	Cooper	T81B	Maserati	V12	84		13	5
11	6	M Fisher	Lotus	33	BRM	V8	81		17	7
r	3	J Clark	Lotus	49	Ford Cosworth	V8	69	ignition wet	1	1
dq	5	E Wietzes	Lotus	49	Ford Cosworth	V8	69	ignition wet / push started	16	7
r	15	J Stewart	BRM	P115	BRM	H16	65	throttle slides	9	4
nc	11	A Pease	Eagle	T1G	Climax	4	47		15	6
r	17	C Irwin	BRM	P83	BRM	H16	18	throttle slides	11	5
r	71	J Rindt	Cooper	T81	Maserati	V12	4	ignition wet	8	3
ns	14	J Siffert	Cooper	T81	Maserati	V12		starter ring		
nq	41	T Jones	Cooper	T82	Climax	V8				

Winning speed 133.007 km/h, 82.647 mph
Pole Position speed 172.895 km/h, 107.432 mph (J Clark, 1 min:22.400 sec)
Fastest Lap speed 171.439 km/h, 106.527 mph (J Clark, 1 min:23.100 sec on lap 54)
Lap Leaders J Clark 1-3,58-67 (13); D Hulme 4-57 (54); J Brabham 68-90 (23).

---

10 Sep 1967 **!TALY: Monza** (Round 9) (Race 159)

68 laps x 5.750 km, 3.573 miles = 391.000 km, 242.956 miles

Pos	No	Driver	Car	Model	Engine		Laps	Time/Reason for Retirement	Grid Pos	Row
1	14	J Surtees	Honda	RA300	Honda	V12	68	1h 43m 45.000s	9	4
2	16	J Brabham	Brabham	BT24	Repco	V8	68	1h 43m 45.200s	2	1
3	20	J Clark	Lotus	49	Ford Cosworth	V8	68	1h 44m 08.100s	1	1
4	30	J Rindt	Cooper	T86	Maserati	V12	68	1h 44m 41.600s	11	5
5	36	M Spence	BRM	P83	BRM	H16	67		12	5
6	32	J Ickx	Cooper	T81B	Maserati	V12	66		15	6
7	2	C Amon	Ferrari	312	Ferrari	V12	64		4	2
r	22	G Hill	Lotus	49	Ford Cosworth	V8	58	engine	8	3
r	24	G Baghetti	Lotus	49	Ford Cosworth	V8	50	engine	17	7
r	6	J Siffert	Cooper	T81	Maserati	V12	50	tyre / accident	13	5
r	4	B McLaren	McLaren	M5A	BRM	V12	46	engine	3	1
r	26	J Bonnier	Cooper	T81	Maserati	V12	46	engine overheating	14	6
r	34	J Stewart	BRM	P115	BRM	H16	45	engine	7	3
r	18	D Hulme	Brabham	BT24	Repco	V8	30	engine overheating	6	3
r	12	G Ligier	Brabham	BT20	Repco	V8	26	valve	18	7
r	38	C Irwin	BRM	P83	BRM	H16	16	fuel pump drive	16	7
r	10	L Scarfiotti	Eagle	T1G	Weslake	V12	5	engine	10	4
r	8	D Gurney	Eagle	T1G	Weslake	V12	4	engine	5	2

Winning speed 226.120 km/h, 140.505 mph
Pole Position speed 233.898 km/h, 145.338 mph (J Clark, 1 min:28.500 sec)
Fastest Lap speed 233.898 km/h, 145.338 mph (J Clark, 1 min:28.500 sec on lap 26)
Lap Leaders D Gurney 1-2 (2); J Clark 3-9,11-12,61-67 (16); D Hulme 10,13-15,17,24-27 (9); J Brabham 16,59-60 (3); G Hill 18-23,28-58 (37); J Surtees 68 (1).

Also the Grand Prix of Europe.

1 Oct 1967   USA: Watkins Glen   (Round 10)   (Race 160)

108 laps x 3.701 km, 2.300 miles = 399.761 km, 248.400 miles

Pos	No	Driver	Car	Model	Engine		Laps	Time/Reason for Retirement	Grid Pos	Row
1	5	J Clark	Lotus	49	Ford Cosworth	V8	108	2h 03m 13.200s	2	1
2	6	G Hill	Lotus	49	Ford Cosworth	V8	108	2h 03m 19.500s	1	1
3	2	D Hulme	Brabham	BT24	Repco	V8	107		6	3
4	15	J Siffert	Cooper	T81	Maserati	V12	106		12	6
5	1	J Brabham	Brabham	BT24	Repco	V8	104		5	3
6	16	J Bonnier	Cooper	T81	Maserati	V12	101		15	8
7	22	J-P Beltoise	Matra	MS7	Ford Cosworth	4	101		18	9
r	3	J Surtees	Honda	RA300	Honda	V12	96	electrics	11	6
r	9	C Amon	Ferrari	312	Ferrari	V12	95	oil pressure	4	2
r	7	J Stewart	BRM	P115	BRM	H16	72	fuel pump drive	10	5
r	21	J Ickx	Cooper	T86	Maserati	V12	45	engine overheating	16	8
r	19	G Ligier	Brabham	BT20	Repco	V8	43	camshaft	17	9
r	17	C Irwin	BRM	P83	BRM	H16	41	connecting rod	14	7
r	8	M Spence	BRM	P83	BRM	H16	35	engine	13	7
r	4	J Rindt	Cooper	T81B	Maserati	V12	33	engine	8	4
r	11	D Gurney	Eagle	T1G	Weslake	V12	24	rear suspension	3	2
r	14	B McLaren	McLaren	M5A	BRM	V12	16	water hose	9	5
r	18	M Solana	Lotus	49	Ford Cosworth	V8	7	ignition	7	4

Winning speed 194.657 km/h, 120.954 mph
Pole Position speed 203.503 km/h, 126.451 mph (G Hill, 1 min: 5.480 sec)
Fastest Lap speed 201.900 km/h, 125.455 mph (G Hill, 1 min: 6.000 sec on lap 81)
Lap Leaders G Hill 1-40 (40); J Clark 41-108 (68).

22 Oct 1967   MEXICO: Mexico City   (Round 11)   (Race 161)

65 laps x 5.000 km, 3.107 miles = 325.000 km, 201.946 miles

Pos	No	Driver	Car	Model	Engine		Laps	Time/Reason for Retirement	Grid Pos	Row
1	5	J Clark	Lotus	49	Ford Cosworth	V8	65	1h 59m 28.700s	1	1
2	1	J Brabham	Brabham	BT24	Repco	V8	65	2h 00m 54.060s	5	3
3	2	D Hulme	Brabham	BT24	Repco	V8	64		6	3
4	3	J Surtees	Honda	RA300	Honda	V12	64		7	4
5	8	M Spence	BRM	P83	BRM	H16	63		11	6
6	21	P Rodríguez	Cooper	T81B	Maserati	V12	63		13	7
7	22	J-P Beltoise	Matra	MS7	Ford Cosworth	4	63		14	7
8	12	J Williams	Ferrari	312	Ferrari	V12	63		16	8
9	9	C Amon	Ferrari	312	Ferrari	V12	62		2	1
10	16	J Bonnier	Cooper	T81	Maserati	V12	61		17	9
11	19	G Ligier	Brabham	BT20	Repco	V8	61		19	10
12r	15	J Siffert	Cooper	T81	Maserati	V12	59	engine	10	5
r	14	B McLaren	McLaren	M5A	BRM	V12	45	oil pressure	8	4
r	17	C Irwin	BRM	P83	BRM	H16	33	oil loss	15	8
r	7	J Stewart	BRM	P115	BRM	H16	24	engine	12	6
r	6	G Hill	Lotus	49	Ford Cosworth	V8	18	universal joint	4	2
r	18	M Solana	Lotus	49	Ford Cosworth	V8	12	front suspension	9	5
r	11	D Gurney	Eagle	T1G	Weslake	V12	4	radiator	3	2
ns	10	M Fisher	Lotus	33	BRM	V8		fuel metering unit on parade lap	18	9

Winning speed 163.210 km/h, 101.414 mph
Pole Position speed 167.348 km/h, 103.986 mph (J Clark, 1 min:47.560 sec)
Fastest Lap speed 166.466 km/h, 103.437 mph (J Clark, 1 min:48.130 sec on lap 52)
Lap Leaders G Hill 1-2 (2); J Clark 3-65 (63).

C Amon finished 5th, having completed 63 laps, but was only credited with 62, as his final lap exceeded twice the time of the race's fastest lap.

Lap Leaders 1967

Pos	Driver	Car-Engine	GPs	laps	km	miles
1	J Clark	Lotus-Ford Cosworth	9	317	1,573.3	977.6
2	D Hulme	Brabham-Repco	5	216	862.6	536.0
3	G Hill	Lotus-Ford Cosworth	6	122	567.0	352.3
4	J Brabham	Brabham-Repco	4	91	394.5	245.2
5	D Gurney	Eagle-Weslake	3	19	329.8	204.9
6	J Stewart	BRM	2	17	141.1	87.7
7	J Love	Cooper-Climax	1	13	53.2	33.1
8	P Rodríguez	Cooper-Maserati	1	7	28.7	17.8
9	J Surtees	Honda	1	1	5.7	3.6
	L Bandini	Ferrari	1	1	3.1	2.0
			11	**804**	**3,959.2**	**2,460.1**

Driver Points 1967

		ZA	MC	NL	B	F	GB	D	CDN	I	USA	MEX	Total
1	D Hulme	3	9	4	-	6	6	9	6	-	4	4	51
2	J Brabham	1	-	6	-	9	3	6	9	6	(2)	6	46 (2)
3	J Clark	-	-	9	1	-	9	-	-	4	9	9	41
4	J Surtees	4	-	-	-	-	1	3	-	9	-	3	20
	C Amon	-	4	3	4	-	4	4	1	-	-	-	20
6	P Rodríguez	9	2	-	-	1	2	-	-	-	-	1	15
	G Hill	-	6	-	-	-	-	-	3	-	6	-	15
8	D Gurney	-	-	-	9	-	-	-	4	-	-	-	13
9	J Stewart	-	-	-	6	4	-	-	-	-	-	-	10
10	M Spence	-	1	-	2	-	-	-	2	2	-	2	9
11	J Love	6	-	-	-	-	-	-	-	-	-	-	6
	J Rindt	-	-	-	3	-	-	-	-	3	-	-	6
	J Siffert	-	-	-	-	3	-	-	-	-	3	-	6
14	B McLaren	-	3	-	-	-	-	-	-	-	-	-	3
	J Bonnier	-	-	-	-	-	-	2	-	-	1	-	3
16	B Anderson	2	-	-	-	-	-	-	-	-	-	-	2
	M Parkes	-	-	2	-	-	-	-	-	-	-	-	2
	C Irwin	-	-	-	-	2	-	-	-	-	-	-	2
19	L Scarfiotti	-	-	1	-	-	-	-	-	-	-	-	1
	G Ligier	-	-	-	-	-	-	1	-	-	-	-	1
	J Ickx	-	-	-	-	-	-	-	-	1	-	-	1

9,6,4,3,2 and 1 point awarded to the first six finishers. Best 5 scores from first 6 races, best 4 from remaining 5 races.

Constructor Points 1967

		ZA	MC	NL	B	F	GB	D	CDN	I	USA	MEX	Total
1	Brabham-Repco	3	9	6	-	9	6	9	9	6	(4)	6	63 (4)
2	Lotus-Ford Cosworth	-	-	9	1	-	9	-	3	4	9	9	44
3	Cooper-Maserati	9	2	-	3	3	2	2	-	3	3	1	28
4	Honda	4	-	-	-	-	1	3	-	9	-	3	20
	Ferrari	-	4	3	4	-	4	4	1	-	-	-	20
6	BRM	-	1	-	6	4	-	-	2	2	-	2	17
7	Eagle-Weslake	-	-	-	9	-	-	-	4	-	-	-	13
8	Cooper-Climax	6	-	-	-	-	-	-	-	-	-	-	6
	Lotus-BRM	-	6	-	-	-	-	-	-	-	-	-	6
10	McLaren-BRM	-	3	-	-	-	-	-	-	-	-	-	3
11	Brabham-Climax	2	-	-	-	-	-	-	-	-	-	-	2

9,6,4,3,2 and 1 point awarded to the first six finishers. Points only for highest placed car. Best 5 scores from first 6 races, best 4 from remaining 5 races.

Race Entrants and Results

The racing world was devastated with the death of Jim Clark at a minor F2 race at Hockenheim. Sponsorship arrived at the very next race in Spain, where Lotus appeared in the red and white colours of Gold Leaf cigarettes. The Cosworth engine was now made available to other teams. Aerodynamic aids appeared at the Belgian Grand Prix, initially manually operated wings.

FERRARI
Scuderia Ferrari SpA SEFAC: Amon, Ickx, Bell, de Adamich

BRM
Owen Racing Organisation: Rodríguez, Spence, Attwood, Unser
Reg Parnell Racing Ltd: Courage
Bernard White Racing: (Gardner)

BRABHAM
Brabham Racing Organisation: Brabham, Rindt, Gurney
Charles Vögele Racing: Moser
Caltex Racing Team Frankfurt: Ahrens
Team Gunston: Love
Scuderia Scribante: Charlton
Team Pretoria: Pretorius

COOPER
Cooper Car Co: Scarfiotti, Bianchi, Redman, Elford, Servoz-Gavin, Widdows
Rob Walker/Jack Durlacher Racing: Siffert
Joakim Bonnier Racing Team: Bonnier
John Love: van Rooyen

LOLA
Bayerische Motoren Werke AG: Hahne

LOTUS
Team Lotus*: Clark, Hill, Oliver, Andretti, Brack, Solana
* Gold Leaf Team Lotus from ZA GP
Rob Walker/Jack Durlacher Racing: Siffert

McLAREN
Bruce McLaren Motor Racing: McLaren, Hulme
Joakim Bonnier Racing Team: Bonnier
Anglo American Racers: Gurney

MATRA
Matra International: Stewart, Servoz-Gavin, Beltoise (E)
Matra Sports: Beltoise, Pescarolo

EAGLE
Anglo American Racers: Gurney
Castrol Oils Ltd: (Pease)

LDS
Team Gunston: Tingle

HONDA
Honda Racing: Surtees, Hobbs
Honda Racing (France): Schlesser
Joakim Bonnier Racing Team: Bonnier

1 Jan 1968			**SOUTH AFRICA: Kyalami**					**(Round 1)**	**(Race 162)**	
			80 laps x 4.104 km, 2.550 miles = 328.306 km, 204.000 miles							
Pos	No	Driver	Car	Model	Engine		Laps	Time/Reason for Retirement	Grid Pos	Row
1	4	J Clark	Lotus	49	Ford Cosworth	V8	80	1h 53m 56.600s	1	1
2	5	G Hill	Lotus	49	Ford Cosworth	V8	80	1h 54m 21.900s	2	1
3	3	J Rindt	Brabham	BT24	Repco	V8	80	1h 54m 27.000s	4	2
4	8	C Amon	Ferrari	312	Ferrari	V12	78		8	3
5	1	D Hulme	McLaren	M5A	BRM	V12	78		9	4
6	21	J-P Beltoise	Matra	MS7	Ford Cosworth	4	77		18	7
7	19	J Siffert	Cooper	T81	Maserati	V12	77		16	7
8	7	J Surtees	Honda	RA300	Honda	V12	75		6	3
9	17	J Love	Brabham	BT20	Repco	V8	75		17	7
nc	23	J Pretorius	Brabham	BT11	Climax	4	71		23	9
r	6	D Gurney	Eagle	T1G	Weslake	V12	58	oil leak / engine overheating	12	5
r	9	J Ickx	Ferrari	312	Ferrari	V12	51	oil tank burst	11	5
r	20	J Bonnier	Cooper	T81	Maserati	V12	47	rear wheel lost	19	8
r	16	J Stewart	Matra	MS9	Ford Cosworth	V8	43	connecting rod	3	1
r	18	S Tingle	LDS	Mk 3B	Repco	V8	35	engine overheating	22	9
r	25	B van Rooyen	Cooper	T79	Climax	4	22	cylinder head gasket	20	8
r	11	P Rodríguez	BRM	P126	BRM	V12	20	ignition / boiling fuel	10	4
r	2	J Brabham	Brabham	BT24	Repco	V8	17	valve spring	5	2
r	10	A de Adamich	Ferrari	312	Ferrari	V12	13	accident	7	3
r	12	M Spence	BRM	P115	BRM	H16	8	boiling fuel	13	5
r	14	B Redman	Cooper	T81B	Maserati	V12	5	camshaft / oil leak / engine	21	9
r	22	D Charlton	Brabham	BT11	Repco	V8	3	crown wheel & pinion	14	6
r	15	L Scarfiotti	Cooper	T86	Maserati	V12	2	brake pipe / accident	15	6

Winning speed 172.879 km/h, 107.422 mph
Pole Position speed 181.051 km/h, 112.500 mph (J Clark, 1 min:21.600 sec)
Fastest Lap speed 176.509 km/h, 109.677 mph (J Clark, 1 min:23.700 sec on lap 73)
Lap Leaders J Stewart 1 (1); J Clark 2-80 (79).

90 laps x 3.404 km, 2.115 miles = 306.360 km, 190.363 miles

Pos	No	Driver	Car	Model	Engine		Laps	Time/Reason for Retirement	Grid Pos	Row
1	10	G Hill	Lotus	49	Ford Cosworth	V8	90	2h 15m 20.100s	6	3
2	1	D Hulme	McLaren	M7A	Ford Cosworth	V8	90	2h 15m 36.000s	3	1
3	14	B Redman	Cooper	T86B	BRM	V12	89		13	5
4	15	L Scarfiotti	Cooper	T86B	BRM	V12	89		12	5
5	6	J-P Beltoise	Matra	MS10	Ford Cosworth	V8	81		5	2
r	2	B McLaren	McLaren	M7A	Ford Cosworth	V8	77	oil loss	4	2
r	7	J Surtees	Honda	RA301	Honda	V12	74	gear linkage	7	3
r	16	J Siffert	Lotus	49	Ford Cosworth	V8	62	transmission	10	4
r	19	C Amon	Ferrari	312	Ferrari	V12	57	fuel pump	1	1
r	5	P Courage	BRM	P126	BRM	V12	52	fuel metering unit	11	5
r	9	P Rodríguez	BRM	P133	BRM	V12	27	accident	2	1
r	21	J Ickx	Ferrari	312	Ferrari	V12	13	ignition	8	3
r	4	J Rindt	Brabham	BT24	Repco	V8	10	oil pressure	9	4
ns	8	J Brabham	Brabham	BT26	Repco	V8		engine		

Winning speed 135.823 km/h, 84.396 mph
Pole Position speed 139.413 km/h, 86.627 mph (C Amon, 1 min:27.900 sec)
Fastest Lap speed 138.781 km/h, 86.235 mph (J-P Beltoise, 1 min:28.300 sec on lap 47)
Lap Leaders P Rodríguez 1-11 (11); J-P Beltoise 12-15 (4); C Amon 16-57 (42); G Hill 58-90 (33).

80 laps x 3.145 km, 1.954 miles = 251.600 km, 156.337 miles

Pos	No	Driver	Car	Model	Engine		Laps	Time/Reason for Retirement	Grid Pos	Row
1	9	G Hill	Lotus	49B	Ford Cosworth	V8	80	2h 00m 32.300s	1	1
2	15	D Attwood	BRM	P126	BRM	V12	80	2h 00m 34.500s	6	3
3	7	L Bianchi	Cooper	T86B	BRM	V12	76		14	7
4	6	L Scarfiotti	Cooper	T86B	BRM	V12	76		15	8
5	12	D Hulme	McLaren	M7A	Ford Cosworth	V8	73		10	5
r	8	J Surtees	Honda	RA301	Honda	V12	16	gearbox	4	2
r	4	P Rodríguez	BRM	P133	BRM	V12	16	accident	9	5
r	16	P Courage	BRM	P126	BRM	V12	12	chassis	11	6
r	1	J-P Beltoise	Matra	MS11	Matra	V12	11	accident	8	4
r	17	J Siffert	Lotus	49	Ford Cosworth	V8	11	crown wheel & pinion	3	2
r	19	D Gurney	Eagle	T1G	Weslake	V12	9	ignition	16	8
r	3	J Rindt	Brabham	BT24	Repco	V8	8	accident	5	3
r	2	J Brabham	Brabham	BT26	Repco	V8	7	rear suspension	12	6
r	11	J Servoz-Gavin	Matra	MS10	Ford Cosworth	V8	3	accident / driveshaft	2	1
r	10	J Oliver	Lotus	49	Ford Cosworth	V8	0	accident	13	7
r	14	B McLaren	McLaren	M7A	Ford Cosworth	V8	0	accident	7	4
nq	18	J Bonnier	McLaren	M5A	BRM	V12				
nq	21	S Moser	Brabham	BT20	Repco	V8				

Winning speed 125.238 km/h, 77.819 mph
Pole Position speed 128.367 km/h, 79.764 mph (G Hill, 1 min:28.200 sec)
Fastest Lap speed 128.513 km/h, 79.854 mph (D Attwood, 1 min:28.100 sec on lap 80)
Lap Leaders J Servoz-Gavin 1-3 (3); G Hill 4-80 (77).

28 laps x 14.100 km, 8.761 miles = 394.800 km, 245.317 miles

Pos	No	Driver	Car	Model	Engine		Laps	Time/Reason for Retirement	Grid Pos	Row
1	5	B McLaren	McLaren	M7A	Ford Cosworth	V8	28	1h 40m 02.100s	6	3
2	11	P Rodríguez	BRM	P133	BRM	V12	28	1h 40m 14.200s	8	3
3	23	J Ickx	Ferrari	312	Ferrari	V12	28	1h 40m 41.700s	3	1
4	7	J Stewart	Matra	MS10	Ford Cosworth	V8	27		2	1
5r	2	J Oliver	Lotus	49B	Ford Cosworth	V8	26	driveshaft	15	6
6	15	L Bianchi	Cooper	T86B	BRM	V12	26		12	5
7r	3	J Siffert	Lotus	49	Ford Cosworth	V8	25	oil pressure	9	4
8	10	J-P Beltoise	Matra	MS11	Matra	V12	25		13	5
r	14	P Courage	BRM	P126	BRM	V12	22	engine	7	3
r	6	D Hulme	McLaren	M7A	Ford Cosworth	V8	18	driveshaft	5	2
r	20	J Surtees	Honda	RA301	Honda	V12	11	rear suspension	4	2
r	22	C Amon	Ferrari	312	Ferrari	V12	8	oil radiator	1	1
r	12	D Attwood	BRM	P126	BRM	V12	6	oil line	11	5
r	18	J Brabham	Brabham	BT26	Repco	V8	6	throttle slides	18	7
r	16	B Redman	Cooper	T86B	BRM	V12	6	accident	10	4
r	19	J Rindt	Brabham	BT26	Repco	V8	5	valve insert	17	7
r	1	G Hill	Lotus	49B	Ford Cosworth	V8	5	universal joint	14	6
r	17	J Bonnier	McLaren	M5A	BRM	V12	1	wheel stud	16	7

Winning speed 236.797 km/h, 147.139 mph
Pole Position speed 243.337 km/h, 151.202 mph (C Amon, 3 min:28.600 sec)
Fastest Lap speed 241.140 km/h, 149.838 mph (J Surtees, 3 min:30.500 sec on lap 5)
Lap Leaders C Amon 1 (1); J Surtees 2-10 (9); D Hulme 11,15 (2); J Stewart 12-14,16-27 (15); B McLaren 28 (1).

J Stewart completed 28 laps, but was only credited with 27, as his final lap exceeded twice the time of the race's fastest lap.

23 Jun 1968   **NETHERLANDS: Zandvoort**   **(Round 5)**   **(Race 166)**

90 laps x 4.193 km, 2.605 miles = 377.370 km, 234.487 miles

Pos	No	Driver	Car	Model	Engine		Laps	Time/Reason for Retirement	Grid Pos	Row
1	8	J Stewart	Matra	MS10	Ford Cosworth	V8	90	2h 46m 11.260s	5	2
2	17	J-P Beltoise	Matra	MS11	Matra	V12	90	2h 47m 45.190s	16	7
3	15	P Rodríguez	BRM	P133	BRM	V12	89		11	5
4	10	J Ickx	Ferrari	312	Ferrari	V12	88		6	3
5	22	S Moser	Brabham	BT20	Repco	V8	87		17	7
6	9	C Amon	Ferrari	312	Ferrari	V12	85		1	1
7	16	D Attwood	BRM	P126	BRM	V12	85		15	6
8	19	J Bonnier	McLaren	M5A	BRM	V12	82		19	8
9r	3	G Hill	Lotus	49B	Ford Cosworth	V8	81	spin	3	1
nc	4	J Oliver	Lotus	49B	Ford Cosworth	V8	80		10	4
r	18	D Gurney	Brabham	BT24	Repco	V8	63	throttle slides	12	5
r	21	J Siffert	Lotus	49	Ford Cosworth	V8	55	gear selection	13	5
r	20	P Courage	BRM	P126	BRM	V12	50	spin	14	6
r	7	J Surtees	Honda	RA301	Honda	V12	50	alternator	9	4
r	6	J Rindt	Brabham	BT26	Repco	V8	39	ignition damp	2	1
r	5	J Brabham	Brabham	BT26	Repco	V8	22	spin	4	2
r	2	B McLaren	McLaren	M7A	Ford Cosworth	V8	19	accident	8	3
r	1	D Hulme	McLaren	M7A	Ford Cosworth	V8	10	ignition damp	7	3
r	14	L Bianchi	Cooper	T86B	BRM	V12	9	accident	18	7

Winning speed 136.245 km/h, 84.659 mph
Pole Position speed 180.689 km/h, 112.275 mph (C Amon, 1 min:23.540 sec)
Fastest Lap speed 142.525 km/h, 88.561 mph (J-P Beltoise, 1 min:45.910 sec on lap 6)
Lap Leaders G Hill 1-3 (3); J Stewart 4-90 (87).

7 Jul 1968   **FRANCE: Rouen-les-Essarts**   **(Round 6)**   **(Race 167)**

60 laps x 6.542 km, 4.065 miles = 392.520 km, 243.901 miles

Pos	No	Driver	Car	Model	Engine		Laps	Time/Reason for Retirement	Grid Pos	Row
1	26	J Ickx	Ferrari	312	Ferrari	V12	60	2h 25m 40.900s	3	1
2	16	J Surtees	Honda	RA301	Honda	V12	60	2h 27m 39.500s	7	3
3	28	J Stewart	Matra	MS10	Ford Cosworth	V8	59		2	1
4	30	V Elford	Cooper	T86B	BRM	V12	58		17	7
5	8	D Hulme	McLaren	M7A	Ford Cosworth	V8	58		4	2
6	36	P Courage	BRM	P126	BRM	V12	57		14	6
7	22	D Attwood	BRM	P126	BRM	V12	57		12	5
8	6	B McLaren	McLaren	M7A	Ford Cosworth	V8	56		6	3
9	6	J-P Beltoise	Matra	MS11	Matra	V12	56		8	3
10	24	C Amon	Ferrari	312	Ferrari	V12	55		5	2
11	34	J Siffert	Lotus	49	Ford Cosworth	V8	54		11	5
nc	20	P Rodríguez	BRM	P133	BRM	V12	53		10	4
r	2	J Rindt	Brabham	BT26	Repco	V8	45	fuel tank	1	1
r	4	J Brabham	Brabham	BT26	Repco	V8	15	fuel pump	13	5
r	32	J Servoz-Gavin	Cooper	T86B	BRM	V12	14	accident	15	6
r	12	G Hill	Lotus	49B	Ford Cosworth	V8	14	driveshaft	9	4
r	18	J Schlesser	Honda	RA302	Honda	V8	2	fatal accident	16	7
ns	14	J Oliver	Lotus	49B	Ford Cosworth	V8		accident		

Winning speed 161.662 km/h, 100.452 mph
Pole Position speed 202.853 km/h, 126.047 mph (J Rindt, 1 min:56.100 sec)
Fastest Lap speed 179.097 km/h, 111.285 mph (P Rodríguez, 2 min:11.500 sec on lap 19)
Lap Leaders J Ickx 1-18,20-60 (59); P Rodríguez 19 (1).

Cars on row 7 lined up in reverse order.

20 Jul 1968   BRITAIN: Brands Hatch   (Round 7)   (Race 168)

80 laps x 4.265 km, 2.650 miles = 341.181 km, 212.000 miles

Pos	No	Driver	Car	Model	Engine		Laps	Time/Reason for Retirement	Grid Pos	Row
1	22	J Siffert	Lotus	49B	Ford Cosworth	V8	80	2h 01m 20.300s	4	2
2	5	C Amon	Ferrari	312	Ferrari	V12	80	2h 01m 24.700s	3	1
3	6	J Ickx	Ferrari	312	Ferrari	V12	79		12	5
4	1	D Hulme	McLaren	M7A	Ford Cosworth	V8	79		11	5
5	7	J Surtees	Honda	RA301	Honda	V12	78		9	4
6	14	J Stewart	Matra	MS10	Ford Cosworth	V8	78		7	3
7	2	B McLaren	McLaren	M7A	Ford Cosworth	V8	77		10	4
8	20	P Courage	BRM	P126	BRM	V12	72		16	7
r	4	J Rindt	Brabham	BT26	Repco	V8	55	fuel system	5	2
r	10	P Rodríguez	BRM	P133	BRM	V12	52	timing chain	13	5
nc	19	S Moser	Brabham	BT20	Repco	V8	52		19	8
r	9	J Oliver	Lotus	49B	Ford Cosworth	V8	43	crown wheel & pinion	2	1
r	16	R Widdows	Cooper	T86	BRM	V12	34	ignition	18	7
r	15	V Elford	Cooper	T86B	BRM	V12	26	engine	17	7
r	8	G Hill	Lotus	49B	Ford Cosworth	V8	26	universal joint	1	1
r	18	J-P Beltoise	Matra	MS11	Matra	V12	11	oil pressure	14	6
r	11	D Attwood	BRM	P126	BRM	V12	10	radiator	15	6
r	24	D Gurney	Eagle	T1G	Weslake	V12	8	fuel pump	6	3
r	23	J Bonnier	McLaren	M5A	BRM	V12	6	dropped valve	20	8
r	3	J Brabham	Brabham	BT26	Repco	V8	0	engine	8	3

Winning speed 168.709 km/h, 104.831 mph
Pole Position speed 172.701 km/h, 107.312 mph (G Hill, 1 min:28.900 sec)
Fastest Lap speed 171.161 km/h, 106.355 mph (J Siffert, 1 min:29.700 sec on lap 42)
Lap Leaders J Oliver 1-3,27-43 (20); G Hill 4-26 (23); J Siffert 44-80 (37).

4 Aug 1968   GERMANY: Nürburgring   (Round 8)   (Race 169)

14 laps x 22.835 km, 14.189 miles = 319.690 km, 198.646 miles

Pos	No	Driver	Car	Model	Engine		Laps	Time/Reason for Retirement	Grid Pos	Row
1	6	J Stewart	Matra	MS10	Ford Cosworth	V8	14	2h 19m 03.200s	6	3
2	3	G Hill	Lotus	49B	Ford Cosworth	V8	14	2h 23m 06.400s	4	2
3	5	J Rindt	Brabham	BT26	Repco	V8	14	2h 23m 12.600s	3	1
4	9	J Ickx	Ferrari	312	Ferrari	V12	14	2h 24m 58.400s	1	1
5	4	J Brabham	Brabham	BT26	Repco	V8	14	2h 25m 24.300s	15	6
6	10	P Rodríguez	BRM	P133	BRM	V12	14	2h 25m 28.200s	14	6
7	1	D Hulme	McLaren	M7A	Ford Cosworth	V8	14	2h 25m 34.200s	11	5
8	22	P Courage	BRM	P126	BRM	V12	14	2h 26m 59.600s	8	3
9	14	D Gurney	Eagle	T1G	Weslake	V12	14	2h 27m 16.900s	10	4
10	18	H Hahne	Lola	T102	BMW	4	14	2h 29m 14.600s	18	7
11	21	J Oliver	Lotus	49B	Ford Cosworth	V8	13		13	5
12	17	K Ahrens	Brabham	BT24	Repco	V8	13		17	7
13	2	B McLaren	McLaren	M7A	Ford Cosworth	V8	13		16	7
14	11	D Attwood	BRM	P126	BRM	V12	13		20	8
r	8	C Amon	Ferrari	312	Ferrari	V12	11	accident	2	1
r	12	J-P Beltoise	Matra	MS11	Matra	V12	8	accident	12	5
r	19	L Bianchi	Cooper	T86B	BRM	V12	7	fuel tank leak	19	8
r	16	J Siffert	Lotus	49B	Ford Cosworth	V8	6	ignition wet	9	4
r	7	J Surtees	Honda	RA301	Honda	V12	3	ignition	7	3
r	20	V Elford	Cooper	T86B	BRM	V12	0	accident	5	2
ns	23	S Moser	Brabham	BT20	Repco	V8		oil pump		

Winning speed 137.943 km/h, 85.714 mph
Pole Position speed 151.114 km/h, 93.898 mph (J Ickx, 9 min: 4.000 sec)
Fastest Lap speed 142.719 km/h, 88.681 mph (J Stewart, 9 min:36.000 sec on lap 8)
Lap Leaders J Stewart 1-14 (14).

Also the Grand Prix of Europe.

| | 8 Sep 1968 | **ITALY: Monza** | | | | | | | (Round 9) | (Race 170) | |

68 laps x 5.750 km, 3.573 miles = 391.000 km, 242.956 miles

Pos	No	Driver	Car	Model	Engine		Laps	Time/Reason for Retirement	Grid Pos	Row
1	1	D Hulme	McLaren	M7A	Ford Cosworth	V8	68	1h 40m 14.800s	7	3
2	5	J Servoz-Gavin	Matra	MS10	Ford Cosworth	V8	68	1h 41m 43.200s	13	5
3	8	J Ickx	Ferrari	312	Ferrari	V12	68	1h 41m 43.400s	4	1
4	27	P Courage	BRM	P126	BRM	V12	67		17	7
5	6	J-P Beltoise	Matra	MS11	Matra	V12	66		18	7
6	3	J Bonnier	McLaren	M5A	BRM	V12	64		19	8
r	20	J Siffert	Lotus	49B	Ford Cosworth	V8	58	rear suspension	9	4
r	10	J Brabham	Brabham	BT26	Repco	V8	56	oil pressure	16	7
r	15	D Hobbs	Honda	RA301	Honda	V12	42	dropped valve	14	6
r	4	J Stewart	Matra	MS10	Ford Cosworth	V8	42	engine	6	3
r	19	J Oliver	Lotus	49B	Ford Cosworth	V8	38	transmission	11	5
r	2	B McLaren	McLaren	M7A	Ford Cosworth	V8	34	oil loss	2	1
r	11	J Rindt	Brabham	BT26	Repco	V8	33	dropped valve	10	4
r	26	P Rodríguez	BRM	P138	BRM	V12	22	timing chain	15	6
r	21	D Gurney	Eagle	T1G	Weslake	V12	19	engine overheating	12	5
r	16	G Hill	Lotus	49B	Ford Cosworth	V8	10	rear wheel lost / accident	5	2
r	14	J Surtees	Honda	RA301	Honda	V12	8	accident	1	1
r	9	C Amon	Ferrari	312	Ferrari	V12	8	accident	3	1
r	7	D Bell	Ferrari	312	Ferrari	V12	4	fuel metering unit	8	3
r	23	V Elford	Cooper	T86B	BRM	V12	2	brakes / accident	20	8
exc	18	M Andretti	Lotus	49B	Ford Cosworth	V8		raced in USA within 24 hours		
exc	25	B Unser	BRM	P126	BRM	V12		raced in USA within 24 hours		
nq	28	F Gardner	BRM	P261	BRM	V12				
nq	12	S Moser	Brabham	BT20	Repco	V8				

Winning speed 234.023 km/h, 145.415 mph
Pole Position speed 240.502 km/h, 149.441 mph (J Surtees, 1 min:26.070 sec)
Fastest Lap speed 239.306 km/h, 148.698 mph (J Oliver, 1 min:26.500 sec on lap 7) *
Lap Leaders B McLaren 1-6,8-12,14 (12); J Surtees 7 (1); J Stewart 13,17-18,27,30,33,40 (7); J Siffert 15-16 (2); D Hulme 19-26,28-29,31-32,34-39,41-68 (46).

* Although J Oliver was credited with fastest lap, this lap time was impossible. Instead, it is clear that J Ickx achieved it in 1 min 26.600s on laps 53 and 63.

| | 22 Sep 1968 | **CANADA: Mont-Tremblant** | | | | | | | (Round 10) | (Race 171) | |

90 laps x 4.265 km, 2.650 miles = 383.829 km, 238.500 miles

Pos	No	Driver	Car	Model	Engine		Laps	Time/Reason for Retirement	Grid Pos	Row
1	1	D Hulme	McLaren	M7A	Ford Cosworth	V8	90	2h 27m 11.200s	6	3
2	2	B McLaren	McLaren	M7A	Ford Cosworth	V8	89		8	3
3	16	P Rodríguez	BRM	P133	BRM	V12	88		12	5
4	3	G Hill	Lotus	49B	Ford Cosworth	V8	86		5	2
5	21	V Elford	Cooper	T86B	BRM	V12	86		16	7
6	14	J Stewart	Matra	MS10	Ford Cosworth	V8	83		11	5
r	18	J-P Beltoise	Matra	MS11	Matra	V12	77	gearbox	15	6
r	9	C Amon	Ferrari	312	Ferrari	V12	72	transmission	2	1
r	15	J Servoz-Gavin	Matra	MS10	Ford Cosworth	V8	71	accident	13	5
nc	20	L Bianchi	Cooper	T86B	BRM	V12	56		18	7
r	19	H Pescarolo	Matra	MS11	Matra	V12	54	oil pressure	19	8
r	6	J Rindt	Brabham	BT26	Repco	V8	39	engine overheating	1	1
r	4	J Oliver	Lotus	49B	Ford Cosworth	V8	32	transmission	9	4
r	5	J Brabham	Brabham	BT26	Repco	V8	31	front suspension	10	4
r	12	J Siffert	Lotus	49B	Ford Cosworth	V8	29	oil leak	3	1
r	11	D Gurney	McLaren	M7A	Ford Cosworth	V8	29	radiator	4	2
r	24	P Courage	BRM	P126	BRM	V12	22	gearbox	14	6
r	27	B Brack	Lotus	49B	Ford Cosworth	V8	18	driveshaft	20	8
r	8	J Surtees	Honda	RA301	Honda	V12	10	gearbox	7	3
r	22	J Bonnier	McLaren	M5A	BRM	V12	0	fuel metering unit on grid	17	7
ns	10	J Ickx	Ferrari	312	Ferrari	V12		accident / injury		
ns	25	A Pease	Eagle	T1G	Climax		4	engine		

Winning speed 156.466 km/h, 97.223 mph
Pole Position speed 163.680 km/h, 101.706 mph (J Rindt, 1 min:33.800 sec)
Fastest Lap speed 161.442 km/h, 100.315 mph (J Siffert, 1 min:35.100 sec on lap 22)
Lap Leaders C Amon 1-72 (72); D Hulme 73-90 (18).

108 laps x 3.701 km, 2.300 miles = 399.761 km, 248.400 miles

Pos	No	Driver	Car	Model	Engine		Laps	Time/Reason for Retirement	Grid Pos	Row
1	15	J Stewart	Matra	MS10	Ford Cosworth	V8	108	1h 59m 20.290s	2	1
2	10	G Hill	Lotus	49B	Ford Cosworth	V8	108	1h 59m 44.970s	3	2
3	5	J Surtees	Honda	RA301	Honda	V12	107		9	5
4	14	D Gurney	McLaren	M7A	Ford Cosworth	V8	107		7	4
5	16	J Siffert	Lotus	49B	Ford Cosworth	V8	105		12	6
6	2	B McLaren	McLaren	M7A	Ford Cosworth	V8	103		10	5
r	22	P Courage	BRM	P126	BRM	V12	93	out of fuel	14	7
r	1	D Hulme	McLaren	M7A	Ford Cosworth	V8	92	accident	5	3
nc	19	L Bianchi	Cooper	T86B	BRM	V12	88		20	10
r	3	J Brabham	Brabham	BT26	Repco	V8	77	cam follower	8	4
r	4	J Rindt	Brabham	BT26	Repco	V8	73	engine	6	3
r	18	V Elford	Cooper	T86B	BRM	V12	71	camshaft	17	9
r	8	P Rodríguez	BRM	P133	BRM	V12	66	rear suspension	11	6
nc	17	J Bonnier	McLaren	M5A	BRM	V12	62		18	9
r	6	C Amon	Ferrari	312	Ferrari	V12	59	water pipe	4	2
r	21	J-P Beltoise	Matra	MS11	Matra	V12	44	driveshaft	13	7
r	9	B Unser	BRM	P138	BRM	V12	35	engine	19	10
r	12	M Andretti	Lotus	49B	Ford Cosworth	V8	32	clutch	1	1
r	7	D Bell	Ferrari	312	Ferrari	V12	14	engine	15	8
ns	11	J Oliver	Lotus	49B	Ford Cosworth	V8		accident	16	8
ns	21	H Pescarolo	Matra	MS11	Matra	V12		engine		

Winning speed 200.989 km/h, 124.889 mph
Pole Position speed 207.560 km/h, 128.972 mph (M Andretti, 1 min: 4.200 sec)
Fastest Lap speed 204.314 km/h, 126.955 mph (J Stewart, 1 min: 5.220 sec on lap 52)
Lap Leaders J Stewart 1-108 (108).

65 laps x 5.000 km, 3.107 miles = 325.000 km, 201.946 miles

Pos	No	Driver	Car	Model	Engine		Laps	Time/Reason for Retirement	Grid Pos	Row
1	10	G Hill	Lotus	49B	Ford Cosworth	V8	65	1h 56m 43.950s	3	2
2	2	B McLaren	McLaren	M7A	Ford Cosworth	V8	65	1h 58m 03.270s	9	5
3	11	J Oliver	Lotus	49B	Ford Cosworth	V8	65	1h 58m 24.600s	14	7
4	8	P Rodríguez	BRM	P133	BRM	V12	65	1h 58m 25.040s	12	6
5	17	J Bonnier	Honda	RA301	Honda	V12	64		18	9
6	16	J Siffert	Lotus	49B	Ford Cosworth	V8	64		1	1
7	15	J Stewart	Matra	MS10	Ford Cosworth	V8	64		7	4
8	18	V Elford	Cooper	T86B	BRM	V12	63		17	9
9	9	H Pescarolo	Matra	MS11	Matra	V12	62		20	10
10r	3	J Brabham	Brabham	BT26	Repco	V8	59	oil pressure	8	4
r	23	J Servoz-Gavin	Matra	MS10	Ford Cosworth	V8	57	ignition	16	8
r	14	D Gurney	McLaren	M7A	Ford Cosworth	V8	28	rear suspension	5	3
r	22	P Courage	BRM	P126	BRM	V12	25	engine overheating	19	10
r	19	L Bianchi	Cooper	T86B	BRM	V12	21	engine	21	11
r	5	J Surtees	Honda	RA301	Honda	V12	17	engine overheating	6	3
r	6	C Amon	Ferrari	312	Ferrari	V12	16	water pump	2	1
r	12	M Solana	Lotus	49B	Ford Cosworth	V8	14	wing collapsed	11	6
r	21	J-P Beltoise	Matra	MS11	Matra	V12	10	rear suspension	13	7
r	1	D Hulme	McLaren	M7A	Ford Cosworth	V8	10	rear suspension / accident	4	2
r	7	J Ickx	Ferrari	312	Ferrari	V12	3	ignition	15	8
r	4	J Rindt	Brabham	BT26	Repco	V8	2	ignition	10	5

Winning speed 167.049 km/h, 103.799 mph
Pole Position speed 171.070 km/h, 106.298 mph (J Siffert, 1 min:45.220 sec)
Fastest Lap speed 172.695 km/h, 107.308 mph (J Siffert, 1 min:44.230 sec on lap 52)
Lap Leaders G Hill 1-4,9-21,25-65 (58); J Stewart 5-8 (4); J Siffert 22-24 (3).

Lap Leaders 1968

Pos	Driver	Car-Engine	GPs	laps	km	miles
1	J Stewart	Matra-Ford Cosworth	7	236	1,360.0	845.1
2	G Hill	Lotus-Ford Cosworth	5	194	755.2	469.2
3	C Amon	Ferrari	3	115	464.1	288.4
4	J Clark	Lotus-Ford Cosworth	1	79	324.2	201.5
5	D Hulme	McLaren-Ford Cosworth	3	66	369.5	229.6
6	J Ickx	Ferrari	1	59	386.0	239.8
7	J Siffert	Lotus-Ford Cosworth	3	42	184.3	114.5
8	J Oliver	Lotus-Ford Cosworth	1	20	85.3	53.0
9	B McLaren	McLaren-Ford Cosworth	2	13	83.1	51.6
10	P Rodríguez	BRM	2	12	44.0	27.3
11	J Surtees	Honda	2	10	132.6	82.4
12	J-P Beltoise	Matra-Ford Cosworth	1	4	13.6	8.5
13	J Servoz-Gavin	Matra-Ford Cosworth	1	3	9.4	5.9
			12	**853**	**4,211.4**	**2,616.9**

Driver Points 1968

		ZA	E	MC	B	NL	F	GB	D	I	CDN	USA	MEX	Total
1	G Hill	6	9	9	-	-	-	-	6	-	3	6	9	48
2	J Stewart	-	-	-	3	9	4	1	9	-	1	9	-	36
3	D Hulme	2	6	2	-	-	2	3	-	9	9	-	-	33
4	J Ickx	-	-	-	4	3	9	4	3	4	-	-	-	27
5	B McLaren	-	-	-	9	-	-	-	-	-	6	1	6	22
6	P Rodríguez	-	-	-	6	4	-	-	1	-	4	-	3	18
7	J Siffert	-	-	-	-	-	-	9	-	-	-	2	1	12
	J Surtees	-	-	-	-	-	6	2	-	-	-	4	-	12
9	J-P Beltoise	1	2	-	-	6	-	-	-	2	-	-	-	11
10	C Amon	3	-	-	-	1	-	6	-	-	-	-	-	10
11	J Clark	9	-	-	-	-	-	-	-	-	-	-	-	9
12	J Rindt	4	-	-	-	-	-	-	4	-	-	-	-	8
13	D Attwood	-	-	6	-	-	-	-	-	-	-	-	-	6
	J Servoz-Gavin	-	-	-	-	-	-	-	-	6	-	-	-	6
	J Oliver	-	-	-	2	-	-	-	-	-	-	-	4	6
	L Scarfiotti	-	3	3	-	-	-	-	-	-	-	-	-	6
17	L Bianchi	-	-	4	1	-	-	-	-	-	-	-	-	5
	V Elford	-	-	-	-	-	3	-	-	-	2	-	-	5
19	B Redman	-	4	-	-	-	-	-	-	-	-	-	-	4
	P Courage	-	-	-	-	-	1	-	-	3	-	-	-	4
21	D Gurney	-	-	-	-	-	-	-	-	-	-	3	-	3
	J Bonnier	-	-	-	-	-	-	-	-	1	-	-	2	3
23	S Moser	-	-	-	2	-	-	-	-	-	-	-	-	2
	J Brabham	-	-	-	-	-	-	-	2	-	-	-	-	2

9,6,4,3,2 and 1 point awarded to the first six finishers. Best 5 scores from first 6 races, best 5 from remaining 6 races.

Constructor Points 1968

		ZA	E	MC	B	NL	F	GB	D	I	CDN	USA	MEX	Total
1	Lotus-Ford Cosworth	9	9	9	2	-	-	9	6	-	3	6	9	62
2	McLaren-Ford Cosworth	-	6	2	9	-	2	3	-	9	9	3	6	49
3	Matra-Ford Cosworth	1	2	-	3	9	4	1	9	6	1	9	-	45
4	Ferrari	3	-	-	4	3	9	6	3	4	-	-	-	32
5	BRM	-	-	6	6	4	1	-	1	3	4	-	3	28
6	Honda	-	-	-	-	-	6	2	-	-	-	4	2	14
	Cooper-BRM	-	4	4	1	-	3	-	-	-	2	-	-	14
8	Brabham-Repco	4	-	-	-	2	-	-	4	-	-	-	-	10
9	Matra	-	-	-	-	6	-	-	-	2	-	-	-	8
10	McLaren-BRM	2	-	-	-	-	-	-	-	1	-	-	-	3

9,6,4,3,2 and 1 point awarded to the first six finishers. Points only for highest placed car. Best 5 scores from first 6 races, best 5 from remaining 6 races.

1969

Race Entrants and Results

Cosworth-engined cars were beginning to dominate the grids. Ferrari effectively withdrew at the end of the season, to concentrate on development work. This was the year of the four-wheel-drive experiments, with Lotus, Matra and McLaren trying out such cars. In June, FIAT bought a 50% stake in Ferrari. Shortly afterwards, Tony Rudd and BRM parted company. Grids fell to their smallest during this season, averaging below 16 starters.

FERRARI
Scuderia Ferrari SpA SEFAC: Amon, Rodríguez, (Brambilla)
North American Racing Team: Rodríguez (CDN,USA,MEX)

BRABHAM
Motor Racing Developments: Brabham, Ickx
Frank Williams Racing Cars: Courage
Silvio Moser Racing Team: Moser
Team Gunston: Tingle
Jack Holme: de Klerk
Paul Seitz: Cordts

BRM
Owen Racing Organisation: Surtees, Oliver, Eaton, Brack
Reg Parnell Racing Ltd: Rodríguez

COOPER
Antique Automobiles: Elford

LOTUS
Gold Leaf Team Lotus: Hill, Rindt, Miles, Andretti, Attwood
Rob Walker/Jack Durlacher Racing: Siffert
Pete Lovely Volkswagen Inc: Lovely
Ecurie Bonnier: Bonnier
Team Gunston: Love

McLAREN
Bruce McLaren Motor Racing: McLaren, Hulme, Bell
Antique Automobiles: Elford
Team Lawson: van Rooyen

MATRA
Matra International: Stewart, Beltoise, Servoz-Gavin

EAGLE
John Maryon: Pease

(Entries for the F2 section are not included)

1 Mar 1969			SOUTH AFRICA: Kyalami						(Round 1)	(Race 174)	
			80 laps x 4.104 km, 2.550 miles = 328.306 km, 204.000 miles								
Pos	No	Driver	Car	Model	Engine			Laps	Time/Reason for Retirement	Grid Pos	Row
1	7	J Stewart	Matra	MS10	Ford Cosworth	V8		80	1h 50m 39.100s	4	2
2	1	G Hill	Lotus	49B	Ford Cosworth	V8		80	1h 50m 57.900s	7	3
3	5	D Hulme	McLaren	M7A	Ford Cosworth	V8		80	1h 51m 10.900s	3	1
4	4	J Siffert	Lotus	49B	Ford Cosworth	V8		80	1h 51m 28.300s	12	5
5	6	B McLaren	McLaren	M7A	Ford Cosworth	V8		79		8	3
6	8	J-P Beltoise	Matra	MS10	Ford Cosworth	V8		78		11	5
7	11	J Oliver	BRM	P133	BRM	V12		77		14	6
8	17	S Tingle	Brabham	BT24	Repco	V8		73		17	7
nc	19	P de Klerk	Brabham	BT20	Repco	V8		67		16	7
r	2	J Rindt	Lotus	49B	Ford Cosworth	V8		44	fuel pump	2	1
r	10	J Surtees	BRM	P138	BRM	V12		40	engine	18	7
r	12	P Rodríguez	BRM	P126	BRM	V12		38	water leak / engine	15	6
r	9	C Amon	Ferrari	312	Ferrari	V12		34	engine	5	2
r	14	J Brabham	Brabham	BT26A	Ford Cosworth	V8		32	rear wing lost	1	1
r	16	J Love	Lotus	49	Ford Cosworth	V8		31	ignition	10	4
r	3	M Andretti	Lotus	49B	Ford Cosworth	V8		31	gearbox	6	3
r	15	J Ickx	Brabham	BT26A	Ford Cosworth	V8		20	ignition	13	5
r	18	B van Rooyen	McLaren	M7A	Ford Cosworth	V8		12	brakes	9	4

Winning speed 178.021 km/h, 110.617 mph
Pole Position speed 184.672 km/h, 114.750 mph (J Brabham, 1 min:20.000 sec)
Fastest Lap speed 181.051 km/h, 112.500 mph (J Stewart, 1 min:21.600 sec on lap 50)
Lap Leaders J Stewart 1-80 (80).

4 May 1969 **SPAIN: Montjuïc** (Round 2) (Race 175)

90 laps x 3.791 km, 2.356 miles = 341.190 km, 212.006 miles

Pos	No	Driver	Car	Model	Engine		Laps	Time/Reason for Retirement	Grid Pos	Row
1	7	J Stewart	Matra	MS80	Ford Cosworth	V8	90	2h 16m 53.990s	4	2
2	6	B McLaren	McLaren	M7C	Ford Cosworth	V8	88		13	5
3	8	J-P Beltoise	Matra	MS80	Ford Cosworth	V8	87		12	5
4	5	D Hulme	McLaren	M7A	Ford Cosworth	V8	87		8	3
5	14	J Surtees	BRM	P138	BRM	V12	84		9	4
6r	4	J Ickx	Brabham	BT26A	Ford Cosworth	V8	83	rear suspension	7	3
r	9	P Rodríguez	BRM	P126	BRM	V12	73	piston	14	6
r	15	C Amon	Ferrari	312	Ferrari	V12	56	engine	2	1
r	3	J Brabham	Brabham	BT26A	Ford Cosworth	V8	51	connecting rod	5	2
r	10	J Siffert	Lotus	49B	Ford Cosworth	V8	30	oil loss / engine	6	3
r	2	J Rindt	Lotus	49B	Ford Cosworth	V8	19	aerofoil / accident / injury	1	1
r	11	P Courage	Brabham	BT26A	Ford Cosworth	V8	18	valve spring	11	5
r	1	G Hill	Lotus	49B	Ford Cosworth	V8	8	aerofoil / accident	3	1
r	12	J Oliver	BRM	P133	BRM	V12	1	oil line	10	4

Winning speed 149.536 km/h, 92.917 mph
Pole Position speed 159.249 km/h, 98.952 mph (J Rindt, 1 min:25.700 sec)
Fastest Lap speed 154.559 km/h, 96.039 mph (J Rindt, 1 min:28.300 sec on lap 15)
Lap Leaders J Rindt 1-19 (19); C Amon 20-56 (37); J Stewart 57-90 (34).

---

18 May 1969 **MONACO: Monte-Carlo** (Round 3) (Race 176)

80 laps x 3.145 km, 1.954 miles = 251.600 km, 156.337 miles

Pos	No	Driver	Car	Model	Engine		Laps	Time/Reason for Retirement	Grid Pos	Row
1	1	G Hill	Lotus	49B	Ford Cosworth	V8	80	1h 56m 59.400s	4	2
2	16	P Courage	Brabham	BT26A	Ford Cosworth	V8	80	1h 57m 16.700s	9	5
3	9	J Siffert	Lotus	49B	Ford Cosworth	V8	80	1h 57m 34.000s	5	3
4	2	D Attwood	Lotus	49B	Ford Cosworth	V8	80	1h 57m 52.300s	10	5
5	4	B McLaren	McLaren	M7C	Ford Cosworth	V8	79		11	6
6	3	D Hulme	McLaren	M7A	Ford Cosworth	V8	78		12	6
7	12	V Elford	Cooper	T86B	Maserati	V12	74		16	8
r	6	J Ickx	Brabham	BT26A	Ford Cosworth	V8	48	rear suspension	7	4
r	7	J Stewart	Matra	MS80	Ford Cosworth	V8	22	universal joint	1	1
r	8	J-P Beltoise	Matra	MS80	Ford Cosworth	V8	20	universal joint	3	2
r	11	C Amon	Ferrari	312	Ferrari	V12	16	differential	2	1
r	17	S Moser	Brabham	BT24	Ford Cosworth	V8	15	universal joint	15	8
r	10	P Rodríguez	BRM	P126	BRM	V12	15	engine	14	7
r	5	J Brabham	Brabham	BT26A	Ford Cosworth	V8	9	accident	8	4
r	14	J Surtees	BRM	P138	BRM	V12	9	accident / gearbox	6	3
r	15	J Oliver	BRM	P133	BRM	V12	0	accident	13	7

Winning speed 129.037 km/h, 80.180 mph
Pole Position speed 133.830 km/h, 83.158 mph (J Stewart, 1 min:24.600 sec)
Fastest Lap speed 133.043 km/h, 82.669 mph (J Stewart, 1 min:25.100 sec on lap 16)
Lap Leaders J Stewart 1-22 (22); G Hill 23-80 (58).

---

21 Jun 1969 **NETHERLANDS: Zandvoort** (Round 4) (Race 177)

90 laps x 4.193 km, 2.605 miles = 377.370 km, 234.487 miles

Pos	No	Driver	Car	Model	Engine		Laps	Time/Reason for Retirement	Grid Pos	Row
1	4	J Stewart	Matra	MS80	Ford Cosworth	V8	90	2h 06m 42.080s	2	1
2	10	J Siffert	Lotus	49B	Ford Cosworth	V8	90	2h 07m 06.600s	10	4
3	8	C Amon	Ferrari	312	Ferrari	V12	90	2h 07m 12.590s	4	2
4	7	D Hulme	McLaren	M7A	Ford Cosworth	V8	90	2h 07m 19.240s	7	3
5	12	J Ickx	Brabham	BT26A	Ford Cosworth	V8	90	2h 07m 19.750s	5	2
6	11	J Brabham	Brabham	BT26A	Ford Cosworth	V8	90	2h 07m 52.890s	8	3
7	1	G Hill	Lotus	49B	Ford Cosworth	V8	88		3	1
8	5	J-P Beltoise	Matra	MS80	Ford Cosworth	V8	87		11	5
9	14	J Surtees	BRM	P138	BRM	V12	87		12	5
10	18	V Elford	McLaren	M7A	Ford Cosworth	V8	84		15	6
r	17	S Moser	Brabham	BT24	Ford Cosworth	V8	54	steering / electrics	14	6
r	6	B McLaren	McLaren	M7C	Ford Cosworth	V8	24	front suspension	6	3
r	2	J Rindt	Lotus	49B	Ford Cosworth	V8	16	cv joint	1	1
r	16	P Courage	Brabham	BT26A	Ford Cosworth	V8	12	clutch	9	4
r	15	J Oliver	BRM	P133	BRM	V12	9	gear selector	13	5

Winning speed 178.705 km/h, 111.042 mph
Pole Position speed 186.701 km/h, 116.011 mph (J Rindt, 1 min:20.850 sec)
Fastest Lap speed 181.997 km/h, 113.087 mph (J Stewart, 1 min:22.940 sec on lap 5)
Lap Leaders G Hill 1-2 (2); J Rindt 3-16 (14); J Stewart 17-90 (74).

6 Jul 1969 **FRANCE: Clermont-Ferrand** **(Round 5)** **(Race 178)**

38 laps x 8.055 km, 5.005 miles = 306.090 km, 190.196 miles

Pos	No	Driver	Car	Model	Engine		Laps	Time/Reason for Retirement	Grid Pos	Row
1	2	J Stewart	Matra	MS80	Ford Cosworth	V8	38	1h 56m 47.400s	1	1
2	7	J-P Beltoise	Matra	MS80	Ford Cosworth	V8	38	1h 57m 44.500s	5	3
3	11	J Ickx	Brabham	BT26A	Ford Cosworth	V8	38	1h 57m 44.700s	4	2
4	5	B McLaren	McLaren	M7C	Ford Cosworth	V8	37		7	4
5	10	V Elford	McLaren	M7A	Ford Cosworth	V8	37		10	5
6	1	G Hill	Lotus	49B	Ford Cosworth	V8	37		8	4
7	12	S Moser	Brabham	BT24	Ford Cosworth	V8	36		13	7
8	4	D Hulme	McLaren	M7A	Ford Cosworth	V8	35		2	1
9	3	J Siffert	Lotus	49B	Ford Cosworth	V8	34		9	5
r	6	C Amon	Ferrari	312	Ferrari	V12	30	engine	6	3
r	15	J Rindt	Lotus	49B	Ford Cosworth	V8	22	driver had double vision	3	2
r	9	P Courage	Brabham	BT26A	Ford Cosworth	V8	21	nose cone mounting	11	6
r	14	J Miles	Lotus	63	Ford Cosworth	V8	1	fuel pump belt	12	6

Winning speed 157.251 km/h, 97.712 mph
Pole Position speed 160.565 km/h, 99.770 mph (J Stewart, 3 min: 0.600 sec)
Fastest Lap speed 158.719 km/h, 98.624 mph (J Stewart, 3 min: 2.700 sec on lap 27)
Lap Leaders J Stewart 1-38 (38).

19 Jul 1969 **BRITAIN: Silverstone** **(Round 6)** **(Race 179)**

84 laps x 4.711 km, 2.927 miles = 395.686 km, 245.868 miles

Pos	No	Driver	Car	Model	Engine		Laps	Time/Reason for Retirement	Grid Pos	Row
1	3	J Stewart	Matra	MS80	Ford Cosworth	V8	84	1h 55m 55.600s	2	1
2	7	J Ickx	Brabham	BT26A	Ford Cosworth	V8	83		4	2
3	6	B McLaren	McLaren	M7C	Ford Cosworth	V8	83		7	3
4	2	J Rindt	Lotus	49B	Ford Cosworth	V8	83		1	1
5	16	P Courage	Brabham	BT26A	Ford Cosworth	V8	83		10	4
6	19	V Elford	McLaren	M7A	Ford Cosworth	V8	82		11	5
7	1	G Hill	Lotus	49B	Ford Cosworth	V8	82		12	5
8	10	J Siffert	Lotus	49B	Ford Cosworth	V8	81		9	4
9	4	J-P Beltoise	Matra	MS84	Ford Cosworth	V8	78		17	7
10	9	J Miles	Lotus	63	Ford Cosworth	V8	75		14	6
r	12	P Rodríguez	Ferrari	312	Ferrari	V12	61	engine	8	3
r	11	C Amon	Ferrari	312	Ferrari	V12	45	gearbox	5	2
r	5	D Hulme	McLaren	M7A	Ford Cosworth	V8	27	camshaft	3	1
r	15	J Oliver	BRM	P133	BRM	V12	19	transmission	13	7
r	18	J Bonnier	Lotus	63	Ford Cosworth	V8	6	engine	16	7
r	20	D Bell	McLaren	M9A	Ford Cosworth	V8	5	rear suspension	15	6
r	14	J Surtees	BRM	P139	BRM	V12	1	front suspension	6	3

Winning speed 204.795 km/h, 127.254 mph
Pole Position speed 209.876 km/h, 130.411 mph (J Rindt, 1 min:20.800 sec)
Fastest Lap speed 208.585 km/h, 129.609 mph (J Stewart, 1 min:21.300 sec on lap 57 & 60)
Lap Leaders J Rindt 1-5,16-61 (51); J Stewart 6-15,62-84 (33).

GERMANY: Nürburgring (Round 7) (Race 180)

14 laps x 22.835 km, 14.189 miles = 319.690 km, 198.646 miles

Pos	No	Driver	Car	Model	Engine		Laps	Time/Reason for Retirement	Grid Pos	Row
1	6	J Ickx	Brabham	BT26A	Ford Cosworth	V8	14	1h 49m 55.400s	1	1
2	7	J Stewart	Matra	MS80	Ford Cosworth	V8	14	1h 50m 53.100s	2	1
3	10	B McLaren	McLaren	M7C	Ford Cosworth	V8	14	1h 53m 17.000s	8	3
4	1	G Hill	Lotus	49B	Ford Cosworth	V8	14	1h 53m 54.200s	9	4
F2: 1	*26*	*H Pescarolo*	*Matra*	*MS7*	*Ford Cosworth*	*4*	*14*	*1h 58m 06.400s*	*17*	*7*
F2: 2	*29*	*D Attwood*	*Brabham*	*BT30*	*Ford Cosworth*	*4*	*13*		*20*	*9*
F2: 3	*20*	*K Ahrens*	*Brabham*	*BT30*	*Ford Cosworth*	*4*	*13*		*19*	*8*
F2: 4	*22*	*R Stommelen*	*Lotus*	*59B*	*Ford Cosworth*	*4*	*13*		*21*	*9*
F2: 5	*31*	*P Westbury*	*Brabham*	*BT30*	*Ford Cosworth*	*4*	*13*		*18*	*8*
F2: 6	*30*	*X Perrot*	*Brabham*	*BT23C*	*Ford Cosworth*	*4*	*13*		*22*	*9*
5r	11	J Siffert	Lotus	49B	Ford Cosworth	V8	12	front suspension	4	2
6r	8	J-P Beltoise	Matra	MS80	Ford Cosworth	V8	12	front suspension	10	4
r	15	J Oliver	BRM	P138	BRM	V12	11	sump	13	5
r	9	D Hulme	McLaren	M7A	Ford Cosworth	V8	11	transmission	5	2
r	2	J Rindt	Lotus	49B	Ford Cosworth	V8	10	ignition	3	1
F2: r	*28*	*F Cevert*	*Tecno*	*TOO*	*Ford Cosworth*	*4*	*9*	*crown wheel & pinion*	*16*	*7*
F2: r	*27*	*J Servoz-Gavin*	*Matra*	*MS7*	*Ford Cosworth*	*4*	*6*	*engine*	*15*	*7*
r	16	J Bonnier	Lotus	49B	Ford Cosworth	V8	4	fuel tank leak	14	6
r	17	P Courage	Brabham	BT26A	Ford Cosworth	V8	1	accident	7	3
r	12	V Elford	McLaren	M7A	Ford Cosworth	V8	0	accident	6	3
r	3	M Andretti	Lotus	63	Ford Cosworth	V8	0	accident	12	5
ns	14	J Surtees	BRM	P139	BRM	V12		front suspension	11	5
F2: ns	*23*	*H Hahne*	*BMW*	*269*	*BMW*	*4*		*withdrew after Mitter accident*		
F2: ns	*25*	*D Quester*	*BMW*	*269*	*BMW*	*4*		*withdrew after Mitter accident*		
F2: ns	*24*	*G Mitter*	*BMW*	*269*	*BMW*	*4*		*fatal accident*		
F2:	*21*	*H Herrmann*	*Lotus*	*59B*	*Ford Cosworth*	*4*		*withdrew after Mitter accident*		

Winning speed 174.498 km/h, 108.428 mph
Pole Position speed 177.897 km/h, 110.540 mph (J Ickx, 7 min:42.100 sec)
Fastest Lap speed 177.245 km/h, 110.135 mph (J Ickx, 7 min:43.800 sec on lap 7)
Lap Leaders J Stewart 1-6 (6); J Ickx 7-14 (8).

Formula 2 cars raced simultaneously with F1, and are shown in italics.
H Pescarolo and D Attwood finished 5th and 6th, but were not eligible for points due to being in the F2 section of the race.

ITALY: Monza (Round 8) (Race 181)

68 laps x 5.750 km, 3.573 miles = 391.000 km, 242.956 miles

Pos	No	Driver	Car	Model	Engine		Laps	Time/Reason for Retirement	Grid Pos	Row
1	20	J Stewart	Matra	MS80	Ford Cosworth	V8	68	1h 39m 11.260s	3	2
2	4	J Rindt	Lotus	49B	Ford Cosworth	V8	68	1h 39m 11.340s	1	1
3	22	J-P Beltoise	Matra	MS80	Ford Cosworth	V8	68	1h 39m 11.430s	6	3
4	18	B McLaren	McLaren	M7C	Ford Cosworth	V8	68	1h 39m 11.450s	5	3
5	32	P Courage	Brabham	BT26A	Ford Cosworth	V8	68	1h 39m 44.700s	4	2
6	10	P Rodríguez	Ferrari	312	Ferrari	V12	66		12	6
7	16	D Hulme	McLaren	M7A	Ford Cosworth	V8	66		2	1
8r	30	J Siffert	Lotus	49B	Ford Cosworth	V8	65	piston	8	4
9r	2	G Hill	Lotus	49B	Ford Cosworth	V8	63	driveshaft	9	5
10r	26	J Ickx	Brabham	BT26A	Ford Cosworth	V8	62	oil pressure	15	8
nc	14	J Surtees	BRM	P139	BRM	V12	60		10	5
r	12	J Oliver	BRM	P139	BRM	V12	49	oil pressure	11	6
r	36	S Moser	Brabham	BT24	Ford Cosworth	V8	10	fuel leak	13	7
r	28	J Brabham	Brabham	BT26A	Ford Cosworth	V8	6	fuel line	7	4
r	6	J Miles	Lotus	63	Ford Cosworth	V8	3	engine	14	7
ns	10	T Brambilla	Ferrari	312	Ferrari	V12		car raced by Rodríguez		

Winning speed 236.521 km/h, 146.968 mph
Pole Position speed 242.162 km/h, 150.472 mph (J Rindt, 1 min:25.480 sec)
Fastest Lap speed 242.958 km/h, 150.967 mph (J-P Beltoise, 1 min:25.200 sec on lap 64)
Lap Leaders J Stewart 1-6,9-17,19-24,28-30,33,35-36,38-68 (58);J Rindt 7,25-27,31,34,37 (7);D Hulme 8 (1);P Courage 18,32 (2).

90 laps x 3.957 km, 2.459 miles = 356.164 km, 221.310 miles

Pos	No	Driver	Car	Model	Engine		Laps	Time/Reason for Retirement	Grid Pos	Row
1	11	J Ickx	Brabham	BT26A	Ford Cosworth	V8	90	1h 59m 25.700s	1	1
2	12	J Brabham	Brabham	BT26A	Ford Cosworth	V8	90	2h 00m 11.900s	6	3
3	2	J Rindt	Lotus	49B	Ford Cosworth	V8	90	2h 00m 17.700s	3	1
4	18	J-P Beltoise	Matra	MS80	Ford Cosworth	V8	89		2	1
5	4	B McLaren	McLaren	M7C	Ford Cosworth	V8	87		9	4
6	19	J Servoz-Gavin	Matra	MS84	Ford Cosworth	V8	84		15	6
7	25	P Lovely	Lotus	49B	Ford Cosworth	V8	81		16	7
nc	16	B Brack	BRM	P138	BRM	V12	80		18	7
r	1	G Hill	Lotus	49B	Ford Cosworth	V8	42	camshaft	7	3
r	9	J Siffert	Lotus	49B	Ford Cosworth	V8	40	driveshaft	8	3
r	3	J Miles	Lotus	63	Ford Cosworth	V8	40	gearbox	11	5
r	6	P Rodríguez	Ferrari	312	Ferrari	V12	37	oil pressure	13	5
r	17	J Stewart	Matra	MS80	Ford Cosworth	V8	32	accident	4	2
dq	69	A Pease	Eagle	T1G	Climax	4	22	too slow	17	7
r	14	J Surtees	BRM	P139	BRM	V12	15	engine	14	6
r	21	P Courage	Brabham	BT26A	Ford Cosworth	V8	13	fuel leak	10	4
r	26	J Cordts	Brabham	BT23B	Climax	4	10	oil leak	19	8
r	5	D Hulme	McLaren	M7A	Ford Cosworth	V8	9	distributor	5	2
r	15	J Oliver	BRM	P139	BRM	V12	2	engine	12	5
r	20	S Moser	Brabham	BT24	Ford Cosworth	V8	0	accident	20	8

Winning speed 178.934 km/h, 111.185 mph
Pole Position speed 184.064 km/h, 114.372 mph (J Ickx, 1 min:17.400 sec)
Fastest Lap speed 182.414 km/h, 113.347 mph (J Ickx / J Brabham, 1 min:18.100 sec on lap 30 / 62)
Lap Leaders J Rindt 1-5 (5); J Stewart 6-32 (27); J Ickx 33-90 (58).

108 laps x 3.701 km, 2.300 miles = 399.761 km, 248.400 miles

Pos	No	Driver	Car	Model	Engine		Laps	Time/Reason for Retirement	Grid Pos	Row
1	2	J Rindt	Lotus	49B	Ford Cosworth	V8	108	1h 57m 56.840s	1	1
2	18	P Courage	Brabham	BT26A	Ford Cosworth	V8	108	1h 58m 43.830s	9	5
3	14	J Surtees	BRM	P139	BRM	V12	106		11	6
4	8	J Brabham	Brabham	BT26A	Ford Cosworth	V8	106		10	5
5	12	P Rodríguez	Ferrari	312	Ferrari	V12	101		12	6
6	19	S Moser	Brabham	BT24	Ford Cosworth	V8	98		17	9
nc	16	J Servoz-Gavin	Matra	MS84	Ford Cosworth	V8	92		15	8
r	1	G Hill	Lotus	49B	Ford Cosworth	V8	90	accident / injury	4	2
r	7	J Ickx	Brabham	BT26A	Ford Cosworth	V8	77	engine	8	4
r	22	G Eaton	BRM	P138	BRM	V12	76	engine	18	9
r	4	J-P Beltoise	Matra	MS80	Ford Cosworth	V8	72	engine	7	4
r	5	D Hulme	McLaren	M7A	Ford Cosworth	V8	52	gear selection	2	1
r	3	J Stewart	Matra	MS80	Ford Cosworth	V8	35	engine	3	2
r	21	P Lovely	Lotus	49B	Ford Cosworth	V8	25	universal joint	16	8
r	15	J Oliver	BRM	P139	BRM	V12	23	engine	14	7
r	9	M Andretti	Lotus	63	Ford Cosworth	V8	3	spin / rear suspension	13	7
r	10	J Siffert	Lotus	49B	Ford Cosworth	V8	3	fuel metering unit	5	3
ns	6	B McLaren	McLaren	M7C	Ford Cosworth	V8		engine	6	3

Winning speed 203.359 km/h, 126.361 mph
Pole Position speed 209.453 km/h, 130.148 mph (J Rindt, 1 min: 3.620 sec)
Fastest Lap speed 207.109 km/h, 128.691 mph (J Rindt, 1 min: 4.340 sec on lap 69)
Lap Leaders J Rindt 1-11,21-108 (99); J Stewart 12-20 (9).

19 Oct 1969		MEXICO: Mexico City				(Round 11)		(Race 184)		

65 laps x 5.000 km, 3.107 miles = 325.000 km, 201.946 miles

Pos	No	Driver	Car	Model	Engine		Laps	Time/Reason for Retirement	Grid Pos	Row
1	5	D Hulme	McLaren	M7A	Ford Cosworth	V8	65	1h 54m 08.800s	4	2
2	7	J Ickx	Brabham	BT26A	Ford Cosworth	V8	65	1h 54m 11.360s	2	1
3	8	J Brabham	Brabham	BT26A	Ford Cosworth	V8	65	1h 54m 47.280s	1	1
4	3	J Stewart	Matra	MS80	Ford Cosworth	V8	65	1h 54m 55.840s	3	2
5	4	J-P Beltoise	Matra	MS80	Ford Cosworth	V8	65	1h 55m 47.320s	8	4
6	15	J Oliver	BRM	P139	BRM	V12	63		12	6
7	12	P Rodríguez	Ferrari	312	Ferrari	V12	63		15	8
8	16	J Servoz-Gavin	Matra	MS84	Ford Cosworth	V8	63		14	7
9	21	P Lovely	Lotus	49B	Ford Cosworth	V8	62		16	8
10	18	P Courage	Brabham	BT26A	Ford Cosworth	V8	61		9	5
11r	19	S Moser	Brabham	BT24	Ford Cosworth	V8	60	fuel leak	13	7
r	14	J Surtees	BRM	P139	BRM	V12	53	gearbox	10	5
r	2	J Rindt	Lotus	49B	Ford Cosworth	V8	21	front suspension	6	3
r	22	G Eaton	BRM	P138	BRM	V12	6	gearbox	17	9
r	10	J Siffert	Lotus	49B	Ford Cosworth	V8	4	accident	5	3
r	9	J Miles	Lotus	63	Ford Cosworth	V8	3	fuel pump	11	6
ns	6	B McLaren	McLaren	M7C	Ford Cosworth	V8		fuel pump on parade lap	7	4

Winning speed 170.833 km/h, 106.151 mph
Pole Position speed 174.927 km/h, 108.695 mph (J Brabham, 1 min:42.900 sec)
Fastest Lap speed 174.672 km/h, 108.536 mph (J Ickx, 1 min:43.050 sec on lap 64)
Lap Leaders J Stewart 1-5 (5); J Ickx 6-9 (4); D Hulme 10-65 (56).

Lap Leaders 1969

Pos	Driver	Car-Engine	GPs	laps	km	miles
1	J Stewart	Matra-Ford Cosworth	11	386	1,933.9	1,201.7
2	J Rindt	Lotus-Ford Cosworth	6	195	797.4	495.5
3	J Ickx	Brabham-Ford Cosworth	3	70	432.2	268.5
4	G Hill	Lotus-Ford Cosworth	2	60	190.8	118.6
5	D Hulme	McLaren-Ford Cosworth	2	57	285.7	177.6
6	C Amon	Ferrari	1	37	140.3	87.2
7	P Courage	Brabham-Ford Cosworth	1	2	11.5	7.1
			11	807	3,791.8	2,356.1

Driver Points 1969

		ZA	E	MC	NL	F	GB	D	I	CDN	USA	MEX	Total
1	J Stewart	9	9	-	9	9	9	6	9	-	-	3	63
2	J Ickx	-	1	-	2	4	6	9	-	9	-	6	37
3	B McLaren	2	6	2	-	3	4	4	3	2	-	-	26
4	J Rindt	-	-	-	-	-	3	-	6	4	9	-	22
5	J-P Beltoise	1	4	-	-	6	-	1	4	3	-	2	21
6	D Hulme	4	3	1	3	-	-	-	-	-	-	9	20
7	G Hill	6	-	9	-	1	-	3	-	-	-	-	19
8	P Courage	-	-	6	-	-	2	-	2	-	6	-	16
9	J Siffert	3	-	4	6	-	-	2	-	-	-	-	15
10	J Brabham	-	-	-	1	-	-	-	-	6	3	4	14
11	J Surtees	-	2	-	-	-	-	-	-	-	4	-	6
12	C Amon	-	-	-	4	-	-	-	-	-	-	-	4
13	D Attwood	-	-	3	-	-	-	-	-	-	-	-	3
	V Elford	-	-	-	-	2	1	-	-	-	-	-	3
	P Rodríguez	-	-	-	-	-	-	-	1	-	2	-	3
16	J Servoz-Gavin	-	-	-	-	-	-	-	-	1	-	-	1
	S Moser	-	-	-	-	-	-	-	-	-	1	-	1
	J Oliver	-	-	-	-	-	-	-	-	-	-	1	1

9,6,4,3,2 and 1 point awarded to the first six finishers. Best 5 scores from first 6 races, best 4 from remaining 5 races.

Constructor Points 1969

		ZA	E	MC	NL	F	GB	D	I	CDN	USA	MEX	Total	
1	Matra-Ford Cosworth	9	9	-	9	9	9	6	9	3	-	3	66	
2	Brabham-Ford Cosworth	-	1	6	2	4	6	9	(2)	9	6	6	49	(2)
3	Lotus-Ford Cosworth	6	-	9	6	1	3	3	6	4	9	-	47	
4	McLaren-Ford Cosworth	4	6	(2)	3	3	4	4	3	2	-	9	38	(2)
5	Ferrari	-	-	-	4	-	-	-	1	-	2	-	7	
	BRM	-	2	-	-	-	-	-	-	-	4	1	7	

9,6,4,3,2 and 1 point awarded to the first six finishers. Points only for highest placed car. Best 5 scores from first 6 races, best 4 from remaining 5 races.

1970

Race Entrants and Results

New entrant March helped increase grids by making their car available to customers, the first of which was Ken Tyrrell, who had split from his successful partnership with Matra. Lotus again introduced an advancement in design, with the wedge-shaped 72 created with radiators alongside the cockpit. Brabham produced its first monocoque, the turquoise BT33, BRM appeared in Yardley cosmetic colours and Dunlop withdrew at the season's end.

FERRARI
Scuderia Ferrari SpA SEFAC: Ickx, Regazzoni, Giunti

BELLASI
Silvio Moser Racing Team: Moser

DE TOMASO
Frank Williams Racing Cars: Courage, Schenken, (Redman)

BRABHAM
Motor Racing Developments: Brabham
Auto Motor Und Sport: Stommelen
Tom Wheatcroft Racing: Bell
Team Gunston: de Klerk
Privateer: Hutchison

BRM
Owen Racing Organisation*: Rodríguez, Oliver, Eaton, (Westbury)
* Yardley Team BRM from E GP

LOTUS
Gold Leaf Team Lotus: Rindt, Miles, Fittipaldi, Wisell
World Wide Racing: (Soler-Roig)
Garvey Team Lotus at E GP
Brooke Bond Oxo Racing/Rob Walker: Hill
Rob Walker Racing Team (first two GPs)
Pete Lovely Volkswagen Inc: Lovely
Team Gunston: Love
Scuderia Scribante: Charlton

MARCH
March Engineering: Amon, Siffert
STP Corporation: Andretti
Tyrrell Racing Organisation: Stewart, Cevert, Servoz-Gavin
Colin Crabbe Racing: Peterson (Antique Automobiles Racing Team at MC & B GPs)
Privateer: (Hahne)

McLAREN
Bruce McLaren Motor Racing: McLaren, Hulme, Gethin, Gurney, de Adamich, (Galli)
Team Surtees: Surtees
Ecurie Bonnier: Bonnier

SURTEES
Team Surtees: Surtees, Bell

TYRRELL
Tyrrell Racing Organisation: Stewart

MATRA SIMCA
Equipe Matra Elf: Beltoise, Pescarolo

7 Mar 1970		SOUTH AFRICA: Kyalami						(Round 1)	(Race 185)	
		80 laps x 4.104 km, 2.550 miles = 328.306 km, 204.000 miles								
Pos	No	Driver	Car	Model	Engine		Laps	Time/Reason for Retirement	Grid Pos	Row
1	12	J Brabham	Brabham	BT33	Ford Cosworth	V8	80	1h 49m 34.600s	3	1
2	6	D Hulme	McLaren	M14A	Ford Cosworth	V8	80	1h 49m 42.700s	6	3
3	1	J Stewart	March	701	Ford Cosworth	V8	80	1h 49m 51.700s	1	1
4	3	J-P Beltoise	Matra Simca	MS120	Matra	V12	80	1h 50m 47.700s	8	3
5	10	J Miles	Lotus	49C	Ford Cosworth	V8	79		14	6
6	11	G Hill	Lotus	49C	Ford Cosworth	V8	79		19	8
7	4	H Pescarolo	Matra Simca	MS120	Matra	V12	78		18	7
8	23	J Love	Lotus	49	Ford Cosworth	V8	78		22	9
9	20	P Rodríguez	BRM	P153	BRM	V12	76		16	7
10	16	J Siffert	March	701	Ford Cosworth	V8	75		9	4
11	24	P de Klerk	Brabham	BT26A	Ford Cosworth	V8	75		21	9
12r	25	D Charlton	Lotus	49C	Ford Cosworth	V8	73	rear tyre / ignition	13	5
13r	9	J Rindt	Lotus	49C	Ford Cosworth	V8	72	engine	4	2
r	7	J Surtees	McLaren	M7C	Ford Cosworth	V8	60	engine	7	3
r	17	J Ickx	Ferrari	312B	Ferrari	F12	60	engine	5	2
r	21	G Eaton	BRM	P139	BRM	V12	58	engine	23	9
r	2	J Servoz-Gavin	March	701	Ford Cosworth	V8	57	engine	17	7
.r	22	P Courage	De Tomaso	505	Ford Cosworth	V8	39	accident / suspension	20	8
r	5	B McLaren	McLaren	M14A	Ford Cosworth	V8	39	engine	10	4
r	8	M Andretti	March	701	Ford Cosworth	V8	26	engine overheating	11	5
r	14	R Stommelen	Brabham	BT33	Ford Cosworth	V8	23	engine	15	6
r	19	J Oliver	BRM	P153	BRM	V12	22	gear selectors	12	5
r	15	C Amon	March	701	Ford Cosworth	V8	14	engine overheating	2	1

Winning speed 179.768 km/h, 111.703 mph
Pole Position speed 186.302 km/h, 115.763 mph (J Stewart, 1 min:19.300 sec)
Fastest Lap speed 182.844 km/h, 113.614 mph (J Surtees / J Brabham, 1 min:20.800 sec on lap 6 / 71)
Lap Leaders J Stewart 1-19 (19); J Brabham 20-80 (61).

19 Apr 1970   SPAIN: Jarama   (Round 2)   (Race 186)

90 laps x 3.404 km, 2.115 miles = 306.360 km, 190.363 miles

Pos	No	Driver	Car	Model	Engine		Laps	Time/Reason for Retirement	Grid Pos	Row
1	1	J Stewart	March	701	Ford Cosworth	V8	90	2h 10m 58.200s	3	1
2	11	B McLaren	McLaren	M14A	Ford Cosworth	V8	89		11	5
3	18	M Andretti	March	701	Ford Cosworth	V8	89		16	7
4	6	G Hill	Lotus	49C	Ford Cosworth	V8	89		15	6
5	16	J Servoz-Gavin	March	701	Ford Cosworth	V8	88		14	6
r	8	J Surtees	McLaren	M7C	Ford Cosworth	V8	76	gearbox	12	5
r	7	J Brabham	Brabham	BT33	Ford Cosworth	V8	61	engine	1	1
r	24	R Stommelen	Brabham	BT33	Ford Cosworth	V8	43	valve spring	17	7
r	22	H Pescarolo	Matra Simca	MS120	Matra	V12	33	connecting rod	9	4
r	4	J-P Beltoise	Matra Simca	MS120	Matra	V12	31	engine	4	2
r	9	C Amon	March	701	Ford Cosworth	V8	10	clutch / engine	6	3
r	5	D Hulme	McLaren	M14A	Ford Cosworth	V8	10	rotor arm shaft	2	1
r	3	J Rindt	Lotus	72	Ford Cosworth	V8	9	ignition	8	3
r	10	P Rodríguez	BRM	P153	BRM	V12	4	withdrew	5	2
r	2	J Ickx	Ferrari	312B	Ferrari	F12	0	accident / injury	7	3
r	15	J Oliver	BRM	P153	BRM	V12	0	accident	10	4
ns	12	P Courage	De Tomaso	505	Ford Cosworth	V8		accident	13	5
nq	20	A de Adamich	McLaren	M7D	Alfa Romeo	V8				
nq	19	J Miles	Lotus	72	Ford Cosworth	V8				
nq	14	J Siffert	March	701	Ford Cosworth	V8				
nq	23	A Soler-Roig	Lotus	49C	Ford Cosworth	V8				
nq	21	G Eaton	BRM	P153	BRM	V12				

Winning speed 140.350 km/h, 87.209 mph
Pole Position speed 146.060 km/h, 90.757 mph (J Brabham, 1 min:23.900 sec)
Fastest Lap speed 145.367 km/h, 90.327 mph (J Brabham, 1 min:24.300 sec on lap 19)
Lap Leaders J Stewart 1-90 (90).

10 May 1970   MONACO: Monte-Carlo   (Round 3)   (Race 187)

80 laps x 3.145 km, 1.954 miles = 251.600 km, 156.337 miles

Pos	No	Driver	Car	Model	Engine		Laps	Time/Reason for Retirement	Grid Pos	Row
1	3	J Rindt	Lotus	49C	Ford Cosworth	V8	80	1h 54m 36.600s	8	4
2	5	J Brabham	Brabham	BT33	Ford Cosworth	V8	80	1h 54m 59.700s	4	2
3	9	H Pescarolo	Matra Simca	MS120	Matra	V12	80	1h 55m 28.000s	7	4
4	11	D Hulme	McLaren	M14A	Ford Cosworth	V8	80	1h 56m 04.900s	3	2
5	1	G Hill	Lotus	49C	Ford Cosworth	V8	79		12	6
6	17	P Rodríguez	BRM	P153	BRM	V12	78		16	8
7	23	R Peterson	March	701	Ford Cosworth	V8	78		13	7
8r	19	J Siffert	March	701	Ford Cosworth	V8	76	fuel injection	11	6
r	28	C Amon	March	701	Ford Cosworth	V8	60	rear suspension	2	1
nc	24	P Courage	De Tomaso	505	Ford Cosworth	V8	58		9	5
r	21	J Stewart	March	701	Ford Cosworth	V8	57	engine	1	1
r	16	J Oliver	BRM	P153	BRM	V12	42	engine	15	8
r	8	J-P Beltoise	Matra Simca	MS120	Matra	V12	21	crown wheel & pinion	6	3
r	12	B McLaren	McLaren	M14A	Ford Cosworth	V8	19	accident / front suspension	10	5
r	14	J Surtees	McLaren	M7C	Ford Cosworth	V8	14	oil pressure	14	7
r	26	J Ickx	Ferrari	312B	Ferrari	F12	11	universal joint	5	3
nq	6	R Stommelen	Brabham	BT33	Ford Cosworth	V8				
nq	10	A de Adamich	McLaren	M7D	Alfa Romeo	V8				
nq	20	J Servoz-Gavin	March	701	Ford Cosworth	V8				
nq	15	G Eaton	BRM	P153	BRM	V12				
nq	2	J Miles	Lotus	72	Ford Cosworth	V8				

Winning speed 131.716 km/h, 81.845 mph
Pole Position speed 134.786 km/h, 83.752 mph (J Stewart, 1 min:24.000 sec)
Fastest Lap speed 136.082 km/h, 84.557 mph (J Rindt, 1 min:23.200 sec on lap 80)
Lap Leaders J Stewart 1-27 (27); J Brabham 28-79 (52); J Rindt 80 (1).

G Hill took over J Miles' car and so had to start from the back of the grid, leaving his slot empty.

7 Jun 1970 — BELGIUM: Spa-Francorchamps (Round 4) (Race 188)

28 laps x 14.100 km, 8.761 miles = 394.800 km, 245.317 miles

Pos	No	Driver	Car	Model	Engine		Laps	Time/Reason for Retirement	Grid Pos	Row
1	1	P Rodríguez	BRM	P153	BRM	V12	28	1h 38m 09.900s	6	3
2	10	C Amon	March	701	Ford Cosworth	V8	28	1h 38m 11.000s	3	1
3	25	J-P Beltoise	Matra Simca	MS120	Matra	V12	28	1h 39m 53.600s	11	5
4	28	I Giunti	Ferrari	312B	Ferrari	F12	28	1h 40m 48.400s	8	3
5	19	R Stommelen	Brabham	BT33	Ford Cosworth	V8	28	1h 41m 41.700s	7	3
6r	26	H Pescarolo	Matra Simca	MS120	Matra	V12	27	out of fuel	17	7
7r	9	J Siffert	March	701	Ford Cosworth	V8	26	fuel injection	10	4
8	27	J Ickx	Ferrari	312B	Ferrari	F12	26		4	2
nc	14	R Peterson	March	701	Ford Cosworth	V8	20		9	4
r	23	G Hill	Lotus	49C	Ford Cosworth	V8	19	engine	16	7
r	18	J Brabham	Brabham	BT33	Ford Cosworth	V8	19	clutch / flywheel	5	2
r	11	J Stewart	March	701	Ford Cosworth	V8	14	engine	1	1
r	21	J Miles	Lotus	72B	Ford Cosworth	V8	13	gear selection	13	5
r	20	J Rindt	Lotus	49C	Ford Cosworth	V8	10	piston	2	1
r	2	J Oliver	BRM	P153	BRM	V12	7	throttle linkage	14	6
r	7	P Courage	De Tomaso	505	Ford Cosworth	V8	4	oil pressure	12	5
r	8	D Bell	Brabham	BT26A	Ford Cosworth	V8	1	gear linkage	15	6
nq	22	A Soler-Roig	Lotus	72C	Ford Cosworth	V8				

Winning speed 241.308 km/h, 149.942 mph
Pole Position speed 244.038 km/h, 151.638 mph (J Stewart, 3 min:28.000 sec)
Fastest Lap speed 244.744 km/h, 152.077 mph (C Amon, 3 min:27.400 sec on lap 28)
Lap Leaders C Amon 1,3-4 (3); J Stewart 2 (1); P Rodríguez 5-28 (24).

21 Jun 1970 — NETHERLANDS: Zandvoort (Round 5) (Race 189)

80 laps x 4.193 km, 2.605 miles = 335.440 km, 208.433 miles

Pos	No	Driver	Car	Model	Engine		Laps	Time/Reason for Retirement	Grid Pos	Row
1	10	J Rindt	Lotus	72C	Ford Cosworth	V8	80	1h 50m 43.410s	1	1
2	5	J Stewart	March	701	Ford Cosworth	V8	80	1h 51m 13.410s	2	1
3	25	J Ickx	Ferrari	312B	Ferrari	F12	79		3	1
4	26	C Regazzoni	Ferrari	312B	Ferrari	F12	79		6	3
5	23	J-P Beltoise	Matra Simca	MS120	Matra	V12	79		10	4
6	16	J Surtees	McLaren	M7C	Ford Cosworth	V8	79		14	6
7	12	J Miles	Lotus	72B	Ford Cosworth	V8	78		8	3
8	24	H Pescarolo	Matra Simca	MS120	Matra	V12	78		13	5
9	22	R Peterson	March	701	Ford Cosworth	V8	78		16	7
10	1	P Rodríguez	BRM	P153	BRM	V12	77		7	3
11	18	J Brabham	Brabham	BT33	Ford Cosworth	V8	76		12	5
nc	15	G Hill	Lotus	49C	Ford Cosworth	V8	71		20	8
r	6	F Cevert	March	701	Ford Cosworth	V8	31	connecting rod	15	6
r	3	G Eaton	BRM	P153	BRM	V12	26	oil tank loose	18	7
r	2	J Oliver	BRM	P153	BRM	V12	23	connecting rod	5	2
r	4	P Courage	De Tomaso	505	Ford Cosworth	V8	22	fatal accident	9	4
r	9	J Siffert	March	701	Ford Cosworth	V8	22	engine	17	7
r	20	P Gethin	McLaren	M14A	Ford Cosworth	V8	18	accident	11	5
r	32	D Gurney	McLaren	M14A	Ford Cosworth	V8	2	timing gear	19	8
r	8	C Amon	March	701	Ford Cosworth	V8	1	clutch	4	2
nq	21	A de Adamich	McLaren	M14D	Alfa Romeo	V8				
nq	19	R Stommelen	Brabham	BT33	Ford Cosworth	V8				
nq	31	P Lovely	Lotus	49B	Ford Cosworth	V8				
nq	29	S Moser	Bellasi		Ford Cosworth	V8				

Winning speed 181.772 km/h, 112.948 mph
Pole Position speed 192.290 km/h, 119.484 mph (J Rindt, 1 min:18.500 sec)
Fastest Lap speed 190.519 km/h, 118.383 mph (J Ickx, 1 min:19.230 sec on lap 22)
Lap Leaders J Ickx 1-2 (2); J Rindt 3-80 (78).

FRANCE: Clermont-Ferrand (Round 6) (Race 190)

38 laps x 8.055 km, 5.005 miles = 306.090 km, 190.196 miles

Pos	No	Driver	Car	Model	Engine		Laps	Time/Reason for Retirement	Grid Pos	Row
1	6	J Rindt	Lotus	72C	Ford Cosworth	V8	38	1h 55m 57.000s	6	3
2	14	C Amon	March	701	Ford Cosworth	V8	38	1h 56m 04.610s	3	2
3	23	J Brabham	Brabham	BT33	Ford Cosworth	V8	38	1h 56m 41.830s	5	3
4	19	D Hulme	McLaren	M14D	Ford Cosworth	V8	38	1h 56m 42.660s	7	4
5	20	H Pescarolo	Matra Simca	MS120	Matra	V12	38	1h 57m 16.420s	8	4
6	17	D Gurney	McLaren	M14A	Ford Cosworth	V8	38	1h 57m 16.650s	17	9
7	22	R Stommelen	Brabham	BT33	Ford Cosworth	V8	38	1h 58m 17.160s	14	7
8	7	J Miles	Lotus	72B	Ford Cosworth	V8	38	1h 58m 44.170s	18	9
9	1	J Stewart	March	701	Ford Cosworth	V8	38	1h 59m 06.610s	4	2
10	8	G Hill	Lotus	49C	Ford Cosworth	V8	37		20	10
11	2	F Cevert	March	701	Ford Cosworth	V8	37		13	7
12	4	G Eaton	BRM	P153	BRM	V12	36		19	10
13r	21	J-P Beltoise	Matra Simca	MS120	Matra	V12	35	fuel pressure	2	1
14	11	I Giunti	Ferrari	312B	Ferrari	F12	35		11	6
nc	16	A de Adamich	McLaren	M7D	Alfa Romeo	V8	29		15	8
r	12	J Siffert	March	701	Ford Cosworth	V8	23	accident	16	8
r	18	R Peterson	March	701	Ford Cosworth	V8	17	crown wheel & pinion	9	5
r	10	J Ickx	Ferrari	312B	Ferrari	F12	16	valve	1	1
r	3	P Rodríguez	BRM	P153	BRM	V12	6	gearbox	10	5
r	5	J Oliver	BRM	P153	BRM	V12	5	timing	12	6
nq	24	S Moser	Bellasi		Ford Cosworth	V8				
nq	9	A Soler-Roig	Lotus	49C	Ford Cosworth	V8				
nq	35	P Lovely	Lotus	49B	Ford Cosworth	V8				

Winning speed 158.391 km/h, 98.419 mph
Pole Position speed 162.709 km/h, 101.103 mph (J Ickx, 2 min:58.220 sec)
Fastest Lap speed 160.432 km/h, 99.688 mph (J Brabham, 3 min: 0.750 sec on lap 29)
Lap Leaders J Ickx 1-14 (14); J-P Beltoise 15-25 (11); J Rindt 26-38 (13).

18 Jul 1970 **BRITAIN: Brands Hatch** (Round 7) (Race 191)

80 laps x 4.265 km, 2.650 miles = 341.181 km, 212.000 miles

Pos	No	Driver	Car	Model	Engine		Laps	Time/Reason for Retirement	Grid Pos	Row
1	5	J Rindt	Lotus	72C	Ford Cosworth	V8	80	1h 57m 02.000s	1	1
2	17	J Brabham	Brabham	BT33	Ford Cosworth	V8	80	1h 57m 34.900s	2	1
3	9	D Hulme	McLaren	M14D	Ford Cosworth	V8	80	1h 57m 56.400s	5	2
4	4	C Regazzoni	Ferrari	312B	Ferrari	F12	80	1h 57m 56.800s	6	3
5	16	C Amon	March	701	Ford Cosworth	V8	79		17	7
6	14	G Hill	Lotus	49C	Ford Cosworth	V8	79		22	9
7	2	F Cevert	March	701	Ford Cosworth	V8	79		14	6
8	28	E Fittipaldi	Lotus	49C	Ford Cosworth	V8	78		21	9
9	27	R Peterson	March	701	Ford Cosworth	V8	72		13	5
nc	29	P Lovely	Lotus	49B	Ford Cosworth	V8	69		23	9
r	10	D Gurney	McLaren	M14A	Ford Cosworth	V8	60	oil pressure	11	5
r	22	P Rodríguez	BRM	P153	BRM	V12	58	accident	15	6
r	23	J Oliver	BRM	P153	BRM	V12	54	engine	4	2
r	1	J Stewart	March	701	Ford Cosworth	V8	52	fire / clutch	8	3
r	20	J Surtees	Surtees	TS7	Ford Cosworth	V8	51	engine	19	8
r	8	H Pescarolo	Matra Simca	MS120	Matra	V12	41	accident	12	5
r	7	J-P Beltoise	Matra Simca	MS120	Matra	V12	24	front wheel bearing	10	4
r	26	M Andretti	March	701	Ford Cosworth	V8	21	rear suspension	9	4
r	15	J Siffert	March	701	Ford Cosworth	V8	19	rear suspension	20	8
r	6	J Miles	Lotus	72B	Ford Cosworth	V8	15	camshaft	7	3
r	24	G Eaton	BRM	P153	BRM	V12	10	oil pressure	16	7
r	3	J Ickx	Ferrari	312B	Ferrari	F12	6	differential	3	1
ns	11	A de Adamich	McLaren	M7D	Alfa Romeo	V8		fuel tank leak	18	7
ns	18	R Stommelen	Brabham	BT33	Ford Cosworth	V8		accident		
ns	25	B Redman	De Tomaso	505	Ford Cosworth	V8		rear hub		

Winning speed 174.915 km/h, 108.687 mph
Pole Position speed 181.051 km/h, 112.500 mph (J Rindt, 1 min:24.800 sec)
Fastest Lap speed 178.733 km/h, 111.059 mph (J Brabham, 1 min:25.900 sec on lap 70)
Lap Leaders J Ickx 1-6 (6); J Rindt 7-68,80 (63); J Brabham 69-79 (11).

J Rindt was originally disqualified for wing being too high, but was later reinstated.

50 laps x 6.789 km, 4.218 miles = 339.450 km, 210.924 miles

Pos	No	Driver	Car	Model	Engine		Laps	Time/Reason for Retirement	Grid Pos	Row
1	2	J Rindt	Lotus	72C	Ford Cosworth	V8	50	1h 42m 00.300s	2	1
2	10	J Ickx	Ferrari	312B	Ferrari	F12	50	1h 42m 01.000s	1	1
3	4	D Hulme	McLaren	M14A	Ford Cosworth	V8	50	1h 43m 22.100s	16	8
4	17	E Fittipaldi	Lotus	49C	Ford Cosworth	V8	50	1h 43m 55.400s	13	7
5	21	R Stommelen	Brabham	BT33	Ford Cosworth	V8	49		11	6
6	14	H Pescarolo	Matra Simca	MS120	Matra	V12	49		5	3
7	23	F Cevert	March	701	Ford Cosworth	V8	49		14	7
8r	12	J Siffert	March	701	Ford Cosworth	V8	47	engine	4	2
9r	7	J Surtees	Surtees	TS7	Ford Cosworth	V8	46	engine	15	8
r	9	G Hill	Lotus	49C	Ford Cosworth	V8	37	engine	20	10
r	5	C Amon	March	701	Ford Cosworth	V8	34	engine	6	3
r	15	C Regazzoni	Ferrari	312B	Ferrari	F12	30	engine	3	2
r	16	J Miles	Lotus	72C	Ford Cosworth	V8	24	engine	10	5
r	1	J Stewart	March	701	Ford Cosworth	V8	20	engine	7	4
r	11	M Andretti	March	701	Ford Cosworth	V8	15	gear selector	9	5
r	22	R Peterson	March	701	Ford Cosworth	V8	11	engine	19	10
r	6	P Rodríguez	BRM	P153	BRM	V12	7	ignition	8	4
r	18	J Oliver	BRM	P153	BRM	V12	5	engine	18	9
r	3	J Brabham	Brabham	BT33	Ford Cosworth	V8	4	oil union leak	12	6
r	8	J-P Beltoise	Matra Simca	MS120	Matra	V12	4	front suspension	21	11
r	24	P Gethin	McLaren	M14A	Ford Cosworth	V8	3	throttle slides	17	9
nq	25	B Redman	De Tomaso	505	Ford Cosworth	V8				
nq	20	A de Adamich	McLaren	M14D	Alfa Romeo	V8				
nq	27	S Moser	Bellasi		Ford Cosworth	V8				
nq	26	H Hahne	March	701	Ford Cosworth	V8				

Winning speed 199.667 km/h, 124.067 mph
Pole Position speed 204.522 km/h, 127.084 mph (J Ickx, 1 min:59.500 sec)
Fastest Lap speed 202.825 km/h, 126.030 mph (J Ickx, 2 min: 0.500 sec on lap 49)
Lap Leaders J Ickx 1-6,10-17,26-31,36-43,45-46,48 (31); J Rindt 7-9,18-21,24-25,32-35,44,47,49-50 (17); C Regazzoni 22-23 (2).

60 laps x 5.911 km, 3.673 miles = 354.660 km, 220.376 miles

Pos	No	Driver	Car	Model	Engine		Laps	Time/Reason for Retirement	Grid Pos	Row
1	12	J Ickx	Ferrari	312B	Ferrari	F12	60	1h 42m 17.320s	3	2
2	27	C Regazzoni	Ferrari	312B	Ferrari	F12	60	1h 42m 17.930s	2	1
3	11	R Stommelen	Brabham	BT33	Ford Cosworth	V8	60	1h 43m 45.200s	17	9
4	17	P Rodríguez	BRM	P153	BRM	V12	59		22	11
5	16	J Oliver	BRM	P153	BRM	V12	59		14	7
6	19	J-P Beltoise	Matra Simca	MS120	Matra	V12	59		7	4
7	14	I Giunti	Ferrari	312B	Ferrari	F12	59		5	3
8	4	C Amon	March	701	Ford Cosworth	V8	59		6	3
9	3	J Siffert	March	701	Ford Cosworth	V8	59		20	10
10	23	P Gethin	McLaren	M14A	Ford Cosworth	V8	59		21	11
11	18	G Eaton	BRM	P153	BRM	V12	58		23	12
12	22	A de Adamich	McLaren	M14D	Alfa Romeo	V8	57		15	8
13	10	J Brabham	Brabham	BT33	Ford Cosworth	V8	56		8	4
14	20	H Pescarolo	Matra Simca	MS120	Matra	V12	56		13	7
15	8	E Fittipaldi	Lotus	49C	Ford Cosworth	V8	55		16	8
r	21	D Hulme	McLaren	M14A	Ford Cosworth	V8	30	engine	11	6
r	15	J Surtees	Surtees	TS7	Ford Cosworth	V8	27	engine	12	6
r	26	T Schenken	De Tomaso	505	Ford Cosworth	V8	25	engine	19	10
r	6	J Rindt	Lotus	72C	Ford Cosworth	V8	21	engine	1	1
r	24	S Moser	Bellasi		Ford Cosworth	V8	13	radiator	24	12
r	5	M Andretti	March	701	Ford Cosworth	V8	13	throttle jammed / accident	18	9
r	1	J Stewart	March	701	Ford Cosworth	V8	7	fuel line	4	2
r	7	J Miles	Lotus	72C	Ford Cosworth	V8	4	brake shaft	10	5
r	2	F Cevert	March	701	Ford Cosworth	V8	0	engine	9	5

Winning speed 208.035 km/h, 129.267 mph
Pole Position speed 214.447 km/h, 133.251 mph (J Rindt, 1 min:39.230 sec)
Fastest Lap speed 211.948 km/h, 131.699 mph (J Ickx / C Regazzoni, 1 min:40.400 sec on lap 45)
Lap Leaders C Regazzoni 1 (1); J Ickx 2-60 (59).

Although J Miles supposedly set a faster time than D Hulme in qualifying, there was confusion among the officials and they lined up in reverse order.

6 Sep 1970   ITALY: Monza   (Round 10)   (Race 194)

68 laps x 5.750 km, 3.573 miles = 391.000 km, 242.956 miles

Pos	No	Driver	Car	Model	Engine		Laps	Time/Reason for Retirement	Grid Pos	Row
1	4	C Regazzoni	Ferrari	312B	Ferrari	F12	68	1h 39m 06.880s	3	2
2	18	J Stewart	March	701	Ford Cosworth	V8	68	1h 39m 12.610s	4	2
3	40	J-P Beltoise	Matra Simca	MS120	Matra	V12	68	1h 39m 12.680s	14	7
4	30	D Hulme	McLaren	M14A	Ford Cosworth	V8	68	1h 39m 13.030s	9	5
5	46	R Stommelen	Brabham	BT33	Ford Cosworth	V8	68	1h 39m 13.290s	17	9
6	20	F Cevert	March	701	Ford Cosworth	V8	68	1h 40m 10.340s	11	6
7	48	C Amon	March	701	Ford Cosworth	V8	67		18	9
8	34	A de Adamich	McLaren	M14D	Alfa Romeo	V8	61		12	6
nc	32	P Gethin	McLaren	M14A	Ford Cosworth	V8	60		16	8
r	8	J Oliver	BRM	P153	BRM	V12	36	engine	6	3
r	52	R Peterson	March	701	Ford Cosworth	V8	35	engine	13	7
r	44	J Brabham	Brabham	BT33	Ford Cosworth	V8	31	engine / accident	8	4
r	2	J Ickx	Ferrari	312B	Ferrari	F12	25	clutch	1	1
r	12	G Eaton	BRM	P153	BRM	V12	21	engine overheating	20	10
r	54	T Schenken	De Tomaso	505	Ford Cosworth	V8	17	engine	19	10
r	6	I Giunti	Ferrari	312B	Ferrari	F12	14	fuel metering unit	5	3
r	42	H Pescarolo	Matra Simca	MS120	Matra	V12	14	valve spring	15	8
r	10	P Rodríguez	BRM	P153	BRM	V12	12	engine	2	1
r	50	J Siffert	March	701	Ford Cosworth	V8	3	engine	7	4
r	14	J Surtees	Surtees	TS7	Ford Cosworth	V8	0	electrics	10	5
ns	22	J Rindt	Lotus	72C	Ford Cosworth	V8		fatal accident		
ns	28	G Hill	Lotus	72C	Ford Cosworth	V8		withdrew after Rindt accident		
ns	24	J Miles	Lotus	72C	Ford Cosworth	V8		withdrew after Rindt accident		
nq	38	J Bonnier	McLaren	M7C	Ford Cosworth	V8				
ns	26	E Fittipaldi	Lotus	72C	Ford Cosworth	V8		withdrew after Rindt accident		
nq	36	N Galli	McLaren	M7D	Alfa Romeo	V8				
nq	56	S Moser	Bellasi		Ford Cosworth	V8				

Winning speed 236.696 km/h, 147.076 mph
Pole Position speed 246.019 km/h, 152.869 mph (J Ickx, 1 min:24.140 sec)
Fastest Lap speed 242.958 km/h, 150.967 mph (C Regazzoni, 1 min:25.200 sec on lap 65)
Lap Leaders J Ickx 1-3,19-20 (5); P Rodríguez 4,7-8 (3); J Stewart 5-6,9,11,14-17,26-27,31,35,37,42-43,51,53 (17);
C Regazzoni 10,12,32-34,36,38-41,44-50,52,54-68 (33); J Oliver 13,18,21-25,28,30 (9); D Hulme 29 (1).

20 Sep 1970   CANADA: Mont-Tremblant   (Round 11)   (Race 195)

90 laps x 4.265 km, 2.650 miles = 383.829 km, 238.500 miles

Pos	No	Driver	Car	Model	Engine		Laps	Time/Reason for Retirement	Grid Pos	Row
1	18	J Ickx	Ferrari	312B	Ferrari	F12	90	2h 21m 18.400s	2	1
2	19	C Regazzoni	Ferrari	312B	Ferrari	F12	90	2h 21m 33.200s	3	2
3	20	C Amon	March	701	Ford Cosworth	V8	90	2h 22m 16.300s	6	3
4	14	P Rodríguez	BRM	P153	BRM	V12	89		7	4
5	4	J Surtees	Surtees	TS7	Ford Cosworth	V8	89		5	3
6	6	P Gethin	McLaren	M14A	Ford Cosworth	V8	88		11	6
7	24	H Pescarolo	Matra Simca	MS120	Matra	V12	87		8	4
8	23	J-P Beltoise	Matra Simca	MS120	Matra	V12	85		13	7
9	2	F Cevert	March	701	Ford Cosworth	V8	85		4	2
10	16	G Eaton	BRM	P153	BRM	V12	85		9	5
nc	10	T Schenken	De Tomaso	505	Ford Cosworth	V8	79		17	9
nc	9	G Hill	Lotus	72C	Ford Cosworth	V8	77		20	10
r	8	A de Adamich	McLaren	M14D	Alfa Romeo	V8	69	oil pressure	12	6
nc	26	R Peterson	March	701	Ford Cosworth	V8	65		16	8
r	5	D Hulme	McLaren	M14A	Ford Cosworth	V8	59	flywheel	15	8
r	11	J Brabham	Brabham	BT33	Ford Cosworth	V8	57	oil leak	19	10
nc	15	J Oliver	BRM	P153	BRM	V12	52		10	5
r	3	J Stewart	Tyrrell	001	Ford Cosworth	V8	31	front stub axle	1	1
r	12	R Stommelen	Brabham	BT33	Ford Cosworth	V8	23	steering	18	9
r	21	J Siffert	March	701	Ford Cosworth	V8	22	engine	14	7

Winning speed 162.977 km/h, 101.269 mph
Pole Position speed 167.794 km/h, 104.262 mph (J Stewart, 1 min:31.500 sec)
Fastest Lap speed 166.520 km/h, 103.471 mph (C Regazzoni, 1 min:32.200 sec on lap 75)
Lap Leaders J Stewart 1-31 (31); J Ickx 32-90 (59).

4 Oct 1970 **USA: Watkins Glen** **(Round 12)** **(Race 196)**

108 laps x 3.701 km, 2.300 miles = 399.761 km, 248.400 miles

Pos	No	Driver	Car	Model	Engine		Laps	Time/Reason for Retirement	Grid Pos	Row
1	24	E Fittipaldi	Lotus	72C	Ford Cosworth	V8	108	1h 57m 32.790s	3	2
2	19	P Rodríguez	BRM	P153	BRM	V12	108	1h 58m 09.180s	4	2
3	23	R Wisell	Lotus	72C	Ford Cosworth	V8	108	1h 58m 17.960s	9	5
4	3	J Ickx	Ferrari	312B	Ferrari	F12	107		1	1
5	12	C Amon	March	701	Ford Cosworth	V8	107		5	3
6	18	D Bell	Surtees	TS7	Ford Cosworth	V8	107		13	7
7	8	D Hulme	McLaren	M14A	Ford Cosworth	V8	106		11	6
8	7	H Pescarolo	Matra Simca	MS120	Matra	V12	105		12	6
9	11	J Siffert	March	701	Ford Cosworth	V8	105		23	12
10	15	J Brabham	Brabham	BT33	Ford Cosworth	V8	105		16	8
11	29	R Peterson	March	701	Ford Cosworth	V8	104		15	8
12	16	R Stommelen	Brabham	BT33	Ford Cosworth	V8	104		19	10
13	4	C Regazzoni	Ferrari	312B	Ferrari	F12	101		6	3
14	9	P Gethin	McLaren	M14A	Ford Cosworth	V8	100		21	11
r	1	J Stewart	Tyrrell	001	Ford Cosworth	V8	82	oil leak	2	1
r	14	G Hill	Lotus	72C	Ford Cosworth	V8	72	clutch	10	5
r	2	F Cevert	March	701	Ford Cosworth	V8	62	rear wheel lost	17	9
r	30	T Schenken	De Tomaso	505	Ford Cosworth	V8	61	rear suspension	20	10
r	27	J Bonnier	McLaren	M7C	Ford Cosworth	V8	50	water pipe	24	12
r	6	J-P Beltoise	Matra Simca	MS120	Matra	V12	27	handling	18	9
r	31	G Hutchison	Brabham	BT26A	Ford Cosworth	V8	21	accident / fuel tank	22	11
r	20	J Oliver	BRM	P153	BRM	V12	14	engine	7	4
r	21	G Eaton	BRM	P153	BRM	V12	10	engine	14	7
r	17	J Surtees	Surtees	TS7	Ford Cosworth	V8	6	flywheel	8	4
nq	32	P Westbury	BRM	P153	BRM	V12				
nq	28	P Lovely	Lotus	49B	Ford Cosworth	V8				
nq	10	A de Adamich	McLaren	M14D	Alfa Romeo	V8				

Winning speed 204.053 km/h, 126.792 mph
Pole Position speed 211.279 km/h, 131.283 mph (J Ickx, 1 min: 3.070 sec)
Fastest Lap speed 212.390 km/h, 131.973 mph (J Ickx, 1 min: 2.740 sec on lap 105)
Lap Leaders J Stewart 1-82 (82); P Rodríguez 83-100 (18); E Fittipaldi 101-108 (8).

25 Oct 1970 **MEXICO: Mexico City** **(Round 13)** **(Race 197)**

65 laps x 5.000 km, 3.107 miles = 325.000 km, 201.946 miles

Pos	No	Driver	Car	Model	Engine		Laps	Time/Reason for Retirement	Grid Pos	Row
1	3	J Ickx	Ferrari	312B	Ferrari	F12	65	1h 53m 28.360s	3	2
2	4	C Regazzoni	Ferrari	312B	Ferrari	F12	65	1h 54m 13.820s	1	1
3	8	D Hulme	McLaren	M14A	Ford Cosworth	V8	65	1h 54m 14.330s	14	7
4	12	C Amon	March	701	Ford Cosworth	V8	65	1h 54m 15.410s	5	3
5	19	J-P Beltoise	Matra Simca	MS120	Matra	V12	65	1h 54m 18.470s	6	3
6	19	P Rodríguez	BRM	P153	BRM	V12	65	1h 54m 53.120s	7	4
7	20	J Oliver	BRM	P153	BRM	V12	64		13	7
8	17	J Surtees	Surtees	TS7	Ford Cosworth	V8	64		15	8
9	7	H Pescarolo	Matra Simca	MS120	Matra	V12	61		11	6
nc	23	R Wisell	Lotus	72C	Ford Cosworth	V8	56		12	6
r	15	J Brabham	Brabham	BT33	Ford Cosworth	V8	52	oil pressure	4	2
r	1	J Stewart	Tyrrell	001	Ford Cosworth	V8	33	front suspension	2	1
r	9	P Gethin	McLaren	M14A	Ford Cosworth	V8	27	engine	10	5
r	16	R Stommelen	Brabham	BT33	Ford Cosworth	V8	15	fuel system	17	9
r	2	F Cevert	March	701	Ford Cosworth	V8	8	engine	9	5
r	14	G Hill	Lotus	72C	Ford Cosworth	V8	4	engine overheating	8	4
r	11	J Siffert	March	701	Ford Cosworth	V8	3	engine	16	8
r	24	E Fittipaldi	Lotus	72C	Ford Cosworth	V8	1	engine	18	9

Winning speed 171.848 km/h, 106.781 mph
Pole Position speed 176.713 km/h, 109.804 mph (C Regazzoni, 1 min:41.860 sec)
Fastest Lap speed 174.571 km/h, 108.473 mph (J Ickx, 1 min:43.110 sec on lap 46)
Lap Leaders C Regazzoni 1 (1); J Ickx 2-65 (64).

Lap Leaders 1970

Pos	Driver	Car-Engine	GPs	laps	km	miles
1	J Stewart	March-Ford Cosworth	5	154	581.1	361.1
		Tyrrell-Ford Cosworth	2	113	435.7	270.7
			7	267	1,016.8	631.8
2	J Ickx	Ferrari	8	240	1,306.3	811.7
3	J Rindt	Lotus-Ford Cosworth	5	172	819.0	508.9
4	J Brabham	Brabham-Ford Cosworth	3	124	460.8	286.3
5	P Rodríguez	BRM	3	45	422.3	262.4
6	C Regazzoni	Ferrari	4	37	214.2	133.1
7	J-P Beltoise	Matra Simca	1	11	88.6	55.1
8	J Oliver	BRM	1	9	51.7	32.2
9	E Fittipaldi	Lotus-Ford Cosworth	1	8	29.6	18.4
10	C Amon	March-Ford Cosworth	1	3	42.3	26.3
11	D Hulme	McLaren-Ford Cosworth	1	1	5.7	3.6
			13	917	4,457.5	2,769.7

Driver Points 1970

		ZA	E	MC	B	NL	F	GB	D	A	I	CDN	USA	MEX	Total
1	J Rindt	-	-	9	-	9	9	9	9	-	-	-	-	-	45
2	J Ickx	-	-	-	-	4	-	-	6	9	-	9	3	9	40
3	C Regazzoni	-	-	-	3	-	3	-	6	9	6	-	6	33
4	D Hulme	6	-	3	-	-	3	4	4	-	3	-	-	4	27
5	J Brabham	9	-	6	-	-	4	6	-	-	-	-	-	-	25
	J Stewart	4	9	-	-	6	-	-	-	-	6	-	-	-	25
7	P Rodríguez	-	-	1	9	-	-	-	-	3	-	3	6	1	23
	C Amon	-	-	-	6	-	6	2	-	-	-	4	2	3	23
9	J-P Beltoise	3	-	4	2	-	-	-	1	4	-	-	2	16
10	E Fittipaldi	-	-	-	-	-	-	-	3	-	-	-	9	-	12
11	R Stommelen	-	-	-	2	-	-	-	2	4	2	-	-	-	10
12	H Pescarolo	-	-	4	1	-	2	-	1	-	-	-	-	-	8
13	G Hill	1	3	2	-	-	-	1	-	-	-	-	-	-	7
14	B McLaren	-	6	-	-	-	-	-	-	-	-	-	-	-	6
15	M Andretti	-	4	-	-	-	-	-	-	-	-	-	-	-	4
	R Wisell	-	-	-	-	-	-	-	-	-	-	-	4	-	4
17	I Giunti	-	-	-	3	-	-	-	-	-	-	-	-	-	3
	J Surtees	-	-	-	-	1	-	-	-	-	-	2	-	-	3
19	J Miles	2	-	-	-	-	-	-	-	-	-	-	-	-	2
	J Servoz-Gavin	-	2	-	-	-	-	-	-	-	-	-	-	-	2
	J Oliver	-	-	-	-	-	-	-	-	2	-	-	-	-	2
22	D Gurney	-	-	-	-	-	1	-	-	-	-	-	-	-	1
	F Cevert	-	-	-	-	-	-	-	-	-	1	-	-	-	1
	P Gethin	-	-	-	-	-	-	-	-	-	-	1	-	-	1
	D Bell	-	-	-	-	-	-	-	-	-	-	1	-	-	1

9,6,4,3,2 and 1 point awarded to the first six finishers. Best 6 scores from first 7 races, best 5 from remaining 6 races.

Constructor Points 1970

		ZA	E	MC	B	NL	F	GB	D	A	I	CDN	USA	MEX	Total
1	Lotus-Ford Cosworth	2	3	9	-	9	9	9	9	-	-	-	9	-	59
2	Ferrari	-	-	-	3	4	-	3	6	9	9	9	(3)	9	52 (3)
3	March-Ford Cosworth	4	9	-	6	6	6	2	-	-	6	4	2	3	48
4	Brabham-Ford Cosworth	9	-	6	2	-	4	6	2	4	2	-	-	-	35
	McLaren-Ford Cosworth	6	6	3	-	1	3	4	4	-	3	1	-	4	35
6	BRM	-	-	1	9	-	-	-	-	3	-	3	6	1	23
	Matra Simca	3	-	4	4	2	2	-	1	1	4	-	-	2	23
8	Surtees-Ford Cosworth	-	-	-	-	-	-	-	-	-	-	2	1	-	3

9,6,4,3,2 and 1 point awarded to the first six finishers. Points only for highest placed car. Best 6 scores from first 7 races, best 5 from remaining 6 races.

1971

Race Entrants and Results

Progress in tyre design led to substantial width increases, as well as the introduction of the treadless slick. Air scoops appeared on some cars and Lotus tried out its turbine car in selected races. The season ended on a sour note when Jo Siffert was killed in a non-championship race at Brands Hatch.

FERRARI
Scuderia Ferrari SpA SEFAC: Ickx, Regazzoni, Andretti

BELLASI
Jolly Club Switzerland: Moser

BRABHAM
Motor Racing Developments: Hill, Schenken, Charlton
Ecurie Evergreen/Alain de Cadenet: Craft
Team Gunston: Pretorius

BRM
Yardley Team BRM: Rodríguez, Siffert, Ganley, Marko, Gethin, Elford, Eaton, Cannon

LOTUS
Gold Leaf Team Lotus: Fittipaldi, Wisell, Charlton, Walker
World Wide Racing: Fittipaldi (I)
Pete Lovely Volkswagen Inc: Lovely

McLAREN
Bruce McLaren Motor Racing: Hulme, Gethin, Oliver
Ecurie Bonnier: Bonnier, (Marko)
Penske-White Racing: Donohue, Hobbs

MARCH
STP March Racing Team: Peterson, Galli, de Adamich, Soler-Roig, Lauda, Beuttler (CDN)
Frank Williams Racing Cars: Pescarolo, Jean
Gene Mason Racing: Barber
Clarke-Mordaunt-Guthrie Racing: Beuttler
Shell Arnold Team: Jarier
Jo Siffert Automobiles: Mazet
Team Gunston: Love

SURTEES
Brooke Bond Oxo-Rob Walker Team Surtees: Surtees
Auto Motor Und Sport-Eifelland Team Surtees: Stommelen
Team Surtees: Redman, Hailwood, Bell, Posey
Stichting Autoraces Nederland: van Lennep

TYRRELL
Elf Team Tyrrell: Stewart, Cevert, Revson

MATRA SIMCA
Equipe Matra Sports: Amon, Beltoise

6 Mar 1971		SOUTH AFRICA: Kyalami						(Round 1)	(Race 198)	
		79 laps x 4.104 km, 2.550 miles = 324.216 km, 201.458 miles								
Pos	No	Driver	Car	Model	Engine		Laps	Time/Reason for Retirement	Grid Pos	Row
1	6	M Andretti	Ferrari	312B	Ferrari	F12	79	1h 47m 35.500s	4	2
2	9	J Stewart	Tyrrell	001	Ford Cosworth	V8	79	1h 47m 56.400s	1	1
3	5	C Regazzoni	Ferrari	312B	Ferrari	F12	79	1h 48m 06.900s	3	1
4	3	R Wisell	Lotus	72C	Ford Cosworth	V8	79	1h 48m 44.900s	14	6
5	19	C Amon	Matra Simca	MS120B	Matra	V12	78		2	1
6	11	D Hulme	McLaren	M19A	Ford Cosworth	V8	78		7	3
7	28	B Redman	Surtees	TS7	Ford Cosworth	V8	78		17	7
8	4	J Ickx	Ferrari	312B	Ferrari	F12	78		8	3
9	14	G Hill	Brabham	BT33	Ford Cosworth	V8	77		19	8
10	7	R Peterson	March	711	Ford Cosworth	V8	77		13	5
11	22	H Pescarolo	March	701	Ford Cosworth	V8	77		18	7
12	21	R Stommelen	Surtees	TS7	Ford Cosworth	V8	77		15	6
13	8	A de Adamich	March	711	Alfa Romeo	V8	75		22	9
r	2	E Fittipaldi	Lotus	72C	Ford Cosworth	V8	58	engine	5	2
r	20	J Surtees	Surtees	TS9	Ford Cosworth	V8	56	gearbox oil pipe	6	3
r	10	F Cevert	Tyrrell	002	Ford Cosworth	V8	45	accident	9	4
r	27	H Ganley	BRM	P153	BRM	V12	42	driver ill	24	10
r	16	P Rodríguez	BRM	P160	BRM	V12	33	engine overheating	10	4
r	17	J Siffert	BRM	P153	BRM	V12	31	engine overheating	16	7
r	15	D Charlton	Brabham	BT33	Ford Cosworth	V8	31	valve spring	12	5
r	24	J Love	March	701	Ford Cosworth	V8	30	differential	21	9
r	25	J Pretorius	Brabham	BT26A	Ford Cosworth	V8	22	camshaft	20	8
r	12	P Gethin	McLaren	M14A	Ford Cosworth	V8	7	fuel line / leak	11	5
r	23	J Bonnier	McLaren	M7C	Ford Cosworth	V8	5	suspension	23	9
r	26	A Soler-Roig	March	711	Ford Cosworth	V8	5	engine	25	10

Winning speed 180.804 km/h, 112.346 mph
Pole Position speed 189.902 km/h, 118.000 mph (J Stewart, 1 min:17.800 sec)
Fastest Lap speed 183.990 km/h, 114.326 mph (M Andretti, 1 min:20.300 sec on lap 73)
Lap Leaders C Regazzoni 1-16 (16); D Hulme 17-75 (59); M Andretti 76-79 (4).

18 Apr 1971 **SPAIN: Montjuïc** (Round 2) (Race 199)

75 laps x 3.791 km, 2.356 miles = 284.325 km, 176.671 miles

Pos	No	Driver	Car	Model	Engine		Laps	Time/Reason for Retirement	Grid Pos	Row
1	11	J Stewart	Tyrrell	003	Ford Cosworth	V8	75	1h 49m 03.400s	4	2
2	4	J Ickx	Ferrari	312B	Ferrari	F12	75	1h 49m 06.800s	1	1
3	20	C Amon	Matra Simca	MS120B	Matra	V12	75	1h 50m 01.500s	3	1
4	14	P Rodríguez	BRM	P160	BRM	V12	75	1h 50m 21.300s	5	2
5	9	D Hulme	McLaren	M19A	Ford Cosworth	V8	75	1h 50m 30.400s	9	4
6	21	J-P Beltoise	Matra Simca	MS120B	Matra	V12	74		6	3
7	12	F Cevert	Tyrrell	002	Ford Cosworth	V8	74		12	5
8	10	P Gethin	McLaren	M14A	Ford Cosworth	V8	73		7	3
9	8	T Schenken	Brabham	BT33	Ford Cosworth	V8	72		21	9
10	16	H Ganley	BRM	P153	BRM	V12	71		17	7
11	24	J Surtees	Surtees	TS9	Ford Cosworth	V8	67		22	9
nc	3	R Wisell	Lotus	72C	Ford Cosworth	V8	58		16	7
r	2	E Fittipaldi	Lotus	72C	Ford Cosworth	V8	54	rear suspension	14	6
r	27	H Pescarolo	March	711	Ford Cosworth	V8	53	engine / rear wing	11	5
r	6	M Andretti	Ferrari	312B	Ferrari	F12	50	fuel pump / oil pressure	8	3
r	19	A Soler-Roig	March	711	Ford Cosworth	V8	46	fuel line	20	8
r	17	A de Adamich	March	711	Alfa Romeo	V8	26	transmission	18	7
r	18	R Peterson	March	711	Ford Cosworth	V8	26	ignition	13	5
r	5	C Regazzoni	Ferrari	312B	Ferrari	F12	13	engine	2	1
r	25	R Stommelen	Surtees	TS9	Ford Cosworth	V8	9	fuel pressure	19	8
r	15	J Siffert	BRM	P160	BRM	V12	5	gear linkage	10	4
r	7	G Hill	Brabham	BT34	Ford Cosworth	V8	5	steering	15	6

Winning speed 156.428 km/h, 97.200 mph
Pole Position speed 158.878 km/h, 98.722 mph (J Ickx, 1 min:25.900 sec)
Fastest Lap speed 160.371 km/h, 99.650 mph (J Ickx, 1 min:25.100 sec on lap 69)
Lap Leaders J Ickx 1-5 (5); J Stewart 6-75 (70).

23 May 1971 **MONACO: Monte-Carlo** (Round 3) (Race 200)

80 laps x 3.145 km, 1.954 miles = 251.600 km, 156.337 miles

Pos	No	Driver	Car	Model	Engine		Laps	Time/Reason for Retirement	Grid Pos	Row
1	11	J Stewart	Tyrrell	003	Ford Cosworth	V8	80	1h 52m 21.300s	1	1
2	17	R Peterson	March	711	Ford Cosworth	V8	80	1h 52m 46.900s	8	4
3	4	J Ickx	Ferrari	312B2	Ferrari	F12	80	1h 53m 14.600s	2	1
4	9	D Hulme	McLaren	M19A	Ford Cosworth	V8	80	1h 53m 28.000s	6	3
5	1	E Fittipaldi	Lotus	72D	Ford Cosworth	V8	79		17	9
6	24	R Stommelen	Surtees	TS9	Ford Cosworth	V8	79		16	8
7	22	J Surtees	Surtees	TS9	Ford Cosworth	V8	79		10	5
8	27	H Pescarolo	March	711	Ford Cosworth	V8	77		13	7
9	15	P Rodríguez	BRM	P160	BRM	V12	76		5	3
10	8	T Schenken	Brabham	BT33	Ford Cosworth	V8	76		18	9
r	14	J Siffert	BRM	P160	BRM	V12	58	oil line	3	2
r	21	J-P Beltoise	Matra Simca	MS120B	Matra	V12	47	crown wheel & pinion	7	4
r	20	C Amon	Matra Simca	MS120B	Matra	V12	45	crown wheel & pinion	4	2
r	3	C Regazzoni	Ferrari	312B2	Ferrari	F12	24	accident / rear suspension	11	6
r	10	P Gethin	McLaren	M14A	Ford Cosworth	V8	22	accident	14	7
r	2	R Wisell	Lotus	72C	Ford Cosworth	V8	21	rear hub bearing	12	6
r	12	F Cevert	Tyrrell	002	Ford Cosworth	V8	5	engine / accident	15	8
r	7	G Hill	Brabham	BT34	Ford Cosworth	V8	1	accident	9	5
nq	16	H Ganley	BRM	P153	BRM	V12				
nq	6	M Andretti	Ferrari	312B	Ferrari	F12				
nq	19	N Galli	March	711	Alfa Romeo	V8				
nq	18	A Soler-Roig	March	711	Ford Cosworth	V8				
nq	28	S Barber	March	711	Ford Cosworth	V8				

Winning speed 134.360 km/h, 83.487 mph
Pole Position speed 136.082 km/h, 84.557 mph (J Stewart, 1 min:23.200 sec)
Fastest Lap speed 137.737 km/h, 85.586 mph (J Stewart, 1 min:22.200 sec on lap 57)
Lap Leaders J Stewart 1-80 (80).

70 laps x 4.193 km, 2.605 miles = 293.510 km, 182.379 miles

Pos	No	Driver	Car	Model	Engine		Laps	Time/Reason for Retirement	Grid Pos	Row
1	2	J Ickx	Ferrari	312B2	Ferrari	F12	70	1h 56m 20.090s	1	1
2	8	P Rodríguez	BRM	P160	BRM	V12	70	1h 56m 28.080s	2	1
3	3	C Regazzoni	Ferrari	312B2	Ferrari	F12	69		4	2
4	16	R Peterson	March	711	Ford Cosworth	V8	68		13	5
5	23	J Surtees	Surtees	TS9	Ford Cosworth	V8	68		7	3
6	9	J Siffert	BRM	P160	BRM	V12	68		8	3
7	10	H Ganley	BRM	P153	BRM	V12	66		9	4
8	30	G van Lennep	Surtees	TS7	Ford Cosworth	V8	65		21	9
9	21	J-P Beltoise	Matra Simca	MS120B	Matra	V12	65		11	5
10	24	G Hill	Brabham	BT34	Ford Cosworth	V8	65		16	7
11	5	J Stewart	Tyrrell	003	Ford Cosworth	V8	65		3	1
12	26	D Hulme	McLaren	M19A	Ford Cosworth	V8	63		14	6
nc	31	H Pescarolo	March	711	Ford Cosworth	V8	62		15	6
nc	22	S Barber	March	711	Ford Cosworth	V8	60		24	10
nc	28	P Gethin	McLaren	M19A	Ford Cosworth	V8	60		23	9
r	19	A Soler-Roig	March	711	Ford Cosworth	V8	57	engine	17	7
r	25	T Schenken	Brabham	BT33	Ford Cosworth	V8	39	accident / suspension	19	8
r	6	F Cevert	Tyrrell	002	Ford Cosworth	V8	29	accident	12	5
dq	29	R Stommelen	Surtees	TS9	Ford Cosworth	V8	19	push start after spin	10	4
dq	14	R Wisell	Lotus	72D	Ford Cosworth	V8	17	reversed into pits	6	3
r	18	N Galli	March	711	Alfa Romeo	V8	7	accident	20	8
r	15	D Walker	Lotus	56B	Pratt & Whitney	tbne	6	accident	22	9
r	4	M Andretti	Ferrari	312B	Ferrari	F12	5	fuel pump / engine	18	7
r	20	C Amon	Matra Simca	MS120B	Matra	V12	2	spin / radiator	5	2

Winning speed 151.379 km/h, 94.062 mph
Pole Position speed 194.973 km/h, 121.151 mph (J Ickx, 1 min:17.420 sec)
Fastest Lap speed 158.976 km/h, 98.783 mph (J Ickx, 1 min:34.950 sec on lap 49)
Lap Leaders J Ickx 1-8,30,32-70 (48); P Rodríguez 9-29,31 (22).

55 laps x 5.810 km, 3.610 miles = 319.550 km, 198.559 miles

Pos	No	Driver	Car	Model	Engine		Laps	Time/Reason for Retirement	Grid Pos	Row
1	11	J Stewart	Tyrrell	003	Ford Cosworth	V8	55	1h 46m 41.680s	1	1
2	12	F Cevert	Tyrrell	002	Ford Cosworth	V8	55	1h 47m 09.800s	7	3
3	1	E Fittipaldi	Lotus	72D	Ford Cosworth	V8	55	1h 47m 15.750s	17	7
4	14	J Siffert	BRM	P160	BRM	V12	55	1h 47m 18.850s	6	3
5	20	C Amon	Matra Simca	MS120B	Matra	V12	55	1h 47m 22.760s	9	4
6	2	R Wisell	Lotus	72D	Ford Cosworth	V8	55	1h 47m 57.766s	15	6
7	21	J-P Beltoise	Matra Simca	MS120B	Matra	V12	55	1h 47m 58.610s	8	3
8	22	J Surtees	Surtees	TS9	Ford Cosworth	V8	55	1h 48m 06.590s	13	5
9	10	P Gethin	McLaren	M19A	Ford Cosworth	V8	54		19	8
10	16	H Ganley	BRM	P153	BRM	V12	54		16	7
11	24	R Stommelen	Surtees	TS9	Ford Cosworth	V8	53		10	4
12r	8	T Schenken	Brabham	BT33	Ford Cosworth	V8	50	oil pressure	14	6
13	34	F Mazet	March	701	Ford Cosworth	V8	50		23	9
nc	28	M Jean	March	701	Ford Cosworth	V8	46		22	9
r	27	H Pescarolo	March	711	Ford Cosworth	V8	45	gearbox	18	7
r	7	G Hill	Brabham	BT34	Ford Cosworth	V8	34	oil line	4	2
r	19	A de Adamich	March	711	Alfa Romeo	V8	31	engine	20	8
r	15	P Rodríguez	BRM	P160	BRM	V12	27	coil	5	2
r	5	C Regazzoni	Ferrari	312B2	Ferrari	F12	20	accident	2	1
r	17	R Peterson	March	711	Alfa Romeo	V8	19	engine	12	5
r	9	D Hulme	McLaren	M19A	Ford Cosworth	V8	16	ignition	11	5
r	4	J Ickx	Ferrari	312B2	Ferrari	F12	4	engine	3	1
r	18	A Soler-Roig	March	711	Ford Cosworth	V8	4	fuel pump	21	9
ns	33	N Galli	March	711	Ford Cosworth	V8		car raced by Soler-Roig		

Winning speed 179.700 km/h, 111.660 mph
Pole Position speed 188.926 km/h, 117.393 mph (J Stewart, 1 min:50.710 sec)
Fastest Lap speed 183.329 km/h, 113.915 mph (J Stewart, 1 min:54.090 sec on lap 2)
Lap Leaders J Stewart 1-55 (55).

17 Jul 1971 — BRITAIN: Silverstone — (Round 6) — (Race 203)

68 laps x 4.711 km, 2.927 miles = 320.317 km, 199.036 miles

Pos	No	Driver	Car	Model	Engine		Laps	Time/Reason for Retirement	Grid Pos	Row
1	12	J Stewart	Tyrrell	003	Ford Cosworth	V8	68	1h 31m 31.500s	2	1
2	18	R Peterson	March	711	Ford Cosworth	V8	68	1h 32m 07.600s	5	2
3	1	E Fittipaldi	Lotus	72D	Ford Cosworth	V8	68	1h 32m 22.000s	4	2
4	26	H Pescarolo	March	711	Ford Cosworth	V8	67		17	7
5	24	R Stommelen	Surtees	TS9	Ford Cosworth	V8	67		12	5
6	23	J Surtees	Surtees	TS9	Ford Cosworth	V8	67		18	7
7	22	J-P Beltoise	Matra Simca	MS120B	Matra	V12	66		15	6
8	17	H Ganley	BRM	P153	BRM	V12	66		11	5
9	16	J Siffert	BRM	P160	BRM	V12	66		3	1
10	14	F Cevert	Tyrrell	002	Ford Cosworth	V8	65		10	4
11	20	N Galli	March	711	Ford Cosworth	V8	65		21	9
12r	8	T Schenken	Brabham	BT33	Ford Cosworth	V8	63	gearbox	7	3
nc	3	R Wisell	Lotus	56B	Pratt & Whitney	tbne	57		19	8
nc	19	A de Adamich	March	711	Alfa Romeo	V8	56		24	10
r	10	P Gethin	McLaren	M19A	Ford Cosworth	V8	53	engine	14	6
r	4	J Ickx	Ferrari	312B2	Ferrari	F12	51	engine	6	3
r	5	C Regazzoni	Ferrari	312B2	Ferrari	F12	48	oil pressure	1	1
r	21	C Amon	Matra Simca	MS120B	Matra	V12	35	dropped valve	9	4
r	9	D Hulme	McLaren	M19A	Ford Cosworth	V8	32	engine	8	3
r	25	D Bell	Surtees	TS9	Ford Cosworth	V8	23	rear suspension	23	9
r	6	M Beuttler	March	711	Ford Cosworth	V8	21	oil pressure	20	8
r	2	D Charlton	Lotus	72D	Ford Cosworth	V8	1	engine	13	5
r	11	J Oliver	McLaren	M14A	Ford Cosworth	V8	0	accident	22	9
r	7	G Hill	Brabham	BT34	Ford Cosworth	V8	0	accident	16	7

Winning speed 209.987 km/h, 130.480 mph
Pole Position speed 217.132 km/h, 134.919 mph (C Regazzoni, 1 min:18.100 sec)
Fastest Lap speed 212.240 km/h, 131.880 mph (J Stewart, 1 min:19.900 sec on lap 45)
Lap Leaders C Regazzoni 1-3 (3); J Stewart 4-68 (65).

1 Aug 1971 — GERMANY: Nürburgring — (Round 7) — (Race 204)

12 laps x 22.835 km, 14.189 miles = 274.020 km, 170.268 miles

Pos	No	Driver	Car	Model	Engine		Laps	Time/Reason for Retirement	Grid Pos	Row
1	2	J Stewart	Tyrrell	003	Ford Cosworth	V8	12	1h 29m 15.700s	1	1
2	3	F Cevert	Tyrrell	002	Ford Cosworth	V8	12	1h 29m 45.800s	5	3
3	6	C Regazzoni	Ferrari	312B2	Ferrari	F12	12	1h 29m 52.800s	4	2
4	5	M Andretti	Ferrari	312B2	Ferrari	F12	12	1h 31m 20.700s	11	6
5	15	R Peterson	March	711	Ford Cosworth	V8	12	1h 31m 44.800s	7	4
6	25	T Schenken	Brabham	BT33	Ford Cosworth	V8	12	1h 32m 14.300s	9	5
7	7	J Surtees	Surtees	TS9	Ford Cosworth	V8	12	1h 32m 34.700s	15	8
8	9	R Wisell	Lotus	72D	Ford Cosworth	V8	12	1h 35m 47.400s	17	9
9	24	G Hill	Brabham	BT34	Ford Cosworth	V8	12	1h 35m 52.700s	13	7
10	12	R Stommelen	Surtees	TS9	Ford Cosworth	V8	11		12	6
11	22	V Elford	BRM	P160	BRM	V12	11		18	9
12	17	N Galli	March	711	Alfa Romeo	V8	10		21	11
r	8	E Fittipaldi	Lotus	72D	Ford Cosworth	V8	8	oil leak	8	4
r/dq	21	J Siffert	BRM	P160	BRM	V12	6	coil / entered pits at rear	3	2
r	10	C Amon	Matra Simca	MS120B	Matra	V12	6	accident / suspension / steering	16	8
r	20	P Gethin	McLaren	M19A	Ford Cosworth	V8	5	accident	19	10
r	14	H Pescarolo	March	711	Ford Cosworth	V8	5	rear suspension	10	5
dq	28	M Beuttler	March	711	Ford Cosworth	V8	3	incorrect route into pits	22	11
r	18	D Hulme	McLaren	M19A	Ford Cosworth	V8	3	fuel leak	6	3
r	16	A de Adamich	March	711	Alfa Romeo	V8	2	fuel injection	20	10
r	23	H Ganley	BRM	P153	BRM	V12	2	engine	14	7
r	4	J Ickx	Ferrari	312B2	Ferrari	F12	1	accident	2	1
nq	27	J Bonnier	McLaren	M7C	Ford Cosworth	V8				
nq	27	H Marko	McLaren	M7C	Ford Cosworth	V8		out of fuel / withdrew		

Winning speed 184.191 km/h, 114.451 mph
Pole Position speed 187.257 km/h, 116.356 mph (J Stewart, 7 min:19.000 sec)
Fastest Lap speed 186.789 km/h, 116.066 mph (F Cevert, 7 min:20.100 sec on lap 10)
Lap Leaders J Stewart 1-12 (12).

15 Aug 1971   AUSTRIA: Österreichring   (Round 8)   (Race 205)

54 laps x 5.911 km, 3.673 miles = 319.194 km, 198.338 miles

Pos	No	Driver	Car	Model	Engine		Laps	Time/Reason for Retirement	Grid Pos	Row
1	14	J Siffert	BRM	P160	BRM	V12	54	1h 30m 23.910s	1	1
2	2	E Fittipaldi	Lotus	72D	Ford Cosworth	V8	54	1h 30m 28.030s	5	3
3	8	T Schenken	Brabham	BT33	Ford Cosworth	V8	54	1h 30m 43.680s	7	4
4	3	R Wisell	Lotus	72D	Ford Cosworth	V8	54	1h 30m 55.780s	10	5
5	7	G Hill	Brabham	BT34	Ford Cosworth	V8	54	1h 31m 12.340s	8	4
6	25	H Pescarolo	March	711	Ford Cosworth	V8	54	1h 31m 48.420s	13	7
7	24	R Stommelen	Surtees	TS9	Ford Cosworth	V8	54	1h 32m 01.330s	12	6
8	17	R Peterson	March	711	Ford Cosworth	V8	53		11	6
9	10	J Oliver	McLaren	M19A	Ford Cosworth	V8	53		22	11
10	23	P Gethin	BRM	P160	BRM	V12	52		16	8
11	16	H Marko	BRM	P153	BRM	V12	52		17	9
12	19	N Galli	March	711	Alfa Romeo	V8	51		15	8
nc	27	M Beuttler	March	711	Ford Cosworth	V8	47		19	10
r	12	F Cevert	Tyrrell	002	Ford Cosworth	V8	42	engine	3	2
r	11	J Stewart	Tyrrell	003	Ford Cosworth	V8	35	rear stub axle / wheel lost	2	1
r	4	J Ickx	Ferrari	312B2	Ferrari	F12	31	spark plug leads	6	3
r	26	N Lauda	March	711	Ford Cosworth	V8	20	handling	21	11
r	22	J Surtees	Surtees	TS9	Ford Cosworth	V8	12	engine	18	9
r	5	C Regazzoni	Ferrari	312B2	Ferrari	F12	8	engine	4	2
r	15	H Ganley	BRM	P160	BRM	V12	6	ignition	14	7
r	9	D Hulme	McLaren	M19A	Ford Cosworth	V8	4	engine	9	5
ns	28	J Bonnier	McLaren	M7C	Ford Cosworth	V8		fuel leak	20	10

Winning speed 211.858 km/h, 131.642 mph
Pole Position speed 218.387 km/h, 135.699 mph (J Siffert, 1 min:37.440 sec)
Fastest Lap speed 216.102 km/h, 134.280 mph (J Siffert, 1 min:38.470 sec on lap 22)
Lap Leaders J Siffert 1-54 (54).

5 Sep 1971   ITALY: Monza   (Round 9)   (Race 206)

55 laps x 5.750 km, 3.573 miles = 316.250 km, 196.509 miles

Pos	No	Driver	Car	Model	Engine		Laps	Time/Reason for Retirement	Grid Pos	Row
1	18	P Gethin	BRM	P160	BRM	V12	55	1h 18m 12.600s	11	6
2	25	R Peterson	March	711	Ford Cosworth	V8	55	1h 18m 12.610s	6	3
3	2	F Cevert	Tyrrell	002	Ford Cosworth	V8	55	1h 18m 12.690s	5	3
4	9	M Hailwood	Surtees	TS9	Ford Cosworth	V8	55	1h 18m 12.780s	17	9
5	19	H Ganley	BRM	P160	BRM	V12	55	1h 18m 13.210s	4	2
6	12	C Amon	Matra Simca	MS120B	Matra	V12	55	1h 18m 44.960s	1	1
7	14	J Oliver	McLaren	M14A	Ford Cosworth	V8	55	1h 19m 37.430s	13	7
8	5	E Fittipaldi	Lotus	56B	Pratt & Whitney	tbne	54		18	9
9	20	J Siffert	BRM	P160	BRM	V12	53		3	2
10	28	J Bonnier	McLaren	M7C	Ford Cosworth	V8	51		21	11
r	10	G Hill	Brabham	BT34	Ford Cosworth	V8	47	gearbox	14	7
nc	26	J-P Jarier	March	701	Ford Cosworth	V8	47		24	12
r	24	M Beuttler	March	711	Ford Cosworth	V8	41	piston / valves	16	8
r	16	H Pescarolo	March	711	Ford Cosworth	V8	40	rear suspension	10	5
r	23	A de Adamich	March	711	Alfa Romeo	V8	33	engine	20	10
r	4	C Regazzoni	Ferrari	312B2	Ferrari	F12	17	engine	8	4
r	30	J Stewart	Tyrrell	003	Ford Cosworth	V8	15	connecting rod	7	4
r	3	J Ickx	Ferrari	312B	Ferrari	F12	15	engine	2	1
r	22	N Galli	March	711	Ford Cosworth	V8	11	electrics	19	10
r	27	S Moser	Bellasi		Ford Cosworth	V8	5	suspension mountings	22	11
r	11	T Schenken	Brabham	BT33	Ford Cosworth	V8	5	rear suspension	9	5
r	21	H Marko	BRM	P153	BRM	V12	3	engine	12	6
r	7	J Surtees	Surtees	TS9	Ford Cosworth	V8	3	engine	15	8
ns	8	R Stommelen	Surtees	TS9	Ford Cosworth	V8		accident	23	12

Winning speed 242.616 km/h, 150.755 mph
Pole Position speed 251.214 km/h, 156.097 mph (C Amon, 1 min:22.400 sec)
Fastest Lap speed 247.017 km/h, 153.489 mph (H Pescarolo, 1 min:23.800 sec on lap 9)
Lap Leaders C Regazzoni 1-3,9 (4); R Peterson 4-7,10-14,17-22,24,26,33,47-50,54 (23); J Stewart 8 (1);
F Cevert 15-16,23,31-32,34,36 (7); M Hailwood 25,27,35,42,51 (5); J Siffert 28-30 (3); C Amon 37-41,43-46 (9); P Gethin 52-53,55 (3).

64 laps x 3.957 km, 2.459 miles = 253.272 km, 157.376 miles

Pos	No	Driver	Car	Model	Engine		Laps	Time/Reason for Retirement	Grid Pos	Row
1	11	J Stewart	Tyrrell	003	Ford Cosworth	V8	64	1h 55m 12.900s	1	1
2	17	R Peterson	March	711	Ford Cosworth	V8	64	1h 55m 51.200s	6	3
3	10	M Donohue	McLaren	M19A	Ford Cosworth	V8	64	1h 56m 48.700s	8	3
4	9	D Hulme	McLaren	M19A	Ford Cosworth	V8	63		10	4
5	3	R Wisell	Lotus	72D	Ford Cosworth	V8	63		7	3
6	12	F Cevert	Tyrrell	002	Ford Cosworth	V8	62		3	1
7	2	E Fittipaldi	Lotus	72D	Ford Cosworth	V8	62		4	2
8	4	J Ickx	Ferrari	312B2	Ferrari	F12	62		12	5
9	14	J Siffert	BRM	P160	BRM	V12	61		2	1
10	20	C Amon	Matra Simca	MS120B	Matra	V12	61		5	2
11	22	J Surtees	Surtees	TS9	Ford Cosworth	V8	60		14	6
12	31	H Marko	BRM	P153	BRM	V12	60		19	8
13	6	M Andretti	Ferrari	312B2	Ferrari	F12	60		13	5
14	15	P Gethin	BRM	P160	BRM	V12	59		16	7
15	28	G Eaton	BRM	P160	BRM	V12	59		21	9
16	18	N Galli	March	711	Ford Cosworth	V8	57		20	8
nc	19	M Beuttler	March	711	Ford Cosworth	V8	56		22	9
nc	35	P Lovely	Lotus	69	Ford Cosworth	V8	55		25	10
r	24	R Stommelen	Surtees	TS9	Ford Cosworth	V8	26	oil pressure / engine overheating	23	9
r	21	J-P Beltoise	Matra Simca	MS120B	Matra	V12	15	accident	11	5
r	33	S Barber	March	711	Ford Cosworth	V8	13	oil pressure	24	10
r	5	C Regazzoni	Ferrari	312B2	Ferrari	F12	7	accident	18	7
r	37	G Hill	Brabham	BT34	Ford Cosworth	V8	2	accident	15	6
r	8	T Schenken	Brabham	BT33	Ford Cosworth	V8	1	ignition	17	7
ns	16	H Ganley	BRM	P160	BRM	V12		accident (familiarisation laps)	9	4
ns	26	C Craft	Brabham	BT33	Ford Cosworth	V8		engine		
ns	27	H Pescarolo	March	711	Ford Cosworth	V8		accident / injury		

Winning speed 131.895 km/h, 81.956 mph
Pole Position speed 189.197 km/h, 117.562 mph (J Stewart, 1 min:15.300 sec)
Fastest Lap speed 137.648 km/h, 85.530 mph (D Hulme, 1 min:43.500 sec on lap 57)
Lap Leaders J Stewart 1-17,31-64 (51); R Peterson 18-30 (13).

Scheduled for 80 laps, but stopped early because of rain.

59 laps x 5.435 km, 3.377 miles = 320.651 km, 199.243 miles

Pos	No	Driver	Car	Model	Engine		Laps	Time/Reason for Retirement	Grid Pos	Row
1	9	F Cevert	Tyrrell	002	Ford Cosworth	V8	59	1h 43m 51.991s	5	2
2	14	J Siffert	BRM	P160	BRM	V12	59	1h 44m 32.053s	6	3
3	25	R Peterson	March	711	Ford Cosworth	V8	59	1h 44m 36.061s	11	5
4	16	H Ganley	BRM	P160	BRM	V12	59	1h 44m 48.740s	12	5
5	8	J Stewart	Tyrrell	003	Ford Cosworth	V8	59	1h 44m 51.994s	1	1
6	5	C Regazzoni	Ferrari	312B2	Ferrari	F12	59	1h 45m 08.417s	4	2
7	22	G Hill	Brabham	BT34	Ford Cosworth	V8	58		18	7
8	12	J-P Beltoise	Matra Simca	MS120B	Matra	V12	58		10	4
9	15	P Gethin	BRM	P160	BRM	V12	58		21	9
10	31	D Hobbs	McLaren	M19A	Ford Cosworth	V8	58		22	9
11	27	A de Adamich	March	711	Alfa Romeo	V8	57		26	11
12	11	C Amon	Matra Simca	MS120B	Matra	V12	57		8	3
13	17	H Marko	BRM	P160	BRM	V12	57		16	7
14	28	J Cannon	BRM	P153	BRM	V12	56		24	10
15r	20	M Hailwood	Surtees	TS9	Ford Cosworth	V8	54	rear tyre / accident	14	6
16r	29	J Bonnier	McLaren	M7C	Ford Cosworth	V8	54	out of fuel	28	11
17	18	J Surtees	Surtees	TS9	Ford Cosworth	V8	54		13	5
nc	33	S Barber	March	711	Ford Cosworth	V8	52		25	10
nc	2	E Fittipaldi	Lotus	72D	Ford Cosworth	V8	49		2	1
nc	30	P Lovely	Lotus	69	Ford Cosworth	V8	49		29	12
r	32	J Ickx	Ferrari	312B	Ferrari	F12	49	alternator	7	3
r	7	D Hulme	McLaren	M19A	Ford Cosworth	V8	47	accident	3	1
r	23	T Schenken	Brabham	BT33	Ford Cosworth	V8	41	engine	15	6
r	24	C Craft	Brabham	BT33	Ford Cosworth	V8	30	rear suspension	27	11
r	21	H Pescarolo	March	711	Ford Cosworth	V8	23	camshaft	20	8
r	19	S Posey	Surtees	TS9	Ford Cosworth	V8	15	piston	17	7
r	26	N Galli	March	711	Ford Cosworth	V8	11	radiator / front wheel / suspension	23	9
r	3	R Wisell	Lotus	72D	Ford Cosworth	V8	5	brakes / accident	9	4
r	10	P Revson	Tyrrell	001	Ford Cosworth	V8	1	clutch	19	8
ns	6	M Andretti	Ferrari	312B2	Ferrari	F12		raced elsewhere		
ns	31	M Donohue	McLaren	M19A	Ford Cosworth	V8		raced elsewhere		
ns	19	G van Lennep	Surtees	TS9	Ford Cosworth	V8		car raced by Posey		

Winning speed 185.228 km/h, 115.096 mph
Pole Position speed 190.615 km/h, 118.443 mph (J Stewart, 1 min:42.642 sec)
Fastest Lap speed 189.082 km/h, 117.490 mph (J Ickx, 1 min:43.474 sec on lap 43)
Lap Leaders J Stewart 1-13 (13); F Cevert 14-59 (46).

Races

Lap Leaders 1971

Pos	Driver	Car-Engine	GPs	laps	km	miles
1	J Stewart	Tyrrell-Ford Cosworth	8	347	1,695.0	1,053.2
2	D Hulme	McLaren-Ford Cosworth	1	59	242.1	150.5
3	J Siffert	BRM	2	57	336.4	209.1
4	F Cevert	Tyrrell-Ford Cosworth	2	53	290.3	180.4
	J Ickx	Ferrari	2	53	220.2	136.8
6	R Peterson	March-Ford Cosworth	2	36	183.7	114.1
7	C Regazzoni	Ferrari	3	23	102.8	63.9
8	P Rodríguez	BRM	1	22	92.2	57.3
9	C Amon	Matra Simca	1	9	51.7	32.2
10	M Hailwood	Surtees-Ford Cosworth	1	5	28.7	17.9
11	M Andretti	Ferrari	1	4	16.4	10.2
12	P Gethin	BRM	1	3	17.2	10.7
			11	**671**	**3,276.9**	**2,036.2**

Driver Points 1971

		ZA	E	MC	NL	F	GB	D	A	I	CDN	USA	Total
1	J Stewart	6	9	9	-	9	9	9	-	-	9	2	62
2	R Peterson	-	-	6	3	-	6	2	-	6	6	4	33
3	F Cevert	-	-	-	-	6	-	6	-	4	1	9	26
4	J Ickx	-	6	4	9	-	-	-	-	-	-	-	19
	J Siffert	-	-	-	1	3	-	-	9	-	-	6	19
6	E Fittipaldi	-	-	2	-	4	4	-	6	-	-	-	16
7	C Regazzoni	4	-	-	4	-	-	4	-	-	-	1	13
8	M Andretti	9	-	-	-	-	-	3	-	-	-	-	12
9	P Gethin	-	-	-	-	-	-	-	-	9	-	-	9
	P Rodríguez	-	3	-	6	-	-	-	-	-	-	-	9
	C Amon	2	4	-	-	2	-	-	-	1	-	-	9
	R Wisell	3	-	-	-	1	-	-	3	-	2	-	9
	D Hulme	1	2	3	-	-	-	-	-	-	3	-	9
14	T Schenken	-	-	-	-	-	-	1	4	-	-	-	5
	H Ganley	-	-	-	-	-	-	-	-	2	-	3	5
16	M Donohue	-	-	-	-	-	-	-	-	-	4	-	4
	H Pescarolo	-	-	-	-	-	3	-	1	-	-	-	4
18	M Hailwood	-	-	-	-	-	-	-	-	3	-	-	3
	J Surtees	-	-	-	2	-	1	-	-	-	-	-	3
	R Stommelen	-	-	1	-	-	2	-	-	-	-	-	3
21	G Hill	-	-	-	-	-	-	-	2	-	-	-	2
22	J-P Beltoise	-	1	-	-	-	-	-	-	-	-	-	1

9,6,4,3,2 and 1 point awarded to the first six finishers. Best 5 scores from first 6 races, best 4 from remaining 5 races.

Constructor Points 1971

		ZA	E	MC	NL	F	GB	D	A	I	CDN	USA	Total
1	Tyrrell-Ford Cosworth	6	9	9	-	9	9	9	-	4	9	9	73
2	BRM	-	3	-	6	3	-	-	9	9	-	6	36
3	Ferrari	9	6	4	9	-	-	4	-	-	-	1	33
	March-Ford Cosworth	-	-	6	3	-	6	2	(1)	6	6	4	33 (1)
5	Lotus-Ford Cosworth	3	-	2	-	4	4	-	6	-	2	-	21
6	McLaren-Ford Cosworth	1	2	3	-	-	-	-	-	-	4	-	10
7	Matra Simca	2	4	-	-	2	-	-	-	1	-	-	9
8	Surtees-Ford Cosworth	-	-	1	2	-	2	-	-	3	-	-	8
9	Brabham-Ford Cosworth	-	-	-	-	-	-	1	4	-	-	-	5

9,6,4,3,2 and 1 point awarded to the first six finishers. Points only for highest placed car. Best 5 scores from first 6 races, best 4 from remaining 5 races.

Race Entrants and Results

The Brabham team was sold to businessman and former entrant Bernie Ecclestone. Sponsorship changes meant that Lotus turned into the black and gold John Player Specials and McLaren inherited Yardley's colours, while BRM created its multiple entry team with Marlboro assistance.

FERRARI
Scuderia Ferrari SpA SEFAC: Ickx, Regazzoni, Andretti, Merzario, Galli

TECNO
Martini Racing Team: Bell, Galli

BRABHAM
Motor Racing Developments: Hill, Reutemann, W Fittipaldi
Team Gunston: (Ferguson)

BRM
Marlboro BRM: Beltoise, Gethin, Ganley, Wisell, Marko, Soler-Roig, Oliver, Redman, Brack, (Schuppan)

CONNEW
Darnval Connew Racing Team: Migault

LOTUS
John Player Team Lotus: E Fittipaldi, Walker, Wisell
World Wide Racing: E Fittipaldi (I)
Scuderia Scribante-Lucky Strike Racing: Charlton

McLAREN
Yardley Team McLaren: Hulme, Revson, Redman, Scheckter

MARCH
STP March Racing Team: Peterson, Lauda
Team Williams-Motul: Pescarolo, Pace
Team Eifelland Caravans: Stommelen
Clarke-Mordaunt-Guthrie Racing: Beuttler
Gene Mason Racing: Barber

SURTEES
Team Surtees: Schenken, Surtees
with Booke Bond Oxo/Rob Walker: Hailwood, Schenken (RA,ZA,E)
with Ceramica Pagnossin: de Adamich
Champcarr Inc: Posey
Team Gunston: Love

TYRRELL
Elf Team Tyrrell: Stewart, Cevert, Depailler

WILLIAMS (POLITOYS)
Team Williams-Motul: Pescarolo

MATRA SIMCA
Equipe Matra: Amon

23 Jan 1972			**ARGENTINA: Buenos Aires No.9**					(Round 1)		(Race 209)	
			95 laps x 3.345 km, 2.078 miles = 317.775 km, 197.456 miles								
Pos	No	Driver	Car	Model	Engine		Laps	Time/Reason for Retirement		Grid Pos	Row
1	21	J Stewart	Tyrrell	003	Ford Cosworth	V8	95	1h 57m 58.820s		2	1
2	17	D Hulme	McLaren	M19A	Ford Cosworth	V8	95	1h 58m 24.780s		4	2
3	8	J Ickx	Ferrari	312B2	Ferrari	F12	95	1h 58m 58.210s		8	4
4	9	C Regazzoni	Ferrari	312B2	Ferrari	F12	95	1h 59m 05.540s		6	3
5	19	T Schenken	Surtees	TS9B	Ford Cosworth	V8	95	1h 59m 07.930s		11	6
6	14	R Peterson	March	721	Ford Cosworth	V8	94			10	5
7	2	C Reutemann	Brabham	BT34	Ford Cosworth	V8	93			1	1
8	23	H Pescarolo	March	721	Ford Cosworth	V8	93			15	8
9	3	H Ganley	BRM	P160B	BRM	V12	93			13	7
10	7	H Marko	BRM	P153	BRM	V12	93			19	10
11	15	N Lauda	March	721	Ford Cosworth	V8	93			22	11
r	11	E Fittipaldi	JPS Lotus	72D	Ford Cosworth	V8	61	rear suspension radius rod		5	3
r	22	F Cevert	Tyrrell	002	Ford Cosworth	V8	59	gearbox oil line		7	4
r	4	R Wisell	BRM	P153	BRM	V12	59	water hose		17	9
r	18	P Revson	McLaren	M19A	Ford Cosworth	V8	49	spin / water pipe / engine		3	2
r	10	M Andretti	Ferrari	312B2	Ferrari	F12	20	misfire		9	5
r	1	G Hill	Brabham	BT33	Ford Cosworth	V8	11	fuel pump		16	8
r	20	A de Adamich	Surtees	TS9B	Ford Cosworth	V8	11	fuel metering unit		14	7
dq	12	D Walker	JPS Lotus	72D	Ford Cosworth	V8	8	used pit tools to repair car		20	10
r	5	P Gethin	BRM	P160B	BRM	V12	1	accident / oil line / spin		18	9
r	6	A Soler-Roig	BRM	P160B	BRM	V12	1	throttle jammed / accident		21	11
ns	16	C Amon	Matra Simca	MS120C	Matra	V12		gearbox on parade lap		12	6

Winning speed 161.607 km/h, 100.418 mph
Pole Position speed 166.188 km/h, 103.265 mph (C Reutemann, 1 min:12.460 sec)
Fastest Lap speed 163.481 km/h, 101.582 mph (J Stewart, 1 min:13.660 sec on lap 25)
Lap Leaders J Stewart 1-95 (95).

79 laps x 4.104 km, 2.550 miles = 324.216 km, 201.458 miles

Pos	No	Driver	Car	Model	Engine		Laps	Time/Reason for Retirement	Grid Pos	Row
1	12	D Hulme	McLaren	M19A	Ford Cosworth	V8	79	1h 45m 49.100s	5	2
2	8	E Fittipaldi	JPS Lotus	72D	Ford Cosworth	V8	79	1h 46m 03.200s	3	1
3	14	P Revson	McLaren	M19A	Ford Cosworth	V8	79	1h 46m 14.900s	12	5
4	7	M Andretti	Ferrari	312B2	Ferrari	F12	79	1h 46m 27.600s	6	3
5	3	R Peterson	March	721	Ford Cosworth	V8	79	1h 46m 38.100s	9	4
6	19	G Hill	Brabham	BT33	Ford Cosworth	V8	78		14	6
7	4	N Lauda	March	721	Ford Cosworth	V8	78		21	9
8	5	J Ickx	Ferrari	312B2	Ferrari	F12	78		7	3
9	2	F Cevert	Tyrrell	002	Ford Cosworth	V8	78		8	3
10	9	D Walker	JPS Lotus	72D	Ford Cosworth	V8	78		19	8
11	21	H Pescarolo	March	721	Ford Cosworth	V8	77		22	9
12	6	C Regazzoni	Ferrari	312B2	Ferrari	F12	77		2	1
13	25	R Stommelen	Eifelland March	721	Ford Cosworth	V8	77		25	10
14	24	H Marko	BRM	P153	BRM	V12	76		23	9
15	15	C Amon	Matra Simca	MS120C	Matra	V12	76		13	5
16r	27	J Love	Surtees	TS9	Ford Cosworth	V8	73	rear tyre burst / accident	26	11
17	22	C Pace	March	711	Ford Cosworth	V8	73		24	10
nc	23	H Ganley	BRM	P160B	BRM	V12	70		16	7
nc	18	A de Adamich	Surtees	TS9B	Ford Cosworth	V8	69		20	8
nc	11	P Gethin	BRM	P160B	BRM	V12	65		18	7
r	10	J-P Beltoise	BRM	P160B	BRM	V12	60	valve springs	11	5
r	1	J Stewart	Tyrrell	003	Ford Cosworth	V8	45	gearbox	1	1
r	17	M Hailwood	Surtees	TS9B	Ford Cosworth	V8	28	rear suspension	4	2
r	20	C Reutemann	Brabham	BT34	Ford Cosworth	V8	27	fuel line	15	6
r	16	T Schenken	Surtees	TS9B	Ford Cosworth	V8	9	cylinder liner / engine	10	4
r	26	D Charlton	Lotus	72D	Ford Cosworth	V8	2	fuel pump	17	7
ns	28	W Ferguson	Brabham	BT33	Ford Cosworth	V8		engine		

Winning speed 183.834 km/h, 114.229 mph
Pole Position speed 191.875 km/h, 119.226 mph (J Stewart, 1 min:17.000 sec)
Fastest Lap speed 187.255 km/h, 116.355 mph (M Hailwood, 1 min:18.900 sec on lap 20)
Lap Leaders D Hulme 1,57-79 (24); J Stewart 2-44 (43); E Fittipaldi 45-56 (12).

W Ferguson also practised in a Surtees TS9-Ford Cosworth V8 (27) which was raced by J Love.

90 laps x 3.404 km, 2.115 miles = 306.360 km, 190.363 miles

Pos	No	Driver	Car	Model	Engine		Laps	Time/Reason for Retirement	Grid Pos	Row
1	5	E Fittipaldi	JPS Lotus	72D	Ford Cosworth	V8	90	2h 03m 41.230s	3	1
2	4	J Ickx	Ferrari	312B2	Ferrari	F12	90	2h 04m 00.150s	1	1
3	6	C Regazzoni	Ferrari	312B2	Ferrari	F12	89		8	3
4	26	A de Adamich	Surtees	TS9B	Ford Cosworth	V8	89		13	5
5	20	P Revson	McLaren	M19A	Ford Cosworth	V8	89		11	5
6	29	C Pace	March	711	Ford Cosworth	V8	89		16	7
7	22	W Fittipaldi	Brabham	BT33	Ford Cosworth	V8	88		14	6
8	12	T Schenken	Surtees	TS9B	Ford Cosworth	V8	88		18	7
9r	21	D Walker	JPS Lotus	72D	Ford Cosworth	V8	87	out of fuel	24	10
10	18	G Hill	Brabham	BT37	Ford Cosworth	V8	86		23	9
11	14	H Pescarolo	March	721	Ford Cosworth	V8	86		19	8
r	1	J Stewart	Tyrrell	003	Ford Cosworth	V8	69	accident	4	2
r	9	C Amon	Matra Simca	MS120C	Matra	V12	66	spin / gearbox pinion bearing	6	3
r	3	F Cevert	Tyrrell	002	Ford Cosworth	V8	65	ignition	12	5
r	8	P Gethin	BRM	P180	BRM	V12	65	engine	21	9
r	11	D Hulme	McLaren	M19A	Ford Cosworth	V8	48	gearbox pinion bearing	2	1
r	25	H Ganley	BRM	P160B	BRM	V12	38	engine	20	8
r	10	R Wisell	BRM	P160B	BRM	V12	24	accident	10	4
r	7	M Andretti	Ferrari	312B2	Ferrari	F12	23	oil pressure / engine	5	2
r	15	M Hailwood	Surtees	TS9B	Ford Cosworth	V8	20	starter solenoid	15	6
r	2	R Peterson	March	721X	Ford Cosworth	V8	16	accident / fuel leak / suspension	9	4
r	16	R Stommelen	Eifelland March	721	Ford Cosworth	V8	15	accident	17	7
r	19	J-P Beltoise	BRM	P160B	BRM	V12	9	gear linkage	7	3
r	24	N Lauda	March	721X	Ford Cosworth	V8	7	throttle jammed	25	10
r	28	A Soler-Roig	BRM	P160B	BRM	V12	6	gear selection / accident	22	9
nq	23	M Beuttler	March	721G	Ford Cosworth	V8				

Winning speed 148.614 km/h, 92.344 mph
Pole Position speed 156.246 km/h, 97.087 mph (J Ickx, 1 min:18.430 sec)
Fastest Lap speed 151.270 km/h, 93.995 mph (J Ickx, 1 min:21.010 sec on lap 52)
Lap Leaders D Hulme 1-4 (4); J Stewart 5-8 (4); E Fittipaldi 9-90 (82).

80 laps x 3.145 km, 1.954 miles = 251.600 km, 156.337 miles

Pos	No	Driver	Car	Model	Engine		Laps	Time/Reason for Retirement	Grid Pos	Row
1	17	J-P Beltoise	BRM	P160B	BRM	V12	80	2h 26m 54.700s	4	2
2	6	J Ickx	Ferrari	312B2	Ferrari	F12	80	2h 27m 32.900s	2	1
3	8	E Fittipaldi	JPS Lotus	72D	Ford Cosworth	V8	79		1	1
4	1	J Stewart	Tyrrell	004	Ford Cosworth	V8	78		8	4
5	15	B Redman	McLaren	M19A	Ford Cosworth	V8	77		10	5
6	16	C Amon	Matra Simca	MS120C	Matra	V12	77		6	3
7	12	A de Adamich	Surtees	TS9B	Ford Cosworth	V8	77		18	9
8	26	H Marko	BRM	P153B	BRM	V12	77		17	9
9	21	W Fittipaldi	Brabham	BT33	Ford Cosworth	V8	77		21	11
10	27	R Stommelen	Eifelland March	721	Ford Cosworth	V8	77		25	13
11	3	R Peterson	March	721X	Ford Cosworth	V8	76		15	8
12	20	G Hill	Brabham	BT37	Ford Cosworth	V8	76		19	10
13	5	M Beuttler	March	721G	Ford Cosworth	V8	76		23	12
14	9	D Walker	JPS Lotus	72D	Ford Cosworth	V8	75		14	7
15	14	D Hulme	McLaren	M19C	Ford Cosworth	V8	74		7	4
16	4	N Lauda	March	721X	Ford Cosworth	V8	74		22	11
17	23	C Pace	March	711	Ford Cosworth	V8	72		24	12
nc	2	F Cevert	Tyrrell	002	Ford Cosworth	V8	70		12	6
r	22	H Pescarolo	March	721	Ford Cosworth	V8	58	accident	9	5
r	7	C Regazzoni	Ferrari	312B2	Ferrari	F12	51	accident	3	2
r	11	M Hailwood	Surtees	TS9B	Ford Cosworth	V8	48	accident	11	6
r	19	H Ganley	BRM	P180	BRM	V12	47	accident	20	10
r	10	T Schenken	Surtees	TS9B	Ford Cosworth	V8	31	accident	13	7
dq	18	P Gethin	BRM	P160B	BRM	V12	27	accident / reversed into pits	5	3
r	28	R Wisell	BRM	P160B	BRM	V12	16	engine	16	8

Winning speed 102.756 km/h, 63.849 mph
Pole Position speed 139.091 km/h, 86.427 mph (E Fittipaldi, 1 min:21.400 sec)
Fastest Lap speed 113.220 km/h, 70.352 mph (J-P Beltoise, 1 min:40.000 sec on lap 9).
Lap Leaders J-P Beltoise 1-80 (80).

85 laps x 3.724 km, 2.314 miles = 316.540 km, 196.689 miles

Pos	No	Driver	Car	Model	Engine		Laps	Time/Reason for Retirement	Grid Pos	Row
1	32	E Fittipaldi	JPS Lotus	72D	Ford Cosworth	V8	85	1h 44m 06.700s	1	1
2	8	F Cevert	Tyrrell	002	Ford Cosworth	V8	85	1h 44m 33.300s	5	2
3	9	D Hulme	McLaren	M19C	Ford Cosworth	V8	85	1h 45m 04.800s	3	1
4	34	M Hailwood	Surtees	TS9B	Ford Cosworth	V8	85	1h 45m 18.700s	8	3
5	16	C Pace	March	711	Ford Cosworth	V8	84		11	5
6	5	C Amon	Matra Simca	MS120C	Matra	V12	84		13	5
7	10	P Revson	McLaren	M19A	Ford Cosworth	V8	83		7	3
8	25	H Ganley	BRM	P160B	BRM	V12	83		15	6
9	11	R Peterson	March	721X	Ford Cosworth	V8	83		14	6
10	27	H Marko	BRM	P153B	BRM	V12	83		23	9
11	6	R Stommelen	Eifelland March	721	Ford Cosworth	V8	83		20	8
12	12	N Lauda	March	721X	Ford Cosworth	V8	82		25	10
13	19	C Reutemann	Brabham	BT37	Ford Cosworth	V8	81		9	4
14	33	D Walker	JPS Lotus	72D	Ford Cosworth	V8	79		12	5
r	17	G Hill	Brabham	BT37	Ford Cosworth	V8	73	rear suspension	16	7
nc	15	H Pescarolo	March	721	Ford Cosworth	V8	59		19	8
r	30	C Regazzoni	Ferrari	312B2	Ferrari	F12	57	accident	2	1
r	36	A de Adamich	Surtees	TS9B	Ford Cosworth	V8	55	connecting rod	10	4
r	22	N Galli	Tecno	PA123	Tecno	F12	54	accident / rear suspension	24	10
r	29	J Ickx	Ferrari	312B2	Ferrari	F12	47	fuel injection	4	2
r	14	M Beuttler	March	721G	Ford Cosworth	V8	31	driveshaft	22	9
r	18	W Fittipaldi	Brabham	BT34	Ford Cosworth	V8	28	gearbox	18	7
r	24	P Gethin	BRM	P160B	BRM	V12	27	fuel pump	17	7
r	23	J-P Beltoise	BRM	P160B	BRM	V12	15	engine overheating	6	3
r	35	T Schenken	Surtees	TS9B	Ford Cosworth	V8	11	engine overheating	21	9
ns	26	V Schuppan	BRM	P153B	BRM	V12		car raced by Marko		

Winning speed 182.423 km/h, 113.353 mph
Pole Position speed 187.686 km/h, 116.623 mph (E Fittipaldi, 1 min:11.430 sec)
Fastest Lap speed 185.890 km/h, 115.507 mph (C Amon, 1 min:12.120 sec on lap 66)
Lap Leaders C Regazzoni 1-8 (8); E Fittipaldi 9-85 (77).

Races

2 Jul 1972   FRANCE: Clermont-Ferrand   (Round 6)   (Race 214)

38 laps x 8.055 km, 5.005 miles = 306.090 km, 190.196 miles

Pos	No	Driver	Car	Model	Engine		Laps	Time/Reason for Retirement	Grid Pos	Row
1	4	J Stewart	Tyrrell	003	Ford Cosworth	V8	38	1h 52m 21.500s	3	2
2	1	E Fittipaldi	JPS Lotus	72D	Ford Cosworth	V8	38	1h 52m 49.200s	8	4
3	9	C Amon	Matra Simca	MS120D	Matra	V12	38	1h 52m 53.400s	1	1
4	7	F Cevert	Tyrrell	002	Ford Cosworth	V8	38	1h 53m 10.800s	7	4
5	12	R Peterson	March	721G	Ford Cosworth	V8	38	1h 53m 18.300s	9	5
6	26	M Hailwood	Surtees	TS9B	Ford Cosworth	V8	38	1h 53m 57.600s	10	5
7	2	D Hulme	McLaren	M19C	Ford Cosworth	V8	38	1h 54m 09.600s	2	1
8	19	W Fittipaldi	Brabham	BT34	Ford Cosworth	V8	38	1h 54m 46.600s	14	7
9	11	B Redman	McLaren	M19A	Ford Cosworth	V8	38	1h 55m 17.000s	13	7
10	18	G Hill	Brabham	BT37	Ford Cosworth	V8	38	1h 55m 21.000s	20	10
11	3	J Ickx	Ferrari	312B2	Ferrari	F12	37		4	2
12	20	C Reutemann	Brabham	BT37	Ford Cosworth	V8	37		17	9
13	30	N Galli	Ferrari	312B2	Ferrari	F12	37		19	10
14	28	A de Adamich	Surtees	TS9B	Ford Cosworth	V8	37		12	6
15	5	J-P Beltoise	BRM	P160B	BRM	V12	37		24	12
16	10	R Stommelen	Eifelland March	721	Ford Cosworth	V8	37		15	8
17	27	T Schenken	Surtees	TS9B	Ford Cosworth	V8	36		5	3
18r	6	D Walker	JPS Lotus	72D	Ford Cosworth	V8	34	crown wheel & pinion	22	11
r	15	M Beuttler	March	721G	Ford Cosworth	V8	33	out of fuel	23	12
nc	8	P Depailler	Tyrrell	004	Ford Cosworth	V8	33		16	8
r	24	R Wisell	BRM	P160B	BRM	V12	25	gear linkage	18	9
r	17	C Pace	March	711	Ford Cosworth	V8	18	connecting rod	11	6
r	25	H Marko	BRM	P160B	BRM	V12	8	eye injury from flying stone	6	3
r	14	N Lauda	March	721G	Ford Cosworth	V8	4	driveshaft	21	11
ns	16	H Pescarolo	March	721	Ford Cosworth	V8		accident		
ns	23	H Ganley	BRM	P160B	BRM	V12		car raced by Beltoise		
ns	22	P Gethin	BRM	P160B	BRM	V12		accident		
ns	21	D Bell	Tecno	PA123	Tecno	F12		chassis		
ns	29	D Charlton	Lotus	72D	Ford Cosworth	V8		car unprepared		

Winning speed 163.454 km/h, 101.566 mph
Pole Position speed 167.232 km/h, 103.913 mph (C Amon, 2 min:53.400 sec)
Fastest Lap speed 166.751 km/h, 103.614 mph (C Amon, 2 min:53.900 sec on lap 32)
Lap Leaders C Amon 1-19 (19); J Stewart 20-38 (19).

15 Jul 1972   BRITAIN: Brands Hatch   (Round 7)   (Race 215)

76 laps x 4.265 km, 2.650 miles = 324.122 km, 201.400 miles

Pos	No	Driver	Car	Model	Engine		Laps	Time/Reason for Retirement	Grid Pos	Row
1	8	E Fittipaldi	JPS Lotus	72D	Ford Cosworth	V8	76	1h 47m 50.200s	2	1
2	1	J Stewart	Tyrrell	003	Ford Cosworth	V8	76	1h 47m 54.300s	4	2
3	19	P Revson	McLaren	M19A	Ford Cosworth	V8	76	1h 49m 02.700s	3	2
4	17	C Amon	Matra Simca	MS120C	Matra	V12	75		17	9
5	18	D Hulme	McLaren	M19C	Ford Cosworth	V8	75		11	6
6	6	A Merzario	Ferrari	312B2	Ferrari	F12	75		9	5
7r	3	R Peterson	March	721G	Ford Cosworth	V8	74	engine / accident	8	4
8	27	C Reutemann	Brabham	BT37	Ford Cosworth	V8	73		10	5
9	4	N Lauda	March	721G	Ford Cosworth	V8	73		19	10
10	33	R Stommelen	Eifelland March	721	Ford Cosworth	V8	71		25	13
11	11	J-P Beltoise	BRM	P160C	BRM	V12	70		6	3
12r	28	W Fittipaldi	Brabham	BT34	Ford Cosworth	V8	69	rear suspension radius rod	22	11
13	31	M Beuttler	March	721G	Ford Cosworth	V8	69		23	12
r	22	T Schenken	Surtees	TS9B	Ford Cosworth	V8	64	rear suspension	5	3
r	2	F Cevert	Tyrrell	002	Ford Cosworth	V8	60	accident	12	6
r	9	D Walker	JPS Lotus	72D	Ford Cosworth	V8	59	rear suspension radius rod	15	8
r	5	J Ickx	Ferrari	312B2	Ferrari	F12	49	oil radiator leak	1	1
r	26	G Hill	Brabham	BT37	Ford Cosworth	V8	47	accident	21	11
r	25	C Pace	March	711	Ford Cosworth	V8	39	differential	13	7
r	14	J Oliver	BRM	P160B	BRM	V12	36	rear suspension radius rod	14	7
r	21	M Hailwood	Surtees	TS9B	Ford Cosworth	V8	31	gear linkage	7	4
r	29	D Charlton	Lotus	72D	Ford Cosworth	V8	21	gear selection	24	12
r	30	N Galli	Tecno	PA123	Tecno	F12	9	accident	18	9
r	24	H Pescarolo	Politoys	FX3	Ford Cosworth	V8	7	suspension / accident	26	13
r	12	P Gethin	BRM	P160B	BRM	V12	5	engine	16	8
r	23	A de Adamich	Surtees	TS9B	Ford Cosworth	V8	3	accident	20	10
ns	34	F Migault	Connew	PC1	Ford Cosworth	V8		rear suspension		

Winning speed 180.340 km/h, 112.058 mph
Pole Position speed 186.778 km/h, 116.058 mph (J Ickx, 1 min:22.200 sec)
Fastest Lap speed 182.775 km/h, 113.571 mph (J Stewart, 1 min:24.000 sec on lap 58 & 60)
Lap Leaders J Ickx 1-48 (48); E Fittipaldi 49-76 (28).

Also the Grand Prix of Europe.

30 Jul 1972		**GERMANY: Nürburgring**							(Round 8)	(Race 216)

14 laps x 22.835 km, 14.189 miles = 319.690 km, 198.646 miles

Pos	No	Driver	Car	Model	Engine		Laps	Time/Reason for Retirement	Grid Pos	Row
1	4	J Ickx	Ferrari	312B2	Ferrari	F12	14	1h 42m 12.300s	1	1
2	9	C Regazzoni	Ferrari	312B2	Ferrari	F12	14	1h 43m 00.600s	7	4
3	10	R Peterson	March	721G	Ford Cosworth	V8	14	1h 43m 19.000s	4	2
4	17	H Ganley	BRM	P160C	BRM	V12	14	1h 44m 32.500s	18	9
5	5	B Redman	McLaren	M19A	Ford Cosworth	V8	14	1h 44m 48.000s	19	10
6	11	G Hill	Brabham	BT37	Ford Cosworth	V8	14	1h 45m 11.900s	15	8
7	26	W Fittipaldi	Brabham	BT34	Ford Cosworth	V8	14	1h 45m 12.400s	21	11
8	28	M Beuttler	March	721G	Ford Cosworth	V8	14	1h 47m 23.000s	27	14
9	6	J-P Beltoise	BRM	P160C	BRM	V12	14	1h 47m 32.500s	13	7
10	7	F Cevert	Tyrrell	002	Ford Cosworth	V8	14	1h 47m 56.000s	5	3
11r	1	J Stewart	Tyrrell	003	Ford Cosworth	V8	13	accident	2	1
12	19	A Merzario	Ferrari	312B2	Ferrari	F12	13		22	11
13	16	A de Adamich	Surtees	TS9B	Ford Cosworth	V8	13		20	10
14	15	T Schenken	Surtees	TS9B	Ford Cosworth	V8	13		12	6
15	8	C Amon	Matra Simca	MS120D	Matra	V12	13		8	4
nc	21	C Pace	March	711	Ford Cosworth	V8	11		11	6
r	20	H Pescarolo	March	721	Ford Cosworth	V8	10	accident	9	5
r	2	E Fittipaldi	JPS Lotus	72D	Ford Cosworth	V8	10	gearbox casing / oil fire	3	2
r	3	D Hulme	McLaren	M19C	Ford Cosworth	V8	8	engine	10	5
r	14	M Hailwood	Surtees	TS9B	Ford Cosworth	V8	8	front suspension	16	8
r	12	C Reutemann	Brabham	BT37	Ford Cosworth	V8	6	crown wheel & pinion	6	3
r	22	R Stommelen	Eifelland March	721	Ford Cosworth	V8	6	electrics	14	7
r	25	D Walker	JPS Lotus	72D	Ford Cosworth	V8	6	oil tank	23	12
r	27	D Bell	Tecno	PA123	Tecno	F12	4	dropped valve	25	13
r	29	D Charlton	Lotus	72D	Ford Cosworth	V8	4	driver ill	26	13
r	23	N Lauda	March	721G	Ford Cosworth	V8	4	oil tank	24	12
r	18	R Wisell	BRM	P160C	BRM	V12	3	engine	17	9

Winning speed 187.676 km/h, 116.616 mph
Pole Position speed 192.520 km/h, 119.626 mph (J Ickx, 7 min: 7.000 sec)
Fastest Lap speed 189.589 km/h, 117.805 mph (J Ickx, 7 min:13.600 sec on lap 10)
Lap Leaders J Ickx 1-14 (14).

13 Aug 1972		**AUSTRIA: Österreichring**							(Round 9)	(Race 217)

54 laps x 5.911 km, 3.673 miles = 319.194 km, 198.338 miles

Pos	No	Driver	Car	Model	Engine		Laps	Time/Reason for Retirement	Grid Pos	Row
1	31	E Fittipaldi	JPS Lotus	72D	Ford Cosworth	V8	54	1h 29m 16.660s	1	1
2	12	D Hulme	McLaren	M19C	Ford Cosworth	V8	54	1h 29m 17.840s	7	4
3	14	P Revson	McLaren	M19C	Ford Cosworth	V8	54	1h 29m 53.190s	4	2
4	25	M Hailwood	Surtees	TS9B	Ford Cosworth	V8	54	1h 30m 01.420s	12	6
5	10	C Amon	Matra Simca	MS120D	Matra	V12	54	1h 30m 02.300s	6	3
6	9	H Ganley	BRM	P160C	BRM	V12	54	1h 30m 17.850s	10	5
7	1	J Stewart	Tyrrell	005	Ford Cosworth	V8	54	1h 30m 25.750s	3	2
8	7	J-P Beltoise	BRM	P160C	BRM	V12	54	1h 30m 38.110s	21	11
9	2	F Cevert	Tyrrell	002	Ford Cosworth	V8	53		20	10
10	4	N Lauda	March	721G	Ford Cosworth	V8	53		22	11
11	24	T Schenken	Surtees	TS9B	Ford Cosworth	V8	52		8	4
12	5	R Peterson	March	721G	Ford Cosworth	V8	52		11	6
13	6	P Gethin	BRM	P160C	BRM	V12	51		16	8
14	11	A de Adamich	Surtees	TS9B	Ford Cosworth	V8	51		13	7
15	27	R Stommelen	Eifelland March	721	Ford Cosworth	V8	48		17	9
nc	23	C Pace	March	711	Ford Cosworth	V8	46		18	9
nc	15	N Galli	Tecno	PA123	Tecno	F12	45		23	12
r	16	G Hill	Brabham	BT37	Ford Cosworth	V8	36	fuel metering unit	14	7
r	28	W Fittipaldi	Brabham	BT34	Ford Cosworth	V8	31	brake pipe	15	8
r	3	M Beuttler	March	721G	Ford Cosworth	V8	24	fuel metering unit	24	12
r	29	F Migault	Connew	PC1	Ford Cosworth	V8	22	rear suspension	25	13
r	18	J Ickx	Ferrari	312B2	Ferrari	F12	20	fuel vaporisation	9	5
r	17	C Reutemann	Brabham	BT37	Ford Cosworth	V8	14	fuel metering unit	5	3
r	19	C Regazzoni	Ferrari	312B2	Ferrari	F12	13	fuel vaporisation	2	1
r	21	D Walker	JPS Lotus	72D	Ford Cosworth	V8	6	connecting rod	19	10
ns	22	H Pescarolo	March	721	Ford Cosworth	V8		accident		

Winning speed 214.518 km/h, 133.295 mph
Pole Position speed 221.732 km/h, 137.778 mph (E Fittipaldi, 1 min:35.970 sec)
Fastest Lap speed 216.432 km/h, 134.485 mph (D Hulme, 1 min:38.320 sec on lap 47)
Lap Leaders J Stewart 1-23 (23); E Fittipaldi 24-54 (31).

10 Sep 1972 **ITALY: Monza** **(Round 10)** **(Race 218)**

55 laps x 5.775 km, 3.588 miles = 317.625 km, 197.363 miles

Pos	No	Driver	Car	Model	Engine		Laps	Time/Reason for Retirement	Grid Pos	Row
1	6	E Fittipaldi	JPS Lotus	72D	Ford Cosworth	V8	55	1h 29m 58.400s	6	3
2	10	M Hailwood	Surtees	TS9B	Ford Cosworth	V8	55	1h 30m 12.900s	9	5
3	14	D Hulme	McLaren	M19C	Ford Cosworth	V8	55	1h 30m 22.200s	5	3
4	15	P Revson	McLaren	M19C	Ford Cosworth	V8	55	1h 30m 34.100s	8	4
5	28	G Hill	Brabham	BT37	Ford Cosworth	V8	55	1h 31m 04.000s	13	7
6	23	P Gethin	BRM	P160C	BRM	V12	55	1h 31m 20.300s	12	6
7	3	M Andretti	Ferrari	312B2	Ferrari	F12	54		7	4
8	21	J-P Beltoise	BRM	P180	BRM	V12	54		16	8
9	19	R Peterson	March	721G	Ford Cosworth	V8	54		24	12
10	16	M Beuttler	March	721G	Ford Cosworth	V8	54		25	13
11	22	H Ganley	BRM	P160C	BRM	V12	52		17	9
12	24	R Wisell	BRM	P160C	BRM	V12	51		10	5
13	18	N Lauda	March	721G	Ford Cosworth	V8	50		20	10
r	4	J Ickx	Ferrari	312B2	Ferrari	F12	46	battery	1	1
r	20	C Amon	Matra Simca	MS120D	Matra	V12	38	brake pads	2	1
r	9	A de Adamich	Surtees	TS9B	Ford Cosworth	V8	33	brake calipers	21	11
r	7	J Surtees	Surtees	TS14	Ford Cosworth	V8	20	fuel vaporisation	19	10
r	8	T Schenken	Surtees	TS9B	Ford Cosworth	V8	20	accident	22	11
r	29	W Fittipaldi	Brabham	BT34	Ford Cosworth	V8	20	rear suspension	15	8
r	5	C Regazzoni	Ferrari	312B2	Ferrari	F12	16	accident	4	2
r	26	C Pace	March	711	Ford Cosworth	V8	15	accident	18	9
r	30	C Reutemann	Brabham	BT37	Ford Cosworth	V8	14	accident / front suspension	11	6
r	2	F Cevert	Tyrrell	002	Ford Cosworth	V8	14	engine	14	7
r	11	N Galli	Tecno	PA123	Tecno	F12	6	engine	23	12
r	1	J Stewart	Tyrrell	005	Ford Cosworth	V8	0	clutch	3	2
nq	25	H Pescarolo	March	721	Ford Cosworth	V8				
nq	12	D Bell	Tecno	PA123	Tecno	F12				

Winning speed 211.813 km/h, 131.614 mph
Pole Position speed 217.355 km/h, 135.058 mph (J Ickx, 1 min:35.650 sec)
Fastest Lap speed 215.888 km/h, 134.146 mph (J Ickx, 1 min:36.300 sec on lap 44)
Lap Leaders J Ickx 1-13,17-45 (42); C Regazzoni 14-16 (3); E Fittipaldi 46-55 (10).

24 Sep 1972 **CANADA: Mosport Park** **(Round 11)** **(Race 219)**

80 laps x 3.957 km, 2.459 miles = 316.590 km, 196.720 miles

Pos	No	Driver	Car	Model	Engine		Laps	Time/Reason for Retirement	Grid Pos	Row
1	1	J Stewart	Tyrrell	005	Ford Cosworth	V8	80	1h 43m 16.900s	5	2
2	19	P Revson	McLaren	M19C	Ford Cosworth	V8	80	1h 44m 05.100s	1	1
3	18	D Hulme	McLaren	M19C	Ford Cosworth	V8	80	1h 44m 11.500s	2	1
4	8	C Reutemann	Brabham	BT37	Ford Cosworth	V8	80	1h 44m 17.600s	9	4
5	11	C Regazzoni	Ferrari	312B2	Ferrari	F12	80	1h 44m 23.900s	7	3
6	4	C Amon	Matra Simca	MS120D	Matra	V12	79		10	4
7	22	T Schenken	Surtees	TS9B	Ford Cosworth	V8	79		13	5
8	7	G Hill	Brabham	BT37	Ford Cosworth	V8	79		17	7
9r	29	C Pace	March	711	Ford Cosworth	V8	78	out of fuel	18	7
10	15	H Ganley	BRM	P160C	BRM	V12	78		14	6
11	5	E Fittipaldi	JPS Lotus	72D	Ford Cosworth	V8	78		4	2
12	10	J Ickx	Ferrari	312B2	Ferrari	F12	77		8	3
13	28	H Pescarolo	March	721	Ford Cosworth	V8	73		21	9
r	6	R Wisell	JPS Lotus	72D	Ford Cosworth	V8	65	valve spring	16	7
dq	26	N Lauda	March	721G	Ford Cosworth	V8	64	push start after spin	19	8
dq	25	R Peterson	March	721G	Ford Cosworth	V8	61	push start after accident	3	1
nc	27	M Beuttler	March	721G	Ford Cosworth	V8	59		24	10
r	2	F Cevert	Tyrrell	006	Ford Cosworth	V8	51	gearbox	6	3
r	16	P Gethin	BRM	P160C	BRM	V12	25	rear suspension radius rod	12	5
nc	33	S Barber	March	711	Ford Cosworth	V8	24		22	9
r	14	J-P Beltoise	BRM	P180	BRM	V12	21	oil radiator leak	20	8
r	17	B Brack	BRM	P180	BRM	V12	20	spin	23	9
r	9	W Fittipaldi	Brabham	BT34	Ford Cosworth	V8	5	gearbox	11	5
r	23	A de Adamich	Surtees	TS9B	Ford Cosworth	V8	2	gearbox	15	6
ns	31	D Bell	Tecno	PA123	Tecno	F12		accident		

Winning speed 183.918 km/h, 114.282 mph
Pole Position speed 193.567 km/h, 120.277 mph (P Revson, 1 min:13.600 sec)
Fastest Lap speed 188.198 km/h, 116.941 mph (J Stewart, 1 min:15.700 sec on lap 25)
Lap Leaders R Peterson 1-3 (3); J Stewart 4-80 (77).

8 Oct 1972　　USA: Watkins Glen　　　　　　　　　　　　　　　　　(Round 12)　　(Race 220)
59 laps x 5.435 km, 3.377 miles = 320.651 km, 199.243 miles

Pos	No	Driver	Car	Model	Engine		Laps	Time/Reason for Retirement	Grid Pos	Row
1	1	J Stewart	Tyrrell	005	Ford Cosworth	V8	59	1h 41m 45.354s	1	1
2	2	F Cevert	Tyrrell	006	Ford Cosworth	V8	59	1h 42m 17.622s	4	2
3	19	D Hulme	McLaren	M19C	Ford Cosworth	V8	59	1h 42m 22.882s	3	1
4	4	R Peterson	March	721G	Ford Cosworth	V8	59	1h 43m 07.870s	26	11
5	7	J Ickx	Ferrari	312B2	Ferrari	F12	59	1h 43m 08.473s	12	5
6	9	M Andretti	Ferrari	312B2	Ferrari	F12	58		10	4
7	3	P Depailler	Tyrrell	004	Ford Cosworth	V8	58		11	5
8	8	C Regazzoni	Ferrari	312B2	Ferrari	F12	58		6	3
9	21	J Scheckter	McLaren	M19A	Ford Cosworth	V8	58		8	3
10	12	R Wisell	JPS Lotus	72D	Ford Cosworth	V8	57		16	7
11	28	G Hill	Brabham	BT37	Ford Cosworth	V8	57		27	11
12	34	S Posey	Surtees	TS9B	Ford Cosworth	V8	57		23	9
13	6	M Beuttler	March	721G	Ford Cosworth	V8	57		21	9
14	26	H Pescarolo	March	721	Ford Cosworth	V8	57		22	9
15	18	C Amon	Matra Simca	MS120D	Matra	V12	57		7	3
16	33	S Barber	March	711	Ford Cosworth	V8	57		20	8
17r	23	M Hailwood	Surtees	TS9B	Ford Cosworth	V8	56	accident	14	6
18r	20	P Revson	McLaren	M19C	Ford Cosworth	V8	54	ignition	2	1
nc	5	N Lauda	March	721G	Ford Cosworth	V8	49		25	10
r	27	C Pace	March	711	Ford Cosworth	V8	48	fuel injection	15	6
r	14	P Gethin	BRM	P160C	BRM	V12	47	engine	28	11
r	11	D Walker	JPS Lotus	72D	Ford Cosworth	V8	44	coil	30	12
r	16	H Ganley	BRM	P160C	BRM	V12	44	cylinder liner	17	7
r	30	W Fittipaldi	Brabham	BT34	Ford Cosworth	V8	43	engine	13	5
r	17	J-P Beltoise	BRM	P180	BRM	V12	40	ignition rotor	18	7
r	15	B Redman	BRM	P180	BRM	V12	34	connecting rod	24	10
r	29	C Reutemann	Brabham	BT37	Ford Cosworth	V8	31	engine	5	2
r	25	A de Adamich	Surtees	TS9B	Ford Cosworth	V8	25	accident	19	8
r	22	T Schenken	Surtees	TS14	Ford Cosworth	V8	22	rear suspension	31	13
r	10	E Fittipaldi	JPS Lotus	72D	Ford Cosworth	V8	17	rear vibration	9	4
r	31	D Bell	Tecno	PA123	Tecno	F12	8	cylinder head gasket	29	12
ns	24	J Surtees	Surtees	TS14	Ford Cosworth	V8		engine shortage		

Winning speed 189.070 km/h, 117.483 mph
Pole Position speed 194.715 km/h, 120.990 mph (J Stewart, 1 min:40.481 sec)
Fastest Lap speed 192.487 km/h, 119.606 mph (J Stewart, 1 min:41.644 sec on lap 33)
Lap Leaders J Stewart 1-59 (59).

C Amon elected to start from the back of the grid (engine problem). 7th slot on the grid remained empty.

Lap Leaders 1972

Pos	Driver	Car-Engine	GPs	laps	km	miles
1	J Stewart	Tyrrell-Ford Cosworth	7	320	1,422.2	883.7
2	E Fittipaldi	Lotus-Ford Cosworth	6	240	975.5	606.2
3	J Ickx	Ferrari	3	104	767.0	476.6
4	J-P Beltoise	BRM	1	80	251.6	156.3
5	D Hulme	McLaren-Ford Cosworth	2	28	112.1	69.7
6	C Amon	Matra Simca	1	19	153.0	95.1
7	C Regazzoni	Ferrari	2	11	47.1	29.3
8	R Peterson	March-Ford Cosworth	1	3	11.9	7.4
			12	805	3,740.5	2,324.2

Driver Points 1972

		RA	ZA	E	MC	B	F	GB	D	A	I	CDN	USA	Total
1	E Fittipaldi	-	6	9	4	9	6	9	-	9	9	-	-	61
2	J Stewart	9	-	-	3	-	9	6	-	-	-	9	9	45
3	D Hulme	6	9	-	-	4	-	2	-	6	4	4	4	39
4	J Ickx	4	-	6	6	-	-	-	9	-	-	-	2	27
5	P Revson	-	4	2	-	-	-	4	-	4	3	6	-	23
6	F Cevert	-	-	-	-	6	3	-	-	-	-	-	6	15
	C Regazzoni	3	-	4	-	-	-	-	6	-	-	2	-	15
8	M Hailwood	-	-	-	-	3	1	-	-	3	6	-	-	13
9	R Peterson	1	2	-	-	-	2	-	4	-	-	-	3	12
	C Amon	-	-	-	1	1	4	3	-	2	-	1	-	12
11	J-P Beltoise	-	-	-	9	-	-	-	-	-	-	-	-	9
12	M Andretti	-	3	-	-	-	-	-	-	-	-	-	1	4
	H Ganley	-	-	-	-	-	-	-	3	1	-	-	-	4
	B Redman	-	-	-	2	-	-	-	2	-	-	-	-	4
	G Hill	-	1	-	-	-	-	-	1	-	2	-	-	4
16	A de Adamich	-	-	3	-	-	-	-	-	-	-	-	-	3
	C Reutemann	-	-	-	-	-	-	-	-	-	-	3	-	3
	C Pace	-	-	1	-	2	-	-	-	-	-	-	-	3
19	T Schenken	2	-	-	-	-	-	-	-	-	-	-	-	2
20	A Merzario	-	-	-	-	-	-	1	-	-	-	-	-	1
	P Gethin	-	-	-	-	-	-	-	-	-	1	-	-	1

9,6,4,3,2 and 1 point awarded to the first six finishers. Best 5 scores from first 6 races, best 5 from remaining 6 races.

Constructor Points 1972

		RA	ZA	E	MC	B	F	GB	D	A	I	CDN	USA	Total
1	Lotus-Ford Cosworth	-	6	9	4	9	6	9	-	9	9	-	-	61
2	Tyrrell-Ford Cosworth	9	-	-	3	6	9	6	-	-	-	9	9	51
3	McLaren-Ford Cosworth	6	9	2	2	4	-	4	(2)	6	4	6	4	47 (2)
4	Ferrari	4	3	6	6	-	-	1	9	-	-	2	2	33
5	Surtees-Ford Cosworth	2	-	3	-	3	1	-	-	3	6	-	-	18
6	March-Ford Cosworth	1	2	1	-	2	2	-	4	-	-	-	3	15
7	BRM	-	-	-	9	-	-	-	3	1	1	-	-	14
8	Matra Simca	-	-	-	1	1	4	3	-	2	-	1	-	12
9	Brabham-Ford Cosworth	-	1	-	-	-	-	-	1	-	2	3	-	7

9,6,4,3,2 and 1 point awarded to the first six finishers. Points only for highest placed car. Best 5 scores from first 6 races, best 5 from remaining 6 races.

Race Entrants and Results

The Formula 1 Constructors Association demanded more start and appearance money. Safety became a major issue; deformable structures were required from the Spanish race and after the Dutch race all grids would be 2 x 2 formation. Frank Williams had his first full season with the Iso Marlboro and Ferrari produced its first full monocoque.

FERRARI
Scuderia Ferrari SpA SEFAC: Ickx, Merzario

BRABHAM
Motor Racing Developments: Reutemann, W Fittipaldi
Ceramica Pagnossin-Team MRD: de Adamich, Stommelen, Watson

ENSIGN
Team Ensign: von Opel

BRM
Marlboro BRM: Beltoise, Regazzoni, Lauda, Gethin

LOTUS
John Player Team Lotus: E Fittipaldi, Peterson
Scuderia Scribante-Lucky Strike Racing: Charlton

MARCH
STP March Racing Team: Jarier, Williamson*, Pescarolo
Clarke-Mordaunt-Guthrie-Durlacher: Beuttler, Wisell (F)
Hesketh Racing: Hunt
Lec Refrigeration Racing: Purley
Team Pierre Robert: (Wisell)
* co-entered by Wheatcroft Racing at GB GP

McLAREN
Yardley Team McLaren: Hulme, Revson, Scheckter, Ickx

SHADOW
UOP Shadow Racing Team: Oliver, Follmer, Redman
Embassy Racing: Hill

SURTEES
Team Surtees-Brooke Bond Oxo/Rob Walker: Hailwood
Team Surtees-Brooke Bond Oxo: Pace
Ceramica Pagnossin-Team Surtees: de Adamich
Team Surtees: Mass, Bueno

TECNO
Martini Racing Team: Amon

TYRRELL
Elf Team Tyrrell: Stewart, Cevert, Amon
Blignaut-Lucky Strike Racing: Keizan

WILLIAMS (ISO MARLBORO)
Frank Williams Racing Cars: Ganley, Galli, Pescarolo, van Lennep, Pretorius, McRae, Schenken, Ickx, (Belsø)

28 Jan 1973		ARGENTINA: Buenos Aires No.9						(Round 1)	(Race 221)	
		96 laps x 3.345 km, 2.078 miles = 321.120 km, 199.535 miles								
Pos	No	Driver	Car	Model	Engine		Laps	Time/Reason for Retirement	Grid Pos	Row
1	2	E Fittipaldi	JPS Lotus	72D	Ford Cosworth	V8	96	1h 56m 18.220s	2	1
2	8	F Cevert	Tyrrell	006	Ford Cosworth	V8	96	1h 56m 22.910s	6	3
3	6	J Stewart	Tyrrell	005	Ford Cosworth	V8	96	1h 56m 51.410s	4	2
4	18	J Ickx	Ferrari	312B2	Ferrari	F12	96	1h 57m 00.790s	3	2
5	14	D Hulme	McLaren	M19C	Ford Cosworth	V8	95		8	4
6	12	W Fittipaldi	Brabham	BT37	Ford Cosworth	V8	95		12	6
7	32	C Regazzoni	BRM	P160D	BRM	V12	93		1	1
8	16	P Revson	McLaren	M19C	Ford Cosworth	V8	92		11	6
9	20	A Merzario	Ferrari	312B2	Ferrari	F12	92		14	7
10r	22	M Beuttler	March	721G	Ford Cosworth	V8	90	rear suspension radius rod	18	9
r	24	J-P Jarier	March	721G	Ford Cosworth	V8	84	gear linkage / radiator	17	9
r	30	J-P Beltoise	BRM	P160D	BRM	V12	79	engine	7	4
nc	38	H Ganley	Iso Marlboro	FX3B	Ford Cosworth	V8	79		19	10
r	4	R Peterson	JPS Lotus	72D	Ford Cosworth	V8	66	oil pressure	5	3
r	34	N Lauda	BRM	P160C	BRM	V12	66	oil pressure	13	7
r	10	C Reutemann	Brabham	BT37	Ford Cosworth	V8	16	gearbox	9	5
r	28	C Pace	Surtees	TS14A	Ford Cosworth	V8	10	suspension / spin	15	8
r	26	M Hailwood	Surtees	TS14A	Ford Cosworth	V8	10	driveshaft	10	5
r	36	N Galli	Iso Marlboro	FX3B	Ford Cosworth	V8	0	water pump belt	16	8

Winning speed 165.663 km/h, 102.938 mph
Pole Position speed 170.712 km/h, 106.075 mph (C Regazzoni, 1 min:10.540 sec)
Fastest Lap speed 169.082 km/h, 105.063 mph (E Fittipaldi, 1 min:11.220 sec on lap 79)
Lap Leaders C Regazzoni 1-28 (28); F Cevert 29-85 (57); E Fittipaldi 86-96 (11).

BRAZIL: Interlagos (Round 2) (Race 222)

40 laps x 7.960 km, 4.946 miles = 318.400 km, 197.845 miles

Pos	No	Driver	Car	Model	Engine		Laps	Time/Reason for Retirement	Grid Pos	Row
1	1	E Fittipaldi	JPS Lotus	72D	Ford Cosworth	V8	40	1h 43m 55.600s	2	1
2	3	J Stewart	Tyrrell	005	Ford Cosworth	V8	40	1h 44m 09.100s	8	3
3	7	D Hulme	McLaren	M19C	Ford Cosworth	V8	40	1h 45m 42.000s	5	2
4	10	A Merzario	Ferrari	312B2	Ferrari	F12	39		17	7
5	9	J Ickx	Ferrari	312B2	Ferrari	F12	39		3	1
6	14	C Regazzoni	BRM	P160D	BRM	V12	39		4	2
7	19	H Ganley	Iso Marlboro	FX3B	Ford Cosworth	V8	39		16	7
8	16	N Lauda	BRM	P160C	BRM	V12	38		13	5
9	20	N Galli	Iso Marlboro	FX3B	Ford Cosworth	V8	38		18	7
10	4	F Cevert	Tyrrell	006	Ford Cosworth	V8	38		9	4
11	17	C Reutemann	Brabham	BT37	Ford Cosworth	V8	38		7	3
12	23	L Bueno	Surtees	TS9B	Ford Cosworth	V8	36		20	8
r	15	J-P Beltoise	BRM	P160D	BRM	V12	23	electrics	10	4
r	12	M Beuttler	March	721G	Ford Cosworth	V8	18	engine overheating	19	8
r	6	C Pace	Surtees	TS14A	Ford Cosworth	V8	9	rear suspension	6	3
r	5	M Hailwood	Surtees	TS14A	Ford Cosworth	V8	6	gearbox pinion bearing	14	6
r	11	J-P Jarier	March	721G	Ford Cosworth	V8	5	gearbox	15	6
r	2	R Peterson	JPS Lotus	72D	Ford Cosworth	V8	5	rear wheel	1	1
r	18	W Fittipaldi	Brabham	BT37	Ford Cosworth	V8	5	cylinder head ring	11	5
r	8	P Revson	McLaren	M19C	Ford Cosworth	V8	3	gearbox	12	5

Winning speed 183.822 km/h, 114.222 mph
Pole Position speed 190.405 km/h, 118.312 mph (R Peterson, 2 min:30.500 sec)
Fastest Lap speed 184.877 km/h, 114.878 mph (E Fittipaldi / D Hulme, 2 min:35.000 sec on lap 14 / 20)
Lap Leaders E Fittipaldi 1-40 (40).

SOUTH AFRICA: Kyalami (Round 3) (Race 223)

79 laps x 4.104 km, 2.550 miles = 324.216 km, 201.458 miles

Pos	No	Driver	Car	Model	Engine		Laps	Time/Reason for Retirement	Grid Pos	Row
1	3	J Stewart	Tyrrell	006	Ford Cosworth	V8	79	1h 43m 11.070s	16	7
2	6	P Revson	McLaren	M19C	Ford Cosworth	V8	79	1h 43m 35.620s	6	3
3	1	E Fittipaldi	JPS Lotus	72D	Ford Cosworth	V8	79	1h 43m 36.130s	2	1
4	9	A Merzario	Ferrari	312B2	Ferrari	F12	78		15	6
5	5	D Hulme	McLaren	M23	Ford Cosworth	V8	77		1	1
6	23	G Follmer	Shadow	DN1	Ford Cosworth	V8	77		21	9
7	18	C Reutemann	Brabham	BT37	Ford Cosworth	V8	77		8	3
8	12	A de Adamich	Surtees	TS9B	Ford Cosworth	V8	77		20	8
9r	7	J Scheckter	McLaren	M19C	Ford Cosworth	V8	75	engine	3	1
10	21	H Ganley	Iso Marlboro	FX3B	Ford Cosworth	V8	73		19	8
11	2	R Peterson	JPS Lotus	72D	Ford Cosworth	V8	73		4	2
r	11	C Pace	Surtees	TS14A	Ford Cosworth	V8	69	front tyre burst / accident	9	4
nc	26	E Keizan	Tyrrell	004	Ford Cosworth	V8	67		22	9
nc	14	J-P Jarier	March	721G	Ford Cosworth	V8	66		18	7
nc	4	F Cevert	Tyrrell	005	Ford Cosworth	V8	66		25	10
nc	24	M Beuttler	March	721G	Ford Cosworth	V8	65		23	9
r	19	W Fittipaldi	Brabham	BT37	Ford Cosworth	V8	52	gear selector	17	7
r	20	J Pretorius	Iso Marlboro	FX3B	Ford Cosworth	V8	35	engine overheating	24	10
r	17	N Lauda	BRM	P160D	BRM	V12	26	engine	10	4
r	22	J Oliver	Shadow	DN1	Ford Cosworth	V8	14	engine	14	6
r	16	J-P Beltoise	BRM	P160D	BRM	V12	4	clutch	7	3
r	25	D Charlton	Lotus	72D	Ford Cosworth	V8	3	accident	13	5
r	15	C Regazzoni	BRM	P160D	BRM	V12	2	accident / fire / injury	5	2
r	8	J Ickx	Ferrari	312B2	Ferrari	F12	2	accident	11	5
r	10	M Hailwood	Surtees	TS14A	Ford Cosworth	V8	2	accident	12	5

Winning speed 188.526 km/h, 117.145 mph
Pole Position speed 193.686 km/h, 120.351 mph (D Hulme, 1 min:16.280 sec)
Fastest Lap speed 191.626 km/h, 119.071 mph (E Fittipaldi, 1 min:17.100 sec on lap 76)
Lap Leaders D Hulme 1-4 (4); J Scheckter 5-6 (2); J Stewart 7-79 (73).

SPAIN: Montjuïc (Round 4) (Race 224)

75 laps x 3.791 km, 2.356 miles = 284.325 km, 176.671 miles

Pos	No	Driver	Car	Model	Engine		Laps	Time/Reason for Retirement	Grid Pos	Row
1	1	E Fittipaldi	JPS Lotus	72E	Ford Cosworth	V8	75	1h 48m 18.700s	7	4
2	4	F Cevert	Tyrrell	006	Ford Cosworth	V8	75	1h 49m 01.400s	3	2
3	20	G Follmer	Shadow	DN1	Ford Cosworth	V8	75	1h 49m 31.800s	14	7
4	6	P Revson	McLaren	M23	Ford Cosworth	V8	74		5	3
5	15	J-P Beltoise	BRM	P160E	BRM	V12	74		10	5
6	5	D Hulme	McLaren	M23	Ford Cosworth	V8	74		2	1
7	12	M Beuttler	March	731	Ford Cosworth	V8	74		19	10
8	11	H Pescarolo	March	731	Ford Cosworth	V8	73		18	9
9	14	C Regazzoni	BRM	P160E	BRM	V12	69		8	4
10	17	W Fittipaldi	Brabham	BT42	Ford Cosworth	V8	69		12	6
11	24	N Galli	Iso Marlboro	IR	Ford Cosworth	V8	69		20	10
12	7	J Ickx	Ferrari	312B3	Ferrari	F12	69		6	3
r	18	C Reutemann	Brabham	BT42	Ford Cosworth	V8	66	driveshaft	15	8
r	23	H Ganley	Iso Marlboro	IR	Ford Cosworth	V8	63	out of fuel	21	11
r	2	R Peterson	JPS Lotus	72E	Ford Cosworth	V8	56	gearbox	1	1
r	3	J Stewart	Tyrrell	006	Ford Cosworth	V8	47	brake disc	4	2
r	16	N Lauda	BRM	P160E	BRM	V12	28	tyres	11	6
r	25	G Hill	Shadow	DN1	Ford Cosworth	V8	27	brakes	22	11
r	9	M Hailwood	Surtees	TS14A	Ford Cosworth	V8	25	oil line	9	5
r	19	J Oliver	Shadow	DN1	Ford Cosworth	V8	23	oil loss / engine	13	7
r	21	A de Adamich	Brabham	BT37	Ford Cosworth	V8	17	rear stub axle / accident	17	9
r	10	C Pace	Surtees	TS14A	Ford Cosworth	V8	13	driveshaft	16	8

Winning speed 157.504 km/h, 97.868 mph
Pole Position speed 166.841 km/h, 103.670 mph (R Peterson, 1 min:21.800 sec)
Fastest Lap speed 162.859 km/h, 101.196 mph (R Peterson, 1 min:23.800 sec on lap 13)
Lap Leaders R Peterson 1-56 (56); E Fittipaldi 57-75 (19).

20 May 1973 **BELGIUM: Zolder** (Round 5) (Race 225)

70 laps x 4.220 km, 2.622 miles = 295.400 km, 183.553 miles

Pos	No	Driver	Car	Model	Engine		Laps	Time/Reason for Retirement	Grid Pos	Row
1	5	J Stewart	Tyrrell	006	Ford Cosworth	V8	70	1h 42m 13.430s	6	3
2	6	F Cevert	Tyrrell	006	Ford Cosworth	V8	70	1h 42m 45.270s	4	2
3	1	E Fittipaldi	JPS Lotus	72E	Ford Cosworth	V8	70	1h 44m 16.220s	9	5
4	9	A de Adamich	Brabham	BT37	Ford Cosworth	V8	69		18	9
5	21	N Lauda	BRM	P160E	BRM	V12	69		14	7
6	22	C Amon	Tecno	PA123	Tecno	F12	67		15	8
7	7	D Hulme	McLaren	M23	Ford Cosworth	V8	67		2	1
8	24	C Pace	Surtees	TS14A	Ford Cosworth	V8	66		8	4
9	12	G Hill	Shadow	DN1	Ford Cosworth	V8	65		23	12
10r	19	C Regazzoni	BRM	P160E	BRM	V12	63	accident	12	6
11r	15	M Beuttler	March	731	Ford Cosworth	V8	63	accident	20	10
r	14	J-P Jarier	March	731	Ford Cosworth	V8	60	accident	16	8
r	20	J-P Beltoise	BRM	P160E	BRM	V12	56	engine	5	3
r	11	W Fittipaldi	Brabham	BT42	Ford Cosworth	V8	46	engine / brakes	19	10
r	2	R Peterson	JPS Lotus	72E	Ford Cosworth	V8	42	accident	1	1
r	8	P Revson	McLaren	M23	Ford Cosworth	V8	33	accident	10	5
r	25	H Ganley	Iso Marlboro	IR	Ford Cosworth	V8	16	throttle jammed / accident	21	11
r	10	C Reutemann	Brabham	BT42	Ford Cosworth	V8	14	oil leak / engine	7	4
r	16	G Follmer	Shadow	DN1	Ford Cosworth	V8	13	throttle slides jammed	11	6
r	17	J Oliver	Shadow	DN1	Ford Cosworth	V8	11	accident	22	11
r	3	J Ickx	Ferrari	312B3	Ferrari	F12	6	oil pump	3	2
r	26	N Galli	Iso Marlboro	IR	Ford Cosworth	V8	6	engine	17	9
r	23	M Hailwood	Surtees	TS14A	Ford Cosworth	V8	4	accident	13	7

Winning speed 173.384 km/h, 107.736 mph
Pole Position speed 184.235 km/h, 114.478 mph (R Peterson, 1 min:22.460 sec)
Fastest Lap speed 177.851 km/h, 110.511 mph (F Cevert, 1 min:25.420 sec on lap 28)
Lap Leaders R Peterson 1 (1); F Cevert 2-19 (18); E Fittipaldi 20-24 (5); J Stewart 25-70 (46).

3 Jun 1973 **MONACO: Monte-Carlo** (Round 6) (Race 226)

78 laps x 3.278 km, 2.037 miles = 255.684 km, 158.875 miles

Pos	No	Driver	Car	Model	Engine		Laps	Time/Reason for Retirement	Grid Pos	Row
1	5	J Stewart	Tyrrell	006	Ford Cosworth	V8	78	1h 57m 44.300s	1	1
2	1	E Fittipaldi	JPS Lotus	72E	Ford Cosworth	V8	78	1h 57m 45.600s	5	3
3	2	R Peterson	JPS Lotus	72E	Ford Cosworth	V8	77		2	1
4	6	F Cevert	Tyrrell	006	Ford Cosworth	V8	77		4	2
5	8	P Revson	McLaren	M23	Ford Cosworth	V8	76		15	8
6	7	D Hulme	McLaren	M23	Ford Cosworth	V8	76		3	2
7	9	A de Adamich	Brabham	BT37	Ford Cosworth	V8	75		25	13
8	23	M Hailwood	Surtees	TS14A	Ford Cosworth	V8	75		13	7
9r	27	J Hunt	March	731	Ford Cosworth	V8	73	engine	18	9
10	17	J Oliver	Shadow	DN1	Ford Cosworth	V8	72		22	11
11r	11	W Fittipaldi	Brabham	BT42	Ford Cosworth	V8	71	fuel line	9	5
r	14	J-P Jarier	March	731	Ford Cosworth	V8	67	gearbox	14	7
r	12	G Hill	Shadow	DN1	Ford Cosworth	V8	62	rear suspension	24	12
r	4	A Merzario	Ferrari	312B3	Ferrari	F12	58	oil pressure	16	8
r	10	C Reutemann	Brabham	BT42	Ford Cosworth	V8	46	gearbox	19	10
r	3	J Ickx	Ferrari	312B3	Ferrari	F12	44	driveshaft	7	4
r	25	H Ganley	Iso Marlboro	IR	Ford Cosworth	V8	41	driveshaft	10	5
r	20	J-P Beltoise	BRM	P160E	BRM	V12	39	accident	11	6
r	18	D Purley	March	731	Ford Cosworth	V8	31	fuel line	23	12
r	24	C Pace	Surtees	TS14A	Ford Cosworth	V8	31	driveshaft	17	9
r	26	N Galli	Iso Marlboro	IR	Ford Cosworth	V8	30	driveshaft	21	11
r	21	N Lauda	BRM	P160E	BRM	V12	24	gearbox	6	3
r	22	C Amon	Tecno	PA123	Tecno	F12	22	engine overheating	12	6
r	19	C Regazzoni	BRM	P160E	BRM	V12	15	brake fluid boiling	8	4
r	15	M Beuttler	March	731	Ford Cosworth	V8	3	engine	20	10
ns	16	G Follmer	Shadow	DN1	Ford Cosworth	V8		accident		

Winning speed 130.298 km/h, 80.963 mph
Pole Position speed 134.866 km/h, 83.802 mph (J Stewart, 1 min:27.500 sec)
Fastest Lap speed 133.948 km/h, 83.231 mph (E Fittipaldi, 1 min:28.100 sec on lap 78)
Lap Leaders F Cevert 1 (1); R Peterson 2-7 (6); J Stewart 8-78 (71).

17 Jun 1973 **SWEDEN: Anderstorp** (Round 7) (Race 227)

80 laps x 4.018 km, 2.497 miles = 321.440 km, 199.734 miles

Pos	No	Driver	Car	Model	Engine		Laps	Time/Reason for Retirement	Grid Pos	Row
1	7	D Hulme	McLaren	M23	Ford Cosworth	V8	80	1h 56m 46.049s	6	3
2	2	R Peterson	JPS Lotus	72E	Ford Cosworth	V8	80	1h 56m 50.088s	1	1
3	6	F Cevert	Tyrrell	006	Ford Cosworth	V8	80	1h 57m 00.716s	2	1
4	10	C Reutemann	Brabham	BT42	Ford Cosworth	V8	80	1h 57m 04.117s	5	3
5	5	J Stewart	Tyrrell	006	Ford Cosworth	V8	80	1h 57m 12.047s	3	2
6	3	J Ickx	Ferrari	312B3	Ferrari	F12	79		8	4
7	8	P Revson	McLaren	M23	Ford Cosworth	V8	79		7	4
8	15	M Beuttler	March	731	Ford Cosworth	V8	77		21	11
9	19	C Regazzoni	BRM	P160E	BRM	V12	77		12	6
10	24	C Pace	Surtees	TS14A	Ford Cosworth	V8	77		16	8
11	25	H Ganley	Iso Marlboro	IR	Ford Cosworth	V8	76		11	6
12r	1	E Fittipaldi	JPS Lotus	72E	Ford Cosworth	V8	76	gearbox / brakes	4	2
13	21	N Lauda	BRM	P160E	BRM	V12	75		15	8
14	16	G Follmer	Shadow	DN1	Ford Cosworth	V8	74		19	10
r	20	J-P Beltoise	BRM	P160E	BRM	V12	57	engine	9	5
r	17	J Oliver	Shadow	DN1	Ford Cosworth	V8	50	rear suspension / gearbox	17	9
r	23	M Hailwood	Surtees	TS14A	Ford Cosworth	V8	41	tyres / vibration	10	5
r	14	J-P Jarier	March	731	Ford Cosworth	V8	36	throttle linkage	20	10
r	12	G Hill	Shadow	DN1	Ford Cosworth	V8	16	ignition	18	9
r	11	W Fittipaldi	Brabham	BT42	Ford Cosworth	V8	0	accident	13	7
ns	27	R Wisell	March	731	Ford Cosworth	V8		front suspension on parade lap	14	7
ns	26	T Belsø	Iso Marlboro	IR	Ford Cosworth	V8		car raced by Ganley		

Winning speed 165.169 km/h, 102.631 mph
Pole Position speed 172.590 km/h, 107.243 mph (R Peterson, 1 min:23.810 sec)
Fastest Lap speed 167.910 km/h, 104.335 mph (D Hulme, 1 min:26.146 sec on lap 7)
Lap Leaders R Peterson 1-78 (78); D Hulme 79-80 (2).

54 laps x 5.810 km, 3.610 miles = 313.740 km, 194.949 miles

Pos	No	Driver	Car	Model	Engine		Laps	Time/Reason for Retirement	Grid Pos	Row
1	2	R Peterson	JPS Lotus	72E	Ford Cosworth	V8	54	1h 41m 36.520s	5	2
2	6	F Cevert	Tyrrell	006	Ford Cosworth	V8	54	1h 42m 17.440s	4	2
3	10	C Reutemann	Brabham	BT42	Ford Cosworth	V8	54	1h 42m 23.000s	8	3
4	5	J Stewart	Tyrrell	006	Ford Cosworth	V8	54	1h 42m 23.400s	1	1
5	3	J Ickx	Ferrari	312B3	Ferrari	F12	54	1h 42m 25.420s	12	5
6	27	J Hunt	March	731	Ford Cosworth	V8	54	1h 42m 59.060s	14	6
7	4	A Merzario	Ferrari	312B3	Ferrari	F12	54	1h 43m 05.710s	10	4
8	7	D Hulme	McLaren	M23	Ford Cosworth	V8	54	1h 43m 06.050s	6	3
9	21	N Lauda	BRM	P160E	BRM	V12	54	1h 43m 22.280s	17	7
10	12	G Hill	Shadow	DN1	Ford Cosworth	V8	53		16	7
11	20	J-P Beltoise	BRM	P160E	BRM	V12	53		15	6
12	19	C Regazzoni	BRM	P160E	BRM	V12	53		9	4
13	24	C Pace	Surtees	TS14A	Ford Cosworth	V8	51		18	7
14	25	H Ganley	Iso Marlboro	IR	Ford Cosworth	V8	51		24	10
15	29	R von Opel	Ensign	N173	Ford Cosworth	V8	51		25	10
16r	11	W Fittipaldi	Brabham	BT42	Ford Cosworth	V8	50	fuel metering unit	19	8
r	8	J Scheckter	McLaren	M23	Ford Cosworth	V8	43	accident / front suspension	2	1
r	1	E Fittipaldi	JPS Lotus	72E	Ford Cosworth	V8	41	accident	3	1
r	23	M Hailwood	Surtees	TS14A	Ford Cosworth	V8	30	oil leak	11	5
r	9	A de Adamich	Brabham	BT37	Ford Cosworth	V8	28	driveshaft	13	5
r	15	R Wisell	March	731	Ford Cosworth	V8	20	engine overheating	22	9
r	16	G Follmer	Shadow	DN1	Ford Cosworth	V8	16	fuel vaporisation	20	8
r	26	H Pescarolo	Iso Marlboro	IR	Ford Cosworth	V8	16	engine overheating	23	9
r	14	J-P Jarier	March	731	Ford Cosworth	V8	7	driveshaft	7	3
r	17	J Oliver	Shadow	DN1	Ford Cosworth	V8	0	clutch	21	9

Winning speed 185.264 km/h, 115.118 mph
Pole Position speed 193.005 km/h, 119.928 mph (J Stewart, 1 min:48.370 sec)
Fastest Lap speed 188.449 km/h, 117.097 mph (D Hulme, 1 min:50.990 sec on lap 52)
Lap Leaders J Scheckter 1-41 (41); R Peterson 42-54 (13).

67 laps x 4.711 km, 2.927 miles = 315.607 km, 196.109 miles

Pos	No	Driver	Car	Model	Engine		Laps	Time/Reason for Retirement	Grid Pos	Row
1	8	P Revson	McLaren	M23	Ford Cosworth	V8	67	1h 29m 18.500s	3	1
2	2	R Peterson	JPS Lotus	72E	Ford Cosworth	V8	67	1h 29m 21.300s	1	1
3	7	D Hulme	McLaren	M23	Ford Cosworth	V8	67	1h 29m 21.500s	2	1
4	27	J Hunt	March	731	Ford Cosworth	V8	67	1h 29m 21.900s	11	5
5	6	F Cevert	Tyrrell	006	Ford Cosworth	V8	67	1h 29m 55.100s	7	3
6	10	C Reutemann	Brabham	BT42	Ford Cosworth	V8	67	1h 30m 03.200s	8	3
7	19	C Regazzoni	BRM	P160E	BRM	V12	67	1h 30m 30.200s	10	4
8	3	J Ickx	Ferrari	312B3	Ferrari	F12	67	1h 30m 35.900s	19	8
9	25	H Ganley	Iso Marlboro	IR	Ford Cosworth	V8	66		18	7
10	5	J Stewart	Tyrrell	006	Ford Cosworth	V8	66		4	2
11	15	M Beuttler	March	731	Ford Cosworth	V8	65		24	10
12	21	N Lauda	BRM	P160E	BRM	V12	63		9	4
13	28	R von Opel	Ensign	N173	Ford Cosworth	V8	61		21	9
r	11	W Fittipaldi	Brabham	BT42	Ford Cosworth	V8	44	oil line	13	5
r	1	E Fittipaldi	JPS Lotus	72E	Ford Cosworth	V8	36	cv joint	5	2
r	29	J Watson	Brabham	BT37	Ford Cosworth	V8	36	fuel metering unit	23	9
r	12	G Hill	Shadow	DN1	Ford Cosworth	V8	24	front sub-frame	27	11
r	22	C Amon	Tecno	PA123	Tecno	F12	6	fuel pressure	29	12
r	26	G McRae	Iso Marlboro	IR	Ford Cosworth	V8	0	throttle slides	28	11
r	20	J-P Beltoise	BRM	P160E	BRM	V12	0	accident *	17	7
r	9	A de Adamich	Brabham	BT42	Ford Cosworth	V8	0	accident / injury *	20	8
r	16	G Follmer	Shadow	DN1	Ford Cosworth	V8	0	accident *	25	10
r	23	M Hailwood	Surtees	TS14A	Ford Cosworth	V8	0	accident *	12	5
r	31	J Mass	Surtees	TS14A	Ford Cosworth	V8	0	accident *	14	6
r	24	C Pace	Surtees	TS14A	Ford Cosworth	V8	0	accident *	15	6
r	30	J Scheckter	McLaren	M23	Ford Cosworth	V8	0	accident *	6	3
r	14	R Williamson	March	731	Ford Cosworth	V8	0	accident *	22	9
r	17	J Oliver	Shadow	DN1	Ford Cosworth	V8	0	accident *	26	11
ns	18	D Purley	March	731	Ford Cosworth	V8		accident	16	7

Winning speed 212.034 km/h, 131.752 mph
Pole Position speed 222.254 km/h, 138.102 mph (R Peterson, 1 min:16.300 sec)
Fastest Lap speed 215.750 km/h, 134.061 mph (J Hunt, 1 min:18.600 sec on lap 63)
Lap Leaders R Peterson 1-38 (38); P Revson 39-67 (29).

*Interrupted after 2nd lap, because of an accident. Restarted for original distance. * Retired after first start.*

29 Jul 1973		NETHERLANDS: Zandvoort						(Round 10)		(Race 230)

72 laps x 4.226 km, 2.626 miles = 304.272 km, 189.066 miles

Pos	No	Driver	Car	Model	Engine		Laps	Time/Reason for Retirement	Grid Pos	Row
1	5	J Stewart	Tyrrell	006	Ford Cosworth	V8	72	1h 39m 12.450s	2	1
2	6	F Cevert	Tyrrell	006	Ford Cosworth	V8	72	1h 39m 28.280s	3	1
3	27	J Hunt	March	731	Ford Cosworth	V8	72	1h 40m 15.460s	7	3
4	8	P Revson	McLaren	M23	Ford Cosworth	V8	72	1h 40m 21.580s	6	3
5	20	J-P Beltoise	BRM	P160E	BRM	V12	72	1h 40m 25.820s	9	4
6	26	G van Lennep	Iso Marlboro	IR	Ford Cosworth	V8	70		20	8
7	24	C Pace	Surtees	TS14A	Ford Cosworth	V8	69		8	3
8	19	C Regazzoni	BRM	P160E	BRM	V12	68		12	5
9	25	H Ganley	Iso Marlboro	IR	Ford Cosworth	V8	68		15	6
10	16	G Follmer	Shadow	DN1	Ford Cosworth	V8	67		22	9
11r	2	R Peterson	JPS Lotus	72E	Ford Cosworth	V8	66	gearbox / engine	1	1
nc	12	G Hill	Shadow	DN1	Ford Cosworth	V8	56		17	7
r	23	M Hailwood	Surtees	TS14A	Ford Cosworth	V8	52	electrics	24	10
r	21	N Lauda	BRM	P160E	BRM	V12	51	fuel pump	11	5
r	7	D Hulme	McLaren	M23	Ford Cosworth	V8	31	engine	4	2
r	11	W Fittipaldi	Brabham	BT42	Ford Cosworth	V8	27	accident	13	5
r	22	C Amon	Tecno	PA123	Tecno	F12	22	fuel pressure	19	8
r	10	C Reutemann	Brabham	BT42	Ford Cosworth	V8	9	front tyre burst	5	2
r	18	D Purley	March	731	Ford Cosworth	V8	8	stopped to help Williamson	21	9
r	14	R Williamson	March	731	Ford Cosworth	V8	7	fatal accident	18	7
r	15	M Beuttler	March	731	Ford Cosworth	V8	2	electrics	23	9
r	1	E Fittipaldi	JPS Lotus	72E	Ford Cosworth	V8	2	driver discomfort	16	7
r	17	J Oliver	Shadow	DN1	Ford Cosworth	V8	1	throttle jammed / accident	10	4
ns	28	R von Opel	Ensign	N173	Ford Cosworth	V8		rear suspension	14	6

Winning speed 184.022 km/h, 114.346 mph
Pole Position speed 191.438 km/h, 118.954 mph (R Peterson, 1 min:19.470 sec)
Fastest Lap speed 189.436 km/h, 117.710 mph (R Peterson, 1 min:20.310 sec on lap 42)
Lap Leaders R Peterson 1-63 (63); J Stewart 64-72 (9).

5 Aug 1973		GERMANY: Nürburgring						(Round 11)		(Race 231)

14 laps x 22.835 km, 14.189 miles = 319.690 km, 198.646 miles

Pos	No	Driver	Car	Model	Engine		Laps	Time/Reason for Retirement	Grid Pos	Row
1	5	J Stewart	Tyrrell	006	Ford Cosworth	V8	14	1h 42m 03.000s	1	1
2	6	F Cevert	Tyrrell	006	Ford Cosworth	V8	14	1h 42m 04.600s	3	2
3	30	J Ickx	McLaren	M23	Ford Cosworth	V8	14	1h 42m 44.200s	4	2
4	24	C Pace	Surtees	TS14A	Ford Cosworth	V8	14	1h 42m 56.800s	11	6
5	11	W Fittipaldi	Brabham	BT42	Ford Cosworth	V8	14	1h 43m 22.900s	13	7
6	1	E Fittipaldi	JPS Lotus	72E	Ford Cosworth	V8	14	1h 43m 27.300s	14	7
7	31	J Mass	Surtees	TS14A	Ford Cosworth	V8	14	1h 43m 28.200s	15	8
8	17	J Oliver	Shadow	DN1	Ford Cosworth	V8	14	1h 43m 28.700s	17	9
9	8	P Revson	McLaren	M23	Ford Cosworth	V8	14	1h 44m 14.800s	7	4
10	26	H Pescarolo	Iso Marlboro	IR	Ford Cosworth	V8	14	1h 44m 25.500s	12	6
11	9	R Stommelen	Brabham	BT42	Ford Cosworth	V8	14	1h 45m 30.300s	16	8
12	7	D Hulme	McLaren	M23	Ford Cosworth	V8	14	1h 45m 41.700s	8	4
13	12	G Hill	Shadow	DN1	Ford Cosworth	V8	14	1h 45m 52.000s	20	10
14	23	M Hailwood	Surtees	TS14A	Ford Cosworth	V8	13		18	9
15	18	D Purley	March	731	Ford Cosworth	V8	13		22	11
16	15	M Beuttler	March	731	Ford Cosworth	V8	13		19	10
r	10	C Reutemann	Brabham	BT42	Ford Cosworth	V8	7	engine	6	3
r	19	C Regazzoni	BRM	P160E	BRM	V12	7	engine	10	5
r	16	G Follmer	Shadow	DN1	Ford Cosworth	V8	5	accident	21	11
r	20	J-P Beltoise	BRM	P160E	BRM	V12	4	tyre / gearbox	9	5
r	21	N Lauda	BRM	P160E	BRM	V12	1	accident / injury	5	3
r	2	R Peterson	JPS Lotus	72E	Ford Cosworth	V8	0	distributor	2	1
ns	25	H Ganley	Iso Marlboro	IR	Ford Cosworth	V8		accident		

Winning speed 187.961 km/h, 116.793 mph
Pole Position speed 192.160 km/h, 119.403 mph (J Stewart, 7 min: 7.800 sec)
Fastest Lap speed 190.556 km/h, 118.406 mph (C Pace, 7 min:11.400 sec on lap 13)
Lap Leaders J Stewart 1-14 (14).

19 Aug 1973 AUSTRIA: Österreichring (Round 12) (Race 232)

54 laps x 5.911 km, 3.673 miles = 319.194 km, 198.338 miles

Pos	No	Driver	Car	Model	Engine		Laps	Time/Reason for Retirement	Grid Pos	Row
1	2	R Peterson	JPS Lotus	72E	Ford Cosworth	V8	54	1h 28m 48.780s	2	1
2	5	J Stewart	Tyrrell	006	Ford Cosworth	V8	54	1h 28m 57.790s	7	4
3	24	C Pace	Surtees	TS14A	Ford Cosworth	V8	54	1h 29m 35.420s	8	4
4	10	C Reutemann	Brabham	BT42	Ford Cosworth	V8	54	1h 29m 36.690s	5	3
5	20	J-P Beltoise	BRM	P160E	BRM	V12	54	1h 30m 10.380s	13	7
6	19	C Regazzoni	BRM	P160E	BRM	V12	54	1h 30m 27.180s	14	7
7	4	A Merzario	Ferrari	312B3	Ferrari	F12	53		6	3
8	7	D Hulme	McLaren	M23	Ford Cosworth	V8	53		3	2
9	26	G van Lennep	Iso Marlboro	IR	Ford Cosworth	V8	52		23	12
10	23	M Hailwood	Surtees	TS14A	Ford Cosworth	V8	49		15	8
11r	1	E Fittipaldi	JPS Lotus	72E	Ford Cosworth	V8	48	fuel line	1	1
nc	25	H Ganley	Iso Marlboro	IR	Ford Cosworth	V8	44		21	11
r	18	J-P Jarier	March	731	Ford Cosworth	V8	37	gearbox / engine	12	6
r	28	R von Opel	Ensign	N173	Ford Cosworth	V8	34	fuel pressure	19	10
r	11	W Fittipaldi	Brabham	BT42	Ford Cosworth	V8	31	fuel metering unit	16	8
r	12	G Hill	Shadow	DN1	Ford Cosworth	V8	28	rear suspension radius rod	22	11
r	16	G Follmer	Shadow	DN1	Ford Cosworth	V8	23	crown wheel & pinion	20	10
r	9	R Stommelen	Brabham	BT42	Ford Cosworth	V8	21	front wheel bearing	17	9
r	17	J Oliver	Shadow	DN1	Ford Cosworth	V8	9	fuel leak	18	9
r	6	F Cevert	Tyrrell	006	Ford Cosworth	V8	6	accident / front suspension	10	5
r	27	J Hunt	March	731	Ford Cosworth	V8	3	fuel metering unit	9	5
r	15	M Beuttler	March	731	Ford Cosworth	V8	0	accident / oil radiator	11	6
r	8	P Revson	McLaren	M23	Ford Cosworth	V8	0	clutch	4	2
ns	22	C Amon	Tecno	E731	Tecno	F12		engine shortage		
ns	21	N Lauda	BRM	P160E	BRM	V12		driver unfit (Germany injury)		

Winning speed 215.640 km/h, 133.993 mph
Pole Position speed 224.043 km/h, 139.214 mph (E Fittipaldi, 1 min:34.980 sec)
Fastest Lap speed 218.723 km/h, 135.908 mph (C Pace, 1 min:37.290 sec on lap 46)
Lap Leaders R Peterson 1-16,49-54 (22); E Fittipaldi 17-48 (32).

9 Sep 1973 ITALY: Monza (Round 13) (Race 233)

55 laps x 5.775 km, 3.588 miles = 317.625 km, 197.363 miles

Pos	No	Driver	Car	Model	Engine		Laps	Time/Reason for Retirement	Grid Pos	Row
1	2	R Peterson	JPS Lotus	72E	Ford Cosworth	V8	55	1h 29m 17.000s	1	1
2	1	E Fittipaldi	JPS Lotus	72E	Ford Cosworth	V8	55	1h 29m 17.800s	4	2
3	8	P Revson	McLaren	M23	Ford Cosworth	V8	55	1h 29m 45.800s	2	1
4	5	J Stewart	Tyrrell	006	Ford Cosworth	V8	55	1h 29m 50.200s	6	3
5	6	F Cevert	Tyrrell	006	Ford Cosworth	V8	55	1h 30m 03.200s	11	6
6	10	C Reutemann	Brabham	BT42	Ford Cosworth	V8	55	1h 30m 16.800s	10	5
7	23	M Hailwood	Surtees	TS14A	Ford Cosworth	V8	55	1h 30m 45.700s	8	4
8	3	J Ickx	Ferrari	312B3	Ferrari	F12	54		14	7
9	29	D Purley	March	731	Ford Cosworth	V8	54		24	12
10	16	G Follmer	Shadow	DN1	Ford Cosworth	V8	54		21	11
11	17	J Oliver	Shadow	DN1	Ford Cosworth	V8	54		19	10
12	9	R Stommelen	Brabham	BT42	Ford Cosworth	V8	54		9	5
13	20	J-P Beltoise	BRM	P160E	BRM	V12	54		13	7
14	12	G Hill	Shadow	DN1	Ford Cosworth	V8	54		22	11
15	7	D Hulme	McLaren	M23	Ford Cosworth	V8	53		3	2
nc	25	H Ganley	Iso Marlboro	IR	Ford Cosworth	V8	44		20	10
r	15	M Beuttler	March	731	Ford Cosworth	V8	34	gear lever	12	6
r	21	N Lauda	BRM	P160E	BRM	V12	33	tyre burst / accident	15	8
r	19	C Regazzoni	BRM	P160E	BRM	V12	31	coil	18	9
r	24	C Pace	Surtees	TS14A	Ford Cosworth	V8	17	front tyre burst	5	3
r	26	G van Lennep	Iso Marlboro	IR	Ford Cosworth	V8	14	engine overheating	23	12
r	28	R von Opel	Ensign	N173	Ford Cosworth	V8	10	engine overheating	17	9
r	11	W Fittipaldi	Brabham	BT42	Ford Cosworth	V8	6	brakes	16	8
r	4	A Merzario	Ferrari	312B3	Ferrari	F12	2	accident / front suspension	7	4
ns	27	J Hunt	March	731	Ford Cosworth	V8		accident		

Winning speed 213.450 km/h, 132.631 mph
Pole Position speed 219.304 km/h, 136.269 mph (R Peterson, 1 min:34.800 sec)
Fastest Lap speed 218.153 km/h, 135.554 mph (J Stewart, 1 min:35.300 sec on lap 51)
Lap Leaders R Peterson 1-55 (55).

23 Sep 1973   CANADA: Mosport Park   (Round 14)   (Race 234)
80 laps x 3.957 km, 2.459 miles = 316.590 km, 196.720 miles

Pos	No	Driver	Car	Model	Engine		Laps	Time/Reason for Retirement	Grid Pos	Row
1	8	P Revson	McLaren	M23	Ford Cosworth	V8	80	1h 59m 04.083s	2	1
2	1	E Fittipaldi	JPS Lotus	72E	Ford Cosworth	V8	80	1h 59m 36.817s	5	3
3	17	J Oliver	Shadow	DN1	Ford Cosworth	V8	80	1h 59m 38.588s	14	7
4	20	J-P Beltoise	BRM	P160E	BRM	V12	80	1h 59m 40.597s	16	8
5	5	J Stewart	Tyrrell	006	Ford Cosworth	V8	79		9	5
6	25	H Ganley	Iso Marlboro	IR	Ford Cosworth	V8	79		22	11
7	27	J Hunt	March	731	Ford Cosworth	V8	78		15	8
8	10	C Reutemann	Brabham	BT42	Ford Cosworth	V8	78		4	2
9	23	M Hailwood	Surtees	TS14A	Ford Cosworth	V8	78		12	6
10	29	C Amon	Tyrrell	005	Ford Cosworth	V8	77		11	6
11	11	W Fittipaldi	Brabham	BT42	Ford Cosworth	V8	77		10	5
12	9	R Stommelen	Brabham	BT42	Ford Cosworth	V8	76		18	9
13	7	D Hulme	McLaren	M23	Ford Cosworth	V8	75		7	4
14	26	T Schenken	Iso Marlboro	IR	Ford Cosworth	V8	75		24	12
15	4	A Merzario	Ferrari	312B3	Ferrari	F12	75		20	10
16	12	G Hill	Shadow	DN1	Ford Cosworth	V8	73		17	9
17	16	G Follmer	Shadow	DN1	Ford Cosworth	V8	73		13	7
18r	24	C Pace	Surtees	TS14A	Ford Cosworth	V8	72	wheel / spin	19	10
nc	18	J-P Jarier	March	731	Ford Cosworth	V8	71		23	12
nc	28	R von Opel	Ensign	N173	Ford Cosworth	V8	68		26	13
r	21	N Lauda	BRM	P160E	BRM	V12	62	transmission	8	4
r	0	J Scheckter	McLaren	M23	Ford Cosworth	V8	32	accident	3	2
r	6	F Cevert	Tyrrell	006	Ford Cosworth	V8	32	accident	6	3
r	15	M Beuttler	March	731	Ford Cosworth	V8	20	engine	21	11
r	2	R Peterson	JPS Lotus	72E	Ford Cosworth	V8	16	rear tyre / accident	1	1
r	19	P Gethin	BRM	P160E	BRM	V12	5	oil pump belt	25	13

Winning speed 159.534 km/h, 99.130 mph
Pole Position speed 193.313 km/h, 120.119 mph (R Peterson, 1 min:13.697 sec)
Fastest Lap speed 188.706 km/h, 117.257 mph (E Fittipaldi, 1 min:15.496 sec)
Lap Leaders R Peterson 1-2 (2); N Lauda 3-19 (17); E Fittipaldi 20-32 (13); J Stewart 33 (1); J-P Beltoise 34-39 (6); J Oliver 40-46 (7); P Revson 47-80 (34).

7 Oct 1973   USA: Watkins Glen   (Round 15)   (Race 235)
59 laps x 5.435 km, 3.377 miles = 320.651 km, 199.243 miles

Pos	No	Driver	Car	Model	Engine		Laps	Time/Reason for Retirement	Grid Pos	Row
1	2	R Peterson	JPS Lotus	72E	Ford Cosworth	V8	59	1h 41m 15.779s	1	1
2	27	J Hunt	March	731	Ford Cosworth	V8	59	1h 41m 16.467s	4	2
3	10	C Reutemann	Brabham	BT42	Ford Cosworth	V8	59	1h 41m 38.729s	2	1
4	7	D Hulme	McLaren	M23	Ford Cosworth	V8	59	1h 42m 06.025s	8	4
5	8	P Revson	McLaren	M23	Ford Cosworth	V8	59	1h 42m 36.166s	7	4
6	1	E Fittipaldi	JPS Lotus	72E	Ford Cosworth	V8	59	1h 43m 03.744s	3	2
7	26	J Ickx	Iso Marlboro	IR	Ford Cosworth	V8	58		23	12
8	19	C Regazzoni	BRM	P160E	BRM	V12	58		15	8
9	20	J-P Beltoise	BRM	P160E	BRM	V12	58		14	7
10	15	M Beuttler	March	731	Ford Cosworth	V8	58		26	13
11r	18	J-P Jarier	March	731	Ford Cosworth	V8	57	accident	17	9
12	25	H Ganley	Iso Marlboro	IR	Ford Cosworth	V8	57		19	10
13	12	G Hill	Shadow	DN1	Ford Cosworth	V8	57		18	9
14	16	G Follmer	Shadow	DN1	Ford Cosworth	V8	57		20	10
15	17	J Oliver	Shadow	DN1	Ford Cosworth	V8	55		22	11
16	4	A Merzario	Ferrari	312B3	Ferrari	F12	55		11	6
nc	11	W Fittipaldi	Brabham	BT42	Ford Cosworth	V8	52		25	13
r	0	J Scheckter	McLaren	M23	Ford Cosworth	V8	39	rear suspension	10	5
r	30	J Mass	Surtees	TS14A	Ford Cosworth	V8	35	engine	16	8
r	21	N Lauda	BRM	P160E	BRM	V12	35	fuel pump	21	11
r	23	M Hailwood	Surtees	TS14A	Ford Cosworth	V8	34	rear suspension	6	3
r	24	C Pace	Surtees	TS14A	Ford Cosworth	V8	32	rear suspension	9	5
r	9	J Watson	Brabham	BT42	Ford Cosworth	V8	7	engine	24	12
dq	31	B Redman	Shadow	DN1	Ford Cosworth	V8	5	push start after spin	13	7
r	28	R von Opel	Ensign	N173	Ford Cosworth	V8	0	throttle slides jammed	27	14
ns	5	J Stewart	Tyrrell	006	Ford Cosworth	V8		withdrew after Cevert accident	5	3
ns	29	C Amon	Tyrrell	005	Ford Cosworth	V8		withdrew after Cevert accident	12	6
ns	6	F Cevert	Tyrrell	006	Ford Cosworth	V8		fatal accident		

Winning speed 189.991 km/h, 118.055 mph
Pole Position speed 196.325 km/h, 121.990 mph (R Peterson, 1 min:39.657 sec)
Fastest Lap speed 192.472 km/h, 119.596 mph (J Hunt, 1 min:41.652 sec on lap 58)
Lap Leaders R Peterson 1-59 (59).

Lap Leaders 1973

Pos	Driver	Car-Engine	GPs	laps	km	miles
1	R Peterson	Lotus-Ford Cosworth	11	393	1,846.6	1,147.4
2	J Stewart	Tyrrell-Ford Cosworth	6	214	1,088.1	676.1
3	E Fittipaldi	Lotus-Ford Cosworth	6	120	688.9	428.1
4	F Cevert	Tyrrell-Ford Cosworth	3	76	269.9	167.7
5	P Revson	McLaren-Ford Cosworth	2	63	271.2	168.5
6	J Scheckter	McLaren-Ford Cosworth	2	43	246.4	153.1
7	C Regazzoni	BRM	1	28	93.7	58.2
8	N Lauda	BRM	1	17	67.3	41.8
9	J Oliver	Shadow-Ford Cosworth	1	7	27.7	17.2
10	D Hulme	McLaren-Ford Cosworth	2	6	24.5	15.2
	J-P Beltoise	BRM	1	6	23.7	14.8
			15	973	4,648.0	2,888.1

Driver Points 1973

	Driver	RA	BR	ZA	E	B	MC	S	F	GB	NL	D	A	I	CDN	USA	Total
1	J Stewart	4	6	9	-	9	9	2	3	-	9	9	6	3	2	-	71
2	E Fittipaldi	9	9	4	9	4	6	-	-	-	1	-	6	6	1	-	55
3	R Peterson	-	-	-	-	-	4	6	9	6	-	-	9	9	-	9	52
4	F Cevert	6	-	-	6	6	3	4	6	2	6	6	-	2	-	-	47
5	P Revson	-	-	6	3	-	2	-	-	9	3	-	-	4	9	2	38
6	D Hulme	2	4	2	1	-	1	9	-	4	-	-	-	-	-	3	26
7	C Reutemann	-	-	-	-	-	-	3	4	1	-	-	3	1	-	4	16
8	J Hunt	-	-	-	-	-	-	-	1	3	4	-	-	-	-	6	14
9	J Ickx	3	2	-	-	-	-	1	2	-	-	4	-	-	-	-	12
10	J-P Beltoise	-	-	-	2	-	-	-	-	-	2	-	2	-	3	-	9
11	C Pace	-	-	-	-	-	-	-	-	-	-	3	4	-	-	-	7
12	A Merzario	-	3	3	-	-	-	-	-	-	-	-	-	-	-	-	6
13	G Follmer	-	-	1	4	-	-	-	-	-	-	-	-	-	-	-	5
14	J Oliver	-	-	-	-	-	-	-	-	-	-	-	-	-	4	-	4
15	A de Adamich	-	-	-	-	3	-	-	-	-	-	-	-	-	-	-	3
	W Fittipaldi	1	-	-	-	-	-	-	-	-	-	2	-	-	-	-	3
17	N Lauda	-	-	-	-	2	-	-	-	-	-	-	-	-	-	-	2
	C Regazzoni	-	1	-	-	-	-	-	-	-	-	-	1	-	-	-	2
19	C Amon	-	-	-	-	1	-	-	-	-	-	-	-	-	-	-	1
	G van Lennep	-	-	-	-	-	-	-	-	-	1	-	-	-	-	-	1
	H Ganley	-	-	-	-	-	-	-	-	-	-	-	-	-	1	-	1

9,6,4,3,2 and 1 point awarded to the first six finishers. Best 7 scores from first 8 races, best 6 from remaining 7 races.

Constructor Points 1973

		RA	BR	ZA	E	B	MC	S	F	GB	NL	D	A	I	CDN	USA	Total
1	Lotus-Ford Cosworth	9	9	4	9	(4)	6	6	9	6	-	1	9	9	6	9	92 (4)
2	Tyrrell-Ford Cosworth	6	6	9	6	9	9	(4)	6	2	9	9	6	3	2	-	82 (4)
3	McLaren-Ford Cosworth	2	4	6	3	-	2	9	-	9	3	4	-	4	9	3	58
4	Brabham-Ford Cosworth	1	-	-	-	3	-	3	4	1	-	2	3	1	-	4	22
5	March-Ford Cosworth	-	-	-	-	-	-	-	1	3	4	-	-	-	-	6	14
6	Ferrari	3	3	3	-	-	-	1	2	-	-	-	-	-	-	-	12
	BRM	-	1	-	2	2	-	-	-	-	2	-	2	-	3	-	12
8	Shadow-Ford Cosworth	-	-	1	4	-	-	-	-	-	-	-	-	-	4	-	9
9	Surtees-Ford Cosworth	-	-	-	-	-	-	-	-	-	-	3	4	-	-	-	7
10	Iso-Ford Cosworth	-	-	-	-	-	-	-	-	-	1	-	-	-	1	-	2
11	Tecno	-	-	-	-	1	-	-	-	-	-	-	-	-	-	-	1

9,6,4,3,2 and 1 point awarded to the first six finishers. Points only for highest placed car. Best 7 scores from first 8 races, best 6 from remaining 7 races.

1974

Race Entrants and Results

There was an increase in the number of participating teams, most notably from Hesketh, Parnelli and Penske, to make a new record total of 18. This led to further restrictions in qualifying. Ferrari introduced the 312T transverse gearbox and Marlboro began their long association with McLaren. From this year, entrants generally held the same numbers throughout the season, and are listed in numerical order of the works teams.

LOTUS
John Player Team Lotus: Peterson, Ickx, Schenken
Team Gunston: I Scheckter, Driver

TYRRELL
Elf Team Tyrrell: J Scheckter, Depailler
Alex Blignaut/Embassy Racing SA: Keizan

McLAREN
Marlboro Team Texaco: E Fittipaldi, Hulme
Yardley Team McLaren: Hailwood, Hobbs, Mass
Scuderia Scribante-Lucky Strike: Charlton

FERRARI
Scuderia Ferrari SpA SEFAC: Regazzoni, Lauda

MARCH
March Engineering: Stuck, Wisell, Ganley, Brambilla
Hesketh Racing: Hunt
Dempster International Racing Team: (Wilds)

BRABHAM
Motor Racing Developments: Reutemann, Robarts, von Opel, Pace, Pilette
John Goldie Racing With Hexagon: Watson, (Pace (F))
Scuderia Finotto: Larrousse, (Koinigg, Facetti)
Team Canada F1 Racing: Weitzes
Chequered Flag: (Ashley)
Allied Polymer Group: (Lombardi)

BRM
Team Motul BRM: Beltoise, Pescarolo, Migault, Amon

SHADOW
UOP Shadow Racing Team: Revson, Redman, Roos, Pryce, Jarier

SURTEES
Bang & Olufsen* Team Surtees: Pace, Dolhem, Bell, Mass, (Jabouille), Koinigg* ZA-D GPs only
Memphis International Team Surtees: Quester
AAW Racing Team: Kinnunen

ENSIGN
Team Ensign: (von Opel), Schuppan, Wilds

WILLIAMS (ISO MARLBORO)
Frank Williams Racing Cars: Merzario, (Robarts), Belsø, van Lennep, (Jabouille), Laffite

TROJAN
Trojan-Tauranac Racing: Schenken

HESKETH
Hesketh Racing: Hunt, (I Scheckter)

MAKI
Maki Engineering: (Ganley)

LOLA
Embassy Racing With Graham Hill: Hill, Edwards, Gethin, Stommelen

AMON
Chris Amon Racing: Amon, (Perkins)

LYNCAR
Pinch (Plant) Ltd: (Nicholson)

TOKEN
Token Racing: Pryce, (Purley), Ashley

PARNELLI
Vel's Parnelli Jones Racing: Andretti

PENSKE
Penske Cars: Donohue

---

13 Jan 1974 **ARGENTINA: Buenos Aires No.15** (Round 1) (Race 236)
53 laps x 5.968 km, 3.708 miles = 316.304 km, 196.542 miles

Pos	No	Driver	Car	Model	Engine		Laps	Time/Reason for Retirement	Grid Pos	Row
1	6	D Hulme	McLaren	M23	Ford Cosworth	V8	53	1h 41m 02.010s	10	5
2	12	N Lauda	Ferrari	312B3	Ferrari	F12	53	1h 41m 11.280s	8	4
3	11	C Regazzoni	Ferrari	312B3	Ferrari	F12	53	1h 41m 22.420s	2	1
4	33	M Hailwood	McLaren	M23	Ford Cosworth	V8	53	1h 41m 33.800s	9	5
5	14	J-P Beltoise	BRM	P160E	BRM	V12	53	1h 41m 53.850s	14	7
6	4	P Depailler	Tyrrell	005	Ford Cosworth	V8	53	1h 42m 54.490s	15	8
7r	7	C Reutemann	Brabham	BT44	Ford Cosworth	V8	52	out of fuel	6	3
8r	10	H Ganley	March	741	Ford Cosworth	V8	52	out of fuel	19	10
9	15	H Pescarolo	BRM	P160E	BRM	V12	52		21	11
10	5	E Fittipaldi	McLaren	M23	Ford Cosworth	V8	51		3	2
11	27	G Edwards	Lola	T370	Ford Cosworth	V8	50		25	13
12	28	J Watson	Brabham	BT42	Ford Cosworth	V8	49		20	10
13	1	R Peterson	JPS Lotus	72E	Ford Cosworth	V8	48		1	1
r	26	G Hill	Lola	T370	Ford Cosworth	V8	45	engine overheating	17	9
r	8	R Robarts	Brabham	BT44	Ford Cosworth	V8	35	gearbox	22	11
r	2	J Ickx	JPS Lotus	72E	Ford Cosworth	V8	35	transmission	7	4
r	9	H-J Stuck	March	741	Ford Cosworth	V8	31	transmission	23	12
r	37	F Migault	BRM	P160E	BRM	V12	31	water leak	24	12
r	3	J Scheckter	Tyrrell	006	Ford Cosworth	V8	25	cylinder head gasket	12	6
r	18	C Pace	Surtees	TS16	Ford Cosworth	V8	21	engine	11	6
r	20	A Merzario	Iso Marlboro	FW	Ford Cosworth	V8	19	engine	13	7
r	24	J Hunt	March	731	Ford Cosworth	V8	11	engine overheating	5	3
r	19	J Mass	Surtees	TS16	Ford Cosworth	V8	10	piston	18	9
r	16	P Revson	Shadow	DN3	Ford Cosworth	V8	1	accident	4	2
r	17	J-P Jarier	Shadow	DN1	Ford Cosworth	V8	0	accident	16	8
ns	22	R von Opel	Ensign	N174	Ford Cosworth	V8		handling	26	13

Winning speed 187.841 km/h, 116.719 mph
Pole Position speed 193.941 km/h, 120.509 mph (R Peterson, 1 min:50.780 sec)
Fastest Lap speed 191.657 km/h, 119.090 mph (C Regazzoni, 1 min:52.100 sec on lap 38)
Lap Leaders R Peterson 1-2 (2); C Reutemann 3-51 (49); D Hulme 52-53 (2).

27 Jan 1974   **BRAZIL: Interlagos**   (Round 2)   (Race 237)

32 laps x 7.960 km, 4.946 miles = 254.720 km, 158.276 miles

Pos	No	Driver	Car	Model	Engine		Laps	Time/Reason for Retirement	Grid Pos	Row
1	5	E Fittipaldi	McLaren	M23	Ford Cosworth	V8	32	1h 24m 37.060s	1	1
2	11	C Regazzoni	Ferrari	312B3	Ferrari	F12	32	1h 24m 50.630s	8	4
3	2	J Ickx	JPS Lotus	72E	Ford Cosworth	V8	31		5	3
4	18	C Pace	Surtees	TS16	Ford Cosworth	V8	31		12	6
5	33	M Hailwood	McLaren	M23	Ford Cosworth	V8	31		7	4
6	1	R Peterson	JPS Lotus	72E	Ford Cosworth	V8	31		4	2
7	7	C Reutemann	Brabham	BT44	Ford Cosworth	V8	31		2	1
8	4	P Depailler	Tyrrell	005	Ford Cosworth	V8	31		16	8
9	24	J Hunt	March	731	Ford Cosworth	V8	31		18	9
10	14	J-P Beltoise	BRM	P160E	BRM	V12	31		17	9
11	26	G Hill	Lola	T370	Ford Cosworth	V8	31		21	11
12	6	D Hulme	McLaren	M23	Ford Cosworth	V8	31		11	6
13	3	J Scheckter	Tyrrell	006	Ford Cosworth	V8	31		14	7
14	15	H Pescarolo	BRM	P160E	BRM	V12	30		22	11
15	8	R Robarts	Brabham	BT44	Ford Cosworth	V8	30		24	12
16	37	F Migault	BRM	P160E	BRM	V12	30		23	12
17	19	J Mass	Surtees	TS16	Ford Cosworth	V8	30		10	5
r	28	J Watson	Brabham	BT42	Ford Cosworth	V8	27	clutch	15	8
r	9	H-J Stuck	March	741	Ford Cosworth	V8	24	cv joint	13	7
r	17	J-P Jarier	Shadow	DN1	Ford Cosworth	V8	22	brakes	19	10
r	20	A Merzario	Iso Marlboro	FW	Ford Cosworth	V8	20	throttle slides	9	5
r	16	P Revson	Shadow	DN3	Ford Cosworth	V8	11	engine overheating	6	3
r	10	H Ganley	March	741	Ford Cosworth	V8	9	ignition switch	20	10
r	27	G Edwards	Lola	T370	Ford Cosworth	V8	3	rear wing	25	13
r	12	N Lauda	Ferrari	312B3	Ferrari	F12	3	engine	3	2

Winning speed 180.615 km/h, 112.229 mph
Pole Position speed 187.331 km/h, 116.402 mph (E Fittipaldi, 2 min:32.970 sec)
Fastest Lap speed 183.633 km/h, 114.105 mph (C Regazzoni, 2 min:36.050 sec on lap 26)
Lap Leaders C Reutemann 1-3 (3); R Peterson 4-15 (12); E Fittipaldi 16-32 (17).

Scheduled for 40 laps, but stopped early because of rain.

---

30 Mar 1974   **SOUTH AFRICA: Kyalami**   (Round 3)   (Race 238)

78 laps x 4.104 km, 2.550 miles = 320.112 km, 198.908 miles

Pos	No	Driver	Car	Model	Engine		Laps	Time/Reason for Retirement	Grid Pos	Row
1	7	C Reutemann	Brabham	BT44	Ford Cosworth	V8	78	1h 42m 40.960s	4	2
2	14	J-P Beltoise	BRM	P201	BRM	V12	78	1h 43m 14.900s	11	6
3	33	M Hailwood	McLaren	M23	Ford Cosworth	V8	78	1h 43m 23.120s	12	6
4	4	P Depailler	Tyrrell	005	Ford Cosworth	V8	78	1h 43m 25.150s	15	8
5	9	H-J Stuck	March	741	Ford Cosworth	V8	78	1h 43m 27.190s	7	4
6	20	A Merzario	Iso Marlboro	FW	Ford Cosworth	V8	78	1h 43m 37.000s	3	2
7	5	E Fittipaldi	McLaren	M23	Ford Cosworth	V8	78	1h 43m 49.350s	5	3
8	3	J Scheckter	Tyrrell	006	Ford Cosworth	V8	78	1h 43m 51.500s	8	4
9	6	D Hulme	McLaren	M23	Ford Cosworth	V8	77		9	5
10	10	V Brambilla	March	741	Ford Cosworth	V8	77		19	10
11	18	C Pace	Surtees	TS16	Ford Cosworth	V8	77		2	1
12	26	G Hill	Lola	T370	Ford Cosworth	V8	77		18	9
13	29	I Scheckter	Lotus	72E	Ford Cosworth	V8	76		22	11
14	32	E Keizan	Tyrrell	004	Ford Cosworth	V8	76		24	12
15	37	F Migault	BRM	P160E	BRM	V12	75		25	13
16r	12	N Lauda	Ferrari	312B3	Ferrari	F12	74	ignition	1	1
17	8	R Robarts	Brabham	BT44	Ford Cosworth	V8	74		23	12
18	15	H Pescarolo	BRM	P160E	BRM	V12	72		21	11
19	23	D Charlton	McLaren	M23	Ford Cosworth	V8	71		20	10
r	11	C Regazzoni	Ferrari	312B3	Ferrari	F12	65	oil pressure	6	3
r	28	J Watson	Brabham	BT42	Ford Cosworth	V8	56	fuel union	13	7
r	2	J Ickx	JPS Lotus	76	Ford Cosworth	V8	31	brakes	10	5
r	24	J Hunt	Hesketh	308	Ford Cosworth	V8	13	cv joint	14	7
r	19	J Mass	Surtees	TS16	Ford Cosworth	V8	11	accident / withdrew	17	9
r	30	P Driver	Lotus	72E	Ford Cosworth	V8	6	clutch	26	13
r	1	R Peterson	JPS Lotus	76	Ford Cosworth	V8	2	accident	16	8
r	21	T Belsø	Iso Marlboro	FW	Ford Cosworth	V8	0	clutch	27	14

Winning speed 187.049 km/h, 116.227 mph
Pole Position speed 192.928 km/h, 119.880 mph (N Lauda, 1 min:16.580 sec)
Fastest Lap speed 189.028 km/h, 117.456 mph (C Reutemann, 1 min:18.160 sec on lap 58)
Lap Leaders N Lauda 1-8 (8); C Reutemann 9-78 (70).

SPAIN: Jarama   (Round 4)   (Race 239)

84 laps x 3.404 km, 2.115 miles = 285.936 km, 177.672 miles

Pos	No	Driver	Car	Model	Engine		Laps	Time/Reason for Retirement	Grid Pos	Row
1	12	N Lauda	Ferrari	312B3	Ferrari	F12	84	2h 00m 29.560s	1	1
2	11	C Regazzoni	Ferrari	312B3	Ferrari	F12	84	2h 01m 05.170s	3	2
3	5	E Fittipaldi	McLaren	M23	Ford Cosworth	V8	83		4	2
4	9	H-J Stuck	March	741	Ford Cosworth	V8	82		13	7
5	3	J Scheckter	Tyrrell	007	Ford Cosworth	V8	82		9	5
6	56	D Hulme	McLaren	M23	Ford Cosworth	V8	82		8	4
7	16	B Redman	Shadow	DN3	Ford Cosworth	V8	81		21	11
8	4	P Depailler	Tyrrell	006	Ford Cosworth	V8	81		16	8
9	33	M Hailwood	McLaren	M23	Ford Cosworth	V8	81		17	9
10	24	J Hunt	Hesketh	308	Ford Cosworth	V8	81		10	5
11	28	J Watson	Brabham	BT42	Ford Cosworth	V8	80		15	8
12	15	H Pescarolo	BRM	P160E	BRM	V12	80		20	10
13	18	C Pace	Surtees	TS16	Ford Cosworth	V8	78		14	7
14r	23	T Schenken	Trojan	T103	Ford Cosworth	V8	76	spin	25	13
nc	17	J-P Jarier	Shadow	DN3	Ford Cosworth	V8	73		12	6
r	26	G Hill	Lola	T370	Ford Cosworth	V8	43	engine	19	10
r	20	A Merzario	Iso Marlboro	FW	Ford Cosworth	V8	37	accident	7	4
r	19	J Mass	Surtees	TS16	Ford Cosworth	V8	35	gearbox	18	9
r	37	F Migault	BRM	P160E	BRM	V12	27	engine	22	11
r	2	J Ickx	JPS Lotus	76	Ford Cosworth	V8	26	brake fluid leak	5	3
r	1	R Peterson	JPS Lotus	76	Ford Cosworth	V8	23	engine overheating	2	1
r	30	C Amon	Amon	AF101	Ford Cosworth	V8	22	brake shaft	23	12
r	8	R von Opel	Brabham	BT44	Ford Cosworth	V8	14	oil leak	24	12
r	7	C Reutemann	Brabham	BT44	Ford Cosworth	V8	12	accident	6	3
r	14	J-P Beltoise	BRM	P201	BRM	V12	2	engine	11	6
ns	10	V Brambilla	March	741	Ford Cosworth	V8		accident		
nq	27	G Edwards	Lola	T370	Ford Cosworth	V8				
nq	21	T Belsø	Iso Marlboro	FW	Ford Cosworth	V8				

Winning speed 142.383 km/h, 88.473 mph
Pole Position speed 156.226 km/h, 97.075 mph (N Lauda, 1 min:18.440 sec)
Fastest Lap speed 151.607 km/h, 94.204 mph (N Lauda, 1 min:20.830 sec on lap 47)
Lap Leaders R Peterson 1-20 (20); N Lauda 21-22,25-84 (62); J Ickx 23-24 (2).

Scheduled for 90 laps, but stopped at 2 hours.

---

12 May 1974   **BELGIUM: Nivelles-Baulers**   (Round 5)   (Race 240)

85 laps x 3.724 km, 2.314 miles = 316.540 km, 196.689 miles

Pos	No	Driver	Car	Model	Engine		Laps	Time/Reason for Retirement	Grid Pos	Row
1	5	E Fittipaldi	McLaren	M23	Ford Cosworth	V8	85	1h 44m 20.570s	4	2
2	12	N Lauda	Ferrari	312B3	Ferrari	F12	85	1h 44m 20.920s	3	2
3	3	J Scheckter	Tyrrell	007	Ford Cosworth	V8	85	1h 45m 06.180s	2	1
4	11	C Regazzoni	Ferrari	312B3	Ferrari	F12	85	1h 45m 12.590s	1	1
5	14	J-P Beltoise	BRM	P201	BRM	V12	85	1h 45m 28.620s	7	4
6	6	D Hulme	McLaren	M23	Ford Cosworth	V8	85	1h 45m 31.110s	12	6
7	33	M Hailwood	McLaren	M23	Ford Cosworth	V8	84		13	7
8	26	G Hill	Lola	T370	Ford Cosworth	V8	83		29	15
9	10	V Brambilla	March	741	Ford Cosworth	V8	83		31	16
10	41	T Schenken	Trojan	T103	Ford Cosworth	V8	83		23	12
11	28	J Watson	Brabham	BT42	Ford Cosworth	V8	83		19	10
12r	27	G Edwards	Lola	T370	Ford Cosworth	V8	82	fuel leak	21	11
13	17	J-P Jarier	Shadow	DN3	Ford Cosworth	V8	82		17	9
14	21	G van Lennep	Iso Marlboro	FW	Ford Cosworth	V8	82		30	15
15	22	V Schuppan	Ensign	N174	Ford Cosworth	V8	82		14	7
16	37	F Migault	BRM	P160E	BRM	V12	82		25	13
17	34	T Pilette	Brabham	BT42	Ford Cosworth	V8	81		27	14
18r	16	B Redman	Shadow	DN3	Ford Cosworth	V8	80	engine	18	9
r	2	J Ickx	JPS Lotus	76	Ford Cosworth	V8	72	brakes	16	8
r	42	T Pryce	Token	RJ02	Ford Cosworth	V8	66	fuel pressure / accident	20	10
r	7	C Reutemann	Brabham	BT44	Ford Cosworth	V8	62	fuel line	24	12
r	1	R Peterson	JPS Lotus	76	Ford Cosworth	V8	56	fuel tank leak	5	3
r	4	P Depailler	Tyrrell	007	Ford Cosworth	V8	53	brake strap	11	6
r	19	J Mass	Surtees	TS16	Ford Cosworth	V8	53	rear suspension	26	13
r	43	G Larrousse	Brabham	BT42	Ford Cosworth	V8	53	tyres	28	14
r	18	C Pace	Surtees	TS16	Ford Cosworth	V8	50	tyres / vibration	8	4
r	8	R von Opel	Brabham	BT44	Ford Cosworth	V8	49	oil pressure	22	11
r	24	J Hunt	Hesketh	308	Ford Cosworth	V8	45	rear suspension	9	5
r	20	A Merzario	Iso Marlboro	FW	Ford Cosworth	V8	29	driveshaft	6	3
r	15	H Pescarolo	BRM	P160E	BRM	V12	12	accident	15	8
r	9	H-J Stuck	March	741	Ford Cosworth	V8	6	clutch	10	5
nq	44	L Kinnunen	Surtees	TS16	Ford Cosworth	V8				

Winning speed 182.019 km/h, 113.101 mph
Pole Position speed 192.014 km/h, 119.312 mph (C Regazzoni, 1 min: 9.820 sec)
Fastest Lap speed 188.002 km/h, 116.819 mph (D Hulme, 1 min:11.310 sec on lap 37)
Lap Leaders C Regazzoni 1-38 (38); E Fittipaldi 39-85 (47).

26 May 1974   **MONACO: Monte-Carlo**   (Round 6)   (Race 241)

78 laps x 3.278 km, 2.037 miles = 255.684 km, 158.875 miles

Pos	No	Driver	Car	Model	Engine		Laps	Time/Reason for Retirement	Grid Pos	Row
1	1	R Peterson	JPS Lotus	72E	Ford Cosworth	V8	78	1h 58m 03.700s	3	2
2	3	J Scheckter	Tyrrell	007	Ford Cosworth	V8	78	1h 58m 32.500s	5	3
3	17	J-P Jarier	Shadow	DN3	Ford Cosworth	V8	78	1h 58m 52.600s	6	3
4	11	C Regazzoni	Ferrari	312B3	Ferrari	F12	78	1h 59m 06.800s	2	1
5	5	E Fittipaldi	McLaren	M23	Ford Cosworth	V8	77		13	7
6	28	J Watson	Brabham	BT42	Ford Cosworth	V8	77		23	12
7	26	G Hill	Lola	T370	Ford Cosworth	V8	76		21	11
8	27	G Edwards	Lola	T370	Ford Cosworth	V8	76		26	13
9	4	P Depailler	Tyrrell	006	Ford Cosworth	V8	75		4	2
r	15	H Pescarolo	BRM	P160E	BRM	V12	62	gearbox	27	14
r	2	J Ickx	JPS Lotus	72E	Ford Cosworth	V8	34	gearbox	19	10
r	12	N Lauda	Ferrari	312B3	Ferrari	F12	32	ignition	1	1
r	24	J Hunt	Hesketh	308	Ford Cosworth	V8	28	driveshaft	7	4
r	33	M Hailwood	McLaren	M23	Ford Cosworth	V8	11	accident	10	5
r	7	C Reutemann	Brabham	BT44	Ford Cosworth	V8	5	accident	8	4
r	37	F Migault	BRM	P160E	BRM	V12	5	brakes / accident	22	11
r	22	V Schuppan	Ensign	N174	Ford Cosworth	V8	4	accident	25	13
r	9	H-J Stuck	March	741	Ford Cosworth	V8	3	accident	9	5
r	10	V Brambilla	March	741	Ford Cosworth	V8	1	accident	15	8
r	14	J-P Beltoise	BRM	P201	BRM	V12	1	accident	11	6
r	23	T Schenken	Trojan	T103	Ford Cosworth	V8	0	accident	24	12
r	18	C Pace	Surtees	TS16	Ford Cosworth	V8	0	accident	18	9
r	16	B Redman	Shadow	DN3	Ford Cosworth	V8	0	accident	16	8
r	20	A Merzario	Iso Marlboro	FW	Ford Cosworth	V8	0	accident	14	7
r	6	D Hulme	McLaren	M23	Ford Cosworth	V8	0	accident	12	6
ns	19	J Mass	Surtees	TS16	Ford Cosworth	V8		shortage of parts	17	9
ns	30	C Amon	Amon	AF101	Ford Cosworth	V8		hub	20	10
nq	8	R von Opel	Brabham	BT44	Ford Cosworth	V8				

Winning speed 129.941 km/h, 80.742 mph
Pole Position speed 136.742 km/h, 84.967 mph (N Lauda, 1 min:26.300 sec)
Fastest Lap speed 134.253 km/h, 83.421 mph (R Peterson, 1 min:27.900 sec on lap 57)
Lap Leaders C Regazzoni 1-20 (20); N Lauda 21-32 (12); R Peterson 33-78 (46).

9 Jun 1974   **SWEDEN: Anderstorp**   (Round 7)   (Race 242)

80 laps x 4.018 km, 2.497 miles = 321.440 km, 199.734 miles

Pos	No	Driver	Car	Model	Engine		Laps	Time/Reason for Retirement	Grid Pos	Row
1	3	J Scheckter	Tyrrell	007	Ford Cosworth	V8	80	1h 58m 31.391s	2	1
2	4	P Depailler	Tyrrell	007	Ford Cosworth	V8	80	1h 58m 31.771s	1	1
3	24	J Hunt	Hesketh	308	Ford Cosworth	V8	80	1h 58m 34.716s	6	3
4	5	E Fittipaldi	McLaren	M23	Ford Cosworth	V8	80	1h 59m 24.898s	9	5
5	17	J-P Jarier	Shadow	DN3	Ford Cosworth	V8	80	1h 59m 47.794s	8	4
6	26	G Hill	Lola	T370	Ford Cosworth	V8	79		15	8
7	27	G Edwards	Lola	T370	Ford Cosworth	V8	79		18	9
8	21	T Belsø	Iso Marlboro	FW	Ford Cosworth	V8	79		21	11
9	8	R von Opel	Brabham	BT44	Ford Cosworth	V8	79		20	10
10r	10	V Brambilla	March	741	Ford Cosworth	V8	79	engine	17	9
11	28	J Watson	Brabham	BT42	Ford Cosworth	V8	77		14	7
dq	22	V Schuppan	Ensign	N174	Ford Cosworth	V8	77	started unofficially	26	13
r	12	N Lauda	Ferrari	312B3	Ferrari	F12	70	transmission	3	2
r	9	R Wisell	March	741	Ford Cosworth	V8	59	rear suspension	16	8
r	6	D Hulme	McLaren	M23	Ford Cosworth	V8	56	rear suspension	12	6
r	19	J Mass	Surtees	TS16	Ford Cosworth	V8	53	front suspension	22	11
r	7	C Reutemann	Brabham	BT44	Ford Cosworth	V8	30	oil leak	10	5
r	2	J Ickx	JPS Lotus	72E	Ford Cosworth	V8	27	oil pressure	7	4
r	11	C Regazzoni	Ferrari	312B3	Ferrari	F12	24	gearbox	4	2
r	18	C Pace	Surtees	TS16	Ford Cosworth	V8	15	handling	24	12
r	23	L Kinnunen	Surtees	TS16	Ford Cosworth	V8	8	electrics	25	13
r	1	R Peterson	JPS Lotus	72E	Ford Cosworth	V8	8	driveshaft	5	3
r	33	M Hailwood	McLaren	M23	Ford Cosworth	V8	5	fuel line	11	6
r	14	J-P Beltoise	BRM	P201	BRM	V12	3	engine	13	7
r	16	B Roos	Shadow	DN3	Ford Cosworth	V8	2	gearbox	23	12
r	15	H Pescarolo	BRM	P201	BRM	V12	0	fire	19	10
ns	20	R Robarts	Iso Marlboro	FW	Ford Cosworth	V8		car raced by Belsø		
ns	20	A Merzario	Iso Marlboro	FW	Ford Cosworth	V8		driver ill		

Winning speed 162.723 km/h, 101.111 mph
Pole Position speed 170.660 km/h, 106.043 mph (P Depailler, 1 min:24.758 sec)
Fastest Lap speed 165.763 km/h, 103.000 mph (P Depailler, 1 min:27.262 sec on lap 72)
Lap Leaders J Scheckter 1-80 (80).

75 laps x 4.226 km, 2.626 miles = 316.950 km, 196.944 miles

Pos	No	Driver	Car	Model	Engine		Laps	Time/Reason for Retirement	Grid Pos	Row
1	12	N Lauda	Ferrari	312B3	Ferrari	F12	75	1h 43m 00.350s	1	1
2	11	C Regazzoni	Ferrari	312B3	Ferrari	F12	75	1h 43m 08.600s	2	1
3	5	E Fittipaldi	McLaren	M23	Ford Cosworth	V8	75	1h 43m 30.620s	3	2
4	33	M Hailwood	McLaren	M23	Ford Cosworth	V8	75	1h 43m 31.640s	4	2
5	3	J Scheckter	Tyrrell	007	Ford Cosworth	V8	75	1h 43m 34.630s	5	3
6	4	P Depailler	Tyrrell	007	Ford Cosworth	V8	75	1h 43m 51.870s	8	4
7	28	J Watson	Brabham	BT42	Ford Cosworth	V8	75	1h 44m 14.300s	13	7
8	1	R Peterson	JPS Lotus	72E	Ford Cosworth	V8	73		10	5
9	8	R von Opel	Brabham	BT44	Ford Cosworth	V8	73		23	12
10	10	V Brambilla	March	741	Ford Cosworth	V8	72		15	8
11	2	J Ickx	JPS Lotus	72E	Ford Cosworth	V8	71		18	9
12	7	C Reutemann	Brabham	BT44	Ford Cosworth	V8	71		12	6
dq	22	V Schuppan	Ensign	N174	Ford Cosworth	V8	69	tyre change outside pits	17	9
r	6	D Hulme	McLaren	M23	Ford Cosworth	V8	65	ignition	9	5
r	37	F Migault	BRM	P201	BRM	V12	60	gear linkage	25	13
r	20	A Merzario	Iso Marlboro	FW	Ford Cosworth	V8	54	gearbox	21	11
r	27	G Edwards	Lola	T370	Ford Cosworth	V8	36	fuel system	14	7
r	17	J-P Jarier	Shadow	DN3	Ford Cosworth	V8	27	clutch	7	4
r	14	J-P Beltoise	BRM	P201	BRM	V12	18	gearbox	16	8
r	26	G Hill	Lola	T370	Ford Cosworth	V8	16	clutch	19	10
r	15	H Pescarolo	BRM	P160E	BRM	V12	15	handling	24	12
r	19	J Mass	Surtees	TS16	Ford Cosworth	V8	8	cv joint	20	10
r	24	J Hunt	Hesketh	308	Ford Cosworth	V8	2	accident / rear suspension	6	3
r	9	H-J Stuck	March	741	Ford Cosworth	V8	0	accident	22	11
r	16	T Pryce	Shadow	DN3	Ford Cosworth	V8	0	accident	11	6
nq	23	T Schenken	Trojan	T103	Ford Cosworth	V8				
nq	21	G van Lennep	Iso Marlboro	FW	Ford Cosworth	V8				

Winning speed 184.621 km/h, 114.718 mph
Pole Position speed 194.274 km/h, 120.716 mph (N Lauda, 1 min:18.310 sec)
Fastest Lap speed 186.807 km/h, 116.077 mph (R Peterson, 1 min:21.440 sec on lap 63)
Lap Leaders N Lauda 1-75 (75).

80 laps x 3.289 km, 2.044 miles = 263.120 km, 163.495 miles

Pos	No	Driver	Car	Model	Engine		Laps	Time/Reason for Retirement	Grid Pos	Row
1	1	R Peterson	JPS Lotus	72E	Ford Cosworth	V8	80	1h 21m 55.020s	2	1
2	12	N Lauda	Ferrari	312B3	Ferrari	F12	80	1h 22m 15.380s	1	1
3	11	C Regazzoni	Ferrari	312B3	Ferrari	F12	80	1h 22m 22.860s	4	2
4	3	J Scheckter	Tyrrell	007	Ford Cosworth	V8	80	1h 22m 23.130s	7	4
5	2	J Ickx	JPS Lotus	72E	Ford Cosworth	V8	80	1h 22m 32.560s	13	7
6	6	D Hulme	McLaren	M23	Ford Cosworth	V8	80	1h 22m 33.160s	11	6
7	33	M Hailwood	McLaren	M23	Ford Cosworth	V8	79		6	3
8	4	P Depailler	Tyrrell	006	Ford Cosworth	V8	79		9	5
9	20	A Merzario	Iso Marlboro	FW	Ford Cosworth	V8	79		15	8
10	14	J-P Beltoise	BRM	P201	BRM	V12	79		17	9
11	10	V Brambilla	March	741	Ford Cosworth	V8	79		16	8
12	17	J-P Jarier	Shadow	DN3	Ford Cosworth	V8	79		12	6
13	26	G Hill	Lola	T370	Ford Cosworth	V8	78		21	11
14	37	F Migault	BRM	P160E	BRM	V12	78		22	11
15	27	G Edwards	Lola	T370	Ford Cosworth	V8	77		20	10
16	28	J Watson	Brabham	BT42	Ford Cosworth	V8	76		14	7
r	5	E Fittipaldi	McLaren	M23	Ford Cosworth	V8	27	engine	5	3
r	7	C Reutemann	Brabham	BT44	Ford Cosworth	V8	24	handling	8	4
r	19	J Mass	Surtees	TS16	Ford Cosworth	V8	4	clutch	18	9
r	16	T Pryce	Shadow	DN3	Ford Cosworth	V8	1	accident	3	2
r	15	H Pescarolo	BRM	P201	BRM	V12	1	clutch	19	10
r	24	J Hunt	Hesketh	308	Ford Cosworth	V8	0	accident	10	5
nq	22	V Schuppan	Ensign	N174	Ford Cosworth	V8				
nq	34	C Pace	Brabham	BT42	Ford Cosworth	V8				
nq	21	J-P Jabouille	Iso Marlboro	FW	Ford Cosworth	V8				
nq	9	H-J Stuck	March	741	Ford Cosworth	V8				
nq	18	J Dolhem	Surtees	TS16	Ford Cosworth	V8				
nq	8	R von Opel	Brabham	BT44	Ford Cosworth	V8				
nq	23	L Kinnunen	Surtees	TS16	Ford Cosworth	V8				
nq	43	G Larrousse	Brabham	BT42	Ford Cosworth	V8				

Winning speed 192.722 km/h, 119.752 mph
Pole Position speed 201.402 km/h, 125.145 mph (N Lauda, 0 min:58.790 sec)
Fastest Lap speed 197.340 km/h, 122.621 mph (J Scheckter, 1 min: 0.000 sec on lap 10)
Lap Leaders N Lauda 1-16 (16); R Peterson 17-80 (64).

laps x 4.265 km, 2.650 miles = 319.857 km, 198.750 miles

Pos	No	Driver	Car	Model	Engine		Laps	Time/Reason for Retirement	Grid Pos	Row
1	3	J Scheckter	Tyrrell	007	Ford Cosworth	V8	75	1h 43m 02.200s	3	2
2	5	E Fittipaldi	McLaren	M23	Ford Cosworth	V8	75	1h 43m 17.500s	8	4
3	2	J Ickx	JPS Lotus	72E	Ford Cosworth	V8	75	1h 44m 03.700s	12	6
4	11	C Regazzoni	Ferrari	312B3	Ferrari	F12	75	1h 44m 09.400s	7	4
5	12	N Lauda	Ferrari	312B3	Ferrari	F12	74		1	1
6	7	C Reutemann	Brabham	BT44	Ford Cosworth	V8	74		4	2
7	6	D Hulme	McLaren	M23	Ford Cosworth	V8	74		19	10
8	16	T Pryce	Shadow	DN3	Ford Cosworth	V8	74		5	3
9	8	C Pace	Brabham	BT44	Ford Cosworth	V8	74		20	10
10	1	R Peterson	JPS Lotus	72E	Ford Cosworth	V8	73		2	1
11	28	J Watson	Brabham	BT42	Ford Cosworth	V8	73		13	7
12	14	J-P Beltoise	BRM	P201	BRM	V12	72		23	12
13	26	G Hill	Lola	T370	Ford Cosworth	V8	69		22	11
14	19	J Mass	Surtees	TS16	Ford Cosworth	V8	68		17	9
r	15	H Pescarolo	BRM	P201	BRM	V12	64	engine	24	12
nc	37	F Migault	BRM	P160E	BRM	V12	62		14	7
r	33	M Hailwood	McLaren	M23	Ford Cosworth	V8	57	spin	11	6
r	17	J-P Jarier	Shadow	DN3	Ford Cosworth	V8	45	rear suspension	16	8
r	9	H-J Stuck	March	741	Ford Cosworth	V8	36	accident	9	5
r	4	P Depailler	Tyrrell	007	Ford Cosworth	V8	35	engine	10	5
r	20	A Merzario	Iso Marlboro	FW	Ford Cosworth	V8	25	engine	15	8
r	10	V Brambilla	March	741	Ford Cosworth	V8	17	fuel pressure	18	9
r	23	T Schenken	Trojan	T103	Ford Cosworth	V8	6	rear suspension	25	13
r	24	J Hunt	Hesketh	308	Ford Cosworth	V8	2	rear suspension / spin	6	3
r	27	P Gethin	Lola	T370	Ford Cosworth	V8	0	driver discomfort	21	11
nq	42	D Purley	Token	RJ02	Ford Cosworth	V8				
nq	39	D Bell	Surtees	TS16	Ford Cosworth	V8				
nq	21	T Belsø	Iso Marlboro	FW	Ford Cosworth	V8				
nq	208	L Lombardi	Brabham	BT42	Ford Cosworth	V8				
nq	22	V Schuppan	Ensign	N174	Ford Cosworth	V8				
nq	29	J Nicholson	Lyncar	006	Ford Cosworth	V8				
nq	25	H Ganley	Maki	F101	Ford Cosworth	V8				
nq	35	M Wilds	March	731	Ford Cosworth	V8				
nq	43	L Kinnunen	Surtees	TS16	Ford Cosworth	V8				
nq	27	G Edwards	Lola	T370	Ford Cosworth	V8		driver unfit (earlier accident)		

Winning speed 186.258 km/h, 115.735 mph
Pole Position speed 192.637 km/h, 119.699 mph (N Lauda, 1 min:19.700 sec)
Fastest Lap speed 189.311 km/h, 117.633 mph (N Lauda, 1 min:21.100 sec on lap 25)
Lap Leaders N Lauda 1-69 (69); J Scheckter 70-75 (6).

N Lauda completed 73 laps and was initially classified 9th, but awarded an extra lap and 5th place on appeal because his exit from a pit stop was blocked.

14 laps x 22.835 km, 14.189 miles = 319.690 km, 198.646 miles

Pos	No	Driver	Car	Model	Engine		Laps	Time/Reason for Retirement	Grid Pos	Row
1	11	C Regazzoni	Ferrari	312B3	Ferrari	F12	14	1h 41m 35.000s	2	1
2	3	J Scheckter	Tyrrell	007	Ford Cosworth	V8	14	1h 42m 25.700s	4	2
3	7	C Reutemann	Brabham	BT44	Ford Cosworth	V8	14	1h 42m 58.300s	6	3
4	1	R Peterson	JPS Lotus	76	Ford Cosworth	V8	14	1h 42m 59.200s	8	4
5	2	J Ickx	JPS Lotus	72E	Ford Cosworth	V8	14	1h 43m 00.000s	9	5
6	16	T Pryce	Shadow	DN3	Ford Cosworth	V8	14	1h 43m 53.100s	11	6
7	9	H-J Stuck	March	741	Ford Cosworth	V8	14	1h 44m 33.700s	20	10
8	17	J-P Jarier	Shadow	DN3	Ford Cosworth	V8	14	1h 45m 00.900s	18	9
9	26	G Hill	Lola	T370	Ford Cosworth	V8	14	1h 45m 01.400s	19	10
10	15	H Pescarolo	BRM	P201	BRM	V12	14	1h 45m 52.700s	24	12
11	18	D Bell	Surtees	TS16	Ford Cosworth	V8	14	1h 46m 52.700s	25	13
12	8	C Pace	Brabham	BT44	Ford Cosworth	V8	14	1h 48m 01.300s	17	9
13	10	V Brambilla	March	741	Ford Cosworth	V8	14	1h 50m 18.100s	23	12
14	32	I Ashley	Token	RJ02	Ford Cosworth	V8	13		26	13
15r	33	M Hailwood	McLaren	M23	Ford Cosworth	V8	12	accident / injury	12	6
r	24	J Hunt	Hesketh	308	Ford Cosworth	V8	11	gearbox	13	7
r	19	J Mass	Surtees	TS16	Ford Cosworth	V8	10	engine	10	5
r	4	P Depailler	Tyrrell	007	Ford Cosworth	V8	5	accident / rear tyre	5	3
r	20	A Merzario	Iso Marlboro	FW	Ford Cosworth	V8	5	throttle linkage	16	8
r	14	J-P Beltoise	BRM	P201	BRM	V12	4	drive belt	15	8
r	22	V Schuppan	Ensign	N174	Ford Cosworth	V8	4	gearbox	22	11
r	5	E Fittipaldi	McLaren	M23	Ford Cosworth	V8	2	accident / rear suspension	3	2
r	21	J Laffite	Iso Marlboro	FW	Ford Cosworth	V8	2	accident / rear suspension	21	11
r/dq	6	D Hulme	McLaren	M23	Ford Cosworth	V8	2	accident / took over spare car	7	4
r	28	J Watson	Brabham	BT44	Ford Cosworth	V8	1	accident / front suspension	14	7
r	12	N Lauda	Ferrari	312B3	Ferrari	F12	0	accident	1	1
nq	37	F Migault	BRM	P160E	BRM	V12				
nq	23	T Schenken	Trojan	T103	Ford Cosworth	V8				
nq	27	G Edwards	Lola	T370	Ford Cosworth	V8				
nq	30	L Perkins	Amon	AF101	Ford Cosworth	V8				
nq	30	C Amon	Amon	AF101	Ford Cosworth	V8		driver ill		
nq	25	H Ganley	Maki	F101	Ford Cosworth	V8		accident / injury		

Winning speed 188.824 km/h, 117.330 mph
Pole Position speed 195.356 km/h, 121.389 mph (N Lauda, 7 min: 0.800 sec)
Fastest Lap speed 190.689 km/h, 118.489 mph (J Scheckter, 7 min:11.100 sec on lap 11)
Lap Leaders C Regazzoni 1-14 (14).

Also the Grand Prix of Europe. D Hulme took over the spare car (no. 5T) after retiring, only to be disqualified.

18 Aug 1974		**AUSTRIA: Österreichring**						**(Round 12)**		**(Race 247)**
		54 laps x 5.911 km, 3.673 miles = 319.194 km, 198.338 miles								

Pos	No	Driver	Car	Model	Engine		Laps	Time/Reason for Retirement	Grid Pos	Row
1	7	C Reutemann	Brabham	BT44	Ford Cosworth	V8	54	1h 28m 44.720s	2	1
2	6	D Hulme	McLaren	M23	Ford Cosworth	V8	54	1h 29m 27.640s	10	5
3	24	J Hunt	Hesketh	308	Ford Cosworth	V8	54	1h 29m 46.260s	7	4
4	28	J Watson	Brabham	BT44	Ford Cosworth	V8	54	1h 29m 54.110s	11	6
5	11	C Regazzoni	Ferrari	312B3	Ferrari	F12	54	1h 29m 57.800s	8	4
6	10	V Brambilla	March	741	Ford Cosworth	V8	54	1h 29m 58.540s	20	10
7	33	D Hobbs	McLaren	M23	Ford Cosworth	V8	53		17	9
8	17	J-P Jarier	Shadow	DN3	Ford Cosworth	V8	52		23	12
9	30	D Quester	Surtees	TS16	Ford Cosworth	V8	51		25	13
10	23	T Schenken	Trojan	T103	Ford Cosworth	V8	50		19	10
11r	9	H-J Stuck	March	741	Ford Cosworth	V8	48	rear suspension / spin	15	8
12	26	G Hill	Lola	T370	Ford Cosworth	V8	48		21	11
nc	35	I Ashley	Token	RJ02	Ford Cosworth	V8	46		24	12
r	1	R Peterson	JPS Lotus	72E	Ford Cosworth	V8	45	universal joint	6	3
r	2	J Ickx	JPS Lotus	76	Ford Cosworth	V8	43	accident	22	11
r	4	P Depailler	Tyrrell	007	Ford Cosworth	V8	42	accident	14	7
r	8	C Pace	Brabham	BT44	Ford Cosworth	V8	41	fuel line	4	2
r	5	E Fittipaldi	McLaren	M23	Ford Cosworth	V8	37	engine	3	2
nc	21	J Laffite	Iso Marlboro	FW	Ford Cosworth	V8	37		12	6
r	20	A Merzario	Iso Marlboro	FW	Ford Cosworth	V8	24	fuel pressure	9	5
r	14	J-P Beltoise	BRM	P201	BRM	V12	22	engine	18	9
r	16	T Pryce	Shadow	DN3	Ford Cosworth	V8	22	spin	16	8
r	12	N Lauda	Ferrari	312B3	Ferrari	F12	17	valve	1	1
r	27	R Stommelen	Lola	T370	Ford Cosworth	V8	14	tyre / accident	13	7
r	3	J Scheckter	Tyrrell	007	Ford Cosworth	V8	8	engine	5	3
nq	31	I Scheckter	Hesketh	308	Ford Cosworth	V8				
nq	43	L Kinnunen	Surtees	TS16	Ford Cosworth	V8				
nq	18	D Bell	Surtees	TS16	Ford Cosworth	V8				
nq	22	M Wilds	Ensign	N174	Ford Cosworth	V8				
nq	19	J-P Jabouille	Surtees	TS16	Ford Cosworth	V8				
nq	32	H Koinigg	Brabham	BT42	Ford Cosworth	V8				

Winning speed 215.804 km/h, 134.095 mph
Pole Position speed 223.057 km/h, 138.601 mph (N Lauda, 1 min:35.400 sec)
Fastest Lap speed 218.881 km/h, 136.006 mph (C Regazzoni, 1 min:37.220 sec on lap 46)
Lap Leaders C Reutemann 1-54 (54).

8 Sep 1974		**ITALY: Monza**						**(Round 13)**		**(Race 248)**
		52 laps x 5.780 km, 3.592 miles = 300.560 km, 186.759 miles								

Pos	No	Driver	Car	Model	Engine		Laps	Time/Reason for Retirement	Grid Pos	Row
1	1	R Peterson	JPS Lotus	72E	Ford Cosworth	V8	52	1h 22m 56.600s	7	4
2	5	E Fittipaldi	McLaren	M23	Ford Cosworth	V8	52	1h 22m 57.400s	6	3
3	3	J Scheckter	Tyrrell	007	Ford Cosworth	V8	52	1h 23m 21.300s	12	6
4	20	A Merzario	Iso Marlboro	FW	Ford Cosworth	V8	52	1h 24m 24.300s	15	8
5	8	C Pace	Brabham	BT44	Ford Cosworth	V8	51		3	2
6	6	D Hulme	McLaren	M23	Ford Cosworth	V8	51		19	10
7	28	J Watson	Brabham	BT44	Ford Cosworth	V8	51		4	2
8	26	G Hill	Lola	T370	Ford Cosworth	V8	51		21	11
9	33	D Hobbs	McLaren	M23	Ford Cosworth	V8	51		23	12
10	16	T Pryce	Shadow	DN3	Ford Cosworth	V8	50		22	11
11	4	P Depailler	Tyrrell	007	Ford Cosworth	V8	50		10	5
r	11	C Regazzoni	Ferrari	312B3	Ferrari	F12	40	oil seal	5	3
r	12	N Lauda	Ferrari	312B3	Ferrari	F12	32	water leak	1	1
r	2	J Ickx	JPS Lotus	76	Ford Cosworth	V8	31	throttle linkage	16	8
r	27	R Stommelen	Lola	T370	Ford Cosworth	V8	25	rear suspension	14	7
r	21	J Laffite	Iso Marlboro	FW	Ford Cosworth	V8	22	engine	17	9
r	17	J-P Jarier	Shadow	DN3	Ford Cosworth	V8	19	engine	9	5
r	10	V Brambilla	March	741	Ford Cosworth	V8	16	accident	13	7
r	29	T Schenken	Trojan	T103	Ford Cosworth	V8	15	gear selection	20	10
r	7	C Reutemann	Brabham	BT44	Ford Cosworth	V8	11	gearbox bearing	2	1
r	9	H-J Stuck	March	741	Ford Cosworth	V8	10	engine mounting bolts	18	9
r	15	H Pescarolo	BRM	P201	BRM	V12	3	engine	25	13
r	24	J Hunt	Hesketh	308	Ford Cosworth	V8	2	engine	8	4
r	37	F Migault	BRM	P201	BRM	V12	1	gearbox	24	12
r	14	J-P Beltoise	BRM	P201	BRM	V12	0	electrics	11	6
nq	19	J Dolhem	Surtees	TS16	Ford Cosworth	V8				
nq	31	C Facetti	Brabham	BT42	Ford Cosworth	V8				
nq	18	D Bell	Surtees	TS16	Ford Cosworth	V8				
nq	25	M Wilds	Ensign	N174	Ford Cosworth	V8				
nq	22	C Amon	Amon	AF101	Ford Cosworth	V8				
nq	23	L Kinnunen	Surtees	TS16	Ford Cosworth	V8				

Winning speed 217.421 km/h, 135.099 mph
Pole Position speed 223.358 km/h, 138.788 mph (N Lauda, 1 min:33.160 sec)
Fastest Lap speed 220.892 km/h, 137.256 mph (C Pace, 1 min:34.200 sec on lap 46)
Lap Leaders N Lauda 1-29 (29); C Regazzoni 30-40 (11); R Peterson 41-52 (12).

Races

80 laps x 3.957 km, 2.459 miles = 316.590 km, 196.720 miles

Pos	No	Driver	Car	Model	Engine		Laps	Time/Reason for Retirement	Grid Pos	Row
1	5	E Fittipaldi	McLaren	M23	Ford Cosworth	V8	80	1h 40m 26.136s	1	1
2	11	C Regazzoni	Ferrari	312B3	Ferrari	F12	80	1h 40m 39.170s	6	3
3	1	R Peterson	JPS Lotus	72E	Ford Cosworth	V8	80	1h 40m 40.630s	10	5
4	24	J Hunt	Hesketh	308	Ford Cosworth	V8	80	1h 40m 41.805s	8	4
5	4	P Depailler	Tyrrell	007	Ford Cosworth	V8	80	1h 41m 21.458s	7	4
6	6	D Hulme	McLaren	M23	Ford Cosworth	V8	79		14	7
7	55	M Andretti	Parnelli	VPJ4	Ford Cosworth	V8	79		16	8
8	8	C Pace	Brabham	BT44	Ford Cosworth	V8	79		9	5
9	7	C Reutemann	Brabham	BT44	Ford Cosworth	V8	79		4	2
10	19	H Koinigg	Surtees	TS16	Ford Cosworth	V8	78		22	11
11	27	R Stommelen	Lola	T370	Ford Cosworth	V8	78		11	6
12	66	M Donohue	Penske	PC1	Ford Cosworth	V8	78		24	12
13	2	J Ickx	JPS Lotus	72E	Ford Cosworth	V8	78		21	11
14	26	G Hill	Lola	T370	Ford Cosworth	V8	77		20	10
15	21	J Laffite	Iso Marlboro	FW	Ford Cosworth	V8	74	in pits at chequered flag	18	9
16	33	J Mass	McLaren	M23	Ford Cosworth	V8	72		12	6
nc	15	C Amon	BRM	P201	BRM	V12	70		25	13
r	12	N Lauda	Ferrari	312B3	Ferrari	F12	67	accident	2	1
r	16	T Pryce	Shadow	DN3	Ford Cosworth	V8	65	engine	13	7
r	28	J Watson	Brabham	BT44	Ford Cosworth	V8	61	front suspension / accident	15	8
nc	14	J-P Beltoise	BRM	P201	BRM	V12	60		17	9
r	3	J Scheckter	Tyrrell	007	Ford Cosworth	V8	48	brakes / accident	3	2
r	17	J-P Jarier	Shadow	DN3	Ford Cosworth	V8	46	driveshaft	5	3
r	20	A Merzario	Iso Marlboro	FW	Ford Cosworth	V8	40	handling	19	10
r	50	E Wietzes	Brabham	BT42	Ford Cosworth	V8	33	transmission	26	13
r	9	H-J Stuck	March	741	Ford Cosworth	V8	12	fuel pressure	23	12
nq	18	D Bell	Surtees	TS16	Ford Cosworth	V8				
nq	22	M Wilds	Ensign	N174	Ford Cosworth	V8				
nq	10	V Brambilla	March	741	Ford Cosworth	V8		accident		
nq	42	I Ashley	Brabham	BT42	Ford Cosworth	V8				

Winning speed 189.130 km/h, 117.520 mph
Pole Position speed 194.657 km/h, 120.954 mph (E Fittipaldi, 1 min:13.188 sec)
Fastest Lap speed 193.412 km/h, 120.181 mph (N Lauda, 1 min:13.659 sec on lap 60)
Lap Leaders N Lauda 1-67 (67); E Fittipaldi 68-80 (13).

59 laps x 5.435 km, 3.377 miles = 320.651 km, 199.243 miles

Pos	No	Driver	Car	Model	Engine		Laps	Time/Reason for Retirement	Grid Pos	Row
1	7	C Reutemann	Brabham	BT44	Ford Cosworth	V8	59	1h 40m 21.439s	1	1
2	8	C Pace	Brabham	BT44	Ford Cosworth	V8	59	1h 40m 32.174s	4	2
3	24	J Hunt	Hesketh	308	Ford Cosworth	V8	59	1h 41m 31.823s	2	1
4	5	E Fittipaldi	McLaren	M23	Ford Cosworth	V8	59	1h 41m 39.192s	8	4
5	28	J Watson	Brabham	BT44	Ford Cosworth	V8	59	1h 41m 47.243s	7	4
6	4	P Depailler	Tyrrell	007	Ford Cosworth	V8	59	1h 41m 48.945s	13	7
7	33	J Mass	McLaren	M23	Ford Cosworth	V8	59	1h 41m 51.451s	20	10
8	26	G Hill	Lola	T370	Ford Cosworth	V8	58		24	12
9	15	C Amon	BRM	P201	BRM	V12	57		12	6
10	17	J-P Jarier	Shadow	DN3	Ford Cosworth	V8	57		10	5
11	11	C Regazzoni	Ferrari	312B3	Ferrari	F12	55		9	5
12	27	R Stommelen	Lola	T370	Ford Cosworth	V8	54		21	11
r	1	R Peterson	JPS Lotus	72E	Ford Cosworth	V8	52	fuel line / engine	19	10
nc	22	M Wilds	Ensign	N174	Ford Cosworth	V8	50		22	11
nc	16	T Pryce	Shadow	DN3	Ford Cosworth	V8	47		18	9
r	3	J Scheckter	Tyrrell	007	Ford Cosworth	V8	44	fuel line	6	3
r	20	A Merzario	Iso Marlboro	FW	Ford Cosworth	V8	43	fire extinguisher discharge	15	8
r	12	N Lauda	Ferrari	312B3	Ferrari	F12	38	front suspension	5	3
r	21	J Laffite	Iso Marlboro	FW	Ford Cosworth	V8	31	rear wheel centre	11	6
r	66	M Donohue	Penske	PC1	Ford Cosworth	V8	27	rear suspension	14	7
r	18	J Dolhem	Surtees	TS16	Ford Cosworth	V8	25	withdrew (after Koinigg's accident)	26	14
r	10	V Brambilla	March	741	Ford Cosworth	V8	21	fuel metering unit	25	13
r	19	H Koinigg	Surtees	TS16	Ford Cosworth	V8	9	fatal accident	23	12
r	2	J Ickx	JPS Lotus	72E	Ford Cosworth	V8	7	accident / front suspension	16	8
dq	31	T Schenken	JPS Lotus	76	Ford Cosworth	V8	6	started unofficially	27	14
r	6	D Hulme	McLaren	M23	Ford Cosworth	V8	4	engine	17	9
dq	55	M Andretti	Parnelli	VPJ4	Ford Cosworth	V8	4	push start on grid	3	2
nq	9	H-J Stuck	March	741	Ford Cosworth	V8				
nq	42	I Ashley	Brabham	BT42	Ford Cosworth	V8				
nq	14	J-P Beltoise	BRM	P201	BRM	V12		accident / injury		

Winning speed 191.705 km/h, 119.120 mph
Pole Position speed 197.671 km/h, 122.827 mph (C Reutemann, 1 min:38.978 sec)
Fastest Lap speed 194.469 km/h, 120.837 mph (C Pace, 1 min:40.608 sec on lap 54)
Lap Leaders C Reutemann 1-59 (59).

Lap Leaders 1974

Pos	Driver	Car-Engine	GPs	laps	km	miles
1	N Lauda	Ferrari	8	338	1,379.8	857.4
2	C Reutemann	Brabham-Ford Cosworth	5	235	1,243.5	772.6
3	R Peterson	Lotus-Ford Cosworth	6	156	606.2	376.7
4	J Scheckter	Tyrrell-Ford Cosworth	2	86	347.0	215.6
5	C Regazzoni	Ferrari	4	83	590.3	366.8
6	E Fittipaldi	McLaren-Ford Cosworth	3	77	361.8	224.8
7	D Hulme	McLaren-Ford Cosworth	1	2	11.9	7.4
8	J Ickx	Lotus-Ford Cosworth	1	2	6.8	4.2
			15	979	4,547.4	2,825.6

Driver Points 1974

	Driver	RA	BR	ZA	E	B	MC	S	NL	F	GB	D	A	I	CDN	USA	Total
1	E Fittipaldi	-	9	-	4	9	2	3	4	-	6	-	-	6	9	3	55
2	C Regazzoni	4	6	-	6	3	3	-	6	4	3	9	2	-	6	-	52
3	J Scheckter	-	-	-	2	4	6	9	2	3	9	6	-	4	-	-	45
4	N Lauda	6	-	-	9	6	-	-	9	6	2	-	-	-	-	-	38
5	R Peterson	-	1	-	-	-	9	-	-	9	-	3	-	9	4	-	35
6	C Reutemann	-	-	9	-	-	-	-	-	-	1	4	9	-	-	9	32
7	D Hulme	9	-	-	1	1	-	-	-	1	-	-	6	1	1	-	20
8	J Hunt	-	-	-	-	-	-	4	-	-	-	-	4	-	3	4	15
9	P Depailler	1	-	3	-	-	-	6	1	-	-	-	-	-	2	1	14
10	J Ickx	-	4	-	-	-	-	-	-	2	4	2	-	-	-	-	12
	M Hailwood	3	2	4	-	-	-	-	3	-	-	-	-	-	-	-	12
12	C Pace	-	3	-	-	-	-	-	-	-	-	-	-	2	-	6	11
13	J-P Beltoise	2	-	6	-	2	-	-	-	-	-	-	-	-	-	-	10
14	J-P Jarier	-	-	-	-	-	4	2	-	-	-	-	-	-	-	-	6
	J Watson	-	-	-	-	-	1	-	-	-	-	-	3	-	-	2	6
16	H-J Stuck	-	-	2	3	-	-	-	-	-	-	-	-	-	-	-	5
17	A Merzario	-	-	1	-	-	-	-	-	-	-	-	-	3	-	-	4
18	G Hill	-	-	-	-	-	1	-	-	-	-	-	-	-	-	-	1
	T Pryce	-	-	-	-	-	-	-	-	-	-	1	-	-	-	-	1
	V Brambilla	-	-	-	-	-	-	-	-	-	-	-	-	1	-	-	1

9,6,4,3,2 and 1 point awarded to the first six finishers. Best 7 scores from first 8 races, best 6 from remaining 7 races.

Constructor Points 1974

		RA	BR	ZA	E	B	MC	S	NL	F	GB	D	A	I	CDN	USA	Total	
1	McLaren-Ford Cosworth	9	9	4	4	9	(2)	3	4	1	6	-	6	6	9	3	73	(2)
2	Ferrari	6	6	-	9	6	3	-	9	6	3	9	2	-	6	-	65	
3	Tyrrell-Ford Cosworth	1	-	3	2	4	6	9	2	3	9	6	-	4	2	1	52	
4	Lotus-Ford Cosworth	-	4	-	-	-	9	-	-	9	4	3	-	9	4	-	42	
5	Brabham-Ford Cosworth	-	-	9	-	-	1	-	-	-	1	4	9	2	-	9	35	
6	Hesketh-Ford Cosworth	-	-	-	-	-	-	4	-	-	-	-	4	-	3	4	15	
7	BRM	2	-	6	-	2	-	-	-	-	-	-	-	-	-	-	10	
8	Shadow-Ford Cosworth	-	-	-	-	-	4	2	-	-	-	1	-	-	-	-	7	
9	March-Ford Cosworth	-	-	2	3	-	-	-	-	-	-	-	-	1	-	-	6	
10	Iso-Ford Cosworth	-	-	1	-	-	-	-	-	-	-	-	-	3	-	-	4	
11	Surtees-Ford Cosworth	-	3	-	-	-	-	-	-	-	-	-	-	-	-	-	3	
12	Lola-Ford Cosworth	-	-	-	-	-	-	1	-	-	-	-	-	-	-	-	1	

9,6,4,3,2 and 1 point awarded to the first six finishers. Points only for highest placed car. Best 7 scores from first 8 races, best 6 from remaining 7 races.

1975

Race Entrants and Results

Firestone withdrew early in the season, leaving a Goodyear tyre monopoly. BRM restructured as Stanley BRM after the withdrawal of Rubery Owen support. The accident-strewn Spanish Grand Prix was prematurely stopped after an accident involving spectators, making it the first event at which half points were awarded.

McLAREN
Marlboro Team McLaren: E Fittipaldi, Mass
Lucky Strike Racing: Charlton

TYRRELL
Elf Team Tyrrell: J Scheckter, Depailler, Jabouille, Leclère
Lexington Racing: I Scheckter

LOTUS
John Player Team Lotus: Peterson, Ickx, Henton, Crawford, Watson
Team Gunston: Keizan, Tunmer

BRABHAM
Martini Racing: Reutemann, Pace

MARCH
Beta Team March: Brambilla
Lavazza March: Lombardi, Stuck
Penske Cars: Donohue

FERRARI
Scuderia Ferrari SpA SEFAC: Regazzoni, Lauda

BRM
Stanley BRM: Wilds, Evans

SHADOW
UOP Shadow Racing Team: Pryce, Jarier

SURTEES
Team Surtees: Watson, Morgan (with National Organs)

WILLIAMS
Frank Williams Racing Cars: Merzario, Magee, (Migault), Vonlanthen, Zorzi, (Lombardi), I Scheckter, Laffite, Brise

LOLA
Embassy Racing with Graham Hill: Hill, Stommelen

HILL
Embassy Racing with Graham Hill: Stommelen, Migault, Schuppan, Jones, (Hill), Brise

HESKETH
Hesketh Racing: Hunt, Lunger
Custom Made Harry Stiller Racing: Jones
Warsteiner Brewery: Ertl
Polar Caravans: Palm

PARNELLI
Vel's Parnelli Jones Racing: Andretti

PENSKE
Penske Cars: Donohue, Watson

FITTIPALDI (COPERSUCAR)
Copersucar-Fittipaldi: W Fittipaldi, Merzario

LYNCAR
Pinch (Plant) Ltd: Nicholson

ENSIGN
HB Bewaking Team Ensign: Wunderink, van Lennep, Amon

MAKI
Maki Engineering: (Fushida, Trimmer)

---

53 laps x 5.968 km, 3.708 miles = 316.304 km, 196.542 miles

Pos	No	Driver	Car	Model	Engine		Laps	Time/Reason for Retirement	Grid Pos	Row
1	1	E Fittipaldi	McLaren	M23	Ford Cosworth	V8	53	1h 39m 26.290s	5	3
2	24	J Hunt	Hesketh	308	Ford Cosworth	V8	53	1h 39m 32.200s	6	3
3	7	C Reutemann	Brabham	BT44B	Ford Cosworth	V8	53	1h 39m 43.350s	3	2
4	11	C Regazzoni	Ferrari	312B3	Ferrari	F12	53	1h 40m 02.080s	7	4
5	4	P Depailler	Tyrrell	007	Ford Cosworth	V8	53	1h 40m 20.540s	8	4
6	12	N Lauda	Ferrari	312B3	Ferrari	F12	53	1h 40m 45.940s	4	2
7	28	M Donohue	Penske	PC1	Ford Cosworth	V8	52		16	8
8	6	J Ickx	JPS Lotus	72E	Ford Cosworth	V8	52		18	9
9	9	V Brambilla	March	741	Ford Cosworth	V8	52		12	6
10	22	G Hill	Lola	T370	Ford Cosworth	V8	52		21	11
11	3	J Scheckter	Tyrrell	007	Ford Cosworth	V8	52		9	5
12r	16	T Pryce	Shadow	DN3B	Ford Cosworth	V8	51	transmission	14	7
13	23	R Stommelen	Lola	T370	Ford Cosworth	V8	51		19	10
14	2	J Mass	McLaren	M23	Ford Cosworth	V8	50		13	7
r	8	C Pace	Brabham	BT44B	Ford Cosworth	V8	46	engine	2	1
nc	20	A Merzario	Williams	FW	Ford Cosworth	V8	44		20	10
r	27	M Andretti	Parnelli	VPJ4	Ford Cosworth	V8	27	cv joint	10	5
r	14	M Wilds	Stanley BRM	P201	BRM	V12	24	oil scavenge pump drive belt	22	11
r	5	R Peterson	JPS Lotus	72E	Ford Cosworth	V8	15	brakes / gearbox	11	6
r	21	J Laffite	Williams	FW	Ford Cosworth	V8	15	gearbox	17	9
r	30	W Fittipaldi	Copersucar	FD01	Ford Cosworth	V8	12	accident	23	12
dq	18	J Watson	Surtees	TS16	Ford Cosworth	V8	6	repaired outside pits	15	8
ns	17	J-P Jarier	Shadow	DN5	Ford Cosworth	V8		crown wheel & pinion	1	1

Winning speed 190.855 km/h, 118.592 mph
Pole Position speed 196.729 km/h, 122.242 mph (J-P Jarier, 1 min:49.210 sec)
Fastest Lap speed 193.714 km/h, 120.368 mph (J Hunt, 1 min:50.910 sec on lap 34)
Lap Leaders C Reutemann 1-25 (25); J Hunt 26-34 (9); E Fittipaldi 35-53 (19).

J-P Jarier qualified for pole position, but did not start due to car failure in warm-up. Pole position left vacant.

26 Jan 1975   **BRAZIL: Interlagos**   (Round 2)   (Race 252)

40 laps x 7.960 km, 4.946 miles = 318.400 km, 197.845 miles

Pos	No	Driver	Car	Model	Engine		Laps	Time/Reason for Retirement	Grid Pos	Row
1	8	C Pace	Brabham	BT44B	Ford Cosworth	V8	40	1h 44m 41.170s	6	3
2	1	E Fittipaldi	McLaren	M23	Ford Cosworth	V8	40	1h 44m 46.960s	2	1
3	2	J Mass	McLaren	M23	Ford Cosworth	V8	40	1h 45m 17.830s	10	5
4	11	C Regazzoni	Ferrari	312B3	Ferrari	F12	40	1h 45m 24.450s	5	3
5	12	N Lauda	Ferrari	312B3	Ferrari	F12	40	1h 45m 43.050s	4	2
6	24	J Hunt	Hesketh	308	Ford Cosworth	V8	40	1h 45m 46.290s	7	4
7	27	M Andretti	Parnelli	VPJ4	Ford Cosworth	V8	40	1h 45m 47.980s	18	9
8	7	C Reutemann	Brabham	BT44B	Ford Cosworth	V8	40	1h 46m 20.790s	3	2
9	6	J Ickx	JPS Lotus	72E	Ford Cosworth	V8	40	1h 46m 33.010s	12	6
10	18	J Watson	Surtees	TS16	Ford Cosworth	V8	40	1h 47m 10.770s	13	7
11	21	J Laffite	Williams	FW	Ford Cosworth	V8	39		19	10
12	22	G Hill	Lola	T370	Ford Cosworth	V8	39		20	10
13	30	W Fittipaldi	Copersucar	FD02	Ford Cosworth	V8	39		21	11
14	23	R Stommelen	Lola	T370	Ford Cosworth	V8	39		23	12
15	5	R Peterson	JPS Lotus	72E	Ford Cosworth	V8	38		16	8
r	17	J-P Jarier	Shadow	DN5	Ford Cosworth	V8	32	fuel metering unit	1	1
r	4	P Depailler	Tyrrell	007	Ford Cosworth	V8	31	front suspension / accident	9	5
r	16	T Pryce	Shadow	DN3B	Ford Cosworth	V8	31	accident	14	7
r	20	A Merzario	Williams	FW	Ford Cosworth	V8	25	fuel metering unit	11	6
r	14	M Wilds	Stanley BRM	P201	BRM	V12	22	clutch nut loose / electrics	22	11
r	28	M Donohue	Penske	PC1	Ford Cosworth	V8	22	handling	15	8
r	3	J Scheckter	Tyrrell	007	Ford Cosworth	V8	18	oil tank	8	4
r	9	V Brambilla	March	741	Ford Cosworth	V8	1	engine	17	9

Winning speed 182.488 km/h, 113.393 mph
Pole Position speed 191.193 km/h, 118.802 mph (J-P Jarier, 2 min:29.880 sec)
Fastest Lap speed 185.885 km/h, 115.503 mph (J-P Jarier, 2 min:34.160 sec on lap 10)
Lap Leaders C Reutemann 1-4 (4); J-P Jarier 5-32 (28); C Pace 33-40 (8).

1 Mar 1975   **SOUTH AFRICA: Kyalami**   (Round 3)   (Race 253)

78 laps x 4.104 km, 2.550 miles = 320.112 km, 198.908 miles

Pos	No	Driver	Car	Model	Engine		Laps	Time/Reason for Retirement	Grid Pos	Row
1	3	J Scheckter	Tyrrell	007	Ford Cosworth	V8	78	1h 43m 16.900s	3	2
2	7	C Reutemann	Brabham	BT44B	Ford Cosworth	V8	78	1h 43m 20.640s	2	1
3	4	P Depailler	Tyrrell	007	Ford Cosworth	V8	78	1h 43m 33.820s	5	3
4	8	C Pace	Brabham	BT44B	Ford Cosworth	V8	78	1h 43m 34.210s	1	1
5	12	N Lauda	Ferrari	312T	Ferrari	F12	78	1h 43m 45.540s	4	2
6	2	J Mass	McLaren	M23	Ford Cosworth	V8	78	1h 44m 20.240s	16	8
7	23	R Stommelen	Lola	T371	Ford Cosworth	V8	78	1h 44m 29.810s	14	7
8	28	M Donohue	Penske	PC1	Ford Cosworth	V8	77		18	9
9	16	T Pryce	Shadow	DN5	Ford Cosworth	V8	77		19	10
10	5	R Peterson	JPS Lotus	72E	Ford Cosworth	V8	77		8	4
11	34	G Tunmer	Lotus	72E	Ford Cosworth	V8	76		25	13
12	6	J Ickx	JPS Lotus	72E	Ford Cosworth	V8	76		21	11
13	33	E Keizan	Lotus	72E	Ford Cosworth	V8	76		22	11
14	31	D Charlton	McLaren	M23	Ford Cosworth	V8	76		20	10
15	14	B Evans	Stanley BRM	P201	BRM	V12	76		24	12
16r	11	C Regazzoni	Ferrari	312T	Ferrari	F12	71	throttle linkage	9	5
17r	27	M Andretti	Parnelli	VPJ4	Ford Cosworth	V8	70	cv joint	6	3
nc	21	J Laffite	Williams	FW	Ford Cosworth	V8	69		23	12
nc	1	E Fittipaldi	McLaren	M23	Ford Cosworth	V8	65		11	6
r	32	I Scheckter	Tyrrell	007	Ford Cosworth	V8	55	accident	17	9
r	24	J Hunt	Hesketh	308	Ford Cosworth	V8	53	fuel metering unit	12	6
r	17	J-P Jarier	Shadow	DN5	Ford Cosworth	V8	37	engine	13	7
r	10	L Lombardi	March	741	Ford Cosworth	V8	23	engine	26	13
r	20	A Merzario	Williams	FW	Ford Cosworth	V8	22	engine	15	8
r	18	J Watson	Surtees	TS16	Ford Cosworth	V8	19	clutch	10	5
r	9	V Brambilla	March	751	Ford Cosworth	V8	16	oil cooler leak	7	4
r	30	W Fittipaldi	Copersucar	FD02	Ford Cosworth	V8	0	withdrew (reserve entry)	27	14
ns	22	G Hill	Lola	T370	Ford Cosworth	V8		accident		

Winning speed 185.964 km/h, 115.553 mph
Pole Position speed 193.357 km/h, 120.146 mph (C Pace, 1 min:16.410 sec)
Fastest Lap speed 191.378 km/h, 118.917 mph (C Pace, 1 min:17.200 sec on lap 11)
Lap Leaders C Pace 1-2 (2); J Scheckter 3-78 (76).

SPAIN: Montjuïc (Round 4) (Race 254)

29 laps x 3.791 km, 2.356 miles = 109.939 km, 68.313 miles

Pos	No	Driver	Car	Model	Engine		Laps	Time/Reason for Retirement	Grid Pos	Row
1	2	J Mass	McLaren	M23	Ford Cosworth	V8	29	42m 53.700s	11	6
2	6	J Ickx	JPS Lotus	72E	Ford Cosworth	V8	29	42m 54.800s	16	8
3	7	C Reutemann	Brabham	BT44B	Ford Cosworth	V8	28		15	8
4	17	J-P Jarier	Shadow	DN5	Ford Cosworth	V8	28		10	5
5	9	V Brambilla	March	751	Ford Cosworth	V8	28		5	3
6	10	L Lombardi	March	751	Ford Cosworth	V8	27		24	12
7	21	T Brise	Williams	FW	Ford Cosworth	V8	27		18	9
8	18	J Watson	Surtees	TS16	Ford Cosworth	V8	26		6	3
r	22	R Stommelen	Hill	GH1	Ford Cosworth	V8	25	rear wing / accident / injury	9	5
r	8	C Pace	Brabham	BT44B	Ford Cosworth	V8	25	accident	14	7
nc	11	C Regazzoni	Ferrari	312T	Ferrari	F12	25		2	1
r	5	R Peterson	JPS Lotus	72E	Ford Cosworth	V8	23	accident	12	6
r	16	T Pryce	Shadow	DN5	Ford Cosworth	V8	23	accident	8	4
r	31	R Wunderink	Ensign	N174	Ford Cosworth	V8	20	cv joint	19	10
nc	23	F Migault	Hill	GH1	Ford Cosworth	V8	18		22	11
r	27	M Andretti	Parnelli	VPJ4	Ford Cosworth	V8	16	accident / rear suspension	4	2
r	14	B Evans	Stanley BRM	P201	BRM	V12	7	fuel metering unit	23	12
r	24	J Hunt	Hesketh	308	Ford Cosworth	V8	6	accident	3	2
r	3	J Scheckter	Tyrrell	007	Ford Cosworth	V8	3	engine	13	7
r	28	M Donohue	Penske	PC1	Ford Cosworth	V8	3	accident	17	9
r	25	A Jones	Hesketh	308	Ford Cosworth	V8	3	accident	20	10
r	4	P Depailler	Tyrrell	007	Ford Cosworth	V8	1	accident	7	4
r	20	A Merzario	Williams	FW04	Ford Cosworth	V8	1	withdrew (protest)	25	13
r	30	W Fittipaldi	Copersucar	FD02	Ford Cosworth	V8	1	withdrew (protest)	21	11
r	12	N Lauda	Ferrari	312T	Ferrari	F12	0	accident	1	1
ns	1	E Fittipaldi	McLaren	M23	Ford Cosworth	V8		considered track unsafe		

Winning speed 153.779 km/h, 95.554 mph
Pole Position speed 163.640 km/h, 101.681 mph (N Lauda, 1 min:23.400 sec)
Fastest Lap speed 160.371 km/h, 99.650 mph (M Andretti, 1 min:25.100 sec on lap 14)
Lap Leaders J Hunt 1-6 (6);M Andretti 7-16 (10);R Stommelen 17-21,23-25 (8);C Pace 22 (1);J Mass 26-27,29 (3);J Ickx 28 (1).

Scheduled for 75 laps, but stopped after R Stommelen's accident which killed 5 spectators. Half points were awarded.
J-P Jarier completed 29 laps but was given a 1 lap penalty for overtaking under a yellow flag.

11 May 1975 **MONACO: Monte-Carlo** (Round 5) (Race 255)

75 laps x 3.278 km, 2.037 miles = 245.850 km, 152.764 miles

Pos	No	Driver	Car	Model	Engine		Laps	Time/Reason for Retirement	Grid Pos	Row
1	12	N Lauda	Ferrari	312T	Ferrari	F12	75	2h 01m 21.310s	1	1
2	1	E Fittipaldi	McLaren	M23	Ford Cosworth	V8	75	2h 01m 24.090s	9	5
3	8	C Pace	Brabham	BT44B	Ford Cosworth	V8	75	2h 01m 39.120s	8	4
4	5	R Peterson	JPS Lotus	72E	Ford Cosworth	V8	75	2h 01m 59.760s	4	2
5	4	P Depailler	Tyrrell	007	Ford Cosworth	V8	75	2h 02m 02.170s	12	6
6	2	J Mass	McLaren	M23	Ford Cosworth	V8	75	2h 02m 03.380s	15	8
7	3	J Scheckter	Tyrrell	007	Ford Cosworth	V8	74		7	4
8	6	J Ickx	JPS Lotus	72E	Ford Cosworth	V8	74		14	7
9	7	C Reutemann	Brabham	BT44B	Ford Cosworth	V8	73		10	5
r	28	M Donohue	Penske	PC1	Ford Cosworth	V8	66	front suspension / accident	16	8
r	24	J Hunt	Hesketh	308	Ford Cosworth	V8	63	accident	11	6
r	26	A Jones	Hesketh	308	Ford Cosworth	V8	61	rear wheel lost	18	9
r	9	V Brambilla	March	751	Ford Cosworth	V8	48	accident / steering	5	3
r	16	T Pryce	Shadow	DN5	Ford Cosworth	V8	39	accident	2	1
r	18	J Watson	Surtees	TS16	Ford Cosworth	V8	36	spin	17	9
r	11	C Regazzoni	Ferrari	312T	Ferrari	F12	36	accident	6	3
r	27	M Andretti	Parnelli	VPJ4	Ford Cosworth	V8	9	oil line / fire	13	7
r	17	J-P Jarier	Shadow	DN5	Ford Cosworth	V8	0	accident	3	2
nq	21	J Laffite	Williams	FW04	Ford Cosworth	V8				
nq	20	A Merzario	Williams	FW	Ford Cosworth	V8				
nq	23	G Hill	Hill	GH1	Ford Cosworth	V8				
nq	14	B Evans	Stanley BRM	P201	BRM	V12				
nq	31	R Wunderink	Ensign	N174	Ford Cosworth	V8				
nq	25	T Palm	Hesketh	308	Ford Cosworth	V8				
nq	10	L Lombardi	March	751	Ford Cosworth	V8				
nq	30	W Fittipaldi	Copersucar	FD02	Ford Cosworth	V8				

Winning speed 121.552 km/h, 75.529 mph
Pole Position speed 136.583 km/h, 84.869 mph (N Lauda, 1 min:26.400 sec)
Fastest Lap speed 133.087 km/h, 82.696 mph (P Depailler, 1 min:28.670 sec on lap 68)
Lap Leaders N Lauda 1-23,25-75 (74); R Peterson 24 (1).

Scheduled for 78 laps, but stopped at 2 hours. G Hill also practised in a Lola T370-Ford Cosworth V8 (22).

70 laps x 4.262 km, 2.648 miles = 298.340 km, 185.380 miles

Pos	No	Driver	Car	Model	Engine		Laps	Time/Reason for Retirement	Grid Pos	Row
1	12	N Lauda	Ferrari	312T	Ferrari	F12	70	1h 43m 53.980s	1	1
2	3	J Scheckter	Tyrrell	007	Ford Cosworth	V8	70	1h 44m 13.200s	9	5
3	7	C Reutemann	Brabham	BT44B	Ford Cosworth	V8	70	1h 44m 35.800s	6	3
4	4	P Depailler	Tyrrell	007	Ford Cosworth	V8	70	1h 44m 54.060s	12	6
5	11	C Regazzoni	Ferrari	312T	Ferrari	F12	70	1h 44m 57.840s	4	2
6	16	T Pryce	Shadow	DN5	Ford Cosworth	V8	70	1h 45m 22.430s	5	3
7	1	E Fittipaldi	McLaren	M23	Ford Cosworth	V8	69		8	4
8	8	C Pace	Brabham	BT44B	Ford Cosworth	V8	69		2	1
9	14	B Evans	Stanley BRM	P201	BRM	V12	68		20	10
10	18	J Watson	Surtees	TS16	Ford Cosworth	V8	68		18	9
11	28	M Donohue	Penske	PC1	Ford Cosworth	V8	67		21	11
12	30	W Fittipaldi	Copersucar	FD02	Ford Cosworth	V8	67		24	12
r	22	F Migault	Hill	GH1	Ford Cosworth	V8	57	rear suspension	22	11
r	9	V Brambilla	March	751	Ford Cosworth	V8	54	brakes	3	2
r	6	J Ickx	JPS Lotus	72E	Ford Cosworth	V8	52	front brake shaft	16	8
r	5	R Peterson	JPS Lotus	72E	Ford Cosworth	V8	36	brakes / accident	14	7
r	10	L Lombardi	March	751	Ford Cosworth	V8	18	oil cooler leak / engine	23	12
r	21	J Laffite	Williams	FW04	Ford Cosworth	V8	18	gearbox	17	9
r	23	T Brise	Hill	GH1	Ford Cosworth	V8	17	piston / spin	7	4
r	24	J Hunt	Hesketh	308	Ford Cosworth	V8	15	gear linkage	11	6
r	17	J-P Jarier	Shadow	DN5	Ford Cosworth	V8	13	spin	10	5
r	20	A Merzario	Williams	FW	Ford Cosworth	V8	2	clutch	19	10
r	26	A Jones	Hesketh	308	Ford Cosworth	V8	0	accident damage	13	7
r	2	J Mass	McLaren	M23	Ford Cosworth	V8	0	accident	15	8

Winning speed 172.285 km/h, 107.053 mph
Pole Position speed 179.600 km/h, 111.598 mph (N Lauda, 1 min:25.430 sec)
Fastest Lap speed 176.846 km/h, 109.887 mph (C Regazzoni, 1 min:26.760 sec on lap 11)
Lap Leaders C Pace 1-3 (3); V Brambilla 4-5 (2); N Lauda 6-70 (65).

80 laps x 4.018 km, 2.497 miles = 321.440 km, 199.734 miles

Pos	No	Driver	Car	Model	Engine		Laps	Time/Reason for Retirement	Grid Pos	Row
1	12	N Lauda	Ferrari	312T	Ferrari	F12	80	1h 59m 18.319s	5	3
2	7	C Reutemann	Brabham	BT44B	Ford Cosworth	V8	80	1h 59m 24.607s	4	2
3	11	C Regazzoni	Ferrari	312T	Ferrari	F12	80	1h 59m 47.414s	12	6
4	27	M Andretti	Parnelli	VPJ4	Ford Cosworth	V8	80	2h 00m 02.699s	15	8
5	28	M Donohue	Penske	PC1	Ford Cosworth	V8	80	2h 00m 49.082s	16	8
6	23	T Brise	Hill	GH1	Ford Cosworth	V8	79		17	9
7	3	J Scheckter	Tyrrell	007	Ford Cosworth	V8	79		8	4
8	1	E Fittipaldi	McLaren	M23	Ford Cosworth	V8	79		11	6
9	5	R Peterson	JPS Lotus	72E	Ford Cosworth	V8	79		9	5
10r	32	T Palm	Hesketh	308	Ford Cosworth	V8	78	out of fuel	21	11
11	26	A Jones	Hesketh	308	Ford Cosworth	V8	78		19	10
12	4	P Depailler	Tyrrell	007	Ford Cosworth	V8	78		2	1
13	14	B Evans	Stanley BRM	P201	BRM	V12	78		23	12
14	20	D Magee	Williams	FW	Ford Cosworth	V8	78		22	11
15	6	J Ickx	JPS Lotus	72E	Ford Cosworth	V8	77		18	9
16	18	J Watson	Surtees	TS16	Ford Cosworth	V8	77		10	5
17	30	W Fittipaldi	Copersucar	FD02	Ford Cosworth	V8	74		25	13
r	16	T Pryce	Shadow	DN5	Ford Cosworth	V8	53	spin	7	4
r	21	I Scheckter	Williams	FW04	Ford Cosworth	V8	49	rear tyre burst / accident	20	10
r	22	V Schuppan	Hill	GH1	Ford Cosworth	V8	47	driveshaft	26	13
r	8	C Pace	Brabham	BT44B	Ford Cosworth	V8	41	accident	6	3
r	17	J-P Jarier	Shadow	DN5	Ford Cosworth	V8	38	engine	3	2
r	9	V Brambilla	March	751	Ford Cosworth	V8	36	universal joint	1	1
r	2	J Mass	McLaren	M23	Ford Cosworth	V8	34	water leak	14	7
r	24	J Hunt	Hesketh	308	Ford Cosworth	V8	21	brake fluid leak	13	7
r	10	L Lombardi	March	751	Ford Cosworth	V8	10	fuel metering unit	24	12

Winning speed 161.656 km/h, 100.448 mph
Pole Position speed 170.918 km/h, 106.204 mph (V Brambilla, 1 min:24.630 sec)
Fastest Lap speed 163.876 km/h, 101.828 mph (N Lauda, 1 min:28.267 sec on lap 61)
Lap Leaders V Brambilla 1-15 (15); C Reutemann 16-69 (54); N Lauda 70-80 (11).

75 laps x 4.226 km, 2.626 miles = 316.950 km, 196.944 miles

Pos	No	Driver	Car	Model	Engine		Laps	Time/Reason for Retirement	Grid Pos	Row
1	24	J Hunt	Hesketh	308	Ford Cosworth	V8	75	1h 46m 57.400s	3	2
2	12	N Lauda	Ferrari	312T	Ferrari	F12	75	1h 46m 58.460s	1	1
3	11	C Regazzoni	Ferrari	312T	Ferrari	F12	75	1h 47m 52.460s	2	1
4	7	C Reutemann	Brabham	BT44B	Ford Cosworth	V8	74		5	3
5	8	C Pace	Brabham	BT44B	Ford Cosworth	V8	74		9	5
6	16	T Pryce	Shadow	DN5	Ford Cosworth	V8	74		12	6
7	23	T Brise	Hill	GH1	Ford Cosworth	V8	74		7	4
8	28	M Donohue	Penske	PC1	Ford Cosworth	V8	74		18	9
9	4	P Depailler	Tyrrell	007	Ford Cosworth	V8	73		13	7
10	31	G van Lennep	Ensign	N174	Ford Cosworth	V8	71		22	11
11	30	W Fittipaldi	Copersucar	FD03	Ford Cosworth	V8	71		24	12
12	20	I Scheckter	Williams	FW	Ford Cosworth	V8	70		19	10
13	22	A Jones	Hill	GH1	Ford Cosworth	V8	70		17	9
14	10	L Lombardi	March	751	Ford Cosworth	V8	70		23	12
15r	5	R Peterson	JPS Lotus	72E	Ford Cosworth	V8	69	out of fuel	16	8
16r	3	J Scheckter	Tyrrell	007	Ford Cosworth	V8	67	engine	4	2
r	21	J Laffite	Williams	FW04	Ford Cosworth	V8	65	engine	15	8
r	2	J Mass	McLaren	M23	Ford Cosworth	V8	61	accident	8	4
r	17	J-P Jarier	Shadow	DN5	Ford Cosworth	V8	44	rear tyre burst / accident	10	5
r	18	J Watson	Surtees	TS16	Ford Cosworth	V8	43	vibration	14	7
r	1	E Fittipaldi	McLaren	M23	Ford Cosworth	V8	40	engine	6	3
r	14	B Evans	Stanley BRM	P201	BRM	V12	23	crown wheel & pinion	20	10
r	6	J Ickx	JPS Lotus	72E	Ford Cosworth	V8	6	engine	21	11
r	9	V Brambilla	March	751	Ford Cosworth	V8	0	accident / rear suspension	11	6
ns	35	H Fushida	Maki	F101C	Ford Cosworth	V8		engine		

Winning speed 177.801 km/h, 110.480 mph
Pole Position speed 189.483 km/h, 117.739 mph (N Lauda, 1 min:20.290 sec)
Fastest Lap speed 186.578 km/h, 115.934 mph (N Lauda, 1 min:21.540 sec on lap 55)
Lap Leaders N Lauda 1-12 (12); C Regazzoni 13-14 (2); J Hunt 15-75 (61).

54 laps x 5.810 km, 3.610 miles = 313.740 km, 194.949 miles

Pos	No	Driver	Car	Model	Engine		Laps	Time/Reason for Retirement	Grid Pos	Row
1	12	N Lauda	Ferrari	312T	Ferrari	F12	54	1h 40m 18.840s	1	1
2	24	J Hunt	Hesketh	308	Ford Cosworth	V8	54	1h 40m 20.430s	3	2
3	2	J Mass	McLaren	M23	Ford Cosworth	V8	54	1h 40m 21.150s	7	4
4	1	E Fittipaldi	McLaren	M23	Ford Cosworth	V8	54	1h 40m 58.610s	10	5
5	27	M Andretti	Parnelli	VPJ4	Ford Cosworth	V8	54	1h 41m 20.920s	15	8
6	4	P Depailler	Tyrrell	007	Ford Cosworth	V8	54	1h 41m 26.240s	13	7
7	23	T Brise	Hill	GH1	Ford Cosworth	V8	54	1h 41m 28.450s	12	6
8	17	J-P Jarier	Shadow	DN5	Ford Cosworth	V8	54	1h 41m 38.620s	4	2
9	3	J Scheckter	Tyrrell	007	Ford Cosworth	V8	54	1h 41m 50.520s	2	1
10	5	R Peterson	JPS Lotus	72E	Ford Cosworth	V8	54	1h 41m 54.860s	17	9
11	21	J Laffite	Williams	FW04	Ford Cosworth	V8	54	1h 41m 55.610s	16	8
12	15	J-P Jabouille	Tyrrell	007	Ford Cosworth	V8	54	1h 41m 55.970s	21	11
13	18	J Watson	Surtees	TS16	Ford Cosworth	V8	53		14	7
14	7	C Reutemann	Brabham	BT44B	Ford Cosworth	V8	53		11	6
15	31	G van Lennep	Ensign	N175	Ford Cosworth	V8	53		22	11
16	22	A Jones	Hill	GH1	Ford Cosworth	V8	53		20	10
17	14	B Evans	Stanley BRM	P201	BRM	V12	52		25	13
18	10	L Lombardi	March	751	Ford Cosworth	V8	50		26	13
r	8	C Pace	Brabham	BT44B	Ford Cosworth	V8	26	cv joint	5	3
r	6	J Ickx	JPS Lotus	72F	Ford Cosworth	V8	17	front brake shaft joint	19	10
r	30	W Fittipaldi	Copersucar	FD03	Ford Cosworth	V8	14	engine	23	12
r	28	M Donohue	Penske	PC1	Ford Cosworth	V8	6	cv joint	18	9
r	9	V Brambilla	March	751	Ford Cosworth	V8	6	rear suspension	8	4
r	11	C Regazzoni	Ferrari	312T	Ferrari	F12	6	engine	9	5
r	16	T Pryce	Shadow	DN5	Ford Cosworth	V8	2	transmission	6	3
ns	20	F Migault	Williams	FW	Ford Cosworth	V8		engine	24	12

Winning speed 187.655 km/h, 116.603 mph
Pole Position speed 193.990 km/h, 120.540 mph (N Lauda, 1 min:47.820 sec)
Fastest Lap speed 189.114 km/h, 117.510 mph (J Mass, 1 min:50.600 sec on lap 38)
Lap Leaders N Lauda 1-54 (54).

Right: *Bob Gerard and his ERA, one of many pre-war cars that competed in the first World Championship Grand Prix, held at Silverstone in 1950. From a field of 23 drivers – including stars such as Juan Manuel Fangio, Louis Chiron, Emanuel de Graffenried and Prince 'B' Bira – Gerard finished sixth. The race was won by Giuseppe Farina. (LAT)*

Below: *The first-ever World Champion, Giuseppe 'Nino' Farina, at Reims, 1951, in the Alfa Romeo 159. (LAT)*

Above: *Alberto Ascari (Ferrari 500), whose record nine consecutive Grand Prix wins began here at Spa-Francorchamps in 1952. He won the title that year and the next. (LAT)*

Left: *German Grand Prix race winner Alberto Ascari (left) and second-placed Nino Farina, on the podium at the Nürburgring, 1952. (LAT)*

Opposite top: *Maurice Trintignant and Stirling Moss at the presentation for the 1954 Belgian Grand Prix, where they finished second and third. Fangio won. (LAT)*

Opposite bottom: *Karl Kling races the new open-wheel Mercedes-Benz W196 at the Nürburgring, 1954. (LAT)*

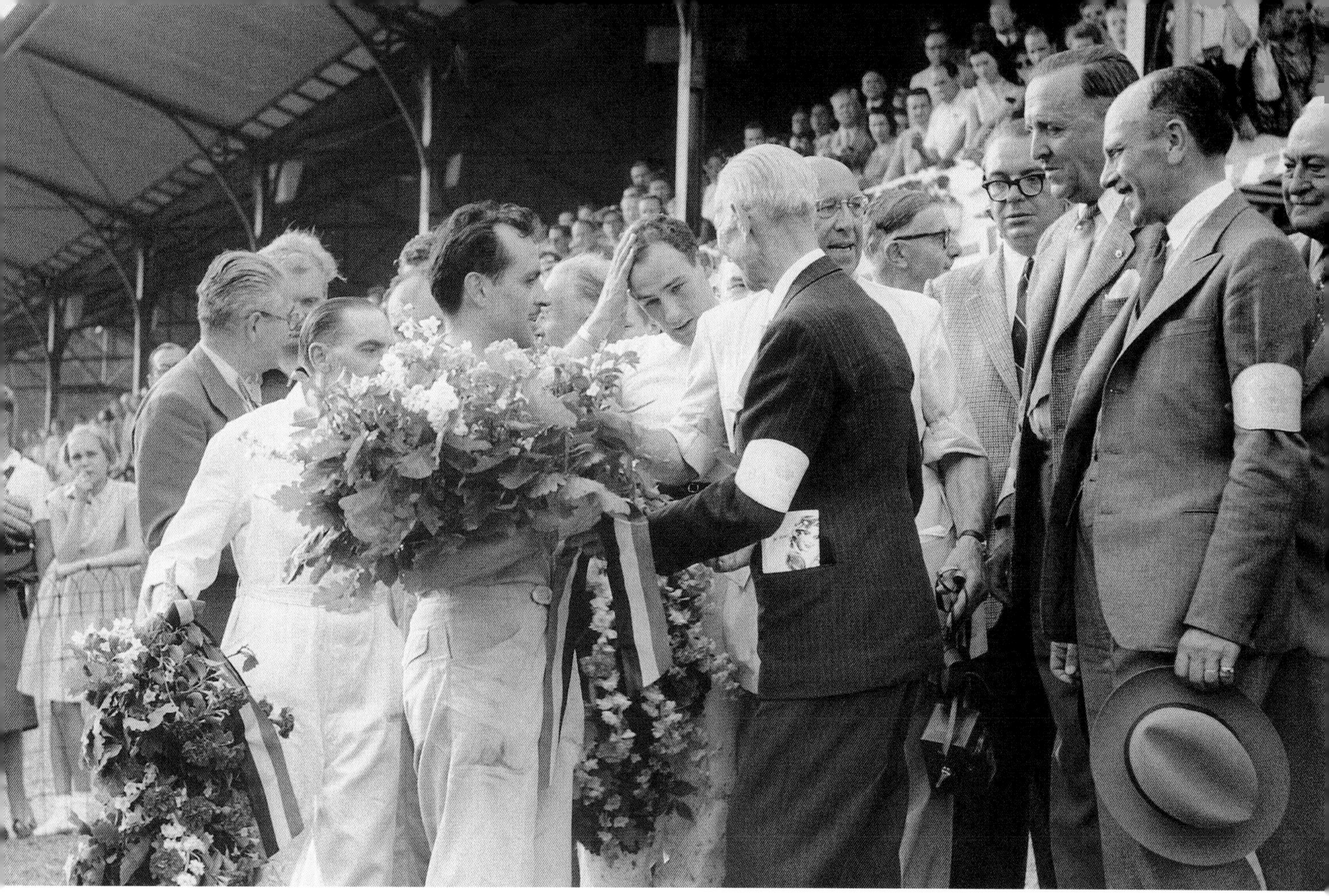

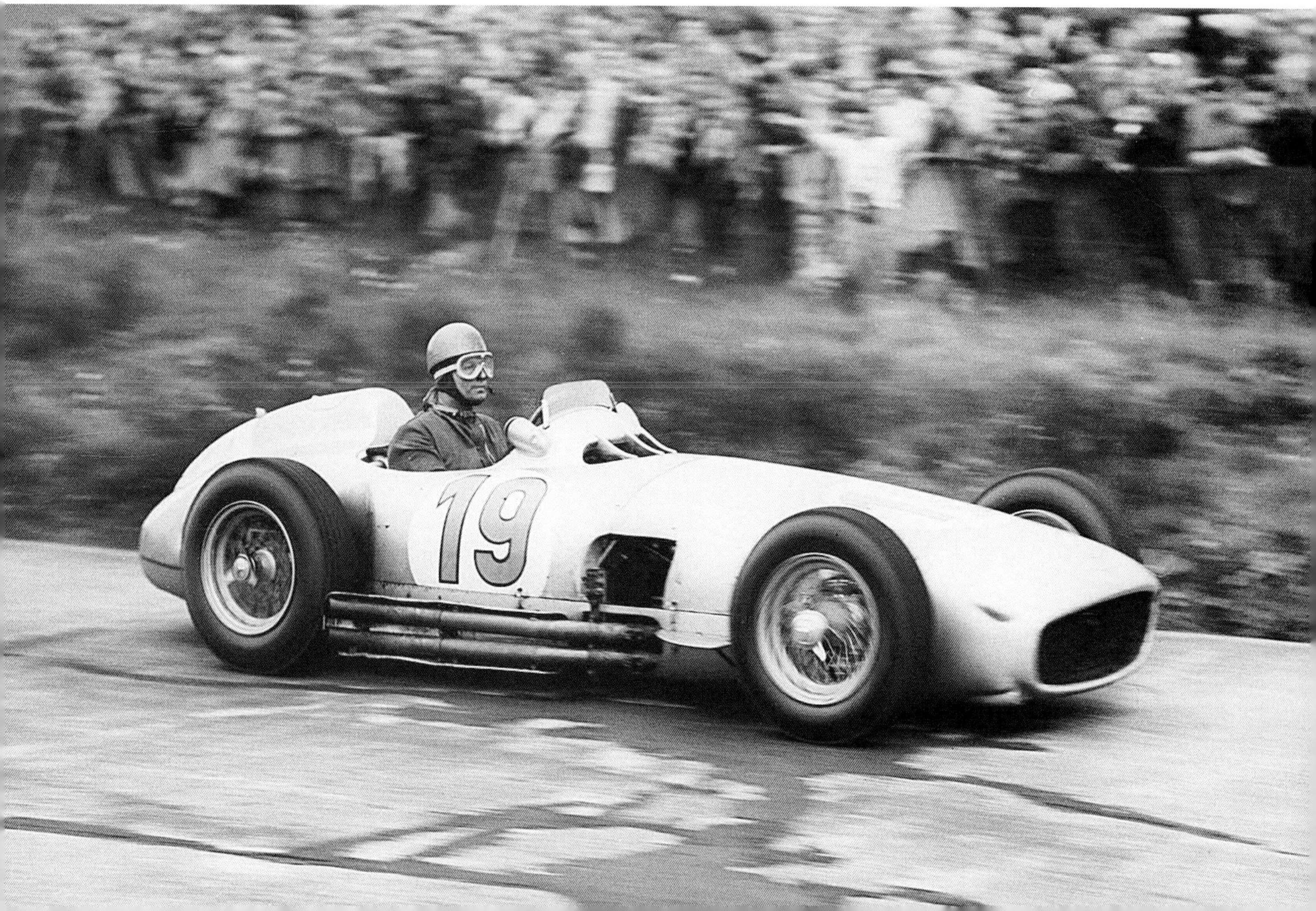
19

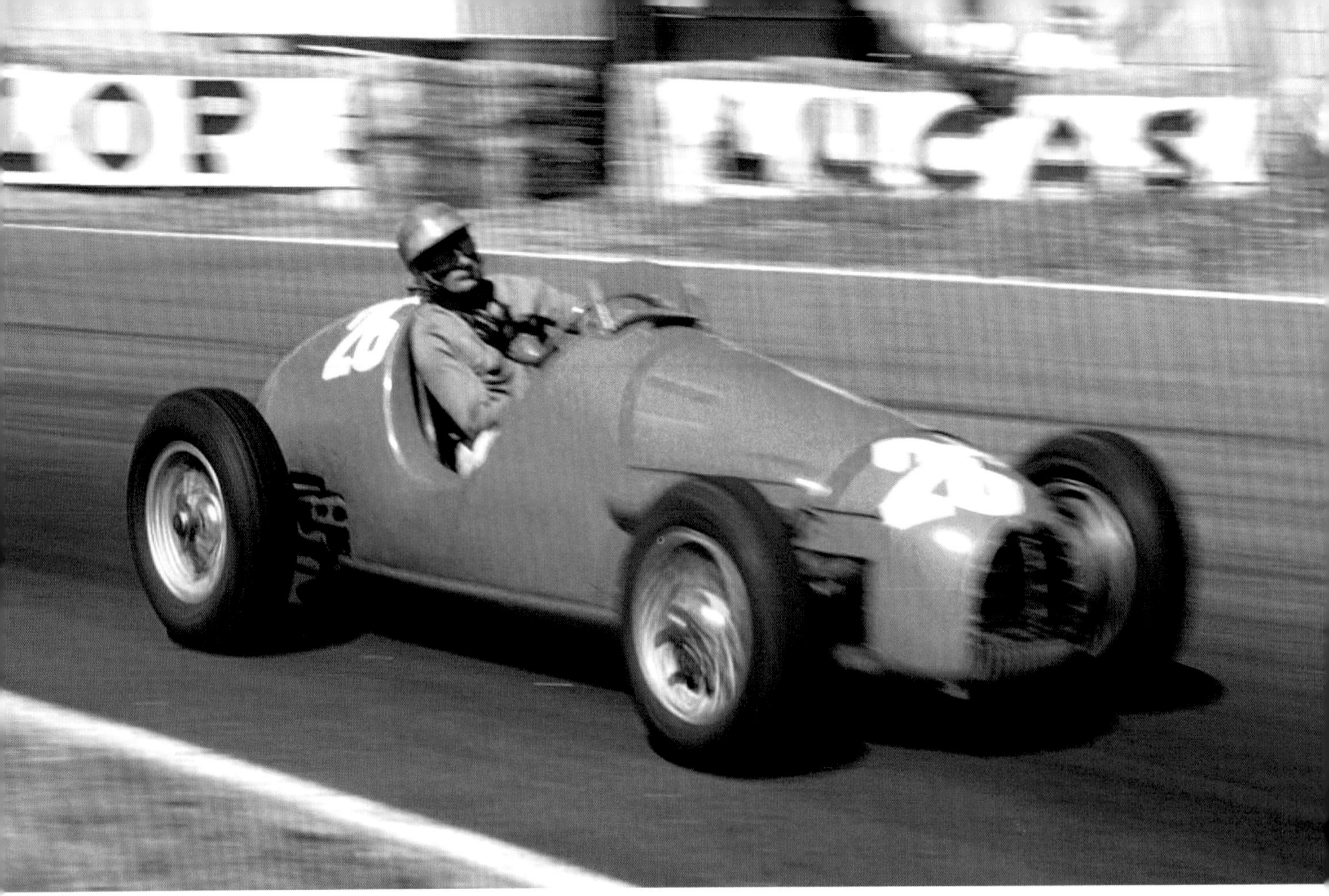
LUCAS

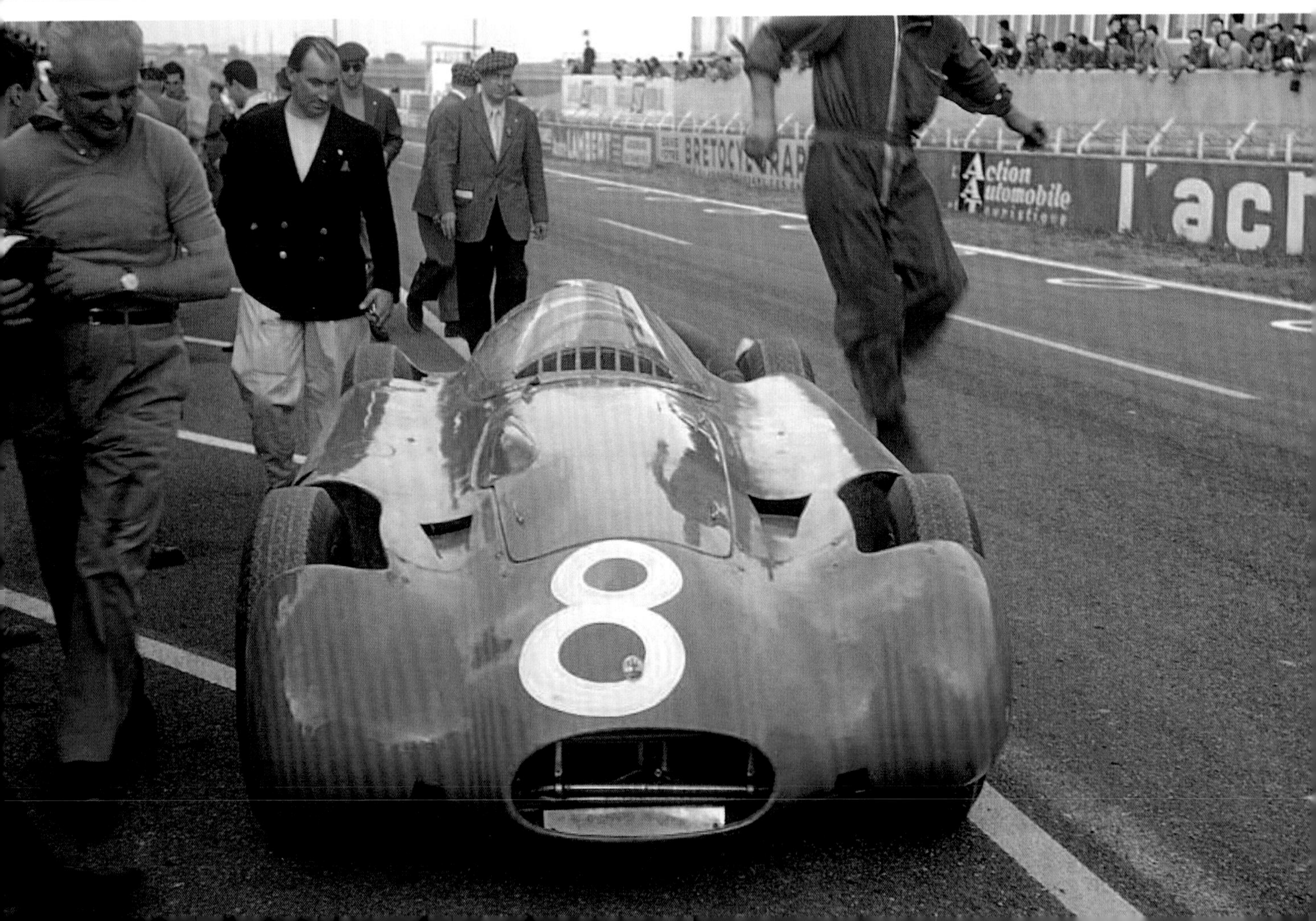
Action
Automobile

Left: *Michel Poberejsky, a French amateur enthusiast who raced sports cars under the name 'Mike Sparken', races a Gordini T16 in his only Formula 1 appearance, the 1955 British Grand Prix. (LAT)*

Right: *Stirling Moss, Cesare Perdisa, Juan Manuel Fangio and Eugenio Castellotti, at the 1956 British Grand Prix. With them is Fangio's companion, Beba. (John Ross)*

Opposite bottom: *Piero Taruffi (far left) drove the streamline Maserati 250F at the 1956 French Grand Prix. Here he seems to be taking a close interest in the experimental variation of this classic design. (LAT)*

Below: *Alfonso de Portago pushing his Lancia-Ferrari D50 over the line at the 1956 British Grand Prix after suffering mechanical woes near the end of the race. However, his original car finished second, in the hands of team-mate Peter Collins. (John Ross)*

Above: *Mike Hawthorn finished third in the 1957 British Grand Prix at Aintree, driving a Lancia Ferrari 801.* (John Ross)

Left: *Peter Collins (Ferrari D246), winner of the 1958 British Grand Prix at Silverstone.* (John Ross)

Below: *The Maserati 250F cars and transporter at the 1957 Italian Grand Prix.* (John Ross)

Above: *Tony Brooks (Vanwall), winner of the 1958 Belgian Grand Prix at the classic Spa circuit.* (LAT)

Right: *Stirling Moss in a Vanwall at the 1958 Italian Grand Prix. The British team went on to win the Constructors' Championship inaugurated that year, with 48 points to Ferrari's 40.* (John Ross)

Left: *Carroll Shelby inspects his Aston Martin DBR4 at the 1959 British Grand Prix.* (John Ross)

Below: *Ferrari colleagues, driver Tony Brooks and designer Carlo Chiti, at the 1959 Italian Grand Prix. The team's fortunes would be very mixed that day.* (John Ross)

Above: *Chuck Daigh in the front-engined Scarab, Riverside, 1960. Although the car looked stunning in its metallic blue colour scheme, the front engine era of GP racing had now passed.* (LAT)

Right: *Reigning World Champion Phil Hill (Ferrari 156) finished third in the 1962 Dutch Grand Prix.* (John Ross)

Above: *Jim Clark in the Lotus 25, on his way to winning the 1962 Belgian Grand Prix.* (John Ross)

Left: *Bruce McLaren walks back to the pits after retiring his Cooper at Spa, 1962.* (John Ross)

Opposite top: *Graham Hill (BRM P57) clinched his first World Championship at the 1962 South African Grand Prix, held at East London.* (LAT)

Opposite bottom: *The grid moves off at East London for the start of the 1963 South African Grand Prix. The race was won by Clark, with Dan Gurney second, Graham Hill third.* (LAT)

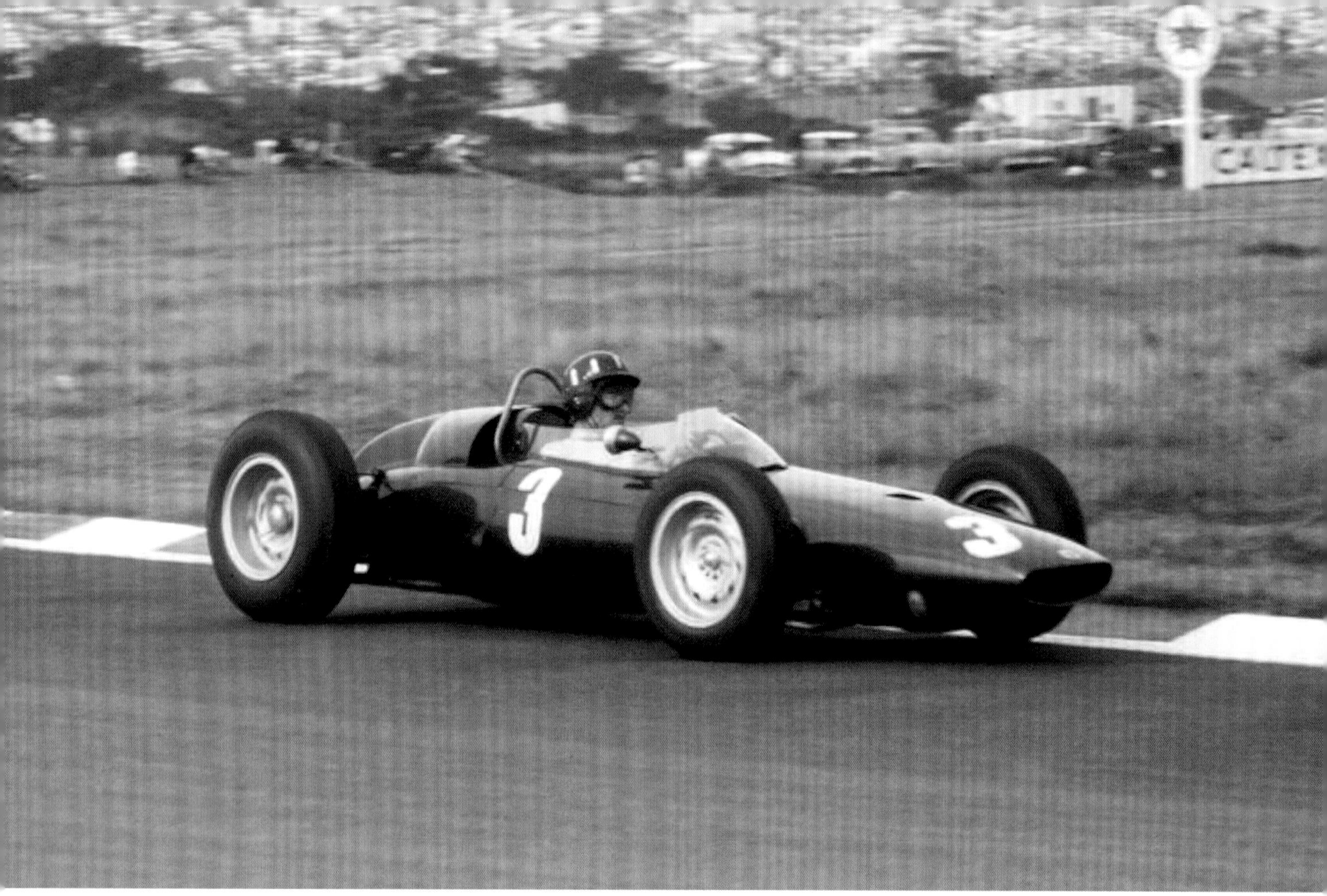

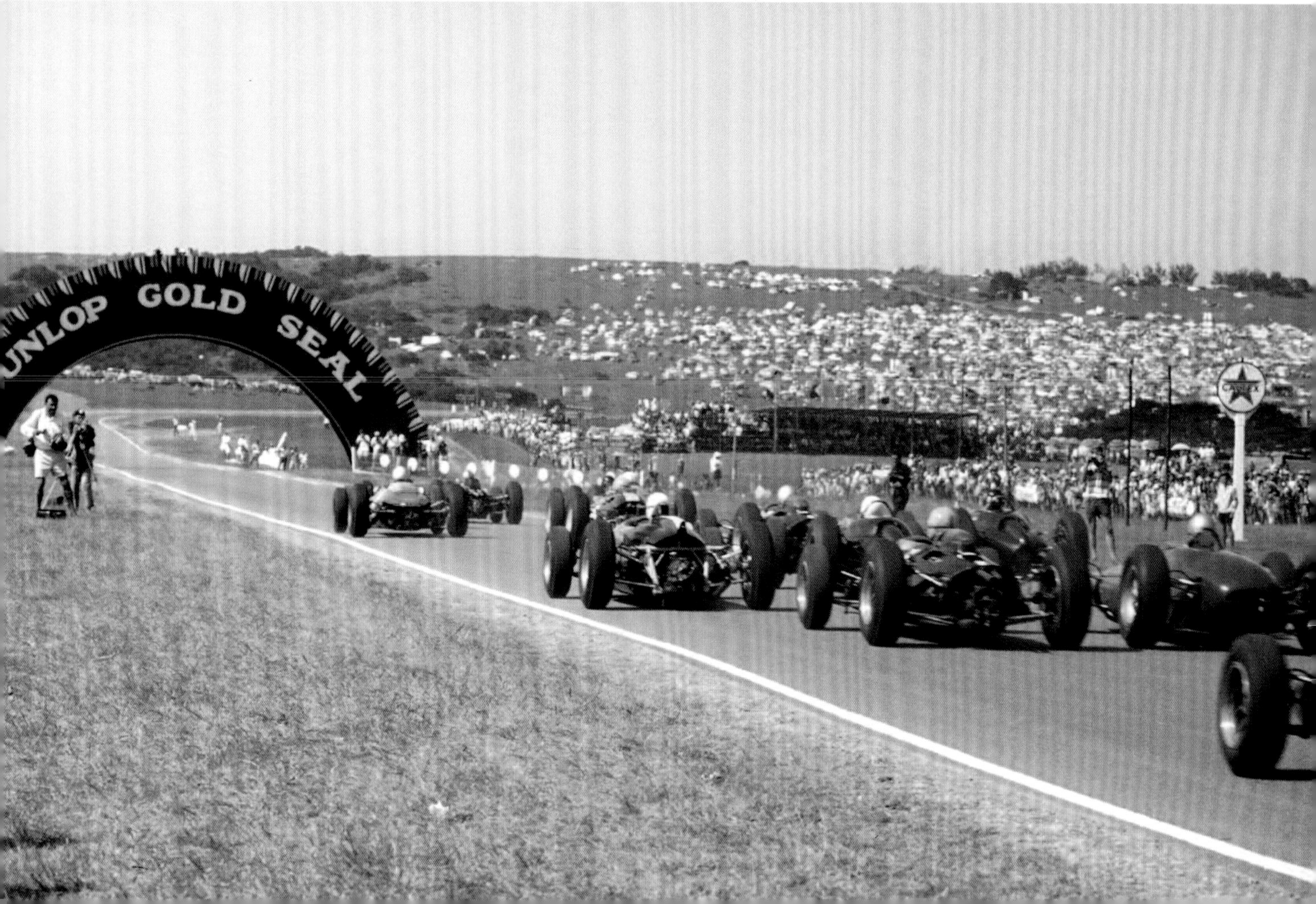
UNLOP GOLD SEAL

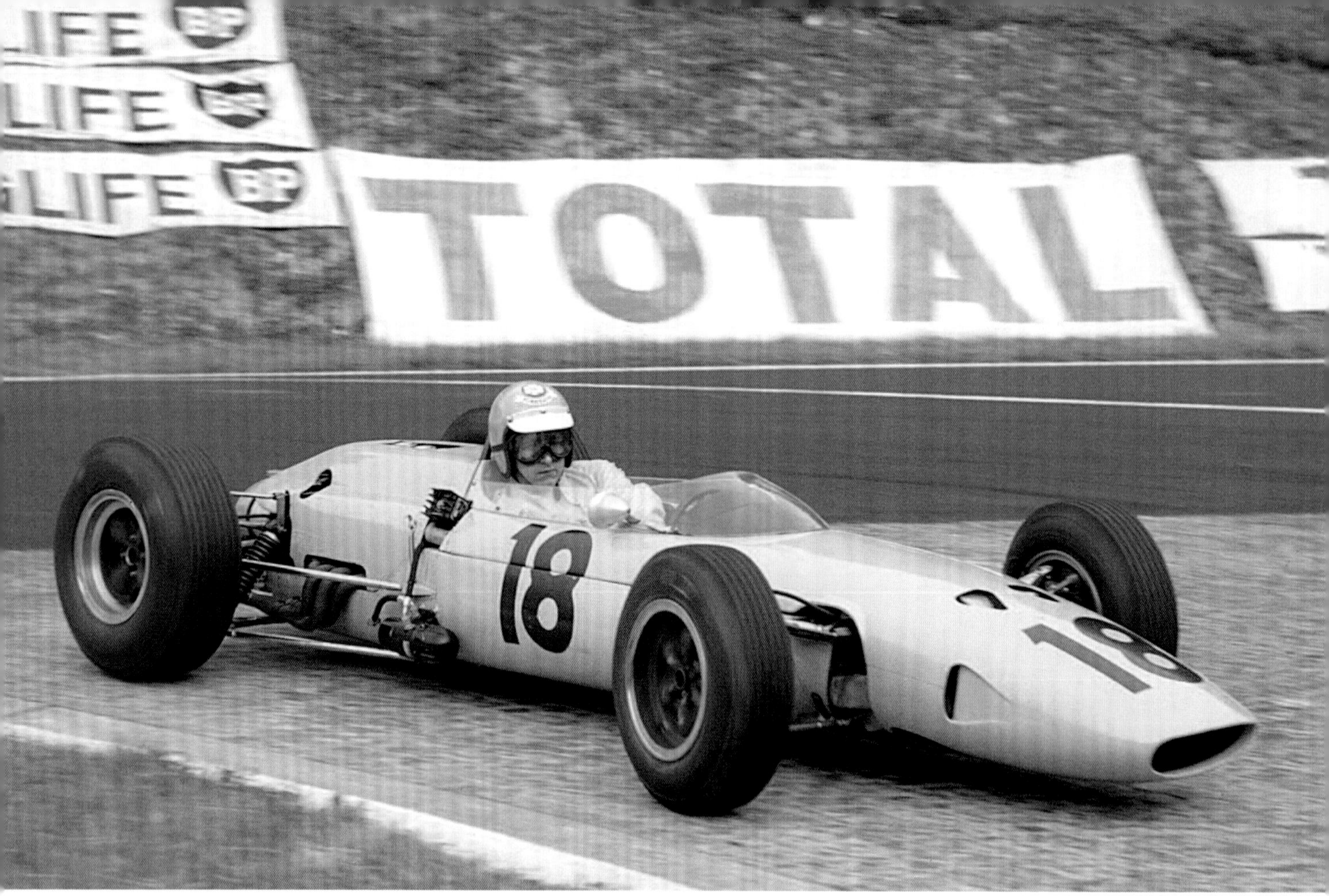
LIFE
LIFE
LIFE
BP
TOTAL
18
18

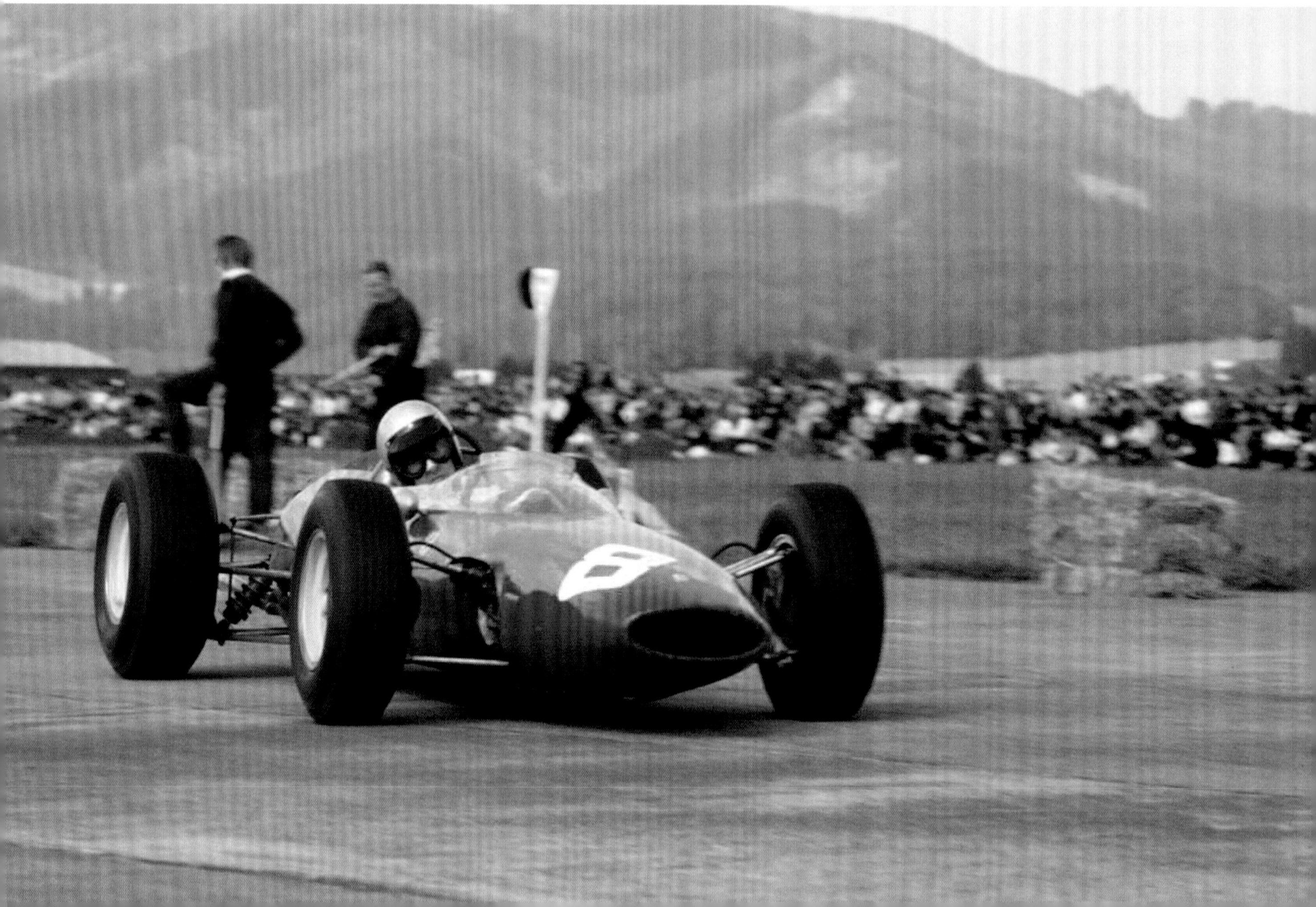
8

Opposite top: *Trevor Taylor (BRP Mk2-BRM), with his trademark yellow overalls and Yorkshire Rose, French Grand Prix, Rouen, 1964. (LAT)*

Opposite bottom: *Lorenzo Bandini (Ferrari 156) at the scene of his only World Championship victory, the 1964 Austrian Grand Prix. (LAT)*

Above: *Denny Hulme (Brabham BT7) in his debut championship race, Monaco, 1965. (LAT)*

Right: *The grid at Watkins Glen in 1965. Graham Hill was on pole and won the race after leading 107 of the 110 laps. (LAT)*

Left: *After seven seasons with the Cooper team, Bruce McLaren launched his own creation, the McLaren M2B, at the 1966 Monaco Grand Prix.* (LAT)

Below: *John Surtees, the only World Champion on two wheels and four, won the last race of the 1966 season, Mexico, in a Cooper-Maserati.* (LAT)

Above: *Reigning champion Jack Brabham in his Brabham BT24-Repco, heading for fourth place in the 1967 British Grand Prix at Silverstone.* (John Ross)

Right: *Denny Hulme (Brabham) overtook Jackie Stewart in the 1967 Monaco Grand Prix, one of his two victories in his championship year.* (LAT)

Below: *Jo Bonnier and John Surtees at the 1967 British Grand Prix. For the Swedish driver, now running his own team, this was a difficult season.* (John Ross)

Left: *Jean-Pierre Beltoise and Lodovico Scarfiotti at Kyalami in 1968 for the South African Grand Prix. This was the scene of Jim Clark's final GP victory and the last race where all cars ran without sponsors.* (LAT)

Below: *Jo Siffert, winner of the 1968 British Grand Prix in Rob Walker's privately entered Lotus 49B.* (LAT)

56 laps x 4.719 km, 2.932 miles = 264.241 km, 164.192 miles

Pos	No	Driver	Car	Model	Engine		Laps	Time/Reason for Retirement	Grid Pos	Row
1	1	E Fittipaldi	McLaren	M23	Ford Cosworth	V8	56	1h 22m 05.000s	7	4
2r	8	C Pace	Brabham	BT44B	Ford Cosworth	V8	55	accident	2	1
3r	3	J Scheckter	Tyrrell	007	Ford Cosworth	V8	55	accident	6	3
4r	24	J Hunt	Hesketh	308	Ford Cosworth	V8	55	accident	9	5
5r	28	M Donohue	March	751	Ford Cosworth	V8	55	accident	15	8
6	9	V Brambilla	March	751	Ford Cosworth	V8	55		5	3
7r	2	J Mass	McLaren	M23	Ford Cosworth	V8	55	accident	10	5
8	12	N Lauda	Ferrari	312T	Ferrari	F12	54		3	2
9r	4	P Depailler	Tyrrell	007	Ford Cosworth	V8	54	accident	17	9
10	22	A Jones	Hill	GH1	Ford Cosworth	V8	54		20	10
11r	18	J Watson	Surtees	TS16	Ford Cosworth	V8	54	accident	18	9
12	27	M Andretti	Parnelli	VPJ4	Ford Cosworth	V8	54		12	6
13	11	C Regazzoni	Ferrari	312T	Ferrari	F12	54		4	2
14r	17	J-P Jarier	Shadow	DN5	Ford Cosworth	V8	53	accident	11	6
15r	23	T Brise	Hill	GH1	Ford Cosworth	V8	53	accident	13	7
16r	15	B Henton	JPS Lotus	72F	Ford Cosworth	V8	53	accident	21	11
17r	32	J Nicholson	Lyncar	006	Ford Cosworth	V8	51	accident	26	13
18r	19	D Morgan	Surtees	TS16	Ford Cosworth	V8	50	accident	23	12
19r	30	W Fittipaldi	Copersucar	FD03	Ford Cosworth	V8	50	accident	24	12
r	10	H-J Stuck	March	751	Ford Cosworth	V8	45	accident	14	7
r	6	J Crawford	JPS Lotus	72F	Ford Cosworth	V8	28	accident	25	13
r	16	T Pryce	Shadow	DN5	Ford Cosworth	V8	20	accident	1	1
r	29	L Lombardi	March	751	Ford Cosworth	V8	18	ignition	22	11
r	5	R Peterson	JPS Lotus	72E	Ford Cosworth	V8	7	engine	16	8
r	21	J Laffite	Williams	FW04	Ford Cosworth	V8	5	gearbox	19	10
r	7	C Reutemann	Brabham	BT44B	Ford Cosworth	V8	4	engine	8	4
nq	31	R Wunderink	Ensign	N175	Ford Cosworth	V8				
nq	35	H Fushida	Maki	F101C	Ford Cosworth	V8				

Winning speed 193.151 km/h, 120.019 mph
Pole Position speed 214.049 km/h, 133.004 mph (T Pryce, 1 min:19.360 sec)
Fastest Lap speed 209.975 km/h, 130.472 mph (C Regazzoni, 1 min:20.900 sec on lap 16)
Lap Leaders C Pace 1-12,22-26 (17); C Regazzoni 13-18 (6); T Pryce 19-20 (2); J Scheckter 21,27-32 (7); J-P Jarier 33-34 (2); J Hunt 35-42 (8); E Fittipaldi 43-56 (14).

Scheduled for 67 laps, but stopped early because of rain.

14 laps x 22.835 km, 14.189 miles = 319.690 km, 198.646 miles

Pos	No	Driver	Car	Model	Engine		Laps	Time/Reason for Retirement	Grid Pos	Row
1	7	C Reutemann	Brabham	BT44B	Ford Cosworth	V8	14	1h 41m 14.100s	10	5
2	21	J Laffite	Williams	FW04	Ford Cosworth	V8	14	1h 42m 51.800s	15	8
3	12	N Lauda	Ferrari	312T	Ferrari	F12	14	1h 43m 37.400s	1	1
4	16	T Pryce	Shadow	DN5	Ford Cosworth	V8	14	1h 44m 45.500s	16	8
5	22	A Jones	Hill	GH1	Ford Cosworth	V8	14	1h 45m 04.400s	21	11
6	19	G van Lennep	Ensign	N175	Ford Cosworth	V8	14	1h 46m 19.600s	24	12
7	29	L Lombardi	March	751	Ford Cosworth	V8	14	1h 48m 44.500s	25	13
8	25	H Ertl	Hesketh	308	Ford Cosworth	V8	14	1h 48m 55.000s	23	12
9	4	P Depailler	Tyrrell	007	Ford Cosworth	V8	13		4	2
10r	27	M Andretti	Parnelli	VPJ4	Ford Cosworth	V8	12	out of fuel (leak)	13	7
r	24	J Hunt	Hesketh	308	Ford Cosworth	V8	10	rear hub	9	5
r	11	C Regazzoni	Ferrari	312T	Ferrari	F12	9	engine	5	3
r	23	T Brise	Hill	GH1	Ford Cosworth	V8	9	rear suspension / accident	17	9
r	3	J Scheckter	Tyrrell	007	Ford Cosworth	V8	7	tyre burst / accident	3	2
r	17	J-P Jarier	Shadow	DN5	Ford Cosworth	V8	7	rear tyre	12	6
r	8	C Pace	Brabham	BT44B	Ford Cosworth	V8	5	rear suspension	2	1
r	30	W Fittipaldi	Copersucar	FD03	Ford Cosworth	V8	4	engine	22	11
r	1	E Fittipaldi	McLaren	M23	Ford Cosworth	V8	3	rear tyre / suspension	8	4
r	10	H-J Stuck	March	751	Ford Cosworth	V8	3	engine	7	4
r	9	V Brambilla	March	751	Ford Cosworth	V8	3	tyres / suspension	11	6
r	6	J Watson	JPS Lotus	72F	Ford Cosworth	V8	2	front suspension	14	7
r	5	R Peterson	JPS Lotus	72E	Ford Cosworth	V8	1	clutch	18	9
r	28	M Donohue	March	751	Ford Cosworth	V8	1	front tyre burst	19	10
r	2	J Mass	McLaren	M23	Ford Cosworth	V8	0	front tyre burst / accident	6	3
ns	20	I Ashley	Williams	FW	Ford Cosworth	V8		accident / injury	20	10
nq	35	T Trimmer	Maki	F101C	Ford Cosworth	V8				

Winning speed 189.474 km/h, 117.734 mph
Pole Position speed 196.383 km/h, 122.027 mph (N Lauda, 6 min:58.600 sec)
Fastest Lap speed 192.791 km/h, 119.795 mph (C Regazzoni, 7 min: 6.400 sec on lap 7)
Lap Leaders N Lauda 1-9 (9); C Reutemann 10-14 (5).

29 laps x 5.911 km, 3.673 miles = 171.419 km, 106.515 miles

Pos	No	Driver	Car	Model	Engine		Laps	Time/Reason for Retirement	Grid Pos	Row
1	9	V Brambilla	March	751	Ford Cosworth	V8	29	57m 56.690s	8	4
2	24	J Hunt	Hesketh	308	Ford Cosworth	V8	29	58m 23.720s	2	1
3	16	T Pryce	Shadow	DN5	Ford Cosworth	V8	29	58m 31.540s	15	8
4	2	J Mass	McLaren	M23	Ford Cosworth	V8	29	59m 09.350s	9	5
5	5	R Peterson	JPS Lotus	72E	Ford Cosworth	V8	29	59m 20.020s	13	7
6	12	N Lauda	Ferrari	312T	Ferrari	F12	29	59m 26.970s	1	1
7	11	C Regazzoni	Ferrari	312T	Ferrari	F12	29	59m 35.760s	5	3
8	3	J Scheckter	Tyrrell	007	Ford Cosworth	V8	28		10	5
9	1	E Fittipaldi	McLaren	M23	Ford Cosworth	V8	28		3	2
10	18	J Watson	Surtees	TS16	Ford Cosworth	V8	28		18	9
11	4	P Depailler	Tyrrell	007	Ford Cosworth	V8	28		7	4
12	31	C Amon	Ensign	N175	Ford Cosworth	V8	28		23	12
13	25	B Lunger	Hesketh	308	Ford Cosworth	V8	28		17	9
14	7	C Reutemann	Brabham	BT44B	Ford Cosworth	V8	28		11	6
15	23	T Brise	Hill	GH1	Ford Cosworth	V8	28		16	8
16	22	R Stommelen	Hill	GH1	Ford Cosworth	V8	27		25	13
17	29	L Lombardi	March	751	Ford Cosworth	V8	26		21	11
nc	33	R Wunderink	Ensign	N174	Ford Cosworth	V8	25		27	14
r	32	H Ertl	Hesketh	308	Ford Cosworth	V8	23	electrics	26	13
r	21	J Laffite	Williams	FW04	Ford Cosworth	V8	21	handling	12	6
r	8	C Pace	Brabham	BT44B	Ford Cosworth	V8	17	engine	6	3
r	20	J Vonlanthen	Williams	FW	Ford Cosworth	V8	15	engine	28	14
r	10	H-J Stuck	March	751	Ford Cosworth	V8	11	accident	4	2
r	17	J-P Jarier	Shadow	DN7	Matra	V12	10	fuel injection	14	7
r	14	B Evans	Stanley BRM	P201	BRM	V12	2	engine	24	12
r	27	M Andretti	Parnelli	VPJ4	Ford Cosworth	V8	1	accident / front suspension	19	10
ns	30	W Fittipaldi	Copersucar	FD03	Ford Cosworth	V8		accident / injury		
ns	28	M Donohue	March	751	Ford Cosworth	V8		front tyre / fatal accident	20	10
ns	6	B Henton	JPS Lotus	72F	Ford Cosworth	V8		accident	22	11
nq	35	T Trimmer	Maki	F101C	Ford Cosworth	V8				

Winning speed 177.499 km/h, 110.293 mph
Pole Position speed 224.350 km/h, 139.405 mph (N Lauda, 1 min:34.850 sec)
Fastest Lap speed 186.827 km/h, 116.089 mph (V Brambilla, 1 min:53.900 sec)
Lap Leaders N Lauda 1-14 (14); J Hunt 15-18 (4); V Brambilla 19-29 (11).

Scheduled for 54 laps, but stopped early because of rain. Half points were awarded. Also the Grand Prix of Europe.

52 laps x 5.780 km, 3.592 miles = 300.560 km, 186.759 miles

Pos	No	Driver	Car	Model	Engine		Laps	Time/Reason for Retirement	Grid Pos	Row
1	11	C Regazzoni	Ferrari	312T	Ferrari	F12	52	1h 22m 42.600s	2	1
2	1	E Fittipaldi	McLaren	M23	Ford Cosworth	V8	52	1h 22m 59.200s	3	2
3	12	N Lauda	Ferrari	312T	Ferrari	F12	52	1h 23m 05.800s	1	1
4	7	C Reutemann	Brabham	BT44B	Ford Cosworth	V8	52	1h 23m 37.700s	7	4
5	24	J Hunt	Hesketh	308C	Ford Cosworth	V8	52	1h 23m 39.700s	8	4
6	16	T Pryce	Shadow	DN5	Ford Cosworth	V8	52	1h 23m 58.500s	14	7
7	4	P Depailler	Tyrrell	007	Ford Cosworth	V8	51		12	6
8	3	J Scheckter	Tyrrell	007	Ford Cosworth	V8	51		4	2
9	34	H Ertl	Hesketh	308	Ford Cosworth	V8	51		17	9
10	25	B Lunger	Hesketh	308	Ford Cosworth	V8	50		21	11
11	30	A Merzario	Copersucar	FD03	Ford Cosworth	V8	48		26	13
12	32	C Amon	Ensign	N175	Ford Cosworth	V8	48		19	10
13	6	J Crawford	JPS Lotus	72F	Ford Cosworth	V8	46		25	13
14	20	R Zorzi	Williams	FW	Ford Cosworth	V8	46		22	11
r	17	J-P Jarier	Shadow	DN7	Matra	V12	32	fuel pump	13	7
r	29	L Lombardi	March	751	Ford Cosworth	V8	21	accident	24	12
r	10	H-J Stuck	March	751	Ford Cosworth	V8	15	accident / rear suspension	16	8
r	21	J Laffite	Williams	FW04	Ford Cosworth	V8	7	gearbox	18	9
r	8	C Pace	Brabham	BT44B	Ford Cosworth	V8	6	throttle linkage	10	5
r	22	R Stommelen	Hill	GH1	Ford Cosworth	V8	3	accident / rear suspension	23	12
r	2	J Mass	McLaren	M23	Ford Cosworth	V8	2	accident	5	3
r	9	V Brambilla	March	751	Ford Cosworth	V8	1	clutch	9	5
r	27	M Andretti	Parnelli	VPJ4	Ford Cosworth	V8	1	accident	15	8
r	23	T Brise	Hill	GH1	Ford Cosworth	V8	1	accident	6	3
r	5	R Peterson	JPS Lotus	72E	Ford Cosworth	V8	1	engine	11	6
r	14	B Evans	Stanley BRM	P201	BRM	V12	0	clutch nut loose / electrics	20	10
nq	31	R Wunderink	Ensign	N174	Ford Cosworth	V8				
nq	35	T Trimmer	Maki	F101C	Ford Cosworth	V8				

Winning speed 218.034 km/h, 135.480 mph
Pole Position speed 225.585 km/h, 140.172 mph (N Lauda, 1 min:32.240 sec)
Fastest Lap speed 223.502 km/h, 138.877 mph (C Regazzoni, 1 min:33.100 sec on lap 47)
Lap Leaders C Regazzoni 1-52 (52).

59 laps x 5.435 km, 3.377 miles = 320.651 km, 199.243 miles

Pos	No	Driver	Car	Model	Engine		Laps	Time/Reason for Retirement	Grid Pos	Row
1	12	N Lauda	Ferrari	312T	Ferrari	F12	59	1h 42m 58.175s	1	1
2	1	E Fittipaldi	McLaren	M23	Ford Cosworth	V8	59	1h 43m 03.118s	2	1
3	2	J Mass	McLaren	M23	Ford Cosworth	V8	59	1h 43m 45.812s	9	5
4	24	J Hunt	Hesketh	308C	Ford Cosworth	V8	59	1h 43m 47.650s	15	8
5	5	R Peterson	JPS Lotus	72E	Ford Cosworth	V8	59	1h 43m 48.161s	14	7
6	3	J Scheckter	Tyrrell	007	Ford Cosworth	V8	59	1h 43m 48.496s	10	5
7	9	V Brambilla	March	751	Ford Cosworth	V8	59	1h 44m 42.206s	6	3
8	10	H-J Stuck	March	751	Ford Cosworth	V8	58		13	7
9	28	J Watson	Penske	PC1	Ford Cosworth	V8	57		12	6
10	30	W Fittipaldi	Copersucar	FD03	Ford Cosworth	V8	55		23	12
nc	16	T Pryce	Shadow	DN5	Ford Cosworth	V8	52		7	4
nc	6	B Henton	JPS Lotus	72F	Ford Cosworth	V8	49		19	10
r	25	B Lunger	Hesketh	308	Ford Cosworth	V8	46	accident	18	9
r	31	R Wunderink	Ensign	N175	Ford Cosworth	V8	41	gearbox	22	11
r	11	C Regazzoni	Ferrari	312T	Ferrari	F12	28	withdrew (protest)	11	6
r	17	J-P Jarier	Shadow	DN5	Ford Cosworth	V8	19	rear wheel bearing	4	2
r	7	C Reutemann	Brabham	BT44B	Ford Cosworth	V8	9	engine	3	2
r	27	M Andretti	Parnelli	VPJ4	Ford Cosworth	V8	9	front suspension	5	3
r	23	T Brise	Hill	GH1	Ford Cosworth	V8	5	accident	17	9
r	15	M Leclère	Tyrrell	007	Ford Cosworth	V8	5	engine	20	10
r	4	P Depailler	Tyrrell	007	Ford Cosworth	V8	2	accident	8	4
r	8	C Pace	Brabham	BT44B	Ford Cosworth	V8	2	accident	16	8
ns	21	J Laffite	Williams	FW04	Ford Cosworth	V8		visor cleaning fluid in eyes	21	11
ns	20	L Lombardi	Williams	FW04	Ford Cosworth	V8		ignition	24	12

Winning speed 186.842 km/h, 116.098 mph
Pole Position speed 191.809 km/h, 119.185 mph (N Lauda, 1 min:42.003 sec)
Fastest Lap speed 189.265 km/h, 117.604 mph (E Fittipaldi, 1 min:43.374 sec on lap 43)
Lap Leaders N Lauda 1-59 (59).

Lap Leaders 1975

Pos	Driver	Car-Engine	GPs	laps	km	miles
1	N Lauda	Ferrari	8	298	1,537.2	955.2
2	J Hunt	Hesketh-Ford Cosworth	5	88	395.6	245.8
	C Reutemann	Brabham-Ford Cosworth	4	88	512.2	318.3
4	J Scheckter	Tyrrell-Ford Cosworth	2	83	344.9	214.3
5	C Regazzoni	Ferrari	3	60	337.3	209.6
6	E Fittipaldi	McLaren-Ford Cosworth	2	33	179.5	111.5
7	C Pace	Brabham-Ford Cosworth	5	31	168.7	104.8
8	J-P Jarier	Shadow-Ford Cosworth	2	30	232.3	144.4
9	V Brambilla	March-Ford Cosworth	3	28	133.8	83.1
10	M Andretti	Parnelli-Ford Cosworth	1	10	37.9	23.6
11	R Stommelen	Hill-Ford Cosworth	1	8	30.3	18.8
12	J Mass	McLaren-Ford Cosworth	1	3	11.4	7.1
13	T Pryce	Shadow-Ford Cosworth	1	2	9.4	5.9
14	J Ickx	Lotus-Ford Cosworth	1	1	3.8	2.4
	R Peterson	Lotus-Ford Cosworth	1	1	3.3	2.0
			14	764	3,937.7	2,446.8

Driver Points 1975

	Driver	RA	BR	ZA	E	MC	B	S	NL	F	GB	D	A	I	USA	Total
1	N Lauda	1	2	2	-	9	9	9	6	9	-	4	0.5	4	9	64.5
2	E Fittipaldi	9	6	-	-	6	-	-	-	3	9	-	-	6	6	45
3	C Reutemann	4	-	6	2	-	4	6	3	-	-	9	-	3	-	37
4	J Hunt	6	1	-	-	-	-	-	9	6	3	-	3	2	3	33
5	C Regazzoni	3	3	-	-	-	2	4	4	-	-	-	-	9	-	25
6	C Pace	-	9	3	-	4	-	-	2	-	6	-	-	-	-	24
7	J Scheckter	-	-	9	-	-	6	-	-	-	4	-	-	-	1	20
	J Mass	-	4	1	4.5	1	-	-	4	-	-	-	1.5	-	4	20
9	P Depailler	2	-	4	-	2	3	-	1	-	-	-	-	-	-	12
10	T Pryce	-	-	-	-	-	1	-	1	-	-	3	2	1	-	8
11	V Brambilla	-	-	-	1	-	-	-	-	-	1	-	4.5	-	-	6.5
12	J Laffite	-	-	-	-	-	-	-	-	-	-	6	-	-	-	6
	R Peterson	-	-	-	3	-	-	-	-	-	-	-	1	-	2	6
14	M Andretti	-	-	-	-	-	-	3	-	2	-	-	-	-	-	5
15	M Donohue	-	-	-	-	-	-	2	-	-	2	-	-	-	-	4
16	J Ickx	-	-	-	3	-	-	-	-	-	-	-	-	-	-	3
17	A Jones	-	-	-	-	-	-	-	-	-	-	2	-	-	-	2
18	J-P Jarier	-	-	-	1.5	-	-	-	-	-	-	-	-	-	-	1.5
19	T Brise	-	-	-	-	-	-	1	-	-	-	-	-	-	-	1
	G van Lennep	-	-	-	-	-	-	-	-	-	-	1	-	-	-	1
21	L Lombardi	-	-	-	0.5	-	-	-	-	-	-	-	-	-	-	0.5

9,6,4,3,2 and 1 point awarded to the first six finishers. Best 7 scores from first 8 races, best 5 from remaining 6 races.
Half points awarded in Spain and Austria where the races were stopped early.

Constructor Points 1975

		RA	BR	ZA	E	MC	B	S	NL	F	GB	D	A	I	USA	Total
1	Ferrari	3	3	2	-	9	9	9	6	9	-	4	0.5	9	9	72.5
2	Brabham-Ford Cosworth	4	9	6	(2)	4	4	6	3	-	6	9	-	3	-	54 (2)
3	McLaren-Ford Cosworth	9	6	1	4.5	6	-	-	-	4	9	-	1.5	6	6	53
4	Hesketh-Ford Cosworth	6	1	-	-	-	-	-	9	6	3	-	3	2	3	33
5	Tyrrell-Ford Cosworth	2	-	9	-	-	2	6	-	-	1	4	-	-	1	25
6	Shadow-Ford Cosworth	-	-	-	1.5	-	1	-	1	-	-	3	2	1	-	9.5
7	Lotus-Ford Cosworth	-	-	-	3	3	-	-	-	-	-	-	1	-	2	9
8	March-Ford Cosworth	-	-	-	1	-	-	-	-	-	2	-	4.5	-	-	7.5
9	Williams-Ford Cosworth	-	-	-	-	-	-	-	-	-	-	6	-	-	-	6
10	Parnelli-Ford Cosworth	-	-	-	-	-	-	3	-	2	-	-	-	-	-	5
11	Hill-Ford Cosworth	-	-	-	-	-	1	-	-	-	-	2	-	-	-	3
12	Penske-Ford Cosworth	-	-	-	-	-	2	-	-	-	-	-	-	-	-	2
13	Ensign-Ford Cosworth	-	-	-	-	-	-	-	-	-	-	1	-	-	-	1

9,6,4,3,2 and 1 point awarded to the first six finishers. Points only for highest placed car. Best 7 scores from first 8 races, best 5 from remaining 6 races.

Race Entrants and Results

At the end of the previous season, the sports world was devastated by the air crash that killed Graham Hill, Tony Brise and four members of their racing team. Emerson Fittipaldi's sudden switch to the family team left a vacancy at McLaren, quickly filled by Hunt after the works Hesketh closure. Alfa and Matra engines made their full return and Tyrrell unveiled its unique 6-wheeler. Lauda was lucky to survive a fiery crash at the Nürburgring, but made an incredibly swift return to the tracks.

FERRARI
Scuderia Ferrari SpA SEFAC: Lauda, Regazzoni, Reutemann

TYRRELL
Elf Team Tyrrell: J Scheckter, Depailler
Scuderia Gulf Rondini: Pesenti-Rossi
Lexington Racing: I Scheckter
Heros Racing: Hoshino
OASC Racing Team: (Stuppacher)

LOTUS
John Player Team Lotus: Peterson, Evans, Andretti, Nilsson

BRABHAM
Martini Racing: Reutemann, Stommelen, Perkins, Pace
RAM Racing: Kessel, Evans, Nève, Lombardi, (de Villota, Nelleman, Magee)

MARCH
Beta Team March: Brambilla
March Engineering: Peterson, Stuck
Ovoro Team March: Merzario
Lavazza March: Lombardi

McLAREN
Marlboro Team McLaren: Hunt, Mass

BRM
Stanley BRM: Ashley

SHADOW
Shadow Racing Team: Pryce, Jarier
Team P R Reilly: (Wilds)

SURTEES
Team Surtees: Jones, Lunger, Andersson, Takahara
Team Norev Racing/BS Fabrications: Pescarolo
Shellsport: (Galica)

WILLIAMS
Walter Wolf Racing*: Ickx, Merzario, Zorzi, Leclère, Brown, Binder (Amon, Kuwashima) * known as Frank Williams Racing Cars for first 3 GPs
Mapfre-Williams: (Zapico)

ENSIGN
Team Ensign: Amon, Nève, Binder, Ickx
HB Bewaking Alarm Systems: Perkins (Boro)

HESKETH
Hesketh Racing: Ertl
Penthouse Rizla Racing with Hesketh: Edwards, Stommelen, Riberio

LIGIER
Ligier Gitanes: Laffite

PARNELLI
Vel's Parnelli Jones Racing: Andretti

PENSKE
Citibank Team Penske: Watson

FITTIPALDI (COPERSUCAR)
Copersucar-Fittipaldi: Fittipaldi, Hoffmann

KOJIMA
Kojima Engineering: Hasemi

MAKI
Maki Engineering: (Trimmer)

| 25 Jan 1976 | | BRAZIL: Interlagos | | | | | | | (Round 1) | (Race 265) |

40 laps x 7.960 km, 4.946 miles = 318.400 km, 197.845 miles

Pos	No	Driver	Car	Model	Engine		Laps	Time/Reason for Retirement	Grid Pos	Row
1	1	N Lauda	Ferrari	312T	Ferrari	F12	40	1h 45m 16.780s	2	1
2	4	P Depailler	Tyrrell	007	Ford Cosworth	V8	40	1h 45m 38.250s	9	5
3	16	T Pryce	Shadow	DN5B	Ford Cosworth	V8	40	1h 45m 40.620s	12	6
4	34	H-J Stuck	March	761	Ford Cosworth	V8	40	1h 46m 44.950s	14	7
5	3	J Scheckter	Tyrrell	007	Ford Cosworth	V8	40	1h 47m 13.240s	13	7
6	12	J Mass	McLaren	M23	Ford Cosworth	V8	40	1h 47m 15.050s	6	3
7	2	C Regazzoni	Ferrari	312T	Ferrari	F12	40	1h 47m 32.020s	4	2
8	20	J Ickx	Wolf Williams	FW05	Ford Cosworth	V8	39		19	10
9	21	R Zorzi	Wolf Williams	FW04	Ford Cosworth	V8	39		17	9
10	8	C Pace	Brabham	BT45	Alfa Romeo	F12	39		10	5
11	31	I Hoffmann	Copersucar	FD03	Ford Cosworth	V8	39		20	10
12r	7	C Reutemann	Brabham	BT45	Alfa Romeo	F12	37	out of fuel	15	8
13	30	E Fittipaldi	Copersucar	FD04	Ford Cosworth	V8	37		5	3
14	10	L Lombardi	March	761	Ford Cosworth	V8	36		22	11
r	17	J-P Jarier	Shadow	DN5B	Ford Cosworth	V8	33	accident	3	2
r	11	J Hunt	McLaren	M23	Ford Cosworth	V8	32	stuck throttle / accident	1	1
r	9	V Brambilla	March	761	Ford Cosworth	V8	15	oil leak	7	4
r	26	J Laffite	Ligier	JS5	Matra	V12	14	gear linkage	11	6
r	5	R Peterson	JPS Lotus	77	Ford Cosworth	V8	10	accident / engine overheating	18	9
r	6	M Andretti	JPS Lotus	77	Ford Cosworth	V8	6	accident / front suspension	16	8
r	28	J Watson	Penske	PC3	Ford Cosworth	V8	2	fuel line / fire	8	4
r	14	I Ashley	Stanley BRM	P201B	BRM	V12	2	oil pump	21	11

Winning speed 181.460 km/h, 112.754 mph
Pole Position speed 187.908 km/h, 116.761 mph (J Hunt, 2 min:32.500 sec)
Fastest Lap speed 184.794 km/h, 114.826 mph (J-P Jarier, 2 min:35.070 sec on lap 31)
Lap Leaders C Regazzoni 1-8 (8); N Lauda 9-40 (32).

SOUTH AFRICA: Kyalami (Round 2) (Race 266)

78 laps x 4.104 km, 2.550 miles = 320.112 km, 198.908 miles

Pos	No	Driver	Car	Model	Engine		Laps	Time/Reason for Retirement	Grid Pos	Row
1	1	N Lauda	Ferrari	312T	Ferrari	F12	78	1h 42m 18.400s	2	1
2	11	J Hunt	McLaren	M23	Ford Cosworth	V8	78	1h 42m 19.700s	1	1
3	12	J Mass	McLaren	M23	Ford Cosworth	V8	78	1h 43m 04.300s	4	2
4	3	J Scheckter	Tyrrell	007	Ford Cosworth	V8	78	1h 43m 26.800s	12	6
5	28	J Watson	Penske	PC3	Ford Cosworth	V8	77		3	2
6	27	M Andretti	Parnelli	VPJ4B	Ford Cosworth	V8	77		13	7
7	16	T Pryce	Shadow	DN5B	Ford Cosworth	V8	77		7	4
8	9	V Brambilla	March	761	Ford Cosworth	V8	77		5	3
9	4	P Depailler	Tyrrell	007	Ford Cosworth	V8	77		6	3
10	5	B Evans	JPS Lotus	77	Ford Cosworth	V8	77		23	12
11	18	B Lunger	Surtees	TS19	Ford Cosworth	V8	77		20	10
12	34	H-J Stuck	March	761	Ford Cosworth	V8	76		17	9
13	21	M Leclère	Wolf Williams	FW05	Ford Cosworth	V8	76		22	11
14	22	C Amon	Ensign	N174	Ford Cosworth	V8	76		18	9
15	24	H Ertl	Hesketh	308D	Ford Cosworth	V8	74		24	12
16	20	J Ickx	Wolf Williams	FW05	Ford Cosworth	V8	73		19	10
17r	30	E Fittipaldi	Copersucar	FD04	Ford Cosworth	V8	70	engine	21	11
r	2	C Regazzoni	Ferrari	312T	Ferrari	F12	52	engine	9	5
r	26	J Laffite	Ligier	JS5	Matra	V12	49	engine	8	4
r	17	J-P Jarier	Shadow	DN5B	Ford Cosworth	V8	28	radiator	15	8
r	8	C Pace	Brabham	BT45	Alfa Romeo	F12	22	engine	14	7
r	6	G Nilsson	JPS Lotus	77	Ford Cosworth	V8	18	clutch	25	13
r	7	C Reutemann	Brabham	BT45	Alfa Romeo	F12	16	engine	11	6
r	10	R Peterson	March	761	Ford Cosworth	V8	15	accident	10	5
r	15	I Scheckter	Tyrrell	007	Ford Cosworth	V8	0	accident	16	8

Winning speed 187.737 km/h, 116.654 mph
Pole Position speed 194.145 km/h, 120.636 mph (J Hunt, 1 min:16.100 sec)
Fastest Lap speed 189.488 km/h, 117.743 mph (N Lauda, 1 min:17.970 sec on lap 6)
Lap Leaders N Lauda 1-78 (78).

First 2 rows of the grid, chose to line up on the other side.

USA West: Long Beach (Round 3) (Race 267)

80 laps x 3.251 km, 2.020 miles = 260.070 km, 161.600 miles

Pos	No	Driver	Car	Model	Engine		Laps	Time/Reason for Retirement	Grid Pos	Row
1	2	C Regazzoni	Ferrari	312T	Ferrari	F12	80	1h 53m 18.471s	1	1
2	1	N Lauda	Ferrari	312T	Ferrari	F12	80	1h 54m 00.885s	4	2
3	4	P Depailler	Tyrrell	007	Ford Cosworth	V8	80	1h 54m 08.443s	2	1
4	26	J Laffite	Ligier	JS5	Matra	V12	80	1h 54m 31.299s	12	6
5	12	J Mass	McLaren	M23	Ford Cosworth	V8	80	1h 54m 40.763s	14	7
6	30	E Fittipaldi	Copersucar	FD04	Ford Cosworth	V8	79		16	8
7	17	J-P Jarier	Shadow	DN5B	Ford Cosworth	V8	79		7	4
8	22	C Amon	Ensign	N174	Ford Cosworth	V8	78		17	9
9	8	C Pace	Brabham	BT45	Alfa Romeo	F12	77		13	7
10	10	R Peterson	March	761	Ford Cosworth	V8	77		6	3
nc	19	A Jones	Surtees	TS19	Ford Cosworth	V8	70		19	10
nc	28	J Watson	Penske	PC3	Ford Cosworth	V8	69		9	5
r	3	J Scheckter	Tyrrell	007	Ford Cosworth	V8	34	front suspension	11	6
r	16	T Pryce	Shadow	DN5B	Ford Cosworth	V8	32	driveshaft	5	3
r	27	M Andretti	Parnelli	VPJ4B	Ford Cosworth	V8	15	water leak	15	8
r	11	J Hunt	McLaren	M23	Ford Cosworth	V8	3	accident	3	2
r	34	H-J Stuck	March	761	Ford Cosworth	V8	2	accident	18	9
r	6	G Nilsson	JPS Lotus	77	Ford Cosworth	V8	0	rear suspension / accident	20	10
r	7	C Reutemann	Brabham	BT45	Alfa Romeo	F12	0	accident	10	5
r	9	V Brambilla	March	761	Ford Cosworth	V8	0	accident	8	4
nq	21	M Leclère	Wolf Williams	FW05	Ford Cosworth	V8				
nq	31	I Hoffmann	Copersucar	FD04	Ford Cosworth	V8				
nq	35	A Merzario	March	761	Ford Cosworth	V8				
nq	5	B Evans	JPS Lotus	77	Ford Cosworth	V8				
nq	20	J Ickx	Wolf Williams	FW05	Ford Cosworth	V8				
nq	24	H Ertl	Hesketh	308D	Ford Cosworth	V8				
nq	18	B Lunger	Surtees	TS19	Ford Cosworth	V8				

Winning speed 137.715 km/h, 85.572 mph
Pole Position speed 140.834 km/h, 87.510 mph (C Regazzoni, 1 min:23.099 sec)
Fastest Lap speed 140.873 km/h, 87.534 mph (C Regazzoni, 1 min:23.076 sec on lap 61)
Lap Leaders C Regazzoni 1-80 (80).

75 laps x 3.404 km, 2.115 miles = 255.300 km, 158.636 miles

Pos	No	Driver	Car	Model	Engine		Laps	Time/Reason for Retirement	Grid Pos	Row
1	11	J Hunt	McLaren	M23	Ford Cosworth	V8	75	1h 42m 20.430s	1	1
2	1	N Lauda	Ferrari	312T2	Ferrari	F12	75	1h 42m 51.400s	2	1
3	6	G Nilsson	JPS Lotus	77	Ford Cosworth	V8	75	1h 43m 08.450s	7	4
4	7	C Reutemann	Brabham	BT45	Alfa Romeo	F12	74		12	6
5	22	C Amon	Ensign	N176	Ford Cosworth	V8	74		10	5
6	8	C Pace	Brabham	BT45	Alfa Romeo	F12	74		11	6
7	20	J Ickx	Wolf Williams	FW05	Ford Cosworth	V8	74		21	11
8	16	T Pryce	Shadow	DN5B	Ford Cosworth	V8	74		22	11
9	19	A Jones	Surtees	TS19	Ford Cosworth	V8	74		20	10
10	21	M Leclère	Wolf Williams	FW05	Ford Cosworth	V8	73		23	12
11	2	C Regazzoni	Ferrari	312T2	Ferrari	F12	72		5	3
12	26	J Laffite	Ligier	JS5	Matra	V12	72		8	4
13	37	L Perkins	Boro	N175	Ford Cosworth	V8	72		24	12
r	12	J Mass	McLaren	M23	Ford Cosworth	V8	65	engine	4	2
r	17	J-P Jarier	Shadow	DN5B	Ford Cosworth	V8	61	electrics	15	8
r	3	J Scheckter	Tyrrell	007	Ford Cosworth	V8	53	oil pump drive	14	7
r	28	J Watson	Penske	PC3	Ford Cosworth	V8	51	engine	13	7
r	35	A Merzario	March	761	Ford Cosworth	V8	36	gear linkage	18	9
r	5	M Andretti	JPS Lotus	77	Ford Cosworth	V8	34	gear selection	9	5
r	4	P Depailler	Tyrrell	P34	Ford Cosworth	V8	25	brakes / accident	3	2
r	9	V Brambilla	March	761	Ford Cosworth	V8	21	accident / rear suspension	6	3
r	34	H-J Stuck	March	761	Ford Cosworth	V8	16	gearbox	17	9
r	10	R Peterson	March	761	Ford Cosworth	V8	11	transmission	16	8
r	30	E Fittipaldi	Copersucar	FD04	Ford Cosworth	V8	3	gear linkage	19	10
nq	18	B Lunger	Surtees	TS19	Ford Cosworth	V8				
nq	32	L Kessel	Brabham	BT44B	Ford Cosworth	V8				
nq	25	E Zapico	Williams	FW04	Ford Cosworth	V8				
nq	33	E de Villota	Brabham	BT44B	Ford Cosworth	V8				
nq	24	H Ertl	Hesketh	308D	Ford Cosworth	V8				
nq	31	I Hoffmann	Copersucar	FD04	Ford Cosworth	V8				

Winning speed 149.677 km/h, 93.005 mph
Pole Position speed 156.067 km/h, 96.976 mph (J Hunt, 1 min:18.520 sec)
Fastest Lap speed 151.420 km/h, 94.088 mph (J Mass, 1 min:20.930 sec on lap 52)
Lap Leaders N Lauda 1-31 (31); J Hunt 32-75 (44).

J Hunt originally disqualified for car being too wide, but reinstated after appeal.
J Laffite originally disqualified for rear aerofoil irregularities, but reinstated after appeal.

70 laps x 4.262 km, 2.648 miles = 298.340 km, 185.380 miles

Pos	No	Driver	Car	Model	Engine		Laps	Time/Reason for Retirement	Grid Pos	Row
1	1	N Lauda	Ferrari	312T2	Ferrari	F12	70	1h 42m 53.230s	1	1
2	2	C Regazzoni	Ferrari	312T2	Ferrari	F12	70	1h 42m 56.690s	2	1
3	26	J Laffite	Ligier	JS5	Matra	V12	70	1h 43m 28.610s	6	3
4	3	J Scheckter	Tyrrell	P34	Ford Cosworth	V8	70	1h 44m 24.310s	7	4
5	19	A Jones	Surtees	TS19	Ford Cosworth	V8	69		16	8
6	12	J Mass	McLaren	M23	Ford Cosworth	V8	69		18	9
7	28	J Watson	Penske	PC3	Ford Cosworth	V8	69		17	9
8	37	L Perkins	Boro	N175	Ford Cosworth	V8	69		20	10
9	17	J-P Jarier	Shadow	DN5B	Ford Cosworth	V8	69		14	7
10	16	T Pryce	Shadow	DN5B	Ford Cosworth	V8	68		13	7
11	21	M Leclère	Wolf Williams	FW05	Ford Cosworth	V8	68		25	13
12	32	L Kessel	Brabham	BT44B	Ford Cosworth	V8	63		23	12
r	18	B Lunger	Surtees	TS19	Ford Cosworth	V8	62	electrics	26	13
r	8	C Pace	Brabham	BT45	Alfa Romeo	F12	58	electrics	9	5
r	22	C Amon	Ensign	N176	Ford Cosworth	V8	51	rear wheel lost / accident	8	4
r	11	J Hunt	McLaren	M23	Ford Cosworth	V8	35	transmission	3	2
r	34	H-J Stuck	March	761	Ford Cosworth	V8	33	rear wheel nut / suspension	15	8
r	24	H Ertl	Hesketh	308D	Ford Cosworth	V8	31	engine	24	12
r	4	P Depailler	Tyrrell	P34	Ford Cosworth	V8	29	engine	4	2
r	5	M Andretti	JPS Lotus	77	Ford Cosworth	V8	28	cv joint	11	6
r	33	P Nève	Brabham	BT44B	Ford Cosworth	V8	26	cv joint	19	10
r	35	A Merzario	March	761	Ford Cosworth	V8	21	engine	21	11
r	7	C Reutemann	Brabham	BT45	Alfa Romeo	F12	17	engine	12	6
r	10	R Peterson	March	761	Ford Cosworth	V8	16	accident	10	5
r	6	G Nilsson	JPS Lotus	77	Ford Cosworth	V8	7	accident	22	11
r	9	V Brambilla	March	761	Ford Cosworth	V8	6	driveshaft	5	3
nq	30	E Fittipaldi	Copersucar	FD04	Ford Cosworth	V8				
nq	20	J Ickx	Wolf Williams	FW05	Ford Cosworth	V8				
nq	25	G Edwards	Hesketh	308D	Ford Cosworth	V8				

Winning speed 173.981 km/h, 108.107 mph
Pole Position speed 177.276 km/h, 110.154 mph (N Lauda, 1 min:26.550 sec)
Fastest Lap speed 178.451 km/h, 110.884 mph (N Lauda, 1 min:25.980 sec)
Lap Leaders N Lauda 1-70 (70).

78 laps x 3.312 km, 2.058 miles = 258.336 km, 160.523 miles

Pos	No	Driver	Car	Model	Engine		Laps	Time/Reason for Retirement	Grid Pos	Row
1	1	N Lauda	Ferrari	312T2	Ferrari	F12	78	1h 59m 51.470s	1	1
2	3	J Scheckter	Tyrrell	P34	Ford Cosworth	V8	78	2h 00m 02.600s	5	3
3	4	P Depailler	Tyrrell	P34	Ford Cosworth	V8	78	2h 00m 56.310s	4	2
4	34	H-J Stuck	March	761	Ford Cosworth	V8	77		6	3
5	12	J Mass	McLaren	M23	Ford Cosworth	V8	77		11	6
6	30	E Fittipaldi	Copersucar	FD04	Ford Cosworth	V8	77		7	4
7	16	T Pryce	Shadow	DN5B	Ford Cosworth	V8	77		15	8
8	17	J-P Jarier	Shadow	DN5B	Ford Cosworth	V8	76		10	5
9	8	C Pace	Brabham	BT45	Alfa Romeo	F12	76		13	7
10	28	J Watson	Penske	PC3	Ford Cosworth	V8	76		17	9
11	21	M Leclère	Wolf Williams	FW05	Ford Cosworth	V8	76		18	9
12r	26	J Laffite	Ligier	JS5	Matra	V12	75	accident	8	4
13	22	C Amon	Ensign	N176	Ford Cosworth	V8	74		12	6
14r	2	C Regazzoni	Ferrari	312T2	Ferrari	F12	73	accident	2	1
r	6	G Nilsson	JPS Lotus	77	Ford Cosworth	V8	39	engine	16	8
r	10	R Peterson	March	761	Ford Cosworth	V8	26	accident	3	2
r	11	J Hunt	McLaren	M23	Ford Cosworth	V8	24	engine	14	7
r	9	V Brambilla	March	761	Ford Cosworth	V8	9	rear suspension / spin	9	5
r	19	A Jones	Surtees	TS19	Ford Cosworth	V8	1	accident	19	10
r	7	C Reutemann	Brabham	BT45	Alfa Romeo	F12	0	accident	20	10
nq	20	J Ickx	Wolf Williams	FW05	Ford Cosworth	V8				
nq	38	H Pescarolo	Surtees	TS19	Ford Cosworth	V8				
nq	37	L Perkins	Boro	N175	Ford Cosworth	V8				
nq	24	H Ertl	Hesketh	308D	Ford Cosworth	V8				
nq	35	A Merzario	March	761	Ford Cosworth	V8				

Winning speed 129.321 km/h, 80.356 mph
Pole Position speed 132.997 km/h, 82.641 mph (N Lauda, 1 min:29.650 sec)
Fastest Lap speed 132.069 km/h, 82.064 mph (C Regazzoni, 1 min:30.280 sec on lap 60)
Lap Leaders N Lauda 1-78 (78).

13 Jun 1976		SWEDEN: Anderstorp						(Round 7)		(Race 271)

72 laps x 4.018 km, 2.497 miles = 289.296 km, 179.760 miles

Pos	No	Driver	Car	Model	Engine		Laps	Time/Reason for Retirement	Grid Pos	Row
1	3	J Scheckter	Tyrrell	P34	Ford Cosworth	V8	72	1h 46m 53.729s	1	1
2	4	P Depailler	Tyrrell	P34	Ford Cosworth	V8	72	1h 47m 13.495s	4	2
3	1	N Lauda	Ferrari	312T2	Ferrari	F12	72	1h 47m 27.595s	5	3
4	26	J Laffite	Ligier	JS5	Matra	V12	72	1h 47m 49.548s	7	4
5	11	J Hunt	McLaren	M23	Ford Cosworth	V8	72	1h 47m 53.212s	8	4
6	2	C Regazzoni	Ferrari	312T2	Ferrari	F12	72	1h 47m 54.095s	11	6
7	10	R Peterson	March	761	Ford Cosworth	V8	72	1h 47m 57.222s	9	5
8	8	C Pace	Brabham	BT45	Alfa Romeo	F12	72	1h 48m 05.342s	10	5
9	16	T Pryce	Shadow	DN5B	Ford Cosworth	V8	71		12	6
10	9	V Brambilla	March	761	Ford Cosworth	V8	71		15	8
11	12	J Mass	McLaren	M23	Ford Cosworth	V8	71		13	7
12	17	J-P Jarier	Shadow	DN5B	Ford Cosworth	V8	71		14	7
13	19	A Jones	Surtees	TS19	Ford Cosworth	V8	71		18	9
14r	35	A Merzario	March	761	Ford Cosworth	V8	70	engine	19	10
15	18	B Lunger	Surtees	TS19	Ford Cosworth	V8	70		24	12
r	24	H Ertl	Hesketh	308D	Ford Cosworth	V8	54	spin	23	12
r	34	H-J Stuck	March	761	Ford Cosworth	V8	52	engine	20	10
r	5	M Andretti	JPS Lotus	77	Ford Cosworth	V8	45	engine	2	1
r	22	C Amon	Ensign	N176	Ford Cosworth	V8	38	front suspension / accident	3	2
r	21	M Leclère	Wolf Williams	FW05	Ford Cosworth	V8	20	engine	25	13
r	37	L Perkins	Boro	N175	Ford Cosworth	V8	18	engine	22	11
r	30	E Fittipaldi	Copersucar	FD04	Ford Cosworth	V8	10	handling	21	11
r	32	L Kessel	Brabham	BT44B	Ford Cosworth	V8	5	accident	26	13
r	6	G Nilsson	JPS Lotus	77	Ford Cosworth	V8	3	accident	6	3
r	7	C Reutemann	Brabham	BT45	Alfa Romeo	F12	2	engine	16	8
r	28	J Watson	Penske	PC4	Ford Cosworth	V8	0	throttle jammed / accident	17	9
nq	33	J Nelleman	Brabham	BT44B	Ford Cosworth	V8				

Winning speed 162.381 km/h, 100.899 mph
Pole Position speed 168.865 km/h, 104.928 mph (J Scheckter, 1 min:25.659 sec)
Fastest Lap speed 164.369 km/h, 102.134 mph (M Andretti, 1 min:28.002 sec on lap 11)
Lap Leaders M Andretti 1-45 (45); J Scheckter 46-72 (27).

M Andretti was given a 1 min penalty for jumping the start but led until lap 45. He is shown as a lap leader 'on the road'.

4 Jul 1976		FRANCE: Paul Ricard						(Round 8)		(Race 272)

54 laps x 5.810 km, 3.610 miles = 313.740 km, 194.949 miles

Pos	No	Driver	Car	Model	Engine		Laps	Time/Reason for Retirement	Grid Pos	Row
1	11	J Hunt	McLaren	M23	Ford Cosworth	V8	54	1h 40m 58.600s	1	1
2	4	P Depailler	Tyrrell	P34	Ford Cosworth	V8	54	1h 41m 11.300s	3	2
3	28	J Watson	Penske	PC4	Ford Cosworth	V8	54	1h 41m 22.150s	8	4
4	8	C Pace	Brabham	BT45	Alfa Romeo	F12	54	1h 41m 23.420s	5	3
5	5	M Andretti	JPS Lotus	77	Ford Cosworth	V8	54	1h 41m 42.520s	7	4
6	3	J Scheckter	Tyrrell	P34	Ford Cosworth	V8	54	1h 41m 53.670s	9	5
7	34	H-J Stuck	March	761	Ford Cosworth	V8	54	1h 42m 20.150s	17	9
8	16	T Pryce	Shadow	DN5B	Ford Cosworth	V8	54	1h 42m 29.270s	16	8
9	35	A Merzario	March	761	Ford Cosworth	V8	54	1h 42m 52.170s	20	10
10	20	J Ickx	Wolf Williams	FW05	Ford Cosworth	V8	53		19	10
11	7	C Reutemann	Brabham	BT45	Alfa Romeo	F12	53		10	5
12	17	J-P Jarier	Shadow	DN5B	Ford Cosworth	V8	53		15	8
13	21	M Leclère	Wolf Williams	FW05	Ford Cosworth	V8	53		22	11
14	26	J Laffite	Ligier	JS5	Matra	V12	53		13	7
15	12	J Mass	McLaren	M23	Ford Cosworth	V8	53		14	7
16	18	B Lunger	Surtees	TS19	Ford Cosworth	V8	53		23	12
17	25	G Edwards	Hesketh	308D	Ford Cosworth	V8	53		25	13
18	22	P Nève	Ensign	N176	Ford Cosworth	V8	53		26	13
19r	10	R Peterson	March	761	Ford Cosworth	V8	51	fuel metering unit	6	3
r	19	A Jones	Surtees	TS19	Ford Cosworth	V8	44	rear suspension	18	9
r	9	V Brambilla	March	761	Ford Cosworth	V8	28	oil pressure	11	6
r	30	E Fittipaldi	Copersucar	FD04	Ford Cosworth	V8	21	oil pressure	21	11
r	38	H Pescarolo	Surtees	TS19	Ford Cosworth	V8	19	rear suspension	24	12
r	2	C Regazzoni	Ferrari	312T2	Ferrari	F12	17	crankshaft / spin	4	2
r	1	N Lauda	Ferrari	312T2	Ferrari	F12	8	crankshaft	2	1
r	6	G Nilsson	JPS Lotus	77	Ford Cosworth	V8	8	transmission	12	6
r	24	H Ertl	Hesketh	308D	Ford Cosworth	V8	4	driveshaft (unofficial starter)	27	14
nq	33	D Magee	Brabham	BT44B	Ford Cosworth	V8				
nq	31	I Hoffmann	Copersucar	FD04	Ford Cosworth	V8				
nq	32	L Kessel	Brabham	BT44B	Ford Cosworth	V8				

Winning speed 186.423 km/h, 115.838 mph
Pole Position speed 193.864 km/h, 120.462 mph (J Hunt, 1 min:47.890 sec)
Fastest Lap speed 188.432 km/h, 117.086 mph (N Lauda, 1 min:51.000 sec on lap 4)
Lap Leaders N Lauda 1-8 (8); J Hunt 9-54 (46).

J Watson originally disqualified for rear aerofoil irregularities, but reinstated after appeal.

Races

76 laps x 4.207 km, 2.614 miles = 319.719 km, 198.664 miles

Pos	No	Driver	Car	Model	Engine		Laps	Time/Reason for Retirement	Grid Pos	Row
dq	11	J Hunt	McLaren	M23	Ford Cosworth	V8	76	used spare car in restart	2	1
1	1	N Lauda	Ferrari	312T2	Ferrari	F12	76	1h 44m 19.660s	1	1
2	3	J Scheckter	Tyrrell	P34	Ford Cosworth	V8	76	1h 44m 35.840s	8	4
3	28	J Watson	Penske	PC4	Ford Cosworth	V8	75		11	6
4	16	T Pryce	Shadow	DN5B	Ford Cosworth	V8	75		20	10
5	19	A Jones	Surtees	TS19	Ford Cosworth	V8	75		19	10
6	30	E Fittipaldi	Copersucar	FD04	Ford Cosworth	V8	74		21	11
7	24	H Ertl	Hesketh	308D	Ford Cosworth	V8	73		24	12
8	8	C Pace	Brabham	BT45	Alfa Romeo	F12	73		16	8
9	17	J-P Jarier	Shadow	DN5B	Ford Cosworth	V8	70		23	12
r	6	G Nilsson	JPS Lotus	77	Ford Cosworth	V8	67	engine	14	7
r	10	R Peterson	March	761	Ford Cosworth	V8	61	fuel pressure	7	4
r	18	B Lunger	Surtees	TS19	Ford Cosworth	V8	55	gearbox	18	9
r	4	P Depailler	Tyrrell	P34	Ford Cosworth	V8	47	engine	5	3
r	7	C Reutemann	Brabham	BT45	Alfa Romeo	F12	46	oil pressure	15	8
r	35	A Merzario	March	761	Ford Cosworth	V8	40	engine	9	5
r/dq	2	C Regazzoni	Ferrari	312T2	Ferrari	F12	37	engine *	4	2
r/dq	26	J Laffite	Ligier	JS5	Matra	V12	32	rear suspension *	13	7
r	32	B Evans	Brabham	BT44B	Ford Cosworth	V8	24	gearbox	22	11
r	9	V Brambilla	March	761	Ford Cosworth	V8	23	accident / front suspension	10	5
r	38	H Pescarolo	Surtees	TS19	Ford Cosworth	V8	16	fuel pressure	26	13
r	22	C Amon	Ensign	N176	Ford Cosworth	V8	9	water leak	6	3
r	5	M Andretti	JPS Lotus	77	Ford Cosworth	V8	5	engine	3	2
r	12	J Mass	McLaren	M23	Ford Cosworth	V8	2	clutch	12	6
r	34	H-J Stuck	March	761	Ford Cosworth	V8	0	accident	17	9
r	25	G Edwards	Hesketh	308D	Ford Cosworth	V8	0	accident	25	13
nq	20	J Ickx	Wolf Williams	FW05	Ford Cosworth	V8				
nq	13	D Galica	Surtees	TS16	Ford Cosworth	V8				
nq	40	M Wilds	Shadow	DN3	Ford Cosworth	V8				
nq	33	L Lombardi	Brabham	BT44B	Ford Cosworth	V8				

Winning speed 183.874 km/h, 114.254 mph
Pole Position speed 190.858 km/h, 118.594 mph (N Lauda, 1 min:19.350 sec)
Fastest Lap speed 189.520 km/h, 117.762 mph (N Lauda, 1 min:19.910 sec on lap 41)
Lap Leaders N Lauda 1-44 (44); J Hunt 45-76 (32).

Interrupted after first lap accident. Restarted for original distance. J Hunt finished 1st in 1h 43m 27.61s (185.416 km/h, 115.212 mph)
and recorded the fastest lap in 1m 19.82s (189.734 km/h, 117.895 mph).
* C Regazzoni and J Laffite disqualified (after their retirement), for restarting in spare cars.
J-P Jarier and H Ertl lined up on the grid in reverse order.

14 laps x 22.835 km, 14.189 miles = 319.690 km, 198.646 miles

Pos	No	Driver	Car	Model	Engine		Laps	Time/Reason for Retirement	Grid Pos	Row
1	11	J Hunt	McLaren	M23	Ford Cosworth	V8	14	1h 41m 42.700s	1	1
2	3	J Scheckter	Tyrrell	P34	Ford Cosworth	V8	14	1h 42m 10.400s	8	4
3	12	J Mass	McLaren	M23	Ford Cosworth	V8	14	1h 42m 35.100s	9	5
4	8	C Pace	Brabham	BT45	Alfa Romeo	F12	14	1h 42m 36.900s	7	4
5	6	G Nilsson	JPS Lotus	77	Ford Cosworth	V8	14	1h 43m 40.000s	16	8
6	77	R Stommelen	Brabham	BT45	Alfa Romeo	F12	14	1h 44m 13.000s	15	8
7	28	J Watson	Penske	PC4	Ford Cosworth	V8	14	1h 44m 16.600s	19	10
8	16	T Pryce	Shadow	DN5B	Ford Cosworth	V8	14	1h 44m 30.900s	18	9
9	2	C Regazzoni	Ferrari	312T2	Ferrari	F12	14	1h 45m 28.700s	5	3
10	19	A Jones	Surtees	TS19	Ford Cosworth	V8	14	1h 45m 30.000s	14	7
11	17	J-P Jarier	Shadow	DN5B	Ford Cosworth	V8	14	1h 46m 34.400s	23	12
12	5	M Andretti	JPS Lotus	77	Ford Cosworth	V8	14	1h 46m 40.800s	12	6
13	30	E Fittipaldi	Copersucar	FD04	Ford Cosworth	V8	14	1h 47m 07.900s	20	10
14	40	S Pesenti-Rossi	Tyrrell	007	Ford Cosworth	V8	13		26	13
15	25	G Edwards	Hesketh	308D	Ford Cosworth	V8	13		25	13
r	20	A Merzario	Wolf Williams	FW05	Ford Cosworth	V8	3	brakes	21	11
r	9	V Brambilla	March	761	Ford Cosworth	V8	1	brakes / accident	13	7
r	4	P Depailler	Tyrrell	P34	Ford Cosworth	V8	0	accident	3	2
r	7	C Reutemann	Brabham	BT45	Alfa Romeo	F12	0	engine	10	5
r	10	R Peterson	March	761	Ford Cosworth	V8	0	accident	11	6
r	34	H-J Stuck	March	761	Ford Cosworth	V8	0	clutch *	4	2
r	26	J Laffite	Ligier	JS5	Matra	V12	0	gearbox *	6	3
r	22	C Amon	Ensign	N176	Ford Cosworth	V8	0	withdrew *	17	9
r	1	N Lauda	Ferrari	312T2	Ferrari	F12	0	accident / injury *	2	1
r	18	B Lunger	Surtees	TS19	Ford Cosworth	V8	0	accident *	24	12
r	24	H Ertl	Hesketh	308D	Ford Cosworth	V8	0	accident *	22	11
nq	33	L Lombardi	Brabham	BT44B	Ford Cosworth	V8		car impounded by police		
nq	38	H Pescarolo	Surtees	TS19	Ford Cosworth	V8				

Winning speed 188.586 km/h, 117.182 mph
Pole Position speed 192.746 km/h, 119.767 mph (J Hunt, 7 min: 6.500 sec)
Fastest Lap speed 190.822 km/h, 118.571 mph (J Scheckter, 7 min:10.800 sec on lap 13)
Lap Leaders J Hunt 1-14 (14).

Interrupted after first lap accident. Restarted for original distance.   ** Retired after first start.*

15 Aug 1976   **AUSTRIA: Österreichring**   **(Round 11)**   **(Race 275)**

54 laps x 5.910 km, 3.672 miles = 319.140 km, 198.304 miles

Pos	No	Driver	Car	Model	Engine		Laps	Time/Reason for Retirement	Grid Pos	Row
1	28	J Watson	Penske	PC4	Ford Cosworth	V8	54	1h 30m 07.860s	2	1
2	26	J Laffite	Ligier	JS5	Matra	V12	54	1h 30m 18.650s	5	3
3	6	G Nilsson	JPS Lotus	77	Ford Cosworth	V8	54	1h 30m 19.840s	4	2
4	11	J Hunt	McLaren	M23	Ford Cosworth	V8	54	1h 30m 20.300s	1	1
5	5	M Andretti	JPS Lotus	77	Ford Cosworth	V8	54	1h 30m 29.350s	9	5
6	10	R Peterson	March	761	Ford Cosworth	V8	54	1h 30m 42.200s	3	2
7	12	J Mass	McLaren	M23	Ford Cosworth	V8	54	1h 31m 07.310s	12	6
8	24	H Ertl	Hesketh	308D	Ford Cosworth	V8	53		20	10
9	38	H Pescarolo	Surtees	TS19	Ford Cosworth	V8	52		22	11
10r	18	B Lunger	Surtees	TS19	Ford Cosworth	V8	51	brakes / accident	16	8
11	39	S Pesenti-Rossi	Tyrrell	007	Ford Cosworth	V8	51		23	12
12	33	L Lombardi	Brabham	BT44B	Ford Cosworth	V8	50		24	12
r	22	H Binder	Ensign	N176	Ford Cosworth	V8	47	throttle linkage	19	10
nc	32	L Kessel	Brabham	BT44B	Ford Cosworth	V8	44		25	13
r	9	V Brambilla	March	761	Ford Cosworth	V8	43	accident	7	4
r	30	E Fittipaldi	Copersucar	FD04	Ford Cosworth	V8	43	accident	17	9
r	17	J-P Jarier	Shadow	DN5B	Ford Cosworth	V8	40	fuel pump	18	9
r	8	C Pace	Brabham	BT45	Alfa Romeo	F12	40	brakes / accident	8	4
r	19	A Jones	Surtees	TS19	Ford Cosworth	V8	30	engine / accident	15	8
r	34	H-J Stuck	March	761	Ford Cosworth	V8	26	fuel pump	11	6
r	4	P Depailler	Tyrrell	P34	Ford Cosworth	V8	24	front suspension	13	7
r	20	A Merzario	Wolf Williams	FW05	Ford Cosworth	V8	17	accident	21	11
r	16	T Pryce	Shadow	DN5B	Ford Cosworth	V8	14	brakes	6	3
r	3	J Scheckter	Tyrrell	P34	Ford Cosworth	V8	14	front suspension / accident	10	5
r	7	C Reutemann	Brabham	BT45	Alfa Romeo	F12	0	clutch	14	7

Winning speed 212.451 km/h, 132.011 mph
Pole Position speed 223.911 km/h, 139.132 mph (J Hunt, 1 min:35.020 sec)
Fastest Lap speed 221.833 km/h, 137.841 mph (J Hunt, 1 min:35.910 sec)
Lap Leaders J Watson 1-2,12-54 (45); R Peterson 3-9,11 (8); J Scheckter 10 (1).

29 Aug 1976   **NETHERLANDS: Zandvoort**   **(Round 12)**   **(Race 276)**

75 laps x 4.226 km, 2.626 miles = 316.950 km, 196.944 miles

Pos	No	Driver	Car	Model	Engine		Laps	Time/Reason for Retirement	Grid Pos	Row
1	11	J Hunt	McLaren	M23	Ford Cosworth	V8	75	1h 44m 52.090s	2	1
2	2	C Regazzoni	Ferrari	312T2	Ferrari	F12	75	1h 44m 53.010s	5	3
3	5	M Andretti	JPS Lotus	77	Ford Cosworth	V8	75	1h 44m 54.180s	6	3
4	16	T Pryce	Shadow	DN8	Ford Cosworth	V8	75	1h 44m 59.030s	3	2
5	3	J Scheckter	Tyrrell	P34	Ford Cosworth	V8	75	1h 45m 14.550s	8	4
6	9	V Brambilla	March	761	Ford Cosworth	V8	75	1h 45m 37.120s	7	4
7	4	P Depailler	Tyrrell	P34	Ford Cosworth	V8	75	1h 45m 48.370s	14	7
8	19	A Jones	Surtees	TS19	Ford Cosworth	V8	74		16	8
9	12	J Mass	McLaren	M26	Ford Cosworth	V8	74		15	8
10	17	J-P Jarier	Shadow	DN5B	Ford Cosworth	V8	74		20	10
11	38	H Pescarolo	Surtees	TS19	Ford Cosworth	V8	74		22	11
12	25	R Stommelen	Hesketh	308D	Ford Cosworth	V8	72		25	13
r	22	J Ickx	Ensign	N176	Ford Cosworth	V8	66	electrics	11	6
r	39	B Hayje	Penske	PC3	Ford Cosworth	V8	63	driveshaft	21	11
r	8	C Pace	Brabham	BT45	Alfa Romeo	F12	53	oil leak	9	5
r	26	J Laffite	Ligier	JS5	Matra	V12	53	oil pressure	10	5
r	10	R Peterson	March	761	Ford Cosworth	V8	52	oil pressure	1	1
r	24	H Ertl	Hesketh	308D	Ford Cosworth	V8	49	spin / gearbox	24	12
r	28	J Watson	Penske	PC4	Ford Cosworth	V8	47	gearbox	4	2
r	37	L Perkins	Boro	N175	Ford Cosworth	V8	44	accident	19	10
r	30	E Fittipaldi	Copersucar	FD04	Ford Cosworth	V8	40	electrics	17	9
r	7	C Reutemann	Brabham	BT45	Alfa Romeo	F12	11	clutch fluid loss	12	6
r	6	G Nilsson	JPS Lotus	77	Ford Cosworth	V8	10	accident	13	7
r	18	C Andersson	Surtees	TS19	Ford Cosworth	V8	9	engine	26	13
r	34	H-J Stuck	March	761	Ford Cosworth	V8	9	engine	18	9
r	20	A Merzario	Wolf Williams	FW05	Ford Cosworth	V8	5	accident	23	12
nq	40	S Pesenti-Rossi	Tyrrell	007	Ford Cosworth	V8				

Winning speed 181.342 km/h, 112.681 mph
Pole Position speed 187.106 km/h, 116.262 mph (R Peterson, 1 min:21.310 sec)
Fastest Lap speed 184.206 km/h, 114.461 mph (C Regazzoni, 1 min:22.590 sec on lap 49)
Lap Leaders R Peterson 1-11 (11); J Hunt 12-75 (64).

Also the Grand Prix of Europe.

12 Sep 1976   **ITALY: Monza**   **(Round 13)**   **(Race 277)**

52 laps x 5.800 km, 3.604 miles = 301.600 km, 187.406 miles

Pos	No	Driver	Car	Model	Engine		Laps	Time/Reason for Retirement	Grid Pos	Row
1	10	R Peterson	March	761	Ford Cosworth	V8	52	1h 30m 35.600s	8	4
2	2	C Regazzoni	Ferrari	312T2	Ferrari	F12	52	1h 30m 37.900s	9	5
3	26	J Laffite	Ligier	JS5	Matra	V12	52	1h 30m 38.600s	1	1
4	1	N Lauda	Ferrari	312T2	Ferrari	F12	52	1h 30m 55.000s	5	3
5	3	J Scheckter	Tyrrell	P34	Ford Cosworth	V8	52	1h 30m 55.100s	2	1
6	4	P Depailler	Tyrrell	P34	Ford Cosworth	V8	52	1h 31m 11.300s	4	2
7	9	V Brambilla	March	761	Ford Cosworth	V8	52	1h 31m 19.500s	16	8
8	16	T Pryce	Shadow	DN8	Ford Cosworth	V8	52	1h 31m 28.500s	15	8
9	35	C Reutemann	Ferrari	312T2	Ferrari	F12	52	1h 31m 33.100s	7	4
10	22	J Ickx	Ensign	N176	Ford Cosworth	V8	52	1h 31m 48.000s	10	5
11	28	J Watson	Penske	PC4	Ford Cosworth	V8	52	1h 32m 17.800s	27	14
12	19	A Jones	Surtees	TS19	Ford Cosworth	V8	51		18	9
13	6	G Nilsson	JPS Lotus	77	Ford Cosworth	V8	51		12	6
14	18	B Lunger	Surtees	TS19	Ford Cosworth	V8	50		24	12
15	30	E Fittipaldi	Copersucar	FD04	Ford Cosworth	V8	50		20	10
16r	24	H Ertl	Hesketh	308D	Ford Cosworth	V8	49	driveshaft	19	10
17	38	H Pescarolo	Surtees	TS19	Ford Cosworth	V8	49		22	11
18	37	S Pesenti-Rossi	Tyrrell	007	Ford Cosworth	V8	49		21	11
19	17	J-P Jarier	Shadow	DN5B	Ford Cosworth	V8	47		17	9
r	7	R Stommelen	Brabham	BT45	Alfa Romeo	F12	41	fuel system	11	6
r	34	H-J Stuck	March	761	Ford Cosworth	V8	23	accident	6	3
r	5	M Andretti	JPS Lotus	77	Ford Cosworth	V8	23	accident	14	7
r	11	J Hunt	McLaren	M23	Ford Cosworth	V8	11	spin	25	13
r	40	L Perkins	Boro	N175	Ford Cosworth	V8	9	connecting rod	13	7
r	8	C Pace	Brabham	BT45	Alfa Romeo	F12	4	piston	3	2
r	12	J Mass	McLaren	M23	Ford Cosworth	V8	3	ignition	26	13
ns	25	G Edwards	Hesketh	308D	Ford Cosworth	V8		allowed Watson to race	23	12
ns	20	A Merzario	Wolf Williams	FW05	Ford Cosworth	V8		withdrew		
ns	39	O Stuppacher	Tyrrell	007	Ford Cosworth	V8		believed he hadn't qualified		

Winning speed 199.750 km/h, 124.119 mph
Pole Position speed 206.019 km/h, 128.014 mph (J Laffite, 1 min:41.350 sec)
Fastest Lap speed 206.120 km/h, 128.077 mph (R Peterson, 1 min:41.300 sec on lap 50)
Lap Leaders J Scheckter 1-10 (10); R Peterson 11-52 (42).

---

3 Oct 1976   **CANADA: Mosport Park**   **(Round 14)**   **(Race 278)**

80 laps x 3.957 km, 2.459 miles = 316.590 km, 196.720 miles

Pos	No	Driver	Car	Model	Engine		Laps	Time/Reason for Retirement	Grid Pos	Row
1	11	J Hunt	McLaren	M23	Ford Cosworth	V8	80	1h 40m 09.626s	1	1
2	4	P Depailler	Tyrrell	P34	Ford Cosworth	V8	80	1h 40m 15.957s	4	2
3	5	M Andretti	JPS Lotus	77	Ford Cosworth	V8	80	1h 40m 19.992s	5	3
4	3	J Scheckter	Tyrrell	P34	Ford Cosworth	V8	80	1h 40m 29.371s	7	4
5	12	J Mass	McLaren	M23	Ford Cosworth	V8	80	1h 40m 51.437s	11	6
6	2	C Regazzoni	Ferrari	312T2	Ferrari	F12	80	1h 40m 55.882s	12	6
7	8	C Pace	Brabham	BT45	Alfa Romeo	F12	80	1h 40m 56.098s	10	5
8	1	N Lauda	Ferrari	312T2	Ferrari	F12	80	1h 41m 22.583s	6	3
9	10	R Peterson	March	761	Ford Cosworth	V8	79		2	1
10	28	J Watson	Penske	PC4	Ford Cosworth	V8	79		14	7
11	16	T Pryce	Shadow	DN8	Ford Cosworth	V8	79		13	7
12	6	G Nilsson	JPS Lotus	77	Ford Cosworth	V8	79		15	8
13	22	J Ickx	Ensign	N176	Ford Cosworth	V8	79		16	8
14	9	V Brambilla	March	761	Ford Cosworth	V8	79		3	2
15	18	B Lunger	Surtees	TS19	Ford Cosworth	V8	78		22	11
16	19	A Jones	Surtees	TS19	Ford Cosworth	V8	78		20	10
17	7	L Perkins	Brabham	BT45	Alfa Romeo	F12	78		19	10
18	17	J-P Jarier	Shadow	DN5B	Ford Cosworth	V8	77		18	9
19	38	H Pescarolo	Surtees	TS19	Ford Cosworth	V8	77		21	11
20	25	G Edwards	Hesketh	308D	Ford Cosworth	V8	75		23	12
r	26	J Laffite	Ligier	JS5	Matra	V12	43	oil pressure	9	5
r	30	E Fittipaldi	Copersucar	FD04	Ford Cosworth	V8	42	exhaust / wing bracket	17	9
r	34	H-J Stuck	March	761	Ford Cosworth	V8	36	handling	8	4
r	20	A Merzario	Wolf Williams	FW05	Ford Cosworth	V8	11	spin	24	12
ns	24	H Ertl	Hesketh	308D	Ford Cosworth	V8		accident		
ns	21	C Amon	Wolf Williams	FW05	Ford Cosworth	V8		accident		
nq	39	O Stuppacher	Tyrrell	007	Ford Cosworth	V8				

Winning speed 189.650 km/h, 117.843 mph
Pole Position speed 196.806 km/h, 122.289 mph (J Hunt, 1 min:12.389 sec)
Fastest Lap speed 192.998 km/h, 119.924 mph (P Depailler, 1 min:13.817 sec on lap 60)
Lap Leaders R Peterson 1-8 (8); J Hunt 9-80 (72).

59 laps x 5.435 km, 3.377 miles = 320.651 km, 199.243 miles

Pos	No	Driver	Car	Model	Engine		Laps	Time/Reason for Retirement	Grid Pos	Row
1	11	J Hunt	McLaren	M23	Ford Cosworth	V8	59	1h 42m 40.741s	1	1
2	3	J Scheckter	Tyrrell	P34	Ford Cosworth	V8	59	1h 42m 48.771s	2	1
3	1	N Lauda	Ferrari	312T2	Ferrari	F12	59	1h 43m 43.065s	5	3
4	12	J Mass	McLaren	M23	Ford Cosworth	V8	59	1h 43m 43.199s	17	9
5	34	H-J Stuck	March	761	Ford Cosworth	V8	59	1h 43m 48.719s	6	3
6	28	J Watson	Penske	PC4	Ford Cosworth	V8	59	1h 43m 48.931s	8	4
7	2	C Regazzoni	Ferrari	312T2	Ferrari	F12	58		14	7
8	19	A Jones	Surtees	TS19	Ford Cosworth	V8	58		18	9
9	30	E Fittipaldi	Copersucar	FD04	Ford Cosworth	V8	57		15	8
10	17	J-P Jarier	Shadow	DN5B	Ford Cosworth	V8	57		16	8
11	18	B Lunger	Surtees	TS19	Ford Cosworth	V8	57		24	12
12	25	A D Ribeiro	Hesketh	308D	Ford Cosworth	V8	57		22	11
13	24	H Ertl	Hesketh	308D	Ford Cosworth	V8	54		21	11
14	21	W Brown	Wolf Williams	FW05	Ford Cosworth	V8	54		23	12
nc	38	H Pescarolo	Surtees	TS19	Ford Cosworth	V8	48		26	13
r	16	T Pryce	Shadow	DN8	Ford Cosworth	V8	45	engine	9	5
r	26	J Laffite	Ligier	JS5	Matra	V12	34	rear tyre burst / suspension	12	6
r	9	V Brambilla	March	761	Ford Cosworth	V8	34	rear tyre burst	4	2
r	8	C Pace	Brabham	BT45	Alfa Romeo	F12	31	accident	10	5
r	7	L Perkins	Brabham	BT45	Alfa Romeo	F12	30	front suspension	13	7
r	5	M Andretti	JPS Lotus	77	Ford Cosworth	V8	23	accident / front suspension	11	6
r	22	J Ickx	Ensign	N176	Ford Cosworth	V8	14	accident	19	10
r	6	G Nilsson	JPS Lotus	77	Ford Cosworth	V8	13	engine	20	10
r	10	R Peterson	March	761	Ford Cosworth	V8	12	front suspension	3	2
r	20	A Merzario	Wolf Williams	FW05	Ford Cosworth	V8	9	spin	25	13
r	4	P Depailler	Tyrrell	P34	Ford Cosworth	V8	7	fuel line	7	4
nq	39	O Stuppacher	Tyrrell	007	Ford Cosworth	V8				

Winning speed 187.371 km/h, 116.427 mph
Pole Position speed 188.812 km/h, 117.323 mph (J Hunt, 1 min:43.622 sec)
Fastest Lap speed 190.228 km/h, 118.202 mph (J Hunt, 1 min:42.851 sec on lap 53)
Lap Leaders J Scheckter 1-36,41-45 (41); J Hunt 37-40,46-59 (18).

73 laps x 4.359 km, 2.709 miles = 318.207 km, 197.725 miles

Pos	No	Driver	Car	Model	Engine		Laps	Time/Reason for Retirement	Grid Pos	Row
1	5	M Andretti	JPS Lotus	77	Ford Cosworth	V8	73	1h 43m 58.860s	1	1
2	4	P Depailler	Tyrrell	P34	Ford Cosworth	V8	72		13	7
3	11	J Hunt	McLaren	M23	Ford Cosworth	V8	72		2	1
4	19	A Jones	Surtees	TS19	Ford Cosworth	V8	72		20	10
5	2	C Regazzoni	Ferrari	312T2	Ferrari	F12	72		7	4
6	6	G Nilsson	JPS Lotus	77	Ford Cosworth	V8	72		16	8
7	26	J Laffite	Ligier	JS5	Matra	V12	72		11	6
8	24	H Ertl	Hesketh	308D	Ford Cosworth	V8	72		22	11
9	18	N Takahara	Surtees	TS19	Ford Cosworth	V8	70		24	12
10	17	J-P Jarier	Shadow	DN5B	Ford Cosworth	V8	69		15	8
11	51	M Hasemi	Kojima	KE007	Ford Cosworth	V8	66		10	5
r	3	J Scheckter	Tyrrell	P34	Ford Cosworth	V8	58	engine overheating	5	3
r	21	H Binder	Wolf Williams	FW05	Ford Cosworth	V8	49	rear wheel bearing	25	13
r	16	T Pryce	Shadow	DN8	Ford Cosworth	V8	46	engine	14	7
r	9	V Brambilla	March	761	Ford Cosworth	V8	38	engine	8	4
r	34	H-J Stuck	March	761	Ford Cosworth	V8	37	electrics	18	9
r	12	J Mass	McLaren	M23	Ford Cosworth	V8	35	accident	12	6
r	28	J Watson	Penske	PC4	Ford Cosworth	V8	33	engine	4	2
r	52	K Hoshino	Tyrrell	007	Ford Cosworth	V8	27	team ran out of tyres	21	11
r	20	A Merzario	Wolf Williams	FW05	Ford Cosworth	V8	23	gearbox	19	10
r	30	E Fittipaldi	Copersucar	FD04	Ford Cosworth	V8	9	withdrew	23	12
r	8	C Pace	Brabham	BT45	Alfa Romeo	F12	7	withdrew	6	3
r	1	N Lauda	Ferrari	312T2	Ferrari	F12	2	withdrew	3	2
r	7	L Perkins	Brabham	BT45	Alfa Romeo	F12	1	withdrew	17	9
r	10	R Peterson	March	761	Ford Cosworth	V8	0	engine	9	5
ns	21	M Kuwashima	Wolf Williams	FW05	Ford Cosworth	V8		sponsors withdrew		
nq	54	T Trimmer	Maki	F102A	Ford Cosworth	V8				

Winning speed 183.615 km/h, 114.093 mph
Pole Position speed 215.644 km/h, 133.995 mph (M Andretti, 1 min:12.770 sec)
Fastest Lap speed 196.229 km/h, 121.931 mph (J Laffite, 1 min:19.970 sec)
Lap Leaders J Hunt 1-61 (61); P Depailler 62-63 (2); M Andretti 64-73 (10).

The organisers originally credited M Hasemi with a fastest lap time of 1 min 18.230 sec, but this was found to be incorrect.

Pos	Driver	Car-Engine	GPs	laps	km	miles
1	J Hunt	McLaren-Ford Cosworth	8	351	1,790.4	1,112.5
2	N Lauda	Ferrari	7	341	1,468.6	912.6
3	C Regazzoni	Ferrari	2	88	323.8	201.2
4	J Scheckter	Tyrrell-Ford Cosworth	4	79	395.2	245.6
5	R Peterson	March-Ford Cosworth	4	69	369.0	229.3
6	M Andretti	Lotus-Ford Cosworth	2	55	224.4	139.4
7	J Watson	Penske-Ford Cosworth	1	45	265.9	165.3
8	P Depailler	Tyrrell-Ford Cosworth	1	2	8.7	5.4
			16	1,030	4,846.1	3,011.3

Driver Points 1976

		BR	ZA	USAW	E	B	MC	S	F	GB	D	A	NL	I	CDN	USAE	J	Total
1	J Hunt	-	6	-	9	-	-	2	9	-	9	3	9	-	9	9	4	69
2	N Lauda	9	9	6	6	9	9	4	-	9	-	-	-	3	-	4	-	68
3	J Scheckter	2	3	-	-	3	6	9	1	6	6	-	2	2	3	6	-	49
4	P Depailler	6	-	4	-	-	4	6	6	-	-	-	-	1	6	-	6	39
5	C Regazzoni	-	-	9	-	6	-	1	-	-	-	-	6	6	1	-	2	31
6	M Andretti	-	1	-	-	-	-	-	2	-	-	2	4	-	4	-	9	22
7	J Watson	-	2	-	-	-	-	-	4	4	-	9	-	-	-	1	-	20
	J Laffite	-	-	3	-	4	-	3	-	-	-	6	-	4	-	-	-	20
9	J Mass	1	4	2	-	1	2	-	-	-	4	-	-	-	2	3	-	19
10	G Nilsson	-	-	-	4	-	-	-	-	-	2	4	-	-	-	-	1	11
11	R Peterson	-	-	-	-	-	-	-	-	-	-	1	-	9	-	-	-	10
	T Pryce	4	-	-	-	-	-	-	3	-	-	-	3	-	-	-	-	10
13	H-J Stuck	3	-	-	-	-	3	-	-	-	-	-	-	-	2	-	-	8
14	C Pace	-	-	-	1	-	-	-	3	-	3	-	-	-	-	-	-	7
	A Jones	-	-	-	-	2	-	-	-	2	-	-	-	-	-	-	3	7
16	C Reutemann	-	-	-	3	-	-	-	-	-	-	-	-	-	-	-	-	3
	E Fittipaldi	-	-	1	-	-	1	-	-	1	-	-	-	-	-	-	-	3
18	C Amon	-	-	-	2	-	-	-	-	-	-	-	-	-	-	-	-	2
19	R Stommelen	-	-	-	-	-	-	-	-	-	1	-	-	-	-	-	-	1
	V Brambilla	-	-	-	-	-	-	-	-	-	-	-	1	-	-	-	-	1

9,6,4,3,2 and 1 point awarded to the first six finishers. Best 7 scores from first 8 races, best 7 from remaining 8 races.

Constructor Points 1976

		BR	ZA	USAW	E	B	MC	S	F	GB	D	A	NL	I	CDN	USAE	J	Total
1	Ferrari	9	9	9	6	9	9	4	-	9	-	-	6	6	1	4	2	83
2	McLaren-Ford Cosworth	1	6	2	9	(1)	2	2	9	-	9	3	9	-	9	9	4	74 (1)
3	Tyrrell-Ford Cosworth	6	3	4	-	3	6	9	6	6	6	-	2	2	6	6	6	71
4	Lotus-Ford Cosworth	-	-	-	4	-	-	-	2	-	2	4	4	-	4	-	9	29
5	Penske-Ford Cosworth	-	2	-	-	-	-	-	4	4	-	9	-	-	-	1	-	20
	Ligier-Matra	-	-	3	-	4	-	3	-	-	-	6	-	4	-	-	-	20
7	March-Ford Cosworth	3	-	-	-	-	3	-	-	-	-	1	1	9	-	2	-	19
8	Shadow-Ford Cosworth	4	-	-	-	-	-	-	-	3	-	-	3	-	-	-	-	10
9	Brabham-Alfa Romeo	-	-	-	3	-	-	-	3	-	3	-	-	-	-	-	-	9
10	Surtees-Ford Cosworth	-	-	-	-	2	-	-	-	2	-	-	-	-	-	-	3	7
11	Copersucar-Ford Cosworth	-	-	1	-	-	1	-	-	1	-	-	-	-	-	-	-	3
12	Ensign-Ford Cosworth	-	-	-	2	-	-	-	-	-	-	-	-	-	-	-	-	2
13	Parnelli-Ford Cosworth	-	1	-	-	-	-	-	-	-	-	-	-	-	-	-	-	1

9,6,4,3,2 and 1 point awarded to the first six finishers. Points only for highest placed car. Best 7 scores from first 8 races, best 7 from remaining 8 races.

Race Entrants and Results

Lotus made another significant step forward, with the 78 wing car, the first successful attempt at ground effects. Renault also introduced the first turbo to World Championship racing, complying with the equivalent formula of 1.5 litres. Ferrari appeared with FIAT advertising for the first time and Wolf introduced their new car, enticing Scheckter away from Tyrrell. BRM finally ran out of steam and Tom Pryce was killed in a bizarre accident, colliding with a marshal crossing the track at Kyalami.

McLAREN
Marlboro Team McLaren: Hunt, Mass, Villeneuve, Giacomelli
Chesterfield Racing: Lunger
Iberia Airlines: de Villota

TYRRELL
Elf Team Tyrrell: Peterson, Depailler
Meritsu Racing Team: Takahashi

LOTUS
John Player Team Lotus: Andretti, Nilsson

BRABHAM
Martini Racing: Watson, Pace, Stuck, (Francia)

MARCH
Hollywood March Racing: Ribeiro
Team Rothmans International: I Scheckter, Stuck, Henton (USAW)
Williams Grand Prix Engineering: Nève
Chesterfield Racing: Lunger
Team Merzario: Merzario
Ram Racing F & S Properties: Hayje, (Sutcliffe, Kozarowitsky, Bleekemolen)
British Formula 1 Racing: (Henton, de Dryver)

FERRARI
Scuderia Ferrari SpA SEFAC: Lauda, Villeneuve, Reutemann

BRM
Rotary Watches-Stanley BRM: Perkins, (Andersson, Edwards, Pilette)

RENAULT
Equipe Renault Elf: Jabouille

SHADOW
Shadow Racing Team: Pryce, Jones, Zorzi, Patrese, Oliver, Merzario, Jarier

SURTEES
Team Surtees: Binder, Brambilla, Perkins, Schuppan, (Tambay, Leoni)
Melchester Racing: (Trimmer)

WOLF
Walter Wolf Racing: J Scheckter

ENSIGN
Team Tissot Ensign with Castrol: Regazzoni, Ickx
Theodore Racing Hong Kong: Tambay
HB Bewaking Alarm Systems: Henton (Boro)

HESKETH
Hesketh Racing: Ertl, Rebaque, Ashley
Penthouse Rizla Racing: Keegan

LIGIER
Ligier Gitanes: Laffite, Jarier

FITTIPALDI (COPERSUCAR)
Copersucar-Fittipaldi: Fittipaldi, Hoffmann

LEC
Lec Refrigeration Racing: Purley

PENSKE
ATS Racing Team: Jarier, Heyer, Binder
Interscope Racing: Ongais

KOJIMA
Kojima Engineering: Takahara
Heros Racing: Hoshino

WILLIAMS
Jolly Club of Switzerland: (Kessel)
Privateer: (McGuire)

---

9 Jan 1977　　**ARGENTINA: Buenos Aires No.15**　　　　　　　　**(Round 1)**　　**(Race 281)**
53 laps x 5.968 km, 3.708 miles = 316.304 km, 196.542 miles

Pos	No	Driver	Car	Model	Engine		Laps	Time/Reason for Retirement	Grid Pos	Row
1	20	J Scheckter	Wolf	WR1	Ford Cosworth	V8	53	1h 40m 11.190s	11	6
2	8	C Pace	Brabham	BT45	Alfa Romeo	F12	53	1h 40m 54.430s	6	3
3	12	C Reutemann	Ferrari	312T2	Ferrari	F12	53	1h 40m 57.210s	7	4
4	28	E Fittipaldi	Copersucar	FD04	Ford Cosworth	V8	53	1h 41m 06.670s	16	8
5r	5	M Andretti	JPS Lotus	78	Ford Cosworth	V8	51	rear wheel bearing	8	4
6	22	C Regazzoni	Ensign	N177	Ford Cosworth	V8	51		12	6
7r	19	V Brambilla	Surtees	TS19	Ford Cosworth	V8	48	fuel injection	13	7
r	10	I Scheckter	March	761B	Ford Cosworth	V8	45	battery terminal	17	9
nc	16	T Pryce	Shadow	DN8	Ford Cosworth	V8	45		9	5
r	7	J Watson	Brabham	BT45	Alfa Romeo	F12	41	rear suspension mounts / gearbox	2	1
r	9	A D Ribeiro	March	761B	Ford Cosworth	V8	39	gear lever	20	10
nc	26	J Laffite	Ligier	JS7	Matra	V12	37		15	8
r	4	P Depailler	Tyrrell	P34	Ford Cosworth	V8	32	engine overheating	3	2
r	1	J Hunt	McLaren	M23	Ford Cosworth	V8	31	rear suspension	1	1
r	2	J Mass	McLaren	M23	Ford Cosworth	V8	28	engine / spin	5	3
r	3	R Peterson	Tyrrell	P34	Ford Cosworth	V8	28	spin	14	7
r	29	I Hoffmann	Copersucar	FD04	Ford Cosworth	V8	22	engine	19	10
r	11	N Lauda	Ferrari	312T2	Ferrari	F12	20	fuel metering unit	4	2
r	18	H Binder	Surtees	TS19	Ford Cosworth	V8	18	nose section	18	9
r	17	R Zorzi	Shadow	DN5B	Ford Cosworth	V8	2	gearbox	21	11
ns	6	G Nilsson	JPS Lotus	78	Ford Cosworth	V8		car raced by Andretti	10	5

Winning speed 189.429 km/h, 117.706 mph
Pole Position speed 197.689 km/h, 122.838 mph (J Hunt, 1 min:48.680 sec)
Fastest Lap speed 193.452 km/h, 120.206 mph (J Hunt, 1 min:51.060 sec on lap 21)
Lap Leaders J Watson 1-10,32-34 (13); J Hunt 11-31 (21); C Pace 35-47 (13); J Scheckter 48-53 (6).

BRAZIL: Interlagos (Round 2) (Race 282)

40 laps x 7.960 km, 4.946 miles = 318.400 km, 197.845 miles

Pos	No	Driver	Car	Model	Engine		Laps	Time/Reason for Retirement	Grid Pos	Row
1	12	C Reutemann	Ferrari	312T2	Ferrari	F12	40	1h 45m 07.720s	2	1
2	1	J Hunt	McLaren	M23	Ford Cosworth	V8	40	1h 45m 18.430s	1	1
3	11	N Lauda	Ferrari	312T2	Ferrari	F12	40	1h 46m 55.230s	13	7
4	28	E Fittipaldi	Copersucar	FD04	Ford Cosworth	V8	39		16	8
5	6	G Nilsson	JPS Lotus	78	Ford Cosworth	V8	39		10	5
6	17	R Zorzi	Shadow	DN5B	Ford Cosworth	V8	39		18	9
7	29	I Hoffmann	Copersucar	FD04	Ford Cosworth	V8	38		19	10
r	16	T Pryce	Shadow	DN8	Ford Cosworth	V8	33	engine	12	6
r	8	C Pace	Brabham	BT45	Alfa Romeo	F12	33	accident	5	3
r	18	H Binder	Surtees	TS19	Ford Cosworth	V8	32	front suspension	20	10
r	7	J Watson	Brabham	BT45	Alfa Romeo	F12	30	accident	7	4
r	26	J Laffite	Ligier	JS7	Matra	V12	26	accident	14	7
r	4	P Depailler	Tyrrell	P34	Ford Cosworth	V8	23	accident	6	3
r	5	M Andretti	JPS Lotus	78	Ford Cosworth	V8	19	ignition	3	2
r	9	A D Ribeiro	March	761B	Ford Cosworth	V8	16	dropped valve	21	11
r	2	J Mass	McLaren	M23	Ford Cosworth	V8	12	accident	4	2
r	22	C Regazzoni	Ensign	N177	Ford Cosworth	V8	12	accident	9	5
r	3	R Peterson	Tyrrell	P34	Ford Cosworth	V8	12	accident	8	4
r	20	J Scheckter	Wolf	WR1	Ford Cosworth	V8	11	engine	15	8
r	19	V Brambilla	Surtees	TS19	Ford Cosworth	V8	11	radiator	11	6
r	10	I Scheckter	March	761B	Ford Cosworth	V8	1	transmission	17	9
r	14	L Perkins	Stanley BRM	P207	BRM	V12	1	water loss / engine	22	11

Winning speed 181.720 km/h, 112.916 mph
Pole Position speed 190.900 km/h, 118.620 mph (J Hunt, 2 min:30.110 sec)
Fastest Lap speed 185.416 km/h, 115.212 mph (J Hunt, 2 min:34.550 sec on lap 33)
Lap Leaders C Pace 1-6 (6); J Hunt 7-22 (16); C Reutemann 23-40 (18).

---

5 Mar 1977 **SOUTH AFRICA: Kyalami** (Round 3) (Race 283)

78 laps x 4.104 km, 2.550 miles = 320.112 km, 198.908 miles

Pos	No	Driver	Car	Model	Engine		Laps	Time/Reason for Retirement	Grid Pos	Row
1	11	N Lauda	Ferrari	312T2	Ferrari	F12	78	1h 42m 21.600s	3	2
2	20	J Scheckter	Wolf	WR1	Ford Cosworth	V8	78	1h 42m 26.800s	5	3
3	4	P Depailler	Tyrrell	P34	Ford Cosworth	V8	78	1h 42m 27.300s	4	2
4	1	J Hunt	McLaren	M23	Ford Cosworth	V8	78	1h 42m 31.100s	1	1
5	2	J Mass	McLaren	M23	Ford Cosworth	V8	78	1h 42m 41.500s	13	7
6	7	J Watson	Brabham	BT45	Alfa Romeo	F12	78	1h 42m 41.800s	11	6
7	19	V Brambilla	Surtees	TS19	Ford Cosworth	V8	78	1h 42m 45.200s	14	7
8	12	C Reutemann	Ferrari	312T2	Ferrari	F12	78	1h 42m 48.300s	8	4
9	22	C Regazzoni	Ensign	N177	Ford Cosworth	V8	78	1h 43m 07.800s	16	8
10	28	E Fittipaldi	Copersucar	FD04	Ford Cosworth	V8	78	1h 43m 33.300s	9	5
11	18	H Binder	Surtees	TS19	Ford Cosworth	V8	77		19	10
12	6	G Nilsson	JPS Lotus	78	Ford Cosworth	V8	77		10	5
13	8	C Pace	Brabham	BT45B	Alfa Romeo	F12	76		2	1
14	30	B Lunger	March	761	Ford Cosworth	V8	76		23	12
15	14	L Perkins	Stanley BRM	P201B	BRM	V12	73		22	11
r	9	A D Ribeiro	March	761B	Ford Cosworth	V8	66	engine	17	9
r	10	H-J Stuck	March	761B	Ford Cosworth	V8	55	engine	18	9
r	5	M Andretti	JPS Lotus	78	Ford Cosworth	V8	43	accident / front suspension	6	3
r	33	B Hayje	March	761	Ford Cosworth	V8	33	gearbox	21	11
r	16	T Pryce	Shadow	DN8	Ford Cosworth	V8	22	fatal accident	15	8
r	26	J Laffite	Ligier	JS7	Matra	V12	22	accident	12	6
r	17	R Zorzi	Shadow	DN8	Ford Cosworth	V8	21	engine	20	10
r	3	R Peterson	Tyrrell	P34	Ford Cosworth	V8	5	fuel pressure	7	4

Winning speed 187.639 km/h, 116.593 mph
Pole Position speed 194.502 km/h, 120.858 mph (J Hunt, 1 min:15.960 sec)
Fastest Lap speed 190.318 km/h, 118.258 mph (J Watson, 1 min:17.630 sec on lap 7)
Lap Leaders J Hunt 1-6 (6); N Lauda 7-78 (72).

3 Apr 1977		USA West: Long Beach						(Round 4)	(Race 284)
		80 laps x 3.251 km, 2.020 miles = 260.070 km, 161.600 miles							

Pos	No	Driver	Car	Model	Engine		Laps	Time/Reason for Retirement	Grid Pos	Row
1	5	M Andretti	JPS Lotus	78	Ford Cosworth	V8	80	1h 51m 35.470s	2	1
2	11	N Lauda	Ferrari	312T2	Ferrari	F12	80	1h 51m 36.243s	1	1
3	20	J Scheckter	Wolf	WR1	Ford Cosworth	V8	80	1h 51m 40.327s	3	2
4	4	P Depailler	Tyrrell	P34	Ford Cosworth	V8	80	1h 52m 49.957s	12	6
5	28	E Fittipaldi	Copersucar	FD04	Ford Cosworth	V8	80	1h 52m 56.378s	7	4
6	34	J-P Jarier	Penske	PC4	Ford Cosworth	V8	79		9	5
7	1	J Hunt	McLaren	M23	Ford Cosworth	V8	79		8	4
8	6	G Nilsson	JPS Lotus	78	Ford Cosworth	V8	79		16	8
9r	26	J Laffite	Ligier	JS7	Matra	V12	78	electrical master switch	5	3
10	10	B Henton	March	761B	Ford Cosworth	V8	77		18	9
11	18	H Binder	Surtees	TS19	Ford Cosworth	V8	77		19	10
r	3	R Peterson	Tyrrell	P34	Ford Cosworth	V8	62	fuel line	10	5
r	22	C Regazzoni	Ensign	N177	Ford Cosworth	V8	58	gearbox	13	7
r	8	H-J Stuck	Brabham	BT45B	Alfa Romeo	F12	54	brakes	17	9
r	17	A Jones	Shadow	DN8	Ford Cosworth	V8	41	gearbox	14	7
r	2	J Mass	McLaren	M23	Ford Cosworth	V8	40	rear vibration	15	8
dq	7	J Watson	Brabham	BT45B	Alfa Romeo	F12	33	push start after engine cut	6	3
r	16	R Zorzi	Shadow	DN8	Ford Cosworth	V8	28	gearbox	20	10
r	9	A D Ribeiro	March	761B	Ford Cosworth	V8	16	gearbox oil leak	22	11
r	12	C Reutemann	Ferrari	312T2	Ferrari	F12	5	accident	4	2
r	30	B Lunger	March	761	Ford Cosworth	V8	4	accident	21	11
r	19	V Brambilla	Surtees	TS19	Ford Cosworth	V8	0	accident	11	6

Winning speed 139.834 km/h, 86.889 mph
Pole Position speed 143.333 km/h, 89.063 mph (N Lauda, 1 min:21.650 sec)
Fastest Lap speed 141.423 km/h, 87.876 mph (N Lauda, 1 min:22.753 sec on lap 62)
Lap Leaders J Scheckter 1-76 (76); M Andretti 77-80 (4).

8 May 1977		SPAIN: Jarama						(Round 5)	(Race 285)
		75 laps x 3.404 km, 2.115 miles = 255.300 km, 158.636 miles							

Pos	No	Driver	Car	Model	Engine		Laps	Time/Reason for Retirement	Grid Pos	Row
1	5	M Andretti	JPS Lotus	78	Ford Cosworth	V8	75	1h 42m 52.220s	1	1
2	12	C Reutemann	Ferrari	312T2	Ferrari	F12	75	1h 43m 08.070s	4	2
3	20	J Scheckter	Wolf	WR2	Ford Cosworth	V8	75	1h 43m 16.730s	5	3
4	2	J Mass	McLaren	M23	Ford Cosworth	V8	75	1h 43m 17.090s	9	5
5	6	G Nilsson	JPS Lotus	78	Ford Cosworth	V8	75	1h 43m 58.050s	12	6
6	8	H-J Stuck	Brabham	BT45B	Alfa Romeo	F12	74		13	7
7	26	J Laffite	Ligier	JS7	Matra	V12	74		2	1
8	3	R Peterson	Tyrrell	P34	Ford Cosworth	V8	74		15	8
9	18	H Binder	Surtees	TS19	Ford Cosworth	V8	73		20	10
10	30	B Lunger	March	761	Ford Cosworth	V8	72		25	13
11	10	I Scheckter	March	761B	Ford Cosworth	V8	72		17	9
12	27	P Nève	March	761	Ford Cosworth	V8	71		22	11
13	36	E de Villota	McLaren	M23	Ford Cosworth	V8	70		23	12
14	28	E Fittipaldi	Copersucar	FD04	Ford Cosworth	V8	70		19	10
r	7	J Watson	Brabham	BT45B	Alfa Romeo	F12	64	fuel metering unit	6	3
r	17	A Jones	Shadow	DN8	Ford Cosworth	V8	56	accident / front suspension	14	7
r	24	R Keegan	Hesketh	308E	Ford Cosworth	V8	32	accident	16	8
r	25	H Ertl	Hesketh	308E	Ford Cosworth	V8	29	radiator	18	9
r	16	R Zorzi	Shadow	DN8	Ford Cosworth	V8	25	engine	24	12
r	37	A Merzario	March	761B	Ford Cosworth	V8	16	front suspension	21	11
r	4	P Depailler	Tyrrell	P34	Ford Cosworth	V8	12	engine	10	5
r	1	J Hunt	McLaren	M26	Ford Cosworth	V8	10	engine	7	4
r	22	C Regazzoni	Ensign	N177	Ford Cosworth	V8	9	accident	8	4
r	19	V Brambilla	Surtees	TS19	Ford Cosworth	V8	9	accident	11	6
ns	11	N Lauda	Ferrari	312T2	Ferrari	F12		accident / injury	3	2
nq	34	J-P Jarier	Penske	PC4	Ford Cosworth	V8				
nq	9	A D Ribeiro	March	761B	Ford Cosworth	V8				
nq	33	B Hayje	March	761	Ford Cosworth	V8				
nq	38	B Henton	March	761	Ford Cosworth	V8				
nq	31	D Purley	Lec	CRP1	Ford Cosworth	V8				
nq	35	C Andersson	Stanley BRM	P207	BRM	V12				

Winning speed 148.906 km/h, 92.526 mph
Pole Position speed 155.710 km/h, 96.754 mph (M Andretti, 1 min:18.700 sec)
Fastest Lap speed 151.645 km/h, 94.228 mph (J Laffite, 1 min:20.810 sec on lap 5)
Lap Leaders M Andretti 1-75 (75).

Races

22 May 1977   MONACO: Monte-Carlo   (Round 6)   (Race 286)

76 laps x 3.312 km, 2.058 miles = 251.712 km, 156.407 miles

Pos	No	Driver	Car	Model	Engine		Laps	Time/Reason for Retirement	Grid Pos	Row
1	20	J Scheckter	Wolf	WR1	Ford Cosworth	V8	76	1h 57m 52.770s	2	1
2	11	N Lauda	Ferrari	312T2	Ferrari	F12	76	1h 57m 53.660s	6	3
3	12	C Reutemann	Ferrari	312T2	Ferrari	F12	76	1h 58m 25.570s	3	2
4	2	J Mass	McLaren	M23	Ford Cosworth	V8	76	1h 58m 27.370s	9	5
5	5	M Andretti	JPS Lotus	78	Ford Cosworth	V8	76	1h 58m 28.320s	10	5
6	17	A Jones	Shadow	DN8	Ford Cosworth	V8	76	1h 58m 29.380s	11	6
7	26	J Laffite	Ligier	JS7	Matra	V12	76	1h 58m 57.210s	16	8
8	19	V Brambilla	Surtees	TS19	Ford Cosworth	V8	76	1h 59m 01.410s	14	7
9	16	R Patrese	Shadow	DN8	Ford Cosworth	V8	75		15	8
10	22	J Ickx	Ensign	N177	Ford Cosworth	V8	75		17	9
11	34	J-P Jarier	Penske	PC4	Ford Cosworth	V8	74		12	6
12	24	R Keegan	Hesketh	308E	Ford Cosworth	V8	73		20	10
r	6	G Nilsson	JPS Lotus	78	Ford Cosworth	V8	51	gearbox	13	7
r	7	J Watson	Brabham	BT45B	Alfa Romeo	F12	48	gearbox	1	1
r	4	P Depailler	Tyrrell	P34	Ford Cosworth	V8	46	brakes / gearbox	8	4
r	18	H Binder	Surtees	TS19	Ford Cosworth	V8	41	fuel injection	19	10
r	28	E Fittipaldi	Copersucar	FD04	Ford Cosworth	V8	37	engine	18	9
r	1	J Hunt	McLaren	M23	Ford Cosworth	V8	25	dropped valve	7	4
r	8	H-J Stuck	Brabham	BT45B	Alfa Romeo	F12	19	electrics / fire	5	3
r	3	R Peterson	Tyrrell	P34	Ford Cosworth	V8	10	brakes	4	2
nq	37	A Merzario	March	761B	Ford Cosworth	V8				
nq	33	B Hayje	March	761	Ford Cosworth	V8				
nq	25	H Ertl	Hesketh	308E	Ford Cosworth	V8				
nq	22	C Regazzoni	Ensign	N177	Ford Cosworth	V8				
nq	9	A D Ribeiro	March	761B	Ford Cosworth	V8				
nq	10	I Scheckter	March	761B	Ford Cosworth	V8		accident / injury		

Winning speed 128.120 km/h, 79.610 mph
Pole Position speed 132.686 km/h, 82.448 mph (J Watson, 1 min:29.860 sec)
Fastest Lap speed 130.923 km/h, 81.352 mph (J Scheckter, 1 min:31.070 sec on lap 35)
Lap Leaders J Scheckter 1-76 (76).

5 Jun 1977   BELGIUM: Zolder   (Round 7)   (Race 287)

70 laps x 4.262 km, 2.648 miles = 298.340 km, 185.380 miles

Pos	No	Driver	Car	Model	Engine		Laps	Time/Reason for Retirement	Grid Pos	Row
1	6	G Nilsson	JPS Lotus	78	Ford Cosworth	V8	70	1h 55m 05.710s	3	2
2	11	N Lauda	Ferrari	312T2	Ferrari	F12	70	1h 55m 19.900s	11	6
3	3	R Peterson	Tyrrell	P34	Ford Cosworth	V8	70	1h 55m 25.660s	8	4
4	19	V Brambilla	Surtees	TS19	Ford Cosworth	V8	70	1h 55m 30.690s	12	6
5	17	A Jones	Shadow	DN8	Ford Cosworth	V8	70	1h 56m 21.180s	17	9
6	8	H-J Stuck	Brabham	BT45B	Alfa Romeo	F12	69		18	9
7	1	J Hunt	McLaren	M26	Ford Cosworth	V8	69		9	5
8	4	P Depailler	Tyrrell	P34	Ford Cosworth	V8	69		5	3
9	25	H Ertl	Hesketh	308E	Ford Cosworth	V8	69		25	13
10	27	P Nève	March	761	Ford Cosworth	V8	68		24	12
11	34	J-P Jarier	Penske	PC4	Ford Cosworth	V8	68		26	13
12	18	L Perkins	Surtees	TS19	Ford Cosworth	V8	67		23	12
13	31	D Purley	Lec	CRP1	Ford Cosworth	V8	67		20	10
14	37	A Merzario	March	761B	Ford Cosworth	V8	65		14	7
15	33	B Hayje	March	761	Ford Cosworth	V8	63		27	14
r	20	J Scheckter	Wolf	WR3	Ford Cosworth	V8	62	fuel pump	4	2
r	2	J Mass	McLaren	M23	Ford Cosworth	V8	39	accident	6	3
r	26	J Laffite	Ligier	JS7	Matra	V12	32	engine	10	5
r	22	C Regazzoni	Ensign	N177	Ford Cosworth	V8	29	engine	13	7
r	24	R Keegan	Hesketh	308E	Ford Cosworth	V8	14	accident	19	10
r	12	C Reutemann	Ferrari	312T2	Ferrari	F12	14	accident	7	4
r	16	R Patrese	Shadow	DN8	Ford Cosworth	V8	12	accident	15	8
r	10	I Scheckter	March	761B	Ford Cosworth	V8	8	accident	21	11
r	28	E Fittipaldi	Copersucar	F5	Ford Cosworth	V8	2	water in electrics	16	8
r	5	M Andretti	JPS Lotus	78	Ford Cosworth	V8	0	accident	1	1
r	7	J Watson	Brabham	BT45B	Alfa Romeo	F12	0	accident	2	1
ns	30	B Lunger	McLaren	M23	Ford Cosworth	V8		car not ready	22	11
nq	36	E de Villota	McLaren	M23	Ford Cosworth	V8				
nq	35	C Andersson	Stanley BRM	P207	BRM	V12				
nq	9	A D Ribeiro	March	761B	Ford Cosworth	V8				
nq	38	B de Dryver	March	761	Ford Cosworth	V8				
nq	39	H Rebaque	Hesketh	308E	Ford Cosworth	V8				

Winning speed 155.527 km/h, 96.640 mph
Pole Position speed 181.276 km/h, 112.640 mph (M Andretti, 1 min:24.640 sec)
Fastest Lap speed 175.271 km/h, 108.908 mph (G Nilsson, 1 min:27.540 sec on lap 53)
Lap Leaders J Scheckter 1-16 (16); J Mass 17-18 (2); N Lauda 23-49 (27); V Brambilla 19-22 (4); G Nilsson 50-70 (21).

72 laps x 4.018 km, 2.497 miles = 289.296 km, 179.760 miles

Pos	No	Driver	Car	Model	Engine		Laps	Time/Reason for Retirement	Grid Pos	Row
1	26	J Laffite	Ligier	JS7	Matra	V12	72	1h 46m 55.520s	8	4
2	2	J Mass	McLaren	M23	Ford Cosworth	V8	72	1h 47m 03.969s	9	5
3	12	C Reutemann	Ferrari	312T2	Ferrari	F12	72	1h 47m 09.889s	12	6
4	4	P Depailler	Tyrrell	P34	Ford Cosworth	V8	72	1h 47m 11.828s	6	3
5	7	J Watson	Brabham	BT45B	Alfa Romeo	F12	72	1h 47m 14.255s	2	1
6	5	M Andretti	JPS Lotus	78	Ford Cosworth	V8	72	1h 47m 20.797s	1	1
7	22	C Regazzoni	Ensign	N177	Ford Cosworth	V8	72	1h 47m 26.786s	14	7
8	34	J-P Jarier	Penske	PC4	Ford Cosworth	V8	72	1h 48m 00.087s	17	9
9	16	J Oliver	Shadow	DN8	Ford Cosworth	V8	72	1h 48m 17.999s	16	8
10	8	H-J Stuck	Brabham	BT45B	Alfa Romeo	F12	71		5	3
11	30	B Lunger	McLaren	M23	Ford Cosworth	V8	71		22	11
12	1	J Hunt	McLaren	M26	Ford Cosworth	V8	71		3	2
13	24	R Keegan	Hesketh	308E	Ford Cosworth	V8	71		24	12
14	31	D Purley	Lec	CRP1	Ford Cosworth	V8	70		19	10
15	27	P Nève	March	761	Ford Cosworth	V8	69		20	10
16	25	H Ertl	Hesketh	308E	Ford Cosworth	V8	68		23	12
17	17	A Jones	Shadow	DN8	Ford Cosworth	V8	67		11	6
18	28	E Fittipaldi	Copersucar	FD04	Ford Cosworth	V8	66		18	9
19r	6	G Nilsson	JPS Lotus	78	Ford Cosworth	V8	64	front wheel bearing	7	4
r	10	I Scheckter	March	761B	Ford Cosworth	V8	61	cv joint	21	11
r	19	V Brambilla	Surtees	TS19	Ford Cosworth	V8	52	fuel pressure	13	7
r	11	N Lauda	Ferrari	312T2	Ferrari	F12	47	handling	15	8
r	20	J Scheckter	Wolf	WR1	Ford Cosworth	V8	29	accident	4	2
r	3	R Peterson	Tyrrell	P34	Ford Cosworth	V8	7	ignition	10	5
nq	9	A D Ribeiro	March	761B	Ford Cosworth	V8				
nq	36	E de Villota	McLaren	M23	Ford Cosworth	V8				
nq	18	L Perkins	Surtees	TS19	Ford Cosworth	V8				
nq	33	B Hayje	March	761	Ford Cosworth	V8				
nq	39	H Rebaque	Hesketh	308E	Ford Cosworth	V8				
nq	35	C Andersson	Stanley BRM	P207	BRM	V12				
nq	32	M Kozarowitsky	March	761	Ford Cosworth	V8				

Winning speed 162.335 km/h, 100.871 mph
Pole Position speed 169.369 km/h, 105.241 mph (M Andretti, 1 min:25.404 sec)
Fastest Lap speed 165.110 km/h, 102.595 mph (M Andretti, 1 min:27.607 sec)
Lap Leaders J Watson 1 (1); M Andretti 2-69 (68); J Laffite 70-72 (3).

80 laps x 3.800 km, 2.361 miles = 304.000 km, 188.897 miles

Pos	No	Driver	Car	Model	Engine		Laps	Time/Reason for Retirement	Grid Pos	Row
1	5	M Andretti	JPS Lotus	78	Ford Cosworth	V8	80	1h 39m 40.130s	1	1
2	7	J Watson	Brabham	BT45B	Alfa Romeo	F12	80	1h 39m 41.680s	4	2
3	1	J Hunt	McLaren	M26	Ford Cosworth	V8	80	1h 40m 14.000s	2	1
4	6	G Nilsson	JPS Lotus	78	Ford Cosworth	V8	80	1h 40m 51.210s	3	2
5	11	N Lauda	Ferrari	312T2	Ferrari	F12	80	1h 40m 54.580s	9	5
6	12	C Reutemann	Ferrari	312T2	Ferrari	F12	79		6	3
7	22	C Regazzoni	Ensign	N177	Ford Cosworth	V8	79		16	8
8	26	J Laffite	Ligier	JS7	Matra	V12	78		5	3
9	2	J Mass	McLaren	M23	Ford Cosworth	V8	78		7	4
10	24	R Keegan	Hesketh	308E	Ford Cosworth	V8	78		14	7
11	28	E Fittipaldi	Copersucar	F5	Ford Cosworth	V8	77		22	11
12	3	R Peterson	Tyrrell	P34	Ford Cosworth	V8	77		17	9
13	19	V Brambilla	Surtees	TS19	Ford Cosworth	V8	77		11	6
nc	10	I Scheckter	March	761B	Ford Cosworth	V8	69		20	10
r	20	J Scheckter	Wolf	WR3	Ford Cosworth	V8	66	accident	8	4
r	8	H-J Stuck	Brabham	BT45B	Alfa Romeo	F12	64	accident	13	7
r	17	A Jones	Shadow	DN8	Ford Cosworth	V8	60	driveshaft	10	5
r	37	A Merzario	March	761B	Ford Cosworth	V8	27	gearbox	18	9
r	4	P Depailler	Tyrrell	P34	Ford Cosworth	V8	21	accident	12	6
r	16	R Patrese	Shadow	DN8	Ford Cosworth	V8	6	clutch / engine	15	8
r	31	D Purley	Lec	CRP1	Ford Cosworth	V8	5	brakes / accident	21	11
r	34	J-P Jarier	Penske	PC4	Ford Cosworth	V8	4	gearbox / accident	19	10
nq	9	A D Ribeiro	March	761B	Ford Cosworth	V8				
nq	27	P Nève	March	761	Ford Cosworth	V8				
nq	30	B Lunger	McLaren	M23	Ford Cosworth	V8				
nq	25	H Ertl	Hesketh	308E	Ford Cosworth	V8				
nq	18	L Perkins	Surtees	TS19	Ford Cosworth	V8				
nq	39	H Rebaque	Hesketh	308E	Ford Cosworth	V8				
nq	18	P Tambay	Surtees	TS19	Ford Cosworth	V8				
nq	35	C Andersson	Stanley BRM	P207	BRM	V12				

Winning speed 183.006 km/h, 113.715 mph
Pole Position speed 189.447 km/h, 117.717 mph (M Andretti, 1 min:12.210 sec)
Fastest Lap speed 185.492 km/h, 115.259 mph (M Andretti, 1 min:13.750 sec on lap 76)
Lap Leaders J Hunt 1-4 (4); J Watson 5-79 (75); M Andretti 80 (1).

Pos	No	Driver	Car	Model	Engine		Laps	Time/Reason for Retirement	Grid Pos	Row
1	1	J Hunt	McLaren	M26	Ford Cosworth	V8	68	1h 31m 46.060s	1	1
2	11	N Lauda	Ferrari	312T2	Ferrari	F12	68	1h 32m 04.370s	3	2
3	6	G Nilsson	JPS Lotus	78	Ford Cosworth	V8	68	1h 32m 05.630s	5	3
4	2	J Mass	McLaren	M26	Ford Cosworth	V8	68	1h 32m 33.820s	11	6
5	8	H-J Stuck	Brabham	BT45B	Alfa Romeo	F12	68	1h 32m 57.790s	7	4
6	26	J Laffite	Ligier	JS7	Matra	V12	67		15	8
7	17	A Jones	Shadow	DN8	Ford Cosworth	V8	67		12	6
8	19	V Brambilla	Surtees	TS19	Ford Cosworth	V8	67		8	4
9	34	J-P Jarier	Penske	PC4	Ford Cosworth	V8	67		20	10
10	27	P Nève	March	761	Ford Cosworth	V8	66		26	13
11	40	G Villeneuve	McLaren	M23	Ford Cosworth	V8	66		9	5
12	18	V Schuppan	Surtees	TS19	Ford Cosworth	V8	66		23	12
13	30	B Lunger	McLaren	M23	Ford Cosworth	V8	64		19	10
14r	5	M Andretti	JPS Lotus	78	Ford Cosworth	V8	62	engine	6	3
15	12	C Reutemann	Ferrari	312T2	Ferrari	F12	62		14	7
r	7	J Watson	Brabham	BT45B	Alfa Romeo	F12	60	fuel injection	2	1
r	20	J Scheckter	Wolf	WR1	Ford Cosworth	V8	59	engine	4	2
r	28	E Fittipaldi	Copersucar	F5	Ford Cosworth	V8	42	engine	22	11
r	37	A Merzario	March	761B	Ford Cosworth	V8	28	driveshaft	17	9
r	16	R Patrese	Shadow	DN8	Ford Cosworth	V8	20	fuel pressure	25	13
r	4	P Depailler	Tyrrell	P34	Ford Cosworth	V8	16	brakes / accident	18	9
r	15	J-P Jabouille	Renault	RS01	Renault	V6t	16	turbo	21	11
r	10	I Scheckter	March	761B	Ford Cosworth	V8	6	accident	24	12
r	23	P Tambay	Ensign	N177	Ford Cosworth	V8	3	electrics	16	8
r	3	R Peterson	Tyrrell	P34	Ford Cosworth	V8	3	engine	10	5
r	24	R Keegan	Hesketh	308E	Ford Cosworth	V8	0	accident	13	7
nq	9	A D Ribeiro	March	761B	Ford Cosworth	V8				
nq	22	C Regazzoni	Ensign	N177	Ford Cosworth	V8				
nq	38	B Henton	March	761	Ford Cosworth	V8				
nq	36	E de Villota	McLaren	M23	Ford Cosworth	V8				
npq	31	D Purley	Lec	CRP1	Ford Cosworth	V8		accident / injury		
npq	33	A Sutcliffe	March	761	Ford Cosworth	V8				
npq	35	G Edwards	Stanley BRM	P207	BRM	V12				
npq	44	T Trimmer	Surtees	TS19	Ford Cosworth	V8				
npq	45	B McGuire	McGuire	BM1	Ford Cosworth	V8				
npq	32	M Kozarowitsky	March	761	Ford Cosworth	V8				

Winning speed 209.789 km/h, 130.357 mph
Pole Position speed 216.422 km/h, 134.478 mph (J Hunt, 1 min:18.490 sec)
Fastest Lap speed 213.404 km/h, 132.603 mph (J Hunt, 1 min:19.600 sec on lap 48)
Lap Leaders J Watson 1-49 (49); J Hunt 50-68 (19).

Also the Grand Prix of Europe.

31 Jul 1977 **GERMANY: Hockenheim** (Round 11) (Race 291)

47 laps x 6.789 km, 4.218 miles = 319.083 km, 198.269 miles

Pos	No	Driver	Car	Model	Engine		Laps	Time/Reason for Retirement	Grid Pos	Row
1	11	N Lauda	Ferrari	312T2	Ferrari	F12	47	1h 31m 48.620s	3	2
2	20	J Scheckter	Wolf	WR2	Ford Cosworth	V8	47	1h 32m 02.950s	1	1
3	8	H-J Stuck	Brabham	BT45B	Alfa Romeo	F12	47	1h 32m 09.520s	5	3
4	12	C Reutemann	Ferrari	312T2	Ferrari	F12	47	1h 32m 48.890s	8	4
5	19	V Brambilla	Surtees	TS19	Ford Cosworth	V8	47	1h 33m 15.990s	10	5
6	23	P Tambay	Ensign	N177	Ford Cosworth	V8	47	1h 33m 18.430s	11	6
7	18	V Schuppan	Surtees	TS19	Ford Cosworth	V8	46		19	10
8	9	A D Ribeiro	March	761B	Ford Cosworth	V8	46		20	10
9r	3	R Peterson	Tyrrell	P34	Ford Cosworth	V8	42	engine	14	7
10r	16	R Patrese	Shadow	DN8	Ford Cosworth	V8	42	rear wheel lost	16	8
r	24	R Keegan	Hesketh	308E	Ford Cosworth	V8	40	accident	23	12
r	5	M Andretti	JPS Lotus	78	Ford Cosworth	V8	34	engine	7	4
r	1	J Hunt	McLaren	M26	Ford Cosworth	V8	32	fuel pump	4	2
r	6	G Nilsson	JPS Lotus	78	Ford Cosworth	V8	31	engine	9	5
r	2	J Mass	McLaren	M26	Ford Cosworth	V8	26	gearbox	13	7
r	4	P Depailler	Tyrrell	P34	Ford Cosworth	V8	22	engine	15	8
r	26	J Laffite	Ligier	JS7	Matra	V12	21	engine	6	3
r	25	H Rebaque	Hesketh	308E	Ford Cosworth	V8	20	battery	24	12
r	30	B Lunger	McLaren	M23	Ford Cosworth	V8	14	accident / gearbox	21	11
r	35	H Heyer	Penske	PC4	Ford Cosworth	V8	9	gear linkage (unofficial starter)	25	13
r	10	I Scheckter	March	761B	Ford Cosworth	V8	9	clutch	18	9
r	7	J Watson	Brabham	BT45B	Alfa Romeo	F12	8	engine	2	1
r	34	J-P Jarier	Penske	PC4	Ford Cosworth	V8	5	accident	12	6
r	17	A Jones	Shadow	DN8	Ford Cosworth	V8	0	accident	17	9
r	22	C Regazzoni	Ensign	N177	Ford Cosworth	V8	0	accident	22	11
nq	27	P Nève	March	761	Ford Cosworth	V8				
nq	36	E de Villota	McLaren	M23	Ford Cosworth	V8				
nq	28	E Fittipaldi	Copersucar	F5	Ford Cosworth	V8				
nq	37	A Merzario	March	761B	Ford Cosworth	V8				
nq	40	T Pilette	Stanley BRM	P207	BRM	V12				

Winning speed 208.528 km/h, 129.573 mph
Pole Position speed 216.153 km/h, 134.311 mph (J Scheckter, 1 min:53.070 sec)
Fastest Lap speed 210.711 km/h, 130.930 mph (N Lauda, 1 min:55.990 sec on lap 28)
Lap Leaders J Scheckter 1-12 (12); N Lauda 13-47 (35).

14 Aug 1977 **AUSTRIA: Österreichring** (Round 12) (Race 292)

54 laps x 5.942 km, 3.692 miles = 320.868 km, 199.378 miles

Pos	No	Driver	Car	Model	Engine		Laps	Time/Reason for Retirement	Grid Pos	Row
1	17	A Jones	Shadow	DN8	Ford Cosworth	V8	54	1h 37m 16.490s	14	7
2	11	N Lauda	Ferrari	312T2	Ferrari	F12	54	1h 37m 36.620s	1	1
3	8	H-J Stuck	Brabham	BT45B	Alfa Romeo	F12	54	1h 37m 50.990s	4	2
4	12	C Reutemann	Ferrari	312T2	Ferrari	F12	54	1h 37m 51.240s	5	3
5	3	R Peterson	Tyrrell	P34	Ford Cosworth	V8	54	1h 38m 18.580s	15	8
6	2	J Mass	McLaren	M26	Ford Cosworth	V8	53		9	5
7	24	R Keegan	Hesketh	308E	Ford Cosworth	V8	53		20	10
8	7	J Watson	Brabham	BT45B	Alfa Romeo	F12	53		12	6
9	27	P Nève	March	761	Ford Cosworth	V8	53		22	11
10	30	B Lunger	McLaren	M23	Ford Cosworth	V8	53		17	9
11	28	E Fittipaldi	Copersucar	F5	Ford Cosworth	V8	53		23	12
12	33	H Binder	Penske	PC4	Ford Cosworth	V8	53		19	10
13	4	P Depailler	Tyrrell	P34	Ford Cosworth	V8	53		10	5
14	34	J-P Jarier	Penske	PC4	Ford Cosworth	V8	52		18	9
15	19	V Brambilla	Surtees	TS19	Ford Cosworth	V8	52		13	7
16	18	V Schuppan	Surtees	TS19	Ford Cosworth	V8	52		25	13
17r	36	E de Villota	McLaren	M23	Ford Cosworth	V8	50	accident	26	13
r	20	J Scheckter	Wolf	WR3	Ford Cosworth	V8	45	spin	8	4
r	1	J Hunt	McLaren	M26	Ford Cosworth	V8	43	engine	2	1
r	23	P Tambay	Ensign	N177	Ford Cosworth	V8	41	engine	7	4
r	6	G Nilsson	JPS Lotus	78	Ford Cosworth	V8	38	engine	16	8
r	16	A Merzario	Shadow	DN8	Ford Cosworth	V8	29	gear linkage	21	11
r	26	J Laffite	Ligier	JS7	Matra	V12	21	oil leak onto tyre / handling	6	3
r	5	M Andretti	JPS Lotus	78	Ford Cosworth	V8	11	engine	3	2
r	10	I Scheckter	March	761B	Ford Cosworth	V8	2	accident	24	12
r	22	C Regazzoni	Ensign	N177	Ford Cosworth	V8	0	accident	11	6
nq	38	B Henton	March	761	Ford Cosworth	V8				
nq	39	I Ashley	Hesketh	308E	Ford Cosworth	V8				
nq	25	H Rebaque	Hesketh	308E	Ford Cosworth	V8				
nq	9	A D Ribeiro	March	761B	Ford Cosworth	V8				

Winning speed 197.914 km/h, 122.978 mph
Pole Position speed 215.377 km/h, 133.829 mph (N Lauda, 1 min:39.320 sec)
Fastest Lap speed 211.878 km/h, 131.655 mph (J Watson, 1 min:40.960 sec on lap 52)
Lap Leaders M Andretti 1-11 (11); J Hunt 12-43 (32); A Jones 44-54 (11).

75 laps x 4.226 km, 2.626 miles = 316.950 km, 196.944 miles

Pos	No	Driver	Car	Model	Engine		Laps	Time/Reason for Retirement	Grid Pos	Row
1	11	N Lauda	Ferrari	312T2	Ferrari	F12	75	1h 41m 45.930s	4	2
2	26	J Laffite	Ligier	JS7	Matra	V12	75	1h 41m 47.820s	2	1
3	20	J Scheckter	Wolf	WR2	Ford Cosworth	V8	74		15	8
4	28	E Fittipaldi	Copersucar	F5	Ford Cosworth	V8	74		17	9
5r	23	P Tambay	Ensign	N177	Ford Cosworth	V8	73	out of fuel	12	6
6	12	C Reutemann	Ferrari	312T2	Ferrari	F12	73		6	3
7	8	H-J Stuck	Brabham	BT45B	Alfa Romeo	F12	73		19	10
8	35	H Binder	Penske	PC4	Ford Cosworth	V8	73		18	9
9	30	B Lunger	McLaren	M23	Ford Cosworth	V8	73		20	10
10	10	I Scheckter	March	771	Ford Cosworth	V8	73		25	13
11	9	A D Ribeiro	March	761B	Ford Cosworth	V8	72		24	12
dq	38	B Henton	Boro	N175	Ford Cosworth	V8	70	push start after spin	23	12
12r	19	V Brambilla	Surtees	TS19	Ford Cosworth	V8	67	accident	22	11
13	16	R Patrese	Shadow	DN8	Ford Cosworth	V8	67		16	8
r	15	J-P Jabouille	Renault	RS01	Renault	V6t	39	rear suspension	10	5
r	6	G Nilsson	JPS Lotus	78	Ford Cosworth	V8	34	accident	5	3
r	17	A Jones	Shadow	DN8	Ford Cosworth	V8	32	engine	13	7
r	4	P Depailler	Tyrrell	P34	Ford Cosworth	V8	31	engine	11	6
r	3	R Peterson	Tyrrell	P34	Ford Cosworth	V8	18	ignition	7	4
r	22	C Regazzoni	Ensign	N177	Ford Cosworth	V8	17	throttle linkage	9	5
r	5	M Andretti	JPS Lotus	78	Ford Cosworth	V8	14	engine	1	1
r	24	R Keegan	Hesketh	308E	Ford Cosworth	V8	8	accident	26	13
r	1	J Hunt	McLaren	M26	Ford Cosworth	V8	5	accident	3	2
r	34	J-P Jarier	Penske	PC4	Ford Cosworth	V8	4	engine	21	11
r	7	J Watson	Brabham	BT45B	Alfa Romeo	F12	2	sump / engine	8	4
r	2	J Mass	McLaren	M26	Ford Cosworth	V8	0	accident	14	7
nq	27	P Nève	March	761	Ford Cosworth	V8				
nq	37	A Merzario	March	761B	Ford Cosworth	V8				
nq	18	V Schuppan	Surtees	TS19	Ford Cosworth	V8				
nq	39	I Ashley	Hesketh	308E	Ford Cosworth	V8				
nq	33	B Hayje	March	761	Ford Cosworth	V8				
nq	25	H Rebaque	Hesketh	308E	Ford Cosworth	V8				
nq	29	T Pilette	Stanley BRM	P207	BRM	V12				
nq	32	M Bleekemolen	March	761	Ford Cosworth	V8				

Winning speed 186.871 km/h, 116.116 mph
Pole Position speed 193.434 km/h, 120.194 mph (M Andretti, 1 min:18.650 sec)
Fastest Lap speed 190.194 km/h, 118.181 mph (N Lauda, 1 min:19.990 sec on lap 72)
Lap Leaders J Hunt 1-5 (5); J Laffite 6-19 (14); N Lauda 20-75 (56).

11 Sep 1977　　**ITALY: Monza**　　　　　　　　　　　　　　　　　　**(Round 14)**　　**(Race 294)**
52 laps x 5.800 km, 3.604 miles = 301.600 km, 187.406 miles

Pos	No	Driver	Car	Model	Engine		Laps	Time/Reason for Retirement	Grid Pos	Row
1	5	M Andretti	JPS Lotus	78	Ford Cosworth	V8	52	1h 27m 50.300s	4	2
2	11	N Lauda	Ferrari	312T2	Ferrari	F12	52	1h 28m 07.260s	5	3
3	17	A Jones	Shadow	DN8	Ford Cosworth	V8	52	1h 28m 13.930s	16	8
4	2	J Mass	McLaren	M26	Ford Cosworth	V8	52	1h 28m 18.780s	9	5
5	22	C Regazzoni	Ensign	N177	Ford Cosworth	V8	52	1h 28m 21.410s	7	4
6	3	R Peterson	Tyrrell	P34	Ford Cosworth	V8	52	1h 29m 09.520s	12	6
7	27	P Nève	March	761	Ford Cosworth	V8	50		24	12
8	26	J Laffite	Ligier	JS7	Matra	V12	50		8	4
9	24	R Keegan	Hesketh	308E	Ford Cosworth	V8	48		23	12
r	10	I Scheckter	March	771	Ford Cosworth	V8	41	half shaft	17	9
r	12	C Reutemann	Ferrari	312T2	Ferrari	F12	39	accident	2	1
r	16	R Patrese	Shadow	DN8	Ford Cosworth	V8	39	accident	6	3
r	14	B Giacomelli	McLaren	M23	Ford Cosworth	V8	38	engine	15	8
r	8	H-J Stuck	Brabham	BT45B	Alfa Romeo	F12	31	engine	11	6
r	1	J Hunt	McLaren	M26	Ford Cosworth	V8	26	brakes / spin	1	1
r	4	P Depailler	Tyrrell	P34	Ford Cosworth	V8	24	engine	13	7
r	20	J Scheckter	Wolf	WR1	Ford Cosworth	V8	23	engine	3	2
r	15	J-P Jabouille	Renault	RS01	Renault	V6t	23	engine	20	10
r	34	J-P Jarier	Penske	PC4	Ford Cosworth	V8	19	engine	18	9
r	23	P Tambay	Ensign	N177	Ford Cosworth	V8	9	engine	21	11
r	19	V Brambilla	Surtees	TS19	Ford Cosworth	V8	5	accident / radiator	10	5
r	30	B Lunger	McLaren	M23	Ford Cosworth	V8	4	engine	22	11
r	6	G Nilsson	JPS Lotus	78	Ford Cosworth	V8	4	front suspension	19	10
r	7	J Watson	Brabham	BT45B	Alfa Romeo	F12	3	accident	14	7
nq	9	A D Ribeiro	March	761B	Ford Cosworth	V8				
nq	28	E Fittipaldi	Copersucar	F5	Ford Cosworth	V8				
nq	18	L Leoni	Surtees	TS19	Ford Cosworth	V8				
nq	38	B Henton	Boro	N175	Ford Cosworth	V8				
nq	36	E de Villota	McLaren	M23	Ford Cosworth	V8				
nq	25	I Ashley	Hesketh	308E	Ford Cosworth	V8				
nq	35	T Pilette	Stanley BRM	P207	BRM	V12				
nq	33	H Binder	Penske	PC4	Ford Cosworth	V8				
nq	41	L Kessel	Williams	FW	Ford Cosworth	V8				
nq	21	G Francia	Brabham	BT45B	Alfa Romeo	F12				

Winning speed 206.015 km/h, 128.012 mph
Pole Position speed 212.887 km/h, 132.282 mph (J Hunt, 1 min:38.080 sec)
Fastest Lap speed 210.696 km/h, 130.921 mph (M Andretti, 1 min:39.100 sec on lap 31)
Lap Leaders J Scheckter 1-9 (9); M Andretti 10-52 (43).

2 Oct 1977　　**USA East: Watkins Glen**　　　　　　　　　　　　　　**(Round 15)**　　**(Race 295)**
59 laps x 5.435 km, 3.377 miles = 320.651 km, 199.243 miles

Pos	No	Driver	Car	Model	Engine		Laps	Time/Reason for Retirement	Grid Pos	Row
1	1	J Hunt	McLaren	M26	Ford Cosworth	V8	59	1h 58m 23.267s	1	1
2	5	M Andretti	JPS Lotus	78	Ford Cosworth	V8	59	1h 58m 25.293s	4	2
3	20	J Scheckter	Wolf	WR2	Ford Cosworth	V8	59	1h 59m 42.146s	9	5
4	11	N Lauda	Ferrari	312T2	Ferrari	F12	59	2h 00m 03.882s	7	4
5	22	C Regazzoni	Ensign	N177	Ford Cosworth	V8	59	2h 00m 11.405s	19	10
6	12	C Reutemann	Ferrari	312T2	Ferrari	F12	58		6	3
7	26	J Laffite	Ligier	JS7	Matra	V12	58		10	5
8	24	R Keegan	Hesketh	308E	Ford Cosworth	V8	58		20	10
9	16	J-P Jarier	Shadow	DN8	Ford Cosworth	V8	58		16	8
10	30	B Lunger	McLaren	M23	Ford Cosworth	V8	57		17	9
11	18	H Binder	Surtees	TS19	Ford Cosworth	V8	57		25	13
12	7	J Watson	Brabham	BT45B	Alfa Romeo	F12	57		3	2
13	28	E Fittipaldi	Copersucar	F5	Ford Cosworth	V8	57		18	9
14	4	P Depailler	Tyrrell	P34	Ford Cosworth	V8	56		8	4
15	9	A D Ribeiro	March	761B	Ford Cosworth	V8	56		23	12
16	3	R Peterson	Tyrrell	P34	Ford Cosworth	V8	56		5	3
17	25	I Ashley	Hesketh	308E	Ford Cosworth	V8	55		22	11
18	27	P Nève	March	761	Ford Cosworth	V8	55		24	12
19	19	V Brambilla	Surtees	TS19	Ford Cosworth	V8	54		11	6
r	15	J-P Jabouille	Renault	RS01	Renault	V6t	30	alternator belt	14	7
r	6	G Nilsson	JPS Lotus	78	Ford Cosworth	V8	17	accident	12	6
r	8	H-J Stuck	Brabham	BT45B	Alfa Romeo	F12	14	accident	2	1
r	10	I Scheckter	March	771	Ford Cosworth	V8	10	accident	21	11
r	2	J Mass	McLaren	M26	Ford Cosworth	V8	8	fuel pump belt	15	8
r	14	D Ongais	Penske	PC4	Ford Cosworth	V8	6	accident	26	13
r	17	A Jones	Shadow	DN8	Ford Cosworth	V8	3	accident	13	7
nq	23	P Tambay	Ensign	N177	Ford Cosworth	V8				

Winning speed 162.509 km/h, 100.978 mph
Pole Position speed 193.977 km/h, 120.532 mph (J Hunt, 1 min:40.863 sec)
Fastest Lap speed 174.917 km/h, 108.688 mph (R Peterson, 1 min:51.854 sec on lap 56)
Lap Leaders H-J Stuck 1-14 (14); J Hunt 15-59 (45).

Races　　　　　　　　　　　　　　　　　　　　　　　　　　　　　　　　　　**199**

9 Oct 1977 **CANADA: Mosport Park** **(Round 16)** **(Race 296)**

80 laps x 3.957 km, 2.459 miles = 316.590 km, 196.720 miles

Pos	No	Driver	Car	Model	Engine		Laps	Time/Reason for Retirement	Grid Pos	Row
1	20	J Scheckter	Wolf	WR1	Ford Cosworth	V8	80	1h 40m 00.000s	9	5
2	4	P Depailler	Tyrrell	P34	Ford Cosworth	V8	80	1h 40m 06.770s	6	3
3	2	J Mass	McLaren	M26	Ford Cosworth	V8	80	1h 40m 15.760s	5	3
4	17	A Jones	Shadow	DN8	Ford Cosworth	V8	80	1h 40m 46.690s	7	4
5	23	P Tambay	Ensign	N177	Ford Cosworth	V8	80	1h 41m 03.260s	16	8
6r	19	V Brambilla	Surtees	TS19	Ford Cosworth	V8	78	accident	15	8
7	14	D Ongais	Penske	PC4	Ford Cosworth	V8	78		22	11
8	9	A D Ribeiro	March	761B	Ford Cosworth	V8	78		23	12
9r	5	M Andretti	JPS Lotus	78	Ford Cosworth	V8	77	engine	1	1
10r	16	R Patrese	Shadow	DN8	Ford Cosworth	V8	76	accident	8	4
11r	30	B Lunger	McLaren	M23	Ford Cosworth	V8	76	engine	20	10
12r	21	G Villeneuve	Ferrari	312T2	Ferrari	F12	76	driveshaft	17	9
r	1	J Hunt	McLaren	M26	Ford Cosworth	V8	61	accident	2	1
r	27	P Nève	March	761	Ford Cosworth	V8	56	oil pressure	21	11
r	3	R Peterson	Tyrrell	P34	Ford Cosworth	V8	34	fuel leak	3	2
r	24	R Keegan	Hesketh	308E	Ford Cosworth	V8	32	accident	25	13
r	18	H Binder	Surtees	TS19	Ford Cosworth	V8	31	accident	24	12
r	28	E Fittipaldi	Copersucar	F5	Ford Cosworth	V8	29	engine	19	10
r	10	I Scheckter	March	771	Ford Cosworth	V8	29	engine	18	9
r	12	C Reutemann	Ferrari	312T2	Ferrari	F12	20	fuel pressure	12	6
r	8	H-J Stuck	Brabham	BT45B	Alfa Romeo	F12	19	engine	13	7
r	6	G Nilsson	JPS Lotus	78	Ford Cosworth	V8	17	throttle jammed / accident	4	2
r	26	J Laffite	Ligier	JS7	Matra	V12	12	driveshaft	11	6
r	7	J Watson	Brabham	BT45B	Alfa Romeo	F12	1	accident	10	5
r	22	C Regazzoni	Ensign	N177	Ford Cosworth	V8	0	accident	14	7
ns	25	I Ashley	Hesketh	308E	Ford Cosworth	V8		accident / injury		
nq	15	J-P Jabouille	Renault	RS01	Renault	V6t				

Winning speed 189.954 km/h, 118.032 mph
Pole Position speed 199.574 km/h, 124.009 mph (M Andretti, 1 min:11.385 sec)
Fastest Lap speed 194.362 km/h, 120.771 mph (M Andretti, 1 min:13.299 sec on lap 56)
Lap Leaders M Andretti 1-60,62-77 (76); J Hunt 61 (1); J Scheckter 78-80 (3).

23 Oct 1977 **JAPAN: Fuji** **(Round 17)** **(Race 297)**

73 laps x 4.359 km, 2.709 miles = 318.207 km, 197.725 miles

Pos	No	Driver	Car	Model	Engine		Laps	Time/Reason for Retirement	Grid Pos	Row
1	1	J Hunt	McLaren	M26	Ford Cosworth	V8	73	1h 31m 51.680s	2	1
2	12	C Reutemann	Ferrari	312T2	Ferrari	F12	73	1h 32m 54.130s	7	4
3	4	P Depailler	Tyrrell	P34	Ford Cosworth	V8	73	1h 32m 58.070s	15	8
4	17	A Jones	Shadow	DN8	Ford Cosworth	V8	73	1h 32m 58.290s	12	6
5r	26	J Laffite	Ligier	JS7	Matra	V12	72	out of fuel	5	3
6	16	R Patrese	Shadow	DN8	Ford Cosworth	V8	72		13	7
7	8	H-J Stuck	Brabham	BT45B	Alfa Romeo	F12	72		4	2
8	19	V Brambilla	Surtees	TS19	Ford Cosworth	V8	71		9	5
9	50	K Takahashi	Tyrrell	007	Ford Cosworth	V8	71		22	11
10	20	J Scheckter	Wolf	WR3	Ford Cosworth	V8	71		6	3
11	52	K Hoshino	Kojima	KE009	Ford Cosworth	V8	71		11	6
12	9	A D Ribeiro	March	761B	Ford Cosworth	V8	69		23	12
r	6	G Nilsson	JPS Lotus	78	Ford Cosworth	V8	63	gearbox linkage	14	7
r	22	C Regazzoni	Ensign	N177	Ford Cosworth	V8	43	oil line	10	5
r	7	J Watson	Brabham	BT45B	Alfa Romeo	F12	29	gearbox	3	2
r	2	J Mass	McLaren	M26	Ford Cosworth	V8	28	engine	8	4
r	23	P Tambay	Ensign	N177	Ford Cosworth	V8	14	engine	16	8
r	3	R Peterson	Tyrrell	P34	Ford Cosworth	V8	5	accident	18	9
r	11	G Villeneuve	Ferrari	312T2	Ferrari	F12	5	accident	20	10
r	27	J-P Jarier	Ligier	JS7	Matra	V12	3	engine	17	9
r	18	H Binder	Surtees	TS19	Ford Cosworth	V8	1	accident	21	11
r	51	N Takahara	Kojima	KE009	Ford Cosworth	V8	1	accident	19	10
r	5	M Andretti	JPS Lotus	78	Ford Cosworth	V8	1	accident	1	1

Winning speed 207.840 km/h, 129.146 mph
Pole Position speed 217.256 km/h, 134.997 mph (M Andretti, 1 min:12.230 sec)
Fastest Lap speed 211.203 km/h, 131.236 mph (J Scheckter, 1 min:14.300 sec on lap 72)
Lap Leaders J Hunt 1-73 (73).

Lap Leaders 1977

Pos	Driver	Car-Engine	GPs	laps	km	miles
1	M Andretti	Lotus-Ford Cosworth	7	278	1,160.8	721.3
2	J Hunt	McLaren-Ford Cosworth	10	222	1,160.2	720.9
3	J Scheckter	Wolf-Ford Cosworth	7	198	748.3	465.0
4	N Lauda	Ferrari	4	190	884.8	549.8
5	J Watson	Brabham-Alfa Romeo	4	138	597.8	371.5
6	G Nilsson	Lotus-Ford Cosworth	1	21	89.5	55.6
7	C Pace	Brabham-Alfa Romeo	2	19	125.3	77.9
8	C Reutemann	Ferrari	1	18	143.3	89.0
9	J Laffite	Ligier-Matra	2	17	71.2	44.3
10	H-J Stuck	Brabham-Alfa Romeo	1	14	76.1	47.3
11	A Jones	Shadow-Ford Cosworth	1	11	65.4	40.6
12	V Brambilla	Surtees-Ford Cosworth	1	4	17.0	10.6
13	J Mass	McLaren-Ford Cosworth	1	2	8.5	5.3
			17	1,132	5,148.4	3,199.0

Driver Points 1977

	Driver	RA	BR	ZA	USAW	E	MC	B	S	F	GB	D	A	NL	I	USAE	CDN	J	Total
1	N Lauda	-	4	9	6	-	6	6	-	2	6	9	6	9	6	3	-	-	72
2	J Scheckter	9	-	6	4	4	9	-	-	-	-	6	-	4	-	4	9	-	55
3	M Andretti	2	-	-	9	9	2	-	1	9	-	-	-	-	9	6	-	-	47
4	C Reutemann	4	9	-	-	6	4	-	4	1	-	3	3	1	-	1	-	6	42
5	J Hunt	-	6	3	-	-	-	-	-	4	9	-	-	-	-	9	-	9	40
6	J Mass	-	-	2	-	3	3	-	6	-	3	-	1	-	3	-	4	-	25
7	A Jones	-	-	-	-	-	1	2	-	-	-	-	9	-	4	-	3	3	22
8	G Nilsson	-	2	-	-	2	-	9	-	3	4	-	-	-	-	-	-	-	20
	P Depailler	-	-	4	3	-	-	-	3	-	-	-	-	-	-	-	6	4	20
10	J Laffite	-	-	-	-	-	-	-	9	-	1	-	-	6	-	-	-	2	18
11	H-J Stuck	-	-	-	-	1	-	1	-	-	2	4	4	-	-	-	-	-	12
12	E Fittipaldi	3	3	-	2	-	-	-	-	-	-	-	-	3	-	-	-	-	11
13	J Watson	-	-	1	-	-	-	2	6	-	-	-	-	-	-	-	-	-	9
14	R Peterson	-	-	-	-	4	-	-	-	-	-	2	-	1	-	-	-	-	7
15	C Pace	6	-	-	-	-	-	-	-	-	-	-	-	-	-	-	-	-	6
	V Brambilla	-	-	-	-	-	3	-	-	-	2	-	-	-	-	-	1	-	6
17	P Tambay	-	-	-	-	-	-	-	-	1	-	-	2	-	-	-	2	-	5
	C Regazzoni	1	-	-	-	-	-	-	-	-	-	-	-	2	2	-	-	-	5
19	R Zorzi	-	1	-	-	-	-	-	-	-	-	-	-	-	-	-	-	-	1
	J-P Jarier	-	-	-	1	-	-	-	-	-	-	-	-	-	-	-	-	-	1
	R Patrese	-	-	-	-	-	-	-	-	-	-	-	-	-	-	-	1	-	1

9,6,4,3,2 and 1 point awarded to the first six finishers. Best 8 scores from first 9 races, best 7 from remaining 8 races.

Constructor Points 1977

	Constructor	RA	BR	ZA	USAW	E	MC	B	S	F	GB	D	A	NL	I	USAE	CDN	J	Total
1	Ferrari	4	9	9	6	6	6	6	4	(2)	6	9	6	9	6	3	-	6	95 (2)
2	Lotus-Ford Cosworth	2	2	-	9	9	2	9	1	9	4	-	-	-	9	6	-	-	62
3	McLaren-Ford Cosworth	-	6	3	-	3	3	-	6	4	9	-	1	-	3	9	4	9	60
4	Wolf-Ford Cosworth	9	-	6	4	4	9	-	-	-	-	6	-	4	-	4	9	-	55
5	Brabham-Alfa Romeo	6	-	1	-	1	-	1	2	6	2	4	4	-	-	-	-	-	27
	Tyrrell-Ford Cosworth	-	-	4	3	-	-	4	3	-	-	-	2	-	1	-	6	4	27
7	Shadow-Ford Cosworth	-	1	-	-	-	1	2	-	-	-	-	9	-	4	-	3	3	23
8	Ligier-Matra	-	-	-	-	-	-	-	9	-	1	-	-	6	-	-	-	2	18
9	Copersucar-Ford Cosworth	3	3	-	2	-	-	-	-	-	-	-	-	3	-	-	-	-	11
10	Ensign-Ford Cosworth	1	-	-	-	-	-	-	-	1	-	-	2	2	2	-	2	-	10
11	Surtees-Ford Cosworth	-	-	-	-	-	-	3	-	-	-	2	-	-	-	-	1	-	6
12	Penske-Ford Cosworth	-	-	-	1	-	-	-	-	-	-	-	-	-	-	-	-	-	1

9,6,4,3,2 and 1 point awarded to the first six finishers. Points only for highest placed car. Best 8 scores from first 9 races, best 7 from remaining 8 races.

1978

Race Entrants and Results

Ferrari turned to Michelin radial tyres as used by Renault, while Goodyear produced the soft qualifying rubber. Lotus developed the wing car, with skirts along the sidepods to avoid escaping air. The Brabham fan-car was created in the same vein but was made illegal after its first win. A new team, Arrows, was created by a splinter group from the ailing Shadow operation.

BRABHAM
Parmalat Racing Team: Lauda, Watson, Piquet

TYRRELL
Elf Team Tyrrell: Pironi, Depailler

LOTUS
John Player Team Lotus: Andretti, Peterson, Jarier
Team Rebaque: Rebaque

McLAREN
Marlboro Team McLaren: Hunt, Tambay, Giacomelli
B & S Fabrications: Lunger, Piquet
Melchester Racing: (Trimmer)
Centro Aseguredor F1: (de Villota)

ATS
ATS Racing Team: Mass, Bleekemolen, Jarier, (Colombo), Rosberg, (Binder, Ertl)

FERRARI
Scuderia Ferrari SpA SEFAC: Reutemann, Villeneuve

FITTIPALDI (COPERSUCAR)
Fittipaldi Automotive: Fittipaldi

RENAULT
Equipe Renault Elf: Jabouille

SHADOW
Shadow Racing Team: Stuck, Regazzoni
Interscope Racing: (Ongais)

SURTEES
Team Surtees: Keegan, Brambilla, (Gimax, Henton), Arnoux, (Gabbiani)

WOLF
Walter Wolf Racing: Scheckter, Rahal
Theodore Racing Hong Kong: Rosberg

HESKETH
Olympus Cameras/Hesketh Racing: (Galica), Cheever, (Daly)

ENSIGN
Team Tissot Ensign: Ongais, Ickx, Daly, Piquet, Leoni, Lunger
Sachs Racing: Ertl
Privateer: (de Dryver)

LIGIER
Ligier Gitanes: Laffite

WILLIAMS
Williams Grand Prix Engineering: Jones

MARTINI
Automobiles Martini: Arnoux

THEODORE
Theodore Racing Hong Kong: (Cheever), Rosberg

ARROWS
Arrows Racing Team: Patrese, Stommelen

MERZARIO
Team Merzario: Merzario, (Colombo)

MARCH
Privateer: (Nève)

---

15 Jan 1978 **ARGENTINA: Buenos Aires No.15** **(Round 1)** **(Race 298)**
52 laps x 5.968 km, 3.708 miles = 310.336 km, 192.834 miles

Pos	No	Driver	Car	Model	Engine		Laps	Time/Reason for Retirement	Grid Pos	Row
1	5	M Andretti	JPS Lotus	78	Ford Cosworth	V8	52	1h 37m 04.470s	1	1
2	1	N Lauda	Brabham	BT45C	Alfa Romeo	F12	52	1h 37m 17.680s	5	3
3	4	P Depailler	Tyrrell	008	Ford Cosworth	V8	52	1h 37m 18.110s	10	5
4	7	J Hunt	McLaren	M26	Ford Cosworth	V8	52	1h 37m 20.520s	6	3
5	6	R Peterson	JPS Lotus	78	Ford Cosworth	V8	52	1h 38m 19.320s	3	2
6	8	P Tambay	McLaren	M26	Ford Cosworth	V8	52	1h 38m 24.370s	9	5
7	11	C Reutemann	Ferrari	312T2	Ferrari	F12	52	1h 38m 27.070s	2	1
8	12	G Villeneuve	Ferrari	312T2	Ferrari	F12	52	1h 38m 43.350s	7	4
9	14	E Fittipaldi	Copersucar	F5A	Ford Cosworth	V8	52	1h 38m 45.070s	17	9
10	20	J Scheckter	Wolf	WR4	Ford Cosworth	V8	52	1h 38m 47.970s	15	8
11	9	J Mass	ATS	HS1	Ford Cosworth	V8	52	1h 38m 53.540s	13	7
12	10	J-P Jarier	ATS	HS1	Ford Cosworth	V8	51		11	6
13	30	B Lunger	McLaren	M23	Ford Cosworth	V8	51		24	12
14	3	D Pironi	Tyrrell	008	Ford Cosworth	V8	51		23	12
15	17	C Regazzoni	Shadow	DN8	Ford Cosworth	V8	51		16	8
16r	26	J Laffite	Ligier	JS7	Matra	V12	50	engine	8	4
17	16	H-J Stuck	Shadow	DN8	Ford Cosworth	V8	50		18	9
18	19	V Brambilla	Surtees	TS19	Ford Cosworth	V8	50		12	6
r	2	J Watson	Brabham	BT45C	Alfa Romeo	F12	41	water leak / engine	4	2
r	27	A Jones	Williams	FW06	Ford Cosworth	V8	36	fuel vaporisation	14	7
r	22	D Ongais	Ensign	N177	Ford Cosworth	V8	35	distributor rotor arm	21	11
r	23	L Leoni	Ensign	N177	Ford Cosworth	V8	28	water leak / engine	22	11
r	37	A Merzario	Merzario	A1	Ford Cosworth	V8	9	differential	20	10
r	18	R Keegan	Surtees	TS19	Ford Cosworth	V8	4	spin / engine overheating	19	10
nq	25	H Rebaque	Lotus	78	Ford Cosworth	V8				
nq	32	E Cheever	Theodore	TR1	Ford Cosworth	V8				
nq	24	D Galica	Hesketh	308E	Ford Cosworth	V8				

Winning speed 191.813 km/h, 119.187 mph
Pole Position speed 199.395 km/h, 123.898 mph (M Andretti, 1 min:47.750 sec)
Fastest Lap speed 195.743 km/h, 121.629 mph (G Villeneuve, 1 min:49.760 sec on lap 3)
Lap Leaders M Andretti 1-52 (52).

29 Jan 1978 **BRAZIL: Rio de Janeiro** (Round 2) (Race 299)

63 laps x 5.031 km, 3.126 miles = 316.953 km, 196.945 miles

Pos	No	Driver	Car	Model	Engine		Laps	Time/Reason for Retirement	Grid Pos	Row
1	11	C Reutemann	Ferrari	312T2	Ferrari	F12	63	1h 49m 59.860s	4	2
2	14	E Fittipaldi	Copersucar	F5A	Ford Cosworth	V8	63	1h 50m 48.990s	7	4
3	1	N Lauda	Brabham	BT45C	Alfa Romeo	F12	63	1h 50m 56.880s	10	5
4	5	M Andretti	JPS Lotus	78	Ford Cosworth	V8	63	1h 51m 32.980s	3	2
5	17	C Regazzoni	Shadow	DN8	Ford Cosworth	V8	62		15	8
6	3	D Pironi	Tyrrell	008	Ford Cosworth	V8	62		19	10
7	9	J Mass	ATS	HS1	Ford Cosworth	V8	62		20	10
8	2	J Watson	Brabham	BT45C	Alfa Romeo	F12	61		21	11
9	26	J Laffite	Ligier	JS7	Matra	V12	61		14	7
10	36	R Patrese	Arrows	FA1	Ford Cosworth	V8	59		18	9
11	27	A Jones	Williams	FW06	Ford Cosworth	V8	58		8	4
r	25	H Rebaque	Lotus	78	Ford Cosworth	V8	40	driver exhausted	22	11
r	12	G Villeneuve	Ferrari	312T2	Ferrari	F12	35	accident	6	3
r	8	P Tambay	McLaren	M26	Ford Cosworth	V8	34	accident	5	3
r	16	H-J Stuck	Shadow	DN8	Ford Cosworth	V8	25	fuel pump	9	5
r	7	J Hunt	McLaren	M26	Ford Cosworth	V8	25	accident	2	1
r	20	J Scheckter	Wolf	WR1	Ford Cosworth	V8	16	accident / suspension	12	6
r	6	R Peterson	JPS Lotus	78	Ford Cosworth	V8	15	accident / rear suspension	1	1
r	22	D Ongais	Ensign	N177	Ford Cosworth	V8	13	brake disc	23	12
r	30	B Lunger	McLaren	M23	Ford Cosworth	V8	11	engine overheating	13	7
r	4	P Depailler	Tyrrell	008	Ford Cosworth	V8	8	spin / brake master cylinder	11	6
r	18	R Keegan	Surtees	TS19	Ford Cosworth	V8	5	accident	24	12
ns	23	L Leoni	Ensign	N177	Ford Cosworth	V8		driveshaft on parade lap	17	9
ns	10	J-P Jarier	ATS	HS1	Ford Cosworth	V8		car raced by Mass	16	8
nq	37	A Merzario	Merzario	A1	Ford Cosworth	V8				
nq	32	E Cheever	Theodore	TR1	Ford Cosworth	V8				
nq	19	V Brambilla	Surtees	TS19	Ford Cosworth	V8				
nq	24	D Galica	Hesketh	308E	Ford Cosworth	V8				

Winning speed 172.887 km/h, 107.427 mph
Pole Position speed 180.305 km/h, 112.036 mph (R Peterson, 1 min:40.450 sec)
Fastest Lap speed 175.721 km/h, 109.188 mph (C Reutemann, 1 min:43.070 sec on lap 35)
Lap Leaders C Reutemann 1-63 (63).

4 Mar 1978 **SOUTH AFRICA: Kyalami** (Round 3) (Race 300)

78 laps x 4.104 km, 2.550 miles = 320.112 km, 198.908 miles

Pos	No	Driver	Car	Model	Engine		Laps	Time/Reason for Retirement	Grid Pos	Row
1	6	R Peterson	JPS Lotus	78	Ford Cosworth	V8	78	1h 42m 15.767s	11	6
2	4	P Depailler	Tyrrell	008	Ford Cosworth	V8	78	1h 42m 16.233s	12	6
3	2	J Watson	Brabham	BT46	Alfa Romeo	F12	78	1h 42m 20.209s	10	5
4	27	A Jones	Williams	FW06	Ford Cosworth	V8	78	1h 42m 54.753s	18	9
5	26	J Laffite	Ligier	JS7	Matra	V12	78	1h 43m 24.985s	14	7
6	3	D Pironi	Tyrrell	008	Ford Cosworth	V8	77		13	7
7	5	M Andretti	JPS Lotus	78	Ford Cosworth	V8	77		2	1
8	10	J-P Jarier	ATS	HS1	Ford Cosworth	V8	77		17	9
9	36	R Stommelen	Arrows	FA1	Ford Cosworth	V8	77		21	11
10	25	H Rebaque	Lotus	78	Ford Cosworth	V8	77		22	11
11	30	B Lunger	McLaren	M23	Ford Cosworth	V8	76		19	10
12	19	V Brambilla	Surtees	TS19	Ford Cosworth	V8	76		20	10
r	35	R Patrese	Arrows	FA1	Ford Cosworth	V8	63	engine	7	4
r	20	J Scheckter	Wolf	WR1	Ford Cosworth	V8	59	accident	5	3
r	8	P Tambay	McLaren	M26	Ford Cosworth	V8	56	accident	4	2
r	11	C Reutemann	Ferrari	312T3	Ferrari	F12	55	accident	9	5
r	12	G Villeneuve	Ferrari	312T3	Ferrari	F12	55	oil leak	8	4
r	18	R Keegan	Surtees	TS19	Ford Cosworth	V8	52	oil line	23	12
r	1	N Lauda	Brabham	BT46	Alfa Romeo	F12	52	engine	1	1
r	9	J Mass	ATS	HS1	Ford Cosworth	V8	43	engine	16	8
r	37	A Merzario	Merzario	A1	Ford Cosworth	V8	39	front suspension radius rod	26	13
r	15	J-P Jabouille	Renault	RS01	Renault	V6t	38	misfire	6	3
r	32	K Rosberg	Theodore	TR1	Ford Cosworth	V8	15	clutch / engine / fuel leak	24	12
r	14	E Fittipaldi	Copersucar	F5A	Ford Cosworth	V8	9	driveshaft	15	8
r	24	E Cheever	Hesketh	308E	Ford Cosworth	V8	8	oil line / engine	25	13
r	7	J Hunt	McLaren	M26	Ford Cosworth	V8	5	engine	3	2
nq	31	R Arnoux	Martini	MK23	Ford Cosworth	V8				
nq	17	C Regazzoni	Shadow	DN8	Ford Cosworth	V8				
nq	22	L Leoni	Ensign	N177	Ford Cosworth	V8				
nq	16	H-J Stuck	Shadow	DN8	Ford Cosworth	V8				

Winning speed 187.817 km/h, 116.704 mph
Pole Position speed 197.916 km/h, 122.979 mph (N Lauda, 1 min:14.650 sec)
Fastest Lap speed 191.651 km/h, 119.087 mph (M Andretti, 1 min:17.090 sec on lap 2)
Lap Leaders M Andretti 1-20 (20); J Scheckter 21-26 (6); R Patrese 27-63 (37); P Depailler 64-77 (14); R Peterson 78 (1).

Cars on rows 6,7,8,10 and 11 lined up on the grid in reverse order, due to N Lauda choosing, at a late stage,
to line up on the other side and causing confusion.

2 Apr 1978 — USA West: Long Beach (Round 4) (Race 301)

80.5 laps x 3.251 km, 2.020 miles = 261.706 km, 162.616 miles

Pos	No	Driver	Car	Model	Engine		Laps	Time/Reason for Retirement	Grid Pos	Row
1	11	C Reutemann	Ferrari	312T3	Ferrari	F12	80	1h 52m 01.301s	1	1
2	5	M Andretti	JPS Lotus	78	Ford Cosworth	V8	80	1h 52m 12.362s	4	2
3	4	P Depailler	Tyrrell	008	Ford Cosworth	V8	80	1h 52m 30.252s	12	6
4	6	R Peterson	JPS Lotus	78	Ford Cosworth	V8	80	1h 52m 46.904s	3	3
5	26	J Laffite	Ligier	JS7	Matra	V12	80	1h 53m 24.185s	14	7
6	35	R Patrese	Arrows	FA1	Ford Cosworth	V8	79		9	5
7	27	A Jones	Williams	FW06	Ford Cosworth	V8	79		8	4
8	14	E Fittipaldi	Copersucar	F5A	Ford Cosworth	V8	79		15	8
9	36	R Stommelen	Arrows	FA1	Ford Cosworth	V8	79		18	9
10	17	C Regazzoni	Shadow	DN8	Ford Cosworth	V8	79		20	10
11	10	J-P Jarier	ATS	HS1	Ford Cosworth	V8	75		19	10
12r	8	P Tambay	McLaren	M26	Ford Cosworth	V8	74	accident	11	6
r	20	J Scheckter	Wolf	WR3	Ford Cosworth	V8	59	accident	10	5
r	19	V Brambilla	Surtees	TS19	Ford Cosworth	V8	50	crown wheel & pinion	17	9
r	15	J-P Jabouille	Renault	RS01	Renault	V6t	43	turbo	13	7
r	12	G Villeneuve	Ferrari	312T3	Ferrari	F12	38	accident	2	1
r	1	N Lauda	Brabham	BT46	Alfa Romeo	F12	27	ignition	3	2
r	3	D Pironi	Tyrrell	008	Ford Cosworth	V8	25	gearbox	22	11
r	37	A Merzario	Merzario	A1	Ford Cosworth	V8	17	gearbox	21	11
r	9	J Mass	ATS	HS1	Ford Cosworth	V8	11	brake master cylinder	16	8
r	2	J Watson	Brabham	BT46	Alfa Romeo	F12	9	oil tank	5	3
r	7	J Hunt	McLaren	M26	Ford Cosworth	V8	5	accident	7	4
ns	18	R Keegan	Surtees	TS19	Ford Cosworth	V8		accident		
ns	16	H-J Stuck	Shadow	DN9	Ford Cosworth	V8		accident		
nq	30	B Lunger	McLaren	M23	Ford Cosworth	V8				
nq	22	L Leoni	Ensign	N177	Ford Cosworth	V8				
npq	32	K Rosberg	Theodore	TR1	Ford Cosworth	V8				
npq	25	H Rebaque	Lotus	78	Ford Cosworth	V8				
npq	39	D Ongais	Shadow	DN9	Ford Cosworth	V8				
npq	24	D Daly	Hesketh	308E	Ford Cosworth	V8				

Winning speed 140.172 km/h, 87.099 mph
Pole Position speed 145.141 km/h, 90.187 mph (C Reutemann, 1 min:20.636 sec)
Fastest Lap speed 142.354 km/h, 88.454 mph (A Jones, 1 min:22.215 sec on lap 27)
Lap Leaders G Villeneuve 1-38 (38.5); C Reutemann 39-80 (42).

The start and finish lines were at different positions on the circuit. The fraction of a lap is credited to the first lap leader.

7 May 1978 — MONACO: Monte-Carlo (Round 5) (Race 302)

75 laps x 3.312 km, 2.058 miles = 248.400 km, 154.349 miles

Pos	No	Driver	Car	Model	Engine		Laps	Time/Reason for Retirement	Grid Pos	Row
1	4	P Depailler	Tyrrell	008	Ford Cosworth	V8	75	1h 55m 14.660s	5	3
2	1	N Lauda	Brabham	BT46	Alfa Romeo	F12	75	1h 55m 37.110s	3	2
3	20	J Scheckter	Wolf	WR1	Ford Cosworth	V8	75	1h 55m 46.950s	9	5
4	2	J Watson	Brabham	BT46	Alfa Romeo	F12	75	1h 55m 48.190s	2	1
5	3	D Pironi	Tyrrell	008	Ford Cosworth	V8	75	1h 56m 22.720s	13	7
6	35	R Patrese	Arrows	FA1	Ford Cosworth	V8	75	1h 56m 23.430s	14	7
7	8	P Tambay	McLaren	M26	Ford Cosworth	V8	74		11	6
8	11	C Reutemann	Ferrari	312T3	Ferrari	F12	74		1	1
9	14	E Fittipaldi	Copersucar	F5A	Ford Cosworth	V8	74		20	10
10	15	J-P Jabouille	Renault	RS01	Renault	V6t	71		12	6
11	5	M Andretti	JPS Lotus	78	Ford Cosworth	V8	69		4	2
r	12	G Villeneuve	Ferrari	312T3	Ferrari	F12	62	front tyre burst / accident	8	4
r	6	R Peterson	JPS Lotus	78	Ford Cosworth	V8	56	gearbox	7	4
r	7	J Hunt	McLaren	M26	Ford Cosworth	V8	43	rear anti-roll bar	6	3
r	36	R Stommelen	Arrows	FA1	Ford Cosworth	V8	38	driver ill	19	10
r	27	A Jones	Williams	FW06	Ford Cosworth	V8	29	oil leak	10	5
r	22	J Ickx	Ensign	N177	Ford Cosworth	V8	27	brakes	16	8
r	16	H-J Stuck	Shadow	DN9	Ford Cosworth	V8	24	accident / steering	17	9
r	26	J Laffite	Ligier	JS9	Matra	V12	13	gearbox	15	8
r	18	R Keegan	Surtees	TS19	Ford Cosworth	V8	8	crown wheel & pinion	18	9
nq	9	J Mass	ATS	HS1	Ford Cosworth	V8				
nq	17	C Regazzoni	Shadow	DN9	Ford Cosworth	V8				
nq	10	J-P Jarier	ATS	HS1	Ford Cosworth	V8				
nq	19	V Brambilla	Surtees	TS20	Ford Cosworth	V8				
npq	32	K Rosberg	Theodore	TR1	Ford Cosworth	V8				
npq	24	D Daly	Hesketh	308E	Ford Cosworth	V8				
npq	31	R Arnoux	Martini	MK23	Ford Cosworth	V8				
npq	25	H Rebaque	Lotus	78	Ford Cosworth	V8				
npq	30	B Lunger	McLaren	M26	Ford Cosworth	V8				
npq	37	A Merzario	Merzario	A1	Ford Cosworth	V8				

Winning speed 129.325 km/h, 80.359 mph
Pole Position speed 134.969 km/h, 83.866 mph (C Reutemann, 1 min:28.340 sec)
Fastest Lap speed 134.497 km/h, 83.573 mph (N Lauda, 1 min:28.650 sec on lap 72)
Lap Leaders J Watson 1-37 (37); P Depailler 38-75 (38).

21 May 1978 **BELGIUM: Zolder** (Round 6) (Race 303)

70 laps x 4.262 km, 2.648 miles = 298.340 km, 185.380 miles

Pos	No	Driver	Car	Model	Engine		Laps	Time/Reason for Retirement	Grid Pos	Row
1	5	M Andretti	JPS Lotus	79	Ford Cosworth	V8	70	1h 39m 52.020s	1	1
2	6	R Peterson	JPS Lotus	78	Ford Cosworth	V8	70	1h 40m 01.920s	7	4
3	11	C Reutemann	Ferrari	312T3	Ferrari	F12	70	1h 40m 16.360s	2	1
4	12	G Villeneuve	Ferrari	312T3	Ferrari	F12	70	1h 40m 39.060s	4	2
5r	26	J Laffite	Ligier	JS7	Matra	V12	69	accident	14	7
6	3	D Pironi	Tyrrell	008	Ford Cosworth	V8	69		23	12
7	30	B Lunger	McLaren	M26	Ford Cosworth	V8	69		24	12
8	33	B Giacomelli	McLaren	M26	Ford Cosworth	V8	69		21	11
9	31	R Arnoux	Martini	MK23	Ford Cosworth	V8	68		19	10
10	27	A Jones	Williams	FW06	Ford Cosworth	V8	68		11	6
11	9	J Mass	ATS	HS1	Ford Cosworth	V8	68		16	8
12	22	J Ickx	Ensign	N177	Ford Cosworth	V8	64		22	11
13r	19	V Brambilla	Surtees	TS20	Ford Cosworth	V8	63	engine	12	6
r	16	H-J Stuck	Shadow	DN9	Ford Cosworth	V8	56	spin	20	10
nc	15	J-P Jabouille	Renault	RS01	Renault	V6t	56		10	5
r	20	J Scheckter	Wolf	WR1	Ford Cosworth	V8	53	accident	5	3
r	4	P Depailler	Tyrrell	008	Ford Cosworth	V8	51	gearbox	13	7
r	17	C Regazzoni	Shadow	DN9	Ford Cosworth	V8	40	differential	18	9
r	35	R Patrese	Arrows	FA1	Ford Cosworth	V8	31	rear suspension	8	4
r	36	R Stommelen	Arrows	FA1	Ford Cosworth	V8	26	accident	17	9
r	2	J Watson	Brabham	BT46	Alfa Romeo	F12	18	accident	9	5
r	14	E Fittipaldi	Copersucar	F5A	Ford Cosworth	V8	0	accident	15	8
r	7	J Hunt	McLaren	M26	Ford Cosworth	V8	0	accident	6	3
r	1	N Lauda	Brabham	BT46	Alfa Romeo	F12	0	accident	3	2
nq	18	R Keegan	Surtees	TS20	Ford Cosworth	V8				
nq	24	D Daly	Hesketh	308E	Ford Cosworth	V8				
nq	32	K Rosberg	Theodore	TR1	Ford Cosworth	V8				
nq	10	A Colombo	ATS	HS1	Ford Cosworth	V8				
npq	25	H Rebaque	Lotus	78	Ford Cosworth	V8				
npq	37	A Merzario	Merzario	A1	Ford Cosworth	V8				
npq	-	P Nève	March	781S	Ford Cosworth	V8				
npq	-	B de Dryver	Ensign	N177	Ford Cosworth	V8				

Winning speed 179.242 km/h, 111.376 mph
Pole Position speed 189.656 km/h, 117.847 mph (M Andretti, 1 min:20.900 sec)
Fastest Lap speed 184.569 km/h, 114.686 mph (R Peterson, 1 min:23.130 sec on lap 66)
Lap Leaders M Andretti 1-70 (70).

4 Jun 1978 **SPAIN: Jarama** (Round 7) (Race 304)

75 laps x 3.404 km, 2.115 miles = 255.300 km, 158.636 miles

Pos	No	Driver	Car	Model	Engine		Laps	Time/Reason for Retirement	Grid Pos	Row
1	5	M Andretti	JPS Lotus	79	Ford Cosworth	V8	75	1h 41m 47.060s	1	1
2	6	R Peterson	JPS Lotus	79	Ford Cosworth	V8	75	1h 42m 06.620s	2	1
3	26	J Laffite	Ligier	JS9	Matra	V12	75	1h 42m 24.300s	10	5
4	20	J Scheckter	Wolf	WR5	Ford Cosworth	V8	75	1h 42m 47.120s	9	5
5	2	J Watson	Brabham	BT46	Alfa Romeo	F12	75	1h 42m 52.980s	7	4
6	7	J Hunt	McLaren	M26	Ford Cosworth	V8	74		4	2
7	19	V Brambilla	Surtees	TS20	Ford Cosworth	V8	74		16	8
8	27	A Jones	Williams	FW06	Ford Cosworth	V8	74		18	9
9	9	J Mass	ATS	HS1	Ford Cosworth	V8	74		17	9
10	12	G Villeneuve	Ferrari	312T3	Ferrari	F12	74		5	3
11	18	R Keegan	Surtees	TS20	Ford Cosworth	V8	73		23	12
12	3	D Pironi	Tyrrell	008	Ford Cosworth	V8	71		13	7
13	15	J-P Jabouille	Renault	RS01	Renault	V6t	71		11	6
14	36	R Stommelen	Arrows	FA1	Ford Cosworth	V8	71		19	10
15r	17	C Regazzoni	Shadow	DN9	Ford Cosworth	V8	67	fuel union	22	11
r	22	J Ickx	Ensign	N177	Ford Cosworth	V8	64	engine	21	11
r	14	E Fittipaldi	Copersucar	F5A	Ford Cosworth	V8	62	throttle linkage	15	8
r	11	C Reutemann	Ferrari	312T3	Ferrari	F12	57	driveshaft / accident	3	2
r	1	N Lauda	Brabham	BT46	Alfa Romeo	F12	56	engine	6	3
r	4	P Depailler	Tyrrell	008	Ford Cosworth	V8	51	engine	12	6
r	16	H-J Stuck	Shadow	DN9	Ford Cosworth	V8	45	rear suspension radius rod	24	12
r	25	H Rebaque	Lotus	78	Ford Cosworth	V8	21	exhaust	20	10
r	35	R Patrese	Arrows	FA1	Ford Cosworth	V8	21	engine	8	4
r	8	P Tambay	McLaren	M26	Ford Cosworth	V8	16	spin / clutch	14	7
nq	37	A Merzario	Merzario	A1	Ford Cosworth	V8				
nq	30	B Lunger	McLaren	M26	Ford Cosworth	V8				
nq	36	E de Villota	McLaren	M23	Ford Cosworth	V8				
nq	10	A Colombo	ATS	HS1	Ford Cosworth	V8				
npq	32	K Rosberg	Theodore	TR1	Ford Cosworth	V8				

Winning speed 150.495 km/h, 93.513 mph
Pole Position speed 160.419 km/h, 99.680 mph (M Andretti, 1 min:16.390 sec)
Fastest Lap speed 153.065 km/h, 95.110 mph (M Andretti, 1 min:20.060 sec on lap 5)
Lap Leaders J Hunt 1-5 (5); M Andretti 6-75 (70).

Races

17 Jun 1978 **SWEDEN: Anderstorp** (Round 8) (Race 305)

70 laps x 4.031 km, 2.505 miles = 282.170 km, 175.332 miles

Pos	No	Driver	Car	Model	Engine		Laps	Time/Reason for Retirement	Grid Pos	Row
1	1	N Lauda	Brabham	BT46B	Alfa Romeo	F12	70	1h 41m 00.606s	3	2
2	35	R Patrese	Arrows	FA1	Ford Cosworth	V8	70	1h 41m 34.625s	5	3
3	6	R Peterson	JPS Lotus	79	Ford Cosworth	V8	70	1h 41m 34.711s	4	2
4	8	P Tambay	McLaren	M26	Ford Cosworth	V8	69		15	8
5	17	C Regazzoni	Shadow	DN9	Ford Cosworth	V8	69		16	8
6	14	E Fittipaldi	Copersucar	F5A	Ford Cosworth	V8	69		13	7
7	26	J Laffite	Ligier	JS9	Matra	V12	69		11	6
8	7	J Hunt	McLaren	M26	Ford Cosworth	V8	69		14	7
9	12	G Villeneuve	Ferrari	312T3	Ferrari	F12	69		7	4
10	11	C Reutemann	Ferrari	312T3	Ferrari	F12	69		8	4
11	16	H-J Stuck	Shadow	DN9	Ford Cosworth	V8	68		20	10
12	25	H Rebaque	Lotus	78	Ford Cosworth	V8	68		21	11
13	9	J Mass	ATS	HS1	Ford Cosworth	V8	68		19	10
14	36	R Stommelen	Arrows	FA1	Ford Cosworth	V8	67		24	12
15	10	K Rosberg	ATS	HS1	Ford Cosworth	V8	63		23	12
nc	37	A Merzario	Merzario	A1	Ford Cosworth	V8	62		22	11
r	27	A Jones	Williams	FW06	Ford Cosworth	V8	47	front wheel bearing	9	5
r	5	M Andretti	JPS Lotus	79	Ford Cosworth	V8	46	piston	1	1
r	4	P Depailler	Tyrrell	008	Ford Cosworth	V8	43	tyre / suspension	12	6
r	15	J-P Jabouille	Renault	RS01	Renault	V6t	29	piston	10	5
r	2	J Watson	Brabham	BT46B	Alfa Romeo	F12	20	spin / throttle jammed	2	1
r	20	J Scheckter	Wolf	WR5	Ford Cosworth	V8	17	water pipe	6	3
r	3	D Pironi	Tyrrell	008	Ford Cosworth	V8	8	accident / rear tyre / oil cooler	17	9
r	19	V Brambilla	Surtees	TS20	Ford Cosworth	V8	8	accident	18	9
nq	18	R Keegan	Surtees	TS20	Ford Cosworth	V8				
nq	30	B Lunger	McLaren	M26	Ford Cosworth	V8				
nq	22	J Ickx	Ensign	N177	Ford Cosworth	V8				

Winning speed 167.609 km/h, 104.147 mph
Pole Position speed 176.846 km/h, 109.887 mph (M Andretti, 1 min:22.058 sec)
Fastest Lap speed 171.055 km/h, 106.288 mph (N Lauda, 1 min:24.836 sec on lap 33)
Lap Leaders M Andretti 1-38 (38); N Lauda 39-70 (32).

2 Jul 1978 **FRANCE: Paul Ricard** (Round 9) (Race 306)

54 laps x 5.810 km, 3.610 miles = 313.740 km, 194.949 miles

Pos	No	Driver	Car	Model	Engine		Laps	Time/Reason for Retirement	Grid Pos	Row
1	5	M Andretti	JPS Lotus	79	Ford Cosworth	V8	54	1h 38m 51.920s	2	1
2	6	R Peterson	JPS Lotus	79	Ford Cosworth	V8	54	1h 38m 54.850s	5	3
3	7	J Hunt	McLaren	M26	Ford Cosworth	V8	54	1h 39m 11.720s	4	2
4	2	J Watson	Brabham	BT46	Alfa Romeo	F12	54	1h 39m 28.800s	1	1
5	27	A Jones	Williams	FW06	Ford Cosworth	V8	54	1h 39m 33.730s	14	7
6	20	J Scheckter	Wolf	WR5	Ford Cosworth	V8	54	1h 39m 46.450s	7	4
7	26	J Laffite	Ligier	JS9	Matra	V12	54	1h 39m 46.660s	10	5
8	35	R Patrese	Arrows	FA1	Ford Cosworth	V8	54	1h 40m 16.800s	12	6
9	8	P Tambay	McLaren	M26	Ford Cosworth	V8	54	1h 40m 18.980s	6	3
10	3	D Pironi	Tyrrell	008	Ford Cosworth	V8	54	1h 40m 21.900s	16	8
11	16	H-J Stuck	Shadow	DN9	Ford Cosworth	V8	53		20	10
12	12	G Villeneuve	Ferrari	312T3	Ferrari	F12	53		9	5
13	9	J Mass	ATS	HS1	Ford Cosworth	V8	53		25	13
14	31	R Arnoux	Martini	MK23	Ford Cosworth	V8	53		18	9
15	36	R Stommelen	Arrows	FA1	Ford Cosworth	V8	53		21	11
16	10	K Rosberg	ATS	HS1	Ford Cosworth	V8	52		26	13
17	19	V Brambilla	Surtees	TS20	Ford Cosworth	V8	52		19	10
18	11	C Reutemann	Ferrari	312T3	Ferrari	F12	49		8	4
r	30	B Lunger	McLaren	M26	Ford Cosworth	V8	45	engine	24	12
r	14	E Fittipaldi	Copersucar	F5A	Ford Cosworth	V8	43	rear suspension	15	8
r	18	R Keegan	Surtees	TS20	Ford Cosworth	V8	40	engine	23	12
r	33	B Giacomelli	McLaren	M26	Ford Cosworth	V8	28	engine	22	11
r	4	P Depailler	Tyrrell	008	Ford Cosworth	V8	10	engine	13	7
r	1	N Lauda	Brabham	BT46	Alfa Romeo	F12	10	engine	3	2
r	17	C Regazzoni	Shadow	DN9	Ford Cosworth	V8	4	electrics	17	9
r	15	J-P Jabouille	Renault	RS01	Renault	V6t	2	engine	11	6
nq	37	A Merzario	Merzario	A1	Ford Cosworth	V8				
nq	22	D Daly	Ensign	N177	Ford Cosworth	V8				
nq	25	H Rebaque	Lotus	78	Ford Cosworth	V8				

Winning speed 190.404 km/h, 118.312 mph
Pole Position speed 200.326 km/h, 124.477 mph (J Watson, 1 min:44.410 sec)
Fastest Lap speed 192.668 km/h, 119.718 mph (C Reutemann, 1 min:48.560 sec on lap 48)
Lap Leaders M Andretti 1-54 (54).

16 Jul 1978 **BRITAIN: Brands Hatch** (Round 10) (Race 307)

76 laps x 4.207 km, 2.614 miles = 319.719 km, 198.664 miles

Pos	No	Driver	Car	Model	Engine		Laps	Time/Reason for Retirement	Grid Pos	Row
1	11	C Reutemann	Ferrari	312T3	Ferrari	F12	76	1h 42m 12.390s	8	4
2	1	N Lauda	Brabham	BT46	Alfa Romeo	F12	76	1h 42m 13.620s	4	2
3	2	J Watson	Brabham	BT46	Alfa Romeo	F12	76	1h 42m 49.640s	9	5
4	4	P Depailler	Tyrrell	008	Ford Cosworth	V8	76	1h 43m 25.660s	10	5
5	16	H-J Stuck	Shadow	DN9	Ford Cosworth	V8	75		18	9
6	8	P Tambay	McLaren	M26	Ford Cosworth	V8	75		20	10
7	33	B Giacomelli	McLaren	M26	Ford Cosworth	V8	75		16	8
8	30	B Lunger	McLaren	M26	Ford Cosworth	V8	75		24	12
9	19	V Brambilla	Surtees	TS20	Ford Cosworth	V8	75		25	13
10	26	J Laffite	Ligier	JS9	Matra	V12	73		7	4
nc	9	J Mass	ATS	HS1	Ford Cosworth	V8	66		26	13
r	10	K Rosberg	ATS	HS1	Ford Cosworth	V8	59	front suspension	22	11
r	17	C Regazzoni	Shadow	DN9	Ford Cosworth	V8	49	gearbox	17	9
r	15	J-P Jabouille	Renault	RS01	Renault	V6t	46	engine	12	6
r	35	R Patrese	Arrows	FA1	Ford Cosworth	V8	40	rear tyre / suspension	5	3
r	3	D Pironi	Tyrrell	008	Ford Cosworth	V8	40	gearbox mounting	19	10
r	20	J Scheckter	Wolf	WR5	Ford Cosworth	V8	36	gearbox	3	2
r	14	E Fittipaldi	Copersucar	F5A	Ford Cosworth	V8	32	engine	11	6
r	37	A Merzario	Merzario	A1	Ford Cosworth	V8	32	fuel pump	23	12
r	22	D Daly	Ensign	N177	Ford Cosworth	V8	30	rear wheel lost / accident	15	8
r	5	M Andretti	JPS Lotus	79	Ford Cosworth	V8	28	engine	2	1
r	27	A Jones	Williams	FW06	Ford Cosworth	V8	26	driveshaft	6	3
r	12	G Villeneuve	Ferrari	312T3	Ferrari	F12	19	driveshaft	13	7
r	25	H Rebaque	Lotus	78	Ford Cosworth	V8	15	gearbox	21	11
r	7	J Hunt	McLaren	M26	Ford Cosworth	V8	8	accident	14	7
r	6	R Peterson	JPS Lotus	79	Ford Cosworth	V8	6	fuel pump	1	1
nq	36	R Stommelen	Arrows	FA1	Ford Cosworth	V8				
nq	23	G Lees	Ensign	N175	Ford Cosworth	V8				
nq	18	R Keegan	Surtees	TS20	Ford Cosworth	V8				
nq	40	T Trimmer	McLaren	M23	Ford Cosworth	V8				

Winning speed 187.690 km/h, 116.625 mph
Pole Position speed 197.195 km/h, 122.531 mph (R Peterson, 1 min:16.800 sec)
Fastest Lap speed 192.679 km/h, 119.725 mph (N Lauda, 1 min:18.600 sec on lap 72)
Lap Leaders M Andretti 1-23 (23); J Scheckter 24-33 (10); N Lauda 34-59 (26); C Reutemann 60-76 (17).

---

30 Jul 1978 **GERMANY: Hockenheim** (Round 11) (Race 308)

45 laps x 6.789 km, 4.218 miles = 305.505 km, 189.832 miles

Pos	No	Driver	Car	Model	Engine		Laps	Time/Reason for Retirement	Grid Pos	Row
1	5	M Andretti	JPS Lotus	79	Ford Cosworth	V8	45	1h 28m 00.900s	1	1
2	20	J Scheckter	Wolf	WR5	Ford Cosworth	V8	45	1h 28m 16.250s	4	2
3	26	J Laffite	Ligier	JS9	Matra	V12	45	1h 28m 28.910s	7	4
4	14	E Fittipaldi	Copersucar	F5A	Ford Cosworth	V8	45	1h 28m 37.780s	10	5
5	3	D Pironi	Tyrrell	008	Ford Cosworth	V8	45	1h 28m 58.160s	16	8
6	25	H Rebaque	Lotus	78	Ford Cosworth	V8	45	1h 29m 38.760s	18	9
7	2	J Watson	Brabham	BT46	Alfa Romeo	F12	45	1h 29m 40.430s	5	3
8	12	G Villeneuve	Ferrari	312T3	Ferrari	F12	45	1h 29m 57.770s	15	8
9	35	R Patrese	Arrows	FA1	Ford Cosworth	V8	44		14	7
10	32	K Rosberg	Wolf	WR3	Ford Cosworth	V8	42		19	10
dq	36	R Stommelen	Arrows	FA1	Ford Cosworth	V8	42	incorrect route into pits	17	9
11r	23	H Ertl	Ensign	N177	Ford Cosworth	V8	41	engine	23	12
r	6	R Peterson	JPS Lotus	79	Ford Cosworth	V8	36	gearbox	2	1
dq	7	J Hunt	McLaren	M26	Ford Cosworth	V8	34	incorrect route into pits	8	4
r	27	A Jones	Williams	FW06	Ford Cosworth	V8	31	fuel vaporisation	6	3
r	22	N Piquet	Ensign	N177	Ford Cosworth	V8	31	engine	21	11
r	19	V Brambilla	Surtees	TS20	Ford Cosworth	V8	24	fuel vaporisation	20	10
r	8	P Tambay	McLaren	M26	Ford Cosworth	V8	16	tyre / suspension / accident	11	6
r	11	C Reutemann	Ferrari	312T3	Ferrari	F12	14	fuel vaporisation	12	6
r	1	N Lauda	Brabham	BT46	Alfa Romeo	F12	11	engine	3	2
r	15	J-P Jabouille	Renault	RS01	Renault	V6t	5	piston rings	9	5
r	16	H-J Stuck	Shadow	DN9	Ford Cosworth	V8	1	accident	24	12
r	9	J Mass	ATS	HS1	Ford Cosworth	V8	1	front suspension / accident	22	11
r	4	P Depailler	Tyrrell	008	Ford Cosworth	V8	0	accident	13	7
nq	17	C Regazzoni	Shadow	DN9	Ford Cosworth	V8				
nq	10	J-P Jarier	ATS	HS1	Ford Cosworth	V8				
nq	18	R Keegan	Surtees	TS20	Ford Cosworth	V8				
nq	37	A Merzario	Merzario	A1	Ford Cosworth	V8				
npq	31	R Arnoux	Martini	MK23	Ford Cosworth	V8				
npq	30	B Lunger	McLaren	M26	Ford Cosworth	V8				

Winning speed 208.263 km/h, 129.409 mph
Pole Position speed 218.413 km/h, 135.715 mph (M Andretti, 1 min:51.900 sec)
Fastest Lap speed 211.386 km/h, 131.349 mph (R Peterson, 1 min:55.620 sec on lap 26)
Lap Leaders R Peterson 1-4 (4); M Andretti 5-45 (41).

Races

207

13 Aug 1978 **AUSTRIA: Österreichring** (Round 12) (Race 309)

54 laps x 5.942 km, 3.692 miles = 320.868 km, 199.378 miles

Pos	No	Driver	Car	Model	Engine		Laps	Time/Reason for Retirement	Grid Pos	Row
1	6	R Peterson	JPS Lotus	79	Ford Cosworth	V8	54	1h 41m 21.570s	1	1
2	4	P Depailler	Tyrrell	008	Ford Cosworth	V8	54	1h 42m 09.010s	13	7
3	12	G Villeneuve	Ferrari	312T3	Ferrari	F12	54	1h 43m 01.330s	11	6
4	14	E Fittipaldi	Copersucar	F5A	Ford Cosworth	V8	53		6	3
5	26	J Laffite	Ligier	JS9	Matra	V12	53		5	3
6	19	V Brambilla	Surtees	TS20	Ford Cosworth	V8	53		21	11
7	2	J Watson	Brabham	BT46	Alfa Romeo	F12	53		10	5
8	30	B Lunger	McLaren	M26	Ford Cosworth	V8	52		17	9
9	31	R Arnoux	Martini	MK23	Ford Cosworth	V8	52		26	13
nc	17	C Regazzoni	Shadow	DN9	Ford Cosworth	V8	50		22	11
nc	32	K Rosberg	Wolf	WR3	Ford Cosworth	V8	49		25	13
dq	22	D Daly	Ensign	N177	Ford Cosworth	V8	43	push start after spin	19	10
r	8	P Tambay	McLaren	M26	Ford Cosworth	V8	40	accident	14	7
r	16	H-J Stuck	Shadow	DN9	Ford Cosworth	V8	33	accident	23	12
r	15	J-P Jabouille	Renault	RS01	Renault	V6t	31	gearbox	3	2
r	1	N Lauda	Brabham	BT46	Alfa Romeo	F12	28	accident	12	6
dq	11	C Reutemann	Ferrari	312T3	Ferrari	F12	27	push start after spin	4	2
r	3	D Pironi	Tyrrell	008	Ford Cosworth	V8	20	accident	9	5
r	7	J Hunt	McLaren	M26	Ford Cosworth	V8	8	accident	8	4
r	27	A Jones	Williams	FW06	Ford Cosworth	V8	7	accident	15	8
r	23	H Ertl	Ensign	N177	Ford Cosworth	V8	6	accident	24	12
r	35	R Patrese	Arrows	A1	Ford Cosworth	V8	6	accident	16	8
r	20	J Scheckter	Wolf	WR5	Ford Cosworth	V8	3	accident	7	4
r	29	N Piquet	McLaren	M23	Ford Cosworth	V8	2	accident	20	10
r	25	H Rebaque	Lotus	78	Ford Cosworth	V8	1	clutch	18	9
r	5	M Andretti	JPS Lotus	79	Ford Cosworth	V8	0	accident	2	1
nq	37	A Merzario	Merzario	A1	Ford Cosworth	V8				
nq	9	J Mass	ATS	HS1	Ford Cosworth	V8				
nq	18	R Keegan	Surtees	TS20	Ford Cosworth	V8				
nq	10	H Binder	ATS	HS1	Ford Cosworth	V8				
nq	18	B Henton	Surtees	TS20	Ford Cosworth	V8		tested only / car raced by Keegan		
npq	36	R Stommelen	Arrows	A1	Ford Cosworth	V8				

Winning speed 189.939 km/h, 118.022 mph
Pole Position speed 218.925 km/h, 136.034 mph (R Peterson, 1 min:37.710 sec)
Fastest Lap speed 207.440 km/h, 128.897 mph (R Peterson, 1 min:43.120 sec)
Lap Leaders R Peterson 1-18,29-54 (44); C Reutemann 19-22 (4); G Villeneuve 23-28 (6).

Interrupted after 7 laps, because of an accident. Restarted for the remaining 47 laps, with results being on aggregate.
Lap leaders are given 'on the road'.

75 laps x 4.226 km, 2.626 miles = 316.950 km, 196.944 miles

Pos	No	Driver	Car	Model	Engine		Laps	Time/Reason for Retirement	Grid Pos	Row
1	5	M Andretti	JPS Lotus	79	Ford Cosworth	V8	75	1h 41m 04.230s	1	1
2	6	R Peterson	JPS Lotus	79	Ford Cosworth	V8	75	1h 41m 04.550s	2	1
3	1	N Lauda	Brabham	BT46	Alfa Romeo	F12	75	1h 41m 16.440s	3	2
4	2	J Watson	Brabham	BT46	Alfa Romeo	F12	75	1h 41m 25.150s	8	4
5	14	E Fittipaldi	Copersucar	F5A	Ford Cosworth	V8	75	1h 41m 25.730s	10	5
6	12	G Villeneuve	Ferrari	312T3	Ferrari	F12	75	1h 41m 50.180s	5	3
7	11	C Reutemann	Ferrari	312T3	Ferrari	F12	75	1h 42m 04.730s	4	2
8	26	J Laffite	Ligier	JS9	Matra	V12	74		6	3
9	8	P Tambay	McLaren	M26	Ford Cosworth	V8	74		14	7
10	7	J Hunt	McLaren	M26	Ford Cosworth	V8	74		7	4
11	25	H Rebaque	Lotus	78	Ford Cosworth	V8	74		20	10
12	20	J Scheckter	Wolf	WR6	Ford Cosworth	V8	73		15	8
r	33	B Giacomelli	McLaren	M26	Ford Cosworth	V8	60	spin	19	10
r	16	H-J Stuck	Shadow	DN9	Ford Cosworth	V8	56	differential	18	9
r	31	R Arnoux	Martini	MK23	Ford Cosworth	V8	40	rear wing mounting	23	12
r	37	A Merzario	Merzario	A1	Ford Cosworth	V8	40	engine	27	14
dq	19	V Brambilla	Surtees	TS20	Ford Cosworth	V8	37	push start after spin	22	11
r	15	J-P Jabouille	Renault	RS01	Renault	V6t	35	piston rings	9	5
r	30	B Lunger	McLaren	M26	Ford Cosworth	V8	35	engine	21	11
r	32	K Rosberg	Wolf	WR4	Ford Cosworth	V8	21	throttle jammed / accident	24	12
r	27	A Jones	Williams	FW06	Ford Cosworth	V8	17	throttle linkage	11	6
r	29	N Piquet	McLaren	M23	Ford Cosworth	V8	16	driveshaft	26	13
r	4	P Depailler	Tyrrell	008	Ford Cosworth	V8	13	engine	12	6
r	22	D Daly	Ensign	N177	Ford Cosworth	V8	10	driveshaft	16	8
r	35	R Patrese	Arrows	A1	Ford Cosworth	V8	0	accident	13	7
r	3	D Pironi	Tyrrell	008	Ford Cosworth	V8	0	accident	17	9
ns	18	R Keegan	Surtees	TS20	Ford Cosworth	V8		accident / injury	25	13
nq	17	C Regazzoni	Shadow	DN9	Ford Cosworth	V8				
nq	10	M Bleekemolen	ATS	HS1	Ford Cosworth	V8				
nq	9	J Mass	ATS	HS1	Ford Cosworth	V8				
npq	23	H Ertl	Ensign	N177	Ford Cosworth	V8				
npq	39	D Ongais	Shadow	DN9	Ford Cosworth	V8				
npq	36	R Stommelen	Arrows	A1	Ford Cosworth	V8				

Winning speed 188.156 km/h, 116.915 mph
Pole Position speed 199.235 km/h, 123.799 mph (M Andretti, 1 min:16.360 sec)
Fastest Lap speed 191.198 km/h, 118.805 mph (N Lauda, 1 min:19.570 sec on lap 57)
Lap Leaders M Andretti 1-75 (75).

10 Sep 1978   **ITALY: Monza**   (Round 14)   (Race 311)

40 laps x 5.800 km, 3.604 miles = 232.000 km, 144.158 miles

Pos	No	Driver	Car	Model	Engine		Laps	Time/Reason for Retirement	Grid Pos	Row
1	1	N Lauda	Brabham	BT46	Alfa Romeo	F12	40	1h 07m 04.540s	4	2
2	2	J Watson	Brabham	BT46	Alfa Romeo	F12	40	1h 07m 06.020s	7	4
3	11	C Reutemann	Ferrari	312T3	Ferrari	F12	40	1h 07m 25.010s	11	6
4	26	J Laffite	Ligier	JS9	Matra	V12	40	1h 07m 42.070s	8	4
5	8	P Tambay	McLaren	M26	Ford Cosworth	V8	40	1h 07m 44.930s	19	10
6	5	M Andretti	JPS Lotus	79	Ford Cosworth	V8	40	1h 07m 50.870s	1	1
7	12	G Villeneuve	Ferrari	312T3	Ferrari	F12	40	1h 07m 53.020s	2	1
8	14	E Fittipaldi	Copersucar	F5A	Ford Cosworth	V8	40	1h 07m 59.780s	13	7
9	29	N Piquet	McLaren	M23	Ford Cosworth	V8	40	1h 08m 11.370s	24	12
10	22	D Daly	Ensign	N177	Ford Cosworth	V8	40	1h 08m 13.650s	18	9
11	4	P Depailler	Tyrrell	008	Ford Cosworth	V8	40	1h 08m 21.110s	16	8
12	20	J Scheckter	Wolf	WR5	Ford Cosworth	V8	39		9	5
13	27	A Jones	Williams	FW06	Ford Cosworth	V8	39		6	3
14	33	B Giacomelli	McLaren	M26	Ford Cosworth	V8	39		20	10
nc	17	C Regazzoni	Shadow	DN9	Ford Cosworth	V8	33		15	8
r	35	R Patrese	Arrows	A1	Ford Cosworth	V8	28	engine	12	6
r	7	J Hunt	McLaren	M26	Ford Cosworth	V8	19	distributor	10	5
r	37	A Merzario	Merzario	A1	Ford Cosworth	V8	13	engine	22	11
r	15	J-P Jabouille	Renault	RS01	Renault	V6t	6	dropped valve	3	2
r	6	R Peterson	JPS Lotus	78	Ford Cosworth	V8	0	fatal accident *	5	3
r	19	V Brambilla	Surtees	TS20	Ford Cosworth	V8	0	accident / injury *	23	12
r	30	B Lunger	McLaren	M26	Ford Cosworth	V8	0	accident *	21	11
r	3	D Pironi	Tyrrell	008	Ford Cosworth	V8	0	accident *	14	7
r	16	H-J Stuck	Shadow	DN9	Ford Cosworth	V8	0	accident / injury *	17	9
nq	25	H Rebaque	Lotus	78	Ford Cosworth	V8				
nq	10	H Ertl	ATS	HS1	Ford Cosworth	V8				
nq	9	M Bleekemolen	ATS	HS1	Ford Cosworth	V8				
nq	18	Gimax	Surtees	TS20	Ford Cosworth	V8				
npq	32	K Rosberg	Wolf	WR4	Ford Cosworth	V8				
npq	36	R Stommelen	Arrows	A1	Ford Cosworth	V8				
npq	34	A Colombo	Merzario	A1	Ford Cosworth	V8				

Winning speed 207.527 km/h, 128.951 mph
Pole Position speed 214.110 km/h, 133.042 mph (M Andretti, 1 min:37.520 sec)
Fastest Lap speed 212.562 km/h, 132.080 mph (M Andretti, 1 min:38.230 sec on lap 33)
Lap Leaders G Villeneuve 1-34 (34); M Andretti 35-40 (6).

Scheduled for 52 laps, but interrupted after first lap accident. Restarted race was shortened. M Andretti finished 1st in
1h 06m 40.39s (208.780 km/h, 129.730 mph), but penalised 1 minute for jumping the start and classified 6th. G Villeneuve
finished 2nd, but penalised 1 minute for jumping the start and classified 7th. These drivers are shown as leaders 'on the road'.
*H Ertl also practised in an Ensign N177-Ford Cosworth V8 (23) but failed to pre-qualify.   * Retired after first start.*

1 Oct 1978   **USA East: Watkins Glen**   (Round 15)   (Race 312)

59 laps x 5.435 km, 3.377 miles = 320.651 km, 199.243 miles

Pos	No	Driver	Car	Model	Engine		Laps	Time/Reason for Retirement	Grid Pos	Row
1	11	C Reutemann	Ferrari	312T3	Ferrari	F12	59	1h 40m 48.800s	2	1
2	27	A Jones	Williams	FW06	Ford Cosworth	V8	59	1h 41m 08.539s	3	2
3	20	J Scheckter	Wolf	WR6	Ford Cosworth	V8	59	1h 41m 34.501s	11	6
4	15	J-P Jabouille	Renault	RS01	Renault	V6t	59	1h 42m 13.807s	9	5
5	14	E Fittipaldi	Copersucar	F5A	Ford Cosworth	V8	59	1h 42m 16.889s	13	7
6	8	P Tambay	McLaren	M26	Ford Cosworth	V8	59	1h 42m 39.010s	18	9
7	7	J Hunt	McLaren	M26	Ford Cosworth	V8	58		6	3
8	22	D Daly	Ensign	N177	Ford Cosworth	V8	58		19	10
9	18	R Arnoux	Surtees	TS20	Ford Cosworth	V8	58		21	11
10	3	D Pironi	Tyrrell	008	Ford Cosworth	V8	58		16	8
11	26	J Laffite	Ligier	JS9	Matra	V12	58		10	5
12	21	B Rahal	Wolf	WR5	Ford Cosworth	V8	58		20	10
13	23	B Lunger	Ensign	N177	Ford Cosworth	V8	58		24	12
14	17	C Regazzoni	Shadow	DN9	Ford Cosworth	V8	56		17	9
15r	55	J-P Jarier	JPS Lotus	79	Ford Cosworth	V8	55	out of fuel	8	4
16	36	R Stommelen	Arrows	A1	Ford Cosworth	V8	54		22	11
r	37	A Merzario	Merzario	A1	Ford Cosworth	V8	46	gearbox oil leak	26	13
r	9	M Bleekemolen	ATS	HS1	Ford Cosworth	V8	43	oil pump leak	25	13
r	1	N Lauda	Brabham	BT46	Alfa Romeo	F12	28	engine	5	3
r	5	M Andretti	JPS Lotus	79	Ford Cosworth	V8	27	engine	1	1
r	2	J Watson	Brabham	BT46	Alfa Romeo	F12	25	engine	7	4
r	4	P Depailler	Tyrrell	008	Ford Cosworth	V8	23	rear hub	12	6
r	12	G Villeneuve	Ferrari	312T3	Ferrari	F12	22	engine	4	2
r	32	K Rosberg	ATS	D1	Ford Cosworth	V8	21	gear linkage	15	8
r	16	H-J Stuck	Shadow	DN9	Ford Cosworth	V8	1	fuel pump	14	7
r	25	H Rebaque	Lotus	78	Ford Cosworth	V8	0	clutch	23	12
nq	19	B Gabbiani	Surtees	TS20	Ford Cosworth	V8				

Winning speed 190.838 km/h, 118.581 mph
Pole Position speed 199.412 km/h, 123.909 mph (M Andretti, 1 min:38.114 sec)
Fastest Lap speed 196.522 km/h, 122.113 mph (J-P Jarier, 1 min:39.557 sec on lap 55)
Lap Leaders M Andretti 1-2 (2); C Reutemann 3-59 (57).

70 laps x 4.500 km, 2.796 miles = 315.000 km, 195.732 miles

Pos	No	Driver	Car	Model	Engine		Laps	Time/Reason for Retirement	Grid Pos	Row
1	12	G Villeneuve	Ferrari	312T3	Ferrari	F12	70	1h 57m 49.196s	3	2
2	20	J Scheckter	Wolf	WR6	Ford Cosworth	V8	70	1h 58m 02.568s	2	1
3	11	C Reutemann	Ferrari	312T3	Ferrari	F12	70	1h 58m 08.604s	11	6
4	35	R Patrese	Arrows	A1	Ford Cosworth	V8	70	1h 58m 13.863s	12	6
5	4	P Depailler	Tyrrell	008	Ford Cosworth	V8	70	1h 58m 17.754s	13	7
6	22	D Daly	Ensign	N177	Ford Cosworth	V8	70	1h 58m 43.672s	15	8
7	3	D Pironi	Tyrrell	008	Ford Cosworth	V8	70	1h 59m 10.446s	18	9
8	8	P Tambay	McLaren	M26	Ford Cosworth	V8	70	1h 59m 15.756s	17	9
9	27	A Jones	Williams	FW06	Ford Cosworth	V8	70	1h 59m 18.138s	5	3
10	5	M Andretti	JPS Lotus	79	Ford Cosworth	V8	69		9	5
11	66	N Piquet	Brabham	BT46	Alfa Romeo	F12	69		14	7
12	15	J-P Jabouille	Renault	RS01	Renault	V6t	65		22	11
nc	32	K Rosberg	ATS	D1	Ford Cosworth	V8	58		21	11
r	26	J Laffite	Ligier	JS9	Matra	V12	52	transmission	10	5
r	7	J Hunt	McLaren	M26	Ford Cosworth	V8	51	accident	19	10
r	55	J-P Jarier	JPS Lotus	79	Ford Cosworth	V8	49	oil radiator leak	1	1
r	18	R Arnoux	Surtees	TS20	Ford Cosworth	V8	37	oil pressure	16	8
r	21	B Rahal	Wolf	WR1	Ford Cosworth	V8	16	fuel system	20	10
r	2	J Watson	Brabham	BT46	Alfa Romeo	F12	8	accident / suspension	4	2
r	1	N Lauda	Brabham	BT46	Alfa Romeo	F12	5	brakes / accident	7	4
r	16	H-J Stuck	Shadow	DN9	Ford Cosworth	V8	1	accident / front suspension	8	4
r	14	E Fittipaldi	Copersucar	F5A	Ford Cosworth	V8	0	accident	6	3
nq	17	C Regazzoni	Shadow	DN9	Ford Cosworth	V8				
nq	19	B Gabbiani	Surtees	TS20	Ford Cosworth	V8				
nq	37	A Merzario	Merzario	A1	Ford Cosworth	V8				
nq	25	H Rebaque	Lotus	78	Ford Cosworth	V8				
nq	36	R Stommelen	Arrows	A1	Ford Cosworth	V8				
nq	9	M Bleekemolen	ATS	HS1	Ford Cosworth	V8				

Winning speed 160.414 km/h, 99.677 mph
Pole Position speed 165.281 km/h, 102.701 mph (J-P Jarier, 1 min:38.015 sec)
Fastest Lap speed 165.185 km/h, 102.641 mph (A Jones, 1 min:38.072 sec on lap 70)
Lap Leaders J-P Jarier 1-49 (49); G Villeneuve 50-70 (21).

Lap Leaders 1978

Pos	Driver	Car-Engine	GPs	laps	km	miles
1	M Andretti	Lotus-Ford Cosworth	11	451	2,133.7	1,325.8
2	C Reutemann	Ferrari	5	183	858.6	533.5
3	G Villeneuve	Ferrari	4	99.5	452.5	281.2
4	N Lauda	Brabham-Alfa Romeo	2	58	238.4	148.1
5	P Depailler	Tyrrell-Ford Cosworth	2	52	183.3	113.9
6	R Peterson	Lotus-Ford Cosworth	3	49	292.7	181.9
	J-P Jarier	Lotus-Ford Cosworth	1	49	220.5	137.0
8	R Patrese	Arrows-Ford Cosworth	1	37	151.8	94.4
	J Watson	Brabham-Alfa Romeo	1	37	122.5	76.1
10	J Scheckter	Wolf-Ford Cosworth	2	16	66.7	41.4
11	J Hunt	McLaren-Ford Cosworth	1	5	17.0	10.6
			16	1,036.5	4,737.8	2,943.9

Driver Points 1978

		RA	BR	ZA	USAW	MC	B	E	S	F	GB	D	A	NL	I	USAE	CDN	Total
1	M Andretti	9	3	-	6	-	9	9	-	9	-	9	-	9	1	-	-	64
2	R Peterson	2	-	9	3	-	6	6	4	6	-	-	9	6	-	-	-	51
3	C Reutemann	-	9	-	9	-	4	-	-	-	9	-	-	-	4	9	4	48
4	N Lauda	6	4	-	-	6	-	-	9	-	6	-	-	4	9	-	-	44
5	P Depailler	4	-	6	4	9	-	-	-	-	3	-	6	-	-	-	2	34
6	J Watson	-	-	4	-	3	-	2	-	3	4	-	-	3	6	-	-	25
7	J Scheckter	-	-	-	4	-	3	-	1	-	6	-	-	-	-	4	6	24
8	J Laffite	-	-	2	2	-	2	4	-	-	-	4	2	-	3	-	-	19
9	G Villeneuve	-	-	-	-	-	3	-	-	-	-	-	4	1	-	-	9	17
	E Fittipaldi	-	6	-	-	-	-	-	1	-	3	3	2	-	2	-	-	17
11	A Jones	-	-	3	-	-	-	-	2	-	-	-	-	-	-	6	-	11
	R Patrese	-	-	-	1	1	-	-	6	-	-	-	-	-	-	-	3	11
13	J Hunt	3	-	-	-	-	-	1	-	4	-	-	-	-	-	-	-	8
	P Tambay	1	-	-	-	-	-	3	-	1	-	-	-	-	2	1	-	8
15	D Pironi	-	1	1	-	2	1	-	-	-	-	2	-	-	-	-	-	7
16	C Regazzoni	-	2	-	-	-	-	-	2	-	-	-	-	-	-	-	-	4
17	J-P Jabouille	-	-	-	-	-	-	-	-	-	-	-	-	-	3	-	-	3
18	H-J Stuck	-	-	-	-	-	-	-	-	2	-	-	-	-	-	-	-	2
19	H Rebaque	-	-	-	-	-	-	-	-	-	1	-	-	-	-	-	-	1
	V Brambilla	-	-	-	-	-	-	-	-	-	-	-	1	-	-	-	-	1
	D Daly	-	-	-	-	-	-	-	-	-	-	-	-	-	-	-	1	1

9,6,4,3,2 and 1 point awarded to the first six finishers. Best 7 scores from first 8 races, best 7 from remaining 8 races.

Constructor Points 1978

		RA	BR	ZA	USAW	MC	B	E	S	F	GB	D	A	NL	I	USAE	CDN	Total
1	Lotus-Ford Cosworth	9	3	9	6	-	9	9	4	9	-	9	9	9	1	-	-	86
2	Ferrari	-	9	-	9	-	4	-	-	-	9	-	4	1	4	9	9	58
3	Brabham-Alfa Romeo	6	4	4	-	6	-	2	9	3	6	-	-	4	9	-	-	53
4	Tyrrell-Ford Cosworth	4	1	6	4	9	1	-	-	3	2	6	-	-	-	-	2	38
5	Wolf-Ford Cosworth	-	-	-	-	4	-	3	-	1	-	6	-	-	-	4	6	24
6	Ligier-Matra	-	-	2	2	-	2	4	-	-	-	4	2	-	3	-	-	19
7	Copersucar-Ford Cosworth	-	6	-	-	-	-	1	-	-	3	3	2	-	2	-	-	17
8	McLaren-Ford Cosworth	3	-	-	-	-	1	3	4	1	-	-	-	2	1	-	-	15
9	Williams-Ford Cosworth	-	-	3	-	-	-	2	-	-	-	-	-	-	6	-	-	11
	Arrows-Ford Cosworth	-	-	-	1	1	-	6	-	-	-	-	-	-	-	-	3	11
11	Shadow-Ford Cosworth	-	2	-	-	-	2	-	2	-	-	-	-	-	-	-	-	6
12	Renault	-	-	-	-	-	-	-	-	-	-	-	-	3	-	-	-	3
13	Surtees-Ford Cosworth	-	-	-	-	-	-	-	-	-	-	-	1	-	-	-	-	1
	Ensign-Ford Cosworth	-	-	-	-	-	-	-	-	-	-	-	-	-	-	-	1	1

9,6,4,3,2 and 1 point awarded to the first six finishers. Points only for highest placed car. Best 7 scores from first 8 races, best 7 from remaining 8 races.

Race Entrants and Results

JPS left as Lotus sponsors and the new model was too advanced to tame. Alfa Romeo returned as a constructor in its own right. The CSI was replaced by La Fédération Internationale du Sport Automobile (FISA) headed by Jean-Marie Balestre. A turbo won for the first time and carbon-fibre formed part of the new Brabham chassis.

LOTUS
Martini Racing Team Lotus: Andretti, Reutemann
Team Rebaque: Rebaque

TYRRELL
Team Tyrrell: Pironi, Jarier, Lees, Daly Candy Team Tyrrell from B GP

BRABHAM
Parmalat Racing Team: Lauda, Zunino, Piquet

McLAREN
Marlboro Team McLaren: Watson, Tambay

ATS
ATS Wheels: Stuck

FERRARI
Scuderia Ferrari SpA SEFAC: Scheckter, Villeneuve

FITTIPALDI (COPERSUCAR)
Fittipaldi Automotive: Fittipaldi, (Ribeiro)

RENAULT
Equipe Renault Elf: Jabouille, Arnoux

SHADOW
Samson Shadow Racing Team: Lammers
Interscope Shadow Racing Team: de Angelis

WOLF
Olympus Cameras Wolf Racing: Hunt, Rosberg

ENSIGN
Team Ensign: Daly, Gaillard, Surer

MERZARIO
Team Merzario: Merzario, (Brancatelli)

LIGIER
Ligier Gitanes: Depailler, Ickx, Laffite

WILLIAMS
Albilad-Saudia Racing Team: Jones, Regazzoni

ARROWS
Warsteiner Arrows Racing Team: Patrese, Mass

REBAQUE
Team Rebaque: Rebaque

ALFA ROMEO
Autodelta: Giacomelli, Brambilla

KAUHSEN
Willi Kauhsen Racing Team: (Brancatelli)

21 Jan 1979		ARGENTINA: Buenos Aires No.15						(Round 1)	(Race 314)	
		53 laps x 5.968 km, 3.708 miles = 316.304 km, 196.542 miles								
Pos	No	Driver	Car	Model	Engine		Laps	Time/Reason for Retirement	Grid Pos	Row
1	26	J Laffite	Ligier	JS11	Ford Cosworth	V8	53	1h 36m 03.210s	1	1
2	2	C Reutemann	Lotus	79	Ford Cosworth	V8	53	1h 36m 18.150s	3	2
3	7	J Watson	McLaren	M28	Ford Cosworth	V8	53	1h 37m 32.020s	6	3
4	25	P Depailler	Ligier	JS11	Ford Cosworth	V8	53	1h 37m 44.930s	2	1
5	1	M Andretti	Lotus	79	Ford Cosworth	V8	52		7	4
6	14	E Fittipaldi	Copersucar	F5A	Ford Cosworth	V8	52		11	6
7	18	E de Angelis	Shadow	DN9	Ford Cosworth	V8	52		16	8
8	30	J Mass	Arrows	A1B	Ford Cosworth	V8	51		14	7
9	27	A Jones	Williams	FW06	Ford Cosworth	V8	51		15	8
10	28	C Regazzoni	Williams	FW06	Ford Cosworth	V8	51		17	9
11	22	D Daly	Ensign	N177	Ford Cosworth	V8	51		24	12
12r	12	G Villeneuve	Ferrari	312T3	Ferrari	F12	48	engine	10	5
r	31	H Rebaque	Lotus	79	Ford Cosworth	V8	46	suspension	19	10
r	17	J Lammers	Shadow	DN9	Ford Cosworth	V8	42	cv joint	21	11
r	20	J Hunt	Wolf	WR7	Ford Cosworth	V8	42	electrics	18	9
r	4	J-P Jarier	Tyrrell	009	Ford Cosworth	V8	15	engine	4	2
r	15	J-P Jabouille	Renault	RS01	Renault	V6t	15	engine	12	6
r	5	N Lauda	Brabham	BT48	Alfa Romeo	V12	8	fuel pressure	23	12
r	16	R Arnoux	Renault	RS01	Renault	V6t	6	engine	25	13
r	11	J Scheckter	Ferrari	312T3	Ferrari	F12	0	accident *	5	3
r	3	D Pironi	Tyrrell	009	Ford Cosworth	V8	0	accident *	8	4
r	8	P Tambay	McLaren	M28	Ford Cosworth	V8	0	accident *	9	5
r	6	N Piquet	Brabham	BT46	Alfa Romeo	F12	0	accident / injury *	20	10
r	24	A Merzario	Merzario	A1B	Ford Cosworth	V8	0	accident *	22	11
ns	29	R Patrese	Arrows	A1B	Ford Cosworth	V8		accident	13	7
ns	9	H-J Stuck	ATS	D2	Ford Cosworth	V8		car unprepared		

Winning speed 197.580 km/h, 122.770 mph
Pole Position speed 206.188 km/h, 128.119 mph (J Laffite, 1 min:44.200 sec)
Fastest Lap speed 200.962 km/h, 124.872 mph (J Laffite, 1 min:46.910 sec on lap 42)
Lap Leaders P Depailler 1-10 (10); J Laffite 11-53 (43).

*Interrupted after first lap accident. Restarted for original distance. * Retired after first start.*

4 Feb 1979   BRAZIL: Interlagos   (Round 2)   (Race 315)
40 laps x 7.874 km, 4.893 miles = 314.960 km, 195.707 miles

Pos	No	Driver	Car	Model	Engine		Laps	Time/Reason for Retirement	Grid Pos	Row
1	26	J Laffite	Ligier	JS11	Ford Cosworth	V8	40	1h 40m 09.640s	1	1
2	25	P Depailler	Ligier	JS11	Ford Cosworth	V8	40	1h 40m 14.920s	2	1
3	2	C Reutemann	Lotus	79	Ford Cosworth	V8	40	1h 40m 53.780s	3	2
4	3	D Pironi	Tyrrell	009	Ford Cosworth	V8	40	1h 41m 35.520s	8	4
5	12	G Villeneuve	Ferrari	312T3	Ferrari	F12	39		5	3
6	11	J Scheckter	Ferrari	312T3	Ferrari	F12	39		6	3
7	30	J Mass	Arrows	A1B	Ford Cosworth	V8	39		19	10
8	7	J Watson	McLaren	M28	Ford Cosworth	V8	39		14	7
9	29	R Patrese	Arrows	A1B	Ford Cosworth	V8	39		16	8
10	15	J-P Jabouille	Renault	RS01	Renault	V6t	39		7	4
11	14	E Fittipaldi	Copersucar	F5A	Ford Cosworth	V8	39		9	5
12	18	E de Angelis	Shadow	DN9	Ford Cosworth	V8	39		20	10
13	22	D Daly	Ensign	N177	Ford Cosworth	V8	39		23	12
14	17	J Lammers	Shadow	DN9	Ford Cosworth	V8	39		21	11
15	28	C Regazzoni	Williams	FW06	Ford Cosworth	V8	38		17	9
r	27	A Jones	Williams	FW06	Ford Cosworth	V8	33	fuel pressure	13	7
r	9	H-J Stuck	ATS	D2	Ford Cosworth	V8	31	steering wheel	24	12
r	16	R Arnoux	Renault	RS01	Renault	V6t	28	spin	11	6
r	8	P Tambay	McLaren	M26	Ford Cosworth	V8	7	accident	18	9
r	20	J Hunt	Wolf	WR7	Ford Cosworth	V8	7	steering rack	10	5
r	6	N Piquet	Brabham	BT48	Alfa Romeo	V12	5	accident / foot injury	22	11
r	5	N Lauda	Brabham	BT48	Alfa Romeo	V12	5	gear linkage	12	6
r	1	M Andretti	Lotus	79	Ford Cosworth	V8	2	misfire / fuel leak / fire	4	2
ns	4	J-P Jarier	Tyrrell	009	Ford Cosworth	V8		electrics on parade lap	15	8
nq	31	H Rebaque	Lotus	79	Ford Cosworth	V8				
nq	24	A Merzario	Merzario	A1B	Ford Cosworth	V8				

Winning speed 188.673 km/h, 117.236 mph
Pole Position speed 198.130 km/h, 123.112 mph (J Laffite, 2 min:23.070 sec)
Fastest Lap speed 190.551 km/h, 118.403 mph (J Laffite, 2 min:28.760 sec on lap 23)
Lap Leaders J Laffite 1-40 (40).

3 Mar 1979   SOUTH AFRICA: Kyalami   (Round 3)   (Race 316)
78 laps x 4.104 km, 2.550 miles = 320.112 km, 198.908 miles

Pos	No	Driver	Car	Model	Engine		Laps	Time/Reason for Retirement	Grid Pos	Row
1	12	G Villeneuve	Ferrari	312T4	Ferrari	F12	78	1h 41m 49.960s	3	2
2	11	J Scheckter	Ferrari	312T4	Ferrari	F12	78	1h 41m 53.380s	2	1
3	4	J-P Jarier	Tyrrell	009	Ford Cosworth	V8	78	1h 42m 12.070s	9	5
4	1	M Andretti	Lotus	79	Ford Cosworth	V8	78	1h 42m 17.840s	8	4
5	2	C Reutemann	Lotus	79	Ford Cosworth	V8	78	1h 42m 56.930s	11	6
6	5	N Lauda	Brabham	BT48	Alfa Romeo	V12	77		4	2
7	6	N Piquet	Brabham	BT48	Alfa Romeo	V12	77		12	6
8	20	J Hunt	Wolf	WR7	Ford Cosworth	V8	77		13	7
9	28	C Regazzoni	Williams	FW06	Ford Cosworth	V8	76		22	11
10	8	P Tambay	McLaren	M28	Ford Cosworth	V8	75		17	9
11	29	R Patrese	Arrows	A1B	Ford Cosworth	V8	75		16	8
12	30	J Mass	Arrows	A1B	Ford Cosworth	V8	74		20	10
13	14	E Fittipaldi	Copersucar	F6	Ford Cosworth	V8	74		18	9
14r	31	H Rebaque	Lotus	79	Ford Cosworth	V8	71	engine	23	12
r	16	R Arnoux	Renault	RS01	Renault	V6t	67	rear tyre / accident	10	5
r	27	A Jones	Williams	FW06	Ford Cosworth	V8	63	rear suspension	19	10
r	7	J Watson	McLaren	M28	Ford Cosworth	V8	61	ignition	14	7
r	9	H-J Stuck	ATS	D2	Ford Cosworth	V8	57	accident	24	12
r	15	J-P Jabouille	Renault	RS01	Renault	V6t	47	valve spring	1	1
r	26	J Laffite	Ligier	JS11	Ford Cosworth	V8	45	accident	6	3
r	3	D Pironi	Tyrrell	009	Ford Cosworth	V8	25	throttle linkage	7	4
r	18	E de Angelis	Shadow	DN9	Ford Cosworth	V8	16	accident	15	8
r	25	P Depailler	Ligier	JS11	Ford Cosworth	V8	4	accident	5	3
r	17	J Lammers	Shadow	DN9	Ford Cosworth	V8	2	accident	21	11
nq	22	D Daly	Ensign	N179	Ford Cosworth	V8				
nq	24	A Merzario	Merzario	A1B	Ford Cosworth	V8				

Winning speed 188.611 km/h, 117.197 mph
Pole Position speed 205.772 km/h, 127.861 mph (J-P Jabouille, 1 min:11.800 sec)
Fastest Lap speed 198.549 km/h, 123.372 mph (G Villeneuve, 1 min:14.412 sec on lap 23)
Lap Leaders J-P Jabouille 1 (1); G Villeneuve 2-14,53-78 (39); J Scheckter 15-52 (38).

Interrupted after 2 laps, because of heavy rain. Restarted for remaining 76 laps, with results being on aggregate.
Lap leaders are given 'on the road'.

8 Apr 1979   USA West: Long Beach   (Round 4)   (Race 317)
80.5 laps x 3.251 km, 2.020 miles = 261.706 km, 162.616 miles

Pos	No	Driver	Car	Model	Engine		Laps	Time/Reason for Retirement	Grid Pos	Row
1	12	G Villeneuve	Ferrari	312T4	Ferrari	F12	80	1h 50m 25.400s	1	1
2	11	J Scheckter	Ferrari	312T4	Ferrari	F12	80	1h 50m 54.780s	3	2
3	27	A Jones	Williams	FW06	Ford Cosworth	V8	80	1h 51m 25.090s	10	5
4	1	M Andretti	Lotus	79	Ford Cosworth	V8	80	1h 51m 29.730s	6	3
5	25	P Depailler	Ligier	JS11	Ford Cosworth	V8	80	1h 51m 48.920s	4	2
6	4	J-P Jarier	Tyrrell	009	Ford Cosworth	V8	79		7	4
7	18	E de Angelis	Shadow	DN9	Ford Cosworth	V8	78		20	10
8	6	N Piquet	Brabham	BT48	Alfa Romeo	V12	78		12	6
9	30	J Mass	Arrows	A1B	Ford Cosworth	V8	78		13	7
dq	3	D Pironi	Tyrrell	009	Ford Cosworth	V8	75	push start after spin	17	9
r	31	H Rebaque	Lotus	79	Ford Cosworth	V8	71	accident	23	12
r	22	D Daly	Ensign	N179	Ford Cosworth	V8	69	accident	24	12
dq	9	H-J Stuck	ATS	D2	Ford Cosworth	V8	66	push start after spin	21	11
r	7	J Watson	McLaren	M28	Ford Cosworth	V8	63	fuel injection	18	9
r	28	C Regazzoni	Williams	FW06	Ford Cosworth	V8	49	engine	15	8
r	17	J Lammers	Shadow	DN9	Ford Cosworth	V8	48	accident	14	7
r	29	R Patrese	Arrows	A1B	Ford Cosworth	V8	40	brake master cylinder	9	5
r	2	C Reutemann	Lotus	79	Ford Cosworth	V8	21	driveshaft	2	1
r	14	E Fittipaldi	Copersucar	F5A	Ford Cosworth	V8	19	driveshaft	16	8
r	24	A Merzario	Merzario	A1B	Ford Cosworth	V8	13	engine	22	11
r	26	J Laffite	Ligier	JS11	Ford Cosworth	V8	9	brakes	5	3
r	20	J Hunt	Wolf	WR8	Ford Cosworth	V8	1	driveshaft joint	8	4
r	5	N Lauda	Brabham	BT48	Alfa Romeo	V12	0	accident	11	6
r	8	P Tambay	McLaren	M28	Ford Cosworth	V8	0	accident	19	10
ns	15	J-P Jabouille	Renault	RS01	Renault	V6t		accident / injury		
ns	16	R Arnoux	Renault	RS01	Renault	V6t		universal joint		

Winning speed 141.313 km/h, 87.808 mph (based on time taken to complete 80 laps)
Pole Position speed 148.476 km/h, 92.259 mph (G Villeneuve, 1 min:18.825 sec)
Fastest Lap speed 144.133 km/h, 89.560 mph (G Villeneuve, 1 min:21.200 sec)
Lap Leaders G Villeneuve 1-80 (80.5).

The start and finish lines were at different positions on the circuit. The fraction of a lap is credited to the first lap leader.

29 Apr 1979   SPAIN: Jarama   (Round 5)   (Race 318)
75 laps x 3.404 km, 2.115 miles = 255.300 km, 158.636 miles

Pos	No	Driver	Car	Model	Engine		Laps	Time/Reason for Retirement	Grid Pos	Row
1	25	P Depailler	Ligier	JS11	Ford Cosworth	V8	75	1h 39m 11.840s	2	1
2	2	C Reutemann	Lotus	79	Ford Cosworth	V8	75	1h 39m 32.780s	8	4
3	1	M Andretti	Lotus	80	Ford Cosworth	V8	75	1h 39m 39.150s	4	2
4	11	J Scheckter	Ferrari	312T4	Ferrari	F12	75	1h 39m 40.520s	5	3
5	4	J-P Jarier	Tyrrell	009	Ford Cosworth	V8	75	1h 39m 42.230s	12	6
6	3	D Pironi	Tyrrell	009	Ford Cosworth	V8	75	1h 40m 00.270s	10	5
7	12	G Villeneuve	Ferrari	312T4	Ferrari	F12	75	1h 40m 04.150s	3	2
8	30	J Mass	Arrows	A1B	Ford Cosworth	V8	75	1h 40m 26.680s	17	9
9	16	R Arnoux	Renault	RS01	Renault	V6t	74		11	6
10	29	R Patrese	Arrows	A1B	Ford Cosworth	V8	74		16	8
11	14	E Fittipaldi	Copersucar	F5A	Ford Cosworth	V8	74		19	10
12	17	J Lammers	Shadow	DN9	Ford Cosworth	V8	73		24	12
13	8	P Tambay	McLaren	M28	Ford Cosworth	V8	72		20	10
14	9	H-J Stuck	ATS	D2	Ford Cosworth	V8	69		21	11
r	5	N Lauda	Brabham	BT48	Alfa Romeo	V12	63	water leak	6	3
r	31	H Rebaque	Lotus	79	Ford Cosworth	V8	58	engine	23	12
r	27	A Jones	Williams	FW07	Ford Cosworth	V8	54	gear selection	13	7
r	18	E de Angelis	Shadow	DN9	Ford Cosworth	V8	52	engine	22	11
r	28	C Regazzoni	Williams	FW07	Ford Cosworth	V8	32	engine	14	7
r	20	J Hunt	Wolf	WR7	Ford Cosworth	V8	26	brakes	15	8
r	7	J Watson	McLaren	M28	Ford Cosworth	V8	21	engine	18	9
r	15	J-P Jabouille	Renault	RS10	Renault	V6t	21	turbo leak	9	5
r	26	J Laffite	Ligier	JS11	Ford Cosworth	V8	15	engine	1	1
r	6	N Piquet	Brabham	BT48	Alfa Romeo	V12	15	fuel metering unit	7	4
nq	22	D Daly	Ensign	N177	Ford Cosworth	V8				
nq	24	A Merzario	Merzario	A2	Ford Cosworth	V8				
nq	36	G Brancatelli	Kauhsen	WK	Ford Cosworth	V8				

Winning speed 154.419 km/h, 95.952 mph
Pole Position speed 164.489 km/h, 102.208 mph (J Laffite, 1 min:14.500 sec)
Fastest Lap speed 160.314 km/h, 99.614 mph (G Villeneuve, 1 min:16.440 sec on lap 72)
Lap Leaders P Depailler 1-75 (75).

13 May 1979   BELGIUM: Zolder   (Round 6)   (Race 319)

70 laps x 4.262 km, 2.648 miles = 298.340 km, 185.380 miles

Pos	No	Driver	Car	Model	Engine		Laps	Time/Reason for Retirement	Grid Pos	Row
1	11	J Scheckter	Ferrari	312T4	Ferrari	F12	70	1h 39m 59.530s	7	4
2	26	J Laffite	Ligier	JS11	Ford Cosworth	V8	70	1h 40m 14.890s	1	1
3	3	D Pironi	Tyrrell	009	Ford Cosworth	V8	70	1h 40m 34.700s	12	6
4	2	C Reutemann	Lotus	79	Ford Cosworth	V8	70	1h 40m 46.020s	10	5
5	29	R Patrese	Arrows	A1B	Ford Cosworth	V8	70	1h 41m 03.840s	16	8
6	7	J Watson	McLaren	M28	Ford Cosworth	V8	70	1h 41m 05.380s	19	10
7r	12	G Villeneuve	Ferrari	312T4	Ferrari	F12	69	out of fuel	6	3
8	9	H-J Stuck	ATS	D2	Ford Cosworth	V8	69		20	10
9	14	E Fittipaldi	Copersucar	F5A	Ford Cosworth	V8	68		23	12
10	17	J Lammers	Shadow	DN9	Ford Cosworth	V8	68		21	11
11	4	J-P Jarier	Tyrrell	009	Ford Cosworth	V8	67		11	6
r	25	P Depailler	Ligier	JS11	Ford Cosworth	V8	46	accident	2	1
r	20	J Hunt	Wolf	WR8	Ford Cosworth	V8	40	accident	9	5
r	27	A Jones	Williams	FW07	Ford Cosworth	V8	39	electrics	4	2
r	1	M Andretti	Lotus	79	Ford Cosworth	V8	27	brakes	5	3
r	6	N Piquet	Brabham	BT48	Alfa Romeo	V12	23	engine	3	2
r	5	N Lauda	Brabham	BT48	Alfa Romeo	V12	23	engine	13	7
r	16	R Arnoux	Renault	RS01	Renault	V6t	22	turbo	18	9
r	35	B Giacomelli	Alfa Romeo	177	Alfa Romeo	F12	21	accident	14	7
r	18	E de Angelis	Shadow	DN9	Ford Cosworth	V8	21	accident	24	12
r	30	J Mass	Arrows	A1B	Ford Cosworth	V8	17	spin	22	11
r	31	H Rebaque	Lotus	79	Ford Cosworth	V8	13	driveshaft	15	8
r	15	J-P Jabouille	Renault	RS10	Renault	V6t	13	turbo	17	9
r	28	C Regazzoni	Williams	FW07	Ford Cosworth	V8	1	accident	8	4
nq	8	P Tambay	McLaren	M26	Ford Cosworth	V8				
nq	24	A Merzario	Merzario	A2	Ford Cosworth	V8				
nq	22	D Daly	Ensign	N177	Ford Cosworth	V8				
nq	36	G Brancatelli	Kauhsen	WK	Ford Cosworth	V8				

Winning speed 179.018 km/h, 111.237 mph
Pole Position speed 189.119 km/h, 117.513 mph (J Laffite, 1 min:21.130 sec)
Fastest Lap speed 184.658 km/h, 114.741 mph (G Villeneuve, 1 min:23.090 sec on lap 63)
Lap Leaders P Depailler 1-18,40-46 (25); J Laffite 19-23,47-53 (12); A Jones 24-39 (16); J Scheckter 54-70 (17).

J Scheckter originally credited with fastest lap, but this was later amended.

27 May 1979   MONACO: Monte-Carlo   (Round 7)   (Race 320)

76 laps x 3.312 km, 2.058 miles = 251.712 km, 156.407 miles

Pos	No	Driver	Car	Model	Engine		Laps	Time/Reason for Retirement	Grid Pos	Row
1	11	J Scheckter	Ferrari	312T4	Ferrari	F12	76	1h 55m 22.480s	1	1
2	28	C Regazzoni	Williams	FW07	Ford Cosworth	V8	76	1h 55m 22.920s	16	8
3	2	C Reutemann	Lotus	79	Ford Cosworth	V8	76	1h 55m 31.050s	11	6
4	7	J Watson	McLaren	M28	Ford Cosworth	V8	76	1h 56m 03.790s	14	7
5r	25	P Depailler	Ligier	JS11	Ford Cosworth	V8	74	engine	3	2
6	30	J Mass	Arrows	A1B	Ford Cosworth	V8	69		8	4
7r	6	N Piquet	Brabham	BT48	Alfa Romeo	V12	68	driveshaft	18	9
8	15	J-P Jabouille	Renault	RS10	Renault	V6t	68		20	10
r	26	J Laffite	Ligier	JS11	Ford Cosworth	V8	55	gearbox	5	3
r	12	G Villeneuve	Ferrari	312T4	Ferrari	F12	54	transmission	2	1
r	27	A Jones	Williams	FW07	Ford Cosworth	V8	43	accident	9	5
r	4	J-P Jarier	Tyrrell	009	Ford Cosworth	V8	34	rear suspension	6	3
r	9	H-J Stuck	ATS	D2	Ford Cosworth	V8	30	wheel lost	12	6
r	5	N Lauda	Brabham	BT48	Alfa Romeo	V12	21	accident	4	2
r	3	D Pironi	Tyrrell	009	Ford Cosworth	V8	21	accident	7	4
r	1	M Andretti	Lotus	80	Ford Cosworth	V8	21	rear suspension	13	7
r	14	E Fittipaldi	Copersucar	F5A	Ford Cosworth	V8	17	engine	17	9
r	16	R Arnoux	Renault	RS10	Renault	V6t	8	accident	19	10
r	20	J Hunt	Wolf	WR7	Ford Cosworth	V8	4	cv joint	10	5
r	29	R Patrese	Arrows	A1B	Ford Cosworth	V8	4	front suspension	15	8
nq	18	E de Angelis	Shadow	DN9	Ford Cosworth	V8				
nq	8	P Tambay	McLaren	M28	Ford Cosworth	V8				
nq	17	J Lammers	Shadow	DN9	Ford Cosworth	V8				
nq	22	D Daly	Ensign	N179	Ford Cosworth	V8				
npq	24	G Brancatelli	Merzario	A2	Ford Cosworth	V8				

Winning speed 130.902 km/h, 81.338 mph
Pole Position speed 137.920 km/h, 85.700 mph (J Scheckter, 1 min:26.450 sec)
Fastest Lap speed 134.240 km/h, 83.413 mph (P Depailler, 1 min:28.820 sec on lap 69)
Lap Leaders J Scheckter 1-76 (76).

Pos	No	Driver	Car	Model	Engine		Laps	Time/Reason for Retirement	Grid Pos	Row
1	15	J-P Jabouille	Renault	RS10	Renault	V6t	80	1h 35m 20.420s	1	1
2	12	G Villeneuve	Ferrari	312T4	Ferrari	F12	80	1h 35m 35.010s	3	2
3	16	R Arnoux	Renault	RS10	Renault	V6t	80	1h 35m 35.250s	2	1
4	27	A Jones	Williams	FW07	Ford Cosworth	V8	80	1h 35m 57.030s	7	4
5	4	J-P Jarier	Tyrrell	009	Ford Cosworth	V8	80	1h 36m 24.930s	10	5
6	28	C Regazzoni	Williams	FW07	Ford Cosworth	V8	80	1h 36m 25.930s	9	5
7	11	J Scheckter	Ferrari	312T4	Ferrari	F12	79		5	3
8	26	J Laffite	Ligier	JS11	Ford Cosworth	V8	79		8	4
9	20	K Rosberg	Wolf	WR8	Ford Cosworth	V8	79		16	8
10	8	P Tambay	McLaren	M28	Ford Cosworth	V8	78		20	10
11	7	J Watson	McLaren	M28	Ford Cosworth	V8	78		15	8
12	31	H Rebaque	Lotus	79	Ford Cosworth	V8	78		23	12
13r	2	C Reutemann	Lotus	79	Ford Cosworth	V8	77	accident	13	7
14	29	R Patrese	Arrows	A2	Ford Cosworth	V8	77		19	10
15	30	J Mass	Arrows	A2	Ford Cosworth	V8	75		22	11
16	18	E de Angelis	Shadow	DN9	Ford Cosworth	V8	75		24	12
17	35	B Giacomelli	Alfa Romeo	177	Alfa Romeo	F12	75		17	9
18	17	J Lammers	Shadow	DN9	Ford Cosworth	V8	73		21	11
r	3	D Pironi	Tyrrell	009	Ford Cosworth	V8	71	rear suspension	11	6
r	14	E Fittipaldi	Copersucar	F5A	Ford Cosworth	V8	53	oil loss / engine	18	9
r	6	N Piquet	Brabham	BT48	Alfa Romeo	V12	52	accident	4	2
r	1	M Andretti	Lotus	80	Ford Cosworth	V8	52	brakes / suspension	12	6
r	25	J Ickx	Ligier	JS11	Ford Cosworth	V8	45	engine	14	7
r	5	N Lauda	Brabham	BT48	Alfa Romeo	V12	23	spin	6	3
ns	9	H-J Stuck	ATS	D2	Ford Cosworth	V8		tyre dispute		
nq	22	P Gaillard	Ensign	N179	Ford Cosworth	V8				
nq	24	A Merzario	Merzario	A2	Ford Cosworth	V8				

Winning speed 191.315 km/h, 118.877 mph
Pole Position speed 203.602 km/h, 126.512 mph (J-P Jabouille, 1 min: 7.190 sec)
Fastest Lap speed 197.802 km/h, 122.909 mph (R Arnoux, 1 min: 9.160 sec on lap 71)
Lap Leaders G Villeneuve 1-46 (46); J-P Jabouille 47-80 (34).

Pos	No	Driver	Car	Model	Engine		Laps	Time/Reason for Retirement	Grid Pos	Row
1	28	C Regazzoni	Williams	FW07	Ford Cosworth	V8	68	1h 26m 11.170s	4	2
2	16	R Arnoux	Renault	RS10	Renault	V6t	68	1h 26m 35.450s	5	3
3	4	J-P Jarier	Tyrrell	009	Ford Cosworth	V8	67		16	8
4	7	J Watson	McLaren	M29	Ford Cosworth	V8	67		7	4
5	11	J Scheckter	Ferrari	312T4	Ferrari	F12	67		11	6
6	25	J Ickx	Ligier	JS11	Ford Cosworth	V8	67		17	9
7r	8	P Tambay	McLaren	M28	Ford Cosworth	V8	66	out of fuel	18	9
8	2	C Reutemann	Lotus	79	Ford Cosworth	V8	66		8	4
9	31	H Rebaque	Lotus	79	Ford Cosworth	V8	66		24	12
10	3	D Pironi	Tyrrell	009	Ford Cosworth	V8	66		15	8
11	17	J Lammers	Shadow	DN9	Ford Cosworth	V8	65		21	11
12	18	E de Angelis	Shadow	DN9	Ford Cosworth	V8	65		12	6
13	22	P Gaillard	Ensign	N179	Ford Cosworth	V8	65		23	12
14r	12	G Villeneuve	Ferrari	312T4	Ferrari	F12	63	fuel vaporisation	13	7
r	29	R Patrese	Arrows	A2	Ford Cosworth	V8	45	gearbox	19	10
r	26	J Laffite	Ligier	JS11	Ford Cosworth	V8	44	spark plug	10	5
r	20	K Rosberg	Wolf	WR7	Ford Cosworth	V8	43	fuel system	14	7
r	27	A Jones	Williams	FW07	Ford Cosworth	V8	38	water pump	1	1
r	30	J Mass	Arrows	A2	Ford Cosworth	V8	37	gearbox / rear suspension	20	10
r	14	E Fittipaldi	Copersucar	F5A	Ford Cosworth	V8	25	oil pressure	22	11
r	15	J-P Jabouille	Renault	RS10	Renault	V6t	21	valve spring	2	1
r	5	N Lauda	Brabham	BT48	Alfa Romeo	V12	12	brakes	6	3
r	1	M Andretti	Lotus	79	Ford Cosworth	V8	3	accident / rear wheel bearing	9	5
r	6	N Piquet	Brabham	BT48	Alfa Romeo	V12	1	spin	3	2
nq	9	H-J Stuck	ATS	D2	Ford Cosworth	V8				
nq	24	A Merzario	Merzario	A4	Ford Cosworth	V8				

Winning speed 223.375 km/h, 138.799 mph
Pole Position speed 236.324 km/h, 146.845 mph (A Jones, 1 min:11.880 sec)
Fastest Lap speed 228.319 km/h, 141.871 mph (C Regazzoni, 1 min:14.400 sec on lap 39)
Lap Leaders A Jones 1-38 (38); C Regazzoni 39-68 (30).

E de Angelis penalised 1 minute for jumping the start.

29 Jul 1979 **GERMANY: Hockenheim** (Round 10) (Race 323)

45 laps x 6.789 km, 4.218 miles = 305.505 km, 189.832 miles

Pos	No	Driver	Car	Model	Engine		Laps	Time/Reason for Retirement	Grid Pos	Row
1	27	A Jones	Williams	FW07	Ford Cosworth	V8	45	1h 24m 48.830s	2	1
2	28	C Regazzoni	Williams	FW07	Ford Cosworth	V8	45	1h 24m 51.740s	6	3
3	26	J Laffite	Ligier	JS11	Ford Cosworth	V8	45	1h 25m 07.220s	3	2
4	11	J Scheckter	Ferrari	312T4	Ferrari	F12	45	1h 25m 20.030s	5	3
5	7	J Watson	McLaren	M29	Ford Cosworth	V8	45	1h 26m 26.630s	12	6
6	30	J Mass	Arrows	A2	Ford Cosworth	V8	44		18	9
7	4	G Lees	Tyrrell	009	Ford Cosworth	V8	44		16	8
8	12	G Villeneuve	Ferrari	312T4	Ferrari	F12	44		9	5
9	3	D Pironi	Tyrrell	009	Ford Cosworth	V8	44		8	4
10	17	J Lammers	Shadow	DN9	Ford Cosworth	V8	44		20	10
11	18	E de Angelis	Shadow	DN9	Ford Cosworth	V8	43		21	11
12r	6	N Piquet	Brabham	BT48	Alfa Romeo	V12	42	engine	4	2
r	29	R Patrese	Arrows	A2	Ford Cosworth	V8	34	rear tyre / suspension	19	10
r	8	P Tambay	McLaren	M29	Ford Cosworth	V8	30	rear suspension	15	8
r	20	K Rosberg	Wolf	WR8	Ford Cosworth	V8	29	engine	17	9
r	5	N Lauda	Brabham	BT48	Alfa Romeo	V12	27	engine	7	4
r	25	J Ickx	Ligier	JS11	Ford Cosworth	V8	24	rear tyre burst	14	7
r	31	H Rebaque	Lotus	79	Ford Cosworth	V8	22	handling	24	12
r	1	M Andretti	Lotus	79	Ford Cosworth	V8	16	cv joint	11	6
r	16	R Arnoux	Renault	RS10	Renault	V6t	9	rear tyre burst	10	5
r	15	J-P Jabouille	Renault	RS10	Renault	V6t	7	spin	1	1
r	14	E Fittipaldi	Copersucar	F6A	Ford Cosworth	V8	4	electrics	22	11
r	2	C Reutemann	Lotus	79	Ford Cosworth	V8	1	accident	13	7
r	9	H-J Stuck	ATS	D2	Ford Cosworth	V8	0	front bulkhead casting	23	12
nq	22	P Gaillard	Ensign	N179	Ford Cosworth	V8				
nq	24	A Merzario	Merzario	A4	Ford Cosworth	V8				

Winning speed 216.124 km/h, 134.293 mph
Pole Position speed 225.299 km/h, 139.994 mph (J-P Jabouille, 1 min:48.480 sec)
Fastest Lap speed 218.432 km/h, 135.728 mph (G Villeneuve, 1 min:51.890 sec on lap 40)
Lap Leaders A Jones 1-45 (45).

12 Aug 1979 **AUSTRIA: Österreichring** (Round 11) (Race 324)

54 laps x 5.942 km, 3.692 miles = 320.868 km, 199.378 miles

Pos	No	Driver	Car	Model	Engine		Laps	Time/Reason for Retirement	Grid Pos	Row
1	27	A Jones	Williams	FW07	Ford Cosworth	V8	54	1h 27m 38.010s	2	1
2	12	G Villeneuve	Ferrari	312T4	Ferrari	F12	54	1h 28m 14.060s	5	3
3	26	J Laffite	Ligier	JS11	Ford Cosworth	V8	54	1h 28m 24.780s	8	4
4	11	J Scheckter	Ferrari	312T4	Ferrari	F12	54	1h 28m 25.220s	9	5
5	28	C Regazzoni	Williams	FW07	Ford Cosworth	V8	54	1h 28m 26.930s	6	3
6	16	R Arnoux	Renault	RS10	Renault	V6t	53		1	1
7	3	D Pironi	Tyrrell	009	Ford Cosworth	V8	53		10	5
8	4	D Daly	Tyrrell	009	Ford Cosworth	V8	53		11	6
9	7	J Watson	McLaren	M29	Ford Cosworth	V8	53		16	8
10	8	P Tambay	McLaren	M29	Ford Cosworth	V8	53		14	7
r	5	N Lauda	Brabham	BT48	Alfa Romeo	V12	45	oil pressure	4	2
r	22	P Gaillard	Ensign	N179	Ford Cosworth	V8	42	front suspension	24	12
r	18	E de Angelis	Shadow	DN9	Ford Cosworth	V8	35	engine	22	11
r	29	R Patrese	Arrows	A2	Ford Cosworth	V8	34	rear suspension	13	7
r	6	N Piquet	Brabham	BT48	Alfa Romeo	V12	32	engine	7	4
r	9	H-J Stuck	ATS	D3	Ford Cosworth	V8	28	engine	18	9
r	25	J Ickx	Ligier	JS11	Ford Cosworth	V8	26	engine	21	11
r	2	C Reutemann	Lotus	79	Ford Cosworth	V8	22	handling	17	9
r	15	J-P Jabouille	Renault	RS10	Renault	V6t	16	clutch / transmission	3	2
r	14	E Fittipaldi	Copersucar	F6A	Ford Cosworth	V8	15	brakes	19	10
r	20	K Rosberg	Wolf	WR9	Ford Cosworth	V8	15	electrics	12	6
r	17	J Lammers	Shadow	DN9	Ford Cosworth	V8	3	accident	23	12
r	30	J Mass	Arrows	A2	Ford Cosworth	V8	1	engine	20	10
r	1	M Andretti	Lotus	79	Ford Cosworth	V8	0	clutch	15	8
nq	31	H Rebaque	Lotus	79	Ford Cosworth	V8				
nq	24	A Merzario	Merzario	A4	Ford Cosworth	V8				

Winning speed 219.689 km/h, 136.508 mph
Pole Position speed 227.397 km/h, 141.298 mph (R Arnoux, 1 min:34.070 sec)
Fastest Lap speed 223.360 km/h, 138.790 mph (R Arnoux, 1 min:35.770 sec on lap 40)
Lap Leaders G Villeneuve 1-3 (3); A Jones 4-54 (51).

26 Aug 1979   **NETHERLANDS: Zandvoort**   **(Round 12)**   **(Race 325)**

75 laps x 4.226 km, 2.626 miles = 316.950 km, 196.944 miles

Pos	No	Driver	Car	Model	Engine		Laps	Time/Reason for Retirement	Grid Pos	Row
1	27	A Jones	Williams	FW07	Ford Cosworth	V8	75	1h 41m 19.775s	2	1
2	11	J Scheckter	Ferrari	312T4	Ferrari	F12	75	1h 41m 41.558s	5	3
3	26	J Laffite	Ligier	JS11	Ford Cosworth	V8	75	1h 42m 23.028s	7	4
4	6	N Piquet	Brabham	BT48	Alfa Romeo	V12	74		11	6
5	25	J Ickx	Ligier	JS11	Ford Cosworth	V8	74		20	10
6	30	J Mass	Arrows	A2	Ford Cosworth	V8	73		18	9
7	31	H Rebaque	Lotus	79	Ford Cosworth	V8	73		24	12
r	3	D Pironi	Tyrrell	009	Ford Cosworth	V8	51	rear suspension	10	5
r	12	G Villeneuve	Ferrari	312T4	Ferrari	F12	49	tyre / rear suspension	6	3
r	18	E de Angelis	Shadow	DN9	Ford Cosworth	V8	40	driveshaft	22	11
r	20	K Rosberg	Wolf	WR9	Ford Cosworth	V8	33	engine	8	4
r	15	J-P Jabouille	Renault	RS10	Renault	V6t	26	clutch	4	2
r	7	J Watson	McLaren	M29	Ford Cosworth	V8	22	engine	12	6
r	4	J-P Jarier	Tyrrell	009	Ford Cosworth	V8	20	throttle slides jammed / spin	16	8
r	9	H-J Stuck	ATS	D3	Ford Cosworth	V8	19	driveshaft	15	8
r	17	J Lammers	Shadow	DN9	Ford Cosworth	V8	12	gearbox linkage	23	12
r	1	M Andretti	Lotus	79	Ford Cosworth	V8	9	rear suspension	17	9
r	29	R Patrese	Arrows	A2	Ford Cosworth	V8	7	brakes / accident	19	10
r	8	P Tambay	McLaren	M29	Ford Cosworth	V8	5	engine	14	7
r	5	N Lauda	Brabham	BT48	Alfa Romeo	V12	3	driver unfit (wrist injury)	9	5
r	14	E Fittipaldi	Copersucar	F6A	Ford Cosworth	V8	2	electrics	21	11
r	2	C Reutemann	Lotus	79	Ford Cosworth	V8	1	accident	13	7
r	16	R Arnoux	Renault	RS10	Renault	V6t	1	accident	1	1
r	28	C Regazzoni	Williams	FW07	Ford Cosworth	V8	0	accident	3	2
nq	22	P Gaillard	Ensign	N179	Ford Cosworth	V8				
nq	24	A Merzario	Merzario	A4	Ford Cosworth	V8				

Winning speed 187.675 km/h, 116.616 mph
Pole Position speed 201.609 km/h, 125.274 mph (R Arnoux, 1 min:15.461 sec)
Fastest Lap speed 191.515 km/h, 119.002 mph (G Villeneuve, 1 min:19.438 sec on lap 39)
Lap Leaders A Jones 1-10,47-75 (39); G Villeneuve 11-46 (36).

9 Sep 1979   **ITALY: Monza**   **(Round 13)**   **(Race 326)**

50 laps x 5.800 km, 3.604 miles = 290.000 km, 180.198 miles

Pos	No	Driver	Car	Model	Engine		Laps	Time/Reason for Retirement	Grid Pos	Row
1	11	J Scheckter	Ferrari	312T4	Ferrari	F12	50	1h 22m 00.220s	3	2
2	12	G Villeneuve	Ferrari	312T4	Ferrari	F12	50	1h 22m 00.680s	5	3
3	28	C Regazzoni	Williams	FW07	Ford Cosworth	V8	50	1h 22m 05.000s	6	3
4	5	N Lauda	Brabham	BT48	Alfa Romeo	V12	50	1h 22m 54.620s	9	5
5	1	M Andretti	Lotus	79	Ford Cosworth	V8	50	1h 22m 59.920s	10	5
6	4	J-P Jarier	Tyrrell	009	Ford Cosworth	V8	50	1h 23m 01.770s	16	8
7	2	C Reutemann	Lotus	79	Ford Cosworth	V8	50	1h 23m 24.360s	13	7
8	14	E Fittipaldi	Copersucar	F6A	Ford Cosworth	V8	49		20	10
9	27	A Jones	Williams	FW07	Ford Cosworth	V8	49		4	2
10	3	D Pironi	Tyrrell	009	Ford Cosworth	V8	49		12	6
11	9	H-J Stuck	ATS	D3	Ford Cosworth	V8	49		15	8
12	36	V Brambilla	Alfa Romeo	177	Alfa Romeo	F12	49		22	11
13	29	R Patrese	Arrows	A2	Ford Cosworth	V8	48		17	9
14r	15	J-P Jabouille	Renault	RS10	Renault	V6t	45	valve	1	1
r	26	J Laffite	Ligier	JS11	Ford Cosworth	V8	42	engine	7	4
r	20	K Rosberg	Wolf	WR8	Ford Cosworth	V8	41	engine	23	12
r	25	J Ickx	Ligier	JS11	Ford Cosworth	V8	40	engine	11	6
r	18	E de Angelis	Shadow	DN9	Ford Cosworth	V8	34	clutch	24	12
r	35	B Giacomelli	Alfa Romeo	179	Alfa Romeo	V12	28	spin	18	9
r	16	R Arnoux	Renault	RS10	Renault	V6t	14	misfire	2	1
r	7	J Watson	McLaren	M29	Ford Cosworth	V8	13	accident	19	10
r	8	P Tambay	McLaren	M29	Ford Cosworth	V8	3	engine	14	7
r	30	J Mass	Arrows	A2	Ford Cosworth	V8	3	rear suspension	21	11
r	6	N Piquet	Brabham	BT48	Alfa Romeo	V12	1	accident	8	4
nq	17	J Lammers	Shadow	DN9	Ford Cosworth	V8				
nq	22	M Surer	Ensign	N179	Ford Cosworth	V8				
nq	24	A Merzario	Merzario	A4	Ford Cosworth	V8				
nq	31	H Rebaque	Rebaque	HR100	Ford Cosworth	V8				

Winning speed 212.186 km/h, 131.846 mph
Pole Position speed 220.765 km/h, 137.177 mph (J-P Jabouille, 1 min:34.580 sec)
Fastest Lap speed 218.410 km/h, 135.714 mph (C Regazzoni, 1 min:35.600 sec on lap 46)
Lap Leaders J Scheckter 1,13-50 (39); R Arnoux 2-12 (11).

30 Sep 1979　　CANADA: Montréal　　(Round 14)　(Race 327)
72 laps x 4.410 km, 2.740 miles = 317.520 km, 197.298 miles

Pos	No	Driver	Car	Model	Engine		Laps	Time/Reason for Retirement	Grid Pos	Row
1	27	A Jones	Williams	FW07	Ford Cosworth	V8	72	1h 52m 06.892s	1	1
2	12	G Villeneuve	Ferrari	312T4	Ferrari	F12	72	1h 52m 07.972s	2	1
3	28	C Regazzoni	Williams	FW07	Ford Cosworth	V8	72	1h 53m 20.548s	3	2
4	11	J Scheckter	Ferrari	312T4	Ferrari	F12	71		9	5
5	3	D Pironi	Tyrrell	009	Ford Cosworth	V8	71		6	3
6	7	J Watson	McLaren	M29	Ford Cosworth	V8	70		17	9
7	5	R Zunino	Brabham	BT49	Ford Cosworth	V8	68		19	10
8	14	E Fittipaldi	Copersucar	F6A	Ford Cosworth	V8	67		15	8
9	17	J Lammers	Shadow	DN9	Ford Cosworth	V8	67		21	11
10r	1	M Andretti	Lotus	79	Ford Cosworth	V8	66	out of fuel	10	5
r	6	N Piquet	Brabham	BT49	Ford Cosworth	V8	61	gearbox	4	2
r	36	V Brambilla	Alfa Romeo	179	Alfa Romeo	V12	52	fuel metering unit	18	9
r	25	J Ickx	Ligier	JS11	Ford Cosworth	V8	47	gearbox	16	8
r	4	J-P Jarier	Tyrrell	009	Ford Cosworth	V8	33	engine	13	7
r	33	D Daly	Tyrrell	009	Ford Cosworth	V8	28	engine	24	12
r	31	H Rebaque	Rebaque	HR100	Ford Cosworth	V8	26	engine mounting	22	11
r	18	E de Angelis	Shadow	DN9	Ford Cosworth	V8	24	distributor rotor arm	23	12
r	15	J-P Jabouille	Renault	RS10	Renault	V6t	24	brakes	7	4
r	2	C Reutemann	Lotus	79	Ford Cosworth	V8	23	rear suspension	11	6
r	29	R Patrese	Arrows	A1B	Ford Cosworth	V8	20	spin	14	7
r	8	P Tambay	McLaren	M29	Ford Cosworth	V8	19	engine	20	10
r	16	R Arnoux	Renault	RS10	Renault	V6t	14	accident	8	4
r	9	H-J Stuck	ATS	D3	Ford Cosworth	V8	14	accident	12	6
r	26	J Laffite	Ligier	JS11	Ford Cosworth	V8	10	engine	5	3
nq	30	J Mass	Arrows	A2	Ford Cosworth	V8				
nq	22	M Surer	Ensign	N179	Ford Cosworth	V8				
nq	20	K Rosberg	Wolf	WR9	Ford Cosworth	V8				
nq	19	A D Ribeiro	Copersucar	F6A	Ford Cosworth	V8				
nq	24	A Merzario	Merzario	A4	Ford Cosworth	V8				
ew	5	N Lauda	Brabham	BT49	Ford Cosworth	V8		sudden retirement from the sport		

Winning speed 169.926 km/h, 105.587 mph
Pole Position speed 176.612 km/h, 109.742 mph (A Jones, 1 min:29.892 sec)
Fastest Lap speed 173.942 km/h, 108.082 mph (A Jones, 1 min:31.272 sec on lap 65)
Lap Leaders G Villeneuve 1-50 (50); A Jones 51-72 (22).

7 Oct 1979　　USA East: Watkins Glen　　(Round 15)　(Race 328)
59 laps x 5.435 km, 3.377 miles = 320.651 km, 199.243 miles

Pos	No	Driver	Car	Model	Engine		Laps	Time/Reason for Retirement	Grid Pos	Row
1	12	G Villeneuve	Ferrari	312T4	Ferrari	F12	59	1h 52m 17.734s	3	2
2	16	R Arnoux	Renault	RS10	Renault	V6t	59	1h 53m 06.521s	7	4
3	3	D Pironi	Tyrrell	009	Ford Cosworth	V8	59	1h 53m 10.933s	10	5
4	18	E de Angelis	Shadow	DN9	Ford Cosworth	V8	59	1h 53m 48.246s	20	10
5	9	H-J Stuck	ATS	D3	Ford Cosworth	V8	59	1h 53m 58.993s	14	7
6	7	J Watson	McLaren	M29	Ford Cosworth	V8	58		13	7
7	14	E Fittipaldi	Copersucar	F6A	Ford Cosworth	V8	55		23	12
8r	6	N Piquet	Brabham	BT49	Ford Cosworth	V8	53	driveshaft	2	1
r	33	D Daly	Tyrrell	009	Ford Cosworth	V8	52	accident	15	8
r	11	J Scheckter	Ferrari	312T4	Ferrari	F12	48	rear tyre burst	16	8
r	29	R Patrese	Arrows	A2	Ford Cosworth	V8	44	rear suspension	19	10
r	27	A Jones	Williams	FW07	Ford Cosworth	V8	36	rear wheel lost	1	1
r	22	M Surer	Ensign	N179	Ford Cosworth	V8	32	engine	21	11
r	28	C Regazzoni	Williams	FW07	Ford Cosworth	V8	29	accident	5	3
r	5	R Zunino	Brabham	BT49	Ford Cosworth	V8	25	accident	9	5
r	15	J-P Jabouille	Renault	RS10	Renault	V6t	24	camshaft belt	8	4
r	8	P Tambay	McLaren	M29	Ford Cosworth	V8	20	engine	22	11
r	20	K Rosberg	Wolf	WR8/9	Ford Cosworth	V8	20	accident / oil line	12	6
r	4	J-P Jarier	Tyrrell	009	Ford Cosworth	V8	18	accident	11	6
r	1	M Andretti	Lotus	79	Ford Cosworth	V8	15	gearbox	17	9
r	2	C Reutemann	Lotus	79	Ford Cosworth	V8	6	accident	6	3
r	26	J Laffite	Ligier	JS11	Ford Cosworth	V8	3	accident	4	2
r	25	J Ickx	Ligier	JS11	Ford Cosworth	V8	2	accident	24	12
r	35	B Giacomelli	Alfa Romeo	179	Alfa Romeo	V12	0	accident	18	9
nq	36	V Brambilla	Alfa Romeo	179	Alfa Romeo	V12				
nq	30	J Mass	Arrows	A2	Ford Cosworth	V8				
nq	17	J Lammers	Shadow	DN9	Ford Cosworth	V8				
nq	31	H Rebaque	Rebaque	HR100	Ford Cosworth	V8				
nq	19	A D Ribeiro	Copersucar	F6A	Ford Cosworth	V8				
nq	24	A Merzario	Merzario	A4	Ford Cosworth	V8				

Winning speed 171.325 km/h, 106.456 mph
Pole Position speed 204.624 km/h, 127.147 mph (A Jones, 1 min:35.615 sec)
Fastest Lap speed 195.546 km/h, 121.506 mph (N Piquet, 1 min:40.054 sec on lap 51)
Lap Leaders G Villeneuve 1-31,37-59 (54); A Jones 32-36 (5).

Lap Leaders 1979

Pos	Driver	Car-Engine	GPs	laps	km	miles
1	G Villeneuve	Ferrari	7	308.5	1,280.5	795.7
2	A Jones	Williams-Ford Cosworth	7	216	1,145.1	711.5
3	J Scheckter	Ferrari	4	170	706.3	438.9
4	P Depailler	Ligier-Ford Cosworth	3	110	421.5	261.9
5	J Laffite	Ligier-Ford Cosworth	3	95	622.7	386.9
6	J-P Jabouille	Renault	2	35	133.3	82.8
7	C Regazzoni	Williams-Ford Cosworth	1	30	141.6	88.0
8	R Arnoux	Renault	1	11	63.8	39.6
			15	**975.5**	**4,514.8**	**2,805.4**

Driver Points 1979

		RA	BR	ZA	USAW	E	B	MC	F	GB	D	A	NL	I	CDN	USAE	Total	
1	J Scheckter	-	(1)	6	6	(3)	9	9	-	(2)	3	3	6	9	(3)	-	51	(9)
2	G Villeneuve	-	2	9	9	-	-	-	6	-	-	6	-	6	(6)	9	47	(6)
3	A Jones	-	-	-	4	-	-	-	(3)	-	9	9	9	-	9	-	40	(3)
4	J Laffite	9	9	-	-	-	6	-	-	-	4	4	4	-	-	-	36	
5	C Regazzoni	-	-	-	-	-	-	6	(1)	9	6	(2)	-	4	4	-	29	(3)
6	P Depailler	3	6	-	2	9	-	(2)	-	-	-	-	-	-	-	-	20	(2)
	C Reutemann	6	4	(2)	-	6	(3)	4	-	-	-	-	-	-	-	-	20	(5)
8	R Arnoux	-	-	-	-	-	-	-	4	6	-	1	-	-	-	6	17	
9	J Watson	4	-	-	-	1	3	-	3	2	-	-	-	1	1	15	
10	D Pironi	-	3	-	-	1	4	-	-	-	-	-	-	2	4	14	
	J-P Jarier	-	-	4	1	2	-	-	2	4	-	-	-	1	-	-	14	
	M Andretti	2	-	3	3	4	-	-	-	-	-	-	-	2	-	-	14	
13	J-P Jabouille	-	-	-	-	-	-	-	9	-	-	-	-	-	-	-	9	
14	N Lauda	-	-	1	-	-	-	-	-	-	-	-	-	3	-	4	
15	N Piquet	-	-	-	-	-	-	-	-	-	-	-	3	-	-	-	3	
	E de Angelis	-	-	-	-	-	-	-	-	-	-	-	-	-	-	3	3	
	J Ickx	-	-	-	-	-	-	-	-	1	-	-	2	-	-	-	3	
	J Mass	-	-	-	-	-	-	1	-	-	1	-	1	-	-	-	3	
19	R Patrese	-	-	-	-	-	2	-	-	-	-	-	-	-	-	-	2	
	H-J Stuck	-	-	-	-	-	-	-	-	-	-	-	-	-	-	2	2	
21	E Fittipaldi	1	-	-	-	-	-	-	-	-	-	-	-	-	-	-	1	

9,6,4,3,2 and 1 point awarded to the first six finishers. Best 4 scores from first 7 races, best 4 from remaining 8 races.

Constructor Points 1979

		RA	BR	ZA	USAW	E	B	MC	F	GB	D	A	NL	I	CDN	USAE	Total
1	Ferrari	-	3	15	15	3	9	9	6	2	3	9	6	15	9	9	113
2	Williams-Ford Cosworth	-	-	-	4	-	-	6	4	9	15	11	9	4	13	-	75
3	Ligier-Ford Cosworth	12	15	-	2	9	6	2	-	1	4	4	6	-	-	-	61
4	Lotus-Ford Cosworth	8	4	5	3	10	3	4	-	-	-	-	-	2	-	-	39
5	Tyrrell-Ford Cosworth	-	3	4	1	3	4	-	2	4	-	-	-	1	2	4	28
6	Renault	-	-	-	-	-	-	-	13	6	-	1	-	-	-	6	26
7	McLaren-Ford Cosworth	4	-	-	-	-	1	3	-	3	2	-	-	-	1	1	15
8	Brabham-Alfa Romeo	-	-	1	-	-	-	-	-	-	-	-	3	3	-	-	7
9	Arrows-Ford Cosworth	-	-	-	-	-	2	1	-	-	1	-	1	-	-	-	5
10	Shadow-Ford Cosworth	-	-	-	-	-	-	-	-	-	-	-	-	-	-	3	3
11	ATS-Ford Cosworth	-	-	-	-	-	-	-	-	-	-	-	-	-	-	2	2
12	Copersucar-Ford Cosworth	1	-	-	-	-	-	-	-	-	-	-	-	-	-	-	1

9,6,4,3,2 and 1 point awarded to the first six finishers.

1980

Race Entrants and Results

A power struggle emerged between FISA and FOCA (the constructors' association headed by Bernie Ecclestone). McLaren merged with Ron Dennis's Project 4 team to produce McLaren International, while Shadow was sold to Teddy Yip. Cornering speeds were causing concern with huge G-forces imposed on the drivers. Williams emerged as the favourites, as Ferrari and Alfa worked on turbo engines.

FERRARI
Scuderia Ferrari SpA SEFAC: Scheckter, Villeneuve

TYRRELL
Candy Team Tyrrell: Jarier, Daly, Thackwell

BRABHAM
Parmalat Racing Team: Piquet, Zunino, Rebaque

McLAREN
Marlboro Team McLaren: Watson, Prost, (South)

ATS
Team ATS: Surer, Lammers, (Ertl)

LOTUS
Team Essex Lotus: Andretti, de Angelis, Mansell

ENSIGN
Unipart Racing Team: Regazzoni, Needell, Lammers, Lees

RENAULT
Equipe Renault Elf: Jabouille, Arnoux

SHADOW
Shadow Cars: (Johansson), Lees, (Kennedy)
Theodore Shadow from MC

FITTIPALDI
Skol Fittipaldi Team: Fittipaldi, Rosberg

ALFA ROMEO
Marlboro Team Alfa Romeo: Depailler, Brambilla, de Cesaris, Giacomelli

LIGIER
Equipe Ligier Gitanes: Pironi, Laffite

WILLIAMS
Albilad Williams Racing Team: Jones, Reutemann
RAM/Penthouse Rizla Racing: Keegan
RAM/Rainbow Jeans Racing: (Cogan, Lees)
Brands Hatch Racing: Wilson

ARROWS
Warsteiner Arrows Racing Team: Patrese, Mass, (Thackwell, Winkelhock)

OSELLA
Osella Squadra Corse: Cheever

13 Jan 1980			ARGENTINA: Buenos Aires No.15							(Round 1)		(Race 329)	
			53 laps x 5.968 km, 3.708 miles = 316.304 km, 196.542 miles										
Pos	No	Driver	Car	Model		Engine			Laps	Time/Reason for Retirement		Grid Pos	Row
1	27	A Jones	Williams	FW07		Ford Cosworth		V8	53	1h 43m 24.380s		1	1
2	5	N Piquet	Brabham	BT49		Ford Cosworth		V8	53	1h 43m 48.970s		4	2
3	21	K Rosberg	Fittipaldi	F7		Ford Cosworth		V8	53	1h 44m 43.020s		13	7
4	4	D Daly	Tyrrell	009		Ford Cosworth		V8	53	1h 44m 47.860s		22	11
5	23	B Giacomelli	Alfa Romeo	179		Alfa Romeo		V12	52			20	10
6	8	A Prost	McLaren	M29		Ford Cosworth		V8	52			12	6
7	6	R Zunino	Brabham	BT49		Ford Cosworth		V8	51			16	8
r	22	P Depailler	Alfa Romeo	179		Alfa Romeo		V12	46	engine		23	12
r	1	J Scheckter	Ferrari	312T5		Ferrari		F12	45	engine		11	6
nc	14	C Regazzoni	Ensign	N180		Ford Cosworth		V8	44			15	8
nc	20	E Fittipaldi	Fittipaldi	F7		Ford Cosworth		V8	37			24	12
r	2	G Villeneuve	Ferrari	312T5		Ferrari		F12	36	steering / accident		8	4
r	26	J Laffite	Ligier	JS11/15		Ford Cosworth		V8	30	engine		2	1
r	9	M Surer	ATS	D3		Ford Cosworth		V8	27	brake fluid on disc / fire		21	11
r	29	R Patrese	Arrows	A3		Ford Cosworth		V8	27	engine		7	4
r	30	J Mass	Arrows	A3		Ford Cosworth		V8	20	gearbox		14	7
r	11	M Andretti	Lotus	81		Ford Cosworth		V8	20	fuel metering unit		6	3
r	28	C Reutemann	Williams	FW07B		Ford Cosworth		V8	12	engine		10	5
r	12	E de Angelis	Lotus	81		Ford Cosworth		V8	7	rear suspension		5	3
r	7	J Watson	McLaren	M29		Ford Cosworth		V8	5	gearbox oil leak		17	9
r	15	J-P Jabouille	Renault	RE20		Renault		V6t	3	clutch / gearbox		9	5
r	16	R Arnoux	Renault	RE20		Renault		V6t	2	front suspension		19	10
r	25	D Pironi	Ligier	JS11/15		Ford Cosworth		V8	1	engine		3	2
r	3	J-P Jarier	Tyrrell	009		Ford Cosworth		V8	1	accident damage		18	9
nq	18	D Kennedy	Shadow	DN11		Ford Cosworth		V8					
nq	10	J Lammers	ATS	D3		Ford Cosworth		V8					
nq	17	S Johansson	Shadow	DN11		Ford Cosworth		V8					
nq	31	E Cheever	Osella	FA1		Ford Cosworth		V8					

Winning speed 183.531 km/h, 114.041 mph
Pole Position speed 206.247 km/h, 128.156 mph (A Jones, 1 min:44.170 sec)
Fastest Lap speed 194.521 km/h, 120.869 mph (A Jones, 1 min:50.450 sec on lap 5)
Lap Leaders A Jones 1-17,30-53 (41); J Laffite 18-29 (12).

27 Jan 1980   BRAZIL: Interlagos   (Round 2)   (Race 330)

40 laps x 7.874 km, 4.893 miles = 314.960 km, 195.707 miles

Pos	No	Driver	Car	Model	Engine		Laps	Time/Reason for Retirement	Grid Pos	Row
1	16	R Arnoux	Renault	RE20	Renault	V6t	40	1h 40m 01.330s	6	3
2	12	E de Angelis	Lotus	81	Ford Cosworth	V8	40	1h 40m 23.190s	7	4
3	27	A Jones	Williams	FW07B	Ford Cosworth	V8	40	1h 41m 07.440s	10	5
4	25	D Pironi	Ligier	JS11/15	Ford Cosworth	V8	40	1h 41m 41.460s	2	1
5	8	A Prost	McLaren	M29	Ford Cosworth	V8	40	1h 42m 26.740s	13	7
6	29	R Patrese	Arrows	A3	Ford Cosworth	V8	39		14	7
7	9	M Surer	ATS	D3	Ford Cosworth	V8	39		20	10
8	6	R Zunino	Brabham	BT49	Ford Cosworth	V8	39		18	9
9	21	K Rosberg	Fittipaldi	F7	Ford Cosworth	V8	39		15	8
10	30	J Mass	Arrows	A3	Ford Cosworth	V8	39		16	8
11	7	J Watson	McLaren	M29	Ford Cosworth	V8	39		23	12
12	3	J-P Jarier	Tyrrell	009	Ford Cosworth	V8	39		22	11
13	23	B Giacomelli	Alfa Romeo	179	Alfa Romeo	V12	39		17	9
14	4	D Daly	Tyrrell	009	Ford Cosworth	V8	38		24	12
15	20	E Fittipaldi	Fittipaldi	F7	Ford Cosworth	V8	38		19	10
16r	2	G Villeneuve	Ferrari	312T5	Ferrari	F12	36	throttle jammed / spin	3	2
r	22	P Depailler	Alfa Romeo	179	Alfa Romeo	V12	33	ignition	21	11
r	15	J-P Jabouille	Renault	RE20	Renault	V6t	25	turbo	1	1
r	5	N Piquet	Brabham	BT49	Ford Cosworth	V8	14	rear suspension / accident	9	5
r	14	C Regazzoni	Ensign	N180	Ford Cosworth	V8	13	handling	12	6
r	26	J Laffite	Ligier	JS11/15	Ford Cosworth	V8	13	coil	5	3
r	1	J Scheckter	Ferrari	312T5	Ferrari	F12	10	engine	8	4
r	28	C Reutemann	Williams	FW07B	Ford Cosworth	V8	1	driveshaft	4	2
r	11	M Andretti	Lotus	81	Ford Cosworth	V8	1	spin	11	6
nq	10	J Lammers	ATS	D3	Ford Cosworth	V8				
nq	18	D Kennedy	Shadow	DN11	Ford Cosworth	V8				
nq	17	S Johansson	Shadow	DN11	Ford Cosworth	V8				
nq	31	E Cheever	Osella	FA1	Ford Cosworth	V8				

Winning speed 188.934 km/h, 117.398 mph
Pole Position speed 200.470 km/h, 124.566 mph (J-P Jabouille, 2 min:21.400 sec)
Fastest Lap speed 192.427 km/h, 119.569 mph (R Arnoux, 2 min:27.310 sec on lap 22)
Lap Leaders G Villeneuve 1 (1); J-P Jabouille 2-24 (23); R Arnoux 25-40 (16).

1 Mar 1980   SOUTH AFRICA: Kyalami   (Round 3)   (Race 331)

78 laps x 4.104 km, 2.550 miles = 320.112 km, 198.908 miles

Pos	No	Driver	Car	Model	Engine		Laps	Time/Reason for Retirement	Grid Pos	Row
1	16	R Arnoux	Renault	RE20	Renault	V6t	78	1h 36m 52.540s	2	1
2	26	J Laffite	Ligier	JS11/15	Ford Cosworth	V8	78	1h 37m 26.610s	4	2
3	25	D Pironi	Ligier	JS11/15	Ford Cosworth	V8	78	1h 37m 45.030s	5	3
4	5	N Piquet	Brabham	BT49	Ford Cosworth	V8	78	1h 37m 53.560s	3	2
5	28	C Reutemann	Williams	FW07B	Ford Cosworth	V8	77		6	3
6	30	J Mass	Arrows	A3	Ford Cosworth	V8	77		19	10
7	3	J-P Jarier	Tyrrell	010	Ford Cosworth	V8	77		13	7
8	20	E Fittipaldi	Fittipaldi	F7	Ford Cosworth	V8	77		18	9
9	14	C Regazzoni	Ensign	N180	Ford Cosworth	V8	77		20	10
10	6	R Zunino	Brabham	BT49	Ford Cosworth	V8	77		17	9
11	7	J Watson	McLaren	M29	Ford Cosworth	V8	76		21	11
12	11	M Andretti	Lotus	81	Ford Cosworth	V8	76		15	8
13r	17	G Lees	Shadow	DN11	Ford Cosworth	V8	70	front suspension / accident	24	12
r	23	B Giacomelli	Alfa Romeo	179	Alfa Romeo	V12	69	engine	12	6
r	15	J-P Jabouille	Renault	RE20	Renault	V6t	61	front tyre	1	1
r	4	D Daly	Tyrrell	010	Ford Cosworth	V8	61	rear tyre burst	16	8
r	21	K Rosberg	Fittipaldi	F7	Ford Cosworth	V8	58	accident	23	12
nc	22	P Depailler	Alfa Romeo	179	Alfa Romeo	V12	53		7	4
r	27	A Jones	Williams	FW07B	Ford Cosworth	V8	34	gearbox oil cooler	8	4
r	2	G Villeneuve	Ferrari	312T5	Ferrari	F12	31	transmission	10	5
r	1	J Scheckter	Ferrari	312T5	Ferrari	F12	14	engine / electrics	9	5
r	29	R Patrese	Arrows	A3	Ford Cosworth	V8	10	accident	11	6
r	31	E Cheever	Osella	FA1	Ford Cosworth	V8	8	accident	22	11
r	12	E de Angelis	Lotus	81	Ford Cosworth	V8	1	accident	14	7
ns	8	A Prost	McLaren	M29	Ford Cosworth	V8		accident / injury		
nq	9	M Surer	ATS	D4	Ford Cosworth	V8		accident / injury		
nq	18	D Kennedy	Shadow	DN11	Ford Cosworth	V8				
nq	9	J Lammers	ATS	D3	Ford Cosworth	V8				

Winning speed 198.262 km/h, 123.194 mph
Pole Position speed 211.063 km/h, 131.148 mph (J-P Jabouille, 1 min:10.000 sec)
Fastest Lap speed 201.974 km/h, 125.501 mph (R Arnoux, 1 min:13.150 sec on lap 51)
Lap Leaders J-P Jabouille 1-61 (61); R Arnoux 62-78 (17).

30 Mar 1980   **USA West: Long Beach**   (Round 4)   (Race 332)

80.5 laps x 3.251 km, 2.020 miles = 261.706 km, 162.616 miles

Pos	No	Driver	Car	Model	Engine		Laps	Time/Reason for Retirement	Grid Pos	Row
1	5	N Piquet	Brabham	BT49	Ford Cosworth	V8	80	1h 50m 18.550s	1	1
2	29	R Patrese	Arrows	A3	Ford Cosworth	V8	80	1h 51m 07.762s	8	4
3	20	E Fittipaldi	Fittipaldi	F7	Ford Cosworth	V8	80	1h 51m 37.113s	24	12
4	7	J Watson	McLaren	M29	Ford Cosworth	V8	79		21	11
5	1	J Scheckter	Ferrari	312T5	Ferrari	F12	79		16	8
6	25	D Pironi	Ligier	JS11/15	Ford Cosworth	V8	79		9	5
7	30	J Mass	Arrows	A3	Ford Cosworth	V8	79		17	9
8	4	D Daly	Tyrrell	010	Ford Cosworth	V8	79		14	7
9	16	R Arnoux	Renault	RE20	Renault	V6t	78		2	1
10	15	J-P Jabouille	Renault	RE20	Renault	V6t	71		11	6
r	21	K Rosberg	Fittipaldi	F7	Ford Cosworth	V8	58	engine overheating	22	11
r	14	C Regazzoni	Ensign	N180	Ford Cosworth	V8	50	accident / injury	23	12
r	23	B Giacomelli	Alfa Romeo	179	Alfa Romeo	V12	49	accident	6	3
r	27	A Jones	Williams	FW07B	Ford Cosworth	V8	47	accident	5	3
r	2	G Villeneuve	Ferrari	312T5	Ferrari	F12	46	driveshaft	10	5
r	22	P Depailler	Alfa Romeo	179	Alfa Romeo	V12	40	rear suspension	3	2
r	26	J Laffite	Ligier	JS11/15	Ford Cosworth	V8	36	rear tyre / suspension	13	7
r	31	E Cheever	Osella	FA1	Ford Cosworth	V8	11	driveshaft	19	10
r	28	C Reutemann	Williams	FW07B	Ford Cosworth	V8	3	driveshaft	7	4
r	3	J-P Jarier	Tyrrell	010	Ford Cosworth	V8	3	accident	12	6
r	12	E de Angelis	Lotus	81	Ford Cosworth	V8	3	accident	20	10
r	6	R Zunino	Brabham	BT49	Ford Cosworth	V8	0	accident	18	9
r	11	M Andretti	Lotus	81	Ford Cosworth	V8	0	accident	15	8
r	9	J Lammers	ATS	D4	Ford Cosworth	V8	0	driveshaft	4	2
nq	18	D Kennedy	Shadow	DN11	Ford Cosworth	V8				
nq	17	G Lees	Shadow	DN11	Ford Cosworth	V8		driver ill		
nq	8	S South	McLaren	M29	Ford Cosworth	V8				

Winning speed 142.348 km/h, 88.451 mph
Pole Position speed 150.637 km/h, 93.602 mph (N Piquet, 1 min:17.694 sec)
Fastest Lap speed 146.607 km/h, 91.097 mph (N Piquet, 1 min:19.830 sec on lap 38)
Lap Leaders N Piquet 1-80 (80.5).

The start and finish lines were at different positions on the circuit. The fraction of a lap is credited to the first lap leader.

4 May 1980   **BELGIUM: Zolder**   (Round 5)   (Race 333)

72 laps x 4.262 km, 2.648 miles = 306.864 km, 190.676 miles

Pos	No	Driver	Car	Model	Engine		Laps	Time/Reason for Retirement	Grid Pos	Row
1	25	D Pironi	Ligier	JS11/15	Ford Cosworth	V8	72	1h 38m 46.510s	2	1
2	27	A Jones	Williams	FW07B	Ford Cosworth	V8	72	1h 39m 33.880s	1	1
3	28	C Reutemann	Williams	FW07B	Ford Cosworth	V8	72	1h 40m 10.630s	4	2
4	16	R Arnoux	Renault	RE20	Renault	V6t	71		6	3
5	3	J-P Jarier	Tyrrell	010	Ford Cosworth	V8	71		9	5
6	2	G Villeneuve	Ferrari	312T5	Ferrari	F12	71		12	6
7	21	K Rosberg	Fittipaldi	F7	Ford Cosworth	V8	71		21	11
8	1	J Scheckter	Ferrari	312T5	Ferrari	F12	70		14	7
9	4	D Daly	Tyrrell	010	Ford Cosworth	V8	70		11	6
10r	12	E de Angelis	Lotus	81	Ford Cosworth	V8	69	accident	8	4
11	26	J Laffite	Ligier	JS11/15	Ford Cosworth	V8	68		3	2
12r	9	J Lammers	ATS	D4	Ford Cosworth	V8	64	engine	15	8
nc	7	J Watson	McLaren	M29	Ford Cosworth	V8	61		20	10
r	29	R Patrese	Arrows	A3	Ford Cosworth	V8	58	accident	16	8
r	11	M Andretti	Lotus	81	Ford Cosworth	V8	41	gear linkage	17	9
r	22	P Depailler	Alfa Romeo	179	Alfa Romeo	V12	38	exhaust	10	5
r	5	N Piquet	Brabham	BT49	Ford Cosworth	V8	32	accident	7	4
r	8	A Prost	McLaren	M29	Ford Cosworth	V8	29	transmission	19	10
r	20	E Fittipaldi	Fittipaldi	F7	Ford Cosworth	V8	16	electrics	24	12
r	14	T Needell	Ensign	N180	Ford Cosworth	V8	12	engine	23	12
r	23	B Giacomelli	Alfa Romeo	179	Alfa Romeo	V12	11	accident / suspension	18	9
r	6	R Zunino	Brabham	BT49	Ford Cosworth	V8	5	clutch / gearbox	22	11
r	15	J-P Jabouille	Renault	RE20	Renault	V6t	1	clutch	5	3
r	30	J Mass	Arrows	A3	Ford Cosworth	V8	1	accident	13	7
nq	17	G Lees	Shadow	DN12	Ford Cosworth	V8				
nq	18	D Kennedy	Shadow	DN11	Ford Cosworth	V8				
nq	31	E Cheever	Osella	FA1	Ford Cosworth	V8				

Winning speed 186.402 km/h, 115.825 mph
Pole Position speed 193.923 km/h, 120.498 mph (A Jones, 1 min:19.120 sec)
Fastest Lap speed 189.703 km/h, 117.876 mph (J Laffite, 1 min:20.880 sec on lap 57)
Lap Leaders D Pironi 1-72 (72).

18 May 1980   **MONACO: Monte-Carlo**   **(Round 6)**   **(Race 334)**

76 laps x 3.312 km, 2.058 miles = 251.712 km, 156.407 miles

Pos	No	Driver	Car	Model	Engine		Laps	Time/Reason for Retirement	Grid Pos	Row
1	28	C Reutemann	Williams	FW07B	Ford Cosworth	V8	76	1h 55m 34.365s	2	1
2	26	J Laffite	Ligier	JS11/15	Ford Cosworth	V8	76	1h 56m 47.994s	5	3
3	5	N Piquet	Brabham	BT49	Ford Cosworth	V8	76	1h 56m 52.091s	4	2
4	30	J Mass	Arrows	A3	Ford Cosworth	V8	75		15	8
5	2	G Villeneuve	Ferrari	312T5	Ferrari	F12	75		6	3
6	20	E Fittipaldi	Fittipaldi	F7	Ford Cosworth	V8	74		18	9
7	11	M Andretti	Lotus	81	Ford Cosworth	V8	73		19	10
8	29	R Patrese	Arrows	A3	Ford Cosworth	V8	73		11	6
9r	12	E de Angelis	Lotus	81	Ford Cosworth	V8	68	accident	14	7
nc	9	J Lammers	ATS	D4	Ford Cosworth	V8	64		13	7
r	25	D Pironi	Ligier	JS11/15	Ford Cosworth	V8	54	accident	1	1
r	16	R Arnoux	Renault	RE20	Renault	V6t	53	accident	20	10
r	22	P Depailler	Alfa Romeo	179	Alfa Romeo	V12	50	engine	7	4
r	1	J Scheckter	Ferrari	312T5	Ferrari	F12	27	handling	17	9
r	15	J-P Jabouille	Renault	RE20	Renault	V6t	25	gearbox	16	8
r	27	A Jones	Williams	FW07B	Ford Cosworth	V8	24	differential	3	2
r	3	J-P Jarier	Tyrrell	010	Ford Cosworth	V8	0	accident	9	5
r	23	B Giacomelli	Alfa Romeo	179	Alfa Romeo	V12	0	accident	8	4
r	8	A Prost	McLaren	M29	Ford Cosworth	V8	0	accident	10	5
r	4	D Daly	Tyrrell	010	Ford Cosworth	V8	0	accident	12	6
nq	7	J Watson	McLaren	M29	Ford Cosworth	V8				
nq	31	E Cheever	Osella	FA1	Ford Cosworth	V8				
nq	17	G Lees	Shadow	DN12	Ford Cosworth	V8				
nq	21	K Rosberg	Fittipaldi	F7	Ford Cosworth	V8				
nq	6	R Zunino	Brabham	BT49	Ford Cosworth	V8				
nq	14	T Needell	Ensign	N180	Ford Cosworth	V8				
nq	18	D Kennedy	Shadow	DN11	Ford Cosworth	V8				

Winning speed 130.677 km/h, 81.199 mph
Pole Position speed 140.582 km/h, 87.354 mph (D Pironi, 1 min:24.813 sec)
Fastest Lap speed 136.393 km/h, 84.751 mph (C Reutemann, 1 min:27.418 sec on lap 40)
Lap Leaders D Pironi 1-54 (54); C Reutemann 55-76 (22).

R Patrese was officially credited with fastest lap in 1m 26.058s (138.548 km/h, 86.090 mph), but this is considered impossible, because of wet conditions on that particular lap.

---

29 Jun 1980   **FRANCE: Paul Ricard**   **(Round 7)**   **(Race 335)**

54 laps x 5.810 km, 3.610 miles = 313.740 km, 194.949 miles

Pos	No	Driver	Car	Model	Engine		Laps	Time/Reason for Retirement	Grid Pos	Row
1	27	A Jones	Williams	FW07B	Ford Cosworth	V8	54	1h 32m 43.420s	4	2
2	25	D Pironi	Ligier	JS11/15	Ford Cosworth	V8	54	1h 32m 47.940s	3	2
3	26	J Laffite	Ligier	JS11/15	Ford Cosworth	V8	54	1h 33m 13.680s	1	1
4	5	N Piquet	Brabham	BT49	Ford Cosworth	V8	54	1h 33m 58.300s	8	4
5	16	R Arnoux	Renault	RE20	Renault	V6t	54	1h 33m 59.570s	2	1
6	28	C Reutemann	Williams	FW07B	Ford Cosworth	V8	54	1h 34m 00.160s	5	3
7	7	J Watson	McLaren	M29	Ford Cosworth	V8	53		13	7
8	2	G Villeneuve	Ferrari	312T5	Ferrari	F12	53		17	9
9	29	R Patrese	Arrows	A3	Ford Cosworth	V8	53		18	9
10	30	J Mass	Arrows	A3	Ford Cosworth	V8	53		15	8
11	4	D Daly	Tyrrell	010	Ford Cosworth	V8	52		20	10
12	1	J Scheckter	Ferrari	312T5	Ferrari	F12	52		19	10
13r	20	E Fittipaldi	Fittipaldi	F7	Ford Cosworth	V8	50	electrics	24	12
14	3	J-P Jarier	Tyrrell	010	Ford Cosworth	V8	50		16	8
r	31	E Cheever	Osella	FA1	Ford Cosworth	V8	43	engine	21	11
r	9	M Surer	ATS	D4	Ford Cosworth	V8	26	gearbox	11	6
r	22	P Depailler	Alfa Romeo	179	Alfa Romeo	V12	25	handling	10	5
r	11	M Andretti	Lotus	81	Ford Cosworth	V8	18	gearbox	12	6
r	21	K Rosberg	Fittipaldi	F7	Ford Cosworth	V8	8	accident	23	12
r	23	B Giacomelli	Alfa Romeo	179	Alfa Romeo	V12	8	handling	9	5
r	8	A Prost	McLaren	M29	Ford Cosworth	V8	6	transmission	7	4
r	12	E de Angelis	Lotus	81	Ford Cosworth	V8	3	clutch	14	7
r	6	R Zunino	Brabham	BT49	Ford Cosworth	V8	0	clutch	22	11
r	15	J-P Jabouille	Renault	RE20	Renault	V6t	0	transmission	6	3
nq	17	G Lees	Shadow	DN12	Ford Cosworth	V8				
nq	14	J Lammers	Ensign	N180	Ford Cosworth	V8				
nq	18	D Kennedy	Shadow	DN12	Ford Cosworth	V8				

Winning speed 203.016 km/h, 126.148 mph
Pole Position speed 211.529 km/h, 131.438 mph (J Laffite, 1 min:38.880 sec)
Fastest Lap speed 206.171 km/h, 128.108 mph (A Jones, 1 min:41.450 sec on lap 48)
Lap Leaders J Laffite 1-34 (34); A Jones 35-54 (20).

Races   **225**

13 Jul 1980 **BRITAIN: Brands Hatch** (Round 8) (Race 336)

76 laps x 4.207 km, 2.614 miles = 319.719 km, 198.664 miles

Pos	No	Driver	Car	Model	Engine		Laps	Time/Reason for Retirement	Grid Pos	Row
1	27	A Jones	Williams	FW07B	Ford Cosworth	V8	76	1h 34m 49.228s	3	2
2	5	N Piquet	Brabham	BT49	Ford Cosworth	V8	76	1h 35m 00.235s	5	3
3	28	C Reutemann	Williams	FW07B	Ford Cosworth	V8	76	1h 35m 02.513s	4	2
4	4	D Daly	Tyrrell	010	Ford Cosworth	V8	75		10	5
5	3	J-P Jarier	Tyrrell	010	Ford Cosworth	V8	75		11	6
6	8	A Prost	McLaren	M29	Ford Cosworth	V8	75		7	4
7	6	H Rebaque	Brabham	BT49	Ford Cosworth	V8	74		17	9
8	7	J Watson	McLaren	M29	Ford Cosworth	V8	74		12	6
9	29	R Patrese	Arrows	A3	Ford Cosworth	V8	73		21	11
10	1	J Scheckter	Ferrari	312T5	Ferrari	F12	73		23	12
11	50	R Keegan	Williams	FW07	Ford Cosworth	V8	73		18	9
12	20	E Fittipaldi	Fittipaldi	F8	Ford Cosworth	V8	72		22	11
13	30	J Mass	Arrows	A3	Ford Cosworth	V8	69		24	12
nc	16	R Arnoux	Renault	RE20	Renault	V6t	67		16	8
r	25	D Pironi	Ligier	JS11/15	Ford Cosworth	V8	63	wheel / rear tyre	1	1
r	9	M Surer	ATS	D4	Ford Cosworth	V8	59	engine	15	8
r	11	M Andretti	Lotus	81	Ford Cosworth	V8	57	gearbox	9	5
r	23	B Giacomelli	Alfa Romeo	179	Alfa Romeo	V12	42	accident	6	3
r	2	G Villeneuve	Ferrari	312T5	Ferrari	F12	35	engine	19	10
r	26	J Laffite	Ligier	JS11/15	Ford Cosworth	V8	30	rear wheel / tyre / accident	2	1
r	22	P Depailler	Alfa Romeo	179	Alfa Romeo	V12	27	valve spring	8	4
r	31	E Cheever	Osella	FA1	Ford Cosworth	V8	17	rear suspension	20	10
r	12	E de Angelis	Lotus	81	Ford Cosworth	V8	16	rear suspension	14	7
r	15	J-P Jabouille	Renault	RE20	Renault	V6t	6	engine	13	7
nq	14	J Lammers	Ensign	N180	Ford Cosworth	V8				
nq	21	K Rosberg	Fittipaldi	F7	Ford Cosworth	V8				
nq	43	D Wilson	Williams	FW07	Ford Cosworth	V8				

Winning speed 202.310 km/h, 125.710 mph
Pole Position speed 213.292 km/h, 132.533 mph (D Pironi, 1 min:11.004 sec)
Fastest Lap speed 209.272 km/h, 130.035 mph (D Pironi, 1 min:12.368 sec on lap 54)
Lap Leaders D Pironi 1-18 (18); J Laffite 19-30 (12); A Jones 31-76 (46).

10 Aug 1980 **GERMANY: Hockenheim** (Round 9) (Race 337)

45 laps x 6.789 km, 4.218 miles = 305.505 km, 189.832 miles

Pos	No	Driver	Car	Model	Engine		Laps	Time/Reason for Retirement	Grid Pos	Row
1	26	J Laffite	Ligier	JS11/15	Ford Cosworth	V8	45	1h 22m 59.730s	5	3
2	28	C Reutemann	Williams	FW07B	Ford Cosworth	V8	45	1h 23m 02.920s	4	2
3	27	A Jones	Williams	FW07B	Ford Cosworth	V8	45	1h 23m 43.260s	1	1
4	5	N Piquet	Brabham	BT49	Ford Cosworth	V8	45	1h 23m 44.210s	6	3
5	23	B Giacomelli	Alfa Romeo	179	Alfa Romeo	V12	45	1h 24m 16.220s	19	10
6	2	G Villeneuve	Ferrari	312T5	Ferrari	F12	45	1h 24m 28.450s	16	8
7	11	M Andretti	Lotus	81	Ford Cosworth	V8	45	1h 24m 32.740s	9	5
8	30	J Mass	Arrows	A3	Ford Cosworth	V8	45	1h 24m 47.480s	17	9
9	29	R Patrese	Arrows	A3	Ford Cosworth	V8	44		10	5
10	4	D Daly	Tyrrell	010	Ford Cosworth	V8	44		22	11
11	8	A Prost	McLaren	M29	Ford Cosworth	V8	44		14	7
12	9	M Surer	ATS	D4	Ford Cosworth	V8	44		13	7
13	1	J Scheckter	Ferrari	312T5	Ferrari	F12	44		21	11
14	14	J Lammers	Ensign	N180	Ford Cosworth	V8	44		24	12
15	3	J-P Jarier	Tyrrell	010	Ford Cosworth	V8	44		23	12
16r	12	E de Angelis	Lotus	81	Ford Cosworth	V8	43	wheel bearing	11	6
r	7	J Watson	McLaren	M29	Ford Cosworth	V8	39	engine	20	10
r	15	J-P Jabouille	Renault	RE20	Renault	V6t	27	valve spring	2	1
r	16	R Arnoux	Renault	RE20	Renault	V6t	26	valve spring	3	2
r	31	E Cheever	Osella	FA1	Ford Cosworth	V8	23	gearbox	18	9
r	25	D Pironi	Ligier	JS11/15	Ford Cosworth	V8	18	driveshaft	7	4
r	20	E Fittipaldi	Fittipaldi	F8	Ford Cosworth	V8	18	skirt	12	6
r	21	K Rosberg	Fittipaldi	F8	Ford Cosworth	V8	8	front wheel bearing	8	4
r	6	H Rebaque	Brabham	BT49	Ford Cosworth	V8	4	gearbox	15	8
nq	50	R Keegan	Williams	FW07B	Ford Cosworth	V8				
nq	10	H Ertl	ATS	D4	Ford Cosworth	V8				

Winning speed 220.859 km/h, 137.235 mph
Pole Position speed 230.897 km/h, 143.472 mph (A Jones, 1 min:45.850 sec)
Fastest Lap speed 225.278 km/h, 139.981 mph (A Jones, 1 min:48.490 sec on lap 43)
Lap Leaders J-P Jabouille 1-26 (26); A Jones 27-40 (14); J Laffite 41-45 (5).

17 Aug 1980   **AUSTRIA: Österreichring**   (Round 10)   (Race 338)

54 laps x 5.942 km, 3.692 miles = 320.868 km, 199.378 miles

Pos	No	Driver	Car	Model	Engine		Laps	Time/Reason for Retirement	Grid Pos	Row
1	15	J-P Jabouille	Renault	RE20	Renault	V6t	54	1h 26m 15.730s	2	1
2	27	A Jones	Williams	FW07B	Ford Cosworth	V8	54	1h 26m 16.550s	3	2
3	28	C Reutemann	Williams	FW07B	Ford Cosworth	V8	54	1h 26m 35.090s	4	2
4	26	J Laffite	Ligier	JS11/15	Ford Cosworth	V8	54	1h 26m 57.750s	5	3
5	5	N Piquet	Brabham	BT49	Ford Cosworth	V8	54	1h 27m 18.540s	7	4
6	12	E de Angelis	Lotus	81	Ford Cosworth	V8	54	1h 27m 30.700s	9	5
7	8	A Prost	McLaren	M29	Ford Cosworth	V8	54	1h 27m 49.140s	12	6
8	2	G Villeneuve	Ferrari	312T5	Ferrari	F12	53		15	8
9	16	R Arnoux	Renault	RE20	Renault	V6t	53		1	1
10	6	H Rebaque	Brabham	BT49	Ford Cosworth	V8	53		14	7
11	20	E Fittipaldi	Fittipaldi	F8	Ford Cosworth	V8	53		23	12
12	9	M Surer	ATS	D4	Ford Cosworth	V8	53		16	8
13	1	J Scheckter	Ferrari	312T5	Ferrari	F12	53		22	11
14	29	R Patrese	Arrows	A3	Ford Cosworth	V8	53		18	9
15	50	R Keegan	Williams	FW07B	Ford Cosworth	V8	52		20	10
16	21	K Rosberg	Fittipaldi	F8	Ford Cosworth	V8	52		11	6
r	43	N Mansell	Lotus	81B	Ford Cosworth	V8	40	engine	24	12
r	7	J Watson	McLaren	M29	Ford Cosworth	V8	34	engine	21	11
r	23	B Giacomelli	Alfa Romeo	179	Alfa Romeo	V12	28	rear wheel loose / suspension	8	4
r	3	J-P Jarier	Tyrrell	010	Ford Cosworth	V8	25	engine	13	7
r	25	D Pironi	Ligier	JS11/15	Ford Cosworth	V8	25	handling	6	3
r	31	E Cheever	Osella	FA1	Ford Cosworth	V8	23	wheel bearing	19	10
r	4	D Daly	Tyrrell	010	Ford Cosworth	V8	12	brake disc / accident	10	5
r	11	M Andretti	Lotus	81	Ford Cosworth	V8	6	engine	17	9
nq	14	J Lammers	Ensign	N180	Ford Cosworth	V8				
nq	30	J Mass	Arrows	A3	Ford Cosworth	V8		accident / injury		

Winning speed 223.181 km/h, 138.678 mph
Pole Position speed 236.969 km/h, 147.246 mph (R Arnoux, 1 min:30.270 sec)
Fastest Lap speed 231.181 km/h, 143.649 mph (R Arnoux, 1 min:32.530 sec on lap 50)
Lap Leaders A Jones 1-2 (2); R Arnoux 3-20 (18); J-P Jabouille 21-54 (34).

31 Aug 1980   **NETHERLANDS: Zandvoort**   (Round 11)   (Race 339)

72 laps x 4.252 km, 2.642 miles = 306.144 km, 190.229 miles

Pos	No	Driver	Car	Model	Engine		Laps	Time/Reason for Retirement	Grid Pos	Row
1	5	N Piquet	Brabham	BT49	Ford Cosworth	V8	72	1h 38m 13.830s	5	3
2	16	R Arnoux	Renault	RE20	Renault	V6t	72	1h 38m 26.760s	1	1
3	26	J Laffite	Ligier	JS11/15	Ford Cosworth	V8	72	1h 38m 27.260s	6	3
4	28	C Reutemann	Williams	FW07B	Ford Cosworth	V8	72	1h 38m 29.120s	3	2
5	3	J-P Jarier	Tyrrell	010	Ford Cosworth	V8	72	1h 39m 13.850s	17	9
6	8	A Prost	McLaren	M30	Ford Cosworth	V8	72	1h 39m 36.450s	18	9
7	2	G Villeneuve	Ferrari	312T5	Ferrari	F12	71		7	4
8r	11	M Andretti	Lotus	81	Ford Cosworth	V8	70	out of fuel	10	5
9	1	J Scheckter	Ferrari	312T5	Ferrari	F12	70		12	6
10	9	M Surer	ATS	D4	Ford Cosworth	V8	69		20	10
11	27	A Jones	Williams	FW07B	Ford Cosworth	V8	69		4	2
r	4	D Daly	Tyrrell	010	Ford Cosworth	V8	60	front brake disc / tyre / accident	23	12
r	23	B Giacomelli	Alfa Romeo	179	Alfa Romeo	V12	58	skirt	8	4
r	31	E Cheever	Osella	FA1	Ford Cosworth	V8	38	engine	19	10
r	29	R Patrese	Arrows	A3	Ford Cosworth	V8	29	engine	14	7
r	15	J-P Jabouille	Renault	RE20	Renault	V6t	23	differential / handling	2	1
r	41	G Lees	Ensign	N180	Ford Cosworth	V8	21	accident	24	12
r	22	V Brambilla	Alfa Romeo	179	Alfa Romeo	V12	21	accident	22	11
r	7	J Watson	McLaren	M29	Ford Cosworth	V8	18	engine	9	5
r	20	E Fittipaldi	Fittipaldi	F8	Ford Cosworth	V8	16	brakes	21	11
r	43	N Mansell	Lotus	81B	Ford Cosworth	V8	15	brakes / accident	16	8
r	25	D Pironi	Ligier	JS11/15	Ford Cosworth	V8	2	accident	15	8
r	12	E de Angelis	Lotus	81	Ford Cosworth	V8	2	accident	11	6
r	6	H Rebaque	Brabham	BT49	Ford Cosworth	V8	1	gearbox	13	7
nq	50	R Keegan	Williams	FW07B	Ford Cosworth	V8				
nq	14	J Lammers	Ensign	N180	Ford Cosworth	V8				
nq	30	M Thackwell	Arrows	A3	Ford Cosworth	V8				
nq	21	K Rosberg	Fittipaldi	F8	Ford Cosworth	V8				
ew	30	J Mass	Arrows	A3	Ford Cosworth	V8		driver unfit (Austria injury)		

Winning speed 186.995 km/h, 116.193 mph
Pole Position speed 197.665 km/h, 122.824 mph (R Arnoux, 1 min:17.440 sec)
Fastest Lap speed 192.907 km/h, 119.867 mph (R Arnoux, 1 min:19.350 sec on lap 67)
Lap Leaders A Jones 1 (1); R Arnoux 2 (1); J Laffite 3-12 (10); N Piquet 13-72 (60).

Races

60 laps x 5.000 km, 3.107 miles = 300.000 km, 186.411 miles

Pos	No	Driver	Car	Model	Engine		Laps	Time/Reason for Retirement	Grid Pos	Row
1	5	N Piquet	Brabham	BT49	Ford Cosworth	V8	60	1h 38m 07.520s	5	3
2	27	A Jones	Williams	FW07B	Ford Cosworth	V8	60	1h 38m 36.450s	6	3
3	28	C Reutemann	Williams	FW07B	Ford Cosworth	V8	60	1h 39m 21.190s	3	2
4	12	E de Angelis	Lotus	81	Ford Cosworth	V8	59		18	9
5	21	K Rosberg	Fittipaldi	F8	Ford Cosworth	V8	59		11	6
6	25	D Pironi	Ligier	JS11/15	Ford Cosworth	V8	59		13	7
7	8	A Prost	McLaren	M30	Ford Cosworth	V8	59		24	12
8	1	J Scheckter	Ferrari	312T5	Ferrari	F12	59		16	8
9	26	J Laffite	Ligier	JS11/15	Ford Cosworth	V8	59		20	10
10	16	R Arnoux	Renault	RE20	Renault	V6t	58		1	1
11	50	R Keegan	Williams	FW07B	Ford Cosworth	V8	58		21	11
12	31	E Cheever	Osella	FA1	Ford Cosworth	V8	57		17	9
13r	3	J-P Jarier	Tyrrell	010	Ford Cosworth	V8	54	brakes	12	6
r	15	J-P Jabouille	Renault	RE20	Renault	V6t	53	gearbox	2	1
r	9	M Surer	ATS	D4	Ford Cosworth	V8	45	engine	23	12
r	11	M Andretti	Lotus	81	Ford Cosworth	V8	40	engine	10	5
r	29	R Patrese	Arrows	A3	Ford Cosworth	V8	38	engine	7	4
r	4	D Daly	Tyrrell	010	Ford Cosworth	V8	33	accident	22	11
r	7	J Watson	McLaren	M29	Ford Cosworth	V8	20	rear wheel bearing / brakes	14	7
r	6	H Rebaque	Brabham	BT49	Ford Cosworth	V8	18	rear suspension	9	5
r	20	E Fittipaldi	Fittipaldi	F8	Ford Cosworth	V8	17	accident	15	8
r	2	G Villeneuve	Ferrari	312T5	Ferrari	F12	5	rear tyre / accident	8	4
r	23	B Giacomelli	Alfa Romeo	179	Alfa Romeo	V12	5	tyre / accident	4	2
r	22	V Brambilla	Alfa Romeo	179	Alfa Romeo	V12	4	accident	19	10
nq	43	N Mansell	Lotus	81B	Ford Cosworth	V8				
nq	30	M Winkelhock	Arrows	A3	Ford Cosworth	V8				
nq	14	J Lammers	Ensign	N180	Ford Cosworth	V8				
nq	41	G Lees	Ensign	N180	Ford Cosworth	V8				

Winning speed 183.439 km/h, 113.984 mph
Pole Position speed 191.514 km/h, 119.001 mph (R Arnoux, 1 min:33.988 sec)
Fastest Lap speed 187.326 km/h, 116.399 mph (A Jones, 1 min:36.089 sec on lap 47)
Lap Leaders R Arnoux 1-2 (2); J-P Jabouille 3 (1); N Piquet 4-60 (57).

28 Sep 1980 **CANADA: Montréal** **(Round 13)** **(Race 341)**
70 laps x 4.410 km, 2.740 miles = 308.700 km, 191.817 miles

Pos	No	Driver	Car	Model	Engine		Laps	Time/Reason for Retirement	Grid Pos	Row
1	27	A Jones	Williams	FW07B	Ford Cosworth	V8	70	1h 46m 45.530s	2	1
2	28	C Reutemann	Williams	FW07B	Ford Cosworth	V8	70	1h 47m 01.070s	5	3
3	25	D Pironi	Ligier	JS11/15	Ford Cosworth	V8	70	1h 47m 04.660s	3	2
4	7	J Watson	McLaren	M29	Ford Cosworth	V8	70	1h 47m 16.510s	7	4
5	2	G Villeneuve	Ferrari	312T5	Ferrari	F12	70	1h 47m 40.760s	22	11
6	6	H Rebaque	Brabham	BT49	Ford Cosworth	V8	69		10	5
7	3	J-P Jarier	Tyrrell	010	Ford Cosworth	V8	69		15	8
8r	26	J Laffite	Ligier	JS11/15	Ford Cosworth	V8	68	out of fuel	9	5
9	21	K Rosberg	Fittipaldi	F8	Ford Cosworth	V8	68		6	3
10	12	E de Angelis	Lotus	81	Ford Cosworth	V8	68		17	9
11	30	J Mass	Arrows	A3	Ford Cosworth	V8	67		21	11
12	14	J Lammers	Ensign	N180	Ford Cosworth	V8	66		19	10
r	8	A Prost	McLaren	M30	Ford Cosworth	V8	41	front suspension / accident	12	6
r	16	R Arnoux	Renault	RE20	Renault	V6t	39	brakes / gearbox	23	12
r	15	J-P Jabouille	Renault	RE20	Renault	V6t	25	front suspension / accident / injury	13	7
r	5	N Piquet	Brabham	BT49	Ford Cosworth	V8	23	engine	1	1
r	11	M Andretti	Lotus	81	Ford Cosworth	V8	11	engine	18	9
r	22	A de Cesaris	Alfa Romeo	179	Alfa Romeo	V12	8	engine	8	4
r	31	E Cheever	Osella	FA1	Ford Cosworth	V8	8	fuel pump	14	7
r	20	E Fittipaldi	Fittipaldi	F8	Ford Cosworth	V8	8	gear linkage	16	8
r	23	B Giacomelli	Alfa Romeo	179	Alfa Romeo	V12	7	skirt	4	2
r	29	R Patrese	Arrows	A3	Ford Cosworth	V8	6	accident	11	6
r	4	D Daly	Tyrrell	010	Ford Cosworth	V8	0	accident *	20	10
r	43	M Thackwell	Tyrrell	010	Ford Cosworth	V8	0	accident *	24	12
nq	9	M Surer	ATS	D4	Ford Cosworth	V8				
nq	1	J Scheckter	Ferrari	312T5	Ferrari	F12				
nq	50	R Keegan	Williams	FW07B	Ford Cosworth	V8				
nq	51	K Cogan	Williams	FW07B	Ford Cosworth	V8				

Winning speed 173.494 km/h, 107.804 mph
Pole Position speed 181.797 km/h, 112.964 mph (N Piquet, 1 min:27.328 sec)
Fastest Lap speed 178.846 km/h, 111.130 mph (D Pironi, 1 min:28.769 sec on lap 62)
Lap Leaders A Jones 1-2,24-43 (22); N Piquet 3-23 (21); D Pironi 44-70 (27).

*Interrupted after first lap accident. Restarted for original distance. * Retired after first start.*
D Pironi finished 1st in 1h 45m 19.06s (175.868 km/h, 109.279 mph), but penalised 1 minute for jumping the second start and classified 3rd.
He is shown as leader 'on the road' but on corrected time, A Jones led laps 44-70.

5 Oct 1980 **USA East: Watkins Glen** **(Round 14)** **(Race 342)**
59 laps x 5.435 km, 3.377 miles = 320.651 km, 199.243 miles

Pos	No	Driver	Car	Model	Engine		Laps	Time/Reason for Retirement	Grid Pos	Row
1	27	A Jones	Williams	FW07B	Ford Cosworth	V8	59	1h 34m 36.050s	5	3
2	28	C Reutemann	Williams	FW07B	Ford Cosworth	V8	59	1h 34m 40.260s	3	2
3	25	D Pironi	Ligier	JS11/15	Ford Cosworth	V8	59	1h 34m 48.620s	7	4
4	12	E de Angelis	Lotus	81	Ford Cosworth	V8	59	1h 35m 05.740s	4	2
5	26	J Laffite	Ligier	JS11/15	Ford Cosworth	V8	58		12	6
6	11	M Andretti	Lotus	81	Ford Cosworth	V8	58		11	6
7	16	R Arnoux	Renault	RE20	Renault	V6t	58		6	3
8	9	M Surer	ATS	D4	Ford Cosworth	V8	57		17	9
9	50	R Keegan	Williams	FW07B	Ford Cosworth	V8	57		15	8
10	21	K Rosberg	Fittipaldi	F8	Ford Cosworth	V8	57		14	7
11	1	J Scheckter	Ferrari	312T5	Ferrari	F12	56		23	12
nc	7	J Watson	McLaren	M29	Ford Cosworth	V8	50		9	5
r	2	G Villeneuve	Ferrari	312T5	Ferrari	F12	49	accident	18	9
nc	3	J-P Jarier	Tyrrell	010	Ford Cosworth	V8	40		22	11
r	30	J Mass	Arrows	A3	Ford Cosworth	V8	36	driveshaft	24	12
r	23	B Giacomelli	Alfa Romeo	179	Alfa Romeo	V12	31	electrics	1	1
r	5	N Piquet	Brabham	BT49	Ford Cosworth	V8	25	spin	2	1
r	31	E Cheever	Osella	FA1	Ford Cosworth	V8	21	front suspension	16	8
r	6	H Rebaque	Brabham	BT49	Ford Cosworth	V8	20	engine	8	4
r	29	R Patrese	Arrows	A3	Ford Cosworth	V8	16	accident	20	10
r	14	J Lammers	Ensign	N180	Ford Cosworth	V8	16	steering mount	25	13
r	20	E Fittipaldi	Fittipaldi	F8	Ford Cosworth	V8	15	rear suspension	19	10
r	4	D Daly	Tyrrell	010	Ford Cosworth	V8	3	rear suspension / accident	21	11
r	22	A de Cesaris	Alfa Romeo	179	Alfa Romeo	V12	2	accident	10	5
ns	8	A Prost	McLaren	M30	Ford Cosworth	V8		accident / injury	13	7
nq	43	M Thackwell	Tyrrell	010	Ford Cosworth	V8				
nq	51	G Lees	Williams	FW07B	Ford Cosworth	V8				

Winning speed 203.371 km/h, 126.369 mph
Pole Position speed 209.721 km/h, 130.315 mph (B Giacomelli, 1 min:33.291 sec)
Fastest Lap speed 207.989 km/h, 129.238 mph (A Jones, 1 min:34.068 sec on lap 44)
Lap Leaders B Giacomelli 1-31 (31); A Jones 32-59 (28).

Races

Lap Leaders 1980

Pos	Driver	Car-Engine	GPs	laps	km	miles
1	N Piquet	Brabham-Ford Cosworth	4	218.5	894.4	555.8
2	A Jones	Williams-Ford Cosworth	8	174	914.8	568.4
3	D Pironi	Ligier-Ford Cosworth	4	171	680.5	422.8
4	J-P Jabouille	Renault	5	145	815.0	506.4
5	J Laffite	Ligier-Ford Cosworth	5	73	396.1	246.1
6	R Arnoux	Renault	5	54	317.0	197.2
7	B Giacomelli	Alfa Romeo	1	31	168.5	104.7
8	C Reutemann	Williams-Ford Cosworth	1	22	72.9	45.3
9	G Villeneuve	Ferrari	1	1	7.9	4.9
			14	889.5	4,267.0	2,651.4

Driver Points 1980

		RA	BR	ZA	USAW	B	MC	F	GB	D	A	NL	I	CDN	USAE	Total	
1	A Jones	9	4	-	-	6	-	9	9	(4)	6	-	6	9	9	67	(4)
2	N Piquet	6	-	3	9	-	4	3	6	3	2	9	9	-	-	54	
3	C Reutemann	-	-	2	-	4	9	1	4	6	4	(3)	(4)	6	6	42	(7)
4	J Laffite	-	-	6	-	-	6	4	-	9	3	4	-	-	2	34	
5	D Pironi	-	3	4	1	9	-	6	-	-	-	-	1	4	4	32	
6	R Arnoux	-	9	9	-	3	-	2	-	-	-	6	-	-	-	29	
7	E de Angelis	-	6	-	-	-	-	-	-	1	-	3	-	-	3	13	
8	J-P Jabouille	-	-	-	-	-	-	-	-	-	9	-	-	-	-	9	
9	R Patrese	-	1	-	6	-	-	-	-	-	-	-	-	-	-	7	
10	K Rosberg	4	-	-	-	-	-	-	-	-	-	-	2	-	-	6	
	D Daly	3	-	-	-	-	-	-	3	-	-	-	-	-	-	6	
	J Watson	-	-	-	3	-	-	-	-	-	-	-	-	3	-	6	
	J-P Jarier	-	-	-	-	2	-	-	2	-	-	2	-	-	-	6	
	G Villeneuve	-	-	-	-	1	2	-	-	1	-	-	-	2	-	6	
15	E Fittipaldi	-	-	-	4	-	1	-	-	-	-	-	-	-	-	5	
	A Prost	1	2	-	-	-	-	-	1	-	-	1	-	-	-	5	
17	J Mass	-	-	1	-	-	3	-	-	-	-	-	-	-	-	4	
	B Giacomelli	2	-	-	-	-	-	-	-	2	-	-	-	-	-	4	
19	J Scheckter	-	-	-	2	-	-	-	-	-	-	-	-	-	-	2	
20	H Rebaque	-	-	-	-	-	-	-	-	-	-	-	-	1	-	1	
	M Andretti	-	-	-	-	-	-	-	-	-	-	-	-	-	1	1	

9,6,4,3,2 and 1 point awarded to the first six finishers. Best 5 scores from first 7 races, best 5 from remaining 7 races.

Constructor Points 1980

		RA	BR	ZA	USAW	B	MC	F	GB	D	A	NL	I	CDN	USAE	Total
1	Williams-Ford Cosworth	9	4	2	-	10	9	10	13	10	10	3	10	15	15	120
2	Ligier-Ford Cosworth	-	3	10	1	9	6	10	-	9	3	4	1	4	6	66
3	Brabham-Ford Cosworth	6	-	3	9	-	4	3	6	3	2	9	9	1	-	55
4	Renault	-	9	9	-	3	-	2	-	-	9	6	-	-	-	38
5	Lotus-Ford Cosworth	-	6	-	-	-	-	-	-	-	1	-	3	-	4	14
6	Tyrrell-Ford Cosworth	3	-	-	-	2	-	-	5	-	-	2	-	-	-	12
7	Arrows-Ford Cosworth	-	1	1	6	-	3	-	-	-	-	-	-	-	-	11
	Fittipaldi-Ford Cosworth	4	-	-	4	-	1	-	-	-	-	-	2	-	-	11
	McLaren-Ford Cosworth	1	2	-	3	-	-	-	1	-	-	1	-	3	-	11
10	Ferrari	-	-	-	2	1	2	-	-	1	-	-	-	2	-	8
11	Alfa Romeo	2	-	-	-	-	-	-	-	2	-	-	-	-	-	4

9,6,4,3,2 and 1 point awarded to the first six finishers.

1981

Race Entrants and Results

Politics stole the headlines with threats of a breakaway series, until all parties talked through their differences to arrive at what was known as the Concorde Agreement. A ban on skirts was eventually agreed, as well as a 6 cm ground clearance – which was soon overcome with various hydraulic devices. In view of the goings-on Goodyear withdrew, only to come back later after Pirelli and Avon re-entered Formula 1. McLaren and Lotus both built carbon-fibre chassis.

WILLIAMS
Albilad Williams Racing Team: Jones, Reutemann
TAG Williams Team from E GP
Equipe Banco Occidental: (de Villota)

TYRRELL
Team Tyrrell: Cheever, (Cogan), Zunino, Alboreto

BRABHAM
Parmalat Racing Team: Piquet, Rebaque

McLAREN
McLaren International: Watson, de Cesaris

ATS
Team ATS: Lammers, Borgudd

LOTUS
Team Essex Lotus: de Angelis, Mansell
John Player Team Lotus from E GP

ENSIGN
Ensign Racing: Surer, Salazar

RENAULT
Equipe Renault Elf: Prost, Arnoux

MARCH
March Grand Prix Team: Daly, Salazar

FITTIPALDI
Fittipaldi Automotive: Rosberg, Serra

ALFA ROMEO
Marlboro Team Alfa Romeo: Andretti, Giacomelli

LIGIER
Equipe Talbot Gitanes: Jarier, Jabouille, Tambay, Laffite

FERRARI
Scuderia Ferrari SpA SEFAC: G Villeneuve, Pironi

ARROWS
Arrows Racing Team: Patrese, Stohr, (J Villeneuve)

OSELLA
Osella Squadra Corse: Gabbiani, Guerra, Ghinzani, (Francia), Jarier

THEODORE
Theodore Racing Team: Tambay, Surer

TOLEMAN
Candy Toleman Motorsport: Henton, Warwick

15 Mar 1981		USA West: Long Beach					(Round 1)		(Race 343)	
		80.5 laps x 3.251 km, 2.020 miles = 261.706 km, 162.616 miles								
Pos	No	Driver	Car	Model	Engine		Laps	Time/Reason for Retirement	Grid Pos	Row
1	1	A Jones	Williams	FW07C	Ford Cosworth	V8	80	1h 50m 41.330s	2	1
2	2	C Reutemann	Williams	FW07C	Ford Cosworth	V8	80	1h 50m 50.520s	3	2
3	5	N Piquet	Brabham	BT49C	Ford Cosworth	V8	80	1h 51m 16.250s	4	2
4	22	M Andretti	Alfa Romeo	179C	Alfa Romeo	V12	80	1h 51m 30.640s	6	3
5	3	E Cheever	Tyrrell	010	Ford Cosworth	V8	80	1h 51m 48.030s	8	4
6	33	P Tambay	Theodore	TY01	Ford Cosworth	V8	79		17	9
7	21	C Serra	Fittipaldi	F8C	Ford Cosworth	V8	78		18	9
8	16	R Arnoux	Renault	RE20B	Renault	V6t	77		20	10
r	14	M Surer	Ensign	N180B	Ford Cosworth	V8	70	ignition	19	10
r	28	D Pironi	Ferrari	126CK	Ferrari	V6t	67	engine	11	6
r	25	J-P Jarier	Talbot Ligier	JS17	Matra	V12	64	fuel pump	10	5
r	6	H Rebaque	Brabham	BT49C	Ford Cosworth	V8	49	accident	15	8
r	26	J Laffite	Talbot Ligier	JS17	Matra	V12	41	accident	12	6
r	23	B Giacomelli	Alfa Romeo	179C	Alfa Romeo	V12	41	accident	9	5
r	9	J Lammers	ATS	D4	Ford Cosworth	V8	41	accident	21	11
r	20	K Rosberg	Fittipaldi	F8C	Ford Cosworth	V8	41	distributor rotor arm	16	8
r	29	R Patrese	Arrows	A3	Ford Cosworth	V8	33	fuel filter	1	1
r	32	B Gabbiani	Osella	FA1B	Ford Cosworth	V8	26	front suspension / accident	24	12
r	12	N Mansell	Lotus	81B	Ford Cosworth	V8	25	accident	7	4
r	27	G Villeneuve	Ferrari	126CK	Ferrari	V6t	17	driveshaft	5	3
r	7	J Watson	McLaren	M29F	Ford Cosworth	V8	16	engine	23	12
r	11	E de Angelis	Lotus	81B	Ford Cosworth	V8	13	accident	13	7
r	15	A Prost	Renault	RE20B	Renault	V6t	0	accident	14	7
r	8	A de Cesaris	McLaren	M29F	Ford Cosworth	V8	0	accident	22	11
nq	4	K Cogan	Tyrrell	010	Ford Cosworth	V8				
nq	17	D Daly	March	811	Ford Cosworth	V8				
nq	31	M A Guerra	Osella	FA1B	Ford Cosworth	V8				
nq	30	S Stohr	Arrows	A3	Ford Cosworth	V8				
nq	18	E Salazar	March	811	Ford Cosworth	V8				

Winning speed 140.974 km/h, 87.597 mph (based on time taken to complete 80 laps)
Pole Position speed 147.402 km/h, 91.592 mph (R Patrese, 1 min:19.399 sec)
Fastest Lap speed 144.666 km/h, 89.891 mph (A Jones, 1 min:20.901 sec on lap 31)
Lap Leaders R Patrese 1-24 (24.5); C Reutemann 25-31 (7); A Jones 32-80 (49).

The start and finish lines were at different positions on the circuit. The fraction of a lap is credited to the first lap leader.

Races
231

62 laps x 5.031 km, 3.126 miles = 311.922 km, 193.819 miles

Pos	No	Driver	Car	Model	Engine		Laps	Time/Reason for Retirement	Grid Pos	Row
1	2	C Reutemann	Williams	FW07C	Ford Cosworth	V8	62	2h 00m 23.660s	2	1
2	1	A Jones	Williams	FW07C	Ford Cosworth	V8	62	2h 00m 28.100s	3	2
3	29	R Patrese	Arrows	A3	Ford Cosworth	V8	62	2h 01m 26.740s	4	2
4	14	M Surer	Ensign	N180B	Ford Cosworth	V8	62	2h 01m 40.690s	18	9
5	11	E de Angelis	Lotus	81B	Ford Cosworth	V8	62	2h 01m 50.080s	10	5
6	26	J Laffite	Talbot Ligier	JS17	Matra	V12	62	2h 01m 50.490s	16	8
7	25	J-P Jarier	Talbot Ligier	JS17	Matra	V12	62	2h 01m 53.910s	23	12
8	7	J Watson	McLaren	M29F	Ford Cosworth	V8	61		15	8
9	20	K Rosberg	Fittipaldi	F8C	Ford Cosworth	V8	61		12	6
10	33	P Tambay	Theodore	TY01	Ford Cosworth	V8	61		19	10
11	12	N Mansell	Lotus	81B	Ford Cosworth	V8	61		13	7
12	5	N Piquet	Brabham	BT49C	Ford Cosworth	V8	60		1	1
13	4	R Zunino	Tyrrell	010	Ford Cosworth	V8	57		24	12
nc	3	E Cheever	Tyrrell	010	Ford Cosworth	V8	49		14	7
nc	23	B Giacomelli	Alfa Romeo	179C	Alfa Romeo	V12	40		6	3
r	27	G Villeneuve	Ferrari	126CK	Ferrari	V6t	25	turbo wastegate	7	4
r	6	H Rebaque	Brabham	BT49C	Ford Cosworth	V8	22	rear suspension	11	6
r	30	S Stohr	Arrows	A3	Ford Cosworth	V8	20	accident	21	11
r	15	A Prost	Renault	RE20B	Renault	V6t	20	accident	5	3
r	28	D Pironi	Ferrari	126CK	Ferrari	V6t	19	accident	17	9
r	8	A de Cesaris	McLaren	M29F	Ford Cosworth	V8	9	electrics	20	10
r	21	C Serra	Fittipaldi	F8C	Ford Cosworth	V8	0	accident	22	11
r	16	R Arnoux	Renault	RE20B	Renault	V6t	0	accident	8	4
r	22	M Andretti	Alfa Romeo	179C	Alfa Romeo	V12	0	accident	9	5
nq	9	J Lammers	ATS	D4	Ford Cosworth	V8				
nq	25	J-P Jabouille	Talbot Ligier	JS17	Matra	V12		car raced by Jarier		
nq	32	B Gabbiani	Osella	FA1B	Ford Cosworth	V8				
nq	31	M A Guerra	Osella	FA1B	Ford Cosworth	V8				
nq	18	E Salazar	March	811	Ford Cosworth	V8				
nq	17	D Daly	March	811	Ford Cosworth	V8				
exc	14	R Londono	Ensign	N180B	Ford Cosworth	V8		super licence refused		

Winning speed 155.450 km/h, 96.592 mph
Pole Position speed 190.490 km/h, 118.365 mph (N Piquet, 1 min:35.079 sec)
Fastest Lap speed 158.454 km/h, 98.459 mph (M Surer, 1 min:54.302 sec on lap 36)
Lap Leaders C Reutemann 1-62 (62).

Scheduled for 63 laps, but stopped at 2 hours.

53 laps x 5.968 km, 3.708 miles = 316.304 km, 196.542 miles

Pos	No	Driver	Car	Model	Engine		Laps	Time/Reason for Retirement	Grid Pos	Row
1	5	N Piquet	Brabham	BT49C	Ford Cosworth	V8	53	1h 34m 32.740s	1	1
2	2	C Reutemann	Williams	FW07C	Ford Cosworth	V8	53	1h 34m 59.350s	4	2
3	15	A Prost	Renault	RE20B	Renault	V6t	53	1h 35m 22.720s	2	1
4	1	A Jones	Williams	FW07C	Ford Cosworth	V8	53	1h 35m 40.620s	3	2
5	16	R Arnoux	Renault	RE20B	Renault	V6t	53	1h 36m 04.590s	5	3
6	11	E de Angelis	Lotus	81B	Ford Cosworth	V8	52		10	5
7	29	R Patrese	Arrows	A3	Ford Cosworth	V8	52		9	5
8	22	M Andretti	Alfa Romeo	179C	Alfa Romeo	V12	52		17	9
9	30	S Stohr	Arrows	A3	Ford Cosworth	V8	52		19	10
10r	23	B Giacomelli	Alfa Romeo	179C	Alfa Romeo	V12	51	out of fuel	22	11
11	8	A de Cesaris	McLaren	M29F	Ford Cosworth	V8	51		18	9
12	9	J Lammers	ATS	D4	Ford Cosworth	V8	51		23	12
13	4	R Zunino	Tyrrell	010	Ford Cosworth	V8	51	1 lap penalty (missed chicane)	24	12
r	27	G Villeneuve	Ferrari	126CK	Ferrari	V6t	40	driveshaft	7	4
r	33	P Tambay	Theodore	TY01	Ford Cosworth	V8	36	oil loss / engine	14	7
r	7	J Watson	McLaren	MP4	Ford Cosworth	V8	36	crown wheel & pinion	11	6
r	6	H Rebaque	Brabham	BT49C	Ford Cosworth	V8	32	distributor rotor arm	6	3
r	21	C Serra	Fittipaldi	F8C	Ford Cosworth	V8	28	gearbox	20	10
r	26	J Laffite	Talbot Ligier	JS17	Matra	V12	19	vibration / handling	21	11
r	14	M Surer	Ensign	N180B	Ford Cosworth	V8	14	engine	16	8
r	20	K Rosberg	Fittipaldi	F8C	Ford Cosworth	V8	4	fuel pump belt	8	4
r	12	N Mansell	Lotus	81B	Ford Cosworth	V8	3	engine	15	8
r	28	D Pironi	Ferrari	126CK	Ferrari	V6t	3	engine	12	6
r	3	E Cheever	Tyrrell	010	Ford Cosworth	V8	1	clutch	13	7
nq	31	M A Guerra	Osella	FA1B	Ford Cosworth	V8				
nq	32	B Gabbiani	Osella	FA1B	Ford Cosworth	V8				
nq	17	D Daly	March	811	Ford Cosworth	V8				
nq	25	J-P Jabouille	Talbot Ligier	JS17	Matra	V12				
nq	18	E Salazar	March	811	Ford Cosworth	V8				

Winning speed 200.731 km/h, 124.728 mph
Pole Position speed 209.271 km/h, 130.035 mph (N Piquet, 1 min:42.665 sec)
Fastest Lap speed 204.059 km/h, 126.797 mph (N Piquet, 1 min:45.287 sec on lap 6)
Lap Leaders N Piquet 1-53 (53).

R Zunino penalised 1 lap for taking a short cut.

3 May 1981   SAN MARINO: Imola   (Round 4)   (Race 346)
60 laps x 5.040 km, 3.132 miles = 302.400 km, 187.903 miles

Pos	No	Driver	Car	Model	Engine		Laps	Time/Reason for Retirement	Grid Pos	Row
1	5	N Piquet	Brabham	BT49C	Ford Cosworth	V8	60	1h 51m 23.970s	5	3
2	29	R Patrese	Arrows	A3	Ford Cosworth	V8	60	1h 51m 28.550s	9	5
3	2	C Reutemann	Williams	FW07C	Ford Cosworth	V8	60	1h 51m 30.310s	2	1
4	6	H Rebaque	Brabham	BT49C	Ford Cosworth	V8	60	1h 51m 46.860s	13	7
5	28	D Pironi	Ferrari	126CK	Ferrari	V6t	60	1h 51m 49.840s	6	3
6	8	A de Cesaris	McLaren	M29F	Ford Cosworth	V8	60	1h 52m 30.580s	14	7
7	27	G Villeneuve	Ferrari	126CK	Ferrari	V6t	60	1h 53m 05.940s	1	1
8	16	R Arnoux	Renault	RE20B	Renault	V6t	59		3	2
9	14	M Surer	Ensign	N180B	Ford Cosworth	V8	59		21	11
10	7	J Watson	McLaren	MP4	Ford Cosworth	V8	58		7	4
11	33	P Tambay	Theodore	TY01	Ford Cosworth	V8	58		16	8
12	1	A Jones	Williams	FW07C	Ford Cosworth	V8	58		8	4
13	10	S Borgudd	ATS	D4	Ford Cosworth	V8	57		24	12
nc	25	J-P Jabouille	Talbot Ligier	JS17	Matra	V12	45		18	9
r	17	E Salazar	March	811	Ford Cosworth	V8	38	oil pressure	23	12
r	4	M Alboreto	Tyrrell	010	Ford Cosworth	V8	31	accident	17	9
r	32	B Gabbiani	Osella	FA1B	Ford Cosworth	V8	31	accident	20	10
r	23	B Giacomelli	Alfa Romeo	179C	Alfa Romeo	V12	28	accident	11	6
r	3	E Cheever	Tyrrell	010	Ford Cosworth	V8	28	accident	19	10
r	22	M Andretti	Alfa Romeo	179C	Alfa Romeo	V12	26	gearbox	12	6
r	20	K Rosberg	Fittipaldi	F8C	Ford Cosworth	V8	14	engine	15	8
r	26	J Laffite	Talbot Ligier	JS17	Matra	V12	7	accident	10	5
r	15	A Prost	Renault	RE20B	Renault	V6t	3	gearbox	4	2
r	31	M A Guerra	Osella	FA1B	Ford Cosworth	V8	0	accident / injury	22	11
nq	30	S Stohr	Arrows	A3	Ford Cosworth	V8				
nq	18	D Daly	March	811	Ford Cosworth	V8				
nq	9	J Lammers	ATS	D4	Ford Cosworth	V8				
nq	21	C Serra	Fittipaldi	F8C	Ford Cosworth	V8				
nq	36	D Warwick	Toleman	TG181	Hart	4t				
nq	35	B Henton	Toleman	TG181	Hart	4t				

Winning speed 162.873 km/h, 101.205 mph
Pole Position speed 191.953 km/h, 119.274 mph (G Villeneuve, 1 min:34.523 sec)
Fastest Lap speed 167.901 km/h, 104.329 mph (G Villeneuve, 1 min:48.064 sec on lap 46)
Lap Leaders G Villeneuve 1-14 (14); D Pironi 15-46 (32); N Piquet 47-60 (14).

17 May 1981   BELGIUM: Zolder   (Round 5)   (Race 347)
54 laps x 4.262 km, 2.648 miles = 230.148 km, 143.007 miles

Pos	No	Driver	Car	Model	Engine		Laps	Time/Reason for Retirement	Grid Pos	Row
1	2	C Reutemann	Williams	FW07C	Ford Cosworth	V8	54	1h 16m 31.610s	1	1
2	26	J Laffite	Talbot Ligier	JS17	Matra	V12	54	1h 17m 07.670s	9	5
3	12	N Mansell	Lotus	81B	Ford Cosworth	V8	54	1h 17m 15.300s	10	5
4	27	G Villeneuve	Ferrari	126CK	Ferrari	V6t	54	1h 17m 19.250s	7	4
5	11	E de Angelis	Lotus	81B	Ford Cosworth	V8	54	1h 17m 20.810s	14	7
6	3	E Cheever	Tyrrell	010	Ford Cosworth	V8	54	1h 17m 24.120s	8	4
7	7	J Watson	McLaren	MP4	Ford Cosworth	V8	54	1h 17m 33.270s	5	3
8	28	D Pironi	Ferrari	126CK	Ferrari	V6t	54	1h 18m 03.650s	3	2
9	23	B Giacomelli	Alfa Romeo	179C	Alfa Romeo	V12	54	1h 18m 07.190s	17	9
10	22	M Andretti	Alfa Romeo	179C	Alfa Romeo	V12	53		18	9
11	14	M Surer	Ensign	N180B	Ford Cosworth	V8	52		15	8
12	4	M Alboreto	Tyrrell	010	Ford Cosworth	V8	52		19	10
13	31	P Ghinzani	Osella	FA1B	Ford Cosworth	V8	50		24	12
r	6	H Rebaque	Brabham	BT49C	Ford Cosworth	V8	39	accident	21	11
r	25	J-P Jabouille	Talbot Ligier	JS17	Matra	V12	35	transmission	16	8
r	21	C Serra	Fittipaldi	F8C	Ford Cosworth	V8	29	engine	20	10
r	32	B Gabbiani	Osella	FA1B	Ford Cosworth	V8	22	engine	22	11
r	1	A Jones	Williams	FW07C	Ford Cosworth	V8	19	accident	6	3
r	8	A de Cesaris	McLaren	M29F	Ford Cosworth	V8	11	gearbox	23	12
r	5	N Piquet	Brabham	BT49C	Ford Cosworth	V8	10	accident	2	1
r	20	K Rosberg	Fittipaldi	F8C	Ford Cosworth	V8	10	gear lever	11	6
r	15	A Prost	Renault	RE20B	Renault	V6t	2	clutch	12	6
r	30	S Stohr	Arrows	A3	Ford Cosworth	V8	0	accident *	13	7
r	29	R Patrese	Arrows	A3	Ford Cosworth	V8	0	stalled on grid / accident *	4	2
nq	16	R Arnoux	Renault	RE30	Renault	V6t				
nq	17	E Salazar	March	811	Ford Cosworth	V8				
nq	9	S Borgudd	ATS	HGS1	Ford Cosworth	V8				
nq	33	P Tambay	Theodore	TY01	Ford Cosworth	V8				
nq	36	D Warwick	Toleman	TG181	Hart	4t				
nq	35	B Henton	Toleman	TG181	Hart	4t				
nq	18	D Daly	March	811	Ford Cosworth	V8				

Winning speed 180.445 km/h, 112.123 mph
Pole Position speed 186.475 km/h, 115.870 mph (C Reutemann, 1 min:22.280 sec)
Fastest Lap speed 184.192 km/h, 114.452 mph (C Reutemann, 1 min:23.300 sec on lap 37)
Lap Leaders D Pironi 1-12 (12); A Jones 13-19 (7); C Reutemann 20-54 (35).

Scheduled for 70 laps, but interrupted after first lap accident. Restarted for original distance, but stopped early because of rain.
* Retired after first start.

Races   233

31 May 1981   MONACO: Monte-Carlo   (Round 6)   (Race 348)
76 laps x 3.312 km, 2.058 miles = 251.712 km, 156.407 miles

Pos	No	Driver	Car	Model	Engine		Laps	Time/Reason for Retirement	Grid Pos	Row
1	27	G Villeneuve	Ferrari	126CK	Ferrari	V6t	76	1h 54m 23.380s	2	1
2	1	A Jones	Williams	FW07C	Ford Cosworth	V8	76	1h 55m 03.290s	7	4
3	26	J Laffite	Talbot Ligier	JS17	Matra	V12	76	1h 55m 52.620s	8	4
4	28	D Pironi	Ferrari	126CK	Ferrari	V6t	75		17	9
5	3	E Cheever	Tyrrell	010	Ford Cosworth	V8	74		15	8
6	14	M Surer	Ensign	N180B	Ford Cosworth	V8	74		19	10
7	33	P Tambay	Theodore	TY01	Ford Cosworth	V8	72		16	8
r	5	N Piquet	Brabham	BT49C	Ford Cosworth	V8	53	accident	1	1
r	7	J Watson	McLaren	MP4	Ford Cosworth	V8	53	engine	10	5
r	4	M Alboreto	Tyrrell	010	Ford Cosworth	V8	50	accident	20	10
r	23	B Giacomelli	Alfa Romeo	179C	Alfa Romeo	V12	50	accident	18	9
r	15	A Prost	Renault	RE30	Renault	V6t	45	engine	9	5
r	2	C Reutemann	Williams	FW07C	Ford Cosworth	V8	34	gearbox	4	2
r	16	R Arnoux	Renault	RE20B	Renault	V6t	32	accident	13	7
r	11	E de Angelis	Lotus	87	Ford Cosworth	V8	32	engine	6	3
r	29	R Patrese	Arrows	A3	Ford Cosworth	V8	29	gearbox	5	3
r	12	N Mansell	Lotus	87	Ford Cosworth	V8	16	rear suspension	3	2
r	30	S Stohr	Arrows	A3	Ford Cosworth	V8	15	electrical misfire	14	7
r	8	A de Cesaris	McLaren	MP4	Ford Cosworth	V8	0	accident	11	6
r	22	M Andretti	Alfa Romeo	179C	Alfa Romeo	V12	0	accident	12	6
nq	20	K Rosberg	Fittipaldi	F8C	Ford Cosworth	V8				
nq	25	J-P Jabouille	Talbot Ligier	JS17	Matra	V12				
nq	6	H Rebaque	Brabham	BT49C	Ford Cosworth	V8				
nq	21	C Serra	Fittipaldi	F8C	Ford Cosworth	V8				
nq	32	P Ghinzani	Osella	FA1B	Ford Cosworth	V8				
nq	31	B Gabbiani	Osella	FA1B	Ford Cosworth	V8				
npq	10	S Borgudd	ATS	D4	Ford Cosworth	V8				
npq	18	D Daly	March	811	Ford Cosworth	V8				
npq	17	E Salazar	March	811	Ford Cosworth	V8				
npq	35	B Henton	Toleman	TG181	Hart	4t				
npq	36	D Warwick	Toleman	TG181	Hart	4t				

Winning speed 132.029 km/h, 82.039 mph
Pole Position speed 139.111 km/h, 86.440 mph (N Piquet, 1 min:25.710 sec)
Fastest Lap speed 136.312 km/h, 84.700 mph (A Jones, 1 min:27.470 sec on lap 48)
Lap Leaders N Piquet 1-53 (53); A Jones 54-72 (19); G Villeneuve 73-76 (4).

21 Jun 1981   SPAIN: Jarama   (Round 7)   (Race 349)
80 laps x 3.312 km, 2.058 miles = 264.960 km, 164.639 miles

Pos	No	Driver	Car	Model	Engine		Laps	Time/Reason for Retirement	Grid Pos	Row
1	27	G Villeneuve	Ferrari	126CK	Ferrari	V6t	80	1h 46m 35.019s	7	4
2	26	J Laffite	Talbot Ligier	JS17	Matra	V12	80	1h 46m 35.230s	1	1
3	7	J Watson	McLaren	MP4	Ford Cosworth	V8	80	1h 46m 35.590s	4	2
4	2	C Reutemann	Williams	FW07C	Ford Cosworth	V8	80	1h 46m 36.020s	3	2
5	11	E de Angelis	Lotus	87	Ford Cosworth	V8	80	1h 46m 36.250s	10	5
6	12	N Mansell	Lotus	87	Ford Cosworth	V8	80	1h 47m 03.590s	11	6
7	1	A Jones	Williams	FW07C	Ford Cosworth	V8	80	1h 47m 31.590s	2	1
8	22	M Andretti	Alfa Romeo	179C	Alfa Romeo	V12	80	1h 47m 35.810s	8	4
9	16	R Arnoux	Renault	RE30	Renault	V6t	80	1h 47m 42.090s	17	9
10	23	B Giacomelli	Alfa Romeo	179C	Alfa Romeo	V12	80	1h 47m 48.660s	6	3
11	21	C Serra	Fittipaldi	F8C	Ford Cosworth	V8	79		21	11
12	20	K Rosberg	Fittipaldi	F8C	Ford Cosworth	V8	78		15	8
13	33	P Tambay	Theodore	TY01	Ford Cosworth	V8	78		16	8
14	14	E Salazar	Ensign	N180B	Ford Cosworth	V8	77		24	12
15	28	D Pironi	Ferrari	126CK	Ferrari	V6t	76		13	7
16	17	D Daly	March	811	Ford Cosworth	V8	75		22	11
nc	3	E Cheever	Tyrrell	010	Ford Cosworth	V8	61		20	10
r	25	J-P Jabouille	Talbot Ligier	JS17	Matra	V12	52	brakes	19	10
r	6	H Rebaque	Brabham	BT49C	Ford Cosworth	V8	46	gearbox	18	9
r	5	N Piquet	Brabham	BT49C	Ford Cosworth	V8	43	accident	9	5
r	30	S Stohr	Arrows	A3	Ford Cosworth	V8	43	engine	23	12
r	15	A Prost	Renault	RE30	Renault	V6t	28	accident	5	3
r	29	R Patrese	Arrows	A3	Ford Cosworth	V8	21	engine	12	6
r	8	A de Cesaris	McLaren	MP4	Ford Cosworth	V8	9	accident	14	7
nq	4	M Alboreto	Tyrrell	010	Ford Cosworth	V8				
nq	31	B Gabbiani	Osella	FA1B	Ford Cosworth	V8				
nq	9	S Borgudd	ATS	HGS1	Ford Cosworth	V8				
nq	35	B Henton	Toleman	TG181	Hart	4t				
nq	36	D Warwick	Toleman	TG181	Hart	4t				
nq	32	G Francia	Osella	FA1B	Ford Cosworth	V8				
exc	37	E de Villota	Williams	FW07	Ford Cosworth	V8		not allowed to practise		

Winning speed 149.156 km/h, 92.681 mph
Pole Position speed 161.662 km/h, 100.452 mph (J Laffite, 1 min:13.754 sec)
Fastest Lap speed 153.219 km/h, 95.206 mph (A Jones, 1 min:17.818 sec on lap 5)
Lap Leaders A Jones 1-13 (13); G Villeneuve 14-80 (67).

80 laps x 3.800 km, 2.361 miles = 304.000 km, 188.897 miles

Pos	No	Driver	Car	Model	Engine		Laps	Time/Reason for Retirement	Grid Pos	Row
1	15	A Prost	Renault	RE30	Renault	V6t	80	1h 35m 48.130s	3	2
2	7	J Watson	McLaren	MP4	Ford Cosworth	V8	80	1h 35m 50.420s	2	1
3	5	N Piquet	Brabham	BT49C	Ford Cosworth	V8	80	1h 36m 12.350s	4	2
4	16	R Arnoux	Renault	RE30	Renault	V6t	80	1h 36m 30.430s	1	1
5	28	D Pironi	Ferrari	126CK	Ferrari	V6t	79		14	7
6	11	E de Angelis	Lotus	87	Ford Cosworth	V8	79		8	4
7	12	N Mansell	Lotus	87	Ford Cosworth	V8	79		13	7
8	22	M Andretti	Alfa Romeo	179C	Alfa Romeo	V12	79		10	5
9	6	H Rebaque	Brabham	BT49C	Ford Cosworth	V8	78		15	8
10	2	C Reutemann	Williams	FW07C	Ford Cosworth	V8	78		7	4
11	8	A de Cesaris	McLaren	MP4	Ford Cosworth	V8	78		5	3
12	33	M Surer	Theodore	TY01	Ford Cosworth	V8	78		21	11
13	3	E Cheever	Tyrrell	010	Ford Cosworth	V8	77		19	10
14	29	R Patrese	Arrows	A3	Ford Cosworth	V8	77		18	9
15	23	B Giacomelli	Alfa Romeo	179C	Alfa Romeo	V12	77		12	6
16	4	M Alboreto	Tyrrell	010	Ford Cosworth	V8	77		23	12
17	1	A Jones	Williams	FW07C	Ford Cosworth	V8	76		9	5
r	26	J Laffite	Talbot Ligier	JS17	Matra	V12	57	accident / front suspension	6	3
r	17	D Daly	March	811	Ford Cosworth	V8	55	engine	20	10
r	27	G Villeneuve	Ferrari	126CK	Ferrari	V6t	41	electrics	11	6
r	25	P Tambay	Talbot Ligier	JS17	Matra	V12	31	rear wheel bearing	16	8
r	20	K Rosberg	Fittipaldi	F8C	Ford Cosworth	V8	12	rear suspension	17	9
r	14	E Salazar	Ensign	N180B	Ford Cosworth	V8	7	rear suspension	22	11
ns	21	C Serra	Fittipaldi	F8C	Ford Cosworth	V8		accident	24	12
nq	30	S Stohr	Arrows	A3	Ford Cosworth	V8				
nq	35	B Henton	Toleman	TG181	Hart	4t				
nq	9	S Borgudd	ATS	HGS1	Ford Cosworth	V8				
nq	31	B Gabbiani	Osella	FA1B	Ford Cosworth	V8				
nq	36	D Warwick	Toleman	TG181	Hart	4t				

Winning speed 190.392 km/h, 118.304 mph
Pole Position speed 207.430 km/h, 128.891 mph (R Arnoux, 1 min: 5.950 sec)
Fastest Lap speed 197.859 km/h, 122.944 mph (A Prost, 1 min: 9.140 sec on lap 64)
Lap Leaders N Piquet 1-58 (58); A Prost 59-80 (22).

Interrupted after 58 laps, because of rain. Restarted for remaining 22 laps, with results being on aggregate.
Lap leaders are given 'on the road'.

68 laps x 4.719 km, 2.932 miles = 320.865 km, 199.376 miles

Pos	No	Driver	Car	Model	Engine		Laps	Time/Reason for Retirement	Grid Pos	Row
1	7	J Watson	McLaren	MP4	Ford Cosworth	V8	68	1h 26m 54.800s	5	3
2	2	C Reutemann	Williams	FW07C	Ford Cosworth	V8	68	1h 27m 35.450s	9	5
3	26	J Laffite	Talbot Ligier	JS17	Matra	V12	67		14	7
4	3	E Cheever	Tyrrell	010	Ford Cosworth	V8	67		23	12
5	6	H Rebaque	Brabham	BT49C	Ford Cosworth	V8	67		13	7
6	9	S Borgudd	ATS	HGS1	Ford Cosworth	V8	67		21	11
7	17	D Daly	March	811	Ford Cosworth	V8	66		17	9
8	32	J-P Jarier	Osella	FA1B	Ford Cosworth	V8	65		20	10
9r	16	R Arnoux	Renault	RE30	Renault	V6t	64	engine	1	1
10r	29	R Patrese	Arrows	A3	Ford Cosworth	V8	64	engine	10	5
11r	33	M Surer	Theodore	TY01	Ford Cosworth	V8	61	out of fuel	24	12
r	22	M Andretti	Alfa Romeo	179D	Alfa Romeo	V12	59	throttle linkage	11	6
r	20	K Rosberg	Fittipaldi	F8C	Ford Cosworth	V8	56	rear suspension	16	8
r	11	E de Angelis	Lotus	87	Ford Cosworth	V8	25	black-flagged / withdrew	22	11
r	15	A Prost	Renault	RE30	Renault	V6t	17	engine	2	1
r	25	P Tambay	Talbot Ligier	JS17	Matra	V12	15	ignition	15	8
r	28	D Pironi	Ferrari	126CK	Ferrari	V6t	13	engine	4	2
r	5	N Piquet	Brabham	BT49C	Ford Cosworth	V8	11	front tyre burst / accident	3	2
r	23	B Giacomelli	Alfa Romeo	179D	Alfa Romeo	V12	5	gearbox	12	6
r	27	G Villeneuve	Ferrari	126CK	Ferrari	V6t	4	accident	8	4
r	1	A Jones	Williams	FW07C	Ford Cosworth	V8	3	accident	7	4
r	8	A de Cesaris	McLaren	MP4	Ford Cosworth	V8	3	accident	6	3
r	4	M Alboreto	Tyrrell	010	Ford Cosworth	V8	0	clutch	19	10
r	30	S Stohr	Arrows	A3	Ford Cosworth	V8	0	accident	18	9
nq	21	C Serra	Fittipaldi	F8C	Ford Cosworth	V8				
nq	35	B Henton	Toleman	TG181	Hart	4t				
nq	12	N Mansell	Lotus	87	Ford Cosworth	V8				
nq	14	E Salazar	Ensign	N180B	Ford Cosworth	V8				
nq	36	D Warwick	Toleman	TG181	Hart	4t				
nq	31	B Gabbiani	Osella	FA1B	Ford Cosworth	V8				

Winning speed 221.507 km/h, 137.638 mph
Pole Position speed 239.253 km/h, 148.665 mph (R Arnoux, 1 min:11.000 sec)
Fastest Lap speed 226.290 km/h, 140.610 mph (R Arnoux, 1 min:15.067 sec on lap 50)
Lap Leaders A Prost 1-16 (16); R Arnoux 17-60 (44); J Watson 61-68 (8).

45 laps x 6.789 km, 4.218 miles = 305.505 km, 189.832 miles

Pos	No	Driver	Car	Model	Engine		Laps	Time/Reason for Retirement	Grid Pos	Row
1	5	N Piquet	Brabham	BT49C	Ford Cosworth	V8	45	1h 25m 55.600s	6	3
2	15	A Prost	Renault	RE30	Renault	V6t	45	1h 26m 07.120s	1	1
3	26	J Laffite	Talbot Ligier	JS17	Matra	V12	45	1h 27m 00.200s	7	4
4	6	H Rebaque	Brabham	BT49C	Ford Cosworth	V8	45	1h 27m 35.290s	16	8
5	3	E Cheever	Tyrrell	011	Ford Cosworth	V8	45	1h 27m 46.120s	18	9
6	7	J Watson	McLaren	MP4	Ford Cosworth	V8	44		9	5
7	11	E de Angelis	Lotus	87	Ford Cosworth	V8	44		14	7
8	32	J-P Jarier	Osella	FA1B	Ford Cosworth	V8	44		17	9
9	22	M Andretti	Alfa Romeo	179E	Alfa Romeo	V12	44		12	6
10	27	G Villeneuve	Ferrari	126CK	Ferrari	V6t	44		8	4
11	1	A Jones	Williams	FW07C	Ford Cosworth	V8	44		4	2
12	30	S Stohr	Arrows	A3	Ford Cosworth	V8	44		24	12
13	16	R Arnoux	Renault	RE30	Renault	V6t	44		2	1
14r	33	M Surer	Theodore	TY01	Ford Cosworth	V8	43	front suspension / accident	22	11
15	23	B Giacomelli	Alfa Romeo	179D	Alfa Romeo	V12	43		19	10
nc	14	E Salazar	Ensign	N180B	Ford Cosworth	V8	39		23	12
r	9	S Borgudd	ATS	HGS1	Ford Cosworth	V8	35	engine	20	10
r	2	C Reutemann	Williams	FW07C	Ford Cosworth	V8	27	engine	3	2
r	29	R Patrese	Arrows	A3	Ford Cosworth	V8	27	engine	13	7
r	25	P Tambay	Talbot Ligier	JS17	Matra	V12	27	rear wheel bearing	11	6
r	17	D Daly	March	811	Ford Cosworth	V8	15	steering tie rod	21	11
r	12	N Mansell	Lotus	87	Ford Cosworth	V8	12	fuel leak	15	8
r	8	A de Cesaris	McLaren	MP4	Ford Cosworth	V8	4	spin	10	5
r	28	D Pironi	Ferrari	126CK	Ferrari	V6t	1	engine	5	3
nq	20	K Rosberg	Fittipaldi	F8C	Ford Cosworth	V8				
nq	35	B Henton	Toleman	TG181	Hart	4t				
nq	31	B Gabbiani	Osella	FA1B	Ford Cosworth	V8				
nq	36	D Warwick	Toleman	TG181	Hart	4t				
nq	4	M Alboreto	Tyrrell	010	Ford Cosworth	V8				
nq	21	C Serra	Fittipaldi	F8C	Ford Cosworth	V8				

Winning speed 213.325 km/h, 132.554 mph
Pole Position speed 227.353 km/h, 141.270 mph (A Prost, 1 min:47.500 sec)
Fastest Lap speed 217.403 km/h, 135.088 mph (A Jones, 1 min:52.420 sec on lap 4)
Lap Leaders A Prost 1-20 (20); A Jones 21-38 (18); N Piquet 39-45 (7).

53 laps x 5.942 km, 3.692 miles = 314.926 km, 195.686 miles

Pos	No	Driver	Car	Model	Engine		Laps	Time/Reason for Retirement	Grid Pos	Row
1	26	J Laffite	Talbot Ligier	JS17	Matra	V12	53	1h 27m 36.470s	4	2
2	16	R Arnoux	Renault	RE30	Renault	V6t	53	1h 27m 41.640s	1	1
3	5	N Piquet	Brabham	BT49C	Ford Cosworth	V8	53	1h 27m 43.810s	7	4
4	1	A Jones	Williams	FW07C	Ford Cosworth	V8	53	1h 27m 48.510s	6	3
5	2	C Reutemann	Williams	FW07C	Ford Cosworth	V8	53	1h 28m 08.320s	5	3
6	7	J Watson	McLaren	MP4	Ford Cosworth	V8	53	1h 29m 07.610s	12	6
7	11	E de Angelis	Lotus	87	Ford Cosworth	V8	52		9	5
8	8	A de Cesaris	McLaren	MP4	Ford Cosworth	V8	52		18	9
9	28	D Pironi	Ferrari	126CK	Ferrari	V6t	52		8	4
10	32	J-P Jarier	Osella	FA1B	Ford Cosworth	V8	51		14	7
11	17	D Daly	March	811	Ford Cosworth	V8	47		19	10
r	22	M Andretti	Alfa Romeo	179E	Alfa Romeo	V12	46	engine	13	7
r	9	S Borgudd	ATS	HGS1	Ford Cosworth	V8	44	transmission	21	11
r	29	R Patrese	Arrows	A3	Ford Cosworth	V8	43	engine	10	5
r	14	E Salazar	Ensign	N180B	Ford Cosworth	V8	43	engine	20	10
r	4	M Alboreto	Tyrrell	010	Ford Cosworth	V8	40	gearbox / valve spring	22	11
r	23	B Giacomelli	Alfa Romeo	179D	Alfa Romeo	V12	35	engine / fire	16	8
r	6	H Rebaque	Brabham	BT49C	Ford Cosworth	V8	31	clutch	15	8
r	30	S Stohr	Arrows	A3	Ford Cosworth	V8	27	engine / spin	24	12
r	15	A Prost	Renault	RE30	Renault	V6t	26	front suspension	2	1
r	25	P Tambay	Talbot Ligier	JS17	Matra	V12	26	engine	17	9
r	12	N Mansell	Lotus	87	Ford Cosworth	V8	23	engine	11	6
r	27	G Villeneuve	Ferrari	126CK	Ferrari	V6t	11	accident	3	2
r	33	M Surer	Theodore	TY01	Ford Cosworth	V8	0	distributor	23	12
nq	3	E Cheever	Tyrrell	011	Ford Cosworth	V8				
nq	36	D Warwick	Toleman	TG181	Hart	4t				
nq	35	B Henton	Toleman	TG181	Hart	4t				
nq	31	B Gabbiani	Osella	FA1B	Ford Cosworth	V8				

Winning speed 215.683 km/h, 134.019 mph
Pole Position speed 232.468 km/h, 144.449 mph (R Arnoux, 1 min:32.018 sec)
Fastest Lap speed 219.127 km/h, 136.159 mph (J Laffite, 1 min:37.620 sec on lap 47)
Lap Leaders G Villeneuve 1 (1); A Prost 2-26 (25); R Arnoux 27-38 (12); J Laffite 39-53 (15).

30 Aug 1981 **NETHERLANDS: Zandvoort** **(Round 12)** **(Race 354)**

72 laps x 4.252 km, 2.642 miles = 306.144 km, 190.229 miles

Pos	No	Driver	Car	Model	Engine		Laps	Time/Reason for Retirement	Grid Pos	Row
1	15	A Prost	Renault	RE30	Renault	V6t	72	1h 40m 22.430s	1	1
2	5	N Piquet	Brabham	BT49C	Ford Cosworth	V8	72	1h 40m 30.670s	3	2
3	1	A Jones	Williams	FW07C	Ford Cosworth	V8	72	1h 40m 57.930s	4	2
4	6	H Rebaque	Brabham	BT49C	Ford Cosworth	V8	71		15	8
5	11	E de Angelis	Lotus	87	Ford Cosworth	V8	71		9	5
6	14	E Salazar	Ensign	N180B	Ford Cosworth	V8	70		24	12
7	30	S Stohr	Arrows	A3	Ford Cosworth	V8	69		21	11
8	33	M Surer	Theodore	TY01	Ford Cosworth	V8	69		20	10
9r	4	M Alboreto	Tyrrell	011	Ford Cosworth	V8	68	engine	25	13
10	9	S Borgudd	ATS	HGS1	Ford Cosworth	V8	68		23	12
r	22	M Andretti	Alfa Romeo	179D	Alfa Romeo	V12	62	front tyre burst / accident	7	4
r	7	J Watson	McLaren	MP4	Ford Cosworth	V8	50	ignition	8	4
r	3	E Cheever	Tyrrell	011	Ford Cosworth	V8	46	front suspension / accident	22	11
r	32	J-P Jarier	Osella	FA1B	Ford Cosworth	V8	29	gearbox	18	9
r	16	R Arnoux	Renault	RE30	Renault	V6t	21	accident	2	1
r	23	B Giacomelli	Alfa Romeo	179C	Alfa Romeo	V12	19	accident	14	7
r	26	J Laffite	Talbot Ligier	JS17	Matra	V12	18	accident	6	3
r	2	C Reutemann	Williams	FW07C	Ford Cosworth	V8	18	accident	5	3
r	29	R Patrese	Arrows	A3	Ford Cosworth	V8	16	active suspension	10	5
r	17	D Daly	March	811	Ford Cosworth	V8	5	rear suspension	19	10
r	28	D Pironi	Ferrari	126CK	Ferrari	V6t	4	accident / rear suspension	12	6
r	12	N Mansell	Lotus	87	Ford Cosworth	V8	1	electrics	17	9
r	25	P Tambay	Talbot Ligier	JS17	Matra	V12	0	accident	11	6
r	27	G Villeneuve	Ferrari	126CK	Ferrari	V6t	0	accident	16	8
ns	8	A de Cesaris	McLaren	MP4	Ford Cosworth	V8		withdrawn by team (accidents)	13	7
nq	35	B Henton	Toleman	TG181	Hart	4t				
nq	20	K Rosberg	Fittipaldi	F8C	Ford Cosworth	V8				
nq	21	C Serra	Fittipaldi	F8C	Ford Cosworth	V8				
nq	31	B Gabbiani	Osella	FA1B	Ford Cosworth	V8				
nq	36	D Warwick	Toleman	TG181	Hart	4t				

Winning speed 183.002 km/h, 113.712 mph
Pole Position speed 195.804 km/h, 121.667 mph (A Prost, 1 min:18.176 sec)
Fastest Lap speed 187.061 km/h, 116.234 mph (A Jones, 1 min:21.830 sec on lap 15)
Lap Leaders A Prost 1-22,24-72 (71); A Jones 23 (1).

13 Sep 1981 **ITALY: Monza** **(Round 13)** **(Race 355)**

52 laps x 5.800 km, 3.604 miles = 301.600 km, 187.406 miles

Pos	No	Driver	Car	Model	Engine		Laps	Time/Reason for Retirement	Grid Pos	Row
1	15	A Prost	Renault	RE30	Renault	V6t	52	1h 26m 33.897s	3	2
2	1	A Jones	Williams	FW07C	Ford Cosworth	V8	52	1h 26m 56.072s	5	3
3	2	C Reutemann	Williams	FW07C	Ford Cosworth	V8	52	1h 27m 24.484s	2	1
4	11	E de Angelis	Lotus	87	Ford Cosworth	V8	52	1h 28m 06.799s	11	6
5	28	D Pironi	Ferrari	126CK	Ferrari	V6t	52	1h 28m 08.419s	8	4
6r	5	N Piquet	Brabham	BT49C	Ford Cosworth	V8	51	engine	6	3
7r	8	A de Cesaris	McLaren	MP4	Ford Cosworth	V8	51	tyre burst / accident	16	8
8	23	B Giacomelli	Alfa Romeo	179C	Alfa Romeo	V12	50		10	5
9	32	J-P Jarier	Osella	FA1C	Ford Cosworth	V8	50		18	9
10	35	B Henton	Toleman	TG181	Hart	4t	49		23	12
r	22	M Andretti	Alfa Romeo	179D	Alfa Romeo	V12	41	flywheel coupling	13	7
r	17	D Daly	March	811	Ford Cosworth	V8	37	gearbox	19	10
r	25	P Tambay	Talbot Ligier	JS17	Matra	V12	22	rear tyre burst / spin	15	8
r	12	N Mansell	Lotus	87	Ford Cosworth	V8	21	handling	12	6
r	7	J Watson	McLaren	MP4	Ford Cosworth	V8	19	accident	7	4
r	29	R Patrese	Arrows	A3	Ford Cosworth	V8	19	gearbox	20	10
r	4	M Alboreto	Tyrrell	011	Ford Cosworth	V8	16	accident	22	11
r	14	E Salazar	Ensign	N180B	Ford Cosworth	V8	13	rear tyre burst / spin	24	12
r	16	R Arnoux	Renault	RE30	Renault	V6t	12	accident	1	1
r	3	E Cheever	Tyrrell	011	Ford Cosworth	V8	11	spin	17	9
r	26	J Laffite	Talbot Ligier	JS17	Matra	V12	11	rear tyre	4	2
r	9	S Borgudd	ATS	HGS1	Ford Cosworth	V8	10	spin	21	11
r	27	G Villeneuve	Ferrari	126CK	Ferrari	V6t	6	turbo	9	5
r	6	H Rebaque	Brabham	BT49C	Ford Cosworth	V8	2	electrics	14	7
nq	33	M Surer	Theodore	TY01	Ford Cosworth	V8				
nq	31	B Gabbiani	Osella	FA1B	Ford Cosworth	V8				
nq	36	D Warwick	Toleman	TG181	Hart	4t				
nq	30	S Stohr	Arrows	A3	Ford Cosworth	V8				
nq	20	K Rosberg	Fittipaldi	F8C	Ford Cosworth	V8				
nq	21	C Serra	Fittipaldi	F8C	Ford Cosworth	V8				

Winning speed 209.045 km/h, 129.895 mph
Pole Position speed 223.394 km/h, 138.811 mph (R Arnoux, 1 min:33.467 sec)
Fastest Lap speed 214.092 km/h, 133.031 mph (C Reutemann, 1 min:37.528 sec on lap 48)
Lap Leaders A Prost 1-52 (52).

63 laps x 4.410 km, 2.740 miles = 277.830 km, 172.636 miles

Pos	No	Driver	Car	Model	Engine		Laps	Time/Reason for Retirement	Grid Pos	Row
1	26	J Laffite	Talbot Ligier	JS17	Matra	V12	63	2h 01m 25.205s	10	5
2	7	J Watson	McLaren	MP4	Ford Cosworth	V8	63	2h 01m 31.438s	9	5
3	27	G Villeneuve	Ferrari	126CK	Ferrari	V6t	63	2h 03m 15.480s	11	6
4	23	B Giacomelli	Alfa Romeo	179C	Alfa Romeo	V12	62		15	8
5	5	N Piquet	Brabham	BT49C	Ford Cosworth	V8	62		1	1
6	11	E de Angelis	Lotus	87	Ford Cosworth	V8	62		7	4
7	22	M Andretti	Alfa Romeo	179D	Alfa Romeo	V12	62		16	8
8	17	D Daly	March	811	Ford Cosworth	V8	61		20	10
9	33	M Surer	Theodore	TY01	Ford Cosworth	V8	61		19	10
10	2	C Reutemann	Williams	FW07C	Ford Cosworth	V8	60		2	1
11	4	M Alboreto	Tyrrell	011	Ford Cosworth	V8	59		22	11
12r	3	E Cheever	Tyrrell	011	Ford Cosworth	V8	56	engine	14	7
r	8	A de Cesaris	McLaren	MP4	Ford Cosworth	V8	51	spin	13	7
r	15	A Prost	Renault	RE30	Renault	V6t	48	accident	4	2
r	12	N Mansell	Lotus	87	Ford Cosworth	V8	45	accident	5	3
r	9	S Borgudd	ATS	HGS1	Ford Cosworth	V8	40	spin	21	11
r	6	H Rebaque	Brabham	BT49C	Ford Cosworth	V8	35	spin	6	3
r	32	J-P Jarier	Osella	FA1C	Ford Cosworth	V8	26	accident	23	12
r	28	D Pironi	Ferrari	126CK	Ferrari	V6t	24	engine	12	6
r	1	A Jones	Williams	FW07C	Ford Cosworth	V8	24	handling	3	2
r	14	E Salazar	Ensign	N180B	Ford Cosworth	V8	8	spin	24	12
r	25	P Tambay	Talbot Ligier	JS17	Matra	V12	6	spin	17	9
r	29	R Patrese	Arrows	A3	Ford Cosworth	V8	6	spin	18	9
r	16	R Arnoux	Renault	RE30	Renault	V6t	0	accident	8	4
nq	20	K Rosberg	Fittipaldi	F8C	Ford Cosworth	V8				
nq	21	C Serra	Fittipaldi	F8C	Ford Cosworth	V8				
nq	35	B Henton	Toleman	TG181	Hart	4t				
nq	30	J Villeneuve	Arrows	A3	Ford Cosworth	V8				
nq	36	D Warwick	Toleman	TG181	Hart	4t				
nq	31	B Gabbiani	Osella	FA1B	Ford Cosworth	V8				

Winning speed 137.290 km/h, 85.308 mph
Pole Position speed 177.960 km/h, 110.579 mph (N Piquet, 1 min:29.211 sec)
Fastest Lap speed 145.019 km/h, 90.111 mph (J Watson, 1 min:49.475 sec on lap 43)
Lap Leaders A Jones 1-6 (6); A Prost 7-12 (6); J Laffite 13-63 (51).

Scheduled for 70 laps, but stopped at 2 hours.

75 laps x 3.650 km, 2.268 miles = 273.749 km, 170.100 miles

Pos	No	Driver	Car	Model	Engine		Laps	Time/Reason for Retirement	Grid Pos	Row
1	1	A Jones	Williams	FW07C	Ford Cosworth	V8	75	1h 44m 09.077s	2	1
2	15	A Prost	Renault	RE30	Renault	V6t	75	1h 44m 29.125s	5	3
3	23	B Giacomelli	Alfa Romeo	179C	Alfa Romeo	V12	75	1h 44m 29.505s	8	4
4	12	N Mansell	Lotus	87	Ford Cosworth	V8	75	1h 44m 56.550s	9	5
5	5	N Piquet	Brabham	BT49C	Ford Cosworth	V8	75	1h 45m 25.515s	4	2
6	26	J Laffite	Talbot Ligier	JS17	Matra	V12	75	1h 45m 27.252s	12	6
7	7	J Watson	McLaren	MP4	Ford Cosworth	V8	75	1h 45m 27.574s	6	3
8	2	C Reutemann	Williams	FW07C	Ford Cosworth	V8	74		1	1
9	28	D Pironi	Ferrari	126CK	Ferrari	V6t	73		18	9
10	20	K Rosberg	Fittipaldi	F8C	Ford Cosworth	V8	73		20	10
11	29	R Patrese	Arrows	A3	Ford Cosworth	V8	71		11	6
12	8	A de Cesaris	McLaren	MP4	Ford Cosworth	V8	69		14	7
13r	4	M Alboreto	Tyrrell	011	Ford Cosworth	V8	67	engine	17	9
nc	14	E Salazar	Ensign	N180B	Ford Cosworth	V8	61		24	12
r	36	D Warwick	Toleman	TG181	Hart	4t	43	gearbox	22	11
r	22	M Andretti	Alfa Romeo	179D	Alfa Romeo	V12	29	rear suspension	10	5
dq	27	G Villeneuve	Ferrari	126CK	Ferrari	V6t	22	started from wrong grid position	3	2
r	6	H Rebaque	Brabham	BT49C	Ford Cosworth	V8	20	spin	16	8
r	33	M Surer	Theodore	TY01	Ford Cosworth	V8	19	rear suspension	23	12
r	3	E Cheever	Tyrrell	011	Ford Cosworth	V8	10	engine	19	10
r	16	R Arnoux	Renault	RE30	Renault	V6t	10	electrics	13	7
r	25	P Tambay	Talbot Ligier	JS17	Matra	V12	2	accident	7	4
r	11	E de Angelis	Lotus	87	Ford Cosworth	V8	2	water leak	15	8
r	32	J-P Jarier	Osella	FA1C	Ford Cosworth	V8	0	transmission	21	11
nq	9	S Borgudd	ATS	HGS1	Ford Cosworth	V8				
nq	21	C Serra	Fittipaldi	F8C	Ford Cosworth	V8				
nq	17	D Daly	March	811	Ford Cosworth	V8				
nq	30	J Villeneuve	Arrows	A3	Ford Cosworth	V8				
nq	35	B Henton	Toleman	TG181	Hart	4t				
nq	31	B Gabbiani	Osella	FA1B	Ford Cosworth	V8				

Winning speed 157.703 km/h, 97.992 mph
Pole Position speed 168.849 km/h, 104.918 mph (C Reutemann, 1 min:17.821 sec)
Fastest Lap speed 163.930 km/h, 101.861 mph (D Pironi, 1 min:20.156 sec on lap 49)
Lap Leaders A Jones 1-75 (75).

Pos	Driver	Car-Engine	GPs	laps	km	miles
1	A Prost	Renault	7	212	1,073.4	667.0
2	A Jones	Williams-Ford Cosworth	8	188	721.8	448.5
3	N Piquet	Brabham-Ford Cosworth	5	185	830.3	515.9
4	C Reutemann	Williams-Ford Cosworth	3	104	483.8	300.6
5	G Villeneuve	Ferrari	4	86	311.7	193.7
6	J Laffite	Talbot Ligier-Matra	2	66	314.0	195.1
7	R Arnoux	Renault	2	56	278.9	173.3
8	D Pironi	Ferrari	2	44	212.4	132.0
9	R Patrese	Arrows-Ford Cosworth	1	24.5	79.6	49.5
10	J Watson	McLaren-Ford Cosworth	1	8	37.8	23.5
			15	**973.5**	**4,343.8**	**2,699.1**

Driver Points 1981

		USAW	BR	RA	RSM	B	MC	E	F	GB	D	A	NL	I	CDN	LV	Total
1	N Piquet	4	-	9	9	-	-	-	4	-	9	4	6	1	2	2	50
2	C Reutemann	6	9	6	4	9	-	3	-	6	-	2	-	4	-	-	49
3	A Jones	9	6	3	-	-	6	-	-	-	-	3	4	6	-	9	46
4	J Laffite	-	1	-	-	6	4	6	-	4	4	9	-	-	9	1	44
5	A Prost	-	-	4	-	-	-	-	9	-	6	-	9	9	-	6	43
6	J Watson	-	-	-	-	-	-	4	6	9	1	1	-	-	6	-	27
7	G Villeneuve	-	-	-	-	3	9	9	-	-	-	-	-	-	4	-	25
8	E de Angelis	-	2	1	-	2	-	2	1	-	-	-	2	3	1	-	14
9	R Arnoux	-	-	2	-	-	-	-	3	-	-	6	-	-	-	-	11
	H Rebaque	-	-	-	3	-	-	-	-	2	3	-	3	-	-	-	11
11	R Patrese	-	4	-	6	-	-	-	-	-	-	-	-	-	-	-	10
	E Cheever	2	-	-	-	1	2	-	-	3	2	-	-	-	-	-	10
13	D Pironi	-	-	-	2	-	3	-	2	-	-	-	-	2	-	-	9
14	N Mansell	-	-	-	-	4	-	1	-	-	-	-	-	-	-	3	8
15	B Giacomelli	-	-	-	-	-	-	-	-	-	-	-	-	-	3	4	7
16	M Surer	-	3	-	-	-	1	-	-	-	-	-	-	-	-	-	4
17	M Andretti	3	-	-	-	-	-	-	-	-	-	-	-	-	-	-	3
18	P Tambay	1	-	-	-	-	-	-	-	-	-	-	-	-	-	-	1
	A de Cesaris	-	-	-	1	-	-	-	-	-	-	-	-	-	-	-	1
	S Borgudd	-	-	-	-	-	-	-	1	-	-	-	-	-	-	-	1
	E Salazar	-	-	-	-	-	-	-	-	-	-	-	1	-	-	-	1

9,6,4,3,2 and 1 point awarded to the first six finishers. Best 11 scores.

Constructor Points 1981

		USAW	BR	RA	RSM	B	MC	E	F	GB	D	A	NL	I	CDN	LV	Total
1	Williams-Ford Cosworth	15	15	9	4	9	6	3	-	6	-	5	4	10	-	9	95
2	Brabham-Ford Cosworth	4	-	9	12	-	-	-	4	2	12	4	9	1	2	2	61
3	Renault	-	-	6	-	-	-	-	12	-	6	6	9	9	-	6	54
4	Talbot Ligier-Matra	-	1	-	-	6	4	6	-	4	4	9	-	-	9	1	44
5	Ferrari	-	-	-	2	3	12	9	2	-	-	-	-	2	4	-	34
6	McLaren-Ford Cosworth	-	-	-	1	-	-	4	6	9	1	1	-	-	6	-	28
7	Lotus-Ford Cosworth	-	2	1	-	6	-	3	1	-	-	-	2	3	1	3	22
8	Arrows-Ford Cosworth	-	4	-	6	-	-	-	-	-	-	-	-	-	-	-	10
	Alfa Romeo	3	-	-	-	-	-	-	-	-	-	-	-	-	3	4	10
	Tyrrell-Ford Cosworth	2	-	-	-	1	2	-	-	3	2	-	-	-	-	-	10
11	Ensign-Ford Cosworth	-	3	-	-	-	1	-	-	-	-	-	1	-	-	-	5
12	Theodore-Ford Cosworth	1	-	-	-	-	-	-	-	-	-	-	-	-	-	-	1
	ATS-Ford Cosworth	-	-	-	-	-	-	-	-	1	-	-	-	-	-	-	1

9,6,4,3,2 and 1 point awarded to the first six finishers.

1982

Race Entrants and Results

Lauda returned after his sudden retirement and promptly organised a drivers strike over licences, at the first race. By now, cars had rigid suspension and were subjected to even higher G-forces, the aluminium chassis was a thing of the past. The lighter Cosworth-engined cars got round the weight limit by topping up water tanks, apparently needed for water cooled brakes. Ferrari had a distraught year with appalling accidents to both Villeneuve and Pironi.

BRABHAM
Parmalat Racing Team: Piquet, Patrese

TYRRELL
Team Tyrrell: Alboreto, Borgudd, Henton

WILLIAMS
TAG Williams Team: Reutemann, Andretti, Daly, Rosberg

McLAREN
Marlboro McLaren International: Watson, Lauda

ATS
Team ATS: Winkelhock, Salazar

LOTUS
John Player Team Lotus: de Angelis, Mansell, (Moreno), Lees

ENSIGN
Ensign Racing: Guerrero

RENAULT
Equipe Renault Elf: Prost, Arnoux

MARCH
Rothmans March Grand Prix Team: Mass, Keegan, Boesel
LBT Team March: (de Villota)

FITTIPALDI
Fittipaldi Automotive: Serra

ALFA ROMEO
Marlboro Team Alfa Romeo: de Cesaris, Giacomelli

LIGIER
Equipe Talbot Gitanes: Cheever, Laffite

FERRARI
Scuderia Ferrari SpA SEFAC: Villeneuve, Tambay, Pironi, Andretti

ARROWS
Arrows Racing Team: Henton, Surer, Baldi

OSELLA
Osella Squadra Corse: Jarier, Paletti

THEODORE
Theodore Racing Team: Daly, Lammers, Lees, Byrne

TOLEMAN
Candy Toleman Motorsport: Warwick, Fabi
Toleman Group Motorsport from RSM GP

23 Jan 1982		SOUTH AFRICA: Kyalami						(Round 1)		(Race 358)
77 laps x 4.104 km, 2.550 miles = 316.008 km, 196.358 miles										

Pos	No	Driver	Car	Model	Engine		Laps	Time/Reason for Retirement	Grid Pos	Row
1	15	A Prost	Renault	RE30B	Renault	V6t	77	1h 32m 08.401s	5	3
2	5	C Reutemann	Williams	FW07C	Ford Cosworth	V8	77	1h 32m 23.347s	8	4
3	16	R Arnoux	Renault	RE30B	Renault	V6t	77	1h 32m 36.301s	1	1
4	8	N Lauda	McLaren	MP4	Ford Cosworth	V8	77	1h 32m 40.514s	13	7
5	6	K Rosberg	Williams	FW07C	Ford Cosworth	V8	77	1h 32m 54.540s	7	4
6	7	J Watson	McLaren	MP4B	Ford Cosworth	V8	77	1h 32m 59.394s	9	5
7	3	M Alboreto	Tyrrell	011	Ford Cosworth	V8	76		10	5
8	11	E de Angelis	Lotus	87B	Ford Cosworth	V8	76		15	8
9	10	E Salazar	ATS	D5	Ford Cosworth	V8	75		12	6
10	9	M Winkelhock	ATS	D5	Ford Cosworth	V8	75		20	10
11	23	B Giacomelli	Alfa Romeo	179D	Alfa Romeo	V12	74		19	10
12	17	J Mass	March	821	Ford Cosworth	V8	74		22	11
13	22	A de Cesaris	Alfa Romeo	179D	Alfa Romeo	V12	73		16	8
14	33	D Daly	Theodore	TY01	Ford Cosworth	V8	73		24	12
15	18	R Boesel	March	821	Ford Cosworth	V8	72		21	11
16	4	S Borgudd	Tyrrell	011	Ford Cosworth	V8	72		23	12
17	20	C Serra	Fittipaldi	F8D	Ford Cosworth	V8	72		25	13
18	28	D Pironi	Ferrari	126C2	Ferrari	V6t	71		6	3
r	26	J Laffite	Talbot Ligier	JS17	Matra	V12	54	fuel vaporisation	11	6
r	35	D Warwick	Toleman	TG181C	Hart	4t	44	accident	14	7
r	2	R Patrese	Brabham	BT50	BMW	4t	18	oil loss / turbo bearing	4	2
r	25	E Cheever	Talbot Ligier	JS17	Matra	V12	11	fuel vaporisation	17	9
r	27	G Villeneuve	Ferrari	126C2	Ferrari	V6t	6	turbo	3	2
r	1	N Piquet	Brabham	BT50	BMW	4t	3	accident	2	1
r	12	N Mansell	Lotus	87B	Ford Cosworth	V8	0	electrics	18	9
r	31	J-P Jarier	Osella	FA1C	Ford Cosworth	V8	0	accident	26	13
nq	30	M Baldi	Arrows	A4	Ford Cosworth	V8				
nq	32	R Paletti	Osella	FA1C	Ford Cosworth	V8				
nq	29	B Henton	Arrows	A4	Ford Cosworth	V8				
nq	36	T Fabi	Toleman	TG181B	Hart	4t				

Winning speed 205.779 km/h, 127.865 mph
Pole Position speed 222.670 km/h, 138.361 mph (R Arnoux, 1 min: 6.351 sec)
Fastest Lap speed 216.386 km/h, 134.456 mph (A Prost, 1 min: 8.278 sec on lap 49)
Lap Leaders R Arnoux 1-13,41-67 (40); A Prost 14-40,68-77 (37).

63 laps x 5.031 km, 3.126 miles = 316.953 km, 196.945 miles

Pos	No	Driver	Car	Model	Engine		Laps	Time/Reason for Retirement	Grid Pos	Row
dq	1	N Piquet	Brabham	BT49D	Ford Cosworth	V8	63	car under weight	7	4
dq	6	K Rosberg	Williams	FW07C	Ford Cosworth	V8	63	car under weight	3	2
1	15	A Prost	Renault	RE30B	Renault	V6t	63	1h 44m 33.134s	1	1
2	7	J Watson	McLaren	MP4B	Ford Cosworth	V8	63	1h 44m 36.124s	12	6
3	12	N Mansell	Lotus	91	Ford Cosworth	V8	63	1h 45m 09.993s	14	7
4	3	M Alboreto	Tyrrell	011	Ford Cosworth	V8	63	1h 45m 23.895s	13	7
5	9	M Winkelhock	ATS	D5	Ford Cosworth	V8	62		15	8
6	28	D Pironi	Ferrari	126C2	Ferrari	V6t	62		8	4
7	4	S Borgudd	Tyrrell	011	Ford Cosworth	V8	61		21	11
8	17	J Mass	March	821	Ford Cosworth	V8	61		22	11
9	31	J-P Jarier	Osella	FA1C	Ford Cosworth	V8	60		23	12
10	30	M Baldi	Arrows	A4	Ford Cosworth	V8	57		19	10
r	10	E Salazar	ATS	D5	Ford Cosworth	V8	37	engine	18	9
r	20	C Serra	Fittipaldi	F8D	Ford Cosworth	V8	36	accident	25	13
r	2	R Patrese	Brabham	BT49D	Ford Cosworth	V8	34	driver exhausted	9	5
r	27	G Villeneuve	Ferrari	126C2	Ferrari	V6t	29	accident	2	1
r	8	N Lauda	McLaren	MP4B	Ford Cosworth	V8	21	accident	5	3
r	16	R Arnoux	Renault	RE30B	Renault	V6t	21	accident	4	2
r	5	C Reutemann	Williams	FW07C	Ford Cosworth	V8	21	accident	6	3
r	11	E de Angelis	Lotus	91	Ford Cosworth	V8	21	accident	11	6
r	25	E Cheever	Talbot Ligier	JS17	Matra	V12	19	water leak	26	13
r	23	B Giacomelli	Alfa Romeo	182	Alfa Romeo	V12	16	engine	16	8
r	26	J Laffite	Talbot Ligier	JS17	Matra	V12	15	misfire / skirt	24	12
r	22	A de Cesaris	Alfa Romeo	182	Alfa Romeo	V12	14	undertray	10	5
r	33	D Daly	Theodore	TY02	Ford Cosworth	V8	12	accident / nose wing / spin	20	10
r	18	R Boesel	March	821	Ford Cosworth	V8	11	rear suspension / accident	17	9
nq	36	T Fabi	Toleman	TG181B	Hart	4t				
nq	14	R Guerrero	Ensign	N181	Ford Cosworth	V8				
nq	29	B Henton	Arrows	A4	Ford Cosworth	V8				
nq	35	D Warwick	Toleman	TG181C	Hart	4t				
npq	32	R Paletti	Osella	FA1C	Ford Cosworth	V8				

Winning speed 181.892 km/h, 113.022 mph
Pole Position speed 203.941 km/h, 126.723 mph (A Prost, 1 min:28.808 sec)
Fastest Lap speed 186.687 km/h, 116.002 mph (A Prost, 1 min:37.016 sec on lap 36)
Lap Leaders G Villeneuve 1-29 (29); N Piquet 30-63 (34).

N Piquet finished 1st in 1m 43m 53.760s (183.041 km/h, 113.736 mph), and recorded the fastest lap in 1m 36.582s (187.526 km/h, 116.523 mph).
K Rosberg finished 2nd in 1h 44m 05.737s.

75.5 laps x 3.428 km, 2.130 miles = 258.807 km, 160.815 miles

Pos	No	Driver	Car	Model	Engine		Laps	Time/Reason for Retirement	Grid Pos	Row
1	8	N Lauda	McLaren	MP4B	Ford Cosworth	V8	75	1h 58m 25.318s	2	1
2	6	K Rosberg	Williams	FW07C	Ford Cosworth	V8	75	1h 58m 39.978s	8	4
dq	27	G Villeneuve	Ferrari	126C2	Ferrari	V6t	75	irregular wing	7	4
3	2	R Patrese	Brabham	BT49C	Ford Cosworth	V8	75	1h 59m 44.461s	18	9
4	3	M Alboreto	Tyrrell	011	Ford Cosworth	V8	75	1h 59m 46.265s	12	6
5	11	E de Angelis	Lotus	91	Ford Cosworth	V8	74		16	8
6	7	J Watson	McLaren	MP4B	Ford Cosworth	V8	74		11	6
7	12	N Mansell	Lotus	91	Ford Cosworth	V8	73		17	9
8	17	J Mass	March	821	Ford Cosworth	V8	73		21	11
9	18	R Boesel	March	821	Ford Cosworth	V8	70		23	12
10	4	S Borgudd	Tyrrell	011	Ford Cosworth	V8	68		24	12
r	25	E Cheever	Talbot Ligier	JS17B	Matra	V12	58	gearbox	13	7
r	22	A de Cesaris	Alfa Romeo	182	Alfa Romeo	V12	33	accident	1	1
r	29	B Henton	Arrows	A4	Ford Cosworth	V8	32	accident	20	10
r	14	R Guerrero	Ensign	N181	Ford Cosworth	V8	27	accident	19	10
r	26	J Laffite	Talbot Ligier	JS17B	Matra	V12	26	spin	15	8
r	31	J-P Jarier	Osella	FA1C	Ford Cosworth	V8	26	gearbox	10	5
r	1	N Piquet	Brabham	BT49D	Ford Cosworth	V8	25	accident	6	3
r	33	D Daly	Theodore	TY02	Ford Cosworth	V8	23	accident	22	11
r	5	M Andretti	Williams	FW07C	Ford Cosworth	V8	18	accident / rear suspension	14	7
r	15	A Prost	Renault	RE30B	Renault	V6t	10	brakes / accident	4	2
r	28	D Pironi	Ferrari	126C2	Ferrari	V6t	6	accident	9	5
r	16	R Arnoux	Renault	RE30B	Renault	V6t	5	accident	3	2
r	23	B Giacomelli	Alfa Romeo	182	Alfa Romeo	V12	5	accident	5	3
r	10	E Salazar	ATS	D5	Ford Cosworth	V8	3	accident	26	13
r	9	M Winkelhock	ATS	D5	Ford Cosworth	V8	1	accident	25	13
nq	36	T Fabi	Toleman	TG181C	Hart	4t				
nq	32	R Paletti	Osella	FA1C	Ford Cosworth	V8				
nq	20	C Serra	Fittipaldi	F8D	Ford Cosworth	V8				
nq	30	M Baldi	Arrows	A4	Ford Cosworth	V8				
npq	35	D Warwick	Toleman	TG181C	Hart	4t				

Winning speed 131.128 km/h, 81.479 mph
Pole Position speed 141.331 km/h, 87.819 mph (A de Cesaris, 1 min:27.316 sec)
Fastest Lap speed 135.862 km/h, 84.421 mph (N Lauda, 1 min:30.831 sec on lap 12)
Lap Leaders A de Cesaris 1-14 (14.5); N Lauda 15-75 (61).

The start and finish lines were at different positions on the circuit. The fraction of a lap is credited to the first lap leader. G Villeneuve finished 3rd in 1h 59m 29.606s.

60 laps x 5.040 km, 3.132 miles = 302.400 km, 187.903 miles

Pos	No	Driver	Car	Model	Engine		Laps	Time/Reason for Retirement	Grid Pos	Row
1	28	D Pironi	Ferrari	126C2	Ferrari	V6t	60	1h 36m 38.887s	4	2
2	27	G Villeneuve	Ferrari	126C2	Ferrari	V6t	60	1h 36m 39.253s	3	2
3	3	M Alboreto	Tyrrell	011	Ford Cosworth	V8	60	1h 37m 46.571s	5	3
4	31	J-P Jarier	Osella	FA1C	Ford Cosworth	V8	59		9	5
5	10	E Salazar	ATS	D5	Ford Cosworth	V8	57		14	7
dq	9	M Winkelhock	ATS	D5	Ford Cosworth	V8	54	car under weight	12	6
nc	36	T Fabi	Toleman	TG181C	Hart	4t	52		10	5
r	16	R Arnoux	Renault	RE30B	Renault	V6t	44	engine	1	1
r	23	B Giacomelli	Alfa Romeo	182	Alfa Romeo	V12	24	engine	6	3
r	32	R Paletti	Osella	FA1C	Ford Cosworth	V8	7	rear suspension	13	7
r	15	A Prost	Renault	RE30B	Renault	V6t	6	engine	2	1
r	22	A de Cesaris	Alfa Romeo	182	Alfa Romeo	V12	4	fuel pump	7	4
r	4	B Henton	Tyrrell	011	Ford Cosworth	V8	0	clutch	11	6
ns	35	D Warwick	Toleman	TG181C	Hart	4t		electrics on parade lap	8	4

Winning speed 187.733 km/h, 116.652 mph
Pole Position speed 202.128 km/h, 125.596 mph (R Arnoux, 1 min:29.765 sec)
Fastest Lap speed 190.917 km/h, 118.630 mph (D Pironi, 1 min:35.036 sec on lap 44)
Lap Leaders R Arnoux 1-26,31-43 (39); G Villeneuve 27-30,44-45,49-52,59 (11); D Pironi 46-48,53-58,60 (10).

70 laps x 4.262 km, 2.648 miles = 298.340 km, 185.380 miles

Pos	No	Driver	Car	Model	Engine		Laps	Time/Reason for Retirement	Grid Pos	Row
1	7	J Watson	McLaren	MP4B	Ford Cosworth	V8	70	1h 35m 41.995s	10	5
2	6	K Rosberg	Williams	FW08	Ford Cosworth	V8	70	1h 35m 49.263s	3	2
dq	8	N Lauda	McLaren	MP4B	Ford Cosworth	V8	70	car under weight	4	2
3	25	E Cheever	Talbot Ligier	JS17B	Matra	V12	69		14	7
4	11	E de Angelis	Lotus	91	Ford Cosworth	V8	68		11	6
5	1	N Piquet	Brabham	BT50	BMW	4t	67		8	4
6	20	C Serra	Fittipaldi	F8D	Ford Cosworth	V8	67		23	12
7	29	M Surer	Arrows	A4	Ford Cosworth	V8	66		22	11
8	18	R Boesel	March	821	Ford Cosworth	V8	66		24	12
9	26	J Laffite	Talbot Ligier	JS17B	Matra	V12	66		17	9
r	5	D Daly	Williams	FW08	Ford Cosworth	V8	60	accident	13	7
r	17	J Mass	March	821	Ford Cosworth	V8	60	engine	25	13
r	15	A Prost	Renault	RE30B	Renault	V6t	59	spin	1	1
r	2	R Patrese	Brabham	BT50	BMW	4t	52	accident	9	5
r	30	M Baldi	Arrows	A4	Ford Cosworth	V8	51	throttle / spin	26	13
r	31	J-P Jarier	Osella	FA1C	Ford Cosworth	V8	37	rear aerofoil	16	8
r	22	A de Cesaris	Alfa Romeo	182	Alfa Romeo	V12	34	gear linkage	6	3
r	4	B Henton	Tyrrell	011	Ford Cosworth	V8	33	engine	20	10
r	3	M Alboreto	Tyrrell	011	Ford Cosworth	V8	29	engine	5	3
r	35	D Warwick	Toleman	TG181C	Hart	4t	29	driveshaft	19	10
r	36	T Fabi	Toleman	TG181C	Hart	4t	13	brakes	21	11
r	12	N Mansell	Lotus	91	Ford Cosworth	V8	9	clutch	7	4
r	16	R Arnoux	Renault	RE30B	Renault	V6t	7	turbo compressor	2	1
r	9	M Winkelhock	ATS	D5	Ford Cosworth	V8	0	clutch	12	6
r	10	E Salazar	ATS	D5	Ford Cosworth	V8	0	accident	18	9
r	23	B Giacomelli	Alfa Romeo	182	Alfa Romeo	V12	0	accident	15	8
ns	28	D Pironi	Ferrari	126C2	Ferrari	V6t		withdrew after Villeneuve accident		
ns	27	G Villeneuve	Ferrari	126C2	Ferrari	V6t		fatal accident		
nq	14	R Guerrero	Ensign	N181	Ford Cosworth	V8				
nq	33	J Lammers	Theodore	TY02	Ford Cosworth	V8				
npq	32	R Paletti	Osella	FA1C	Ford Cosworth	V8				
npq	19	E de Villota	March	821	Ford Cosworth	V8				

Winning speed 187.047 km/h, 116.226 mph
Pole Position speed 202.682 km/h, 125.941 mph (A Prost, 1 min:15.701 sec)
Fastest Lap speed 191.278 km/h, 118.855 mph (J Watson, 1 min:20.214 sec on lap 67)
Lap Leaders R Arnoux 1-4 (4); K Rosberg 5-68 (64); J Watson 69-70 (2).

N Lauda finished 3rd in 1h 36m 50.132s.

23 May 1982   MONACO: Monte-Carlo   (Round 6)   (Race 363)

76 laps x 3.312 km, 2.058 miles = 251.712 km, 156.407 miles

Pos	No	Driver	Car	Model	Engine		Laps	Time/Reason for Retirement	Grid Pos	Row
1	2	R Patrese	Brabham	BT49D	Ford Cosworth	V8	76	1h 54m 11.259s	2	1
2r	28	D Pironi	Ferrari	126C2	Ferrari	V6t	75	electrics	5	3
3r	22	A de Cesaris	Alfa Romeo	182	Alfa Romeo	V12	75	out of fuel	7	4
4	12	N Mansell	Lotus	91	Ford Cosworth	V8	75		11	6
5	11	E de Angelis	Lotus	91	Ford Cosworth	V8	75		15	8
6r	5	D Daly	Williams	FW08	Ford Cosworth	V8	74	accident / gearbox	8	4
7r	15	A Prost	Renault	RE30B	Renault	V6t	73	accident	4	2
8	4	B Henton	Tyrrell	011	Ford Cosworth	V8	72		17	9
9	29	M Surer	Arrows	A4	Ford Cosworth	V8	70		19	10
10r	3	M Alboreto	Tyrrell	011	Ford Cosworth	V8	69	front suspension	9	5
r	6	K Rosberg	Williams	FW08	Ford Cosworth	V8	65	front suspension	6	3
r	8	N Lauda	McLaren	MP4B	Ford Cosworth	V8	57	engine	12	6
r	1	N Piquet	Brabham	BT50	BMW	4t	50	gearbox	13	7
r	7	J Watson	McLaren	MP4B	Ford Cosworth	V8	36	oil leak / battery	10	5
r	9	M Winkelhock	ATS	D5	Ford Cosworth	V8	31	differential	14	7
r	26	J Laffite	Talbot Ligier	JS19	Matra	V12	30	handling	18	9
r	25	E Cheever	Talbot Ligier	JS19	Matra	V12	28	engine	16	8
r	10	E Salazar	ATS	D5	Ford Cosworth	V8	22	fire extinguisher	20	10
r	16	R Arnoux	Renault	RE30B	Renault	V6t	14	spin	1	1
r	23	B Giacomelli	Alfa Romeo	182	Alfa Romeo	V12	5	transmission	3	2
nq	30	M Baldi	Arrows	A4	Ford Cosworth	V8				
nq	33	J Lammers	Theodore	TY02	Ford Cosworth	V8				
nq	17	J Mass	March	821	Ford Cosworth	V8				
nq	35	D Warwick	Toleman	TG181C	Hart	4t				
nq	31	J-P Jarier	Osella	FA1C	Ford Cosworth	V8				
nq	14	R Guerrero	Ensign	N181	Ford Cosworth	V8				
npq	36	T Fabi	Toleman	TG181C	Hart	4t				
npq	32	R Paletti	Osella	FA1C	Ford Cosworth	V8				
npq	18	R Boesel	March	821	Ford Cosworth	V8				
npq	20	C Serra	Fittipaldi	F8D	Ford Cosworth	V8				
npq	19	E de Villota	March	821	Ford Cosworth	V8				

Winning speed 132.262 km/h, 82.184 mph
Pole Position speed 143.168 km/h, 88.961 mph (R Arnoux, 1 min:23.281 sec)
Fastest Lap speed 138.074 km/h, 85.795 mph (R Patrese, 1 min:26.354 sec on lap 69)
Lap Leaders R Arnoux 1-14 (14); A Prost 15-73 (59); R Patrese 74,76 (2); D Pironi 75 (1).

6 Jun 1982   USA: Detroit   (Round 7)   (Race 364)

62 laps x 4.012 km, 2.493 miles = 248.750 km, 154.566 miles

Pos	No	Driver	Car	Model	Engine		Laps	Time/Reason for Retirement	Grid Pos	Row
1	7	J Watson	McLaren	MP4B	Ford Cosworth	V8	62	1h 58m 41.043s	17	9
2	25	E Cheever	Talbot Ligier	JS17B	Matra	V12	62	1h 58m 56.769s	9	5
3	28	D Pironi	Ferrari	126C2	Ferrari	V6t	62	1h 59m 09.120s	4	2
4	6	K Rosberg	Williams	FW08	Ford Cosworth	V8	62	1h 59m 53.019s	3	2
5	5	D Daly	Williams	FW08	Ford Cosworth	V8	62	2h 00m 04.800s	12	6
6	26	J Laffite	Talbot Ligier	JS17B	Matra	V12	61		13	7
7	17	J Mass	March	821	Ford Cosworth	V8	61		18	9
8	29	M Surer	Arrows	A4	Ford Cosworth	V8	61		19	10
9	4	B Henton	Tyrrell	011	Ford Cosworth	V8	60		20	10
10	16	R Arnoux	Renault	RE30B	Renault	V6t	59		15	8
11	20	C Serra	Fittipaldi	F8D	Ford Cosworth	V8	59		26	13
nc	15	A Prost	Renault	RE30B	Renault	V6t	54		1	1
r	12	N Mansell	Lotus	91	Ford Cosworth	V8	44	engine	7	4
r	8	N Lauda	McLaren	MP4B	Ford Cosworth	V8	40	accident	10	5
r	3	M Alboreto	Tyrrell	011	Ford Cosworth	V8	40	accident	16	8
r	23	B Giacomelli	Alfa Romeo	182	Alfa Romeo	V12	30	accident	6	3
r	11	E de Angelis	Lotus	91	Ford Cosworth	V8	17	gearbox	8	4
r	10	E Salazar	ATS	D5	Ford Cosworth	V8	13	accident	25	13
r	14	R Guerrero	Ensign	N181	Ford Cosworth	V8	6	accident	11	6
r	2	R Patrese	Brabham	BT49D	Ford Cosworth	V8	6	accident / fire	14	7
r	22	A de Cesaris	Alfa Romeo	182	Alfa Romeo	V12	2	transmission	2	1
r	31	J-P Jarier	Osella	FA1C	Ford Cosworth	V8	2	ignition	22	11
r	9	M Winkelhock	ATS	D5	Ford Cosworth	V8	1	accident	5	3
r	18	R Boesel	March	821	Ford Cosworth	V8	1	accident	21	11
r	30	M Baldi	Arrows	A4	Ford Cosworth	V8	0	accident	24	12
ns	32	R Paletti	Osella	FA1C	Ford Cosworth	V8		accident	23	12
nq	19	E de Villota	March	821	Ford Cosworth	V8				
nq	1	N Piquet	Brabham	BT50	BMW	4t				
nq	33	J Lammers	Theodore	TY02	Ford Cosworth	V8		accident / injury		

Winning speed 125.754 km/h, 78.140 mph
Pole Position speed 133.075 km/h, 82.689 mph (A Prost, 1 min:48.537 sec)
Fastest Lap speed 130.784 km/h, 81.266 mph (A Prost, 1 min:50.438 sec on lap 45)
Lap Leaders A Prost 1-22 (22); K Rosberg 23-36 (14); J Watson 37-62 (26).

Scheduled for 70 laps but interrupted after 6 laps, because of an accident. Restart scheduled for a further 64 laps, but stopped at 2 hours, with results being an aggregate of 6 and 56 laps. Lap leaders are given 'on the road'.

70 laps x 4.410 km, 2.740 miles = 308.700 km, 191.817 miles

Pos	No	Driver	Car	Model	Engine		Laps	Time/Reason for Retirement	Grid Pos	Row
1	1	N Piquet	Brabham	BT50	BMW	4t	70	1h 46m 39.577s	4	2
2	2	R Patrese	Brabham	BT49D	Ford Cosworth	V8	70	1h 46m 53.376s	8	4
3	7	J Watson	McLaren	MP4B	Ford Cosworth	V8	70	1h 47m 41.413s	6	3
4	11	E de Angelis	Lotus	91	Ford Cosworth	V8	69		10	5
5	29	M Surer	Arrows	A4	Ford Cosworth	V8	69		16	8
6r	22	A de Cesaris	Alfa Romeo	182	Alfa Romeo	V12	68	out of fuel	9	5
7r	5	D Daly	Williams	FW08	Ford Cosworth	V8	68	out of fuel	13	7
8	30	M Baldi	Arrows	A4	Ford Cosworth	V8	68		17	9
9	28	D Pironi	Ferrari	126C2	Ferrari	V6t	67		1	1
10r	25	E Cheever	Talbot Ligier	JS17B	Matra	V12	66	out of fuel	12	6
11	17	J Mass	March	821	Ford Cosworth	V8	66		22	11
nc	4	B Henton	Tyrrell	011	Ford Cosworth	V8	59		26	13
r	6	K Rosberg	Williams	FW08	Ford Cosworth	V8	52	gearbox	7	4
r	18	R Boesel	March	821	Ford Cosworth	V8	47	engine	21	11
r	3	M Alboreto	Tyrrell	011	Ford Cosworth	V8	41	gearbox / fuel pressure	15	8
r	15	A Prost	Renault	RE30B	Renault	V6t	30	engine	3	2
r	16	R Arnoux	Renault	RE30B	Renault	V6t	28	spin	2	1
r	10	E Salazar	ATS	D5	Ford Cosworth	V8	20	transmission	24	12
r	8	N Lauda	McLaren	MP4B	Ford Cosworth	V8	17	clutch	11	6
r	26	J Laffite	Talbot Ligier	JS17B	Matra	V12	8	handling	19	10
r	14	R Guerrero	Ensign	N181	Ford Cosworth	V8	2	clutch	20	10
r	23	B Giacomelli	Alfa Romeo	182	Alfa Romeo	V12	1	accident	5	3
r	12	N Mansell	Lotus	91	Ford Cosworth	V8	1	accident / injury	14	7
r	33	G Lees	Theodore	TY02	Ford Cosworth	V8	0	accident *	25	13
r	31	J-P Jarier	Osella	FA1C	Ford Cosworth	V8	0	withdrew after Paletti accident*	18	9
r	32	R Paletti	Osella	FA1C	Ford Cosworth	V8	0	fatal accident on grid *	23	12
nq	9	M Winkelhock	ATS	D5	Ford Cosworth	V8				
nq	19	E de Villota	March	821	Ford Cosworth	V8				
nq	20	C Serra	Fittipaldi	F8D	Ford Cosworth	V8				

Winning speed 173.655 km/h, 107.904 mph
Pole Position speed 181.421 km/h, 112.730 mph (D Pironi, 1 min:27.509 sec)
Fastest Lap speed 179.749 km/h, 111.691 mph (D Pironi, 1 min:28.323 sec on lap 66)
Lap Leaders D Pironi 1 (1); R Arnoux 2-8 (7); N Piquet 9-70 (62).

Interrupted after first lap accident. Restarted for original distance.   * *Retired after first start.*

72 laps x 4.252 km, 2.642 miles = 306.144 km, 190.229 miles

Pos	No	Driver	Car	Model	Engine		Laps	Time/Reason for Retirement	Grid Pos	Row
1	28	D Pironi	Ferrari	126C2	Ferrari	V6t	72	1h 38m 03.254s	4	2
2	1	N Piquet	Brabham	BT50	BMW	4t	72	1h 38m 24.903s	3	2
3	6	K Rosberg	Williams	FW08	Ford Cosworth	V8	72	1h 38m 25.619s	7	4
4	8	N Lauda	McLaren	MP4B	Ford Cosworth	V8	72	1h 39m 26.974s	5	3
5	5	D Daly	Williams	FW08	Ford Cosworth	V8	71		12	6
6	30	M Baldi	Arrows	A4	Ford Cosworth	V8	71		16	8
7	3	M Alboreto	Tyrrell	011	Ford Cosworth	V8	71		14	7
8	27	P Tambay	Ferrari	126C2	Ferrari	V6t	71		6	3
9	7	J Watson	McLaren	MP4B	Ford Cosworth	V8	71		11	6
10	29	M Surer	Arrows	A4	Ford Cosworth	V8	71		17	9
11	23	B Giacomelli	Alfa Romeo	182	Alfa Romeo	V12	70		8	4
12	9	M Winkelhock	ATS	D5	Ford Cosworth	V8	70		18	9
13	10	E Salazar	ATS	D5	Ford Cosworth	V8	70		25	13
14	31	J-P Jarier	Osella	FA1C	Ford Cosworth	V8	69		23	12
15	2	R Patrese	Brabham	BT50	BMW	4t	69		10	5
r	17	J Mass	March	821	Ford Cosworth	V8	60	engine	24	12
r	33	J Lammers	Theodore	TY02	Ford Cosworth	V8	41	engine	26	13
r	11	E de Angelis	Lotus	91	Ford Cosworth	V8	40	handling	15	8
r	22	A de Cesaris	Alfa Romeo	182	Alfa Romeo	V12	35	electrics	9	5
r	15	A Prost	Renault	RE30B	Renault	V6t	33	engine	2	1
r	16	R Arnoux	Renault	RE30B	Renault	V6t	21	front suspension / accident	1	1
r	4	B Henton	Tyrrell	011	Ford Cosworth	V8	21	throttle linkage	20	10
r	18	R Boesel	March	821	Ford Cosworth	V8	21	engine	22	11
r	20	C Serra	Fittipaldi	F8D	Ford Cosworth	V8	18	fuel pump	19	10
r	35	D Warwick	Toleman	TG181C	Hart	4t	15	oil union leak	13	7
r	26	J Laffite	Talbot Ligier	JS19	Matra	V12	4	handling	21	11
nq	14	R Guerrero	Ensign	N181	Ford Cosworth	V8				
nq	36	T Fabi	Toleman	TG181C	Hart	4t				
nq	25	E Cheever	Talbot Ligier	JS19	Matra	V12				
nq	12	R Moreno	Lotus	91	Ford Cosworth	V8				
npq	19	E de Villota	March	821	Ford Cosworth	V8				

Winning speed 187.331 km/h, 116.402 mph
Pole Position speed 206.205 km/h, 128.130 mph (R Arnoux, 1 min:14.233 sec)
Fastest Lap speed 191.868 km/h, 119.221 mph (D Warwick, 1 min:19.780 sec on lap 13)
Lap Leaders A Prost 1-4 (4); D Pironi 5-72 (68).

18 Jul 1982 **BRITAIN: Brands Hatch** (Round 10) (Race 367)

76 laps x 4.207 km, 2.614 miles = 319.719 km, 198.664 miles

Pos	No	Driver	Car	Model	Engine		Laps	Time/Reason for Retirement	Grid Pos	Row
1	8	N Lauda	McLaren	MP4B	Ford Cosworth	V8	76	1h 35m 33.812s	5	3
2	28	D Pironi	Ferrari	126C2	Ferrari	V6t	76	1h 35m 59.538s	4	2
3	27	P Tambay	Ferrari	126C2	Ferrari	V6t	76	1h 36m 12.248s	13	7
4	11	E de Angelis	Lotus	91	Ford Cosworth	V8	76	1h 36m 15.054s	7	4
5	5	D Daly	Williams	FW08	Ford Cosworth	V8	76	1h 36m 15.242s	10	5
6	15	A Prost	Renault	RE30B	Renault	V6t	76	1h 36m 15.448s	8	4
7	23	B Giacomelli	Alfa Romeo	182	Alfa Romeo	V12	75		14	7
8	4	B Henton	Tyrrell	011	Ford Cosworth	V8	75		17	9
9	30	M Baldi	Arrows	A4	Ford Cosworth	V8	74		26	13
10	17	J Mass	March	821	Ford Cosworth	V8	73		25	13
r	22	A de Cesaris	Alfa Romeo	182	Alfa Romeo	V12	66	electrics	11	6
r	25	E Cheever	Talbot Ligier	JS19	Matra	V12	60	engine	24	12
r	29	M Surer	Arrows	A4	Ford Cosworth	V8	59	engine	22	11
r	6	K Rosberg	Williams	FW08	Ford Cosworth	V8	50	fuel pressure	1	1
nc	3	M Alboreto	Tyrrell	011	Ford Cosworth	V8	44		9	5
r	26	J Laffite	Talbot Ligier	JS19	Matra	V12	41	gearbox	20	10
r	35	D Warwick	Toleman	TG181C	Hart	4t	40	cv joint	16	8
r	12	N Mansell	Lotus	91	Ford Cosworth	V8	29	broken skirt / driver discomfort	23	12
r	1	N Piquet	Brabham	BT50	BMW	4t	9	fuel injection pump belt	3	2
r	14	R Guerrero	Ensign	N181	Ford Cosworth	V8	3	accident / oil line / engine	19	10
r	31	J-P Jarier	Osella	FA1C	Ford Cosworth	V8	2	accident	18	9
r	20	C Serra	Fittipaldi	F8D	Ford Cosworth	V8	2	accident / fire	21	11
r	7	J Watson	McLaren	MP4B	Ford Cosworth	V8	2	spin	12	6
r	36	T Fabi	Toleman	TG181C	Hart	4t	0	accident	15	8
r	16	R Arnoux	Renault	RE30B	Renault	V6t	0	accident	6	3
r	2	R Patrese	Brabham	BT50	BMW	4t	0	stalled on grid / accident	2	1
nq	9	M Winkelhock	ATS	D5	Ford Cosworth	V8				
nq	33	J Lammers	Theodore	TY02	Ford Cosworth	V8				
nq	10	E Salazar	ATS	D5	Ford Cosworth	V8				
nq	18	R Boesel	March	821	Ford Cosworth	V8				

Winning speed 200.737 km/h, 124.732 mph
Pole Position speed 217.782 km/h, 135.324 mph (K Rosberg, 1 min: 9.540 sec)
Fastest Lap speed 207.380 km/h, 128.860 mph (B Henton, 1 min:13.028 sec on lap 63)
Lap Leaders N Piquet 1-9 (9); N Lauda 10-76 (67).

25 Jul 1982 **FRANCE: Paul Ricard** (Round 11) (Race 368)

54 laps x 5.810 km, 3.610 miles = 313.740 km, 194.949 miles

Pos	No	Driver	Car	Model	Engine		Laps	Time/Reason for Retirement	Grid Pos	Row
1	16	R Arnoux	Renault	RE30B	Renault	V6t	54	1h 33m 33.217s	1	1
2	15	A Prost	Renault	RE30B	Renault	V6t	54	1h 33m 50.525s	2	1
3	28	D Pironi	Ferrari	126C2	Ferrari	V6t	54	1h 34m 15.345s	3	2
4	27	P Tambay	Ferrari	126C2	Ferrari	V6t	54	1h 34m 49.458s	5	3
5	6	K Rosberg	Williams	FW08	Ford Cosworth	V8	54	1h 35m 04.211s	10	5
6	3	M Alboreto	Tyrrell	011	Ford Cosworth	V8	54	1h 35m 05.556s	15	8
7	5	D Daly	Williams	FW08	Ford Cosworth	V8	53		11	6
8	8	N Lauda	McLaren	MP4B	Ford Cosworth	V8	53		9	5
9	23	B Giacomelli	Alfa Romeo	182	Alfa Romeo	V12	53		8	4
10	4	B Henton	Tyrrell	011	Ford Cosworth	V8	53		23	12
11	9	M Winkelhock	ATS	D5	Ford Cosworth	V8	52		18	9
12	12	G Lees	Lotus	91	Ford Cosworth	V8	52		24	12
13	29	M Surer	Arrows	A4	Ford Cosworth	V8	52		20	10
14	26	J Laffite	Talbot Ligier	JS19	Matra	V12	51		16	8
15	35	D Warwick	Toleman	TG181C	Hart	4t	50		14	7
16	25	E Cheever	Talbot Ligier	JS19	Matra	V12	49		19	10
r	22	A de Cesaris	Alfa Romeo	182	Alfa Romeo	V12	25	front tyre / accident	7	4
r	1	N Piquet	Brabham	BT50	BMW	4t	23	engine	6	3
r	11	E de Angelis	Lotus	91	Ford Cosworth	V8	17	fuel pressure	13	7
r	7	J Watson	McLaren	MP4B	Ford Cosworth	V8	13	battery lead	12	6
r	17	J Mass	March	821	Ford Cosworth	V8	10	accident	26	13
r	30	M Baldi	Arrows	A4	Ford Cosworth	V8	10	accident	25	13
r	2	R Patrese	Brabham	BT50	BMW	4t	8	engine / fire	4	2
r	10	E Salazar	ATS	D5	Ford Cosworth	V8	2	accident	22	11
r	36	T Fabi	Toleman	TG181C	Hart	4t	0	oil pump drive	21	11
r	31	J-P Jarier	Osella	FA1C	Ford Cosworth	V8	0	driveshaft	17	9
nq	33	J Lammers	Theodore	TY02	Ford Cosworth	V8				
nq	14	R Guerrero	Ensign	N181	Ford Cosworth	V8				
nq	20	C Serra	Fittipaldi	F9	Ford Cosworth	V8				
nq	18	R Boesel	March	821	Ford Cosworth	V8				

Winning speed 201.215 km/h, 125.029 mph
Pole Position speed 221.554 km/h, 137.667 mph (R Arnoux, 1 min:34.406 sec)
Fastest Lap speed 209.003 km/h, 129.869 mph (R Patrese, 1 min:40.075 sec on lap 4)
Lap Leaders R Arnoux 1-2,24-54 (33); R Patrese 3-7 (5); N Piquet 8-23 (16).

8 Aug 1982		GERMANY: Hockenheim						(Round 12)	(Race 369)	

45 laps x 6.797 km, 4.223 miles = 305.865 km, 190.056 miles

Pos	No	Driver	Car	Model	Engine		Laps	Time/Reason for Retirement	Grid Pos	Row
1	27	P Tambay	Ferrari	126C2	Ferrari	V6t	45	1h 27m 25.178s	5	3
2	16	R Arnoux	Renault	RE30B	Renault	V6t	45	1h 27m 41.557s	3	2
3	6	K Rosberg	Williams	FW08	Ford Cosworth	V8	44		9	5
4	3	M Alboreto	Tyrrell	011	Ford Cosworth	V8	44		7	4
5	23	B Giacomelli	Alfa Romeo	182	Alfa Romeo	V12	44		11	6
6	29	M Surer	Arrows	A4	Ford Cosworth	V8	44		26	13
7	4	B Henton	Tyrrell	011	Ford Cosworth	V8	44		17	9
8	14	R Guerrero	Ensign	N181	Ford Cosworth	V8	44		21	11
9	12	N Mansell	Lotus	91	Ford Cosworth	V8	43		18	9
10	35	D Warwick	Toleman	TG181C	Hart	4t	43		14	7
11	20	C Serra	Fittipaldi	F9	Ford Cosworth	V8	43		25	13
r	7	J Watson	McLaren	MP4B	Ford Cosworth	V8	36	front suspension	10	5
r	26	J Laffite	Talbot Ligier	JS19	Matra	V12	36	handling	15	8
r	5	D Daly	Williams	FW08	Ford Cosworth	V8	25	engine	19	10
r	18	R Boesel	March	821	Ford Cosworth	V8	22	tyre / accident	24	12
r	11	E de Angelis	Lotus	91	Ford Cosworth	V8	21	transmission	13	7
r	1	N Piquet	Brabham	BT50	BMW	4t	18	accident	4	2
r	10	E Salazar	ATS	D5	Ford Cosworth	V8	17	accident	22	11
r	15	A Prost	Renault	RE30B	Renault	V6t	14	fuel injection	2	1
r	2	R Patrese	Brabham	BT50	BMW	4t	13	piston	6	3
r	22	A de Cesaris	Alfa Romeo	182	Alfa Romeo	V12	9	accident	8	4
r	25	E Cheever	Talbot Ligier	JS19	Matra	V12	8	handling	12	6
r	30	M Baldi	Arrows	A4	Ford Cosworth	V8	6	misfire	23	12
r	31	J-P Jarier	Osella	FA1D	Ford Cosworth	V8	3	steering	20	10
r	9	M Winkelhock	ATS	D5	Ford Cosworth	V8	3	clutch / gearbox	16	8
ns	28	D Pironi	Ferrari	126C2	Ferrari	V6t		accident / injury	1	1
ns	8	N Lauda	McLaren	MP4B	Ford Cosworth	V8		accident / injury		
nq	33	T Byrne	Theodore	TY02	Ford Cosworth	V8				
nq	17	R Keegan	March	821	Ford Cosworth	V8				
nq	36	T Fabi	Toleman	TG181C	Hart	4t				

Winning speed 209.929 km/h, 130.444 mph
Pole Position speed 226.678 km/h, 140.851 mph (D Pironi, 1 min:47.947 sec)
Fastest Lap speed 214.576 km/h, 133.331 mph (N Piquet, 1 min:54.035 sec on lap 7)
Lap Leaders R Arnoux 1 (1); N Piquet 2-18 (17); P Tambay 19-45 (27).

D Pironi qualified for pole position, but did not start, because of an accident in qualifying. Pole position left vacant.

15 Aug 1982		AUSTRIA: Österreichring						(Round 13)	(Race 370)	

53 laps x 5.942 km, 3.692 miles = 314.926 km, 195.686 miles

Pos	No	Driver	Car	Model	Engine		Laps	Time/Reason for Retirement	Grid Pos	Row
1	11	E de Angelis	Lotus	91	Ford Cosworth	V8	53	1h 25m 02.212s	7	4
2	6	K Rosberg	Williams	FW08	Ford Cosworth	V8	53	1h 25m 02.262s	6	3
3	26	J Laffite	Talbot Ligier	JS19	Matra	V12	52		14	7
4	27	P Tambay	Ferrari	126C2	Ferrari	V6t	52		4	2
5	8	N Lauda	McLaren	MP4B	Ford Cosworth	V8	52		10	5
6	30	M Baldi	Arrows	A4	Ford Cosworth	V8	52		23	12
7	20	C Serra	Fittipaldi	F9	Ford Cosworth	V8	51		20	10
8r	15	A Prost	Renault	RE30B	Renault	V6t	48	fuel injection	3	2
r	7	J Watson	McLaren	MP4B	Ford Cosworth	V8	44	water pipe	18	9
r	4	B Henton	Tyrrell	011	Ford Cosworth	V8	32	valve spring	19	10
r	1	N Piquet	Brabham	BT50	BMW	4t	31	camshaft drive	1	1
r	33	T Byrne	Theodore	TY02	Ford Cosworth	V8	28	spin	26	13
r	29	M Surer	Arrows	A4	Ford Cosworth	V8	28	fuel system	21	11
r	2	R Patrese	Brabham	BT50	BMW	4t	27	engine gudgeon pin / spin	2	1
r	25	E Cheever	Talbot Ligier	JS19	Matra	V12	22	valve	22	11
r	12	N Mansell	Lotus	91	Ford Cosworth	V8	17	engine	12	6
r	16	R Arnoux	Renault	RE30B	Renault	V6t	16	turbo	5	3
r	9	M Winkelhock	ATS	D5	Ford Cosworth	V8	15	spin	25	13
r	35	D Warwick	Toleman	TG181C	Hart	4t	7	rear suspension	15	8
r	36	T Fabi	Toleman	TG181C	Hart	4t	7	driveshaft	17	9
r	14	R Guerrero	Ensign	N181	Ford Cosworth	V8	6	driveshaft	16	8
r	3	M Alboreto	Tyrrell	011	Ford Cosworth	V8	1	accident	8	4
r	17	R Keegan	March	821	Ford Cosworth	V8	1	accident	24	12
r	22	A de Cesaris	Alfa Romeo	182	Alfa Romeo	V12	0	accident	11	6
r	5	D Daly	Williams	FW08	Ford Cosworth	V8	0	accident	9	5
r	23	B Giacomelli	Alfa Romeo	182	Alfa Romeo	V12	0	accident	13	7
nq	18	R Boesel	March	821	Ford Cosworth	V8				
nq	31	J-P Jarier	Osella	FA1D	Ford Cosworth	V8				
nq	10	E Salazar	ATS	D5	Ford Cosworth	V8				

Winning speed 222.204 km/h, 138.071 mph
Pole Position speed 244.158 km/h, 151.713 mph (N Piquet, 1 min:27.612 sec)
Fastest Lap speed 228.297 km/h, 141.857 mph (N Piquet, 1 min:33.699 sec on lap 5)
Lap Leaders N Piquet 1 (1); R Patrese 2-27 (26); A Prost 28-48 (21); E de Angelis 49-53 (5).

Races

80 laps x 3.800 km, 2.361 miles = 304.000 km, 188.897 miles

Pos	No	Driver	Car	Model	Engine		Laps	Time/Reason for Retirement	Grid Pos	Row
1	6	K Rosberg	Williams	FW08	Ford Cosworth	V8	80	1h 32m 41.087s	8	4
2	15	A Prost	Renault	RE30B	Renault	V6t	80	1h 32m 45.529s	1	1
3	8	N Lauda	McLaren	MP4B	Ford Cosworth	V8	80	1h 33m 41.430s	4	2
4	1	N Piquet	Brabham	BT50	BMW	4t	79		6	3
5	2	R Patrese	Brabham	BT50	BMW	4t	79		3	2
6	11	E de Angelis	Lotus	91	Ford Cosworth	V8	79		15	8
7	3	M Alboreto	Tyrrell	011	Ford Cosworth	V8	79		12	6
8	12	N Mansell	Lotus	91	Ford Cosworth	V8	79		26	13
9	5	D Daly	Williams	FW08	Ford Cosworth	V8	79		7	4
10	22	A de Cesaris	Alfa Romeo	182	Alfa Romeo	V12	78		5	3
11	4	B Henton	Tyrrell	011	Ford Cosworth	V8	78		18	9
12	23	B Giacomelli	Alfa Romeo	182	Alfa Romeo	V12	78		9	5
13	7	J Watson	McLaren	MP4B	Ford Cosworth	V8	77		11	6
14	10	E Salazar	ATS	D5	Ford Cosworth	V8	77		25	13
15	29	M Surer	Arrows	A5	Ford Cosworth	V8	76		14	7
16r	16	R Arnoux	Renault	RE30B	Renault	V6t	75	fuel injection	2	1
nc	25	E Cheever	Talbot Ligier	JS19	Matra	V12	70		16	8
r	9	M Winkelhock	ATS	D5	Ford Cosworth	V8	56	engine mounting	20	10
r	31	J-P Jarier	Osella	FA1D	Ford Cosworth	V8	44	engine	17	9
r	26	J Laffite	Talbot Ligier	JS19	Matra	V12	33	skirts / handling	13	7
r	36	T Fabi	Toleman	TG181C	Hart	4t	31	engine overheating	23	12
r	18	R Boesel	March	821	Ford Cosworth	V8	31	gearbox oil leak	24	12
r	17	R Keegan	March	821	Ford Cosworth	V8	25	spin	22	11
r	35	D Warwick	Toleman	TG181C	Hart	4t	24	engine	21	11
r	14	R Guerrero	Ensign	N181	Ford Cosworth	V8	4	engine	19	10
ns	27	P Tambay	Ferrari	126C2	Ferrari	V6t		driver unfit (neck injury)	10	5
nq	20	C Serra	Fittipaldi	F9	Ford Cosworth	V8				
nq	33	T Byrne	Theodore	TY02	Ford Cosworth	V8				
nq	30	M Baldi	Arrows	A4	Ford Cosworth	V8				

Winning speed 196.796 km/h, 122.283 mph
Pole Position speed 222.874 km/h, 138.487 mph (A Prost, 1 min: 1.380 sec)
Fastest Lap speed 202.736 km/h, 125.974 mph (A Prost, 1 min: 7.477 sec on lap 2)
Lap Leaders R Arnoux 1 (1); A Prost 2-78 (77); K Rosberg 79-80 (2).

The chequered flag was shown a lap late, ie at the end of the 81st lap. Nevertheless, the results were officially recorded as at the end of the 80th lap.

12 Sep 1982		ITALY: Monza						(Round 15)	(Race 372)	

52 laps x 5.800 km, 3.604 miles = 301.600 km, 187.406 miles

Pos	No	Driver	Car	Model	Engine		Laps	Time/Reason for Retirement	Grid Pos	Row
1	16	R Arnoux	Renault	RE30B	Renault	V6t	52	1h 22m 25.734s	6	3
2	27	P Tambay	Ferrari	126C2	Ferrari	V6t	52	1h 22m 39.798s	3	2
3	28	M Andretti	Ferrari	126C2	Ferrari	V6t	52	1h 23m 14.186s	1	1
4	7	J Watson	McLaren	MP4B	Ford Cosworth	V8	52	1h 23m 53.579s	12	6
5	3	M Alboreto	Tyrrell	011	Ford Cosworth	V8	51		11	6
6	25	E Cheever	Talbot Ligier	JS19	Matra	V12	51		14	7
7	12	N Mansell	Lotus	91	Ford Cosworth	V8	51		23	12
8	6	K Rosberg	Williams	FW08	Ford Cosworth	V8	50		7	4
9	10	E Salazar	ATS	D5	Ford Cosworth	V8	50		25	13
10	22	A de Cesaris	Alfa Romeo	182	Alfa Romeo	V12	50		9	5
11	20	C Serra	Fittipaldi	F9	Ford Cosworth	V8	49		26	13
12	30	M Baldi	Arrows	A5	Ford Cosworth	V8	49		24	12
nc	14	R Guerrero	Ensign	N181	Ford Cosworth	V8	40		18	9
r	11	E de Angelis	Lotus	91	Ford Cosworth	V8	34	throttle jammed	17	9
r	23	B Giacomelli	Alfa Romeo	182	Alfa Romeo	V12	33	side-pod / handling	8	4
r	29	M Surer	Arrows	A4	Ford Cosworth	V8	29	ignition	19	10
r	15	A Prost	Renault	RE30B	Renault	V6t	27	fuel injection	5	3
r	8	N Lauda	McLaren	MP4B	Ford Cosworth	V8	22	brakes / handling	10	5
r	31	J-P Jarier	Osella	FA1D	Ford Cosworth	V8	10	rear wheel lost	15	8
r	1	N Piquet	Brabham	BT50	BMW	4t	7	clutch / engine	2	1
r	2	R Patrese	Brabham	BT50	BMW	4t	6	clutch	4	2
r	26	J Laffite	Talbot Ligier	JS19	Matra	V12	5	gearbox	21	11
r	36	T Fabi	Toleman	TG181C	Hart	4t	2	engine	22	11
r	5	D Daly	Williams	FW08	Ford Cosworth	V8	1	accident / rear suspension	13	7
r	35	D Warwick	Toleman	TG183	Hart	4t	0	accident	16	8
r	4	B Henton	Tyrrell	011	Ford Cosworth	V8	0	accident	20	10
nq	17	R Keegan	March	821	Ford Cosworth	V8				
nq	9	M Winkelhock	ATS	D5	Ford Cosworth	V8				
nq	18	R Boesel	March	821	Ford Cosworth	V8				
nq	33	T Byrne	Theodore	TY02	Ford Cosworth	V8				

Winning speed 219.535 km/h, 136.413 mph
Pole Position speed 236.004 km/h, 146.646 mph (M Andretti, 1 min:28.473 sec)
Fastest Lap speed 223.032 km/h, 138.585 mph (R Arnoux, 1 min:33.619 sec on lap 25)
Lap Leaders R Arnoux 1-52 (52).

25 Sep 1982		CAESARS PALACE: Las Vegas						(Round 16)	(Race 373)	

75 laps x 3.650 km, 2.268 miles = 273.749 km, 170.100 miles

Pos	No	Driver	Car	Model	Engine		Laps	Time/Reason for Retirement	Grid Pos	Row
1	3	M Alboreto	Tyrrell	011	Ford Cosworth	V8	75	1h 41m 56.888s	3	2
2	7	J Watson	McLaren	MP4B	Ford Cosworth	V8	75	1h 42m 24.180s	9	5
3	25	E Cheever	Talbot Ligier	JS19	Matra	V12	75	1h 42m 53.338s	4	2
4	15	A Prost	Renault	RE30B	Renault	V6t	75	1h 43m 05.536s	1	1
5	6	K Rosberg	Williams	FW08	Ford Cosworth	V8	75	1h 43m 08.263s	6	3
6	5	D Daly	Williams	FW08	Ford Cosworth	V8	74		14	7
7	29	M Surer	Arrows	A5	Ford Cosworth	V8	74		17	9
8	4	B Henton	Tyrrell	011	Ford Cosworth	V8	74		19	10
9	22	A de Cesaris	Alfa Romeo	182	Alfa Romeo	V12	73		18	9
10	23	B Giacomelli	Alfa Romeo	182	Alfa Romeo	V12	73		16	8
11	30	M Baldi	Arrows	A4	Ford Cosworth	V8	73		23	12
12	17	R Keegan	March	821	Ford Cosworth	V8	73		25	13
13	18	R Boesel	March	821	Ford Cosworth	V8	69		24	12
nc	9	M Winkelhock	ATS	D5	Ford Cosworth	V8	62		22	11
r	8	N Lauda	McLaren	MP4B	Ford Cosworth	V8	53	engine	13	7
r	33	T Byrne	Theodore	TY02	Ford Cosworth	V8	39	spin	26	13
r	35	D Warwick	Toleman	TG183	Hart	4t	32	spark plugs	10	5
r	11	E de Angelis	Lotus	91	Ford Cosworth	V8	28	engine	20	10
r	28	M Andretti	Ferrari	126C2	Ferrari	V6t	26	rear suspension	7	4
r	1	N Piquet	Brabham	BT50	BMW	4t	26	spark plug	12	6
r	16	R Arnoux	Renault	RE30B	Renault	V6t	20	engine	2	1
r	2	R Patrese	Brabham	BT50	BMW	4t	17	clutch	5	3
r	12	N Mansell	Lotus	91	Ford Cosworth	V8	8	accident	21	11
r	26	J Laffite	Talbot Ligier	JS19	Matra	V12	5	ignition	11	6
ns	27	P Tambay	Ferrari	126C2	Ferrari	V6t		driver unfit	8	4
ns	14	R Guerrero	Ensign	N181	Ford Cosworth	V8		engine	15	8
ns	31	J-P Jarier	Osella	FA1D	Ford Cosworth	V8		accident		
nq	36	T Fabi	Toleman	TG181C	Hart	4t				
nq	10	E Salazar	ATS	D5	Ford Cosworth	V8				
nq	20	C Serra	Fittipaldi	F9	Ford Cosworth	V8				

Winning speed 161.111 km/h, 100.110 mph
Pole Position speed 172.088 km/h, 106.931 mph (A Prost, 1 min:16.356 sec)
Fastest Lap speed 164.994 km/h, 102.523 mph (M Alboreto, 1 min:19.639 sec on lap 59)
Lap Leaders A Prost 1,15-51 (38); R Arnoux 2-14 (13); M Alboreto 52-75 (24).

Races

Lap Leaders 1982

Pos	Driver	Car-Engine	GPs	laps	km	miles
1	A Prost	Renault	7	258	1,008.6	626.7
2	R Arnoux	Renault	10	204	1,006.4	625.3
3	N Piquet	Brabham-BMW	5	105	525.7	326.7
		Brabham-Ford Cosworth	1	34	171.1	106.3
			6	139	696.8	433.0
4	N Lauda	McLaren-Ford Cosworth	2	128	491.0	305.1
5	D Pironi	Ferrari	4	80	347.3	215.8
	K Rosberg	Williams-Ford Cosworth	3	80	336.5	209.1
7	G Villeneuve	Ferrari	2	40	201.3	125.1
8	R Patrese	Brabham-BMW	2	31	183.5	114.0
		Brabham-Ford Cosworth	1	2	6.6	4.1
			3	33	190.2	118.2
9	J Watson	McLaren-Ford Cosworth	2	28	112.8	70.1
10	P Tambay	Ferrari	1	27	183.5	114.0
11	M Alboreto	Tyrrell-Ford Cosworth	1	24	87.6	54.4
12	A de Cesaris	Alfa Romeo	1	14.5	49.7	30.9
13	E de Angelis	Lotus-Ford Cosworth	1	5	29.7	18.5
			16	1,060.5	4,741.4	2,946.2

Driver Points 1982

Pos	Driver	ZA	BR	USAW	RSM	B	MC	DET	CDN	NL	GB	F	D	A	CH	I	LV	Total
1	K Rosberg	2	-	6	-	6	-	3	-	4	-	2	4	6	9	-	2	44
2	D Pironi	-	1	-	9	-	6	4	-	9	6	4	-	-	-	-	-	39
	J Watson	1	6	1	-	9	-	9	4	-	-	-	-	-	-	3	6	39
4	A Prost	9	9	-	-	-	-	-	-	-	1	6	-	-	6	-	3	34
5	N Lauda	3	-	9	-	-	-	-	-	3	9	-	-	2	4	-	-	30
6	R Arnoux	4	-	-	-	-	-	-	-	-	-	9	6	-	-	9	-	28
7	P Tambay	-	-	-	-	-	-	-	-	4	3	9	3	-	6	-	-	25
	M Alboreto	-	3	3	4	-	-	-	-	-	-	1	3	-	-	2	9	25
9	E de Angelis	-	-	2	-	3	2	-	3	-	3	-	-	9	1	-	-	23
10	R Patrese	-	-	4	-	-	9	-	6	-	-	-	-	-	2	-	-	21
11	N Piquet	-	-	-	-	2	-	-	9	6	-	-	-	-	3	-	-	20
12	E Cheever	-	-	-	-	4	-	6	-	-	-	-	-	-	-	1	4	15
13	D Daly	-	-	-	-	-	1	2	-	2	2	-	-	-	-	-	1	8
14	N Mansell	-	4	-	-	-	3	-	-	-	-	-	-	-	-	-	-	7
15	C Reutemann	6	-	-	-	-	-	-	-	-	-	-	-	-	-	-	-	6
	G Villeneuve	-	-	-	6	-	-	-	-	-	-	-	-	-	-	-	-	6
17	A de Cesaris	-	-	-	-	-	4	-	1	-	-	-	-	-	-	-	-	5
	J Laffite	-	-	-	-	-	1	-	-	-	-	-	4	-	-	-	-	5
19	M Andretti	-	-	-	-	-	-	-	-	-	-	-	-	-	-	4	-	4
20	J-P Jarier	-	-	-	3	-	-	-	-	-	-	-	-	-	-	-	-	3
	M Surer	-	-	-	-	-	-	-	2	-	-	-	1	-	-	-	-	3
22	M Winkelhock	-	2	-	-	-	-	-	-	-	-	-	-	-	-	-	-	2
	E Salazar	-	-	-	2	-	-	-	-	-	-	-	-	-	-	-	-	2
	B Giacomelli	-	-	-	-	-	-	-	-	-	-	-	2	-	-	-	-	2
	M Baldi	-	-	-	-	-	-	-	-	1	-	-	-	1	-	-	-	2
26	C Serra	-	-	-	1	-	-	-	-	-	-	-	-	-	-	-	-	1

9,6,4,3,2 and 1 point awarded to the first six finishers. Best 11 scores.

Constructor Points 1982

Pos	Constructor	ZA	BR	USAW	RSM	B	MC	DET	CDN	NL	GB	F	D	A	CH	I	LV	Total
1	Ferrari	-	1	-	15	-	6	4	-	9	10	7	9	3	-	10	-	74
2	McLaren-Ford Cosworth	4	6	10	-	9	-	9	4	3	9	-	-	2	4	3	6	69
3	Renault	13	9	-	-	-	-	-	-	-	1	15	6	-	6	9	3	62
4	Williams-Ford Cosworth	8	-	6	-	6	1	5	-	6	2	2	4	6	9	-	3	58
5	Lotus-Ford Cosworth	-	4	2	-	3	5	-	3	-	3	-	-	9	1	-	-	30
6	Tyrrell-Ford Cosworth	-	3	3	4	-	-	-	-	-	-	1	3	-	-	2	9	25
7	Brabham-BMW	-	-	-	-	2	-	-	9	6	-	-	-	-	5	-	-	22
8	Talbot Ligier-Matra	-	-	-	-	4	-	7	-	-	-	-	-	4	-	1	4	20
9	Brabham-Ford Cosworth	-	-	4	-	-	9	-	6	-	-	-	-	-	-	-	-	19
10	Alfa Romeo	-	-	-	-	-	4	-	1	-	-	-	2	-	-	-	-	7
11	Arrows-Ford Cosworth	-	-	-	-	-	-	-	2	1	-	-	1	1	-	-	-	5
12	ATS-Ford Cosworth	-	2	-	2	-	-	-	-	-	-	-	-	-	-	-	-	4
13	Osella-Ford Cosworth	-	-	-	3	-	-	-	-	-	-	-	-	-	-	-	-	3
14	Fittipaldi-Ford Cosworth	-	-	-	-	1	-	-	-	-	-	-	-	-	-	-	-	1

9,6,4,3,2 and 1 point awarded to the first six finishers.

Race Entrants and Results

Colin Chapman, the genius behind Lotus, died suddenly at the end of 1982. New rules insisted on flat-bottomed cars with no skirts. Fuel stops, tried out by Brabham in 1992, were a major new strategy tried by all teams. Alfa Romeo transferred its racing operation to Euroracing.

WILLIAMS
TAG Williams Team: Rosberg, Laffite, Palmer

TYRRELL
Benetton Tyrrell Team: Alboreto, Sullivan

BRABHAM
Fila Sport: Piquet, Patrese

McLAREN
Marlboro McLaren International: Watson, Lauda

ATS
Team ATS: Winkelhock

LOTUS
John Player Team Lotus: de Angelis, Mansell

RENAULT
Equipe Renault Elf: Prost, Cheever

RAM
RAM Automotive Team March: Salazar, (Villeneuve), Acheson, (Schlesser)

ALFA ROMEO
Marlboro Team Alfa Romeo: de Cesaris, Baldi

LIGIER
Equipe Ligier Gitanes: Jarier, Boesel

FERRARI
Scuderia Ferrari SpA SEFAC: Tambay, Arnoux

ARROWS
Arrows Racing Team: Surer, Serra, Jones, Boutsen

OSELLA
Osella Squadra Corse: Fabi, Ghinzani

THEODORE
Theodore Racing Team: Guerrero, Cecotto

TOLEMAN
Candy Toleman Motorsport: Warwick, Giacomelli

SPIRIT
Spirit Racing: Johansson

13 Mar 1983		BRAZIL: Rio de Janeiro						(Round 1)	(Race 374)	
		63 laps x 5.031 km, 3.126 miles = 316.953 km, 196.945 miles								
Pos	No	Driver	Car	Model	Engine		Laps	Time/Reason for Retirement	Grid Pos	Row
1	5	N Piquet	Brabham	BT52	BMW	4t	63	1h 48m 27.731s	4	2
dq	1	K Rosberg	Williams	FW08C	Ford Cosworth	V8	63	push start in pits	1	1
3	8	N Lauda	McLaren	MP4/1C	Ford Cosworth	V8	63	1h 49m 19.614s	9	5
4	2	J Laffite	Williams	FW08C	Ford Cosworth	V8	63	1h 49m 41.682s	18	9
5	27	P Tambay	Ferrari	126C2B	Ferrari	V6t	63	1h 49m 45.848s	3	2
6	29	M Surer	Arrows	A6	Ford Cosworth	V8	63	1h 49m 45.938s	20	10
7	15	A Prost	Renault	RE30C	Renault	V6t	62		2	1
8	35	D Warwick	Toleman	TG183B	Hart	4t	62		5	3
9	30	C Serra	Arrows	A6	Ford Cosworth	V8	62		23	12
10	28	R Arnoux	Ferrari	126C2B	Ferrari	V6t	62		6	3
11	4	D Sullivan	Tyrrell	011	Ford Cosworth	V8	62		21	11
12	12	N Mansell	Lotus	92	Ford Cosworth	V8	61		22	11
dq	11	E de Angelis	Lotus	91	Ford Cosworth	V8	60	changed car after parade lap	13	7
14	34	J Cecotto	Theodore	N183	Ford Cosworth	V8	60		19	10
15	17	E Salazar	RAM March	01	Ford Cosworth	V8	59		26	13
16	9	M Winkelhock	ATS	D6	BMW	4t	59		25	13
nc	33	R Guerrero	Theodore	N183	Ford Cosworth	V8	53		14	7
r	16	E Cheever	Renault	RE30C	Renault	V6t	41	turbo	8	4
r	7	J Watson	McLaren	MP4/1C	Ford Cosworth	V8	34	engine	16	8
r	26	R Boesel	Ligier	JS21	Ford Cosworth	V8	25	electrics	17	9
r	23	M Baldi	Alfa Romeo	183T	Alfa Romeo	V8t	23	accident / front suspension	10	5
r	25	J-P Jarier	Ligier	JS21	Ford Cosworth	V8	22	rear suspension	12	6
r	6	R Patrese	Brabham	BT52	BMW	4t	19	exhaust	7	4
r	31	C Fabi	Osella	FA1D	Ford Cosworth	V8	17	engine	24	12
r	36	B Giacomelli	Toleman	TG183B	Hart	4t	16	spin	15	8
r	3	M Alboreto	Tyrrell	011	Ford Cosworth	V8	7	accident / oil cooler	11	6
nq	32	P Ghinzani	Osella	FA1D	Ford Cosworth	V8				
exc	22	A de Cesaris	Alfa Romeo	183T	Alfa Romeo	V8t		missed weight check		

Winning speed 175.335 km/h, 108.948 mph
Pole Position speed 191.604 km/h, 119.057 mph (K Rosberg, 1 min:34.526 sec)
Fastest Lap speed 181.426 km/h, 112.733 mph (N Piquet, 1 min:39.829 sec on lap 4)
Lap Leaders K Rosberg 1-6 (6); N Piquet 7-63 (57).

K Rosberg finished 2nd in 1h 48m 48.362s. E de Angelis retired his Lotus 93T-Renault V6t on the parade lap with a turbo failure and proceeded to race in the Ford Cosworth powered car, being consequently disqualified. Lower positions were not moved up.

27 Mar 1983 USA West: Long Beach (Round 2) (Race 375)

75 laps x 3.275 km, 2.035 miles = 245.626 km, 152.625 miles

Pos	No	Driver	Car	Model	Engine		Laps	Time/Reason for Retirement	Grid Pos	Row
1	7	J Watson	McLaren	MP4/1C	Ford Cosworth	V8	75	1h 53m 34.889s	22	11
2	8	N Lauda	McLaren	MP4/1C	Ford Cosworth	V8	75	1h 54m 02.882s	23	12
3	28	R Arnoux	Ferrari	126C2B	Ferrari	V6t	75	1h 54m 48.527s	2	1
4	2	J Laffite	Williams	FW08C	Ford Cosworth	V8	74		4	2
5	29	M Surer	Arrows	A6	Ford Cosworth	V8	74		16	8
6	34	J Cecotto	Theodore	N183	Ford Cosworth	V8	74		17	9
7	26	R Boesel	Ligier	JS21	Ford Cosworth	V8	73		26	13
8	4	D Sullivan	Tyrrell	011	Ford Cosworth	V8	73		9	5
9	3	M Alboreto	Tyrrell	011	Ford Cosworth	V8	73		7	4
10r	6	R Patrese	Brabham	BT52	BMW	4t	72	distributor	11	6
11	15	A Prost	Renault	RE40	Renault	V6t	72		8	4
12	12	N Mansell	Lotus	92	Ford Cosworth	V8	72		13	7
13r	16	E Cheever	Renault	RE30C	Renault	V6t	67	gearbox	15	8
r	30	A Jones	Arrows	A6	Ford Cosworth	V8	58	driver discomfort	12	6
r	5	N Piquet	Brabham	BT52	BMW	4t	51	throttle jammed	20	10
r	22	A de Cesaris	Alfa Romeo	183T	Alfa Romeo	V8t	48	gearbox	19	10
r	11	E de Angelis	Lotus	93T	Renault	V6t	29	team ran out of tyres	5	3
r	33	R Guerrero	Theodore	N183	Ford Cosworth	V8	27	gearbox	18	9
r	25	J-P Jarier	Ligier	JS21	Ford Cosworth	V8	26	accident	10	5
r	36	B Giacomelli	Toleman	TG183B	Hart	4t	26	battery	14	7
r	23	M Baldi	Alfa Romeo	183T	Alfa Romeo	V8t	26	accident	21	11
r	27	P Tambay	Ferrari	126C2B	Ferrari	V6t	25	accident	1	1
r	1	K Rosberg	Williams	FW08C	Ford Cosworth	V8	25	accident	3	2
r	17	E Salazar	RAM March	01	Ford Cosworth	V8	25	gear linkage	25	13
r	35	D Warwick	Toleman	TG183B	Hart	4t	11	rear tyre burst / accident	6	3
r	9	M Winkelhock	ATS	D6	BMW	4t	3	accident	24	12
nq	31	C Fabi	Osella	FA1D	Ford Cosworth	V8				
nq	32	P Ghinzani	Osella	FA1D	Ford Cosworth	V8				

Winning speed 129.753 km/h, 80.625 mph
Pole Position speed 136.907 km/h, 85.070 mph (P Tambay, 1 min:26.117 sec)
Fastest Lap speed 133.477 km/h, 82.939 mph (N Lauda, 1 min:28.330 sec on lap 42)
Lap Leaders P Tambay 1-25 (25); J Laffite 26-44 (19); J Watson 45-75 (31).

17 Apr 1983 FRANCE: Paul Ricard (Round 3) (Race 376)

54 laps x 5.810 km, 3.610 miles = 313.740 km, 194.949 miles

Pos	No	Driver	Car	Model	Engine		Laps	Time/Reason for Retirement	Grid Pos	Row
1	15	A Prost	Renault	RE40	Renault	V6t	54	1h 34m 13.913s	1	1
2	5	N Piquet	Brabham	BT52	BMW	4t	54	1h 34m 43.633s	6	3
3	16	E Cheever	Renault	RE40	Renault	V6t	54	1h 34m 54.145s	2	1
4	27	P Tambay	Ferrari	126C2B	Ferrari	V6t	54	1h 35m 20.793s	11	6
5	1	K Rosberg	Williams	FW08C	Ford Cosworth	V8	53		16	8
6	2	J Laffite	Williams	FW08C	Ford Cosworth	V8	53		19	10
7	28	R Arnoux	Ferrari	126C2B	Ferrari	V6t	53		4	2
8	3	M Alboreto	Tyrrell	011	Ford Cosworth	V8	53		15	8
9	25	J-P Jarier	Ligier	JS21	Ford Cosworth	V8	53		20	10
10	29	M Surer	Arrows	A6	Ford Cosworth	V8	53		21	11
11	34	J Cecotto	Theodore	N183	Ford Cosworth	V8	52		17	9
12	22	A de Cesaris	Alfa Romeo	183T	Alfa Romeo	V8t	50		7	4
13r	36	B Giacomelli	Toleman	TG183B	Hart	4t	49	gearbox	13	7
r	26	R Boesel	Ligier	JS21	Ford Cosworth	V8	47	engine	25	13
r	31	C Fabi	Osella	FA1D	Ford Cosworth	V8	36	engine	23	12
r	9	M Winkelhock	ATS	D6	BMW	4t	36	engine / exhaust	10	5
r	8	N Lauda	McLaren	MP4/1C	Ford Cosworth	V8	29	rear wheel bearing / spin	12	6
r	23	M Baldi	Alfa Romeo	183T	Alfa Romeo	V8t	28	accident	8	4
r	30	C Serra	Arrows	A6	Ford Cosworth	V8	26	gearbox	26	13
r	33	R Guerrero	Theodore	N183	Ford Cosworth	V8	23	engine	22	11
r	4	D Sullivan	Tyrrell	011	Ford Cosworth	V8	21	clutch	24	12
r	11	E de Angelis	Lotus	93T	Renault	V6t	20	electrics	5	3
r	6	R Patrese	Brabham	BT52	BMW	4t	19	water leak / engine overheating	3	2
r	35	D Warwick	Toleman	TG183B	Hart	4t	14	water pipe / engine	9	5
r	12	N Mansell	Lotus	92	Ford Cosworth	V8	6	driver discomfort	18	9
r	7	J Watson	McLaren	MP4/1C	Ford Cosworth	V8	3	throttle linkage	14	7
nq	17	E Salazar	RAM March	01	Ford Cosworth	V8				
nq	32	P Ghinzani	Osella	FA1D	Ford Cosworth	V8				
nq	18	J-L Schlesser	RAM March	01	Ford Cosworth	V8				

Winning speed 199.767 km/h, 124.129 mph
Pole Position speed 216.360 km/h, 134.440 mph (A Prost, 1 min:36.672 sec)
Fastest Lap speed 203.671 km/h, 126.555 mph (A Prost, 1 min:42.695 sec on lap 34)
Lap Leaders A Prost 1-29,33-54 (51); N Piquet 30-32 (3).

		1 May 1983	SAN MARINO: Imola			(Round 4)	(Race 377)		

60 laps x 5.040 km, 3.132 miles = 302.400 km, 187.903 miles

Pos	No	Driver	Car	Model	Engine		Laps	Time/Reason for Retirement	Grid Pos	Row
1	27	P Tambay	Ferrari	126C2B	Ferrari	V6t	60	1h 37m 52.460s	3	2
2	15	A Prost	Renault	RE40	Renault	V6t	60	1h 38m 41.241s	4	2
3	28	R Arnoux	Ferrari	126C2B	Ferrari	V6t	59		1	1
4	1	K Rosberg	Williams	FW08C	Ford Cosworth	V8	59		11	6
5	7	J Watson	McLaren	MP4/1C	Ford Cosworth	V8	59		24	12
6	29	M Surer	Arrows	A6	Ford Cosworth	V8	59		12	6
7	2	J Laffite	Williams	FW08C	Ford Cosworth	V8	59		16	8
8	30	C Serra	Arrows	A6	Ford Cosworth	V8	58		20	10
9	26	R Boesel	Ligier	JS21	Ford Cosworth	V8	58		25	13
10r	23	M Baldi	Alfa Romeo	183T	Alfa Romeo	V8t	57	engine	10	5
11	9	M Winkelhock	ATS	D6	BMW	4t	57		7	4
12r	12	N Mansell	Lotus	92	Ford Cosworth	V8	56	rear wing / accident	15	8
13r	6	R Patrese	Brabham	BT52	BMW	4t	54	accident	5	3
r	22	A de Cesaris	Alfa Romeo	183T	Alfa Romeo	V8t	45	distributor	8	4
r	11	E de Angelis	Lotus	93T	Renault	V6t	43	handling	9	5
r	5	N Piquet	Brabham	BT52	BMW	4t	41	engine	2	1
r	25	J-P Jarier	Ligier	JS21	Ford Cosworth	V8	39	radiator	19	10
r	4	D Sullivan	Tyrrell	011	Ford Cosworth	V8	37	accident	22	11
r	35	D Warwick	Toleman	TG183B	Hart	4t	27	accident	14	7
r	36	B Giacomelli	Toleman	TG183B	Hart	4t	20	rear suspension	17	9
r	31	C Fabi	Osella	FA1D	Ford Cosworth	V8	20	accident	26	13
r	8	N Lauda	McLaren	MP4/1C	Ford Cosworth	V8	11	accident	18	9
r	34	J Cecotto	Theodore	N183	Ford Cosworth	V8	11	accident	23	12
r	3	M Alboreto	Tyrrell	011	Ford Cosworth	V8	10	accident / rear suspension	13	7
r	33	R Guerrero	Theodore	N183	Ford Cosworth	V8	3	accident	21	11
r	16	E Cheever	Renault	RE40	Renault	V6t	1	turbo	6	3
nq	17	E Salazar	RAM March	01	Ford Cosworth	V8				
nq	32	P Ghinzani	Osella	FA1E	Alfa Romeo	V12				

Winning speed 185.381 km/h, 115.190 mph
Pole Position speed 198.865 km/h, 123.569 mph (R Arnoux, 1 min:31.238 sec)
Fastest Lap speed 192.128 km/h, 119.383 mph (R Patrese, 1 min:34.437 sec on lap 47)
Lap Leaders R Arnoux 1-5 (5); R Patrese 6-33 (28); P Tambay 34-60 (27).

		15 May 1983	MONACO: Monte-Carlo			(Round 5)	(Race 378)		

76 laps x 3.312 km, 2.058 miles = 251.712 km, 156.407 miles

Pos	No	Driver	Car	Model	Engine		Laps	Time/Reason for Retirement	Grid Pos	Row
1	1	K Rosberg	Williams	FW08C	Ford Cosworth	V8	76	1h 56m 38.121s	5	3
2	5	N Piquet	Brabham	BT52	BMW	4t	76	1h 56m 56.596s	6	3
3	15	A Prost	Renault	RE40	Renault	V6t	76	1h 57m 09.487s	1	1
4	27	P Tambay	Ferrari	126C2B	Ferrari	V6t	76	1h 57m 42.418s	4	2
5	4	D Sullivan	Tyrrell	011	Ford Cosworth	V8	74		20	10
6	23	M Baldi	Alfa Romeo	183T	Alfa Romeo	V8t	74		13	7
7	30	C Serra	Arrows	A6	Ford Cosworth	V8	74		15	8
r	6	R Patrese	Brabham	BT52	BMW	4t	64	electrics	17	9
r	2	J Laffite	Williams	FW08C	Ford Cosworth	V8	53	gearbox	8	4
r	29	M Surer	Arrows	A6	Ford Cosworth	V8	49	accident	12	6
r	35	D Warwick	Toleman	TG183B	Hart	4t	49	accident	10	5
r	11	E de Angelis	Lotus	93T	Renault	V6t	49	driveshaft	19	10
r	25	J-P Jarier	Ligier	JS21	Ford Cosworth	V8	32	suspension hydraulics	9	5
r	16	E Cheever	Renault	RE40	Renault	V6t	30	electrics	3	2
r	22	A de Cesaris	Alfa Romeo	183T	Alfa Romeo	V8t	13	gearbox	7	4
r	28	R Arnoux	Ferrari	126C2B	Ferrari	V6t	6	accident / rear wheel / tyre	2	1
r	26	R Boesel	Ligier	JS21	Ford Cosworth	V8	3	accident	18	9
r	9	M Winkelhock	ATS	D6	BMW	4t	3	accident	16	8
r	3	M Alboreto	Tyrrell	011	Ford Cosworth	V8	0	accident	11	6
r	12	N Mansell	Lotus	92	Ford Cosworth	V8	0	accident	14	7
nq	36	B Giacomelli	Toleman	TG183B	Hart	4t				
nq	8	N Lauda	McLaren	MP4/1C	Ford Cosworth	V8				
nq	7	J Watson	McLaren	MP4/1C	Ford Cosworth	V8				
nq	31	C Fabi	Osella	FA1D	Ford Cosworth	V8				
nq	17	E Salazar	RAM March	01	Ford Cosworth	V8				
nq	32	P Ghinzani	Osella	FA1E	Alfa Romeo	V12				
npq	34	J Cecotto	Theodore	N183	Ford Cosworth	V8				
npq	33	R Guerrero	Theodore	N183	Ford Cosworth	V8				

Winning speed 129.487 km/h, 80.459 mph
Pole Position speed 140.537 km/h, 87.326 mph (A Prost, 1 min:24.840 sec)
Fastest Lap speed 136.604 km/h, 84.882 mph (N Piquet, 1 min:27.283 sec on lap 69)
Lap Leaders K Rosberg 1-76 (76).

Pos	No	Driver	Car	Model	Engine		Laps	Time/Reason for Retirement	Grid Pos	Row
								22 May 1983 BELGIUM: Spa-Francorchamps	**(Round 6)**	**(Race 379)**

40.0953 laps x 6.949 km, 4.318 miles = 278.620 km, 173.126 miles

Pos	No	Driver	Car	Model	Engine		Laps	Time/Reason for Retirement	Grid Pos	Row
1	15	A Prost	Renault	RE40	Renault	V6t	40	1h 27m 11.502s	1	1
2	27	P Tambay	Ferrari	126C2B	Ferrari	V6t	40	1h 27m 34.684s	2	1
3	16	E Cheever	Renault	RE40	Renault	V6t	40	1h 27m 51.371s	8	4
4	5	N Piquet	Brabham	BT52	BMW	4t	40	1h 27m 53.797s	4	2
5	1	K Rosberg	Williams	FW08C	Ford Cosworth	V8	40	1h 28m 01.982s	9	5
6	2	J Laffite	Williams	FW08C	Ford Cosworth	V8	40	1h 28m 44.609s	11	6
7	35	D Warwick	Toleman	TG183B	Hart	4t	40	1h 29m 10.041s	22	11
8	36	B Giacomelli	Toleman	TG183B	Hart	4t	40	1h 29m 49.775s	16	8
9	11	E de Angelis	Lotus	93T	Renault	V6t	39		13	7
10	34	J Cecotto	Theodore	N183	Ford Cosworth	V8	39		25	13
11	29	M Surer	Arrows	A6	Ford Cosworth	V8	39		10	5
12	4	D Sullivan	Tyrrell	011	Ford Cosworth	V8	39		23	12
13	26	R Boesel	Ligier	JS21	Ford Cosworth	V8	39		26	13
14	3	M Alboreto	Tyrrell	011	Ford Cosworth	V8	38		17	9
r	8	N Lauda	McLaren	MP4/1C	Ford Cosworth	V8	33	engine	15	8
r	12	N Mansell	Lotus	92	Ford Cosworth	V8	30	gearbox	19	10
r	22	A de Cesaris	Alfa Romeo	183T	Alfa Romeo	V8t	25	engine	3	2
r	33	R Guerrero	Theodore	N183	Ford Cosworth	V8	23	engine	14	7
r	28	R Arnoux	Ferrari	126C2B	Ferrari	V6t	22	engine	5	3
r	31	C Fabi	Osella	FA1D	Ford Cosworth	V8	19	rear suspension	24	12
r	9	M Winkelhock	ATS	D6	BMW	4t	18	rear wheel lost / accident	7	4
r	7	J Watson	McLaren	MP4/1C	Ford Cosworth	V8	8	accident	20	10
r	25	J-P Jarier	Ligier	JS21	Ford Cosworth	V8	8	accident	21	11
r	30	T Boutsen	Arrows	A6	Ford Cosworth	V8	4	rear suspension	18	9
r	23	M Baldi	Alfa Romeo	183T	Alfa Romeo	V8t	3	throttle linkage	12	6
r	6	R Patrese	Brabham	BT52	BMW	4t	0	engine	6	3
nq	32	P Ghinzani	Osella	FA1E	Alfa Romeo	V12				
nq	17	E Salazar	RAM March	01	Ford Cosworth	V8				

Winning speed 191.729 km/h, 119.135 mph
Pole Position speed 200.750 km/h, 124.740 mph (A Prost, 2 min: 4.615 sec)
Fastest Lap speed 196.218 km/h, 121.924 mph (A de Cesaris, 2 min: 7.493 sec on lap 17)
Lap Leaders A de Cesaris 1-18 (18.1); A Prost 19-22,24-40 (21); N Piquet 23 (1).

The start and finish lines were at different positions on the circuit. The fraction of a lap is credited to the first lap leader.

								5 Jun 1983 USA: Detroit	**(Round 7)**	**(Race 380)**

60 laps x 4.023 km, 2.500 miles = 241.402 km, 150.000 miles

Pos	No	Driver	Car	Model	Engine		Laps	Time/Reason for Retirement	Grid Pos	Row
1	3	M Alboreto	Tyrrell	011	Ford Cosworth	V8	60	1h 50m 53.669s	6	3
2	1	K Rosberg	Williams	FW08C	Ford Cosworth	V8	60	1h 51m 01.371s	12	6
3	7	J Watson	McLaren	MP4/1C	Ford Cosworth	V8	60	1h 51m 02.952s	21	11
4	5	N Piquet	Brabham	BT52	BMW	4t	60	1h 52m 05.854s	2	1
5	2	J Laffite	Williams	FW08C	Ford Cosworth	V8	60	1h 52m 26.272s	20	10
6	12	N Mansell	Lotus	92	Ford Cosworth	V8	59		14	7
7	30	T Boutsen	Arrows	A6	Ford Cosworth	V8	59		10	5
8	15	A Prost	Renault	RE40	Renault	V6t	59		13	7
9	36	B Giacomelli	Toleman	TG183B	Hart	4t	58		17	9
10	26	R Boesel	Ligier	JS21	Ford Cosworth	V8	58		23	12
11	29	M Surer	Arrows	A6	Ford Cosworth	V8	58		5	3
12	23	M Baldi	Alfa Romeo	183T	Alfa Romeo	V8t	56		25	13
r	8	N Lauda	McLaren	MP4/1C	Ford Cosworth	V8	49	suspension / handling	18	9
nc	33	R Guerrero	Theodore	N183	Ford Cosworth	V8	38		11	6
r	34	J Cecotto	Theodore	N183	Ford Cosworth	V8	34	gear linkage	26	13
r	22	A de Cesaris	Alfa Romeo	183T	Alfa Romeo	V8t	33	turbo	8	4
r	28	R Arnoux	Ferrari	126C2B	Ferrari	V6t	31	electrics	1	1
r	4	D Sullivan	Tyrrell	011	Ford Cosworth	V8	30	electrics	16	8
r	25	J-P Jarier	Ligier	JS21	Ford Cosworth	V8	29	front wheel nut	19	10
r	9	M Winkelhock	ATS	D6	BMW	4t	26	accident	22	11
r	35	D Warwick	Toleman	TG183B	Hart	4t	25	water leak / engine	9	5
r	6	R Patrese	Brabham	BT52	BMW	4t	24	brakes	15	8
r	11	E de Angelis	Lotus	93T	Renault	V6t	5	transmission	4	2
r	16	E Cheever	Renault	RE40	Renault	V6t	4	distributor	7	4
r	32	P Ghinzani	Osella	FA1E	Alfa Romeo	V12	4	oil cooler	24	12
r	27	P Tambay	Ferrari	126C2B	Ferrari	V6t	0	stalled on grid	3	2
nq	31	C Fabi	Osella	FA1D	Ford Cosworth	V8				

Winning speed 130.612 km/h, 81.158 mph
Pole Position speed 138.294 km/h, 85.932 mph (R Arnoux, 1 min:44.734 sec)
Fastest Lap speed 134.526 km/h, 83.590 mph (J Watson, 1 min:47.668 sec on lap 55)
Lap Leaders N Piquet 1-9,32-50 (28); R Arnoux 10-31 (22); M Alboreto 51-60 (10).

CANADA: Montréal (Round 8) (Race 381)

70 laps x 4.410 km, 2.740 miles = 308.700 km, 191.817 miles

Pos	No	Driver	Car	Model	Engine		Laps	Time/Reason for Retirement	Grid Pos	Row
1	28	R Arnoux	Ferrari	126C2B	Ferrari	V6t	70	1h 48m 31.838s	1	1
2	16	E Cheever	Renault	RE40	Renault	V6t	70	1h 49m 13.867s	6	3
3	27	P Tambay	Ferrari	126C2B	Ferrari	V6t	70	1h 49m 24.448s	4	2
4	1	K Rosberg	Williams	FW08C	Ford Cosworth	V8	70	1h 49m 48.886s	9	5
5	15	A Prost	Renault	RE40	Renault	V6t	69		2	1
6	7	J Watson	McLaren	MP4/1C	Ford Cosworth	V8	69		20	10
7	30	T Boutsen	Arrows	A6	Ford Cosworth	V8	69		15	8
8	3	M Alboreto	Tyrrell	011	Ford Cosworth	V8	68		17	9
dq	4	D Sullivan	Tyrrell	011	Ford Cosworth	V8	68	car under weight	22	11
9r	9	M Winkelhock	ATS	D6	BMW	4t	67	fuel system	7	4
10	23	M Baldi	Alfa Romeo	183T	Alfa Romeo	V8t	67		26	13
r	6	R Patrese	Brabham	BT52	BMW	4t	56	gearbox	5	3
r	35	D Warwick	Toleman	TG183B	Hart	4t	47	turbo	12	6
r	36	B Giacomelli	Toleman	TG183B	Hart	4t	43	engine overheating	10	5
r	12	N Mansell	Lotus	92	Ford Cosworth	V8	43	handling / team ran out of tyres	18	9
r	22	A de Cesaris	Alfa Romeo	183T	Alfa Romeo	V8t	42	engine	8	4
r	2	J Laffite	Williams	FW08C	Ford Cosworth	V8	37	gearbox	13	7
r	26	R Boesel	Ligier	JS21	Ford Cosworth	V8	32	rear wheel bearing	24	12
r	33	R Guerrero	Theodore	N183	Ford Cosworth	V8	27	engine	21	11
r	31	C Fabi	Osella	FA1D	Ford Cosworth	V8	26	engine	25	13
r	34	J Cecotto	Theodore	N183	Ford Cosworth	V8	17	crown wheel & pinion	23	12
r	5	N Piquet	Brabham	BT52	BMW	4t	15	throttle linkage	3	2
r	8	N Lauda	McLaren	MP4/1C	Ford Cosworth	V8	11	spin	19	10
r	11	E de Angelis	Lotus	93T	Renault	V6t	1	throttle linkage	11	6
r	25	J-P Jarier	Ligier	JS21	Ford Cosworth	V8	0	gearbox	16	8
r	29	M Surer	Arrows	A6	Ford Cosworth	V8	0	differential	14	7
nq	17	J Villeneuve	RAM March	01	Ford Cosworth	V8				
nq	32	P Ghinzani	Osella	FA1E	Alfa Romeo	V12				

Winning speed 170.661 km/h, 106.044 mph
Pole Position speed 178.927 km/h, 111.180 mph (R Arnoux, 1 min:28.729 sec)
Fastest Lap speed 174.748 km/h, 108.583 mph (P Tambay, 1 min:30.851 sec on lap 42)
Lap Leaders R Arnoux 1-34,39-70 (66); R Patrese 35-37 (3); P Tambay 38 (1).

BRITAIN: Silverstone (Round 9) (Race 382)

67 laps x 4.719 km, 2.932 miles = 316.146 km, 196.444 miles

Pos	No	Driver	Car	Model	Engine		Laps	Time/Reason for Retirement	Grid Pos	Row
1	15	A Prost	Renault	RE40	Renault	V6t	67	1h 24m 39.780s	3	2
2	5	N Piquet	Brabham	BT52B	BMW	4t	67	1h 24m 58.941s	6	3
3	27	P Tambay	Ferrari	126C3	Ferrari	V6t	67	1h 25m 06.026s	2	1
4	12	N Mansell	Lotus	94T	Renault	V6t	67	1h 25m 18.732s	18	9
5	28	R Arnoux	Ferrari	126C3	Ferrari	V6t	67	1h 25m 38.654s	1	1
6	8	N Lauda	McLaren	MP4/1C	Ford Cosworth	V8	66		15	8
7	23	M Baldi	Alfa Romeo	183T	Alfa Romeo	V8t	66		11	6
8	22	A de Cesaris	Alfa Romeo	183T	Alfa Romeo	V8t	66		9	5
9	7	J Watson	McLaren	MP4/1C	Ford Cosworth	V8	66		24	12
10	25	J-P Jarier	Ligier	JS21	Ford Cosworth	V8	65		25	13
11	1	K Rosberg	Williams	FW08C	Ford Cosworth	V8	65		13	7
12	2	J Laffite	Williams	FW08C	Ford Cosworth	V8	65		20	10
13	3	M Alboreto	Tyrrell	011	Ford Cosworth	V8	65		16	8
14	4	D Sullivan	Tyrrell	011	Ford Cosworth	V8	65		23	12
15	30	T Boutsen	Arrows	A6	Ford Cosworth	V8	65		17	9
16	33	R Guerrero	Theodore	N183	Ford Cosworth	V8	64		21	11
17	29	M Surer	Arrows	A6	Ford Cosworth	V8	64		19	10
r	9	M Winkelhock	ATS	D6	BMW	4t	49	engine overheating	8	4
r	26	R Boesel	Ligier	JS21	Ford Cosworth	V8	48	suspension hydraulics	22	11
r	32	P Ghinzani	Osella	FA1E	Alfa Romeo	V12	46	fuel pressure	26	13
r	35	D Warwick	Toleman	TG183B	Hart	4t	27	gearbox	10	5
r	6	R Patrese	Brabham	BT52B	BMW	4t	9	turbo	5	3
r	40	S Johansson	Spirit	201	Honda	V6t	5	fuel pump belt	14	7
r	16	E Cheever	Renault	RE40	Renault	V6t	3	cylinder head gasket	7	4
r	36	B Giacomelli	Toleman	TG183B	Hart	4t	3	turbo	12	6
r	11	E de Angelis	Lotus	94T	Renault	V6t	1	distributor	4	2
nq	34	J Cecotto	Theodore	N183	Ford Cosworth	V8				
nq	31	C Fabi	Osella	FA1E	Alfa Romeo	V12				
nq	17	K Acheson	RAM March	01	Ford Cosworth	V8				

Winning speed 224.050 km/h, 139.218 mph
Pole Position speed 244.550 km/h, 151.956 mph (R Arnoux, 1 min: 9.462 sec)
Fastest Lap speed 228.898 km/h, 142.230 mph (A Prost, 1 min:14.212 sec on lap 32)
Lap Leaders P Tambay 1-19 (19); A Prost 20-36,42-67 (43); N Piquet 37-41 (5).

45 laps x 6.797 km, 4.223 miles = 305.865 km, 190.056 miles

Pos	No	Driver	Car	Model	Engine		Laps	Time/Reason for Retirement	Grid Pos	Row
1	28	R Arnoux	Ferrari	126C3	Ferrari	V6t	45	1h 27m 10.319s	2	1
2	22	A de Cesaris	Alfa Romeo	183T	Alfa Romeo	V8t	45	1h 28m 20.971s	3	2
3	6	R Patrese	Brabham	BT52B	BMW	4t	45	1h 28m 54.412s	8	4
4	15	A Prost	Renault	RE40	Renault	V6t	45	1h 29m 11.069s	5	3
dq	8	N Lauda	McLaren	MP4/1C	Ford Cosworth	V8	44	reversed in pits	18	9
5	7	J Watson	McLaren	MP4/1C	Ford Cosworth	V8	44		23	12
6	2	J Laffite	Williams	FW08C	Ford Cosworth	V8	44		15	8
7	29	M Surer	Arrows	A6	Ford Cosworth	V8	44		20	10
8	25	J-P Jarier	Ligier	JS21	Ford Cosworth	V8	44		19	10
9	30	T Boutsen	Arrows	A6	Ford Cosworth	V8	44		14	7
10	1	K Rosberg	Williams	FW08C	Ford Cosworth	V8	44		12	6
11	34	J Cecotto	Theodore	N183	Ford Cosworth	V8	44		22	11
12	4	D Sullivan	Tyrrell	011	Ford Cosworth	V8	43		21	11
13r	5	N Piquet	Brabham	BT52B	BMW	4t	42	fuel filter leak / fire	4	2
r	16	E Cheever	Renault	RE40	Renault	V6t	38	fuel injection pump	6	3
r	32	P Ghinzani	Osella	FA1E	Alfa Romeo	V12	34	engine	26	13
r	26	R Boesel	Ligier	JS21	Ford Cosworth	V8	27	engine	25	13
r	23	M Baldi	Alfa Romeo	183T	Alfa Romeo	V8t	24	engine	7	4
r	36	B Giacomelli	Toleman	TG183B	Hart	4t	19	turbo	10	5
r	35	D Warwick	Toleman	TG183B	Hart	4t	17	engine	9	5
r	40	S Johansson	Spirit	201C	Honda	V6t	11	engine	13	7
r	27	P Tambay	Ferrari	126C3	Ferrari	V6t	11	engine	1	1
r	11	E de Angelis	Lotus	94T	Renault	V6t	10	engine overheating	11	6
r	3	M Alboreto	Tyrrell	011	Ford Cosworth	V8	4	fuel pump drive	16	8
r	12	N Mansell	Lotus	94T	Renault	V6t	1	engine	17	9
r	33	R Guerrero	Theodore	N183	Ford Cosworth	V8	0	engine	24	12
nq	17	K Acheson	RAM March	01	Ford Cosworth	V8				
nq	31	C Fabi	Osella	FA1E	Alfa Romeo	V12				
nq	9	M Winkelhock	ATS	D6	BMW	4t				

Winning speed 210.525 km/h, 130.814 mph
Pole Position speed 223.815 km/h, 139.072 mph (P Tambay, 1 min:49.328 sec)
Fastest Lap speed 214.759 km/h, 133.445 mph (R Arnoux, 1 min:53.938 sec on lap 12)
Lap Leaders P Tambay 1 (1); R Arnoux 2-23,31-45 (37); N Piquet 24-30 (7).

53 laps x 5.942 km, 3.692 miles = 314.926 km, 195.686 miles

Pos	No	Driver	Car	Model	Engine		Laps	Time/Reason for Retirement	Grid Pos	Row
1	15	A Prost	Renault	RE40	Renault	V6t	53	1h 24m 32.745s	5	3
2	28	R Arnoux	Ferrari	126C3	Ferrari	V6t	53	1h 24m 39.580s	2	1
3	5	N Piquet	Brabham	BT52B	BMW	4t	53	1h 25m 00.404s	4	2
4	16	E Cheever	Renault	RE40	Renault	V6t	53	1h 25m 01.140s	8	4
5	12	N Mansell	Lotus	94T	Renault	V6t	52		3	2
6	8	N Lauda	McLaren	MP4/1C	Ford Cosworth	V8	51		14	7
7	25	J-P Jarier	Ligier	JS21	Ford Cosworth	V8	51		20	10
8	1	K Rosberg	Williams	FW08C	Ford Cosworth	V8	51		15	8
9	7	J Watson	McLaren	MP4/1C	Ford Cosworth	V8	51		17	9
10	31	C Fabi	Osella	FA1E	Alfa Romeo	V12	50		26	13
11	32	P Ghinzani	Osella	FA1E	Alfa Romeo	V12	49		25	13
12	40	S Johansson	Spirit	201	Honda	V6t	48		16	8
13	30	T Boutsen	Arrows	A6	Ford Cosworth	V8	48		19	10
r	9	M Winkelhock	ATS	D6	BMW	4t	33	engine overheating	13	7
r	22	A de Cesaris	Alfa Romeo	183T	Alfa Romeo	V8t	31	out of fuel	11	6
r	27	P Tambay	Ferrari	126C3	Ferrari	V6t	30	oil union / engine	1	1
r	6	R Patrese	Brabham	BT52B	BMW	4t	29	engine overheating	6	3
r	33	R Guerrero	Theodore	N183	Ford Cosworth	V8	25	gearbox	21	11
r	2	J Laffite	Williams	FW08C	Ford Cosworth	V8	21	accident / handling	24	12
r	23	M Baldi	Alfa Romeo	183T	Alfa Romeo	V8t	13	engine	9	5
r	3	M Alboreto	Tyrrell	011	Ford Cosworth	V8	8	accident	18	9
r	35	D Warwick	Toleman	TG183B	Hart	4t	2	turbo	10	5
r	36	B Giacomelli	Toleman	TG183B	Hart	4t	1	accident	7	4
r	4	D Sullivan	Tyrrell	011	Ford Cosworth	V8	0	accident	23	12
r	29	M Surer	Arrows	A6	Ford Cosworth	V8	0	accident	22	11
r	11	E de Angelis	Lotus	94T	Renault	V6t	0	accident	12	6
nq	26	R Boesel	Ligier	JS21	Ford Cosworth	V8				
nq	34	J Cecotto	Theodore	N183	Ford Cosworth	V8				
nq	17	K Acheson	RAM March	01	Ford Cosworth	V8				

Winning speed 223.495 km/h, 138.873 mph
Pole Position speed 238.021 km/h, 147.899 mph (P Tambay, 1 min:29.871 sec)
Fastest Lap speed 227.660 km/h, 141.462 mph (A Prost, 1 min:33.961 sec on lap 20)
Lap Leaders P Tambay 1-21 (21); R Arnoux 22-27,38-47 (16); N Piquet 28-37 (10); A Prost 48-53 (6).

72 laps x 4.252 km, 2.642 miles = 306.144 km, 190.229 miles

Pos	No	Driver	Car	Model	Engine		Laps	Time/Reason for Retirement	Grid Pos	Row
1	28	R Arnoux	Ferrari	126C3	Ferrari	V6t	72	1h 38m 41.950s	10	5
2	27	P Tambay	Ferrari	126C3	Ferrari	V6t	72	1h 39m 02.789s	2	1
3	7	J Watson	McLaren	MP4/1C	Ford Cosworth	V8	72	1h 39m 25.691s	15	8
4	35	D Warwick	Toleman	TG183B	Hart	4t	72	1h 39m 58.789s	7	4
5	23	M Baldi	Alfa Romeo	183T	Alfa Romeo	V8t	72	1h 40m 06.242s	12	6
6	3	M Alboreto	Tyrrell	012	Ford Cosworth	V8	71		18	9
7	40	S Johansson	Spirit	201C	Honda	V6t	70		16	8
8	29	M Surer	Arrows	A6	Ford Cosworth	V8	70		14	7
9	6	R Patrese	Brabham	BT52B	BMW	4t	70		6	3
10	26	R Boesel	Ligier	JS21	Ford Cosworth	V8	70		24	12
11r	31	C Fabi	Osella	FA1E	Alfa Romeo	V12	68	engine	25	13
12	33	R Guerrero	Theodore	N183	Ford Cosworth	V8	68		20	10
13	36	B Giacomelli	Toleman	TG183B	Hart	4t	68		13	7
14r	30	T Boutsen	Arrows	A6	Ford Cosworth	V8	65	engine	21	11
r	1	K Rosberg	Williams	FW08C	Ford Cosworth	V8	53	misfire	23	12
dq	9	M Winkelhock	ATS	D6	BMW	4t	50	overtook on parade lap	9	5
r	5	N Piquet	Brabham	BT52B	BMW	4t	41	accident	1	1
r	15	A Prost	Renault	RE40	Renault	V6t	41	accident / front wing	4	2
r	16	E Cheever	Renault	RE40	Renault	V6t	39	electrics / turbo	11	6
r	2	J Laffite	Williams	FW08C	Ford Cosworth	V8	37	tyres / handling	17	9
r	12	N Mansell	Lotus	94T	Renault	V6t	26	spin	5	3
r	8	N Lauda	McLaren	MP4/1E	TAG Porsche	V6t	25	brakes	19	10
r	4	D Sullivan	Tyrrell	011	Ford Cosworth	V8	20	engine	26	13
r	11	E de Angelis	Lotus	94T	Renault	V6t	12	fuel metering unit	3	2
r	22	A de Cesaris	Alfa Romeo	183T	Alfa Romeo	V8t	5	engine	8	4
r	25	J-P Jarier	Ligier	JS21	Ford Cosworth	V8	3	accident / front suspension	22	11
nq	32	P Ghinzani	Osella	FA1E	Alfa Romeo	V12				
nq	34	J Cecotto	Theodore	N183	Ford Cosworth	V8				
nq	17	K Acheson	RAM March	01	Ford Cosworth	V8				

Winning speed 186.107 km/h, 115.642 mph
Pole Position speed 202.396 km/h, 125.763 mph (N Piquet, 1 min:15.630 sec)
Fastest Lap speed 191.668 km/h, 119.097 mph (R Arnoux, 1 min:19.863 sec on lap 33)
Lap Leaders N Piquet 1-41 (41); R Arnoux 42-72 (31).

52 laps x 5.800 km, 3.604 miles = 301.600 km, 187.406 miles

Pos	No	Driver	Car	Model	Engine		Laps	Time/Reason for Retirement	Grid Pos	Row
1	5	N Piquet	Brabham	BT52B	BMW	4t	52	1h 23m 10.880s	4	2
2	28	R Arnoux	Ferrari	126C3	Ferrari	V6t	52	1h 23m 21.092s	3	2
3	16	E Cheever	Renault	RE40	Renault	V6t	52	1h 23m 29.492s	7	4
4	27	P Tambay	Ferrari	126C3	Ferrari	V6t	52	1h 23m 39.903s	2	1
5	11	E de Angelis	Lotus	94T	Renault	V6t	52	1h 24m 04.560s	8	4
6	35	D Warwick	Toleman	TG183B	Hart	4t	52	1h 24m 24.228s	12	6
7	36	B Giacomelli	Toleman	TG183B	Hart	4t	52	1h 24m 44.802s	14	7
8	12	N Mansell	Lotus	94T	Renault	V6t	52	1h 24m 46.915s	11	6
9	25	J-P Jarier	Ligier	JS21	Ford Cosworth	V8	51		19	10
10	29	M Surer	Arrows	A6	Ford Cosworth	V8	51		20	10
11	1	K Rosberg	Williams	FW08C	Ford Cosworth	V8	51		16	8
12	34	J Cecotto	Theodore	N183	Ford Cosworth	V8	50		26	13
13	33	R Guerrero	Theodore	N183	Ford Cosworth	V8	50		21	11
r	31	C Fabi	Osella	FA1E	Alfa Romeo	V12	45	oil union	25	13
r	4	D Sullivan	Tyrrell	011	Ford Cosworth	V8	44	fuel pump drive	22	11
r	30	T Boutsen	Arrows	A6	Ford Cosworth	V8	41	engine	18	9
r	9	M Winkelhock	ATS	D6	BMW	4t	35	exhaust	9	5
r	3	M Alboreto	Tyrrell	012	Ford Cosworth	V8	28	clutch	24	12
r	15	A Prost	Renault	RE40	Renault	V6t	26	turbo	5	3
r	8	N Lauda	McLaren	MP4/1E	TAG Porsche	V6t	24	electrics	13	7
r	7	J Watson	McLaren	MP4/1E	TAG Porsche	V6t	13	engine	15	8
r	32	P Ghinzani	Osella	FA1E	Alfa Romeo	V12	10	gearbox	23	12
r	23	M Baldi	Alfa Romeo	183T	Alfa Romeo	V8t	4	turbo	10	5
r	40	S Johansson	Spirit	201	Honda	V6t	4	distributor	17	9
r	6	R Patrese	Brabham	BT52B	BMW	4t	2	electrics	1	1
r	22	A de Cesaris	Alfa Romeo	183T	Alfa Romeo	V8t	2	spin	6	3
nq	26	R Boesel	Ligier	JS21	Ford Cosworth	V8				
nq	2	J Laffite	Williams	FW08C	Ford Cosworth	V8				
nq	17	K Acheson	RAM March	01	Ford Cosworth	V8				

Winning speed 217.549 km/h, 135.179 mph
Pole Position speed 234.286 km/h, 145.578 mph (R Patrese, 1 min:29.122 sec)
Fastest Lap speed 221.114 km/h, 137.394 mph (N Piquet, 1 min:34.431 sec on lap 20)
Lap Leaders R Patrese 1-2 (2); N Piquet 3-52 (50).

K Rosberg finished 9th, but penalised 1 minute for infringement at the start.

76 laps x 4.207 km, 2.614 miles = 319.719 km, 198.664 miles

Pos	No	Driver	Car	Model	Engine		Laps	Time/Reason for Retirement	Grid Pos	Row
1	5	N Piquet	Brabham	BT52B	BMW	4t	76	1h 36m 45.865s	4	2
2	15	A Prost	Renault	RE40	Renault	V6t	76	1h 36m 52.436s	8	4
3	12	N Mansell	Lotus	94T	Renault	V6t	76	1h 37m 16.180s	3	2
4	22	A de Cesaris	Alfa Romeo	183T	Alfa Romeo	V8t	76	1h 37m 20.261s	14	7
5	35	D Warwick	Toleman	TG183B	Hart	4t	76	1h 37m 30.780s	11	6
6	36	B Giacomelli	Toleman	TG183B	Hart	4t	76	1h 37m 38.055s	12	6
7	6	R Patrese	Brabham	BT52B	BMW	4t	76	1h 37m 58.549s	2	1
8	9	M Winkelhock	ATS	D6	BMW	4t	75		9	5
9	28	R Arnoux	Ferrari	126C3	Ferrari	V6t	75		5	3
10	16	E Cheever	Renault	RE40	Renault	V6t	75		7	4
11	30	T Boutsen	Arrows	A6	Ford Cosworth	V8	75		18	9
12	33	R Guerrero	Theodore	N183	Ford Cosworth	V8	75		21	11
13	42	J Palmer	Williams	FW08C	Ford Cosworth	V8	74		25	13
14	40	S Johansson	Spirit	201	Honda	V6t	74		19	10
15	26	R Boesel	Ligier	JS21	Ford Cosworth	V8	73		23	12
r	27	P Tambay	Ferrari	126C3	Ferrari	V6t	67	accident / brake fluid loss	6	3
r	3	M Alboreto	Tyrrell	012	Ford Cosworth	V8	64	engine	26	13
nc	32	P Ghinzani	Osella	FA1E	Alfa Romeo	V12	63		24	12
r	29	M Surer	Arrows	A6	Ford Cosworth	V8	50	engine	17	9
r	1	K Rosberg	Williams	FW08C	Ford Cosworth	V8	43	valve springs	16	8
r	23	M Baldi	Alfa Romeo	183T	Alfa Romeo	V8t	39	clutch	15	8
r	7	J Watson	McLaren	MP4/1E	TAG Porsche	V6t	36	accident / wing	10	5
r	4	D Sullivan	Tyrrell	012	Ford Cosworth	V8	27	oil line / fire	20	10
r	8	N Lauda	McLaren	MP4/1E	TAG Porsche	V6t	25	engine	13	7
r	11	E de Angelis	Lotus	94T	Renault	V6t	12	engine	1	1
r	25	J-P Jarier	Ligier	JS21	Ford Cosworth	V8	0	gearbox on grid	22	11
nq	17	K Acheson	RAM March	01	Ford Cosworth	V8				
nq	31	C Fabi	Osella	FA1E	Alfa Romeo	V12				
nq	2	J Laffite	Williams	FW08C	Ford Cosworth	V8				

Winning speed 198.246 km/h, 123.184 mph
Pole Position speed 210.073 km/h, 130.533 mph (E de Angelis, 1 min:12.092 sec)
Fastest Lap speed 203.715 km/h, 126.583 mph (N Mansell, 1 min:14.342 sec on lap 70)
Lap Leaders R Patrese 1-10 (10); N Piquet 11-76 (66).

77 laps x 4.104 km, 2.550 miles = 316.008 km, 196.358 miles

Pos	No	Driver	Car	Model	Engine		Laps	Time/Reason for Retirement	Grid Pos	Row
1	6	R Patrese	Brabham	BT52B	BMW	4t	77	1h 33m 25.708s	3	2
2	22	A de Cesaris	Alfa Romeo	183T	Alfa Romeo	V8t	77	1h 33m 35.027s	9	5
3	5	N Piquet	Brabham	BT52B	BMW	4t	77	1h 33m 47.677s	2	1
4	35	D Warwick	Toleman	TG183B	Hart	4t	76		13	7
5	1	K Rosberg	Williams	FW09	Honda	V6t	76		6	3
6	16	E Cheever	Renault	RE40	Renault	V6t	76		14	7
7	4	D Sullivan	Tyrrell	012	Ford Cosworth	V8	75		19	10
8	29	M Surer	Arrows	A6	Ford Cosworth	V8	75		22	11
9	30	T Boutsen	Arrows	A6	Ford Cosworth	V8	74		20	10
10	25	J-P Jarier	Ligier	JS21	Ford Cosworth	V8	73		21	11
11r	8	N Lauda	McLaren	MP4/1E	TAG Porsche	V6t	71	electrics	12	6
12	17	K Acheson	RAM March	01	Ford Cosworth	V8	71		24	12
nc	12	N Mansell	Lotus	94T	Renault	V6t	68		7	4
nc	26	R Boesel	Ligier	JS21	Ford Cosworth	V8	66		23	12
r	3	M Alboreto	Tyrrell	012	Ford Cosworth	V8	60	engine	18	9
r	27	P Tambay	Ferrari	126C3	Ferrari	V6t	56	turbo	1	1
r	36	B Giacomelli	Toleman	TG183B	Hart	4t	56	turbo / fire	16	8
r	15	A Prost	Renault	RE40	Renault	V6t	35	turbo	5	3
r	31	C Fabi	Osella	FA1E	Alfa Romeo	V12	28	engine	25	13
r	11	E de Angelis	Lotus	94T	Renault	V6t	20	misfire	11	6
dq	7	J Watson	McLaren	MP4/1E	TAG Porsche	V6t	18	overtook on parade lap	15	8
r	28	R Arnoux	Ferrari	126C3	Ferrari	V6t	9	engine	4	2
r	23	M Baldi	Alfa Romeo	183T	Alfa Romeo	V8t	5	engine	17	9
r	9	M Winkelhock	ATS	D6	BMW	4t	1	engine	8	4
r	2	J Laffite	Williams	FW09	Honda	V6t	1	accident	10	5
r	32	P Ghinzani	Osella	FA1E	Alfa Romeo	V12	1	engine	26	13

Winning speed 202.941 km/h, 126.102 mph
Pole Position speed 221.991 km/h, 137.939 mph (P Tambay, 1 min: 6.554 sec)
Fastest Lap speed 211.220 km/h, 131.246 mph (N Piquet, 1 min: 9.948 sec on lap 6)
Lap Leaders N Piquet 1-59 (59); R Patrese 60-77 (18).

Pos	Driver	Car-Engine	GPs	laps	km	miles
1	N Piquet	Brabham-BMW	11	327	1,538.5	956.0
2	R Arnoux	Ferrari	6	177	883.1	548.8
3	A Prost	Renault	4	121	680.8	423.0
4	P Tambay	Ferrari	6	94	443.6	275.6
5	K Rosberg	Williams-Ford Cosworth	2	82	281.9	175.2
6	R Patrese	Brabham-BMW	5	61	281.9	175.2
7	J Watson	McLaren-Ford Cosworth	1	31	101.5	63.1
8	J Laffite	Williams-Ford Cosworth	1	19	62.2	38.7
9	A de Cesaris	Alfa Romeo	1	18.1	125.7	78.1
10	M Alboreto	Tyrrell-Ford Cosworth	1	10	40.2	25.0
			15	940.1	4,439.6	2,758.6

Driver Points 1983

		BR	USAW	F	RSM	MC	B	DET	CDN	GB	D	A	NL	I	EUR	ZA	Total
1	N Piquet	9	-	6	-	6	3	3	-	6	-	4	-	9	9	4	59
2	A Prost	-	-	9	6	4	9	-	2	9	3	9	-	-	6	-	57
3	R Arnoux	-	4	-	4	-	-	-	9	2	9	6	9	6	-	-	49
4	P Tambay	2	-	3	9	3	6	-	4	4	-	-	6	3	-	-	40
5	K Rosberg	-	-	2	3	9	2	6	3	-	-	-	-	-	-	2	27
6	J Watson	-	9	-	2	-	-	4	1	-	2	-	4	-	-	-	22
	E Cheever	-	-	4	-	-	4	-	6	-	-	3	-	4	-	1	22
8	A de Cesaris	-	-	-	-	-	-	-	-	-	6	-	-	-	3	6	15
9	R Patrese	-	-	-	-	-	-	-	-	-	4	-	-	-	-	9	13
10	N Lauda	4	6	-	-	-	-	-	-	1	-	1	-	-	-	-	12
11	J Laffite	3	3	1	-	-	1	2	-	-	1	-	-	-	-	-	11
12	M Alboreto	-	-	-	-	-	-	9	-	-	-	-	1	-	-	-	10
	N Mansell	-	-	-	-	-	1	-	3	-	2	-	-	4	-		10
14	D Warwick	-	-	-	-	-	-	-	-	-	-	3	1	2	3		9
15	M Surer	1	2	-	1	-	-	-	-	-	-	-	-	-	-	-	4
16	M Baldi	-	-	-	-	1	-	-	-	-	-	2	-	-	-		3
17	D Sullivan	-	-	-	-	2	-	-	-	-	-	-	-	-	-		2
	E de Angelis	-	-	-	-	-	-	-	-	-	-	-	2	-	-		2
19	J Cecotto	-	1	-	-	-	-	-	-	-	-	-	-	-	-	-	1
	B Giacomelli	-	-	-	-	-	-	-	-	-	-	-	-	1	-		1

9,6,4,3,2 and 1 point awarded to the first six finishers. Best 11 scores.

Constructor Points 1983

		BR	USAW	F	RSM	MC	B	DET	CDN	GB	D	A	NL	I	EUR	ZA	Total
1	Ferrari	2	4	3	13	3	6	-	13	6	9	6	15	9	-	-	89
2	Renault	-	-	13	6	4	13	-	8	9	3	12	-	4	6	1	79
3	Brabham-BMW	9	-	6	-	6	3	3	-	6	4	4	-	9	9	13	72
4	Williams-Ford Cosworth	3	3	3	3	9	3	8	3	-	1	-	-	-	-	-	36
5	McLaren-Ford Cosworth	4	15	-	2	-	-	4	1	1	2	1	4	-	-	-	34
6	Alfa Romeo	-	-	-	-	1	-	-	-	-	6	-	2	-	3	6	18
7	Tyrrell-Ford Cosworth	-	-	-	-	2	-	9	-	-	-	-	1	-	-	-	12
8	Lotus-Renault	-	-	-	-	-	-	-	-	3	-	2	-	2	4	-	11
9	Toleman-Hart	-	-	-	-	-	-	-	-	-	-	-	3	1	3	3	10
10	Arrows-Ford Cosworth	1	2	-	1	-	-	-	-	-	-	-	-	-	-	-	4
11	Williams-Honda	-	-	-	-	-	-	-	-	-	-	-	-	-	-	2	2
12	Theodore-Ford Cosworth	-	1	-	-	-	-	-	-	-	-	-	-	-	-	-	1
	Lotus-Ford Cosworth	-	-	-	-	-	-	1	-	-	-	-	-	-	-	-	1

9,6,4,3,2 and 1 point awarded to the first six finishers.

1984

Race Entrants and Results

Safety issues forced a refuelling ban as teams now had a fuel limit of 220 litres. After the first turbo champion, virtually all entries followed this route, with the TAG Porsche powered McLaren emerging dominant. Tyrrell was the only normally aspirated car but they found themselves banned for weight deception after ball bearings were found in tanks at post-race scrutineering.

BRABHAM
MRD International: Piquet, T Fabi, C Fabi, Winkelhock

TYRRELL
Tyrrell Racing Organisation: Brundle, Johansson, Bellof, (Thackwell)

WILLIAMS
Williams Grand Prix Engineering: Laffite, Rosberg

McLAREN
Marlboro McLaren International: Prost, Lauda

RAM
Skoal Bandit Formula 1 Team: Alliot, Palmer, Thackwell

LOTUS
John Player Team Lotus: de Angelis, Mansell

ATS
Team ATS: Winkelhock, Berger

RENAULT
Equipe Renault Elf: Tambay, Warwick, Streiff

ARROWS
Barclay Nordica Arrows BMW: Surer, Boutsen

TOLEMAN
Toleman Group Motorsport: Senna, (Martini), Cecotto, Johansson

SPIRIT
Spirit Racing: Baldi, Rothengatter

ALFA ROMEO
Benetton Team Alfa Romeo: Patrese, Cheever

OSELLA
Osella Squadra Corse: Ghinzani, Gartner

LIGIER
Ligier Loto: Hesnault, de Cesaris

FERRARI
Scuderia Ferrari SpA SEFAC: Alboreto, Arnoux

25 Mar 1984		BRAZIL: Rio de Janeiro							(Round 1)		(Race 389)
		61 laps x 5.031 km, 3.126 miles = 306.891 km, 190.693 miles									
Pos	No	Driver	Car	Model	Engine		Laps	Time/Reason for Retirement		Grid Pos	Row
1	7	A Prost	McLaren	MP4/2	TAG Porsche	V6t	61	1h 42m 34.492s		4	2
2	6	K Rosberg	Williams	FW09	Honda	V6t	61	1h 43m 15.006s		9	5
3	11	E de Angelis	Lotus	95T	Renault	V6t	61	1h 43m 33.620s		1	1
4	23	E Cheever	Alfa Romeo	184T	Alfa Romeo	V8t	60			12	6
dq	3	M Brundle	Tyrrell	012	Ford Cosworth	V8	60	(1)		18	9
5r	15	P Tambay	Renault	RE50	Renault	V6t	59	out of fuel		8	4
6	18	T Boutsen	Arrows	A6	Ford Cosworth	V8	59			20	10
7	17	M Surer	Arrows	A6	Ford Cosworth	V8	59			24	12
8	10	J Palmer	RAM	01	Hart	4t	58			26	13
r	16	D Warwick	Renault	RE50	Renault	V6t	51	front suspension		3	2
r	26	A de Cesaris	Ligier	JS23	Renault	V6t	42	gear linkage		14	7
r	22	R Patrese	Alfa Romeo	184T	Alfa Romeo	V8t	41	gearbox		11	6
r	8	N Lauda	McLaren	MP4/2	TAG Porsche	V6t	38	ignition		6	3
r	12	N Mansell	Lotus	95T	Renault	V6t	35	accident		5	3
r	1	N Piquet	Brabham	BT53	BMW	4t	32	turbo		7	4
r	2	T Fabi	Brabham	BT53	BMW	4t	32	turbo		15	8
r	28	R Arnoux	Ferrari	126C4	Ferrari	V6t	30	battery		10	5
r	24	P Ghinzani	Osella	FA1F	Alfa Romeo	V8t	28	gearbox		21	11
r	25	F Hesnault	Ligier	JS23	Renault	V6t	25	engine overheating		19	10
r	9	P Alliot	RAM	02	Hart	4t	24	battery mounting		25	13
r	20	J Cecotto	Toleman	TG183B	Hart	4t	18	turbo boost pressure		17	9
r	5	J Laffite	Williams	FW09	Honda	V6t	15	electrics / turbo		13	7
r	27	M Alboreto	Ferrari	126C4	Ferrari	V6t	14	brake caliper		2	1
r	21	M Baldi	Spirit	101	Hart	4t	12	distributor rotor arm		23	12
dq	4	S Bellof	Tyrrell	012	Ford Cosworth	V8	11	throttle linkage / (1)		22	11
r	19	A Senna	Toleman	TG183B	Hart	4t	8	turbo boost pressure		16	8
exc	14	M Winkelhock	ATS	D7	BMW	4t		mechanics pushed car into pits			

Winning speed 179.512 km/h, 111.544 mph
Pole Position speed 204.901 km/h, 127.320 mph (E de Angelis, 1 min:28.392 sec)
Fastest Lap speed 187.687 km/h, 116.623 mph (A Prost, 1 min:36.499 sec on lap 42)
Lap Leaders M Alboreto 1-11 (11); N Lauda 12-37 (26); A Prost 38,51-61 (12); D Warwick 39-50 (12).

(1) On 18 July 1984, due to infringing the rules, Tyrrell were disqualified from all the races they had competed in during the season, and refused entry to all remaining races, although the team was allowed to continue until their appeal was heard.

75 laps x 4.104 km, 2.550 miles = 307.800 km, 191.258 miles

Pos	No	Driver	Car	Model	Engine		Laps	Time/Reason for Retirement	Grid Pos	Row
1	8	N Lauda	McLaren	MP4/2	TAG Porsche	V6t	75	1h 29m 23.430s	8	4
2	7	A Prost	McLaren	MP4/2	TAG Porsche	V6t	75	1h 30m 29.380s	5	3
3	16	D Warwick	Renault	RE50	Renault	V6t	74		9	5
4	22	R Patrese	Alfa Romeo	184T	Alfa Romeo	V8t	73		18	9
5	26	A de Cesaris	Ligier	JS23	Renault	V6t	73		14	7
6	19	A Senna	Toleman	TG183B	Hart	4t	72		13	7
7	11	E de Angelis	Lotus	95T	Renault	V6t	71		7	4
8	21	M Baldi	Spirit	101	Hart	4t	71		20	10
9	17	M Surer	Arrows	A6	Ford Cosworth	V8	71		23	12
10	25	F Hesnault	Ligier	JS23	Renault	V6t	71		17	9
dq	3	M Brundle	Tyrrell	012	Ford Cosworth	V8	71	(1)	25	13
11r	27	M Alboreto	Ferrari	126C4	Ferrari	V6t	70	ignition	10	5
12	18	T Boutsen	Arrows	A6	Ford Cosworth	V8	70		26	13
r	15	P Tambay	Renault	RE50	Renault	V6t	66	fuel metering unit	4	2
r	5	J Laffite	Williams	FW09	Honda	V6t	60	rear wheel nut / wheel lost	11	6
dq	4	S Bellof	Tyrrell	012	Ford Cosworth	V8	59	front hub / brakes / spin (1)	24	12
r	14	M Winkelhock	ATS	D7	BMW	4t	53	battery	12	6
r	6	K Rosberg	Williams	FW09	Honda	V6t	51	brake overheating / cv joint	2	1
r	12	N Mansell	Lotus	95T	Renault	V6t	51	turbo inlet duct	3	2
r	28	R Arnoux	Ferrari	126C4	Ferrari	V6t	40	fuel injection	15	8
r	1	N Piquet	Brabham	BT53	BMW	4t	29	turbo compressor	1	1
r	20	J Cecotto	Toleman	TG183B	Hart	4t	26	rear tyre burst / suspension	19	10
r	9	P Alliot	RAM	02	Hart	4t	24	water leak / engine	22	11
r	10	J Palmer	RAM	01	Hart	4t	22	gearbox / electrics	21	11
r	2	T Fabi	Brabham	BT53	BMW	4t	18	turbo compressor	6	3
r	23	E Cheever	Alfa Romeo	184T	Alfa Romeo	V8t	4	radiator	16	8
ns	24	P Ghinzani	Osella	FA1F	Alfa Romeo	V8t		accident / injury		

Winning speed 206.599 km/h, 128.375 mph
Pole Position speed 227.750 km/h, 141.518 mph (N Piquet, 1 min: 4.871 sec)
Fastest Lap speed 214.504 km/h, 133.287 mph (P Tambay, 1 min: 8.877 sec on lap 64)
Lap Leaders K Rosberg 1 (1); N Piquet 2-20 (19); N Lauda 21-75 (55).

T Boutsen should have been placed 9th (71 laps) but a lap charting error cost him a lap. Protest by team was too late to correct the error.

70 laps x 4.262 km, 2.648 miles = 298.340 km, 185.380 miles

Pos	No	Driver	Car	Model	Engine		Laps	Time/Reason for Retirement	Grid Pos	Row
1	27	M Alboreto	Ferrari	126C4	Ferrari	V6t	70	1h 36m 32.048s	1	1
2	16	D Warwick	Renault	RE50	Renault	V6t	70	1h 37m 14.434s	4	2
3	28	R Arnoux	Ferrari	126C4	Ferrari	V6t	70	1h 37m 41.851s	2	1
4r	6	K Rosberg	Williams	FW09	Honda	V6t	69	out of fuel	3	2
5	11	E de Angelis	Lotus	95T	Renault	V6t	69		5	3
dq	4	S Bellof	Tyrrell	012	Ford Cosworth	V8	69	(1)	21	11
6	19	A Senna	Toleman	TG183B	Hart	4t	68		19	10
7	15	P Tambay	Renault	RE50	Renault	V6t	68		12	6
8	17	M Surer	Arrows	A6	Ford Cosworth	V8	68		24	12
9r	1	N Piquet	Brabham	BT53	BMW	4t	66	engine	9	5
10	10	J Palmer	RAM	02	Hart	4t	64		26	13
r	21	M Baldi	Spirit	101	Hart	4t	53	suspension mounting	25	13
dq	3	M Brundle	Tyrrell	012	Ford Cosworth	V8	51	front hub / wheel lost / (1)	22	11
r	2	T Fabi	Brabham	BT53	BMW	4t	42	spin	18	9
r	26	A de Cesaris	Ligier	JS23	Renault	V6t	42	accident	13	7
r	14	M Winkelhock	ATS	D7	BMW	4t	39	exhaust / electrics	6	3
r	8	N Lauda	McLaren	MP4/2	TAG Porsche	V6t	35	water pump / engine overheating	14	7
r	23	E Cheever	Alfa Romeo	184T	Alfa Romeo	V8t	28	piston	11	6
r	5	J Laffite	Williams	FW09	Honda	V6t	15	electrics	15	8
r	25	F Hesnault	Ligier	JS23	Renault	V6t	15	radiator	23	12
r	18	T Boutsen	Arrows	A7	BMW	4t	15	wire loose / misfire	17	9
r	24	P Ghinzani	Osella	FA1F	Alfa Romeo	V8t	14	differential	20	10
r	12	N Mansell	Lotus	95T	Renault	V6t	14	clutch	10	5
r	7	A Prost	McLaren	MP4/2	TAG Porsche	V6t	5	distributor	8	4
r	22	R Patrese	Alfa Romeo	184T	Alfa Romeo	V8t	2	ignition	7	4
r	20	J Cecotto	Toleman	TG183B	Hart	4t	1	clutch	16	8
nq	9	P Alliot	RAM	02	Hart	4t				

Winning speed 185.431 km/h, 115.221 mph
Pole Position speed 204.997 km/h, 127.379 mph (M Alboreto, 1 min:14.846 sec)
Fastest Lap speed 193.498 km/h, 120.234 mph (R Arnoux, 1 min:19.294 sec on lap 64)
Lap Leaders M Alboreto 1-70 (70).

6 May 1984   **SAN MARINO: Imola**   **(Round 4)   (Race 392)**

60 laps x 5.040 km, 3.132 miles = 302.400 km, 187.903 miles

Pos	No	Driver	Car	Model	Engine		Laps	Time/Reason for Retirement	Grid Pos	Row
1	7	A Prost	McLaren	MP4/2	TAG Porsche	V6t	60	1h 36m 53.679s	2	1
2	28	R Arnoux	Ferrari	126C4	Ferrari	V6t	60	1h 37m 07.095s	6	3
3r	11	E de Angelis	Lotus	95T	Renault	V6t	59		11	6
4	16	D Warwick	Renault	RE50	Renault	V6t	59		4	2
dq	4	S Bellof	Tyrrell	012	Ford Cosworth	V8	59	(1)	21	11
5	18	T Boutsen	Arrows	A6	Ford Cosworth	V8	59		20	10
6r	26	A de Cesaris	Ligier	JS23	Renault	V6t	58	out of fuel	12	6
7r	23	E Cheever	Alfa Romeo	184T	Alfa Romeo	V8t	58	out of fuel	8	4
8	21	M Baldi	Spirit	101	Hart	4t	58		24	12
9	10	J Palmer	RAM	02	Hart	4t	57		25	13
dq	3	M Brundle	Tyrrell	012	Ford Cosworth	V8	55	fuel injection / (1)	22	11
r	9	P Alliot	RAM	02	Hart	4t	53	turbo boost pressure	23	12
nc	20	J Cecotto	Toleman	TG183B	Hart	4t	52		19	10
r	1	N Piquet	Brabham	BT53	BMW	4t	48	turbo	1	1
r	2	T Fabi	Brabham	BT53	BMW	4t	48	turbo	9	5
r	30	J Gartner	Osella	FA1E	Alfa Romeo	V12	46	engine	26	13
r	17	M Surer	Arrows	A7	BMW	4t	40	turbo	16	8
r	14	M Winkelhock	ATS	D7	BMW	4t	31	turbo	7	4
r	27	M Alboreto	Ferrari	126C4	Ferrari	V6t	23	exhaust	13	7
r	8	N Lauda	McLaren	MP4/2	TAG Porsche	V6t	15	engine	5	3
r	5	J Laffite	Williams	FW09	Honda	V6t	11	engine	15	8
r	22	R Patrese	Alfa Romeo	184T	Alfa Romeo	V8t	6	electrics	10	5
r	12	N Mansell	Lotus	95T	Renault	V6t	2	brakes / spin	18	9
r	6	K Rosberg	Williams	FW09	Honda	V6t	2	electrics	3	2
r	15	P Tambay	Renault	RE50	Renault	V6t	0	accident	14	7
r	25	F Hesnault	Ligier	JS23	Renault	V6t	0	accident	17	9
nq	24	P Ghinzani	Osella	FA1F	Alfa Romeo	V8t				
nq	19	A Senna	Toleman	TG183B	Hart	4t				

Winning speed 187.255 km/h, 116.355 mph
Pole Position speed 204.978 km/h, 127.367 mph (N Piquet, 1 min:28.517 sec)
Fastest Lap speed 194.522 km/h, 120.870 mph (N Piquet, 1 min:33.275 sec on lap 48)
Lap Leaders A Prost 1-60 (60).

20 May 1984   **FRANCE: Dijon-Prenois**   **(Round 5)   (Race 393)**

79 laps x 3.887 km, 2.415 miles = 307.073 km, 190.806 miles

Pos	No	Driver	Car	Model	Engine		Laps	Time/Reason for Retirement	Grid Pos	Row
1	8	N Lauda	McLaren	MP4/2	TAG Porsche	V6t	79	1h 31m 11.951s	9	5
2	15	P Tambay	Renault	RE50	Renault	V6t	79	1h 31m 19.105s	1	1
3	12	N Mansell	Lotus	95T	Renault	V6t	79	1h 31m 35.920s	6	3
4	28	R Arnoux	Ferrari	126C4	Ferrari	V6t	79	1h 31m 55.657s	11	6
5	11	E de Angelis	Lotus	95T	Renault	V6t	79	1h 32m 18.076s	2	1
6	6	K Rosberg	Williams	FW09	Honda	V6t	78		4	2
7	7	A Prost	McLaren	MP4/2	TAG Porsche	V6t	78		5	3
8	5	J Laffite	Williams	FW09	Honda	V6t	78		12	6
9	2	T Fabi	Brabham	BT53	BMW	4t	78		17	9
10	26	A de Cesaris	Ligier	JS23	Renault	V6t	77		26	13
11	18	T Boutsen	Arrows	A7	BMW	4t	77		14	7
dq	3	M Brundle	Tyrrell	012	Ford Cosworth	V8	76	(1)	23	12
12	24	P Ghinzani	Osella	FA1F	Alfa Romeo	V8t	74		25	13
13	10	J Palmer	RAM	02	Hart	4t	72		21	11
r	21	M Baldi	Spirit	101	Hart	4t	61	engine	24	12
r	16	D Warwick	Renault	RE50	Renault	V6t	53	accident	7	4
r	17	M Surer	Arrows	A6	Ford Cosworth	V8	51	accident	19	10
r	23	E Cheever	Alfa Romeo	184T	Alfa Romeo	V8t	51	engine	16	8
r	19	A Senna	Toleman	TG184	Hart	4t	35	turbo	13	7
r	27	M Alboreto	Ferrari	126C4	Ferrari	V6t	33	engine	10	5
r	20	J Cecotto	Toleman	TG184	Hart	4t	22	turbo	18	9
r	22	R Patrese	Alfa Romeo	184T	Alfa Romeo	V8t	15	engine	15	8
r	1	N Piquet	Brabham	BT53	BMW	4t	11	turbo	3	2
dq	4	S Bellof	Tyrrell	012	Ford Cosworth	V8	11	thought engine had failed / (1)	20	10
r	14	M Winkelhock	ATS	D7	BMW	4t	5	clutch / brakes	8	4
r	9	P Alliot	RAM	02	Hart	4t	4	electrics	22	11
ns	25	F Hesnault	Ligier	JS23	Renault	V6t		car raced by de Cesaris		

Winning speed 202.024 km/h, 125.532 mph
Pole Position speed 224.971 km/h, 139.791 mph (P Tambay, 1 min: 2.200 sec)
Fastest Lap speed 214.432 km/h, 133.242 mph (A Prost, 1 min: 5.257 sec on lap 59)
Lap Leaders P Tambay 1-38,40,54-61 (47); N Lauda 39,41-53,62-79 (32).

3 Jun 1984 **MONACO: Monte-Carlo** (Round 6) (Race 394)

31 laps x 3.312 km, 2.058 miles = 102.672 km, 63.797 miles

Pos	No	Driver	Car	Model	Engine		Laps	Time/Reason for Retirement	Grid Pos	Row
1	7	A Prost	McLaren	MP4/2	TAG Porsche	V6t	31	1h 01m 07.740s	1	1
2	19	A Senna	Toleman	TG184	Hart	4t	31	1h 01m 15.186s	13	7
dq	4	S Bellof	Tyrrell	012	Ford Cosworth	V8	31	1h 01m 28.881s / (1)	20	10
3	28	R Arnoux	Ferrari	126C4	Ferrari	V6t	31	1h 01m 36.817s	3	2
4	6	K Rosberg	Williams	FW09	Honda	V6t	31	1h 01m 42.986s	10	5
5	11	E de Angelis	Lotus	95T	Renault	V6t	31	1h 01m 52.179s	11	6
6	27	M Alboreto	Ferrari	126C4	Ferrari	V6t	30		4	2
7	24	P Ghinzani	Osella	FA1F	Alfa Romeo	V8t	30		19	10
8	5	J Laffite	Williams	FW09	Honda	V6t	30		16	8
r	22	R Patrese	Alfa Romeo	184T	Alfa Romeo	V8t	24	spin / steering	14	7
r	8	N Lauda	McLaren	MP4/2	TAG Porsche	V6t	23	spin	8	4
r	14	M Winkelhock	ATS	D7	BMW	4t	22	spin	12	6
r	12	N Mansell	Lotus	95T	Renault	V6t	15	accident	2	1
r	1	N Piquet	Brabham	BT53	BMW	4t	14	ignition	9	5
r	25	F Hesnault	Ligier	JS23	Renault	V6t	12	ignition	17	9
r	2	C Fabi	Brabham	BT53	BMW	4t	9	spin	15	8
r	20	J Cecotto	Toleman	TG184	Hart	4t	1	spin	18	9
r	26	A de Cesaris	Ligier	JS23	Renault	V6t	0	accident damage	7	4
r	16	D Warwick	Renault	RE50	Renault	V6t	0	accident	5	3
r	15	P Tambay	Renault	RE50	Renault	V6t	0	accident / injury	6	3
nq	17	M Surer	Arrows	A6	Ford Cosworth	V8				
nq	3	M Brundle	Tyrrell	012	Ford Cosworth	V8				
nq	23	E Cheever	Alfa Romeo	184T	Alfa Romeo	V8t				
nq	18	T Boutsen	Arrows	A7	BMW	4t				
nq	10	J Palmer	RAM	02	Hart	4t				
nq	21	M Baldi	Spirit	101	Hart	4t				
nq	9	P Alliot	RAM	02	Hart	4t				

Winning speed 100.776 km/h, 62.619 mph
Pole Position speed 144.242 km/h, 89.628 mph (A Prost, 1 min:22.661 sec)
Fastest Lap speed 104.284 km/h, 64.799 mph (A Senna, 1 min:54.334 sec on lap 24)
Lap Leaders A Prost 1-10,16-31 (26); N Mansell 11-15 (5).

Scheduled for 77 laps, but stopped early because of rain. Half points were awarded.

17 Jun 1984 **CANADA: Montréal** (Round 7) (Race 395)

70 laps x 4.410 km, 2.740 miles = 308.700 km, 191.817 miles

Pos	No	Driver	Car	Model	Engine		Laps	Time/Reason for Retirement	Grid Pos	Row
1	1	N Piquet	Brabham	BT53	BMW	4t	70	1h 46m 23.748s	1	1
2	8	N Lauda	McLaren	MP4/2	TAG Porsche	V6t	70	1h 46m 26.360s	8	4
3	7	A Prost	McLaren	MP4/2	TAG Porsche	V6t	70	1h 47m 51.780s	2	1
4	11	E de Angelis	Lotus	95T	Renault	V6t	69		3	2
5	28	R Arnoux	Ferrari	126C4	Ferrari	V6t	68		5	3
6	12	N Mansell	Lotus	95T	Renault	V6t	68		7	4
7	19	A Senna	Toleman	TG184	Hart	4t	68		9	5
8	14	M Winkelhock	ATS	D7	BMW	4t	68		12	6
dq	3	M Brundle	Tyrrell	012	Ford Cosworth	V8	68	(1)	21	11
9	20	J Cecotto	Toleman	TG184	Hart	4t	68		20	10
10	9	P Alliot	RAM	02	Hart	4t	65		26	13
11r	23	E Cheever	Alfa Romeo	184T	Alfa Romeo	V8t	63	out of fuel	11	6
r	17	M Surer	Arrows	A6	Ford Cosworth	V8	59	engine	23	12
r	16	D Warwick	Renault	RE50	Renault	V6t	57	undertray	4	2
nc	21	H Rothengatter	Spirit	101	Hart	4t	56		24	12
dq	4	S Bellof	Tyrrell	012	Ford Cosworth	V8	52	driveshaft / (1)	22	11
r	26	A de Cesaris	Ligier	JS23	Renault	V6t	40	brakes	10	5
r	2	C Fabi	Brabham	BT53	BMW	4t	39	turbo boost pressure	16	8
r	18	T Boutsen	Arrows	A7	BMW	4t	38	engine	18	9
r	22	R Patrese	Alfa Romeo	184T	Alfa Romeo	V8t	37	accident	14	7
r	6	K Rosberg	Williams	FW09	Honda	V6t	32	fuel system	15	8
r	5	J Laffite	Williams	FW09	Honda	V6t	31	turbo boost pressure	17	9
r	10	M Thackwell	RAM	02	Hart	4t	29	turbo wastegate	25	13
r	24	P Ghinzani	Osella	FA1F	Alfa Romeo	V8t	11	gearbox	19	10
r	27	M Alboreto	Ferrari	126C4	Ferrari	V6t	10	engine	6	3
r	25	F Hesnault	Ligier	JS23	Renault	V6t	7	turbo	13	7
ew	15	P Tambay	Renault	RE50	Renault	V6t		driver unfit (Monaco injury)		

Winning speed 174.086 km/h, 108.172 mph
Pole Position speed 185.810 km/h, 115.457 mph (N Piquet, 1 min:25.442 sec)
Fastest Lap speed 178.858 km/h, 111.137 mph (N Piquet, 1 min:28.763 sec on lap 55)
Lap Leaders N Piquet 1-70 (70).

24 Jun 1984   USA: Detroit   (Round 8)   (Race 396)

63 laps x 4.023 km, 2.500 miles = 253.472 km, 157.500 miles

Pos	No	Driver	Car	Model	Engine		Laps	Time/Reason for Retirement	Grid Pos	Row
1	1	N Piquet	Brabham	BT53	BMW	4t	63	1h 55m 41.842s	1	1
dq	3	M Brundle	Tyrrell	012	Ford Cosworth	V8	63	1h 55m 42.679s / (1)	11	6
2	11	E de Angelis	Lotus	95T	Renault	V6t	63	1h 56m 14.480s	5	3
3	2	T Fabi	Brabham	BT53	BMW	4t	63	1h 57m 08.370s	23	12
4	7	A Prost	McLaren	MP4/2	TAG Porsche	V6t	63	1h 57m 37.100s	2	1
5	5	J Laffite	Williams	FW09	Honda	V6t	62		19	10
r	27	M Alboreto	Ferrari	126C4	Ferrari	V6t	49	engine	4	2
r	6	K Rosberg	Williams	FW09	Honda	V6t	47	exhaust / turbo	21	11
r	16	D Warwick	Renault	RE50	Renault	V6t	40	gearbox	6	3
dq	4	S Bellof	Tyrrell	012	Ford Cosworth	V8	33	accident / (1)	16	8
r	15	P Tambay	Renault	RE50	Renault	V6t	33	transmission	9	5
r	9	P Alliot	RAM	02	Hart	4t	33	brakes / accident	20	10
r	8	N Lauda	McLaren	MP4/2	TAG Porsche	V6t	33	electronics	10	5
r	12	N Mansell	Lotus	95T	Renault	V6t	27	gearbox	3	2
r	18	T Boutsen	Arrows	A7	BMW	4t	27	engine	13	7
r	26	A de Cesaris	Ligier	JS23	Renault	V6t	24	engine overheating	12	6
r	20	J Cecotto	Toleman	TG184	Hart	4t	23	clutch	17	9
r	23	E Cheever	Alfa Romeo	184T	Alfa Romeo	V8t	21	turbo intercooler	8	4
r	19	A Senna	Toleman	TG184	Hart	4t	21	front suspension / accident	7	4
r	22	R Patrese	Alfa Romeo	184T	Alfa Romeo	V8t	20	spin	25	13
r	25	F Hesnault	Ligier	JS23	Renault	V6t	3	accident	18	9
r	24	P Ghinzani	Osella	FA1F	Alfa Romeo	V8t	3	accident	26	13
r	28	R Arnoux	Ferrari	126C4	Ferrari	V6t	2	accident	15	8
r	10	J Palmer	RAM	02	Hart	4t	2	rear tyre burst / accident	24	12
r	14	M Winkelhock	ATS	D7	BMW	4t	0	accident	14	7
r	17	M Surer	Arrows	A6	Ford Cosworth	V8	0	accident *	22	11
nq	21	H Rothengatter	Spirit	101	Ford Cosworth	V8				

Winning speed 131.449 km/h, 81.679 mph
Pole Position speed 143.435 km/h, 89.127 mph (N Piquet, 1 min:40.980 sec)
Fastest Lap speed 136.358 km/h, 84.729 mph (D Warwick, 1 min:46.221 sec on lap 32)
Lap Leaders N Piquet 1-63 (63).

*Interrupted after first lap accident. Restarted for original distance. * Retired after first start.*
It was at this race that a water sample from M Brundle's car was found to infringe the regulations, resulting in Tyrrell's disqualification from the season.

8 Jul 1984   USA: Dallas   (Round 9)   (Race 397)

67 laps x 3.901 km, 2.424 miles = 261.370 km, 162.408 miles

Pos	No	Driver	Car	Model	Engine		Laps	Time/Reason for Retirement	Grid Pos	Row
1	6	K Rosberg	Williams	FW09	Honda	V6t	67	2h 01m 22.617s	8	4
2	28	R Arnoux	Ferrari	126C4	Ferrari	V6t	67	2h 01m 45.081s	4	2
3	11	E de Angelis	Lotus	95T	Renault	V6t	66		2	1
4	5	J Laffite	Williams	FW09	Honda	V6t	65		24	12
5	24	P Ghinzani	Osella	FA1F	Alfa Romeo	V8t	65		18	9
6r	12	N Mansell	Lotus	95T	Renault	V6t	64	gearbox	1	1
7	2	C Fabi	Brabham	BT53	BMW	4t	64		11	6
8	14	M Winkelhock	ATS	D7	BMW	4t	64		13	7
9r	8	N Lauda	McLaren	MP4/2	TAG Porsche	V6t	60	accident	5	3
r	7	A Prost	McLaren	MP4/2	TAG Porsche	V6t	56	accident	7	4
r	18	T Boutsen	Arrows	A7	BMW	4t	55	accident	20	10
r	27	M Alboreto	Ferrari	126C4	Ferrari	V6t	54	accident	9	5
r	17	M Surer	Arrows	A7	BMW	4t	54	accident	22	11
r	19	A Senna	Toleman	TG184	Hart	4t	47	driveshaft	6	3
r	10	J Palmer	RAM	02	Hart	4t	46	electrics	25	13
r	1	N Piquet	Brabham	BT53	BMW	4t	45	throttle jammed / accident	12	6
r	20	J Cecotto	Toleman	TG184	Hart	4t	25	accident	15	8
r	15	P Tambay	Renault	RE50	Renault	V6t	25	accident	10	5
r	26	A de Cesaris	Ligier	JS23	Renault	V6t	15	accident	16	8
r	21	H Rothengatter	Spirit	101	Hart	4t	15	fuel leak into cockpit	23	12
r	22	R Patrese	Alfa Romeo	184T	Alfa Romeo	V8t	12	accident	21	11
r	16	D Warwick	Renault	RE50	Renault	V6t	10	spin	3	2
dq	4	S Bellof	Tyrrell	012	Ford Cosworth	V8	9	accident / (1)	17	9
r	23	E Cheever	Alfa Romeo	184T	Alfa Romeo	V8t	8	accident	14	7
r	25	F Hesnault	Ligier	JS23	Renault	V6t	0	accident	19	10
ns	9	P Alliot	RAM	02	Hart	4t		accident		
nq	3	M Brundle	Tyrrell	012	Ford Cosworth	V8		accident / injury		

Winning speed 129.203 km/h, 80.283 mph
Pole Position speed 144.720 km/h, 89.925 mph (N Mansell, 1 min:37.041 sec)
Fastest Lap speed 133.302 km/h, 82.830 mph (N Lauda, 1 min:45.353 sec on lap 22)
Lap Leaders N Mansell 1-35 (35); K Rosberg 36-48,57-67 (24); A Prost 49-56 (8).

Scheduled for 78 laps, but stopped at 2 hours.

71 laps x 4.207 km, 2.614 miles = 298.685 km, 185.594 miles

Pos	No	Driver	Car	Model	Engine		Laps	Time/Reason for Retirement	Grid Pos	Row
1	8	N Lauda	McLaren	MP4/2	TAG Porsche	V6t	71	1h 29m 28.532s	3	2
2	16	D Warwick	Renault	RE50	Renault	V6t	71	1h 30m 10.655s	6	3
3	19	A Senna	Toleman	TG184	Hart	4t	71	1h 30m 31.860s	7	4
4	11	E de Angelis	Lotus	95T	Renault	V6t	70		4	2
5	27	M Alboreto	Ferrari	126C4	Ferrari	V6t	70		9	5
6	28	R Arnoux	Ferrari	126C4	Ferrari	V6t	70		13	7
7	1	N Piquet	Brabham	BT53	BMW	4t	70		1	1
8r	15	P Tambay	Renault	RE50	Renault	V6t	69	turbo	10	5
9	24	P Ghinzani	Osella	FA1F	Alfa Romeo	V8t	68		21	11
10	26	A de Cesaris	Ligier	JS23	Renault	V6t	68		19	10
dq	4	S Bellof	Tyrrell	012	Ford Cosworth	V8	68	(1)	26	13
11	17	M Surer	Arrows	A7	BMW	4t	67		15	8
12r	22	R Patrese	Alfa Romeo	184T	Alfa Romeo	V8t	66	out of fuel	17	9
nc	21	H Rothengatter	Spirit	101	Hart	4t	62		22	11
r	25	F Hesnault	Ligier	JS23	Renault	V6t	43	electrics	20	10
r	7	A Prost	McLaren	MP4/2	TAG Porsche	V6t	37	gearbox pinion	2	1
r	12	N Mansell	Lotus	95T	Renault	V6t	24	gearbox	8	4
r	18	T Boutsen	Arrows	A7	BMW	4t	24	electrics	12	6
r	5	J Laffite	Williams	FW09B	Honda	V6t	14	water pump	16	8
r	10	J Palmer	RAM	02	Hart	4t	10	steering / accident	23	12
r	2	T Fabi	Brabham	BT53	BMW	4t	9	electrics	14	7
r	14	M Winkelhock	ATS	D7	BMW	4t	8	spin	11	6
r	6	K Rosberg	Williams	FW09B	Honda	V6t	5	engine	5	3
r	23	E Cheever	Alfa Romeo	184T	Alfa Romeo	V8t	0	accident	18	9
dq	3	S Johansson	Tyrrell	012	Ford Cosworth	V8	0	accident / (1)	25	13
r	9	P Alliot	RAM	02	Hart	4t	0	accident	24	12
r	30	J Gartner	Osella	FA1F	Alfa Romeo	V8t	0	accident	27	14
nq	20	J Cecotto	Toleman	TG184	Hart	4t		accident / injury		

Winning speed 200.290 km/h, 124.455 mph
Pole Position speed 213.698 km/h, 132.786 mph (N Piquet, 1 min:10.869 sec)
Fastest Lap speed 206.918 km/h, 128.573 mph (N Lauda, 1 min:13.191 sec on lap 57)
Lap Leaders N Piquet 1-11 (11); A Prost 12-37 (26); N Lauda 38-71 (34).

Scheduled for 75 laps, but interrupted after 11 laps, because of an accident. Restarted for a further 60 laps, with results being on aggregate.
Lap leaders are given 'on the road'.

44 laps x 6.797 km, 4.223 miles = 299.068 km, 185.832 miles

Pos	No	Driver	Car	Model	Engine		Laps	Time/Reason for Retirement	Grid Pos	Row
1	7	A Prost	McLaren	MP4/2	TAG Porsche	V6t	44	1h 24m 43.210s	1	1
2	8	N Lauda	McLaren	MP4/2	TAG Porsche	V6t	44	1h 24m 46.359s	7	4
3	16	D Warwick	Renault	RE50	Renault	V6t	44	1h 25m 19.633s	3	2
4	12	N Mansell	Lotus	95T	Renault	V6t	44	1h 25m 34.873s	16	8
5	15	P Tambay	Renault	RE50	Renault	V6t	44	1h 25m 55.159s	4	2
6	28	R Arnoux	Ferrari	126C4	Ferrari	V6t	43		10	5
7	26	A de Cesaris	Ligier	JS23	Renault	V6t	43		11	6
8	25	F Hesnault	Ligier	JS23	Renault	V6t	43		17	9
dq	3	S Johansson	Tyrrell	012	Ford Cosworth	V8	42	(1)	26	13
9	21	H Rothengatter	Spirit	101	Hart	4t	40		24	12
r	14	M Winkelhock	ATS	D7	BMW	4t	31	turbo boost pressure / gearbox	13	7
r	23	E Cheever	Alfa Romeo	184T	Alfa Romeo	V8t	29	engine	18	9
r	2	T Fabi	Brabham	BT53	BMW	4t	28	turbo boost pressure	8	4
r	1	N Piquet	Brabham	BT53	BMW	4t	23	gearbox pinion	5	3
r	22	R Patrese	Alfa Romeo	184T	Alfa Romeo	V8t	16	fuel metering unit	20	10
r	24	P Ghinzani	Osella	FA1F	Alfa Romeo	V8t	14	electrics	21	11
r	30	J Gartner	Osella	FA1F	Alfa Romeo	V8t	13	turbo	23	12
r	27	M Alboreto	Ferrari	126C4	Ferrari	V6t	13	misfire	6	3
r	10	J Palmer	RAM	02	Hart	4t	11	turbo	25	13
r	6	K Rosberg	Williams	FW09B	Honda	V6t	10	ignition	19	10
r	5	J Laffite	Williams	FW09B	Honda	V6t	10	engine	12	6
r	18	T Boutsen	Arrows	A7	BMW	4t	8	oil pressure	15	8
r	11	E de Angelis	Lotus	95T	Renault	V6t	8	turbo	2	1
r	9	P Alliot	RAM	02	Hart	4t	7	engine overheating	22	11
r	19	A Senna	Toleman	TG184	Hart	4t	4	rear wing failure / accident	9	5
r	17	M Surer	Arrows	A7	BMW	4t	1	turbo	14	7
nq	4	M Thackwell	Tyrrell	012	Ford Cosworth	V8				

Winning speed 211.804 km/h, 131.609 mph
Pole Position speed 228.658 km/h, 142.082 mph (A Prost, 1 min:47.012 sec)
Fastest Lap speed 215.516 km/h, 133.915 mph (A Prost, 1 min:53.538 sec on lap 31)
Lap Leaders E de Angelis 1-7 (7); N Piquet 8-21 (14); A Prost 22-44 (23).

19 Aug 1984 **AUSTRIA: Österreichring** (Round 12) (Race 400)

51 laps x 5.942 km, 3.692 miles = 303.042 km, 188.302 miles

Pos	No	Driver	Car	Model	Engine		Laps	Time/Reason for Retirement	Grid Pos	Row
1	8	N Lauda	McLaren	MP4/2	TAG Porsche	V6t	51	1h 21m 12.851s	4	2
2	1	N Piquet	Brabham	BT53	BMW	4t	51	1h 21m 36.376s	1	1
3	27	M Alboreto	Ferrari	126C4	Ferrari	V6t	51	1h 22m 01.849s	12	6
4	2	T Fabi	Brabham	BT53	BMW	4t	51	1h 22m 09.163s	7	4
5	18	T Boutsen	Arrows	A7	BMW	4t	50		17	9
6	17	M Surer	Arrows	A7	BMW	4t	50		19	10
7	28	R Arnoux	Ferrari	126C4	Ferrari	V6t	50		15	8
8	25	F Hesnault	Ligier	JS23	Renault	V6t	49		21	11
9	10	J Palmer	RAM	02	Hart	4t	49		24	12
10r	22	R Patrese	Alfa Romeo	184T	Alfa Romeo	V8t	48	out of fuel	13	7
11	9	P Alliot	RAM	02	Hart	4t	48		25	13
12r	31	G Berger	ATS	D7	BMW	4t	48	gearbox	20	10
r	15	P Tambay	Renault	RE50	Renault	V6t	42	engine	5	3
r	19	A Senna	Toleman	TG184	Hart	4t	35	oil pressure	10	5
r	12	N Mansell	Lotus	95T	Renault	V6t	32	engine	8	4
r	7	A Prost	McLaren	MP4/2	TAG Porsche	V6t	28	spin	2	1
r	11	E de Angelis	Lotus	95T	Renault	V6t	28	engine	3	2
nc	21	H Rothengatter	Spirit	101	Hart	4t	23		26	13
r	23	E Cheever	Alfa Romeo	184T	Alfa Romeo	V8t	18	engine	16	8
r	16	D Warwick	Renault	RE50	Renault	V6t	17	engine	6	3
r	26	A de Cesaris	Ligier	JS23	Renault	V6t	15	fuel metering unit	18	9
r	6	K Rosberg	Williams	FW09B	Honda	V6t	15	handling	9	5
r	5	J Laffite	Williams	FW09B	Honda	V6t	12	engine	11	6
r	30	J Gartner	Osella	FA1F	Alfa Romeo	V8t	6	engine	22	11
r	24	P Ghinzani	Osella	FA1F	Alfa Romeo	V8t	4	gearbox	23	12
ns	14	M Winkelhock	ATS	D7	BMW	4t		gearbox	14	7
nq	3	S Johansson	Tyrrell	012	Ford Cosworth	V8				
nq	4	S Bellof	Tyrrell	012	Ford Cosworth	V8				

Winning speed 223.884 km/h, 139.115 mph
Pole Position speed 248.236 km/h, 154.246 mph (N Piquet, 1 min:26.173 sec)
Fastest Lap speed 230.305 km/h, 143.105 mph (N Lauda, 1 min:32.882 sec on lap 23)
Lap Leaders N Piquet 1-39 (39); N Lauda 40-51 (12).

Interrupted after first lap, because of a mis-start. Restarted for original distance.

26 Aug 1984 **NETHERLANDS: Zandvoort** (Round 13) (Race 401)

71 laps x 4.252 km, 2.642 miles = 301.892 km, 187.587 miles

Pos	No	Driver	Car	Model	Engine		Laps	Time/Reason for Retirement	Grid Pos	Row
1	7	A Prost	McLaren	MP4/2	TAG Porsche	V6t	71	1h 37m 21.468s	1	1
2	8	N Lauda	McLaren	MP4/2	TAG Porsche	V6t	71	1h 37m 31.751s	6	3
3	12	N Mansell	Lotus	95T	Renault	V6t	71	1h 38m 41.012s	12	6
4	11	E de Angelis	Lotus	95T	Renault	V6t	70		3	2
5	2	T Fabi	Brabham	BT53	BMW	4t	70		10	5
6	15	P Tambay	Renault	RE50	Renault	V6t	70		5	3
7	25	F Hesnault	Ligier	JS23	Renault	V6t	69		20	10
dq	3	S Johansson	Tyrrell	012	Ford Cosworth	V8	69	(1)	25	13
dq	4	S Bellof	Tyrrell	012	Ford Cosworth	V8	69	(1)	24	12
8r	6	K Rosberg	Williams	FW09B	Honda	V6t	68	out of fuel	7	4
9	10	J Palmer	RAM	02	Hart	4t	67		22	11
10	9	P Alliot	RAM	02	Hart	4t	67		26	13
11r	28	R Arnoux	Ferrari	126C4	Ferrari	V6t	66	electrics	15	8
12	30	J Gartner	Osella	FA1F	Alfa Romeo	V8t	66		23	12
13r	23	E Cheever	Alfa Romeo	184T	Alfa Romeo	V8t	65	out of fuel	17	9
r	18	T Boutsen	Arrows	A7	BMW	4t	59	accident	11	6
r	21	H Rothengatter	Spirit	101	Hart	4t	53	throttle linkage	27	14
r	22	R Patrese	Alfa Romeo	184T	Alfa Romeo	V8t	51	engine	18	9
r	26	A de Cesaris	Ligier	JS23	Renault	V6t	31	engine	14	7
r	5	J Laffite	Williams	FW09B	Honda	V6t	23	engine	8	4
r	16	D Warwick	Renault	RE50	Renault	V6t	23	spin	4	2
r	14	M Winkelhock	ATS	D7	BMW	4t	22	spin	16	8
r	19	A Senna	Toleman	TG184	Hart	4t	19	engine	13	7
r	17	M Surer	Arrows	A7	BMW	4t	17	wheel bearing	19	10
r	1	N Piquet	Brabham	BT53	BMW	4t	10	oil union	2	1
r	24	P Ghinzani	Osella	FA1F	Alfa Romeo	V8t	8	fuel pump	21	11
r	27	M Alboreto	Ferrari	126C4	Ferrari	V6t	7	engine	9	5

Winning speed 186.051 km/h, 115.607 mph
Pole Position speed 208.072 km/h, 129.290 mph (A Prost, 1 min:13.567 sec)
Fastest Lap speed 192.628 km/h, 119.694 mph (R Arnoux, 1 min:19.465 sec on lap 64)
Lap Leaders N Piquet 1-10 (10); A Prost 11-71 (61).

9 Sep 1984		**ITALY: Monza**						**(Round 14)**		**(Race 402)**
		51 laps x 5.800 km, 3.604 miles = 295.800 km, 183.802 miles								

Pos	No	Driver	Car	Model	Engine		Laps	Time/Reason for Retirement	Grid Pos	Row
1	8	N Lauda	McLaren	MP4/2	TAG Porsche	V6t	51	1h 20m 29.065s	4	2
2	27	M Alboreto	Ferrari	126C4	Ferrari	V6t	51	1h 20m 53.314s	11	6
3	22	R Patrese	Alfa Romeo	184T	Alfa Romeo	V8t	50		9	5
4	19	S Johansson	Toleman	TG184	Hart	4t	49		17	9
5	30	J Gartner	Osella	FA1F	Alfa Romeo	V8t	49		24	12
6	31	G Berger	ATS	D7	BMW	4t	49		20	10
7r	24	P Ghinzani	Osella	FA1F	Alfa Romeo	V8t	48	out of fuel	22	11
8	21	H Rothengatter	Spirit	101	Hart	4t	48		25	13
9r	23	E Cheever	Alfa Romeo	184T	Alfa Romeo	V8t	45	out of fuel	10	5
10	18	T Boutsen	Arrows	A7	BMW	4t	45		19	10
r	15	P Tambay	Renault	RE50	Renault	V6t	43	throttle linkage	8	4
r	2	T Fabi	Brabham	BT53	BMW	4t	43	oil union / engine	5	3
r	17	M Surer	Arrows	A7	BMW	4t	43	engine	15	8
r	16	D Warwick	Renault	RE50	Renault	V6t	31	oil pressure	12	6
r	10	J Palmer	RAM	02	Hart	4t	20	oil pressure	26	13
r	1	N Piquet	Brabham	BT53	BMW	4t	15	radiator / engine	1	1
r	11	E de Angelis	Lotus	95T	Renault	V6t	14	gearbox	3	2
r	12	N Mansell	Lotus	95T	Renault	V6t	13	spin	7	4
r	5	J Laffite	Williams	FW09B	Honda	V6t	10	turbo	13	7
r	6	K Rosberg	Williams	FW09B	Honda	V6t	8	engine	6	3
r	26	A de Cesaris	Ligier	JS23	Renault	V6t	7	engine	16	8
r	25	F Hesnault	Ligier	JS23	Renault	V6t	7	spin	18	9
r	9	P Alliot	RAM	02	Hart	4t	6	electrics	23	12
r	28	R Arnoux	Ferrari	126C4	Ferrari	V6t	5	gearbox	14	7
r	7	A Prost	McLaren	MP4/2	TAG Porsche	V6t	3	engine	2	1
ns	14	M Winkelhock	ATS	D7	BMW	4t		gearbox on parade lap	21	11
nq	20	P Martini	Toleman	TG184	Hart	4t				

Winning speed 220.515 km/h, 137.022 mph
Pole Position speed 241.153 km/h, 149.846 mph (N Piquet, 1 min:26.584 sec)
Fastest Lap speed 227.174 km/h, 141.159 mph (N Lauda, 1 min:31.912 sec on lap 42)
Lap Leaders N Piquet 1-15 (15); P Tambay 16-42 (27); N Lauda 43-51 (9).

7 Oct 1984		**EUROPE: Nürburgring**						**(Round 15)**		**(Race 403)**
		67 laps x 4.542 km, 2.822 miles = 304.314 km, 189.092 miles								

Pos	No	Driver	Car	Model	Engine		Laps	Time/Reason for Retirement	Grid Pos	Row
1	7	A Prost	McLaren	MP4/2	TAG Porsche	V6t	67	1h 35m 13.284s	2	1
2	27	M Alboreto	Ferrari	126C4	Ferrari	V6t	67	1h 35m 37.195s	5	3
3	1	N Piquet	Brabham	BT53	BMW	4t	67	1h 35m 38.206s	1	1
4	8	N Lauda	McLaren	MP4/2	TAG Porsche	V6t	67	1h 35m 56.370s	15	8
5	28	R Arnoux	Ferrari	126C4	Ferrari	V6t	67	1h 36m 14.714s	6	3
6	22	R Patrese	Alfa Romeo	184T	Alfa Romeo	V8t	66		9	5
7	26	A de Cesaris	Ligier	JS23	Renault	V6t	65		17	9
8	21	M Baldi	Spirit	101	Hart	4t	65		24	12
9r	18	T Boutsen	Arrows	A7	BMW	4t	64	electrics / ignition	11	6
10	25	F Hesnault	Ligier	JS23	Renault	V6t	64		19	10
11r	16	D Warwick	Renault	RE50	Renault	V6t	61	valve / engine overheating	7	4
12r	30	J Gartner	Osella	FA1F	Alfa Romeo	V8t	60	out of fuel	22	11
r	2	T Fabi	Brabham	BT53	BMW	4t	57	gearbox	10	5
r	12	N Mansell	Lotus	95T	Renault	V6t	51	engine	8	4
r	15	P Tambay	Renault	RE50	Renault	V6t	47	fuel injection	3	2
r	23	E Cheever	Alfa Romeo	184T	Alfa Romeo	V8t	37	fuel pump	13	7
r	9	P Alliot	RAM	02	Hart	4t	37	turbo	25	13
r	10	J Palmer	RAM	02	Hart	4t	35	turbo	21	11
r	5	J Laffite	Williams	FW09B	Honda	V6t	27	engine	14	7
r	11	E de Angelis	Lotus	95T	Renault	V6t	25	turbo	23	12
r	20	S Johansson	Toleman	TG184	Hart	4t	17	water pump / engine overheating	26	13
r	6	K Rosberg	Williams	FW09B	Honda	V6t	0	accident	4	2
r	31	G Berger	ATS	D7	BMW	4t	0	accident	18	9
r	17	M Surer	Arrows	A7	BMW	4t	0	accident	16	8
r	24	P Ghinzani	Osella	FA1F	Alfa Romeo	V8t	0	accident	20	10
r	19	A Senna	Toleman	TG184	Hart	4t	0	accident	12	6

Winning speed 191.751 km/h, 119.149 mph
Pole Position speed 207.316 km/h, 128.820 mph (N Piquet, 1 min:18.871 sec)
Fastest Lap speed 196.656 km/h, 122.197 mph (M Alboreto / N Piquet, 1 min:23.146 sec on lap 62)
Lap Leaders A Prost 1-67 (67).

Pos	No	Driver	Car	Model	Engine		Laps	Time/Reason for Retirement	Grid Pos	Row
1	7	A Prost	McLaren	MP4/2	TAG Porsche	V6t	70	1h 41m 11.753s	2	1
2	8	N Lauda	McLaren	MP4/2	TAG Porsche	V6t	70	1h 41m 25.178s	11	6
3	19	A Senna	Toleman	TG184	Hart	4t	70	1h 41m 31.795s	3	2
4	27	M Alboreto	Ferrari	126C4	Ferrari	V6t	70	1h 41m 32.070s	8	4
5	11	E de Angelis	Lotus	95T	Renault	V6t	70	1h 42m 43.922s	5	3
6	1	N Piquet	Brabham	BT53	BMW	4t	69		1	1
7	15	P Tambay	Renault	RE50	Renault	V6t	69		7	4
8	22	R Patrese	Alfa Romeo	184T	Alfa Romeo	V8t	69		12	6
9	28	R Arnoux	Ferrari	126C4	Ferrari	V6t	69		17	9
10	2	M Winkelhock	Brabham	BT53	BMW	4t	69		19	10
11	20	S Johansson	Toleman	TG184	Hart	4t	69		10	5
12	26	A de Cesaris	Ligier	JS23	Renault	V6t	69		20	10
13	14	G Berger	ATS	D7	BMW	4t	68		23	12
14	5	J Laffite	Williams	FW09B	Honda	V6t	67		15	8
15	21	M Baldi	Spirit	101	Hart	4t	66		25	13
16r	30	J Gartner	Osella	FA1F	Alfa Romeo	V8t	65	out of fuel	24	12
17	23	E Cheever	Alfa Romeo	184T	Alfa Romeo	V8t	64		14	7
r	24	P Ghinzani	Osella	FA1F	Alfa Romeo	V8t	60	engine	22	11
r	12	N Mansell	Lotus	95T	Renault	V6t	52	brake fluid loss / spin	6	3
r	16	D Warwick	Renault	RE50	Renault	V6t	51	gearbox	9	5
r	33	P Streiff	Renault	RE50	Renault	V6t	48	driveshaft	13	7
r	6	K Rosberg	Williams	FW09B	Honda	V6t	39	engine	4	2
r	25	F Hesnault	Ligier	JS23	Renault	V6t	31	electrics	21	11
r	18	T Boutsen	Arrows	A7	BMW	4t	24	driveshaft	18	9
r	10	J Palmer	RAM	02	Hart	4t	19	gearbox	26	13
r	17	M Surer	Arrows	A7	BMW	4t	8	electrics	16	8
r	9	P Alliot	RAM	02	Hart	4t	2	engine	27	14

Winning speed 180.541 km/h, 112.183 mph
Pole Position speed 191.670 km/h, 119.098 mph (N Piquet, 1 min:21.703 sec)
Fastest Lap speed 188.684 km/h, 117.243 mph (N Lauda, 1 min:22.996 sec on lap 51)
Lap Leaders K Rosberg 1-8 (8); A Prost 9-70 (62).

Lap Leaders 1984

Pos	Driver	Car-Engine	GPs	laps	km	miles
1	A Prost	McLaren-TAG Porsche	9	345	1,579.2	981.3
2	N Piquet	Brabham-BMW	8	241	1,142.8	710.1
3	N Lauda	McLaren-TAG Porsche	6	168	747.5	464.4
4	M Alboreto	Ferrari	2	81	353.7	219.8
5	P Tambay	Renault	2	74	339.3	210.8
6	N Mansell	Lotus-Renault	2	40	153.1	95.1
7	K Rosberg	Williams-Honda	3	33	132.5	82.3
8	D Warwick	Renault	1	12	60.4	37.5
9	E de Angelis	Lotus-Renault	1	7	47.6	29.6
			16	**1,001**	**4,556.0**	**2,831.0**

Driver Points 1984

	Driver	BR	ZA	B	RSM	F	MC	CDN	DET	DAL	GB	D	A	NL	I	EUR	P	Total
1	N Lauda	-	9	-	-	9	-	6	-	-	9	6	9	6	9	3	6	72
2	A Prost	9	6	-	9	-	4.5	4	3	-	-	9	-	9	-	9	9	71.5
3	E de Angelis	4	-	2	4	2	1	3	6	4	3	-	4	-	3	-	2	34
4	M Alboreto	-	-	9	-	-	0.5	-	-	-	2	-	4	-	6	6	3	30.5
5	N Piquet	-	-	-	-	-	-	9	9	-	-	-	6	-	-	4	1	29
6	R Arnoux	-	-	4	6	3	2	2	-	6	1	1	-	-	-	2	-	27
7	D Warwick	-	4	6	3	-	-	-	-	-	6	4	-	-	-	-	-	23
8	K Rosberg	6	-	3	-	1	1.5	-	-	9	-	-	-	-	-	-	-	20.5
9	N Mansell	-	-	-	-	4	-	1	-	1	-	3	-	4	-	-	-	13
	A Senna	-	1	1	-	-	3	-	-	-	4	-	-	-	-	-	4	13
11	P Tambay	2	-	-	-	6	-	-	-	-	-	2	-	1	-	-	-	11
12	T Fabi	-	-	-	-	-	-	-	4	-	-	-	3	2	-	-	-	9
13	R Patrese	-	3	-	-	-	-	-	-	-	-	-	-	-	4	1	-	8
14	J Laffite	-	-	-	-	-	-	2	3	-	-	-	-	-	-	-	-	5
	T Boutsen	1	-	-	2	-	-	-	-	-	-	-	2	-	-	-	-	5
16	E Cheever	3	-	-	-	-	-	-	-	-	-	-	-	-	-	-	-	3
	S Johansson	-	-	-	-	-	-	-	-	-	-	-	-	-	3	-	-	3
	A de Cesaris	-	2	-	1	-	-	-	-	-	-	-	-	-	-	-	-	3
19	P Ghinzani	-	-	-	-	-	-	-	-	2	-	-	-	-	-	-	-	2
20	M Surer	-	-	-	-	-	-	-	-	-	-	-	1	-	-	-	-	1
21	J Gartner	-	-	-	-	-	-	-	-	-	-	-	-	-	(2)	-	-	(2)
	G Berger	-	-	-	-	-	-	-	-	-	-	-	-	-	(1)	-	-	(1)

9,6,4,3,2 and 1 point awarded to the first six finishers. Best 11 scores. Half points awarded in Monaco where race was stopped early. J Gartner (Osella-Alfa Romeo) and G Berger (ATS-BMW) finished 5th and 6th respectively in Italy, but points not valid for Championship because these constructors had only entered one car each for the season. All points scored by Tyrrell were redistributed due to an infringement of the rules. Points originally scored were Brundle 8, Bellof, 7, Tyrrell-Ford Cosworth 15.

Constructor Points 1984

		BR	ZA	B	RSM	F	MC	CDN	DET	DAL	GB	D	A	NL	I	EUR	P	Total
1	McLaren-TAG Porsche	9	15	-	9	9	4.5	10	3	-	9	15	9	15	9	12	15	143.5
2	Ferrari	-	-	13	6	3	2.5	2	-	6	3	1	4	-	6	8	3	57.5
3	Lotus-Renault	4	-	2	4	6	1	4	6	5	3	3	-	7	-	-	2	47
4	Brabham-BMW	-	-	-	-	-	-	9	13	-	-	-	9	2	-	4	1	38
5	Renault	2	4	6	3	6	-	-	-	-	6	6	-	1	-	-	-	34
6	Williams-Honda	6	-	3	-	1	1.5	-	2	12	-	-	-	-	-	-	-	25.5
7	Toleman-Hart	-	1	1	-	-	3	-	-	-	4	-	-	-	3	-	4	16
8	Alfa Romeo	3	3	-	-	-	-	-	-	-	-	-	-	-	4	1	-	11
9	Arrows-BMW	-	-	-	-	-	-	-	-	-	-	-	3	-	-	-	-	3
	Ligier-Renault	-	2	-	1	-	-	-	-	-	-	-	-	-	-	-	-	3
	Arrows-Ford Cosworth	1	-	-	2	-	-	-	-	-	-	-	-	-	-	-	-	3
12	Osella-Alfa Romeo	-	-	-	-	-	-	-	-	2	-	-	-	-	(2)	-	-	2 (2)
13	ATS-BMW	-	-	-	-	-	-	-	-	-	-	-	-	-	(1)	-	-	(1)

9,6,4,3,2 and 1 point awarded to the first six finishers.

1985

Race Entrants and Results

Michelin withdrew at the end of 1984. McLaren merged with the TAG group. The ever increasing power from the turbo brigade, at the time, appeared to signal the end of the most successful Formula 1 engine: the Ford Cosworth V8. At season's end, Renault announced its intentions to withdraw.

McLAREN
Marlboro McLaren International: Lauda, Watson, Prost

TYRRELL
Tyrrell Racing Organisation: Brundle, Johansson, Bellof, Capelli, Streiff

WILLIAMS
Canon Williams Team: Mansell, Rosberg

BRABHAM
Motor Racing Developments: Piquet, Hesnault, Surer

RAM
Skoal Bandit Formula 1 Team: Winkelhock, Acheson, Alliot

LOTUS
John Player Special Team Lotus: de Angelis, Senna

RENAULT
Equipe Renault Elf: Tambay, Warwick, Hesnault

ARROWS
Barclay Arrows BMW: Berger, Boutsen

TOLEMAN
Toleman Group Motorsport: Fabi, Ghinzani

SPIRIT
Spirit Enterprises Ltd: Baldi

ALFA ROMEO
Benetton Team Alfa Romeo: Patrese, Cheever

OSELLA
Osella Squadra Corse: Ghinzani, /Rothengatter

LIGIER
Equipe Ligier Gitanes: de Cesaris, Streiff, Laffite

FERRARI
Scuderia Ferrari SpA SEFAC: Alboreto, Arnoux, Johansson

MINARDI
Minardi Team: Martini

ZAKSPEED
West Zakspeed Racing: Palmer, Danner

LOLA
Team Haas (USA) Ltd: Jones

7 Apr 1985		**BRAZIL: Rio de Janeiro**					(Round 1)	(Race 405)	

61 laps x 5.031 km, 3.126 miles = 306.891 km, 190.693 miles

Pos	No	Driver	Car	Model	Engine		Laps	Time/Reason for Retirement	Grid Pos	Row
1	2	A Prost	McLaren	MP4/2B	TAG Porsche	V6t	61	1h 41m 26.115s	6	3
2	27	M Alboreto	Ferrari	156/85	Ferrari	V6t	61	1h 41m 29.374s	1	1
3	11	E de Angelis	Lotus	97T	Renault	V6t	60		3	2
4	28	R Arnoux	Ferrari	156/85	Ferrari	V6t	59		7	4
5	15	P Tambay	Renault	RE60	Renault	V6t	59		11	6
6	26	J Laffite	Ligier	JS25	Renault	V6t	59		15	8
7	4	S Johansson	Tyrrell	012	Ford Cosworth	V8	58		23	12
8	3	M Brundle	Tyrrell	012	Ford Cosworth	V8	58		21	11
9	10	P Alliot	RAM	03	Hart	4t	58		20	10
10	16	D Warwick	Renault	RE60	Renault	V6t	57		10	5
11	18	T Boutsen	Arrows	A8	BMW	4t	57		12	6
12	24	P Ghinzani	Osella	FA1F	Alfa Romeo	V8t	57		22	11
13	9	M Winkelhock	RAM	03	Hart	4t	57		16	8
r	17	G Berger	Arrows	A8	BMW	4t	51	rear suspension	19	10
r	12	A Senna	Lotus	97T	Renault	V6t	48	ignition	4	2
r	23	E Cheever	Alfa Romeo	185T	Alfa Romeo	V8t	42	engine	18	9
r	29	P Martini	Minardi	M185	Ford Cosworth	V8	41	electronics	25	13
r	1	N Lauda	McLaren	MP4/2B	TAG Porsche	V6t	27	fuel metering unit	9	5
r	25	A de Cesaris	Ligier	JS25	Renault	V6t	26	accident damage	13	7
r	22	R Patrese	Alfa Romeo	185T	Alfa Romeo	V8t	20	accident / rear tyre	14	7
r	6	K Rosberg	Williams	FW10	Honda	V6t	10	turbo	2	1
r	8	F Hesnault	Brabham	BT54	BMW	4t	9	accident damage	17	9
r	5	N Mansell	Williams	FW10	Honda	V6t	8	accident / exhaust	5	3
r	21	M Baldi	Spirit	101D	Hart	4t	7	turbo / misfire	24	12
r	7	N Piquet	Brabham	BT54	BMW	4t	2	accident	8	4

Winning speed 181.529 km/h, 112.797 mph
Pole Position speed 206.358 km/h, 128.225 mph (M Alboreto, 1 min:27.768 sec)
Fastest Lap speed 187.293 km/h, 116.378 mph (A Prost, 1 min:36.702 sec on lap 34)
Lap Leaders K Rosberg 1-9 (9); M Alboreto 10-17 (8); A Prost 18-61 (44).

21 Apr 1985   PORTUGAL: Estoril   (Round 2)   (Race 406)

67 laps x 4.350 km, 2.703 miles = 291.450 km, 181.099 miles

Pos	No	Driver	Car	Model	Engine		Laps	Time/Reason for Retirement	Grid Pos	Row
1	12	A Senna	Lotus	97T	Renault	V6t	67	2h 00m 28.006s	1	1
2	27	M Alboreto	Ferrari	156/85	Ferrari	V6t	67	2h 01m 30.984s	5	3
3	15	P Tambay	Renault	RE60	Renault	V6t	66		12	6
4	11	E de Angelis	Lotus	97T	Renault	V6t	66		4	2
5	5	N Mansell	Williams	FW10	Honda	V6t	65		9	5
6	4	S Bellof	Tyrrell	012	Ford Cosworth	V8	65		21	11
7	16	D Warwick	Renault	RE60	Renault	V6t	65		6	3
8	28	S Johansson	Ferrari	156/85	Ferrari	V6t	62		11	6
9	24	P Ghinzani	Osella	FA1F	Alfa Romeo	V8t	61		26	13
nc	9	M Winkelhock	RAM	03	Hart	4t	50		15	8
r	1	N Lauda	McLaren	MP4/2B	TAG Porsche	V6t	49	piston	7	4
r	23	E Cheever	Alfa Romeo	185T	Alfa Romeo	V8t	36	misfire	14	7
r	2	A Prost	McLaren	MP4/2B	TAG Porsche	V6t	30	spin	2	1
r	25	A de Cesaris	Ligier	JS25	Renault	V6t	29	tyres / handling	8	4
r	18	T Boutsen	Arrows	A8	BMW	4t	28	electrics	16	8
r	7	N Piquet	Brabham	BT54	BMW	4t	28	tyres / handling	10	5
r	3	M Brundle	Tyrrell	012	Ford Cosworth	V8	20	gear linkage	22	11
r	21	M Baldi	Spirit	101D	Hart	4t	19	spin	24	12
r	6	K Rosberg	Williams	FW10	Honda	V6t	16	spin	3	2
r	26	J Laffite	Ligier	JS25	Renault	V6t	15	tyres / handling	18	9
r	17	G Berger	Arrows	A8	BMW	4t	12	spin	17	9
r	29	P Martini	Minardi	M185	Ford Cosworth	V8	12	spin	25	13
r	22	R Patrese	Alfa Romeo	185T	Alfa Romeo	V8t	4	spin	13	7
r	10	P Alliot	RAM	03	Hart	4t	3	spin	20	10
r	8	F Hesnault	Brabham	BT54	BMW	4t	3	electrics	19	10
r	30	J Palmer	Zakspeed	841	Zakspeed	4t	2	accident / front suspension	23	12

Winning speed 145.160 km/h, 90.198 mph
Pole Position speed 193.317 km/h, 120.121 mph (A Senna, 1 min:21.007 sec)
Fastest Lap speed 150.402 km/h, 93.455 mph (A Senna, 1 min:44.121 sec on lap 15)
Lap Leaders A Senna 1-67 (67).

Scheduled for 69 laps, but stopped at 2 hours.

5 May 1985   SAN MARINO: Imola   (Round 3)   (Race 407)

60 laps x 5.040 km, 3.132 miles = 302.400 km, 187.903 miles

Pos	No	Driver	Car	Model	Engine		Laps	Time/Reason for Retirement	Grid Pos	Row
dq	2	A Prost	McLaren	MP4/2B	TAG Porsche	V6t	60	car under weight	6	3
1	11	E de Angelis	Lotus	97T	Renault	V6t	60	1h 34m 35.955s	3	2
2	18	T Boutsen	Arrows	A8	BMW	4t	59		5	3
3	15	P Tambay	Renault	RE60	Renault	V6t	59		11	6
4	1	N Lauda	McLaren	MP4/2B	TAG Porsche	V6t	59		8	4
5	5	N Mansell	Williams	FW10	Honda	V6t	58		7	4
6r	28	S Johansson	Ferrari	156/85	Ferrari	V6t	57	out of fuel	15	8
7r	12	A Senna	Lotus	97T	Renault	V6t	57	out of fuel	1	1
8r	7	N Piquet	Brabham	BT54	BMW	4t	57	out of fuel	9	5
9	3	M Brundle	Tyrrell	012	Ford Cosworth	V8	56		25	13
10	16	D Warwick	Renault	RE60	Renault	V6t	56		14	7
r	23	E Cheever	Alfa Romeo	185T	Alfa Romeo	V8t	50	engine	12	6
nc	24	P Ghinzani	Osella	FA1G	Alfa Romeo	V8t	46		22	11
r	27	M Alboreto	Ferrari	156/85	Ferrari	V6t	29	electrics	4	2
r	9	M Winkelhock	RAM	03	Hart	4t	27	engine	23	12
r	10	P Alliot	RAM	03	Hart	4t	24	turbo	21	11
r	6	K Rosberg	Williams	FW10	Honda	V6t	23	throttle linkage / brakes	2	1
r	26	J Laffite	Ligier	JS25	Renault	V6t	22	turbo	16	8
r	29	P Martini	Minardi	M185	Motori Moderni	V6t	14	turbo	19	10
r	25	A de Cesaris	Ligier	JS25	Renault	V6t	11	spin	13	7
r	21	M Baldi	Spirit	101D	Hart	4t	9	electrics	26	13
r	8	F Hesnault	Brabham	BT54	BMW	4t	5	engine	20	10
r	4	S Bellof	Tyrrell	012	Ford Cosworth	V8	5	engine	24	12
r	17	G Berger	Arrows	A8	BMW	4t	4	electrics	10	5
r	22	R Patrese	Alfa Romeo	185T	Alfa Romeo	V8t	4	turbo	18	9
ns	30	J Palmer	Zakspeed	841	Zakspeed	4t		misfire on parade lap	17	9

Winning speed 191.799 km/h, 119.178 mph
Pole Position speed 207.771 km/h, 129.103 mph (A Senna, 1 min:27.327 sec)
Fastest Lap speed 199.470 km/h, 123.945 mph (M Alboreto, 1 min:30.961 sec on lap 29)
Lap Leaders A Senna 1-56 (56); S Johansson 57 (1); A Prost 58-60 (3).

A Prost finished 1st in 1h 33m 57.118s (193.120 km/h, 119.999 mph).

Races   271

19 May 1985 — MONACO: Monte-Carlo — (Round 4) — (Race 408)

78 laps x 3.312 km, 2.058 miles = 258.336 km, 160.523 miles

Pos	No	Driver	Car	Model	Engine		Laps	Time/Reason for Retirement	Grid Pos	Row
1	2	A Prost	McLaren	MP4/2B	TAG Porsche	V6t	78	1h 51m 58.034s	5	3
2	27	M Alboreto	Ferrari	156/85	Ferrari	V6t	78	1h 52m 05.575s	3	2
3	11	E de Angelis	Lotus	97T	Renault	V6t	78	1h 53m 25.205s	9	5
4	25	A de Cesaris	Ligier	JS25	Renault	V6t	77		8	4
5	16	D Warwick	Renault	RE60	Renault	V6t	77		10	5
6	26	J Laffite	Ligier	JS25	Renault	V6t	77		16	8
7	5	N Mansell	Williams	FW10	Honda	V6t	77		2	1
8	6	K Rosberg	Williams	FW10	Honda	V6t	76		7	4
9	18	T Boutsen	Arrows	A8	BMW	4t	76		6	3
10	3	M Brundle	Tyrrell	012	Ford Cosworth	V8	74		18	9
11	30	J Palmer	Zakspeed	841	Zakspeed	4t	74		19	10
r	1	N Lauda	McLaren	MP4/2B	TAG Porsche	V6t	17	spin	14	7
r	22	R Patrese	Alfa Romeo	185T	Alfa Romeo	V8t	16	accident	12	6
r	7	N Piquet	Brabham	BT54	BMW	4t	16	accident	13	7
r	19	T Fabi	Toleman	TG185	Hart	4t	16	turbo	20	10
r	12	A Senna	Lotus	97T	Renault	V6t	13	engine	1	1
r	23	E Cheever	Alfa Romeo	185T	Alfa Romeo	V8t	10	alternator	4	2
r	28	S Johansson	Ferrari	156/85	Ferrari	V6t	1	accident / rear suspension	15	8
r	15	P Tambay	Renault	RE60	Renault	V6t	0	accident	17	9
r	17	G Berger	Arrows	A8	BMW	4t	0	accident	11	6
nq	24	P Ghinzani	Osella	FA1G	Alfa Romeo	V8t				
nq	4	S Bellof	Tyrrell	012	Ford Cosworth	V8				
nq	10	P Alliot	RAM	03	Hart	4t				
nq	9	M Winkelhock	RAM	03	Hart	4t				
nq	8	F Hesnault	Brabham	BT54	BMW	4t				
nq	29	P Martini	Minardi	M185	Motori Moderni	V6t		accident / injury		

Winning speed 138.435 km/h, 86.019 mph
Pole Position speed 148.206 km/h, 92.091 mph (A Senna, 1 min:20.450 sec)
Fastest Lap speed 144.284 km/h, 89.654 mph (M Alboreto, 1 min:22.637 sec on lap 60)
Lap Leaders A Senna 1-13 (13); M Alboreto 14-17,24-31 (12); A Prost 18-23,32-78 (53).

16 Jun 1985 — CANADA: Montréal — (Round 5) — (Race 409)

70 laps x 4.410 km, 2.740 miles = 308.700 km, 191.817 miles

Pos	No	Driver	Car	Model	Engine		Laps	Time/Reason for Retirement	Grid Pos	Row
1	27	M Alboreto	Ferrari	156/85	Ferrari	V6t	70	1h 46m 01.813s	3	2
2	28	S Johansson	Ferrari	156/85	Ferrari	V6t	70	1h 46m 03.770s	4	2
3	2	A Prost	McLaren	MP4/2B	TAG Porsche	V6t	70	1h 46m 06.154s	5	3
4	6	K Rosberg	Williams	FW10	Honda	V6t	70	1h 46m 29.634s	8	4
5	11	E de Angelis	Lotus	97T	Renault	V6t	70	1h 46m 45.162s	1	1
6	5	N Mansell	Williams	FW10	Honda	V6t	70	1h 47m 19.691s	16	8
7	15	P Tambay	Renault	RE60	Renault	V6t	69		10	5
8	26	J Laffite	Ligier	JS25	Renault	V6t	69	*	19	10
9	18	T Boutsen	Arrows	A8	BMW	4t	68		7	4
10	22	R Patrese	Alfa Romeo	185T	Alfa Romeo	V8t	68		13	7
11	4	S Bellof	Tyrrell	012	Ford Cosworth	V8	68		23	12
12	3	M Brundle	Tyrrell	012	Ford Cosworth	V8	68		24	12
13	17	G Berger	Arrows	A8	BMW	4t	67		12	6
14	25	A de Cesaris	Ligier	JS25	Renault	V6t	67		15	8
15	8	M Surer	Brabham	BT54	BMW	4t	67		20	10
16	12	A Senna	Lotus	97T	Renault	V6t	65		2	1
17	23	E Cheever	Alfa Romeo	185T	Alfa Romeo	V8t	64		11	6
r	29	P Martini	Minardi	M185	Motori Moderni	V6t	57	accident	25	13
r	1	N Lauda	McLaren	MP4/2B	TAG Porsche	V6t	37	engine	17	9
r	24	P Ghinzani	Osella	FA1G	Alfa Romeo	V8t	35	vapour lock	22	11
r	10	P Alliot	RAM	03	Hart	4t	28	accident	21	11
r	16	D Warwick	Renault	RE60	Renault	V6t	25	accident	6	3
r	9	M Winkelhock	RAM	03	Hart	4t	5	accident	14	7
r	19	T Fabi	Toleman	TG185	Hart	4t	3	turbo	18	9
r	7	N Piquet	Brabham	BT54	BMW	4t	0	transmission	9	5

Winning speed 174.686 km/h, 108.545 mph
Pole Position speed 187.733 km/h, 116.652 mph (E de Angelis, 1 min:24.567 sec)
Fastest Lap speed 181.554 km/h, 112.812 mph (A Senna, 1 min:27.445 sec on lap 45)
Lap Leaders E de Angelis 1-15 (15); M Alboreto 16-70 (55).

* Includes 1 minute penalty for jumping the start.

	23 Jun 1985		USA: Detroit						(Round 6)		(Race 410)	

63 laps x 4.023 km, 2.500 miles = 253.472 km, 157.500 miles

Pos	No	Driver	Car	Model	Engine		Laps	Time/Reason for Retirement	Grid Pos	Row
1	6	K Rosberg	Williams	FW10	Honda	V6t	63	1h 55m 39.851s	5	3
2	28	S Johansson	Ferrari	156/85	Ferrari	V6t	63	1h 56m 37.400s	9	5
3	27	M Alboreto	Ferrari	156/85	Ferrari	V6t	63	1h 56m 43.021s	3	2
4	4	S Bellof	Tyrrell	012	Ford Cosworth	V8	63	1h 56m 46.076s	19	10
5	11	E de Angelis	Lotus	97T	Renault	V6t	63	1h 57m 06.817s	8	4
6	7	N Piquet	Brabham	BT54	BMW	4t	62		10	5
7	18	T Boutsen	Arrows	A8	BMW	4t	62		21	11
8	8	M Surer	Brabham	BT54	BMW	4t	62		11	6
9	23	E Cheever	Alfa Romeo	185T	Alfa Romeo	V8t	61		7	4
10	25	A de Cesaris	Ligier	JS25	Renault	V6t	61		17	9
11	17	G Berger	Arrows	A8	BMW	4t	60		24	12
12	26	J Laffite	Ligier	JS25	Renault	V6t	58		16	8
r	12	A Senna	Lotus	97T	Renault	V6t	51	accident	1	1
r	3	M Brundle	Tyrrell	012	Ford Cosworth	V8	30	accident	18	9
r	10	P Alliot	RAM	03	Hart	4t	27	accident	23	12
r	5	N Mansell	Williams	FW10	Honda	V6t	26	brakes / accident	2	1
r	2	A Prost	McLaren	MP4/2B	TAG Porsche	V6t	19	brakes / accident	4	2
r	22	R Patrese	Alfa Romeo	185T	Alfa Romeo	V8t	19	electrics	14	7
r	16	D Warwick	Renault	RE60	Renault	V6t	18	gearbox	6	3
r	15	P Tambay	Renault	RE60	Renault	V6t	15	accident	15	8
r	29	P Martini	Minardi	M185	Motori Moderni	V6t	11	turbo	25	13
r	1	N Lauda	McLaren	MP4/2B	TAG Porsche	V6t	10	brakes	12	6
r	19	T Fabi	Toleman	TG185	Hart	4t	4	clutch	13	7
r	9	M Winkelhock	RAM	03	Hart	4t	3	turbo	20	10
r	24	P Ghinzani	Osella	FA1G	Alfa Romeo	V8t	0	accident	22	11

Winning speed 131.487 km/h, 81.702 mph
Pole Position speed 141.930 km/h, 88.191 mph (A Senna, 1 min:42.051 sec)
Fastest Lap speed 137.144 km/h, 85.218 mph (A Senna, 1 min:45.612 sec on lap 51)
Lap Leaders A Senna 1-7 (7); K Rosberg 8-63 (56).

	7 Jul 1985		FRANCE: Paul Ricard						(Round 7)		(Race 411)	

53 laps x 5.810 km, 3.610 miles = 307.930 km, 191.339 miles

Pos	No	Driver	Car	Model	Engine		Laps	Time/Reason for Retirement	Grid Pos	Row
1	7	N Piquet	Brabham	BT54	BMW	4t	53	1h 31m 46.266s	5	3
2	6	K Rosberg	Williams	FW10	Honda	V6t	53	1h 31m 52.926s	1	1
3	2	A Prost	McLaren	MP4/2B	TAG Porsche	V6t	53	1h 31m 55.551s	4	2
4	28	S Johansson	Ferrari	156/85	Ferrari	V6t	53	1h 32m 39.757s	15	8
5	11	E de Angelis	Lotus	97T	Renault	V6t	53	1h 32m 39.956s	7	4
6	15	P Tambay	Renault	RE60B	Renault	V6t	53	1h 33m 01.433s	9	5
7	16	D Warwick	Renault	RE60	Renault	V6t	53	1h 33m 30.478s	10	5
8	8	M Surer	Brabham	BT54	BMW	4t	52		13	7
9	18	T Boutsen	Arrows	A8	BMW	4t	52		11	6
10	23	E Cheever	Alfa Romeo	185T	Alfa Romeo	V8t	52		17	9
11	22	R Patrese	Alfa Romeo	185T	Alfa Romeo	V8t	52		16	8
12	9	M Winkelhock	RAM	03	Hart	4t	50		19	10
13	4	S Bellof	Tyrrell	012	Ford Cosworth	V8	50		25	13
14r	19	T Fabi	Toleman	TG185	Hart	4t	49	fuel pressure	18	9
15	24	P Ghinzani	Osella	FA1G	Alfa Romeo	V8t	49		23	12
r	3	M Brundle	Tyrrell	014	Renault	V6t	32	gear lever	20	10
r	1	N Lauda	McLaren	MP4/2B	TAG Porsche	V6t	30	gearbox	6	3
r	12	A Senna	Lotus	97T	Renault	V6t	26	engine / accident	2	1
r	17	G Berger	Arrows	A8	BMW	4t	20	accident	8	4
r	29	P Martini	Minardi	M185	Motori Moderni	V6t	19	accident	24	12
r	10	P Alliot	RAM	03	Hart	4t	8	fuel pressure	22	11
r	30	J Palmer	Zakspeed	841	Zakspeed	4t	6	electronics	21	11
r	27	M Alboreto	Ferrari	156/85	Ferrari	V6t	5	turbo	3	2
r	25	A de Cesaris	Ligier	JS25	Renault	V6t	4	driveshaft	12	6
r	26	J Laffite	Ligier	JS25	Renault	V6t	2	turbo	14	7
ns	5	N Mansell	Williams	FW10	Honda	V6t		accident / injury		

Winning speed 201.325 km/h, 125.097 mph
Pole Position speed 226.212 km/h, 140.562 mph (K Rosberg, 1 min:32.462 sec)
Fastest Lap speed 209.340 km/h, 130.078 mph (K Rosberg, 1 min:39.914 sec on lap 46)
Lap Leaders K Rosberg 1-10 (10); N Piquet 11-53 (43).

21 Jul 1985   BRITAIN: Silverstone   (Round 8)   (Race 412)

65 laps x 4.719 km, 2.932 miles = 306.709 km, 190.580 miles

Pos	No	Driver	Car	Model	Engine		Laps	Time/Reason for Retirement	Grid Pos	Row
1	2	A Prost	McLaren	MP4/2B	TAG Porsche	V6t	65	1h 18m 10.436s	3	2
2	27	M Alboreto	Ferrari	156/85	Ferrari	V6t	64		6	3
3	26	J Laffite	Ligier	JS25	Renault	V6t	64		16	8
4	7	N Piquet	Brabham	BT54	BMW	4t	64		2	1
5	16	D Warwick	Renault	RE60B	Renault	V6t	64		12	6
6	8	M Surer	Brabham	BT54	BMW	4t	63		15	8
7	3	M Brundle	Tyrrell	014	Renault	V6t	63		20	10
8	17	G Berger	Arrows	A8	BMW	4t	63		17	9
9	22	R Patrese	Alfa Romeo	185T	Alfa Romeo	V8t	62		14	7
10r	12	A Senna	Lotus	97T	Renault	V6t	60	fuel injection	4	2
11	4	S Bellof	Tyrrell	012	Ford Cosworth	V8	59		26	13
r	1	N Lauda	McLaren	MP4/2B	TAG Porsche	V6t	57	electrics	10	5
r	18	T Boutsen	Arrows	A8	BMW	4t	57	throttle / spin	19	10
r	25	A de Cesaris	Ligier	JS25	Renault	V6t	41	clutch	7	4
r	29	P Martini	Minardi	M185	Motori Moderni	V6t	38	transmission	23	12
nc	11	E de Angelis	Lotus	97T	Renault	V6t	37		8	4
r	9	M Winkelhock	RAM	03	Hart	4t	28	turbo	18	9
r	6	K Rosberg	Williams	FW10	Honda	V6t	21	exhaust	1	1
r	5	N Mansell	Williams	FW10	Honda	V6t	17	clutch	5	3
r	23	E Cheever	Alfa Romeo	185T	Alfa Romeo	V8t	17	turbo	22	11
r	30	J Palmer	Zakspeed	841	Zakspeed	4t	6	camshaft drive pinion	24	12
r	19	T Fabi	Toleman	TG185	Hart	4t	4	crown wheel & pinion	9	5
r	28	S Johansson	Ferrari	156/85	Ferrari	V6t	1	accident / intercooler	11	6
r	15	P Tambay	Renault	RE60B	Renault	V6t	0	accident	13	7
r	10	P Alliot	RAM	03	Hart	4t	0	accident	21	11
r	24	P Ghinzani	Osella	FA1G	Alfa Romeo	V8t	0	accident	25	13

Winning speed 235.405 km/h, 146.274 mph
Pole Position speed 258.983 km/h, 160.925 mph (K Rosberg, 1 min: 5.591 sec)
Fastest Lap speed 243.067 km/h, 151.035 mph (A Prost, 1 min: 9.886 sec on lap 43)
Lap Leaders A Senna 1-57,59 (58); A Prost 58,60-65 (7).

Scheduled for 66 laps, but stopped 1 lap early in error.

4 Aug 1985   GERMANY: Nürburgring   (Round 9)   (Race 413)

67 laps x 4.542 km, 2.822 miles = 304.314 km, 189.092 miles

Pos	No	Driver	Car	Model	Engine		Laps	Time/Reason for Retirement	Grid Pos	Row
1	27	M Alboreto	Ferrari	156/85	Ferrari	V6t	67	1h 35m 31.337s	8	4
2	2	A Prost	McLaren	MP4/2B	TAG Porsche	V6t	67	1h 35m 42.998s	3	2
3	26	J Laffite	Ligier	JS25	Renault	V6t	67	1h 36m 22.491s	13	7
4	18	T Boutsen	Arrows	A8	BMW	4t	67	1h 36m 26.616s	15	8
5	1	N Lauda	McLaren	MP4/2B	TAG Porsche	V6t	67	1h 36m 45.309s	12	6
6	5	N Mansell	Williams	FW10	Honda	V6t	67	1h 36m 48.157s	10	5
7	17	G Berger	Arrows	A8	BMW	4t	66		17	9
8	3	S Bellof	Tyrrell	014	Renault	V6t	66		19	10
9	28	S Johansson	Ferrari	156/85	Ferrari	V6t	66		2	1
10	4	M Brundle	Tyrrell	012	Ford Cosworth	V8	63		26	13
11r	29	P Martini	Minardi	M185	Motori Moderni	V6t	62	engine	27	14
12r	6	K Rosberg	Williams	FW10	Honda	V6t	61	brake caliper	4	2
r	23	E Cheever	Alfa Romeo	184T	Alfa Romeo	V8t	45	turbo	18	9
r	11	E de Angelis	Lotus	97T	Renault	V6t	40	engine	7	4
r	24	H Rothengatter	Osella	FA1G	Alfa Romeo	V8t	32	gearbox	25	13
r	19	T Fabi	Toleman	TG185	Hart	4t	29	clutch	1	1
r	12	A Senna	Lotus	97T	Renault	V6t	27	cv joint	5	3
r	16	D Warwick	Renault	RE60B	Renault	V6t	25	ignition	20	10
r	7	N Piquet	Brabham	BT54	BMW	4t	23	turbo	6	3
r	15	P Tambay	Renault	RE60B	Renault	V6t	19	spin	16	8
r	8	M Surer	Brabham	BT54	BMW	4t	15	valve	11	6
r	9	M Winkelhock	RAM	03	Hart	4t	8	engine	22	11
r	22	R Patrese	Alfa Romeo	184T	Alfa Romeo	V8t	8	gearbox	9	5
r	14	F Hesnault	Renault	RE60	Renault	V6t	8	clutch	23	12
r	10	P Alliot	RAM	03	Hart	4t	8	oil pressure / electrics	21	11
r	30	J Palmer	Zakspeed	841	Zakspeed	4t	7	alternator belt	24	12
r	25	A de Cesaris	Ligier	JS25	Renault	V6t	0	accident / steering	14	7

Winning speed 191.147 km/h, 118.774 mph
Pole Position speed 211.177 km/h, 131.219 mph (T Fabi, 1 min:17.429 sec)
Fastest Lap speed 197.464 km/h, 122.698 mph (N Lauda, 1 min:22.806 sec on lap 53)
Lap Leaders K Rosberg 1-15,27-44 (33); A Senna 16-26 (11); M Alboreto 45-67 (23).

18 Aug 1985　　**AUSTRIA: Österreichring**　　　　　　　　　　　　　**(Round 10)**　　**(Race 414)**

52 laps x 5.942 km, 3.692 miles = 308.984 km, 191.994 miles

Pos	No	Driver	Car	Model	Engine		Laps	Time/Reason for Retirement	Grid Pos	Row
1	2	A Prost	McLaren	MP4/2B	TAG Porsche	V6t	52	1h 20m 12.583s	1	1
2	12	A Senna	Lotus	97T	Renault	V6t	52	1h 20m 42.585s	14	7
3	27	M Alboreto	Ferrari	156/85	Ferrari	V6t	52	1h 20m 46.939s	9	5
4	28	S Johansson	Ferrari	156/85	Ferrari	V6t	52	1h 20m 51.656s	12	6
5	11	E de Angelis	Lotus	97T	Renault	V6t	52	1h 21m 34.675s	7	4
6	8	M Surer	Brabham	BT54	BMW	4t	51		11	6
7r	3	S Bellof	Tyrrell	014	Renault	V6t	49	out of fuel	22	11
8	18	T Boutsen	Arrows	A8	BMW	4t	49		16	8
9	24	H Rothengatter	Osella	FA1G	Alfa Romeo	V8t	48		24	12
10r	15	P Tambay	Renault	RE60B	Renault	V6t	46	engine	8	4
r	26	J Laffite	Ligier	JS25	Renault	V6t	43	front wheel lost	15	8
r	29	P Martini	Minardi	M185	Motori Moderni	V6t	40	engine	26	13
r	1	N Lauda	McLaren	MP4/2B	TAG Porsche	V6t	39	turbo	3	2
r	17	G Berger	Arrows	A8	BMW	4t	33	turbo	17	9
r	19	T Fabi	Toleman	TG185	Hart	4t	31	electrics	6	3
r	16	D Warwick	Renault	RE60B	Renault	V6t	29	engine	13	7
r	10	K Acheson	RAM	03	Hart	4t	28	engine	23	12
r	7	N Piquet	Brabham	BT54	BMW	4t	26	exhaust	5	3
r	5	N Mansell	Williams	FW10	Honda	V6t	25	oil pressure / engine	2	1
r	22	R Patrese	Alfa Romeo	184T	Alfa Romeo	V8t	25	turbo	10	5
r	30	J Palmer	Zakspeed	841	Zakspeed	4t	17	alternator belt	25	13
r	9	P Alliot	RAM	03	Hart	4t	16	turbo	21	11
r	25	A de Cesaris	Ligier	JS25	Renault	V6t	13	accident	18	9
r	23	E Cheever	Alfa Romeo	184T	Alfa Romeo	V8t	6	turbo	20	10
r	6	K Rosberg	Williams	FW10	Honda	V6t	4	engine	4	2
r	20	P Ghinzani	Toleman	TG185	Hart	4t	0	engine *	19	10
nq	4	M Brundle	Tyrrell	012	Ford Cosworth	V8				

Winning speed 231.132 km/h, 143.619 mph
Pole Position speed 250.219 km/h, 155.479 mph (A Prost, 1 min:25.490 sec)
Fastest Lap speed 239.701 km/h, 148.944 mph (A Prost, 1 min:29.241 sec on lap 39)
Lap Leaders A Prost 1-25,40-52 (38); N Lauda 26-39 (14).

Interrupted after first lap accident. Restarted for original distance.　　　　　* *Retired after first start.*

---

25 Aug 1985　　**NETHERLANDS: Zandvoort**　　　　　　　　　　　　　**(Round 11)**　　**(Race 415)**

70 laps x 4.252 km, 2.642 miles = 297.640 km, 184.945 miles

Pos	No	Driver	Car	Model	Engine		Laps	Time/Reason for Retirement	Grid Pos	Row
1	1	N Lauda	McLaren	MP4/2B	TAG Porsche	V6t	70	1h 32m 29.263s	10	5
2	2	A Prost	McLaren	MP4/2B	TAG Porsche	V6t	70	1h 32m 29.495s	3	2
3	12	A Senna	Lotus	97T	Renault	V6t	70	1h 33m 17.754s	4	2
4	27	M Alboreto	Ferrari	156/85	Ferrari	V6t	70	1h 33m 18.100s	16	8
5	11	E de Angelis	Lotus	97T	Renault	V6t	69		11	6
6	5	N Mansell	Williams	FW10	Honda	V6t	69		7	4
7	3	M Brundle	Tyrrell	014	Renault	V6t	69		21	11
8	7	N Piquet	Brabham	BT54	BMW	4t	69		1	1
9	17	G Berger	Arrows	A8	BMW	4t	68		14	7
10r	8	M Surer	Brabham	BT54	BMW	4t	65	exhaust	9	5
nc	24	H Rothengatter	Osella	FA1G	Alfa Romeo	V8t	56		26	13
r	18	T Boutsen	Arrows	A8	BMW	4t	54	rear suspension	8	4
r	9	P Alliot	RAM	03	Hart	4t	52	engine	25	13
r	4	S Bellof	Tyrrell	014	Renault	V6t	39	oil pressure	22	11
r	16	D Warwick	Renault	RE60B	Renault	V6t	27	gearbox	12	6
r	25	A de Cesaris	Ligier	JS25	Renault	V6t	25	turbo	18	9
r	15	P Tambay	Renault	RE60B	Renault	V6t	22	transmission	6	3
r	6	K Rosberg	Williams	FW10	Honda	V6t	20	engine	2	1
r	19	T Fabi	Toleman	TG185	Hart	4t	18	rear wheel bearings	5	3
r	26	J Laffite	Ligier	JS25	Renault	V6t	17	ignition	13	7
r	30	J Palmer	Zakspeed	841	Zakspeed	4t	13	oil pressure	23	12
r	20	P Ghinzani	Toleman	TG185	Hart	4t	12	engine	15	8
r	28	S Johansson	Ferrari	156/85	Ferrari	V6t	9	engine	17	9
r	29	P Martini	Minardi	M185	Motori Moderni	V6t	1	accident	24	12
r	23	E Cheever	Alfa Romeo	184T	Alfa Romeo	V8t	1	turbo	20	10
r	22	R Patrese	Alfa Romeo	184T	Alfa Romeo	V8t	1	turbo	19	10
nq	10	K Acheson	RAM	03	Hart	4t				

Winning speed 193.089 km/h, 119.980 mph
Pole Position speed 215.370 km/h, 133.825 mph (N Piquet, 1 min:11.074 sec)
Fastest Lap speed 199.995 km/h, 124.271 mph (A Prost, 1 min:16.538 sec on lap 57)
Lap Leaders K Rosberg 1-19 (19); A Prost 20-33 (14); N Lauda 34-70 (37).

51 laps x 5.800 km, 3.604 miles = 295.800 km, 183.802 miles

Pos	No	Driver	Car	Model	Engine		Laps	Time/Reason for Retirement	Grid Pos	Row
1	2	A Prost	McLaren	MP4/2B	TAG Porsche	V6t	51	1h 17m 59.451s	5	3
2	7	N Piquet	Brabham	BT54	BMW	4t	51	1h 18m 51.086s	4	2
3	12	A Senna	Lotus	97T	Renault	V6t	51	1h 18m 59.841s	1	1
4	8	M Surer	Brabham	BT54	BMW	4t	51	1h 19m 00.060s	9	5
5r	28	S Johansson	Ferrari	156/85	Ferrari	V6t	50	out of fuel	10	5
6	11	E de Angelis	Lotus	97T	Renault	V6t	50		6	3
7	15	P Tambay	Renault	RE60B	Renault	V6t	50		8	4
8	3	M Brundle	Tyrrell	014	Renault	V6t	50		18	9
9	18	T Boutsen	Arrows	A8	BMW	4t	50		14	7
10	25	P Streiff	Ligier	JS25	Renault	V6t	49		19	10
11r	5	N Mansell	Williams	FW10	Honda	V6t	47	engine	3	2
12	19	T Fabi	Toleman	TG185	Hart	4t	47		15	8
13r	27	M Alboreto	Ferrari	156/85	Ferrari	V6t	45	engine	7	4
r	6	K Rosberg	Williams	FW10	Honda	V6t	44	engine	2	1
r	26	J Laffite	Ligier	JS25	Renault	V6t	40	engine	20	10
r	1	N Lauda	McLaren	MP4/2B	TAG Porsche	V6t	33	transmission	16	8
r	22	R Patrese	Alfa Romeo	184T	Alfa Romeo	V8t	31	exhaust	13	7
r	24	H Rothengatter	Osella	FA1G	Alfa Romeo	V8t	26	engine	22	11
r	9	P Alliot	RAM	03	Hart	4t	19	turbo	26	13
r	17	G Berger	Arrows	A8	BMW	4t	13	gearbox	11	6
r	16	D Warwick	Renault	RE60B	Renault	V6t	9	crown wheel & pinion	12	6
r	33	A Jones	Lola	THL1	Hart	4t	6	distributor	25	13
r	23	E Cheever	Alfa Romeo	184T	Alfa Romeo	V8t	3	engine	17	9
r	10	K Acheson	RAM	03	Hart	4t	2	transmission	24	12
r	29	P Martini	Minardi	M185	Motori Moderni	V6t	0	fuel pump	23	12
r	20	P Ghinzani	Toleman	TG185	Hart	4t	0	stalled on grid	21	11

Winning speed 227.565 km/h, 141.402 mph
Pole Position speed 245.405 km/h, 152.487 mph (A Senna, 1 min:25.084 sec)
Fastest Lap speed 236.512 km/h, 146.962 mph (N Mansell, 1 min:28.283 sec on lap 38)
Lap Leaders K Rosberg 1-27,40-44 (32); A Prost 28-39,45-51 (19).

43 laps x 6.940 km, 4.312 miles = 298.420 km, 185.430 miles

Pos	No	Driver	Car	Model	Engine		Laps	Time/Reason for Retirement	Grid Pos	Row
1	12	A Senna	Lotus	97T	Renault	V6t	43	1h 34m 19.893s	2	1
2	5	N Mansell	Williams	FW10	Honda	V6t	43	1h 34m 48.315s	7	4
3	2	A Prost	McLaren	MP4/2B	TAG Porsche	V6t	43	1h 35m 15.002s	1	1
4	6	K Rosberg	Williams	FW10	Honda	V6t	43	1h 35m 35.183s	10	5
5	7	N Piquet	Brabham	BT54	BMW	4t	42		3	2
6	16	D Warwick	Renault	RE60B	Renault	V6t	42		14	7
7	17	G Berger	Arrows	A8	BMW	4t	42		8	4
8	8	M Surer	Brabham	BT54	BMW	4t	42		12	6
9	25	P Streiff	Ligier	JS25	Renault	V6t	42		18	9
10r	18	T Boutsen	Arrows	A8	BMW	4t	40	gearbox	6	3
11r	26	J Laffite	Ligier	JS25	Renault	V6t	38	accident	17	9
12	29	P Martini	Minardi	M185	Motori Moderni	V6t	38		24	12
13	3	M Brundle	Tyrrell	014	Renault	V6t	38		21	11
nc	24	H Rothengatter	Osella	FA1G	Alfa Romeo	V8t	37		23	12
r	22	R Patrese	Alfa Romeo	184T	Alfa Romeo	V8t	31	ignition	15	8
r	23	E Cheever	Alfa Romeo	184T	Alfa Romeo	V8t	26	gearbox	19	10
r	15	P Tambay	Renault	RE60B	Renault	V6t	24	oil line / gearbox	13	7
r	19	T Fabi	Toleman	TG185	Hart	4t	23	throttle linkage	11	6
r	11	E de Angelis	Lotus	97T	Renault	V6t	17	turbo	9	5
r	30	C Danner	Zakspeed	841	Zakspeed	4t	16	gearbox	22	11
r	9	P Alliot	RAM	03	Hart	4t	10	accident	20	10
r	28	S Johansson	Ferrari	156/85	Ferrari	V6t	7	engine / spin	5	3
r	20	P Ghinzani	Toleman	TG185	Hart	4t	7	accident	16	8
r	27	M Alboreto	Ferrari	156/85	Ferrari	V6t	3	clutch	4	2
ns	1	N Lauda	McLaren	MP4/2B	TAG Porsche	V6t		accident / injury		

Winning speed 189.811 km/h, 117.943 mph
Pole Position speed 216.676 km/h, 134.636 mph (A Prost, 1 min:55.306 sec)
Fastest Lap speed 205.241 km/h, 127.531 mph (A Prost, 2 min: 1.730 sec on lap 38)
Lap Leaders A Senna 1-8,10-43 (42); E de Angelis 9 (1).

Race originally scheduled for 2 June but postponed after Friday's qualifying due to track surface disintegration.

6 Oct 1985　　　　**EUROPE: Brands Hatch**　　　　　　　　　　　　　　　**(Round 14)**　　**(Race 418)**

75 laps x 4.207 km, 2.614 miles = 315.512 km, 196.050 miles

Pos	No	Driver	Car	Model	Engine		Laps	Time/Reason for Retirement	Grid Pos	Row
1	5	N Mansell	Williams	FW10	Honda	V6t	75	1h 32m 58.109s	3	2
2	12	A Senna	Lotus	97T	Renault	V6t	75	1h 33m 19.505s	1	1
3	6	K Rosberg	Williams	FW10	Honda	V6t	75	1h 33m 56.642s	4	2
4	2	A Prost	McLaren	MP4/2B	TAG Porsche	V6t	75	1h 34m 04.230s	6	3
5	11	E de Angelis	Lotus	97T	Renault	V6t	74		9	5
6	18	T Boutsen	Arrows	A8	BMW	4t	73		12	6
7	1	J Watson	McLaren	MP4/2B	TAG Porsche	V6t	73		21	11
8	25	P Streiff	Ligier	JS25	Renault	V6t	73		5	3
9	22	R Patrese	Alfa Romeo	184T	Alfa Romeo	V8t	73		11	6
10	17	G Berger	Arrows	A8	BMW	4t	73		19	10
11	23	E Cheever	Alfa Romeo	184T	Alfa Romeo	V8t	73		18	9
12	15	P Tambay	Renault	RE60B	Renault	V6t	72		17	9
r	8	M Surer	Brabham	BT54	BMW	4t	62	turbo / fire	7	4
r	28	S Johansson	Ferrari	156/85	Ferrari	V6t	59	alternator	13	7
r	26	J Laffite	Ligier	JS25	Renault	V6t	58	engine	10	5
r	30	C Danner	Zakspeed	841	Zakspeed	4t	55	turbo	25	13
r	4	I Capelli	Tyrrell	014	Renault	V6t	44	accident	24	12
r	3	M Brundle	Tyrrell	014	Renault	V6t	40	water pipe	16	8
r	19	T Fabi	Toleman	TG185	Hart	4t	33	engine	20	10
r	9	P Alliot	RAM	03	Hart	4t	31	engine overheating	23	12
r	20	P Ghinzani	Toleman	TG185	Hart	4t	16	engine	14	7
r	33	A Jones	Lola	THL1	Hart	4t	13	radiator / engine overheating	22	11
r	27	M Alboreto	Ferrari	156/85	Ferrari	V6t	13	turbo / fire	15	8
r	7	N Piquet	Brabham	BT54	BMW	4t	6	accident	2	1
r	16	D Warwick	Renault	RE60B	Renault	V6t	4	fuel injection	8	4
r	29	P Martini	Minardi	M185	Motori Moderni	V6t	3	accident	26	13
nq	24	H Rothengatter	Osella	FA1G	Alfa Romeo	V8t				

Winning speed 203.625 km/h, 126.527 mph
Pole Position speed 225.470 km/h, 140.100 mph (A Senna, 1 min: 7.169 sec)
Fastest Lap speed 211.735 km/h, 131.566 mph (J Laffite, 1 min:11.526 sec on lap 55)
Lap Leaders A Senna 1-8 (8); N Mansell 9-75 (67).

---

19 Oct 1985　　　　**SOUTH AFRICA: Kyalami**　　　　　　　　　　　　　　　**(Round 15)**　　**(Race 419)**

75 laps x 4.104 km, 2.550 miles = 307.800 km, 191.258 miles

Pos	No	Driver	Car	Model	Engine		Laps	Time/Reason for Retirement	Grid Pos	Row
1	5	N Mansell	Williams	FW10	Honda	V6t	75	1h 28m 22.866s	1	1
2	6	K Rosberg	Williams	FW10	Honda	V6t	75	1h 28m 30.438s	3	2
3	2	A Prost	McLaren	MP4/2B	TAG Porsche	V6t	74		9	5
4	28	S Johansson	Ferrari	156/85	Ferrari	V6t	74		16	8
5	17	G Berger	Arrows	A8	BMW	4t	74		11	6
6	18	T Boutsen	Arrows	A8	BMW	4t	74		10	5
7	3	M Brundle	Tyrrell	014	Renault	V6t	73		17	9
r	11	E de Angelis	Lotus	97T	Renault	V6t	52	engine	6	3
r	29	P Martini	Minardi	M185	Motori Moderni	V6t	45	radiator	19	10
r	1	N Lauda	McLaren	MP4/2B	TAG Porsche	V6t	37	turbo	8	4
r	4	P Streiff	Tyrrell	014	Renault	V6t	16	accident	18	9
r	12	A Senna	Lotus	97T	Renault	V6t	8	engine	4	2
r	27	M Alboreto	Ferrari	156/85	Ferrari	V6t	8	turbo	15	8
r	7	N Piquet	Brabham	BT54	BMW	4t	6	engine	2	1
r	20	P Ghinzani	Toleman	TG185	Hart	4t	4	engine	13	7
r	19	T Fabi	Toleman	TG185	Hart	4t	3	valves	7	4
r	8	M Surer	Brabham	BT54	BMW	4t	3	valves	5	3
r	24	H Rothengatter	Osella	FA1G	Alfa Romeo	V8t	1	electrics	20	10
r	23	E Cheever	Alfa Romeo	184T	Alfa Romeo	V8t	0	accident	14	7
r	22	R Patrese	Alfa Romeo	184T	Alfa Romeo	V8t	0	accident	12	6
ns	33	A Jones	Lola	THL1	Hart	4t		driver ill		

Winning speed 208.959 km/h, 129.841 mph
Pole Position speed 236.898 km/h, 147.202 mph (N Mansell, 1 min: 2.366 sec)
Fastest Lap speed 216.796 km/h, 134.711 mph (K Rosberg, 1 min: 8.149 sec on lap 74)
Lap Leaders N Mansell 1-7,9-75 (74); K Rosberg 8 (1).

Alain Prost's final lap (75) was too slow and disallowed for the classification.

Pos	No	Driver	Car	Model	Engine		Laps	Time/Reason for Retirement	Grid Pos	Row
1	6	K Rosberg	Williams	FW10	Honda	V6t	82	2h 00m 40.473s	3	2
2	26	J Laffite	Ligier	JS25	Renault	V6t	82	2h 01m 26.603s	20	10
3	25	P Streiff	Ligier	JS25	Renault	V6t	82	2h 02m 09.009s	18	9
4	4	I Capelli	Tyrrell	014	Renault	V6t	81		22	11
5	28	S Johansson	Ferrari	156/85	Ferrari	V6t	81		15	8
6	17	G Berger	Arrows	A8	BMW	4t	81		7	4
7	24	H Rothengatter	Osella	FA1G	Alfa Romeo	V8t	78		25	13
8	29	P Martini	Minardi	M185	Motori Moderni	V6t	78		23	12
r	12	A Senna	Lotus	97T	Renault	V6t	62	engine	1	1
r	27	M Alboreto	Ferrari	156/85	Ferrari	V6t	61	gear linkage	5	3
r	1	N Lauda	McLaren	MP4/2B	TAG Porsche	V6t	57	brakes / accident	16	8
r	16	D Warwick	Renault	RE60B	Renault	V6t	57	transmission	12	6
nc	3	M Brundle	Tyrrell	014	Renault	V6t	49		17	9
r	8	M Surer	Brabham	BT54	BMW	4t	42	engine	6	3
r	22	R Patrese	Alfa Romeo	184T	Alfa Romeo	V8t	42	exhaust	14	7
r	19	T Fabi	Toleman	TG185	Hart	4t	40	engine	24	12
r	18	T Boutsen	Arrows	A8	BMW	4t	37	oil leak / spin	11	6
r	20	P Ghinzani	Toleman	TG185	Hart	4t	28	clutch	21	11
r	2	A Prost	McLaren	MP4/2B	TAG Porsche	V6t	26	engine	4	2
r	15	P Tambay	Renault	RE60B	Renault	V6t	20	differential	8	4
r	33	A Jones	Lola	THL1	Hart	4t	20	electrics	19	10
dq	11	E de Angelis	Lotus	97T	Renault	V6t	19	started from wrong grid position	10	5
r	7	N Piquet	Brabham	BT54	BMW	4t	14	electrics / fire	9	5
r	23	E Cheever	Alfa Romeo	184T	Alfa Romeo	V8t	5	engine	13	7
r	5	N Mansell	Williams	FW10	Honda	V6t	1	crown wheel & pinion	2	1

Winning speed 154.032 km/h, 95.711 mph
Pole Position speed 170.344 km/h, 105.847 mph (A Senna, 1 min:19.843 sec)
Fastest Lap speed 162.382 km/h, 100.900 mph (K Rosberg, 1 min:23.758 sec on lap 57)
Lap Leaders K Rosberg 1-41,44-52,62-82 (71); A Senna 42-43,53-55,58-61 (9); N Lauda 56-57 (2).

Lap Leaders 1985

Pos	Driver	Car-Engine	GPs	laps	km	miles
1	A Senna	Lotus-Renault	9	271	1,327.7	825.0
2	K Rosberg	Williams-Honda	8	231	1,017.3	632.1
3	A Prost	McLaren-TAG Porsche	7	178	841.5	522.9
4	N Mansell	Williams-Honda	2	141	585.6	363.9
5	M Alboreto	Ferrari	4	98	427.0	265.3
6	N Lauda	McLaren-TAG Porsche	3	53	248.1	154.1
7	N Piquet	Brabham-BMW	1	43	249.8	155.2
8	E de Angelis	Lotus-Renault	2	16	73.1	45.4
9	S Johansson	Ferrari	1	1	5.0	3.1
			16	**1,032**	**4,774.2**	**2,966.5**

Driver Points 1985

	Driver	BR	P	RSM	MC	CDN	USA	F	GB	D	A	NL	I	B	EUR	ZA	AUS	Total	
1	A Prost	9	-	-	9	4	-	4	9	6	9	6	9	4	(3)	4	-	73	(3)
2	M Alboreto	6	6	-	6	9	4	-	6	9	4	3	-	-	-	-	-	53	
3	K Rosberg	-	-	-	-	3	9	6	-	-	-	-	-	3	4	6	9	40	
4	A Senna	-	9	-	-	-	-	-	-	-	6	4	4	9	6	-	-	38	
5	E de Angelis	4	3	9	4	2	2	2	-	-	2	2	1	-	2	-	-	33	
6	N Mansell	-	2	2	-	1	-	-	-	1	-	1	-	6	9	9	-	31	
7	S Johansson	-	-	1	-	6	6	3	-	-	3	-	2	-	-	3	2	26	
8	N Piquet	-	-	-	-	-	1	9	3	-	-	-	6	2	-	-	-	21	
9	J Laffite	1	-	-	1	-	-	-	4	4	-	-	-	-	-	-	6	16	
10	N Lauda	-	-	3	-	-	-	-	-	2	-	9	-	-	-	-	-	14	
11	T Boutsen	-	-	6	-	-	-	-	-	3	-	-	-	-	1	1	-	11	
	P Tambay	2	4	4	-	-	-	1	-	-	-	-	-	-	-	-	-	11	
13	M Surer	-	-	-	-	-	-	-	1	-	1	-	3	-	-	-	-	5	
	D Warwick	-	-	-	2	-	-	-	2	-	-	-	-	1	-	-	-	5	
15	P Streiff	-	-	-	-	-	-	-	-	-	-	-	-	-	-	-	4	4	
	S Bellof	-	1	-	-	-	3	-	-	-	-	-	-	-	-	-	-	4	
17	R Arnoux	3	-	-	-	-	-	-	-	-	-	-	-	-	-	-	-	3	
	A de Cesaris	-	-	-	3	-	-	-	-	-	-	-	-	-	-	-	-	3	
	I Capelli	-	-	-	-	-	-	-	-	-	-	-	-	-	-	3	-	3	
	G Berger	-	-	-	-	-	-	-	-	-	-	-	-	-	-	2	1	3	

9,6,4,3,2 and 1 point awarded to the first six finishers. Best 11 scores.

Constructor Points 1985

	Constructor	BR	P	RSM	MC	CDN	USA	F	GB	D	A	NL	I	B	EUR	ZA	AUS	Total
1	McLaren-TAG Porsche	9	-	3	9	4	-	4	9	8	9	15	9	4	3	4	-	90
2	Ferrari	9	6	1	6	15	10	3	6	9	7	3	2	-	-	3	2	82
3	Williams-Honda	-	2	2	-	4	9	6	-	1	-	1	-	9	13	15	9	71
	Lotus-Renault	4	12	9	4	2	2	2	-	-	8	6	5	9	8	-	-	71
5	Brabham-BMW	-	-	-	-	-	1	9	4	-	1	-	9	2	-	-	-	26
6	Ligier-Renault	1	-	-	4	-	-	-	4	4	-	-	-	-	-	-	10	23
7	Renault	2	4	4	2	-	-	1	2	-	-	-	-	1	-	-	-	16
8	Arrows-BMW	-	-	6	-	-	-	-	-	3	-	-	-	-	1	3	1	14
9	Tyrrell-Ford Cosworth	-	1	-	-	-	3	-	-	-	-	-	-	-	-	-	-	4
10	Tyrrell-Renault	-	-	-	-	-	-	-	-	-	-	-	-	-	-	-	3	3

9,6,4,3,2 and 1 point awarded to the first six finishers.

1986

Race Entrants and Results

Only turbos (1.5-litre) were permitted with a new fuel allowance of 195 litres. The Williams FW11 was the car to have, but the team had a dreadful setback when Frank Williams was paralysed in a road accident after pre-season testing in the South of France. Toleman was purchased and re-named by Benetton. Gordon Murray produced the ultra low-line BT55, only to leave at the end of the year, as did Pirelli.

McLAREN
Marlboro McLaren International: Prost, Rosberg

TYRRELL
Data General Team Tyrrell: Brundle, Streiff

WILLIAMS
Canon Williams Team: Mansell, Piquet

BRABHAM
Motor Racing Developments: Patrese, de Angelis, Warwick

LOTUS
John Player Special Team Lotus: Dumfries, Senna

ZAKSPEED
West Zakspeed Racing: Palmer, Rothengatter

LOLA
Team Haas (USA) Ltd: Jones, Tambay, Cheever

ARROWS
Barclay Arrows BMW: Surer, Danner, Boutsen

BENETTON
Benetton Formula: Fabi, Berger

OSELLA
Osella Squadra Corse: Ghinzani, Danner, Berg, Caffi

MINARDI
Minardi Team: de Cesaris, Nannini

LIGIER
Equipe Ligier: Arnoux, Laffite, Alliot

FERRARI
Scuderia Ferrari SpA SEFAC: Alboreto, Johansson

AGS
Jolly Club SpA: Capelli

23 Mar 1986		**BRAZIL: Rio de Janeiro**							**(Round 1)**		**(Race 421)**
		61 laps x 5.031 km, 3.126 miles = 306.891 km, 190.693 miles									
Pos	No	Driver	Car	Model	Engine		Laps	Time/Reason for Retirement		Grid Pos	Row
1	6	N Piquet	Williams	FW11	Honda	V6t	61	1h 39m 32.583s		2	1
2	12	A Senna	Lotus	98T	Renault	V6t	61	1h 40m 07.410s		1	1
3	26	J Laffite	Ligier	JS27	Renault	V6t	61	1h 40m 32.342s		5	3
4	25	R Arnoux	Ligier	JS27	Renault	V6t	61	1h 41m 01.012s		4	2
5	3	M Brundle	Tyrrell	014	Renault	V6t	60			17	9
6	20	G Berger	Benetton	B186	BMW	4t	59			16	8
7	4	P Streiff	Tyrrell	014	Renault	V6t	59			18	9
8	8	E de Angelis	Brabham	BT55	BMW	4t	58			14	7
9	11	J Dumfries	Lotus	98T	Renault	V6t	58			11	6
10	19	T Fabi	Benetton	B186	BMW	4t	56			12	6
r	18	T Boutsen	Arrows	A8	BMW	4t	37	turbo wastegate		15	8
r	27	M Alboreto	Ferrari	F1-86	Ferrari	V6t	35	fuel pump drive		6	3
r	1	A Prost	McLaren	MP4/2C	TAG Porsche	V6t	30	engine		9	5
r	22	C Danner	Osella	FA1F	Alfa Romeo	V8t	29	engine		24	12
r	28	S Johansson	Ferrari	F1-86	Ferrari	V6t	26	brakes / spin		8	4
r	16	P Tambay	Lola	THL1	Hart	4t	24	alternator		13	7
r	7	R Patrese	Brabham	BT55	BMW	4t	21	water pipe		10	5
r	14	J Palmer	Zakspeed	861	Zakspeed	4t	20	airbox		21	11
r	17	M Surer	Arrows	A8	BMW	4t	19	engine overheating		20	10
r	24	A Nannini	Minardi	M185B	Motori Moderni	V6t	18	clutch		25	13
r	23	A de Cesaris	Minardi	M185B	Motori Moderni	V6t	16	turbo		22	11
r	21	P Ghinzani	Osella	FA1G	Alfa Romeo	V8t	16	engine		23	12
r	2	K Rosberg	McLaren	MP4/2C	TAG Porsche	V6t	6	engine		7	4
r	15	A Jones	Lola	THL1	Hart	4t	5	distributor rotor arm		19	10
r	5	N Mansell	Williams	FW11	Honda	V6t	0	accident		3	2

Winning speed 184.980 km/h, 114.941 mph
Pole Position speed 211.829 km/h, 131.625 mph (A Senna, 1 min:25.501 sec)
Fastest Lap speed 193.612 km/h, 120.305 mph (N Piquet, 1 min:33.546 sec on lap 46)
Lap Leaders A Senna 1-2,19,41 (4); N Piquet 3-18,27-40,42-61 (50); A Prost 20-26 (7).

13 Apr 1986 **SPAIN: Jerez de la Frontera** **(Round 2)** **(Race 422)**

72 laps x 4.218 km, 2.621 miles = 303.696 km, 188.708 miles

Pos	No	Driver	Car	Model	Engine		Laps	Time/Reason for Retirement	Grid Pos	Row
1	12	A Senna	Lotus	98T	Renault	V6t	72	1h 48m 47.735s	1	1
2	5	N Mansell	Williams	FW11	Honda	V6t	72	1h 48m 47.749s	3	2
3	1	A Prost	McLaren	MP4/2C	TAG Porsche	V6t	72	1h 49m 09.287s	4	2
4	2	K Rosberg	McLaren	MP4/2C	TAG Porsche	V6t	71		5	3
5	19	T Fabi	Benetton	B186	BMW	4t	71		9	5
6	20	G Berger	Benetton	B186	BMW	4t	71		7	4
7	18	T Boutsen	Arrows	A8	BMW	4t	68		19	10
8	16	P Tambay	Lola	THL1	Hart	4t	66		18	9
r	11	J Dumfries	Lotus	98T	Renault	V6t	52	gearbox	10	5
r	3	M Brundle	Tyrrell	014	Renault	V6t	41	oil loss	12	6
r	26	J Laffite	Ligier	JS27	Renault	V6t	40	driveshaft	8	4
r	6	N Piquet	Williams	FW11	Honda	V6t	39	engine overheating	2	1
r	17	M Surer	Arrows	A8	BMW	4t	39	fuel leak	22	11
r	8	E de Angelis	Brabham	BT55	BMW	4t	29	gearbox	15	8
r	25	R Arnoux	Ligier	JS27	Renault	V6t	29	driveshaft	6	3
r	27	M Alboreto	Ferrari	F1-86	Ferrari	V6t	22	front wheel bearing	13	7
r	4	P Streiff	Tyrrell	014	Renault	V6t	22	oil loss	20	10
r	22	C Danner	Osella	FA1F	Alfa Romeo	V8t	14	engine	23	12
r	28	S Johansson	Ferrari	F1-86	Ferrari	V6t	11	brakes / accident	11	6
r	21	P Ghinzani	Osella	FA1G	Alfa Romeo	V8t	10	engine	21	11
r	7	R Patrese	Brabham	BT55	BMW	4t	8	gearbox	14	7
r	23	A de Cesaris	Minardi	M185B	Motori Moderni	V6t	1	differential	24	12
r	14	J Palmer	Zakspeed	861	Zakspeed	4t	0	accident	16	8
r	15	A Jones	Lola	THL1	Hart	4t	0	accident	17	9
ns	24	A Nannini	Minardi	M185B	Motori Moderni	V6t		differential on parade lap	25	13

Winning speed 167.486 km/h, 104.071 mph
Pole Position speed 186.077 km/h, 115.623 mph (A Senna, 1 min:21.605 sec)
Fastest Lap speed 174.186 km/h, 108.234 mph (N Mansell, 1 min:27.176 sec on lap 65)
Lap Leaders A Senna 1-39,63-72 (49); N Mansell 40-62 (23).

27 Apr 1986 **SAN MARINO: Imola** **(Round 3)** **(Race 423)**

60 laps x 5.040 km, 3.132 miles = 302.400 km, 187.903 miles

Pos	No	Driver	Car	Model	Engine		Laps	Time/Reason for Retirement	Grid Pos	Row
1	1	A Prost	McLaren	MP4/2C	TAG Porsche	V6t	60	1h 32m 28.408s	4	2
2	6	N Piquet	Williams	FW11	Honda	V6t	60	1h 32m 36.053s	2	1
3	20	G Berger	Benetton	B186	BMW	4t	59		9	5
4	28	S Johansson	Ferrari	F1-86	Ferrari	V6t	59		7	4
5r	2	K Rosberg	McLaren	MP4/2C	TAG Porsche	V6t	58	out of fuel	6	3
6r	7	R Patrese	Brabham	BT55	BMW	4t	58	out of fuel	16	8
7	18	T Boutsen	Arrows	A8	BMW	4t	58		12	6
8	3	M Brundle	Tyrrell	014	Renault	V6t	58		13	7
9r	17	M Surer	Arrows	A8	BMW	4t	57	out of fuel	15	8
10r	27	M Alboreto	Ferrari	F1-86	Ferrari	V6t	56	turbo boost pressure	5	3
r	21	P Ghinzani	Osella	FA1G	Alfa Romeo	V8t	52	out of fuel	26	13
r	25	R Arnoux	Ligier	JS27	Renault	V6t	46	front wheel lost	8	4
r	4	P Streiff	Tyrrell	014	Renault	V6t	41	transmission	22	11
r	19	T Fabi	Benetton	B186	BMW	4t	39	engine	10	5
r	14	J Palmer	Zakspeed	861	Zakspeed	4t	38	brakes	20	10
r	22	C Danner	Osella	FA1F	Alfa Romeo	V8t	31	electrics	25	13
r	15	A Jones	Lola	THL2	Ford Cosworth	V6t	28	radiator / engine overheating	21	11
r	23	A de Cesaris	Minardi	M185B	Motori Moderni	V6t	20	engine	23	12
r	8	E de Angelis	Brabham	BT55	BMW	4t	19	engine	19	10
r	26	J Laffite	Ligier	JS27	Renault	V6t	14	turbo boost pressure	14	7
r	12	A Senna	Lotus	98T	Renault	V6t	11	wheel bearing	1	1
r	5	N Mansell	Williams	FW11	Honda	V6t	8	engine	3	2
r	11	J Dumfries	Lotus	98T	Renault	V6t	8	rear wheel bearing	17	9
r	29	H Rothengatter	Zakspeed	861	Zakspeed	4t	7	turbo boost pressure	24	12
r	16	P Tambay	Lola	THL1	Hart	4t	5	engine	11	6
r	24	A Nannini	Minardi	M185B	Motori Moderni	V6t	0	accident	18	9

Winning speed 196.208 km/h, 121.918 mph
Pole Position speed 213.333 km/h, 132.559 mph (A Senna, 1 min:25.050 sec)
Fastest Lap speed 204.631 km/h, 127.152 mph (N Piquet, 1 min:28.667 sec on lap 57)
Lap Leaders N Piquet 1-28 (28); K Rosberg 29-32 (4); A Prost 33-60 (28).

11 May 1986　MONACO: Monte-Carlo　(Round 4)　(Race 424)
78 laps x 3.328 km, 2.068 miles = 259.584 km, 161.298 miles

Pos	No	Driver	Car	Model	Engine		Laps	Time/Reason for Retirement	Grid Pos	Row
1	1	A Prost	McLaren	MP4/2C	TAG Porsche	V6t	78	1h 55m 41.060s	1	1
2	2	K Rosberg	McLaren	MP4/2C	TAG Porsche	V6t	78	1h 56m 06.082s	9	5
3	12	A Senna	Lotus	98T	Renault	V6t	78	1h 56m 34.706s	3	2
4	5	N Mansell	Williams	FW11	Honda	V6t	78	1h 56m 52.462s	2	1
5	25	R Arnoux	Ligier	JS27	Renault	V6t	77		12	6
6	26	J Laffite	Ligier	JS27	Renault	V6t	77		7	4
7	6	N Piquet	Williams	FW11	Honda	V6t	77		11	6
8	18	T Boutsen	Arrows	A8	BMW	4t	75		14	7
9	17	M Surer	Arrows	A8	BMW	4t	75		17	9
10	28	S Johansson	Ferrari	F1-86	Ferrari	V6t	75		15	8
11	4	P Streiff	Tyrrell	015	Renault	V6t	74		13	7
12	14	J Palmer	Zakspeed	861	Zakspeed	4t	74		19	10
r	3	M Brundle	Tyrrell	015	Renault	V6t	67	accident	10	5
r	16	P Tambay	Lola	THL2	Ford Cosworth	V6t	67	accident	8	4
r	20	G Berger	Benetton	B186	BMW	4t	42	front wheel drive pegs	5	3
r	27	M Alboreto	Ferrari	F1-86	Ferrari	V6t	38	turbo	4	2
r	7	R Patrese	Brabham	BT55	BMW	4t	38	fuel pump	6	3
r	8	E de Angelis	Brabham	BT55	BMW	4t	31	turbo boost pressure	20	10
r	19	T Fabi	Benetton	B186	BMW	4t	17	brakes	16	8
r	15	A Jones	Lola	THL2	Ford Cosworth	V6t	2	accident	18	9
nq	21	P Ghinzani	Osella	FA1G	Alfa Romeo	V8t				
nq	11	J Dumfries	Lotus	98T	Renault	V6t				
nq	29	H Rothengatter	Zakspeed	861	Zakspeed	4t				
nq	22	C Danner	Osella	FA1F	Alfa Romeo	V8t				
nq	23	A de Cesaris	Minardi	M185B	Motori Moderni	V6t				
nq	24	A Nannini	Minardi	M185B	Motori Moderni	V6t				

Winning speed 134.634 km/h, 83.658 mph
Pole Position speed 144.999 km/h, 90.098 mph (A Prost, 1 min:22.627 sec)
Fastest Lap speed 138.335 km/h, 85.958 mph (A Prost, 1 min:26.607 sec on lap 51)
Lap Leaders A Prost 1-34,42-78 (71); A Senna 35-41 (7).

25 May 1986　BELGIUM: Spa-Francorchamps　(Round 5)　(Race 425)
43 laps x 6.940 km, 4.312 miles = 298.420 km, 185.430 miles

Pos	No	Driver	Car	Model	Engine		Laps	Time/Reason for Retirement	Grid Pos	Row
1	5	N Mansell	Williams	FW11	Honda	V6t	43	1h 27m 57.925s	5	3
2	12	A Senna	Lotus	98T	Renault	V6t	43	1h 28m 17.752s	4	2
3	28	S Johansson	Ferrari	F1-86	Ferrari	V6t	43	1h 28m 24.517s	11	6
4	27	M Alboreto	Ferrari	F1-86	Ferrari	V6t	43	1h 28m 27.559s	9	5
5	26	J Laffite	Ligier	JS27	Renault	V6t	43	1h 29m 08.615s	17	9
6	1	A Prost	McLaren	MP4/2C	TAG Porsche	V6t	43	1h 30m 15.697s	3	2
7	19	T Fabi	Benetton	B186	BMW	4t	42		6	3
8	7	R Patrese	Brabham	BT55	BMW	4t	42		15	8
9	17	M Surer	Arrows	A8	BMW	4t	41		21	11
10	20	G Berger	Benetton	B186	BMW	4t	41		2	1
11r	15	A Jones	Lola	THL2	Ford Cosworth	V6t	40	out of fuel	16	8
12	4	P Streiff	Tyrrell	015	Renault	V6t	40	*	18	9
13	14	J Palmer	Zakspeed	861	Zakspeed	4t	37		20	10
r	23	A de Cesaris	Minardi	M185B	Motori Moderni	V6t	35	out of fuel	19	10
r	3	M Brundle	Tyrrell	015	Renault	V6t	25	gearbox	12	6
r	29	H Rothengatter	Zakspeed	861	Zakspeed	4t	25	alternator	23	12
r	24	A Nannini	Minardi	M185B	Motori Moderni	V6t	24	gearbox	22	11
r	25	R Arnoux	Ligier	JS27	Renault	V6t	23	engine	7	4
r	6	N Piquet	Williams	FW11	Honda	V6t	16	turbo boost control	1	1
r	18	T Boutsen	Arrows	A8	BMW	4t	7	electrics	14	7
r	11	J Dumfries	Lotus	98T	Renault	V6t	7	spin / radiator	13	7
r	2	K Rosberg	McLaren	MP4/2C	TAG Porsche	V6t	6	engine	8	4
r	21	P Ghinzani	Osella	FA1G	Alfa Romeo	V8t	3	engine	24	12
r	22	C Danner	Osella	FA1F	Alfa Romeo	V8t	2	engine	25	13
r	16	P Tambay	Lola	THL2	Ford Cosworth	V6t	0	accident	10	5

Winning speed 203.548 km/h, 126.479 mph
Pole Position speed 218.523 km/h, 135.784 mph (N Piquet, 1 min:54.331 sec)
Fastest Lap speed 209.453 km/h, 130.148 mph (A Prost, 1 min:59.282 sec on lap 31)
Lap Leaders N Piquet 1-16 (16); A Senna 17-21 (5); S Johansson 22-23 (2); N Mansell 24-43 (20).

* Although J Palmer completed less than 90% of the race distance, he was classified due to being prevented from leaving the pits to complete an extra lap.

15 Jun 1986 **CANADA: Montréal** (Round 6) (Race 426)

69 laps x 4.410 km, 2.740 miles = 304.290 km, 189.077 miles

Pos	No	Driver	Car	Model	Engine		Laps	Time/Reason for Retirement	Grid Pos	Row
1	5	N Mansell	Williams	FW11	Honda	V6t	69	1h 42m 26.415s	1	1
2	1	A Prost	McLaren	MP4/2C	TAG Porsche	V6t	69	1h 42m 47.074s	4	2
3	6	N Piquet	Williams	FW11	Honda	V6t	69	1h 43m 02.677s	3	2
4	2	K Rosberg	McLaren	MP4/2C	TAG Porsche	V6t	69	1h 44m 02.088s	6	3
5	12	A Senna	Lotus	98T	Renault	V6t	68		2	1
6	25	R Arnoux	Ligier	JS27	Renault	V6t	68		5	3
7	26	J Laffite	Ligier	JS27	Renault	V6t	68		8	4
8	27	M Alboreto	Ferrari	F1-86	Ferrari	V6t	68		11	6
9	3	M Brundle	Tyrrell	015	Renault	V6t	67		18	9
10	15	A Jones	Lola	THL2	Ford Cosworth	V6t	66		13	7
11	4	P Streiff	Tyrrell	014	Renault	V6t	65		16	8
12	29	H Rothengatter	Zakspeed	861	Zakspeed	4t	63		23	12
r	7	R Patrese	Brabham	BT55	BMW	4t	44	turbo	9	5
r	21	P Ghinzani	Osella	FA1G	Alfa Romeo	V8t	43	gearbox	22	11
r	23	A de Cesaris	Minardi	M185B	Motori Moderni	V6t	40	gearbox	20	10
r	18	T Boutsen	Arrows	A8	BMW	4t	38	electrics	12	6
r	20	G Berger	Benetton	B186	BMW	4t	34	turbo boost pressure	7	4
r	28	S Johansson	Ferrari	F1-86	Ferrari	V6t	29	accident	17	9
r	11	J Dumfries	Lotus	98T	Renault	V6t	28	accident	15	8
r	14	J Palmer	Zakspeed	861	Zakspeed	4t	24	engine	21	11
r	8	D Warwick	Brabham	BT55	BMW	4t	20	engine	10	5
r	24	A Nannini	Minardi	M185B	Motori Moderni	V6t	17	turbo	19	10
r	19	T Fabi	Benetton	B186	BMW	4t	13	battery	14	7
r	22	C Danner	Osella	FA1F	Alfa Romeo	V8t	6	turbo	24	12
ns	16	P Tambay	Lola	THL2	Ford Cosworth	V6t		accident / injury		

Winning speed 178.225 km/h, 110.744 mph
Pole Position speed 188.735 km/h, 117.274 mph (N Mansell, 1 min:24.118 sec)
Fastest Lap speed 185.808 km/h, 115.456 mph (N Piquet, 1 min:25.443 sec on lap 63)
Lap Leaders N Mansell 1-16,22-30,32-69 (63); K Rosberg 17-21 (5); A Prost 31 (1).

22 Jun 1986 **USA: Detroit** (Round 7) (Race 427)

63 laps x 4.023 km, 2.500 miles = 253.472 km, 157.500 miles

Pos	No	Driver	Car	Model	Engine		Laps	Time/Reason for Retirement	Grid Pos	Row
1	12	A Senna	Lotus	98T	Renault	V6t	63	1h 51m 12.847s	1	1
2	26	J Laffite	Ligier	JS27	Renault	V6t	63	1h 51m 43.864s	6	3
3	1	A Prost	McLaren	MP4/2C	TAG Porsche	V6t	63	1h 51m 44.671s	7	4
4	27	M Alboreto	Ferrari	F1-86	Ferrari	V6t	63	1h 52m 43.783s	11	6
5	5	N Mansell	Williams	FW11	Honda	V6t	62		2	1
6	7	R Patrese	Brabham	BT55	BMW	4t	62		8	4
7	11	J Dumfries	Lotus	98T	Renault	V6t	61		14	7
8	14	J Palmer	Zakspeed	861	Zakspeed	4t	61		20	10
9	4	P Streiff	Tyrrell	015	Renault	V6t	61		18	9
10	8	D Warwick	Brabham	BT55	BMW	4t	60		15	8
r	17	C Danner	Arrows	A8	BMW	4t	51	fuel metering unit	19	10
r	25	R Arnoux	Ligier	JS27	Renault	V6t	46	accident	4	2
r	18	T Boutsen	Arrows	A8	BMW	4t	44	accident	13	7
r	23	A de Cesaris	Minardi	M185B	Motori Moderni	V6t	43	gearbox	23	12
r	6	N Piquet	Williams	FW11	Honda	V6t	41	accident	3	2
r	28	S Johansson	Ferrari	F1-86	Ferrari	V6t	40	alternator	5	3
r	19	T Fabi	Benetton	B186	BMW	4t	38	gearbox	17	9
r	16	E Cheever	Lola	THL2	Ford Cosworth	V6t	37	drive pegs	10	5
r	15	A Jones	Lola	THL2	Ford Cosworth	V6t	33	drive pegs	21	11
r	22	A Berg	Osella	FA1F	Alfa Romeo	V8t	28	electrics	25	13
r	3	M Brundle	Tyrrell	015	Renault	V6t	15	electronics	16	8
r	21	P Ghinzani	Osella	FA1G	Alfa Romeo	V8t	14	turbo	22	11
r	2	K Rosberg	McLaren	MP4/2C	TAG Porsche	V6t	12	gearbox	9	5
r	20	G Berger	Benetton	B186	BMW	4t	8	ignition	12	6
r	24	A Nannini	Minardi	M185B	Motori Moderni	V6t	3	turbo	24	12
ns	29	H Rothengatter	Zakspeed	861	Zakspeed	4t		electrics on parade lap	26	13

Winning speed 136.748 km/h, 84.971 mph
Pole Position speed 147.344 km/h, 91.556 mph (A Senna, 1 min:38.301 sec)
Fastest Lap speed 143.077 km/h, 88.904 mph (N Piquet, 1 min:41.233 sec on lap 41)
Lap Leaders A Senna 1,8-13,39-63 (32); N Mansell 2-7 (6); R Arnoux 14-17 (4); J Laffite 18-30 (13); N Piquet 31-38 (8).

6 Jul 1986   FRANCE: Paul Ricard   (Round 8)   (Race 428)

80 laps x 3.813 km, 2.369 miles = 305.040 km, 189.543 miles

Pos	No	Driver	Car	Model	Engine		Laps	Time/Reason for Retirement	Grid Pos	Row
1	5	N Mansell	Williams	FW11	Honda	V6t	80	1h 37m 19.272s	2	1
2	1	A Prost	McLaren	MP4/2C	TAG Porsche	V6t	80	1h 37m 36.400s	5	3
3	6	N Piquet	Williams	FW11	Honda	V6t	80	1h 37m 56.817s	3	2
4	2	K Rosberg	McLaren	MP4/2C	TAG Porsche	V6t	80	1h 38m 07.975s	7	4
5	25	R Arnoux	Ligier	JS27	Renault	V6t	79		4	2
6	26	J Laffite	Ligier	JS27	Renault	V6t	79		11	6
7	7	R Patrese	Brabham	BT55	BMW	4t	78		16	8
8	27	M Alboreto	Ferrari	F1-86	Ferrari	V6t	78		6	3
9	8	D Warwick	Brabham	BT55	BMW	4t	77		14	7
10	3	M Brundle	Tyrrell	015	Renault	V6t	77		15	8
11	17	C Danner	Arrows	A8	BMW	4t	76		18	9
nc	18	T Boutsen	Arrows	A8	BMW	4t	67		1	11
r	16	P Tambay	Lola	THL2	Ford Cosworth	V6t	64	brake caliper	13	7
r	11	J Dumfries	Lotus	98T	Renault	V6t	56	engine	12	6
r	14	J Palmer	Zakspeed	861	Zakspeed	4t	46	engine	22	11
r	4	P Streiff	Tyrrell	015	Renault	V6t	43	fuel injection / fire	17	9
r	29	H Rothengatter	Zakspeed	861	Zakspeed	4t	32	accident	24	12
r	22	A Berg	Osella	FA1G	Alfa Romeo	V8t	25	turbo	26	13
r	20	G Berger	Benetton	B186	BMW	4t	22	accident / gear selector	8	4
r	19	T Fabi	Benetton	B186	BMW	4t	7	misfire	9	5
r	28	S Johansson	Ferrari	F1-86	Ferrari	V6t	5	turbo	10	5
r	12	A Senna	Lotus	98T	Renault	V6t	3	accident	1	1
r	21	P Ghinzani	Osella	FA1H	Alfa Romeo	V8t	3	accident	25	13
r	24	A Nannini	Minardi	M185B	Motori Moderni	V6t	3	accident	19	10
r	23	A de Cesaris	Minardi	M185B	Motori Moderni	V6t	3	turbo	23	12
r	15	A Jones	Lola	THL2	Ford Cosworth	V6t	2	accident	20	10

Winning speed 188.062 km/h, 116.856 mph
Pole Position speed 206.337 km/h, 128.212 mph (A Senna, 1 min: 6.526 sec)
Fastest Lap speed 196.117 km/h, 121.861 mph (N Mansell, 1 min: 9.993 sec on lap 57)
Lap Leaders N Mansell 1-25,37-53,59-80 (64); A Prost 26-36,54-58 (16).

13 Jul 1986   BRITAIN: Brands Hatch   (Round 9)   (Race 429)

75 laps x 4.207 km, 2.614 miles = 315.512 km, 196.050 miles

Pos	No	Driver	Car	Model	Engine		Laps	Time/Reason for Retirement	Grid Pos	Row
1	5	N Mansell	Williams	FW11	Honda	V6t	75	1h 30m 38.471s	2	1
2	6	N Piquet	Williams	FW11	Honda	V6t	75	1h 30m 44.045s	1	1
3	1	A Prost	McLaren	MP4/2C	TAG Porsche	V6t	74		6	3
4	25	R Arnoux	Ligier	JS27	Renault	V6t	73		8	4
5	3	M Brundle	Tyrrell	015	Renault	V6t	72		11	6
6	4	P Streiff	Tyrrell	015	Renault	V6t	72		16	8
7	11	J Dumfries	Lotus	98T	Renault	V6t	72		10	5
8	8	D Warwick	Brabham	BT55	BMW	4t	72		9	5
9	14	J Palmer	Zakspeed	861	Zakspeed	4t	69		22	11
nc	18	T Boutsen	Arrows	A8	BMW	4t	62		13	7
r	16	P Tambay	Lola	THL2	Ford Cosworth	V6t	60	gearbox pinion bearing	17	9
r	27	M Alboreto	Ferrari	F1-86	Ferrari	V6t	51	turbo	12	6
r	24	A Nannini	Minardi	M185B	Motori Moderni	V6t	50	cv joint	20	10
r	19	T Fabi	Benetton	B186	BMW	4t	45	fuel pump	7	4
r	7	R Patrese	Brabham	BT54	BMW	4t	39	engine	15	8
r	12	A Senna	Lotus	98T	Renault	V6t	27	gearbox	3	2
r	29	H Rothengatter	Zakspeed	861	Zakspeed	4t	24	engine	25	13
r	23	A de Cesaris	Minardi	M185B	Motori Moderni	V6t	23	alternator	21	11
r	20	G Berger	Benetton	B186	BMW	4t	22	electrics	4	2
r	15	A Jones	Lola	THL2	Ford Cosworth	V6t	22	throttle linkage	14	7
r	28	S Johansson	Ferrari	F1-86	Ferrari	V6t	20	radiator	18	9
r	2	K Rosberg	McLaren	MP4/2C	TAG Porsche	V6t	7	gearbox	5	3
r	26	J Laffite	Ligier	JS27	Renault	V6t	0	accident / injury *	19	10
r	17	C Danner	Arrows	A8	BMW	4t	0	accident *	23	12
r	21	P Ghinzani	Osella	FA1G	Alfa Romeo	V8t	0	accident *	24	12
r	22	A Berg	Osella	FA1H	Alfa Romeo	V8t	0	accident *	26	13

Winning speed 208.853 km/h, 129.775 mph
Pole Position speed 226.170 km/h, 140.536 mph (N Piquet, 1 min: 6.961 sec)
Fastest Lap speed 217.616 km/h, 135.220 mph (N Mansell, 1 min: 9.593 sec on lap 69)
Lap Leaders N Piquet 1-22 (22); N Mansell 23-75 (53).

Interrupted after first lap accident. Restarted for original distance.   * *Retired after first start.*

27 Jul 1986   GERMANY: Hockenheim   (Round 10)   (Race 430)
44 laps x 6.797 km, 4.223 miles = 299.068 km, 185.832 miles

Pos	No	Driver	Car	Model	Engine		Laps	Time/Reason for Retirement	Grid Pos	Row
1	6	N Piquet	Williams	FW11	Honda	V6t	44	1h 22m 08.263s	5	3
2	12	A Senna	Lotus	98T	Renault	V6t	44	1h 22m 23.700s	3	2
3	5	N Mansell	Williams	FW11	Honda	V6t	44	1h 22m 52.843s	6	3
4	25	R Arnoux	Ligier	JS27	Renault	V6t	44	1h 23m 23.439s	8	4
5r	2	K Rosberg	McLaren	MP4/2C	TAG Porsche	V6t	43	out of fuel	1	1
6r	1	A Prost	McLaren	MP4/2C	TAG Porsche	V6t	43	out of fuel	2	1
7	8	D Warwick	Brabham	BT55	BMW	4t	43		20	10
8	16	P Tambay	Lola	THL2	Ford Cosworth	V6t	43		13	7
9	15	A Jones	Lola	THL2	Ford Cosworth	V6t	42		19	10
10	20	G Berger	Benetton	B186	BMW	4t	42		4	2
11r	28	S Johansson	Ferrari	F1-86	Ferrari	V6t	41	rear wing	11	6
12	22	A Berg	Osella	FA1F	Alfa Romeo	V8t	40		26	13
r	17	C Danner	Arrows	A8	BMW	4t	38	turbo	17	9
nc	29	H Rothengatter	Zakspeed	861	Zakspeed	4t	38		24	12
r	14	J Palmer	Zakspeed	861	Zakspeed	4t	37	engine	16	8
r	3	M Brundle	Tyrrell	015	Renault	V6t	34	electrics / fire	15	8
r	7	R Patrese	Brabham	BT55	BMW	4t	22	spark plug	7	4
r	23	A de Cesaris	Minardi	M185B	Motori Moderni	V6t	20	gearbox	23	12
r	24	A Nannini	Minardi	M185B	Motori Moderni	V6t	19	engine overheating	22	11
r	11	J Dumfries	Lotus	98T	Renault	V6t	17	radiator leak	12	6
r	18	T Boutsen	Arrows	A9	BMW	4t	13	turbo / fire	21	11
r	26	P Alliot	Ligier	JS27	Renault	V6t	11	engine	14	7
r	21	P Ghinzani	Osella	FA1G	Alfa Romeo	V8t	10	clutch	25	13
r	4	P Streiff	Tyrrell	015	Renault	V6t	7	engine	18	9
r	27	M Alboreto	Ferrari	F1-86	Ferrari	V6t	6	gearbox	10	5
r	19	T Fabi	Benetton	B186	BMW	4t	0	accident	9	5

Winning speed 218.463 km/h, 135.747 mph
Pole Position speed 239.864 km/h, 149.044 mph (K Rosberg, 1 min:42.013 sec)
Fastest Lap speed 229.534 km/h, 142.626 mph (G Berger, 1 min:46.604 sec on lap 35)
Lap Leaders A Senna 1 (1); K Rosberg 2-5,15-19,27-38 (21); N Piquet 6-14,21-26,39-44 (21); A Prost 20 (1).

10 Aug 1986   HUNGARY: Hungaroring   (Round 11)   (Race 431)
76 laps x 4.014 km, 2.494 miles = 305.064 km, 189.558 miles

Pos	No	Driver	Car	Model	Engine		Laps	Time/Reason for Retirement	Grid Pos	Row
1	6	N Piquet	Williams	FW11	Honda	V6t	76	2h 00m 34.508s	2	1
2	12	A Senna	Lotus	98T	Renault	V6t	76	2h 00m 52.181s	1	1
3	5	N Mansell	Williams	FW11	Honda	V6t	75		4	2
4	28	S Johansson	Ferrari	F1-86	Ferrari	V6t	75		7	4
5	11	J Dumfries	Lotus	98T	Renault	V6t	74		8	4
6	3	M Brundle	Tyrrell	015	Renault	V6t	74		16	8
7	16	P Tambay	Lola	THL2	Ford Cosworth	V6t	74		6	3
8	4	P Streiff	Tyrrell	015	Renault	V6t	74		18	9
9	26	P Alliot	Ligier	JS27	Renault	V6t	73		12	6
10	14	J Palmer	Zakspeed	861	Zakspeed	4t	70		24	12
r	25	R Arnoux	Ligier	JS27	Renault	V6t	48	engine	9	5
r	15	A Jones	Lola	THL2	Ford Cosworth	V6t	46	differential	10	5
r	20	G Berger	Benetton	B186	BMW	4t	44	fuel leak / gearbox	11	6
r	18	T Boutsen	Arrows	A8	BMW	4t	40	fuel metering unit	22	11
r	2	K Rosberg	McLaren	MP4/2C	TAG Porsche	V6t	34	rear suspension	5	3
r	19	T Fabi	Benetton	B186	BMW	4t	32	spin / clutch	13	7
r	24	A Nannini	Minardi	M185B	Motori Moderni	V6t	30	engine	17	9
r	27	M Alboreto	Ferrari	F1-86	Ferrari	V6t	29	accident	15	8
r	8	D Warwick	Brabham	BT55	BMW	4t	28	accident	19	10
r	1	A Prost	McLaren	MP4/2C	TAG Porsche	V6t	23	accident / suspension	3	2
r	21	P Ghinzani	Osella	FA1G	Alfa Romeo	V8t	15	rear suspension	23	12
r	17	C Danner	Arrows	A9	BMW	4t	7	rear suspension	21	11
r	7	R Patrese	Brabham	BT55	BMW	4t	5	accident	14	7
r	23	A de Cesaris	Minardi	M186	Motori Moderni	V6t	5	engine	20	10
r	29	H Rothengatter	Zakspeed	861	Zakspeed	4t	2	oil cooler	25	13
r	22	A Berg	Osella	FA1F	Alfa Romeo	V8t	1	turbo	26	13

Winning speed 151.804 km/h, 94.327 mph
Pole Position speed 161.547 km/h, 100.381 mph (A Senna, 1 min:29.450 sec)
Fastest Lap speed 158.794 km/h, 98.670 mph (N Piquet, 1 min:31.001 sec on lap 73)
Lap Leaders A Senna 1-11,36-56 (32); N Piquet 12-35,57-76 (44).

Scheduled for 77 laps, but stopped at 2 hours.

AUSTRIA: Österreichring (Round 12) (Race 432)

52 laps x 5.942 km, 3.692 miles = 308.984 km, 191.994 miles

Pos	No	Driver	Car	Model	Engine		Laps	Time/Reason for Retirement	Grid Pos	Row
1	1	A Prost	McLaren	MP4/2C	TAG Porsche	V6t	52	1h 21m 22.531s	5	3
2	27	M Alboreto	Ferrari	F1-86	Ferrari	V6t	51		9	5
3	28	S Johansson	Ferrari	F1-86	Ferrari	V6t	50		14	7
4	15	A Jones	Lola	THL2	Ford Cosworth	V6t	50		16	8
5	16	P Tambay	Lola	THL2	Ford Cosworth	V6t	50		13	7
6	17	C Danner	Arrows	A8	BMW	4t	49		22	11
7	20	G Berger	Benetton	B186	BMW	4t	49		2	1
8	29	H Rothengatter	Zakspeed	861	Zakspeed	4t	48		24	12
9r	2	K Rosberg	McLaren	MP4/2C	TAG Porsche	V6t	47	electrics	3	2
10	25	R Arnoux	Ligier	JS27	Renault	V6t	47		12	6
11	21	P Ghinzani	Osella	FA1G	Alfa Romeo	V8t	46		25	13
r	5	N Mansell	Williams	FW11	Honda	V6t	32	cv joint	6	3
r	6	N Piquet	Williams	FW11	Honda	V6t	29	engine overheating	7	4
r	18	T Boutsen	Arrows	A9	BMW	4t	25	turbo	18	9
r	19	T Fabi	Benetton	B186	BMW	4t	17	engine	1	1
r	26	P Alliot	Ligier	JS27	Renault	V6t	16	engine	11	6
r	24	A Nannini	Minardi	M185B	Motori Moderni	V6t	13	rear suspension / spin	19	10
r	23	A de Cesaris	Minardi	M186	Motori Moderni	V6t	13	driveshaft	23	12
r	12	A Senna	Lotus	98T	Renault	V6t	13	misfire	8	4
r	3	M Brundle	Tyrrell	015	Renault	V6t	12	turbo	17	9
r	4	P Streiff	Tyrrell	015	Renault	V6t	10	engine	20	10
r	11	J Dumfries	Lotus	98T	Renault	V6t	9	spark plug	15	8
r	14	J Palmer	Zakspeed	861	Zakspeed	4t	8	engine	21	11
r	22	A Berg	Osella	FA1F	Alfa Romeo	V8t	6	electrics	26	13
r	7	R Patrese	Brabham	BT55	BMW	4t	2	engine	4	2
ns	8	D Warwick	Brabham	BT55	BMW	4t		car raced by Patrese	10	5

Winning speed 227.821 km/h, 141.561 mph
Pole Position speed 256.032 km/h, 159.091 mph (T Fabi, 1 min:23.549 sec)
Fastest Lap speed 239.157 km/h, 148.606 mph (G Berger, 1 min:29.444 sec on lap 49)
Lap Leaders G Berger 1-25 (25); N Mansell 26-28 (3); A Prost 29-52 (24).

7 Sep 1986 **ITALY: Monza** (Round 13) (Race 433)

51 laps x 5.800 km, 3.604 miles = 295.800 km, 183.802 miles

Pos	No	Driver	Car	Model	Engine		Laps	Time/Reason for Retirement	Grid Pos	Row
1	6	N Piquet	Williams	FW11	Honda	V6t	51	1h 17m 42.889s	6	3
2	5	N Mansell	Williams	FW11	Honda	V6t	51	1h 17m 52.717s	3	2
3	28	S Johansson	Ferrari	F1-86	Ferrari	V6t	51	1h 18m 05.804s	12	6
4	2	K Rosberg	McLaren	MP4/2C	TAG Porsche	V6t	51	1h 18m 36.698s	8	4
5	20	G Berger	Benetton	B186	BMW	4t	50		4	2
6	15	A Jones	Lola	THL2	Ford Cosworth	V6t	49		18	9
7	18	T Boutsen	Arrows	A8	BMW	4t	49		13	7
8	17	C Danner	Arrows	A8	BMW	4t	49		16	8
9	4	P Streiff	Tyrrell	015	Renault	V6t	49		23	12
10	3	M Brundle	Tyrrell	015	Renault	V6t	49		20	10
11	22	A Caffi	Osella	FA1F	Alfa Romeo	V8t	45		27	14
r	19	T Fabi	Benetton	B186	BMW	4t	44	front tyre / spin	1	1
r	27	M Alboreto	Ferrari	F1-86	Ferrari	V6t	33	engine	9	5
r	23	A de Cesaris	Minardi	M186	Motori Moderni	V6t	33	engine	21	11
r	31	I Capelli	AGS	JH21C	Motori Moderni	V6t	31	rear tyre	25	13
r	25	R Arnoux	Ligier	JS27	Renault	V6t	30	gearbox	11	6
r/dq	1	A Prost	McLaren	MP4/2C	TAG Porsche	V6t	27	engine *	2	1
r	14	J Palmer	Zakspeed	861	Zakspeed	4t	27	alternator	22	11
r	26	P Alliot	Ligier	JS27	Renault	V6t	22	engine	14	7
r	11	J Dumfries	Lotus	98T	Renault	V6t	18	gearbox	17	9
r	8	D Warwick	Brabham	BT55	BMW	4t	16	brakes / accident	7	4
r	24	A Nannini	Minardi	M185B	Motori Moderni	V6t	15	alternator belt	19	10
r	21	P Ghinzani	Osella	FA1G	Alfa Romeo	V8t	12	rear suspension / spin	26	13
r	16	P Tambay	Lola	THL2	Ford Cosworth	V6t	2	accident	15	8
r	7	R Patrese	Brabham	BT55	BMW	4t	2	accident	10	5
r	29	H Rothengatter	Zakspeed	861	Zakspeed	4t	1	electrics	24	12
r	12	A Senna	Lotus	98T	Renault	V6t	0	clutch	5	3

Winning speed 228.373 km/h, 141.905 mph
Pole Position speed 248.341 km/h, 154.312 mph (T Fabi, 1 min:24.078 sec)
Fastest Lap speed 237.006 km/h, 147.269 mph (T Fabi, 1 min:28.099 sec on lap 35)
Lap Leaders G Berger 1-6,25-26 (8); N Mansell 7-24,27-37 (29); N Piquet 38-51 (14).

* A Prost was belatedly disqualified for changing to the spare car after the start of the parade lap.

21 Sep 1986 **PORTUGAL: Estoril** **(Round 14)** **(Race 434)**

70 laps x 4.350 km, 2.703 miles = 304.500 km, 189.208 miles

Pos	No	Driver	Car	Model	Engine		Laps	Time/Reason for Retirement	Grid Pos	Row
1	5	N Mansell	Williams	FW11	Honda	V6t	70	1h 37m 21.900s	2	1
2	1	A Prost	McLaren	MP4/2C	TAG Porsche	V6t	70	1h 37m 40.672s	3	2
3	6	N Piquet	Williams	FW11	Honda	V6t	70	1h 38m 11.174s	6	3
4r	12	A Senna	Lotus	98T	Renault	V6t	69	out of fuel	1	1
5	27	M Alboreto	Ferrari	F1-86	Ferrari	V6t	69		13	7
6	28	S Johansson	Ferrari	F1-86	Ferrari	V6t	69		8	4
7	25	R Arnoux	Ligier	JS27	Renault	V6t	69		10	5
8	19	T Fabi	Benetton	B186	BMW	4t	68		5	3
9	11	J Dumfries	Lotus	98T	Renault	V6t	68		15	8
10	18	T Boutsen	Arrows	A8	BMW	4t	67		21	11
11	17	C Danner	Arrows	A8	BMW	4t	67		22	11
12	14	J Palmer	Zakspeed	861	Zakspeed	4t	67		20	10
13	22	A Berg	Osella	FA1F	Alfa Romeo	V8t	63		27	14
r	7	R Patrese	Brabham	BT55	BMW	4t	62	engine	9	5
nc	16	P Tambay	Lola	THL2	Ford Cosworth	V6t	62		14	7
r	24	A Nannini	Minardi	M185B	Motori Moderni	V6t	60	gearbox	18	9
r	20	G Berger	Benetton	B186	BMW	4t	44	accident	4	2
r	23	A de Cesaris	Minardi	M186	Motori Moderni	V6t	43	accident	16	8
r	2	K Rosberg	McLaren	MP4/2C	TAG Porsche	V6t	41	engine	7	4
r	8	D Warwick	Brabham	BT55	BMW	4t	41	electrics	12	6
r	26	P Alliot	Ligier	JS27	Renault	V6t	39	engine	11	6
r	4	P Streiff	Tyrrell	015	Renault	V6t	28	engine	23	12
r	3	M Brundle	Tyrrell	015	Renault	V6t	18	engine	19	10
r	15	A Jones	Lola	THL2	Ford Cosworth	V6t	10	brakes / spin	17	9
r	29	H Rothengatter	Zakspeed	861	Zakspeed	4t	9	crown wheel & pinion	26	13
r	21	P Ghinzani	Osella	FA1G	Alfa Romeo	V8t	8	electrics	24	12
r	31	I Capelli	AGS	JH21C	Motori Moderni	V6t	6	gearbox	25	13

Winning speed 187.644 km/h, 116.597 mph
Pole Position speed 204.244 km/h, 126.911 mph (A Senna, 1 min:16.673 sec)
Fastest Lap speed 193.469 km/h, 120.216 mph (N Mansell, 1 min:20.943 sec on lap 53)
Lap Leaders N Mansell 1-70 (70).

12 Oct 1986 **MEXICO: Mexico City** **(Round 15)** **(Race 435)**

68 laps x 4.421 km, 2.747 miles = 300.628 km, 186.802 miles

Pos	No	Driver	Car	Model	Engine		Laps	Time/Reason for Retirement	Grid Pos	Row
1	20	G Berger	Benetton	B186	BMW	4t	68	1h 33m 18.700s	4	2
2	1	A Prost	McLaren	MP4/2C	TAG Porsche	V6t	68	1h 33m 44.138s	6	3
3	12	A Senna	Lotus	98T	Renault	V6t	68	1h 34m 11.213s	1	1
4	6	N Piquet	Williams	FW11	Honda	V6t	67		2	1
5	5	N Mansell	Williams	FW11	Honda	V6t	67		3	2
6	26	P Alliot	Ligier	JS27	Renault	V6t	67		10	5
7	18	T Boutsen	Arrows	A8	BMW	4t	66		21	11
8	23	A de Cesaris	Minardi	M186	Motori Moderni	V6t	66		22	11
9	17	C Danner	Arrows	A8	BMW	4t	66		20	10
10r	14	J Palmer	Zakspeed	861	Zakspeed	4t	65	out of fuel	18	9
11	3	M Brundle	Tyrrell	015	Renault	V6t	65		16	8
12r	28	S Johansson	Ferrari	F1-86	Ferrari	V6t	64	turbo / fire	14	7
13r	7	R Patrese	Brabham	BT55	BMW	4t	64	accident	5	3
14	24	A Nannini	Minardi	M185B	Motori Moderni	V6t	64		24	12
15r	25	R Arnoux	Ligier	JS27	Renault	V6t	63	engine	13	7
16	22	A Berg	Osella	FA1F	Alfa Romeo	V8t	61		26	13
r	11	J Dumfries	Lotus	98T	Renault	V6t	53	battery	17	9
r	8	D Warwick	Brabham	BT55	BMW	4t	37	engine	7	4
r	15	A Jones	Lola	THL2	Ford Cosworth	V6t	35	gear selection / radiator	15	8
r	2	K Rosberg	McLaren	MP4/2C	TAG Porsche	V6t	32	rear tyre	11	6
r	27	M Alboreto	Ferrari	F1-86	Ferrari	V6t	10	turbo	12	6
r	4	P Streiff	Tyrrell	015	Renault	V6t	8	turbo	19	10
r	21	P Ghinzani	Osella	FA1G	Alfa Romeo	V8t	8	turbo	25	13
r	19	T Fabi	Benetton	B186	BMW	4t	4	engine	9	5
r	16	P Tambay	Lola	THL2	Ford Cosworth	V6t	0	accident	8	4
ns	29	H Rothengatter	Zakspeed	861	Zakspeed	4t		accident	23	12

Winning speed 193.306 km/h, 120.115 mph
Pole Position speed 206.723 km/h, 128.452 mph (A Senna, 1 min:16.990 sec)
Fastest Lap speed 200.549 km/h, 124.616 mph (N Piquet, 1 min:19.360 sec on lap 64)
Lap Leaders N Piquet 1-31 (31); A Senna 32-35 (4); G Berger 36-68 (33).

Races

82 laps x 3.779 km, 2.348 miles = 309.878 km, 192.549 miles

Pos	No	Driver	Car	Model	Engine		Laps	Time/Reason for Retirement	Grid Pos	Row
1	1	A Prost	McLaren	MP4/2C	TAG Porsche	V6t	82	1h 54m 20.388s	4	2
2	6	N Piquet	Williams	FW11	Honda	V6t	82	1h 54m 24.593s	2	1
3	28	S Johansson	Ferrari	F1-86	Ferrari	V6t	81		12	6
4	3	M Brundle	Tyrrell	015	Renault	V6t	81		16	8
5r	4	P Streiff	Tyrrell	015	Renault	V6t	80	out of fuel	10	5
6	11	J Dumfries	Lotus	98T	Renault	V6t	80		14	7
7	25	R Arnoux	Ligier	JS27	Renault	V6t	79		5	3
8	26	P Alliot	Ligier	JS27	Renault	V6t	79		8	4
9	14	J Palmer	Zakspeed	861	Zakspeed	4t	77		21	11
10	19	T Fabi	Benetton	B186	BMW	4t	77		13	7
nc	16	P Tambay	Lola	THL2	Ford Cosworth	V6t	70		17	9
r	5	N Mansell	Williams	FW11	Honda	V6t	63	rear tyre burst / accident	1	1
r	7	R Patrese	Brabham	BT55	BMW	4t	63	electrics	19	10
r	2	K Rosberg	McLaren	MP4/2C	TAG Porsche	V6t	62	rear tyre	7	4
nc	22	A Berg	Osella	FA1F	Alfa Romeo	V8t	61		26	13
r	8	D Warwick	Brabham	BT55	BMW	4t	57	brakes	20	10
r	17	C Danner	Arrows	A8	BMW	4t	52	engine	24	12
r	18	T Boutsen	Arrows	A8	BMW	4t	50	throttle spring	22	11
r	12	A Senna	Lotus	98T	Renault	V6t	43	engine	3	2
r	20	G Berger	Benetton	B186	BMW	4t	40	clutch / engine	6	3
r	23	A de Cesaris	Minardi	M186	Motori Moderni	V6t	40	fire extinguisher	11	6
r	29	H Rothengatter	Zakspeed	861	Zakspeed	4t	29	rear suspension	23	12
r	15	A Jones	Lola	THL2	Ford Cosworth	V6t	16	engine	15	8
r	24	A Nannini	Minardi	M185B	Motori Moderni	V6t	10	accident	18	9
r	21	P Ghinzani	Osella	FA1G	Alfa Romeo	V8t	2	crown wheel & pinion	25	13
r	27	M Alboreto	Ferrari	F1-86	Ferrari	V6t	0	accident / rear suspension	9	5

Winning speed 162.609 km/h, 101.041 mph
Pole Position speed 173.519 km/h, 107.820 mph (N Mansell, 1 min:18.403 sec)
Fastest Lap speed 168.398 km/h, 104.638 mph (N Piquet, 1 min:20.787 sec on lap 82)
Lap Leaders N Piquet 1-6,63-64 (8); K Rosberg 7-62 (56); A Prost 65-82 (18).

Lap Leaders 1986

Pos	Driver	Car-Engine	GPs	laps	km	miles
1	N Mansell	Williams-Honda	9	331	1,495.3	929.1
2	N Piquet	Williams-Honda	10	242	1,196.3	743.3
3	A Prost	McLaren-TAG Porsche	8	166	695.5	432.1
4	A Senna	Lotus-Renault	8	134	566.5	352.0
5	K Rosberg	McLaren-TAG Porsche	4	86	396.6	246.4
6	G Berger	Benetton-BMW	3	66	340.8	211.8
7	J Laffite	Ligier-Renault	1	13	52.3	32.5
8	R Arnoux	Ligier-Renault	1	4	16.1	10.0
9	S Johansson	Ferrari	1	2	13.9	8.6
			16	1,044	4,773.2	2,965.9

Driver Points 1986

		BR	E	RSM	MC	B	CDN	USA	F	GB	D	H	A	I	P	MEX	AUS	Total	
1	A Prost	-	4	9	9	(1)	6	4	6	4	(1)	-	9	-	6	6	9	72	(2)
2	N Mansell	-	6	-	3	9	9	2	9	9	4	4	-	6	9	(2)	-	70	(2)
3	N Piquet	9	-	6	-	-	4	-	4	6	9	9	-	9	4	3	6	69	
4	A Senna	6	9	-	4	6	2	9	-	-	6	6	-	-	3	4	-	55	
5	S Johansson	-	-	3	-	4	-	-	-	-	-	3	4	4	1	-	4	23	
6	K Rosberg	-	3	2	6	-	3	-	3	-	2	-	-	3	-	-	-	22	
7	G Berger	1	1	4	-	-	-	-	-	-	-	-	-	2	-	9	-	17	
8	J Laffite	4	-	-	1	2	-	6	1	-	-	-	-	-	-	-	-	14	
	M Alboreto	-	-	-	-	3	-	3	-	-	-	-	6	-	2	-	-	14	
	R Arnoux	3	-	-	2	-	1	-	2	3	3	-	-	-	-	-	-	14	
11	M Brundle	2	-	-	-	-	-	-	-	2	-	1	-	-	-	-	3	8	
12	A Jones	-	-	-	-	-	-	-	-	-	-	-	3	1	-	-	-	4	
13	P Streiff	-	-	-	-	-	-	-	-	1	-	-	-	-	-	-	2	3	
	J Dumfries	-	-	-	-	-	-	-	-	-	-	2	-	-	-	-	1	3	
15	T Fabi	-	2	-	-	-	-	-	-	-	-	-	-	-	-	-	-	2	
	P Tambay	-	-	-	-	-	-	-	-	-	-	-	2	-	-	-	-	2	
	R Patrese	-	-	1	-	-	1	-	-	-	-	-	-	-	-	-	-	2	
18	P Alliot	-	-	-	-	-	-	-	-	-	-	-	-	-	-	1	-	1	
	C Danner	-	-	-	-	-	-	-	-	-	-	-	-	1	-	-	-	1	

9,6,4,3,2 and 1 point awarded to the first six finishers. Best 11 scores.

Constructor Points 1986

		BR	P	RSM	MC	CDN	USA	F	GB	D	A	NL	I	B	EUR	ZA	AUS	Total
1	Williams-Honda	9	6	6	3	9	13	2	13	15	13	13	-	15	13	5	6	141
2	McLaren-TAG Porsche	-	7	11	15	1	9	4	9	4	3	-	9	3	6	6	9	96
3	Lotus-Renault	6	9	-	4	6	2	9	-	-	6	8	-	-	3	4	1	58
4	Ferrari	-	-	3	-	7	-	3	-	-	-	3	10	4	3	-	4	37
5	Ligier-Renault	7	-	-	3	2	1	6	3	3	3	-	-	-	-	1	-	29
6	Benetton-BMW	1	3	4	-	-	-	-	-	-	-	-	-	2	-	9	-	19
7	Tyrrell-Renault	2	-	-	-	-	-	-	-	3	-	1	-	-	-	-	5	11
8	Lola-Ford Cosworth	-	-	-	-	-	-	-	-	-	-	-	5	1	-	-	-	6
9	Brabham-BMW	-	-	1	-	-	-	1	-	-	-	-	-	-	-	-	-	2
10	Arrows-BMW	-	-	-	-	-	-	-	-	-	-	-	1	-	-	-	-	1

9,6,4,3,2 and 1 point awarded to the first six finishers.

1987

Race Entrants and Results

March returned to compete in the newly created 3.5-litre normally aspirated division. Turbos would be limited to a maximum boost to 4.0 bar by compulsory pop-off valves. Lotus raced its active suspension system utilising computer controlled hydraulics. Ligier was left without a suitable engine when the new Alfa unit was suddenly withdrawn.

McLAREN
Marlboro McLaren International: Prost, Johansson

TYRRELL
Data General Team Tyrrell: Palmer, Streiff

WILLIAMS
Canon Williams Team: Mansell, Patrese, Piquet

BRABHAM
Motor Racing Developments: Patrese, Modena, de Cesaris

ZAKSPEED
West Zakspeed Racing: Brundle, Danner

LOTUS
Camel Team Lotus Honda: Nakajima, Senna

AGS
Team El Charro AGS: Fabre, Moreno

MARCH
Leyton House March Racing Team: Capelli

ARROWS
USF&G Arrows Megatron: Warwick, Cheever

BENETTON
Benetton Formula: Fabi, Boutsen

OSELLA
Osella Squadra Corse: Caffi, Tarquini, Forini

MINARDI
Minardi Team: Campos, Nannini

LIGIER
Ligier Loto: Arnoux, Ghinzani

FERRARI
Scuderia Ferrari SpA SEFAC: Alboreto, Berger

LOLA
Larrousse Calmels: Dalmas, Alliot

COLONI
Enzo Coloni Racing Car System: Larini

12 Apr 1987		BRAZIL: Rio de Janeiro						(Round 1)	(Race 437)	
		61 laps x 5.031 km, 3.126 miles = 306.891 km, 190.693 miles								
Pos	No	Driver	Car	Model	Engine		Laps	Time/Reason for Retirement	Grid Pos	Row
1	1	A Prost	McLaren	MP4/3	TAG Porsche	V6t	61	1h 39m 45.141s	5	3
2	6	N Piquet	Williams	FW11B	Honda	V6t	61	1h 40m 25.688s	2	1
3	2	S Johansson	McLaren	MP4/3	TAG Porsche	V6t	61	1h 40m 41.899s	10	5
4	28	G Berger	Ferrari	F1-87	Ferrari	V6t	61	1h 41m 24.376s	7	4
5	20	T Boutsen	Benetton	B187	Ford Cosworth	V6t	60		6	3
6	5	N Mansell	Williams	FW11B	Honda	V6t	60		1	1
7	11	S Nakajima	Lotus	99T	Honda	V6t	59		12	6
8r	27	M Alboreto	Ferrari	F1-87	Ferrari	V6t	58	rear undertray / spin	9	5
9	10	C Danner	Zakspeed	861	Zakspeed	4t	58		17	9
10	3	J Palmer	Tyrrell	DG016	Ford Cosworth	V8	58		18	9
11	4	P Streiff	Tyrrell	DG016	Ford Cosworth	V8	57		20	10
12	14	P Fabre	AGS	JH22	Ford Cosworth	V8	55		22	11
r	18	E Cheever	Arrows	A10	Megatron	4t	52	engine	14	7
r	12	A Senna	Lotus	99T	Honda	V6t	50	engine	3	2
r	7	R Patrese	Brabham	BT56	BMW	4t	48	battery loose	11	6
r	8	A de Cesaris	Brabham	BT56	BMW	4t	21	differential	13	7
r	17	D Warwick	Arrows	A10	Megatron	4t	20	engine overheating	8	4
r	21	A Caffi	Osella	FA1I	Alfa Romeo	V8t	20	driver exhausted	21	11
r	24	A Nannini	Minardi	M187	Motori Moderni	V6t	17	suspension / accident	15	8
r	9	M Brundle	Zakspeed	861	Zakspeed	4t	15	turbo	19	10
r	19	T Fabi	Benetton	B187	Ford Cosworth	V6t	9	turbo	4	2
dq	23	A Campos	Minardi	M187	Motori Moderni	V6t	3	overtook on parade lap	16	8
ns	16	I Capelli	March	87P	Ford Cosworth	V8		no engine	23	12

Winning speed 184.592 km/h, 114.700 mph
Pole Position speed 210.287 km/h, 130.666 mph (N Mansell, 1 min:26.128 sec)
Fastest Lap speed 192.962 km/h, 119.901 mph (N Piquet, 1 min:33.861 sec on lap 42)
Lap Leaders N Piquet 1-7,17-20 (11); A Senna 8-12 (5); A Prost 13-16,21-61 (45).

3 May 1987   SAN MARINO: Imola   (Round 2)   (Race 438)

59 laps x 5.040 km, 3.132 miles = 297.360 km, 184.771 miles

Pos	No	Driver	Car	Model	Engine		Laps	Time/Reason for Retirement	Grid Pos	Row
1	5	N Mansell	Williams	FW11B	Honda	V6t	59	1h 31m 24.076s	2	1
2	12	A Senna	Lotus	99T	Honda	V6t	59	1h 31m 51.621s	1	1
3	27	M Alboreto	Ferrari	F1-87	Ferrari	V6t	59	1h 32m 03.220s	6	3
4	2	S Johansson	McLaren	MP4/3	TAG Porsche	V6t	59	1h 32m 24.664s	8	4
5	9	M Brundle	Zakspeed	871	Zakspeed	4t	57		14	7
6	11	S Nakajima	Lotus	99T	Honda	V6t	57		12	6
7	10	C Danner	Zakspeed	861	Zakspeed	4t	57		17	9
8	4	P Streiff	Tyrrell	DG016	Ford Cosworth	V8	57		20	10
9	7	R Patrese	Brabham	BT56	BMW	4t	57		7	4
10	30	P Alliot	Lola	LC87	Ford Cosworth	V8	56		21	11
11r	17	D Warwick	Arrows	A10	Megatron	4t	55	out of fuel	10	5
12r	21	A Caffi	Osella	FA1I	Alfa Romeo	V8t	54	out of fuel	19	10
13	14	P Fabre	AGS	JH22	Ford Cosworth	V8	53		24	12
r	19	T Fabi	Benetton	B187	Ford Cosworth	V6t	51	turbo	4	2
r	20	T Boutsen	Benetton	B187	Ford Cosworth	V6t	48	engine	11	6
r	18	E Cheever	Arrows	A10	Megatron	4t	48	engine overheating	9	5
r	3	J Palmer	Tyrrell	DG016	Ford Cosworth	V8	48	clutch	23	12
r	8	A de Cesaris	Brabham	BT56	BMW	4t	39	spin	13	7
r	23	A Campos	Minardi	M187	Motori Moderni	V6t	30	gearbox	16	8
r	22	G Tarquini	Osella	FA1G	Alfa Romeo	V8t	26	gearbox	25	13
r	24	A Nannini	Minardi	M187	Motori Moderni	V6t	25	engine	15	8
r	16	I Capelli	March	871	Ford Cosworth	V8	18	distributor rotor arm	22	11
r	28	G Berger	Ferrari	F1-87	Ferrari	V6t	16	electronics	5	3
r	1	A Prost	McLaren	MP4/3	TAG Porsche	V6t	14	alternator belt	3	2
r	26	P Ghinzani	Ligier	JS29B	Megatron	4t	7	handling	18	9
ns	6	N Piquet	Williams	FW11B	Honda	V6t		accident / injury		
ns	25	R Arnoux	Ligier	JS29B	Megatron	4t		front suspension		

Winning speed 195.201 km/h, 121.292 mph
Pole Position speed 211.404 km/h, 131.361 mph (A Senna, 1 min:25.826 sec)
Fastest Lap speed 203.303 km/h, 126.327 mph (T Fabi, 1 min:29.246 sec on lap 51)
Lap Leaders A Senna 1,25-26 (3); N Mansell 2-21,27-59 (53); M Alboreto 22-24 (3).

Published results at the time were based incorrectly on a circuit length of 5.004 km.

17 May 1987   BELGIUM: Spa-Francorchamps   (Round 3)   (Race 439)

43 laps x 6.940 km, 4.312 miles = 298.420 km, 185.430 miles

Pos	No	Driver	Car	Model	Engine		Laps	Time/Reason for Retirement	Grid Pos	Row
1	1	A Prost	McLaren	MP4/3	TAG Porsche	V6t	43	1h 27m 03.217s	6	3
2	2	S Johansson	McLaren	MP4/3	TAG Porsche	V6t	43	1h 27m 27.981s	10	5
3r	8	A de Cesaris	Brabham	BT56	BMW	4t	42	out of fuel	13	7
4	18	E Cheever	Arrows	A10	Megatron	4t	42		11	6
5	11	S Nakajima	Lotus	99T	Honda	V6t	42		15	8
6	25	R Arnoux	Ligier	JS29B	Megatron	4t	41		16	8
7r	26	P Ghinzani	Ligier	JS29B	Megatron	4t	40	out of fuel	17	9
8	30	P Alliot	Lola	LC87	Ford Cosworth	V8	40		22	11
9	4	P Streiff	Tyrrell	DG016	Ford Cosworth	V8	39		23	12
10r	14	P Fabre	AGS	JH22	Ford Cosworth	V8	38	electrics	25	13
r	19	T Fabi	Benetton	B187	Ford Cosworth	V6t	34	oil pump drive	9	5
r	9	M Brundle	Zakspeed	871	Zakspeed	4t	19	engine	18	9
r	20	T Boutsen	Benetton	B187	Ford Cosworth	V6t	18	cv joint	7	4
r	5	N Mansell	Williams	FW11B	Honda	V6t	17	accident / undertray	1	1
r	16	I Capelli	March	871	Ford Cosworth	V8	14	oil pressure	21	11
r	6	N Piquet	Williams	FW11B	Honda	V6t	11	turbo sensor	2	1
r	21	A Caffi	Osella	FA1I	Alfa Romeo	V8t	11	engine	26	13
r	27	M Alboreto	Ferrari	F1-87	Ferrari	V6t	9	transmission	5	3
r	10	C Danner	Zakspeed	871	Zakspeed	4t	9	brakes / spin	20	10
r	17	D Warwick	Arrows	A10	Megatron	4t	8	water hose / engine overheating	12	6
r	7	R Patrese	Brabham	BT56	BMW	4t	5	clutch	8	4
r	28	G Berger	Ferrari	F1-87	Ferrari	V6t	2	turbo	4	2
r	24	A Nannini	Minardi	M187	Motori Moderni	V6t	1	turbo	14	7
r	12	A Senna	Lotus	99T	Honda	V6t	0	accident	3	2
r	23	A Campos	Minardi	M187	Motori Moderni	V6t	0	clutch	19	10
r	3	J Palmer	Tyrrell	DG016	Ford Cosworth	V8	0	accident *	24	12

Winning speed 205.680 km/h, 127.804 mph
Pole Position speed 223.020 km/h, 138.578 mph (N Mansell, 1 min:52.026 sec)
Fastest Lap speed 213.260 km/h, 132.513 mph (A Prost, 1 min:57.153 sec on lap 26)
Lap Leaders N Piquet 1-9 (9); A Prost 10-43 (34).

*Interrupted after 2nd lap accident. Restarted for original distance. * Retired after first start.*

31 May 1987   **MONACO: Monte-Carlo**   (Round 4)   (Race 440)

78 laps x 3.328 km, 2.068 miles = 259.584 km, 161.298 miles

Pos	No	Driver	Car	Model	Engine		Laps	Time/Reason for Retirement	Grid Pos	Row
1	12	A Senna	Lotus	99T	Honda	V6t	78	1h 57m 54.085s	2	1
2	6	N Piquet	Williams	FW11B	Honda	V6t	78	1h 58m 27.297s	3	2
3	27	M Alboreto	Ferrari	F1-87	Ferrari	V6t	78	1h 59m 06.924s	5	3
4	28	G Berger	Ferrari	F1-87	Ferrari	V6t	77		8	4
5	3	J Palmer	Tyrrell	DG016	Ford Cosworth	V8	76		15	8
6	16	I Capelli	March	871	Ford Cosworth	V8	76		19	10
7	9	M Brundle	Zakspeed	871	Zakspeed	4t	76		14	7
8	19	T Fabi	Benetton	B187	Ford Cosworth	V6t	76		12	6
9r	1	A Prost	McLaren	MP4/3	TAG Porsche	V6t	75	engine	4	2
10	11	S Nakajima	Lotus	99T	Honda	V6t	75		17	9
11	25	R Arnoux	Ligier	JS29B	Megatron	4t	74		22	11
12	26	P Ghinzani	Ligier	JS29B	Megatron	4t	74		20	10
13	14	P Fabre	AGS	JH22	Ford Cosworth	V8	71		24	12
r	18	E Cheever	Arrows	A10	Megatron	4t	59	cylinder head gasket	6	3
r	17	D Warwick	Arrows	A10	Megatron	4t	58	gear linkage	11	6
r	2	S Johansson	McLaren	MP4/3	TAG Porsche	V6t	57	engine	7	4
r	30	P Alliot	Lola	LC87	Ford Cosworth	V8	42	engine	18	9
r	7	R Patrese	Brabham	BT56	BMW	4t	41	electronics	10	5
r	21	A Caffi	Osella	FA1I	Alfa Romeo	V8t	39	electrics	16	8
r	8	A de Cesaris	Brabham	BT56	BMW	4t	38	accident / suspension	21	11
r	5	N Mansell	Williams	FW11B	Honda	V6t	29	turbo wastegate	1	1
r	24	A Nannini	Minardi	M187	Motori Moderni	V6t	21	electrics	13	7
r	4	P Streiff	Tyrrell	DG016	Ford Cosworth	V8	9	accident	23	12
r	20	T Boutsen	Benetton	B187	Ford Cosworth	V6t	5	cv joint	9	5
ns	23	A Campos	Minardi	M187	Motori Moderni	V6t		accident / injury		
exc	10	C Danner	Zakspeed	871	Zakspeed	4t		dangerous driving		

Winning speed 132.102 km/h, 82.085 mph
Pole Position speed 144.279 km/h, 89.651 mph (N Mansell, 1 min:23.039 sec)
Fastest Lap speed 136.635 km/h, 84.901 mph (A Senna, 1 min:27.685 sec on lap 72)
Lap Leaders N Mansell 1-29 (29); A Senna 30-78 (49).

---

21 Jun 1987   **USA: Detroit**   (Round 5)   (Race 441)

63 laps x 4.023 km, 2.500 miles = 253.472 km, 157.500 miles

Pos	No	Driver	Car	Model	Engine		Laps	Time/Reason for Retirement	Grid Pos	Row
1	12	A Senna	Lotus	99T	Honda	V6t	63	1h 50m 16.358s	2	1
2	6	N Piquet	Williams	FW11B	Honda	V6t	63	1h 50m 50.177s	3	2
3	1	A Prost	McLaren	MP4/3	TAG Porsche	V6t	63	1h 51m 01.685s	5	3
4	28	G Berger	Ferrari	F1-87	Ferrari	V6t	63	1h 51m 18.959s	12	6
5	5	N Mansell	Williams	FW11B	Honda	V6t	62		1	1
6r	18	E Cheever	Arrows	A10	Megatron	4t	60	out of fuel	6	3
7	2	S Johansson	McLaren	MP4/3	TAG Porsche	V6t	60		11	6
8	10	C Danner	Zakspeed	871	Zakspeed	4t	60		16	8
9	7	R Patrese	Brabham	BT56	BMW	4t	60		9	5
10	25	R Arnoux	Ligier	JS29B	Megatron	4t	60		21	11
11	3	J Palmer	Tyrrell	DG016	Ford Cosworth	V8	60		13	7
12	14	P Fabre	AGS	JH22	Ford Cosworth	V8	58		26	13
r	20	T Boutsen	Benetton	B187	Ford Cosworth	V6t	52	brake disc	4	2
nc	26	P Ghinzani	Ligier	JS29B	Megatron	4t	51		23	12
r	4	P Streiff	Tyrrell	DG016	Ford Cosworth	V8	44	accident	14	7
r	30	P Alliot	Lola	LC87	Ford Cosworth	V8	38	rear wheel lost / accident	20	10
r	27	M Alboreto	Ferrari	F1-87	Ferrari	V6t	25	gear linkage	7	4
r	24	A Nannini	Minardi	M187	Motori Moderni	V6t	22	gearbox	18	9
r	9	M Brundle	Zakspeed	871	Zakspeed	4t	16	turbo / fire	15	8
r	17	D Warwick	Arrows	A10	Megatron	4t	12	accident	10	5
r	16	I Capelli	March	871	Ford Cosworth	V8	9	battery	22	11
r	19	T Fabi	Benetton	B187	Ford Cosworth	V6t	6	accident / nose cone	8	4
r	21	A Caffi	Osella	FA1I	Alfa Romeo	V8t	3	gear lever	19	10
r	8	A de Cesaris	Brabham	BT56	BMW	4t	2	gearbox	17	9
r	23	A Campos	Minardi	M187	Motori Moderni	V6t	1	accident	25	13
r	11	S Nakajima	Lotus	99T	Honda	V6t	0	accident	24	12

Winning speed 137.915 km/h, 85.697 mph
Pole Position speed 145.915 km/h, 90.667 mph (N Mansell, 1 min:39.264 sec)
Fastest Lap speed 144.172 km/h, 89.584 mph (A Senna, 1 min:40.464 sec on lap 39)
Lap Leaders N Mansell 1-33 (33); A Senna 34-63 (30).

	5 Jul 1987	FRANCE: Paul Ricard						(Round 6)	(Race 442)	

80 laps x 3.813 km, 2.369 miles = 305.040 km, 189.543 miles

Pos	No	Driver	Car	Model	Engine		Laps	Time/Reason for Retirement	Grid Pos	Row
1	5	N Mansell	Williams	FW11B	Honda	V6t	80	1h 37m 03.839s	1	1
2	6	N Piquet	Williams	FW11B	Honda	V6t	80	1h 37m 11.550s	4	2
3	1	A Prost	McLaren	MP4/3	TAG Porsche	V6t	80	1h 37m 59.094s	2	1
4	12	A Senna	Lotus	99T	Honda	V6t	79		3	2
5r	19	T Fabi	Benetton	B187	Ford Cosworth	V6t	77	driveshaft	7	4
6	4	P Streiff	Tyrrell	DG016	Ford Cosworth	V8	76		25	13
7	3	J Palmer	Tyrrell	DG016	Ford Cosworth	V8	76		24	12
8r	2	S Johansson	McLaren	MP4/3	TAG Porsche	V6t	74	alternator belt	9	5
9	14	P Fabre	AGS	JH22	Ford Cosworth	V8	74		26	13
r	28	G Berger	Ferrari	F1-87	Ferrari	V6t	71	suspension / spin	6	3
nc	11	S Nakajima	Lotus	99T	Honda	V6t	71		16	8
r	27	M Alboreto	Ferrari	F1-87	Ferrari	V6t	64	engine	8	4
r	17	D Warwick	Arrows	A10	Megatron	4t	62	turbo	10	5
r	30	P Alliot	Lola	LC87	Ford Cosworth	V8	57	transmission	23	12
r	16	I Capelli	March	871	Ford Cosworth	V8	52	engine	22	11
r	23	A Campos	Minardi	M187	Motori Moderni	V6t	52	turbo	21	11
r	25	R Arnoux	Ligier	JS29C	Megatron	4t	33	exhaust	13	7
r	20	T Boutsen	Benetton	B187	Ford Cosworth	V6t	31	distributor	5	3
r	10	C Danner	Zakspeed	871	Zakspeed	4t	26	engine overheating	19	10
r	26	P Ghinzani	Ligier	JS29C	Megatron	4t	24	engine	17	9
r	24	A Nannini	Minardi	M187	Motori Moderni	V6t	23	turbo	15	8
r	7	R Patrese	Brabham	BT56	BMW	4t	19	crown wheel & pinion	12	6
r	9	M Brundle	Zakspeed	871	Zakspeed	4t	18	rear wheel lost	18	9
r	21	A Caffi	Osella	FA1I	Alfa Romeo	V8t	11	gearbox	20	10
r	8	A de Cesaris	Brabham	BT56	BMW	4t	2	turbo / fire	11	6
r	18	E Cheever	Arrows	A10	Megatron	4t	0	driver turned off ignition	14	7

Winning speed 188.560 km/h, 117.166 mph
Pole Position speed 206.561 km/h, 128.351 mph (N Mansell, 1 min: 6.454 sec)
Fastest Lap speed 197.372 km/h, 122.641 mph (N Piquet, 1 min: 9.548 sec on lap 68)
Lap Leaders N Mansell 1-35,46-80 (70); N Piquet 36-45 (10).

	12 Jul 1987	BRITAIN: Silverstone						(Round 7)	(Race 443)	

65 laps x 4.778 km, 2.969 miles = 310.579 km, 192.985 miles

Pos	No	Driver	Car	Model	Engine		Laps	Time/Reason for Retirement	Grid Pos	Row
1	5	N Mansell	Williams	FW11B	Honda	V6t	65	1h 19m 11.780s	2	1
2	6	N Piquet	Williams	FW11B	Honda	V6t	65	1h 19m 13.698s	1	1
3	12	A Senna	Lotus	99T	Honda	V6t	64		3	2
4	11	S Nakajima	Lotus	99T	Honda	V6t	63		12	6
5	17	D Warwick	Arrows	A10	Megatron	4t	63		13	7
6	19	T Fabi	Benetton	B187	Ford Cosworth	V6t	63		6	3
7	20	T Boutsen	Benetton	B187	Ford Cosworth	V6t	62		5	3
8	3	J Palmer	Tyrrell	DG016	Ford Cosworth	V8	60		23	12
9	14	P Fabre	AGS	JH22	Ford Cosworth	V8	59		25	13
r	4	P Streiff	Tyrrell	DG016	Ford Cosworth	V8	57	engine	22	11
nc	9	M Brundle	Zakspeed	871	Zakspeed	4t	54		17	9
r	1	A Prost	McLaren	MP4/3	TAG Porsche	V6t	53	clutch bearing / electrics	4	2
r	27	M Alboreto	Ferrari	F1-87	Ferrari	V6t	52	rear suspension	7	4
r	18	E Cheever	Arrows	A10	Megatron	4t	45	engine overheating	14	7
r	23	A Campos	Minardi	M187	Motori Moderni	V6t	34	fuel pump	19	10
r	21	A Caffi	Osella	FA1I	Alfa Romeo	V8t	32	turbo	20	10
r	10	C Danner	Zakspeed	871	Zakspeed	4t	32	gearbox	18	9
r	7	R Patrese	Brabham	BT56	BMW	4t	28	fuel metering unit	11	6
r	2	S Johansson	McLaren	MP4/3	TAG Porsche	V6t	18	engine	10	5
r	24	A Nannini	Minardi	M187	Motori Moderni	V6t	10	engine	15	8
r	8	A de Cesaris	Brabham	BT56	BMW	4t	8	fuel line / fire	9	5
r	28	G Berger	Ferrari	F1-87	Ferrari	V6t	7	accident	8	4
r	30	P Alliot	Lola	LC87	Ford Cosworth	V8	7	gearbox	21	11
r	25	R Arnoux	Ligier	JS29C	Megatron	4t	3	electrics	16	8
r	16	I Capelli	March	871	Ford Cosworth	V8	3	gearbox	24	12
exc	26	P Ghinzani	Ligier	JS29C	Megatron	4t		refuelled on circuit		

Winning speed 235.298 km/h, 146.208 mph
Pole Position speed 256.315 km/h, 159.267 mph (N Piquet, 1 min: 7.110 sec)
Fastest Lap speed 246.324 km/h, 153.059 mph (N Mansell, 1 min: 9.832 sec on lap 58)
Lap Leaders N Piquet 1-62 (62); N Mansell 63-65 (3).

26 Jul 1987   GERMANY: Hockenheim   (Round 8)   (Race 444)

44 laps x 6.797 km, 4.223 miles = 299.068 km, 185.832 miles

Pos	No	Driver	Car	Model	Engine		Laps	Time/Reason for Retirement	Grid Pos	Row
1	6	N Piquet	Williams	FW11B	Honda	V6t	44	1h 21m 25.091s	4	2
2	2	S Johansson	McLaren	MP4/3	TAG Porsche	V6t	44	1h 23m 04.682s	8	4
3	12	A Senna	Lotus	99T	Honda	V6t	43		2	1
4	4	P Streiff	Tyrrell	DG016	Ford Cosworth	V8	43		22	11
5	3	J Palmer	Tyrrell	DG016	Ford Cosworth	V8	43		23	12
6	30	P Alliot	Lola	LC87	Ford Cosworth	V8	42		21	11
7r	1	A Prost	McLaren	MP4/3	TAG Porsche	V6t	39	alternator belt	3	2
nc	9	M Brundle	Zakspeed	871	Zakspeed	4t	34		19	10
r	26	P Ghinzani	Ligier	JS29C	Megatron	4t	32	engine	17	9
r	23	A Campos	Minardi	M187	Motori Moderni	V6t	28	engine	18	9
r	20	T Boutsen	Benetton	B187	Ford Cosworth	V6t	26	engine	6	3
r	5	N Mansell	Williams	FW11B	Honda	V6t	25	engine	1	1
r	24	A Nannini	Minardi	M187	Motori Moderni	V6t	25	engine	16	8
r	17	D Warwick	Arrows	A10	Megatron	4t	23	turbo	13	7
r	10	C Danner	Zakspeed	871	Zakspeed	4t	21	input shaft	20	10
r	28	G Berger	Ferrari	F1-87	Ferrari	V6t	19	turbo	10	5
r	19	T Fabi	Benetton	B187	Ford Cosworth	V6t	18	engine	9	5
r	21	A Caffi	Osella	FA1I	Alfa Romeo	V8t	17	engine	26	13
r	8	A de Cesaris	Brabham	BT56	BMW	4t	12	engine	7	4
r	27	M Alboreto	Ferrari	F1-87	Ferrari	V6t	10	turbo	5	3
r	14	P Fabre	AGS	JH22	Ford Cosworth	V8	10	valve	25	13
r	18	E Cheever	Arrows	A10	Megatron	4t	9	throttle linkage	15	8
r	11	S Nakajima	Lotus	99T	Honda	V6t	9	suspension	14	7
r	16	I Capelli	March	871	Ford Cosworth	V8	7	distributor rotor arm	24	12
r	25	R Arnoux	Ligier	JS29C	Megatron	4t	6	electrics	12	6
r	7	R Patrese	Brabham	BT56	BMW	4t	5	engine	11	6

Winning speed 220.394 km/h, 136.946 mph
Pole Position speed 238.454 km/h, 148.168 mph (N Mansell, 1 min:42.616 sec)
Fastest Lap speed 231.462 km/h, 143.824 mph (N Mansell, 1 min:45.716 sec on lap 24)
Lap Leaders A Senna 1 (1); N Mansell 2-7,19-22 (10); A Prost 8-18,23-39 (28); N Piquet 40-44 (5).

9 Aug 1987   HUNGARY: Hungaroring   (Round 9)   (Race 445)

76 laps x 4.014 km, 2.494 miles = 305.064 km, 189.558 miles

Pos	No	Driver	Car	Model	Engine		Laps	Time/Reason for Retirement	Grid Pos	Row
1	6	N Piquet	Williams	FW11B	Honda	V6t	76	1h 59m 26.793s	3	2
2	12	A Senna	Lotus	99T	Honda	V6t	76	2h 00m 04.520s	6	3
3	1	A Prost	McLaren	MP4/3	TAG Porsche	V6t	76	2h 00m 54.249s	4	2
4	20	T Boutsen	Benetton	B187	Ford Cosworth	V6t	75		7	4
5	7	R Patrese	Brabham	BT56	BMW	4t	75		10	5
6	17	D Warwick	Arrows	A10	Megatron	4t	74		9	5
7	3	J Palmer	Tyrrell	DG016	Ford Cosworth	V8	74		16	8
8	18	E Cheever	Arrows	A10	Megatron	4t	74		11	6
9	4	P Streiff	Tyrrell	DG016	Ford Cosworth	V8	74		14	7
10	16	I Capelli	March	871	Ford Cosworth	V8	74		18	9
11	24	A Nannini	Minardi	M187	Motori Moderni	V6t	73		20	10
12	26	P Ghinzani	Ligier	JS29C	Megatron	4t	73		25	13
13	14	P Fabre	AGS	JH22	Ford Cosworth	V8	71		26	13
14r	5	N Mansell	Williams	FW11B	Honda	V6t	70	rear wheel nut lost	1	1
r	21	A Caffi	Osella	FA1I	Alfa Romeo	V8t	64	out of fuel	21	11
r	25	R Arnoux	Ligier	JS29C	Megatron	4t	57	electrics	19	10
r	30	P Alliot	Lola	LC87	Ford Cosworth	V8	48	rear suspension / accident	15	8
r	9	M Brundle	Zakspeed	871	Zakspeed	4t	45	turbo	22	11
r	27	M Alboreto	Ferrari	F1-87	Ferrari	V6t	43	engine	5	3
r	8	A de Cesaris	Brabham	BT56	BMW	4t	43	gearbox	13	7
r	2	S Johansson	McLaren	MP4/3	TAG Porsche	V6t	14	differential / spin	8	4
r	19	T Fabi	Benetton	B187	Ford Cosworth	V6t	14	gearbox	12	6
r	23	A Campos	Minardi	M187	Motori Moderni	V6t	14	accident	24	12
r	28	G Berger	Ferrari	F1-87	Ferrari	V6t	13	cv joint	2	1
r	10	C Danner	Zakspeed	871	Zakspeed	4t	3	electrics	23	12
r	11	S Nakajima	Lotus	99T	Honda	V6t	1	driveshaft	17	9

Winning speed 153.239 km/h, 95.218 mph
Pole Position speed 164.121 km/h, 101.980 mph (N Mansell, 1 min:28.047 sec)
Fastest Lap speed 160.295 km/h, 99.602 mph (N Piquet, 1 min:30.149 sec on lap 63)
Lap Leaders N Mansell 1-70 (70); N Piquet 71-76 (6).

16 Aug 1987 **AUSTRIA: Österreichring** (Round 10) (Race 446)

52 laps x 5.942 km, 3.692 miles = 308.984 km, 191.994 miles

Pos	No	Driver	Car	Model	Engine		Laps	Time/Reason for Retirement	Grid Pos	Row
1	5	N Mansell	Williams	FW11B	Honda	V6t	52	1h 18m 44.898s	2	1
2	6	N Piquet	Williams	FW11B	Honda	V6t	52	1h 19m 40.602s	1	1
3	19	T Fabi	Benetton	B187	Ford Cosworth	V6t	51		5	3
4	20	T Boutsen	Benetton	B187	Ford Cosworth	V6t	51		4	2
5	12	A Senna	Lotus	99T	Honda	V6t	50		7	4
6	1	A Prost	McLaren	MP4/3	TAG Porsche	V6t	50		9	5
7	2	S Johansson	McLaren	MP4/3	TAG Porsche	V6t	50		14	7
8	26	P Ghinzani	Ligier	JS29C	Megatron	4t	50		18	9
9	10	C Danner	Zakspeed	871	Zakspeed	4t	49		20	10
10	25	R Arnoux	Ligier	JS29C	Megatron	4t	49		16	8
11	16	I Capelli	March	871	Ford Cosworth	V8	49		23	12
12	30	P Alliot	Lola	LC87	Ford Cosworth	V8	49		22	11
13	11	S Nakajima	Lotus	99T	Honda	V6t	49		13	7
dq	9	M Brundle	Zakspeed	871	Zakspeed	4t	48	bodywork infringement	17	9
14	3	J Palmer	Tyrrell	DG016	Ford Cosworth	V8	47		24	12
nc	14	P Fabre	AGS	JH22	Ford Cosworth	V8	45		26	13
r	7	R Patrese	Brabham	BT56	BMW	4t	43	engine	8	4
r	27	M Alboreto	Ferrari	F1-87	Ferrari	V6t	42	exhaust	6	3
r	8	A de Cesaris	Brabham	BT56	BMW	4t	35	turbo	10	5
r	17	D Warwick	Arrows	A10	Megatron	4t	35	engine	11	6
r	18	E Cheever	Arrows	A10	Megatron	4t	31	tyre / spin	12	6
r	28	G Berger	Ferrari	F1-87	Ferrari	V6t	5	turbo	3	2
r	23	A Campos	Minardi	M187	Motori Moderni	V6t	3	distributor belt	19	10
r	24	A Nannini	Minardi	M187	Motori Moderni	V6t	1	engine	15	8
r	21	A Caffi	Osella	FA1I	Alfa Romeo	V8t	0	electrics on 3rd parade lap *	21	11
r	4	P Streiff	Tyrrell	DG016	Ford Cosworth	V8	0	accident *	25	13

Winning speed 235.421 km/h, 146.284 mph
Pole Position speed 256.622 km/h, 159.457 mph (N Piquet, 1 min:23.357 sec)
Fastest Lap speed 242.207 km/h, 150.500 mph (N Mansell, 1 min:28.318 sec on lap 31)
Lap Leaders N Piquet 1-20 (20); N Mansell 21-52 (32).

*Interrupted twice after first lap accidents. Restarted for original distance. * Retired after second start.*

6 Sep 1987 **ITALY: Monza** (Round 11) (Race 447)

50 laps x 5.800 km, 3.604 miles = 290.000 km, 180.198 miles

Pos	No	Driver	Car	Model	Engine		Laps	Time/Reason for Retirement	Grid Pos	Row
1	6	N Piquet	Williams	FW11B	Honda	V6t	50	1h 14m 47.707s	1	1
2	12	A Senna	Lotus	99T	Honda	V6t	50	1h 14m 49.513s	4	2
3	5	N Mansell	Williams	FW11B	Honda	V6t	50	1h 15m 36.743s	2	1
4	28	G Berger	Ferrari	F1-87	Ferrari	V6t	50	1h 15m 45.686s	3	2
5	20	T Boutsen	Benetton	B187	Ford Cosworth	V6t	50	1h 16m 09.026s	6	3
6	2	S Johansson	McLaren	MP4/3	TAG Porsche	V6t	50	1h 16m 16.494s	11	6
7	19	T Fabi	Benetton	B187	Ford Cosworth	V6t	49		7	4
8	26	P Ghinzani	Ligier	JS29C	Megatron	4t	48		19	10
9	10	C Danner	Zakspeed	871	Zakspeed	4t	48		16	8
10	25	R Arnoux	Ligier	JS29C	Megatron	4t	48		15	8
11	11	S Nakajima	Lotus	99T	Honda	V6t	47		14	7
12	4	P Streiff	Tyrrell	DG016	Ford Cosworth	V8	47		24	12
13	16	I Capelli	March	871	Ford Cosworth	V8	47		25	13
14	3	J Palmer	Tyrrell	DG016	Ford Cosworth	V8	47		22	11
15	1	A Prost	McLaren	MP4/3	TAG Porsche	V6t	46		5	3
16r	24	A Nannini	Minardi	M187	Motori Moderni	V6t	45	out of fuel	18	9
r	9	M Brundle	Zakspeed	871	Zakspeed	4t	43	gearbox	17	9
r	30	P Alliot	Lola	LC87	Ford Cosworth	V8	37	accident	23	12
r	23	A Campos	Minardi	M187	Motori Moderni	V6t	34	fuel filter / fire	20	10
r	18	E Cheever	Arrows	A10	Megatron	4t	27	cv joint	13	7
r	22	F Forini	Osella	FA1I	Alfa Romeo	V8t	27	turbo	26	13
r	21	A Caffi	Osella	FA1I	Alfa Romeo	V8t	16	rear suspension	21	11
r	27	M Alboreto	Ferrari	F1-87	Ferrari	V6t	13	turbo	8	4
r	17	D Warwick	Arrows	A10	Megatron	4t	9	fuel metering unit	12	6
r	8	A de Cesaris	Brabham	BT56	BMW	4t	7	front suspension	10	5
r	7	R Patrese	Brabham	BT56	BMW	4t	5	engine	9	5
nq	32	N Larini	Coloni	FC187	Ford Cosworth	V8				
nq	14	P Fabre	AGS	JH22	Ford Cosworth	V8				

Winning speed 232.636 km/h, 144.553 mph
Pole Position speed 250.180 km/h, 155.454 mph (N Piquet, 1 min:23.460 sec)
Fastest Lap speed 240.564 km/h, 149.480 mph (A Senna, 1 min:26.796 sec on lap 49)
Lap Leaders N Piquet 1-23,43-50 (31); A Senna 24-42 (19).

Races 295

20 Sep 1987   PORTUGAL: Estoril   (Round 12)   (Race 448)

70 laps x 4.350 km, 2.703 miles = 304.500 km, 189.208 miles

Pos	No	Driver	Car	Model	Engine		Laps	Time/Reason for Retirement	Grid Pos	Row
1	1	A Prost	McLaren	MP4/3	TAG Porsche	V6t	70	1h 37m 03.906s	3	2
2	28	G Berger	Ferrari	F1-87	Ferrari	V6t	70	1h 37m 24.399s	1	1
3	6	N Piquet	Williams	FW11B	Honda	V6t	70	1h 38m 07.201s	4	2
4r	19	T Fabi	Benetton	B187	Ford Cosworth	V6t	69	out of fuel	10	5
5	2	S Johansson	McLaren	MP4/3	TAG Porsche	V6t	69		8	4
6	18	E Cheever	Arrows	A10	Megatron	4t	68		11	6
7	12	A Senna	Lotus	99T	Honda	V6t	68		5	3
8	11	S Nakajima	Lotus	99T	Honda	V6t	68		15	8
9	16	I Capelli	March	871	Ford Cosworth	V8	67		22	11
10	3	J Palmer	Tyrrell	DG016	Ford Cosworth	V8	67		24	12
11r	24	A Nannini	Minardi	M187	Motori Moderni	V6t	66	out of fuel	14	7
12	4	P Streiff	Tyrrell	DG016	Ford Cosworth	V8	66		21	11
13	17	D Warwick	Arrows	A10	Megatron	4t	66		12	6
14	20	T Boutsen	Benetton	B187	Ford Cosworth	V6t	64		9	5
r	8	A de Cesaris	Brabham	BT56	BMW	4t	54	injector pipe	13	7
r	27	M Alboreto	Ferrari	F1-87	Ferrari	V6t	38	gear linkage	6	3
r	9	M Brundle	Zakspeed	871	Zakspeed	4t	35	gearbox	17	9
r	22	F Forini	Osella	FA1I	Alfa Romeo	V8t	32	rear wheel bearing	26	13
r	30	P Alliot	Lola	LC87	Ford Cosworth	V8	31	fuel pump	19	10
r	25	R Arnoux	Ligier	JS29C	Megatron	4t	29	intercooler	18	9
r	21	A Caffi	Osella	FA1I	Alfa Romeo	V8t	27	turbo	25	13
r	26	P Ghinzani	Ligier	JS29C	Megatron	4t	24	clutch / ignition	23	12
r	23	A Campos	Minardi	M187	Motori Moderni	V6t	24	intercooler	20	10
r	5	N Mansell	Williams	FW11B	Honda	V6t	13	electrics	2	1
r	7	R Patrese	Brabham	BT56	BMW	4t	13	engine	7	4
r	10	C Danner	Zakspeed	871	Zakspeed	4t	0	accident *	16	8
nq	14	P Fabre	AGS	JH22	Ford Cosworth	V8				

Winning speed 188.224 km/h, 116.957 mph
Pole Position speed 201.752 km/h, 125.363 mph (G Berger, 1 min:17.620 sec)
Fastest Lap speed 197.523 km/h, 122.735 mph (G Berger, 1 min:19.282 sec on lap 66)
Lap Leaders N Mansell 1 (1); G Berger 2-33,36-67 (64); M Alboreto 34-35 (2); A Prost 68-70 (3).

*Interrupted after 2nd lap, because of an accident. Restarted for original distance. * Retired after first start.*

27 Sep 1987   SPAIN: Jerez de la Frontera   (Round 13)   (Race 449)

72 laps x 4.218 km, 2.621 miles = 303.696 km, 188.708 miles

Pos	No	Driver	Car	Model	Engine		Laps	Time/Reason for Retirement	Grid Pos	Row
1	5	N Mansell	Williams	FW11B	Honda	V6t	72	1h 49m 12.692s	2	1
2	1	A Prost	McLaren	MP4/3	TAG Porsche	V6t	72	1h 49m 34.917s	7	4
3	2	S Johansson	McLaren	MP4/3	TAG Porsche	V6t	72	1h 49m 43.510s	11	6
4	6	N Piquet	Williams	FW11B	Honda	V6t	72	1h 49m 44.142s	1	1
5	12	A Senna	Lotus	99T	Honda	V6t	72	1h 50m 26.199s	5	3
6	30	P Alliot	Lola	LC87	Ford Cosworth	V8	71		17	9
7	4	P Streiff	Tyrrell	DG016	Ford Cosworth	V8	71		15	8
8r	18	E Cheever	Arrows	A10	Megatron	4t	70	out of fuel	13	7
9	11	S Nakajima	Lotus	99T	Honda	V6t	70		18	9
10	17	D Warwick	Arrows	A10	Megatron	4t	70		12	6
11	9	M Brundle	Zakspeed	871	Zakspeed	4t	70		20	10
12	16	I Capelli	March	871	Ford Cosworth	V8	70		19	10
13	7	R Patrese	Brabham	BT56	BMW	4t	68		9	5
14	23	A Campos	Minardi	M187	Motori Moderni	V6t	68		24	12
15r	27	M Alboreto	Ferrari	F1-87	Ferrari	V6t	67	engine	4	2
16r	20	T Boutsen	Benetton	B187	Ford Cosworth	V6t	66	brakes / spin	8	4
r	28	G Berger	Ferrari	F1-87	Ferrari	V6t	62	oil radiator / engine	3	2
r	3	J Palmer	Tyrrell	DG016	Ford Cosworth	V8	55	accident	16	8
r	25	R Arnoux	Ligier	JS29C	Megatron	4t	55	engine	14	7
r	10	C Danner	Zakspeed	871	Zakspeed	4t	50	gearbox	22	11
r	24	A Nannini	Minardi	M187	Motori Moderni	V6t	45	turbo	21	11
r	19	T Fabi	Benetton	B187	Ford Cosworth	V6t	40	engine	6	3
r	8	A de Cesaris	Brabham	BT56	BMW	4t	26	gearbox	10	5
r	26	P Ghinzani	Ligier	JS29C	Megatron	4t	24	ignition	23	12
r	14	P Fabre	AGS	JH22	Ford Cosworth	V8	10	clutch	25	13
r	32	N Larini	Coloni	FC187	Ford Cosworth	V8	8	engine	26	13
nq	21	A Caffi	Osella	FA1I	Alfa Romeo	V8t				
nq	22	F Forini	Osella	FA1I	Alfa Romeo	V8t				

Winning speed 166.848 km/h, 103.675 mph
Pole Position speed 184.145 km/h, 114.423 mph (N Piquet, 1 min:22.461 sec)
Fastest Lap speed 174.566 km/h, 108.470 mph (G Berger, 1 min:26.986 sec on lap 49)
Lap Leaders N Mansell 1-72 (72).

18 Oct 1987   **MEXICO: Mexico City**   **(Round 14)**   **(Race 450)**

63 laps x 4.421 km, 2.747 miles = 278.523 km, 173.066 miles

Pos	No	Driver	Car	Model	Engine		Laps	Time/Reason for Retirement	Grid Pos	Row
1	5	N Mansell	Williams	FW11B	Honda	V6t	63	1h 26m 24.207s	1	1
2	6	N Piquet	Williams	FW11B	Honda	V6t	63	1h 26m 50.383s	3	2
3	7	R Patrese	Brabham	BT56	BMW	4t	63	1h 27m 51.086s	8	4
4	18	E Cheever	Arrows	A10	Megatron	4t	63	1h 28m 05.559s	12	6
5	19	T Fabi	Benetton	B187	Ford Cosworth	V6t	61		6	3
6	30	P Alliot	Lola	LC87	Ford Cosworth	V8	60		24	12
7	3	J Palmer	Tyrrell	DG016	Ford Cosworth	V8	60		22	11
8	4	P Streiff	Tyrrell	DG016	Ford Cosworth	V8	60		25	13
9	29	Y Dalmas	Lola	LC87	Ford Cosworth	V8	59		23	12
r	12	A Senna	Lotus	99T	Honda	V6t	54	spin	7	4
r	16	I Capelli	March	871	Ford Cosworth	V8	51	engine	20	10
r	21	A Caffi	Osella	FA1I	Alfa Romeo	V8t	50	engine	26	13
r	26	P Ghinzani	Ligier	JS29C	Megatron	4t	43	engine overheating	21	11
r	23	A Campos	Minardi	M187	Motori Moderni	V6t	32	gear linkage	19	10
r	25	R Arnoux	Ligier	JS29C	Megatron	4t	29	ignition	18	9
r	17	D Warwick	Arrows	A10	Megatron	4t	26	accident	11	6
r	8	A de Cesaris	Brabham	BT56	BMW	4t	22	spin	10	5
r	28	G Berger	Ferrari	F1-87	Ferrari	V6t	20	engine	2	1
r	20	T Boutsen	Benetton	B187	Ford Cosworth	V6t	15	electronics	4	2
r	24	A Nannini	Minardi	M187	Motori Moderni	V6t	13	turbo	14	7
r	27	M Alboreto	Ferrari	F1-87	Ferrari	V6t	12	engine	9	5
r	9	M Brundle	Zakspeed	871	Zakspeed	4t	3	turbo	13	7
r	2	S Johansson	McLaren	MP4/3	TAG Porsche	V6t	1	accident	15	8
r	11	S Nakajima	Lotus	99T	Honda	V6t	1	accident	16	8
r	10	C Danner	Zakspeed	871	Zakspeed	4t	1	accident	17	9
r	1	A Prost	McLaren	MP4/3	TAG Porsche	V6t	0	accident	5	3
nq	14	P Fabre	AGS	JH22	Ford Cosworth	V8				

Winning speed 193.411 km/h, 120.180 mph
Pole Position speed 203.049 km/h, 126.169 mph (N Mansell, 1 min:18.383 sec)
Fastest Lap speed 201.127 km/h, 124.975 mph (N Piquet, 1 min:19.132 sec on lap 57)
Lap Leaders G Berger 1,15-20 (7); T Boutsen 2-14 (13); N Mansell 21-30 (10); N Piquet 31-63 (33).

Scheduled for 68 laps, but interrupted after 30 laps, because of an accident. Restarted for a further 33 laps, with results being on aggregate and lap leaders 'on the road'.

1 Nov 1987   **JAPAN: Suzuka**   **(Round 15)**   **(Race 451)**

51 laps x 5.859 km, 3.641 miles = 298.809 km, 185.671 miles

Pos	No	Driver	Car	Model	Engine		Laps	Time/Reason for Retirement	Grid Pos	Row
1	28	G Berger	Ferrari	F1-87	Ferrari	V6t	51	1h 32m 58.072s	1	1
2	12	A Senna	Lotus	99T	Honda	V6t	51	1h 33m 15.456s	7	4
3	2	S Johansson	McLaren	MP4/3	TAG Porsche	V6t	51	1h 33m 15.766s	9	5
4	27	M Alboreto	Ferrari	F1-87	Ferrari	V6t	51	1h 34m 18.513s	4	2
5	20	T Boutsen	Benetton	B187	Ford Cosworth	V6t	51	1h 34m 23.648s	3	2
6	11	S Nakajima	Lotus	99T	Honda	V6t	51	1h 34m 34.551s	11	6
7	1	A Prost	McLaren	MP4/3	TAG Porsche	V6t	50		2	1
8	3	J Palmer	Tyrrell	DG016	Ford Cosworth	V8	50		19	10
9	18	E Cheever	Arrows	A10	Megatron	4t	50		12	6
10	17	D Warwick	Arrows	A10	Megatron	4t	50		13	7
11r	7	R Patrese	Brabham	BT56	BMW	4t	49	engine	8	4
12	4	P Streiff	Tyrrell	DG016	Ford Cosworth	V8	49		25	13
13r	26	P Ghinzani	Ligier	JS29C	Megatron	4t	48	out of fuel	24	12
14r	29	Y Dalmas	Lola	LC87	Ford Cosworth	V8	47	electrics	22	11
15r	6	N Piquet	Williams	FW11B	Honda	V6t	46	engine	5	3
r	25	R Arnoux	Ligier	JS29C	Megatron	4t	44	out of fuel	17	9
r	21	A Caffi	Osella	FA1I	Alfa Romeo	V8t	43	out of fuel	23	12
r	14	R Moreno	AGS	JH22	Ford Cosworth	V8	38	fuel injection	26	13
r	24	A Nannini	Minardi	M187	Motori Moderni	V6t	35	engine	14	7
r	9	M Brundle	Zakspeed	871	Zakspeed	4t	32	engine overheating	15	8
r	8	A de Cesaris	Brabham	BT56	BMW	4t	26	turbo	10	5
r	19	T Fabi	Benetton	B187	Ford Cosworth	V6t	16	engine	6	3
r	10	C Danner	Zakspeed	871	Zakspeed	4t	13	engine / oil on tyres / accident	16	8
r	16	I Capelli	March	871	Ford Cosworth	V8	13	accident	20	10
r	23	A Campos	Minardi	M187	Motori Moderni	V6t	2	engine	21	11
r	30	P Alliot	Lola	LC87	Ford Cosworth	V8	0	accident	18	9
ns	5	N Mansell	Williams	FW11B	Honda	V6t		accident / injury		

Winning speed 192.847 km/h, 119.829 mph
Pole Position speed 210.835 km/h, 131.007 mph (G Berger, 1 min:40.042 sec)
Fastest Lap speed 203.116 km/h, 126.211 mph (A Prost, 1 min:43.844 sec on lap 35)
Lap Leaders G Berger 1-24,26-51 (50); A Senna 25 (1).

82 laps x 3.779 km, 2.348 miles = 309.878 km, 192.549 miles

Pos	No	Driver	Car	Model	Engine		Laps	Time/Reason for Retirement	Grid Pos	Row
1	28	G Berger	Ferrari	F1-87	Ferrari	V6t	82	1h 52m 56.144s	1	1
dq	12	A Senna	Lotus	99T	Honda	V6t	82	brake duct irregularities	4	2
2	27	M Alboreto	Ferrari	F1-87	Ferrari	V6t	82	1h 54m 04.028s	6	3
3	20	T Boutsen	Benetton	B187	Ford Cosworth	V6t	81		5	3
4	3	J Palmer	Tyrrell	DG016	Ford Cosworth	V8	80		19	10
5	29	Y Dalmas	Lola	LC87	Ford Cosworth	V8	79		21	11
6	14	R Moreno	AGS	JH22	Ford Cosworth	V8	79		25	13
7	10	C Danner	Zakspeed	871	Zakspeed	4t	79		24	12
8r	8	A de Cesaris	Brabham	BT56	BMW	4t	78	spin	10	5
9r	5	R Patrese	Williams	FW11B	Honda	V6t	76	engine	7	4
r	6	N Piquet	Williams	FW11B	Honda	V6t	58	brakes / gear linkage	3	2
r	16	I Capelli	March	871	Ford Cosworth	V6t	58	spin	23	12
r	1	A Prost	McLaren	MP4/3	TAG Porsche	V6t	53	brakes / accident	2	1
r	18	E Cheever	Arrows	A10	Megatron	4t	53	engine overheating	11	6
r	2	S Johansson	McLaren	MP4/3	TAG Porsche	V6t	48	brakes	8	4
r	19	T Fabi	Benetton	B187	Ford Cosworth	V6t	46	brakes	9	5
r	23	A Campos	Minardi	M187	Motori Moderni	V6t	46	gearbox	26	13
r	30	P Alliot	Lola	LC87	Ford Cosworth	V8	45	electrics	17	9
r	25	R Arnoux	Ligier	JS29C	Megatron	4t	41	electrics	20	10
r	7	S Modena	Brabham	BT56	BMW	4t	31	driver exhausted	15	8
r	26	P Ghinzani	Ligier	JS29C	Megatron	4t	26	engine	22	11
r	11	S Nakajima	Lotus	99T	Honda	V6t	22	suspension hydraulics	14	7
r	17	D Warwick	Arrows	A10	Megatron	4t	19	transmission	12	6
r	9	M Brundle	Zakspeed	871	Zakspeed	4t	18	gear selection / turbo	16	8
r	4	P Streiff	Tyrrell	DG016	Ford Cosworth	V8	6	spin	18	9
r	24	A Nannini	Minardi	M187	Motori Moderni	V6t	0	accident	13	7
nq	21	A Caffi	Osella	FA1I	Alfa Romeo	V8t				

Winning speed 164.631 km/h, 102.297 mph
Pole Position speed 176.070 km/h, 109.405 mph (G Berger, 1 min:17.267 sec)
Fastest Lap speed 169.175 km/h, 105.121 mph (G Berger, 1 min:20.416 sec on lap 72)
Lap Leaders G Berger 1-82 (82).

A Senna finished 2nd in 1h 53m 30.989s.

Lap Leaders 1987

Pos	Driver	Car-Engine	GPs	laps	km	miles
1	N Mansell	Williams-Honda	11	383	1,669.0	1,037.1
2	G Berger	Ferrari	4	203	912.2	566.8
3	N Piquet	Williams-Honda	9	187	954.8	593.3
4	A Prost	McLaren-TAG Porsche	4	110	665.7	413.7
5	A Senna	Lotus-Honda	7	108	446.9	277.7
6	T Boutsen	Benetton-Ford Cosworth	1	13	57.5	35.7
7	M Alboreto	Ferrari	2	5	23.8	14.8
			16	1,009	4,729.8	2,939.0

Driver Points 1987

	Driver	BR	RSM	B	MC	USA	F	GB	D	H	A	I	P	E	MEX	J	AUS	Total	
1	N Piquet	6	-	-	6	6	6	6	9	9	6	9	4	(3)	6	-	-	73	(3)
2	N Mansell	1	9	-	-	2	9	9	-	-	9	4	-	9	9	-	-	61	
3	A Senna	-	6	-	9	9	3	4	4	6	2	6	-	2	-	6	-	57	
4	A Prost	9	-	9	-	4	4	-	-	4	1	-	9	6	-	-	-	46	
5	G Berger	3	-	-	3	3	-	-	-	-	-	3	6	-	-	9	9	36	
6	S Johansson	4	3	6	-	-	-	-	6	-	-	1	2	4	-	4	-	30	
7	M Alboreto	-	4	-	4	-	-	-	-	-	-	-	-	-	-	3	6	17	
8	T Boutsen	2	-	-	-	-	-	-	-	3	3	2	-	-	-	2	4	16	
9	T Fabi	-	-	-	-	-	-	2	1	-	-	4	-	3	-	2	-	12	
10	E Cheever	-	-	-	3	-	1	-	-	-	-	-	1	-	3	-	-	8	
11	J Palmer	-	-	-	2	-	-	-	2	-	-	-	-	-	-	-	3	7	
	S Nakajima	-	1	2	-	-	-	3	-	-	-	-	-	-	-	1	-	7	
13	R Patrese	-	-	-	-	-	-	-	-	2	-	-	-	-	4	-	-	6	
14	A de Cesaris	-	-	4	-	-	-	-	-	-	-	-	-	-	-	-	-	4	
	P Streiff	-	-	-	-	-	1	-	3	-	-	-	-	-	-	-	-	4	
16	D Warwick	-	-	-	-	-	-	2	-	1	-	-	-	-	-	-	-	3	
	P Alliot	-	-	-	-	-	-	-	1	-	-	-	-	1	1	-	-	3	
18	M Brundle	-	2	-	-	-	-	-	-	-	-	-	-	-	-	-	-	2	
19	R Arnoux	-	-	1	-	-	-	-	-	-	-	-	-	-	-	-	-	1	
	I Capelli	-	-	-	1	-	-	-	-	-	-	-	-	-	-	-	-	1	
	R Moreno	-	-	-	-	-	-	-	-	-	-	-	-	-	-	-	1	1	
22	Y Dalmas	-	-	-	-	-	-	-	-	-	-	-	-	-	-	(2)	-	(2)	

Jim Clark Trophy

	Driver	BR	RSM	B	MC	USA	F	GB	D	H	A	I	P	E	MEX	J	AUS	Total	
1	J Palmer	9	-	-	9	9	6	9	6	9	(4)	(4)	6	-	6	9	9	87	(8)
2	P Streiff	6	9	6	-	-	9	-	9	6	-	9	4	6	4	6	-	74	
3	P Alliot	-	6	9	-	-	-	-	4	-	6	-	-	9	9	-	-	43	
4	I Capelli	-	-	-	6	-	-	-	-	4	9	6	9	4	-	-	-	38	
5	P Fabre	-	4	4	4	4	6	4	6	-	3	-	-	-	-	-	-	35	
6	R Moreno	-	-	-	-	-	-	-	-	-	-	-	-	-	-	-	4	4	
7	Y Dalmas	-	-	-	-	-	-	-	-	-	-	-	-	-	-	(6)	-	(6)	

9,6,4,3,2 and 1 point awarded to the first six finishers. Best 11 scores. Y Dalmas (Lola-Ford Cosworth) finished 5th in Australia, but points not valid for Championship because constructor had only entered one car for the season.

In an effort to promote interest in the power disadvantaged normally aspirated cars, separate championships were created (Jim Clark and Colin Chapman Trophies) and points distributed in the usual manner. Drivers were eligible for World Championship points, if they finished in the top six overall.

Constructor Points 1987

		BR	RSM	B	MC	USA	F	GB	D	H	A	I	P	E	MEX	J	AUS	Total	
1	Williams-Honda	7	9	-	6	8	15	15	9	9	15	13	4	12	15	-	-	137	
2	McLaren-TAG Porsche	13	3	15	-	4	4	-	6	4	1	1	11	10	-	4	-	76	
3	Lotus-Honda	-	7	2	9	9	3	7	4	6	2	6	-	2	-	7	-	64	
4	Ferrari	3	4	-	7	3	-	-	-	-	-	3	6	-	-	12	15	53	
5	Benetton-Ford Cosworth	2	-	-	-	-	2	1	-	3	7	2	3	-	2	2	4	28	
6	Tyrrell-Ford Cosworth	-	-	-	2	-	1	-	5	-	-	-	-	-	-	-	3	11	
	Arrows-Megatron	-	-	3	-	1	-	2	-	1	-	-	1	-	3	-	-	11	
8	Brabham-BMW	-	-	4	-	-	-	-	-	2	-	-	-	-	4	-	-	10	
9	Lola-Ford Cosworth	-	-	-	-	-	-	-	1	-	-	-	-	1	1	-	(2)	3	(2)
10	Zakspeed	-	2	-	-	-	-	-	-	-	-	-	-	-	-	-	-	2	
11	Ligier-Megatron	-	-	1	-	-	-	-	-	-	-	-	-	-	-	-	-	1	
	March-Ford Cosworth	-	-	-	1	-	-	-	-	-	-	-	-	-	-	-	-	1	
	AGS-Ford Cosworth	-	-	-	-	-	-	-	-	-	-	-	-	-	-	-	1	1	

Colin Chapman Trophy

		BR	RSM	B	MC	USA	F	GB	D	H	A	I	P	E	MEX	J	AUS	Total	
1	Tyrrell-Ford Cosworth	15	9	(6)	9	9	15	(9)	15	15	(4)	13	10	(6)	10	10	(9)	130	(34)
2	Lola-Ford Cosworth	-	6	9	-	-	-	-	4	-	6	-	-	9	9	9	(6)	52	(6)
3	AGS-Ford Cosworth	4	4	4	4	6	4	6	-	3	-	-	-	-	-	-	4	39	
4	March-Ford Cosworth	-	-	-	6	-	-	-	-	4	9	6	6	4	-	-	-	35	

9,6,4,3,2 and 1 point awarded to the first six finishers.

1988

Race Entrants and Results

The turbos were further regulated with 2.5 bar pressure and only 150 litres of fuel. Honda took their engine from Williams to McLaren. Enzo Ferrari died in August of this year at the age of 90. Pre-qualifying re-emerged in a small way and it was to become an early morning ritual for some teams in years to come.

LOTUS
Camel Team Lotus Honda: Piquet, Nakajima

TYRRELL
Tyrrell Racing Organisation: Palmer, Bailey

WILLIAMS
Canon Williams Team: Mansell, Brundle, Schlesser, Patrese

ZAKSPEED
West Zakspeed Racing: Ghinzani, Schneider

McLAREN
Honda Marlboro McLaren: Prost, Senna

AGS
Automobiles Gonfaronaises Sportives: Streiff

MARCH
Leyton House March Racing Team: Gugelmin, Capelli

ARROWS
USF&G Arrows Megatron: Warwick, Cheever

BENETTON
Benetton Formula: Nannini, Boutsen

OSELLA
Osella Squadra Corse: Larini

RIAL
Rial Racing: de Cesaris

MINARDI
Lois Minardi Team: Campos, Martini, Sala

LIGIER
Ligier Loto: Arnoux, Johansson

FERRARI
Scuderia Ferrari SpA SEFAC: Alboreto, Berger

LOLA
Larrousse Calmels: Dalmas, Suzuki, (Raphanel), Alliot

COLONI
Coloni SpA: Tarquini

EUROBRUN
EuroBrun Racing: Larrauri, Modena

DALLARA
Scuderia Italia: Caffi

3 Apr 1988			**BRAZIL: Rio de Janeiro**					(Round 1)		(Race 453)	
			60 laps x 5.031 km, 3.126 miles = 301.860 km, 187.567 miles								
Pos	**No**	**Driver**	**Car**	**Model**	**Engine**		**Laps**	**Time/Reason for Retirement**		**Grid Pos**	**Row**
1	11	A Prost	McLaren	MP4/4	Honda	V6t	60	1h 36m 06.857s		3	2
2	28	G Berger	Ferrari	F1-87/88C	Ferrari	V6t	60	1h 36m 16.730s		4	2
3	1	N Piquet	Lotus	100T	Honda	V6t	60	1h 37m 15.438s		5	3
4	17	D Warwick	Arrows	A10B	Megatron	4t	60	1h 37m 20.205s		11	6
5	27	M Alboreto	Ferrari	F1-87/88C	Ferrari	V6t	60	1h 37m 21.413s		6	3
6	2	S Nakajima	Lotus	100T	Honda	V6t	59			10	5
7	20	T Boutsen	Benetton	B188	Ford Cosworth	V8	59			7	4
8	18	E Cheever	Arrows	A10B	Megatron	4t	59			15	8
9	26	S Johansson	Ligier	JS31	Judd	V8	57			21	11
r	22	A de Cesaris	Rial	ARC1	Ford Cosworth	V8	53	engine		14	7
r	3	J Palmer	Tyrrell	017	Ford Cosworth	V8	47	driveshaft		22	11
r	24	L Sala	Minardi	M188	Ford Cosworth	V8	46	rear wing mounting		20	10
r	30	P Alliot	Lola	LC88	Ford Cosworth	V8	40	rear suspension / accident		16	8
r	31	G Tarquini	Coloni	FC188	Ford Cosworth	V8	35	rear suspension		25	13
r	14	P Streiff	AGS	JH23	Ford Cosworth	V8	35	brakes / spin		19	10
r	29	Y Dalmas	Lola	LC88	Ford Cosworth	V8	32	engine		17	9
dq	12	A Senna	McLaren	MP4/4	Honda	V6t	31	changed car after parade lap		1	1
r	25	R Arnoux	Ligier	JS31	Judd	V8	23	clutch		18	9
r	33	S Modena	EuroBrun	ER188	Ford Cosworth	V8	20	fuel pump / engine		24	12
r	5	N Mansell	Williams	FW12	Judd	V8	18	electrics / engine overheating		2	1
r	19	A Nannini	Benetton	B188	Ford Cosworth	V8	7	engine overheating		12	6
r	6	R Patrese	Williams	FW12	Judd	V8	6	engine overheating		8	4
r	16	I Capelli	March	881	Judd	V8	6	engine overheating		9	5
r	23	A Campos	Minardi	M188	Ford Cosworth	V8	5	rear wing mounting		23	12
r	15	M Gugelmin	March	881	Judd	V8	0	transmission		13	7
ns	32	O Larrauri	EuroBrun	ER188	Ford Cosworth	V8		electrics on parade lap		26	13
nq	4	J Bailey	Tyrrell	017	Ford Cosworth	V8					
nq	9	P Ghinzani	Zakspeed	881	Zakspeed	4t					
nq	21	N Larini	Osella	FA1I	Alfa Romeo	V8t					
nq	10	B Schneider	Zakspeed	881	Zakspeed	4t					
npq	36	A Caffi	Dallara	3087	Ford Cosworth	V8					

Winning speed 188.438 km/h, 117.090 mph
Pole Position speed 205.589 km/h, 127.747 mph (A Senna, 1 min:28.096 sec)
Fastest Lap speed 194.868 km/h, 121.085 mph (G Berger, 1 min:32.943 sec on lap 45)
Lap Leaders A Prost 1-60 (60).

Scheduled for 61 laps but reduced after second parade lap, due to gearbox problems on Senna's car.

60 laps x 5.040 km, 3.132 miles = 302.400 km, 187.903 miles

Pos	No	Driver	Car	Model	Engine		Laps	Time/Reason for Retirement	Grid Pos	Row
1	12	A Senna	McLaren	MP4/4	Honda	V6t	60	1h 32m 41.264s	1	1
2	11	A Prost	McLaren	MP4/4	Honda	V6t	60	1h 32m 43.598s	2	1
3	1	N Piquet	Lotus	100T	Honda	V6t	59		3	2
4	20	T Boutsen	Benetton	B188	Ford Cosworth	V8	59		8	4
5	28	G Berger	Ferrari	F1-87/88C	Ferrari	V6t	59		5	3
6	19	A Nannini	Benetton	B188	Ford Cosworth	V8	59		4	2
7	18	E Cheever	Arrows	A10B	Megatron	4t	59		7	4
8	2	S Nakajima	Lotus	100T	Honda	V6t	59		12	6
9	17	D Warwick	Arrows	A10B	Megatron	4t	58		14	7
10	14	P Streiff	AGS	JH23	Ford Cosworth	V8	58		13	7
11	24	L Sala	Minardi	M188	Ford Cosworth	V8	58		18	9
12	29	Y Dalmas	Lola	LC88	Ford Cosworth	V8	58		19	10
13	6	R Patrese	Williams	FW12	Judd	V8	58		6	3
14	3	J Palmer	Tyrrell	017	Ford Cosworth	V8	58		23	12
15	15	M Gugelmin	March	881	Judd	V8	58		20	10
16	23	A Campos	Minardi	M188	Ford Cosworth	V8	57		22	11
17	30	P Alliot	Lola	LC88	Ford Cosworth	V8	57		15	8
18r	27	M Alboreto	Ferrari	F1-87/88C	Ferrari	V6t	54	engine	10	5
nc	33	S Modena	EuroBrun	ER188	Ford Cosworth	V8	52		26	13
r	4	J Bailey	Tyrrell	017	Ford Cosworth	V8	48	gearbox	21	11
r	5	N Mansell	Williams	FW12	Judd	V8	42	electrics	11	6
r	31	G Tarquini	Coloni	FC188	Ford Cosworth	V8	40	throttle linkage	17	9
r	36	A Caffi	Dallara	188	Ford Cosworth	V8	18	gearbox	24	12
r	9	P Ghinzani	Zakspeed	881	Zakspeed	4t	16	electrics	25	13
r	16	I Capelli	March	881	Judd	V8	2	gearbox	9	5
r	22	A de Cesaris	Rial	ARC1	Ford Cosworth	V8	0	front suspension	16	8
nq	32	O Larrauri	EuroBrun	ER188	Ford Cosworth	V8				
nq	26	S Johansson	Ligier	JS31	Judd	V8				
nq	25	R Arnoux	Ligier	JS31	Judd	V8				
nq	10	B Schneider	Zakspeed	881	Zakspeed	4t				
exc	21	N Larini	Osella	FA1L	Alfa Romeo	V8t		failed scrutineering		

Winning speed 195.754 km/h, 121.636 mph
Pole Position speed 208.198 km/h, 129.368 mph (A Senna, 1 min:27.148 sec)
Fastest Lap speed 202.308 km/h, 125.708 mph (A Prost, 1 min:29.685 sec on lap 53)
Lap Leaders A Senna 1-60 (60).

78 laps x 3.328 km, 2.068 miles = 259.584 km, 161.298 miles

Pos	No	Driver	Car	Model	Engine		Laps	Time/Reason for Retirement	Grid Pos	Row
1	11	A Prost	McLaren	MP4/4	Honda	V6t	78	1h 57m 17.077s	2	1
2	28	G Berger	Ferrari	F1-87/88C	Ferrari	V6t	78	1h 57m 37.530s	3	2
3	27	M Alboreto	Ferrari	F1-87/88C	Ferrari	V6t	78	1h 57m 58.306s	4	2
4	17	D Warwick	Arrows	A10B	Megatron	4t	77		7	4
5	3	J Palmer	Tyrrell	017	Ford Cosworth	V8	77		10	5
6	6	R Patrese	Williams	FW12	Judd	V8	77		8	4
7	29	Y Dalmas	Lola	LC88	Ford Cosworth	V8	77		21	11
8	20	T Boutsen	Benetton	B188	Ford Cosworth	V8	76		16	8
9	21	N Larini	Osella	FA1L	Alfa Romeo	V8t	75		25	13
10	16	I Capelli	March	881	Judd	V8	72		22	11
r	12	A Senna	McLaren	MP4/4	Honda	V6t	66	accident	1	1
r	30	P Alliot	Lola	LC88	Ford Cosworth	V8	50	accident	13	7
r	15	M Gugelmin	March	881	Judd	V8	45	fuel pump	14	7
r	9	P Ghinzani	Zakspeed	881	Zakspeed	4t	43	gearbox	23	12
r	19	A Nannini	Benetton	B188	Ford Cosworth	V8	38	gearbox / clutch	6	3
r	24	L Sala	Minardi	M188	Ford Cosworth	V8	36	driveshaft	15	8
r	5	N Mansell	Williams	FW12	Judd	V8	32	accident	5	3
r	22	A de Cesaris	Rial	ARC1	Ford Cosworth	V8	28	oil pressure	19	10
r	25	R Arnoux	Ligier	JS31	Judd	V8	17	electrics	20	10
r	32	O Larrauri	EuroBrun	ER188	Ford Cosworth	V8	14	accident	18	9
r	18	E Cheever	Arrows	A10B	Megatron	4t	8	electrics	9	5
r	26	S Johansson	Ligier	JS31	Judd	V8	6	electrics	26	13
r	31	G Tarquini	Coloni	FC188	Ford Cosworth	V8	5	engine	24	12
r	1	N Piquet	Lotus	100T	Honda	V6t	0	accident	11	6
r	36	A Caffi	Dallara	188	Ford Cosworth	V8	0	accident	17	9
ns	14	P Streiff	AGS	JH23	Ford Cosworth	V8		throttle linkage on parade lap	12	6
nq	2	S Nakajima	Lotus	100T	Honda	V6t				
nq	10	B Schneider	Zakspeed	881	Zakspeed	4t				
nq	23	A Campos	Minardi	M188	Ford Cosworth	V8				
nq	4	J Bailey	Tyrrell	017	Ford Cosworth	V8				
exc	33	S Modena	EuroBrun	ER188	Ford Cosworth	V8		missed weight check		

Winning speed 132.797 km/h, 82.516 mph
Pole Position speed 142.632 km/h, 88.627 mph (A Senna, 1 min:23.998 sec)
Fastest Lap speed 138.794 km/h, 86.242 mph (A Senna, 1 min:26.321 sec on lap 59)
Lap Leaders A Senna 1-66 (66); A Prost 67-78 (12).

29 May 1988   MEXICO: Mexico City   (Round 4)   (Race 456)

67 laps x 4.421 km, 2.747 miles = 296.207 km, 184.054 miles

Pos	No	Driver	Car	Model	Engine		Laps	Time/Reason for Retirement	Grid Pos	Row
1	11	A Prost	McLaren	MP4/4	Honda	V6t	67	1h 30m 15.737s	2	1
2	12	A Senna	McLaren	MP4/4	Honda	V6t	67	1h 30m 22.841s	1	1
3	28	G Berger	Ferrari	F1-87/88C	Ferrari	V6t	67	1h 31m 13.051s	3	2
4	27	M Alboreto	Ferrari	F1-87/88C	Ferrari	V6t	66		5	3
5	17	D Warwick	Arrows	A10B	Megatron	4t	66		9	5
6	18	E Cheever	Arrows	A10B	Megatron	4t	66		7	4
7	19	A Nannini	Benetton	B188	Ford Cosworth	V8	65		8	4
8	20	T Boutsen	Benetton	B188	Ford Cosworth	V8	64		11	6
9	29	Y Dalmas	Lola	LC88	Ford Cosworth	V8	64		22	11
10	26	S Johansson	Ligier	JS31	Judd	V8	63		24	12
11	24	L Sala	Minardi	M188	Ford Cosworth	V8	63		25	13
12	14	P Streiff	AGS	JH23	Ford Cosworth	V8	63		19	10
13	32	O Larrauri	EuroBrun	ER188	Ford Cosworth	V8	63		26	13
14	31	G Tarquini	Coloni	FC188	Ford Cosworth	V8	62		21	11
15	9	P Ghinzani	Zakspeed	881	Zakspeed	4t	61		18	9
16	16	I Capelli	March	881	Judd	V8	61		10	5
r	1	N Piquet	Lotus	100T	Honda	V6t	58	engine	4	2
r	22	A de Cesaris	Rial	ARC1	Ford Cosworth	V8	52	gearbox	12	6
r	2	S Nakajima	Lotus	100T	Honda	V6t	27	turbo	6	3
r	5	N Mansell	Williams	FW12	Judd	V8	20	engine	14	7
r	10	B Schneider	Zakspeed	881	Zakspeed	4t	16	engine overheating	15	8
r	6	R Patrese	Williams	FW12	Judd	V8	16	engine	17	9
r	25	R Arnoux	Ligier	JS31	Judd	V8	13	accident / rear wing	20	10
r	36	A Caffi	Dallara	188	Ford Cosworth	V8	13	brakes / accident	23	12
r	15	M Gugelmin	March	881	Judd	V8	10	electrics	16	8
r	30	P Alliot	Lola	LC88	Ford Cosworth	V8	0	rear suspension / handling	13	7
nq	3	J Palmer	Tyrrell	017	Ford Cosworth	V8				
nq	21	N Larini	Osella	FA1L	Alfa Romeo	V8t				
nq	4	J Bailey	Tyrrell	017	Ford Cosworth	V8				
nq	23	A Campos	Minardi	M188	Ford Cosworth	V8				
exc	33	S Modena	EuroBrun	ER188	Ford Cosworth	V8		rear wing infringement		

Winning speed 196.898 km/h, 122.346 mph
Pole Position speed 205.447 km/h, 127.659 mph (A Senna, 1 min:17.468 sec)
Fastest Lap speed 202.468 km/h, 125.808 mph (A Prost, 1 min:18.608 sec on lap 52)
Lap Leaders A Prost 1-67 (67).

12 Jun 1988   CANADA: Montréal   (Round 5)   (Race 457)

69 laps x 4.390 km, 2.728 miles = 302.910 km, 188.220 miles

Pos	No	Driver	Car	Model	Engine		Laps	Time/Reason for Retirement	Grid Pos	Row
1	12	A Senna	McLaren	MP4/4	Honda	V6t	69	1h 39m 46.618s	1	1
2	11	A Prost	McLaren	MP4/4	Honda	V6t	69	1h 39m 52.552s	2	1
3	20	T Boutsen	Benetton	B188	Ford Cosworth	V8	69	1h 40m 38.027s	7	4
4	1	N Piquet	Lotus	100T	Honda	V6t	68		6	3
5	16	I Capelli	March	881	Judd	V8	68		14	7
6	3	J Palmer	Tyrrell	017	Ford Cosworth	V8	67		19	10
7	17	D Warwick	Arrows	A10B	Megatron	4t	67		16	8
8	31	G Tarquini	Coloni	FC188	Ford Cosworth	V8	67		26	13
9r	22	A de Cesaris	Rial	ARC1	Ford Cosworth	V8	66	out of fuel	12	6
10r	30	P Alliot	Lola	LC88	Ford Cosworth	V8	66	fuel system	17	9
11	2	S Nakajima	Lotus	100T	Honda	V6t	66		13	7
12	33	S Modena	EuroBrun	ER188	Ford Cosworth	V8	66		15	8
13	24	L Sala	Minardi	M188	Ford Cosworth	V8	64		21	11
14r	9	P Ghinzani	Zakspeed	881	Zakspeed	4t	63	engine overheating	22	11
r	15	M Gugelmin	March	881	Judd	V8	54	gearbox	18	9
r	14	P Streiff	AGS	JH23	Ford Cosworth	V8	41	rear suspension	10	5
r	25	R Arnoux	Ligier	JS31	Judd	V8	36	gearbox	20	10
r	27	M Alboreto	Ferrari	F1-87/88C	Ferrari	V6t	33	engine	4	2
r	6	R Patrese	Williams	FW12	Judd	V8	32	engine	11	6
r	18	E Cheever	Arrows	A10B	Megatron	4t	31	throttle spring	8	4
r	5	N Mansell	Williams	FW12	Judd	V8	28	engine	9	5
r	26	S Johansson	Ligier	JS31	Judd	V8	24	engine	25	13
r	28	G Berger	Ferrari	F1-87/88C	Ferrari	V6t	22	ignition	3	2
r	19	A Nannini	Benetton	B188	Ford Cosworth	V8	15	water leak / electrics	5	3
r	32	O Larrauri	EuroBrun	ER188	Ford Cosworth	V8	8	accident / nose mounting	24	12
r	4	J Bailey	Tyrrell	017	Ford Cosworth	V8	0	accident / front suspension	23	12
nq	23	A Campos	Minardi	M188	Ford Cosworth	V8				
nq	21	N Larini	Osella	FA1L	Alfa Romeo	V8t				
nq	29	Y Dalmas	Lola	LC88	Ford Cosworth	V8				
nq	10	B Schneider	Zakspeed	881	Zakspeed	4t				
npq	36	A Caffi	Dallara	188	Ford Cosworth	V8				

Winning speed 182.152 km/h, 113.184 mph
Pole Position speed 193.484 km/h, 120.226 mph (A Senna, 1 min:21.681 sec)
Fastest Lap speed 185.988 km/h, 115.568 mph (A Senna, 1 min:24.973 sec on lap 53)
Lap Leaders A Prost 1-18 (18); A Senna 19-69 (51).

19 Jun 1988	USA: Detroit						(Round 6)		(Race 458)

63 laps x 4.023 km, 2.500 miles = 253.472 km, 157.500 miles

Pos	No	Driver	Car	Model	Engine		Laps	Time/Reason for Retirement	Grid Pos	Row
1	12	A Senna	McLaren	MP4/4	Honda	V6t	63	1h 54m 56.035s	1	1
2	11	A Prost	McLaren	MP4/4	Honda	V6t	63	1h 55m 34.748s	4	2
3	20	T Boutsen	Benetton	B188	Ford Cosworth	V8	62		5	3
4	22	A de Cesaris	Rial	ARC1	Ford Cosworth	V8	62		12	6
5	3	J Palmer	Tyrrell	017	Ford Cosworth	V8	62		17	9
6	23	P Martini	Minardi	M188	Ford Cosworth	V8	62		16	8
7	29	Y Dalmas	Lola	LC88	Ford Cosworth	V8	61		24	12
8	36	A Caffi	Dallara	188	Ford Cosworth	V8	61		21	11
9r	4	J Bailey	Tyrrell	017	Ford Cosworth	V8	59	accident	22	11
r	24	L Sala	Minardi	M188	Ford Cosworth	V8	54	gearbox	25	13
r	30	P Alliot	Lola	LC88	Ford Cosworth	V8	46	gearbox	14	7
r	33	S Modena	EuroBrun	ER188	Ford Cosworth	V8	46	accident	19	10
r	27	M Alboreto	Ferrari	F1-87/88C	Ferrari	V6t	45	spin	3	2
r	25	R Arnoux	Ligier	JS31	Judd	V8	45	engine	20	10
r	15	M Gugelmin	March	881	Judd	V8	34	engine	13	7
r	6	R Patrese	Williams	FW12	Judd	V8	26	electrics	10	5
r	1	N Piquet	Lotus	100T	Honda	V6t	26	accident	8	4
r	32	O Larrauri	EuroBrun	ER188	Ford Cosworth	V8	26	gearbox	23	12
r	17	D Warwick	Arrows	A10B	Megatron	4t	24	accident	9	5
r	5	N Mansell	Williams	FW12	Judd	V8	18	electrics	6	3
r	14	P Streiff	AGS	JH23	Ford Cosworth	V8	15	accident	11	6
r	19	A Nannini	Benetton	B188	Ford Cosworth	V8	14	accident / front suspension	7	4
r	18	E Cheever	Arrows	A10B	Megatron	4t	14	electronics	15	8
r	21	N Larini	Osella	FA1L	Alfa Romeo	V8t	7	engine	26	13
r	28	G Berger	Ferrari	F1-87/88C	Ferrari	V6t	6	accident / rear tyre	2	1
r	26	S Johansson	Ligier	JS31	Judd	V8	2	engine overheating	18	9
ns	16	I Capelli	March	881	Judd	V8		accident / injury		
nq	2	S Nakajima	Lotus	100T	Honda	V6t				
nq	10	B Schneider	Zakspeed	881	Zakspeed	4t				
nq	9	P Ghinzani	Zakspeed	881	Zakspeed	4t				
npq	31	G Tarquini	Coloni	FC188	Ford Cosworth	V8				

Winning speed 132.322 km/h, 82.221 mph
Pole Position speed 143.969 km/h, 89.458 mph (A Senna, 1 min:40.606 sec)
Fastest Lap speed 138.160 km/h, 85.848 mph (A Prost, 1 min:44.836 sec on lap 4)
Lap Leaders A Senna 1-63 (63).

3 Jul 1988	FRANCE: Paul Ricard						(Round 7)		(Race 459)

80 laps x 3.813 km, 2.369 miles = 305.040 km, 189.543 miles

Pos	No	Driver	Car	Model	Engine		Laps	Time/Reason for Retirement	Grid Pos	Row
1	11	A Prost	McLaren	MP4/4	Honda	V6t	80	1h 37m 37.328s	1	1
2	12	A Senna	McLaren	MP4/4	Honda	V6t	80	1h 38m 09.080s	2	1
3	27	M Alboreto	Ferrari	F1-87/88C	Ferrari	V6t	80	1h 38m 43.833s	4	2
4	28	G Berger	Ferrari	F1-87/88C	Ferrari	V6t	79		3	2
5	1	N Piquet	Lotus	100T	Honda	V6t	79		7	4
6	19	A Nannini	Benetton	B188	Ford Cosworth	V8	79		6	3
7	2	S Nakajima	Lotus	100T	Honda	V6t	79		8	4
8	15	M Gugelmin	March	881	Judd	V8	79		16	8
9	16	I Capelli	March	881	Judd	V8	79		10	5
10	22	A de Cesaris	Rial	ARC1	Ford Cosworth	V8	78		12	6
11	18	E Cheever	Arrows	A10B	Megatron	4t	78		13	7
12	36	A Caffi	Dallara	188	Ford Cosworth	V8	78		14	7
13	29	Y Dalmas	Lola	LC88	Ford Cosworth	V8	78		19	10
14	33	S Modena	EuroBrun	ER188	Ford Cosworth	V8	77		20	10
15	23	P Martini	Minardi	M188	Ford Cosworth	V8	77		22	11
nc	24	L Sala	Minardi	M188	Ford Cosworth	V8	70		25	13
r	32	O Larrauri	EuroBrun	ER188	Ford Cosworth	V8	64	clutch	26	13
r	21	N Larini	Osella	FA1L	Alfa Romeo	V8t	56	driveshaft	24	12
r	10	B Schneider	Zakspeed	881	Zakspeed	4t	55	gearbox	21	11
r	5	N Mansell	Williams	FW12	Judd	V8	48	rear suspension	9	5
r	30	P Alliot	Lola	LC88	Ford Cosworth	V8	46	electrics	18	9
r	3	J Palmer	Tyrrell	017	Ford Cosworth	V8	40	engine	23	12
r	6	R Patrese	Williams	FW12	Judd	V8	35	brakes	15	8
r	20	T Boutsen	Benetton	B188	Ford Cosworth	V8	28	electrics	5	3
r	14	P Streiff	AGS	JH23	Ford Cosworth	V8	20	fuel leak	17	9
r	17	D Warwick	Arrows	A10B	Megatron	4t	11	spin	11	6
exc	9	P Ghinzani	Zakspeed	881	Zakspeed	4t		missed weight check		
nq	25	R Arnoux	Ligier	JS31	Judd	V8				
nq	4	J Bailey	Tyrrell	017	Ford Cosworth	V8				
nq	26	S Johansson	Ligier	JS31	Judd	V8				
npq	31	G Tarquini	Coloni	FC188	Ford Cosworth	V8				

Winning speed 187.482 km/h, 116.496 mph
Pole Position speed 203.092 km/h, 126.196 mph (A Prost, 1 min: 7.589 sec)
Fastest Lap speed 191.349 km/h, 118.899 mph (A Prost, 1 min:11.737 sec on lap 45)
Lap Leaders A Prost 1-36,61-80 (56); A Senna 37-60 (24).

65 laps x 4.778 km, 2.969 miles = 310.579 km, 192.985 miles

Pos	No	Driver	Car	Model	Engine		Laps	Time/Reason for Retirement	Grid Pos	Row
1	12	A Senna	McLaren	MP4/4	Honda	V6t	65	1h 33m 16.367s	3	2
2	5	N Mansell	Williams	FW12	Judd	V8	65	1h 33m 39.711s	11	6
3	19	A Nannini	Benetton	B188	Ford Cosworth	V8	65	1h 34m 07.581s	8	4
4	15	M Gugelmin	March	881	Judd	V8	65	1h 34m 27.745s	5	3
5	1	N Piquet	Lotus	100T	Honda	V6t	65	1h 34m 37.202s	7	4
6	17	D Warwick	Arrows	A10B	Megatron	4t	64		9	5
7	18	E Cheever	Arrows	A10B	Megatron	4t	64		13	7
8	6	R Patrese	Williams	FW12	Judd	V8	64		15	8
9	28	G Berger	Ferrari	F1-87/88C	Ferrari	V6t	64		1	1
10	2	S Nakajima	Lotus	100T	Honda	V6t	64		10	5
11	36	A Caffi	Dallara	188	Ford Cosworth	V8	64		21	11
12	33	S Modena	EuroBrun	ER188	Ford Cosworth	V8	64		20	10
13	29	Y Dalmas	Lola	LC88	Ford Cosworth	V8	63		23	12
14	30	P Alliot	Lola	LC88	Ford Cosworth	V8	63		22	11
15	23	P Martini	Minardi	M188	Ford Cosworth	V8	63		19	10
16	4	J Bailey	Tyrrell	017	Ford Cosworth	V8	63		24	12
17r	27	M Alboreto	Ferrari	F1-87/88C	Ferrari	V6t	62	out of fuel	2	1
18	25	R Arnoux	Ligier	JS31	Judd	V8	62		25	13
19r	21	N Larini	Osella	FA1L	Alfa Romeo	V8t	60	out of fuel	26	13
r	20	T Boutsen	Benetton	B188	Ford Cosworth	V8	38	cv joint	12	6
r	16	I Capelli	March	881	Judd	V8	34	alternator	6	3
r	11	A Prost	McLaren	MP4/4	Honda	V6t	24	handling	4	2
r	3	J Palmer	Tyrrell	017	Ford Cosworth	V8	14	transmission	17	9
r	22	A de Cesaris	Rial	ARC1	Ford Cosworth	V8	9	clutch	14	7
r	14	P Streiff	AGS	JH23	Ford Cosworth	V8	8	accident / rear wing	16	8
r	24	L Sala	Minardi	M188	Ford Cosworth	V8	0	accident	18	9
nq	32	O Larrauri	EuroBrun	ER188	Ford Cosworth	V8				
nq	9	P Ghinzani	Zakspeed	881	Zakspeed	4t				
nq	26	S Johansson	Ligier	JS31	Judd	V8				
nq	10	B Schneider	Zakspeed	881	Zakspeed	4t				
npq	31	G Tarquini	Coloni	FC188	Ford Cosworth	V8				

Winning speed 199.788 km/h, 124.142 mph
Pole Position speed 245.267 km/h, 152.402 mph (G Berger, 1 min:10.133 sec)
Fastest Lap speed 206.479 km/h, 128.300 mph (N Mansell, 1 min:23.308 sec on lap 48)
Lap Leaders G Berger 1-13 (13); A Senna 14-65 (52).

44 laps x 6.797 km, 4.223 miles = 299.068 km, 185.832 miles

Pos	No	Driver	Car	Model	Engine		Laps	Time/Reason for Retirement	Grid Pos	Row
1	12	A Senna	McLaren	MP4/4	Honda	V6t	44	1h 32m 54.188s	1	1
2	11	A Prost	McLaren	MP4/4	Honda	V6t	44	1h 33m 07.797s	2	1
3	28	G Berger	Ferrari	F1-87/88C	Ferrari	V6t	44	1h 33m 46.283s	3	2
4	27	M Alboreto	Ferrari	F1-87/88C	Ferrari	V6t	44	1h 34m 35.100s	4	2
5	16	I Capelli	March	881	Judd	V8	44	1h 34m 43.794s	7	4
6	20	T Boutsen	Benetton	B188	Ford Cosworth	V8	43		9	5
7	17	D Warwick	Arrows	A10B	Megatron	4t	43		12	6
8	15	M Gugelmin	March	881	Judd	V8	43		10	5
9	2	S Nakajima	Lotus	100T	Honda	V6t	43		8	4
10	18	E Cheever	Arrows	A10B	Megatron	4t	43		15	8
11	3	J Palmer	Tyrrell	017	Ford Cosworth	V8	43		24	12
12	10	B Schneider	Zakspeed	881	Zakspeed	4t	43		22	11
13	22	A de Cesaris	Rial	ARC1	Ford Cosworth	V8	42		14	7
14	9	P Ghinzani	Zakspeed	881	Zakspeed	4t	42		23	12
15	36	A Caffi	Dallara	188	Ford Cosworth	V8	42		19	10
16	32	O Larrauri	EuroBrun	ER188	Ford Cosworth	V8	42		26	13
17	25	R Arnoux	Ligier	JS31	Judd	V8	41		17	9
18	19	A Nannini	Benetton	B188	Ford Cosworth	V8	40		6	3
19r	29	Y Dalmas	Lola	LC88	Ford Cosworth	V8	39	clutch	21	11
r	14	P Streiff	AGS	JH23	Ford Cosworth	V8	38	throttle linkage	16	8
r	6	R Patrese	Williams	FW12	Judd	V8	34	accident	13	7
r	21	N Larini	Osella	FA1L	Alfa Romeo	V8t	27	heat exchange pipe	18	9
r	5	N Mansell	Williams	FW12	Judd	V8	16	accident	11	6
r	33	S Modena	EuroBrun	ER188	Ford Cosworth	V8	15	electrics	25	13
r	30	P Alliot	Lola	LC88	Ford Cosworth	V8	8	accident	20	10
r	1	N Piquet	Lotus	100T	Honda	V6t	1	accident	5	3
nq	24	L Sala	Minardi	M188	Ford Cosworth	V8				
nq	26	S Johansson	Ligier	JS31	Judd	V8				
nq	4	J Bailey	Tyrrell	017	Ford Cosworth	V8				
nq	23	P Martini	Minardi	M188	Ford Cosworth	V8				
npq	31	G Tarquini	Coloni	FC188	Ford Cosworth	V8				

Winning speed 193.148 km/h, 120.017 mph
Pole Position speed 233.940 km/h, 145.364 mph (A Senna, 1 min:44.596 sec)
Fastest Lap speed 198.885 km/h, 123.581 mph (A Nannini, 2 min: 3.032 sec on lap 40)
Lap Leaders A Senna 1-44 (44).

7 Aug 1988 HUNGARY: Hungaroring (Round 10) (Race 462)

76 laps x 4.014 km, 2.494 miles = 305.064 km, 189.558 miles

Pos	No	Driver	Car	Model	Engine		Laps	Time/Reason for Retirement	Grid Pos	Row
1	12	A Senna	McLaren	MP4/4	Honda	V6t	76	1h 57m 47.081s	1	1
2	11	A Prost	McLaren	MP4/4	Honda	V6t	76	1h 57m 47.610s	7	4
3	20	T Boutsen	Benetton	B188	Ford Cosworth	V8	76	1h 58m 18.491s	3	2
4	28	G Berger	Ferrari	F1-87/88C	Ferrari	V6t	76	1h 59m 15.751s	9	5
5	15	M Gugelmin	March	881	Judd	V8	75		8	4
6	6	R Patrese	Williams	FW12	Judd	V8	75		6	3
7	2	S Nakajima	Lotus	100T	Honda	V6t	73		19	10
8	1	N Piquet	Lotus	100T	Honda	V6t	73		13	7
9	29	Y Dalmas	Lola	LC88	Ford Cosworth	V8	73		17	9
10	24	L Sala	Minardi	M188	Ford Cosworth	V8	72		11	6
11	33	S Modena	EuroBrun	ER188	Ford Cosworth	V8	72		26	13
12	30	P Alliot	Lola	LC88	Ford Cosworth	V8	72		20	10
13	31	G Tarquini	Coloni	FC188	Ford Cosworth	V8	71		22	11
r	17	D Warwick	Arrows	A10B	Megatron	4t	65	brakes	12	6
r	5	N Mansell	Williams	FW12	Judd	V8	60	driver exhausted	2	1
r	18	E Cheever	Arrows	A10B	Megatron	4t	55	brakes	14	7
r	27	M Alboreto	Ferrari	F1-87/88C	Ferrari	V6t	40	electronics	15	8
r	25	R Arnoux	Ligier	JS31	Judd	V8	32	engine	25	13
r	22	A de Cesaris	Rial	ARC1	Ford Cosworth	V8	28	cv joint	18	9
r	19	A Nannini	Benetton	B188	Ford Cosworth	V8	24	water pipe	5	3
r	36	A Caffi	Dallara	188	Ford Cosworth	V8	22	engine	10	5
r	26	S Johansson	Ligier	JS31	Judd	V8	19	throttle jammed	24	12
r	23	P Martini	Minardi	M188	Ford Cosworth	V8	8	accident	16	8
r	14	P Streiff	AGS	JH23	Ford Cosworth	V8	8	accident / front suspension	23	12
r	16	I Capelli	March	881	Judd	V8	5	misfire	4	2
r	3	J Palmer	Tyrrell	017	Ford Cosworth	V8	3	engine	21	11
nq	32	O Larrauri	EuroBrun	ER188	Ford Cosworth	V8				
nq	10	B Schneider	Zakspeed	881	Zakspeed	4t				
nq	4	J Bailey	Tyrrell	017	Ford Cosworth	V8				
nq	9	P Ghinzani	Zakspeed	881	Zakspeed	4t				
npq	21	N Larini	Osella	FA1L	Alfa Romeo	V8t				

Winning speed 155.401 km/h, 96.562 mph
Pole Position speed 164.893 km/h, 102.460 mph (A Senna, 1 min:27.635 sec)
Fastest Lap speed 159.428 km/h, 99.064 mph (A Prost, 1 min:30.639 sec on lap 51)
Lap Leaders A Senna 1-76 (76).

28 Aug 1988 BELGIUM: Spa-Francorchamps (Round 11) (Race 463)

43 laps x 6.940 km, 4.312 miles = 298.420 km, 185.430 miles

Pos	No	Driver	Car	Model	Engine		Laps	Time/Reason for Retirement	Grid Pos	Row
1	12	A Senna	McLaren	MP4/4	Honda	V6t	43	1h 28m 00.549s	1	1
2	11	A Prost	McLaren	MP4/4	Honda	V6t	43	1h 28m 31.019s	2	1
dq	20	T Boutsen	Benetton	B188	Ford Cosworth	V8	43	fuel irregularities	6	3
dq	19	A Nannini	Benetton	B188	Ford Cosworth	V8	43	fuel irregularities	7	4
3	16	I Capelli	March	881	Judd	V8	43	1h 29m 16.317s	14	7
4	1	N Piquet	Lotus	100T	Honda	V6t	43	1h 29m 24.177s	9	5
5	17	D Warwick	Arrows	A10B	Megatron	4t	43	1h 29m 25.904s	10	5
6	18	E Cheever	Arrows	A10B	Megatron	4t	42		11	6
7	5	M Brundle	Williams	FW12	Judd	V8	42		12	6
8	36	A Caffi	Dallara	188	Ford Cosworth	V8	42		15	8
9	30	P Alliot	Lola	LC88	Ford Cosworth	V8	42		16	8
10	14	P Streiff	AGS	JH23	Ford Cosworth	V8	42		18	9
11r	26	S Johansson	Ligier	JS31	Judd	V8	39	crown wheel & pinion	20	10
12r	3	J Palmer	Tyrrell	017	Ford Cosworth	V8	39	throttle linkage	21	11
13r	10	B Schneider	Zakspeed	881	Zakspeed	4t	38	gearbox	25	13
nc	31	G Tarquini	Coloni	FC188	Ford Cosworth	V8	36		22	11
r	27	M Alboreto	Ferrari	F1-87/88C	Ferrari	V6t	35	engine	4	2
r	6	R Patrese	Williams	FW12	Judd	V8	30	engine	5	3
r	15	M Gugelmin	March	881	Judd	V8	29	clutch / accident	13	7
r	9	P Ghinzani	Zakspeed	881	Zakspeed	4t	25	oil leak	24	12
r	2	S Nakajima	Lotus	100T	Honda	V6t	22	engine	8	4
r	21	N Larini	Osella	FA1L	Alfa Romeo	V8t	14	fuel pump	26	13
r	28	G Berger	Ferrari	F1-87/88C	Ferrari	V6t	11	electronics	3	2
r	29	Y Dalmas	Lola	LC88	Ford Cosworth	V8	9	engine	23	12
r	22	A de Cesaris	Rial	ARC1	Ford Cosworth	V8	2	accident	19	10
r	25	R Arnoux	Ligier	JS31	Judd	V8	2	accident	17	9
nq	24	L Sala	Minardi	M188	Ford Cosworth	V8				
nq	23	P Martini	Minardi	M188	Ford Cosworth	V8				
nq	33	S Modena	EuroBrun	ER188	Ford Cosworth	V8				
nq	4	J Bailey	Tyrrell	017	Ford Cosworth	V8				
npq	32	O Larrauri	EuroBrun	ER188	Ford Cosworth	V8				

Winning speed 203.447 km/h, 126.416 mph
Pole Position speed 219.701 km/h, 136.516 mph (A Senna, 1 min:53.718 sec)
Fastest Lap speed 206.869 km/h, 128.543 mph (G Berger, 2 min: 0.772 sec on lap 10)
Lap Leaders A Senna 1-43 (43).

T Boutsen finished 3rd in 1h 29m 00.230s and A Nannini finished 4th in 1h 29m 09.143s but both were disqualified after analysis of fuel later in the year.

Races

11 Sep 1988   ITALY: Monza   (Round 12)   (Race 464)

51 laps x 5.800 km, 3.604 miles = 295.800 km, 183.802 miles

Pos	No	Driver	Car	Model	Engine		Laps	Time/Reason for Retirement	Grid Pos	Row
1	28	G Berger	Ferrari	F1-87/88C	Ferrari	V6t	51	1h 17m 39.744s	3	2
2	27	M Alboreto	Ferrari	F1-87/88C	Ferrari	V6t	51	1h 17m 40.246s	4	2
3	18	E Cheever	Arrows	A10B	Megatron	4t	51	1h 18m 15.276s	5	3
4	17	D Warwick	Arrows	A10B	Megatron	4t	51	1h 18m 15.858s	6	3
5	16	I Capelli	March	881	Judd	V8	51	1h 18m 32.266s	11	6
6	20	T Boutsen	Benetton	B188	Ford Cosworth	V8	51	1h 18m 39.622s	8	4
7	6	R Patrese	Williams	FW12	Judd	V8	51	1h 18m 54.487s	10	5
8	15	M Gugelmin	March	881	Judd	V8	51	1h 19m 12.310s	13	7
9	19	A Nannini	Benetton	B188	Ford Cosworth	V8	50		9	5
10r	12	A Senna	McLaren	MP4/4	Honda	V6t	49	accident	1	1
11	5	J-L Schlesser	Williams	FW12	Judd	V8	49		22	11
12	4	J Bailey	Tyrrell	017	Ford Cosworth	V8	49		26	13
13	25	R Arnoux	Ligier	JS31	Judd	V8	49		24	12
r	11	A Prost	McLaren	MP4/4	Honda	V6t	34	engine	2	1
r	30	P Alliot	Lola	LC88	Ford Cosworth	V8	33	engine	20	10
r	14	P Streiff	AGS	JH23	Ford Cosworth	V8	31	gear linkage	23	12
r	10	B Schneider	Zakspeed	881	Zakspeed	4t	28	engine	15	8
r	22	A de Cesaris	Rial	ARC1	Ford Cosworth	V8	27	accident / front suspension	18	9
r	9	P Ghinzani	Zakspeed	881	Zakspeed	4t	25	engine	16	8
r	36	A Caffi	Dallara	188	Ford Cosworth	V8	24	electrics	21	11
r	29	Y Dalmas	Lola	LC88	Ford Cosworth	V8	17	spin / radiator	25	13
r	23	P Martini	Minardi	M188	Ford Cosworth	V8	15	engine	14	7
r	2	S Nakajima	Lotus	100T	Honda	V6t	14	engine	12	6
r	24	L Sala	Minardi	M188	Ford Cosworth	V8	12	gearbox	19	10
r	1	N Piquet	Lotus	100T	Honda	V6t	11	clutch / spin	7	4
r	21	N Larini	Osella	FA1L	Alfa Romeo	V8t	2	engine	17	9
nq	3	J Palmer	Tyrrell	017	Ford Cosworth	V8				
nq	26	S Johansson	Ligier	JS31	Judd	V8				
nq	31	G Tarquini	Coloni	FC188B	Ford Cosworth	V8				
nq	33	S Modena	EuroBrun	ER188	Ford Cosworth	V8				
npq	32	O Larrauri	EuroBrun	ER188	Ford Cosworth	V8				

Winning speed 228.528 km/h, 142.000 mph
Pole Position speed 242.864 km/h, 150.909 mph (A Senna, 1 min:25.974 sec)
Fastest Lap speed 234.422 km/h, 145.663 mph (M Alboreto, 1 min:29.070 sec on lap 44)
Lap Leaders A Senna 1-49 (49); G Berger 50-51 (2).

25 Sep 1988   PORTUGAL: Estoril   (Round 13)   (Race 465)

70 laps x 4.350 km, 2.703 miles = 304.500 km, 189.208 miles

Pos	No	Driver	Car	Model	Engine		Laps	Time/Reason for Retirement	Grid Pos	Row
1	11	A Prost	McLaren	MP4/4	Honda	V6t	70	1h 37m 40.958s	1	1
2	16	I Capelli	March	881	Judd	V8	70	1h 37m 50.511s	3	2
3	20	T Boutsen	Benetton	B188	Ford Cosworth	V8	70	1h 38m 25.577s	13	7
4	17	D Warwick	Arrows	A10B	Megatron	4t	70	1h 38m 48.377s	10	5
5	27	M Alboreto	Ferrari	F1-87/88C	Ferrari	V6t	70	1h 38m 52.842s	7	4
6	12	A Senna	McLaren	MP4/4	Honda	V6t	70	1h 38m 59.227s	2	1
7	36	A Caffi	Dallara	188	Ford Cosworth	V8	69		17	9
8	24	L Sala	Minardi	M188	Ford Cosworth	V8	68		19	10
9	14	P Streiff	AGS	JH23	Ford Cosworth	V8	68		21	11
10	25	R Arnoux	Ligier	JS31	Judd	V8	68		23	12
11	31	G Tarquini	Coloni	FC188B	Ford Cosworth	V8	65		26	13
12	21	N Larini	Osella	FA1L	Alfa Romeo	V8t	63		25	13
r	15	M Gugelmin	March	881	Judd	V8	59	engine	5	3
r	5	N Mansell	Williams	FW12	Judd	V8	54	accident	6	3
r	3	J Palmer	Tyrrell	017	Ford Cosworth	V8	53	engine overheating	22	11
r	19	A Nannini	Benetton	B188	Ford Cosworth	V8	52	vibration / driver exhausted	9	5
r	28	G Berger	Ferrari	F1-87/88C	Ferrari	V6t	35	fire extinguisher / accident	4	2
r	1	N Piquet	Lotus	100T	Honda	V6t	34	clutch	8	4
r	6	R Patrese	Williams	FW12	Judd	V8	29	radiator	11	6
r	23	P Martini	Minardi	M188	Ford Cosworth	V8	27	engine	14	7
r	29	Y Dalmas	Lola	LC88	Ford Cosworth	V8	20	alternator belt	15	8
r	2	S Nakajima	Lotus	100T	Honda	V6t	16	accident	16	8
r	22	A de Cesaris	Rial	ARC1	Ford Cosworth	V8	11	driveshaft	12	6
r	18	E Cheever	Arrows	A10B	Megatron	4t	10	turbo	18	9
r	30	P Alliot	Lola	LC88	Ford Cosworth	V8	7	engine	20	10
r	26	S Johansson	Ligier	JS31	Judd	V8	4	engine	24	12
nq	4	J Bailey	Tyrrell	017	Ford Cosworth	V8				
nq	9	P Ghinzani	Zakspeed	881	Zakspeed	4t				
nq	33	S Modena	EuroBrun	ER188	Ford Cosworth	V8				
nq	10	B Schneider	Zakspeed	881	Zakspeed	4t				
npq	32	O Larrauri	EuroBrun	ER188	Ford Cosworth	V8				

Winning speed 187.034 km/h, 116.218 mph
Pole Position speed 202.297 km/h, 125.701 mph (A Prost, 1 min:17.411 sec)
Fastest Lap speed 191.066 km/h, 118.723 mph (G Berger, 1 min:21.961 sec on lap 31)
Lap Leaders A Senna 1 (1); A Prost 2-70 (69).

Pos	No	Driver	Car	Model	Engine		Laps	Time/Reason for Retirement	Grid Pos	Row
								2 Oct 1988 **SPAIN: Jerez de la Frontera** (Round 14) (Race 466)		
								72 laps x 4.218 km, 2.621 miles = 303.696 km, 188.708 miles		
1	11	A Prost	McLaren	MP4/4	Honda	V6t	72	1h 48m 43.851s	2	1
2	5	N Mansell	Williams	FW12	Judd	V8	72	1h 49m 10.083s	3	2
3	19	A Nannini	Benetton	B188	Ford Cosworth	V8	72	1h 49m 19.297s	5	3
4	12	A Senna	McLaren	MP4/4	Honda	V6t	72	1h 49m 30.561s	1	1
5	6	R Patrese	Williams	FW12	Judd	V8	72	1h 49m 31.281s	7	4
6	28	G Berger	Ferrari	F1-87/88C	Ferrari	V6t	72	1h 49m 35.664s	8	4
7	15	M Gugelmin	March	881	Judd	V8	72	1h 49m 59.815s	11	6
8	1	N Piquet	Lotus	100T	Honda	V6t	72	1h 50m 01.160s	9	5
9	20	T Boutsen	Benetton	B188	Ford Cosworth	V8	72	1h 50m 01.506s	4	2
10	36	A Caffi	Dallara	188	Ford Cosworth	V8	71		18	9
11	29	Y Dalmas	Lola	LC88	Ford Cosworth	V8	71		16	8
12	24	L Sala	Minardi	M188	Ford Cosworth	V8	70		24	12
13	33	S Modena	EuroBrun	ER188	Ford Cosworth	V8	70		26	13
14	30	P Alliot	Lola	LC88	Ford Cosworth	V8	69		12	6
r	26	S Johansson	Ligier	JS31	Judd	V8	62	rear wheel lost	21	11
r	18	E Cheever	Arrows	A10B	Megatron	4t	60	handling	25	13
r	16	I Capelli	March	881	Judd	V8	45	engine	6	3
r	17	D Warwick	Arrows	A10B	Megatron	4t	41	accident / chassis	17	9
r	22	A de Cesaris	Rial	ARC1	Ford Cosworth	V8	37	engine	23	12
r	14	P Streiff	AGS	JH23	Ford Cosworth	V8	16	engine	13	7
r	27	M Alboreto	Ferrari	F1-87/88C	Ferrari	V6t	15	engine	10	5
r	23	P Martini	Minardi	M188	Ford Cosworth	V8	15	gearbox	20	10
r	2	S Nakajima	Lotus	100T	Honda	V6t	14	spin	15	8
r	21	N Larini	Osella	FA1L	Alfa Romeo	V8t	9	front suspension	14	7
r	3	J Palmer	Tyrrell	017	Ford Cosworth	V8	4	accident / radiator	22	11
r	25	R Arnoux	Ligier	JS31	Judd	V8	0	throttle jammed	19	10
nq	10	B Schneider	Zakspeed	881	Zakspeed	4t				
nq	32	O Larrauri	EuroBrun	ER188	Ford Cosworth	V8				
nq	4	J Bailey	Tyrrell	017	Ford Cosworth	V8				
nq	9	P Ghinzani	Zakspeed	881	Zakspeed	4t				
npq	31	G Tarquini	Coloni	FC188B	Ford Cosworth	V8				

Winning speed 167.586 km/h, 104.133 mph
Pole Position speed 180.627 km/h, 112.237 mph (A Senna, 1 min:24.067 sec)
Fastest Lap speed 172.859 km/h, 107.410 mph (A Prost, 1 min:27.845 sec on lap 60)
Lap Leaders A Prost 1-72 (72).

Pos	No	Driver	Car	Model	Engine		Laps	Time/Reason for Retirement	Grid Pos	Row
								30 Oct 1988 **JAPAN: Suzuka** (Round 15) (Race 467)		
								51 laps x 5.859 km, 3.641 miles = 298.809 km, 185.671 miles		
1	12	A Senna	McLaren	MP4/4	Honda	V6t	51	1h 33m 26.173s	1	1
2	11	A Prost	McLaren	MP4/4	Honda	V6t	51	1h 33m 39.536s	2	1
3	20	T Boutsen	Benetton	B188	Ford Cosworth	V8	51	1h 34m 02.282s	10	5
4	28	G Berger	Ferrari	F1-87/88C	Ferrari	V6t	51	1h 34m 52.887s	3	2
5	19	A Nannini	Benetton	B188	Ford Cosworth	V8	51	1h 34m 56.776s	12	6
6	6	R Patrese	Williams	FW12	Judd	V8	51	1h 35m 03.788s	11	6
7	2	S Nakajima	Lotus	100T	Honda	V6t	50		6	3
8	14	P Streiff	AGS	JH23	Ford Cosworth	V8	50		18	9
9	30	P Alliot	Lola	LC88	Ford Cosworth	V8	50		19	10
10	15	M Gugelmin	March	881	Judd	V8	50		13	7
11	27	M Alboreto	Ferrari	F1-87/88C	Ferrari	V6t	50		9	5
12	3	J Palmer	Tyrrell	017	Ford Cosworth	V8	50		16	8
13	23	P Martini	Minardi	M188	Ford Cosworth	V8	49		17	9
14	4	J Bailey	Tyrrell	017	Ford Cosworth	V8	49		26	13
15	24	L Sala	Minardi	M188	Ford Cosworth	V8	49		22	11
16	29	A Suzuki	Lola	LC88	Ford Cosworth	V8	48		20	10
17	25	R Arnoux	Ligier	JS31	Judd	V8	48		23	12
r	22	A de Cesaris	Rial	ARC1	Ford Cosworth	V8	36	radiator	14	7
r	18	E Cheever	Arrows	A10B	Megatron	4t	35	turbo	15	8
r	21	N Larini	Osella	FA1L	Alfa Romeo	V8t	34	wheel nut / wheel lost	24	12
r	1	N Piquet	Lotus	100T	Honda	V6t	34	driver ill	5	3
r	5	N Mansell	Williams	FW12	Judd	V8	24	accident	8	4
r	36	A Caffi	Dallara	188	Ford Cosworth	V8	22	accident	21	11
r	16	I Capelli	March	881	Judd	V8	19	electrics	4	2
r	17	D Warwick	Arrows	A10B	Megatron	4t	16	spin	7	4
r	10	B Schneider	Zakspeed	881	Zakspeed	4t	14	driver unfit (practice accident)	25	13
nq	26	S Johansson	Ligier	JS31	Judd	V8				
nq	32	O Larrauri	EuroBrun	ER188	Ford Cosworth	V8				
nq	9	P Ghinzani	Zakspeed	881	Zakspeed	4t				
nq	33	S Modena	EuroBrun	ER188	Ford Cosworth	V8				
npq	31	G Tarquini	Coloni	FC188B	Ford Cosworth	V8				

Winning speed 191.880 km/h, 119.229 mph
Pole Position speed 207.087 km/h, 128.678 mph (A Senna, 1 min:41.853 sec)
Fastest Lap speed 198.375 km/h, 123.264 mph (A Senna, 1 min:46.326 sec on lap 33)
Lap Leaders A Prost 1-15,17-27 (26); I Capelli 16 (1); A Senna 28-51 (24).

Races

Pos	No	Driver	Car	Model	Engine		Laps	Time/Reason for Retirement	Grid Pos	Row
1	11	A Prost	McLaren	MP4/4	Honda	V6t	82	1h 53m 14.676s	2	1
2	12	A Senna	McLaren	MP4/4	Honda	V6t	82	1h 53m 51.463s	1	1
3	1	N Piquet	Lotus	100T	Honda	V6t	82	1h 54m 02.222s	5	3
4	6	R Patrese	Williams	FW12	Judd	V8	82	1h 54m 34.764s	6	3
5	20	T Boutsen	Benetton	B188	Ford Cosworth	V8	81		10	5
6	16	I Capelli	March	881	Judd	V8	81		9	5
7	23	P Martini	Minardi	M188	Ford Cosworth	V8	80		14	7
8r	22	A de Cesaris	Rial	ARC1	Ford Cosworth	V8	77	out of fuel	15	8
9r	26	S Johansson	Ligier	JS31	Judd	V8	76	out of fuel	22	11
10r	30	P Alliot	Lola	LC88	Ford Cosworth	V8	75	out of fuel	24	12
11r	14	P Streiff	AGS	JH23	Ford Cosworth	V8	73	electrics	16	8
r	9	P Ghinzani	Zakspeed	881	Zakspeed	4t	69	fuel pump	26	13
r	5	N Mansell	Williams	FW12	Judd	V8	65	brakes / accident	3	2
r	19	A Nannini	Benetton	B188	Ford Cosworth	V8	63	handling / spin	8	4
r	33	S Modena	EuroBrun	ER188	Ford Cosworth	V8	63	half shaft	20	10
r	17	D Warwick	Arrows	A10B	Megatron	4t	52	engine	7	4
r	18	E Cheever	Arrows	A10B	Megatron	4t	51	engine	18	9
r	15	M Gugelmin	March	881	Judd	V8	46	accident	19	10
r	2	S Nakajima	Lotus	100T	Honda	V6t	45	accident	13	7
r	24	L Sala	Minardi	M188	Ford Cosworth	V8	41	engine	21	11
r	36	A Caffi	Dallara	188	Ford Cosworth	V8	32	clutch	11	6
r	28	G Berger	Ferrari	F1-87/88C	Ferrari	V6t	25	accident	4	2
r	25	R Arnoux	Ligier	JS31	Judd	V8	24	accident	23	12
r	3	J Palmer	Tyrrell	017	Ford Cosworth	V8	16	crown wheel & pinion	17	9
r	32	O Larrauri	EuroBrun	ER188	Ford Cosworth	V8	12	half shaft / accident	25	13
r	27	M Alboreto	Ferrari	F1-87/88C	Ferrari	V6t	0	accident	12	6
nq	31	G Tarquini	Coloni	FC188B	Ford Cosworth	V8				
nq	4	J Bailey	Tyrrell	017	Ford Cosworth	V8				
nq	29	P-H Raphanel	Lola	LC88	Ford Cosworth	V8				
nq	10	B Schneider	Zakspeed	881	Zakspeed	4t				
npq	21	N Larini	Osella	FA1L	Alfa Romeo	V8t				

Winning speed 164.225 km/h, 102.045 mph
Pole Position speed 175.027 km/h, 108.757 mph (A Senna, 1 min:17.748 sec)
Fastest Lap speed 167.553 km/h, 104.113 mph (A Prost, 1 min:21.216 sec on lap 59)
Lap Leaders A Prost 1-13,26-82 (70); G Berger 14-25 (12).

Lap Leaders 1988

Pos	Driver	Car-Engine	GPs	laps	km	miles
1	A Senna	McLaren-Honda	12	553	2,671.1	1,659.7
2	A Prost	McLaren-Honda	9	450	1,951.3	1,212.5
3	G Berger	Ferrari	3	27	119.1	74.0
4	I Capelli	March-Judd	1	1	5.9	3.6
			16	**1,031**	**4,747.3**	**2,949.9**

Driver Points 1988

		BR	RSM	MC	MEX	CDN	USA	F	GB	D	H	B	I	P	E	J	AUS	Total	
1	A Senna	-	9	-	6	9	9	6	9	9	9	9	-	(1)	(3)	9	6	90	(4)
2	A Prost	9	6	9	9	6	6	9	-	6	(6)	(6)	-	9	9	(6)	9	87	(18)
3	G Berger	6	2	6	4	-	-	3	-	4	3	-	9	-	1	3	-	41	
4	T Boutsen	-	3	-	-	4	4	-	-	1	4	-	1	4	-	4	2	27	
5	M Alboreto	2	-	4	3	-	-	4	-	3	-	-	6	2	-	-	-	24	
6	N Piquet	4	4	-	-	3	-	2	2	-	-	3	-	-	-	-	4	22	
7	I Capelli	-	-	-	-	2	-	-	-	2	-	4	2	6	-	-	1	17	
	D Warwick	3	-	3	2	-	-	-	1	-	-	2	3	3	-	-	-	17	
9	N Mansell	-	-	-	-	-	-	-	6	-	-	-	-	-	6	-	-	12	
	A Nannini	-	1	-	-	-	-	1	4	-	-	-	-	-	4	2	-	12	
11	R Patrese	-	-	1	-	-	-	-	-	-	1	-	-	-	2	1	3	8	
12	E Cheever	-	-	-	1	-	-	-	-	-	-	1	4	-	-	-	-	6	
13	M Gugelmin	-	-	-	-	-	-	-	3	-	2	-	-	-	-	-	-	5	
	J Palmer	-	-	2	-	1	2	-	-	-	-	-	-	-	-	-	-	5	
15	A de Cesaris	-	-	-	-	3	-	-	-	-	-	-	-	-	-	-	-	3	
16	S Nakajima	1	-	-	-	-	-	-	-	-	-	-	-	-	-	-	-	1	
	P Martini	-	-	-	-	-	1	-	-	-	-	-	-	-	-	-	-	1	

9,6,4,3,2 and 1 point awarded to the first six finishers. Best 11 scores.

Constructor Points 1988

		BR	RSM	MC	MEX	CDN	USA	F	GB	D	H	B	I	P	E	J	AUS	Total
1	McLaren-Honda	9	15	9	15	15	15	15	9	15	15	15	-	10	12	15	15	199
2	Ferrari	8	2	10	7	-	-	7	-	7	3	-	15	2	1	3	-	65
3	Benetton-Ford Cosworth	-	4	-	-	4	4	1	4	1	4	-	1	4	4	6	2	39
4	Arrows-Megatron	3	-	3	3	-	-	-	1	-	-	3	7	3	-	-	-	23
	Lotus-Honda	5	4	-	-	3	-	2	2	-	-	3	-	-	-	-	4	23
6	March-Judd	-	-	-	2	-	-	-	3	2	2	4	2	6	-	-	1	22
7	Williams-Judd	-	-	1	-	-	-	-	6	-	1	-	-	-	8	1	3	20
8	Tyrrell-Ford Cosworth	-	-	2	-	1	2	-	-	-	-	-	-	-	-	-	-	5
9	Rial-Ford Cosworth	-	-	-	-	3	-	-	-	-	-	-	-	-	-	-	-	3
10	Minardi-Ford Cosworth	-	-	-	-	-	1	-	-	-	-	-	-	-	-	-	-	1

9,6,4,3,2 and 1 point awarded to the first six finishers.

1989

Turbo engines were banned, with only 3.5-litre atmospheric engines being permitted. There was a record entry of 20 teams with new engines from Lamborghini and Yamaha as well as a return for Pirelli. Brabham also returned after a year away, now owned by Joachim Luhti. Ferrari produced the revolutionary semi-automatic gearbox, controlled by switches on the steering wheel. The AGS driver Philippe Streiff was paralysed after a pre-season testing crash at Rio.

McLAREN
Honda Marlboro McLaren: Senna, Prost

TYRRELL
Tyrrell Racing Organisation: Palmer, Alboreto, Alesi, Herbert

WILLIAMS
Canon Williams Team: Boutsen, Patrese

BRABHAM
Motor Racing Developments: Brundle, Modena

ARROWS
USF&G Arrows: Warwick, Donnelly, Cheever

LOTUS
Camel Team Lotus: Piquet, Nakajima

MARCH
Leyton House March Racing Team: Gugelmin, Capelli

OSELLA
Osella Squadra Corse: Larini, Ghinzani

BENETTON
Benetton Formula: Nannini, Herbert, Pirro

DALLARA
Scuderia Italia: Caffi, de Cesaris

MINARDI
Lois Minardi Team: Martini, Barilla, Sala

LIGIER
Ligier Loto: Arnoux, Grouillard

FERRARI
Scuderia Ferrari SpA SEFAC: Mansell, Berger

LOLA
Equipe Larrousse: Dalmas, Bernard, Alboreto, Alliot

COLONI
Coloni SpA: Moreno, Raphanel, (Bertaggia)

EUROBRUN
EuroBrun Racing: (Foitek, Larrauri)

ZAKSPEED
West Zakspeed Racing: Schneider, (Suzuki)

ONYX
Moneytron Onyx: Johansson, Gachot, Lehto

RIAL
Rial Racing: Danner, (Foitek, Gachot, Weidler, Raphanel)

AGS
Automobiles Gonfaronaises Sportives: Tarquini, (Winkelhock, Dalmas)

26 Mar 1989		BRAZIL: Rio de Janeiro							(Round 1)	(Race 469)	
		61 laps x 5.031 km, 3.126 miles = 306.891 km, 190.693 miles									
Pos	No	Driver	Car	Model	Engine		Laps	Time/Reason for Retirement		Grid Pos	Row
1	27	N Mansell	Ferrari	640	Ferrari	V12	61	1h 38m 58.744s		6	3
2	2	A Prost	McLaren	MP4/5	Honda	V10	61	1h 39m 06.553s		5	3
3	15	M Gugelmin	March	881	Judd	V8	61	1h 39m 08.114s		12	6
4	20	J Herbert	Benetton	B188	Ford Cosworth	V8	61	1h 39m 09.237s		10	5
5	9	D Warwick	Arrows	A11	Ford Cosworth	V8	61	1h 39m 16.610s		8	4
6	19	A Nannini	Benetton	B188	Ford Cosworth	V8	61	1h 39m 16.985s		11	6
7	3	J Palmer	Tyrrell	017B	Ford Cosworth	V8	60			18	9
8	12	S Nakajima	Lotus	101	Judd	V8	60			21	11
9	26	O Grouillard	Ligier	JS33	Ford Cosworth	V8	60			22	11
10	4	M Alboreto	Tyrrell	017B	Ford Cosworth	V8	59			20	10
11	1	A Senna	McLaren	MP4/5	Honda	V10	59			1	1
12	30	P Alliot	Lola	LC88B	Lamborghini	V12	58			26	13
13r	22	A de Cesaris	Dallara	189	Ford Cosworth	V8	57	engine		15	8
14r	38	C Danner	Rial	ARC2	Ford Cosworth	V8	56	gearbox		17	9
r	6	R Patrese	Williams	FW12C	Renault	V10	51	camshaft pulley		2	1
r	10	E Cheever	Arrows	A11	Ford Cosworth	V8	37	accident		24	12
r	34	B Schneider	Zakspeed	891	Yamaha	V8	36	front suspension / accident		25	13
r	7	M Brundle	Brabham	BT58	Judd	V8	27	wiring loom		13	7
r	16	I Capelli	March	881	Judd	V8	22	rear suspension		7	4
r	11	N Piquet	Lotus	101	Judd	V8	10	fuel pump		9	5
dq	17	N Larini	Osella	FA1M	Ford Cosworth	V8	10	started from wrong grid position		19	10
r	8	S Modena	Brabham	BT58	Judd	V8	9	cv joint		14	7
r	5	T Boutsen	Williams	FW12C	Renault	V10	3	engine		4	2
r	23	P Martini	Minardi	M188B	Ford Cosworth	V8	2	engine mounting		16	8
r	24	L Sala	Minardi	M188B	Ford Cosworth	V8	0	accident		23	12
r	28	G Berger	Ferrari	640	Ferrari	V12	0	accident		3	2
nq	29	Y Dalmas	Lola	LC88B	Lamborghini	V12					
nq	25	R Arnoux	Ligier	JS33	Ford Cosworth	V8					
nq	33	G Foitek	EuroBrun	ER188B	Judd	V8					
nq	31	R Moreno	Coloni	FC188B	Ford Cosworth	V8					
npq	21	A Caffi	Dallara	189	Ford Cosworth	V8					
npq	18	P Ghinzani	Osella	FA1M	Ford Cosworth	V8					
npq	39	V Weidler	Rial	ARC2	Ford Cosworth	V8					
npq	32	P-H Raphanel	Coloni	FC188B	Ford Cosworth	V8					
npq	41	J Winkelhock	AGS	JH23B	Ford Cosworth	V8					
npq	35	A Suzuki	Zakspeed	891	Yamaha	V8					
npq	36	S Johansson	Onyx	ORE-1	Ford Cosworth	V8					
npq	37	B Gachot	Onyx	ORE-1	Ford Cosworth	V8					

Winning speed 186.034 km/h, 115.596 mph
Pole Position speed 212.323 km/h, 131.932 mph (A Senna, 1 min:25.302 sec)
Fastest Lap speed 195.786 km/h, 121.656 mph (R Patrese, 1 min:32.507 sec on lap 47)
Lap Leaders R Patrese 1-15,21-22 (17); N Mansell 16-20,28-44,47-61 (37); A Prost 23-27,45-46 (7).

23 Apr 1989   **SAN MARINO: Imola**   (Round 2)   (Race 470)

58 laps x 5.040 km, 3.132 miles = 292.320 km, 181.639 miles

Pos	No	Driver	Car	Model	Engine		Laps	Time/Reason for Retirement	Grid Pos	Row
1	1	A Senna	McLaren	MP4/5	Honda	V10	58	1h 26m 51.245s	1	1
2	2	A Prost	McLaren	MP4/5	Honda	V10	58	1h 27m 31.470s	2	1
3	19	A Nannini	Benetton	B188	Ford Cosworth	V8	57		7	4
4	5	T Boutsen	Williams	FW12C	Renault	V10	57		6	3
5	9	D Warwick	Arrows	A11	Ford Cosworth	V8	57		12	6
6	3	J Palmer	Tyrrell	018	Ford Cosworth	V8	57		25	13
7	21	A Caffi	Dallara	189	Ford Cosworth	V8	57		9	5
8	40	G Tarquini	AGS	JH23B	Ford Cosworth	V8	57		18	9
9	10	E Cheever	Arrows	A11	Ford Cosworth	V8	56		21	11
10	22	A de Cesaris	Dallara	189	Ford Cosworth	V8	56		16	8
11	20	J Herbert	Benetton	B188	Ford Cosworth	V8	56		23	12
12r	17	N Larini	Osella	FA1M	Ford Cosworth	V8	52	hub / accident	14	7
r	7	M Brundle	Brabham	BT58	Judd	V8	51	fuel pump	22	11
nc	12	S Nakajima	Lotus	101	Judd	V8	46		24	12
r	24	L Sala	Minardi	M188B	Ford Cosworth	V8	43	accident	15	8
r	15	M Gugelmin	March	881	Judd	V8	39	clutch	19	10
r	11	N Piquet	Lotus	101	Judd	V8	29	engine	8	4
r	27	N Mansell	Ferrari	640	Ferrari	V12	23	gearbox	3	2
r	6	R Patrese	Williams	FW12C	Renault	V10	21	camshaft belt	4	2
r	8	S Modena	Brabham	BT58	Judd	V8	19	accident	17	9
r	23	P Martini	Minardi	M188B	Ford Cosworth	V8	6	gearbox	11	6
dq	26	O Grouillard	Ligier	JS33	Ford Cosworth	V8	4	car worked on between starts	10	5
r	28	G Berger	Ferrari	640	Ferrari	V12	3	accident / fire / injury	5	3
r	16	I Capelli	March	881	Judd	V8	1	accident	13	7
r	30	P Alliot	Lola	LC89	Lamborghini	V12	0	fuel injection	20	10
ns	29	Y Dalmas	Lola	LC89	Lamborghini	V12		stalled on dummy grid	26	13
nq	4	M Alboreto	Tyrrell	018	Ford Cosworth	V8				
nq	25	R Arnoux	Ligier	JS33	Ford Cosworth	V8				
nq	38	C Danner	Rial	ARC2	Ford Cosworth	V8				
nq	31	R Moreno	Coloni	FC188B	Ford Cosworth	V8				
npq	37	B Gachot	Onyx	ORE-1	Ford Cosworth	V8				
npq	33	G Foitek	EuroBrun	ER188B	Judd	V8				
npq	18	P Ghinzani	Osella	FA1M	Ford Cosworth	V8				
npq	36	S Johansson	Onyx	ORE-1	Ford Cosworth	V8				
npq	41	J Winkelhock	AGS	JH23B	Ford Cosworth	V8				
npq	32	P-H Raphanel	Coloni	FC188B	Ford Cosworth	V8				
npq	35	A Suzuki	Zakspeed	891	Yamaha	V8				
npq	34	B Schneider	Zakspeed	891	Yamaha	V8				
npq	39	V Weidler	Rial	ARC2	Ford Cosworth	V8				

Winning speed 201.939 km/h, 125.479 mph
Pole Position speed 210.952 km/h, 131.080 mph (A Senna, 1 min:26.010 sec)
Fastest Lap speed 209.044 km/h, 129.894 mph (A Prost, 1 min:26.795 sec on lap 45)
Lap Leaders A Senna 1-58 (58).

Scheduled for 61 laps, but interrupted after 3 laps, because of an accident.
Restarted for a further 55 laps, with results being on aggregate.

Races

77 laps x 3.328 km, 2.068 miles = 256.256 km, 159.230 miles

Pos	No	Driver	Car	Model	Engine		Laps	Time/Reason for Retirement	Grid Pos	Row
1	1	A Senna	McLaren	MP4/5	Honda	V10	77	1h 53m 33.251s	1	1
2	2	A Prost	McLaren	MP4/5	Honda	V10	77	1h 54m 25.780s	2	1
3	8	S Modena	Brabham	BT58	Judd	V8	76		8	4
4	21	A Caffi	Dallara	189	Ford Cosworth	V8	75		9	5
5	4	M Alboreto	Tyrrell	018	Ford Cosworth	V8	75		12	6
6	7	M Brundle	Brabham	BT58	Judd	V8	75		4	2
7	10	E Cheever	Arrows	A11	Ford Cosworth	V8	75		20	10
8	19	A Nannini	Benetton	B188	Ford Cosworth	V8	74		15	8
9	3	J Palmer	Tyrrell	018	Ford Cosworth	V8	74		23	12
10	5	T Boutsen	Williams	FW12C	Renault	V10	74		3	2
11r	16	I Capelli	March	CG891	Judd	V8	73	electrics / fire	22	11
12	25	R Arnoux	Ligier	JS33	Ford Cosworth	V8	73		21	11
13	22	A de Cesaris	Dallara	189	Ford Cosworth	V8	73		10	5
14	20	J Herbert	Benetton	B188	Ford Cosworth	V8	73		24	12
15	6	R Patrese	Williams	FW12C	Renault	V10	73		7	4
r	24	L Sala	Minardi	M188B	Ford Cosworth	V8	48	engine / fire	26	13
r	40	G Tarquini	AGS	JH23B	Ford Cosworth	V8	46	electrics	13	7
r	31	R Moreno	Coloni	FC188B	Ford Cosworth	V8	44	gearbox pinion	25	13
r	30	P Alliot	Lola	LC89	Lamborghini	V12	38	engine	17	9
r	15	M Gugelmin	March	CG891	Judd	V8	36	engine	14	7
r	11	N Piquet	Lotus	101	Judd	V8	32	accident	19	10
r	27	N Mansell	Ferrari	640	Ferrari	V12	30	gearbox	5	3
r	32	P-H Raphanel	Coloni	FC188B	Ford Cosworth	V8	19	gearbox	18	9
r	26	O Grouillard	Ligier	JS33	Ford Cosworth	V8	4	gearbox	16	8
r	23	P Martini	Minardi	M188B	Ford Cosworth	V8	3	clutch	11	6
r	9	D Warwick	Arrows	A11	Ford Cosworth	V8	2	electrics / fire	6	3
nq	38	C Danner	Rial	ARC2	Ford Cosworth	V8				
nq	29	Y Dalmas	Lola	LC89	Lamborghini	V12				
nq	12	S Nakajima	Lotus	101	Judd	V8				
npq	18	P Ghinzani	Osella	FA1M	Ford Cosworth	V8				
npq	36	S Johansson	Onyx	ORE-1	Ford Cosworth	V8				
npq	17	N Larini	Osella	FA1M	Ford Cosworth	V8				
npq	34	B Schneider	Zakspeed	891	Yamaha	V8				
npq	37	B Gachot	Onyx	ORE-1	Ford Cosworth	V8				
npq	33	G Foitek	EuroBrun	ER188B	Judd	V8				
npq	39	V Weidler	Rial	ARC2	Ford Cosworth	V8				
npq	35	A Suzuki	Zakspeed	891	Yamaha	V8				
npq	41	J Winkelhock	AGS	JH23B	Ford Cosworth	V8				

Winning speed 135.401 km/h, 84.134 mph
Pole Position speed 145.561 km/h, 90.447 mph (A Senna, 1 min:22.308 sec)
Fastest Lap speed 140.125 km/h, 87.069 mph (A Prost, 1 min:25.501 sec on lap 59)
Lap Leaders A Senna 1-77 (77).

69 laps x 4.421 km, 2.747 miles = 305.049 km, 189.549 miles

Pos	No	Driver	Car	Model	Engine		Laps	Time/Reason for Retirement	Grid Pos	Row
1	1	A Senna	McLaren	MP4/5	Honda	V10	69	1h 35m 21.431s	1	1
2	6	R Patrese	Williams	FW12C	Renault	V10	69	1h 35m 36.991s	5	3
3	4	M Alboreto	Tyrrell	018	Ford Cosworth	V8	69	1h 35m 52.685s	7	4
4	19	A Nannini	Benetton	B188	Ford Cosworth	V8	69	1h 36m 06.926s	13	7
5	2	A Prost	McLaren	MP4/5	Honda	V10	69	1h 36m 17.544s	2	1
6	40	G Tarquini	AGS	JH23B	Ford Cosworth	V8	68		17	9
7	10	E Cheever	Arrows	A11	Ford Cosworth	V8	68		24	12
8	26	O Grouillard	Ligier	JS33	Ford Cosworth	V8	68		11	6
9	7	M Brundle	Brabham	BT58	Judd	V8	68		20	10
10	8	S Modena	Brabham	BT58	Judd	V8	68		9	5
11	11	N Piquet	Lotus	101	Judd	V8	68		26	13
12	38	C Danner	Rial	ARC2	Ford Cosworth	V8	67		23	12
13	21	A Caffi	Dallara	189	Ford Cosworth	V8	67		19	10
14	25	R Arnoux	Ligier	JS33	Ford Cosworth	V8	66		25	13
15	20	J Herbert	Benetton	B188	Ford Cosworth	V8	66		18	9
r	23	P Martini	Minardi	M189	Ford Cosworth	V8	53	engine	22	11
r	27	N Mansell	Ferrari	640	Ferrari	V12	43	hydraulics	3	2
r	9	D Warwick	Arrows	A11	Ford Cosworth	V8	35	electrics	10	5
r	12	S Nakajima	Lotus	101	Judd	V8	35	gearbox / spin	15	8
nc	30	P Alliot	Lola	LC89	Lamborghini	V12	28		16	8
r	22	A de Cesaris	Dallara	189	Ford Cosworth	V8	20	fuel pump	12	6
r	28	G Berger	Ferrari	640	Ferrari	V12	16	hydraulics	6	3
r	36	S Johansson	Onyx	ORE-1	Ford Cosworth	V8	16	clutch	21	11
r	5	T Boutsen	Williams	FW12C	Renault	V10	15	electrics	8	4
r	3	J Palmer	Tyrrell	018	Ford Cosworth	V8	9	throttle linkage	14	7
r	16	I Capelli	March	CG891	Judd	V8	1	cv joint	4	2
nq	24	L Sala	Minardi	M189	Ford Cosworth	V8				
nq	15	M Gugelmin	March	CG891	Judd	V8				

Pos	No	Driver	Car	Model	Engine		Laps	Time/Reason for Retirement	Grid Pos	Row
nq	29	Y Dalmas	Lola	LC89	Lamborghini	V12				
nq	31	R Moreno	Coloni	FC188B	Ford Cosworth	V8				
npq	37	B Gachot	Onyx	ORE-1	Ford Cosworth	V8				
npq	33	G Foitek	EuroBrun	ER188B	Judd	V8				
npq	17	N Larini	Osella	FA1M	Ford Cosworth	V8				
npq	39	V Weidler	Rial	ARC2	Ford Cosworth	V8				
npq	34	B Schneider	Zakspeed	891	Yamaha	V8				
npq	35	A Suzuki	Zakspeed	891	Yamaha	V8				
exc	18	P Ghinzani	Osella	FA1M	Ford Cosworth	V8		missed weight check		
npq	41	J Winkelhock	AGS	JH23B	Ford Cosworth	V8				
npq	32	P-H Raphanel	Coloni	FC188B	Ford Cosworth	V8				

Winning speed 191.941 km/h, 119.267 mph
Pole Position speed 204.371 km/h, 126.990 mph (A Senna, 1 min:17.876 sec)
Fastest Lap speed 197.906 km/h, 122.973 mph (N Mansell, 1 min:20.420 sec on lap 41)
Lap Leaders A Senna 1-69 (69).

Interrupted after 2nd lap, because of an accident. Restarted for original distance.

4 Jun 1989		**USA: Phoenix**							(Round 5)	(Race 473)
		75 laps x 3.798 km, 2.360 miles = 284.854 km, 177.000 miles								

Pos	No	Driver	Car	Model	Engine		Laps	Time/Reason for Retirement	Grid Pos	Row
1	2	A Prost	McLaren	MP4/5	Honda	V10	75	2h 01m 33.133s	2	1
2	6	R Patrese	Williams	FW12C	Renault	V10	75	2h 02m 12.829s	14	7
3	10	E Cheever	Arrows	A11	Ford Cosworth	V8	75	2h 02m 16.343s	17	9
4	38	C Danner	Rial	ARC2	Ford Cosworth	V8	74		26	13
5	20	J Herbert	Benetton	B188	Ford Cosworth	V8	74		25	13
6	5	T Boutsen	Williams	FW12C	Renault	V10	74		16	8
7r	40	G Tarquini	AGS	JH23B	Ford Cosworth	V8	73	engine	24	12
8r	22	A de Cesaris	Dallara	189	Ford Cosworth	V8	70	fuel pump	13	7
9r	3	J Palmer	Tyrrell	018	Ford Cosworth	V8	69	fuel injection	21	11
r	28	G Berger	Ferrari	640	Ferrari	V12	61	alternator	8	4
r	21	A Caffi	Dallara	189	Ford Cosworth	V8	52	accident	6	3
r	11	N Piquet	Lotus	101	Judd	V8	52	accident / rear suspension	22	11
r	36	S Johansson	Onyx	ORE-1	Ford Cosworth	V8	50	tyre / suspension	19	10
r	24	L Sala	Minardi	M189	Ford Cosworth	V8	46	engine overheating	20	10
r	1	A Senna	McLaren	MP4/5	Honda	V10	44	electronics	1	1
r	7	M Brundle	Brabham	BT58	Judd	V8	43	brakes	5	3
r	8	S Modena	Brabham	BT58	Judd	V8	37	brakes	7	4
r	27	N Mansell	Ferrari	640	Ferrari	V12	31	gearbox	4	2
r	23	P Martini	Minardi	M189	Ford Cosworth	V8	26	engine overheating	15	8
r	12	S Nakajima	Lotus	101	Judd	V8	24	throttle linkage	23	12
r	16	I Capelli	March	CG891	Judd	V8	22	gearbox	11	6
dq	15	M Gugelmin	March	CG891	Judd	V8	20	brake fluid refilled during race	18	9
r	4	M Alboreto	Tyrrell	018	Ford Cosworth	V8	17	gearbox	9	5
r	19	A Nannini	Benetton	B188	Ford Cosworth	V8	10	driver exhausted	3	2
r	9	D Warwick	Arrows	A11	Ford Cosworth	V8	7	accident	10	5
r	30	P Alliot	Lola	LC89	Lamborghini	V12	3	spin	12	6
nq	26	O Grouillard	Ligier	JS33	Ford Cosworth	V8				
nq	31	R Moreno	Coloni	FC188B	Ford Cosworth	V8				
nq	25	R Arnoux	Ligier	JS33	Ford Cosworth	V8				
nq	29	Y Dalmas	Lola	LC89	Lamborghini	V12				
npq	18	P Ghinzani	Osella	FA1M	Ford Cosworth	V8				
npq	32	P-H Raphanel	Coloni	FC188B	Ford Cosworth	V8				
npq	33	G Foitek	EuroBrun	ER188B	Judd	V8				
npq	17	N Larini	Osella	FA1M	Ford Cosworth	V8				
npq	41	J Winkelhock	AGS	JH23B	Ford Cosworth	V8				
npq	39	V Weidler	Rial	ARC2	Ford Cosworth	V8				
npq	34	B Schneider	Zakspeed	891	Yamaha	V8				
npq	35	A Suzuki	Zakspeed	891	Yamaha	V8				
npq	37	B Gachot	Onyx	ORE-1	Ford Cosworth	V8				

Winning speed 140.608 km/h, 87.370 mph
Pole Position speed 151.740 km/h, 94.287 mph (A Senna, 1 min:30.108 sec)
Fastest Lap speed 145.505 km/h, 90.413 mph (A Senna, 1 min:33.969 sec on lap 38)
Lap Leaders A Senna 1-33 (33); A Prost 34-75 (42).

Scheduled for 81 laps, but stopped at 2 hours.

18 Jun 1989   **CANADA: Montréal**   **(Round 6)**   **(Race 474)**

69 laps x 4.390 km, 2.728 miles = 302.910 km, 188.220 miles

Pos	No	Driver	Car	Model	Engine		Laps	Time/Reason for Retirement	Grid Pos	Row
1	5	T Boutsen	Williams	FW12C	Renault	V10	69	2h 01m 24.073s	6	3
2	6	R Patrese	Williams	FW12C	Renault	V10	69	2h 01m 54.080s	3	2
3	22	A de Cesaris	Dallara	189	Ford Cosworth	V8	69	2h 03m 00.722s	9	5
4	11	N Piquet	Lotus	101	Judd	V8	69	2h 03m 05.557s	19	10
5	25	R Arnoux	Ligier	JS33	Ford Cosworth	V8	68		22	11
6	21	A Caffi	Dallara	189	Ford Cosworth	V8	67		8	4
7r	1	A Senna	McLaren	MP4/5	Honda	V10	66	engine	2	1
8	38	C Danner	Rial	ARC2	Ford Cosworth	V8	66		23	12
r	31	R Moreno	Coloni	FC189	Ford Cosworth	V8	57	gearbox	26	13
r	9	D Warwick	Arrows	A11	Ford Cosworth	V8	40	engine	12	6
r	3	J Palmer	Tyrrell	018	Ford Cosworth	V8	35	accident	14	7
r	17	N Larini	Osella	FA1M	Ford Cosworth	V8	33	electrics	15	8
r	16	I Capelli	March	CG891	Judd	V8	28	accident	21	11
r	30	P Alliot	Lola	LC89	Lamborghini	V12	26	accident	10	5
dq	36	S Johansson	Onyx	ORE-1	Ford Cosworth	V8	13	ignored black flag	18	9
r	24	L Sala	Minardi	M189	Ford Cosworth	V8	11	accident	24	12
r	15	M Gugelmin	March	CG891	Judd	V8	11	electrics	17	9
r	28	G Berger	Ferrari	640	Ferrari	V12	6	alternator belt	4	2
r	40	G Tarquini	AGS	JH23B	Ford Cosworth	V8	6	accident	25	13
r	10	E Cheever	Arrows	A11	Ford Cosworth	V8	3	electrics	16	8
r	2	A Prost	McLaren	MP4/5	Honda	V10	2	front suspension	1	1
r	4	M Alboreto	Tyrrell	018	Ford Cosworth	V8	0	electrics	20	10
r	8	S Modena	Brabham	BT58	Judd	V8	0	accident	7	4
r	23	P Martini	Minardi	M189	Ford Cosworth	V8	0	accident	11	6
dq	27	N Mansell	Ferrari	640	Ferrari	V12	0	started from pits too soon	5	3
dq	19	A Nannini	Benetton	B188	Ford Cosworth	V8	0	started from pits too soon	13	7
nq	12	S Nakajima	Lotus	101	Judd	V8				
nq	29	Y Dalmas	Lola	LC89	Lamborghini	V12				
nq	20	J Herbert	Benetton	B188	Ford Cosworth	V8				
nq	26	O Grouillard	Ligier	JS33	Ford Cosworth	V8				
npq	7	M Brundle	Brabham	BT58	Judd	V8				
npq	37	B Gachot	Onyx	ORE-1	Ford Cosworth	V8				
npq	33	G Foitek	EuroBrun	ER188B	Judd	V8				
npq	18	P Ghinzani	Osella	FA1M	Ford Cosworth	V8				
npq	34	B Schneider	Zakspeed	891	Yamaha	V8				
npq	41	J Winkelhock	AGS	JH23B	Ford Cosworth	V8				
npq	39	V Weidler	Rial	ARC2	Ford Cosworth	V8				
npq	35	A Suzuki	Zakspeed	891	Yamaha	V8				
npq	32	P-H Raphanel	Coloni	FC189	Ford Cosworth	V8				

Winning speed 149.707 km/h, 93.024 mph
Pole Position speed 195.176 km/h, 121.277 mph (A Prost, 1 min:20.973 sec)
Fastest Lap speed 171.923 km/h, 106.828 mph (J Palmer, 1 min:31.925 sec on lap 11)
Lap Leaders A Prost 1 (1); A Senna 2-3,39-66 (30); R Patrese 4-34 (31); D Warwick 35-38 (4); T Boutsen 67-69 (3).

9 Jul 1989   **FRANCE: Paul Ricard**   **(Round 7)**   **(Race 475)**

80 laps x 3.813 km, 2.369 miles = 305.040 km, 189.543 miles

Pos	No	Driver	Car	Model	Engine		Laps	Time/Reason for Retirement	Grid Pos	Row
1	2	A Prost	McLaren	MP4/5	Honda	V10	80	1h 38m 29.411s	1	1
2	27	N Mansell	Ferrari	640	Ferrari	V12	80	1h 39m 13.428s	3	2
3	6	R Patrese	Williams	FW12C	Renault	V10	80	1h 39m 36.332s	8	4
4	4	J Alesi	Tyrrell	018	Ford Cosworth	V8	80	1h 39m 42.643s	16	8
5	36	S Johansson	Onyx	ORE-1	Ford Cosworth	V8	79		13	7
6	26	O Grouillard	Ligier	JS33	Ford Cosworth	V8	79		17	9
7	10	E Cheever	Arrows	A11	Ford Cosworth	V8	79		25	13
8	11	N Piquet	Lotus	101	Judd	V8	78		20	10
9	20	E Pirro	Benetton	B188	Ford Cosworth	V8	78		24	12
10	3	J Palmer	Tyrrell	018	Ford Cosworth	V8	78		9	5
11r	29	É Bernard	Lola	LC89	Lamborghini	V12	77	engine	15	8
12	9	M Donnelly	Arrows	A11	Ford Cosworth	V8	77		14	7
13	37	B Gachot	Onyx	ORE-1	Ford Cosworth	V8	76		11	6
nc	15	M Gugelmin	March	CG891	Judd	V8	71		10	5
r	8	S Modena	Brabham	BT58	Judd	V8	67	engine	22	11
r	5	T Boutsen	Williams	FW12C	Renault	V10	50	gearbox	5	3
r	12	S Nakajima	Lotus	101	Judd	V8	49	electrics	19	10
r	16	I Capelli	March	CG891	Judd	V8	43	engine	12	6
r	19	A Nannini	Benetton	B189	Ford Cosworth	V8	40	rear suspension	4	2
r	23	P Martini	Minardi	M189	Ford Cosworth	V8	31	oil pressure	23	12
r	30	P Alliot	Lola	LC89	Lamborghini	V12	30	engine	7	4
r	40	G Tarquini	AGS	JH23B	Ford Cosworth	V8	30	engine	21	11
r	28	G Berger	Ferrari	640	Ferrari	V12	29	gearbox oil leak	6	3
r	21	A Caffi	Dallara	189	Ford Cosworth	V8	27	accident / clutch master cylinder	26	13
r	25	R Arnoux	Ligier	JS33	Ford Cosworth	V8	14	gearbox	18	9
r	1	A Senna	McLaren	MP4/5	Honda	V10	0	differential	2	1
nq	22	A de Cesaris	Dallara	189	Ford Cosworth	V8				

Pos	No	Driver	Car	Model	Engine		Laps	Time/Reason for Retirement	Grid Pos	Row
nq	24	L Sala	Minardi	M189	Ford Cosworth	V8				
nq	38	C Danner	Rial	ARC2	Ford Cosworth	V8				
nq	31	R Moreno	Coloni	FC189	Ford Cosworth	V8				
npq	17	N Larini	Osella	FA1M	Ford Cosworth	V8				
npq	7	M Brundle	Brabham	BT58	Judd	V8				
npq	39	V Weidler	Rial	ARC2	Ford Cosworth	V8				
npq	34	B Schneider	Zakspeed	891	Yamaha	V8				
npq	18	P Ghinzani	Osella	FA1M	Ford Cosworth	V8				
npq	32	P-H Raphanel	Coloni	FC189	Ford Cosworth	V8				
npq	35	A Suzuki	Zakspeed	891	Yamaha	V8				
npq	33	G Foitek	EuroBrun	ER188B	Judd	V8				
npq	41	J Winkelhock	AGS	JH23B	Ford Cosworth	V8				

Winning speed 185.830 km/h, 115.469 mph
Pole Position speed 204.259 km/h, 126.920 mph (A Prost, 1 min: 7.203 sec)
Fastest Lap speed 190.412 km/h, 118.317 mph (M Gugelmin, 1 min:12.090 sec on lap 29)
Lap Leaders A Prost 1-80 (80).

Interrupted after first lap accident. Restarted for original distance.

16 Jul 1989		**BRITAIN: Silverstone**							**(Round 8)**	**(Race 476)**

64 laps x 4.780 km, 2.970 miles = 305.904 km, 190.080 miles

Pos	No	Driver	Car	Model	Engine		Laps	Time/Reason for Retirement	Grid Pos	Row
1	2	A Prost	McLaren	MP4/5	Honda	V10	64	1h 19m 22.131s	2	1
2	27	N Mansell	Ferrari	640	Ferrari	V12	64	1h 19m 41.500s	3	2
3	19	A Nannini	Benetton	B189	Ford Cosworth	V8	64	1h 20m 10.150s	9	5
4	11	N Piquet	Lotus	101	Judd	V8	64	1h 20m 28.866s	10	5
5	23	P Martini	Minardi	M189	Ford Cosworth	V8	63		11	6
6	24	L Sala	Minardi	M189	Ford Cosworth	V8	63		15	8
7	26	O Grouillard	Ligier	JS33	Ford Cosworth	V8	63		24	12
8	12	S Nakajima	Lotus	101	Judd	V8	63		16	8
9	9	D Warwick	Arrows	A11	Ford Cosworth	V8	62		19	10
10	5	T Boutsen	Williams	FW12C	Renault	V10	62		7	4
11	20	E Pirro	Benetton	B188	Ford Cosworth	V8	62		26	13
12	37	B Gachot	Onyx	ORE-1	Ford Cosworth	V8	62		21	11
r	15	M Gugelmin	March	CG891	Judd	V8	54	gearbox	6	3
r	7	M Brundle	Brabham	BT58	Judd	V8	49	engine	20	10
r	28	G Berger	Ferrari	640	Ferrari	V12	49	gearbox	4	2
r	29	É Bernard	Lola	LC89	Lamborghini	V12	46	gearbox	13	7
r	30	P Alliot	Lola	LC89	Lamborghini	V12	39	engine	12	6
r	3	J Palmer	Tyrrell	018	Ford Cosworth	V8	32	accident	18	9
r	8	S Modena	Brabham	BT58	Judd	V8	31	engine	14	7
r	4	J Alesi	Tyrrell	018	Ford Cosworth	V8	28	accident	22	11
r	17	N Larini	Osella	FA1M	Ford Cosworth	V8	23	handling	17	9
r	6	R Patrese	Williams	FW12C	Renault	V10	19	water leak / accident	5	3
r	16	I Capelli	March	CG891	Judd	V8	15	differential	8	4
r	22	A de Cesaris	Dallara	189	Ford Cosworth	V8	14	gearbox	25	13
r	1	A Senna	McLaren	MP4/5	Honda	V10	11	gearbox / spin	1	1
r	31	R Moreno	Coloni	FC189	Ford Cosworth	V8	2	gearbox	23	12
nq	25	R Arnoux	Ligier	JS33	Ford Cosworth	V8				
nq	10	E Cheever	Arrows	A11	Ford Cosworth	V8				
nq	40	G Tarquini	AGS	JH24	Ford Cosworth	V8				
nq	38	C Danner	Rial	ARC2	Ford Cosworth	V8				
npq	36	S Johansson	Onyx	ORE-1	Ford Cosworth	V8				
npq	21	A Caffi	Dallara	189	Ford Cosworth	V8				
npq	33	G Foitek	EuroBrun	ER188B	Judd	V8				
npq	18	P Ghinzani	Osella	FA1M	Ford Cosworth	V8				
npq	41	Y Dalmas	AGS	JH23B	Ford Cosworth	V8				
npq	34	B Schneider	Zakspeed	891	Yamaha	V8				
npq	32	P-H Raphanel	Coloni	FC189	Ford Cosworth	V8				
npq	35	A Suzuki	Zakspeed	891	Yamaha	V8				
npq	39	V Weidler	Rial	ARC2	Ford Cosworth	V8				

Winning speed 231.253 km/h, 143.694 mph
Pole Position speed 249.021 km/h, 154.735 mph (A Senna, 1 min: 9.099 sec)
Fastest Lap speed 238.931 km/h, 148.465 mph (N Mansell, 1 min:12.017 sec on lap 57)
Lap Leaders A Senna 1-11 (11); A Prost 12-64 (53).

30 Jul 1989 **GERMANY: Hockenheim** **(Round 9)** **(Race 477)**

45 laps x 6.797 km, 4.223 miles = 305.865 km, 190.056 miles

Pos	No	Driver	Car	Model	Engine		Laps	Time/Reason for Retirement	Grid Pos	Row
1	1	A Senna	McLaren	MP4/5	Honda	V10	45	1h 21m 43.302s	1	1
2	2	A Prost	McLaren	MP4/5	Honda	V10	45	1h 22m 01.453s	2	1
3	27	N Mansell	Ferrari	640	Ferrari	V12	45	1h 23m 06.556s	3	2
4	6	R Patrese	Williams	FW12C	Renault	V10	44		5	3
5	11	N Piquet	Lotus	101	Judd	V8	44		8	4
6	9	D Warwick	Arrows	A11	Ford Cosworth	V8	44		17	9
7	22	A de Cesaris	Dallara	189	Ford Cosworth	V8	44		21	11
8	7	M Brundle	Brabham	BT58	Judd	V8	44		12	6
9	23	P Martini	Minardi	M189	Ford Cosworth	V8	44		13	7
10	4	J Alesi	Tyrrell	018	Ford Cosworth	V8	43		10	5
11	25	R Arnoux	Ligier	JS33	Ford Cosworth	V8	42		23	12
12r	10	E Cheever	Arrows	A11	Ford Cosworth	V8	40	fuel pick-up	25	13
r	8	S Modena	Brabham	BT58	Judd	V8	37	engine	16	8
r	12	S Nakajima	Lotus	101	Judd	V8	36	spin	18	9
r	16	I Capelli	March	CG891	Judd	V8	32	electronics	22	11
r	15	M Gugelmin	March	CG891	Judd	V8	28	gearbox	14	7
r	20	E Pirro	Benetton	B189	Ford Cosworth	V8	26	accident / injury	9	5
r	30	P Alliot	Lola	LC89	Lamborghini	V12	20	oil leak / fire	15	8
r	3	J Palmer	Tyrrell	018	Ford Cosworth	V8	16	throttle linkage	19	10
r	28	G Berger	Ferrari	640	Ferrari	V12	13	accident / rear suspension	4	2
r	36	S Johansson	Onyx	ORE-1	Ford Cosworth	V8	8	rear wheel bearing	24	12
r	19	A Nannini	Benetton	B189	Ford Cosworth	V8	6	electrical sensor	7	4
r	5	T Boutsen	Williams	FW12C	Renault	V10	4	accident	6	3
r	21	A Caffi	Dallara	189	Ford Cosworth	V8	2	electrics	20	10
r	29	M Alboreto	Lola	LC89	Lamborghini	V12	1	electrics	26	13
r	26	O Grouillard	Ligier	JS33	Ford Cosworth	V8	0	gearbox	11	6
nq	24	L Sala	Minardi	M189	Ford Cosworth	V8				
nq	37	B Gachot	Onyx	ORE-1	Ford Cosworth	V8				
nq	38	C Danner	Rial	ARC2	Ford Cosworth	V8				
exc	39	V Weidler	Rial	ARC2	Ford Cosworth	V8		push start after spin		
npq	41	Y Dalmas	AGS	JH24	Ford Cosworth	V8				
npq	17	N Larini	Osella	FA1M	Ford Cosworth	V8				
npq	40	G Tarquini	AGS	JH23B	Ford Cosworth	V8				
npq	18	P Ghinzani	Osella	FA1M	Ford Cosworth	V8				
npq	31	R Moreno	Coloni	FC189	Ford Cosworth	V8				
npq	32	P-H Raphanel	Coloni	FC189	Ford Cosworth	V8				
npq	33	G Foitek	EuroBrun	ER189	Judd	V8				
npq	35	A Suzuki	Zakspeed	891	Yamaha	V8				
npq	34	B Schneider	Zakspeed	891	Yamaha	V8				

Winning speed 224.566 km/h, 139.539 mph
Pole Position speed 239.191 km/h, 148.626 mph (A Senna, 1 min:42.300 sec)
Fastest Lap speed 231.094 km/h, 143.595 mph (A Senna, 1 min:45.884 sec on lap 43)
Lap Leaders A Senna 1-19,43-45 (22); A Prost 20-42 (23).

---

13 Aug 1989 **HUNGARY: Hungaroring** **(Round 10)** **(Race 478)**

77 laps x 3.968 km, 2.466 miles = 305.536 km, 189.851 miles

Pos	No	Driver	Car	Model	Engine		Laps	Time/Reason for Retirement	Grid Pos	Row
1	27	N Mansell	Ferrari	640	Ferrari	V12	77	1h 49m 38.650s	12	6
2	1	A Senna	McLaren	MP4/5	Honda	V10	77	1h 50m 04.617s	2	1
3	5	T Boutsen	Williams	FW12C	Renault	V10	77	1h 50m 17.004s	4	2
4	2	A Prost	McLaren	MP4/5	Honda	V10	77	1h 50m 22.827s	5	3
5	10	E Cheever	Arrows	A11	Ford Cosworth	V8	77	1h 50m 23.756s	16	8
6	11	N Piquet	Lotus	101	Judd	V8	77	1h 50m 50.689s	17	9
7	21	A Caffi	Dallara	189	Ford Cosworth	V8	77	1h 51m 02.875s	3	2
8	20	E Pirro	Benetton	B189	Ford Cosworth	V8	76		25	13
9	4	J Alesi	Tyrrell	018	Ford Cosworth	V8	76		11	6
10	9	D Warwick	Arrows	A11	Ford Cosworth	V8	76		9	5
11	8	S Modena	Brabham	BT58	Judd	V8	76		8	4
12	7	M Brundle	Brabham	BT58	Judd	V8	75		15	8
13	3	J Palmer	Tyrrell	018	Ford Cosworth	V8	73		19	10
r	24	L Sala	Minardi	M189	Ford Cosworth	V8	57	accident	23	12
r	28	G Berger	Ferrari	640	Ferrari	V12	56	gearbox	6	3
r	6	R Patrese	Williams	FW12C	Renault	V10	54	radiator	1	1
r	36	S Johansson	Onyx	ORE-1	Ford Cosworth	V8	48	gearbox	24	12
r	19	A Nannini	Benetton	B189	Ford Cosworth	V8	46	gear linkage	7	4
r	37	B Gachot	Onyx	ORE-1	Ford Cosworth	V8	38	gear linkage	21	11
r	12	S Nakajima	Lotus	101	Judd	V8	33	accident	20	10
r	15	M Gugelmin	March	CG891	Judd	V8	27	electrics	13	7
r	16	I Capelli	March	CG891	Judd	V8	26	rear wheel drive pegs	14	7
r	29	M Alboreto	Lola	LC89	Lamborghini	V12	26	engine	26	13
r	18	P Ghinzani	Osella	FA1M	Ford Cosworth	V8	20	electrics	22	11
r	23	P Martini	Minardi	M189	Ford Cosworth	V8	19	wheel bearings / brake fire	10	5
r	22	A de Cesaris	Dallara	189	Ford Cosworth	V8	0	clutch	18	9
nq	25	R Arnoux	Ligier	JS33	Ford Cosworth	V8				

Pos	No	Driver	Car	Model	Engine		Laps	Time/Reason for Retirement	Grid Pos	Row
nq	26	O Grouillard	Ligier	JS33	Ford Cosworth	V8				
nq	38	C Danner	Rial	ARC2	Ford Cosworth	V8				
nq	39	V Weidler	Rial	ARC2	Ford Cosworth	V8				
npq	17	N Larini	Osella	FA1M	Ford Cosworth	V8				
npq	30	P Alliot	Lola	LC89	Lamborghini	V12				
npq	41	Y Dalmas	AGS	JH23B	Ford Cosworth	V8				
npq	34	B Schneider	Zakspeed	891	Yamaha	V8				
npq	40	G Tarquini	AGS	JH24	Ford Cosworth	V8				
npq	31	R Moreno	Coloni	FC189	Ford Cosworth	V8				
npq	33	G Foitek	EuroBrun	ER189	Judd	V8				
npq	35	A Suzuki	Zakspeed	891	Yamaha	V8				
npq	32	P-H Raphanel	Coloni	FC189	Ford Cosworth	V8				

Winning speed 167.197 km/h, 103.891 mph
Pole Position speed 179.174 km/h, 111.333 mph (R Patrese, 1 min:19.726 sec)
Fastest Lap speed 172.862 km/h, 107.411 mph (N Mansell, 1 min:22.637 sec on lap 66)
Lap Leaders R Patrese 1-52 (52); A Senna 53-57 (5); N Mansell 58-77 (20).

27 Aug 1989		BELGIUM: Spa-Francorchamps							(Round 11)	(Race 479)

44 laps x 6.940 km, 4.312 miles = 305.360 km, 189.742 miles

Pos	No	Driver	Car	Model	Engine		Laps	Time/Reason for Retirement	Grid Pos	Row
1	1	A Senna	McLaren	MP4/5	Honda	V10	44	1h 40m 54.196s	1	1
2	2	A Prost	McLaren	MP4/5	Honda	V10	44	1h 40m 55.500s	2	1
3	27	N Mansell	Ferrari	640	Ferrari	V12	44	1h 40m 56.020s	6	3
4	5	T Boutsen	Williams	FW12C	Renault	V10	44	1h 41m 48.614s	4	2
5	19	A Nannini	Benetton	B189	Ford Cosworth	V8	44	1h 42m 03.001s	7	4
6	9	D Warwick	Arrows	A11	Ford Cosworth	V8	44	1h 42m 12.512s	10	5
7	15	M Gugelmin	March	CG891	Judd	V8	43		9	5
8	36	S Johansson	Onyx	ORE-1	Ford Cosworth	V8	43		15	8
9	23	P Martini	Minardi	M189	Ford Cosworth	V8	43		14	7
10	20	E Pirro	Benetton	B189	Ford Cosworth	V8	43		13	7
11	22	A de Cesaris	Dallara	189	Ford Cosworth	V8	43		18	9
12	16	I Capelli	March	CG891	Judd	V8	43		19	10
13	26	O Grouillard	Ligier	JS33	Ford Cosworth	V8	43		26	13
14	3	J Palmer	Tyrrell	018	Ford Cosworth	V8	42		21	11
15	24	L Sala	Minardi	M189	Ford Cosworth	V8	41		25	13
16r	30	P Alliot	Lola	LC89	Lamborghini	V12	39	oil pressure	11	6
r	10	E Cheever	Arrows	A11	Ford Cosworth	V8	38	wheel nut / wheel lost	24	12
r	37	B Gachot	Onyx	ORE-1	Ford Cosworth	V8	21	rear wheel bearing / accident	23	12
r	6	R Patrese	Williams	FW12C	Renault	V10	20	accident	5	3
r	29	M Alboreto	Lola	LC89	Lamborghini	V12	19	accident	22	11
r	21	A Caffi	Dallara	189	Ford Cosworth	V8	13	spin	12	6
r	7	M Brundle	Brabham	BT58	Judd	V8	12	brakes	20	10
r	28	G Berger	Ferrari	640	Ferrari	V12	9	spin	3	2
r	8	S Modena	Brabham	BT58	Judd	V8	9	handling	8	4
r	25	R Arnoux	Ligier	JS33	Ford Cosworth	V8	4	accident	17	9
r	4	J Herbert	Tyrrell	018	Ford Cosworth	V8	3	spin	16	8
nq	12	S Nakajima	Lotus	101	Judd	V8				
nq	11	N Piquet	Lotus	101	Judd	V8				
nq	38	C Danner	Rial	ARC2	Ford Cosworth	V8				
nq	39	P-H Raphanel	Rial	ARC2	Ford Cosworth	V8				
npq	17	N Larini	Osella	FA1M	Ford Cosworth	V8				
npq	18	P Ghinzani	Osella	FA1M	Ford Cosworth	V8				
npq	31	R Moreno	Coloni	FC189	Ford Cosworth	V8				
npq	40	G Tarquini	AGS	JH24	Ford Cosworth	V8				
npq	34	B Schneider	Zakspeed	891	Yamaha	V8				
npq	35	A Suzuki	Zakspeed	891	Yamaha	V8				
npq	41	Y Dalmas	AGS	JH23B	Ford Cosworth	V8				
npq	33	G Foitek	EuroBrun	ER188B	Judd	V8				
npq	32	E Bertaggia	Coloni	FC189	Ford Cosworth	V8				

Winning speed 181.576 km/h, 112.826 mph
Pole Position speed 225.351 km/h, 140.027 mph (A Senna, 1 min:50.867 sec)
Fastest Lap speed 189.890 km/h, 117.992 mph (A Prost, 2 min:11.571 sec on lap 44)
Lap Leaders A Senna 1-44 (44).

Races

53 laps x 5.800 km, 3.604 miles = 307.400 km, 191.010 miles

Pos	No	Driver	Car	Model	Engine		Laps	Time/Reason for Retirement	Grid Pos	Row
1	2	A Prost	McLaren	MP4/5	Honda	V10	53	1h 19m 27.550s	4	2
2	28	G Berger	Ferrari	640	Ferrari	V12	53	1h 19m 34.876s	2	1
3	5	T Boutsen	Williams	FW12C	Renault	V10	53	1h 19m 42.525s	6	3
4	6	R Patrese	Williams	FW12C	Renault	V10	53	1h 20m 06.272s	5	3
5	4	J Alesi	Tyrrell	018	Ford Cosworth	V8	52		10	5
6	7	M Brundle	Brabham	BT58	Judd	V8	52		12	6
7	23	P Martini	Minardi	M189	Ford Cosworth	V8	52		15	8
8	24	L Sala	Minardi	M189	Ford Cosworth	V8	51		26	13
9	25	R Arnoux	Ligier	JS33	Ford Cosworth	V8	51		23	12
10	12	S Nakajima	Lotus	101	Judd	V8	51		19	10
11r	21	A Caffi	Dallara	189	Ford Cosworth	V8	47	engine	20	10
r	22	A de Cesaris	Dallara	189	Ford Cosworth	V8	45	engine	17	9
r	1	A Senna	McLaren	MP4/5	Honda	V10	44	engine / spin	1	1
r	27	N Mansell	Ferrari	640	Ferrari	V12	41	gearbox	3	2
r	37	B Gachot	Onyx	ORE-1	Ford Cosworth	V8	38	accident / radiator	22	11
r	19	A Nannini	Benetton	B189	Ford Cosworth	V8	33	brakes	8	4
r	16	I Capelli	March	CG891	Judd	V8	30	engine	18	9
r	26	O Grouillard	Ligier	JS33	Ford Cosworth	V8	30	exhaust	21	11
r	11	N Piquet	Lotus	101	Judd	V8	23	spin	11	6
r	3	J Palmer	Tyrrell	018	Ford Cosworth	V8	18	engine	14	7
r	9	D Warwick	Arrows	A11	Ford Cosworth	V8	18	engine	16	8
r	17	N Larini	Osella	FA1M	Ford Cosworth	V8	16	gearbox	24	12
r	29	M Alboreto	Lola	LC89	Lamborghini	V12	14	electrics	13	7
r	15	M Gugelmin	March	CG891	Judd	V8	14	throttle jammed	25	13
r	30	P Alliot	Lola	LC89	Lamborghini	V12	1	throttle jammed / spin	7	4
r	20	E Pirro	Benetton	B189	Ford Cosworth	V8	0	gearbox	9	5
nq	10	E Cheever	Arrows	A11	Ford Cosworth	V8				
nq	38	C Danner	Rial	ARC2	Ford Cosworth	V8				
nq	39	P-H Raphanel	Rial	ARC2	Ford Cosworth	V8				
exc	8	S Modena	Brabham	BT58	Judd	V8		missed weight check		
npq	36	S Johansson	Onyx	ORE-1	Ford Cosworth	V8				
npq	40	G Tarquini	AGS	JH24	Ford Cosworth	V8				
npq	31	R Moreno	Coloni	FC189	Ford Cosworth	V8				
npq	18	P Ghinzani	Osella	FA1M	Ford Cosworth	V8				
npq	34	B Schneider	Zakspeed	891	Yamaha	V8				
npq	35	A Suzuki	Zakspeed	891	Yamaha	V8				
npq	33	O Larrauri	EuroBrun	ER189	Judd	V8				
npq	41	Y Dalmas	AGS	JH24	Ford Cosworth	V8				
npq	32	E Bertaggia	Coloni	FC189	Ford Cosworth	V8				

Winning speed 232.119 km/h, 144.232 mph
Pole Position speed 249.403 km/h, 154.972 mph (A Senna, 1 min:23.720 sec)
Fastest Lap speed 236.985 km/h, 147.255 mph (A Prost, 1 min:28.107 sec on lap 43)
Lap Leaders A Senna 1-44 (44); A Prost 45-53 (9).

71 laps x 4.350 km, 2.703 miles = 308.850 km, 191.910 miles

Pos	No	Driver	Car	Model	Engine		Laps	Time/Reason for Retirement	Grid Pos	Row
1	28	G Berger	Ferrari	640	Ferrari	V12	71	1h 36m 48.546s	2	1
2	2	A Prost	McLaren	MP4/5	Honda	V10	71	1h 37m 21.183s	4	2
3	36	S Johansson	Onyx	ORE-1	Ford Cosworth	V8	71	1h 37m 43.871s	12	6
4	19	A Nannini	Benetton	B189	Ford Cosworth	V8	71	1h 38m 10.915s	13	7
5	23	P Martini	Minardi	M189	Ford Cosworth	V8	70		5	3
6	3	J Palmer	Tyrrell	018	Ford Cosworth	V8	70		18	9
7	12	S Nakajima	Lotus	101	Judd	V8	70		25	13
8	7	M Brundle	Brabham	BT58	Judd	V8	70		10	5
9	30	P Alliot	Lola	LC89	Lamborghini	V12	70		17	9
10	15	M Gugelmin	March	CG891	Judd	V8	69		14	7
11	29	M Alboreto	Lola	LC89	Lamborghini	V12	69		21	11
12	24	L Sala	Minardi	M189	Ford Cosworth	V8	69		9	5
13	25	R Arnoux	Ligier	JS33	Ford Cosworth	V8	69		23	12
14	8	S Modena	Brabham	BT58	Judd	V8	69		11	6
r	6	R Patrese	Williams	FW13	Renault	V10	60	radiator	6	3
r	5	T Boutsen	Williams	FW13	Renault	V10	60	radiator	8	4
r	1	A Senna	McLaren	MP4/5	Honda	V10	48	accident	1	1
r/dq	27	N Mansell	Ferrari	640	Ferrari	V12	48	accident (disqualified for push)	3	2
r	9	D Warwick	Arrows	A11	Ford Cosworth	V8	37	accident	22	11
r	11	N Piquet	Lotus	101	Judd	V8	33	accident	20	10
r	21	A Caffi	Dallara	189	Ford Cosworth	V8	33	accident	7	4
r	20	E Pirro	Benetton	B189	Ford Cosworth	V8	29	suspension	16	8
r	16	I Capelli	March	CG891	Judd	V8	25	engine	24	12
r	10	E Cheever	Arrows	A11	Ford Cosworth	V8	24	engine / spin	26	13
r	22	A de Cesaris	Dallara	189	Ford Cosworth	V8	17	electronics	19	10
r	31	R Moreno	Coloni	FC189	Ford Cosworth	V8	11	electrics	15	8
nq	4	J Herbert	Tyrrell	018	Ford Cosworth	V8				

Pos	No	Driver	Car	Model	Engine		Laps	Time/Reason for Retirement	Grid Pos	Row
nq	26	O Grouillard	Ligier	JS33	Ford Cosworth	V8				
nq	39	P-H Raphanel	Rial	ARC2	Ford Cosworth	V8				
nq	38	C Danner	Rial	ARC2	Ford Cosworth	V8				
npq	37	J J Lehto	Onyx	ORE-1	Ford Cosworth	V8				
npq	18	P Ghinzani	Osella	FA1M	Ford Cosworth	V8				
npq	33	O Larrauri	EuroBrun	ER189	Judd	V8				
npq	40	G Tarquini	AGS	JH24	Ford Cosworth	V8				
npq	35	A Suzuki	Zakspeed	891	Yamaha	V8				
npq	34	B Schneider	Zakspeed	891	Yamaha	V8				
npq	32	E Bertaggia	Coloni	FC189	Ford Cosworth	V8				
exc	41	Y Dalmas	AGS	JH24	Ford Cosworth	V8		tyre infringement		
exc	17	N Larini	Osella	FA1M	Ford Cosworth	V8		missed weight check		

Winning speed 191.418 km/h, 118.942 mph
Pole Position speed 207.505 km/h, 128.938 mph (A Senna, 1 min:15.468 sec)
Fastest Lap speed 198.263 km/h, 123.195 mph (G Berger, 1 min:18.986 sec on lap 49)
Lap Leaders G Berger 1-23,41-71 (54); N Mansell 24-39 (16); P Martini 40 (1).

1 Oct 1989		SPAIN: Jerez de la Frontera							(Round 14)	(Race 482)
		73 laps x 4.218 km, 2.621 miles = 307.914 km, 191.329 miles								

Pos	No	Driver	Car	Model	Engine		Laps	Time/Reason for Retirement	Grid Pos	Row
1	1	A Senna	McLaren	MP4/5	Honda	V10	73	1h 47m 48.264s	1	1
2	28	G Berger	Ferrari	640	Ferrari	V12	73	1h 48m 15.315s	2	1
3	2	A Prost	McLaren	MP4/5	Honda	V10	73	1h 48m 42.052s	3	2
4	4	J Alesi	Tyrrell	018	Ford Cosworth	V8	72		9	5
5	6	R Patrese	Williams	FW12C	Renault	V10	72		6	3
6	30	P Alliot	Lola	LC89	Lamborghini	V12	72		5	3
7	22	A de Cesaris	Dallara	189	Ford Cosworth	V8	72		15	8
8	11	N Piquet	Lotus	101	Judd	V8	71		7	4
9	9	D Warwick	Arrows	A11	Ford Cosworth	V8	71		16	8
10	3	J Palmer	Tyrrell	018	Ford Cosworth	V8	71		13	7
r	10	E Cheever	Arrows	A11	Ford Cosworth	V8	61	engine	22	11
r	20	E Pirro	Benetton	B189	Ford Cosworth	V8	59	driver discomfort (cramp) / spin	10	5
r	21	A Caffi	Dallara	189	Ford Cosworth	V8	55	engine	23	12
r	7	M Brundle	Brabham	BT58	Judd	V8	51	rear suspension / spin	8	4
r	15	M Gugelmin	March	CG891	Judd	V8	47	accident	26	13
r	24	L Sala	Minardi	M189	Ford Cosworth	V8	47	accident	20	10
r	5	T Boutsen	Williams	FW13	Renault	V10	40	fuel pump	21	11
r	26	O Grouillard	Ligier	JS33	Ford Cosworth	V8	34	engine	24	12
r	23	P Martini	Minardi	M189	Ford Cosworth	V8	27	spin	4	2
r	16	I Capelli	March	CG891	Judd	V8	23	differential	19	10
r	37	J J Lehto	Onyx	ORE-1	Ford Cosworth	V8	20	gearbox	17	9
r	18	P Ghinzani	Osella	FA1M	Ford Cosworth	V8	17	gearbox	25	13
r	19	A Nannini	Benetton	B189	Ford Cosworth	V8	14	spin	14	7
r	8	S Modena	Brabham	BT58	Judd	V8	11	electrics	12	6
r	17	N Larini	Osella	FA1M	Ford Cosworth	V8	6	rear suspension / accident	11	6
r	12	S Nakajima	Lotus	101	Judd	V8	0	accident	18	9
nq	25	R Arnoux	Ligier	JS33	Ford Cosworth	V8				
nq	39	P-H Raphanel	Rial	ARC2	Ford Cosworth	V8				
nq	38	G Foitek	Rial	ARC2	Ford Cosworth	V8				
npq	40	G Tarquini	AGS	JH24	Ford Cosworth	V8				
npq	36	S Johansson	Onyx	ORE-1	Ford Cosworth	V8				
npq	31	R Moreno	Coloni	FC189	Ford Cosworth	V8				
npq	29	M Alboreto	Lola	LC89	Lamborghini	V12				
npq	34	B Schneider	Zakspeed	891	Yamaha	V8				
npq	41	Y Dalmas	AGS	JH24	Ford Cosworth	V8				
npq	35	A Suzuki	Zakspeed	891	Yamaha	V8				
npq	33	O Larrauri	EuroBrun	ER189	Judd	V8				
npq	32	E Bertaggia	Coloni	FC189	Ford Cosworth	V8				

Winning speed 171.374 km/h, 106.487 mph
Pole Position speed 189.122 km/h, 117.515 mph (A Senna, 1 min:20.291 sec)
Fastest Lap speed 177.022 km/h, 109.997 mph (A Senna, 1 min:25.779 sec on lap 55)
Lap Leaders A Senna 1-73 (73).

Pos	No	Driver	Car	Model	Engine		Laps	Time/Reason for Retirement	Grid Pos	Row
dq	1	A Senna	McLaren	MP4/5	Honda	V10	53	push start after accident	1	1
1	19	A Nannini	Benetton	B189	Ford Cosworth	V8	53	1h 35m 06.277s	6	3
2	6	R Patrese	Williams	FW13	Renault	V10	53	1h 35m 18.181s	5	3
3	5	T Boutsen	Williams	FW13	Renault	V10	53	1h 35m 19.723s	7	4
4	11	N Piquet	Lotus	101	Judd	V8	53	1h 36m 50.502s	11	6
5	7	M Brundle	Brabham	BT58	Judd	V8	52		13	7
6	9	D Warwick	Arrows	A11	Ford Cosworth	V8	52		25	13
7	15	M Gugelmin	March	CG891	Judd	V8	52		20	10
8	10	E Cheever	Arrows	A11	Ford Cosworth	V8	52		24	12
9	21	A Caffi	Dallara	189	Ford Cosworth	V8	52		15	8
10	22	A de Cesaris	Dallara	189	Ford Cosworth	V8	51		16	8
r	2	A Prost	McLaren	MP4/5	Honda	V10	46	accident	2	1
r	8	S Modena	Brabham	BT58	Judd	V8	46	alternator	9	5
r	27	N Mansell	Ferrari	640	Ferrari	V12	43	engine	4	2
r	12	S Nakajima	Lotus	101	Judd	V8	41	engine	12	6
r	4	J Alesi	Tyrrell	018	Ford Cosworth	V8	37	gearbox	18	9
r	30	P Alliot	Lola	LC89	Lamborghini	V12	36	engine	8	4
r	28	G Berger	Ferrari	640	Ferrari	V12	34	gear selector	3	2
r	20	E Pirro	Benetton	B189	Ford Cosworth	V8	33	accident	22	11
r	26	O Grouillard	Ligier	JS33	Ford Cosworth	V8	31	engine	23	12
r	16	I Capelli	March	CG891	Judd	V8	27	front suspension	17	9
r	17	N Larini	Osella	FA1M	Ford Cosworth	V8	21	brakes	10	5
r	3	J Palmer	Tyrrell	018	Ford Cosworth	V8	20	fuel leak	26	13
r	34	B Schneider	Zakspeed	891	Yamaha	V8	1	driveshaft	21	11
r	23	P Barilla	Minardi	M189	Ford Cosworth	V8	0	clutch	19	10
r	24	L Sala	Minardi	M189	Ford Cosworth	V8	0	accident	14	7
nq	25	R Arnoux	Ligier	JS33	Ford Cosworth	V8				
nq	29	M Alboreto	Lola	LC89	Lamborghini	V12				
nq	38	P-H Raphanel	Rial	ARC2	Ford Cosworth	V8				
nq	39	B Gachot	Rial	ARC2	Ford Cosworth	V8				
npq	18	P Ghinzani	Osella	FA1M	Ford Cosworth	V8				
npq	31	R Moreno	Coloni	FC189	Ford Cosworth	V8				
npq	36	S Johansson	Onyx	ORE-1	Ford Cosworth	V8				
npq	35	A Suzuki	Zakspeed	891	Yamaha	V8				
npq	33	O Larrauri	EuroBrun	ER189	Judd	V8				
npq	37	J J Lehto	Onyx	ORE-1	Ford Cosworth	V8				
npq	40	G Tarquini	AGS	JH24	Ford Cosworth	V8				
npq	41	Y Dalmas	AGS	JH24	Ford Cosworth	V8				
npq	32	E Bertaggia	Coloni	FC189	Ford Cosworth	V8				

Winning speed 195.907 km/h, 121.731 mph
Pole Position speed 215.139 km/h, 133.681 mph (A Senna, 1 min:38.041 sec)
Fastest Lap speed 203.779 km/h, 126.623 mph (A Prost, 1 min:43.506 sec on lap 43)
Lap Leaders A Prost 1-20,24-46 (43); A Senna 21-23,47-48,51-53 (8); A Nannini 49-50 (2).

A Senna finished 1st in 1h 35m 03.980s (195.985 km/h,121.780 mph) and recorded the fastest lap in 1m 43.025s (204.731 km/h,127.214 mph).

70 laps x 3.780 km, 2.349 miles = 264.600 km, 164.415 miles

Pos	No	Driver	Car	Model	Engine		Laps	Time/Reason for Retirement	Grid Pos	Row
1	5	T Boutsen	Williams	FW13	Renault	V10	70	2h 00m 17.421s	5	3
2	19	A Nannini	Benetton	B189	Ford Cosworth	V8	70	2h 00m 46.079s	4	2
3	6	R Patrese	Williams	FW13	Renault	V10	70	2h 00m 55.104s	6	3
4	12	S Nakajima	Lotus	101	Judd	V8	70	2h 00m 59.752s	23	12
5	20	E Pirro	Benetton	B189	Ford Cosworth	V8	68		13	7
6	23	P Martini	Minardi	M189	Ford Cosworth	V8	67		3	2
7	15	M Gugelmin	March	CG891	Judd	V8	66		5	13
8	8	S Modena	Brabham	BT58	Judd	V8	64		8	4
r	10	E Cheever	Arrows	A11	Ford Cosworth	V8	42	misfire / spin	22	11
r	37	J J Lehto	Onyx	ORE-1	Ford Cosworth	V8	27	electrics / spin	17	9
r	26	O Grouillard	Ligier	JS33	Ford Cosworth	V8	22	accident	24	12
r	11	N Piquet	Lotus	101	Judd	V8	19	accident	18	9
r	18	P Ghinzani	Osella	FA1M	Ford Cosworth	V8	18	accident	21	11
r	27	N Mansell	Ferrari	640	Ferrari	V12	17	accident	7	4
r	1	A Senna	McLaren	MP4/5	Honda	V10	13	accident	1	1
r	21	A Caffi	Dallara	189	Ford Cosworth	V8	13	spin	10	5
r	16	I Capelli	March	CG891	Judd	V8	13	radiator	16	8
r	22	A de Cesaris	Dallara	189	Ford Cosworth	V8	12	accident	9	5
r	7	M Brundle	Brabham	BT58	Judd	V8	12	accident	12	6
r	9	D Warwick	Arrows	A11	Ford Cosworth	V8	7	engine / accident	20	10
r	28	G Berger	Ferrari	640	Ferrari	V12	6	accident	14	7
r	30	P Alliot	Lola	LC89	Lamborghini	V12	6	accident	19	10
r	4	J Alesi	Tyrrell	018	Ford Cosworth	V8	5	electrics	15	8
r	25	R Arnoux	Ligier	JS33	Ford Cosworth	V8	4	accident	26	13
r	17	N Larini	Osella	FA1M	Ford Cosworth	V8	0	engine on 2nd parade lap *	11	6
r	2	A Prost	McLaren	MP4/5	Honda	V10	0	withdrew *	2	1
nq	3	J Palmer	Tyrrell	018	Ford Cosworth	V8				
nq	24	L Sala	Minardi	M189	Ford Cosworth	V8				
nq	39	B Gachot	Rial	ARC2	Ford Cosworth	V8				
nq	38	P-H Raphanel	Rial	ARC2	Ford Cosworth	V8				
npq	36	S Johansson	Onyx	ORE-1	Ford Cosworth	V8				
npq	29	M Alboreto	Lola	LC89	Lamborghini	V12				
npq	34	B Schneider	Zakspeed	891	Yamaha	V8				
npq	31	R Moreno	Coloni	FC189	Ford Cosworth	V8				
npq	33	O Larrauri	EuroBrun	ER189	Judd	V8				
npq	35	A Suzuki	Zakspeed	891	Yamaha	V8				
npq	41	Y Dalmas	AGS	JH24	Ford Cosworth	V8				
npq	40	G Tarquini	AGS	JH24	Ford Cosworth	V8				
npq	32	E Bertaggia	Coloni	FC189	Ford Cosworth	V8				

Winning speed 131.981 km/h, 82.009 mph
Pole Position speed 177.500 km/h, 110.293 mph (A Senna, 1 min:16.665 sec)
Fastest Lap speed 138.180 km/h, 85.861 mph (S Nakajima, 1 min:38.480 sec on lap 64)
Lap Leaders A Senna 1-13 (13); T Boutsen 14-70 (57).

Scheduled for 81 laps, but interrupted after first lap, because of rain. Restarted for original distance, but stopped at 2 hours.
* Retired after first start.

Lap Leaders 1989

Pos	Driver	Car-Engine	GPs	laps	km	miles
1	A Senna	McLaren-Honda	13	487	2,297.1	1,427.4
2	A Prost	McLaren-Honda	8	258	1,218.0	756.8
3	R Patrese	Williams-Renault	3	100	428.0	265.9
4	N Mansell	Ferrari	3	73	335.1	208.2
5	T Boutsen	Williams-Renault	2	60	228.6	142.1
6	G Berger	Ferrari	1	54	234.9	146.0
7	D Warwick	Arrows-Ford Cosworth	1	4	17.6	10.9
8	A Nannini	Benetton-Ford Cosworth	1	2	11.7	7.3
9	P Martini	Minardi-Ford Cosworth	1	1	4.3	2.7
			16	1,039	4,775.3	2,967.2

Driver Points 1989

		BR	RSM	MC	MEX	USA	CDN	F	GB	D	H	B	I	P	E	J	AUS	Total
1	A Prost	6	6	6	(2)	9	-	9	9	6	(3)	6	9	6	4	-	-	76 (5)
2	A Senna	-	9	9	9	-	-	-	-	9	6	9	-	-	-	-	-	60
3	R Patrese	-	-	-	6	6	6	4	-	3	-	-	3	-	2	6	4	40
4	N Mansell	9	-	-	-	-	-	6	6	4	9	4	-	-	-	-	-	38
5	T Boutsen	-	3	-	-	1	9	-	-	4	3	4	-	-	-	4	9	37
6	A Nannini	1	4	-	3	-	-	-	4	-	-	2	-	3	-	9	6	32
7	G Berger	-	-	-	-	-	-	-	-	-	-	-	6	9	6	-	-	21
8	N Piquet	-	-	-	-	-	3	-	3	2	1	-	-	-	-	3	-	12
9	J Alesi	-	-	-	-	-	-	3	-	-	-	-	2	-	3	-	-	8
10	D Warwick	2	2	-	-	-	-	-	-	1	-	1	-	-	-	1	-	7
11	M Alboreto	-	-	2	4	-	-	-	-	-	-	-	-	-	-	-	-	6
	E Cheever	-	-	-	-	4	-	-	-	2	-	-	-	-	-	-	-	6
	S Johansson	-	-	-	-	-	-	2	-	-	-	-	-	4	-	-	-	6
14	J Herbert	3	-	-	-	2	-	-	-	-	-	-	-	-	-	-	-	5
	P Martini	-	-	-	-	-	-	-	2	-	-	-	-	2	-	-	1	5
16	M Gugelmin	4	-	-	-	-	-	-	-	-	-	-	-	-	-	-	-	4
	S Modena	-	-	4	-	-	-	-	-	-	-	-	-	-	-	-	-	4
	A de Cesaris	-	-	-	-	-	4	-	-	-	-	-	-	-	-	-	-	4
	A Caffi	-	-	3	-	-	1	-	-	-	-	-	-	-	-	-	-	4
	M Brundle	-	-	1	-	-	-	-	-	-	-	-	1	-	-	2	-	4
21	C Danner	-	-	-	3	-	-	-	-	-	-	-	-	-	-	-	-	3
	S Nakajima	-	-	-	-	-	-	-	-	-	-	-	-	-	-	-	3	3
23	R Arnoux	-	-	-	-	-	2	-	-	-	-	-	-	-	-	-	-	2
	E Pirro	-	-	-	-	-	-	-	-	-	-	-	-	-	-	-	2	2
	J Palmer	-	1	-	-	-	-	-	-	-	-	-	-	1	-	-	-	2
26	G Tarquini	-	-	-	1	-	-	-	-	-	-	-	-	-	-	-	-	1
	O Grouillard	-	-	-	-	-	-	1	-	-	-	-	-	-	-	-	-	1
	L Sala	-	-	-	-	-	-	-	1	-	-	-	-	-	-	-	-	1
	P Alliot	-	-	-	-	-	-	-	-	-	-	-	-	-	1	-	-	1

9,6,4,3,2 and 1 point awarded to the first six finishers. Best 11 scores.

Constructor Points 1989

		BR	RSM	MC	MEX	USA	CDN	F	GB	D	H	B	I	P	E	J	AUS	Total
1	McLaren-Honda	6	15	15	11	9	-	9	9	15	9	15	9	6	13	-	-	141
2	Williams-Renault	-	3	-	6	7	15	4	-	3	4	3	7	-	2	10	13	77
3	Ferrari	9	-	-	-	-	-	6	6	4	9	4	6	9	6	-	-	59
4	Benetton-Ford Cosworth	4	4	-	3	2	-	-	4	-	-	2	-	3	-	9	8	39
5	Tyrrell-Ford Cosworth	-	1	2	4	-	-	3	-	-	-	-	2	1	3	-	-	16
6	Lotus-Judd	-	-	-	-	-	3	-	3	2	1	-	-	-	-	3	3	15
7	Arrows-Ford Cosworth	2	2	-	-	4	-	-	-	1	2	1	-	-	-	1	-	13
8	Dallara-Ford Cosworth	-	-	3	-	-	5	-	-	-	-	-	-	-	-	-	-	8
	Brabham-Judd	-	-	5	-	-	-	-	-	-	-	-	1	-	-	2	-	8
10	Onyx-Ford Cosworth	-	-	-	-	-	-	2	-	-	-	-	-	4	-	-	-	6
	Minardi-Ford Cosworth	-	-	-	-	-	-	-	3	-	-	-	-	2	-	-	1	6
12	March-Judd	4	-	-	-	-	-	-	-	-	-	-	-	-	-	-	-	4
13	Rial-Ford Cosworth	-	-	-	3	-	-	-	-	-	-	-	-	-	-	-	-	3
	Ligier-Ford Cosworth	-	-	-	-	2	1	-	-	-	-	-	-	-	-	-	-	3
15	AGS-Ford Cosworth	-	-	-	1	-	-	-	-	-	-	-	-	-	-	-	-	1
	Lola-Lamborghini	-	-	-	-	-	-	-	-	-	-	-	-	-	1	-	-	1

9,6,4,3,2 and 1 point awarded to the first six finishers.

Race Entrants and Results

Senna and FISA were still in dispute over the crash at Suzuka and this would rumble on for the early part of the year. David Brabham became the first son of a World Champion to start a Grand Prix when he took to the grid at Monte Carlo in a Brabham-Judd. Subaru entered with its Flat 12 engine while Life introduced their unusual W12 engine (neither would qualify).

FERRARI
Scuderia Ferrari SpA: Prost, Mansell

TYRRELL
Tyrrell Racing Organisation: Nakajima, Alesi

WILLIAMS
Canon Williams Team: Boutsen, Patrese

BRABHAM
Motor Racing Developments: Foitek, D Brabham, Modena

ARROWS
Footwork Arrows Racing: Alboreto, Caffi, Schneider

LOTUS
Camel Team Lotus: Warwick, Donnelly, Herbert

OSELLA
Fondmetal Osella: Grouillard

LEYTON HOUSE
Leyton House Racing: Gugelmin, Capelli

AGS
Automobiles Gonfaronaises Sportives: Tarquini, Dalmas

BENETTON
Benetton Formula: Nannini, Moreno, Piquet

DALLARA
Scuderia Italia SpA: Pirro, Morbidelli, de Cesaris

MINARDI
SCM Minardi Team: Martini, Barilla, Morbidelli

LIGIER
Ligier Gitanes: Larini, Alliot

McLAREN
Honda Marlboro McLaren: Senna, Berger

LOLA
Espo Larrousse F1: Bernard, Suzuki

COLONI
Coloni Racing: (Gachot)

EUROBRUN
EuroBrun Racing: Moreno, (Langes)

ONYX
Monteverdi Onyx Formula One: (Johansson), Foitek, Lehto

LIFE
Life Racing Engines: (G Brabham, Giacomelli)

11 Mar 1990		USA: Phoenix							(Round 1)	(Race 485)	
		72 laps x 3.798 km, 2.360 miles = 273.460 km, 169.920 miles									
Pos	No	Driver	Car	Model	Engine		Laps	Time/Reason for Retirement		Grid Pos	Row
1	27	A Senna	McLaren	MP4/5B	Honda	V10	72	1h 52m 32.829s		5	3
2	4	J Alesi	Tyrrell	018	Ford Cosworth	V8	72	1h 52m 41.514s		4	2
3	5	T Boutsen	Williams	FW13B	Renault	V10	72	1h 53m 26.909s		9	5
4	20	N Piquet	Benetton	B189B	Ford Cosworth	V8	72	1h 53m 41.187s		6	3
5	8	S Modena	Brabham	BT58	Judd	V8	72	1h 53m 42.332s		10	5
6	3	S Nakajima	Tyrrell	018	Ford Cosworth	V8	71			11	6
7	23	P Martini	Minardi	M189	Ford Cosworth	V8	71			2	1
8	29	É Bernard	Lola	LC89	Lamborghini	V12	71			15	8
9	6	R Patrese	Williams	FW13B	Renault	V10	71			12	6
10	9	M Alboreto	Arrows	A11B	Ford Cosworth	V8	70			21	11
11	19	A Nannini	Benetton	B189B	Ford Cosworth	V8	70			22	11
12	10	B Schneider	Arrows	A11	Ford Cosworth	V8	70			20	10
13	33	R Moreno	EuroBrun	ER189	Judd	V8	67			16	8
14	15	M Gugelmin	Leyton House	CG901	Judd	V8	66			25	13
r	24	P Barilla	Minardi	M189	Ford Cosworth	V8	54	driver discomfort (arm cramp)		14	7
r	30	A Suzuki	Lola	LC89	Lamborghini	V12	53	brakes		18	9
r	2	N Mansell	Ferrari	641	Ferrari	V12	49	engine / clutch / spin / fire		17	9
r	28	G Berger	McLaren	MP4/5B	Honda	V10	44	clutch		1	1
r	7	G Foitek	Brabham	BT58	Judd	V8	39	accident		23	12
r	14	O Grouillard	Osella	FA1M	Ford Cosworth	V8	39	accident / front suspension		8	4
r	22	A de Cesaris	Dallara	190	Ford Cosworth	V8	25	brakes / engine		3	2
r	1	A Prost	Ferrari	641	Ferrari	V12	21	oil leak		7	4
r	16	I Capelli	Leyton House	CG901	Judd	V8	20	electrics		26	13
r	11	D Warwick	Lotus	102	Lamborghini	V12	6	rear suspension		24	12
r	25	N Larini	Ligier	JS33B	Ford Cosworth	V8	4	throttle jammed		13	7
ns	12	M Donnelly	Lotus	102	Lamborghini	V12		ignition on dummy grid		19	10
nq	35	S Johansson	Onyx	ORE-1	Ford Cosworth	V8					
nq	21	G Morbidelli	Dallara	190	Ford Cosworth	V8					
nq	36	J J Lehto	Onyx	ORE-1	Ford Cosworth	V8					
exc	26	P Alliot	Ligier	JS33B	Ford Cosworth	V8		push start during practice			
npq	17	G Tarquini	AGS	JH24	Ford Cosworth	V8					
npq	18	Y Dalmas	AGS	JH24	Ford Cosworth	V8					
npq	34	C Langes	EuroBrun	ER189	Judd	V8					
npq	39	G Brabham	Life	L190	Life	W12					
npq	31	B Gachot	Coloni	FC189B	Subaru	F12					

Winning speed 145.784 km/h, 90.586 mph
Pole Position speed 154.211 km/h, 95.822 mph (G Berger, 1 min:28.664 sec)
Fastest Lap speed 150.170 km/h, 93.311 mph (G Berger, 1 min:31.050 sec on lap 34)
Lap Leaders J Alesi 1-34 (34); A Senna 35-72 (38).

25 Mar 1990   **BRAZIL: Interlagos**   **(Round 2)**   **(Race 486)**

71 laps x 4.325 km, 2.687 miles = 307.075 km, 190.808 miles

Pos	No	Driver	Car	Model	Engine		Laps	Time/Reason for Retirement	Grid Pos	Row
1	1	A Prost	Ferrari	641	Ferrari	V12	71	1h 37m 21.258s	6	3
2	28	G Berger	McLaren	MP4/5B	Honda	V10	71	1h 37m 34.822s	2	1
3	27	A Senna	McLaren	MP4/5B	Honda	V10	71	1h 37m 58.980s	1	1
4	2	N Mansell	Ferrari	641	Ferrari	V12	71	1h 38m 08.524s	5	3
5	5	T Boutsen	Williams	FW13B	Renault	V10	70		3	2
6	20	N Piquet	Benetton	B189B	Ford Cosworth	V8	70		13	7
7	4	J Alesi	Tyrrell	018	Ford Cosworth	V8	70		7	4
8	3	S Nakajima	Tyrrell	018	Ford Cosworth	V8	70		19	10
9	23	P Martini	Minardi	M189	Ford Cosworth	V8	69		8	4
10	19	A Nannini	Benetton	B189B	Ford Cosworth	V8	68	in pits at chequered flag	15	8
11	25	N Larini	Ligier	JS33B	Ford Cosworth	V8	68		20	10
12	26	P Alliot	Ligier	JS33B	Ford Cosworth	V8	68		10	5
13r	6	R Patrese	Williams	FW13B	Renault	V10	65	oil radiator leak	4	2
14	21	G Morbidelli	Dallara	190	Ford Cosworth	V8	64		16	8
r	10	A Caffi	Arrows	A11B	Ford Cosworth	V8	49	driver exhausted	25	13
r	12	M Donnelly	Lotus	102	Lamborghini	V12	43	spin	14	7
r	8	S Modena	Brabham	BT58	Judd	V8	39	spin	12	6
r	24	P Barilla	Minardi	M189	Ford Cosworth	V8	38	engine	17	9
r	18	Y Dalmas	AGS	JH24	Ford Cosworth	V8	28	front suspension	26	13
r	11	D Warwick	Lotus	102	Lamborghini	V12	25	electrics	24	12
r	30	A Suzuki	Lola	LC89	Lamborghini	V12	24	suspension	18	9
r	9	M Alboreto	Arrows	A11B	Ford Cosworth	V8	24	rear suspension	23	12
r	7	G Foitek	Brabham	BT58	Judd	V8	14	gear selection	22	11
r	29	É Bernard	Lola	LC89	Lamborghini	V12	13	gearbox	11	6
r	14	O Grouillard	Osella	FA1M	Ford Cosworth	V8	8	accident	21	11
r	22	A de Cesaris	Dallara	190	Ford Cosworth	V8	0	throttle jammed / accident	9	5
nq	35	S Johansson	Onyx	ORE-1	Ford Cosworth	V8				
nq	36	J J Lehto	Onyx	ORE-1	Ford Cosworth	V8				
nq	16	I Capelli	Leyton House	CG901	Judd	V8				
nq	15	M Gugelmin	Leyton House	CG901	Judd	V8				
npq	17	G Tarquini	AGS	JH24	Ford Cosworth	V8				
npq	33	R Moreno	EuroBrun	ER189	Judd	V8				
npq	31	B Gachot	Coloni	FC189B	Subaru	F12				
npq	34	C Langes	EuroBrun	ER189	Judd	V8				
npq	39	G Brabham	Life	L190	Life	W12				

Winning speed 189.252 km/h, 117.596 mph
Pole Position speed 201.483 km/h, 125.196 mph (A Senna, 1 min:17.277 sec)
Fastest Lap speed 194.871 km/h, 121.087 mph (G Berger, 1 min:19.899 sec on lap 55)
Lap Leaders A Senna 1-32,35-40 (38); G Berger 33-34 (2); A Prost 41-71 (31).

I Capelli also practised in a March CG891-Judd V8 (16).

13 May 1990   **SAN MARINO: Imola**   **(Round 3)**   **(Race 487)**

61 laps x 5.040 km, 3.132 miles = 307.440 km, 191.034 miles

Pos	No	Driver	Car	Model	Engine		Laps	Time/Reason for Retirement	Grid Pos	Row
1	6	R Patrese	Williams	FW13B	Renault	V10	61	1h 30m 55.478s	3	2
2	28	G Berger	McLaren	MP4/5B	Honda	V10	61	1h 31m 00.595s	2	1
3	19	A Nannini	Benetton	B190	Ford Cosworth	V8	61	1h 31m 01.718s	9	5
4	1	A Prost	Ferrari	641/2	Ferrari	V12	61	1h 31m 02.321s	6	3
5	20	N Piquet	Benetton	B190	Ford Cosworth	V8	61	1h 31m 48.590s	8	4
6	4	J Alesi	Tyrrell	019	Ford Cosworth	V8	60		7	4
7	11	D Warwick	Lotus	102	Lamborghini	V12	60		10	5
8	12	M Donnelly	Lotus	102	Lamborghini	V12	60		11	6
9	26	P Alliot	Ligier	JS33B	Ford Cosworth	V8	60		16	8
10	25	N Larini	Ligier	JS33B	Ford Cosworth	V8	59		20	10
11	24	P Barilla	Minardi	M190	Ford Cosworth	V8	59		26	13
12	36	J J Lehto	Onyx	ORE-2	Ford Cosworth	V8	59		25	13
13r	29	É Bernard	Lola	90	Lamborghini	V12	56	gearbox	13	7
r	14	O Grouillard	Osella	FA1M-E	Ford Cosworth	V8	52	wheel bearing	22	11
r	2	N Mansell	Ferrari	641/2	Ferrari	V12	38	engine	5	3
r	35	G Foitek	Onyx	ORE-2	Ford Cosworth	V8	35	engine	23	12
r	8	S Modena	Brabham	BT59	Judd	V8	31	brakes / spin	14	7
r	22	A de Cesaris	Dallara	190	Ford Cosworth	V8	29	hub	17	9
r	15	M Gugelmin	Leyton House	CG901	Judd	V8	24	electrics	12	6
r	5	T Boutsen	Williams	FW13B	Renault	V10	17	engine	4	2
r	30	A Suzuki	Lola	90	Lamborghini	V12	17	clutch	15	8
r	27	A Senna	McLaren	MP4/5B	Honda	V10	3	rear wheel rim / brakes / spin	1	1
r	21	E Pirro	Dallara	190	Ford Cosworth	V8	2	spin	21	11
r	16	I Capelli	Leyton House	CG901	Judd	V8	0	accident	18	9
r	3	S Nakajima	Tyrrell	019	Ford Cosworth	V8	0	accident	19	10
r	33	R Moreno	EuroBrun	ER189	Judd	V8	0	throttle slides	24	12

Pos	No	Driver	Car	Model	Engine		Laps	Time/Reason for Retirement	Grid Pos	Row
ns	23	P Martini	Minardi	M190	Ford Cosworth	V8		accident / injury		
nq	10	A Caffi	Arrows	A11B	Ford Cosworth	V8				
nq	9	M Alboreto	Arrows	A11B	Ford Cosworth	V8				
nq	7	D Brabham	Brabham	BT59	Judd	V8				
npq	31	B Gachot	Coloni	FC189B	Subaru	F12				
npq	34	C Langes	EuroBrun	ER189B	Judd	V8				
npq	39	B Giacomelli	Life	L190	Life	W12				
npq	17	G Tarquini	AGS	JH25	Ford Cosworth	V8				

Winning speed 202.876 km/h, 126.061 mph
Pole Position speed 218.025 km/h, 135.474 mph (A Senna, 1 min:23.220 sec)
Fastest Lap speed 208.178 km/h, 129.356 mph (A Nannini, 1 min:27.156 sec on lap 60)
Lap Leaders A Senna 1-3 (3); T Boutsen 4-17 (14); G Berger 18-50 (33); R Patrese 51-61 (11).

27 May 1990		**MONACO: Monte-Carlo**						**(Round 4)**	**(Race 488)**	
		78 laps x 3.328 km, 2.068 miles = 259.584 km, 161.298 miles								

Pos	No	Driver	Car	Model	Engine		Laps	Time/Reason for Retirement	Grid Pos	Row
1	27	A Senna	McLaren	MP4/5B	Honda	V10	78	1h 52m 46.982s	1	1
2	4	J Alesi	Tyrrell	019	Ford Cosworth	V8	78	1h 52m 48.069s	3	2
3	28	G Berger	McLaren	MP4/5B	Honda	V10	78	1h 52m 49.055s	5	3
4	5	T Boutsen	Williams	FW13B	Renault	V10	77		6	3
5	10	A Caffi	Arrows	A11B	Ford Cosworth	V8	76		22	11
6	29	É Bernard	Lola	90	Lamborghini	V12	76		24	12
7r	35	G Foitek	Onyx	ORE-2	Ford Cosworth	V8	72	accident	20	10
r	11	D Warwick	Lotus	102	Lamborghini	V12	66	brakes / spin	13	7
r	2	N Mansell	Ferrari	641/2	Ferrari	V12	63	battery / gearbox electronics	7	4
r	24	P Barilla	Minardi	M190	Ford Cosworth	V8	52	gearbox	19	10
r	36	J J Lehto	Onyx	ORE-2	Ford Cosworth	V8	52	gearbox	26	13
r	26	P Alliot	Ligier	JS33B	Ford Cosworth	V8	47	gearbox	18	9
r	6	R Patrese	Williams	FW13B	Renault	V10	41	valve gear	4	2
r	22	A de Cesaris	Dallara	190	Ford Cosworth	V8	38	throttle linkage	12	6
r	3	S Nakajima	Tyrrell	019	Ford Cosworth	V8	36	spin	21	11
dq	20	N Piquet	Benetton	B190	Ford Cosworth	V8	35	push start after spin	10	5
r	1	A Prost	Ferrari	641/2	Ferrari	V12	30	battery	2	1
r	19	A Nannini	Benetton	B190	Ford Cosworth	V8	20	oil pressure / engine	16	8
r	7	D Brabham	Brabham	BT59	Judd	V8	16	cv joint	25	13
r	16	I Capelli	Leyton House	CG901	Judd	V8	13	brakes	23	12
r	25	N Larini	Ligier	JS33B	Ford Cosworth	V8	12	differential	17	9
r	30	A Suzuki	Lola	90	Lamborghini	V12	11	electrics	15	8
r	23	P Martini	Minardi	M190	Ford Cosworth	V8	7	ignition	8	4
r	12	M Donnelly	Lotus	102	Lamborghini	V12	6	transmission	11	6
r	8	S Modena	Brabham	BT59	Judd	V8	3	differential	14	7
r	21	E Pirro	Dallara	190	Ford Cosworth	V8	0	fuel vaporisation on 2nd parade lap *	9	5
nq	9	M Alboreto	Arrows	A11B	Ford Cosworth	V8				
nq	14	O Grouillard	Osella	FA1M-E	Ford Cosworth	V8				
nq	15	M Gugelmin	Leyton House	CG901	Judd	V8				
nq	33	R Moreno	EuroBrun	ER189	Judd	V8				
npq	17	G Tarquini	AGS	JH25	Ford Cosworth	V8				
npq	18	Y Dalmas	AGS	JH25	Ford Cosworth	V8				
npq	34	C Langes	EuroBrun	ER189B	Judd	V8				
npq	31	B Gachot	Coloni	FC189B	Subaru	F12				
npq	39	B Giacomelli	Life	L190	Life	W12				

Winning speed 138.097 km/h, 85.810 mph
Pole Position speed 147.340 km/h, 91.553 mph (A Senna, 1 min:21.314 sec)
Fastest Lap speed 141.838 km/h, 88.134 mph (A Senna, 1 min:24.468 sec on lap 59)
Lap Leaders A Senna 1-78 (78).

*Interrupted after first lap accident. Restarted for original distance. * Retired after first start.*

70 laps x 4.390 km, 2.728 miles = 307.300 km, 190.947 miles

Pos	No	Driver	Car	Model	Engine		Laps	Time/Reason for Retirement	Grid Pos	Row
1	27	A Senna	McLaren	MP4/5B	Honda	V10	70	1h 42m 56.400s	1	1
2	20	N Piquet	Benetton	B190	Ford Cosworth	V8	70	1h 43m 06.897s	5	3
3	2	N Mansell	Ferrari	641/2	Ferrari	V12	70	1h 43m 09.785s	7	4
4	28	G Berger	McLaren	MP4/5B	Honda	V10	70	1h 43m 11.254s *	2	1
5	1	A Prost	Ferrari	641/2	Ferrari	V12	70	1h 43m 12.220s	3	2
6	11	D Warwick	Lotus	102	Lamborghini	V12	68		11	6
7	8	S Modena	Brabham	BT59	Judd	V8	68		10	5
8	10	A Caffi	Arrows	A11B	Ford Cosworth	V8	68		26	13
9	29	É Bernard	Lola	90	Lamborghini	V12	67		23	12
10	16	I Capelli	Leyton House	CG901	Judd	V8	67		24	12
11	3	S Nakajima	Tyrrell	019	Ford Cosworth	V8	67		13	7
12	30	A Suzuki	Lola	90	Lamborghini	V12	66		18	9
13	14	O Grouillard	Osella	FA1M-E	Ford Cosworth	V8	65		15	8
r	12	M Donnelly	Lotus	102	Lamborghini	V12	57	valve	12	6
r	35	G Foitek	Onyx	ORE-2	Ford Cosworth	V8	53	valve	21	11
r	22	A de Cesaris	Dallara	190	Ford Cosworth	V8	50	input shaft	25	13
r	36	J J Lehto	Onyx	ORE-2	Ford Cosworth	V8	46	misfire	22	11
r	6	R Patrese	Williams	FW13B	Renault	V10	44	brakes	9	5
r	26	P Alliot	Ligier	JS33B	Ford Cosworth	V8	34	engine	17	9
r	4	J Alesi	Tyrrell	019	Ford Cosworth	V8	26	accident	8	4
r	19	A Nannini	Benetton	B190	Ford Cosworth	V8	21	accident	4	2
r	5	T Boutsen	Williams	FW13B	Renault	V10	19	accident	6	3
r	25	N Larini	Ligier	JS33B	Ford Cosworth	V8	18	accident	20	10
r	21	E Pirro	Dallara	190	Ford Cosworth	V8	11	accident	19	10
r	9	M Alboreto	Arrows	A11B	Ford Cosworth	V8	11	accident	14	7
r	23	P Martini	Minardi	M190	Ford Cosworth	V8	0	spin	16	8
nq	33	R Moreno	EuroBrun	ER189	Judd	V8				
nq	15	M Gugelmin	Leyton House	CG901	Judd	V8				
nq	24	P Barilla	Minardi	M190	Ford Cosworth	V8				
nq	7	D Brabham	Brabham	BT59	Judd	V8				
npq	17	G Tarquini	AGS	JH25	Ford Cosworth	V8				
npq	18	Y Dalmas	AGS	JH25	Ford Cosworth	V8				
npq	31	B Gachot	Coloni	FC189B	Subaru	F12				
npq	34	C Langes	EuroBrun	ER189B	Judd	V8				
npq	39	B Giacomelli	Life	L190	Life	W12				

Winning speed 179.114 km/h, 111.296 mph
Pole Position speed 196.570 km/h, 122.143 mph (A Senna, 1 min:20.399 sec)
Fastest Lap speed 192.551 km/h, 119.646 mph (G Berger, 1 min:22.077 sec on lap 70)
Lap Leaders A Senna 1-11 (11); A Nannini 12-14 (3); G Berger 15-70 (56).

* G Berger finished 1st but was classified 4th, after 1 minute penalty for jumping the start. Lap leaders are shown 'on the road', but on corrected time, A Senna led laps 15-70.

69 laps x 4.421 km, 2.747 miles = 305.049 km, 189.549 miles

Pos	No	Driver	Car	Model	Engine		Laps	Time/Reason for Retirement	Grid Pos	Row
1	1	A Prost	Ferrari	641/2	Ferrari	V12	69	1h 32m 35.783s	13	7
2	2	N Mansell	Ferrari	641/2	Ferrari	V12	69	1h 33m 01.134s	4	2
3	28	G Berger	McLaren	MP4/5B	Honda	V10	69	1h 33m 01.313s	1	1
4	19	A Nannini	Benetton	B190	Ford Cosworth	V8	69	1h 33m 16.882s	14	7
5	5	T Boutsen	Williams	FW13B	Renault	V10	69	1h 33m 22.452s	5	3
6	20	N Piquet	Benetton	B190	Ford Cosworth	V8	69	1h 33m 22.726s	8	4
7	4	J Alesi	Tyrrell	019	Ford Cosworth	V8	69	1h 33m 24.860s	6	3
8	12	M Donnelly	Lotus	102	Lamborghini	V12	69	1h 33m 41.925s	12	6
9	6	R Patrese	Williams	FW13B	Renault	V10	69	1h 33m 45.701s	2	1
10	11	D Warwick	Lotus	102	Lamborghini	V12	68		11	6
11	8	S Modena	Brabham	BT59	Judd	V8	68		10	5
12	23	P Martini	Minardi	M190	Ford Cosworth	V8	68		7	4
13	22	A de Cesaris	Dallara	190	Ford Cosworth	V8	68		15	8
14	24	P Barilla	Minardi	M190	Ford Cosworth	V8	67		16	8
15	35	G Foitek	Onyx	ORE-2	Ford Cosworth	V8	67		23	12
16	25	N Larini	Ligier	JS33B	Ford Cosworth	V8	67		24	12
17	9	M Alboreto	Arrows	A11B	Ford Cosworth	V8	66		17	9
18	26	P Alliot	Ligier	JS33B	Ford Cosworth	V8	66		22	11
19	14	O Grouillard	Osella	FA1M-E	Ford Cosworth	V8	65		20	10
20r	27	A Senna	McLaren	MP4/5B	Honda	V10	63	rear tyre	3	2
r	36	J J Lehto	Onyx	ORE-2	Ford Cosworth	V8	26	engine	26	13
r	29	É Bernard	Lola	90	Lamborghini	V12	12	brakes / spin	25	13
r	30	A Suzuki	Lola	90	Lamborghini	V12	11	accident	19	10
r	3	S Nakajima	Tyrrell	019	Ford Cosworth	V8	11	accident	9	5
r	7	D Brabham	Brabham	BT59	Judd	V8	11	electrics	21	11
r	21	E Pirro	Dallara	190	Ford Cosworth	V8	10	engine	18	9
exc	33	R Moreno	EuroBrun	ER189B	Judd	V8		push start after spin		

Pos	No	Driver	Car	Model	Engine		Laps	Time/Reason for Retirement	Grid Pos	Row
nq	16	I Capelli	Leyton House	CG901	Judd	V8				
nq	15	M Gugelmin	Leyton House	CG901	Judd	V8				
nq	10	A Caffi	Arrows	A11B	Ford Cosworth	V8				
npq	18	Y Dalmas	AGS	JH25	Ford Cosworth	V8				
npq	17	G Tarquini	AGS	JH25	Ford Cosworth	V8				
npq	31	B Gachot	Coloni	FC189B	Subaru	F12				
npq	34	C Langes	EuroBrun	ER189B	Judd	V8				
npq	39	B Giacomelli	Life	L190	Life	W12				

Winning speed 197.664 km/h, 122.823 mph
Pole Position speed 206.089 km/h, 128.057 mph (G Berger, 1 min:17.227 sec)
Fastest Lap speed 204.156 km/h, 126.857 mph (A Prost, 1 min:17.958 sec on lap 58)
Lap Leaders A Senna 1-60 (60); A Prost 61-69 (9).

8 Jul 1990		FRANCE: Paul Ricard						(Round 7)	(Race 491)	

80 laps x 3.813 km, 2.369 miles = 305.040 km, 189.543 miles

Pos	No	Driver	Car	Model	Engine		Laps	Time/Reason for Retirement	Grid Pos	Row
1	1	A Prost	Ferrari	641/2	Ferrari	V12	80	1h 33m 29.606s	4	2
2	16	I Capelli	Leyton House	CG901	Judd	V8	80	1h 33m 38.232s	7	4
3	27	A Senna	McLaren	MP4/5B	Honda	V10	80	1h 33m 41.212s	3	2
4	20	N Piquet	Benetton	B190	Ford Cosworth	V8	80	1h 34m 10.813s	9	5
5	28	G Berger	McLaren	MP4/5B	Honda	V10	80	1h 34m 11.825s	2	1
6	6	R Patrese	Williams	FW13B	Renault	V10	80	1h 34m 38.957s	6	3
7	30	A Suzuki	Lola	90	Lamborghini	V12	79		14	7
8	29	É Bernard	Lola	90	Lamborghini	V12	79		11	6
9	26	P Alliot	Ligier	JS33B	Ford Cosworth	V8	79		12	6
10	9	M Alboreto	Arrows	A11B	Ford Cosworth	V8	79		18	9
11	11	D Warwick	Lotus	102	Lamborghini	V12	79		16	8
12	12	M Donnelly	Lotus	102	Lamborghini	V12	79		17	9
13	8	S Modena	Brabham	BT59	Judd	V8	78		20	10
14	25	N Larini	Ligier	JS33B	Ford Cosworth	V8	78		19	10
dq	22	A de Cesaris	Dallara	190	Ford Cosworth	V8	78	car under weight	21	11
15	7	D Brabham	Brabham	BT59	Judd	V8	77		25	13
16r	19	A Nannini	Benetton	B190	Ford Cosworth	V8	75	electrics	5	3
17	18	Y Dalmas	AGS	JH25	Ford Cosworth	V8	75		26	13
18r	2	N Mansell	Ferrari	641/2	Ferrari	V12	72	engine	1	1
r	3	S Nakajima	Tyrrell	019	Ford Cosworth	V8	63	gear linkage	15	8
r	15	M Gugelmin	Leyton House	CG901	Judd	V8	58	engine	10	5
r	23	P Martini	Minardi	M190	Ford Cosworth	V8	40	electrics	23	12
r	4	J Alesi	Tyrrell	019	Ford Cosworth	V8	23	differential	13	7
r	10	A Caffi	Arrows	A11B	Ford Cosworth	V8	22	rear suspension	22	11
r	5	T Boutsen	Williams	FW13B	Renault	V10	8	engine	8	4
r	21	E Pirro	Dallara	190	Ford Cosworth	V8	7	brake disc / spin	24	12
nq	24	P Barilla	Minardi	M190	Ford Cosworth	V8				
nq	17	G Tarquini	AGS	JH25	Ford Cosworth	V8				
nq	35	G Foitek	Onyx	ORE-2	Ford Cosworth	V8				
nq	36	J J Lehto	Onyx	ORE-2	Ford Cosworth	V8				
npq	14	O Grouillard	Osella	FA1M-E	Ford Cosworth	V8				
npq	33	R Moreno	EuroBrun	ER189B	Judd	V8				
npq	34	C Langes	EuroBrun	ER189B	Judd	V8				
npq	31	B Gachot	Coloni	FC189B	Subaru	F12				
npq	39	B Giacomelli	Life	L190	Life	W12				

Winning speed 195.761 km/h, 121.640 mph
Pole Position speed 213.142 km/h, 132.441 mph (N Mansell, 1 min: 4.402 sec)
Fastest Lap speed 201.829 km/h, 125.411 mph (N Mansell, 1 min: 8.012 sec on lap 64)
Lap Leaders G Berger 1-27 (27);A Senna 28-29 (2);N Mansell 30-31 (2);R Patrese 32 (1);I Capelli 33-77 (45);A Prost 78-80 (3).

15 Jul 1990 BRITAIN: Silverstone (Round 8) (Race 492)

64 laps x 4.780 km, 2.970 miles = 305.904 km, 190.080 miles

Pos	No	Driver	Car	Model	Engine		Laps	Time/Reason for Retirement	Grid Pos	Row
1	1	A Prost	Ferrari	641/2	Ferrari	V12	64	1h 18m 30.999s	5	3
2	5	T Boutsen	Williams	FW13B	Renault	V10	64	1h 19m 10.091s	4	2
3	27	A Senna	McLaren	MP4/5B	Honda	V10	64	1h 19m 14.087s	2	1
4	29	É Bernard	Lola	90	Lamborghini	V12	64	1h 19m 46.301s	8	4
5	20	N Piquet	Benetton	B190	Ford Cosworth	V8	64	1h 19m 55.002s	11	6
6	30	A Suzuki	Lola	90	Lamborghini	V12	63		9	5
7	10	A Caffi	Arrows	A11B	Ford Cosworth	V8	63		17	9
8	4	J Alesi	Tyrrell	019	Ford Cosworth	V8	63		6	3
9	8	S Modena	Brabham	BT59	Judd	V8	62		20	10
10	25	N Larini	Ligier	JS33B	Ford Cosworth	V8	62		21	11
11	21	E Pirro	Dallara	190	Ford Cosworth	V8	62		19	10
12	24	P Barilla	Minardi	M190	Ford Cosworth	V8	62		24	12
13	26	P Alliot	Ligier	JS33B	Ford Cosworth	V8	61		22	11
14r	28	G Berger	McLaren	MP4/5B	Honda	V10	60	throttle linkage	3	2
r	2	N Mansell	Ferrari	641/2	Ferrari	V12	55	gearbox	1	1
r	16	I Capelli	Leyton House	CG901	Judd	V8	48	fuel line	10	5
r	12	M Donnelly	Lotus	102	Lamborghini	V12	48	engine	14	7
r	11	D Warwick	Lotus	102	Lamborghini	V12	46	engine	16	8
r	17	G Tarquini	AGS	JH25	Ford Cosworth	V8	41	engine	26	13
r	9	M Alboreto	Arrows	A11B	Ford Cosworth	V8	37	electrics	25	13
r	6	R Patrese	Williams	FW13B	Renault	V10	26	accident / undertray	7	4
r	3	S Nakajima	Tyrrell	019	Ford Cosworth	V8	20	electrics	12	6
r	19	A Nannini	Benetton	B190	Ford Cosworth	V8	15	accident	13	7
r	22	A de Cesaris	Dallara	190	Ford Cosworth	V8	12	gearbox	23	12
r	23	P Martini	Minardi	M190	Ford Cosworth	V8	3	alternator	18	9
ns	15	M Gugelmin	Leyton House	CG901	Judd	V8		fuel pump on dummy grid	15	8
nq	14	O Grouillard	Osella	FA1M-E	Ford Cosworth	V8				
nq	7	D Brabham	Brabham	BT59	Judd	V8				
nq	36	J J Lehto	Onyx	ORE-2	Ford Cosworth	V8				
nq	35	G Foitek	Onyx	ORE-2	Ford Cosworth	V8				
npq	33	R Moreno	EuroBrun	ER189B	Judd	V8				
npq	18	Y Dalmas	AGS	JH25	Ford Cosworth	V8				
npq	34	C Langes	EuroBrun	ER189B	Judd	V8				
npq	31	B Gachot	Coloni	FC189B	Subaru	F12				
npq	39	B Giacomelli	Life	L190	Life	W12				

Winning speed 233.762 km/h, 145.253 mph
Pole Position speed 255.192 km/h, 158.569 mph (N Mansell, 1 min: 7.428 sec)
Fastest Lap speed 241.364 km/h, 149.977 mph (N Mansell, 1 min:11.291 sec on lap 51)
Lap Leaders A Senna 1-11 (11); N Mansell 12-21,28-42 (25); G Berger 22-27 (6); A Prost 43-64 (22).

29 Jul 1990 GERMANY: Hockenheim (Round 9) (Race 493)

45 laps x 6.802 km, 4.227 miles = 306.090 km, 190.196 miles

Pos	No	Driver	Car	Model	Engine		Laps	Time/Reason for Retirement	Grid Pos	Row
1	27	A Senna	McLaren	MP4/5B	Honda	V10	45	1h 20m 47.164s	1	1
2	19	A Nannini	Benetton	B190	Ford Cosworth	V8	45	1h 20m 53.684s	9	5
3	28	G Berger	McLaren	MP4/5B	Honda	V10	45	1h 20m 55.717s	2	1
4	1	A Prost	Ferrari	641/2	Ferrari	V12	45	1h 21m 32.434s	3	2
5	6	R Patrese	Williams	FW13B	Renault	V10	45	1h 21m 35.192s	5	3
6	5	T Boutsen	Williams	FW13B	Renault	V10	45	1h 22m 08.655s	6	3
7	16	I Capelli	Leyton House	CG901	Judd	V8	44		10	5
8	11	D Warwick	Lotus	102	Lamborghini	V12	44		16	8
9	10	A Caffi	Arrows	A11B	Ford Cosworth	V8	44		18	9
10	25	N Larini	Ligier	JS33B	Ford Cosworth	V8	43		22	11
11r	4	J Alesi	Tyrrell	019	Ford Cosworth	V8	40	cv joint	8	4
nc	36	J J Lehto	Monteverdi	ORE-2	Ford Cosworth	V8	39		25	13
r	29	É Bernard	Lola	90	Lamborghini	V12	35	fuel pressure	12	6
r	30	A Suzuki	Lola	90	Lamborghini	V12	33	clutch	11	6
r	3	S Nakajima	Tyrrell	019	Ford Cosworth	V8	24	engine	13	7
r	20	N Piquet	Benetton	B190	Ford Cosworth	V8	23	engine	7	4
r	23	P Martini	Minardi	M190	Ford Cosworth	V8	20	engine	15	8
r	35	G Foitek	Monteverdi	ORE-2	Ford Cosworth	V8	19	spin	26	13
r	2	N Mansell	Ferrari	641/2	Ferrari	V12	15	undertray damage	4	2
r	15	M Gugelmin	Leyton House	CG901	Judd	V8	12	valve	14	7
r	7	D Brabham	Brabham	BT59	Judd	V8	12	valve	21	11
dq	26	P Alliot	Ligier	JS33B	Ford Cosworth	V8	12	push start after accident	24	12
r	9	M Alboreto	Arrows	A11B	Ford Cosworth	V8	10	engine	19	10
r	12	M Donnelly	Lotus	102	Lamborghini	V12	1	clutch	20	10
r	21	E Pirro	Dallara	190	Ford Cosworth	V8	0	accident / injury	23	12
r	8	S Modena	Brabham	BT59	Judd	V8	0	clutch	17	9
nq	14	O Grouillard	Osella	FA1M-E	Ford Cosworth	V8				

Pos	No	Driver	Car	Model	Engine		Laps	Time/Reason for Retirement	Grid Pos	Row
nq	24	P Barilla	Minardi	M190	Ford Cosworth	V8				
nq	18	Y Dalmas	AGS	JH25	Ford Cosworth	V8				
nq	22	A de Cesaris	Dallara	190	Ford Cosworth	V8				
npq	17	G Tarquini	AGS	JH25	Ford Cosworth	V8				
npq	33	R Moreno	EuroBrun	ER189B	Judd	V8				
npq	31	B Gachot	Coloni	FC189C	Ford Cosworth	V8				
npq	34	C Langes	EuroBrun	ER189B	Judd	V8				
npq	39	B Giacomelli	Life	L190	Life	W12				

Winning speed 227.334 km/h, 141.259 mph
Pole Position speed 244.388 km/h, 151.856 mph (A Senna, 1 min:40.198 sec)
Fastest Lap speed 231.882 km/h, 144.085 mph (T Boutsen, 1 min:45.602 sec on lap 31)
Lap Leaders A Senna 1-17,34-45 (29); A Nannini 18-33 (16).

12 Aug 1990		HUNGARY: Hungaroring							(Round 10)	(Race 494)

77 laps x 3.968 km, 2.466 miles = 305.536 km, 189.851 miles

Pos	No	Driver	Car	Model	Engine		Laps	Time/Reason for Retirement	Grid Pos	Row
1	5	T Boutsen	Williams	FW13B	Renault	V10	77	1h 49m 30.597s	1	1
2	27	A Senna	McLaren	MP4/5B	Honda	V10	77	1h 49m 30.885s	4	2
3	20	N Piquet	Benetton	B190	Ford Cosworth	V8	77	1h 49m 58.490s	9	5
4	6	R Patrese	Williams	FW13B	Renault	V10	77	1h 50m 02.430s	2	1
5	11	D Warwick	Lotus	102	Lamborghini	V12	77	1h 50m 44.841s	11	6
6	29	É Bernard	Lola	90	Lamborghini	V12	77	1h 50m 54.905s	12	6
7	12	M Donnelly	Lotus	102	Lamborghini	V12	76		18	9
8	15	M Gugelmin	Leyton House	CG901	Judd	V8	76		17	9
9	10	A Caffi	Arrows	A11B	Ford Cosworth	V8	76		26	13
10	21	E Pirro	Dallara	190	Ford Cosworth	V8	76		13	7
11	25	N Larini	Ligier	JS33B	Ford Cosworth	V8	76		25	13
12	9	M Alboreto	Arrows	A11B	Ford Cosworth	V8	75		22	11
13	17	G Tarquini	AGS	JH25	Ford Cosworth	V8	74		24	12
14	26	P Alliot	Ligier	JS33B	Ford Cosworth	V8	74		21	11
15	24	P Barilla	Minardi	M190	Ford Cosworth	V8	74		23	12
16r	28	G Berger	McLaren	MP4/5B	Honda	V10	72	accident	3	2
17r	2	N Mansell	Ferrari	641/2	Ferrari	V12	71	accident	5	3
r	19	A Nannini	Benetton	B190	Ford Cosworth	V8	64	accident	7	4
r	16	I Capelli	Leyton House	CG901	Judd	V8	56	gearbox	16	8
r	30	A Suzuki	Lola	90	Lamborghini	V12	37	oil filter / engine	19	10
r	1	A Prost	Ferrari	641/2	Ferrari	V12	36	gearbox / spin	8	4
r	4	J Alesi	Tyrrell	019	Ford Cosworth	V8	36	accident	6	3
r	8	S Modena	Brabham	BT59	Judd	V8	35	engine	20	10
r	23	P Martini	Minardi	M190	Ford Cosworth	V8	35	accident	14	7
r	22	A de Cesaris	Dallara	190	Ford Cosworth	V8	22	engine	10	5
r	3	S Nakajima	Tyrrell	019	Ford Cosworth	V8	9	brakes / accident	15	8
nq	18	Y Dalmas	AGS	JH25	Ford Cosworth	V8				
nq	7	D Brabham	Brabham	BT59	Judd	V8				
nq	36	J J Lehto	Monteverdi	ORE-2	Ford Cosworth	V8				
nq	35	G Foitek	Monteverdi	ORE-2	Ford Cosworth	V8				
npq	14	O Grouillard	Osella	FA1M-E	Ford Cosworth	V8				
npq	31	B Gachot	Coloni	FC189C	Ford Cosworth	V8				
npq	33	R Moreno	EuroBrun	ER189B	Judd	V8				
npq	34	C Langes	EuroBrun	ER189B	Judd	V8				
npq	39	B Giacomelli	Life	L190	Life	W12				

Winning speed 167.402 km/h, 104.019 mph
Pole Position speed 183.329 km/h, 113.915 mph (T Boutsen, 1 min:17.919 sec)
Fastest Lap speed 174.082 km/h, 108.169 mph (R Patrese, 1 min:22.058 sec on lap 63)
Lap Leaders T Boutsen 1-77 (77).

26 Aug 1990   BELGIUM: Spa-Francorchamps   (Round 11)   (Race 495)

44 laps x 6.940 km, 4.312 miles = 305.360 km, 189.742 miles

Pos	No	Driver	Car	Model	Engine		Laps	Time/Reason for Retirement	Grid Pos	Row
1	27	A Senna	McLaren	MP4/5B	Honda	V10	44	1h 26m 31.997s	1	1
2	1	A Prost	Ferrari	641/2	Ferrari	V12	44	1h 26m 35.547s	3	2
3	28	G Berger	McLaren	MP4/5B	Honda	V10	44	1h 27m 00.459s	2	1
4	19	A Nannini	Benetton	B190	Ford Cosworth	V8	44	1h 27m 21.334s	6	3
5	20	N Piquet	Benetton	B190	Ford Cosworth	V8	44	1h 28m 01.647s	8	4
6	15	M Gugelmin	Leyton House	CG901	Judd	V8	44	1h 28m 20.848s	14	7
7	16	I Capelli	Leyton House	CG901	Judd	V8	43		12	6
8	4	J Alesi	Tyrrell	019	Ford Cosworth	V8	43		9	5
9	29	É Bernard	Lola	90	Lamborghini	V12	43		15	8
10	10	A Caffi	Arrows	A11B	Ford Cosworth	V8	43		19	10
11	11	D Warwick	Lotus	102	Lamborghini	V12	43		18	9
12	12	M Donnelly	Lotus	102	Lamborghini	V12	43		22	11
13	9	M Alboreto	Arrows	A11B	Ford Cosworth	V8	43		26	13
14	25	N Larini	Ligier	JS33B	Ford Cosworth	V8	42		21	11
15	23	P Martini	Minardi	M190	Ford Cosworth	V8	42		16	8
16	14	O Grouillard	Osella	FA1M-E	Ford Cosworth	V8	42		23	12
17r	8	S Modena	Brabham	BT59	Judd	V8	39	engine	13	7
r	7	D Brabham	Brabham	BT59	Judd	V8	36	electrics	24	12
r	22	A de Cesaris	Dallara	190	Ford Cosworth	V8	27	oil leak / engine	20	10
r	5	T Boutsen	Williams	FW13B	Renault	V10	21	cv joint	4	2
r	2	N Mansell	Ferrari	641/2	Ferrari	V12	19	handling	5	3
r	6	R Patrese	Williams	FW13B	Renault	V10	18	gearbox	7	4
r	21	E Pirro	Dallara	190	Ford Cosworth	V8	5	water pipe	17	9
r	3	S Nakajima	Tyrrell	019	Ford Cosworth	V8	4	engine	10	5
r	24	P Barilla	Minardi	M190	Ford Cosworth	V8	0	accident **	25	13
r	30	A Suzuki	Lola	90	Lamborghini	V12	0	accident *	11	6
nq	26	P Alliot	Ligier	JS33B	Ford Cosworth	V8				
nq	17	G Tarquini	AGS	JH25	Ford Cosworth	V8				
nq	18	Y Dalmas	AGS	JH25	Ford Cosworth	V8				
nq	31	B Gachot	Coloni	FC189C	Ford Cosworth	V8				
npq	33	R Moreno	EuroBrun	ER189B	Judd	V8				
npq	34	C Langes	EuroBrun	ER189B	Judd	V8				
npq	39	B Giacomelli	Life	L190	Life	W12				

Winning speed 211.729 km/h, 131.562 mph
Pole Position speed 226.376 km/h, 140.664 mph (A Senna, 1 min:50.365 sec)
Fastest Lap speed 217.088 km/h, 134.892 mph (A Prost, 1 min:55.087 sec on lap 38)
Lap Leaders A Senna 1-44 (44).

*Interrupted twice after first lap accidents. Restarted for original distance. * Retired after first start. ** Retired after second start.*

9 Sep 1990   ITALY: Monza   (Round 12)   (Race 496)

53 laps x 5.800 km, 3.604 miles = 307.400 km, 191.010 miles

Pos	No	Driver	Car	Model	Engine		Laps	Time/Reason for Retirement	Grid Pos	Row
1	27	A Senna	McLaren	MP4/5B	Honda	V10	53	1h 17m 57.878s	1	1
2	1	A Prost	Ferrari	641/2	Ferrari	V12	53	1h 18m 03.932s	2	1
3	28	G Berger	McLaren	MP4/5B	Honda	V10	53	1h 18m 05.282s	3	2
4	2	N Mansell	Ferrari	641/2	Ferrari	V12	53	1h 18m 54.097s	4	2
5	6	R Patrese	Williams	FW13B	Renault	V10	53	1h 19m 23.152s	7	4
6	3	S Nakajima	Tyrrell	019	Ford Cosworth	V8	52		14	7
7	20	N Piquet	Benetton	B190	Ford Cosworth	V8	52		9	5
8	19	A Nannini	Benetton	B190	Ford Cosworth	V8	52		8	4
9	10	A Caffi	Arrows	A11B	Ford Cosworth	V8	51		21	11
10	22	A de Cesaris	Dallara	190	Ford Cosworth	V8	51		25	13
11	25	N Larini	Ligier	JS33B	Ford Cosworth	V8	51		26	13
12r	9	M Alboreto	Arrows	A11B	Ford Cosworth	V8	50	spin	22	11
13	26	P Alliot	Ligier	JS33B	Ford Cosworth	V8	50		20	10
nc	18	Y Dalmas	AGS	JH25	Ford Cosworth	V8	45		24	12
r	16	I Capelli	Leyton House	CG901	Judd	V8	36	engine	16	8
r	30	A Suzuki	Lola	90	Lamborghini	V12	36	electrics	18	9
r	14	O Grouillard	Osella	FA1M-E	Ford Cosworth	V8	27	wheel bearing	23	12
r	15	M Gugelmin	Leyton House	CG901	Judd	V8	24	engine	10	5
r	8	S Modena	Brabham	BT59	Judd	V8	21	valve	17	9
r	5	T Boutsen	Williams	FW13B	Renault	V10	18	rear suspension	6	3
r	11	D Warwick	Lotus	102	Lamborghini	V12	15	clutch	12	6
r	21	E Pirro	Dallara	190	Ford Cosworth	V8	14	gearbox / spin	19	10
r	12	M Donnelly	Lotus	102	Lamborghini	V12	13	engine	11	6
r	29	É Bernard	Lola	90	Lamborghini	V12	10	clutch	13	7
r	23	P Martini	Minardi	M190	Ford Cosworth	V8	7	spin / rear suspension	15	8
r	4	J Alesi	Tyrrell	019	Ford Cosworth	V8	4	spin	5	3
nq	17	G Tarquini	AGS	JH25	Ford Cosworth	V8				

Pos	No	Driver	Car	Model	Engine		Laps	Time/Reason for Retirement	Grid Pos	Row
nq	24	P Barilla	Minardi	M190	Ford Cosworth	V8				
nq	7	D Brabham	Brabham	BT59	Judd	V8				
nq	31	B Gachot	Coloni	FC189C	Ford Cosworth	V8				
npq	33	R Moreno	EuroBrun	ER189B	Judd	V8				
npq	34	C Langes	EuroBrun	ER189B	Judd	V8				
npq	39	B Giacomelli	Life	L190	Life	W12				

Winning speed 236.569 km/h, 146.997 mph
Pole Position speed 252.990 km/h, 157.201 mph (A Senna, 1 min:22.533 sec)
Fastest Lap speed 242.076 km/h, 150.419 mph (A Senna, 1 min:26.254 sec on lap 46)
Lap Leaders A Senna 1-53 (53).

Interrupted after first lap accident. Restarted for original distance.

23 Sep 1990		**PORTUGAL: Estoril**							**(Round 13)**	**(Race 497)**
		61 laps x 4.350 km, 2.703 miles = 265.350 km, 164.881 miles								

Pos	No	Driver	Car	Model	Engine		Laps	Time/Reason for Retirement	Grid Pos	Row
1	2	N Mansell	Ferrari	641/2	Ferrari	V12	61	1h 22m 11.014s	1	1
2	27	A Senna	McLaren	MP4/5B	Honda	V10	61	1h 22m 13.822s	3	2
3	1	A Prost	Ferrari	641/2	Ferrari	V12	61	1h 22m 15.203s	2	1
4	28	G Berger	McLaren	MP4/5B	Honda	V10	61	1h 22m 16.910s	4	2
5	20	N Piquet	Benetton	B190	Ford Cosworth	V8	61	1h 23m 08.432s	6	3
6	19	A Nannini	Benetton	B190	Ford Cosworth	V8	61	1h 23m 09.263s	9	5
7	6	R Patrese	Williams	FW13B	Renault	V10	60		5	3
8	4	J Alesi	Tyrrell	019	Ford Cosworth	V8	60		8	4
9	9	M Alboreto	Arrows	A11B	Ford Cosworth	V8	60		19	10
10	25	N Larini	Ligier	JS33B	Ford Cosworth	V8	59		22	11
11	23	P Martini	Minardi	M190	Ford Cosworth	V8	59		16	8
12	15	M Gugelmin	Leyton House	CG901	Judd	V8	59		14	7
13r	10	A Caffi	Arrows	A11B	Ford Cosworth	V8	58	accident / injury	17	9
14r	30	A Suzuki	Lola	90	Lamborghini	V12	58	accident	11	6
15	21	E Pirro	Dallara	190	Ford Cosworth	V8	58		13	7
r	26	P Alliot	Ligier	JS33B	Ford Cosworth	V8	52	accident	20	10
r	7	D Brabham	Brabham	BT59	Judd	V8	52	gearbox	25	13
r	16	I Capelli	Leyton House	CG901	Judd	V8	51	engine	12	6
r	5	T Boutsen	Williams	FW13B	Renault	V10	30	gearbox	7	4
r	29	É Bernard	Lola	90	Lamborghini	V12	24	gearbox	10	5
r	8	S Modena	Brabham	BT59	Judd	V8	21	gearbox	23	12
r	12	M Donnelly	Lotus	102	Lamborghini	V12	14	alternator	15	8
r	11	D Warwick	Lotus	102	Lamborghini	V12	5	throttle slides jammed	21	11
r	18	Y Dalmas	AGS	JH25	Ford Cosworth	V8	3	driveshaft	24	12
r	22	A de Cesaris	Dallara	190	Ford Cosworth	V8	0	throttle jammed / spin	18	9
ns	3	S Nakajima	Tyrrell	019	Ford Cosworth	V8		driver ill (earlier accident)		
nq	14	O Grouillard	Osella	FA1M-E	Ford Cosworth	V8				
nq	24	P Barilla	Minardi	M190	Ford Cosworth	V8				
nq	17	G Tarquini	AGS	JH25	Ford Cosworth	V8				
nq	31	B Gachot	Coloni	FC189C	Ford Cosworth	V8				
npq	33	R Moreno	EuroBrun	ER189B	Judd	V8				
npq	34	C Langes	EuroBrun	ER189B	Judd	V8				
npq	39	B Giacomelli	Life	L190	Judd	V8				

Winning speed 193.725 km/h, 120.375 mph
Pole Position speed 212.896 km/h, 132.288 mph (N Mansell, 1 min:13.557 sec)
Fastest Lap speed 199.985 km/h, 124.265 mph (R Patrese, 1 min:18.306 sec on lap 56)
Lap Leaders A Senna 1-28,32-49 (46); G Berger 29-31 (3); N Mansell 50-61 (12).

Scheduled for 71 laps, but stopped early, because of an accident.

30 Sep 1990   SPAIN: Jerez de la Frontera   (Round 14)   (Race 498)

73 laps x 4.218 km, 2.621 miles = 307.914 km, 191.329 miles

Pos	No	Driver	Car	Model	Engine		Laps	Time/Reason for Retirement	Grid Pos	Row
1	1	A Prost	Ferrari	641/2	Ferrari	V12	73	1h 48m 01.461s	2	1
2	2	N Mansell	Ferrari	641/2	Ferrari	V12	73	1h 48m 23.525s	3	2
3	19	A Nannini	Benetton	B190	Ford Cosworth	V8	73	1h 48m 36.335s	9	5
4	5	T Boutsen	Williams	FW13B	Renault	V10	73	1h 48m 44.757s	7	4
5	6	R Patrese	Williams	FW13B	Renault	V10	73	1h 48m 58.991s	6	3
6	30	A Suzuki	Lola	90	Lamborghini	V12	73	1h 49m 05.189s	15	8
7	25	N Larini	Ligier	JS33B	Ford Cosworth	V8	72		20	10
8	15	M Gugelmin	Leyton House	CG901	Judd	V8	72		12	6
9	18	Y Dalmas	AGS	JH25	Ford Cosworth	V8	72		23	12
10	9	M Alboreto	Arrows	A11B	Ford Cosworth	V8	71		25	13
r	11	D Warwick	Lotus	102	Lamborghini	V12	63	gearbox	10	5
r	16	I Capelli	Leyton House	CG901	Judd	V8	59	driver discomfort (leg cramp)	19	10
r	28	G Berger	McLaren	MP4/5B	Honda	V10	56	accident	5	3
r	27	A Senna	McLaren	MP4/5B	Honda	V10	53	radiator	1	1
r	20	N Piquet	Benetton	B190	Ford Cosworth	V8	47	alternator	8	4
r	22	A de Cesaris	Dallara	190	Ford Cosworth	V8	47	dropped valve	17	9
r	14	O Grouillard	Osella	FA1M-E	Ford Cosworth	V8	45	rear wheel bearing	21	11
r	23	P Martini	Minardi	M190	Ford Cosworth	V8	41	wheel nut loose / spin	11	6
r	26	P Alliot	Ligier	JS33B	Ford Cosworth	V8	22	spin	13	7
r	29	É Bernard	Lola	90	Lamborghini	V12	20	gearbox	18	9
r	3	S Nakajima	Tyrrell	019	Ford Cosworth	V8	13	spin	14	7
r	17	G Tarquini	AGS	JH25	Ford Cosworth	V8	5	electrics	22	11
r	8	S Modena	Brabham	BT59	Judd	V8	5	accident	24	12
r	21	E Pirro	Dallara	190	Ford Cosworth	V8	0	throttle slides / spin	16	8
r	4	J Alesi	Tyrrell	019	Ford Cosworth	V8	0	accident	4	2
ns	12	M Donnelly	Lotus	102	Lamborghini	V12		accident / injury		
nq	7	D Brabham	Brabham	BT59	Judd	V8				
nq	24	P Barilla	Minardi	M190	Ford Cosworth	V8				
nq	10	B Schneider	Arrows	A11B	Ford Cosworth	V8				
nq	31	B Gachot	Coloni	FC189C	Ford Cosworth	V8				
npq	33	R Moreno	EuroBrun	ER189B	Judd	V8				
npq	34	C Langes	EuroBrun	ER189B	Judd	V8				
npq	39	B Giacomelli	Life	L190	Judd	V8				

Winning speed 171.025 km/h, 106.270 mph
Pole Position speed 193.716 km/h, 120.369 mph (A Senna, 1 min:18.387 sec)
Fastest Lap speed 179.674 km/h, 111.644 mph (R Patrese, 1 min:24.513 sec on lap 53)
Lap Leaders A Senna 1-26 (26); N Piquet 27-28 (2); A Prost 29-73 (45).

21 Oct 1990   JAPAN: Suzuka   (Round 15)   (Race 499)

53 laps x 5.859 km, 3.641 miles = 310.527 km, 192.953 miles

Pos	No	Driver	Car	Model	Engine		Laps	Time/Reason for Retirement	Grid Pos	Row
1	20	N Piquet	Benetton	B190	Ford Cosworth	V8	53	1h 34m 36.824s	6	3
2	19	R Moreno	Benetton	B190	Ford Cosworth	V8	53	1h 34m 44.047s	8	4
3	30	A Suzuki	Lola	90	Lamborghini	V12	53	1h 34m 59.293s	9	5
4	6	R Patrese	Williams	FW13B	Renault	V10	53	1h 35m 13.082s	7	4
5	5	T Boutsen	Williams	FW13B	Renault	V10	53	1h 35m 23.708s	5	3
6	3	S Nakajima	Tyrrell	019	Ford Cosworth	V8	53	1h 35m 49.174s	13	7
7	25	N Larini	Ligier	JS33B	Ford Cosworth	V8	52		17	9
8	23	P Martini	Minardi	M190	Ford Cosworth	V8	52		10	5
9	10	A Caffi	Arrows	A11B	Ford Cosworth	V8	52		23	12
10	26	P Alliot	Ligier	JS33B	Ford Cosworth	V8	52		20	10
r	11	D Warwick	Lotus	102	Lamborghini	V12	38	gearbox	11	6
r	12	J Herbert	Lotus	102	Lamborghini	V12	31	engine	14	7
r	9	M Alboreto	Arrows	A11B	Ford Cosworth	V8	28	engine	24	12
r	2	N Mansell	Ferrari	641/2	Ferrari	V12	26	driveshaft	3	2
r	21	E Pirro	Dallara	190	Ford Cosworth	V8	24	alternator	18	9
r	29	É Bernard	Lola	90	Lamborghini	V12	24	oil leak / fire	16	8
r	24	G Morbidelli	Minardi	M190	Ford Cosworth	V8	18	spin	19	10
r	16	I Capelli	Leyton House	CG901	Judd	V8	16	electrics	12	6
r	22	A de Cesaris	Dallara	190	Ford Cosworth	V8	13	spin	25	13
r	15	M Gugelmin	Leyton House	CG901	Judd	V8	5	engine	15	8
r	7	D Brabham	Brabham	BT59	Judd	V8	2	clutch	22	11
r	28	G Berger	McLaren	MP4/5B	Honda	V10	1	spin	4	2
r	8	S Modena	Brabham	BT59	Judd	V8	0	accident	21	11
r	1	A Prost	Ferrari	641/2	Ferrari	V12	0	accident	2	1
r	27	A Senna	McLaren	MP4/5B	Honda	V10	0	accident	1	1
ns	4	J Alesi	Tyrrell	019	Ford Cosworth	V8		driver unfit (earlier accident)		
nq	14	O Grouillard	Osella	FA1M-E	Ford Cosworth	V8				
nq	17	G Tarquini	AGS	JH25	Ford Cosworth	V8				
nq	18	Y Dalmas	AGS	JH25	Ford Cosworth	V8				
nq	31	B Gachot	Coloni	FC189C	Ford Cosworth	V8				

Winning speed 196.923 km/h, 122.362 mph
Pole Position speed 217.456 km/h, 135.121 mph (A Senna, 1 min:36.996 sec)
Fastest Lap speed 202.358 km/h, 125.740 mph (R Patrese, 1 min:44.233 sec on lap 40)
Lap Leaders G Berger 1 (1); N Mansell 2-26 (25); N Piquet 27-53 (27).

81 laps x 3.780 km, 2.349 miles = 306.180 km, 190.251 miles

Pos	No	Driver	Car	Model	Engine		Laps	Time/Reason for Retirement	Grid Pos	Row
1	20	N Piquet	Benetton	B190	Ford Cosworth	V8	81	1h 49m 44.570s	7	4
2	2	N Mansell	Ferrari	641/2	Ferrari	V12	81	1h 49m 47.699s	3	2
3	1	A Prost	Ferrari	641/2	Ferrari	V12	81	1h 50m 21.829s	4	2
4	28	G Berger	McLaren	MP4/5B	Honda	V10	81	1h 50m 31.432s	2	1
5	5	T Boutsen	Williams	FW13B	Renault	V10	81	1h 51m 35.730s	9	5
6	6	R Patrese	Williams	FW13B	Renault	V10	80		6	3
7	19	R Moreno	Benetton	B190	Ford Cosworth	V8	80		8	4
8	4	J Alesi	Tyrrell	019	Ford Cosworth	V8	80		5	3
9	23	P Martini	Minardi	M190	Ford Cosworth	V8	79		10	5
10	25	N Larini	Ligier	JS33B	Ford Cosworth	V8	79		12	6
11	26	P Alliot	Ligier	JS33B	Ford Cosworth	V8	78		19	10
12	8	S Modena	Brabham	BT59	Judd	V8	77		17	9
13	14	O Grouillard	Osella	FA1M-E	Ford Cosworth	V8	74		22	11
r	21	E Pirro	Dallara	190	Ford Cosworth	V8	68	electrics	21	11
r	27	A Senna	McLaren	MP4/5B	Honda	V10	61	accident	1	1
r	17	G Tarquini	AGS	JH25	Ford Cosworth	V8	58	engine / oil fire	26	13
r	12	J Herbert	Lotus	102	Lamborghini	V12	57	clutch	18	9
r	3	S Nakajima	Tyrrell	019	Ford Cosworth	V8	53	accident	13	7
r	16	I Capelli	Leyton House	CG901	Judd	V8	46	throttle jammed	14	7
r	11	D Warwick	Lotus	102	Lamborghini	V12	43	gearbox	11	6
r	15	M Gugelmin	Leyton House	CG901	Judd	V8	27	brakes / spin	16	8
r	22	A de Cesaris	Dallara	190	Ford Cosworth	V8	23	electrics	15	8
r	29	É Bernard	Lola	90	Lamborghini	V12	21	gear selection	23	12
r	24	G Morbidelli	Minardi	M190	Ford Cosworth	V8	20	gearbox	20	10
r	7	D Brabham	Brabham	BT59	Judd	V8	18	spin	25	13
r	30	A Suzuki	Lola	90	Lamborghini	V12	6	differential	24	12
nq	9	M Alboreto	Arrows	A11B	Ford Cosworth	V8				
nq	18	Y Dalmas	AGS	JH25	Ford Cosworth	V8				
nq	10	A Caffi	Arrows	A11B	Ford Cosworth	V8				
nq	31	B Gachot	Coloni	FC189C	Ford Cosworth	V8				

Winning speed 167.399 km/h, 104.017 mph
Pole Position speed 179.831 km/h, 111.742 mph (A Senna, 1 min:15.671 sec)
Fastest Lap speed 174.009 km/h, 108.124 mph (N Mansell, 1 min:18.203 sec on lap 75)
Lap Leaders A Senna 1-61 (61); N Piquet 62-81 (20).

Pos	Driver	Car-Engine	GPs	laps	km	miles
1	A Senna	McLaren-Honda	14	500	2,307.5	1,433.8
2	G Berger	McLaren-Honda	7	128	571.3	355.0
3	A Prost	Ferrari	5	110	480.3	298.4
4	T Boutsen	Williams-Renault	2	91	376.1	233.7
5	N Mansell	Ferrari	4	64	325.8	202.4
6	N Piquet	Benetton-Ford Cosworth	3	49	242.2	150.5
7	I Capelli	Leyton House-Judd	1	45	171.6	106.6
8	J Alesi	Tyrrell-Ford Cosworth	1	34	129.1	80.2
9	A Nannini	Benetton-Ford Cosworth	2	19	122.0	75.8
10	R Patrese	Williams-Renault	2	12	59.3	36.8
			16	1,052	4,785.2	2,973.4

Driver Points 1990

	Driver	USA	BR	RSM	MC	CDN	MEX	F	GB	D	H	B	I	P	E	J	AUS	Total	
1	A Senna	9	4	-	9	9	-	4	4	9	6	9	9	6	-	-	-	78	
2	A Prost	-	9	3	-	(2)	9	9	9	3	-	6	6	4	9	-	4	71	(2)
3	N Piquet	3	1	2	-	6	(1)	3	2	-	4	2	-	2	-	9	9	43	(1)
	G Berger	-	6	6	4	3	4	2	-	4	-	4	4	3	-	-	3	43	
5	N Mansell	-	3	-	-	4	6	-	-	-	-	-	3	9	6	-	6	37	
6	T Boutsen	4	2	-	3	-	2	-	6	1	9	-	-	-	3	2	2	34	
7	R Patrese	-	-	9	-	-	-	1	-	2	3	-	2	-	2	3	1	23	
8	A Nannini	-	-	4	-	-	3	-	-	6	-	3	-	1	4	-	-	21	
9	J Alesi	6	-	1	6	-	-	-	-	-	-	-	-	-	-	-	-	13	
10	I Capelli	-	-	-	-	-	-	6	-	-	-	-	-	-	-	-	-	6	
	R Moreno	-	-	-	-	-	-	-	-	-	-	-	-	-	6	-	-	6	
	A Suzuki	-	-	-	-	-	-	1	-	-	-	-	-	1	4	-	-	6	
13	É Bernard	-	-	-	1	-	-	-	3	-	1	-	-	-	-	-	-	5	
14	D Warwick	-	-	-	-	1	-	-	-	2	-	-	-	-	-	-	-	3	
	S Nakajima	1	-	-	-	-	-	-	-	-	-	-	1	-	-	1	-	3	
16	S Modena	2	-	-	-	-	-	-	-	-	-	-	-	-	-	-	-	2	
	A Caffi	-	-	-	2	-	-	-	-	-	-	-	-	-	-	-	-	2	
18	M Gugelmin	-	-	-	-	-	-	-	-	-	1	-	-	-	-	-	-	1	

9,6,4,3,2 and 1 point awarded to the first six finishers. Best 11 scores.

Constructor Points 1990

	Constructor	USA	BR	RSM	MC	CDN	MEX	F	GB	D	H	B	I	P	E	J	AUS	Total	
1	McLaren-Honda	9	10	6	13	12	4	6	4	13	6	13	13	9	-	-	3	121	
2	Ferrari	-	12	3	-	6	15	9	9	3	-	6	9	13	15	-	10	110	
3	Benetton-Ford Cosworth	3	1	6	-	6	4	3	2	6	4	5	-	3	4	15	9	71	
4	Williams-Renault	4	2	9	3	-	2	1	6	3	12	-	2	-	5	5	3	57	
5	Tyrrell-Ford Cosworth	7	-	1	6	-	-	-	-	-	-	-	1	-	-	1	-	16	
6	Lola-Lamborghini	-	-	-	1	-	-	-	4	-	1	-	-	-	1	4	-	11	*
7	Leyton House-Judd	-	-	-	-	-	-	6	-	-	-	1	-	-	-	-	-	7	
8	Lotus-Lamborghini	-	-	-	-	1	-	-	-	-	2	-	-	-	-	-	-	3	
9	Brabham-Judd	2	-	-	-	-	-	-	-	-	-	-	-	-	-	-	-	2	
	Arrows-Ford Cosworth	-	-	-	2	-	-	-	-	-	-	-	-	-	-	-	-	2	

*9,6,4,3,2 and 1 point awarded to the first six finishers. * Points disallowed by FISA at end of season, due to entry irregularity.*

Race Entrants and Results

Honda raced its new V12 engine and Porsche returned with the Footwork Arrows team. Jordan made an impressive debut although Gachot found himself in a British jail after a traffic argument. Tom Walkinshaw purchased a share of the Benetton operation. 10 points were now awarded to race winners.

McLAREN
Honda Marlboro McLaren: Senna, Berger

TYRRELL
Braun Tyrrell Honda: Nakajima, Modena

WILLIAMS
Canon Williams Team: Mansell, Patrese

BRABHAM
Motor Racing Developments: Brundle, Blundell

FOOTWORK
Footwork (Porsche): Alboreto, Caffi, Johansson

LOTUS
Team Lotus: Häkkinen, Bailey, Herbert, (Bartels)

FOMET
Fondmetal F1 SpA: Grouillard, Tarquini

LEYTON HOUSE
Leyton House Racing: Gugelmin, Capelli, Wendlinger

AGS
Automobiles Gonfaronaises Sportives: Tarquini, (Grouillard, Johansson, Barbazza)

BENETTON
Camel Benetton Ford: Moreno, Schumacher, Piquet

DALLARA
Scuderia Italia SpA: Pirro, Lehto

MINARDI
SCM Minardi Team: Martini, Morbidelli, Moreno

LIGIER
Ligier Gitanes: Boutsen, Comas

FERRARI
Scuderia Ferrari SpA: Prost, Morbidelli, Alesi

LOLA
Larrousse: Bernard, (Gachot), Suzuki

COLONI
Coloni Racing Srl: (Chaves, Hattori)

JORDAN
Team 7UP Jordan: Gachot, Schumacher, Moreno, Zanardi, de Cesaris

LAMBORGHINI
Modena Team SpA: Larini, van de Poele

10 Mar 1991   USA: Phoenix   (Round 1)   (Race 501)
81 laps x 3.721 km, 2.312 miles = 301.385 km, 187.272 miles

Pos	No	Driver	Car	Model	Engine		Laps	Time/Reason for Retirement	Grid Pos	Row
1	1	A Senna	McLaren	MP4/6	Honda	V12	81	2h 00m 47.828s	1	1
2	27	A Prost	Ferrari	642	Ferrari	V12	81	2h 01m 04.150s	2	1
3	20	N Piquet	Benetton	B190B	Ford Cosworth	V8	81	2h 01m 05.204s	5	3
4	4	S Modena	Tyrrell	020	Honda	V10	81	2h 01m 13.237s	11	6
5	3	S Nakajima	Tyrrell	020	Honda	V10	80		16	8
6	30	A Suzuki	Lola	L91	Ford Cosworth	V8	79		21	11
7	34	N Larini	Lamborghini	291	Lamborghini	V12	78		17	9
8	17	G Tarquini	AGS	JH25	Ford Cosworth	V8	77		22	11
9r	23	P Martini	Minardi	M191	Ferrari	V12	75	engine	15	8
10r	32	B Gachot	Jordan	191	Ford Cosworth	V8	75	engine	14	7
11	7	M Brundle	Brabham	BT59Y	Yamaha	V12	73		12	6
12r	28	J Alesi	Ferrari	642	Ferrari	V12	72	gearbox	6	3
r	11	M Häkkinen	Lotus	102B	Judd	V8	59	engine / fire	13	7
r	6	R Patrese	Williams	FW14	Renault	V10	49	gearbox / accident	3	2
r	19	R Moreno	Benetton	B190B	Ford Cosworth	V8	49	accident	8	4
r	9	M Alboreto	Footwork	A11C	Porsche	V12	41	gearbox	25	13
r	16	I Capelli	Leyton House	CG911	Ilmor	V10	40	gearbox oil pump	18	9
r	25	T Boutsen	Ligier	JS35	Lamborghini	V12	40	electronics	20	10
r	2	G Berger	McLaren	MP4/6	Honda	V12	36	fuel pump	7	4
r	5	N Mansell	Williams	FW14	Renault	V10	35	gearbox	4	2
r	15	M Gugelmin	Leyton House	CG911	Ilmor	V10	34	gearbox	23	12
r	8	M Blundell	Brabham	BT59Y	Yamaha	V12	32	accident	24	12
r	21	E Pirro	Dallara	191	Judd	V10	16	clutch	9	5
r	24	G Morbidelli	Minardi	M191	Ferrari	V12	15	gearbox	26	13
r	22	J J Lehto	Dallara	191	Judd	V10	12	clutch	10	5
r	29	É Bernard	Lola	L91	Ford Cosworth	V8	4	engine	19	10
nq	26	E Comas	Ligier	JS35	Lamborghini	V12				
nq	10	A Caffi	Footwork	A11C	Porsche	V12				
nq	18	S Johansson	AGS	JH25	Ford Cosworth	V8				
nq	12	J Bailey	Lotus	102B	Judd	V8				
npq	33	A de Cesaris	Jordan	191	Ford Cosworth	V8				
npq	31	P Chaves	Coloni	C4	Ford Cosworth	V8				
npq	14	O Grouillard	Fomet	FA1M-E	Ford Cosworth	V8				
npq	35	E van de Poele	Lamborghini	291	Lamborghini	V12				

Winning speed 149.698 km/h, 93.018 mph
Pole Position speed 164.488 km/h, 102.208 mph (A Senna, 1 min:21.434 sec)
Fastest Lap speed 154.394 km/h, 95.936 mph (J Alesi, 1 min:26.758 sec on lap 49)
Lap Leaders A Senna 1-81 (81).

Scheduled for 82 laps, but stopped at 2 hours.

BRAZIL: Interlagos (Round 2) (Race 502)

71 laps x 4.325 km, 2.687 miles = 307.075 km, 190.808 miles

Pos	No	Driver	Car	Model	Engine		Laps	Time/Reason for Retirement	Grid Pos	Row
1	1	A Senna	McLaren	MP4/6	Honda	V12	71	1h 38m 28.128s	1	1
2	6	R Patrese	Williams	FW14	Renault	V10	71	1h 38m 31.119s	2	1
3	2	G Berger	McLaren	MP4/6	Honda	V12	71	1h 38m 33.544s	4	2
4	27	A Prost	Ferrari	642	Ferrari	V12	71	1h 38m 47.497s	6	3
5	20	N Piquet	Benetton	B190B	Ford Cosworth	V8	71	1h 38m 50.088s	7	4
6	28	J Alesi	Ferrari	642	Ferrari	V12	71	1h 38m 51.769s	5	3
7	19	R Moreno	Benetton	B190B	Ford Cosworth	V8	70		14	7
8	24	G Morbidelli	Minardi	M191	Ferrari	V12	69		21	11
9	11	M Häkkinen	Lotus	102B	Judd	V8	68		22	11
10	25	T Boutsen	Ligier	JS35	Lamborghini	V12	68		18	9
11	21	E Pirro	Dallara	191	Judd	V10	68		12	6
12	7	M Brundle	Brabham	BT59Y	Yamaha	V12	67		26	13
13r	32	B Gachot	Jordan	191	Ford Cosworth	V8	63	exhaust / fuel pick-up	10	5
r	5	N Mansell	Williams	FW14	Renault	V10	59	gearbox	3	2
r	26	E Comas	Ligier	JS35	Lamborghini	V12	50	oil radiator fire / spin	23	12
r	23	P Martini	Minardi	M191	Ferrari	V12	47	spin	20	10
r	8	M Blundell	Brabham	BT59Y	Yamaha	V12	34	engine	25	13
r	29	É Bernard	Lola	L91	Ford Cosworth	V8	33	clutch hydraulic pipe	11	6
r	22	J J Lehto	Dallara	191	Judd	V10	22	alternator	19	10
r	33	A de Cesaris	Jordan	191	Ford Cosworth	V8	20	electronics / accident	13	7
r	4	S Modena	Tyrrell	020	Honda	V10	19	gear linkage	9	5
r	16	I Capelli	Leyton House	CG911	Ilmor	V10	16	engine	15	8
r	3	S Nakajima	Tyrrell	020	Honda	V10	12	spin	16	8
r	15	M Gugelmin	Leyton House	CG911	Ilmor	V10	9	driver unfit (burnt in warm-up)	8	4
r	17	G Tarquini	AGS	JH25	Ford Cosworth	V8	0	spin	24	12
ns	30	A Suzuki	Lola	L91	Ford Cosworth	V8		fuel pump on dummy grid	17	9
nq	10	A Caffi	Footwork	A11C	Porsche	V12				
nq	18	S Johansson	AGS	JH25	Ford Cosworth	V8				
nq	9	M Alboreto	Footwork	A11C	Porsche	V12				
nq	12	J Bailey	Lotus	102B	Judd	V8				
npq	35	E van de Poele	Lamborghini	291	Lamborghini	V12				
npq	34	N Larini	Lamborghini	291	Lamborghini	V12				
npq	31	P Chaves	Coloni	C4	Ford Cosworth	V8				
npq	14	O Grouillard	Fomet	FA1M-E	Ford Cosworth	V8				

Winning speed 187.110 km/h, 116.265 mph
Pole Position speed 203.817 km/h, 126.646 mph (A Senna, 1 min:16.392 sec)
Fastest Lap speed 193.570 km/h, 120.279 mph (N Mansell, 1 min:20.436 sec on lap 35)
Lap Leaders A Senna 1-71 (71).

---

28 Apr 1991 **SAN MARINO: Imola** (Round 3) (Race 503)

61 laps x 5.040 km, 3.132 miles = 307.440 km, 191.034 miles

Pos	No	Driver	Car	Model	Engine		Laps	Time/Reason for Retirement	Grid Pos	Row
1	1	A Senna	McLaren	MP4/6	Honda	V12	61	1h 35m 14.750s	1	1
2	2	G Berger	McLaren	MP4/6	Honda	V12	61	1h 35m 16.425s	5	3
3	22	J J Lehto	Dallara	191	Judd	V10	60		16	8
4	23	P Martini	Minardi	M191	Ferrari	V12	59		9	5
5	11	M Häkkinen	Lotus	102B	Judd	V8	58		25	13
6	12	J Bailey	Lotus	102B	Judd	V8	58		26	13
7	25	T Boutsen	Ligier	JS35	Lamborghini	V12	58		24	12
8	8	M Blundell	Brabham	BT60Y	Yamaha	V12	58		23	12
9r	35	E van de Poele	Lamborghini	291	Lamborghini	V12	57	fuel pump	21	11
10	26	E Comas	Ligier	JS35	Lamborghini	V12	57		19	10
11	7	M Brundle	Brabham	BT60Y	Yamaha	V12	57		18	9
12r	15	M Gugelmin	Leyton House	CG911	Ilmor	V10	55	engine	15	8
13r	19	R Moreno	Benetton	B191	Ford Cosworth	V8	54	gearbox / engine	13	7
r	4	S Modena	Tyrrell	020	Honda	V10	41	transmission	6	3
r	33	A de Cesaris	Jordan	191	Ford Cosworth	V8	37	gear linkage	11	6
r	32	B Gachot	Jordan	191	Ford Cosworth	V8	37	spin / suspension	12	6
r	16	I Capelli	Leyton House	CG911	Ilmor	V10	24	tyre / spin	22	11
r	29	É Bernard	Lola	L91	Ford Cosworth	V8	17	engine	17	9

Grand Prix Data Book

Pos	No	Driver	Car	Model	Engine		Laps	Time/Reason for Retirement	Grid Pos	Row
r	6	R Patrese	Williams	FW14	Renault	V10	17	electrics / engine	2	1
r	3	S Nakajima	Tyrrell	020	Honda	V10	15	transmission	10	5
r	24	G Morbidelli	Minardi	M191	Ferrari	V12	10	gearbox	8	4
r	28	J Alesi	Ferrari	642	Ferrari	V12	2	spin	7	4
r	30	A Suzuki	Lola	L91	Ford Cosworth	V8	2	spin	20	10
r	20	N Piquet	Benetton	B191	Ford Cosworth	V8	1	spin	14	7
r	5	N Mansell	Williams	FW14	Renault	V10	0	gearbox / accident	4	2
ns	27	A Prost	Ferrari	642	Ferrari	V12		spin on parade lap	3	2
nq	17	G Tarquini	AGS	JH25	Ford Cosworth	V8				
nq	18	F Barbazza	AGS	JH25	Ford Cosworth	V8				
nq	10	A Caffi	Footwork	FA12	Porsche	V12				
nq	9	M Alboreto	Footwork	A11C	Porsche	V12				
npq	21	E Pirro	Dallara	191	Judd	V10				
npq	14	O Grouillard	Fomet	F1	Ford Cosworth	V8				
npq	34	N Larini	Lamborghini	291	Lamborghini	V12				
npq	31	P Chaves	Coloni	C4	Ford Cosworth	V8				

Winning speed 193.671 km/h, 120.342 mph
Pole Position speed 221.601 km/h, 137.696 mph (A Senna, 1 min:21.877 sec)
Fastest Lap speed 209.682 km/h, 130.290 mph (G Berger, 1 min:26.531 sec on lap 55)
Lap Leaders R Patrese 1-9 (9); A Senna 10-61 (52).

12 May 1991		**MONACO: Monte-Carlo**						**(Round 4)**	**(Race 504)**	
		78 laps x 3.328 km, 2.068 miles = 259.584 km, 161.298 miles								

Pos	No	Driver	Car	Model	Engine		Laps	Time/Reason for Retirement	Grid Pos	Row
1	1	A Senna	McLaren	MP4/6	Honda	V12	78	1h 53m 02.334s	1	1
2	5	N Mansell	Williams	FW14	Renault	V10	78	1h 53m 20.682s	5	3
3	28	J Alesi	Ferrari	642	Ferrari	V12	78	1h 53m 49.789s	9	5
4	19	R Moreno	Benetton	B191	Ford Cosworth	V8	77		8	4
5	27	A Prost	Ferrari	642	Ferrari	V12	77		7	4
6	21	E Pirro	Dallara	191	Judd	V10	77		12	6
7	25	T Boutsen	Ligier	JS35	Lamborghini	V12	76		16	8
8	32	B Gachot	Jordan	191	Ford Cosworth	V8	76		24	12
9	29	É Bernard	Lola	L91	Ford Cosworth	V8	76		21	11
10	26	E Comas	Ligier	JS35	Lamborghini	V12	76		23	12
11	22	J J Lehto	Dallara	191	Judd	V10	75		13	7
12	23	P Martini	Minardi	M191	Ferrari	V12	72		14	7
r	11	M Häkkinen	Lotus	102B	Judd	V8	64	oil leak / fire	26	13
r	24	G Morbidelli	Minardi	M191	Ferrari	V12	49	gearbox	17	9
r	15	M Gugelmin	Leyton House	CG911	Ilmor	V10	43	throttle linkage	15	8
r	4	S Modena	Tyrrell	020	Honda	V10	42	engine	2	1
r	6	R Patrese	Williams	FW14	Renault	V10	42	accident	3	2
r	8	M Blundell	Brabham	BT60Y	Yamaha	V12	41	accident	22	11
r	9	M Alboreto	Footwork	FA12	Porsche	V12	39	engine	25	13
r	3	S Nakajima	Tyrrell	020	Honda	V10	35	spin	11	6
r	30	A Suzuki	Lola	L91	Ford Cosworth	V8	24	brakes / accident	19	10
r	33	A de Cesaris	Jordan	191	Ford Cosworth	V8	21	throttle linkage	10	5
r	16	I Capelli	Leyton House	CG911	Ilmor	V10	12	brake fluid loss	18	9
r	17	G Tarquini	AGS	JH25	Ford Cosworth	V8	9	gearbox	20	10
r	2	G Berger	McLaren	MP4/6	Honda	V12	9	accident	6	3
r	20	N Piquet	Benetton	B191	Ford Cosworth	V8	0	accident / rear suspension	4	2
nq	12	J Bailey	Lotus	102B	Judd	V8				
nq	18	F Barbazza	AGS	JH25	Ford Cosworth	V8				
nq	10	A Caffi	Footwork	FA12	Porsche	V12		accident / injury		
npq	34	N Larini	Lamborghini	291	Lamborghini	V12				
npq	35	E van de Poele	Lamborghini	291	Lamborghini	V12				
npq	31	P Chaves	Coloni	C4	Ford Cosworth	V8				
npq	14	O Grouillard	Fomet	F1	Ford Cosworth	V8				
exc	7	M Brundle	Brabham	BT60Y	Yamaha	V12		missed weight check		

Winning speed 137.785 km/h, 85.615 mph
Pole Position speed 149.119 km/h, 92.658 mph (A Senna, 1 min:20.344 sec)
Fastest Lap speed 142.006 km/h, 88.239 mph (A Prost, 1 min:24.368 sec on lap 77)
Lap Leaders A Senna 1-78 (78).

Races

CANADA: Montréal (Round 5) (Race 505)

69 laps x 4.430 km, 2.753 miles = 305.670 km, 189.935 miles

Pos	No	Driver	Car	Model	Engine		Laps	Time/Reason for Retirement	Grid Pos	Row
1	20	N Piquet	Benetton	B191	Ford Cosworth	V8	69	1h 38m 51.490s	8	4
2	4	S Modena	Tyrrell	020	Honda	V10	69	1h 39m 23.322s	9	5
3	6	R Patrese	Williams	FW14	Renault	V10	69	1h 39m 33.707s	1	1
4	33	A de Cesaris	Jordan	191	Ford Cosworth	V8	69	1h 40m 11.700s	11	6
5	32	B Gachot	Jordan	191	Ford Cosworth	V8	69	1h 40m 13.841s	14	7
6r	5	N Mansell	Williams	FW14	Renault	V10	68	gearbox / engine	2	1
7	23	P Martini	Minardi	M191	Ferrari	V12	68		18	9
8	26	E Comas	Ligier	JS35	Lamborghini	V12	68		26	13
9	21	E Pirro	Dallara	191	Judd	V10	68		10	5
10	3	S Nakajima	Tyrrell	020	Honda	V10	67		12	6
r	15	M Gugelmin	Leyton House	CG911	Ilmor	V10	61	engine	23	12
r	22	J J Lehto	Dallara	191	Judd	V10	50	engine	17	9
r	10	S Johansson	Footwork	FA12	Porsche	V12	48	gearbox / engine	25	13
r	16	I Capelli	Leyton House	CG911	Ilmor	V10	42	engine	13	7
r	28	J Alesi	Ferrari	642	Ferrari	V12	34	engine	7	4
r	29	É Bernard	Lola	L91	Ford Cosworth	V8	29	gearbox	19	10
r	27	A Prost	Ferrari	642	Ferrari	V12	27	gearbox	4	2
r	25	T Boutsen	Ligier	JS35	Lamborghini	V12	27	engine	16	8
r	1	A Senna	McLaren	MP4/6	Honda	V12	25	alternator	3	2
r	11	M Häkkinen	Lotus	102B	Judd	V8	21	spin	24	12
r	7	M Brundle	Brabham	BT60Y	Yamaha	V12	21	engine	20	10
r	24	G Morbidelli	Minardi	M191	Ferrari	V12	20	spin	15	8
r	19	R Moreno	Benetton	B191	Ford Cosworth	V8	10	spin / rear suspension	5	3
r	2	G Berger	McLaren	MP4/6	Honda	V12	4	electronics	6	3
r	30	A Suzuki	Lola	L91	Ford Cosworth	V8	3	fuel line / fire	22	11
r	9	M Alboreto	Footwork	FA12	Porsche	V12	2	throttle / engine	21	11
nq	18	F Barbazza	AGS	JH25	Ford Cosworth	V8				
nq	17	G Tarquini	AGS	JH25	Ford Cosworth	V8				
nq	8	M Blundell	Brabham	BT60Y	Yamaha	V12				
nq	12	J Herbert	Lotus	102B	Judd	V8				
npq	14	O Grouillard	Fomet	F1	Ford Cosworth	V8				
npq	34	N Larini	Lamborghini	291	Lamborghini	V12				
npq	35	E van de Poele	Lamborghini	291	Lamborghini	V12				
npq	31	P Chaves	Coloni	C4	Ford Cosworth	V8				

Winning speed 185.520 km/h, 115.277 mph
Pole Position speed 199.757 km/h, 124.123 mph (R Patrese, 1 min:19.837 sec)
Fastest Lap speed 193.579 km/h, 120.284 mph (N Mansell, 1 min:22.385 sec on lap 65)
Lap Leaders N Mansell 1-68 (68); N Piquet 69 (1).

---

16 Jun 1991 **MEXICO: Mexico City** (Round 6) (Race 506)

67 laps x 4.421 km, 2.747 miles = 296.207 km, 184.054 miles

Pos	No	Driver	Car	Model	Engine		Laps	Time/Reason for Retirement	Grid Pos	Row
1	6	R Patrese	Williams	FW14	Renault	V10	67	1h 29m 52.205s	1	1
2	5	N Mansell	Williams	FW14	Renault	V10	67	1h 29m 53.541s	2	1
3	1	A Senna	McLaren	MP4/6	Honda	V12	67	1h 30m 49.561s	3	2
4r	33	A de Cesaris	Jordan	191	Ford Cosworth	V8	66	throttle potentiometer	11	6
5	19	R Moreno	Benetton	B191	Ford Cosworth	V8	66		9	5
6	29	É Bernard	Lola	L91	Ford Cosworth	V8	66		18	9
7	24	G Morbidelli	Minardi	M191	Ferrari	V12	66		23	12
8	25	T Boutsen	Ligier	JS35	Lamborghini	V12	65		14	7
9	11	M Häkkinen	Lotus	102B	Judd	V8	65		24	12
10	12	J Herbert	Lotus	102B	Judd	V8	65		25	13
11	4	S Modena	Tyrrell	020	Honda	V10	65		8	4
12	3	S Nakajima	Tyrrell	020	Honda	V10	64		13	7
r	8	M Blundell	Brabham	BT60Y	Yamaha	V12	54	engine	12	6
r	32	B Gachot	Jordan	191	Ford Cosworth	V8	51	spin	20	10
r	30	A Suzuki	Lola	L91	Ford Cosworth	V8	48	gearbox	19	10
r	20	N Piquet	Benetton	B191	Ford Cosworth	V8	44	rear wheel bearing	6	3
r	28	J Alesi	Ferrari	642	Ferrari	V12	42	clutch	4	2
r	22	J J Lehto	Dallara	191	Judd	V10	30	engine	16	8

Pos	No	Driver	Car	Model	Engine		Laps	Time/Reason for Retirement	Grid Pos	Row
r	9	M Alboreto	Footwork	FA12	Porsche	V12	24	oil pressure	26	13
r	7	M Brundle	Brabham	BT60Y	Yamaha	V12	20	rear wheel lost	17	9
r	16	I Capelli	Leyton House	CG911	Ilmor	V10	19	engine	22	11
r	27	A Prost	Ferrari	642	Ferrari	V12	16	alternator	7	4
r	15	M Gugelmin	Leyton House	CG911	Ilmor	V10	15	engine	21	11
r	14	O Grouillard	Fomet	F1	Ford Cosworth	V8	13	oil leak	10	5
r	2	G Berger	McLaren	MP4/6	Honda	V12	5	radiator / engine	5	3
r	23	P Martini	Minardi	M191	Ferrari	V12	4	spin	15	8
nq	26	E Comas	Ligier	JS35	Lamborghini	V12				
nq	17	G Tarquini	AGS	JH25	Ford Cosworth	V8				
nq	10	S Johansson	Footwork	FA12	Porsche	V12				
nq	18	F Barbazza	AGS	JH25	Ford Cosworth	V8				
exc	34	N Larini	Lamborghini	291	Lamborghini	V12		rear wing infringement		
npq	35	E van de Poele	Lamborghini	291	Lamborghini	V12				
npq	31	P Chaves	Coloni	C4	Ford Cosworth	V8				
npq	21	E Pirro	Dallara	191	Judd	V10				

Winning speed 197.757 km/h, 122.880 mph
Pole Position speed 207.515 km/h, 128.944 mph (R Patrese, 1 min:16.696 sec)
Fastest Lap speed 207.267 km/h, 128.790 mph (N Mansell, 1 min:16.788 sec on lap 61)
Lap Leaders N Mansell 1-14 (14); R Patrese 15-67 (53).

7 Jul 1991	FRANCE: Magny-Cours								(Round 7)	(Race 507)
		72 laps x 4.271 km, 2.654 miles = 307.512 km, 191.079 miles								

Pos	No	Driver	Car	Model	Engine		Laps	Time/Reason for Retirement	Grid Pos	Row
1	5	N Mansell	Williams	FW14	Renault	V10	72	1h 38m 00.056s	4	2
2	27	A Prost	Ferrari	643	Ferrari	V12	72	1h 38m 05.059s	2	1
3	1	A Senna	McLaren	MP4/6	Honda	V12	72	1h 38m 34.990s	3	2
4	28	J Alesi	Ferrari	643	Ferrari	V12	72	1h 38m 35.976s	6	3
5	6	R Patrese	Williams	FW14	Renault	V10	71		1	1
6	33	A de Cesaris	Jordan	191	Ford Cosworth	V8	71		13	7
7	15	M Gugelmin	Leyton House	CG911	Ilmor	V10	70		9	5
8	20	N Piquet	Benetton	B191	Ford Cosworth	V8	70		7	4
9	23	P Martini	Minardi	M191	Ferrari	V12	70		12	6
10	12	J Herbert	Lotus	102B	Judd	V8	70		20	10
11	26	E Comas	Ligier	JS35B	Lamborghini	V12	70		14	7
12	25	T Boutsen	Ligier	JS35B	Lamborghini	V12	69		16	8
r	19	R Moreno	Benetton	B191	Ford Cosworth	V8	63	driver ill	8	4
r	4	S Modena	Tyrrell	020	Honda	V10	57	gearbox	11	6
r	14	O Grouillard	Fomet	F1	Ford Cosworth	V8	47	oil leak	21	11
r	29	É Bernard	Lola	L91	Ford Cosworth	V8	43	crown wheel & pinion	23	12
r	22	J J Lehto	Dallara	191	Judd	V10	39	tyre	26	13
r	8	M Blundell	Brabham	BT60Y	Yamaha	V12	36	accident	17	9
r	30	A Suzuki	Lola	L91	Ford Cosworth	V8	32	clutch	22	11
r	9	M Alboreto	Footwork	FA12	Ford Cosworth	V8	31	gearbox	25	13
r	7	M Brundle	Brabham	BT60Y	Yamaha	V12	21	gearbox	24	12
r	3	S Nakajima	Tyrrell	020	Honda	V10	12	spin	18	9
r	24	G Morbidelli	Minardi	M191	Ferrari	V12	8	accident	10	5
r	16	I Capelli	Leyton House	CG911	Ilmor	V10	7	spin	15	8
r	2	G Berger	McLaren	MP4/6	Honda	V12	6	engine	5	3
r	32	B Gachot	Jordan	191	Ford Cosworth	V8	0	spin	19	10
nq	11	M Häkkinen	Lotus	102B	Judd	V8				
nq	18	F Barbazza	AGS	JH25B	Ford Cosworth	V8				
nq	17	G Tarquini	AGS	JH25B	Ford Cosworth	V8				
nq	10	S Johansson	Footwork	FA12	Ford Cosworth	V8				
npq	21	E Pirro	Dallara	191	Judd	V10				
npq	34	N Larini	Lamborghini	291	Lamborghini	V12				
npq	35	E van de Poele	Lamborghini	291	Lamborghini	V12				
npq	31	P Chaves	Coloni	C4	Ford Cosworth	V8				

Winning speed 188.271 km/h, 116.986 mph
Pole Position speed 206.221 km/h, 128.140 mph (R Patrese, 1 min:14.559 sec)
Fastest Lap speed 194.215 km/h, 120.680 mph (N Mansell, 1 min:19.168 sec on lap 49)
Lap Leaders A Prost 1-21,32-54 (44); N Mansell 22-31,55-72 (28).

14 Jul 1991   BRITAIN: Silverstone   (Round 8)   (Race 508)

59 laps x 5.226 km, 3.247 miles = 308.307 km, 191.573 miles

Pos	No	Driver	Car	Model	Engine		Laps	Time/Reason for Retirement	Grid Pos	Row
1	5	N Mansell	Williams	FW14	Renault	V10	59	1h 27m 35.479s	1	1
2	2	G Berger	McLaren	MP4/6	Honda	V12	59	1h 28m 17.772s	4	2
3	27	A Prost	Ferrari	643	Ferrari	V12	59	1h 28m 35.629s	5	3
4r	1	A Senna	McLaren	MP4/6	Honda	V12	58	out of fuel	2	1
5	20	N Piquet	Benetton	B191	Ford Cosworth	V8	58		8	4
6	32	B Gachot	Jordan	191	Ford Cosworth	V8	58		17	9
7	4	S Modena	Tyrrell	020	Honda	V10	58		10	5
8	3	S Nakajima	Tyrrell	020	Honda	V10	58		15	8
9	23	P Martini	Minardi	M191	Ferrari	V12	58		23	12
10	21	E Pirro	Dallara	191	Judd	V10	57		18	9
11	24	G Morbidelli	Minardi	M191	Ferrari	V12	57		20	10
12	11	M Häkkinen	Lotus	102B	Judd	V8	57		25	13
13	22	J J Lehto	Dallara	191	Judd	V10	56		11	6
14r	12	J Herbert	Lotus	102B	Judd	V8	55	engine	24	12
r	8	M Blundell	Brabham	BT60Y	Yamaha	V12	52	engine	12	6
r	33	A de Cesaris	Jordan	191	Ford Cosworth	V8	41	rear suspension / accident	13	7
r	28	J Alesi	Ferrari	643	Ferrari	V12	31	accident	6	3
r	30	A Suzuki	Lola	L91	Ford Cosworth	V8	29	accident	22	11
r	25	T Boutsen	Ligier	JS35B	Lamborghini	V12	29	engine	19	10
r	7	M Brundle	Brabham	BT60Y	Yamaha	V12	28	throttle linkage	14	7
r	9	M Alboreto	Footwork	FA12	Ford Cosworth	V8	25	gearbox	26	13
r	15	M Gugelmin	Leyton House	CG911	Ilmor	V10	24	chassis vibration / driver cramp	9	5
r	19	R Moreno	Benetton	B191	Ford Cosworth	V8	21	gearbox	7	4
r	29	É Bernard	Lola	L91	Ford Cosworth	V8	21	crown wheel & pinion	21	11
r	16	I Capelli	Leyton House	CG911	Ilmor	V10	16	spin	16	8
r	6	R Patrese	Williams	FW14	Renault	V10	1	accident	3	2
nq	26	E Comas	Ligier	JS35B	Lamborghini	V12				
nq	10	S Johansson	Footwork	FA12	Ford Cosworth	V8				
nq	18	F Barbazza	AGS	JH25B	Ford Cosworth	V8				
nq	17	G Tarquini	AGS	JH25B	Ford Cosworth	V8				
npq	14	O Grouillard	Fomet	F1	Ford Cosworth	V8				
npq	34	N Larini	Lamborghini	291	Lamborghini	V12				
npq	35	E van de Poele	Lamborghini	291	Lamborghini	V12				
npq	31	P Chaves	Coloni	C4	Ford Cosworth	V8				

Winning speed 211.189 km/h, 131.227 mph
Pole Position speed 232.421 km/h, 144.420 mph (N Mansell, 1 min:20.939 sec)
Fastest Lap speed 217.784 km/h, 135.325 mph (N Mansell, 1 min:26.379 sec on lap 43)
Lap Leaders N Mansell 1-59 (59).

28 Jul 1991   GERMANY: Hockenheim   (Round 9)   (Race 509)

45 laps x 6.802 km, 4.227 miles = 306.090 km, 190.196 miles

Pos	No	Driver	Car	Model	Engine		Laps	Time/Reason for Retirement	Grid Pos	Row
1	5	N Mansell	Williams	FW14	Renault	V10	45	1h 19m 29.661s	1	1
2	6	R Patrese	Williams	FW14	Renault	V10	45	1h 19m 43.440s	4	2
3	28	J Alesi	Ferrari	643	Ferrari	V12	45	1h 19m 47.279s	6	3
4	2	G Berger	McLaren	MP4/6	Honda	V12	45	1h 20m 02.312s	3	2
5	33	A de Cesaris	Jordan	191	Ford Cosworth	V8	45	1h 20m 47.198s	7	4
6	32	B Gachot	Jordan	191	Ford Cosworth	V8	45	1h 21m 10.266s	11	6
7r	1	A Senna	McLaren	MP4/6	Honda	V12	44	out of fuel	2	1
8	19	R Moreno	Benetton	B191	Ford Cosworth	V8	44		9	5
9	25	T Boutsen	Ligier	JS35B	Lamborghini	V12	44		17	9
10	21	E Pirro	Dallara	191	Judd	V10	44		18	9
11	7	M Brundle	Brabham	BT60Y	Yamaha	V12	43		15	8
12	8	M Blundell	Brabham	BT60Y	Yamaha	V12	43		21	11
13	4	S Modena	Tyrrell	020	Honda	V10	41		14	7
r	27	A Prost	Ferrari	643	Ferrari	V12	37	accident	5	3
r	16	I Capelli	Leyton House	CG911	Ilmor	V10	36	misfire	12	6
r	22	J J Lehto	Dallara	191	Judd	V10	35	engine	20	10
r	20	N Piquet	Benetton	B191	Ford Cosworth	V8	27	engine	8	4
r	3	S Nakajima	Tyrrell	020	Honda	V10	26	gearbox	13	7

Pos	No	Driver	Car	Model	Engine		Laps	Time/Reason for Retirement	Grid Pos	Row
r	26	E Comas	Ligier	JS35B	Lamborghini	V12	22	oil pressure	26	13
r	15	M Gugelmin	Leyton House	CG911	Ilmor	V10	21	gearbox	16	8
r	11	M Häkkinen	Lotus	102B	Judd	V8	19	engine	23	12
r	30	A Suzuki	Lola	L91	Ford Cosworth	V8	15	engine	22	11
r	24	G Morbidelli	Minardi	M191	Ferrari	V12	14	engine	19	10
r	23	P Martini	Minardi	M191	Ferrari	V12	11	engine / spin	10	5
r	29	É Bernard	Lola	L91	Ford Cosworth	V8	9	crown wheel & pinion	25	13
r	34	N Larini	Lamborghini	291	Lamborghini	V12	0	spin	24	12
nq	9	M Alboreto	Footwork	FA12	Ford Cosworth	V8				
nq	12	M Bartels	Lotus	102B	Judd	V8				
nq	17	G Tarquini	AGS	JH25B	Ford Cosworth	V8				
nq	35	E van de Poele	Lamborghini	291	Lamborghini	V12				
npq	14	O Grouillard	Fomet	F1	Ford Cosworth	V8				
npq	10	A Caffi	Footwork	FA12	Ford Cosworth	V8				
npq	18	F Barbazza	AGS	JH25B	Ford Cosworth	V8				
npq	31	P Chaves	Coloni	C4	Ford Cosworth	V8				

Winning speed 231.028 km/h, 143.554 mph
Pole Position speed 252.219 km/h, 156.722 mph (N Mansell, 1 min:37.087 sec)
Fastest Lap speed 236.434 km/h, 146.913 mph (R Patrese, 1 min:43.569 sec on lap 35)
Lap Leaders N Mansell 1-18,21-45 (43); J Alesi 19-20 (2).

11 Aug 1991		**HUNGARY: Hungaroring**							**(Round 10)**	**(Race 510)**
		77 laps x 3.968 km, 2.466 miles = 305.536 km, 189.851 miles								

Pos	No	Driver	Car	Model	Engine		Laps	Time/Reason for Retirement	Grid Pos	Row
1	1	A Senna	McLaren	MP4/6	Honda	V12	77	1h 49m 12.796s	1	1
2	5	N Mansell	Williams	FW14	Renault	V10	77	1h 49m 17.395s	3	2
3	6	R Patrese	Williams	FW14	Renault	V10	77	1h 49m 28.390s	2	1
4	2	G Berger	McLaren	MP4/6	Honda	V12	77	1h 49m 34.652s	5	3
5	28	J Alesi	Ferrari	643	Ferrari	V12	77	1h 49m 44.185s	6	3
6	16	I Capelli	Leyton House	CG911	Ilmor	V10	76		9	5
7	33	A de Cesaris	Jordan	191	Ford Cosworth	V8	76		17	9
8	19	R Moreno	Benetton	B191	Ford Cosworth	V8	76		15	8
9	32	B Gachot	Jordan	191	Ford Cosworth	V8	76		16	8
10	26	E Comas	Ligier	JS35B	Lamborghini	V12	75		25	13
11	15	M Gugelmin	Leyton House	CG911	Ilmor	V10	75		13	7
12	4	S Modena	Tyrrell	020	Honda	V10	75		8	4
13	24	G Morbidelli	Minardi	M191	Ferrari	V12	75		23	12
14	11	M Häkkinen	Lotus	102B	Judd	V8	74		26	13
15	3	S Nakajima	Tyrrell	020	Honda	V10	74		14	7
16	34	N Larini	Lamborghini	291	Lamborghini	V12	74		24	12
17r	25	T Boutsen	Ligier	JS35B	Lamborghini	V12	71	engine	19	10
r	23	P Martini	Minardi	M191	Ferrari	V12	65	engine	18	9
r	8	M Blundell	Brabham	BT60Y	Yamaha	V12	62	spin	20	10
r	7	M Brundle	Brabham	BT60Y	Yamaha	V12	59	driver discomfort (cramp)	10	5
r	22	J J Lehto	Dallara	191	Judd	V10	49	oil pressure	12	6
r	20	N Piquet	Benetton	B191	Ford Cosworth	V8	38	gearbox	11	6
r	29	É Bernard	Lola	L91	Ford Cosworth	V8	38	engine	21	11
r	30	A Suzuki	Lola	L91	Ford Cosworth	V8	38	engine	22	11
r	21	E Pirro	Dallara	191	Judd	V10	37	oil pressure	7	4
r	27	A Prost	Ferrari	643	Ferrari	V12	28	engine	4	2
nq	14	O Grouillard	Fomet	F1	Ford Cosworth	V8				
nq	9	M Alboreto	Footwork	FA12	Ford Cosworth	V8				
nq	35	E van de Poele	Lamborghini	291	Lamborghini	V12				
nq	12	M Bartels	Lotus	102B	Judd	V8				
npq	17	G Tarquini	AGS	JH25B	Ford Cosworth	V8				
npq	10	A Caffi	Footwork	FA12	Ford Cosworth	V8				
npq	18	F Barbazza	AGS	JH25B	Ford Cosworth	V8				
npq	31	P Chaves	Coloni	C4	Ford Cosworth	V8				

Winning speed 167.857 km/h, 104.301 mph
Pole Position speed 187.595 km/h, 116.566 mph (A Senna, 1 min:16.147 sec)
Fastest Lap speed 175.173 km/h, 108.847 mph (B Gachot, 1 min:21.547 sec on lap 71)
Lap Leaders A Senna 1-77 (77).

25 Aug 1991 **BELGIUM: Spa-Francorchamps** (Round 11) (Race 511)

44 laps x 6.940 km, 4.312 miles = 305.360 km, 189.742 miles

Pos	No	Driver	Car	Model	Engine		Laps	Time/Reason for Retirement	Grid Pos	Row
1	1	A Senna	McLaren	MP4/6	Honda	V12	44	1h 27m 17.669s	1	1
2	2	G Berger	McLaren	MP4/6	Honda	V12	44	1h 27m 19.570s	4	2
3	20	N Piquet	Benetton	B191	Ford Cosworth	V8	44	1h 27m 49.845s	6	3
4	19	R Moreno	Benetton	B191	Ford Cosworth	V8	44	1h 27m 54.979s	8	4
5	6	R Patrese	Williams	FW14	Renault	V10	44	1h 28m 14.856s	17	9
6	8	M Blundell	Brabham	BT60Y	Yamaha	V12	44	1h 28m 57.704s	13	7
7	12	J Herbert	Lotus	102B	Judd	V8	44	1h 29m 02.268s	21	11
8	21	E Pirro	Dallara	191	Judd	V10	43		25	13
9	7	M Brundle	Brabham	BT60Y	Yamaha	V12	43		16	8
10	14	O Grouillard	Fomet	F1	Ford Cosworth	V8	43		23	12
11	25	T Boutsen	Ligier	JS35B	Lamborghini	V12	43		18	9
12	23	P Martini	Minardi	M191	Ferrari	V12	42		9	5
13r	33	A de Cesaris	Jordan	191	Ford Cosworth	V8	41	radiator / engine	11	6
r	4	S Modena	Tyrrell	020	Honda	V10	33	oil leak / fire	10	5
r	22	J J Lehto	Dallara	191	Judd	V10	33	engine	14	7
r	28	J Alesi	Ferrari	643	Ferrari	V12	30	engine	5	3
r	24	G Morbidelli	Minardi	M191	Ferrari	V12	29	engine	19	10
r	11	M Häkkinen	Lotus	102B	Judd	V8	25	engine	24	12
r	26	E Comas	Ligier	JS35B	Lamborghini	V12	25	engine	26	13
r	5	N Mansell	Williams	FW14	Renault	V10	22	voltage regulator	3	2
r	29	É Bernard	Lola	L91	Ford Cosworth	V8	21	gearbox	20	10
r	16	I Capelli	Leyton House	CG911	Ilmor	V10	13	engine	12	6
r	3	S Nakajima	Tyrrell	020	Honda	V10	7	accident	22	11
r	27	A Prost	Ferrari	643	Ferrari	V12	2	engine	2	1
r	15	M Gugelmin	Leyton House	CG911	Ilmor	V10	1	engine	15	8
r	32	M Schumacher	Jordan	191	Ford Cosworth	V8	0	clutch	7	4
nq	30	A Suzuki	Lola	L91	Ford Cosworth	V8				
nq	34	N Larini	Lamborghini	291	Lamborghini	V12				
nq	10	A Caffi	Footwork	FA12	Ford Cosworth	V8				
nq	35	E van de Poele	Lamborghini	291	Lamborghini	V12				
npq	9	M Alboreto	Footwork	FA12	Ford Cosworth	V8				
npq	17	G Tarquini	AGS	JH25B	Ford Cosworth	V8				
npq	31	P Chaves	Coloni	C4	Ford Cosworth	V8				
npq	18	F Barbazza	AGS	JH25B	Ford Cosworth	V8				

Winning speed 209.883 km/h, 130.415 mph
Pole Position speed 231.739 km/h, 143.996 mph (A Senna, 1 min:47.811 sec)
Fastest Lap speed 216.948 km/h, 134.806 mph (R Moreno, 1 min:55.161 sec on lap 40)
Lap Leaders A Senna 1-14,31-44 (28); N Mansell 15-16,18-21 (6); N Piquet 17 (1); J Alesi 22-30 (9).

---

8 Sep 1991 **ITALY: Monza** (Round 12) (Race 512)

53 laps x 5.800 km, 3.604 miles = 307.400 km, 191.010 miles

Pos	No	Driver	Car	Model	Engine		Laps	Time/Reason for Retirement	Grid Pos	Row
1	5	N Mansell	Williams	FW14	Renault	V10	53	1h 17m 54.319s	2	1
2	1	A Senna	McLaren	MP4/6	Honda	V12	53	1h 18m 10.581s	1	1
3	27	A Prost	Ferrari	643	Ferrari	V12	53	1h 18m 11.148s	5	3
4	2	G Berger	McLaren	MP4/6	Honda	V12	53	1h 18m 22.038s	3	2
5	19	M Schumacher	Benetton	B191	Ford Cosworth	V8	53	1h 18m 28.782s	7	4
6	20	N Piquet	Benetton	B191	Ford Cosworth	V8	53	1h 18m 39.919s	8	4
7	33	A de Cesaris	Jordan	191	Ford Cosworth	V8	53	1h 18m 45.455s	14	7
8	16	I Capelli	Leyton House	CG911	Ilmor	V10	53	1h 19m 09.338s	12	6
9	24	G Morbidelli	Minardi	M191	Ferrari	V12	52		17	9
10	21	E Pirro	Dallara	191	Judd	V10	52		16	8
11	26	E Comas	Ligier	JS35B	Lamborghini	V12	52		22	11
12	8	M Blundell	Brabham	BT60Y	Yamaha	V12	52		11	6
13	7	M Brundle	Brabham	BT60Y	Yamaha	V12	52		19	10
14	11	M Häkkinen	Lotus	102B	Judd	V8	49		25	13
15	15	M Gugelmin	Leyton House	CG911	Ilmor	V10	49		18	9
16	34	N Larini	Lamborghini	291	Lamborghini	V12	48		23	12
r	14	O Grouillard	Fomet	F1	Ford Cosworth	V8	46	engine	26	13
r	22	J J Lehto	Dallara	191	Judd	V10	35	tyre / suspension	20	10
r	4	S Modena	Tyrrell	020	Honda	V10	32	engine	13	7
r	28	J Alesi	Ferrari	643	Ferrari	V12	29	engine	6	3

Pos	No	Driver	Car	Model	Engine		Laps	Time/Reason for Retirement	Grid Pos	Row
r	6	R Patrese	Williams	FW14	Renault	V10	27	gearbox / clutch	4	2
r	3	S Nakajima	Tyrrell	020	Honda	V10	24	throttle jammed	15	8
r	29	É Bernard	Lola	L91	Ford Cosworth	V8	21	engine	24	12
r	23	P Martini	Minardi	M191	Ferrari	V12	8	brakes / spin	10	5
r	32	R Moreno	Jordan	191	Ford Cosworth	V8	2	brakes / spin	9	5
r	25	T Boutsen	Ligier	JS35B	Lamborghini	V12	1	spin	21	11
nq	9	M Alboreto	Footwork	FA12	Ford Cosworth	V8				
nq	12	M Bartels	Lotus	102B	Judd	V8				
nq	35	E van de Poele	Lamborghini	291	Lamborghini	V12				
nq	30	A Suzuki	Lola	L91	Ford Cosworth	V8				
npq	18	F Barbazza	AGS	JH25B	Ford Cosworth	V8				
npq	17	G Tarquini	AGS	JH27	Ford Cosworth	V8				
npq	10	A Caffi	Footwork	FA12	Ford Cosworth	V8				
npq	31	P Chaves	Coloni	C4	Ford Cosworth	V8				

Winning speed 236.749 km/h, 147.109 mph
Pole Position speed 257.415 km/h, 159.951 mph (A Senna, 1 min:21.114 sec)
Fastest Lap speed 242.619 km/h, 150.756 mph (A Senna, 1 min:26.061 sec on lap 41)
Lap Leaders A Senna 1-25,27-33 (32); R Patrese 26 (1); N Mansell 34-53 (20).

22 Sep 1991	PORTUGAL: Estoril	(Round 13)	(Race 513)

71 laps x 4.350 km, 2.703 miles = 308.850 km, 191.910 miles

Pos	No	Driver	Car	Model	Engine		Laps	Time/Reason for Retirement	Grid Pos	Row
1	6	R Patrese	Williams	FW14	Renault	V10	71	1h 35m 42.304s	1	1
2	1	A Senna	McLaren	MP4/6	Honda	V12	71	1h 36m 03.245s	3	2
3	28	J Alesi	Ferrari	643	Ferrari	V12	71	1h 36m 35.858s	6	3
4	23	P Martini	Minardi	M191	Ferrari	V12	71	1h 36m 45.802s	8	4
5	20	N Piquet	Benetton	B191	Ford Cosworth	V8	71	1h 36m 52.337s	11	6
6	19	M Schumacher	Benetton	B191	Ford Cosworth	V8	71	1h 36m 58.886s	10	5
7	15	M Gugelmin	Leyton House	CG911	Ilmor	V10	70		7	4
8	33	A de Cesaris	Jordan	191	Ford Cosworth	V8	70		14	7
9	24	G Morbidelli	Minardi	M191	Ferrari	V12	70		13	7
10	32	R Moreno	Jordan	191	Ford Cosworth	V8	70		16	8
11	26	E Comas	Ligier	JS35B	Lamborghini	V12	70		23	12
12	7	M Brundle	Brabham	BT60Y	Yamaha	V12	69		19	10
13	3	S Nakajima	Tyrrell	020	Honda	V10	68		21	11
14	11	M Häkkinen	Lotus	102B	Judd	V8	68		26	13
15	9	M Alboreto	Footwork	FA12	Ford Cosworth	V8	68		24	12
16	25	T Boutsen	Ligier	JS35B	Lamborghini	V12	68		20	10
17r	16	I Capelli	Leyton House	CG911	Ilmor	V10	64	nose cone	9	5
r	4	S Modena	Tyrrell	020	Honda	V10	56	visor into air intake / engine	12	6
r/dq	5	N Mansell	Williams	FW14	Renault	V10	51	wheel change outside pit / accid.	4	2
r	30	A Suzuki	Lola	L91	Ford Cosworth	V8	40	gearbox	25	13
r	27	A Prost	Ferrari	643	Ferrari	V12	39	engine	5	3
r	2	G Berger	McLaren	MP4/6	Honda	V12	37	engine	2	1
r	21	E Pirro	Dallara	191	Judd	V10	18	engine	17	9
r	22	J J Lehto	Dallara	191	Judd	V10	18	gear linkage	18	9
r	8	M Blundell	Brabham	BT60Y	Yamaha	V12	12	rear suspension	15	8
r	12	J Herbert	Lotus	102B	Judd	V8	1	engine / transmission	22	11
nq	29	É Bernard	Lola	L91	Ford Cosworth	V8				
nq	17	G Tarquini	AGS	JH27	Ford Cosworth	V8				
nq	34	N Larini	Lamborghini	291	Lamborghini	V12				
nq	35	E van de Poele	Lamborghini	291	Lamborghini	V12				
npq	18	F Barbazza	AGS	JH27	Ford Cosworth	V8				
npq	14	O Grouillard	Fomet	F1	Ford Cosworth	V8				
npq	10	A Caffi	Footwork	FA12	Ford Cosworth	V8				
npq	31	P Chaves	Coloni	C4	Ford Cosworth	V8				

Winning speed 193.626 km/h, 120.314 mph
Pole Position speed 214.518 km/h, 133.295 mph (R Patrese, 1 min:13.001 sec)
Fastest Lap speed 200.310 km/h, 124.467 mph (N Mansell, 1 min:18.179 sec on lap 36)
Lap Leaders R Patrese 1-17,30-71 (59); N Mansell 18-29 (12).

Although N Mansell was disqualified, the authorities appeared to forget to withdraw his fastest lap.
Second fastest was set by R Patrese on lap 38 (1m 18.350s, 199.872 km/h, 124.195 mph).

Races

65 laps x 4.747 km, 2.950 miles = 308.555 km, 191.727 miles

Pos	No	Driver	Car	Model	Engine		Laps	Time/Reason for Retirement	Grid Pos	Row
1	5	N Mansell	Williams	FW14	Renault	V10	65	1h 38m 41.541s	2	1
2	27	A Prost	Ferrari	643	Ferrari	V12	65	1h 38m 52.872s	6	3
3	6	R Patrese	Williams	FW14	Renault	V10	65	1h 38m 57.450s	4	2
4	28	J Alesi	Ferrari	643	Ferrari	V12	65	1h 39m 04.313s	7	4
5	1	A Senna	McLaren	MP4/6	Honda	V12	65	1h 39m 43.943s	3	2
6	19	M Schumacher	Benetton	B191	Ford Cosworth	V8	65	1h 40m 01.009s	5	3
7	15	M Gugelmin	Leyton House	CG911	Ilmor	V10	64		13	7
8	22	J J Lehto	Dallara	191	Judd	V10	64		15	8
9	32	A Zanardi	Jordan	191	Ford Cosworth	V8	64		20	10
10	7	M Brundle	Brabham	BT60Y	Yamaha	V12	63		11	6
11	20	N Piquet	Benetton	B191	Ford Cosworth	V8	63		10	5
12	14	G Tarquini	Fomet	F1	Ford Cosworth	V8	63		22	11
13	23	P Martini	Minardi	M191	Ferrari	V12	63		19	10
14r	24	G Morbidelli	Minardi	M191	Ferrari	V12	62	accident	16	8
15	21	E Pirro	Dallara	191	Judd	V10	62		9	5
16	4	S Modena	Tyrrell	020	Honda	V10	62		14	7
17	3	S Nakajima	Tyrrell	020	Honda	V10	62		18	9
r	8	M Blundell	Brabham	BT60Y	Yamaha	V12	49	engine	12	6
r	26	E Comas	Ligier	JS35B	Lamborghini	V12	36	electronics	25	13
r	2	G Berger	McLaren	MP4/6	Honda	V12	33	engine	1	1
r	9	M Alboreto	Footwork	FA12	Ford Cosworth	V8	23	engine	24	12
r	33	A de Cesaris	Jordan	191	Ford Cosworth	V8	22	electrics	17	9
r	11	M Häkkinen	Lotus	102B	Judd	V8	5	accident	21	11
r	16	I Capelli	Leyton House	CG911	Ilmor	V10	1	accident	8	4
r	29	É Bernard	Lola	L91	Ford Cosworth	V8	0	accident	23	12
r	25	T Boutsen	Ligier	JS35B	Lamborghini	V12	0	accident	26	13
nq	30	A Suzuki	Lola	L91	Ford Cosworth	V8				
nq	34	N Larini	Lamborghini	291	Lamborghini	V12				
nq	12	M Bartels	Lotus	102B	Judd	V8				
nq	35	E van de Poele	Lamborghini	291	Lamborghini	V12				
npq	10	A Caffi	Footwork	FA12	Ford Cosworth	V8				
npq	18	F Barbazza	AGS	JH27	Ford Cosworth	V8				
npq	17	O Grouillard	AGS	JH27	Ford Cosworth	V8				

Winning speed 187.586 km/h, 116.561 mph
Pole Position speed 217.003 km/h, 134.839 mph (G Berger, 1 min:18.751 sec)
Fastest Lap speed 206.299 km/h, 128.188 mph (R Patrese, 1 min:22.837 sec on lap 63)
Lap Leaders G Berger 1-8,12-20 (17); N Mansell 9,21-65 (46); R Patrese 10 (1); A Senna 11 (1).

53 laps x 5.864 km, 3.644 miles = 310.792 km, 193.117 miles

Pos	No	Driver	Car	Model	Engine		Laps	Time/Reason for Retirement	Grid Pos	Row
1	2	G Berger	McLaren	MP4/6	Honda	V12	53	1h 32m 10.695s	1	1
2	1	A Senna	McLaren	MP4/6	Honda	V12	53	1h 32m 11.039s	2	1
3	6	R Patrese	Williams	FW14	Renault	V10	53	1h 33m 07.426s	5	3
4	27	A Prost	Ferrari	643	Ferrari	V12	53	1h 33m 31.456s	4	2
5	7	M Brundle	Brabham	BT60Y	Yamaha	V12	52		19	10
6	4	S Modena	Tyrrell	020	Honda	V10	52		14	7
7	20	N Piquet	Benetton	B191	Ford Cosworth	V8	52		10	5
8	15	M Gugelmin	Leyton House	CG911	Ilmor	V10	52		18	9
9	25	T Boutsen	Ligier	JS35B	Lamborghini	V12	52		17	9
10	10	A Caffi	Footwork	FA12	Ford Cosworth	V8	51		26	13
11	14	G Tarquini	Fomet	F1	Ford Cosworth	V8	50		24	12
r	26	E Comas	Ligier	JS35B	Lamborghini	V12	41	alternator	20	10
r	23	P Martini	Minardi	M191	Ferrari	V12	39	clutch	7	4
r	19	M Schumacher	Benetton	B191	Ford Cosworth	V8	34	engine	9	5
r	12	J Herbert	Lotus	102B	Judd	V8	31	earth wire / engine	23	12
r	3	S Nakajima	Tyrrell	020	Honda	V10	30	suspension / accident	15	8
r	30	A Suzuki	Lola	L91	Ford Cosworth	V8	26	engine	25	13
r	24	G Morbidelli	Minardi	M191	Ferrari	V12	15	wheel bearing	8	4
r	5	N Mansell	Williams	FW14	Renault	V10	9	brakes / spin	3	2
r	32	A Zanardi	Jordan	191	Ford Cosworth	V8	7	gearbox	13	7

Pos	No	Driver	Car	Model	Engine		Laps	Time/Reason for Retirement	Grid Pos	Row
r	11	M Häkkinen	Lotus	102B	Judd	V8	4	spin	21	11
r	33	A de Cesaris	Jordan	191	Ford Cosworth	V8	1	accident	11	6
r	22	J J Lehto	Dallara	191	Judd	V10	1	accident	12	6
r	21	E Pirro	Dallara	191	Judd	V10	1	accident	16	8
r	16	K Wendlinger	Leyton House	CG911	Ilmor	V10	1	accident	22	11
r	28	J Alesi	Ferrari	643	Ferrari	V12	0	engine	6	3
nq	9	M Alboreto	Footwork	FA12	Ford Cosworth	V8				
nq	34	N Larini	Lamborghini	291	Lamborghini	V12				
nq	35	E van de Poele	Lamborghini	291	Lamborghini	V12				
nq	29	É Bernard	Lola	L91	Ford Cosworth	V8		accident / injury		
npq	8	M Blundell	Brabham	BT60Y	Yamaha	V12				
npq	31	N Hattori	Coloni	C4	Ford Cosworth	V8				

Winning speed 202.298 km/h, 125.702 mph
Pole Position speed 222.919 km/h, 138.515 mph (G Berger, 1 min:34.700 sec)
Fastest Lap speed 207.919 km/h, 129.195 mph (A Senna, 1 min:41.532 sec on lap 39)
Lap Leaders G Berger 1-17,53 (18); A Senna 18-21,24-52 (33); R Patrese 22-23 (2).

3 Nov 1991　AUSTRALIA: Adelaide　(Round 16)　(Race 516)
14 laps x 3.780 km, 2.349 miles = 52.920 km, 32.883 miles

Pos	No	Driver	Car	Model	Engine		Laps	Time/Reason for Retirement	Grid Pos	Row
1	1	A Senna	McLaren	MP4/6	Honda	V12	14	24m 34.899s	1	1
2	5	N Mansell	Williams	FW14	Renault	V10	14	24m 36.158s	3	2
3	2	G Berger	McLaren	MP4/6	Honda	V12	14	24m 40.019s	2	1
4	20	N Piquet	Benetton	B191	Ford Cosworth	V8	14	25m 05.002s	5	3
5	6	R Patrese	Williams	FW14	Renault	V10	14	25m 25.436s	4	2
6	27	G Morbidelli	Ferrari	643	Ferrari	V12	14	25m 25.968s	8	4
7	21	E Pirro	Dallara	191	Judd	V10	14	25m 27.260s	13	7
8	33	A de Cesaris	Jordan	191	Ford Cosworth	V8	14	25m 35.330s	12	6
9	32	A Zanardi	Jordan	191	Ford Cosworth	V8	14	25m 50.466s	16	8
10	4	S Modena	Tyrrell	020	Honda	V10	14	25m 55.269s	9	5
11	12	J Herbert	Lotus	102B	Judd	V8	14	25m 56.972s	21	11
12	22	J J Lehto	Dallara	191	Judd	V10	14	26m 13.418s	11	6
13	9	M Alboreto	Footwork	FA12	Ford Cosworth	V8	14	26m 14.202s	15	8
14r	15	M Gugelmin	Leyton House	CG911	Ilmor	V10	13	accident in pit lane	14	7
15	10	A Caffi	Footwork	FA12	Ford Cosworth	V8	13		23	12
16	24	R Moreno	Minardi	M191	Ferrari	V12	13		18	9
17	8	M Blundell	Brabham	BT60Y	Yamaha	V12	13		17	9
18	26	E Comas	Ligier	JS35B	Lamborghini	V12	13		22	11
19	11	M Häkkinen	Lotus	102B	Judd	V8	13		25	13
20	16	K Wendlinger	Leyton House	CG911	Ilmor	V10	12		26	13
r	23	P Martini	Minardi	M191	Ferrari	V12	8	accident	10	5
r	19	M Schumacher	Benetton	B191	Ford Cosworth	V8	5	accident	6	3
r	28	J Alesi	Ferrari	643	Ferrari	V12	5	accident	7	4
r	34	N Larini	Lamborghini	291	Lamborghini	V12	5	accident	19	10
r	25	T Boutsen	Ligier	JS35B	Lamborghini	V12	5	accident	20	10
r	3	S Nakajima	Tyrrell	020	Honda	V10	4	accident	24	12
nq	30	A Suzuki	Lola	L91	Ford Cosworth	V8				
nq	7	M Brundle	Brabham	BT60Y	Yamaha	V12				
nq	35	E van de Poele	Lamborghini	291	Lamborghini	V12				
nq	29	B Gachot	Lola	L91	Ford Cosworth	V8				
npq	14	G Tarquini	Fomet	F1	Ford Cosworth	V8				
npq	31	N Hattori	Coloni	C4	Ford Cosworth	V8				

Winning speed 129.170 km/h, 80.262 mph
Pole Position speed 183.790 km/h, 114.202 mph (A Senna, 1 min:14.041 sec)
Fastest Lap speed 134.545 km/h, 83.602 mph (G Berger, 1 min:41.141 sec on lap 14)
Lap Leaders A Senna 1-14 (14).

Scheduled for 81 laps, but stopped early, because of rain. Half points awarded.

Pos	Driver	Car-Engine	GPs	laps	km	miles
1	A Senna	McLaren-Honda	10	467	2,066.8	1,284.2
2	N Mansell	Williams-Renault	9	296	1,511.7	939.4
3	R Patrese	Williams-Renault	6	125	558.6	347.1
4	A Prost	Ferrari	1	44	187.9	116.8
5	G Berger	McLaren-Honda	2	35	186.3	115.7
6	J Alesi	Ferrari	2	11	76.1	47.3
7	N Piquet	Benetton-Ford Cosworth	2	2	11.4	7.1
			16	980	4,598.7	2,857.5

Driver Points 1991

		USA	BR	RSM	MC	CDN	MEX	F	GB	D	H	B	I	P	E	J	AUS	Total
1	A Senna	10	10	10	10	-	4	4	3	-	10	10	6	6	2	6	5	96
2	N Mansell	-	-	-	6	1	6	10	10	10	6	-	10	-	10	-	3	72
3	R Patrese	-	6	-	-	4	10	2	-	6	4	2	-	10	4	4	1	53
4	G Berger	-	4	6	-	-	-	-	6	3	3	6	3	-	-	10	2	43
5	A Prost	6	3	-	2	-	-	6	4	-	-	-	4	-	6	3	-	34
6	N Piquet	4	2	-	-	10	-	-	2	-	-	4	1	2	-	-	1.5	26.5
7	J Alesi	-	1	-	4	-	-	3	-	4	2	-	-	4	3	-	-	21
8	S Modena	3	-	-	-	6	-	-	-	-	-	-	-	-	-	1	-	10
9	A de Cesaris	-	-	-	-	3	3	1	-	2	-	-	-	-	-	-	-	9
10	R Moreno	-	-	-	3	-	2	-	-	-	3	-	-	-	-	-	-	8
11	P Martini	-	-	3	-	-	-	-	-	-	-	-	-	3	-	-	-	6
12	J J Lehto	-	-	4	-	-	-	-	-	-	-	-	-	-	-	-	-	4
	B Gachot	-	-	-	-	2	-	-	1	1	-	-	-	-	-	-	-	4
	M Schumacher	-	-	-	-	-	-	-	-	-	-	-	2	1	1	-	-	4
15	S Nakajima	2	-	-	-	-	-	-	-	-	-	-	-	-	-	-	-	2
	M Häkkinen	-	-	2	-	-	-	-	-	-	-	-	-	-	-	-	-	2
	M Brundle	-	-	-	-	-	-	-	-	-	-	-	-	-	-	2	-	2
18	A Suzuki	1	-	-	-	-	-	-	-	-	-	-	-	-	-	-	-	1
	J Bailey	-	-	1	-	-	-	-	-	-	-	-	-	-	-	-	-	1
	E Pirro	-	-	-	1	-	-	-	-	-	-	-	-	-	-	-	-	1
	É Bernard	-	-	-	-	-	1	-	-	-	-	-	-	-	-	-	-	1
	I Capelli	-	-	-	-	-	-	-	-	-	1	-	-	-	-	-	-	1
	M Blundell	-	-	-	-	-	-	-	-	-	-	1	-	-	-	-	-	1
24	G Morbidelli	-	-	-	-	-	-	-	-	-	-	-	-	-	-	-	0.5	0.5

10,6,4,3,2 and 1 point awarded to the first six finishers. Half points awarded in Australia where race was stopped early.

Constructor Points 1991

		USA	BR	RSM	MC	CDN	MEX	F	GB	D	H	B	I	P	E	J	AUS	Total
1	McLaren-Honda	10	14	16	10	-	4	4	9	3	13	16	9	6	2	16	7	139
2	Williams-Renault	-	6	-	6	5	16	12	10	16	10	2	10	10	14	4	4	125
3	Ferrari	6	4	-	6	-	-	9	4	4	2	-	4	4	9	3	0.5	55.5
4	Benetton-Ford Cosworth	4	2	-	3	10	2	-	2	-	-	7	3	3	1	-	1.5	38.5
5	Jordan-Ford Cosworth	-	-	-	-	5	3	1	1	3	-	-	-	-	-	-	-	13
6	Tyrrell-Honda	5	-	-	-	6	-	-	-	-	-	-	-	-	-	1	-	12
7	Minardi-Ferrari	-	-	3	-	-	-	-	-	-	-	-	-	3	-	-	-	6
8	Dallara-Judd	-	-	4	1	-	-	-	-	-	-	-	-	-	-	-	-	5
9	Lotus-Judd	-	-	3	-	-	-	-	-	-	-	-	-	-	-	-	-	3
	Brabham-Yamaha	-	-	-	-	-	-	-	-	-	-	1	-	-	-	2	-	3
11	Lola-Ford Cosworth	1	-	-	-	-	1	-	-	-	-	-	-	-	-	-	-	2
12	Leyton House-Ilmor	-	-	-	-	-	-	-	-	-	1	-	-	-	-	-	-	1

10,6,4,3,2 and 1 point awarded to the first six finishers.

1992

Race Entrants and Results

Max Mosley became the new president of FISA. Giovanna Amati caused a lot of the pre-season interest as there hadn't been a woman driver in Formula 1 since 1980. Honda withdrew at season's end, but retained a presence with their related company Mugen. March returned to its original name and Larrousse built its own car with help from the Venturi concern. Pirelli left Formula 1 again. Denny Hulme became the first World Champion to die of natural causes.

McLAREN
Honda Marlboro McLaren: Senna, Berger

TYRRELL
Tyrrell Racing Organisation: Grouillard, de Cesaris

WILLIAMS
Canon Williams Team: Mansell, Patrese

BRABHAM
Motor Racing Developments: van de Poele, (Amati), Hill

FOOTWORK
Footwork Mugen Honda: Alboreto, Suzuki

LOTUS
Team Lotus: Häkkinen, Herbert

FONDMETAL
Fondmetal: Chiesa, van de Poele, Tarquini

MARCH
March F1: Wendlinger, Lammers, Belmondo, Naspetti

BENETTON
Camel Benetton Ford: Schumacher, Brundle

DALLARA
Scuderia Italia SpA: Lehto, Martini

MINARDI
Minardi Team: Fittipaldi, Zanardi, Morbidelli

LIGIER
Ligier Gitanes Blondes: Boutsen, Comas

FERRARI
Scuderia Ferrari SpA: Alesi, Capelli, Larini

VENTURI LARROUSSE
Central Park Venturi Larrousse: Gachot, Katayama

JORDAN
Sasol Jordan Yamaha: Modena, Gugelmin

ANDREA MODA
Andrea Moda Formula: Moreno, (McCarthy)

1 Mar 1992		SOUTH AFRICA: Kyalami							(Round 1)	(Race 517)	
		72 laps x 4.261 km, 2.648 miles = 306.792 km, 190.632 miles									
Pos	No	Driver	Car	Model	Engine		Laps	Time/Reason for Retirement		Grid Pos	Row
1	5	N Mansell	Williams	FW14B	Renault	V10	72	1h 36m 45.320s		1	1
2	6	R Patrese	Williams	FW14B	Renault	V10	72	1h 37m 09.680s		4	2
3	1	A Senna	McLaren	MP4/6B	Honda	V12	72	1h 37m 19.995s		2	1
4	19	M Schumacher	Benetton	B191B	Ford Cosworth	V8	72	1h 37m 33.183s		6	3
5	2	G Berger	McLaren	MP4/6B	Honda	V12	72	1h 37m 58.954s		3	2
6	12	J Herbert	Lotus	102D	Ford Cosworth	V8	71			11	6
7	26	E Comas	Ligier	JS37	Renault	V10	71			13	7
8	10	A Suzuki	Footwork	FA13	Mugen Honda	V10	70			16	8
9	11	M Häkkinen	Lotus	102D	Ford Cosworth	V8	70			21	11
10	9	M Alboreto	Footwork	FA13	Mugen Honda	V10	70			17	9
11	33	M Gugelmin	Jordan	192	Yamaha	V12	70			23	12
12	30	U Katayama	Venturi Larrousse	LC92	Lamborghini	V12	68			18	9
13	7	E van de Poele	Brabham	BT60B	Judd	V10	68			26	13
r	3	O Grouillard	Tyrrell	020B	Ilmor	V10	62	clutch		12	6
r	25	T Boutsen	Ligier	JS37	Renault	V10	60	engine		14	7
r	22	P Martini	Dallara	192	Ferrari	V12	56	clutch		25	13
r	24	G Morbidelli	Minardi	M191B	Lamborghini	V12	55	engine		19	10
r	21	J J Lehto	Dallara	192	Ferrari	V12	46	differential		24	12
r	23	C Fittipaldi	Minardi	M191B	Lamborghini	V12	43	electrics		20	10
r	4	A de Cesaris	Tyrrell	020B	Ilmor	V10	41	engine		10	5
r	27	J Alesi	Ferrari	F92A	Ferrari	V12	40	engine		5	3
r	28	I Capelli	Ferrari	F92A	Ferrari	V12	28	engine		9	5
r	15	G Tarquini	Fondmetal	GR01	Ford Cosworth	V8	23	engine		15	8
r	16	K Wendlinger	March	CG911	Ilmor	V10	13	engine overheating		7	4
r	29	B Gachot	Venturi Larrousse	LC92	Lamborghini	V12	8	accident / steering		22	11
r	20	M Brundle	Benetton	B191B	Ford Cosworth	V8	1	accident / clutch		8	4
nq	17	P Belmondo	March	CG911	Ilmor	V10					
nq	14	A Chiesa	Fondmetal	GR01	Ford Cosworth	V8					
nq	32	S Modena	Jordan	192	Yamaha	V12					
nq	8	G Amati	Brabham	BT60B	Judd	V10					

Winning speed 190.248 km/h, 118.215 mph
Pole Position speed 203.211 km/h, 126.270 mph (N Mansell, 1 min:15.486 sec)
Fastest Lap speed 197.731 km/h, 122.865 mph (N Mansell, 1 min:17.578 sec on lap 70)
Lap Leaders N Mansell 1-72 (72).

69 laps x 4.421 km, 2.747 miles = 305.049 km, 189.549 miles

Pos	No	Driver	Car	Model	Engine		Laps	Time/Reason for Retirement	Grid Pos	Row
1	5	N Mansell	Williams	FW14B	Renault	V10	69	1h 31m 53.587s	1	1
2	6	R Patrese	Williams	FW14B	Renault	V10	69	1h 32m 06.558s	2	1
3	19	M Schumacher	Benetton	B191B	Ford Cosworth	V8	69	1h 32m 15.016s	3	2
4	2	G Berger	McLaren	MP4/6B	Honda	V12	69	1h 32m 26.934s	5	3
5	4	A de Cesaris	Tyrrell	020B	Ilmor	V10	68		11	6
6	11	M Häkkinen	Lotus	102D	Ford Cosworth	V8	68		18	9
7	12	J Herbert	Lotus	102D	Ford Cosworth	V8	68		12	6
8	21	J J Lehto	Dallara	192	Ferrari	V12	68		7	4
9	26	E Comas	Ligier	JS37	Renault	V10	67		26	13
10	25	T Boutsen	Ligier	JS37	Renault	V10	67		22	11
11	29	B Gachot	Venturi Larrousse	LC92	Lamborghini	V12	66		13	7
12	30	U Katayama	Venturi Larrousse	LC92	Lamborghini	V12	66		24	12
13	9	M Alboreto	Footwork	FA13	Mugen Honda	V10	65		25	13
r	20	M Brundle	Benetton	B191B	Ford Cosworth	V8	47	radiator / engine overheating	4	2
r	15	G Tarquini	Fondmetal	GR01	Ford Cosworth	V8	45	clutch	14	7
r	14	A Chiesa	Fondmetal	GR01	Ford Cosworth	V8	37	spin	23	12
r	22	P Martini	Dallara	192	Ferrari	V12	36	handling	9	5
r	27	J Alesi	Ferrari	F92A	Ferrari	V12	31	engine	10	5
r	24	G Morbidelli	Minardi	M191B	Lamborghini	V12	29	spin	21	11
r	32	S Modena	Jordan	192	Yamaha	V12	17	gearbox	15	8
r	3	O Grouillard	Tyrrell	020B	Ilmor	V10	12	engine	16	8
r	1	A Senna	McLaren	MP4/6B	Honda	V12	11	transmission	6	3
r	23	C Fittipaldi	Minardi	M191B	Lamborghini	V12	2	spin	17	9
r	33	M Gugelmin	Jordan	192	Yamaha	V12	0	engine	8	4
r	28	I Capelli	Ferrari	F92A	Ferrari	V12	0	accident	20	10
r	16	K Wendlinger	March	CG911	Ilmor	V10	0	accident	19	10
nq	10	A Suzuki	Footwork	FA13	Mugen Honda	V10				
nq	17	P Belmondo	March	CG911	Ilmor	V10				
nq	7	E van de Poele	Brabham	BT60B	Judd	V10				
nq	8	G Amati	Brabham	BT60B	Judd	V10				

Winning speed 199.176 km/h, 123.762 mph
Pole Position speed 208.467 km/h, 129.535 mph (N Mansell, 1 min:16.346 sec)
Fastest Lap speed 204.805 km/h, 127.260 mph (G Berger, 1 min:17.711 sec on lap 60)
Lap Leaders N Mansell 1-69 (69).

71 laps x 4.325 km, 2.687 miles = 307.075 km, 190.808 miles

Pos	No	Driver	Car	Model	Engine		Laps	Time/Reason for Retirement	Grid Pos	Row
1	5	N Mansell	Williams	FW14B	Renault	V10	71	1h 36m 51.856s	1	1
2	6	R Patrese	Williams	FW14B	Renault	V10	71	1h 37m 21.186s	2	1
3	19	M Schumacher	Benetton	B191B	Ford Cosworth	V8	70		5	3
4	27	J Alesi	Ferrari	F92A	Ferrari	V12	70		6	3
5	28	I Capelli	Ferrari	F92A	Ferrari	V12	70		11	6
6	9	M Alboreto	Footwork	FA13	Mugen Honda	V10	70		14	7
7	24	G Morbidelli	Minardi	M191B	Lamborghini	V12	69		23	12
8	21	J J Lehto	Dallara	192	Ferrari	V12	69		16	8
9	30	U Katayama	Venturi Larrousse	LC92	Lamborghini	V12	68		25	13
10	11	M Häkkinen	Lotus	102D	Ford Cosworth	V8	67		24	12
r	15	G Tarquini	Fondmetal	GR01	Ford Cosworth	V8	62	radiator	19	10
r	16	K Wendlinger	March	CG911	Ilmor	V10	55	clutch	9	5
r	23	C Fittipaldi	Minardi	M191B	Lamborghini	V12	54	gearbox	20	10
r	3	O Grouillard	Tyrrell	020B	Ilmor	V10	52	engine	17	9
r	26	E Comas	Ligier	JS37	Renault	V10	42	engine	15	8
r	12	J Herbert	Lotus	102D	Ford Cosworth	V8	36	accident	26	13
r	25	T Boutsen	Ligier	JS37	Renault	V10	36	accident	10	5
r	33	M Gugelmin	Jordan	192	Yamaha	V12	36	gearbox	21	11
r	20	M Brundle	Benetton	B191B	Ford Cosworth	V8	30	accident	7	4
r	22	P Martini	Dallara	192	Ferrari	V12	24	clutch	8	4
r	29	B Gachot	Venturi Larrousse	LC92	Lamborghini	V12	23	rear suspension	18	9
r	4	A de Cesaris	Tyrrell	020B	Ilmor	V10	21	electrics	13	7
r	1	A Senna	McLaren	MP4/7A	Honda	V12	17	electrics	3	2
r	2	G Berger	McLaren	MP4/7A	Honda	V12	4	engine overheating	4	2
r	10	A Suzuki	Footwork	FA13	Mugen Honda	V10	2	oil system	22	11
r	32	S Modena	Jordan	192	Yamaha	V12	1	gearbox	12	6
nq	14	A Chiesa	Fondmetal	GR01	Ford Cosworth	V8				
nq	17	P Belmondo	March	CG911	Ilmor	V10				
nq	7	E van de Poele	Brabham	BT60B	Judd	V10				
nq	8	G Amati	Brabham	BT60B	Judd	V10				
npq	34	R Moreno	Andrea Moda	S921	Judd	V10				

Winning speed 190.209 km/h, 118.191 mph
Pole Position speed 205.672 km/h, 127.799 mph (N Mansell, 1 min:15.703 sec)
Fastest Lap speed 195.874 km/h, 121.710 mph (R Patrese, 1 min:19.490 sec on lap 34)
Lap Leaders R Patrese 1-31 (31); N Mansell 32-71 (40).

3 May 1992 **SPAIN: Montmeló** (Round 4) (Race 520)

65 laps x 4.747 km, 2.950 miles = 308.555 km, 191.727 miles

Pos	No	Driver	Car	Model	Engine		Laps	Time/Reason for Retirement	Grid Pos	Row
1	5	N Mansell	Williams	FW14B	Renault	V10	65	1h 56m 10.674s	1	1
2	19	M Schumacher	Benetton	B192	Ford Cosworth	V8	65	1h 56m 34.588s	2	1
3	27	J Alesi	Ferrari	F92A	Ferrari	V12	65	1h 56m 37.136s	8	4
4	2	G Berger	McLaren	MP4/7A	Honda	V12	65	1h 57m 31.321s	7	4
5	9	M Alboreto	Footwork	FA13	Mugen Honda	V10	64		16	8
6	22	P Martini	Dallara	192	Ferrari	V12	63		13	7
7	10	A Suzuki	Footwork	FA13	Mugen Honda	V10	63		19	10
8	16	K Wendlinger	March	CG911	Ilmor	V10	63		9	5
9r	1	A Senna	McLaren	MP4/7A	Honda	V12	62	spin	3	2
10r	28	I Capelli	Ferrari	F92A	Ferrari	V12	62	spin	5	3
11	23	C Fittipaldi	Minardi	M191B	Lamborghini	V12	61		22	11
12	17	P Belmondo	March	CG911	Ilmor	V10	61		23	12
r	21	J J Lehto	Dallara	192	Ferrari	V12	56	spin	12	6
r	15	G Tarquini	Fondmetal	GR01	Ford Cosworth	V8	56	spin	18	9
r	11	M Häkkinen	Lotus	102D	Ford Cosworth	V8	56	spin	21	11
r	26	E Comas	Ligier	JS37	Renault	V10	55	spin	10	5
r	29	B Gachot	Venturi Larrousse	LC92	Lamborghini	V12	35	engine	24	12
r	3	O Grouillard	Tyrrell	020B	Ilmor	V10	30	spin	15	8
r	24	G Morbidelli	Minardi	M191B	Lamborghini	V12	26	handling	25	13
r	33	M Gugelmin	Jordan	192	Yamaha	V12	24	spin	17	9
r	14	A Chiesa	Fondmetal	GR01	Ford Cosworth	V8	22	spin	20	10
r	6	R Patrese	Williams	FW14B	Renault	V10	19	spin	4	2
r	12	J Herbert	Lotus	102D	Ford Cosworth	V8	13	spin	26	13
r	25	T Boutsen	Ligier	JS37	Renault	V10	11	engine	14	7
r	20	M Brundle	Benetton	B192	Ford Cosworth	V8	4	spin	6	3
r	4	A de Cesaris	Tyrrell	020B	Ilmor	V10	2	oil pressure / spin	11	6
nq	30	U Katayama	Venturi Larrousse	LC92	Lamborghini	V12				
nq	7	E van de Poele	Brabham	BT60B	Judd	V10				
nq	32	S Modena	Jordan	192	Yamaha	V12				
nq	8	D Hill	Brabham	BT60B	Judd	V10				
npq	34	R Moreno	Andrea Moda	S921	Judd	V10				
npq	35	P McCarthy	Andrea Moda	S921	Judd	V10				

Winning speed 159.353 km/h, 99.017 mph
Pole Position speed 213.109 km/h, 132.420 mph (N Mansell, 1 min:20.190 sec)
Fastest Lap speed 166.719 km/h, 103.594 mph (N Mansell, 1 min:42.503 sec on lap 10)
Lap Leaders N Mansell 1-65 (65).

17 May 1992 **SAN MARINO: Imola** (Round 5) (Race 521)

60 laps x 5.040 km, 3.132 miles = 302.400 km, 187.903 miles

Pos	No	Driver	Car	Model	Engine		Laps	Time/Reason for Retirement	Grid Pos	Row
1	5	N Mansell	Williams	FW14B	Renault	V10	60	1h 28m 40.927s	1	1
2	6	R Patrese	Williams	FW14B	Renault	V10	60	1h 28m 50.378s	2	1
3	1	A Senna	McLaren	MP4/7A	Honda	V12	60	1h 29m 29.911s	3	2
4	20	M Brundle	Benetton	B192	Ford Cosworth	V8	60	1h 29m 33.934s	6	3
5	9	M Alboreto	Footwork	FA13	Mugen Honda	V10	59		9	5
6	22	P Martini	Dallara	192	Ferrari	V12	59		15	8
7	33	M Gugelmin	Jordan	192	Yamaha	V12	58		18	9
8	3	O Grouillard	Tyrrell	020B	Ilmor	V10	58		20	10
9	26	E Comas	Ligier	JS37	Renault	V10	58		13	7
10	10	A Suzuki	Footwork	FA13	Mugen Honda	V10	58		11	6
11r	21	J J Lehto	Dallara	192	Ferrari	V12	57	engine overheating	16	8
12	16	K Wendlinger	March	CG911	Ilmor	V10	57		12	6
13	17	P Belmondo	March	CG911	Ilmor	V10	57		24	12
14r	4	A de Cesaris	Tyrrell	020B	Ilmor	V10	55	fuel pressure	14	7
r	30	U Katayama	Venturi Larrousse	LC92	Lamborghini	V12	40	spin	17	9
r	27	J Alesi	Ferrari	F92A	Ferrari	V12	39	accident	7	4
r	2	G Berger	McLaren	MP4/7A	Honda	V12	39	accident	4	2
r	29	B Gachot	Venturi Larrousse	LC92	Lamborghini	V12	32	spin	19	10
r	25	T Boutsen	Ligier	JS37	Renault	V10	29	fuel pump	10	5
r	32	S Modena	Jordan	192	Yamaha	V12	25	gearbox	23	12
r	24	G Morbidelli	Minardi	M192	Lamborghini	V12	24	transmission	21	11
r	15	G Tarquini	Fondmetal	GR01	Ford Cosworth	V8	24	engine overheating	22	11
r	19	M Schumacher	Benetton	B192	Ford Cosworth	V8	20	accident / front suspension	5	3
r	28	I Capelli	Ferrari	F92A	Ferrari	V12	11	spin	8	4
r	23	C Fittipaldi	Minardi	M192	Lamborghini	V12	8	transmission	25	13
r	12	J Herbert	Lotus	107	Ford Cosworth	V8	8	gearbox	26	13
nq	11	M Häkkinen	Lotus	102D	Ford Cosworth	V8				
nq	14	A Chiesa	Fondmetal	GR01	Ford Cosworth	V8				
nq	8	D Hill	Brabham	BT60B	Judd	V10				
nq	7	E van de Poele	Brabham	BT60B	Judd	V10				
npq	34	R Moreno	Andrea Moda	S921	Judd	V10				
npq	35	P McCarthy	Andrea Moda	S921	Judd	V10				

Winning speed 204.596 km/h, 127.130 mph
Pole Position speed 221.695 km/h, 137.755 mph (N Mansell, 1 min:21.842 sec)
Fastest Lap speed 210.732 km/h, 130.943 mph (R Patrese, 1 min:26.100 sec on lap 60)
Lap Leaders N Mansell 1-60 (60).

78 laps x 3.328 km, 2.068 miles = 259.584 km, 161.298 miles

Pos	No	Driver	Car	Model	Engine		Laps	Time/Reason for Retirement	Grid Pos	Row
1	1	A Senna	McLaren	MP4/7A	Honda	V12	78	1h 50m 59.372s	3	2
2	5	N Mansell	Williams	FW14B	Renault	V10	78	1h 50m 59.587s	1	1
3	6	R Patrese	Williams	FW14B	Renault	V10	78	1h 51m 31.215s	2	1
4	19	M Schumacher	Benetton	B192	Ford Cosworth	V8	78	1h 51m 38.666s	6	3
5	20	M Brundle	Benetton	B192	Ford Cosworth	V8	78	1h 52m 20.719s	7	4
6	29	B Gachot	Venturi Larrousse	LC92	Lamborghini	V12	77		15	8
7	9	M Alboreto	Footwork	FA13	Mugen Honda	V10	77		11	6
8	23	C Fittipaldi	Minardi	M192	Lamborghini	V12	77		17	9
9	21	J J Lehto	Dallara	192	Ferrari	V12	76		20	10
10	26	E Comas	Ligier	JS37	Renault	V10	76		23	12
11	10	A Suzuki	Footwork	FA13	Mugen Honda	V10	76		19	10
12	25	T Boutsen	Ligier	JS37	Renault	V10	75		22	11
r	28	I Capelli	Ferrari	F92A	Ferrari	V12	60	accident / steering / spin	8	4
r	2	G Berger	McLaren	MP4/7A	Honda	V12	32	gearbox	5	3
r	11	M Häkkinen	Lotus	107	Ford Cosworth	V8	30	clutch / gearbox	14	7
r	27	J Alesi	Ferrari	F92A	Ferrari	V12	28	gearbox	4	2
r	33	M Gugelmin	Jordan	192	Yamaha	V12	18	transmission	13	7
r	12	J Herbert	Lotus	107	Ford Cosworth	V8	17	accident	9	5
r	34	R Moreno	Andrea Moda	S921	Judd	V10	11	engine	26	13
r	4	A de Cesaris	Tyrrell	020B	Ilmor	V10	9	gearbox	10	5
r	15	G Tarquini	Fondmetal	GR01	Ford Cosworth	V8	9	engine overheating	25	13
r	32	S Modena	Jordan	192	Yamaha	V12	6	accident	21	11
r	3	O Grouillard	Tyrrell	020B	Ilmor	V10	4	transmission	24	12
r	16	K Wendlinger	March	CG911	Ilmor	V10	1	gearbox	16	8
r	24	G Morbidelli	Minardi	M192	Lamborghini	V12	1	battery	12	6
r	22	P Martini	Dallara	192	Ferrari	V12	0	accident	18	9
nq	7	E van de Poele	Brabham	BT60B	Judd	V10				
nq	8	D Hill	Brabham	BT60B	Judd	V10				
nq	14	A Chiesa	Fondmetal	GR01	Ford Cosworth	V8				
nq	17	P Belmondo	March	CG911	Ilmor	V10				
npq	30	U Katayama	Venturi Larrousse	LC92	Lamborghini	V12				
npq	35	P McCarthy	Andrea Moda	S921	Judd	V10				

Winning speed 140.329 km/h, 87.196 mph
Pole Position speed 150.711 km/h, 93.648 mph (N Mansell, 1 min:19.495 sec)
Fastest Lap speed 146.827 km/h, 91.234 mph (N Mansell, 1 min:21.598 sec on lap 74)
Lap Leaders N Mansell 1-70 (70); A Senna 71-78 (8).

69 laps x 4.430 km, 2.753 miles = 305.670 km, 189.935 miles

Pos	No	Driver	Car	Model	Engine		Laps	Time/Reason for Retirement	Grid Pos	Row
1	2	G Berger	McLaren	MP4/7A	Honda	V12	69	1h 37m 08.299s	4	2
2	19	M Schumacher	Benetton	B192	Ford Cosworth	V8	69	1h 37m 20.700s	5	3
3	27	J Alesi	Ferrari	F92A	Ferrari	V12	69	1h 38m 15.626s	8	4
4	16	K Wendlinger	March	CG911	Ilmor	V10	68		12	6
5	4	A de Cesaris	Tyrrell	020B	Ilmor	V10	68		14	7
6	26	E Comas	Ligier	JS37	Renault	V10	68		22	11
7	9	M Alboreto	Footwork	FA13	Mugen Honda	V10	68		16	8
8	22	P Martini	Dallara	192	Ferrari	V12	68		15	8
9	21	J J Lehto	Dallara	192	Ferrari	V12	68		23	12
10	25	T Boutsen	Ligier	JS37	Renault	V10	67		21	11
11	24	G Morbidelli	Minardi	M192	Lamborghini	V12	67		13	7
12	3	O Grouillard	Tyrrell	020B	Ilmor	V10	67		26	13
13r	23	C Fittipaldi	Minardi	M192	Lamborghini	V12	65	gearbox oil fire	25	13
14	17	P Belmondo	March	CG911	Ilmor	V10	64		20	10
r	30	U Katayama	Venturi Larrousse	LC92	Lamborghini	V12	61	engine	11	6
r	20	M Brundle	Benetton	B192	Ford Cosworth	V8	45	transmission	7	4
r	6	R Patrese	Williams	FW14B	Renault	V10	43	gearbox	2	1
r	1	A Senna	McLaren	MP4/7A	Honda	V12	37	electrics	1	1
r	32	S Modena	Jordan	192	Yamaha	V12	36	transmission	17	9
r	11	M Häkkinen	Lotus	107	Ford Cosworth	V8	35	gearbox	10	5
r	12	J Herbert	Lotus	107	Ford Cosworth	V8	34	clutch	6	3
r	28	I Capelli	Ferrari	F92A	Ferrari	V12	18	accident	9	5
r	5	N Mansell	Williams	FW14B	Renault	V10	14	accident	3	2
r	33	M Gugelmin	Jordan	192	Yamaha	V12	14	transmission	24	12
dq	29	B Gachot	Venturi Larrousse	LC92	Lamborghini	V12	14	push start after accident	19	10
r	15	G Tarquini	Fondmetal	GR02	Ford Cosworth	V8	0	gearbox	18	9
nq	10	A Suzuki	Footwork	FA13	Mugen Honda	V10				
nq	7	E van de Poele	Brabham	BT60B	Judd	V10				
nq	14	A Chiesa	Fondmetal	GR01	Ford Cosworth	V8				
nq	8	D Hill	Brabham	BT60B	Judd	V10				
npq	34	R Moreno	Andrea Moda	S921	Judd	V10				

Winning speed 188.805 km/h, 117.318 mph
Pole Position speed 199.912 km/h, 124.220 mph (A Senna, 1 min:19.775 sec)
Fastest Lap speed 193.720 km/h, 120.372 mph (G Berger, 1 min:22.325 sec on lap 61)
Lap Leaders A Senna 1-37 (37); G Berger 38-69 (32).

5 Jul 1992　　　**FRANCE: Magny-Cours**　　　**(Round 8)**　　**(Race 524)**

69 laps x 4.250 km, 2.641 miles = 293.250 km, 182.217 miles

Pos	No	Driver	Car	Model	Engine		Laps	Time/Reason for Retirement	Grid Pos	Row
1	5	N Mansell	Williams	FW14B	Renault	V10	69	1h 38m 08.459s	1	1
2	6	R Patrese	Williams	FW14B	Renault	V10	69	1h 38m 54.906s	2	1
3	20	M Brundle	Benetton	B192	Ford Cosworth	V8	69	1h 39m 21.038s	7	4
4	11	M Häkkinen	Lotus	107	Ford Cosworth	V8	68		11	6
5	26	E Comas	Ligier	JS37	Renault	V10	68		10	5
6	12	J Herbert	Lotus	107	Ford Cosworth	V8	68		12	6
7	9	M Alboreto	Footwork	FA13	Mugen Honda	V10	68		14	7
8	24	G Morbidelli	Minardi	M192	Lamborghini	V12	68		16	8
9	21	J J Lehto	Dallara	192	Ferrari	V12	67		17	9
10	22	P Martini	Dallara	192	Ferrari	V12	67		25	13
11	3	O Grouillard	Tyrrell	020B	Ilmor	V10	66		22	11
r	27	J Alesi	Ferrari	F92A	Ferrari	V12	61	engine	6	3
r	4	A de Cesaris	Tyrrell	020B	Ilmor	V10	51	spin	19	10
r	30	U Katayama	Venturi Larrousse	LC92	Lamborghini	V12	49	engine	18	9
r	25	T Boutsen	Ligier	JS37	Renault	V10	46	spin	9	5
r	28	I Capelli	Ferrari	F92A	Ferrari	V12	38	engine	8	4
r	16	K Wendlinger	March	CG911	Ilmor	V10	33	gearbox	21	11
r	32	S Modena	Jordan	192	Yamaha	V12	25	engine	20	10
r	10	A Suzuki	Footwork	FA13	Mugen Honda	V10	20	spin	15	8
r	19	M Schumacher	Benetton	B192	Ford Cosworth	V8	17	accident	5	3
r	2	G Berger	McLaren	MP4/7A	Honda	V12	10	engine	4	2
r	15	G Tarquini	Fondmetal	GR02	Ford Cosworth	V8	6	throttle linkage	23	12
r	29	B Gachot	Venturi Larrousse	LC92	Lamborghini	V12	0	accident	13	7
r	33	M Gugelmin	Jordan	192	Yamaha	V12	0	accident	24	12
r	14	A Chiesa	Fondmetal	GR02	Ford Cosworth	V8	0	accident	26	13
r	1	A Senna	McLaren	MP4/7A	Honda	V12	0	accident	3	2
nq	17	P Belmondo	March	CG911	Ilmor	V10				
nq	23	C Fittipaldi	Minardi	M192	Lamborghini	V12		accident / injury		
nq	7	E van de Poele	Brabham	BT60B	Judd	V10				
nq	8	D Hill	Brabham	BT60B	Judd	V10				

Winning speed 179.283 km/h, 111.401 mph
Pole Position speed 207.137 km/h, 128.709 mph (N Mansell, 1 min:13.864 sec)
Fastest Lap speed 198.521 km/h, 123.355 mph (N Mansell, 1 min:17.070 sec on lap 37)
Lap Leaders R Patrese 1-19 (19); N Mansell 20-69 (50).
Scheduled for 72 laps, but interrupted after 18 laps, because of rain. Restarted for a further 51 laps, with results being given on aggregate. Lap leaders are shown 'on the road'.

12 Jul 1992　　　**BRITAIN: Silverstone**　　　**(Round 9)**　　**(Race 525)**

59 laps x 5.226 km, 3.247 miles = 308.334 km, 191.590 miles

Pos	No	Driver	Car	Model	Engine		Laps	Time/Reason for Retirement	Grid Pos	Row
1	5	N Mansell	Williams	FW14B	Renault	V10	59	1h 25m 42.991s	1	1
2	6	R Patrese	Williams	FW14B	Renault	V10	59	1h 26m 22.085s	2	1
3	20	M Brundle	Benetton	B192	Ford Cosworth	V8	59	1h 26m 31.386s	6	3
4	19	M Schumacher	Benetton	B192	Ford Cosworth	V8	59	1h 26m 36.258s	4	2
5	2	G Berger	McLaren	MP4/7A	Honda	V12	59	1h 26m 38.786s	5	3
6	11	M Häkkinen	Lotus	107	Ford Cosworth	V8	59	1h 27m 03.129s	9	5
7	9	M Alboreto	Footwork	FA13	Mugen Honda	V10	58		12	6
8	26	E Comas	Ligier	JS37	Renault	V10	58		10	5
9	28	I Capelli	Ferrari	F92A	Ferrari	V12	58		14	7
10	25	T Boutsen	Ligier	JS37	Renault	V10	57		13	7
11	3	O Grouillard	Tyrrell	020B	Ilmor	V10	57		20	10
12	10	A Suzuki	Footwork	FA13	Mugen Honda	V10	57		17	9
13	21	J J Lehto	Dallara	192	Ferrari	V12	57		19	10
14	15	G Tarquini	Fondmetal	GR02	Ford Cosworth	V8	57		15	8
15	22	P Martini	Dallara	192	Ferrari	V12	56		22	11
16	8	D Hill	Brabham	BT60B	Judd	V10	55		26	13
17r	24	G Morbidelli	Minardi	M192	Lamborghini	V12	53	oil pressure	25	13
r	1	A Senna	McLaren	MP4/7A	Honda	V12	52	gearbox	3	2
r	4	A de Cesaris	Tyrrell	020B	Ilmor	V10	46	suspension / spin	18	9
r	27	J Alesi	Ferrari	F92A	Ferrari	V12	43	fire extinguisher	8	4
r	32	S Modena	Jordan	192	Yamaha	V12	43	engine	23	12
r	33	M Gugelmin	Jordan	192	Yamaha	V12	37	engine	24	12
r	29	B Gachot	Venturi Larrousse	LC92	Lamborghini	V12	32	rear wheel bearing	11	6
r	12	J Herbert	Lotus	107	Ford Cosworth	V8	31	gearbox	7	4
r	16	K Wendlinger	March	CG911	Ilmor	V10	27	gearbox	21	11
r	30	U Katayama	Venturi Larrousse	LC92	Lamborghini	V12	27	gear linkage	16	8
nq	23	A Zanardi	Minardi	M192	Lamborghini	V12				
nq	17	P Belmondo	March	CG911	Ilmor	V10				
nq	14	A Chiesa	Fondmetal	GR01	Ford Cosworth	V8				
nq	7	E van de Poele	Brabham	BT60B	Judd	V10				
npq	34	R Moreno	Andrea Moda	S921	Judd	V10				
npq	35	P McCarthy	Andrea Moda	S921	Judd	V10				

Winning speed 215.828 km/h, 134.109 mph
Pole Position speed 238.252 km/h, 148.043 mph (N Mansell, 1 min:18.965 sec)
Fastest Lap speed 227.936 km/h, 141.633 mph (N Mansell, 1 min:22.539 sec on lap 57)
Lap Leaders N Mansell 1-59 (59).

Races

GERMANY: Hockenheim (Round 10) (Race 526)

45 laps x 6.815 km, 4.235 miles = 306.675 km, 190.559 miles

Pos	No	Driver	Car	Model	Engine		Laps	Time/Reason for Retirement	Grid Pos	Row
1	5	N Mansell	Williams	FW14B	Renault	V10	45	1h 18m 22.032s	1	1
2	1	A Senna	McLaren	MP4/7A	Honda	V12	45	1h 18m 26.532s	3	2
3	19	M Schumacher	Benetton	B192	Ford Cosworth	V8	45	1h 18m 56.494s	6	3
4	20	M Brundle	Benetton	B192	Ford Cosworth	V8	45	1h 18m 58.991s	9	5
5	27	J Alesi	Ferrari	F92A	Ferrari	V12	45	1h 19m 34.639s	5	3
6	26	E Comas	Ligier	JS37	Renault	V10	45	1h 19m 58.530s	7	4
7	25	T Boutsen	Ligier	JS37	Renault	V10	45	1h 19m 59.212s	8	4
8r	6	R Patrese	Williams	FW14B	Renault	V10	44	spin	2	1
9	9	M Alboreto	Footwork	FA13	Mugen Honda	V10	44		17	9
10	21	J J Lehto	Dallara	192	Ferrari	V12	44		21	11
11	22	P Martini	Dallara	192	Ferrari	V12	44		18	9
12	24	G Morbidelli	Minardi	M192	Lamborghini	V12	44		26	13
13	17	P Belmondo	March	CG911	Ilmor	V10	44		22	11
14	29	B Gachot	Venturi Larrousse	LC92	Lamborghini	V12	44		25	13
15	33	M Gugelmin	Jordan	192	Yamaha	V12	43		23	12
16	16	K Wendlinger	March	CG911	Ilmor	V10	42		10	5
r	15	G Tarquini	Fondmetal	GR02	Ford Cosworth	V8	33	engine	19	10
r	4	A de Cesaris	Tyrrell	020B	Ilmor	V10	25	engine	20	10
r	12	J Herbert	Lotus	107	Ford Cosworth	V8	23	engine	11	6
r	28	I Capelli	Ferrari	F92A	Ferrari	V12	21	engine	12	6
r	11	M Häkkinen	Lotus	107	Ford Cosworth	V8	21	engine	13	7
r	2	G Berger	McLaren	MP4/7A	Honda	V12	16	misfire	4	2
r	3	O Grouillard	Tyrrell	020B	Ilmor	V10	8	engine overheating	14	7
r	30	U Katayama	Venturi Larrousse	LC92	Lamborghini	V12	8	accident	16	8
r	10	A Suzuki	Footwork	FA13	Mugen Honda	V10	1	spin	15	8
r	23	A Zanardi	Minardi	M192	Lamborghini	V12	1	clutch	24	12
nq	32	S Modena	Jordan	192	Yamaha	V12				
nq	7	E van de Poele	Brabham	BT60B	Judd	V10				
nq	14	A Chiesa	Fondmetal	GR02	Ford Cosworth	V8				
nq	8	D Hill	Brabham	BT60B	Judd	V10				
npq	34	R Moreno	Andrea Moda	S921	Judd	V10				
exc	35	P McCarthy	Andrea Moda	S921	Judd	V10		missed weight check		

Winning speed 234.798 km/h, 145.897 mph
Pole Position speed 250.449 km/h, 155.622 mph (N Mansell, 1 min:37.960 sec)
Fastest Lap speed 241.498 km/h, 150.060 mph (R Patrese, 1 min:41.591 sec on lap 36)
Lap Leaders N Mansell 1-14,20-45 (40); R Patrese 15-19 (5).

HUNGARY: Hungaroring (Round 11) (Race 527)

77 laps x 3.968 km, 2.466 miles = 305.536 km, 189.851 miles

Pos	No	Driver	Car	Model	Engine		Laps	Time/Reason for Retirement	Grid Pos	Row
1	1	A Senna	McLaren	MP4/7A	Honda	V12	77	1h 46m 19.216s	3	2
2	5	N Mansell	Williams	FW14B	Renault	V10	77	1h 46m 59.355s	2	1
3	2	G Berger	McLaren	MP4/7A	Honda	V12	77	1h 47m 09.998s	5	3
4	11	M Häkkinen	Lotus	107	Ford Cosworth	V8	77	1h 47m 13.529s	16	8
5	20	M Brundle	Benetton	B192	Ford Cosworth	V8	77	1h 47m 16.714s	6	3
6	28	I Capelli	Ferrari	F92A	Ferrari	V12	76		10	5
7	9	M Alboreto	Footwork	FA13	Mugen Honda	V10	75		7	4
8	4	A de Cesaris	Tyrrell	020B	Ilmor	V10	75		19	10
9	17	P Belmondo	March	CG911	Ilmor	V10	74		17	9
10	33	M Gugelmin	Jordan	192	Yamaha	V12	73		21	11
11	8	D Hill	Brabham	BT60B	Judd	V10	73		25	13
r	19	M Schumacher	Benetton	B192	Ford Cosworth	V8	63	accident / rear wing lost / spin	4	2
r	6	R Patrese	Williams	FW14B	Renault	V10	55	engine	1	1
r	22	P Martini	Dallara	192	Ferrari	V12	40	gearbox	26	13
r	30	U Katayama	Venturi Larrousse	LC92	Lamborghini	V12	35	engine	20	10
r	27	J Alesi	Ferrari	F92A	Ferrari	V12	14	spin	9	5
r	29	B Gachot	Venturi Larrousse	LC92	Lamborghini	V12	13	accident	15	8
r	10	A Suzuki	Footwork	FA13	Mugen Honda	V10	13	accident	14	7
r	3	O Grouillard	Tyrrell	020B	Ilmor	V10	13	accident	22	11
r	16	K Wendlinger	March	CG911	Ilmor	V10	13	accident	23	12
r	32	S Modena	Jordan	192	Yamaha	V12	13	accident	24	12
r	14	E van de Poele	Fondmetal	GR02	Ford Cosworth	V8	2	spin	18	9
r	26	E Comas	Ligier	JS37	Renault	V10	0	accident	11	6
r	25	T Boutsen	Ligier	JS37	Renault	V10	0	accident	8	4
r	12	J Herbert	Lotus	107	Ford Cosworth	V8	0	accident	13	7
r	15	G Tarquini	Fondmetal	GR02	Ford Cosworth	V8	0	accident	12	6
nq	24	G Morbidelli	Minardi	M192	Lamborghini	V12				
nq	21	J J Lehto	Dallara	192	Ferrari	V12				
nq	23	A Zanardi	Minardi	M192	Lamborghini	V12				
nq	34	R Moreno	Andrea Moda	S921	Judd	V10				
npq	35	P McCarthy	Andrea Moda	S921	Judd	V10				

Winning speed 172.424 km/h, 107.139 mph
Pole Position speed 189.263 km/h, 117.602 mph (R Patrese, 1 min:15.476 sec)
Fastest Lap speed 182.418 km/h, 113.349 mph (N Mansell, 1 min:18.308 sec on lap 63)
Lap Leaders R Patrese 1-38 (38); A Senna 39-77 (39).

30 Aug 1992   BELGIUM: Spa-Francorchamps   (Round 12)   (Race 528)

44 laps x 6.974 km, 4.333 miles = 306.856 km, 190.671 miles

Pos	No	Driver	Car	Model	Engine		Laps	Time/Reason for Retirement	Grid Pos	Row
1	19	M Schumacher	Benetton	B192	Ford Cosworth	V8	44	1h 36m 10.721s	3	2
2	5	N Mansell	Williams	FW14B	Renault	V10	44	1h 36m 47.316s	1	1
3	6	R Patrese	Williams	FW14B	Renault	V10	44	1h 36m 54.618s	4	2
4	20	M Brundle	Benetton	B192	Ford Cosworth	V8	44	1h 36m 56.780s	9	5
5	1	A Senna	McLaren	MP4/7A	Honda	V12	44	1h 37m 19.090s	2	1
6	11	M Häkkinen	Lotus	107	Ford Cosworth	V8	44	1h 37m 20.751s	8	4
7	21	J J Lehto	Dallara	192	Ferrari	V12	44	1h 37m 48.958s	16	8
8	4	A de Cesaris	Tyrrell	020B	Ilmor	V10	43		13	7
9	10	A Suzuki	Footwork	FA13	Mugen Honda	V10	43		25	13
10	14	E van de Poele	Fondmetal	GR02	Ford Cosworth	V8	43		15	8
11	16	K Wendlinger	March	CG911	Ilmor	V10	43		18	9
12	17	E Naspetti	March	CG911	Ilmor	V10	43		21	11
13r	12	J Herbert	Lotus	107	Ford Cosworth	V8	42	engine	10	5
14	33	M Gugelmin	Jordan	192	Yamaha	V12	42		24	12
15	32	S Modena	Jordan	192	Yamaha	V12	42		17	9
16	24	G Morbidelli	Minardi	M192	Lamborghini	V12	42		23	12
17	30	U Katayama	Venturi Larrousse	LC92	Lamborghini	V12	42		26	13
18r	29	B Gachot	Venturi Larrousse	LC92	Lamborghini	V12	40	spin	20	10
r	25	T Boutsen	Ligier	JS37	Renault	V10	27	accident	7	4
r	28	I Capelli	Ferrari	F92A	Ferrari	V12	25	engine	12	6
r	15	G Tarquini	Fondmetal	GR02	Ford Cosworth	V8	25	engine	11	6
r	9	M Alboreto	Footwork	FA13	Mugen Honda	V10	20	gearbox	14	7
r	27	J Alesi	Ferrari	F92AT	Ferrari	V12	7	spin	5	3
r	3	O Grouillard	Tyrrell	020B	Ilmor	V10	1	accident	22	11
r	22	P Martini	Dallara	192	Ferrari	V12	0	spin	19	10
r	2	G Berger	McLaren	MP4/7A	Honda	V12	0	transmission	6	3
nq	23	C Fittipaldi	Minardi	M192	Lamborghini	V12				
nq	34	R Moreno	Andrea Moda	S921	Judd	V10				
nq	35	P McCarthy	Andrea Moda	S921	Judd	V10				
nq	26	E Comas	Ligier	JS37	Renault	V10		accident / injury		

Winning speed 191.429 km/h, 118.948 mph
Pole Position speed 227.115 km/h, 141.123 mph (N Mansell, 1 min:50.545 sec)
Fastest Lap speed 220.636 km/h, 137.097 mph (M Schumacher, 1 min:53.791 sec on lap 39)
Lap Leaders A Senna 1,7-10 (5); N Mansell 2-3,11-33 (25); R Patrese 4-6 (3); M Schumacher 34-44 (11).

13 Sep 1992   ITALY: Monza   (Round 13)   (Race 529)

53 laps x 5.800 km, 3.604 miles = 307.400 km, 191.010 miles

Pos	No	Driver	Car	Model	Engine		Laps	Time/Reason for Retirement	Grid Pos	Row
1	1	A Senna	McLaren	MP4/7A	Honda	V12	53	1h 18m 15.349s	2	1
2	20	M Brundle	Benetton	B192	Ford Cosworth	V8	53	1h 18m 32.399s	9	5
3	19	M Schumacher	Benetton	B192	Ford Cosworth	V8	53	1h 18m 39.722s	6	3
4	2	G Berger	McLaren	MP4/7A	Honda	V12	53	1h 19m 40.839s	5	3
5	6	R Patrese	Williams	FW14B	Renault	V10	53	1h 19m 48.507s	4	2
6	4	A de Cesaris	Tyrrell	020B	Ilmor	V10	52		21	11
7	9	M Alboreto	Footwork	FA13	Mugen Honda	V10	52		16	8
8	22	P Martini	Dallara	192	Ferrari	V12	52		22	11
9r	30	U Katayama	Venturi Larrousse	LC92	Lamborghini	V12	50	transmission / spin	23	12
10	16	K Wendlinger	March	CG911	Ilmor	V10	50		17	9
11r	21	J J Lehto	Dallara	192	Ferrari	V12	47	electrics	14	7
r	33	M Gugelmin	Jordan	192	Yamaha	V12	46	transmission	26	13
r	5	N Mansell	Williams	FW14B	Renault	V10	41	hydraulics	1	1
r	25	T Boutsen	Ligier	JS37	Renault	V10	41	electronics	8	4
r	26	E Comas	Ligier	JS37	Renault	V10	35	accident	15	8
r	15	G Tarquini	Fondmetal	GR02	Ford Cosworth	V8	30	gearbox	20	10
r	3	O Grouillard	Tyrrell	020B	Ilmor	V10	26	engine	18	9
r	12	J Herbert	Lotus	107	Ford Cosworth	V8	18	engine	13	7
r	17	E Naspetti	March	CG911	Ilmor	V10	17	accident	24	12
r	27	J Alesi	Ferrari	F92AT	Ferrari	V12	12	fuel pressure	3	2
r	28	I Capelli	Ferrari	F92AT	Ferrari	V12	12	spin	7	4
r	24	G Morbidelli	Minardi	M192	Lamborghini	V12	12	engine	12	6
r	29	B Gachot	Venturi Larrousse	LC92	Lamborghini	V12	11	engine	10	5
r	11	M Häkkinen	Lotus	107	Ford Cosworth	V8	5	electrics	11	6
r	10	A Suzuki	Footwork	FA13	Mugen Honda	V10	2	accident / rear suspension	19	10
r	14	E van de Poele	Fondmetal	GR02	Ford Cosworth	V8	0	clutch	25	13
nq	23	C Fittipaldi	Minardi	M192	Lamborghini	V12				
nq	32	S Modena	Jordan	192	Yamaha	V12				

Winning speed 235.689 km/h, 146.450 mph
Pole Position speed 253.950 km/h, 157.797 mph (N Mansell, 1 min:22.221 sec)
Fastest Lap speed 242.455 km/h, 150.655 mph (N Mansell, 1 min:26.119 sec on lap 39)
Lap Leaders N Mansell 1-19 (19); R Patrese 20-47 (28); A Senna 48-53 (6).

27 Sep 1992   PORTUGAL: Estoril   (Round 14)   (Race 530)

71 laps x 4.350 km, 2.703 miles = 308.850 km, 191.910 miles

Pos	No	Driver	Car	Model	Engine		Laps	Time/Reason for Retirement	Grid Pos	Row
1	5	N Mansell	Williams	FW14B	Renault	V10	71	1h 34m 46.659s	1	1
2	2	G Berger	McLaren	MP4/7A	Honda	V12	71	1h 35m 24.192s	4	2
3	1	A Senna	McLaren	MP4/7A	Honda	V12	70		3	2
4	20	M Brundle	Benetton	B192	Ford Cosworth	V8	70		6	3
5	11	M Häkkinen	Lotus	107	Ford Cosworth	V8	70		7	4
6	9	M Alboreto	Footwork	FA13	Mugen Honda	V10	70		8	4
7	19	M Schumacher	Benetton	B192	Ford Cosworth	V8	69		5	3
8	25	T Boutsen	Ligier	JS37	Renault	V10	69		11	6
9	4	A de Cesaris	Tyrrell	020B	Ilmor	V10	69		12	6
10	10	A Suzuki	Footwork	FA13	Mugen Honda	V10	68		17	9
11	17	E Naspetti	March	CG911	Ilmor	V10	68		23	12
12	23	C Fittipaldi	Minardi	M192	Lamborghini	V12	68		26	13
13	32	S Modena	Jordan	192	Yamaha	V12	68		24	12
14	24	G Morbidelli	Minardi	M192	Lamborghini	V12	68		18	9
r	21	J J Lehto	Dallara	192	Ferrari	V12	51	accident / chassis	19	10
r	16	K Wendlinger	March	CG911	Ilmor	V10	48	oil radiator / gearbox	22	11
r	26	E Comas	Ligier	JS37	Renault	V10	47	engine	14	7
r	30	U Katayama	Venturi Larrousse	LC92	Lamborghini	V12	46	spin	25	13
r	6	R Patrese	Williams	FW14B	Renault	V10	43	accident	2	1
r	22	P Martini	Dallara	192	Ferrari	V12	43	tyre burst	21	11
r	28	I Capelli	Ferrari	F92AT	Ferrari	V12	34	engine	16	8
r	3	O Grouillard	Tyrrell	020B	Ilmor	V10	27	gearbox	15	8
r	29	B Gachot	Venturi Larrousse	LC92	Lamborghini	V12	25	fuel pressure	13	7
r	33	M Gugelmin	Jordan	192	Yamaha	V12	19	electrics	20	10
r	27	J Alesi	Ferrari	F92AT	Ferrari	V12	12	spin	10	5
r	12	J Herbert	Lotus	107	Ford Cosworth	V8	2	accident / steering	9	5

Winning speed 195.521 km/h, 121.491 mph
Pole Position speed 214.400 km/h, 133.222 mph (N Mansell, 1 min:13.041 sec)
Fastest Lap speed 205.318 km/h, 127.579 mph (A Senna, 1 min:16.272 sec on lap 66)
Lap Leaders N Mansell 1-71 (71).

25 Oct 1992   JAPAN: Suzuka   (Round 15)   (Race 531)

53 laps x 5.864 km, 3.644 miles = 310.792 km, 193.117 miles

Pos	No	Driver	Car	Model	Engine		Laps	Time/Reason for Retirement	Grid Pos	Row
1	6	R Patrese	Williams	FW14B	Renault	V10	53	1h 33m 09.553s	2	1
2	2	G Berger	McLaren	MP4/7A	Honda	V12	53	1h 33m 23.282s	4	2
3	20	M Brundle	Benetton	B192	Ford Cosworth	V8	53	1h 34m 25.056s	13	7
4	4	A de Cesaris	Tyrrell	020B	Ilmor	V10	52		9	5
5	27	J Alesi	Ferrari	F92AT	Ferrari	V12	52		15	8
6	23	C Fittipaldi	Minardi	M192	Lamborghini	V12	52		12	6
7	32	S Modena	Jordan	192	Yamaha	V12	52		17	9
8	10	A Suzuki	Footwork	FA13	Mugen Honda	V10	52		16	8
9	21	J J Lehto	Dallara	192	Ferrari	V12	52		22	11
10	22	P Martini	Dallara	192	Ferrari	V12	52		19	10
11	30	U Katayama	Venturi Larrousse	LC92	Lamborghini	V12	52		20	10
12	28	N Larini	Ferrari	F9200	Ferrari	V12	52		11	6
13	17	E Naspetti	March	CG911	Ilmor	V10	51		26	13
14	24	G Morbidelli	Minardi	M192	Lamborghini	V12	51		14	7
15	9	M Alboreto	Footwork	FA13	Mugen Honda	V10	51		24	12
r	5	N Mansell	Williams	FW14B	Renault	V10	44	engine	1	1
r	11	M Häkkinen	Lotus	107	Ford Cosworth	V8	44	engine	7	4
r	29	B Gachot	Venturi Larrousse	LC92	Lamborghini	V12	39	accident	18	9
r	26	E Comas	Ligier	JS37	Renault	V10	36	engine	8	4
r	16	J Lammers	March	CG911	Ilmor	V10	27	clutch	23	12
r	33	M Gugelmin	Jordan	192	Yamaha	V12	22	accident	25	13
r	12	J Herbert	Lotus	107	Ford Cosworth	V8	15	gearbox	6	3
r	19	M Schumacher	Benetton	B192	Ford Cosworth	V8	13	gearbox	5	3
r	3	O Grouillard	Tyrrell	020B	Ilmor	V10	6	accident	21	11
r	25	T Boutsen	Ligier	JS37	Renault	V10	3	gearbox	10	5
r	1	A Senna	McLaren	MP4/7A	Honda	V12	2	engine	3	2

Winning speed 200.168 km/h, 124.379 mph
Pole Position speed 216.828 km/h, 134.731 mph (N Mansell, 1 min:37.360 sec)
Fastest Lap speed 209.749 km/h, 130.332 mph (N Mansell, 1 min:40.646 sec on lap 44)
Lap Leaders N Mansell 1-35 (35); R Patrese 36-53 (18).

8 Nov 1992   **AUSTRALIA: Adelaide**   (Round 16)   (Race 532)

81 laps x 3.780 km, 2.349 miles = 306.180 km, 190.251 miles

Pos	No	Driver	Car	Model	Engine		Laps	Time/Reason for Retirement	Grid Pos	Row
1	2	G Berger	McLaren	MP4/7A	Honda	V12	81	1h 46m 54.786s	4	2
2	19	M Schumacher	Benetton	B192	Ford Cosworth	V8	81	1h 46m 55.527s	5	3
3	20	M Brundle	Benetton	B192	Ford Cosworth	V8	81	1h 47m 48.942s	8	4
4	27	J Alesi	Ferrari	F92AT	Ferrari	V12	80		6	3
5	25	T Boutsen	Ligier	JS37	Renault	V10	80		22	11
6	32	S Modena	Jordan	192	Yamaha	V12	80		15	8
7	11	M Häkkinen	Lotus	107	Ford Cosworth	V8	80		10	5
8	10	A Suzuki	Footwork	FA13	Mugen Honda	V10	79		18	9
9	23	C Fittipaldi	Minardi	M192	Lamborghini	V12	79		17	9
10	24	G Morbidelli	Minardi	M192	Lamborghini	V12	79		16	8
11	28	N Larini	Ferrari	F9200	Ferrari	V12	79		19	10
12	16	J Lammers	March	CG911	Ilmor	V10	78		25	13
13	12	J Herbert	Lotus	107	Ford Cosworth	V8	77		12	6
r	21	J J Lehto	Dallara	192	Ferrari	V12	70	gearbox	24	12
r	17	E Naspetti	March	CG911	Ilmor	V10	55	gearbox	23	12
r	29	B Gachot	Venturi Larrousse	LC92	Lamborghini	V12	51	engine	21	11
r	6	R Patrese	Williams	FW14B	Renault	V10	50	fuel pressure	3	2
r	30	U Katayama	Venturi Larrousse	LC92	Lamborghini	V12	35	differential	26	13
r	4	A de Cesaris	Tyrrell	020B	Ilmor	V10	29	fuel pressure / fire	7	4
r	5	N Mansell	Williams	FW14B	Renault	V10	18	accident	1	1
r	1	A Senna	McLaren	MP4/7A	Honda	V12	18	accident	2	1
r	33	M Gugelmin	Jordan	192	Yamaha	V12	7	brakes / accident	20	10
r	26	E Comas	Ligier	JS37	Renault	V10	4	engine	9	5
r	9	M Alboreto	Footwork	FA13	Mugen Honda	V10	0	accident	11	6
r	22	P Martini	Dallara	192	Ferrari	V12	0	accident	14	7
r	3	O Grouillard	Tyrrell	020B	Ilmor	V10	0	accident	13	7

Winning speed 171.829 km/h, 106.770 mph
Pole Position speed 184.560 km/h, 114.680 mph (N Mansell, 1 min:13.732 sec)
Fastest Lap speed 178.869 km/h, 111.144 mph (M Schumacher, 1 min:16.078 sec on lap 68)
Lap Leaders N Mansell 1-18 (18); R Patrese 19-50 (32); G Berger 51-81 (31).

Lap Leaders 1992

Pos	Driver	Car-Engine	GPs	laps	km	miles
1	N Mansell	Williams-Renault	14	693	3,288.9	2,043.6
2	R Patrese	Williams-Renault	8	174	809.5	503.0
3	A Senna	McLaren-Honda	5	95	415.0	257.8
4	G Berger	McLaren-Honda	2	63	258.9	160.9
5	M Schumacher	Benetton-Ford Cosworth	1	11	76.7	47.7
			16	1,036	4,849.0	3,013.0

Driver Points 1992

		ZA	MEX	BR	E	RSM	MC	CDN	F	GB	D	H	B	I	P	J	AUS	Total
1	N Mansell	10	10	10	10	10	6	-	10	10	10	6	6	-	10	-	-	108
2	R Patrese	6	6	6	-	6	4	-	6	6	-	-	4	2	-	10	-	56
3	M Schumacher	3	4	4	6	-	3	6	-	3	4	-	10	4	-	-	6	53
4	A Senna	4	-	-	-	4	10	-	-	-	6	10	2	10	4	-	-	50
5	G Berger	2	3	-	3	-	-	10	-	2	-	4	-	3	6	6	10	49
6	M Brundle	-	-	-	-	3	2	-	4	4	3	2	3	6	3	4	4	38
7	J Alesi	-	-	3	4	-	-	4	-	-	-	2	-	-	-	2	3	18
8	M Häkkinen	-	1	-	-	-	-	-	3	1	-	3	1	-	2	-	-	11
9	A de Cesaris	-	2	-	-	-	-	2	-	-	-	-	1	-	-	3	-	8
10	M Alboreto	-	-	1	2	2	-	-	-	-	-	-	-	1	-	-	-	6
11	E Comas	-	-	-	-	-	-	1	2	-	1	-	-	-	-	-	-	4
12	K Wendlinger	-	-	-	-	-	3	-	-	-	-	-	-	-	-	-	-	3
	I Capelli	-	-	2	-	-	-	-	-	-	-	1	-	-	-	-	-	3
14	T Boutsen	-	-	-	-	-	-	-	-	-	-	-	-	-	-	-	2	2
	J Herbert	1	-	-	-	-	-	-	1	-	-	-	-	-	-	-	-	2
	P Martini	-	-	-	1	1	-	-	-	-	-	-	-	-	-	-	-	2
17	B Gachot	-	-	-	-	-	1	-	-	-	-	-	-	-	-	-	-	1
	C Fittipaldi	-	-	-	-	-	-	-	-	-	-	-	-	-	-	1	-	1
	S Modena	-	-	-	-	-	-	-	-	-	-	-	-	-	-	-	1	1

10,6,4,3,2 and 1 point awarded to the first six finishers.

Constructor Points 1992

		ZA	MEX	BR	E	RSM	MC	CDN	F	GB	D	H	B	I	P	J	AUS	Total
1	Williams-Renault	16	16	16	10	16	10	-	16	16	10	6	10	2	10	10	-	164
2	McLaren-Honda	6	3	-	3	4	10	10	-	2	6	14	2	13	10	6	10	99
3	Benetton-Ford Cosworth	3	4	4	6	3	5	6	4	7	7	2	13	10	3	4	10	91
4	Ferrari	-	-	5	4	-	-	4	-	-	2	1	-	-	-	2	3	21
5	Lotus-Ford Cosworth	1	1	-	-	-	-	-	4	1	-	3	1	-	2	-	-	13
6	Tyrrell-Ilmor	-	2	-	-	-	-	2	-	-	-	-	-	1	-	3	-	8
7	Footwork-Mugen Honda	-	-	1	2	2	-	-	-	-	-	-	-	-	1	-	-	6
	Ligier-Renault	-	-	-	-	-	-	1	2	-	1	-	-	-	-	-	2	6
9	March-Ilmor	-	-	-	-	-	-	3	-	-	-	-	-	-	-	-	-	3
10	Dallara-Ferrari	-	-	-	1	1	-	-	-	-	-	-	-	-	-	-	-	2
11	Venturi Larrousse-Lamborghini	-	-	-	-	-	1	-	-	-	-	-	-	-	-	-	-	1
	Minardi-Lamborghini	-	-	-	-	-	-	-	-	-	-	-	-	-	-	1	-	1
	Jordan-Yamaha	-	-	-	-	-	-	-	-	-	-	-	-	-	-	1	-	1

10,6,4,3,2 and 1 point awarded to the first six finishers..

Race Entrants and Results

The new World Champion left after a team dispute to race in the American IndyCar series. A safety and cost reduction package called for narrower tyres, smaller wings and tyre and spare car restrictions. Safety cars were re-introduced in an effort to improve the movement of damaged cars from dangerous positions. Traction control and other computer aids were the major technical progression. Sauber entered with backing from Mercedes-Benz. The racing world was stunned by the sudden death of James Hunt from a heart attack at the early age of 45.

WILLIAMS
Canon Williams Team: Hill, Prost

TYRRELL
Tyrrell Racing Organisation: Katayama, de Cesaris

BENETTON
Camel Benetton Ford: Schumacher, Patrese

McLAREN
Marlboro McLaren: Andretti, Häkkinen, Senna

FOOTWORK
Footwork Mugen Honda: Warwick, A Suzuki

LOTUS
Team Lotus: Zanardi, Lamy, Herbert

LARROUSSE
Larrousse F1: Alliot, T Suzuki, Comas

JORDAN
Sasol Jordan: Barrichello, Capelli, Boutsen, Apicella, Naspetti, Irvine

LOLA
Lola BMS Scuderia Italia: Alboreto, Badoer

MINARDI
Minardi Team: Fittipaldi, Gounon, Barbazza, Martini

LIGIER
Ligier Gitanes Blondes: Brundle, Blundell

FERRARI
Scuderia Ferrari SpA: Alesi, Berger

SAUBER
Sauber: Wendlinger, Lehto

14 Mar 1993		SOUTH AFRICA: Kyalami						(Round 1)	(Race 533)	
		72 laps x 4.261 km, 2.648 miles = 306.792 km, 190.632 miles								
Pos	No	Driver	Car	Model	Engine		Laps	Time/Reason for Retirement	Grid Pos	Row
1	2	A Prost	Williams	FW15C	Renault	V10	72	1h 38m 45.082s	1	1
2	8	A Senna	McLaren	MP4/8	Ford Cosworth	V8	72	1h 40m 04.906s	2	1
3	26	M Blundell	Ligier	JS39	Renault	V10	71		8	4
4	23	C Fittipaldi	Minardi	M193	Ford Cosworth	V8	71		13	7
5	30	J J Lehto	Sauber	C12	Ilmor	V10	70		6	3
6r	28	G Berger	Ferrari	F93A	Ferrari	V12	69	engine	15	8
7r	9	D Warwick	Footwork	FA13B	Mugen Honda	V10	69	spin	22	11
r	25	M Brundle	Ligier	JS39	Renault	V10	57	spin	12	6
r	21	M Alboreto	Lola	T93/30	Ferrari	V12	55	engine	25	13
r	20	E Comas	Larrousse	LH93	Lamborghini	V12	51	engine	19	10
r	6	R Patrese	Benetton	B192B	Ford Cosworth	V8	46	spin	7	4
r	5	M Schumacher	Benetton	B192B	Ford Cosworth	V8	39	accident	3	2
r	12	J Herbert	Lotus	107B	Ford Cosworth	V8	38	fuel pressure	17	9
r	29	K Wendlinger	Sauber	C12	Ilmor	V10	33	electrics	10	5
r	14	R Barrichello	Jordan	193	Hart	V10	31	gearbox	14	7
r	27	J Alesi	Ferrari	F93A	Ferrari	V12	30	hydraulics	5	3
r	19	P Alliot	Larrousse	LH93	Lamborghini	V12	27	spin	11	6
r	24	F Barbazza	Minardi	M193	Ford Cosworth	V8	21	accident	24	12
r	10	A Suzuki	Footwork	FA13B	Mugen Honda	V10	21	accident	20	10
r	22	L Badoer	Lola	T93/30	Ferrari	V12	20	gearbox	26	13
r	0	D Hill	Williams	FW15C	Renault	V10	16	accident	4	2
r	11	A Zanardi	Lotus	107B	Ford Cosworth	V8	16	accident	16	8
r	7	M Andretti	McLaren	MP4/8	Ford Cosworth	V8	4	accident	9	5
r	15	I Capelli	Jordan	193	Hart	V10	2	accident	18	9
r	3	U Katayama	Tyrrell	020C	Yamaha	V10	1	transmission	21	11
r	4	A de Cesaris	Tyrrell	020C	Yamaha	V10	0	transmission	23	12

Winning speed 186.403 km/h, 115.825 mph
Pole Position speed 202.647 km/h, 125.919 mph (A Prost, 1 min:15.696 sec)
Fastest Lap speed 192.970 km/h, 119.906 mph (A Prost, 1 min:19.492 sec on lap 40)
Lap Leaders A Senna 1-23 (23); A Prost 24-72 (49).

71 laps x 4.325 km, 2.687 miles = 307.075 km, 190.808 miles

Pos	No	Driver	Car	Model	Engine		Laps	Time/Reason for Retirement	Grid Pos	Row
1	8	A Senna	McLaren	MP4/8	Ford Cosworth	V8	71	1h 51m 15.485s	3	2
2	0	D Hill	Williams	FW15C	Renault	V10	71	1h 51m 32.110s	2	1
3	5	M Schumacher	Benetton	B192B	Ford Cosworth	V8	71	1h 52m 00.921s	4	2
4	12	J Herbert	Lotus	107B	Ford Cosworth	V8	71	1h 52m 02.042s	12	6
5	26	M Blundell	Ligier	JS39	Renault	V10	71	1h 52m 07.612s	10	5
6	11	A Zanardi	Lotus	107B	Ford Cosworth	V8	70		15	8
7	19	P Alliot	Larrousse	LH93	Lamborghini	V12	70		11	6
8	27	J Alesi	Ferrari	F93A	Ferrari	V12	70		9	5
9	9	D Warwick	Footwork	FA13B	Mugen Honda	V10	69		18	9
10	20	E Comas	Larrousse	LH93	Lamborghini	V12	69		17	9
11	21	M Alboreto	Lola	T93/30	Ferrari	V12	68		25	13
12	22	L Badoer	Lola	T93/30	Ferrari	V12	68		21	11
r	29	K Wendlinger	Sauber	C12	Ilmor	V10	61	engine overheating	8	4
r	30	J J Lehto	Sauber	C12	Ilmor	V10	52	electrics	7	4
r	4	A de Cesaris	Tyrrell	020C	Yamaha	V10	48	electrics	23	12
r	2	A Prost	Williams	FW15C	Renault	V10	29	accident	1	1
r	23	C Fittipaldi	Minardi	M193	Ford Cosworth	V8	28	accident	20	10
r	10	A Suzuki	Footwork	FA13B	Mugen Honda	V10	27	accident	19	10
r	3	U Katayama	Tyrrell	020C	Yamaha	V10	26	accident	22	11
r	14	R Barrichello	Jordan	193	Hart	V10	13	gearbox	14	7
r	6	R Patrese	Benetton	B192B	Ford Cosworth	V8	3	suspension oil cooler	6	3
r	25	M Brundle	Ligier	JS39	Renault	V10	0	accident	16	8
r	24	F Barbazza	Minardi	M193	Ford Cosworth	V8	0	accident	24	12
r	7	M Andretti	McLaren	MP4/8	Ford Cosworth	V8	0	accident	5	3
r	28	G Berger	Ferrari	F93A	Ferrari	V12	0	accident	13	7
nq	15	I Capelli	Jordan	193	Hart	V10				

Winning speed 165.601 km/h, 102.900 mph
Pole Position speed 205.230 km/h, 127.524 mph (A Prost, 1 min:15.866 sec)
Fastest Lap speed 194.567 km/h, 120.898 mph (M Schumacher, 1 min:20.024 sec on lap 61)
Lap Leaders A Prost 1-29 (29); D Hill 30-41 (12); A Senna 42-71 (30).

76 laps x 4.023 km, 2.500 miles = 305.748 km, 189.983 miles

Pos	No	Driver	Car	Model	Engine		Laps	Time/Reason for Retirement	Grid Pos	Row
1	8	A Senna	McLaren	MP4/8	Ford Cosworth	V8	76	1h 50m 46.570s	4	2
2	0	D Hill	Williams	FW15C	Renault	V10	76	1h 52m 09.769s	2	1
3	2	A Prost	Williams	FW15C	Renault	V10	75		1	1
4	12	J Herbert	Lotus	107B	Ford Cosworth	V8	75		11	6
5	6	R Patrese	Benetton	B193B	Ford Cosworth	V8	74		10	5
6	24	F Barbazza	Minardi	M193	Ford Cosworth	V8	74		20	10
7	23	C Fittipaldi	Minardi	M193	Ford Cosworth	V8	73		16	8
8	11	A Zanardi	Lotus	107B	Ford Cosworth	V8	72		13	7
9	20	E Comas	Larrousse	LH93	Lamborghini	V12	72		17	9
10r	14	R Barrichello	Jordan	193	Hart	V10	70	fuel pressure	12	6
11	21	M Alboreto	Lola	T93/30	Ferrari	V12	70		24	12
r	9	D Warwick	Footwork	FA14	Mugen Honda	V10	66	gearbox	14	7
r	15	T Boutsen	Jordan	193	Hart	V10	61	throttle jammed	19	10
r	4	A de Cesaris	Tyrrell	020C	Yamaha	V10	55	gearbox	25	13
r	27	J Alesi	Ferrari	F93A	Ferrari	V12	36	suspension hydraulics	9	5
r	10	A Suzuki	Footwork	FA14	Mugen Honda	V10	29	gearbox	23	12
r	19	P Alliot	Larrousse	LH93	Lamborghini	V12	27	accident	15	8
r	5	M Schumacher	Benetton	B193B	Ford Cosworth	V8	22	accident	3	2
r	26	M Blundell	Ligier	JS39	Renault	V10	20	accident	21	11
r	28	G Berger	Ferrari	F93A	Ferrari	V12	19	suspension hydraulics	8	4
r	30	J J Lehto	Sauber	C12	Ilmor	V10	13	handling	7	4
r	3	U Katayama	Tyrrell	020C	Yamaha	V10	11	clutch	18	9
r	25	M Brundle	Ligier	JS39	Renault	V10	7	accident	22	11
r	7	M Andretti	McLaren	MP4/8	Ford Cosworth	V8	0	accident	6	3
r	29	K Wendlinger	Sauber	C12	Ilmor	V10	0	accident	5	3
nq	22	L Badoer	Lola	T93/30	Ferrari	V12				

Winning speed 165.603 km/h, 102.901 mph
Pole Position speed 205.552 km/h, 127.724 mph (A Prost, 1 min:10.458 sec)
Fastest Lap speed 185.608 km/h, 115.331 mph (A Senna, 1 min:18.029 sec on lap 57)
Lap Leaders A Senna 1-18,20-34,39-76 (71); A Prost 19,35-38 (5).

The official fastest lap credited to A Senna was set via the pit lane. The fastest complete lap was set by D Hill on lap 55 (1m 19.379s, 182.451 km/h, 113.370 mph).

25 Apr 1993 **SAN MARINO: Imola** (Round 4) (Race 536)

61 laps x 5.040 km, 3.132 miles = 307.440 km, 191.034 miles

Pos	No	Driver	Car	Model	Engine		Laps	Time/Reason for Retirement	Grid Pos	Row
1	2	A Prost	Williams	FW15C	Renault	V10	61	1h 33m 20.413s	1	1
2	5	M Schumacher	Benetton	B193B	Ford Cosworth	V8	61	1h 33m 52.823s	3	2
3	25	M Brundle	Ligier	JS39	Renault	V10	60		10	5
4r	30	J J Lehto	Sauber	C12	Ilmor	V10	59	engine	16	8
5	19	P Alliot	Larrousse	LH93	Lamborghini	V12	59		14	7
6	24	F Barbazza	Minardi	M193	Ford Cosworth	V8	59		25	13
7	22	L Badoer	Lola	T93/30	Ferrari	V12	58		24	12
8r	12	J Herbert	Lotus	107B	Ford Cosworth	V8	57	engine	12	6
9	10	A Suzuki	Footwork	FA14	Mugen Honda	V10	54		21	11
r	11	A Zanardi	Lotus	107B	Ford Cosworth	V8	53	accident	20	10
r	29	K Wendlinger	Sauber	C12	Ilmor	V10	48	engine	5	3
r	8	A Senna	McLaren	MP4/8	Ford Cosworth	V8	42	hydraulics	4	2
r	27	J Alesi	Ferrari	F93A	Ferrari	V12	40	clutch	9	5
r	23	C Fittipaldi	Minardi	M193	Ford Cosworth	V8	36	steering	23	12
r	7	M Andretti	McLaren	MP4/8	Ford Cosworth	V8	32	brakes / spin	6	3
r	9	D Warwick	Footwork	FA14	Mugen Honda	V10	29	spin	15	8
r	3	U Katayama	Tyrrell	020C	Yamaha	V10	22	engine	22	11
r	0	D Hill	Williams	FW15C	Renault	V10	20	spin	2	1
r	20	E Comas	Larrousse	LH93	Lamborghini	V12	18	oil pressure	17	9
r	4	A de Cesaris	Tyrrell	020C	Yamaha	V10	18	gearbox	18	9
r	14	R Barrichello	Jordan	193	Hart	V10	17	spin	13	7
r	28	G Berger	Ferrari	F93A	Ferrari	V12	8	gearbox	8	4
r	15	T Boutsen	Jordan	193	Hart	V10	1	gearbox	19	10
r	6	R Patrese	Benetton	B193B	Ford Cosworth	V8	0	accident	11	6
r	26	M Blundell	Ligier	JS39	Renault	V10	0	accident	7	4
nq	21	M Alboreto	Lola	T93/30	Ferrari	V12				

Winning speed 197.625 km/h, 122.799 mph
Pole Position speed 221.080 km/h, 137.372 mph (A Prost, 1 min:22.070 sec)
Fastest Lap speed 210.663 km/h, 130.900 mph (A Prost, 1 min:26.128 sec on lap 42)
Lap Leaders D Hill 1-11 (11); A Prost 12-61 (50).

9 May 1993 **SPAIN: Montmeló** (Round 5) (Race 537)

65 laps x 4.747 km, 2.950 miles = 308.555 km, 191.727 miles

Pos	No	Driver	Car	Model	Engine		Laps	Time/Reason for Retirement	Grid Pos	Row
1	2	A Prost	Williams	FW15C	Renault	V10	65	1h 32m 27.685s	1	1
2	8	A Senna	McLaren	MP4/8	Ford Cosworth	V8	65	1h 32m 44.558s	3	2
3	5	M Schumacher	Benetton	B193B	Ford Cosworth	V8	65	1h 32m 54.810s	4	2
4	6	R Patrese	Benetton	B193B	Ford Cosworth	V8	64		5	3
5	7	M Andretti	McLaren	MP4/8	Ford Cosworth	V8	64		7	4
6	28	G Berger	Ferrari	F93A	Ferrari	V12	63		11	6
7	26	M Blundell	Ligier	JS39	Renault	V10	63		12	6
8	23	C Fittipaldi	Minardi	M193	Ford Cosworth	V8	63		20	10
9	20	E Comas	Larrousse	LH93	Lamborghini	V12	63		14	7
10	10	A Suzuki	Footwork	FA14	Mugen Honda	V10	63		19	10
11	15	T Boutsen	Jordan	193	Hart	V10	62		21	11
12	14	R Barrichello	Jordan	193	Hart	V10	62		17	9
13	9	D Warwick	Footwork	FA14	Mugen Honda	V10	62		16	8
14r	11	A Zanardi	Lotus	107B	Ford Cosworth	V8	60	engine	15	8
r	30	J J Lehto	Sauber	C12	Ilmor	V10	53	engine	9	5
r	22	L Badoer	Lola	T93/30	Ferrari	V12	43	clutch	22	11
r	29	K Wendlinger	Sauber	C12	Ilmor	V10	42	fuel pressure	6	3
dq	4	A de Cesaris	Tyrrell	020C	Yamaha	V10	42	push start after engine cut	24	12
r	0	D Hill	Williams	FW15C	Renault	V10	41	engine	2	1
r	27	J Alesi	Ferrari	F93A	Ferrari	V12	40	engine	8	4
r	24	F Barbazza	Minardi	M193	Ford Cosworth	V8	37	accident	25	13
r	19	P Alliot	Larrousse	LH93	Lamborghini	V12	26	gearbox	13	7
r	25	M Brundle	Ligier	JS39	Renault	V10	11	rear tyre / accident	18	9
r	3	U Katayama	Tyrrell	020C	Yamaha	V10	11	accident	23	12
r	12	J Herbert	Lotus	107B	Ford Cosworth	V8	2	active suspension	10	5
nq	21	M Alboreto	Lola	T93/30	Ferrari	V12				

Winning speed 200.227 km/h, 124.415 mph
Pole Position speed 219.630 km/h, 136.472 mph (A Prost, 1 min:17.809 sec)
Fastest Lap speed 211.006 km/h, 131.113 mph (M Schumacher, 1 min:20.989 sec on lap 61)
Lap Leaders D Hill 1-10 (10); A Prost 11-65 (55).

78 laps x 3.328 km, 2.068 miles = 259.584 km, 161.298 miles

Pos	No	Driver	Car	Model	Engine		Laps	Time/Reason for Retirement	Grid Pos	Row
1	8	A Senna	McLaren	MP4/8	Ford Cosworth	V8	78	1h 52m 10.947s	3	2
2	0	D Hill	Williams	FW15C	Renault	V10	78	1h 53m 03.065s	4	2
3	27	J Alesi	Ferrari	F93A	Ferrari	V12	78	1h 53m 14.309s	5	3
4	2	A Prost	Williams	FW15C	Renault	V10	77		1	1
5	23	C Fittipaldi	Minardi	M193	Ford Cosworth	V8	76		17	9
6	25	M Brundle	Ligier	JS39	Renault	V10	76		13	7
7	11	A Zanardi	Lotus	107B	Ford Cosworth	V8	76		20	10
8	7	M Andretti	McLaren	MP4/8	Ford Cosworth	V8	76		9	5
9	14	R Barrichello	Jordan	193	Hart	V10	76		16	8
10	4	A de Cesaris	Tyrrell	020C	Yamaha	V10	76		19	10
11	24	F Barbazza	Minardi	M193	Ford Cosworth	V8	75		25	13
12	19	P Alliot	Larrousse	LH93	Lamborghini	V12	75		15	8
13	29	K Wendlinger	Sauber	C12	Ilmor	V10	74		8	4
14r	28	G Berger	Ferrari	F93A	Ferrari	V12	70	accident	7	4
r	12	J Herbert	Lotus	107B	Ford Cosworth	V8	61	accident	14	7
r	6	R Patrese	Benetton	B193B	Ford Cosworth	V8	53	engine	6	3
r	20	E Comas	Larrousse	LH93	Lamborghini	V12	51	accident	10	5
r	10	A Suzuki	Footwork	FA14	Mugen Honda	V10	46	accident	18	9
r	9	D Warwick	Footwork	FA14	Mugen Honda	V10	43	throttle	12	6
r	5	M Schumacher	Benetton	B193B	Ford Cosworth	V8	32	suspension hydraulics	2	1
r	3	U Katayama	Tyrrell	020C	Yamaha	V10	31	oil leak	22	11
r	21	M Alboreto	Lola	T93/30	Ferrari	V12	28	gearbox	24	12
r	30	J J Lehto	Sauber	C12	Ilmor	V10	23	accident	11	6
r	15	T Boutsen	Jordan	193	Hart	V10	12	suspension	23	12
r	26	M Blundell	Ligier	JS39	Renault	V10	3	accident / rear suspension/spin	21	11
nq	22	L Badoer	Lola	T93/30	Ferrari	V12				

Winning speed 138.837 km/h, 86.269 mph
Pole Position speed 148.725 km/h, 92.413 mph (A Prost, 1 min:20.557 sec)
Fastest Lap speed 143.304 km/h, 89.045 mph (A Prost, 1 min:23.604 sec on lap 52)
Lap Leaders A Prost 1-11 (11); M Schumacher 12-32 (21); A Senna 33-78 (46).

69 laps x 4.430 km, 2.753 miles = 305.670 km, 189.935 miles

Pos	No	Driver	Car	Model	Engine		Laps	Time/Reason for Retirement	Grid Pos	Row
1	2	A Prost	Williams	FW15C	Renault	V10	69	1h 36m 41.822s	1	1
2	5	M Schumacher	Benetton	B193B	Ford Cosworth	V8	69	1h 36m 56.349s	3	2
3	0	D Hill	Williams	FW15C	Renault	V10	69	1h 37m 34.507s	2	1
4	28	G Berger	Ferrari	F93A	Ferrari	V12	68		5	3
5	25	M Brundle	Ligier	JS39	Renault	V10	68		7	4
6	29	K Wendlinger	Sauber	C12	Ilmor	V10	68		9	5
7	30	J J Lehto	Sauber	C12	Ilmor	V10	68		11	6
8	20	E Comas	Larrousse	LH93	Lamborghini	V12	68		13	7
9	23	C Fittipaldi	Minardi	M193	Ford Cosworth	V8	67		17	9
10	12	J Herbert	Lotus	107B	Ford Cosworth	V8	67		20	10
11	11	A Zanardi	Lotus	107B	Ford Cosworth	V8	67		21	11
12	15	T Boutsen	Jordan	193	Hart	V10	67		24	12
13	10	A Suzuki	Footwork	FA14	Mugen Honda	V10	66		16	8
14	7	M Andretti	McLaren	MP4/8	Ford Cosworth	V8	66		12	6
15	22	L Badoer	Lola	T93/30	Ferrari	V12	65		25	13
16	9	D Warwick	Footwork	FA14	Mugen Honda	V10	65		18	9
17	3	U Katayama	Tyrrell	020C	Yamaha	V10	64		22	11
18r	8	A Senna	McLaren	MP4/8	Ford Cosworth	V8	62	alternator	8	4
r	6	R Patrese	Benetton	B193B	Ford Cosworth	V8	52	driver discomfort	4	2
r	4	A de Cesaris	Tyrrell	020C	Yamaha	V10	45	accident	19	10
r	24	F Barbazza	Minardi	M193	Ford Cosworth	V8	33	gearbox	23	12
r	27	J Alesi	Ferrari	F93A	Ferrari	V12	23	water leak / engine	6	3
r	26	M Blundell	Ligier	JS39	Renault	V10	13	accident	10	5
r	14	R Barrichello	Jordan	193	Hart	V10	10	electrics	14	7
r	19	P Alliot	Larrousse	LH93	Lamborghini	V12	8	gear lever	15	8
nq	21	M Alboreto	Lola	T93/30	Ferrari	V12				

Winning speed 189.667 km/h, 117.853 mph
Pole Position speed 201.907 km/h, 125.459 mph (A Prost, 1 min:18.987 sec)
Fastest Lap speed 195.681 km/h, 121.591 mph (M Schumacher, 1 min:21.500 sec on lap 57)
Lap Leaders D Hill 1-5 (5); A Prost 6-69 (64).

4 Jul 1993   FRANCE: Magny-Cours   (Round 8)   (Race 540)
72 laps x 4.250 km, 2.641 miles = 306.000 km, 190.140 miles

Pos	No	Driver	Car	Model	Engine		Laps	Time/Reason for Retirement	Grid Pos	Row
1	2	A Prost	Williams	FW15C	Renault	V10	72	1h 38m 35.241s	2	1
2	0	D Hill	Williams	FW15C	Renault	V10	72	1h 38m 35.583s	1	1
3	5	M Schumacher	Benetton	B193B	Ford Cosworth	V8	72	1h 38m 56.450s	7	4
4	8	A Senna	McLaren	MP4/8	Ford Cosworth	V8	72	1h 39m 07.646s	5	3
5	25	M Brundle	Ligier	JS39	Renault	V10	72	1h 39m 09.036s	3	2
6	7	M Andretti	McLaren	MP4/8	Ford Cosworth	V8	71		16	8
7	14	R Barrichello	Jordan	193	Hart	V10	71		8	4
8	23	C Fittipaldi	Minardi	M193	Ford Cosworth	V8	71		23	12
9	19	P Alliot	Larrousse	LH93	Lamborghini	V12	70		10	5
10	6	R Patrese	Benetton	B193B	Ford Cosworth	V8	70		12	6
11	15	T Boutsen	Jordan	193	Hart	V10	70		20	10
12	10	A Suzuki	Footwork	FA14	Mugen Honda	V10	70		13	7
13	9	D Warwick	Footwork	FA14	Mugen Honda	V10	70		15	8
14	28	G Berger	Ferrari	F93A	Ferrari	V12	70		14	7
15	4	A de Cesaris	Tyrrell	020C	Yamaha	V10	68		25	13
16r	20	E Comas	Larrousse	LH93	Lamborghini	V12	66	gearbox	9	5
r	27	J Alesi	Ferrari	F93A	Ferrari	V12	47	engine	6	3
r	22	L Badoer	Lola	T93/30	Ferrari	V12	28	suspension	22	11
r	29	K Wendlinger	Sauber	C12	Ilmor	V10	25	gearbox	11	6
r	30	J J Lehto	Sauber	C12	Ilmor	V10	22	gearbox	18	9
r	26	M Blundell	Ligier	JS39	Renault	V10	20	spin	4	2
r	12	J Herbert	Lotus	107B	Ford Cosworth	V8	16	spin	19	10
r	24	F Barbazza	Minardi	M193	Ford Cosworth	V8	16	gearbox	24	12
r	3	U Katayama	Tyrrell	020C	Yamaha	V10	9	sump / oil leak	21	11
r	11	A Zanardi	Lotus	107B	Ford Cosworth	V8	3	active suspension	17	9
nq	21	M Alboreto	Lola	T93/30	Ferrari	V12				

Winning speed 186.231 km/h, 115.718 mph
Pole Position speed 205.695 km/h, 127.813 mph (D Hill, 1 min:14.382 sec)
Fastest Lap speed 193.045 km/h, 119.953 mph (M Schumacher, 1 min:19.256 sec on lap 47)
Lap Leaders D Hill 1-26 (26); A Prost 27-72 (46).

11 Jul 1993   BRITAIN: Silverstone   (Round 9)   (Race 541)
59 laps x 5.226 km, 3.247 miles = 308.334 km, 191.590 miles

Pos	No	Driver	Car	Model	Engine		Laps	Time/Reason for Retirement	Grid Pos	Row
1	2	A Prost	Williams	FW15C	Renault	V10	59	1h 25m 38.189s	1	1
2	5	M Schumacher	Benetton	B193B	Ford Cosworth	V8	59	1h 25m 45.849s	3	2
3	6	R Patrese	Benetton	B193B	Ford Cosworth	V8	59	1h 26m 55.671s	5	3
4	12	J Herbert	Lotus	107B	Ford Cosworth	V8	59	1h 26m 56.596s	7	4
5r	8	A Senna	McLaren	MP4/8	Ford Cosworth	V8	58	out of fuel	4	2
6	9	D Warwick	Footwork	FA14	Mugen Honda	V10	58		8	4
7	26	M Blundell	Ligier	JS39	Renault	V10	58		9	5
8	30	J J Lehto	Sauber	C12	Ilmor	V10	58		16	8
9	27	J Alesi	Ferrari	F93A	Ferrari	V12	58		12	6
10	14	R Barrichello	Jordan	193	Hart	V10	58		15	8
11	19	P Alliot	Larrousse	LH93	Lamborghini	V12	57		24	12
12r	23	C Fittipaldi	Minardi	M193	Ford Cosworth	V8	56	gearbox	19	10
13	3	U Katayama	Tyrrell	020C	Yamaha	V10	55		22	11
14r	25	M Brundle	Ligier	JS39	Renault	V10	53	gearbox	6	3
r	4	A de Cesaris	Tyrrell	021	Yamaha	V10	43	steering	21	11
r	0	D Hill	Williams	FW15C	Renault	V10	41	engine	2	1
r	11	A Zanardi	Lotus	107B	Ford Cosworth	V8	41	spin	14	7
r	15	T Boutsen	Jordan	193	Hart	V10	41	wheel bearing	23	12
r	22	L Badoer	Lola	T93/30	Ferrari	V12	32	electrics	25	13
r	24	P Martini	Minardi	M193	Ford Cosworth	V8	31	driver discomfort	20	10
r	29	K Wendlinger	Sauber	C12	Ilmor	V10	24	accident	18	9
r	28	G Berger	Ferrari	F93A	Ferrari	V12	10	active suspension	13	7
r	10	A Suzuki	Footwork	FA14	Mugen Honda	V10	8	spin	10	5
r	7	M Andretti	McLaren	MP4/8	Ford Cosworth	V8	0	spin	11	6
r	20	E Comas	Larrousse	LH93	Lamborghini	V12	0	driveshaft	17	9
nq	21	M Alboreto	Lola	T93/30	Ferrari	V12				

Winning speed 216.030 km/h, 134.235 mph
Pole Position speed 238.129 km/h, 147.966 mph (A Prost, 1 min:19.006 sec)
Fastest Lap speed 228.002 km/h, 141.674 mph (D Hill, 1 min:22.515 sec on lap 41)
Lap Leaders D Hill 1-41 (41); A Prost 42-59 (18).

Races   361

GERMANY: Hockenheim   (Round 10)   (Race 542)
45 laps x 6.815 km, 4.235 miles = 306.675 km, 190.559 miles

Pos	No	Driver	Car	Model	Engine		Laps	Time/Reason for Retirement	Grid Pos	Row
1	2	A Prost	Williams	FW15C	Renault	V10	45	1h 18m 40.885s	1	1
2	5	M Schumacher	Benetton	B193B	Ford Cosworth	V8	45	1h 18m 57.549s	3	2
3	26	M Blundell	Ligier	JS39	Renault	V10	45	1h 19m 40.234s	5	3
4	8	A Senna	McLaren	MP4/8	Ford Cosworth	V8	45	1h 19m 49.114s	4	2
5	6	R Patrese	Benetton	B193B	Ford Cosworth	V8	45	1h 20m 12.401s	7	4
6	28	G Berger	Ferrari	F93A	Ferrari	V12	45	1h 20m 15.639s	9	5
7	27	J Alesi	Ferrari	F93A	Ferrari	V12	45	1h 20m 16.726s	10	5
8	25	M Brundle	Ligier	JS39	Renault	V10	44		6	3
9	29	K Wendlinger	Sauber	C12	Ilmor	V10	44		14	7
10	12	J Herbert	Lotus	107B	Ford Cosworth	V8	44		13	7
11	23	C Fittipaldi	Minardi	M193	Ford Cosworth	V8	44		20	10
12	19	P Alliot	Larrousse	LH93	Lamborghini	V12	44		23	12
13	15	T Boutsen	Jordan	193	Hart	V10	44		24	12
14	24	P Martini	Minardi	M193	Ford Cosworth	V8	44		22	11
15r	0	D Hill	Williams	FW15C	Renault	V10	43	rear tyre	2	1
16	21	M Alboreto	Lola	T93/30	Ferrari	V12	43		26	13
17	9	D Warwick	Footwork	FA14	Mugen Honda	V10	42		11	6
r	14	R Barrichello	Jordan	193	Hart	V10	34	wheel bearing	17	9
r	3	U Katayama	Tyrrell	021	Yamaha	V10	28	spin / driveshaft	21	11
r	30	J J Lehto	Sauber	C12	Ilmor	V10	22	throttle jammed / spin	18	9
r	11	A Zanardi	Lotus	107B	Ford Cosworth	V8	19	spin	15	8
r	10	A Suzuki	Footwork	FA14	Mugen Honda	V10	9	gearbox	8	4
r	7	M Andretti	McLaren	MP4/8	Ford Cosworth	V8	4	accident / steering	12	6
r	22	L Badoer	Lola	T93/30	Ferrari	V12	4	accident / rear suspension	25	13
r	4	A de Cesaris	Tyrrell	021	Yamaha	V10	1	gearbox	19	10
r	20	E Comas	Larrousse	LH93	Lamborghini	V12	0	clutch	16	8

Winning speed 233.861 km/h, 145.314 mph
Pole Position speed 248.451 km/h, 154.380 mph (A Prost, 1 min:38.748 sec)
Fastest Lap speed 240.862 km/h, 149.665 mph (M Schumacher, 1 min:41.859 sec on lap 40)
Lap Leaders D Hill 1-7,10-43 (41); A Prost 8-9,44-45 (4).

HUNGARY: Hungaroring   (Round 11)   (Race 543)
77 laps x 3.968 km, 2.466 miles = 305.536 km, 189.851 miles

Pos	No	Driver	Car	Model	Engine		Laps	Time/Reason for Retirement	Grid Pos	Row
1	0	D Hill	Williams	FW15C	Renault	V10	77	1h 47m 39.098s	2	1
2	6	R Patrese	Benetton	B193B	Ford Cosworth	V8	77	1h 48m 51.013s	5	3
3	28	G Berger	Ferrari	F93A	Ferrari	V12	77	1h 48m 57.140s	6	3
4	9	D Warwick	Footwork	FA14	Mugen Honda	V10	76		9	5
5	25	M Brundle	Ligier	JS39	Renault	V10	76		13	7
6	29	K Wendlinger	Sauber	C12	Ilmor	V10	76		17	9
7	26	M Blundell	Ligier	JS39	Renault	V10	76		12	6
8	19	P Alliot	Larrousse	LH93	Lamborghini	V12	75		19	10
9	15	T Boutsen	Jordan	193	Hart	V10	75		24	12
10	3	U Katayama	Tyrrell	021	Yamaha	V10	73		23	12
11	4	A de Cesaris	Tyrrell	021	Yamaha	V10	72		22	11
12	2	A Prost	Williams	FW15C	Renault	V10	70		1	1
r	24	P Martini	Minardi	M193	Ford Cosworth	V8	59	accident	7	4
r	20	E Comas	Larrousse	LH93	Lamborghini	V12	54	oil leak	18	9
r	11	A Zanardi	Lotus	107B	Ford Cosworth	V8	45	gearbox	21	11
r	10	A Suzuki	Footwork	FA14	Mugen Honda	V10	41	spin	10	5
r	21	M Alboreto	Lola	T93/30	Ferrari	V12	39	radiator / engine overheating	25	13
r	12	J Herbert	Lotus	107B	Ford Cosworth	V8	38	spin	20	10
r	22	L Badoer	Lola	T93/30	Ferrari	V12	37	spin	26	13
r	5	M Schumacher	Benetton	B193B	Ford Cosworth	V8	26	fuel pump	3	2
r	23	C Fittipaldi	Minardi	M193	Ford Cosworth	V8	22	accident	14	7
r	27	J Alesi	Ferrari	F93A	Ferrari	V12	22	accident	8	4
r	30	J J Lehto	Sauber	C12	Ilmor	V10	18	engine	15	8
r	8	A Senna	McLaren	MP4/8	Ford Cosworth	V8	17	throttle	4	2
r	7	M Andretti	McLaren	MP4/8	Ford Cosworth	V8	15	throttle linkage	11	6
r	14	R Barrichello	Jordan	193	Hart	V10	0	accident	16	8

Winning speed 170.292 km/h, 105.814 mph
Pole Position speed 191.406 km/h, 118.934 mph (A Prost, 1 min:14.631 sec)
Fastest Lap speed 179.383 km/h, 111.463 mph (A Prost, 1 min:19.633 sec on lap 52)
Lap Leaders D Hill 1-77 (77).

29 Aug 1993   BELGIUM: Spa-Francorchamps   (Round 12)   (Race 544)

44 laps x 6.974 km, 4.333 miles = 306.856 km, 190.671 miles

Pos	No	Driver	Car	Model	Engine		Laps	Time/Reason for Retirement	Grid Pos	Row
1	0	D Hill	Williams	FW15C	Renault	V10	44	1h 24m 32.124s	2	1
2	5	M Schumacher	Benetton	B193B	Ford Cosworth	V8	44	1h 24m 35.792s	3	2
3	2	A Prost	Williams	FW15C	Renault	V10	44	1h 24m 47.112s	1	1
4	8	A Senna	McLaren	MP4/8	Ford Cosworth	V8	44	1h 26m 11.887s	5	3
5	12	J Herbert	Lotus	107B	Ford Cosworth	V8	43		10	5
6	6	R Patrese	Benetton	B193B	Ford Cosworth	V8	43		8	4
7	25	M Brundle	Ligier	JS39	Renault	V10	43		11	6
8	7	M Andretti	McLaren	MP4/8	Ford Cosworth	V8	43		14	7
9	30	J J Lehto	Sauber	C12	Ilmor	V10	43		9	5
10r	28	G Berger	Ferrari	F93A	Ferrari	V12	42	accident	16	8
11r	26	M Blundell	Ligier	JS39	Renault	V10	42	accident	15	8
12	19	P Alliot	Larrousse	LH93	Lamborghini	V12	42		18	9
13	22	L Badoer	Lola	T93/30	Ferrari	V12	42		24	12
14	21	M Alboreto	Lola	T93/30	Ferrari	V12	41		25	13
15	3	U Katayama	Tyrrell	021	Yamaha	V10	40		23	12
r	20	E Comas	Larrousse	LH93	Lamborghini	V12	37	ignition	19	10
r	9	D Warwick	Footwork	FA14	Mugen Honda	V10	28	electrics	7	4
r	29	K Wendlinger	Sauber	C12	Ilmor	V10	27	engine	12	6
r	4	A de Cesaris	Tyrrell	021	Yamaha	V10	24	engine	17	9
r	23	C Fittipaldi	Minardi	M193	Ford Cosworth	V8	15	accident	22	11
r	24	P Martini	Minardi	M193	Ford Cosworth	V8	15	spin	21	11
r	10	A Suzuki	Footwork	FA14	Mugen Honda	V10	14	gearbox	6	3
r	14	R Barrichello	Jordan	193	Hart	V10	11	rear wheel bearing	13	7
r	27	J Alesi	Ferrari	F93A	Ferrari	V12	4	rear suspension / handling	4	2
r	15	T Boutsen	Jordan	193	Hart	V10	0	gearbox	20	10
ns	11	A Zanardi	Lotus	107B	Ford Cosworth	V8		accident / injury		

Winning speed 217.795 km/h, 135.331 mph
Pole Position speed 233.394 km/h, 145.024 mph (A Prost, 1 min:47.571 sec)
Fastest Lap speed 225.990 km/h, 140.424 mph (A Prost, 1 min:51.095 sec on lap 41)
Lap Leaders A Prost 1-30 (30); D Hill 31-44 (14).

12 Sep 1993   ITALY: Monza   (Round 13)   (Race 545)

53 laps x 5.800 km, 3.604 miles = 307.400 km, 191.010 miles

Pos	No	Driver	Car	Model	Engine		Laps	Time/Reason for Retirement	Grid Pos	Row
1	0	D Hill	Williams	FW15C	Renault	V10	53	1h 17m 07.509s	2	1
2	27	J Alesi	Ferrari	F93A	Ferrari	V12	53	1h 17m 47.521s	3	2
3	7	M Andretti	McLaren	MP4/8	Ford Cosworth	V8	52		9	5
4	29	K Wendlinger	Sauber	C12	Ilmor	V10	52		15	8
5	6	R Patrese	Benetton	B193B	Ford Cosworth	V8	52		10	5
6	20	E Comas	Larrousse	LH93	Lamborghini	V12	51		20	10
7	24	P Martini	Minardi	M193	Ford Cosworth	V8	51		22	11
8	23	C Fittipaldi	Minardi	M193	Ford Cosworth	V8	51		24	12
9	19	P Alliot	Larrousse	LH93	Lamborghini	V12	51		16	8
10	22	L Badoer	Lola	T93/30	Ferrari	V12	51		25	13
11r	11	P Lamy	Lotus	107B	Ford Cosworth	V8	49	engine	26	13
12r	2	A Prost	Williams	FW15C	Renault	V10	48	engine	1	1
13r	4	A de Cesaris	Tyrrell	021	Yamaha	V10	47	oil pressure	18	9
14	3	U Katayama	Tyrrell	021	Yamaha	V10	47		17	9
r	21	M Alboreto	Lola	T93/30	Ferrari	V12	23	rear suspension	21	11
r	5	M Schumacher	Benetton	B193B	Ford Cosworth	V8	21	engine	5	3
r	26	M Blundell	Ligier	JS39	Renault	V10	20	accident	14	7
r	28	G Berger	Ferrari	F93A	Ferrari	V12	15	active suspension	6	3
r	12	J Herbert	Lotus	107B	Ford Cosworth	V8	14	accident	7	4
r	25	M Brundle	Ligier	JS39	Renault	V10	8	accident	12	6
r	8	A Senna	McLaren	MP4/8	Ford Cosworth	V8	8	accident	4	2
r	10	A Suzuki	Footwork	FA14	Mugen Honda	V10	0	accident	8	4
r	9	D Warwick	Footwork	FA14	Mugen Honda	V10	0	accident	11	6
r	30	J J Lehto	Sauber	C12	Ilmor	V10	0	accident	13	7
r	14	R Barrichello	Jordan	193	Hart	V10	0	accident	19	10
r	15	M Apicella	Jordan	193	Hart	V10	0	accident	23	12

Winning speed 239.144 km/h, 148.597 mph
Pole Position speed 257.209 km/h, 159.822 mph (A Prost, 1 min:21.179 sec)
Fastest Lap speed 249.835 km/h, 155.241 mph (D Hill, 1 min:23.575 sec on lap 45)
Lap Leaders A Prost 1-48 (48); D Hill 49-53 (5).

P Martini and C Fittipaldi had an accident at the end of the race, but both reached the chequered flag.

71 laps x 4.350 km, 2.703 miles = 308.850 km, 191.910 miles

Pos	No	Driver	Car	Model	Engine		Laps	Time/Reason for Retirement	Grid Pos	Row
1	5	M Schumacher	Benetton	B193B	Ford Cosworth	V8	71	1h 32m 46.309s	6	3
2	2	A Prost	Williams	FW15C	Renault	V10	71	1h 32m 47.291s	2	1
3	0	D Hill	Williams	FW15C	Renault	V10	71	1h 32m 54.515s	1	1
4	27	J Alesi	Ferrari	F93A	Ferrari	V12	71	1h 33m 53.914s	5	3
5	29	K Wendlinger	Sauber	C12	Ilmor	V10	70		13	7
6	25	M Brundle	Ligier	JS39	Renault	V10	70		11	6
7	30	J J Lehto	Sauber	C12	Ilmor	V10	69		12	6
8	24	P Martini	Minardi	M193	Ford Cosworth	V8	69		19	10
9	23	C Fittipaldi	Minardi	M193	Ford Cosworth	V8	69		24	12
10	19	P Alliot	Larrousse	LH93	Lamborghini	V12	69		20	10
11	20	E Comas	Larrousse	LH93	Lamborghini	V12	68		22	11
12	4	A de Cesaris	Tyrrell	021	Yamaha	V10	68		17	9
13	14	R Barrichello	Jordan	193	Hart	V10	68		15	8
14	22	L Badoer	Lola	T93/30	Ferrari	V12	68		26	13
15r	9	D Warwick	Footwork	FA14	Mugen Honda	V10	63	accident	9	5
16r	6	R Patrese	Benetton	B193B	Ford Cosworth	V8	63	accident	7	4
r	11	P Lamy	Lotus	107B	Ford Cosworth	V8	61	accident	18	9
r	12	J Herbert	Lotus	107B	Ford Cosworth	V8	60	accident	14	7
r	26	M Blundell	Ligier	JS39	Renault	V10	51	accident	10	5
r	21	M Alboreto	Lola	T93/30	Ferrari	V12	38	gearbox / accident	25	13
r	28	G Berger	Ferrari	F93A	Ferrari	V12	35	active suspension / accident	8	4
r	7	M Häkkinen	McLaren	MP4/8	Ford Cosworth	V8	32	accident	3	2
r	10	A Suzuki	Footwork	FA14	Mugen Honda	V10	27	gearbox	16	8
r	8	A Senna	McLaren	MP4/8	Ford Cosworth	V8	19	engine	4	2
r	3	U Katayama	Tyrrell	021	Yamaha	V10	12	accident	21	11
r	15	E Naspetti	Jordan	193	Hart	V10	8	engine	23	12

Winning speed 199.748 km/h, 124.118 mph
Pole Position speed 219.039 km/h, 136.105 mph (D Hill, 1 min:11.494 sec)
Fastest Lap speed 209.193 km/h, 129.987 mph (D Hill, 1 min:14.859 sec on lap 68)
Lap Leaders J Alesi 1-19 (19); A Prost 20-29 (10); M Schumacher 30-71 (42).

53 laps x 5.864 km, 3.644 miles = 310.792 km, 193.117 miles

Pos	No	Driver	Car	Model	Engine		Laps	Time/Reason for Retirement	Grid Pos	Row
1	8	A Senna	McLaren	MP4/8	Ford Cosworth	V8	53	1h 40m 27.912s	2	1
2	2	A Prost	Williams	FW15C	Renault	V10	53	1h 40m 39.347s	1	1
3	7	M Häkkinen	McLaren	MP4/8	Ford Cosworth	V8	53	1h 40m 54.041s	3	2
4	0	D Hill	Williams	FW15C	Renault	V10	53	1h 41m 51.450s	6	3
5	14	R Barrichello	Jordan	193	Hart	V10	53	1h 42m 03.013s	12	6
6	15	E Irvine	Jordan	193	Hart	V10	53	1h 42m 14.333s	8	4
7	26	M Blundell	Ligier	JS39	Renault	V10	52		17	9
8	30	J J Lehto	Sauber	C12	Ilmor	V10	52		11	6
9r	25	M Brundle	Ligier	JS39	Renault	V10	51	accident	15	8
10	24	P Martini	Minardi	M193	Ford Cosworth	V8	51		22	11
11	12	J Herbert	Lotus	107B	Ford Cosworth	V8	51		19	10
12	19	T Suzuki	Larrousse	LH93	Lamborghini	V12	51		23	12
13r	11	P Lamy	Lotus	107B	Ford Cosworth	V8	49	accident	20	10
14r	9	D Warwick	Footwork	FA14	Mugen Honda	V10	48	accident	7	4
r	6	R Patrese	Benetton	B193B	Ford Cosworth	V8	45	accident	10	5
r	28	G Berger	Ferrari	F93A	Ferrari	V12	40	engine	5	3
r	10	A Suzuki	Footwork	FA14	Mugen Honda	V10	28	spin	9	5
r	3	U Katayama	Tyrrell	021	Yamaha	V10	26	engine	13	7
r	23	J-M Gounon	Minardi	M193	Ford Cosworth	V8	26	engine	24	12
r	29	K Wendlinger	Sauber	C12	Ilmor	V10	25	throttle jammed	16	8
r	20	E Comas	Larrousse	LH93	Lamborghini	V12	17	engine	21	11
r	5	M Schumacher	Benetton	B193B	Ford Cosworth	V8	10	accident	4	2
r	27	J Alesi	Ferrari	F93A	Ferrari	V12	7	electrics	14	7
r	4	A de Cesaris	Tyrrell	021	Yamaha	V10	0	accident / rear tyre	18	9

Winning speed 185.612 km/h, 115.334 mph
Pole Position speed 217.288 km/h, 135.017 mph (A Prost, 1 min:37.154 sec)
Fastest Lap speed 208.650 km/h, 129.649 mph (A Prost, 1 min:41.176 sec on lap 53)
Lap Leaders A Senna 1-13,21-53 (46); A Prost 14-20 (7).

79 laps x 3.780 km, 2.349 miles = 298.620 km, 185.554 miles

Pos	No	Driver	Car	Model	Engine		Laps	Time/Reason for Retirement	Grid Pos	Row
1	8	A Senna	McLaren	MP4/8	Ford Cosworth	V8	79	1h 43m 27.476s	1	1
2	2	A Prost	Williams	FW15C	Renault	V10	79	1h 43m 36.735s	2	1
3	0	D Hill	Williams	FW15C	Renault	V10	79	1h 44m 01.378s	3	2
4	27	J Alesi	Ferrari	F93A	Ferrari	V12	78		7	4
5	28	G Berger	Ferrari	F93A	Ferrari	V12	78		6	3
6	25	M Brundle	Ligier	JS39	Renault	V10	78		8	4
7	10	A Suzuki	Footwork	FA14	Mugen Honda	V10	78		10	5
8r	6	R Patrese	Benetton	B193B	Ford Cosworth	V8	77	fuel pressure	9	5
9	26	M Blundell	Ligier	JS39	Renault	V10	77		14	7
10	9	D Warwick	Footwork	FA14	Mugen Honda	V10	77		17	9
11	14	R Barrichello	Jordan	193	Hart	V10	76		13	7
12	20	E Comas	Larrousse	LH93	Lamborghini	V12	76		21	11
13	4	A de Cesaris	Tyrrell	021	Yamaha	V10	75		15	8
14	19	T Suzuki	Larrousse	LH93	Lamborghini	V12	74		24	12
15r	29	K Wendlinger	Sauber	C12	Ilmor	V10	73	brake disc / accident	11	6
r	30	J J Lehto	Sauber	C12	Ilmor	V10	56	throttle jammed / accident	12	6
r	23	J-M Gounon	Minardi	M193	Ford Cosworth	V8	34	spin	22	11
r	7	M Häkkinen	McLaren	MP4/8	Ford Cosworth	V8	28	brake pipe	5	3
r	5	M Schumacher	Benetton	B193B	Ford Cosworth	V8	19	engine	4	2
r	3	U Katayama	Tyrrell	021	Yamaha	V10	11	accident	18	9
r	15	E Irvine	Jordan	193	Hart	V10	10	accident / suspension	19	10
r	12	J Herbert	Lotus	107B	Ford Cosworth	V8	9	hydraulics	20	10
r	24	P Martini	Minardi	M193	Ford Cosworth	V8	5	gearbox	16	8
r	11	P Lamy	Lotus	107B	Ford Cosworth	V8	0	accident	23	12

Winning speed 173.183 km/h, 107.611 mph
Pole Position speed 185.468 km/h, 115.245 mph (A Senna, 1 min:13.371 sec)
Fastest Lap speed 180.523 km/h, 112.172 mph (D Hill, 1 min:15.381 sec on lap 64)
Lap Leaders A Senna 1-23,29-79 (74); A Prost 24-28 (5).

Races

Pos	Driver	Car-Engine	GPs	laps	km	miles
1	A Prost	Williams-Renault	15	431	2,095.4	1,302.0
2	A Senna	McLaren-Ford Cosworth	6	290	1,215.9	755.5
3	D Hill	Williams-Renault	10	242	1,213.3	753.9
4	M Schumacher	Benetton-Ford Cosworth	2	63	252.6	157.0
5	J Alesi	Ferrari	1	19	82.6	51.4
			16	1,045	4,859.9	3,019.8

Driver Points 1993

	Driver	ZA	BR	EUR	RSM	E	MC	CDN	F	GB	D	H	B	I	P	J	AUS	Total
1	A Prost	10	-	4	10	10	3	10	10	10	10	-	4	-	6	6	6	99
2	A Senna	6	10	10	-	6	10	-	3	2	3	-	3	-	-	10	10	73
3	D Hill	-	6	6	-	-	6	4	6	-	-	10	10	10	4	3	4	69
4	M Schumacher	-	4	-	6	4	-	6	4	6	6	-	6	-	10	-	-	52
5	R Patrese	-	-	2	-	3	-	-	-	4	2	6	1	2	-	-	-	20
6	J Alesi	-	-	-	-	-	4	-	-	-	-	-	-	6	3	-	3	16
7	M Brundle	-	-	-	4	-	1	2	2	-	-	2	-	-	1	-	1	13
8	G Berger	1	-	-	-	1	-	3	-	-	1	4	-	-	-	-	2	12
9	J Herbert	-	3	3	-	-	-	-	-	3	-	-	2	-	-	-	-	11
10	M Blundell	4	2	-	-	-	-	-	-	-	4	-	-	-	-	-	-	10
11	M Andretti	-	-	-	2	-	-	1	-	-	-	-	-	4	-	-	-	7
	K Wendlinger	-	-	-	-	-	-	1	-	-	-	1	-	3	2	-	-	7
13	C Fittipaldi	3	-	-	-	2	-	-	-	-	-	-	-	-	-	-	-	5
	J J Lehto	2	-	-	3	-	-	-	-	-	-	-	-	-	-	-	-	5
15	M Häkkinen	-	-	-	-	-	-	-	-	-	-	-	-	-	-	4	-	4
	D Warwick	-	-	-	-	-	-	-	1	-	3	-	-	-	-	-	-	4
17	P Alliot	-	-	-	2	-	-	-	-	-	-	-	-	-	-	-	-	2
	R Barrichello	-	-	-	-	-	-	-	-	-	-	-	-	-	-	2	-	2
	F Barbazza	-	-	1	1	-	-	-	-	-	-	-	-	-	-	-	-	2
20	A Zanardi	-	1	-	-	-	-	-	-	-	-	-	-	-	-	-	-	1
	E Comas	-	-	-	-	-	-	-	-	-	-	-	-	1	-	-	-	1
	E Irvine	-	-	-	-	-	-	-	-	-	-	-	-	-	-	1	-	1

10,6,4,3,2 and 1 point awarded to the first six finishers.

Constructor Points 1993

		ZA	BR	EUR	RSM	E	MC	CDN	F	GB	D	H	B	I	P	J	AUS	Total
1	Williams-Renault	10	6	10	10	10	9	14	16	10	10	10	14	10	10	9	10	168
2	McLaren-Ford Cosworth	6	10	10	-	8	10	-	4	2	3	-	3	4	-	14	10	84
3	Benetton-Ford Cosworth	-	4	2	6	7	-	6	4	10	8	6	7	2	10	-	-	72
4	Ferrari	1	-	-	-	1	4	3	-	-	1	4	-	6	3	-	5	28
5	Ligier-Renault	4	2	-	4	-	1	2	2	-	4	2	-	-	1	-	1	23
6	Lotus-Ford Cosworth	-	4	3	-	-	-	-	-	3	-	-	2	-	-	-	-	12
	Sauber-Ilmor	2	-	-	3	-	-	1	-	-	-	1	-	3	2	-	-	12
8	Minardi-Ford Cosworth	3	-	1	1	-	2	-	-	-	-	-	-	-	-	-	-	7
9	Footwork-Mugen Honda	-	-	-	-	-	-	-	-	1	-	3	-	-	-	-	-	4
10	Jordan-Hart	-	-	-	-	-	-	-	-	-	-	-	-	-	-	3	-	3
	Larrousse-Lamborghini	-	-	-	2	-	-	-	-	-	-	-	-	1	-	-	-	3

10,6,4,3,2 and 1 point awarded to the first six finishers.

Race Entrants and Results

Traction control and other driver aids were banned in an attempt to emphasise the driver's input. Refuelling returned, to increase the strategic aspect of racing. Camel and Canon left Formula 1 as high profile sponsors. Once again the World Champion departed, this time to retirement. Frank Williams finally got his man, only for Ayrton Senna to die on the traumatic weekend of Imola, a day after Roland Ratzenberger.

WILLIAMS
Rothmans Williams Renault: Hill, Senna, Coulthard, Mansell

TYRRELL
Tyrrell Racing Organisation: Katayama, Blundell

BENETTON
Mild Seven Benetton Ford: Schumacher, Lehto, Verstappen, Herbert

McLAREN
Marlboro McLaren Peugeot: Häkkinen, Alliot, Brundle

FOOTWORK
Arrows Grand Prix International: Fittipaldi, Morbidelli

LOTUS
Team Lotus: Lamy, Zanardi, Adams, Herbert, Bernard, Salo

JORDAN
Sasol Jordan: Barrichello, Irvine, Suzuki, de Cesaris

LARROUSSE
Tourtel Larrousse F1: Beretta, Alliot, Dalmas, Noda, Comas, Deletraz

MINARDI
Minardi Scuderia Italia: Martini, Alboreto

LIGIER
Ligier Gitanes Blondes: Bernard, Herbert, Lagorce, Panis

FERRARI
Scuderia Ferrari SpA: Alesi, Larini, Berger

SAUBER
PP Sauber AG: Wendlinger, de Cesaris, Lehto, Frentzen

SIMTEK
MTV Simtek Ford: Brabham, Ratzenberger, (Montermini), Gounon, Schiattarella, Inoue

PACIFIC
Pacific Grand Prix: Belmondo, Gachot

27 Mar 1994		BRAZIL: Interlagos							(Round 1)	(Race 549)	
		71 laps x 4.325 km, 2.687 miles = 307.075 km, 190.808 miles									
Pos	No	Driver	Car	Model	Engine		Laps	Time/Reason for Retirement		Grid Pos	Row
1	5	M Schumacher	Benetton	B194	Ford Cosworth	V8	71	1h 35m 38.759s		2	1
2	0	D Hill	Williams	FW16	Renault	V10	70			4	2
3	27	J Alesi	Ferrari	412T1	Ferrari	V12	70			3	2
4	14	R Barrichello	Jordan	194	Hart	V10	70			14	7
5	3	U Katayama	Tyrrell	022	Yamaha	V10	69			10	5
6	29	K Wendlinger	Sauber	C13	Mercedes-Benz	V10	69			7	4
7	12	J Herbert	Lotus	107C	Mugen Honda	V10	69			21	11
8	23	P Martini	Minardi	M193B	Ford Cosworth	V8	69			15	8
9	20	E Comas	Larrousse	LH94	Ford Cosworth	V8	68			13	7
10	11	P Lamy	Lotus	107C	Mugen Honda	V10	68			24	12
11	26	O Panis	Ligier	JS39B	Renault	V10	68			19	10
12	31	D Brabham	Simtek	S941	Ford Cosworth	V8	67			26	13
r	2	A Senna	Williams	FW16	Renault	V10	55	spin		1	1
r	8	M Brundle	McLaren	MP4/9	Peugeot	V10	34	accident		18	9
r	15	E Irvine	Jordan	194	Hart	V10	34	accident		16	8
r	6	J Verstappen	Benetton	B194	Ford Cosworth	V8	34	accident		9	5
r	25	É Bernard	Ligier	JS39B	Renault	V10	33	accident		20	10
r	4	M Blundell	Tyrrell	022	Yamaha	V10	21	accident		12	6
r	9	C Fittipaldi	Footwork	FA15	Ford Cosworth	V8	21	gearbox		11	6
r	30	H-H Frentzen	Sauber	C13	Mercedes-Benz	V10	15	spin		5	3
r	7	M Häkkinen	McLaren	MP4/9	Peugeot	V10	13	airbox fire / electrics		8	4
r	24	M Alboreto	Minardi	M193B	Ford Cosworth	V8	7	electrics		22	11
r	10	G Morbidelli	Footwork	FA15	Ford Cosworth	V8	5	gearbox		6	3
r	28	G Berger	Ferrari	412T1	Ferrari	V12	5	engine		17	9
r	19	O Beretta	Larrousse	LH94	Ford Cosworth	V8	2	accident		23	12
r	34	B Gachot	Pacific	PR01	Ilmor	V10	1	accident		25	13
nq	32	R Ratzenberger	Simtek	S941	Ford Cosworth	V8					
nq	33	P Belmondo	Pacific	PR01	Ilmor	V10					

Winning speed 192.632 km/h, 119.696 mph
Pole Position speed 204.970 km/h, 127.363 mph (A Senna, 1 min:15.962 sec)
Fastest Lap speed 198.457 km/h, 123.316 mph (M Schumacher, 1 min:18.455 sec on lap 7)
Lap Leaders A Senna 1-21 (21); M Schumacher 22-71 (50).

17 Apr 1994 PACIFIC: Aida (Round 2) (Race 550)
83 laps x 3.703 km, 2.301 miles = 307.349 km, 190.978 miles

Pos	No	Driver	Car	Model	Engine		Laps	Time/Reason for Retirement	Grid Pos	Row
1	5	M Schumacher	Benetton	B194	Ford Cosworth	V8	83	1h 46m 01.693s	2	1
2	28	G Berger	Ferrari	412T1	Ferrari	V12	83	1h 47m 16.993s	5	3
3	14	R Barrichello	Jordan	194	Hart	V10	82		8	4
4	9	C Fittipaldi	Footwork	FA15	Ford Cosworth	V8	82		9	5
5	30	H-H Frentzen	Sauber	C13	Mercedes-Benz	V10	82		11	6
6	20	E Comas	Larrousse	LH94	Ford Cosworth	V8	80		16	8
7	12	J Herbert	Lotus	107C	Mugen Honda	V10	80		23	12
8	11	P Lamy	Lotus	107C	Mugen Honda	V10	79		24	12
9	26	O Panis	Ligier	JS39B	Renault	V10	78		22	11
10	25	É Bernard	Ligier	JS39B	Renault	V10	78		18	9
11	32	R Ratzenberger	Simtek	S941	Ford Cosworth	V8	78		26	13
r	10	G Morbidelli	Footwork	FA15	Ford Cosworth	V8	69	engine	13	7
r	29	K Wendlinger	Sauber	C13	Mercedes-Benz	V10	69	accident	19	10
r	24	M Alboreto	Minardi	M193B	Ford Cosworth	V8	69	accident	15	8
r	8	M Brundle	McLaren	MP4/9	Peugeot	V10	67	radiator / engine overheating	6	3
r	23	P Martini	Minardi	M193B	Ford Cosworth	V8	63	electrics	17	9
r	6	J Verstappen	Benetton	B194	Ford Cosworth	V8	54	spin	10	5
r	0	D Hill	Williams	FW16	Renault	V10	49	transmission	3	2
r	15	A Suzuki	Jordan	194	Hart	V10	44	steering upright / accident	20	10
r	3	U Katayama	Tyrrell	022	Yamaha	V10	42	engine	14	7
r	7	M Häkkinen	McLaren	MP4/9	Peugeot	V10	19	hydraulics	4	2
r	19	O Beretta	Larrousse	LH94	Ford Cosworth	V8	14	electrics	21	11
r	31	D Brabham	Simtek	S941	Ford Cosworth	V8	2	engine	25	13
r	2	A Senna	Williams	FW16	Renault	V10	0	accident	1	1
r	4	M Blundell	Tyrrell	022	Yamaha	V10	0	accident	12	6
r	27	N Larini	Ferrari	412T1	Ferrari	V12	0	accident	7	4
nq	34	B Gachot	Pacific	PR01	Ilmor	V10				
nq	33	P Belmondo	Pacific	PR01	Ilmor	V10				

Winning speed 173.924 km/h, 108.072 mph
Pole Position speed 189.848 km/h, 117.967 mph (A Senna, 1 min:10.218 sec)
Fastest Lap speed 180.089 km/h, 111.903 mph (M Schumacher, 1 min:14.023 sec on lap 10)
Lap Leaders M Schumacher 1-83 (83).

1 May 1994 SAN MARINO: Imola (Round 3) (Race 551)
58 laps x 5.040 km, 3.132 miles = 292.320 km, 181.639 miles

Pos	No	Driver	Car	Model	Engine		Laps	Time/Reason for Retirement	Grid Pos	Row
1	5	M Schumacher	Benetton	B194	Ford Cosworth	V8	58	1h 28m 28.642s	2	1
2	27	N Larini	Ferrari	412T1	Ferrari	V12	58	1h 29m 23.584s	6	3
3	7	M Häkkinen	McLaren	MP4/9	Peugeot	V10	58	1h 29m 39.321s	8	4
4	29	K Wendlinger	Sauber	C13	Mercedes-Benz	V10	58	1h 29m 42.300s	10	5
5	3	U Katayama	Tyrrell	022	Yamaha	V10	57		9	5
6	0	D Hill	Williams	FW16	Renault	V10	57		4	2
7	30	H-H Frentzen	Sauber	C13	Mercedes-Benz	V10	57		7	4
8	8	M Brundle	McLaren	MP4/9	Peugeot	V10	57		13	7
9	4	M Blundell	Tyrrell	022	Yamaha	V10	56		12	6
10	12	J Herbert	Lotus	107C	Mugen Honda	V10	56		20	10
11	26	O Panis	Ligier	JS39B	Renault	V10	56		19	10
12	25	É Bernard	Ligier	JS39B	Renault	V10	56		17	9
13r	9	C Fittipaldi	Footwork	FA15	Ford Cosworth	V8	54	brakes / spin	16	8
r	15	A de Cesaris	Jordan	194	Hart	V10	49	accident	21	11
r	24	M Alboreto	Minardi	M193B	Ford Cosworth	V8	44	rear wheel lost	15	8
r	10	G Morbidelli	Footwork	FA15	Ford Cosworth	V8	40	engine	11	6
r	23	P Martini	Minardi	M193B	Ford Cosworth	V8	37	spin	14	7
r	31	D Brabham	Simtek	S941	Ford Cosworth	V8	27	tyre / accident	24	12
r	34	B Gachot	Pacific	PR01	Ilmor	V10	23	oil pressure	25	13
r	19	O Beretta	Larrousse	LH94	Ford Cosworth	V8	17	engine	23	12
r	28	G Berger	Ferrari	412T1	Ferrari	V12	16	handling	3	2
r	2	A Senna	Williams	FW16	Renault	V10	5	fatal accident	1	1
r	20	E Comas	Larrousse	LH94	Ford Cosworth	V8	5	accident / under-wing	18	9
r	6	J J Lehto	Benetton	B194	Ford Cosworth	V8	0	accident	5	3
r	11	P Lamy	Lotus	107C	Mugen Honda	V10	0	accident	22	11
ns	32	R Ratzenberger	Simtek	S941	Ford Cosworth	V8		fatal accident	26	13
nq	33	P Belmondo	Pacific	PR01	Ilmor	V10				
nq	14	R Barrichello	Jordan	194	Hart	V10		accident / injury		

Winning speed 198.233 km/h, 123.177 mph
Pole Position speed 222.494 km/h, 138.252 mph (A Senna, 1 min:21.548 sec)
Fastest Lap speed 215.141 km/h, 133.683 mph (D Hill, 1 min:24.335 sec on lap 10)
Lap Leaders A Senna 1-5 (5); G Berger 6-14 (9); M Häkkinen 15-18 (4); N Larini 19-23 (5); M Schumacher 24-58 (35).

Scheduled for 61 laps, but interrupted after 5 laps, because of an accident. Restarted for a further 53 laps, with results being on aggregate.
Lap leaders are given 'on the road'.

Right: *Derek Bell, Silverstone, 1969, in the four-wheel-drive McLaren M9A, painted the traditional orange colours of McLaren's early days. (LAT)*

Below: *Johnny Servoz-Gavin in the four-wheel-drive Matra MS84, heading for sixth place at the 1969 Canadian Grand Prix. (LAT)*

Above: *Jack Brabham finished second in the Brabham BT33-Ford Cosworth at Brands Hatch, 1970. (Maureen Magee)*

Left: *Jochen Rindt (Lotus 72C-Ford Cosworth), winner of the 1970 British Grand Prix, the third of four consecutive victories. He became World Champion posthumously that year, after a fatal accident in practice for the Italian Grand Prix. It was a year of tragedies. Formula 1 was already mourning the deaths of Bruce McLaren and Piers Courage. (Maureen Magee)*

Below: *Chris Amon (Matra Simca MS120B) who retired after just six laps at the Nürburgring, 1971. (Maureen Magee)*

Above: *Jackie Stewart (Tyrrell) passes the famous Silverstone corn on his way to winning the 1971 British Grand Prix. (LAT)*

Right: *Emerson Fittipaldi (right), winner of the 1972 Belgian Grand Prix, celebrates with second-placed François Cevert. The race was held at Nivelles as the regular long Spa track, used until 1970, did not meet modern safety standards. (Maureen Magee)*

Below: *Nanni Galli in the Tecno PA123 which lasted 54 laps at Nivelles, 1972. He spun at the hairpin and Clay Regazzoni, who was following closely, had no chance of avoiding him. (Maureen Magee)*

Left: *Triple World Champion Jackie Stewart in his final year, 1973, seen here at Silverstone.* (Maureen Magee)

Below: *Henri Pescarolo, in his second outing in the Iso Marlboro IR-Ford Cosworth, finished tenth at the 1973 German Grand Prix.* (Maureen Magee)

Above: *James Hunt (Hesketh 308-Ford Cosworth) at Brands Hatch in 1974. In his first full F1 season he finished third three times.* (Maureen Magee)

Right: *Carlos Reutemann (Brabham) with his boss Bernie Ecclestone, owner of the Brabham team, Silverstone, 1975. Bernie was once a driver in the 50s, then manager of Stuart Lewis-Evans and Jochen Rindt. He would go on to form the Formula One Constructors Association, ending up as the 'ringmaster' in the F1 circus.* (Maureen Magee)

Marlboro
TEAM McLAREN
James Hunt
TEXACO
CHAMPION

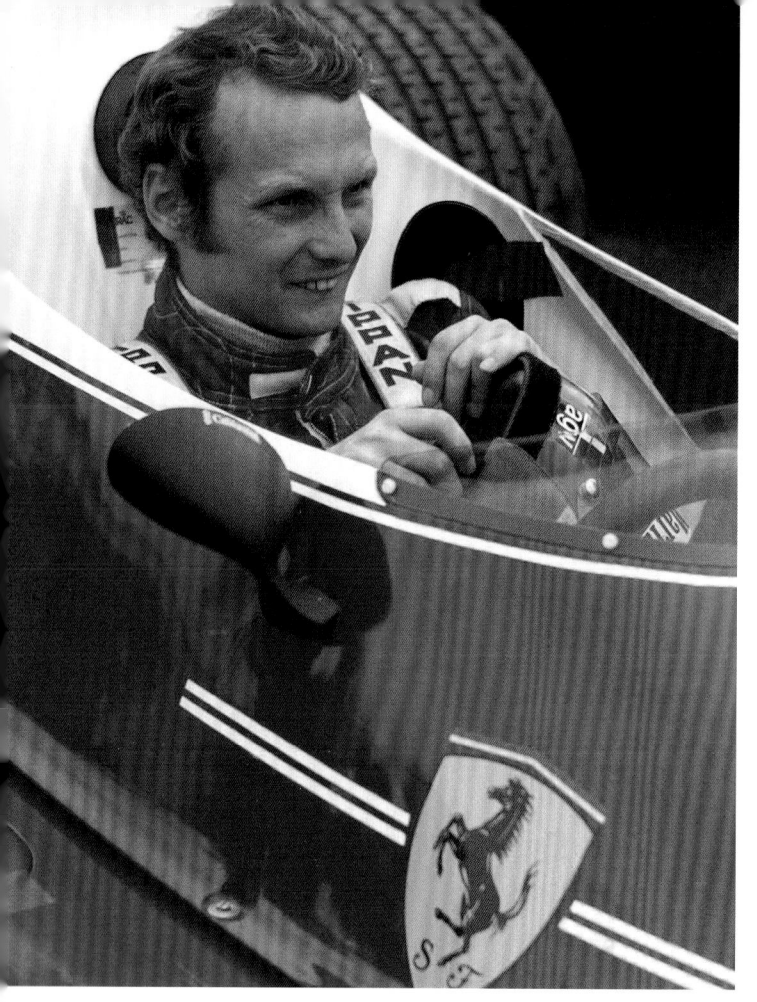

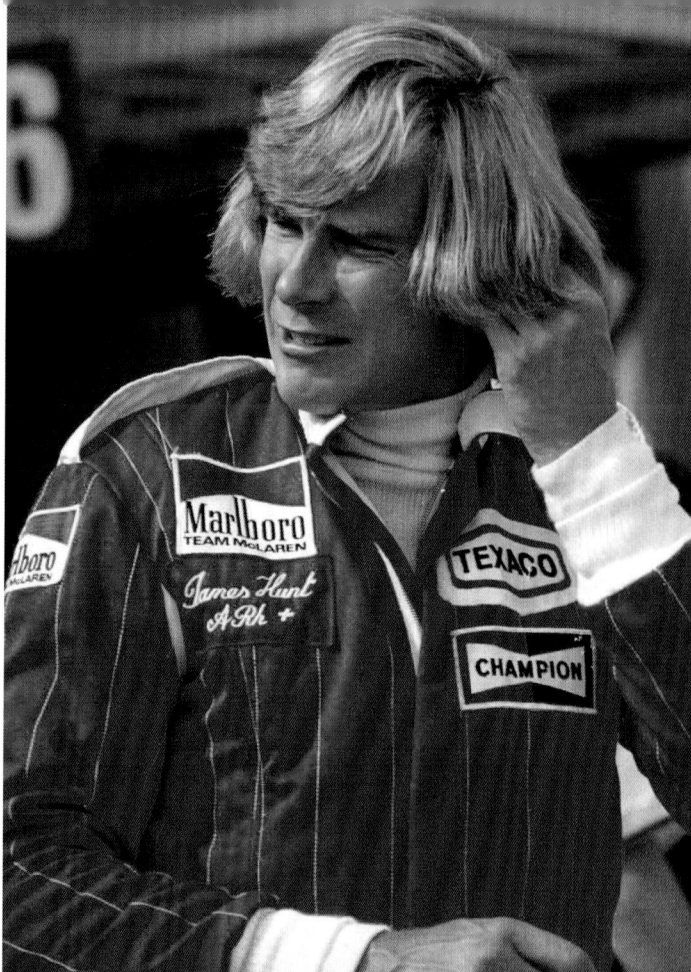

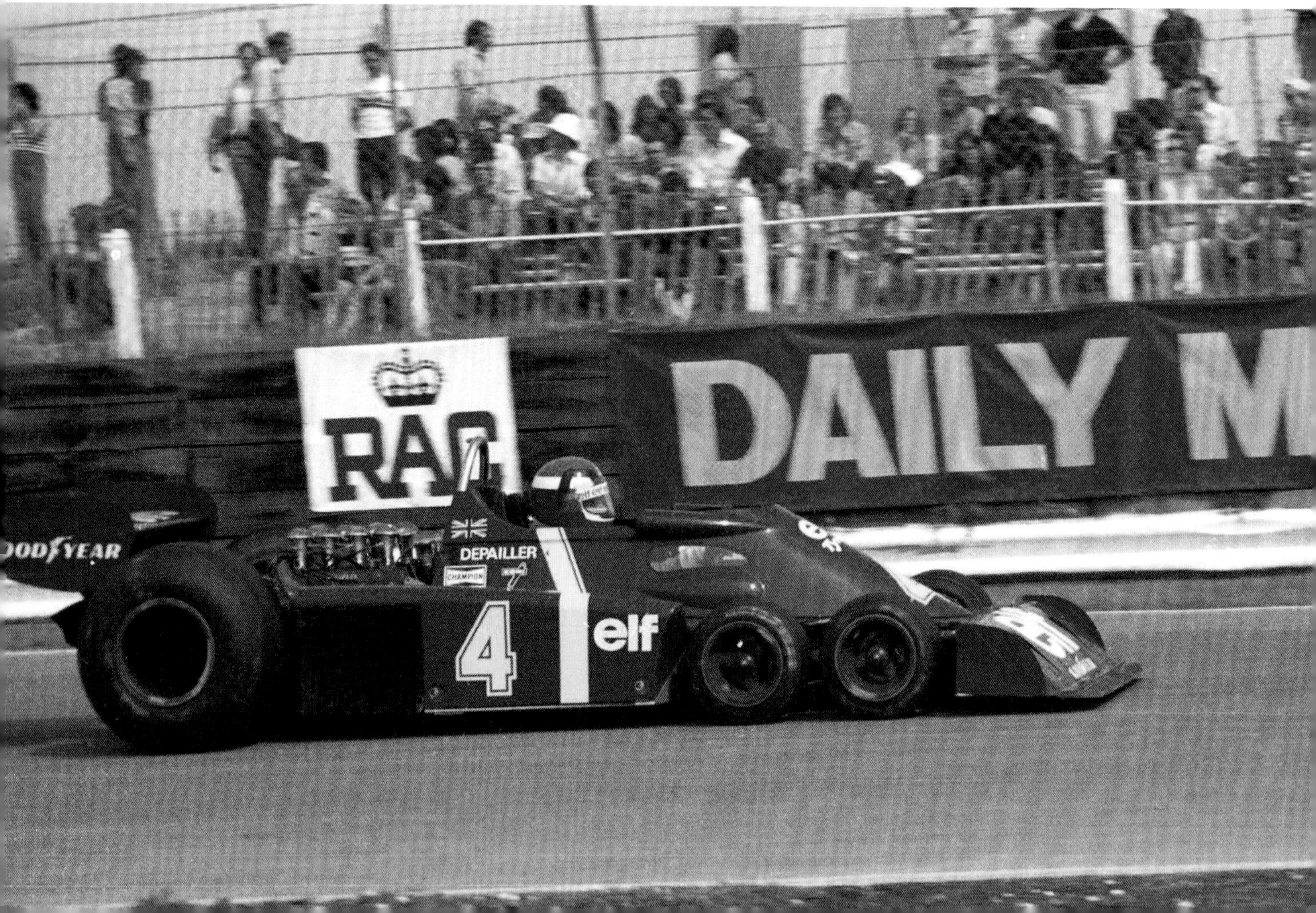
RAC
DAILY M
DEPAILLER
4
elf

Opposite top left: *Niki Lauda (Ferrari) in 1975, when he achieved nine pole positions, five wins and the first of three World Championships. In 1976 he would be runner-up to the title, despite a fiery accident that left his head terribly scarred.* (Maureen Magee)

Opposite top right: *The controversial and colourful James Hunt won the World Championship in 1976 at the wheel of a McLaren M23-Ford Cosworth.* (Maureen Magee)

Opposite bottom: *Patrick Depailler, in the Tyrrell P34-Ford Cosworth six-wheeler, achieved five second places in 1976.* (Maureen Magee)

Right *Ronnie Peterson in 1977, when he was driving for Tyrrell.* (Maureen Magee)

Below: *Gunnar Nilsson at the scene of his only F1 victory, the 1977 Belgian Grand Prix. He was driving a JPS Lotus 78.* (Maureen Magee)

John Player Special
John Player Special
Valvoline
Valvoline
5
Valvoline
Valvoline

AL BILAD
27

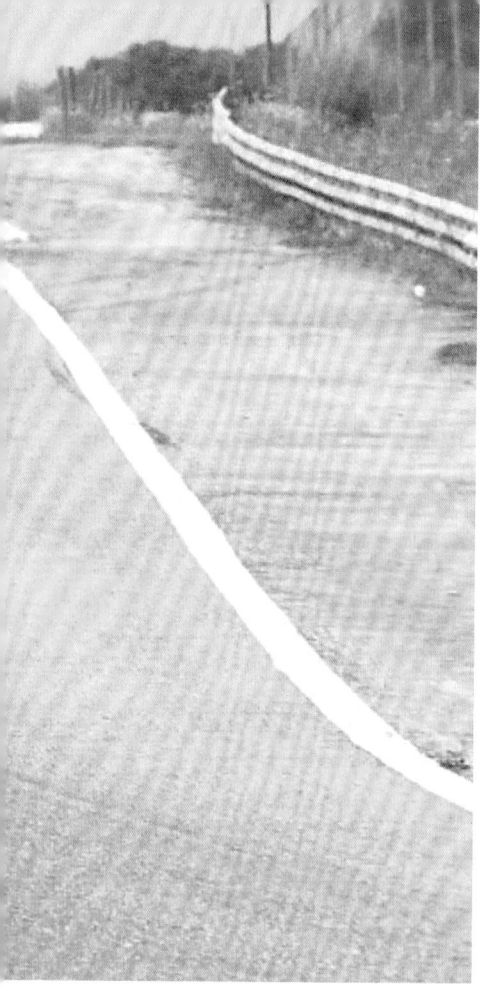

Above: *Mario Andretti and Ronnie Peterson had a 1-2 victory in their JPS Lotus 79s at the 1978 Spanish Grand Prix. (LAT)*

Above right: *Two of the seven French drivers in the 1979 Spanish Grand Prix: Jean-Pierre Jabouille (Renault) and Jean-Pierre Jarier (Tyrrell). (Maureen Magee)*

Left: *In 1980, his World Championship year, Williams-Ford Cosworth driver Alan Jones had three pole positions, five fastest laps, and five victories – at the French, British, Canadian and US East Grands Prix, and here, the first race of the season, in Argentina. (LAT)*

Right: *Ferrari drivers, Jody Scheckter and Gilles Villeneuve, 1980. (Maureen Magee)*

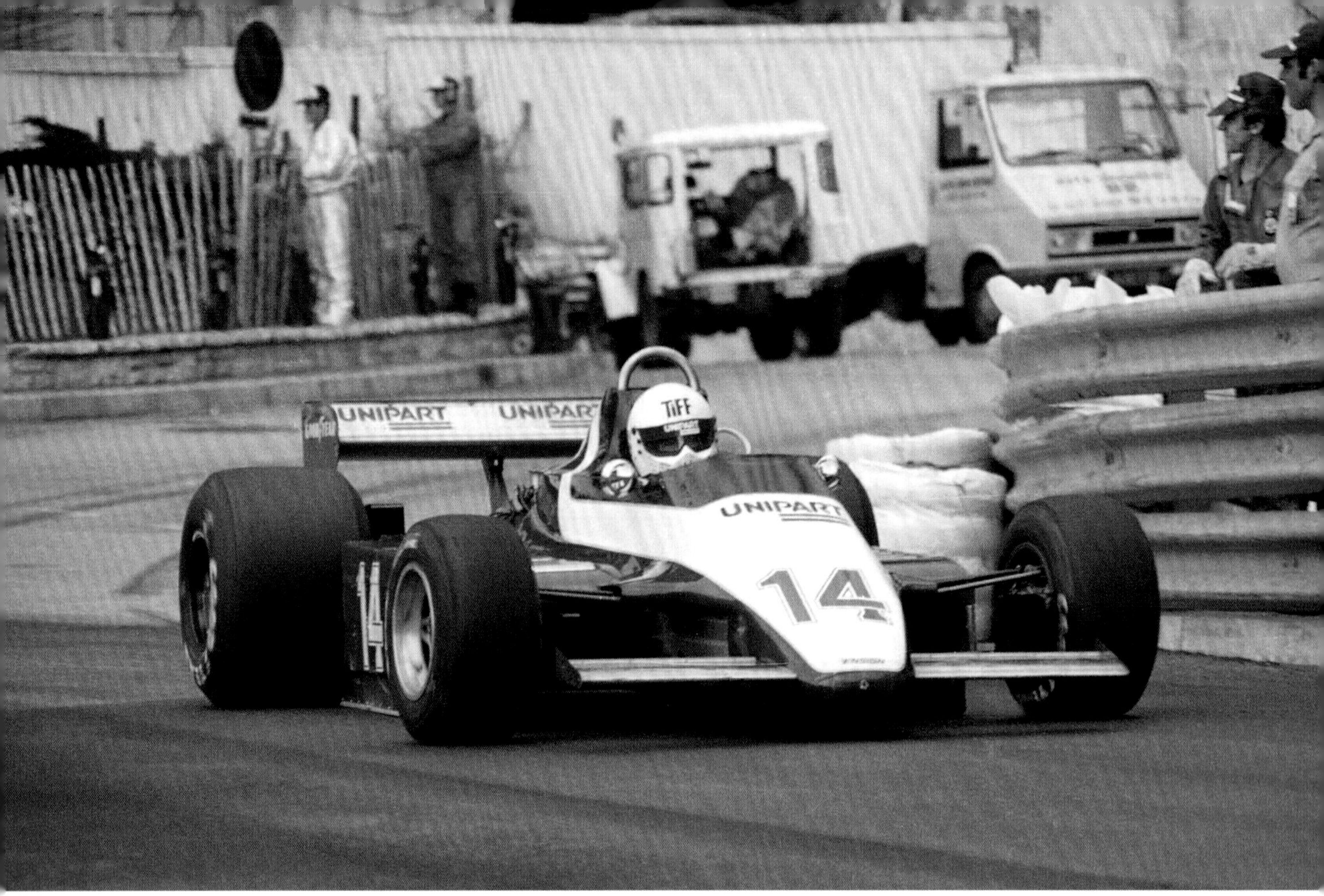
UNIPART
UNIPART
TiFF
UNIPART
14

FIAT
RITMO
parmalat
5
parmalat
BRABHAM
MICHELIN
MICHELIN

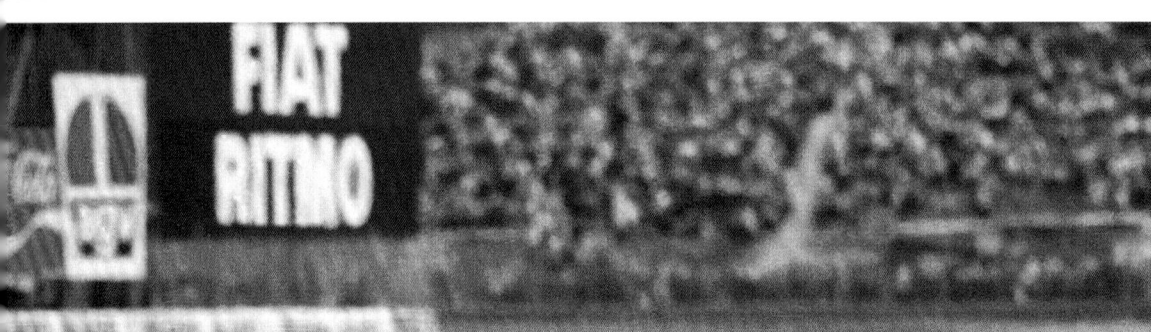

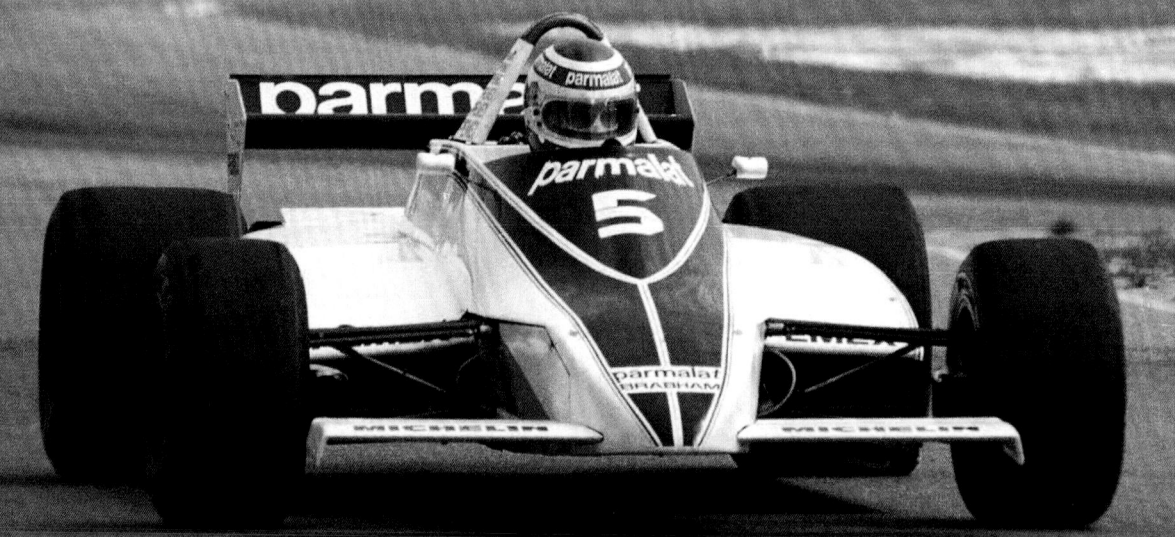

Opposite top: *Tiff Needell at his second and final Grand Prix, Monaco, 1980. He failed to qualify in the Ensign N180-Ford Cosworth.* (Maureen Magee)

Opposite bottom: *Nelson Piquet (Brabham BT49C-Ford Cosworth) won three races in 1981, including the San Marino Grand Prix, and was crowned World Champion. He also won the title in 1983 and 1987.* (Maureen Magee)

Top left: *Reigning World Champion Alan Jones won the first and last races of the 1981 season.* (Maureen Magee)

Top right: *Keke Rosberg (Williams) took the 1982 title with just one victory – the Swiss Grand Prix at Dijon. (*Maureen Magee)

Right: *Didier Pironi and Patrick Tambay (Ferrari) finished third and fourth at the 1982 French Grand Prix.* (Maureen Magee)

TAG
TAG
saudia
TAG
6
John Player Special
GOODYEAR
11

Marlboro
SAIMA
SAIMA
SAIMA
Marlboro
8
HERCULES
HERCULES
UNIPART

Opposite top: *Elio de Angelis (Lotus) wins by 5/100ths of a second over Keke Rosberg (Williams) at the 1982 Austrian Grand Prix.* (LAT)

Left: *Niki Lauda (McLaren MP4/2) wins the Austrian GP in 1984, the year he won his final title. This was the only home victory of his Grand Prix career.* (LAT)

Above: *The presentation ceremony at the 1984 Portuguese Grand Prix, featuring Alain Prost, new World Champion Niki Lauda, and young Toleman driver Ayrton Senna who, in only his first Formula 1 season, achieved three podium positions. FISA President Jean-Marie Balestre is in the foreground.* (Maureen Magee)

Right: *In a frustrating two years with the Benetton Alfa team, Eddie Cheever (Alfa Romeo 185T) had engine problems at the 1985 San Marino Grand Prix, which was one of his 12 retirements that season.* (Maureen Magee)

Opposite top left: *Pierluigi Martini (Minardi M185) at Monza in 1985, the first of his eight seasons with the team.* (Maureen Magee)

Opposite top right: *Martin Brundle, whose best result in the 1986 Tyrrell was fourth in Adelaide.* (David Hayhoe)

Opposite bottom: *Michele Alboreto (Ferrari F186), 1986 Italian Grand Prix.* (David Hayhoe)

Above: *Keke Rosberg in the unusually coloured McLaren MP4/2C-TAG at the 1986 Portuguese Grand Prix.* (David Hayhoe)

Right: *René Arnoux, Ligier JS29B-Megatron, 1987 Monaco Grand Prix.* (David Hayhoe)

Above: *Nigel Mansell drives the Williams FW11B-Honda to fifth place in the 1987 USA Grand Prix.* (David Hayhoe)

Left: *Alain Prost in his second term as World Champion, 1987.* (David Hayhoe)

Below: *The most experienced racer of them all, Riccardo Patrese, a Formula 1 campaigner from 1977 to 1993. In 1989, his second season with Williams, he played a major part in the development work that was to bring the team such success in the 1990s.* (David Hayhoe)

15 May 1994 **MONACO: Monte-Carlo** **(Round 4)** **(Race 552)**

78 laps x 3.328 km, 2.068 miles = 259.584 km, 161.298 miles

Pos	No	Driver	Car	Model	Engine		Laps	Time/Reason for Retirement	Grid Pos	Row
1	5	M Schumacher	Benetton	B194	Ford Cosworth	V8	78	1h 49m 55.372s	1	1
2	8	M Brundle	McLaren	MP4/9	Peugeot	V10	78	1h 50m 32.650s	8	4
3	28	G Berger	Ferrari	412T1	Ferrari	V12	78	1h 51m 12.196s	3	2
4	15	A de Cesaris	Jordan	194	Hart	V10	77		14	7
5	27	J Alesi	Ferrari	412T1	Ferrari	V12	77		5	3
6	24	M Alboreto	Minardi	M193B	Ford Cosworth	V8	77		12	6
7	6	J J Lehto	Benetton	B194	Ford Cosworth	V8	77		17	9
8	19	O Beretta	Larrousse	LH94	Ford Cosworth	V8	76		18	9
9	26	O Panis	Ligier	JS39B	Renault	V10	76		20	10
10	20	E Comas	Larrousse	LH94	Ford Cosworth	V8	75		13	7
11	11	P Lamy	Lotus	107C	Mugen Honda	V10	73		19	10
r	12	J Herbert	Lotus	107C	Mugen Honda	V10	68	gearbox	16	8
r	33	P Belmondo	Pacific	PR01	Ilmor	V10	53	driver discomfort	24	12
r	34	B Gachot	Pacific	PR01	Ilmor	V10	49	gearbox	23	12
r	9	C Fittipaldi	Footwork	FA15	Ford Cosworth	V8	47	gearbox	6	3
r	31	D Brabham	Simtek	S941	Ford Cosworth	V8	45	accident / front suspension	22	11
r	4	M Blundell	Tyrrell	022	Yamaha	V10	40	engine	10	5
r	3	U Katayama	Tyrrell	022	Yamaha	V10	38	gearbox	11	6
r	25	É Bernard	Ligier	JS39B	Renault	V10	34	spin	21	11
r	14	R Barrichello	Jordan	194	Hart	V10	27	electrics	15	8
r	0	D Hill	Williams	FW16	Renault	V10	0	accident	4	2
r	7	M Häkkinen	McLaren	MP4/9	Peugeot	V10	0	accident	2	1
r	10	G Morbidelli	Footwork	FA15	Ford Cosworth	V8	0	accident	7	4
r	23	P Martini	Minardi	M193B	Ford Cosworth	V8	0	accident	9	5
ns	30	H-H Frentzen	Sauber	C13	Mercedes-Benz	V10		withdrew after Wendlinger accid.		
ns	29	K Wendlinger	Sauber	C13	Mercedes-Benz	V10		accident / injury		

Winning speed 141.690 km/h, 88.042 mph
Pole Position speed 152.505 km/h, 94.762 mph (M Schumacher, 1 min:18.560 sec)
Fastest Lap speed 147.772 km/h, 91.822 mph (M Schumacher, 1 min:21.076 sec on lap 35)
Lap Leaders M Schumacher 1-78 (78).

The usual front row of the grid was left vacant, in memory of Ayrton Senna and Roland Ratzenberger.

29 May 1994 **SPAIN: Montmeló** **(Round 5)** **(Race 553)**

65 laps x 4.747 km, 2.950 miles = 308.555 km, 191.727 miles

Pos	No	Driver	Car	Model	Engine		Laps	Time/Reason for Retirement	Grid Pos	Row
1	0	D Hill	Williams	FW16	Renault	V10	65	1h 36m 14.374s	2	1
2	5	M Schumacher	Benetton	B194	Ford Cosworth	V8	65	1h 36m 38.540s	1	1
3	4	M Blundell	Tyrrell	022	Yamaha	V10	65	1h 37m 41.343s	11	6
4	27	J Alesi	Ferrari	412T1	Ferrari	V12	64		6	3
5	23	P Martini	Minardi	M193B	Ford Cosworth	V8	64		18	9
6	15	E Irvine	Jordan	194	Hart	V10	64		13	7
7	26	O Panis	Ligier	JS39B	Renault	V10	63		19	10
8	25	É Bernard	Ligier	JS39B	Renault	V10	62		20	10
9	11	A Zanardi	Lotus	107C	Mugen Honda	V10	62		23	12
10	31	D Brabham	Simtek	S941	Ford Cosworth	V8	61		24	12
11r	8	M Brundle	McLaren	MP4/9	Peugeot	V10	59	transmission	8	4
r	6	J J Lehto	Benetton	B194	Ford Cosworth	V8	53	engine	4	2
r	7	M Häkkinen	McLaren	MP4/9	Peugeot	V10	48	engine	3	2
r	12	J Herbert	Lotus	109	Mugen Honda	V10	41	spin	22	11
r	14	R Barrichello	Jordan	194	Hart	V10	39	engine	5	3
r	9	C Fittipaldi	Footwork	FA15	Ford Cosworth	V8	35	engine	21	11
r	2	D Coulthard	Williams	FW16	Renault	V10	32	electrics	9	5
r	34	B Gachot	Pacific	PR01	Ilmor	V10	32	rear wing	25	13
r	28	G Berger	Ferrari	412T1	Ferrari	V12	27	gearbox	7	4
r	10	G Morbidelli	Footwork	FA15	Ford Cosworth	V8	24	fuel valve fell into tank	15	8
r	30	H-H Frentzen	Sauber	C13	Mercedes-Benz	V10	21	gearbox	12	6
r	20	E Comas	Larrousse	LH94	Ford Cosworth	V8	19	radiator	16	8
r	3	U Katayama	Tyrrell	022	Yamaha	V10	16	engine	10	5
r	24	M Alboreto	Minardi	M193B	Ford Cosworth	V8	4	engine	14	7
r	33	P Belmondo	Pacific	PR01	Ilmor	V10	2	spin	26	13
ns	19	O Beretta	Larrousse	LH94	Ford Cosworth	V8		engine on parade lap	17	9
nq	32	A Montermini	Simtek	S941	Ford Cosworth	V8		accident / injury		

Winning speed 192.366 km/h, 119.531 mph
Pole Position speed 208.638 km/h, 129.642 mph (M Schumacher, 1 min:21.908 sec)
Fastest Lap speed 200.683 km/h, 124.699 mph (M Schumacher, 1 min:25.155 sec on lap 18)
Lap Leaders M Schumacher 1-22,41-45 (27); M Häkkinen 23-30 (8); D Hill 31-40,46-65 (30).

12 Jun 1994   CANADA: Montréal   (Round 6)   (Race 554)
69 laps x 4.450 km, 2.765 miles = 307.050 km, 190.792 miles

Pos	No	Driver	Car	Model	Engine		Laps	Time/Reason for Retirement	Grid Pos	Row
1	5	M Schumacher	Benetton	B194	Ford Cosworth	V8	69	1h 44m 31.887s	1	1
2	0	D Hill	Williams	FW16	Renault	V10	69	1h 45m 11.547s	4	2
3	27	J Alesi	Ferrari	412T1	Ferrari	V12	69	1h 45m 45.275s	2	1
4	28	G Berger	Ferrari	412T1	Ferrari	V12	69	1h 45m 47.496s	3	2
5	2	D Coulthard	Williams	FW16	Renault	V10	68		5	3
dq	9	C Fittipaldi	Footwork	FA15	Ford Cosworth	V8	68	car under weight	16	8
6	6	J J Lehto	Benetton	B194	Ford Cosworth	V8	68		20	10
7	14	R Barrichello	Jordan	194	Hart	V10	68		6	3
8	12	J Herbert	Lotus	109	Mugen Honda	V10	68		17	9
9	23	P Martini	Minardi	M194	Ford Cosworth	V8	68		15	8
10r	4	M Blundell	Tyrrell	022	Yamaha	V10	67	accident	13	7
11	24	M Alboreto	Minardi	M194	Ford Cosworth	V8	67		18	9
12	26	O Panis	Ligier	JS39B	Renault	V10	67		19	10
13	25	É Bernard	Ligier	JS39B	Renault	V10	66		24	12
14	31	D Brabham	Simtek	S941	Ford Cosworth	V8	65		25	13
15r	11	A Zanardi	Lotus	107C	Mugen Honda	V10	62	engine	23	12
r	7	M Häkkinen	McLaren	MP4/9	Peugeot	V10	61	engine	7	4
r	19	O Beretta	Larrousse	LH94	Ford Cosworth	V8	57	engine	22	11
r	10	G Morbidelli	Footwork	FA15	Ford Cosworth	V8	50	gearbox	11	6
r	34	B Gachot	Pacific	PR01	Ilmor	V10	47	oil pressure	26	13
r	20	E Comas	Larrousse	LH94	Ford Cosworth	V8	45	clutch	21	11
r	3	U Katayama	Tyrrell	022	Yamaha	V10	44	spin	9	5
r	15	E Irvine	Jordan	194	Hart	V10	40	accident	8	4
r	29	A de Cesaris	Sauber	C13	Mercedes-Benz	V10	24	oil leak	14	7
r	30	H-H Frentzen	Sauber	C13	Mercedes-Benz	V10	5	accident	10	5
r	8	M Brundle	McLaren	MP4/9	Peugeot	V10	3	engine	12	6
nq	33	P Belmondo	Pacific	PR01	Ilmor	V10				

Winning speed 176.243 km/h, 109.513 mph
Pole Position speed 185.894 km/h, 115.509 mph (M Schumacher, 1 min:26.178 sec)
Fastest Lap speed 180.147 km/h, 111.939 mph (M Schumacher, 1 min:28.927 sec on lap 31)
Lap Leaders M Schumacher 1-69 (69).

3 Jul 1994   FRANCE: Magny-Cours   (Round 7)   (Race 555)
72 laps x 4.250 km, 2.641 miles = 306.000 km, 190.140 miles

Pos	No	Driver	Car	Model	Engine		Laps	Time/Reason for Retirement	Grid Pos	Row
1	5	M Schumacher	Benetton	B194	Ford Cosworth	V8	72	1h 38m 35.704s	3	2
2	0	D Hill	Williams	FW16	Renault	V10	72	1h 38m 48.346s	1	1
3	28	G Berger	Ferrari	412T1B	Ferrari	V12	72	1h 39m 28.469s	5	3
4	30	H-H Frentzen	Sauber	C13	Mercedes-Benz	V10	71		10	5
5	23	P Martini	Minardi	M194	Ford Cosworth	V8	70		16	8
6	29	A de Cesaris	Sauber	C13	Mercedes-Benz	V10	70		11	6
7	12	J Herbert	Lotus	109	Mugen Honda	V10	70		19	10
8	9	C Fittipaldi	Footwork	FA15	Ford Cosworth	V8	70		18	9
9	32	J-M Gounon	Simtek	S941	Ford Cosworth	V8	68		26	13
10	4	M Blundell	Tyrrell	022	Yamaha	V10	67		17	9
11r	20	E Comas	Larrousse	LH94	Ford Cosworth	V8	66	engine	20	10
r	3	U Katayama	Tyrrell	022	Yamaha	V10	53	spin	14	7
r	7	M Häkkinen	McLaren	MP4/9	Peugeot	V10	48	engine	9	5
r	2	N Mansell	Williams	FW16	Renault	V10	45	transmission	2	1
r	27	J Alesi	Ferrari	412T1B	Ferrari	V12	41	accident	4	2
r	14	R Barrichello	Jordan	194	Hart	V10	41	accident	7	4
r	25	É Bernard	Ligier	JS39B	Renault	V10	40	gearbox	15	8
r	19	O Beretta	Larrousse	LH94	Ford Cosworth	V8	36	engine	25	13
r	8	M Brundle	McLaren	MP4/9	Peugeot	V10	29	engine	12	6
r	10	G Morbidelli	Footwork	FA15	Ford Cosworth	V8	28	accident	22	11
r	26	O Panis	Ligier	JS39B	Renault	V10	28	accident	13	7
r	31	D Brabham	Simtek	S941	Ford Cosworth	V8	28	gearbox	24	12
r	6	J Verstappen	Benetton	B194	Ford Cosworth	V8	25	spin	8	4
r	15	E Irvine	Jordan	194	Hart	V10	24	gearbox	6	3
r	24	M Alboreto	Minardi	M194	Ford Cosworth	V8	21	engine	21	11
r	11	A Zanardi	Lotus	109	Mugen Honda	V10	20	engine / fire	23	12
nq	34	B Gachot	Pacific	PR01	Ilmor	V10				
nq	33	P Belmondo	Pacific	PR01	Ilmor	V10				

Winning speed 186.216 km/h, 115.709 mph
Pole Position speed 200.571 km/h, 124.629 mph (D Hill, 1 min:16.282 sec)
Fastest Lap speed 192.022 km/h, 119.317 mph (D Hill, 1 min:19.678 sec on lap 4)
Lap Leaders M Schumacher 1-37,45-72 (65); D Hill 38-44 (7).

10 Jul 1994 — BRITAIN: Silverstone — (Round 8) (Race 556)

60 laps x 5.057 km, 3.142 miles = 303.420 km, 188.536 miles

Pos	No	Driver	Car	Model	Engine		Laps	Time/Reason for Retirement	Grid Pos	Row
1	0	D Hill	Williams	FW16	Renault	V10	60	1h 30m 03.640s	1	1
dq	5	M Schumacher	Benetton	B194	Ford Cosworth	V8	60	overtook on parade lap	2	1
2	27	J Alesi	Ferrari	412T1B	Ferrari	V12	60	1h 31m 11.768s	4	2
3	7	M Häkkinen	McLaren	MP4/9	Peugeot	V10	60	1h 31m 44.299s	5	3
4	14	R Barrichello	Jordan	194	Hart	V10	60	1h 31m 45.391s	6	3
5	2	D Coulthard	Williams	FW16	Renault	V10	59		7	4
6	3	U Katayama	Tyrrell	022	Yamaha	V10	59		8	4
7	30	H-H Frentzen	Sauber	C13	Mercedes-Benz	V10	59		13	7
8	6	J Verstappen	Benetton	B194	Ford Cosworth	V8	59		10	5
9	9	C Fittipaldi	Footwork	FA15	Ford Cosworth	V8	58		20	10
10	23	P Martini	Minardi	M194	Ford Cosworth	V8	58		14	7
11	12	J Herbert	Lotus	109	Mugen Honda	V10	58		21	11
12	26	O Panis	Ligier	JS39B	Renault	V10	58		15	8
13	25	É Bernard	Ligier	JS39B	Renault	V10	58		23	12
14	19	O Beretta	Larrousse	LH94	Ford Cosworth	V8	58		24	12
15	31	D Brabham	Simtek	S941	Ford Cosworth	V8	57		25	13
16	32	J-M Gounon	Simtek	S941	Ford Cosworth	V8	57		26	13
r	24	M Alboreto	Minardi	M194	Ford Cosworth	V8	48	engine	17	9
r	28	G Berger	Ferrari	412T1B	Ferrari	V12	32	engine	3	2
r	4	M Blundell	Tyrrell	022	Yamaha	V10	20	gearbox	11	6
r	20	E Comas	Larrousse	LH94	Ford Cosworth	V8	12	engine	22	11
r	29	A de Cesaris	Sauber	C13	Mercedes-Benz	V10	11	engine	18	9
r	10	G Morbidelli	Footwork	FA15	Ford Cosworth	V8	5	fuel line	16	8
r	11	A Zanardi	Lotus	109	Mugen Honda	V10	4	engine	19	10
r	8	M Brundle	McLaren	MP4/9	Peugeot	V10	0	engine	9	5
ns	15	E Irvine	Jordan	194	Hart	V10		engine on parade lap	12	6
nq	34	B Gachot	Pacific	PR01	Ilmor	V10				
nq	33	P Belmondo	Pacific	PR01	Ilmor	V10				

Winning speed 202.143 km/h, 125.606 mph
Pole Position speed 214.279 km/h, 133.147 mph (D Hill, 1 min:24.960 sec)
Fastest Lap speed 209.014 km/h, 129.876 mph (D Hill, 1 min:27.100 sec on lap 11)
Lap Leaders D Hill 1-14,27-60 (48); M Schumacher 15-17,22-26 (8); G Berger 18-21 (4).

M Schumacher finished 2nd in 1h 30m 22.418s.

31 Jul 1994 — GERMANY: Hockenheim — (Round 9) (Race 557)

45 laps x 6.823 km, 4.240 miles = 307.035 km, 190.783 miles

Pos	No	Driver	Car	Model	Engine		Laps	Time/Reason for Retirement	Grid Pos	Row
1	28	G Berger	Ferrari	412T1B	Ferrari	V12	45	1h 22m 37.272s	1	1
2	26	O Panis	Ligier	JS39B	Renault	V10	45	1h 23m 32.051s	12	6
3	25	É Bernard	Ligier	JS39B	Renault	V10	45	1h 23m 42.314s	14	7
4	9	C Fittipaldi	Footwork	FA15	Ford Cosworth	V8	45	1h 23m 58.881s	17	9
5	10	G Morbidelli	Footwork	FA15	Ford Cosworth	V8	45	1h 24m 07.816s	16	8
6	20	E Comas	Larrousse	LH94	Ford Cosworth	V8	45	1h 24m 22.717s	22	11
7	19	O Beretta	Larrousse	LH94	Ford Cosworth	V8	44		24	12
8	0	D Hill	Williams	FW16B	Renault	V10	44		3	2
r	32	J-M Gounon	Simtek	S941	Ford Cosworth	V8	39	gearbox	26	13
r	31	D Brabham	Simtek	S941	Ford Cosworth	V8	37	clutch	25	13
r	5	M Schumacher	Benetton	B194	Ford Cosworth	V8	20	engine	4	2
r	8	M Brundle	McLaren	MP4/9	Peugeot	V10	19	engine	13	7
r	2	D Coulthard	Williams	FW16B	Renault	V10	17	electronics / gearbox	6	3
r	6	J Verstappen	Benetton	B194	Ford Cosworth	V8	15	refuelling fire	19	10
r	3	U Katayama	Tyrrell	022	Yamaha	V10	6	throttle jammed	5	3
r	27	J Alesi	Ferrari	412T1B	Ferrari	V12	0	electrics	2	1
r	30	H-H Frentzen	Sauber	C13	Mercedes-Benz	V10	0	accident	9	5
r	12	J Herbert	Lotus	109	Mugen Honda	V10	0	accident	15	8
r	14	R Barrichello	Jordan	194	Hart	V10	0	accident	11	6
r	15	E Irvine	Jordan	194	Hart	V10	0	accident	10	5
r	4	M Blundell	Tyrrell	022	Yamaha	V10	0	accident	7	4
r	7	M Häkkinen	McLaren	MP4/9	Peugeot	V10	0	accident	8	4
r	11	A Zanardi	Lotus	109	Mugen Honda	V10	0	accident	21	11
r	23	P Martini	Minardi	M194	Ford Cosworth	V8	0	accident	20	10
r	24	M Alboreto	Minardi	M194	Ford Cosworth	V8	0	accident	23	12
r	29	A de Cesaris	Sauber	C13	Mercedes-Benz	V10	0	accident	18	9
nq	33	P Belmondo	Pacific	PR01	Ilmor	V10				
nq	34	B Gachot	Pacific	PR01	Ilmor	V10				

Winning speed 222.970 km/h, 138.548 mph
Pole Position speed 237.133 km/h, 147.348 mph (G Berger, 1 min:43.582 sec)
Fastest Lap speed 231.264 km/h, 143.701 mph (D Coulthard, 1 min:46.211 sec on lap 11)
Lap Leaders G Berger 1-45 (45).

HUNGARY: Hungaroring (Round 10) (Race 558)

77 laps x 3.968 km, 2.466 miles = 305.536 km, 189.851 miles

Pos	No	Driver	Car	Model	Engine		Laps	Time/Reason for Retirement	Grid Pos	Row
1	5	M Schumacher	Benetton	B194	Ford Cosworth	V8	77	1h 48m 00.185s	1	1
2	0	D Hill	Williams	FW16B	Renault	V10	77	1h 48m 21.012s	2	1
3	6	J Verstappen	Benetton	B194	Ford Cosworth	V8	77	1h 49m 10.514s	12	6
4r	8	M Brundle	McLaren	MP4/9	Peugeot	V10	76	alternator	3	3
5	4	M Blundell	Tyrrell	022	Yamaha	V10	76		11	6
6	26	O Panis	Ligier	JS39B	Renault	V10	76		9	5
7	24	M Alboreto	Minardi	M194	Ford Cosworth	V8	75		20	10
8	20	E Comas	Larrousse	LH94	Ford Cosworth	V8	75		21	11
9	19	O Beretta	Larrousse	LH94	Ford Cosworth	V8	75		25	13
10	25	É Bernard	Ligier	JS39B	Renault	V10	75		18	9
11	31	D Brabham	Simtek	S941	Ford Cosworth	V8	74		23	12
12r	28	G Berger	Ferrari	412T1B	Ferrari	V12	72	pneumatic valve air pressure	4	2
13	11	A Zanardi	Lotus	109	Mugen Honda	V10	72		22	11
14r	9	C Fittipaldi	Footwork	FA15	Ford Cosworth	V8	69		16	8
r	2	D Coulthard	Williams	FW16B	Renault	V10	59	accident	3	2
r	27	J Alesi	Ferrari	412T1B	Ferrari	V12	58	gearbox	13	7
r	23	P Martini	Minardi	M194	Ford Cosworth	V8	58	spin	15	8
r	30	H-H Frentzen	Sauber	C13	Mercedes-Benz	V10	39	gearbox	8	4
r	12	J Herbert	Lotus	109	Mugen Honda	V10	34	electrics	24	12
r	29	A de Cesaris	Sauber	C13	Mercedes-Benz	V10	30	accident	17	9
r	10	G Morbidelli	Footwork	FA15	Ford Cosworth	V8	30	accident	19	10
r	7	P Alliot	McLaren	MP4/9	Peugeot	V10	21	water leak / engine	14	7
r	32	J-M Gounon	Simtek	S941	Ford Cosworth	V8	9	handling	26	13
r	3	U Katayama	Tyrrell	022	Yamaha	V10	0	accident	5	3
r	14	R Barrichello	Jordan	194	Hart	V10	0	accident	10	5
r	15	E Irvine	Jordan	194	Hart	V10	0	accident	7	4
nq	34	B Gachot	Pacific	PR01	Ilmor	V10				
nq	33	P Belmondo	Pacific	PR01	Ilmor	V10				

Winning speed 169.737 km/h, 105.470 mph
Pole Position speed 182.534 km/h, 113.422 mph (M Schumacher, 1 min:18.258 sec)
Fastest Lap speed 176.615 km/h, 109.743 mph (M Schumacher, 1 min:20.881 sec on lap 5)
Lap Leaders M Schumacher 1-16,26-77 (68); D Hill 17-25 (9).

BELGIUM: Spa-Francorchamps (Round 11) (Race 559)

44 laps x 7.001 km, 4.350 miles = 308.044 km, 191.410 miles

Pos	No	Driver	Car	Model	Engine		Laps	Time/Reason for Retirement	Grid Pos	Row
dq	5	M Schumacher	Benetton	B194	Ford Cosworth	V8	44	illegal skidblock wear	2	1
1	0	D Hill	Williams	FW16B	Renault	V10	44	1h 28m 47.170s	3	2
2	7	M Häkkinen	McLaren	MP4/9	Peugeot	V10	44	1h 29m 38.551s	8	4
3	6	J Verstappen	Benetton	B194	Ford Cosworth	V8	44	1h 29m 57.623s	6	3
4	2	D Coulthard	Williams	FW16B	Renault	V10	44	1h 30m 32.957s	7	4
5	4	M Blundell	Tyrrell	022	Yamaha	V10	43		12	6
6	10	G Morbidelli	Footwork	FA15	Ford Cosworth	V8	43		14	7
7	26	O Panis	Ligier	JS39B	Renault	V10	43		17	9
8	23	P Martini	Minardi	M194	Ford Cosworth	V8	43		10	5
9	24	M Alboreto	Minardi	M194	Ford Cosworth	V8	43		18	9
10	25	É Bernard	Ligier	JS39B	Renault	V10	42		16	8
11	32	J-M Gounon	Simtek	S941	Ford Cosworth	V8	42		25	13
12	12	J Herbert	Lotus	109	Mugen Honda	V10	41		20	10
13r	15	E Irvine	Jordan	194	Hart	V10	40	alternator	4	2
r	9	C Fittipaldi	Footwork	FA15	Ford Cosworth	V8	33	engine	24	12
r	31	D Brabham	Simtek	S941	Ford Cosworth	V8	29	rear wheel lost / accident	21	11
r	29	A de Cesaris	Sauber	C13	Mercedes-Benz	V10	27	throttle jammed / accident	15	8
r	8	M Brundle	McLaren	MP4/9	Peugeot	V10	24	spin	13	7
r	14	R Barrichello	Jordan	194	Hart	V10	19	spin	1	1
r	3	U Katayama	Tyrrell	022	Yamaha	V10	18	engine / spin	23	12
r	11	P Adams	Lotus	109	Mugen Honda	V10	15	spin	26	13
r	28	G Berger	Ferrari	412T1B	Ferrari	V12	11	engine	11	6
r	19	P Alliot	Larrousse	LH94	Ford Cosworth	V8	11	engine	19	10
r	30	H-H Frentzen	Sauber	C13	Mercedes-Benz	V10	10	spin	9	5
r	20	E Comas	Larrousse	LH94	Ford Cosworth	V8	3	engine	22	11
r	27	J Alesi	Ferrari	412T1B	Ferrari	V12	2	engine	5	3
nq	34	B Gachot	Pacific	PR01	Ilmor	V10				
nq	33	P Belmondo	Pacific	PR01	Ilmor	V10				

Winning speed 208.170 km/h, 129.351 mph
Pole Position speed 178.542 km/h, 110.941 mph (R Barrichello, 2 min:21.163 sec)
Fastest Lap speed 215.200 km/h, 133.719 mph (D Hill, 1 min:57.117 sec on lap 41)
Lap Leaders M Schumacher 1-28,30-44 (43); D Coulthard 29 (1).

M Schumacher finished 1st in 1h 28m 33.508s (208.706 km/h, 129.684 mph).

11 Sep 1994   **ITALY: Monza**   **(Round 12)**   **(Race 560)**

53 laps x 5.800 km, 3.604 miles = 307.400 km, 191.010 miles

Pos	No	Driver	Car	Model	Engine		Laps	Time/Reason for Retirement	Grid Pos	Row
1	0	D Hill	Williams	FW16B	Renault	V10	53	1h 18m 02.754s	3	2
2	28	G Berger	Ferrari	412T1B	Ferrari	V12	53	1h 18m 07.684s	2	1
3	7	M Häkkinen	McLaren	MP4/9	Peugeot	V10	53	1h 18m 28.394s	7	4
4	14	R Barrichello	Jordan	194	Hart	V10	53	1h 18m 53.388s	16	8
5	8	M Brundle	McLaren	MP4/9	Peugeot	V10	53	1h 19m 28.329s	15	8
6r	2	D Coulthard	Williams	FW16B	Renault	V10	52	out of fuel	5	3
7	25	É Bernard	Ligier	JS39B	Renault	V10	52		12	6
8	20	E Comas	Larrousse	LH94	Ford Cosworth	V8	52		24	12
9	5	J J Lehto	Benetton	B194	Ford Cosworth	V8	52		20	10
10	26	O Panis	Ligier	JS39B	Renault	V10	51		6	3
r	31	D Brabham	Simtek	S941	Ford Cosworth	V8	46	brakes	26	13
r	3	U Katayama	Tyrrell	022	Yamaha	V10	45	brake disc / accident	14	7
r	9	C Fittipaldi	Footwork	FA15	Ford Cosworth	V8	43	engine	19	10
r	15	E Irvine	Jordan	194	Hart	V10	41	engine	9	5
r	4	M Blundell	Tyrrell	022	Yamaha	V10	39	brake disc / accident	21	11
r	23	P Martini	Minardi	M194	Ford Cosworth	V8	30	spin	18	9
r	24	M Alboreto	Minardi	M194	Ford Cosworth	V8	28	gearbox	22	11
r	30	H-H Frentzen	Sauber	C13	Mercedes-Benz	V10	22	engine	11	6
r	29	A de Cesaris	Sauber	C13	Mercedes-Benz	V10	20	engine	8	4
r	32	J-M Gounon	Simtek	S941	Ford Cosworth	V8	20	transmission	25	13
r	19	Y Dalmas	Larrousse	LH94	Ford Cosworth	V8	18	spin	23	12
r	27	J Alesi	Ferrari	412T1B	Ferrari	V12	14	gearbox	1	1
r	12	J Herbert	Lotus	109	Mugen Honda	V10	13	alternator	4	2
r	6	J Verstappen	Benetton	B194	Ford Cosworth	V8	0	accident / rear tyre	10	5
r	11	A Zanardi	Lotus	109	Mugen Honda	V10	0	accident	13	7
r	10	G Morbidelli	Footwork	FA15	Ford Cosworth	V8	0	accident	17	9
nq	34	B Gachot	Pacific	PR01	Ilmor	V10				
nq	33	P Belmondo	Pacific	PR01	Ilmor	V10				

Winning speed 236.322 km/h, 146.844 mph
Pole Position speed 249.033 km/h, 154.743 mph (J Alesi, 1 min:23.844 sec)
Fastest Lap speed 242.988 km/h, 150.986 mph (D Hill, 1 min:25.930 sec on lap 24)
Lap Leaders J Alesi 1-14 (14); G Berger 15-23 (9); D Hill 24,29-53 (26); D Coulthard 25,27-28 (3); M Häkkinen 26 (1).

25 Sep 1994   **PORTUGAL: Estoril**   **(Round 13)**   **(Race 561)**

71 laps x 4.360 km, 2.709 miles = 309.560 km, 192.352 miles

Pos	No	Driver	Car	Model	Engine		Laps	Time/Reason for Retirement	Grid Pos	Row
1	0	D Hill	Williams	FW16B	Renault	V10	71	1h 41m 10.165s	2	1
2	2	D Coulthard	Williams	FW16B	Renault	V10	71	1h 41m 10.768s	3	2
3	7	M Häkkinen	McLaren	MP4/9	Peugeot	V10	71	1h 41m 30.358s	4	2
4	14	R Barrichello	Jordan	194	Hart	V10	71	1h 41m 38.168s	8	4
5	6	J Verstappen	Benetton	B194	Ford Cosworth	V8	71	1h 41m 39.550s	10	5
6	8	M Brundle	McLaren	MP4/9	Peugeot	V10	71	1h 42m 02.867s	7	4
7	15	E Irvine	Jordan	194	Hart	V10	70		13	7
8	9	C Fittipaldi	Footwork	FA15	Ford Cosworth	V8	70		11	6
dq	26	O Panis	Ligier	JS39B	Renault	V10	70	illegal skidblock wear	15	8
9	10	G Morbidelli	Footwork	FA15	Ford Cosworth	V8	70		16	8
10	25	É Bernard	Ligier	JS39B	Renault	V10	70		21	11
11	12	J Herbert	Lotus	109	Mugen Honda	V10	70		20	10
12	23	P Martini	Minardi	M194	Ford Cosworth	V8	69		18	9
13	24	M Alboreto	Minardi	M194	Ford Cosworth	V8	69		19	10
14	19	Y Dalmas	Larrousse	LH94	Ford Cosworth	V8	69		23	12
15	32	J-M Gounon	Simtek	S941	Ford Cosworth	V8	67		26	13
16	11	P Adams	Lotus	109	Mugen Honda	V10	67		25	13
r	4	M Blundell	Tyrrell	022	Yamaha	V10	61	engine	12	6
r	5	J J Lehto	Benetton	B194	Ford Cosworth	V8	60	spin	14	7
r	29	A de Cesaris	Sauber	C13	Mercedes-Benz	V10	54	spin	17	9
r	27	J Alesi	Ferrari	412T1B	Ferrari	V12	38	accident	5	3
r	31	D Brabham	Simtek	S941	Ford Cosworth	V8	36	accident	24	12
r	30	H-H Frentzen	Sauber	C13	Mercedes-Benz	V10	31	transmission	9	5
r	20	E Comas	Larrousse	LH94	Ford Cosworth	V8	27	accident	22	11
r	3	U Katayama	Tyrrell	022	Yamaha	V10	26	gearbox	6	3
r	28	G Berger	Ferrari	412T1B	Ferrari	V12	7	hydraulics	1	1
nq	34	B Gachot	Pacific	PR01	Ilmor	V10				
nq	33	P Belmondo	Pacific	PR01	Ilmor	V10				

Winning speed 183.589 km/h, 114.077 mph
Pole Position speed 194.720 km/h, 120.993 mph (G Berger, 1 min:20.608 sec)
Fastest Lap speed 190.379 km/h, 118.296 mph (D Coulthard, 1 min:22.446 sec on lap 12)
Lap Leaders G Berger 1-7 (7); D Coulthard 8-17,26-27 (12); D Hill 18,28-71 (45); J Alesi 19-22 (4); R Barrichello 23-25 (3).

Races   **373**

69 laps x 4.428 km, 2.751 miles = 305.532 km, 189.849 miles

Pos	No	Driver	Car	Model	Engine		Laps	Time/Reason for Retirement	Grid Pos	Row
1	5	M Schumacher	Benetton	B194	Ford Cosworth	V8	69	1h 40m 26.689s	1	1
2	0	D Hill	Williams	FW16B	Renault	V10	69	1h 40m 51.378s	2	1
3	7	M Häkkinen	McLaren	MP4/9	Peugeot	V10	69	1h 41m 36.337s	9	5
4	15	E Irvine	Jordan	194	Hart	V10	69	1h 41m 45.135s	10	5
5	28	G Berger	Ferrari	412T1B	Ferrari	V12	68		6	3
6	30	H-H Frentzen	Sauber	C13	Mercedes-Benz	V10	68		4	2
7	3	U Katayama	Tyrrell	022	Yamaha	V10	68		13	7
8	25	J Herbert	Ligier	JS39B	Renault	V10	68		7	4
9	26	O Panis	Ligier	JS39B	Renault	V10	68		11	6
10	27	J Alesi	Ferrari	412T1B	Ferrari	V12	68		16	8
11	10	G Morbidelli	Footwork	FA15	Ford Cosworth	V8	68		8	4
12	14	R Barrichello	Jordan	194	Hart	V10	68		5	3
13	4	M Blundell	Tyrrell	022	Yamaha	V10	68		14	7
14	24	M Alboreto	Minardi	M194	Ford Cosworth	V8	67		20	10
15	23	P Martini	Minardi	M194	Ford Cosworth	V8	67		17	9
16	12	A Zanardi	Lotus	109	Mugen Honda	V10	67		21	11
17	9	C Fittipaldi	Footwork	FA15	Ford Cosworth	V8	66		19	10
18	11	É Bernard	Lotus	109	Mugen Honda	V10	66		22	11
19	32	M Schiattarella	Simtek	S941	Ford Cosworth	V8	64		26	13
r	2	N Mansell	Williams	FW16B	Renault	V10	47	spin	3	2
r	31	D Brabham	Simtek	S941	Ford Cosworth	V8	42	engine	25	13
r	29	A de Cesaris	Sauber	C13	Mercedes-Benz	V10	37	throttle linkage	18	9
r	20	E Comas	Larrousse	LH94	Ford Cosworth	V8	37	electrics	23	12
r	6	J Verstappen	Benetton	B194	Ford Cosworth	V8	15	spin	12	6
r	19	H Noda	Larrousse	LH94	Ford Cosworth	V8	10	gearbox	24	12
r	8	M Brundle	McLaren	MP4/9	Peugeot	V10	8	engine	15	8
nq	34	B Gachot	Pacific	PR01	Ilmor	V10				
nq	33	P Belmondo	Pacific	PR01	Ilmor	V10				

Winning speed 182.507 km/h, 113.405 mph
Pole Position speed 192.610 km/h, 119.682 mph (M Schumacher, 1 min:22.762 sec)
Fastest Lap speed 187.450 km/h, 116.476 mph (M Schumacher, 1 min:25.040 sec on lap 17)
Lap Leaders D Hill 1-17,33-34 (19); M Schumacher 18-32,35-69 (50).

50 laps x 5.864 km, 3.644 miles = 293.200 km, 182.186 miles

Pos	No	Driver	Car	Model	Engine		Laps	Time/Reason for Retirement	Grid Pos	Row
1	0	D Hill	Williams	FW16B	Renault	V10	50	1h 55m 53.532s	2	1
2	5	M Schumacher	Benetton	B194	Ford Cosworth	V8	50	1h 55m 56.897s	1	1
3	27	J Alesi	Ferrari	412T1B	Ferrari	V12	50	1h 56m 45.577s	7	4
4	2	N Mansell	Williams	FW16B	Renault	V10	50	1h 56m 49.606s	4	2
5	15	E Irvine	Jordan	194	Hart	V10	50	1h 57m 35.639s	6	3
6	30	H-H Frentzen	Sauber	C13	Mercedes-Benz	V10	50	1h 57m 53.395s	3	2
7	7	M Häkkinen	McLaren	MP4/9	Peugeot	V10	50	1h 57m 56.517s	8	4
8	9	C Fittipaldi	Footwork	FA15	Ford Cosworth	V8	49		18	9
9	20	E Comas	Larrousse	LH94	Ford Cosworth	V8	49		22	11
10	11	M Salo	Lotus	109	Mugen Honda	V10	49		25	13
11	26	O Panis	Ligier	JS39B	Renault	V10	49		19	10
12	31	D Brabham	Simtek	S941	Ford Cosworth	V8	48		24	12
13	12	A Zanardi	Lotus	109	Mugen Honda	V10	48		17	9
r	4	M Blundell	Tyrrell	022	Yamaha	V10	26	engine	13	7
r	14	R Barrichello	Jordan	194	Hart	V10	16	gearbox	10	5
r	8	M Brundle	McLaren	MP4/9	Peugeot	V10	13	accident	9	5
r	10	G Morbidelli	Footwork	FA15	Ford Cosworth	V8	13	accident	12	6
r	28	G Berger	Ferrari	412T1B	Ferrari	V12	10	coil	11	6
r	25	F Lagorce	Ligier	JS39B	Renault	V10	10	accident	20	10
r	23	P Martini	Minardi	M194	Ford Cosworth	V8	10	accident	16	8
r	24	M Alboreto	Minardi	M194	Ford Cosworth	V8	10	spin	21	11
r	6	J Herbert	Benetton	B194	Ford Cosworth	V8	3	spin	5	3
r	3	U Katayama	Tyrrell	022	Yamaha	V10	3	accident	14	7
r	32	T Inoue	Simtek	S941	Ford Cosworth	V8	3	accident	26	13
r	19	H Noda	Larrousse	LH94	Ford Cosworth	V8	0	fuel injection	23	12
r	29	J J Lehto	Sauber	C13	Mercedes-Benz	V10	0	engine	15	8
nq	34	B Gachot	Pacific	PR01	Ilmor	V10				
nq	33	P Belmondo	Pacific	PR01	Ilmor	V10				

Winning speed 151.796 km/h, 94.322 mph
Pole Position speed 217.165 km/h, 134.940 mph (M Schumacher, 1 min:37.209 sec)
Fastest Lap speed 181.054 km/h, 112.502 mph (D Hill, 1 min:56.597 sec on lap 24)
Lap Leaders M Schumacher 1-18 (18); D Hill 19-50 (32).

Scheduled for 53 laps, but interrupted after 13 laps, because of an accident. Restarted for a further 37 laps, with results being given on aggregate. Lap leaders are given 'on the road', although on aggregated time, Schumacher took the lead for 5 laps on lap 36.

81 laps x 3.780 km, 2.349 miles = 306.180 km, 190.251 miles

Pos	No	Driver	Car	Model	Engine		Laps	Time/Reason for Retirement	Grid Pos	Row
1	2	N Mansell	Williams	FW16B	Renault	V10	81	1h 47m 51.480s	1	1
2	28	G Berger	Ferrari	412T1B	Ferrari	V12	81	1h 47m 53.991s	11	6
3	8	M Brundle	McLaren	MP4/9	Peugeot	V10	81	1h 48m 43.967s	9	5
4	14	R Barrichello	Jordan	194	Hart	V10	81	1h 49m 02.010s	5	3
5	26	O Panis	Ligier	JS39B	Renault	V10	80		12	6
6	27	J Alesi	Ferrari	412T1B	Ferrari	V12	80		8	4
7	30	H-H Frentzen	Sauber	C13	Mercedes-Benz	V10	80		10	5
8	9	C Fittipaldi	Footwork	FA15	Ford Cosworth	V8	80		19	10
9	23	P Martini	Minardi	M194	Ford Cosworth	V8	79		18	9
10	29	J J Lehto	Sauber	C13	Mercedes-Benz	V10	79		17	9
11	25	F Lagorce	Ligier	JS39B	Renault	V10	79		20	10
12r	7	M Häkkinen	McLaren	MP4/9	Peugeot	V10	76	brakes / accident	4	2
r	24	M Alboreto	Minardi	M194	Ford Cosworth	V8	69	accident / rear suspension	16	8
r	4	M Blundell	Tyrrell	022	Yamaha	V10	66	accident	13	7
r	20	J-D Deletraz	Larrousse	LH94	Ford Cosworth	V8	56	gearbox	25	13
r	11	M Salo	Lotus	109	Mugen Honda	V10	49	electrics	22	11
r	31	D Brabham	Simtek	S941	Ford Cosworth	V8	49	engine	24	12
r	12	A Zanardi	Lotus	109	Mugen Honda	V10	40	throttle	14	7
r	0	D Hill	Williams	FW16B	Renault	V10	35	accident / front suspension	3	2
r	5	M Schumacher	Benetton	B194	Ford Cosworth	V8	35	accident	2	1
r	32	M Schiattarella	Simtek	S941	Ford Cosworth	V8	21	gear lever	26	13
r	3	U Katayama	Tyrrell	022	Yamaha	V10	19	spin	15	8
r	19	H Noda	Larrousse	LH94	Ford Cosworth	V8	18	oil leak / fire	23	12
r	10	G Morbidelli	Footwork	FA15	Ford Cosworth	V8	17	oil scavenge pump	21	11
r	15	E Irvine	Jordan	194	Hart	V10	15	spin	6	3
r	6	J Herbert	Benetton	B194	Ford Cosworth	V8	13	gearbox	7	4
nq	33	P Belmondo	Pacific	PR01	Ilmor	V10				
nq	34	B Gachot	Pacific	PR01	Ilmor	V10				

Winning speed 170.323 km/h, 105.834 mph
Pole Position speed 178.631 km/h, 110.997 mph (N Mansell, 1 min:16.179 sec)
Fastest Lap speed 176.406 km/h, 109.614 mph (M Schumacher, 1 min:17.140 sec on lap 29)
Lap Leaders M Schumacher 1-35 (35); N Mansell 36-53,64-81 (36); G Berger 54-63 (10).

Lap Leaders 1994

Pos	Driver	Car-Engine	GPs	laps	km	miles
1	M Schumacher	Benetton-Ford Cosworth	13	629	2,741.6	1,703.6
2	D Hill	Williams-Renault	8	216	1,069.4	664.5
3	G Berger	Ferrari	6	84	493.1	306.4
4	N Mansell	Williams-Renault	1	36	136.1	84.6
5	A Senna	Williams-Renault	2	26	116.0	72.1
6	J Alesi	Ferrari	2	18	98.6	61.3
7	D Coulthard	Williams-Renault	3	16	76.7	47.7
8	M Häkkinen	McLaren-Peugeot	3	13	63.9	39.7
9	N Larini	Ferrari	1	5	25.2	15.7
10	R Barrichello	Jordan-Hart	1	3	13.1	8.1
			16	**1,046**	**4,833.8**	**3,003.6**

Driver Points 1994

		BR	PAC	RSM	MC	E	CDN	F	GB	D	H	B	I	P	EUR	J	AUS	Total
1	M Schumacher	10	10	10	10	6	10	10	-	-	10	-	-	-	10	6	-	92
2	D Hill	6	-	1	-	10	6	6	10	-	6	10	10	10	6	10	-	91
3	G Berger	-	6	-	4	-	3	4	-	10	-	-	6	-	2	-	6	41
4	M Häkkinen	-	-	4	-	-	-	-	4	-	-	6	4	4	4	-	-	26
5	J Alesi	4	-	-	2	3	4	-	6	-	-	-	-	-	-	4	1	24
6	R Barrichello	3	4	-	-	-	-	3	-	-	-	-	3	3	-	-	3	19
7	M Brundle	-	-	6	-	-	-	-	-	-	3	-	2	1	-	-	4	16
8	D Coulthard	-	-	-	-	-	2	-	2	-	-	3	1	6	-	-	-	14
9	N Mansell	-	-	-	-	-	-	-	-	-	-	-	-	-	-	3	10	13
10	J Verstappen	-	-	-	-	-	-	-	-	-	4	4	-	2	-	-	-	10
11	O Panis	-	-	-	-	-	-	-	-	6	1	-	-	-	-	-	2	9
12	M Blundell	-	-	-	4	-	-	-	-	-	2	2	-	-	-	-	-	8
13	H-H Frentzen	-	2	-	-	-	-	3	-	-	-	-	-	1	-	1	-	7
14	N Larini	-	-	6	-	-	-	-	-	-	-	-	-	-	-	-	-	6
	C Fittipaldi	-	3	-	-	-	-	-	-	3	-	-	-	-	-	-	-	6
	E Irvine	-	-	-	-	1	-	-	-	-	-	-	-	-	3	2	-	6
17	U Katayama	2	-	2	-	-	-	1	-	-	-	-	-	-	-	-	-	5
18	É Bernard	-	-	-	-	-	-	-	-	4	-	-	-	-	-	-	-	4
	K Wendlinger	1	-	3	-	-	-	-	-	-	-	-	-	-	-	-	-	4
	A de Cesaris	-	-	-	3	-	-	1	-	-	-	-	-	-	-	-	-	4
	P Martini	-	-	-	2	-	2	-	-	-	-	-	-	-	-	-	-	4
22	G Morbidelli	-	-	-	-	-	-	-	-	2	-	1	-	-	-	-	-	3
23	E Comas	-	1	-	-	-	-	-	-	1	-	-	-	-	-	-	-	2
24	M Alboreto	-	-	-	1	-	-	-	-	-	-	-	-	-	-	-	-	1
	J J Lehto	-	-	-	-	-	1	-	-	-	-	-	-	-	-	-	-	1

10,6,4,3,2 and 1 point awarded to the first six finishers.

Constructor Points 1994

		BR	PAC	RSM	MC	E	CDN	F	GB	D	H	B	I	P	EUR	J	AUS	Total
1	Williams-Renault	6	-	1	-	10	8	6	12	-	6	13	11	16	6	13	10	118
2	Benetton-Ford Cosworth	10	10	10	10	6	11	10	-	-	14	4	-	2	10	6	-	103
3	Ferrari	4	6	6	6	3	7	4	6	10	-	-	6	-	2	4	7	71
4	McLaren-Peugeot	-	-	4	6	-	-	-	4	-	3	6	6	5	4	-	4	42
5	Jordan-Hart	3	4	-	3	1	-	-	3	-	-	-	3	3	3	2	3	28
6	Ligier-Renault	-	-	-	-	-	-	-	-	10	1	-	-	-	-	-	2	13
	Tyrrell-Yamaha	2	-	2	-	4	-	-	1	-	2	2	-	-	-	-	-	13
8	Sauber-Mercedes-Benz	1	2	3	-	-	-	4	-	-	-	-	-	-	1	1	-	12
9	Footwork-Ford Cosworth	-	3	-	-	-	-	-	-	5	-	1	-	-	-	-	-	9
10	Minardi-Ford Cosworth	-	-	-	1	2	-	2	-	-	-	-	-	-	-	-	-	5
11	Larrousse-Ford Cosworth	-	1	-	-	-	-	-	1	-	-	-	-	-	-	-	-	2

10,6,4,3,2 and 1 point awarded to the first six finishers.

Race Entrants and Results

The final safety measures came into effect with the reduction in engine size to 3 litres and a fully stepped chassis bottom to help reduce speeds. Benetton moved from Ford to Renault, with McLaren, Jordan and Sauber all negotiating new engine deals. With the addition of Argentina, there would be 17 races for only the second time ever. The motor racing world mourned the death of the man who epitomised all that was good in motorsport – the great Juan Manuel Fangio.

BENETTON
Mild Seven Benetton Renault: Schumacher, Herbert

TYRRELL
Nokia Tyrrell Yamaha: Katayama, Tarquini, Salo

WILLIAMS
Rothmans Williams Renault: Hill, Coulthard

McLAREN
Marlboro McLaren Mercedes: Blundell, Mansell, Häkkinen, Magnussen

FOOTWORK
Footwork Hart: Morbidelli, Papis, Inoue

SIMTEK
MTV Simtek Ford: Schiattarella, Verstappen

JORDAN
Total Jordan Peugeot: Barrichello, Irvine

PACIFIC
Pacific Grand Prix: Gachot, Lavaggi, Deletraz, Montermini

FORTI
Parmalat Forti Ford: Diniz, Moreno

MINARDI
Minardi-Scuderia Italia: Martini, Lamy, Badoer

LIGIER
Ligier Gitanes Blondes: Suzuki, Brundle, Panis

FERRARI
Scuderia Ferrari SpA: Alesi, Berger

SAUBER
Red Bull Sauber Ford: Wendlinger, Boullion, Frentzen

26 Mar 1995		BRAZIL: Interlagos							(Round 1)	(Race 565)	
		71 laps x 4.325 km, 2.687 miles = 307.075 km, 190.808 miles									
Pos	No	Driver	Car	Model	Engine		Laps	Time/Reason for Retirement		Grid Pos	Row
1	1	M Schumacher	Benetton	B195	Renault	V10	71	1h 38m 34.154s		2	1
2	6	D Coulthard	Williams	FW17	Renault	V10	71	1h 38m 42.214s		3	2
3	28	G Berger	Ferrari	412T2	Ferrari	V12	70			5	3
4	8	M Häkkinen	McLaren	MP4/10	Mercedes-Benz	V10	70			7	4
5	27	J Alesi	Ferrari	412T2	Ferrari	V12	70			6	3
6	7	M Blundell	McLaren	MP4/10	Mercedes-Benz	V10	70			9	5
7	4	M Salo	Tyrrell	023	Yamaha	V10	69			12	6
8	25	A Suzuki	Ligier	JS41	Mugen Honda	V10	69			15	8
9	17	A Montermini	Pacific	PR02	Ford Cosworth	V8	65			22	11
10	21	P Diniz	Forti	FG01-95	Ford Cosworth	V8	64			25	13
r	9	G Morbidelli	Footwork	FA16	Hart	V8	62	fuel pressure valve		13	7
r	10	T Inoue	Footwork	FA16	Hart	V8	48	fuel leak / engine fire		21	11
r	24	L Badoer	Minardi	M195	Ford Cosworth	V8	47	gearbox		18	9
r	22	R Moreno	Forti	FG01-95	Ford Cosworth	V8	47	spin		23	12
r	29	K Wendlinger	Sauber	C14	Ford Cosworth	V8	41	heat shield loss / battery wire		19	10
r	5	D Hill	Williams	FW17	Renault	V10	30	rear suspension / spin		1	1
r	2	J Herbert	Benetton	B195	Renault	V10	30	accident		4	2
r	16	B Gachot	Pacific	PR02	Ford Cosworth	V8	23	gearbox		20	10
r	14	R Barrichello	Jordan	195	Peugeot	V10	16	gearbox		16	8
r	12	J Verstappen	Simtek	S951	Ford Cosworth	V8	16	clutch		24	12
r	3	U Katayama	Tyrrell	023	Yamaha	V10	15	spin		11	6
r	15	E Irvine	Jordan	195	Peugeot	V10	15	hydraulics		8	4
r	11	M Schiattarella	Simtek	S951	Ford Cosworth	V8	12	steering box loose		26	13
r	30	H-H Frentzen	Sauber	C14	Ford Cosworth	V8	10	electrics		14	7
r	26	O Panis	Ligier	JS41	Mugen Honda	V10	0	accident		10	5
ns	23	P Martini	Minardi	M195	Ford Cosworth	V8		gearbox on parade lap		17	9

Winning speed 186.919 km/h, 116.146 mph
Pole Position speed 194.428 km/h, 120.812 mph (D Hill, 1 min:20.081 sec)
Fastest Lap speed 192.409 km/h, 119.558 mph (M Schumacher, 1 min:20.921 sec on lap 51)
Lap Leaders M Schumacher 1-17,31-35,47-71 (47); D Hill 18-21,23-30 (12); D Coulthard 22,36-46 (12).

Benetton (finishing 1st) and Williams (finishing 2nd) received no points towards the Constructors' Championship, due to fuel irregularities.

ARGENTINA: Buenos Aires (Round 2) (Race 566)

72 laps x 4.259 km, 2.646 miles = 306.482 km, 190.439 miles

Pos	No	Driver	Car	Model	Engine		Laps	Time/Reason for Retirement	Grid Pos	Row
1	5	D Hill	Williams	FW17	Renault	V10	72	1h 53m 14.532s	2	1
2	27	J Alesi	Ferrari	412T2	Ferrari	V12	72	1h 53m 20.939s	6	3
3	1	M Schumacher	Benetton	B195	Renault	V10	72	1h 53m 47.908s	3	2
4	2	J Herbert	Benetton	B195	Renault	V10	71		11	6
5	30	H-H Frentzen	Sauber	C14	Ford Cosworth	V8	70		9	5
6	28	G Berger	Ferrari	412T2	Ferrari	V12	70		8	4
7	26	O Panis	Ligier	JS41	Mugen Honda	V10	70		18	9
8	3	U Katayama	Tyrrell	023	Yamaha	V10	69		15	8
9	11	M Schiattarella	Simtek	S951	Ford Cosworth	V8	68		20	10
nc	21	P Diniz	Forti	FG01-95	Ford Cosworth	V8	63		25	13
nc	22	R Moreno	Forti	FG01-95	Ford Cosworth	V8	63		24	12
r	4	M Salo	Tyrrell	023	Yamaha	V10	48	accident	7	4
r	25	A Suzuki	Ligier	JS41	Mugen Honda	V10	47	accident	19	10
r	23	P Martini	Minardi	M195	Ford Cosworth	V8	44	spin	16	8
r	9	G Morbidelli	Footwork	FA16	Hart	V8	43	electrics	12	6
r	10	T Inoue	Footwork	FA16	Hart	V8	40	spin	26	13
r	14	R Barrichello	Jordan	195	Peugeot	V10	33	oil leak / engine	10	5
r	12	J Verstappen	Simtek	S951	Ford Cosworth	V8	23	gearbox	14	7
r	6	D Coulthard	Williams	FW17	Renault	V10	16	clutch / electrics	1	1
r	7	M Blundell	McLaren	MP4/10	Mercedes-Benz	V10	9	gearbox casing / oil loss	17	9
r	15	E Irvine	Jordan	195	Peugeot	V10	6	engine	4	2
r	17	A Montermini	Pacific	PR02	Ford Cosworth	V8	1	accident / front suspension	22	11
r	8	M Häkkinen	McLaren	MP4/10	Mercedes-Benz	V10	0	accident	5	3
r	16	B Gachot	Pacific	PR02	Ford Cosworth	V8	0	accident	23	12
r	29	K Wendlinger	Sauber	C14	Ford Cosworth	V8	0	accident	21	11
r	24	L Badoer	Minardi	M195	Ford Cosworth	V8	0	accident *	13	7

Winning speed 162.385 km/h, 100.902 mph
Pole Position speed 135.396 km/h, 84.131 mph (D Coulthard, 1 min:53.241 sec)
Fastest Lap speed 169.377 km/h, 105.246 mph (M Schumacher, 1 min:30.522 sec on lap 55)
Lap Leaders D Coulthard 1-5 (5); M Schumacher 6-10,17 (6); D Hill 11-16,26-72 (53); J Alesi 18-25 (8).

*Interrupted after first lap accident. Restarted for original distance. * Retired after first start.*

SAN MARINO: Imola (Round 3) (Race 567)

63 laps x 4.895 km, 3.042 miles = 308.385 km, 191.622 miles

Pos	No	Driver	Car	Model	Engine		Laps	Time/Reason for Retirement	Grid Pos	Row
1	5	D Hill	Williams	FW17	Renault	V10	63	1h 41m 42.552s	4	2
2	27	J Alesi	Ferrari	412T2	Ferrari	V12	63	1h 42m 01.062s	5	3
3	28	G Berger	Ferrari	412T2	Ferrari	V12	63	1h 42m 25.668s	2	1
4	6	D Coulthard	Williams	FW17	Renault	V10	63	1h 42m 34.442s	3	2
5	8	M Häkkinen	McLaren	MP4/10	Mercedes-Benz	V10	62		6	3
6	30	H-H Frentzen	Sauber	C14	Ford Cosworth	V8	62		14	7
7	2	J Herbert	Benetton	B195	Renault	V10	61		8	4
8	15	E Irvine	Jordan	195	Peugeot	V10	61		7	4
9	26	O Panis	Ligier	JS41	Mugen Honda	V10	61		12	6
10	7	N Mansell	McLaren	MP4/10B	Mercedes-Benz	V10	61		9	5
11	25	A Suzuki	Ligier	JS41	Mugen Honda	V10	60		16	8
12	23	P Martini	Minardi	M195	Ford Cosworth	V8	59		18	9
13	9	G Morbidelli	Footwork	FA16	Hart	V8	59		11	6
14	24	L Badoer	Minardi	M195	Ford Cosworth	V8	59		20	10
15	21	P Diniz	Forti	FG01-95	Ford Cosworth	V8	56		26	13
16	22	R Moreno	Forti	FG01-95	Ford Cosworth	V8	56		25	13
r	29	K Wendlinger	Sauber	C14	Ford Cosworth	V8	43	rear wheel nut jammed	21	11
r	16	B Gachot	Pacific	PR02	Ford Cosworth	V8	36	hydraulics	22	11
r	11	M Schiattarella	Simtek	S951	Ford Cosworth	V8	35	accident / rear suspension	23	12
r	14	R Barrichello	Jordan	195	Peugeot	V10	31	gearbox	10	5
r	3	U Katayama	Tyrrell	023	Yamaha	V10	23	spin	15	8
r	4	M Salo	Tyrrell	023	Yamaha	V10	19	engine	13	7
r	17	A Montermini	Pacific	PR02	Ford Cosworth	V8	15	hydraulics	24	12
r	12	J Verstappen	Simtek	S951	Ford Cosworth	V8	14	gearbox	17	9
r	10	T Inoue	Footwork	FA16	Hart	V8	12	spin	19	10
r	1	M Schumacher	Benetton	B195	Renault	V10	10	accident	1	1

Winning speed 181.921 km/h, 113.041 mph
Pole Position speed 201.915 km/h, 125.465 mph (M Schumacher, 1 min:27.274 sec)
Fastest Lap speed 196.744 km/h, 122.251 mph (G Berger, 1 min:29.568 sec on lap 57)
Lap Leaders M Schumacher 1-9 (9); D Coulthard 10 (1); G Berger 11-21 (11); D Hill 22-63 (42).

14 May 1995 **SPAIN: Montmeló** (Round 4) (Race 568)

65 laps x 4.727 km, 2.937 miles = 307.114 km, 190.832 miles

Pos	No	Driver	Car	Model	Engine		Laps	Time/Reason for Retirement	Grid Pos	Row
1	1	M Schumacher	Benetton	B195	Renault	V10	65	1h 34m 20.507s	1	1
2	2	J Herbert	Benetton	B195	Renault	V10	65	1h 35m 12.495s	7	4
3	28	G Berger	Ferrari	412T2	Ferrari	V12	65	1h 35m 25.744s	3	2
4	5	D Hill	Williams	FW17	Renault	V10	65	1h 36m 22.256s	5	3
5	15	E Irvine	Jordan	195	Peugeot	V10	64		6	3
6	26	O Panis	Ligier	JS41	Mugen Honda	V10	64		15	8
7	14	R Barrichello	Jordan	195	Peugeot	V10	64		8	4
8	30	H-H Frentzen	Sauber	C14	Ford Cosworth	V8	64		12	6
9	25	M Brundle	Ligier	JS41	Mugen Honda	V10	64		11	6
10	4	M Salo	Tyrrell	023	Yamaha	V10	64		13	7
11	9	G Morbidelli	Footwork	FA16	Hart	V8	63		14	7
12	12	J Verstappen	Simtek	S951	Ford Cosworth	V8	63		16	8
13	29	K Wendlinger	Sauber	C14	Ford Cosworth	V8	63		20	10
14	23	P Martini	Minardi	M195	Ford Cosworth	V8	62		19	10
15	11	M Schiattarella	Simtek	S951	Ford Cosworth	V8	61		22	11
r	3	U Katayama	Tyrrell	023	Yamaha	V10	56	engine pneumatic valve system	17	9
r	6	D Coulthard	Williams	FW17	Renault	V10	54	gearbox	4	2
r	8	M Häkkinen	McLaren	MP4/10	Mercedes-Benz	V10	53	fuel pressure	9	5
r	10	T Inoue	Footwork	FA16	Hart	V8	43	engine fire	18	9
r	16	B Gachot	Pacific	PR02	Ford Cosworth	V8	43	refuelling valve / fire	24	12
r	22	R Moreno	Forti	FG01-95	Ford Cosworth	V8	39	water pump	25	13
r	27	J Alesi	Ferrari	412T2	Ferrari	V12	25	engine	2	1
r	24	L Badoer	Minardi	M195	Ford Cosworth	V8	21	hydraulics	21	11
r	7	N Mansell	McLaren	MP4/10B	Mercedes-Benz	V10	18	handling	10	5
r	21	P Diniz	Forti	FG01-95	Ford Cosworth	V8	17	exhaust / gearbox cable	26	13
ns	17	A Montermini	Pacific	PR02	Ford Cosworth	V8		hydraulics on parade lap	23	12

Winning speed 195.320 km/h, 121.367 mph
Pole Position speed 208.923 km/h, 129.819 mph (M Schumacher, 1 min:21.452 sec)
Fastest Lap speed 201.313 km/h, 125.090 mph (D Hill, 1 min:24.531 sec on lap 46)
Lap Leaders M Schumacher 1-65 (65).

28 May 1995 **MONACO: Monte-Carlo** (Round 5) (Race 569)

78 laps x 3.328 km, 2.068 miles = 259.584 km, 161.298 miles

Pos	No	Driver	Car	Model	Engine		Laps	Time/Reason for Retirement	Grid Pos	Row
1	1	M Schumacher	Benetton	B195	Renault	V10	78	1h 53m 11.258s	2	1
2	5	D Hill	Williams	FW17	Renault	V10	78	1h 53m 46.075s	1	1
3	28	G Berger	Ferrari	412T2	Ferrari	V12	78	1h 54m 22.705s	4	2
4	2	J Herbert	Benetton	B195	Renault	V10	77		7	4
5	7	M Blundell	McLaren	MP4/10B	Mercedes-Benz	V10	77		10	5
6	30	H-H Frentzen	Sauber	C14	Ford Cosworth	V8	76		14	7
7	23	P Martini	Minardi	M195	Ford Cosworth	V8	76		18	9
8r	29	J-C Boullion	Sauber	C14	Ford Cosworth	V8	74	accident	19	10
9	9	G Morbidelli	Footwork	FA16	Hart	V8	74		13	7
10	21	P Diniz	Forti	FG01-95	Ford Cosworth	V8	72		22	11
r	24	L Badoer	Minardi	M195	Ford Cosworth	V8	68	accident / driveshaft / suspension	16	8
r	26	O Panis	Ligier	JS41	Mugen Honda	V10	65	accident	12	6
r	4	M Salo	Tyrrell	023	Yamaha	V10	63	engine	17	9
r	14	R Barrichello	Jordan	195	Peugeot	V10	60	throttle jammed open	11	6
r	16	B Gachot	Pacific	PR02	Ford Cosworth	V8	42	hydraulics	21	11
r	27	J Alesi	Ferrari	412T2	Ferrari	V12	41	accident	5	3
r	25	M Brundle	Ligier	JS41	Mugen Honda	V10	40	accident	8	4
r	10	T Inoue	Footwork	FA16	Hart	V8	27	gearbox	26	13
r	23	U Katayama	Tyrrell	023	Yamaha	V10	26	accident	15	8
dq	17	A Montermini	Pacific	PR02	Ford Cosworth	V8	23	late for stop-go penalty	25	13
r	15	E Irvine	Jordan	195	Peugeot	V10	22	wheel rim	9	5
r	6	D Coulthard	Williams	FW17	Renault	V10	16	throttle / gearbox	3	2
r	22	R Moreno	Forti	FG01-95	Ford Cosworth	V8	9	brakes / accident	24	12
r	8	M Häkkinen	McLaren	MP4/10B	Mercedes-Benz	V10	8	oil pump / engine	6	3
r	11	M Schiattarella	Simtek	S951	Ford Cosworth	V8	0	accident *	20	10
r	12	J Verstappen	Simtek	S951	Ford Cosworth	V8	0	gearbox *	23	12

Winning speed 137.603 km/h, 85.503 mph
Pole Position speed 146.192 km/h, 90.840 mph (D Hill, 1 min:21.952 sec)
Fastest Lap speed 141.581 km/h, 87.975 mph (J Alesi, 1 min:24.621 sec on lap 36)
Lap Leaders D Hill 1-23 (23); M Schumacher 24-35,37-78 (54); J Alesi 36 (1).

*Interrupted after first lap accident. Restarted for original distance. * Retired after first start.*

11 Jun 1995   **CANADA: Montréal**   (Round 6)   (Race 570)

68 laps x 4.430 km, 2.753 miles = 301.240 km, 187.182 miles

Pos	No	Driver	Car	Model	Engine		Laps	Time/Reason for Retirement	Grid Pos	Row
1	27	J Alesi	Ferrari	412T2	Ferrari	V12	68	1h 46m 31.333s	5	3
2	14	R Barrichello	Jordan	195	Peugeot	V10	68	1h 47m 03.020s	9	5
3	15	E Irvine	Jordan	195	Peugeot	V10	68	1h 47m 04.603s	8	4
4	26	O Panis	Ligier	JS41	Mugen Honda	V10	68	1h 47m 07.839s	11	6
5	1	M Schumacher	Benetton	B195	Renault	V10	68	1h 47m 08.393s	1	1
6	9	G Morbidelli	Footwork	FA16	Hart	V8	67		13	7
7	4	M Salo	Tyrrell	023	Yamaha	V10	67		15	8
8	24	L Badoer	Minardi	M195	Ford Cosworth	V8	67		19	10
9	10	T Inoue	Footwork	FA16	Hart	V8	66		22	11
10r	25	M Brundle	Ligier	JS41	Mugen Honda	V10	61	accident	14	7
11r	28	G Berger	Ferrari	412T2	Ferrari	V12	61	accident	4	2
r	23	P Martini	Minardi	M195	Ford Cosworth	V8	60	throttle linkage	17	9
r	22	R Moreno	Forti	FG01-95	Ford Cosworth	V8	54	out of fuel (refuelling failure)	23	12
r	5	D Hill	Williams	FW17	Renault	V10	50	hydraulics	2	1
r	7	M Blundell	McLaren	MP4/10B	Mercedes-Benz	V10	47	engine	10	5
r	3	U Katayama	Tyrrell	023	Yamaha	V10	42	engine air pressure	16	8
r	16	B Gachot	Pacific	PR02	Ford Cosworth	V8	36	battery	20	10
r	30	H-H Frentzen	Sauber	C14	Ford Cosworth	V8	26	engine	12	6
r	21	P Diniz	Forti	FG01-95	Ford Cosworth	V8	26	gearbox	24	12
r	29	J-C Boullion	Sauber	C14	Ford Cosworth	V8	19	spin	18	9
r	17	A Montermini	Pacific	PR02	Ford Cosworth	V8	5	hydraulics	21	11
r	6	D Coulthard	Williams	FW17	Renault	V10	1	spin	3	2
r	2	J Herbert	Benetton	B195	Renault	V10	0	accident	6	3
r	8	M Häkkinen	McLaren	MP4/10B	Mercedes-Benz	V10	0	accident	7	4

Winning speed 172.296 km/h, 107.060 mph
Pole Position speed 181.928 km/h, 113.045 mph (M Schumacher, 1 min:27.661 sec)
Fastest Lap speed 178.841 km/h, 111.127 mph (M Schumacher, 1 min:29.174 sec on lap 67)
Lap Leaders M Schumacher 1-57 (57); J Alesi 58-68 (11).

Scheduled for 69 laps but results declared after 68 laps due to a crowd invasion of the track.

2 Jul 1995   **FRANCE: Magny-Cours**   (Round 7)   (Race 571)

72 laps x 4.250 km, 2.641 miles = 305.814 km, 190.024 miles

Pos	No	Driver	Car	Model	Engine		Laps	Time/Reason for Retirement	Grid Pos	Row
1	1	M Schumacher	Benetton	B195	Renault	V10	72	1h 38m 28.429s	2	1
2	5	D Hill	Williams	FW17	Renault	V10	72	1h 38m 59.738s	1	1
3	6	D Coulthard	Williams	FW17	Renault	V10	72	1h 39m 31.255s	3	2
4	25	M Brundle	Ligier	JS41	Mugen Honda	V10	72	1h 39m 31.722s	9	5
5	27	J Alesi	Ferrari	412T2	Ferrari	V12	72	1h 39m 46.298s	4	2
6	14	R Barrichello	Jordan	195	Peugeot	V10	71		5	3
7	8	M Häkkinen	McLaren	MP4/10B	Mercedes-Benz	V10	71		8	4
8	26	O Panis	Ligier	JS41	Mugen Honda	V10	71		6	3
9	15	E Irvine	Jordan	195	Peugeot	V10	71		11	6
10	30	H-H Frentzen	Sauber	C14	Ford Cosworth	V8	71		12	6
11	7	M Blundell	McLaren	MP4/10B	Mercedes-Benz	V10	70		13	7
12	28	G Berger	Ferrari	412T2	Ferrari	V12	70		7	4
13	24	L Badoer	Minardi	M195	Ford Cosworth	V8	69		17	9
14	9	G Morbidelli	Footwork	FA16	Hart	V8	69		16	8
15	4	M Salo	Tyrrell	023	Yamaha	V10	69		14	7
16	22	R Moreno	Forti	FG01-95	Ford Cosworth	V8	66		24	12
nc	17	A Montermini	Pacific	PR02	Ford Cosworth	V8	62		21	11
r	29	J-C Boullion	Sauber	C14	Ford Cosworth	V8	48	transmission	15	8
r	16	B Gachot	Pacific	PR02	Ford Cosworth	V8	24	gearbox	22	11
r	23	P Martini	Minardi	M195	Ford Cosworth	V8	23	gearbox	20	10
r	2	J Herbert	Benetton	B195	Renault	V10	2	accident	10	5
r	3	U Katayama	Tyrrell	023	Yamaha	V10	0	accident	19	10
r	10	T Inoue	Footwork	FA16	Hart	V8	0	accident	18	9
r	21	P Diniz	Forti	FG01-95	Ford Cosworth	V8	0	accident	23	12

Winning speed 186.332 km/h, 115.781 mph
Pole Position speed 198.122 km/h, 123.108 mph (D Hill, 1 min:17.225 sec)
Fastest Lap speed 190.730 km/h, 118.514 mph (M Schumacher, 1 min:20.218 sec on lap 51)
Lap Leaders D Hill 1-21 (21); M Schumacher 22-72 (51).

16 Jul 1995 **BRITAIN: Silverstone** (Round 8) (Race 572)

61 laps x 5.057 km, 3.142 miles = 308.477 km, 191.679 miles

Pos	No	Driver	Car	Model	Engine		Laps	Time/Reason for Retirement	Grid Pos	Row
1	2	J Herbert	Benetton	B195	Renault	V10	61	1h 34m 35.093s	5	3
2	27	J Alesi	Ferrari	412T2	Ferrari	V12	61	1h 34m 51.572s	6	3
3	6	D Coulthard	Williams	FW17	Renault	V10	61	1h 34m 58.981s	3	2
4	26	O Panis	Ligier	JS41	Mugen Honda	V10	61	1h 36m 08.261s	13	7
5	7	M Blundell	McLaren	MP4/10B	Mercedes-Benz	V10	61	1h 36m 23.265s	10	5
6	30	H-H Frentzen	Sauber	C14	Ford Cosworth	V8	60		12	6
7	23	P Martini	Minardi	M195	Ford Cosworth	V8	60		15	8
8	4	M Salo	Tyrrell	023	Yamaha	V10	60		23	12
9	29	J-C Boullion	Sauber	C14	Ford Cosworth	V8	60		16	8
10	24	L Badoer	Minardi	M195	Ford Cosworth	V8	60		18	9
11r	14	R Barrichello	Jordan	195	Peugeot	V10	59	accident / front suspension	9	5
12	16	B Gachot	Pacific	PR02	Ford Cosworth	V8	58		21	11
r	22	R Moreno	Forti	FG01-95	Ford Cosworth	V8	48	pneumatic valve fluid pressure	22	11
r	1	M Schumacher	Benetton	B195	Renault	V10	45	accident	2	1
r	5	D Hill	Williams	FW17	Renault	V10	45	accident	1	1
r	9	M Papis	Footwork	FA16	Hart	V8	28	accident / front suspension	17	9
r	3	U Katayama	Tyrrell	023	Yamaha	V10	22	fuel starvation	14	7
r	17	A Montermini	Pacific	PR02	Ford Cosworth	V8	21	spin	24	12
r	8	M Häkkinen	McLaren	MP4/10B	Mercedes-Benz	V10	20	gearbox electronic control unit	8	4
r	28	G Berger	Ferrari	412T2	Ferrari	V12	20	front wheel loose	4	2
r	25	M Brundle	Ligier	JS41	Mugen Honda	V10	16	spin	11	6
r	10	T Inoue	Footwork	FA16	Hart	V8	16	spin	19	10
r	21	P Diniz	Forti	FG01-95	Ford Cosworth	V8	13	gearbox	20	10
r	15	E Irvine	Jordan	195	Peugeot	V10	2	crankshaft sensor	7	4

Winning speed 195.682 km/h, 121.592 mph
Pole Position speed 206.586 km/h, 128.367 mph (D Hill, 1 min:28.124 sec)
Fastest Lap speed 202.838 km/h, 126.038 mph (D Hill, 1 min:29.752 sec on lap 37)
Lap Leaders D Hill 1-22,32-41 (32); M Schumacher 23-31,42-45 (13); J Herbert 46-48,51-61 (14); D Coulthard 49-50 (2).

30 Jul 1995 **GERMANY: Hockenheim** (Round 9) (Race 573)

45 laps x 6.823 km, 4.240 miles = 307.022 km, 190.775 miles

Pos	No	Driver	Car	Model	Engine		Laps	Time/Reason for Retirement	Grid Pos	Row
1	1	M Schumacher	Benetton	B195	Renault	V10	45	1h 22m 56.043s	2	1
2	6	D Coulthard	Williams	FW17	Renault	V10	45	1h 23m 02.031s	3	2
3	28	G Berger	Ferrari	412T2	Ferrari	V12	45	1h 24m 04.140s	4	2
4	2	J Herbert	Benetton	B195	Renault	V10	45	1h 24m 19.479s	9	5
5	29	J-C Boullion	Sauber	C14	Ford Cosworth	V8	44		14	7
6	25	A Suzuki	Ligier	JS41	Mugen Honda	V10	44		18	9
7	3	U Katayama	Tyrrell	023	Yamaha	V10	44		17	9
8	17	A Montermini	Pacific	PR02	Ford Cosworth	V8	42		23	12
9r	15	E Irvine	Jordan	195	Peugeot	V10	41	throttle potentiometer	6	3
r	8	M Häkkinen	McLaren	MP4/10B	Mercedes-Benz	V10	33	pneumatic pressure / engine	7	4
r	30	H-H Frentzen	Sauber	C14	Ford Cosworth	V8	32	engine	11	6
r	24	L Badoer	Minardi	M195	Ford Cosworth	V8	28	gearbox actuator oil leak	16	8
r	16	G Lavaggi	Pacific	PR02	Ford Cosworth	V8	27	gearbox	24	12
r	22	R Moreno	Forti	FG01-95	Ford Cosworth	V8	27	driveshaft	22	11
r	14	R Barrichello	Jordan	195	Peugeot	V10	20	pneumatic pressure / engine	5	3
r	7	M Blundell	McLaren	MP4/10B	Mercedes-Benz	V10	17	engine	8	4
r	26	O Panis	Ligier	JS41	Mugen Honda	V10	13	water pipe split	12	6
r	27	J Alesi	Ferrari	412T2	Ferrari	V12	12	engine	10	5
r	23	P Martini	Minardi	M195	Ford Cosworth	V8	11	engine	20	10
r	10	T Inoue	Footwork	FA16	Hart	V8	9	gearbox	19	10
r	21	P Diniz	Forti	FG01-95	Ford Cosworth	V8	8	brakes	21	11
r	5	D Hill	Williams	FW17	Renault	V10	1	accident	1	1
r	4	M Salo	Tyrrell	023	Yamaha	V10	0	driveshaft	13	7
r	9	M Papis	Footwork	FA16	Hart	V8	0	gearbox electrics	15	8

Winning speed 222.120 km/h, 138.019 mph
Pole Position speed 235.309 km/h, 146.215 mph (D Hill, 1 min:44.385 sec)
Fastest Lap speed 225.711 km/h, 140.250 mph (M Schumacher, 1 min:48.824 sec on lap 22)
Lap Leaders D Hill 1 (1); M Schumacher 2-19,24-45 (40); D Coulthard 20-23 (4).

13 Aug 1995　　**HUNGARY: Hungaroring**　　　　　　　　　　　　**(Round 10)**　　**(Race 574)**

77 laps x 3.968 km, 2.466 miles = 305.536 km, 189.851 miles

Pos	No	Driver	Car	Model	Engine		Laps	Time/Reason for Retirement	Grid Pos	Row
1	5	D Hill	Williams	FW17	Renault	V10	77	1h 46m 25.721s	1	1
2	6	D Coulthard	Williams	FW17	Renault	V10	77	1h 46m 59.119s	2	1
3	28	G Berger	Ferrari	412T2	Ferrari	V12	76		4	2
4	2	J Herbert	Benetton	B195	Renault	V10	76		9	5
5	30	H-H Frentzen	Sauber	C14	Ford Cosworth	V8	76		11	6
6	26	O Panis	Ligier	JS41	Mugen Honda	V10	76		10	5
7	14	R Barrichello	Jordan	195	Peugeot	V10	76		14	7
8	24	L Badoer	Minardi	M195	Ford Cosworth	V8	75		12	6
9	23	P Lamy	Minardi	M195	Ford Cosworth	V8	74		15	8
10	29	J-C Boullion	Sauber	C14	Ford Cosworth	V8	74		19	10
11r	1	M Schumacher	Benetton	B195	Renault	V10	73	fuel pump	3	2
12	17	A Montermini	Pacific	PR02	Ford Cosworth	V8	73		22	11
13r	15	E Irvine	Jordan	195	Peugeot	V10	70	clutch	7	4
r	25	M Brundle	Ligier	JS41	Mugen Honda	V10	67	engine	8	4
r	4	M Salo	Tyrrell	023	Yamaha	V10	58	throttle potentiometer	16	8
r	7	M Blundell	McLaren	MP4/10B	Mercedes-Benz	V10	54	engine	13	7
r	3	U Katayama	Tyrrell	023	Yamaha	V10	46	accident	17	9
r	9	M Papis	Footwork	FA16	Hart	V8	45	brake fluid loss	20	10
r	27	J Alesi	Ferrari	412T2	Ferrari	V12	42	spark plug / piston	6	3
r	21	P Diniz	Forti	FG01-95	Ford Cosworth	V8	32	oil pressure / engine	23	12
r	10	T Inoue	Footwork	FA16	Hart	V8	13	engine / fire / injured by safety car	18	9
r	22	R Moreno	Forti	FG01-95	Ford Cosworth	V8	8	gear lever	21	11
r	16	G Lavaggi	Pacific	PR02	Ford Cosworth	V8	5	spin	24	12
r	8	M Häkkinen	McLaren	MP4/10B	Mercedes-Benz	V10	3	engine	5	3

Winning speed 172.248 km/h, 107.030 mph
Pole Position speed 185.560 km/h, 115.302 mph (D Hill, 1 min:16.982 sec)
Fastest Lap speed 178.010 km/h, 110.611 mph (D Hill, 1 min:20.247 sec on lap 34)
Lap Leaders D Hill 1-77 (77).

---

27 Aug 1995　　**BELGIUM: Spa-Francorchamps**　　　　　　　　　　**(Round 11)**　　**(Race 575)**

44 laps x 6.974 km, 4.333 miles = 306.856 km, 190.671 miles

Pos	No	Driver	Car	Model	Engine		Laps	Time/Reason for Retirement	Grid Pos	Row
1	1	M Schumacher	Benetton	B195	Renault	V10	44	1h 36m 47.875s	16	8
2	5	D Hill	Williams	FW17	Renault	V10	44	1h 37m 07.368s	8	4
3	25	M Brundle	Ligier	JS41	Mugen Honda	V10	44	1h 37m 12.873s	13	7
4	30	H-H Frentzen	Sauber	C14	Ford Cosworth	V8	44	1h 37m 14.847s	10	5
5	7	M Blundell	McLaren	MP4/10B	Mercedes-Benz	V10	44	1h 37m 21.647s	6	3
6	14	R Barrichello	Jordan	195	Peugeot	V10	44	1h 37m 27.549s	12	6
7	2	J Herbert	Benetton	B195	Renault	V10	44	1h 37m 41.923s	4	2
8	4	M Salo	Tyrrell	023	Yamaha	V10	44	1h 37m 42.423s	11	6
9	26	O Panis	Ligier	JS41	Mugen Honda	V10	44	1h 37m 54.045s	9	5
10	23	P Lamy	Minardi	M195	Ford Cosworth	V8	44	1h 38m 07.664s	17	9
11	29	J-C Boullion	Sauber	C14	Ford Cosworth	V8	43		14	7
12	10	T Inoue	Footwork	FA16	Hart	V8	43		18	9
13	21	P Diniz	Forti	FG01-95	Ford Cosworth	V8	42		24	12
14	22	R Moreno	Forti	FG01-95	Ford Cosworth	V8	42		22	11
r	3	U Katayama	Tyrrell	023	Yamaha	V10	28	spin	15	8
r	16	G Lavaggi	Pacific	PR02	Ford Cosworth	V8	27	gearbox	23	12
r	24	L Badoer	Minardi	M195	Ford Cosworth	V8	23	accident	19	10
r	28	G Berger	Ferrari	412T2	Ferrari	V12	22	electrics	1	1
r	15	E Irvine	Jordan	195	Peugeot	V10	21	refuelling fire	7	4
r	9	M Papis	Footwork	FA16	Hart	V8	20	spin	20	10
r	17	A Montermini	Pacific	PR02	Ford Cosworth	V8	18	fuel pressure	21	11
r	6	D Coulthard	Williams	FW17	Renault	V10	13	gearbox oil loss	5	3
r	27	J Alesi	Ferrari	412T2	Ferrari	V12	4	rear suspension	2	1
r	8	M Häkkinen	McLaren	MP4/10B	Mercedes-Benz	V10	1	spin	3	2

Winning speed 190.204 km/h, 118.187 mph
Pole Position speed 219.476 km/h, 136.377 mph (G Berger, 1 min:54.392 sec)
Fastest Lap speed 221.373 km/h, 137.555 mph (D Coulthard, 1 min:53.412 sec on lap 11)
Lap Leaders J Herbert 1,4-5 (3); J Alesi 2-3 (2); D Coulthard 6-13 (8); D Hill 14-15,19-21,24 (6); M Schumacher 16-18,22-23,25-44 (25).

10 Sep 1995　　**ITALY: Monza**　　　　　　　　　　　　　　　　**(Round 12)**　　**(Race 576)**

53 laps x 5.770 km, 3.585 miles = 305.772 km, 189.998 miles

Pos	No	Driver	Car	Model	Engine		Laps	Time/Reason for Retirement	Grid Pos	Row
1	2	J Herbert	Benetton	B195	Renault	V10	53	1h 18m 27.916s	8	4
2	8	M Häkkinen	McLaren	MP4/10B	Mercedes-Benz	V10	53	1h 18m 45.695s	7	4
3	30	H-H Frentzen	Sauber	C14	Ford Cosworth	V8	53	1h 18m 52.237s	10	5
4	7	M Blundell	McLaren	MP4/10B	Mercedes-Benz	V10	53	1h 18m 56.139s	9	5
5	4	M Salo	Tyrrell	023	Yamaha	V10	52		16	8
6	29	J-C Boullion	Sauber	C14	Ford Cosworth	V8	52		14	7
7	9	M Papis	Footwork	FA16	Hart	V8	52		15	8
8	10	T Inoue	Footwork	FA16	Hart	V8	52		20	10
9	21	P Diniz	Forti	FG01-95	Ford Cosworth	V8	50		23	12
10	3	U Katayama	Tyrrell	023	Yamaha	V10	47		17	9
r	27	J Alesi	Ferrari	412T2	Ferrari	V12	45	rear wheel bearing	5	3
r	14	R Barrichello	Jordan	195	Peugeot	V10	43	hydraulics	6	3
r	15	E Irvine	Jordan	195	Peugeot	V10	40	oil pressure / engine	12	6
r	28	G Berger	Ferrari	412T2	Ferrari	V12	32	front suspension (Alesi's camera)	3	2
r	24	L Badoer	Minardi	M195	Ford Cosworth	V8	26	accident	18	9
r	1	M Schumacher	Benetton	B195	Renault	V10	23	accident	2	1
r	5	D Hill	Williams	FW17	Renault	V10	23	accident	4	2
r	26	O Panis	Ligier	JS41	Mugen Honda	V10	20	spin	13	7
r	6	D Coulthard	Williams	FW17	Renault	V10	13	front wheel bearing / spin	1	1
r	25	M Brundle	Ligier	JS41	Mugen Honda	V10	10	rear tyre	11	6
r	16	G Lavaggi	Pacific	PR02	Ford Cosworth	V8	6	spin	24	12
r	23	P Lamy	Minardi	M195	Ford Cosworth	V8	0	differential	19	10
r	22	R Moreno	Forti	FG01-95	Ford Cosworth	V8	0	accident *	22	11
r	17	A Montermini	Pacific	PR02	Ford Cosworth	V8	0	accident *	21	11

Winning speed 233.814 km/h, 145.286 mph
Pole Position speed 245.933 km/h, 152.816 mph (D Coulthard, 1 min:24.462 sec)
Fastest Lap speed 240.363 km/h, 149.355 mph (G Berger, 1 min:26.419 sec on lap 24)
Lap Leaders D Coulthard 1-13 (13); G Berger 14-24 (11); J Alesi 25,30-45 (17); R Barrichello 26 (1); M Häkkinen 27 (1); J Herbert 28-29,46-53 (10).

*Interrupted after first lap accident. Restarted for original distance. * Retired after first start.*

---

24 Sep 1995　　**PORTUGAL: Estoril**　　　　　　　　　　　　　　**(Round 13)**　　**(Race 577)**

71 laps x 4.360 km, 2.709 miles = 309.545 km, 192.342 miles

Pos	No	Driver	Car	Model	Engine		Laps	Time/Reason for Retirement	Grid Pos	Row
1	6	D Coulthard	Williams	FW17	Renault	V10	71	1h 41m 52.145s	1	1
2	1	M Schumacher	Benetton	B195	Renault	V10	71	1h 41m 59.393s	3	2
3	5	D Hill	Williams	FW17	Renault	V10	71	1h 42m 14.266s	2	1
4	28	G Berger	Ferrari	412T2	Ferrari	V12	71	1h 43m 17.024s	4	2
5	27	J Alesi	Ferrari	412T2	Ferrari	V12	71	1h 43m 17.574s	7	4
6	30	H-H Frentzen	Sauber	C14	Ford Cosworth	V8	70		5	3
7	2	J Herbert	Benetton	B195	Renault	V10	70		6	3
8	25	M Brundle	Ligier	JS41	Mugen Honda	V10	70		9	5
9	7	M Blundell	McLaren	MP4/10C	Mercedes-Benz	V10	70		12	6
10	15	E Irvine	Jordan	195	Peugeot	V10	70		10	5
11	14	R Barrichello	Jordan	195	Peugeot	V10	70		8	4
12	29	J-C Boullion	Sauber	C14	Ford Cosworth	V8	70		14	7
13	4	M Salo	Tyrrell	023	Yamaha	V10	69		15	8
14	24	L Badoer	Minardi	M195	Ford Cosworth	V8	68		18	9
15	10	T Inoue	Footwork	FA16	Hart	V8	68		19	10
16	21	P Diniz	Forti	FG01-95	Ford Cosworth	V8	66		22	11
17	22	R Moreno	Forti	FG01-95	Ford Cosworth	V8	64		23	12
r	17	A Montermini	Pacific	PR02	Ford Cosworth	V8	53	gearbox	21	11
r	8	M Häkkinen	McLaren	MP4/10B	Mercedes-Benz	V10	44	engine	13	7
r	16	J-D Deletraz	Pacific	PR02	Ford Cosworth	V8	14	driver discomfort (cramp)	24	12
r	26	O Panis	Ligier	JS41	Mugen Honda	V10	10	spin	11	6
r	23	P Lamy	Minardi	M195	Ford Cosworth	V8	7	hydraulics	17	9
r	3	U Katayama	Tyrrell	023	Yamaha	V10	0	accident *	16	8
r	9	M Papis	Footwork	FA16	Hart	V8	0	gearbox *	20	10

Winning speed 182.319 km/h, 113.288 mph
Pole Position speed 194.891 km/h, 121.100 mph (D Coulthard, 1 min:20.537 sec)
Fastest Lap speed 188.608 km/h, 117.196 mph (D Coulthard, 1 min:23.220 sec on lap 2)
Lap Leaders D Coulthard 1-38,44-71 (66); D Hill 39-43 (5).

*Interrupted after first lap accident. Restarted for original distance. * Retired after first start.*

1 Oct 1995	EUROPE: Nürburgring						(Round 14)	(Race 578)	

67 laps x 4.556 km, 2.831 miles = 305.252 km, 189.675 miles

Pos	No	Driver	Car	Model	Engine		Laps	Time/Reason for Retirement	Grid Pos	Row
1	1	M Schumacher	Benetton	B195	Renault	V10	67	1h 39m 59.044s	3	2
2	27	J Alesi	Ferrari	412T2	Ferrari	V12	67	1h 40m 01.728s	6	3
3	6	D Coulthard	Williams	FW17B	Renault	V10	67	1h 40m 34.426s	1	1
4	14	R Barrichello	Jordan	195	Peugeot	V10	66		11	6
5	2	J Herbert	Benetton	B195	Renault	V10	66		7	4
6	15	E Irvine	Jordan	195	Peugeot	V10	66		5	3
7	25	M Brundle	Ligier	JS41	Mugen Honda	V10	66		12	6
8	8	M Häkkinen	McLaren	MP4/10C	Mercedes-Benz	V10	65		9	5
9	23	P Lamy	Minardi	M195	Ford Cosworth	V8	64		16	8
10	4	M Salo	Tyrrell	023	Yamaha	V10	64		15	8
11	24	L Badoer	Minardi	M195	Ford Cosworth	V8	64		18	9
12	9	M Papis	Footwork	FA16	Hart	V8	64		17	9
13	21	P Diniz	Forti	FG01-95	Ford Cosworth	V8	62		22	11
14	3	G Tarquini	Tyrrell	023	Yamaha	V10	61		19	10
15	16	J-D Deletraz	Pacific	PR02	Ford Cosworth	V8	60		24	12
r	5	D Hill	Williams	FW17B	Renault	V10	58	accident	2	1
r	17	A Montermini	Pacific	PR02	Ford Cosworth	V8	45	out of fuel	20	10
r	29	J-C Boullion	Sauber	C14	Ford Cosworth	V8	44	accident	13	7
r	28	G Berger	Ferrari	412T2	Ferrari	V12	40	electronics	4	2
r	22	R Moreno	Forti	FG01-95	Ford Cosworth	V8	22	driveshaft	23	12
r	30	H-H Frentzen	Sauber	C14	Ford Cosworth	V8	17	accident	8	4
r	26	O Panis	Ligier	JS41	Mugen Honda	V10	14	spin	14	7
r	7	M Blundell	McLaren	MP4/10C	Mercedes-Benz	V10	14	spin	10	5
r	10	T Inoue	Footwork	FA16	Hart	V8	0	electronic control system on grid	21	11

Winning speed 183.180 km/h, 113.823 mph
Pole Position speed 208.306 km/h, 129.435 mph (D Coulthard, 1 min:18.738 sec)
Fastest Lap speed 202.039 km/h, 125.542 mph (M Schumacher, 1 min:21.180 sec on lap 57)
Lap Leaders D Coulthard 1-12 (12); J Alesi 13-64 (52); M Schumacher 65-67 (3).

Scheduled for 68 laps but reduced to 67 due to aborted start and extra parade lap.

22 Oct 1995	PACIFIC: Aida						(Round 15)	(Race 579)	

83 laps x 3.703 km, 2.301 miles = 307.349 km, 190.978 miles

Pos	No	Driver	Car	Model	Engine		Laps	Time/Reason for Retirement	Grid Pos	Row
1	1	M Schumacher	Benetton	B195	Renault	V10	83	1h 48m 49.972s	3	2
2	6	D Coulthard	Williams	FW17B	Renault	V10	83	1h 49m 04.892s	1	1
3	5	D Hill	Williams	FW17B	Renault	V10	83	1h 49m 38.305s	2	1
4	28	G Berger	Ferrari	412T2	Ferrari	V12	82		5	3
5	27	J Alesi	Ferrari	412T2	Ferrari	V12	82		4	2
6	2	J Herbert	Benetton	B195	Renault	V10	82		7	4
7	30	H-H Frentzen	Sauber	C14	Ford Cosworth	V8	82		8	4
8	26	O Panis	Ligier	JS41	Mugen Honda	V10	81		9	5
9	7	M Blundell	McLaren	MP4/10B	Mercedes-Benz	V10	81		10	5
10	8	J Magnussen	McLaren	MP4/10B	Mercedes-Benz	V10	81		12	6
11	15	E Irvine	Jordan	195	Peugeot	V10	81		6	3
12	4	M Salo	Tyrrell	023	Yamaha	V10	80		18	9
13	23	P Lamy	Minardi	M195	Ford Cosworth	V8	80		14	7
14	3	U Katayama	Tyrrell	023	Yamaha	V10	80		17	9
15	24	L Badoer	Minardi	M195	Ford Cosworth	V8	80		16	8
16	22	R Moreno	Forti	FG01-95	Ford Cosworth	V8	78		22	11
17	21	P Diniz	Forti	FG01-95	Ford Cosworth	V8	77		21	11
r	14	R Barrichello	Jordan	195	Peugeot	V10	67	engine	11	6
r	9	G Morbidelli	Footwork	FA16	Hart	V8	53	engine	19	10
r	10	T Inoue	Footwork	FA16	Hart	V8	38	engine	20	10
r	17	A Montermini	Pacific	PR02	Ford Cosworth	V8	14	gearbox	23	12
r	25	A Suzuki	Ligier	JS41	Mugen Honda	V10	10	spin	13	7
r	29	J-C Boullion	Sauber	C14	Ford Cosworth	V8	7	spin	15	8
r	16	B Gachot	Pacific	PR02	Ford Cosworth	V8	2	hydraulics	24	12

Winning speed 169.442 km/h, 105.287 mph
Pole Position speed 180.114 km/h, 111.918 mph (D Coulthard, 1 min:14.013 sec)
Fastest Lap speed 174.546 km/h, 108.458 mph (M Schumacher, 1 min:16.374 sec on lap 40)
Lap Leaders D Coulthard 1-49 (49); M Schumacher 50-83 (34).

29 Oct 1995   JAPAN: Suzuka   (Round 16)   (Race 580)

53 laps x 5.864 km, 3.644 miles = 310.588 km, 192.989 miles

Pos	No	Driver	Car	Model	Engine		Laps	Time/Reason for Retirement	Grid Pos	Row
1	1	M Schumacher	Benetton	B195	Renault	V10	53	1h 36m 52.930s	1	1
2	8	M Häkkinen	McLaren	MP4/10B	Mercedes-Benz	V10	53	1h 37m 12.267s	3	2
3	2	J Herbert	Benetton	B195	Renault	V10	53	1h 38m 16.734s	9	5
4	15	E Irvine	Jordan	195	Peugeot	V10	53	1h 38m 35.066s	7	4
5	26	O Panis	Ligier	JS41	Mugen Honda	V10	52		11	6
6	4	M Salo	Tyrrell	023	Yamaha	V10	52		12	6
7	7	M Blundell	McLaren	MP4/10B	Mercedes-Benz	V10	52		23	12
8	30	H-H Frentzen	Sauber	C14	Ford Cosworth	V8	52		8	4
9	24	L Badoer	Minardi	M195	Ford Cosworth	V8	51		17	9
10	29	K Wendlinger	Sauber	C14	Ford Cosworth	V8	51		15	8
11	23	P Lamy	Minardi	M195	Ford Cosworth	V8	51		16	8
12	10	T Inoue	Footwork	FA16	Hart	V8	51		18	9
r	5	D Hill	Williams	FW17B	Renault	V10	40	spin	4	2
r	6	D Coulthard	Williams	FW17B	Renault	V10	39	accident	6	3
r	21	P Diniz	Forti	FG01-95	Ford Cosworth	V8	32	spin	20	10
r	27	J Alesi	Ferrari	412T2	Ferrari	V12	24	differential	2	1
r	17	A Montermini	Pacific	PR02	Ford Cosworth	V8	23	spin	19	10
r	28	G Berger	Ferrari	412T2	Ferrari	V12	16	electronics sensor	5	3
r	14	R Barrichello	Jordan	195	Peugeot	V10	15	accident	10	5
r	3	U Katayama	Tyrrell	023	Yamaha	V10	12	accident	13	7
r	16	B Gachot	Pacific	PR02	Ford Cosworth	V8	6	driveshaft bearing	22	11
r	22	R Moreno	Forti	FG01-95	Ford Cosworth	V8	1	gearbox	21	11
r	9	G Morbidelli	Footwork	FA16	Hart	V8	0	spin	14	7
ns	25	A Suzuki	Ligier	JS41	Mugen Honda	V10		accident / injury		

Winning speed 192.349 km/h, 119.521 mph
Pole Position speed 215.361 km/h, 133.820 mph (M Schumacher, 1 min:38.023 sec)
Fastest Lap speed 205.003 km/h, 127.383 mph (M Schumacher, 1 min:42.976 sec on lap 33)
Lap Leaders M Schumacher 1-10,12-31;36-53 (48); M Häkkinen 11 (1); D Hill 32-35 (4).

12 Nov 1995   AUSTRALIA: Adelaide   (Round 17)   (Race 581)

81 laps x 3.780 km, 2.349 miles = 306.180 km, 190.251 miles

Pos	No	Driver	Car	Model	Engine		Laps	Time/Reason for Retirement	Grid Pos	Row
1	5	D Hill	Williams	FW17B	Renault	V10	81	1h 49m 15.946s	1	1
2	26	O Panis	Ligier	JS41	Mugen Honda	V10	79		12	6
3	9	G Morbidelli	Footwork	FA16	Hart	V8	79		13	7
4	7	M Blundell	McLaren	MP4/10B	Mercedes-Benz	V10	79		10	5
5	4	M Salo	Tyrrell	023	Yamaha	V10	78		14	7
6	23	P Lamy	Minardi	M195	Ford Cosworth	V8	78		17	9
7	21	P Diniz	Forti	FG01-95	Ford Cosworth	V8	77		21	11
8	16	B Gachot	Pacific	PR02	Ford Cosworth	V8	76		23	12
r	3	U Katayama	Tyrrell	023	Yamaha	V10	70	oil pressure / engine	16	8
r	2	J Herbert	Benetton	B195	Renault	V10	69	driveshaft	8	4
r	15	E Irvine	Jordan	195	Peugeot	V10	62	hydraulics	9	5
r	30	H-H Frentzen	Sauber	C14	Ford Cosworth	V8	39	gearbox	6	3
r	28	G Berger	Ferrari	412T2	Ferrari	V12	34	engine	4	2
r	25	M Brundle	Ligier	JS41	Mugen Honda	V10	29	accident	11	6
r	1	M Schumacher	Benetton	B195	Renault	V10	25	accident / rear suspension	3	2
r	27	J Alesi	Ferrari	412T2	Ferrari	V12	23	accident / front suspension	5	3
r	22	R Moreno	Forti	FG01-95	Ford Cosworth	V8	21	accident	20	10
r	14	R Barrichello	Jordan	195	Peugeot	V10	20	accident	7	4
r	6	D Coulthard	Williams	FW17B	Renault	V10	19	accident	2	1
r	10	T Inoue	Footwork	FA16	Hart	V8	15	accident	19	10
r	29	K Wendlinger	Sauber	C14	Ford Cosworth	V8	8	withdrew (neck injury)	18	9
r	17	A Montermini	Pacific	PR02	Ford Cosworth	V8	2	gearbox / spin	22	11
ns	24	L Badoer	Minardi	M195	Ford Cosworth	V8		electrics on dummy grid	15	8
ns	8	M Häkkinen	McLaren	MP4/10B	Mercedes-Benz	V10		rear tyre / accident / injury		

Winning speed 168.129 km/h, 104.471 mph
Pole Position speed 180.226 km/h, 111.988 mph (D Hill, 1 min:15.505 sec)
Fastest Lap speed 174.589 km/h, 108.485 mph (D Hill, 1 min:17.943 sec on lap 16)
Lap Leaders D Coulthard 1-19 (19); M Schumacher 20-21 (2); D Hill 22-81 (60).

Lap Leaders 1995

Pos	Driver	Car-Engine	GPs	laps	km	miles
1	M Schumacher	Benetton-Renault	14	454	2,170.7	1,348.8
2	D Hill	Williams-Renault	12	336	1,437.1	893.0
3	D Coulthard	Williams-Renault	11	191	842.0	523.2
4	J Alesi	Ferrari	6	91	435.1	270.3
5	J Herbert	Benetton-Renault	3	27	149.4	92.8
6	G Berger	Ferrari	2	22	117.3	72.9
7	M Häkkinen	McLaren-Mercedes-Benz	2	2	11.6	7.2
8	R Barrichello	Jordan-Peugeot	1	1	5.8	3.6
			17	1,124	5,169.0	3,211.9

Driver Points 1995

	Driver	BR	RA	RSM	E	MC	CDN	F	GB	D	H	B	I	P	EUR	PAC	J	AUS	Total
1	M Schumacher	10	4	-	10	10	2	10	-	10	-	10	-	6	10	10	10	-	102
2	D Hill	-	10	10	3	6	-	6	-	-	10	6	-	4	-	4	-	10	69
3	D Coulthard	6	-	3	-	-	-	4	4	6	6	-	-	10	4	6	-	-	49
4	J Herbert	-	3	-	6	3	-	-	10	3	3	-	10	-	2	1	4	-	45
5	J Alesi	2	6	6	-	-	10	2	6	-	-	-	-	2	6	2	-	-	42
6	G Berger	4	1	4	4	4	-	-	-	4	4	-	-	3	-	3	-	-	31
7	M Häkkinen	3	-	2	-	-	-	-	-	-	-	-	6	-	-	-	6	-	17
8	O Panis	-	-	-	1	-	3	-	3	-	1	-	-	-	-	-	2	6	16
9	H-H Frentzen	-	2	1	-	1	-	-	1	-	2	3	4	1	-	-	-	-	15
10	M Blundell	1	-	-	-	2	-	-	2	-	-	2	3	-	-	-	-	3	13
11	R Barrichello	-	-	-	-	-	6	1	-	-	-	1	-	-	3	-	-	-	11
12	E Irvine	-	-	-	2	-	4	-	-	-	-	-	-	-	1	-	3	-	10
13	M Brundle	-	-	-	-	-	-	3	-	-	-	4	-	-	-	-	-	-	7
14	M Salo	-	-	-	-	-	-	-	-	-	-	-	2	-	-	-	1	2	5
	G Morbidelli	-	-	-	-	-	1	-	-	-	-	-	-	-	-	-	-	4	5
16	J-C Boullion	-	-	-	-	-	-	-	-	2	-	-	1	-	-	-	-	-	3
17	A Suzuki	-	-	-	-	-	-	-	1	-	-	-	-	-	-	-	-	-	1
	P Lamy	-	-	-	-	-	-	-	-	-	-	-	-	-	-	-	-	1	1

10,6,4,3,2 and 1 point awarded to the first six finishers.

Constructor Points 1995

	Constructor	BR	RA	RSM	E	MC	CDN	F	GB	D	H	B	I	P	EUR	PAC	J	AUS	Total
1	Benetton-Renault	-	7	-	16	13	2	10	10	13	3	10	10	6	12	11	14	-	137
2	Williams-Renault	-	10	13	3	6	-	10	4	6	16	6	-	14	4	10	-	10	112
3	Ferrari	6	7	10	4	4	10	2	6	4	4	-	-	5	6	5	-	-	73
4	McLaren-Mercedes-Benz	4	-	2	-	2	-	-	2	-	-	2	9	-	-	-	6	3	30
5	Ligier-Mugen Honda	-	-	-	1	-	3	3	3	1	1	4	-	-	-	-	2	6	24
6	Jordan-Peugeot	-	-	-	2	-	10	1	-	-	-	1	-	-	4	-	3	-	21
7	Sauber-Ford Cosworth	-	2	1	-	1	-	-	1	2	2	3	5	1	-	-	-	-	18
8	Footwork-Hart	-	-	-	-	-	1	-	-	-	-	-	-	-	-	-	-	4	5
	Tyrrell-Yamaha	-	-	-	-	-	-	-	-	-	-	-	2	-	-	-	1	2	5
10	Minardi-Ford Cosworth	-	-	-	-	-	-	-	-	-	-	-	-	-	-	-	-	1	1

10,6,4,3,2 and 1 point awarded to the first six finishers.

Race Entrants and Results

Safety was still very high on the priority list and driver protection continued with higher cockpit sides and removable padding around the drivers' heads. Jacques Villeneuve, the reigning IndyCar champion, landed a plum drive with the best team and his results were eagerly anticipated. The World Champion switched teams and joined Ferrari, knowing this first season would be spent developing the new V10 engine into a potential championship-winning car. The entry list was down to eleven teams and some races started with less than 20 cars on the grid. In an attempt to improve the television spectacle in the event of a wash-out, qualifying became restricted to one hour on the Saturday.

FERRARI
Scuderia Ferrari SpA: Schumacher, Irvine

BENETTON
Mild Seven Benetton Renault: Alesi, Berger

WILLIAMS
Rothmans Williams Renault: Hill, Villeneuve

McLAREN
Marlboro McLaren Mercedes: Häkkinen, Coulthard

LIGIER
Equipe Ligier Gauloises Blondes: Panis, Diniz

JORDAN
Benson & Hedges Jordan Peugeot: Barrichello, Brundle

SAUBER
Red Bull Sauber Ford: Herbert, Frentzen

FOOTWORK
Footwork Hart / TWR Arrows: Rosset, Verstappen

TYRRELL
Tyrrell Yamaha: Katayama, Salo

MINARDI
Minardi Team: Lamy, Fisichella, Marques, Lavaggi

FORTI
Forti Grand Prix: Badoer, Montermini

10 Mar 1996		AUSTRALIA: Melbourne							(Round 1)	(Race 582)	
		58 laps x 5.302 km, 3.295 miles = 307.516 km, 191.082 miles									
Pos	No	Driver	Car	Model	Engine		Laps	Time/Reason for Retirement		Grid Pos	Row
1	5	D Hill	Williams	FW18	Renault	V10	58	1h 32m 50.491s		2	1
2	6	J Villeneuve	Williams	FW18	Renault	V10	58	1h 33m 28.511s		1	1
3	2	E Irvine	Ferrari	F310	Ferrari	V10	58	1h 33m 53.062s		3	2
4	4	G Berger	Benetton	B196	Renault	V10	58	1h 34m 07.528s		7	4
5	7	M Häkkinen	McLaren	MP4/11	Mercedes-Benz	V10	58	1h 34m 25.562s		5	3
6	19	M Salo	Tyrrell	024	Yamaha	V10	57			10	5
7	9	O Panis	Ligier	JS43	Mugen Honda	V10	57			11	6
8	15	H-H Frentzen	Sauber	C15	Ford Cosworth	V10	57			9	5
9	16	R Rosset	Footwork	FA17	Hart	V8	56			18	9
10	10	P Diniz	Ligier	JS43	Mugen Honda	V10	56			20	10
11	18	U Katayama	Tyrrell	024	Yamaha	V10	55			15	8
r	20	P Lamy	Minardi	M195B	Ford Cosworth	V8	42	accident / loose seat belts		17	9
r	1	M Schumacher	Ferrari	F310	Ferrari	V10	32	brake fluid loss		4	2
r	21	G Fisichella	Minardi	M195B	Ford Cosworth	V8	32	clutch		16	8
r	11	R Barrichello	Jordan	196	Peugeot	V10	29	engine		8	4
r	8	D Coulthard	McLaren	MP4/11	Mercedes-Benz	V10	24	throttle jammed		13	7
r	17	J Verstappen	Footwork	FA17	Hart	V8	15	engine		12	6
r	3	J Alesi	Benetton	B196	Renault	V10	9	accident		6	3
r	12	M Brundle	Jordan	196	Peugeot	V10	1	spin		19	10
r	14	J Herbert	Sauber	C15	Ford Cosworth	V10	0	accident *		14	7
nq	22	L Badoer	Forti	FG01-95B	Ford Cosworth	V8					
nq	23	A Montermini	Forti	FG01-95B	Ford Cosworth	V8					

Winning speed 198.736 km/h, 123.489 mph
Pole Position speed 206.636 km/h, 128.398 mph (J Villeneuve, 1 min:32.371 sec)
Fastest Lap speed 204.313 km/h, 126.955 mph (J Villeneuve, 1 min:33.421 sec on lap 27)
Lap Leaders J Villeneuve 1-29,33-53 (50); D Hill 30-32,54-58 (8).

*Interrupted after first lap accident. Restarted for original distance. * Retired after first start.*

BRAZIL: Interlagos (Round 2) (Race 583)

71 laps x 4.325 km, 2.687 miles = 307.075 km, 190.808 miles

Pos	No	Driver	Car	Model	Engine		Laps	Time/Reason for Retirement	Grid Pos	Row
1	5	D Hill	Williams	FW18	Renault	V10	71	1h 49m 52.976s	1	1
2	3	J Alesi	Benetton	B196	Renault	V10	71	1h 50m 10.958s	5	3
3	1	M Schumacher	Ferrari	F310	Ferrari	V10	70		4	2
4	7	M Häkkinen	McLaren	MP4/11	Mercedes-Benz	V10	70		7	4
5	19	M Salo	Tyrrell	024	Yamaha	V10	70		11	6
6	9	O Panis	Ligier	JS43	Mugen Honda	V10	70		15	8
7	2	E Irvine	Ferrari	F310	Ferrari	V10	70		10	5
8	10	P Diniz	Ligier	JS43	Mugen Honda	V10	69		22	11
9	18	U Katayama	Tyrrell	024	Yamaha	V10	69		16	8
10	20	P Lamy	Minardi	M195B	Ford Cosworth	V8	68		18	9
11	22	L Badoer	Forti	FG01-95B	Ford Cosworth	V8	67		19	10
12r	12	M Brundle	Jordan	196	Peugeot	V10	64	spin	6	3
r	11	R Barrichello	Jordan	196	Peugeot	V10	59	spin	2	1
r	15	H-H Frentzen	Sauber	C15	Ford Cosworth	V10	36	engine	9	5
r	8	D Coulthard	McLaren	MP4/11	Mercedes-Benz	V10	29	spin	14	7
r	14	J Herbert	Sauber	C15	Ford Cosworth	V10	28	engine	12	6
r	6	J Villeneuve	Williams	FW18	Renault	V10	26	spin	3	2
r	4	G Berger	Benetton	B196	Renault	V10	26	hydraulics	8	4
r	23	A Montermini	Forti	FG01-95B	Ford Cosworth	V8	26	spin	20	10
r	16	R Rosset	Footwork	FA17	Hart	V8	24	accident	17	9
r	17	J Verstappen	Footwork	FA17	Hart	V8	19	engine	13	7
r	21	T Marques	Minardi	M195B	Ford Cosworth	V8	0	spin	21	11

Winning speed 167.673 km/h, 104.188 mph
Pole Position speed 199.331 km/h, 123.859 mph (D Hill, 1 min:18.111 sec)
Fastest Lap speed 190.932 km/h, 118.640 mph (D Hill, 1 min:21.547 sec on lap 65)
Lap Leaders D Hill 1-39,43-71 (68); J Alesi 40-42 (3).

P Diniz (qualified 18th) and T Marques (qualified 19th) were penalised for irregularities and demoted to the back row of the grid.

---

7 Apr 1996 **ARGENTINA: Buenos Aires** (Round 3) (Race 584)

72 laps x 4.259 km, 2.646 miles = 306.484 km, 190.440 miles

Pos	No	Driver	Car	Model	Engine		Laps	Time/Reason for Retirement	Grid Pos	Row
1	5	D Hill	Williams	FW18	Renault	V10	72	1h 54m 55.322s	1	1
2	6	J Villeneuve	Williams	FW18	Renault	V10	72	1h 55m 07.489s	3	2
3	3	J Alesi	Benetton	B196	Renault	V10	72	1h 55m 10.076s	4	2
4	11	R Barrichello	Jordan	196	Peugeot	V10	72	1h 55m 50.453s	6	3
5	2	E Irvine	Ferrari	F310	Ferrari	V10	72	1h 56m 00.313s	10	5
6	17	J Verstappen	Footwork	FA17	Hart	V8	72	1h 56m 04.235s	7	4
7	8	D Coulthard	McLaren	MP4/11	Mercedes-Benz	V10	72	1h 56m 08.722s	9	5
8	9	O Panis	Ligier	JS43	Mugen Honda	V10	72	1h 56m 09.617s	12	6
9	14	J Herbert	Sauber	C15	Ford Cosworth	V10	71		17	9
10	23	A Montermini	Forti	FG01-95B	Ford Cosworth	V8	69		22	11
r	4	G Berger	Benetton	B196	Renault	V10	56	rear suspension	5	3
r	1	M Schumacher	Ferrari	F310	Ferrari	V10	46	rear wing / handling	2	1
r	20	P Lamy	Minardi	M195B	Ford Cosworth	V8	39	differential	19	10
r	19	M Salo	Tyrrell	024	Yamaha	V10	36	throttle jammed	16	8
r	12	M Brundle	Jordan	196	Peugeot	V10	34	accident / rear wing	15	8
r	21	T Marques	Minardi	M195B	Ford Cosworth	V8	33	accident	14	7
r	15	H-H Frentzen	Sauber	C15	Ford Cosworth	V10	32	spin	11	6
r	10	P Diniz	Ligier	JS43	Mugen Honda	V10	29	fuel leak / fire	18	9
r	18	U Katayama	Tyrrell	024	Yamaha	V10	28	transmission	13	7
r	16	R Rosset	Footwork	FA17	Hart	V8	24	fuel pump	20	10
r	22	L Badoer	Forti	FG01-95B	Ford Cosworth	V8	24	accident	21	11
r	7	M Häkkinen	McLaren	MP4/11	Mercedes-Benz	V10	19	throttle valve	8	4

Winning speed 160.013 km/h, 99.428 mph
Pole Position speed 169.707 km/h, 105.451 mph (D Hill, 1 min:30.346 sec)
Fastest Lap speed 171.478 km/h, 106.552 mph (J Alesi, 1 min:29.413 sec on lap 66)
Lap Leaders D Hill 1-72 (72).

---

28 Apr 1996 **EUROPE: Nürburgring** (Round 4) (Race 585)

67 laps x 4.556 km, 2.831 miles = 305.252 km, 189.675 miles

Pos	No	Driver	Car	Model	Engine		Laps	Time/Reason for Retirement	Grid Pos	Row
1	6	J Villeneuve	Williams	FW18	Renault	V10	67	1h 33m 26.473s	2	1
2	1	M Schumacher	Ferrari	F310	Ferrari	V10	67	1h 33m 27.235s	3	2
3	8	D Coulthard	McLaren	MP4/11	Mercedes-Benz	V10	67	1h 33m 59.307s	6	3
4	5	D Hill	Williams	FW18	Renault	V10	67	1h 33m 59.984s	1	1
5	11	R Barrichello	Jordan	196	Peugeot	V10	67	1h 34m 00.186s	5	3
6	12	M Brundle	Jordan	196	Peugeot	V10	67	1h 34m 22.040s	11	6
7	14	J Herbert	Sauber	C15	Ford Cosworth	V10	67	1h 34m 44.500s	12	6
8	7	M Häkkinen	McLaren	MP4/11	Mercedes-Benz	V10	67	1h 34m 44.911s	9	5
9	4	G Berger	Benetton	B196	Renault	V10	67	1h 34m 47.534s	8	4
dq	19	M Salo	Tyrrell	024	Yamaha	V10	66	car under weight	14	7
10	10	P Diniz	Ligier	JS43	Mugen Honda	V10	66		17	9
dq	18	U Katayama	Tyrrell	024	Yamaha	V10	65	push start on grid	16	8

Grand Prix Data Book

Pos	No	Driver	Car	Model	Engine		Laps	Time/Reason for Retirement	Grid Pos	Row
11	16	R Rosset	Footwork	FA17	Hart	V8	65		20	10
12	20	P Lamy	Minardi	M195B	Ford Cosworth	V8	65		19	10
13	21	G Fisichella	Minardi	M195B	Ford Cosworth	V8	65		18	9
r	15	H-H Frentzen	Sauber	C15	Ford Cosworth	V10	59	handling / spin	10	5
r	17	J Verstappen	Footwork	FA17	Hart	V8	38	gearbox	13	7
r	9	O Panis	Ligier	JS43	Mugen Honda	V10	6	accident	15	8
r	2	E Irvine	Ferrari	F310	Ferrari	V10	6	spin	7	4
r	3	J Alesi	Benetton	B196	Renault	V10	1	accident	4	2
nq	23	A Montermini	Forti	FG03-96	Ford Cosworth	V8				
nq	22	L Badoer	Forti	FG03-96	Ford Cosworth	V8				

Winning speed 196.006 km/h, 121.793 mph
Pole Position speed 207.770 km/h, 129.103 mph (D Hill, 1 min:18.941 sec)
Fastest Lap speed 201.585 km/h, 125.259 mph (D Hill, 1 min:21.363 sec on lap 55)
Lap Leaders J Villeneuve 1-67 (67).

5 May 1996		**SAN MARINO: Imola**							**(Round 5)**	**(Race 586)**
		63 laps x 4.892 km, 3.040 miles = 308.196 km, 191.504 miles								
Pos	No	Driver	Car	Model	Engine		Laps	Time/Reason for Retirement	Grid Pos	Row
1	5	D Hill	Williams	FW18	Renault	V10	63	1h 35m 26.156s	2	1
2	1	M Schumacher	Ferrari	F310	Ferrari	V10	63	1h 35m 42.616s	1	1
3	4	G Berger	Benetton	B196	Renault	V10	63	1h 36m 13.047s	7	4
4	2	E Irvine	Ferrari	F310	Ferrari	V10	63	1h 36m 27.739s	6	3
5	11	R Barrichello	Jordan	196	Peugeot	V10	63	1h 36m 44.646s	9	5
6	3	J Alesi	Benetton	B196	Renault	V10	62		5	3
7	10	P Diniz	Ligier	JS43	Mugen Honda	V10	62		17	9
8r	7	M Häkkinen	McLaren	MP4/11	Mercedes-Benz	V10	61	engine	11	6
9	20	P Lamy	Minardi	M195B	Ford Cosworth	V8	61		18	9
10	22	L Badoer	Forti	FG03-96	Ford Cosworth	V8	59		21	11
11r	6	J Villeneuve	Williams	FW18	Renault	V10	57	rear suspension	3	2
r	9	O Panis	Ligier	JS43	Mugen Honda	V10	54	gearbox	13	7
r	18	U Katayama	Tyrrell	024	Yamaha	V10	45	transmission	16	8
r	8	D Coulthard	McLaren	MP4/11	Mercedes-Benz	V10	44	hydraulics	4	2
r	16	R Rosset	Footwork	FA17	Hart	V8	40	engine	20	10
r	17	J Verstappen	Footwork	FA17	Hart	V8	38	refuelling hose attached	14	7
r	12	M Brundle	Jordan	196	Peugeot	V10	36	spin	12	6
r	15	H-H Frentzen	Sauber	C15	Ford Cosworth	V10	32	brakes	10	5
r	21	G Fisichella	Minardi	M195B	Ford Cosworth	V8	30	engine	19	10
r	14	J Herbert	Sauber	C15	Ford Cosworth	V10	25	electronics / misfire	15	8
r	19	M Salo	Tyrrell	024	Yamaha	V10	23	engine	8	4
nq	23	A Montermini	Forti	FG01-95B	Ford Cosworth	V8				

Winning speed 193.760 km/h, 120.397 mph
Pole Position speed 202.683 km/h, 125.942 mph (M Schumacher, 1 min:26.890 sec)
Fastest Lap speed 198.032 km/h, 123.051 mph (D Hill, 1 min:28.931 sec on lap 49)
Lap Leaders D Coulthard 1-19 (19); M Schumacher 20 (1); D Hill 21-63 (43).

19 May 1996		**MONACO: Monte-Carlo**							**(Round 6)**	**(Race 587)**
		75 laps x 3.328 km, 2.068 miles = 249.600 km, 155.094 miles								
Pos	No	Driver	Car	Model	Engine		Laps	Time/Reason for Retirement	Grid Pos	Row
1	9	O Panis	Ligier	JS43	Mugen Honda	V10	75	2h 00m 45.629s	14	7
2	8	D Coulthard	McLaren	MP4/11B	Mercedes-Benz	V10	75	2h 00m 50.457s	5	3
3	14	J Herbert	Sauber	C15	Ford Cosworth	V10	75	2h 01m 23.132s	13	7
4	15	H-H Frentzen	Sauber	C15	Ford Cosworth	V10	74	in pits at chequered flag	9	5
5r	19	M Salo	Tyrrell	024	Yamaha	V10	70	accident	11	6
6r	7	M Häkkinen	McLaren	MP4/11B	Mercedes-Benz	V10	70	accident	8	4
7r	2	E Irvine	Ferrari	F310	Ferrari	V10	68	accident	7	4
r	6	J Villeneuve	Williams	FW18	Renault	V10	66	accident	10	5
r	3	J Alesi	Benetton	B196	Renault	V10	60	rear suspension	3	2
r	22	L Badoer	Forti	FG03-96	Ford Cosworth	V8	60	accident	21	11
r	5	D Hill	Williams	FW18	Renault	V10	40	oil pump / engine	2	1
r	12	M Brundle	Jordan	196	Peugeot	V10	30	accident	16	8
r	4	G Berger	Benetton	B196	Renault	V10	9	gearbox sensor	4	2
r	10	P Diniz	Ligier	JS43	Mugen Honda	V10	5	transmission / spin	17	9
r	16	R Rosset	Footwork	FA17	Hart	V8	3	accident	20	10
r	18	U Katayama	Tyrrell	024	Yamaha	V10	2	throttle jammed / accident	15	8
r	1	M Schumacher	Ferrari	F310	Ferrari	V10	0	accident	1	1
r	11	R Barrichello	Jordan	196	Peugeot	V10	0	accident	6	3
r	17	J Verstappen	Footwork	FA17	Hart	V8	0	spin	12	6
r	20	P Lamy	Minardi	M195B	Ford Cosworth	V8	0	accident	19	10
r	21	G Fisichella	Minardi	M195B	Ford Cosworth	V8	0	accident	18	9
ns	23	A Montermini	Forti	FG03-96	Ford Cosworth	V8		accident	22	11

Winning speed 124.014 km/h, 77.059 mph
Pole Position speed 149.096 km/h, 92.644 mph (M Schumacher, 1 min:20.356 sec)
Fastest Lap speed 140.611 km/h, 87.372 mph (J Alesi, 1 min:25.205 sec on lap 59)
Lap Leaders D Hill 1-27,30-40 (38); J Alesi 28-29,41-59 (21); O Panis 60-75 (16).

Scheduled for 78 laps, but stopped at 2 hours.

2 Jun 1996   SPAIN: Montmeló   (Round 7)   (Race 588)

65 laps x 4.727 km, 2.937 miles = 307.114 km, 190.832 miles

Pos	No	Driver	Car	Model	Engine		Laps	Time/Reason for Retirement	Grid Pos	Row
1	1	M Schumacher	Ferrari	F310	Ferrari	V10	65	1h 59m 49.307s	3	2
2	3	J Alesi	Benetton	B196	Renault	V10	65	2h 00m 34.609s	4	2
3	6	J Villeneuve	Williams	FW18	Renault	V10	65	2h 00m 37.695s	2	1
4	15	H-H Frentzen	Sauber	C15	Ford Cosworth	V10	64		11	6
5	7	M Häkkinen	McLaren	MP4/11	Mercedes-Benz	V10	64		10	5
6	10	P Diniz	Ligier	JS43	Mugen Honda	V10	63		17	9
r	17	J Verstappen	Footwork	FA17	Hart	V8	47	spin	13	7
r	11	R Barrichello	Jordan	196	Peugeot	V10	45	differential	7	4
r	4	G Berger	Benetton	B196	Renault	V10	44	spin	5	3
r	14	J Herbert	Sauber	C15	Ford Cosworth	V10	20	spin	9	5
r	12	M Brundle	Jordan	196	Peugeot	V10	17	differential	15	8
dq	19	M Salo	Tyrrell	024	Yamaha	V10	16	changed car after parade lap	12	6
r	5	D Hill	Williams	FW18	Renault	V10	10	spin	1	1
r	18	U Katayama	Tyrrell	024	Yamaha	V10	8	electrics	16	8
r	2	E Irvine	Ferrari	F310	Ferrari	V10	1	spin	6	3
r	9	O Panis	Ligier	JS43	Mugen Honda	V10	1	accident damage	8	4
r	21	G Fisichella	Minardi	M195B	Ford Cosworth	V8	1	accident damage	19	10
r	8	D Coulthard	McLaren	MP4/11	Mercedes-Benz	V10	0	accident	14	7
r	16	R Rosset	Footwork	FA17	Hart	V8	0	accident	20	10
r	20	P Lamy	Minardi	M195B	Ford Cosworth	V8	0	accident	18	9
nq	22	L Badoer	Forti	FG01-95B	Ford Cosworth	V8				
nq	23	A Montermini	Forti	FG01-95B	Ford Cosworth	V8				

Winning speed 153.785 km/h, 95.558 mph
Pole Position speed 211.000 km/h, 131.110 mph (D Hill, 1 min:20.650 sec)
Fastest Lap speed 161.274 km/h, 100.211 mph (M Schumacher, 1 min:45.517 sec on lap 14)
Lap Leaders J Villeneuve 1-11 (11); M Schumacher 12-65 (54).

16 Jun 1996   CANADA: Montréal   (Round 8)   (Race 589)

69 laps x 4.421 km, 2.747 miles = 305.049 km, 189.549 miles

Pos	No	Driver	Car	Model	Engine		Laps	Time/Reason for Retirement	Grid Pos	Row
1	5	D Hill	Williams	FW18	Renault	V10	69	1h 36m 03.465s	1	1
2	6	J Villeneuve	Williams	FW18	Renault	V10	69	1h 36m 07.648s	2	1
3	3	J Alesi	Benetton	B196	Renault	V10	69	1h 36m 58.121s	4	2
4	8	D Coulthard	McLaren	MP4/11	Mercedes-Benz	V10	69	1h 37m 07.138s	10	5
5	7	M Häkkinen	McLaren	MP4/11	Mercedes-Benz	V10	68		6	3
6	12	M Brundle	Jordan	196	Peugeot	V10	68		9	5
7	14	J Herbert	Sauber	C15	Ford Cosworth	V10	68		15	8
8	21	G Fisichella	Minardi	M195B	Ford Cosworth	V8	67		16	8
r	20	P Lamy	Minardi	M195B	Ford Cosworth	V8	44	accident	19	10
r	22	L Badoer	Forti	FG03-96	Ford Cosworth	V8	44	gearbox	20	10
r	4	G Berger	Benetton	B196	Renault	V10	42	spin	7	4
r	1	M Schumacher	Ferrari	F310	Ferrari	V10	41	driveshaft	3	2
r	9	O Panis	Ligier	JS43	Mugen Honda	V10	39	alternator	11	6
r	19	M Salo	Tyrrell	024	Yamaha	V10	39	engine	14	7
r	10	P Diniz	Ligier	JS43	Mugen Honda	V10	38	engine	18	9
r	11	R Barrichello	Jordan	196	Peugeot	V10	22	clutch	8	4
r	23	A Montermini	Forti	FG03-96	Ford Cosworth	V8	22	loose ballast	22	11
r	15	H-H Frentzen	Sauber	C15	Ford Cosworth	V10	19	gearbox	12	6
r	17	J Verstappen	Footwork	FA17	Hart	V8	10	engine	13	7
r	16	R Rosset	Footwork	FA17	Hart	V8	6	accident	21	11
r	18	U Katayama	Tyrrell	024	Yamaha	V10	6	accident	17	9
r	2	E Irvine	Ferrari	F310	Ferrari	V10	1	steering push-rod	5	3

Winning speed 190.541 km/h, 118.397 mph
Pole Position speed 196.345 km/h, 122.004 mph (D Hill, 1 min:21.059 sec)
Fastest Lap speed 194.291 km/h, 120.727 mph (J Villeneuve, 1 min:21.916 sec on lap 67)
Lap Leaders D Hill 1-27,36-69 (61); J Villeneuve 28-35 (8).

30 Jun 1996   FRANCE: Magny-Cours   (Round 9)   (Race 590)

72 laps x 4.250 km, 2.641 miles = 305.814 km, 190.024 miles

Pos	No	Driver	Car	Model	Engine		Laps	Time/Reason for Retirement	Grid Pos	Row
1	5	D Hill	Williams	FW18	Renault	V10	72	1h 36m 28.795s	2	1
2	6	J Villeneuve	Williams	FW18	Renault	V10	72	1h 36m 36.922s	6	3
3	3	J Alesi	Benetton	B196	Renault	V10	72	1h 37m 15.237s	3	2
4	4	G Berger	Benetton	B196	Renault	V10	72	1h 37m 15.654s	4	2
5	7	M Häkkinen	McLaren	MP4/11	Mercedes-Benz	V10	72	1h 37m 31.569s	5	3
6	8	D Coulthard	McLaren	MP4/11	Mercedes-Benz	V10	71		7	4
7	9	O Panis	Ligier	JS43	Mugen Honda	V10	71		9	5
8	12	M Brundle	Jordan	196	Peugeot	V10	71		8	4
9	11	R Barrichello	Jordan	196	Peugeot	V10	71		10	5
10	19	M Salo	Tyrrell	024	Yamaha	V10	70		13	7
dq	14	J Herbert	Sauber	C15	Ford Cosworth	V10	70	bodywork infringement	16	8
11	16	R Rosset	Footwork	FA17	Hart	V8	69		19	10
12	20	P Lamy	Minardi	M195B	Ford Cosworth	V8	69		18	9

Pos	No	Driver	Car	Model	Engine		Laps	Time/Reason for Retirement	Grid Pos	Row
r	15	H-H Frentzen	Sauber	C15	Ford Cosworth	V10	56	throttle jammed / spin	12	6
r	18	U Katayama	Tyrrell	024	Yamaha	V10	33	engine	14	7
r	22	L Badoer	Forti	FG03-96	Ford Cosworth	V8	29	fuel pump	20	10
r	10	P Diniz	Ligier	JS43	Mugen Honda	V10	28	engine pneumatic valve system	11	6
r	17	J Verstappen	Footwork	FA17	Hart	V8	10	front steering / accident	15	8
r	2	E Irvine	Ferrari	F310	Ferrari	V10	5	gearbox	22	11
r	21	G Fisichella	Minardi	M195B	Ford Cosworth	V8	2	fuel pump	17	9
r	23	A Montermini	Forti	FG03-96	Ford Cosworth	V8	2	electrics	21	11
ns	1	M Schumacher	Ferrari	F310	Ferrari	V10		engine on parade lap	1	1

Winning speed 190.183 km/h, 118.174 mph
Pole Position speed 201.344 km/h, 125.110 mph (M Schumacher, 1 min:15.989 sec)
Fastest Lap speed 194.631 km/h, 120.939 mph (J Villeneuve, 1 min:18.610 sec on lap 48)
Lap Leaders D Hill 1-27,31-72 (69); J Villeneuve 28-30 (3).

E Irvine qualified 10th, but was placed at the back of the grid, due to a bodywork infringement.

14 Jul 1996   BRITAIN: Silverstone   (Round 10)   (Race 591)
61 laps x 5.072 km, 3.152 miles = 309.392 km, 192.247 miles

Pos	No	Driver	Car	Model	Engine		Laps	Time/Reason for Retirement	Grid Pos	Row
1	6	J Villeneuve	Williams	FW18	Renault	V10	61	1h 33m 00.874s	2	1
2	4	G Berger	Benetton	B196	Renault	V10	61	1h 33m 19.900s	7	4
3	7	M Häkkinen	McLaren	MP4/11B	Mercedes-Benz	V10	61	1h 33m 51.704s	4	2
4	11	R Barrichello	Jordan	196	Peugeot	V10	61	1h 34m 07.590s	6	3
5	8	D Coulthard	McLaren	MP4/11B	Mercedes-Benz	V10	61	1h 34m 23.381s	9	5
6	12	M Brundle	Jordan	196	Peugeot	V10	60		8	4
7	19	M Salo	Tyrrell	024	Yamaha	V10	60		14	7
8	15	H-H Frentzen	Sauber	C15	Ford Cosworth	V10	60		11	6
9	14	J Herbert	Sauber	C15	Ford Cosworth	V10	60		13	7
10	17	J Verstappen	Footwork	FA17	Hart	V8	60		15	8
11	21	G Fisichella	Minardi	M195B	Ford Cosworth	V8	59		18	9
r	3	J Alesi	Benetton	B196	Renault	V10	44	rear wheel bearing	5	3
r	9	O Panis	Ligier	JS43	Mugen Honda	V10	40	handling	16	8
r	10	P Diniz	Ligier	JS43	Mugen Honda	V10	38	engine	17	9
r	5	D Hill	Williams	FW18	Renault	V10	26	front wheel nut loose / spin	1	1
r	20	P Lamy	Minardi	M195B	Ford Cosworth	V8	21	hydraulics	19	10
r	16	R Rosset	Footwork	FA17	Hart	V8	13	alternator	20	10
r	18	U Katayama	Tyrrell	024	Yamaha	V10	12	engine overheating	12	6
r	2	E Irvine	Ferrari	F310	Ferrari	V10	5	differential bearing	10	5
r	1	M Schumacher	Ferrari	F310	Ferrari	V10	3	hydraulics	3	2
nq	23	A Montermini	Forti	FG03-96	Ford Cosworth	V8				
nq	22	L Badoer	Forti	FG03-96	Ford Cosworth	V8				

Winning speed 199.576 km/h, 124.011 mph
Pole Position speed 210.177 km/h, 130.598 mph (D Hill, 1 min:26.875 sec)
Fastest Lap speed 204.497 km/h, 127.069 mph (J Villeneuve, 1 min:29.288 sec on lap 21)
Lap Leaders J Villeneuve 1-23,31-61 (54); J Alesi 24-30 (7).

R Rosset qualified 17th, but was placed at the back of the grid, for failing to stop for scrutineering.

28 Jul 1996   GERMANY: Hockenheim   (Round 11)   (Race 592)
45 laps x 6.823 km, 4.240 miles = 307.022 km, 190.775 miles

Pos	No	Driver	Car	Model	Engine		Laps	Time/Reason for Retirement	Grid Pos	Row
1	5	D Hill	Williams	FW18	Renault	V10	45	1h 21m 43.417s	1	1
2	3	J Alesi	Benetton	B196	Renault	V10	45	1h 21m 54.869s	5	3
3	6	J Villeneuve	Williams	FW18	Renault	V10	45	1h 22m 17.343s	6	3
4	1	M Schumacher	Ferrari	F310	Ferrari	V10	45	1h 22m 24.934s	3	2
5	8	D Coulthard	McLaren	MP4/11B	Mercedes-Benz	V10	45	1h 22m 25.613s	7	4
6	11	R Barrichello	Jordan	196	Peugeot	V10	45	1h 23m 25.516s	9	5
7	9	O Panis	Ligier	JS43	Mugen Honda	V10	45	1h 23m 27.329s	12	6
8	15	H-H Frentzen	Sauber	C15	Ford Cosworth	V10	44		13	7
9	19	M Salo	Tyrrell	024	Yamaha	V10	44		15	8
10	12	M Brundle	Jordan	196	Peugeot	V10	44		10	5
11	16	R Rosset	Footwork	FA17	Hart	V8	44		19	10
12	20	P Lamy	Minardi	M195B	Ford Cosworth	V8	43		18	9
13r	4	G Berger	Benetton	B196	Renault	V10	42	engine	2	1
r	2	E Irvine	Ferrari	F310	Ferrari	V10	34	gearbox oil loss	8	4
r	14	J Herbert	Sauber	C15	Ford Cosworth	V10	25	gearbox	14	7
r	10	P Diniz	Ligier	JS43	Mugen Honda	V10	19	engine	11	6
r	18	U Katayama	Tyrrell	024	Yamaha	V10	19	accident	16	8
r	7	M Häkkinen	McLaren	MP4/11B	Mercedes-Benz	V10	13	gearbox	4	2
r	17	J Verstappen	Footwork	FA17	Hart	V8	0	accident	17	9
nq	21	G Lavaggi	Minardi	M195B	Ford Cosworth	V8				

Winning speed 225.409 km/h, 140.063 mph
Pole Position speed 236.380 km/h, 146.880 mph (D Hill, 1 min:43.912 sec)
Fastest Lap speed 230.627 km/h, 143.306 mph (D Hill, 1 min:46.504 sec on lap 26)
Lap Leaders G Berger 1-23,35-42 (31); D Hill 24-34,43-45 (14).

Races

11 Aug 1996   HUNGARY: Hungaroring   (Round 12)   (Race 593)

77 laps x 3.968 km, 2.466 miles = 305.536 km, 189.851 miles

Pos	No	Driver	Car	Model	Engine		Laps	Time/Reason for Retirement	Grid Pos	Row
1	6	J Villeneuve	Williams	FW18	Renault	V10	77	1h 46m 21.134s	3	2
2	5	D Hill	Williams	FW18	Renault	V10	77	1h 46m 21.905s	2	1
3	3	J Alesi	Benetton	B196	Renault	V10	77	1h 47m 45.346s	5	3
4	7	M Häkkinen	McLaren	MP4/11B	Mercedes-Benz	V10	76		7	4
5	9	O Panis	Ligier	JS43	Mugen Honda	V10	76		11	6
6	11	R Barrichello	Jordan	196	Peugeot	V10	75		13	7
7	18	U Katayama	Tyrrell	024	Yamaha	V10	74		14	7
8	16	R Rosset	Footwork	FA17	Hart	V8	74		18	9
9r	1	M Schumacher	Ferrari	F310	Ferrari	V10	70	throttle control unit	1	1
10r	21	G Lavaggi	Minardi	M195B	Ford Cosworth	V8	69	spin	20	10
r	4	G Berger	Benetton	B196	Renault	V10	64	engine	6	3
r	15	H-H Frentzen	Sauber	C15	Ford Cosworth	V10	50	engine	10	5
r	14	J Herbert	Sauber	C15	Ford Cosworth	V10	35	engine	8	4
r	2	E Irvine	Ferrari	F310	Ferrari	V10	31	gearbox oil temperature	4	2
r	20	P Lamy	Minardi	M195B	Ford Cosworth	V8	24	accident / rear suspension	19	10
r	8	D Coulthard	McLaren	MP4/11B	Mercedes-Benz	V10	23	water pump / engine / spin	9	5
r	17	J Verstappen	Footwork	FA17	Hart	V8	10	spin	17	9
r	12	M Brundle	Jordan	196	Peugeot	V10	5	accident	12	6
r	10	P Diniz	Ligier	JS43	Mugen Honda	V10	1	accident / rear suspension	15	8
r	19	M Salo	Tyrrell	024	Yamaha	V10	0	accident	16	8

Winning speed 172.372 km/h, 107.107 mph
Pole Position speed 185.206 km/h, 115.082 mph (M Schumacher, 1 min:17.129 sec)
Fastest Lap speed 178.352 km/h, 110.823 mph (D Hill, 1 min:20.093 sec on lap 67)
Lap Leaders M Schumacher 1-18 (18); J Villeneuve 19-21,25-58,64-77 (51); D Hill 22-24,59-63 (8).

25 Aug 1996   BELGIUM: Spa-Francorchamps   (Round 13)   (Race 594)

44 laps x 6.968 km, 4.330 miles = 306.592 km, 190.507 miles

Pos	No	Driver	Car	Model	Engine		Laps	Time/Reason for Retirement	Grid Pos	Row
1	1	M Schumacher	Ferrari	F310	Ferrari	V10	44	1h 28m 15.125s	3	2
2	6	J Villeneuve	Williams	FW18	Renault	V10	44	1h 28m 20.727s	1	1
3	7	M Häkkinen	McLaren	MP4/11B	Mercedes-Benz	V10	44	1h 28m 30.835s	6	3
4	3	J Alesi	Benetton	B196	Renault	V10	44	1h 28m 34.250s	7	4
5	5	D Hill	Williams	FW18	Renault	V10	44	1h 28m 44.304s	2	1
6	4	G Berger	Benetton	B196	Renault	V10	44	1h 28m 45.021s	5	3
7	19	M Salo	Tyrrell	024	Yamaha	V10	44	1h 29m 15.879s	13	7
8	18	U Katayama	Tyrrell	024	Yamaha	V10	44	1h 29m 55.352s	17	9
9	16	R Rosset	Footwork	FA17	Hart	V8	43		18	9
10	20	P Lamy	Minardi	M195B	Ford Cosworth	V8	43		19	10
r	8	D Coulthard	McLaren	MP4/11B	Mercedes-Benz	V10	37	spin	4	2
r	12	M Brundle	Jordan	196	Peugeot	V10	34	engine	8	4
r	2	E Irvine	Ferrari	F310	Ferrari	V10	29	gearbox	9	5
r	11	R Barrichello	Jordan	196	Peugeot	V10	29	accident / front suspension	10	5
r	10	P Diniz	Ligier	JS43	Mugen Honda	V10	22	ignition	15	8
r	17	J Verstappen	Footwork	FA17	Hart	V8	11	stub axle / accident	16	8
r	9	O Panis	Ligier	JS43	Mugen Honda	V10	0	accident	14	7
r	14	J Herbert	Sauber	C15	Ford Cosworth	V10	0	accident	12	6
r	15	H-H Frentzen	Sauber	C15	Ford Cosworth	V10	0	accident	11	6
nq	21	G Lavaggi	Minardi	M195B	Ford Cosworth	V8				

Winning speed 208.442 km/h, 129.520 mph
Pole Position speed 226.859 km/h, 140.964 mph (J Villeneuve, 1 min:50.574 sec)
Fastest Lap speed 221.857 km/h, 137.856 mph (G Berger, 1 min:53.067 sec on lap 42)
Lap Leaders J Villeneuve 1-14,30-32 (17); D Coulthard 15-21 (7); M Häkkinen 22-23 (2); M Schumacher 24-29,33-44 (18).

8 Sep 1996		ITALY: Monza					(Round 14)		(Race 595)	

53 laps x 5.770 km, 3.585 miles = 305.772 km, 189.998 miles

Pos	No	Driver	Car	Model	Engine		Laps	Time/Reason for Retirement	Grid Pos	Row
1	1	M Schumacher	Ferrari	F310	Ferrari	V10	53	1h 17m 43.632s	3	2
2	3	J Alesi	Benetton	B196	Renault	V10	53	1h 18m 01.897s	6	3
3	7	M Häkkinen	McLaren	MP4/11B	Mercedes-Benz	V10	53	1h 18m 50.267s	4	2
4	12	M Brundle	Jordan	196	Peugeot	V10	53	1h 19m 08.849s	9	5
5	11	R Barrichello	Jordan	196	Peugeot	V10	53	1h 19m 09.107s	10	5
6	10	P Diniz	Ligier	JS43	Mugen Honda	V10	52		14	7
7	6	J Villeneuve	Williams	FW18	Renault	V10	52		2	1
8	17	J Verstappen	Footwork	FA17	Hart	V8	52		15	8
9r	14	J Herbert	Sauber	C15	Ford Cosworth	V10	51	engine	12	6
10	18	U Katayama	Tyrrell	024	Yamaha	V10	51		16	8
r	16	R Rosset	Footwork	FA17	Hart	V8	36	accident	19	10
r	2	E Irvine	Ferrari	F310	Ferrari	V10	23	accident	7	4
r	20	P Lamy	Minardi	M195B	Ford Cosworth	V8	12	engine	18	9
r	19	M Salo	Tyrrell	024	Yamaha	V10	9	engine	17	9
r	15	H-H Frentzen	Sauber	C15	Ford Cosworth	V10	7	accident	13	7
r	5	D Hill	Williams	FW18	Renault	V10	5	accident	1	1
r	21	G Lavaggi	Minardi	M195B	Ford Cosworth	V8	5	engine	20	10
r	4	G Berger	Benetton	B196	Renault	V10	4	hydraulics	8	4
r	9	O Panis	Ligier	JS43	Mugen Honda	V10	2	accident	11	6
r	8	D Coulthard	McLaren	MP4/11B	Mercedes-Benz	V10	1	accident	5	3

Winning speed 236.034 km/h, 146.665 mph
Pole Position speed 246.686 km/h, 153.284 mph (D Hill, 1 min:24.204 sec)
Fastest Lap speed 241.226 km/h, 149.891 mph (M Schumacher, 1 min:26.110 sec on lap 50)
Lap Leaders D Hill 1-5 (5); J Alesi 6-30 (25); M Schumacher 31-53 (23).

22 Sep 1996		PORTUGAL: Estoril					(Round 15)		(Race 596)	

70 laps x 4.360 km, 2.709 miles = 305.200 km, 189.642 miles

Pos	No	Driver	Car	Model	Engine		Laps	Time/Reason for Retirement	Grid Pos	Row
1	6	J Villeneuve	Williams	FW18	Renault	V10	70	1h 40m 22.915s	2	1
2	5	D Hill	Williams	FW18	Renault	V10	70	1h 40m 42.881s	1	1
3	1	M Schumacher	Ferrari	F310	Ferrari	V10	70	1h 41m 16.680s	4	2
4	3	J Alesi	Benetton	B196	Renault	V10	70	1h 41m 18.024s	3	2
5	2	E Irvine	Ferrari	F310	Ferrari	V10	70	1h 41m 50.304s	6	3
6	4	G Berger	Benetton	B196	Renault	V10	70	1h 41m 56.056s	5	3
7	15	H-H Frentzen	Sauber	C15	Ford Cosworth	V10	69		11	6
8	14	J Herbert	Sauber	C15	Ford Cosworth	V10	69		12	6
9	12	M Brundle	Jordan	196	Peugeot	V10	69		10	5
10	9	O Panis	Ligier	JS43	Mugen Honda	V10	69		15	8
11	19	M Salo	Tyrrell	024	Yamaha	V10	69		13	7
12	18	U Katayama	Tyrrell	024	Yamaha	V10	68		14	7
13	8	D Coulthard	McLaren	MP4/11B	Mercedes-Benz	V10	68		8	4
14	16	R Rosset	Footwork	FA17	Hart	V8	67		17	9
15	21	G Lavaggi	Minardi	M195B	Ford Cosworth	V8	65		20	10
16	20	P Lamy	Minardi	M195B	Ford Cosworth	V8	65		19	10
r	7	M Häkkinen	McLaren	MP4/11B	Mercedes-Benz	V10	52	accident / handling	7	4
r	17	J Verstappen	Footwork	FA17	Hart	V8	47	engine	16	8
r	10	P Diniz	Ligier	JS43	Mugen Honda	V10	46	spin	18	9
r	11	R Barrichello	Jordan	196	Peugeot	V10	41	spin	9	5

Winning speed 182.423 km/h, 113.353 mph
Pole Position speed 195.393 km/h, 121.412 mph (D Hill, 1 min:20.330 sec)
Fastest Lap speed 189.398 km/h, 117.687 mph (J Villeneuve, 1 min:22.873 sec on lap 37)
Lap Leaders D Hill 1-17,22-33,36-48 (42); J Alesi 18-21 (4); J Villeneuve 34-35,49-70 (24).

13 Oct 1996 JAPAN: Suzuka (Round 16) (Race 597)

52 laps x 5.864 km, 3.644 miles = 304.718 km, 189.343 miles

Pos	No	Driver	Car	Model	Engine		Laps	Time/Reason for Retirement	Grid Pos	Row
1	5	D Hill	Williams	FW18	Renault	V10	52	1h 32m 33.791s	2	1
2	1	M Schumacher	Ferrari	F310	Ferrari	V10	52	1h 32m 35.674s	3	2
3	7	M Häkkinen	McLaren	MP4/11B	Mercedes-Benz	V10	52	1h 32m 37.003s	5	3
4	4	G Berger	Benetton	B196	Renault	V10	52	1h 33m 00.317s	4	2
5	12	M Brundle	Jordan	196	Peugeot	V10	52	1h 33m 40.911s	10	5
6	15	H-H Frentzen	Sauber	C15	Ford Cosworth	V10	52	1h 33m 54.977s	7	4
7	9	O Panis	Ligier	JS43	Mugen Honda	V10	52	1h 33m 58.301s	12	6
8	8	D Coulthard	McLaren	MP4/11B	Mercedes-Benz	V10	52	1h 33m 59.024s	8	4
9	11	R Barrichello	Jordan	196	Peugeot	V10	52	1h 34m 14.856s	11	6
10	14	J Herbert	Sauber	C15	Ford Cosworth	V10	52	1h 34m 15.590s	13	7
11	17	J Verstappen	Footwork	FA17	Hart	V8	51		17	9
12	20	P Lamy	Minardi	M195B	Ford Cosworth	V8	50		18	9
13	16	R Rosset	Footwork	FA17	Hart	V8	50		19	10
r	2	E Irvine	Ferrari	F310	Ferrari	V10	39	accident	6	3
r	18	U Katayama	Tyrrell	024	Yamaha	V10	37	engine	14	7
r	6	J Villeneuve	Williams	FW18	Renault	V10	36	rear wheel lost / accident	1	1
r	19	M Salo	Tyrrell	024	Yamaha	V10	20	engine	15	8
r	10	P Diniz	Ligier	JS43	Mugen Honda	V10	13	spin	16	8
r	3	J Alesi	Benetton	B196	Renault	V10	0	accident	9	5
nq	21	G Lavaggi	Minardi	M195B	Ford Cosworth	V8				

Winning speed 197.520 km/h, 122.733 mph
Pole Position speed 213.432 km/h, 132.621 mph (J Villeneuve, 1 min:38.909 sec)
Fastest Lap speed 202.900 km/h, 126.077 mph (J Villeneuve, 1 min:44.043 sec on lap 34)
Lap Leaders D Hill 1-52 (52).

Lap Leaders 1996

Pos	Driver	Car-Engine	GPs	laps	km	miles
1	D Hill	Williams-Renault	12	480	2,187.1	1,359.0
2	J Villeneuve	Williams-Renault	9	285	1,369.8	851.2
3	M Schumacher	Ferrari	5	114	589.7	366.4
4	J Alesi	Benetton-Renault	5	60	280.1	174.0
5	G Berger	Benetton-Renault	1	31	211.5	131.4
6	D Coulthard	McLaren-Mercedes-Benz	2	26	141.7	88.1
7	O Panis	Ligier-Mugen Honda	1	16	53.2	33.1
8	M Häkkinen	McLaren-Mercedes-Benz	1	2	13.9	8.7
			16	**1,014**	**4,847.1**	**3,011.8**

Driver Points 1996

		AUS	BR	RA	EUR	RSM	MC	E	CDN	F	GB	D	H	B	I	P	J	Total
1	D Hill	10	10	10	3	10	-	-	10	10	-	10	6	2	-	6	10	97
2	J Villeneuve	6	-	6	10	-	-	4	6	6	10	4	10	6	-	10	-	78
3	M Schumacher	-	4	-	6	6	-	10	-	-	-	3	-	10	10	4	6	59
4	J Alesi	-	6	4	-	1	-	6	4	4	-	6	4	3	6	3	-	47
5	M Häkkinen	2	3	-	-	-	1	2	2	2	4	-	3	4	4	-	4	31
6	G Berger	3	-	-	4	-	-	-	-	3	6	-	-	1	-	1	3	21
7	D Coulthard	-	-	-	4	-	6	-	3	1	2	2	-	-	-	-	-	18
8	R Barrichello	-	-	3	2	2	-	-	-	-	3	1	1	-	2	-	-	14
9	O Panis	-	1	-	-	-	10	-	-	-	-	-	2	-	-	-	-	13
10	E Irvine	4	-	2	-	3	-	-	-	-	-	-	-	-	-	2	-	11
11	M Brundle	-	-	-	1	-	-	-	1	-	1	-	-	-	3	-	2	8
12	H-H Frentzen	-	-	-	-	3	3	-	-	-	-	-	-	-	-	-	1	7
13	M Salo	1	2	-	-	2	-	-	-	-	-	-	-	-	-	-	-	5
14	J Herbert	-	-	-	-	4	-	-	-	-	-	-	-	-	-	-	-	4
15	P Diniz	-	-	-	-	-	-	1	-	-	-	-	-	-	1	-	-	2
16	J Verstappen	-	-	1	-	-	-	-	-	-	-	-	-	-	-	-	-	1

10,6,4,3,2 and 1 point awarded to the first six finishers.

Constructor Points 1996

		AUS	BR	RA	EUR	RSM	MC	E	CDN	F	GB	D	H	B	I	P	J	Total
1	Williams-Renault	16	10	16	13	10	-	4	16	16	10	14	16	8	-	16	10	175
2	Ferrari	4	4	2	6	9	-	10	-	-	-	3	-	10	10	6	6	70
3	Benetton-Renault	3	6	4	-	5	-	6	4	7	6	6	4	4	6	4	3	68
4	McLaren-Mercedes-Benz	2	3	-	4	-	7	2	5	3	6	2	3	4	4	-	4	49
5	Jordan-Peugeot	-	-	3	3	2	-	-	1	-	4	1	1	-	5	-	2	22
6	Ligier-Mugen Honda	-	1	-	-	-	10	1	-	-	-	-	2	-	1	-	-	15
7	Sauber-Ford Cosworth	-	-	-	-	-	-	7	3	-	-	-	-	-	-	-	1	11
8	Tyrrell-Yamaha	1	2	-	-	-	-	2	-	-	-	-	-	-	-	-	-	5
9	Footwork-Hart	-	-	1	-	-	-	-	-	-	-	-	-	-	-	-	-	1

10,6,4,3,2 and 1 point awarded to the first six finishers.

Grand Prix Data Book

1997

Race Entrants and Results

The new World Champion joined Tom Walkinshaw's Arrows team to help them find the elusive victory. Bridgestone tyres entered Grands Prix on a full time basis with Arrows, Prost, Minardi, Stewart and Lola. Former World Champions Alain Prost and Jackie Stewart became the newest team owners, with the Frenchman taking over Ligier and the Scotsman entering a new team with the help of Ford. Renault left victorious at the end of a season, which concluded in Europe for the first time since 1984.

ARROWS
Danka Arrows Yamaha: Hill, Diniz

WILLIAMS
Rothmans Williams Renault: Villeneuve, Frentzen

FERRARI
Scuderia Ferrari Marlboro: M Schumacher, Irvine

BENETTON
Mild Seven Benetton Renault: Alesi, Berger, Wurz

McLAREN
West McLaren Mercedes: Häkkinen, Coulthard

JORDAN
Benson & Hedges Total Jordan Peugeot: R Schumacher, Fisichella

PROST
Prost Gauloises Blondes: Panis, Nakano, Trulli

SAUBER
Red Bull Sauber Petronas: Herbert, Larini, Morbidelli, Fontana

TYRRELL
Tyrrell: Verstappen, Salo

MINARDI
Minardi Team: Katayama, Trulli, Marques

STEWART
Stewart Ford: Barrichello, Magnussen

LOLA
MasterCard Lola Formula One Team: Sospiri, Rosset

9 Mar 1997		AUSTRALIA: Melbourne							(Round 1)		(Race 598)
		58 laps x 5.302 km, 3.295 miles = 307.516 km, 191.082 miles									
Pos	No	Driver	Car	Model	Engine		Laps	Time/Reason for Retirement		Grid Pos	Row
1	10	D Coulthard	McLaren	MP4/12	Mercedes-Benz	V10	58	1h 30m 28.718s		4	2
2	5	M Schumacher	Ferrari	F310B	Ferrari	V10	58	1h 30m 48.764s		3	2
3	9	M Häkkinen	McLaren	MP4/12	Mercedes	V10	58	1h 30m 50.895s		6	3
4	8	G Berger	Benetton	B197	Renault	V10	58	1h 30m 51.559s		10	5
5	14	O Panis	Prost	JS45	Mugen Honda	V10	58	1h 31m 29.026s		9	5
6	17	N Larini	Sauber	C16	Petronas	V10	58	1h 32m 04.758s		13	7
7	15	S Nakano	Prost	JS45	Mugen Honda	V10	56			16	8
8r	4	H-H Frentzen	Williams	FW19	Renault	V10	55	front brake disc / spin		2	1
9	21	J Trulli	Minardi	M197	Hart	V8	55			17	9
10	2	P Diniz	Arrows	A18	Yamaha	V10	54			22	11
r	22	R Barrichello	Stewart	SF-1	Cosworth	V10	49	engine		11	6
r	19	M Salo	Tyrrell	025	Cosworth	V8	42	electrics		18	9
r	23	J Magnussen	Stewart	SF-1	Cosworth	V10	36	rear suspension		19	10
r	7	J Alesi	Benetton	B197	Renault	V10	34	out of fuel		8	4
r	20	U Katayama	Minardi	M197	Hart	V8	32	fuel pump		15	8
r	12	G Fisichella	Jordan	197	Peugeot	V10	14	spin		14	7
r	18	J Verstappen	Tyrrell	025	Cosworth	V8	2	accident		21	11
r	11	R Schumacher	Jordan	197	Peugeot	V10	1	gearbox		12	6
r	6	E Irvine	Ferrari	F310B	Ferrari	V10	0	accident / front tyre		5	3
r	3	J Villeneuve	Williams	FW19	Renault	V10	0	accident		1	1
r	16	J Herbert	Sauber	C16	Petronas	V10	0	accident		7	4
ns	1	D Hill	Arrows	A18	Yamaha	V10		throttle sensor on parade lap		20	10
nq	24	V Sospiri	Lola	T97/30	Cosworth	V8					
nq	25	R Rosset	Lola	T97/30	Cosworth	V8					

Winning speed 203.926 km/h, 126.714 mph
Pole Position speed 213.577 km/h, 132.711 mph (J Villeneuve, 1 min:29.369 sec)
Fastest Lap speed 210.710 km/h, 130.929 mph (H-H Frentzen, 1 min:30.585 sec on lap 36)
Lap Leaders H-H Frentzen 1-17,33-39 (24); D Coulthard 18-32,40-58 (34).

30 Mar 1997   BRAZIL: Interlagos   (Round 2)   (Race 599)

72 laps x 4.292 km, 2.667 miles = 309.024 km, 192.019 miles

Pos	No	Driver	Car	Model	Engine		Laps	Time/Reason for Retirement	Grid Pos	Row
1	3	J Villeneuve	Williams	FW19	Renault	V10	72	1h 36m 06.990s	1	1
2	8	G Berger	Benetton	B197	Renault	V10	72	1h 36m 11.180s	3	2
3	14	O Panis	Prost	JS45	Mugen Honda	V10	72	1h 36m 22.860s	5	3
4	9	M Häkkinen	McLaren	MP4/12	Mercedes	V10	72	1h 36m 40.023s	4	2
5	5	M Schumacher	Ferrari	F310B	Ferrari	V10	72	1h 36m 40.721s	2	1
6	7	J Alesi	Benetton	B197	Renault	V10	72	1h 36m 41.010s	6	3
7	16	J Herbert	Sauber	C16	Petronas	V10	72	1h 36m 57.902s	13	7
8	12	G Fisichella	Jordan	197	Peugeot	V10	72	1h 37m 07.629s	7	4
9	4	H-H Frentzen	Williams	FW19	Renault	V10	72	1h 37m 22.392s	8	4
10	10	D Coulthard	McLaren	MP4/12	Mercedes	V10	71		12	6
11	17	N Larini	Sauber	C16	Petronas	V10	71		19	10
12	21	J Trulli	Minardi	M197	Hart	V8	71		17	9
13	19	M Salo	Tyrrell	025	Cosworth	V8	71		22	11
14	15	S Nakano	Prost	JS45	Mugen Honda	V10	71		15	8
15	18	J Verstappen	Tyrrell	025	Cosworth	V8	70		21	11
16	6	E Irvine	Ferrari	F310B	Ferrari	V10	70		14	7
17r	1	D Hill	Arrows	A18	Yamaha	V10	68	oil leak / fire	9	5
18	20	U Katayama	Minardi	M197	Hart	V8	67		18	9
r	11	R Schumacher	Jordan	197	Peugeot	V10	52	electrics / fuel pump	10	5
r	22	R Barrichello	Stewart	SF-1	Cosworth	V10	16	rear suspension	11	6
r	2	P Diniz	Arrows	A18	Yamaha	V10	15	spin	16	8
r	23	J Magnussen	Stewart	SF-1	Cosworth	V10	0	accident *	20	10

Winning speed 192.905 km/h, 119.866 mph
Pole Position speed 203.294 km/h, 126.321 mph (J Villeneuve, 1 min:16.004 sec)
Fastest Lap speed 197.089 km/h, 122.466 mph (J Villeneuve, 1 min:18.397 sec on lap 28)
Lap Leaders J Villeneuve 1-45,49-72 (69); G Berger 46-48 (3).

*Race stopped and restarted for original distance after accidents on first lap. * Retired after first start.*

13 Apr 1997   ARGENTINA: Buenos Aires   (Round 3)   (Race 600)

72 laps x 4.259 km, 2.646 miles = 306.502 km, 190.452 miles

Pos	No	Driver	Car	Model	Engine		Laps	Time/Reason for Retirement	Grid Pos	Row
1	3	J Villeneuve	Williams	FW19	Renault	V10	72	1h 52m 01.715s	1	1
2	6	E Irvine	Ferrari	F310B	Ferrari	V10	72	1h 52m 02.694s	7	4
3	11	R Schumacher	Jordan	197	Peugeot	V10	72	1h 52m 13.804s	6	3
4	16	J Herbert	Sauber	C16	Petronas	V10	72	1h 52m 31.634s	8	4
5	9	M Häkkinen	McLaren	MP4/12	Mercedes	V10	72	1h 52m 32.066s	17	9
6	8	G Berger	Benetton	B197	Renault	V10	72	1h 52m 33.108s	12	6
7	7	J Alesi	Benetton	B197	Renault	V10	72	1h 52m 48.074s	11	6
8	19	M Salo	Tyrrell	025	Cosworth	V8	71		19	10
9	21	J Trulli	Minardi	M197	Hart	V8	71		18	9
10r	23	J Magnussen	Stewart	SF-1	Cosworth	V10	66	oil pressure / engine	15	8
r	17	N Larini	Sauber	C16	Petronas	V10	63	spin	14	7
r	2	P Diniz	Arrows	A18	Yamaha	V10	50	gearbox	22	11
r	15	S Nakano	Prost	JS45	Mugen Honda	V10	49	engine	20	10
r	18	J Verstappen	Tyrrell	025	Cosworth	V8	43	fuel pressure	16	8
r	20	U Katayama	Minardi	M197	Hart	V8	37	throttle stuck / spin	21	11
r	1	D Hill	Arrows	A18	Yamaha	V10	33	engine air pressure	13	7
r	12	G Fisichella	Jordan	197	Peugeot	V10	24	accident	9	5
r	22	R Barrichello	Stewart	SF-1	Cosworth	V10	24	hydraulics	5	3
r	14	O Panis	Prost	JS45	Mugen Honda	V10	18	pneumatic valve system	3	2
r	4	H-H Frentzen	Williams	FW19	Renault	V10	5	clutch	2	1
r	5	M Schumacher	Ferrari	F310B	Ferrari	V10	0	accident	4	2
r	10	D Coulthard	McLaren	MP4/12	Mercedes	V10	0	accident	10	5

Winning speed 164.155 km/h, 102.002 mph
Pole Position speed 181.506 km/h, 112.783 mph (J Villeneuve, 1 min:24.473 sec)
Fastest Lap speed 174.269 km/h, 108.286 mph (G Berger, 1 min:27.981 sec on lap 63)
Lap Leaders J Villeneuve 1-38,45-72 (66); E Irvine 39-44 (6).

27 Apr 1997   SAN MARINO: Imola   (Round 4)   (Race 601)

62 laps x 4.930 km, 3.063 miles = 305.660 km, 189.928 miles

Pos	No	Driver	Car	Model	Engine		Laps	Time/Reason for Retirement	Grid Pos	Row
1	4	H-H Frentzen	Williams	FW19	Renault	V10	62	1h 31m 00.673s	2	1
2	5	M Schumacher	Ferrari	F310B	Ferrari	V10	62	1h 31m 01.910s	3	2
3	6	E Irvine	Ferrari	F310B	Ferrari	V10	62	1h 32m 19.016s	9	5
4	12	G Fisichella	Jordan	197	Peugeot	V10	62	1h 32m 24.061s	6	3
5	7	J Alesi	Benetton	B197	Renault	V10	61		14	7
6	9	M Häkkinen	McLaren	MP4/12	Mercedes	V10	61		8	4
7	17	N Larini	Sauber	C16	Petronas	V10	61		12	6
8	14	O Panis	Prost	JS45	Mugen Honda	V10	61		4	2
9	19	M Salo	Tyrrell	025	Cosworth	V8	60		19	10
10	18	J Verstappen	Tyrrell	025	Cosworth	V8	60		21	11
11	20	U Katayama	Minardi	M197	Hart	V8	59		22	11
r	2	P Diniz	Arrows	A18	Yamaha	V10	53	hydraulics	17	9
r	3	J Villeneuve	Williams	FW19	Renault	V10	40	gearbox	1	1
r	10	D Coulthard	McLaren	MP4/12	Mercedes	V10	38	engine	10	5
r	22	R Barrichello	Stewart	SF-1	Cosworth	V10	32	engine	13	7
r	16	J Herbert	Sauber	C16	Petronas	V10	18	electrics	7	4
r	11	R Schumacher	Jordan	197	Peugeot	V10	17	driveshaft	5	3
r	15	S Nakano	Prost	JS45	Mugen Honda	V10	11	accident	18	9
r	1	D Hill	Arrows	A18	Yamaha	V10	11	accident	15	8
r	8	G Berger	Benetton	B197	Renault	V10	4	spin	11	6
r	23	J Magnussen	Stewart	SF-1	Cosworth	V10	2	spin	16	8
ns	21	J Trulli	Minardi	M197	Hart	V8		hydraulics on parade lap	20	10

Winning speed 201.509 km/h, 125.212 mph
Pole Position speed 213.053 km/h, 132.385 mph (J Villeneuve, 1 min:23.303 sec)
Fastest Lap speed 207.503 km/h, 128.937 mph (H-H Frentzen, 1 min:25.531 sec on lap 42)
Lap Leaders J Villeneuve 1-25 (25); H-H Frentzen 26-43,45-62 (36); M Schumacher 44 (1).

11 May 1997   MONACO: Monte-Carlo   (Round 5)   (Race 602)

62 laps x 3.366 km, 2.092 miles = 208.692 km, 129.675 miles

Pos	No	Driver	Car	Model	Engine		Laps	Time/Reason for Retirement	Grid Pos	Row
1	5	M Schumacher	Ferrari	F310B	Ferrari	V10	62	2h 00m 05.654s	2	1
2	22	R Barrichello	Stewart	SF-1	Cosworth	V10	62	2h 00m 58.960s	10	5
3	6	E Irvine	Ferrari	F310B	Ferrari	V10	62	2h 01m 27.762s	15	8
4	14	O Panis	Prost	JS45	Mugen Honda	V10	62	2h 01m 50.056s	12	6
5	19	M Salo	Tyrrell	025	Cosworth	V8	61		14	7
6	12	G Fisichella	Jordan	197	Peugeot	V10	61		4	2
7	23	J Magnussen	Stewart	SF-1	Cosworth	V10	61		19	10
8	18	J Verstappen	Tyrrell	025	Cosworth	V8	60		22	11
9	8	G Berger	Benetton	B197	Renault	V10	60		17	9
10	20	U Katayama	Minardi	M197	Hart	V8	60		20	10
r	4	H-H Frentzen	Williams	FW19	Renault	V10	39	accident	1	1
r	15	S Nakano	Prost	JS45	Mugen Honda	V10	36	accident	21	11
r	17	N Larini	Sauber	C16	Petronas	V10	24	accident	11	6
r	7	J Alesi	Benetton	B197	Renault	V10	16	spin	9	5
r	3	J Villeneuve	Williams	FW19	Renault	V10	16	accident / rear suspension	3	2
r	11	R Schumacher	Jordan	197	Peugeot	V10	10	accident	6	3
r	16	J Herbert	Sauber	C16	Petronas	V10	9	accident	7	4
r	21	J Trulli	Minardi	M197	Hart	V8	7	accident	18	9
r	10	D Coulthard	McLaren	MP4/12	Mercedes	V10	1	accident	5	3
r	9	M Häkkinen	McLaren	MP4/12	Mercedes	V10	1	accident	8	4
r	1	D Hill	Arrows	A18	Yamaha	V10	1	accident	13	7
r	2	P Diniz	Arrows	A18	Yamaha	V10	0	spin	16	8

Winning speed 104.264 km/h, 64.787 mph
Pole Position speed 154.924 km/h, 96.266 mph (H-H Frentzen, 1 min:18.216 sec)
Fastest Lap speed 106.937 km/h, 66.448 mph (M Schumacher, 1 min:53.315 sec on lap 26)
Lap Leaders M Schumacher 1-62 (62).

Races   397

25 May 1997   SPAIN: Montmeló   (Round 6)   (Race 603)

64 laps x 4.728 km, 2.938 miles = 302.469 km, 187.946 miles

Pos	No	Driver	Car	Model	Engine		Laps	Time/Reason for Retirement	Grid Pos	Row
1	3	J Villeneuve	Williams	FW19	Renault	V10	64	1h 30m 35.896s	1	1
2	14	O Panis	Prost	JS45	Mugen Honda	V10	64	1h 30m 41.700s	12	6
3	7	J Alesi	Benetton	B197	Renault	V10	64	1h 30m 48.430s	4	2
4	5	M Schumacher	Ferrari	F310B	Ferrari	V10	64	1h 30m 53.875s	7	4
5	16	J Herbert	Sauber	C16	Petronas	V10	64	1h 31m 03.882s	10	5
6	10	D Coulthard	McLaren	MP4/12	Mercedes	V10	64	1h 31m 05.640s	3	2
7	9	M Häkkinen	McLaren	MP4/12	Mercedes	V10	64	1h 31m 24.681s	5	3
8	4	H-H Frentzen	Williams	FW19	Renault	V10	64	1h 31m 40.035s	2	1
9	12	G Fisichella	Jordan	197	Peugeot	V10	64	1h 31m 40.663s	8	4
10	8	G Berger	Benetton	B197	Renault	V10	64	1h 31m 41.566s	6	3
11	18	J Verstappen	Tyrrell	025	Cosworth	V8	63		19	10
12	6	E Irvine	Ferrari	F310B	Ferrari	V10	63		11	6
13	23	J Magnussen	Stewart	SF-1	Cosworth	V10	63		22	11
14	17	G Morbidelli	Sauber	C16	Petronas	V10	62		13	7
15	21	J Trulli	Minardi	M197	Hart	V8	62		18	9
r	2	P Diniz	Arrows	A18	Yamaha	V10	53	engine	21	11
r	11	R Schumacher	Jordan	197	Peugeot	V10	50	oil leak / engine	9	5
r	22	R Barrichello	Stewart	SF-1	Cosworth	V10	37	engine	17	9
r	19	M Salo	Tyrrell	025	Cosworth	V8	35	rear tyre	14	7
r	15	S Nakano	Prost	JS45	Mugen Honda	V10	34	gearbox	16	8
r	1	D Hill	Arrows	A18	Yamaha	V10	18	oil pressure / engine	15	8
r	20	U Katayama	Minardi	M197	Hart	V8	11	hydraulics	20	10

Winning speed 200.314 km/h, 124.469 mph
Pole Position speed 222.421 km/h, 138.206 mph (J Villeneuve, 1 min:16.525 sec)
Fastest Lap speed 206.959 km/h, 128.599 mph (G Fisichella, 1 min:22.242 sec on lap 20)
Lap Leaders J Villeneuve 1-20,22-45,47-64 (62); J Alesi 21 (1); M Schumacher 46 (1).

Scheduled for 65 laps, but reduced by a lap, following G Berger and R Schumacher stalling on grid. Restarted for 64 laps.

15 Jun 1997   CANADA: Montréal   (Round 7)   (Race 604)

54 laps x 4.421 km, 2.747 miles = 238.734 km, 148.342 miles

Pos	No	Driver	Car	Model	Engine		Laps	Time/Reason for Retirement	Grid Pos	Row
1	5	M Schumacher	Ferrari	F310B	Ferrari	V10	54	1h 17m 40.646s	1	1
2	7	J Alesi	Benetton	B197	Renault	V10	54	1h 17m 43.211s	8	4
3	12	G Fisichella	Jordan	197	Peugeot	V10	54	1h 17m 43.865s	6	3
4	4	H-H Frentzen	Williams	FW19	Renault	V10	54	1h 17m 44.414s	4	2
5	16	J Herbert	Sauber	C16	Petronas	V10	54	1h 17m 45.362s	13	7
6	15	S Nakano	Prost	JS45	Mugen Honda	V10	54	1h 18m 17.347s	19	10
7	10	D Coulthard	McLaren	MP4/12	Mercedes	V10	54	1h 18m 18.399s	5	3
8	2	P Diniz	Arrows	A18	Yamaha	V10	53		16	8
9	1	D Hill	Arrows	A18	Yamaha	V10	53		15	8
10	17	G Morbidelli	Sauber	C16	Petronas	V10	53		18	9
11r	14	O Panis	Prost	JS45	Mugen Honda	V10	51	accident / injury	10	5
r	19	M Salo	Tyrrell	025	Cosworth	V8	46	engine	17	9
r	18	J Verstappen	Tyrrell	025	Cosworth	V8	42	gearbox	14	7
r	8	A Wurz	Benetton	B197	Renault	V10	35	transmission	11	6
r	22	R Barrichello	Stewart	SF-1	Cosworth	V10	33	gearbox	3	2
r	21	J Trulli	Minardi	M197	Hart	V8	32	engine	20	10
r	11	R Schumacher	Jordan	197	Peugeot	V10	14	accident	7	4
r	20	U Katayama	Minardi	M197	Hart	V8	5	throttle jammed / accident	22	11
r	3	J Villeneuve	Williams	FW19	Renault	V10	1	accident	2	1
r	6	E Irvine	Ferrari	F310B	Ferrari	V10	0	spin	12	6
r	9	M Häkkinen	McLaren	MP4/12	Mercedes	V10	0	accident / rear wing	9	5
r	23	J Magnussen	Stewart	SF-1	Cosworth	V10	0	accident	21	11

Winning speed 184.404 km/h, 114.583 mph
Pole Position speed 203.797 km/h, 126.634 mph (M Schumacher, 1 min:18.095 sec)
Fastest Lap speed 199.856 km/h, 124.185 mph (D Coulthard, 1 min:19.635 sec on lap 37)
Lap Leaders M Schumacher 1-27,40-43,52-54 (34); D Coulthard 28-39,44-51 (20).

Scheduled for 69 laps, but stopped early due to O Panis' accident.

FRANCE: Magny-Cours (Round 8) (Race 605)

72 laps x 4.250 km, 2.641 miles = 305.814 km, 190.024 miles

Pos	No	Driver	Car	Model	Engine		Laps	Time/Reason for Retirement	Grid Pos	Row
1	5	M Schumacher	Ferrari	F310B	Ferrari	V10	72	1h 38m 50.492s	1	1
2	4	H-H Frentzen	Williams	FW19	Renault	V10	72	1h 39m 14.029s	2	1
3	6	E Irvine	Ferrari	F310B	Ferrari	V10	72	1h 40m 05.293s	5	3
4	3	J Villeneuve	Williams	FW19	Renault	V10	72	1h 40m 12.276s	4	2
5	7	J Alesi	Benetton	B197	Renault	V10	72	1h 40m 13.227s	8	4
6	11	R Schumacher	Jordan	197	Peugeot	V10	72	1h 40m 20.363s	3	2
7r	10	D Coulthard	McLaren	MP4/12	Mercedes	V10	71	accident	9	5
8	16	J Herbert	Sauber	C16	Petronas	V10	71		14	7
9	12	G Fisichella	Jordan	197	Peugeot	V10	71		11	6
10	14	J Trulli	Prost	JS45	Mugen Honda	V10	70		6	3
11	20	U Katayama	Minardi	M197	Hart	V8	70		21	11
12	1	D Hill	Arrows	A18	Yamaha	V10	69		17	9
r	19	M Salo	Tyrrell	025	Cosworth	V8	61	electronics	19	10
r	8	A Wurz	Benetton	B197	Renault	V10	60	spin	7	4
r	2	P Diniz	Arrows	A18	Yamaha	V10	58	spin	16	8
r	17	N Fontana	Sauber	C16	Petronas	V10	40	spin	20	10
r	22	R Barrichello	Stewart	SF-1	Cosworth	V10	36	engine	13	7
r	23	J Magnussen	Stewart	SF-1	Cosworth	V10	33	brake duct loose / fire	15	8
r	9	M Häkkinen	McLaren	MP4/12	Mercedes	V10	18		10	5
r	18	J Verstappen	Tyrrell	025	Cosworth	V8	15	throttle stuck / accident	18	9
r	15	S Nakano	Prost	JS45	Mugen Honda	V10	7	spin	12	6
r	21	T Marques	Minardi	M197	Hart	V8	5	engine	22	11

Winning speed 185.638 km/h, 115.351 mph
Pole Position speed 205.236 km/h, 127.528 mph (M Schumacher, 1 min:14.548 sec)
Fastest Lap speed 196.380 km/h, 122.025 mph (M Schumacher, 1 min:17.910 sec on lap 37)
Lap Leaders M Schumacher 1-22,24-46,48-72 (70); H-H Frentzen 23,47 (2).

13 Jul 1997 **BRITAIN: Silverstone** (Round 9) (Race 606)

59 laps x 5.140 km, 3.194 miles = 303.260 km, 188.437 miles

Pos	No	Driver	Car	Model	Engine		Laps	Time/Reason for Retirement	Grid Pos	Row
1	3	J Villeneuve	Williams	FW19	Renault	V10	59	1h 28m 01.665s	1	1
2	7	J Alesi	Benetton	B197	Renault	V10	59	1h 28m 11.870s	11	6
3	8	A Wurz	Benetton	B197	Renault	V10	59	1h 28m 12.961s	8	4
4	10	D Coulthard	McLaren	MP4/12	Mercedes	V10	59	1h 28m 32.894s	6	3
5	11	R Schumacher	Jordan	197	Peugeot	V10	59	1h 28m 33.545s	5	3
6	1	D Hill	Arrows	A18	Yamaha	V10	59	1h 29m 15.217s	12	6
7	12	G Fisichella	Jordan	197	Peugeot	V10	58		10	5
8	14	J Trulli	Prost	JS45	Mugen Honda	V10	58		13	7
9	17	N Fontana	Sauber	C16	Petronas	V10	58		22	11
10	21	T Marques	Minardi	M197	Hart	V8	58		20	10
11r	15	S Nakano	Prost	JS45	Mugen Honda	V10	57	engine	14	7
r	9	M Häkkinen	McLaren	MP4/12	Mercedes	V10	52	engine	3	2
r	23	J Magnussen	Stewart	SF-1	Cosworth	V10	50	engine	15	8
r	18	J Verstappen	Tyrrell	025	Cosworth	V8	45	engine	19	10
r	6	E Irvine	Ferrari	F310B	Ferrari	V10	44	transmission	7	4
r	19	M Salo	Tyrrell	025	Cosworth	V8	44	engine	17	9
r	16	J Herbert	Sauber	C16	Petronas	V10	42	electronics	9	5
r	5	M Schumacher	Ferrari	F310B	Ferrari	V10	38	rear wheel bearing	4	2
r	22	R Barrichello	Stewart	SF-1	Cosworth	V10	37	engine	21	11
r	2	P Diniz	Arrows	A18	Yamaha	V10	29	engine	16	8
r	4	H-H Frentzen	Williams	FW19	Renault	V10	0	accident	2	1
r	20	U Katayama	Minardi	M197	Hart	V8	0	accident	18	9

Winning speed 206.702 km/h, 128.439 mph
Pole Position speed 226.770 km/h, 140.909 mph (J Villeneuve, 1 min:21.598 sec)
Fastest Lap speed 219.047 km/h, 136.110 mph (M Schumacher, 1 min:24.475 sec on lap 34)
Lap Leaders J Villeneuve 1-22,38-44,53-59 (36); M Schumacher 23-37 (15); M Häkkinen 45-52 (8).

27 Jul 1997   **GERMANY: Hockenheim**   **(Round 10)**   **(Race 607)**

45 laps x 6.823 km, 4.240 miles = 307.035 km, 190.783 miles

Pos	No	Driver	Car	Model	Engine		Laps	Time/Reason for Retirement	Grid Pos	Row
1	8	G Berger	Benetton	B197	Renault	V10	45	1h 20m 59.046s	1	1
2	5	M Schumacher	Ferrari	F310B	Ferrari	V10	45	1h 21m 16.573s	4	2
3	9	M Häkkinen	McLaren	MP4/12	Mercedes	V10	45	1h 21m 23.816s	3	2
4	14	J Trulli	Prost	JS45	Mugen Honda	V10	45	1h 21m 26.211s	11	6
5	11	R Schumacher	Jordan	197	Peugeot	V10	45	1h 21m 29.041s	7	4
6	7	J Alesi	Benetton	B197	Renault	V10	45	1h 21m 33.763s	6	3
7	15	S Nakano	Prost	JS45	Mugen Honda	V10	45	1h 22m 18.768s	17	9
8	1	D Hill	Arrows	A18	Yamaha	V10	44		13	7
9	17	N Fontana	Sauber	C16	Petronas	V10	44		18	9
10	18	J Verstappen	Tyrrell	025	Cosworth	V8	44		20	10
11r	12	G Fisichella	Jordan	197	Peugeot	V10	40	oil cooler	2	1
r	3	J Villeneuve	Williams	FW19	Renault	V10	33	spin	9	5
r	22	R Barrichello	Stewart	SF-1	Cosworth	V10	33	camshaft drivetrain	12	6
r	19	M Salo	Tyrrell	025	Cosworth	V8	33	clutch	19	10
r	23	J Magnussen	Stewart	SF-1	Cosworth	V10	27	engine overheating	15	8
r	20	U Katayama	Minardi	M197	Hart	V8	23	out of fuel	22	11
r	16	J Herbert	Sauber	C16	Petronas	V10	8	accident	14	7
r	2	P Diniz	Arrows	A18	Yamaha	V10	8	accident	16	8
r	10	D Coulthard	McLaren	MP4/12	Mercedes	V10	1	accident / transmission	8	4
r	4	H-H Frentzen	Williams	FW19	Renault	V10	1	accident damage	5	3
r	6	E Irvine	Ferrari	F310B	Ferrari	V10	1	accident damage	10	5
r	21	T Marques	Minardi	M197	Hart	V8	0	transmission	21	11

Winning speed 227.477 km/h, 141.348 mph
Pole Position speed 241.111 km/h, 149.820 mph (G Berger, 1 min:41.873 sec)
Fastest Lap speed 232.278 km/h, 144.331 mph (G Berger, 1 min:45.747 sec on lap 9)
Lap Leaders G Berger 1-17,25-45 (38); G Fisichella 18-24 (7).

---

10 Aug 1997   **HUNGARY: Hungaroring**   **(Round 11)**   **(Race 608)**

77 laps x 3.968 km, 2.466 miles = 305.536 km, 189.851 miles

Pos	No	Driver	Car	Model	Engine		Laps	Time/Reason for Retirement	Grid Pos	Row
1	3	J Villeneuve	Williams	FW19	Renault	V10	77	1h 45m 47.149s	2	1
2	1	D Hill	Arrows	A18	Yamaha	V10	77	1h 45m 56.228s	3	2
3	16	J Herbert	Sauber	C16	Petronas	V10	77	1h 46m 07.594s	10	5
4	5	M Schumacher	Ferrari	F310B	Ferrari	V10	77	1h 46m 17.650s	1	1
5	11	R Schumacher	Jordan	197	Peugeot	V10	77	1h 46m 17.864s	14	7
6	15	S Nakano	Prost	JS45	Mugen Honda	V10	77	1h 46m 28.661s	16	8
7	14	J Trulli	Prost	JS45	Mugen Honda	V10	77	1h 47m 02.701s	12	6
8	8	G Berger	Benetton	B197	Renault	V10	77	1h 47m 03.558s	7	4
9r	6	E Irvine	Ferrari	F310B	Ferrari	V10	76	accident	5	3
10	20	U Katayama	Minardi	M197	Hart	V8	76		20	10
11	7	J Alesi	Benetton	B197	Renault	V10	76		9	5
12	21	T Marques	Minardi	M197	Hart	V8	75		22	11
13	19	M Salo	Tyrrell	025	Cosworth	V8	75		21	11
r	10	D Coulthard	McLaren	MP4/12	Mercedes	V10	65	alternator	8	4
r	18	J Verstappen	Tyrrell	025	Cosworth	V8	61	hydraulics	18	9
r	2	P Diniz	Arrows	A18	Yamaha	V10	53	alternator	19	10
r	12	G Fisichella	Jordan	197	Peugeot	V10	42	spin	13	7
r	4	H-H Frentzen	Williams	FW19	Renault	V10	29	fuel filler valve	6	3
r	22	R Barrichello	Stewart	SF-1	Cosworth	V10	29	engine	11	6
r	9	M Häkkinen	McLaren	MP4/12	Mercedes	V10	12	hydraulics	4	2
r	17	G Morbidelli	Sauber	C16	Petronas	V10	7	engine	15	8
r	23	J Magnussen	Stewart	SF-1	Cosworth	V10	5	accident / steering	17	9

Winning speed 173.295 km/h, 107.681 mph
Pole Position speed 191.300 km/h, 118.869 mph (M Schumacher, 1 min:14.672 sec)
Fastest Lap speed 182.269 km/h, 113.257 mph (H-H Frentzen, 1 min:18.372 sec on lap 25)
Lap Leaders M Schumacher 1-10 (10); D Hill 11-25,30-76 (62); H-H Frentzen 26-29 (4); J Villeneuve 77 (1).

44 laps x 6.968 km, 4.330 miles = 306.577 km, 190.498 miles

Pos	No	Driver	Car	Model	Engine		Laps	Time/Reason for Retirement	Grid Pos	Row
1	5	M Schumacher	Ferrari	F310B	Ferrari	V10	44	1h 33m 46.717s	3	2
2	12	G Fisichella	Jordan	197	Peugeot	V10	44	1h 34m 13.470s	4	2
dq	9	M Häkkinen	McLaren	MP4/12	Mercedes	V10	44	1h 34m 17.573s	5	3
3	4	H-H Frentzen	Williams	FW19	Renault	V10	44	1h 34m 18.864s	7	4
4	16	J Herbert	Sauber	C16	Petronas	V10	44	1h 34m 25.742s	11	6
5	3	J Villeneuve	Williams	FW19	Renault	V10	44	1h 34m 28.820s	1	1
6	8	G Berger	Benetton	B197	Renault	V10	44	1h 34m 50.458s	15	8
7	2	P Diniz	Arrows	A18	Yamaha	V10	44	1h 35m 12.648s	8	4
8	7	J Alesi	Benetton	B197	Renault	V10	44	1h 35m 28.725s	2	1
9	17	G Morbidelli	Sauber	C16	Petronas	V10	44	1h 35m 29.299s	13	7
10r	6	E Irvine	Ferrari	F310B	Ferrari	V10	43	accident	17	9
11	19	M Salo	Tyrrell	025	Cosworth	V8	43		19	10
12	23	J Magnussen	Stewart	SF-1	Cosworth	V10	43		18	9
13r	1	D Hill	Arrows	A18	Yamaha	V10	42	front wheel nut	9	5
14r	20	U Katayama	Minardi	M197	Hart	V8	42	engine	20	10
15	14	J Trulli	Prost	JS45	Mugen Honda	V10	42		14	7
r	18	J Verstappen	Tyrrell	025	Cosworth	V8	25	spin	21	11
r	11	R Schumacher	Jordan	197	Peugeot	V10	21	accident	6	3
r	10	D Coulthard	McLaren	MP4/12	Mercedes	V10	19	spin	10	5
r	21	T Marques	Minardi	M197	Hart	V8	18	spin	22	11
r	22	R Barrichello	Stewart	SF-1	Cosworth	V10	8	accident	12	6
r	15	S Nakano	Prost	JS45	Mugen Honda	V10	5	gearbox electronics / spin	16	8

Winning speed 196.149 km/h, 121.882 mph
Pole Position speed 229.189 km/h, 142.412 mph (J Villeneuve, 1 min:49.450 sec)
Fastest Lap speed 222.596 km/h, 138.315 mph (J Villeneuve, 1 min:52.692 sec on lap 43)
Lap Leaders J Villeneuve 1-4 (4); M Schumacher 5-44 (40).

M Häkkinen disqualified for using illegal fuel.

53 laps x 5.770 km, 3.585 miles = 305.785 km, 190.006 miles

Pos	No	Driver	Car	Model	Engine		Laps	Time/Reason for Retirement	Grid Pos	Row
1	10	D Coulthard	McLaren	MP4/12	Mercedes	V10	53	1h 17m 04.609s	6	3
2	7	J Alesi	Benetton	B197	Renault	V10	53	1h 17m 06.546s	1	1
3	4	H-H Frentzen	Williams	FW19	Renault	V10	53	1h 17m 08.952s	2	1
4	12	G Fisichella	Jordan	197	Peugeot	V10	53	1h 17m 10.480s	3	2
5	3	J Villeneuve	Williams	FW19	Renault	V10	53	1h 17m 11.025s	4	2
6	5	M Schumacher	Ferrari	F310B	Ferrari	V10	53	1h 17m 16.090s	9	5
7	8	G Berger	Benetton	B197	Renault	V10	53	1h 17m 17.080s	7	4
8	6	E Irvine	Ferrari	F310B	Ferrari	V10	53	1h 17m 22.248s	10	5
9	9	M Häkkinen	McLaren	MP4/12	Mercedes	V10	53	1h 17m 53.982s	5	3
10	14	J Trulli	Prost	JS45	Mugen Honda	V10	53	1h 18m 07.315s	16	8
11	15	S Nakano	Prost	JS45	Mugen Honda	V10	53	1h 18m 07.936s	15	8
12	17	G Morbidelli	Sauber	C16	Petronas	V10	52		18	9
13	22	R Barrichello	Stewart	SF-1	Cosworth	V10	52		11	6
14	21	T Marques	Minardi	M197	Hart	V8	50		22	11
r	1	D Hill	Arrows	A18	Yamaha	V10	46	engine	14	7
r	11	R Schumacher	Jordan	197	Peugeot	V10	39	accident / rear suspension	8	4
r	16	J Herbert	Sauber	C16	Petronas	V10	38	accident	12	6
r	19	M Salo	Tyrrell	025	Cosworth	V8	33	engine	19	10
r	23	J Magnussen	Stewart	SF-1	Cosworth	V10	31	transmission	13	7
r	18	J Verstappen	Tyrrell	025	Cosworth	V8	12	hydraulics	20	10
r	20	U Katayama	Minardi	M197	Hart	V8	8	front wheel rim / tyre / accident	21	11
r	2	P Diniz	Arrows	A18	Yamaha	V10	4	rear suspension / spin	17	9

Winning speed 238.036 km/h, 147.909 mph
Pole Position speed 250.295 km/h, 155.526 mph (J Alesi, 1 min:22.990 sec)
Fastest Lap speed 244.929 km/h, 152.192 mph (M Häkkinen, 1 min:24.808 sec on lap 49)
Lap Leaders J Alesi 1-31 (31); M Häkkinen 32-33 (2); M Schumacher 34 (1); D Coulthard 35-53 (19).

21 Sep 1997   AUSTRIA: A1-Ring   (Round 14)   (Race 611)

71 laps x 4.323 km, 2.686 miles = 306.933 km, 190.719 miles

Pos	No	Driver	Car	Model	Engine		Laps	Time/Reason for Retirement	Grid Pos	Row
1	3	J Villeneuve	Williams	FW19	Renault	V10	71	1h 27m 35.999s	1	1
2	10	D Coulthard	McLaren	MP4/12	Mercedes	V10	71	1h 27m 38.908s	10	5
3	4	H-H Frentzen	Williams	FW19	Renault	V10	71	1h 27m 39.961s	4	2
4	12	G Fisichella	Jordan	197	Peugeot	V10	71	1h 27m 48.126s	14	7
5	11	R Schumacher	Jordan	197	Peugeot	V10	71	1h 28m 07.858s	11	6
6	5	M Schumacher	Ferrari	F310B	Ferrari	V10	71	1h 28m 09.409s	9	5
7	1	D Hill	Arrows	A18	Yamaha	V10	71	1h 28m 13.206s	7	4
8	16	J Herbert	Sauber	C16	Petronas	V10	71	1h 28m 25.056s	12	6
9	17	G Morbidelli	Sauber	C16	Petronas	V10	71	1h 28m 42.454s	13	7
10	8	G Berger	Benetton	B197	Renault	V10	70		18	9
11	20	U Katayama	Minardi	M197	Hart	V8	69		19	10
12	18	J Verstappen	Tyrrell	025	Cosworth	V8	69		20	10
13r	2	P Diniz	Arrows	A18	Yamaha	V10	67	rear suspension	17	9
14r	22	R Barrichello	Stewart	SF-1	Cosworth	V10	64	spin	5	3
r	14	J Trulli	Prost	JS45	Mugen Honda	V10	58	engine	3	2
r	23	J Magnussen	Stewart	SF-1	Cosworth	V10	58	engine	6	3
r	15	S Nakano	Prost	JS45	Mugen Honda	V10	57	engine	16	8
r	19	M Salo	Tyrrell	025	Cosworth	V8	48	gearbox	21	11
r	6	E Irvine	Ferrari	F310B	Ferrari	V10	38	accident / front suspension	8	4
r	7	J Alesi	Benetton	B197	Renault	V10	37	accident	15	8
r	9	M Häkkinen	McLaren	MP4/12	Mercedes	V10	1	engine	2	1
exc	21	T Marques	Minardi	M197	Hart	V8		car under weight during practice		

Winning speed 210.228 km/h, 130.630 mph
Pole Position speed 221.364 km/h, 137.549 mph (J Villeneuve, 1 min:10.304 sec)
Fastest Lap speed 216.709 km/h, 134.657 mph (J Villeneuve, 1 min:11.814 sec on lap 36)
Lap Leaders J Trulli 1-37 (37); J Villeneuve 38-40,44-71 (31); M Schumacher 41-42 (2); D Coulthard 43 (1).

T Marques qualified 21st but was excluded for car being under weight.

28 Sep 1997   LUXEMBOURG: Nürburgring   (Round 15)   (Race 612)

67 laps x 4.556 km, 2.831 miles = 305.235 km, 189.664 miles

Pos	No	Driver	Car	Model	Engine		Laps	Time/Reason for Retirement	Grid Pos	Row
1	3	J Villeneuve	Williams	FW19	Renault	V10	67	1h 31m 27.843s	2	1
2	7	J Alesi	Benetton	B197	Renault	V10	67	1h 31m 39.613s	10	5
3	4	H-H Frentzen	Williams	FW19	Renault	V10	67	1h 31m 41.323s	3	2
4	8	G Berger	Benetton	B197	Renault	V10	67	1h 31m 44.259s	7	4
5	2	P Diniz	Arrows	A18	Yamaha	V10	67	1h 32m 10.990s	15	8
6	14	O Panis	Prost	JS45	Mugen Honda	V10	67	1h 32m 11.593s	11	6
7	16	J Herbert	Sauber	C16	Petronas	V10	67	1h 32m 12.197s	16	8
8	1	D Hill	Arrows	A18	Yamaha	V10	67	1h 32m 12.620s	13	7
9	17	G Morbidelli	Sauber	C16	Petronas	V10	66		19	10
10	19	M Salo	Tyrrell	025	Cosworth	V8	66		20	10
r	18	J Verstappen	Tyrrell	025	Cosworth	V8	50	engine / spin	21	11
r	9	M Häkkinen	McLaren	MP4/12	Mercedes	V10	43	engine	1	1
r	22	R Barrichello	Stewart	SF-1	Cosworth	V10	43	hydraulics	9	5
r	10	D Coulthard	McLaren	MP4/12	Mercedes	V10	42	engine	6	3
r	23	J Magnussen	Stewart	SF-1	Cosworth	V10	40	driveshaft	12	6
r	6	E Irvine	Ferrari	F310B	Ferrari	V10	22	engine	14	7
r	15	S Nakano	Prost	JS45	Mugen Honda	V10	16	engine	17	9
r	5	M Schumacher	Ferrari	F310B	Ferrari	V10	2	accident / front suspension	5	3
r	21	T Marques	Minardi	M197	Hart	V8	1	engine	18	9
r	20	U Katayama	Minardi	M197	Hart	V8	1	accident damage	22	11
r	11	R Schumacher	Jordan	197	Peugeot	V10	0	accident	8	4
r	12	G Fisichella	Jordan	197	Peugeot	V10	0	accident	4	2

Winning speed 200.232 km/h, 124.419 mph
Pole Position speed 214.114 km/h, 133.045 mph (M Häkkinen, 1 min:16.602 sec)
Fastest Lap speed 208.128 km/h, 129.325 mph (H-H Frentzen, 1 min:18.805 sec on lap 32)
Lap Leaders M Häkkinen 1-28,32-43 (40); D Coulthard 29-31 (3); J Villeneuve 44-67 (24).

12 Oct 1997 — JAPAN: Suzuka — (Round 16) — (Race 613)

53 laps x 5.864 km, 3.644 miles = 310.596 km, 192.987 miles

Pos	No	Driver	Car	Model	Engine		Laps	Time/Reason for Retirement	Grid Pos	Row
1	5	M Schumacher	Ferrari	F310B	Ferrari	V10	53	1h 29m 48.446s	2	1
2	4	H-H Frentzen	Williams	FW19	Renault	V10	53	1h 29m 49.824s	6	3
3	6	E Irvine	Ferrari	F310B	Ferrari	V10	53	1h 30m 14.830s	3	2
4	9	M Häkkinen	McLaren	MP4/12	Mercedes	V10	53	1h 30m 15.575s	4	2
dq	3	J Villeneuve	Williams	FW19	Renault	V10	53	1h 30m 28.222s	1	1
5	7	J Alesi	Benetton	B197	Renault	V10	53	1h 30m 28.849s	7	4
6	16	J Herbert	Sauber	C16	Petronas	V10	53	1h 30m 30.076s	8	4
7	12	G Fisichella	Jordan	197	Peugeot	V10	53	1h 30m 45.271s	9	5
8	8	G Berger	Benetton	B197	Renault	V10	53	1h 30m 48.875s	5	3
9	11	R Schumacher	Jordan	197	Peugeot	V10	53	1h 31m 10.482s	13	7
10r	10	D Coulthard	McLaren	MP4/12	Mercedes	V10	52	engine / accident	11	6
11	1	D Hill	Arrows	A18	Yamaha	V10	52		17	9
12	2	P Diniz	Arrows	A18	Yamaha	V10	52		16	8
13	18	J Verstappen	Tyrrell	025	Cosworth	V8	52		20	10
r	21	T Marques	Minardi	M197	Hart	V8	46	gearbox	19	10
r	19	M Salo	Tyrrell	025	Cosworth	V8	46	engine	21	11
r	14	O Panis	Prost	JS45	Mugen Honda	V10	36	engine	10	5
r	15	S Nakano	Prost	JS45	Mugen Honda	V10	22	rear wheel bearing	15	8
r	20	U Katayama	Minardi	M197	Hart	V8	8	engine	18	9
r	22	R Barrichello	Stewart	SF-1	Cosworth	V10	6	spin	12	6
r	23	J Magnussen	Stewart	SF-1	Cosworth	V10	3	spin	14	7
ns	17	G Morbidelli	Sauber	C16	Petronas	V10		accident / injury		

Winning speed 207.507 km/h, 128.939 mph
Pole Position speed 219.737 km/h, 136.539 mph (J Villeneuve, 1 min:36.071 sec)
Fastest Lap speed 213.361 km/h, 132.577 mph (H-H Frentzen, 1 min:38.942 sec on lap 48)
Lap Leaders J Villeneuve 1-2,17-20 (6); E Irvine 3-16,22-24 (17); H-H Frentzen 21,34-37 (5); M Schumacher 25-33,38-53 (25).

J Villeneuve disqualified for failing to slow down under a waved yellow flag during practice.

26 Oct 1997 — EUROPE: Jerez de la Frontera — (Round 17) — (Race 614)

69 laps x 4.428 km, 2.751 miles = 305.532 km, 189.849 miles

Pos	No	Driver	Car	Model	Engine		Laps	Time/Reason for Retirement	Grid Pos	Row
1	9	M Häkkinen	McLaren	MP4/12	Mercedes	V10	69	1h 38m 57.771s	5	3
2	10	D Coulthard	McLaren	MP4/12	Mercedes	V10	69	1h 38m 59.425s	6	3
3	3	J Villeneuve	Williams	FW19	Renault	V10	69	1h 38m 59.574s	1	1
4	8	G Berger	Benetton	B197	Renault	V10	69	1h 38m 59.690s	8	4
5	6	E Irvine	Ferrari	F310B	Ferrari	V10	69	1h 39m 01.560s	7	4
6	4	H-H Frentzen	Williams	FW19	Renault	V10	69	1h 39m 02.308s	3	2
7	14	O Panis	Prost	JS45	Mugen Honda	V10	69	1h 40m 04.916s	9	5
8	16	J Herbert	Sauber	C16	Petronas	V10	69	1h 40m 10.732s	14	7
9	23	J Magnussen	Stewart	SF-1	Cosworth	V10	69	1h 40m 15.258s	11	6
10	15	S Nakano	Prost	JS45	Mugen Honda	V10	69	1h 40m 15.986s	15	8
11	12	G Fisichella	Jordan	197	Peugeot	V10	68		17	9
12	19	M Salo	Tyrrell	025	Cosworth	V8	68		21	11
13	7	J Alesi	Benetton	B197	Renault	V10	68		10	5
14	17	N Fontana	Sauber	C16	Petronas	V10	68		18	9
15	21	T Marques	Minardi	M197	Hart	V8	68		20	10
16	18	J Verstappen	Tyrrell	025	Cosworth	V8	68		22	11
17	20	U Katayama	Minardi	M197	Hart	V8	68		19	10
r	5	M Schumacher	Ferrari	F310B	Ferrari	V10	47	accident	2	1
r	1	D Hill	Arrows	A18	Yamaha	V10	47	hydraulics	4	2
r	11	R Schumacher	Jordan	197	Peugeot	V10	44	alternator	16	8
r	22	R Barrichello	Stewart	SF-1	Cosworth	V10	30	gearbox	12	6
r	2	P Diniz	Arrows	A18	Yamaha	V10	11	spin	13	7

Winning speed 185.240 km/h, 115.103 mph
Pole Position speed 196.625 km/h, 122.177 mph (J Villeneuve, 1 min:21.072 sec)
Fastest Lap speed 191.745 km/h, 119.145 mph (H-H Frentzen, 1 min:23.135 sec on lap 30)
Lap Leaders M Schumacher 1-21,28-42,45-47 (39); J Villeneuve 22,43-44,48-68 (24); H-H Frentzen 23-27 (5); M Häkkinen 69 (1).

Lap Leaders 1997

Pos	Driver	Car-Engine	GPs	laps	km	miles
1	J Villeneuve	Williams-Renault	11	348	1,595.3	991.3
2	M Schumacher	Ferrari	12	300	1,395.4	867.0
3	D Coulthard	McLaren-Mercedes-Benz	5	77	396.3	246.3
4	H-H Frentzen	Williams-Renault	6	76	380.6	236.5
5	D Hill	Arrows-Yamaha	1	62	246.0	152.9
6	M Häkkinen	McLaren-Mercedes-Benz	4	51	239.3	148.7
7	G Berger	Benetton-Renault	2	41	272.2	169.1
8	J Trulli	Prost-Mugen Honda	1	37	160.0	99.4
9	J Alesi	Benetton-Renault	2	32	183.6	114.1
10	E Irvine	Ferrari	2	23	125.2	77.8
11	G Fisichella	Jordan-Peugeot	1	7	47.8	29.7
			17	1,054	5,041.6	3,132.7

Driver Points 1997

		AUS	BR	RA	RSM	MC	E	CDN	F	GB	D	H	B	I	A	L	J	EUR	Total
1	J Villeneuve	-	10	10	-	-	10	-	3	10	-	10	2	2	10	10	-	4	81
2	H-H Frentzen	-	-	-	10	-	-	3	6	-	-	-	4	4	4	4	6	1	42
3	D Coulthard	10	-	-	-	-	1	-	-	3	-	-	-	10	6	-	-	6	36
	J Alesi	-	1	-	2	-	4	6	2	6	1	-	-	6	-	6	2	-	36
5	G Berger	3	6	1	-	-	-	-	-	-	10	-	1	-	-	3	-	3	27
	M Häkkinen	4	3	2	1	-	-	-	-	-	4	-	-	-	-	-	3	10	27
7	E Irvine	-	-	6	4	4	-	-	4	-	-	-	-	-	-	-	4	2	24
8	G Fisichella	-	-	-	3	1	-	4	-	-	-	-	6	3	3	-	-	-	20
9	O Panis	2	4	-	-	3	6	-	-	-	-	-	-	-	-	1	-	-	16
10	J Herbert	-	-	3	-	-	2	2	-	-	-	4	3	-	-	-	1	-	15
11	R Schumacher	-	-	4	-	-	-	-	1	2	2	2	-	-	2	-	-	-	13
12	D Hill	-	-	-	-	-	-	-	1	-	-	6	-	-	-	-	-	-	7
13	R Barrichello	-	-	-	-	6	-	-	-	-	-	-	-	-	-	-	-	-	6
14	A Wurz	-	-	-	-	-	-	-	-	4	-	-	-	-	-	-	-	-	4
15	J Trulli	-	-	-	-	-	-	-	-	-	3	-	-	-	-	-	-	-	3
16	P Diniz	-	-	-	-	-	-	-	-	-	-	-	-	-	-	2	-	-	2
	M Salo	-	-	-	2	-	-	-	-	-	-	-	-	-	-	-	-	-	2
	S Nakano	-	-	-	-	-	-	1	-	-	-	1	-	-	-	-	-	-	2
19	N Larini	1	-	-	-	-	-	-	-	-	-	-	-	-	-	-	-	-	1
	M Schumacher	6	2	-	6	10	3	10	10	-	6	3	10	1	1	-	10	-	78

10,6,4,3,2 and 1 point awarded to the first six finishers.
M Schumacher finished 2nd in the Championship but he was removed from the overall placings as punishment for the Jerez incident where he collided with J Villeneuve.

Constructor Points 1997

		AUS	BR	RA	RSM	MC	E	CDN	F	GB	D	H	B	I	A	L	J	EUR	Total
1	Williams-Renault	-	10	10	10	-	10	3	9	10	-	10	6	6	14	14	6	5	123
2	Ferrari	6	2	6	10	14	3	10	14	-	6	3	10	1	1	-	14	2	102
3	Benetton-Renault	3	7	1	2	-	4	6	2	10	11	-	1	6	-	9	2	3	67
4	McLaren-Mercedes-Benz	14	3	2	1	-	1	-	-	3	4	-	-	10	6	-	3	16	63
5	Jordan-Peugeot	-	-	4	3	1	-	4	1	2	2	2	6	3	5	-	-	-	33
6	Prost-Mugen Honda	2	4	-	-	3	6	1	-	-	3	1	-	-	-	1	-	-	21
7	Sauber-Petronas	1	-	3	-	-	2	2	-	-	-	4	3	-	-	-	1	-	16
8	Arrows-Yamaha	-	-	-	-	-	-	-	1	-	-	6	-	-	-	2	-	-	9
9	Stewart-Ford Cosworth	-	-	-	-	6	-	-	-	-	-	-	-	-	-	-	-	-	6
10	Tyrrell-Ford Cosworth	-	-	-	-	2	-	-	-	-	-	-	-	-	-	-	-	-	2

10,6,4,3,2 and 1 point awarded to the first six finishers.

Race Entrants and Results

In further attempts to reduce speed, cars were limited to a much narrower track whilst grooved tyres were introduced to reduce grip and promote closer racing. Two major players left at the end of the season when Goodyear and Tyrrell ended their long associations with Formula 1. Arrows built their own Brian Hart designed V10 engine to become the first British team since BRM to construct the entire car.

WILLIAMS
Winfield Williams: Villeneuve, Frentzen

FERRARI
Scuderia Ferrari Marlboro: M Schumacher, Irvine

BENETTON
Mild Seven Benetton Playlife: Fisichella, Wurz

McLAREN
West McLaren Mercedes: Häkkinen, Coulthard

PROST
Gauloises Prost Peugeot: Panis, Trulli

SAUBER
Red Bull Sauber Petronas: Alesi, Herbert

JORDAN
Benson & Hedges Jordan Mugen Honda: Hill, R Schumacher

ARROWS
Danka Zepter Arrows: Diniz, Salo

STEWART
Stewart Ford: Barrichello, Magnussen, Verstappen

TYRRELL
Tyrrell Ford: Rosset, Takagi

MINARDI
Fondmetal Minardi Ford: Nakano, Tuero

8 Mar 1998		AUSTRALIA: Melbourne						(Round 1)	(Race 615)	
		58 laps x 5.303 km, 3.295 miles = 307.574 km, 191.118 miles								
Pos	No	Driver	Car	Model	Engine		Laps	Time/Reason for Retirement	Grid Pos	Row
1	8	M Häkkinen	McLaren	MP4/13	Mercedes-Benz	V10	58	1h 31m 45.996s	1	1
2	7	D Coulthard	McLaren	MP4/13	Mercedes-Benz	V10	58	1h 31m 46.698s	2	1
3	2	H-H Frentzen	Williams	FW20	Mecachrome	V10	57		6	3
4	4	E Irvine	Ferrari	F300	Ferrari	V10	57		8	4
5	1	J Villeneuve	Williams	FW20	Mecachrome	V10	57		4	2
6	15	J Herbert	Sauber	C17	Petronas	V10	57		5	3
7	6	A Wurz	Benetton	B198	Playlife	V10	57		11	6
8	9	D Hill	Jordan	198	Mugen Honda	V10	57		10	5
9	11	O Panis	Prost	AP01	Peugeot	V10	57		21	11
r	5	G Fisichella	Benetton	B198	Playlife	V10	43	rear wing support	7	4
r	14	J Alesi	Sauber	C17	Petronas	V10	41	engine	12	6
r	12	J Trulli	Prost	AP01	Peugeot	V10	26	gearbox	15	8
r	20	R Rosset	Tyrrell	026	Ford Cosworth	V10	25	gearbox	19	10
r	17	M Salo	Arrows	A19	Arrows	V10	23	transmission	16	8
r	23	E Tuero	Minardi	M198	Ford Cosworth	V10	22	engine	17	9
r	22	S Nakano	Minardi	M198	Ford Cosworth	V10	8	driveshaft	22	11
r	3	M Schumacher	Ferrari	F300	Ferrari	V10	5	engine	3	2
r	16	P Diniz	Arrows	A19	Arrows	V10	2	hydraulics	20	10
r	10	R Schumacher	Jordan	198	Mugen Honda	V10	1	accident	9	5
r	19	J Magnussen	Stewart	SF-2	Ford Cosworth	V10	1	accident	18	9
r	21	T Takagi	Tyrrell	026	Ford Cosworth	V10	1	spin	13	7
r	18	R Barrichello	Stewart	SF-2	Ford Cosworth	V10	0	gearbox	14	7

Winning speed 201.101 km/h, 124.959 mph
Pole Position speed 212.096 km/h, 131.791 mph (M Häkkinen, 1 min:30.010 sec)
Fastest Lap speed 208.303 km/h, 129.434 mph (M Häkkinen, 1 min:31.649 sec on lap 39)
Lap Leaders M Häkkinen 1-23,25-35,56-58 (37); D Coulthard 24,36-55 (21).

29 Mar 1998   BRAZIL: Interlagos   (Round 2)   (Race 616)

72 laps x 4.292 km, 2.667 miles = 309.024 km, 192.019 miles

Pos	No	Driver	Car	Model	Engine		Laps	Time/Reason for Retirement	Grid Pos	Row
1	8	M Häkkinen	McLaren	MP4/13	Mercedes-Benz	V10	72	1h 37m 11.747s	1	1
2	7	D Coulthard	McLaren	MP4/13	Mercedes-Benz	V10	72	1h 37m 12.849s	2	1
3	3	M Schumacher	Ferrari	F300	Ferrari	V10	72	1h 38m 12.297s	4	2
4	6	A Wurz	Benetton	B198	Playlife	V10	72	1h 38m 19.200s	5	3
5	2	H-H Frentzen	Williams	FW20	Mecachrome	V10	71		3	2
6	5	G Fisichella	Benetton	B198	Playlife	V10	71		7	4
7	1	J Villeneuve	Williams	FW20	Mecachrome	V10	71		10	5
8	4	E Irvine	Ferrari	F300	Ferrari	V10	71		6	3
9	14	J Alesi	Sauber	C17	Petronas	V10	71		15	8
dq	9	D Hill	Jordan	198	Mugen Honda	V10	70	under weight	11	6
10	19	J Magnussen	Stewart	SF-2	Ford Cosworth	V10	70		16	8
11r	15	J Herbert	Sauber	C17	Petronas	V10	67	driver discomfort / neck injury	14	7
r	11	O Panis	Prost	AP01	Peugeot	V10	63	gearbox oil cap lost	9	5
r	18	R Barrichello	Stewart	SF-2	Ford Cosworth	V10	56	gearbox	13	7
r	20	R Rosset	Tyrrell	026	Ford Cosworth	V10	52	gear selector / spin	21	11
r	23	E Tuero	Minardi	M198	Ford Cosworth	V10	44	gearbox	19	10
r	16	P Diniz	Arrows	A19	Arrows	V10	26	gearbox	22	11
r	21	T Takagi	Tyrrell	026	Ford Cosworth	V10	19	engine	17	9
r	17	M Salo	Arrows	A19	Arrows	V10	18	engine	20	10
r	12	J Trulli	Prost	AP01	Peugeot	V10	17	fuel pressure	12	6
r	22	S Nakano	Minardi	M198	Ford Cosworth	V10	3	spin	18	9
r	10	R Schumacher	Jordan	198	Mugen Honda	V10	0	spin	8	4

Winning speed 190.763 km/h, 118.535 mph
Pole Position speed 200.425 km/h, 124.539 mph (M Häkkinen, 1 min:17.092 sec)
Fastest Lap speed 194.754 km/h, 121.015 mph (M Häkkinen, 1 min:19.337 sec on lap 64)
Lap Leaders M Häkkinen 1-72 (72).

12 Apr 1998   ARGENTINA: Buenos Aires   (Round 3)   (Race 617)

72 laps x 4.259 km, 2.646 miles = 306.449 km, 190.419 miles

Pos	No	Driver	Car	Model	Engine		Laps	Time/Reason for Retirement	Grid Pos	Row
1	3	M Schumacher	Ferrari	F300	Ferrari	V10	72	1h 48m 36.175s	2	1
2	8	M Häkkinen	McLaren	MP4/13	Mercedes-Benz	V10	72	1h 48m 59.073s	3	2
3	4	E Irvine	Ferrari	F300	Ferrari	V10	72	1h 49m 33.920s	4	2
4	6	A Wurz	Benetton	B198	Playlife	V10	72	1h 49m 44.309s	8	4
5	14	J Alesi	Sauber	C17	Petronas	V10	72	1h 49m 54.461s	11	6
6	7	D Coulthard	McLaren	MP4/13	Mercedes-Benz	V10	72	1h 49m 55.926s	1	1
7	5	G Fisichella	Benetton	B198	Playlife	V10	72	1h 50m 04.612s	10	5
8	9	D Hill	Jordan	198	Mugen Honda	V10	71		9	5
9	2	H-H Frentzen	Williams	FW20	Mecachrome	V10	71		6	3
10	18	R Barrichello	Stewart	SF-2	Ford Cosworth	V10	70		14	7
11	12	J Trulli	Prost	AP01	Peugeot	V10	70		16	8
12	21	T Takagi	Tyrrell	026	Ford Cosworth	V10	70		13	7
13	22	S Nakano	Minardi	M198	Ford Cosworth	V10	69		19	10
14	20	R Rosset	Tyrrell	026	Ford Cosworth	V10	68		21	11
15r	11	O Panis	Prost	AP01	Peugeot	V10	65	engine	15	8
r	23	E Tuero	Minardi	M198	Ford Cosworth	V10	63	accident	20	10
r	1	J Villeneuve	Williams	FW20	Mecachrome	V10	52	accident	7	4
r	15	J Herbert	Sauber	C17	Petronas	V10	46	accident damage	12	6
r	10	R Schumacher	Jordan	198	Mugen Honda	V10	22	rear suspension / spin	5	3
r	17	M Salo	Arrows	A19	Arrows	V10	18	gearbox	17	9
r	19	J Magnussen	Stewart	SF-2	Ford Cosworth	V10	17	transmission	22	11
r	16	P Diniz	Arrows	A19	Arrows	V10	13	gearbox	18	9

Winning speed 169.304 km/h, 105.201 mph
Pole Position speed 178.591 km/h, 110.971 mph (D Coulthard, 1 min:25.852 sec)
Fastest Lap speed 173.878 km/h, 108.043 mph (A Wurz, 1 min:28.179 sec on lap 39)
Lap Leaders D Coulthard 1-4 (4); M Schumacher 5-28,43-72 (54); M Häkkinen 29-42 (14).

26 Apr 1998   SAN MARINO: Imola   (Round 4)   (Race 618)

62 laps x 4.930 km, 3.063 miles = 305.443 km, 189.794 miles

Pos	No	Driver	Car	Model	Engine		Laps	Time/Reason for Retirement	Grid Pos	Row
1	7	D Coulthard	McLaren	MP4/13	Mercedes-Benz	V10	62	1h 34m 24.593s	1	1
2	3	M Schumacher	Ferrari	F300	Ferrari	V10	62	1h 34m 29.147s	3	2
3	4	E Irvine	Ferrari	F300	Ferrari	V10	62	1h 35m 16.368s	4	2
4	1	J Villeneuve	Williams	FW20	Mecachrome	V10	62	1h 35m 19.183s	6	3
5	2	H-H Frentzen	Williams	FW20	Mecachrome	V10	62	1h 35m 42.069s	8	4
6	14	J Alesi	Sauber	C17	Petronas	V10	61		12	6
7	10	R Schumacher	Jordan	198	Mugen Honda	V10	60		9	5
8	23	E Tuero	Minardi	M198	Ford Cosworth	V10	60		19	10
9	17	M Salo	Arrows	A19	Arrows	V10	60		14	7
10r	9	D Hill	Jordan	198	Mugen Honda	V10	57	air valve leak / engine	7	4
11r	11	O Panis	Prost	AP01	Peugeot	V10	56	engine	13	7
r	20	R Rosset	Tyrrell	026	Ford Cosworth	V10	48	engine air valve pressure	22	11

Pos	No	Driver	Car	Model	Engine		Laps	Time/Reason for Retirement	Grid Pos	Row
r	21	T Takagi	Tyrrell	026	Ford Cosworth	V10	40	engine air valve pressure	15	8
r	12	J Trulli	Prost	AP01	Peugeot	V10	34	throttle stuck / spin	16	8
r	22	S Nakano	Minardi	M198	Ford Cosworth	V10	27	engine / fire	21	11
r	16	P Diniz	Arrows	A19	Arrows	V10	18	engine	18	9
r	8	M Häkkinen	McLaren	MP4/13	Mercedes-Benz	V10	17	gearbox	2	1
r	5	G Fisichella	Benetton	B198	Playlife	V10	17	accident	10	5
r	6	A Wurz	Benetton	B198	Playlife	V10	17	oil pressure / engine	5	3
r	15	J Herbert	Sauber	C17	Petronas	V10	12	rear tyre	11	6
r	19	J Magnussen	Stewart	SF-2	Ford Cosworth	V10	8	gearbox	20	10
r	18	R Barrichello	Stewart	SF-2	Ford Cosworth	V10	0	accident	17	9

Winning speed 194.117 km/h, 120.619 mph
Pole Position speed 206.436 km/h, 128.274 mph (D Coulthard, 1 min:25.973 sec)
Fastest Lap speed 198.645 km/h, 123.433 mph (M Schumacher, 1 min:29.345 sec on lap 48)
Lap Leaders D Coulthard 1-62 (62).

10 May 1998		SPAIN: Montmeló							(Round 5)	(Race 619)
		65 laps x 4.728 km, 2.938 miles = 307.196 km, 190.883 miles								

Pos	No	Driver	Car	Model	Engine		Laps	Time/Reason for Retirement	Grid Pos	Row
1	8	M Häkkinen	McLaren	MP4/13	Mercedes-Benz	V10	65	1h 33m 37.621s	1	1
2	7	D Coulthard	McLaren	MP4/13	Mercedes-Benz	V10	65	1h 33m 47.060s	2	1
3	3	M Schumacher	Ferrari	F300	Ferrari	V10	65	1h 34m 24.716s	3	2
4	6	A Wurz	Benetton	B198	Playlife	V10	65	1h 34m 40.159s	5	3
5	18	R Barrichello	Stewart	SF-2	Ford Cosworth	V10	64		9	5
6	1	J Villeneuve	Williams	FW20	Mecachrome	V10	64		10	5
7	15	J Herbert	Sauber	C17	Petronas	V10	64		7	4
8	2	H-H Frentzen	Williams	FW20	Mecachrome	V10	63		13	7
9	12	J Trulli	Prost	AP01	Peugeot	V10	63		16	8
10	14	J Alesi	Sauber	C17	Petronas	V10	63		14	7
11	10	R Schumacher	Jordan	198	Mugen Honda	V10	63		11	6
12	19	J Magnussen	Stewart	SF-2	Ford Cosworth	V10	63		18	9
13	21	T Takagi	Tyrrell	026	Ford Cosworth	V10	63		21	11
14	22	S Nakano	Minardi	M198	Ford Cosworth	V10	63		20	10
15	23	E Tuero	Minardi	M198	Ford Cosworth	V10	63		19	10
16r	11	O Panis	Prost	AP01	Peugeot	V10	60	hydraulics	12	6
r	9	D Hill	Jordan	198	Mugen Honda	V10	46	engine	8	4
r	4	E Irvine	Ferrari	F300	Ferrari	V10	28	accident	6	3
r	5	G Fisichella	Benetton	B198	Playlife	V10	28	accident	4	2
r	17	M Salo	Arrows	A19	Arrows	V10	21	engine	17	9
r	16	P Diniz	Arrows	A19	Arrows	V10	20	engine	15	8
nq	20	R Rosset	Tyrrell	026	Ford Cosworth	V10				

Winning speed 196.863 km/h, 122.325 mph
Pole Position speed 212.065 km/h, 131.771 mph (M Häkkinen, 1 min:20.262 sec)
Fastest Lap speed 201.967 km/h, 125.497 mph (M Häkkinen, 1 min:24.275 sec on lap 25)
Lap Leaders M Häkkinen 1-26,28-45,47-65 (63); D Coulthard 27,46 (2).

24 May 1998		MONACO: Monte-Carlo							(Round 6)	(Race 620)
		78 laps x 3.367 km, 2.092 miles = 262.626 km, 163.188 miles								

Pos	No	Driver	Car	Model	Engine		Laps	Time/Reason for Retirement	Grid Pos	Row
1	8	M Häkkinen	McLaren	MP4/13	Mercedes-Benz	V10	78	1h 51m 23.595s	1	1
2	5	G Fisichella	Benetton	B198	Playlife	V10	78	1h 51m 35.070s	3	2
3	4	E Irvine	Ferrari	F300	Ferrari	V10	78	1h 52m 04.973s	7	4
4	17	M Salo	Arrows	A19	Arrows	V10	78	1h 52m 23.958s	8	4
5	1	J Villeneuve	Williams	FW20	Mecachrome	V10	77		13	7
6	16	P Diniz	Arrows	A19	Arrows	V10	77		12	6
7	15	J Herbert	Sauber	C17	Petronas	V10	77		9	5
8	9	D Hill	Jordan	198	Mugen Honda	V10	76		15	8
9	22	S Nakano	Minardi	M198	Ford Cosworth	V10	76		19	10
10	3	M Schumacher	Ferrari	F300	Ferrari	V10	76		4	2
11	21	T Takagi	Tyrrell	026	Ford Cosworth	V10	76		20	10
12r	14	J Alesi	Sauber	C17	Petronas	V10	72	gearbox	11	6
r	12	J Trulli	Prost	AP01	Peugeot	V10	56	gearbox	10	5
r	11	O Panis	Prost	AP01	Peugeot	V10	49	wheel loose	18	9
r	10	R Schumacher	Jordan	198	Mugen Honda	V10	44	accident / suspension	16	8
r	6	A Wurz	Benetton	B198	Playlife	V10	42	accident	6	3
r	19	J Magnussen	Stewart	SF-2	Ford Cosworth	V10	30	rear suspension	17	9
r	7	D Coulthard	McLaren	MP4/13	Mercedes-Benz	V10	17	engine	2	1
r	18	R Barrichello	Stewart	SF-2	Ford Cosworth	V10	11	rear suspension	14	7
r	2	H-H Frentzen	Williams	FW20	Mecachrome	V10	9	accident	5	3
r	23	E Tuero	Minardi	M198	Ford Cosworth	V10	0	accident	21	11
nq	20	R Rosset	Tyrrell	026	Ford Cosworth	V10				

Winning speed 141.458 km/h, 87.898 mph
Pole Position speed 151.898 km/h, 94.385 mph (M Häkkinen, 1 min:19.798 sec)
Fastest Lap speed 146.130 km/h, 90.801 mph (M Häkkinen, 1 min:22.948 sec on lap 29)
Lap Leaders M Häkkinen 1-78 (78).

Races

407

7 Jun 1998   CANADA: Montréal   (Round 7)   (Race 621)

69 laps x 4.421 km, 2.747 miles = 305.049 km, 189.549 miles

Pos	No	Driver	Car	Model	Engine		Laps	Time/Reason for Retirement	Grid Pos	Row
1	3	M Schumacher	Ferrari	F300	Ferrari	V10	69	1h 40m 57.355s	3	2
2	5	G Fisichella	Benetton	B198	Playlife	V10	69	1h 41m 14.017s	4	2
3	4	E Irvine	Ferrari	F300	Ferrari	V10	69	1h 41m 57.414s	8	4
4	6	A Wurz	Benetton	B198	Playlife	V10	69	1h 42m 00.587s	11	6
5	18	R Barrichello	Stewart	SF-2	Ford Cosworth	V10	69	1h 42m 18.868s	13	7
6	19	J Magnussen	Stewart	SF-2	Ford Cosworth	V10	68		20	10
7	22	S Nakano	Minardi	M198	Ford Cosworth	V10	68		18	9
8	20	R Rosset	Tyrrell	026	Ford Cosworth	V10	68		22	11
9	16	P Diniz	Arrows	A19	Arrows	V10	68		19	10
10	1	J Villeneuve	Williams	FW20	Mecachrome	V10	63		6	3
r	23	E Tuero	Minardi	M198	Ford Cosworth	V10	53	electrics	21	11
r	9	D Hill	Jordan	198	Mugen Honda	V10	42	electrics	10	5
r	11	O Panis	Prost	AP01	Peugeot	V10	39	engine	15	8
r	2	H-H Frentzen	Williams	FW20	Mecachrome	V10	20	accident	7	4
r	7	D Coulthard	McLaren	MP4/13	Mercedes-Benz	V10	18	throttle linkage	1	1
r	15	J Herbert	Sauber	C17	Petronas	V10	18	spin	12	6
r	17	M Salo	Arrows	A19	Arrows	V10	18	steering / accident	17	9
r	8	M Häkkinen	McLaren	MP4/13	Mercedes-Benz	V10	0	gearbox	2	1
r	10	R Schumacher	Jordan	198	Mugen Honda	V10	0	clutch / spin	5	3
r	14	J Alesi	Sauber	C17	Petronas	V10	0	accident	9	5
r	12	J Trulli	Prost	AP01	Peugeot	V10	0	accident	14	7
r	21	T Takagi	Tyrrell	026	Ford Cosworth	V10	0	clutch	16	8

Winning speed 181.296 km/h, 112.652 mph
Pole Position speed 203.490 km/h, 126.443 mph (D Coulthard, 1 min:18.213 sec)
Fastest Lap speed 200.501 km/h, 124.586 mph (M Schumacher, 1 min:19.379 sec on lap 48)
Lap Leaders D Coulthard 1-18 (18); M Schumacher 19,44-69 (27); G Fisichella 20-43 (24).

28 Jun 1998   FRANCE: Magny-Cours   (Round 8)   (Race 622)

71 laps x 4.250 km, 2.641 miles = 301.564 km, 187.383 miles

Pos	No	Driver	Car	Model	Engine		Laps	Time/Reason for Retirement	Grid Pos	Row
1	3	M Schumacher	Ferrari	F300	Ferrari	V10	71	1h 34m 45.026s	2	1
2	4	E Irvine	Ferrari	F300	Ferrari	V10	71	1h 35m 04.601s	4	2
3	8	M Häkkinen	McLaren	MP4/13	Mercedes-Benz	V10	71	1h 35m 04.773s	1	1
4	1	J Villeneuve	Williams	FW20	Mecachrome	V10	71	1h 35m 51.991s	5	3
5	6	A Wurz	Benetton	B198	Playlife	V10	70		10	5
6	7	D Coulthard	McLaren	MP4/13	Mercedes-Benz	V10	70		3	2
7	14	J Alesi	Sauber	C17	Petronas	V10	70		11	6
8	15	J Herbert	Sauber	C17	Petronas	V10	70		13	7
9	5	G Fisichella	Benetton	B198	Playlife	V10	70		9	5
10	18	R Barrichello	Stewart	SF-2	Ford Cosworth	V10	69		14	7
11	11	O Panis	Prost	AP01	Peugeot	V10	69		16	8
12	19	J Verstappen	Stewart	SF-2	Ford Cosworth	V10	69		15	8
13	17	M Salo	Arrows	A19	Arrows	V10	69		19	10
14	16	P Diniz	Arrows	A19	Arrows	V10	69		17	9
15r	2	H-H Frentzen	Williams	FW20	Mecachrome	V10	68	accident / steering	8	4
16	10	R Schumacher	Jordan	198	Mugen Honda	V10	68		6	3
17r	22	S Nakano	Minardi	M198	Ford Cosworth	V10	65	engine	21	11
r	21	T Takagi	Tyrrell	026	Ford Cosworth	V10	60	engine	20	10
r	12	J Trulli	Prost	AP01	Peugeot	V10	55	spin	12	6
r	23	E Tuero	Minardi	M198	Ford Cosworth	V10	41	gearbox	22	11
r	9	D Hill	Jordan	198	Mugen Honda	V10	19	hydraulics	7	4
r	20	R Rosset	Tyrrell	026	Ford Cosworth	V10	16	engine	18	9

Winning speed 190.963 km/h, 118.659 mph
Pole Position speed 204.193 km/h, 126.880 mph (M Häkkinen, 1 min:14.929 sec)
Fastest Lap speed 197.360 km/h, 122.634 mph (D Coulthard, 1 min:17.523 sec on lap 59)
Lap Leaders M Schumacher 1-22,24-71 (70); E Irvine 23 (1).

Scheduled for 72 laps but stopped on first lap due to stalled car and restarted for 71 laps.

12 Jul 1998 **BRITAIN: Silverstone** (Round 9) (Race 623)

60 laps x 5.140 km, 3.194 miles = 308.296 km, 191.566 miles

Pos	No	Driver	Car	Model	Engine		Laps	Time/Reason for Retirement	Grid Pos	Row
1	3	M Schumacher	Ferrari	F300	Ferrari	V10	60	1h 47m 02.450s	2	1
2	8	M Häkkinen	McLaren	MP4/13	Mercedes-Benz	V10	60	1h 47m 24.915s	1	1
3	4	E Irvine	Ferrari	F300	Ferrari	V10	60	1h 47m 31.649s	5	3
4	6	A Wurz	Benetton	B198	Playlife	V10	59		11	6
5	5	G Fisichella	Benetton	B198	Playlife	V10	59		10	5
6	10	R Schumacher	Jordan	198	Mugen Honda	V10	59		21	11
7	1	J Villeneuve	Williams	FW20	Mecachrome	V10	59		3	2
8	22	S Nakano	Minardi	M198	Ford Cosworth	V10	58		19	10
9	21	T Takagi	Tyrrell	026	Ford Cosworth	V10	56		17	9
r	14	J Alesi	Sauber	C17	Petronas	V10	53	gearbox electrics	8	4
r	16	P Diniz	Arrows	A19	Arrows	V10	45	spin	12	6
r	11	O Panis	Prost	AP01	Peugeot	V10	40	spin	22	11
r	18	R Barrichello	Stewart	SF-2	Ford Cosworth	V10	39	spin	16	8
r	19	J Verstappen	Stewart	SF-2	Ford Cosworth	V10	38	engine	15	8
r	7	D Coulthard	McLaren	MP4/13	Mercedes-Benz	V10	37	spin	4	2
r	12	J Trulli	Prost	AP01	Peugeot	V10	37	spin	14	7
r	20	R Rosset	Tyrrell	026	Ford Cosworth	V10	29	spin	20	10
r	23	E Tuero	Minardi	M198	Ford Cosworth	V10	29	spin	18	9
r	15	J Herbert	Sauber	C17	Petronas	V10	27	accident damage / spin	9	5
r	17	M Salo	Arrows	A19	Arrows	V10	27	spin	13	7
r	2	H-H Frentzen	Williams	FW20	Mecachrome	V10	15	spin	6	3
r	9	D Hill	Jordan	198	Mugen Honda	V10	13	spin	7	4

Winning speed 172.810 km/h, 107.379 mph
Pole Position speed 222.214 km/h, 138.078 mph (M Häkkinen, 1 min:23.271 sec)
Fastest Lap speed 193.346 km/h, 120.140 mph (M Schumacher, 1 min:35.704 sec on lap 12)
Lap Leaders M Häkkinen 1-50 (50); M Schumacher 51-60 (10).

M Schumacher was brought into pits to serve a penalty for overtaking behind the pace car. He was able to delay this until the final lap and was instead given a 10 seconds penalty. This was withdrawn due to it being awarded incorrectly. R Schumacher and O Panis failed the driver egress check and were relegated to the back row, after qualifying 10th and 16th respectively.

26 Jul 1998 **AUSTRIA: A1-Ring** (Round 10) (Race 624)

71 laps x 4.319 km, 2.684 miles = 306.649 km, 190.543 miles

Pos	No	Driver	Car	Model	Engine		Laps	Time/Reason for Retirement	Grid Pos	Row
1	8	M Häkkinen	McLaren	MP4/13	Mercedes-Benz	V10	71	1h 30m 44.086s	3	2
2	7	D Coulthard	McLaren	MP4/13	Mercedes-Benz	V10	71	1h 30m 49.375s	14	7
3	3	M Schumacher	Ferrari	F300	Ferrari	V10	71	1h 31m 23.178s	4	2
4	4	E Irvine	Ferrari	F300	Ferrari	V10	71	1h 31m 28.062s	8	4
5	10	R Schumacher	Jordan	198	Mugen Honda	V10	71	1h 31m 34.740s	9	5
6	1	J Villeneuve	Williams	FW20	Mecachrome	V10	71	1h 31m 37.288s	11	6
7	9	D Hill	Jordan	198	Mugen Honda	V10	71	1h 31m 57.710s	15	8
8	15	J Herbert	Sauber	C17	Petronas	V10	70		18	9
9	6	A Wurz	Benetton	B198	Playlife	V10	70		17	9
10	12	J Trulli	Prost	AP01	Peugeot	V10	70		16	8
11	22	S Nakano	Minardi	M198	Ford Cosworth	V10	70		21	11
12	20	R Rosset	Tyrrell	026	Ford Cosworth	V10	69		22	11
r	19	J Verstappen	Stewart	SF-2	Ford Cosworth	V10	51	engine	12	6
r	23	E Tuero	Minardi	M198	Ford Cosworth	V10	30	spin	19	10
r	5	G Fisichella	Benetton	B198	Playlife	V10	21	accident	1	1
r	14	J Alesi	Sauber	C17	Petronas	V10	21	accident	2	1
r	2	H-H Frentzen	Williams	FW20	Mecachrome	V10	16	engine	7	4
r	18	R Barrichello	Stewart	SF-2	Ford Cosworth	V10	8	brakes	5	3
r	16	P Diniz	Arrows	A19	Arrows	V10	3	accident damage	13	7
r	17	M Salo	Arrows	A19	Arrows	V10	1	accident damage	6	3
r	11	O Panis	Prost	AP01	Peugeot	V10	0	clutch	10	5
r	21	T Takagi	Tyrrell	026	Ford Cosworth	V10	0	accident	20	10

Winning speed 202.777 km/h, 126.000 mph
Pole Position speed 173.535 km/h, 107.830 mph (G Fisichella, 1 min:29.598 sec)
Fastest Lap speed 213.348 km/h, 132.569 mph (D Coulthard, 1 min:12.878 sec on lap 30)
Lap Leaders M Häkkinen 1-34,37-71 (69); D Coulthard 35-36 (2).

2 Aug 1998 — GERMANY: Hockenheim — (Round 11) (Race 625)

45 laps x 6.823 km, 4.240 miles = 307.035 km, 190.783 miles

Pos	No	Driver	Car	Model	Engine		Laps	Time/Reason for Retirement	Grid Pos	Row
1	8	M Häkkinen	McLaren	MP4/13	Mercedes-Benz	V10	45	1h 20m 47.984s	1	1
2	7	D Coulthard	McLaren	MP4/13	Mercedes-Benz	V10	45	1h 20m 48.410s	2	1
3	1	J Villeneuve	Williams	FW20	Mecachrome	V10	45	1h 20m 50.561s	3	2
4	9	D Hill	Jordan	198	Mugen Honda	V10	45	1h 20m 55.169s	5	3
5	3	M Schumacher	Ferrari	F300	Ferrari	V10	45	1h 21m 00.597s	9	5
6	10	R Schumacher	Jordan	198	Mugen Honda	V10	45	1h 21m 17.722s	4	2
7	5	G Fisichella	Benetton	B198	Playlife	V10	45	1h 21m 19.010s	8	4
8	4	E Irvine	Ferrari	F300	Ferrari	V10	45	1h 21m 19.633s	6	3
9	2	H-H Frentzen	Williams	FW20	Mecachrome	V10	45	1h 21m 20.768s	10	5
10	14	J Alesi	Sauber	C17	Petronas	V10	45	1h 21m 36.355s	11	6
11	6	A Wurz	Benetton	B198	Playlife	V10	45	1h 21m 45.978s	7	4
12	12	J Trulli	Prost	AP01	Peugeot	V10	44		14	7
13	21	T Takagi	Tyrrell	026	Ford Cosworth	V10	44		15	8
14	17	M Salo	Arrows	A19	Arrows	V10	44		17	9
15	11	O Panis	Prost	AP01	Peugeot	V10	44		16	8
16	23	E Tuero	Minardi	M198	Ford Cosworth	V10	43		21	11
r	15	J Herbert	Sauber	C17	Petronas	V10	37	gearbox	12	6
r	22	S Nakano	Minardi	M198	Ford Cosworth	V10	36	gearbox	20	10
r	18	R Barrichello	Stewart	SF-2	Ford Cosworth	V10	27	gearbox	13	7
r	19	J Verstappen	Stewart	SF-2	Ford Cosworth	V10	24	transmission	19	10
r	16	P Diniz	Arrows	A19	Arrows	V10	2	throttle	18	9
ns	20	R Rosset	Tyrrell	026	Ford Cosworth	V10		accident / unwell		

Winning speed 227.997 km/h, 141.671 mph
Pole Position speed 241.194 km/h, 149.872 mph (M Häkkinen, 1 min:41.838 sec)
Fastest Lap speed 231.471 km/h, 143.830 mph (D Coulthard, 1 min:46.116 sec on lap 17)
Lap Leaders M Häkkinen 1-25,28-45 (43); D Coulthard 26-27 (2).

16 Aug 1998 — HUNGARY: Hungaroring — (Round 12) (Race 626)

77 laps x 3.972 km, 2.468 miles = 305.844 km, 190.043 miles

Pos	No	Driver	Car	Model	Engine		Laps	Time/Reason for Retirement	Grid Pos	Row
1	3	M Schumacher	Ferrari	F300	Ferrari	V10	77	1h 45m 25.550s	3	2
2	7	D Coulthard	McLaren	MP4/13	Mercedes-Benz	V10	77	1h 45m 34.983s	2	1
3	1	J Villeneuve	Williams	FW20	Mecachrome	V10	77	1h 46m 09.994s	6	3
4	9	D Hill	Jordan	198	Mugen Honda	V10	77	1h 46m 20.626s	4	2
5	2	H-H Frentzen	Williams	FW20	Mecachrome	V10	77	1h 46m 22.060s	7	4
6	8	M Häkkinen	McLaren	MP4/13	Mercedes-Benz	V10	76		1	1
7	14	J Alesi	Sauber	C17	Petronas	V10	76		11	6
8	5	G Fisichella	Benetton	B198	Playlife	V10	76		8	4
9	10	R Schumacher	Jordan	198	Mugen Honda	V10	76		10	5
10	15	J Herbert	Sauber	C17	Petronas	V10	76		15	8
11	16	P Diniz	Arrows	A19	Arrows	V10	74		12	6
12	11	O Panis	Prost	AP01	Peugeot	V10	74		20	10
13	19	J Verstappen	Stewart	SF-2	Ford Cosworth	V10	74		17	9
14	21	T Takagi	Tyrrell	026	Ford Cosworth	V10	74		18	9
15	22	S Nakano	Minardi	M198	Ford Cosworth	V10	74		19	10
16r	6	A Wurz	Benetton	B198	Playlife	V10	69	gearbox	9	5
r	18	R Barrichello	Stewart	SF-2	Ford Cosworth	V10	54	gearbox	14	7
r	12	J Trulli	Prost	AP01	Peugeot	V10	28	engine	16	8
r	17	M Salo	Arrows	A19	Arrows	V10	18	gearbox	13	7
r	4	E Irvine	Ferrari	F300	Ferrari	V10	13	gearbox	5	3
r	23	E Tuero	Minardi	M198	Ford Cosworth	V10	13	gearbox	21	11
nq	20	R Rosset	Tyrrell	026	Ford Cosworth	V10				

Winning speed 174.062 km/h, 108.157 mph
Pole Position speed 185.769 km/h, 115.432 mph (M Häkkinen, 1 min:16.973 sec)
Fastest Lap speed 180.349 km/h, 112.064 mph (M Schumacher, 1 min:19.286 sec on lap 60)
Lap Leaders M Häkkinen 1-46 (46); M Schumacher 47-77 (31).

30 Aug 1998 — BELGIUM: Spa-Francorchamps — (Round 13) (Race 627)

44 laps x 6.968 km, 4.330 miles = 306.577 km, 190.498 miles

Pos	No	Driver	Car	Model	Engine		Laps	Time/Reason for Retirement	Grid Pos	Row
1	9	D Hill	Jordan	198	Mugen Honda	V10	44	1h 43m 47.407s	3	2
2	10	R Schumacher	Jordan	198	Mugen Honda	V10	44	1h 43m 48.339s	8	4
3	14	J Alesi	Sauber	C17	Petronas	V10	44	1h 43m 54.647s	10	5
4	2	H-H Frentzen	Williams	FW20	Mecachrome	V10	44	1h 44m 19.650s	9	5
5	16	P Diniz	Arrows	A19	Arrows	V10	44	1h 44m 39.089s	16	8
6	12	J Trulli	Prost	AP01	Peugeot	V10	42		13	7
7	7	D Coulthard	McLaren	MP4/13	Mercedes-Benz	V10	39		2	1
8	22	S Nakano	Minardi	M198	Ford Cosworth	V10	39		21	11
r	5	G Fisichella	Benetton	B198	Playlife	V10	26	accident	7	4
r	3	M Schumacher	Ferrari	F300	Ferrari	V10	25	accident	4	2
r	4	E Irvine	Ferrari	F300	Ferrari	V10	25	accident	5	3
r	23	E Tuero	Minardi	M198	Ford Cosworth	V10	17	electrics	22	11
r	1	J Villeneuve	Williams	FW20	Mecachrome	V10	16	accident	6	3
r	21	T Takagi	Tyrrell	026	Ford Cosworth	V10	10	accident	19	10

Pos	No	Driver	Car	Model	Engine		Laps	Time/Reason for Retirement	Grid Pos	Row
r	19	J Verstappen	Stewart	SF-2	Ford Cosworth	V10	8	engine	17	9
r	8	M Häkkinen	McLaren	MP4/13	Mercedes-Benz	V10	0	accident	1	1
r	6	A Wurz	Benetton	B198	Playlife	V10	0	accident	11	6
r	15	J Herbert	Sauber	C17	Petronas	V10	0	accident	12	6
r	11	O Panis	Prost	AP01	Peugeot	V10	0	accident *	15	8
r	18	R Barrichello	Stewart	SF-2	Ford Cosworth	V10	0	accident *	14	7
r	17	M Salo	Arrows	A19	Arrows	V10	0	accident *	18	9
r	20	R Rosset	Tyrrell	026	Ford Cosworth	V10	0	accident *	20	10

Winning speed 177.229 km/h, 110.125 mph
Pole Position speed 230.809 km/h, 143.418 mph (M Häkkinen, 1 min:48.682 sec)
Fastest Lap speed 202.679 km/h, 125.939 mph (M Schumacher, 2 min: 3.766 sec on lap 9)
Lap Leaders D Hill 1-7,26-44 (26); M Schumacher 8-25 (18).

*Race stopped and restarted for original distance after first lap pile-up. * Retired after first start.*

13 Sep 1998   ITALY: Monza   (Round 14)   (Race 628)
53 laps x 5.770 km, 3.585 miles = 305.548 km, 189.859 miles

Pos	No	Driver	Car	Model	Engine		Laps	Time/Reason for Retirement	Grid Pos	Row
1	3	M Schumacher	Ferrari	F300	Ferrari	V10	53	1h 17m 09.672s	1	1
2	4	E Irvine	Ferrari	F300	Ferrari	V10	53	1h 17m 47.649s	5	3
3	10	R Schumacher	Jordan	198	Mugen Honda	V10	53	1h 17m 50.824s	6	3
4	8	M Häkkinen	McLaren	MP4/13	Mercedes-Benz	V10	53	1h 18m 05.343s	3	2
5	14	J Alesi	Sauber	C17	Petronas	V10	53	1h 18m 11.544s	8	4
6	9	D Hill	Jordan	198	Mugen Honda	V10	53	1h 18m 16.360s	14	7
7	2	H-H Frentzen	Williams	FW20	Mecachrome	V10	52		12	6
8	5	G Fisichella	Benetton	B198	Playlife	V10	52		11	6
9	21	T Takagi	Tyrrell	026	Ford Cosworth	V10	52		19	10
10	18	R Barrichello	Stewart	SF-2	Ford Cosworth	V10	52		13	7
11	23	E Tuero	Minardi	M198	Ford Cosworth	V10	51		22	11
12	20	R Rosset	Tyrrell	026	Ford Cosworth	V10	51		18	9
13	12	J Trulli	Prost	AP01	Peugeot	V10	50		10	5
r	19	J Verstappen	Stewart	SF-2	Ford Cosworth	V10	39	gearbox	17	9
r	1	J Villeneuve	Williams	FW20	Mecachrome	V10	37	spin	2	1
r	17	M Salo	Arrows	A19	Arrows	V10	32	hydraulics	16	8
r	6	A Wurz	Benetton	B198	Playlife	V10	24	gearbox	7	4
r	7	D Coulthard	McLaren	MP4/13	Mercedes-Benz	V10	16	engine	4	2
r	11	O Panis	Prost	AP01	Peugeot	V10	15	rear suspension	9	5
r	22	S Nakano	Minardi	M198	Ford Cosworth	V10	13	engine / fire	21	11
r	15	J Herbert	Sauber	C17	Petronas	V10	12	spin	15	8
r	16	P Diniz	Arrows	A19	Arrows	V10	10	brakes / spin	20	10

Winning speed 237.591 km/h, 147.633 mph
Pole Position speed 243.548 km/h, 151.334 mph (M Schumacher, 1 min:25.289 sec)
Fastest Lap speed 243.977 km/h, 151.601 mph (M Häkkinen, 1 min:25.139 sec on lap 45)
Lap Leaders M Häkkinen 1-7,32-34 (10); D Coulthard 8-16 (9); M Schumacher 17-31,35-53 (34).

27 Sep 1998   LUXEMBOURG: Nürburgring   (Round 15)   (Race 629)
67 laps x 4.556 km, 2.831 miles = 305.235 km, 189.664 miles

Pos	No	Driver	Car	Model	Engine		Laps	Time/Reason for Retirement	Grid Pos	Row
1	8	M Häkkinen	McLaren	MP4/13	Mercedes-Benz	V10	67	1h 32m 14.789s	3	2
2	3	M Schumacher	Ferrari	F300	Ferrari	V10	67	1h 32m 17.000s	1	1
3	7	D Coulthard	McLaren	MP4/13	Mercedes-Benz	V10	67	1h 32m 48.952s	5	3
4	4	E Irvine	Ferrari	F300	Ferrari	V10	67	1h 33m 12.971s	2	1
5	2	H-H Frentzen	Williams	FW20	Mecachrome	V10	67	1h 33m 15.036s	7	4
6	5	G Fisichella	Benetton	B198	Playlife	V10	67	1h 33m 16.148s	4	2
7	6	A Wurz	Benetton	B198	Playlife	V10	67	1h 33m 19.578s	8	4
8	1	J Villeneuve	Williams	FW20	Mecachrome	V10	66		9	5
9	9	D Hill	Jordan	198	Mugen Honda	V10	66		10	5
10	14	J Alesi	Sauber	C17	Petronas	V10	66		11	6
11	18	R Barrichello	Stewart	SF-2	Ford Cosworth	V10	65		12	6
12	11	O Panis	Prost	AP01	Peugeot	V10	65		15	8
13	19	J Verstappen	Stewart	SF-2	Ford Cosworth	V10	65		18	9
14	17	M Salo	Arrows	A19	Arrows	V10	65		16	8
15	22	S Nakano	Minardi	M198	Ford Cosworth	V10	65		20	10
16	21	T Takagi	Tyrrell	026	Ford Cosworth	V10	65		19	10
nc	23	E Tuero	Minardi	M198	Ford Cosworth	V10	56		21	11
r	10	R Schumacher	Jordan	198	Mugen Honda	V10	53	front brake disc	6	3
r	15	J Herbert	Sauber	C17	Petronas	V10	37	engine	13	7
r	20	R Rosset	Tyrrell	026	Ford Cosworth	V10	36	engine	22	11
r	12	J Trulli	Prost	AP01	Peugeot	V10	6	gearbox	14	7
r	16	P Diniz	Arrows	A19	Arrows	V10	6	hydraulics	17	9

Winning speed 198.534 km/h, 123.364 mph
Pole Position speed 208.775 km/h, 129.727 mph (M Schumacher, 1 min:18.561 sec)
Fastest Lap speed 203.873 km/h, 126.681 mph (M Häkkinen, 1 min:20.450 sec on lap 25)
Lap Leaders M Schumacher 1-24 (24); M Häkkinen 25-67 (43).

Races 411

1 Nov 1998   JAPAN: Suzuka   (Round 16)   (Race 630)

51 laps x 5.864 km, 3.644 miles = 298.868 km, 185.708 miles

Pos	No	Driver	Car	Model	Engine		Laps	Time/Reason for Retirement	Grid Pos	Row
1	8	M Häkkinen	McLaren	MP4/13	Mercedes-Benz	V10	51	1h 27m 22.535s	2	1
2	4	E Irvine	Ferrari	F300	Ferrari	V10	51	1h 27m 29.026s	4	2
3	7	D Coulthard	McLaren	MP4/13	Mercedes-Benz	V10	51	1h 27m 50.197s	3	2
4	9	D Hill	Jordan	198	Mugen Honda	V10	51	1h 28m 36.026s	8	4
5	2	H-H Frentzen	Williams	FW20	Mecachrome	V10	51	1h 28m 36.392s	5	3
6	1	J Villeneuve	Williams	FW20	Mecachrome	V10	51	1h 28m 38.402s	6	3
7	14	J Alesi	Sauber	C17	Petronas	V10	51	1h 28m 58.588s	12	6
8	5	G Fisichella	Benetton	B198	Playlife	V10	51	1h 29m 03.837s	10	5
9	6	A Wurz	Benetton	B198	Playlife	V10	50		9	5
10	15	J Herbert	Sauber	C17	Petronas	V10	50		11	6
11	11	O Panis	Prost	AP01	Peugeot	V10	50		13	7
12r	12	J Trulli	Prost	AP01B	Peugeot	V10	48	engine	14	7
r	22	S Nakano	Minardi	M198	Ford Cosworth	V10	40	throttle	20	10
r	3	M Schumacher	Ferrari	F300	Ferrari	V10	31	rear tyre	1	1
r	21	T Takagi	Tyrrell	026	Ford Cosworth	V10	28	accident	17	9
r	23	E Tuero	Minardi	M198	Ford Cosworth	V10	28	accident	21	11
r	18	R Barrichello	Stewart	SF-2	Ford Cosworth	V10	25	differential	16	8
r	19	J Verstappen	Stewart	SF-2	Ford Cosworth	V10	21	gearbox	19	10
r	17	M Salo	Arrows	A19	Arrows	V10	14	hydraulics	15	8
r	10	R Schumacher	Jordan	198	Mugen Honda	V10	13	engine	7	4
r	16	P Diniz	Arrows	A19	Arrows	V10	2	brakes / spin	18	9
nq	20	R Rosset	Tyrrell	026	Ford Cosworth	V10				

Winning speed 205.229 km/h, 127.524 mph
Pole Position speed 219.230 km/h, 136.224 mph (M Schumacher, 1 min:36.293 sec)
Fastest Lap speed 210.703 km/h, 130.925 mph (M Schumacher, 1 min:40.190 sec on lap 19)
Lap Leaders M Häkkinen 1-51 (51).

Race abandoned twice due to stalled cars on the grid. Race consequently reduced by two laps.

Lap Leaders 1998

Pos	Driver	Car-Engine	GPs	laps	km	miles
1	M Häkkinen	McLaren-Mercedes-Benz	12	576	2,709.1	1,683.4
2	M Schumacher	Ferrari	8	268	1,252.3	778.2
3	D Coulthard	McLaren-Mercedes-Benz	8	120	597.3	371.1
4	D Hill	Jordan-Mugen Honda	1	26	181.2	112.6
5	G Fisichella	Benetton-Playlife	1	24	106.1	65.9
6	E Irvine	Ferrari	1	1	4.3	2.6
			16	**1,015**	**4,850.3**	**3,013.8**

Driver Points 1998

		AUS	BR	RA	RSM	E	MC	CDN	F	GB	A	D	H	B	I	L	J	Total
1	M Häkkinen	10	10	6	-	10	10	-	4	6	10	10	1	-	3	10	10	100
2	M Schumacher	-	4	10	6	4	-	10	10	10	4	2	10	-	10	6	-	86
3	D Coulthard	6	6	1	10	6	-	-	1	-	6	6	6	-	-	4	4	56
4	E Irvine	3	-	4	4	-	4	4	6	4	3	-	-	-	6	3	6	47
5	J Villeneuve	2	-	-	3	1	2	3	3	-	1	4	4	-	-	-	1	21
6	D Hill	-	-	-	-	-	-	-	-	-	-	3	3	10	1	-	3	20
7	H-H Frentzen	4	2	-	2	-	-	-	-	-	-	-	2	3	-	2	2	17
	A Wurz	-	3	3	-	3	-	-	2	3	-	-	-	-	-	-	-	17
9	G Fisichella	-	1	-	-	-	6	6	-	2	-	-	-	-	-	1	-	16
10	R Schumacher	-	-	-	-	-	-	-	1	2	1	-	6	4	-	-	-	14
11	J Alesi	-	-	2	1	-	-	-	-	-	-	-	-	4	2	-	-	9
12	R Barrichello	-	-	-	-	2	-	2	-	-	-	-	-	-	-	-	-	4
13	M Salo	-	-	-	-	-	3	-	-	-	-	-	-	-	-	-	-	3
	P Diniz	-	-	-	-	-	1	-	-	-	-	-	2	-	-	-	-	3
15	J Herbert	1	-	-	-	-	-	-	-	-	-	-	-	-	-	-	-	1
	J Magnussen	-	-	-	-	-	-	1	-	-	-	-	-	-	-	-	-	1
	J Trulli	-	-	-	-	-	-	-	-	-	-	-	-	1	-	-	-	1

10,6,4,3,2 and 1 point awarded to the first six finishers.

Constructor Points 1998

		AUS	BR	RA	RSM	E	MC	CDN	F	GB	A	D	H	B	I	L	J	Total
1	McLaren-Mercedes-Benz	16	16	7	10	16	10	-	5	6	16	16	7	-	3	14	14	156
2	Ferrari	3	4	14	10	4	4	4	16	14	7	2	10	-	16	9	6	133
3	Williams-Mecachrome	6	2	-	5	1	2	3	3	-	1	4	4	3	-	2	3	38
4	Jordan-Mugen Honda	-	-	-	-	-	-	-	1	2	4	3	16	5	-	3	34
5	Benetton-Playlife	-	4	3	-	3	6	6	2	5	-	-	-	-	-	1	-	33
6	Sauber-Petronas	1	-	2	1	-	-	-	-	-	-	-	-	4	2	-	-	10
7	Arrows	-	-	-	-	-	4	-	-	-	-	-	-	2	-	-	-	6
8	Stewart-Ford Cosworth	-	-	-	2	-	3	-	-	-	-	-	-	-	-	-	5
9	Prost-Peugeot	-	-	-	-	-	-	-	-	-	-	-	-	1	-	-	-	1

10,6,4,3,2 and 1 point awarded to the first six finishers.

Race Entrants and Results

Williams signed as their lead driver Alex Zanardi who returned to Formula 1 after winning back to back championships in Champ Cars (formerly IndyCars). British American Racing made a controversial entrance to the sport with promises of a victory first time out and a provocative dual cigarette branding colour scheme. In June, Ford announced that they were to purchase the Stewart team outright and rumours immediately began that they would be rebadged as Jaguar. Meanwhile, in April, the motorsport world mourned the death of designer Harvey Postlethwaite which resulted in the Honda F1 car project being disbanded.

McLAREN
West McLaren Mercedes: Häkkinen, Coulthard

FERRARI
Scuderia Ferrari Marlboro: M Schumacher, Irvine, Salo

WILLIAMS
Winfield Williams: Zanardi, R Schumacher

JORDAN
Benson & Hedges Jordan: Hill, Frentzen

BENETTON
Mild Seven Benetton Playlife: Fisichella, Wurz

SAUBER
Red Bull Sauber Petronas: Alesi, Diniz

ARROWS
Arrows: de la Rosa, Takagi

STEWART
Stewart Ford: Barrichello, Herbert

PROST
Gauloises Prost Peugeot: Panis, Trulli

MINARDI
Fondmetal Minardi Ford: Badoer, Gené, Sarrazin

BAR
British American Racing: Villeneuve, Zonta, Salo

7 Mar 1999		AUSTRALIA: Melbourne						(Round 1)	(Race 631)	
		57 laps x 5.303 km, 3.295 miles = 302.271 km, 187.822 miles								
Pos	No	Driver	Car	Model	Engine		Laps	Time/Reason for Retirement	Grid Pos	Row
1	4	E Irvine	Ferrari	F399	Ferrari	V10	57	1h 35m 01.659s	6	3
2	8	H-H Frentzen	Jordan	199	Mugen Honda	V10	57	1h 35m 02.686s	5	3
3	6	R Schumacher	Williams	FW21	Supertec	V10	57	1h 35m 08.671s	8	4
4	9	G Fisichella	Benetton	B199	Playlife	V10	57	1h 35m 35.077s	7	4
5	16	R Barrichello	Stewart	SF-3	Ford Cosworth	V10	57	1h 35m 56.357s	4	2
6	14	P de la Rosa	Arrows	A20	Arrows	V10	57	1h 36m 25.976s	18	9
7	15	T Takagi	Arrows	A20	Arrows	V10	57	1h 36m 27.947s	17	9
8	3	M Schumacher	Ferrari	F399	Ferrari	V10	56		3	2
r	23	R Zonta	BAR	01	Supertec	V10	48	engine	19	10
r	20	L Badoer	Minardi	M01	Ford Cosworth	V10	42	gearbox	21	11
r	10	A Wurz	Benetton	B199	Playlife	V10	28	rear suspension / spin	10	5
r	12	P Diniz	Sauber	C18	Petronas	V10	27	gearbox	14	7
r	21	M Gené	Minardi	M01	Ford Cosworth	V10	25	accident	22	11
r	19	J Trulli	Prost	AP02	Peugeot	V10	25	accident	12	6
r	18	O Panis	Prost	AP02	Peugeot	V10	23	jammed wheel nut	20	10
r	1	M Häkkinen	McLaren	MP4/14	Mercedes-Benz	V10	21	throttle linkage	1	1
r	5	A Zanardi	Williams	FW21	Supertec	V10	20	accident	15	8
r	2	D Coulthard	McLaren	MP4/14	Mercedes-Benz	V10	13	hydraulics	2	1
r	22	J Villeneuve	BAR	01	Supertec	V10	13	rear wing / accident	11	6
r	7	D Hill	Jordan	199	Mugen Honda	V10	0	accident	9	5
r	11	J Alesi	Sauber	C18	Petronas	V10	0	gearbox	16	8
ns	17	J Herbert	Stewart	SF-3	Ford Cosworth	V10		oil leak / fire on parade lap	13	7

Winning speed 190.852 km/h, 118.590 mph
Pole Position speed 211.036 km/h, 131.132 mph (M Häkkinen, 1 min:30.462 sec)
Fastest Lap speed 207.256 km/h, 128.783 mph (M Schumacher, 1 min:32.112 sec on lap 55)
Lap Leaders M Häkkinen 1-17 (17); E Irvine 18-57 (40).

11 Apr 1999   BRAZIL: Interlagos   (Round 2)   (Race 632)

72 laps x 4.292 km, 2.667 miles = 308.994 km, 192.000 miles

Pos	No	Driver	Car	Model	Engine		Laps	Time/Reason for Retirement	Grid Pos	Row
1	1	M Häkkinen	McLaren	MP4/14	Mercedes-Benz	V10	72	1h 36m 03.785s	1	1
2	3	M Schumacher	Ferrari	F399	Ferrari	V10	72	1h 36m 08.710s	4	2
3r	8	H-H Frentzen	Jordan	199	Mugen Honda	V10	71	out of fuel	8	4
4	6	R Schumacher	Williams	FW21	Supertec	V10	71		11	6
5	4	E Irvine	Ferrari	F399	Ferrari	V10	71		6	3
6	18	O Panis	Prost	AP02	Peugeot	V10	71		12	6
7	10	A Wurz	Benetton	B199	Playlife	V10	70		9	5
8	15	T Takagi	Arrows	A20	Arrows	V10	69		19	10
9	21	M Gené	Minardi	M01	Ford Cosworth	V10	69		20	10
r	14	P de la Rosa	Arrows	A20	Arrows	V10	52	hydraulics	18	9
r	22	J Villeneuve	BAR	01	Supertec	V10	49	hydraulics	21	11
r	5	A Zanardi	Williams	FW21	Supertec	V10	43	transmission	16	8
r	16	R Barrichello	Stewart	SF-3	Ford Cosworth	V10	42	engine	3	2
r	12	P Diniz	Sauber	C18	Petronas	V10	42	accident	15	8
r	9	G Fisichella	Benetton	B199	Playlife	V10	38	clutch	5	3
r	20	S Sarrazin	Minardi	M01	Ford Cosworth	V10	31	throttle / accident	17	9
r	11	J Alesi	Sauber	C18	Petronas	V10	27	gearbox	14	7
r	2	D Coulthard	McLaren	MP4/14	Mercedes-Benz	V10	22	gearbox	2	1
r	19	J Trulli	Prost	AP02	Peugeot	V10	21	gearbox	13	7
r	17	J Herbert	Stewart	SF-3	Ford Cosworth	V10	15	hydraulics	10	5
r	7	D Hill	Jordan	199	Mugen Honda	V10	10	accident / steering	7	4
ns	23	R Zonta	BAR	01	Supertec	V10		accident / injury		

Winning speed 192.994 km/h, 119.921 mph
Pole Position speed 201.797 km/h, 125.391 mph (M Häkkinen, 1 min:16.568 sec)
Fastest Lap speed 196.961 km/h, 122.386 mph (M Häkkinen, 1 min:18.448 sec on lap 70)
Lap Leaders M Häkkinen 1-3,38-72 (38); R Barrichello 4-26 (23); M Schumacher 27-37 (11).

2 May 1999   SAN MARINO: Imola   (Round 3)   (Race 633)

62 laps x 4.930 km, 3.063 miles = 305.428 km, 189.784 miles

Pos	No	Driver	Car	Model	Engine		Laps	Time/Reason for Retirement	Grid Pos	Row
1	3	M Schumacher	Ferrari	F399	Ferrari	V10	62	1h 33m 44.792s	3	2
2	2	D Coulthard	McLaren	MP4/14	Mercedes-Benz	V10	62	1h 33m 49.057s	2	1
3	16	R Barrichello	Stewart	SF-3	Ford Cosworth	V10	61		6	3
4	7	D Hill	Jordan	199	Mugen Honda	V10	61		8	4
5	9	G Fisichella	Benetton	B199	Playlife	V10	61		16	8
6	11	J Alesi	Sauber	C18	Petronas	V10	61		13	7
7r	23	M Salo	BAR	01	Supertec	V10	59	electrics	19	10
8	20	L Badoer	Minardi	M01	Ford Cosworth	V10	59		22	11
9	21	M Gené	Minardi	M01	Ford Cosworth	V10	59		21	11
10r	17	J Herbert	Stewart	SF-3	Ford Cosworth	V10	58	engine	12	6
11r	5	A Zanardi	Williams	FW21	Supertec	V10	58	spin	10	5
r	12	P Diniz	Sauber	C18	Petronas	V10	49	spin	15	8
r	18	O Panis	Prost	AP02	Peugeot	V10	48	engine	11	6
r	4	E Irvine	Ferrari	F399	Ferrari	V10	46	engine	4	2
r	8	H-H Frentzen	Jordan	199	Mugen Honda	V10	46	spin	7	4
r	15	T Takagi	Arrows	A20	Arrows	V10	29	fuel pressure	20	10
r	6	R Schumacher	Williams	FW21	Supertec	V10	28	electrics / fire	9	5
r	1	M Häkkinen	McLaren	MP4/14	Mercedes-Benz	V10	17	accident	1	1
r	14	P de la Rosa	Arrows	A20	Arrows	V10	5	accident	18	9
r	10	A Wurz	Benetton	B199	Playlife	V10	5	accident	17	9
r	19	J Trulli	Prost	AP02	Peugeot	V10	0	accident	14	7
r	22	J Villeneuve	BAR	01	Supertec	V10	0	gearbox	5	3

Winning speed 195.481 km/h, 121.466 mph
Pole Position speed 205.507 km/h, 127.696 mph (M Häkkinen, 1 min:26.362 sec)
Fastest Lap speed 200.435 km/h, 124.545 mph (M Schumacher, 1 min:28.547 sec on lap 45)
Lap Leaders M Häkkinen 1-17 (17); D Coulthard 18-35 (18); M Schumacher 36-62 (27).

16 May 1999   MONACO: Monte-Carlo   (Round 4)   (Race 634)

78 laps x 3.367 km, 2.092 miles = 262.626 km, 163.188 miles

Pos	No	Driver	Car	Model	Engine		Laps	Time/Reason for Retirement	Grid Pos	Row
1	3	M Schumacher	Ferrari	F399	Ferrari	V10	78	1h 49m 31.812s	2	1
2	4	E Irvine	Ferrari	F399	Ferrari	V10	78	1h 50m 02.288s	4	2
3	1	M Häkkinen	McLaren	MP4/14	Mercedes-Benz	V10	78	1h 50m 09.295s	1	1
4	8	H-H Frentzen	Jordan	199	Mugen Honda	V10	78	1h 50m 25.821s	6	3
5	9	G Fisichella	Benetton	B199	Playlife	V10	77		9	5
6	10	A Wurz	Benetton	B199	Playlife	V10	77		10	5
7	19	J Trulli	Prost	AP02	Peugeot	V10	77		7	4
8	5	A Zanardi	Williams	FW21	Supertec	V10	76		11	6
9r	16	R Barrichello	Stewart	SF-3	Ford Cosworth	V10	71	rear suspension / accident	5	3
r	6	R Schumacher	Williams	FW21	Supertec	V10	54	accident	16	8
r	11	J Alesi	Sauber	C18	Petronas	V10	50	accident / rear suspension	14	7
r	12	P Diniz	Sauber	C18	Petronas	V10	49	brakes / accident	15	8

Pos	No	Driver	Car	Model	Engine		Laps	Time/Reason for Retirement	Grid Pos	Row
r	18	O Panis	Prost	AP02	Peugeot	V10	40	engine	18	9
r	2	D Coulthard	McLaren	MP4/14	Mercedes-Benz	V10	36	gearbox oil leak	3	2
r	23	M Salo	BAR	01	Supertec	V10	36	brakes / accident	12	6
r	15	T Takagi	Arrows	A20	Arrows	V10	36	engine	19	10
r	22	J Villeneuve	BAR	01	Supertec	V10	32	oil leak	8	4
r	17	J Herbert	Stewart	SF-3	Ford Cosworth	V10	32	rear suspension	13	7
r	14	P de la Rosa	Arrows	A20	Arrows	V10	30	gearbox	21	11
r	21	M Gené	Minardi	M01	Ford Cosworth	V10	24	accident	22	11
r	20	L Badoer	Minardi	M01	Ford Cosworth	V10	10	gearbox	20	10
r	7	D Hill	Jordan	199	Mugen Honda	V10	3	accident	17	9

Winning speed 143.864 km/h, 89.394 mph
Pole Position speed 150.486 km/h, 93.508 mph (M Häkkinen, 1 min:20.547 sec)
Fastest Lap speed 147.354 km/h, 91.562 mph (M Häkkinen, 1 min:22.259 sec on lap 67)
Lap Leaders M Schumacher 1-78 (78).

30 May 1999   SPAIN: Montmeló   (Round 5)   (Race 635)

65 laps x 4.728 km, 2.938 miles = 307.196 km, 190.883 miles

Pos	No	Driver	Car	Model	Engine		Laps	Time/Reason for Retirement	Grid Pos	Row
1	1	M Häkkinen	McLaren	MP4/14	Mercedes-Benz	V10	65	1h 34m 13.665s	1	1
2	2	D Coulthard	McLaren	MP4/14	Mercedes-Benz	V10	65	1h 34m 19.903s	3	2
3	3	M Schumacher	Ferrari	F399	Ferrari	V10	65	1h 34m 24.510s	4	2
4	4	E Irvine	Ferrari	F399	Ferrari	V10	65	1h 34m 43.847s	2	1
5	6	R Schumacher	Williams	FW21	Supertec	V10	65	1h 35m 40.873s	10	5
6	19	J Trulli	Prost	AP02	Peugeot	V10	64		9	5
7	7	D Hill	Jordan	199	Mugen Honda	V10	64		11	6
dq	16	R Barrichello	Stewart	SF-3	Ford Cosworth	V10	64	used wrong undertray fittings	7	4
8	23	M Salo	BAR	01	Supertec	V10	64		16	8
9	9	G Fisichella	Benetton	B199	Playlife	V10	64		13	7
10	10	A Wurz	Benetton	B199	Playlife	V10	64		18	9
11	14	P de la Rosa	Arrows	A20	Arrows	V10	63		19	10
12	15	T Takagi	Arrows	A20	Arrows	V10	62		20	10
r	20	L Badoer	Minardi	M01	Ford Cosworth	V10	50	spin	22	11
r	22	J Villeneuve	BAR	01	Supertec	V10	40	gearbox	6	3
r	12	P Diniz	Sauber	C18	Petronas	V10	40	gearbox	12	6
r	17	J Herbert	Stewart	SF-3	Ford Cosworth	V10	40	transmission	14	7
r	8	H-H Frentzen	Jordan	199	Mugen Honda	V10	35	differential	8	4
r	11	J Alesi	Sauber	C18	Petronas	V10	27	electrics	5	3
r	5	A Zanardi	Williams	FW21	Supertec	V10	24	gearbox	17	9
r	18	O Panis	Prost	AP02	Peugeot	V10	24	gearbox oil pressure	15	8
r	21	M Gené	Minardi	M01	Ford Cosworth	V10	0	gearbox	21	11

Winning speed 195.608 km/h, 121.546 mph
Pole Position speed 207.348 km/h, 128.840 mph (M Häkkinen, 1 min:22.088 sec)
Fastest Lap speed 200.287 km/h, 124.453 mph (M Schumacher, 1 min:24.982 sec on lap 29)
Lap Leaders M Häkkinen 1-23,27-44,46-65 (61); D Coulthard 24-26,45 (4).

13 Jun 1999   CANADA: Montréal   (Round 6)   (Race 636)

69 laps x 4.421 km, 2.747 miles = 305.049 km, 189.549 miles

Pos	No	Driver	Car	Model	Engine		Laps	Time/Reason for Retirement	Grid Pos	Row
1	1	M Häkkinen	McLaren	MP4/14	Mercedes-Benz	V10	69	1h 41m 35.727s	2	1
2	9	G Fisichella	Benetton	B199	Playlife	V10	69	1h 41m 36.509s	7	4
3	4	E Irvine	Ferrari	F399	Ferrari	V10	69	1h 41m 37.524s	3	2
4	6	R Schumacher	Williams	FW21	Supertec	V10	69	1h 41m 38.119s	13	7
5	17	J Herbert	Stewart	SF-3	Ford Cosworth	V10	69	1h 41m 38.532s	10	5
6	12	P Diniz	Sauber	C18	Petronas	V10	69	1h 41m 39.438s	18	9
7	2	D Coulthard	McLaren	MP4/14	Mercedes-Benz	V10	69	1h 41m 40.731s	4	2
8	21	M Gené	Minardi	M01	Ford Cosworth	V10	68		22	11
9	18	O Panis	Prost	AP02	Peugeot	V10	68		15	8
10	20	L Badoer	Minardi	M01	Ford Cosworth	V10	67		21	11
11r	8	H-H Frentzen	Jordan	199	Mugen Honda	V10	65	brake disc / accident	6	3
r	5	A Zanardi	Williams	FW21	Supertec	V10	50	gearbox / spin	12	6
r	15	T Takagi	Arrows	A20	Arrows	V10	41	transmission	19	10
r	22	J Villeneuve	BAR	01	Supertec	V10	34	accident	16	8
r	3	M Schumacher	Ferrari	F399	Ferrari	V10	29	accident	1	1
r	14	P de la Rosa	Arrows	A20	Arrows	V10	22	transmission	20	10
r	7	D Hill	Jordan	199	Mugen Honda	V10	14	accident	14	7
r	16	R Barrichello	Stewart	SF-3	Ford Cosworth	V10	14	accident / steering	5	3
r	23	R Zonta	BAR	01	Supertec	V10	2	accident	17	9
r	11	J Alesi	Sauber	C18	Petronas	V10	0	accident	8	4
r	19	J Trulli	Prost	AP02	Peugeot	V10	0	accident	9	5
r	10	A Wurz	Benetton	B199	Playlife	V10	0	driveshaft	11	6

Winning speed 180.155 km/h, 111.943 mph
Pole Position speed 200.706 km/h, 124.713 mph (M Schumacher, 1 min:19.298 sec)
Fastest Lap speed 197.999 km/h, 123.031 mph (E Irvine, 1 min:20.382 sec on lap 62)
Lap Leaders M Schumacher 1-29 (29); M Häkkinen 30-69 (40).

27 Jun 1999   FRANCE: Magny-Cours   (Round 7)   (Race 637)

72 laps x 4.250 km, 2.641 miles = 305.814 km, 190.024 miles

Pos	No	Driver	Car	Model	Engine		Laps	Time/Reason for Retirement	Grid Pos	Row
1	8	H-H Frentzen	Jordan	199	Mugen Honda	V10	72	1h 58m 24.343s	5	3
2	1	M Häkkinen	McLaren	MP4/14	Mercedes-Benz	V10	72	1h 58m 35.435s	14	7
3	16	R Barrichello	Stewart	SF-3	Ford Cosworth	V10	72	1h 59m 07.775s	1	1
4	6	R Schumacher	Williams	FW21	Supertec	V10	72	1h 59m 09.818s	16	8
5	3	M Schumacher	Ferrari	F399	Ferrari	V10	72	1h 59m 12.224s	6	3
6	4	E Irvine	Ferrari	F399	Ferrari	V10	72	1h 59m 13.244s	17	9
7	19	J Trulli	Prost	AP02	Peugeot	V10	72	1h 59m 22.114s	8	4
8	18	O Panis	Prost	AP02	Peugeot	V10	72	1h 59m 22.874s	3	2
9	23	R Zonta	BAR	01	Supertec	V10	72	1h 59m 53.107s	10	5
10	20	L Badoer	Minardi	M01	Ford Cosworth	V10	71		21	11
dq	15	T Takagi	Arrows	A20	Arrows	V10	71	used illegal tyres	19	10
11	14	P de la Rosa	Arrows	A20	Arrows	V10	71		20	10
r	9	G Fisichella	Benetton	B199	Playlife	V10	42	spin	7	4
r	7	D Hill	Jordan	199	Mugen Honda	V10	31	ignition	18	9
r	5	A Zanardi	Williams	FW21	Supertec	V10	26	spin / engine	15	8
r	22	J Villeneuve	BAR	01	Supertec	V10	25	spin	12	6
r	10	A Wurz	Benetton	B199	Playlife	V10	25	spin	13	7
r	21	M Gené	Minardi	M01	Ford Cosworth	V10	25	spin	22	11
r	11	J Alesi	Sauber	C18	Petronas	V10	24	spin	2	1
r	2	D Coulthard	McLaren	MP4/14	Mercedes-Benz	V10	9	alternator	4	2
r	12	P Diniz	Sauber	C18	Petronas	V10	6	transmission	11	6
r	17	J Herbert	Stewart	SF-3	Ford Cosworth	V10	4	gearbox	9	5

Winning speed 154.965 km/h, 96.291 mph
Pole Position speed 155.423 km/h, 96.575 mph (R Barrichello, 1 min:38.441 sec)
Fastest Lap speed 193.115 km/h, 119.997 mph (D Coulthard, 1 min:19.227 sec on lap 8)
Lap Leaders R Barrichello 1-5,10-43,55-59 (44); D Coulthard 6-9 (4); M Schumacher 44-54 (11); M Häkkinen 60-65 (6); H-H Frentzen 66-72 (7).

11 Jul 1999   BRITAIN: Silverstone   (Round 8)   (Race 638)

60 laps x 5.140 km, 3.194 miles = 308.296 km, 191.566 miles

Pos	No	Driver	Car	Model	Engine		Laps	Time/Reason for Retirement	Grid Pos	Row
1	2	D Coulthard	McLaren	MP4/14	Mercedes-Benz	V10	60	1h 32m 30.144s	3	2
2	4	E Irvine	Ferrari	F399	Ferrari	V10	60	1h 32m 31.973s	4	2
3	6	R Schumacher	Williams	FW21	Supertec	V10	60	1h 32m 57.555s	8	4
4	8	H-H Frentzen	Jordan	199	Mugen Honda	V10	60	1h 32m 57.933s	5	3
5	7	D Hill	Jordan	199	Mugen Honda	V10	60	1h 33m 08.750s	6	3
6	12	P Diniz	Sauber	C18	Petronas	V10	60	1h 33m 23.787s	12	6
7	9	G Fisichella	Benetton	B199	Playlife	V10	60	1h 33m 24.758s	17	9
8	16	R Barrichello	Stewart	SF-3	Ford Cosworth	V10	60	1h 33m 38.734s	7	4
9	19	J Trulli	Prost	AP02	Peugeot	V10	60	1h 33m 42.189s	14	7
10	10	A Wurz	Benetton	B199	Playlife	V10	60	1h 33m 42.267s	18	9
11	5	A Zanardi	Williams	FW21	Supertec	V10	60	1h 33m 47.268s	13	7
12	17	J Herbert	Stewart	SF-3	Ford Cosworth	V10	60	1h 33m 47.853s	11	6
13	18	O Panis	Prost	AP02	Peugeot	V10	60	1h 33m 50.636s	15	8
14	11	J Alesi	Sauber	C18	Petronas	V10	59		10	5
15	21	M Gené	Minardi	M01	Ford Cosworth	V10	58		22	11
16	15	T Takagi	Arrows	A20	Arrows	V10	58		19	10
r	23	R Zonta	BAR	01	Supertec	V10	41	suspension / spin	16	8
r	1	M Häkkinen	McLaren	MP4/14	Mercedes-Benz	V10	35	rear hub / brakes	1	1
r	22	J Villeneuve	BAR	01	Supertec	V10	29	gearbox	9	5
r	20	L Badoer	Minardi	M01	Ford Cosworth	V10	6	gearbox	21	11
r	14	P de la Rosa	Arrows	A20	Arrows	V10	0	gearbox	20	10
r	3	M Schumacher	Ferrari	F399	Ferrari	V10	0	accident / injury *	2	1

Winning speed 199.970 km/h, 124.256 mph
Pole Position speed 218.197 km/h, 135.581 mph (M Häkkinen, 1 min:24.804 sec)
Fastest Lap speed 209.536 km/h, 130.200 mph (M Häkkinen, 1 min:28.309 sec on lap 28)
Lap Leaders M Häkkinen 1-24 (24); E Irvine 25-26 (2); D Coulthard 27-42,46-60 (31); H-H Frentzen 43-44 (2); D Hill 45 (1).

* Retired after first start.

25 Jul 1999   AUSTRIA: A1-Ring   (Round 9)   (Race 639)

71 laps x 4.319 km, 2.684 miles = 306.649 km, 190.543 miles

Pos	No	Driver	Car	Model	Engine		Laps	Time/Reason for Retirement	Grid Pos	Row
1	4	E Irvine	Ferrari	F399	Ferrari	V10	71	1h 28m 12.438s	3	2
2	2	D Coulthard	McLaren	MP4/14	Mercedes-Benz	V10	71	1h 28m 12.751s	2	1
3	1	M Häkkinen	McLaren	MP4/14	Mercedes-Benz	V10	71	1h 28m 34.720s	1	1
4	8	H-H Frentzen	Jordan	199	Mugen Honda	V10	71	1h 29m 05.241s	4	2
5	10	A Wurz	Benetton	B199	Playlife	V10	71	1h 29m 18.796s	10	5
6	12	P Diniz	Sauber	C18	Petronas	V10	71	1h 29m 23.371s	16	8
7	19	J Trulli	Prost	AP02	Peugeot	V10	70		13	7
8	7	D Hill	Jordan	199	Mugen Honda	V10	70		11	6
9	3	M Salo	Ferrari	F399	Ferrari	V10	70		7	4
10	18	O Panis	Prost	AP02	Peugeot	V10	70		18	9
11	21	M Gené	Minardi	M01	Ford Cosworth	V10	70		22	11
12r	9	G Fisichella	Benetton	B199	Playlife	V10	68	engine	12	6

Pos	No	Driver	Car	Model	Engine		Laps	Time/Reason for Retirement	Grid Pos	Row
13	20	L Badoer	Minardi	M01	Ford Cosworth	V10	68		19	10
14	17	J Herbert	Stewart	SF-3	Ford Cosworth	V10	67		6	3
15r	23	R Zonta	BAR	01	Supertec	V10	63	clutch	15	8
r	16	R Barrichello	Stewart	SF-3	Ford Cosworth	V10	55	engine	5	3
r	11	J Alesi	Sauber	C18	Petronas	V10	49	out of fuel	17	9
r	14	P de la Rosa	Arrows	A20	Arrows	V10	38	brakes / spin	21	11
r	5	A Zanardi	Williams	FW21	Supertec	V10	35	out of fuel	14	7
r	22	J Villeneuve	BAR	01	Supertec	V10	34	driveshaft	9	5
r	15	T Takagi	Arrows	A20	Arrows	V10	25	engine	20	10
r	6	R Schumacher	Williams	FW21	Supertec	V10	8	spin	8	4

Winning speed 208.587 km/h, 129.610 mph
Pole Position speed 219.133 km/h, 136.163 mph (M Häkkinen, 1 min:10.954 sec)
Fastest Lap speed 215.629 km/h, 133.986 mph (M Häkkinen, 1 min:12.107 sec on lap 39)
Lap Leaders D Coulthard 1-39 (39); E Irvine 40-71 (32).

1 Aug 1999		**GERMANY: Hockenheim**							**(Round 10)**	**(Race 640)**
		45 laps x 6.823 km, 4.240 miles = 307.035 km, 190.783 miles								

Pos	No	Driver	Car	Model	Engine		Laps	Time/Reason for Retirement	Grid Pos	Row
1	4	E Irvine	Ferrari	F399	Ferrari	V10	45	1h 21m 58.594s	5	3
2	3	M Salo	Ferrari	F399	Ferrari	V10	45	1h 21m 59.601s	4	2
3	8	H-H Frentzen	Jordan	199	Mugen Honda	V10	45	1h 22m 03.789s	2	1
4	6	R Schumacher	Williams	FW21	Supertec	V10	45	1h 22m 11.403s	11	6
5	2	D Coulthard	McLaren	MP4/14	Mercedes-Benz	V10	45	1h 22m 15.417s	3	2
6	18	O Panis	Prost	AP02	Peugeot	V10	45	1h 22m 28.473s	7	4
7	10	A Wurz	Benetton	B199	Playlife	V10	45	1h 22m 31.927s	13	7
8	11	J Alesi	Sauber	C18	Petronas	V10	45	1h 23m 09.885s	21	11
9	21	M Gené	Minardi	M01	Ford Cosworth	V10	45	1h 23m 46.912s	15	8
10	20	L Badoer	Minardi	M01	Ford Cosworth	V10	44		19	10
11r	17	J Herbert	Stewart	SF-3	Ford Cosworth	V10	40	gearbox	17	9
r	14	P de la Rosa	Arrows	A20	Arrows	V10	37	accident	20	10
r	1	M Häkkinen	McLaren	MP4/14	Mercedes-Benz	V10	25	rear tyre / accident	1	1
r	5	A Zanardi	Williams	FW21	Supertec	V10	21	differential	14	7
r	23	R Zonta	BAR	01	Supertec	V10	20	engine	18	9
r	15	T Takagi	Arrows	A20	Arrows	V10	15	engine	22	11
r	7	D Hill	Jordan	199	Mugen Honda	V10	13	brakes	8	4
r	19	J Trulli	Prost	AP02	Peugeot	V10	10	engine	9	5
r	9	G Fisichella	Benetton	B199	Playlife	V10	7	front suspension	10	5
r	16	R Barrichello	Stewart	SF-3	Ford Cosworth	V10	6	hydraulics	6	3
r	22	J Villeneuve	BAR	01	Supertec	V10	0	accident	12	6
r	12	P Diniz	Sauber	C18	Petronas	V10	0	accident	16	8

Winning speed 224.723 km/h, 139.637 mph
Pole Position speed 238.589 km/h, 148.253 mph (M Häkkinen, 1 min:42.950 sec)
Fastest Lap speed 233.331 km/h, 144.985 mph (D Coulthard, 1 min:45.270 sec on lap 43)
Lap Leaders M Häkkinen 1-24 (24); M Salo 25 (1); E Irvine 26-45 (20).

15 Aug 1999		**HUNGARY: Hungaroring**							**(Round 11)**	**(Race 641)**
		77 laps x 3.973 km, 2.469 miles = 305.921 km, 190.090 miles								

Pos	No	Driver	Car	Model	Engine		Laps	Time/Reason for Retirement	Grid Pos	Row
1	1	M Häkkinen	McLaren	MP4/14	Mercedes-Benz	V10	77	1h 46m 23.536s	1	1
2	2	D Coulthard	McLaren	MP4/14	Mercedes-Benz	V10	77	1h 46m 33.242s	3	2
3	4	E Irvine	Ferrari	F399	Ferrari	V10	77	1h 46m 50.764s	2	1
4	8	H-H Frentzen	Jordan	199	Mugen Honda	V10	77	1h 46m 55.351s	5	3
5	16	R Barrichello	Stewart	SF-3	Ford Cosworth	V10	77	1h 47m 07.344s	8	4
6	7	D Hill	Jordan	199	Mugen Honda	V10	77	1h 47m 19.262s	6	3
7	10	A Wurz	Benetton	B199	Playlife	V10	77	1h 47m 24.548s	7	4
8	19	J Trulli	Prost	AP02	Peugeot	V10	76		13	7
9	6	R Schumacher	Williams	FW21	Supertec	V10	76		16	8
10	18	O Panis	Prost	AP02	Peugeot	V10	76		14	7
11	17	J Herbert	Stewart	SF-3	Ford Cosworth	V10	76		10	5
12	3	M Salo	Ferrari	F399	Ferrari	V10	75		18	9
13	23	R Zonta	BAR	01	Supertec	V10	75		17	9
14	20	L Badoer	Minardi	M01	Ford Cosworth	V10	75		19	10
15	14	P de la Rosa	Arrows	A20	Arrows	V10	75		20	10
16r	11	J Alesi	Sauber	C18	Petronas	V10	74	fuel pressure	11	6
17	21	M Gené	Minardi	M01	Ford Cosworth	V10	74		22	11
r	22	J Villeneuve	BAR	01	Supertec	V10	60	clutch	9	5
r	9	G Fisichella	Benetton	B199	Playlife	V10	52	fuel pressure	4	2
r	15	T Takagi	Arrows	A20	Arrows	V10	26	transmission	21	11
r	12	P Diniz	Sauber	C18	Petronas	V10	19	spin	12	6
r	5	A Zanardi	Williams	FW21	Supertec	V10	10	differential	15	8

Winning speed 172.524 km/h, 107.202 mph
Pole Position speed 183.003 km/h, 113.713 mph (M Häkkinen, 1 min:18.156 sec)
Fastest Lap speed 177.236 km/h, 110.130 mph (D Coulthard, 1 min:20.699 sec on lap 69)
Lap Leaders M Häkkinen 1-77 (77).

Races 417

29 Aug 1999   BELGIUM: Spa-Francorchamps   (Round 12)   (Race 642)

44 laps x 6.968 km, 4.330 miles = 306.577 km, 190.498 miles

Pos	No	Driver	Car	Model	Engine		Laps	Time/Reason for Retirement	Grid Pos	Row
1	2	D Coulthard	McLaren	MP4/14	Mercedes-Benz	V10	44	1h 25m 43.057s	2	1
2	1	M Häkkinen	McLaren	MP4/14	Mercedes-Benz	V10	44	1h 25m 53.526s	1	1
3	8	H-H Frentzen	Jordan	199	Mugen Honda	V10	44	1h 26m 16.490s	3	2
4	4	E Irvine	Ferrari	F399	Ferrari	V10	44	1h 26m 28.005s	6	3
5	6	R Schumacher	Williams	FW21	Supertec	V10	44	1h 26m 31.124s	5	3
6	7	D Hill	Jordan	199	Mugen Honda	V10	44	1h 26m 37.973s	4	2
7	3	M Salo	Ferrari	F399	Ferrari	V10	44	1h 26m 39.306s	9	5
8	5	A Zanardi	Williams	FW21	Supertec	V10	44	1h 26m 50.079s	8	4
9	11	J Alesi	Sauber	C18	Petronas	V10	44	1h 26m 56.905s	16	8
10	16	R Barrichello	Stewart	SF-3	Ford Cosworth	V10	44	1h 27m 03.799s	7	4
11	9	G Fisichella	Benetton	B199	Playlife	V10	44	1h 27m 15.252s	13	7
12	19	J Trulli	Prost	AP02	Peugeot	V10	44	1h 27m 19.211s	12	6
13	18	O Panis	Prost	AP02	Peugeot	V10	44	1h 27m 24.600s	17	9
14	10	A Wurz	Benetton	B199	Playlife	V10	44	1h 27m 40.802s	15	8
15	22	J Villeneuve	BAR	01	Supertec	V10	43		11	6
16	21	M Gené	Minardi	M01	Ford Cosworth	V10	43		21	11
r	14	P de la Rosa	Arrows	A20	Arrows	V10	35	transmission	22	11
r	20	L Badoer	Minardi	M01	Ford Cosworth	V10	33	brakes / suspension	20	10
r	23	R Zonta	BAR	01	Supertec	V10	33	gearbox	14	7
r	17	J Herbert	Stewart	SF-3	Ford Cosworth	V10	27	wheel bearing / brakes / accident	10	5
r	12	P Diniz	Sauber	C18	Petronas	V10	19	accident	18	9
r	15	T Takagi	Arrows	A20	Arrows	V10	0	clutch	19	10

Winning speed 214.595 km/h, 133.343 mph
Pole Position speed 227.364 km/h, 141.277 mph (M Häkkinen, 1 min:50.329 sec)
Fastest Lap speed 220.129 km/h, 136.782 mph (M Häkkinen, 1 min:53.955 sec on lap 23)
Lap Leaders D Coulthard 1-44 (44).

12 Sep 1999   ITALY: Monza   (Round 13)   (Race 643)

53 laps x 5.770 km, 3.585 miles = 305.548 km, 189.859 miles

Pos	No	Driver	Car	Model	Engine		Laps	Time/Reason for Retirement	Grid Pos	Row
1	8	H-H Frentzen	Jordan	199	Mugen Honda	V10	53	1h 17m 02.923s	2	1
2	6	R Schumacher	Williams	FW21	Supertec	V10	53	1h 17m 06.195s	5	3
3	3	M Salo	Ferrari	F399	Ferrari	V10	53	1h 17m 14.855s	6	3
4	16	R Barrichello	Stewart	SF-3	Ford Cosworth	V10	53	1h 17m 20.553s	7	4
5	2	D Coulthard	McLaren	MP4/14	Mercedes-Benz	V10	53	1h 17m 21.065s	3	2
6	4	E Irvine	Ferrari	F399	Ferrari	V10	53	1h 17m 30.325s	8	4
7	5	A Zanardi	Williams	FW21	Supertec	V10	53	1h 17m 30.970s	4	2
8	22	J Villeneuve	BAR	01	Supertec	V10	53	1h 17m 44.720s	11	6
9	11	J Alesi	Sauber	C18	Petronas	V10	53	1h 17m 45.121s	13	7
10	7	D Hill	Jordan	199	Mugen Honda	V10	53	1h 17m 59.182s	9	5
11r	18	O Panis	Prost	AP02	Peugeot	V10	52	engine	10	5
r	17	J Herbert	Stewart	SF-3	Ford Cosworth	V10	40	clutch	15	8
r	15	T Takagi	Arrows	A20	Arrows	V10	35	spin	22	11
r	14	P de la Rosa	Arrows	A20	Arrows	V10	35	accident / front suspension	21	11
r	1	M Häkkinen	McLaren	MP4/14	Mercedes-Benz	V10	29	spin	1	1
r	19	J Trulli	Prost	AP02	Peugeot	V10	29	gearbox	12	6
r	23	R Zonta	BAR	01	Supertec	V10	25	front wheel bearing	18	9
r	20	L Badoer	Minardi	M01	Ford Cosworth	V10	23	accident	19	10
r	10	A Wurz	Benetton	B199	Playlife	V10	11	gearbox	14	7
r	12	P Diniz	Sauber	C18	Petronas	V10	1	spin	16	8
r	9	G Fisichella	Benetton	B199	Playlife	V10	1	accident	17	9
r	21	M Gené	Minardi	M01	Ford Cosworth	V10	0	accident	20	10

Winning speed 237.938 km/h, 147.848 mph
Pole Position speed 251.989 km/h, 156.579 mph (M Häkkinen, 1 min:22.432 sec)
Fastest Lap speed 242.723 km/h, 150.821 mph (R Schumacher, 1 min:25.579 sec on lap 48)
Lap Leaders M Häkkinen 1-29 (29); H-H Frentzen 30-35,37-53 (23); M Salo 36 (1).

26 Sep 1999   EUROPE: Nürburgring   (Round 14)   (Race 644)

66 laps x 4.556 km, 2.831 miles = 300.679 km, 186.833 miles

Pos	No	Driver	Car	Model	Engine		Laps	Time/Reason for Retirement	Grid Pos	Row
1	17	J Herbert	Stewart	SF-3	Ford Cosworth	V10	66	1h 41m 54.314s	14	7
2	19	J Trulli	Prost	AP02	Peugeot	V10	66	1h 42m 16.933s	10	5
3	16	R Barrichello	Stewart	SF-3	Ford Cosworth	V10	66	1h 42m 17.180s	15	8
4	6	R Schumacher	Williams	FW21	Supertec	V10	66	1h 42m 33.822s	4	2
5	1	M Häkkinen	McLaren	MP4/14	Mercedes-Benz	V10	66	1h 42m 57.264s	3	2
6	21	M Gené	Minardi	M01	Ford Cosworth	V10	66	1h 42m 59.468s	20	10
7	4	E Irvine	Ferrari	F399	Ferrari	V10	66	1h 43m 00.997s	9	5
8	23	R Zonta	BAR	01	Supertec	V10	65		17	9
9	18	O Panis	Prost	AP02	Peugeot	V10	65		5	3
10r	22	J Villeneuve	BAR	01	Supertec	V10	61	clutch	8	4
r	20	L Badoer	Minardi	M01	Ford Cosworth	V10	53	gearbox	19	10
r	14	P de la Rosa	Arrows	A20	Arrows	V10	52	gearbox	22	11
r	9	G Fisichella	Benetton	B199	Playlife	V10	48	spin	6	3
r	3	M Salo	Ferrari	F399	Ferrari	V10	44	spin / brakes	12	6

Pos	No	Driver	Car	Model	Engine		Laps	Time/Reason for Retirement	Grid Pos	Row
r	15	T Takagi	Arrows	A20	Arrows	V10	42	accident	21	11
r	2	D Coulthard	McLaren	MP4/14	Mercedes-Benz	V10	37	accident	2	1
r	11	J Alesi	Sauber	C18	Petronas	V10	35	transmission	16	8
r	8	H-H Frentzen	Jordan	199	Mugen Honda	V10	32	electrics	1	1
r	5	A Zanardi	Williams	FW21	Supertec	V10	10	accident / transmission	18	9
r	7	D Hill	Jordan	199	Mugen Honda	V10	0	electrics	7	4
r	10	A Wurz	Benetton	B199	Playlife	V10	0	accident	11	6
r	12	P Diniz	Sauber	C18	Petronas	V10	0	accident	13	7

Winning speed 177.034 km/h, 110.004 mph
Pole Position speed 205.250 km/h, 127.537 mph (H-H Frentzen, 1 min:19.910 sec)
Fastest Lap speed 201.786 km/h, 125.384 mph (M Häkkinen, 1 min:21.282 sec on lap 64)
Lap Leaders H-H Frentzen 1-32 (32); D Coulthard 33-37 (5); R Schumacher 38-44,49 (8); G Fisichella 45-48 (4); J Herbert 50-66 (17).

Scheduled for 67 laps but aborted after first lap accident. Restarted for 66 laps.

17 Oct 1999	MALAYSIA: Sepang	(Round 15)	(Race 645)

56 laps x 5.542 km, 3.444 miles = 310.352 km, 192.844 miles

Pos	No	Driver	Car	Model	Engine		Laps	Time/Reason for Retirement	Grid Pos	Row
1	4	E Irvine	Ferrari	F399	Ferrari	V10	56	1h 36m 38.494s	2	1
2	3	M Schumacher	Ferrari	F399	Ferrari	V10	56	1h 36m 39.534s	1	1
3	1	M Häkkinen	McLaren	MP4/14	Mercedes-Benz	V10	56	1h 36m 48.237s	4	2
4	17	J Herbert	Stewart	SF-3	Ford Cosworth	V10	56	1h 36m 56.032s	5	3
5	16	R Barrichello	Stewart	SF-3	Ford Cosworth	V10	56	1h 37m 10.790s	6	3
6	8	H-H Frentzen	Jordan	199	Mugen Honda	V10	56	1h 37m 13.378s	14	7
7	11	J Alesi	Sauber	C18	Petronas	V10	56	1h 37m 32.902s	15	8
8	10	A Wurz	Benetton	B199	Playlife	V10	56	1h 37m 39.428s	7	4
9	21	M Gené	Minardi	M01	Ford Cosworth	V10	55		19	10
10	5	A Zanardi	Williams	FW21	Supertec	V10	55		16	8
11	9	G Fisichella	Benetton	B199	Playlife	V10	52		11	6
r	22	J Villeneuve	BAR	01	Supertec	V10	48	hydraulics	10	5
r	12	P Diniz	Sauber	C18	Petronas	V10	44	spin	17	9
r	14	P de la Rosa	Arrows	A20	Arrows	V10	30	engine	20	10
r	20	L Badoer	Minardi	M01	Ford Cosworth	V10	15	engine overheating	21	11
r	2	D Coulthard	McLaren	MP4/14	Mercedes-Benz	V10	14	fuel pump	3	2
r	6	R Schumacher	Williams	FW21	Supertec	V10	7	spin	8	4
r	15	T Takagi	Arrows	A20	Arrows	V10	7	driveshaft	22	11
r	23	R Zonta	BAR	01	Supertec	V10	6	oil leak / engine	13	7
r	18	O Panis	Prost	AP02	Peugeot	V10	5	engine	12	6
r	7	D Hill	Jordan	199	Mugen Honda	V10	0	accident	9	5
ns	19	J Trulli	Prost	AP02	Peugeot	V10		engine on parade lap	18	9

Winning speed 192.682 km/h, 119.727 mph
Pole Position speed 200.136 km/h, 124.359 mph (M Schumacher, 1 min:39.688 sec)
Fastest Lap speed 198.980 km/h, 123.641 mph (M Schumacher, 1 min:40.267 sec on lap 25)
Lap Leaders M Schumacher 1-3,26-28,42-52 (17); E Irvine 4-25,29-41,53-56 (39).

M Schumacher and E Irvine were originally disqualified for having illegal bargeboards, but were reinstated following an appeal.

31 Oct 1999	JAPAN: Suzuka	(Round 16)	(Race 646)

53 laps x 5.864 km, 3.644 miles = 310.596 km, 192.995 miles

Pos	No	Driver	Car	Model	Engine		Laps	Time/Reason for Retirement	Grid Pos	Row
1	1	M Häkkinen	McLaren	MP4/14	Mercedes-Benz	V10	53	1h 31m 18.785s	2	1
2	3	M Schumacher	Ferrari	F399	Ferrari	V10	53	1h 31m 23.800s	1	1
3	4	E Irvine	Ferrari	F399	Ferrari	V10	53	1h 32m 54.473s	5	3
4	8	H-H Frentzen	Jordan	199	Mugen Honda	V10	53	1h 32m 57.420s	4	2
5	6	R Schumacher	Williams	FW21	Supertec	V10	53	1h 32m 58.279s	9	5
6	11	J Alesi	Sauber	C18	Petronas	V10	52		10	5
7	17	J Herbert	Stewart	SF-3	Ford Cosworth	V10	52		8	4
8	16	R Barrichello	Stewart	SF-3	Ford Cosworth	V10	52		13	7
9	22	J Villeneuve	BAR	01	Supertec	V10	52		11	6
10	10	A Wurz	Benetton	B199	Playlife	V10	52		15	8
11	12	P Diniz	Sauber	C18	Petronas	V10	52		17	9
12	23	R Zonta	BAR	01	Supertec	V10	52		18	9
13	14	P de la Rosa	Arrows	A20	Arrows	V10	51		21	11
14r	9	G Fisichella	Benetton	B199	Playlife	V10	47	engine	14	7
r	15	T Takagi	Arrows	A20	Arrows	V10	43	gearbox	19	10
r	20	L Badoer	Minardi	M01	Ford Cosworth	V10	43	engine	22	11
r	2	D Coulthard	McLaren	MP4/14	Mercedes-Benz	V10	39	hydraulics	3	2
r	21	M Gené	Minardi	M01	Ford Cosworth	V10	31	gearbox	20	10
r	7	D Hill	Jordan	199	Mugen Honda	V10	21	driver gave up	12	6
r	18	O Panis	Prost	AP02	Peugeot	V10	19	gearbox	6	3
r	19	J Trulli	Prost	AP02	Peugeot	V10	3	engine	7	4
r	5	A Zanardi	Williams	FW21	Supertec	V10	0	electrics	16	8

Winning speed 204.086 km/h, 126.813 mph
Pole Position speed 216.583 km/h, 134.579 mph (M Schumacher, 1 min:37.470 sec)
Fastest Lap speed 208.355 km/h, 129.466 mph (M Schumacher, 1 min:41.319 sec on lap 31)
Lap Leaders M Häkkinen 1-19,23-53 (50); M Schumacher 20-22 (3).

Races

Lap Leaders 1999

Pos	Driver	Car-Engine	GPs	laps	km	miles
1	M Häkkinen	McLaren-Mercedes-Benz	11	383	1,881.4	1,169.0
2	M Schumacher	Ferrari	7	176	729.7	453.4
3	D Coulthard	McLaren-Mercedes-Benz	7	145	781.8	485.8
4	E Irvine	Ferrari	5	133	713.2	443.2
5	R Barrichello	Stewart-Ford Cosworth	2	67	285.7	177.5
6	H-H Frentzen	Jordan-Mugen Honda	4	64	318.5	197.9
7	J Herbert	Stewart-Ford Cosworth	1	17	77.5	48.1
8	R Schumacher	Williams-Supertec	1	8	36.4	22.6
9	G Fisichella	Benetton-Playlife	1	4	18.2	11.3
10	M Salo	Ferrari	2	2	12.6	7.8
11	D Hill	Jordan-Mugen Honda	1	1	5.1	3.2
			16	1,000	4,860.2	3,020.0

Driver Points 1999

		AUS	BR	RSM	MC	E	CDN	F	GB	A	D	H	B	I	EUR	MAL	J	Total
1	M Häkkinen	-	10	-	4	10	10	6	-	4	-	10	6	-	2	4	10	76
2	E Irvine	10	2	-	6	3	4	1	6	10	10	4	3	1	-	10	4	74
3	H-H Frentzen	6	4	-	3	-	-	10	3	3	4	3	4	10	-	1	3	54
4	D Coulthard	-	-	6	-	6	-	-	10	6	2	6	10	2	-	-	-	48
5	M Schumacher	-	6	10	10	4	-	2	-	-	-	-	-	-	-	6	6	44
6	R Schumacher	4	3	-	-	2	3	3	4	-	3	-	2	6	3	-	2	35
7	R Barrichello	2	-	4	-	-	-	4	-	-	-	2	-	3	4	2	-	21
8	J Herbert	-	-	-	-	-	2	-	-	-	-	-	-	-	10	3	-	15
9	G Fisichella	3	-	2	2	-	6	-	-	-	-	-	-	-	-	-	-	13
10	M Salo	-	-	-	-	-	-	-	-	-	6	-	-	4	-	-	-	10
11	J Trulli	-	-	-	-	1	-	-	-	-	-	-	-	-	6	-	-	7
	D Hill	-	-	3	-	-	-	-	2	-	-	1	1	-	-	-	-	7
13	A Wurz	-	-	-	1	-	-	-	-	2	-	-	-	-	-	-	-	3
	P Diniz	-	-	-	-	-	1	-	1	1	-	-	-	-	-	-	-	3
15	J Alesi	-	-	1	-	-	-	-	-	-	-	-	-	-	-	-	1	2
	O Panis	-	1	-	-	-	-	-	-	-	1	-	-	-	-	-	-	2
17	P de la Rosa	1	-	-	-	-	-	-	-	-	-	-	-	-	-	-	-	1
	M Gené	-	-	-	-	-	-	-	-	-	-	-	-	-	1	-	-	1

10,6,4,3,2 and 1 point awarded to the first six finishers.

Constructor Points 1999

		AUS	BR	RSM	MC	E	CDN	F	GB	A	D	H	B	I	EUR	MAL	J	Total
1	Ferrari	10	8	10	16	7	4	3	6	10	16	4	3	5	-	16	10	128
2	McLaren-Mercedes-Benz	-	10	6	4	16	10	6	10	10	2	16	16	2	2	4	10	124
3	Jordan-Mugen Honda	6	4	3	3	-	-	10	5	3	4	4	5	10	-	1	3	61
4	Stewart-Ford Cosworth	2	-	4	-	-	2	4	-	-	-	2	-	3	14	5	-	36
5	Williams-Supertec	4	3	-	-	2	3	3	4	-	3	-	2	6	3	-	2	35
6	Benetton-Playlife	3	-	2	3	-	6	-	-	2	-	-	-	-	-	-	-	16
7	Prost-Peugeot	-	1	-	-	1	-	-	-	-	1	-	-	-	6	-	-	9
8	Sauber-Petronas	-	-	1	-	-	1	-	1	1	-	-	-	-	-	-	1	5
9	Arrows	1	-	-	-	-	-	-	-	-	-	-	-	-	-	-	-	1
	Minardi-Ford Cosworth	-	-	-	-	-	-	-	-	-	-	-	-	-	1	-	-	1

10,6,4,3,2 and 1 point awarded to the first six finishers.

Race Entrants and Results

The main points of interest on the driver front was the arrival of 20-year-old Jenson Button at Williams, with Rubens Barrichello moving to Ferrari to replace the Jaguar-bound Eddie Irvine. The famous Jaguar marque was making its first-ever attempt at single-seater racing after effectively taking over the Stewart concern. Grand Prix racing would return to America for the first time since 1991, on a new road course at the historic Indianapolis Speedway. During the year it was confirmed that Michelin rubber would return in 2001 and a full works effort from Toyota would begin testing in a run up to entering Formula 1 in 2002.

McLAREN
West McLaren Mercedes: Häkkinen, Coulthard

FERRARI
Scuderia Ferrari Marlboro: M Schumacher, Barrichello

JORDAN
Benson & Hedges Jordan: Frentzen, Trulli

JAGUAR
Jaguar Racing: Irvine, Herbert, Burti

WILLIAMS
BMW WilliamsF1 Team: R Schumacher, Button

BENETTON
Mild Seven Benetton Playlife: Fisichella, Wurz

PROST
Gauloises Prost Peugeot: Alesi, Heidfeld

SAUBER
Red Bull Sauber Petronas: Diniz, Salo

ARROWS
Orange Arrows Supertec: de la Rosa, Verstappen

MINARDI
Telefonica Minardi Fondmetal: Gené, Mazzacane

BAR
Lucky Strike British American Racing Honda: Villeneuve, Zonta

12 Mar 2000		AUSTRALIA: Melbourne							(Round 1)	(Race 647)	
		58 laps x 5.303 km, 3.295 miles = 307.574 km, 191.118 miles									
Pos	No	Driver	Car	Model	Engine		Laps	Time/Reason for Retirement		Grid Pos	Row
1	3	M Schumacher	Ferrari	F1 2000	Ferrari	V10	58	1h 34m 01.987s		3	2
2	4	R Barrichello	Ferrari	F1 2000	Ferrari	V10	58	1h 34m 13.402s		4	2
3	9	R Schumacher	Williams	FW22	BMW	V10	58	1h 34m 21.996s		11	6
4	22	J Villeneuve	BAR	002	Honda	V10	58	1h 34m 46.434s		8	4
dq	17	M Salo	Sauber	C19	Petronas	V10	58	1h 34m 47.611s		10	5
5	11	G Fisichella	Benetton	B200	Playlife	V10	58	1h 34m 47.152s		9	5
6	23	R Zonta	BAR	002	Honda	V10	58	1h 34m 48.455s		16	8
7	12	A Wurz	Benetton	B200	Playlife	V10	58	1h 34m 48.902s		14	7
8	20	M Gené	Minardi	M02	Fondmetal	V10	57			18	9
9	15	N Heidfeld	Prost	AP03	Peugeot	V10	56			15	8
r	10	J Button	Williams	FW22	BMW	V10	46	engine		21	11
r	16	P Diniz	Sauber	C19	Petronas	V10	41	gearbox		19	10
r	21	G Mazzacane	Minardi	M02	Fondmetal	V10	40	gearbox		22	11
r	5	H-H Frentzen	Jordan	EJ10	Mugen Honda	V10	39	hydraulics		5	3
r	6	J Trulli	Jordan	EJ10	Mugen Honda	V10	35	exhaust		6	3
r	14	J Alesi	Prost	AP03	Peugeot	V10	27	hydraulics		17	9
r	1	M Häkkinen	McLaren	MP4/15	Mercedes-Benz	V10	18	engine		1	1
r	19	J Verstappen	Arrows	A21	Supertec	V10	16	front track rod		13	7
r	2	D Coulthard	McLaren	MP4/15	Mercedes-Benz	V10	11	engine		2	1
r	18	P de la Rosa	Arrows	A21	Supertec	V10	6	front track rod / accident		12	6
r	7	E Irvine	Jaguar	R1	Ford Cosworth	V10	6	spin		7	4
r	8	J Herbert	Jaguar	R1	Ford Cosworth	V10	1	clutch		20	10

Winning speed 196.254 km/h, 121.947 mph
Pole Position speed 210.817 km/h, 130.996 mph (M Häkkinen, 1 min:30.556 sec)
Fastest Lap speed 208.685 km/h, 129.671 mph (R Barricello, 1 min:31.481 sec on lap 41)
Lap Leaders M Häkkinen 1-18 (18); M Schumacher 19-29,36-44,46-58 (33); H-H Frentzen 30-35 (6); R Barrichello 45 (1).

M Salo finished 5th but was disqualified due to a bodywork infringement.

26 Mar 2000　　　**BRAZIL: Interlagos**　　　　　　　　　　　　　　　　　　**(Round 2)**　　**(Race 648)**

71 laps x 4.309 km, 2.677 miles = 305.909 km, 190.083 miles

Pos	No	Driver	Car	Model	Engine		Laps	Time/Reason for Retirement	Grid Pos	Row
1	3	M Schumacher	Ferrari	F1 2000	Ferrari	V10	71	1h 31m 35.271s	3	2
dq	2	D Coulthard	McLaren	MP4/15	Mercedes-Benz	V10	71	1h 31m 39.573s	2	1
2	11	G Fisichella	Benetton	B200	Playlife	V10	71	1h 32m 15.169s	5	3
3	5	H-H Frentzen	Jordan	EJ10	Mugen Honda	V10	71	1h 32m 17.539s	7	4
4	6	J Trulli	Jordan	EJ10	Mugen Honda	V10	71	1h 32m 48.051s	12	6
5	9	R Schumacher	Williams	FW22	BMW	V10	70		11	6
6	10	J Button	Williams	FW22	BMW	V10	70		9	5
7	19	J Verstappen	Arrows	A21	Supertec	V10	70		14	7
8	18	P de la Rosa	Arrows	A21	Supertec	V10	70		16	8
9	23	R Zonta	BAR	002	Honda	V10	69		8	4
10	21	G Mazzacane	Minardi	M02	Fondmetal	V10	69		20	10
r	8	J Herbert	Jaguar	R1	Ford Cosworth	V10	51	gearbox	17	9
r	20	M Gené	Minardi	M02	Fondmetal	V10	31	engine	18	9
r	1	M Häkkinen	McLaren	MP4/15	Mercedes-Benz	V10	30	oil pressure	1	1
r	4	R Barrichello	Ferrari	F1 2000	Ferrari	V10	27	hydraulics	4	2
r	7	E Irvine	Jaguar	R1	Ford Cosworth	V10	20	accident	6	3
r	22	J Villeneuve	BAR	002	Honda	V10	16	gearbox	10	5
r	14	J Alesi	Prost	AP03	Peugeot	V10	11	electrics	15	8
r	15	N Heidfeld	Prost	AP03	Peugeot	V10	9	engine	19	10
r	12	A Wurz	Benetton	B200	Playlife	V10	6	engine	13	7
ns	16	P Diniz	Sauber	C19	Petronas	V10		withdrawn/rear wing failure		
ns	17	M Salo	Sauber	C19	Petronas	V10		withdrawn/rear wing failure		

Winning speed 200.403 km/h, 124.525 mph
Pole Position speed 209.313 km/h, 130.061 mph (M Häkkinen, 1 min:14.111 sec)
Fastest Lap speed 207.509 km/h, 128.941 mph (M Schumacher, 1 min:14.755 sec on lap 48)
Lap Leaders M Häkkinen 1,23-29 (8); M Schumacher 2-20,30-71 (61); R Barrichello 21-22 (2).

D Coulthard finished 2nd but was disqualified due to the front wing end plates being lower than permitted.
P Diniz qualified 20th and Mika Salo 22nd but were withdrawn by the team due to rear wing failures.

9 Apr 2000　　　**SAN MARINO: Imola**　　　　　　　　　　　　　　　　　**(Round 3)**　　**(Race 649)**

62 laps x 4.933 km, 3.065 miles = 305.609 km, 189.897 miles

Pos	No	Driver	Car	Model	Engine		Laps	Time/Reason for Retirement	Grid Pos	Row
1	3	M Schumacher	Ferrari	F1 2000	Ferrari	V10	62	1h 31m 39.776s	2	1
2	1	M Häkkinen	McLaren	MP4/15	Mercedes-Benz	V10	62	1h 31m 40.944s	1	1
3	2	D Coulthard	McLaren	MP4/15	Mercedes-Benz	V10	62	1h 32m 30.784s	3	2
4	4	R Barrichello	Ferrari	F1 2000	Ferrari	V10	62	1h 33m 09.052s	4	2
5	22	J Villeneuve	BAR	002	Honda	V10	61		9	5
6	17	M Salo	Sauber	C19	Petronas	V10	61		12	6
7	7	E Irvine	Jaguar	R1	Ford Cosworth	V10	61		7	4
8	16	P Diniz	Sauber	C19	Petronas	V10	61		10	5
9	12	A Wurz	Benetton	B200	Playlife	V10	61		11	6
10	8	J Herbert	Jaguar	R1	Ford Cosworth	V10	61		17	9
11	11	G Fisichella	Benetton	B200	Playlife	V10	61		19	10
12	23	R Zonta	BAR	002	Honda	V10	61		14	7
13	21	G Mazzacane	Minardi	M02	Fondmetal	V10	60		20	10
14	19	J Verstappen	Arrows	A21	Supertec	V10	59		16	8
15r	6	J Trulli	Jordan	EJ10	Mugen Honda	V10	58	gearbox	8	4
r	18	P de la Rosa	Arrows	A21	Supertec	V10	49	gearbox / spin	13	7
r	9	R Schumacher	Williams	FW22	BMW	V10	45	fuel pump	5	3
r	14	J Alesi	Prost	AP03	Peugeot	V10	25	hydraulics	15	8
r	15	N Heidfeld	Prost	AP03	Peugeot	V10	22	hydraulics	22	11
r	10	J Button	Williams	FW22	BMW	V10	5	engine	18	9
r	20	M Gené	Minardi	M02	Fondmetal	V10	5	spin	21	11
r	5	H-H Frentzen	Jordan	EJ10	Mugen Honda	V10	4	gearbox	6	3

Winning speed 200.043 km/h, 124.301 mph
Pole Position speed 209.632 km/h, 130.260 mph (M Häkkinen, 1 min:24.714 sec)
Fastest Lap speed 205.249 km/h, 127.536 mph (M Häkkinen, 1 min:26.523 sec on lap 60)
Lap Leaders M Häkkinen 1-44 (44); M Schumacher 45-62 (18).

23 Apr 2000   BRITAIN: Silverstone   (Round 4)   (Race 650)

60 laps x 5.141 km, 3.194 miles = 308.356 km, 191.604 miles

Pos	No	Driver	Car	Model	Engine		Laps	Time/Reason for Retirement	Grid Pos	Row
1	2	D Coulthard	McLaren	MP4/15	Mercedes-Benz	V10	60	1h 28m 50.108s	4	2
2	1	M Häkkinen	McLaren	MP4/15	Mercedes-Benz	V10	60	1h 28m 51.585s	3	2
3	3	M Schumacher	Ferrari	F1 2000	Ferrari	V10	60	1h 29m 10.025s	5	3
4	9	R Schumacher	Williams	FW22	BMW	V10	60	1h 29m 31.420s	7	4
5	10	J Button	Williams	FW22	BMW	V10	60	1h 29m 47.867s	6	3
6	6	J Trulli	Jordan	EJ10	Mugen Honda	V10	60	1h 30m 09.381s	11	6
7	11	G Fisichella	Benetton	B200	Playlife	V10	59		12	6
8	17	M Salo	Sauber	C19	Petronas	V10	59		18	9
9	12	A Wurz	Benetton	B200	Playlife	V10	59		20	10
10	14	J Alesi	Prost	AP03	Peugeot	V10	59		15	8
11	16	P Diniz	Sauber	C19	Petronas	V10	59		13	7
12	8	J Herbert	Jaguar	R1	Ford Cosworth	V10	59		14	7
13	7	E Irvine	Jaguar	R1	Ford Cosworth	V10	59		9	5
14	20	M Gené	Minardi	M02	Fondmetal	V10	59		21	11
15	21	G Mazzacane	Minardi	M02	Fondmetal	V10	59		22	11
16r	22	J Villeneuve	BAR	002	Honda	V10	56	gearbox	10	5
17r	5	H-H Frentzen	Jordan	EJ10	Mugen Honda	V10	54	gearbox	2	1
r	15	N Heidfeld	Prost	AP03	Peugeot	V10	51	oil pressure	17	9
r	23	R Zonta	BAR	002	Honda	V10	36	spin	16	8
r	4	R Barrichello	Ferrari	F1 2000	Ferrari	V10	35	hydraulic / spin	1	1
r	18	P de la Rosa	Arrows	A21	Supertec	V10	26	electronics	19	10
r	19	J Verstappen	Arrows	A21	Supertec	V10	20	electrics	8	4

Winning speed 208.266 km/h, 129.410 mph
Pole Position speed 215.950 km/h, 134.185 mph (R Barrichello, 1 min:25.703 sec)
Fastest Lap speed 214.663 km/h, 133.385 mph (M Häkkinen, 1 min:26.217 sec on lap 56)
Lap Leaders R Barrichello 1-30,33-35 (33); D Coulthard 31-32,42-60 (21); M Schumacher 36-38 (3); H-H Frentzen 39-41 (3).

7 May 2000   SPAIN: Montmeló   (Round 5)   (Race 651)

65 laps x 4.730 km, 2.939 miles = 307.323 km, 128.825 miles

Pos	No	Driver	Car	Model	Engine		Laps	Time/Reason for Retirement	Grid Pos	Row
1	1	M Häkkinen	McLaren	MP4/15	Mercedes-Benz	V10	65	1h 33m 55.390s	2	1
2	2	D Coulthard	McLaren	MP4/15	Mercedes-Benz	V10	65	1h 34m 11.456s	4	2
3	4	R Barrichello	Ferrari	F1 2000	Ferrari	V10	65	1h 34m 24.502s	3	2
4	9	R Schumacher	Williams	FW22	BMW	V10	65	1h 34m 32.701s	5	3
5	3	M Schumacher	Ferrari	F1 2000	Ferrari	V10	65	1h 34m 43.373s	1	1
6	5	H-H Frentzen	Jordan	EJ10	Mugen Honda	V10	65	1h 35m 17.315s	8	4
7	17	M Salo	Sauber	C19	Petronas	V10	64		12	6
8	23	R Zonta	BAR	002	Honda	V10	64		16	8
9	11	G Fisichella	Benetton	B200	Playlife	V10	64		13	7
10	12	A Wurz	Benetton	B200	Playlife	V10	64		18	9
11	7	E Irvine	Jaguar	R1	Ford Cosworth	V10	64		9	5
12	6	J Trulli	Jordan	EJ10	Mugen Honda	V10	64		7	4
13	8	J Herbert	Jaguar	R1	Ford Cosworth	V10	64		14	7
14	20	M Gené	Minardi	M02	Fondmetal	V10	63		20	10
15	21	G Mazzacane	Minardi	M02	Fondmetal	V10	63		21	11
16	15	N Heidfeld	Prost	AP03	Peugeot	V10	62		19	10
17r	10	J Button	Williams	FW22	BMW	V10	61	engine	10	5
r	19	J Verstappen	Arrows	A21	Supertec	V10	25	gearbox	11	6
r	22	J Villeneuve	BAR	002	Honda	V10	21	oil pressure / engine	6	3
r	14	J Alesi	Prost	AP03	Peugeot	V10	1	accident	17	9
r	18	P de la Rosa	Arrows	A21	Supertec	V10	1	accident	22	11
r	16	P Diniz	Sauber	C19	Petronas	V10	0	spin	15	8

Winning speed 196.324 km/h, 121.990 mph
Pole Position speed 210.289 km/h, 130.668 mph (M Schumacher, 1 min:20.974 sec)
Fastest Lap speed 201.586 km/h, 125.260 mph (M Häkkinen, 1 min:24.470 sec on lap 28)
Lap Leaders M Schumacher 1-23,27-41 (38); M Häkkinen 24-26,42-65 (27).

P de la Rosa qualified 9th but time disallowed due to a fuel irregularity.

21 May 2000   EUROPE: Nürburgring   (Round 6)   (Race 652)
67 laps x 4.556 km, 2.831 miles = 305.235 km, 189.664 miles

Pos	No	Driver	Car	Model	Engine		Laps	Time/Reason for Retirement	Grid Pos	Row
1	3	M Schumacher	Ferrari	F1 2000	Ferrari	V10	67	1h 42m 00.307s	2	1
2	1	M Häkkinen	McLaren	MP4/15	Mercedes-Benz	V10	67	1h 42m 14.129s	3	2
3	2	D Coulthard	McLaren	MP4/15	Mercedes-Benz	V10	66		1	1
4	4	R Barrichello	Ferrari	F1 2000	Ferrari	V10	66		4	2
5	11	G Fisichella	Benetton	B200	Playlife	V10	66		7	4
6	18	P de la Rosa	Arrows	A21	Supertec	V10	66		12	6
7	16	P Diniz	Sauber	C19	Petronas	V10	65		15	8
8	21	G Mazzacane	Minardi	M02	Fondmetal	V10	65		21	11
9	14	J Alesi	Prost	AP03	Peugeot	V10	65		17	9
10r	10	J Button	Williams	FW22	BMW	V10	62	electrics	11	6
11r	8	J Herbert	Jaguar	R1	Ford Cosworth	V10	61	accident	16	8
12r	12	A Wurz	Benetton	B200	Playlife	V10	61	accident	14	7
r	23	R Zonta	BAR	002	Honda	V10	51	gearbox / spin	18	9
r	20	M Gené	Minardi	M02	Fondmetal	V10	47	throttle pedal	20	10
r	22	J Villeneuve	BAR	002	Honda	V10	46	engine	9	5
r	7	E Irvine	Jaguar	R1	Ford Cosworth	V10	29	accident / rear wing	8	4
r	19	J Verstappen	Arrows	A21	Supertec	V10	29	accident	13	7
r	9	R Schumacher	Williams	FW22	BMW	V10	29	accident	5	3
r	17	M Salo	Sauber	C19	Petronas	V10	27	driveshaft / spin	19	10
r	5	H-H Frentzen	Jordan	EJ10	Mugen Honda	V10	2	engine	10	5
r	6	J Trulli	Jordan	EJ10	Mugen Honda	V10	0	accident	6	3
exc	15	N Heidfeld	Prost	AP03	Peugeot	V10		car under legal weight limit		

Winning speed 179.540 km/h, 111.561 mph
Pole Position speed 211.554 km/h, 131.454 mph (D Coulthard, 1 min:17.529 sec)
Fastest Lap speed 199.365 km/h, 123.880 mph (M Schumacher, 1 min:22.269 sec on lap 8)
Lap Leaders M Häkkinen 1-10,36-45 (20); M Schumacher 11-15,17-35,46-67 (46); R Barrichello 16 (1).

N Heidfeld qualified 13th but was excluded due to the car being under the legal weight limit.

4 Jun 2000   MONACO: Monte-Carlo   (Round 7)   (Race 653)
78 laps x 3.370 km, 2.094 miles = 262.860 km, 163.334 miles

Pos	No	Driver	Car	Model	Engine		Laps	Time/Reason for Retirement	Grid Pos	Row
1	2	D Coulthard	McLaren	MP4/15	Mercedes-Benz	V10	78	1h 49m 28.213s	3	2
2	4	R Barrichello	Ferrari	F1 2000	Ferrari	V10	78	1h 49m 44.102s	6	3
3	11	G Fisichella	Benetton	B200	Playlife	V10	78	1h 49m 46.735s	8	4
4	7	E Irvine	Jaguar	R1	Ford Cosworth	V10	78	1h 50m 34.137s	10	5
5	17	M Salo	Sauber	C19	Petronas	V10	78	1h 50m 48.988s	13	7
6	1	M Häkkinen	McLaren	MP4/15	Mercedes-Benz	V10	77		5	3
7	22	J Villeneuve	BAR	002	Honda	V10	77		17	9
8	15	N Heidfeld	Prost	AP03	Peugeot	V10	77		18	9
9	8	J Herbert	Jaguar	R1	Ford Cosworth	V10	76		11	6
10r	5	H-H Frentzen	Jordan	EJ10	Mugen Honda	V10	70	accident	4	2
r	19	J Verstappen	Arrows	A21	Supertec	V10	60	accident	15	8
r	3	M Schumacher	Ferrari	F1 2000	Ferrari	V10	55	exhaust / rear suspension	1	1
r	23	R Zonta	BAR	002	Honda	V10	48	accident	20	10
r	9	R Schumacher	Williams	FW22	BMW	V10	37	accident / injury	9	5
r	6	J Trulli	Jordan	EJ10	Mugen Honda	V10	36	gearbox	2	1
r	16	P Diniz	Sauber	C19	Petronas	V10	30	accident	19	10
r	14	J Alesi	Prost	AP03	Peugeot	V10	29	transmission	7	4
r	21	G Mazzacane	Minardi	M02	Fondmetal	V10	22	accident	22	11
r	20	M Gené	Minardi	M02	Fondmetal	V10	21	gearbox	21	11
r	12	A Wurz	Benetton	B200	Playlife	V10	18	accident	12	6
r	10	J Button	Williams	FW22	BMW	V10	16	oil pressure	14	7
r	18	P de la Rosa	Arrows	A21	Supertec	V10	0	accident *	16	8

Winning speed 144.072 km/h, 89.522 mph
Pole Position speed 152.651 km/h, 94.853 mph (M Schumacher, 1 min:19.475 sec)
Fastest Lap speed 148.729 km/h, 92.416 mph (M Häkkinen, 1 min:21.571 sec on lap 57)
Lap Leaders M Schumacher 1-55 (55); D Coulthard 56-78 (23).

Interrupted after an accident. Restarted for original distance.
* Retired after first start.

18 Jun 2000   **CANADA: Montréal**   **(Round 8)**   **(Race 654)**

69 laps x 4.421 km, 2.747 miles = 305.049 km, 189.549 miles

Pos	No	Driver	Car	Model	Engine		Laps	Time/Reason for Retirement	Grid Pos	Row
1	3	M Schumacher	Ferrari	F1 2000	Ferrari	V10	69	1h 41m 12.313s	1	1
2	4	R Barrichello	Ferrari	F1 2000	Ferrari	V10	69	1h 41m 12.487s	3	2
3	11	G Fisichella	Benetton	B200	Playlife	V10	69	1h 41m 27.678s	10	5
4	1	M Häkkinen	McLaren	MP4/15	Mercedes-Benz	V10	69	1h 41m 30.874s	4	2
5	19	J Verstappen	Arrows	A21	Supertec	V10	69	1h 42m 04.521s	13	7
6	6	J Trulli	Jordan	EJ10	Mugen Honda	V10	69	1h 42m 14.000s	7	4
7	2	D Coulthard	McLaren	MP4/15	Mercedes-Benz	V10	69	1h 42m 14.529s	2	1
8	23	R Zonta	BAR	002	Honda	V10	69	1h 42m 22.768s	8	4
9	12	A Wurz	Benetton	B200	Playlife	V10	69	1h 42m 32.212s	14	7
10	16	P Diniz	Sauber	C19	Petronas	V10	69	1h 42m 41.857s	19	10
11	10	J Button	Williams	FW22	BMW	V10	68		18	9
12	21	G Mazzacane	Minardi	M02	Fondmetal	V10	68		22	11
13	7	E Irvine	Jaguar	R1	Ford Cosworth	V10	66		16	8
14r	9	R Schumacher	Williams	FW22	BMW	V10	64	accident	12	6
15r	22	J Villeneuve	BAR	002	Honda	V10	64	accident	6	3
16r	20	M Gené	Minardi	M02	Fondmetal	V10	64	spin	20	10
r	18	P de la Rosa	Arrows	A21	Supertec	V10	48	accident	9	5
r	17	M Salo	Sauber	C19	Petronas	V10	42	engine	15	8
r	14	J Alesi	Prost	AP03	Peugeot	V10	38	hydraulics	17	9
r	15	N Heidfeld	Prost	AP03	Peugeot	V10	34	engine fire	21	11
r	5	H-H Frentzen	Jordan	EJ10	Mugen Honda	V10	32	brake master cylinder	5	3
r	8	J Herbert	Jaguar	R1	Ford Cosworth	V10	14	gearbox	11	6

Winning speed 180.849 km/h, 112.375 mph
Pole Position speed 202.904 km/h, 126.079 mph (M Schumacher, 1 min:18.439 sec)
Fastest Lap speed 201.338 km/h, 125.106 mph (M Häkkinen, 1 min:19.049 sec on lap 37)
Lap Leaders M Schumacher 1-34, 43-69 (61); R Barrichello 35-42 (8).

2 Jul 2000   **FRANCE: Magny-Cours**   **(Round 9)**   **(Race 655)**

72 laps x 4.251 km, 2.641 miles = 305.886 km, 190.069 miles

Pos	No	Driver	Car	Model	Engine		Laps	Time/Reason for Retirement	Grid Pos	Row
1	2	D Coulthard	McLaren	MP4/15	Mercedes-Benz	V10	72	1h 38m 05.538s	2	1
2	1	M Häkkinen	McLaren	MP4/15	Mercedes-Benz	V10	72	1h 38m 20.286s	4	2
3	4	R Barrichello	Ferrari	F1 2000	Ferrari	V10	72	1h 38m 37.947s	3	2
4	22	J Villeneuve	BAR	002	Honda	V10	72	1h 39m 06.860s	7	4
5	9	R Schumacher	Williams	FW22	BMW	V10	72	1h 39m 09.519s	5	3
6	6	J Trulli	Jordan	EJ10	Mugen Honda	V10	72	1h 39m 21.142s	9	5
7	5	H-H Frentzen	Jordan	EJ10	Mugen Honda	V10	71		8	4
8	10	J Button	Williams	FW22	BMW	V10	71		10	5
9	11	G Fisichella	Benetton	B200	Playlife	V10	71		14	7
10	17	M Salo	Sauber	C19	Petronas	V10	71		12	6
11	16	P Diniz	Sauber	C19	Petronas	V10	71		15	8
12	15	N Heidfeld	Prost	AP03	Peugeot	V10	71		16	8
13	7	E Irvine	Jaguar	R1	Ford Cosworth	V10	70		6	3
14	14	J Alesi	Prost	AP03	Peugeot	V10	70		18	9
15	20	M Gené	Minardi	M02	Fondmetal	V10	70		21	11
r	3	M Schumacher	Ferrari	F1 2000	Ferrari	V10	58	engine	1	1
r	18	P de la Rosa	Arrows	A21	Supertec	V10	45	gearbox	13	7
r	12	A Wurz	Benetton	B200	Playlife	V10	34	spin	17	9
r	21	G Mazzacane	Minardi	M02	Fondmetal	V10	31	spin	22	11
r	19	J Verstappen	Arrows	A21	Supertec	V10	25	gearbox	20	10
r	8	J Herbert	Jaguar	R1	Ford Cosworth	V10	20	gearbox	11	6
r	23	R Zonta	BAR	002	Honda	V10	16	brakes / accident	19	10

Winning speed 187.100 km/h, 116.259 mph
Pole Position speed 202.342 km/h, 125.730 mph (M Schumacher, 1 min:15.632 sec)
Fastest Lap speed 192.548 km/h, 119.644 mph (D Coulthard, 1 min:19.479 sec on lap 28)
Lap Leaders M Schumacher 1-24,26-39 (38); D Coulthard 25,40-72 (34).

16 Jul 2000 — AUSTRIA: A1-Ring (Round 10) (Race 656)

71 laps x 4.326 km, 2.688 miles = 307.146 km, 190.852 miles

Pos	No	Driver	Car	Model	Engine		Laps	Time/Reason for Retirement	Grid Pos	Row
1	1	M Häkkinen	McLaren	MP4/15	Mercedes-Benz	V10	71	1h 28m 15.818s	1	1
2	2	D Coulthard	McLaren	MP4/15	Mercedes-Benz	V10	71	1h 28m 28.353s	2	1
3	4	R Barrichello	Ferrari	F1 2000	Ferrari	V10	71	1h 28m 46.613s	3	2
4	22	J Villeneuve	BAR	002	Honda	V10	70		7	4
5	10	J Button	Williams	FW22	BMW	V10	70		18	9
6	17	M Salo	Sauber	C19	Petronas	V10	70		9	5
7	8	J Herbert	Jaguar	R1	Ford Cosworth	V10	70		16	8
8	20	M Gené	Minardi	M02	Fondmetal	V10	70		20	10
9	16	P Diniz	Sauber	C19	Petronas	V10	70		11	6
10	12	A Wurz	Benetton	B200	Playlife	V10	70		14	7
11	7	L Burti	Jaguar	R1	Ford Cosworth	V10	69		21	11
12	21	G Mazzacane	Minardi	M02	Fondmetal	V10	68		22	11
r	23	R Zonta	BAR	002	Honda	V10	58	engine	6	3
r	9	R Schumacher	Williams	FW22	BMW	V10	52	brakes	19	10
r	15	N Heidfeld	Prost	AP03	Peugeot	V10	41	accident	13	7
r	14	J Alesi	Prost	AP03	Peugeot	V10	41	accident	17	9
r	18	P de la Rosa	Arrows	A21	Supertec	V10	32	gearbox	12	6
r	19	J Verstappen	Arrows	A21	Supertec	V10	14	engine	10	5
r	5	H-H Frentzen	Jordan	EJ10	Mugen Honda	V10	4	engine / spin	15	8
r	3	M Schumacher	Ferrari	F1 2000	Ferrari	V10	0	accident	4	2
r	6	J Trulli	Jordan	EJ10	Mugen Honda	V10	0	accident	5	3
r	11	G Fisichella	Benetton	B200	Playlife	V10	0	accident	8	4
ew	7	E Irvine	Jaguar	R1	Ford Cosworth	V10		driver ill		

Winning speed 208.792 km/h, 129.737 mph
Pole Position speed 221.184 km/h, 137.438 mph (M Häkkinen, 1 min:10.410 sec)
Fastest Lap speed 216.953 km/h, 134.809 mph (D Coulthard, 1 min:11.783 sec on lap 67)
Lap Leaders M Häkkinen 1-38,43-71 (67); D Coulthard 39-42 (4).

30 Jul 2000 — GERMANY: Hockenheim (Round 11) (Race 657)

45 laps x 6.825 km, 4.241 miles = 307.125 km, 190.839 miles

Pos	No	Driver	Car	Model	Engine		Laps	Time/Reason for Retirement	Grid Pos	Row
1	4	R Barrichello	Ferrari	F1 2000	Ferrari	V10	45	1h 25m 34.418s	18	9
2	1	M Häkkinen	McLaren	MP4/15	Mercedes-Benz	V10	45	1h 25m 41.870s	4	2
3	2	D Coulthard	McLaren	MP4/15	Mercedes-Benz	V10	45	1h 25m 55.586s	1	1
4	10	J Button	Williams	FW22	BMW	V10	45	1h 25m 57.103s	16	8
5	17	M Salo	Sauber	C19	Petronas	V10	45	1h 26m 01.530s	15	8
6	18	P de la Rosa	Arrows	A21	Supertec	V10	45	1h 26m 03.497s	5	3
7	9	R Schumacher	Williams	FW22	BMW	V10	45	1h 26m 05.315s	14	7
8	22	J Villeneuve	BAR	002	Honda	V10	45	1h 26m 21.955s	9	5
9	6	J Trulli	Jordan	EJ10	Mugen Honda	V10	45	1h 26m 25.319s	6	3
10	7	E Irvine	Jaguar	R1	Ford Cosworth	V10	45	1h 27m 54.082s	10	5
11	21	G Mazzacane	Minardi	M02	Fondmetal	V10	45	1h 28m 03.922s	21	11
12r	15	N Heidfeld	Prost	AP03	Peugeot	V10	40	alternator	13	7
r	5	H-H Frentzen	Jordan	EJ10	Mugen Honda	V10	39	electronics	17	9
r	19	J Verstappen	Arrows	A21	Supertec	V10	39	spin	11	6
r	23	R Zonta	BAR	002	Honda	V10	37	spin	12	6
r	20	M Gené	Minardi	M02	Fondmetal	V10	33	engine	22	11
r	12	A Wurz	Benetton	B200	Playlife	V10	31	gearbox / spin	7	4
r	16	P Diniz	Sauber	C19	Petronas	V10	29	accident	19	10
r	14	J Alesi	Prost	AP03	Peugeot	V10	29	accident	20	10
r	8	J Herbert	Jaguar	R1	Ford Cosworth	V10	12	gearbox	8	4
r	3	M Schumacher	Ferrari	F1 2000	Ferrari	V10	0	accident	2	1
r	11	G Fisichella	Benetton	B200	Playlife	V10	0	accident	3	2

Winning speed 215.340 km/h, 133.807 mph
Pole Position speed 232.456 km/h, 144.442 mph (D Coulthard, 1 min:45.697 sec)
Fastest Lap speed 235.570 km/h, 146.377 mph (R Barrichello, 1 min:44.300 sec on lap 20)
Lap Leaders M Häkkinen 1-25,28-35 (33); D Coulthard 26-27 (2); R Barrichello 36-45 (10).

13 Aug 2000 — HUNGARY: Hungaroring (Round 12) (Race 658)

77 laps x 3.975 km, 2.470 miles = 306.075 km, 190.186 miles

Pos	No	Driver	Car	Model	Engine		Laps	Time/Reason for Retirement	Grid Pos	Row
1	1	M Häkkinen	McLaren	MP4/15	Mercedes-Benz	V10	77	1h 45m 33.869s	3	2
2	3	M Schumacher	Ferrari	F1 2000	Ferrari	V10	77	1h 45m 41.786s	1	1
3	2	D Coulthard	McLaren	MP4/15	Mercedes-Benz	V10	77	1h 45m 42.324s	2	1
4	4	R Barrichello	Ferrari	F1 2000	Ferrari	V10	77	1h 46m 18.026s	5	3
5	9	R Schumacher	Williams	FW22	BMW	V10	77	1h 46m 24.306s	4	2
6	5	H-H Frentzen	Jordan	EJ10	Mugen Honda	V10	77	1h 46m 41.968s	6	3
7	6	J Trulli	Jordan	EJ10	Mugen Honda	V10	76		12	6
8	7	E Irvine	Jaguar	R1	Ford Cosworth	V10	76		10	5
9	10	J Button	Williams	FW22	BMW	V10	76		8	4
10	17	M Salo	Sauber	C19	Petronas	V10	76		9	5
11	12	A Wurz	Benetton	B200	Playlife	V10	76		11	6

Pos	No	Driver	Car	Model	Engine		Laps	Time/Reason for Retirement	Grid Pos	Row
12	22	J Villeneuve	BAR	002	Honda	V10	75		16	8
13	19	J Verstappen	Arrows	A21	Supertec	V10	75		20	10
14	23	R Zonta	BAR	002	Honda	V10	75		18	9
15	20	M Gené	Minardi	M02	Fondmetal	V10	74		21	11
16	18	P de la Rosa	Arrows	A21	Supertec	V10	73		15	8
r	21	G Mazzacane	Minardi	M02	Fondmetal	V10	68	engine	22	11
r	8	J Herbert	Jaguar	R1	Ford Cosworth	V10	67	gear shift	17	9
r	16	P Diniz	Sauber	C19	Petronas	V10	62	engine	13	7
r	11	G Fisichella	Benetton	B200	Playlife	V10	31	brakes	7	4
r	15	N Heidfeld	Prost	AP03	Peugeot	V10	22	battery	19	10
r	14	J Alesi	Prost	AP03	Peugeot	V10	11	rear suspension / steering	14	7

Winning speed 173.964 km/h, 108.097 mph
Pole Position speed 184.611 km/h, 114.712 mph (M Schumacher, 1 min:17.514 sec)
Fastest Lap speed 178.812 km/h, 111.109 mph (M Häkkinen, 1 min:20.028 sec on lap 33)
Lap Leaders M Häkkinen 1-31,33-77 (76); D Coulthard 32 (1).

27 Aug 2000	BELGIUM: Spa-Francorchamps	(Round 13)	(Race 659)

44 laps x 6.968 km, 4.330 miles = 306.592 km, 190.507 miles

Pos	No	Driver	Car	Model	Engine		Laps	Time/Reason for Retirement	Grid Pos	Row
1	1	M Häkkinen	McLaren	MP4/15	Mercedes-Benz	V10	44	1h 28m 14.494s	1	1
2	3	M Schumacher	Ferrari	F1 2000	Ferrari	V10	44	1h 28m 15.598s	4	2
3	9	R Schumacher	Williams	FW22	BMW	V10	44	1h 28m 52.590s	6	3
4	2	D Coulthard	McLaren	MP4/15	Mercedes-Benz	V10	44	1h 28m 57.775s	5	3
5	10	J Button	Williams	FW22	BMW	V10	44	1h 29m 04.408s	3	2
6	5	H-H Frentzen	Jordan	EJ10	Mugen Honda	V10	44	1h 29m 10.478s	8	4
7	22	J Villeneuve	BAR	002	Honda	V10	44	1h 29m 26.874s	7	4
8	8	J Herbert	Jaguar	R1	Ford Cosworth	V10	44	1h 29m 42.302s	9	5
9	17	M Salo	Sauber	C19	Petronas	V10	44	1h 29m 43.164s	18	9
10	7	E Irvine	Jaguar	R1	Ford Cosworth	V10	44	1h 29m 46.049s	12	6
11	16	P Diniz	Sauber	C19	Petronas	V10	44	1h 29m 48.617s	15	8
12	23	R Zonta	BAR	002	Honda	V10	43		13	7
13	12	A Wurz	Benetton	B200	Playlife	V10	43		19	10
14	20	M Gené	Minardi	M02	Fondmetal	V10	43		21	11
15	19	J Verstappen	Arrows	A21	Supertec	V10	43		20	10
16	18	P de la Rosa	Arrows	A21	Supertec	V10	42		16	8
17	21	G Mazzacane	Minardi	M02	Fondmetal	V10	42		22	11
r	4	R Barrichello	Ferrari	F1 2000	Ferrari	V10	32	fuel pressure	10	5
r	14	J Alesi	Prost	AP03	Peugeot	V10	32	fuel pressure	17	9
r	15	N Heidfeld	Prost	AP03	Peugeot	V10	12	engine	14	7
r	11	G Fisichella	Benetton	B200	Playlife	V10	8	electrics / accident	11	6
r	6	J Trulli	Jordan	EJ10	Mugen Honda	V10	4	accident	2	1

Winning speed 208.467 km/h, 129.536 mph
Pole Position speed 226.712 km/h, 140.872 mph (M Häkkinen, 1 min:50.646 sec)
Fastest Lap speed 220.423 km/h, 136.965 mph (R Barrichello, 1 min:53.803 sec on lap 30)
Lap Leaders M Häkkinen 1-12,23-27,41-44 (21); M Schumacher 13-22,28-40 (23).

10 Sep 2000	ITALY: Monza	(Round 14)	(Race 660)

53 laps x 5.793 km, 3.600 miles = 306.764 km, 190.614 miles

Pos	No	Driver	Car	Model	Engine		Laps	Time/Reason for Retirement	Grid Pos	Row
1	3	M Schumacher	Ferrari	F1 2000	Ferrari	V10	53	1h 27m 31.638s	1	1
2	1	M Häkkinen	McLaren	MP4/15	Mercedes-Benz	V10	53	1h 27m 35.448s	3	2
3	9	R Schumacher	Williams	FW22	BMW	V10	53	1h 28m 24.070s	7	4
4	19	J Verstappen	Arrows	A21	Supertec	V10	53	1h 28m 31.576s	11	6
5	12	A Wurz	Benetton	B200	Playlife	V10	53	1h 28m 39.064s	13	7
6	23	R Zonta	BAR	002	Honda	V10	53	1h 28m 40.931s	17	9
7	17	M Salo	Sauber	C19	Petronas	V10	52		15	8
8	16	P Diniz	Sauber	C19	Petronas	V10	52		16	8
9	20	M Gené	Minardi	M02	Fondmetal	V10	52		21	11
10	21	G Mazzacane	Minardi	M02	Fondmetal	V10	52		22	11
11	11	G Fisichella	Benetton	B200	Playlife	V10	52		9	5
12	14	J Alesi	Prost	AP03	Peugeot	V10	51		19	10
r	15	N Heidfeld	Prost	AP03	Peugeot	V10	15	spin	20	10
r	22	J Villeneuve	BAR	002	Honda	V10	14	electrics	4	2
r	10	J Button	Williams	FW22	BMW	V10	10	accident	12	6
r	8	J Herbert	Jaguar	R1	Ford Cosworth	V10	1	accident	18	9
r	4	R Barrichello	Ferrari	F1 2000	Ferrari	V10	0	accident	2	1
r	2	D Coulthard	McLaren	MP4/15	Mercedes-Benz	V10	0	accident	5	3
r	6	J Trulli	Jordan	EJ10	Mugen Honda	V10	0	accident	6	3
r	5	H-H Frentzen	Jordan	EJ10	Mugen Honda	V10	0	accident	8	4
r	18	P de la Rosa	Arrows	A21	Supertec	V10	0	accident	10	5
r	7	E Irvine	Jaguar	R1	Ford Cosworth	V10	0	accident	14	7

Winning speed 210.286 km/h, 130.665 mph
Pole Position speed 248.953 km/h, 154.692 mph (M Schumacher, 1 min:23.770 sec)
Fastest Lap speed 243.645 km/h, 151.394 mph (M Häkkinen, 1 min:25.595 sec on lap 50)
Lap Leaders M Schumacher 1-39,43-53 (50); M Häkkinen 40-42 (3).

Races

24 Sep 2000 — USA: Indianapolis (Round 15) (Race 661)

73 laps x 4.192 km, 2.605 miles = 306.016 km, 190.150 miles

Pos	No	Driver	Car	Model	Engine		Laps	Time/Reason for Retirement	Grid Pos	Row
1	3	M Schumacher	Ferrari	F1 2000	Ferrari	V10	73	1h 36m 30.883s	1	1
2	4	R Barrichello	Ferrari	F1 2000	Ferrari	V10	73	1h 36m 43.001s	4	2
3	5	H-H Frentzen	Jordan	EJ10	Mugen Honda	V10	73	1h 36m 48.251s	7	4
4	22	J Villeneuve	BAR	002	Honda	V10	73	1h 36m 48.819s	8	4
5	2	D Coulthard	McLaren	MP4/15	Mercedes-Benz	V10	73	1h 36m 59.696s	2	1
6	23	R Zonta	BAR	002	Honda	V10	73	1h 37m 22.577s	12	6
7	7	E Irvine	Jaguar	R1	Ford Cosworth	V10	73	1h 37m 41.998s	17	9
8	16	P Diniz	Sauber	C19	Petronas	V10	72		9	5
9	15	N Heidfeld	Prost	AP03	Peugeot	V10	72		16	8
10	12	A Wurz	Benetton	B200	Playlife	V10	72		11	6
11	8	J Herbert	Jaguar	R1	Ford Cosworth	V10	72		19	10
12	20	M Gené	Minardi	M02	Fondmetal	V10	72		22	11
r	14	J Alesi	Prost	AP03	Peugeot	V10	64	engine / spin	20	10
r	21	G Mazzacane	Minardi	M02	Fondmetal	V10	59	engine	21	11
r	9	R Schumacher	Williams	FW22	BMW	V10	58	engine	10	5
r	18	P de la Rosa	Arrows	A21	Supertec	V10	45	gearbox	18	9
r	11	G Fisichella	Benetton	B200	Playlife	V10	44	engine	15	8
r	19	J Verstappen	Arrows	A21	Supertec	V10	34	brakes / accident	13	7
r	1	M Häkkinen	McLaren	MP4/15	Mercedes-Benz	V10	25		3	2
r	17	M Salo	Sauber	C19	Petronas	V10	18	spin	14	7
r	10	J Button	Williams	FW22	BMW	V10	14	engine	6	3
r	6	J Trulli	Jordan	EJ10	Mugen Honda	V10	12	gearbox	5	3

Winning speed 190.240 km/h, 118.210 mph
Pole Position speed 203.204 km/h, 126.266 mph (M Schumacher, 1 min:14.266 sec)
Fastest Lap speed 201.994 km/h, 125.513 mph (D Coulthard, 1 min:14.711 sec on lap 40)
Lap Leaders D Coulthard 1-6 (6); M Schumacher 7-73 (67).

8 Oct 2000 — JAPAN: Suzuka (Round 16) (Race 662)

53 laps x 5.864 km, 3.644 miles = 310.594 km, 192.994 miles

Pos	No	Driver	Car	Model	Engine		Laps	Time/Reason for Retirement	Grid Pos	Row
1	3	M Schumacher	Ferrari	F1 2000	Ferrari	V10	53	1h 29m 53.435s	1	1
2	1	M Häkkinen	McLaren	MP4/15	Mercedes-Benz	V10	53	1h 29m 55.272s	2	1
3	2	D Coulthard	McLaren	MP4/15	Mercedes-Benz	V10	53	1h 30m 03.349s	3	2
4	4	R Barrichello	Ferrari	F1 2000	Ferrari	V10	53	1h 30m 12.625s	4	2
5	10	J Button	Williams	FW22	BMW	V10	53	1h 30m 19.129s	5	3
6	22	J Villeneuve	BAR	002	Honda	V10	52		9	5
7	8	J Herbert	Jaguar	R1	Ford Cosworth	V10	52		10	5
8	7	E Irvine	Jaguar	R1	Ford Cosworth	V10	52		7	4
9	23	R Zonta	BAR	002	Honda	V10	52		18	9
10	17	M Salo	Sauber	C19	Petronas	V10	52		19	10
11	16	P Diniz	Sauber	C19	Petronas	V10	52		20	10
12	18	P de la Rosa	Arrows	A21	Supertec	V10	52		13	7
13	6	J Trulli	Jordan	EJ10	Mugen Honda	V10	52		15	8
14	11	G Fisichella	Benetton	B200	Playlife	V10	52		12	6
15	21	G Mazzacane	Minardi	M02	Fondmetal	V10	51		22	11
r	20	M Gené	Minardi	M02	Fondmetal	V10	46	engine	21	11
r	9	R Schumacher	Williams	FW22	BMW	V10	41	spin	6	3
r	15	N Heidfeld	Prost	AP03	Peugeot	V10	41	rear suspension	16	8
r	12	A Wurz	Benetton	B200	Playlife	V10	37	spin	11	6
r	5	H-H Frentzen	Jordan	EJ10	Mugen Honda	V10	29	hydraulics	8	4
r	14	J Alesi	Prost	AP03	Peugeot	V10	19	engine / spin	17	9
r	19	J Verstappen	Arrows	A21	Supertec	V10	9	electrics / gearbox	14	7

Winning speed 207.315 km/h, 128.819 mph
Pole Position speed 220.301 km/h, 136.889 mph (M Schumacher, 1 min:35.825 sec)
Fastest Lap speed 212.830 km/h, 132.246 mph (M Häkkinen, 1 min:39.189 sec on lap 26)
Lap Leaders M Häkkinen 1-21,25-36 (33); M Schumacher 22-23,37-53 (19); D Coulthard 24 (1).

56 laps x 5.543 km, 3.444 miles = 310.408 km, 192.879 miles

Pos	No	Driver	Car	Model	Engine		Laps	Time/Reason for Retirement	Grid Pos	Row
1	3	M Schumacher	Ferrari	F1 2000	Ferrari	V10	56	1h 35m 54.235s	1	1
2	2	D Coulthard	McLaren	MP4/15	Mercedes-Benz	V10	56	1h 35m 54.967s	3	2
3	4	R Barrichello	Ferrari	F1 2000	Ferrari	V10	56	1h 36m 12.679s	4	2
4	1	M Häkkinen	McLaren	MP4/15	Mercedes-Benz	V10	56	1h 36m 29.504s	2	1
5	22	J Villeneuve	BAR	002	Honda	V10	56	1h 37m 04.927s	6	3
6	7	E Irvine	Jaguar	R1	Ford Cosworth	V10	56	1h 37m 06.803s	7	4
7	12	A Wurz	Benetton	B200	Playlife	V10	56	1h 37m 23.549s	5	3
8	17	M Salo	Sauber	C19	Petronas	V10	55		17	9
9	11	G Fisichella	Benetton	B200	Playlife	V10	55		13	7
10	19	J Verstappen	Arrows	A21	Supertec	V10	55		15	8
11	14	J Alesi	Prost	AP03	Peugeot	V10	55		18	9
12	6	J Trulli	Jordan	EJ10	Mugen Honda	V10	55		9	5
13r	21	G Mazzacane	Minardi	M02	Fondmetal	V10	50		22	11
r	8	J Herbert	Jaguar	R1	Ford Cosworth	V10	48	rear suspension / accident	12	6
r	23	R Zonta	BAR	002	Honda	V10	46	engine	11	6
r	9	R Schumacher	Williams	FW22	BMW	V10	43	oil pressure / engine	8	4
r	20	M Gené	Minardi	M02	Fondmetal	V10	36	rear wheel	21	11
r	10	J Button	Williams	FW22	BMW	V10	18	engine	16	8
r	5	H-H Frentzen	Jordan	EJ10	Mugen Honda	V10	7	hydraulics	10	5
r	18	P de la Rosa	Arrows	A21	Supertec	V10	0	accident	14	7
r	15	N Heidfeld	Prost	AP03	Peugeot	V10	0	accident	19	10
r	16	P Diniz	Sauber	C19	Petronas	V10	0	accident	20	10

Winning speed 194.199 km/h, 120.670 mph
Pole Position speed 204.881 km/h, 127.307 mph (M Schumacher, 1 min:37.397 sec)
Fastest Lap speed 202.498 km/h, 125.827 mph (M Häkkinen, 1 min:38.543 sec on lap 34)
Lap Leaders M Häkkinen 1-2 (2); D Coulthard 3-17 (15); M Schumacher 18-24,26-39,42-56 (36); R Barrichello 25,40-41 (3).

Lap Leaders 2000

Pos	Driver	Car-Engine	GPs	laps	km	miles
1	M Schumacher	Ferrari	14	548	2,589.7	1,609.1
2	M Häkkinen	McLaren-Mercedes-Benz	12	352	1,751.3	1,088.2
3	D Coulthard	McLaren-Mercedes-Benz	9	107	479.1	297.7
4	R Barrichello	Ferrari	7	58	308.4	191.6
5	H-H Frentzen	Jordan-Mugen Honda	2	9	47.2	29.4
			17	1,074	5,175.7	3,216.0

Driver Points 2000

		AUS	BR	RSM	GB	E	EUR	MC	CDN	F	A	D	H	B	I	USA	J	MAL	Total
1	M Schumacher	10	10	10	4	2	10	-	10	-	-	-	6	6	10	10	10	10	108
2	M Häkkinen	-	-	6	6	10	6	1	3	6	10	6	10	10	6	-	6	3	89
3	D Coulthard	-	-	4	10	6	4	10	-	10	6	4	4	3	-	2	4	6	73
4	R Barrichello	6	-	3	-	4	3	6	6	4	4	10	3	-	-	6	3	4	62
5	R Schumacher	4	2	-	3	3	-	-	-	2	-	-	-	2	4	-	-	-	24
6	G Fisichella	2	6	-	-	-	2	4	4	-	-	-	-	-	-	-	-	-	18
7	J Villeneuve	3	-	2	-	-	-	-	-	3	3	-	-	-	-	3	1	2	17
8	J Button	-	1	-	2	-	-	-	-	2	3	-	-	2	-	-	2	-	12
9	H-H Frentzen	-	4	-	-	-	1	-	-	-	-	-	1	1	-	4	-	-	11
10	J Trulli	-	3	-	1	-	-	-	1	1	-	-	-	-	-	-	-	-	6
	M Salo	-	-	1	-	-	-	2	-	-	1	2	-	-	-	-	-	-	5
12	J Verstappen	-	-	-	-	-	-	-	2	-	-	-	-	-	3	-	-	-	5
13	E Irvine	-	-	-	-	-	3	-	-	-	-	-	-	-	-	-	-	1	4
14	R Zonta	1	-	-	-	-	-	-	-	-	-	-	-	1	1	-	-	-	3
15	A Wurz	-	-	-	-	-	-	-	-	-	-	-	-	-	2	-	-	-	2
	P de la Rosa	-	-	-	-	1	-	-	-	-	1	-	-	-	-	-	-	-	2

10,6,4,3,2 and 1 point awarded to the first six finishers.

Constructor Points 2000

		AUS	BR	RSM	GB	E	EUR	MC	CDN	F	A	D	H	B	I	USA	J	MAL	Total
1	Ferrari	16	10	13	4	6	13	6	16	4	4	10	9	6	10	16	13	14	170
2	McLaren-Mercedes-Benz	-	-	10	16	16	10	11	3	16	6	10	14	13	6	2	10	9	152
3	Williams-BMW	4	3	-	5	3	-	-	-	2	2	3	2	6	4	-	2	-	36
4	Benetton-Playlife	2	6	-	-	-	2	4	4	-	-	-	-	-	2	-	-	-	20
	BAR-Honda	4	-	2	-	-	-	-	-	3	3	-	-	1	4	1	2	-	20
6	Jordan-Mugen Honda	-	7	-	1	1	-	-	1	1	-	-	1	1	-	4	-	-	17
7	Arrows-Supertec	-	-	-	-	1	-	-	2	-	-	1	-	-	3	-	-	-	7
8	Sauber-Petronas	-	-	1	-	-	-	2	-	-	1	2	-	-	-	-	-	-	6
9	Jaguar-Ford Cosworth	-	-	-	-	-	3	-	-	-	-	-	-	-	-	-	-	1	4

10,6,4,3,2 and 1 point awarded to the first six finishers.
In Austria, McLaren were stripped of 10 points for Häkkinen's win, due to a missing seal from the black box.

2001

Race Entrants and Results

Michelin returned to F1 after a fifteen year gap. Electronic driver aids such as traction control and launch control were reintroduced at the fifth race of the season. A lot of interest centred on Williams new driver Juan Pablo Montoya who came with an impressive pedigree of Indy 500 winner and ChampCar champion of 1999. The Italian GP saw the first two new nationalities to enter F1 since Venezuela in 1983. During the course of the season the German media group Kirch bought a major share in the broadcasting rights of Formula 1 and in return the major manufacturers talked of a breakaway championship at the end of the present Concorde Agreement in 2008.

FERRARI
Scuderia Ferrari Marlboro: M Schumacher, Barrichello

McLAREN
West McLaren Mercedes: Häkkinen, Coulthard

WILLIAMS
BMW WilliamsF1 Team: R Schumacher, Montoya

BENETTON
Mild Seven Benetton Renault: Fisichella, Button

BAR
Lucky Strike B.A.R. Honda: Panis, Villeneuve

JORDAN
Benson & Hedges Jordan Honda: Frentzen, Trulli, Zonta, Alesi

ARROWS
Orange Arrows Asiatech: Verstappen, Bernoldi

SAUBER
Red Bull Sauber Petronas: Heidfeld, Räikkönen

JAGUAR
Jaguar Racing: Irvine, Burti, de la Rosa

MINARDI
European Minardi F1: Marques, Yoong, Alonso

PROST
Prost Acer: Alesi, Frentzen, Mazzacane, Burti, Enge

4 Mar 2001		AUSTRALIA: Melbourne							(Round 1)	(Race 664)	

58 laps x 5.303 km, 3.295 miles = 307.574 km, 191.118 miles

Pos	No	Driver	Car	Model	Engine		Laps	Time/Reason for Retirement	Grid Pos	Row
1	1	M Schumacher	Ferrari	F2001	Ferrari	V10	58	1h 38m 26.533s	1	1
2	4	D Coulthard	McLaren	MP4-16	Mercedes-Benz	V10	58	1h 38m 28.251s	6	3
3	2	R Barrichello	Ferrari	F2001	Ferrari	V10	58	1h 39m 00.024s	2	1
4	16	N Heidfeld	Sauber	C20	Petronas	V10	58	1h 39m 38.012s	10	5
5	11	H-H Frentzen	Jordan	EJ11	Honda	V10	58	1h 39m 39.340s	4	2
6	17	K Räikkönen	Sauber	C20	Petronas	V10	58	1h 39m 50.676s	13	7
7	9	O Panis	BAR	003	Honda	V10	58	1h 39m 53.583s	9	5
8	19	L Burti	Jaguar	R2	Ford Cosworth	V10	57		21	11
9	14	J Verstappen	Arrows	A22	Asiatech	V10	57		15	8
10	22	J Alesi	Prost	AP04	Acer	V10	57		14	7
11	18	E Irvine	Jaguar	R2	Ford Cosworth	V10	57		12	6
12	21	F Alonso	Minardi	PS01	European	V10	56		19	10
13	7	G Fisichella	Benetton	B201	Renault	V10	55		17	9
14r	8	J Button	Benetton	B201	Renault	V10	52	exhaust / electrics	16	8
r	6	J P Montoya	Williams	FW23	BMW	V10	40	engine	11	6
r	12	J Trulli	Jordan	EJ11	Honda	V10	38	misfire	7	4
r	3	M Häkkinen	McLaren	MP4-16	Mercedes-Benz	V10	25	front suspension / accident	3	2
r	5	R Schumacher	Williams	FW23	BMW	V10	4	accident	5	3
r	10	J Villeneuve	BAR	003	Honda	V10	4	accident	8	4
r	20	T Marques	Minardi	PS01	European	V10	3	electrics	22	11
r	15	E Bernoldi	Arrows	A22	Asiatech	V10	2	accident	18	9
r	23	G Mazzacane	Prost	AP04	Acer	V10	0	brakes	20	10

Winning speed 187.464 km/h, 116.485 mph
Pole Position speed 219.707 km/h, 136.520 mph (M Schumacher, 1 min:26.892 sec)
Fastest Lap speed 216.414 km/h, 134.474 mph (M Schumacher, 1 min:28.214 sec on lap 34)
Lap Leaders M Schumacher 1-36,41-58 (54); D Coulthard 37-40 (4).

O Panis finished 4th in 1h 39m 28.583s, but was given a 25s penalty, due to overtaking under yellow flags.

18 Mar 2001   MALAYSIA: Sepang   (Round 2)   (Race 665)

55 laps x 5.543 km, 3.444 miles = 304.865 km, 189.434 miles

Pos	No	Driver	Car	Model	Engine		Laps	Time/Reason for Retirement	Grid Pos	Row
1	1	M Schumacher	Ferrari	F2001	Ferrari	V10	55	1h 47m 34.801s	1	1
2	2	R Barrichello	Ferrari	F2001	Ferrari	V10	55	1h 47m 58.461s	2	1
3	4	D Coulthard	McLaren	MP4-16	Mercedes-Benz	V10	55	1h 48m 03.356s	8	4
4	11	H-H Frentzen	Jordan	EJ11	Honda	V10	55	1h 48m 21.344s	9	5
5	5	R Schumacher	Williams	FW23	BMW	V10	55	1h 48m 23.034s	3	2
6	3	M Häkkinen	McLaren	MP4-16	Mercedes-Benz	V10	55	1h 48m 23.407s	4	2
7	14	J Verstappen	Arrows	A22	Asiatech	V10	55	1h 48m 56.361s	18	9
8	12	J Trulli	Jordan	EJ11	Honda	V10	54		5	3
9	22	J Alesi	Prost	AP04	Acer	V10	54		13	7
10	19	L Burti	Jaguar	R2	Ford Cosworth	V10	54		15	8
11	8	J Button	Benetton	B201	Renault	V10	53		17	9
12	23	G Mazzacane	Prost	AP04	Acer	V10	53		19	10
13	21	F Alonso	Minardi	PS01	European	V10	52		21	11
14	20	T Marques	Minardi	PS01	European	V10	51		20	10
r	7	G Fisichella	Benetton	B201	Renault	V10	31	fuel pressure	16	8
r	10	J Villeneuve	BAR	003	Honda	V10	3	spin	7	4
r	16	N Heidfeld	Sauber	C20	Petronas	V10	3	spin	11	6
r	15	E Bernoldi	Arrows	A22	Asiatech	V10	3	spin	22	11
r	6	J P Montoya	Williams	FW23	BMW	V10	3	spin	6	3
r	18	E Irvine	Jaguar	R2	Ford Cosworth	V10	3	accident / radiator	12	6
r	9	O Panis	BAR	003	Honda	V10	1	oil system / engine fire	10	5
r	17	K Räikkönen	Sauber	C20	Petronas	V10	0	clutch	14	7

Winning speed 170.030 km/h, 105.652 mph
Pole Position speed 209.565 km/h, 130.218 mph (M Schumacher, 1 min:35.220 sec)
Fastest Lap speed 197.646 km/h, 122.812 mph (M Häkkinen, 1 min:40.962 sec on lap 48)
Lap Leaders M Schumacher 1-2,16-55 (42); J Trulli 3 (1); D Coulthard 4-15 (12).

Scheduled for 56 laps but reduced by a lap due to the first start being abandoned.
E Bernoldi qualified 19th in 1m 38.708s, but his time was disallowed due to a rear wing infringement. He started from the back of the grid.

1 Apr 2001   BRAZIL: Interlagos   (Round 3)   (Race 666)

71 laps x 4.309 km, 2.677 miles = 305.909 km, 190.083 miles

Pos	No	Driver	Car	Model	Engine		Laps	Time/Reason for Retirement	Grid Pos	Row
1	4	D Coulthard	McLaren	MP4-16	Mercedes-Benz	V10	71	1h 39m 00.834s	5	3
2	1	M Schumacher	Ferrari	F2001	Ferrari	V10	71	1h 39m 16.998s	1	1
3	16	N Heidfeld	Sauber	C20	Petronas	V10	70		9	5
4	9	O Panis	BAR	003	Honda	V10	70		11	6
5	12	J Trulli	Jordan	EJ11	Honda	V10	70		7	4
6	7	G Fisichella	Benetton	B201	Renault	V10	70		18	9
7	10	J Villeneuve	BAR	003	Honda	V10	70		12	6
8	22	J Alesi	Prost	AP04	Acer	V10	70		15	8
9	20	T Marques	Minardi	PS01	European	V10	68		22	11
10	8	J Button	Benetton	B201	Renault	V10	64		20	10
11r	11	H-H Frentzen	Jordan	EJ11	Honda	V10	63	electronics	8	4
r	17	K Räikkönen	Sauber	C20	Petronas	V10	55	spin / rear tyre lost	10	5
r	23	G Mazzacane	Prost	AP04	Acer	V10	54	clutch	21	11
r	5	R Schumacher	Williams	FW23	BMW	V10	54	spin	2	1
r	18	E Irvine	Jaguar	R2	Ford Cosworth	V10	52	spin	13	7
r	6	J P Montoya	Williams	FW23	BMW	V10	38	accident	4	2
r	14	J Verstappen	Arrows	A22	Asiatech	V10	37	accident	17	9
r	19	L Burti	Jaguar	R2	Ford Cosworth	V10	30	water seal / engine	14	7
r	21	F Alonso	Minardi	PS01	European	V10	25	throttle potentiometer	19	10
r	15	E Bernoldi	Arrows	A22	Asiatech	V10	15	hydraulics	16	8
r	2	R Barrichello	Ferrari	F2001	Ferrari	V10	2	accident	6	3
r	3	M Häkkinen	McLaren	MP4-16	Mercedes-Benz	V10	0	hydraulics	3	2

Winning speed 185.373 km/h, 115.186 mph
Pole Position speed 210.252 km/h, 130.645 mph (M Schumacher, 1 min:13.780 sec)
Fastest Lap speed 204.938 km/h, 127.343 mph (R Schumacher, 1 min:15.693 sec on lap 38)
Lap Leaders M Schumacher 1-2,48-49 (4); J P Montoya 3-38 (36); D Coulthard 39-47,50-71 (31).

15 Apr 2001   SAN MARINO: Imola   (Round 4)   (Race 667)

62 laps x 4.933 km, 3.065 miles = 305.609 km, 189.897 miles

Pos	No	Driver	Car	Model	Engine		Laps	Time/Reason for Retirement	Grid Pos	Row
1	5	R Schumacher	Williams	FW23	BMW	V10	62	1h 30m 44.817s	3	2
2	4	D Coulthard	McLaren	MP4-16	Mercedes-Benz	V10	62	1h 30m 49.169s	1	1
3	2	R Barrichello	Ferrari	F2001	Ferrari	V10	62	1h 31m 19.583s	6	3
4	3	M Häkkinen	McLaren	MP4-16	Mercedes-Benz	V10	62	1h 31m 21.132s	2	1
5	12	J Trulli	Jordan	EJ11	Honda	V10	62	1h 32m 10.375s	5	3
6	11	H-H Frentzen	Jordan	EJ11	Honda	V10	61		9	5
7	16	N Heidfeld	Sauber	C20	Petronas	V10	61		12	6
8	9	O Panis	BAR	003	Honda	V10	61		8	4
9	22	J Alesi	Prost	AP04	Acer	V10	61		14	7
10	15	E Bernoldi	Arrows	A22	Asiatech	V10	60		16	8
11	19	L Burti	Jaguar	R2	Ford Cosworth	V10	60		15	8
12	8	J Button	Benetton	B201	Renault	V10	60		21	11
r	20	T Marques	Minardi	PS01	European	V10	50	engine	22	11
r	6	J P Montoya	Williams	FW23	BMW	V10	48	clutch	7	4
r	18	E Irvine	Jaguar	R2	Ford Cosworth	V10	42	engine	13	7
r	7	G Fisichella	Benetton	B201	Renault	V10	31	misfire	19	10
r	10	J Villeneuve	BAR	003	Honda	V10	30	engine	11	6
r	23	G Mazzacane	Prost	AP04	Acer	V10	28	engine	20	10
r	1	M Schumacher	Ferrari	F2001	Ferrari	V10	24	front brake caliper / wheel / tyre	4	2
r	17	K Räikkönen	Sauber	C20	Petronas	V10	17	steering wheel / spin	10	5
r	14	J Verstappen	Arrows	A22	Asiatech	V10	6	exhaust	17	9
r	21	F Alonso	Minardi	PS01	European	V10	5	accident	18	9

Winning speed 202.062 km/h, 125.556 mph
Pole Position speed 213.822 km/h, 132.863 mph (D Coulthard, 1 min:23.054 sec)
Fastest Lap speed 207.646 km/h, 129.026 mph (R Schumacher, 1 min:25.524 sec on lap 27)
Lap Leaders R Schumacher 1-62 (62).

29 Apr 2001   SPAIN: Montmeló   (Round 5)   (Race 668)

65 laps x 4.730 km, 2.939 miles = 307.323 km, 190.962 miles

Pos	No	Driver	Car	Model	Engine		Laps	Time/Reason for Retirement	Grid Pos	Row
1	1	M Schumacher	Ferrari	F2001	Ferrari	V10	65	1h 31m 03.305s	1	1
2	6	J P Montoya	Williams	FW23	BMW	V10	65	1h 31m 44.042s	12	6
3	10	J Villeneuve	BAR	003	Honda	V10	65	1h 31m 52.930s	7	4
4	12	J Trulli	Jordan	EJ11	Honda	V10	65	1h 31m 54.557s	6	3
5	4	D Coulthard	McLaren	MP4-16	Mercedes-Benz	V10	65	1h 31m 54.920s	3	2
6	16	N Heidfeld	Sauber	C20	Petronas	V10	65	1h 32m 05.197s	10	5
7	9	O Panis	BAR	003	Honda	V10	65	1h 32m 08.281s	11	6
8	17	K Räikkönen	Sauber	C20	Petronas	V10	65	1h 32m 23.112s	9	5
9r	3	M Häkkinen	McLaren	MP4-16	Mercedes-Benz	V10	64	clutch	2	1
10	22	J Alesi	Prost	AP04	Acer	V10	64		15	8
11	23	L Burti	Prost	AP04	Acer	V10	64		14	7
12	14	J Verstappen	Arrows	A22	Asiatech	V10	63		17	9
13	21	F Alonso	Minardi	PS01	European	V10	63		18	9
14	7	G Fisichella	Benetton	B201	Renault	V10	63		19	10
15	8	J Button	Benetton	B201	Renault	V10	62		21	11
16	20	T Marques	Minardi	PS01	European	V10	62		22	11
r	2	R Barrichello	Ferrari	F2001	Ferrari	V10	49	rear suspension	4	2
r	18	E Irvine	Jaguar	R2	Ford Cosworth	V10	48	engine	13	7
r	5	R Schumacher	Williams	FW23	BMW	V10	20	rear brakes / spin	5	3
r	15	E Bernoldi	Arrows	A22	Asiatech	V10	8	fuel pressure	16	8
r	19	P de la Rosa	Jaguar	R2	Ford Cosworth	V10	5	accident	20	10
r	11	H-H Frentzen	Jordan	EJ11	Honda	V10	5	accident	8	4

Winning speed 202.507 km/h, 125.833 mph
Pole Position speed 217.746 km/h, 135.301 mph (M Schumacher, 1 min:18.201 sec)
Fastest Lap speed 209.831 km/h, 130.383 mph (M Schumacher, 1 min:21.151 sec on lap 25)
Lap Leaders M Schumacher 1-22,28-43,65 (39); M Häkkinen 23-27,44-64 (26).

13 May 2001   AUSTRIA: A1-Ring   (Round 6)   (Race 669)

71 laps x 4.326 km, 2.688 miles = 307.146 km, 190.852 miles

Pos	No	Driver	Car	Model	Engine		Laps	Time/Reason for Retirement	Grid Pos	Row
1	4	D Coulthard	McLaren	MP4-16	Mercedes-Benz	V10	71	1h 27m 45.927s	7	4
2	1	M Schumacher	Ferrari	F2001	Ferrari	V10	71	1h 27m 48.117s	1	1
3	2	R Barrichello	Ferrari	F2001	Ferrari	V10	71	1h 27m 48.454s	4	2
4	17	K Räikkönen	Sauber	C20	Petronas	V10	71	1h 28m 27.520s	9	5
5	9	O Panis	BAR	003	Honda	V10	71	1h 28m 39.702s	10	5
6	14	J Verstappen	Arrows	A22	Asiatech	V10	70		16	8
7	18	E Irvine	Jaguar	R2	Ford Cosworth	V10	70		13	7
8	10	J Villeneuve	BAR	003	Honda	V10	70		12	6
9	16	N Heidfeld	Sauber	C20	Petronas	V10	69		6	3
10	22	J Alesi	Prost	AP04	Acer	V10	69		20	10
11	23	L Burti	Prost	AP04	Acer	V10	69		17	9
r	8	J Button	Benetton	B201	Renault	V10	60	engine / spin	21	11
r	19	P de la Rosa	Jaguar	R2	Ford Cosworth	V10	48	transmission	14	7
r	6	J P Montoya	Williams	FW23	BMW	V10	41	hydraulics	2	1
r	21	F Alonso	Minardi	PS01	European	V10	38	clutch / gearbox	18	9
r	20	T Marques	Minardi	PS01	European	V10	25	gearbox	22	11
r	15	E Bernoldi	Arrows	A22	Asiatech	V10	17	hydraulics	15	8
dq	12	J Trulli	Jordan	EJ11	Honda	V10	14	left pit lane under red light	5	3
r	5	R Schumacher	Williams	FW23	BMW	V10	10	brakes	3	2
r	7	G Fisichella	Benetton	B201	Renault	V10	3	engine	19	10
r	3	M Häkkinen	McLaren	MP4-16	Mercedes-Benz	V10	1	electronics	8	4
r	11	H-H Frentzen	Jordan	EJ11	Honda	V10	0	gearbox	11	6

Winning speed 209.977 km/h, 130.474 mph
Pole Position speed 223.880 km/h, 139.113 mph (M Schumacher, 1 min: 9.562 sec)
Fastest Lap speed 219.832 km/h, 136.598 mph (D Coulthard, 1 min:10.843 sec on lap 48)
Lap Leaders J P Montoya 1-15 (15); R Barrichello 16-46 (31); D Coulthard 47-71 (25).

27 May 2001   MONACO: Monte-Carlo   (Round 7)   (Race 670)

78 laps x 3.370 km, 2.094 miles = 262.860 km, 163.334 miles

Pos	No	Driver	Car	Model	Engine		Laps	Time/Reason for Retirement	Grid Pos	Row
1	1	M Schumacher	Ferrari	F2001	Ferrari	V10	78	1h 47m 22.561s	2	1
2	2	R Barrichello	Ferrari	F2001	Ferrari	V10	78	1h 47m 22.992s	4	2
3	18	E Irvine	Jaguar	R2	Ford Cosworth	V10	78	1h 47m 53.259s	6	3
4	10	J Villeneuve	BAR	003	Honda	V10	78	1h 47m 55.015s	9	5
5	4	D Coulthard	McLaren	MP4-16	Mercedes-Benz	V10	77		1	1
6	22	J Alesi	Prost	AP04	Acer	V10	77		11	6
7	8	J Button	Benetton	B201	Renault	V10	77		17	9
8	14	J Verstappen	Arrows	A22	Asiatech	V10	77		19	10
9	15	E Bernoldi	Arrows	A22	Asiatech	V10	76		20	10
10	17	K Räikkönen	Sauber	C20	Petronas	V10	73		15	8
r	5	R Schumacher	Williams	FW23	BMW	V10	57	electrics	5	3
r	20	T Marques	Minardi	PS01	European	V10	56	driveshaft	22	11
r	21	F Alonso	Minardi	PS01	European	V10	54	gearbox	18	9
r	11	H-H Frentzen	Jordan	EJ11	Honda	V10	49	accident / injury	13	7
r	7	G Fisichella	Benetton	B201	Renault	V10	43	gearbox / accident	10	5
r	12	J Trulli	Jordan	EJ11	Honda	V10	30	hydraulics	8	4
r	23	L Burti	Prost	AP04	Acer	V10	24	brakes / gearbox	21	11
r	19	P de la Rosa	Jaguar	R2	Ford Cosworth	V10	18	hydraulics	14	7
r	3	M Häkkinen	McLaren	MP4-16	Mercedes-Benz	V10	15	suspension / handling	3	2
r	9	O Panis	BAR	003	Honda	V10	13	steering	12	6
r	6	J P Montoya	Williams	FW23	BMW	V10	2	accident	7	4
r	16	N Heidfeld	Sauber	C20	Petronas	V10	0	accident	16	8

Winning speed 146.881 km/h, 91.268 mph
Pole Position speed 156.683 km/h, 97.359 mph (D Coulthard, 1 min:17.430 sec)
Fastest Lap speed 152.749 km/h, 94.914 mph (D Coulthard, 1 min:19.424 sec on lap 68)
Lap Leaders M Schumacher 1-54,60-78 (73); R Barrichello 55-59 (5).

69 laps x 4.421 km, 2.747 miles = 305.049 km, 189.549 miles

Pos	No	Driver	Car	Model	Engine		Laps	Time/Reason for Retirement	Grid Pos	Row
1	5	R Schumacher	Williams	FW23	BMW	V10	69	1h 34m 31.522s	2	1
2	1	M Schumacher	Ferrari	F2001	Ferrari	V10	69	1h 34m 51.757s	1	1
3	3	M Häkkinen	McLaren	MP4-16	Mercedes-Benz	V10	69	1h 35m 12.194s	8	4
4	17	K Räikkönen	Sauber	C20	Petronas	V10	69	1h 35m 39.638s	7	4
5	22	J Alesi	Prost	AP04	Acer	V10	69	1h 35m 41.957s	16	8
6	19	P de la Rosa	Jaguar	R2	Ford Cosworth	V10	68		14	7
7	11	R Zonta	Jordan	EJ11	Honda	V10	68		12	6
8	23	L Burti	Prost	AP04	Acer	V10	68		19	10
9	20	T Marques	Minardi	PS01	European	V10	66		21	11
10r	14	J Verstappen	Arrows	A22	Asiatech	V10	65	brakes / spin	13	7
11r	12	J Trulli	Jordan	EJ11	Honda	V10	63	brakes	4	2
r	4	D Coulthard	McLaren	MP4-16	Mercedes-Benz	V10	54	engine	3	2
r	9	O Panis	BAR	003	Honda	V10	38	brakes	6	3
r	10	J Villeneuve	BAR	003	Honda	V10	34	driveshaft	9	5
r	15	E Bernoldi	Arrows	A22	Asiatech	V10	24	radiator / engine overheating	17	9
r	6	J P Montoya	Williams	FW23	BMW	V10	19	accident	10	5
r	2	R Barrichello	Ferrari	F2001	Ferrari	V10	19	accident	5	3
r	8	J Button	Benetton	B201	Renault	V10	17	oil leak	20	10
r	21	F Alonso	Minardi	PS01	European	V10	7	driveshaft	22	11
r	16	N Heidfeld	Sauber	C20	Petronas	V10	1	accident	11	6
r	18	E Irvine	Jaguar	R2	Ford Cosworth	V10	1	accident	15	8
r	7	G Fisichella	Benetton	B201	Renault	V10	0	accident	18	9
ew	11	H-H Frentzen	Jordan	EJ11	Honda	V10		discomfort from Monaco injury		

Winning speed 193.629 km/h, 120.316 mph
Pole Position speed 210.018 km/h, 130.499 mph (M Schumacher, 1 min:15.782 sec)
Fastest Lap speed 206.147 km/h, 128.094 mph (R Schumacher, 1 min:17.205 sec on lap 50)
Lap Leaders M Schumacher 1-45 (45); R Schumacher 46-69 (24).

F Alonso qualified 21st in 1m 19.454s, but his time was disallowed due to front wing being below the regulated height.

67 laps x 4.556 km, 2.831 miles = 305.235 km, 189.664 miles

Pos	No	Driver	Car	Model	Engine		Laps	Time/Reason for Retirement	Grid Pos	Row
1	1	M Schumacher	Ferrari	F2001	Ferrari	V10	67	1h 29m 42.724s	1	1
2	6	J P Montoya	Williams	FW23	BMW	V10	67	1h 29m 46.941s	3	2
3	4	D Coulthard	McLaren	MP4-16	Mercedes-Benz	V10	67	1h 30m 07.717s	5	3
4	5	R Schumacher	Williams	FW23	BMW	V10	67	1h 30m 16.069s	2	1
5	2	R Barrichello	Ferrari	F2001	Ferrari	V10	67	1h 30m 28.219s	4	2
6	3	M Häkkinen	McLaren	MP4-16	Mercedes-Benz	V10	67	1h 30m 47.592s	6	3
7	18	E Irvine	Jaguar	R2	Ford Cosworth	V10	67	1h 30m 48.922s	12	6
8	19	P de la Rosa	Jaguar	R2	Ford Cosworth	V10	66		16	8
9	10	J Villeneuve	BAR	003	Honda	V10	66		11	6
10	17	K Räikkönen	Sauber	C20	Petronas	V10	66		9	5
11	7	G Fisichella	Benetton	B201	Renault	V10	66		15	8
12	23	L Burti	Prost	AP04	Acer	V10	65		17	9
13	8	J Button	Benetton	B201	Renault	V10	65		20	10
14	21	F Alonso	Minardi	PS01	European	V10	65		21	11
15r	22	J Alesi	Prost	AP04	Acer	V10	64	spin	14	7
r	14	J Verstappen	Arrows	A22	Asiatech	V10	58	engine	19	10
r	16	N Heidfeld	Sauber	C20	Petronas	V10	54	driveshaft	10	5
r	11	H-H Frentzen	Jordan	EJ11	Honda	V10	48	traction control / spin	8	4
r	12	J Trulli	Jordan	EJ11	Honda	V10	44	hydraulics	7	4
r	15	E Bernoldi	Arrows	A22	Asiatech	V10	29	gearbox	18	9
r	9	O Panis	BAR	003	Honda	V10	23	electronics / spin	13	7
r	20	T Marques	Minardi	PS01	European	V10	7	gearbox	22	11

Winning speed 204.143 km/h, 126.849 mph
Pole Position speed 218.804 km/h, 135.959 mph (M Schumacher, 1 min:14.960 sec)
Fastest Lap speed 209.326 km/h, 130.070 mph (J P Montoya, 1 min:18.354 sec on lap 27)
Lap Leaders M Schumacher 1-28,30-67 (66); J P Montoya 29 (1).

1 Jul 2001		**FRANCE: Magny-Cours**							**(Round 10)**	**(Race 673)**

72 laps x 4.251 km, 2.641 miles = 305.886 km, 190.069 miles

Pos	No	Driver	Car	Model	Engine		Laps	Time/Reason for Retirement	Grid Pos	Row
1	1	M Schumacher	Ferrari	F2001	Ferrari	V10	72	1h 33m 35.636s	2	1
2	5	R Schumacher	Williams	FW23	BMW	V10	72	1h 33m 46.035s	1	1
3	2	R Barrichello	Ferrari	F2001	Ferrari	V10	72	1h 33m 52.017s	8	4
4	4	D Coulthard	McLaren	MP4-16	Mercedes-Benz	V10	72	1h 33m 52.742s	3	2
5	12	J Trulli	Jordan	EJ11	Honda	V10	72	1h 34m 43.921s	5	3
6	16	N Heidfeld	Sauber	C20	Petronas	V10	71		9	5
7	17	K Räikkönen	Sauber	C20	Petronas	V10	71		13	7
8	11	H-H Frentzen	Jordan	EJ11	Honda	V10	71		7	4
9	9	O Panis	BAR	003	Honda	V10	71		11	6
10	23	L Burti	Prost	AP04	Acer	V10	71		15	8
11	7	G Fisichella	Benetton	B201	Renault	V10	71		16	8
12	22	J Alesi	Prost	AP04	Acer	V10	70		19	10
13	14	J Verstappen	Arrows	A22	Asiatech	V10	70		18	9
14	19	P de la Rosa	Jaguar	R2	Ford Cosworth	V10	70		14	7
15	20	T Marques	Minardi	PS01	European	V10	69		22	11
16r	8	J Button	Benetton	B201	Renault	V10	68	fuel pressure / spin	17	9
17r	21	F Alonso	Minardi	PS01	European	V10	65	engine	21	11
r	18	E Irvine	Jaguar	R2	Ford Cosworth	V10	54	engine	12	6
r	6	J P Montoya	Williams	FW23	BMW	V10	52	engine	6	3
r	15	E Bernoldi	Arrows	A22	Asiatech	V10	17	engine	20	10
r	10	J Villeneuve	BAR	003	Honda	V10	5	electrics	10	5
ns	3	M Häkkinen	McLaren	MP4-16	Mercedes-Benz	V10		gearbox on dummy grid	4	2

Winning speed 196.093 km/h, 121.847 mph
Pole Position speed 209.669 km/h, 130.283 mph (R Schumacher, 1 min:12.989 sec)
Fastest Lap speed 201.130 km/h, 124.977 mph (D Coulthard, 1 min:16.088 sec on lap 53)
Lap Leaders R Schumacher 1-23 (23); M Schumacher 24-25,31-45,51-72 (39); D Coulthard 26 (1); J P Montoya 27-30,46-50 (9).

15 Jul 2001		**BRITAIN: Silverstone**							**(Round 11)**	**(Race 674)**

60 laps x 5.141 km, 3.194 miles = 308.356 km, 191.604 miles

Pos	No	Driver	Car	Model	Engine		Laps	Time/Reason for Retirement	Grid Pos	Row
1	3	M Häkkinen	McLaren	MP4-16	Mercedes-Benz	V10	60	1h 25m 33.770s	2	1
2	1	M Schumacher	Ferrari	F2001	Ferrari	V10	60	1h 26m 07.416s	1	1
3	2	R Barrichello	Ferrari	F2001	Ferrari	V10	60	1h 26m 33.051s	6	3
4	6	J P Montoya	Williams	FW23	BMW	V10	60	1h 26m 42.542s	8	4
5	17	K Räikkönen	Sauber	C20	Petronas	V10	59		7	4
6	16	N Heidfeld	Sauber	C20	Petronas	V10	59		9	5
7	11	H-H Frentzen	Jordan	EJ11	Honda	V10	59		5	3
8	10	J Villeneuve	BAR	003	Honda	V10	59		12	6
9	18	E Irvine	Jaguar	R2	Ford Cosworth	V10	59		15	8
10	14	J Verstappen	Arrows	A22	Asiatech	V10	58		17	9
11	22	J Alesi	Prost	AP04	Acer	V10	58		14	7
12	19	P de la Rosa	Jaguar	R2	Ford Cosworth	V10	58		13	7
13	7	G Fisichella	Benetton	B201	Renault	V10	58		19	10
14	15	E Bernoldi	Arrows	A22	Asiatech	V10	58		20	10
15	8	J Button	Benetton	B201	Renault	V10	58		18	9
16	21	F Alonso	Minardi	PS01	European	V10	57		21	11
r	5	R Schumacher	Williams	FW23	BMW	V10	36	engine	10	5
r	23	L Burti	Prost	AP04	Acer	V10	6	engine	16	8
r	4	D Coulthard	McLaren	MP4-16	Mercedes-Benz	V10	2	accident / rear suspension / spin	3	2
r	12	J Trulli	Jordan	EJ11	Honda	V10	0	accident	4	2
r	9	O Panis	BAR	003	Honda	V10	0	accident	11	6
nq	20	T Marques	Minardi	PS01	European	V10				

Winning speed 216.231 km/h, 134.360 mph
Pole Position speed 230.059 km/h, 142.952 mph (M Schumacher, 1 min:20.447 sec)
Fastest Lap speed 221.900 km/h, 137.882 mph (M Häkkinen, 1 min:23.405 sec on lap 34)
Lap Leaders M Schumacher 1-4 (4); M Häkkinen 5-21,25-60 (53); J P Montoya 22-24 (3).

29 Jul 2001   GERMANY: Hockenheim   (Round 12)   (Race 675)

45 laps x 6.825 km, 4.241 miles = 307.125 km, 190.839 miles

Pos	No	Driver	Car	Model	Engine		Laps	Time/Reason for Retirement	Grid Pos	Row
1	5	R Schumacher	Williams	FW23	BMW	V10	45	1h 18m 17.873s	2	1
2	2	R Barrichello	Ferrari	F2001	Ferrari	V10	45	1h 19m 03.990s	6	3
3	10	J Villeneuve	BAR	003	Honda	V10	45	1h 19m 20.679s	12	6
4	7	G Fisichella	Benetton	B201	Renault	V10	45	1h 19m 21.350s	17	9
5	8	J Button	Benetton	B201	Renault	V10	45	1h 19m 23.327s	18	9
6	22	J Alesi	Prost	AP04	Acer	V10	45	1h 19m 23.823s	14	7
7	9	O Panis	BAR	003	Honda	V10	45	1h 19m 35.400s	13	7
8	15	E Bernoldi	Arrows	A22	Asiatech	V10	44		19	10
9	14	J Verstappen	Arrows	A22	Asiatech	V10	44		20	10
10	21	F Alonso	Minardi	PS01	European	V10	44		21	11
r	12	J Trulli	Jordan	EJ11	Honda	V10	34	hydraulics	10	5
r	4	D Coulthard	McLaren	MP4-16	Mercedes-Benz	V10	27	engine	5	3
r	20	T Marques	Minardi	PS01	European	V10	26	gearbox	22	11
r	6	J P Montoya	Williams	FW23	BMW	V10	24	engine	1	1
r	1	M Schumacher	Ferrari	F2001	Ferrari	V10	23	fuel blockage	4	2
r	23	L Burti	Prost	AP04	Acer	V10	23	spin	16	8
r	17	K Räikkönen	Sauber	C20	Petronas	V10	16	driveshaft	8	4
r	18	E Irvine	Jaguar	R2	Ford Cosworth	V10	16	fuel pressure	11	6
r	3	M Häkkinen	McLaren	MP4-16	Mercedes-Benz	V10	13	engine	3	2
r	11	R Zonta	Jordan	EJ11	Honda	V10	7	accident damage	15	8
r	16	N Heidfeld	Sauber	C20	Petronas	V10	0	accident	7	4
r	19	P de la Rosa	Jaguar	R2	Ford Cosworth	V10	0	accident	9	5

Winning speed 235.351 km/h, 146.240 mph
Pole Position speed 250.415 km/h, 155.601 mph (J P Montoya, 1 min:38.117 sec)
Fastest Lap speed 241.336 km/h, 149.960 mph (J P Montoya, 1 min:41.808 sec on lap 20)
Lap Leaders J P Montoya 1-22 (22); R Schumacher 23-45 (23).

Restarted after first lap accident.

19 Aug 2001   HUNGARY: Hungaroring   (Round 13)   (Race 676)

77 laps x 3.975 km, 2.470 miles = 306.075 km, 190.186 miles

Pos	No	Driver	Car	Model	Engine		Laps	Time/Reason for Retirement	Grid Pos	Row
1	1	M Schumacher	Ferrari	F2001	Ferrari	V10	77	1h 41m 49.675s	1	1
2	2	R Barrichello	Ferrari	F2001	Ferrari	V10	77	1h 41m 53.038s	3	2
3	4	D Coulthard	McLaren	MP4-16	Mercedes-Benz	V10	77	1h 41m 53.615s	2	1
4	5	R Schumacher	Williams	FW23	BMW	V10	77	1h 42m 39.362s	4	2
5	3	M Häkkinen	McLaren	MP4-16	Mercedes-Benz	V10	77	1h 42m 59.968s	6	3
6	16	N Heidfeld	Sauber	C20	Petronas	V10	76		7	4
7	17	K Räikkönen	Sauber	C20	Petronas	V10	76		9	5
8	6	J P Montoya	Williams	FW23	BMW	V10	76		8	4
9	10	J Villeneuve	BAR	003	Honda	V10	75		10	5
10	12	J Alesi	Jordan	EJ11	Honda	V10	75		12	6
11	19	P de la Rosa	Jaguar	R2	Ford Cosworth	V10	75		13	7
12	14	J Verstappen	Arrows	A22	Asiatech	V10	74		21	11
r	7	G Fisichella	Benetton	B201	Renault	V10	67	engine	15	8
r	22	H-H Frentzen	Prost	AP04	Acer	V10	63	spin	16	8
r	20	T Marques	Minardi	PS01	European	V10	63	oil leak / engine	22	11
r	9	O Panis	BAR	003	Honda	V10	58	electronics	11	6
r	11	J Trulli	Jordan	EJ11	Honda	V10	53	hydraulics	5	3
r	21	F Alonso	Minardi	PS01	European	V10	37	brakes / spin	18	9
r	8	J Button	Benetton	B201	Renault	V10	34	spin	17	9
r	15	E Bernoldi	Arrows	A22	Asiatech	V10	11	spin	20	10
r	23	L Burti	Prost	AP04	Acer	V10	8	spin	19	10
r	18	E Irvine	Jaguar	R2	Ford Cosworth	V10	0	spin	14	7

Winning speed 180.348 km/h, 112.063 mph
Pole Position speed 193.224 km/h, 120.064 mph (M Schumacher, 1 min:14.059 sec)
Fastest Lap speed 186.515 km/h, 115.895 mph (M Häkkinen, 1 min:16.723 sec on lap 51)
Lap Leaders M Schumacher 1-28,33-52,55-77 (71); R Barrichello 29-30 (2); D Coulthard 31-32,53-54 (4).

2 Sep 2001 **BELGIUM: Spa-Francorchamps** **(Round 14)** **(Race 677)**

36 laps x 6.968 km, 4.330 miles = 250.831 km, 155.859 miles

Pos	No	Driver	Car	Model	Engine		Laps	Time/Reason for Retirement	Grid Pos	Row
1	1	M Schumacher	Ferrari	F2001	Ferrari	V10	36	1h 08m 05.002s	3	2
2	4	D Coulthard	McLaren	MP4-16	Mercedes-Benz	V10	36	1h 08m 15.100s	9	5
3	7	G Fisichella	Benetton	B201	Renault	V10	36	1h 08m 32.744s	8	4
4	3	M Häkkinen	McLaren	MP4-16	Mercedes-Benz	V10	36	1h 08m 41.089s	7	4
5	2	R Barrichello	Ferrari	F2001	Ferrari	V10	36	1h 08m 59.523s	5	3
6	12	J Alesi	Jordan	EJ11	Honda	V10	36	1h 09m 04.686s	13	7
7	5	R Schumacher	Williams	FW23	BMW	V10	36	1h 09m 04.988s	2	1
8	10	J Villeneuve	BAR	003	Honda	V10	36	1h 09m 09.972s	6	3
9	22	H-H Frentzen	Prost	AP04	Acer	V10	35		4	2
10	14	J Verstappen	Arrows	A22	Asiatech	V10	35		19	10
11	9	O Panis	BAR	003	Honda	V10	35		11	6
12	15	E Bernoldi	Arrows	A22	Asiatech	V10	35		21	11
13	20	T Marques	Minardi	PS01	European	V10	32		22	11
r	11	J Trulli	Jordan	EJ11	Honda	V10	31	engine	16	8
r	8	J Button	Benetton	B201	Renault	V10	17	accident	15	8
r	6	J P Montoya	Williams	FW23	BMW	V10	1	engine	1	1
r	19	P de la Rosa	Jaguar	R2	Ford Cosworth	V10	1	accident	10	5
r	16	N Heidfeld	Sauber	C20	Petronas	V10	0	accident damage	14	7
r	17	K Räikkönen	Sauber	C20	Petronas	V10	0	transmission *	12	6
r	18	E Irvine	Jaguar	R2	Ford Cosworth	V10	0	accident *	17	9
r	23	L Burti	Prost	AP04	Acer	V10	0	accident / injury *	18	9
r	21	F Alonso	Minardi	PS01	European	V10	0	gearbox *	20	10

Winning speed 221.050 km/h, 137.354 mph
Pole Position speed 223.827 km/h, 139.080 mph (J P Montoya, 1 min:52.072 sec)
Fastest Lap speed 228.546 km/h, 142.012 mph (M Schumacher, 1 min:49.758 sec on lap 3)
Lap Leaders M Schumacher 1-36 (36).

Scheduled for 44 laps but shortened to 36 after Burti's crash on lap 4 of the original race.
* Retired after first start.

16 Sep 2001 **ITALY: Monza** **(Round 15)** **(Race 678)**

53 laps x 5.793 km, 3.600 miles = 306.749 km, 190.605 miles

Pos	No	Driver	Car	Model	Engine		Laps	Time/Reason for Retirement	Grid Pos	Row
1	6	J P Montoya	Williams	FW23	BMW	V10	53	1h 16m 58.493s	1	1
2	2	R Barrichello	Ferrari	F2001	Ferrari	V10	53	1h 17m 03.668s	2	1
3	5	R Schumacher	Williams	FW23	BMW	V10	53	1h 17m 15.828s	4	2
4	1	M Schumacher	Ferrari	F2001	Ferrari	V10	53	1h 17m 23.484s	3	2
5	19	P de la Rosa	Jaguar	R2	Ford Cosworth	V10	53	1h 18m 13.477s	10	5
6	10	J Villeneuve	BAR	003	Honda	V10	53	1h 18m 20.962s	15	8
7	17	K Räikkönen	Sauber	C20	Petronas	V10	53	1h 18m 21.600s	9	5
8	12	J Alesi	Jordan	EJ11	Honda	V10	52		16	8
9	9	O Panis	BAR	003	Honda	V10	52		17	9
10	7	G Fisichella	Benetton	B201	Renault	V10	52		14	7
11	16	N Heidfeld	Sauber	C20	Petronas	V10	52		8	4
12	23	T Enge	Prost	AP04	Acer	V10	52		20	10
13	21	F Alonso	Minardi	PS01	European	V10	51		21	11
r	15	E Bernoldi	Arrows	A22	Asiatech	V10	46	crankshaft sensor	18	9
r	20	A Yoong	Minardi	PS01	European	V10	44	spin	22	11
r	22	H-H Frentzen	Prost	AP04	Acer	V10	28	transmission	12	6
r	14	J Verstappen	Arrows	A22	Asiatech	V10	25	fuel pressure	19	10
r	3	M Häkkinen	McLaren	MP4-16	Mercedes-Benz	V10	19	gearbox	7	4
r	18	E Irvine	Jaguar	R2	Ford Cosworth	V10	14	oil leak / engine misfire	13	7
r	4	D Coulthard	McLaren	MP4-16	Mercedes-Benz	V10	6	engine	6	3
r	8	J Button	Benetton	B201	Renault	V10	4	engine	11	6
r	11	J Trulli	Jordan	EJ11	Honda	V10	0	accident	5	3

Winning speed 239.103 km/h, 148.572 mph
Pole Position speed 253.658 km/h, 157.616 mph (J P Montoya, 1 min:22.216 sec)
Fastest Lap speed 245.140 km/h, 152.323 mph (R Schumacher, 1 min:25.073 sec on lap 39)
Lap Leaders J P Montoya 1-8,20-28,42-53 (29); R Barrichello 9-19,36-41 (17); R Schumacher 29-35 (7).

USA: Indianapolis (Round 16) (Race 679)

73 laps x 4.192 km, 2.605 miles = 306.016 km, 190.150 miles

Pos	No	Driver	Car	Model	Engine		Laps	Time/Reason for Retirement	Grid Pos	Row
1	3	M Häkkinen	McLaren	MP4-16	Mercedes-Benz	V10	73	1h 32m 42.840s	4	2
2	1	M Schumacher	Ferrari	F2001	Ferrari	V10	73	1h 32m 53.886s	1	1
3	4	D Coulthard	McLaren	MP4-16	Mercedes-Benz	V10	73	1h 32m 54.883s	7	4
4	11	J Trulli	Jordan	EJ11	Honda	V10	73	1h 33m 40.263s	8	4
5	18	E Irvine	Jaguar	R2	Ford Cosworth	V10	73	1h 33m 55.274s	14	7
6	16	N Heidfeld	Sauber	C20	Petronas	V10	73	1h 33m 55.836s	6	3
7	12	J Alesi	Jordan	EJ11	Honda	V10	72		9	5
8	7	G Fisichella	Benetton	B201	Renault	V10	72		12	6
9	8	J Button	Benetton	B201	Renault	V10	72		10	5
10	22	H-H Frentzen	Prost	AP04	Acer	V10	72		15	8
11	9	O Panis	BAR	003	Honda	V10	72		13	7
12	19	P de la Rosa	Jaguar	R2	Ford Cosworth	V10	72		16	8
13	15	E Bernoldi	Arrows	A22	Asiatech	V10	72		19	10
14	23	T Enge	Prost	AP04	Acer	V10	72		21	11
15r	2	R Barrichello	Ferrari	F2001	Ferrari	V10	71	engine	5	3
r	10	J Villeneuve	BAR	003	Honda	V10	45	accident / rear suspension	18	9
r	14	J Verstappen	Arrows	A22	Asiatech	V10	44	engine	20	10
r	6	J P Montoya	Williams	FW23	BMW	V10	38	hydraulics	3	2
r	20	A Yoong	Minardi	PS01	European	V10	38	gearbox	22	11
r	5	R Schumacher	Williams	FW23	BMW	V10	36	spin	2	1
r	21	F Alonso	Minardi	PS01	European	V10	36	driveshaft	17	9
r	17	K Räikkönen	Sauber	C20	Petronas	V10	2	accident / driveshaft	11	6

Winning speed 198.038 km/h, 123.056 mph
Pole Position speed 210.453 km/h, 130.770 mph (M Schumacher, 1 min:11.708 sec)
Fastest Lap speed 202.707 km/h, 125.957 mph (J P Montoya, 1 min:14.448 sec on lap 35)
Lap Leaders M Schumacher 1-4,27-33,36-38 (14); R Barrichello 5-26,46-49 (26); J P Montoya 34-35 (2); M Häkkinen 39-45,50-73 (31).

J Trulli originally disqualified for worn underbody plank, but reinstated following an appeal.
M Häkkinen qualified 2nd in 1m 11.945s, but this time was disallowed due to leaving the pit lane on race morning during a red light.

JAPAN: Suzuka (Round 17) (Race 680)

53 laps x 5.859 km, 3.641 miles = 310.331 km, 192.831 miles

Pos	No	Driver	Car	Model	Engine		Laps	Time/Reason for Retirement	Grid Pos	Row
1	1	M Schumacher	Ferrari	F2001	Ferrari	V10	53	1h 27m 33.298s	1	1
2	6	J P Montoya	Williams	FW23	BMW	V10	53	1h 27m 36.452s	2	1
3	4	D Coulthard	McLaren	MP4-16	Mercedes-Benz	V10	53	1h 27m 56.560s	7	4
4	3	M Häkkinen	McLaren	MP4-16	Mercedes-Benz	V10	53	1h 28m 08.837s	5	3
5	2	R Barrichello	Ferrari	F2001	Ferrari	V10	53	1h 28m 09.842s	4	2
6	5	R Schumacher	Williams	FW23	BMW	V10	53	1h 28m 10.420s	3	2
7	8	J Button	Benetton	B201	Renault	V10	53	1h 29m 10.400s	9	5
8	11	J Trulli	Jordan	EJ11	Honda	V10	52		8	4
9	16	N Heidfeld	Sauber	C20	Petronas	V10	52		10	5
10	10	J Villeneuve	BAR	003	Honda	V10	52		14	7
11	21	F Alonso	Minardi	PS01	European	V10	52		18	9
12	22	H-H Frentzen	Prost	AP04	Acer	V10	52		15	8
13	9	O Panis	BAR	003	Honda	V10	51		17	9
14	15	E Bernoldi	Arrows	A22	Asiatech	V10	51		20	10
15	14	J Verstappen	Arrows	A22	Asiatech	V10	51		21	11
16	20	A Yoong	Minardi	PS01	European	V10	50		22	11
17r	7	G Fisichella	Benetton	B201	Renault	V10	47	gearbox	6	3
r	19	P de la Rosa	Jaguar	R2	Ford Cosworth	V10	45	oil leak	16	8
r	23	T Enge	Prost	AP04	Acer	V10	42	brakes	19	10
r	18	E Irvine	Jaguar	R2	Ford Cosworth	V10	24	fuel rig failure	13	7
r	17	K Räikkönen	Sauber	C20	Petronas	V10	5	spin	12	6
r	12	J Alesi	Jordan	EJ11	Honda	V10	5	accident	11	6

Winning speed 212.664 km/h, 132.144 mph
Pole Position speed 228.065 km/h, 141.713 mph (M Schumacher, 1 min:32.484 sec)
Fastest Lap speed 217.573 km/h, 135.194 mph (R Schumacher, 1 min:36.944 sec on lap 46)
Lap Leaders M Schumacher 1-18,24-36,39-53 (46); J P Montoya 19-21,37-38 (5); R Schumacher 22-23 (2).

Lap Leaders 2001

Pos	Driver	Car-Engine	GPs	laps	km	miles
1	M Schumacher	Ferrari	13	533	2,514.2	1,562.2
2	R Schumacher	Williams-BMW	6	141	719.0	446.7
3	J P Montoya	Williams-BMW	9	122	634.1	394.0
4	M Häkkinen	McLaren-Mercedes-Benz	3	110	525.4	326.5
5	R Barrichello	Ferrari	5	81	366.4	227.7
6	D Coulthard	McLaren-Mercedes-Benz	6	77	349.6	217.2
7	J Trulli	Jordan-Honda	1	1	5.5	3.4
			17	1,065	5,114.1	3,177.8

Driver Points 2001

		AUS	MAL	BR	RSM	E	A	MC	CDN	EUR	F	GB	D	H	B	I	USA	J	Total
1	M Schumacher	10	10	6	-	10	6	10	6	10	10	6	-	10	10	3	6	10	123
2	D Coulthard	6	4	10	6	2	10	2	-	4	3	-	-	4	6	-	4	4	65
3	R Barrichello	4	6	-	4	-	4	6	-	2	4	4	6	6	2	6	-	2	56
4	R Schumacher	-	2	-	10	-	-	-	10	3	6	-	10	3	-	4	-	1	49
5	M Häkkinen	-	1	-	3	-	-	4	1	-	10	-	2	3	-	10	3	37
6	J P Montoya	-	-	-	-	6	-	-	-	6	-	3	-	-	-	10	-	6	31
7	J Villeneuve	-	-	-	-	4	-	3	-	-	-	-	4	-	-	1	-	-	12
	N Heidfeld	3	-	4	-	1	-	-	-	1	1	-	1	-	-	1	-	12
	J Trulli	-	-	2	2	3	-	-	-	-	2	-	-	-	-	-	3	-	12
10	K Räikkönen	1	-	-	-	-	3	-	3	-	-	2	-	-	-	-	-	-	9
11	G Fisichella	-	-	1	-	-	-	-	-	-	-	-	3	-	4	-	-	-	8
12	E Irvine	-	-	-	-	-	-	4	-	-	-	-	-	-	-	-	2	-	6
	H-H Frentzen	2	3	-	1	-	-	-	-	-	-	-	-	-	-	-	-	-	6
14	O Panis	-	-	3	-	-	2	-	-	-	-	-	-	-	-	-	-	-	5
	J Alesi	-	-	-	-	-	-	1	2	-	-	-	1	-	1	-	-	-	5
16	P de la Rosa	-	-	-	-	-	-	-	1	-	-	-	-	-	-	2	-	-	3
17	J Button	-	-	-	-	-	-	-	-	-	-	-	2	-	-	-	-	-	2
18	J Verstappen	-	-	-	-	-	1	-	-	-	-	-	-	-	-	-	-	-	1

10,6,4,3,2 and 1 point awarded to the first six finishers.

Constructor Points 2001

		AUS	MAL	BR	RSM	E	A	MC	CDN	EUR	F	GB	D	H	B	I	USA	J	Total
1	Ferrari	14	16	6	4	10	10	16	6	12	14	10	6	16	12	9	6	12	179
2	McLaren-Mercedes-Benz	6	5	10	9	2	10	2	4	5	3	10	-	6	9	-	14	7	102
3	Williams-BMW	-	2	-	10	6	-	-	10	9	6	3	10	3	-	14	-	7	80
4	Sauber-Petronas	4	-	4	-	1	3	-	3	-	1	3	-	1	-	-	1	-	21
5	Jordan-Honda	2	3	2	3	3	-	-	-	-	2	-	-	-	1	-	3	-	19
6	BAR-Honda	-	-	3	-	4	2	3	-	-	-	-	4	-	-	1	-	-	17
7	Benetton-Renault	-	-	1	-	-	-	-	-	-	-	-	5	-	4	-	-	-	10
8	Jaguar-Ford Cosworth	-	-	-	-	-	-	4	1	-	-	-	-	-	-	2	2	-	9
9	Prost-Acer	-	-	-	-	-	-	1	2	-	-	-	1	-	-	-	-	-	4
10	Arrows-Asiatech	-	-	-	-	-	1	-	-	-	-	-	-	-	-	-	-	-	1

10,6,4,3,2 and 1 point awarded to the first six finishers.

2002

Race Entrants and Results

Formula 1 was not immune to the financial troubles that crept around the world. The Prost team was declared bankrupt before the season started and Arrows fell by the wayside before the year was out. Ferrari totally dominated the season with Michael Schumacher setting new records at almost every race, although their glory was tainted by team orders and formation finishes in Austria and the US. At the end of the season, radical rules were outlined that included a new one-lap qualifying procedure, an extended points system and testing restrictions to help even the field.

FERRARI
Scuderia Ferrari Marlboro: M Schumacher, Barrichello

McLAREN
West McLaren Mercedes: Coulthard, Räikkönen

WILLIAMS
BMW WilliamsF1 Team: R Schumacher, Montoya

SAUBER
Sauber Petronas: Heidfeld, Massa, Frentzen

JORDAN
DHL Jordan Honda: Fisichella, Sato

BAR
Lucky Strike B.A.R. Honda: Villeneuve, Panis

RENAULT
Mild Seven Renault F1 Team: Trulli, Button

JAGUAR
Jaguar Racing: Irvine, de la Rosa

ARROWS
Orange Arrows: Frentzen, Bernoldi

MINARDI
KL Minardi Asiatech: Webber, Yoong, Davidson

TOYOTA
Panasonic Toyota Racing: Salo, McNish

---

3 March 2002   AUSTRALIA: Melbourne   (Round 1)   (Race 681)

58 laps x 5.303 km, 3.295 miles = 307.574 km, 191.118 miles

Pos	No	Driver	Car	Model	Engine		Laps	Time/Reason for Retirement	Grid Pos	Row
1	1	M Schumacher	Ferrari	F2001	Ferrari	V10	58	1h 35m 36.792s	2	1
2	6	J P Montoya	Williams	FW24	BMW	V10	58	1h 35m 55.419s	6	3
3	4	K Räikkönen	McLaren	MP4-17	Mercedes-Benz	V10	58	1h 36m 01.858s	5	3
4	16	E Irvine	Jaguar	R3	Ford Cosworth	V10	57		19	10
5	23	M Webber	Minardi	PS02	Asiatech	V10	56		18	9
6	24	M Salo	Toyota	TF102	Toyota	V10	56		14	7
7	22	A Yoong	Minardi	PS02	Asiatech	V10	55		21	11
8	17	P de la Rosa	Jaguar	R3	Ford Cosworth	V10	53		20	10
r	3	D Coulthard	McLaren	MP4-17	Mercedes-Benz	V10	33	gearbox	4	2
r	11	J Villeneuve	BAR	004	Honda	V10	27	rear wing / accident	13	7
dq	20	H-H Frentzen	Arrows	A23	Ford Cosworth	V10	16	ignored pit lane red light	15	8
dq	21	E Bernoldi	Arrows	A23	Ford Cosworth	V10	15	switched to spare car	17	9
r	10	T Sato	Jordan	EJ12	Honda	V10	12	electronics	22	11
r	14	J Trulli	Renault	R202	Renault	V10	8	accident	7	4
r	2	R Barrichello	Ferrari	F2001	Ferrari	V10	0	accident	1	1
r	5	R Schumacher	Williams	FW24	BMW	V10	0	accident	3	2
r	9	G Fisichella	Jordan	EJ12	Honda	V10	0	accident	8	4
r	8	F Massa	Sauber	C21	Petronas	V10	0	accident	9	5
r	7	N Heidfeld	Sauber	C21	Petronas	V10	0	accident	10	5
r	15	J Button	Renault	R202	Renault	V10	0	accident	11	6
r	12	O Panis	BAR	004	Honda	V10	0	accident	12	6
r	25	A McNish	Toyota	TF102	Toyota	V10	0	accident	16	8

Winning speed 193.011 km/h, 119.932 mph
Pole Position speed 222.392 km/h, 138.188 mph (R Barrichello, 1 min:25.843 sec)
Fastest Lap speed 215.615 km/h, 133.977 mph (K Räikkönen, 1 min:28.541 sec on lap 37)
Lap Leaders D Coulthard 1-10 (10); M Schumacher 11,17-58 (43); J P Montoya 12-16 (5).

17 Mar 2002 **MALAYSIA: Sepang** (Round 2) (Race 682)

56 laps x 5.543 km, 3.444 miles = 310.408 km, 192.879 miles

Pos	No	Driver	Car	Model	Engine		Laps	Time/Reason for Retirement	Grid Pos	Row
1	5	R Schumacher	Williams	FW24	BMW	V10	56	1h 34m 12.912s	4	2
2	6	J P Montoya	Williams	FW24	BMW	V10	56	1h 34m 52.611s	2	1
3	1	M Schumacher	Ferrari	F2001	Ferrari	V10	56	1h 35m 14.706s	1	1
4	15	J Button	Renault	R202	Renault	V10	56	1h 35m 22.678s	8	4
5	7	N Heidfeld	Sauber	C21	Petronas	V10	55		7	4
6	8	F Massa	Sauber	C21	Petronas	V10	55		14	7
7	25	A McNish	Toyota	TF102	Toyota	V10	55		19	10
8	11	J Villeneuve	BAR	004	Honda	V10	55		13	7
9	10	T Sato	Jordan	EJ12	Honda	V10	54		15	8
10	17	P de la Rosa	Jaguar	R3	Ford Cosworth	V10	54		17	9
11	20	H-H Frentzen	Arrows	A23	Ford Cosworth	V10	54		11	6
12	24	M Salo	Toyota	TF102	Toyota	V10	53		10	5
13	9	G Fisichella	Jordan	EJ12	Honda	V10	53		9	5
r	2	R Barrichello	Ferrari	F2001	Ferrari	V10	39	engine	3	2
r	23	M Webber	Minardi	PS02	Asiatech	V10	34	electrics	21	11
r	16	E Irvine	Jaguar	R3	Ford Cosworth	V10	30	hydraulics	20	10
r	22	A Yoong	Minardi	PS02	Asiatech	V10	29	gearbox	22	11
r	4	K Räikkönen	McLaren	MP4-17	Mercedes-Benz	V10	24	engine	5	3
r	21	E Bernoldi	Arrows	A23	Ford Cosworth	V10	20	fuel system	16	8
r	3	D Coulthard	McLaren	MP4-17	Mercedes-Benz	V10	15	engine	6	3
r	12	O Panis	BAR	004	Honda	V10	9	clutch bearing	18	9
r	14	J Trulli	Renault	R202	Renault	V10	9	engine overheating	12	6

Winning speed 197.680 km/h, 122.833 mph
Pole Position speed 209.464 km/h, 130.155 mph (M Schumacher, 1 min:35.266 sec)
Fastest Lap speed 203.518 km/h, 126.461 mph (J P Montoya, 1 min:38.049 sec on lap 38)
Lap Leaders R Barrichello 1-21, 32-35 (25); R Schumacher 22-31,36-56 (31).

31 Mar 2002 **BRAZIL: Interlagos** (Round 3) (Race 683)

71 laps x 4.309 km, 2.677 miles = 305.909 km, 190.083 miles

Pos	No	Driver	Car	Model	Engine		Laps	Time/Reason for Retirement	Grid Pos	Row
1	1	M Schumacher	Ferrari	F2002	Ferrari	V10	71	1h 31m 43.663s	2	1
2	5	R Schumacher	Williams	FW24	BMW	V10	71	1h 31m 44.251s	3	2
3	3	D Coulthard	McLaren	MP4-17	Mercedes-Benz	V10	71	1h 32m 42.773s	4	2
4	15	J Button	Renault	R202	Renault	V10	71	1h 32m 50.546s	7	4
5	6	J P Montoya	Williams	FW24	BMW	V10	71	1h 32m 51.226s	1	1
6	24	M Salo	Toyota	TF102	Toyota	V10	70		10	5
7	16	E Irvine	Jaguar	R3	Ford Cosworth	V10	70		13	7
8	17	P de la Rosa	Jaguar	R3	Ford Cosworth	V10	70		11	6
9	10	T Sato	Jordan	EJ12	Honda	V10	69		19	10
10r	11	J Villeneuve	BAR	004	Honda	V10	68	engine	15	8
11	23	M Webber	Minardi	PS02	Asiatech	V10	68		20	10
12r	4	K Räikkönen	McLaren	MP4-17	Mercedes-Benz	V10	67	rear hub	5	3
13	22	A Yoong	Minardi	PS02	Asiatech	V10	67		22	11
r	7	N Heidfeld	Sauber	C21	Petronas	V10	61	front brake disc	9	5
r	14	J Trulli	Renault	R202	Renault	V10	60	engine	6	3
r	8	F Massa	Sauber	C21	Petronas	V10	41	accident	12	6
r	25	A McNish	Toyota	TF102	Toyota	V10	40	rear wheel bearing / spin	16	8
r	12	O Panis	BAR	004	Honda	V10	25	gearbox	17	9
r	20	H-H Frentzen	Arrows	A23	Ford Cosworth	V10	25	rear suspension	18	9
r	21	E Bernoldi	Arrows	A23	Ford Cosworth	V10	19	rear suspension	21	11
r	2	R Barrichello	Ferrari	F2001	Ferrari	V10	16	hydraulics	8	4
r	9	G Fisichella	Jordan	EJ12	Honda	V10	6	engine	14	7

Winning speed 200.098 km/h, 124.335 mph
Pole Position speed 212.167 km/h, 131.835 mph (J P Montoya, 1 min:13.114 sec)
Fastest Lap speed 203.898 km/h, 126.697 mph (J P Montoya, 1 min:16.079 sec on lap 60)
Lap Leaders M Schumacher 1-13,17-39,45-71 (63); R Barrichello 14-16 (3); R Schumacher 40-44 (5).

Races

14 Apr 2002   SAN MARINO: Imola   (Round 4)   (Race 684)

62 laps x 4.933 km, 3.065 miles = 305.609 km, 189.897 miles

Pos	No	Driver	Car	Model	Engine		Laps	Time/Reason for Retirement	Grid Pos	Row
1	1	M Schumacher	Ferrari	F2002	Ferrari	V10	62	1h 29m 10.789s	1	1
2	2	R Barrichello	Ferrari	F2002	Ferrari	V10	62	1h 29m 28.696s	2	1
3	5	R Schumacher	Williams	FW24	BMW	V10	62	1h 29m 30.544s	3	2
4	6	J P Montoya	Williams	FW24	BMW	V10	62	1h 29m 55.514s	4	2
5	15	J Button	Renault	R202	Renault	V10	62	1h 30m 34.184s	9	5
6	3	D Coulthard	McLaren	MP4-17	Mercedes-Benz	V10	61		6	3
7	11	J Villeneuve	BAR	004	Honda	V10	61		10	5
8	8	F Massa	Sauber	C21	Petronas	V10	61		11	6
9	14	J Trulli	Renault	R202	Renault	V10	61		8	4
10	7	N Heidfeld	Sauber	C21	Petronas	V10	61		7	4
11	23	M Webber	Minardi	PS02	Asiatech	V10	60		19	10
r	21	E Bernoldi	Arrows	A23	Ford Cosworth	V10	50	engine	20	10
r	16	E Irvine	Jaguar	R3	Ford Cosworth	V10	45	driveshaft	18	9
r	4	K Räikkönen	McLaren	MP4-17	Mercedes-Benz	V10	44	exhaust / rear suspension	5	3
r	12	O Panis	BAR	004	Honda	V10	44	throttle linkage	12	6
r	17	P de la Rosa	Jaguar	R3	Ford Cosworth	V10	30	driveshaft	21	11
r	24	M Salo	Toyota	TF102	Toyota	V10	26	gearbox	16	8
r	20	H-H Frentzen	Arrows	A23	Ford Cosworth	V10	25	fuel pressure	13	7
r	9	G Fisichella	Jordan	EJ12	Honda	V10	19	hydraulics	15	8
r	10	T Sato	Jordan	EJ12	Honda	V10	5	gearbox	14	7
r	25	A McNish	Toyota	TF102	Toyota	V10	0	transmission	17	9
nq	22	A Yoong	Minardi	PS02	Asiatech	V10				

Winning speed 205.613 km/h, 127.762 mph
Pole Position speed 218.998 km/h, 136.079 mph (M Schumacher, 1 min:21.091 sec)
Fastest Lap speed 210.987 km/h, 131.101 mph (R Barrichello, 1 min:24.170 sec on lap 38)
Lap Leaders M Schumacher 1-31,33-46,48-62 (60); R Barrichello 32,47 (2).

28 Apr 2002   SPAIN: Montmeló   (Round 5)   (Race 685)

65 laps x 4.730 km, 2.939 miles = 307.327 km, 190.964 miles

Pos	No	Driver	Car	Model	Engine		Laps	Time/Reason for Retirement	Grid Pos	Row
1	1	M Schumacher	Ferrari	F2002	Ferrari	V10	65	1h 30m 29.981s	1	1
2	6	J P Montoya	Williams	FW24	BMW	V10	65	1h 31m 05.610s	4	2
3	3	D Coulthard	McLaren	MP4-17	Mercedes-Benz	V10	65	1h 31m 12.604s	7	4
4	7	N Heidfeld	Sauber	C21	Petronas	V10	65	1h 31m 36.677s	8	4
5	8	F Massa	Sauber	C21	Petronas	V10	65	1h 31m 48.954s	11	6
6	20	H-H Frentzen	Arrows	A23	Ford Cosworth	V10	65	1h 31m 50.410s	10	5
7	11	J Villeneuve	BAR	004	Honda	V10	64		15	8
8	25	A McNish	Toyota	TF102	Toyota	V10	64		19	10
9	24	M Salo	Toyota	TF102	Toyota	V10	64		17	9
10r	14	J Trulli	Renault	R202	Renault	V10	63	engine	9	5
11r	5	R Schumacher	Williams	FW24	BMW	V10	63	engine	3	2
12r	15	J Button	Renault	R202	Renault	V10	60	hydraulics	6	3
r	12	O Panis	BAR	004	Honda	V10	43	exhaust	13	7
r	16	E Irvine	Jaguar	R3	Ford Cosworth	V10	41	hydraulics	20	10
r	21	E Bernoldi	Arrows	A23	Ford Cosworth	V10	40	hydraulics	14	7
r	10	T Sato	Jordan	EJ12	Honda	V10	10	spin	18	9
r	9	G Fisichella	Jordan	EJ12	Honda	V10	5	hydraulics	12	6
r	4	K Räikkönen	McLaren	MP4-17	Mercedes-Benz	V10	4	rear wing	5	3
r	17	P de la Rosa	Jaguar	R3	Ford Cosworth	V10	2	spin	16	8
ns	2	R Barrichello	Ferrari	F2002	Ferrari	V10		gearbox before parade lap	2	1
ew	23	M Webber	Minardi	PS02	Asiatech	V10		safety concern re wing failures		
ew	22	A Yoong	Minardi	PS02	Asiatech	V10		safety concern re wing failures		

Winning speed 203.753 km/h, 126.607 mph
Pole Position speed 222.984 km/h, 138.556 mph (M Schumacher, 1 min:16.364 sec)
Fastest Lap speed 211.909 km/h, 131.675 mph (M Schumacher, 1 min:20.355 sec on lap 49)
Lap Leaders M Schumacher 1-65 (65).

12 May 2002   AUSTRIA: A1-Ring   (Round 6)   (Race 686)

71 laps x 4.326 km, 2.688 miles = 307.146 km, 190.852 miles

Pos	No	Driver	Car	Model	Engine		Laps	Time/Reason for Retirement	Grid Pos	Row
1	1	M Schumacher	Ferrari	F2002	Ferrari	V10	71	1h 33m 51.562s	3	2
2	2	R Barrichello	Ferrari	F2002	Ferrari	V10	71	1h 33m 51.744s	1	1
3	6	J P Montoya	Williams	FW24	BMW	V10	71	1h 34m 09.292s	4	2
4	5	R Schumacher	Williams	FW24	BMW	V10	71	1h 34m 10.010s	2	1
5	9	G Fisichella	Jordan	EJ12	Honda	V10	71	1h 34m 41.527s	15	8
6	3	D Coulthard	McLaren	MP4-17	Mercedes-Benz	V10	71	1h 34m 42.234s	8	4
7	15	J Button	Renault	R202	Renault	V10	71	1h 34m 42.791s	13	7
8	24	M Salo	Toyota	TF102	Toyota	V10	71	1h 35m 00.987s	10	5
9	25	A McNish	Toyota	TF102	Toyota	V10	71	1h 35m 01.281s	14	7
10r	11	J Villeneuve	BAR	004	Honda	V10	70	engine	17	9
11	20	H-H Frentzen	Arrows	A23	Ford Cosworth	V10	69		11	6
12	23	M Webber	Minardi	PS02	Asiatech	V10	69		21	11

Pos	No	Driver	Car	Model	Engine		Laps	Time/Reason for Retirement	Grid Pos	Row
r	14	J Trulli	Renault	R202	Renault	V10	44	fuel connector	16	8
r	22	A Yoong	Minardi	PS02	Asiatech	V10	42	engine	22	11
r	16	E Irvine	Jaguar	R3	Ford Cosworth	V10	38	hydraulics	20	10
r	7	N Heidfeld	Sauber	C21	Petronas	V10	27	accident	5	3
r	10	T Sato	Jordan	EJ12	Honda	V10	26	accident	18	9
r	12	O Panis	BAR	004	Honda	V10	22	engine / spin	9	5
r	8	F Massa	Sauber	C21	Petronas	V10	7	accident / rear suspension	7	4
r	4	K Räikkönen	McLaren	MP4-17	Mercedes-Benz	V10	5	engine	6	3
r	21	E Bernoldi	Arrows	A23	Ford Cosworth	V10	2	accident / front suspension	12	6
r	17	P de la Rosa	Jaguar	R3	Ford Cosworth	V10	0	throttle	19	10

Winning speed 196.344 km/h, 122.003 mph
Pole Position speed 228.747 km/h, 142.137 mph (R Barrichello, 1 min: 8.082 sec)
Fastest Lap speed 224.733 km/h, 139.643 mph (M Schumacher, 1 min: 9.298 sec on lap 68)
Lap Leaders R Barrichello 1-61,63-70 (69); M Schumacher 62,71 (2).

26 May 2002		**MONACO: Monte-Carlo**							**(Round 7)**	**(Race 687)**
		78 laps x 3.370 km, 2.094 miles = 262.860 km, 163.334 miles								

Pos	No	Driver	Car	Model	Engine		Laps	Time/Reason for Retirement	Grid Pos	Row
1	3	D Coulthard	McLaren	MP4-17	Mercedes-Benz	V10	78	1h 45m 39.055s	2	1
2	1	M Schumacher	Ferrari	F2002	Ferrari	V10	78	1h 45m 40.104s	3	2
3	5	R Schumacher	Williams	FW24	BMW	V10	78	1h 46m 56.504s	4	2
4	14	J Trulli	Renault	R202	Renault	V10	77		7	4
5	9	G Fisichella	Jordan	EJ12	Honda	V10	77		11	6
6	20	H-H Frentzen	Arrows	A23	Ford Cosworth	V10	77		12	6
7	2	R Barrichello	Ferrari	F2002	Ferrari	V10	77		5	3
8	7	N Heidfeld	Sauber	C21	Petronas	V10	76		17	9
9	16	E Irvine	Jaguar	R3	Ford Cosworth	V10	76		21	11
10	17	P de la Rosa	Jaguar	R3	Ford Cosworth	V10	76		20	10
11	23	M Webber	Minardi	PS02	Asiatech	V10	76		19	10
12	21	E Bernoldi	Arrows	A23	Ford Cosworth	V10	76		15	8
r	24	M Salo	Toyota	TF102	Toyota	V10	69	brakes / accident	9	5
r	8	F Massa	Sauber	C21	Petronas	V10	63	brakes / accident	13	7
r	12	O Panis	BAR	004	Honda	V10	51	accident	18	9
r	15	J Button	Renault	R202	Renault	V10	51	accident	8	4
r	6	J P Montoya	Williams	FW24	BMW	V10	46	engine	1	1
r	11	J Villeneuve	BAR	004	Honda	V10	44	engine	14	7
r	4	K Räikkönen	McLaren	MP4-17	Mercedes-Benz	V10	41	accident damage	6	3
r	22	A Yoong	Minardi	PS02	Asiatech	V10	29	accident	22	11
r	10	T Sato	Jordan	EJ12	Honda	V10	22	accident	16	8
r	25	A McNish	Toyota	TF102	Toyota	V10	15	accident	10	5

Winning speed 149.280 km/h, 92.758 mph
Pole Position speed 158.224 km/h, 98.316 mph (J P Montoya, 1 min:16.676 sec)
Fastest Lap speed 155.492 km/h, 96.619 mph (R Barrichello, 1 min:18.023 sec on lap 68)
Lap Leaders D Coulthard 1-78 (78).

9 Jun 2002		**CANADA: Montréal**							**(Round 8)**	**(Race 688)**
		70 laps x 4.361 km, 2.710 miles = 305.270 km, 189.686 miles								

Pos	No	Driver	Car	Model	Engine		Laps	Time/Reason for Retirement	Grid Pos	Row
1	1	M Schumacher	Ferrari	F2002	Ferrari	V10	70	1h 33m 36.111s	2	1
2	3	D Coulthard	McLaren	MP4-17	Mercedes-Benz	V10	70	1h 33m 37.243s	8	4
3	2	R Barrichello	Ferrari	F2002	Ferrari	V10	70	1h 33m 43.193s	3	2
4	4	K Räikkönen	McLaren	MP4-17	Mercedes-Benz	V10	70	1h 34m 13.674s	5	3
5	9	G Fisichella	Jordan	EJ12	Honda	V10	70	1h 34m 18.923s	6	3
6	14	J Trulli	Renault	R202	Renault	V10	70	1h 34m 25.059s	10	5
7	5	R Schumacher	Williams	FW24	BMW	V10	70	1h 34m 27.629s	4	2
8	12	O Panis	BAR	004	Honda	V10	69		11	6
9	8	F Massa	Sauber	C21	Petronas	V10	69		12	6
10	10	T Sato	Jordan	EJ12	Honda	V10	69		15	8
11	23	M Webber	Minardi	PS02	Asiatech	V10	69		21	11
12	7	N Heidfeld	Sauber	C21	Petronas	V10	69		7	4
13	20	H-H Frentzen	Arrows	A23	Ford Cosworth	V10	69		19	10
14	22	A Yoong	Minardi	PS02	Asiatech	V10	68		22	11
15r	15	J Button	Renault	R202	Renault	V10	65	engine	13	7
r	6	J P Montoya	Williams	FW24	BMW	V10	56	engine	1	1
r	25	A McNish	Toyota	TF102	Toyota	V10	45	spin	20	10
r	16	E Irvine	Jaguar	R3	Ford Cosworth	V10	41	engine overheating	14	7
r	24	M Salo	Toyota	TF102	Toyota	V10	41	front tyre / brakes	18	9
r	17	P de la Rosa	Jaguar	R3	Ford Cosworth	V10	29	gearbox	16	8
r	21	E Bernoldi	Arrows	A23	Ford Cosworth	V10	16	vibration	17	9
r	11	J Villeneuve	BAR	004	Honda	V10	8	engine	9	5

Winning speed 195.682 km/h, 121.591 mph
Pole Position speed 215.547 km/h, 133.935 mph (J P Montoya, 1 min:12.836 sec)
Fastest Lap speed 206.682 km/h, 128.427 mph (J P Montoya, 1 min:15.960 sec on lap 50)
Lap Leaders R Barrichello 1-25 (25); M Schumacher 26-37, 51-70 (32); J P Montoya 38-50 (13).

Races

23 Jun 2002 **EUROPE: Nürburgring** (Round 9) (Race 689)

60 laps x 5.146 km, 3.198 miles = 308.743 km, 191.844 miles

Pos	No	Driver	Car	Model	Engine		Laps	Time/Reason for Retirement	Grid Pos	Row
1	2	R Barrichello	Ferrari	F2002	Ferrari	V10	60	1h 35m 07.426s	4	2
2	1	M Schumacher	Ferrari	F2002	Ferrari	V10	60	1h 35m 07.720s	3	2
3	4	K Räikkönen	McLaren	MP4-17	Mercedes-Benz	V10	60	1h 35m 53.861s	6	3
4	5	R Schumacher	Williams	FW24	BMW	V10	60	1h 36m 14.389s	2	1
5	15	J Button	Renault	R202	Renault	V10	60	1h 36m 24.370s	8	4
6	8	F Massa	Sauber	C21	Petronas	V10	59		11	6
7	7	N Heidfeld	Sauber	C21	Petronas	V10	59		9	5
8	14	J Trulli	Renault	R202	Renault	V10	59		7	4
9	12	O Panis	BAR	004	Honda	V10	59		12	6
10	21	E Bernoldi	Arrows	A23	Ford Cosworth	V10	59		21	11
11	17	P de la Rosa	Jaguar	R3	Ford Cosworth	V10	59		16	8
12	11	J Villeneuve	BAR	004	Honda	V10	59		19	10
13	20	H-H Frentzen	Arrows	A23	Ford Cosworth	V10	59		15	8
14	25	A McNish	Toyota	TF102	Toyota	V10	59		13	7
15	23	M Webber	Minardi	PS02	Asiatech	V10	58		20	10
16	10	T Sato	Jordan	EJ12	Honda	V10	58		14	7
r	24	M Salo	Toyota	TF102	Toyota	V10	51	gearbox	10	5
r	22	A Yoong	Minardi	PS02	Asiatech	V10	48	hydraulics	22	11
r	16	E Irvine	Jaguar	R3	Ford Cosworth	V10	41	hydraulics	17	9
r	6	J P Montoya	Williams	FW24	BMW	V10	27	accident	1	1
r	3	D Coulthard	McLaren	MP4-17	Mercedes-Benz	V10	27	accident	5	3
r	9	G Fisichella	Jordan	EJ12	Honda	V10	26	accident / steering	18	9

Winning speed 194.741 km/h, 121.007 mph
Pole Position speed 206.055 km/h, 128.037 mph (J P Montoya, 1 min:29.906 sec)
Fastest Lap speed 200.871 km/h, 124.816 mph (M Schumacher, 1 min:32.226 sec on lap 26)
Lap Leaders R Barrichello, 1-60 (60).

7 Jul 2002 **BRITAIN: Silverstone** (Round 10) (Race 690)

60 laps x 5.141 km, 3.194 miles = 308.356 km, 191.604 miles

Pos	No	Driver	Car	Model	Engine		Laps	Time/Reason for Retirement	Grid Pos	Row
1	1	M Schumacher	Ferrari	F2002	Ferrari	V10	60	1h 31m 45.015s	3	2
2	2	R Barrichello	Ferrari	F2002	Ferrari	V10	60	1h 31m 59.593s	2	1
3	6	J P Montoya	Williams	FW24	BMW	V10	60	1h 32m 16.676s	1	1
4	11	J Villeneuve	BAR	004	Honda	V10	59		9	5
5	12	O Panis	BAR	004	Honda	V10	59		13	7
6	7	N Heidfeld	Sauber	C21	Petronas	V10	59		10	5
7	9	G Fisichella	Jordan	EJ12	Honda	V10	59		17	9
8	5	R Schumacher	Williams	FW24	BMW	V10	59		4	2
9	8	F Massa	Sauber	C21	Petronas	V10	59		11	6
10	3	D Coulthard	McLaren	MP4-17	Mercedes-Benz	V10	58		6	3
11	17	P de la Rosa	Jaguar	R3	Ford Cosworth	V10	58		21	11
12r	15	J Button	Renault	R202	Renault	V10	54	front wheel loose	12	6
r	10	T Sato	Jordan	EJ12	Honda	V10	50	engine	14	7
r	4	K Räikkönen	McLaren	MP4-17	Mercedes-Benz	V10	44	engine	5	3
r	14	J Trulli	Renault	R202	Renault	V10	29	electronics	7	4
r	21	E Bernoldi	Arrows	A23	Ford Cosworth	V10	28	driveshaft	18	9
r	16	E Irvine	Jaguar	R3	Ford Cosworth	V10	23	spin	19	10
r	20	H-H Frentzen	Arrows	A23	Ford Cosworth	V10	20	engine	16	8
r	24	M Salo	Toyota	TF102	Toyota	V10	15	driveshaft	8	4
r	23	M Webber	Minardi	PS02	Asiatech	V10	9	clutch / spin	20	10
r	25	A McNish	Toyota	TF102	Toyota	V10	0	clutch	15	8
nq	22	A Yoong	Minardi	PS02	Asiatech	V10				

Winning speed 201.649 km/h, 125.299 mph
Pole Position speed 234.279 km/h, 145.574 mph (J P Montoya, 1 min:18.998 sec)
Fastest Lap speed 222.760 km/h, 138.417 mph (R Barrichello, 1 min:23.083 sec on lap 58)
Lap Leaders J P Montoya 1-15 (15); M Schumacher 16-60 (45).

21 Jul 2002 FRANCE: Magny-Cours (Round 11) (Race 691)

72 laps x 4.251 km, 2.641 miles = 305.886 km, 190.069 miles

Pos	No	Driver	Car	Model	Engine		Laps	Time/Reason for Retirement	Grid Pos	Row
1	1	M Schumacher	Ferrari	F2002	Ferrari	V10	72	1h 32m 09.837s	2	1
2	4	K Räikkönen	McLaren	MP4-17	Mercedes-Benz	V10	72	1h 32m 10.941s	4	2
3	3	D Coulthard	McLaren	MP4-17	Mercedes-Benz	V10	72	1h 32m 41.812s	6	3
4	6	J P Montoya	Williams	FW24	BMW	V10	72	1h 32m 50.512s	1	1
5	5	R Schumacher	Williams	FW24	BMW	V10	72	1h 32m 51.609s	5	3
6	15	J Button	Renault	R202	Renault	V10	71		7	4
7	7	N Heidfeld	Sauber	C21	Petronas	V10	71		10	5
8	23	M Webber	Minardi	PS02	Asiatech	V10	71		18	9
9	17	P de la Rosa	Jaguar	R3	Ford Cosworth	V10	70		15	8
10	22	A Yoong	Minardi	PS02	Asiatech	V10	68		19	10
11r	25	A McNish	Toyota	TF102	Toyota	V10	65	engine	17	9
r	16	E Irvine	Jaguar	R3	Ford Cosworth	V10	52	rear wing / spin	9	5
r	14	J Trulli	Renault	R202	Renault	V10	49	engine	8	4
r	8	F Massa	Sauber	C21	Petronas	V10	48	transmission	12	6
r	24	M Salo	Toyota	TF102	Toyota	V10	48	engine	16	8
r	11	J Villeneuve	BAR	004	Honda	V10	35	engine	13	7
r	12	O Panis	BAR	004	Honda	V10	29	accident / vibration	11	6
r	10	T Sato	Jordan	EJ12	Honda	V10	23	spin	14	7
ns	2	R Barrichello	Ferrari	F2002	Ferrari	V10		electrics	3	2
nq	20	H-H Frentzen	Arrows	A23	Ford Cosworth	V10		deliberate non-qualification		
nq	21	E Bernoldi	Arrows	A23	Ford Cosworth	V10		deliberate non-qualification		
ew	9	G Fisichella	Jordan	EJ12	Honda	V10		accident / injury		

Winning speed 199.135 km/h, 123.737 mph
Pole Position speed 212.594 km/h, 132.100 mph (J P Montoya, 1 min:11.985 sec)
Fastest Lap speed 203.925 km/h, 126.714 mph (D Coulthard, 1 min:15.045 sec on lap 62)
Lap Leaders J P Montoya 1-23,36-42 (30); M Schumacher 24-25,29-35,68-72 (14); D Coulthard 27-28,50-54 (7); K Räikkönen 26,43-49,55-67 (21).

28 Jul 2002 GERMANY: Hockenheim (Round 12) (Race 692)

67 laps x 4.574 km, 2.842 miles = 306.458 km, 190.424 miles

Pos	No	Driver	Car	Model	Engine		Laps	Time/Reason for Retirement	Grid Pos	Row
1	1	M Schumacher	Ferrari	F2002	Ferrari	V10	67	1h 27m 52.078s	1	1
2	6	J P Montoya	Williams	FW24	BMW	V10	67	1h 28m 02.581s	4	2
3	5	R Schumacher	Williams	FW24	BMW	V10	67	1h 28m 06.544s	2	1
4	2	R Barrichello	Ferrari	F2002	Ferrari	V10	67	1h 28m 15.273s	3	2
5	3	D Coulthard	McLaren	MP4-17	Mercedes-Benz	V10	66		9	5
6	7	N Heidfeld	Sauber	C21	Petronas	V10	66		10	5
7	8	F Massa	Sauber	C21	Petronas	V10	66		14	7
8	10	T Sato	Jordan	EJ12	Honda	V10	66		12	6
9	24	M Salo	Toyota	TF102	Toyota	V10	66		19	10
r	9	G Fisichella	Jordan	EJ12	Honda	V10	59	engine	6	3
r	4	K Räikkönen	McLaren	MP4-17	Mercedes-Benz	V10	59	rear tyre / brake ducts / spin	5	3
r	16	E Irvine	Jaguar	R3	Ford Cosworth	V10	57	brakes	16	8
r	21	E Bernoldi	Arrows	A23	Ford Cosworth	V10	48	engine	18	9
r	12	O Panis	BAR	004	Honda	V10	39	engine / spin	7	4
r	14	J Trulli	Renault	R202	Renault	V10	36	spin	8	4
r	11	J Villeneuve	BAR	004	Honda	V10	27	gearbox	11	6
r	15	J Button	Renault	R202	Renault	V10	24	engine	13	7
r	25	A McNish	Toyota	TF102	Toyota	V10	23	hydraulics	17	9
r	23	M Webber	Minardi	PS02	Asiatech	V10	23	hydraulics	21	11
r	20	H-H Frentzen	Arrows	A23	Ford Cosworth	V10	18	hydraulics	15	8
r	17	P de la Rosa	Jaguar	R3	Ford Cosworth	V10	0	transmission	20	10
nq	22	A Yoong	Minardi	PS02	Asiatech	V10				

Winning speed 209.262 km/h, 130.030 mph
Pole Position speed 221.355 km/h, 137.544 mph (M Schumacher, 1 min:14.389 sec)
Fastest Lap speed 215.354 km/h, 133.815 mph (M Schumacher, 1 min:16.462 sec on lap 44)
Lap Leaders M Schumacher 1-26,31-47,49-67 (62); R Schumacher 27-29,48 (4); J P Montoya 30 (1).

18 Aug 2002   HUNGARY: Hungaroring   (Round 13)   (Race 693)
77 laps x 3.975 km, 2.470 miles = 306.069 km, 190.182 miles

Pos	No	Driver	Car	Model	Engine		Laps	Time/Reason for Retirement	Grid Pos	Row
1	2	R Barrichello	Ferrari	F2002	Ferrari	V10	77	1h 41m 49.001s	1	1
2	1	M Schumacher	Ferrari	F2002	Ferrari	V10	77	1h 41m 49.435s	2	1
3	5	R Schumacher	Williams	FW24	BMW	V10	77	1h 42m 02.357s	3	2
4	4	K Räikkönen	McLaren	MP4-17	Mercedes-Benz	V10	77	1h 42m 18.480s	11	6
5	3	D Coulthard	McLaren	MP4-17	Mercedes-Benz	V10	77	1h 42m 26.801s	10	5
6	9	G Fisichella	Jordan	EJ12	Honda	V10	77	1h 42m 57.805s	5	3
7	8	F Massa	Sauber	C21	Petronas	V10	77	1h 43m 02.613s	7	4
8	14	J Trulli	Renault	R202	Renault	V10	76		6	3
9	7	N Heidfeld	Sauber	C21	Petronas	V10	76		8	4
10	10	T Sato	Jordan	EJ12	Honda	V10	76		14	7
11	6	J P Montoya	Williams	FW24	BMW	V10	76		4	2
12	12	O Panis	BAR	004	Honda	V10	76		12	6
13	17	P de la Rosa	Jaguar	R3	Ford Cosworth	V10	75		15	8
14	25	A McNish	Toyota	TF102	Toyota	V10	75		18	9
15	24	M Salo	Toyota	TF102	Toyota	V10	75		17	9
16	23	M Webber	Minardi	PS02	Asiatech	V10	75		19	10
r	22	A Davidson	Minardi	PS02	Asiatech	V10	58	spin	20	10
r	15	J Button	Renault	R202	Renault	V10	30	spin	9	5
r	16	E Irvine	Jaguar	R3	Ford Cosworth	V10	23	misfire	16	8
r	11	J Villeneuve	BAR	004	Honda	V10	20	transmission	13	7

Winning speed 180.364 km/h, 112.073 mph
Pole Position speed 195.137 km/h, 121.253 mph (R Barrichello, 1 min:13.333 sec)
Fastest Lap speed 187.778 km/h, 116.680 mph (M Schumacher, 1 min:16.207 sec on lap 72)
Lap Leaders R Barrichello 1-32,34-77 (76); R Schumacher 33 (1).

1 Sep 2002   BELGIUM: Spa-Francorchamps   (Round 14)   (Race 694)
44 laps x 6.963 km, 4.327 miles = 306.355 km, 190.360 miles

Pos	No	Driver	Car	Model	Engine		Laps	Time/Reason for Retirement	Grid Pos	Row
1	1	M Schumacher	Ferrari	F2002	Ferrari	V10	44	1h 21m 20.634s	1	1
2	2	R Barrichello	Ferrari	F2002	Ferrari	V10	44	1h 21m 22.611s	3	2
3	6	J P Montoya	Williams	FW24	BMW	V10	44	1h 21m 39.079s	5	3
4	3	D Coulthard	McLaren	MP4-17	Mercedes-Benz	V10	44	1h 21m 39.992s	6	3
5	5	R Schumacher	Williams	FW24	BMW	V10	44	1h 22m 17.074s	4	2
6	16	E Irvine	Jaguar	R3	Ford Cosworth	V10	44	1h 22m 38.004s	8	4
7	24	M Salo	Toyota	TF102	Toyota	V10	44	1h 22m 38.443s	9	5
8	11	J Villeneuve	BAR	004	Honda	V10	44	1h 22m 40.489s	12	6
9	25	A McNish	Toyota	TF102	Toyota	V10	43		13	7
10	7	N Heidfeld	Sauber	C21	Petronas	V10	43		18	9
11	10	T Sato	Jordan	EJ12	Honda	V10	43		16	8
12r	12	O Panis	BAR	004	Honda	V10	39	engine	15	8
r	9	G Fisichella	Jordan	EJ12	Honda	V10	38	engine	14	7
r	17	P de la Rosa	Jaguar	R3	Ford Cosworth	V10	37	rear suspension	11	6
r	8	F Massa	Sauber	C21	Petronas	V10	37	engine	17	9
r	4	K Räikkönen	McLaren	MP4-17	Mercedes-Benz	V10	35	engine	2	1
r	14	J Trulli	Renault	R202	Renault	V10	35	engine	7	4
r	22	A Davidson	Minardi	PS02	Asiatech	V10	17	spin	20	10
r	15	J Button	Renault	R202	Renault	V10	10	engine	10	5
r	23	M Webber	Minardi	PS02	Asiatech	V10	4	gearbox	19	10

Winning speed 225.970 km/h, 140.411 mph
Pole Position speed 241.663 km/h, 150.163 mph (M Schumacher, 1 min:43.726 sec)
Fastest Lap speed 233.884 km/h, 145.329 mph (M Schumacher, 1 min:47.176 sec on lap 15)
Lap Leaders M Schumacher 1-16,18-44 (43); R Barrichello 17 (1).

15 Sep 2002   **ITALY: Monza**   **(Round 15)**   **(Race 695)**

53 laps x 5.793 km, 3.600 miles = 306.719 km, 190.586 miles

Pos	No	Driver	Car	Model	Engine		Laps	Time/Reason for Retirement	Grid Pos	Row
1	2	R Barrichello	Ferrari	F2002	Ferrari	V10	53	1h 16m 19.982s	4	2
2	1	M Schumacher	Ferrari	F2002	Ferrari	V10	53	1h 16m 20.237s	2	1
3	16	E Irvine	Jaguar	R3	Ford Cosworth	V10	53	1h 17m 12.561s	5	3
4	14	J Trulli	Renault	R202	Renault	V10	53	1h 17m 18.201s	11	6
5	15	J Button	Renault	R202	Renault	V10	53	1h 17m 27.752s	17	9
6	12	O Panis	BAR	004	Honda	V10	53	1h 17m 28.473s	16	8
7	3	D Coulthard	McLaren	MP4-17	Mercedes-Benz	V10	53	1h 17m 29.030s	7	4
8	9	G Fisichella	Jordan	EJ12	Honda	V10	53	1h 17m 30.874s	12	6
9	11	J Villeneuve	BAR	004	Honda	V10	53	1h 17m 41.051s	9	5
10	7	N Heidfeld	Sauber	C21	Petronas	V10	53	1h 17m 42.028s	15	8
11	24	M Salo	Toyota	TF102	Toyota	V10	52		10	5
12	10	T Sato	Jordan	EJ12	Honda	V10	52		18	9
13	22	A Yoong	Minardi	PS02	Asiatech	V10	47		20	10
r	6	J P Montoya	Williams	FW24	BMW	V10	33	front suspension	1	1
r	4	K Räikkönen	McLaren	MP4-17	Mercedes-Benz	V10	29	engine	6	3
r	23	M Webber	Minardi	PS02	Asiatech	V10	20	electrics	19	10
r	8	F Massa	Sauber	C21	Petronas	V10	16	accident	14	7
r	17	P de la Rosa	Jaguar	R3	Ford Cosworth	V10	15	accident	8	4
r	25	A McNish	Toyota	TF102	Toyota	V10	13	rear suspension	13	7
r	5	R Schumacher	Williams	FW24	BMW	V10	4	engine	3	2

Winning speed 241.090 km/h, 149.806 mph
Pole Position speed 259.828 km/h, 161.449 mph (J P Montoya, 1 min:20.264 sec)
Fastest Lap speed 249.289 km/h, 154.901 mph (R Barrichello, 1 min:23.657 sec on lap 15)
Lap Leaders R Schumacher 1-3 (3); J P Montoya 4 (1); R Barrichello 5-19,29-53 (40); M Schumacher 20-28 (9).

29 Sep 2002   **USA: Indianapolis**   **(Round 16)**   **(Race 696)**

73 laps x 4.192 km, 2.605 miles = 306.016 km, 190.150 miles

Pos	No	Driver	Car	Model	Engine		Laps	Time/Reason for Retirement	Grid Pos	Row
1	2	R Barrichello	Ferrari	F2002	Ferrari	V10	73	1h 31m 07.934s	2	1
2	1	M Schumacher	Ferrari	F2002	Ferrari	V10	73	1h 31m 07.945s	1	1
3	3	D Coulthard	McLaren	MP4-17	Mercedes-Benz	V10	73	1h 31m 15.733s	3	2
4	6	J P Montoya	Williams	FW24	BMW	V10	73	1h 31m 17.845s	4	2
5	14	J Trulli	Renault	R202	Renault	V10	73	1h 32m 04.781s	8	4
6	11	J Villeneuve	BAR	004	Honda	V10	73	1h 32m 06.146s	7	4
7	9	G Fisichella	Jordan	EJ12	Honda	V10	72		9	5
8	15	J Button	Renault	R202	Renault	V10	72		14	7
9	7	N Heidfeld	Sauber	C21	Petronas	V10	72		10	5
10	16	E Irvine	Jaguar	R3	Ford Cosworth	V10	72		13	7
11	10	T Sato	Jordan	EJ12	Honda	V10	72		15	8
12	12	O Panis	BAR	004	Honda	V10	72		12	6
13	8	H-H Frentzen	Sauber	C21	Petronas	V10	71		11	6
14	24	M Salo	Toyota	TF102	Toyota	V10	71		19	10
15	25	A McNish	Toyota	TF102	Toyota	V10	71		16	8
16	5	R Schumacher	Williams	FW24	BMW	V10	71		5	3
r	4	K Räikkönen	McLaren	MP4-17	Mercedes-Benz	V10	50	engine	6	3
r	22	A Yoong	Minardi	PS02	Asiatech	V10	46	oil pump / engine	20	10
r	23	M Webber	Minardi	PS02	Asiatech	V10	38	steering	18	9
r	17	P de la Rosa	Jaguar	R3	Ford Cosworth	V10	27	transmission	17	9

Winning speed 201.475 km/h, 125.191 mph
Pole Position speed 213.182 km/h, 132.466 mph (M Schumacher, 1 min:10.790 sec)
Fastest Lap speed 207.473 km/h, 128.918 mph (R Barrichello, 1 min:12.738 sec on lap 27)
Lap Leaders M Schumacher 1-26,29-48,51-72 (68); R Barrichello 27-28,49-50,73 (5).

53 laps x 5.821 km, 3.617 miles = 308.317 km, 191.579 miles

Pos	No	Driver	Car	Model	Engine		Laps	Time/Reason for Retirement	Grid Pos	Row
1	1	M Schumacher	Ferrari	F2002	Ferrari	V10	53	1h 26m 59.698s	1	1
2	2	R Barrichello	Ferrari	F2002	Ferrari	V10	53	1h 27m 00.205s	2	1
3	4	K Räikkönen	McLaren	MP4-17	Mercedes-Benz	V10	53	1h 27m 22.990s	4	2
4	6	J P Montoya	Williams	FW24	BMW	V10	53	1h 27m 35.973s	6	3
5	10	T Sato	Jordan	EJ12	Honda	V10	53	1h 28m 22.392s	7	4
6	15	J Button	Renault	R202	Renault	V10	52		10	5
7	7	N Heidfeld	Sauber	C21	Petronas	V10	52		12	6
8	24	M Salo	Toyota	TF102	Toyota	V10	52		13	7
9	16	E Irvine	Jaguar	R3	Ford Cosworth	V10	52		14	7
10	23	M Webber	Minardi	PS02	Asiatech	V10	51		18	9
11r	5	R Schumacher	Williams	FW24	BMW	V10	48	engine	5	3
r	17	P de la Rosa	Jaguar	R3	Ford Cosworth	V10	39	transmission	17	9
r	9	G Fisichella	Jordan	EJ12	Honda	V10	37	engine	8	4
r	14	J Trulli	Renault	R202	Renault	V10	32	engine	11	6
r	11	J Villeneuve	BAR	004	Honda	V10	27	engine	9	5
r	22	A Yoong	Minardi	PS02	Asiatech	V10	14	spin	19	10
r	12	O Panis	BAR	004	Honda	V10	8	throttle	16	8
r	3	D Coulthard	McLaren	MP4-17	Mercedes-Benz	V10	7	throttle	3	2
r	8	F Massa	Sauber	C21	Petronas	V10	3	spin	15	8
ew	25	A McNish	Toyota	TF102	Toyota	V10		accident / injury		

Winning speed 212.644 km/h, 132.131 mph
Pole Position speed 229.481 km/h, 142.593 mph (M Schumacher, 1 min:31.317 sec)
Fastest Lap speed 218.003 km/h, 135.461 mph (M Schumacher, 1 min:36.125 sec on lap 15)
Lap Leaders M Schumacher 1-20,22-53 (52); R Barrichello 21 (1).

Lap Leaders 2002

Pos	Driver	Car-Engine	GPs	laps	km	miles
1	M Schumacher	Ferrari	13	558	2,764.9	1,718.0
2	R Barrichello	Ferrari	11	307	1,445.2	898.0
3	D Coulthard	McLaren-Mercedes-Benz	3	95	345.6	214.8
4	J P Montoya	Williams-BMW	6	65	298.2	185.3
5	R Schumacher	Williams-BMW	5	44	233.0	144.8
6	K Räikkönen	McLaren-Mercedes-Benz	1	21	89.3	55.5
			17	**1,090**	**5,176.2**	**3,216.4**

Driver Points 2002

		AUS	MAL	BR	RSM	E	A	MC	CDN	EUR	GB	F	D	H	B	I	USA	J	Total
1	M Schumacher	10	4	10	10	10	10	6	10	10	10	10	10	6	10	6	6	10	144
2	R Barrichello	-	6	-	6	-	6	-	4	6	6	-	3	10	6	10	10	6	77
3	J P Montoya	6	6	2	3	6	4	-	-	-	4	3	6	-	4	-	3	3	50
4	R Schumacher	-	10	6	4	-	3	4	-	3	-	2	4	4	2	-	-	-	42
5	D Coulthard	-	-	4	1	4	1	10	6	-	-	4	2	2	3	-	4	-	41
6	K Räikkönen	4	-	-	-	-	-	-	3	4	-	6	-	3	-	-	-	4	24
7	J Button	-	3	3	2	-	-	-	-	2	-	1	-	-	-	2	-	1	14
8	J Trulli	-	-	-	-	-	-	3	1	-	-	-	-	-	-	3	2	-	9
9	E Irvine	3	-	-	-	-	-	-	-	-	-	-	-	1	4	-	-	-	8
10	N Heidfeld	-	2	-	3	-	-	-	-	-	1	-	1	-	-	-	-	-	7
	G Fisichella	-	-	-	-	2	2	2	-	-	-	-	-	1	-	-	-	-	7
12	J Villeneuve	-	-	-	-	-	-	-	-	-	3	-	-	-	-	-	1	-	4
	F Massa	-	1	-	2	-	-	-	-	1	-	-	-	-	-	-	-	-	4
14	O Panis	-	-	-	-	-	-	-	-	2	-	-	-	-	1	-	-	-	3
15	M Webber	2	-	-	-	-	-	-	-	-	-	-	-	-	-	-	-	-	2
	T Sato	-	-	-	-	-	-	-	-	-	-	-	-	-	-	-	-	2	2
	M Salo	1	-	1	-	-	-	-	-	-	-	-	-	-	-	-	-	-	2
	H-H Frentzen	-	-	-	1	-	1	-	-	-	-	-	-	-	-	-	-	-	2

10,6,4,3,2 and 1 point awarded to the first six finishers.

Constructor Points 2002

		AUS	MAL	BR	RSM	E	A	MC	CDN	EUR	GB	F	D	H	B	I	USA	J	Total
1	Ferrari	10	4	10	16	10	16	6	14	16	16	10	13	16	16	16	16	16	221
2	Williams-BMW	6	16	8	7	6	7	4	-	3	4	5	10	4	6	-	3	3	92
3	McLaren-Mercedes-Benz	4	-	4	1	4	1	10	9	4	-	10	2	5	3	-	4	4	65
4	Renault	-	3	3	2	-	-	3	1	2	-	1	-	-	-	5	2	1	23
5	Sauber-Petronas	-	3	-	-	5	-	-	-	1	1	-	1	-	-	-	-	-	11
6	Jordan-Honda	-	-	-	-	-	2	2	2	-	-	-	-	1	-	-	-	2	9
7	Jaguar-Ford Cosworth	3	-	-	-	-	-	-	-	-	-	-	-	1	4	-	-	-	8
8	BAR-Honda	-	-	-	-	-	-	-	-	-	5	-	-	-	1	1	-	7
9	Minardi-Asiatech	2	-	-	-	-	-	-	-	-	-	-	-	-	-	-	-	-	2
	Toyota	1	-	1	-	-	-	-	-	-	-	-	-	-	-	-	-	-	2
	Arrows-Ford Cosworth	-	-	-	-	-	1	-	1	-	-	-	-	-	-	-	-	-	2

10,6,4,3,2 and 1 point awarded to the first six finishers.

Race Entrants and Results

Grand Prix racing had its biggest shake up of rules for quite some time after a predictable 2002 season resulted in many televiewers worldwide switching off. Qualifying was reduced to a one lap shoot-out in an attempt to mix up the grid with the cars using their race fuel and then being left in parc fermé until Sunday afternoon. Max Mosley also introduced a new points system rewarding drivers down to eighth place, the intention being to keep the championship alive as long as possible. Traction control was to be banned at the half way point in the season, but this new regulation failed to materialise. Four new drivers lined up in Melbourne making it a total of 600 drivers to have raced in the World Championship since its inception in 1950.

FERRARI
Scuderia Ferrari Marlboro: M Schumacher, Barrichello

WILLIAMS
BMW WilliamsF1 Team: Montoya, R Schumacher, Gené

McLAREN
West McLaren Mercedes: Coulthard, Räikkönen

RENAULT
Mild Seven Renault F1 Team: Trulli, Alonso

SAUBER
Sauber Petronas: Heidfeld, Frentzen

JORDAN
Jordan Ford: Fisichella, Firman, Baumgartner

JAGUAR
Jaguar Racing: Webber, Pizzonia, Wilson

BAR
Lucky Strike B.A.R. Honda: Villeneuve, Button, Sato

MINARDI
European Minardi Cosworth: Wilson, Verstappen, Kiesa

TOYOTA
Panasonic Toyota Racing: Panis, da Matta

9 Mar 2003		AUSTRALIA: Melbourne							(Round 1)	(Race 698)	
		58 laps x 5.303 km, 3.295 miles = 307.574 km, 191.118 miles									
Pos	**No**	**Driver**	**Car**	**Model**	**Engine**		**Laps**	**Time/Reason for Retirement**		**Grid Pos**	**Row**
1	5	D Coulthard	McLaren	MP4-17D	Mercedes-Benz	V10	58	1h 34m 42.124s		11	6
2	3	J P Montoya	Williams	FW25	BMW	V10	58	1h 34m 50.799s		3	2
3	6	K Räikkönen	McLaren	MP4-17D	Mercedes-Benz	V10	58	1h 34m 51.316s		15	8
4	1	M Schumacher	Ferrari	F2002	Ferrari	V10	58	1h 34m 51.606s		1	1
5	7	J Trulli	Renault	R23	Renault	V10	58	1h 35m 20.925s		12	6
6	10	H-H Frentzen	Sauber	C22	Petronas	V10	58	1h 35m 26.052s		4	2
7	8	F Alonso	Renault	R23	Renault	V10	58	1h 35m 27.198s		10	5
8	4	R Schumacher	Williams	FW25	BMW	V10	58	1h 35m 27.869s		9	5
9	16	J Villeneuve	BAR	005	Honda	V10	58	1h 35m 47.660s		6	3
10	17	J Button	BAR	005	Honda	V10	58	1h 35m 48.098s		8	4
11	19	J Verstappen	Minardi	PS03	Ford Cosworth	V10	57			20	10
12r	11	G Fisichella	Jordan	EJ13	Ford Cosworth	V10	52	gearbox		13	7
13r	15	A Pizzonia	Jaguar	R4	Ford Cosworth	V10	52	suspension		18	9
r	20	O Panis	Toyota	TF103	Toyota	V10	31	fuel pressure		5	3
r	9	N Heidfeld	Sauber	C22	Petronas	V10	20	accident / suspension		7	4
r	18	J Wilson	Minardi	PS03	Ford Cosworth	V10	16	radiator		19	10
r	14	M Webber	Jaguar	R4	Ford Cosworth	V10	15	suspension		14	7
r	21	C da Matta	Toyota	TF103	Toyota	V10	7	accident		16	8
r	12	R Firman	Jordan	EJ13	Ford Cosworth	V10	6	accident		17	9
r	2	R Barrichello	Ferrari	F2002	Ferrari	V10	5	accident		2	1
ap	*34*	*A McNish*	*Renault*	*R23*	*Renault*	*V10*					

Winning speed 194.868 km/h, 121.086 mph
Pole Position speed 218.999 km/h, 136.080 mph (M Schumacher, 1 min:27.173 sec)
Fastest Lap speed 217.623 km/h, 135.225 mph (K Räikkönen, 1 min:27.724 sec on lap 32)
Lap Leaders M Schumacher 1-6,42-45 (10); J P Montoya 7-16,33-41,46-47 (21); K Räikkönen 17-32 (16); D Coulthard 48-58 (11).

23 Mar 2003   MALAYSIA: Sepang   (Round 2)   (Race 699)

56 laps x 5.543 km, 3.444 miles = 310.408 km, 192.879 miles

Pos	No	Driver	Car	Model	Engine		Laps	Time/Reason for Retirement	Grid Pos	Row
1	6	K Räikkönen	McLaren	MP4-17D	Mercedes-Benz	V10	56	1h 32m 22.195s	7	4
2	2	R Barrichello	Ferrari	F2002	Ferrari	V10	56	1h 33m 01.481s	5	3
3	8	F Alonso	Renault	R23	Renault	V10	56	1h 33m 26.202s	1	1
4	4	R Schumacher	Williams	FW25	BMW	V10	56	1h 33m 50.221s	17	9
5	7	J Trulli	Renault	R23	Renault	V10	55		2	1
6	1	M Schumacher	Ferrari	F2002	Ferrari	V10	55		3	2
7	17	J Button	BAR	005	Honda	V10	55		9	5
8	9	N Heidfeld	Sauber	C22	Petronas	V10	55		6	3
9	10	H-H Frentzen	Sauber	C22	Petronas	V10	55		13	7
10	12	R Firman	Jordan	EJ13	Ford Cosworth	V10	55		20	10
11	21	C da Matta	Toyota	TF103	Toyota	V10	55		11	6
12	3	J P Montoya	Williams	FW25	BMW	V10	53		8	4
13	19	J Verstappen	Minardi	PS03	Ford Cosworth	V10	52		18	9
r	15	A Pizzonia	Jaguar	R4	Ford Cosworth	V10	42	brakes / spin	15	8
r	18	J Wilson	Minardi	PS03	Ford Cosworth	V10	41	driver discomfort	19	10
r	14	M Webber	Jaguar	R4	Ford Cosworth	V10	35	oil leak	16	8
r	20	O Panis	Toyota	TF103	Toyota	V10	12	fuel pressure	10	5
r	5	D Coulthard	McLaren	MP4-17D	Mercedes-Benz	V10	2	spark box	4	2
r	11	G Fisichella	Jordan	EJ13	Ford Cosworth	V10	0	clutch	14	7
ns	16	J Villeneuve	BAR	005	Honda	V10		electrics / gearbox on dummy grid	12	6
ap	*34*	*A McNish*	*Renault*	*R23*	*Renault*	*V10*				

Winning speed 201.629 km/h, 125.287 mph
Pole Position speed 205.626 km/h, 127.770 mph (F Alonso, 1 min:37.044 sec)
Fastest Lap speed 206.974 km/h, 128.608 mph (M Schumacher, 1 min:36.412 sec on lap 45)
Lap Leaders F Alonso 1-13 (13); K Räikkönen 14-19,23-56 (40); R Barrichello 20-22 (3).

6 Apr 2003   BRAZIL: Interlagos   (Round 3)   (Race 700)

54 laps x 4.309 km, 2.677 miles = 232.656 km, 144.566 miles

Pos	No	Driver	Car	Model	Engine		Laps	Time/Reason for Retirement	Grid Pos	Row
1	11	G Fisichella	Jordan	EJ13	Ford Cosworth	V10	54	1h 31m 17.748s	8	4
2	6	K Räikkönen	McLaren	MP4-17D	Mercedes-Benz	V10	54	1h 31m 18.693s	4	2
3	8	F Alonso	Renault	R23	Renault	V10	54	1h 31m 24.096s	10	5
4	5	D Coulthard	McLaren	MP4-17D	Mercedes-Benz	V10	54	1h 31m 25.844s	2	1
5	10	H-H Frentzen	Sauber	C22	Petronas	V10	54	1h 31m 26.390s	14	7
6	16	J Villeneuve	BAR	005	Honda	V10	54	1h 31m 33.802s	13	7
7	4	R Schumacher	Williams	FW25	BMW	V10	54	1h 31m 56.274s	6	3
8	7	J Trulli	Renault	R23	Renault	V10	54	1h 32m 03.675s	5	3
9r	14	M Webber	Jaguar	R4	Ford Cosworth	V10	53	accident	3	2
10	21	C da Matta	Toyota	TF103	Toyota	V10	53		18	9
r	2	R Barrichello	Ferrari	F2002	Ferrari	V10	46	fuel system	1	1
r	17	J Button	BAR	005	Honda	V10	32	accident	11	6
r	19	J Verstappen	Minardi	PS03	Ford Cosworth	V10	30	accident	19	10
r	1	M Schumacher	Ferrari	F2002	Ferrari	V10	26	accident	7	4
r	3	J P Montoya	Williams	FW25	BMW	V10	24	accident	9	5
r	15	A Pizzonia	Jaguar	R4	Ford Cosworth	V10	24	accident	17	9
r	20	O Panis	Toyota	TF103	Toyota	V10	17	accident	15	8
r	12	R Firman	Jordan	EJ13	Ford Cosworth	V10	17	front suspension / accident	16	8
r	18	J Wilson	Minardi	PS03	Ford Cosworth	V10	15	spin	20	10
r	9	N Heidfeld	Sauber	C22	Petronas	V10	8	engine	12	6
ap	*34*	*A McNish*	*Renault*	*R23*	*Renault*	*V10*				

Winning speed 152.902 km/h, 95.009 mph
Pole Position speed 210.175 km/h, 130.597 mph (R Barrichello, 1 min:13.807 sec)
Fastest Lap speed 189.101 km/h, 117.502 mph (R Barrichello, 1 min:22.032 sec on lap 46)
Lap Leaders R Barrichello 1-8,45-46 (10); D Coulthard 9-10,27-44,47-52 (26); K Räikkönen 11-26,53 (17); G Fisichella 54 (1).

Race scheduled for 71 laps, but stopped prematurely after Alonso's accident. Results originally based on 53 laps, with K Räikkönen winning in 1h 29m 53.179s (152.423 km/h), G Fisichella 2nd in 1h 29m 54.010s and F Alonso 3rd in 1h 29m 59.874s, but later amended with results declared at 54 laps.

20 Apr 2003   SAN MARINO: Imola   (Round 4)   (Race 701)

62 laps x 4.933 km, 3.065 miles = 305.609 km, 189.897 miles

Pos	No	Driver	Car	Model	Engine		Laps	Time/Reason for Retirement	Grid Pos	Row
1	1	M Schumacher	Ferrari	F2002	Ferrari	V10	62	1h 28m 12.058s	1	1
2	6	K Räikkönen	McLaren	MP4-17D	Mercedes-Benz	V10	62	1h 28m 13.940s	6	3
3	2	R Barrichello	Ferrari	F2002	Ferrari	V10	62	1h 28m 14.349s	3	2
4	4	R Schumacher	Williams	FW25	BMW	V10	62	1h 28m 20.861s	2	1
5	5	D Coulthard	McLaren	MP4-17D	Mercedes-Benz	V10	62	1h 28m 21.469s	12	6
6	8	F Alonso	Renault	R23	Renault	V10	62	1h 28m 55.747s	8	4
7	3	J P Montoya	Williams	FW25	BMW	V10	62	1h 28m 57.329s	4	2
8	17	J Button	BAR	005	Honda	V10	61		9	5
9	20	O Panis	Toyota	TF103	Toyota	V10	61		10	5
10	9	N Heidfeld	Sauber	C22	Petronas	V10	61		11	6
11	10	H-H Frentzen	Sauber	C22	Petronas	V10	61		14	7

Pos	No	Driver	Car	Model	Engine		Laps	Time/Reason for Retirement	Grid Pos	Row
12	21	C da Matta	Toyota	TF103	Toyota	V10	61		13	7
13	7	J Trulli	Renault	R23	Renault	V10	61		16	8
14	15	A Pizzonia	Jaguar	R4	Ford Cosworth	V10	60		15	8
15r	11	G Fisichella	Jordan	EJ13	Ford Cosworth	V10	57	engine	17	9
r	14	M Webber	Jaguar	R4	Ford Cosworth	V10	54	driveshaft	5	3
r	12	R Firman	Jordan	EJ13	Ford Cosworth	V10	51	engine	19	10
r	19	J Verstappen	Minardi	PS03	Ford Cosworth	V10	38	electrics	20	10
r	18	J Wilson	Minardi	PS03	Ford Cosworth	V10	23	fuel rig	18	9
r	16	J Villeneuve	BAR	005	Honda	V10	19	oil fire / electrics	7	4
ap	34	A McNish	Renault	R23	Renault	V10				
ap	39	M Bobbi	Minardi	PS03	Ford Cosworth	V10				

Winning speed 207.894 km/h, 129.180 mph
Pole Position speed 215.710 km/h, 134.036 mph (M Schumacher, 1 min:22.327 sec)
Fastest Lap speed 215.281 km/h, 133.770 mph (M Schumacher, 1 min:22.491 sec on lap 17)
Lap Leaders R Schumacher 1-15 (15); M Schumacher 16-18,23-49,51-62 (42); K Räikkönen 19-22 (4); R Barrichello 50 (1).

4 May 2003		SPAIN: Montmeló							(Round 5)	(Race 702)
		65 laps x 4.730 km, 2.939 miles = 307.324 km, 190.962 miles								

Pos	No	Driver	Car	Model	Engine		Laps	Time/Reason for Retirement	Grid Pos	Row
1	1	M Schumacher	Ferrari	F2003-GA	Ferrari	V10	65	1h 33m 46.933s	1	1
2	8	F Alonso	Renault	R23	Renault	V10	65	1h 33m 52.649s	3	2
3	2	R Barrichello	Ferrari	F2003-GA	Ferrari	V10	65	1h 34m 04.934s	2	1
4	3	J P Montoya	Williams	FW25	BMW	V10	65	1h 34m 48.955s	9	5
5	4	R Schumacher	Williams	FW25	BMW	V10	64		7	4
6	21	C da Matta	Toyota	TF103	Toyota	V10	64		13	7
7	14	M Webber	Jaguar	R4	Ford Cosworth	V10	64		12	6
8	12	R Firman	Jordan	EJ13	Ford Cosworth	V10	63		15	8
9	17	J Button	BAR	005	Honda	V10	63		5	3
10	9	N Heidfeld	Sauber	C22	Petronas	V10	63		14	7
11	18	J Wilson	Minardi	PS03	Ford Cosworth	V10	63		18	9
12	19	J Verstappen	Minardi	PS03	Ford Cosworth	V10	62		19	10
r	11	G Fisichella	Jordan	EJ13	Ford Cosworth	V10	43	engine	17	9
r	20	O Panis	Toyota	TF103	Toyota	V10	41	gearbox	6	3
r	10	H-H Frentzen	Sauber	C22	Petronas	V10	38	front suspension	10	5
r	5	D Coulthard	McLaren	MP4-17D	Mercedes-Benz	V10	17	accident	8	4
r	16	J Villeneuve	BAR	005	Honda	V10	12	engine / fire	11	6
r	7	J Trulli	Renault	R23	Renault	V10	0	accident	4	2
r	15	A Pizzonia	Jaguar	R4	Ford Cosworth	V10	0	stalled / accident	16	8
r	6	K Räikkönen	McLaren	MP4-17D	Mercedes-Benz	V10	0	accident	20	10
ap	34	A McNish	Renault	R23	Renault	V10				

Winning speed 196.619 km/h, 122.174 mph
Pole Position speed 218.975 km/h, 136.065 mph (M Schumacher, 1 min:17.762 sec)
Fastest Lap speed 212.470 km/h, 132.023 mph (R Barrichello, 1 min:20.143 sec on lap 52)
Lap Leaders M Schumacher 1-18,21-35,38-49,51-65 (60); R Barrichello 19-20 (2); F Alonso 36-37,50 (3).

18 May 2003		AUSTRIA: A1-Ring							(Round 6)	(Race 703)
		69 laps x 4.326 km, 2.688 miles = 298.494 km, 185.476 miles								

Pos	No	Driver	Car	Model	Engine		Laps	Time/Reason for Retirement	Grid Pos	Row
1	1	M Schumacher	Ferrari	F2003-GA	Ferrari	V10	69	1h 24m 04.888s	1	1
2	6	K Räikkönen	McLaren	MP4-17D	Mercedes-Benz	V10	69	1h 24m 08.250s	2	1
3	2	R Barrichello	Ferrari	F2003-GA	Ferrari	V10	69	1h 24m 08.839s	5	3
4	17	J Button	BAR	005	Honda	V10	69	1h 24m 47.131s	7	4
5	5	D Coulthard	McLaren	MP4-17D	Mercedes-Benz	V10	69	1h 25m 04.628s	14	7
6	4	R Schumacher	Williams	FW25	BMW	V10	68		10	5
7	14	M Webber	Jaguar	R4	Ford Cosworth	V10	68		17	9
8	7	J Trulli	Renault	R23	Renault	V10	68		6	3
9	15	A Pizzonia	Jaguar	R4	Ford Cosworth	V10	68		8	4
10	21	C da Matta	Toyota	TF103	Toyota	V10	68		13	7
11	12	R Firman	Jordan	EJ13	Ford Cosworth	V10	68		16	8
12	16	J Villeneuve	BAR	005	Honda	V10	68		12	6
13	18	J Wilson	Minardi	PS03	Ford Cosworth	V10	67		18	9
r	11	G Fisichella	Jordan	EJ13	Ford Cosworth	V10	60	fuel system	9	5
r	9	N Heidfeld	Sauber	C22	Petronas	V10	46	engine	4	2
r	8	F Alonso	Renault	R23	Renault	V10	44	engine	19	10
r	3	J P Montoya	Williams	FW25	BMW	V10	32	water leak / engine	3	2
r	20	O Panis	Toyota	TF103	Toyota	V10	6	front tyre / suspension	11	6
r	19	J Verstappen	Minardi	PS03	Ford Cosworth	V10	0	launch control *	20	10
r	10	H-H Frentzen	Sauber	C22	Petronas	V10	0	clutch *	15	8
ap	34	A McNish	Renault	R23	Renault	V10				

Winning speed 213.003 km/h, 132.354 mph
Pole Position speed 225.214 km/h, 139.942 mph (M Schumacher, 1 min: 9.150 sec)
Fastest Lap speed 227.894 km/h, 141.607 mph (M Schumacher, 1 min: 8.337 sec on lap 41)
Lap Leaders M Schumacher 1-23,32-42,51-69 (53); J P Montoya 24-31 (8); K Räikkönen 43-49 (7); R Barrichello 50 (1).

*Scheduled for 71 laps but reduced to 69, due to two aborted starts. * Retired after first start.*

Races

1 Jun 2003   MONACO: Monte-Carlo   (Round 7)   (Race 704)

78 laps x 3.340 km, 2.075 miles = 260.520 km, 161.880 miles

Pos	No	Driver	Car	Model	Engine		Laps	Time/Reason for Retirement	Grid Pos	Row
1	3	J P Montoya	Williams	FW25	BMW	V10	78	1h 42m 19.010s	3	2
2	6	K Räikkönen	McLaren	MP4-17D	Mercedes-Benz	V10	78	1h 42m 19.612s	2	1
3	1	M Schumacher	Ferrari	F2003-GA	Ferrari	V10	78	1h 42m 20.730s	5	3
4	4	R Schumacher	Williams	FW25	BMW	V10	78	1h 42m 47.528s	1	1
5	8	F Alonso	Renault	R23	Renault	V10	78	1h 42m 55.261s	8	4
6	7	J Trulli	Renault	R23	Renault	V10	78	1h 42m 59.982s	4	2
7	5	D Coulthard	McLaren	MP4-17D	Mercedes-Benz	V10	78	1h 43m 00.237s	6	3
8	2	R Barrichello	Ferrari	F2003-GA	Ferrari	V10	78	1h 43m 12.276s	7	4
9	21	C da Matta	Toyota	TF103	Toyota	V10	77		10	5
10	11	G Fisichella	Jordan	EJ13	Ford Cosworth	V10	77		12	6
11	9	N Heidfeld	Sauber	C22	Petronas	V10	76		14	7
12	12	R Firman	Jordan	EJ13	Ford Cosworth	V10	76		16	8
13	20	O Panis	Toyota	TF103	Toyota	V10	74		17	9
r	16	J Villeneuve	BAR	005	Honda	V10	63	engine	11	6
r	18	J Wilson	Minardi	PS03	Ford Cosworth	V10	29	fuel feed	19	10
r	19	J Verstappen	Minardi	PS03	Ford Cosworth	V10	28	fuel feed	18	9
r	14	M Webber	Jaguar	R4	Ford Cosworth	V10	16	hydraulics	9	5
r	15	A Pizzonia	Jaguar	R4	Ford Cosworth	V10	10	electrics	13	7
r	10	H-H Frentzen	Sauber	C22	Petronas	V10	0	accident	15	8
ns	17	J Button	BAR	005	Honda	V10		accident / injury		
ap	34	A McNish	Renault	R23	Renault	V10				

Winning speed 152.772 km/h, 94.928 mph
Pole Position speed 159.768 km/h, 99.275 mph (R Schumacher, 1 min:15.259 sec)
Fastest Lap speed 161.298 km/h, 100.226 mph (K Räikkönen, 1 min:14.545 sec on lap 49)
Lap Leaders R Schumacher 1-20 (20); J P Montoya 21-22,31-48,59-78 (40); J Trulli 25-26 (2); K Räikkönen 23-24,49-52 (6); M Schumacher 27-30,53-58 (10).

15 Jun 2003   CANADA: Montréal   (Round 8)   (Race 705)

70 laps x 4.361 km, 2.710 miles = 305.270 km, 189.686 miles

Pos	No	Driver	Car	Model	Engine		Laps	Time/Reason for Retirement	Grid Pos	Row
1	1	M Schumacher	Ferrari	F2003-GA	Ferrari	V10	70	1h 31m 13.591s	3	2
2	4	R Schumacher	Williams	FW25	BMW	V10	70	1h 31m 14.375s	1	1
3	3	J P Montoya	Williams	FW25	BMW	V10	70	1h 31m 14.946s	2	1
4	8	F Alonso	Renault	R23	Renault	V10	70	1h 31m 18.072s	4	2
5	2	R Barrichello	Ferrari	F2003-GA	Ferrari	V10	70	1h 32m 17.852s	5	3
6	6	K Räikkönen	McLaren	MP4-17D	Mercedes-Benz	V10	70	1h 32m 24.093s	20	10
7	14	M Webber	Jaguar	R4	Ford Cosworth	V10	69		6	3
8	20	O Panis	Toyota	TF103	Toyota	V10	69		7	4
9	19	J Verstappen	Minardi	PS03	Ford Cosworth	V10	68		15	8
10r	15	A Pizzonia	Jaguar	R4	Ford Cosworth	V10	66	brakes	13	7
11r	21	C da Matta	Toyota	TF103	Toyota	V10	64	suspension	9	5
r	18	J Wilson	Minardi	PS03	Ford Cosworth	V10	60	gearbox	18	9
r	17	J Button	BAR	005	Honda	V10	51	gearbox	17	9
r	5	D Coulthard	McLaren	MP4-17D	Mercedes-Benz	V10	47	gearbox	11	6
r	9	N Heidfeld	Sauber	C22	Petronas	V10	47	engine	12	6
r	7	J Trulli	Renault	R23	Renault	V10	22	accident / traction control	8	4
r	11	G Fisichella	Jordan	EJ13	Ford Cosworth	V10	20	gearbox	16	8
r	12	R Firman	Jordan	EJ13	Ford Cosworth	V10	20	oil leak / engine	19	10
r	16	J Villeneuve	BAR	005	Honda	V10	14	brake fluid loss	14	7
r	10	H-H Frentzen	Sauber	C22	Petronas	V10	6	electronics	10	5
ap	34	A McNish	Renault	R23	Renault	V10				

Winning speed 200.777 km/h, 124.757 mph
Pole Position speed 207.861 km/h, 129.159 mph (R Schumacher, 1 min:15.529 sec)
Fastest Lap speed 206.465 km/h, 128.291 mph (F Alonso, 1 min:16.040 sec on lap 53)
Lap Leaders R Schumacher 1-19 (19); M Schumacher 20,26-48,55-70 (40); F Alonso 21-25,49-54 (11).

29 Jun 2003   EUROPE: Nürburgring   (Round 9)   (Race 706)

60 laps x 5.148 km, 3.199 miles = 308.863 km, 191.919 miles

Pos	No	Driver	Car	Model	Engine		Laps	Time/Reason for Retirement	Grid Pos	Row
1	4	R Schumacher	Williams	FW25	BMW	V10	60	1h 34m 43.622s	3	2
2	3	J P Montoya	Williams	FW25	BMW	V10	60	1h 35m 00.443s	4	2
3	2	R Barrichello	Ferrari	F2003-GA	Ferrari	V10	60	1h 35m 23.295s	5	3
4	8	F Alonso	Renault	R23	Renault	V10	60	1h 35m 49.353s	8	4
5	1	M Schumacher	Ferrari	F2003-GA	Ferrari	V10	60	1h 35m 49.784s	2	1
6	14	M Webber	Jaguar	R4	Ford Cosworth	V10	59		11	6
7	17	J Button	BAR	005	Honda	V10	59		12	6
8	9	N Heidfeld	Sauber	C22	Petronas	V10	59		20	10
9	10	H-H Frentzen	Sauber	C22	Petronas	V10	59		15	8
10	15	A Pizzonia	Jaguar	R4	Ford Cosworth	V10	59		16	8
11	12	R Firman	Jordan	EJ13	Ford Cosworth	V10	58		14	7
12	11	G Fisichella	Jordan	EJ13	Ford Cosworth	V10	58		13	7
13	18	J Wilson	Minardi	PS03	Ford Cosworth	V10	58		19	10

Pos	No	Driver	Car	Model	Engine		Laps	Time/Reason for Retirement	Grid Pos	Row
14	19	J Verstappen	Minardi	PS03	Ford Cosworth	V10	57		18	9
15r	5	D Coulthard	McLaren	MP4-17D	Mercedes-Benz	V10	56	accident	9	5
r	21	C da Matta	Toyota	TF103	Toyota	V10	53	engine	10	5
r	16	J Villeneuve	BAR	005	Honda	V10	51	gearbox	17	9
r	7	J Trulli	Renault	R23	Renault	V10	37	fuel pump	6	3
r	20	O Panis	Toyota	TF103	Toyota	V10	37	brakes / spin	7	4
r	6	K Räikkönen	McLaren	MP4-17D	Mercedes-Benz	V10	25	engine	1	1
ap	34	A McNish	Renault	R23	Renault	V10				

Winning speed 195.633 km/h, 121.561 mph
Pole Position speed 202.493 km/h, 125.824 mph (K Räikkönen, 1 min:31.523 sec)
Fastest Lap speed 200.092 km/h, 124.332 mph (K Räikkönen, 1 min:32.621 sec on lap 14)
Lap Leaders K Räikkönen 1-16,22-25 (30); R Schumacher 17-21,26-60 (30).

6 Jul 2003		**FRANCE: Magny-Cours**						**(Round 10)**	**(Race 707)**	
		70 laps x 4.411 km, 2.741 miles = 308.586 km, 191.746 miles								
Pos	No	Driver	Car	Model	Engine		Laps	Time/Reason for Retirement	Grid Pos	Row
1	4	R Schumacher	Williams	FW25	BMW	V10	70	1h 30m 49.213s	1	1
2	3	J P Montoya	Williams	FW25	BMW	V10	70	1h 31m 03.026s	2	1
3	1	M Schumacher	Ferrari	F2003-GA	Ferrari	V10	70	1h 31m 08.781s	3	2
4	6	K Räikkönen	McLaren	MP4-17D	Mercedes-Benz	V10	70	1h 31m 27.260s	4	2
5	5	D Coulthard	McLaren	MP4-17D	Mercedes-Benz	V10	70	1h 31m 29.502s	5	3
6	14	M Webber	Jaguar	R4	Ford Cosworth	V10	70	1h 31m 55.593s	9	5
7	2	R Barrichello	Ferrari	F2003-GA	Ferrari	V10	69		8	4
8	20	O Panis	Toyota	TF103	Toyota	V10	69		10	5
9	16	J Villeneuve	BAR	005	Honda	V10	69		12	6
10	15	A Pizzonia	Jaguar	R4	Ford Cosworth	V10	69		11	6
11	21	C da Matta	Toyota	TF103	Toyota	V10	69		13	7
12	10	H-H Frentzen	Sauber	C22	Petronas	V10	68		16	8
13	9	N Heidfeld	Sauber	C22	Petronas	V10	68		15	8
14	18	J Wilson	Minardi	PS03	Ford Cosworth	V10	67		20	10
15	12	R Firman	Jordan	EJ13	Ford Cosworth	V10	67		18	9
16	19	J Verstappen	Minardi	PS03	Ford Cosworth	V10	66		19	10
r	7	J Trulli	Renault	R23	Renault	V10	45	engine	6	3
r	8	F Alonso	Renault	R23	Renault	V10	43	engine	7	4
r	11	G Fisichella	Jordan	EJ13	Ford Cosworth	V10	42	engine	17	9
r	17	J Button	BAR	005	Honda	V10	21	fuel rig / out of fuel	14	7
ap	34	F Montagny	Renault	R23	Renault	V10				

Winning speed 203.866 km/h, 126.676 mph
Pole Position speed 211.674 km/h, 131.528 mph (R Schumacher, 1 min:15.019 sec)
Fastest Lap speed 210.292 km/h, 130.670 mph (J P Montoya, 1 min:15.512 sec on lap 36)
Lap Leaders R Schumacher 1-70 (70).

20 Jul 2003		**BRITAIN: Silverstone**						**(Round 11)**	**(Race 708)**	
		60 laps x 5.141 km, 3.194 miles = 308.355 km, 191.603 miles								
Pos	No	Driver	Car	Model	Engine		Laps	Time/Reason for Retirement	Grid Pos	Row
1	2	R Barrichello	Ferrari	F2003-GA	Ferrari	V10	60	1h 28m 37.554s	1	1
2	3	J P Montoya	Williams	FW25	BMW	V10	60	1h 28m 43.016s	7	4
3	6	K Räikkönen	McLaren	MP4-17D	Mercedes-Benz	V10	60	1h 28m 48.210s	3	2
4	1	M Schumacher	Ferrari	F2003-GA	Ferrari	V10	60	1h 29m 03.202s	5	3
5	5	D Coulthard	McLaren	MP4-17D	Mercedes-Benz	V10	60	1h 29m 14.381s	12	6
6	7	J Trulli	Renault	R23B	Renault	V10	60	1h 29m 20.621s	2	1
7	21	C da Matta	Toyota	TF103	Toyota	V10	60	1h 29m 22.639s	6	3
8	17	J Button	BAR	005	Honda	V10	60	1h 29m 23.032s	20	10
9	4	R Schumacher	Williams	FW25	BMW	V10	60	1h 29m 35.586s	4	2
10	16	J Villeneuve	BAR	005	Honda	V10	60	1h 29m 41.123s	9	5
11	20	O Panis	Toyota	TF103	Toyota	V10	60	1h 29m 42.761s	13	7
12	10	H-H Frentzen	Sauber	C22	Petronas	V10	60	1h 29m 43.118s	14	7
13	12	R Firman	Jordan	EJ13	Ford Cosworth	V10	59		17	9
14	14	M Webber	Jaguar	R4	Ford Cosworth	V10	59		11	6
15	19	J Verstappen	Minardi	PS03	Ford Cosworth	V10	58		19	10
16	18	J Wilson	Minardi	PS03	Ford Cosworth	V10	58		18	9
17	9	N Heidfeld	Sauber	C22	Petronas	V10	58		16	8
r	8	F Alonso	Renault	R23B	Renault	V10	52	electrics / gearbox	8	4
r	11	G Fisichella	Jordan	EJ13	Ford Cosworth	V10	44	rear suspension / spin	15	8
r	15	A Pizzonia	Jaguar	R4	Ford Cosworth	V10	32	engine	10	5
ap	34	A McNish	Renault	R23B	Renault	V10				

Winning speed 208.757 km/h, 129.716 mph
Pole Position speed 227.900 km/h, 141.611 mph (R Barrichello, 1 min:21.209 sec)
Fastest Lap speed 225.054 km/h, 139.843 mph (R Barrichello, 1 min:22.236 sec on lap 38)
Lap Leaders J Trulli 1-12 (12); C da Matta 13-29 (17); K Räikkönen 30-35,40-41 (8); R Barrichello 36-39,42-60 (23).

GERMANY: Hockenheim (Round 12) (Race 709)

67 laps x 4.574 km, 2.842 miles = 306.458 km, 190.424 miles

Pos	No	Driver	Car	Model	Engine		Laps	Time/Reason for Retirement	Grid Pos	Row
1	3	J P Montoya	Williams	FW25	BMW	V10	67	1h 28m 48.769s	1	1
2	5	D Coulthard	McLaren	MP4-17D	Mercedes-Benz	V10	67	1h 29m 54.228s	10	5
3	7	J Trulli	Renault	R23B	Renault	V10	67	1h 29m 57.829s	4	2
4	8	F Alonso	Renault	R23B	Renault	V10	67	1h 29m 58.113s	8	4
5	20	O Panis	Toyota	TF103	Toyota	V10	66		7	4
6	21	C da Matta	Toyota	TF103	Toyota	V10	66		9	5
7	1	M Schumacher	Ferrari	F2003-GA	Ferrari	V10	66		6	3
8	17	J Button	BAR	005	Honda	V10	66		17	9
9	16	J Villeneuve	BAR	005	Honda	V10	65		13	7
10	9	N Heidfeld	Sauber	C22	Petronas	V10	65		15	8
11r	14	M Webber	Jaguar	R4	Ford Cosworth	V10	64	accident	11	6
12	18	N Kiesa	Minardi	PS03	Ford Cosworth	V10	62		20	10
13r	11	G Fisichella	Jordan	EJ13	Ford Cosworth	V10	60	water leak	12	6
r	19	J Verstappen	Minardi	PS03	Ford Cosworth	V10	23	hydraulics	19	10
r	15	J Wilson	Jaguar	R4	Ford Cosworth	V10	6	gearbox	16	8
r	4	R Schumacher	Williams	FW25	BMW	V10	1	accident	2	1
r	10	H-H Frentzen	Sauber	C22	Petronas	V10	1	accident	14	7
r	2	R Barrichello	Ferrari	F2003-GA	Ferrari	V10	0	accident	3	2
r	6	K Räikkönen	McLaren	MP4-17D	Mercedes-Benz	V10	0	accident	5	3
r	12	R Firman	Jordan	EJ13	Ford Cosworth	V10	0	accident	18	9
ap	34	*A McNish*	*Renault*	*R23B*	*Renault*	*V10*				
ap	36	*Z Baumgartner*	*Jordan*	*EJ13*	*Ford Cosworth*	*V10*				
ap	39	*G Bruni*	*Minardi*	*PS03*	*Ford Cosworth*	*V10*				

Winning speed 207.036 km/h, 128.646 mph
Pole Position speed 219.064 km/h, 136.120 mph (J P Montoya, 1 min:15.167 sec)
Fastest Lap speed 219.795 km/h, 136.574 mph (J P Montoya, 1 min:14.917 sec on lap 14)
Lap Leaders J P Montoya 1-17,19-67 (66); F Alonso 18 (1).

HUNGARY: Hungaroring (Round 13) (Race 710)

70 laps x 4.381 km, 2.722 miles = 306.663 km, 190.552 miles

Pos	No	Driver	Car	Model	Engine		Laps	Time/Reason for Retirement	Grid Pos	Row
1	8	F Alonso	Renault	R23B	Renault	V10	70	1h 39m 01.460s	1	1
2	6	K Räikkönen	McLaren	MP4-17D	Mercedes-Benz	V10	70	1h 39m 18.228s	7	4
3	3	J P Montoya	Williams	FW25	BMW	V10	70	1h 39m 35.997s	4	2
4	4	R Schumacher	Williams	FW25	BMW	V10	70	1h 39m 37.080s	2	1
5	5	D Coulthard	McLaren	MP4-17D	Mercedes-Benz	V10	70	1h 39m 57.995s	9	5
6	14	M Webber	Jaguar	R4	Ford Cosworth	V10	70	1h 40m 14.103s	3	2
7	7	J Trulli	Renault	R23B	Renault	V10	69		6	3
8	1	M Schumacher	Ferrari	F2003-GA	Ferrari	V10	69		8	4
9	9	N Heidfeld	Sauber	C22	Petronas	V10	69		11	6
10	17	J Button	BAR	005	Honda	V10	69		14	7
11	21	C da Matta	Toyota	TF103	Toyota	V10	68		15	8
12	19	J Verstappen	Minardi	PS03	Ford Cosworth	V10	67		18	9
13	18	N Kiesa	Minardi	PS03	Ford Cosworth	V10	66		20	10
r	10	H-H Frentzen	Sauber	C22	Petronas	V10	47	out of fuel	17	9
r	15	J Wilson	Jaguar	R4	Ford Cosworth	V10	42	engine	12	6
r	12	Z Baumgartner	Jordan	EJ13	Ford Cosworth	V10	34	engine	19	10
r	20	O Panis	Toyota	TF103	Toyota	V10	33	gearbox	10	5
r	11	G Fisichella	Jordan	EJ13	Ford Cosworth	V10	28	engine	13	7
r	2	R Barrichello	Ferrari	F2003-GA	Ferrari	V10	19	rear suspension / accident	5	3
r	16	J Villeneuve	BAR	005	Honda	V10	14	hydraulics	16	8
ns	12	R Firman	Jordan	EJ13	Ford Cosworth	V10		accident / injury		
ap	34	*A McNish*	*Renault*	*R23B*	*Renault*	*V10*				
ap	39	*G Bruni*	*Minardi*	*PS03*	*Ford Cosworth*	*V10*				

Winning speed 185.810 km/h, 115.458 mph
Pole Position speed 193.071 km/h, 119.969 mph (F Alonso, 1 min:21.688 sec)
Fastest Lap speed 192.114 km/h, 119.374 mph (J P Montoya, 1 min:22.095 sec on lap 37)
Lap Leaders F Alonso, 1-13,15-70 (69); K Räikkönen, 14 (1).

Z Baumgartner practised in car no.36 but took over no.12 for qualifying and the race, after R Firman's accident.

14 Sep 2003   **ITALY: Monza**   **(Round 14)**   **(Race 711)**

53 laps x 5.793 km, 3.600 miles = 306.720 km, 190.587 miles

Pos	No	Driver	Car	Model	Engine		Laps	Time/Reason for Retirement	Grid Pos	Row
1	1	M Schumacher	Ferrari	F2003-GA	Ferrari	V10	53	1h 14m 19.838s	1	1
2	3	J P Montoya	Williams	FW25	BMW	V10	53	1h 14m 25.132s	2	1
3	2	R Barrichello	Ferrari	F2003-GA	Ferrari	V10	53	1h 14m 31.673s	3	2
4	6	K Räikkönen	McLaren	MP4-17D	Mercedes-Benz	V10	53	1h 14m 32.672s	4	2
5	4	M Gené	Williams	FW25	BMW	V10	53	1h 14m 47.729s	5	3
6	16	J Villeneuve	BAR	005	Honda	V10	52		10	5
7	14	M Webber	Jaguar	R4	Ford Cosworth	V10	52		11	6
8	8	F Alonso	Renault	R23B	Renault	V10	52		20	10
9	9	N Heidfeld	Sauber	C22	Petronas	V10	52		16	8
10	11	G Fisichella	Jordan	EJ13	Ford Cosworth	V10	52		13	7
11	12	Z Baumgartner	Jordan	EJ13	Ford Cosworth	V10	51		18	9
12	18	N Kiesa	Minardi	PS03	Ford Cosworth	V10	51		19	10
13r	10	H-H Frentzen	Sauber	C22	Petronas	V10	50	gearbox	14	7
r	5	D Coulthard	McLaren	MP4-17D	Mercedes-Benz	V10	45	fuel pressure	8	4
r	20	O Panis	Toyota	TF103	Toyota	V10	35	brakes	9	5
r	19	J Verstappen	Minardi	PS03	Ford Cosworth	V10	27	oil leak	17	9
r	17	J Button	BAR	005	Honda	V10	24	gearbox	7	4
r	21	C da Matta	Toyota	TF103	Toyota	V10	3	rear tyre / spin	12	6
r	15	J Wilson	Jaguar	R4	Ford Cosworth	V10	2	gearbox	15	8
r	7	J Trulli	Renault	R23B	Renault	V10	0	hydraulics	6	3
ns	4	R Schumacher	Williams	FW25	BMW	V10		unwell from previous injury		
ap	34	A McNish	Renault	R23B	Renault	V10				
ap	39	G Bruni	Minardi	PS03	Ford Cosworth	V10				

Winning speed 247.585 km/h, 153.843 mph
Pole Position speed 257.584 km/h, 160.055 mph (M Schumacher, 1 min:20.963 sec)
Fastest Lap speed 254.848 km/h, 158.356 mph (M Schumacher, 1 min:21.832 sec on lap 14)
Lap Leaders M Schumacher 1-15,17-53 (52); J P Montoya 16 (1).

Z Baumgartner practised in car no. 36 but took no.12 for qualifying and the race.
R Schumacher participated in the initial practice session, but withdrew from the rest of the meeting, being replaced by M Gené.

28 Sep 2003   **USA: Indianapolis**   **(Round 15)**   **(Race 712)**

73 laps x 4.192 km, 2.605 miles = 306.016 km, 190.150 miles

Pos	No	Driver	Car	Model	Engine		Laps	Time/Reason for Retirement	Grid Pos	Row
1	1	M Schumacher	Ferrari	F2003-GA	Ferrari	V10	73	1h 33m 35.997s	7	4
2	6	K Räikkönen	McLaren	MP4-17D	Mercedes-Benz	V10	73	1h 33m 54.255s	1	1
3	10	H-H Frentzen	Sauber	C22	Petronas	V10	73	1h 34m 13.961s	15	8
4	7	J Trulli	Renault	R23B	Renault	V10	73	1h 34m 24.326s	10	5
5	9	N Heidfeld	Sauber	C22	Petronas	V10	73	1h 34m 32.400s	13	7
6	3	J P Montoya	Williams	FW25	BMW	V10	72		4	2
7	11	G Fisichella	Jordan	EJ13	Ford Cosworth	V10	72		17	9
8	15	J Wilson	Jaguar	R4	Ford Cosworth	V10	71		16	8
9	21	C da Matta	Toyota	TF103	Toyota	V10	71		9	5
10	19	J Verstappen	Minardi	PS03	Ford Cosworth	V10	69		19	10
11	18	N Kiesa	Minardi	PS03	Ford Cosworth	V10	69		20	10
r	16	J Villeneuve	BAR	005	Honda	V10	63	engine	12	6
r	12	R Firman	Jordan	EJ13	Ford Cosworth	V10	48	spin	18	9
r	5	D Coulthard	McLaren	MP4-17D	Mercedes-Benz	V10	45	gearbox	8	4
r	8	F Alonso	Renault	R23B	Renault	V10	44	engine	6	3
r	17	J Button	BAR	005	Honda	V10	41	hydraulics	11	6
r	20	O Panis	Toyota	TF103	Toyota	V10	27	accident	3	2
r	14	M Webber	Jaguar	R4	Ford Cosworth	V10	21	accident	14	7
r	4	R Schumacher	Williams	FW25	BMW	V10	21	accident	5	3
r	2	R Barrichello	Ferrari	F2003-GA	Ferrari	V10	2	accident	2	1
ap	34	A McNish	Renault	R23B	Renault	V10				
ap	39	G Bruni	Minardi	PS03	Ford Cosworth	V10				
ap	36	B Wirdheim	Jordan	EJ13	Ford Cosworth	V10				

Winning speed 196.164 km/h, 121.891 mph
Pole Position speed 210.565 km/h, 130.839 mph (K Räikkönen, 1 min:11.670 sec)
Fastest Lap speed 211.145 km/h, 131.200 mph (M Schumacher, 1 min:11.473 sec on lap 13)
Lap Leaders K Räikkönen 1-18 (18); M Schumacher 19,38-47,49-73 (36); M Webber, 20-21 (2); D Coulthard 22 (1); J Button 23-37 (15); H-H Frentzen 48 (1).

12 Oct 2003   JAPAN: Suzuka   (Round 16)   (Race 713)
53 laps x 5.807 km, 3.608 miles = 307.573 km, 191.117 miles

Pos	No	Driver	Car	Model	Engine		Laps	Time/Reason for Retirement	Grid Pos	Row
1	2	R Barrichello	Ferrari	F2003-GA	Ferrari	V10	53	1h 25m 11.743s	1	1
2	6	K Räikkönen	McLaren	MP4-17D	Mercedes-Benz	V10	53	1h 25m 22.828s	8	4
3	5	D Coulthard	McLaren	MP4-17D	Mercedes-Benz	V10	53	1h 25m 23.357s	7	4
4	17	J Button	BAR	005	Honda	V10	53	1h 25m 44.849s	9	5
5	7	J Trulli	Renault	R23B	Renault	V10	53	1h 25m 46.012s	19	10
6	16	T Sato	BAR	005	Honda	V10	53	1h 26m 03.435s	13	7
7	21	C da Matta	Toyota	TF103	Toyota	V10	53	1h 26m 08.537s	3	2
8	1	M Schumacher	Ferrari	F2003-GA	Ferrari	V10	53	1h 26m 11.230s	14	7
9	9	N Heidfeld	Sauber	C22	Petronas	V10	53	1h 26m 11.902s	11	6
10	20	O Panis	Toyota	TF103	Toyota	V10	53	1h 26m 13.587s	4	2
11	14	M Webber	Jaguar	R4	Ford Cosworth	V10	53	1h 26m 22.748s	6	3
12	4	R Schumacher	Williams	FW25	BMW	V10	52		20	10
13	15	J Wilson	Jaguar	R4	Ford Cosworth	V10	52		10	5
14	12	R Firman	Jordan	EJ13	Ford Cosworth	V10	51		15	8
15	19	J Verstappen	Minardi	PS03	Ford Cosworth	V10	51		17	9
16	18	N Kiesa	Minardi	PS03	Ford Cosworth	V10	50		18	9
r	11	G Fisichella	Jordan	EJ13	Ford Cosworth	V10	33	engine	16	8
r	8	F Alonso	Renault	R23B	Renault	V10	17	engine	5	3
r	10	H-H Frentzen	Sauber	C22	Petronas	V10	9	engine	12	6
r	3	J P Montoya	Williams	FW25	BMW	V10	9	hydraulics	2	1
ap	34	A McNish	Renault	R23B	Renault	V10				
ap	36	S Motoyama	Jordan	EJ13	Ford Cosworth	V10				
ap	39	G Bruni	Minardi	PS03	Ford Cosworth	V10				

Winning speed 216.611 km/h, 134.596 mph
Pole Position speed 227.941 km/h, 141.636 mph (R Barrichello, 1 min:31.713 sec)
Fastest Lap speed 223.805 km/h, 139.066 mph (R Schumacher, 1 min:33.408 sec on lap 43)
Lap Leaders J P Montoya 1-8 (8); R Barrichello 9-12,17-40,42-53 (40); K Räikkönen 13 (1); J Button 14-16 (3); D Coulthard 41 (1).

Lap Leaders 2003

Pos	Driver	Car-Engine	GPs	laps	km	miles
1	M Schumacher	Ferrari	8	303	1,433.3	890.6
2	R Schumacher	Williams-BMW	5	164	738.3	458.8
3	J P Montoya	Williams-BMW	6	144	633.7	393.8
4	K Räikkönen	McLaren-Mercedes-Benz	11	138	679.6	422.3
5	F Alonso	Renault	5	97	441.1	274.1
6	R Barrichello	Ferrari	7	80	429.0	266.5
7	D Coulthard	McLaren-Mercedes-Benz	4	39	180.4	112.1
8	J Button	BAR-Honda	2	18	80.3	49.9
9	C da Matta	Toyota	1	17	87.4	54.3
10	J Trulli	Renault	2	14	68.4	42.5
11	M Webber	Jaguar-Ford Cosworth	1	2	8.4	5.2
12	G Fisichella	Jordan-Ford Cosworth	1	1	4.3	2.7
	H-H Frentzen	Sauber-Petronas	1	1	4.2	2.6
			16	1,018	4,788.3	2,975.3

Driver Points 2003

		AUS	MAL	BR	RSM	E	A	MC	CDN	EUR	F	GB	D	H	I	USA	J	Total
1	M Schumacher	5	3	-	10	10	10	6	10	4	6	5	2	1	10	10	1	93
2	K Räikkönen	6	10	8	8	-	8	8	3	-	5	6	-	8	5	8	8	91
3	J P Montoya	8	-	-	2	5	-	10	6	8	8	8	10	6	8	3	-	82
4	R Barrichello	-	8	-	6	6	6	1	4	6	2	10	-	-	6	-	10	65
5	R Schumacher	1	5	2	5	4	3	5	8	10	10	-	-	5	-	-	-	58
6	F Alonso	2	6	6	3	8	-	4	5	5	-	-	5	10	1	-	-	55
7	D Coulthard	10	-	5	4	-	4	2	-	4	4	8	4	-	-	6	51
8	J Trulli	4	4	1	-	-	1	3	-	-	-	3	6	2	-	5	4	33
9	J Button	-	2	-	1	-	5	-	-	2	-	1	1	-	-	-	5	17
	M Webber	-	-	-	-	2	2	-	2	3	3	-	-	3	2	-	-	17
11	H-H Frentzen	3	-	-	4	-	-	-	-	-	-	-	-	-	-	6	-	13
12	G Fisichella	-	-	10	-	-	-	-	-	-	-	-	-	-	-	2	-	12
13	C da Matta	-	-	-	-	3	-	-	-	-	-	-	2	3	-	-	2	10
14	N Heidfeld	-	1	-	-	-	-	-	-	1	-	-	-	-	-	4	-	6
	O Panis	-	-	-	-	-	-	-	1	-	1	-	4	-	-	-	-	6
	J Villeneuve	-	-	3	-	-	-	-	-	-	-	-	-	-	3	-	-	6
17	M Gené	-	-	-	-	-	-	-	-	-	-	-	-	-	4	-	-	4
18	T Sato	-	-	-	-	-	-	-	-	-	-	-	-	-	-	-	3	3
19	R Firman	-	-	-	-	1	-	-	-	-	-	-	-	-	-	-	-	1
	J Wilson	-	-	-	-	-	-	-	-	-	-	-	-	-	-	1	-	1

10,8,6,5,4,3,2 and 1 point awarded to the first eight finishers.

Constructor Points 2003

		AUS	MAL	BR	RSM	E	A	MC	CDN	EUR	F	GB	D	H	I	USA	J	Total
1	Ferrari	5	11	-	16	16	16	7	14	10	8	15	2	1	16	10	11	158
2	Williams-BMW	9	5	2	7	9	3	15	14	18	18	8	10	11	12	3	-	144
3	McLaren-Mercedes-Benz	16	10	13	12	-	12	10	3	-	9	10	8	12	5	8	14	142
4	Renault	6	10	7	3	8	1	7	5	5	-	3	11	12	1	5	4	88
5	BAR-Honda	-	2	3	1	-	5	-	-	2	-	1	1	-	3	-	8	26
6	Sauber-Petronas	3	1	4	-	-	-	-	-	1	-	-	-	-	-	10	-	19
7	Jaguar-Ford Cosworth	-	-	-	-	2	2	-	2	3	3	-	-	3	2	1	-	18
8	Toyota	-	-	-	-	3	-	-	1	-	-	1	2	7	-	-	2	16
9	Jordan-Ford Cosworth	-	-	10	-	1	-	-	-	-	-	-	-	-	-	2	-	13

10,8,6,5,4,3,2 and 1 point awarded to the first eight finishers.

2004

Race Entrants and Results

The championship expanded to 18 races for the first time, with two new countries hosting F1 with brand new venues in Bahrain and China. Timetables changed again with teams outside the top four permitted to use their test or third driver on Fridays. Qualifying sessions took place back to back on a Saturday with any engine failure during the practice sessions resulting in a 10-place grid penalty. Ferrari dominated from the onset and Ford announced its withdrawal from Formula 1 in September leaving Jaguar and other Cosworth-powered teams looking at alternative options for 2005.

FERRARI
Scuderia Ferrari Marlboro: M Schumacher, Barrichello

WILLIAMS
BMW WilliamsF1 Team: Montoya, R Schumacher, Gené, Pizzonia

McLAREN
West McLaren Mercedes: Coulthard, Räikkönen

RENAULT
Mild Seven Renault F1 Team: Trulli, Alonso, Villeneuve

BAR
Lucky Strike B.A.R. Honda: Button, Sato

SAUBER
Sauber Petronas: Fisichella, Massa

JAGUAR
Jaguar Racing: Webber, Klien

TOYOTA
Panasonic Toyota Racing: da Matta, Panis, Zonta, Trulli

JORDAN
Jordan Ford: Heidfeld, Pantano, Glock

MINARDI
European Minardi Cosworth: Bruni, Baumgartner.

7 Mar 2004		AUSTRALIA: Melbourne						(Round 1)		(Race 714)
		58 laps x 5.303 km, 3.295 miles = 307.574 km, 191.118 miles								

Pos	No	Driver	Car	Model	Engine		Laps	Time/Reason for Retirement	Grid Pos	Row
1	1	M Schumacher	Ferrari	F2004	Ferrari	V10	58	1h 24m 15.757s	1	1
2	2	R Barrichello	Ferrari	F2004	Ferrari	V10	58	1h 24m 29.362s	2	1
3	8	F Alonso	Renault	R24	Renault	V10	58	1h 24m 50.430s	5	3
4	4	R Schumacher	Williams	FW26	BMW	V10	58	1h 25m 16.180s	8	4
5	3	J P Montoya	Williams	FW26	BMW	V10	58	1h 25m 24.293s	3	2
6	9	J Button	BAR	006	Honda	V10	58	1h 25m 26.355s	4	2
7	7	J Trulli	Renault	R24	Renault	V10	57		9	5
8	5	D Coulthard	McLaren	MP4-19	Mercedes-Benz	V10	57		12	6
9	10	T Sato	BAR	006	Honda	V10	57		7	4
10	11	G Fisichella	Sauber	C23	Petronas	V10	57		14	7
11	15	C Klien	Jaguar	R5	Ford Cosworth	V10	56		19	10
12	16	C da Matta	Toyota	TF104	Toyota	V10	56		13	7
13	17	O Panis	Toyota	TF104	Toyota	V10	56		18	9
14	19	G Pantano	Jordan	EJ14	Ford Cosworth	V10	55		16	8
r	12	F Massa	Sauber	C23	Petronas	V10	44	engine	11	6
r	18	N Heidfeld	Jordan	EJ14	Ford Cosworth	V10	43	accident	15	8
nc	20	G Bruni	Minardi	PS04B	Ford Cosworth	V10	43		20	10
r	14	M Webber	Jaguar	R5	Ford Cosworth	V10	29	gearbox	6	3
r	21	Z Baumgartner	Minardi	PS04B	Ford Cosworth	V10	13	electronics	17	9
r	6	K Räikkönen	McLaren	MP4-19	Mercedes-Benz	V10	9	engine	10	5
ap	38	*R Zonta*	*Toyota*	*TF104*	*Toyota*	*V10*				
ap	35	*A Davidson*	*BAR*	*006*	*Honda*	*V10*				
ap	37	*B Wirdheim*	*Jaguar*	*R5*	*Ford Cosworth*	*V10*				
ap	39	*T Glock*	*Jordan*	*EJ14*	*Ford Cosworth*	*V10*				

Winning speed 219.011 km/h, 136.087 mph
Pole Position speed 226.172 km/h, 140.537 mph (M Schumacher, 1 min:24.408 sec)
Fastest Lap speed 226.933 km/h, 141.010 mph (M Schumacher, 1 min:24.125 sec on lap 29)
Lap Leaders M Schumacher 1-58 (58).

21 Mar 2004 **MALAYSIA: Sepang** (Round 2) (Race 715)

56 laps x 5.543 km, 3.444 miles = 310.408 km, 192.879 miles

Pos	No	Driver	Car	Model	Engine		Laps	Time/Reason for Retirement	Grid Pos	Row
1	1	M Schumacher	Ferrari	F2004	Ferrari	V10	56	1h 31m 07.490s	1	1
2	3	J P Montoya	Williams	FW26	BMW	V10	56	1h 31m 12.512s	4	2
3	9	J Button	BAR	006	Honda	V10	56	1h 31m 19.058s	6	3
4	2	R Barrichello	Ferrari	F2004	Ferrari	V10	56	1h 31m 21.106s	3	2
5	7	J Trulli	Renault	R24	Renault	V10	56	1h 31m 44.850s	8	4
6	5	D Coulthard	McLaren	MP4-19	Mercedes-Benz	V10	56	1h 32m 00.588s	9	5
7	8	F Alonso	Renault	R24	Renault	V10	56	1h 32m 15.367s	19	10
8	12	F Massa	Sauber	C23	Petronas	V10	55		11	6
9	16	C da Matta	Toyota	TF104	Toyota	V10	55		10	5
10	15	C Klien	Jaguar	R5	Ford Cosworth	V10	55		13	7
11	11	G Fisichella	Sauber	C23	Petronas	V10	55		12	6
12	17	O Panis	Toyota	TF104	Toyota	V10	55		14	7
13	19	G Pantano	Jordan	EJ14	Ford Cosworth	V10	54		18	9
14	20	G Bruni	Minardi	PS04B	Ford Cosworth	V10	53		16	8
15r	10	T Sato	BAR	006	Honda	V10	52	engine	20	10
16	21	Z Baumgartner	Minardi	PS04B	Ford Cosworth	V10	52		17	9
r	6	K Räikkönen	McLaren	MP4-19	Mercedes-Benz	V10	40	transmission	5	3
r	18	N Heidfeld	Jordan	EJ14	Ford Cosworth	V10	34	gearbox	15	8
r	4	R Schumacher	Williams	FW26	BMW	V10	27	engine	7	4
r	14	M Webber	Jaguar	R5	Ford Cosworth	V10	23	spin	2	1
ap	38	R Zonta	Toyota	TF104	Toyota	V10				
ap	35	A Davidson	BAR	006	Honda	V10				
ap	37	B Wirdheim	Jaguar	R5	Ford Cosworth	V10				
ap	39	T Glock	Jordan	EJ14	Ford Cosworth	V10				
ap	40	B Leinders	Minardi	PS04B	Ford Cosworth	V10				

Winning speed 204.384 km/h, 126.998 mph
Pole Position speed 214.397 km/h, 133.220 mph (M Schumacher, 1 min:33.074 sec)
Fastest Lap speed 211.782 km/h, 131.596 mph (J P Montoya, 1 min:34.223 sec on lap 28)
Lap Leaders M Schumacher 1-9,13-26,28-56 (52); J P Montoya 10-12 (3); R Barrichello 27 (1).

4 Apr 2004 **BAHRAIN: Sakhir** (Round 3) (Race 716)

57 laps x 5.417 km, 3.366 miles = 308.523 km, 191.707 miles

Pos	No	Driver	Car	Model	Engine		Laps	Time/Reason for Retirement	Grid Pos	Row
1	1	M Schumacher	Ferrari	F2004	Ferrari	V10	57	1h 28m 34.875s	1	1
2	2	R Barrichello	Ferrari	F2004	Ferrari	V10	57	1h 28m 36.242s	2	1
3	9	J Button	BAR	006	Honda	V10	57	1h 29m 01.562s	6	3
4	7	J Trulli	Renault	R24	Renault	V10	57	1h 29m 07.089s	7	4
5	10	T Sato	BAR	006	Honda	V10	57	1h 29m 27.335s	5	3
6	8	F Alonso	Renault	R24	Renault	V10	57	1h 29m 28.031s	16	8
7	4	R Schumacher	Williams	FW26	BMW	V10	57	1h 29m 33.030s	4	2
8	14	M Webber	Jaguar	R5	Ford Cosworth	V10	56		14	7
9	17	O Panis	Toyota	TF104	Toyota	V10	56		8	4
10	16	C da Matta	Toyota	TF104	Toyota	V10	56		9	5
11	11	G Fisichella	Sauber	C23	Petronas	V10	56		11	6
12	12	F Massa	Sauber	C23	Petronas	V10	56		13	7
13	3	J P Montoya	Williams	FW26	BMW	V10	56		3	2
14	15	C Klien	Jaguar	R5	Ford Cosworth	V10	56		12	6
15	18	N Heidfeld	Jordan	EJ14	Ford Cosworth	V10	56		18	9
16	19	G Pantano	Jordan	EJ14	Ford Cosworth	V10	55		15	8
17	20	G Bruni	Minardi	PS04B	Ford Cosworth	V10	52		17	9
r	5	D Coulthard	McLaren	MP4-19	Mercedes-Benz	V10	50	pneumatic valve system	10	5
r	21	Z Baumgartner	Minardi	PS04B	Ford Cosworth	V10	44	engine	20	10
r	6	K Räikkönen	McLaren	MP4-19	Mercedes-Benz	V10	7	engine	19	10
ap	35	A Davidson	BAR	006	Honda	V10				
ap	38	R Zonta	Toyota	TF104	Toyota	V10				
ap	39	T Glock	Jordan	EJ14	Ford Cosworth	V10				
ap	37	B Wirdheim	Jaguar	R5	Ford Cosworth	V10				
ap	40	B Leinders	Minardi	PS04B	Ford Cosworth	V10				

Winning speed 208.976 km/h, 129.852 mph
Pole Position speed 216.345 km/h, 134.431 mph (M Schumacher, 1 min:30.139 sec)
Fastest Lap speed 216.074 km/h, 134.263 mph (M Schumacher, 1 min:30.252 sec on lap 7)
Lap Leaders M Schumacher 1-9,12-24,28-41,44-57 (50); R Barrichello, 10,25-27,42-43 (6); J Button, 11 (1).

Engine change grid penalty: N Heidfeld.

25 Apr 2004   SAN MARINO: Imola   (Round 4)   (Race 717)

62 laps x 4.933 km, 3.065 miles = 305.609 km, 189.897 miles

Pos	No	Driver	Car	Model	Engine		Laps	Time/Reason for Retirement	Grid Pos	Row
1	1	M Schumacher	Ferrari	F2004	Ferrari	V10	62	1h 26m 19.670s	2	1
2	9	J Button	BAR	006	Honda	V10	62	1h 26m 29.372s	1	1
3	3	J P Montoya	Williams	FW26	BMW	V10	62	1h 26m 41.287s	3	2
4	8	F Alonso	Renault	R24	Renault	V10	62	1h 26m 43.324s	6	3
5	7	J Trulli	Renault	R24	Renault	V10	62	1h 26m 55.886s	9	5
6	2	R Barrichello	Ferrari	F2004	Ferrari	V10	62	1h 26m 56.353s	4	2
7	4	R Schumacher	Williams	FW26	BMW	V10	62	1h 27m 15.400s	5	3
8	6	K Räikkönen	McLaren	MP4-19	Mercedes-Benz	V10	61		20	10
9	11	G Fisichella	Sauber	C23	Petronas	V10	61		19	10
10	12	F Massa	Sauber	C23	Petronas	V10	61		12	6
11	17	O Panis	Toyota	TF104	Toyota	V10	61		13	7
12	5	D Coulthard	McLaren	MP4-19	Mercedes-Benz	V10	61		11	6
13	14	M Webber	Jaguar	R5	Ford Cosworth	V10	61		8	4
14	15	C Klien	Jaguar	R5	Ford Cosworth	V10	60		14	7
15	21	Z Baumgartner	Minardi	PS04B	Ford Cosworth	V10	58		18	9
16r	10	T Sato	BAR	006	Honda	V10	56	engine	7	4
r	18	N Heidfeld	Jordan	EJ14	Ford Cosworth	V10	48	driveshaft	16	8
r	16	C da Matta	Toyota	TF104	Toyota	V10	32	accident	10	5
r	20	G Bruni	Minardi	PS04B	Ford Cosworth	V10	22	brakes	17	9
r	19	G Pantano	Jordan	EJ14	Ford Cosworth	V10	6	hydraulics	15	8
ap	35	A Davidson	BAR	006	Honda	V10				
ap	38	R Zonta	Toyota	TF104	Toyota	V10				
ap	37	B Wirdheim	Jaguar	R5	Ford Cosworth	V10				
ap	39	T Glock	Jordan	EJ14	Ford Cosworth	V10				
ap	40	B Leinders	Minardi	PS04B	Ford Cosworth	V10				

Winning speed 212.405 km/h, 131.983 mph
Pole Position speed 222.672 km/h, 138.362 mph (J Button, 1 min:19.753 sec)
Fastest Lap speed 220.850 km/h, 137.230 mph (M Schumacher, 1 min:20.411 sec on lap 10)
Lap Leaders J Button 1-8 (8); M Schumacher 9-62 (54).

9 May 2004   SPAIN: Montmeló   (Round 5)   (Race 718)

66 laps x 4.627 km, 2.875 miles = 305.256 km, 189.677 miles

Pos	No	Driver	Car	Model	Engine		Laps	Time/Reason for Retirement	Grid Pos	Row
1	1	M Schumacher	Ferrari	F2004	Ferrari	V10	66	1h 27m 32.841s	1	1
2	2	R Barrichello	Ferrari	F2004	Ferrari	V10	66	1h 27m 46.131s	5	3
3	7	J Trulli	Renault	R24	Renault	V10	66	1h 28m 05.135s	4	2
4	8	F Alonso	Renault	R24	Renault	V10	66	1h 28m 05.793s	8	4
5	10	T Sato	BAR	006	Honda	V10	66	1h 28m 15.168s	3	2
6	4	R Schumacher	Williams	FW26	BMW	V10	66	1h 28m 46.645s	6	3
7	11	G Fisichella	Sauber	C23	Petronas	V10	66	1h 28m 49.949s	12	6
8	9	J Button	BAR	006	Honda	V10	65		14	7
9	12	F Massa	Sauber	C23	Petronas	V10	65		17	9
10	5	D Coulthard	McLaren	MP4-19	Mercedes-Benz	V10	65		10	5
11	6	K Räikkönen	McLaren	MP4-19	Mercedes-Benz	V10	65		13	7
12	14	M Webber	Jaguar	R5	Ford Cosworth	V10	65		9	5
13	16	C da Matta	Toyota	TF104	Toyota	V10	65		11	6
r	19	G Pantano	Jordan	EJ14	Ford Cosworth	V10	51	power steering seal	19	10
r	3	J P Montoya	Williams	FW26	BMW	V10	46	brakes	2	1
r	15	C Klien	Jaguar	R5	Ford Cosworth	V10	43	throttle	16	8
r	17	O Panis	Toyota	TF104	Toyota	V10	33	hydraulics	7	4
r	18	N Heidfeld	Jordan	EJ14	Ford Cosworth	V10	33	hydraulics	15	8
r	20	G Bruni	Minardi	PS04B	Ford Cosworth	V10	31	brakes / spin	18	9
r	21	Z Baumgartner	Minardi	PS04B	Ford Cosworth	V10	17	spin	20	10
ap	35	A Davidson	BAR	006	Honda	V10				
ap	38	R Zonta	Toyota	TF104	Toyota	V10				
ap	39	T Glock	Jordan	EJ14	Ford Cosworth	V10				
ap	37	B Wirdheim	Jaguar	R5	Ford Cosworth	V10				
ap	40	B Leinders	Minardi	PS04B	Ford Cosworth	V10				

Winning speed 209.205 km/h, 129.994 mph
Pole Position speed 222.030 km/h, 137.964 mph (M Schumacher, 1 min:15.022 sec)
Fastest Lap speed 215.070 km/h, 133.639 mph (M Schumacher, 1 min:17.450 sec on lap 12)
Lap Leaders J Trulli 1-8 (8); M Schumacher 9-10,18-66 (51); R Barrichello 11-17 (7).

MONACO: Monte-Carlo (Round 6) (Race 719)

77 laps x 3.340 km, 2.075 miles = 257.180 km, 159.804 miles

Pos	No	Driver	Car	Model	Engine		Laps	Time/Reason for Retirement	Grid Pos	Row
1	7	J Trulli	Renault	R24	Renault	V10	77	1h 45m 46.601s	1	1
2	9	J Button	BAR	006	Honda	V10	77	1h 45m 47.098s	2	1
3	2	R Barrichello	Ferrari	F2004	Ferrari	V10	77	1h 47m 02.367s	6	3
4	3	J P Montoya	Williams	FW26	BMW	V10	76		9	5
5	12	F Massa	Sauber	C23	Petronas	V10	76		16	8
6	16	C da Matta	Toyota	TF104	Toyota	V10	76		15	8
7	18	N Heidfeld	Jordan	EJ14	Ford Cosworth	V10	75		17	9
8	17	O Panis	Toyota	TF104	Toyota	V10	74		13	7
9	21	Z Baumgartner	Minardi	PS04B	Ford Cosworth	V10	71		19	10
10r	4	R Schumacher	Williams	FW26	BMW	V10	69	gearbox	12	6
r	1	M Schumacher	Ferrari	F2004	Ferrari	V10	45	accident	4	2
r	8	F Alonso	Renault	R24	Renault	V10	41	accident	3	2
r	6	K Räikkönen	McLaren	MP4-19	Mercedes-Benz	V10	27	engine pneumatics	5	3
r	20	G Bruni	Minardi	PS04B	Ford Cosworth	V10	15	gearbox	20	10
r	19	G Pantano	Jordan	EJ14	Ford Cosworth	V10	12	gearbox	18	9
r	14	M Webber	Jaguar	R5	Ford Cosworth	V10	11	electronics	11	6
r	10	T Sato	BAR	006	Honda	V10	2	engine	7	4
r	5	D Coulthard	McLaren	MP4-19	Mercedes-Benz	V10	2	accident	8	4
r	11	G Fisichella	Sauber	C23	Petronas	V10	2	accident	10	5
r	15	C Klien	Jaguar	R5	Ford Cosworth	V10	0	accident	14	7
ap	35	A Davidson	BAR	006	Honda	V10				
ap	38	R Zonta	Toyota	TF104	Toyota	V10				
ap	39	T Glock	Jordan	EJ14	Ford Cosworth	V10				
ap	40	B Leinders	Minardi	PS04B	Ford Cosworth	V10				
ap	37	B Wirdheim	Jaguar	R5	Ford Cosworth	V10				

Winning speed 145.880 km/h, 90.646 mph
Pole Position speed 162.519 km/h, 100.985 mph (J Trulli, 1 min:13.985 sec)
Fastest Lap speed 161.528 km/h, 100.369 mph (M Schumacher, 1 min:14.439 sec on lap 23)
Lap Leaders J Trulli 1-23,26-42,46-77 (72); F Alonso 24 (1); M Schumacher 25,43-45 (4).

Engine change grid penalty: R Schumacher.

EUROPE: Nürburgring (Round 7) (Race 720)

60 laps x 5.148 km, 3.199 miles = 308.863 km, 191.919 miles

Pos	No	Driver	Car	Model	Engine		Laps	Time/Reason for Retirement	Grid Pos	Row
1	1	M Schumacher	Ferrari	F2004	Ferrari	V10	60	1h 32m 35.101s	1	1
2	2	R Barrichello	Ferrari	F2004	Ferrari	V10	60	1h 32m 53.090s	7	4
3	9	J Button	BAR	006	Honda	V10	60	1h 32m 57.634s	5	3
4	7	J Trulli	Renault	R24	Renault	V10	60	1h 33m 28.774s	3	2
5	8	F Alonso	Renault	R24	Renault	V10	60	1h 33m 36.088s	6	3
6	11	G Fisichella	Sauber	C23	Petronas	V10	60	1h 33m 48.549s	18	9
7	14	M Webber	Jaguar	R5	Ford Cosworth	V10	60	1h 33m 51.307s	14	7
8	3	J P Montoya	Williams	FW26	BMW	V10	59		8	4
9	12	F Massa	Sauber	C23	Petronas	V10	59		16	8
10	18	N Heidfeld	Jordan	EJ14	Ford Cosworth	V10	59		13	7
11	17	O Panis	Toyota	TF104	Toyota	V10	59		10	5
12	15	C Klien	Jaguar	R5	Ford Cosworth	V10	59		12	6
13	19	G Pantano	Jordan	EJ14	Ford Cosworth	V10	58		15	8
14	20	G Bruni	Minardi	PS04B	Ford Cosworth	V10	57		19	10
15	21	Z Baumgartner	Minardi	PS04B	Ford Cosworth	V10	57		17	9
r	10	T Sato	BAR	006	Honda	V10	47	engine	2	1
r	5	D Coulthard	McLaren	MP4-19	Mercedes-Benz	V10	25	engine	20	10
r	6	K Räikkönen	McLaren	MP4-19	Mercedes-Benz	V10	9	engine	4	2
r	4	R Schumacher	Williams	FW26	BMW	V10	0	accident	9	5
r	16	C da Matta	Toyota	TF104	Toyota	V10	0	accident	11	6
ap	35	A Davidson	BAR	006	Honda	V10				
ap	38	R Zonta	Toyota	TF104	Toyota	V10				
ap	37	B Wirdheim	Jaguar	R5	Ford Cosworth	V10				
ap	39	T Glock	Jordan	EJ14	Ford Cosworth	V10				
ap	40	B Leinders	Minardi	PS04B	Ford Cosworth	V10				

Winning speed 200.159 km/h, 124.373 mph
Pole Position speed 209.763 km/h, 130.341 mph (M Schumacher, 1 min:28.351 sec)
Fastest Lap speed 207.144 km/h, 128.714 mph (M Schumacher, 1 min:29.468 sec on lap 7)
Lap Leaders M Schumacher 1-8,16-60 (53); Alonso 9 (1); T Sato 10-11 (2); R Barrichello 12-15 (4).

Engine change grid penalty: D Coulthard. M Webber received a 1 sec penalty in qualifying due to setting his time under waved yellow flags.

CANADA: Montréal **(Round 8)** **(Race 721)**

70 laps x 4.361 km, 2.710 miles = 305.270 km, 189.686 miles

Pos	No	Driver	Car	Model	Engine		Laps	Time/Reason for Retirement	Grid Pos	Row
1	1	M Schumacher	Ferrari	F2004	Ferrari	V10	70	1h 28m 24.803s	6	3
dq	4	R Schumacher	Williams	FW26	BMW	V10	70	1h 28m 25.865s	1	1
2	2	R Barrichello	Ferrari	F2004	Ferrari	V10	70	1h 28m 29.911s	7	4
3	9	J Button	BAR	006	Honda	V10	70	1h 28m 45.212s	2	1
dq	3	J P Montoya	Williams	FW26	BMW	V10	70	1h 28m 46.003s	4	2
4	11	G Fisichella	Sauber	C23	Petronas	V10	69		11	6
5	6	K Räikkönen	McLaren	MP4-19	Mercedes-Benz	V10	69		8	4
dq	16	C da Matta	Toyota	TF104	Toyota	V10	69		12	6
6	5	D Coulthard	McLaren	MP4-19	Mercedes-Benz	V10	69		9	5
dq	17	O Panis	Toyota	TF104	Toyota	V10	69		13	7
7	19	T Glock	Jordan	EJ14	Ford Cosworth	V10	68		16	8
8	18	N Heidfeld	Jordan	EJ14	Ford Cosworth	V10	68		15	8
9	15	C Klien	Jaguar	R5	Ford Cosworth	V10	67		10	5
10	21	Z Baumgartner	Minardi	PS04B	Ford Cosworth	V10	66		18	9
r	12	F Massa	Sauber	C23	Petronas	V10	62	brake disc / rear wheel / accident	17	9
r	10	T Sato	BAR	006	Honda	V10	48	engine	20	10
r	8	F Alonso	Renault	R24	Renault	V10	44	driveshaft	5	3
r	20	G Bruni	Minardi	PS04B	Ford Cosworth	V10	30	gearbox	19	10
r	14	M Webber	Jaguar	R5	Ford Cosworth	V10	6	accident / front suspension	14	7
r	7	J Trulli	Renault	R24	Renault	V10	0	driveshaft / rear suspension	3	2
ap	35	A Davidson	BAR	006	Honda	V10				
ap	38	R Zonta	Toyota	TF104	Toyota	V10				
ap	40	B Leinders	Minardi	PS04B	Ford Cosworth	V10				
ap	37	B Wirdheim	Jaguar	R5	Ford Cosworth	V10				

Winning speed 207.165 km/h, 128.727 mph
Pole Position speed 217.220 km/h, 134.974 mph (R Schumacher, 1 min:12.275 sec)
Fastest Lap speed 213.246 km/h, 132.505 mph (R Barrichello, 1 min:13.622 sec on lap 68)
Lap Leaders R Schumacher 1-14,19-32,47 (29); F Alonso 15-16 (2); M Schumacher 17-18,33-46,48-70 (39).

Williams and Toyota cars all disqualified for brake duct infringements.
Engine change grid penalty: Z Baumgartner; Refuelling grid penalty: T Sato.
T Glock also practised in car no. 39.

20 Jun 2004 **USA: Indianapolis** **(Round 9)** **(Race 722)**

73 laps x 4.192 km, 2.605 miles = 306.016 km, 190.150 miles

Pos	No	Driver	Car	Model	Engine		Laps	Time/Reason for Retirement	Grid Pos	Row
1	1	M Schumacher	Ferrari	F2004	Ferrari	V10	73	1h 40m 29.914s	2	1
2	2	R Barrichello	Ferrari	F2004	Ferrari	V10	73	1h 40m 32.864s	1	1
3	10	T Sato	BAR	006	Honda	V10	73	1h 40m 51.950s	3	2
4	7	J Trulli	Renault	R24	Renault	V10	73	1h 41m 04.458s	20	10
5	17	O Panis	Toyota	TF104	Toyota	V10	73	1h 41m 07.448s	8	4
6	6	K Räikkönen	McLaren	MP4-19	Mercedes-Benz	V10	72		7	4
7	5	D Coulthard	McLaren	MP4-19	Mercedes-Benz	V10	72		12	6
8	21	Z Baumgartner	Minardi	PS04B	Ford Cosworth	V10	70		19	10
9r	11	G Fisichella	Sauber	C23	Petronas	V10	65	hydraulics	14	7
r	14	M Webber	Jaguar	R5	Ford Cosworth	V10	60	engine oil leak / fire	10	5
dq	3	J P Montoya	Williams	FW26	BMW	V10	59	switched cars too late	5	3
r	18	N Heidfeld	Jordan	EJ14	Ford Cosworth	V10	43	engine	16	8
r	9	J Button	BAR	006	Honda	V10	26	gearbox	4	2
r	16	C da Matta	Toyota	TF104	Toyota	V10	17	accident / gearbox	11	6
r	4	R Schumacher	Williams	FW26	BMW	V10	9	rear tyre / accident	6	3
r	8	F Alonso	Renault	R24	Renault	V10	8	rear tyre burst / accident	9	5
r	15	C Klien	Jaguar	R5	Ford Cosworth	V10	0	accident	13	7
r	12	F Massa	Sauber	C23	Petronas	V10	0	accident	15	8
r	19	G Pantano	Jordan	EJ14	Ford Cosworth	V10	0	accident	17	9
r	20	G Bruni	Minardi	PS04B	Ford Cosworth	V10	0	accident	18	9
ap	35	A Davidson	BAR	006	Honda	V10				
ap	38	R Zonta	Toyota	TF104	Toyota	V10				
ap	37	B Wirdheim	Jaguar	R5	Ford Cosworth	V10				
ap	39	T Glock	Jordan	EJ14	Ford Cosworth	V10				
ap	40	B Leinders	Minardi	PS04B	Ford Cosworth	V10				

Winning speed 182.698 km/h, 113.524 mph
Pole Position speed 214.903 km/h, 133.535 mph (R Barrichello, 1 min:10.223 sec)
Fastest Lap speed 214.366 km/h, 133.201 mph (R Barrichello, 1 min:10.399 sec on lap 7)
Lap Leaders R Barrichello 1-5,42-50 (14); M Schumacher 6-41,51-73 (59).

4 Jul 2004   FRANCE: Magny-Cours   (Round 10)   (Race 723)

70 laps x 4.411 km, 2.741 miles = 308.586 km, 191.746 miles

Pos	No	Driver	Car	Model	Engine		Laps	Time/Reason for Retirement	Grid Pos	Row
1	1	M Schumacher	Ferrari	F2004	Ferrari	V10	70	1h 30m 18.133s	2	1
2	8	F Alonso	Renault	R24	Renault	V10	70	1h 30m 26.462s	1	1
3	2	R Barrichello	Ferrari	F2004	Ferrari	V10	70	1h 30m 49.755s	10	5
4	7	J Trulli	Renault	R24	Renault	V10	70	1h 30m 50.215s	5	3
5	9	J Button	BAR	006	Honda	V10	70	1h 30m 50.617s	4	2
6	5	D Coulthard	McLaren	MP4-19B	Mercedes-Benz	V10	70	1h 30m 53.653s	3	2
7	6	K Räikkönen	McLaren	MP4-19B	Mercedes-Benz	V10	70	1h 30m 54.363s	9	5
8	3	J P Montoya	Williams	FW26	BMW	V10	70	1h 31m 01.552s	6	3
9	14	M Webber	Jaguar	R5	Ford Cosworth	V10	70	1h 31m 10.527s	12	6
10	4	M Gené	Williams	FW26	BMW	V10	70	1h 31m 16.299s	8	4
11	15	C Klien	Jaguar	R5	Ford Cosworth	V10	69		13	7
12	11	G Fisichella	Sauber	C23	Petronas	V10	69		15	8
13	12	F Massa	Sauber	C23	Petronas	V10	69		16	8
14	16	C da Matta	Toyota	TF104	Toyota	V10	69		11	6
15	17	O Panis	Toyota	TF104	Toyota	V10	68		14	7
16	18	N Heidfeld	Jordan	EJ14	Ford Cosworth	V10	68		17	9
17	19	G Pantano	Jordan	EJ14	Ford Cosworth	V10	67		18	9
18r	20	G Bruni	Minardi	PS04B	Ford Cosworth	V10	65	gearbox oil leak	19	10
r	21	Z Baumgartner	Minardi	PS04B	Ford Cosworth	V10	31	accident	20	10
r	10	T Sato	BAR	006	Honda	V10	15	engine	7	4
ap	35	A Davidson	BAR	006	Honda	V10				
ap	38	R Zonta	Toyota	TF104	Toyota	V10				
ap	37	B Wirdheim	Jaguar	R5	Ford Cosworth	V10				
ap	39	T Glock	Jordan	EJ14	Ford Cosworth	V10				
ap	40	B Leinders	Minardi	PS04B	Ford Cosworth	V10				

Winning speed 205.035 km/h, 127.403 mph
Pole Position speed 215.468 km/h, 133.886 mph (F Alonso, 1 min:13.698 sec)
Fastest Lap speed 210.669 km/h, 130.904 mph (M Schumacher, 1 min:15.377 sec on lap 32)
Lap Leaders F Alonso 1-32,43-46 (36); M Schumacher 33-42,47-70 (34).

11 Jul 2004   BRITAIN: Silverstone   (Round 11)   (Race 724)

60 laps x 5.141 km, 3.194 miles = 308.355 km, 191.603 miles

Pos	No	Driver	Car	Model	Engine		Laps	Time/Reason for Retirement	Grid Pos	Row
1	1	M Schumacher	Ferrari	F2004	Ferrari	V10	60	1h 24m 42.700s	4	2
2	6	K Räikkönen	McLaren	MP4-19B	Mercedes-Benz	V10	60	1h 24m 44.830s	1	1
3	2	R Barrichello	Ferrari	F2004	Ferrari	V10	60	1h 24m 45.814s	2	1
4	9	J Button	BAR	006	Honda	V10	60	1h 24m 53.383s	3	2
5	3	J P Montoya	Williams	FW26	BMW	V10	60	1h 24m 54.873s	7	4
6	11	G Fisichella	Sauber	C23	Petronas	V10	60	1h 24m 55.588s	20	10
7	5	D Coulthard	McLaren	MP4-19B	Mercedes-Benz	V10	60	1h 25m 02.368s	6	3
8	14	M Webber	Jaguar	R5	Ford Cosworth	V10	60	1h 25m 06.401s	9	5
9	12	F Massa	Sauber	C23	Petronas	V10	60	1h 25m 06.723s	10	5
10	8	F Alonso	Renault	R24	Renault	V10	60	1h 25m 07.535s	16	8
11	10	T Sato	BAR	006	Honda	V10	60	1h 25m 16.436s	8	4
12	4	M Gené	Williams	FW26	BMW	V10	60	1h 25m 17.003s	11	6
13	16	C da Matta	Toyota	TF104	Toyota	V10	59		12	6
14	15	C Klien	Jaguar	R5	Ford Cosworth	V10	59		13	7
15	18	N Heidfeld	Jordan	EJ14	Ford Cosworth	V10	59		15	8
16	20	G Bruni	Minardi	PS04B	Ford Cosworth	V10	56		18	9
r	19	G Pantano	Jordan	EJ14	Ford Cosworth	V10	47	spin	14	7
r	7	J Trulli	Renault	R24	Renault	V10	39	accident	5	3
r	21	Z Baumgartner	Minardi	PS04B	Ford Cosworth	V10	29	engine	19	10
r	17	O Panis	Toyota	TF104	Toyota	V10	16	fire extinguisher / spin	17	9
ap	35	A Davidson	BAR	006	Honda	V10				
ap	38	R Zonta	Toyota	TF104	Toyota	V10				
ap	37	B Wirdheim	Jaguar	R5	Ford Cosworth	V10				
ap	39	T Glock	Jordan	EJ14	Ford Cosworth	V10				
ap	40	B Leinders	Minardi	PS04B	Ford Cosworth	V10				

Winning speed 218.403 km/h, 135.709 mph
Pole Position speed 236.570 km/h, 146.998 mph (K Räikkönen, 1 min:18.233 sec)
Fastest Lap speed 235.049 km/h, 146.053 mph (M Schumacher, 1 min:18.739 sec on lap 14)
Lap Leaders K Räikkönen 1-11 (11); M Schumacher 12-60 (49).

Engine change grid penalty: F Alonso. O Panis received a grid penalty for impeding F Massa.

25 Jul 2004 GERMANY: Hockenheim (Round 12) (Race 725)

66 laps x 4.574 km, 2.842 miles = 301.884 km, 187.582 miles

Pos	No	Driver	Car	Model	Engine		Laps	Time/Reason for Retirement	Grid Pos	Row
1	1	M Schumacher	Ferrari	F2004	Ferrari	V10	66	1h 23m 54.848s	1	1
2	9	J Button	BAR	006	Honda	V10	66	1h 24m 03.236s	13	7
3	8	F Alonso	Renault	R24	Renault	V10	66	1h 24m 11.199s	5	3
4	5	D Coulthard	McLaren	MP4-19B	Mercedes-Benz	V10	66	1h 24m 14.079s	4	2
5	3	J P Montoya	Williams	FW26	BMW	V10	66	1h 24m 17.903s	2	1
6	14	M Webber	Jaguar	R5	Ford Cosworth	V10	66	1h 24m 35.956s	11	6
7	4	A Pizzonia	Williams	FW26	BMW	V10	66	1h 24m 36.804s	10	5
8	10	T Sato	BAR	006	Honda	V10	66	1h 24m 41.690s	8	4
9	11	G Fisichella	Sauber	C23	Petronas	V10	66	1h 25m 01.950s	14	7
10	15	C Klien	Jaguar	R5	Ford Cosworth	V10	66	1h 25m 03.426s	12	6
11	7	J Trulli	Renault	R24	Renault	V10	66	1h 25m 05.106s	6	3
12	2	R Barrichello	Ferrari	F2004	Ferrari	V10	66	1h 25m 08.100s	7	4
13	12	F Massa	Sauber	C23	Petronas	V10	65		16	8
14	17	O Panis	Toyota	TF104	Toyota	V10	65		9	5
15	19	G Pantano	Jordan	EJ14	Ford Cosworth	V10	63		17	9
16	21	Z Baumgartner	Minardi	PS04B	Ford Cosworth	V10	62		20	10
17	20	G Bruni	Minardi	PS04B	Ford Cosworth	V10	62		19	10
r	18	N Heidfeld	Jordan	EJ14	Ford Cosworth	V10	42	handling	18	9
r	16	C da Matta	Toyota	TF104	Toyota	V10	38	rear tyre / spin	15	8
r	6	K Räikkönen	McLaren	MP4-19B	Mercedes-Benz	V10	13	rear wing / accident	3	2
ap	35	A Davidson	BAR	006	Honda	V10				
ap	38	R Zonta	Toyota	TF104	Toyota	V10				
ap	37	B Wirdheim	Jaguar	R5	Ford Cosworth	V10				
ap	39	T Glock	Jordan	EJ14	Ford Cosworth	V10				
ap	40	B Leinders	Minardi	PS04B	Ford Cosworth	V10				

Winning speed 215.852 km/h, 134.124 mph
Pole Position speed 224.625 km/h, 139.576 mph (M Schumacher, 1 min:13.306 sec)
Fastest Lap speed 223.182 km/h, 138.679 mph (K Räikkönen, 1 min:13.780 sec on lap 10)
Lap Leaders M Schumacher 1-10,15-28,35-47,51-66 (53); K Räikkönen 11 (1); J Button 12-14,30-34,48-50 (11); F Alonso 29 (1).

Scheduled for 67 laps but reduced due to an aborted start.
Engine change grid penalty: J Button.

15 Aug 2004 HUNGARY: Hungaroring (Round 13) (Race 726)

70 laps x 4.381 km, 2.722 miles = 306.663 km, 190.552 miles

Pos	No	Driver	Car	Model	Engine		Laps	Time/Reason for Retirement	Grid Pos	Row
1	1	M Schumacher	Ferrari	F2004	Ferrari	V10	70	1h 35m 26.131s	1	1
2	2	R Barrichello	Ferrari	F2004	Ferrari	V10	70	1h 35m 30.827s	2	1
3	8	F Alonso	Renault	R24	Renault	V10	70	1h 36m 10.730s	5	3
4	3	J P Montoya	Williams	FW26	BMW	V10	70	1h 36m 28.744s	7	4
5	9	J Button	BAR	006	Honda	V10	70	1h 36m 33.570s	4	2
6	10	T Sato	BAR	006	Honda	V10	69		3	2
7	4	A Pizzonia	Williams	FW26	BMW	V10	69		6	3
8	11	G Fisichella	Sauber	C23	Petronas	V10	69		8	4
9	5	D Coulthard	McLaren	MP4-19B	Mercedes-Benz	V10	69		12	6
10	14	M Webber	Jaguar	R5	Ford Cosworth	V10	69		11	6
11	17	O Panis	Toyota	TF104	Toyota	V10	69		13	7
12	18	N Heidfeld	Jordan	EJ14	Ford Cosworth	V10	68		16	8
13	15	C Klien	Jaguar	R5	Ford Cosworth	V10	68		14	7
14	20	G Bruni	Minardi	PS04B	Ford Cosworth	V10	66		19	10
15	21	Z Baumgartner	Minardi	PS04B	Ford Cosworth	V10	65		18	9
r	19	G Pantano	Jordan	EJ14	Ford Cosworth	V10	48	gearbox	17	9
r	7	J Trulli	Renault	R24	Renault	V10	41	oil pressure	9	5
r	16	R Zonta	Toyota	TF104	Toyota	V10	31	electronics	15	8
r	12	F Massa	Sauber	C23	Petronas	V10	21	brakes	20	10
r	6	K Räikkönen	McLaren	MP4-19B	Mercedes-Benz	V10	13	electrics	10	5
ap	35	A Davidson	BAR	006	Honda	V10				
ap	37	B Wirdheim	Jaguar	R5	Ford Cosworth	V10				
ap	39	T Glock	Jordan	EJ14	Ford Cosworth	V10				
ap	38	R Briscoe	Toyota	TF104	Toyota	V10				
ap	40	B Leinders	Minardi	PS04B	Ford Cosworth	V10				

Winning speed 192.798 km/h, 119.799 mph
Pole Position speed 199.272 km/h, 123.822 mph (M Schumacher, 1 min:19.146 sec)
Fastest Lap speed 199.461 km/h, 123.939 mph (M Schumacher, 1 min:19.071 sec on lap 29)
Lap Leaders M Schumacher 1-70 (70).

29 Aug 2004 **BELGIUM: Spa-Francorchamps** **(Round 14)** **(Race 727)**

44 laps x 6.976 km, 4.335 miles = 306.927 km, 190.716 miles

Pos	No	Driver	Car	Model	Engine		Laps	Time/Reason for Retirement	Grid Pos	Row
1	6	K Räikkönen	McLaren	MP4-19B	Mercedes-Benz	V10	44	1h 32m 35.274s	10	5
2	1	M Schumacher	Ferrari	F2004	Ferrari	V10	44	1h 32m 38.406s	2	1
3	2	R Barrichello	Ferrari	F2004	Ferrari	V10	44	1h 32m 39.645s	6	3
4	12	F Massa	Sauber	C23	Petronas	V10	44	1h 32m 47.778s	8	4
5	11	G Fisichella	Sauber	C23	Petronas	V10	44	1h 32m 49.378s	5	3
6	15	C Klien	Jaguar	R5	Ford Cosworth	V10	44	1h 32m 49.888s	13	7
7	5	D Coulthard	McLaren	MP4-19B	Mercedes-Benz	V10	44	1h 32m 53.244s	4	2
8	17	O Panis	Toyota	TF104	Toyota	V10	44	1h 32m 53.967s	9	5
9	7	J Trulli	Renault	R24	Renault	V10	44	1h 32m 57.389s	1	1
10r	16	R Zonta	Toyota	TF104	Toyota	V10	41	engine	20	10
11	18	N Heidfeld	Jordan	EJ14	Ford Cosworth	V10	40		16	8
r	3	J P Montoya	Williams	FW26	BMW	V10	37	rear tyre / suspension / spin	11	6
r	4	A Pizzonia	Williams	FW26	BMW	V10	31	gearbox	14	7
r	9	J Button	BAR	006	Honda	V10	29	rear tyre burst / accident	12	6
r	21	Z Baumgartner	Minardi	PS04B	Ford Cosworth	V10	28	accident	18	9
r	8	F Alonso	Renault	R24	Renault	V10	11	oil leak / accident	3	2
r	14	M Webber	Jaguar	R5	Ford Cosworth	V10	0	accident	7	4
r	10	T Sato	BAR	006	Honda	V10	0	accident	15	8
r	20	G Bruni	Minardi	PS04B	Ford Cosworth	V10	0	accident	17	9
r	19	G Pantano	Jordan	EJ14	Ford Cosworth	V10	0	accident	19	10
ap	35	A Davidson	BAR	006	Honda	V10				
ap	37	B Wirdheim	Jaguar	R5	Ford Cosworth	V10				
ap	38	R Briscoe	Toyota	TF104	Toyota	V10				
ap	39	T Glock	Jordan	EJ14	Ford Cosworth	V10				
ap	40	B Leinders	Minardi	PS04B	Ford Cosworth	V10				

Winning speed 198.898 km/h, 123.590 mph
Pole Position speed 216.064 km/h, 134.256 mph (J Trulli, 1 min:56.232 sec)
Fastest Lap speed 238.931 km/h, 148.465 mph (K Räikkönen, 1 min:45.108 sec on lap 42)
Lap Leaders J Trulli 1-9 (9); F Alonso 10-11 (2); K Räikkönen 12-13,17-29,31-44 (29); J P Montoya 14 (1); M Schumacher 15,30 (2); A Pizzonia 16 (1).

---

12 Sep 2004 **ITALY: Monza** **(Round 15)** **(Race 728)**

53 laps x 5.793 km, 3.600 miles = 306.720 km, 190.587 miles

Pos	No	Driver	Car	Model	Engine		Laps	Time/Reason for Retirement	Grid Pos	Row
1	2	R Barrichello	Ferrari	F2004	Ferrari	V10	53	1h 15m 18.448s	1	1
2	1	M Schumacher	Ferrari	F2004	Ferrari	V10	53	1h 15m 19.795s	3	2
3	9	J Button	BAR	006	Honda	V10	53	1h 15m 28.645s	6	3
4	10	T Sato	BAR	006	Honda	V10	53	1h 15m 33.818s	5	3
5	3	J P Montoya	Williams	FW26	BMW	V10	53	1h 15m 50.800s	2	1
6	5	D Coulthard	McLaren	MP4-19B	Mercedes-Benz	V10	53	1h 15m 51.887s	10	5
7	4	A Pizzonia	Williams	FW26	BMW	V10	53	1h 15m 52.200s	8	4
8	11	G Fisichella	Sauber	C23	Petronas	V10	53	1h 15m 53.879s	15	8
9	14	M Webber	Jaguar	R5	Ford Cosworth	V10	53	1h 16m 15.209s	12	6
10	7	J Trulli	Renault	R24	Renault	V10	53	1h 16m 24.764s	9	5
11	16	R Zonta	Toyota	TF104	Toyota	V10	53	1h 16m 40.979s	11	6
12	12	F Massa	Sauber	C23	Petronas	V10	52		16	8
13	15	C Klien	Jaguar	R5	Ford Cosworth	V10	52		14	7
14	18	N Heidfeld	Jordan	EJ14	Ford Cosworth	V10	52		20	10
15	21	Z Baumgartner	Minardi	PS04B	Ford Cosworth	V10	50		19	10
r	8	F Alonso	Renault	R24	Renault	V10	40	spin	4	2
r	19	G Pantano	Jordan	EJ14	Ford Cosworth	V10	33	spin	17	9
r	20	G Bruni	Minardi	PS04B	Ford Cosworth	V10	29	breathing problem after pit fire	18	9
r	6	K Räikkönen	McLaren	MP4-19B	Mercedes-Benz	V10	13	water pressure	7	4
r	17	O Panis	Toyota	TF104	Toyota	V10	0	accident	13	7
ap	35	A Davidson	BAR	006	Honda	V10				
ap	37	B Wirdheim	Jaguar	R5	Ford Cosworth	V10				
ap	38	R Briscoe	Toyota	TF104	Toyota	V10				
ap	39	T Glock	Jordan	EJ14	Ford Cosworth	V10				
ap	40	B Leinders	Minardi	PS04B	Ford Cosworth	V10				

Winning speed 244.374 km/h, 151.847 mph
Pole Position speed 260.395 km/h, 161.802 mph (R Barrichello, 1 min:20.089 sec)
Fastest Lap speed 257.320 km/h, 159.892 mph (R Barrichello, 1 min:21.046 sec on lap 41)
Lap Leaders R Barrichello 1-4,37-53 (21); F Alonso 5-10 (6); J Button 11-34 (24); M Schumacher 35-36 (2).

Engine change grid penalty: N Heidfeld.

26 Sep 2004　　**CHINA: Shanghai**　　　　　　　　**(Round 16)**　　**(Race 729)**

56 laps x 5.451 km, 3.387 miles = 305.066 km, 189.559 miles

Pos	No	Driver	Car	Model	Engine		Laps	Time/Reason for Retirement	Grid Pos	Row
1	2	R Barrichello	Ferrari	F2004	Ferrari	V10	56	1h 29m 12.420s	1	1
2	9	J Button	BAR	006	Honda	V10	56	1h 29m 13.455s	3	2
3	6	K Räikkönen	McLaren	MP4-19B	Mercedes-Benz	V10	56	1h 29m 13.889s	2	1
4	8	F Alonso	Renault	R24	Renault	V10	56	1h 29m 44.930s	6	3
5	3	J P Montoya	Williams	FW26	BMW	V10	56	1h 29m 57.613s	10	5
6	10	T Sato	BAR	006	Honda	V10	56	1h 30m 07.211s	18	9
7	11	G Fisichella	Sauber	C23	Petronas	V10	56	1h 30m 17.884s	7	4
8	12	F Massa	Sauber	C23	Petronas	V10	56	1h 30m 32.500s	4	2
9	5	D Coulthard	McLaren	MP4-19B	Mercedes-Benz	V10	56	1h 30m 33.039s	9	5
10	14	M Webber	Jaguar	R5	Ford Cosworth	V10	55		11	6
11	7	J Villeneuve	Renault	R24	Renault	V10	55		12	6
12	1	M Schumacher	Ferrari	F2004	Ferrari	V10	55		20	10
13	18	N Heidfeld	Jordan	EJ14	Ford Cosworth	V10	55		14	7
14	17	O Panis	Toyota	TF104	Toyota	V10	55		8	4
15	19	T Glock	Jordan	EJ14	Ford Cosworth	V10	55		16	8
16	21	Z Baumgartner	Minardi	PS04B	Ford Cosworth	V10	53		19	10
r	20	G Bruni	Minardi	PS04B	Ford Cosworth	V10	38	front wheel lost	17	9
r	4	R Schumacher	Williams	FW26	BMW	V10	37	accident damage	5	3
r	16	R Zonta	Toyota	TF104	Toyota	V10	35	gearbox	13	7
r	15	C Klien	Jaguar	R5	Ford Cosworth	V10	11	accident / suspension	15	8
ap	35	A Davidson	BAR	006	Honda	V10				
ap	38	R Briscoe	Toyota	TF104	Toyota	V10				
ap	37	B Wirdheim	Jaguar	R5	Ford Cosworth	V10				
ap	40	B Leinders	Minardi	PS04B	Ford Cosworth	V10				
ap	39	R Doornbos	Jordan	EJ14	Ford Cosworth	V10				

Winning speed 205.185 km/h, 127.496 mph
Pole Position speed 208.735 km/h, 129.702 mph (R Barrichello, 1 min:34.012 sec)
Fastest Lap speed 212.749 km/h, 132.196 mph (M Schumacher, 1 min:32.238 sec on lap 55)
Lap Leaders R Barrichello 1-12,16-29,36-56 (47); J Button 13-14,30-35 (8); R Schumacher 15 (1).

Engine change grid penalty: T Sato; Z Baumgartner.

10 Oct 2004　　**JAPAN: Suzuka**　　　　　　　　**(Round 17)**　　**(Race 730)**

53 laps x 5.807 km, 3.608 miles = 307.573 km, 191.117 miles

Pos	No	Driver	Car	Model	Engine		Laps	Time/Reason for Retirement	Grid Pos	Row
1	1	M Schumacher	Ferrari	F2004	Ferrari	V10	53	1h 24m 26.985s	1	1
2	4	R Schumacher	Williams	FW26	BMW	V10	53	1h 24m 41.083s	2	1
3	9	J Button	BAR	006	Honda	V10	53	1h 24m 46.647s	5	3
4	10	T Sato	BAR	006	Honda	V10	53	1h 24m 58.766s	4	2
5	8	F Alonso	Renault	R24	Renault	V10	53	1h 25m 04.752s	11	6
6	6	K Räikkönen	McLaren	MP4-19B	Mercedes-Benz	V10	53	1h 25m 06.347s	12	6
7	3	J P Montoya	Williams	FW26	BMW	V10	53	1h 25m 22.332s	13	7
8	11	G Fisichella	Sauber	C23	Petronas	V10	53	1h 25m 23.261s	7	4
9	12	F Massa	Sauber	C23	Petronas	V10	53	1h 25m 56.641s	19	10
10	7	J Villeneuve	Renault	R24	Renault	V10	52		9	5
11	16	J Trulli	Toyota	TF104	Toyota	V10	52		6	3
12	15	C Klien	Jaguar	R5	Ford Cosworth	V10	52		14	7
13	18	N Heidfeld	Jordan	EJ14	Ford Cosworth	V10	52		16	8
14	17	O Panis	Toyota	TF104	Toyota	V10	51		10	5
15	19	T Glock	Jordan	EJ14	Ford Cosworth	V10	51		17	9
16	20	G Bruni	Minardi	PS04B	Ford Cosworth	V10	50		18	9
r	21	Z Baumgartner	Minardi	PS04B	Ford Cosworth	V10	41	accident	20	10
r	5	D Coulthard	McLaren	MP4-19B	Mercedes-Benz	V10	38	accident / front wheel	8	4
r	2	R Barrichello	Ferrari	F2004	Ferrari	V10	38	accident / front wheel	15	8
r	14	M Webber	Jaguar	R5	Ford Cosworth	V10	20	cockpit overheating	3	2
ap	35	A Davidson	BAR	006	Honda	V10				
ap	39	R Doornbos	Jordan	EJ14	Ford Cosworth	V10				
ap	40	B Leinders	Minardi	PS04B	Ford Cosworth	V10				
ap	38	R Briscoe	Toyota	TF104	Toyota	V10				

Winning speed 218.524 km/h, 135.785 mph
Pole Position speed 223.484 km/h, 138.867 mph (M Schumacher, 1 min:33.542 sec)
Fastest Lap speed 225.441 km/h, 140.083 mph (R Barrichello, 1 min:32.730 sec on lap 30)
Lap Leaders M Schumacher 1-53 (53).

71 laps x 4.309 km, 2.677 miles = 305.909 km, 190.083 miles

Pos	No	Driver	Car	Model	Engine		Laps	Time/Reason for Retirement	Grid Pos	Row
1	3	J P Montoya	Williams	FW26	BMW	V10	71	1h 28m 01.451s	2	1
2	6	K Räikkönen	McLaren	MP4-19B	Mercedes-Benz	V10	71	1h 28m 02.473s	3	2
3	2	R Barrichello	Ferrari	F2004	Ferrari	V10	71	1h 28m 25.550s	1	1
4	8	F Alonso	Renault	R24	Renault	V10	71	1h 28m 50.359s	8	4
5	4	R Schumacher	Williams	FW26	BMW	V10	71	1h 28m 51.191s	7	4
6	10	T Sato	BAR	006	Honda	V10	71	1h 28m 51.699s	6	3
7	1	M Schumacher	Ferrari	F2004	Ferrari	V10	71	1h 28m 52.077s	18	9
8	12	F Massa	Sauber	C23	Petronas	V10	71	1h 29m 03.761s	4	2
9	11	G Fisichella	Sauber	C23	Petronas	V10	71	1h 29m 05.293s	10	5
10	7	J Villeneuve	Renault	R24	Renault	V10	70		13	7
11	5	D Coulthard	McLaren	MP4-19B	Mercedes-Benz	V10	70		12	6
12	16	J Trulli	Toyota	TF104	Toyota	V10	70		9	5
13	17	R Zonta	Toyota	TF104	Toyota	V10	70		14	7
14	15	C Klien	Jaguar	R5	Ford Cosworth	V10	69		15	8
15	19	T Glock	Jordan	EJ14	Ford Cosworth	V10	69		17	9
16	21	Z Baumgartner	Minardi	PS04B	Ford Cosworth	V10	67		20	10
17	20	G Bruni	Minardi	PS04B	Ford Cosworth	V10	67		19	10
r	14	M Webber	Jaguar	R5	Ford Cosworth	V10	23	accident	11	6
r	18	N Heidfeld	Jordan	EJ14	Ford Cosworth	V10	15	transmission	16	8
r	9	J Button	BAR	006	Honda	V10	3	engine	5	3
ap	35	A Davidson	BAR	006	Honda	V10				
ap	38	R Briscoe	Toyota	TF104	Toyota	V10				
ap	39	R Doornbos	Jordan	EJ14	Ford Cosworth	V10				
ap	37	B Wirdheim	Jaguar	R5	Ford Cosworth	V10				
ap	40	B Leinders	Minardi	PS04B	Ford Cosworth	V10				

Winning speed 208.517 km/h, 129.566 mph
Pole Position speed 219.579 km/h, 136.440 mph (R Barrichello, 1 min:10.646 sec)
Fastest Lap speed 217.038 km/h, 134.862 mph (J P Montoya, 1 min:11.473 sec on lap 49)
Lap Leaders K Räikkönen 1-3,29,51-55 (9); R Barrichello 4-5 (2); F Massa 6-7 (2); F Alonso 8-18 (11); J P Montoya 19-28,30-50,56-71 (47).

Engine change grid penalty: M Schumacher, Z Baumgartner.

Lap Leaders 2004

Pos	Driver	Car-Engine	GPs	laps	km	miles
1	M Schumacher	Ferrari	16	683	3,356.9	2,085.9
2	R Barrichello	Ferrari	8	102	536.2	333.2
3	J Trulli	Renault	3	89	340.3	211.4
4	F Alonso	Renault	8	60	276.7	171.9
5	J Button	BAR-Honda	5	52	277.8	172.6
6	J P Montoya	Williams-BMW	3	51	226.1	140.5
7	K Räikkönen	McLaren-Mercedes-Benz	4	50	302.2	187.8
8	R Schumacher	Williams-BMW	2	30	131.9	82.0
9	T Sato	BAR-Honda	1	2	10.3	6.4
10	F Massa	Sauber-Petronas	1	2	8.6	5.4
11	A Pizzonia	Williams-BMW	1	1	7.0	4.3
			18	1,122	5,474.0	3,401.4

Driver Points 2004

Pos	Driver	AUS	MAL	BRN	RSM	E	MC	EUR	CDN	USA	F	GB	D	H	B	I	CHN	J	BR	Total
1	M Schumacher	10	10	10	10	10	-	10	10	10	10	10	10	10	8	8	-	10	2	148
2	R Barrichello	8	5	8	3	8	6	8	8	8	6	6	-	8	6	10	10	-	6	114
3	J Button	3	6	6	8	1	8	6	6	-	4	5	8	4	-	6	8	6	-	85
4	F Alonso	6	2	3	5	5	-	4	-	-	8	-	6	6	-	-	5	4	5	59
5	J P Montoya	4	8	-	6	-	5	1	-	-	1	4	4	5	-	4	4	2	10	58
6	J Trulli	2	4	5	4	6	10	5	-	5	5	-	-	-	-	-	-	-	-	46
7	K Räikkönen	-	-	-	1	-	-	-	4	3	2	8	-	-	10	-	6	3	8	45
8	T Sato	-	-	4	-	4	-	-	-	6	-	-	1	3	-	5	3	5	3	34
9	R Schumacher	5	-	2	2	3	-	-	-	-	-	-	-	-	-	-	-	8	4	24
	D Coulthard	1	3	-	-	-	-	3	2	3	2	5	-	2	3	-	-	-	-	24
11	G Fisichella	-	-	-	-	2	-	3	5	-	-	3	-	1	4	1	2	1	-	22
12	F Massa	-	1	-	-	-	4	-	-	-	-	-	-	5	-	-	-	-	1	12
13	M Webber	-	-	1	-	-	-	2	-	-	-	3	-	-	-	1	-	-	-	7
14	O Panis	-	-	-	-	-	1	-	4	-	-	-	-	-	1	-	-	-	-	6
	A Pizzonia	-	-	-	-	-	-	-	-	-	-	-	2	2	2	-	-	-	-	6
16	C Klien	-	-	-	-	-	-	-	-	-	-	-	-	-	3	-	-	-	-	3
	C da Matta	-	-	-	-	3	-	-	-	-	-	-	-	-	-	-	-	-	-	3
	N Heidfeld	-	-	-	-	-	2	-	1	-	-	-	-	-	-	-	-	-	-	3
19	T Glock	-	-	-	-	-	-	-	2	-	-	-	-	-	-	-	-	-	-	2
20	Z Baumgartner	-	-	-	-	-	-	-	-	1	-	-	-	-	-	-	-	-	-	1

10,8,6,5,4,3,2 and 1 point awarded to the first eight finishers.

Constructor Points 2004

Pos	Constructor	AUS	MAL	BRN	RSM	E	MC	EUR	CDN	USA	F	GB	D	H	B	I	CHN	J	BR	Total
1	Ferrari	18	15	18	13	18	6	18	18	18	16	16	10	18	14	18	10	10	8	262
2	BAR-Honda	3	6	10	8	5	8	6	6	6	4	5	9	7	-	11	11	11	3	119
3	Renault	8	6	8	9	11	10	9	-	5	13	-	6	6	-	-	5	4	5	105
4	Williams-BMW	9	8	2	8	3	5	1	-	-	1	4	6	7	-	6	4	10	14	88
5	McLaren-Mercedes-Benz	1	3	-	1	-	-	-	7	5	5	10	5	-	12	3	6	3	8	69
6	Sauber-Petronas	-	1	-	-	2	4	3	5	-	-	3	-	1	9	1	3	1	1	34
7	Jaguar-Ford Cosworth	-	-	1	-	-	-	2	-	-	1	3	-	-	3	-	-	-	-	10
8	Toyota	-	-	-	-	-	4	-	-	4	-	-	-	1	-	-	-	-	-	9
9	Jordan-Ford Cosworth	-	-	-	-	-	2	-	3	-	-	-	-	-	-	-	-	-	-	5
10	Minardi-Ford Cosworth	-	-	-	-	-	-	-	-	1	-	-	-	-	-	-	-	-	-	1

10,8,6,5,4,3,2 and 1 point awarded to the first eight finishers.

Race Entrants and Results

Ford's decision to leave F1 meant that Jaguar were purchased by Red Bull to form a new team while Honda increased their stake in BAR. The season expanded yet again to 19 races with the addition of Turkey to the calendar. There was an extension to the Concorde Agreement with engines now being required to last for two race weekends and tyre changes not permitted during the race unless damaged or the race declared wet. For the first time, qualifying times over two sessions were aggregated, with the final session being held on raceday morning. This proved unpopular and was abandoned after the Monaco event, resulting in single lap qualifying on Saturday, as before. The final race of the season saw four team names leave Formula 1 with the take-overs of BAR, Jordan, Minardi and Sauber.

FERRARI
Scuderia Ferrari Marlboro: M Schumacher, Barrichello

BAR
Lucky Strike B.A.R. Honda: Button, Sato, Davidson

RENAULT
Mild Seven Renault F1 Team: Alonso, Fisichella

WILLIAMS
BMW WilliamsF1 Team: Webber, Heidfeld, Pizzonia

McLAREN
West McLaren Mercedes: Räikkönen, Montoya, de la Rosa, Wurz

SAUBER
Sauber Petronas: Villeneuve, Massa

RED BULL
Red Bull Racing: Coulthard, Klien, Liuzzi

TOYOTA
Panasonic Toyota Racing: Trulli, R Schumacher, Zonta

JORDAN
Jordan Ford: Monteiro, Karthikeyan

MINARDI
European Minardi Cosworth: Friesacher, Albers, Doornbos

6 Mar 2005		AUSTRALIA: Melbourne							(Round 1)	(Race 732)
		57 laps x 5.303 km, 3.295 miles = 302.271 km, 187.822 miles								
Pos	No	Driver	Car	Model	Engine		Laps	Time/Reason for Retirement	Grid Pos	Row
1	6	G Fisichella	Renault	R25	Renault	V10	57	1h 24m 17.336s	1	1
2	2	R Barrichello	Ferrari	F2004M	Ferrari	V10	57	1h 24m 22.889s	11	6
3	5	F Alonso	Renault	R25	Renault	V10	57	1h 24m 24.048s	13	7
4	14	D Coulthard	Red Bull	RB1	Cosworth	V10	57	1h 24m 33.467s	5	3
5	7	M Webber	Williams	FW27	BMW	V10	57	1h 24m 34.244s	3	2
6	10	J P Montoya	McLaren	MP4-20	Mercedes-Benz	V10	57	1h 24m 52.369s	9	5
7	15	C Klien	Red Bull	RB1	Cosworth	V10	57	1h 24m 56.333s	6	3
8	9	K Räikkönen	McLaren	MP4-20	Mercedes-Benz	V10	57	1h 24m 56.969s	10	5
9	16	J Trulli	Toyota	TF105	Toyota	V10	57	1h 25m 20.444s	2	1
10	12	F Massa	Sauber	C24	Petronas	V10	57	1h 25m 21.729s	18	9
11r	3	J Button	BAR	007	Honda	V10	56	withdrew to permit engine change	8	4
12	17	R Schumacher	Toyota	TF105	Toyota	V10	56		15	8
13	11	J Villeneuve	Sauber	C24	Petronas	V10	56		4	2
14r	4	T Sato	BAR	007	Honda	V10	55	withdrew to permit engine change	20	10
15	19	N Karthikeyan	Jordan	EJ15	Toyota	V10	55		12	6
16	18	T Monteiro	Jordan	EJ15	Toyota	V10	55		14	7
17	20	P Friesacher	Minardi	PS04B	Cosworth	V10	53		16	8
r	1	M Schumacher	Ferrari	F2004M	Ferrari	V10	42	accident damage	19	10
r	8	N Heidfeld	Williams	FW27	BMW	V10	42	accident	7	4
r	21	C Albers	Minardi	PS04B	Cosworth	V10	16	gearbox	17	9
ap	35	P de la Rosa	McLaren	MP4-20	Mercedes-Benz	V10				
ap	37	V Liuzzi	Red Bull	RB1	Cosworth	V10				
ap	38	R Zonta	Toyota	TF105	Toyota	V10				
ap	39	R Doornbos	Jordan	EJ15	Toyota	V10				

Winning speed 215.167 km/h, 133.699 mph
Pole Position speed 210.413 km/h, 130.744 mph (G Fisichella, 3 min: 1.460 sec)
Fastest Lap speed 222.807 km/h, 138.446 mph (F Alonso, 1 min: 25.683 sec on lap 24)
Lap Leaders G Fisichella 1-23, 25-42, 45-57 (54); R Barrichello 24 (1); F Alonso 43-44 (2).

Engine change grid penalty: M Schumacher, T Sato.

20 Mar 2005   **MALAYSIA: Sepang**   **(Round 2)**   **(Race 733)**

56 laps x 5.543 km, 3.444 miles = 310.408 km, 192.879 miles

Pos	No	Driver	Car	Model	Engine		Laps	Time/Reason for Retirement	Grid Pos	Row
1	5	F Alonso	Renault	R25	Renault	V10	56	1h 31m 33.736s	1	1
2	16	J Trulli	Toyota	TF105	Toyota	V10	56	1h 31m 58.063s	2	1
3	8	N Heidfeld	Williams	FW27	BMW	V10	56	1h 32m 05.924s	10	5
4	10	J P Montoya	McLaren	MP4-20	Mercedes-Benz	V10	56	1h 32m 15.367s	11	6
5	17	R Schumacher	Toyota	TF105	Toyota	V10	56	1h 32m 25.590s	5	3
6	14	D Coulthard	Red Bull	RB1	Cosworth	V10	56	1h 32m 46.279s	8	4
7	1	M Schumacher	Ferrari	F2004M	Ferrari	V10	56	1h 32m 53.724s	13	7
8	15	C Klien	Red Bull	RB1	Cosworth	V10	56	1h 32m 54.571s	7	4
9	9	K Räikkönen	McLaren	MP4-20	Mercedes-Benz	V10	56	1h 32m 55.316s	6	3
10	12	F Massa	Sauber	C24	Petronas	V10	55		14	7
11	19	N Karthikeyan	Jordan	EJ15	Toyota	V10	54		17	9
12	18	T Monteiro	Jordan	EJ15	Toyota	V10	53		18	9
13	21	C Albers	Minardi	PS04B	Cosworth	V10	52		19	10
r	2	R Barrichello	Ferrari	F2004M	Ferrari	V10	49	tyres/ handling/ withdrawn	12	6
r	6	G Fisichella	Renault	R25	Renault	V10	36	accident	3	2
r	7	M Webber	Williams	FW27	BMW	V10	36	accident	4	2
r	11	J Villeneuve	Sauber	C24	Petronas	V10	26	spin	16	8
r	3	J Button	BAR	007	Honda	V10	2	engine	9	5
r	4	A Davidson	BAR	007	Honda	V10	2	engine	15	8
r	20	P Friesacher	Minardi	PS04B	Cosworth	V10	2	spin	20	10
ap	38	R Zonta	Toyota	TF105	Toyota	V10				
ap	35	P de la Rosa	McLaren	MP4-20	Mercedes-Benz	V10				
ap	37	V Liuzzi	Red Bull	RB1	Cosworth	V10				
ap	39	R Doornbos	Jordan	EJ15	Toyota	V10				

Winning speed 203.407 km/h, 126.392 mph
Pole Position speed 212.656 km/h, 132.138 mph (F Alonso, 3 min: 7.672 sec)
Fastest Lap speed 208.987 km/h, 129.859 mph (K Räikkönen, 1 min:35.483 sec on lap 23)
Lap Leaders F Alonso 1-21,25-40,43-56 (51); G Fisichella 22 (1); K Räikkönen 23-24 (2); J Trulli 41-42 (2).

Engine change grid penalty: P Friesacher.

---

3 Apr 2005   **BAHRAIN: Sakhir**   **(Round 3)**   **(Race 734)**

57 laps x 5.412 km, 3.363 miles = 308.238 km, 191.530 miles

Pos	No	Driver	Car	Model	Engine		Laps	Time/Reason for Retirement	Grid Pos	Row
1	5	F Alonso	Renault	R25	Renault	V10	57	1h 29m 18.531s	1	1
2	16	J Trulli	Toyota	TF105	Toyota	V10	57	1h 29m 31.940s	3	2
3	9	K Räikkönen	McLaren	MP4-20	Mercedes-Benz	V10	57	1h 29m 50.594s	9	5
4	17	R Schumacher	Toyota	TF105	Toyota	V10	57	1h 30m 11.803s	6	3
5	10	P de la Rosa	McLaren	MP4-20	Mercedes-Benz	V10	57	1h 30m 23.519s	8	4
6	7	M Webber	Williams	FW27	BMW	V10	57	1h 30m 33.232s	5	3
7	12	F Massa	Sauber	C24	Petronas	V10	56		12	6
8	14	D Coulthard	Red Bull	RB1	Cosworth	V10	56		14	7
9	2	R Barrichello	Ferrari	F2005	Ferrari	V10	56		20	10
10	18	T Monteiro	Jordan	EJ15	Toyota	V10	55		16	8
11r	11	J Villeneuve	Sauber	C24	Petronas	V10	54	accident	15	8
12	20	P Friesacher	Minardi	PS04B	Cosworth	V10	54		19	10
13	21	C Albers	Minardi	PS04B	Cosworth	V10	53		18	9
r	3	J Button	BAR	007	Honda	V10	46	clutch	11	6
r	4	T Sato	BAR	007	Honda	V10	27	brakes	13	7
r	8	N Heidfeld	Williams	FW27	BMW	V10	25	engine	4	2
r	1	M Schumacher	Ferrari	F2005	Ferrari	V10	12	hydraulics	2	1
r	6	G Fisichella	Renault	R25	Renault	V10	4	engine	10	5
r	19	N Karthikeyan	Jordan	EJ15	Toyota	V10	2	electrics	17	9
ns	15	C Klien	Red Bull	RB1	Cosworth	V10		electrics in pit-lane	7	4
ap	35	A Wurz	McLaren	MP4-20	Mercedes-Benz	V10				
ap	38	R Zonta	Toyota	TF105	Toyota	V10				
ap	37	V Liuzzi	Red Bull	RB1	Cosworth	V10				
ap	39	R Doornbos	Jordan	EJ15	Toyota	V10				

Winning speed 207.082 km/h, 128.675 mph
Pole Position speed 214.216 km/h, 133.108 mph (F Alonso, 3 min: 1.902 sec)
Fastest Lap speed 213.054 km/h, 132.386 mph (P de la Rosa, 1 min:31.447 sec on lap 43)
Lap Leaders F Alonso 1-20,22-41,43-57 (55); J Trulli 21,42 (2).

Engine change grid penalty: R Barrichello.

24 Apr 2005   **SAN MARINO: Imola**   **(Round 4)**   **(Race 735)**

62 laps x 4.933 km, 3.065 miles = 305.609 km, 189.896 miles

Pos	No	Driver	Car	Model	Engine		Laps	Time/Reason for Retirement	Grid Pos	Row
1	5	F Alonso	Renault	R25	Renault	V10	62	1h 27m 41.921s	2	1
2	1	M Schumacher	Ferrari	F2005	Ferrari	V10	62	1h 27m 42.136s	13	7
dq	3	J Button	BAR	007	Honda	V10	62	car under weight	3	2
3	10	A Wurz	McLaren	MP4-20	Mercedes-Benz	V10	62	1h 28m 09.475s	7	4
dq	4	T Sato	BAR	007	Honda	V10	62	car under weight	6	3
4	11	J Villeneuve	Sauber	C24	Petronas	V10	62	1h 28m 46.363s	11	6
5	16	J Trulli	Toyota	TF105	Toyota	V10	62	1h 28m 52.179s	5	3
6	8	N Heidfeld	Williams	FW27	BMW	V10	62	1h 28m 53.203s	8	4
7	7	M Webber	Williams	FW27	BMW	V10	62	1h 29m 05.218s	4	2
8	15	V Liuzzi	Red Bull	RB1	Cosworth	V10	62	1h 29m 05.685s	15	8
9	17	R Schumacher	Toyota	TF105	Toyota	V10	62	1h 29m 17.762s *	10	5
10	12	F Massa	Sauber	C24	Petronas	V10	61		18	9
11	14	D Coulthard	Red Bull	RB1	Cosworth	V10	61		14	7
12	19	N Karthikeyan	Jordan	EJ15	Toyota	V10	61		16	8
13	18	T Monteiro	Jordan	EJ15	Toyota	V10	60		17	9
r	21	C Albers	Minardi	PS05	Cosworth	V10	20	gearbox fluid leak	20	10
r	2	R Barrichello	Ferrari	F2005	Ferrari	V10	18	electronics	9	5
r	9	K Räikkönen	McLaren	MP4-20	Mercedes-Benz	V10	9	cv joint	1	1
r	20	P Friesacher	Minardi	PS05	Cosworth	V10	8	gearbox shaft	19	10
r	6	G Fisichella	Renault	R25	Renault	V10	5	rear end / accident	12	6
ap	35	P de la Rosa	McLaren	MP4-20	Mercedes-Benz	V10				
ap	38	R Zonta	Toyota	TF105	Toyota	V10				
ap	37	C Klien	Red Bull	RB1	Cosworth	V10				
ap	39	R Doornbos	Jordan	EJ15	Toyota	V10				

Winning speed 209.085 km/h, 129.920 mph
Pole Position speed 218.059 km/h, 135.496 mph (K Räikkönen, 2 min:42.880 sec)
Fastest Lap speed 216.946 km/h, 134.804 mph (M Schumacher, 1 min:21.858 sec on lap 48)
Lap Leaders K Räikkönen 1-8 (8); F Alonso 9-23,25-42,50-62 (46); J Button 24,43-46 (5); M Schumacher 47-49 (3).

J Button and T Sato completed the 62 laps in 1h 27m 52.402s (3rd) and 1h 28m 16.704s (5th) respectively, but were disqualified.
The BAR team was barred from taking part in the subsequent Grands Prix in Spain and Monaco.
* R Schumacher finished 8th in 1h 28m 52.762s, but was awarded a 25 sec penalty for dangerous driving.
Engine change grid penalty: F Massa.

---

8 May 2005   **SPAIN: Montmeló**   **(Round 5)**   **(Race 736)**

66 laps x 4.627 km, 2.875 miles = 305.256 km, 189.677 miles

Pos	No	Driver	Car	Model	Engine		Laps	Time/Reason for Retirement	Grid Pos	Row
1	9	K Räikkönen	McLaren	MP4-20	Mercedes-Benz	V10	66	1h 27m 16.830s	1	1
2	5	F Alonso	Renault	R25	Renault	V10	66	1h 27m 44.482s	3	2
3	16	J Trulli	Toyota	TF105	Toyota	V10	66	1h 28m 02.777s	5	3
4	17	R Schumacher	Toyota	TF105	Toyota	V10	66	1h 28m 03.549s	4	2
5	6	G Fisichella	Renault	R25	Renault	V10	66	1h 28m 14.766s	6	3
6	7	M Webber	Williams	FW27	BMW	V10	66	1h 28m 25.372s	2	1
7	10	J P Montoya	McLaren	MP4-20	Mercedes-Benz	V10	65		7	4
8	14	D Coulthard	Red Bull	RB1	Cosworth	V10	65		9	5
9	2	R Barrichello	Ferrari	F2005	Ferrari	V10	65		16	8
10	8	N Heidfeld	Williams	FW27	BMW	V10	65		17	9
11r	12	F Massa	Sauber	C24	Petronas	V10	63	rear wheel rim	10	5
12	18	T Monteiro	Jordan	EJ15	Toyota	V10	63		18	9
13	19	N Karthikeyan	Jordan	EJ15	Toyota	V10	63		13	7
r	11	J Villeneuve	Sauber	C24	Petronas	V10	51	water leak	12	6
r	1	M Schumacher	Ferrari	F2005	Ferrari	V10	46	tyre / front suspension	8	4
r	21	C Albers	Minardi	PS05	Cosworth	V10	19	gearbox	14	7
r	20	P Friesacher	Minardi	PS05	Cosworth	V10	11	spin	15	8
r	15	V Liuzzi	Red Bull	RB1	Cosworth	V10	9	engine / spin	11	6
ap	35	P de la Rosa	McLaren	MP4-20	Mercedes-Benz	V10				
ap	38	R Zonta	Toyota	TF105	Toyota	V10				
ap	37	C Klien	Red Bull	RB1	Cosworth	V10				
ap	39	R Doornbos	Jordan	EJ15	Toyota	V10				

Winning speed 209.844 km/h, 130.392 mph
Pole Position speed 220.011 km/h, 136.708 mph (K Räikkönen, 2 min:31.421 sec)
Fastest Lap speed 220.213 km/h, 136.835 mph (G Fisichella, 1 min:15.641 sec on lap 66)
Lap Leaders K Räikkönen 1-66 (66).

Engine change grid penalty: R Barrichello, N Heidfeld, T Monteiro.

Races

22 May 2005 **MONACO: Monte-Carlo** (Round 6) (Race 737)

78 laps x 3.340 km, 2.075 miles = 260.520 km, 161.880 miles

Pos	No	Driver	Car	Model	Engine		Laps	Time/Reason for Retirement	Grid Pos	Row
1	9	K Räikkönen	McLaren	MP4-20	Mercedes-Benz	V10	78	1h 45m 15.556s	1	1
2	8	N Heidfeld	Williams	FW27	BMW	V10	78	1h 45m 29.433s	6	3
3	7	M Webber	Williams	FW27	BMW	V10	78	1h 45m 34.040s	3	2
4	5	F Alonso	Renault	R25	Renault	V10	78	1h 45m 52.043s	2	1
5	10	J P Montoya	McLaren	MP4-20	Mercedes-Benz	V10	78	1h 45m 52.203s	16	8
6	17	R Schumacher	Toyota	TF105	Toyota	V10	78	1h 45m 52.733s	18	9
7	1	M Schumacher	Ferrari	F2005	Ferrari	V10	78	1h 45m 52.779s	8	4
8	2	R Barrichello	Ferrari	F2005	Ferrari	V10	78	1h 45m 53.126s	10	5
9	12	F Massa	Sauber	C24	Petronas	V10	77		11	6
10	16	J Trulli	Toyota	TF105	Toyota	V10	77		5	3
11	11	J Villeneuve	Sauber	C24	Petronas	V10	77		9	5
12	6	G Fisichella	Renault	R25	Renault	V10	77		4	2
13	18	T Monteiro	Jordan	EJ15	Toyota	V10	75		15	8
14	21	C Albers	Minardi	PS05	Cosworth	V10	73		14	7
r	15	V Liuzzi	Red Bull	RB1	Cosworth	V10	59	rear tyres / accident / suspension	12	6
r	20	P Friesacher	Minardi	PS05	Cosworth	V10	29	accident	13	7
r	14	D Coulthard	Red Bull	RB1	Cosworth	V10	23	accident / rear suspension	7	4
r	19	N Karthikeyan	Jordan	EJ15	Toyota	V10	18	accident / hydraulics	17	9
ap	35	A Wurz	McLaren	MP4-20	Mercedes-Benz	V10				
ap	38	R Zonta	Toyota	TF105	Toyota	V10				
ap	37	C Klien	Red Bull	RB1	Cosworth	V10				
ap	39	R Doornbos	Jordan	EJ15	Toyota	V10				

Winning speed 148.501 km/h,92.275 mph
Pole Position speed 159.975 km/h,99.404 mph (K Räikkönen,2 min:30.323 sec)
Fastest Lap speed 158.540 km/h,98.512 mph (M Schumacher,1 min:15.842 sec on lap 40)
Lap Leaders K Räikkönen 1-78 (78).

Engine change grid penalty: N Karthikeyan, R Schumacher.
J P Montoya's qualifying time was deleted, due to causing an accident.

29 May 2005 **EUROPE: Nürburgring** (Round 7) (Race 738)

59 laps x 5.148 km, 3.199 miles = 303.715 km, 188.730 miles

Pos	No	Driver	Car	Model	Engine		Laps	Time/Reason for Retirement	Grid Pos	Row
1	5	F Alonso	Renault	R25	Renault	V10	59	1h 31m 46.648s	6	3
2	8	N Heidfeld	Williams	FW27	BMW	V10	59	1h 32m 03.215s	1	1
3	2	R Barrichello	Ferrari	F2005	Ferrari	V10	59	1h 32m 05.197s	7	4
4	14	D Coulthard	Red Bull	RB1	Cosworth	V10	59	1h 32m 18.236s	12	6
5	1	M Schumächer	Ferrari	F2005	Ferrari	V10	59	1h 32m 37.093s	10	5
6	6	G Fisichella	Renault	R25	Renault	V10	59	1h 32m 38.580s	9	5
7	10	J P Montoya	McLaren	MP4-20	Mercedes-Benz	V10	59	1h 32m 44.821s	5	3
8	16	J Trulli	Toyota	TF105	Toyota	V10	59	1h 32m 57.739s	4	2
9	15	V Liuzzi	Red Bull	RB1	Cosworth	V10	59	1h 32m 58.177s	14	7
10	3	J Button	BAR	007	Honda	V10	59	1h 33m 22.434s	13	7
11r	9	K Räikkönen	McLaren	MP4-20	Mercedes-Benz	V10	58	front tyre / suspension / accident	2	1
12	4	T Sato	BAR	007	Honda	V10	58		16	8
13	11	J Villeneuve	Sauber	C24	Petronas	V10	58		15	8
14	12	F Massa	Sauber	C24	Petronas	V10	58		11	6
15	18	T Monteiro	Jordan	EJ15	Toyota	V10	58		17	9
16	19	N Karthikeyan	Jordan	EJ15	Toyota	V10	58		19	10
17	21	C Albers	Minardi	PS05	Cosworth	V10	57		20	10
18	20	P Friesacher	Minardi	PS05	Cosworth	V10	56		18	9
r	17	R Schumacher	Toyota	TF105	Toyota	V10	33	accident	8	4
r	7	M Webber	Williams	FW27	BMW	V10	0	accident	3	2
ap	35	A Wurz	McLaren	MP4-20	Mercedes-Benz	V10				
ap	38	R Zonta	Toyota	TF105	Toyota	V10				
ap	37	C Klien	Red Bull	RB1	Cosworth	V10				
ap	39	F Montagny	Jordan	EJ15	Toyota	V10				

Winning speed 198.555 km/h, 123.377 mph
Pole Position speed 205.734 km/h, 127.838 mph (N Heidfeld,1 min:30.081 sec)
Fastest Lap speed 204.305 km/h, 126.950 mph (F Alonso,1 min:30.711 sec on lap 44)
Lap Leaders K Räikkönen 1-18,24-29,31-43,48-58 (48); D Coulthard 19 (1); F Alonso 20-23,44-47,59 (9); N Heidfeld 30 (1).

Race scheduled for 60 laps, but reduced by 1 lap due to an aborted start.

CANADA: Montréal (Round 8) (Race 739)

70 laps x 4.361 km, 2.710 miles = 305.270 km, 189.686 miles

Pos	No	Driver	Car	Model	Engine		Laps	Time/Reason for Retirement	Grid Pos	Row
1	9	K Räikkönen	McLaren	MP4-20	Mercedes-Benz	V10	70	1h 32m 09.290s	7	4
2	1	M Schumacher	Ferrari	F2005	Ferrari	V10	70	1h 32m 10.427s	2	1
3	2	R Barrichello	Ferrari	F2005	Ferrari	V10	70	1h 32m 49.773s	20	10
4	12	F Massa	Sauber	C24	Petronas	V10	70	1h 33m 04.429s	11	6
5	7	M Webber	Williams	FW27	BMW	V10	70	1h 33m 05.069s	14	7
6	17	R Schumacher	Toyota	TF105	Toyota	V10	69		10	5
7	14	D Coulthard	Red Bull	RB1	Cosworth	V10	69		12	6
8	15	C Klien	Red Bull	RB1	Cosworth	V10	69		16	8
9	11	J Villeneuve	Sauber	C24	Petronas	V10	69		8	4
10	18	T Monteiro	Jordan	EJ15	Toyota	V10	67		18	9
11	21	C Albers	Minardi	PS05	Cosworth	V10	67		15	8
r	16	J Trulli	Toyota	TF105	Toyota	V10	62	front brake disc	9	5
r	10	J P Montoya	McLaren	MP4-20	Mercedes-Benz	V10	52	left pit lane on red light	5	3
r	3	J Button	BAR	007	Honda	V10	46	accident	1	1
r	8	N Heidfeld	Williams	FW27	BMW	V10	43	engine	13	7
r	4	T Sato	BAR	007	Honda	V10	40	rear drive / spin	6	3
r	20	P Friesacher	Minardi	PS05	Cosworth	V10	39	hydraulics	19	10
r	5	F Alonso	Renault	R25	Renault	V10	38	accident / rear suspension	3	2
r	6	G Fisichella	Renault	R25	Renault	V10	32	hydraulics	4	2
r	19	N Karthikeyan	Jordan	EJ15	Toyota	V10	24	accident	17	9
ap	35	P de la Rosa	McLaren	MP4-20	Mercedes-Benz	V10				
ap	38	R Zonta	Toyota	TF105	Toyota	V10				
ap	37	S Speed	Red Bull	RB1	Cosworth	V10				

Winning speed 198.754 km/h, 123.500 mph
Pole Position speed 208.724 km/h, 129.695 mph (J Button, 1 min:15.217 sec)
Fastest Lap speed 211.061 km/h, 131.148 mph (K Räikkönen, 1 min:14.384 sec on lap 23)
Lap Leaders G Fisichella 1-32 (32); F Alonso 33-38 (6); J P Montoya 39-48 (10); K Räikkönen 49-70 (32).

USA: Indianapolis (Round 9) (Race 740)

73 laps x 4.192 km, 2.605 miles = 306.016 km, 190.150 miles

Pos	No	Driver	Car	Model	Engine		Laps	Time/Reason for Retirement	Grid Pos	Row
1	1	M Schumacher	Ferrari	F2005	Ferrari	V10	73	1h 29m 43.181s	5	3
2	2	R Barrichello	Ferrari	F2005	Ferrari	V10	73	1h 29m 44.703s	7	4
3	18	T Monteiro	Jordan	EJ15	Toyota	V10	72		17	9
4	19	N Karthikeyan	Jordan	EJ15	Toyota	V10	72		19	10
5	21	C Albers	Minardi	PS05	Cosworth	V10	71		18	9
6	20	P Friesacher	Minardi	PS05	Cosworth	V10	71		20	10
ns	16	J Trulli	Toyota	TF105	Toyota	V10		withdrawn on parade lap	1	1
ns	9	K Räikkönen	McLaren	MP4-20	Mercedes-Benz	V10		withdrawn on parade lap	2	1
ns	3	J Button	BAR	007	Honda	V10		withdrawn on parade lap	3	2
ns	6	G Fisichella	Renault	R25	Renault	V10		withdrawn on parade lap	4	2
ns	5	F Alonso	Renault	R25	Renault	V10		withdrawn on parade lap	6	3
ns	4	T Sato	BAR	007	Honda	V10		withdrawn on parade lap	8	4
ns	7	M Webber	Williams	FW27	BMW	V10		withdrawn on parade lap	9	5
ns	12	F Massa	Sauber	C24	Petronas	V10		withdrawn on parade lap	10	5
ns	10	J P Montoya	McLaren	MP4-20	Mercedes-Benz	V10		withdrawn on parade lap	11	6
ns	11	J Villeneuve	Sauber	C24	Petronas	V10		withdrawn on parade lap	12	6
ns	17	R Zonta	Toyota	TF105	Toyota	V10		withdrawn on parade lap	13	7
ns	15	C Klien	Red Bull	RB1	Cosworth	V10		withdrawn on parade lap	14	7
ns	8	N Heidfeld	Williams	FW27	BMW	V10		withdrawn on parade lap	15	8
ns	14	D Coulthard	Red Bull	RB1	Cosworth	V10		withdrawn on parade lap	16	8
ns	17	R Schumacher	Toyota	TF105	Toyota	V10		accident / injury		
ap	35	P de la Rosa	McLaren	MP4-20	Mercedes-Benz	V10				
ap	37	S Speed	Red Bull	RB1	Cosworth	V10				
ap	39	R Doornbos	Jordan	EJ15	Toyota	V10				

Winning speed 204.648 km/h, 127.162 mph
Pole Position speed 213.680 km/h, 132.775 mph (J Trulli, 1 min:10.625 sec)
Fastest Lap speed 211.074 km/h, 131.156 mph (M Schumacher, 1 min:11.497 sec on lap 48)
Lap Leaders M Schumacher 1-26, 49-73 (51); R Barrichello 27-48 (22).

The 14 Michelin runners pulled into the pits after the parade lap, due to the tyres being declared unsafe by the tyre company.
R Zonta also practised in car no. 38.

3 Jul 2005   FRANCE: Magny-Cours   (Round 10)   (Race 741)

70 laps x 4.411 km, 2.741 miles = 308.586 km, 191.746 miles

Pos	No	Driver	Car	Model	Engine		Laps	Time/Reason for Retirement	Grid Pos	Row
1	5	F Alonso	Renault	R25	Renault	V10	70	1h 31m 22.233s	1	1
2	9	K Räikkönen	McLaren	MP4-20	Mercedes-Benz	V10	70	1h 31m 34.038s	13	7
3	1	M Schumacher	Ferrari	F2005	Ferrari	V10	70	1h 32m 44.147s	3	2
4	3	J Button	BAR	007	Honda	V10	69		7	4
5	16	J Trulli	Toyota	TF105	Toyota	V10	69		2	1
6	6	G Fisichella	Renault	R25	Renault	V10	69		6	3
7	17	R Schumacher	Toyota	TF105	Toyota	V10	69		11	6
8	11	J Villeneuve	Sauber	C24	Petronas	V10	69		10	5
9	2	R Barrichello	Ferrari	F2005	Ferrari	V10	69		5	3
10	14	D Coulthard	Red Bull	RB1	Cosworth	V10	69		15	8
11	4	T Sato	BAR	007	Honda	V10	69		4	2
12	7	M Webber	Williams	FW27	BMW	V10	68		12	6
13	18	T Monteiro	Jordan	EJ15	Toyota	V10	67		19	10
14	8	N Heidfeld	Williams	FW27	BMW	V10	66		14	7
15	19	N Karthikeyan	Jordan	EJ15	Toyota	V10	66		17	9
r	10	J P Montoya	McLaren	MP4-20	Mercedes-Benz	V10	46	hydraulics	8	4
r	21	C Albers	Minardi	PS05	Cosworth	V10	37	tyre	20	10
r	20	P Friesacher	Minardi	PS05	Cosworth	V10	33	tyre	18	9
r	12	F Massa	Sauber	C24	Petronas	V10	30	hydraulics	9	5
r	15	C Klien	Red Bull	RB1	Cosworth	V10	1	fuel pressure	16	8
ap	35	P de la Rosa	McLaren	MP4-20	Mercedes-Benz	V10				
ap	38	O Panis	Toyota	TF105	Toyota	V10				
ap	37	V Liuzzi	Red Bull	RB1	Cosworth	V10				
ap	39	R Doornbos	Jordan	EJ15	Toyota	V10				

Winning speed 202.638 km/h, 125.914 mph
Pole Position speed 213.401 km/h, 132.601 mph (F Alonso,1 min:14.412 sec)
Fastest Lap speed 207.785 km/h, 129.112 mph (K Räikkönen,1 min:16.423 sec on lap 25)
Lap Leaders F Alonso 1-70 (70).

Engine change grid penalty: K Räikkönen.

10 Jul 2005   BRITAIN: Silverstone   (Round 11)   (Race 742)

60 laps x 5.141 km, 3.194 miles = 308.355 km, 191.603 miles

Pos	No	Driver	Car	Model	Engine		Laps	Time/Reason for Retirement	Grid Pos	Row
1	10	J P Montoya	McLaren	MP4-20	Mercedes-Benz	V10	60	1h 24m 29.588s	3	2
2	5	F Alonso	Renault	R25	Renault	V10	60	1h 24m 32.327s	1	1
3	9	K Räikkönen	McLaren	MP4-20	Mercedes-Benz	V10	60	1h 24m 44.024s	12	6
4	6	G Fisichella	Renault	R25	Renault	V10	60	1h 24m 47.502s	6	3
5	3	J Button	BAR	007	Honda	V10	60	1h 25m 09.852s	2	1
6	1	M Schumacher	Ferrari	F2005	Ferrari	V10	60	1h 25m 44.910s	9	5
7	2	R Barrichello	Ferrari	F2005	Ferrari	V10	60	1h 25m 46.155s	5	3
8	17	R Schumacher	Toyota	TF105	Toyota	V10	60	1h 25m 48.800s	8	4
9	16	J Trulli	Toyota	TF105	Toyota	V10	60	1h 25m 50.439s	4	2
10	12	F Massa	Sauber	C24	Petronas	V10	59		16	8
11	7	M Webber	Williams	FW27	BMW	V10	59		11	6
12	8	N Heidfeld	Williams	FW27	BMW	V10	59		14	7
13	14	D Coulthard	Red Bull	RB1	Cosworth	V10	59		13	7
14	11	J Villeneuve	Sauber	C24	Petronas	V10	59		10	5
15	15	C Klien	Red Bull	RB1	Cosworth	V10	59		15	8
16	4	T Sato	BAR	007	Honda	V10	58		7	4
17	18	T Monteiro	Jordan	EJ15	Toyota	V10	58		20	10
18	21	C Albers	Minardi	PS05	Cosworth	V10	57		18	9
19	20	P Friesacher	Minardi	PS05	Cosworth	V10	56		19	10
r	19	N Karthikeyan	Jordan	EJ15	Toyota	V10	10	electrics	17	9
ap	35	P de la Rosa	McLaren	MP4-20	Mercedes-Benz	V10				
ap	38	R Zonta	Toyota	TF105	Toyota	V10				
ap	37	V Liuzzi	Red Bull	RB1	Cosworth	V10				
ap	39	R Doornbos	Jordan	EJ15	Toyota	V10				

Winning speed 218.968 km/h, 136.060 mph
Pole Position speed 231.620 km/h, 143.922 mph (F Alonso,1 min:19.905 sec)
Fastest Lap speed 229.902 km/h, 142.855 mph (K Räikkönen,1 min:20.502 sec on lap 60)
Lap Leaders J P Montoya 1-21,26-44,50-60 (51); F Alonso 22-23,45-49 (7); G Fisichella 24-25 (2).

Engine change grid penalty: T Monteiro, K Räikkönen.

67 laps x 4.574 km, 2.842 miles = 306.458 km, 190.424 miles

Pos	No	Driver	Car	Model	Engine		Laps	Time/Reason for Retirement	Grid Pos	Row
1	5	F Alonso	Renault	R25	Renault	V10	67	1h 26m 28.599s	3	2
2	10	J P Montoya	McLaren	MP4-20	Mercedes-Benz	V10	67	1h 26m 51.168s	20	10
3	3	J Button	BAR	007	Honda	V10	67	1h 26m 53.021s	2	1
4	6	G Fisichella	Renault	R25	Renault	V10	67	1h 27m 19.186s	4	2
5	1	M Schumacher	Ferrari	F2005	Ferrari	V10	67	1h 27m 20.289s	5	3
6	17	R Schumacher	Toyota	TF105	Toyota	V10	67	1h 27m 20.841s	12	6
7	14	D Coulthard	Red Bull	RB1	Cosworth	V10	67	1h 27m 21.299s	11	6
8	12	F Massa	Sauber	C24	Petronas	V10	67	1h 27m 25.169s	13	7
9	15	C Klien	Red Bull	RB1	Cosworth	V10	67	1h 27m 38.417s	10	5
10	2	R Barrichello	Ferrari	F2005	Ferrari	V10	66		15	8
11	8	N Heidfeld	Williams	FW27	BMW	V10	66		7	4
12	4	T Sato	BAR	007	Honda	V10	66		8	4
13	21	C Albers	Minardi	PS05	Cosworth	V10	65		16	8
14r	16	J Trulli	Toyota	TF105	Toyota	V10	64	pneumatics	9	5
15	11	J Villeneuve	Sauber	C24	Petronas	V10	64		14	7
16	19	N Karthikeyan	Jordan	EJ15	Toyota	V10	64		19	10
17	18	T Monteiro	Jordan	EJ15	Toyota	V10	64		18	9
18	20	R Doornbos	Minardi	PS05	Cosworth	V10	63		17	9
nc	7	M Webber	Williams	FW27	BMW	V10	55		6	3
r	9	K Räikkönen	McLaren	MP4-20	Mercedes-Benz	V10	35	hydraulics	1	1
ap	35	A Wurz	McLaren	MP4-20	Mercedes-Benz	V10				
ap	38	R Zonta	Toyota	TF105	Toyota	V10				
ap	37	V Liuzzi	Red Bull	RB1	Cosworth	V10				
ap	39	N Kiesa	Jordan	EJ15	Toyota	V10				

Winning speed 212.629 km/h, 132.122 mph
Pole Position speed 221.560 km/h, 137.672 mph (K Räikkönen,1 min:14.320 sec)
Fastest Lap speed 219.924 km/h, 136.655 mph (K Räikkönen,1 min:14.873 sec on lap 24)
Lap Leaders K Räikkönen 1-35 (35); F Alonso 36-67 (32).

Engine change grid penalty: J P Montoya.

70 laps x 4.381 km, 2.722 miles = 306.663 km, 190.552 miles

Pos	No	Driver	Car	Model	Engine		Laps	Time/Reason for Retirement	Grid Pos	Row
1	9	K Räikkönen	McLaren	MP4-20	Mercedes-Benz	V10	70	1h 37m 25.552s	4	2
2	1	M Schumacher	Ferrari	F2005	Ferrari	V10	70	1h 38m 01.133s	1	1
3	17	R Schumacher	Toyota	TF105	Toyota	V10	70	1h 38m 01.681s	5	3
4	16	J Trulli	Toyota	TF105	Toyota	V10	70	1h 38m 19.773s	3	2
5	3	J Button	BAR	007	Honda	V10	70	1h 38m 24.384s	8	4
6	8	N Heidfeld	Williams	FW27	BMW	V10	70	1h 38m 33.927s	12	6
7	7	M Webber	Williams	FW27	BMW	V10	69		16	8
8	4	T Sato	BAR	007	Honda	V10	69		10	5
9	6	G Fisichella	Renault	R25	Renault	V10	69		9	5
10	2	R Barrichello	Ferrari	F2005	Ferrari	V10	69		7	4
11	5	F Alonso	Renault	R25	Renault	V10	69		6	3
12	19	N Karthikeyan	Jordan	EJ15	Toyota	V10	67		18	9
13	18	T Monteiro	Jordan	EJ15	Toyota	V10	66		20	10
14	12	F Massa	Sauber	C24	Petronas	V10	63		14	7
r	21	C Albers	Minardi	PS05	Cosworth	V10	59	hydraulics	17	9
r	11	J Villeneuve	Sauber	C24	Petronas	V10	56	engine overheating	15	8
r	10	J P Montoya	McLaren	MP4-20	Mercedes-Benz	V10	41	driveshaft	2	1
r	20	R Doornbos	Minardi	PS05	Cosworth	V10	26	hydraulics	19	10
r	15	C Klien	Red Bull	RB1	Cosworth	V10	0	accident	11	6
r	14	D Coulthard	Red Bull	RB1	Cosworth	V10	0	accident	13	7
ap	38	R Zonta	Toyota	TF105	Toyota	V10				
ap	35	A Wurz	McLaren	MP4-20	Mercedes-Benz	V10				
ap	37	V Liuzzi	Red Bull	RB1	Cosworth	V10				
ap	39	N Kiesa	Jordan	EJ15	Toyota	V10				
ap	40	C Nissany	Minardi	PS05	Cosworth	V10				

Winning speed 188.859 km/h, 117.352 mph
Pole Position speed 197.436 km/h, 122.681 mph (M Schumacher,1 min:19.882 sec)
Fastest Lap speed 194.186 km/h, 120.662 mph (K Räikkönen,1 min:21.219 sec on lap 40)
Lap Leaders M Schumacher 1-15,23-35 (28); J P Montoya 16-22,38-40 (10); K Räikkönen 36-37,41-70 (32).

Engine change grid penalty: T Monteiro.

21 Aug 2005   TURKEY: Istanbul   (Round 14)   (Race 745)

58 laps x 5.338 km, 3.317 miles = 309.396 km, 192.250 miles

Pos	No	Driver	Car	Model	Engine		Laps	Time/Reason for Retirement	Grid Pos	Row
1	9	K Räikkönen	McLaren	MP4-20	Mercedes-Benz	V10	58	1h 24m 34.454s	1	1
2	5	F Alonso	Renault	R25	Renault	V10	58	1h 24m 53.063s	3	2
3	10	J P Montoya	McLaren	MP4-20	Mercedes-Benz	V10	58	1h 24m 54.089s	4	2
4	6	G Fisichella	Renault	R25	Renault	V10	58	1h 25m 12.427s	2	1
5	3	J Button	BAR	007	Honda	V10	58	1h 25m 13.758s	13	7
6	16	J Trulli	Toyota	TF105	Toyota	V10	58	1h 25m 29.874s	5	3
7	14	D Coulthard	Red Bull	RB1	Cosworth	V10	58	1h 25m 43.750s	12	6
8	15	C Klien	Red Bull	RB1	Cosworth	V10	58	1h 25m 46.076s	10	5
9	4	T Sato	BAR	007	Honda	V10	58	1h 26m 24.441s	20	10
10	2	R Barrichello	Ferrari	F2005	Ferrari	V10	57		11	6
11	11	J Villeneuve	Sauber	C24	Petronas	V10	57		16	8
12	17	R Schumacher	Toyota	TF105	Toyota	V10	57		9	5
13	20	R Doornbos	Minardi	PS05	Cosworth	V10	55		17	9
14	19	N Karthikeyan	Jordan	EJ15	Toyota	V10	55		18	9
15	18	T Monteiro	Jordan	EJ15	Toyota	V10	55		14	7
r	21	C Albers	Minardi	PS05	Cosworth	V10	48	withdrawn	15	8
r	1	M Schumacher	Ferrari	F2005	Ferrari	V10	32	accident damage	19	10
r	8	N Heidfeld	Williams	FW27	BMW	V10	29	out of tyres	6	3
r	12	F Massa	Sauber	C24	Petronas	V10	28	engine	8	4
r	7	M Webber	Williams	FW27	BMW	V10	20	out of tyres	7	4
ap	38	R Zonta	Toyota	TF105	Toyota	V10				
ap	35	P de la Rosa	McLaren	MP4-20	Mercedes-Benz	V10				
ap	37	V Liuzzi	Red Bull	RB1	Cosworth	V10				
ap	39	N Kiesa	Jordan	EJ15	Toyota	V10				
ap	40	E Toccacelo	Minardi	PS05	Cosworth	V10				

Winning speed 219.496 km/h, 136.389 mph
Pole Position speed 221.399 km/h, 137.571 mph (K Räikkönen, 1 min:26.797 sec)
Fastest Lap speed 226.693 km/h, 140.861 mph (J P Montoya, 1 min:24.770 sec on lap 39)
Lap Leaders K Räikkönen 1-58 (58).

Engine change grid penalty: N Karthikeyan, M Schumacher, T Sato.

4 Sep 2005   ITALY: Monza   (Round 15)   (Race 746)

53 laps x 5.793 km, 3.600 miles = 306.720 km, 190.587 miles

Pos	No	Driver	Car	Model	Engine		Laps	Time/Reason for Retirement	Grid Pos	Row
1	10	J P Montoya	McLaren	MP4-20	Mercedes-Benz	V10	53	1h 14m 28.659s	1	1
2	5	F Alonso	Renault	R25	Renault	V10	53	1h 14m 31.138s	2	1
3	6	G Fisichella	Renault	R25	Renault	V10	53	1h 14m 46.634s	8	4
4	9	K Räikkönen	McLaren	MP4-20	Mercedes-Benz	V10	53	1h 14m 51.434s	11	6
5	16	J Trulli	Toyota	TF105	Toyota	V10	53	1h 15m 02.445s	5	3
6	17	R Schumacher	Toyota	TF105	Toyota	V10	53	1h 15m 12.584s	9	5
7	8	A Pizzonia	Williams	FW27	BMW	V10	53	1h 15m 13.302s	16	8
8	3	J Button	BAR	007	Honda	V10	53	1h 15m 32.294s	3	2
9	12	F Massa	Sauber	C24	Petronas	V10	53	1h 15m 44.072s	15	8
10	1	M Schumacher	Ferrari	F2005	Ferrari	V10	53	1h 16m 04.729s	6	3
11	11	J Villeneuve	Sauber	C24	Petronas	V10	52		12	6
12	2	R Barrichello	Ferrari	F2005	Ferrari	V10	52		7	4
13	15	C Klien	Red Bull	RB1	Cosworth	V10	52		13	7
14	7	M Webber	Williams	FW27	BMW	V10	52		14	7
15	14	D Coulthard	Red Bull	RB1	Cosworth	V10	52		10	5
16	4	T Sato	BAR	007	Honda	V10	52		4	2
17	18	T Monteiro	Jordan	EJ15B	Toyota	V10	51		17	9
18	20	R Doornbos	Minardi	PS05	Cosworth	V10	51		18	9
19	21	C Albers	Minardi	PS05	Cosworth	V10	51		20	10
20	19	N Karthikeyan	Jordan	EJ15	Toyota	V10	50		19	10
ap	35	P de la Rosa	McLaren	MP4-20	Mercedes-Benz	V10				
ap	38	R Zonta	Toyota	TF105	Toyota	V10				
ap	37	V Liuzzi	Red Bull	RB1	Cosworth	V10				
ap	40	E Toccacelo	Minardi	PS05	Cosworth	V10				
ap	39	N Kiesa	Jordan	EJ15	Toyota	V10				

Winning speed 247.096 km/h, 153.539 mph
Pole Position speed 257.295 km/h, 159.876 mph (J P Montoya, 1 min:21.054 sec)
Fastest Lap speed 255.874 km/h, 158.993 mph (K Räikkönen, 1 min:21.504 sec on lap 51)
Lap Leaders J P Montoya 1-53 (53).

Engine change grid penalty: K Räikkönen (original time was fast enough for pole position).

11 Sep 2005   **BELGIUM: Spa-Francorchamps**   **(Round 16)**   **(Race 747)**

44 laps x 6.976 km, 4.335 miles = 306.927 km, 190.716 miles

Pos	No	Driver	Car	Model	Engine		Laps	Time/Reason for Retirement	Grid Pos	Row
1	9	K Räikkönen	McLaren	MP4-20	Mercedes-Benz	V10	44	1h 30m 01.295s	2	1
2	5	F Alonso	Renault	R25	Renault	V10	44	1h 30m 29.689s	4	2
3	3	J Button	BAR	007	Honda	V10	44	1h 30m 33.372s	8	4
4	7	M Webber	Williams	FW27	BMW	V10	44	1h 31m 10.462s	9	5
5	2	R Barrichello	Ferrari	F2005	Ferrari	V10	44	1h 31m 19.431s	12	6
6	11	J Villeneuve	Sauber	C24	Petronas	V10	44	1h 31m 28.730s	14	7
7	17	R Schumacher	Toyota	TF105	Toyota	V10	44	1h 31m 28.869s	5	3
8	18	T Monteiro	Jordan	EJ15B	Toyota	V10	43		19	10
9	15	C Klien	Red Bull	RB1	Cosworth	V10	43		16	8
10	12	F Massa	Sauber	C24	Petronas	V10	43		7	4
11	19	N Karthikeyan	Jordan	EJ15B	Toyota	V10	43		20	10
12	21	C Albers	Minardi	PS05	Cosworth	V10	42		18	9
13	20	R Doornbos	Minardi	PS05	Cosworth	V10	41		17	9
14r	10	J P Montoya	McLaren	MP4-20	Mercedes-Benz	V10	40	accident	1	1
15r	8	A Pizzonia	Williams	FW27	BMW	V10	39	accident	15	8
r	16	J Trulli	Toyota	TF105	Toyota	V10	34	accident	3	2
r	14	D Coulthard	Red Bull	RB1	Cosworth	V10	18	engine	11	6
r	1	M Schumacher	Ferrari	F2005	Ferrari	V10	13	accident	6	3
r	4	T Sato	BAR	007	Honda	V10	13	accident	10	5
r	6	G Fisichella	Renault	R25	Renault	V10	10	accident	13	7
ap	35	A Wurz	McLaren	MP4-20	Mercedes-Benz	V10				
ap	38	R Zonta	Toyota	TF105	Toyota	V10				
ap	37	V Liuzzi	Red Bull	RB1	Cosworth	V10				
ap	39	N Kiesa	Jordan	EJ15	Toyota	V10				
ap	40	E Toccacelo	Minardi	PS05	Cosworth	V10				

Winning speed 204.568 km/h, 127.113 mph
Pole Position speed 236.050 km/h, 146.675 mph (J P Montoya,1 min:46.391 sec)
Fastest Lap speed 225.329 km/h, 140.013 mph (R Schumacher,1 min:51.453 sec on lap 43)
Lap Leaders J P Montoya 1-32 (32); K Räikkönen 33-44 (12).

Engine change grid penalty: G Fisichella.

25 Sep 2005   **BRAZIL: Interlagos**   **(Round 17)**   **(Race 748)**

71 laps x 4.309 km, 2.677 miles = 305.909 km, 190.083 miles

Pos	No	Driver	Car	Model	Engine		Laps	Time/Reason for Retirement	Grid Pos	Row
1	10	J P Montoya	McLaren	MP4-20	Mercedes-Benz	V10	71	1h 29m 20.574s	2	1
2	9	K Räikkönen	McLaren	MP4-20	Mercedes-Benz	V10	71	1h 29m 23.101s	5	3
3	5	F Alonso	Renault	R25	Renault	V10	71	1h 29m 45.414s	1	1
4	1	M Schumacher	Ferrari	F2005	Ferrari	V10	71	1h 29m 56.242s	7	4
5	6	G Fisichella	Renault	R25	Renault	V10	71	1h 30m 00.792s	3	2
6	2	R Barrichello	Ferrari	F2005	Ferrari	V10	71	1h 30m 29.747s	9	5
7	3	J Button	BAR	007	Honda	V10	70		4	2
8	17	R Schumacher	Toyota	TF105	Toyota	V10	70		10	5
9	15	C Klien	Red Bull	RB1	Cosworth	V10	70		6	3
10	4	T Sato	BAR	007	Honda	V10	70		19	10
11	12	F Massa	Sauber	C24	Petronas	V10	70		8	4
12	11	J Villeneuve	Sauber	C24	Petronas	V10	70		20	10
13	16	J Trulli	Toyota	TF105	Toyota	V10	69		17	9
14	21	C Albers	Minardi	PS05	Cosworth	V10	69		16	8
15	19	N Karthikeyan	Jordan	EJ15B	Toyota	V10	68		15	8
r	18	T Monteiro	Jordan	EJ15B	Toyota	V10	55	driveshaft	11	6
nc	7	M Webber	Williams	FW27	BMW	V10	45		12	6
r	20	R Doornbos	Minardi	PS05	Cosworth	V10	34	oil pipe	18	9
r	8	A Pizzonia	Williams	FW27	BMW	V10	0	accident	13	7
r	14	D Coulthard	Red Bull	RB1	Cosworth	V10	0	accident	14	7
ap	35	A Wurz	McLaren	MP4-20	Mercedes-Benz	V10				
ap	38	R Zonta	Toyota	TF105	Toyota	V10				
ap	37	V Liuzzi	Red Bull	RB1	Cosworth	V10				
ap	39	N Kiesa	Jordan	EJ15B	Toyota	V10				

Winning speed 205.439 km/h, 127.654 mph
Pole Position speed 215.485 km/h, 133.897 mph (F Alonso,1 min:11.988 sec)
Fastest Lap speed 214.651 km/h, 133.378 mph (K Räikkönen,1 min:12.268 sec on lap 29)
Lap Leaders F Alonso 1-2 (2); J P Montoya 3-28,32-54,60-71 (61); K Räikkönen 29-31,55-59 (8).

Engine change grid penalty: J Trulli. T Sato received a 10 place grid penalty for dangerous driving in Belgium.
J Villeneuve had to start from the back of the field (from the pit lane) due to a parc fermé infringement.

Races

JAPAN: Suzuka

(Round 18) **(Race 749)**

53 laps x 5.807 km, 3.608 miles = 307.573 km, 191.117 miles

Pos	No	Driver	Car	Model	Engine		Laps	Time/Reason for Retirement	Grid Pos	Row
1	9	K Räikkönen	McLaren	MP4-20	Mercedes-Benz	V10	53	1h 29m 02.212s	17	9
2	6	G Fisichella	Renault	R25	Renault	V10	53	1h 29m 03.845s	3	2
3	5	F Alonso	Renault	R25	Renault	V10	53	1h 29m 19.668s	16	8
4	7	M Webber	Williams	FW27	BMW	V10	53	1h 29m 24.486s	7	4
5	3	J Button	BAR	007	Honda	V10	53	1h 29m 31.719s	2	1
6	14	D Coulthard	Red Bull	RB1	Cosworth	V10	53	1h 29m 33.813s	6	3
7	1	M Schumacher	Ferrari	F2005	Ferrari	V10	53	1h 29m 36.091s	14	7
8	17	R Schumacher	Toyota	TF105B	Toyota	V10	53	1h 29m 51.760s	1	1
9	15	C Klien	Red Bull	RB1	Cosworth	V10	53	1h 29m 54.137s	4	2
10	12	F Massa	Sauber	C24	Petronas	V10	53	1h 29m 59.721s	10	5
11	2	R Barrichello	Ferrari	F2005	Ferrari	V10	53	1h 30m 02.845s	9	5
12	11	J Villeneuve	Sauber	C24	Petronas	V10	53	1h 30m 25.433s	8	4
13	18	T Monteiro	Jordan	EJ15B	Toyota	V10	52		20	10
dq	4	T Sato	BAR	007	Honda	V10	52	forced J Trulli off track	5	3
14	20	R Doornbos	Minardi	PS05	Cosworth	V10	51		15	8
15	19	N Karthikeyan	Jordan	EJ15B	Toyota	V10	51		11	6
16	21	C Albers	Minardi	PS05	Cosworth	V10	49		13	7
r	8	A Pizzonia	Williams	FW27	BMW	V10	9	accident	12	6
r	16	J Trulli	Toyota	TF105B	Toyota	V10	9	accident	19	10
r	10	J P Montoya	McLaren	MP4-20	Mercedes-Benz	V10	0	accident	18	9
ap	35	P de la Rosa	McLaren	MP4-20	Mercedes-Benz	V10				
ap	38	R Zonta	Toyota	TF105	Toyota	V10				
ap	37	V Liuzzi	Red Bull	RB1	Cosworth	V10				
ap	39	S Yamamoto	Jordan	EJ15B	Toyota	V10				

Winning speed 207.266 km/h, 128.790 mph
Pole Position speed 197.021 km/h, 122.424 mph (R Schumacher,1 min:46.106 sec)
Fastest Lap speed 228.372 km/h, 141.904 mph (K Räikkönen,1 min:31.540 sec on lap 44)
Lap Leaders R Schumacher 1-12 (12); G Fisichella 13-20,27-38,46-52 (27); J Button 21-22,39-40 (4); D Coulthard 23 (1); M Schumacher 24-26 (3); K Räikkönen 41-45,53 (6).

Engine change grid penalty: K Räikkönen.
T Sato completed 42 laps but was disqualified for forcing J P Montoya off the track.
J Villeneuve was penalised 25 seconds for forcing J Trulli off the track.

CHINA: Shanghai

(Round 19) **(Race 750)**

56 laps x 5.451 km, 3.387 miles = 305.066 km, 189.559 miles

Pos	No	Driver	Car	Model	Engine		Laps	Time/Reason for Retirement	Grid Pos	Row
1	5	F Alonso	Renault	R25	Renault	V10	56	1h 39m 53.618s	1	1
2	9	K Räikkönen	McLaren	MP4-20	Mercedes-Benz	V10	56	1h 39m 57.633s	3	2
3	17	R Schumacher	Toyota	TF105B	Toyota	V10	56	1h 40m 18.994s	9	5
4	6	G Fisichella	Renault	R25	Renault	V10	56	1h 40m 19.732s	2	1
5	15	C Klien	Red Bull	RB1	Cosworth	V10	56	1h 40m 25.457s	14	7
6	12	F Massa	Sauber	C24	Petronas	V10	56	1h 40m 30.018s	11	6
7	7	M Webber	Williams	FW27	BMW	V10	56	1h 40m 30.460s	10	5
8	3	J Button	BAR	007	Honda	V10	56	1h 40m 34.867s	4	2
9	14	D Coulthard	Red Bull	RB1	Cosworth	V10	56	1h 40m 37.865s	7	4
10	11	J Villeneuve	Sauber	C24	Petronas	V10	56	1h 40m 53.595s	16	8
11	18	T Monteiro	Jordan	EJ15B	Toyota	V10	56	1h 41m 18.266s	19	10
12	2	R Barrichello	Ferrari	F2005	Ferrari	V10	56	1h 41m 26.430s	8	4
13	8	A Pizzonia	Williams	FW27	BMW	V10	55		13	7
14	20	R Doornbos	Minardi	PS05	Cosworth	V10	55		20	10
15	16	J Trulli	Toyota	TF105B	Toyota	V10	55		12	6
16	21	C Albers	Minardi	PS05	Cosworth	V10	51		18	9
r	4	T Sato	BAR	007	Honda	V10	34	gearbox	17	9
r	19	N Karthikeyan	Jordan	EJ15B	Toyota	V10	28	accident	15	8
r	10	J P Montoya	McLaren	MP4-20	Mercedes-Benz	V10	24	hit drain cover / engine	5	3
r	1	M Schumacher	Ferrari	F2005	Ferrari	V10	22	spin	6	3
ap	35	P de la Rosa	McLaren	MP4-20	Mercedes-Benz	V10				
ap	38	R Zonta	Toyota	TF105	Toyota	V10				
ap	37	V Liuzzi	Red Bull	RB1	Cosworth	V10				
ap	39	N Kiesa	Jordan	EJ15B	Toyota	V10				

Winning speed 183.234 km/h, 113.857 mph
Pole Position speed 208.584 km/h, 129.608 mph (F Alonso,1 min:34.080 sec)
Fastest Lap speed 210.458 km/h, 130.773 mph (K Räikkönen,1 min:33.242 sec on lap 56)
Lap Leaders F Alonso 1-56 (56).

Lap Leaders 2005

Pos	Driver	Car-Engine	GPs	laps	km	miles
1	K Räikkönen	McLaren-Mercedes-Benz	12	375	1,722.4	1,070.3
2	F Alonso	Renault	11	336	1,695.4	1,053.5
3	J P Montoya	McLaren-Mercedes-Benz	6	217	1,142.7	710.1
4	G Fisichella	Renault	5	116	598.5	371.9
5	M Schumacher	Ferrari	4	85	368.7	229.1
6	R Barrichello	Ferrari	2	23	97.5	60.6
7	R Schumacher	Toyota	1	12	69.7	43.3
8	J Button	BAR-Honda	2	9	47.9	29.8
9	J Trulli	Toyota	2	4	21.9	13.6
10	D Coulthard	Red Bull-Cosworth	2	2	11.0	6.8
11	N Heidfeld	Williams-BMW	1	1	5.1	3.2
			19	1,180	5,780.8	3,592.0

Driver Points 2005

		AUS	MAL	BRN	RSM	E	MC	EUR	CDN	USA	F	GB	D	H	TR	I	B	BR	J	CHN	Total
1	F Alonso	6	10	10	10	8	5	10	-	-	10	8	10	-	8	8	8	6	6	10	133
2	K Räikkönen	1	-	6	-	10	10	-	10	-	8	6	-	10	10	5	10	8	10	8	112
3	M Schumacher	-	2	-	8	-	2	4	8	10	6	3	4	8	-	-	-	5	2	-	62
4	J P Montoya	3	5	-	-	2	4	2	-	-	-	10	8	-	6	10	-	10	-	-	60
5	G Fisichella	10	-	-	-	4	-	3	-	-	3	5	5	-	5	6	-	4	8	5	58
6	R Schumacher	-	4	5	-	5	3	-	3	-	2	1	3	6	-	3	2	1	1	6	45
7	J Trulli	-	8	8	4	6	-	1	-	-	4	-	-	5	3	4	-	-	-	-	43
8	R Barrichello	8	-	-	-	-	1	6	6	8	-	2	-	-	-	-	4	3	-	-	38
9	J Button	-	-	-	-	-	-	-	-	-	5	4	6	4	4	1	6	2	4	1	37
10	M Webber	4	-	3	2	3	6	-	4	-	-	-	-	2	-	-	5	-	5	2	36
11	N Heidfeld	-	6	-	3	-	8	8	-	-	-	-	-	3	-	-	-	-	-	-	28
12	D Coulthard	5	3	1	-	1	-	5	2	-	-	-	2	-	2	-	-	-	3	-	24
13	F Massa	-	-	2	-	-	-	-	5	-	-	-	1	-	-	-	-	-	-	3	11
14	J Villeneuve	-	-	-	5	-	-	-	-	-	1	-	-	-	-	-	3	-	-	-	9
	C Klien	2	1	-	-	-	-	-	1	-	-	-	-	-	1	-	-	-	-	4	9
16	T Monteiro	-	-	-	-	-	-	-	6	-	-	-	-	-	-	-	1	-	-	-	7
17	A Wurz	-	-	-	6	-	-	-	-	-	-	-	-	-	-	-	-	-	-	-	6
18	N Karthikeyan	-	-	-	-	-	-	-	-	5	-	-	-	-	-	-	-	-	-	-	5
19	C Albers	-	-	-	-	-	-	-	-	4	-	-	-	-	-	-	-	-	-	-	4
	P de la Rosa	-	-	4	-	-	-	-	-	-	-	-	-	-	-	-	-	-	-	-	4
21	P Friesacher	-	-	-	-	-	-	-	-	3	-	-	-	-	-	-	-	-	-	-	3
22	A Pizzonia	-	-	-	-	-	-	-	-	-	-	-	-	-	-	-	2	-	-	-	2
23	V Liuzzi	-	-	-	1	-	-	-	-	-	-	-	-	-	-	-	-	-	-	-	1
	T Sato	-	-	-	-	-	-	-	-	-	-	-	-	1	-	-	-	-	-	-	1

10,8,6,5,4,3,2 and 1 point awarded to the first eight finishers.

Constructor Points 2005

		AUS	MAL	BRN	RSM	E	MC	EUR	CDN	USA	F	GB	D	H	TR	I	B	BR	J	CHN	Total
1	Renault	16	10	10	10	12	5	13	-	-	13	13	15	-	13	14	8	10	14	15	191
2	McLaren-Mercedes-Benz	4	5	10	6	12	14	2	10	-	8	16	8	10	16	15	10	18	10	8	182
3	Ferrari	8	2	-	8	-	3	10	14	18	6	5	4	8	-	-	4	8	2	-	100
4	Toyota	-	12	13	4	11	3	1	3	-	6	1	3	11	3	7	2	1	1	6	88
5	Williams-BMW	4	6	3	5	3	14	8	4	-	-	-	-	5	-	2	5	-	5	2	66
6	BAR-Honda	-	-	-	-	-	-	-	-	-	5	4	6	5	4	1	6	2	4	1	38
7	Red Bull-Cosworth	7	4	1	1	1	-	5	3	-	-	-	2	-	3	-	-	-	3	4	34
8	Sauber-Petronas	-	-	2	5	-	-	-	5	-	1	-	1	-	-	-	3	-	-	3	20
9	Jordan-Toyota	-	-	-	-	-	-	-	11	-	-	-	-	-	-	-	1	-	-	-	12
10	Minardi-Cosworth	-	-	-	-	-	-	-	7	-	-	-	-	-	-	-	-	-	-	-	7

10,8,6,5,4,3,2 and 1 point awarded to the first eight finishers.

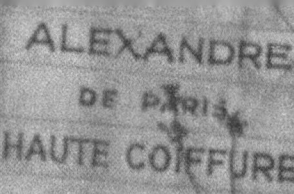

2

SEASON-BY-SEASON SUMMARY

Grands Prix (1950 to 2005)
Race Results and Grid Positions

Indianapolis 500 (1950 to 1960)
Race Results and Grid Positions

Left: *In 1978 Alan Jones was regularly up among the race leaders, but he retired at Monaco when his Williams FW06-Ford Cosworth developed an oil leak. His best result that year was a second at Watkins Glen.* (Maureen Magee)

1950 RACE RESULTS & GRID POSITIONS

	GB	MC	CH	B	F	I
Alberto ASCARI	-	2	r	5	-	r/2=
(Ferrari)	-	7	5	8	ns	2
Clemente BIONDETTI	-	-	-	-	-	r
(Ferrari-Jaguar)	-	-	-	-	-	25
B BIRA	r	5	4	-	-	r
(Maserati)	5	15	8	-	-	15
Felice BONETTO	-	-	5	-	r	-
(Maserati Milano)	-	-	12	-	11	-
(Milano-Speluzzi)	-	-	-	-	-	23ns
Toni BRANCA	-	-	11	10	-	-
(Maserati)	-	-	17	13	-	-
Eugène CHABOUD	-	-	-	r	5=	-
(Talbot Lago)	-	-	-	11	10ns	-
Louis CHIRON	r	3	9	-	r	r
(Maserati)	11	8	16	-	14	19
Johnny CLAES	11	7	10	8	r	r
(Talbot Lago)	21	19	14	14	15	22
Franco COMOTTI	-	-	-	-	-	r
(Maserati Milano)	-	-	-	-	-	26
Geoffrey CROSSLEY	r	-	-	9	-	-
(Alta)	17	-	-	12	-	-
Emmanuel de GRAFFENRIED	r	r	6	-	-	6
(Maserati)	8	11	11	-	-	17
Philippe ÉTANÇELIN	8	r	r	r	5=	5
(Talbot Lago)	14	4	6	7	4	16
Luigi FAGIOLI	2	r	2	2	2	3
(Alfa Romeo)	2	5	3	3	3	5
Juan Manuel FANGIO	r	1f	r	1	1f	rf/r=
(Alfa Romeo)	3	1	1	2	1	1
Giuseppe FARINA	1f	r	1f	4f	7r	1
(Alfa Romeo)	1	2	2	1	2	3
Joe FRY †	10=	-	-	-	-	-
(Maserati)	20	-	-	-	-	-
Bob GERARD	6	6	-	-	-	-
(ERA)	13	16	-	-	-	-
Yves GIRAUD-CABANTOUS	4	-	r	r	8	-
(Talbot Lago)	6	-	7	9	5	-
Froilán GONZÁLEZ	-	r	-	-	r	-
(Maserati)	-	3	-	-	8	-
David HAMPSHIRE	9	-	-	-	r	-
(Maserati)	16	-	-	-	18	-
Cuth HARRISON	7	r	-	-	-	r
(ERA)	15	14	-	-	-	21
Leslie JOHNSON	r	-	-	-	-	-
(ERA)	12	-	-	-	-	-
Joe KELLY	nc	-	-	-	-	-
(Alta)	19	-	-	-	-	-
Pierre LEVEGH	-	-	-	7	r	r
(Talbot Lago)	-	-	-	10	9	20

	GB	MC	CH	B	F	I
Henri LOUVEAU	-	-	-	-	-	r
(Talbot Lago)	-	-	-	-	-	14
Guy MAIRESSE	-	-	-	-	-	r
(Talbot Lago)	-	-	-	-	-	11
Robert MANZON	-	r	-	-	4	r
(Simca Gordini)	-	12	-	-	13	10
Eugène MARTIN	r	-	r	-	-	-
(Talbot Lago)	7	-	9	-	-	-
David MURRAY	r	-	-	-	-	r
(Maserati)	18	-	-	-	-	24
Nello PAGANI	-	-	7	-	-	-
(Maserati)	-	-	15	-	-	-
Reg PARNELL	3	-	-	-	r	-
(Alfa Romeo)	4	-	-	-	-	-
(Maserati)	-	-	-	-	12	-
Alfredo PIÁN	-	18ns	-	-	-	-
(Maserati)	-	-	-	-	-	-
Paul PIETSCH	-	-	-	-	-	r
(Maserati)	-	-	-	-	-	27
Charles POZZI	-	-	-	-	6=	-
(Talbot Lago)	-	-	-	-	16	-
Franco ROL	-	r	-	-	r	r
(Maserati)	-	17	-	-	7	9
Tony ROLT	r=	-	-	-	-	-
(ERA)	-	-	-	-	-	-
Louis ROSIER	5	r	3	3	r/6=	4
(Talbot Lago)	9	10	10	6	6	13
Consalvo SANESI	-	-	-	-	-	r
(Alfa Romeo)	-	-	-	-	-	4
Harry SCHELL	-	r	8	-	-	-
(Cooper-JAP)	-	20	-	-	-	-
(Talbot Lago)	-	-	18	-	-	-
Dorino SERAFINI	-	-	-	-	-	2=
(Ferrari)	-	-	-	-	-	6
Brian SHAWE-TAYLOR	10=	-	-	-	-	-
(Maserati)	-	-	-	-	-	-
Raymond SOMMER †	-	4	r	r	r	r
(Ferrari)	-	9	13	-	-	-
(Talbot Lago)	-	-	-	5	17	8
Piero TARUFFI	-	-	-	-	-	r=
(Alfa Romeo)	-	-	-	-	-	7
Maurice TRINTIGNANT	-	r	-	-	-	r
(Simca Gordini)	-	13	-	-	-	12
Luigi VILLORESI	-	r	r	6	-	-
(Ferrari)	-	6	4	4	ns	-
Peter WALKER	r=	-	-	-	-	-
(ERA)	10	-	-	-	-	-
Peter WHITEHEAD	-	-	-	-	3	7
(Ferrari)	-	ns	-	-	19	18

	CH	B	F	GB	D	I	E
George ABECASSIS	r	-	-	-	-	-	-
(HWM)	20	-	-	-	-	-	-
Alberto ASCARI	6	2	r/2=	r	1	1	4
(Ferrari)	7	4	3	4	1	3	1
B BIRA	-	-	-	-	-	-	r
(Maserati-OSCA)	-	-	-	-	-	-	19
Felice BONETTO	-	-	-	4	r	3=	5
(Alfa Romeo)	-	-	-	7	10	7	8
Toni BRANCA	-	-	-	-	r	-	-
(Maserati)	-	-	-	-	17	-	-
Eugène CHABOUD	-	-	8	-	-	-	-
(Talbot Lago)	-	-	14	-	-	-	-
Louis CHIRON	7	r	6	r	r	r	r
(Maserati)	19	-	-	-	-	-	-
(Talbot Lago)	-	9	8	13	13	17	12
Johnny CLAES	13	7	r	13	11	r	r
(Talbot Lago)	18	11	12	14	18	21	15
Emmanuel de GRAFFENRIED	5	-	r	-	r	r	6
(Alfa Romeo)	5	-	-	-	-	-	-
(Maserati)	-	-	16	-	16	-	-
Philippe ÉTANÇELIN	10	r	r	-	r	-	8
(Talbot Lago)	12	10	10	-	21	-	13
Luigi FAGIOLI	-	-	1=/11=	-	-	-	-
(Alfa Romeo)	-	-	7	-	-	-	-
Juan Manuel FANGIO	1f	9f	11=/1=f	2	2f	r	1f
(Alfa Romeo)	1	1	1	2	3	1	2
Giuseppe FARINA	3	1	5	rf	r	r/3=f	3
(Alfa Romeo)	2	2	2	3	4	2	4
Rudi FISCHER	11	-	-	-	6	-	-
(Ferrari)	10	-	-	-	8	ns	-
Philip FOTHERINGHAM-PARKER	-	-	-	r	-	-	-
(Maserati)	-	-	-	16	-	-	-
Bob GERARD	-	-	-	11	-	-	-
(ERA)	-	-	-	10	-	-	-
Yves GIRAUD-CABANTOUS	r	5	7	-	r	8	r
(Talbot Lago)	15	8	11	-	11	14	14
Chico GODIA	-	-	-	-	-	-	10
(Maserati)	-	-	-	-	-	-	17
Froilán GONZÁLEZ	r	-	2=	1	3	2	2
(Talbot Lago)	13	-	-	-	-	-	-
(Ferrari)	-	-	6	1	2	4	3
Aldo GORDINI	-	-	r	-	-	-	-
(Simca Gordini)	-	-	17	-	-	-	-
Georges GRIGNARD	-	-	-	-	-	-	r
(Talbot Lago)	-	-	-	-	-	-	16
Duncan HAMILTON	-	-	-	12	r	-	-
(Talbot Lago)	-	-	-	11	20	-	-
Peter HIRT	r	-	-	-	-	-	-
(Veritas)	16	-	-	-	-	-	-
John JAMES	-	-	-	r	-	-	-
(Maserati)	-	-	-	17	-	-	-
Juan JOVER	-	-	-	-	-	-	-
(Maserati)	-	-	-	-	-	-	18ns
Joe KELLY	-	-	-	nc	-	-	-
(Alta)	-	-	-	18	-	-	-

	CH	B	F	GB	D	I	E
Chico LANDI	-	-	-	-	-	r	-
(Ferrari)	-	-	-	-	-	16	-
Pierre LEVEGH	-	8	-	-	9	r	-
(Talbot Lago)	-	13	-	-	19	20	-
Henri LOUVEAU	r	-	-	-	-	-	-
(Talbot Lago)	11	-	-	-	-	-	-
Guy MAIRESSE	14	-	9	-	-	-	-
(Talbot Lago)	21	-	19	-	-	-	-
Robert MANZON	-	-	r	-	7	r	9
(Simca Gordini)	-	-	23	-	9	13	9
Onofré MARIMÓN	-	-	r	-	-	-	-
(Maserati Milano)	-	-	15	-	-	-	-
Stirling MOSS	8	-	-	-	-	-	-
(HWM)	14	-	-	-	-	-	-
David MURRAY	-	-	-	r	-	-	-
(Maserati)	-	-	-	15	ns	-	-
Reg PARNELL	-	-	4	5	-	-	-
(Thin Wall Ferrari)	-	-	9	-	-	-	-
(BRM)	-	-	-	20	8ns	-	-
Paul PIETSCH	-	-	-	-	r	-	-
(Alfa Romeo)	-	-	-	-	7	-	-
André PILETTE	-	6	-	-	-	-	-
(Talbot Lago)	-	12	-	-	-	-	-
Ken RICHARDSON	-	-	-	-	-	-	-
(BRM)	-	-	-	-	10ns	-	-
Franco ROL	-	-	-	-	-	9	-
(OSCA)	-	-	-	-	-	18	-
Louis ROSIER	9	4	r	10	8	7	7
(Talbot Lago)	8	7	13	9	15	15	20
Consalvo SANESI	4	r	10	6	-	-	-
(Alfa Romeo)	4	6	5	6	-	-	-
Harry SCHELL	12	-	r	-	-	-	-
(Maserati)	17	-	22	-	-	-	-
Brian SHAWE-TAYLOR	-	-	-	8	-	-	-
(Thin Wall Ferrari)	-	ns	-	-	-	-	-
(ERA)	-	-	-	12	-	-	-
André SIMON	-	-	r	-	r	6	r
(Simca Gordini)	-	-	21	-	12	11	10
Hans STUCK	-	-	-	-	-	-	-
(BRM)	-	-	-	-	-	ns	-
Jacques SWATERS	-	-	-	-	10	r	-
(Talbot Lago)	-	-	-	-	22	22	-
Piero TARUFFI	2	r	-	-	5	5	r
(Ferrari)	6	5	-	-	6	6	7
Maurice TRINTIGNANT	-	-	r	-	r	r	r
(Simca Gordini)	-	-	18	-	14	12	11
Luigi VILLORESI	r	3	3	3	4	4	r
(Ferrari)	3	3	4	5	5	5	5
Peter WALKER	-	-	-	7	-	-	-
(BRM)	-	-	-	19	-	-	-
Peter WHITEHEAD	r	-	r	9	-	r	-
(Ferrari)	9	-	20	-	-	19	-
(Thin Wall Ferrari)	-	-	-	8	-	-	-

	CH	B	F	GB	D	NL	I
George ABECASSIS	r	-	-	-	-	-	-
(HWM)	10	-	-	-	-	-	-
Alberto ASCARI	-	1f	1f	1f	1f	1f	1f=
(Ferrari)	-	1	1	2	1	1	1
Bill ASTON	-	-	-	-	r	-	-
(Aston-Butterworth)	-	-	-	30ns	21	-	nq
Marcel BALSA	-	-	-	-	r	-	-
(BMW)	-	-	-	-	25	-	-
Elie BAYOL	-	-	-	-	-	-	r
(OSCA)	-	-	-	-	-	-	10
Jean BEHRA	3	r	7	-	5	r	r
(Gordini)	7	5	4	-	11	6	11
Gino BIANCO	-	-	-	18	r	r	r
(Maserati)	-	-	-	28	16	12	24
B BIRA	r	10	r	11	-	-	-
(Gordini) *	11	18	7	10	-	-	-
Felice BONETTO	-	-	-	-	dq	-	5
(Maserati)	-	-	-	-	10	-	13
Eric BRANDON	8	9	-	20	-	-	13
(Cooper-Bristol)	17	12	-	18	-	-	20
Alan BROWN	5	6	-	22	-	-	15
(Cooper-Bristol)	15	9	-	13	-	-	21
Adolf BRUDES	-	-	-	-	r	-	-
(Veritas)	-	-	-	-	19	-	-
Eitel CANTONI	-	-	-	r	r	-	11
(Maserati)	-	-	-	27	26	-	23
Piero CARINI	-	-	r	-	r	-	-
(Ferrari)	-	-	19	-	27	-	-
Johnny CLAES	-	8	r	14	10	-	-
(Gordini) *	-	19	20	23	-	-	nq
(HWM)	-	-	-	-	32	-	-
Peter COLLINS	r	r	6	r	-	-	-
(HWM)	6	11	8	14	ns	-	nq
Franco COMOTTI	-	-	12	-	-	-	-
(Ferrari)	-	-	16	-	-	-	-
Alberto CRESPO	-	-	-	-	-	-	-
(Maserati Platé)	-	-	-	-	-	-	nq
Tony CROOK	-	-	-	21	-	-	-
(Frazer Nash-Bristol)	-	-	-	25	-	-	-
Emmanuel de GRAFFENRIED	6	-	r=	19	-	-	-
(Maserati Platé)	8	-	12	31	-	-	nq
Max de TERRA	r	-	-	-	-	-	-
(Simca Gordini)	21	-	-	-	-	-	-
Charles de TORNACO	-	7	-	-	-	r	-
(Ferrari)	-	13	-	-	-	17	nq
Ken DOWNING	-	-	-	9	-	r	-
(Connaught)	-	-	-	5	-	13	-
Piero DUSIO	-	-	-	-	-	-	-
(Cisitalia-BPM)	-	-	-	-	-	-	nq
Philippe ÉTANÇELIN	-	-	8	-	-	-	-
(Maserati)	-	-	18	-	-	-	-
Giuseppe FARINA	r/r=	2	2	6	2	2	4
(Ferrari)	1	2	2	1	2	2	3
Ludwig FISCHER	-	-	-	-	-	-	-
(AFM-BMW)	-	-	-	-	31ns	-	-
Rudi FISCHER	2	-	11=	13	3	-	r
(Ferrari)	5	-	17	15	6	-	14
Jan FLINTERMAN	-	-	-	-	-	r/9=	-
(Maserati)	-	-	-	-	-	15	-
Paul FRÈRE	-	5	-	-	r	r	-
(HWM)	-	8	-	-	13	-	-
(Simca Gordini)	-	-	-	-	-	11	-
Tony GAZE	-	15	-	r	r	-	-
(HWM)	-	16	-	26	14	-	nq
Yves GIRAUD-CABANTOUS	-	-	10	-	-	-	-
(HWM)	-	-	10	-	-	-	-
Froilán GONZÁLEZ	-	-	-	-	-	-	2f=
(Maserati)	-	-	-	-	-	-	5
Duncan HAMILTON	-	-	-	r	-	7	-
(HWM)	-	-	-	11	-	10	-
Mike HAWTHORN	-	4	r	3	-	4	nc
(Cooper-Bristol)	-	6	15	7	-	3	12
Willi HEEKS	-	-	-	-	r	-	-
(AFM-BMW)	-	-	-	-	9	-	-
Theo HELFRICH	-	-	-	-	r	-	-
(Veritas)	-	-	-	-	18	-	-
Peter HIRT	7	-	11=	r	-	-	-
(Ferrari)	19	-	-	24	-	-	-
Hans KLENK	-	-	-	-	11	-	-
(Veritas)	-	-	-	-	8	-	-
Ernst KLODWIG	-	-	-	-	12	-	-
(BMW)	-	-	-	-	29	-	-
Willi KRAKAU	-	-	-	-	r	-	-
(AFM-BMW)	-	-	-	-	28ns	-	-
Rudolf KRAUSE	-	-	-	-	r	-	-
(BMW)	-	-	-	-	23	-	-
Chico LANDI	-	-	-	-	-	9=	8
(Maserati)	-	-	-	-	-	16	18
Roger LAURENT	-	12	-	-	6	-	-
(HWM)	-	20	-	-	-	-	-
(Ferrari)	-	-	-	-	17	-	-
Arthur LEGAT	-	13	-	-	-	-	-
(Veritas)	-	21	-	-	-	-	-
Lance MACKLIN	r	11	9	15	-	8	-
(HWM)	12	14	14	29	-	9	nq
Robert MANZON	r	3	4	r	r	5	14
(Gordini)	3	4	5	4	4	8	7
Kenneth McALPINE	-	-	-	16	-	-	r
(Connaught)	-	-	-	17	-	-	22
Harry MERKEL	-	-	-	-	-	-	-
(BMW)	-	-	-	-	ns	-	-
Robin MONTGOMERIE-CHARRINGTON	-	r	-	-	-	-	-
(Aston-Butterworth)	-	15	-	-	-	-	-
Stirling MOSS	r	r	-	r	-	r	r
(HWM)	9	-	-	-	-	-	-
(ERA-Bristol)	-	10	-	16	-	18	-
(Connaught)	-	-	-	-	-	-	9
David MURRAY	-	-	-	r	-	-	-
(Cooper-Bristol)	-	-	-	22	-	-	-
Bernd NACKE @	-	-	-	-	r	-	-
(BMW)	-	-	-	-	30	-	-
Helmut NIEDERMAYR	-	-	-	-	9	-	-
(AFM-BMW)	-	-	-	-	22	-	-
Robert O'BRIEN	-	14	-	-	-	-	-
(Simca Gordini)	-	22	-	-	-	-	-
Reg PARNELL	-	-	-	7	-	-	-
(Cooper-Bristol)	-	-	-	6	-	-	-
Josef PETERS	-	-	-	-	r	-	-
(Veritas)	-	-	-	-	20	-	-
Paul PIETSCH	-	-	-	-	r	-	-
(Veritas)	-	-	-	-	7	-	-
Dennis POORE	-	-	-	4	-	-	12
(Connaught)	-	-	-	8	-	-	19
Fritz RIESS	-	-	-	-	7	-	-
(Veritas)	-	-	-	-	12	-	-
Franco ROL	-	-	-	-	-	-	r
(Maserati)	-	-	-	-	-	-	16

	CH	B	F	GB	D	NL	I
Louis ROSIER	r	r	r	-	-	-	10
(Ferrari)	20	17	9	-	-	-	17
Roy SALVADORI	-	-	-	8	-	-	-
(Ferrari)	-	-	-	19	-	-	-
Harry SCHELL	r	-	r/r=	17	-	-	-
(Maserati Platé)	18	-	11	32	-	-	-
Rudolf SCHOELLER	-	-	-	-	r	-	-
(Ferrari)	-	-	-	-	24	-	-
André SIMON	r=	-	-	-	-	-	6
(Ferrari)	4	-	-	-	-	-	8
Hans STUCK	r	-	-	-	-	-	-
(AFM-Küchen)	14	-	-	-	-	-	-
(Ferrari)	-	-	-	-	-	-	nq
Piero TARUFFI	1f	r	3	2	4	-	7
(Ferrari)	2	3	3	3	5	-	6
Eric THOMPSON	-	-	-	5	-	-	-
(Connaught)	-	-	-	9	-	-	-
Maurice TRINTIGNANT	-	-	5	r	r	6	r
(Ferrari)	ns	-	-	-	-	-	-
(Gordini) *	-	-	6	21	3	5	4

	CH	B	F	GB	D	NL	I
Toni ULMEN	r	-	-	-	8	-	-
(Veritas)	16	-	-	-	15	-	-
Dries van der LOF	-	-	-	-	-	nc	-
(HWM)	-	-	-	-	-	14	-
Luigi VILLORESI	-	-	-	-	-	3	3
(Ferrari)	-	-	-	-	-	4	2
Ken WHARTON	4	r	-	-	-	r	9
(Frazer Nash-Bristol)	13	7	-	-	-	7	-
(Cooper-Bristol)	-	-	-	-	-	-	15
Graham WHITEHEAD	-	-	-	12	-	-	-
(Alta)	-	-	-	12	-	-	-
Peter WHITEHEAD	-	-	r	10	-	-	-
(Alta)	-	-	13	-	-	-	-
(Ferrari)	-	-	-	20	-	-	nq

@ pseudonym of Günther BECHEM who also raced in 1953.
* Although the Simca Gordini partnership was dissolved in 1951, B Bira, J Claes and M Trintignant drove one or more of those cars in 1952. The car was a Gordini for the remainder of the season.

1953 RACE RESULTS & GRID POSITIONS

	RA	NL	B	F	GB	D	CH	I
Kurt ADOLFF	-	-	-	-	-	r	-	-
(Ferrari)	-	-	-	-	-	27	-	-
Alberto ASCARI	1f	1	1	4f=	1f=	8=/r=f	1f	r
(Ferrari)	1	1	2	1	1	1	2	1
John BARBER	8	-	-	-	-	-	-	-
(Cooper-Bristol)	16	-	-	-	-	-	-	-
Edgar BARTH	-	-	-	-	-	r	-	-
(EMW)	-	-	-	-	-	24	-	-
Erwin BAUER	-	-	-	-	-	r	-	-
(Veritas)	-	-	-	-	-	33	-	-
Elie BAYOL	-	-	-	r	-	-	-	r
(OSCA)	-	-	-	15	-	-	ns	13
Günther BECHEM	-	-	-	-	-	r	-	-
(AFM-BMW)	-	-	-	-	-	30	-	-
Jean BEHRA	6	-	r	10	r	r	r	-
(Gordini)	11	-	14	22	22	9	12	-
Georges BERGER	-	-	r	-	-	-	-	-
(Simca Gordini)	-	-	20	-	-	-	-	-
B BIRA	-	-	-	r	7	r	-	11
(Connaught)	-	-	-	11	19	15	-	-
(Maserati)	-	-	-	-	-	-	-	23
Pablo BIRGER	r	-	-	-	-	-	-	-
(Simca Gordini)	14	-	-	-	-	-	-	-
Felice BONETTO †	r	3=	-	r	6	4	r=/4=	r
(Maserati)	15	13	-	2	16	7	10	7
Alan BROWN	9	-	-	-	r	r	-	12
(Cooper-Bristol)	12	-	-	-	21	17	-	24
Piero CARINI	-	-	-	-	-	-	-	r
(Ferrari)	-	-	-	-	-	-	-	20
Louis CHIRON	-	-	-	15	-	-	-	10
(OSCA)	-	-	-	25	ns	-	ns	25
Johnny CLAES	-	nc	r=	12	-	r	-	r
(Connaught)	-	17	-	21	-	25	-	30
(Maserati)	-	-	10	-	-	-	-	-
Peter COLLINS	-	8	r	13	r	-	-	-
(HWM)	-	16	16	17	23	-	-	-
Tony CROOK	-	-	-	-	r	-	-	-
(Cooper-Bristol)	-	-	-	-	25	-	-	-
Emmanuel de GRAFFENRIED	-	5	4	7	r	5	r	r
(Maserati)	-	7	9	9	26	11	8	9
Max de TERRA	-	-	-	-	-	-	8	-
(Ferrari)	-	-	-	-	-	-	19	-

	RA	NL	B	F	GB	D	CH	I
Charles de TORNACO	-	-	-	-	-	-	-	-
(Ferrari)	-	-	ns	-	-	-	-	-
Jack FAIRMAN	-	-	-	r	-	-	-	nc
(HWM)	-	-	-	27	-	-	-	-
(Connaught)	-	-	-	-	-	-	-	22
Juan Manuel FANGIO	r	r	r/r=	2f=	2	2	4=/r=	1f
(Maserati)	2	2	1	4	4	2	1	2
Giuseppe FARINA	r	2	r	5	3	1	2	2
(Ferrari)	4	3	4	6	5	3	3	3
John FITCH	-	-	-	-	-	-	-	r
(HWM)	-	-	-	-	-	-	-	26
Theo FITZAU	-	-	-	-	-	r	-	-
(AFM-BMW)	-	-	-	-	-	21	-	-
Paul FRÈRE	-	-	10	-	-	-	r	-
(HWM)	-	-	11	-	-	-	16	-
Oscar GÁLVEZ	5	-	-	-	-	-	-	-
(Maserati)	9	-	-	-	-	-	-	-
Bob GERARD	-	-	-	11	r	-	-	-
(Cooper-Bristol)	-	-	-	12	18	-	-	-
Yves GIRAUD-CABANTOUS	-	-	-	14	-	-	-	15
(HWM)	-	-	-	18	-	-	-	28
Helm GLÖCKLER	-	-	-	-	-	ns	-	-
(Cooper-Bristol)	-	-	-	-	-	-	-	-
Froilán GONZÁLEZ	3	r/3=	rf	3	4f=	-	-	-
(Maserati)	5	5	3	5	2	-	-	-
Duncan HAMILTON	-	-	-	-	r	-	-	-
(HWM)	-	-	-	-	17	-	-	-
Mike HAWTHORN	4	4	6	1	5	3	3	4
(Ferrari)	6	6	7	7	3	4	7	6
Willi HEEKS	-	-	-	-	-	r	-	-
(Veritas)	-	-	-	-	-	18	-	-
Theo HELFRICH	-	-	-	-	-	12	-	-
(Veritas)	-	-	-	-	-	28	-	-
Hans HERRMANN	-	-	-	-	-	9	-	-
(Veritas)	-	-	-	-	-	14	-	-
Peter HIRT	-	-	-	-	-	-	r	-
(Ferrari)	-	-	-	-	-	-	17	-
Oswald KARCH	-	-	-	-	-	r	-	-
(Veritas)	-	-	-	-	-	34	-	-
Ernst KLODWIG	-	-	-	-	-	15	-	-
(BMW)	-	-	-	-	-	32	-	-

	RA	NL	B	F	GB	D	CH	I
Rudolf KRAUSE	-	-	-	-	-	14	-	-
(BMW)	-	-	-	-	-	26	-	-
Chico LANDI	-	-	-	-	-	-	r	r
(Maserati)	-	-	-	-	-	-	20	21
Hermann LANG	-	-	-	-	-	-	5	-
(Maserati)	-	-	-	-	-	-	11	-
Arthur LEGAT	-	-	r	-	-	-	-	-
(Veritas)	-	-	19	-	-	-	-	-
Ernst LOOF	-	-	-	-	-	r	-	-
(Veritas)	-	-	-	-	-	31	-	-
Lance MACKLIN	-	r	r	r	r	-	r	r
(HWM)	-	15	17	16	12	-	15	27
Umberto MAGLIOLI	-	-	-	-	-	-	-	8
(Ferrari)	-	-	-	-	-	-	-	11
Sergio MANTOVANI	-	-	-	-	-	-	-	7=
(Maserati)	-	-	-	-	-	-	-	12
Robert MANZON	r	-	-	-	-	-	-	-
(Gordini)	8	-	-	-	-	-	-	-
Onofré MARIMÓN	-	-	3	9	r	r	r	r
(Maserati)	-	-	6	8	7	8	5	4
Kenneth McALPINE	-	r	-	-	r	13	-	nc
(Connaught)	-	14	-	-	13	16	-	18
Carlos MENDITÉGUY	r	-	-	-	-	-	-	-
(Gordini)	10	-	-	-	-	-	-	-
Roberto MIÈRES	-	r	-	r	-	-	-	6
(Gordini)	-	19	-	24	-	-	-	16
Stirling MOSS	-	9	-	r	-	6	-	13
(Connaught)	-	9	-	-	-	-	-	-
(Cooper-Alta)	-	-	-	13	-	12	-	10
Luigi MUSSO	-	-	-	-	-	-	-	7=
(Maserati)	-	-	-	-	-	-	-	-
Rodney NUCKEY	-	-	-	-	-	11	-	-
(Cooper-Bristol)	-	-	-	-	-	20	-	-
André PILETTE	-	-	11	-	-	-	-	-
(Connaught)	-	-	18	-	-	-	-	-

	RA	NL	B	F	GB	D	CH	I
Tony ROLT	-	-	-	-	r	-	-	-
(Connaught)	-	-	-	-	10	-	-	-
Louis ROSIER	-	7	8	8	10	10	r	16
(Ferrari)	-	8	13	10	24	22	14	17
Roy SALVADORI	-	r	-	r	r	r	-	r
(Connaught)	-	11	-	19	28	13	-	14
Harry SCHELL	7=	r	7	r	r	r	-	9
(Gordini)	-	10	12	20	9	10	-	15
Albert SCHERRER	-	-	-	-	-	-	9	-
(HWM)	-	-	-	-	-	-	18	-
Adolfo SCHWELM CRUZ	r	-	-	-	-	-	-	-
(Cooper-Bristol)	13	-	-	-	-	-	-	-
Wolfgang SEIDEL	-	-	-	-	-	16	-	-
(Veritas)	-	-	-	-	-	29	-	-
Ian STEWART	-	-	-	-	r	-	-	-
(Connaught)	-	-	-	-	20	-	-	-
Jimmy STEWART	-	-	-	-	r	-	-	-
(Cooper-Bristol)	-	-	-	-	15	-	-	-
Hans STUCK	-	-	-	-	-	r	-	14
(AFM-Bristol)	-	-	-	-	-	23	-	29
Jacques SWATERS	-	-	-	-	-	7	r	-
(Ferrari)	-	-	ns	-	-	19	13	-
Maurice TRINTIGNANT	7=	6	5	r	r	r	r	5
(Gordini)	7	12	8	23	8	5	4	8
Luigi VILLORESI	2	rf	2	6	r	r=/8=	6	3
(Ferrari)	3	4	5	3	6	6	6	5
Fred WACKER	-	-	9	-	-	-	-	-
(Gordini)	-	ns	15	-	-	-	ns	-
Ken WHARTON	-	r	-	r	8	-	7	nc
(Cooper-Bristol)	-	18	-	14	11	-	9	19
Peter WHITEHEAD	-	-	-	-	9	-	-	-
(Cooper-Alta)	-	-	-	-	14	-	-	-

	RA	B	F	GB	D	CH	I	E
Alberto ASCARI	-	-	r	r/r=f=	-	-	r	rf
(Maserati)	-	-	3	30	-	-	-	-
(Ferrari)	-	-	-	-	-	-	2	-
(Lancia)	-	-	-	-	-	-	-	1
Elie BAYOL	5	-	-	-	-	-	-	-
(Gordini)	14	-	-	-	-	-	-	-
Don BEAUMAN	-	-	-	11	-	-	-	-
(Connaught)	-	-	-	17	-	-	-	-
Jean BEHRA	dq	r	6	rf=	10	r	r	r
(Gordini)	16	7	17	5	9	14	12	18
Georges BERGER	-	-	r	-	-	-	-	-
(Gordini)	-	-	20	-	-	-	-	-
B BIRA	7	6	4	r=	r	-	-	9
(Maserati)	9	13	6	10	19	-	-	15
Eric BRANDON	-	-	-	r	-	-	-	-
(Cooper-Bristol)	-	-	-	25	-	-	-	-
Alan BROWN	-	-	-	26ns	-	-	-	-
(Cooper-Bristol)	-	-	-	-	-	-	-	-
Clemar BUCCI	-	-	-	r	r	r	r	-
(Gordini)	-	-	-	13	16	10	17	-
Peter COLLINS	-	-	-	r	-	-	7	-
(Vanwall)	-	-	-	11	-	-	16	ns
Jorge DAPONTE	r	-	-	-	-	-	11	-
(Maserati)	17	-	-	-	-	-	19	-
Emmanuel de GRAFFENRIED	8	-	-	-	-	-	-	r=
(Maserati)	12	-	-	-	-	-	-	21
Giovanni de RIU	-	-	-	-	-	-	-	-
(Maserati)	-	-	-	-	-	-	ns	-
Juan Manuel FANGIO	1	1f	1	4f=	1	1f	1	3
(Maserati)	3	1	-	-	-	-	-	-
(Mercedes-Benz)	-	-	1	1	1	2	1	2
Giuseppe FARINA	2	r	-	-	-	-	-	-
(Ferrari)	1	3	-	-	-	-	-	-
Ron FLOCKHART	-	-	-	r=	-	-	-	-
(Maserati)	-	-	-	-	-	-	-	-
Paul FRÈRE	-	r	r	-	r	-	-	-
(Gordini)	-	10	19	-	6	-	-	-
Bob GERARD	-	-	-	10	-	-	-	-
(Cooper-Bristol)	-	-	-	18	-	-	-	-
Chico GODIA	-	-	-	-	-	-	-	6
(Maserati)	-	-	-	-	-	-	-	13
Froilán GONZÁLEZ	3f	r/4=	r	1f=	2=	2	r/3=f	-
(Ferrari)	2	2	4	2	5	1	5	-
Horace GOULD	-	-	-	15	-	-	-	-
(Cooper-Bristol)	-	-	-	20	-	-	-	-
Mike HAWTHORN	dq	4=	r	2f=	r/2=	r	2	1
(Ferrari)	4	5	8	3	2	6	7	3
Theo HELFRICH	-	-	-	-	r	-	-	-
(Klenk-BMW)	-	-	-	-	21	-	-	-
Hans HERRMANN	-	-	rf	-	r	3	4	r
(Mercedes-Benz)	-	-	7	-	4	7	8	9
Karl KLING	-	-	2	7	4f	r	r	5
(Mercedes-Benz)	-	-	2	6	23	5	4	12
Hermann LANG	-	-	-	-	r	-	-	-
(Mercedes-Benz)	-	-	-	-	11	-	-	-
Roger LOYER	r	-	-	-	-	-	-	-
(Gordini)	15	-	-	-	-	-	-	-
Lance MACKLIN	-	-	r	-	-	-	-	-
(HWM)	-	-	15	-	-	-	-	-

	RA	B	F	GB	D	CH	I	E
Umberto MAGLIOLI	9	-	-	-	-	7	3=	-
(Ferrari)	11	-	-	-	-	11	13	-
Sergio MANTOVANI	-	7	-	-	5	5	9	r
(Maserati)	-	11	ns	-	15	9	9	10
Robert MANZON	-	-	3	r	9	-	r	r
(Ferrari)	-	-	12	15	12	ns	15	17
Onofré MARIMÓN †	r	r	r	3f=	-	-	-	-
(Maserati)	6	4	5	28	8ns	-	-	-
Leslie MARR	-	-	-	13	-	-	-	-
(Connaught)	-	-	-	22	-	-	-	-
Carlos MENDITÉGUY	-	-	-	-	-	-	-	-
(Maserati)	ns	-	-	-	-	-	-	-
Roberto MIÈRES	r	r	r	6	r	4	r	4
(Maserati)	8	12	11	31	17	12	10	11
Stirling MOSS	-	3	-	rf=	r	r	10	r
(Maserati)	-	9	4	3	3	3	3	6
Luigi MUSSO	-	-	-	-	-	-	r	2
(Maserati)	7ns	-	-	-	-	-	14	7
Rodney NUCKEY	-	-	-	ns	-	-	-	-
(Cooper-Bristol)	-	-	-	ns	-	-	-	-
Reg PARNELL	-	-	-	r	-	-	-	-
(Ferrari)	-	-	-	14	-	-	-	-
André PILETTE	-	5	-	9	r	-	-	-
(Gordini)	-	8	-	12	20	-	-	-
Jacques POLLET	-	-	r	-	-	-	-	r
(Gordini)	-	-	18	-	-	-	-	16
John RISELEY-PRICHARD	-	-	-	r	-	-	-	-
(Connaught)	-	-	-	21	-	-	-	-
Louis ROSIER	r	-	r	r	8	-	8	7
(Ferrari)	13	-	13	29	18	-	-	-
(Maserati)	-	-	-	-	-	-	20	20
Roy SALVADORI	-	-	r	r	-	-	-	-
(Maserati)	-	-	10	7	-	-	-	-
Harry SCHELL	6	-	r	12	7	r	-	r
(Maserati)	10	-	21	16	14	13	-	4
Jacques SWATERS	-	r	-	-	8	-	-	r
(Ferrari)	-	14	-	-	16	-	-	19
Piero TARUFFI	-	-	-	-	6	-	-	-
(Ferrari)	-	-	-	-	13	-	-	-
Leslie THORNE	-	-	-	14	-	-	-	-
(Connaught)	-	-	-	23	-	-	-	-
Maurice TRINTIGNANT	4	2	r	5	3	r	5	r
(Ferrari)	5	6	9	8	7	4	11	8
Luigi VILLORESI	-	-	5	r=	-	-	r	r
(Maserati)	-	-	14	27	10ns	-	6	-
(Lancia)	-	-	-	-	-	-	-	5
Ottorino VOLONTERIO	-	-	-	-	-	-	-	r=
(Maserati)	-	-	-	-	-	-	-	-
Fred WACKER	-	-	-	-	r	6	-	-
(Gordini)	-	-	-	-	15	18	-	-
Ken WHARTON	-	-	r	8	-	6	-	8
(Maserati)	-	-	16	9	22ns	8	-	14
Peter WHITEHEAD	-	-	-	r	-	-	-	-
(Cooper-Alta)	-	-	-	24	-	-	-	-
Bill WHITEHOUSE	-	-	-	r	-	-	-	-
(Connaught)	-	-	-	19	-	-	-	-

	RA	MC	B	NL	GB	I
Alberto ASCARI †	r	r	-	-	-	-
(Lancia)	2	2	-	-	-	-
Elie BAYOL	r	r	-	-	-	-
(Gordini)	15	16	-	-	-	-
Jean BEHRA	r/r=/6=	3=/r=	r/5=	6	r	4
(Maserati)	4	5	5	6	3	6
Pablo BIRGER	r	-	-	-	-	-
(Gordini)	9	-	-	-	-	-
Jack BRABHAM	-	-	-	r	-	-
(Cooper-Bristol)	-	-	-	25	-	-
Clemar BUCCI	r=	-	-	-	-	-
(Maserati)	20	-	-	-	-	-
Eugenio CASTELLOTTI	r=	2	r	5	r/6=	3
(Lancia)	12	4	1	-	-	-
(Ferrari)	-	-	-	9	10	4
Louis CHIRON	-	6	-	-	-	-
(Lancia)	-	19	-	-	-	-
Johnny CLAES	-	-	-	11	-	-
(Maserati)	-	-	ns	-	-	-
(Ferrari)	-	-	-	16	-	-
Peter COLLINS	-	-	-	-	r	r
(Maserati)	-	-	-	-	24	11
Nano da SILVA RAMOS	-	-	-	8	r	r
(Gordini)	-	-	-	14	18	18
Jack FAIRMAN	-	-	-	-	-	-
(Connaught)	-	-	-	-	21ns	-
Juan Manuel FANGIO	1f	rf	1f	1	2	1
(Mercedes-Benz)	3	1	2	1	2	1
Giuseppe FARINA	3=/2=	4	3	-	-	-
(Ferrari)	5	14	4	-	-	-
(Lancia)	-	-	-	-	-	5ns
John FITCH	-	-	-	-	-	9
(Maserati)	-	-	-	-	-	20
Paul FRÈRE	-	8=	4	-	-	-
(Ferrari)	-	-	8	-	-	-
Froilán GONZÁLEZ	2=	-	-	-	-	-
(Ferrari)	1	-	-	-	-	-
Horace GOULD	-	-	-	r	r	r
(Maserati)	-	-	-	15	22	21
Mike HAWTHORN	-	r	r	7	6=	r
(Vanwall)	-	12	9	-	-	-
(Ferrari)	-	-	-	5	12	14
Hans HERRMANN	4=	-	-	-	-	-
(Mercedes-Benz)	10	ns	-	-	-	-
Jesús IGLESIAS	r	-	-	-	-	-
(Gordini)	17	-	-	-	-	-
Karl KLING	r/4=	-	r	r	3	r
(Mercedes-Benz)	6	-	6	3	4	3
Jean LUCAS	-	-	-	-	-	r
(Gordini)	-	-	-	-	-	22
Lance MACKLIN	-	-	-	-	8	-
(Maserati)	-	nq	-	-	16	-
Umberto MAGLIOLI	3=	-	-	-	-	6
(Ferrari)	-	-	-	-	-	12

	RA	MC	B	NL	GB	I
Sergio MANTOVANI	r=/7=	-	-	-	-	-
(Maserati)	19	-	-	-	-	-
Robert MANZON	-	r	-	r	r	-
(Gordini)	-	13	-	11	11	-
Leslie MARR	-	-	-	-	r	-
(Connaught)	-	-	-	-	19	-
Kenneth McALPINE	-	-	-	-	r	-
(Connaught)	-	-	-	-	17	-
Carlos MENDITÉGUY	r/r=	-	-	-	-	5
(Maserati)	13	-	-	-	-	16
Roberto MIÈRES	5	r	5=	4f	r	7
(Maserati)	16	6	13	7	6	7
Stirling MOSS	r/4=	9	2	2	1f	rf
(Mercedes-Benz)	8	3	3	2	1	2
Luigi MUSSO	7=/r=	r	7	3	5	r
(Maserati)	18	8	7	4	9	10
Cesare PERDISA	-	r=/3=	8	-	-	-
(Maserati)	-	11	11	-	-	-
Luigi PIOTTI	-	-	-	-	-	ns
(Arzani Volpini-Maserati)	-	-	-	-	-	-
Jacques POLLET	-	7	-	10	-	r
(Gordini)	-	20	-	12	-	19
Tony ROLT	-	-	-	-	r=	-
(Connaught)	-	-	-	-	14	-
Louis ROSIER	-	r	9	9	-	-
(Maserati)	-	17	12	13	-	-
Roy SALVADORI	-	-	-	-	r	-
(Maserati)	-	-	-	-	20	-
Harry SCHELL	6=/r=/7=	r	-	-	r/9=	r
(Maserati)	7	-	-	-	-	-
(Ferrari)	-	18	-	-	-	-
(Vanwall)	-	-	-	-	7	13
André SIMON	-	r	-	-	r	-
(Mercedes-Benz)	-	10	-	-	-	-
(Maserati)	-	-	-	-	8	-
Mike SPARKEN	-	-	-	-	7	-
(Gordini)	-	-	-	-	23	-
Piero TARUFFI	-	8=	-	-	4	2
(Ferrari)	-	15	-	-	-	-
(Mercedes-Benz)	-	-	-	-	5	9
Maurice TRINTIGNANT	r/2=/3=	1	6	r	r	8
(Ferrari)	14	9	10	8	13	15
Alfredo URIA	r	-	-	-	-	-
(Maserati)	21	-	-	-	-	-
Luigi VILLORESI	r/r=	5	-	-	-	-
(Lancia)	11	7	-	-	-	8ns
Peter WALKER	-	-	-	r	r=	-
(Maserati)	-	-	10	-	-	-
(Connaught)	-	-	-	-	°	-
Ken WHARTON	-	-	-	-	9=	r
(Vanwall)	-	-	-	-	15	17
Ted WHITEAWAY	-	-	-	-	-	-
(HWM)	-	nq	-	-	-	-

° Took over in a shared drive and was not on the grid

	RA	MC	B	F	GB	D	I
Elie BAYOL	-	6=	-	-	-	-	-
(Gordini)	-	11	-	-	-	-	-
Jean BEHRA	2	3	7	3	3	3	r/r=
(Maserati)	4	4	4	7	13	8	5
Jo BONNIER	-	-	-	-	-	-	r=
(Maserati)	-	-	-	-	-	-	-
Jack BRABHAM	-	-	-	-	r	-	-
(Maserati)	-	-	-	-	28	-	-
Tony BROOKS	-	-	-	-	r	-	-
(BRM)	-	ns	-	-	9	-	-
Eugenio CASTELLOTTI	r	r/4=	r	2	10=	r/r=	r/8=
(Lancia Ferrari)	2	3	5	2	8	3	2
Colin CHAPMAN	-	-	-	-	-	-	-
(Vanwall)	-	-	-	5ns	-	-	-
Louis CHIRON	-	-	-	-	-	-	-
(Maserati)	-	ns	-	-	-	-	-
Peter COLLINS	r	2=	1	1	r/2=	r/r=	2=
(Ferrari)	9	-	-	-	-	-	-
(Lancia Ferrari)	-	9	3	3	4	2	7
Nano da SILVA RAMOS	-	5	-	8	r	-	r
(Gordini)	-	10	-	14	26	-	20
Emmanuel de GRAFFENRIED	-	-	-	-	-	-	7
(Maserati)	-	-	-	-	-	-	18
Alfonso de PORTAGO	-	-	-	r	2=/10=	r=	r
(Lancia Ferrari)	-	-	-	9	12	10	9
Paul EMERY	-	-	-	-	r	-	-
(Emeryson-Alta)	-	-	-	-	23	-	-
Jack FAIRMAN	-	-	-	-	4	-	5
(Connaught)	-	-	-	-	21	-	15
Juan Manuel FANGIO	r/1=f	4=/2=f	r	4f	1	1f	8=/2=
(Lancia Ferrari)	1	1	1	1	2	1	1
Ron FLOCKHART	-	-	-	-	r	-	3
(BRM)	-	-	-	-	17	-	-
(Connaught)	-	-	-	-	-	-	23
Paul FRÈRE	-	-	2	-	-	-	-
(Lancia Ferrari)	-	-	8	-	-	-	-
Olivier GENDEBIEN	5	-	-	r	-	-	-
(Ferrari-Lancia Ferrari)	10	-	-	-	-	-	-
(Lancia Ferrari)	-	-	-	11	-	-	-
Bob GERARD	-	-	-	-	11	-	-
(Cooper-Bristol)	-	-	-	-	22	-	-
Gerino GERINI	4=	-	-	-	-	-	10
(Maserati)	-	-	-	-	-	-	16
Chico GODIA	-	-	r	7	8	4	4
(Maserati)	-	-	13	17	25	16	17
Froilán GONZÁLEZ	r	-	-	-	r	-	-
(Maserati)	5	-	-	-	-	-	-
(Vanwall)	-	-	-	-	6	-	-
Oscar GONZÁLEZ	6=	-	-	-	-	-	-
(Maserati)	-	-	-	-	-	-	-
Horace GOULD	-	8	r	-	5	r	-
(Maserati)	-	14	14	-	14	13	-
Bruce HALFORD	-	-	-	-	r	dq	r
(Maserati)	-	-	-	-	20	11	21
Mike HAWTHORN	3	-	-	10=	r	-	-
(Maserati)	8	-	ns	-	-	-	-
(BRM)	-	ns	-	-	3	-	-
(Vanwall)	-	-	-	6	-	-	-
Chico LANDI	4=	-	-	-	-	-	-
(Maserati)	11	-	-	-	-	-	-
Les LESTON	-	-	-	-	-	-	r
(Connaught)	-	-	-	-	-	-	19
Umberto MAGLIOLI	-	-	-	-	r	r	r=
(Maserati)	-	-	-	-	24	7	12
Robert MANZON	-	r	-	9	9	r	r
(Gordini)	-	12	-	15	18	15	22
Carlos MENDITÉGUY	r	-	-	-	-	-	-
(Maserati)	6	-	-	-	-	-	-
André MILHOUX	-	-	-	-	-	r	-
(Gordini)	-	-	-	-	-	17	-
Stirling MOSS	r	1	r/3=f	r/5=	rf	2	1f
(Maserati)	7	2	2	8	1	4	6
Luigi MUSSO	1=	r	-	-	-	r=	r
(Lancia Ferrari)	3	8	-	-	-	5	3
Cesare PERDISA	-	7	3=	5=	7	-	-
(Maserati)	-	7	9	16	15	6ns	-
André PILETTE	-	6=	6	11	-	-	-
(Gordini)	-	o	-	19	-	ns	-
(Lancia Ferrari)	-	-	15	-	-	-	-
Luigi PIOTTI	r	-	-	-	-	-	6
(Maserati)	12	-	-	-	-	ns	14
Louis ROSIER †	-	r	8	6	r	5	-
(Maserati)	-	13	10	13	27	14	-
Roy SALVADORI	-	-	-	-	r	r	11
(Maserati)	-	-	-	-	7	9	13
Giorgio SCARLATTI	-	nq	-	-	-	r	-
(Ferrari)	-	-	-	-	-	18	-
Harry SCHELL	-	r	4	r/10=	r	r	r
(Vanwall)	-	5	6	4	5	-	10
(Maserati)	-	-	-	-	-	12	-
Archie SCOTT BROWN	-	-	-	-	r	-	-
(Connaught)	-	-	-	-	10	-	ns
Piero SCOTTI	-	r	-	-	-	-	-
(Connaught)	-	12	-	-	-	-	-
André SIMON	-	-	-	r	-	-	9
(Maserati)	-	-	-	20	-	-	-
(Gordini)	-	-	-	-	-	-	24
Piero TARUFFI	-	-	-	r	-	-	r
(Maserati)	-	-	-	12	-	-	-
(Vanwall)	-	-	-	-	-	-	4
Desmond TITTERINGTON	-	-	-	-	r	-	-
(Connaught)	-	-	-	-	11	-	-
Maurice TRINTIGNANT	-	r	r	r	r	-	r
(Vanwall)	-	6	7	-	16	-	11
(Bugatti)	-	-	18	-	-	-	-
Alfredo URIA	6=	-	-	-	-	-	-
(Maserati)	13	-	-	-	-	-	-
Luigi VILLORESI	-	-	5	r	6	r	r=
(Maserati)	-	-	11	10	19	19	8
Ottorino VOLONTERIO	-	-	-	-	-	nc	-
(Maserati)	-	-	-	-	-	20	-
Wolfgang von TRIPS	-	-	-	-	-	-	ns
(Lancia Ferrari)	-	-	-	-	-	-	ns

o Took over in a shared drive and was not on the grid

	RA	MC	F	GB	D	PES	I
Edgar BARTH	-	-	-	-	F2:1	-	-
(Porsche)	-	-	-	-	12	-	-
Jean BEHRA	2	-	6	r	6	r	r
(Maserati)	3	-	2	2	3	4	5
Jo BONNIER	7	-	-	r	-	r	r
(Maserati)	13	-	-	17	-	9	13
Jack BRABHAM	-	6	r/7=	r	r	7	-
(Cooper-Climax)	-	15	13	13	18	16	-
Tony BROOKS	-	2	-	1=/r=	9	r	7f
(Vanwall)	-	4	-	3	5	6	3
Ivor BUEB	-	r	-	8	-	-	-
(Connaught)	-	16	-	-	-	-	-
(Maserati)	-	-	-	19	-	-	-
Eugenio CASTELLOTTI †	r	-	-	-	-	-	-
(Lancia Ferrari)	4	-	-	-	-	-	-
Peter COLLINS	r/6=	r	3	r/4=	3	-	r
(Lancia Ferrari)	5	2	5	8	4	-	7
Carel Godin de BEAUFORT	-	-	-	-	F2:3	-	-
(Porsche)	-	-	-	-	20	-	-
Alfonso de PORTAGO †	5=	-	-	-	-	-	-
(Lancia Ferrari)	-	-	-	-	-	-	-
Alessandro de TOMASO	9	-	-	-	-	-	-
(Ferrari)	12	-	-	-	-	-	-
Paul ENGLAND	-	-	-	-	r	-	-
(Cooper-Climax)	-	-	-	-	23	-	-
Jack FAIRMAN	-	-	-	r	-	-	-
(BRM)	-	-	-	16	-	-	-
Juan Manuel FANGIO	1	1f	1	r	1f	2	2
(Maserati)	2	1	1	4	1	1	4
Ron FLOCKHART	-	r	r	-	-	-	-
(BRM)	-	11	11	-	-	-	-
Bob GERARD	-	-	-	6	-	-	-
(Cooper-Bristol)	-	-	-	18	-	-	-
Dick GIBSON	-	-	-	-	r	-	-
(Cooper-Climax)	-	-	-	-	24	-	-
Chico GODIA	-	-	-	-	r	r	9
(Maserati)	-	-	-	-	21	12	15
Froilán GONZÁLEZ	5=	-	-	-	-	-	-
(Lancia Ferrari)	10	-	-	-	-	-	-
Horace GOULD	-	r	r	-	r	r	10
(Maserati)	-	12	14	14ns	19	11	18
Masten GREGORY	-	3	-	-	8	4	4
(Maserati)	-	10	-	-	10	7	11
Bruce HALFORD	-	-	-	-	11	r	r
(Maserati)	-	-	-	-	16	14	14
Mike HAWTHORN	r	r/7r=	4	3	2	-	6
(Lancia Ferrari)	7	5	7	5	2	-	10

	RA	MC	F	GB	D	PES	I
Hans HERRMANN	-	nq	-	-	r	-	-
(Maserati)	-	-	-	-	11	-	-
Les LESTON	-	nq	-	r	-	-	-
(Cooper-Climax)	-	-	-	-	-	-	-
(BRM)	-	-	-	12	-	-	-
Stuart LEWIS-EVANS	-	4	r	7	r	5	r
(Connaught)	-	13	-	-	-	-	-
(Vanwall)	-	-	10	6	9	8	1
Mike MacDOWEL	-	-	7=	-	-	-	-
(Cooper-Climax)	-	-	15	-	-	-	-
Herbert MacKAY-FRASER †	-	-	r	-	-	-	-
(BRM)	-	-	12	-	-	-	-
Umberto MAGLIOLI	-	-	-	-	r	-	-
(Porsche)	-	-	-	-	15	-	-
Tony MARSH	-	-	-	-	F2:4	-	-
(Cooper-Climax)	-	-	-	-	22	-	-
Carlos MENDITÉGUY	3	r	r	r	-	-	-
(Maserati)	8	7	9	11	-	-	-
Stirling MOSS	8f	r	-	r=/1=f	5	1f	1
(Maserati)	1	-	-	-	-	-	-
(Vanwall)	-	3	-	1	7	2	2
Luigi MUSSO	r	-	2f	2	4	r	8
(Lancia-Ferrari)	6	-	3	10	8	3	9
Brian NAYLOR	-	-	-	-	F2:2	-	-
(Cooper-Climax)	-	-	-	-	17	-	-
Cesare PERDISA	6=	-	-	-	-	-	-
(Lancia-Ferrari)	11	-	-	-	-	-	-
Luigi PIOTTI	10	-	-	-	-	r	r
(Maserati)	14	nq	-	-	-	13	17
Roy SALVADORI	-	-	r	5	r	r	-
(BRM)	-	nq	-	-	-	-	-
(Vanwall)	-	-	6	-	-	-	-
(Cooper-Climax)	-	-	-	15	14	15	-
Giorgio SCARLATTI	-	r=	-	-	10	6	5=
(Maserati)	-	14	-	-	13	10	12
Harry SCHELL	4	r/r=	5	r	7	3	r/5=
(Maserati)	9	8	4	7	6	5	6
André SIMON	-	-	-	-	-	-	11=
(Maserati)	-	nq	-	-	-	-	16
Maurice TRINTIGNANT	-	5	r	4=	-	-	-
(Lancia-Ferrari)	-	6	8	9	-	-	-
Ottorino VOLONTERIO	-	-	-	-	-	-	11=
(Maserati)	-	-	-	-	-	-	-
Wolfgang von TRIPS	6=	7r=	-	-	-	-	3
(Lancia-Ferrari)	-	9	-	-	-	-	8

Driver / Car	RA	MC	NL	B	F	GB	D	P	I	MA
Cliff ALLISON	-	6	6	4	r	r	5	r	7	10
(Lotus-Climax)	-	13	11	12	20	5	24	-	16	16
(Maserati)	-	-	-	-	-	-	-	13	-	-
Edgar BARTH	-	-	-	-	-	-	F2:2	-	-	-
(Porsche)	-	-	-	-	-	-	13	-	-	-
Jean BEHRA	5	r	3	r	r	r	r	4	r	r
(Maserati)	4	-	-	-	-	-	-	-	-	-
(BRM)	-	2	4	10	9	8	9	4	8	4
Jo BONNIER	-	r	10	9	8	r	r	r	r	4
(Maserati)	-	16	15	14	16	13	21	14	-	-
(BRM)	-	-	-	-	-	-	-	-	10	8
Jack BRABHAM	-	4	8	r	6	6	F2:r	7	r	F2:1
(Cooper-Climax)	-	3	5	8	12	10	19	8	15	19
Tom BRIDGER	-	-	-	-	-	-	-	-	-	r
(Cooper-Climax)	-	-	-	-	-	-	-	-	-	22
Tony BROOKS	-	r	r	1	r/r=	7	1	r	1	r
(Vanwall)	-	1	3	5	5	9	2	5	2	7
Ivor BUEB	-	-	-	-	-	r	r	-	-	-
(Connaught)	-	-	-	-	-	17	-	-	-	-
(Lotus-Climax)	-	-	-	-	-	-	16	-	-	-
Ian BURGESS	-	-	-	-	-	r	F2:3	-	-	-
(Cooper-Climax)	-	-	-	-	-	16	11	-	-	-
Giulio CABIANCA	-	-	-	-	-	-	-	-	r	-
(OSCA)	-	nq	-	-	-	-	-	-	-	-
(Maserati)	-	-	-	-	-	-	-	-	20	-
Louis CHIRON	-	-	-	-	-	-	-	-	-	-
(Maserati)	-	nq	-	-	-	-	-	-	-	-
Peter COLLINS †	r	3	r	r	5	1	r	-	-	-
(Ferrari)	3	9	10	4	4	6	4	-	-	-
Carel Godin de BEAUFORT	-	-	11	-	-	-	r	-	-	-
(Porsche)	-	-	17	-	-	-	15	-	-	-
Maria Teresa de FILIPPIS	-	-	-	10	-	-	-	r	r	-
(Maserati)	-	nq	-	19	-	-	-	15	21	-
Bernie ECCLESTONE	-	-	-	-	-	-	-	-	-	-
(Connaught)	-	nq	-	-	-	-	-	-	-	-
Paul EMERY	-	-	-	-	-	-	-	-	-	-
(Connaught)	-	nq	-	-	-	-	-	-	-	-
Jack FAIRMAN	-	-	-	-	r	-	-	-	-	8
(Connaught)	-	-	-	-	19	-	-	-	-	-
(Cooper-Climax)	-	-	-	-	-	-	-	-	-	11
Juan Manuel FANGIO	4f	-	-	-	4	-	-	-	-	-
(Maserati)	1	-	-	-	8	-	-	-	-	-
Ron FLOCKHART	-	-	-	-	-	-	-	-	-	r
(Cooper-Climax)	-	nq	-	-	-	-	-	-	-	-
(BRM)	-	-	-	-	-	-	-	-	-	15
Olivier GENDEBIEN	-	-	-	6	-	-	-	-	r	r
(Ferrari)	-	-	-	6	-	-	-	-	5	6
Gerino GERINI	-	-	-	-	9	r	-	-	r	11
(Maserati)	-	nq	-	-	15	18	-	-	19	17
Dick GIBSON	-	-	-	-	-	-	r	-	-	-
(Cooper-Climax)	-	-	-	-	-	-	18	-	-	-
Chico GODIA	8	-	r	r	-	-	-	-	-	-
(Maserati)	9	nq	-	18	11	-	-	-	-	-
Christian GOETHALS	-	-	-	-	-	-	r	-	-	-
(Cooper-Climax)	-	-	-	-	-	-	23	-	-	-
Horace GOULD	9	-	-	-	-	-	-	-	-	-
(Maserati)	10	nq	ns	-	-	-	-	-	-	-
Masten GREGORY	-	-	r	r	-	-	-	-	4=	6
(Maserati)	-	-	14	9	-	-	-	-	11	13
André GUELFI	-	-	-	-	-	-	-	-	-	F2:4
(Cooper-Climax)	-	-	-	-	-	-	-	-	-	25

Driver / Car	RA	MC	NL	B	F	GB	D	P	I	MA
Mike HAWTHORN	3	rf	5	2f	1f	2f	r	2f	2	2
(Ferrari)	2	6	6	1	1	4	1	2	3	1
Hans HERRMANN	-	-	-	-	-	-	r	-	-	9
(Maserati)	-	-	-	-	-	-	20	-	18	18
Graham HILL	-	r	r	r	r	r	r	r	6	12
(Lotus-Climax)	-	15	13	15	19	14	22	12	12	12
Phil HILL	-	-	-	-	7	-	F2:5	-	3f	3
(Maserati)	-	-	-	-	13	-	-	-	-	-
(Ferrari)	-	-	-	-	-	-	10	-	7	5
Ken KAVANAGH	-	-	-	-	-	-	-	-	-	-
(Maserati)	-	nq	-	ns	-	-	-	-	-	-
Bruce KESSLER	-	-	-	-	-	-	-	-	-	-
(Connaught)	-	nq	-	-	-	-	-	-	-	-
Robert La CAZE	-	-	-	-	-	-	-	-	-	F2:3
(Cooper-Climax)	-	-	-	-	-	-	-	-	-	23
Stuart LEWIS-EVANS †	-	r	r	3	r=	4	-	3	r	r
(Vanwall)	-	7	1	11	10	7	-	3	4	3
Tony MARSH	-	-	-	-	-	-	F2:4	-	-	-
(Cooper-Climax)	-	-	-	-	-	-	14	-	-	-
Bruce McLAREN	-	-	-	-	-	-	F2:1	-	-	F2:2
(Cooper-Climax)	-	-	-	-	-	-	12	-	-	21
Carlos MENDITÉGUY	7	-	-	-	-	-	-	-	-	-
(Maserati)	6	-	-	-	-	-	-	-	-	-
Stirling MOSS	1	r	1f	r	2	r	rf	1	r	1f
(Cooper-Climax)	7	-	-	-	-	-	-	-	-	-
(Vanwall)	-	8	2	3	6	1	3	1	1	2
Luigi MUSSO †	2	2	7	r	r	-	-	-	-	-
(Ferrari)	5	10	12	2	2	-	-	-	-	-
Brian NAYLOR	-	-	-	-	-	-	r	-	-	-
(Cooper-Climax)	-	-	-	-	-	-	25	-	-	-
François PICARD	-	-	-	-	-	-	-	-	-	r
(Cooper-Climax)	-	-	-	-	-	-	-	-	-	24
Luigi PIOTTI	-	-	-	-	-	-	-	-	-	-
(OSCA)	-	nq	-	-	-	-	-	-	-	-
Troy RUTTMAN	-	-	-	-	10	-	-	-	-	-
(Maserati)	-	-	-	-	18	ns	-	-	-	-
Roy SALVADORI	-	r	4	8	11	3	2	9	5	7
(Cooper-Climax)	-	4	9	13	14	3	6	11	14	14
Giorgio SCARLATTI	-	r	r	-	-	-	-	-	-	-
(Maserati)	-	14	16	-	-	-	-	-	-	-
Harry SCHELL	6	5	2	5	r	5	r	6	r	5
(Maserati)	8	-	-	-	-	-	-	-	-	-
(BRM)	-	12	7	7	3	2	8	7	9	10
Wolfgang SEIDEL	-	-	-	r	-	-	r	-	-	r
(Maserati)	-	-	-	17	-	-	-	-	-	-
(Cooper-Climax)	-	-	-	-	-	-	17	-	-	20
Carroll SHELBY	-	-	-	-	r	9	-	r	r/4=	-
(Maserati)	-	-	-	-	17	15	-	10	17	-
Alan STACEY	-	-	-	-	-	-	r	-	-	-
(Lotus-Climax)	-	-	-	-	-	-	20	-	-	-
Luigi TARAMAZZO	-	-	-	-	-	-	-	-	-	-
(Maserati)	-	nq	-	-	-	-	-	-	-	-
André TESTUT	-	-	-	-	-	-	-	-	-	-
(Maserati)	-	nq	-	-	-	-	-	-	-	-
Maurice TRINTIGNANT	-	1	9	7	r	8	3	8	r	r
(Cooper-Climax)	-	5	8	-	12	7	-	9	13	9
(Maserati)	-	-	-	16	-	-	-	-	-	-
(BRM)	-	-	-	-	-	-	7	-	-	-
Wolfgang von TRIPS	-	r	-	-	3	r	4	5	r	-
(Ferrari)	-	11	-	-	21	11	5	6	6	-

	MC	NL	F	GB	D	P	I	USA
Cliff ALLISON	r	9	-	-	r	-	5	r
(Ferrari)	15	15	-	-	14	-	8	7
Peter ASHDOWN	-	-	-	12	-	-	-	-
(Cooper-Climax)	-	-	-	23	-	-	-	-
Astrubel BAYARDO	-	-	nq	-	-	-	-	-
(Maserati)	-	-	nq	-	-	-	-	-
Jean BEHRA †	r	5	r	-	-	-	-	-
(Ferrari)	2	4	5	-	-	-	-	-
(Behra Porsche)	-	-	-	-	ns	-	-	-
Lucien BIANCHI	-	-	-	-	-	-	-	-
(Cooper-Climax)	nq	-	-	-	-	-	-	-
Harry BLANCHARD	-	-	-	-	-	-	-	7
(Porsche)	-	-	-	-	-	-	-	16
Jo BONNIER	r	1	r	r	5	r	8	-
(BRM)	7	1	6	10	7	5	11	-
Jack BRABHAM	1f	2	3	1	r	r	3	4
(Cooper-Climax)	3	2	2	1	4	2	3	2
Chris BRISTOW	-	-	-	10	-	-	-	-
(Cooper-Borgward)	-	-	-	16	-	-	-	-
Tony BROOKS	2	r	1	r	1f	9	r	3
(Ferrari)	4	8	1	-	1	10	2	4
(Vanwall)	-	-	-	17	-	-	-	-
Ivor BUEB †	-	-	-	13	-	-	-	-
(Cooper-Climax)	nq	-	-	-	-	-	-	-
(Cooper-Borgward)	-	-	-	18	-	-	-	-
Ian BURGESS	-	-	r	r	6	-	14	-
(Cooper-Maserati)	-	-	19	13	15	-	16	-
Giulio CABIANCA	-	-	-	-	-	-	15	-
(Maserati)	-	-	-	-	-	-	21	-
Mário CABRAL	-	-	-	-	-	10	-	-
(Cooper-Maserati)	-	-	-	-	-	14	-	-
Phil CADE	-	-	-	-	-	-	-	18ns
(Maserati)	-	-	-	-	-	-	-	-
George CONSTANTINE	-	-	-	-	-	-	-	r
(Cooper-Climax)	-	-	-	-	-	-	-	15
Fritz d'OREY	-	-	10	r	-	-	-	r
(Maserati)	-	-	18	20	-	-	-	-
(Tec Mec)	-	-	-	-	-	-	-	17
Colin DAVIS	-	-	r	-	-	-	11	-
(Cooper-Maserati)	-	-	17	-	-	-	18	-
Carel Godin de BEAUFORT	-	10	9	-	-	-	-	-
(Porsche)	-	14	-	-	-	-	-	-
(Maserati)	-	-	20	-	-	-	-	-
Alain de CHANGY	-	-	-	-	-	-	-	-
(Cooper-Climax)	nq	-	-	-	-	-	-	-
Maria Teresa de FILIPPIS	-	-	-	-	-	-	-	-
(Behra Porsche)	nq	-	-	-	-	-	-	-
Alessandro de TOMASO	-	-	-	-	-	-	-	r
(Cooper-OSCA)	-	-	-	-	-	-	-	14
Jack FAIRMAN	-	-	-	r	-	-	r	-
(Cooper-Climax)	-	-	-	15	-	-	-	-
(Cooper-Maserati)	-	-	-	-	-	-	20	-
Ron FLOCKHART	r	-	6	r	-	7	13	-
(BRM)	10	-	13	11	-	11	15	-
Olivier GENDEBIEN	-	-	4	-	-	-	6	-
(Ferrari)	-	-	11	-	-	-	6	-
Keith GREENE	-	-	-	-	-	-	-	-
(Cooper-Climax)	-	-	-	nq	-	-	-	-
Masten GREGORY	r	3	r	7	r	2	-	-
(Cooper-Climax)	11	7	7	5	5	3	-	-
Dan GURNEY	-	-	r	-	2	3	4	-
(Ferrari)	-	-	12	-	3	6	4	-

	MC	NL	F	GB	D	P	I	USA
Bruce HALFORD	r	-	-	-	-	-	-	-
(Lotus-Climax)	16	-	-	-	-	-	-	-
Hans HERRMANN	-	-	-	r	r	-	-	-
(Cooper-Maserati)	-	-	-	19	-	-	-	-
(BRM)	-	-	-	-	11	-	-	-
Graham HILL	r	7	r	9	r	r	r	-
(Lotus-Climax)	14	5	14	9	10	15	10	-
Phil HILL	4	6	2	-	3	r	2f	r
(Ferrari)	5	12	3	-	6	7	5	8
Innes IRELAND	-	4	r	-	r	r	r	5
(Lotus-Climax)	-	9	15	ns	13	16	14	9
Pete LOVELY	-	-	-	-	-	-	-	-
(Lotus-Climax)	nq	-	-	-	-	-	-	-
Jean LUCIENBONNET	-	-	-	-	-	-	-	-
(Cooper-Climax)	nq	-	-	-	-	-	-	-
Bruce McLAREN	5	-	5	3f=	r	r	r	1
(Cooper-Climax)	13	-	10	8	9	8	9	10
Bill MOSS	-	-	-	-	-	-	-	-
(Cooper-Climax)	-	-	-	nq	-	-	-	-
Stirling MOSS	r	rf	dqf	2f=	r	1f	1	r
(Cooper-Climax)	1	3	-	-	2	1	1	1
(BRM)	-	-	4	7	-	-	-	-
Brian NAYLOR	-	-	-	r	-	-	-	-
(JBW-Maserati)	-	-	-	14	-	-	-	-
Mike PARKES	-	-	-	nq	-	-	-	-
(Fry-Climax)	-	-	-	nq	-	-	-	-
Tim PARNELL	-	-	-	nq	-	-	-	-
(Cooper-Climax)	-	-	-	nq	-	-	-	-
David PIPER	-	-	-	r	-	-	-	-
(Lotus-Climax)	-	-	-	22	-	-	-	-
Bob SAID	-	-	-	-	-	-	-	r
(Connaught)	-	-	-	-	-	-	-	13
Roy SALVADORI	6	r	r	6	-	6	r	r
(Cooper-Maserati)	8	-	16	-	-	-	-	11
(Aston Martin)	-	13	-	2	-	12	17	-
Giorgio SCARLATTI	-	-	8	-	-	-	12	-
(Maserati)	nq	-	21	-	-	-	-	-
(Cooper-Climax)	-	-	-	-	-	-	12	-
Harry SCHELL	r	r	7	4	7	5	7	r
(BRM)	9	6	9	3	8	9	7	-
(Cooper-Climax)	-	-	-	-	-	-	-	3
Carroll SHELBY	-	r	-	r	-	8	10	-
(Aston Martin)	-	10	-	6	-	13	19	-
Alan STACEY	-	-	-	8	-	-	-	r
(Lotus-Climax)	-	-	-	12	-	-	-	12
Dennis TAYLOR	-	-	-	nq	-	-	-	-
(Lotus-Climax)	-	-	-	nq	-	-	-	-
Henry TAYLOR	-	-	-	11	-	-	-	-
(Cooper-Climax)	-	-	-	21	-	-	-	-
Mike TAYLOR	-	-	-	r	-	-	-	-
(Cooper-Climax)	-	-	-	24	-	-	-	-
Trevor TAYLOR	-	-	-	nq	-	-	-	-
(Cooper-Climax)	-	-	-	nq	-	-	-	-
André TESTUT	-	-	-	-	-	-	-	-
(Maserati)	nq	-	-	-	-	-	-	-
Maurice TRINTIGNANT	3	8	11	5	4	4	9	2f
(Cooper-Climax)	6	11	8	4	12	4	13	5
Wolfgang von TRIPS	r	-	-	-	-	-	-	6
(Porsche)	12	-	-	-	ns	-	-	-
(Ferrari)	-	-	-	-	-	-	-	6
Rodger WARD	-	-	-	-	-	-	-	r
(Kurtis Kraft-Offenhauser)	-	-	-	-	-	-	-	19

	RA	MC	NL	B	F	GB	P	I	USA
Cliff ALLISON	**2**	-	-	-	-	-	-	-	-
(Ferrari)	7	nq	-	-	-	-	-	-	-
Edgar BARTH	-	-	-	-	-	-	**7**	-	-
(Porsche)	-	-	-	-	-	-	12	-	-
Lucien BIANCHI	-	-	-	**6**	**r**	**r**	-	-	-
(Cooper-Climax)	-	-	-	14	15	17	-	-	-
Jo BONNIER	**7**	**5**	**r**	**r**	**r**	**r**	**r**	-	**5**
(BRM)	4	5	4	6	10	4	13	-	4
Roberto BONOMI	**11**	-	-	-	-	-	-	-	-
(Cooper-Maserati)	17	-	-	-	-	-	-	-	-
Jack BRABHAM	**r**	**dq**	**1**	**1f=**	**1f**	**1**	**1**	-	**4f**
(Cooper-Climax)	10	2	2	1	1	1	3	-	2
Chris BRISTOW †	-	**r**	**r**	**r**	-	-	-	-	-
(Cooper-Climax)	-	4	7	8	-	-	-	-	-
Tony BROOKS	-	**4**	**r**	**r**	**r**	**5**	**5**	-	**r**
(Cooper-Climax)	-	3	10	2	-	9	12	-	9
(Vanwall)	-	-	-	-	14	-	-	-	-
Ian BURGESS	-	-	-	-	**10**	**r**	-	-	**r**
(Cooper-Climax)	-	nq	-	-	-	-	-	-	-
(Cooper-Maserati)	-	-	-	-	20	20	-	-	23
Giulio CABIANCA	-	-	-	-	-	-	-	**4**	-
(Cooper-Castellotti)	-	-	-	-	-	-	-	4	-
Mário CABRAL	-	-	-	-	-	-	**r**	-	-
(Cooper-Maserati)	-	-	-	-	-	-	15	-	-
Ettore CHIMERI †	**r**	-	-	-	-	-	-	-	-
(Maserati)	21	-	-	-	-	-	-	-	-
Jim CLARK	-	-	**r**	**5**	**5**	**16**	**3**	-	**16**
(Lotus-Climax)	-	-	11	9	12	8	8	-	5
Antonio CREUS	**r**	-	-	-	-	-	-	-	-
(Maserati)	22	-	-	-	-	-	-	-	-
Chuck DAIGH	-	-	-	**r**	-	**r**	-	-	**10**
(Scarab)	-	nq	ns	17	ns	-	-	-	18
(Cooper-Climax)	-	-	-	-	-	19	-	-	-
Carel Godin de BEAUFORT	-	-	**8**	-	-	-	-	-	-
(Cooper-Climax)	-	-	17	-	-	-	-	-	-
Bob DRAKE	-	-	-	-	-	-	-	-	**13**
(Maserati)	-	-	-	-	-	-	-	-	22
Piero DROGO	-	-	-	-	-	-	-	**8**	-
(Cooper-Climax)	-	-	-	-	-	-	-	15	-
Nasif ESTÉFANO	**14**	-	-	-	-	-	-	-	-
(Maserati)	20	-	-	-	-	-	-	-	-
Jack FAIRMAN	-	-	-	-	-	**r**	-	-	-
(Cooper-Climax)	-	-	-	-	-	15	-	-	-
Ron FLOCKHART	-	-	-	-	**6**	-	-	-	**r**
(Lotus-Climax)	-	-	-	-	8	-	-	-	-
(Cooper-Climax)	-	-	-	-	-	-	-	-	21
Fred GAMBLE	-	-	-	-	-	-	-	**10**	-
(Behra Porsche)	-	-	-	-	-	-	-	14	-
Olivier GENDEBIEN	-	-	-	**3**	**2**	**9**	**7**	-	**12**
(Cooper-Climax)	-	-	-	4	11	12	14	-	8
Richie GINTHER	-	**6**	**6**	-	-	-	-	**2**	-
(Ferrari)	-	9	12	-	-	-	-	2	-
(Scarab)	-	-	-	-	ns	-	-	-	-
Froilán GONZÁLEZ	**10**	-	-	-	-	-	-	-	-
(Ferrari)	11	-	-	-	-	-	-	-	-
Horace GOULD	-	-	-	-	-	-	-	-	-
(Maserati)	-	-	-	-	-	-	-	ns	-
Keith GREENE	-	-	-	-	-	**r**	-	-	-
(Cooper-Maserati)	-	-	-	-	-	22	-	-	-
Masten GREGORY	**12**	-	-	-	**9**	**14**	**r**	-	-
(Behra Porsche)	16	-	-	-	-	-	-	-	-
(Cooper-Maserati)	-	nq	ns	-	17	14	11	-	-
Dan GURNEY	-	**r**	**r**	**r**	**r**	**10**	**r**	-	**r**
(BRM)	-	14	6	11	7	6	2	-	3
Bruce HALFORD	-	-	-	-	**8r**	-	-	-	-
(Cooper-Climax)	-	nq	-	-	16	-	-	-	-

	RA	MC	NL	B	F	GB	P	I	USA
Jim HALL	-	-	-	-	-	-	-	-	**7**
(Lotus-Climax)	-	-	-	-	-	-	-	-	12
Hans HERRMANN	-	-	-	-	-	-	**6**	-	-
(Porsche)	-	-	-	-	-	-	10	-	-
Graham HILL	**r**	**7r**	**3**	**r**	**r**	**rf**	**r**	-	**r**
(BRM)	3	6	5	5	3	2	5	-	11
Phil HILL	**8**	**3**	**r**	**4f=**	**12r**	**7**	**r**	**1f**	**6**
(Ferrari)	6	10	13	3	2	10	10	1	-
(Cooper-Climax)	-	-	-	-	-	-	-	-	13
Innes IRELAND	**6**	**9**	**2**	**rf=**	**7**	**3**	**6**	-	**2**
(Lotus-Climax)	2	7	3	7	4	5	7	-	7
Rodríguez LARRETA	**9**	-	-	-	-	-	-	-	-
(Lotus-Climax)	15	-	-	-	-	-	-	-	-
Pete LOVELY	-	-	-	-	-	-	-	-	**11**
(Cooper-Castellotti)	-	-	-	-	-	-	-	-	20
Willy MAIRESSE	-	-	-	**r**	**r**	-	**3**	-	-
(Ferrari)	-	-	-	12	5	-	3	-	-
Bruce McLAREN	**1**	**2f**	**r**	**2**	**3**	**4**	**2**	-	**3**
(Cooper-Climax)	13	11	9	13	9	3	6	-	10
Carlos MENDITÉGUY	**4**	-	-	-	-	-	-	-	-
(Cooper-Maserati)	12	-	-	-	-	-	-	-	-
Stirling MOSS	**r/3=f**	**1**	**4f**	-	-	-	**dq**	-	**1**
(Cooper-Climax)	1	-	-	-	-	-	-	-	-
(Lotus-Climax)	-	1	1	ns	-	4	-	-	1
Gino MUNARON	**13**	-	-	**r**	**15**	-	**r**	-	-
(Maserati)	19	-	-	-	-	-	-	-	-
(Cooper-Castellotti)	-	nq	-	19	24	-	8	-	-
Brian NAYLOR	-	-	-	-	**13**	-	**r**	-	**r**
(JBW-Maserati)	-	nq	-	-	18	-	7	-	17
Arthur OWEN	-	-	-	-	-	-	**r**	-	-
(Cooper-Climax)	-	-	-	-	-	-	11	-	-
David PIPER	-	-	-	-	-	**12**	-	-	-
(Lotus-Climax)	-	-	-	-	ns	23	-	-	-
Lance REVENTLOW	-	-	**r**	-	-	-	-	-	-
(Scarab)	-	nq	ns	15	-	-	-	-	-
(Cooper-Climax)	-	-	-	-	-	ns	-	-	-
Roy SALVADORI	-	**r**	-	-	-	**r**	-	-	**8**
(Cooper-Climax)	-	12	-	-	-	-	-	-	15
(Aston Martin)	-	-	ns	-	-	13	-	-	-
Giorgio SCARLATTI	**r**	-	-	-	-	-	**r**	-	-
(Maserati)	18	-	-	-	-	-	-	-	-
(Cooper-Castellotti)	-	nq	-	-	-	-	-	-	-
(Cooper-Maserati)	-	-	-	-	-	-	5	-	-
Harry SCHELL †	**r**	-	-	-	-	-	-	-	-
(Cooper-Climax)	9	-	-	-	-	-	-	-	-
Wolfgang SEIDEL	-	-	-	-	-	-	**9**	-	-
(Cooper-Maserati)	-	-	-	-	-	-	13	-	-
Alan STACEY †	**r**	**r**	**r**	**r**	-	-	-	-	-
(Lotus-Climax)	14	13	8	16	-	-	-	-	-
John SURTEES	-	**r**	-	-	-	**2**	**rf**	-	**r**
(Lotus-Climax)	-	15	-	-	-	11	1	-	6
Henry TAYLOR	-	-	**7**	-	**4**	**8**	-	-	**14**
(Cooper-Climax)	-	-	14	-	13	16	ns	-	14
Mike TAYLOR	-	-	-	-	-	-	-	-	-
(Lotus-Climax)	-	-	-	ns	-	-	-	-	-
Alfonse THIELE	-	-	-	-	-	-	-	**r**	-
(Cooper-Maserati)	-	-	-	-	-	-	-	9	-
Maurice TRINTIGNANT	**3=**	**r**	**r**	-	**r**	**11**	-	-	**15**
(Cooper-Climax)	8	-	-	-	-	-	-	-	-
(Cooper-Maserati)	-	16	16	-	18	-	-	-	19
(Aston Martin)	-	-	-	-	-	21	-	-	-
Wolfgang von TRIPS	**5**	**8r**	**5**	**r**	**11r**	**6**	**4**	**5**	**9**
(Ferrari)	5	8	15	10	6	7	9	6	-
(Cooper-Maserati)	-	-	-	-	-	-	-	-	16
Vic WILSON	-	-	-	-	-	-	-	**r**	-
(Cooper-Maserati)	-	-	-	-	-	-	-	16	-

	MC	NL	B	F	GB	D	I	USA
Cliff ALLISON	8	-	-	-	-	-	-	-
(Lotus-Climax)	14	-	ns	-	-	-	-	-
Gerry ASHMORE	-	-	-	-	r	16	r	-
(Lotus-Climax)	-	-	-	-	26	25	25	-
Giancarlo BAGHETTI	-	-	-	1	r	-	rf	-
(Ferrari)	-	-	-	12	19	-	6	-
Lorenzo BANDINI	-	-	r	-	12	r	8	-
(Cooper-Maserati)	-	-	17	-	21	19	21	-
Lucien BIANCHI	-	-	r	r	r	-	-	-
(Emeryson-Maserati)	nq	-	-	-	-	-	-	-
(Lotus-Climax)	-	-	21	19	30	-	-	-
Jo BONNIER	12r	11	7	7	5	r	r	6
(Porsche)	9	11	9	13	3	4	8	10
Juan Manuel BORDEU	-	-	-	ns	-	-	-	-
(Lotus-Climax)								
Jack BRABHAM	r	6	r	r	4	r	r	rf
(Cooper-Climax)	16	7	11	14	9	2	10	1
Tony BROOKS	13r	9	13	r	9f	r	5	3
(BRM-Climax)	8	8	7	11	6	9	13	6
Ian BURGESS	-	-	-	14	14	12	-	-
(Lotus-Climax)	-	ns	ns	24	25	-	-	-
(Cooper-Climax)	-	-	-	-	-	24	-	-
Roberto BUSSINELLO	-	-	-	-	-	-	r	-
(De Tomaso-Conrero)	-	-	-	-	-	-	24	-
Jim CLARK	10	3f	12	3	r	4	r	7
(Lotus-Climax)	3	10	16	5	8	8	7	5
Bernard COLLOMB	-	-	-	r	-	r	-	-
(Cooper-Climax)	-	-	-	21	-	26	-	-
Carel Godin de BEAUFORT	-	14	11	r	16	14	7	-
(Porsche)	-	15	14	17	18	17	15	-
Jack FAIRMAN	-	-	-	-	dq=	-	r	-
(Ferguson-Climax)	-	-	-	-	20	-	-	-
(Cooper-Climax)	-	-	-	-	-	-	26	-
Olivier GENDEBIEN	-	-	4	-	-	-	-	11=
(Emeryson-Maserati)	nq	-	-	-	-	-	-	-
(Ferrari)	-	-	3	-	-	-	-	-
(Lotus-Climax)	-	-	-	-	-	-	-	15
Richie GINTHER	2f=	5	3f	15r	3	8	r	-
(Ferrari)	2	3	5	3	2	14	3	-
Keith GREENE	-	-	-	-	15	-	-	-
(Gilby-Climax)	-	-	-	-	23	-	-	-
Masten GREGORY	-	-	10	12	11	-	r	r/11=
(Cooper-Climax)	nq	ns	12	16	16	-	-	-
(Lotus-Climax)	-	-	-	-	-	-	17	11
Dan GURNEY	5	10	6	2	7	7	2	2
(Porsche)	10	6	10	9	12	7	12	7
Jim HALL	-	-	-	-	-	-	-	r
(Lotus-Climax)	-	-	-	-	-	-	-	18
Walt HANSGEN	-	-	-	-	-	-	-	r
(Cooper-Climax)	-	-	-	-	-	-	-	14
Hans HERRMANN	9	15	-	-	-	13	-	-
(Porsche)	12	12	-	-	-	11	-	-
Graham HILL	r	8	r	6	r	r	r	5
(BRM-Climax)	4	5	6	6	11	6	5	2
Phil HILL	3	2	1	9f	2	3f	1	-
(Ferrari)	5	1	1	1	1	1	4	-
Innes IRELAND	-	-	r	4	10	r	r	1
(Lotus-Climax)	ns	-	18	10	7	16	9	8
Jack LEWIS	-	-	9	r	r	9	4	-
(Cooper-Climax)	-	-	13	18	15	18	16	-
Roberto LIPPI	-	-	-	-	-	-	r	-
(De Tomaso-OSCA)	-	-	-	-	-	-	32	-
Tony MAGGS	-	-	-	-	13	11	-	-
(Lotus-Climax)	-	-	-	-	24	22	-	-
Willy MAIRESSE	-	-	r	r	-	r	-	-
(Lotus-Climax)	-	-	19	20	-	-	-	-
(Ferrari)	-	-	-	-	-	13	-	-
Tony MARSH	-	-	-	-	r	15	-	-
(Lotus-Climax)	-	-	ns	-	27	20	-	-
Michael MAY	r	-	-	11	-	-	-	-
(Lotus-Climax)	13	-	-	22	-	ns	-	-
Bruce McLAREN	6	12	r	5	8	6	3	4
(Cooper-Climax)	7	13	15	8	14	12	14	4
Stirling MOSS	1f=	4	8	r	r/dq=	1	r	r
(Lotus-Climax)	1	4	8	4	5/-	3	11	3
(Ferguson-Climax)	-	-	-	-	-/°	-	-	-
Massimo NATILI	-	-	-	-	r	-	-	-
(Cooper-Maserati)	-	-	-	-	28	-	ns	-
Brian NAYLOR	-	-	-	-	-	-	r	-
(JBW-Climax)	-	-	-	-	-	-	31	-
Tim PARNELL	-	-	-	-	r	-	10	-
(Lotus-Climax)	-	-	-	-	29	-	27	-
Roger PENSKE	-	-	-	-	-	-	-	8
(Cooper-Climax)	-	-	-	-	-	-	-	16
André PILETTE	-	-	-	-	-	nq	-	-
(Emeryson-Climax)								
Renato PIROCCHI	-	-	-	-	-	-	12	-
(Cooper-Maserati)	-	-	-	-	-	-	29	-
Ricardo RODRÍGUEZ	-	-	-	-	-	-	r	-
(Ferrari)	-	-	-	-	-	-	2	-
Lloyd RUBY	-	-	-	-	-	-	-	r
(Lotus-Climax)	-	-	-	-	-	-	-	19
Peter RYAN	-	-	-	-	-	-	-	9
(Lotus-Climax)	-	-	-	-	-	-	-	13
Roy SALVADORI	-	-	-	8	6	10	6	r
(Cooper-Climax)	-	-	-	15	13	15	18	12
Giorgio SCARLATTI	-	-	-	r	-	-	-	-
(De Tomaso-OSCA)	-	-	-	26	-	-	-	-
Wolfgang SEIDEL	-	-	-	-	17	r	r	-
(Lotus-Climax)	-	-	ns	-	22	23	28	-
Hap SHARP	-	-	-	-	-	-	-	10
(Cooper-Climax)	-	-	-	-	-	-	-	17
Gaetano STARRABBA	-	-	-	-	-	-	r	-
(Lotus-Maserati)	-	-	-	-	-	-	30	-
John SURTEES	11r	7	5	r	r	5	r	r
(Cooper-Climax)	11	9	4	7	10	10	19	9
Henry TAYLOR	-	-	-	10	r	-	11	-
(Lotus-Climax)	nq	-	-	25	17	-	23	-
Trevor TAYLOR	-	13	-	-	-	-	-	-
(Lotus-Climax)	-	14	-	-	-	-	-	-
Maurice TRINTIGNANT	7	-	r	13	-	17	9	-
(Cooper-Maserati)	15	-	20	23	-	21	22	-
Nino VACCARELLA	-	-	-	-	-	-	r	-
(De Tomaso-Conrero)	-	-	-	-	-	-	20	-
Wolfgang von TRIPS †	4r	1	2	r	1	2	r	-
(Ferrari)	6	2	2	2	4	5	1	-

° Took over in a shared drive and was not on the grid in this car

	NL	MC	B	F	GB	D	I	USA	ZA
Gerry ASHMORE (Lotus-Climax)	-	-	-	-	-	-	-	-	-
	-	-	-	-	-	-	nq	-	-
Giancarlo BAGHETTI (Ferrari)	4	-	r	-	-	10	5	-	-
	12	-	14	-	-	13	18	-	-
Lorenzo BANDINI (Ferrari)	-	3	-	-	-	r	8	-	-
	-	10	-	-	-	18	17	-	-
Lucien BIANCHI (Lotus-Climax)	-	-	9	-	-	16	-	-	-
	-	-	18	-	-	-	-	-	-
(ENB-Maserati)	-	-	-	-	-	25	-	-	-
Jo BONNIER (Porsche)	7	5	-	10r	r	7	6	13	-
	13	15	-	9	7	6	9	9	-
Jack BRABHAM (Lotus-Climax)	r	8r	6	r	5	r	-	4	4
	4	6	15	4	9	-	-	-	-
(Brabham-Climax)	-	-	-	-	-	24	-	5	3
Ian BURGESS (Cooper-Climax)	-	-	-	-	12	11	-	-	-
	-	-	-	-	16	16	nq	-	-
John CAMPBELL-JONES (Lotus-Climax)	-	-	11	-	-	-	-	-	-
	-	-	19	-	-	-	-	-	-
Jay CHAMBERLAIN (Lotus-Climax)	-	-	-	-	15	-	-	-	-
	-	-	-	-	20	nq	nq	-	-
Jim CLARK (Lotus-Climax)	9	rf	1f	r	1f	4	r	1f	rf
	3	1	12	1	1	3	1	1	1
Bernard COLLOMB (Cooper-Climax)	-	-	-	-	-	r	-	-	-
	-	-	-	-	-	22	-	-	-
Carel Godin de BEAUFORT (Porsche)	6	-	7	6	14	13	10	r	11r
	14	nq	13	17	17	8	20	13	16
Nasif ESTÉFANO (De Tomaso)	-	-	-	-	-	-	-	-	-
	-	-	-	-	-	-	nq	-	-
Richie GINTHER (BRM)	r	r	r	3	13	8	2	r	7
	7	13	9	10	8	7	3	2	7
Keith GREENE (Lotus-Climax)	-	-	-	-	-	r	-	-	-
	-	-	-	-	ns	-	-	-	-
(Gilby-BRM)	-	-	-	-	-	19	nq	-	-
Masten GREGORY (Lotus-Climax)	r	-	r	r	7	-	12	6	-
	16	-	-	-	14	-	-	-	-
(Lotus-BRM)	-	nq	8	7	-	-	6	7	-
Dan GURNEY (Porsche)	r	r	-	1	9	3	13r	5	-
	8	5	-	6	6	1	7	4	-
(Lotus-BRM)	-	-	ns	-	-	-	-	-	-
Jim HALL (Lotus-Climax)	-	-	-	-	-	-	-	r	-
	-	-	-	-	-	-	-	ns	-
Mike HARRIS (Cooper-Alfa Romeo)	-	-	-	-	-	-	-	-	r
	-	-	-	-	-	-	-	-	15
Graham HILL (BRM)	1	6r	2	9f	4	1f	1f	2	1
	2	2	1	2	5	2	2	3	2
Phil HILL (Ferrari)	3	2	3	-	r	r	11	-	-
	9	9	4	-	12	12	15	-	-
(Porsche)	-	-	-	-	-	-	-	ns	-
Innes IRELAND (Lotus-Climax)	r	r	r	r	16	-	r	8	5
	6	8	5	8	3	-	5	15	4
Bruce JOHNSTONE (BRM)	-	-	-	-	-	-	-	-	9
	-	-	-	-	-	-	-	-	17
Neville LEDERLE (Lotus-Climax)	-	-	-	-	-	-	-	-	6
	-	-	-	-	-	-	-	-	10
Jack LEWIS (Cooper-Climax)	8	-	-	r	10	17r	-	-	-
	19	-	-	16	15	21	-	-	-
(BRM)	-	nq	-	-	-	-	-	-	-
Roberto LIPPI (De Tomaso-OSCA)	-	-	-	-	-	-	-	-	-
	-	-	-	-	-	-	nq	-	-
John LOVE (Cooper-Climax)	-	-	-	-	-	-	-	-	8
	-	-	-	-	-	-	-	-	12
Tony MAGGS (Cooper-Climax)	5	r	r	2	6	9	7	7	3
	15	16	10	11	13	23	12	10	6
Willy MAIRESSE (Ferrari)	-	7r	r	-	-	-	4	-	-
	-	4	6	-	-	-	10	-	-
Timmy MAYER (Cooper-Climax)	-	-	-	-	-	-	-	r	-
	-	-	-	-	-	-	-	11	-
Bruce McLAREN (Cooper-Climax)	rf	1	r	4	3	5	3	3	2
	5	3	2	3	4	5	4	6	8
Roger PENSKE (Lotus-Climax)	-	-	-	-	-	-	-	9	-
	-	-	-	-	-	-	-	12	-
Ernie PIETERSE (Lotus-Climax)	-	-	-	-	-	-	-	-	10
	-	-	-	-	-	-	-	-	13
Ben PON (Porsche)	r	-	-	-	-	-	-	-	-
	18	-	-	-	-	-	-	-	-
Ernesto PRINOTH (Lotus-Climax)	-	-	-	-	-	-	-	-	-
	-	-	-	-	-	nq	-	-	-
Ricardo RODRÍGUEZ † (Ferrari)	r	-	4	-	-	6	14r	-	-
	11	ns	7	-	-	10	11	-	-
Roy SALVADORI (Lola-Climax)	r	r	-	r	r	r	r	r	r
	17	12	-	14	11	9	13	ns	11
Heinz SCHILLER (Lotus-BRM)	-	-	-	-	-	r	-	-	-
	-	-	-	-	-	20	-	-	-
Rob SCHROEDER (Lotus-Climax)	-	-	-	-	-	-	-	10	-
	-	-	-	-	-	-	-	16	-
Wolfgang SEIDEL (Emeryson-Climax)	nc	-	-	r	-	-	-	-	-
	20	-	-	-	-	-	-	-	-
(Lotus-BRM)	-	-	-	21	nq	-	-	-	-
Günther SEIFERT (Lotus-BRM)	-	-	-	-	-	-	-	-	-
	-	-	-	-	nq	-	-	-	-
Doug SERRURIER (LDS-Alfa Romeo)	-	-	-	-	-	-	-	-	r
	-	-	-	-	-	-	-	-	14
Tony SETTEMBER (Emeryson-Climax)	-	-	-	-	11	-	r	-	-
	-	-	-	-	19	-	21	-	-
Hap SHARP (Cooper-Climax)	-	-	-	-	-	-	-	11	-
	-	-	-	-	-	-	-	14	-
Tony SHELLY (Lotus-Climax)	-	-	-	-	r	-	-	-	-
	-	-	-	-	18	nq	-	-	-
(Lotus-BRM)	-	-	-	-	-	nq	-	-	-
Jo SIFFERT (Lotus-Climax)	-	-	10	r	-	12	-	-	-
	-	nq	17	-	-	17	-	-	-
(Lotus-BRM)	-	-	-	15	-	nq	-	-	-
John SURTEES (Lola-Climax)	r	4	5	5	2	2	r	r	r
	1	11	11	5	2	4	8	18	5
Trevor TAYLOR (Lotus-Climax)	2	r	r	8	8	r	r	12	r
	10	14	3	12	10	26	16	8	9
Maurice TRINTIGNANT (Lotus-Climax)	-	r	8	7	-	r	r	r	-
	-	7	16	13	-	11	19	17	-
Nino VACCARELLA (Lotus-Climax)	-	-	-	-	-	15	9	-	-
	-	nq	-	-	-	14	-	-	-
(Porsche)	-	-	-	-	-	15	-	-	-
Heini WALTER (Porsche)	-	-	-	-	-	14	-	-	-
	-	-	-	-	-	14	-	-	-

	MC	B	NL	F	GB	D	I	USA	MEX	ZA
Chris AMON	-	r	r	7	7	r	-	-	r	-
(Lola-Climax)	ns	15	12	15	14	14	ns	-	-	-
(Lotus-BRM)	-	-	-	-	-	-	-	-	19	-
Bob ANDERSON	-	-	-	-	12	-	12	-	-	-
(Lola-Climax)	-	-	-	-	16	-	18	-	-	-
Peter ARUNDELL	-	-	-	-	-	-	-	-	-	-
(Lotus-Climax)	-	-	-	ns	-	-	-	-	-	-
Giancarlo BAGHETTI	-	r	r	-	-	-	15	r	r	-
(ATS)	-	20	15	-	-	-	20	20	21	-
Lorenzo BANDINI	-	-	-	10	5	r	r	5	r	5
(BRM)	-	-	-	19	8	3	-	-	-	-
(Ferrari)	-	-	-	-	-	-	6	9	7	5
Lucien BIANCHI	-	r	-	-	-	-	-	-	-	-
(Lola-Climax)	-	16	-	-	-	-	-	-	-	-
Trevor BLOKDYK	-	-	-	-	-	-	-	-	-	12
(Cooper-Maserati)	-	-	-	-	-	-	-	-	-	19
Jo BONNIER	7	5	11	nc	r	6	7	8	5	6
(Cooper-Climax)	11	13	8	11	12	12	11	12	8	11
Jack BRABHAM	9	r	r	4	r	7	5	4	2	13r
(Lotus-Climax)	15	-	-	-	-	-	-	-	-	-
(Brabham-Climax)	-	6	4	5	4	8	7	5	10	2
Tino BRAMBILLA	-	-	-	-	-	-	-	-	-	-
(Cooper-Maserati)	-	-	-	-	-	-	nq	-	-	-
Peter BROEKER	-	-	-	-	-	-	-	7	-	-
(Stebro-Ford)	-	-	-	-	-	-	-	21	-	-
Ian BURGESS	-	-	-	-	r	r	-	-	-	-
(Scirocco-BRM)	-	-	-	-	20	19	-	-	-	-
Mário CABRAL	-	-	-	-	-	r	-	-	-	-
(Cooper-Climax)	-	-	-	-	-	20	nq	-	-	-
John CAMPBELL-JONES	-	-	-	-	13	-	-	-	-	-
(Lola-Climax)	-	-	-	-	23	-	-	-	-	-
Jim CLARK	8r	1f	1f	1f	1	2	1f	3f	1f	1
(Lotus-Climax)	1	8	1	1	1	1	3	2	1	1
Bernard COLLOMB	-	-	-	-	-	10	-	-	-	-
(Lotus-Climax)	nq	-	-	-	-	21	-	-	-	-
Carel Godin de BEAUFORT	-	6	9	-	10	r	-	6	10	10
(Porsche)	-	18	19	-	21	17	nq	19	18	20
Peter de KLERK	-	-	-	-	-	-	-	-	-	r
(Alfa Special)	-	-	-	-	-	-	-	-	-	16
Frank DOCHNAL	-	-	-	-	-	-	-	-	-	-
(Cooper-Climax)	-	-	-	-	-	-	-	-	ns	-
Paddy DRIVER	-	-	-	-	-	-	-	-	-	-
(Lotus-BRM)	-	-	-	-	-	-	-	-	-	ns
Richie GINTHER	2	4	5	r	4	3	2	2	3	r
(BRM)	4	9	6	12	9	6	4	4	5	7
Masten GREGORY	-	-	-	r	11	-	r	r	r	-
(Lotus-BRM)	-	-	-	17	22	-	12	-	-	-
(Lola-Climax)	-	-	-	-	-	-	-	8	14	-
Dan GURNEY	r	3	2	5	r	r	14r	r	6	2f
(Brabham-Climax)	6	2	14	3	2	13	5	6	4	3
Mike HAILWOOD	-	-	-	-	8	-	10	-	-	-
(Lotus-Climax)	-	-	-	-	17	-	-	-	-	-
(Lola-Climax)	-	-	-	-	-	-	17	-	-	-
Jim HALL	r	r	8	11	6	5	8	10r	8	-
(Lotus-BRM)	13	12	18	16	13	16	16	16	15	-
Graham HILL	1	r	r	3	3	r	16r	1	4	3
(BRM)	2	1	2	2	3	4	2	1	3	6
Phil HILL	-	r	r	nc	-	-	11	r	r	-
(ATS)	-	17	13	-	-	-	14	15	17	-
(Lotus-BRM)	-	-	-	13	-	-	-	-	-	-

	MC	B	NL	F	GB	D	I	USA	MEX	ZA
Innes IRELAND	r	r	4	9	dq	r	4r	-	-	-
(Lotus-BRM)	5	-	-	-	11	-	-	-	-	-
(BRP-BRM)	-	7	7	9	11	-	10	-	-	-
Kurt KUHNKE	-	-	-	-	-	-	-	-	-	-
(Lotus-Borgward)	-	-	-	-	-	nq	-	-	-	-
Roberto LIPPI	-	-	-	-	-	-	-	-	-	-
(De Tomaso-Ferrari)	-	-	-	-	-	-	nq	-	-	-
John LOVE	-	-	-	-	-	-	-	-	-	9
(Cooper-Climax)	-	-	-	-	-	-	-	-	-	13
Tony MAGGS	5	7r	r	2	9	r	6	r	r	7
(Cooper-Climax)	10	4	9	8	7	10	13	10	13	10
Willy MAIRESSE	r	r	-	-	-	r	-	-	-	-
(Ferrari)	7	3	-	-	-	7	-	-	-	-
Bruce McLAREN	3	2	r	12r	r	r	3	11r	r	4
(Cooper-Climax)	8	5	3	6	6	5	8	11	6	9
Gerhard MITTER	-	-	r	-	-	4	-	-	-	-
(Porsche)	-	-	16	-	-	15	-	-	-	-
Brausch NIEMANN	-	-	-	-	-	-	-	-	-	14
(Lotus-Ford)	-	-	-	-	-	-	-	-	-	15
Tim PARNELL	-	-	-	-	-	-	-	-	-	-
(Lotus-Climax)	-	-	-	-	-	nq	-	-	-	-
Ernie PIETERSE	-	-	-	-	-	-	-	-	-	r
(Lotus-Climax)	-	-	-	-	-	-	-	-	-	12
André PILETTE	-	-	-	-	-	-	-	-	-	-
(Lotus-Climax)	-	-	-	-	-	nq	nq	-	-	-
David PROPHET	-	-	-	-	-	-	-	-	-	r
(Brabham-Ford)	-	-	-	-	-	-	-	-	-	14
Ian RABY	-	-	-	r	-	-	-	-	-	-
(Gilby-BRM)	-	-	-	-	19	nq	nq	-	-	-
Pedro RODRÍGUEZ	-	-	-	-	-	-	-	r	r	-
(Lotus-Climax)	-	-	-	-	-	-	-	13	20	-
Lodovico SCARFIOTTI	-	-	6	-	-	-	-	-	-	-
(Ferrari)	-	-	11	ns	-	-	-	-	-	-
Doug SERRURIER	-	-	-	-	-	-	-	-	-	11
(LDS-Alfa Romeo)	-	-	-	-	-	-	-	-	-	18
Tony SETTEMBER	-	8r	-	r	r	r	-	-	-	-
(Scirocco-BRM)	-	19	-	18	18	22	nq	-	-	-
Hap SHARP	-	-	-	-	-	-	-	r	7	-
(Lotus-BRM)	-	-	-	-	-	-	-	18	16	-
Jo SIFFERT	r	r	7	6	r	9r	r	r	9	-
(Lotus-BRM)	12	14	17	10	15	9	15	14	9	-
Moisés SOLANA	-	-	-	-	-	-	-	-	11r	-
(BRM)	-	-	-	-	-	-	-	-	11	-
Mike SPENCE	-	-	-	-	-	13r	-	-	-	-
(Lotus-Climax)	-	-	-	-	-	9	-	-	-	-
John SURTEES	4f	r	3	r	2f	1f	r	9r	dq	r
(Ferrari)	3	10	5	4	5	2	1	3	2	4
Trevor TAYLOR	6	r	10	13r	dq	8	-	r	r	8
(Lotus-Climax)	9	11	10	7	10	18	-	7	12	8
Sam TINGLE	-	-	-	-	-	-	-	-	-	r
(LDS-Alfa Romeo)	-	-	-	-	-	-	-	-	-	17
Maurice TRINTIGNANT	r	-	-	8	-	9	-	-	-	-
(Lola-Climax)	14	-	-	-	-	-	-	-	-	-
(Lotus-Climax)	-	-	14	-	-	-	-	-	-	-
(BRM)	-	-	-	-	-	19	-	-	-	-
Rodger WARD	-	-	-	-	-	-	-	r	-	-
(Lotus-BRM)	-	-	-	-	-	-	-	17	-	-

1964 RACE RESULTS & GRID POSITIONS

	MC	NL	B	F	GB	D	A	I	USA	MEX
Chris AMON	-	5	r	10	r	11r	r	-	r	r
(Lotus-BRM)	nq	13	11	14	11	9	-	-	11	12
(Lotus-Climax)	-	-	-	-	-	-	17	-	-	-
Bob ANDERSON	7r	6	-	12	7	r	3	11	-	-
(Brabham-Climax)	12	11	ns	15	7	15	14	14	-	-
Peter ARUNDELL	3	3	9	4	-	-	-	-	-	-
(Lotus-Climax)	6	6	4	4	-	-	-	-	-	-
Dickie ATTWOOD	-	-	-	-	ns	-	-	-	-	-
(BRM)	-	-	-	-	-	-	-	-	-	-
Giancarlo BAGHETTI	-	10	8	-	12	r	7	8	-	-
(BRM)	-	16	17	-	21	21	15	15	-	-
Lorenzo BANDINI	10r	r	r	9	5	3	1	3	r	3
(Ferrari)	7	10	9	8	8	4	7	7	8	3
Edgar BARTH	-	-	-	-	-	r	-	-	-	-
(Cooper-Climax)	-	-	-	-	-	20	-	-	-	-
Jo BONNIER	5	9	r	-	r	r	6	12	r	r
(Cooper-Climax)	11									
(Brabham-BRM)	-	12	14	-	9	12	-	-	-	-
(Brabham-Climax)	-	-	-	-	-	-	10	12	9	8
Jack BRABHAM	r	r	3	3f	4	12r	9	14r	r	r
(Brabham-Climax)	2	7	3	5	4	6	6	11	7	7
Ronnie BUCKNUM	-	-	-	-	-	13r	-	r	r	-
(Honda)	-	-	-	-	-	22	-	10	14	-
Mário CABRAL	-	-	-	-	-	-	-	r	-	-
(Derrington Francis-ATS)	-	-	-	-	-	-	-	19	-	-
Jim CLARK	4r	1f	1	r	1f	r	r	r	r=/7r=f	5rf
(Lotus-Climax)	1	2	6	1	1	2	3	4	1	1
Bernard COLLOMB	-	-	-	-	-	-	-	-	-	-
(Lotus-Climax)	nq									
Carel Godin de BEAUFORT †	-	r	-	-	-	-	-	-	-	-
(Porsche)	-	17	-	-	ns	-	-	-	-	-
Frank GARDNER	-	-	-	r	-	-	-	-	-	-
(Brabham-Ford)	-	-	-	-	19	-	-	-	-	-
GEKI	-	-	-	-	-	-	-	r	-	-
(Brabham-BRM)	-	-	-	-	-	-	-	nq	-	-
Richie GINTHER	2	11	4	5	8	7	2	4	4	8
(BRM)	8	8	8	9	14	11	5	9	13	11
Dan GURNEY	r	r	6rf	1	13	10	rf	10	r	1
(Brabham-Climax)	5	1	1	2	3	3	4	2	3	2
Mike HAILWOOD	6	12r	-	8	r	r	8	r	8r	r
(Lotus-BRM)	15	14	-	13	12	13	18	17	16	17
Walt HANSGEN	-	-	-	-	-	-	-	-	5	-
(Lotus-Climax)	-	-	-	-	-	-	-	-	17	-
Graham HILL	1f	4	5r	2	2	2	r	r	1	11
(BRM)	3	3	2	6	2	5	1	3	4	6
Phil HILL	9r	8	r	7	6	r	r	-	r	9r
(Cooper-Climax)	9	9	15	10	15	8	20	-	19	15
Innes IRELAND	-	-	10	r	10	-	5	5	r	12
(Lotus-BRM)	ns									
(BRP-BRM)	-	-	16	11	10	-	11	13	10	16
John LOVE	-	-	-	-	-	-	-	-	-	-
(Cooper-Climax)	-	-	-	-	-	-	-	nq	-	-
Tony MAGGS	-	-	-	-	r	6	4	-	-	-
(BRM)	-	15ns	ns	-	23	16	19	-	-	-
Bruce McLAREN	r	7	2	6	r	r	r	2	r	7
(Cooper-Climax)	10	5	7	7	6	7	9	5	5	10
Gerhard MITTER	-	-	-	-	-	9	-	-	-	-
(Lotus-Climax)	-	-	-	-	-	19	-	-	-	-
André PILETTE	-	-	r	-	-	-	-	-	-	-
(Scirocco-Climax)	-	-	18	-	nq	-	-	-	-	-
Ian RABY	-	-	-	-	r	-	-	-	-	-
(Brabham-BRM)	-	-	-	-	17	-	nq	-	-	-
Peter REVSON	-	-	dq	-	r	14r	-	13	-	-
(Lotus-BRM)	nq	-	10	ns	22	18	-	18	-	-
Jochen RINDT	-	-	-	-	-	-	r	-	-	-
(Brabham-BRM)	-	-	-	-	-	-	13	-	-	-
Pedro RODRÍGUEZ	-	-	-	-	-	-	-	-	-	6
(Ferrari)	-	-	-	-	-	-	-	-	-	9
Jean-Claude RUDAZ	-	-	-	-	-	-	-	ns	-	-
(Cooper-Climax)	-	-	-	-	-	-	-	ns	-	-
Lodovico SCARFIOTTI	-	-	-	-	-	-	9	-	-	-
(Ferrari)	-	-	-	-	-	-	16	-	-	-
Hap SHARP	-	-	-	-	-	-	-	-	nc	13
(Brabham-BRM)	-	-	-	-	-	-	-	-	18	19
Jo SIFFERT	8	13	r	r	11	4	r	7	3	r
(Lotus-BRM)	16									
(Brabham-BRM)	-	18	13	17	16	10	12	6	12	13
Moisés SOLANA	-	-	-	-	-	-	-	-	-	10
(Lotus-Climax)	-	-	-	-	-	-	-	-	-	14
Mike SPENCE	-	-	-	-	9	8	r	6	7r=/r=	4
(Lotus-Climax)	-	-	-	-	13	17	8	8	6	5
John SURTEES	r	2	r	r	3	1f	r	1f	2	2
(Ferrari)	4	4	5	3	5	1	2	1	2	4
John TAYLOR	-	-	-	-	14	-	-	-	-	-
(Cooper-Ford)	-	-	-	-	20	-	-	-	-	-
Trevor TAYLOR	r	-	7	r	r	-	r	-	6	r
(BRP-BRM)	14	-	12	12	-	-	16	nq	15	18
(Lotus-BRM)	-	-	-	-	18	-	-	-	-	-
Maurice TRINTIGNANT	r	-	-	11	-	5r	-	r	-	-
(BRM)	13	-	-	16	nq	14	-	20	-	-

1965 RACE RESULTS & GRID POSITIONS

	ZA	MC	B	F	GB	NL	D	I	USA	MEX
Chris AMON	-	-	-	r	-	-	r	-	-	-
(Lotus-BRM)	-	-	-	8	-	-	15	-	-	-
(Brabham-BRM)	-	-	-	-	ns	-	-	-	-	-
Bob ANDERSON	nc	9	-	9r	r	r	-	-	-	-
(Brabham-Climax)	12	9	19ns	15	17	16	ns	-	-	-
Dickie ATTWOOD	-	r	14r	-	13	12	r	6	10	6
(Lotus-BRM)	-	6	13	-	16	17	16	13	16	16
Giancarlo BAGHETTI	-	-	-	-	-	-	-	r	-	-
(Brabham-Climax)	-	-	-	-	-	-	-	19	-	-
Lorenzo BANDINI	15r	2	9	8r	r	9	6	4	4	8
(Ferrari)	6	4	15	3	9	12	7	5	5	7
Giorgio BASSI	-	-	-	-	-	-	-	r	-	-
(BRM)	-	-	-	-	-	-	-	22	-	-
Lucien BIANCHI	-	-	12	-	-	-	-	-	-	-
(BRM)	-	-	17	-	-	-	-	-	-	-
Trevor BLOKDYK	-	-	-	-	-	-	-	-	-	-
(Cooper-Ford)	nq	-	-	-	-	-	-	-	-	-
Bob BONDURANT	-	-	-	-	-	-	-	-	9	r
(Ferrari)	-	-	-	-	-	-	-	-	14	-
(Lotus-BRM)	-	-	-	-	-	-	-	-	-	17
Jo BONNIER	r	7	r	r	7	r	7	7	8	r
(Brabham-Climax)	7	13	7	11	14	15	9	14	10	12
Jack BRABHAM	8	r	4	-	-	-	5	-	3	r
(Brabham-Climax)	3	2	10	-	8ns	-	14	-	7	4
Ronnie BUCKNUM	-	r	r	r	-	-	-	r	13	5
(Honda)	-	15	11	16	-	-	-	6	12	10
Roberto BUSSINELLO	-	-	-	-	-	-	-	13r	-	-
(BRM)	-	-	-	-	-	-	nq	21	-	-
Dave CHARLTON	-	-	-	-	-	-	-	-	-	-
(Lotus-Ford)	npq	-	-	-	-	-	-	-	-	-

Season-by-Season Summary 497

	ZA	MC	B	F	GB	NL	D	I	USA	MEX
Jim CLARK	1f	-	1f	1f	1	1f	1f	10rf	r	r
(Lotus-Climax)	1	-	2	1	1	2	1	1	2	1
Peter de KLERK	10	-	-	-	-	-	-	-	-	-
(Alfa Special)	17	-	-	-	-	-	-	-	-	-
Frank GARDNER	12	r	r	-	8	11	r	r	-	-
(Brabham-BRM)	15	11	18	-	13	11	17	16	-	-
GEKI	-	-	-	-	-	-	-	r	-	-
(Lotus-Climax)	-	-	-	-	-	-	-	20	-	-
Richie GINTHER	-	r	6	r	r	6	-	14r	7	1
(Honda)	-	16	4	7	3	3	-	17	3	3
Masten GREGORY	-	-	r	-	12	-	8	r	-	-
(BRM)	-	-	20	-	19	-	18	23	-	-
Brian GUBBY	-	-	-	-	nq	-	-	-	-	-
(Lotus-Climax)										
Dan GURNEY	r	-	10	r	6	3	3	3	2	2f
(Brabham-Climax)	9	-	5	5	7	5	5	9	8	2
Mike HAILWOOD	-	r	-	-	-	-	-	-	-	-
(Lotus-BRM)	-	12	-	-	-	-	-	-	-	-
Paul HAWKINS	9	10r	-	-	-	-	r	-	-	-
(Brabham-Ford)	16									
(Lotus-Climax)	-	14	-	-	-	-	19	-	-	-
Graham HILL	3	1f	5	5	2f	4	2	2	1f	r
(BRM)	5	1	1	13	2	1	3	4	1	5
Denny HULME	-	8	-	4	r	5	r	r	-	-
(Brabham-Climax)	-	8	-	6	10	7	13	12	-	-
Innes IRELAND	-	-	13	r	r	10	-	9	r	-
(Lotus-BRM)	-	-	16	17	15	13	-	18	18	ns
Neville LEDERLE	nq	-	-	-	-	-	-	-	-	-
(Lotus-Climax)										
John LOVE	r	-	-	-	-	-	-	-	-	-
(Cooper-Climax)	18	-	-	-	-	-	-	-	-	-
Tony MAGGS	11	-	-	-	-	-	-	-	-	-
(Lotus-BRM)	13	-	-	-	-	-	-	-	-	-
Willy MAIRESSE	-	-	ns	-	-	-	-	-	-	-
(BRM)										
Bruce McLAREN	5	5	3	r	10	r	r	5	r	r
(Cooper-Climax)	8	7	9	9	11	9	10	11	9	14
Gerhard MITTER	-	-	-	-	-	-	r	-	-	-
(Lotus-Climax)	-	-	-	-	-	-	12	-	-	-
Brausch NIEMANN	-	-	-	-	-	-	-	-	-	-
(Lotus-Ford)	nq	-	-	-	-	-	-	-	-	-
Ernie PIETERSE	-	-	-	-	-	-	-	-	-	-
(Lotus-Climax)	nq	-	-	-	-	-	-	-	-	-
Jackie PRETORIUS	-	-	-	-	-	-	-	-	-	-
(LDS-Alfa Romeo)	npq	-	-	-	-	-	-	-	-	-
David PROPHET	14	-	-	-	-	-	-	-	-	-
(Brabham-Ford)	19	-	-	-	-	-	-	-	-	-
Clive PUZEY	-	-	-	-	-	-	-	-	-	-
(Lotus-Climax)	npq	-	-	-	-	-	-	-	-	-
Ian RABY	-	-	-	-	11	-	-	-	-	-
(Brabham-BRM)	-	-	-	-	20	nq	-	-	-	-
John RHODES	-	-	-	r	-	-	-	-	-	-
(Cooper-Climax)	-	-	-	21	-	-	-	-	-	-
Jochen RINDT	r	-	11	r	14r	r	4	8	6	r
(Cooper-Climax)	10	nq	14	12	12	14	8	7	13	15
Pedro RODRÍGUEZ	-	-	-	-	-	-	-	-	5	7
(Ferrari)	-	-	-	-	-	-	-	-	15	13
Alan ROLLINSON	-	-	-	-	nq	-	-	-	-	-
(Cooper-Ford)										
Lodovico SCARFIOTTI	-	-	-	-	-	-	-	-	-	ns
(Ferrari)										
Doug SERRURIER	-	-	-	-	-	-	-	-	-	-
(LDS-Climax)	nq	-	-	-	-	-	-	-	-	-
Jo SIFFERT	7	6	8	6	9	13	r	r	11	4
(Brabham-BRM)	14	10	8	14	18	10	11	10	11	11
Moisés SOLANA	-	-	-	-	-	-	-	-	12	r
(Lotus-Climax)	-	-	-	-	-	-	-	-	17	9
Mike SPENCE	4	-	7	7	4	8	r	11r	r	3
(Lotus-Climax)	4	-	12	10	6	8	6	8	4	6
Jackie STEWART	6	3	2	2	5	2	r	1	r	r
(BRM)	11	3	3	2	4	6	2	3	6	8
John SURTEES	2	4r	r	3	3	7	r	r	-	-
(Ferrari)	2	5	6	4	5	4	4	2	-	-
Sam TINGLE	13	-	-	-	-	-	-	-	-	-
(LDS-Alfa Romeo)	20	-	-	-	-	-	-	-	-	-
Nino VACCARELLA	-	-	-	-	-	-	-	12r	-	-
(Ferrari)	-	-	-	-	-	-	-	15	-	-

1966 RACE RESULTS & GRID POSITIONS

	MC	B	F	GB	NL	D	I	USA	MEX
Kurt AHRENS	-	-	-	-	-	r	-	-	-
(Brabham-Ford Cosworth)	-	-	-	-	-	21	-	-	-
Chris AMON	-	-	8	-	-	-	-	-	-
(Cooper-Maserati)	-	-	7	-	-	-	-	-	-
(Brabham-BRM)	-	-	-	-	-	-	nq	-	-
Bob ANDERSON	r	-	7	nc	r	r	6	-	-
(Brabham-Climax)	8	-	13	10	14	14	15	-	-
Peter ARUNDELL	-	-	r	r	r	8	8r	6	7
(Lotus-BRM)	-	ns	16	20	15	17	13	-	17
(Lotus-Climax)	-	-	-	-	-	-	-	19	-
Giancarlo BAGHETTI	-	-	-	-	-	-	nc	-	-
(Ferrari)	-	-	-	-	-	-	16	-	-
Lorenzo BANDINI	2f	3	ncf	-	6	6	r	r	-
(Ferrari)	5	5	1	-	9	6	5	3	-
Jean-Pierre BELTOISE	-	-	-	-	-	F2:1	-	-	-
(Matra-Ford Cosworth)	-	-	-	-	-	18	-	-	-
Bob BONDURANT	4	r	-	9	-	r	7	dq	r
(BRM)	16	11	-	14	-	11	18	-	-
(Eagle-Climax)	-	-	-	-	-	-	-	16	-
(Eagle-Weslake)	-	-	-	-	-	-	-	-	18
Jo BONNIER	nc	r	nc	r	7	r	r	nc	6
(Cooper-Maserati)	14	6	-	-	13	12	12	15	12
(Brabham-Climax)	-	-	17	15	-	-	-	-	-
Jack BRABHAM	r	4	1	1f	1	1	r	r	2
(Brabham-Repco)	11	4	4	1	1	5	6	1	4
Ronnie BUCKNUM	-	-	-	-	-	-	-	r	8
(Honda)	-	-	-	-	-	-	-	18	13
Jim CLARK	r	r	-	4	3	r	r	1	r
(Lotus-Climax)	1	10	ns	5	3	1	-	-	-
(Lotus-BRM)	-	-	-	-	-	-	3	2	2
Piers COURAGE	-	-	-	-	-	r	-	-	-
(Lotus-Ford Cosworth)	-	-	-	-	-	23	-	-	-
GEKI	-	-	-	-	-	-	9	-	-
(Lotus-Climax)	-	-	-	-	-	-	20	-	-
Richie GINTHER	r	5	-	-	-	-	r	nc	4f
(Cooper-Maserati)	9	8	-	-	-	-	-	-	-
(Honda)	-	-	-	-	-	-	7	8	3
Dan GURNEY	-	nc	5	r	r	7	r	r	5
(Eagle-Climax)	-	15	14	3	4	8	-	-	9
(Eagle-Weslake)	-	-	-	-	-	-	19	14	-
Hubert HAHNE	-	-	-	-	-	F2:2	-	-	-
(Matra-BRM)	-	-	-	-	-	27	-	-	-
Hans HERRMANN	-	-	-	-	-	F2:4	-	-	-
(Brabham-Ford Cosworth)	-	-	-	-	-	22	-	-	-
Graham HILL	3	r	r	3	2	4	r	r	r
(BRM)	4	9	8	4	7	10	11	5	7
Phil HILL	-	-	-	-	-	-	-	nq	-
(Eagle-Climax)									

	MC	B	F	GB	NL	D	I	USA	MEX
Denny HULME	r	r	3	2	rf	r	3	r	3
(Brabham-Climax)	6	13	-	-	-	-	-	-	-
(Brabham-Repco)	-	-	9	2	2	15	10	7	6
Jacky ICKX	-	-	-	-	-	r	-	-	-
(Matra-Ford Cosworth)	-	-	-	-	-	16	-	-	-
Innes IRELAND	-	-	-	-	-	-	-	r	r
(BRM)	-	-	-	-	-	-	-	17	16
Chris IRWIN	-	-	-	7	-	-	-	-	-
(Brabham-Climax)	-	-	-	12	-	-	-	-	-
Chris LAWRENCE	-	-	-	11	-	r	-	-	-
(Cooper-Ferrari)	-	-	-	19	-	26	-	-	-
Guy LIGIER	nc	nc	nc	10	9	-	-	-	-
(Cooper-Maserati)	15	12	11	17	16	ns	-	-	-
Bruce McLAREN	r	-	-	6	-	-	-	5	r
(McLaren-Ford)	10	-	-	-	-	-	-	11	14
(McLaren-Serenissima)	-	ns	-	13	ns	-	-	-	-
Gerhard MITTER	-	-	-	-	-	-	-	-	-
(Lotus-Ford Cosworth)	-	-	-	-	-	ns	-	-	-
Silvio MOSER	-	-	-	-	-	-	-	-	-
(Brabham-Ford Cosworth)	-	-	-	-	-	ns	-	-	-
Mike PARKES	-	-	2	-	r	r	2	-	-
(Ferrari)	-	-	3	-	5	7	1	-	-
Alan REES	-	-	-	-	-	r	-	-	-
(Brabham-Ford Cosworth)	-	-	-	-	-	24	-	-	-
Jochen RINDT	r	2	4	5	r	3	4	2	r
(Cooper-Maserati)	7	2	5	7	6	9	8	9	5

	MC	B	F	GB	NL	D	I	USA	MEX
Pedro RODRÍGUEZ	-	-	r	-	-	r	-	r	r
(Lotus-Climax)	-	-	12	-	-	-	-	-	8
(Lotus-Ford Cosworth)	-	-	-	-	-	20	-	-	-
(Lotus-BRM)	-	-	-	-	-	-	-	10	-
Lodovico SCARFIOTTI	-	-	-	-	-	r	1f	-	-
(Ferrari)	-	-	-	-	-	4	2	-	-
Jo SCHLESSER	-	-	-	-	-	F2:3	-	-	-
(Matra-Ford Cosworth)	-	-	-	-	-	19	-	-	-
Jo SIFFERT	r	r	r	nc	r	-	r	4	r
(Brabham-BRM)	13	-	-	-	-	-	-	-	-
(Cooper-Maserati)	-	14	6	11	11	-	17	13	11
Moisés SOLANA	-	-	-	-	-	-	-	-	r
(Cooper-Maserati)	-	-	-	-	-	-	-	-	15
Mike SPENCE	r	r	r	r	5	r	5	r	-
(Lotus-BRM)	12	7	10	9	12	13	14	12	ns
Jackie STEWART	1	r	-	r	4	5	r	r	r
(BRM)	3	3	-	8	8	3	9	6	10
John SURTEES	r	1f	r	r	r	2f	r	3f	1
(Ferrari)	2	1	-	-	-	-	-	-	-
(Cooper-Maserati)	-	-	2	6	10	2	4	4	1
John TAYLOR †	-	-	6	8	8	r	-	-	-
(Brabham-BRM)	-	-	15	16	17	25	-	-	-
Trevor TAYLOR	-	-	-	r	-	-	-	-	-
(Shannon-Climax)	-	-	-	18	-	-	-	-	-
Vic WILSON	-	-	-	-	-	-	-	-	-
(BRM)	-	ns	-	-	-	-	-	-	-

1967 RACE RESULTS & GRID POSITIONS

	ZA	MC	NL	B	F	GB	D	CDN	I	USA	MEX
Kurt AHRENS	-	-	-	-	-	-	r	-	-	-	-
(Protos-Ford Cosworth)	-	-	-	-	-	-	23	-	-	-	-
Chris AMON	-	3	4	3	r	3	3	6	7	r	9
(Ferrari)	-	14	9	5	7	6	8	4	4	4	2
Bob ANDERSON †	5	-	9	8	r	r	-	-	-	-	-
(Brabham-Climax)	10	nq	17	17	14	17	-	-	-	-	-
Dickie ATTWOOD	-	-	-	-	-	-	-	10	-	-	-
(Cooper-Maserati)	-	-	-	-	-	-	-	13	-	-	-
Giancarlo BAGHETTI	-	-	-	-	-	-	-	-	r	-	-
(Lotus-Ford Cosworth)	-	-	-	-	-	-	-	-	17	-	-
Lorenzo BANDINI †	-	r	-	-	-	-	-	-	-	-	-
(Ferrari)	-	2	-	-	-	-	-	-	-	-	-
Jean-Pierre BELTOISE	-	-	-	-	-	-	-	-	-	7	7
(Matra-Ford Cosworth)	-	nq	-	-	-	-	-	-	-	18	14
Jo BONNIER	r	-	-	r	-	r	5	8	r	6	10
(Cooper-Maserati)	12	-	-	12	-	19	16	14	14	15	17
Luki BOTHA	nc	-	-	-	-	-	-	-	-	-	-
(Brabham-Climax)	17	-	-	-	-	-	-	-	-	-	-
Jack BRABHAM	6	r	2	r	1	4	2	1	2	5	2
(Brabham-Repco)	1	1	3	7	2	3	7	7	2	5	5
Dave CHARLTON	nc	-	-	-	-	-	-	-	-	-	-
(Brabham-Climax)	8	-	-	-	-	-	-	-	-	-	-
Jim CLARK	r	rf	1f	6	r	1	r	rf	3f	1	1f
(Lotus-BRM)	3	-	-	-	-	-	-	-	-	-	-
(Lotus-Climax)	-	5	-	-	-	-	-	-	-	-	-
(Lotus-Ford Cosworth)	-	-	8	1	4	1	1	1	1	2	1
Piers COURAGE	r	r	-	-	-	-	-	-	-	-	-
(Lotus-BRM)	18	-	-	-	-	-	-	-	-	-	-
(BRM)	-	13	-	-	-	16ns	-	-	-	-	-
Mike FISHER	-	-	-	-	-	-	-	11	-	-	-
(Lotus-BRM)	-	-	-	-	-	-	-	17	-	-	18ns
Richie GINTHER	-	-	-	-	-	-	-	-	-	-	-
(Eagle-Weslake)	-	nq	-	-	-	-	-	-	-	-	-
Dan GURNEY	r	r	r	1f	r	r	rf	3	r	r	r
(Eagle-Climax)	11	-	-	-	-	-	-	-	-	-	-
(Eagle-Weslake)	-	7	2	2	3	5	4	5	5	3	3

	ZA	MC	NL	B	F	GB	D	CDN	I	USA	MEX
Hubert HAHNE	-	-	-	-	-	-	r	-	-	-	-
(Lola-BMW)	-	-	-	-	-	-	14	-	-	-	-
Brian HART	-	-	-	-	-	-	nc	-	-	-	-
(Protos-Ford Cosworth)	-	-	-	-	-	-	25	-	-	-	-
Graham HILL	r	2	r	r	rf	r	r	4	r	2f	r
(Lotus-BRM)	15	8	-	-	-	-	-	-	-	-	-
(Lotus-Ford Cosworth)	-	-	1	3	1	2	13	2	8	1	4
David HOBBS	-	-	-	-	-	8	F2:3	9	-	-	-
(BRM)	-	-	-	-	-	14	-	12	-	-	-
(Lola-BMW)	-	-	-	-	-	-	22	-	-	-	-
Denny HULME	4f	1	3	r	2	2f	1	2	r	3	3
(Brabham-Repco)	2	4	7	14	6	4	2	3	6	6	6
Jacky ICKX	-	-	-	-	-	-	r	-	6	r	-
(Matra-Ford Cosworth)	-	-	-	-	-	-	18	-	-	-	-
(Cooper-Maserati)	-	-	-	-	-	-	-	-	15	16	-
Chris IRWIN	-	-	7	r	5r	7	7	r	r	r	r
(Lotus-BRM)	-	-	13	-	-	-	-	-	-	-	-
(BRM)	-	-	-	15	9	13	15	11	16	14	15
Tom JONES	-	-	-	-	-	-	-	-	-	-	-
(Cooper-Climax)	-	-	-	-	-	-	-	nq	-	-	-
Guy LIGIER	-	-	-	10	nc	10	6	-	r	r	11
(Cooper-Maserati)	-	-	-	18	15	-	-	-	-	-	-
(Brabham-Repco)	-	-	-	-	-	21	17	-	18	17	19
John LOVE	2	-	-	-	-	-	-	-	-	-	-
(Cooper-Climax)	5	-	-	-	-	-	-	-	-	-	-
Bruce McLAREN	-	4	r	-	r	r	r	7	r	r	r
(McLaren-BRM)	-	10	14	-	-	-	-	6	3	9	8
(Eagle-Weslake)	-	-	-	-	5	10	5	-	-	-	-
Gerhard MITTER	-	-	-	-	-	-	r	-	-	-	-
(Brabham-Ford Cosworth)	-	-	-	-	-	-	24	-	-	-	-
Silvio MOSER	-	-	-	-	-	r	-	-	-	-	-
(Cooper-ATS)	-	-	-	-	-	20	-	-	-	-	-
Jackie OLIVER	-	-	-	-	-	-	F2:1	-	-	-	-
(Lotus-Ford Cosworth)	-	-	-	-	-	-	19	-	-	-	-
Mike PARKES	-	-	5	r	-	-	-	-	-	-	-
(Ferrari)	-	-	10	8	-	-	-	-	-	-	-
Al PEASE	-	-	-	-	-	-	-	nc	-	-	-
(Eagle-Climax)	-	-	-	-	-	-	-	15	-	-	-
Brian REDMAN	-	-	-	-	-	-	-	-	-	-	-
(Lola-Ford Cosworth)	-	-	-	-	-	-	ns	-	-	-	-
Alan REES	-	-	-	-	-	9	F2:2	-	-	-	-
(Cooper-Maserati)	-	-	-	-	-	15	-	-	-	-	-
(Brabham-Ford Cosworth)	-	-	-	-	-	-	20	-	-	-	-
Jochen RINDT	r	r	r	4	r	r	r	r	4	r	-
(Cooper-Maserati)	7	15	4	4	8	8	9	8	11	8	-
Pedro RODRÍGUEZ	1	5	r	9r	6	5	8	-	-	-	6
(Cooper-Maserati)	4	16	5	13	13	9	10	-	-	-	13
Lodovico SCARFIOTTI	-	-	6	nc	-	-	-	-	r	-	-
(Ferrari)	-	-	15	9	-	-	-	-	-	-	-
(Eagle-Weslake)	-	-	-	-	-	-	-	-	10	-	-
Jo SCHLESSER	-	-	-	-	-	-	r	-	-	-	-
(Matra-Ford Cosworth)	-	-	-	-	-	-	21	-	-	-	-
Johnny SERVOZ-GAVIN	-	r	-	-	-	-	-	-	-	-	-
(Matra-Ford Cosworth)	-	11	-	-	-	-	-	-	-	-	-
Jo SIFFERT	r	r	10	7	4	r	nc	-	r	4	12r
(Cooper-Maserati)	16	9	16	16	11	18	12	ns	13	12	10
Moisés SOLANA	-	-	-	-	-	-	-	-	-	r	r
(Lotus-Ford Cosworth)	-	-	-	-	-	-	-	-	-	7	9
Mike SPENCE	r	6	8	5	r	r	r	5	5	r	5
(BRM)	13	12	12	11	12	11	11	10	12	13	11
Jackie STEWART	r	r	r	2	3	r	r	r	r	r	r
(BRM)	9	6	11	6	10	12	3	9	7	10	12
John SURTEES	3	r	r	r	-	6	4	-	1	r	4
(Honda)	6	3	6	10	-	7	6	-	9	11	7
Sam TINGLE	r	-	-	-	-	-	-	-	-	-	-
(LDS-Climax)	14	-	-	-	-	-	-	-	-	-	-
Eppie WIETZES	-	-	-	-	-	-	-	dq	-	-	-
(Lotus-Ford Cosworth)	-	-	-	-	-	-	-	16	-	-	-
Jonathan WILLIAMS	-	-	-	-	-	-	-	-	-	-	8
(Ferrari)	-	-	-	-	-	-	-	-	-	-	16

	ZA	E	MC	B	NL	F	GB	D	I	CDN	USA	MEX
Kurt AHRENS	-	-	-	-	-	-	-	12	-	-	-	-
(Brabham-Repco)	-	-	-	-	-	-	-	17	-	-	-	-
Chris AMON	4	r	-	r	6	10	2	r	r	r	r	r
(Ferrari)	8	1	-	1	1	5	3	2	3	2	4	2
Mario ANDRETTI	-	-	-	-	-	-	-	-	-	-	r	-
(Lotus-Ford Cosworth)	-	-	-	-	-	-	-	-	exc	-	1	-
Dickie ATTWOOD	-	-	2f	r	7	7	r	14	-	-	-	-
(BRM)	-	-	6	11	15	12	15	20	-	-	-	-
Derek BELL	-	-	-	-	-	-	-	-	r	-	r	-
(Ferrari)	-	-	-	-	-	-	-	-	8	-	15	-
Jean-Pierre BELTOISE	6	5f	r	8	2f	9	r	r	5	r	r	r
(Matra-Ford Cosworth)	18	5	-	-	-	-	-	-	-	-	-	-
(Matra)	-	-	8	13	16	8	14	12	18	15	13	13
Lucien BIANCHI	-	-	3	6	r	-	-	r	-	nc	nc	r
(Cooper-BRM)	-	-	14	12	18	-	-	19	-	18	20	21
Jo BONNIER	r	-	-	r	8	-	r	-	6	r	nc	5
(Cooper-Maserati)	19											
(McLaren-BRM)	-	-	nq	16	19	-	20	-	19	17	18	-
(Honda)	-	-	-	-	-	-	-	-	-	-	-	18
Jack BRABHAM	r	-	r	r	r	r	r	5	r	r	r	10r
(Brabham-Repco)	5	ns	12	18	4	13	8	15	16	10	8	8
Bill BRACK	-	-	-	-	-	-	-	-	-	r	-	-
(Lotus-Ford Cosworth)	-	-	-	-	-	-	-	-	-	20	-	-
Dave CHARLTON	r	-	-	-	-	-	-	-	-	-	-	-
(Brabham-Repco)	14	-	-	-	-	-	-	-	-	-	-	-
Jim CLARK †	1f	-	-	-	-	-	-	-	-	-	-	-
(Lotus-Ford Cosworth)	1	-	-	-	-	-	-	-	-	-	-	-
Piers COURAGE	-	r	r	r	r	6	8	8	4	r	r	r
(BRM)	-	11	11	7	14	14	16	8	17	14	14	19
Andrea de ADAMICH	r	-	-	-	-	-	-	-	-	-	-	-
(Ferrari)	7	-	-	-	-	-	-	-	-	-	-	-
Vic ELFORD	-	-	-	-	-	4	r	r	r	5	r	8
(Cooper-BRM)	-	-	-	-	-	17	17	5	20	16	17	17
Frank GARDNER	-	-	-	-	-	-	-	-	r	-	-	-
(BRM)	-	-	-	-	-	-	-	-	nq	-	-	-
Dan GURNEY	r	-	r	-	r	-	r	9	r	r	r	r
(Eagle-Weslake)	12	-	16	-	-	-	6	10	12	-	-	-
(Brabham-Repco)	-	-	-	-	12	-	-	-	-	-	-	-
(McLaren-Ford Cosworth)	-	-	-	-	-	-	-	-	-	4	7	5
Hubert HAHNE	-	-	-	-	-	-	-	10	-	-	-	-
(Lola-BMW)	-	-	-	-	-	-	-	18	-	-	-	-
Graham HILL	2	1	1	r	9r	r	r	2	r	4	2	1
(Lotus-Ford Cosworth)	2	6	1	14	3	9	1	4	5	5	3	3
David HOBBS	-	-	-	-	-	-	-	-	r	-	-	-
(Honda)	-	-	-	-	-	-	-	-	14	-	-	-
Denny HULME	5	2	5	r	r	5	4	7	1	1	r	r
(McLaren-BRM)	9	-	-	-	-	-	-	-	-	-	-	-
(McLaren-Ford Cosworth)	-	3	10	5	7	4	11	11	7	6	5	4
Jacky ICKX	r	r	-	3	4	1	3	4	3	-	-	r
(Ferrari)	11	8	-	3	6	3	12	1	4	ns	-	15
John LOVE	9	-	-	-	-	-	-	-	-	-	-	-
(Brabham-Repco)	17	-	-	-	-	-	-	-	-	-	-	-
Bruce McLAREN	-	r	r	1	r	8	7	13	r	2	6	2
(McLaren-Ford Cosworth)	-	4	7	6	8	6	10	16	2	8	10	9
Silvio MOSER	-	-	-	-	5	-	nc	-	-	-	-	-
(Brabham-Repco)	-	-	nq	-	17	-	19	ns	nq	-	-	-
Jackie OLIVER	-	-	r	5r	nc	-	r	11	rf	r	-	3
(Lotus-Ford Cosworth)	-	-	13	15	10	ns	2	13	11	9	16ns	14
Al PEASE	-	-	-	-	-	-	-	-	-	-	-	-
(Eagle-Climax)	-	-	-	-	-	-	-	-	-	ns	-	-
Henri PESCAROLO	-	-	-	-	-	-	-	-	-	r	-	9
(Matra)	-	-	-	-	-	-	-	-	-	19	ns	20
Jackie PRETORIUS	nc	-	-	-	-	-	-	-	-	-	-	-
(Brabham-Climax)	23	-	-	-	-	-	-	-	-	-	-	-

	ZA	E	MC	B	NL	F	GB	D	I	CDN	USA	MEX
Brian REDMAN	r	3	-	r	-	-	-	-	-	-	-	-
(Cooper-Maserati)	21	-	-	-	-	-	-	-	-	-	-	-
(Cooper-BRM)	-	13	-	10	-	-	-	-	-	-	-	-
Jochen RINDT	3	r	r	r	r	r	r	3	r	r	r	r
(Brabham-Repco)	4	9	5	17	2	1	5	3	10	1	6	10
Pedro RODRÍGUEZ	r	r	r	2	3	ncf	r	6	r	3	r	4
(BRM)	10	2	9	8	11	10	13	14	15	12	11	12
Lodovico SCARFIOTTI †	r	4	4	-	-	-	-	-	-	-	-	-
(Cooper-Maserati)	15	-	-	-	-	-	-	-	-	-	-	-
(Cooper-BRM)	-	12	15	-	-	-	-	-	-	-	-	-
Jo SCHLESSER †	-	-	-	-	-	r	-	-	-	-	-	-
(Honda)	-	-	-	-	-	16	-	-	-	-	-	-
Johnny SERVOZ-GAVIN	-	-	r	-	-	r	-	-	2	r	-	r
(Matra-Ford Cosworth)	-	-	2	-	-	-	-	-	13	13	-	16
(Cooper-BRM)	-	-	-	-	-	15	-	-	-	-	-	-
Jo SIFFERT	7	r	r	7r	r	11	1f	r	r	rf	5	6f
(Cooper-Maserati)	16	-	-	-	-	-	-	-	-	-	-	-
(Lotus-Ford Cosworth)	-	10	3	9	13	11	4	9	9	3	12	1
Moisés SOLANA	-	-	-	-	-	-	-	-	-	-	-	r
(Lotus-Ford Cosworth)	-	-	-	-	-	-	-	-	-	-	-	11
Mike SPENCE †	r	-	-	-	-	-	-	-	-	-	-	-
(BRM)	13	-	-	-	-	-	-	-	-	-	-	-
Jackie STEWART	r	-	-	4	1	3	6	1f	r	6	1f	7
(Matra-Ford Cosworth)	3	-	-	2	5	2	7	6	6	11	2	7
John SURTEES	8	r	r	rf	r	2	5	r	r	r	3	r
(Honda)	6	7	4	4	9	7	9	7	1	7	9	6
Sam TINGLE	r	-	-	-	-	-	-	-	-	-	-	-
(LDS-Repco)	22	-	-	-	-	-	-	-	-	-	-	-
Bobby UNSER	-	-	-	-	-	-	-	-	-	-	r	-
(BRM)	-	-	-	-	-	-	-	-	-	exc	19	-
Basil van ROOYEN	r	-	-	-	-	-	-	-	-	-	-	-
(Cooper-Climax)	20	-	-	-	-	-	-	-	-	-	-	-
Robin WIDDOWS	-	-	-	-	-	-	r	-	-	-	-	-
(Cooper-BRM)	-	-	-	-	-	-	18	-	-	-	-	-

1969 RACE RESULTS & GRID POSITIONS

	ZA	E	MC	NL	F	GB	D	I	CDN	USA	MEX
Kurt AHRENS	-	-	-	-	-	-	F2:3	-	-	-	-
(Brabham-Ford Cosworth)	-	-	-	-	-	-	19	-	-	-	-
Chris AMON	r	r	r	3	r	r	-	-	-	-	-
(Ferrari)	5	2	2	4	6	5	-	-	-	-	-
Mario ANDRETTI	r	-	-	-	-	-	r	-	-	r	-
(Lotus-Ford Cosworth)	6	-	-	-	-	-	12	-	-	13	-
Dickie ATTWOOD	-	-	4	-	-	-	F2:2	-	-	-	-
(Lotus-Ford Cosworth)	-	-	10	-	-	-	-	-	-	-	-
(Brabham-Ford Cosworth)	-	-	-	-	-	-	20	-	-	-	-
Derek BELL	-	-	-	-	-	r	-	-	-	-	-
(McLaren-Ford Cosworth)	-	-	-	-	-	15	-	-	-	-	-
Jean-Pierre BELTOISE	6	3	r	8	2	9	6r	3f	4	r	5
(Matra-Ford Cosworth)	11	12	3	11	5	17	10	6	2	7	8
Jo BONNIER	-	-	-	-	-	r	r	-	-	-	-
(Lotus-Ford Cosworth)	-	-	-	-	-	16	14	-	-	-	-
Jack BRABHAM	r	r	r	6	-	-	-	r	2f=	4	3
(Brabham-Ford Cosworth)	1	5	8	8	-	-	-	7	6	10	1
Bill BRACK	-	-	-	-	-	-	-	-	nc	-	-
(BRM)	-	-	-	-	-	-	-	-	18	-	-
Tino BRAMBILLA	-	-	-	-	-	-	-	-	-	-	-
(Ferrari)	-	-	-	-	-	-	-	ns	-	-	-
François CEVERT	-	-	-	-	-	-	r	-	-	-	-
(Tecno-Ford Cosworth)	-	-	-	-	-	-	16	-	-	-	-
John CORDTS	-	-	-	-	-	-	-	-	-	r	-
(Brabham-Climax)	-	-	-	-	-	-	-	-	-	19	-

Grand Prix Data Book

	ZA	E	MC	NL	F	GB	D	I	CDN	USA	MEX
Piers COURAGE	-	r	2	r	r	5	r	5	r	2	10
(Brabham-Ford Cosworth)	-	11	9	9	11	10	7	4	10	9	9
Peter de KLERK	nc	-	-	-	-	-	-	-	-	-	-
(Brabham-Repco)	16	-	-	-	-	-	-	-	-	-	-
George EATON	-	-	-	-	-	-	-	-	-	r	r
(BRM)	-	-	-	-	-	-	-	-	-	18	17
Vic ELFORD	-	-	7	10	5	6	r	-	-	-	-
(Cooper-Maserati)	-	-	16	-	-	-	-	-	-	-	-
(McLaren-Ford Cosworth)	-	-	-	15	10	11	6	-	-	-	-
Hubert HAHNE	-	-	-	-	-	-	-	-	-	-	-
(BMW)	-	-	-	-	-	-	ns	-	-	-	-
Hans HERRMANN	-	-	-	-	-	-	-	-	-	-	-
(Lotus-Ford Cosworth)	-	-	-	-	-	-	ns	-	-	-	-
Graham HILL	2	r	1	7	6	7	4	9r	r	r	-
(Lotus-Ford Cosworth)	7	3	4	3	8	12	9	9	7	4	-
Denny HULME	3	4	6	4	8	r	r	7	r	r	1
(McLaren-Ford Cosworth)	3	8	12	7	2	3	5	2	5	2	4
Jacky ICKX	r	6r	r	5	3	2	1f	10r	1f=	r	2f
(Brabham-Ford Cosworth)	13	7	7	5	4	4	1	15	1	8	2
John LOVE	r	-	-	-	-	-	-	-	-	-	-
(Lotus-Ford Cosworth)	10	-	-	-	-	-	-	-	-	-	-
Pete LOVELY	-	-	-	-	-	-	-	-	7	r	9
(Lotus-Ford Cosworth)	-	-	-	-	-	-	-	-	16	16	16
Bruce McLAREN	5	2	5	r	4	3	3	4	5	-	-
(McLaren-Ford Cosworth)	8	13	11	6	7	7	8	5	9	6ns	7ns
John MILES	-	-	-	-	r	10	-	r	r	-	r
(Lotus-Ford Cosworth)	-	-	-	-	12	14	-	14	11	-	11
Gerhard MITTER †	-	-	-	-	-	-	-	-	-	-	-
(BMW)	-	-	-	-	-	-	ns	-	-	-	-
Silvio MOSER	-	-	r	r	7	-	-	r	r	6	11r
(Brabham-Ford Cosworth)	-	-	15	14	13	-	-	13	20	17	13
Jackie OLIVER	7	r	r	r	-	r	r	r	r	r	6
(BRM)	14	10	13	13	-	13	13	11	12	14	12
Al PEASE	-	-	-	-	-	-	-	-	dq	-	-
(Eagle-Climax)	-	-	-	-	-	-	-	-	17	-	-
Xavier PERROT	-	-	-	-	-	-	F2:6	-	-	-	-
(Brabham-Ford Cosworth)	-	-	-	-	-	-	22	-	-	-	-
Henri PESCAROLO	-	-	-	-	-	-	F2:1	-	-	-	-
(Matra-Ford Cosworth)	-	-	-	-	-	-	17	-	-	-	-
Dieter QUESTER	-	-	-	-	-	-	-	-	-	-	-
(BMW)	-	-	-	-	-	-	ns	-	-	-	-
Jochen RINDT	r	rf	-	r	r	4	r	2	3	1f	r
(Lotus-Ford Cosworth)	2	1	-	1	3	1	3	1	3	1	6
Pedro RODRÍGUEZ	r	r	r	-	-	r	-	6	r	5	7
(BRM)	15	14	14	-	-	-	-	-	-	-	-
(Ferrari)	-	-	-	-	-	8	-	12	13	12	15
Johnny SERVOZ-GAVIN	-	-	-	-	-	-	r	-	6	nc	8
(Matra-Ford Cosworth)	-	-	-	-	-	-	15	-	15	15	14
Jo SIFFERT	4	r	3	2	9	8	5r	8r	r	r	r
(Lotus-Ford Cosworth)	12	6	5	10	9	9	4	8	8	5	5
Jackie STEWART	1f	1	rf	1f	1f	1f	2	1	r	r	4
(Matra-Ford Cosworth)	4	4	1	2	1	2	2	3	4	3	3
Rolf STOMMELEN	-	-	-	-	-	-	F2:4	-	-	-	-
(Lotus-Ford Cosworth)	-	-	-	-	-	-	21	-	-	-	-
John SURTEES	r	5	r	9	-	r	-	nc	r	3	r
(BRM)	18	9	6	12	-	6	11ns	10	14	11	10
Sam TINGLE	8	-	-	-	-	-	-	-	-	-	-
(Brabham-Repco)	17	-	-	-	-	-	-	-	-	-	-
Basil van ROOYEN	r	-	-	-	-	-	-	-	-	-	-
(McLaren-Ford Cosworth)	9	-	-	-	-	-	-	-	-	-	-
Peter WESTBURY	-	-	-	-	-	-	F2:5	-	-	-	-
(Brabham-Ford Cosworth)	-	-	-	-	-	-	18	-	-	-	-

	ZA	E	MC	B	NL	F	GB	D	A	I	CDN	USA	MEX
Chris AMON	r	r	r	2f	r	2	5	r	8	7	3	5	4
(March-Ford Cosworth)	2	6	2	3	4	3	17	6	6	18	6	5	5
Mario ANDRETTI	r	3	-	-	-	-	r	r	r	-	-	-	-
(March-Ford Cosworth)	11	16	-	-	-	-	9	9	18	-	-	-	-
Derek BELL	-	-	-	r	-	-	-	-	-	-	-	6	-
(Brabham-Ford Cosworth)	-	-	-	15	-	-	-	-	-	-	-	-	-
(Surtees-Ford Cosworth)	-	-	-	-	-	-	-	-	-	-	-	13	-
Jean-Pierre BELTOISE	4	r	r	3	5	13r	r	r	6	3	8	r	5
(Matra Simca)	8	4	6	11	10	2	10	21	7	14	13	18	6
Jo BONNIER	-	-	-	-	-	-	-	-	-	-	-	r	-
(McLaren-Ford Cosworth)	-	-	-	-	-	-	-	-	-	nq	-	24	-
Jack BRABHAM	1f=	rf	2	r	11	3f	2f	r	13	r	r	10	r
(Brabham-Ford Cosworth)	3	1	4	5	12	5	2	12	8	8	19	16	4
François CEVERT	-	-	-	-	r	11	7	7	r	6	9	r	r
(March-Ford Cosworth)	-	-	-	-	15	13	14	14	9	11	4	17	9
Dave CHARLTON	12r	-	-	-	-	-	-	-	-	-	-	-	-
(Lotus-Ford Cosworth)	13	-	-	-	-	-	-	-	-	-	-	-	-
Piers COURAGE †	r	-	nc	r	r	-	-	-	-	-	-	-	-
(De Tomaso-Ford Cosworth)	20	13ns	9	12	9	-	-	-	-	-	-	-	-
Andrea de ADAMICH	-	-	-	-	-	nc	-	-	12	8	r	-	-
(McLaren-Alfa Romeo)	-	nq	nq	-	nq	15	18ns	nq	15	12	12	nq	-
Peter de KLERK	11	-	-	-	-	-	-	-	-	-	-	-	-
(Brabham-Ford Cosworth)	21	-	-	-	-	-	-	-	-	-	-	-	-
George EATON	r	-	-	-	r	12	r	-	11	r	10	r	-
(BRM)	23	nq	nq	-	18	19	16	-	23	20	9	14	-
Emerson FITTIPALDI	-	-	-	-	-	-	8	4	15	-	-	1	r
(Lotus-Ford Cosworth)	-	-	-	-	-	-	21	13	16	ns	-	3	18
Nanni GALLI	-	-	-	-	-	-	-	-	-	-	-	-	-
(McLaren-Alfa Romeo)	-	-	-	-	-	-	-	-	-	nq	-	-	-
Peter GETHIN	-	-	-	-	r	-	-	r	10	nc	6	14	r
(McLaren-Ford Cosworth)	-	-	-	-	11	-	-	17	21	16	11	21	10
Ignazio GIUNTI	-	-	-	4	-	14	-	-	7	r	-	-	-
(Ferrari)	-	-	-	8	-	11	-	-	5	5	-	-	-
Dan GURNEY	-	-	-	-	r	6	r	-	-	-	-	-	-
(McLaren-Ford Cosworth)	-	-	-	-	19	17	11	-	-	-	-	-	-
Hubert HAHNE	-	-	-	-	-	-	-	-	-	-	-	-	-
(March-Ford Cosworth)	-	-	-	-	-	-	-	nq	-	-	-	-	-
Graham HILL	6	4	5	r	nc	10	6	r	-	-	nc	r	r
(Lotus-Ford Cosworth)	19	15	12	16	20	20	22	20	-	ns	20	10	8
Denny HULME	2	r	4	-	-	4	3	3	r	4	r	7	3
(McLaren-Ford Cosworth)	6	2	3	-	-	7	5	16	11	9	15	11	14
Gus HUTCHISON	-	-	-	-	-	-	-	-	-	-	-	r	-
(Brabham-Ford Cosworth)	-	-	-	-	-	-	-	-	-	-	-	22	-
Jacky ICKX	r	r	r	8	3f	r	r	2f	1f=	r	1	4f	1f
(Ferrari)	5	7	5	4	3	1	3	1	3	1	2	1	3
John LOVE	8	-	-	-	-	-	-	-	-	-	-	-	-
(Lotus-Ford Cosworth)	22	-	-	-	-	-	-	-	-	-	-	-	-
Pete LOVELY	-	-	-	-	-	-	nc	-	-	-	-	-	-
(Lotus-Ford Cosworth)	-	-	-	-	nq	nq	23	-	-	-	-	nq	-
Bruce McLAREN †	r	2	r	-	-	-	-	-	-	-	-	-	-
(McLaren-Ford Cosworth)	10	11	10	-	-	-	-	-	-	-	-	-	-
John MILES	5	-	-	r	7	8	r	r	r	-	-	-	-
(Lotus-Ford Cosworth)	14	nq	nq	13	8	18	7	10	10	ns	-	-	-
Silvio MOSER	-	-	-	-	-	-	-	-	r	-	-	-	-
(Bellasi-Ford Cosworth)	-	-	-	-	nq	nq	-	nq	24	nq	-	-	-
Jackie OLIVER	r	r	r	r	r	r	r	r	5	r	nc	r	7
(BRM)	12	10	15	14	5	12	4	18	14	6	10	7	13
Henri PESCAROLO	7	r	3	6r	8	5	r	6	14	r	7	8	9
(Matra Simca)	18	9	7	17	13	8	12	5	13	15	8	12	11
Ronnie PETERSON	-	-	7	nc	9	r	9	r	-	r	nc	11	-
(March-Ford Cosworth)	-	-	13	9	16	9	13	19	-	13	16	15	-
Brian REDMAN	-	-	-	-	-	-	ns	nq	-	-	-	-	-
(De Tomaso-Ford Cosworth)	-	-	-	-	-	-	-	-	-	-	-	-	-
Clay REGAZZONI	-	-	-	-	4	-	4	r	2f=	1f	2f	13	2
(Ferrari)	-	-	-	-	6	-	6	3	2	3	3	6	1

	ZA	E	MC	B	NL	F	GB	D	A	I	CDN	USA	MEX
Jochen RINDT †	13r	r	1f	r	1	1	1	1	r	-	-	-	-
(Lotus-Ford Cosworth)	4	8	8	2	1	6	1	2	1	ns	-	-	-
Pedro RODRÍGUEZ	9	r	6	1	10	r	r	r	4	r	4	2	6
(BRM)	16	5	16	6	7	10	15	8	22	2	7	4	7
Tim SCHENKEN	-	-	-	-	-	-	-	-	r	r	nc	r	-
(De Tomaso-Ford Cosworth)	-	-	-	-	-	-	-	-	19	19	17	20	-
Johnny SERVOZ-GAVIN	r	5	-	-	-	-	-	-	-	-	-	-	-
(March-Ford Cosworth)	17	14	nq	-	-	-	-	-	-	-	-	-	-
Jo SIFFERT	10	-	8r	7r	r	r	r	8r	9	r	r	9	r
(March-Ford Cosworth)	9	nq	11	10	17	16	20	4	20	7	14	23	16
Alex SOLER-ROIG	-	nq	-	nq	-	nq	-	-	-	-	-	-	-
(Lotus-Ford Cosworth)	-	-	-	-	-	-	-	-	-	-	-	-	-
Jackie STEWART	3	1	r	r	2	9	r	r	r	2	r	r	r
(March-Ford Cosworth)	1	3	1	1	2	4	8	7	4	4	-	-	-
(Tyrrell-Ford Cosworth)	-	-	-	-	-	-	-	-	-	-	1	2	2
Rolf STOMMELEN	r	r	-	5	-	7	-	5	3	5	r	12	r
(Brabham-Ford Cosworth)	15	17	nq	7	nq	14	ns	11	17	17	18	19	17
John SURTEES	rf=	r	r	-	6	-	r	9r	r	r	5	r	8
(McLaren-Ford Cosworth)	7	12	14	-	14	-	-	-	-	-	-	-	-
(Surtees-Ford Cosworth)	-	-	-	-	-	-	19	15	12	10	5	8	15
Peter WESTBURY	-	-	-	-	-	-	-	-	-	-	-	-	-
(BRM)	-	-	-	-	-	-	-	-	-	-	-	nq	-
Reine WISELL	-	-	-	-	-	-	-	-	-	-	-	3	nc
(Lotus-Ford Cosworth)	-	-	-	-	-	-	-	-	-	-	-	9	12

1971 RACE RESULTS & GRID POSITIONS

	ZA	E	MC	NL	F	GB	D	A	I	CDN	USA
Chris AMON	5	3	r	r	5	r	r	-	6	10	12
(Matra Simca)	2	3	4	5	9	9	16	-	1	5	8
Mario ANDRETTI	1f	r	-	r	-	-	4	-	-	13	-
(Ferrari)	4	8	nq	18	-	-	11	-	-	13	ns
Skip BARBER	-	-	-	nc	-	-	-	-	-	r	nc
(March-Ford Cosworth)	-	-	nq	24	-	-	-	-	-	24	25
Derek BELL	-	-	-	-	-	r	-	-	-	-	-
(Surtees-Ford Cosworth)	-	-	-	-	-	23	-	-	-	-	-
Jean-Pierre BELTOISE	-	6	r	9	7	7	-	-	-	r	8
(Matra Simca)	-	6	7	11	8	15	-	-	-	11	10
Mike BEUTTLER	-	-	-	-	-	r	dq	nc	r	nc	-
(March-Ford Cosworth)	-	-	-	-	-	20	22	19	16	22	-
Jo BONNIER	r	-	-	-	-	-	-	-	10	-	16r
(McLaren-Ford Cosworth)	23	-	-	-	-	-	nq	20ns	21	-	28
John CANNON	-	-	-	-	-	-	-	-	-	-	14
(BRM)	-	-	-	-	-	-	-	-	-	-	24
François CEVERT	r	7	r	r	2	10	2f	r	3	6	1
(Tyrrell-Ford Cosworth)	9	12	15	12	7	10	5	3	5	3	5
Dave CHARLTON	r	-	-	-	-	r	-	-	-	-	-
(Brabham-Ford Cosworth)	12	-	-	-	-	-	-	-	-	-	-
(Lotus-Ford Cosworth)	-	-	-	-	-	13	-	-	-	-	-
Chris CRAFT	-	-	-	-	-	-	-	-	-	-	r
(Brabham-Ford Cosworth)	-	-	-	-	-	-	-	-	-	ns	27
Andrea de ADAMICH	13	r	-	-	r	nc	r	-	r	-	11
(March-Alfa Romeo)	22	18	-	-	20	24	20	-	20	-	26
Mark DONOHUE	-	-	-	-	-	-	-	-	-	3	-
(McLaren-Ford Cosworth)	-	-	-	-	-	-	-	-	-	8	ns
George EATON	-	-	-	-	-	-	-	-	-	15	-
(BRM)	-	-	-	-	-	-	-	-	-	21	-
Vic ELFORD	-	-	-	-	-	-	11	-	-	-	-
(BRM)	-	-	-	-	-	-	18	-	-	-	-
Emerson FITTIPALDI	r	r	5	-	3	3	r	2	8	7	nc
(Lotus-Ford Cosworth)	5	14	17	-	17	4	8	5	-	4	2
(Lotus-Pratt & Whitney)	-	-	-	-	-	-	-	-	18	-	-
Nanni GALLI	-	-	-	r	-	11	12	12	r	16	r
(March-Alfa Romeo)	-	-	nq	20	-	-	21	15	-	-	-
(March-Ford Cosworth)	-	-	-	-	ns	21	-	-	19	20	23
Howden GANLEY	r	10	-	7	10	8	r	r	5	-	4
(BRM)	24	17	nq	9	16	11	14	14	4	9ns	12

	ZA	E	MC	NL	F	GB	D	A	I	CDN	USA
Peter GETHIN	r	8	r	nc	9	r	r	10	1	14	9
(McLaren-Ford Cosworth)	11	7	14	23	19	14	19	-	-	-	-
(BRM)	-	-	-	-	-	-	-	16	11	16	21
Mike HAILWOOD	-	-	-	-	-	-	-	-	4	-	15r
(Surtees-Ford Cosworth)	-	-	-	-	-	-	-	-	17	-	14
Graham HILL	9	r	r	10	r	r	9	5	r	r	7
(Brabham-Ford Cosworth)	19	15	9	16	4	16	13	8	14	15	18
David HOBBS	-	-	-	-	-	-	-	-	-	-	10
(McLaren-Ford Cosworth)	-	-	-	-	-	-	-	-	-	-	22
Denny HULME	6	5	4	12	r	r	r	r	-	4f	r
(McLaren-Ford Cosworth)	7	9	6	14	11	8	6	9	-	10	3
Jacky ICKX	8	2f	3	1f	r	r	r	r	r	8	rf
(Ferrari)	8	1	2	1	3	6	2	6	2	12	7
Jean-Pierre JARIER	-	-	-	-	-	-	-	-	nc	-	-
(March-Ford Cosworth)	-	-	-	-	-	-	-	-	24	-	-
Max JEAN	-	-	-	-	nc	-	-	-	-	-	-
(March-Ford Cosworth)	-	-	-	-	22	-	-	-	-	-	-
Niki LAUDA	-	-	-	-	-	-	-	r	-	-	-
(March-Ford Cosworth)	-	-	-	-	-	-	-	21	-	-	-
John LOVE	r	-	-	-	-	-	-	-	-	-	-
(March-Ford Cosworth)	21	-	-	-	-	-	-	-	-	-	-
Pete LOVELY	-	-	-	-	-	-	-	-	-	nc	nc
(Lotus-Ford Cosworth)	-	-	-	-	-	-	-	-	-	25	29
Helmut MARKO	-	-	-	-	-	-	-	11	r	12	13
(McLaren-Ford Cosworth)	-	-	-	-	-	-	nq	-	-	-	-
(BRM)	-	-	-	-	-	-	-	17	12	19	16
François MAZET	-	-	-	-	13	-	-	-	-	-	-
(March-Ford Cosworth)	-	-	-	-	23	-	-	-	-	-	-
Silvio MOSER	-	-	-	-	-	-	-	-	r	-	-
(Bellasi-Ford Cosworth)	-	-	-	-	-	-	-	-	22	-	-
Jackie OLIVER	-	-	-	-	-	r	-	9	7	-	-
(McLaren-Ford Cosworth)	-	-	-	-	-	22	-	22	13	-	-
Henri PESCAROLO	11	r	8	nc	r	4	r	6	rf	-	r
(March-Ford Cosworth)	18	11	13	15	18	17	10	13	10	ns	20
Ronnie PETERSON	10	r	2	4	r	2	5	8	2	2	3
(March-Ford Cosworth)	13	13	8	13	-	5	7	11	6	6	11
(March-Alfa Romeo)	-	-	-	-	12	-	-	-	-	-	-
Sam POSEY	-	-	-	-	-	-	-	-	-	-	r
(Surtees-Ford Cosworth)	-	-	-	-	-	-	-	-	-	-	17
Jackie PRETORIUS	r	-	-	-	-	-	-	-	-	-	-
(Brabham-Ford Cosworth)	20	-	-	-	-	-	-	-	-	-	-
Brian REDMAN	7	-	-	-	-	-	-	-	-	-	-
(Surtees-Ford Cosworth)	17	-	-	-	-	-	-	-	-	-	-
Clay REGAZZONI	3	r	r	3	r	r	3	r	r	r	6
(Ferrari)	3	2	11	4	2	1	4	4	8	18	4
Peter REVSON	-	-	-	-	-	-	-	-	-	-	r
(Tyrrell-Ford Cosworth)	-	-	-	-	-	-	-	-	-	-	19
Pedro RODRÍGUEZ †	r	4	9	2	r	-	-	-	-	-	-
(BRM)	10	5	5	2	5	-	-	-	-	-	-
Tim SCHENKEN	-	9	10	r	12r	12r	6	3	r	r	r
(Brabham-Ford Cosworth)	-	21	18	19	14	7	9	7	9	17	15
Jo SIFFERT †	r	r	r	6	4	9	r/dq	1f	9	9	2
(BRM)	16	10	3	8	6	3	3	1	3	2	6
Alex SOLER-ROIG	r	r	-	r	r	-	-	-	-	-	-
(March-Ford Cosworth)	25	20	nq	17	21	-	-	-	-	-	-
Jackie STEWART	2	1	1f	11	1f	1f	1	r	r	1	5
(Tyrrell-Ford Cosworth)	1	4	1	3	1	2	1	2	7	1	1
Rolf STOMMELEN	12	r	6	dq	11	5	10	7	-	r	-
(Surtees-Ford Cosworth)	15	19	16	10	10	12	12	12	23ns	23	-
John SURTEES	r	11	7	5	8	6	7	r	r	11	17
(Surtees-Ford Cosworth)	6	22	10	7	13	18	15	18	15	14	13
Gijs van LENNEP	-	-	-	8	-	-	-	-	-	-	-
(Surtees-Ford Cosworth)	-	-	-	21	-	-	-	-	-	-	ns
Dave WALKER	-	-	-	r	-	-	-	-	-	-	-
(Lotus-Pratt & Whitney)	-	-	-	22	-	-	-	-	-	-	-
Reine WISELL	4	nc	r	dq	6	nc	8	4	-	5	r
(Lotus-Ford Cosworth)	14	16	12	6	15	-	17	10	-	7	9
(Lotus-Pratt & Whitney)	-	-	-	-	-	19	-	-	-	-	-

	RA	ZA	E	MC	B	F	GB	D	A	I	CDN	USA
Chris AMON	-	15	r	6	6f	3f	4	15	5	r	6	15
(Matra Simca)	12ns	13	6	6	13	1	17	8	6	2	10	7
Mario ANDRETTI	r	4	r	-	-	-	-	-	-	7	-	6
(Ferrari)	9	6	5	-	-	-	-	-	-	7	-	10
Skip BARBER	-	-	-	-	-	-	-	-	-	-	nc	16
(March-Ford Cosworth)	-	-	-	-	-	-	-	-	-	-	22	20
Derek BELL	-	-	-	-	-	ns	-	r	-	-	ns	r
(Tecno)	-	-	-	-	-	-	-	25	-	nq	ns	29
Jean-Pierre BELTOISE	-	r	r	1f	r	15	11	9	8	8	r	r
(BRM)	-	11	7	4	6	24	6	13	21	16	20	18
Mike BEUTTLER	-	-	-	13	r	r	13	8	r	10	nc	13
(March-Ford Cosworth)	-	-	nq	23	22	23	23	27	24	25	24	21
Bill BRACK	-	-	-	-	-	-	-	-	-	-	r	-
(BRM)	-	-	-	-	-	-	-	-	-	-	23	-
François CEVERT	r	9	r	nc	2	4	r	10	9	r	r	2
(Tyrrell-Ford Cosworth)	7	8	12	12	5	7	12	5	20	14	6	4
Dave CHARLTON	-	r	-	-	-	-	r	r	-	-	-	-
(Lotus-Ford Cosworth)	-	17	-	-	-	ns	24	26	-	-	-	-
Andrea de ADAMICH	r	nc	4	7	r	14	r	13	14	r	r	r
(Surtees-Ford Cosworth)	14	20	13	18	10	12	20	20	13	21	15	19
Patrick DEPAILLER	-	-	-	-	-	nc	-	-	-	-	-	7
(Tyrrell-Ford Cosworth)	-	-	-	-	-	16	-	-	-	-	-	11
Willie FERGUSON	-	-	-	-	-	-	-	-	-	-	-	-
(Brabham-Ford Cosworth)	-	ns	-	-	-	-	-	-	-	-	-	-
Emerson FITTIPALDI	r	2	1	3	1	2	1	r	1	1	11	r
(JPS Lotus-Ford Cosworth)	5	3	3	1	1	8	2	3	1	6	4	9
Wilson FITTIPALDI	-	-	7	9	r	8	12r	7	r	r	r	r
(Brabham-Ford Cosworth)	-	-	14	21	18	14	22	21	15	15	11	13
Nanni GALLI	-	-	-	-	r	13	r	-	nc	r	-	-
(Tecno)	-	-	-	-	24	-	18	-	23	23	-	-
(Ferrari)	-	-	-	-	-	19	-	-	-	-	-	-
Howden GANLEY	9	nc	r	r	8	-	-	4	6	11	10	r
(BRM)	13	16	20	20	15	ns	-	18	10	17	14	17
Peter GETHIN	r	nc	r	dq	r	-	r	-	13	6	r	r
(BRM)	18	18	21	5	17	ns	16	-	16	12	12	28
Mike HAILWOOD	-	rf	r	r	4	6	r	r	4	2	-	17r
(Surtees-Ford Cosworth)	-	4	15	11	8	10	7	16	12	9	-	14
Graham HILL	r	6	10	12	r	10	r	6	r	5	8	11
(Brabham-Ford Cosworth)	16	14	23	19	16	20	21	15	14	13	17	27
Denny HULME	2	1	r	15	3	7	5	r	2f	3	3	3
(McLaren-Ford Cosworth)	4	5	2	7	3	2	11	10	7	5	2	3
Jacky ICKX	3	8	2f	2	r	11	r	1f	r	rf	12	5
(Ferrari)	8	7	1	2	4	4	1	1	9	1	8	12
Niki LAUDA	11	7	r	16	12	r	9	r	10	13	dq	nc
(March-Ford Cosworth)	22	21	25	22	25	21	19	24	22	20	19	25
John LOVE	-	16r	-	-	-	-	-	-	-	-	-	-
(Surtees-Ford Cosworth)	-	26	-	-	-	-	-	-	-	-	-	-
Helmut MARKO	10	14	-	8	10	r	-	-	-	-	-	-
(BRM)	19	23	-	17	23	6	-	-	-	-	-	-
Arturo MERZARIO	-	-	-	-	-	-	6	12	-	-	-	-
(Ferrari)	-	-	-	-	-	-	9	22	-	-	-	-
François MIGAULT	-	-	-	-	-	-	-	-	r	-	-	-
(Connew-Ford Cosworth)	-	-	-	-	-	-	ns	-	25	-	-	-
Jackie OLIVER	-	-	-	-	-	-	r	-	-	-	-	-
(BRM)	-	-	-	-	-	-	14	-	-	-	-	-
Carlos PACE	-	17	6	17	5	r	r	nc	nc	r	9r	r
(March-Ford Cosworth)	-	24	16	24	11	11	13	11	18	18	18	15
Henri PESCAROLO	8	11	11	r	nc	-	r	r	-	-	13	14
(March-Ford Cosworth)	15	22	19	9	19	ns	-	9	ns	nq	21	22
(Politoys-Ford Cosworth)	-	-	-	-	-	-	26	-	-	-	-	-
Ronnie PETERSON	6	5	r	11	9	5	7r	3	12	9	dq	4
(March-Ford Cosworth)	10	9	9	15	14	9	8	4	11	24	3	26
Sam POSEY	-	-	-	-	-	-	-	-	-	-	-	12
(Surtees-Ford Cosworth)	-	-	-	-	-	-	-	-	-	-	-	23

	RA	ZA	E	MC	B	F	GB	D	A	I	CDN	USA
Brian REDMAN	-	-	-	5	-	9	-	5	-	-	-	r
(McLaren-Ford Cosworth)	-	-	-	10	-	13	-	19	-	-	-	-
(BRM)	-	-	-	-	-	-	-	-	-	-	-	24
Clay REGAZZONI	4	12	3	r	r	-	-	2	r	r	5	8
(Ferrari)	6	2	8	3	2	-	-	7	2	4	7	6
Carlos REUTEMANN	7	r	-	-	13	12	8	r	r	r	4	r
(Brabham-Ford Cosworth)	1	15	-	-	9	17	10	6	5	11	9	5
Peter REVSON	r	3	5	-	7	-	3	-	3	4	2	18r
(McLaren-Ford Cosworth)	3	12	11	-	7	-	3	-	4	8	1	2
Jody SCHECKTER	-	-	-	-	-	-	-	-	-	-	-	9
(McLaren-Ford Cosworth)	-	-	-	-	-	-	-	-	-	-	-	8
Tim SCHENKEN	5	r	8	r	r	17	r	14	11	r	7	r
(Surtees-Ford Cosworth)	11	10	18	13	21	5	5	12	8	22	13	31
Vern SCHUPPAN	-	-	-	-	ns	-	-	-	-	-	-	-
(BRM)	-	-	-	-	-	-	-	-	-	-	-	-
Alex SOLER-ROIG	r	-	r	-	-	-	-	-	-	-	-	-
(BRM)	21	-	22	-	-	-	-	-	-	-	-	-
Jackie STEWART	1f	r	r	4	-	1	2f	11r	7	r	1f	1f
(Tyrrell-Ford Cosworth)	2	1	4	8	-	3	4	2	3	3	5	1
Rolf STOMMELEN	-	13	r	10	11	16	10	r	15	-	-	-
(Eiffeland March-Ford Cosworth)	-	25	17	25	20	15	25	14	17	-	-	-
John SURTEES	-	-	-	-	-	-	-	-	-	r	-	-
(Surtees-Ford Cosworth)	-	-	-	-	-	-	-	-	-	19	-	ns
Dave WALKER	dq	10	9r	14	14	18r	r	r	r	-	-	r
(JPS Lotus-Ford Cosworth)	20	19	24	14	12	22	15	23	19	-	-	30
Reine WISELL	r	-	r	r	-	r	-	r	-	12	r	10
(BRM)	17	-	10	16	-	18	-	17	-	10	-	-
(JPS Lotus-Ford Cosworth)	-	-	-	-	-	-	-	-	-	-	16	16

1973 RACE RESULTS & GRID POSITIONS

	RA	BR	ZA	E	B	MC	S	F	GB	NL	D	A	I	CDN	USA
Chris AMON	-	-	-	-	6	r	-	-	r	r	-	-	-	10	-
(Tecno)	-	-	-	-	15	12	-	-	29	19	-	ns	-	-	-
(Tyrrell-Ford Cosworth)	-	-	-	-	-	-	-	-	-	-	-	-	-	11	12ns
Tom BELSØ	-	-	-	-	-	-	-	-	-	-	-	-	-	-	-
(Iso Marlboro-Ford Cosworth)	-	-	-	-	-	-	ns	-	-	-	-	-	-	-	-
Jean-Pierre BELTOISE	r	r	r	5	r	r	r	11	r	5	r	5	13	4	9
(BRM)	7	10	7	10	5	11	9	15	17	9	9	13	13	16	14
Mike BEUTTLER	10r	r	nc	7	11r	r	8	-	11	r	16	r	r	r	10
(March-Ford Cosworth)	18	19	23	19	20	20	21	-	24	23	19	11	12	21	26
Luiz BUENO	-	12	-	-	-	-	-	-	-	-	-	-	-	-	-
(Surtees-Ford Cosworth)	-	20	-	-	-	-	-	-	-	-	-	-	-	-	-
François CEVERT †	2	10	nc	2	2f	4	3	2	5	2	2	r	5	r	-
(Tyrrell-Ford Cosworth)	6	9	25	3	4	4	2	4	7	3	3	10	11	6	ns
Dave CHARLTON	-	-	r	-	-	-	-	-	-	-	-	-	-	-	-
(Lotus-Ford Cosworth)	-	-	13	-	-	-	-	-	-	-	-	-	-	-	-
Andrea de ADAMICH	-	-	8	r	4	7	-	r	r	-	-	-	-	-	-
(Surtees-Ford Cosworth)	-	-	20	-	-	-	-	-	-	-	-	-	-	-	-
(Brabham-Ford Cosworth)	-	-	-	17	18	25	-	13	20	-	-	-	-	-	-
Emerson FITTIPALDI	1f	1f=	3f	1	3	2f	12r	r	r	r	6	11r	2	2f	6
(JPS Lotus-Ford Cosworth)	2	2	2	7	9	5	4	3	5	16	14	1	4	5	3
Wilson FITTIPALDI	6	r	r	10	r	11r	r	16r	r	r	5	r	r	11	nc
(Brabham-Ford Cosworth)	12	11	17	12	19	9	13	19	13	13	13	16	16	10	25
George FOLLMER	-	-	6	3	r	-	14	r	r	10	r	r	10	17	14
(Shadow-Ford Cosworth)	-	-	21	14	11	ns	19	20	25	22	21	20	21	13	20
Nanni GALLI	r	9	-	11	r	r	-	-	-	-	-	-	-	-	-
(Iso Marlboro-Ford Cosworth)	16	18	-	20	17	21	-	-	-	-	-	-	-	-	-
Howden GANLEY	nc	7	10	r	r	r	11	14	9	9	-	nc	nc	6	12
(Iso Marlboro-Ford Cosworth)	19	16	19	21	21	10	11	24	18	15	ns	21	20	22	19
Peter GETHIN	-	-	-	-	-	-	-	-	-	-	-	-	-	r	-
(BRM)	-	-	-	-	-	-	-	-	-	-	-	-	-	25	-
Mike HAILWOOD	r	r	r	r	r	8	r	r	r	r	14	10	7	9	r
(Surtees-Ford Cosworth)	10	14	12	9	13	13	10	11	12	24	18	15	8	12	6

	RA	BR	ZA	E	B	MC	S	F	GB	NL	D	A	I	CDN	USA
Graham HILL	-	-	-	r	9	r	r	10	r	nc	13	r	14	16	13
(Shadow-Ford Cosworth)	-	-	-	22	23	24	18	16	27	17	20	22	22	17	18
Denny HULME	5	3f=	5	6	7	6	1f	8f	3	r	12	8	15	13	4
(McLaren-Ford Cosworth)	8	5	1	2	2	3	6	6	2	4	8	3	3	7	8
James HUNT	-	-	-	-	-	9r	-	6	4f	3	-	r	-	7	2f
(March-Ford Cosworth)	-	-	-	-	-	18	-	14	11	7	-	9	ns	15	4
Jacky ICKX	4	5	r	12	r	r	6	5	8	-	3	-	8	-	7
(Ferrari)	3	3	11	6	3	7	8	12	19	-	-	-	14	-	-
(McLaren-Ford Cosworth)	-	-	-	-	-	-	-	-	-	-	-	4	-	-	-
(Iso Marlboro-Ford Cosworth)	-	-	-	-	-	-	-	-	-	-	-	-	-	-	23
Jean-Pierre JARIER	r	r	nc	-	r	r	r	r	-	-	-	r	-	nc	11r
(March-Ford Cosworth)	17	15	18	-	16	14	20	7	-	-	-	12	-	23	17
Eddie KEIZAN	-	-	nc	-	-	-	-	-	-	-	-	-	-	-	-
(Tyrrell-Ford Cosworth)	-	-	22	-	-	-	-	-	-	-	-	-	-	-	-
Niki LAUDA	r	8	r	r	5	r	13	9	12	r	r	-	r	r	r
(BRM)	13	13	10	11	14	6	15	17	9	11	5	ns	15	8	21
Jochen MASS	-	-	-	-	-	-	-	r	-	-	7	-	-	-	r
(Surtees-Ford Cosworth)	-	-	-	-	-	-	-	14	-	-	15	-	-	-	16
Graham McRAE	-	-	-	-	-	-	-	r	-	-	-	-	-	-	-
(Iso Marlboro-Ford Cosworth)	-	-	-	-	-	-	-	28	-	-	-	-	-	-	-
Arturo MERZARIO	9	4	4	-	-	r	-	7	-	-	-	7	r	15	16
(Ferrari)	14	17	15	-	-	16	-	10	-	-	-	6	7	20	11
Jackie OLIVER	-	-	r	r	r	10	r	r	r	r	8	r	11	3	15
(Shadow-Ford Cosworth)	-	-	14	13	22	22	17	21	26	10	17	18	19	14	22
Carlos PACE	r	r	r	r	8	r	10	13	r	7	4f	3f	r	18r	r
(Surtees-Ford Cosworth)	15	6	9	16	8	17	16	18	15	8	11	8	5	19	9
Henri PESCAROLO	-	-	-	8	-	-	-	-	-	-	-	-	-	-	-
(March-Ford Cosworth)	-	-	-	18	-	-	-	-	-	-	-	-	-	-	-
(Iso Marlboro-Ford Cosworth)	-	-	-	-	-	-	-	r	-	-	10	-	-	-	-
	-	-	-	-	-	-	-	23	-	-	12	-	-	-	-
Ronnie PETERSON	r	r	11	rf	r	3	2	1	2	11rf	r	1	1	r	1
(JPS Lotus-Ford Cosworth)	5	1	4	1	1	2	1	5	1	1	2	2	1	1	1
Jackie PRETORIUS	-	-	r	-	-	-	-	-	-	-	-	-	-	-	-
(Iso Marlboro-Ford Cosworth)	-	-	24	-	-	-	-	-	-	-	-	-	-	-	-
David PURLEY	-	-	-	-	-	r	-	-	-	r	15	-	9	-	-
(March-Ford Cosworth)	-	-	-	-	-	23	-	-	16ns	21	22	-	24	-	-
Brian REDMAN	-	-	-	-	-	-	-	-	-	-	-	-	-	-	dq
(Shadow-Ford Cosworth)	-	-	-	-	-	-	-	-	-	-	-	-	-	-	13
Clay REGAZZONI	7	6	r	9	10r	r	9	12	7	8	r	6	r	-	8
(BRM)	1	4	5	8	12	8	12	9	10	12	10	14	18	-	15
Carlos REUTEMANN	r	11	7	r	r	r	4	3	6	r	r	4	6	8	3
(Brabham-Ford Cosworth)	9	7	8	15	7	19	5	8	8	5	6	5	10	4	2
Peter REVSON	8	r	2	4	r	5	7	-	1	4	9	r	3	1	5
(McLaren-Ford Cosworth)	11	12	6	5	10	15	7	-	3	6	7	4	2	2	7
Jody SCHECKTER	-	-	9r	-	-	-	-	r	r	-	-	-	-	r	r
(McLaren-Ford Cosworth)	-	-	3	-	-	-	-	2	6	-	-	-	-	3	10
Tim SCHENKEN	-	-	-	-	-	-	-	-	-	-	-	-	-	14	-
(Iso Marlboro-Ford Cosworth)	-	-	-	-	-	-	-	-	-	-	-	-	-	24	-
Jackie STEWART	3	2	1	r	1	1	5	4	10	1	1	2	4f	5	-
(Tyrrell-Ford Cosworth)	4	8	16	4	6	1	3	1	4	2	1	7	6	9	5ns
Rolf STOMMELEN	-	-	-	-	-	-	-	-	-	-	11	r	12	12	-
(Brabham-Ford Cosworth)	-	-	-	-	-	-	-	-	-	-	16	17	9	18	-
Gijs van LENNEP	-	-	-	-	-	-	-	-	-	6	-	9	r	-	-
(Iso Marlboro-Ford Cosworth)	-	-	-	-	-	-	-	-	-	20	-	23	23	-	-
Rikky von OPEL	-	-	-	-	-	-	-	15	13	-	-	r	r	nc	r
(Ensign-Ford Cosworth)	-	-	-	-	-	-	-	25	21	14ns	-	19	17	26	27
John WATSON	-	-	-	-	-	-	-	-	r	-	-	-	-	-	r
(Brabham-Ford Cosworth)	-	-	-	-	-	-	-	-	23	-	-	-	-	-	24
Roger WILLIAMSON †	-	-	-	-	-	-	-	-	r	r	-	-	-	-	-
(March-Ford Cosworth)	-	-	-	-	-	-	-	-	22	18	-	-	-	-	-
Reine WISELL	-	-	-	-	-	-	-	r	-	-	-	-	-	-	-
(March-Ford Cosworth)	-	-	-	-	-	-	14ns	22	-	-	-	-	-	-	-

	RA	BR	ZA	E	B	MC	S	NL	F	GB	D	A	I	CDN	USA
Chris AMON	-	-	-	r	-	-	-	-	-	-	-	-	-	nc	9
(Amon-Ford Cosworth)	-	-	-	23	-	20ns	-	-	-	-	nq	-	nq		
(BRM)	-	-	-	-	-	-	-	-	-	-	-	-	-	25	12
Mario ANDRETTI	-	-	-	-	-	-	-	-	-	-	-	-	-	7	dq
(Parnelli-Ford Cosworth)	-	-	-	-	-	-	-	-	-	-	-	-	-	16	3
Ian ASHLEY	-	-	-	-	-	-	-	-	-	-	14	nc	-	-	-
(Token-Ford Cosworth)	-	-	-	-	-	-	-	-	-	-	26	24	-	-	-
(Brabham-Ford Cosworth)	-	-	-	-	-	-	-	-	-	-	-	-	-	nq	nq
Derek BELL	-	-	-	-	-	-	-	-	-	-	11	-	-	-	-
(Surtees-Ford Cosworth)	-	-	-	-	-	-	-	-	-	nq	25	nq	nq	nq	-
Tom BELSØ	-	-	r	-	-	-	8	-	-	-	-	-	-	-	-
(Iso Marlboro-Ford Cosworth)	-	-	27	nq	-	-	21	-	-	nq	-	-	-	-	-
Jean-Pierre BELTOISE	5	10	2	r	5	r	r	r	10	12	r	r	r	nc	-
(BRM)	14	17	11	11	7	11	13	16	17	23	15	18	11	17	nq
Vittorio BRAMBILLA	-	-	10	-	9	r	10r	10	11	r	13	6	r	-	r
(March-Ford Cosworth)	-	-	19	ns	31	15	17	15	16	18	23	20	13	nq	25
Dave CHARLTON	-	-	19	-	-	-	-	-	-	-	-	-	-	-	-
(McLaren-Ford Cosworth)	-	-	20	-	-	-	-	-	-	-	-	-	-	-	-
Patrick DEPAILLER	6	8	4	8	r	9	2f	6	8	r	r	r	11	5	6
(Tyrrell-Ford Cosworth)	15	16	15	16	11	4	1	8	9	10	5	14	10	7	13
José DOLHEM	-	-	-	-	-	-	-	-	-	-	-	-	-	-	r
(Surtees-Ford Cosworth)	-	-	-	-	-	-	-	-	nq	-	-	-	nq	-	26
Mark DONOHUE	-	-	-	-	-	-	-	-	-	-	-	-	-	12	r
(Penske-Ford Cosworth)	-	-	-	-	-	-	-	-	-	-	-	-	-	24	14
Paddy DRIVER	-	-	r	-	-	-	-	-	-	-	-	-	-	-	-
(Lotus-Ford Cosworth)	-	-	26	-	-	-	-	-	-	-	-	-	-	-	-
Guy EDWARDS	11	r	-	-	12r	8	7	r	15	-	-	-	-	-	-
(Lola-Ford Cosworth)	25	25	-	nq	21	26	18	14	20	nq	nq	-	-	-	-
Carlo FACETTI	-	-	-	-	-	-	-	-	-	-	-	-	-	-	-
(Brabham-Ford Cosworth)	-	-	-	-	-	-	-	-	-	-	-	-	nq	-	-
Emerson FITTIPALDI	10	1	7	3	1	5	4	3	r	2	r	r	2	1	4
(McLaren-Ford Cosworth)	3	1	5	4	4	13	9	3	5	8	3	3	6	1	8
Howden GANLEY	8r	r	-	-	-	-	-	-	-	-	-	-	-	-	-
(March-Ford Cosworth)	19	20	-	-	-	-	-	-	-	-	-	-	-	-	-
(Maki-Ford Cosworth)	-	-	-	-	-	-	-	-	-	-	nq	nq	-	-	-
Peter GETHIN	-	-	-	-	-	-	-	-	-	-	r	-	-	-	-
(Lola-Ford Cosworth)	-	-	-	-	-	-	-	-	-	-	21	-	-	-	-
Mike HAILWOOD	4	5	3	9	7	r	r	4	7	r	15r	-	-	-	-
(McLaren-Ford Cosworth)	9	7	12	17	13	10	11	4	6	11	12	-	-	-	-
Graham HILL	r	11	12	r	8	7	6	r	13	13	9	12	8	14	8
(Lola-Ford Cosworth)	17	21	18	19	29	21	15	19	21	22	19	21	21	20	24
David HOBBS	-	-	-	-	-	-	-	-	-	-	-	7	9	-	-
(McLaren-Ford Cosworth)	-	-	-	-	-	-	-	-	-	-	-	17	23	-	-
Denny HULME	1	12	9	6	6f	r	r	r	6	7	r/dq	2	6	6	r
(McLaren-Ford Cosworth)	10	11	9	8	12	12	12	9	11	19	7	10	19	14	17
James HUNT	r	9	r	10	r	r	3	r	r	r	r	3	r	4	3
(March-Ford Cosworth)	5	18	-	-	-	-	-	-	-	-	-	-	-	-	-
(Hesketh-Ford Cosworth)	-	-	14	10	9	7	6	6	10	6	13	7	8	8	2
Jacky ICKX	r	3	r	r	r	r	r	11	5	3	5	r	r	13	r
(JPS Lotus-Ford Cosworth)	7	5	10	5	16	19	7	18	13	12	9	22	16	21	16
Jean-Pierre JABOUILLE	-	-	-	-	-	-	-	-	-	-	-	-	-	-	-
(Iso Marlboro-Ford Cosworth)	-	-	-	-	-	-	-	-	nq	-	-	-	-	-	-
(Surtees-Ford Cosworth)	-	-	-	-	-	-	-	-	-	-	-	-	nq	-	-

	RA	BR	ZA	E	B	MC	S	NL	F	GB	D	A	I	CDN	USA
Jean-Pierre JARIER	r	r	-	nc	13	3	5	r	12	r	8	8	r	r	10
(Shadow-Ford Cosworth)	16	19	-	12	17	6	8	7	12	16	18	23	9	5	10
Eddie KEIZAN	-	-	14	-	-	-	-	-	-	-	-	-	-	-	-
(Tyrrell-Ford Cosworth)	-	-	24	-	-	-	-	-	-	-	-	-	-	-	-
Leo KINNUNEN	-	-	-	-	-	-	r	-	-	-	-	-	-	-	-
(Surtees-Ford Cosworth)	-	-	-	-	nq	-	25	-	nq	nq	-	nq	nq	-	-
Helmut KOINIGG †	-	-	-	-	-	-	-	-	-	-	-	-	-	10	r
(Brabham-Ford Cosworth)	-	-	-	-	-	-	-	-	-	-	-	nq	-	-	-
(Surtees-Ford Cosworth)	-	-	-	-	-	-	-	-	-	-	-	-	-	22	23
Jacques LAFFITE	-	-	-	-	-	-	-	-	-	-	r	nc	r	15	r
(Iso Marlboro-Ford Cosworth)	-	-	-	-	-	-	-	-	-	-	21	12	17	18	11
Gérard LARROUSSE	-	-	-	-	r	-	-	-	nq	-	-	-	-	-	-
(Brabham-Ford Cosworth)	-	-	-	-	28	-	-	-	-	-	-	-	-	-	-
Niki LAUDA	2	r	16r	1f	2	r	r	1	2	5f	r	r	r	rf	r
(Ferrari)	8	3	1	1	3	1	3	1	1	1	1	1	1	2	5
Lella LOMBARDI	-	-	-	-	-	-	-	-	-	-	-	-	-	-	-
(Brabham-Ford Cosworth)	-	-	-	-	-	-	-	-	-	nq	-	-	-	-	-
Jochen MASS	r	17	r	r	r	-	r	r	r	14	r	-	-	16	7
(Surtees-Ford Cosworth)	18	10	17	18	26	17ns	22	20	18	17	10	-	-	-	-
(McLaren-Ford Cosworth)	-	-	-	-	-	-	-	-	-	-	-	-	-	12	20
Arturo MERZARIO	r	r	6	r	r	r	-	r	9	r	r	r	4	r	r
(Iso Marlboro-Ford Cosworth)	13	9	3	7	6	14	ns	21	15	15	16	9	15	19	15
François MIGAULT	r	16	15	r	16	r	-	r	14	nc	-	-	r	-	-
(BRM)	24	23	25	22	25	22	-	25	22	14	nq	-	24	-	-
John NICHOLSON	-	-	-	-	-	-	-	-	-	-	-	-	-	-	-
(Lyncar-Ford Cosworth)	-	-	-	-	-	-	-	-	-	nq	-	-	-	-	-
Carlos PACE	r	4	11	13	r	r	r	-	-	9	12	r	5f	8	2f
(Surtees-Ford Cosworth)	11	12	2	14	8	18	24	-	-	-	-	-	-	-	-
(Brabham-Ford Cosworth)	-	-	-	-	-	-	-	-	nq	20	17	4	3	9	4
Larry PERKINS	-	-	-	-	-	-	-	-	-	-	-	-	-	-	-
(Amon-Ford Cosworth)	-	-	-	-	-	-	-	-	-	-	nq	-	-	-	-
Henri PESCAROLO	9	14	18	12	r	r	r	r	r	r	10	-	r	-	-
(BRM)	21	22	21	20	15	27	19	24	19	24	24	-	25	-	-
Ronnie PETERSON	13	6	r	r	r	1f	r	8f	1	10	4	r	1	3	r
(JPS Lotus-Ford Cosworth)	1	4	16	2	5	3	5	10	2	2	8	6	7	10	19
Teddy PILETTE	-	-	-	-	17	-	-	-	-	-	-	-	-	-	-
(Brabham-Ford Cosworth)	-	-	-	-	27	-	-	-	-	-	-	-	-	-	-
Tom PRYCE	-	-	-	-	r	-	-	r	r	8	6	r	10	r	nc
(Token-Ford Cosworth)	-	-	-	-	20	-	-	-	-	-	-	-	-	-	-
(Shadow-Ford Cosworth)	-	-	-	-	-	-	-	11	3	5	11	16	22	13	18
David PURLEY	-	-	-	-	-	-	-	-	-	-	-	-	-	-	-
(Token-Ford Cosworth)	-	-	-	-	-	-	-	-	-	-	nq	-	-	-	-
Dieter QUESTER	-	-	-	-	-	-	-	-	-	-	-	9	-	-	-
(Surtees-Ford Cosworth)	-	-	-	-	-	-	-	-	-	-	-	25	-	-	-
Brian REDMAN	-	-	-	7	18r	r	-	-	-	-	-	-	-	-	-
(Shadow-Ford Cosworth)	-	-	-	21	18	16	-	-	-	-	-	-	-	-	-
Clay REGAZZONI	3f	2f	r	2	4	4	r	2	3	4	1	5f	r	2	11
(Ferrari)	2	8	6	3	1	2	4	2	4	7	2	8	5	6	9
Carlos REUTEMANN	7r	7	1f	r	r	r	r	12	r	6	3	1	r	9	1
(Brabham-Ford Cosworth)	6	2	4	6	24	8	10	12	8	4	6	2	2	4	1
Peter REVSON †	r	r	-	-	-	-	-	-	-	-	-	-	-	-	-
(Shadow-Ford Cosworth)	4	6	-	-	-	-	-	-	-	-	-	-	-	-	-
Richard ROBARTS	r	15	17	-	-	-	-	-	-	-	-	-	-	-	-
(Brabham-Ford Cosworth)	22	24	23	-	-	-	-	-	-	-	-	-	-	-	-
(Iso Marlboro-Ford Cosworth)	-	-	-	-	-	-	ns	-	-	-	-	-	-	-	-
Bertil ROOS	-	-	-	-	-	-	r	-	-	-	-	-	-	-	-
(Shadow-Ford Cosworth)	-	-	-	-	-	-	23	-	-	-	-	-	-	-	-
Ian SCHECKTER	-	-	13	-	-	-	-	-	-	-	-	-	-	-	-
(Lotus-Ford Cosworth)	-	-	22	-	-	-	-	-	-	-	-	-	-	-	-
(Hesketh-Ford Cosworth)	-	-	-	-	-	-	-	-	-	-	-	nq	-	-	-
Jody SCHECKTER	r	13	8	5	3	2	1	5	4f	1	2f	r	3	r	r
(Tyrrell-Ford Cosworth)	12	14	8	9	2	5	2	5	7	3	4	5	12	3	6
Tim SCHENKEN	-	-	-	14r	10	r	-	-	-	r	-	10	r	-	dq
(Trojan-Ford Cosworth)	-	-	-	25	23	24	-	nq	-	25	nq	19	20	-	-
(JPS Lotus-Ford Cosworth)	-	-	-	-	-	-	-	-	-	-	-	-	-	-	27
Vern SCHUPPAN	-	-	-	-	15	r	dq	dq	-	-	-	r	-	-	-
(Ensign-Ford Cosworth)	-	-	-	-	14	25	26	17	nq	nq	-	22	-	-	-
Rolf STOMMELEN	-	-	-	-	-	-	-	-	-	-	-	r	r	11	12
(Lola-Ford Cosworth)	-	-	-	-	-	-	-	-	-	-	-	13	14	11	21

Season-by-Season Summary

	RA	BR	ZA	E	B	MC	S	NL	F	GB	D	A	I	CDN	USA
Hans-Joachim STUCK	r	r	5	4	r	r	-	r	-	r	7	11r	r	r	-
(March-Ford Cosworth)	23	13	7	13	10	9	-	22	nq	9	20	15	18	23	nq
Gijs van LENNEP	-	-	-	-	14	-	-	-	-	-	-	-	-	-	-
(Iso Marlboro-Ford Cosworth)	-	-	-	-	30	-	-	nq	-	-	-	-	-	-	-
Rikky von OPEL	-	-	-	r	r	-	9	9	-	-	-	-	-	-	-
(Ensign-Ford Cosworth)	26ns	-	-	-	-	-	-	-	-	-	-	-	-	-	-
(Brabham-Ford Cosworth)	-	-	-	24	22	nq	20	23	nq	-	-	-	-	-	-
John WATSON	12	r	r	11	11	6	11	7	16	11	r	4	7	r	5
(Brabham-Ford Cosworth)	20	15	13	15	19	23	14	13	14	13	14	11	4	15	7
Eppie WIETZES	-	-	-	-	-	-	-	-	-	-	-	-	-	r	-
(Brabham-Ford Cosworth)	-	-	-	-	-	-	-	-	-	-	-	-	-	26	-
Mike WILDS	-	-	-	-	-	-	-	-	-	-	-	-	-	-	nc
(March-Ford Cosworth)	-	-	-	-	-	-	-	-	-	nq	-	-	-	-	-
(Ensign-Ford Cosworth)	-	-	-	-	-	-	-	-	-	-	-	nq	nq	nq	22
Reine WISELL	-	-	-	-	-	-	r	-	-	-	-	-	-	-	-
(March-Ford Cosworth)	-	-	-	-	-	-	16	-	-	-	-	-	-	-	-

1975 RACE RESULTS & GRID POSITIONS

	RA	BR	ZA	E	MC	B	S	NL	F	GB	D	A	I	USA
Chris AMON	-	-	-	-	-	-	-	-	-	-	-	12	12	-
(Ensign-Ford Cosworth)	-	-	-	-	-	-	-	-	-	-	-	23	19	-
Mario ANDRETTI	r	7	17r	rf	r	-	4	-	5	12	10r	r	r	r
(Parnelli-Ford Cosworth)	10	18	6	4	13	-	15	-	15	12	13	19	15	5
Ian ASHLEY	-	-	-	-	-	-	-	-	-	-	-	-	-	-
(Williams-Ford Cosworth)	-	-	-	-	-	-	-	-	-	-	20ns	-	-	-
Vittorio BRAMBILLA	9	r	r	5	r	r	r	r	r	6	r	1f	r	7
(March-Ford Cosworth)	12	17	7	5	5	3	1	11	8	5	11	8	9	6
Tony BRISE †	-	-	-	7	-	r	6	7	7	15r	r	15	r	r
(Williams-Ford Cosworth)	-	-	-	18	-	-	-	-	-	-	-	-	-	-
(Hill-Ford Cosworth)	-	-	-	-	-	7	17	7	12	13	17	16	6	17
Dave CHARLTON	-	-	14	-	-	-	-	-	-	-	-	-	-	-
(McLaren-Ford Cosworth)	-	-	20	-	-	-	-	-	-	-	-	-	-	-
Jim CRAWFORD	-	-	-	-	-	-	-	-	-	r	-	-	13	-
(JPS Lotus-Ford Cosworth)	-	-	-	-	-	-	-	-	-	25	-	-	25	-
Patrick DEPAILLER	5	r	3	r	5f	4	12	9	6	9r	9	11	7	r
(Tyrrell-Ford Cosworth)	8	9	5	7	12	12	2	13	13	17	4	7	12	8
Mark DONOHUE †	7	r	8	r	r	11	5	8	r	5r	r	-	-	-
(Penske-Ford Cosworth)	16	15	18	17	16	21	16	18	18	-	-	-	-	-
(March-Ford Cosworth)	-	-	-	-	-	-	-	-	-	15	19	20ns	-	-
Harald ERTL	-	-	-	-	-	-	-	-	-	-	8	r	9	-
(Hesketh-Ford Cosworth)	-	-	-	-	-	-	-	-	-	-	23	26	17	-
Bob EVANS	-	-	15	r	-	9	13	r	17	-	-	r	r	-
(Stanley BRM)	-	-	24	23	nq	20	23	20	25	-	-	24	20	-
Emerson FITTIPALDI	1	2	nc	-	2	7	8	r	4	1	r	9	2	2f
(McLaren-Ford Cosworth)	5	2	11	ns	9	8	11	6	10	7	8	3	3	2
Wilson FITTIPALDI	r	13	r	r	-	12	17	11	r	19r	r	-	-	10
(Copersucar-Ford Cosworth)	23	21	27	21	nq	24	25	24	23	24	22	ns	-	23
Hiroshi FUSHIDA	-	-	-	-	-	-	-	-	-	-	-	-	-	-
(Maki-Ford Cosworth)	-	-	-	-	-	-	-	ns	nq	-	-	-	-	-
Brian HENTON	-	-	-	-	-	-	-	-	-	16r	-	-	-	nc
(JPS Lotus-Ford Cosworth)	-	-	-	-	-	-	-	-	-	21	-	22ns	-	19
Graham HILL	10	12	-	-	-	-	-	-	-	-	-	-	-	-
(Lola-Ford Cosworth)	21	20	ns	-	-	-	-	-	-	-	-	-	-	-
(Hill-Ford Cosworth)	-	-	-	-	nq	-	-	-	-	-	-	-	-	-
James HUNT	2f	6	r	r	r	r	r	1	2	4r	r	2	5	4
(Hesketh-Ford Cosworth)	6	7	12	3	11	11	13	3	3	9	9	2	8	15
Jacky ICKX	8	9	12	2	8	r	15	r	r	-	-	-	-	-
(JPS Lotus-Ford Cosworth)	18	12	21	16	14	16	18	21	19	-	-	-	-	-
Jean-Pierre JABOUILLE	-	-	-	-	-	-	-	-	12	-	-	-	-	-
(Tyrrell-Ford Cosworth)	-	-	-	-	-	-	-	-	21	-	-	-	-	-
Jean-Pierre JARIER	-	rf	r	4	r	r	r	r	8	14r	r	r	r	r
(Shadow-Ford Cosworth)	1ns	1	13	10	3	10	3	10	4	11	12	-	-	4
(Shadow-Matra)	-	-	-	-	-	-	-	-	-	-	-	14	13	-
Alan JONES	-	-	-	r	r	r	11	13	16	10	5	-	-	-
(Hesketh-Ford Cosworth)	-	-	-	20	18	13	19	-	-	-	-	-	-	-
(Hill-Ford Cosworth)	-	-	-	-	-	-	-	17	20	20	21	-	-	-

	RA	BR	ZA	E	MC	B	S	NL	F	GB	D	A	I	USA
Eddie KEIZAN	-	-	13	-	-	-	-	-	-	-	-	-	-	-
(Lotus-Ford Cosworth)	-	-	22	-	-	-	-	-	-	-	-	-	-	-
Jacques LAFFITE	r	11	nc	-	-	r	-	r	11	r	2	r	r	-
(Williams-Ford Cosworth)	17	19	23	-	nq	17	-	15	16	19	15	12	18	21ns
Niki LAUDA	6	5	5	r	1	1	1f	2f	1	8	3	6	3	1
(Ferrari)	4	4	4	1	1	1	5	1	1	3	1	1	1	1
Michel LECLÈRE	-	-	-	-	-	-	-	-	-	-	-	-	-	r
(Tyrrell-Ford Cosworth)	-	-	-	-	-	-	-	-	-	-	-	-	-	20
Lella LOMBARDI	-	-	r	6	-	r	r	14	18	r	7	17	r	-
(March-Ford Cosworth)	-	-	26	24	nq	23	24	23	26	22	25	21	24	-
(Williams-Ford Cosworth)	-	-	-	-	-	-	-	-	-	-	-	-	-	24ns
Brett LUNGER	-	-	-	-	-	-	-	-	-	-	-	13	10	r
(Hesketh-Ford Cosworth)	-	-	-	-	-	-	-	-	-	-	-	17	21	18
Damien MAGEE	-	-	-	-	-	-	14	-	-	-	-	-	-	-
(Williams-Ford Cosworth)	-	-	-	-	-	-	22	-	-	-	-	-	-	-
Jochen MASS	14	3	6	1	6	r	r	r	3f	7r	r	4	r	3
(McLaren-Ford Cosworth)	13	10	16	11	15	15	14	8	7	10	6	9	5	9
Arturo MERZARIO	nc	r	r	r	-	r	-	-	-	-	-	-	11	-
(Williams-Ford Cosworth)	20	11	15	25	nq	19	-	-	-	-	-	-	-	-
(Copersucar-Ford Cosworth)	-	-	-	-	-	-	-	-	-	-	-	-	26	-
François MIGAULT	-	-	-	nc	-	r	-	-	-	-	-	-	-	-
(Hill-Ford Cosworth)	-	-	-	22	-	22	-	-	-	-	-	-	-	-
(Williams-Ford Cosworth)	-	-	-	-	-	-	-	-	24ns	-	-	-	-	-
Dave MORGAN	-	-	-	-	-	-	-	-	-	18r	-	-	-	-
(Surtees-Ford Cosworth)	-	-	-	-	-	-	-	-	-	23	-	-	-	-
John NICHOLSON	-	-	-	-	-	-	-	-	-	17r	-	-	-	-
(Lyncar-Ford Cosworth)	-	-	-	-	-	-	-	-	-	26	-	-	-	-
Carlos PACE	r	1	4f	r	3	8	r	5	r	2r	r	r	r	r
(Brabham-Ford Cosworth)	2	6	1	14	8	2	6	9	5	2	2	6	10	16
Torsten PALM	-	-	-	-	-	-	10r	-	-	-	-	-	-	-
(Hesketh-Ford Cosworth)	-	-	-	-	nq	-	21	-	-	-	-	-	-	-
Ronnie PETERSON	r	15	10	r	4	r	9	15r	10	r	r	5	r	5
(JPS Lotus-Ford Cosworth)	11	16	8	12	4	14	9	16	17	16	18	13	11	14
Tom PRYCE	12r	r	9	r	r	6	r	6	r	r	4	3	6	nc
(Shadow-Ford Cosworth)	14	14	19	8	2	5	7	12	6	1	16	15	14	7
Clay REGAZZONI	4	4	16r	nc	r	5f	3	3	r	13f	rf	7	1f	r
(Ferrari)	7	5	9	2	6	4	12	2	9	4	5	5	2	11
Carlos REUTEMANN	3	8	2	3	9	3	2	4	14	r	1	14	4	r
(Brabham-Ford Cosworth)	3	3	2	15	10	6	4	5	11	8	10	11	7	3
Ian SCHECKTER	-	-	r	-	-	-	r	12	-	-	-	-	-	-
(Tyrrell-Ford Cosworth)	-	-	17	-	-	-	-	-	-	-	-	-	-	-
(Williams-Ford Cosworth)	-	-	-	-	-	-	20	19	-	-	-	-	-	-
Jody SCHECKTER	11	r	1	r	7	2	7	16r	9	3r	r	8	8	6
(Tyrrell-Ford Cosworth)	9	8	3	13	7	9	8	4	2	6	3	10	4	10
Vern SCHUPPAN	-	-	-	-	-	-	r	-	-	-	-	-	-	-
(Hill-Ford Cosworth)	-	-	-	-	-	-	26	-	-	-	-	-	-	-
Rolf STOMMELEN	13	14	7	r	-	-	-	-	-	-	-	16	r	-
(Lola-Ford Cosworth)	19	23	14	-	-	-	-	-	-	-	-	-	-	-
(Hill-Ford Cosworth)	-	-	-	9	-	-	-	-	-	-	-	25	23	-
Hans-Joachim STUCK	-	-	-	-	-	-	-	-	-	r	r	r	r	8
(March-Ford Cosworth)	-	-	-	-	-	-	-	-	-	14	7	4	16	13
Tony TRIMMER	-	-	-	-	-	-	-	-	-	-	-	-	-	-
(Maki-Ford Cosworth)	-	-	-	-	-	-	-	-	-	-	nq	nq	nq	-
Guy TUNMER	-	-	11	-	-	-	-	-	-	-	-	-	-	-
(Lotus-Ford Cosworth)	-	-	25	-	-	-	-	-	-	-	-	-	-	-
Gijs van LENNEP	-	-	-	-	-	-	-	10	15	-	6	-	-	-
(Ensign-Ford Cosworth)	-	-	-	-	-	-	-	22	22	-	24	-	-	-
Jo VONLANTHEN	-	-	-	-	-	-	-	-	-	-	-	r	-	-
(Williams-Ford Cosworth)	-	-	-	-	-	-	-	-	-	-	-	28	-	-
John WATSON	dq	10	r	8	r	10	16	r	13	11r	r	10	-	9
(Surtees-Ford Cosworth)	15	13	10	6	17	18	10	14	14	18	-	18	-	-
(JPS Lotus-Ford Cosworth)	-	-	-	-	-	-	-	-	-	-	14	-	-	-
(Penske-Ford Cosworth)	-	-	-	-	-	-	-	-	-	-	-	-	-	12
Mike WILDS	r	r	-	-	-	-	-	-	-	-	-	-	-	-
(Stanley BRM)	22	22	-	-	-	-	-	-	-	-	-	-	-	-
Roelof WUNDERINK	-	-	-	r	-	-	-	-	-	-	-	nc	-	r
(Ensign-Ford Cosworth)	-	-	-	19	nq	-	-	-	-	nq	-	27	nq	22
Renzo ZORZI	-	-	-	-	-	-	-	-	-	-	-	-	14	-
(Williams-Ford Cosworth)	-	-	-	-	-	-	-	-	-	-	-	-	22	-

	BR	ZA	USAW	E	B	MC	S	F	GB	D	A	NL	I	CDN	USAE	J
Chris AMON	-	14	8	5	r	13	r	-	r	r	-	-	-	-	-	-
(Ensign-Ford Cosworth)	-	18	17	10	8	12	3	-	6	17	-	-	-	-	-	-
(Wolf Williams-Ford Cosworth)	-	-	-	-	-	-	-	-	-	-	-	-	-	ns	-	-
Conny ANDERSSON	-	-	-	-	-	-	-	-	-	-	-	r	-	-	-	-
(Surtees-Ford Cosworth)	-	-	-	-	-	-	-	-	-	-	-	26	-	-	-	-
Mario ANDRETTI	r	6	r	r	r	-	rf	5	r	12	5	3	r	3	r	1
(JPS Lotus-Ford Cosworth)	16	-	-	9	11	-	2	7	3	12	9	6	14	5	11	1
(Parnelli-Ford Cosworth)	-	13	15	-	-	-	-	-	-	-	-	-	-	-	-	-
Ian ASHLEY	r	-	-	-	-	-	-	-	-	-	-	-	-	-	-	-
(Stanley BRM)	21	-	-	-	-	-	-	-	-	-	-	-	-	-	-	-
Hans BINDER	-	-	-	-	-	-	-	-	-	-	-	r	-	-	-	r
(Ensign-Ford Cosworth)	-	-	-	-	-	-	-	-	-	-	-	19	-	-	-	-
(Wolf Williams-Ford Cosworth)	-	-	-	-	-	-	-	-	-	-	-	-	-	-	-	25
Vittorio BRAMBILLA	r	8	r	r	r	r	10	r	r	r	r	6	7	14	r	r
(March-Ford Cosworth)	7	5	8	6	5	9	15	11	10	13	7	7	16	3	4	8
Warwick BROWN	-	-	-	-	-	-	-	-	-	-	-	-	-	-	14	-
(Wolf Williams-Ford Cosworth)	-	-	-	-	-	-	-	-	-	-	-	-	-	-	23	-
Emilio de VILLOTA	-	-	-	-	-	-	-	-	-	-	-	-	-	-	-	-
(Brabham-Ford Cosworth)	-	-	-	nq	-	-	-	-	-	-	-	-	-	-	-	-
Patrick DEPAILLER	2	9	3	r	r	3	2	2	r	r	r	7	6	2f	r	2
(Tyrrell-Ford Cosworth)	9	6	2	3	4	4	4	3	5	3	13	14	4	4	7	13
Guy EDWARDS	-	-	-	-	-	-	-	17	r	15	-	-	-	20	-	-
(Hesketh-Ford Cosworth)	-	-	-	-	nq	-	-	25	25	25	-	-	23ns	23	-	-
Harald ERTL	-	15	-	-	r	-	r	r	7	r	8	r	16r	-	13	8
(Hesketh-Ford Cosworth)	-	24	nq	nq	24	nq	23	27	24	22	20	24	19	ns	21	22
Bob EVANS	-	10	-	-	-	-	-	-	r	-	-	-	-	-	-	-
(JPS Lotus-Ford Cosworth)	-	23	nq	-	-	-	-	-	-	-	-	-	-	-	-	-
(Brabham-Ford Cosworth)	-	-	-	-	-	-	-	-	22	-	-	-	-	-	-	-
Emerson FITTIPALDI	13	17r	6	r	-	6	r	r	6	13	r	r	15	r	9	r
(Copersucar-Ford Cosworth)	5	21	16	19	nq	7	21	21	21	20	17	17	20	17	15	23
Divina GALICA	-	-	-	-	-	-	-	-	-	-	-	-	-	-	-	-
(Surtees-Ford Cosworth)	-	-	-	-	-	-	-	-	nq	-	-	-	-	-	-	-
Masahiro HASEMI	-	-	-	-	-	-	-	-	-	-	-	-	-	-	-	11
(Kojima-Ford Cosworth)	-	-	-	-	-	-	-	-	-	-	-	-	-	-	-	10
Boy HAYJE	-	-	-	-	-	-	-	-	-	-	-	r	-	-	-	-
(Penske-Ford Cosworth)	-	-	-	-	-	-	-	-	-	-	-	21	-	-	-	-
Ingo HOFFMANN	11	-	-	-	-	-	-	-	-	-	-	-	-	-	-	-
(Copersucar-Ford Cosworth)	20	-	nq	nq	-	-	-	nq	-	-	-	-	-	-	-	-
Kazuyoshi HOSHINO	-	-	-	-	-	-	-	-	-	-	-	-	-	-	-	r
(Tyrrell-Ford Cosworth)	-	-	-	-	-	-	-	-	-	-	-	-	-	-	-	21
James HUNT	r	2	r	1	r	r	5	1	dq	1	4f	1	r	1	1f	3
(McLaren-Ford Cosworth)	1	1	3	1	3	14	8	1	2	1	1	2	25	1	1	2
Jacky ICKX	8	16	-	7	-	-	-	10	-	-	-	r	10	13	r	-
(Wolf Williams-Ford Cosworth)	19	19	nq	21	nq	nq	-	19	nq	-	-	-	-	-	-	-
(Ensign-Ford Cosworth)	-	-	-	-	-	-	-	-	-	-	-	11	10	16	19	-
Jean-Pierre JARIER	rf	r	7	r	9	8	12	12	9	11	r	10	19	18	10	10
(Shadow-Ford Cosworth)	3	15	7	15	14	10	14	15	23	23	18	20	17	18	16	15
Alan JONES	-	-	nc	9	5	r	13	r	5	10	r	8	12	16	8	4
(Surtees-Ford Cosworth)	-	-	19	20	16	19	18	18	19	14	15	16	18	20	18	20
Loris KESSEL	-	-	-	-	12	-	r	-	-	-	-	nc	-	-	-	-
(Brabham-Ford Cosworth)	-	-	-	nq	23	-	26	nq	-	-	-	25	-	-	-	-
Masami KUWASHIMA	-	-	-	-	-	-	-	-	-	-	-	-	-	-	-	-
(Wolf Williams-Ford Cosworth)	-	-	-	-	-	-	-	-	-	-	-	-	-	-	-	ns
Jacques LAFFITE	r	r	4	12	3	12r	4	14	r/dq	r	2	r	3	r	r	7f
(Ligier-Matra)	11	8	12	8	6	8	7	13	13	6	5	10	1	9	12	11
Niki LAUDA	1	1f	2	2	1f	1	3	rf	1f	r	-	-	4	8	3	r
(Ferrari)	2	2	4	2	1	1	5	2	1	2	-	-	5	6	5	3
Michel LECLÈRE	-	13	-	10	11	11	r	13	-	-	-	-	-	-	-	-
(Wolf Williams-Ford Cosworth)	-	22	nq	23	25	18	25	22	-	-	-	-	-	-	-	-
Lella LOMBARDI	14	-	-	-	-	-	-	-	-	-	-	12	-	-	-	-
(March-Ford Cosworth)	22	-	-	-	-	-	-	-	-	-	-	-	-	-	-	-
(Brabham-Ford Cosworth)	-	-	-	-	-	-	-	-	-	nq	nq	24	-	-	-	-
Brett LUNGER	-	11	-	-	r	-	15	16	r	r	10r	-	14	15	11	-
(Surtees-Ford Cosworth)	-	20	nq	nq	26	-	24	23	18	24	16	-	24	22	24	-

	BR	ZA	USAW	E	B	MC	S	F	GB	D	A	NL	I	CDN	USAE	J
Damien MAGEE	-	-	-	-	-	-	-		-	-	-	-	-	-	-	-
(Brabham-Ford Cosworth)	-	-	-	-	-	-	-	nq	-	-	-	-	-	-	-	-
Jochen MASS	6	3	5	rf	6	5	11	15	r	3	7	9	r	5	4	r
(McLaren-Ford Cosworth)	6	4	14	4	18	11	13	14	12	9	12	15	26	11	17	12
Arturo MERZARIO	-	-	-	r	r	-	14r	9	r	r	r	r	-	r	r	r
(March-Ford Cosworth)	-	-	nq	18	21	nq	19	20	9	-	-	-	-	-	-	-
(Wolf Williams-Ford Cosworth)	-	-	-	-	-	-	-	-	-	21	21	23	ns	24	25	19
Jac NELLEMAN	-	-	-	-	-	-	-	-	-	-	-	-	-	-	-	-
(Brabham-Ford Cosworth)	-	-	-	-	-	-	nq	-	-	-	-	-	-	-	-	-
Patrick NÈVE	-	-	-	-	r	-	-	18	-	-	-	-	-	-	-	-
(Brabham-Ford Cosworth)	-	-	-	-	19	-	-	-	-	-	-	-	-	-	-	-
(Ensign-Ford Cosworth)	-	-	-	-	-	-	-	26	-	-	-	-	-	-	-	-
Gunnar NILSSON	-	r	r	3	r	r	r	r	r	5	3	r	13	12	r	6
(JPS Lotus-Ford Cosworth)	-	25	20	7	22	16	6	12	14	16	4	13	12	15	20	16
Carlos PACE	10	r	9	6	r	9	8	4	8	4	r	r	r	7	r	r
(Brabham-Alfa Romeo)	10	14	13	11	9	13	10	5	16	7	8	9	3	10	10	6
Larry PERKINS	-	-	-	13	8	-	r	-	-	-	-	r	r	17	r	r
(Boro-Ford Cosworth)	-	-	-	24	20	nq	22	-	-	-	-	19	13	-	-	-
(Brabham-Alfa Romeo)	-	-	-	-	-	-	-	-	-	-	-	-	-	19	13	17
Henri PESCAROLO	-	-	-	-	-	-	-	r	r	-	9	11	17	19	nc	-
(Surtees-Ford Cosworth)	-	-	-	-	-	nq	-	24	26	nq	22	22	22	21	26	-
Sandro PESENTI-ROSSI	-	-	-	-	-	-	-	-	-	14	11	-	18	-	-	-
(Tyrrell-Ford Cosworth)	-	-	-	-	-	-	-	-	-	26	23	nq	21	-	-	-
Ronnie PETERSON	r	r	10	r	r	r	7	19r	r	r	6	r	1f	9	r	r
(JPS Lotus-Ford Cosworth)	18	-	-	-	-	-	-	-	-	-	-	-	-	-	-	-
(March-Ford Cosworth)	-	10	6	16	10	3	9	6	7	11	3	1	8	2	3	9
Tom PRYCE	3	7	r	8	10	7	9	8	4	8	r	4	8	11	r	r
(Shadow-Ford Cosworth)	12	7	5	22	13	15	12	16	20	18	6	3	15	13	9	14
Clay REGAZZONI	7	r	1f	11	2	14rf	6	r	r/dq	9	-	2f	2	6	7	5
(Ferrari)	4	9	1	5	2	2	11	4	4	5	-	5	9	12	14	7
Carlos REUTEMANN	12r	r	r	4	r	r	r	11	r	r	r	r	9	-	-	-
(Brabham-Alfa Romeo)	15	11	10	12	12	20	16	10	15	10	14	12	-	-	-	-
(Ferrari)	-	-	-	-	-	-	-	-	-	-	-	-	7	-	-	-
Alex Dias RIBEIRO	-	-	-	-	-	-	-	-	-	-	-	-	-	-	12	-
(Hesketh-Ford Cosworth)	-	-	-	-	-	-	-	-	-	-	-	-	-	-	22	-
Ian SCHECKTER	-	r	-	-	-	-	-	-	-	-	-	-	-	-	-	-
(Tyrrell-Ford Cosworth)	-	16	-	-	-	-	-	-	-	-	-	-	-	-	-	-
Jody SCHECKTER	5	4	r	r	4	2	1	6	2	2f	r	5	5	4	2	r
(Tyrrell-Ford Cosworth)	13	12	11	14	7	5	1	9	8	8	10	8	2	7	2	5
Rolf STOMMELEN	-	-	-	-	-	-	-	-	-	6	-	12	r	-	-	-
(Brabham-Alfa Romeo)	-	-	-	-	-	-	-	-	-	15	-	11	-	-	-	-
(Hesketh-Ford Cosworth)	-	-	-	-	-	-	-	-	-	-	-	-	25	-	-	-
Hans-Joachim STUCK	4	12	r	r	r	4	r	7	r	r	r	r	r	r	5	r
(March-Ford Cosworth)	14	17	18	17	15	6	20	17	17	4	11	18	6	8	6	18
Otto STUPPACHER	-	-	-	-	-	-	-	-	-	-	-	-	ns	nq	nq	-
(Tyrrell-Ford Cosworth)	-	-	-	-	-	-	-	-	-	-	-	-	-	-	-	-
Noritake TAKAHARA	-	-	-	-	-	-	-	-	-	-	-	-	-	-	-	9
(Surtees-Ford Cosworth)	-	-	-	-	-	-	-	-	-	-	-	-	-	-	-	24
Tony TRIMMER	-	-	-	-	-	-	-	-	-	-	-	-	-	-	-	-
(Maki-Ford Cosworth)	-	-	-	-	-	-	-	-	-	-	-	-	-	-	-	nq
John WATSON	r	5	nc	r	7	10	r	3	3	7	1	r	11	10	6	r
(Penske-Ford Cosworth)	8	3	9	13	17	17	17	8	11	19	2	4	27	14	8	4
Mike WILDS	-	-	-	-	-	-	-	-	-	-	-	-	-	-	-	-
(Shadow-Ford Cosworth)	-	-	-	-	-	-	nq	-	-	-	-	-	-	-	-	-
Emilio ZAPICO	-	-	-	-	-	-	-	-	-	-	-	-	-	-	-	-
(Williams-Ford Cosworth)	-	-	-	nq	-	-	-	-	-	-	-	-	-	-	-	-
Renzo ZORZI	9	-	-	-	-	-	-	-	-	-	-	-	-	-	-	-
(Wolf Williams-Ford Cosworth)	17	-	-	-	-	-	-	-	-	-	-	-	-	-	-	-

	RA	BR	ZA	USAW	E	MC	B	S	F	GB	D	A	NL	I	USAE	CDN	J
Conny ANDERSSON	-	-	-	-	-	-	-	-	-	-	-	-	-	-	-	-	-
(Stanley BRM)	-	-	-	-	nq	-	nq	nq	nq	-	-	-	-	-	-	-	-
Mario ANDRETTI	5r	r	r	1	1	5	r	6f	1f	14r	r	r	r	1f	2	9rf	r
(JPS Lotus-Ford Cosworth)	8	3	6	2	1	10	1	1	1	6	7	3	1	4	4	4	1
Ian ASHLEY	-	-	-	-	-	-	-	-	-	-	-	-	-	-	17	-	-
(Hesketh-Ford Cosworth)	-	-	-	-	-	-	-	-	-	-	-	nq	nq	nq	22	ns	-
Hans BINDER	r	r	11	11	9	r	-	-	-	-	-	12	8	-	11	r	r
(Surtees-Ford Cosworth)	18	20	19	19	20	19	-	-	-	-	-	-	-	-	25	24	21
(Penske-Ford Cosworth)	-	-	-	-	-	-	-	-	-	-	-	19	18	nq	-	-	-
Michael BLEEKEMOLEN	-	-	-	-	-	-	-	-	-	-	-	-	-	-	-	-	-
(March-Ford Cosworth)	-	-	-	-	-	-	-	-	-	-	-	-	nq	-	-	-	-
Vittorio BRAMBILLA	7r	r	7	r	r	8	4	r	13	8	5	15	12r	r	19	6r	8
(Surtees-Ford Cosworth)	13	11	14	11	11	14	12	13	11	8	10	13	22	10	11	15	9
Bernard de DRYVER	-	-	-	-	-	-	-	-	-	-	-	-	-	-	-	-	-
(March-Ford Cosworth)	-	-	-	-	-	-	nq	-	-	-	-	-	-	-	-	-	-
Emilio de VILLOTA	-	-	-	-	13	-	-	-	-	-	-	17r	-	-	-	-	-
(McLaren-Ford Cosworth)	-	-	-	-	23	-	nq	nq	-	nq	nq	26	-	nq	-	-	-
Patrick DEPAILLER	r	r	3	4	r	r	8	4	r	r	r	13	r	r	14	2	3
(Tyrrell-Ford Cosworth)	3	6	4	12	10	8	5	6	12	18	15	10	11	13	8	6	15
Guy EDWARDS	-	-	-	-	-	-	-	-	-	-	-	-	-	-	-	-	-
(Stanley BRM)	-	-	-	-	-	-	-	-	-	-	npq	-	-	-	-	-	-
Harald ERTL	-	-	-	-	r	-	9	16	-	-	-	-	-	-	-	-	-
(Hesketh-Ford Cosworth)	-	-	-	-	18	nq	25	23	nq	-	-	-	-	-	-	-	-
Emerson FITTIPALDI	4	4	10	5	14	r	r	18	11	r	-	11	4	-	13	r	-
(Copersucar-Ford Cosworth)	16	16	9	7	19	18	16	18	22	22	nq	23	17	nq	18	19	-
Giorgio FRANCIA	-	-	-	-	-	-	-	-	-	-	-	-	-	-	-	-	-
(Brabham-Alfa Romeo)	-	-	-	-	-	-	-	-	-	-	-	-	-	nq	-	-	-
Bruno GIACOMELLI	-	-	-	-	-	-	-	-	-	-	-	-	-	r	-	-	-
(McLaren-Ford Cosworth)	-	-	-	-	-	-	-	-	-	-	-	-	-	15	-	-	-
Boy HAYJE	-	-	r	-	-	-	15	-	-	-	-	-	-	-	-	-	-
(March-Ford Cosworth)	-	-	21	-	nq	nq	27	nq	-	-	-	-	nq	-	-	-	-
Brian HENTON	-	-	-	10	-	-	-	-	-	-	-	-	dq	-	-	-	-
(March-Ford Cosworth)	-	-	-	18	nq	-	-	-	-	nq	-	nq	-	-	-	-	-
(Boro-Ford Cosworth)	-	-	-	-	-	-	-	-	-	-	-	-	23	nq	-	-	-
Hans HEYER	-	-	-	-	-	-	-	-	-	-	r	-	-	-	-	-	-
(Penske-Ford Cosworth)	-	-	-	-	-	-	-	-	-	-	25	-	-	-	-	-	-
Ingo HOFFMANN	r	7	-	-	-	-	-	-	-	-	-	-	-	-	-	-	-
(Copersucar-Ford Cosworth)	19	19	-	-	-	-	-	-	-	-	-	-	-	-	-	-	-
Kazuyoshi HOSHINO	-	-	-	-	-	-	-	-	-	-	-	-	-	-	-	-	11
(Kojima-Ford Cosworth)	-	-	-	-	-	-	-	-	-	-	-	-	-	-	-	-	11
James HUNT	rf	2f	4	7	r	r	7	12	3	1f	r	r	r	r	1	r	1
(McLaren-Ford Cosworth)	1	1	1	8	7	7	9	3	2	1	4	2	3	1	1	2	2
Jacky ICKX	-	-	-	-	-	10	-	-	-	-	-	-	-	-	-	-	-
(Ensign-Ford Cosworth)	-	-	-	-	-	17	-	-	-	-	-	-	-	-	-	-	-
Jean-Pierre JABOUILLE	-	-	-	-	-	-	-	-	-	r	-	-	r	r	r	-	-
(Renault)	-	-	-	-	-	-	-	-	-	21	-	-	10	20	14	nq	-
Jean-Pierre JARIER	-	-	-	6	-	11	11	8	r	9	r	14	r	r	9	-	r
(Penske-Ford Cosworth)	-	-	-	9	nq	12	26	17	19	20	12	18	21	18	-	-	-
(Shadow-Ford Cosworth)	-	-	-	-	-	-	-	-	-	-	-	-	-	-	16	-	-
(Ligier-Matra)	-	-	-	-	-	-	-	-	-	-	-	-	-	-	-	-	17
Alan JONES	-	-	-	r	r	6	5	17	r	7	r	1	r	3	r	4	4
(Shadow-Ford Cosworth)	-	-	-	14	14	11	17	11	10	12	17	14	13	16	13	7	12
Rupert KEEGAN	-	-	-	r	12	r	13	10	r	r	7	r	9	8	r	-	-
(Hesketh-Ford Cosworth)	-	-	-	16	20	19	24	14	13	23	20	26	23	20	25	-	-
Loris KESSEL	-	-	-	-	-	-	-	-	-	-	-	-	-	-	-	-	-
(Williams-Ford Cosworth)	-	-	-	-	-	-	-	-	-	-	-	-	-	nq	-	-	-
Mikko KOZAROWITSKY	-	-	-	-	-	-	-	-	-	-	-	-	-	-	-	-	-
(March-Ford Cosworth)	-	-	-	-	-	-	-	nq	-	npq	-	-	-	-	-	-	-
Jacques LAFFITE	nc	r	r	9r	7f	7	r	1	8	6	r	r	2	8	7	r	5r
(Ligier-Matra)	15	14	12	5	2	16	10	8	5	15	6	6	2	8	10	11	5
Niki LAUDA	r	3	1	2f	-	2	2	r	5	2	1f	2	1f	2	4	-	-
(Ferrari)	4	13	3	1	3ns	6	11	15	9	3	3	1	4	5	7	-	-
Lamberto LEONI	-	-	-	-	-	-	-	-	-	-	-	-	-	-	-	-	-
(Surtees-Ford Cosworth)	-	-	-	-	-	-	-	-	-	-	-	-	-	nq	-	-	-

	RA	BR	ZA	USAW	E	MC	B	S	F	GB	D	A	NL	I	USAE	CDN	J
Brett LUNGER	-	-	14	r	10	-	-	11	-	13	r	10	9	r	10	11r	-
(March-Ford Cosworth)	-	-	23	21	25	-	-	-	-	-	-	-	-	-	-	-	-
(McLaren-Ford Cosworth)	-	-	-	-	-	-	22ns	22	nq	19	21	17	20	22	17	20	-
Jochen MASS	r	r	5	r	4	4	r	2	9	4	r	6	r	4	r	3	r
(McLaren-Ford Cosworth)	5	4	13	15	9	9	6	9	7	11	13	9	14	9	15	5	8
Brian McGUIRE	-	-	-	-	-	-	-	-	-	-	-	-	-	-	-	-	-
(McGuire-Ford Cosworth)	-	-	-	-	-	-	-	-	-	npq	-	-	-	-	-	-	-
Arturo MERZARIO	-	-	-	-	r	-	14	-	r	r	-	r	-	-	-	-	-
(March-Ford Cosworth)	-	-	-	-	21	nq	14	-	18	17	nq	-	nq	-	-	-	-
(Shadow-Ford Cosworth)	-	-	-	-	-	-	-	-	-	-	-	21	-	-	-	-	-
Patrick NÈVE	-	-	-	-	12	-	10	15	-	10	-	9	-	7	18	r	-
(March-Ford Cosworth)	-	-	-	-	22	-	24	20	nq	26	nq	22	nq	24	24	21	-
Gunnar NILSSON	-	5	12	8	5	r	1f	19r	4	3	r	r	r	r	r	r	r
(JPS Lotus-Ford Cosworth)	10ns	10	10	16	12	13	3	7	3	5	9	16	5	19	12	4	14
Jackie OLIVER	-	-	-	-	-	-	-	9	-	-	-	-	-	-	-	-	-
(Shadow-Ford Cosworth)	-	-	-	-	-	-	-	16	-	-	-	-	-	-	-	-	-
Danny ONGAIS	-	-	-	-	-	-	-	-	-	-	-	-	-	-	r	7	-
(Penske-Ford Cosworth)	-	-	-	-	-	-	-	-	-	-	-	-	-	-	26	22	-
Carlos PACE †	2	r	13	-	-	-	-	-	-	-	-	-	-	-	-	-	-
(Brabham-Alfa Romeo)	6	5	2	-	-	-	-	-	-	-	-	-	-	-	-	-	-
Riccardo PATRESE	-	-	-	-	-	9	r	-	r	r	10r	-	13	r	-	10r	6
(Shadow-Ford Cosworth)	-	-	-	-	-	15	15	-	15	25	16	-	16	6	-	8	13
Larry PERKINS	-	r	15	-	-	-	12	-	-	-	-	-	-	-	-	-	-
(Stanley BRM)	-	22	22	-	-	-	-	-	-	-	-	-	-	-	-	-	-
(Surtees-Ford Cosworth)	-	-	-	-	-	-	23	nq	nq	-	-	-	-	-	-	-	-
Ronnie PETERSON	r	r	r	r	8	r	3	r	12	r	9r	5	r	6	16f	r	r
(Tyrrell-Ford Cosworth)	14	8	7	10	15	4	8	10	17	10	14	15	7	12	5	3	18
Teddy PILETTE	-	-	-	-	-	-	-	-	-	-	-	-	-	-	-	-	-
(Stanley BRM)	-	-	-	-	-	-	-	-	-	-	nq	-	nq	nq	-	-	-
Tom PRYCE †	nc	r	r	-	-	-	-	-	-	-	-	-	-	-	-	-	-
(Shadow-Ford Cosworth)	9	12	15	-	-	-	-	-	-	-	-	-	-	-	-	-	-
David PURLEY	-	-	-	-	-	-	13	14	r	-	-	-	-	-	-	-	-
(Lec-Ford Cosworth)	-	-	-	-	nq	-	20	19	21	npq	-	-	-	-	-	-	-
Hector REBAQUE	-	-	-	-	-	-	-	-	-	-	r	-	-	-	-	-	-
(Hesketh-Ford Cosworth)	-	-	-	-	-	-	nq	nq	nq	-	24	nq	nq	-	-	-	-
Clay REGAZZONI	6	r	9	r	r	-	r	7	7	-	r	r	r	5	5	r	r
(Ensign-Ford Cosworth)	12	9	16	13	8	nq	13	14	16	nq	22	11	9	7	19	14	10
Carlos REUTEMANN	3	1	8	r	2	3	r	3	6	15	4	4	6	r	6	r	2
(Ferrari)	7	2	8	4	4	3	7	12	6	14	8	5	6	2	6	12	7
Alex Dias RIBEIRO	r	r	r	r	-	-	-	-	-	-	8	-	11	-	15	8	12
(March-Ford Cosworth)	20	21	17	22	nq	nq	nq	nq	nq	nq	20	nq	24	nq	23	23	23
Ian SCHECKTER	r	r	-	-	11	-	r	r	nc	r	r	r	10	r	r	r	-
(March-Ford Cosworth)	17	17	-	-	17	nq	21	21	20	24	18	24	25	17	21	18	-
Jody SCHECKTER	1	r	2	3	3	1f	r	r	r	r	2	r	3	r	3	1	10f
(Wolf-Ford Cosworth)	11	15	5	3	5	2	4	4	8	4	1	8	15	3	9	9	6
Vern SCHUPPAN	-	-	-	-	-	-	-	-	-	12	7	16	-	-	-	-	-
(Surtees-Ford Cosworth)	-	-	-	-	-	-	-	-	-	23	19	25	nq	-	-	-	-
Hans-Joachim STUCK	-	-	r	r	6	r	6	10	r	5	3	3	7	r	r	r	7
(March-Ford Cosworth)	-	-	18	-	-	-	-	-	-	-	-	-	-	-	-	-	-
(Brabham-Alfa Romeo)	-	-	-	17	13	5	18	5	13	7	5	4	19	11	2	13	4
Andy SUTCLIFFE	-	-	-	-	-	-	-	-	-	-	-	-	-	-	-	-	-
(March-Ford Cosworth)	-	-	-	-	-	-	-	-	-	npq	-	-	-	-	-	-	-
Noritake TAKAHARA	-	-	-	-	-	-	-	-	-	-	-	-	-	-	-	-	r
(Kojima-Ford Cosworth)	-	-	-	-	-	-	-	-	-	-	-	-	-	-	-	-	19
Kunimitsu TAKAHASHI	-	-	-	-	-	-	-	-	-	-	-	-	-	-	-	-	9
(Tyrrell-Ford Cosworth)	-	-	-	-	-	-	-	-	-	-	-	-	-	-	-	-	22
Patrick TAMBAY	-	-	-	-	-	-	-	-	-	r	6	r	5r	r	-	5	r
(Surtees-Ford Cosworth)	-	-	-	-	-	-	-	-	nq	-	-	-	-	-	-	-	-
(Ensign-Ford Cosworth)	-	-	-	-	-	-	-	-	-	16	11	7	12	21	nq	16	16
Tony TRIMMER	-	-	-	-	-	-	-	-	-	-	-	-	-	-	-	-	-
(Surtees-Ford Cosworth)	-	-	-	-	-	-	-	-	-	npq	-	-	-	-	-	-	-
Gilles VILLENEUVE	-	-	-	-	-	-	-	-	-	11	-	-	-	-	-	12r	r
(McLaren-Ford Cosworth)	-	-	-	-	-	-	-	-	-	9	-	-	-	-	-	-	-
(Ferrari)	-	-	-	-	-	-	-	-	-	-	-	-	-	-	-	17	20
John WATSON	r	r	6f	dq	r	r	r	5	2	r	r	8f	r	r	12	r	r
(Brabham-Alfa Romeo)	2	7	11	6	6	1	2	2	4	2	2	12	8	14	3	10	3
Renzo ZORZI	r	6	r	r	r	-	-	-	-	-	-	-	-	-	-	-	-
(Shadow-Ford Cosworth)	21	18	20	20	24	-	-	-	-	-	-	-	-	-	-	-	-

Season-by-Season Summary

	RA	BR	ZA	USAW	MC	B	E	S	F	GB	D	A	NL	I	USAE	CDN
Mario ANDRETTI	1	4	7f	2	11	1	1f	r	1	r	1	r	1	6f	r	10
(JPS Lotus-Ford Cosworth)	1	3	2	4	4	1	1	1	2	2	1	2	1	1	1	9
René ARNOUX	-	-	-	-	-	9	-	-	14	-	-	9	r	-	9	r
(Martini-Ford Cosworth)	-	-	nq	-	npq	19	-	-	18	-	npq	26	23	-	-	-
(Surtees-Ford Cosworth)	-	-	-	-	-	-	-	-	-	-	-	-	-	-	21	16
Hans BINDER	-	-	-	-	-	-	-	-	-	-	-	-	-	-	-	-
(ATS-Ford Cosworth)	-	-	-	-	-	-	-	-	-	-	-	-	nq	-	-	-
Michael BLEEKEMOLEN	-	-	-	-	-	-	-	-	-	-	-	-	-	-	r	-
(ATS-Ford Cosworth)	-	-	-	-	-	-	-	-	-	-	-	-	nq	nq	25	nq
Vittorio BRAMBILLA	18	-	12	r	-	13r	7	r	17	9	r	6	dq	r	-	-
(Surtees-Ford Cosworth)	12	nq	20	17	nq	12	16	18	19	25	20	21	22	23	-	-
Eddie CHEEVER	-	-	r	-	-	-	-	-	-	-	-	-	-	-	-	-
(Theodore-Ford Cosworth)	nq	nq	-	-	-	-	-	-	-	-	-	-	-	-	-	-
(Hesketh-Ford Cosworth)	-	-	25	-	-	-	-	-	-	-	-	-	-	-	-	-
Alberto COLOMBO	-	-	-	-	-	-	-	-	-	-	-	-	-	-	-	-
(ATS-Ford Cosworth)	-	-	-	-	-	nq	nq	-	-	-	-	-	-	-	-	-
(Merzario-Ford Cosworth)	-	-	-	-	-	-	-	-	-	-	-	-	-	npq	-	-
Derek DALY	-	-	-	-	-	-	-	-	-	r	-	dq	r	10	8	6
(Hesketh-Ford Cosworth)	-	-	-	npq	npq	nq	-	-	-	-	-	-	-	-	-	-
(Ensign-Ford Cosworth)	-	-	-	-	-	-	-	-	nq	15	-	19	16	18	19	15
Bernard de DRYVER	-	-	-	-	-	-	-	-	-	-	-	-	-	-	-	-
(Ensign-Ford Cosworth)	-	-	-	-	-	npq	-	-	-	-	-	-	-	-	-	-
Emilio de VILLOTA	-	-	-	-	-	-	-	-	-	-	-	-	-	-	-	-
(McLaren-Ford Cosworth)	-	-	-	-	-	nq	-	-	-	-	-	-	-	-	-	-
Patrick DEPAILLER	3	r	2	3	1	r	r	r	r	4	r	2	r	11	r	5
(Tyrrell-Ford Cosworth)	10	11	12	12	5	13	12	12	13	10	13	13	12	16	12	13
Harald ERTL	-	-	-	-	-	-	-	-	-	-	11r	r	-	-	-	-
(Ensign-Ford Cosworth)	-	-	-	-	-	-	-	-	-	-	23	24	npq	-	-	-
(ATS-Ford Cosworth)	-	-	-	-	-	-	-	-	-	-	-	-	nq	-	-	-
Emerson FITTIPALDI	9	2	r	8	9	r	r	6	r	r	4	4	5	8	5	r
(Copersucar-Ford Cosworth)	17	7	15	15	20	15	15	13	15	11	10	6	10	13	13	6
Beppe GABBIANI	-	-	-	-	-	-	-	-	-	-	-	-	-	-	-	-
(Surtees-Ford Cosworth)	-	-	-	-	-	-	-	-	-	-	-	-	-	-	nq	nq
Divina GALICA	-	-	-	-	-	-	-	-	-	-	-	-	-	-	-	-
(Hesketh-Ford Cosworth)	nq	nq	-	-	-	-	-	-	-	-	-	-	-	-	-	-
Bruno GIACOMELLI	-	-	-	-	-	8	-	-	r	7	-	-	r	14	-	-
(McLaren-Ford Cosworth)	-	-	-	-	-	21	-	-	22	16	-	-	19	20	-	-
GIMAX	-	-	-	-	-	-	-	-	-	-	-	-	-	-	-	-
(Surtees-Ford Cosworth)	-	-	-	-	-	-	-	-	-	-	-	-	-	nq	-	-
Brian HENTON	-	-	-	-	-	-	-	-	-	-	-	-	-	-	-	-
(Surtees-Ford Cosworth)	-	-	-	-	-	-	-	-	-	-	-	-	nq	-	-	-
James HUNT	4	r	r	r	r	r	6	8	3	r	dq	r	10	r	7	r
(McLaren-Ford Cosworth)	6	2	3	7	6	6	4	14	4	14	8	8	7	10	6	19
Jacky ICKX	-	-	-	-	r	12	r	-	-	-	-	-	-	-	-	-
(Ensign-Ford Cosworth)	-	-	-	-	16	22	21	nq	-	-	-	-	-	-	-	-
Jean-Pierre JABOUILLE	-	-	r	r	10	nc	13	r	r	r	r	r	r	r	4	12
(Renault)	-	-	6	13	12	10	11	10	11	12	9	3	9	3	9	22
Jean-Pierre JARIER	12	-	8	11	-	-	-	-	-	-	-	-	-	-	15rf	r
(ATS-Ford Cosworth)	11	16ns	17	19	nq	-	-	-	-	-	nq	-	-	-	-	-
(JPS Lotus-Ford Cosworth)	-	-	-	-	-	-	-	-	-	-	-	-	-	-	8	1
Alan JONES	r	11	4	7f	r	10	8	r	5	r	r	r	r	13	2	9f
(Williams-Ford Cosworth)	14	8	18	8	10	11	18	9	14	6	6	15	11	6	3	5
Rupert KEEGAN	r	r	r	-	r	-	11	-	r	-	-	-	-	-	-	-
(Surtees-Ford Cosworth)	19	24	23	ns	18	nq	23	nq	23	nq	nq	nq	25ns	-	-	-
Jacques LAFFITE	16r	9	5	5	r	5r	3	7	7	10	3	5	8	4	11	r
(Ligier-Matra)	8	14	14	14	15	14	10	11	10	7	7	5	6	8	10	10
Niki LAUDA	2	3	r	r	2f	r	r	1f	r	2f	r	r	3f	1	r	r
(Brabham-Alfa Romeo)	5	10	1	3	3	3	6	3	3	4	3	12	3	4	5	7
Geoff LEES	-	-	-	-	-	-	-	-	-	-	-	-	-	-	-	-
(Ensign-Ford Cosworth)	-	-	-	-	-	-	-	-	-	-	nq	-	-	-	-	-
Lamberto LEONI	r	-	-	-	-	-	-	-	-	-	-	-	-	-	-	-
(Ensign-Ford Cosworth)	22	17ns	nq	nq	-	-	-	-	-	-	-	-	-	-	-	-
Brett LUNGER	13	r	11	-	-	7	-	-	r	8	-	8	r	r	13	-
(McLaren-Ford Cosworth)	24	13	19	nq	npq	24	nq	nq	24	24	npq	17	21	21	-	-
(Ensign-Ford Cosworth)	-	-	-	-	-	-	-	-	-	-	-	-	-	-	-	24

	RA	BR	ZA	USAW	MC	B	E	S	F	GB	D	A	NL	I	USAE	CDN
Jochen MASS (ATS-Ford Cosworth)	11	7	r	r	-	11	9	13	13	nc	r	-	-	-	-	-
	13	20	16	16	nq	16	17	19	25	26	22	nq	nq	-	-	-
Arturo MERZARIO (Merzario-Ford Cosworth)	r	-	r	r	-	-	-	nc	-	r	-	-	r	r	r	-
	20	nq	26	21	npq	npq	nq	22	nq	23	nq	nq	27	22	26	nq
Patrick NÈVE (March-Ford Cosworth)	-	-	-	-	-	-	-	-	-	-	-	-	-	-	-	-
	-	-	-	-	-	npq	-	-	-	-	-	-	-	-	-	-
Danny ONGAIS (Ensign-Ford Cosworth)	r	r	-	-	-	-	-	-	-	-	-	-	-	-	-	-
	21	23	-	-	-	-	-	-	-	-	-	-	-	-	-	-
(Shadow-Ford Cosworth)	-	-	-	npq	-	-	-	-	-	-	-	-	npq	-	-	-
Riccardo PATRESE (Arrows-Ford Cosworth)	-	10	r	6	6	r	r	2	8	r	9	r	r	r	-	4
	-	18	7	9	14	8	8	5	12	5	14	16	13	12	-	12
Ronnie PETERSON † (Lotus-Ford Cosworth)	5	r	1	4	r	2f	2	3	2	r	rf	1f	2	r	-	-
	3	1	11	6	7	7	2	4	5	1	2	1	2	5	-	-
Nelson PIQUET	-	-	-	-	-	-	-	-	-	-	r	r	r	9	-	11
(Ensign-Ford Cosworth)	-	-	-	-	-	-	-	-	-	-	21	-	-	-	-	-
(McLaren-Ford Cosworth)	-	-	-	-	-	-	-	-	-	-	-	20	26	24	-	-
(Brabham-Alfa Romeo)	-	-	-	-	-	-	-	-	-	-	-	-	-	-	-	14
Didier PIRONI (Tyrrell-Ford Cosworth)	14	6	6	r	5	6	12	r	10	r	5	r	r	r	10	7
	23	19	13	22	13	23	13	17	16	19	16	9	17	14	16	18
Bobby RAHAL (Wolf-Ford Cosworth)	-	-	-	-	-	-	-	-	-	-	-	-	-	-	12	r
	-	-	-	-	-	-	-	-	-	-	-	-	-	-	20	20
Hector REBAQUE (Lotus-Ford Cosworth)	-	r	10	-	-	-	r	12	-	r	6	r	11	-	r	-
	nq	22	22	npq	npq	npq	20	21	nq	21	18	18	20	nq	23	nq
Clay REGAZZONI (Shadow-Ford Cosworth)	15	5	-	10	-	r	15r	5	r	r	-	nc	-	nc	14	-
	16	15	nq	20	nq	18	22	16	17	17	nq	22	nq	15	17	nq
Carlos REUTEMANN (Ferrari)	7	1f	r	1	8	3	r	10	18f	1	r	dq	7	3	1	3
	2	4	9	1	1	2	3	8	8	8	12	4	4	11	2	11
Keke ROSBERG	-	-	r	-	-	-	-	15	16	r	10	nc	r	-	r	nc
(Theodore-Ford Cosworth)	-	-	24	npq	npq	nq	npq	-	-	-	-	-	-	-	-	-
(ATS-Ford Cosworth)	-	-	-	-	-	-	-	23	26	22	-	-	-	-	15	21
(Wolf-Ford Cosworth)	-	-	-	-	-	-	-	-	-	-	19	25	24	npq	-	-
Jody SCHECKTER (Wolf-Ford Cosworth)	10	r	r	r	3	r	4	r	6	r	2	r	12	12	3	2
	15	12	5	10	9	5	9	6	7	3	4	7	15	9	11	2
Rolf STOMMELEN (Arrows-Ford Cosworth)	-	-	9	9	r	r	14	14	15	-	dq	-	-	-	16	-
	-	-	21	18	19	17	19	24	21	nq	17	npq	npq	npq	22	nq
Hans-Joachim STUCK (Shadow-Ford Cosworth)	17	r	-	-	r	r	r	11	11	5	r	r	r	r	r	r
	18	9	nq	ns	17	20	24	20	20	18	24	23	18	17	14	8
Patrick TAMBAY (McLaren-Ford Cosworth)	6	r	r	12r	7	-	r	4	9	6	r	r	9	5	6	8
	9	5	4	11	11	-	14	15	6	20	11	14	14	19	18	17
Tony TRIMMER (McLaren-Ford Cosworth)	-	-	-	-	-	-	-	-	-	-	-	-	-	-	-	-
	-	-	-	-	-	-	-	-	-	nq	-	-	-	-	-	-
Gilles VILLENEUVE (Ferrari)	8f	r	r	r	r	4	10	9	12	r	8	3	6	7	r	1
	7	6	8	2	8	4	5	7	9	13	15	11	5	2	4	3
John WATSON (Brabham-Alfa Romeo)	r	8	3	r	4	r	5	r	4	3	7	7	4	2	r	r
	4	21	10	5	2	9	7	2	1	9	5	10	8	7	7	4

1979 RACE RESULTS & GRID POSITIONS

	RA	BR	ZA	USAW	E	B	MC	F	GB	D	A	NL	I	CDN	USAE
Mario ANDRETTI (Lotus-Ford Cosworth)	5	r	4	4	3	r	r	r	r	r	r	r	5	10r	r
	7	4	8	6	4	5	13	12	9	11	15	17	10	10	17
René ARNOUX (Renault)	r	r	r	-	9	r	r	3f	2	r	6f	r	r	r	2
	25	11	10	ns	11	18	19	2	5	10	1	1	2	8	7
Vittorio BRAMBILLA (Alfa Romeo)	-	-	-	-	-	-	-	-	-	-	-	-	12	r	r
	-	-	-	-	-	-	-	-	-	-	-	-	22	18	nq
Gianfranco BRANCATELLI	-	-	-	-	-	-	-	-	-	-	-	-	-	-	-
(Kauhsen-Ford Cosworth)	-	-	-	-	nq	nq	-	-	-	-	-	-	-	-	-
(Merzario-Ford Cosworth)	-	-	-	-	-	-	npq	-	-	-	-	-	-	-	-
Derek DALY	11	13	-	r	-	-	-	-	-	-	8	-	-	r	r
(Ensign-Ford Cosworth)	24	23	nq	24	nq	nq	nq	-	-	-	-	-	-	-	-
(Tyrrell-Ford Cosworth)	-	-	-	-	-	-	-	-	-	-	-	11	-	24	15
Elio de ANGELIS (Shadow-Ford Cosworth)	7	12	r	7	r	r	-	16	12	11	r	r	r	r	4
	16	20	15	20	22	24	nq	24	12	21	22	22	24	23	20
Patrick DEPAILLER (Ligier-Ford Cosworth)	4	2	r	5	1	r	5rf	-	-	-	-	-	-	-	-
	2	2	5	4	2	2	3	-	-	-	-	-	-	-	-

	RA	BR	ZA	USAW	E	B	MC	F	GB	D	A	NL	I	CDN	USAE
Emerson FITTIPALDI	6	11	13	r	11	9	r	r	r	r	r	r	8	8	7
(Copersucar-Ford Cosworth)	11	9	18	16	19	23	17	18	22	22	19	21	20	15	23
Patrick GAILLARD	-	-	-	-	-	-	-	-	13	-	r	-	-	-	-
(Ensign-Ford Cosworth)	-	-	-	-	-	-	-	nq	23	nq	24	nq	-	-	-
Bruno GIACOMELLI	-	-	-	-	-	r	-	17	-	-	-	-	r	-	r
(Alfa Romeo)	-	-	-	-	-	14	-	17	-	-	-	-	18	-	18
James HUNT	r	r	8	r	r	r	r	-	-	-	-	-	-	-	-
(Wolf-Ford Cosworth)	18	10	13	8	15	9	10	-	-	-	-	-	-	-	-
Jacky ICKX	-	-	-	-	-	-	-	r	6	r	r	5	r	r	r
(Ligier-Ford Cosworth)	-	-	-	-	-	-	-	14	17	14	21	20	11	16	24
Jean-Pierre JABOUILLE	r	10	r	-	r	r	8	1	r	r	r	r	14r	r	r
(Renault)	12	7	1	ns	9	17	20	1	2	1	3	4	1	7	8
Jean-Pierre JARIER	r	-	3	6	5	11	r	5	3	-	-	r	6	r	r
(Tyrrell-Ford Cosworth)	4	15ns	9	7	12	11	6	10	16	-	-	16	16	13	11
Alan JONES	9	r	r	3	r	r	r	4	r	1	1	1	9	1f	r
(Williams-Ford Cosworth)	15	13	19	10	13	4	9	7	1	2	2	2	4	1	1
Jacques LAFFITE	1f	1f	r	r	r	2	r	8	r	3	3	3	r	r	r
(Ligier-Ford Cosworth)	1	1	6	5	1	1	5	8	10	3	8	7	7	5	4
Jan LAMMERS	r	14	r	r	12	10	-	18	11	10	r	r	-	9	-
(Shadow-Ford Cosworth)	21	21	21	14	24	21	nq	21	21	20	23	23	nq	21	nq
Niki LAUDA	r	r	6	r	r	r	r	r	r	r	r	r	4	-	-
(Brabham-Alfa Romeo)	23	12	4	11	6	13	4	6	6	7	4	9	9	-	-
(Brabham-Ford Cosworth)	-	-	-	-	-	-	-	-	-	-	-	-	-	ew	-
Geoff LEES	-	-	-	-	-	-	-	-	-	7	-	-	-	-	-
(Tyrrell-Ford Cosworth)	-	-	-	-	-	-	-	-	-	16	-	-	-	-	-
Jochen MASS	8	7	12	9	8	r	6	15	r	6	r	6	r	-	-
(Arrows-Ford Cosworth)	14	19	20	13	17	22	8	22	20	18	20	18	21	nq	nq
Arturo MERZARIO	r	-	-	r	-	-	-	-	-	-	-	-	-	-	-
(Merzario-Ford Cosworth)	22	nq	nq	22	nq	nq	-	nq	nq	nq	nq	nq	nq	nq	nq
Riccardo PATRESE	-	9	11	r	10	5	r	14	r	r	r	r	13	r	r
(Arrows-Ford Cosworth)	13ns	16	16	9	16	16	15	19	19	19	13	19	17	14	19
Nelson PIQUET	r	r	7	8	r	r	7r	r	r	12r	r	4	r	r	8rf
(Brabham-Alfa Romeo)	20	22	12	12	7	3	18	4	3	4	7	11	8	-	-
(Brabham-Ford Cosworth)	-	-	-	-	-	-	-	-	-	-	-	-	-	4	2
Didier PIRONI	r	4	r	dq	6	3	r	r	10	9	7	r	10	5	3
(Tyrrell-Ford Cosworth)	8	8	7	17	10	12	7	11	15	8	10	10	12	6	10
Hector REBAQUE	r	-	14r	r	r	r	-	12	9	r	-	7	-	r	-
(Lotus-Ford Cosworth)	19	nq	23	23	23	15	-	23	24	24	nq	24	-	-	-
(Rebaque-Ford Cosworth)	-	-	-	-	-	-	-	-	-	-	-	-	nq	22	nq
Clay REGAZZONI	10	15	9	r	r	r	2	6	1f	2	5	r	3f	3	r
(Williams-Ford Cosworth)	17	17	22	15	14	8	16	9	4	6	6	3	6	3	5
Carlos REUTEMANN	2	3	5	r	2	4	3	13r	8	r	r	r	7	r	r
(Lotus-Ford Cosworth)	3	3	11	2	8	10	11	13	8	13	17	13	13	11	6
Alex Dias RIBEIRO	-	-	-	-	-	-	-	-	-	-	-	-	-	nq	nq
(Copersucar-Ford Cosworth)	-	-	-	-	-	-	-	-	-	-	-	-	-	-	-
Keke ROSBERG	-	-	-	-	-	-	-	9	r	r	r	r	r	r	r
(Wolf-Ford Cosworth)	-	-	-	-	-	-	-	16	14	17	12	8	23	nq	12
Jody SCHECKTER	r	6	2	2	4	1	1	7	5	4	4	2	1	4	r
(Ferrari)	5	6	2	3	5	7	1	5	11	5	9	5	3	9	16
Hans-Joachim STUCK	-	r	r	dq	14	8	r	-	-	r	r	r	11	r	5
(ATS-Ford Cosworth)	ns	24	24	21	21	20	12	ns	nq	23	18	15	15	12	14
Marc SURER	-	-	-	-	-	-	-	-	-	-	-	-	-	-	r
(Ensign-Ford Cosworth)	-	-	-	-	-	-	-	-	-	-	-	-	nq	nq	21
Patrick TAMBAY	r	r	10	r	13	-	-	10	7r	r	10	r	r	r	r
(McLaren-Ford Cosworth)	9	18	17	19	20	nq	nq	20	18	15	14	14	14	20	22
Gilles VILLENEUVE	12r	5	1f	1f	7f	7rf	r	2	14r	8f	2	rf	2	2	1
(Ferrari)	10	5	3	1	3	6	2	3	13	9	5	6	5	2	3
John WATSON	3	8	r	r	r	6	4	11	4	5	9	r	r	6	6
(McLaren-Ford Cosworth)	6	14	14	18	18	19	14	15	7	12	16	12	19	17	13
Ricardo ZUNINO	-	-	-	-	-	-	-	-	-	-	-	-	-	7	r
(Brabham-Ford Cosworth)	-	-	-	-	-	-	-	-	-	-	-	-	-	19	9

	RA	BR	ZA	USAW	B	MC	F	GB	D	A	NL	I	CDN	USAE
Mario ANDRETTI	r	r	12	r	r	7	r	r	7	r	8r	r	r	6
(Lotus-Ford Cosworth)	6	11	15	15	17	19	12	9	9	17	10	10	18	11
René ARNOUX	r	1f	1f	9	4	r	5	nc	r	9f	2f	10	r	7
(Renault)	19	6	2	2	6	20	2	16	3	1	1	1	23	6
Vittorio BRAMBILLA	-	-	-	-	-	-	-	-	-	-	r	r	-	-
(Alfa Romeo)	-	-	-	-	-	-	-	-	-	-	22	19	-	-
Eddie CHEEVER	-	-	r	r	-	-	r	r	r	r	r	12	r	r
(Osella-Ford Cosworth)	nq	nq	22	19	nq	nq	21	20	18	19	19	17	14	16
Kevin COGAN	-	-	-	-	-	-	-	-	-	-	-	-	-	-
(Williams-Ford Cosworth)	-	-	-	-	-	-	-	-	-	-	-	-	nq	-
Derek DALY	4	14	r	8	9	r	11	4	10	r	r	r	r	r
(Tyrrell-Ford Cosworth)	22	24	16	14	11	12	20	10	22	10	23	22	20	21
Elio de ANGELIS	r	2	r	r	10r	9r	r	r	16r	6	r	4	10	4
(Lotus-Ford Cosworth)	5	7	14	20	8	14	14	14	11	9	11	18	17	4
Andrea de CESARIS	-	-	-	-	-	-	-	-	-	-	-	-	r	r
(Alfa Romeo)	-	-	-	-	-	-	-	-	-	-	-	-	8	10
Patrick DEPAILLER †	r	r	nc	r	r	r	r	r	-	-	-	-	-	-
(Alfa Romeo)	23	21	7	3	10	7	10	8	-	-	-	-	-	-
Harald ERTL	-	-	-	-	-	-	-	-	r	-	-	-	-	-
(ATS-Ford Cosworth)	-	-	-	-	-	-	-	-	nq	-	-	-	-	-
Emerson FITTIPALDI	nc	15	8	3	r	6	13r	12	r	11	r	r	r	r
(Fittipaldi-Ford Cosworth)	24	19	18	24	24	18	24	22	12	23	21	15	16	19
Bruno GIACOMELLI	5	13	r	r	r	r	r	r	5	r	r	r	r	r
(Alfa Romeo)	20	17	12	6	18	8	9	6	19	8	8	4	4	1
Jean-Pierre JABOUILLE	r	r	r	10	r	r	r	r	r	1	r	r	r	-
(Renault)	9	1	1	11	5	16	6	13	2	2	2	2	13	-
Jean-Pierre JARIER	r	12	7	r	5	r	14	5	15	r	5	13r	7	nc
(Tyrrell-Ford Cosworth)	18	22	13	12	9	9	16	11	23	13	17	12	15	22
Stefan JOHANSSON	-	-	-	-	-	-	-	-	-	-	-	-	-	-
(Shadow-Ford Cosworth)	nq	nq	-	-	-	-	-	-	-	-	-	-	-	-
Alan JONES	1f	3	r	r	2	r	1f	1	3f	2	11	2f	1	1f
(Williams-Ford Cosworth)	1	10	8	5	1	3	4	3	1	3	4	6	2	5
Rupert KEEGAN	-	-	-	-	-	-	-	11	-	15	-	11	-	9
(Williams-Ford Cosworth)	-	-	-	-	-	-	-	18	nq	20	nq	21	nq	15
David KENNEDY	-	-	-	-	-	-	-	-	-	-	-	-	-	-
(Shadow-Ford Cosworth)	nq	nq	nq	nq	nq	nq	nq	-	-	-	-	-	-	-
Jacques LAFFITE	r	r	2	r	11f	2	3	r	1	4	3	9	8r	5
(Ligier-Ford Cosworth)	2	5	4	13	3	5	1	2	5	5	6	20	9	12
Jan LAMMERS	-	-	-	r	12r	nc	-	-	14	-	-	-	12	r
(ATS-Ford Cosworth)	nq	nq	nq	4	15	13	-	-	-	-	-	-	-	-
(Ensign-Ford Cosworth)	-	-	-	-	-	-	nq	nq	24	nq	nq	nq	19	25
Geoff LEES	-	-	13r	-	-	-	-	-	-	-	r	-	-	-
(Shadow-Ford Cosworth)	-	-	24	nq	nq	nq	nq	-	-	-	-	-	-	-
(Ensign-Ford Cosworth)	-	-	-	-	-	-	-	-	-	-	24	nq	-	-
(Williams-Ford Cosworth)	-	-	-	-	-	-	-	-	-	-	-	-	-	nq
Nigel MANSELL	-	-	-	-	-	-	-	-	-	r	r	-	-	-
(Lotus-Ford Cosworth)	-	-	-	-	-	-	-	-	-	24	16	nq	-	-
Jochen MASS	r	10	6	7	r	4	10	13	8	-	-	-	11	r
(Arrows-Ford Cosworth)	14	16	19	17	13	15	15	24	17	nq	ew	-	21	24
Tiff NEEDELL	-	-	-	-	r	-	-	-	-	-	-	-	-	-
(Ensign-Ford Cosworth)	-	-	-	-	23	nq	-	-	-	-	-	-	-	-
Riccardo PATRESE	r	6	r	2	r	8	9	9	9	14	r	r	r	r
(Arrows-Ford Cosworth)	7	14	11	8	16	11	18	21	10	18	14	7	11	20
Nelson PIQUET	2	r	4	1f	r	3	4	2	4	5	1	1	r	r
(Brabham-Ford Cosworth)	4	9	3	1	7	4	8	5	6	7	5	5	1	2
Didier PIRONI	r	4	3	6	1	r	2	rf	r	r	r	6	3f	3
(Ligier-Ford Cosworth)	3	2	5	9	2	1	3	1	7	6	15	13	3	7
Alain PROST	6	5	-	-	r	r	r	6	11	7	6	7	r	-
(McLaren-Ford Cosworth)	12	13	ns	-	19	10	7	7	14	12	18	24	12	13ns
Hector REBAQUE	-	-	-	-	-	-	-	7	r	10	r	r	6	r
(Brabham-Ford Cosworth)	-	-	-	-	-	-	-	17	15	14	13	9	10	8
Clay REGAZZONI	nc	r	9	r	-	-	-	-	-	-	-	-	-	-
(Ensign-Ford Cosworth)	15	12	20	23	-	-	-	-	-	-	-	-	-	-
Carlos REUTEMANN	r	r	5	r	3	1f	6	3	2	3	4	3	2	2
(Williams-Ford Cosworth)	10	4	6	7	4	2	5	4	4	4	3	3	5	3

	RA	BR	ZA	USAW	B	MC	F	GB	D	A	NL	I	CDN	USAE
Keke ROSBERG	3	9	r	r	7	-	r	-	r	16	-	5	9	10
(Fittipaldi-Ford Cosworth)	13	15	23	22	21	nq	23	nq	8	11	nq	11	6	14
Jody SCHECKTER	r	r	r	5	8	r	12	10	13	13	9	8	-	11
(Ferrari)	11	8	9	16	14	17	19	23	21	22	12	16	nq	23
Stephen SOUTH	-	-	-	-	-	-	-	-	-	-	-	-	-	-
(McLaren-Ford Cosworth)	-	-	-	nq	-	-	-	-	-	-	-	-	-	-
Marc SURER	r	7	-	-	-	-	r	r	12	12	10	r	-	8
(ATS-Ford Cosworth)	21	20	nq	-	-	-	11	15	13	16	20	23	nq	17
Mike THACKWELL	-	-	-	-	-	-	-	-	-	-	-	-	r	-
(Arrows-Ford Cosworth)	-	-	-	-	-	-	-	-	-	-	nq	-	-	-
(Tyrrell-Ford Cosworth)	-	-	-	-	-	-	-	-	-	-	-	-	24	nq
Gilles VILLENEUVE	r	16r	r	r	6	5	8	r	6	8	7	r	5	r
(Ferrari)	8	3	10	10	12	6	17	19	16	15	7	8	22	18
John WATSON	r	11	11	4	nc	-	7	8	r	r	r	r	4	nc
(McLaren-Ford Cosworth)	17	23	21	21	20	nq	13	12	20	21	9	14	7	9
Desiré WILSON	-	-	-	-	-	-	-	-	-	-	-	-	-	-
(Williams-Ford Cosworth)	-	-	-	-	-	-	-	nq	-	-	-	-	-	-
Manfred WINKELHOCK	-	-	-	-	-	-	-	-	-	-	-	-	-	-
(Arrows-Ford Cosworth)	-	-	-	-	-	-	-	-	-	-	-	nq	-	-
Ricardo ZUNINO	7	8	10	r	r	-	r	-	-	-	-	-	-	-
(Brabham-Ford Cosworth)	16	18	17	18	22	nq	22	-	-	-	-	-	-	-

1981 RACE RESULTS & GRID POSITIONS

	USAW	BR	RA	RSM	B	MC	E	F	GB	D	A	NL	I	CDN	LV
Michele ALBORETO	-	-	-	r	12	r	-	16	r	-	r	9r	r	11	13r
(Tyrrell-Ford Cosworth)	-	-	-	17	19	20	nq	23	19	nq	22	25	22	22	17
Mario ANDRETTI	4	r	8	r	10	r	8	8	r	9	r	r	r	7	r
(Alfa Romeo)	6	9	17	12	18	12	8	10	11	12	13	7	13	16	10
René ARNOUX	8	r	5	8	-	r	9	4	9rf	13	2	r	r	r	r
(Renault)	20	8	5	3	nq	13	17	1	1	2	1	2	1	8	13
Slim BORGUDD	-	-	-	13	-	-	-	-	6	r	r	10	r	r	-
(ATS-Ford Cosworth)	-	-	-	24	nq	npq	nq	nq	21	20	21	23	21	21	nq
Eddie CHEEVER	5	nc	r	r	6	5	nc	13	4	5	-	r	r	12r	r
(Tyrrell-Ford Cosworth)	8	14	13	19	8	15	20	19	23	18	nq	22	17	14	19
Kevin COGAN	-	-	-	-	-	-	-	-	-	-	-	-	-	-	-
(Tyrrell-Ford Cosworth)	nq	-	-	-	-	-	-	-	-	-	-	-	-	-	-
Derek DALY	-	-	-	-	-	-	16	r	7	r	11	r	r	8	-
(March-Ford Cosworth)	nq	nq	nq	nq	nq	npq	22	20	17	21	19	19	19	20	nq
Elio de ANGELIS	r	5	6	-	5	r	5	6	r	7	7	5	4	6	r
(Lotus-Ford Cosworth)	13	10	10	-	14	6	10	8	22	14	9	9	11	7	15
Andrea de CESARIS	r	r	11	6	r	r	r	11	r	r	8	-	7r	r	12
(McLaren-Ford Cosworth)	22	20	18	14	23	11	14	5	6	10	18	13ns	16	13	14
Emilio de VILLOTA	-	-	-	-	-	-	-	-	-	-	-	-	-	-	-
(Williams-Ford Cosworth)	-	-	-	-	-	-	exc	-	-	-	-	-	-	-	-
Giorgio FRANCIA	-	-	-	-	-	-	-	-	-	-	-	-	-	-	-
(Osella-Ford Cosworth)	-	-	-	-	-	-	nq	-	-	-	-	-	-	-	-
Beppe GABBIANI	r	-	-	r	r	-	-	-	-	-	-	-	-	-	-
(Osella-Ford Cosworth)	24	nq	nq	20	22	nq	nq	nq	nq	nq	nq	nq	nq	nq	nq
Piercarlo GHINZANI	-	-	-	-	13	-	-	-	-	-	-	-	-	-	-
(Osella-Ford Cosworth)	-	-	-	-	24	nq	-	-	-	-	-	-	-	-	-
Bruno GIACOMELLI	r	nc	10r	r	9	r	10	15	r	15	r	r	8	4	3
(Alfa Romeo)	9	6	22	11	17	18	6	12	12	19	16	14	10	15	8
Miguel Angel GUERRA	-	-	-	r	-	-	-	-	-	-	-	-	-	-	-
(Osella-Ford Cosworth)	nq	nq	nq	22	-	-	-	-	-	-	-	-	-	-	-
Brian HENTON	-	-	-	-	-	-	-	-	-	-	-	-	10	-	-
(Toleman-Hart)	-	-	-	nq	nq	npq	nq	nq	nq	nq	nq	nq	23	nq	nq
Jean-Pierre JABOUILLE	-	-	-	nc	r	-	r	-	-	-	-	-	-	-	-
(Talbot Ligier-Matra)	-	nq	nq	18	16	nq	19	-	-	-	-	-	-	-	-
Jean-Pierre JARIER	r	7	-	-	-	-	-	-	8	8	10	r	9	r	r
(Talbot Ligier-Matra)	10	23	-	-	-	-	-	-	-	-	-	-	-	-	-
(Osella-Ford Cosworth)	-	-	-	-	-	-	-	-	20	17	14	18	18	23	21
Alan JONES	1f	2	4	12	r	2f	7f	17	r	11f	4	3f	2	r	1
(Williams-Ford Cosworth)	2	3	3	8	6	7	2	9	7	4	6	4	5	3	2

	USAW	BR	RA	RSM	B	MC	E	F	GB	D	A	NL	I	CDN	LV
Jacques LAFFITE	r	6	r	r	2	3	2	r	3	3	1f	r	r	1	6
(Talbot Ligier-Matra)	12	16	21	10	9	8	1	6	14	7	4	6	4	10	12
Jan LAMMERS	r	-	12	-	-	-	-	-	-	-	-	-	-	-	-
(ATS-Ford Cosworth)	21	nq	23	nq	-	-	-	-	-	-	-	-	-	-	-
Ricardo LONDONO	-	-	-	-	-	-	-	-	-	-	-	-	-	-	-
(Ensign-Ford Cosworth)	-	exc	-	-	-	-	-	-	-	-	-	-	-	-	-
Nigel MANSELL	r	11	r	-	3	r	6	7	-	r	r	r	r	r	4
(Lotus-Ford Cosworth)	7	13	15	-	10	3	11	13	nq	15	11	17	12	5	9
Riccardo PATRESE	r	3	7	2	r	r	r	14	10r	r	r	r	r	r	11
(Arrows-Ford Cosworth)	1	4	9	9	4	5	12	18	10	13	10	10	20	18	11
Nelson PIQUET	3	12	1f	1	r	r	r	3	r	1	3	2	6r	5	5
(Brabham-Ford Cosworth)	4	1	1	5	2	1	9	4	3	6	7	3	6	1	4
Didier PIRONI	r	r	r	5	8	4	15	5	r	r	9	r	5	r	9f
(Ferrari)	11	17	12	6	3	17	13	14	4	5	8	12	8	12	18
Alain PROST	r	r	3	r	r	r	r	1f	r	2	r	1	1	r	2
(Renault)	14	5	2	4	12	9	5	3	2	1	2	1	3	4	5
Hector REBAQUE	r	r	r	4	r	-	r	9	5	4	r	4	r	r	r
(Brabham-Ford Cosworth)	15	11	6	13	21	nq	18	15	13	16	15	15	14	6	16
Carlos REUTEMANN	2	1	2	3	1f	r	4	10	2	r	5	r	3f	10	8
(Williams-Ford Cosworth)	3	2	4	2	1	4	3	7	9	3	5	5	2	2	1
Keke ROSBERG	r	9	r	r	r	-	12	r	r	-	-	-	-	-	10
(Fittipaldi-Ford Cosworth)	16	12	8	15	11	nq	15	17	16	nq	-	nq	nq	nq	20
Eliseo SALAZAR	-	-	-	r	-	-	14	r	-	nc	r	6	r	r	nc
(March-Ford Cosworth)	nq	nq	nq	23	nq	npq	-	-	-	-	-	-	-	-	-
(Ensign-Ford Cosworth)	-	-	-	-	-	-	24	22	nq	23	20	24	24	24	24
Chico SERRA	7	r	r	-	r	-	11	-	-	-	-	-	-	-	-
(Fittipaldi-Ford Cosworth)	18	22	20	nq	20	nq	21	24ns	nq	nq	-	nq	nq	nq	nq
Siegfried STOHR	-	r	9	-	r	r	r	-	r	12	r	7	-	-	-
(Arrows-Ford Cosworth)	nq	21	19	nq	13	14	23	nq	18	24	24	21	nq	-	-
Marc SURER	r	4f	r	9	11	6	-	12	11r	14r	r	8	-	9	r
(Ensign-Ford Cosworth)	19	18	16	21	15	19	-	-	-	-	-	-	-	-	-
(Theodore-Ford Cosworth)	-	-	-	-	-	-	-	21	24	22	23	20	nq	19	23
Patrick TAMBAY	6	10	r	11	-	7	13	r	r	r	r	r	r	r	r
(Theodore-Ford Cosworth)	17	19	14	16	nq	16	16	-	-	-	-	-	-	-	-
(Talbot Ligier-Matra)	-	-	-	-	-	-	-	16	15	11	17	11	15	17	7
Gilles VILLENEUVE	r	r	r	7f	4	1	1	r	r	10	r	r	r	3	dq
(Ferrari)	5	7	7	1	7	2	7	11	8	8	3	16	9	11	3
Jacques VILLENEUVE	-	-	-	-	-	-	-	-	-	-	-	-	-	-	-
(Arrows-Ford Cosworth)	-	-	-	-	-	-	-	-	-	-	-	-	-	nq	nq
Derek WARWICK	-	-	-	-	-	-	-	-	-	-	-	-	-	-	r
(Toleman-Hart)	-	-	-	nq	nq	npq	nq	nq	nq	nq	nq	nq	nq	nq	22
John WATSON	r	8	r	10	7	r	3	2	1	6	6	r	r	2f	7
(McLaren-Ford Cosworth)	23	15	11	7	5	10	4	2	5	9	12	8	7	9	6
Ricardo ZUNINO	-	13	13	-	-	-	-	-	-	-	-	-	-	-	-
(Tyrrell-Ford Cosworth)	-	24	24	-	-	-	-	-	-	-	-	-	-	-	-

1982 RACE RESULTS & GRID POSITIONS

	ZA	BR	USAW	RSM	B	MC	DET	CDN	NL	GB	F	D	A	CH	I	LV
Michele ALBORETO	7	4	4	3	r	10r	r	r	7	nc	6	4	r	7	5	1f
(Tyrrell-Ford Cosworth)	10	13	12	5	5	9	16	15	14	9	15	7	8	12	11	3
Mario ANDRETTI	-	-	r	-	-	-	-	-	-	-	-	-	-	-	3	r
(Williams-Ford Cosworth)	-	-	14	-	-	-	-	-	-	-	-	-	-	-	-	-
(Ferrari)	-	-	-	-	-	-	-	-	-	-	-	-	-	-	1	7
René ARNOUX	3	r	r	r	r	r	10	r	r	r	1	2	r	16r	1f	r
(Renault)	1	4	3	1	2	1	15	2	1	6	1	3	5	2	6	2
Mauro BALDI	-	10	-	-	r	r	r	8	6	9	r	r	6	-	12	11
(Arrows-Ford Cosworth)	nq	19	nq	-	26	nq	24	17	16	26	25	23	23	nq	24	23
Raul BOESEL	15	r	9	-	8	r	r	r	r	-	-	r	-	r	-	13
(March-Ford Cosworth)	21	17	23	-	24	npq	21	21	22	nq	nq	24	nq	24	nq	24
Slim BORGUDD	16	7	10	-	-	-	-	-	-	-	-	-	-	-	-	-
(Tyrrell-Ford Cosworth)	23	21	24	-	-	-	-	-	-	-	-	-	-	-	-	-
Tommy BYRNE	-	-	-	-	-	-	-	-	-	-	-	-	r	-	-	r
(Theodore-Ford Cosworth)	-	-	-	-	-	-	-	-	-	-	-	nq	26	nq	nq	26
Eddie CHEEVER	r	r	r	-	3	r	2	10r	-	r	16	r	r	nc	6	3
(Talbot Ligier-Matra)	17	26	13	-	14	16	9	12	nq	24	19	12	22	16	14	4

	ZA	BR	USAW	RSM	B	MC	DET	CDN	NL	GB	F	D	A	CH	I	LV
Derek DALY	14	r	r	-	r	6r	5	7r	5	5	7	r	r	9	r	6
(Theodore-Ford Cosworth)	24	20	22	-	-	-	-	-	-	-	-	-	-	-	-	-
(Williams-Ford Cosworth)	-	-	-	-	13	8	12	13	12	10	11	19	9	7	13	14
Elio de ANGELIS	8	r	5	-	4	5	r	4	r	4	r	r	1	6	r	r
(Lotus-Ford Cosworth)	15	11	16	-	11	15	8	10	15	7	13	13	7	15	17	20
Andrea de CESARIS	13	r	r	r	r	3r	r	6r	r	r	r	r	r	10	10	9
(Alfa Romeo)	16	10	1	7	6	7	2	9	9	11	7	8	11	5	9	18
Emilio de VILLOTA	-	-	-	-	-	-	-	-	-	-	-	-	-	-	-	-
(March-Ford Cosworth)	-	-	-	-	npq	npq	nq	nq	npq	-	-	-	-	-	-	-
Teo FABI	-	-	-	nc	r	-	-	-	-	r	r	-	r	r	r	-
(Toleman-Hart)	nq	nq	nq	10	21	npq	-	-	nq	15	21	nq	17	23	22	nq
Bruno GIACOMELLI	11	r	r	r	r	r	r	r	11	7	9	5	r	12	r	10
(Alfa Romeo)	19	16	5	6	15	3	6	5	8	14	8	11	13	9	8	16
Roberto GUERRERO	-	-	r	-	-	-	r	r	-	r	-	8	r	r	nc	-
(Ensign-Ford Cosworth)	-	nq	19	-	nq	nq	11	20	nq	19	nq	21	16	19	18	15ns
Brian HENTON	-	-	r	r	r	8	9	nc	r	8f	10	7	r	11	r	8
(Arrows-Ford Cosworth)	nq	nq	20	-	-	-	-	-	-	-	-	-	-	-	-	-
(Tyrrell-Ford Cosworth)	-	-	-	11	20	17	20	26	20	17	23	17	19	18	20	19
Jean-Pierre JARIER	r	9	r	4	r	-	r	r	14	r	r	r	-	r	r	-
(Osella-Ford Cosworth)	26	23	10	9	16	nq	22	18	23	18	17	20	nq	17	15	ns
Rupert KEEGAN	-	-	-	-	-	-	-	-	-	-	-	-	r	r	-	12
(March-Ford Cosworth)	-	-	-	-	-	-	-	-	-	-	-	nq	24	22	nq	25
Jacques LAFFITE	r	r	r	-	9	r	6	r	r	r	14	r	r	3	r	r
(Talbot Ligier-Matra)	11	24	15	-	17	18	13	19	21	20	16	15	14	13	21	11
Jan LAMMERS	-	-	-	-	-	-	-	-	r	-	r	-	-	-	-	-
(Theodore-Ford Cosworth)	-	-	-	-	nq	nq	nq	-	26	nq	nq	-	-	-	-	-
Niki LAUDA	4	r	1f	-	dq	r	r	r	4	1	8	-	5	3	r	r
(McLaren-Ford Cosworth)	13	5	2	-	4	12	10	11	5	5	9	ns	10	4	10	13
Geoff LEES	-	-	-	-	-	-	-	r	-	-	12	-	-	-	-	-
(Theodore-Ford Cosworth)	-	-	-	-	-	-	-	25	-	-	-	-	-	-	-	-
(Lotus-Ford Cosworth)	-	-	-	-	-	-	-	-	-	-	24	-	-	-	-	-
Nigel MANSELL	r	3	7	-	r	4	r	r	-	r	-	9	r	8	7	r
(Lotus-Ford Cosworth)	18	14	17	-	7	11	7	14	-	23	-	18	12	26	23	21
Jochen MASS	12	8	8	-	r	-	7	11	r	10	r	-	-	-	-	-
(March-Ford Cosworth)	22	22	21	-	25	nq	18	22	24	25	26	-	-	-	-	-
Roberto MORENO	-	-	-	-	-	-	-	-	-	-	-	-	-	-	-	-
(Lotus-Ford Cosworth)	-	-	-	-	-	-	-	-	nq	-	-	-	-	-	-	-
Riccardo PALETTI †	-	-	-	r	-	-	-	r	-	-	-	-	-	-	-	-
(Osella-Ford Cosworth)	nq	npq	nq	13	npq	npq	23ns	23	-	-	-	-	-	-	-	-
Riccardo PATRESE	r	r	3	-	r	1f	r	2	15	r	rf	r	r	5	r	r
(Brabham-BMW)	4	-	-	-	9	-	-	-	10	2	4	6	2	3	4	5
(Brabham-Ford Cosworth)	-	9	18	-	-	2	14	8	-	-	-	-	-	-	-	-
Nelson PIQUET	r	dq	r	-	5	r	-	1	2	r	r	rf	rf	4	r	r
(Brabham-BMW)	2	-	-	-	8	13	nq	4	3	3	6	4	1	6	2	12
(Brabham-Ford Cosworth)	-	7	6	-	-	-	-	-	-	-	-	-	-	-	-	-
Didier PIRONI	18	6	r	1f	-	2r	3	9f	1	2	3	-	-	-	-	-
(Ferrari)	6	8	9	4	ns	5	4	1	4	4	3	1ns	-	-	-	-
Alain PROST	1f	1f	r	r	r	7r	ncf	r	r	6	2	r	8r	2f	r	4
(Renault)	5	1	4	2	1	4	1	3	2	8	2	2	3	1	5	1
Carlos REUTEMANN	2	r	-	-	-	-	-	-	-	-	-	-	-	-	-	-
(Williams-Ford Cosworth)	8	6	-	-	-	-	-	-	-	-	-	-	-	-	-	-
Keke ROSBERG	5	dq	2	-	2	r	4	r	3	r	5	3	2	1	8	5
(Williams-Ford Cosworth)	7	3	8	-	3	6	3	7	7	1	10	9	6	8	7	6
Eliseo SALAZAR	9	r	r	5	r	r	r	r	13	-	r	r	-	14	9	-
(ATS-Ford Cosworth)	12	18	26	14	18	20	25	24	25	nq	22	22	nq	25	25	nq
Chico SERRA	17	r	-	-	6	-	11	-	r	r	-	11	7	-	11	-
(Fittipaldi-Ford Cosworth)	25	25	nq	-	23	npq	26	nq	19	21	nq	25	20	nq	26	nq
Marc SURER	-	-	-	-	7	9	8	5	10	r	13	6	r	15	r	7
(Arrows-Ford Cosworth)	-	-	-	-	22	19	19	16	17	22	20	26	21	14	19	17
Patrick TAMBAY	-	-	-	-	-	-	-	-	8	3	4	1	4	-	2	-
(Ferrari)	-	-	-	-	-	-	-	-	6	13	5	5	4	10ns	3	8ns
Gilles VILLENEUVE †	r	r	dq	2	-	-	-	-	-	-	-	-	-	-	-	-
(Ferrari)	3	2	7	3	ns	-	-	-	-	-	-	-	-	-	-	-
Derek WARWICK	r	-	-	-	r	-	-	-	rf	r	15	10	r	r	r	r
(Toleman-Hart)	14	nq	npq	8ns	19	nq	-	-	13	16	14	14	15	21	16	10
John WATSON	6	2	6	-	1f	r	1	3	9	r	r	r	r	13	4	2
(McLaren-Ford Cosworth)	9	12	11	-	10	10	17	6	11	12	12	10	18	11	12	9
Manfred WINKELHOCK	10	5	r	dq	r	r	r	-	12	-	11	r	r	r	-	nc
(ATS-Ford Cosworth)	20	15	25	12	12	14	5	nq	18	nq	18	16	25	20	nq	22

	BR	USAW	F	RSM	MC	B	DET	CDN	GB	D	A	NL	I	EUR	ZA
Kenny ACHESON	-	-	-	-	-	-	-	-	-	-	-	-	-	-	12
(RAM March-Ford Cosworth)	-	-	-	-	-	-	-	-	nq	nq	nq	nq	nq	nq	24
Michele ALBORETO	r	9	8	r	r	14	1	8	13	r	r	6	r	r	r
(Tyrrell-Ford Cosworth)	11	7	15	13	11	17	6	17	16	16	18	18	24	26	18
René ARNOUX	10	3	7	3	r	r	r	1	5	1f	2	1f	2	9	r
(Ferrari)	6	2	4	1	2	5	1	1	1	2	2	10	3	5	4
Mauro BALDI	r	r	r	10r	6	r	12	10	7	r	r	5	r	r	r
(Alfa Romeo)	10	21	8	10	13	12	25	26	11	7	9	12	10	15	17
Raul BOESEL	r	7	r	9	r	13	10	r	r	r	-	10	-	15	nc
(Ligier-Ford Cosworth)	17	26	25	25	18	26	23	24	22	25	nq	24	nq	23	23
Thierry BOUTSEN	-	-	-	-	-	r	7	7	15	9	13	14r	r	11	9
(Arrows-Ford Cosworth)	-	-	-	-	-	18	10	15	17	14	19	21	18	18	20
Johnny CECOTTO	14	6	11	r	-	10	r	r	-	11	-	-	12	-	-
(Theodore-Ford Cosworth)	19	17	17	23	npq	25	26	23	nq	22	nq	nq	26	-	-
Eddie CHEEVER	r	13r	3	r	r	3	r	2	r	r	4	r	3	10	6
(Renault)	8	15	2	6	3	8	7	6	7	6	8	11	7	7	14
Elio de ANGELIS	dq	r	r	r	r	9	r	r	r	r	r	r	5	r	r
(Lotus-Ford Cosworth)	13														
(Lotus-Renault)	-	5	5	9	19	13	4	11	4	11	12	3	8	1	11
Andrea de CESARIS	-	r	12	r	r	rf	r	r	8	2	r	r	r	4	2
(Alfa Romeo)	exc	19	7	8	7	3	8	8	9	3	11	8	6	14	9
Corrado FABI	r	-	r	r	nq	r	-	r	-	-	10	11r	r	-	-
(Osella-Ford Cosworth)	24	nq	23	26	nq	24	nq	25							
(Osella-Alfa Romeo)	-	-	-	-	-	-	-	-	nq	nq	26	25	25	nq	25
Piercarlo GHINZANI	-	-	-	-	-	-	r	-	r	r	11	-	r	nc	r
(Osella-Ford Cosworth)	nq	nq	nq												
(Osella-Alfa Romeo)	-	-	-	-	-	-	24	nq	26	26	25	nq	23	24	26
Bruno GIACOMELLI	r	r	13r	r	-	8	9	r	r	r	r	13	7	6	r
(Toleman-Hart)	15	14	13	17	nq	16	17	10	12	10	7	13	14	12	16
Roberto GUERRERO	nc	r	r	r	-	r	nc	r	16	r	r	12	13	12	-
(Theodore-Ford Cosworth)	14	18	22	21	npq	14	11	21	21	24	21	20	21	21	-
Jean-Pierre JARIER	r	r	9	r	r	r	r	r	10	8	7	r	9	r	10
(Ligier-Ford Cosworth)	12	10	20	19	9	21	19	16	25	19	20	22	19	22	21
Stefan JOHANSSON	-	-	-	-	-	-	-	-	r	r	12	7	r	14	-
(Spirit-Honda)	-	-	-	-	-	-	-	-	14	13	16	16	17	19	-
Alan JONES	-	r	-	-	-	-	-	-	-	-	-	-	-	-	-
(Arrows-Ford Cosworth)	-	12													
Jacques LAFFITE	4	4	6	7	r	6	5	r	12	6	r	r	r	r	r
(Williams-Ford Cosworth)	18	4	19	16	8	11	20	13	20	15	24	17	nq	nq	-
(Williams-Honda)	-	-	-	-	-	-	-	-	-	-	-	-	-	-	10
Niki LAUDA	3	2f	r	r	-	r	r	r	6	dq	6	r	r	r	11r
(McLaren-Ford Cosworth)	9	23	12	18	nq	15	18	19	15	18	14	-	-	-	-
(McLaren-TAG Porsche)	-	-	-	-	-	-	-	-	-	-	-	19	13	13	12
Nigel MANSELL	12	12	r	12r	r	r	6	r	4	r	5	r	8	3f	nc
(Lotus-Ford Cosworth)	22	13	18	15	14	19	14	18	-	-	-	-	-	-	-
(Lotus-Renault)	-	-	-	-	-	-	-	-	18	17	3	5	11	3	7
Jonathan PALMER	-	-	-	-	-	-	-	-	-	-	-	-	-	13	-
(Williams-Ford Cosworth)	-	-	-	-	-	-	-	-	-	-	-	-	-	25	-
Riccardo PATRESE	r	10r	r	13rf	r	r	r	r	r	3	r	9	r	7	1
(Brabham-BMW)	7	11	3	5	17	6	15	5	5	8	6	6	1	2	3
Nelson PIQUET	1f	r	2	r	2f	4	4	r	2	13r	3	r	1f	1	3f
(Brabham-BMW)	4	20	6	2	6	4	2	3	6	4	4	1	4	4	
Alain PROST	7	11	1f	2	3	1	8	5	1f	4	1f	r	r	2	r
(Renault)	2	8	1	4	1	1	13	2	3	5	5	4	5	8	5
Keke ROSBERG	dq	r	5	4	1	5	2	4	11	10	8	r	11	r	5
(Williams-Ford Cosworth)	1	3	16	11	5	9	12	9	13	12	15	23	16	16	-
(Williams-Honda)	-	-	-	-	-	-	-	-	-	-	-	-	-	-	6
Eliseo SALAZAR	15	r	-	-	-	-	-	-	-	-	-	-	-	-	-
(RAM March-Ford Cosworth)	26	25	nq	nq	nq	nq	-	-	-	-	-	-	-	-	-
Jean-Louis SCHLESSER	-	-	-	-	-	-	-	-	-	-	-	-	-	-	-
(RAM March-Ford Cosworth)	-	-	nq	-	-	-	-	-	-	-	-	-	-	-	-
Chico SERRA	9	-	r	8	7	-	-	-	-	-	-	-	-	-	-
(Arrows-Ford Cosworth)	23	-	26	20	15	-	-	-	-	-	-	-	-	-	-
Danny SULLIVAN	11	8	r	r	5	12	r	dq	14	12	r	r	r	r	7
(Tyrrell-Ford Cosworth)	21	9	24	22	20	23	16	22	23	21	23	26	22	20	19

Season-by-Season Summary

	BR	USAW	F	RSM	MC	B	DET	CDN	GB	D	A	NL	I	EUR	ZA
Marc SURER	6	5	10	6	r	11	11	r	17	7	r	8	10	r	8
(Arrows-Ford Cosworth)	20	16	21	12	12	10	5	14	19	20	22	14	20	17	22
Patrick TAMBAY	5	r	4	1	4	2	r	3f	3	r	r	2	4	r	r
(Ferrari)	3	1	11	3	4	2	3	4	2	1	1	2	2	6	1
Jacques VILLENEUVE	-	-	-	-	-	-	-	-	-	-	-	-	-	-	-
(RAM March-Ford Cosworth)	-	-	-	-	-	-	-	nq	-	-	-	-	-	-	-
Derek WARWICK	8	r	r	r	r	7	r	r	r	r	r	4	6	5	4
(Toleman-Hart)	5	6	9	14	10	22	9	12	10	9	10	7	12	11	13
John WATSON	r	1	r	5	-	r	3f	6	9	5	9	3	r	r	dq
(McLaren-Ford Cosworth)	16	22	14	24	nq	20	21	20	24	23	17	15	-	-	-
(McLaren-TAG Porsche)	-	-	-	-	-	-	-	-	-	-	-	-	15	10	15
Manfred WINKELHOCK	16	r	r	11	r	r	r	9r	r	-	r	dq	r	8	r
(ATS-BMW)	25	24	10	7	16	7	22	7	8	nq	13	9	9	9	8

1984 RACE RESULTS & GRID POSITIONS

	BR	ZA	B	RSM	F	MC	CDN	DET	DAL	GB	D	A	NL	I	EUR	P
Michele ALBORETO	r	11r	1	r	r	6	r	r	r	5	r	3	r	2	2f=	4
(Ferrari)	2	10	1	13	10	4	6	4	9	9	6	12	9	11	5	8
Philippe ALLIOT	r	r	-	r	r	-	10	r	-	r	r	11	10	r	r	r
(RAM-Hart)	25	22	nq	23	22	nq	26	20	ns	24	22	25	26	23	25	27
René ARNOUX	r	r	3f	2	4	3	5	r	2	6	6	7	11rf	r	5	9
(Ferrari)	10	15	2	6	11	3	5	15	4	13	10	15	15	14	6	17
Mauro BALDI	r	8	r	8	r	-	-	-	-	-	-	-	-	-	8	15
(Spirit-Hart)	23	20	25	24	24	nq	-	-	-	-	-	-	-	-	24	25
Stefan BELLOF	dq	dq	dq	dq	dq	dq	dq	dq	dq	dq	-	-	dq	-	-	-
(Tyrrell-Ford Cosworth)	22	24	21	21	20	20	22	16	17	26	-	nq	24	-	-	-
Gerhard BERGER	-	-	-	-	-	-	-	-	-	-	-	12r	-	6	r	13
(ATS-BMW)	-	-	-	-	-	-	-	-	-	-	-	20	-	20	18	23
Thierry BOUTSEN	6	12	r	5	11	-	r	r	r	r	r	5	r	10	9r	r
(Arrows-Ford Cosworth)	20	26	-	20	-	-	-	-	-	-	-	-	-	-	-	-
(Arrows-BMW)	-	-	17	-	14	nq	18	13	20	12	15	17	11	19	11	18
Martin BRUNDLE	dq	dq	dq	dq	dq	-	dq	dq	-	-	-	-	-	-	-	-
(Tyrrell-Ford Cosworth)	18	25	22	22	23	nq	21	11	nq	-	-	-	-	-	-	-
Johnny CECOTTO	r	r	r	nc	r	r	9	r	r	-	-	-	-	-	-	-
(Toleman-Hart)	17	19	16	19	18	18	20	17	15	nq	-	-	-	-	-	-
Eddie CHEEVER	4	r	r	7r	r	-	11r	r	r	r	r	r	13r	9r	r	17
(Alfa Romeo)	12	16	11	8	16	nq	11	8	14	18	18	16	17	10	13	14
Elio de ANGELIS	3	7	5	3r	5	5	4	2	3	4	r	r	4	r	r	5
(Lotus-Renault)	1	7	5	11	2	11	3	5	2	4	2	3	3	3	23	5
Andrea de CESARIS	r	5	r	6r	10	r	r	r	r	10	7	r	r	r	7	12
(Ligier-Renault)	14	14	13	12	26	7	10	12	16	19	11	18	14	16	17	20
Corrado FABI	-	-	-	-	-	r	r	-	7	-	-	-	-	-	-	-
(Brabham-BMW)	-	-	-	-	-	15	16	-	11	-	-	-	-	-	-	-
Teo FABI	r	r	r	r	9	-	-	3	-	r	r	4	5	r	r	-
(Brabham-BMW)	15	6	18	9	17	-	-	23	-	14	8	7	10	5	10	-
Jo GARTNER	-	-	-	r	-	-	-	-	-	r	r	r	12	5	12r	16r
(Osella-Alfa Romeo)	-	-	-	26	-	-	-	-	-	27	23	22	23	24	22	24
Piercarlo GHINZANI	r	-	r	-	12	7	r	r	5	9	r	r	r	7r	r	r
(Osella-Alfa Romeo)	21	ns	20	nq	25	19	19	26	18	21	21	23	21	22	20	22
François HESNAULT	r	10	r	r	-	r	r	r	r	r	8	8	7	r	10	r
(Ligier-Renault)	19	17	23	17	ns	17	13	18	19	20	17	21	20	18	19	21
Stefan JOHANSSON	-	-	-	-	-	-	-	-	-	dq	dq	-	dq	4	r	11
(Tyrrell-Ford Cosworth)	-	-	-	-	-	-	-	-	-	25	26	nq	25	-	-	-
(Toleman-Hart)	-	-	-	-	-	-	-	-	-	-	-	-	-	17	26	10
Jacques LAFFITE	r	r	r	r	8	8	r	5	4	r	r	r	r	r	r	14
(Williams-Honda)	13	11	15	15	12	16	17	19	24	16	12	11	8	13	14	15
Niki LAUDA	r	1	r	r	1	r	2	r	9rf	1f	2	1f	2	1f	4	2f
(McLaren-TAG Porsche)	6	8	14	5	9	8	8	10	5	3	7	4	6	4	15	11
Nigel MANSELL	r	r	r	r	3	r	6	r	6r	r	4	r	3	r	r	r
(Lotus-Renault)	5	3	10	18	6	2	7	3	1	8	16	8	12	7	8	6
Pierluigi MARTINI	-	-	-	-	-	-	-	-	-	-	-	-	-	nq	-	-
(Toleman-Hart)	-	-	-	-	-	-	-	-	-	-	-	-	-	-	-	-
Jonathan PALMER	8	r	10	9	13	-	-	r	r	r	r	9	9	r	r	r
(RAM-Hart)	26	21	26	25	21	nq	-	24	25	23	25	24	22	26	21	26

Grand Prix Data Book

	BR	ZA	B	RSM	F	MC	CDN	DET	DAL	GB	D	A	NL	I	EUR	P
Riccardo PATRESE	r	4	r	r	r	r	r	r	r	12r	r	10r	r	3	6	8
(Alfa Romeo)	11	18	7	10	15	14	14	25	21	17	20	13	18	9	9	12
Nelson PIQUET	r	r	9r	rf	r	r	1f	1	r	7	r	2	r	r	3f=	6
(Brabham-BMW)	7	1	9	1	3	9	1	1	12	1	5	1	2	1	1	1
Alain PROST	1f	2	r	1	7f	1	3	4	r	r	1f	r	1	r	1	1
(McLaren-TAG Porsche)	4	5	8	2	5	1	2	2	7	2	1	2	1	2	2	2
Keke ROSBERG	2	r	4r	r	6	4	r	r	1	r	r	r	8r	r	r	r
(Williams-Honda)	9	2	3	3	4	10	15	21	8	5	19	9	7	6	4	4
Huub ROTHENGATTER	-	-	-	-	-	-	nc	-	r	nc	9	nc	r	8	-	-
(Spirit-Hart)																
(Spirit-Ford Cosworth)	-	-	-	-	-	-	24	nq	23	22	24	26	27	25	-	-
Ayrton SENNA	r	6	6	-	r	2f	7	r	r	3	r	r	r	-	r	3
(Toleman-Hart)	16	13	19	nq	13	13	9	7	6	7	9	10	13	-	12	3
Philippe STREIFF	-	-	-	-	-	-	-	-	-	-	-	-	-	-	-	r
(Renault)	-	-	-	-	-	-	-	-	-	-	-	-	-	-	-	13
Marc SURER	7	9	8	r	r	-	r	r	r	11	r	6	r	r	r	r
(Arrows-Ford Cosworth)	24	23	24	-	19	nq	23	22	-	-	-	-	-	-	-	-
(Arrows-BMW)	-	-	-	16	-	-	-	-	22	15	14	19	19	15	16	16
Patrick TAMBAY	5r	rf	7	r	2	r	-	r	r	8r	5	r	6	r	r	7
(Renault)	8	4	12	14	1	6	ew	9	10	10	4	5	5	8	3	7
Mike THACKWELL	-	-	-	-	-	-	r	-	-	-	-	-	-	-	-	-
(RAM-Hart)	-	-	-	-	-	-	25	-	-	-	-	-	-	-	-	-
(Tyrrell-Ford Cosworth)	-	-	-	-	-	-	-	-	-	-	-	nq	-	-	-	-
Derek WARWICK	r	3	2	4	r	r	r	rf	r	2	3	r	r	r	11r	r
(Renault)	3	9	4	4	7	5	4	6	3	6	3	6	4	12	7	9
Manfred WINKELHOCK	-	r	r	r	r	r	8	r	8	r	r	r	-	r	-	10
(ATS-BMW)	exc	12	6	7	8	12	12	14	13	11	13	14ns	16	21ns	-	-
(Brabham-BMW)	-	-	-	-	-	-	-	-	-	-	-	-	-	-	-	19

1985 RACE RESULTS & GRID POSITIONS

	BR	P	RSM	MC	CDN	USA	F	GB	D	A	NL	I	B	EUR	ZA	AUS
Kenny ACHESON	-	-	-	-	-	-	-	-	-	r	-	r	-	-	-	-
(RAM-Hart)	-	-	-	-	-	-	-	-	-	23	nq	24	-	-	-	-
Michele ALBORETO	2	2	rf	2f	1	3	r	2	1	3	4	13r	r	r	r	r
(Ferrari)	1	5	4	3	3	3	3	6	8	9	16	7	4	15	15	5
Philippe ALLIOT	9	r	r	-	r	r	r	r	r	r	r	r	r	r	-	-
(RAM-Hart)	20	20	21	nq	21	23	22	21	21	21	25	26	20	23	-	-
René ARNOUX	4	-	-	-	-	-	-	-	-	-	-	-	-	-	-	-
(Ferrari)	7	-	-	-	-	-	-	-	-	-	-	-	-	-	-	-
Mauro BALDI	r	r	r	-	-	-	-	-	-	-	-	-	-	-	-	-
(Spirit-Hart)	24	24	26	-	-	-	-	-	-	-	-	-	-	-	-	-
Stefan BELLOF †	-	6	r	-	11	4	13	11	8	7r	r	-	-	-	-	-
(Tyrrell-Ford Cosworth)	-	21	24	nq	23	19	25	26	-	-	-	-	-	-	-	-
(Tyrrell-Renault)	-	-	-	-	-	-	-	-	19	22	22	-	-	-	-	-
Gerhard BERGER	r	r	r	r	13	11	r	8	7	r	9	r	7	10	5	6
(Arrows-BMW)	19	17	10	11	12	24	8	17	17	17	14	11	8	19	11	7
Thierry BOUTSEN	11	r	2	9	9	7	9	r	4	8	r	9	10r	6	6	r
(Arrows-BMW)	12	16	5	6	7	21	11	19	15	16	8	14	6	12	10	11
Martin BRUNDLE	8	r	9	10	12	r	r	7	10	-	7	8	13	r	7	nc
(Tyrrell-Ford Cosworth)	21	22	25	18	24	18	-	-	26	nq	-	-	-	-	-	-
(Tyrrell-Renault)	-	-	-	-	-	-	20	20	-	-	21	18	21	16	17	17
Ivan CAPELLI	-	-	-	-	-	-	-	-	-	-	-	-	-	r	-	4
(Tyrrell-Renault)	-	-	-	-	-	-	-	-	-	-	-	-	-	24	-	22
Eddie CHEEVER	r	r	r	r	17	9	10	r	r	r	r	r	r	11	r	r
(Alfa Romeo)	18	14	12	4	11	7	17	22	18	20	20	17	19	18	14	13
Christian DANNER	-	-	-	-	-	-	-	-	-	-	-	-	r	r	-	-
(Zakspeed)	-	-	-	-	-	-	-	-	-	-	-	-	22	25	-	-
Elio de ANGELIS	3	4	1	3	5	5	5	nc	r	5	5	6	r	5	r	dq
(Lotus-Renault)	3	4	3	9	1	8	7	8	7	7	11	6	9	9	6	10
Andrea de CESARIS	r	r	r	r	4	14	10	r	r	r	r	-	-	-	-	-
(Ligier-Renault)	13	8	13	8	15	17	12	7	14	18	18	-	-	-	-	-
Teo FABI	-	-	-	r	r	r	14r	r	r	r	r	12	r	r	r	r
(Toleman-Hart)	-	-	-	20	18	13	18	9	1	6	5	15	11	20	7	24
Piercarlo GHINZANI	12	9	nc	-	r	r	15	r	r	r	r	r	r	r	r	r
(Osella-Alfa Romeo)	22	26	22	nq	22	22	23	25	-	-	-	-	-	-	-	-
(Toleman-Hart)	-	-	-	-	-	-	-	-	-	19	15	21	16	14	13	21

	BR	P	RSM	MC	CDN	USA	F	GB	D	A	NL	I	B	EUR	ZA	AUS
François HESNAULT	r	r	r	-	-	-	-	-	r	-	-	-	-	-	-	-
(Brabham-BMW)	17	19	20	nq	-	-	-	-	-	-	-	-	-	-	-	-
(Renault)	-	-	-	-	-	-	-	-	23	-	-	-	-	-	-	-
Stefan JOHANSSON	7	8	6r	r	2	2	4	r	9	4	r	5r	r	r	4	5
(Tyrrell-Ford Cosworth)	23	-	-	-	-	-	-	-	-	-	-	-	-	-	-	-
(Ferrari)	-	11	15	15	4	9	15	11	2	12	17	10	5	13	16	15
Alan JONES	-	-	-	-	-	-	-	-	-	-	-	r	-	r	-	r
(Lola-Hart)	-	-	-	-	-	-	-	-	-	-	-	25	-	22	ns	19
Jacques LAFFITE	6	r	r	6	8	12	r	3	3	r	r	r	11r	rf	-	2
(Ligier-Renault)	15	18	16	16	19	16	14	16	13	15	13	20	17	10	-	20
Niki LAUDA	r	r	4	r	r	r	r	r	5f	r	1	r	-	-	r	r
(McLaren-TAG Porsche)	9	7	8	14	17	12	6	10	12	3	10	16	ns	-	8	16
Nigel MANSELL	r	5	5	7	6	r	-	r	6	r	6	11rf	2	1	1	r
(Williams-Honda)	5	9	7	2	16	2	ns	5	10	2	7	3	7	3	1	2
Pierluigi MARTINI	r	r	r	-	r	r	r	r	11r	r	r	r	12	r	r	8
(Minardi-Ford Cosworth)	25	25	-	-	-	-	-	-	-	-	-	-	-	-	-	-
(Minardi-Motori Moderni)	-	-	19	nq	25	25	24	23	27	26	24	23	24	26	19	23
Jonathan PALMER	-	r	-	11	-	-	r	r	r	r	r	-	-	-	-	-
(Zakspeed)	-	23	17ns	19	-	-	21	24	24	25	23	-	-	-	-	-
Riccardo PATRESE	r	r	r	r	10	r	11	9	r	r	r	r	r	9	r	r
(Alfa Romeo)	14	13	18	12	13	14	16	14	9	10	19	13	15	11	12	14
Nelson PIQUET	r	r	8r	r	r	6	1	4	r	r	8	2	5	r	r	r
(Brabham-BMW)	8	10	9	13	9	10	5	2	6	5	1	4	3	2	2	9
Alain PROST	1f	r	dq	1	3	r	3	1f	2	1f	2f	1	3f	4	3	r
(McLaren-TAG Porsche)	6	2	6	5	5	4	4	4	3	3	3	5	1	6	9	4
Keke ROSBERG	r	r	r	8	4	1	2f	r	12r	r	r	r	4	3	2f	1f
(Williams-Honda)	2	3	2	7	8	5	1	1	4	4	2	2	10	4	3	3
Huub ROTHENGATTER	-	-	-	-	-	-	-	-	r	9	nc	r	nc	-	r	7
(Osella-Alfa Romeo)	-	-	-	-	-	-	-	-	25	24	26	22	23	nq	20	25
Ayrton SENNA	r	1f	7r	r	16f	rf	r	10r	r	2	3	3	1	2	r	r
(Lotus-Renault)	4	1	1	1	2	1	2	4	5	14	4	1	2	1	4	1
Philippe STREIFF	-	-	-	-	-	-	-	-	-	-	-	10	9	8	r	3
(Ligier-Renault)	-	-	-	-	-	-	-	-	-	-	-	19	18	5	-	18
(Tyrrell-Renault)	-	-	-	-	-	-	-	-	-	-	-	-	-	-	18	-
Marc SURER	-	-	-	-	15	8	8	6	r	6	10r	4	8	r	r	r
(Brabham-BMW)	-	-	-	-	20	11	13	15	11	11	9	9	12	7	5	6
Patrick TAMBAY	5	3	3	r	7	r	6	r	r	10r	r	7	r	12	-	r
(Renault)	11	12	11	17	10	15	9	13	16	8	6	8	13	17	-	8
Derek WARWICK	10	7	10	5	r	r	7	5	r	r	r	r	6	r	-	r
(Renault)	10	6	14	10	6	6	10	12	20	13	12	12	14	8	-	12
John WATSON	-	-	-	-	-	-	-	-	-	-	-	-	-	7	-	-
(McLaren-TAG Porsche)	-	-	-	-	-	-	-	-	-	-	-	-	-	21	-	-
Manfred WINKELHOCK †	13	nc	r	-	r	r	12	r	r	-	-	-	-	-	-	-
(RAM-Hart)	16	15	23	nq	14	20	19	18	22	-	-	-	-	-	-	-

	BR	E	RSM	MC	B	CDN	USA	F	GB	D	H	A	I	P	MEX	AUS
Michele ALBORETO	r	r	10r	r	4	8	4	8	r	r	r	2	r	5	r	r
(Ferrari)	6	13	5	4	9	11	11	6	12	10	15	9	9	13	12	9
Philippe ALLIOT	-	-	-	-	-	-	-	-	-	r	9	r	r	r	6	8
(Ligier-Renault)	-	-	-	-	-	-	-	-	-	14	12	11	14	11	10	8
René ARNOUX	4	r	r	5	r	6	r	5	4	4	r	10	r	7	15r	7
(Ligier-Renault)	4	6	8	12	7	5	4	4	8	8	9	12	11	10	13	5
Allen BERG	-	-	-	-	-	-	r	r	r	12	r	r	-	13	16	nc
(Osella-Alfa Romeo)	-	-	-	-	-	-	25	26	26	26	26	26	-	27	26	26
Gerhard BERGER	6	6	3	r	10	r	r	r	r	10f	r	7f	5	r	1	r
(Benetton-BMW)	16	7	9	5	2	7	12	8	4	4	11	2	4	4	4	6
Thierry BOUTSEN	r	7	7	8	r	r	r	nc	nc	r	r	r	7	10	7	r
(Arrows-BMW)	15	19	12	14	14	12	13	21	13	21	22	18	13	21	21	22
Martin BRUNDLE	5	r	8	r	r	9	r	10	5	r	6	r	10	r	11	4
(Tyrrell-Renault)	17	12	13	10	12	18	16	15	11	15	16	17	20	19	16	16
Alex CAFFI	-	-	-	-	-	-	-	-	-	-	-	-	11	-	-	-
(Osella-Alfa Romeo)	-	-	-	-	-	-	-	-	-	-	-	-	27	-	-	-
Ivan CAPELLI	-	-	-	-	-	-	-	-	-	-	-	-	r	r	-	-
(AGS-Motori Moderni)	-	-	-	-	-	-	-	-	-	-	-	-	25	25	-	-
Eddie CHEEVER	-	-	-	-	-	-	r	-	-	-	-	-	-	-	-	-
(Lola-Ford Cosworth)	-	-	-	-	-	-	10	-	-	-	-	-	-	-	-	-
Christian DANNER	r	r	r	-	r	r	r	11	r	r	r	6	8	11	9	r
(Osella-Alfa Romeo)	24	23	25	nq	25	24	-	-	-	-	-	-	-	-	-	-
(Arrows-BMW)	-	-	-	-	-	-	19	18	23	17	21	22	16	22	20	24
Elio de ANGELIS †	8	r	r	r	-	-	-	-	-	-	-	-	-	-	-	-
(Brabham-BMW)	14	15	19	20	-	-	-	-	-	-	-	-	-	-	-	-
Andrea de CESARIS	r	r	r	-	r	r	r	r	r	r	r	r	r	r	8	r
(Minardi-Motori Moderni)	22	24	23	nq	19	20	23	23	21	23	20	23	21	16	22	11
Johnny DUMFRIES	9	r	r	-	r	r	7	r	7	r	5	r	r	9	r	6
(Lotus-Renault)	11	10	17	nq	13	15	14	12	10	12	8	15	17	15	17	14
Teo FABI	10	5	r	r	7	r	r	r	r	r	r	r	rf	8	r	10
(Benetton-BMW)	12	9	10	16	6	14	17	9	7	9	13	1	1	5	9	13
Piercarlo GHINZANI	r	r	r	-	r	r	r	r	r	r	r	11	r	r	r	r
(Osella-Alfa Romeo)	23	21	26	nq	24	22	22	25	24	25	23	25	26	24	25	25
Stefan JOHANSSON	r	r	4	10	3	r	r	r	r	11r	4	3	3	6	12r	3
(Ferrari)	8	11	7	15	11	17	5	10	18	11	7	14	12	8	14	12
Alan JONES	r	r	r	r	11r	10	r	r	r	9	r	4	6	r	r	r
(Lola-Hart)	19	17	-	-	-	-	-	-	-	-	-	-	-	-	-	-
(Lola-Ford Cosworth)	-	-	21	18	16	13	21	20	14	19	10	16	18	17	15	15
Jacques LAFFITE	3	r	r	6	5	7	2	6	r	-	-	-	-	-	-	-
(Ligier-Renault)	5	8	14	7	17	8	6	11	19	-	-	-	-	-	-	-
Nigel MANSELL	r	2f	r	4	1	1	5	1f	1f	3	3	r	2	1f	5	r
(Williams-Honda)	3	3	3	2	5	1	2	2	2	6	4	6	3	2	3	1
Alessandro NANNINI	r	-	r	-	r	r	r	r	r	r	r	r	r	r	14	r
(Minardi-Motori Moderni)	25	25ns	18	nq	22	19	24	19	20	22	17	19	19	18	24	18
Jonathan PALMER	r	r	r	12	13	r	8	r	9	r	10	r	r	12	10r	9
(Zakspeed)	21	16	20	19	20	21	20	22	22	16	24	21	22	20	18	21
Riccardo PATRESE	r	r	6r	r	8	r	6	7	r	r	r	r	r	r	13r	r
(Brabham-BMW)	10	14	16	6	15	9	8	16	15	7	14	4	10	9	5	19
Nelson PIQUET	1f	r	2f	7	r	3f	rf	3	2	1	1f	r	1	3	4f	2f
(Williams-Honda)	2	2	2	11	1	3	3	3	1	5	2	7	6	6	2	2
Alain PROST	r	3	1	1f	6f	2	3	2	3	6r	r	1	r/dq	2	2	1
(McLaren-TAG Porsche)	9	4	4	1	3	4	7	5	6	2	3	5	2	3	6	4
Keke ROSBERG	r	4	5r	2	r	4	r	4	r	5r	r	9r	4	r	r	r
(McLaren-TAG Porsche)	7	5	6	9	8	6	9	7	5	1	5	3	8	7	11	7
Huub ROTHENGATTER	-	-	r	-	r	12	r	r	r	nc	r	r	8	r	r	r
(Zakspeed)	-	-	24	nq	23	23	26ns	24	25	24	25	24	24	26	23ns	23
Ayrton SENNA	2	1	r	3	2	5	1	r	r	2	2	r	r	4r	3	r
(Lotus-Renault)	1	1	1	3	4	2	1	1	3	3	1	8	5	1	1	3
Philippe STREIFF	7	r	r	11	12	11	9	r	6	r	8	r	9	r	r	5r
(Tyrrell-Renault)	18	20	22	13	18	16	18	17	16	18	18	20	23	23	19	10
Marc SURER	r	r	9r	9	9	-	-	-	-	-	-	-	-	-	-	-
(Arrows-BMW)	20	22	15	17	21	-	-	-	-	-	-	-	-	-	-	-
Patrick TAMBAY	r	8	r	r	r	-	-	r	r	8	7	5	r	nc	r	nc
(Lola-Hart)	13	18	11	-	-	-	-	-	-	-	-	-	-	-	-	-
(Lola-Ford Cosworth)	-	-	-	8	10	ns	-	13	17	13	6	13	15	14	8	17
Derek WARWICK	-	-	-	-	-	r	10	9	8	7	r	r	-	r	r	r
(Brabham-BMW)	-	-	-	-	-	10	15	14	9	20	19	10ns	7	12	7	20

	BR	RSM	B	MC	USA	F	GB	D	H	A	I	P	E	MEX	J	AUS
Michele ALBORETO (Ferrari)	8r	3	r	3	r	r	r	r	r	r	r	r	15r	r	4	2
	9	6	5	5	7	8	7	5	5	6	8	6	4	9	4	6
Philippe ALLIOT (Lola-Ford Cosworth)	-	10	8	r	r	r	r	6	r	12	r	r	6	6	r	r
	-	21	22	18	20	23	21	21	15	22	23	19	17	24	18	17
René ARNOUX (Ligier-Megatron)	-	-	6	11	10	r	r	r	r	10	10	r	r	r	r	r
	-	ns	16	22	21	13	16	12	19	16	15	18	14	18	17	20
Gerhard BERGER (Ferrari)	4	r	r	4	4	r	r	r	r	r	4	2f	rf	r	1	1f
	7	5	4	8	12	6	8	10	2	3	3	1	3	2	1	1
Thierry BOUTSEN (Benetton-Ford Cosworth)	5	r	r	r	r	r	7	r	4	4	5	14	16r	r	5	3
	6	11	7	9	4	5	5	6	7	4	6	9	8	4	3	5
Martin BRUNDLE (Zakspeed)	r	5	r	7	r	r	nc	nc	r	dq	r	r	11	r	r	r
	19	14	18	14	15	18	17	19	22	17	17	17	20	13	15	16
Alex CAFFI (Osella-Alfa Romeo)	r	12r	r	r	r	r	r	r	r	r	r	r	-	r	r	-
	21	19	26	16	19	20	20	26	21	21	21	25	nq	26	23	nq
Adrian CAMPOS (Minardi-Motori Moderni)	dq	r	r	-	r	r	r	r	r	r	r	r	14	r	r	r
	16	16	19	ns	25	21	19	18	24	19	20	20	24	19	21	26
Ivan CAPELLI (March-Ford Cosworth)	-	r	r	6	r	r	r	r	10	11	13	9	12	r	r	r
	23ns	22	21	19	22	22	24	24	18	23	25	22	19	20	20	23
Eddie CHEEVER (Arrows-Megatron)	r	r	4	r	6r	r	r	r	8	r	r	6	8r	4	9	r
	14	9	11	6	6	14	14	15	11	12	13	11	13	12	12	11
Yannick DALMAS (Lola-Ford Cosworth)	-	-	-	-	-	-	-	-	-	-	-	-	-	9	14r	5
	-	-	-	-	-	-	-	-	-	-	-	-	-	23	22	21
Christian DANNER (Zakspeed)	9	7	r	-	8	r	r	r	r	9	9	r	r	r	r	7
	17	17	20	exc	16	19	18	20	23	20	16	16	22	17	16	24
Andrea de CESARIS (Brabham-BMW)	r	r	3r	r	r	r	r	r	r	r	r	r	r	r	r	8r
	13	13	13	21	17	11	9	7	13	10	10	13	10	10	10	10
Teo FABI (Benetton-Ford Cosworth)	r	rf	r	8	r	5r	6	r	r	3	7	4r	r	5	r	r
	4	4	9	12	8	7	6	9	12	5	7	10	6	6	6	9
Pascal FABRE (AGS-Ford Cosworth)	12	13	10r	13	12	9	9	r	13	nc	-	-	r	-	-	-
	22	24	25	24	26	26	25	25	26	26	nq	nq	25	nq	-	-
Franco FORINI (Osella-Alfa Romeo)	-	-	-	-	-	-	-	-	-	-	r	r	-	-	-	-
	-	-	-	-	-	-	-	-	-	-	26	26	nq	-	-	-
Piercarlo GHINZANI (Ligier-Megatron)	-	r	7r	12	nc	r	-	r	12	8	8	r	r	r	13r	r
	-	18	17	20	23	17	exc	17	25	18	19	23	23	21	24	22
Stefan JOHANSSON (McLaren-TAG Porsche)	3	4	2	r	7	8r	r	2	r	7	6	5	3	r	3	r
	10	8	10	7	11	9	10	8	8	14	11	8	11	15	9	8
Nicola LARINI (Coloni-Ford Cosworth)	-	-	-	-	-	-	-	-	-	-	-	-	r	-	-	-
	-	-	-	-	-	-	-	-	-	-	nq	-	26	-	-	-
Nigel MANSELL (Williams-Honda)	6	1	r	r	5	1	1f	rf	14r	1f	3	r	1	1	-	-
	1	2	1	1	1	1	2	1	1	2	2	2	2	1	ns	-
Stefano MODENA (Brabham-BMW)	-	-	-	-	-	-	-	-	-	-	-	-	-	-	-	r
	-	-	-	-	-	-	-	-	-	-	-	-	-	-	-	15
Roberto MORENO (AGS-Ford Cosworth)	-	-	-	-	-	-	-	-	-	-	-	-	-	-	r	6
	-	-	-	-	-	-	-	-	-	-	-	-	-	-	26	25
Satoru NAKAJIMA (Lotus-Honda)	7	6	5	10	r	nc	4	r	r	13	11	8	9	r	6	r
	12	12	15	17	24	16	12	14	17	13	14	15	18	16	11	14
Alessandro NANNINI (Minardi-Motori Moderni)	r	r	r	r	r	r	r	r	11	r	16r	11r	r	r	r	r
	15	15	14	13	18	15	15	16	20	15	18	14	21	14	14	13
Jonathan PALMER (Tyrrell-Ford Cosworth)	10	r	r	5	11	7	8	5	7	14	14	10	r	7	8	4
	18	23	24	15	13	24	23	23	16	24	22	24	16	22	19	19
Riccardo PATRESE (Brabham-BMW)	r	9	r	r	9	r	r	r	5	r	r	r	13	3	11r	9r
	11	7	8	10	9	12	11	11	10	8	9	7	9	8	8	-
(Williams-Honda)	-	-	-	-	-	-	-	-	-	-	-	-	-	-	-	7
Nelson PIQUET (Williams-Honda)	2f	-	r	2	2	2f	2	1	1f	2	1	3	4	2f	15r	r
	2	ns	2	3	3	4	1	4	3	1	1	4	1	3	5	3
Alain PROST (McLaren-TAG Porsche)	1	r	1f	9r	3	3	r	7r	3	6	15	1	2	r	7f	r
	5	3	6	4	5	2	4	3	4	9	5	3	7	5	2	2
Ayrton SENNA (Lotus-Honda)	r	2	r	1f	1f	4	3	3	2	5	2f	7	5	r	2	dq
	3	1	3	2	2	3	3	2	6	7	4	5	5	7	7	4
Philippe STREIFF (Tyrrell-Ford Cosworth)	11	8	9	r	r	6	r	4	9	r	12	12	7	8	12	r
	20	20	23	23	14	25	22	22	14	25	24	21	15	25	25	18
Gabriele TARQUINI (Osella-Alfa Romeo)	-	r	-	-	-	-	-	-	-	-	-	-	-	-	-	-
	-	25	-	-	-	-	-	-	-	-	-	-	-	-	-	-
Derek WARWICK (Arrows-Megatron)	r	11r	r	r	r	r	5	r	6	r	r	13	10	r	10	r
	8	10	12	11	10	10	13	13	9	11	12	12	12	11	13	12

	BR	RSM	MC	MEX	CDN	USA	F	GB	D	H	B	I	P	E	J	AUS
Michele ALBORETO	5	18r	3	4	r	r	3	17r	4	r	r	2f	5	r	11	r
(Ferrari)	6	10	4	5	4	3	4	2	4	15	4	4	7	10	9	12
Philippe ALLIOT	r	17	r	r	10r	r	r	14	r	12	9	r	r	14	9	10r
(Lola-Ford Cosworth)	16	15	13	13	17	14	18	22	20	20	16	20	20	12	19	24
René ARNOUX	r	-	r	r	r	r	-	18	17	r	r	13	10	r	17	r
(Ligier-Judd)	18	nq	20	20	20	20	nq	25	17	25	17	24	23	19	23	23
Julian BAILEY	-	r	-	-	r	9r	-	16	-	-	-	12	-	-	14	-
(Tyrrell-Ford Cosworth)	nq	21	nq	nq	23	22	nq	24	nq	nq	nq	26	nq	nq	26	nq
Gerhard BERGER	2f	5	2	3	r	r	4	9	3	4	rf	1	rf	6	4	r
(Ferrari)	4	5	3	3	3	2	3	1	3	9	3	3	4	8	3	4
Thierry BOUTSEN	7	4	8	8	3	3	r	r	6	3	dq	6	3	9	3	5
(Benetton-Ford Cosworth)	7	8	16	11	7	5	5	12	9	3	6	8	13	4	10	10
Martin BRUNDLE	-	-	-	-	-	-	-	-	-	-	7	-	-	-	-	-
(Williams-Judd)	-	-	-	-	-	-	-	-	-	-	12	-	-	-	-	-
Alex CAFFI	-	r	r	r	-	8	12	11	15	r	8	r	7	10	r	r
(Dallara-Ford Cosworth)	npq	24	17	23	npq	21	14	21	19	10	15	21	17	18	21	11
Adrian CAMPOS	r	16	-	-	-	-	-	-	-	-	-	-	-	-	-	-
(Minardi-Ford Cosworth)	23	22	nq	nq	-	-	-	-	-	-	-	-	-	-	-	-
Ivan CAPELLI	r	r	10	16	5	r	9	r	5	r	3	5	2	r	r	6
(March-Judd)	9	9	22	10	14	ns	10	6	7	4	14	11	3	6	4	9
Eddie CHEEVER	8	7	r	6	r	r	11	7	10	r	6	3	r	r	r	r
(Arrows-Megatron)	15	7	9	7	8	15	13	13	15	14	11	5	18	25	15	18
Yannick DALMAS	r	12	7	9	-	7	13	13	19r	9	r	r	r	11	-	-
(Lola-Ford Cosworth)	17	19	21	22	nq	24	19	23	21	17	23	25	15	16	-	-
Andrea de CESARIS	r	r	r	r	9r	4	10	r	13	r	r	r	r	r	r	8r
(Rial-Ford Cosworth)	14	16	19	12	12	12	12	14	14	18	19	18	12	23	14	15
Piercarlo GHINZANI	-	r	r	15	14r	-	-	-	14	-	r	r	-	-	-	r
(Zakspeed)	nq	25	23	18	22	nq	exc	nq	23	nq	24	16	nq	nq	nq	26
Mauricio GUGELMIN	r	15	r	r	r	r	8	4	8	5	r	8	r	7	10	r
(March-Judd)	13	20	14	16	18	13	16	5	10	8	13	13	5	11	13	19
Stefan JOHANSSON	9	-	r	10	r	r	-	-	-	r	11r	-	r	r	-	9r
(Ligier-Judd)	21	nq	26	24	25	18	nq	nq	nq	24	20	nq	24	21	nq	22
Nicola LARINI	-	-	9	-	-	r	r	19r	r	-	r	r	12	r	r	-
(Osella-Alfa Romeo)	nq	exc	25	nq	nq	26	24	26	18	npq	26	17	25	14	24	npq
Oscar LARRAURI	-	-	r	13	r	r	r	-	16	-	-	-	-	-	-	r
(EuroBrun-Ford Cosworth)	26ns	nq	18	26	24	23	26	nq	26	nq	npq	npq	npq	nq	nq	25
Nigel MANSELL	r	r	r	r	r	r	r	2f	r	r	-	-	r	2	r	r
(Williams-Judd)	2	11	5	14	9	6	9	11	11	2	-	-	6	3	8	3
Pierluigi MARTINI	-	-	-	-	-	6	15	15	-	r	-	r	r	r	13	7
(Minardi-Ford Cosworth)	-	-	-	-	-	16	22	19	nq	16	nq	14	14	20	17	14
Stefano MODENA	r	nc	-	-	12	r	14	12	r	11	-	-	-	13	-	r
(EuroBrun-Ford Cosworth)	24	26	exc	exc	15	19	20	20	25	26	nq	nq	nq	26	nq	20
Satoru NAKAJIMA	6	8	-	r	11	-	7	10	9	7	r	r	r	r	7	r
(Lotus-Honda)	10	12	nq	6	13	nq	8	10	8	19	8	12	16	15	6	13
Alessandro NANNINI	r	6	r	7	r	r	6	3	18f	r	dq	9	r	3	5	r
(Benetton-Ford Cosworth)	12	4	6	8	5	7	6	8	6	5	7	9	9	5	12	8
Jonathan PALMER	r	14	5	-	6	5	r	r	11	r	12r	-	r	r	12	r
(Tyrrell-Ford Cosworth)	22	23	10	nq	19	17	23	17	24	21	21	nq	22	22	16	17
Riccardo PATRESE	r	13	6	r	r	r	r	8	r	6	r	7	r	5	6	4
(Williams-Judd)	8	6	8	17	11	10	15	15	13	6	5	10	11	7	11	6
Nelson PIQUET	3	3	r	r	4	r	5	5	r	8	4	r	r	8	r	3
(Lotus-Honda)	5	3	11	4	6	8	7	7	5	13	9	7	8	9	5	5
Alain PROST	1	2f	1	1f	2	2f	1f	r	2	2f	2	r	1	1f	2	1f
(McLaren-Honda)	3	2	2	2	2	4	1	4	2	7	2	2	1	2	2	2
Pierre-Henri RAPHANEL	-	-	-	-	-	-	-	-	-	-	-	-	-	-	-	-
(Lola-Ford Cosworth)	-	-	-	-	-	-	-	-	-	-	-	-	-	-	-	nq
Luis SALA	r	11	r	11	13	r	nc	r	-	10	-	r	8	12	15	r
(Minardi-Ford Cosworth)	20	18	15	25	21	25	25	18	nq	11	nq	19	19	24	22	21
Jean-Louis SCHLESSER	-	-	-	-	-	-	-	-	-	-	-	11	-	-	-	-
(Williams-Judd)	-	-	-	-	-	-	-	-	-	-	-	22	-	-	-	-
Bernd SCHNEIDER	-	-	-	r	-	-	r	-	12	-	13r	r	-	-	r	-
(Zakspeed)	nq	nq	nq	15	nq	nq	21	nq	22	nq	25	15	nq	nq	25	nq
Ayrton SENNA	dq	1	rf	2	1f	1	2	1	1	1	1	10r	6	4	1f	2
(McLaren-Honda)	1	1	1	1	1	1	2	3	1	1	1	1	2	1	1	1

Season-by-Season Summary

	BR	RSM	MC	MEX	CDN	USA	F	GB	D	H	B	I	P	E	J	AUS
Philippe STREIFF	r	10	-	12	r	r	r	r	r	r	10	r	9	r	8	11r
(AGS-Ford Cosworth)	19	13	12ns	19	10	11	17	16	16	23	18	23	21	13	18	16
Aguri SUZUKI	-	-	-	-	-	-	-	-	-	-	-	-	-	-	16	-
(Lola-Ford Cosworth)	-	-	-	-	-	-	-	-	-	-	-	-	-	-	20	-
Gabriele TARQUINI	r	r	r	14	8	-	npq	npq	npq	13	nc	-	11	npq	npq	-
(Coloni-Ford Cosworth)	25	17	24	21	26	npq	npq	npq	npq	22	22	nq	26	npq	npq	nq
Derek WARWICK	4	9	4	5	7	r	r	6	7	r	5	4	4	r	r	r
(Arrows-Megatron)	11	14	7	9	16	9	11	9	12	12	10	6	10	17	7	7

1989 RACE RESULTS & GRID POSITIONS

	BR	RSM	MC	MEX	USA	CDN	F	GB	D	H	B	I	P	E	J	AUS
Michele ALBORETO	10	-	5	3	r	r	-	-	r	r	r	r	11	-	-	-
(Tyrrell-Ford Cosworth)	20	nq	12	7	9	20										
(Lola-Lamborghini)									26	26	22	13	21	npq	nq	npq
Jean ALESI	-	-	-	-	-	-	4	r	10	9	-	5	-	4	r	r
(Tyrrell-Ford Cosworth)							16	22	10	11	-	10	-	9	18	15
Philippe ALLIOT	12	r	r	nc	r	r	r	r	r	r	16r	r	9	6	r	r
(Lola-Lamborghini)	26	20	17	16	12	10	7	12	15	npq	11	7	17	5	8	19
René ARNOUX	-	-	12	14	-	5	r	-	11	-	r	9	13	-	-	r
(Ligier-Ford Cosworth)	nq	nq	21	25	nq	22	18	nq	23	nq	17	23	23	npq	nq	26
Paulo BARILLA	-	-	-	-	-	-	-	-	-	-	-	-	-	-	r	-
(Minardi-Ford Cosworth)	-	-	-	-	-	-	-	-	-	-	-	-	-	-	19	-
Gerhard BERGER	r	r	-	r	r	r	r	r	r	r	r	2	1f	2	r	r
(Ferrari)	3	5	-	6	8	4	6	4	4	6	3	2	2	2	3	14
Éric BERNARD	-	-	-	-	-	-	11r	r	-	-	-	-	-	-	-	-
(Lola-Lamborghini)	-	-	-	-	-	-	15	13	-	-	-	-	-	-	-	-
Enrico BERTAGGIA	-	-	-	-	-	-	-	-	-	-	-	-	-	-	-	-
(Coloni-Ford Cosworth)	-	-	-	-	-	-	-	-	-	-	npq	npq	npq	npq	npq	npq
Thierry BOUTSEN	r	4	10	r	6	1	r	10	r	3	4	3	r	r	3	1
(Williams-Renault)	4	6	3	8	16	6	5	7	6	4	4	6	8	21	7	5
Martin BRUNDLE	r	r	6	9	r	-	-	r	8	12	r	6	8	r	5	r
(Brabham-Judd)	13	22	4	20	5	npq	npq	20	12	15	20	12	10	8	13	12
Alex CAFFI	-	7	4	13	r	6	r	-	r	7	r	11r	r	r	9	r
(Dallara-Ford Cosworth)	npq	9	9	19	6	8	26	npq	20	3	12	20	7	23	15	10
Ivan CAPELLI	r	r	11r	r	r	r	r	r	r	r	12	r	r	r	r	r
(March-Judd)	7	13	22	4	11	21	12	8	22	14	19	18	24	19	17	16
Eddie CHEEVER	r	9	7	7	3	r	7	-	12r	5	r	-	r	r	8	r
(Arrows-Ford Cosworth)	24	21	20	24	17	16	25	nq	25	16	24	nq	26	22	24	25
Yannick DALMAS	-	-	-	-	-	-	-	-	-	-	-	-	-	-	-	-
(Lola-Lamborghini)	nq	26ns	nq	nq	nq	nq										
(AGS-Ford Cosworth)							npq	npq	npq	npq	npq	exc	npq	npq	npq	npq
Christian DANNER	14r	-	-	12	4	8	-	-	-	-	-	-	-	-	-	-
(Rial-Ford Cosworth)	17	nq	nq	23	26	23	nq	nq	nq	nq	nq	nq	nq	-	-	-
Andrea de CESARIS	13r	10	13	r	8r	3	-	r	7	r	11	r	r	7	10	r
(Dallara-Ford Cosworth)	15	16	10	12	13	9	nq	25	21	18	18	17	19	15	16	9
Martin DONNELLY	-	-	-	-	-	-	12	-	-	-	-	-	-	-	-	-
(Arrows-Ford Cosworth)	-	-	-	-	-	-	14	-	-	-	-	-	-	-	-	-
Gregor FOITEK	-	-	-	-	-	-	-	-	-	-	-	-	-	-	-	-
(EuroBrun-Judd)	nq	npq	npq	npq	npq	npq	npq	npq	npq	npq	npq					
(Rial-Ford Cosworth)	-	-	-	-	-	-	-	-	-	-	-	-	-	npq	-	-
Bertrand GACHOT	-	-	-	-	-	-	13	12	-	r	r	r	-	-	-	-
(Onyx-Ford Cosworth)	npq	npq	npq	npq	npq	npq	11	21	nq	21	23	22				
(Rial-Ford Cosworth)													-	-	nq	nq
Piercarlo GHINZANI	-	-	-	-	-	-	-	-	-	r	-	-	-	r	-	r
(Osella-Ford Cosworth)	npq	npq	npq	exc	npq	npq	npq	npq	npq	22	npq	npq	npq	25	npq	21
Olivier GROUILLARD	9	dq	r	8	-	-	6	7	r	-	13	r	-	r	r	r
(Ligier-Ford Cosworth)	22	10	16	11	nq	nq	17	24	11	nq	26	21	nq	24	23	24
Mauricio GUGELMIN	3	r	r	-	dq	r	ncf	r	r	r	7	r	10	r	7	7
(March-Judd)	12	19	14	nq	18	17	10	6	14	13	9	25	14	26	20	25
Johnny HERBERT	4	11	14	15	5	-	-	-	-	-	r	-	-	-	-	-
(Benetton-Ford Cosworth)	10	23	24	18	25	nq	-	-	-	-	-	-	-	-	-	-
(Tyrrell-Ford Cosworth)	-	-	-	-	-	-	-	-	-	-	16	-	nq	-	-	-
Stefan JOHANSSON	-	-	-	r	r	dq	5	-	r	r	8	-	3	-	-	-
(Onyx-Ford Cosworth)	npq	npq	npq	21	19	18	13	npq	24	24	15	npq	12	npq	npq	npq

	BR	RSM	MC	MEX	USA	CDN	F	GB	D	H	B	I	P	E	J	AUS
Nicola LARINI	dq	12r	-	-	-	r	-	r	-	-	-	r	-	r	r	r
(Osella-Ford Cosworth)	19	14	npq	npq	npq	15	npq	17	npq	npq	npq	24	exc	11	10	11
Oscar LARRAURI	-	-	-	-	-	-	-	-	-	-	-	-	-	-	-	-
(EuroBrun-Judd)	-	-	-	-	-	-	-	-	-	-	-	npq	npq	npq	npq	npq
J J LEHTO	-	-	-	-	-	-	-	-	-	-	-	-	-	r	-	r
(Onyx-Ford Cosworth)	-	-	-	-	-	-	-	-	-	-	-	-	npq	17	npq	17
Nigel MANSELL	1	r	r	rf	r	dq	2	2f	3	1f	3	r	r/dq	-	r	r
(Ferrari)	6	3	5	3	4	5	3	3	3	12	6	3	3	-	4	7
Pierluigi MARTINI	r	r	r	r	r	r	r	5	9	r	9	7	5	r	-	6
(Minardi-Ford Cosworth)	16	11	11	22	15	11	23	11	13	10	14	15	5	4	-	3
Stefano MODENA	r	r	3	10	r	r	r	r	r	r	11	r	-	14	r	8
(Brabham-Judd)	14	17	8	9	7	7	22	14	16	8	8	exc	11	12	9	8
Roberto MORENO	-	-	r	-	-	r	-	r	-	-	-	-	r	-	-	-
(Coloni-Ford Cosworth)	nq	nq	25	nq	nq	26	nq	23	npq	npq	npq	npq	15	npq	npq	npq
Satoru NAKAJIMA	8	nc	-	r	r	-	r	8	r	r	-	10	7	r	r	4f
(Lotus-Judd)	21	24	nq	15	23	nq	19	16	18	20	nq	19	25	18	12	23
Alessandro NANNINI	6	3	8	4	r	dq	r	3	r	r	5	r	4	r	1	2
(Benetton-Ford Cosworth)	11	7	15	13	3	13	4	9	7	7	7	8	13	14	6	4
Jonathan PALMER	7	6	9	r	9r	rf	10	r	r	13	14	r	6	10	r	-
(Tyrrell-Ford Cosworth)	18	25	23	14	21	14	9	18	19	19	21	14	18	13	26	nq
Riccardo PATRESE	rf	r	15	2	2	2	3	r	4	r	r	4	r	5	2	3
(Williams-Renault)	2	4	7	5	14	3	8	5	5	1	5	5	6	6	5	6
Nelson PIQUET	r	r	r	11	r	4	8	4	5	6	-	r	r	8	4	r
(Lotus-Judd)	9	8	19	26	22	19	20	10	8	17	nq	11	20	7	11	18
Emanuele PIRRO	-	-	-	-	-	-	9	11	r	8	10	r	r	r	r	5
(Benetton-Ford Cosworth)	-	-	-	-	-	-	24	26	9	25	13	9	16	10	22	13
Alain PROST	2	2f	2f	5	1	r	1	1	2	4	2f	1f	2	3	rf	r
(McLaren-Honda)	5	2	2	2	2	1	1	2	2	5	2	4	4	3	2	2
Pierre-Henri RAPHANEL	-	-	r	-	-	-	-	-	-	-	-	-	-	-	-	-
(Coloni-Ford Cosworth)	npq	npq	18	npq	npq	npq	npq	npq	npq	npq						
(Rial-Ford Cosworth)	-	-	-	-	-	-	-	-	-	-	nq	nq	nq	nq	nq	nq
Luis SALA	r	r	r	-	r	r	r	6	-	r	15	8	12	r	r	-
(Minardi-Ford Cosworth)	23	15	26	nq	20	24	nq	15	nq	23	25	26	9	20	14	nq
Bernd SCHNEIDER	r	-	-	-	-	-	-	-	-	-	-	-	-	-	r	-
(Zakspeed-Yamaha)	25	npq	npq	npq	npq	npq	npq	npq	npq	npq	npq	npq	npq	npq	21	npq
Ayrton SENNA	11	1	1	1	rf	7r	r	r	1f	2	1	r	r	1f	dq	r
(McLaren-Honda)	1	1	1	1	1	2	2	1	1	2	1	1	1	1	1	1
Aguri SUZUKI	-	-	-	-	-	-	-	-	-	-	-	-	-	-	-	-
(Zakspeed-Yamaha)	npq	npq	npq	npq	npq	npq	npq	npq	npq	npq	npq	npq	npq	npq	npq	npq
Gabriele TARQUINI	-	8	r	6	7r	r	r	-	-	-	-	-	-	-	-	-
(AGS-Ford Cosworth)	-	18	13	17	24	25	21	nq	npq	npq	npq	npq	npq	npq	npq	npq
Derek WARWICK	5	5	r	r	r	r	-	9	6	10	6	r	r	9	6	r
(Arrows-Ford Cosworth)	8	12	6	10	10	12	-	19	17	9	10	16	22	16	25	20
Volker WEIDLER	-	-	-	-	-	-	-	-	-	-	-	-	-	-	-	-
(Rial-Ford Cosworth)	npq	npq	npq	npq	npq	npq	npq	npq	exc	nq	-	-	-	-	-	-
Joachim WINKELHOCK	-	-	-	-	-	-	-	-	-	-	-	-	-	-	-	-
(AGS-Ford Cosworth)	npq	npq	npq	npq	npq	npq	npq	-	-	-	-	-	-	-	-	-

1990 RACE RESULTS & GRID POSITIONS

	USA	BR	RSM	MC	CDN	MEX	F	GB	D	H	B	I	P	E	J	AUS
Michele ALBORETO	10	r	-	-	r	17	10	r	r	12	13	12r	9	10	r	-
(Arrows-Ford Cosworth)	21	23	nq	nq	14	17	18	25	19	22	26	22	19	25	24	nq
Jean ALESI	2	7	6	2	r	7	r	8	11r	r	8	r	8	r	-	8
(Tyrrell-Ford Cosworth)	4	7	7	3	8	6	13	6	8	6	9	5	8	4	ns	5
Philippe ALLIOT	-	12	9	r	r	18	9	13	dq	14	-	13	r	r	10	11
(Ligier-Ford Cosworth)	exc	10	16	18	17	22	12	22	24	21	nq	20	20	13	20	19
Paulo BARILLA	r	r	11	r	-	14	-	12	-	15	r	-	-	-	-	-
(Minardi-Ford Cosworth)	14	17	26	19	nq	16	nq	24	nq	23	25	nq	nq	nq	-	-
Gerhard BERGER	rf	2f	2	3	4f	3	5	14r	3	16r	3	3	4	r	r	4
(McLaren-Honda)	1	2	2	5	2	1	2	3	2	3	2	3	4	5	4	2
Éric BERNARD	8	r	13r	6	9	r	8	4	r	6	9	r	r	r	r	r
(Lola-Lamborghini)	15	11	13	24	23	25	11	8	12	12	15	13	10	18	16	23
Thierry BOUTSEN	3	5	r	4	r	5	r	2	6f	1	r	r	r	4	5	5
(Williams-Renault)	9	3	4	6	6	5	8	4	6	1	4	6	7	7	5	9
David BRABHAM	-	-	-	r	-	r	15	-	r	-	r	-	r	-	r	r
(Brabham-Judd)	-	-	nq	25	nq	21	25	nq	21	nq	24	nq	25	nq	22	25

	USA	BR	RSM	MC	CDN	MEX	F	GB	D	H	B	I	P	E	J	AUS
Gary BRABHAM	-	-	-	-	-	-	-	-	-	-	-	-	-	-	-	-
(Life)	npq	npq	-	-	-	-	-	-	-	-	-	-	-	-	-	-
Alex CAFFI	-	r	-	5	8	-	r	7	9	9	10	9	13r	-	9	-
(Arrows-Ford Cosworth)	-	25	nq	22	26	nq	22	17	18	26	19	21	17	-	23	nq
Ivan CAPELLI	r	-	r	r	10	-	2	r	7	r	7	r	r	r	r	r
(Leyton House-Judd)	26	nq	18	23	24	-	7	10	10	16	12	16	12	19	12	14
Yannick DALMAS	-	r	-	-	-	-	17	-	-	-	-	nc	r	9	-	-
(AGS-Ford Cosworth)	npq	26	-	npq	npq	npq	26	npq	nq	nq	nq	24	24	23	nq	nq
Andrea de CESARIS	r	r	r	r	r	13	dq	r	-	r	r	10	r	r	r	r
(Dallara-Ford Cosworth)	3	9	17	12	25	15	21	23	nq	10	20	25	18	17	25	15
Martin DONNELLY	-	r	8	r	r	8	12	r	r	7	12	r	r	-	-	-
(Lotus-Lamborghini)	19ns	14	11	11	12	12	17	14	20	18	22	11	15	ns	-	-
Gregor FOITEK	r	r	r	7r	r	15	-	-	r	-	-	-	-	-	-	-
(Brabham-Judd)	23	22	-	-	-	-	-	-	-	-	-	-	-	-	-	-
(Onyx-Ford Cosworth)	-	-	23	20	21	23	nq	nq	26	nq	-	-	-	-	-	-
Bertrand GACHOT	-	-	-	-	-	-	-	-	-	-	-	-	-	-	-	-
(Coloni-Subaru)	npq	npq	npq	npq	npq	npq	npq	npq	-	-	-	-	-	-	-	-
(Coloni-Ford Cosworth)	-	-	-	-	-	-	-	-	npq	npq	nq	nq	nq	nq	nq	nq
Bruno GIACOMELLI	-	-	-	-	-	-	-	-	-	-	-	-	-	-	-	-
(Life)	-	-	npq	npq	npq	npq	npq	npq	npq	npq	npq	npq	-	-	-	-
(Life-Judd)	-	-	-	-	-	-	-	-	-	-	-	-	npq	npq	-	-
Olivier GROUILLARD	r	r	r	-	13	19	-	-	-	-	16	r	-	r	-	13
(Osella-Ford Cosworth)	8	21	22	nq	15	20	npq	nq	nq	npq	23	23	nq	21	nq	22
Mauricio GUGELMIN	14	-	r	-	-	-	r	-	r	8	6	r	12	8	r	r
(Leyton House-Judd)	25	nq	12	nq	nq	nq	10	15ns	14	17	14	10	14	12	15	16
Johnny HERBERT	-	-	-	-	-	-	-	-	-	-	-	-	-	-	r	r
(Lotus-Lamborghini)	-	-	-	-	-	-	-	-	-	-	-	-	-	-	14	18
Stefan JOHANSSON	-	-	-	-	-	-	-	-	-	-	-	-	-	-	-	-
(Onyx-Ford Cosworth)	nq	nq	-	-	-	-	-	-	-	-	-	-	-	-	-	-
Claudio LANGES	-	-	-	-	-	-	-	-	-	-	-	-	-	-	-	-
(EuroBrun-Judd)	npq	npq	npq	npq	npq	npq	npq	npq	npq	npq	npq	npq	npq	npq	-	-
Nicola LARINI	r	11	10	r	r	16	14	10	10	11	14	11	10	7	7	10
(Ligier-Ford Cosworth)	13	20	20	17	20	24	19	21	22	25	21	26	22	20	17	12
J J LEHTO	-	-	12	r	r	r	-	-	nc	-	-	-	-	-	-	-
(Onyx-Ford Cosworth)	nq	nq	25	26	22	26	nq	nq	25	nq	-	-	-	-	-	-
Nigel MANSELL	r	4	r	r	3	2	18rf	rf	r	17r	r	4	1	2	r	2f
(Ferrari)	17	5	5	7	7	4	1	1	4	5	5	4	1	3	3	3
Pierluigi MARTINI	7	9	-	r	r	12	r	r	r	r	15	r	11	r	8	9
(Minardi-Ford Cosworth)	2	8	ns	8	16	7	23	18	15	14	16	15	16	11	10	10
Stefano MODENA	5	r	r	r	7	11	13	9	r	r	17r	r	r	r	r	12
(Brabham-Judd)	10	12	14	14	10	10	20	20	17	20	13	17	23	24	21	17
Gianni MORBIDELLI	-	14	-	-	-	-	-	-	-	-	-	-	-	-	r	r
(Dallara-Ford Cosworth)	nq	16	-	-	-	-	-	-	-	-	-	-	-	-	-	-
(Minardi-Ford Cosworth)	-	-	-	-	-	-	-	-	-	-	-	-	-	-	19	20
Roberto MORENO	13	-	r	-	-	-	-	-	-	-	-	-	-	-	2	7
(EuroBrun-Judd)	16	npq	24	nq	nq	exc	npq	npq	npq	npq	npq	npq	npq	npq	-	-
(Benetton-Ford Cosworth)	-	-	-	-	-	-	-	-	-	-	-	-	-	-	8	8
Satoru NAKAJIMA	6	8	r	r	11	r	r	r	r	r	r	6	-	r	6	r
(Tyrrell-Ford Cosworth)	11	19	19	21	13	9	15	12	13	15	10	14	ns	14	13	13
Alessandro NANNINI	11	10	3f	r	r	4	16r	r	2	r	4	8	6	3	-	-
(Benetton-Ford Cosworth)	22	15	9	16	4	14	5	13	9	7	6	8	9	9	-	-
Riccardo PATRESE	9	13r	1	r	r	9	6	r	5	4f	r	5	7f	5f	4f	6
(Williams-Renault)	12	4	3	4	9	2	6	7	5	2	7	7	5	6	7	6
Nelson PIQUET	4	6	5	dq	2	6	4	5	r	3	5	7	5	r	1	1
(Benetton-Ford Cosworth)	6	13	8	10	5	8	9	11	7	9	8	9	6	8	6	7
Emanuele PIRRO	-	-	r	r	r	r	r	11	r	10	r	17	r	15	r	r
(Dallara-Ford Cosworth)	-	-	21	9	19	18	24	19	23	13	17	19	13	16	18	21
Alain PROST	r	1	4	r	5	1f	1	1	4	r	2f	2	3	1	r	3
(Ferrari)	7	6	6	2	3	13	4	5	3	8	3	2	2	2	2	4
Bernd SCHNEIDER	12	-	-	-	-	-	-	-	-	-	-	-	-	-	-	-
(Arrows-Ford Cosworth)	20	-	-	-	-	-	-	-	-	-	-	-	-	nq	-	-
Ayrton SENNA	1	3	r	1f	1	20r	3	3	1	2	1	1f	2	r	r	r
(McLaren-Honda)	5	1	1	1	1	3	3	2	1	4	1	1	3	1	1	1
Aguri SUZUKI	r	r	r	r	12	r	7	6	r	r	r	r	14r	6	3	r
(Lola-Lamborghini)	18	18	15	15	18	19	14	9	11	19	11	18	11	15	9	24
Gabriele TARQUINI	-	-	-	-	-	-	-	r	-	13	-	-	-	r	-	r
(AGS-Ford Cosworth)	npq	npq	npq	npq	npq	npq	nq	26	npq	24	nq	nq	nq	22	nq	26
Derek WARWICK	r	r	7	r	6	10	11	r	8	5	11	r	r	r	r	r
(Lotus-Lamborghini)	24	24	10	13	11	11	16	16	16	11	18	12	21	10	11	11

Onyx renamed Monteverdi for Germany and Hungary

	USA	BR	RSM	MC	CDN	MEX	F	GB	D	H	B	I	P	E	J	AUS
Michele ALBORETO	r	-	-	r	r	r	r	r	-	-	-	-	15	r	-	13
(Footwork-Porsche)	25	nq	nq	25	21	26	-	-	-	-	-	-	-	-	-	-
(Footwork-Ford Cosworth)	-	-	-	-	-	-	25	26	nq	nq	npq	nq	24	24	nq	15
Jean ALESI	12rf	6	r	3	r	r	4	r	3	5	r	r	3	4	r	r
(Ferrari)	6	5	7	9	7	4	6	6	6	6	5	6	6	7	6	7
Julian BAILEY	-	-	6	-	-	-	-	-	-	-	-	-	-	-	-	-
(Lotus-Judd)	nq	nq	26	nq	-	-	-	-	-	-	-	-	-	-	-	-
Fabrizio BARBAZZA	-	-	-	-	-	-	-	-	-	-	-	-	-	-	-	-
(AGS-Ford Cosworth)	-	-	nq	nq	nq	nq	nq	nq	npq	npq	npq	npq	npq	npq	-	-
Michael BARTELS	-	-	-	-	-	-	-	-	-	-	-	-	-	-	-	-
(Lotus-Judd)	-	-	-	-	-	-	-	-	nq	nq	-	nq	-	nq	-	-
Gerhard BERGER	r	3	2f	r	r	r	r	2	4	4	2	4	r	r	1	3f
(McLaren-Honda)	7	4	5	6	6	5	5	4	3	5	4	3	2	1	1	2
Éric BERNARD	r	r	r	9	r	6	r	r	r	r	r	r	-	r	-	-
(Lola-Ford Cosworth)	19	11	17	21	19	18	23	21	25	21	20	24	nq	23	nq	-
Mark BLUNDELL	r	r	8	r	-	r	r	r	12	r	6	12	r	r	-	17
(Brabham-Yamaha)	24	25	23	22	nq	12	17	12	21	20	13	11	15	12	npq	17
Thierry BOUTSEN	r	10	7	7	r	8	12	r	9	17r	11	r	16	r	9	r
(Ligier-Lamborghini)	20	18	24	16	16	14	16	19	17	19	18	21	20	26	17	20
Martin BRUNDLE	11	12	11	-	r	r	r	r	11	r	9	13	12	10	5	-
(Brabham-Yamaha)	12	26	18	exc	20	17	24	14	15	10	16	19	19	11	19	nq
Alex CAFFI	-	-	-	-	-	-	-	-	-	-	-	-	-	-	10	15
(Footwork-Porsche)	nq	nq	nq	nq	-	-	-	-	-	-	-	-	-	-	-	-
(Footwork-Ford Cosworth)	-	-	-	-	-	-	-	-	npq	npq	nq	npq	npq	npq	26	23
Ivan CAPELLI	r	r	r	r	r	r	r	r	r	6	r	8	17r	r	-	-
(Leyton House-Ilmor)	18	15	22	18	13	22	15	16	12	9	12	12	9	8	-	-
Pedro CHAVES	-	-	-	-	-	-	-	-	-	-	-	-	-	-	-	-
(Coloni-Ford Cosworth)	npq	npq	npq	npq	npq	npq	npq	npq	npq	npq	npq	npq	npq	-	-	-
Erik COMAS	-	r	10	10	8	-	11	-	r	10	r	11	11	r	r	18
(Ligier-Lamborghini)	nq	23	19	23	26	nq	14	nq	26	25	26	22	23	25	20	22
Andrea de CESARIS	-	r	r	r	4	4r	6	r	5	7	13r	7	8	r	r	8
(Jordan-Ford Cosworth)	npq	13	11	10	11	11	13	13	7	17	11	14	14	17	11	12
Bertrand GACHOT	10r	13r	r	8	5	r	r	6	6	9f	-	-	-	-	-	-
(Jordan-Ford Cosworth)	14	10	12	24	14	20	19	17	11	16	-	-	-	-	-	-
(Lola-Ford Cosworth)	-	-	-	-	-	-	-	-	-	-	-	-	-	-	-	nq
Olivier GROUILLARD	-	-	-	-	-	r	r	-	-	-	10	r	-	-	-	-
(Fomet-Ford Cosworth)	npq	npq	npq	npq	npq	10	21	npq	npq	nq	23	26	npq	-	-	-
(AGS-Ford Cosworth)	-	-	-	-	-	-	-	-	-	-	-	-	-	npq	-	-
Mauricio GUGELMIN	r	r	12r	r	r	r	7	r	r	11	r	15	7	7	8	14r
(Leyton House-Ilmor)	23	8	15	15	23	21	9	9	16	13	15	18	7	13	18	14
Mika HÄKKINEN	r	9	5	r	r	9	-	12	r	14	r	14	14	r	r	19
(Lotus-Judd)	13	22	25	26	24	24	nq	25	23	26	24	25	26	21	21	25
Naoki HATTORI	-	-	-	-	-	-	-	-	-	-	-	-	-	-	-	-
(Coloni-Ford Cosworth)	-	-	-	-	-	-	-	-	-	-	-	-	-	-	npq	npq
Johnny HERBERT	-	-	-	-	-	10	10	14r	-	-	7	-	r	-	r	11
(Lotus-Judd)	-	-	-	-	nq	25	20	24	-	-	21	-	22	-	23	21
Stefan JOHANSSON	-	-	-	-	r	-	-	-	-	-	-	-	-	-	-	-
(AGS-Ford Cosworth)	nq	nq	-	-	-	-	-	-	-	-	-	-	-	-	-	-
(Footwork-Porsche)	-	-	-	-	25	nq	-	-	-	-	-	-	-	-	-	-
(Footwork-Ford Cosworth)	-	-	-	-	-	-	nq	nq	-	-	-	-	-	-	-	-
Nicola LARINI	7	-	-	-	-	-	-	-	r	16	-	16	-	-	-	r
(Lamborghini)	17	npq	npq	npq	npq	exc	npq	npq	24	24	nq	23	nq	nq	nq	19
J J LEHTO	r	r	3	11	r	r	r	r	13	r	r	r	r	8	r	12
(Dallara-Judd)	10	19	16	13	17	16	26	11	20	12	14	20	18	15	12	11
Nigel MANSELL	r	rf	r	2	6rf	2f	1f	1f	1	2	r	1	dqf	1	r	2
(Williams-Renault)	4	3	4	5	2	2	4	1	1	3	3	2	4	2	3	3
Pierluigi MARTINI	9r	r	4	12	7	r	9	9	r	r	12	r	4	13	r	r
(Minardi-Ferrari)	15	20	9	14	18	15	12	23	10	18	9	10	8	19	7	10
Stefano MODENA	4	r	r	r	2	11	r	7	13	12	r	r	r	16	6	10
(Tyrrell-Honda)	11	9	6	2	9	8	11	10	14	8	10	13	12	14	14	9
Gianni MORBIDELLI	r	8	r	r	r	7	r	11	r	13	r	9	9	14r	r	6
(Minardi-Ferrari)	26	21	8	17	15	23	10	20	19	23	19	17	13	16	8	-
(Ferrari)	-	-	-	-	-	-	-	-	-	-	-	-	-	-	-	8
Roberto MORENO	r	7	13r	4	r	5	r	r	8	8	4f	r	10	-	-	16
(Benetton-Ford Cosworth)	8	14	13	8	5	9	8	7	9	15	8	-	-	-	-	-
(Jordan-Ford Cosworth)	-	-	-	-	-	-	-	-	-	-	-	-	9	16	-	-
(Minardi-Ferrari)	-	-	-	-	-	-	-	-	-	-	-	-	-	-	-	18

Season-by-Season Summary

	USA	BR	RSM	MC	CDN	MEX	F	GB	D	H	B	I	P	E	J	AUS
Satoru NAKAJIMA	5	r	r	r	10	12	r	8	r	15	r	r	13	17	r	r
(Tyrrell-Honda)	16	16	10	11	12	13	18	15	13	14	22	15	21	18	15	24
Riccardo PATRESE	r	2	r	r	3	1	5	r	2f	3	5	r	1	3f	3	5
(Williams-Renault)	3	2	2	3	1	1	1	3	4	2	17	4	1	4	5	4
Nelson PIQUET	3	5	r	r	1	r	8	5	r	r	3	6	5	11	7	4
(Benetton-Ford Cosworth)	5	7	14	4	8	6	7	8	8	11	6	8	11	10	10	5
Emanuele PIRRO	r	11	-	r	6	9	-	-	10	10	r	8	10	r	15	7
(Dallara-Judd)	9	12	npq	12	10	npq	npq	18	18	7	25	16	17	9	16	13
Alain PROST	2	4	-	5f	r	r	2	3	r	r	r	3	r	2	4	-
(Ferrari)	2	6	3ns	7	4	7	2	5	5	4	2	5	5	6	4	-
Michael SCHUMACHER	-	-	-	-	-	-	-	-	-	-	r	5	6	6	r	r
(Jordan-Ford Cosworth)	-	-	-	-	-	-	-	-	-	-	7	-	-	-	-	-
(Benetton-Ford Cosworth)	-	-	-	-	-	-	-	-	-	-	-	7	10	5	9	6
Ayrton SENNA	1	1	1	1	r	3	3	4r	7r	1	1	2f	2	5	2f	1
(McLaren-Honda)	1	1	1	1	3	3	3	2	2	1	1	1	3	3	2	1
Aguri SUZUKI	6	-	r	r	r	r	r	r	r	r	-	-	r	-	r	-
(Lola-Ford Cosworth)	21	17ns	20	19	22	19	22	22	22	22	nq	nq	25	nq	25	nq
Gabriele TARQUINI	8	r	-	r	-	-	-	-	-	-	-	-	-	12	11	-
(AGS-Ford Cosworth)	22	24	nq	20	nq	nq	nq	nq	nq	npq	npq	npq	nq	-	-	-
(Fomet-Ford Cosworth)	-	-	-	-	-	-	-	-	-	-	-	-	-	22	24	npq
Eric van de POELE	-	-	9r	-	-	-	-	-	-	-	-	-	-	-	-	-
(Lamborghini)	npq	npq	21	npq	npq	npq	npq	npq	nq	nq	nq	nq	nq	nq	nq	nq
Karl WENDLINGER	-	-	-	-	-	-	-	-	-	-	-	-	-	-	r	20
(Leyton House-Ilmor)	-	-	-	-	-	-	-	-	-	-	-	-	-	-	22	26
Alessandro ZANARDI	-	-	-	-	-	-	-	-	-	-	-	-	-	9	r	9
(Jordan-Ford Cosworth)	-	-	-	-	-	-	-	-	-	-	-	-	-	20	13	16

1992 RACE RESULTS & GRID POSITIONS

	ZA	MEX	BR	E	RSM	MC	CDN	F	GB	D	H	B	I	P	J	AUS
Michele ALBORETO	10	13	6	5	5	7	7	7	7	9	7	r	7	6	15	r
(Footwork-Mugen Honda)	17	25	14	16	9	11	16	14	12	17	7	14	16	8	24	11
Jean ALESI	r	r	4	3	r	r	3	r	r	5	r	r	r	r	5	4
(Ferrari)	5	10	6	8	7	4	8	6	8	5	9	5	3	10	15	6
Giovanna AMATI	-	-	-	-	-	-	-	-	-	-	-	-	-	-	-	-
(Brabham-Judd)	nq	nq	nq	-	-	-	-	-	-	-	-	-	-	-	-	-
Paul BELMONDO	-	-	-	12	13	-	14	-	-	13	9	-	-	-	-	-
(March-Ilmor)	nq	nq	nq	23	24	nq	20	nq	nq	22	17	-	-	-	-	-
Gerhard BERGER	5	4f	r	4	r	r	1f	r	5	r	3	r	4	2	2	1
(McLaren-Honda)	3	5	4	7	4	5	4	4	5	4	5	6	5	4	4	4
Thierry BOUTSEN	r	10	r	r	r	12	10	r	10	7	r	r	r	r	r	5
(Ligier-Renault)	14	22	10	14	10	22	21	9	13	8	8	7	8	11	10	22
Martin BRUNDLE	r	r	r	r	4	5	r	3	3	4	5	4	2	4	3	3
(Benetton-Ford Cosworth)	8	4	7	6	6	7	7	7	6	9	6	9	9	6	13	8
Ivan CAPELLI	r	r	5	10r	r	r	r	r	9	r	6	r	r	r	-	-
(Ferrari)	9	20	11	5	8	8	9	8	14	12	10	12	7	16	-	-
Andrea CHIESA	-	r	-	r	-	-	-	r	-	-	-	-	-	-	-	-
(Fondmetal-Ford Cosworth)	nq	23	nq	20	nq	nq	nq	26	nq	nq	-	-	-	-	-	-
Erik COMAS	7	9	r	r	9	10	6	5	8	6	r	-	r	r	r	r
(Ligier-Renault)	13	26	15	10	13	23	22	10	10	7	11	nq	15	14	8	9
Andrea de CESARIS	r	5	r	r	14r	r	5	r	r	r	8	8	6	9	4	r
(Tyrrell-Ilmor)	10	11	13	11	14	10	14	19	18	20	19	13	21	12	9	7
Christian FITTIPALDI	r	r	r	11	r	8	13r	-	-	-	-	-	12	6	9	
(Minardi-Lamborghini)	20	17	20	22	25	17	25	nq	-	-	-	nq	nq	26	12	17
Bertrand GACHOT	r	11	r	r	r	6	dq	r	r	14	r	18r	r	r	r	r
(Venturi Larrousse-Lamborghini)	22	13	18	24	19	15	19	13	11	25	15	20	10	13	18	21
Olivier GROUILLARD	r	r	r	r	8	r	12	11	11	r	r	r	r	r	r	r
(Tyrrell-Ilmor)	12	16	17	15	20	24	26	22	20	14	22	22	18	15	21	13
Mauricio GUGELMIN	11	r	r	r	7	r	r	r	r	15	10	14	r	r	r	r
(Jordan-Yamaha)	23	8	21	17	18	13	24	24	24	23	21	24	26	20	25	20
Mika HÄKKINEN	9	6	10	r	-	r	r	4	6	r	4	6	r	5	r	7
(Lotus-Ford Cosworth)	21	18	24	21	nq	14	10	11	9	13	16	8	11	7	7	10
Johnny HERBERT	6	7	r	r	r	r	r	6	r	r	r	13r	r	r	r	13
(Lotus-Ford Cosworth)	11	12	26	26	26	9	6	12	7	11	13	10	13	9	6	12
Damon HILL	-	-	-	-	-	-	-	-	16	-	11	-	-	-	-	-
(Brabham-Judd)	-	-	-	nq	nq	nq	nq	nq	26	nq	25	-	-	-	-	-

	ZA	MEX	BR	E	RSM	MC	CDN	F	GB	D	H	B	I	P	J	AUS
Ukyo KATAYAMA	12	12	9	-	r	-	r	r	r	r	r	17	9r	r	11	r
(Venturi Larrousse-Lamborghini)	18	24	25	nq	17	npq	11	18	16	16	20	26	23	25	20	26
Jan LAMMERS	-	-	-	-	-	-	-	-	-	-	-	-	-	-	r	12
(March-Ilmor)	-	-	-	-	-	-	-	-	-	-	-	-	-	-	23	25
Nicola LARINI	-	-	-	-	-	-	-	-	-	-	-	-	-	-	12	11
(Ferrari)	-	-	-	-	-	-	-	-	-	-	-	-	-	-	11	19
J J LEHTO	r	8	8	r	11r	9	9	9	13	10	-	7	11r	r	9	r
(Dallara-Ferrari)	24	7	16	12	16	20	23	17	19	21	nq	16	14	19	22	24
Nigel MANSELL	1f	1	1	1f	1	2f	r	1f	1f	1	2f	2	rf	1	rf	r
(Williams-Renault)	1	1	1	1	1	1	3	1	1	1	2	1	1	1	1	1
Pierluigi MARTINI	r	r	r	6	6	r	8	10	15	11	r	r	8	r	10	r
(Dallara-Ferrari)	25	9	8	13	15	18	15	25	22	18	26	19	22	21	19	14
Perry McCARTHY	-	-	-	npq	npq	npq	-	-	npq	exc	npq	nq	-	-	-	-
(Andrea Moda-Judd)	-	-	-	-	-	-	-	-	-	-	-	-	-	-	-	-
Stefano MODENA	-	r	r	-	r	r	r	r	r	-	r	15	-	13	7	6
(Jordan-Yamaha)	nq	15	12	nq	23	21	17	20	23	nq	24	17	nq	24	17	15
Gianni MORBIDELLI	r	r	7	r	r	r	11	8	17r	12	-	16	r	14	14	10
(Minardi-Lamborghini)	19	21	23	25	21	12	13	16	25	26	nq	23	12	18	14	16
Roberto MORENO	-	-	-	-	-	r	-	-	-	-	-	-	-	-	-	-
(Andrea Moda-Judd)	-	-	npq	npq	npq	26	npq	-	npq	npq	nq	nq	-	-	-	-
Emanuele NASPETTI	-	-	-	-	-	-	-	-	-	-	-	12	r	11	13	r
(March-Ilmor)	-	-	-	-	-	-	-	-	-	-	-	21	24	23	26	23
Riccardo PATRESE	2	2	2f	r	2f	3	r	2	2	8rf	r	3	5	r	1	r
(Williams-Renault)	4	2	2	4	2	2	2	2	2	2	1	4	4	2	2	3
Michael SCHUMACHER	4	3	3	2	r	4	2	r	4	3	r	1f	3	7	r	2f
(Benetton-Ford Cosworth)	6	3	5	2	5	6	5	5	4	6	4	3	6	5	5	5
Ayrton SENNA	3	r	r	9r	3	1	r	r	r	2	1	5	1	3f	r	r
(McLaren-Honda)	2	6	3	3	3	3	1	3	3	3	3	2	2	3	3	2
Aguri SUZUKI	8	-	r	7	10	11	-	r	12	r	r	9	r	10	8	8
(Footwork-Mugen Honda)	16	nq	22	19	11	19	nq	15	17	15	14	25	19	17	16	18
Gabriele TARQUINI	r	r	r	r	r	r	r	r	14	r	r	r	r	-	-	-
(Fondmetal-Ford Cosworth)	15	14	19	18	22	25	18	23	15	19	12	11	20	-	-	-
Eric van de POELE	13	-	-	-	-	-	-	-	-	-	r	10	r	-	-	-
(Brabham-Judd)	26	nq	nq	nq	nq	nq	nq	nq	nq	nq	-	-	-	-	-	-
(Fondmetal-Ford Cosworth)	-	-	-	-	-	-	-	-	-	-	18	15	25	-	-	-
Karl WENDLINGER	r	r	r	8	12	r	4	r	r	16	r	11	10	r	-	-
(March-Ilmor)	7	19	9	9	12	16	12	21	21	10	23	18	17	22	-	-
Alessandro ZANARDI	-	-	-	-	-	-	-	-	-	r	-	-	-	-	-	-
(Minardi-Lamborghini)	-	-	-	-	-	-	-	nq	24	nq	-	-	-	-	-	-

1993 RACE RESULTS & GRID POSITIONS

	ZA	BR	EUR	RSM	E	MC	CDN	F	GB	D	H	B	I	P	J	AUS
Michele ALBORETO	r	11	11	-	-	r	-	-	-	16	r	14	r	r	-	-
(Lola-Ferrari)	25	25	24	nq	nq	24	nq	nq	nq	26	25	25	21	25	-	-
Jean ALESI	r	8	r	r	r	3	r	r	9	7	r	r	2	4	r	4
(Ferrari)	5	9	9	9	8	5	6	6	12	10	8	4	3	5	14	7
Philippe ALLIOT	r	7	r	5	r	12	r	9	11	12	8	12	9	10	-	-
(Larrousse-Lamborghini)	11	11	15	14	13	15	15	10	24	23	19	18	16	20	-	-
Michael ANDRETTI	r	r	r	r	5	8	14	6	r	r	r	8	3	-	-	-
(McLaren-Ford Cosworth)	9	5	6	6	7	9	12	16	11	12	11	14	9	-	-	-
Marco APICELLA	-	-	-	-	-	-	-	-	-	-	-	-	r	-	-	-
(Jordan-Hart)	-	-	-	-	-	-	-	-	-	-	-	-	23	-	-	-
Luca BADOER	r	12	-	7	r	-	15	r	r	r	r	13	10	14	-	-
(Lola-Ferrari)	26	21	nq	24	22	nq	25	22	25	25	26	24	25	26	-	-
Fabrizio BARBAZZA	r	r	6	6	r	11	r	r	-	-	-	-	-	-	-	-
(Minardi-Ford Cosworth)	24	24	20	25	25	25	23	24	-	-	-	-	-	-	-	-
Rubens BARRICHELLO	r	r	10r	r	12	9	r	7	10	r	r	r	r	13	5	11
(Jordan-Hart)	14	14	12	13	17	16	14	8	15	17	16	13	19	15	12	13
Gerhard BERGER	6r	r	r	r	6	14r	4	14	r	6	3	10r	r	r	r	5
(Ferrari)	15	13	8	8	11	7	5	14	13	9	6	16	6	8	5	6
Mark BLUNDELL	3	5	r	r	7	r	r	r	7	3	7	11r	r	r	7	9
(Ligier-Renault)	8	10	21	7	12	21	10	4	9	5	12	15	14	10	17	14
Thierry BOUTSEN	-	-	r	r	11	r	12	11	r	13	9	r	-	-	-	-
(Jordan-Hart)	-	-	19	19	21	23	24	20	23	24	24	20	-	-	-	-

	ZA	BR	EUR	RSM	E	MC	CDN	F	GB	D	H	B	I	P	J	AUS
Martin BRUNDLE	r	r	r	3	r	6	5	5	14r	8	5	7	r	6	9r	6
(Ligier-Renault)	12	16	22	10	18	13	7	3	6	6	13	11	12	11	15	8
Ivan CAPELLI	r	-	-	-	-	-	-	-	-	-	-	-	-	-	-	-
(Jordan-Hart)	18	nq	-	-	-	-	-	-	-	-	-	-	-	-	-	-
Erik COMAS	r	10	9	r	9	r	8	16r	r	r	r	r	6	11	r	12
(Larrousse-Lamborghini)	19	17	17	17	14	10	13	9	17	16	18	19	20	22	21	21
Andrea de CESARIS	r	r	r	r	dq	10	r	15	r	r	11	r	13r	12	r	13
(Tyrrell-Yamaha)	23	23	25	18	24	19	19	25	21	19	22	17	18	17	18	15
Christian FITTIPALDI	4	r	7	r	8	5	9	8	12r	11	r	r	8	9	-	-
(Minardi-Ford Cosworth)	13	20	16	23	20	17	17	23	19	20	14	22	24	24	-	-
Jean-Marc GOUNON	-	-	-	-	-	-	-	-	-	-	-	-	-	-	r	r
(Minardi-Ford Cosworth)	-	-	-	-	-	-	-	-	-	-	-	-	-	-	24	22
Mika HÄKKINEN	-	-	-	-	-	-	-	-	-	-	-	-	-	r	3	r
(McLaren-Ford Cosworth)	-	-	-	-	-	-	-	-	-	-	-	-	-	3	3	5
Johnny HERBERT	r	4	4	8r	r	r	10	r	4	10	r	5	r	r	11	r
(Lotus-Ford Cosworth)	17	12	11	12	10	14	20	19	7	13	20	10	7	14	19	20
Damon HILL	r	2	2	r	r	2	3	2	rf	15r	1	1	1f	3f	4	3f
(Williams-Renault)	4	2	2	2	2	4	2	1	2	2	2	2	2	1	6	3
Eddie IRVINE	-	-	-	-	-	-	-	-	-	-	-	-	-	-	6	r
(Jordan-Hart)	-	-	-	-	-	-	-	-	-	-	-	-	-	-	8	19
Ukyo KATAYAMA	r	r	r	r	r	r	17	r	13	r	10	15	14	r	r	r
(Tyrrell-Yamaha)	21	22	18	22	23	22	22	21	22	21	23	23	17	21	13	18
Pedro LAMY	-	-	-	-	-	-	-	-	-	-	-	-	11r	r	13r	r
(Lotus-Ford Cosworth)	-	-	-	-	-	-	-	-	-	-	-	-	26	18	20	23
J J LEHTO	5	r	r	4r	r	r	7	r	8	r	r	9	r	7	8	r
(Sauber-Ilmor)	6	7	7	16	9	11	11	18	16	18	15	9	13	12	11	12
Pierluigi MARTINI	-	-	-	-	-	-	-	-	r	14	r	r	7	8	10	r
(Minardi-Ford Cosworth)	-	-	-	-	-	-	-	-	20	22	7	21	22	19	22	16
Emanuele NASPETTI	-	-	-	-	-	-	-	-	-	-	-	-	-	r	-	-
(Jordan-Hart)	-	-	-	-	-	-	-	-	-	-	-	-	-	23	-	-
Riccardo PATRESE	r	r	5	r	4	r	r	10	3	5	2	6	5	16r	r	8r
(Benetton-Ford Cosworth)	7	6	10	11	5	6	4	12	5	7	5	8	10	7	10	9
Alain PROST	1f	r	3	1f	1	4f	1	1	1	1	12f	3f	12r	2	2f	2
(Williams-Renault)	1	1	1	1	1	1	1	2	1	1	1	1	1	2	1	2
Michael SCHUMACHER	r	3f	r	2	3f	r	2f	3f	2	2f	r	2	r	1	r	r
(Benetton-Ford Cosworth)	3	4	3	3	4	2	3	7	3	3	3	3	5	6	4	4
Ayrton SENNA	2	1	1f	r	2	1	18r	4	5r	4	r	4	r	r	1	1
(McLaren-Ford Cosworth)	2	3	4	4	3	3	8	5	4	4	4	5	4	4	2	1
Aguri SUZUKI	r	r	r	9	10	r	13	12	r	r	r	r	r	r	r	7
(Footwork-Mugen Honda)	20	19	23	21	19	18	16	13	10	8	10	6	8	16	9	10
Toshio SUZUKI	-	-	-	-	-	-	-	-	-	-	-	-	-	-	12	14
(Larrousse-Lamborghini)	-	-	-	-	-	-	-	-	-	-	-	-	-	-	23	24
Derek WARWICK	7r	9	r	r	13	r	16	13	6	17	4	r	r	15r	14r	10
(Footwork-Mugen Honda)	22	18	14	15	16	12	18	15	8	11	9	7	11	9	7	17
Karl WENDLINGER	r	r	r	r	r	13	6	r	r	9	6	r	4	5	r	15r
(Sauber-Ilmor)	10	8	5	5	6	8	9	11	18	14	17	12	15	13	16	11
Alessandro ZANARDI	r	6	8	r	14r	7	11	r	r	r	r	ns	-	-	-	-
(Lotus-Ford Cosworth)	16	15	13	20	15	20	21	17	14	15	21	ns	-	-	-	-

1994 RACE RESULTS & GRID POSITIONS

	BR	PAC	RSM	MC	E	CDN	F	GB	D	H	B	I	P	EUR	J	AUS
Philippe ADAMS	-	-	-	-	-	-	-	-	-	-	r	-	16	-	-	-
(Lotus-Mugen Honda)	-	-	-	-	-	-	-	-	-	-	26	-	25	-	-	-
Michele ALBORETO	r	r	r	6	r	11	r	r	r	7	9	r	13	14	r	r
(Minardi-Ford Cosworth)	22	15	15	12	14	18	21	17	23	20	18	22	19	20	21	16
Jean ALESI	3	-	-	5	4	3	r	2	r	r	r	r	10	3	6	
(Ferrari)	3	-	-	5	6	2	4	4	2	13	5	1	5	16	7	8
Philippe ALLIOT																
(McLaren-Peugeot)	-	-	-	-	-	-	-	-	-	r	-	-	-	-	-	-
	-	-	-	-	-	-	-	-	-	14	-	-	-	-	-	-
(Larrousse-Ford Cosworth)	-	-	-	-	-	-	-	-	-	-	-	r	-	-	-	-
	-	-	-	-	-	-	-	-	-	-	-	19	-	-	-	-
Rubens BARRICHELLO	4	3	-	r	r	7	r	4	r	r	r	4	4	12	r	4
(Jordan-Hart)	14	8	nq	15	5	6	7	6	11	10	1	16	8	5	10	5
Paul BELMONDO	-	-	-	r	r	-	-	-	-	-	-	-	-	-	-	-
(Pacific-Ilmor)	nq	nq	nq	24	26	nq	nq	nq	nq	nq	nq	nq	nq	nq	nq	nq

	BR	PAC	RSM	MC	E	CDN	F	GB	D	H	B	I	P	EUR	J	AUS
Olivier BERETTA	r	r	r	8	-	r	r	14	7	9	-	-	-	-	-	-
(Larrousse-Ford Cosworth)	23	21	23	18	17ns	22	25	24	24	25	-	-	-	-	-	-
Gerhard BERGER	r	2	r	3	r	4	3	r	1	12r	r	2	r	5	r	2
(Ferrari)	17	5	3	3	7	3	5	3	1	4	11	2	1	6	11	11
Éric BERNARD	r	10	12	r	8	13	r	13	3	10	10	7	10	18	-	-
(Ligier-Renault)	20	18	17	21	20	24	15	23	14	18	16	12	21	-	-	-
(Lotus-Mugen Honda)	-	-	-	-	-	-	-	-	-	-	-	-	-	22	-	-
Mark BLUNDELL	r	r	9	r	3	10r	10	r	r	5	5	r	r	13	r	r
(Tyrrell-Yamaha)	12	12	12	10	11	13	17	11	7	11	12	21	12	14	13	13
David BRABHAM	12	r	r	r	10	14	r	15	r	11	r	r	r	r	12	r
(Simtek-Ford Cosworth)	26	25	24	22	24	25	24	25	25	23	21	26	24	25	24	24
Martin BRUNDLE	r	r	8	2	11r	r	r	r	r	4r	r	5	6	r	r	3
(McLaren-Peugeot)	18	6	13	8	8	12	12	9	13	6	13	15	7	15	9	9
Erik COMAS	9	6	r	10	r	r	11r	r	6	8	r	8	r	r	9	-
(Larrousse-Ford Cosworth)	13	16	18	13	16	21	20	22	22	21	22	24	22	23	22	-
David COULTHARD	-	-	-	-	r	5	-	5	rf	r	4	6r	2f	-	-	-
(Williams-Renault)	-	-	-	-	9	5	-	7	6	3	7	5	3	-	-	-
Yannick DALMAS	-	-	-	-	-	-	-	-	-	-	-	r	14	-	-	-
(Larrousse-Ford Cosworth)	-	-	-	-	-	-	-	-	-	-	-	23	23	-	-	-
Andrea de CESARIS	-	-	r	4	-	r	6	r	r	r	r	r	r	r	-	-
(Jordan-Hart)	-	-	21	14	-	-	-	-	-	-	-	-	-	-	-	-
(Sauber-Mercedes Benz)	-	-	-	-	-	14	11	18	18	17	15	8	17	18	-	-
Jean-Denis DELÉTRAZ	-	-	-	-	-	-	-	-	-	-	-	-	-	-	-	r
(Larrousse-Ford Cosworth)	-	-	-	-	-	-	-	-	-	-	-	-	-	-	-	25
Christian FITTIPALDI	r	4	13r	r	r	dq	8	9	4	14r	r	r	8	17	8	8
(Footwork-Ford Cosworth)	11	9	16	6	21	16	18	20	17	16	24	19	11	19	18	19
Heinz-Harald FRENTZEN	r	5	7	-	r	r	4	7	r	r	r	r	r	6	6	7
(Sauber-Mercedes Benz)	5	11	7	ns	12	10	10	13	9	8	9	11	9	4	3	10
Bertrand GACHOT	r	-	r	r	r	r	-	-	-	-	-	-	-	-	-	-
(Pacific-Ilmor)	25	nq	25	23	25	26	nq	nq	nq	nq	nq	nq	nq	nq	nq	nq
Jean-Marc GOUNON	-	-	-	-	-	-	9	16	r	r	11	r	15	-	-	-
(Simtek-Ford Cosworth)	-	-	-	-	-	-	26	26	26	26	25	25	26	-	-	-
Mika HÄKKINEN	r	r	3	r	r	r	r	3	r	-	2	3	3	3	7	12r
(McLaren-Peugeot)	8	4	8	2	3	7	9	5	8	-	8	7	4	9	8	4
Johnny HERBERT	7	7	10	r	r	8	7	11	r	r	12	r	11	8	r	r
(Lotus-Mugen Honda)	21	23	20	16	22	17	19	21	15	24	20	4	20	-	-	-
(Ligier-Renault)	-	-	-	-	-	-	-	-	-	-	-	-	-	7	-	-
(Benetton-Ford Cosworth)	-	-	-	-	-	-	-	-	-	-	-	-	-	-	5	7
Damon HILL	2	r	6f	r	1	2	2f	1f	8	2	1f	1f	1	2	1f	r
(Williams-Renault)	4	3	4	4	2	4	1	1	3	2	3	3	2	2	2	3
Taki INOUE	-	-	-	-	-	-	-	-	-	-	-	-	-	r	-	-
(Simtek-Ford Cosworth)	-	-	-	-	-	-	-	-	-	-	-	-	-	26	-	-
Eddie IRVINE	r	-	-	-	6	r	r	-	r	r	13r	r	7	4	5	r
(Jordan-Hart)	16	-	-	-	13	8	6	12ns	10	7	4	9	13	10	6	6
Ukyo KATAYAMA	5	r	5	r	r	r	r	6	r	r	r	r	r	7	r	r
(Tyrrell-Yamaha)	10	14	9	11	10	9	14	8	5	5	23	14	6	13	14	15
Franck LAGORCE	-	-	-	-	-	-	-	-	-	-	-	-	-	-	r	11
(Ligier-Renault)	-	-	-	-	-	-	-	-	-	-	-	-	-	-	20	20
Pedro LAMY	10	8	r	11	-	-	-	-	-	-	-	-	-	-	-	-
(Lotus-Mugen Honda)	24	24	22	19	-	-	-	-	-	-	-	-	-	-	-	-
Nicola LARINI	-	r	2	-	-	-	-	-	-	-	-	-	-	-	-	-
(Ferrari)	-	7	6	-	-	-	-	-	-	-	-	-	-	-	-	-
J J LEHTO	-	-	r	7	r	6	-	-	-	-	-	9	r	-	r	10
(Benetton-Ford Cosworth)	-	-	5	17	4	20	-	-	-	-	-	20	14	-	-	-
(Sauber-Mercedes Benz)	-	-	-	-	-	-	-	-	-	-	-	-	-	-	15	17
Nigel MANSELL	-	-	-	-	-	-	r	-	-	-	-	-	-	r	4	1
(Williams-Renault)	-	-	-	-	-	-	2	-	-	-	-	-	-	3	4	1
Pierluigi MARTINI	8	r	r	r	5	9	5	10	r	r	8	r	12	15	r	9
(Minardi-Ford Cosworth)	15	17	14	9	18	15	16	14	20	15	10	18	18	17	16	18
Andrea MONTERMINI	-	-	-	-	-	-	-	-	-	-	-	-	-	-	-	-
(Simtek-Ford Cosworth)	-	-	-	-	nq	-	-	-	-	-	-	-	-	-	-	-
Gianni MORBIDELLI	r	r	r	r	r	r	r	r	5	r	6	r	9	11	r	r
(Footwork-Ford Cosworth)	6	13	11	7	15	11	22	16	16	19	14	17	16	8	12	21
Hideki NODA	-	-	-	-	-	-	-	-	-	-	-	-	-	r	r	r
(Larrousse-Ford Cosworth)	-	-	-	-	-	-	-	-	-	-	-	-	-	24	23	23
Olivier PANIS	11	9	11	9	7	12	r	12	2	6	7	10	dq	9	11	5
(Ligier-Renault)	19	22	19	20	19	19	13	15	12	9	17	6	15	11	19	12

Season-by-Season Summary

	BR	PAC	RSM	MC	E	CDN	F	GB	D	H	B	I	P	EUR	J	AUS
Roland RATZENBERGER †	-	11	-	-	-	-	-	-	-	-	-	-	-	-	-	-
(Simtek-Ford Cosworth)	nq	26	26ns	-	-	-	-	-	-	-	-	-	-	-	-	-
Mika SALO	-	-	-	-	-	-	-	-	-	-	-	-	-	-	10	r
(Lotus-Mugen Honda)	-	-	-	-	-	-	-	-	-	-	-	-	-	-	25	22
Mimmo SCHIATTARELLA	-	-	-	-	-	-	-	-	-	-	-	-	-	19	-	r
(Simtek-Ford Cosworth)	-	-	-	-	-	-	-	-	-	-	-	-	-	26	-	26
Michael SCHUMACHER	1f	1f	1	1f	2f	1f	1	dq	r	1f	dq	-	-	1f	2	rf
(Benetton-Ford Cosworth)	2	2	2	1	1	1	3	2	4	1	2	-	-	1	1	2
Ayrton SENNA †	r	r	r	-	-	-	-	-	-	-	-	-	-	-	-	-
(Williams-Renault)	1	1	1	-	-	-	-	-	-	-	-	-	-	-	-	-
Aguri SUZUKI	-	r	-	-	-	-	-	-	-	-	-	-	-	-	-	-
(Jordan-Hart)	-	20	-	-	-	-	-	-	-	-	-	-	-	-	-	-
Jos VERSTAPPEN	r	r	-	-	-	-	r	8	r	3	3	r	5	r	-	-
(Benetton-Ford Cosworth)	9	10	-	-	-	-	8	10	19	12	6	10	10	12	-	-
Karl WENDLINGER	6	r	4	-	-	-	-	-	-	-	-	-	-	-	-	-
(Sauber-Mercedes Benz)	7	19	10	ns	-	-	-	-	-	-	-	-	-	-	-	-
Alessandro ZANARDI	-	-	-	-	9	15r	r	r	r	13	-	r	-	16	13	r
(Lotus-Mugen Honda)	-	-	-	-	23	23	23	19	21	22	-	13	-	21	17	14

1995 RACE RESULTS & GRID POSITIONS

	BR	RA	RSM	E	MC	CDN	F	GB	D	H	B	I	P	EUR	PAC	J	AUS
Jean ALESI	5	2	2	r	rf	1	5	2	r	r	r	r	5	2	5	r	r
(Ferrari)	6	6	5	2	5	5	4	6	10	6	2	5	7	6	4	2	5
Luca BADOER	r	r	14	r	r	8	13	10	r	8	r	r	14	11	15	9	-
(Minardi-Ford Cosworth)	18	13	20	21	16	19	17	18	16	12	19	18	18	18	16	17	15ns
Rubens BARRICHELLO	r	r	r	7	r	2	6	11r	r	7	6	r	11	4	r	r	r
(Jordan-Peugeot)	16	10	10	8	11	9	5	9	5	14	12	6	8	11	11	10	7
Gerhard BERGER	3	6	3f	3	3	11r	12	r	3	3	r	rf	4	r	4	r	r
(Ferrari)	5	8	2	3	4	4	7	4	4	4	1	3	4	4	5	5	4
Mark BLUNDELL	6	r	-	-	5	r	11	5	r	r	5	4	9	r	9	7	4
(McLaren-Mercedes Benz)	9	17	-	-	10	10	13	10	8	13	6	9	12	10	10	23	10
Jean-Christophe BOULLION	-	-	-	-	8r	r	r	9	5	10	11	6	12	r	r	-	-
(Sauber-Ford Cosworth)	-	-	-	-	19	18	15	16	14	19	14	14	14	13	15	-	-
Martin BRUNDLE	-	-	-	9	r	10r	4	r	r	-	r	3	r	8	7	-	r
(Ligier-Mugen Honda)	-	-	-	11	8	14	9	11	-	8	13	11	9	12	-	-	11
David COULTHARD	2	r	4	r	r	r	3	3	2	2	rf	r	1f	3	2	r	r
(Williams-Renault)	3	1	3	4	3	3	3	3	3	2	5	1	1	1	1	6	2
Jean-Denis DELÉTRAZ	-	-	-	-	-	-	-	-	-	-	-	-	r	15	-	-	-
(Pacific-Ford Cosworth)	-	-	-	-	-	-	-	-	-	-	-	-	24	24	-	-	-
Pedro DINIZ	10	nc	15	r	10	r	r	r	r	r	13	9	16	13	17	r	7
(Forti-Ford Cosworth)	25	25	26	26	22	24	23	20	21	23	24	23	22	22	21	20	21
Heinz-Harald FRENTZEN	r	5	6	8	6	r	10	6	r	5	4	3	6	r	7	8	r
(Sauber-Ford Cosworth)	14	9	14	12	14	12	12	12	11	11	10	10	5	8	8	8	6
Bertrand GACHOT	r	r	r	r	r	r	r	12	-	-	-	-	-	-	r	r	8
(Pacific-Ford Cosworth)	20	23	22	24	21	20	22	21	-	-	-	-	-	-	24	22	23
Mika HÄKKINEN	4	r	5	r	r	r	7	r	r	r	r	2	r	8	-	2	-
(McLaren-Mercedes Benz)	7	5	6	9	6	7	8	8	7	5	3	7	13	9	-	3	ns
Johnny HERBERT	r	4	7	2	4	r	r	1	4	4	7	1	7	5	6	3	r
(Benetton-Renault)	4	11	8	7	7	6	10	5	9	9	4	8	6	7	7	9	8
Damon HILL	r	1	1	4f	2	r	2	rf	r	1f	2	r	3	r	3	r	1f
(Williams-Renault)	1	2	4	5	1	2	1	1	1	1	8	4	2	2	2	4	1
Taki INOUE	r	r	r	r	r	9	r	r	r	r	12	8	15	r	r	12	r
(Footwork-Hart)	21	26	19	18	26	22	18	19	19	18	18	20	19	21	20	18	19
Eddie IRVINE	r	r	8	5	r	3	9	r	9r	13r	r	r	10	6	11	4	r
(Jordan-Peugeot)	8	4	7	6	9	8	11	7	6	7	7	7	12	10	5	6	9
Ukyo KATAYAMA	r	8	r	r	r	r	r	r	7	r	r	10	r	r	14	r	r
(Tyrrell-Yamaha)	11	15	15	17	15	16	19	14	17	17	15	17	16	-	17	13	16
Pedro LAMY	-	-	-	-	-	-	-	-	-	9	10	r	r	9	13	11	6
(Minardi-Ford Cosworth)	-	-	-	-	-	-	-	-	-	15	17	19	17	16	14	16	17
Giovanni LAVAGGI	-	-	-	-	-	-	-	-	r	r	r	r	-	-	-	-	-
(Pacific-Ford Cosworth)	-	-	-	-	-	-	-	-	24	24	23	24	-	-	-	-	-
Jan MAGNUSSEN	-	-	-	-	-	-	-	-	-	-	-	-	-	-	10	-	-
(McLaren-Mercedes Benz)	-	-	-	-	-	-	-	-	-	-	-	-	-	-	12	-	-
Nigel MANSELL	-	-	10	r	-	-	-	-	-	-	-	-	-	-	-	-	-
(McLaren-Mercedes Benz)	-	-	9	10	-	-	-	-	-	-	-	-	-	-	-	-	-

	BR	RA	RSM	E	MC	CDN	F	GB	D	H	B	I	P	EUR	PAC	J	AUS
Pierluigi MARTINI (Minardi-Ford Cosworth)	-	r	12	14	7	r	r	7	r	-	-	-	-	-	-	-	-
	17ns	16	18	19	18	17	20	15	20	-	-	-	-	-	-	-	-
Andrea MONTERMINI (Pacific-Ford Cosworth)	9	r	r	-	dq	r	nc	r	8	12	r	r	r	r	r	r	r
	22	22	24	23ns	25	21	21	24	23	22	21	21	21	20	23	19	22
Gianni MORBIDELLI (Footwork-Hart)	r	r	13	11	9	6	14	-	-	-	-	-	-	-	r	r	3
	13	12	11	14	13	13	16	-	-	-	-	-	-	-	19	14	13
Roberto MORENO (Forti-Ford Cosworth)	r	nc	16	r	r	r	16	r	r	r	14	r	17	r	16	r	r
	23	24	25	25	24	23	24	22	22	21	22	22	23	23	22	21	20
Olivier PANIS (Ligier-Mugen Honda)	r	7	9	6	r	4	8	4	r	6	9	r	r	r	8	5	2
	10	18	12	15	12	11	6	13	12	10	9	13	11	14	9	11	12
Max PAPIS (Footwork-Hart)	-	-	-	-	-	-	-	r	r	r	r	7	r	12	-	-	-
	-	-	-	-	-	-	-	17	15	20	20	15	20	17	-	-	-
Mika SALO (Tyrrell-Yamaha)	7	r	r	10	r	7	15	8	r	r	8	5	13	10	12	6	5
	12	7	13	13	17	15	14	23	13	16	11	16	15	15	18	12	14
Mimmo SCHIATTARELLA (Simtek-Ford Cosworth)	r	9	r	15	r	-	-	-	-	-	-	-	-	-	-	-	-
	26	20	23	22	20	-	-	-	-	-	-	-	-	-	-	-	-
Michael SCHUMACHER (Benetton-Renault)	1f	3f	r	1	1	5f	1f	r	1f	11r	1	r	2	1f	1f	1f	r
	2	3	1	1	2	1	2	2	2	3	16	2	3	3	3	1	3
Aguri SUZUKI (Ligier-Mugen Honda)	8	r	11	-	-	-	-	-	6	-	-	-	-	-	r	-	-
	15	19	16	-	-	-	-	-	18	-	-	-	-	-	13	ns	-
Gabriele TARQUINI (Tyrrell-Yamaha)	-	-	-	-	-	-	-	-	-	-	-	-	-	14	-	-	-
	-	-	-	-	-	-	-	-	-	-	-	-	-	19	-	-	-
Jos VERSTAPPEN (Simtek-Ford Cosworth)	r	r	r	12	r	-	-	-	-	-	-	-	-	-	-	-	-
	24	14	17	16	23	-	-	-	-	-	-	-	-	-	-	-	-
Karl WENDLINGER (Sauber-Ford Cosworth)	r	r	r	13	-	-	-	-	-	-	-	-	-	-	10	r	-
	19	21	21	20	-	-	-	-	-	-	-	-	-	-	15	18	-

1996 RACE RESULTS & GRID POSITIONS

	AUS	BR	RA	EUR	RSM	MC	E	CDN	F	GB	D	H	B	I	P	J
Jean ALESI (Benetton-Renault)	r	2	3f	r	6	rf	2	3	3	r	2	3	4	2	4	r
	6	5	4	4	5	3	4	4	3	5	5	5	7	6	3	9
Luca BADOER (Forti-Ford Cosworth)	-	11	r	-	10	r	-	r	r	-	-	-	-	-	-	-
	nq	19	21	nq	21	21	nq	20	20	nq	-	-	-	-	-	-
Rubens BARRICHELLO (Jordan-Peugeot)	r	r	4	5	5	r	r	r	9	4	6	6	r	5	r	9
	8	2	6	5	9	6	7	8	10	6	9	13	10	10	9	11
Gerhard BERGER (Benetton-Renault)	4	r	r	9	3	r	r	r	4	2	13r	r	6f	r	6	4
	7	8	5	8	7	4	5	7	4	7	2	6	5	8	5	4
Martin BRUNDLE (Jordan-Peugeot)	r	12r	r	6	r	r	r	6	8	6	10	r	r	4	9	5
	19	6	15	11	12	16	15	9	8	8	10	12	8	9	10	10
David COULTHARD (McLaren-Mercedes Benz)	r	r	7	3	r	2	r	4	6	5	5	r	r	r	13	8
	13	14	9	6	4	5	14	10	7	9	7	9	4	5	8	8
Pedro DINIZ (Ligier-Mugen Honda)	10	8	r	10	7	r	6	r	r	r	r	r	r	6	r	r
	20	22	18	17	17	17	17	18	11	17	11	15	15	14	18	16
Giancarlo FISICHELLA (Minardi-Ford Cosworth)	r	-	-	13	r	r	r	8	r	11	-	-	-	-	-	-
	16	-	-	18	19	18	19	16	17	18	-	-	-	-	-	-
Heinz-Harald FRENTZEN (Sauber-Ford Cosworth)	8	r	r	r	r	4	4	r	r	8	8	r	r	r	7	6
	9	9	11	10	10	9	11	12	12	11	13	10	11	13	11	7
Mika HÄKKINEN (McLaren-Mercedes Benz)	5	4	r	8	8r	6r	5	5	5	3	r	4	3	3	r	3
	5	7	8	9	11	8	10	6	5	4	4	7	6	4	7	5
Johnny HERBERT (Sauber-Ford Cosworth)	r	r	9	7	r	3	r	7	dq	9	r	r	r	9r	8	10
	14	12	17	12	15	13	9	15	16	13	14	8	12	12	12	13
Damon HILL (Williams-Renault)	1	1f	1	4f	1f	r	r	1	1	r	1f	2f	5	r	2	1
	2	1	1	1	2	2	1	1	2	1	1	2	2	1	1	2
Eddie IRVINE (Ferrari)	3	7	5	r	4	7r	r	r	r	r	r	r	r	r	5	r
	3	10	10	7	6	7	6	5	22	10	8	4	9	7	6	6
Ukyo KATAYAMA (Tyrrell-Yamaha)	11	9	r	dq	r	r	r	r	r	r	r	7	8	10	12	r
	15	16	13	16	16	15	16	17	14	12	16	14	17	16	14	14
Pedro LAMY (Minardi-Ford Cosworth)	r	10	r	12	9	r	r	r	12	r	12	r	10	r	16	12
	17	18	19	19	18	19	18	19	18	19	18	19	19	18	19	18
Giovanni LAVAGGI (Minardi-Ford Cosworth)	-	-	-	-	-	-	-	-	-	-	-	10r	-	r	15	-
	-	-	-	-	-	-	-	-	-	-	nq	20	nq	20	20	nq
Tarso MARQUES (Minardi-Ford Cosworth)	-	r	r	-	-	-	-	-	-	-	-	-	-	-	-	-
	-	21	14	-	-	-	-	-	-	-	-	-	-	-	-	-
Andrea MONTERMINI (Forti-Ford Cosworth)	-	r	10	-	-	-	-	r	r	-	-	-	-	-	-	-
	nq	20	22	nq	nq	22ns	nq	22	21	nq	-	-	-	-	-	-

	AUS	BR	RA	EUR	RSM	MC	E	CDN	F	GB	D	H	B	I	P	J
Olivier PANIS	7	6	8	r	r	1	r	r	7	r	7	5	r	r	10	7
(Ligier-Mugen Honda)	11	15	12	15	13	14	8	11	9	16	12	11	14	11	15	12
Ricardo ROSSET	9	r	r	11	r	r	r	r	11	r	11	8	9	r	14	13
(Footwork-Hart)	18	17	20	20	20	20	20	21	19	20	19	18	18	19	17	19
Mika SALO	6	5	r	dq	r	5r	dq	r	10	7	9	r	7	r	11	r
(Tyrrell-Yamaha)	10	11	16	14	8	11	12	14	13	14	15	16	13	17	13	15
Michael SCHUMACHER	r	3	r	2	2	r	1f	r	-	r	4	9r	1	1f	3	2
(Ferrari)	4	4	2	3	1	1	3	3	1ns	3	3	1	3	3	4	3
Jos VERSTAPPEN	r	r	6	r	r	r	r	r	r	10	r	r	r	8	r	11
(Footwork-Hart)	12	13	7	13	14	12	13	13	15	15	17	17	16	15	16	17
Jacques VILLENEUVE	2f	r	2	1	11r	r	3	2f	2f	1f	3	1	2	7	1f	rf
(Williams-Renault)	1	3	3	2	3	10	2	2	6	2	6	3	1	2	2	1

1997 RACE RESULTS & GRID POSITIONS

	AUS	BR	RA	RSM	MC	E	CDN	F	GB	D	H	B	I	A	L	J	EUR
Jean ALESI	r	6	7	5	r	3	2	5	2	6	11	8	2	r	2	5	13
(Benetton-Renault)	8	6	11	14	9	4	8	8	11	6	9	2	1	15	10	7	10
Rubens BARRICHELLO	r	r	r	r	2	r	r	r	r	r	r	r	13	14r	r	r	r
(Stewart-Ford Cosworth)	11	11	5	13	10	17	3	13	21	12	11	12	11	5	9	12	12
Gerhard BERGER	4	2	6f	r	9	10	-	-	-	1f	8	6	7	10	4	8	4
(Benetton-Renault)	10	3	12	11	17	6	-	-	-	1	7	15	7	18	7	5	8
David COULTHARD	1	10	r	r	r	6	7f	7r	4	r	r	r	1	2	r	10r	2
(McLaren-Mercedes Benz)	4	12	10	10	5	3	5	9	6	8	8	10	6	10	6	11	6
Pedro DINIZ	10	r	r	r	r	r	8	r	r	r	r	7	r	13r	5	12	r
(Arrows-Yamaha)	22	16	22	17	16	21	16	16	16	16	19	8	17	17	15	16	13
Giancarlo FISICHELLA	r	8	r	4	6	9f	3	9	7	11r	r	2	4	4	r	7	11
(Jordan-Peugeot)	14	7	9	6	4	8	6	11	10	2	13	4	3	14	4	9	17
Norberto FONTANA	-	-	-	-	-	-	-	r	9	9	-	-	-	-	-	-	14
(Sauber-Petronas)	-	-	-	-	-	-	-	20	22	18	-	-	-	-	-	-	18
Heinz-Harald FRENTZEN	8rf	9	r	1f	r	8	4	2	r	r	rf	3	3	3	3f	2f	6f
(Williams-Renault)	2	8	2	2	1	2	4	2	2	5	6	7	2	4	3	6	3
Mika HÄKKINEN	3	4	5	6	r	7	r	r	r	3	r	dq	9f	r	r	4	1
(McLaren-Mercedes Benz)	6	4	17	8	8	5	9	10	3	3	4	5	5	2	1	4	5
Johnny HERBERT	r	7	4	r	r	5	5	8	r	r	3	4	r	8	7	6	8
(Sauber-Petronas)	7	13	8	7	7	10	13	14	9	14	10	11	12	12	16	8	14
Damon HILL	-	17r	r	r	r	r	9	12	6	8	2	13r	r	7	8	11	r
(Arrows-Yamaha)	20ns	9	13	15	13	15	15	17	12	13	3	9	14	7	13	17	4
Eddie IRVINE	r	16	2	3	3	12	r	3	r	r	9r	10r	8	r	r	3	5
(Ferrari)	5	14	7	9	15	11	12	5	7	10	5	17	10	8	14	3	7
Ukyo KATAYAMA	r	18	r	11	10	r	r	11	r	r	10	14r	r	11	r	r	17
(Minardi-Hart)	15	18	21	22	20	20	22	21	18	22	20	20	21	19	22	18	19
Nicola LARINI	6	11	r	7	r	-	-	-	-	-	-	-	-	-	-	-	-
(Sauber-Petronas)	13	19	14	12	11	-	-	-	-	-	-	-	-	-	-	-	-
Jan MAGNUSSEN	r	r	10r	r	7	13	r	r	r	r	r	12	r	r	r	r	9
(Stewart-Ford Cosworth)	19	20	15	16	19	22	21	15	15	15	17	18	13	6	12	14	11
Tarso MARQUES	-	-	-	-	-	-	-	r	10	r	12	r	14	-	r	r	15
(Minardi-Hart)	-	-	-	-	-	-	-	22	20	21	22	22	22	exc	18	19	20
Gianni MORBIDELLI	-	-	-	-	-	14	10	-	-	-	r	9	12	9	9	-	-
(Sauber-Petronas)	-	-	-	-	-	13	18	-	-	-	15	13	18	13	19	ns	-
Shinji NAKANO	7	14	r	r	r	r	6	r	11r	7	6	r	11	r	r	r	10
(Prost-Mugen Honda)	16	15	20	18	21	16	19	12	14	17	16	16	15	17	15	15	15
Olivier PANIS	5	3	r	8	4	2	11r	-	-	-	-	-	-	-	6	r	7
(Prost-Mugen Honda)	9	5	3	4	12	12	10	-	-	-	-	-	-	-	11	10	9
Ricardo ROSSET	-	-	-	-	-	-	-	-	-	-	-	-	-	-	-	-	-
(Lola-Ford Cosworth)	nq	-	-	-	-	-	-	-	-	-	-	-	-	-	-	-	-
Mika SALO	r	13	8	9	5	r	r	r	r	r	13	11	r	r	10	r	12
(Tyrrell-Ford Cosworth)	18	22	19	19	14	14	17	19	17	19	21	19	19	21	20	21	21
Michael SCHUMACHER	2	5	r	2	1f	4	1	1f	rf	2	4	1	6	6	r	1	r
(Ferrari)	3	2	4	3	2	7	1	1	4	4	1	3	9	9	5	2	2
Ralf SCHUMACHER	r	r	3	r	r	r	r	6	5	5	5	r	r	5	r	9	r
(Jordan-Peugeot)	12	10	6	5	6	9	7	3	5	7	14	6	8	11	8	13	16
Vincenzo SOSPIRI	-	-	-	-	-	-	-	-	-	-	-	-	-	-	-	-	-
(Lola-Ford Cosworth)	nq	-	-	-	-	-	-	-	-	-	-	-	-	-	-	-	-
Jarno TRULLI	9	12	9	-	r	15	r	10	8	4	7	15	10	r	-	-	-
(Minardi-Hart)	17	17	18	20ns	18	18	20	-	-	-	-	-	-	-	-	-	-
(Prost-Mugen Honda)	-	-	-	-	-	-	-	6	13	11	12	14	16	3	-	-	-

	AUS	BR	RA	RSM	MC	E	CDN	F	GB	D	H	B	I	A	L	J	EUR
Jos VERSTAPPEN	r	15	r	10	8	11	r	r	r	10	r	r	r	12	r	13	16
(Tyrrell-Ford Cosworth)	21	21	16	21	22	19	14	18	19	20	18	21	20	20	21	20	22
Jacques VILLENEUVE	r	1f	1	r	r	1	r	4	1	r	1	5f	5	1f	1	dq	3
(Williams-Renault)	1	1	1	1	3	1	2	4	1	9	2	1	4	1	2	1	1
Alexander WURZ	-	-	-	-	-	-	r	r	3	-	-	-	-	-	-	-	-
(Benetton-Renault)	-	-	-	-	-	-	11	7	8	-	-	-	-	-	-	-	-

1998 RACE RESULTS & GRID POSITIONS

	AUS	BR	RA	RSM	E	MC	CDN	F	GB	A	D	H	B	I	L	J
Jean ALESI	r	9	5	6	10	12r	r	7	r	r	10	7	3	5	10	7
(Sauber-Petronas)	12	15	11	12	14	11	9	11	8	2	11	11	10	8	11	12
Rubens BARRICHELLO	r	r	10	r	5	r	5	10	r	r	r	r	r	10	11	r
(Stewart-Ford Cosworth)	14	13	14	17	9	14	13	14	16	5	13	14	14	13	12	16
David COULTHARD	2	2	6	1	2	r	r	6f	r	2f	2f	2	7	r	3	3
(McLaren-Mercedes Benz)	2	2	1	1	2	2	1	3	4	14	2	2	2	4	5	3
Pedro DINIZ	r	r	r	r	r	6	9	14	r	r	r	11	5	r	r	r
(Arrows)	20	22	18	18	15	12	19	17	12	13	18	12	16	20	17	18
Giancarlo FISICHELLA	r	6	7	r	r	2	2	9	5	r	7	8	r	8	6	8
(Benetton-Playlife)	7	7	10	10	4	3	4	9	10	1	8	8	7	11	4	10
Heinz-Harald FRENTZEN	3	5	9	5	8	r	r	15r	r	r	9	5	4	7	5	5
(Williams-Mecachrome)	6	3	6	8	13	5	7	8	6	7	10	7	9	12	7	5
Mika HÄKKINEN	1f	1f	2	r	1f	1f	r	3	2	1	1	6	r	4f	1f	1
(McLaren-Mercedes Benz)	1	1	3	2	1	1	2	1	1	3	1	1	1	3	3	2
Johnny HERBERT	6	11r	r	r	7	7	r	8	r	8	r	10	r	r	r	10
(Sauber-Petronas)	5	14	12	11	7	9	12	13	9	18	12	15	12	15	13	11
Damon HILL	8	dq	8	10r	r	8	r	r	r	7	4	4	1	6	9	4
(Jordan-Mugen Honda)	10	11	9	7	8	15	10	7	7	15	5	4	3	14	10	8
Eddie IRVINE	4	8	3	3	r	3	3	2	3	4	8	r	r	2	4	2
(Ferrari)	8	6	4	4	6	7	8	4	5	8	6	5	5	5	2	4
Jan MAGNUSSEN	r	10	r	r	12	r	6	-	-	-	-	-	-	-	-	-
(Stewart-Ford Cosworth)	18	16	22	20	18	17	20	-	-	-	-	-	-	-	-	-
Shinji NAKANO	r	r	13	r	14	9	7	17r	8	11	r	15	8	r	15	r
(Minardi-Ford Cosworth)	22	18	19	21	20	19	18	21	19	21	20	19	21	21	20	20
Olivier PANIS	9	r	15r	11r	16r	r	r	11	r	r	15	12	r	r	12	11
(Prost-Peugeot)	21	9	15	13	12	18	15	16	22	10	16	20	15	9	15	13
Ricardo ROSSET	r	r	14	r	-	-	8	r	r	12	-	-	r	12	r	-
(Tyrrell-Ford Cosworth)	19	21	21	22	nq	nq	22	18	20	22	ns	nq	20	18	22	nq
Mika SALO	r	r	r	9	r	4	r	13	r	r	14	r	r	r	14	r
(Arrows)	16	20	17	14	17	8	17	19	13	6	17	13	18	16	16	15
Michael SCHUMACHER	r	3	1	2f	3	10	1f	1	1f	3	5	1f	rf	1	2	rf
(Ferrari)	3	4	2	3	3	4	3	2	2	4	9	3	4	1	1	1
Ralf SCHUMACHER	r	r	r	7	11	r	r	16	6	5	6	9	2	3	r	r
(Jordan-Mugen Honda)	9	8	5	9	11	16	5	6	21	9	4	10	8	6	6	7
Tora TAKAGI	r	r	12	r	13	11	r	r	9	r	13	14	r	9	16	r
(Tyrrell-Ford Cosworth)	13	17	13	15	21	20	16	20	17	20	15	18	19	19	19	17
Jarno TRULLI	r	r	11	r	9	r	r	r	r	10	12	r	6	13	r	12r
(Prost-Peugeot)	15	12	16	16	16	10	14	12	14	16	14	16	13	10	14	14
Esteban TUERO	r	r	r	8	15	r	r	r	r	r	16	r	r	11	nc	r
(Minardi-Ford Cosworth)	17	19	20	19	19	21	21	22	18	19	21	21	22	22	21	21
Jos VERSTAPPEN	-	-	-	-	-	-	-	12	r	r	r	13	r	r	13	r
(Stewart-Ford Cosworth)	-	-	-	-	-	-	-	15	15	12	19	17	17	17	18	19
Jacques VILLENEUVE	5	7	r	4	6	5	10	4	7	6	3	3	r	r	8	6
(Williams-Mecachrome)	4	10	7	6	10	13	6	5	3	11	3	6	6	2	9	6
Alexander WURZ	7	4	4f	r	4	r	4	5	4	9	11	16r	r	r	7	9
(Benetton-Playlife)	11	5	8	5	5	6	11	10	11	17	7	9	11	7	8	9

1999 RACE RESULTS & GRID POSITIONS

	AUS	BR	RSM	MC	E	CDN	F	GB	A	D	H	B	I	EUR	MAL	J
Jean ALESI	r	r	6	r	r	r	r	14	r	8	16r	9	9	r	7	6
(Sauber-Petronas)	16	14	13	14	5	8	2	10	17	21	11	16	13	16	15	10
Luca BADOER	r	-	8	r	r	10	10	r	13	10	14	r	r	r	r	r
(Minardi-Ford Cosworth)	21	-	22	20	22	21	21	21	19	19	19	20	19	19	21	22

	AUS	BR	RSM	MC	E	CDN	F	GB	A	D	H	B	I	EUR	MAL	J
Rubens BARRICHELLO	5	r	3	9r	dq	r	3	8	r	r	5	10	4	3	5	8
(Stewart-Ford Cosworth)	4	3	6	5	7	5	1	7	5	6	8	7	7	15	6	13
David COULTHARD	r	r	2	r	2	7	rf	1	2	5f	2f	1	5	r	r	r
(McLaren-Mercedes Benz)	2	2	2	3	3	4	4	3	2	3	3	2	3	2	3	3
Pedro de la ROSA	6	r	r	r	11	r	11	r	r	r	15	r	r	r	r	13
(Arrows)	18	18	18	21	19	20	20	20	21	20	20	22	21	22	20	21
Pedro DINIZ	r	r	r	r	r	6	r	6	6	r	r	r	r	r	r	11
(Sauber-Petronas)	14	15	15	15	12	18	11	12	16	16	12	18	16	13	17	17
Giancarlo FISICHELLA	4	r	5	5	9	2	r	7	12r	r	r	11	r	r	11	14r
(Benetton-Playlife)	7	5	16	9	13	7	7	17	12	10	4	13	17	6	11	14
Heinz-Harald FRENTZEN	2	3r	r	4	r	11r	6	1	4	4	3	4	3	1	6	4
(Jordan-Mugen Honda)	5	8	7	6	8	6	5	5	4	2	5	3	2	1	14	4
Marc GENÉ	r	9	9	r	r	8	r	15	11	9	17	16	r	6	9	r
(Minardi-Ford Cosworth)	22	20	21	22	21	22	22	22	22	15	22	21	20	20	19	20
Mika HÄKKINEN	r	1f	r	3f	1	1	2	rf	3f	r	1	2f	r	5f	3	1
(McLaren-Mercedes Benz)	1	1	1	1	1	2	14	1	1	1	1	1	1	3	4	2
Johnny HERBERT	-	r	10r	r	r	5	r	12	14	11r	11	r	r	1	4	7
(Stewart-Ford Cosworth)	13ns	10	12	13	14	10	9	11	6	17	10	10	15	14	5	8
Damon HILL	r	r	4	r	7	r	r	5	8	r	6	6	10	r	r	r
(Jordan-Mugen Honda)	9	7	8	17	11	14	18	6	11	8	6	4	9	7	9	12
Eddie IRVINE	1	5	r	2	4	3f	6	2	1	1	3	4	6	7	1	3
(Ferrari)	6	6	4	4	2	3	17	4	3	5	2	6	8	9	2	5
Olivier PANIS	r	6	r	r	r	9	8	13	10	6	10	13	11r	9	r	r
(Prost-Peugeot)	20	12	11	18	15	15	3	15	18	7	14	17	10	5	12	6
Mika SALO	-	-	7r	r	8	-	-	-	9	2	12	7	3	r	-	-
(BAR-Supertec)	-	-	19	12	16	-	-	-	-	-	-	-	-	-	-	-
(Ferrari)	-	-	-	-	-	-	-	-	7	4	18	9	6	-	-	-
Stéphane SARRAZIN	-	r	-	-	-	-	-	-	-	-	-	-	-	-	-	-
(Minardi-Ford Cosworth)	-	17	-	-	-	-	-	-	-	-	-	-	-	-	-	-
Michael SCHUMACHER	8f	2	1f	1	3f	r	5	r	-	-	-	-	-	-	2f	2f
(Ferrari)	3	4	3	2	4	1	6	2	-	-	-	-	-	-	1	1
Ralf SCHUMACHER	3	4	r	r	5	4	4	3	r	4	9	5	2f	4	r	5
(Williams-Supertec)	8	11	9	16	10	13	16	8	8	11	16	5	5	4	8	9
Tora TAKAGI	7	8	r	r	12	r	dq	16	r	r	r	r	r	r	r	r
(Arrows)	17	19	20	19	20	19	19	19	20	22	21	19	22	21	22	19
Jarno TRULLI	r	r	r	7	6	r	7	9	7	r	8	12	r	2	-	r
(Prost-Peugeot)	12	13	14	7	9	9	8	14	13	9	13	12	12	10	18ns	7
Jacques VILLENEUVE	r	r	r	r	r	r	r	r	r	r	r	15	8	10r	r	9
(BAR-Supertec)	11	21	5	8	6	16	12	9	9	12	9	11	11	8	10	11
Alexander WURZ	r	7	r	6	10	r	r	10	5	7	7	14	r	r	8	10
(Benetton-Playlife)	10	9	17	10	18	11	13	18	10	13	7	15	14	11	7	15
Alessandro ZANARDI	r	r	11r	8	r	r	r	11	r	r	r	8	7	r	10	r
(Williams-Supertec)	15	16	10	11	17	12	15	13	14	14	15	8	4	18	16	16
Ricardo ZONTA	r	-	-	-	-	r	9	r	15r	r	13	r	r	8	r	12
(BAR-Supertec)	19	ns	-	-	-	17	10	16	15	18	17	14	18	17	13	18

2000 RACE RESULTS & GRID POSITIONS

	AUS	BR	RSM	GB	E	EUR	MC	CDN	F	A	D	H	B	I	USA	J	MAL
Jean ALESI	r	r	r	10	r	9	r	r	14	r	r	r	r	12	r	r	11
(Prost-Peugeot)	17	15	15	15	17	17	7	17	18	17	20	14	17	19	20	17	18
Rubens BARRICHELLO	2f	r	4	r	3	4	2	2	3	3	1f	4	rf	r	2	4	3
(Ferrari)	4	4	4	1	3	4	6	3	3	3	18	5	10	2	4	4	4
Luciano BURTI	-	-	-	-	-	-	-	-	-	11	-	-	-	-	-	-	-
(Jaguar-Ford Cosworth)	-	-	-	-	-	-	-	-	-	21	-	-	-	-	-	-	-
Jenson BUTTON	r	6	r	5	17r	10r	r	11	8	5	4	9	5	r	r	5	r
(Williams-BMW)	21	9	18	6	10	11	14	18	10	18	16	8	3	12	6	5	16
David COULTHARD	r	dq	3	1	2	3	1	7	1f	2f	3	3	4	r	5f	3	2
(McLaren-Mercedes Benz)	2	2	3	4	4	1	3	2	2	2	1	2	5	5	2	3	3
Pedro de la ROSA	r	8	r	r	r	6	r	r	r	r	6	16	16	r	r	12	r
(Arrows-Supertec)	12	16	13	19	22	12	16	9	13	12	5	15	16	10	18	13	14
Pedro DINIZ	r	-	8	11	r	7	r	10	11	9	r	r	11	8	8	11	r
(Sauber-Petronas)	19	ns	10	13	15	15	19	19	15	11	19	13	15	16	9	20	20
Giancarlo FISICHELLA	5	2	11	7	9	5	3	3	9	r	r	r	r	11	r	14	9
(Benetton-Playlife)	9	5	19	12	13	7	8	10	14	8	3	7	11	9	15	12	13
Heinz-Harald FRENTZEN	r	3	r	17r	6	r	10r	r	7	r	r	6	6	r	3	r	r
(Jordan-Mugen Honda)	5	7	6	2	8	10	4	5	8	15	17	6	8	8	7	8	10

	AUS	BR	RSM	GB	E	EUR	MC	CDN	F	A	D	H	B	I	USA	J	MAL
Marc GENÉ	8	r	r	14	14	r	r	16r	15	8	r	15	14	9	12	r	r
(Minardi-Fondmetal)	18	18	21	21	20	20	21	20	21	20	22	21	21	21	22	21	21
Mika HÄKKINEN	r	r	2f	2f	1f	2	6f	4f	2	1	2	1f	1	2f	r	2f	4f
(McLaren-Mercedes Benz)	1	1	1	3	2	3	5	4	4	1	4	3	1	3	3	2	2
Nick HEIDFELD	9	r	r	r	16	-	8	r	12	r	12r	r	r	r	9	r	r
(Prost-Peugeot)	15	19	22	17	19	exc	18	21	16	13	13	19	14	20	16	16	19
Johnny HERBERT	r	r	10	12	13	11r	9	r	r	7	r	r	8	r	11	7	r
(Jaguar-Ford Cosworth)	20	17	17	14	14	16	11	11	11	16	8	17	9	18	19	10	12
Eddie IRVINE	r	r	7	13	11	r	4	13	13	-	10	8	10	r	7	8	6
(Jaguar-Ford Cosworth)	7	6	7	9	9	8	10	16	6	ew	10	10	12	14	17	7	7
Gastón MAZZACANE	r	10	13	15	15	8	r	12	r	12	11	r	17	10	r	15	13r
(Minardi-Fondmetal)	22	20	20	22	21	21	22	22	22	22	21	22	22	22	21	22	22
Mika SALO	dq	-	6	8	7	r	5	r	10	6	5	10	9	7	r	10	8
(Sauber-Petronas)	10	ns	12	18	12	19	13	15	12	9	15	9	18	15	14	19	17
Michael SCHUMACHER	1	1f	1	3	5	1f	r	1	r	r	r	2	2	1	1	1	1
(Ferrari)	3	3	2	5	1	2	1	1	1	4	2	1	4	1	1	1	1
Ralf SCHUMACHER	3	5	r	4	4	r	r	14r	5	r	7	5	3	3	r	r	r
(Williams-BMW)	11	11	5	7	5	5	9	12	5	19	14	4	6	7	10	6	8
Jarno TRULLI	r	4	15r	6	12	r	r	6	6	r	9	7	r	r	r	13	12
(Jordan-Mugen Honda)	6	12	8	11	7	6	2	7	9	5	6	12	2	6	5	15	9
Jos VERSTAPPEN	r	7	14	r	r	r	r	5	r	r	r	13	15	4	r	r	10
(Arrows-Supertec)	13	14	16	8	11	13	15	13	20	10	11	20	20	11	13	14	15
Jacques VILLENEUVE	4	r	5	16r	r	r	7	15r	4	4	8	12	7	r	4	6	5
(BAR-Honda)	8	10	9	10	6	9	17	6	7	7	9	16	7	4	8	9	6
Alexander WURZ	7	r	9	9	10	12r	r	9	r	10	r	11	13	5	10	r	7
(Benetton-Playlife)	14	13	11	20	18	14	12	14	17	14	7	11	19	13	11	11	5
Ricardo ZONTA	6	9	12	r	8	r	r	8	r	r	r	14	12	6	6	9	r
(BAR-Honda)	16	8	14	16	16	18	20	8	19	6	12	18	13	17	12	18	11

2001 RACE RESULTS & GRID POSITIONS

	AUS	MAL	BR	RSM	E	A	MC	CDN	EUR	F	GB	D	H	B	I	USA	J
Jean ALESI	10	9	8	9	10	10	6	5	15r	12	11	6	10	6	8	7	r
(Prost-Acer)	14	13	15	14	15	20	11	16	14	19	14	14	-	-	-	-	-
(Jordan-Honda)	-	-	-	-	-	-	-	-	-	-	-	-	12	13	16	9	11
Fernando ALONSO	12	13	r	r	13	r	r	r	14	17r	16	10	r	r	13	r	11
(Minardi-European)	19	21	19	18	18	18	18	22	21	21	21	21	18	20	21	17	18
Rubens BARRICHELLO	3	2	r	3	r	3	2	r	5	3	3	2	2	5	2	15r	5
(Ferrari)	2	2	6	6	4	4	4	5	4	8	6	6	3	5	2	5	4
Enrique BERNOLDI	r	r	r	10	r	r	9	r	r	r	14	8	r	12	r	13	14
(Arrows-Asiatech)	18	22	16	16	16	15	20	17	18	20	20	19	20	21	18	19	20
Luciano BURTI	8	10	r	11	11	11	r	8	12	10	r	r	r	r	-	-	-
(Jaguar-Ford Cosworth)	21	15	14	15	-	-	-	-	-	-	-	-	-	-	-	-	-
(Prost-Acer)	-	-	-	-	14	17	21	19	17	15	16	16	19	18	-	-	-
Jenson BUTTON	14r	11	10	12	15	r	7	r	13	16r	15	5	r	r	r	9	7
(Benetton-Renault)	16	17	20	21	21	21	17	20	20	17	18	18	17	15	11	10	9
David COULTHARD	2	3	1	2	5	1f	5f	r	3	4f	r	r	3	2	r	3	3
(McLaren-Mercedes Benz)	6	8	5	1	3	7	1	3	5	3	3	5	2	9	6	7	7
Pedro de la ROSA	-	-	-	-	r	r	r	6	8	14	12	r	11	r	5	12	r
(Jaguar-Ford Cosworth)	-	-	-	-	20	14	14	16	16	14	13	9	13	10	10	16	16
Tomáš ENGE	-	-	-	-	-	-	-	-	-	-	-	-	-	-	12	14	r
(Prost-Acer)	-	-	-	-	-	-	-	-	-	-	-	-	-	-	20	21	19
Giancarlo FISICHELLA	13	r	6	r	14	r	r	r	11	11	13	4	r	3	10	8	17r
(Benetton-Renault)	17	16	18	19	19	19	10	18	15	16	19	17	15	8	14	12	6
Heinz-Harald FRENTZEN	5	4	11r	6	r	r	r	-	r	8	7	-	r	9	r	10	12
(Jordan-Honda)	4	9	8	9	8	11	13	ew	8	7	5	-	-	-	-	-	-
(Prost-Acer)	-	-	-	-	-	-	-	-	-	-	-	-	16	4	12	15	15
Mika HÄKKINEN	r	6f	r	4	9r	r	r	3	6	-	1f	r	5f	4	r	1	4
(McLaren-Mercedes Benz)	3	4	3	2	2	8	3	8	6	4ns	2	3	6	7	7	4	5
Nick HEIDFELD	4	r	3	7	6	9	r	r	r	6	6	r	6	r	11	6	9
(Sauber-Petronas)	10	11	9	12	10	6	16	11	10	9	9	7	7	14	8	6	10
Eddie IRVINE	11	r	r	r	r	7	3	r	7	r	9	r	r	r	r	5	r
(Jaguar-Ford Cosworth)	12	12	13	13	13	13	6	15	12	12	15	11	14	17	13	14	13
Tarso MARQUES	r	14	9	r	16	r	r	9	r	15	-	r	r	13	-	-	-
(Minardi-European)	22	20	22	22	22	22	22	21	22	22	nq	22	22	22	-	-	-
Gastón MAZZACANE	r	12	r	r	-	-	-	-	-	-	-	-	-	-	-	-	-
(Prost-Acer)	20	19	21	20	-	-	-	-	-	-	-	-	-	-	-	-	-

	AUS	MAL	BR	RSM	E	A	MC	CDN	EUR	F	GB	D	H	B	I	USA	J
Juan Pablo MONTOYA	r	r	r	r	2	r	r	r	2f	r	4	rf	8	r	1	rf	2
(Williams-BMW)	11	6	4	7	12	2	7	10	3	6	8	1	8	1	1	3	2
Olivier PANIS	7	r	4	8	7	5	r	r	r	9	r	7	r	11	9	11	13
(BAR-Honda)	9	10	11	8	11	10	12	6	13	11	11	13	11	11	17	13	17
Kimi RÄIKKÖNEN	6	r	r	r	8	4	10	4	10	7	5	r	7	r	7	r	r
(Sauber-Petronas)	13	14	10	10	9	9	15	7	9	13	7	8	9	12	9	11	12
Michael SCHUMACHER	1f	1	2	r	1f	2	1	2	1	1	2	r	1	1f	4	2	1
(Ferrari)	1	1	1	4	1	1	2	1	1	2	1	4	1	3	3	1	1
Ralf SCHUMACHER	r	5	rf	1f	r	r	r	1f	4	2	r	1	4	7	3f	r	6f
(Williams-BMW)	5	3	2	3	5	3	5	2	2	1	10	2	4	2	4	2	3
Jarno TRULLI	r	8	5	5	4	dq	r	11r	r	5	r	r	r	r	r	4	8
(Jordan-Honda)	7	5	7	5	6	5	8	4	7	5	4	10	5	16	5	8	8
Jos VERSTAPPEN	9	7	r	r	12	6	8	10r	r	13	10	9	12	10	r	r	15
(Arrows-Asiatech)	15	18	17	17	17	16	19	13	19	18	17	20	21	19	19	20	21
Jacques VILLENEUVE	r	r	7	r	3	8	4	r	9	r	8	3	9	8	6	r	10
(BAR-Honda)	8	7	12	11	7	12	9	9	11	10	12	12	10	6	15	18	14
Alex YOONG	-	-	-	-	-	-	-	-	-	-	-	-	-	-	r	r	16
(Minardi-European)	-	-	-	-	-	-	-	-	-	-	-	-	-	-	22	22	22
Ricardo ZONTA	-	-	-	-	-	-	-	7	-	-	-	r	-	-	-	-	-
(Jordan-Honda)	-	-	-	-	-	-	-	12	-	-	-	15	-	-	-	-	-

2002 RACE RESULTS & GRID POSITIONS

	AUS	MAL	BR	RSM	E	A	MC	CDN	EUR	GB	F	D	H	B	I	USA	J
Rubens BARRICHELLO	r	r	r	2f	-	2	7f	3	1	2f	-	4	1	2	1f	1f	2
(Ferrari)	1	3	8	2	2ns	1	5	3	4	2	3ns	3	1	3	4	2	2
Enrique BERNOLDI	dq	r	r	r	r	r	12	r	10	r	-	r	-	-	-	-	-
(Arrows-Ford Cosworth)	17	16	21	20	14	12	15	17	21	18	nq	18	-	-	-	-	-
Jenson BUTTON	r	4	4	5	12r	7	r	15r	5	12r	6	r	r	r	5	8	6
(Renault)	11	8	7	9	6	13	8	13	8	12	7	13	9	10	17	14	10
David COULTHARD	r	r	3	6	3	6	1	2	r	10	3f	5	5	4	7	3	r
(McLaren-Mercedes Benz)	4	6	4	6	7	8	2	8	5	6	6	9	10	6	7	3	3
Anthony DAVIDSON	-	-	-	-	-	-	-	-	-	-	-	-	r	r	-	-	-
(Minardi-Asiatech)	-	-	-	-	-	-	-	-	-	-	-	-	20	20	-	-	-
Pedro de la ROSA	8	10	8	r	r	r	10	r	11	11	9	r	13	r	r	r	r
(Jaguar-Ford Cosworth)	20	17	11	21	16	19	20	16	16	21	15	20	15	11	8	17	17
Giancarlo FISICHELLA	r	13	r	r	r	5	5	5	r	7	-	r	6	r	8	7	r
(Jordan-Honda)	8	9	14	15	12	15	11	6	18	17	ew	6	5	14	12	9	8
Heinz-Harald FRENTZEN	dq	11	r	r	6	11	6	13	13	r	-	r	-	-	-	13	-
(Arrows-Ford Cosworth)	15	11	18	13	10	11	12	19	15	16	nq	15	-	-	-	-	-
(Sauber-Petronas)	-	-	-	-	-	-	-	-	-	-	-	-	-	-	-	11	-
Nick HEIDFELD	r	5	r	10	4	r	8	12	7	6	7	6	9	10	10	9	7
(Sauber-Petronas)	10	7	9	7	8	5	17	7	9	10	10	10	8	18	15	10	12
Eddie IRVINE	4	r	7	r	r	r	9	r	r	r	r	r	r	6	3	10	9
(Jaguar-Ford Cosworth)	19	20	13	18	20	20	21	14	17	19	9	16	16	8	5	13	14
Felipe MASSA	r	6	r	8	5	r	r	9	6	9	r	7	7	r	r	-	r
(Sauber-Petronas)	9	14	12	11	11	7	13	12	11	11	12	14	7	17	14	-	15
Allan McNISH	r	7	r	r	8	9	r	r	14	r	11r	r	14	9	r	15	-
(Toyota)	16	19	16	17	19	14	10	20	13	15	17	17	18	13	13	16	ew
Juan Pablo MONTOYA	2	2f	5f	4	2	3	r	rf	r	3	4	2	11	3	r	4	4
(Williams-BMW)	6	2	1	4	4	4	4	1	1	1	1	4	4	5	1	4	6
Olivier PANIS	r	r	r	r	r	r	8	9	5	r	r	12	12r	6	12	r	r
(BAR-Honda)	12	18	17	12	13	9	18	11	12	13	11	7	12	15	16	12	16
Kimi RÄIKKÖNEN	3f	r	12r	r	r	r	r	4	3	r	2	r	4	r	r	r	3
(McLaren-Mercedes Benz)	5	5	5	5	5	6	6	5	6	5	4	5	11	2	6	6	4
Mika SALO	6	12	6	r	9	8	r	r	r	r	r	9	15	7	11	14	8
(Toyota)	14	10	10	16	17	10	9	18	10	8	16	19	17	9	10	19	13
Takuma SATO	r	9	9	r	r	r	r	10	16	r	r	8	10	11	12	11	5
(Jordan-Honda)	22	15	19	14	18	18	16	15	14	14	14	12	14	16	18	15	7
Michael SCHUMACHER	1	3	1	1	1f	1f	2	1	2f	1	1	1f	2f	1f	2	2	1f
(Ferrari)	2	1	2	1	1	3	3	2	3	3	2	1	2	1	2	1	1
Ralf SCHUMACHER	r	1	2	3	11r	4	3	7	4	8	5	3	3	5	r	16	11r
(Williams-BMW)	3	4	3	3	3	2	4	4	2	4	5	2	3	4	3	5	5
Jarno TRULLI	r	r	r	9	10r	r	4	6	8	r	r	r	8	r	4	5	r
(Renault)	7	12	6	8	9	16	7	10	7	7	8	8	6	7	11	4	11
Jacques VILLENEUVE	r	8	10r	7	7	10r	r	r	12	4	r	r	r	8	9	6	r
(BAR-Honda)	13	13	15	10	15	17	14	9	19	9	13	11	13	12	9	7	9
Mark WEBBER	5	r	11	11	-	12	11	11	15	r	8	r	16	r	r	r	10
(Minardi-Asiatech)	18	21	20	19	ew	21	19	21	20	20	18	21	19	19	19	18	18

    Grand Prix Data Book

	AUS	MAL	BR	RSM	E	A	MC	CDN	EUR	GB	F	D	H	B	I	USA	J
Alex YOONG	7	r	13	-	-	r	r	14	r	-	10	-	-	-	13	18	r
(Minardi-Asiatech)	21	22	22	nq	ew	22	22	22	22	nq	19	nq	-	-	20	20	19

2003 RACE RESULTS & GRID POSITIONS

	AUS	MAL	BR	RSM	E	A	MC	CDN	EUR	F	GB	D	H	I	USA	J
Fernando ALONSO	7	3	3	6	2	r	5	4f	4	r	r	4	1	8	r	r
(Renault)	10	1	10	8	3	19	8	4	8	7	8	8	1	20	6	5
Rubens BARRICHELLO	r	2	rf	3	3f	3	8	5	3	7	1f	r	r	3	r	1
(Ferrari)	2	5	1	3	2	5	7	5	5	8	1	3	5	3	2	1
Zsolt BAUMGARTNER	-	-	-	-	-	-	-	-	-	-	-	-	r	11	-	-
(Jordan-Ford Cosworth)	-	-	-	-	-	-	-	-	-	-	-	ap	19	18	-	-
Matteo BOBBI	-	-	-	-	-	-	-	-	-	-	-	-	-	-	-	-
(Minardi-Ford Cosworth)	-	-	-	ap	-	-	-	-	-	-	-	-	-	-	-	-
Gianmaria BRUNI	-	-	-	-	-	-	-	-	-	-	-	-	-	-	-	-
(Minardi-Ford Cosworth)	-	-	-	-	-	-	-	-	-	-	-	ap	ap	ap	ap	ap
Jenson BUTTON	10	7	r	8	9	4	-	r	7	r	8	8	10	r	r	4
(BAR-Honda)	8	9	11	9	5	7	ns	17	12	14	20	17	14	7	11	9
David COULTHARD	1	r	4	5	r	5	7	r	15r	5	5	2	5	r	r	3
(McLaren-Mercedes Benz)	11	4	2	12	8	14	6	11	9	5	12	10	9	8	8	7
Cristiano da MATTA	r	11	10	12	6	10	9	11r	r	11	7	6	11	r	9	7
(Toyota)	16	11	18	13	13	13	10	9	10	13	6	9	15	12	9	3
Ralph FIRMAN	r	10	r	r	8	11	12	r	11	15	13	r	-	-	r	14
(Jordan-Ford Cosworth)	17	20	16	19	15	16	16	19	14	18	17	18	ns	-	18	15
Giancarlo FISICHELLA	12r	r	1	15r	r	r	10	r	12	r	r	13r	r	10	7	r
(Jordan-Ford Cosworth)	13	14	8	17	17	9	12	16	13	17	15	12	13	13	17	16
Heinz-Harald FRENTZEN	6	9	5	11	r	r	r	r	9	12	12	r	r	13r	3	r
(Sauber-Petronas)	4	13	14	14	10	15	15	10	15	16	14	14	17	14	15	12
Marc GENÉ	-	-	-	-	-	-	-	-	-	-	-	-	-	5	-	-
(Williams-BMW)	-	-	-	-	-	-	-	-	-	-	-	-	-	5	-	-
Nick HEIDFELD	r	8	r	10	10	r	11	r	8	13	17	10	9	9	5	9
(Sauber-Petronas)	7	6	12	11	14	4	14	12	20	15	16	15	11	16	13	11
Nicolas KIESA	-	-	-	-	-	-	-	-	-	-	-	12	13	12	11	16
(Minardi-Ford Cosworth)	-	-	-	-	-	-	-	-	-	-	-	20	20	19	20	18
Allan McNISH	-	-	-	-	-	-	-	-	-	-	-	-	-	-	-	-
(Renault)	ap	ap	ap	ap	ap	ap	ap	ap	ap	-	ap	ap	ap	ap	ap	ap
Franck MONTAGNY	-	-	-	-	-	-	-	-	-	-	-	-	-	-	-	-
(Renault)	-	-	-	-	-	-	-	-	-	ap	-	-	-	-	-	-
Juan Pablo MONTOYA	2	12	r	7	4	r	1	3	2	2f	2	1f	3f	2	6	r
(Williams-BMW)	3	8	9	4	9	3	3	2	4	2	7	1	4	2	4	2
Satoshi MOTOYAMA	-	-	-	-	-	-	-	-	-	-	-	-	-	-	-	-
(Jordan-Ford Cosworth)	-	-	-	-	-	-	-	-	-	-	-	-	-	-	-	ap
Olivier PANIS	r	r	r	9	r	r	13	8	r	8	11	5	r	r	r	10
(Toyota)	5	10	15	10	6	11	17	7	7	10	13	7	10	9	3	4
Antonio PIZZONIA	13r	r	r	14	r	9	r	10r	10	10	r	-	-	-	-	-
(Jaguar-Ford Cosworth)	18	15	17	15	16	8	13	13	16	11	10	-	-	-	-	-
Kimi RÄIKKÖNEN	3f	1	2	2	r	2	2f	6	rf	4	3	r	2	4	2	2
(McLaren-Mercedes Benz)	15	7	4	6	20	2	2	20	1	4	3	5	7	4	1	8
Takuma SATO	-	-	-	-	-	-	-	-	-	-	-	-	-	-	-	6
(BAR-Honda)	-	-	-	-	-	-	-	-	-	-	-	-	-	-	-	13
Michael SCHUMACHER	4	6f	r	1f	1	1f	3	1	5	3	4	7	8	1	1f	8
(Ferrari)	1	3	7	1	1	1	5	3	2	3	3	6	8	1	7	14
Ralf SCHUMACHER	8	4	7	4	5	6	4	2	1	1	9	r	4	-	r	12f
(Williams-BMW)	9	17	6	2	7	10	1	1	3	1	4	2	2	ns	5	20
Jarno TRULLI	5	5	8	13	r	8	6	r	r	r	6	3	7	r	4	5
(Renault)	12	2	5	16	4	6	4	8	6	6	2	4	6	6	10	19
Jos VERSTAPPEN	11	13	r	r	12	r	r	9	14	16	15	r	12	r	10	15
(Minardi-Ford Cosworth)	20	18	19	20	19	20	18	15	18	19	19	19	18	17	19	17
Jacques VILLENEUVE	9	-	6	r	r	12	r	r	r	9	10	9	r	6	r	-
(BAR-Honda)	6	12ns	13	7	11	12	11	14	17	12	9	13	16	10	12	-
Mark WEBBER	r	r	9r	r	7	7	r	7	6	6	14	11r	6	7	r	11
(Jaguar-Ford Cosworth)	14	16	3	5	12	17	9	6	11	9	11	11	3	11	14	6
Justin WILSON	r	r	r	r	11	13	r	r	13	14	16	r	r	r	8	13
(Minardi-Ford Cosworth)	19	19	20	18	18	18	19	18	19	20	18	-	-	-	-	-
(Jaguar-Ford Cosworth)	-	-	-	-	-	-	-	-	-	-	-	16	12	15	16	10
Björn WIRDHEIM	-	-	-	-	-	-	-	-	-	-	-	-	-	-	-	-
(Jordan-Ford Cosworth)	-	-	-	-	-	-	-	-	-	-	-	-	-	-	ap	-

Season-by-Season Summary

	AUS	MAL	BRN	RSM	E	MC	EUR	CDN	USA	F	GB	D	H	B	I	CHN	J	BR
Fernando ALONSO	3	7	6	4	4	r	5	r	r	2	10	3	3	r	r	4	5	4
(Renault)	5	19	16	6	8	3	6	5	9	1	16	5	5	3	4	6	11	8
Rubens BARRICHELLO	2	4	2	6	2	3	2	2f	2f	3	3	12	2	3	1f	1	rf	3
(Ferrari)	2	3	2	4	5	6	7	7	1	10	2	7	2	6	1	1	15	1
Zsolt BAUMGARTNER	r	16	r	15	r	9	15	10	8	r	r	16	15	r	15	16	r	16
(Minardi-Ford Cosworth)	17	17	20	18	20	19	17	18	19	20	19	20	18	18	19	19	20	20
Ryan BRISCOE	-	-	-	-	-	-	-	-	-	-	-	-	ap	ap	ap	ap	ap	ap
(Toyota)																		
Gianmaria BRUNI	nc	14	17	r	r	r	14	r	r	18r	16	17	14	r	r	r	16	17
(Minardi-Ford Cosworth)	20	16	17	17	18	20	19	19	18	19	18	19	19	17	18	17	18	19
Jenson BUTTON	6	3	3	2	8	2	3	3	r	5	4	2	5	r	3	2	3	r
(BAR-Honda)	4	6	6	1	14	2	5	2	4	4	3	13	4	12	6	3	5	5
David COULTHARD	8	6	r	12	10	r	r	6	7	6	7	4	9	7	6	9	r	11
(McLaren-Mercedes Benz)	12	9	10	11	10	8	20	9	12	3	6	4	12	4	10	9	8	12
Cristiano da MATTA	12	9	10	r	13	6	r	dq	r	14	13	r	-	-	-	-	-	-
(Toyota)	13	10	9	10	11	15	11	12	11	11	12	15	-	-	-	-	-	-
Anthony DAVIDSON	-	-	-	-	-	-	-	-	-	-	-	-	-	-	-	-	-	-
(BAR-Honda)	ap	ap	ap	ap	ap	ap	ap	ap	ap	ap	ap	ap	ap	ap	ap	ap	ap	ap
Robert DOORNBOS	-	-	-	-	-	-	-	-	-	-	-	-	-	-	-	ap	ap	ap
(Jordan-Ford Cosworth)																		
Giancarlo FISICHELLA	10	11	11	9	7	r	6	4	9r	12	6	9	8	5	8	7	8	9
(Sauber-Petronas)	14	12	11	19	12	10	18	11	14	15	20	14	8	5	15	7	7	10
Marc GENÉ	-	-	-	-	-	-	-	-	-	10	12	-	-	-	-	-	-	-
(Williams-BMW)	-	-	-	-	-	-	-	-	-	8	11	-	-	-	-	-	-	-
Timo GLOCK	-	-	-	-	-	-	-	7	-	-	-	-	-	-	-	15	15	15
(Jordan-Ford Cosworth)	ap	ap	ap	ap	ap	ap	ap	16	ap	ap	ap	ap	ap	ap	ap	16	17	17
Nick HEIDFELD	r	r	15	r	r	7	10	8	r	16	15	r	12	11	14	13	13	r
(Jordan-Ford Cosworth)	15	15	18	16	15	17	13	15	16	17	15	18	16	16	20	14	16	16
Christian KLIEN	11	10	14	14	r	r	12	9	r	11	14	10	13	6	13	r	12	14
(Jaguar-Ford Cosworth)	19	13	12	14	16	14	12	10	13	13	13	12	14	13	14	15	14	15
Bas LEINDERS	-	-	-	-	-	-	-	-	-	-	-	-	-	-	-	-	-	-
(Minardi-Ford Cosworth)	-	ap	ap	ap	ap	ap	ap	ap	ap	ap	ap	ap	ap	ap	ap	ap	ap	ap
Felipe MASSA	r	8	12	10	9	5	9	r	r	13	9	13	r	4	12	8	9	8
(Sauber-Petronas)	11	11	13	12	17	16	16	17	15	16	10	16	20	8	16	4	19	4
Juan Pablo MONTOYA	5	2f	13	3	r	4	8	dq	dq	8	5	5	4	r	5	5	7	1f
(Williams-BMW)	3	4	3	3	2	9	8	4	5	6	7	2	7	11	2	10	13	2
Olivier PANIS	13	12	9	11	r	8	11	dq	5	15	r	14	11	8	r	14	14	-
(Toyota)	18	14	8	13	7	13	10	13	8	14	17	9	13	9	13	8	10	-
Giorgio PANTANO	14	13	16	r	r	r	13	-	r	17	r	15	r	r	r	-	-	-
(Jordan-Ford Cosworth)	16	18	15	15	19	18	15	-	17	18	14	17	17	19	17	-	-	-
Antonio PIZZONIA	-	-	-	-	-	-	-	-	-	-	-	7	7	r	7	-	-	-
(Williams-BMW)	-	-	-	-	-	-	-	-	-	-	-	10	6	14	8	-	-	-
Kimi RÄIKKÖNEN	r	r	r	8	11	r	r	5	6	7	2	rf	r	1f	r	3	6	2
(McLaren-Mercedes Benz)	10	5	19	20	13	5	4	8	7	9	1	3	10	10	7	2	12	3
Takuma SATO	9	15r	5	16r	5	r	r	r	3	r	11	8	6	r	4	6	4	6
(BAR-Honda)	7	20	5	7	3	7	2	20	3	7	8	8	3	15	5	18	4	6
Michael SCHUMACHER	1f	1	1f	1f	1f	rf	1f	1	1	1f	1f	1	1f	2	2	12f	1	7
(Ferrari)	1	1	1	2	1	4	1	6	2	2	4	1	1	2	3	20	1	18
Ralf SCHUMACHER	4	r	7	7	6	10r	r	dq	r	-	-	-	-	-	-	r	2	5
(Williams-BMW)	8	7	4	5	6	12	9	1	6	-	-	-	-	-	-	5	2	7
Jarno TRULLI	7	5	4	5	3	1	4	r	4	4	r	11	r	9	10	-	11	12
(Renault)	9	8	7	9	4	1	3	3	20	5	5	6	9	1	9	-	-	-
(Toyota)	-	-	-	-	-	-	-	-	-	-	-	-	-	-	-	-	6	9
Jacques VILLENEUVE	-	-	-	-	-	-	-	-	-	-	-	-	-	-	-	11	10	10
(Renault)	-	-	-	-	-	-	-	-	-	-	-	-	-	-	-	12	9	13
Mark WEBBER	r	r	8	13	12	r	7	r	r	9	8	6	10	r	9	10	r	r
(Jaguar-Ford Cosworth)	6	2	14	8	9	11	14	14	10	12	9	11	11	7	12	11	3	11
Björn WIRDHEIM	-	-	-	-	-	-	-	-	-	-	-	-	-	-	-	-	-	-
(Jaguar-Ford Cosworth)	ap	ap	ap	ap	ap	ap	ap	ap	ap	ap	ap	ap	ap	ap	ap	ap	-	ap
Ricardo ZONTA	-	-	-	-	-	-	-	-	-	-	-	-	r	10r	11	r	-	13
(Toyota)	ap	ap	ap	ap	ap	ap	ap	ap	ap	ap	ap	ap	15	20	11	13	-	14

	AUS	MAL	BRN	RSM	E	MC	EUR	CDN	USA	F	GB	D	H	TR	I	B	BR	J	CHN
Christijan ALBERS	r	13	13	r	r	14	17	11	5	r	18	13	r	r	19	12	14	16	16
(Minardi-Cosworth)	17	19	18	20	14	14	20	15	18	20	18	16	17	15	20	18	16	13	18

	AUS	MAL	BRN	RSM	E	MC	EUR	CDN	USA	F	GB	D	H	TR	I	B	BR	J	CHN
Fernando ALONSO	3f	1	1	1	2	4	1f	r	-	1	2	1	11	2	2	2	3	3	1
(Renault)	13	1	1	2	3	2	6	3	6ns	1	1	3	6	3	2	4	1	16	1
Rubens BARRICHELLO	2	r	9	r	9	8	3	3	2	9	7	10	10	10	12	5	6	11	12
(Ferrari)	11	12	20	9	16	10	7	20	7	5	5	15	7	11	7	12	9	9	8
Jenson BUTTON	11r	r	r	dq	-	-	10	r	-	4	5	3	5	5	8	3	7	5	8
(BAR-Honda)	8	9	11	3	-	-	13	1	3ns	7	2	2	8	13	3	8	4	2	4
David COULTHARD	4	6	8	11	8	r	4	7	-	10	13	7	r	7	15	r	r	6	9
(Red Bull-Cosworth)	5	8	14	14	9	7	12	12	16ns	15	13	11	13	12	10	11	14	6	7
Anthony DAVIDSON	-	r	-	-	-	-	-	-	-	-	-	-	-	-	-	-	-	-	-
(BAR-Honda)	-	15	-	-	-	-	-	-	-	-	-	-	-	-	-	-	-	-	-
Pedro de la ROSA	-	-	5f	-	-	-	-	-	-	-	-	-	-	-	-	-	-	-	-
(McLaren-Mercedes Benz)	ap	ap	8	ap	ap	-	-	ap	ap	ap	ap	-	-	ap	ap	-	-	ap	ap
Robert DOORNBOS	-	-	-	-	-	-	-	-	-	-	-	18	r	13	18	13	r	14	14
(Jordan-Toyota)	ap	ap	ap	ap	ap	ap	-	-	ap	ap	-	-	-	-	-	-	-	-	-
(Minardi-Cosworth)	-	-	-	-	-	-	-	-	-	-	-	17	19	17	18	17	18	15	20
Giancarlo FISICHELLA	1	r	r	r	5f	12	6	r	-	6	4	4	9	4	3	r	5	2	4
(Renault)	1	3	10	12	6	4	9	4	4ns	6	6	4	9	2	8	13	3	3	2
Patrick FREISACHER	17	r	12	r	r	r	18	r	6	r	19	-	-	-	-	-	-	-	-
(Minardi-Cosworth)	16	20	19	19	15	13	18	19	20	18	19	-	-	-	-	-	-	-	-
Nick HEIDFELD	r	3	r	6	10	2	2	r	-	14	12	11	6	r	-	-	-	-	-
(Williams-BMW)	7	10	4	8	17	6	1	13	15ns	14	14	7	12	6	-	-	-	-	-
Narain KARTHIKEYAN	15	11	r	12	13	r	16	r	4	15	r	16	12	14	20	11	15	15	r
(Jordan-Toyota)	12	17	17	16	13	17	19	17	19	17	17	19	18	18	19	20	15	11	15
Nicolas KIESA	-	-	-	-	-	-	-	-	-	-	-	-	-	-	-	-	-	-	-
(Jordan-Toyota)	-	-	-	-	-	-	-	-	-	-	-	ap	ap	ap	ap	ap	ap	-	ap
Christian KLIEN	7	8	-	-	-	-	-	8	-	r	15	9	r	8	13	9	9	9	5
(Red Bull-Cosworth)	6	7	7ns	ap	ap	ap	ap	16	14ns	16	15	10	11	10	13	16	6	4	14
Vitantonio LIUZZI	-	-	-	8	r	r	9	-	-	-	-	-	-	-	-	-	-	-	-
(Red Bull-Cosworth)	ap	ap	ap	15	11	12	14	-	-	ap	ap	ap	ap	ap	ap	ap	ap	ap	ap
Felipe MASSA	10	10	7	10	11r	9	14	4	-	r	10	8	14	r	9	10	11	10	6
(Sauber-Petronas)	18	14	12	18	10	11	11	11	10ns	9	16	13	14	8	15	7	8	10	11
Franck MONTAGNY	-	-	-	-	-	-	-	-	-	-	-	-	-	-	-	-	-	-	-
(Jordan-Toyota)	-	-	-	-	-	ap	-	-	-	-	-	-	-	-	-	-	-	-	-
Tiago MONTEIRO	16	12	10	13	12	13	15	10	3	13	17	17	13	15	17	8	r	13	11
(Jordan-Toyota)	14	18	16	17	18	15	17	18	17	19	20	18	20	14	17	19	11	20	19
Juan Pablo MONTOYA	6	4	-	-	7	5	7	r	-	r	1	2	r	3f	1	14r	1	r	r
(McLaren-Mercedes Benz)	9	11	-	-	7	16	5	5	11ns	8	3	20	2	4	1	1	2	18	5
Chanoch NISSANY	-	-	-	-	-	-	-	-	-	-	-	-	-	-	-	-	-	-	-
(Minardi-Cosworth)	-	-	-	-	-	-	-	-	-	-	-	-	ap	-	-	-	-	-	-
Olivier PANIS	-	-	-	-	-	-	-	-	-	-	-	-	-	-	-	-	-	-	-
(Toyota)	-	-	-	-	-	-	-	-	-	ap	-	-	-	-	-	-	-	-	-
Antonio PIZZONIA	-	-	-	-	-	-	-	-	-	-	-	-	-	-	7	15r	r	r	13
(Williams-BMW)	-	-	-	-	-	-	-	-	-	-	-	-	-	-	16	15	13	12	13
Kimi RÄIKKÖNEN	8	9f	3	r	1	1	11r	1f	-	2f	3f	rf	1f	1	4f	1	2f	1f	2f
(McLaren-Mercedes Benz)	10	6	9	1	1	1	2	7	2ns	13	12	1	4	1	11	2	5	17	3
Takuma SATO	14r	-	r	dq	-	-	12	r	-	11	16	12	8	9	16	r	10	dq	r
(BAR-Honda)	20	-	13	6	-	-	16	6	8ns	4	7	8	10	20	4	10	19	5	17
Michael SCHUMACHER	r	7	r	2f	r	7f	5	2	1f	3	6	5	2	r	10	r	4	7	r
(Ferrari)	19	13	2	13	8	8	10	2	5	3	9	5	1	19	6	6	7	14	6
Ralf SCHUMACHER	12	5	4	9	4	6	r	6	-	7	8	6	3	12	6	7f	8	8	3
(Toyota)	15	5	6	10	4	18	8	10	ns	11	8	12	5	9	9	5	10	1	9
Scott SPEED	-	-	-	-	-	-	-	-	-	-	-	-	-	-	-	-	-	-	-
(Red Bull-Cosworth)	-	-	-	-	-	-	-	ap	ap	-	-	-	-	-	-	-	-	-	-
Enrico TOCCACELO	-	-	-	-	-	-	-	-	-	-	-	-	-	ap	ap	ap	-	-	-
(Minardi-Cosworth)	-	-	-	-	-	-	-	-	-	-	-	-	-	-	-	-	-	-	-
Jarno TRULLI	9	2	2	5	3	10	8	r	-	5	9	14r	4	6	5	r	13	r	15
(Toyota)	2	2	3	5	5	5	4	9	1ns	2	4	9	3	5	5	3	17	19	12
Jacques VILLENEUVE	13	r	11r	4	r	11	13	9	-	8	14	15	r	11	11	6	12	12	10
(Sauber-Petronas)	4	16	15	11	12	9	15	8	12ns	10	10	14	15	16	12	14	11	8	16
Mark WEBBER	5	r	6	7	6	3	r	5	-	12	11	nc	7	r	14	4	nc	4	7
(Williams-BMW)	3	4	5	4	2	3	3	14	9ns	12	11	6	16	7	14	9	12	7	10
Alex WURZ	-	-	-	3	-	-	-	-	-	-	-	-	-	-	-	-	-	-	-
(McLaren-Mercedes Benz)	-	-	ap	7	-	ap	ap	-	-	-	ap	ap	-	-	ap	ap	-	-	-
Sakon YAMAMOTO	-	-	-	-	-	-	-	-	-	-	-	-	-	-	-	-	-	ap	-
(Jordan-Toyota)	-	-	-	-	-	-	-	-	-	-	-	-	-	-	-	-	-	-	-
Ricardo ZONTA	-	-	-	-	-	-	-	-	-	-	-	-	-	-	-	-	-	-	-
(Toyota)	ap	ap	ap	ap	ap	ap	ap	ap	13ns	-	ap	ap	ap	ap	ap	ap	ap	ap	ap

Season-by-Season Summary

Indianapolis 500
(1950 to 1960)

	1950	1951	1952	1953	1954	1955	1956	1957	1958	1959	1960
Walt ADER	22	-	-	-	-	-	-	-	-	-	-
	29	-	-	-	-	-	-	-	-	-	-
Freddie AGABASHIAN	28r/25=	17r	27r	4=	6	32r	12	22r	-	-	-
	2	11	1	2	24	4	7	4	nq	-	-
George AMICK †	-	-	-	-	-	-	-	-	2	-	-
	-	-	-	-	-	-	-	nq	25	-	-
Red AMICK	-	-	-	-	-	-	-	-	-	31r	11
	-	-	-	-	-	-	-	-	-	-	-
Keith ANDREWS †	-	-	-	-	-	20r	26r	-	-	-	-
	-	-	-	-	-	28	20	nq	-	-	-
Frank ARMI	-	-	-	-	19=	-	-	-	-	-	-
	-	nq	-	nq	33	-	-	-	-	-	-
Chuck ARNOLD	-	-	-	-	-	-	-	-	-	15	-
	-	-	-	-	-	-	-	-	-	21	nq
Alberto ASCARI †	-	-	31r	-	-	-	-	-	-	-	-
	-	-	19	-	-	-	-	-	-	-	-
Manny AYULO †	-	3=	20	13r	13	-	-	-	-	-	-
	nq	-	28	4	22	nq	-	-	-	-	-
Bobby BALL †	-	5	32r	-	-	-	-	-	-	-	-
	-	29	17	-	-	-	-	-	-	-	-
Henry BANKS	25=	6	19	-	-	-	-	-	-	-	-
	21	17	12	nq	-	-	-	-	-	-	-
Tony BETTENHAUSEN	31r/5=	9r	24r	9r=	29r/15=	2=	22r	15	4f	4	23r
	8	9	30	6	21	2	5	22	9	15	18
Art BISCH †	-	-	-	-	-	-	-	-	33r	-	-
	-	-	-	-	-	-	-	-	28	-	-
Johnny BOYD	-	-	-	-	-	29r	30r	6	3	6	27r
	-	-	-	-	-	26	12	5	8	11	13
Don BRANSON	-	-	-	-	-	-	-	-	-	24r	4
	-	-	-	-	-	-	-	-	-	10	8
Walt BROWN †	19	26r	-	-	-	-	-	-	-	-	-
	20	13	-	-	-	-	-	-	-	-	-
Jimmy BRYAN †	-	-	6	14	2	24r	19	3	1	33r	19r
	-	nq	21	31	3	11	19	15	7	20	10
Bill CANTRELL	27r=	-	-	-	-	-	-	-	-	-	-
	-	nq	nq	-	-	-	-	-	-	-	-
Duane CARTER	12	8	4	24r/3=	15=/4=	11	-	-	-	7	12
	13	4	6	27	8	18	-	-	-	12	27
Bill CHEESBOURG	-	-	-	-	-	-	-	26r	10	21r	-
	-	-	-	-	-	-	nq	23	33	30	nq
Joie CHITWOOD	5=	-	-	-	-	-	-	-	-	-	-
	9	-	-	-	-	-	-	-	-	-	-
Bob CHRISTIE	-	-	-	-	-	-	13	13	14r	25r	10
	-	-	-	-	nq	nq	25	33	17	24	14
George CONNOR	8	30r	8	-	-	-	-	-	-	-	-
	4	21	14	nq	-	-	-	-	-	-	-
Ray CRAWFORD	-	-	-	-	-	23r	29r	-	-	23r	-
	-	-	-	-	-	23	17	nq	nq	32	-
Larry CROCKETT †	-	-	-	-	9	-	-	-	-	-	-
	-	-	-	-	25	-	-	-	-	-	-
Art CROSS	-	-	5	2	11=	17r	-	-	-	-	-
	-	-	20	12	27	24	-	-	-	-	-

	1950	1951	1952	1953	1954	1955	1956	1957	1958	1959	1960
Jimmy DAVIES	17	16r	-	10	11=/20r=	3	-	-	-	-	-
	27	27	-	32	-	10	nq	nq	-	nq	nq
Jimmy DAYWALT	-	-	-	6	27r	9	24r	28r	-	14	-
	-	nq	nq	21	2	17	16	29	nq	13	-
Duke DINSMORE	33r	24r	-	16r=	-	-	17	-	-	-	-
	7	32	nq	-	nq	-	33	-	-	-	nq
Len DUNCAN	-	-	-	-	31r=	-	-	-	-	-	-
	-	-	-	nq	26	nq	nq	-	-	-	-
Don EDMUNDS	-	-	-	-	-	-	-	19r	-	-	-
	-	-	-	-	-	-	-	27	nq	nq	-
Ed ELISIAN †	-	-	-	-	18r=	30r	23r=	29r	28r	-	-
	-	-	-	-	31	29	14	7	2	-	-
Walt FAULKNER †	7	15r	-	17=	12=	5=	-	-	-	-	-
	1	14	nq	14	-	7	-	-	-	-	-
Pat FLAHERTY	10	-	-	22r	28r=	10	1	-	-	19r	-
	11	-	-	24	-	12	1	-	-	18	-
Myron FOHR	11	-	-	-	-	-	-	-	-	-	-
	16	nq	-	-	-	-	-	-	-	-	-
George FONDER †	-	-	15	-	19=/31r=	-	-	-	-	-	-
	nq	nq	13	nq	-	-	-	-	-	-	-
Carl FORBERG	-	7	-	-	-	-	-	-	-	-	-
	nq	24	nq	-	-	-	-	-	-	-	-
Gene FORCE	-	11r	-	-	-	-	-	-	-	-	28r
	-	22	nq	-	-	-	-	nq	-	nq	20
A J FOYT	-	-	-	-	-	-	-	-	16r	10	25r
	-	-	-	-	-	-	-	-	12	17	16
Don FREELAND	-	-	-	27r	7	15r	3	17	7	22r	22r
	-	-	-	15	6	21	26	21	13	25	11
Billy GARRETT	-	-	-	-	-	-	16	-	21r	-	-
	-	-	-	-	-	-	29	nq	15	-	-
Elmer GEORGE	-	-	-	-	-	-	-	33r	-	-	-
	-	-	-	-	-	nq	-	9	nq	nq	-
Paul GOLDSMITH	-	-	-	-	-	-	-	-	30r	5	3
	-	-	-	-	-	-	-	-	16	16	26
Cecil GREEN †	4	22r	-	-	-	-	-	-	-	-	-
	12	10	-	-	-	-	-	-	-	-	-
Cliff GRIFFITH	-	28r	9	-	-	-	10	-	-	-	-
	nq	18	9	nq	nq	nq	30	nq	-	-	nq
Bobby GRIM	-	-	-	-	-	-	-	-	-	26r	16
	-	-	-	-	-	-	-	-	-	5	21
Sam HANKS	30r	12r	3	3=	20r=/11=	19r	2	1	-	-	-
	25	12	5	9	10	6	13	13	-	-	-
Gene HARTLEY	16	-	28r	28r/9r=	23r=	-	11	10	-	11	14
	31	-	18	13	17	nq	22	14	nq	9	24
Mack HELLINGS †	13	31r	-	-	-	-	-	-	-	-	-
	26	23	-	-	-	-	-	-	-	-	-
Al HERMAN †	-	-	-	-	-	7	28r	21r	-	13	32r
	-	-	-	nq	nq	16	27	30	nq	23	30
Bill HOLLAND	2f	-	-	15r=	-	-	-	-	-	-	-
	10	-	-	28	nq	-	nq	-	-	-	-
Jackie HOLMES	23r	-	-	19r=	-	-	-	-	-	-	-
	30	nq	nq	-	-	-	-	-	-	-	-
Bill HOMEIER	-	-	-	-	33r/24r=	5=	-	-	-	-	13
	-	-	-	nq	18	-	-	-	nq	nq	31
Jerry HOYT †	21	-	-	23r=	26r/8=	31r	-	-	-	-	-
	15	nq	-	7	30	1	-	-	-	-	-
Jim HURTUBISE	-	-	-	-	-	-	-	-	-	-	18r
	-	-	-	-	-	-	-	-	-	-	23
Jimmy JACKSON	29r	-	-	-	15=	-	-	-	-	-	-
	32	-	nq	-	-	-	-	-	-	-	-
Joe JAMES †	-	33r	13	-	-	-	-	-	-	-	-
	nq	30	16	-	-	-	-	-	-	-	-
Eddie JOHNSON	-	-	16	7=	22r=	13	15	25r	9	8	6
	-	-	24	-	-	32	32	20	26	8	7
Al KELLER	-	-	-	-	-	27r	14	27r	11	18r	-
	-	-	-	-	-	22	28	8	21	28	nq

	1950	1951	1952	1953	1954	1955	1956	1957	1958	1959	1960
Danny KLADIS	-	-	-	-	30r=	-	-	-	-	-	-
	nq	nq	nq	-	-	nq	nq	nq	-	-	-
Jud LARSON	-	-	-	-	-	-	-	-	8	29r	-
	-	-	nq	nq	-	-	-	nq	19	19	-
Bayliss LEVRETT	27r=	-	-	-	-	-	-	-	-	-	-
	17	nq	nq	-	-	-	-	-	-	-	-
Andy LINDEN	-	4	33r	33r/16r=/23r=	25r=/11=/24r=	6	27r	5	-	-	-
	nq	31	2	5	23	8	9	12	-	-	-
Bill MACKEY †	-	19r	-	-	-	-	-	-	-	-	-
	-	33	-	-	-	-	-	-	-	-	-
Mike MAGILL	-	-	-	-	-	-	-	24r	17	30r	-
	-	-	-	-	-	-	nq	18	31	31	nq
Johnny MANTZ	-	-	-	17=	-	-	-	-	-	-	-
	-	-	-	-	-	-	-	-	-	-	-
Ernie McCOY	-	-	-	8	16	-	-	-	-	-	-
	-	-	-	20	20	nq	nq	-	-	-	-
Johnny McDOWELL †	18	32r	21	-	-	-	-	-	-	-	-
	33	26	33	-	-	-	-	-	-	-	-
Jack McGRATH †	14r	3=	11	5	3f	26r	-	-	-	-	-
	6	3	3	3	1	3	-	-	-	-	-
Jim McWiTHEY	-	-	-	-	-	-	-	-	-	16	29r
	-	-	-	-	-	-	nq	nq	nq	33	32
Chet MILLER †	-	25r	30r	-	-	-	-	-	-	-	-
	nq	28	27	nq	-	-	-	-	-	-	-
Duke NALON	-	10r	25r	11r	-	-	-	-	-	-	-
	nq	1	4	26	nq	-	-	-	-	-	-
Mike NAZARUK †	-	2	-	21r	5	-	-	-	-	-	-
	-	7	nq	23	14	-	-	-	-	-	-
Cal NIDAY	-	-	-	30r	10	16r	-	-	-	-	-
	-	-	-	30	13	9	nq	nq	-	-	-
Pat O'CONNOR †	-	-	-	-	21r	8	18	8	29r	-	-
	-	-	-	nq	12	19	3	1	5	-	-
Johnnie PARSONS	1	21r	10	26r	32r/11=	21r	4	16	12	-	-
	5	8	31	8	15	27	6	17	6	-	-
Dick RATHMANN	32r	-	-	-	-	-	5	-	27r	20r	31r
	18	-	-	-	-	-	4	-	1	4	4
Jim RATHMANN	24	-	2	7=/15r=	28r=/20r=	14	20r	2f	5	2	1f
	28	-	10	25	28	20	2	32	20	3	2
Jimmy REECE †	-	-	7	-	17	33r	9	18r	6	-	-
	-	-	23	nq	7	15	21	6	3	-	-
Jim RIGSBY †	-	-	12	-	-	-	-	-	-	-	-
	nq	-	26	-	-	-	-	-	-	-	-
Mauri ROSE	3	14r	-	-	-	-	-	-	-	-	-
	3	5	-	-	-	-	-	-	-	-	-
Lloyd RUBY	-	-	-	-	-	-	-	-	-	-	7
	-	-	-	-	-	-	-	-	-	-	12
Eddie RUSSO	-	-	-	-	-	22r	23r=	32r	-	-	26r
	-	-	-	-	nq	13	-	26	nq	nq	29
Paul RUSSO	9	-	-	25r/4=	8=	2=	33rf	4	18r	9	-
	19	nq	nq	17	32	-	8	10	14	27	nq
Troy RUTTMAN	15	23r	1	-	4=	-	31r	31r	-	-	20r
	24	6	7	-	11	nq	11	3	nq	-	6
Eddie SACHS	-	-	-	-	-	-	-	23r	22r	17r	21r
	-	-	-	nq	nq	-	nq	2	18	2	1
Carl SCARBOROUGH †	-	18r	-	12=	-	-	-	-	-	-	-
	-	15	nq	19	-	-	-	-	-	-	-
Bill SCHINDLER †	26r	13r	14	-	-	-	-	-	-	-	-
	22	16	15	-	-	-	-	-	-	-	-
Bob SCOTT †	-	-	29r	31r/12=	18r=/25r=	-	-	-	-	-	-
	-	nq	25	11	-	-	-	-	-	-	-
Chuck STEVENSON	-	20r	18	29r/9r=/23=	12=	-	-	-	-	-	15
	-	19	11	16	5	-	-	-	-	-	9
Len SUTTON	-	-	-	-	-	-	-	-	32r	32r	30r
	-	-	-	-	-	-	nq	-	27	22	5
Bob SWEIKERT †	-	-	26r	20r	14	1	6	-	-	-	-
	nq	nq	32	29	9	14	10	-	-	-	-

	1950	1951	1952	1953	1954	1955	1956	1957	1958	1959	1960
Marshall TEAGUE †	-	-	-	18r	23r=/15=	-	-	7	-	-	-
	-	-	-	22	-	-	nq	28	nq	-	-
Shorty TEMPLEMAN	-	-	-	-	-	18r	-	-	19r	-	17
	-	-	-	-	-	31	nq	-	23	nq	19
Johnny THOMSON †	-	-	-	32r/19r=	24r=	4	32r	12	23r	3f	5
	-	-	-	33	4	33	18	11	22	1	17
Bud TINGELSTAD	-	-	-	-	-	-	-	-	-	-	9
	-	-	-	-	-	-	-	-	-	-	28
Johnnie TOLAN	-	-	-	-	-	-	21	20r	13	-	-
	-	nq	nq	nq	nq	nq	31	31	30	nq	nq
Jack TURNER	-	-	-	-	-	-	25r	11	25r	27r	-
	-	-	-	-	-	-	24	19	10	14	nq
Jerry UNSER †	-	-	-	-	-	-	-	-	31r	-	-
	-	-	-	-	-	-	-	-	24	nq	-
Bob VEITH	-	-	-	-	-	-	7	9	26r	12	8
	-	-	-	-	-	-	23	16	4	7	25
Bill VUKOVICH †	-	29r	17rf	1f	1	25rf	-	-	-	-	-
	nq	20	8	1	19	5	-	-	-	-	-
Lee WALLARD	6	1f	-	-	-	-	-	-	-	-	-
	23	2	nq	-	-	-	-	-	-	-	-
Rodger WARD	-	27r	23r	16r=	22r=	28r	8	30r	20r	1	2
	-	25	22	10	16	30	15	24	11	6	3
Spider WEBB	20	-	22r	19r=	30r=	-	-	-	-	-	-
	14	-	29	18	29	nq	-	-	-	-	-
Wayne WEILER	-	-	-	-	-	-	-	-	-	-	24r
	-	-	-	-	-	-	-	-	-	-	15
Chuck WEYANT	-	-	-	-	-	12	-	14	24r	28r	-
	-	-	-	-	nq	25	-	25	29	29	nq
Dempsey WILSON	-	-	-	-	-	-	-	-	15r	-	33r
	-	-	-	-	-	-	nq	nq	32	nq	33

Additionally, the drivers who failed at all attempts to qualify for the Indianapolis 500 are listed on page 577.

3

DRIVERS

Grand Prix Starters

Grand Prix Non-Starters

Grand Prix Meeting Testers

Indianapolis 500 Starters

Indianapolis 500 Non-Starters

Drivers often not known by their real name

Left: *Stirling Moss (Lotus), winner of the 1961 German Grand Prix, celebrates with second-placed Wolfgang von Trips (Ferrari), who was at that point leading the championship.* (LAT)

Where drivers have competed in more than one car in any race,
only the best finishing position has been counted in the table.
Therefore, the total placings and non-classifications figures
tally with the number of starts.

Six Formula 2 races were held simultaneously with Grands Prix
(Germany 57, 58, 66, 67 & 69 and Morocco 58), in which drivers
were classified separately and were ineligible for points.
These starts are included in 'GPs' column. F2 drivers in these races
who finished in the top 6 'on the road', have been credited in the
other placings column, as they were not eligible for championship points.

The total points shown, includes those scored but not taken into account for the
Championship.

Places are shown in their native spellings, eg Köln for Cologne, Wien for Vienna.

Key to column headings:

GPs	- Grand Prix starts
PP	- Pole Positions
FL	- Fastest Laps
OP	- Other Placings
NC etc	- Non Classifications (DQ + NC + R)
NS etc	- Non Starts (EW + EXC + NPQ + NQ + NS)
AP	- Also Practised (Grand Prix Meeting Testers table)
R	- Retirements (Indianapolis 500 table)

Grand Prix Starters

Name	Nat	Born / Died	Place of Birth / Place of Death	Years Entered	No. of Years	GPs	Points	PP	FL	Win	2nd	3rd	4th	5th	6th	OP	NC etc	NS etc
ABECASSIS, George	GB	21 Mar 1913 / 18 Dec 1991	Walton-on-Thames, Surrey / Ibstone, Buckinghamshire	1951-52	2	2	0	-	-	-	-	-	-	-	-	-	2	-
ACHESON, Kenny	GB	27 Nov 1957	Cookstown, Tyrone, N Ireland	1983-85	2	3	0	-	-	-	-	-	-	-	-	1	2	7
ADAMS, Philippe	B	19 Nov 1969	Mouscron	1994	1	2	0	-	-	-	-	-	-	-	-	1	1	-
ADOLFF, Kurt	D	5 Nov 1921	Stuttgart	1953	1	1	0	-	-	-	-	-	-	-	-	-	1	-
AHRENS, Kurt	D	19 Apr 1940	Braunschweig, nr Hannover	1966-69	4	4	0	-	-	-	-	-	-	-	-	2	2	-
ALBERS, Christijan	NL	16 Apr 1979	Eindhoven	2005	1	19	4	-	-	-	-	-	-	1	-	12	6	-
ALBORETO, Michele	I	23 Dec 1956 / 25 Apr 2001	Milano / Lausitz, nr Dresden, D	1981-94	14	194	186.5	2	5	5	9	9	10	8	6	55	92	21
ALESI, Jean	F	11 Jun 1964	Montfavet, nr Avignon	1989-01	13	201	241	2	4	1	16	15	11	15	12	49	82	1
ALLIOT, Philippe	F	27 Jul 1954	Voves, nr Chartres	1984-94	9	109	7	-	-	-	-	-	-	1	5	38	65	7
ALLISON, Cliff	GB	8 Feb 1932 / 7 Apr 2005	Brough, Westmorland / Brough, (now Cumbria)	1958-61	4	16	11	-	-	-	1	-	1	2	2	4	6	2
ALONSO, Fernando	E	29 Jul 1981	Oviedo	2001-05	4	69	247	9	3	8	7	8	8	3	2	14	19	1
AMON, Chris	NZ	20 Jul 1943	Palmerston North	1963-76	14	96	83	5	3	-	3	8	4	7	7	22	45	12
ANDERSON, Bob	GB	19 May 1931 / 14 Aug 1967	Hendon, London / Northampton	1963-67	5	25	8	-	-	-	-	1	-	1	2	11	10	4
ANDERSSON, Conny	S	28 Dec 1939	Alingsås	1976-77	2	1	0	-	-	-	-	-	-	-	-	-	1	4
ANDRETTI, Mario	USA	28 Feb 1940	Montona, I (Motovun, Croatia)	1968-82	14	128	180	18	10	12	2	5	7	7	5	24	66	3
ANDRETTI, Michael	USA	5 Oct 1962	Bethlehem, Pennsylvania	1993	1	13	7	-	-	-	-	1	-	1	1	3	7	-
APICELLA, Marco	I	7 Oct 1965	Bologna	1993	1	1	0	-	-	-	-	-	-	-	-	-	1	-
ARNOUX, René	F	4 Jul 1948	Pontcharra, nr Grenoble	1978-89	12	149	181	18	12	7	9	6	7	8	5	40	67	15
ARUNDELL, Peter	GB	8 Nov 1933	Ilford, Essex	1963-66	3	11	12	-	-	-	-	2	1	-	1	4	3	2
ASCARI, Alberto	I	13 Jul 1918 / 26 May 1955	Milano / Monza	1950-55	6	31	140.64	14	13	13	4	-	2	1	1	1	9	1
ASHDOWN, Peter	GB	16 Oct 1934	Danbury, Essex	1959	1	1	0	-	-	-	-	-	-	-	-	1	-	-
ASHLEY, Ian	GB	26 Oct 1947	Wuppertal, D	1974-77	4	4	0	-	-	-	-	-	-	-	-	2	2	7
ASHMORE, Gerry	GB	25 Jul 1936	West Bromwich, Staffordshire	1961-62	2	3	0	-	-	-	-	-	-	-	-	1	2	1
ASTON, Bill	GB	29 Mar 1900 / 4 Mar 1974	Hopton, nr Stafford / Lingfield, Surrey	1952	1	1	0	-	-	-	-	-	-	-	-	-	1	2
ATTWOOD, Dickie	GB	4 Apr 1940	Wolverhampton, Staffordshire	1964-69	5	17	11	-	1	-	1	-	1	-	2	9	4	1
BADOER, Luca	I	25 Jan 1971	Montebelluna, Treviso	1993-99	4	49	0	-	-	-	-	-	-	-	-	23	26	7
BAGHETTI, Giancarlo	I	25 Dec 1934 / 27 Nov 1995	Milano / Milano	1961-67	7	21	14	-	1	1	-	-	1	1	-	7	11	-
BAILEY, Julian	GB	9 Oct 1961	Woolwich, London	1988-91	2	7	1	-	-	-	-	-	-	-	1	4	2	13
BALDI, Mauro	I	31 Jan 1954	Reggio-Emilia	1982-85	4	36	5	-	-	-	-	-	-	1	3	13	19	5
BALSA, Marcel	F	1 Jan 1909 / 11 Aug 1984	Saint-Frion / Maisons-Alfort, Val-de-Marne	1952	1	1	0	-	-	-	-	-	-	-	-	-	1	-
BANDINI, Lorenzo	I	21 Dec 1935 / 10 May 1967	Barce, Cyrenaica (Libya) / Monte-Carlo, MC	1961-67	7	42	58	1	2	1	2	5	2	4	3	11	14	-
BARBAZZA, Fabrizio	I	2 Apr 1963	Monza	1991-93	2	8	2	-	-	-	-	-	-	-	2	1	5	12
BARBER, John	GB	22 Jul 1929	Little Marlow, Buckinghamshire	1953	1	1	0	-	-	-	-	-	-	-	-	1	-	-
BARBER, Skip	USA	16 Nov 1936	Philadelphia, Pennsylvania	1971-72	2	5	0	-	-	-	-	-	-	-	-	1	4	-
BARILLA, Paolo	I	20 Apr 1961	Milano	1989-90	2	9	0	-	-	-	-	-	-	-	-	4	5	6
BARRICHELLO, Rubens	BR	23 May 1972	São Paulo	1993-05	13	215	489	13	15	9	26	26	15	14	6	41	78	3
BARTH, Edgar	D	26 Jan 1917 / 20 May 1965	Herold-Erzegeberge / Ludwigsburg, nr Stuttgart	1953-64	5	5	0	-	-	-	-	-	-	-	-	3	2	-
BASSI, Giorgio	I	20 Jan 1934	Milano	1965	1	1	0	-	-	-	-	-	-	-	-	-	1	-
BAUER, Erwin	D	17 Jul 1912 / 3 Jun 1958	Stuttgart / Köln	1953	1	1	0	-	-	-	-	-	-	-	-	-	1	-
BAUMGARTNER, Zsolt	H	1 Jan 1981	Debrecen	2003-04	2	20	1	-	-	-	-	-	-	-	-	12	8	-
BAYOL, Élie	F	28 Feb 1914 / 25 May 1995	Marseille / La Ciotat	1952-56	5	7	2	-	-	-	-	-	-	1	1	-	5	1
BEAUMAN, Don	GB	26 Jul 1928 / 9 Jul 1955	Farnborough, Hampshire / Rathnew, Co Wicklow, IRL	1954	1	1	0	-	-	-	-	-	-	-	-	1	-	-
BECHEM, Günther (also known as Bernd NACKE)	D	21 Dec 1921	Hagen	1952-53	2	2	0	-	-	-	-	-	-	-	-	-	2	-

	Nat	Born / Died	Place of Birth / Place of Death	Years Entered	No. of Years	GPs	Points	PP	FL	Win	2nd	3rd	4th	5th	6th	OP	NC etc	NS etc
BEHRA, Jean	F	16 Feb 1921 / 1 Aug 1959	Nice / AVUS, Berlin, D	1952-59	8	52	51.14	-	1	-	2	7	2	4	6	4	27	1
BELL, Derek	GB	31 Oct 1941	Pinner, Middlesex	1968-74	6	9	1	-	-	-	-	-	-	-	1	1	7	7
BELLOF, Stefan	D	20 Nov 1957 / 1 Sep 1985	Giessen / Spa-Francorchamps, B	1984-85	2	20	4	-	-	-	-	-	1	-	1	5	13	2
BELMONDO, Paul	F	23 Apr 1963	Boulogne-Billancourt	1992-94	2	7	0	-	-	-	-	-	-	-	-	5	2	20
BELSØ, Tom	DK	27 Aug 1942	Gladsaxe-Søburg, København	1973-74	2	2	0	-	-	-	-	-	-	-	-	1	1	3
BELTOISE, Jean-Pierre	F	26 Apr 1937	Boulogne-Billancourt	1966-74	9	86	77	-	4	1	3	4	3	10	4	25	36	2
BERETTA, Olivier	MC	23 Nov 1969	Monte-Carlo	1994	1	9	0	-	-	-	-	-	-	-	-	4	5	1
BERG, Allen	CDN	1 Aug 1961	Calgary, Alberta	1986	1	9	0	-	-	-	-	-	-	-	-	3	6	-
BERGER, Georges	B	14 Sep 1918 / 23 Aug 1967	Molenbeek-St.-Jean, Bruxelles / Nürburgring, D	1953-54	2	2	0	-	-	-	-	-	-	-	-	-	2	-
BERGER, Gerhard	A	27 Aug 1959	Wörgl, nr Innsbruck	1984-97	14	210	386	12	21	10	17	21	26	8	13	29	86	-
BERNARD, Éric	F	24 Aug 1964	Istres, Martigues	1989-94	4	45	10	-	-	-	-	1	1	-	3	17	23	2
BERNOLDI, Enrique	BR	19 Oct 1978	Curitiba	2001-02	2	28	0	-	-	-	-	-	-	-	-	9	19	1
BEUTTLER, Mike	GB	13 Apr 1940 / 29 Dec 1988	Cairo, Egypt / Los Angeles, California, USA	1971-73	3	28	0	-	-	-	-	-	-	-	-	12	16	1
BIANCHI, Lucien	B	10 Nov 1934 / 30 Mar 1969	Milano, I / Le Mans, F	1959-68	7	17	6	-	-	-	-	1	-	-	2	3	11	2
BIANCO, Gino	BR	22 Jul 1916 / 17 Jan 1983	Torino, I / Rio de Janeiro	1952	1	4	0	-	-	-	-	-	-	-	-	1	3	-
BINDER, Hans	A	12 Jun 1948	Zell am Ziller, nr Innsbruck	1976-78	3	13	0	-	-	-	-	-	-	-	-	6	7	2
BIONDETTI, Clemente	I	18 Aug 1898 / 24 Feb 1955	Buddusó, Sardegna / Firenze	1950	1	1	0	-	-	-	-	-	-	-	-	-	1	-
BIRA, B	T	15 Jul 1914 / 23 Dec 1985	Bangkok / Baron's Court, London, GB	1950-54	5	19	8	-	-	-	-	-	2	1	1	6	9	-
BIRGER, Pablo	RA	6 Jan 1924 / 9 Mar 1966	Buenos Aires / Buenos Aires	1953-55	2	2	0	-	-	-	-	-	-	-	-	-	2	-
BLANCHARD, Harry	USA	30 Jun 1929 / 31 Jan 1960	Burlington, Vermont / Buenos Aires, RA	1959	1	1	0	-	-	-	-	-	-	-	-	1	-	-
BLEEKEMOLEN, Michael	NL	2 Oct 1949	Amsterdam	1977-78	2	1	0	-	-	-	-	-	-	-	-	-	1	4
BLOKDYK, Trevor	ZA	30 Nov 1935 / 19 Mar 1995	Krugersdorp, Transvaal / Hekpoort, nr Krugersdorp	1963-65	2	1	0	-	-	-	-	-	-	-	-	1	-	1
BLUNDELL, Mark	GB	8 Apr 1966	Barnet, Hertfordshire	1991-95	4	61	32	-	-	-	-	3	2	6	2	18	30	2
BOESEL, Raul	BR	4 Dec 1957	Curitiba	1982-83	2	23	0	-	-	-	-	-	-	-	-	10	13	7
BONDURANT, Bob	USA	27 Apr 1933	Evanston, Illinois	1965-66	2	9	3	-	-	-	-	-	1	-	-	3	5	-
BONETTO, Felice	I	9 Jun 1903 / 21 Nov 1953	Manerbio, Brescia / Silao, MEX	1950-53	4	15	17.5	-	-	-	-	2	3	3	1	-	6	1
BONNIER, Jo	S	31 Jan 1930 / 11 Jun 1972	Stockholm / Le Mans, F	1956-71	16	104	39	1	-	1	-	-	1	10	8	31	53	4
BONOMI, Roberto	RA	30 Sep 1919 / 10 Jan 1992	Buenos Aires / Buenos Aires	1960	1	1	0	-	-	-	-	-	-	-	-	1	-	-
BORGUDD, Slim	S	25 Nov 1946	Borgholm, Öland	1981-82	2	10	1	-	-	-	-	-	-	-	1	5	4	5
BOTHA, Luki	ZA	16 Jan 1930	Pretoria	1967	1	1	0	-	-	-	-	-	-	-	-	-	1	-
BOULLION, Jean-Christophe	F	27 Dec 1969	Saint-Brieuc, Côtes-d'Armor	1995	1	11	3	-	-	-	-	-	-	1	1	5	4	-
BOUTSEN, Thierry	B	13 Jul 1957	Bruxelles	1983-93	11	163	132	1	1	3	2	10	8	11	7	56	66	1
BRABHAM, David	AUS	5 Sep 1965	Wimbledon, London, GB	1990-94	2	24	0	-	-	-	-	-	-	-	-	7	17	6
BRABHAM, Jack	AUS	2 Apr 1926	Hurstville, Sydney, NSW	1955-70	16	126	261	13	12	14	10	7	13	5	7	17	53	2
BRACK, Bill	CDN	26 Dec 1935	Toronto, Ontario	1968-72	3	3	0	-	-	-	-	-	-	-	-	-	3	-
BRAMBILLA, Vittorio	I	11 Nov 1937 / 26 May 2001	Monza / Camparada di Lesmo, Brianza	1974-80	7	74	15.5	1	1	1	-	-	1	2	5	28	37	5
BRANCA, Toni	CH	15 Sep 1916 / 10 May 1985	Sierre / Sierre	1950-51	2	3	0	-	-	-	-	-	-	-	-	2	1	-
BRANDON, Eric	GB	18 Jul 1920 / 8 Aug 1982	East Ham, London / Gosport, Hampshire	1952-54	2	5	0	-	-	-	-	-	-	-	-	4	1	-
BRIDGER, Tom	GB	24 Jun 1934 / 30 Jul 1991	Woolmer Green, nr Welwyn, Herts / Aboyne, Aberdeenshire, Scotland	1958	1	1	0	-	-	-	-	-	-	-	-	-	1	-
BRISE, Tony	GB	28 Mar 1952 / 29 Nov 1975	Erith, Dartford, Kent / Arkley, nr Barnet, Hertfordshire	1975	1	10	1	-	-	-	-	-	-	-	1	5	4	-

	Nat	Born / Died	Place of Birth / Place of Death	Years Entered	No. of Years	GPs	Points	PP	FL	Win	2nd	3rd	4th	5th	6th	OP	NC etc	NS etc
BRISTOW, Chris	GB	2 Dec 1937 / 19 Jun 1960	Lambeth, London / Spa-Francorchamps, B	1959-60	2	4	0	-	-	-	-	-	-	-	-	-	1	3	-
BROEKER, Peter	CDN	15 May 1929 / 1980	Hamilton, Ontario	1963	1	1	0	-	-	-	-	-	-	-	:	1	-	-
BROOKS, Tony	GB	25 Feb 1932	Dukinfield, Cheshire	1956-61	6	38	75	3	3	6	2	2	1	3	-	8	16	1
BROWN, Alan	GB	20 Nov 1919 / 20 Jan 2004	Malton, Yorkshire / Guildford, Surrey	1952-54	3	8	2	-	-	-	-	-	1	1	4	2	1
BROWN, Warwick	AUS	24 Dec 1949	Sydney, New South Wales	1976	1	1	0	-	-	-	-	-	-	-	-	1	-	-
BRUDES, Adolf	D	15 Oct 1899 / 5 Nov 1986	Kotulin, nr Breslau (Wroclaw, PL) / Bremen	1952	1	1	0	-	-	-	-	-	-	-	-	-	1	-
BRUNDLE, Martin	GB	1 Jun 1959	King's Lynn, Norfolk	1984-96	12	158	98	-	-	-	2	7	8	12	10	44	75	7
BRUNI, Gianmaria	I	30 May 1981	Roma	2004	1	18	0	-	-	-	-	-	-	-	-	9	9	-
BUCCI, Clemar	RA	4 Sep 1920	Zenón Pereyra, Santa Fe	1954-55	2	5	0	-	-	-	-	-	-	-	-	-	5	-
BUCKNUM, Ronnie	USA	5 Apr 1936 / 23 Apr 1992	Alhambra, California / San Luis Obispo, California	1964-66	3	11	2	-	-	-	-	-	-	1	-	3	7	-
BUEB, Ivor	GB	6 Jun 1923 / 1 Aug 1959	East Ham, London / Clermont-Ferrand, F	1957-59	3	5	0	-	-	-	-	-	-	-	-	3	2	1
BUENO, Luiz	BR	16 Jan 1937	São Paulo	1973	1	1	0	-	-	-	-	-	-	-	-	1	-	-
BURGESS, Ian	GB	6 Jul 1930	London	1958-63	6	16	0	-	-	-	-	-	-	-	1	8	7	4
BURTI, Luciano	BR	5 Mar 1975	São Paulo	2000-01	2	15	0	-	-	-	-	-	-	-	-	9	6	-
BUSSINELLO, Roberto	I	4 Oct 1927 / 24 Aug 1999	Pistoïa / Vicenza	1961-65	2	2	0	-	-	-	-	-	-	-	-	1	1	1
BUTTON, Jenson	GB	19 Jan 1980	Frome, Somerset	2000-05	6	100	167	2	-	-	4	8	7	14	4	35	28	2
BYRNE, Tommy	IRL	6 May 1958	Drogheda, Co. Louth	1982	1	2	0	-	-	-	-	-	-	-	-	-	2	3
CABIANCA, Giulio	I	19 Feb 1923 / 15 Jun 1961	Verona / Modena Aerautodromo	1958-60	3	3	3	-	-	-	-	-	1	-	-	1	1	1
CABRAL, Mário	P	15 Jan 1934	Cedofeita, Porto	1959-64	4	4	0	-	-	-	-	-	-	-	-	1	3	1
CAFFI, Alex	I	18 Mar 1964	Rovato, Brescia	1986-92	7	56	6	-	-	-	-	-	1	1	1	24	29	19
CAMPBELL-JONES, John	GB	21 Jan 1930	Leatherhead, Surrey	1962-63	2	2	0	-	-	-	-	-	-	-	-	2	-	-
CAMPOS, Adrian	E	17 Jun 1960	Alcira, nr Valencia	1987-88	2	17	0	-	-	-	-	-	-	-	-	2	15	4
CANNON, John	CDN	21 Jun 1933 / 18 Oct 1999	Hammersmith, London, GB / nr. Quemado, New Mexico, USA	1971	1	1	0	-	-	-	-	-	-	-	-	1	-	-
CANTONI, Eitel	ROU	4 Oct 1906 / 6 Jun 1997	Montevideo / Montevideo	1952	1	3	0	-	-	-	-	-	-	-	-	1	2	-
CAPELLI, Ivan	I	24 May 1963	Milano	1985-93	9	93	31	-	-	-	2	1	1	4	4	17	64	5
CARINI, Piero	I	6 Mar 1921 / 30 May 1957	Genova / Saint-Étienne, F	1952-53	2	3	0	-	-	-	-	-	-	-	-	-	3	-
CASTELLOTTI, Eugenio	I	10 Oct 1930 / 14 Mar 1957	Lodi, nr Milano / Modena Aerautodromo	1955-57	3	14	19.5	1	-	-	2	1	1	1	1	2	6	-
CECOTTO, Johnny	YV	25 Jan 1956	Caracas	1983-84	2	18	1	-	-	-	-	-	-	-	1	6	11	5
CEVERT, François	F	25 Feb 1944 / 6 Oct 1973	Paris / Watkins Glen, New York, USA	1969-73	5	47	89	-	2	1	10	2	2	2	2	10	18	1
CHABOUD, Eugène	F	12 Apr 1907 / 28 Dec 1983	Lyon / Montfermeil	1950-51	2	3	1	-	-	-	-	-	1	-	-	1	1	-
CHAMBERLAIN, Jay	USA	29 Dec 1925 / 1 Aug 2001	Hollywood, California / Tucson, Arizona	1962	1	1	0	-	-	-	-	-	-	-	-	1	-	2
CHARLTON, Dave	ZA	27 Oct 1936	Brotton, Yorkshire, GB	1965-75	9	11	0	-	-	-	-	-	-	-	-	3	8	2
CHEEVER, Eddie	USA	10 Jan 1958	Phoenix, Arizona	1978-89	11	132	70	-	-	-	2	7	5	4	7	30	77	11
CHIESA, Andrea	CH	6 May 1964	Milano	1992	1	3	0	-	-	-	-	-	-	-	-	-	3	7
CHIMERI, Ettore	I	4 Jun 1921 / 27 Feb 1960	Lodi, nr Milano / Playas, Cuba	1960	1	1	0	-	-	-	-	-	-	-	-	-	1	-
CHIRON, Louis	MC	3 Aug 1899 / 22 Jun 1979	Monte-Carlo / Monte-Carlo	1950-58	6	15	4	-	-	-	-	1	-	-	2	4	8	4
CLAES, Johnny	B	11 Aug 1916 / 3 Feb 1956	Fulham, London, GB / Bruxelles	1950-55	5	23	0	-	-	-	-	-	-	-	-	13	10	2
CLARK, Jim	GB	4 Mar 1936 / 7 Apr 1968	Kilmany, Fifeshire, Scotland / Hockenheim, D	1960-68	9	72	274	33	28	25	1	6	4	3	1	9	23	1
COLLINS, Peter	GB	6 Nov 1931 / 3 Aug 1958	Kidderminster, Worcestershire / Bonn, D	1952-58	7	32	47	-	-	3	3	3	1	1	2	3	16	3

Drivers

	Nat	Born / Died	Place of Birth / Place of Death	Years Entered	No. of Years	GPs	Points	PP	FL	Win	2nd	3rd	4th	5th	6th	OP	NC etc	NS etc
COLLOMB, Bernard	F	7 Oct 1930	Annecy	1961-64	4	4	0	-	-	-	-	-	-	-	-	1	3	2
COMAS, Erik	F	28 Sep 1963	Romans-sur-Isère, nr Valence	1991-94	4	59	7	-	-	-	-	-	-	1	5	26	27	4
COMOTTI, Franco	I	24 Jul 1906 / 10 May 1963	Brescia / Bergamo	1950-52	2	2	0	-	-	-	-	-	-	-	-	1	1	-
CONSTANTINE, George	USA	22 Feb 1918 / 7 Jan 1968	Southbridge, Massachusetts / Massachusetts	1959	1	1	0	-	-	-	-	-	-	-	-	-	1	-
CORDTS, John	CDN	23 Jul 1935	Sweden	1969	1	1	0	-	-	-	-	-	-	-	-	-	1	-
COULTHARD, David	GB	27 Mar 1971	Twynholm, Dumfries, Scotland	1994-05	12	193	499	12	18	13	26	21	11	16	13	33	60	1
COURAGE, Piers	GB	27 May 1942 / 21 Jun 1970	Colchester, Essex / Zandvoort, NL	1966-70	5	28	20	-	-	-	2	-	1	2	1	3	19	2
CRAFT, Chris	GB	17 Nov 1939	Porthleven, Cornwall	1971	1	1	0	-	-	-	-	-	-	-	-	-	1	1
CRAWFORD, Jim	GB	13 Feb 1948 / 6 Aug 2002	Dunfermline, Scotland / Tierre Verde, Florida, USA	1975	1	2	0	-	-	-	-	-	-	-	-	-	1	1
CREUS, Antonio	E	28 Oct 1924 / 19 Feb 1996	Madrid / Madrid	1960	1	1	0	-	-	-	-	-	-	-	-	-	1	-
CROOK, Tony	GB	16 Feb 1920	Chorlton, Manchester	1952-53	2	2	0	-	-	-	-	-	-	-	-	1	1	-
CROSSLEY, Geoffrey	GB	11 May 1921 / 7 Jan 2002	Baslow, nr Bakewell, Derbyshire / Headington, Oxfordshire	1950	1	2	0	-	-	-	-	-	-	-	-	1	1	-
d'OREY, Fritz	BR	25 Mar 1938	São Paulo	1959	1	3	0	-	-	-	-	-	-	-	-	1	2	-
da MATTA, Cristiano	BR	19 Sep 1973	Belo Horizonte	2003-04	2	28	13	-	-	-	-	-	-	-	3	17	8	-
da SILVA RAMOS, Nano	F/BR	7 Dec 1925	Paris	1955-56	2	7	2	-	-	-	-	-	1	-	2	4	-
DAIGH, Chuck	USA	29 Nov 1923	Long Beach, California	1960	1	3	0	-	-	-	-	-	-	-	-	1	2	3
DALMAS, Yannick	F	28 Jul 1961	Le Beausset, nr Toulon	1987-94	5	23	2	-	-	-	-	-	-	1	-	14	8	26
DALY, Derek	IRL	11 Mar 1953	Dundrum, Dublin	1978-82	5	49	15	-	-	-	-	-	2	3	3	18	23	15
DANNER, Christian	D	4 Apr 1958	München	1985-89	4	36	4	-	-	-	-	-	1	-	1	13	21	11
DAPONTE, Jorge	RA	5 Jun 1923 / 9 Mar 1963	Buenos Aires / Buenos Aires	1954	1	2	0	-	-	-	-	-	-	-	-	1	1	-
DAVIDSON, Anthony	GB	18 Apr 1979	Hemel Hempstead, Hertfordshire	2002-05	2	3	0	-	-	-	-	-	-	-	-	-	3	-
DAVIS, Colin	GB	29 Jul 1933	Marylebone, London	1959	1	2	0	-	-	-	-	-	-	-	-	1	1	-
de ADAMICH, Andrea	I	3 Oct 1941	Trieste	1968-73	5	30	6	-	-	-	-	-	2	-	-	10	18	6
de ANGELIS, Elio	I	26 Mar 1958 / 15 May 1986	Roma / Marseille, F	1979-86	8	108	122	3	-	2	2	5	11	17	6	16	49	1
de BEAUFORT, Carel Godin	NL	10 Apr 1934 / 2 Aug 1964	Maarsbergen / Köln, D	1957-64	8	28	4	-	-	-	-	-	-	-	4	19	5	3
de CESARIS, Andrea	I	31 May 1959	Roma	1980-94	15	208	59	1	1	-	2	3	7	4	6	49	137	6
de FILIPPIS, Maria Teresa	I	11 Nov 1926	Napoli	1958-59	2	3	0	-	-	-	-	-	-	-	-	1	2	2
de GRAFFENRIED, Emmanuel	CH	18 May 1914	Paris, F	1950-56	6	22	9	-	-	-	-	-	1	3	4	4	10	1
de KLERK, Peter	ZA	16 Mar 1935	Pilgrims Rest, Transvaal	1963-70	4	4	0	-	-	-	-	-	-	-	-	2	2	-
de la ROSA, Pedro	E	24 Feb 1971	Barcelona	1999-05	5	64	6	-	1	-	-	-	-	2	4	21	37	-
de PORTAGO, Alfonso	E	11 Oct 1928 / 12 May 1957	Marylebone, London, GB / Guidizzolo,nr Montichiari,I	1956-57	2	5	4	-	-	-	1	-	-	1	-	-	3	-
de TERRA, Max	CH	6 Oct 1918 / 29 Dec 1982	Zürich / Zollikon, Zürich	1952-53	2	2	0	-	-	-	-	-	-	-	-	1	1	-
de TOMASO, Alejandro	RA	10 Jul 1928 / 21 May 2003	Buenos Aires / Modena, I	1957-59	2	2	0	-	-	-	-	-	-	-	-	1	1	-
de TORNACO, Charles	B	7 Jun 1927 / 18 Sep 1953	Bruxelles / Modena Aerautodromo, I	1952-53	2	2	0	-	-	-	-	-	-	-	-	1	1	2
de VILLOTA, Emilio	E	26 Jul 1946	Madrid	1976-82	5	2	0	-	-	-	-	-	-	-	-	2	-	13
DELÉTRAZ, Jean-Denis	CH	1 Oct 1963	Genève	1994-95	2	3	0	-	-	-	-	-	-	-	-	1	2	-
DEPAILLER, Patrick	F	9 Aug 1944 / 1 Aug 1980	Clermont-Ferrand / Hockenheim, D	1972-80	8	95	141	1	4	2	10	7	6	6	5	18	41	-
DINIZ, Pedro	BR	22 May 1970	São Paulo	1995-00	6	98	10	-	-	-	-	-	-	2	6	32	58	1
DOLHEM, José	F	26 Apr 1944 / 16 Apr 1988	Paris / St.-Just-St.-Rambert, nr St. Étienne	1974	1	1	0	-	-	-	-	-	-	-	-	-	1	2
DONNELLY, Martin	GB	26 Mar 1964	Belfast, Northern Ireland	1989-90	2	13	0	-	-	-	-	-	-	-	-	6	7	2
DONOHUE, Mark	USA	18 Mar 1937 / 19 Aug 1975	Summit, New Jersey / Graz, A	1971-75	3	14	8	-	-	-	-	1	-	2	-	5	6	2
DOORNBOS, Robert	NL	23 Sep 1981	Rotterdam	2005	1	8	0	-	-	-	-	-	-	-	-	6	2	-
DOWNING, Ken	GB	5 Dec 1917 / 3 May 2004	Chesterton, Staffordshire / Monte-Carlo, MC	1952	1	2	0	-	-	-	-	-	-	-	-	1	1	-

Above: *Thierry Boutsen, Benetton B188-Ford, Silverstone, 1988. That season he achieved five third places and finished fourth in the driver points behind Senna, Prost and Berger.* (David Hayhoe)

Right: *After a disappointing start to 1989, Williams-Ford Cosworth driver Riccardo Patrese finished second three times in a row – Mexico, here in the USA, and Canada. He also inherited second place in Japan when the winner, Ayrton Senna, was disqualified because his McLaren-Honda was push-started after an accident and second-placed Alessandro Nannini (Benetton-Ford Cosworth) was elevated to take his only Formula 1 victory.* (LAT)

Above: *Ayrton Senna, McLaren MP4/5-Honda, 1989 British Grand Prix. It would be his fourth retirement in a row.* (David Hayhoe)

Left: *Jean Alesi was a new star with the Tyrrell 019-Ford, 1990.* (David Hayhoe)

Opposite top: *Alessandro Nannini, Benetton B190-Ford, 1990 Monaco Grand Prix. This final season of his career was curtailed by severe arm injuries sustained in a helicopter crash.* (David Hayhoe)

Right: *In 1990, the sixth of his 13 full seasons in Formula 1, Gerhard Berger (McLaren-Honda) came second in Brazil (pictured) and San Marino. He was on the podium seven times that season, and finished joint third in the driver points.* (LAT)

UNITED COLORS OF BENETTON
Mobil 1
Ford
SANYO
RIELLO
Heating Equipment
AUTOPOLIS
UNITED COLORS OF BENETTON
GOODYEAR
TECHOCAST
19

Marlboro
28
SHOWA
BOSS
Marlboro
HONDA
Marlboro
GOODYEAR

Above left: *The first full-time Japanese driver in F1 was Satoru Nakajima. Initially partnered with Senna at Lotus, he joined Tyrrell Honda in 1991 but had a disappointing year, his best result being a fifth place at Phoenix.* (David Hayhoe)

Above: *Michele Alboreto had a tough year with Footwork in 1991.* (David Hayhoe)

Left: *Roberto Moreno, Benetton B191-Ford, 1991 British Grand Prix. He would soon find himself pushed out of the team following the arrival of a new young talent by the name of Michael Schumacher.* (David Hayhoe)

Opposite top left: *After getting so close three times before, Nigel Mansell became World Champion in 1992, driving a Williams-Renault. He totalled 108 points overall, compared with the 56 scored by his team-mate Riccardo Patrese as runner-up.* (David Hayhoe)

Opposite top right: *Mika Häkkinen (left) and Johnny Herbert looking pensive in 1992.* (David Hayhoe)

Right: *Luca Badoer and the striking Lola T93/30-Ferrari, 1993.* (David Hayhoe)

Marlboro

ABAC
7
McLaren
Mercedes-Benz
Mobil
1

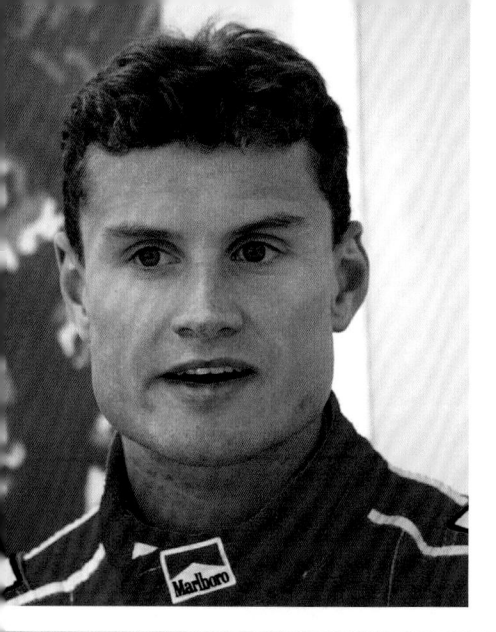

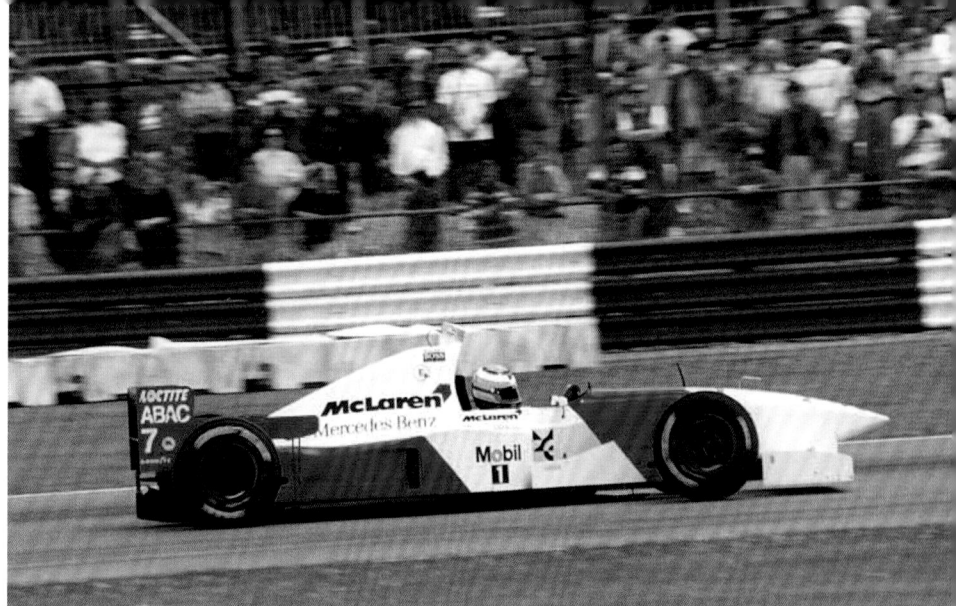

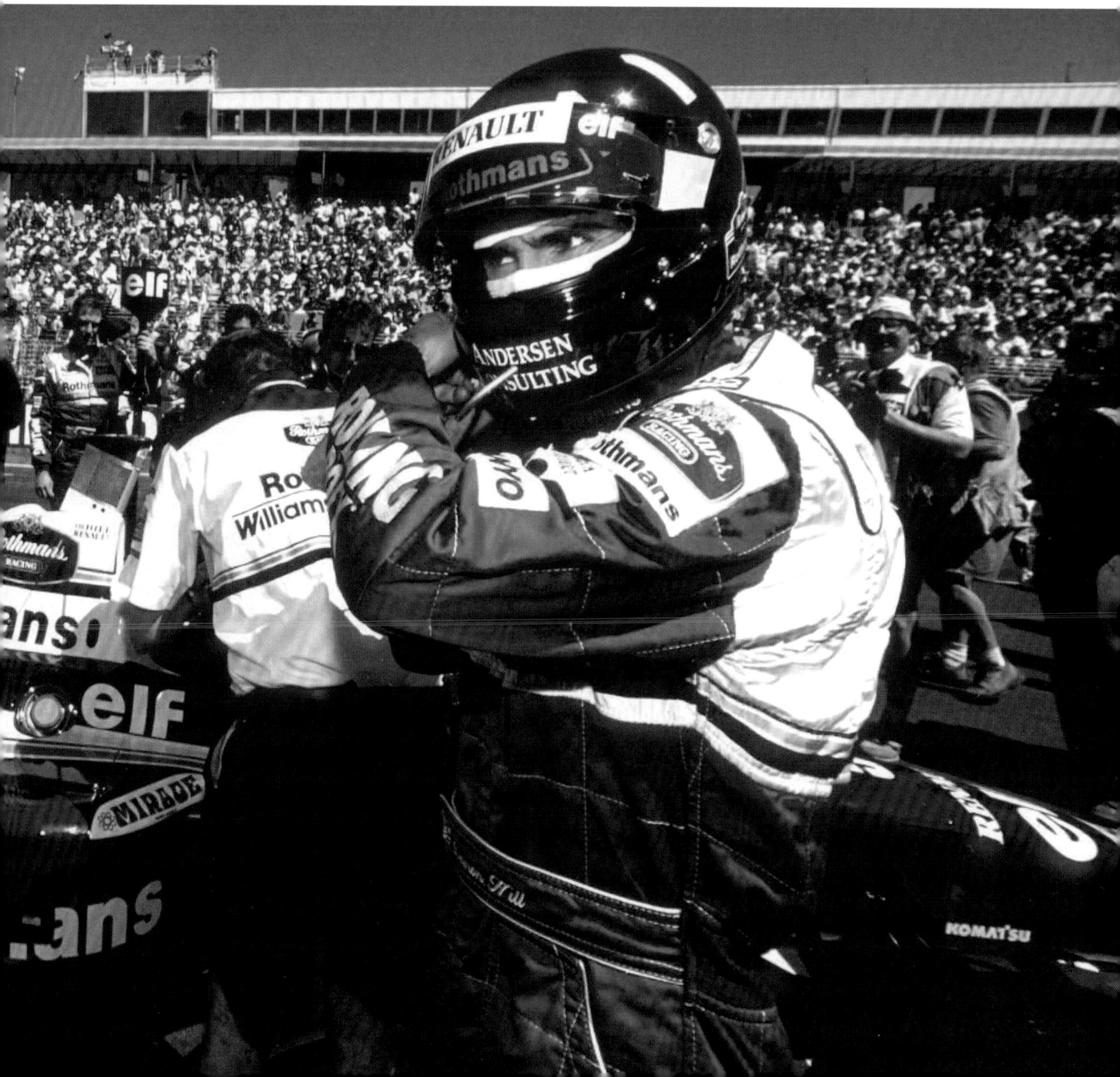
elf
Williams
elf
MIRAGE
KOMATSU

MILD
SEVEN
A1
Agip RENAULT
EDS
Gillette
Gillette
Gillette
MILD SEVEN
FONDMETAL
MILD SEVEN
KOREAN AIR
FedEx
Federal Express
MILD SEVEN
AKAI
RIPA
GOODYEAR
INFORMIX

Rothmans
RENAULT
Rothmans
SONAX

Opposite top: *Jean Alesi (Benetton-Renault) finished second four times in 1997 – Canada, Britain, Italy and Luxembourg – and was joint third, with David Coulthard, in the World Championship. (LAT)*

Left: *Jacques Villeneuve (Williams FW19-Renault) won at Silverstone in 1997, his World Championship year. (David Hayhoe)*

Above: *Damon Hill scored the first win for Jordan, in 1998 at Spa, driving the Jordan 198-Mugen Honda. Bowing to tobacco advertising restrictions, the team came up with cheeky ways to amend their livery that season. (David Hayhoe)*

Right: *Michael Schumacher joined Ferrari for 1996. He is pictured in 1998, when he won six Grands Prix and finished second to Mika Häkkinen in the World Championship. (David Hayhoe)*

Opposite top: *Although Häkkinen finished fourth at Monza in 1998, he won eight races that year and his first World Championship.* (David Hayhoe)

Opposite bottom: *There was great rejoicing in the British camp when Johnny Herbert gave Stewart Grand Prix its maiden victory, at the 1999 European Grand Prix. Herbert is pictured with team owner Jackie Stewart and third-placed Rubens Barrichello.* (LAT)

Right: *Jacques Villeneuve and Ricardo Zonta showing off their dual branding at the BAR 001 launch in Brackley, 1999. This was the first car from the team that took over the famous Tyrrell organisation.* (David Hayhoe)

Bottom: *Johnny Herbert in the Jaguar R1-Ford Cosworth at Silverstone in 2000, his last Grand Prix season. He achieved three wins in 12 seasons.* (David Hayhoe)

Below: *Rubens Barrichello (Ferrari) in 2000 – he had his first victory that year in Germany.* (David Hayhoe)

Above left: *The podium at Silverstone in 2001: winner Mika Häkkinen (McLaren), with Ferrari pair Michael Schumacher and Rubens Barrichello.* (David Hayhoe)

Above right: *Jenson Button, who partnered Jarno Trulli at Renault in 2002.* (David Hayhoe)

Left: *In 2002 Allan McNish's best placing in the Toyota TF102 was seventh in Kuala Lumpur.* (David Hayhoe)

Opposite top: *Nick Heidfeld's best result in the 2003 Sauber C22-Petronas was a fifth at Indianapolis. He is seen here at Silverstone.* (David Hayhoe)

Opposite bottom: *In 2003, a season that saw him second in the World Championship, just two points below the mighty Michael Schumacher, Kimi Räikkönen (McLaren-Mercedes) won the Malaysian Grand Prix and finished second seven times.* (LAT)

FOSTER'S
CREDIT SUISSE
PETRONAS
Red Bull
Red Bull
CREDIT SUISSE

Mobil
West
West
BOSS

Left: *Michael Schumacher in the Ferrari F2003-GA at Silverstone. He had six victories in 2003 and won his sixth World Championship, beating the record of the great Juan Manuel Fangio whose tally of five titles had until then been the benchmark.* (David Hayhoe)

Below: *Williams-BMW driver Juan Pablo Montoya won the 2003 Monaco and German Grands Prix and finished third in the title fight with 82 points.* (LAT)

Far Right: *Michael Schumacher collects his seventh world title at Spa in 2004, the venue of his first race, in 1991, and his maiden victory the year after. His Ferrari team-mate Rubens Barrichello seems underwhelmed.* (LAT)

Right: *The world's media confront Kimi Räikkönen (McLaren) at Silverstone in 2004 after he claimed pole position. He finished second in the race.* (David Hayhoe)

Below: *In 2004 two new countries hosted Grands Prix – Bahrain and China – bringing the number of races per season to 18 for the first time. At Shanghai, Jenson Button (BAR-Honda) had the fourth of his second-place finishes that season.* (LAT)

Above: *Fernando Alonso leads Michael Schumacher at the 2005 Bahrain Grand Prix. The German's days of utter domination seemed now to be over. (LAT)*

Below: *The 2005 Brazilian Grand Prix where Fernando Alonso became the youngest ever World Champion aged just 24. During this race the 50,000th Grand Prix lap was run. (LAT)*

Name	Nat	Born / Died	Place of Birth / Place of Death	Years Entered	No. of Years	GPs	Points	PP	FL	Win	2nd	3rd	4th	5th	6th	OP	NC etc	NS etc
DRAKE, Bob	USA	14 Dec 1919 / 18 Apr 1990	San Francisco, California / Woodland Hills, California	1960	1	1	0	-	-	-	-	-	-	-	-	1		
DRIVER, Paddy	ZA	13 May 1934	Johannesburg	1963-74	2	1	0	-	-	-	-	-	-	-	-	-	1	1
DROGO, Piero	I	8 Aug 1926 / 28 Apr 1973	Vignale Monferrato / Bologna	1960	1	1	0	-	-	-	-	-	-	-	-	1		
DUMFRIES, Johnny	GB	26 Apr 1958	Rothesay, Bute, Scotland	1986	1	15	3	-	-	-	-	-	-	1	1	4	9	1
EATON, George	CDN	12 Nov 1945	Toronto, Ontario	1969-71	3	11	0	-	-	-	-	-	-	-	-	4	7	2
EDWARDS, Guy	GB	30 Dec 1942	Macclesfield, Cheshire	1974-77	3	11	0	-	-	-	-	-	-	-	-	8	3	6
ELFORD, Vic	GB	10 Jun 1935	Peckham, London	1968-71	3	13	8	-	-	-	-	-	1	2	1	4	5	-
EMERY, Paul	GB	12 Nov 1916 / 3 Feb 1993	Chiswick, London / Epsom, Surrey	1956-58	2	1	0	-	-	-	-	-	-	-	-	-	1	1
ENGE, Tomáš	CZ	11 Sep 1976	Liberec	2001	1	3	0	-	-	-	-	-	-	-	-	2	1	-
ENGLAND, Paul	AUS	28 Mar 1929	Melbourne, Victoria	1957	1	1	0	-	-	-	-	-	-	-	-	-	1	
ERTL, Harald	A	31 Aug 1948 / 7 Apr 1982	Zell am See / Hohenahr, nr Giessen, D	1975-80	5	19	0	-	-	-	-	-	-	-	-	11	8	9
ESTÉFANO, Nasif	RA	18 Nov 1932 / 21 Oct 1973	Concepción-Tucumán / Aimogasta, nr Concepción-Tucumán	1960-62	2	1	0	-	-	-	-	-	-	-	-	1	-	1
ÉTANÇELIN, Philippe	F	28 Dec 1896 / 13 Oct 1981	Rouen / Neuilly-sur-Seine, nr Paris	1950-52	3	12	3	-	-	-	-	-	-	2	-	4	6	-
EVANS, Bob	GB	11 Jun 1947	Waddington, Lincolnshire	1975-76	2	10	0	-	-	-	-	-	-	-	-	5	5	2
FABI, Corrado	I	12 Apr 1961	Milano	1983-84	2	12	0	-	-	-	-	-	-	-	-	3	9	6
FABI, Teo	I	9 Mar 1955	Milano	1982-87	5	64	23	3	2	-	-	2	2	4	1	9	46	7
FABRE, Pascal	F	9 Jan 1960	Lyon	1987	1	11	0	-	-	-	-	-	-	-	-	8	3	3
FAGIOLI, Luigi	I	9 Jun 1898 / 20 Jun 1952	Osimo, nr Ancona / Monte-Carlo, MC	1950-51	2	7	32	-	-	1	4	1	-	-	-	-	1	-
FAIRMAN, Jack	GB	15 Mar 1913 / 7 Feb 2002	Smallfield, Surrey / Rugby, Warwickshire	1953-61	8	12	5	-	-	-	-	-	1	1	-	1	9	1
FANGIO, Juan Manuel	RA	24 Jun 1911 / 17 Jul 1995	Balcarce, Buenos Aires / Buenos Aires	1950-58	8	51	277.14	29	23	24	10	1	5	-	-	1	10	-
FARINA, Giuseppe	I	30 Oct 1906 / 30 Jun 1966	Torino / Argentine, nr Aiguebelle, F	1950-55	6	33	127.33	5	5	5	9	5	3	2	1	1	7	1
FIRMAN, Ralph	GB	20 May 1975	Norwich, Norfolk	2003	1	14	1	-	-	-	-	-	-	-	-	8	6	-
FISCHER, Rudi	CH	19 Apr 1912 / 30 Dec 1976	Stuttgart, D / Luzern	1951-52	2	7	10	-	-	-	1	1	-	-	1	3	1	1
FISHER, Mike	USA	13 Mar 1943	Hollywood, California	1967	1	1	0	-	-	-	-	-	-	-	-	1	-	1
FISICHELLA, Giancarlo	I	14 Jan 1973	Roma	1996-05	10	159	174	2	2	2	6	5	10	11	9	63	53	2
FITCH, John	USA	4 Aug 1917	Indianapolis, Indiana	1953-55	2	2	0	-	-	-	-	-	-	-	-	1	1	-
FITTIPALDI, Christian	BR	18 Jan 1971	São Paulo	1992-94	3	40	12	-	-	-	-	-	3	1	1	21	14	3
FITTIPALDI, Emerson	BR	12 Dec 1946	São Paulo	1970-80	11	144	281	6	6	14	13	8	9	5	8	39	48	5
FITTIPALDI, Wilson	BR	25 Dec 1943	São Paulo	1972-75	3	36	3	-	-	-	-	-	-	1	1	15	19	2
FITZAU, Theo	D	10 Feb 1923 / 18 Mar 1982	Köthen / Gross-Gerau	1953	1	1	0	-	-	-	-	-	-	-	-	-	1	-
FLINTERMAN, Jan	NL	2 Oct 1919 / 26 Dec 1992	Den Haag / Leiden	1952	1	1	0	-	-	-	-	-	-	-	-	1	-	-
FLOCKHART, Ron	GB	16 Jun 1923 / 12 Apr 1962	Edinburgh, Scotland / Dandenong Ranges, Victoria, AUS	1954-60	6	13	5	-	-	-	-	1	-	-	2	2	8	1
FOITEK, Gregor	CH	27 Mar 1965	Zürich	1989-90	2	7	0	-	-	-	-	-	-	-	-	2	5	15
FOLLMER, George	USA	27 Jan 1934	Phoenix, Arizona	1973	1	12	5	-	-	-	-	1	-	-	1	5	5	1
FONTANA, Norberto	RA	20 Jan 1975	Arrecifes	1997	1	4	0	-	-	-	-	-	-	-	-	3	1	-
FORINI, Franco	CH	22 Sep 1958	Muralto, nr Locarno	1987	1	2	0	-	-	-	-	-	-	-	-	-	2	1
FOTHERINGHAM-PARKER, Philip	GB	22 Sep 1907 / 15 Oct 1981	Beckenham, Kent / Beckley, nr Rye, East Sussex	1951	1	1	0	-	-	-	-	-	-	-	-	-	1	-
FRENTZEN, Heinz-Harald	D	18 May 1967	Mönchengladbach	1994-03	10	157	174	2	6	3	3	12	12	10	16	40	61	3
FRÈRE, Paul	B	30 Jan 1917	Sainte-Adresse, Le Havre, F	1952-56	5	11	11	-	-	-	1	-	1	1	-	-	2	6
FRIESACHER, Patrick	A	26 Sep 1980	Wolfsberg	2005	1	11	3	-	-	-	-	-	-	-	1	4	6	-
FRY, Joe	GB	26 Oct 1915 / 29 Jul 1950	Winterbourne, Gloucestershire / Blandford Camp, Dorset	1950	1	1	0	-	-	-	-	-	-	-	-	1	-	-
GABBIANI, Beppe	I	2 Jan 1957	Piacenza	1978-81	2	3	0	-	-	-	-	-	-	-	-	-	3	14
GACHOT, Bertrand	F	23 Dec 1962	Luxembourg	1989-95	6	47	5	-	1	-	-	-	-	1	3	11	32	37
GAILLARD, Patrick	F	12 Feb 1952	Paris	1979	1	2	0	-	-	-	-	-	-	-	-	1	1	3

	Nat	Born / Died	Place of Birth / Place of Death	Years Entered	No. of Years	GPs	Points	PP	FL	Win	2nd	3rd	4th	5th	6th	OP	NC etc	NS etc
GALLI, Nanni	I	2 Oct 1940	Bologna	1970-73	4	17	0	-	-	-	-	-	-	-	-	7	10	3
GÁLVEZ, Oscar	RA	17 Aug 1913 / 16 Dec 1989	Buenos Aires / Buenos Aires	1953	1	1	2	-	-	-	-	-	-	1	-	-	-	-
GAMBLE, Fred	USA	17 Mar 1932	Pittsburgh, Pennsylvania	1960	1	1	0	-	-	-	-	-	-	-	-	1	-	-
GANLEY, Howden	NZ	24 Dec 1941	Hamilton	1971-74	4	35	10	-	-	-	-	-	2	1	2	16	14	6
GARDNER, Frank	AUS	1 Oct 1930	Sydney, New South Wales	1964-68	3	8	0	-	-	-	-	-	-	-	-	3	5	1
GARTNER, Jo	A	24 Jan 1954 / 1 Jun 1986	Wien / Le Mans, F	1984	1	8	2	-	-	-	-	-	-	1	-	3	4	-
GAZE, Tony	AUS	3 Feb 1920	Prahran, Melbourne, Victoria	1952	1	3	0	-	-	-	-	-	-	-	-	1	2	1
GEKI	I	23 Oct 1937 / 18 Jun 1967	Milano / Caserta, nr Napoli	1964-66	3	2	0	-	-	-	-	-	-	-	-	1	1	1
GENDEBIEN, Olivier	B	12 Jan 1924 / 2 Oct 1998	Bruxelles / Tarascon, F	1956-61	5	14	18	-	-	-	1	1	2	1	2	4	3	1
GENÉ, Marc	E	29 Mar 1974	Sabadell, nr Barcelona	1999-04	4	36	5	-	-	-	-	-	-	1	1	21	13	-
GERARD, Bob	GB	19 Jan 1914 / 26 Jan 1990	Leicester / South Croxton, Leicester	1950-57	6	8	0	-	-	-	-	-	-	-	-	3	4	1
GERINI, Gerino	I	10 Aug 1928	Roma	1956-58	2	6	1.5	-	-	-	-	-	1	-	-	3	2	1
GETHIN, Peter	GB	21 Feb 1940	Ewell, Surrey	1970-74	5	30	11	-	-	1	-	-	-	-	2	8	19	1
GHINZANI, Piercarlo	I	16 Jan 1952	Riviera d'Adda, Bergamo	1981-89	8	76	2	-	-	-	-	-	-	1	-	19	56	35
GIACOMELLI, Bruno	I	10 Sep 1952	Borgo Poncarale, Brescia	1977-90	8	69	14	1	-	-	-	1	1	3	1	22	41	13
GIBSON, Dick	GB	16 Apr 1918	Bourne, Lincolnshire	1957-58	2	2	0	-	-	-	-	-	-	-	-	-	2	-
GINTHER, Richie	USA	5 Aug 1930 / 20 Sep 1989	Hollywood, California / Touzac, nr Bordeaux, F	1960-67	8	52	107	-	3	1	8	5	6	4	4	11	13	2
GIRAUD-CABANTOUS, Yves	F	8 Oct 1904 / 30 Mar 1973	Saint-Gaudens / Paris	1950-53	4	13	5	-	-	-	-	-	1	1	-	6	5	-
GIUNTI, Ignazio	I	30 Aug 1941 / 10 Jan 1971	Roma / Buenos Aires, RA	1970	1	4	3	-	-	-	-	-	1	-	-	2	1	-
GLOCK, Timo	D	18 Mar 1982	Lindenfels	2004	1	4	2	-	-	-	-	-	-	-	-	4	-	-
GODIA, Chico	E	21 Mar 1921 / 28 Nov 1990	Barcelona / Barcelona	1951-58	5	13	6	-	-	-	-	-	2	-	1	5	5	1
GOETHALS, Christian	B	4 Aug 1928 / 26 Feb 2003	Heule, Kortrijk / Kortrijk	1958	1	1	0	-	-	-	-	-	-	-	-	-	1	-
GONZÁLEZ, Froilán	RA	5 Oct 1922	Arrecifes	1950-60	9	26	77.64	3	6	2	7	6	2	1	-	1	7	-
GONZÁLEZ, Oscar	ROU	7 Nov 1923 / 24 Feb 1999	Montevideo / Montevideo	1956	1	1	0	-	-	-	-	-	-	-	1	-	-	-
GORDINI, Aldo	F	20 May 1921 / 28 Jan 1995	Bologna, I / Paris	1951	1	1	0	-	-	-	-	-	-	-	-	-	1	-
GOULD, Horace	GB	20 Sep 1921 / 4 Nov 1968	Southmead, Bristol / Southmead, Bristol	1954-60	6	14	2	-	-	-	-	-	-	1	-	4	9	4
GOUNON, Jean-Marc	F	1 Jan 1963	Aubenas	1993-94	2	9	0	-	-	-	-	-	-	-	-	4	5	-
GREENE, Keith	GB	5 Jan 1938	Leytonstone, London	1959-62	4	3	0	-	-	-	-	-	-	-	-	1	2	3
GREGORY, Masten	USA	29 Feb 1932 / 8 Nov 1985	Kansas City, Missouri / Porto Ercole, I	1957-65	8	38	21	-	-	-	1	2	3	-	2	14	16	5
GRIGNARD, Georges	F	25 Jul 1905 / 7 Dec 1977	Villeneuve-St-Georges, Paris / Le Port-Marly, nr Versailles	1951	1	1	0	-	-	-	-	-	-	-	-	-	1	-
GROUILLARD, Olivier	F	2 Sep 1958	Fenouillet, Toulouse	1989-92	4	41	1	-	-	-	-	-	-	-	1	13	27	21
GUELFI, André	MA	6 May 1919	Mazagan (El Jadida)	1958	1	1	0	-	-	-	-	-	-	-	-	1	-	-
GUERRA, Miguel Angel	RA	31 Aug 1953	Buenos Aires	1981	1	1	0	-	-	-	-	-	-	-	-	-	1	3
GUERRERO, Roberto	CO	16 Nov 1958	Medellin	1982-83	2	21	0	-	-	-	-	-	-	-	-	5	16	7
GUGELMIN, Mauricio	BR	20 Apr 1963	Joinville	1988-92	5	74	10	-	1	-	-	1	1	1	-	27	43	6
GURNEY, Dan	USA	13 Apr 1931	Port Jefferson, Long Is., New York	1959-70	11	86	133	3	6	4	8	7	2	5	5	13	42	1
HAHNE, Hubert	D	28 Mar 1935	Moers	1966-70	5	3	0	-	-	-	-	-	-	-	-	2	1	2
HAILWOOD, Mike	GB	2 Apr 1940 / 23 Mar 1981	Great Milton, Oxford / Selly Oak, Birmingham	1963-74	7	50	29	-	1	-	1	1	5	-	2	17	23	-
HÄKKINEN, Mika	FIN	28 Sep 1968	Vantaa, Helsinki	1991-01	11	161	420	26	25	20	14	17	13	10	9	19	59	4
HALFORD, Bruce	GB	18 May 1931 / 2 Dec 2001	Hampton-in-Arden, Warwicks / Churston Ferrers, Devon	1956-60	4	8	0	-	-	-	-	-	-	-	-	2	6	1
HALL, Jim	USA	23 Jul 1935	Abilene, Texas	1960-63	4	11	3	-	-	-	-	-	-	1	1	6	3	1
HAMILTON, Duncan	GB	30 Apr 1920 / 13 May 1994	Cork, IRL / Sherborne, Dorset	1951-53	3	5	0	-	-	-	-	-	-	-	-	2	3	-

	Nat	Born / Died	Place of Birth / Place of Death	Years Entered	No. of Years	GPs	Points	PP	FL	Win	2nd	3rd	4th	5th	6th	OP	NC etc	NS etc
HAMPSHIRE, David	GB	29 Dec 1917 / 25 Aug 1990	Mickleover, nr Derby / Newton Solney, Derbyshire	1950	1	2	0	-	-	-	-	-	-	-	-	1	1	-
HANSGEN, Walt	USA	28 Oct 1919 / 7 Apr 1966	Westfield, New Jersey / La Chapelle-St.-Mesmin, nr Orléans, F	1961-64	2	2	2	-	-	-	-	-	-	1	-	-	1	-
HARRIS, Mike	RSR	25 May 1939	Mufulira, N. Rhodesia	1962	1	1	0	-	-	-	-	-	-	-	-	-	1	-
HARRISON, Cuth	GB	6 Jul 1906 / 21 Jan 1981	Ecclesall, Sheffield / Sheffield	1950	1	3	0	-	-	-	-	-	-	-	-	1	2	-
HART, Brian	GB	7 Sep 1936	Enfield, Middlesex	1967	1	1	0	-	-	-	-	-	-	-	-	-	1	-
HASEMI, Masahiro	J	13 Nov 1945	Tokyo	1976	1	1	0	-	-	-	-	-	-	-	-	1	-	-
HAWKINS, Paul	AUS	12 Oct 1937 / 26 May 1969	Richmond, Melbourne, Victoria / Oulton Park, Cheshire, GB	1965	1	3	0	-	-	-	-	-	-	-	-	2	1	-
HAWTHORN, Mike	GB	10 Apr 1929 / 22 Jan 1959	Mexborough, Yorkshire / Guildford-by-pass, Surrey	1952-58	7	45	127.64	4	6	3	9	6	7	2	3	3	12	2
HAYJE, Boy	NL	3 May 1949	Amsterdam	1976-77	2	3	0	-	-	-	-	-	-	-	-	1	2	4
HEEKS, Willi	D	13 Feb 1922 / 13 Aug 1996	Moorlage, nr Detmold / Bocholt	1952-53	2	2	0	-	-	-	-	-	-	-	-	-	2	-
HEIDFELD, Nick	D	10 May 1977	Mönchengladbach	2000-05	6	97	56	1	-	-	2	2	2	2	9	46	34	2
HELFRICH, Theo	D	13 May 1913 / 28 Apr 1978	Frankfurt-am-Main / Ludwigshafen	1952-54	3	3	0	-	-	-	-	-	-	-	-	1	2	-
HENTON, Brian	GB	19 Sep 1946	Castle Donington, Derbyshire	1975-82	5	19	0	-	1	-	-	-	-	-	-	10	9	19
HERBERT, Johnny	GB	25 Jun 1964	Brentwood, Essex	1989-00	12	161	98	-	-	3	1	3	11	6	5	61	71	4
HERRMANN, Hans	D	23 Feb 1928	Stuttgart	1953-69	10	18	10	-	1	-	-	1	2	-	1	6	8	3
HESNAULT, François	F	30 Dec 1956	Neuilly-sur-Seine, nr Paris	1984-85	2	19	0	-	-	-	-	-	-	-	-	5	14	2
HEYER, Hans	D	16 Mar 1943	Mönchengladbach	1977	1	1	0	-	-	-	-	-	-	-	-	-	1	-
HILL, Damon	GB	17 Sep 1960	Hampstead, London	1992-99	8	115	360	20	19	22	15	5	7	2	5	21	38	7
HILL, Graham	GB	15 Feb 1929 / 29 Nov 1975	Hampstead, London / Arkley, nr Barnet, Hertfordshire	1958-75	18	176	289	13	10	14	15	7	9	7	9	41	74	3
HILL, Phil	USA	20 Apr 1927	Miami, Florida	1958-66	8	48	98	6	6	3	5	8	2	-	3	12	15	2
HIRT, Peter	CH	30 Mar 1910 / 28 Jun 1992	Zürich / Küsnacht, Zürich	1951-53	3	5	0	-	-	-	-	-	-	-	-	-	2	3
HOBBS, David	GB	9 Jun 1939	Leamington Spa, Warwickshire	1967-74	4	7	0	-	-	-	-	-	-	-	-	6	1	-
HOFFMANN, Ingo	BR	28 Feb 1953	São Paulo	1976-77	2	3	0	-	-	-	-	-	-	-	-	2	1	3
HOSHINO, Kazuyoshi	J	1 Jul 1947	Shizuoka	1976-77	2	2	0	-	-	-	-	-	-	-	-	1	1	-
HULME, Denny	NZ	18 Jun 1936 / 4 Oct 1992	Nelson / Bathurst, New South Wales, AUS	1965-74	10	112	248	1	9	8	9	16	11	8	9	17	34	-
HUNT, James	GB	29 Aug 1947 / 15 Jun 1993	Belmont, nr Epsom, Surrey / Wimbledon, London	1973-79	7	92	179	14	8	10	6	7	7	2	3	11	46	1
HUTCHISON, Gus	USA	26 Apr 1937	Atlanta, Georgia	1970	1	1	0	-	-	-	-	-	-	-	-	-	1	-
ICKX, Jacky	B	1 Jan 1945	Ixelles, Bruxelles	1966-79	14	116	181	13	14	8	7	10	4	7	4	26	50	6
IGLESIAS, Jesús	RA	22 Feb 1922 / 11 Jul 2005	Pergamino, nr Buenos Aires / Pergamino, nr Buenos Aires	1955	1	1	0	-	-	-	-	-	-	-	-	-	1	-
INOUE, Taki	J	5 Sep 1963	Kobe	1994-95	2	18	0	-	-	-	-	-	-	-	-	5	13	-
IRELAND, Innes	GB	12 Jun 1930 / 23 Oct 1993	Mytholmroyd, Yorkshire / Reading, Berkshire	1959-66	8	50	47	-	1	1	2	1	4	4	2	12	24	4
IRVINE, Eddie	GB	10 Nov 1965	Conlig, Co. Down, N Ireland	1993-02	10	146	191	-	1	4	6	16	10	7	7	36	60	2
IRWIN, Chris	GB	27 Jun 1942	Wandsworth, London	1966-67	2	10	2	-	-	-	-	-	-	1	-	4	5	-
JABOUILLE, Jean-Pierre	F	1 Oct 1942	Paris	1974-81	7	49	21	6	-	2	-	-	1	-	-	8	38	7
JAMES, John	GB	10 May 1914 / 27 Jan 2002	Packwood, Warwickshire / Sliema, Malta	1951	1	1	0	-	-	-	-	-	-	-	-	-	1	-
JARIER, Jean-Pierre	F	10 Jul 1946	Charenton-Le-Pont, nr Paris	1971-83	12	134	31.5	3	3	-	-	3	2	6	3	50	70	9
JEAN, Max	F	27 Jul 1943	Marseille	1971	1	1	0	-	-	-	-	-	-	-	-	-	1	-
JOHANSSON, Stefan	S	8 Sep 1956	Växjö	1983-91	10	79	88	-	-	-	-	4	8	4	3	18	35	24
JOHNSON, Leslie	GB	22 Mar 1912 / 8 Jun 1959	Walthamstow, London / Foxcote, Withington, Glos	1950	1	1	0	-	-	-	-	-	-	-	-	-	1	-
JOHNSTONE, Bruce	ZA	30 Jan 1937	Durban	1962	1	1	0	-	-	-	-	-	-	-	-	1	-	-
JONES, Alan	AUS	2 Nov 1946	Melbourne, Victoria	1975-86	10	116	206	6	13	12	7	5	8	5	2	29	48	1
KARCH, Oswald	D	6 Mar 1917	Ludwigshafen	1953	1	1	0	-	-	-	-	-	-	-	-	-	1	-
KARTHIKEYAN, Narain	IND	14 Jan 1977	Madras (Chennai)	2005	1	19	5	-	-	-	-	-	1	-	-	13	5	-
KATAYAMA, Ukyo	J	29 May 1963	Tokyo	1992-97	6	95	5	-	-	-	-	-	-	2	1	30	62	2
KEEGAN, Rupert	GB	26 Feb 1955	Westcliff-on-Sea, Essex	1977-82	4	25	0	-	-	-	-	-	-	-	-	12	13	12

	Nat	Born / Died	Place of Birth / Place of Death	Years Entered	No. of Years	GPs	Points	PP	FL	Win	2nd	3rd	4th	5th	6th	OP	NC etc	NS etc
KEIZAN, Eddie	ZA	12 Sep 1944	Johannesburg	1973-75	3	3	0	-	-	-	-	-	-	-	-	2	1	-
KELLY, Joe	IRL	13 Mar 1913 / 28 Nov 1993	Dublin / Neston, Cheshire, GB	1950-51	2	2	0	-	-	-	-	-	-	-	-	-	2	-
KESSEL, Loris	CH	1 Apr 1950	Massagno, Lugano	1976-77	2	3	0	-	-	-	-	-	-	-	-	1	2	3
KIESA, Nicolas	DK	3 Mar 1978	København	2003	1	5	0	-	-	-	-	-	-	-	-	5	-	-
KINNUNEN, Leo	FIN	5 Aug 1943	Tampere	1974	1	1	0	-	-	-	-	-	-	-	-	-	1	5
KLENK, Hans	D	28 Oct 1919	Künzelsau	1952	1	1	0	-	-	-	-	-	-	-	-	1	-	-
KLIEN, Christian	A	7 Feb 1983	Hohenems, Vorarlberg	2004-05	2	31	12	-	-	-	-	-	-	1	1	23	6	2
KLING, Karl	D	16 Sep 1910 / 18 Mar 2003	Giessen / Gaienhofen	1954-55	2	11	17	-	1	-	1	1	2	1	-	1	5	-
KLODWIG, Ernst	D	23 May 1903 / 15 Apr 1973	Aschersleben / Hamburg	1952-53	2	2	0	-	-	-	-	-	-	-	-	2	-	-
KOINIGG, Helmut	A	3 Nov 1948 / 6 Oct 1974	Wien / Watkins Glen, New York, USA	1974	1	2	0	-	-	-	-	-	-	-	-	1	1	1
KRAUSE, Rudolf	D	30 Mar 1907 / 11 Apr 1987	Oberreichenbach / Reichenbach	1952-53	2	2	0	-	-	-	-	-	-	-	-	1	1	-
La CAZE, Robert	MA	26 Feb 1917	Paris, F	1958	1	1	0	-	-	-	-	-	-	-	-	1	-	-
LAFFITE, Jacques	F	21 Nov 1943	Paris	1974-86	13	176	228	7	7	6	10	16	7	9	11	35	82	4
LAGORCE, Franck	F	1 Sep 1968	L'Haÿ-les-Roses, nr Paris	1994	1	2	0	-	-	-	-	-	-	-	-	1	1	-
LAMMERS, Jan	NL	2 Jun 1956	Zandvoort	1979-92	5	23	0	-	-	-	-	-	-	-	-	12	11	18
LAMY, Pedro	P	20 Mar 1972	Aldeia Galega Da Merceana	1993-96	4	32	1	-	-	-	-	-	-	-	1	18	13	-
LANDI, Chico	BR	14 Jul 1907 / 7 Jun 1989	São Paulo / São Paulo	1951-56	4	6	1.5	-	-	-	-	1	-	-	-	2	3	-
LANG, Hermann	D	6 Apr 1909 / 19 Oct 1987	Bad Cannstatt, nr Stuttgart / Bad Cannstatt, nr Stuttgart	1953-54	2	2	2	-	-	-	-	-	1	-	-	-	1	-
LARINI, Nicola	I	19 Mar 1964	Lido di Camaiore	1987-97	8	49	7	-	-	-	-	1	-	-	1	24	23	26
LARRAURI, Oscar	RA	19 Aug 1954	Granaderio Baigorria, nr Rosario	1988-89	2	7	0	-	-	-	-	-	-	-	-	2	5	14
LARRETA, Rodríguez	RA	14 Jan 1934 / 11 Mar 1977	Buenos Aires / Buenos Aires	1960	1	1	0	-	-	-	-	-	-	-	-	1	-	-
LARROUSSE, Gérard	F	23 May 1940	Lyon	1974	1	1	0	-	-	-	-	-	-	-	-	-	1	1
LAUDA, Niki	A	22 Feb 1949	Wien	1971-85	13	171	420.5	24	24	25	20	9	7	7	5	17	81	6
LAURENT, Roger	B	21 Feb 1913 / 6 Feb 1997	Liège / Uccle	1952	1	2	0	-	-	-	-	-	1	1	-	-	-	-
LAVAGGI, Giovanni	I	18 Feb 1958	Augusta, Sicilia	1995-96	2	7	0	-	-	-	-	-	-	-	-	2	5	3
LAWRENCE, Chris	GB	27 Jul 1933	Ealing, London	1966	1	2	0	-	-	-	-	-	-	-	-	1	1	-
LECLÈRE, Michel	F	18 Mar 1946	Mantes-la-Jolie, nr Paris	1975-76	2	7	0	-	-	-	-	-	-	-	-	5	2	1
LEDERLE, Neville	ZA	25 Sep 1938	Theunissen, Winburg	1962-65	2	1	1	-	-	-	-	-	-	1	-	-	-	1
LEES, Geoff	GB	1 May 1951	Atherstone, Warwickshire	1978-82	4	5	0	-	-	-	-	-	-	-	-	3	2	7
LEGAT, Arthur	B	1 Nov 1898 / 23 Feb 1960	Haine-Saint-Paul / Haine-Saint-Pierre	1952-53	2	2	0	-	-	-	-	-	-	-	-	1	1	-
LEHTO, J J	FIN	31 Jan 1966	Espoo	1989-94	6	62	10	-	-	-	-	1	1	1	1	24	34	8
LEONI, Lamberto	I	24 May 1953	Argenta	1977-78	2	1	0	-	-	-	-	-	-	-	-	-	1	4
LESTON, Les	GB	16 Dec 1920	Bulwell, Nottingham	1956-57	2	2	0	-	-	-	-	-	-	-	-	-	2	1
LEVEGH, Pierre	F	22 Dec 1905 / 11 Jun 1955	Paris / Le Mans	1950-51	2	6	0	-	-	-	-	-	-	-	-	3	3	-
LEWIS, Jack	GB	1 Nov 1936	Stroud, Gloucestershire	1961-62	2	9	3	-	-	-	-	-	1	-	-	5	3	1
LEWIS-EVANS, Stuart	GB	20 Apr 1930 / 25 Oct 1958	Luton, Bedfordshire / East Grinstead, Sussex	1957-58	2	14	16	2	-	-	-	2	2	1	-	1	8	-
LIGIER, Guy	F	12 Jul 1930	Vichy	1966-67	2	12	1	-	-	-	-	-	-	-	1	5	6	1
LIPPI, Roberto	I	17 Oct 1926	Roma	1961-63	3	1	0	-	-	-	-	-	-	-	-	-	1	2
LIUZZI, Vitantonio	I	6 Aug 1980	Locorotondo, nr Bari	2005	1	4	1	-	-	-	-	-	-	-	-	2	2	-
LOMBARDI, Lella	I	26 Mar 1941 / 3 Mar 1992	Frugarolo, nr Alessándria / Milano	1974-76	3	12	0.5	-	-	-	-	-	-	-	1	6	5	5
LOOF, Ernst	D	4 Jul 1907 / 3 Mar 1956	Neindorf / Bonn	1953	1	1	0	-	-	-	-	-	-	-	-	-	1	-
LOUVEAU, Henri	F	25 Jan 1910 / 7 Jan 1991	Suresnes / Orléans	1950-51	2	2	0	-	-	-	-	-	-	-	-	-	2	-
LOVE, John	RSR	7 Dec 1924 / 25 Apr 2005	Bulawayo / Bulawayo (now Zimbabwe)	1962-72	10	9	6	-	-	-	1	-	-	-	-	5	3	1
LOVELY, Pete	USA	11 Apr 1926	Livingston, Montana	1959-71	5	7	0	-	-	-	-	-	-	-	-	3	4	4

	Nat	Born / Died	Place of Birth / Place of Death	Years Entered	No. of Years	GPs	Points	PP	FL	Win	2nd	3rd	4th	5th	6th	OP	NC etc	NS etc
LOYER, Roger	F	5 Aug 1907 / 24 Mar 1988	Paris / Boulogne-Billancourt	1954	1	1	0	-	-	-	-	-	-	-	-	-	1	-
LUCAS, Jean	F	25 Apr 1917 / 27 Sep 2003	Le Mans / Saint-Martin-de-Ré	1955	1	1	0	-	-	-	-	-	-	-	-	-	1	-
LUNGER, Brett	USA	14 Nov 1945	Wilmington, Delaware	1975-78	4	34	0	-	-	-	-	-	-	-	-	23	11	9
MacDOWEL, Mike	GB	13 Sep 1932	Great Yarmouth, Norfolk	1957	1	1	0	-	-	-	-	-	-	-	-	1	-	-
MacKAY-FRASER, Herbert	USA	23 Jun 1927 / 14 Jul 1957	Pernambuco, BR / Reims, F	1957	1	1	0	-	-	-	-	-	-	-	-	-	1	-
MACKLIN, Lance	GB	2 Sep 1919 / 29 Aug 2002	Kensington, London / Tenterden, Kent	1952-55	4	13	0	-	-	-	-	-	-	-	-	5	8	2
MAGEE, Damien	GB	17 Nov 1945	Belfast, Northern Ireland	1975-76	2	1	0	-	-	-	-	-	-	-	-	1	-	1
MAGGS, Tony	ZA	9 Feb 1937	Pretoria	1961-65	5	25	26	-	-	-	2	1	1	2	3	9	7	2
MAGLIOLI, Umberto	I	5 Jun 1928 / 7 Feb 1999	Bioglio, Vercelli / Monza	1953-57	5	10	3.33	-	-	-	-	2	-	-	1	3	4	-
MAGNUSSEN, Jan	DK	4 Jul 1973	Roskilde	1995-98	3	25	1	-	-	-	-	-	-	-	1	8	16	-
MAIRESSE, Guy	F	10 Aug 1910 / 24 Apr 1954	La Capelle, l'Aisne / Arpajon	1950-51	2	3	0	-	-	-	-	-	-	-	-	2	1	-
MAIRESSE, Willy	B	1 Oct 1928 / 2 Sep 1969	Momignies / Oostende	1960-65	5	12	7	-	-	-	-	1	1	-	-	1	9	1
MANSELL, Nigel	GB	8 Aug 1953	Baughton, Upton upon Severn	1980-95	15	187	482	32	30	31	17	11	8	6	9	16	89	4
MANTOVANI, Sergio	I	22 May 1929 / 23 Feb 2001	Cusano Milanino, Milano / Milano	1953-55	3	7	4	-	-	-	-	-	-	2	-	4	1	1
MANZON, Robert	F	12 Apr 1917	Marseille	1950-56	7	28	16	-	-	-	-	2	2	1	-	6	17	1
MARIMÓN, Onofré	RA	19 Dec 1923 / 31 Jul 1954	Zarate, nr Buenos Aires / Nürburgring, D	1951-54	3	11	8.14	-	1	-	-	2	-	-	-	1	8	1
MARKO, Helmut	A	27 Apr 1943	Graz	1971-72	2	9	0	-	-	-	-	-	-	-	-	7	2	1
MARQUES, Tarso	BR	19 Jan 1976	Curitiba	1996-01	3	24	0	-	-	-	-	-	-	-	-	10	14	2
MARR, Leslie	GB	14 Aug 1922	Durham	1954-55	2	2	0	-	-	-	-	-	-	-	-	1	1	-
MARSH, Tony	GB	20 Jul 1931	Stourbridge, Worcestershire	1957-61	3	4	0	-	-	-	-	-	-	-	-	3	1	1
MARTIN, Eugène	F	24 Mar 1915	Suresnes	1950	1	2	0	-	-	-	-	-	-	-	-	-	2	-
MARTINI, Pierluigi	I	23 Apr 1961	Lugo di Romagna, nr Ravenna	1984-95	10	118	18	-	-	-	-	-	2	4	4	45	63	6
MASS, Jochen	D	30 Sep 1946	Dorfen, nr München	1973-82	9	105	71	-	2	1	1	6	7	4	9	36	41	9
MASSA, Felipe	BR	25 Apr 1981	São Paulo	2002-05	3	52	27	-	-	-	-	-	2	2	3	31	14	1
MAY, Michael	CH	18 Aug 1934	Stuttgart, D	1961	1	2	0	-	-	-	-	-	-	-	-	1	1	1
MAYER, Timmy	USA	22 Feb 1938 / 28 Feb 1964	Dalton, Pennsylvania / Longford, Tasmania, AUS	1962	1	1	0	-	-	-	-	-	-	-	-	-	1	-
MAZET, François	F	26 Feb 1943	Paris	1971	1	1	0	-	-	-	-	-	-	-	-	1	-	-
MAZZACANE, Gastón	RA	8 May 1975	La Plata	2000-01	2	21	0	-	-	-	-	-	-	-	-	13	8	-
McALPINE, Kenneth	GB	21 Sep 1920	Cobham, Surrey	1952-55	3	7	0	-	-	-	-	-	-	-	-	2	5	-
McLAREN, Bruce	NZ	30 Aug 1937 / 2 Jun 1970	Auckland / Goodwood, Sussex, GB	1958-70	13	100	196.5	-	3	4	11	12	7	11	5	13	37	4
McNISH, Allan	GB	29 Dec 1969	Dumfries, Scotland	2002	1	16	0	-	-	-	-	-	-	-	-	8	8	1
McRAE, Graham	NZ	5 Mar 1940	Wellington	1973	1	1	0	-	-	-	-	-	-	-	-	-	1	-
MENDITÉGUY, Carlos	RA	10 Aug 1915 / 27 Apr 1973	Buenos Aires / Buenos Aires	1953-60	7	10	9	-	-	-	-	1	1	1	-	1	6	1
MERZARIO, Arturo	I	11 Mar 1943	Civenna, Como	1972-79	8	57	11	-	-	-	-	-	3	-	2	11	41	28
MIÈRES, Roberto	RA	3 Dec 1924	Mar del Plata	1953-55	3	17	13	-	1	-	-	-	3	2	2	1	9	-
MIGAULT, François	F	4 Dec 1944	Le Mans	1972-75	3	13	0	-	-	-	-	-	-	-	-	4	9	3
MILES, John	GB	14 Jun 1943	Islington, London	1969-70	2	12	2	-	-	-	-	-	-	1	-	3	8	3
MILHOUX, André	B	9 Dec 1928	Bressoux, Liège	1956	1	1	0	-	-	-	-	-	-	-	-	-	1	-
MITTER, Gerhard	D	30 Aug 1935 / 1 Aug 1969	Schönlinde (Krásná Lipa, CZ) / Nürburgring	1963-69	6	5	3	-	-	-	-	-	1	-	-	1	3	2
MODENA, Stefano	I	12 May 1963	Modena	1987-92	6	70	17	-	-	-	1	1	1	1	2	24	40	11
MONTEIRO, Tiago	P	24 Jul 1976	Massarelos, Porto	2005	1	19	7	-	-	-	-	1	-	-	-	17	1	-
MONTERMINI, Andrea	I	30 May 1964	Sassuolo, Modena	1994-96	3	20	0	-	-	-	-	-	-	-	-	4	16	8
MONTGOMERIE-CHARRINGTON, Robin	GB	23 Jun 1915	Mayfair, London	1952	1	1	0	-	-	-	-	-	-	-	-	-	1	-
MONTOYA, Juan Pablo	CO	20 Sep 1975	Bogotá	2001-05	5	84	281	13	12	7	14	7	9	7	2	11	27	1
MORBIDELLI, Gianni	I	13 Jan 1968	Pesaro, nr Rimini	1990-97	6	67	8.5	-	-	-	-	1	-	1	3	29	33	3
MORENO, Roberto	BR	11 Feb 1959	Rio de Janeiro	1982-95	7	42	15	-	1	-	1	-	2	1	1	13	24	33

Name	Nat	Born / Died	Place of Birth / Place of Death	Years Entered	No. of Years	GPs	Points	PP	FL	Win	2nd	3rd	4th	5th	6th	OP	NC etc	NS etc
MORGAN, Dave	GB	7 Aug 1944	Shepton Mallet, Somerset	1975	1	1	0	-	-	-	-	-	-	-	-	-	1	-
MOSER, Silvio	CH	24 Apr 1941 / 26 May 1974	Zürich / Locarno	1966-71	6	12	3	-	-	-	-	-	-	1	1	2	8	8
MOSS, Stirling	GB	17 Sep 1929	West Kensington, London	1951-61	11	66	186.64	16	19	16	5	3	3	2	1	7	29	1
MUNARON, Gino	I	2 Apr 1928	Torino	1960	1	4	0	-	-	-	-	-	-	-	-	2	2	1
MURRAY, David	GB	28 Dec 1909 / 5 Apr 1973	Edinburgh, Scotland / Las Palmas de Gran Canaria, E	1950-52	3	4	0	-	-	-	-	-	-	-	-	-	4	1
MUSSO, Luigi	I	28 Jul 1924 / 6 Jul 1958	Roma / Reims, F	1953-58	6	24	44	-	1	1	5	1	1	1	-	5	10	1
NACKE, Bernd. pseudonym of Günther BECHEM																		
NAKAJIMA, Satoru	J	23 Feb 1953	Okazaki City	1987-91	5	74	16	-	1	-	-	2	2	6	25	39	6	
NAKANO, Shinji	J	1 Apr 1971	Osaka	1997-98	2	33	2	-	-	-	-	-	-	2	16	15	-	
NANNINI, Alessandro	I	7 Jul 1959	Siena	1986-90	5	76	65	-	2	1	2	6	4	2	4	12	45	2
NASPETTI, Emanuele	I	24 Feb 1968	Ancona	1992-93	2	6	0	-	-	-	-	-	-	-	-	3	3	-
NATILI, Massimo	I	28 Jul 1935	Ronciglione, Viterbo	1961	1	1	0	-	-	-	-	-	-	-	-	-	1	1
NAYLOR, Brian	GB	24 Mar 1923 / 8 Aug 1989	Salford, Manchester / Marbella, E	1957-61	5	7	0	-	-	-	-	-	-	-	-	2	5	1
NEEDELL, Tiff	GB	29 Oct 1951	Havant, Hampshire	1980	1	1	0	-	-	-	-	-	-	-	-	-	1	1
NÈVE, Patrick	B	13 Oct 1949	Liège	1976-78	3	10	0	-	-	-	-	-	-	-	-	8	2	4
NICHOLSON, John	NZ	6 Oct 1941	Auckland	1974-75	2	1	0	-	-	-	-	-	-	-	-	1	-	1
NIEDERMAYR, Helmut	D	29 Nov 1915 / 3 Apr 1985	München / Cristiansted, Virgin Is., USA	1952	1	1	0	-	-	-	-	-	-	-	-	1	-	-
NIEMANN, Brausch	ZA	7 Jan 1939	Durban	1963-65	2	1	0	-	-	-	-	-	-	-	-	1	-	1
NILSSON, Gunnar	S	20 Nov 1948 / 20 Oct 1978	Helsingborg / Hammersmith, London, GB	1976-77	2	31	31	-	1	1	-	3	1	3	1	5	17	1
NODA, Hideki	J	7 Mar 1969	Osaka	1994	1	3	0	-	-	-	-	-	-	-	-	-	3	-
NUCKEY, Rodney	GB	26 Jun 1929 / 29 Jun 2000	Wood Green, London / Manila, Philippines	1953-54	2	1	0	-	-	-	-	-	-	-	-	1	-	1
O'BRIEN, Robert	USA			1952	1	1	0	-	-	-	-	-	-	-	-	1	-	-
OLIVER, Jackie	GB	14 Aug 1942	Chadwell Heath, Essex	1967-77	8	50	13	-	1	-	-	2	-	2	11	34	2	
ONGAIS, Danny	USA	21 May 19j42	Honolulu, Hawaii	1977-78	2	4	0	-	-	-	-	-	-	-	-	1	3	2
OWEN, Arthur	GB	23 Mar 1915 / 13 Apr 2000	Forest Gate, London / Wexham Street, nr Slough	1960	1	1	0	-	-	-	-	-	-	-	-	1	-	-
PACE, Carlos	BR	6 Oct 1944 / 18 Mar 1977	São Paulo / nr São Paulo	1972-77	6	72	58	1	5	1	3	2	5	3	2	21	35	1
PAGANI, Nello	I	11 Oct 1911 / 19 Oct 2003	Milano / Miazzina	1950	1	1	0	-	-	-	-	-	-	-	-	1	-	-
PALETTI, Riccardo	I	15 Jun 1958 / 13 Jun 1982	Milano / Montréal, CDN	1982	1	2	0	-	-	-	-	-	-	-	-	-	2	6
PALM, Torsten	S	23 Jul 1947	Kristinehamn	1975	1	1	0	-	-	-	-	-	-	-	-	1	-	1
PALMER, Jonathan	GB	7 Nov 1956	Lewisham, London	1983-89	7	83	14	-	1	-	-	-	1	4	3	37	38	5
PANIS, Olivier	F	2 Sep 1966	Oullins, Lyon	1994-04	10	158	76	-	-	1	3	1	4	8	8	74	59	-
PANTANO, Giorgio	I	4 Feb 1979	Conselve, nr Padova	2004	1	14	0	-	-	-	-	-	-	-	-	6	8	-
PAPIS, Max	I	3 Oct 1969	Como	1995	1	7	0	-	-	-	-	-	-	-	-	2	5	-
PARKES, Mike	GB	24 Sep 1931 / 28 Aug 1977	Richmond, Surrey / Riva Presso Chieri, nr Torino, I	1959-67	3	6	14	1	-	-	2	-	-	1	-	-	3	1
PARNELL, Reg	GB	2 Jul 1911 / 7 Jan 1964	Derby / Derby	1950-54	4	6	9	-	-	-	-	1	1	1	-	1	2	1
PARNELL, Tim	GB	25 Jun 1932	Derby	1959-63	3	2	0	-	-	-	-	-	-	-	-	1	1	2
PATRESE, Riccardo	I	17 Apr 1954	Padova	1977-93	17	256	281	8	13	6	17	14	8	15	13	53	130	1
PEASE, Al	CDN	15 Oct 1921	Darlington, Durham, GB	1967-69	3	2	0	-	-	-	-	-	-	-	-	-	2	1
PENSKE, Roger	USA	20 Feb 1937	Shaker Heights, Ohio	1961-62	2	2	0	-	-	-	-	-	-	-	-	2	-	-
PERDISA, Cesare	I	21 Oct 1932 / 10 May 1998	Bologna / Bologna	1955-57	3	7	5	-	-	-	-	2	-	1	1	3	-	1
PERKINS, Larry	AUS	18 Mar 1950	Murrayville, Victoria	1974-77	3	11	0	-	-	-	-	-	-	-	-	5	6	4
PERROT, Xavier	CH	1 Feb 1932	Zürich	1969	1	1	0	-	-	-	-	-	-	-	-	1	-	-
PESCAROLO, Henri	F	25 Sep 1942	Montfermeil, nr Paris	1968-76	8	57	12	-	1	-	-	1	1	1	3	26	25	7
PESENTI-ROSSI, Sandro	I	31 Aug 1942	Gerosa, nr Bergamo	1976	1	3	0	-	-	-	-	-	-	-	-	3	-	1
PETERS, Josef	D	16 Sep 1914 / 24 Apr 2001	Düsseldorf / Düsseldorf	1952	1	1	0	-	-	-	-	-	-	-	-	-	1	-

	Nat	Born Died	Place of Birth Place of Death	Years Entered	No. of Years	GPs	Points	PP	FL	Win	2nd	3rd	4th	5th	6th	OP	NC etc	NS etc
PETERSON, Ronnie	S	14 Feb 1944 11 Sep 1978	Örebro Milano, I	1970-78	9	123	206	14	9	10	10	6	5	7	4	29	52	-
PICARD, François	F	26 Apr 1921 29 Apr 1996	Villefranche-sur-Saône Nice	1958	1	1	0	-	-	-	-	-	-	-	-	-	1	-
PIETERSE, Ernie	ZA	4 Jul 1938	Parow, Bellville	1962-65	3	2	0	-	-	-	-	-	-	-	-	1	1	1
PIETSCH, Paul	D	20 Jun 1911	Freiburg im Breisgau	1950-52	3	3	0	-	-	-	-	-	-	-	-	-	3	-
PILETTE, André	B	6 Oct 1918 27 Dec 1993	Paris, F Etterbeek, Bruxelles	1951-64	7	9	2	-	-	-	-	-	-	1	3	3	2	5
PILETTE, Teddy	B	26 Jul 1942	Bruxelles	1974-77	2	1	0	-	-	-	-	-	-	-	-	1	-	3
PIOTTI, Luigi	I	27 Oct 1913 19 Apr 1971	Milano Godiasco	1955-58	4	5	0	-	-	-	-	-	-	-	1	1	3	4
PIPER, David	GB	2 Dec 1930	Edgware, Middlesex	1959-60	2	2	0	-	-	-	-	-	-	-	-	1	1	1
PIQUET, Nelson	BR	17 Aug 1952	Rio de Janeiro	1978-91	14	204	485.5	24	23	23	20	17	18	15	7	24	80	3
PIROCCHI, Renato	I	23 Jun 1933 29 Jul 2002	Notaresco, Teramo Chieti, Pescara	1961	1	1	0	-	-	-	-	-	-	-	-	1	-	-
PIRONI, Didier	F	26 Mar 1952 23 Aug 1987	Villecresnes, nr Paris off Isle of Wight, GB	1978-82	5	70	101	4	5	3	3	7	3	6	7	15	26	2
PIRRO, Emanuele	I	12 Jan 1962	Roma	1989-91	3	37	3	-	-	-	-	-	-	1	1	15	20	3
PIZZONIA, Antonio	BR	11 Sep 1980	Manaus	2003-05	3	20	8	-	-	-	-	-	-	-	-	12	8	-
POLLET, Jacques	F	28 Jul 1922 16 Aug 1997	Roubaix Paris	1954-55	2	5	0	-	-	-	-	-	-	-	-	2	3	-
PON, Ben	NL	9 Dec 1936	Leiden	1962	1	1	0	-	-	-	-	-	-	-	-	-	1	-
POORE, Dennis	GB	19 Aug 1916 12 Feb 1987	Paddington, London Kensington, London	1952	1	2	3	-	-	-	-	-	1	-	-	1	-	-
POSEY, Sam	USA	26 May 1944	New York	1971-72	2	2	0	-	-	-	-	-	-	-	-	1	1	-
POZZI, Charles	F	27 Aug 1909 28 Feb 2001	Paris Levallois-Perret, Paris	1950	1	1	0	-	-	-	-	-	-	1	-	-	-	-
PRETORIUS, Jackie	ZA	22 Nov 1934	Potchefstroom, Transvaal	1965-73	4	3	0	-	-	-	-	-	-	-	-	-	3	1
PROPHET, David	GB	9 Oct 1937 29 Mar 1981	Hong Kong Silverstone, Northants	1963-65	2	2	0	-	-	-	-	-	-	-	-	1	1	-
PROST, Alain	F	24 Feb 1955	Lorette, Saint-Chamond	1980-93	13	199	798.5	33	41	51	35	20	10	5	7	15	56	3
PRYCE, Tom	GB	11 Jun 1949 5 Mar 1977	Ruthin, Denbighshire, Wales Kyalami, ZA	1974-77	4	42	19	1	-	-	-	2	3	-	4	13	20	-
PURLEY, David	GB	26 Jan 1945 2 Jul 1985	Bognor Regis, Sussex off Bognor Regis, Sussex	1973-77	3	7	0	-	-	-	-	-	-	-	-	4	3	4
QUESTER, Dieter	A	30 May 1939	Wien	1969-74	2	1	0	-	-	-	-	-	-	-	-	1	-	1
RABY, Ian	GB	22 Sep 1921 7 Nov 1967	Woolwich, London Waterloo, London	1963-65	3	3	0	-	-	-	-	-	-	-	-	1	2	4
RAHAL, Bobby	USA	10 Jan 1953	Medina, Ohio	1978	1	2	0	-	-	-	-	-	-	-	-	1	1	-
RÄIKKÖNEN, Kimi	FIN	17 Oct 1979	Espoo	2001-05	5	86	281	8	16	9	13	8	7	2	4	13	30	1
RAPHANEL, Pierre-Henri	F	27 May 1961	Algiers, Algeria	1988-89	2	1	0	-	-	-	-	-	-	-	-	-	1	16
RATZENBERGER, Roland	A	4 Jul 1960 30 Apr 1994	Salzburg Bologna, I	1994	1	1	0	-	-	-	-	-	-	-	-	1	-	2
REBAQUE, Hector	MEX	5 Feb 1956	Mexico City	1977-81	5	41	13	-	-	-	-	-	3	1	2	10	25	17
REDMAN, Brian	GB	9 Mar 1937	Colne, Lancashire	1967-74	7	12	8	-	-	-	-	1	-	2	-	4	5	3
REES, Alan	GB	12 Jan 1938	Langstone, Monmouthshire	1966-67	2	3	0	-	-	-	-	-	-	-	-	2	1	-
REGAZZONI, Clay	CH	5 Sep 1939	Mendrisio, nr Lugano	1970-80	11	132	212	5	15	5	13	10	8	9	7	31	49	7
REUTEMANN, Carlos	RA	12 Apr 1942	Santa Fe	1972-82	11	146	310	6	6	12	13	20	11	3	7	31	49	-
REVENTLOW, Lance	USA	24 Feb 1936 24 Jul 1972	Paddington, London, GB nr Aspen, Colorado	1960	1	1	0	-	-	-	-	-	-	-	-	-	1	3
REVSON, Peter	USA	27 Feb 1939 22 Mar 1974	New York Kyalami, ZA	1964-74	5	30	61	1	-	2	2	4	3	3	-	7	9	2
RHODES, John	GB	18 Aug 1927	Wolverhampton, Staffordshire	1965	1	1	0	-	-	-	-	-	-	-	-	-	1	-
RIBEIRO, Alex Dias	BR	7 Nov 1948	Belo Horizonte	1976-79	3	10	0	-	-	-	-	-	-	-	-	6	4	10
RIESS, Fritz	D	11 Jul 1922 15 May 1991	Nürnberg Samedan, CH	1952	1	1	0	-	-	-	-	-	-	-	-	1	-	-
RINDT, Jochen	A	18 Apr 1942 5 Sep 1970	Mainz-am-Rhein, D Milano, I	1964-70	7	60	109	10	3	6	3	4	6	1	1	4	35	2
RISELEY-PRICHARD, John	GB	17 Jan 1924 8 Jul 1993	Hereford Baan Kai Thuan, T	1954	1	1	0	-	-	-	-	-	-	-	-	-	1	-

	Nat	Born Died	Place of Birth Place of Death	Years Entered	No. of Years	GPs	Points	PP	FL	Win	2nd	3rd	4th	5th	6th	OP	NC etc	NS etc
ROBARTS, Richard	GB	22 Sep 1944	Bicknacre, nr Chelmsford, Essex	1974	1	3	0	-	-	-	-	-	-	-	-	2	1	1
RODRÍGUEZ, Pedro	MEX	18 Jan 1940	Mexico City	1963-71	9	55	71	-	1	2	3	2	4	4	7	7	26	-
		11 Jul 1971	Norisring, D															
RODRÍGUEZ, Ricardo	MEX	14 Feb 1942	Mexico City	1961-62	2	5	4	-	-	-	-	-	1	-	1	1	2	1
		1 Nov 1962	Mexico City															
ROL, Franco	I	5 Jun 1908	Torino	1950-52	3	5	0	-	-	-	-	-	-	-	-	1	4	-
		18 Jun 1977	Rapallo															
ROLT, Tony	GB	16 Oct 1918	Bordon, Hampshire	1950-55	3	3	0	-	-	-	-	-	-	-	-	-	3	-
ROOS, Bertil	S	12 Oct 1943	Göteborg	1974	1	1	0	-	-	-	-	-	-	-	-	-	1	-
ROSBERG, Keke	FIN	6 Dec 1948	Stockholm, S	1978-86	9	114	159.5	5	3	5	8	4	11	9	1	21	55	14
ROSIER, Louis	F	5 Nov 1905	Chapdes-Beaufort	1950-56	7	38	18	-	-	-	-	2	2	2	2	18	12	-
		29 Oct 1956	Montlhéry, nr Paris															
ROSSET, Ricardo	BR	27 Jul 1968	São Paulo	1996-98	3	27	0	-	-	-	-	-	-	-	-	12	15	6
ROTHENGATTER, Huub	NL	8 Oct 1954	Bussum, nr Hilversum	1984-86	3	25	0	-	-	-	-	-	-	-	-	6	19	5
RUBY, Lloyd	USA	12 Jan 1928	Wichita Falls, Texas	1961	1	1	0	-	-	-	-	-	-	-	-	-	1	-
RUSSO, Giacomo. see GEKI																		
RUTTMAN, Troy	USA	11 Mar 1930	Mooreland, Oklahoma	1958	1	1	0	-	-	-	-	-	-	-	-	1	-	1
		19 May 1997	Lake Havasu City, Arizona															
RYAN, Peter	CDN	10 Jun 1940	Philadelphia, Pennsylvania, USA	1961	1	1	0	-	-	-	-	-	-	-	-	1	-	-
		2 Jul 1962	Paris, F															
SAID, Bob	USA	5 May 1932	Greenwich, New York	1959	1	1	0	-	-	-	-	-	-	-	-	-	1	-
		24 Mar 2002	Kirkland, Washington															
SALA, Luis	E	15 May 1959	Barcelona	1988-89	2	26	1	-	-	-	-	-	-	-	1	10	15	6
SALAZAR, Eliseo	RCH	14 Nov 1954	Santiago	1981-83	3	24	3	-	-	-	-	-	-	1	1	6	16	13
SALO, Mika	FIN	30 Nov 1966	Helsinki	1994-02	8	110	33	-	-	-	1	1	1	7	6	48	46	1
SALVADORI, Roy	GB	12 May 1922	Dovercourt, Essex	1952-62	11	47	19	-	-	-	1	1	1	2	5	9	28	3
SANESI, Consalvo	I	28 Mar 1911	Terranuova Bracciolini, nr Arezzo	1950-51	2	5	3	-	-	-	-	-	1	-	1	1	2	-
		28 Jul 1998	Milano															
SARRAZIN, Stéphane	F	2 Nov 1974	Alès	1999	1	1	0	-	-	-	-	-	-	-	-	-	1	-
SATO, Takuma	J	28 Jan 1977	Tokyo	2002-05	4	51	40	-	-	-	-	1	2	3	4	23	18	1
SCARFIOTTI, Lodovico	I	18 Oct 1933	Torino	1963-68	6	10	17	-	1	1	-	-	2	-	2	1	4	2
		8 Jun 1968	Rossfeld, D															
SCARLATTI, Giorgio	I	2 Oct 1921	Roma	1956-61	6	12	1	-	-	-	-	-	-	1	1	3	7	3
		26 Jul 1990	Roma															
SCHECKTER, Ian	ZA	22 Aug 1947	East London	1974-77	4	18	0	-	-	-	-	-	-	-	-	4	14	2
SCHECKTER, Jody	ZA	29 Jan 1950	East London	1972-80	9	112	255	3	5	10	14	9	9	7	4	24	35	1
SCHELL, Harry	USA	29 Jun 1921	Paris, F	1950-60	11	56	32	-	-	-	1	1	3	7	4	14	26	-
		13 May 1960	Silverstone, GB															
SCHENKEN, Tim	AUS	26 Sep 1943	Gordon, Sydney, NSW	1970-74	5	34	7	-	-	-	-	1	-	1	1	13	18	2
SCHERRER, Albert	CH	28 Feb 1908	Riehen	1953	1	1	0	-	-	-	-	-	-	-	-	1	-	-
		5 Jul 1986	Basel															
SCHIATTARELLA, Mimmo	I	17 Nov 1967	Milano	1994-95	2	7	0	-	-	-	-	-	-	-	-	3	4	-
SCHILLER, Heinz	CH	25 Jan 1930	Frauenfeld	1962	1	1	0	-	-	-	-	-	-	-	-	-	1	-
SCHLESSER, Jean-Louis	F	12 Sep 1948	Nancy	1983-88	2	1	0	-	-	-	-	-	-	-	-	1	-	1
SCHLESSER, Jo	F	18 May 1928	Liouville, nr Nancy	1966-68	3	3	0	-	-	-	-	-	-	-	-	1	2	-
		7 Jul 1968	Rouen															
SCHNEIDER, Bernd	D	20 Jul 1964	St. Ingbert, Saarbrücken	1988-90	3	9	0	-	-	-	-	-	-	-	-	3	6	25
SCHOELLER, Rudolf	CH	27 Apr 1902	Düren, D	1952	1	1	0	-	-	-	-	-	-	-	-	-	1	-
		7 Mar 1978	Grabs															
SCHROEDER, Rob	USA	11 May 1926		1962	1	1	-	0	-	-	-	-	-	-	-	1	-	-
SCHUMACHER, Michael	D	3 Jan 1969	Hürth-Hermühlheim	1991-05	15	231	1248	64	69	84	39	19	10	9	6	14	50	1
SCHUMACHER, Ralf	D	30 Jun 1975	Hürth-Hermühlheim	1997-05	9	145	304	6	8	6	6	14	18	17	10	29	45	2
SCHUPPAN, Vern	AUS	19 Mar 1943	Booleroo Whyalla, South Aus.	1972-77	4	9	0	-	-	-	-	-	-	-	-	4	5	4
SCHWELM CRUZ, Adolfo	RA	28 Jun 1923	Buenos Aires	1953	1	1	0	-	-	-	-	-	-	-	-	-	1	-
SCOTT BROWN, Archie	GB	13 May 1927	Paisley, Scotland	1956	1	1	0	-	-	-	-	-	-	-	-	-	1	1
		19 May 1958	Heusy, nr Spa, B															
SCOTTI, Piero	I	11 Nov 1909	Firenze	1956	1	1	0	-	-	-	-	-	-	-	-	-	1	-
		14 Feb 1976	Samedan, CH															
SEIDEL, Wolfgang	D	4 Jul 1926	Düsseldorf	1953-62	5	10	0	-	-	-	-	-	-	-	-	3	7	2
		1 Mar 1987	München															

	Nat	Born / Died	Place of Birth / Place of Death	Years Entered	No. of Years	GPs	Points	PP	FL	Win	2nd	3rd	4th	5th	6th	OP	NC etc	NS etc
SENNA, Ayrton	BR	21 Mar 1960 / 1 May 1994	São Paulo / Bologna, I	1984-94	11	161	614	65	19	41	23	16	7	6	3	12	53	1
SERAFINI, Dorino	I	22 Jul 1909 / 5 Jul 2000	Pesaro / Pesaro	1950	1	1	3	-	-	-	1	-	-	-	-	-	-	-
SERRA, Chico	BR	3 Feb 1957	São Paulo	1981-83	3	18	1	-	-	-	-	-	-	-	1	10	7	15
SERRURIER, Doug	ZA	9 Dec 1920	Germiston, Transvaal	1962-65	3	2	0	-	-	-	-	-	-	-	-	1	1	1
SERVOZ-GAVIN, Johnny	F	18 Jan 1942	Grenoble	1967-70	4	12	9	-	-	-	1	-	-	1	1	1	8	1
SETTEMBER, Tony	USA	10 Jul 1926	Manila, Philippines	1962-63	2	6	0	-	-	-	-	-	-	-	-	2	4	1
SHARP, Hap	USA	1 Jan 1928 / 11 May 1992	Tulsa, Oklahoma / San Martín de los Andes, RA	1961-64	4	6	0	-	-	-	-	-	-	-	-	4	2	-
SHAWE-TAYLOR, Brian	GB	29 Jan 1915 / 1 May 1999	Dublin, IRL / Dowdeswell, Cheltenham, Glos	1950-51	2	2	0	-	-	-	-	-	-	-	-	2	-	1
SHELBY, Carroll	USA	11 Jan 1923	Leesburg, Texas	1958-59	2	8	0	-	-	-	-	-	1	-	-	3	4	-
SHELLY, Tony	NZ	2 Feb 1937 / 4 Oct 1998	Wellington / Taupo	1962	1	1	0	-	-	-	-	-	-	-	-	-	1	2
SIFFERT, Jo	CH	7 Jul 1936 / 24 Oct 1971	Fribourg / Brands Hatch, Kent, GB	1962-71	10	96	68	2	4	2	2	2	7	2	5	32	44	4
SIMON, André	F	5 Jan 1920	Paris	1951-57	5	11	0	-	-	-	-	-	-	2	2	7	1	
SOLANA, Moisés	MEX	26 Dec 1935 / 27 Jul 1969	Mexico City / Valle de Bravo, nr Mexico City	1963-68	6	8	0	-	-	-	-	-	-	-	3	5	-	
SOLER-ROIG, Alex	E	29 Oct 1932	Barcelona	1970-72	3	6	0	-	-	-	-	-	-	-	-	6	4	
SOMMER, Raymond	F	31 Aug 1906 / 10 Sep 1950	Paris / Cadours, nr Toulouse	1950	1	5	3	-	-	-	-	1	-	-	-	4	-	
SPARKEN, Mike	F	16 Jun 1930	Neuilly-sur-Seine, nr Paris	1955	1	1	0	-	-	-	-	-	-	-	1	-	-	
SPENCE, Mike	GB	30 Dec 1936 / 7 May 1968	Croydon, Surrey / Indianapolis, Indiana, USA	1963-68	6	36	27	-	-	-	1	3	6	2	9	15	1	
STACEY, Alan	GB	29 Aug 1933 / 19 Jun 1960	Broomfield, Essex / Spa-Francorchamps, B	1958-60	3	7	0	-	-	-	-	-	-	-	1	6	-	
STARRABBA, Gaetano	I	3 Dec 1932	Palermo, Sicilia	1961	1	1	0	-	-	-	-	-	-	-	-	1	-	
STEWART, Ian	GB	15 Jul 1929	Edinburgh, Scotland	1953	1	1	0	-	-	-	-	-	-	-	-	1	-	
STEWART, Jackie	GB	11 Jun 1939	Dumbuck, Dumbarton, Scotland	1965-73	9	99	360	17	15	27	11	5	6	5	3	6	36	1
STEWART, Jimmy	GB	6 Mar 1931	Dumbuck, Dumbarton, Scotland	1953	1	1	0	-	-	-	-	-	-	-	-	1	-	
STOHR, Siegfried	I	10 Oct 1952	Rimini	1981	1	9	0	-	-	-	-	-	-	-	-	3	6	4
STOMMELEN, Rolf	D	11 Jul 1943 / 24 Apr 1983	Siegen, nr Köln / Riverside, California, USA	1969-78	9	54	14	-	-	-	-	1	-	4	2	29	18	9
STREIFF, Philippe	F	26 Jun 1955	La Tronche, nr Grenoble	1984-88	5	53	11	-	-	-	-	1	1	1	2	25	23	1
STUCK, Hans	D/A	27 Dec 1900 / 8 Feb 1978	Warszawa, PL / Grainau, D	1951-53	3	3	0	-	-	-	-	-	-	-	1	2	2	
STUCK, Hans-Joachim	D	1 Jan 1951	Grainau	1974-79	6	74	29	-	-	-	-	2	3	5	2	14	48	7
SULLIVAN, Danny	USA	9 Mar 1950	Louisville, Kentucky	1983	1	15	2	-	-	-	-	-	-	1	-	6	8	-
SURER, Marc	CH	18 Sep 1951	Füllinsdorf, nr Basel	1979-86	8	82	17	-	1	-	-	-	2	2	7	39	32	6
SURTEES, John	GB	11 Feb 1934	Tatsfield, Surrey	1960-72	13	111	180	8	11	6	10	8	5	8	3	14	57	2
SUZUKI, Aguri	J	8 Sep 1960	Tokyo	1988-95	8	64	8	-	-	-	-	1	-	-	4	20	39	24
SUZUKI, Toshio	J	10 Mar 1955	Saitama	1993	1	2	0	-	-	-	-	-	-	-	-	2	-	1
SWATERS, Jacques	B	30 Oct 1926	Woluwe-Saint-Lambert, Bruxelles	1951-54	3	7	0	-	-	-	-	-	-	-	-	3	4	-
TAKAGI, Tora	J	12 Feb 1974	Shizuoka	1998-99	2	32	0	-	-	-	-	-	-	-	-	12	20	
TAKAHARA, Noritake	J	6 Jun 1951	Tokyo	1976-77	2	2	0	-	-	-	-	-	-	-	-	1	1	
TAKAHASHI, Kunimitsu	J	29 Jan 1940	Tokyo	1977	1	1	0	-	-	-	-	-	-	-	-	1	-	
TAMBAY, Patrick	F	25 Jun 1949	Paris	1977-86	9	114	103	5	2	2	4	5	6	8	7	25	57	9
TARQUINI, Gabriele	I	2 Mar 1962	Guilianova Lido, nr Pescara	1987-95	7	38	1	-	-	-	-	-	-	-	1	12	25	40
TARUFFI, Piero	I	12 Oct 1906 / 12 Jan 1988	Albano Laziale, Roma / Roma	1950-56	6	18	41	-	1	1	3	1	2	2	1	2	6	-
TAYLOR, Henry	GB	16 Dec 1932	Shefford, Bedfordshire	1959-61	3	8	3	-	-	-	-	-	1	-	-	6	1	2
TAYLOR, John	GB	23 Mar 1933 / 8 Sep 1966	Anstey, nr Leicester / Koblenz, D	1964-66	2	5	1	-	-	-	-	-	-	1	3	1	-	
TAYLOR, Mike	GB	24 Apr 1934	Westminster, London	1959-60	2	1	0	-	-	-	-	-	-	-	-	1	1	
TAYLOR, Trevor	GB	26 Dec 1936	Gleadless, Sheffield, Yorkshire	1959-66	6	27	8	-	-	-	1	-	-	2	9	15	2	
THACKWELL, Mike	NZ	30 Mar 1961	Auckland	1980-84	2	2	0	-	-	-	-	-	-	-	-	2	3	
THIELE, Alfonso	I/USA	5 Apr 1922		1960	1	1	0	-	-	-	-	-	-	-	-	1	-	
THOMPSON, Eric	GB	4 Nov 1919	Ditton Hill, Surrey	1952	1	1	2	-	-	-	-	-	1	-	-	-	-	

Drivers

Name	Nat	Born Died	Place of Birth Place of Death	Years Entered	No. of Years	GPs	Points	PP	FL	Win	2nd	3rd	4th	5th	6th	OP	NC etc	NS etc
THORNE, Leslie	GB	23 Jun 1916 13 Jul 1993	Greenock,Renfrews.,Scotland Troon, Ayrshire, Scotland	1954	1	1	0	-	-	-	-	-	-	-	-	-	1	-
TINGLE, Sam	RSR	24 Aug 1921	Chorlton, Manchester, GB	1963-69	5	5	0	-	-	-	-	-	-	-	-	2	3	-
TITTERINGTON, Desmond	GB	1 May 1928 13 Apr 2002	Cultra, Co. Down, N Ireland Dundee, Scotland	1956	1	1	0	-	-	-	-	-	-	-	-	-	1	-
TRINTIGNANT, Maurice	F	30 Oct 1917 13 Feb 2005	Sainte-Cécile-les-Vignes Nîmes	1950-64	15	82	72.33	-	1	2	3	4	4	8	3	20	38	-
TRULLI, Jarno	I	13 Jul 1974	Pescara	1997-05	9	146	160	3	-	1	3	3	12	12	9	51	55	3
TUERO, Esteban	RA	22 Apr 1978	Buenos Aires	1998	1	16	0	-	-	-	-	-	-	-	-	4	12	-
TUNMER, Guy	ZA	1 Dec 1948 22 Jun 1999	Ficksburg Sandton, Johannesburg	1975	1	1	0	-	-	-	-	-	-	-	-	-	1	-
ULMEN, Toni	D	25 Jan 1906 4 Nov 1976	Düsseldorf Düsseldorf	1952	1	2	0	-	-	-	-	-	-	-	-	1	1	-
UNSER, Bobby	USA	20 Feb 1934	Colorado Springs, Colorado	1968	1	1	0	-	-	-	-	-	-	-	-	-	1	1
URíA, Alberto	ROU	11 Jul 1924 4 Dec 1988	Montevideo Montevideo	1955-56	2	2	0	-	-	-	-	-	-	1	-	-	1	-
VACCARELLA, Nino	I	4 Mar 1933	Palermo, Sicilia	1961-65	3	4	0	-	-	-	-	-	-	-	-	3	1	1
van de POELE, Eric	B	30 Sep 1961	Verviers	1991-92	2	5	0	-	-	-	-	-	-	-	-	3	2	24
van der LOF, Dries	NL	23 Aug 1919 24 May 1990	Emmen Enschede	1952	1	1	0	-	-	-	-	-	-	-	-	-	1	-
van LENNEP, Gijs	NL	16 Mar 1942	Bloemendaal	1971-75	4	8	2	-	-	-	-	-	-	-	2	5	1	2
van ROOYEN, Basil	ZA	19 Apr 1939	Johannesburg	1968-69	2	2	0	-	-	-	-	-	-	-	-	-	2	-
VERSTAPPEN, Jos	NL	4 Mar 1972	Montfort, nr Roermond	1994-03	8	107	17	-	-	-	-	2	1	2	2	42	58	-
VILLENEUVE, Gilles	CDN	18 Jan 1950 8 May 1982	St-Jean-sur-Richelieu,Québec Louvain, nr Zolder, B	1977-82	6	67	107	2	8	6	5	2	2	3	3	19	27	1
VILLENEUVE, Jacques	CDN	9 Apr 1971	St-Jean-sur-Richelieu,Québec	1996-05	10	151	228	13	9	11	5	7	10	6	9	52	51	2
VILLORESI, Luigi	I	16 May 1909 24 Aug 1997	Milano Modena	1950-56	7	31	49	-	1	-	2	6	2	3	4	1	13	3
VOLONTERIO, Ottorino	CH	7 Dec 1917 10 Mar 2003	Orselina, Locarno Lugano	1954-57	3	3	0	-	-	-	-	-	-	-	-	1	2	-
von OPEL, Rikky	FL	14 Oct 1947	New York, USA	1973-74	2	10	0	-	-	-	-	-	-	-	-	4	6	4
von TRIPS, Wolfgang	D	4 May 1928 10 Sep 1961	Horrem, nr Köln Monza, I	1956-61	6	27	56	1	-	2	2	2	3	4	3	4	7	2
VONLANTHEN, Jo	CH	31 May 1942	St Ursen, nr Fribourg	1975	1	1	0	-	-	-	-	-	-	-	-	-	1	-
WACKER, Fred	USA	10 Jul 1918 16 Jun 1998	Chicago, Illinois Lake Bluff, Illinois	1953-54	2	3	0	-	-	-	-	-	-	-	-	1	1	2
WALKER, Dave	AUS	10 Jun 1941	Sydney, New South Wales	1971-72	2	11	0	-	-	-	-	-	-	-	-	5	6	-
WALKER, Peter	GB	7 Oct 1912 1 Mar 1984	Huby, Leeds, Yorkshire Newtown, Worcester	1950-55	3	4	0	-	-	-	-	-	-	-	-	1	3	-
WALTER, Heini	CH	28 Jul 1927	Alpthal	1962	1	1	0	-	-	-	-	-	-	-	-	-	1	-
WARD, Rodger	USA	10 Jan 1921 5 Jul 2004	Beloit, Kansas Anaheim, California	1959-63	2	2	0	-	-	-	-	-	-	-	-	-	2	-
WARWICK, Derek	GB	27 Aug 1954	New Alresford, Hampshire	1981-93	11	146	71	-	2	-	2	2	8	9	9	37	79	16
WATSON, John	GB	4 May 1946	Belfast, Northern Ireland	1973-85	12	152	169	2	5	5	6	9	9	7	11	42	63	2
WEBBER, Mark	AUS	27 Aug 1976	Queanbeyan, New South Wales	2002-05	4	68	62	-	-	-	-	1	2	3	6	32	24	2
WENDLINGER, Karl	A	20 Dec 1968	Kufstein	1991-95	5	41	14	-	-	-	-	-	3	1	3	11	23	1
WESTBURY, Peter	GB	26 May 1938	Roehampton, London	1969-70	2	1	0	-	-	-	-	-	-	-	-	1	-	1
WHARTON, Ken	GB	21 Mar 1916 12 Jan 1957	Smethwick, Worcestershire Auckland, NZ	1952-55	4	15	3	-	-	-	-	-	1	-	1	6	7	1
WHITEHEAD, Graham	GB	15 Apr 1922 15 Jan 1981	Harrogate, Yorkshire Lower Basildon, Berkshire	1952	1	1	0	-	-	-	-	-	-	-	-	-	1	-
WHITEHEAD, Peter	GB	12 Nov 1914 20 Sep 1958	Menston, nr Ikley, Yorkshire Lasalle, nr Nîmes, F	1950-54	5	10	4	-	-	-	-	1	-	-	-	4	5	2
WHITEHOUSE, Bill	GB	1 Apr 1909 14 Jul 1957	Plumstead, London Reims, F	1954	1	1	0	-	-	-	-	-	-	-	-	-	1	-
WIDDOWS, Robin	GB	27 May 1942	Cowley, nr Uxbridge, Middx	1968	1	1	0	-	-	-	-	-	-	-	-	-	1	-
WIETZES, Eppie	CDN	28 May 1938	Assen, NL	1967-74	2	2	0	-	-	-	-	-	-	-	-	-	2	-
WILDS, Mike	GB	7 Jan 1946	Chiswick, London	1974-76	3	3	0	-	-	-	-	-	-	-	-	-	3	5
WILLIAMS, Jonathan	GB	26 Oct 1942	Cairo, Egypt	1967	1	1	0	-	-	-	-	-	-	-	-	-	1	-

	Nat	Born / Died	Place of Birth / Place of Death	Years Entered	No. of Years	GPs	Points	PP	FL	Win	2nd	3rd	4th	5th	6th	OP	NC etc	NS etc
WILLIAMSON, Roger	GB	4 Feb 1949 / 29 Jul 1973	Leicester / Zandvoort, NL	1973	1	2	0	-	-	-	-	-	-	-	-	-	2	-
WILSON, Justin	GB	31 Jul 1978	Sheffield, South Yorkshire	2003	1	16	1	-	-	-	-	-	-	-	-	7	9	-
WILSON, Vic	GB	14 Apr 1931 / 14 Jan 2001	Drypool, Kingston-upon-Hull / Gerrards Cross, Buckinghamshire	1960-66	2	1	0	-	-	-	-	-	-	-	-	-	1	1
WINKELHOCK, Manfred	D	6 Oct 1951 / 12 Aug 1985	Waiblingen, nr Stuttgart / North York, Toronto, Ontario, CDN	1980-85	5	47	2	-	-	-	-	-	-	1	-	12	34	9
WISELL, Reine	S	30 Sep 1941	Motala	1970-74	5	22	13	-	-	-	-	1	2	1	1	3	14	1
WUNDERINK, Roelof	NL	12 Dec 1948	Eindhoven	1975	1	3	0	-	-	-	-	-	-	-	-	-	3	3
WURZ, Alexander	A	15 Feb 1974	Waidhofen an der Thaya	1997-05	5	53	32	-	1	-	-	2	5	3	1	25	17	-
YOONG, Alex	MAL	20 Jul 1976	Kuala Lumpur	2001-02	2	14	0	-	-	-	-	-	-	-	-	6	8	4
ZANARDI, Alessandro	I	23 Oct 1966	Bologna	1991-99	5	41	1	-	-	-	-	-	-	-	1	17	23	3
ZONTA, Ricardo	BR	23 Mar 1976	Curitiba	1999-05	5	36	3	-	-	-	-	-	-	-	3	16	17	2
ZORZI, Renzo	I	12 Dec 1946	Ziano di Fiemme, nr Torino	1975-77	3	7	1	-	-	-	-	-	-	-	1	2	4	-
ZUNINO, Ricardo	RA	13 Apr 1949	San Juan	1979-81	3	10	0	-	-	-	-	-	-	-	-	6	4	1

The following drivers also took part in Friday test sessions:
Zsolt Baumgartner - 2003; Gianmaria Bruni - 2003; Anthony Davidson - 2004 ; Pedro de la Rosa - 2005 ; Robert Doornbos - 2004,05; Timo Glock - 2004
Nicolas Kiesa - 2005; Christian Klien - 2005; Vitantonio Liuzzi - 2005 ; Allan McNish - 2003; Olivier Panis - 2005; Alexander Wurz - 2005; Ricardo Zonta - 2004,05

Grand Prix Non-Starters

	Nat	Born Died	Place of Birth Place of Death	Years Entered	No. of Years	NS etc
AMATI, Giovanna	I	20 Jul 1962	Roma	1992	1	3
BARTELS, Michael	D	8 Mar 1968	Plettenberg	1991	1	4
BAYARDO, Asdrúbal	ROU	26 Dec 1922	Pan de Azucar	1959	1	1
BERTAGGIA, Enrico	I	19 Sep 1964	Noale, nr Venezia	1989-92	2	6
BORDEU, Juan Manuel	RA	28 Jan 1934 24 Nov 1990	Balcarce Buenos Aires	1961	1	1
BRABHAM, Gary	AUS	29 Mar 1961	Wimbledon, London, GB	1990	1	2
BRAMBILLA, Tino	I	31 Jan 1934	Monza	1963-69	2	2
BRANCATELLI, Gianfranco	I	18 Jan 1950	Torino	1979	1	3
CADE, Phil	USA	12 Jun 1916 28 Aug 2001	Charles City, Iowa Winchester, Massachusetts	1959	1	1
CHAPMAN, Colin	GB	19 May 1928 16 Dec 1982	Richmond, Surrey East Carleton, Norfolk	1956	1	1
CHAVES, Pedro	P	27 Feb 1965	Bonfim, Porto	1991	1	13
COGAN, Kevin	USA	31 Mar 1956	Culver City, California	1980-81	2	2
COLOMBO, Alberto	I	23 Feb 1946	Veredo, nr Milano	1978	1	3
CRESPO, Alberto	RA	16 Jan 1930 14 Aug 1991	Buenos Aires Buenos Aires	1952	1	1
de CHANGY, Alain	B	5 Feb 1922 5 Aug 1994	Bruxelles Etterbeek, Bruxelles	1959	1	1
de DRYVER, Bernard	B	19 Sep 1952	Bruxelles	1977-78	2	2
de RIU, Giovanni	I	10 Mar 1925	Macomer, Nuoro, Sardegna	1954	1	1
DOCHNAL, Frank	USA	8 Oct 1920	St. Louis, Missouri	1963	1	1
DUSIO, Piero	I	13 Oct 1899 7 Nov 1975	Scurzolengo d'Asti Victoria, Buenos Aires, RA	1952	1	1
ECCLESTONE, Bernie	GB	28 Oct 1930	St.Peters, nr Bungay, Suffolk	1958	1	1
FACETTI, Carlo	I	26 Jun 1935	Cormano, Milano	1974	1	1
FERGUSON, Willie	ZA	6 Mar 1940	Johannesburg	1972	1	1
FISCHER, Ludwig	D	17 Dec 1915 8 Mar 1991	Straubing Bad Reichenhall	1952	1	1
FRANCIA, Giorgio	I	8 Nov 1947	San Giorgio di Piano, Bologna	1977-81	2	2
FUSHIDA, Hiroshi	J	10 Mar 1946	Kyoto	1975	1	2
GALICA, Divina	GB	13 Aug 1944	Bushey Heath, Hertfordshire	1976-78	2	3
GIMAX	I	1 Jan 1938	Lainate, nr Milano	1978	1	1
GLÖCKLER, Helm	D	13 Jan 1909 18 Dec 1993	Frankfurt Frankfurt	1953	1	1
GUBBY, Brian	GB	17 Apr 1934	Epsom, Surrey	1965	1	1
HATTORI, Naoki	J	13 Jun 1966	Yokkaichi, Mie	1991	1	2
JONES, Tom	USA	26 Apr 1943	Dallas, Texas	1967	1	1
JOVER, Juan	E	23 Nov 1923 28 Jun 1960	Barcelona Sitges, nr Barcelona	1951	1	1
KAVANAGH, Ken	AUS	12 Dec 1923	Melbourne, Victoria	1958	1	2
KENNEDY, David	IRL	15 Jan 1953	Sligo	1980	1	7
KESSLER, Bruce	USA	23 Mar 1936	Seattle, Washington	1958	1	1
KOZAROWITSKY, Mikko	FIN	17 May 1948	Helsinki	1977	1	2
KRAKAU, Willi	D	4 Dec 1911 26 Apr 1995	Schönebeck-Felgeleben Peine	1952	1	1
KUHNKE, Kurt	D	30 Apr 1910 8 Feb 1969	Stettin (Szczecin, PL) Braunschweig	1963	1	1
KUWASHIMA, Masami	J	14 Sep 1950	Kumagaya	1976	1	1
LANGES, Claudio	I	20 Jul 1960	Brescia	1990	1	14
LONDONO, Ricardo	CO	8 Aug 1949	Medellin	1981	1	1

	Nat	Born Died	Place of Birth Place of Death	Years Entered	No. of Years	NS etc
LUCIENBONNET, Jean	F	7 Jan 1923 19 Aug 1962	Nice Enna, Sicilia, I	1959	1	1
McCARTHY, Perry	GB	3 Mar 1961	Stepney, London	1992	1	7
McGUIRE, Brian	AUS	13 Dec 1945 29 Aug 1977	Melbourne, Victoria Brands Hatch, Kent, GB	1977	1	1
MERKEL, Harry	D	10 Jan 1918 11 Feb 1995	Taucha, Leipzig Killarney Vale, NSW, AUS	1952	1	1
MOSS, Bill	GB	4 Sep 1933	Luton, Bedfordshire	1959	1	1
NELLEMAN, Jac	DK	19 Apr 1944	København	1976	1	1
PIÁN, Alfredo	RA	21 Oct 1912 25 Jul 1990	Las Rosas, nr Santa Fe Las Rosas, nr Santa Fe	1950	1	1
PRINOTH, Ernesto	I	15 Apr 1923 26 Nov 1981	Ortisei, Bolzano Innsbruck, A	1962	1	1
PUZEY, Clive	RSR	11 Jul 1941	Bulawayo	1965	1	1
RICHARDSON, Ken	GB	21 Aug 1911 27 Jun 1997	Bourne, Lincolnshire Bourne, Lincolnshire	1951	1	1
ROLLINSON, Alan	GB	15 May 1943	Walsall, Staffordshire	1965	1	1
RUDAZ, Jean-Claude	CH	7 Jul 1942	La Grande Dixence, Sion	1964	1	1
SEIFERT, Günther	D	18 Oct 1937	Oldenburg	1962	1	1
SOSPIRI, Vincenzo	I	7 Oct 1966	Forli	1997	1	1
SOUTH, Stephen	GB	19 Feb 1952	Harrow, Middlesex	1980	1	1
STUPPACHER, Otto	A	3 Mar 1947 13 Aug 2001	Wien Wien	1976	1	3
SUTCLIFFE, Andy	GB	9 May 1947	Mildenhall, Suffolk	1977	1	1
TARAMAZZO, Luigi	I	5 May 1932 15 Feb 2004	Ceva Vallecrosia	1958	1	1
TAYLOR, Dennis	GB	12 Jun 1921 2 Jun 1962	Sidcup, Kent Monte-Carlo, MC	1959	1	1
TESTUT, André	F	13 Apr 1926	Lyon	1958-59	2	2
TRIMMER, Tony	GB	24 Jan 1943	Maidenhead, Berkshire	1975-78	4	6
VILLENEUVE Sr., Jacques	CDN	4 Nov 1953	St-Jean-sur-Richelieu,Québec	1981-83	2	3
WEIDLER, Volker	D	18 Mar 1962	Weinheim, nr Mannheim	1989	1	10
WHITEAWAY, Ted	GB	1 Nov 1928 18 Oct 1995	Feltham, Middlesex Perth, Western Australia, AUS	1955	1	1
WILSON, Desiré	ZA	26 Nov 1953	Brakpan, Johannesburg	1980	1	1
WINKELHOCK, Joachim	D	24 Oct 1960	Waiblingen, nr Stuttgart	1989	1	7
ZAPICO, Emilio	E	21 May 1944 6 Aug 1996	Léon Huete	1976	1	1

Grand Prix Meeting Testers

	Nat	Born	Place of Birth	Years Entered	No. of Years	AP
BOBBI, Matteo	I	2 Jul 1978	Milano	2003	1	1
BRISCOE, Ryan	AUS	24 Sep 1981	Sydney, New South Wales	2004	1	6
LEINDERS, Bas	B	16 Jul 1975	Bree	2004	1	17
MONTAGNY, Franck	F	5 Jan 1978	Feurs	2003-05	2	2
MOTOYAMA, Satoshi	J	4 Mar 1971	Tokyo	2003	1	1
NISSANY, Chanoch	IL	29 Jul 1963	Tel Aviv	2005	1	1
SPEED, Scott	USA	24 Jan 1983	Manteca, California	2005	1	2
TOCCACELO, Enrico	I	12 Dec 1978	Roma	2005	1	3
WIRDHEIM, Björn	S	4 Apr 1980	Växjö	2003-04	2	18
YAMAMOTO, Sakon	J	9 Jul 1982	Toyohashi City, Aichi	2005	1	1

The above drivers are those who have not started a Grand Prix, but taken part in Friday test sessions.

Indianapolis 500 Starters

	Nat	Born / Died	Place of Birth / Place of Death	Years Entered	No. of Years	Races	Pts	PP	FL	Win	2nd	3rd	4th	5th	6th	OP	R	NS
ADER, Walt	USA	15 Dec 1913 / 25 Nov 1982	Long Valley, New Jersey / Califon, New Jersey	1950	1	1	0	-	-	-	-	-	-	-	-	1	-	-
AGABASHIAN, Freddie	USA	21 Aug 1913 / 13 Oct 1989	Modesto, California / Alamo, California	1950-58	9	8	1.5	1	-	-	-	-	1	-	1	2	4	1
AMICK, George	USA	24 Oct 1924 / 4 Apr 1959	Vernonia, Oregon / Daytona Beach, Florida	1957-58	2	1	6	-	-	-	1	-	-	-	-	-	-	1
AMICK, Red	USA	19 Jan 1929 / 16 May 1995	Kansas City, Missouri / Crystal River, Florida	1959-60	2	2	0	-	-	-	-	-	-	-	-	1	1	-
ANDREWS, Keith	USA	15 Jun 1920 / 15 May 1957	Denver, Colorado / Indianapolis, Indiana	1955-57	3	2	0	-	-	-	-	-	-	-	-	-	2	1
ARMI, Frank	USA	12 Oct 1918 / 28 Nov 1992	Portland, Oregon / Hanford, California	1951-54	3	1	0	-	-	-	-	-	-	-	-	1	-	2
ARNOLD, Chuck	USA	30 May 1926 / 4 Sep 1997	Stamford, Connecticut / California	1959-60	2	1	0	-	-	-	-	-	-	-	-	1	-	1
ASCARI, Alberto	I	13 Jul 1918 / 26 May 1955	Milano / Monza	1952	1	1	0	-	-	-	-	-	-	-	-	-	1	-
AYULO, Manny	USA	20 Oct 1921 / 16 May 1955	Los Angeles, California / Indianapolis, Indiana	1950-55	6	4	2	-	-	-	-	1	-	-	-	2	1	2
BALL, Bobby	USA	26 Aug 1925 / 27 Feb 1954	Phoenix, Arizona / Phoenix, Arizona	1951-52	2	2	2	-	-	-	-	-	-	1	-	-	1	-
BANKS, Henry	USA	14 Jun 1913 / 18 Dec 1994	Croydon, Surrey, GB / Michigan	1950-53	4	3	0	-	-	-	-	-	-	-	1	2	-	1
BETTENHAUSEN, Tony	USA	12 Sep 1916 / 12 May 1961	Tinley Park, Illinois / Indianapolis, Indiana	1950-60	11	11	11	-	1	-	1	-	2	1	-	2	5	-
BISCH, Art	USA	10 Nov 1926 / 4 Jul 1958	Mesa, Arizona / Lakewood Speedway, Georgia	1958	1	1	0	-	-	-	-	-	-	-	-	1	-	-
BOYD, Johnny	USA	19 Aug 1926 / 27 Oct 2003	Fresno, California / Fresno, California	1955-60	6	6	4	-	-	-	-	1	-	2	-	3	-	-
BRANSON, Don	USA	2 Jun 1920 / 12 Nov 1966	Rantoul, Illinois / Gardena, California	1959-60	2	2	3	-	-	-	-	-	1	-	-	1	-	-
BROWN, Walt	USA	30 Dec 1911 / 29 Jul 1951	Springfield, New York / Williams Grove, Pennsylvania	1950-51	2	2	0	-	-	-	-	-	-	-	-	1	1	-
BRYAN, Jimmy	USA	28 Jan 1926 / 19 Jun 1960	Phoenix, Arizona / Langhorne, Pennsylvania	1951-60	10	9	18	-	-	1	1	1	-	-	1	2	3	1
CANTRELL, Bill	USA	31 Jan 1908 / 22 Jan 1996	Hardin County, Kentucky / Madison, Indiana	1950-52	3	1	0	-	-	-	-	-	-	-	-	-	1	2
CARTER, Duane	USA	5 May 1913 / 8 Mar 1993	Fresno, California / Indianapolis, Indiana	1950-60	8	8	6.5	-	-	-	-	1	2	-	-	5	-	-
CHEESBOURG, Bill	USA	12 Jun 1927 / 6 Nov 1995	Tucson, Arizona / Tucson, Arizona	1956-60	5	3	0	-	-	-	-	-	-	-	-	1	2	2
CHITWOOD, Joie	USA	14 Apr 1912 / 3 Jan 1988	Denison, Texas / Tampa, Florida	1950	1	1	1	-	-	-	-	-	1	-	-	-	-	-
CHRISTIE, Bob	USA	4 Apr 1924	Grants Pass, Oregon	1954-60	7	5	0	-	-	-	-	-	-	-	-	3	2	2
CONNOR, George	USA	16 Aug 1908 / 29 Mar 2001	San Bernardino, California / Hesperia, California	1950-53	4	3	0	-	-	-	-	-	-	-	-	2	1	1
CRAWFORD, Ray	USA	26 Oct 1915 / 1 Feb 1996	Roswell, New Mexico / Los Angeles, California	1955-59	5	3	0	-	-	-	-	-	-	-	-	-	3	2
CROCKETT, Larry	USA	23 Oct 1926 / 20 Mar 1955	Cambridge City, Indiana / Langhorne, Pennsylvania	1954	1	1	0	-	-	-	-	-	-	-	-	1	-	-
CROSS, Art	USA	24 Jan 1918 / 15 Apr 2005	Jersey City, New Jersey / La Porte, Indiana	1952-55	4	4	8	-	-	-	1	-	-	1	-	1	1	-
DAVIES, Jimmy	USA	18 Aug 1929 / 11 Jun 1966	Glendale, California / Chicago, Illinois	1950-60	9	5	4	-	-	-	-	1	-	-	-	3	1	4
DAYWALT, Jimmy	USA	28 Aug 1924 / 4 Apr 1966	Wabash, Indiana / Indianapolis, Indiana	1951-59	9	6	0	-	-	-	-	-	-	-	1	2	3	3
DINSMORE, Duke	USA	10 Apr 1913 / 12 Oct 1985	Williamstown, West Virgina / Daytona Beach, Florida	1950-56	7	4	0	-	-	-	-	-	-	-	-	1	3	3

Name	Nat	Born / Died	Place of Birth / Place of Death	Years Entered	No. of Years	Races	Pts	PP	FL	Win	2nd	3rd	4th	5th	6th	OP	R	NS
DUNCAN, Len	USA	25 Jul 1911 / 1 Aug 1998	New York City, New York / Lansdale, Pennsylvania	1953-56	4	1	0	-	-	-	-	-	-	-	-	-	1	3
EDMUNDS, Don	USA	23 Sep 1930	Santa Ana, California	1957-59	3	1	0	-	-	-	-	-	-	-	-	-	1	2
ELISIAN, Ed	USA	9 Dec 1926 / 30 Aug 1959	Oakland, California / Milwaukee, Wisconsin	1954-58	5	5	0	-	-	-	-	-	-	-	-	-	5	-
FAULKNER, Walt	USA	16 Feb 1920 / 22 Apr 1956	Tell, Texas / Vallejo, California	1950-55	6	5	1	1	-	-	-	-	-	1	-	3	1	1
FLAHERTY, Pat	USA	6 Jan 1926 / 9 Apr 2002	Glendale, California / Oxnard, California	1950-59	6	6	8	1	-	1	-	-	-	-	-	2	3	-
FOHR, Myron	USA	17 Jun 1912 / 14 Jan 1994	Milwaukee, Wisconsin / Milwaukee, Wisconsin	1950-51	2	1	0	-	-	-	-	-	-	-	-	1	-	1
FONDER, George	USA	22 Jun 1917 / 14 Jun 1958	Elmhurst, Pennsylvania / Hatfield, Pennsylvania	1950-54	5	2	0	-	-	-	-	-	-	-	-	2	-	3
FORBERG, Carl	USA	4 Mar 1911 / 17 Jan 2000	Omaha, Nebraska / Brownsburg, Indiana	1950-52	3	1	0	-	-	-	-	-	-	-	-	1	-	2
FORCE, Gene	USA	15 Jun 1916 / 21 Aug 1983	New Madison, Ohio / Richmond, Indiana	1951-60	5	2	0	-	-	-	-	-	-	-	-	-	2	3
FOYT, A J	USA	16 Jan 1935	Houston, Texas	1958-60	3	3	0	-	-	-	-	-	-	-	-	1	2	-
FREELAND, Don	USA	25 Mar 1925	Los Angeles, California	1953-60	8	8	4	-	-	-	-	1	-	-	-	3	4	-
GARRETT, Billy	USA	24 Apr 1933 / 15 Feb 1999	Princeton, Illinois / Glendale, California	1956-58	3	2	0	-	-	-	-	-	-	-	-	1	1	1
GEORGE, Elmer	USA	5 Jul 1928 / 30 May 1976	Hockerville, Oklahoma / Terre Haute, Indiana	1955-59	4	1	0	-	-	-	-	-	-	-	-	-	1	3
GOLDSMITH, Paul	USA	2 Oct 1925	Parkersburg, West Virginia	1958-60	3	3	6	-	-	-	-	1	-	1	-	-	1	-
GREEN, Cecil	USA	30 Sep 1919 / 29 Jul 1951	Dallas, Texas / Winchester, Indiana	1950-51	2	2	3	-	-	-	-	-	1	-	-	-	1	-
GRIFFITH, Cliff	USA	6 Feb 1916 / 23 Jan 1996	Nineveh, Indiana / Rochester, Indiana	1950-60	9	3	0	-	-	-	-	-	-	-	-	2	1	6
GRIM, Bobby	USA	4 Sep 1924 / 14 Jun 1995	Coal City, Indiana / Indianapolis, Indiana	1959-60	2	2	0	-	-	-	-	-	-	-	-	-	1	1
HANKS, Sam	USA	13 Jul 1914 / 27 Jun 1994	Columbus, Ohio / Pacific Palisades, California	1950-57	8	8	20	-	-	1	1	2	-	-	-	1	3	-
HARTLEY, Gene	USA	28 Jan 1926 / 13 Mar 1994	Roanoke, Indiana / Roanoke, Indiana	1950-60	10	8	0	-	-	-	-	-	-	-	-	5	3	2
HELLINGS, Mack	USA	14 Sep 1917 / 11 Nov 1951	Fort Dodge, Iowa / California	1950-51	2	2	0	-	-	-	-	-	-	-	-	1	1	-
HERMAN, Al	USA	15 Mar 1927 / 18 Jun 1960	Topton, Pennsylvania / West Haven, Connecticut	1955-60	8	5	0	-	-	-	-	-	-	-	-	2	3	3
HOLLAND, Bill	USA	18 Dec 1907 / 20 May 1984	Philadelphia, Pennsylvania / Tucson, Arizona	1950-56	4	2	6	-	-	-	1	-	-	-	-	-	1	2
HOLMES, Jackie	USA	4 Sep 1920 / 1 Mar 1995	Indianapolis, Indiana / Indianapolis, Indiana	1950-53	4	2	0	-	-	-	-	-	-	-	-	-	2	2
HOMEIER, Bill	USA	31 Aug 1918 / 2 May 2001	Rock Island, Texas / Houston, Texas	1953-60	6	3	1	-	-	-	-	-	-	1	-	1	1	3
HOYT, Jerry	USA	29 Jan 1929 / 10 Jul 1955	Chicago, Illinois / Oklahoma City, Oklahoma	1950-55	5	4	0	1	-	-	-	-	-	-	-	2	2	1
HURTUBISE, Jim	USA	5 Dec 1932 / 6 Jan 1989	North Tonawanda, New York / Port Arthur, Texas	1960	1	1	0	-	-	-	-	-	-	-	-	-	1	-
JACKSON, Jimmy	USA	25 Jul 1910 / 25 Nov 1984	Indianapolis, Indiana / Desert Hot Springs, California	1950-54	3	2	0	-	-	-	-	-	-	-	-	1	1	1
JAMES, Joe	USA	23 May 1925 / 5 Nov 1952	Saucier, Mississippi / San Jose, California	1950-52	3	2	0	-	-	-	-	-	-	-	-	1	1	1
JOHNSON, Eddie	USA	10 Feb 1919 / 30 Jun 1974	Richmond, Virginia / Cleveland, Ohio	1952-60	9	9	1	-	-	-	-	-	-	-	1	6	2	-
KELLER, Al	USA	11 Apr 1920 / 19 Nov 1961	Alexander, New York / Phoenix, Arizona	1955-60	6	5	0	-	-	-	-	-	-	-	-	2	3	1
KLADIS, Danny	USA	10 Feb 1917	Crystal City, Missouri	1950-57	7	1	0	-	-	-	-	-	-	-	-	-	1	6
LARSON, Jud	USA	21 Jan 1923 / 11 Jun 1966	Grand Prairie, Texas / Reading, Pennsylvania	1952-59	5	2	0	-	-	-	-	-	-	-	-	1	1	3

Drivers

Name	Nat	Born / Died	Place of Birth / Place of Death	Years Entered	No. of Years	Races	Pts	PP	FL	Win	2nd	3rd	4th	5th	6th	OP	R	NS
LEVRETT, Bayliss	USA	14 Feb 1913 / 13 Mar 2002	Jacksonville, Florida / Reno, Nevada	1950-52	3	1	0	-	-	-	-	-	-	-	-	-	1	2
LINDEN, Andy	USA	5 Apr 1922 / 10 Feb 1987	Brownsville, Pennsylvania / Torrance, California	1950-57	8	7	5	-	-	-	-	-	1	1	1	1	3	1
MACKEY, Bill	USA	15 Dec 1927 / 29 Jul 1951	Dayton, Ohio / Winchester, Indiana	1951	1	1	0	-	-	-	-	-	-	-	-	-	1	-
MAGILL, Mike	USA	8 Feb 1920	Haddonfield, New Jersey	1956-59	5	3	0	-	-	-	-	-	-	-	-	1	2	2
MANTZ, Johnny	USA	18 Sep 1918 / 25 Oct 1972	Hebron, Indiana / Ojai, California	1953	1	1	0	-	-	-	-	-	-	-	-	1	-	-
McCOY, Ernie	USA	19 Feb 1921 / 4 Feb 2001	Reading, Pennsylvania / Port Orange, Forida	1953-56	4	2	0	-	-	-	-	-	-	-	-	2	-	2
McDOWELL, Johnny	USA	29 Jan 1915 / 8 Jun 1952	Delavan, Illinois / Milwaukee, Wisconsin	1950-52	3	3	0	-	-	-	-	-	-	-	-	2	1	-
McGRATH, Jack	USA	8 Oct 1919 / 6 Nov 1955	Los Angeles, California / Phoenix, Arizona	1950-55	6	6	9	1	1	-	-	2	-	1	-	1	2	-
McWITHEY, Jim	USA	4 Jul 1927	Grammer, Indiana	1956-60	5	2	0	-	-	-	-	-	-	-	-	1	1	3
MILLER, Chet	USA	19 Jul 1902 / 15 May 1953	Detroit, Michigan / Indianapolis, Indiana	1950-53	4	2	0	-	-	-	-	-	-	-	-	-	2	2
NALON, Duke	USA	2 Mar 1913 / 26 Feb 2001	Chicago, Illinois / Indianapolis, Indiana	1950-54	5	3	0	1	-	-	-	-	-	-	-	-	3	2
NAZARUK, Mike	USA	2 Oct 1921 / 1 May 1955	Newark, New Jersey / Langhorne, Pennsylvania	1951-54	4	3	8	-	-	-	1	-	1	-	-	-	1	1
NIDAY, Cal	USA	29 Apr 1916 / 14 Feb 1988	Turlock, California / Lancaster, California	1953-57	5	3	0	-	-	-	-	-	-	-	-	1	2	2
O'CONNOR, Pat	USA	9 Oct 1928 / 30 May 1958	North Vernon, Indiana / Indianapolis, Indiana	1953-58	6	5	0	1	-	-	-	-	-	-	-	3	2	1
PARSONS, Johnnie	USA	4 Jul 1918 / 8 Sep 1984	Los Angeles, California / Van Nuys, California	1950-58	9	9	12	-	1	1	-	-	1	-	-	4	3	-
RATHMANN, Dick	USA	6 Jan 1926 / 1 Feb 2000	Los Angeles, California / Melbourne, Florida	1950-60	5	5	2	1	-	-	-	-	-	1	-	4	-	-
RATHMANN, Jim	USA	16 Jul 1928	Valparaiso, Indiana	1950-60	10	10	29	-	2	1	3	-	-	1	-	3	2	-
REECE, Jimmy	USA	17 Nov 1929 / 22 Sep 1958	Oklahoma City, Oklahoma / Trenton, New Jersey	1952-58	7	6	0	-	-	-	-	-	-	1	-	3	2	1
RIGSBY, Jim	USA	6 Jun 1923 / 31 Aug 1952	Spadry, Arkansas / Dayton, Ohio	1950-52	2	1	0	-	-	-	-	-	-	-	-	1	-	1
ROSE, Mauri	USA	26 May 1906 / 1 Jan 1981	Columbus, Ohio / Royal Oak, Michigan	1950-51	2	2	4	-	-	-	-	1	-	-	-	-	1	-
RUBY, Lloyd	USA	12 Jan 1928	Wichita Falls, Texas	1960	1	1	0	-	-	-	-	-	-	-	-	1	-	-
RUSSO, Eddie	USA	19 Nov 1925	Chicago, Illinois	1954-60	7	4	0	-	-	-	-	-	-	-	-	-	4	3
RUSSO, Paul	USA	10 Apr 1914 / 13 Feb 1976	Kenosha, Wisconsin / Daytona Beach, Florida	1950-60	11	8	8.5	-	1	-	1	-	2	-	-	3	2	3
RUTTMAN, Troy	USA	11 Mar 1930 / 19 May 1997	Mooreland, Oklahoma / Lake Havasu City, Arizona	1950-60	9	7	9.5	-	-	1	-	-	1	-	-	1	4	2
SACHS, Eddie	USA	28 May 1927 / 30 May 1964	Bethlehem, Pennsylvania / Indianapolis, Indiana	1953-60	7	4	0	1	-	-	-	-	-	-	-	-	4	3
SCARBOROUGH, Carl	USA	3 Jul 1914 / 30 May 1953	Benton, Illinois / Indianapolis, Indiana	1951-53	3	2	0	-	-	-	-	-	-	-	-	1	1	1
SCHINDLER, Bill	USA	6 Mar 1909 / 20 Sep 1952	Middletown, New York / Allentown, Pennsylvania	1950-52	3	3	0	-	-	-	-	-	-	-	-	1	2	-
SCOTT, Bob	USA	4 Oct 1928 / 5 Jul 1954	Watsonville, California / Darlington, South Carolina	1951-54	4	3	0	-	-	-	-	-	-	-	-	1	2	1
STEVENSON, Chuck	USA	15 Oct 1919 / 21 Aug 1995	Sidney, Montana / Benson, Arizona	1951-60	5	5	0	-	-	-	-	-	-	-	-	3	2	-
SUTTON, Len	USA	9 Aug 1925	Aims, Oregon	1956-60	4	3	0	-	-	-	-	-	-	-	-	-	3	1
SWEIKERT, Bob	USA	20 May 1926 / 17 Jun 1956	Los Angeles, California / Salem, Indiana	1950-56	7	5	8	-	-	1	-	-	-	-	1	1	2	2
TEAGUE, Marshall	USA	22 May 1921 / 11 Feb 1959	Daytona Beach, Florida / Daytona Beach, Florida	1953-58	5	3	0	-	-	-	-	-	-	-	-	2	1	2
TEMPLEMAN, Shorty	USA	12 Aug 1919 / 24 Aug 1962	Pueblo, Colorado / Marion, Ohio	1955-60	5	3	0	-	-	-	-	-	-	-	-	1	2	2

	Nat	Born Died	Place of Birth Place of Death	Years Entered	No. of Years	Races	Pts	PP	FL	Win	2nd	3rd	4th	5th	6th	OP	R	NS
THOMSON, Johnny	USA	9 Apr 1922 24 Sep 1960	Lowell, Massachusetts Allentown, Pennsylvania	1953-60	8	8	10	1	1	-	-	1	1	1	-	1	4	-
TINGELSTAD, Bud	USA	4 Apr 1928 30 Jul 1981	Frazee, Minnesota Indianapolis, Indiana	1960	1	1	0	-	-	-	-	-	-	-	-	1	-	-
TOLAN, Johnnie	USA	22 Oct 1918 2 Jun 1986	Victor, Colorado Redondo Beach, California	1951-60	10	3	0	-	-	-	-	-	-	-	-	2	1	7
TURNER, Jack	USA	12 Feb 1920 12 Sep 2004	Seattle, Washington Renton, Washington	1956-60	5	4	0	-	-	-	-	-	-	-	-	1	3	1
UNSER, Jerry	USA	15 Nov 1932 17 May 1959	Colorado Springs, Colorado Indianapolis, Indiana	1958-59	2	1	0	-	-	-	-	-	-	-	-	-	1	1
VEITH, Bob	USA	1 Nov 1926	Tulare, California	1956-60	5	5	0	-	-	-	-	-	-	-	-	4	1	-
VUKOVICH, Bill	USA	13 Dec 1918 30 May 1955	Fresno, California Indianapolis, Indiana	1950-55	6	5	19	1	3	2	-	-	-	-	-	-	3	1
WALLARD, Lee	USA	8 Sep 1911 28 Nov 1963	Schenectady, New York St. Petersburg, Florida	1950-52	3	2	9	-	1	1	-	-	-	1	-	-	-	1
WARD, Rodger	USA	10 Jan 1921 5 Jul 2004	Beloit, Kansas Anaheim, California	1951-60	10	10	14	-	-	1	1	-	-	-	-	1	7	-
WEBB, Spider	USA	8 Oct 1910 29 Jan 1990	Joplin, Missouri McMinnville, Oregon	1950-55	5	4	0	-	-	-	-	-	-	-	-	1	3	1
WEILER, Wayne	USA	9 Dec 1934 13 Oct 2005	Phoenix, Arizona Phoenix, Arizona	1960	1	1	0	-	-	-	-	-	-	-	-	-	1	-
WEYANT, Chuck	USA	3 Apr 1923	St. Marys, nr Lima, Ohio	1954-60	6	4	0	-	-	-	-	-	-	-	-	2	2	2
WILSON, Dempsey	USA	11 Mar 1927 23 Apr 1971	Los Angeles, California Los Angeles, California	1956-60	5	2	0	-	-	-	-	-	-	-	-	-	2	3

Indianapolis 500 Non-Starters

Drivers who attended but never started

Emil ANDRES - 1950
John BALDWIN - 1956,57
Buzz BARTON - 1952,53
Joe BARZDA - 1951,52,53
Tony BONADIES - 1955,56,57
Bill BOYD - 1951,52,53
Mike BURCH - 1950
Marvin BURKE - 1950
Buddy CAGLE - 1956
Wally CAMPBELL - 1954
Billy CANTRELL - 1953
Neal CARTER - 1951,52,53
Bob CLEBERG 1960
Bud CLEMONS - 1957,58
Hal COLE - 1950
Russ CONGDON 1959,60
Bob CORTNER - 1958,59
Chuck DAIGH - 1959
Jorge DAPONTE - 1953
Billy DEVORE - 1950,54
Lee DROLLINGER 1960
Ted DUNCAN - 1950
Billy EARL - 1950
Rex EASTON - 1958,59
Kenny EATON - 1950,51
Jack ENSLEY - 1958,59,60
Juan Manuel FANGIO - 1958
Milt FANKHOUSER - 1950
Giuseppe FARINA - 1956,57

Cotton FARMER 1960
Johnny FEDRICKS - 1950,53,54,57
John FITCH - 1953
Dick FRAZIER - 1950,51,52
Andy FURCI - 1957,59
Joe GIBA - 1958
Potsy GOACHER - 1950,51,52,53,54
Bob GREGG - 1950
Peter HAHN - 1952
Norm HALL 1960
Red HAMILTON - 1953
Allen HEATH - 1952,53
Norm HOUSER - 1950,51
Chuck HULSE 1960
Van JOHNSON - 1957,58,59
Johnny KAY - 1953,55,56,59
Russ KLAR - 1955
Ray KNEPPER - 1951
Chuck LEIGHTON - 1950
Mark LIGHT - 1950
Ralph LIGUORI - 1959
Frank LUPTOW - 1952
George LYNCH - 1950,51
Cy MARSHALL - 1950
Johnny MAURO - 1950,52
Jim MAYES - 1953
Al MILLER - 1950
John MOORHOUSE - 1959
Earl MOTTER - 1955,56,58,59

Frank MUNDY - 1954
Roy NEUMAN - 1953,55
Danny OAKES - 1952,53,54
Jim PACKARD - 1959,60
Jiggs PETERS - 1955
Marvin PIFER - 1956,60
Ralph PRATT - 1950
Roscoe RANN - 1951
Dick REESE - 1956
Gordon REID - 1951
Johnny ROBERTS - 1953
Hal ROBSON - 1953
Chuck RODEE - 1959,60
Bud ROSE - 1950
Ebb ROSE 1960
Jack ROUNDS 1960
Mike SALAY - 1951
Rob SCHROEDER - 1959
Wayne SELSER - 1953
Bud SENNETT - 1951
Doc SHANEBROOK - 1951,52
Joe SOSTILLO - 1953,54
Gig STEPHENS - 1956
Harry STOCKMAN - 1953
Bill TAYLOR - 1952,53
Joel THORNE - 1950,51
George TICHENOR - 1952,53,54,55
Charles van ACKER - 1950
LeRoy WARRINER - 1951,52,53,56,57,58

Drivers often not known by their real name

(Grand Prix and Indianapolis 500 drivers)

	Real Name			Real Name
Kenny ACHESON	- Kenneth ACHESON		Tom BRIDGER	- Thomas BRIDGER
Walt ADER	- Walter ADER		Tony BRISE	- Anthony BRISE
Freddie AGABASHIAN	- Frederick AGABASHIAN		Chris BRISTOW	- Christopher BRISTOW
Kurt AHRENS	- Karl AHRENS		Tony BROOKS	- Charles Anthony Standish BROOKS
Jean ALESI	- Gianni ALESI		Walt BROWN	- Walter BROWN
Cliff ALLISON	- Henry Clifford ALLISON		Adolf BRUDES	- Adolf BRUDES von BRESLAU
Fernando ALONSO	- Fernando ALONSO DÍAZ		Jimmy BRYAN	- James BRYAN
Red AMICK	- Richard AMICK		Ronnie BUCKNUM	- Ronald BUCKNUM
Chris AMON	- Christopher AMON		Luiz BUENO	- Luiz-Pereira BUENO
Bob ANDERSON	- Robert ANDERSON		Tommy BYRNE	- Thomas BYRNE
Conny ANDERSSON	- Leif Conny ANDERSSON		Mário CABRAL	- Mário VELOSO de ARAÚJO CABRAL
Gerry ASHMORE	- Joseph F H Gerald ASHMORE		Phil CADE	- Philip CADE
Bill ASTON	- William ASTON		Alex CAFFI	- Alessandro CAFFI
Dickie ATTWOOD	- Richard ATTWOOD		John CAMPBELL-JONES	- Michael John CAMPBELL-JONES
Manny AYULO	- Manuel AYULO		Adrian CAMPOS	- Adrián CAMPOS SUÑER
Bobby BALL	- Robert BALL		Bill CANTRELL	- William CANTRELL
Skip BARBER	- John BARBER		Piero CARINI	- Pietro CARINI
Asdrúbal BAYARDO	- Asdrúbal FONTES BAYARDO		Johnny CECOTTO	- Alberton CECOTTO
Don BEAUMAN	- Donald BEAUMAN		François CEVERT	- Albert François CEVERT
Günther BECHEM	- Karl-Günther BECHEM		Eugène CHABOUD	- Marius Eugène CHABOUD
Jean BEHRA	- Jean Marie BEHRA		Colin CHAPMAN	- Anthony Colin Bruce CHAPMAN
Enrique BERNOLDI	- Enrique LANGUE de SILVÉRIO E BERNOLDI		Dave CHARLTON	- David CHARLTON
Tony BETTENHAUSEN	- Melvin Eugene BETTENHAUSEN		Pedro CHAVES	- Pedro MATOS-CHAVES
Mike BEUTTLER	- Michael BEUTTLER		Bill CHEESBOURG	- William CHEESBOURG
Lucien BIANCHI	- Luciano BIANCHI		Eddie CHEEVER	- Edward McKay CHEEVER Jr.
Gino BIANCO	- Luigi Bertetti BIANCO		Louis CHIRON	- Alexandre Louis CHIRON
B BIRA	- Prince BIRABONGSE BHANUDEJ BHANUBANDH OF SIAM		Joie CHITWOOD	- George CHITWOOD
Art BISCH	- Arthur BISCH		Bob CHRISTIE	- Robert CHRISTIE
Trevor BLOKDYK	- John Trevor BLOKDYK		Johnny CLAES	- Octave John CLAES
Raul BOESEL	- Raul de MESQUITA BOESEL		Jim CLARK	- James CLARK
Bob BONDURANT	- Robert BONDURANT		Bernard COLLOMB	- Nicois Bernard COLLOMB-CLERC
Jo BONNIER	- Joakim BONNIER		Franco COMOTTI	- Gianfranco COMOTTI
Slim BORGUDD	- Karl Edward Tommy BORGUDD		Chris CRAFT	- Christopher CRAFT
Johnny BOYD	- John BOYD		Jim CRAWFORD	- James CRAWFORD
Jack BRABHAM	- John BRABHAM		Ray CRAWFORD	- Raymond CRAWFORD
Bill BRACK	- William BRACK		Alberto CRESPO	- Murío Alberto CRESPO
Tino BRAMBILLA	- Ernesto BRAMBILLA		Antonio CREUS	- Antonio CREUS y RUBÍN de CELIS
Toni BRANCA	- Antonio BRANCA		Tony CROOK	- Thomas Anthony CROOK
Don BRANSON	- Donald BRANSON		Art CROSS	- Arthur CROSS

	Real Name		Real Name
Fritz d'OREY	- Frederico d'OREY	Christian GOETHALS	- Kurt Christian GOETHALS
Nano da SILVA RAMOS	- Hermano da SILVA RAMOS	Froilán GONZÁLEZ	- José Froilán GONZÁLEZ
Chuck DAIGH	- Charles DAIGH	Horace GOULD	- Horace TWIGG
Cristiano da MATTA	- Cristiano MONTEIRO da MATTA	Cliff GRIFFITH	- Clifton GRIFFITH
Jimmy DAVIES	- James DAVIES	Georges GRIGNARD	- Auguste Georges GRIGNARD
Jimmy DAYWALT	- James DAYWALT	Bobby GRIM	- Robert GRIM
Carel Godin de BEAUFORT	- Count Jonkheer Carel Pieter Anthonie	Roberto GUERRERO	- Roberto GUERRERO ISAZA
	Jan Hubertus Godin de BEAUFORT	Dan GURNEY	- Daniel GURNEY
Alain de CHANGY	- Alain CARPENTIER de CHANGY	Mike HAILWOOD	- Stanley Michael HAILWOOD
Toulo de GRAFFENRIED	- Baron Emmanuel de GRAFFENRIED	Jim HALL	- James HALL
Peter de KLERK	- Piet de KLERK	Duncan HAMILTON	- James Duncan HAMILTON
Pedro de la ROSA	- Pedro MARTINEZ de la ROSA	Sam HANKS	- Samuel HANKS
Fon de PORTAGO	- Don Alfonso Cabeza de Vacade y Leighton, Carvajal y Are,	Walt HANSGEN	- Walter HANSGEN
	XIII Conde de la Majorada, XV11 Marqués de PORTAGO	Mike HARRIS	- Michael HARRIS
Charles de TORNACO	- Baron Charles de TORNACO	Cuth HARRISON	- Thomas Cuthbert HARRISON
Pedro DINIZ	- Pedro Paulo DINIZ	Gene HARTLEY	- Leslie HARTLEY
Duke DINSMORE	- J. Carlyle DINSMORE	Paul HAWKINS	- Robert Paul HAWKINS
Martin DONNELLY	- Hugh Peter Martin DONNELLY	Mike HAWTHORN	- John Michael HAWTHORN
Ken DOWNING	- Kenneth DOWNING	Boy HAYJE	- Johan Gerard HAIJJE
Bob DRAKE	- Robert DRAKE	Willi HEEKS	- Wilhelm HEEKS
Paddy DRIVER	- Ernest Gould DRIVER	Nick HEIDFELD	- Nicklaus HEIDFELD
Johnny DUMFRIES	- John Colum CRICHTON-STUART, the Earl of Dumfries	Theo HELFRICH	- Theodor HELFRICH
Len DUNCAN	- Leonard DUNCAN	Johnny HERBERT	- John HERBERT
Bernie ECCLESTONE	- Bernard ECCLESTONE	Al HERMAN	- Gerald HERMAN
Don EDMUNDS	- Donald EDMUNDS	Graham HILL	- Norman Graham HILL
Vic ELFORD	- Victor ELFORD	Phil HILL	- Philip HILL Jr.
Bob EVANS	- Robert EVANS	Bill HOLLAND	- William HOLLAND
Teo FABI	- Teodorico FABI	Jackie HOLMES	- John HOLMES
Jack FAIRMAN	- John FAIRMAN	Bill HOMEIER	- William HOMEIER
Nino FARINA	- Dr. Giuseppe FARINA	Jerry HOYT	- Gerald HOYT
Walt FAULKNER	- Walter FAULKNER	Denny HULME	- Denis HULME
Willie FERGUSON	- William FERGUSON	Jim HURTUBISE	- James HURTUBISE
Rudi FISCHER	- Rudolf FISCHER	Gus HUTCHISON	- Augustus HUTCHISON
Mike FISHER	- Michael FISHER	Jacky ICKX	- Jacques-Bernard ICKX
Theo FITZAU	- Theodor FITZAU	Taki INOUE	- Takachiho INOUE
Pat FLAHERTY	- George Francis Patrick FLAHERTY	Innes IRELAND	- Robert McGregor Innes IRELAND
Jan FLINTERMAN	- Johannes FLINTERMAN	Eddie IRVINE	- Edmund IRVINE
Ron FLOCKHART	- William Ronald FLOCKHART	Chris IRWIN	- Christopher IRWIN
Philip FOTHERINGHAM-		Jimmy JACKSON	- James JACKSON
PARKER	- Philip Fotheringham PARKER	Joe JAMES	- Joseph JAMES
A J FOYT	- Anthony Joseph FOYT Jr.	Eddie JOHNSON	- Edward JOHNSON
Don FREELAND	- Donald FREELAND	Bruce JOHNSTONE	- William Bruce JOHNSTONE
Joe FRY	- Joseph FRY	Tom JONES	- Thomas JONES
Beppe GABBIANI	- Giuseppe GABBIANI	Juan JOVER	- Juan JOVER SAÑÉS
Nanni GALLI	- Giovanni Giuseppe Gilberto GALLI	Narain KARTHIKEYAN	- Kumar Ram Narain KARTHIKEYAN
Fred GAMBLE	- Frederick GAMBLE	Ken KAVANAGH	- Kamrick KAVANAGH
Howden GANLEY	- James Howden GANLEY	Eddie KEIZAN	- Edward KEIZAN
Billy GARRETT	- William GARRETT	Joe KELLY	- Joseph KELLY
Jo GARTNER	- Josef GARTNER	Danny KLADIS	- Daniel KLADIS
Tony GAZE	- Frederick Anthony Owen GAZE	Mikko KOZAROWITSKY	- Michael KOZAROWITSKY
GEKI	- Giacomo RUSSO	Rudolf KRAUSE	- Eric Rudolf KRAUSE
Marc GENÉ	- Marc GENÉ GUERRERO	Jacques LAFFITE	- Jacques-Henri LAFFITE
Bob GERARD	- Frederick Roberts GERARD	Jan LAMMERS	- Johannes LAMMERS
Dick GIBSON	- Richard GIBSON	Pedro LAMY	- José Pedro Mourão Nunes LAMY VIÇOSO
GIMAX	- Carlo FRANCHI	Chico LANDI	- Francisco SACCO LANDI
Richie GINTHER	- Paul Richard GINTHER	Rodríguez LARRETA	- Alberto RODRÍGUEZ LARRETA
Yves		Jud LARSON	- Judson LARSON
GIRAUD-CABANTOUS	- Marius Aristide Yves GIRAUD	Niki LAUDA	- Andreas-Nikolaus LAUDA
Helm GLÖCKLER	- Wilhelm GLÖCKLER	Chris LAWRENCE	- Christopher LAWRENCE
Chico GODIA	- Francisco GODIA-SALES	Geoff LEES	- Geoffrey LEES

Drivers

	Real Name
J J LEHTO	- Jyrki JÄRVILEHTO
Les LESTON	- Alfred Lazarus FINGLESTON
Pierre LEVEGH	- Pierre BOUILLIN
Andy LINDEN	- Andrew LINDEN
Lella LOMBARDI	- Maria Grazia LOMBARDI
Ricardo LONDONO	- Ricardo LONDONO-BRIDGE
Henri LOUVEAU	- Ernst Henri LOUVEAU
Pete LOVELY	- Gerard Carlton LOVELY
Jean LUCIENBONNET	- Jean BONNET
Brett LUNGER	- Robert Brett LUNGER
Mike MacDOWEL	- Michael MacDOWEL
Bill MACKEY	- William C. GRETSINGER Jr.
Lance MACKLIN	- Francis Noel Lancelot MACKLIN
Tony MAGGS	- Anthony MAGGS
Mike MAGILL	- Michael MAGILL
Johnny MANTZ	- John MANTZ
Helmut MARKO	- Dr. Helmut MARKO
Tarso MARQES	- Tarso SANT'ANNA MARQUES
Tony MARSH	- Anthony MARSH
Jochen MASS	- Joachim MASS
Timmy MAYER	- Timothy MAYER
Ernie McCOY	- Ernest McCOY
Johnny McDOWELL	- John McDOWELL
Jack McGRATH	- John McGRATH
Jim McWITHEY	- James McWITHEY
Harry MERKEL	- Harald MERKEL
Chet MILLER	- Chester MILLER
Robin MONTGOMERIE-CHARRINGTON	- Robert MONTGOMERIE-CHARRINGTON
Juan Pablo MONTOYA	- Juan Pablo MONTOYA ROLDAN
Roberto MORENO	- Roberto PUPO MORENO
Dave MORGAN	- David MORGAN
Bill MOSS	- William MOSS
Bernd NACKE	- Karl-Günther BECHEM
Duke NALON	- Dennis C. NALON
Brian NAYLOR	- John Brian NAYLOR
Mike NAZARUK	- Michael NAZARUK
Tiff NEEDELL	- Timothy NEEDELL
Jac NELLEMAN	- Jacob NELLEMAN
Patrick NÈVE	- Patrick NÈVE de MÉVERGNIES
Cal NIDAY	- Calvin NIDAY
Brausch NIEMANN	- Ambraüsus NIEMANN
Pat O'CONNOR	- Patrick O'CONNOR
Jackie OLIVER	- Keith Jack OLIVER
Danny ONGAIS	- Daniel ONGAIS
Carlos PACE	- José-Carlos PACE
Nello PAGANI	- Cirillo PAGANI
Max PAPIS	- Massimiliano PAPIS
Mike PARKES	- Michael PARKES
Reg PARNELL	- Reginald PARNELL
Tim PARNELL	- Reginald PARNELL
Johnnie PARSONS	- John PARSONS
Al PEASE	- Victor PEASE
Sandro PESENTI-ROSSI	- Alessandro PESENTI-ROSSI
Ronnie PETERSON	- Bengt Ronnie PETERSON
Ernie PIETERSE	- Ernest PIETERSE
Teddy PILETTE	- Theodore PILETTE-VLUG
Nelson PIQUET	- Nelson PIQUET SOUTO MAIOR
Ben PON	- Bernardus Marinus PON
Dennis POORE	- Roger Dennistoun POORE
Sam POSEY	- Samuel POSEY

	Real Name
Charles POZZI	- Carlos Alberto POZZI
Jackie PRETORIUS	- Jacobus PRETORIUS
Tom PRYCE	- Thomas PRYCE
Dieter QUESTER	- Dietrich QUESTER
Bobby RAHAL	- Robert RAHAL
Kimi RÄIKKÖNEN	- Kimi-Matias RÄIKKÖNEN
Dick RATHMANN	- James RATHMANN
Jim RATHMANN	- Richard RATHMANN
Jimmy REECE	- James REECE
Clay REGAZZONI	- Gianclaudio Giuseppe REGAZZONI
Lance REVENTLOW	- Lance HAUGWITZ-REVENTLOW
Ken RICHARDSON	- William Kenneth RICHARDSON
Fritz RIESS	- Friedrich RIESS
Jim RIGSBY	- James RIGSBY
Jochen RINDT	- Karl-Jochen RINDT
John RISELEY-PRICHARD	- John Henry Estlin PRICHARD
Pedro RODRIGUEZ	- Pedro RODRIGUEZ de la VEGA
Ricardo RODRIGUEZ	- Ricardo RODRIGUEZ de la VEGA
Tony ROLT	- Anthony ROLT
Keke ROSBERG	- Keijo ROSBERG
Mauri ROSE	- Maurice ROSE
Huub ROTHENGATTER	- Hubertus ROTHENGATTER
Eddie RUSSO	- Edward RUSSO
Eddie SACHS	- Edward SACHS
Bob SAID	- Boris SAID
Luis SALA	- Luis PÉREZ-SALA VALLS-TABERNER
Eliseo SALAZAR	- Eliseo SALAZAR VALENZUELA
Harry SCHELL	- Harry O'REILLY SCHELL
Tim SCHENKEN	- Timothy SCHENKEN
Mimmo SCHIATTARELLA	- Domenico SCHIATTARELLA
Bill SCHINDLER	- William SCHINDLER
Jo SCHLESSER	- Joseph SCHLESSER
Rob SCHROEDER	- Robert SCHROEDER
Vern SCHUPPAN	- Vernon SCHUPPAN
Adolfo SCHWELM CRUZ	- Adolf SCHWELM
Bob SCOTT	- Robert SCOTT
Archie SCOTT-BROWN	- William Archibald SCOTT-BROWN
Ayrton SENNA	- Ayrton SENNA da SILVA
Dorino SERAFINI	- Teodoro SERAFINI
Chico SERRA	- Francisco SERRA
Doug SERRURIER	- Louis Douglas SERRURIER
Johnny SERVOZ-GAVIN	- Georges-Francis SERVOZ-GAVIN
Tony SETTEMBER	- Anthony SETTEMBER
Hap SHARP	- James SHARP
Tony SHELLY	- Anthony SHELLY
Jo SIFFERT	- Joseph SIFFERT
Moisés SOLANA	- Moisés SOLANA ARCINIEGA
Alex SOLER-ROIG	- Alejandro SOLER-ROIG
Mike SPARKEN	- Michel POBEREJSKY
Mike SPENCE	- Michael SPENCE
Gaetano STARRABBA	- Prince Gaetano STARRABBA DI GIARDINELLI
Chuck STEVENSON	- John STEVENSON
Jackie STEWART	- John STEWART
Jimmy STEWART	- James STEWART
Rolf STOMMELEN	- Rolf-Johann STOMMELEN
Hans STUCK	- Hans Villiez von STUCK
Danny SULLIVAN	- Daniel SULLIVAN
John SURTEES	- Norman John SURTEES
Andy SUTCLIFFE	- Andrew SUTCLIFFE
Len SUTTON	- Lenard SUTTON
Bob SWEIKERT	- Robert SWEIKERT

Real Name	
Tora TAKAGI	- Toranosuke TAKAGI
Piero TARUFFI	- Pierino TARUFFI
Mike TAYLOR	- Michael TAYLOR
Shorty TEMPLEMAN	- Clark TEMPLEMAN
Mike THACKWELL	- Michael THACKWELL
Johnny THOMSON	- John THOMSON
Leslie THORNE	- William Roberts Leslie THORNE
Sam TINGLE	- Samuel TINGLE
Desmond TITTERINGTON	- John Desmond TITTERINGTON
Johnnie TOLAN	- John TOLAN
Tony TRIMMER	- Anthony TRIMMER
Guy TUNMER	- Percival Guy TUNMER
Toni ULMEN	- Anton ULMEN
Bobby UNSER	- Robert UNSER
Jerry UNSER	- Jerome UNSER
Dries van der LOF	- Andries van der LOF
Gijs van LENNEP	- Gijsbert van LENNEP
Bob VEITH	- Robert VEITH
Jos VERSTAPPEN	- Johannes VERSTAPPEN

Real Name	
Gilles VILLENEUVE	- Joseph Gilles VILLENEUVE
Gigi VILLORESI	- Luigi VILLORESI
Rikky von OPEL	- Frederick von OPEL
Wolfgang 'Taffy' von TRIPS	- Wolfgang Reichsgraf Berghe von TRIPS
Jo VONLANTHEN	- Joseph VONLANTHEN
Bill VUKOVICH	- William VUKOVICH
Fred WACKER	- Frederick WACKER Jr.
Dave WALKER	- David WALKER
Heini WALTER	- Heinrich WALTER
Spider WEBB	- Travis WEBB
Ken WHARTON	- Kenneth WHARTON
Ted WHITEAWAY	- Edward WHITEAWAY
Graham WHITEHEAD	- Alfred Graham WHITEHEAD
Bill WHITEHOUSE	- William WHITEHOUSE
Eppie WIETZES	- Egbert WIETZES
Mike WILDS	- William Michael WILDS
Vic WILSON	- Victor WILSON
Alex YOONG	- Alexander YOONG

4

CONSTRUCTORS

Left: *Jim Clark and his Lotus boss Colin Chapman celebrate at Zandvoort in 1963. That season Clark won seven of the 10 races he started and took the first of his two World Championships. (LAT)*

AFM	FOOTWORK *see ARROWS*	OSCA
AGS	FORTI	OSELLA
ALFA ROMEO	FRAZER NASH	PACIFIC
ALFA SPECIAL	FRY	PARNELLI
ALTA	GILBY	PENSKE
AMON	GORDINI	POLITOYS *see WILLIAMS*
ANDREA MODA	HESKETH	PORSCHE
ARROWS	HILL	PROST *see LIGIER*
ARZANI VOLPINI *see MASERATI*	HONDA	PROTOS
ASTON-BUTTERWORTH	HWM	RAM
ASTON MARTIN	ISO MARLBORO *see WILLIAMS*	RAM MARCH *see RAM*
ATS (Germany)	JAGUAR	REBAQUE
ATS (Italy)	JBW	RED BULL
BAR	JORDAN	RENAULT
BEHRA PORSCHE *see PORSCHE*	JPS LOTUS *see LOTUS*	RIAL
BELLASI	KAUHSEN	SAUBER
BENETTON	KLENK	SCARAB
BMW specials	KOJIMA	SCIROCCO
BORO *see ENSIGN*	KURTIS KRAFT	SHADOW
BRABHAM	LAMBORGHINI	SHANNON
BRM	LANCIA	SIMCA GORDINI *see GORDINI*
BRP	LANCIA FERRARI *see FERRARI*	SIMTEK
BUGATTI	LARROUSSE	SPIRIT
CISITALIA	LDS	STANLEY BRM *see BRM*
COLONI	LEC	STEBRO
CONNAUGHT	LEYTON HOUSE *see MARCH*	STEWART
CONNEW	LIFE	SURTEES
COOPER	LIGIER	TALBOT LAGO
COPERSUCAR *see FITTIPALDI*	LOLA	TALBOT LIGIER *see LIGIER*
DALLARA	LOTUS	TEC MEC
DE TOMASO	LYNCAR	TECNO
DERRINGTON-FRANCIS *see ATS* (Italy)	MAKI	THEODORE
EAGLE	MARCH	THIN WALL FERRARI *see FERRARI*
EIFELLAND MARCH *see MARCH*	MARTINI	TOKEN
EMERYSON	MASERATI	TOLEMAN *see BENETTON*
EMW	MATRA	TOYOTA
ENB	MATRA SIMCA *see MATRA*	TROJAN
ENSIGN	McGUIRE *see WILLIAMS*	TYRRELL
ERA	McLAREN	VANWALL
EUROBRUN	MERCEDES-BENZ	VENTURI LARROUSSE *see LARROUSSE*
FERGUSON	MERZARIO	VERITAS
FERRARI	MILANO *see MASERATI*	WILLIAMS
FITTIPALDI	MINARDI	WOLF
FOMET *see OSELLA*	MONTEVERDI *see ONYX*	WOLF WILLIAMS *see WILLIAMS*
FONDMETAL *see OSELLA*	ONYX	ZAKSPEED

Where a model achieved fastest lap in a race with more than
one car, this is counted as one fastest lap. This occurred at
GB 54 – Maserati 250F (3 cars) and Ferrari 625 (2 cars),
CDN 69 – Brabham BT26A (2) and A 70 – Ferrari 312B (2).

Total points scored relates to those scored by drivers and not
by constructors for their championship.
Indianapolis 500 entrants are excluded.
Note that Maserati made three starts at Indy and Ferrari started
on one occasion, whilst Kurtis Kraft was a regular entrant.

AFM (D)

Principal: Alex von Falkenhausen.
Base: Munich.
Founded: 1948.

Falkenhausen's connections with BMW led to the foundation of Alex von Falkenhausen Motorenbau soon after the Second World War, basing his developments on the 328 sports car. He built single seaters from 1949, although by 1950 he was virtually working full time for BMW once again. From 1951 his cars used the new Küchen V8 engine, but active support was withdrawn soon after, when the workshop closed and the owner returned to BMW.

Totals	GPs	Starts	Points	Poles	F.Laps	Wins			
	4	7	-	-	-	-			
Seasons							Colour	Main Driver(s)	
1952	2	3	-	-	-	-	silver	Stuck	
1953	2	4	-	-	-	-	silver	Stuck	
Models							Year(s)	Chief Designer	Engine
-	4	7	-	-	-	-	52-53	A von Falkenhausen	BMW,Küchen,Bristol

AGS (F)

Principal: Henri Julien.
Base: Gonfaron, nr Toulon/Le Luc-en-Provence (1990).
Founded: 1970.

Automobiles Gonfaronaises Sportives was founded by Henri Julien, a driver and car-builder during the 60s. The first AGS (JH1) was built in 1970 for Formula France, the team progressing through other formulae until their Formula 1 debut in 1986 using a revamped Renault chassis. In 1988 most of the team defected to Coloni and in 1990 it was restructured under the direction of Hughes de Chaunac and relocated from the original Gonfaron base to the Var circuit near Le Luc-en-Provence. June 1990 saw another change – de Chaunac left the team and ownership passed to Cyril de Rouvre who in turn, sold the majority shareholdings to Italians Gabriele Rafanelli and Patrizio Cantu in April 1991, only to see the team close before the end of that year.

Totals	GPs	Starts	Points	Poles	F.Laps	Wins			
	47	48	2	-	-	-			
Seasons							Sponsor(s)	Main Driver(s)	
1986	2	2	-	-	-	-	Charro	Capelli	
1987	13	13	1	-	-	-	Charro	Fabre/Moreno	
1988	15	15	-	-	-	-	Bouygues	Streiff	
1989	6	6	1	-	-	-	Faure	Tarquini,Dalmas	
1990	8	9	-	-	-	-	Lapidus	Tarquini,Dalmas	
1991	3	3	-	-	-	-	Filling	Tarquini,Barbazza	
Models							Year(s)	Chief Designer	Engine
JH21C	2	2	-	-	-	-	86	C Vanderpleyn	Motori Moderni
JH22	13	13	1	-	-	-	87	C Vanderpleyn	Ford Cosworth
JH23-B	21	21	1	-	-	-	88-89	C Vanderpleyn	Ford Cosworth
JH24	1	1	-	-	-	-	90	C Galopin	Ford Cosworth
JH25-B	10	11	-	-	-	-	90-91	M Costa	Ford Cosworth

The JH26 was never completed and the JH27 never qualified in 1991.

ALFA ROMEO (I)

Principals: Alfa Corse, Autodelta & Euroracing.
Base: Portello, Milano.
Founded: 1918.

Societa Anonima Lombarda Fabbrica Automobili (ALFA) was formed in 1909. Nicola Romeo later took over the factory and the company finally became known as Alfa Romeo in 1918. From its earliest days, Alfa Romeo has celebrated many years of successful racing – Enzo Ferrari ran the racing team in the 30s. The first championship car began life in 1938 as a Voiturette (Formula 2) and was stored during the war to be developed over the years and become virtually unbeatable. The team withdrew as the first grand prix formula came to an end, and after a period of engine supply returned as a fully fledged team in the late 70s. Its racing operation passed from Carlo Chiti's Autodelta operation to Paolo Pavanello's Euroracing team in 1983, before the now FIAT owned equipe finally wound down its Formula 1 activity.

Drivers' Championships: 2 (1950,51).

Totals	GPs	Starts	Points	Poles	F.Laps	Wins		
	110	234	214	12	14	10		
Seasons							Sponsor(s)/(Colour)	Main Driver(s)
1950	6	21	89	6	6	6	(red)	Farina*,Fangio,Fagioli *Champion*
1951	7	27	75	4	7	4	(red)	Farina,Fangio*,Sanesi,Bonetto *Champion*
1952-78 did not participate								
1979	5	6	-	-	-	-	Scaini	Giacomelli,Brambilla
1980	14	26	4	1	-	-	Marlboro,Scaini	Depailler,Giacomelli
1981	15	30	10	-	-	-	Marlboro,Scaini	Andretti,Giacomelli
1982	16	32	7	1	-	-	Marlboro	de Cesaris,Giacomelli
1983	15	29	18	-	1	-	Marlboro,Nordica	de Cesaris,Baldi
1984	16	31	11	-	-	-	Benetton	Patrese,Cheever
1985	16	32	-	-	-	-	Benetton	Patrese,Cheever
Models							Year(s)	Chief Designer	Engine
158/159	13	48	164	10	13	10	50-51	G Colombo	8s
177	3	3	-	-	-	-	79	C Chiti	F12
179-C,D,E	33	61	14	1	-	-	79-82	C Chiti	V12
182	15	30	7	1	-	-	82	G Ducarouge	V12
183T	15	29	18	-	1	-	83	G Ducarouge	V8t
184T	24	47	11	-	-	-	84-85	L Marmiroli	V8t
185T	8	16	-	-	-	-	85	L Marmiroli	V8t

ALFA SPECIAL (ZA)

Principal: Peter de Klerk.
Base: South Africa.
Founded: 1962.

Not an Alfa Romeo at all, other than the use of the old Alfa 4-cylinder engine mated to a home built chassis. Created by former Lotus mechanic Peter de Klerk for local races, these cars nevertheless performed well against more contemporary cars in two South African Grands Prix during the 1.5-litre formula.

Totals	GPs	Starts	Points	Poles	F.Laps	Wins		
	2	2	-	-	-	-		
Seasons							Colour	Main Driver(s)
1963	1	1	-	-	-	-	red	de Klerk
1965	1	1	-	-	-	-	red	de Klerk
Models							Year(s)	Chief Designer	Engine
-	2	2	-	-	-	-	63-65	P de Klerk	Alfa Romeo

ALTA (GB)

Principal: Geoffrey Taylor.
Base: Tolworth, Surrey.
Founded: 1928.

Initially formed as an engineering concern, Alta began by building sports cars before moving on to single seaters in the 30s. After the war, Taylor built one-off chassis to order for both Formula 1 and later Formula 2. The company also sold its 4-cylinder, 2-litre engine to the likes of HWM, Cooper and Connaught. After Connaught's demise, there was no call for the engines and the company was wound up. Geoffrey Taylor died in 1966.

Totals	GPs	Starts	Points	Poles	F.Laps	Wins				
	5	6	-	-	-	-				
Seasons							Colour	Main Driver(s)		
1950	2	3	-	-	-	-	green	Kelly, Crossley		
1951	1	1	-	-	-	-	green	Kelly		
1952	2	2	-	-	-	-	green	P & G Whitehead		
Models							Year(s)	Chief Designer	Engine	
GP	3	4	-	-	-	-	50-51	G Taylor	4s	
F2	2	2	-	-	-	-	52	G Taylor	4	

AMON (GB)

Principal: Chris Amon.
Base: Reading.
Founded: 1974.

Amon ventured into the world of driver-constructors with this kit car based around the Ford Cosworth and Hewland gearbox package, financed by John Dalton. The car had unusual features such as titanium suspension and the fuel tank between driver and engine, but unfortunately proved difficult to drive – it only qualified once.

Totals	GPs	Starts	Points	Poles	F.Laps	Wins				
	1	1	-	-	-	-				
Seasons							Colour	Main Driver(s)		
1974	1	1	-	-	-	-	light blue	Amon		
Models							Year(s)	Chief Designer	Engine	
AF101	1	1	-	-	-	-	74	G Fowell	Ford Cosworth	

ANDREA MODA (I)

Principal: Andrea Sassetti.
Base: Trodica di Morovalle, Perugia.
Founded: 1991.

Created from the ashes of Coloni, whose assets were purchased by shoe magnate Andrea Sassetti. The team tried to use the previous year's Coloni chassis but as it was entered as a new team it could only race its own design. This was rushed through but inevitably it failed to qualify apart from a fine effort by Moreno at Monaco. The team suffered the indignity of being expelled from the championship after Sassetti was arrested at Spa for financial irregularities.

Totals	GPs	Starts	Points	Poles	F.Laps	Wins				
	1	1	-	-	-	-				
Seasons							Sponsor(s)	Main Driver(s)		
1992	1	1	-	-	-	-	Ellesse	Moreno		
Models							Year(s)	Chief Designer	Engine	
S921	1	1	-	-	-	-	92	N Wirth	Judd	

ARROWS (GB)

Principals: Jackie Oliver, Alan Rees/Tom Walkinshaw.
Base: Bletchley, Milton Keynes/Leafield, Oxfordshire.
Founded: 1977.

Created as a breakaway from the Shadow team which later contested the design of the first Arrows FA1. The outfit took its name from the instigators – Franco Ambrosio, Alan Rees, Jackie Oliver, Dave Wass and Tony Southgate. The team promised much, but has so far failed to notch up that all-important first win after a record number of attempts. In 1990 Wataru Ohashi's Japanese Footwork corporation tookover, renaming the cars Footwork from the beginning of the 1991 season and effectively reducing the remaining Rees and Oliver to employees. For the 1994 season Oliver and Rees were back in control and the old Arrows name returned to the team although the cars still raced as Footworks in the new livery. 1996 saw another change in ownership as Tom Walkinshaw took over the team in the early part of the season and began the move to a new headquarters in Leafield. In 1997 the team reverted to the original name with World Champion Damon Hill as main driver, together with Yamaha and Bridgestone tyres. During the 2002 season the team struggled with mounting financial problems and finally bowed out after the German Grand Prix.

Totals	GPs	Starts	Points	Poles	F.Laps	Wins		
	382	724	167	1	-	-		
Seasons							**Sponsor(s)**	**Main Driver(s)**
1978	15	23	11	-	-	-	Warsteiner	Patrese, Stommelen
1979	15	27	5	-	-	-	Warsteiner	Patrese, Mass
1980	14	25	11	-	-	-	Warsteiner	Patrese, Mass
1981	15	24	10	1	-	-	Ragno, Penthouse	Patrese, Stohr
1982	14	24	5	-	-	-	Ragno, Nordica	Baldi, Surer
1983	15	30	4	-	-	-	Barclay, Rizla	Surer, Boutsen
1984	15	30	6	-	-	-	Barclay	Surer, Boutsen
1985	16	32	14	-	-	-	Barclay	Berger, Boutsen
1986	16	31	1	-	-	-	USF&G, Barclay	Surer/Danner, Boutsen
1987	16	32	11	-	-	-	USF&G	Warwick, Cheever
1988	16	32	23	-	-	-	USF&G	Warwick, Cheever
1989	16	30	13	-	-	-	USF&G	Warwick, Cheever
1990	14	25	2	-	-	-	Footwork, USF&G	Alboreto, Caffi
1991	10	12	-	-	-	-	Footwork	Alboreto, Caffi
1992	16	30	6	-	-	-	Footwork, Hamacher	Alboreto, Suzuki
1993	16	32	4	-	-	-	Footwork, Japan	Warwick, Suzuki
1994	16	32	9	-	-	-	Uliveto	Fittipaldi, Morbidelli
1995	17	34	5	-	-	-	Sasol, Unimat	Morbidelli, Inoue
1996	16	32	1	-	-	-	Power Horse, Philips	Rosset, Verstappen
1997	17	33	9	-	-	-	Danka, Parmalat	Hill, Diniz
1998	16	32	6	-	-	-	Danka, Parmalat	Salo, Diniz
1999	16	32	1	-	-	-	Repsol	de la Rosa, Takagi
2000	17	34	7	-	-	-	Orange, Repsol YPF	de la Rosa, Verstappen
2001	17	34	1	-	-	-	Orange, Eurobet	Verstappen, Bernoldi
2002	11	22	2	-	-	-	Orange, Red Bull	Frentzen, Bernoldi
Models							**Year(s)**	**Chief Designer**	**Engine**
FA1	10	18	8	-	-	-	78	T Southgate	Ford Cosworth
A1-B	13	19	6	-	-	-	78-79	T Southgate	Ford Cosworth
A2	7	13	2	-	-	-	79	T Southgate	Ford Cosworth
A3	29	49	21	1	-	-	80-81	T Southgate	Ford Cosworth
A4	13	21	5	-	-	-	82	D Wass	Ford Cosworth
A5	3	3	-	-	-	-	82	D Wass	Ford Cosworth
A6	22	39	7	-	-	-	83-84	D Wass	Ford Cosworth
A7	13	21	3	-	-	-	84	D Wass	BMW
A8	32	60	15	-	-	-	85-86	D Wass	BMW
A9	3	3	-	-	-	-	86	D Wass	BMW
A10-B	32	64	34	-	-	-	87-88	R Brawn	Megatron
A11-B,C	31	56	15	-	-	-	89-91	R Brawn	Ford Cosworth, Porsche
FA12	9	11	-	-	-	-	91	A Jenkins	Porsche, Ford Cosworth
FA13-B	18	34	6	-	-	-	92-93	A Jenkins	Mugen Honda
FA14	14	28	4	-	-	-	93	A Jenkins	Mugen Honda

Seasons	GPs	Starts	Points	Poles	F.Laps	Wins	Year(s)	Chief Designer	Engine
FA15	16	32	9	-	-	-	94	A Jenkins	Ford Cosworth
FA16	17	34	5	-	-	-	95	A Jenkins	Hart
FA17	16	32	1	-	-	-	96	A Jenkins	Hart
A18	17	33	9	-	-	-	97	F Dernie	Yamaha
A19	16	32	6	-	-	-	98	J Barnard	Arrows
A20	16	32	1	-	-	-	99	M Coughlan	Arrows
A21	17	34	7	-	-	-	00	M Coughlan	Supertec
A22	17	34	1	-	-	-	01	M Coughlan	Asiatech
A23	11	22	2	-	-	-	02	M Coughlan	Ford Cosworth

ASTON-BUTTERWORTH (GB)

Principal: Bill Aston.
Base: Frimley, Surrey.
Founded: 1952.

The Aston-Butterworth cars were a combination of Bill Aston's Cooper-inspired chassis with Archie Butterworth's flat 4 air-cooled engine, more accurately referred to as an AJB unit. Two were built, the first for Aston himself, and both were raced privately.

Totals	GPs	Starts	Points	Poles	F.Laps	Wins		
	2	2	-	-	-	-		
Seasons						Colour	Main Driver(s)	
1952	2	2	-	-	-	-	green	Aston,Montgomerie-Charrington
Models						Year(s)	Chief Designer	Engine
NB	2	2	-	-	-	-	52	B Aston	Butterworth

ASTON MARTIN (GB)

Principal: David Brown.
Base: Feltham, Middlesex.
Founded: 1914.

Founder Lionel Martin built sports cars for the Aston Clinton hill-climb which gave this new marque its name. The company changed ownership many times before David Brown bought it in 1947. The team re-entered grand prix racing in 1959, with the project delayed due to the company's sports car race successes, which unfortunately meant these front-engined cars were outdated before they had a chance to prove themselves. Now owned by Ford, Aston Martin has produced many successful attempts at sports car racing, the latest beginning in 2005.

Totals	GPs	Starts	Points	Poles	F.Laps	Wins		
	5	10	-	-	-	-		
Seasons						Colour	Main Driver(s)	
1959	4	8	-	-	-	-	green	Salvadori,Shelby
1960	1	2	-	-	-	-	green	Salvadori,Trintignant
Models						Year(s)	Chief Designer	Engine
DBR4	4	8	-	-	-	-	59	T Cutting	6
DBR5	1	2	-	-	-	-	60	T Cutting	6

ATS (D)

Principal: Hans Gunter Schmid.
Base: Bicester, Oxfordshire, GB.
Founded: 1972.

Auto Technisches Spezialzubehör was the company name of German wheel magnate Schmid who entered Formula 1 with the Penske PC4 in 1977. This was later developed into the first proper ATS entry and the team took over the facilities of the departing March operation in Bicester. ATS struggled at this level, with a succession of different designers and team managers before Schmid called it a day, only to return with his new Rial outfit four years later.

Totals	GPs	Starts	Points	Poles	F.Laps	Wins
	89	107	8	-	-	-

Seasons							Sponsor(s)	Main Driver(s)
1978	12	19	-	-	-	-	ATS,Fina	Mass,Jarier/Rosberg
1979	12	12	2	-	-	-	ATS,Hotel Arawak	Stuck
1980	12	12	-	-	-	-	ATS,Hotel Arawak	Surer
1981	9	9	1	-	-	-	ATS,ABBA	Borgudd
1982	15	26	4	-	-	-	ATS,Liqui Moly	Winkelhock,Salazar
1983	14	14	-	-	-	-	ATS,Steinbock	Winkelhock
1984	15	15	1	-	-	-	ATS	Winkelhock

Models							Year(s)	Chief Designer	Engine
HS1	11	17	-	-	-	-	78	G Ferris/R Herd	Ford Cosworth
D1	2	2	-	-	-	-	78	J Gentry/G Brunner	Ford Cosworth
D2	7	7	-	-	-	-	79	G Caliri	Ford Cosworth
D3	7	7	2	-	-	-	79-80	N Stroud	Ford Cosworth
D4	13	13	-	-	-	-	80-81	G Brunner	Ford Cosworth
D5 (HGS1)	21	32	5	-	-	-	81-82	H Guilpin	Ford Cosworth
D6	14	14	-	-	-	-	83	G Brunner	BMW t
D7	15	15	1	-	-	-	84	G Brunner	BMW t

ATS (I)

Principal: Carlo Chiti.
Base: Bologna.
Founded: 1961.

Automobili Turismo e Sport was formed by ex-Ferrari personnel, led by Carlo Chiti (who died in 1994) and Romolo Tavoni, with the backing of Jaime Ortiz Patino, Giorgio Billi and Count Giovanni Volpi (who left early on to form Scuderia Serenissima). The team based itself at Sasso Marconi, Bologna, and appeared unprepared for the rigours of Formula 1 racing and effectively finished after the 1963 season, although it continued as an engineering concern.

Totals	GPs	Starts	Points	Poles	F.Laps	Wins
	6	11	-	-	-	-

Seasons							Colour	Main Driver(s)
1963	5	10	-	-	-	-	red	P Hill,Baghetti
1964	1	1	-	-	-	-	red	Cabral

Models							Year(s)	Chief Designer	Engine
100	5	10	-	-	-	-	63	C Chiti	V8
(D-F)*	1	1	-	-	-	-	64	V Derrington	V8

Derrington-Francis – a development of the first chassis by Vic Derrington and Alf Francis.

BAR (GB)

Principal: Craig Pollock & Adrian Reynard/David Richards/Nick Fry.
Base: Brackley, Northamptonshire.
Founded: 1997.

British American Racing was the brainchild of Craig Pollock, the business manager of Jacques Villeneuve. He joined forces with respected chassis constructor Adrian Reynard and arrived with American tobacco money to challenge the Formula 1 establishment. After buying out Tyrrell, they created a state-of-the-art factory and upset the FIA with a controversial dual sponsorship car livery. Reynard's cars had previously won the first time out in each category but, despite optimism, failed to score a point in this first season. At the launch of the 2002 car, there was a surprise announcement that Craig Pollock had left the team, with David Richards taking control. After a successful 2004 campaign David Richards was relinquished from his team leader role, being replaced by Nick Fry as Honda initially took a bigger share of the company, buying it completely at the end of the 2005 season..

Totals	GPs	Starts	Points	Poles	F.Laps	Wins			
	117	231	227	2	-	-			
Seasons							Sponsor(s)	Main Driver(s)	
1999	16	31	-	-	-	-	Lucky Strike,555	Villeneuve,Zonta	
2000	17	34	20	-	-	-	Lucky Strike,Teleglobe	Villeneuve,Zonta	
2001	17	34	17	-	-	-	Lucky Strike,Tiscali	Villeneuve,Panis	
2002	17	34	7	-	-	-	Lucky Strike,Tiscali	Villeneuve,Panis	
2003	16	30	26	-	-	-	Lucky Strike	Villeneuve,Button	
2004	18	36	119	1	-	-	Lucky Strike	Button,Sato	
2005	16	32	38	1	-	-	Lucky Strike	Button,Sato	
Models							Year(s)	Chief Designer	Engine
01	16	31	-	-	-	-	99	M Oastler	Supertec
002	17	34	20	-	-	-	00	M Oastler	Honda
003	17	34	17	-	-	-	01	M Oastler	Honda
004	17	34	7	-	-	-	02	G Willis	Honda
005	16	30	26	-	-	-	03	G Willis	Honda
006	18	36	119	1	-	-	04	G Willis	Honda
007	16	32	38	1	-	-	05	G Willis	Honda

BELLASI (I)

Principal: Vittorio Bellasi.
Base: Novara, nr Milano.
Founded: 1966.

Bellasi designs were created for the domestic Italian market, the first of many designs being a Formula 3 car. The only Formula 1 design was commissioned by Silvio Moser and was not a great success.

Totals	GPs	Starts	Points	Poles	F.Laps	Wins			
	2	2	-	-	-	-			
Seasons							Colour	Main Driver(s)	
1970	1	1	-	-	-	-	red	Moser	
1971	1	1	-	-	-	-	red	Moser	
Models							Year(s)	Chief Designer	Engine
-	2	2	-	-	-	-	70-71	V Bellasi	Ford Cosworth

BENETTON (GB/I) formerly Toleman (1981 to 1985)

Principals: Ted Toleman/Alessandro Benetton.
Base: Witney, Oxfordshire/Enstone, Oxfordshire (1993).
Founded: 1970.

Ted Toleman and his company took part in British club motorsport, building their first car for Formula 2 in 1980 and entering the big time the following year. In 1985, the Witney-based team ran into difficulties and was rescued by Benetton sponsorship which resulted in a full takeover by the Italian company the following season. A succession of team managers has seen Peter Collins, Davide Paolini, Flavio Briatore, Dave Richards and, since 1998, Rocco Benetton take control of the racing operations. In 1993 the team moved to new Oxfordshire premises and became the team to beat, the following year. The combination of Schumacher and intelligent team strategy paid off with both titles in 1995, although they seemed to miss their superstar the following season when the team officially changed their nationality to Italian. The Benetton family sold out to Renault in 2000 and the following season saw the final Benetton chassis using an experimental Renault engine before the team reverted to the famous French marque's name for the 2002 season.

Constructors' Championships: 1 (1995). **Drivers' Championships:** 2 (1994,95).

Totals	GPs	Starts	Points	Poles	F.Laps	Wins		
	317	613	887.5	16	38	27		
Seasons							Sponsor(s)	Main Driver(s)
1981	2	2	-	-	-	-	Candy	Henton, Warwick
1982	11	17	-	-	1	-	Cougar	Warwick, Fabi
1983	15	29	10	-	-	-	Candy, Magirus	Warwick, Giacomelli
1984	16	26	16	-	1	-	Segafredo, Magirus	Senna, Cecotto
1985	13	20	-	1	-	-	Benetton	Fabi, Ghinzani
1986	16	32	19	2	3	1	Benetton, Sisley	Fabi, Berger
1987	16	32	28	-	1	-	Benetton, Riello	Fabi, Boutsen
1988	16	32	39	-	1	-	Benetton, Riello	Nannini, Boutsen
1989	16	31	39	-	-	1	Benetton, Riello	Nannini, Herbert/Pirro
1990	16	32	71	-	1	2	Benetton, Riello	Nannini, Piquet
1991	16	32	38.5	-	1	1	Camel, Autopolis	Moreno/Schumacher, Piquet
1992	16	32	91	-	2	1	Camel, Benetton	Schumacher, Brundle
1993	16	32	72	-	5	1	Camel, Benetton	Schumacher, Patrese
1994	16	32	103	6	8	8	Mild Seven, Benetton	Schumacher*, Verstappen *Champion*
1995	17	34	147	4	8	11	Mild Seven, Bitburger	Schumacher*, Herbert *Champion*
1996	16	32	68	-	3	-	Mild Seven, Benetton	Alesi, Berger
1997	17	34	67	2	2	1	Mild Seven, FedEx	Alesi, Berger
1998	16	32	33	1	1	-	Mild Seven, FedEx	Fisichella, Wurz
1999	16	32	16	-	-	-	Mild Seven, Playlife	Fisichella, Wurz
2000	17	34	20	-	-	-	Mild Seven, Marconi	Fisichella, Wurz
2001	17	34	10	-	-	-	Mild Seven, Marconi	Fisichella, Button
Models							Year(s)	Chief Designer	Engine
TG181-B,C	12	17	-	-	1	-	81-82	R Byrne	Hart t
TG183-B	21	38	12	-	-	-	82-84	R Byrne	Hart t
TG184	12	19	14	-	1	-	84	R Byrne	Hart t
TG185	13	20	-	1	-	-	85	R Byrne	Hart t
B186	16	32	19	2	3	1	86	R Byrne	BMW t
B187	16	32	28	-	1	-	87	R Byrne	Ford Cosworth t
B188	24	45	52	-	1	-	88-89	R Byrne	Ford Cosworth
B189-B	12	22	30	-	-	1	89-90	R Byrne	Ford Cosworth
B190-B	16	32	73	-	1	2	90-91	R Byrne	Ford Cosworth
B191-B	17	34	43.5	-	1	1	91-92	J Barnard	Ford Cosworth
B192-B	15	30	84	-	3	1	92-93	R Brawn	Ford Cosworth
B193B	14	28	68	-	4	1	93	R Brawn	Ford Cosworth
B194	16	32	103	6	8	8	94	R Brawn	Ford Cosworth
B195	17	34	147	4	8	11	95	R Brawn	Renault
B196	16	32	68	-	3	-	96	R Byrne	Renault
B197	17	34	67	2	2	1	97	P Symonds	Renault
B198	16	32	33	1	1	-	98	P Symonds	Playlife
B199	16	32	16	-	-	-	99	P Symonds	Playlife
B200	17	34	20	-	-	-	00	P Symonds	Playlife
B201	17	34	10	-	-	-	01	M Gascoyne	Renault

BMW specials (D)

Principal: no works involvement.
Base: München (Munich).
Founded: 1916 (aero engines).

Bayerische Motoren Werke of Munich never entered Formula 1 in their own right, although there were entries for the various home-built specials which raced in Germany in the early fifties.

Totals	GPs	Starts	Points	Poles	F.Laps	Wins			
	2	6	-	-	-	-			
Seasons							**Colour**	**Main Driver(s)**	
1952	1	4	-	-	-	-	silver	Krause, Klodwig	
1953	1	2	-	-	-	-	silver	Krause, Klodwig	
Models							**Year(s)**	**Chief Designer**	**Engine**
Greifzu	2	2	-	-	-	-	52-53	P Greifzu	4
Heck	2	2	-	-	-	-	52-53	E Klodwig	4 (rear engine)
Eigenbau	1	1	-	-	-	-	52	G Bechem	4
Speciale	1	1	-	-	-	-	52	M Balsa	4 (Gordini type body)

The Len Terry designed 269 failed to start in the Formula 2 class of the 1969 German Grand Prix.

BRABHAM (GB)

Principals: Jack Brabham, Ron Tauranac/Bernie Ecclestone.
Base: Guildford/New Haw, Weybridge/Chessington/Tilbrook, Milton Keynes.
Founded: 1961.

The first car, known as MRD, appeared in 1961 and the early years up until 1970 saw Brabham and Tauranac produce a succession of winners in Formula 1 and lower formulae, as well as providing customer cars from the New Haw factory. Ecclestone purchased the team in 1972 and from new premises continued the team's winning ways, building Formula 1 team cars only. After a year out of the championship (1988), the team was sold to the Swiss financier Joachim Luhti and the marque began its slow decline until closing in late 1992 when owned by the Middlebridge group.

Constructors' Championships: 2 (1966,67). **Drivers' Championships:** 4 (1966,67,81,83).

Totals	GPs	Starts	Points	Poles	F.Laps	Wins		
	394	932	983	39	41	35		
Seasons							**Sponsor(s)/(Colour)**	**Main Driver(s)**
1962	3	3	6				(green)	Brabham
1963	10	20	33	-	1	-	(green)	Brabham, Gurney
1964	10	49	43	2	3	2	(green)	Brabham, Gurney
1965	10	57	44	-	1	-	(green)	Brabham, Gurney, Hulme
1966	9	35	65	3	2	4	(green)	Brabham*, Hulme *Champion*
1967	11	36	102	2	2	4	(green)	Brabham, Hulme* *Champion*
1968	12	30	12	2	-	-	(green)	Brabham, Rindt
1969	11	43	68	4	3	2	(green)	Brabham, Ickx
1970	13	26	35	1	4	1	(turquoise)	Brabham, Stommelen
1971	11	24	7	-	-	-	(white)	Hill, Schenken
1972	12	32	7	1	-	-	YPF, Bardahl	Hill, Reutemann, W Fittipaldi
1973	15	41	22	-	-	-	YPF, Bardahl	Reutemann, W Fittipaldi
1974	15	46	46	1	3	3	Elan, Stroh	Reutemann, von Opel/Pace
1975	14	28	61	1	1	2	Martini	Reutemann, Pace
1976	16	39	11	-	-	-	Martini	Reutemann, Pace
1977	17	34	27	1	2	-	Martini	Watson, Pace/Stuck
1978	16	33	69	2	4	2	Parmalat	Lauda, Watson
1979	15	30	7	-	1	-	Parmalat	Lauda, Piquet
1980	14	27	55	2	1	3	Parmalat	Piquet, Zunino/Rebaque
1981	15	29	61	4	1	3	Parmalat	Piquet*, Rebaque *Champion*
1982	15	29	41	1	4	2	Parmalat	Piquet, Patrese

Seasons	GPs	Starts	Points	Poles	F.Laps	Wins	Sponsor(s)/(Colour)	Main Driver(s)
1983	15	30	72	2	5	4	Parmalat	Piquet*,Patrese *Champion*
1984	16	32	38	9	3	2	Parmalat	Piquet,T & C Fabi
1985	16	31	26	1	-	1	Olivetti	Piquet,Surer
1986	16	30	2	-	-	-	Olivetti	Patrese,de Angelis/Warwick
1987	16	32	10	-	-	-	Olivetti	Patrese,de Cesaris
1988 did not participate								
1989	16	29	8	-	-	-	Bioptron, Nippon Shinpan	Brundle,Modena
1990	16	26	2	-	-	-	Carvico	Brabham,Modena
1991	16	28	3	-	-	-	Mitsukoshi	Brundle,Blundell
1992	3	3	-	-	-	-	Yamazen	van de Poele,Hill

Models							Year(s)	Chief Designer	Engine
BT3	7	7	8	-	-	-	62-65	R Tauranac	Climax,BRM
BT6	1	1	-	-	-	-	63	R Tauranac	Ford
BT7	32	51	62	2	4	2	63-66	R Tauranac	Climax
BT10	2	3	-	-	-	-	64-65	R Tauranac	Ford
BT11	32	88	60	-	1	-	64-68	R Tauranac	Climax,BRM,Repco
BT18	1	3	-	-	-	-	66	R Tauranac	Ford Cosworth
BT19	10	10	45	3	1	4	66-67	R Tauranac	Repco
BT20	19	22	44	2	2	1	66-69	R Tauranac	Repco
BT22	4	4	-	-	-	-	66	R Tauranac	Climax
BT23-B,C	3	4	-	-	-	-	67-69	R Tauranac	Ford Cosworth,Climax
BT24	21	29	81	-	1	3	67-69	R Tauranac	Repco,Ford Cosworth
BT26-A	25	52	73	6	3	2	68-71	R Tauranac	Repco,Ford Cosworth
BT30	1	3	-	-	-	-	69	R Tauranac	Ford Cosworth
BT33	28	40	41	1	4	1	70-72	R Tauranac	Ford Cosworth
BT34	20	20	2	1	-	-	71-72	R Tauranac	Ford Cosworth
BT37	18	29	10	-	-	-	72-73	R Bellamy	Ford Cosworth
BT42	23	43	19	-	-	-	73-74	G Murray	Ford Cosworth
BT44-B	33	67	106	2	4	5	74-76	G Murray	Ford Cosworth
BT45-B,C	35	71	48	1	2	-	76-78	G Murray	Alfa Romeo F12
BT46-B	15	30	59	2	4	2	78-79	G Murray	Alfa Romeo F12
BT48	13	25	7	-	-	-	79	G Murray	Alfa Romeo V12
BT49-C,D	36	67	135	6	4	7	79-82	G Murray	Ford Cosworth
BT50	12	22	22	1	3	1	82	G Murray	BMW t
BT52-B	15	30	72	2	5	4	83	G Murray	BMW t
BT53	16	32	38	9	3	2	84	G Murray	BMW t
BT54	17	32	26	1	-	1	85-86	G Murray	BMW t
BT55	16	29	2	-	-	-	86	G Murray	BMW t
BT56	16	32	10	-	-	-	87	D North	BMW t
BT58	18	33	10	-	-	-	89-90	S Rinland	Judd
BT59-Y	16	26	-	-	-	-	90-91	S Rinland	Judd,Yamaha
BT60Y,B	17	27	3	-	-	-	91-92	S Rinland	Yamaha,Judd

The BT16-Ford Cosworth did not start in 1966.

BRM (GB)

Principals: Raymond Mays, Alfred Owen, Louis Stanley.
Base: Bourne, Lincolnshire.
Founded: 1945.

British Racing Motors was founded as a trust by Raymond Mays to help establish Britain as a major force in motor racing – a follow up to his earlier ERA set-up. The first V16 supercharged car was over-ambitious and didn't appear at the circuits until 1950. The trust was taken over by Alfred Owen (of Rubery Owen) in 1952, and success gradually came, culminating in winning the drivers' and constructors' championships in 1962. Louis Stanley took control in the later years as BRM slowly ceased to exist as a racing operation, finally closing its doors in the late 70s.

Constructors' Championships: 1 (1962). **Drivers' Championships:** 1 (1962).

Totals	GPs	Starts	Points	Poles	F.Laps	Wins		
	197	522	537.5	11	15	17		
Seasons							Sponsor(s)/(Colour)	Main Driver(s)
1951	1	2	2	-	-	-	(green)	Parnell, Walker
1952-55 did not participate								
1956	1	3	-	-	-	-	(green)	Hawthorn, Brooks, Flockhart
1957	3	5	-	-	-	-	(green)	Flockhart, MacKay-Fraser
1958	9	22	24	-	-	-	(green)	Schell, Behra
1959	7	22	22.5	1	2	1	(green)	Schell, Bonnier, Flockhart
1960	8	23	8	-	1	-	(green)	G Hill, Bonnier, Gurney
1961	8	16	9	-	1	-	(green)	G Hill, Brooks
1962	9	19	62	1	3	4	(green)	G Hill*, Ginther *Champion*
1963	10	25	65	2	-	2	(green)	G Hill, Ginther
1964	10	33	70	1	1	2	(green)	G Hill, Ginther
1965	10	27	81	4	3	3	(green)	G Hill, Stewart
1966	9	24	34	-	-	1	(green)	G Hill, Stewart
1967	11	33	21	-	-	-	(green)	Stewart, Spence
1968	12	31	28	-	2	-	(green)	Rodriguez, Attwood
1969	10	25	7	-	-	-	(green)	Surtees, Oliver
1970	13	34	25	-	-	1	Yardley	Rodriguez, Oliver, Eaton
1971	11	36	42	1	1	2	Yardley	Rodriguez, Siffert, Ganley
1972	12	47	14	-	1	1	Marlboro	Beltoise, Gethin, Ganley, Wisell
1973	15	44	13	1	-	-	Marlboro	Beltoise, Regazzoni, Lauda
1974	15	38	10	-	-	-	Motul	Beltoise, Pescarolo, Migault
1975	10	10	-	-	-	-	(red/white/blue)	Evans
1976	1	1	-	-	-	-	(red/white/blue)	Ashley
1977	2	2	-	-	-	-	Rotary	Perkins
Models							Year(s)	Chief Designer	Engine
P15	1	2	2	-	-	-	51	P Berthon	V16s
P25	21	54	46.5	1	2	1	56-60	P Berthon	4
P48	7	21	8	-	1	-	60	P Berthon	4
P48/57	11	19	9	-	1	-	61-62	P Berthon	4, Climax
P57	31	59	133	3	3	6	62-65	T Rudd	V8
P61	2	2	-	-	-	-	63	T Rudd	V8
P261	34	65	183	5	4	6	64-67	T Rudd	V8
P83	14	27	17	-	-	-	66-67	T Rudd	H16
P115	6	6	-	-	-	-	67-68	T Rudd	H16
P126	15	21	10	-	1	-	68-69	L Terry	V12
P133	15	15	18	-	1	-	68-69	T Rudd	V12
P138	10	10	2	-	-	-	68-69	T Rudd	V12
P139	6	10	5	-	-	-	69-70	A Osborne	V12
P153-B	27	49	25	-	-	1	70-72	T Southgate	V12
P160-B,C,D,E	47	121	71	2	2	3	71-74	T Southgate	V12
P180	5	7	-	-	-	-	72	T Southgate	V12
P201-B	25	33	8	-	-	-	74-77	M Pilbeam	V12
P207	1	1	-	-	-	-	77	L Terry	V12

The P67 did not start in 1964.

Constructors

BRP (GB)

Principals: Alfred Moss, Ken Gregory.
Base: Highgate, London.
Founded: 1959.

British Racing Partnership was formed by Stirling Moss's father and his business manager. It initially ran a BRM P25 until destroyed at AVUS in 1959. After running customer cars with help from Yeoman Credit/UDT-Laystall, a Formula 1 car appeared in 1963. The outfit folded in 1966 after attempts at the Indianapolis 500.

Totals	GPs	Starts	Points	Poles	F.Laps	Wins			
	13	18	11	-	-	-			
Seasons							Colour	Main Driver(s)	
1963	5	5	6	-	-	-	green	Ireland	
1964	8	13	5	-	-	-	green	Ireland, T Taylor	
Models							Year(s)	Chief Designer	Engine
Mk 1	9	9	6	-	-	-	63-64	T Robinson	BRM
Mk 2	7	9	5	-	-	-	64	T Robinson	BRM

BUGATTI (F)

Principal: Roland Bugatti.
Base: Molsheim, nr Strasbourg.
Founded: 1909.

This legendary marque made one last attempt at grand prix racing with Ettore's son Roland now in control. Two cars were built with the unusual transverse engine layout and one made an isolated appearance at the French GP.

Totals	GPs	Starts	Points	Poles	F.Laps	Wins			
	1	1	-	-	-	-			
Seasons							Colour	Main Driver(s)	
1956	1	1	-	-	-	-	blue	Trintignant	
Models							Year(s)	Chief Designer	Engine
T251	1	1	-	-	-	-	56	G Colombo	8

CISITALIA (I)

Compagnia Industriale Sportiva Italia was founded by Piero Dusio and Piero Taruffi who created a simple small car for an early forerunner of one-make racing, immediately after the war. Over thirty of these Giacosa-designed chassis were built at the Turin workshops, one of which (the BPM-powered D46) suffered engine failure during practice for the 1952 Italian Grand Prix.

COLONI (I)

Principal: Enzo Coloni.
Base: Passignano sul Trasimeno, Perugia.
Founded: 1983.

This little team from Perugia initially ran Formula 3 Ralts and built its first car for F1. Always struggling, the team was acquired by the Andrea Moda concern after Subaru had purchased a stake in the team and then promptly sold it back again during the 1991 season.

Totals	GPs	Starts	Points	Poles	F.Laps	Wins			
	13	14	-	-	-	-			
Seasons							Sponsor(s)	Main Driver(s)	
1987	1	1	-	-	-	-	Himont, Renzacci	Larini	
1988	8	8	-	-	-	-	Himont	Tarquini	

Seasons	GPs	Starts	Points	Poles	F.Laps	Wins	Sponsor(s)	Main Driver(s)	
1989	4	5	-	-	-	-	Himont	Moreno, Raphanel	
1990	-	-	-	-	-	-	Agip, Magnabosco	Gachot	
1991	-	-	-	-	-	-	Mateus	Chaves	
Models							Year(s)	Chief Designer	Engine
FC187	1	1	-	-	-	-	87	R Ori	Ford Cosworth
FC188-B	9	10	-	-	-	-	88-89	R Ori	Ford Cosworth
FC189	3	3	-	-	-	-	89	C Vanderpleyn	Ford Cosworth

Models also known as C1,C2,C3. The FC189B (Subaru engine) and FC189C (Ford Cosworth engine) did not qualify in 1990, as was the fate of the C4 in 1991.

CONNAUGHT (GB)

Principals: Rodney Clarke, Mike Oliver, Kenneth McAlpine.
Base: Send, nr Guildford, Surrey.
Founded: 1948.

Financed by Kenneth McAlpine, the Surrey concern built successful designs for both Formula 2 and later Formula 1, which included the unusual streamlined 'B' version. Connaught were renowned for their engineering excellence and durability which also included reliable modifications of Lea Francis and Alta engines within Connaught designs. The team came so close to real success but reluctantly closed after Monaco 1957, and the cars were sold off in September of that year with Bernie Ecclestone purchasing some of the proceeds.

Totals	GPs	Starts	Points	Poles	F.Laps	Wins			
	17	49	17	-	-	-			
Seasons							Colour	Main Driver(s)	
1952	3	8	5	-	-	-	green	McAlpine, Poore, Thompson	
1953	6	21	-	-	-	-	green	McAlpine, Salvadori, Bira	
1954	1	5	-	-	-	-	green	Marr, Whitehouse (privateers)	
1955	1	3	-	-	-	-	green	McAlpine	
1956	3	7	9	-	-	-	green	Fairman, Flockhart	
1957	1	2	3	-	-	-	green	Lewis-Evans, Bueb	
1958	1	2	-	-	-	-	green	Bueb, Fairman (B Ecclestone)	
1959	1	1	-	-	-	-	green	Said (P Emery)	
Models							Year(s)	Chief Designer	Engine
A	10	34	5	-	-	-	52-54	R Clarke	Lea Francis
B	6	14	12	-	-	-	55-58	R Clarke	Alta
C	1	1	-	-	-	-	59	R Clarke	Alta

Models sometimes referred to as 'A-type' etc.

CONNEW (GB)

Principal: Peter Connew.
Base: Chadwell Heath, Essex.
Founded: 1971.

Former Surtees draughtsman, Peter Connew, took on the might of Formula 1 with what was basically a lock-up special. Although only qualifying for one race it remains a remarkable achievement on what was such a financial shoestring.

Totals	GPs	Starts	Points	Poles	F.Laps	Wins			
	1	1	-	-	-	-			
Seasons							Sponsor(s)	Main Driver(s)	
1972	1	1	-	-	-	-	Capricorn	Migault	
Models							Year(s)	Chief Designer	Engine
PC1	1	1	-	-	-	-	72	P Connew	Ford Cosworth

COOPER (GB)

Principals: Charles & John Cooper.
Base: Surbiton/Byfleet, Surrey.
Founded: 1946.

In the immediate post-war years, Charles Cooper and his son John were supporters of the burgeoning Formula 3 500cc racing. They built small rear-engined cars (one of which appeared at Monaco in 1950), that set a trend for the Formula 2 models of the late fifties, although the first Formula 2 Coopers were conventional front-engined cars. Their pinnacle came with back to back championships in 1959-60. Charles died in 1964, and with John suffering from the effects of a serious road accident, the team was sold to the Chipstead Group and later relocated to Canada Road, Byfleet. In the final years Cooper reintroduced the V12 Maserati engine but the writing was on the wall and they closed soon after.

Constructors' Championships: 2 (1959,60). **Drivers' Championships:** 2 (1959,60).

Totals	GPs	Starts	Points	Poles	F.Laps	Wins			
	129	499	484.5	11	14	16			
Seasons							Colour	Main Driver(s)	
1950	1	1	-	-	-	-	blue/white	Schell (privateer)	
1952	6	16	12	-	-	-	green	Hawthorn,Brown (privateers)	
1953	7	20	-	-	-	-	green	Moss,Wharton,Brown	
1954	1	4	-	-	-	-	green	Gerard (privateer)	
1955	1	1	-	-	-	-	green	Brabham	
1956	1	1	-	-	-	-	green	Gerard (privateer)	
1957	5	14	2	-	-	-	green	Brabham,Salvadori,MacDowel	
1958	10	40	38	-	-	2	green	Brabham,Salvadori,Fairman	
1959	8	57	97.5	5	5	5	green	Brabham*,McLaren,Gregory *Champion*	
1960	9	74	108	4	5	6	green	Brabham*,McLaren *Champion*	
1961	8	55	24	1	1	-	green	Brabham,McLaren	
1962	9	29	45	-	1	1	green	McLaren,Maggs	
1963	10	33	32	-	-	-	green	McLaren,Maggs	
1964	10	22	16	-	-	-	green	McLaren,P Hill	
1965	10	21	14	-	-	-	green	McLaren,Rindt	
1966	9	41	39	1	2	1	green	Rindt,Surtees,Ginther	
1967	11	44	37	-	-	1	green	Rindt,Rodriguez,Ickx	
1968	12	25	20	-	-	-	green	Bianchi,Elford	
1969	1	1	-	-	-	-	maroon	Elford (Antique Automobiles)	
Models							Year(s)	Chief Designer	Engine
T12	1	1	-	-	-	-	50	O Maddock	JAP
T20	8	20	12	-	-	-	52-53	O Maddock	Bristol
T23	9	18	-	-	-	-	53-56	O Maddock	Bristol,Alta
Spl.	1	1	-	-	-	-	53	R Martin	Alta
T24	2	2	-	-	-	-	53-54	O Maddock	Alta
T40	1	1	-	-	-	-	55	J Brabham	Bristol
T41	1	1	-	-	-	-	57	O Maddock	Climax
T43	12	23	10	-	-	1	57-60	O Maddock	Climax,OSCA
T44 (T43-BG)	1	1	-	-	-	-	57	B Gerard	Bristol
T45	18	45	30	-	-	1	58-61	O Maddock	Climax,Maserati,Castellotti
T51	24	110	133.5	6	6	6	59-63	O Maddock	Climax,Maserati, Borgward,Castellotti
T53	21	55	81	3	4	5	60-62	O Maddock	Climax,Maserati,Alfa Romeo
T55	14	19	17	-	-	-	61-65	O Maddock	Climax
T58	3	3	-	1	1	-	61	O Maddock	Climax
T60	15	21	45	-	1	1	62-65	O Maddock	Climax
T66	13	30	32	-	-	-	63-64	O Maddock	Climax
T73	13	21	16	-	-	-	64-66	E Stait	Climax,Ford,Ferrari
T77	11	19	12	-	-	-	65-67	E Stait	Climax,ATS
T79	2	2	6	-	-	-	67-68	E Stait	Climax
T81-B	21	80	67	1	2	2	66-68	D White	Maserati
T86-B	17	26	23	-	-	-	67-69	D White	Maserati,BRM

The T59-Ford (1965), T76-Ford (1965) and T82-Climax (1967) did not start.

DALLARA (I)

Principal: Gianpaolo Dallara.
Base: Parma.
Founded: 1972.

Commissioned by Beppe Lucchini's Brescia Motor Sport operation to build a chassis for his Scuderia Italia team, Dallara's first car was the Wolf-Dallara Formula 3 car of 1978. Prior to this he was a successful consultant designer, his work including the de Tomaso Formula 1 car and various road cars. Gianpaolo Dallara retains an active role in chassis design and assisted in all the following grand prix designs. Dallara chassis are still widely used in European lower formula racing and also build chassis for the Indy Racing League series.

Totals	GPs	Starts	Points	Poles	F.Laps	Wins		
	78	133	15	-	-	-		
Seasons							Sponsor(s)	Main Driver(s)
1988	14	14	-	-	-	-	Marlboro	Caffi
1989	16	29	8	-	-	-	Marlboro	Caffi,de Cesaris
1990	16	30	-	-	-	-	Marlboro	Pirro,de Cesaris
1991	16	29	5	-	-	-	Marlboro,Lucchini	Pirro,Lehto
1992	16	31	2	-	-	-	Lucchini,Marlboro	Martini,Lehto
Models							Year(s)	Chief Designer	Engine
188	14	14	-	-	-	-	88	S Rinland	Ford Cosworth
189	16	29	8	-	-	-	89	M Tolentino	Ford Cosworth
190	16	30	-	-	-	-	90	C Vanderpleyn	Ford Cosworth
191	16	29	5	-	-	-	91	N Couperthwaite	Judd
192	16	31	2	-	-	-	92	N Couperthwaite	Ferrari

The 3087 Formula 3000 car did not pre-qualify for the first race of 1988.

DE TOMASO (I)

Principal: Alejandro de Tomaso.
Base: Modena.
Founded: 1959.

De Tomaso Automobili began in October 1959 building Formula Junior and Formula 2 cars at its Modena base. Argentinian racing driver, Alejandro de Tomaso commissioned Gianpaolo Dallara to build an F2 design in 1969 which formed the basis of the Frank Williams-entered Formula 1 car the following year. The company went on to produce exotic Ford-engined road cars, before amalgamating with Maserati.

Totals	GPs	Starts	Points	Poles	F.Laps	Wins		
	10	12	-	-	-	-		
Seasons							Colour	Main Driver(s)
1961	2	4	-	-	-	-	red	Bussinello,Lippi
1962	-	-	-	-	-	-		Estefano
1963	-	-	-	-	-	-		Lippi (privateer)
1964-69 did not participate								
1970	8	8	-	-	-	-	Ward	Courage/Schenken (Williams)
Models							Year(s)	Chief Designer	Engine
F1	2	4	-	-	-	-	61	A Massimino	OSCA,Conrero
505	8	8	-	-	-	-	70	G Dallara	Ford Cosworth

The De Tomaso-powered 801 did not qualify in 1962.

EAGLE (USA)

Principal: Dan Gurney.
Base: Santa Ana, California (GB base: Rye, Sussex).
Founded: 1964.

Initially formed with Carroll Shelby to attack Indianapolis, and known as All American Racers. Gurney still had ambitions in grand prix and formed Anglo American Racers on the other side of the Atlantic, at Weslake's engine workshop. In 1968 Gurney severed his links with the engine builders and moved to a new workshop in Ashford, Kent, to develop his own engines. Funds became very tight and Gurney abandoned his Formula 1 aspirations and returned to America where he has achieved many successes, most notably with Toyota.

Totals	GPs	Starts	Points	Poles	F.Laps	Wins			
	25	32	17	-	2	1			
Seasons							Sponsor(s)/(Colour)	Main Driver(s)	
1966	8	10	4	-	-	-	(blue)	Gurney,Bondurant	
1967	11	16	13	-	2	1	(blue)	Gurney,McLaren	
1968	5	5	-	-	-	-	Harvey Titanium	Gurney	
1969	1	1	-	-	-	-	(yellow)	Pease (privateer)	
Models							Year(s)	Chief Designer	Engine
T1G	25	32	17	-	2	1	66-69	L Terry	Climax,Weslake

The models are sometimes known by their chassis numbers 101-104.

EMERYSON (GB)

Principal: Paul Emery.
Base: Send and Worplesdon, Surrey/Fulham, London.
Founded: 1949.

Paul Emery was a typical 'specials' builder of his era, moving from front-engined 500cc cars to build his first front-line racer in 1953. Using the old Connaught works, a batch of rear-engined cars was created. These in turn were used by others such as ENB and later Scirocco, who took over the Emeryson project in 1962. Paul Emery went on to many more projects including a successful series of oval track midget cars.

Totals	GPs	Starts	Points	Poles	F.Laps	Wins			
	4	4	-	-	-	-			
Seasons							Colour	Main Driver(s)	
1956	1	1	-	-	-	-	green	Emery	
1961	-	-	-	-	-	-	yellow	ENB team	
1962	3	3	-	-	-	-	green	Settember	
Models							Year(s)	Chief Designer	Engine
(56)	1	1	-	-	-	-	56	P Emery	Alta
(61)	3	3	-	-	-	-	62	P Emery	Climax

EMW (D)

Principal: no factory involvement.
Base: Eisenach, Thüringen, East Germany.
Founded: 1945.

Eisenacher Motoren Werke began after the Second World War at Eisenach in the Russian zone of the BMW group. Production cars were built from 1947, with a name change to AWE in 1956. Competition cars were soon forgotten and the company concentrated on producing Wartburg saloons.

Totals	GPs	Starts	Points	Poles	F.Laps	Wins
	1	1	-	-	-	-

Seasons	GPs	Starts	Points	Poles	F.Laps	Wins	Colour	Main Driver(s)	
1953	1	1	-	-	-	-	silver	Barth	
Models							Year(s)	Engine	
-	1	1	-	-	-	-	53	EMW	

ENB (B)

Principal: Jacques Swaters.
Base: Bruxelles.
Founded: 1950s.

Equipe Nationale Belge was a racing organisation for home drivers and was an entrant for many years. In 1961 the team raced Emeryson cars and after various mishaps decided to rebuild a chassis as the one-off ENB-Maserati.

Totals	GPs	Starts	Points	Poles	F.Laps	Wins			
	1	1	-	-	-	-			
Seasons							Colour	Main Driver(s)	
1962	1	1	-	-	-	-	yellow	Bianchi	
Models							Year(s)	Chief Designer	Engine
-	1	1	-	-	-	-	62	P Emery	Maserati

ENSIGN (GB)

Principal: Morris Nunn.
Base: Chasetown, Staffordshire/Lichfield, Staffordshire (1981).
Founded: 1970.

Former racer Nunn started building Formula 3 cars with considerable success and from this, Rikky von Opel commissioned Nunn to build a Formula 1 car for 1973. Nunn stayed with F1 when Opel moved on, but money was always going to be tight. After falling out with his Dutch sponsor, HB Bewaking took the N175 and entered it as a Boro for a couple of seasons. With a shortage of funds, Nunn welcomed a merger with Teddy Yip's Theodore concern and the recently acquired Shadow cars. Morris Nunn then transferred his interests to American racing where he achieved great success as an engineer in IndyCar racing.

Totals	GPs	Starts	Points	Poles	F.Laps	Wins			
	99	116	19	-	1	-			
Seasons							Sponsor(s)/(Colour)	Main Driver(s)	
1973	6	6	-	-	-	-	(green)	von Opel	
1974	6	6	-	-	-	-	Dempster	Schuppan	
1975	7	8	1	-	-	-	HB Alarmsystemen	Wunderink/van Lennep	
1976	14	19	2	-	-	-	F&S Properties, Valvoline	Amon	
1977	17	24	10	-	-	-	Tissot, Castrol	Regazzoni, Tambay	
1978	12	16	1	-	-	-	Tissot	Ickx/Daly, Ertl	
1979	6	6	-	-	-	-	Hi-Line	Daly/Gaillard	
1980	9	9	-	-	-	-	Unipart	Regazzoni/Lammers	
1981	14	14	5	-	1	-	Din, Toyota	Surer/Salazar	
1982	8	8	-	-	-	-	Cafe de Colombia	Guerrero	
Models							Year(s)	Chief Designer	Engine
N173	6	6	-	-	-	-	73	M Nunn	Ford Cosworth
N174	11	11	-	-	-	-	74-76	M Nunn	Ford Cosworth
N175	11	11	1	-	-	-	75-77	D Baldwin	Ford Cosworth
N176	12	12	2	-	-	-	76	D Baldwin	Ford Cosworth
N177	31	41	11	-	-	-	77-79	D Baldwin	Ford Cosworth
N179	4	4	-	-	-	-	79	M Nunn	Ford Cosworth
N180-B	23	23	5	-	1	-	80-81	R Bellamy	Ford Cosworth
N181	8	8	-	-	-	-	82	N Bennett	Ford Cosworth

Models were sometimes known by their chassis numbers, eg MN01.

Constructors

ERA (GB)

Principal: Leslie Johnson.
Base: Dunstable, Bedfordshire.
Founded: 1934.

English Racing Automobiles was originated by Raymond Mays at his Bourne home in Lincolnshire, with the help of his friend, Peter Berthon. The outfit was sold and relocated pre-war, before being purchased by Leslie Johnson in November 1947. Johnson was only interested in the E-type cars and later models and eventually sold out to Bristol. Many of the earlier chassis carried on in private hands and are still racing and winning today in historic series, making them one of the most successful groups of racing cars ever built.

Totals	GPs	Starts	Points	Poles	F.Laps	Wins			
	7	12	-	-	-	-			
Seasons							Colour	Main Driver(s)	
1950	3	7	-	-	-	-	green	Johnson	
1951	1	2	-	-	-	-	green	Gerard (privateer)	
1952	3	3	-	-	-	-	green	Moss	
Models							Year(s)	Chief Designer	Engine
A	1	1	-	-	-	-	50	R Railton	6s
B,B/C	4	6	-	-	-	-	50-51	R Railton	6s
E	1	2	-	-	-	-	50	A Barratt	6s
G	3	3	-	-	-	-	52	D Hodkin	Bristol

EUROBRUN (I)

Principal: Walter Brun.
Base: Senago, Milano.
Founded: 1987.

Successful Swiss sports car driver and entrant Walter Brun teamed up with Paolo Pavanello's Euroracing operation and built the cars at the latter's workshops. The team struggled in its first year but things didn't get any better, the orange cars failing to qualify the next year, finally winding up before the end of the 1990 season.

Totals	GPs	Starts	Points	Poles	F.Laps	Wins			
	14	19	-	-	-	-			
Seasons							Sponsor(s)	Main Driver(s)	
1988	12	17	-	-	-	-	Tommasini	Modena, Larrauri	
1989	-	-	-	-	-	-	Jagermeister	Foitek/Larrauri	
1990	2	2	-	-	-	-	JSK	Moreno, Langes	
Models							Year(s)	Chief Designer	Engine
ER188	12	17	-	-	-	-	88	M Tolentino	Ford Cosworth
ER189	2	2	-	-	-	-	90	G Ryton	Judd

The ER188B-Judd (1989) and ER189B-Judd (1990) did not qualify.

FERGUSON (GB)

Principals: Harry Ferguson.
Base: Coventry.
Founded: 1950.

After financial success with his tractors and devices, Harry Ferguson Research experimented with a 4-wheel-drive racing car, helped by former racer, Major Tony Rolt. It raced only once at championship level and became the last front-engined car in the World Championship. Its traction was useful in its next career step as a hill-climb car.

Totals	GPs	Starts	Points	Poles	F.Laps	Wins			
	1	1	-	-	-	-			
Seasons							Colour	Main Driver(s)	
1961	1	1	-	-	-	-	blue	Fairman, Moss	
Models							Year(s)	Chief Designer	Engine
P99	1	1	-	-	-	-	61	C Hill	Climax

FERRARI (I)

Principal: Enzo Ferrari/Luca di Montezemolo.
Base: Maranello, Modena.
Founded: 1946.

The most evocative name in grand prix, and the only team to have contested every year of the championship, always in the traditional red colour. Enzo Ferrari was a former racer and manager of Alfa Romeo's racing team from 1930-37 but a disagreement saw him leave in 1938. Although he built his first car in 1940, Enzo had agreed not to race under his own name for a further five years so the first true Ferrari did not appear until 1946. Early models were known by the displacement size of each cylinder and it is fair to say that Ferrari's priority lay with engine first and chassis second. The Prancing Horse adapted to each formula change quickly and has been a pace setter throughout most of its lifespan, teaming up with FIAT in 1969. Enzo Ferrari died in August 1988 and apart from a close championship call with Prost, overall success eluded this famous marque. With Luca di Montezemolo back in charge and a design base in England, FIAT and Marlboro bought in double World Champion Michael Schumacher for 1996, as they developed their very first V10 grand prix engine. As this team of Jean Todt, Ross Brawn, Rory Byrne and Schumacher gained momentum it continued to break all records in an unprecedented run of success that simply left the others behind.

Constructors' Championships: 14 (1961,64,75,76,77,79,82,83,99,2000,01,02,03,04).
Drivers' Championships: 14 (1952,53,56,58,61,64,75,77,79,2000,01,02,03,04).

Totals	GPs	Starts	Points	Poles	F.Laps	Wins		
	722	1632	4349.8	179	185	183		
Seasons							Sponsor(s)/(Colour)	Main Driver(s)
1950	5	13	21	-	-	-	(red)	Ascari,Villoresi,Sommer
1951	7	32	86	3	-	3	(red)	Ascari,Villoresi,González
1952	7	43	120.5	7	7	7	(red)	Ascari*,Farina,Taruffi *Champion*
1953	8	46	122.5	6	6	7	(red)	Ascari*,Farina,Hawthorn,Villoresi *Champion*
1954	8	43	80.3	2	3	2	(red)	González,Hawthorn,Trintignant
1955	6	21	34	1	-	1	(red)	Trintignant,Farina,Castellotti
1956	7	34	82	6	4	5	(red)	Fangio*,Collins,Castellotti *Champion*
1957	7	27	48	-	1	-	(red)	Hawthorn,Collins,Musso
1958	10	34	93	4	6	2	(red)	Hawthorn*,Collins,Musso *Champion*
1959	7	29	67	2	2	2	(red)	Brooks,P Hill,Allison
1960	8	24	43	1	2	1	(red)	P Hill,von Trips
1961	7	27	99	6	5	5	(red)	P Hill*,von Trips,Ginther *Champion*
1962	6	20	30	-	-	-	(red)	P Hill,Baghetti,R Rodriguez
1963	10	18	27	1	3	1	(red)	Surtees,Bandini
1964	10	22	64	2	2	3	(red)	Surtees*,Bandini *Champion*
1965	10	22	32	-	-	-	(red)	Surtees,Bandini
1966	7	16	42	3	4	2	(red)	Bandini,Parkes
1967	10	16	23	-	-	-	Shell	Amon,Parkes
1968	11	23	37	4	-	1	Shell	Amon,Ickx
1969	10	11	7	-	-	-	Shell	Amon/P Rodriguez
1970	13	25	76	5	7	4	Shell	Ickx,Regazzoni
1971	11	27	44	3	4	2	Shell	Ickx,Regazzoni
1972	12	30	47	4	3	1	Heuer,FIAT	Ickx,Regazzoni
1973	13	19	14	-	-	-	Ferodo	Ickx,Merzario
1974	15	30	90	10	6	3	Agip	Lauda,Regazzoni
1975	14	28	89.5	9	6	6	Agip,Heuer	Lauda*,Regazzoni *Champion*
1976	15	30	99	4	7	6	Agip,Heuer	Lauda,Regazzoni
1977	17	33	114	2	3	4	FIAT,Agip	Lauda*,Reutemann *Champion*
1978	16	32	65	2	3	5	FIAT,Agip	Reutemann,Villeneuve
1979	15	30	113	2	6	6	FIAT,Agip	Scheckter*,Villeneuve *Champion*
1980	14	27	8	-	-	-	FIAT,Agip	Scheckter,Villeneuve
1981	15	30	34	1	2	2	FIAT,Agip	Villeneuve,Pironi
1982	14	22	74	3	2	3	FIAT,Agip	Villeneuve/Tambay,Pironi
1983	15	30	89	8	3	4	FIAT,Agip	Tambay,Arnoux
1984	16	32	57.5	1	3	1	FIAT,Agip	Alboreto,Arnoux
1985	16	32	82	1	2	2	FIAT,Agip	Alboreto,Johansson
1986	16	32	37	-	-	-	FIAT,Agip	Alboreto,Johansson
1987	16	32	53	3	3	2	FIAT,Agip	Alboreto,Berger
1988	16	32	65	1	4	1	FIAT,Agip	Alboreto,Berger

Seasons (cont.)							Sponsor(s)/(Colour)	Main Driver(s)	
1989	16	30	59	-	4	3	FIAT,Agip	Mansell,Berger	
1990	16	32	110	3	5	6	FIAT,Agip	Prost,Mansell	
1991	16	31	55.5	-	2	-	FIAT,Agip	Prost,Alesi	
1992	16	32	21	-	-	-	FIAT,Agip	Alesi,Capelli	
1993	16	32	28	-	-	-	FIAT,Agip	Alesi,Berger	
1994	16	32	71	3	-	1	Agip	Alesi,Berger	
1995	17	34	73	1	3	1	Marlboro	Alesi,Berger	
1996	16	31	70	4	2	3	Marlboro	Schumacher,Irvine	
1997	17	34	102	3	3	5	Marlboro	Schumacher,Irvine	
1998	16	32	133	3	6	6	Marlboro	Schumacher,Irvine	
1999	16	32	128	3	6	6	Marlboro	Schumacher,Irvine	
2000	17	34	170	10	5	10	Marlboro	Schumacher*,Barrichello	*Champion*
2001	17	34	179	11	3	9	Marlboro	Schumacher*,Barrichello	*Champion*
2002	17	32	221	10	12	15	Marlboro	Schumacher*,Barrichello	*Champion*
2003	16	32	158	8	8	8	Marlboro	Schumacher*,Barrichello	*Champion*
2004	18	36	262	12	14	15	Marlboro	Schumacher*,Barrichello	*Champion*
2005	19	38	100	1	3	1	Marlboro	Schumacher,Barrichello	
Models							Year(s)	Chief Designer	Engine
125	9	12	13	-	-	-	50-52	G Colombo	V12s
275,375	9	30	94	3	-	3	50-51	A Lampredi	V12
212	6	6	-	-	-	-	51-52	A Lampredi	V12
500	26	88	243	13	13	14	52-57	A Lampredi	4
166-S	6	7	-	-	-	-	50-53	A Lampredi	V12,Jaguar
553	6	9	9	-	-	1	53-54	A Lampredi	4
625	11	36	92.3	3	3	2	54-55	A Lampredi	4
555	5	14	15	-	-	-	55-56	A Lampredi	4,Lancia-Ferrari
801 & D50	14	57	128	6	5	5	56-57	V Jano	Lancia-Ferrari
Dino 246-P, MP	25	85	203	7	10	5	58-60	V Jano	V6
Dino 156	2	2	-	-	-	-	58-59	V Jano	V6
156	29	71	172	7	8	7	61-64	C Chiti	V6
158	19	23	58	2	2	2	64-65	M Forghieri	V8
1512	12	15	22	-	-	-	64-65	M Forghieri	F12
246	4	4	10	-	1	-	66	M Forghieri	V6
312	38	62	99	7	3	3	66-69	M Forghieri	V12
312B	18	34	95	6	10	5	70-71	M Forghieri	F12
312B2	24	54	83	6	4	2	71-73	M Forghieri	F12
312B3	27	47	102	10	6	3	73-75	M Forghieri	F12
312T	15	30	113.5	10	8	9	75-76	M Forghieri	F12
312T2	31	61	189	5	10	8	76-78	M Forghieri	F12
312T3	16	32	59	2	1	4	78-79	M Forghieri	F12
312T4	13	26	110	2	6	6	79	M Forghieri	F12
312T5	14	27	8	-	-	-	80	M Forghieri	F12
126CK	15	30	34	1	2	2	81	M Forghieri	V6t
126C2-B	22	38	118	7	3	5	82-83	H Postlethwaite	V6t
126C3	7	14	45	4	2	2	83	H Postlethwaite	V6t
126C4	16	32	57.5	1	3	1	84	H Postlethwaite	V6t
156/85	16	32	82	1	2	2	85	H Postlethwaite	V6t
F1-86	16	32	37	-	-	-	86	H Postlethwaite	V6t
F1-87	16	32	53	3	3	2	87	J Barnard	V6t
F1-87/88C	16	32	65	1	4	1	88	J Barnard	V6t
640	16	30	59	-	4	3	89	J Barnard	V12
641-/2	16	32	110	3	5	6	90	J Barnard	V12
642	6	11	16	-	2	-	91	S Nichols	V12
643	10	20	39.5	-	-	-	91	S Nichols	V12
F92-A,AT,00	16	32	21	-	-	-	92	S Nichols	V12
F93A	16	32	28	-	-	-	93	J Barnard	V12
412T1-B	16	32	71	3	-	1	94	J Barnard	V12
412T2	17	34	73	1	3	1	95	J Barnard	V12
F310	16	31	70	4	2	3	96	J Barnard	V10
F310B	17	34	102	3	3	5	97	J Barnard	V10
F300	16	32	133	3	6	6	98	R Brawn	V10

Models (cont.)							Year(s)	Chief Designer	Engine
F399	16	32	128	3	6	6	99	R Brawn	V10
F1 2000	17	34	170	10	5	10	00	R Brawn	V10
F2001	20	39	193	13	3	10	01	R Brawn	V10
F2002	19	35	239	11	15	15	02-03	R Brawn	V10
F2003-GA	12	24	126	5	5	7	03	R Brawn	V10
F2004-M	20	40	272	12	14	15	04-05	R Brawn	V10
F2005	17	34	90	1	3	1	05	R Brawn	V10

The modified Thin Wall Ferrari appears under the model number 375, referred to in the RACES chapter as 375tw.

FITTIPALDI (BR/GB) formerly Copersucar (1975 to 1979)

Principals: Wilson & Emerson Fittipaldi.
Base: Säo Paulo (GB base: Caversham/Slough/Reading).
Founded: 1973.

Set up by Wilson Fittipaldi, with backing from the Brazilian Copersucar sugar organisation, it gained momentum when brother Emerson joined as driver. In 1980, Copersucar had gone and Fittipaldi merged with Wolf, using their third series models (WR7-9) as the Fittipaldi F7s. As the turbo era approached, lack of sponsorship meant the end of this ambitious and colourful project.

Totals	GPs	Starts	Points	Poles	F.Laps	Wins			
	104	123	44	-	-	-			
Seasons							Sponsor(s)	Main Driver(s)	
1975	12	12	-	-	-	-	Copersucar	W Fittipaldi	
1976	15	16	3	-	-	-	Copersucar	E Fittipaldi	
1977	14	16	11	-	-	-	Copersucar	E Fittipaldi	
1978	16	16	17	-	-	-	Copersucar	E Fittipaldi	
1979	15	15	1	-	-	-	Copersucar	E Fittipaldi	
1980	14	25	11	-	-	-	Skol	Rosberg, Fittipaldi	
1981	9	14	-	-	-	-	Pasta Matic	Rosberg, Serra	
1982	9	9	1	-	-	-	Brasilinvest	Serra	
Models							Year(s)	Chief Designer	Engine
FD01-03	13	13	-	-	-	-	75-76	R Divila	Ford Cosworth
FD04	22	24	11	-	-	-	76-77	R Divila	Ford Cosworth
F5-A	31	31	21	-	-	-	77-79	D Baldwin	Ford Cosworth
F6-A	7	7	-	-	-	-	79	G Caliri	Ford Cosworth
F7	7	13	9	-	-	-	80	H Postlethwaite	Ford Cosworth
F8-C,D	22	32	3	-	-	-	80-82	H Postlethwaite	Ford Cosworth
F9	3	3	-	-	-	-	82	R Divila	Ford Cosworth

FORTI (I)

Principal: Guido Forti.
Base: Alessandria.
Founded: 1975.

A team with an impeccable reputation in Formula 3 and Formula 3000, found its first season very hard going and after back of grid and non-qualifying performances, together with sponsor and ownership disputes, the Italian courts finally wound the team up in August 1996.

Totals	GPs	Starts	Points	Poles	F.Laps	Wins			
	23	44	-	-	-	-			
Seasons							Sponsor(s)	Main Driver(s)	
1995	17	34	-	-	-	-	Parmalat, Arisco	Diniz, Moreno	
1996	6	10	-	-	-	-	Hudson, Shannon	Badoer, Montermini	
Models							Year(s)	Chief Designer	Engine
FG01-95,B	19	38	-	-	-	-	95-96	G Stirano	Ford Cosworth
FG03-96	4	6	-	-	-	-	96	P Guerci	Ford Cosworth

FRAZER NASH (GB)

Principal: Archie Frazer-Nash.
Base: Isleworth, Middlesex.
Founded: 1922.

Archie Frazer-Nash began production of his own cars in the 1920s as a development of the GN cars he helped to create. Taken over by H J Aldington in 1929, the firm moved to London Road, Isleworth where mainly sports cars were produced, although six single seaters were made, including Wharton's car in 1952. The last Frazer Nash was built in 1957 and the firm went on to be the British concessionaires for Porsche.

Totals	GPs	Starts	Points	Poles	F.Laps	Wins			
	4	4	3	-	-	-			
Seasons							Colour	Main Driver(s)	
1952	4	4	3	-	-	-	green	Wharton	
Models							Year(s)	Chief Designer	Engine
FN48	2	2	3	-	-	-	52	H Aldington	Bristol
421 *	2	2	-	-	-	-	52	H Aldington	Bristol

* This model was in fact a stripped down Sports car, the Le Mans Replica Mark II.

FRY (GB)

David Fry created this unusual rear-engined design in the late 50s but it failed to qualify for the British Grand Prix in 1959.

GILBY (GB)

Principal: Syd Greene.
Base: Barking, Essex.
Founded: 1953.

Syd Greene and his Gilby Engineering Company from Ongar entered and raced many cars in the 50s. From 1960 the company decided to build its own single seaters with son Keith as the main driver. A Climax-engined car was built in 1960, followed by a BRM V8 version in 1962, the year in which the firm wound up.

Totals	GPs	Starts	Points	Poles	F.Laps	Wins			
	3	3	-	-	-	-			
Seasons							Colour	Main Driver(s)	
1961	1	1	-	-	-	-	green	Greene	
1962	1	1	-	-	-	-	green	Greene	
1963	1	1	-	-	-	-	green	Raby (privateer)	
Models							Year(s)	Chief Designer	Engine
(61)	1	1	-	-	-	-	61	L Terry	Climax
(62)	2	2	-	-	-	-	62-63	L Terry	BRM

GORDINI (F)

Principal: Amédée Gordini.
Base: Paris.
Founded: 1945.

Amédée Gordini built his first Simca-FIAT based single seater in 1946 at his Boulevard Victor workshop. These were developed into 1.5-litre versions, known as Simca-Gordinis. This collaboration ended in 1951, and from then on the Paris-based concern dropped the Simca connection from its cars. Always struggling financially, the team faded away in the late fifties, while Amédée began experimental work for Renault.

Totals	GPs	Starts	Points	Poles	F.Laps	Wins		Colour	Main Driver(s)	
	40	127	30.1	-	1	-				
Seasons								Colour	Main Driver(s)	
1950	3	5	3	-	-	-		blue	Manzon, Trintignant	
1951	4	13	-	-	-	-		blue	Manzon, Trintignant, Simon	
1952	7	28	17	-	-	-		blue	Manzon, Trintignant, Behra	
1953	8	28	4	-	-	-		blue	Trintignant, Behra, Schell	
1954	8	25	4.1	-	1	-		blue	Behra, Bucci, Pilette	
1955	5	15	-	-	-	-		blue	Manzon, Pollet, da Silva Ramos	
1956	5	13	2	-	-	-		blue	Manzon, da Silva Ramos, Pilette	
Models								Year(s)	Chief Designer	Engine
T11	2	2	-	-	-	-		51-52	A Gordini	4s
T15	14	26	5	-	-	-		50-53	A Gordini	4s
T16	31	88	25.1	-	1	-		52-56	A Gordini	6
T16S	1	1	-	-	-	-		52	A Gordini	6
T32	6	10	-	-	-	-		55-56	A Gordini	8

HESKETH (GB)

Principal: Lord Alexander Hesketh.
Base: Easton Neston, nr Towcester, Northamptonshire.
Founded: 1972.

Lord Alexander Hesketh set up the team in 1972 from his stately home Easton Neston. Quickly rising from Formula 3 to a Formula 1 March in 1973, the team entered as a constructor the following year. At the end of 1975, struggling without sponsorship, Lord Hesketh called a halt, although Anthony Horsley the former team manager, continued a few years more on a rent-a-drive basis.

Totals	GPs	Starts	Points	Poles	F.Laps	Wins		Sponsor(s)/(Colour)	Main Driver(s)	
	52	73	48	-	1	1				
Seasons								Sponsor(s)/(Colour)	Main Driver(s)	
1974	13	13	15	-	-	-		(white)	Hunt	
1975	14	25	33	-	1	1		(white)	Hunt, Lunger	
1976	12	17	-	-	-	-		Rizla, Penthouse	Ertl, Edwards	
1977	12	17	-	-	-	-		Rizla, Penthouse	Ertl, Keegan	
1978	1	1	-	-	-	-		Olympus	Cheever	
Models								Year(s)	Chief Designer	Engine
308	27	36	43	-	1	1		74-75	H Postlethwaite	Ford Cosworth
308C	2	2	5	-	-	-		75	H Postlethwaite	Ford Cosworth
308D	12	17	-	-	-	-		76	H Postlethwaite	Ford Cosworth
308E	13	18	-	-	-	-		77-78	F Dernie	Ford Cosworth

HILL (GB)

Principal: Graham Hill.
Base: Feltham, Middlesex.
Founded: 1972.

Graham Hill started his own team from a Feltham factory unit in 1973. Initially using a Shadow chassis, the team moved on to build Lola chassis in 1974. By the following year, the Lola T370 had evolved into the T371 and further modifications justified the car to be renamed the first Hill – GH1. The following year's GH2 model was undergoing winter testing at Paul Ricard when tragedy struck the team. On 29 November, the plane which Graham Hill was piloting, crashed on Arkley Golf Course, killing all six team members on board, including his promising young driver, Tony Brise.

Totals	GPs	Starts	Points	Poles	F.Laps	Wins		Sponsor(s)	Main Driver(s)	
	10	19	3	-	-	-				
Seasons								Sponsor(s)	Main Driver(s)	
1975	10	19	3	-	-	-		Embassy	Brise, Jones	
Models								Year(s)	Chief Designer	Engine
GH1	10	19	3	-	-	-		75	A Smallman	Ford Cosworth

HONDA (J)

Principal: Soichiro Honda.
Base: Tokyo (European base: Amsterdam/Slough).
Founded: 1948.

Honda became world leaders in motorcycle production and racing, and by 1962 their attention had turned to cars. A low profile entrance was arranged with engineer Yoshio Nakamura and a new base in Amsterdam. From 1967, John Surtees assumed responsibility for the racing side and moved the team base to Slough, enlisting the help of Lola's Eric Broadley. The new RA300 (dubbed Hondola) won first time out, but tragedy struck the following year when Jo Schlesser was killed in the air-cooled V8 model. Honda's first Formula 1 entry came to a sad end but it would return in glory during the 80s, supplying engines in the turbo years. At the end of 2004 Honda bought a larger share of the BAR team with a possible takeover in coming years.

Totals	GPs	Starts	Points	Poles	F.Laps	Wins				
	35	46	50	1	2	2				
Seasons							Colour	Main Driver(s)		
1964	3	3	-	-	-	-	white	Bucknum		
1965	8	14	13	-	-	1	white	Ginther, Bucknum		
1966	3	5	3	-	1	-	white	Ginther, Bucknum		
1967	9	9	20	-	-	1	white	Surtees		
1968	12	15	14	1	1	-	white	Surtees, Schlesser		
Models							Year(s)	Chief Designer	Engine	
RA271	3	3	-	-	-	-	64	Y Nakamura	V12	
RA272	8	14	13	-	-	1	65	Y Nakamura	V12	
RA273	9	11	11	-	1	-	66-67	Y Nakamura	V12	
RA300	4	4	12	-	-	1	67-68	E Broadley	V12	
RA301	11	13	14	1	1	-	68	Y Nakamura	V12	
RA302	1	1	-	-	-	-	68	Y Nakamura	V8	

HWM (GB)

Principals: John Heath, George Abecassis.
Base: Walton-on-Thames, Surrey.
Founded: 1948.

In 1946 George Abecassis and John Heath bought a garage together and went racing with Alta-engined offset cars as HWM (Hersham & Walton Motors). Single seaters were produced from 1951 and this small team travelled Europe entering as many races as they could. For 1953, the car was lower, causing a different appearance in the once upright front grille. From the start of the 2.5-litre formula, the team began to concentrate on sports car racing, but John Heath was killed in the 1956 Mille Miglia and George Abecassis ended the operation soon after.

Totals	GPs	Starts	Points	Poles	F.Laps	Wins				
	14	43	2	-	-	-				
Seasons							Colour	Main Driver(s)		
1951	1	2	-	-	-	-	green	Abecassis, Moss		
1952	6	22	2	-	-	-	green	Macklin, Collins, Frère		
1953	6	18	-	-	-	-	green	Macklin, Collins, Frère		
1954	1	1	-	-	-	-	green	Macklin		
1955	-	-	-	-	-	-	green	Whiteaway (privateer)		
Models							Year(s)	Chief Designer	Engine	
(51)	2	3	-	-	-	-	51-52	J Heath	Alta	
(52)	6	21	2	-	-	-	52	J Heath	Alta	
(53)	7	19	-	-	-	-	53-54	J Heath	Alta	

JAGUAR (GB)

Principals: Neil Ressler/Bobby Rahal/Niki Lauda/Tony Purnell.
Base: Milton Keynes, Buckinghamshire.
Founded: 1935.

The name Jaguar first appeared in 1935 as a new model name in the Coventry based SS concern, but became synonymous with luxury and prestige sporting cars post-war. During the 1950s Jaguar was a dominant name in sports car racing with five wins at Le Mans, followed by a welcome victorious return in the late 1980s. Jaguar became part of the Ford empire and when the Stewart team was sold to Ford in June 1999 it was soon clear that the Jaguar name would emerge in its first attempt at the F1 World Championship. After a tricky first season, the Ford hierarchy brought in Bobby Rahal and then Niki Lauda in an attempt to capture the success it enjoyed in sports car racing. Further personnel changes saw Tony Purnell brought in to oversee the operation in 2003 but the team never lived up to its promise and was bought out by Red Bull at the end of 2004.

Totals	GPs	Starts	Points	Poles	F.Laps	Wins		
	85	170	49	-	-	-		
Seasons							Sponsor(s)	Main Driver(s)
2000	17	34	4	-	-	-	HSBC,Beck's	Irvine,Herbert
2001	17	34	9	-	-	-	HSBC,Beck's	Irvine,de la Rosa
2002	17	34	8	-	-	-	HSBC,Beck's	Irvine,de la Rosa
2003	16	32	18	-	-	-	HSBC	Webber,Pizzonia/Wilson
2004	18	36	10	-	-	-	HSBC	Webber,Klien
Models							Year(s)	Chief Designer	Engine
R1	17	34	4	-	-	-	00	G Anderson	Ford Cosworth
R2	17	34	9	-	-	-	01	J Russell	Ford Cosworth
R3	17	34	8	-	-	-	02	J Russell	Ford Cosworth
R4	16	32	18	-	-	-	03	x	Ford Cosworth
R5	18	36	10	-	-	-	04	x	Ford Cosworth

JBW (GB)

Principal: Brian Naylor.
Base: Stockport, Cheshire.
Founded: 1957.

Stockport motor dealer Brian Naylor, arranged for his chief mechanic Fred Wilkinson to build a Lotus-based sports car in the late 50s, moving on to a Cooper-based single seater in 1959, which was succeeded by a further model in 1961. The name was a combination of Naylor's initials J B and Wilkinson's surname.

Totals	GPs	Starts	Points	Poles	F.Laps	Wins		
	5	5	-	-	-	-		
Seasons							Colour	Main Driver(s)
1959	1	1	-	-	-	-	green	Naylor
1960	3	3	-	-	-	-	green	Naylor
1961	1	1	-	-	-	-	green	Naylor
Models							Year(s)	Chief Designer	Engine
(59)	4	4	-	-	-	-	59-60	F Wilkinson	Maserati
(61)	1	1	-	-	-	-	61	F Wilkinson	Climax

JORDAN (IRL/GB)

Principal: Eddie Jordan.
Base: Silverstone, Northamptonshire.
Founded: 1983.

Irishman Eddie Jordan followed up a successful racing career as an entrant, to become a manager of promising talent. After Formula 3 from 1983 to 1987 the team progressed swiftly through Formula 3000 in 1988-90, to make an impressive impact on Formula 1 in 1991. Based at Silverstone, the team moved into its new factory just across the road from the circuit gates at the beginning of 1992. After a glorious 1999 season, when the yellow cars finished third in the championship, Eddie Jordan found it harder to compete as a private owner and finally sold out to the Midland group in early 2005, with the Jordan name retained for one last season.

Totals	GPs	Starts	Points	Poles	F.Laps	Wins		
	250	491	291	2	2	4		
Seasons							Sponsor(s)	Main Driver(s)
1991	16	31	13	-	1	-	7UP, Fuji Film	de Cesaris, Gachot
1992	16	28	1	-	-	-	Sasol, Barclay	Modena, Gugelmin
1993	16	31	3	-	-	-	Sasol, Barclay	Barrichello, Boutsen
1994	16	30	28	1	-	-	Sasol, Arisco	Barrichello, Irvine
1995	17	34	21	-	-	-	Total, Peugeot	Barrichello, Irvine
1996	16	32	22	-	-	-	B&H, Total	Barrichello, Brundle
1997	17	34	33	-	1	-	B&H, Total	Fisichella, R Schumacher
1998	16	32	34	-	-	1	B&H, MasterCard	Hill, R Schumacher
1999	16	32	61	1	-	2	B&H, MasterCard	Hill, Frentzen
2000	17	34	17	-	-	-	B&H, MasterCard	Frentzen, Trulli
2001	17	34	19	-	-	-	B&H, Deutsche Post	Frentzen, Trulli
2002	17	33	9	-	-	-	DHL, Deutsche Post	Fisichella, Sato
2003	16	32	13	-	-	1	B&H, CCTV	Fisichella, Firman
2004	18	36	5	-	-	-	B&H	Heidfeld, Pantano
2005	19	38	12	-	-	-	B&H, Tata	Karthikeyan, Monteiro
Models							Year(s)	Chief Designer	Engine
191	16	31	13	-	1	-	91	G Anderson	Ford Cosworth
192	16	28	1	-	-	-	92	G Anderson	Yamaha
193	16	31	3	-	-	-	93	G Anderson	Hart
194	16	30	28	1	-	-	94	G Anderson	Hart
195	17	34	21	-	-	-	95	G Anderson	Peugeot
196	16	32	22	-	-	-	96	G Anderson	Peugeot
197	17	34	33	-	1	-	97	G Anderson	Peugeot
198	16	32	34	-	-	1	98	G Anderson	Mugen Honda
199	16	32	61	1	-	2	99	M Gascoyne	Mugen Honda
EJ10	17	34	17	-	-	-	00	M Gascoyne	Mugen Honda
EJ11	17	34	19	-	-	-	01	T Holloway	Honda
EJ12	17	33	9	-	-	-	02	E Hamidy	Honda
EJ13	16	32	13	-	-	1	03	J McQuilliam	Ford Cosworth
EJ14	18	36	5	-	-	-	04	J McQuilliam	Ford Cosworth
EJ15-B	19	38	12	-	-	-	05	J McQuilliam	Toyota

(B & H = Benson & Hedges)

KAUHSEN (D)

Willi Kauhsen built Formula 2 cars in 1977 and went on to create five Formula 1 chassis – the WK – designed by Klaus Kapitza which passed onto the Merzario team after unsuccessful attempts to qualify in the early part of the 1979 season.

KLENK (D)

Principal: Hans Klenk.
Base: Stuttgart.
Founded: 1953.

One time Mercedes test driver and talented engineer, Hans Klenk produced his own special along Veritas lines. It was a typical BMW-based single seater, with a noticeably large intake bulge in the bonnet.

Totals	GPs	Starts	Points	Poles	F.Laps	Wins			
	1	1	-	-	-	-			
Seasons							Colour	Main Driver(s)	
1954	1	1	-	-	-	-	silver	Helfrich	
Models							Year(s)	Chief Designer	Engine
Meteor	1	1	-	-	-	-	54	H Klenk	BMW

KOJIMA (J)

Principal: Matsuhisa Kojima.
Base: Kyoto.

Matsuhisa Kojima, banana importer and moto-cross rider, ran this engineering firm concentrating on Japanese motorsport events. Two versions of a Formula 1 design were produced for the Japanese Grands Prix of the mid-seventies and they equipped themselves well in their home events.

Totals	GPs	Starts	Points	Poles	F.Laps	Wins			
	2	3	-	-	-	-			
Seasons							Sponsor(s)/(Colour)	Main Driver(s)	
1976	1	1	-	-	-	-	(black)	Hasemi	
1977	1	2	-	-	-	-	Uni-Pex	Hoshino, Takahara	
Models							Year(s)	Chief Designer	Engine
KE007	1	1	-	-	-	-	76	M Ono	Ford Cosworth
KE009	1	2	-	-	-	-	77	M Ono	Ford Cosworth

KURTIS KRAFT (USA)

Principal: Frank Kurtis.
Base: Glendale, California.
Founded: 1941 (first Indy entry).

Californian, Frank Kurtis, built front-engined roadsters for Indianapolis and midgets for US-style oval racing. One such design was entered for the first World Championship USA GP in an attempt at an early grand prix versus IndyCar showdown, but was clearly unsuitable for the demands.

Totals	GPs	Starts	Points	Poles	F.Laps	Wins			
	1	1	-	-	-	-			
Seasons							Sponsor(s)	Main Driver(s)	
1959	1	1	-	-	-	-	Leader Cards	Ward	
Models							Year(s)	Chief Designer	Engine
Midget	1	1	-	-	-	-	59	F Kurtis	Offenhauser

LAMBORGHINI (I)

Principal: Carlo Patrucco.
Base: Modena.
Founded: 1963 (car manufacturer).

Originally tractor manufacturers, Lamborghini built road going sports cars in 1963 and were taken over by Chrysler in 1987. After supplying engines to Larrousse, Lola and Lotus, president Carlo Patrucco decided to create a complete package with the remains of the abandoned Glas project. Modena Team was formed in 1990, with Mauro Forghieri as co-ordinator and the chassis renamed as Lambo, although it only raced at this level for one difficult season.

Totals	GPs	Starts	Points	Poles	F.Laps	Wins			
	6	6	-	-	-	-			
Seasons							Sponsor(s)	Main Driver(s)	
1991	6	6	-	-	-	-	Central Park	Larini, van de Poele	
Models							Year(s)	Chief Designer	Engine
291	6	6	-	-	-	-	91	M Forghieri	V12

LANCIA (I)

Principal: Gianni Lancia.
Base: Torìno.
Founded: 1906.

Upon the death of Vincenzo Lancia, his son Gianni formed plans for a racing programme, initially with sports cars. Financial problems led to FIAT taking over the company in 1955 and handing the cars to Ferrari, which continued to modify and race them as the 801. Lancia went on to represent FIAT in rally and sports cars.

Totals	GPs	Starts	Points	Poles	F.Laps	Wins			
	4	10	9	2	1	-			
Seasons							Colour	Main Driver(s)	
1954	1	2	1	1	1	-	red	Ascari, Villoresi	
1955	3	8	8	1	-	-	red	Ascari, Villoresi, Castellotti	
Models							Year(s)	Chief Designer	Engine
D50	4	10	9	2	1	-	54-55	V Jano	V8

LARROUSSE (F)

Principal: Gérard Larrousse.
Base: Toulon.
Founded: 1986.

After five years as an entrant of Lola chassis, former racer Gérard Larrousse took the plunge into Formula 1 as a constructor with a brand new chassis designed by Robin Herd's team in the UK. Funded by Venturi Industrie of France, the new cars were known as Venturi-Larrousse during the debut year. Venturi withdrew its financial support at the end of 1992 and the cars were then known simply as Larrousse. Although entered for 1995 with nominated drivers Bouchut and Hélary, the team never showed and quietly faded away.

Totals	GPs	Starts	Points	Poles	F.Laps	Wins			
	48	93	6	-	-	-			
Seasons							Sponsor(s)	Main Driver(s)	
1992	16	30	1	-	-	-	Cabin, Central Park	Gachot, Katayama	
1993	16	32	3	-	-	-	Central Park, Charro	Comas, Alliot	
1994	16	31	2	-	-	-	Tourtel, Kronenbourg	Comas, Beretta	
Models							Year(s)	Chief Designer	Engine
LC92	16	30	1	-	-	-	92	T Belli	Lamborghini
LH93	16	32	3	-	-	-	93	T Belli	Lamborghini
LH94	16	31	2	-	-	-	94	T Belli	Ford Cosworth

LDS (ZA)

Principal: Doug Serrurier.
Base: Alberton, Transvaal, South Africa.
Founded: 1960.

LDS was named after its South African founder, speedway rider, Louis Douglas Serrurier who built his first car, the Speedy Engineering Special in 1956. Various LDS models were built for local races, the Mk 1 and 2 being based on Cooper designs, whilst the Mk 3B was based on the Brabham BT11.

Totals	GPs	Starts	Points	Poles	F.Laps	Wins			
	5	6	-	-	-	-			
Seasons							Colour	Main Driver(s)	
1962	1	1	-	-	-	-	blue	Serrurier	
1963	1	2	-	-	-	-	blue	Serrurier, Tingle	
1965	1	1	-	-	-	-	green	Tingle	
1967	1	1	-	-	-	-	green	Tingle	
1968	1	1	-	-	-	-	brown	Tingle	
Models							Year(s)	Chief Designer	Engine
Mk 1	2	2	-	-	-	-	63-65	D Serrurier	Alfa Romeo
Mk 2	2	2	-	-	-	-	62-63	D Serrurier	Alfa Romeo
Mk 3B	2	2	-	-	-	-	67-68	D Serrurier	Climax, Repco

LEC (GB)

Principal: David Purley.
Base: Bognor Regis, West Sussex.
Founded: 1973.

David Purley commissioned Mike Pilbeam to design a new grand prix car which was built at his father's Lec refrigeration firm. The project came to an abrupt end when Purley was lucky to survive a massive practice accident at Silverstone. When fully recovered another car was used in domestic racing.

Totals	GPs	Starts	Points	Poles	F.Laps	Wins			
	3	3	-	-	-	-			
Seasons							Sponsor(s)	Main Driver(s)	
1977	3	3	-	-	-	-	Lec	Purley	
Models							Year(s)	Chief Designer	Engine
CRP1	3	3	-	-	-	-	77	M Pilbeam	Ford Cosworth

LIFE (I)

Ernesto Vita's unique W12 engine was mated to the abandoned First chassis to create this 1990 entrant (the L190), which never managed to pass through pre-qualifying, before trying out a Judd engine with equally poor results.

LIGIER (F) latterly Prost (1997 to 2001)

Principal: Guy Ligier/Alain Prost.
Base: Abrest-Vichy/Magny-Cours (1989)/Guyancourt (1997).
Founded: 1969.

Successful businessman and sportsman, Guy Ligier, initially built electric road cars until the JS3 became the first Ligier racing car in 1971. The model number JS is used in memory of Guy Ligier's good friend Jo Schlesser. The company was taken over by Cyril de Rouvre in 1993 but after his arrest, Benetton's Flavio Briatore took control during 1994, finally buying out Guy Ligier's remaining 15% stake in August 1996. Alain Prost took over the team in its entirity from the 1997 season and with no objections from his rival teams, renamed this very French operation. Within weeks of the opening race of 2002, it was announced that the long battle against bankruptcy had failed.

Totals	GPs	Starts	Points	Poles	F.Laps	Wins
	409	742	423	9	10	9

Seasons							Sponsor(s)	Main Driver(s)
1976	16	16	20	1	1	-	Gitanes	Laffite
1977	17	18	18	-	1	1	Gitanes	Laffite
1978	16	16	19	-	-	-	Gitanes	Laffite
1979	15	30	61	4	3	3	Gitanes	Laffite,Depailler/Ickx
1980	14	28	66	3	3	2	Gitanes	Laffite,Pironi
1981	15	28	44	1	1	2	Gitanes,Talbot	Laffite,Tambay
1982	15	29	20	-	-	-	Gitanes,Talbot	Laffite,Cheever
1983	15	28	-	-	-	-	Gitanes,Loto	Jarier,Boesel
1984	16	31	3	-	-	-	Gitanes,Loto	Hesnault,de Cesaris
1985	15	30	23	-	1	-	Gitanes,Candy	Laffite,de Cesaris
1986	16	32	29	-	-	-	Gitanes,Loto	Laffite,Arnoux
1987	15	28	1	-	-	-	Gitanes,Loto	Arnoux,Ghinzani
1988	14	24	-	-	-	-	Gitanes,Loto	Arnoux,Johansson
1989	14	21	3	-	-	-	Gitanes,Loto	Arnoux,Grouillard
1990	16	30	-	-	-	-	Gitanes,Loto	Alliot,Larini
1991	16	29	-	-	-	-	Gitanes	Boutsen,Comas
1992	16	31	6	-	-	-	Gitanes	Boutsen,Comas
1993	16	32	23	-	-	-	Gitanes	Brundle,Blundell
1994	16	32	13	-	-	-	Gitanes	Bernard,Panis
1995	17	33	24	-	-	-	Gitanes	Brundle,Panis
1996	16	32	15	-	-	1	Gauloises,Parmalat	Panis,Diniz
1997	17	34	21	-	-	-	Gauloises	Panis,Nakano
1998	16	32	1	-	-	-	Gauloises	Panis,Trulli
1999	16	31	9	-	-	-	Gauloises	Panis,Trulli
2000	17	33	-	-	-	-	Gauloises,Yahoo!	Alesi,Heidfeld
2001	17	34	4	-	-	-	PSN,Adecco	Alesi,Burti

Models							Year(s)	Chief Designer	Engine
JS5	16	16	20	1	1	-	76	G Ducarouge	Matra
JS7	22	23	24	-	1	1	77-78	G Ducarouge	Matra
JS9	11	11	13	-	-	-	78	G Ducarouge	Matra
JS11	15	30	61	4	3	3	79	G Ducarouge	Ford Cosworth
JS11/15	14	28	66	3	3	2	80	G Ducarouge	Ford Cosworth
JS17-B	21	40	55	1	1	2	81-82	G Ducarouge	Matra
JS19	9	17	9	-	-	-	82	M Beaujon	Matra
JS21	15	28	-	-	-	-	83	M Beaujon	Ford Cosworth
JS23	16	31	3	-	-	-	84	M Beaujon	Renault t
JS25	15	30	23	-	1	-	85	M Beaujon	Renault t
JS27	16	32	29	-	-	-	86	M Têtu	Renault t
JS29B,C	15	28	1	-	-	-	87	M Têtu	Megatron t
JS31	14	24	-	-	-	-	88	M Têtu	Judd
JS33-B	30	51	3	-	-	-	89-90	M Beaujon	Ford Cosworth
JS35-B	16	29	-	-	-	-	91	M Beaujon	Lamborghini
JS37	16	31	6	-	-	-	92	F Dernie	Renault
JS39-B	32	64	36	-	-	-	93-94	G Ducarouge	Renault
JS41	17	33	24	-	-	-	95	F Dernie	Mugen Honda

Models	GPs	Starts	Points	Poles	F.Laps	Wins	Year(s)	Chief Designer	Engine
JS43	16	32	15	-	-	1	96	A de Cortanze	Mugen Honda
JS45	17	34	21	-	-	-	97	L Bigois	Mugen Honda
AP01-B	16	32	1	-	-	-	98	B Dudot	Peugeot
AP02	16	31	9	-	-	-	99	A Jenkins	Peugeot
AP03	17	33	-	-	-	-	00	A Jenkins	Peugeot
AP04	17	34	4	-	-	-	01	A Jenkins	Acer

LOLA (GB)

Principal: Eric Broadley.
Base: Bromley/Slough/Huntingdon.
Founded: 1957.

Eric Broadley built his first sports car behind 137 High Street, Bromley, and the model was so quick he was soon in demand to build copies. The company went on to produce cars for many categories of racing, its most well known successes being in IndyCar and sports car racing. Very probably the most successful racing car manufacturer ever, Lola have never really tackled Formula 1 full on. The first foray came at the instigation of the Yeoman Credit team, and later that decade BMW commissioned a chassis that was mainly used in Formula 2. Graham Hill used Lola as a base for his own model in the 70s and Carl Haas named his own Force built cars in deference to his American Lola import agency. The Larrousse team used a Lola design for five seasons with limited success, while the Scuderia Italia venture of 1993 petered out before the year's end. In spite of this, Lola re-entered under their own name in a unique sponsorship deal with MasterCard which floundered at the second race of the 1997 season.

Totals	GPs	Starts	Points	Poles	F.Laps	Wins			
	149	245	45	1	-	-			
Seasons							**Sponsor(s)/(Colour)**	**Main Driver(s)**	
1962	9	16	19	1	-	-	(green)	Surtees, Salvadori	
1963	9	13	-	-	-	-	(green)	Amon, Anderson	
1964-66 did not participate									
1967	1	2	-	-	-	-	(white)	Hahne	
1968	1	1	-	-	-	-	(white)	Hahne	
1969-73 did not participate									
1974	15	27	1	-	-	-	Embassy	Hill, Edwards	
1975	3	5	-	-	-	-	Embassy	Hill, Stommelen	
1976-84 did not participate									
1985	3	3	-	-	-	-	Beatrice	Jones	
1986	16	31	6	-	-	-	Beatrice	Jones, Tambay	
1987	15	18	5	-	-	-	Elkron	Alliot, Dalmas	
1988	16	30	-	-	-	-	Elkron	Alliot, Dalmas	
1989	16	22	1	-	-	-	BP, Rhône-Poulenc	Alliot, Alboreto	
1990	16	32	11	-	-	-	Espo	Bernard, Suzuki	
1991	15	24	2	-	-	-	Toshiba	Bernard, Suzuki	
1992 did not participate									
1993	14	21	-	-	-	-	Chesterfield	Alboreto, Badoer	
1994-96 did not participate									
1997	-	-	-	-	-	-	MasterCard	Sospiri, Rosset	
Models							**Year(s)**	**Chief Designer**	**Engine**
Mk 4-A	18	29	19	1	-	-	62-63	E Broadley	Climax
T100	1	2	-	-	-	-	67	E Broadley	BMW
T102	1	1	-	-	-	-	68	E Broadley	BMW
T370,371	18	32	1	-	-	-	74-75	E Broadley	Ford Cosworth
THL1	6	8	-	-	-	-	85-86	N Oatley	Hart t
THL2	14	26	6	-	-	-	86	N Oatley	Ford Cosworth t
LC87	15	18	5	-	-	-	87	R Bellamy	Ford Cosworth
LC88-B	17	31	-	-	-	-	88-89	C Murphy	Ford Cosworth, Lamborghini
LC89	17	25	1	-	-	-	89-90	G Ducarouge	Lamborghini
90	14	28	11	-	-	-	90	C Murphy	Lamborghini
L91	15	24	2	-	-	-	91	E Broadley	Ford Cosworth
T93/30	14	21	-	-	-	-	93	E Broadley	Ferrari
T97/30	-	-	-	-	-	-	97	E Broadley	Ford Cosworth

LOTUS (GB)

Principal: Colin Chapman/Peter Warr/Peter Collins.
Base: Hornsey, London/Cheshunt, Hertfordshire/Ketteringham Hall, Norfolk.
Founded: 1952.

Colin Chapman created Lotus Engineering, later forming Team Lotus in 1954, building sports cars from a small workshop at 7 Tottenham Lane, Hornsey, North London. After design work for Vanwall, Chapman produced his own single-seaters that soon revolutionised grand prix racing. On the back of Cooper's rear engine designs, Chapman re-introduced the monocoque chassis with the 25, as well as introducing Ford Cosworth to power the all conquering Lotus 49. The 72 emphasised a new era in lay down designs, removing the bulky radiators to side pods and in so doing produced the streamlined chisel nose. Ground Effects was the next big breakthrough with the first real effective designs in the 78 and 79. Unfortunately, the twin chassis 88 got no further than practice, falling foul of technical regulations. Colin Chapman died suddenly in December 1982, and under the guidance of Peter Warr the team carried on, but apart from the input of Ayrton Senna, never looked like regular winners again. Peter Collins led a buy-out of the famous marque in 1991 but at the end of 1994 the receivers were called in and the team folded in January 1995.

Constructors' Championships: 7 (1963,65,68,70,72,73,78). **Drivers' Championships:** 6 (1963,65,68,70,72,78).

Totals	GPs	Starts	Points	Poles	F.Laps	Wins		
	491	1237	1514	107	71	79		
Seasons							Sponsor(s)/(Colour)	Main Driver(s)
1958	9	19	3	-	-	-	(green)	Allison,G Hill
1959	8	17	5	-	-	-	(green)	G Hill,Ireland
1960	8	30	52	4	3	2	(green)	Ireland,Clark,Stacey
1961	8	55	44	1	2	3	(green)	Clark,Ireland
1962	9	57	43	6	5	3	(green)	Clark,T Taylor
1963	10	56	78	7	6	7	(green)	Clark*,T Taylor *Champion*
1964	10	46	52	5	4	3	(green)	Clark,Arundell/Spence
1965	10	43	66	6	6	6	(green)	Clark*,Spence *Champion*
1966	9	29	21	2	-	1	(green)	Clark,Arundell
1967	11	30	56	9	7	4	(green)	Clark,G Hill
1968	12	35	75	5	5	5	Gold Leaf	G Hill*,Oliver *Champion*
1969	11	47	59	5	2	2	Gold Leaf	G Hill,Rindt
1970	12	37	70	3	1	6	Gold Leaf	Rindt*,Miles *Champion*
1971	11	24	25	-	-	-	Gold Leaf	Fittipaldi,Wisell
1972	12	27	61	3	-	5	JPS	Fittipaldi*,Walker *Champion*
1973	15	31	107	10	7	7	JPS	Fittipaldi,Peterson
1974	15	33	47	1	2	3	JPS	Peterson,Ickx
1975	14	30	9	-	-	-	JPS	Peterson,Ickx
1976	16	30	32	1	1	1	JPS	Andretti,Nilsson
1977	17	33	67	7	5	5	JPS	Andretti,Nilsson
1978	16	41	116	12	7	8	JPS	Andretti*,Peterson *Champion*
1979	15	39	39	-	-	-	Martini,Essex	Andretti,Reutemann
1980	14	30	14	-	-	-	Essex,Tissot	Andretti,de Angelis
1981	14	27	22	-	-	-	JPS,Essex	de Angelis,Mansell
1982	15	29	30	-	-	1	JPS	de Angelis,Mansell
1983	15	30	12	1	1	-	JPS	de Angelis,Mansell
1984	16	32	47	2	-	-	JPS,Elf	de Angelis,Mansell
1985	16	32	71	8	3	3	JPS,Olympus	Senna,de Angelis
1986	16	31	58	8	-	2	JPS,De Longhi	Senna,Dumfries
1987	16	32	64	1	3	2	Camel,De Longhi	Senna,Nakajima
1988	16	30	23	-	-	-	Camel	Piquet,Nakajima
1989	15	28	15	-	1	-	Camel,Epson	Piquet,Nakajima
1990	16	30	3	-	-	-	Camel	Warwick,Donnelly
1991	16	23	3	-	-	-	Tamiya,Komatsu	Häkkinen,Bailey/Herbert
1992	16	31	13	-	-	-	Castrol,Komatsu	Häkkinen,Herbert
1993	16	31	12	-	-	-	Castrol,Hitachi	Zanardi,Herbert
1994	16	32	-	-	-	-	Loctite,Shionogi	Lamy/Zanardi,Herbert

JPS = John Player Special.

Models	GPs	Starts	Points	Poles	F.Laps	Wins	Year(s)	Chief Designer	Engine
12	8	11	3	-	-	-	58	C Chapman	Climax
16	16	28	5	-	-	-	58-60	C Chapman	Climax
18,18/21	19	72	73	5	4	4	60-62	C Chapman	Climax, Maserati
21	12	20	24	-	1	1	61-63	C Chapman	Climax
22	1	1	-	-	-	-	63-65	C Chapman	Ford
24	23	72	16	-	-	-	62-64	C Chapman	Climax, BRM
25	49	101	156	18	14	14	62-67	C Chapman	Climax, BRM
33	26	46	84	8	8	5	64-67	C Chapman	Climax, BRM
43	5	6	9	-	-	1	66-67	C Chapman	BRM
44	1	2	-	-	-	-	66	C Chapman	Ford Cosworth
48	1	1	-	-	-	-	67	C Chapman	Ford Cosworth
49-B,C	41	113	205	19	14	12	67-70	M Phillippe	Ford Cosworth
56B	3	3	-	-	-	-	71	M Phillippe	Pratt & Whitney
59B	1	1	-	-	-	-	69	M Phillippe	Ford Cosworth
63	7	8	-	-	-	-	69	M Phillippe	Ford Cosworth
69	2	2	-	-	-	-	71	M Phillippe	Ford Cosworth
72-B,C,D,E,F	74	149	295	17	9	20	70-75	M Phillippe	Ford Cosworth
76	7	10	3	-	-	-	74	R Bellamy	Ford Cosworth
77	16	30	32	1	1	1	76	R Bellamy	Ford Cosworth
78	31	54	106	9	7	7	77-78	R Bellamy	Ford Cosworth
79	26	56	112	10	5	6	78-79	M Ogilvie	Ford Cosworth
80	3	3	4	-	-	-	79	M Ogilvie	Ford Cosworth
81-B	18	38	23	-	-	-	80-81	M Ogilvie	Ford Cosworth
87-B	11	21	13	-	-	-	81-82	M Ogilvie	Ford Cosworth
91	15	28	30	-	-	1	82-83	M Ogilvie	Ford Cosworth
92	8	8	1	-	-	-	83	M Ogilvie	Ford Cosworth
93T	7	7	-	-	-	-	83	M Ogilvie	Renault t
94T	7	14	11	1	1	-	83	G Ducarouge	Renault t
95T	16	32	47	2	-	-	84	G Ducarouge	Renault t
97T	16	32	71	8	3	3	85	G Ducarouge	Renault t
98T	16	31	58	8	-	2	86	G Ducarouge	Renault t
99T	16	32	64	1	3	2	87	G Ducarouge	Honda t
100T	16	30	23	-	-	-	88	G Ducarouge	Honda t
101	15	28	15	-	1	-	89	F Dernie	Judd
102-B,D	36	61	8	-	-	-	90-92	F Dernie	Lamborghini, Judd, Ford Cosworth
107-B,C	34	64	23	-	-	-	92-94	C Murphy	Ford Cosworth, Mugen Honda
109	12	22	-	-	-	-	94	C Murphy	Mugen Honda

The Lotus 20-Ford did not pre-qualify in South Africa 1965.

LYNCAR (GB)

Principal: Martin Slater.
Base: Slough.
Founded: 1971.

Martin Slater built his first Lyncar for Formula Atlantic in 1971 and successful customer John Nicholson commissioned a Formula 1 car for the 1974 season. After the 1975 season, the car passed into other hands and Nicholson concentrated on his successful engine business in Finchampstead.

Totals	GPs	Starts	Points	Poles	F.Laps	Wins		
	1	1	-	-	-	-		
Seasons							Sponsor(s)	Main Driver(s)
1974	-	-	-	-	-	-	Pinch	Nicholson
1975	1	1	-	-	-	-	Pinch	Nicholson
Models							Year(s)	Chief Designer	Engine
006	1	1	-	-	-	-	75	M Slater	Ford Cosworth

MAKI (J)

The F101 and F102-A models designed by Kenji Mimura, never managed to start a race despite noble efforts in 1974, '75 and '76.

MARCH (GB)

Principals: Robin Herd, Max Mosley.
Base: Bicester, Oxfordshire.
Founded: 1969.

Created as an assault on the Formula 1 establishment by a quartet that gave the car its name; Max Mosley, Alan Rees, Graham Coaker and Robin Herd. They established a works team in F1 and produced customer cars for most of the top single-seater formulae. Mosley left the team at the end of 1977, while Herd continued alone, building customer cars including a very productive period in IndyCar Racing. March became a public limited company at the time of its third F1 entry and sold the F1 operation to the sponsors Leyton House in 1989, with new owner Akira Akagi assuming control. After a financial scandal in Japan, the team resumed the familar March name once again in 1992 and under the guidence of Ken Marrable struggled through one final season.

Totals	GPs	Starts	Points	Poles	F.Laps	Wins		
	227	557	193	5	7	3		
Seasons							Sponsor(s)	Main Driver(s)
1970	13	60	55	3	1	1	STP	Amon, Siffert
1971	11	52	37	-	1	-	STP	Peterson, Soler-Roig
1972	12	62	15	-	-	-	STP	Peterson, Lauda
1973	15	39	14	-	2	-	STP	Jarier, Williamson
1974	15	28	6	-	-	-	Beta	Stuck, Brambilla
1975	14	31	9	1	1	1	Beta	Brambilla, Lombardi
1976	16	53	19	1	1	1	Beta	Brambilla, Peterson, Stuck
1977	16	41	-	-	-	-	Rothmans	Ribeiro, I Scheckter
1978	-	-	-	-	-	-		Neve (privateer)
1979-80 did not participate								
1981	9	9	-	-	-	-	Guinness	Daly, Salazar (RAM)
1982	13	22	-	-	-	-	Rothmans	Mass, Boesel (RAM)
1983-86 did not participate								
1987	15	15	1	-	-	-	Leyton House	Capelli
1988	16	31	22	-	-	-	Leyton House	Capelli, Gugelmin
1989	16	31	4	-	1	-	Leyton House	Capelli, Gugelmin
1990	14	25	7	-	-	-	Leyton House	Capelli, Gugelmin
1991	16	32	1	-	-	-	Leyton House	Capelli, Gugelmin
1992	16	26	3	-	-	-	Uliveto, Rial	Wendlinger, Belmondo
Models							Year(s)	Chief Designer	Engine
701	16	65	55	3	1	1	70-71	R Herd	Ford Cosworth
711	22	60	40	-	1	-	71-72	R Herd	Ford Cosworth, Alfa Romeo
721-X, G	15	55	12	-	-	-	72-73	R Herd	Ford Cosworth
731	14	35	14	-	2	-	73-74	R Herd	Ford Cosworth
741	18	29	6	-	-	-	74-75	R Herd	Ford Cosworth
751	12	28	9	1	1	1	75	R Herd	Ford Cosworth
761-B	32	90	19	1	1	1	76-77	R Herd	Ford Cosworth
771	4	4	-	-	-	-	77	R Herd	Ford Cosworth
811	9	9	-	-	-	-	81	A Reynard	Ford Cosworth
821	13	22	-	-	-	-	82	A Reynard	Ford Cosworth
871	15	15	1	-	-	-	87	G Coppuck	Ford Cosworth
881	18	35	26	-	-	-	88-89	A Newey	Judd
CG891	14	27	-	-	1	-	89	A Newey	Judd
CG901	14	25	7	-	-	-	90	A Newey	Judd
CG911	32	58	4	-	-	-	91-92	C Murphy	Ilmor

The 781S (1978) and 87P (1987) with Ford Cosworth engines, did not start.

MARTINI (F)

Principal: Tico Martini.
Base: Magny-Cours.
Founded: 1962.

The first car was built in 1963 for the race track base of the Knight brothers' Winfield racing school. The cars designation MK refers to the collaboration between the two businesses. Most French formulae were successfully catered for including Formula 2, until the venture in Formula 1 in 1978. Martini pulled out at year's end and returned to build cars for the French domestic market.

Totals	GPs	Starts	Points	Poles	F.Laps	Wins			
	4	4	-	-	-	-			
Seasons							Sponsor(s)	Main Driver(s)	
1978	4	4	-	-	-	-	Silver Match, RMO	Arnoux	
Models							Year(s)	Chief Designer	Engine
MK23	4	4	-	-	-	-	78	T Martini	Ford Cosworth

MASERATI (I)

Principals: Adolfo and Omer Orsi.
Base: Modena.
Founded: 1914.

Alfieri Maserati (1887-1932) started building cars at his Bologna engineering firm back in 1926; the business also included his brothers Bindo, Ettore and Ernesto. In 1937, Maserati was sold to the Orsi family, and the remaining brothers stayed in a consulting role until returning to Bologna to form OSCA. Maserati was a leading light in the 50s scene and produced one of the greatest cars of the era in the 250F. The factory team withdrew at the end of 1957, but the name returned later as an engine supplier to the Cooper team. The Milano and Platé cars were early refinements of Maserati chassis (4CLT), separate from the factory. Once a part of the Citroën group and now under the FIAT banner the company still produces classic road cars.

Drivers' Championships: 2 (1954*,57). * Fangio also raced a Mercedes-Benz during the season

Totals	GPs	Starts	Points	Poles	F.Laps	Wins			
	68	368	313.4	10	15	9			
Seasons							Colour	Main Driver(s)	
1950	6	31	11	-	-	-	red	Chiron, Rol	
1951	5	12	-	-	-	-	red	de Graffenried, Schell (Platé)	
1952	6	21	8.5	-	1	-	red	Bonetto, Rol, González	
1953	8	40	65.5	2	4	1	red	Fangio, Bonetto, González, Marimón	
1954	8	57	46.4	1	2	2	red	Fangio*, Marimón, Mantovani, Mières *Champion*	
1955	6	39	23	-	1	-	red	Behra, Musso, Mières, Perdisa	
1956	7	60	72	1	3	2	red	Moss, Behra, Perdisa, Godia	
1957	7	54	78	5	3	4	red	Fangio*, Behra, Schell, Menditéguy *Champion*	
1958	10	43	9	1	1	-	red	Gregory, Shelby (Centro Sud)	
1959	3	5	-	-	-	-	red	d'Orey (Centro Sud)	
1960	2	6	-	-	-	-	red	Drake (privateer)	
Models							Year(s)	Chief Designer	Engine
4CL	4	4	-	-	-	-	50-51	E Maserati	4s
4CLT-/48, /50	10	35	9	-	-	-	50-51	A Massimino	4s, OSCA
Milano	4	4	2	-	-	-	50-51	Ruggeri brothers	4s
Platé	3	6	-	-	-	-	52	E Platé	4
A6GCM	23	71	74	2	5	1	52-56	A Massimino	6
250F	43	248	228.4	8	10	8	54-60	G Colombo	6, V12

The Arzani Volpini was a further refinement of the Milano (a non-starter in 1950) and failed to start the 1955 Italian GP.

MATRA (F)

Principal: Jean-Luc Lagardère.
Base: Vichy.
Founded: 1942.

Mécanique Aviation Traction was originally a military hardware company which acquired the René Bonnet car company in 1964. Under the Matra Sports subsidiary they contested Formula 3 in 1965, Formula 2 in 1966, until entering grand prix via the back door of the F2 class. A two pronged attack on the championship was established with Ken Tyrrell's team using a chassis mated to the Ford Cosworth DFV, and the factory producing a variation to take its own V12 engine. Victory eluded the factory operation but the howling V12 engine continued for some time with Shadow and Ligier. Matra withdrew from Formula 1 to continue with its sports car successes for a few more years.

Constructors' Championships: 1 (1969). **Drivers' Championships:** 1 (1969).

Totals	GPs	Starts	Points	Poles	F.Laps	Wins			
	62	118	184	4	12	9			
Seasons							Sponsor(s)/ (Colour)	Main Driver(s)	
1966	1	4	-	-	-	-	(blue)	(F2 class entry only)	
1967	4	5	-	-	-	-	Elf	Beltoise	
1968	12	28	53	-	4	3	Elf	Beltoise, Pescarolo	
1969	11	27	85	2	6	6	Elf	Stewart*, Beltoise (Tyrrell)	*Champion*
1970	13	26	24	-	-	-	Elf	Beltoise, Pescarolo	
1971	10	17	10	1	-	-	Elf	Amon, Beltoise	
1972	11	11	12	1	2	-	Shell	Amon	
Models							Year(s)	Chief Designer	Engine
MS5	2	5	-	-	-	-	66-67	B Boyer	Ford Cosworth, BRM
MS7	6	7	1	-	-	-	67-69	B Boyer	Ford Cosworth
MS9	1	1	-	-	-	-	68	B Boyer	Ford Cosworth
MS10	12	16	54	-	4	4	68-69	B Boyer	Ford Cosworth
MS11	10	12	8	-	1	-	68	B Boyer	V12
MS80	10	19	74	2	5	5	69	B Boyer	Ford Cosworth
MS84	4	4	1	-	-	-	69	B Boyer	Ford Cosworth
MS120-B,C,D	34	54	46	2	2	-	70-72	B Boyer	V12

McLAREN (GB)

Principals: Bruce McLaren, Teddy Mayer, Ron Dennis.
Base: Colnbrook, nr Slough/Woking, Surrey.
Founded: 1963.

Formed initially for Tasman racing, the team built its first sports cars in 1964 and 1965 before Bruce left Cooper to tackle Formula 1 on his own. Initial success turned to tragedy when Bruce was killed testing a Can-Am car at Goodwood in 1970. With the help of Denny Hulme the team struggled on and established itself at the top during the mid 70s. A steady decline left the team floundering as the decade turned to a close, and sponsors Marlboro instigated a merger with Ron Dennis's Project Four Formula 2 operation. Teddy Mayer left soon after, whilst with the help of John Barnard's revolutionary carbon-fibre monocoque, McLaren not only returned to the very top, but led the next major innovation in chassis design. With the departure of Prost and Senna, who scored six championships between them, the team entered a barren period culminating in the loss of the longest running sponsorship deal in Formula 1, switching from Marlboro to West from 1997. McLaren built up a formidable partnership with Mercedes culminating in the constructors' title in 1998 and two drivers' championships before moving to new state-of-the-art facilities in 2004.

Constructors' Championships: 8 (1974,84,85,88,89,90,91,98).
Drivers' Championships: 11 (1974,76,84,85,86,88,89,90,91,98,99).

Totals	GPs	Starts	Points	Poles	F.Laps	Wins		
	595	1243	3139.5	122	126	148		
Seasons							Sponsor(s)/ (Colour)	Main Driver(s)
1966	4	4	3	-	-	-	(white)	McLaren
1967	6	6	3	-	-	-	(red)	McLaren
1968	12	32	59	-	-	3	(orange)	McLaren, Hulme
1969	11	26	49	-	-	1	(orange)	McLaren, Hulme
1970	12	33	36	-	1	-	(orange)	McLaren, Hulme
1971	11	25	13	-	1	-	(orange)	Hulme, Gethin
1972	12	25	66	1	1	1	Yardley	Hulme, Revson

Seasons	GPs	Starts	Points	Poles	F.Laps	Wins	Sponsor(s)/(Colour)	Main Driver(s)
1973	15	35	68	1	3	3	Yardley	Hulme,Revson
1974	15	46	87	2	1	4	Marlboro	Hulme,Fittipaldi* *Champion*
1975	14	28	65	-	2	3	Marlboro	Fittipaldi,Mass
1976	16	32	88	8	3	6	Marlboro	Hunt*,Mass *Champion*
1977	17	46	65	6	3	3	Marlboro	Hunt,Mass
1978	16	48	16	-	-	-	Marlboro	Hunt,Tambay
1979	15	28	15	-	-	-	Marlboro	Watson,Tambay
1980	14	24	11	-	-	-	Marlboro	Watson,Prost
1981	15	29	28	-	1	1	Marlboro	Watson,de Cesaris
1982	15	29	69	-	2	4	Marlboro	Watson,Lauda
1983	14	28	34	-	2	1	Marlboro	Watson,Lauda
1984	16	32	143.5	3	8	12	Marlboro	Prost,Lauda* *Champion*
1985	16	31	90	2	6	6	Marlboro	Prost*,Lauda *Champion*
1986	16	32	96	2	2	4	Marlboro	Prost*,Rosberg *Champion*
1987	16	32	76	-	2	3	Marlboro	Prost,Johansson
1988	16	32	199	15	10	15	Marlboro	Prost,Senna* *Champion*
1989	16	32	141	15	8	10	Marlboro	Prost*,Senna *Champion*
1990	16	32	121	12	5	6	Marlboro	Senna*,Berger *Champion*
1991	16	32	139	10	4	8	Marlboro	Senna*,Berger *Champion*
1992	16	32	99	1	3	5	Marlboro	Senna,Berger
1993	16	32	84	1	1	5	Marlboro	Senna,Andretti
1994	16	32	42	-	-	-	Marlboro	Häkkinen,Brundle
1995	17	33	30	-	-	-	Marlboro	Häkkinen,Blundell
1996	16	32	49	-	-	-	Marlboro	Häkkinen,Coulthard
1997	17	34	63	1	2	3	West,Mobil	Häkkinen,Coulthard
1998	16	32	156	12	9	9	West,Mobil	Häkkinen*,Coulthard *Champion*
1999	16	32	124	11	9	7	West,Mobil	Häkkinen*,Coulthard *Champion*
2000	17	34	152	7	12	7	West,Mobil	Häkkinen,Coulthard
2001	17	33	102	2	6	4	West,Mobil	Häkkinen,Coulthard
2002	17	34	65	-	2	1	West,Mobil	Coulthard,Räikkönen
2003	16	32	142	2	3	2	West,Mobil	Coulthard,Räikkönen
2004	18	36	69	1	2	1	West,Mobil	Coulthard,Räikkönen
2005	18	36	182	7	12	10	West,Mobil	Montoya,Räikkönen

Models	GPs	Starts	Points	Poles	F.Laps	Wins	Year(s)	Chief Designer	Engine
M2B	4	4	3	-	-	-	66	R Herd	Ford,Serenissima
M4B	2	2	3	-	-	-	67	R Herd	BRM
M5A	11	11	3	-	-	-	67-68	R Herd	BRM
M7A,C,D	30	59	106	-	1	4	68-71	R Herd	Ford Cosworth,Alfa Romeo
M9A	1	1	-	-	-	-	69	J Marquart	Ford Cosworth
M14A,D	17	32	35	-	-	-	70-71	J Marquart	Ford Cosworth,Alfa Romeo
M19A,C	25	48	91	1	3	1	71-73	R Bellamy	Ford Cosworth
M23	80	166	319	14	10	16	73-78	G Coppuck	Ford Cosworth
M26	30	64	58	3	1	3	76-79	G Coppuck	Ford Cosworth
M28	9	14	8	-	-	-	79	G Coppuck	Ford Cosworth
M29-F	26	41	17	-	-	-	79-81	G Coppuck	Ford Cosworth
M30	3	3	1	-	-	-	80	G Coppuck	Ford Cosworth
MP4-B,/1C,/1E	42	79	131	-	5	6	81-83	J Barnard	Ford Cosworth,TAG Porsche t
MP4/2-B,C	48	95	329.5	7	16	22	84-86	J Barnard	TAG Porsche t
MP4/3	16	32	76	-	2	3	87	S Nichols	TAG Porsche t
MP4/4	16	32	199	15	10	15	88	S Nichols	Honda t
MP4/5-B	16	64	262	27	13	16	89-90	N Oatley	Honda
MP4/6-B	18	36	148	10	5	8	91-92	N Oatley	Honda
MP4/7A	14	28	90	1	2	5	92	N Oatley	Honda
MP4/8	16	32	84	1	1	5	93	N Oatley	Ford Cosworth
MP4/9	16	32	42	-	-	-	94	N Oatley	Peugeot
MP4/10-B,C	17	33	30	-	-	-	95	N Oatley	Mercedes-Benz
MP4/11-B	16	32	49	-	-	-	96	N Oatley	Mercedes-Benz
MP4-12	17	34	63	1	2	3	97	N Oatley	Mercedes-Benz
MP4-13	16	32	156	12	9	9	98	A Newey	Mercedes-Benz
MP4-14	16	32	124	11	9	7	99	A Newey	Mercedes-Benz
MP4-15	17	34	152	7	12	7	00	A Newey	Mercedes-Benz
MP4-16	17	33	102	2	6	4	01	A Newey	Mercedes-Benz
MP4-17-D	33	66	207	2	5	3	02-03	A Newey	Mercedes-Benz
MP4-19-B	18	36	69	1	2	1	04	A Newey	Mercedes-Benz
MP4-20	18	36	182	7	12	10	05	A Newey	Mercedes-Benz

Constructors

MERCEDES-BENZ (D)

Principal: Walter Kostelezky.
Base: Unterturkheim, Stuttgart.
Re-formed: 1926 (as Mercedes-Benz).

Mercedes, initially founded in 1901, was one of the great racing car constructors of the early part of the century, their 1930s cars dominating many grands prix. After a low key entry post-war, the three-pointed star reappeared on the grid in its startling stromlinienwagen (streamlined) form. A combination of a revolutionary design, Alfred Neubauer's team management and the talents of the current World Champion, meant Mercedes started where they left off. With nothing further to prove and the Le Mans disaster very much in the public eye, the team made a tearful exit at the end of 1955. Mercedes returned to sports car racing with Peter Sauber and featured in the engine development on their Formula 1 debut before forming a partnership with McLaren in 1995.

Drivers' Championships: 2 (1954*,55). * Fangio also raced a Maserati during the season

Totals	GPs	Starts	Points	Poles	F.Laps	Wins			
	12	39	139.1	8	9	9			
Seasons							Colour	Main Driver(s)	
1954	6	18	60.1	4	4	4	silver	Fangio*,Kling,Herrmann *Champion*	
1955	6	21	79	4	5	5	silver	Fangio*,Moss,Kling *Champion*	
Models							Year(s)	Chief Designer	Engine
W196	12	39	139.1	8	9	9	54-55	R Uhlenhaut	8
Streamliner	5	10	33.1	4	3	3	54-55		
Open-wheeler	10	29	106.0	4	6	6	54-55		

MERZARIO (I)

Principal: Arturo Merzario.
Base: Milano.
Founded: 1977.

Former driver Merzario turned his hand as a constructor when his driving career waned, but these cars proved ineffective. A merger with the Kauhsen operation was equally unsuccessful and the A2 and A4 designs never made the grid. Merzario turned his attention to Formula 2 and continued with this series until it became the Formula 3000 Championship.

Totals	GPs	Starts	Points	Poles	F.Laps	Wins			
	10	10	-	-	-	-			
Seasons							Sponsor(s)	Main Driver(s)	
1978	8	8	-	-	-	-	Flor Bath	Merzario	
1979	2	2	-	-	-	-	Flor Bath	Merzario	
Models							Year(s)	Chief Designer	Engine
A1-B	10	10	-	-	-	-	78-79	A Merzario	Ford Cosworth

The A2 and the A4 never qualified in 1979.

MINARDI (I)

Principal: Gian Carlo Minardi/Gabriele Rumi/Paul Stoddart.
Base: Faenza, Ravenna.
Founded: 1972.

Based near his FIAT dealership, Minardi entered Italian Formula 3 and Formula 2, building his first Formula 2 car in 1980. Entering with the Carlo Chiti Motori Moderni engine, the team found Formula 1 a struggle. Minardi persevered with very few highs, before merging with Scuderia Italia for the 1994 season. Lucchini reduced his involvement and at the end of 1997 Gabriele Rumi became part of an alliance in acquiring a majority stake in the team. In 1998, Gabriele Rumi became a sole majority shareholder but sold out towards the end of the 2000 season to Australian businessman Paul Stoddart, who set up a British base in Ledbury. The team may have won many fans over the years but success on the track has continued to elude this popular outfit. The team finally bowed to financial pressure and sold out to Red Bull in September 2005, becoming their junior team Squadra Toro Rosso.

Totals	GPs	Starts	Points	Poles	F.Laps	Wins
	340	634	38	-	-	-

Models	GPs	Starts	Points	Poles	F.Laps	Wins	Sponsor(s)	Main Driver(s)
1985	15	15	-	-	-	-	Simod	Martini
1986	15	29	-	-	-	-	Simod	de Cesaris, Nannini
1987	16	31	-	-	-	-	Lois, Simod	Campos, Nannini
1988	14	25	1	-	-	-	Lois, Cimarron	Martini, Sala
1989	16	28	6	-	-	-	SCM, Lois	Martini, Sala
1990	16	25	-	-	-	-	SCM	Martini, Barilla
1991	16	32	6	-	-	-	SCM	Martini, Morbidelli
1992	15	26	1	-	-	-	Sabiem, Mercatone Uno	Fittipaldi, Morbidelli
1993	16	32	7	-	-	-	Beta, Cocif	Fittipaldi, Barbazza/Martini
1994	16	32	5	-	-	-	Lucchini, Beta	Martini, Alboreto
1995	17	32	1	-	-	-	Doimo, Valleverde	Martini/Lamy, Badoer
1996	16	29	-	-	-	-	Doimo, Bossini	Lamy, Fisichella
1997	17	33	-	-	-	-	Mild Seven, Fondmetal	Katayama, Trulli
1998	16	32	-	-	-	-	Fondmetal, Roces	Nakano, Tuero
1999	16	31	1	-	-	-	Fondmetal, Telefonica	Gené, Badoer
2000	17	34	-	-	-	-	Telefonica, Fondmetal	Gené, Mazzacane
2001	17	33	-	-	-	-	European, Magnum	Alonso, Marques
2002	16	29	2	-	-	-	KL, European	Webber, Yoong
2003	16	32	-	-	-	-	Trust, European	Verstappen, Wilson/Kiesa
2004	18	36	1	-	-	-	Superfund/Wilux	Bruni, Baumgartner
2005	19	38	7	-	-	-	Ozjet	Albers, Friesacher/Doornbos

Models	GPs	Starts	Points	Poles	F.Laps	Wins	Year(s)	Chief Designer	Engine
M185-B	30	38	-	-	-	-	85-86	G Caliri	Ford Cosworth, Motori Moderni
M186	6	6	-	-	-	-	86	G Caliri	Motori Moderni
M187	16	31	-	-	-	-	87	G Caliri	Motori Moderni
M188-B	17	31	1	-	-	-	88-89	G Caliri	Ford Cosworth
M189	15	26	6	-	-	-	89-90	A Costa	Ford Cosworth
M190	14	21	-	-	-	-	90	A Costa	Ford Cosworth
M191-B	20	40	6	-	-	-	91-92	A Costa	Ferrari, Lamborghini
M192	11	18	1	-	-	-	92	A Costa	Lamborghini
M193-B	21	42	10	-	-	-	93-94	A Costa	Ford Cosworth
M194	11	22	2	-	-	-	94	A Costa	Ford Cosworth
M195-B	33	61	1	-	-	-	95-96	A Costa	Ford Cosworth
M197	17	32	-	-	-	-	97	G Tredozi	Hart
M198	16	32	-	-	-	-	98	G Brunner	Ford Cosworth
M01	16	32	1	-	-	-	99	G Brunner	Ford Cosworth
M02	17	34	-	-	-	-	00	G Brunner	Fondmetal
PS01	17	33	-	-	-	-	01	G Brunner	European
PS02	16	29	2	-	-	-	02	G Tredozi	Asiatech
PS03	16	32	-	-	-	-	03	G Tredozi	Ford Cosworth
PS04B	21	42	1	-	-	-	04-05	G Tredozi	Ford Cosworth
PS05	16	32	7	-	-	-	05	G Tredozi	Cosworth

ONYX (GB)

Principal: Mike Earle / Peter Monteverdi.
Base: Fontwell, nr Arundel, West Sussex.
Founded: 1979.

This operation began as Onyx Engineering at Littlehampton and achieved many successful years in Formula 3000. An eventful Formula 1 baptism saw the team initially failing to qualify and then ending with a podium finish. The colourful Jean-Pierre van Rossem (of sponsor's Moneytron) bought out Mike Earle in December 1989, but sold the team to Peter Monteverdi early the next year. He relocated to Switzerland in July and renamed the cars Monteverdi, before folding altogether in August of that year.

Totals	GPs	Starts	Points	Poles	F.Laps	Wins		
	17	25	6	-	-	-		
Seasons							Sponsor(s)	Main Driver(s)
1989	12	15	6	-	-	-	Moneytron	Johansson, Gachot
1990	5	10	-	-	-	-	Marlboro	Foitek, Lehto
Models							Year(s)	Chief Designer	Engine
ORE-1	12	15	6	-	-	-	89	A Jenkins	Ford Cosworth
ORE-2	5	10	-	-	-	-	90	A Jenkins	Ford Cosworth

OSCA (I)

Principals: Ernesto, Ettore & Bindo Maserati.
Base: Bologna.
Founded: 1947.

Officine Specializate Costruzione Automobili Fratelli Maserati
The three Maserati brothers left Maserati after their ten year contract with Orsi, to reform their car construction business. They specialised in sports cars but built three types of single seaters; the last of which, a Formula 2 design failed to qualify at Monaco in 1958. The company was sold to MV in 1962.

Totals	GPs	Starts	Points	Poles	F.Laps	Wins			
	4	6	-	-	-	-			
Seasons							Colour	Main Driver(s)	
1951	1	1	-	-	-	-	red	Rol	
1952	1	1	-	-	-	-	red	Bayol	
1953	2	4	-	-	-	-	red	Bayol,Chiron	
Models							Year(s)	Chief Designer	Engine
4500G	1	1	-	-	-	-	51	Maserati brothers	V12
20	3	5	-	-	-	-	52-53	Maserati brothers	6

The 1958 model entered by Cabianca and Piotti, did not start in Monaco.

OSELLA (I)

Principal: Enzo Osella.
Base: Volpiano, Torino/Palosco, Bergamo (1990).
Founded: 1972.

Initially running Abarth sports cars, Osella built its first car for Formula 2 in 1974. Ever the enthusiast, Osella mainly ran a one car team usually found at the back of the grid. Taken over by Gabriele Rumi's Fondmetal in 1990 and renamed the following year, the team finally closed after the Italian Grand Prix in 1992.

Totals	GPs	Starts	Points	Poles	F.Laps	Wins			
	151	191	7	-	-	-			
Seasons							Sponsor(s)	Main Driver(s)	
1980	10	10	-	-	-	-	Denim	Cheever	
1981	10	12	-	-	-	-	Denim	Gabbiani,Jarier	
1982	13	15	3	-	-	-	Denim	Jarier,Paletti	
1983	13	16	-	-	-	-	Kelémata	Ghinzani,C Fabi	
1984	15	22	4	-	-	-	Kelémata	Ghinzani,Gartner	
1985	14	14	-	-	-	-	Kelémata	Ghinzani,Rothengatter	
1986	15	30	-	-	-	-	Landis & Gyr	Ghinzani,Berg	
1987	14	17	-	-	-	-	Landis & Gyr	Caffi	
1988	10	10	-	-	-	-	Stievani	Larini	
1989	9	11	-	-	-	-	Fondmetal	Larini,Ghinzani	
1990	9	9	-	-	-	-	Fondmetal,Spal	Grouillard	
1991	6	6	-	-	-	-	Fondmetal	Grouillard	
1992	13	19	-	-	-	-	Fondmetal,Sgomma Tutto	Tarquini,Chiesa	
Models							Year(s)	Chief Designer	Engine
FA1	10	10	-	-	-	-	80	E Osella	Ford Cosworth
FA1B	7	9	-	-	-	-	81	G Valentini	Ford Cosworth
FA1C	13	15	3	-	-	-	81-82	G Valentini	Ford Cosworth
FA1D	8	8	-	-	-	-	82-83	G Petrotta	Ford Cosworth
FA1E	9	12	-	-	-	-	83-84	T Southgate	Alfa Romeo
FA1F	29	36	4	-	-	-	84-86	G Petrotta	Alfa Romeo t
FA1G	28	28	-	-	-	-	85-87	G Petrotta	Alfa Romeo t
FA1H	2	2	-	-	-	-	86	G Petrotta	Alfa Romeo t
FA1I	14	16	-	-	-	-	87	G Petrotta	Alfa Romeo t
FA1L	10	10	-	-	-	-	88	A Tomaini	Alfa Romeo t
FA1M-E	18	20	-	-	-	-	89-90	A Tomaini	Ford Cosworth
F1 & GRO1	12	14	-	-	-	-	91-92	T Belli	Ford Cosworth
GRO2	7	11	-	-	-	-	92	S Rinland	Ford Cosworth

In 1988 the Alfa Romeo engines had the Osella name on the cam covers.

Principal: Keith Wiggins.
Base: Thetford, Norfolk.
Founded: 1984.

Pacific achieved major success in all levels the team entered, although it suffered from the outdated chassis that was originally part of the abortive Reynard Formula 1 entry. Pacific joined with the moribund Team Lotus for 1995 but its lack of success sealed its fate as a grand prix concern during the winter.

Totals	GPs	Starts	Points	Poles	F.Laps	Wins			
	22	40	-	-	-	-			
Seasons							Sponsor(s)	Main Driver(s)	
1994	5	7	-	-	-	-	Ursus	Gachot,Belmondo	
1995	17	33	-	-	-	-	Ursus	Gachot,Montermini	
Models							Year(s)	Chief Designer	Engine
PRO1	5	7	-	-	-	-	94	R Byrne	Ilmor
PRO2	17	33	-	-	-	-	95	F Coppuck	Ford Cosworth

PARNELLI (USA)

Principals: Velco Miletich, Rufus Parnelli Jones.
Base: Torrance, California (GB Base: Griston, Norfolk).
Founded: 1969.

With backing from Firestone, Parnelli entered the Formula 1 fray but it was soon apparent that American racing was their priority and when Firestone withdrew, the team soon followed back to the United States.

Totals	GPs	Starts	Points	Poles	F.Laps	Wins			
	16	16	6	-	1	-			
Seasons							Sponsor(s)	Main Driver(s)	
1974	2	2	-	-	-	-	Viceroy,Firestone	Andretti	
1975	12	12	5	-	1	-	Viceroy	Andretti	
1976	2	2	1	-	-	-	American Wheels	Andretti	
Models							Year(s)	Chief Designer	Engine
VPJ4-B	16	16	6	-	1	-	74-76	M Phillippe	Ford Cosworth

PENSKE (USA)

Principal: Roger Penske.
Base: Reading, Pennsylvania (GB Base: Poole, Dorset).
Founded: 1966.

After a career as driver and entrant in America, wealthy businessman Roger Penske decided to tackle Formula 1 using Graham McRae's old workshop as his base. After a successful but tragic period, in which his friend and regular driver Mark Donohue was killed, Penske sold his cars to the ATS team and returned to the US racing scene. He has since become a mainstay of the IndyCar movement, owning various circuits and going on to be the most successful IndyCar entrant of all time.

Totals	GPs	Starts	Points	Poles	F.Laps	Wins			
	40	44	23	-	-	1			
Seasons							Sponsor(s)	Main Driver(s)	
1974	2	2	-	-	-	-	First National City	Donohue	
1975	10	10	2	-	-	-	First National City	Donohue	
1976	16	17	20	-	-	1	First National City	Watson	
1977	12	15	1	-	-	-	ATS	Jarier (ATS)	
Models							Year(s)	Chief Designer	Engine
PC1	12	12	2	-	-	-	74-75	G Ferris	Ford Cosworth
PC3	7	7	2	-	-	-	76	G Ferris	Ford Cosworth
PC4	22	25	19	-	-	1	76-77	G Ferris	Ford Cosworth

PORSCHE (D)

Principal: Ferry Porsche.
Base: Stuttgart-Zuffenhausen.
Founded: 1948.

The company's vast racing success has been built upon sports car racing and it was through this medium that the Porsche name appeared as modified two seaters in Formula 2 racing. A true Formula 1 entry didn't materialise until 1961, and the team soon withdrew and concentrated on the racing it knew best. The TAG-backed turbo engine of the mid eighties was a great success, but this was tempered by the disastrous V12 produced for Footwork in 1991.

Totals	GPs	Starts	Points	Poles	F.Laps	Wins			
	33	73	50	1	-	1			
Seasons							Colour	Main Driver(s)	
1957	1	3	-	-	-	-	silver	(F2 class entry only)	
1958	2	3	-	-	-	-	silver	de Beaufort (Maarsbergen)	
1959	3	3	-	-	-	-	silver	von Trips	
1960	2	4	1	-	-	-	silver	Barth, Herrmann	
1961	8	25	24	-	-	-	silver	Gurney, Bonnier	
1962	9	25	20	1	-	1	silver	Gurney, Bonnier	
1963	7	9	5	-	-	-	orange	de Beaufort (Maarsbergen)	
1964	1	1	-	-	-	-	orange	de Beaufort (Maarsbergen)	
Models							Year(s)	Chief Designer	Engine
RS550	2	4	-	-	-	-	57-58	W Hild	F4
RSK	4	4	-	-	-	-	58-59	W Hild	F4
Behra	2	2	-	-	-	-	59-60	V Colloti	F4
718	27	46	34	-	-	-	59-64	W Hild	F4
787	3	4	-	-	-	-	61-62	W Hild	F4
804	7	13	16	1	-	1	62	H Bott	F8

PROTOS (GB)

Principals: Frank Costin.
Base:
Founded: 1967.

Not really a Formula 1 car at all, this unusual design took part in the Formula 2 class of the German Grand Prix.

Totals	GPs	Starts	Points	Poles	F.Laps	Wins			
	1	2	-	-	-	-			
Seasons							Colour	Main Driver(s)	
1967	1	2	-	-	-	-	green	(F2 class entry only)	
Models							Year(s)	Chief Designer	Engine
-	1	2	-	-	-	-	67	F Costin	Ford Cosworth

RAM (GB)

Principals: John MacDonald, Mick Ralph.
Base: Bicester, Oxfordshire.
Founded: 1975.

One time Formula 1 entrants with March and Williams chassis, the team had strong March connections and brought the constructor back into grand prix in 1981-82. The March name was retained the following year but these were the first true RAM cars. An unsuccessful period followed, and although Mike Thackwell tested in Rio prior to the 1986 season, the team folded through lack of funds.

Totals	GPs	Starts	Points	Poles	F.Laps	Wins			
	31	54	-	-	-	-			
Seasons							Sponsor(s)	Main Driver(s)	
1983	3	3	-	-	-	-	Rizla	Salazar,Acheson	
1984	15	28	-	-	-	-	Skoal Bandit	Palmer,Alliot	
1985	13	23	-	-	-	-	Skoal Bandit	Alliot,Winkelhock	
Models							Year(s)	Chief Designer	Engine
01	5	5	-	-	-	-	83-84	D Kelly	Ford Cosworth,Hart t
02	15	26	-	-	-	-	84	D Kelly	Hart t
03	13	23	-	-	-	-	85	G Brunner	Hart t

REBAQUE (MEX/GB)

Principal: Hector Rebaque.
Base: Leamington Spa, Warwickshire.
Founded: 1977.

Built at Penske in Poole and based on the Lotus he previously entered, the car was soon discarded when the wealthy Mexican managed a works Brabham drive the following year.

Totals	GPs	Starts	Points	Poles	F.Laps	Wins			
	1	1	-	-	-	-			
Seasons							Sponsor(s)	Main Driver(s)	
1979	1	1	-	-	-	-	Carta Blanca	Rebaque	
Models							Year(s)	Chief Designer	Engine
HR100	1	1	-	-	-	-	79	G Ferris	Ford Cosworth

RED BULL (A/GB)

Principal: Dietrich Mateschitz.
Base: Milton Keynes, Buckinghamshire, GB.
Founded: 2004.

Energy drink manufacturer Red Bull bought the ailing Jaguar team from Ford at the end of the 2004 season, and after a transition period, Christian Horner was brought in as team boss. The team added a lot of colour to the 2005 paddock and produced a successful driver development programme.

Totals	GPs	Starts	Points	Poles	F.Laps	Wins			
	18	35	34	-	-	-			
Seasons							Sponsor(s)	Main Driver(s)	
2005	18	35	34	-	-	-	Red Bull	Coulthard,Klien	
Models							Year(s)	Chief Designer	Engine
RB1	18	35	34	-	-	-	05	G Steiner	Cosworth

RENAULT (F)

Principal: Bernard Dudot/Flavio Briatore.
Base: Viry-Châtillon, nr Paris. GB Base: Enstone, Oxfordshire.
Founded: 1898.

Renault began manufacturing racing cars back in 1899 and went on to win the first ever Grand Prix in 1906. After establishing itself as France's leading motor manufacturer, a sporting division was created for sports car racing with the Alpine-Renault. After Formula 2 success, Renault went on to introduce one of the major Formula 1 innovations – the turbo engine, based on a Renault-Gordini design. Following their failure to win the World Championship, after coming so close, the company concentrated on engine supply which came to fruition with the Williams partnership of the 1990s. In 2000, Renault bought the Benetton team and from the 2002 season ran under their own name once again. Under the guidance of Flavio Briatore, the team returned to the winner's circle in 2003 and finally clinched both titles in 2005.

Constructors' Championships: 1 (2005). **Drivers' Championships:** 1 (2005).

Totals	GPs	Starts	Points	Poles	F.Laps	Wins			
	192	365	719	43	22	25			
Seasons							Sponsor(s)	Main Driver(s)	
1977	4	4	-	-	-	-	Elf	Jabouille	
1978	14	14	3	-	-	-	Elf	Jabouille	
1979	14	28	26	6	2	1	Elf	Jabouille,Arnoux	
1980	14	27	38	5	4	3	Elf	Jabouille,Arnoux	
1981	15	29	54	6	2	3	Elf	Prost,Arnoux	
1982	16	32	62	10	5	4	Elf	Prost,Arnoux	
1983	15	30	79	3	3	4	Elf	Prost,Cheever	
1984	16	32	34	1	2	-	Elf	Tambay,Warwick	
1985	15	31	16	-	-	-	Elf	Tambay,Warwick	
2002	17	34	23	-	-	-	Mild Seven	Trulli,Button	
2003	16	32	88	2	1	1	Mild Seven	Trulli,Alonso	
2004	18	36	105	3	-	1	Mild Seven	Trulli,Alonso	
2005	18	36	191	7	3	8	Mild Seven	Alonso*,Fisichella *Champion *	
Models							Year(s)	Chief Designer	Engine
RS01	23	26	3	1	-	-	77-79	F Castaing	V6t
RS10	11	20	26	5	2	1	79	F Castaing	V6t
RE20-B	20	37	44	5	4	3	80-81	M Têtu	V6t
RE30-B,C	28	54	110	16	7	7	81-83	M Têtu	V6t
RE40	14	27	79	3	3	4	83	M Têtu	V6t
RE50	16	32	34	1	2	-	84	M Têtu	V6t
RE60-B	15	31	16	-	-	-	85	M Têtu	V6t
R202	17	34	23	-	-	-	02	M Gascoyne	V10
R23-B	16	32	88	2	1	1	03	M Gascoyne	V10
R24	18	36	105	3	-	1	04	B Bell	V10
R25	18	36	191	7	3	8	05	B Bell	V10

The early cars are often referred to by their chassis numbers incorporated into the model number, eg RE23.

RIAL (D)

Principal: Hans Günter Schmid.
Base: Fussgönheim, nr Ludwigshafen.
Founded: 1987.

The founder of ATS returned to Formula 1 with his team renamed after his wheel company. Schmid withdrew yet again at the end of his second season.

Totals	GPs	Starts	Points	Poles	F.Laps	Wins			
	20	20	6	-	-	-			
Seasons							Sponsor(s)	Main Driver(s)	
1988	16	16	3	-	-	-	Rial	de Cesaris	
1989	4	4	3	-	-	-	Rial	Danner,Weidler	
Models							Year(s)	Chief Designer	Engine
ARC1	16	16	3	-	-	-	88	G Brunner	Ford Cosworth
ARC2	4	4	3	-	-	-	89	R Bell	Ford Cosworth

SAUBER (CH)

Principal: Peter Sauber.
Base: Hinwil, nr Zürich.
Founded: 1970.

Former racer, Peter Sauber, built his first car in 1970 and continued with sports cars, achieving many successes including Le Mans and Sportscar World Championships in 1989-90. Peter Sauber moved from Beetle tuning to building two-seater open sportscars, beginning with the C1. He has used the first initial of his wife's name Christiane to name all of his cars, a tribute to her patience in accepting her husband's frequent absences from home. Sauber helped bring Mercedes back to front line motorsport with the C8 sports car in 1984 although their relationship finished at the end of the 1994 season. A Ford works deal was lost to the new Stewart Grand Prix operation and the team went on to use re-badged Ferrari engines under the name of their sponsor Petronas. In August 2005 BMW announced their split with Williams and their purchase of the Sauber operation in its entirety.

Totals	GPs	Starts	Points	Poles	F.Laps	Wins			
	215	428	195	-	-	-			
Seasons							Sponsor(s)	Main Driver(s)	
1993	16	32	12	-	-	-	Lighthouse, Liqui Moly	Wendlinger, Lehto	
1994	15	29	12	-	-	-	Tissot	Wendlinger/de Cesaris, Frentzen	
1995	17	34	18	-	-	-	Red Bull, Petronas	Wendlinger/Boullion, Frentzen	
1996	16	32	11	-	-	-	Red Bull, Petronas	Herbert, Frentzen	
1997	17	33	16	-	-	-	Red Bull, Petronas	Herbert, Morbidelli	
1998	16	32	10	-	-	-	Red Bull, Petronas	Herbert, Alesi	
1999	16	32	5	-	-	-	Red Bull, Petronas	Alesi, Diniz	
2000	16	32	6	-	-	-	Red Bull, Petronas	Diniz, Salo	
2001	17	34	21	-	-	-	Red Bull, Petronas	Heidfeld, Räikkönen	
2002	17	34	11	-	-	-	Petronas, Red Bull	Heidfeld, Massa	
2003	16	32	19	-	-	-	Petronas, Red Bull	Heidfeld, Frentzen	
2004	18	36	34	-	-	-	Petronas, Red Bull	Fisichella, Massa	
2005	18	36	20	-	-	-	Petronas, Credit Suisse	Villeneuve, Massa	
Models							Year(s)	Chief Designer	Engine
C12	16	32	12	-	-	-	93	L Ress	Ilmor
C13	15	29	12	-	-	-	94	L Ress	Mercedes-Benz
C14	17	34	18	-	-	-	95	L Ress	Ford Cosworth
C15	16	32	11	-	-	-	96	L Ress	Ford Cosworth
C16	17	33	16	-	-	-	97	L Ress	Petronas (Ferrari)
C17	16	32	10	-	-	-	98	L Ress	Petronas (Ferrari)
C18	16	32	5	-	-	-	99	L Ress	Petronas (Ferrari)
C19	16	32	6	-	-	-	00	L Ress	Petronas (Ferrari)
C20	17	34	21	-	-	-	01	S Rinland	Petronas (Ferrari)
C21	17	34	11	-	-	-	02	W Rampf	Petronas (Ferrari)
C22	16	32	19	-	-	-	03	W Rampf	Petronas (Ferrari)
C23	18	36	34	-	-	-	04	W Rampf	Petronas (Ferrari)
C24	18	36	20	-	-	-	05	W Rampf	Petronas (Ferrari)

SCARAB (USA)

Principal: Lance Reventlow.
Base: Culver City, California.
Founded: 1957.

Multi-millionaire and heir to the Woolworth empire, Reventlow decided to take on the might of Europe with a front-engined car based on his successful sports car design. Basing itself in Kingston-upon-Thames the team soon realised their Goodyear shod cars were outdated and returned to America, closing down in 1962.

Totals	GPs	Starts	Points	Poles	F.Laps	Wins			
	2	3	-	-	-	-			
Seasons							Colour	Main Driver(s)	
1960	2	3	-	-	-	-	blue/white	Daigh, Reventlow	
Models							Year(s)	Chief Designer	Engine
-	2	3	-	-	-	-	60	M Whitfield	4

SCIROCCO (USA)

Principal: Hugh Powell.
Base: Shepherds Bush, London, GB.
Founded: 1962.

American enthusiast Hugh Powell, acquired the assets of the Emeryson Company in 1962. After racing with these chassis it was decided to build new cars for the 1963 season. They raced in American blue and white colours, although based in Goldhawk Road, Shepherds Bush, London.

Totals	GPs	Starts	Points	Poles	F.Laps	Wins			
	5	7	-	-	-	-			
Seasons							Colour	Main Driver(s)	
1963	4	6	-	-	-	-	blue/white	Settember, Burgess	
1964	1	1	-	-	-	-	yellow	Pilette	
Models							Year(s)	Chief Designer	Engine
SP	5	7	-	-	-	-	63-64	H Aiden-Jones	BRM, Climax

SHADOW (USA)

Principal: Don Nicholls.
GB Base: Northampton.
Founded: 1968.

Don Nicholls, the founder of Advanced Vehicle Systems, built his first car for CanAm racing in 1970 and whilst continuing to race back home, set up an English establishment for a serious, and occasionally successful, Formula 1 venture. In 1980, Teddy Yip's Theodore operation took over the Shadow team and the latest design was absorbed into the new outfit.

Totals	GPs	Starts	Points	Poles	F.Laps	Wins			
	104	211	68.5	3	2	1			
Seasons							Sponsor(s)	Main Driver(s)	
1973	13	38	9	-	-	-	UOP	Follmer, Oliver	
1974	14	28	7	-	-	-	UOP	Revson/Pryce, Jarier	
1975	14	27	9.5	3	1	-	UOP	Pryce, Jarier	
1976	16	32	10	-	1	-	Tabatip, Valvoline	Pryce, Jarier	
1977	17	34	24	-	-	1	Ambrosio, Tabatip	Pryce/Jones, Patrese	
1978	15	25	6	-	-	-	Villiger, Tabatip	Stuck, Regazzoni	
1979	14	26	3	-	-	-	Samson	Lammers, de Angelis	
1980	1	1	-	-	-	-	Interlekt	Lees, Kennedy	
Models							Year(s)	Chief Designer	Engine
DN1	15	40	9	-	-	-	73-74	T Southgate	Ford Cosworth
DN3-B	16	28	7	-	-	-	74-75	T Southgate	Ford Cosworth
DN5-B	31	52	17.5	3	2	-	75-77	T Southgate	Ford Cosworth
DN7	2	2	-	-	-	-	75	T Southgate	Matra
DN8	25	42	28	-	-	1	76-78	T Southgate	Ford Cosworth
DN9	26	46	7	-	-	-	78-79	T Southgate	Ford Cosworth
DN11	1	1	-	-	-	-	80	J Gentry	Ford Cosworth

The DN12-Ford Cosworth (1980) did not start in the World Championship and became the Theodore TR2.

SHANNON (GB)

Principals: Hugh Aiden-Jones, Paul Emery.
Base: Fulham, London.
Founded: 1966.

This one-off design used the unraced Climax FPE V8 engine. It retired after a quarter of a lap of its only race at Brands Hatch, which gives it the record of the shortest grand prix race career.

Totals	GPs	Starts	Points	Poles	F.Laps	Wins			
	1	1	-	-	-	-			
Seasons							Colour	Main Driver(s)	
1966	1	1	-	-	-	-	green	T Taylor	
Models							Year(s)	Chief Designer	Engine
Mk 1	1	1	-	-	-	-	66	H Aiden-Jones	Climax

SIMTEK (GB)

Principal: Nick Wirth.
Base: Banbury, Oxfordshire.
Founded: 1989.

Nick Wirth had undertaken design work on many recent Formula 1 cars when Max Mosley was a part owner of Simtek Research. With the backing of the Brabham family their debut year was especially fraught with the death of newcomer Roland Ratzenberger. The team pushed on but found themselves without the funds to continue during the 1995 season and sold its assets at auction later that year with Nick Wirth going on to work for Benetton in F1.

Totals	GPs	Starts	Points	Poles	F.Laps	Wins			
	21	37	-	-	-	-			
Seasons							Sponsor(s)	Main Driver(s)	
1994	16	27	-	-	-	-	MTV,Barbara MC	Brabham,Ratzenberger/Gounon	
1995	5	10	-	-	-	-	MTV,Barbara MC	Schiattarella,Verstappen	
Models							Year(s)	Chief Designer	Engine
S941	16	27	-	-	-	-	94	N Wirth	Ford Cosworth
S951	5	10	-	-	-	-	95	P Crooks	Ford Cosworth

SPIRIT (GB)

Principals: John Wickham, Gordon Coppuck.
Base: Slough.
Founded: 1981.

The first Formula 2 car was built in 1982 and the following year they reintroduced Honda to Formula 1 in a hybrid chassis. Honda soon took their engines to Williams and the team struggled without them, withdrawing during the 1985 season.

Totals	GPs	Starts	Points	Poles	F.Laps	Wins			
	23	23	-	-	-	-			
Seasons							Sponsor(s)	Main Driver(s)	
1983	6	6	-	-	-	-	Honda	Johansson	
1984	14	14	-	-	-	-	Australian	Baldi,Rothengatter	
1985	3	3	-	-	-	-	Australian	Baldi	
Models							Year(s)	Chief Designer	Engine
201-C	6	6	-	-	-	-	83	G Coppuck	Honda t
101-D	17	17	-	-	-	-	84-85	G Coppuck	Hart t

STEBRO (CDN)

Principals: John Stephens/Peter Broeker.
Base: Montréal, Quebec.
Founded: 1959.

This company began as a repair shop and developed into a specialist exhaust manufacturer that gave the means for owner Peter Broeker to go motor racing. After building earlier front-engined models the Formula Junior mark IV model complied with the current F1 formula and managed to reach the grid in the United States Grand Prix, giving the Ford engine its debut at World Championship level.

Totals	GPs	Starts	Points	Poles	F.Laps	Wins			
	1	1	-	-	-	-			
Seasons							Colour	Main Driver(s)	
1963	1	1	-	-	-	-	black/white	Broeker	
Models							Year(s)	Engine	
Mk IV	1	1	-	-	-	-	63	Ford	

STEWART (GB)

Principals: Jackie Stewart & Paul Stewart.
Base: Milton Keynes, Buckinghamshire.
Founded: 1988.

Paul Stewart and his father Jackie founded Paul Stewart Racing back in 1988 to contest the lower British formulae. It was always their intention to progress to the top level which came to fruition with the founding of Stewart Grand Prix in 1996. Ford was always a major backer and bought the team out in June 1999 before creating the foundations for a new Jaguar operation.

Totals	GPs	Starts	Points	Poles	F.Laps	Wins			
	49	97	47	1	-	1			
Seasons							Sponsor(s)	Main Driver(s)	
1997	17	34	6	-	-	-	HSBC,Malaysia	Barrichello,Magnussen	
1998	16	32	5	-	-	-	HSBC,MCI	Barrichello,Magnussen	
1999	16	31	36	1	-	1	HSBC,MCI	Barrichello,Herbert	
Models							Year(s)	Chief Designer	Engine
SF-1	17	34	6	-	-	-	97	A Jenkins	Ford Cosworth
SF-2	16	32	5	-	-	-	98	A Jenkins	Ford Cosworth
SF-3	16	31	36	1	-	1	99	G Anderson	Ford Cosworth

SURTEES (GB)

Principal: John Surtees.
Base: Edenbridge, Kent.
Founded: 1966.

Surtees first car was a Formula 5000 design originating from the Leda project which formed the basis of the first proper Formula 1 car. Although successful in F5000 and Formula 2, grand prix glory eluded the team and somewhat disillusioned, the operation closed at the end of 1978. What made this constructor most remarkable, was that the team principal, John Surtees, was also a designer and driver.

Totals	GPs	Starts	Points	Poles	F.Laps	Wins			
	118	224	54	-	3	-			
Seasons							Sponsor(s)/ (Colour)	Main Driver(s)	
1970	7	8	3	-	-	-	(red)	Surtees	
1971	11	26	9	-	-	-	Brooke Bond Oxo	Surtees,Stommelen	
1972	12	37	18	-	1	-	Brooke Bond Oxo	Hailwood,Schenken,de Adamich	
1973	15	35	7	-	2	-	Brooke Bond Oxo	Hailwood,Pace	

Seasons	GPs	Starts	Points	Poles	F.Laps	Wins	Sponsor(s)	Main Driver(s)	
1974	14	23	3	-	-	-	Fina	Pace, Mass	
1975	11	12	-	-	-	-	Matchbox	Watson	
1976	15	33	7	-	-	-	Durex, Chesterfield	Jones, Lunger	
1977	17	30	6	-	-	-	Durex, Beta	Binder, Brambilla	
1978	16	20	1	-	-	-	Durex, Beta, BAF	Keegan, Brambilla	
Models							Year(s)	Chief Designer	Engine
TS7	9	11	3	-	-	-	70-71	J Surtees	Ford Cosworth
TS9-B	25	60	27	-	1	-	71-73	J Surtees	Ford Cosworth
TS14-A	17	35	7	-	2	-	72-73	J Surtees	Ford Cosworth
TS16	25	35	3	-	-	-	74-75	J Surtees	Ford Cosworth
TS19	37	70	13	-	-	-	76-78	K Sears	Ford Cosworth
TS20	11	13	1	-	-	-	78	K Sears	Ford Cosworth

TALBOT LAGO (F)

Principal: Anthony Lago.
Base: Suresnes, Paris.
Founded: 1935.

After taking over the Sunbeam-Talbot-Darracq concern, Lago developed the sports cars and produced their first single seater in 1939. The works operation withdrew in early 1951 but cars raced on in private hands.

Totals	GPs	Starts	Points	Poles	F.Laps	Wins			
	13	80	25	-	-	-			
Seasons							Colour	Main Driver(s)	
1950	6	35	20	-	-	-	blue	Giraud-Cabantous, Martin	
1951	7	45	5	-	-	-	blue	Rosier, Claes (privateers)	
Models							Year(s)	Chief Designer	Engine
T26C-DA, GS	13	80	25	-	-	-	50-51	A Lago	6

TEC MEC (I)

Principal: Valerio Colotti.
Base: Modena.
Founded: 1958.

Tecnica Mecanica, derived from the Maserati 250F, was a one-off evolution of that famous marque. Originated by Valerio Colotti at his Modena studio, the design passed into the hands of a syndicate led by Gordon Pennington, after Giorgio Scarlatti lost interest in the project. It raced only once at World Championship level.

Totals	GPs	Starts	Points	Poles	F.Laps	Wins			
	1	1	-	-	-	-			
Seasons							Colour	Main Driver(s)	
1959	1	1	-	-	-	-	red	d'Orey	
Models							Year(s)	Chief Designer	Engine
F415	1	1	-	-	-	-	59	V Colotti	'Maserati'

TECNO (I)

Principals: Luciano & Gianfranco Pederzani.
Base: Bologna.
Founded: 1962.

The Pederzani brothers created Tecnokart, initially building karts until their first Formula 4 car in 1964. They progressed through the lower formulae, until finance by Martini drinks enabled them to enter the top flight.

Totals	GPs	Starts	Points	Poles	F.Laps	Wins			
	11	11	1	-	-	-			
Seasons							Sponsor(s)	Main Driver(s)	
1969	1	1	-	-	-	-		(F2 class entry only)	
1972	6	6	-	-	-	-	Martini	Galli,Bell	
1973	4	4	1	-	-	-	Martini	Amon	
Models							Year(s)	Chief Designer	Engine
TOO	1	1	-	-	-	-	69	L&G Pederzani	Ford Cosworth
PA123	6	6	-	-	-	-	72	L&G Pederzani	F12
PA123	4	4	1	-	-	-	73	A McCall	F12

Although carrying the same name, the latest two models were different chassis designs, a fourth, the E731 (1973) never raced.

THEODORE (GB)

Principal: Teddy Yip.
Base: Woking, Surrey.
Founded: 1978.

Founded by millionaire businessman Teddy Yip and based at Ralt's old works at Woking. Yip had previously backed drivers such as Tambay and Jones and decided to enter his own design. A second attempt with the Shadow design didn't fair much better, and neither did a final attempt with an amalgamation of the struggling Ensign team, after which this Macau-based entrepeneur turned his attention to the IndyCar scene.

Totals	GPs	Starts	Points	Poles	F.Laps	Wins			
	34	43	2	-	-	-			
Seasons							Sponsor(s)	Main Driver(s)	
1978	1	1	-	-	-	-	Hi-Line	Rosberg	
1979-80 did not participate									
1981	13	13	1	-	-	-	Moulin Rouge,Penthouse	Tambay/Surer	
1982	7	7	-	-	-	-	Rizla	Daly/Byrne	
1983	13	22	1	-	-	-	Cafe de Colombia	Guerrero,Cecotto	
Models							Year(s)	Chief Designer	Engine
TR1	1	1	-	-	-	-	78	R Tauranac	Ford Cosworth
TY01	14	14	1	-	-	-	81-82	T Southgate	Ford Cosworth
TY02	6	6	-	-	-	-	82	T Southgate	Ford Cosworth
N183	13	22	1	-	-	-	83	N Bennett	Ford Cosworth

TOKEN (GB)

Principals: Tony Vlassopoulo, Ken Grob.
Base: Woking, Surrey.
Founded: 1973.

Originally built for Rondel Racing run by Ron Dennis and Neil Trundle. Finance problems resulted in this being taken over by Tony Vlassopoulo and Ken Grob who gave their name to the team. This car went on to become the Safir in 1975 British domestic racing.

Totals	GPs	Starts	Points	Poles	F.Laps	Wins			
	3	3	-	-	-	-			
Seasons							Sponsor(s)	Main Driver(s)	
1974	3	3	-	-	-	-	Shell	Pryce/Ashley	
Models							Year(s)	Chief Designer	Engine
RJ02	3	3	-	-	-	-	74	R Jessop	Ford Cosworth

TOYOTA (J)

Principal: Ove Andersson/Tsutomu Tomita.
Base: Tokyo [European base: Köln (Cologne), D].
Founded: 1937 (as a manufacturer).

Toyota finally made the top step of motor sport after many years in lower formulae and success in rally. Swedish rally star of the 1970s, Ove Andersson was placed in charge of this new operation, based in Cologne, where both chassis and engine are produced. After a full year of testing with initial drivers Mika Salo and Allan McNish, the team did very well to score points first time out, but found the rest of their debut year as hard as they anticipated. With an extensive budget the team have changed drivers, designers and team leaders but success still seems out of reach.

Totals	GPs	Starts	Points	Poles	F.Laps	Wins			
	69	137	115	2	1	-			
Seasons							Sponsor(s)	Main Driver(s)	
2002	17	33	2	-	-	-	Panasonic	Salo,McNish	
2003	16	32	16	-	-	-	Panasonic	Panis,da Matta	
2004	18	36	9	-	-	-	Panasonic	Panis,da Matta/Zonta	
2005	18	36	88	2	1	-	Panasonic	R Schumacher,Trulli	
Models							Year(s)	Chief Designer	Engine
TF102	17	33	2	-	-	-	02	G Brunner	V10
TF103	16	32	16	-	-	-	03	G Brunner	V10
TF104	18	36	9	-	-	-	04	M Gascoyne	V10
TF105-B	18	36	88	2	1	-	05	M Gascoyne	V10

TROJAN (GB)

Principal: Peter Agg.
Base: Croydon, Surrey.
Founded: 1964.

After taking over the Elva concern, the Beddington Lane-based company forged a deal to reconstruct McLaren sports cars during the 60s and early 70s. From this they established their own Formula 5000 designs in 1973 before venturing into Formula 1.

Totals	GPs	Starts	Points	Poles	F.Laps	Wins			
	6	6	-	-	-	-			
Seasons							Sponsor(s)	Main Driver(s)	
1974	6	6	-	-	-	-	Suzuki,Homelite	Schenken	
Models							Year(s)	Chief Designer	Engine
T103	6	6	-	-	-	-	74	R Tauranac	Ford Cosworth

TYRRELL (GB)

Principal: Ken Tyrrell.
Base: Ockham, Woking, Surrey.
Founded: 1960.

Former wood merchant and one time Formula 3 racer, Ken Tyrrell, moved towards team management, first with a Cooper Formula 2 and then with his own team. Successful years with Matra in F2/F3 led to a grand prix entry in 1968 with Matra's first Formula 1 chassis. Reacquainted with Jackie Stewart, the team had two successful years with the Matra-Cosworth DFV combination including a debut World Championship in 1969. With Matra using its own engine, Tyrrell stayed with Ford Cosworth power and needed a new chassis for 1970. The new March organisation became the stop-gap until the first Tyrrell, built in utmost secrecy, was ready to race late that season. The passing years haven't been kind to the Tyrrell organisation. After such a high flying start, the team's results declined with its nadir being the disqualification from the World Championship in 1984 for alleged fuel irregularities. Ken Tyrrell sold the team and left before the 1998 season started, although by that time they had been absorbed into the new British American Racing operation.

Constructors' Championships: 1 (1971). **Drivers' Championships:** 2 (1971,73).

Totals	GPs	Starts	Points	Poles	F.Laps	Wins		
	430	842	711	14	20	23		
Seasons							Sponsor(s)	Main Driver(s)
1970	3	3	-	1	-	-	Elf	Stewart
1971	11	23	88	6	4	7	Elf	Stewart*,Cevert *Champion*
1972	12	25	60	2	4	4	Elf	Stewart,Cevert
1973	14	30	118	3	2	5	Elf	Stewart*,Cevert *Champion*
1974	15	31	59	1	3	2	Elf	J Scheckter,Depailler
1975	14	31	32	-	1	1	Elf	J Scheckter,Depailler
1976	16	37	88	1	2	1	Elf	J Scheckter,Depailler
1977	17	35	27	-	1	-	Elf,First Nat City	Peterson,Depailler
1978	16	32	41	-	-	1	Elf,First Nat City	Pironi,Depailler
1979	15	31	28	-	-	-	Candy	Pironi,Jarier
1980	14	29	12	-	-	-	Candy	Jarier,Daly
1981	15	26	10	-	-	-	Ceramica Imola	Cheever,Alboreto
1982	16	32	25	-	2	1	Denim,Candy	Alboreto,Henton
1983	15	30	12	-	-	1	Benetton	Alboreto,Sullivan
1984	12	21	0	-	-	-	Systime,De Longhi	Brundle,Bellof
1985	16	28	7	-	-	-	Maredo,Porchester	Brundle,Bellof
1986	16	32	11	-	-	-	Data General	Brundle,Streiff
1987	16	32	11	-	-	-	Data General	Palmer,Streiff
1988	15	20	5	-	-	-	Courtaulds	Palmer,Bailey
1989	16	29	16	-	1	-	Camel	Palmer,Alboreto
1990	16	30	16	-	-	-	Epson	Nakajima,Alesi
1991	16	32	12	-	-	-	Braun,Epson	Nakajima,Modena
1992	16	32	8	-	-	-	Calbee,Club Angle	Grouillard,de Cesaris
1993	16	32	-	-	-	-	Cabin,Calbee	Katayama,de Cesaris
1994	16	32	13	-	-	-	Mild Seven,Calbee	Katayama,Blundell
1995	17	34	5	-	-	-	Nokia,Mild Seven	Katayama,Salo
1996	16	32	5	-	-	-	Mild Seven,Korean Air	Katayama,Salo
1997	17	34	2	-	-	-	PIAA	Verstappen,Salo
1998	16	27	-	-	-	-	PIAA	Takagi,Rosset
Models							Year(s)	Chief Designer	Engine
001-004	27	47	124	8	6	9	70-74	D Gardner	Ford Cosworth
005-006	24	44	146	4	4	7	72-74	D Gardner	Ford Cosworth
007	35	65	102	1	4	3	74-77	D Gardner	Ford Cosworth
P34	30	59	100	1	3	1	76-77	D Gardner	Ford Cosworth
008	16	32	41	-	-	1	78	M Phillippe	Ford Cosworth
009	17	35	31	-	-	-	79-80	M Phillippe	Ford Cosworth
010	22	42	17	-	-	-	80-81	M Phillippe	Ford Cosworth
011	34	65	38	-	2	2	81-83	M Phillippe	Ford Cosworth
012	26	41	5	-	-	-	83-85	M Phillippe	Ford Cosworth
014	14	21	5	-	-	-	85-86	M Phillippe	Renault t
015	13	25	9	-	-	-	86	M Phillippe	Renault t
DG016	16	32	11	-	-	-	87	M Phillippe	Ford Cosworth
017-B	16	22	5	-	-	-	88-89	B Lisles	Ford Cosworth
018	17	31	23	-	1	-	89-90	H Postlethwaite	Ford Cosworth
019	14	26	9	-	-	-	90	H Postlethwaite	Ford Cosworth

Models	GPs	Starts	Points	Poles	F.Laps	Wins	Year(s)	Chief Designer	Engine
020-B,C	41	81	20	-	-	-	91-93	G Ryton	Honda, Ilmor, Yamaha
021	8	15	-	-	-	-	93	M Coughlan	Yamaha
022	16	32	13	-	-	-	94	H Postlethwaite	Yamaha
023	17	34	5	-	-	-	95	H Postlethwaite	Yamaha
024	16	32	5	-	-	-	96	H Postlethwaite	Yamaha
025	17	34	2	-	-	-	97	H Postlethwaite	Ford Cosworth
026	16	27	-	-	-	-	98	H Postlethwaite	Ford Cosworth

* Team disqualified in 1984 and all points from that season removed. It wasn't until the 007 that the model number was attributed to a type of car. Prior to this, they related to chassis numbers over two distinct model types.

VANWALL (GB)

Principal: Tony Vandervell.
Base: Acton, London.
Founded: 1949.

Guy Anthony Vandervell, owner of VP bearings, began racing with the Thin Wall Ferrari but soon moved on to his own designs. A very thorough organisation, each year the cars were dismantled and completely revised and rebuilt (hence the difficulty with model numbers, as all cars were known by the chassis number). Upset by the death of Stuart Lewis-Evans, the team withdrew from extensive racing and finally closed due to ill health of the owner.

Constructors' Championships: 1 (1958)

Totals	GPs	Starts	Points	Poles	F.Laps	Wins			
	28	64	108	7	6	9			
Seasons							Colour	Main Driver(s)	
1954	2	2	-	-	-	-	green	Collins	
1955	4	6	-	-	-	-	green	Hawthorn, Wharton, Schell	
1956	5	12	3	-	-	-	green	Schell, Trintignant	
1957	6	16	37	2	3	3	green	Moss, Brooks, Lewis-Evans	
1958	9	26	68	5	3	6	green	Moss, Brooks, Lewis-Evans	
1959	1	1	-	-	-	-	green	Brooks	
1960	1	1	-	-	-	-	green	Brooks	
Models							Year(s)	Chief Designer	Engine
Spl.	2	2	-	-	-	-	54	O Maddock	4
VW (55)	4	6	-	-	-	-	55	O Maddock	4
VW (56)	5	12	3	-	-	-	56	C Chapman	4
VW (57)	15	42	105	7	6	9	57-58	F Costin	4
VW (59)	1	1	-	-	-	-	59	F Costin	4
VW11	1	1	-	-	-	-	60	F Costin	4

Prior to the VW11, the cars were referred to by chassis numbers only, although each year's model was a slight variation on the predecessor.

VERITAS (D)

Principal: Ernst Loof.
Base: Nürburgring.
Founded: 1948.

Formed by BMW engineers Ernst Loof and Lorenz Dietrich to build BMW-based sports cars (RS) and later single seaters (Meteor). Financial problems in 1950 moved the firm to a small workshop at the Nürburgring but it finally closed in 1953 when Loof returned to BMW.

Totals	GPs	Starts	Points	Poles	F.Laps	Wins			
	6	18	-	-	-	-			
Seasons							Colour	Main Driver(s)	
1951	1	1	-	-	-	-	silver	Hirt	
1952	3	9	-	-	-	-	silver	Ulmen, Legat, Riess	
1953	2	8	-	-	-	-	silver	Herrmann, Helfrich, Loof	
Models							Year(s)	Chief Designer	Engine
Meteor	6	10	-	-	-	-	51-53	E Loof	6
RS	2	8	-	-	-	-	52-53	E Loof	6

WILLIAMS (GB)

Principal: Frank Williams.
Base: Reading, Berkshire/Didcot, Oxfordshire (1976)/Grove, Wantage, Oxfordshire (1996).
Founded: 1968.

Frank Williams, one time racer and racing car dealer, took the step up to Formula 1 with his good friend Piers Courage. Racing a Brabham very successfully in 1969 turned to disaster when Piers perished in a de Tomaso car the following year. The team struggled on using March chassis, until the finance was available for their own car. The first true Williams appeared in 1972 and was known as a Politoys in deference to the sponsors. Future cars would follow this trend as with the Iso-Marlboros the following year. After the 1976 season when they were called Wolf Williams, Frank split from Walter Wolf and virtually started again. Moving from the Reading base, a new factory was found and Williams Grand Prix Engineering came into being. After a first season with the March chassis once again, the team has never looked back with the Patrick Head designed cars winning driver and constructor championships on a regular basis. The team battled on from the major setback of Frank Williams being paralysed in a road accident near the Paul Ricard circuit in March 1986. The combination of Renault engines and Adrian Newey's design expertise made the 90's cars virtually unstoppable, although this partnership concluded at the end of 1997. Damon Hill became the fourth World Champion at Williams to vacate the number one seat in the wake of Prost, Mansell and Piquet. After a lean spell BMW forged a strong partnership with the team in 2000 which brought wins but no championships. This engine partnership dissolved in 2005 resulting in Williams reuniting with Cosworth for the immediate future.

Constructors' Championships: 9 (1980,81,86,87,92,93,94,96,97). **Drivers' Championships:** 7 (1980,82,87,92,93,96,97).

Totals	GPs	Starts	Points	Poles	F.Laps	Wins		
	507	976	2507.5	125	128	113		
Seasons							Sponsor(s)	Main Driver(s)
1972	1	1	-	-	-	-	Politoys	Pescarolo
1973	15	28	2	-	-	-	Iso,Marlboro	Ganley,Galli
1974	15	22	4	-	-	-	Iso,Marlboro	Merzario,Laffite
1975	12	21	6	-	-	-	Fina,Ambrozium	Laffite,Merzario
1976	13	19	-	-	-	-	Marlboro	Ickx,Leclère/Merzario
1977 used March chassis								
1978	16	16	11	-	2	-	Saudia,Albilad	Jones
1979	15	30	75	3	3	5	Saudia,Albilad	Jones,Regazzoni
1980	14	32	120	3	6	6	Saudia,Leyland	Jones*,Reutemann *Champion*
1981	15	30	95	2	7	4	Saudia,Leyland	Jones,Reutemann
1982	15	30	58	1	-	1	Saudia,TAG	Rosberg*,Daly *Champion*
1983	15	29	38	1	-	1	Denim,Saudia	Rosberg,Laffite
1984	16	32	25.5	-	-	1	Saudia,Denim	Rosberg,Laffite
1985	16	31	71	3	4	4	Canon,Denim	Rosberg,Mansell
1986	16	32	141	4	11	9	Canon,Mobil	Piquet,Mansell
1987	16	30	137	12	7	9	Canon	Piquet*,Mansell *Champion*
1988	16	32	20	-	1	-	Canon	Mansell,Patrese
1989	16	32	77	1	1	2	Canon	Boutsen,Patrese
1990	16	32	57	1	5	2	Canon	Boutsen,Patrese
1991	16	32	125	6	8	7	Canon,Labatt's	Mansell,Patrese
1992	16	32	164	15	11	10	Canon,Labatt's	Mansell*,Patrese *Champion*
1993	16	32	168	15	10	10	Canon,Camel	Prost*,Hill *Champion*
1994	16	31	118	6	8	7	Rothmans	Hill,Senna/Coulthard
1995	17	34	118	12	6	5	Rothmans	Hill,Coulthard
1996	16	32	175	12	11	12	Rothmans	Hill*,Villeneuve *Champion*
1997	17	34	123	11	9	8	Rothmans	Villeneuve*,Frentzen *Champion*
1998	16	32	38	-	-	-	Winfield	Villeneuve,Frentzen
1999	16	32	35	-	1	-	Winfield	R Schumacher,Zanardi
2000	17	34	36	-	-	-	Compaq,Allianz	R Schumacher,Button
2001	17	34	80	4	8	4	Compaq,Allianz	R Schumacher,Montoya
2002	17	34	92	7	3	1	Compaq,Allianz	R Schumacher,Montoya
2003	16	32	144	4	4	4	HP,Allianz	R Schumacher,Montoya
2004	18	36	88	1	2	1	HP,Allianz	R Schumacher,Montoya
2005	18	36	66	1	-	-	HP,RBS	Webber, Heidfeld
Models							Year(s)	Chief Designer	Engine
FX3-B	4	7	-	-	-	-	72-73	L Bailey	Ford Cosworth
IR	12	22	2	-	-	-	73	J Clarke	Ford Cosworth
FW	24	34	4	-	-	-	74-75	J Clarke	Ford Cosworth
FW04	10	10	6	-	-	-	75-76	R Stokoe	Ford Cosworth
FW05	13	18	-	-	-	-	76	H Postlethwaite	Ford Cosworth
FW06	20	24	15	-	2	-	78-79	P Head	Ford Cosworth
FW07-B,C	43	90	300	8	16	15	79-82	P Head	Ford Cosworth
FW08-C	26	51	80	2	-	2	82-83	P Head	Ford Cosworth
FW09-B	17	34	27.5	-	-	1	83-84	P Head	Honda t

Models	GPs	Starts	Points	Poles	F.Laps	Wins	Year(s)	Chief Designer	Engine
FW10	16	31	71	3	4	4	85	P Head	Honda t
FW11-B	32	62	278	16	18	18	86-87	P Head	Honda t
FW12-C	29	57	74	1	2	1	88-89	P Head	Judd, Renault
FW13-B	20	39	80	1	5	3	89-90	P Head	Renault
FW14-B	32	64	289	21	19	17	91-92	P Head	Renault
FW15C	16	32	168	15	10	10	93	P Head	Renault
FW16-B	16	31	118	6	8	7	94	P Head	Renault
FW17-B	17	34	118	12	6	5	95	P Head	Renault
FW18	16	32	175	12	11	12	96	P Head	Renault
FW19	17	34	123	11	9	8	97	P Head	Renault
FW20	16	32	38	-	-	-	98	P Head	Mecachrome
FW21	16	32	35	-	1	-	99	P Head	Supertec
FW22	17	34	36	-	-	-	00	P Head	BMW
FW23	17	34	80	4	8	4	01	P Head	BMW
FW24	17	34	92	7	3	1	02	P Head	BMW
FW25	16	32	144	4	4	4	03	P Head	BMW
FW26	18	36	88	1	2	1	04	P Head	BMW
FW27	18	36	66	1	-	-	05	S Michael	BMW

The McGuire BM1 which was a modification of the FW04 failed to pre-qualify in 1977. It wasn't until the FW04 that the model number was attributed to a type of car. Prior to this, they were related to different chassis. The cars named FW02 & 03 in 1975 were the FW model from the previous year.

WOLF (CDN/GB)

Principal: Walter Wolf.
Base: Reading, Berkshire.
Founded: 1975.

Canadian oil businessman, Walter Wolf, financed the Williams Formula 1 operation in 1976. Disappointed, he bought out Williams and set up his own Walter Wolf Racing. The new car was an instant success, winning first time out. After a great first season, the team faded quickly and by the end of 1979 had withdrawn from racing completely.

Totals	GPs	Starts	Points	Poles	F.Laps	Wins			
	47	52	79	1	2	3			
Seasons							Sponsor(s)	Main Driver(s)	
1977	17	17	55	1	2	3	Castrol, Fina	J Scheckter	
1978	16	21	24	-	-	-	Castrol	J Scheckter, Rahal	
1979	14	14	-	-	-	-	Olympus	Hunt/Rosberg	
Models							Year(s)	Chief Designer	Engine
WR1,2,3,4	27	27	59	1	2	3	77-78	H Postlethwaite	Ford Cosworth
WR5,6	10	11	20	-	-	-	78	H Postlethwaite	Ford Cosworth
WR7,8,8/9,9	14	14	-	-	-	-	79	H Postlethwaite	Ford Cosworth

Cars were not given separate model numbers and were known by chassis numbers. They are grouped here in their three distinct model variations.

ZAKSPEED (D)

Principal: Erich Zakowski.
Base: Niederzissen, nr Koblenz.
Founded: 1968.

Formed from a saloon car team from which Zakowski helped develop the Ford Capri and Escort, after taking over the factory team in 1976. In a bold move, this ambitious team built both chassis and turbo engine, with the car completed late in 1984. After no real results with either its own turbo or the Yamaha unit it introduced to Grands Prix, Zakowski returned to the German Touring Car series.

Totals	GPs	Starts	Points	Poles	F.Laps	Wins			
	53	83	2	-	-	-			
Seasons							Sponsor(s)	Main Driver(s)	
1985	9	9	-	-	-	-	West	Palmer	
1986	16	27	-	-	-	-	West	Palmer, Rothengatter	
1987	16	31	2	-	-	-	West	Brundle, Danner	
1988	10	14	-	-	-	-	West	Schneider, Ghinzani	
1989	2	2	-	-	-	-	West	Schneider, Suzuki	
Models							Year(s)	Chief Designer	Engine
841	9	9	-	-	-	-	85	P Brown	4t
861	18	30	-	-	-	-	86-87	P Brown	4t
871	15	28	2	-	-	-	87	H Zollinir	4t
881	10	14	-	-	-	-	88	H Zollinir	4t
891	2	2	-	-	-	-	89	G Brunner	Yamaha

Constructors

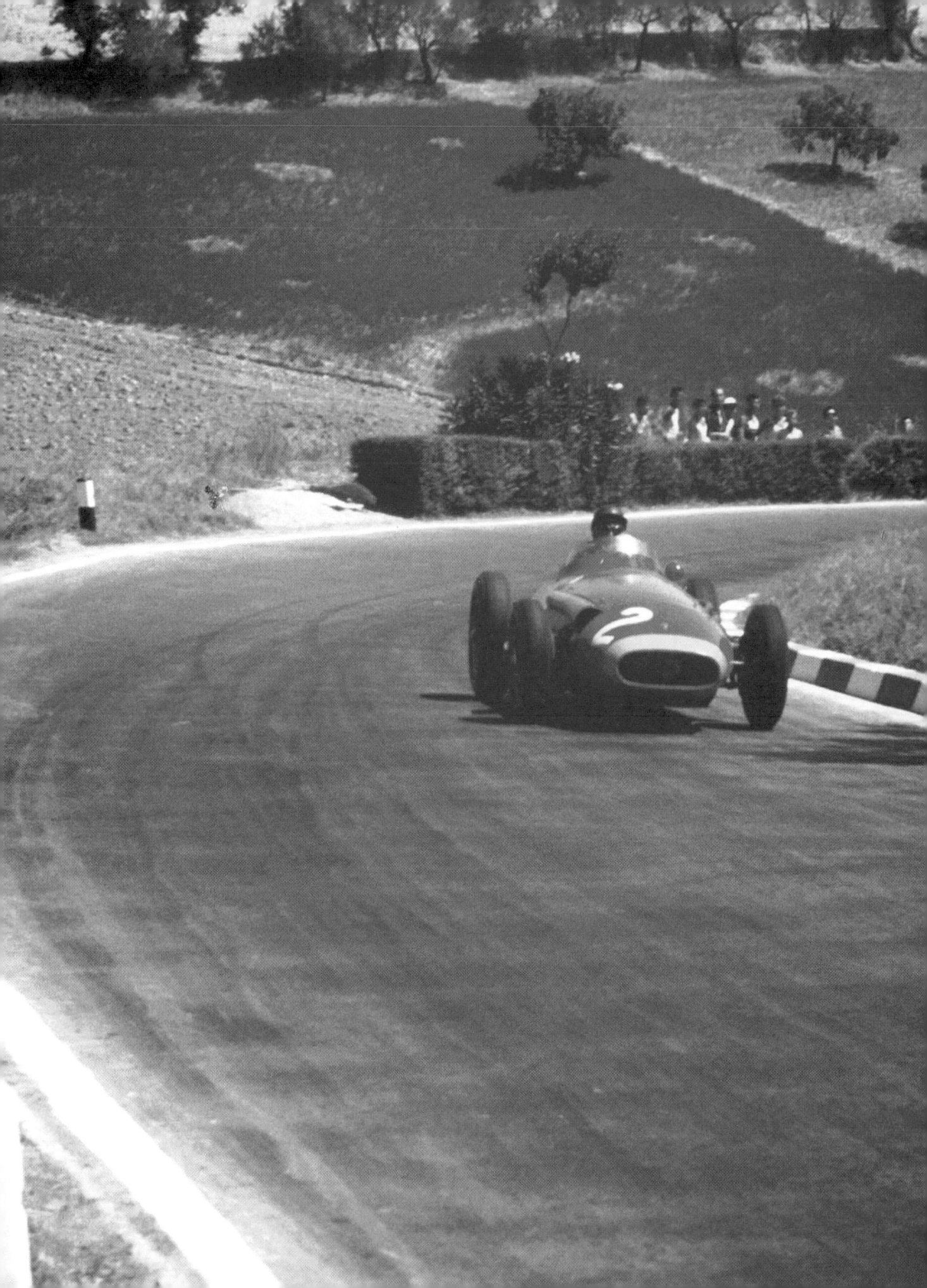

5

CIRCUITS

Circuit History
Circuit Summary

Left: *Juan Manuel Fangio (Maserati 250F) in 1957 at Pescara, the longest circuit ever to feature in the World Championship. He finished second. (LAT)*

COUNTRIES

ARGENTINA
AUSTRALIA
AUSTRIA
BAHRAIN
BELGIUM
BRAZIL
CANADA
CHINA
FRANCE
GERMANY
GREAT BRITAIN
HUNGARY
ITALY
JAPAN
MALAYSIA
MEXICO
MONACO
MOROCCO
NETHERLANDS
PORTUGAL
SOUTH AFRICA
SPAIN
SWEDEN
SWITZERLAND
TURKEY
UNITED STATES OF AMERICA

Where circuits have changed their layout, the darker line depicts the most recent configuration. They are not drawn to scale.

CIRCUITS

A1-Ring
Adelaide
Aida
Âin-Diab
Aintree
Anderstorp
Avus
Brands Hatch
Bremgarten
Buenos Aires
Bugatti Au Mans
Clermont-Ferrand
Dallas
Detroit
Dijon-Prenois
Donington Park
East London
Estoril
Fuji
Hockenheim
Hungaroring
Imola
Indianapolis
Interlagos
Istanbul
Jarama
Jerez de la Frontera
Kylami
Las Vegas
Long Beach
Magny-Cours
Melbourne
Mexico City
Monsanto Park
Mont-Tremblant
Monte-Carlo

Montjuïc
Montmeló
Montréal
Monza
Mosport Park
Nivelles-Baulers
Nürburgring
Paul Richard
Pedralbes
Pescara
Phoenix
Porto
Reims & Reims-Gueux
Rio de Janeiro
Riverside
Rouen-les-Essarts
Sakhir
Sebring
Sepang
Shanghai
Silverstone
Spa-Francorchamps
Suzuka
Watkins Glen
Zandvoort
Zeltweg
Zolder

Circuit History

Argentina (RA)

BUENOS AIRES

Location: Buenos Aires (southern outskirts).
First Used: 1952.

Overseen by President Juan Domingo Peron and named El Autódromo 17 de Octubre, the date of Peron's accession. The circuit includes various permutations, but was involved in an accident that killed nine spectators in 1953. A much faster extension was later added on swamp land around the lake, when the circuit was known as the Autódromo Almirante (Admiral) Brown. Further redevelopment in the 1990s and another new name, Autódromo Oscar Alfredo Gálvez, after the Argentinian driver, saw the circuit emerge as a Championship venue once again. The lake extension has been lost to a power station, but the track now uses the existing infield and the new Senna's 'S' section.

World Championship races: 20

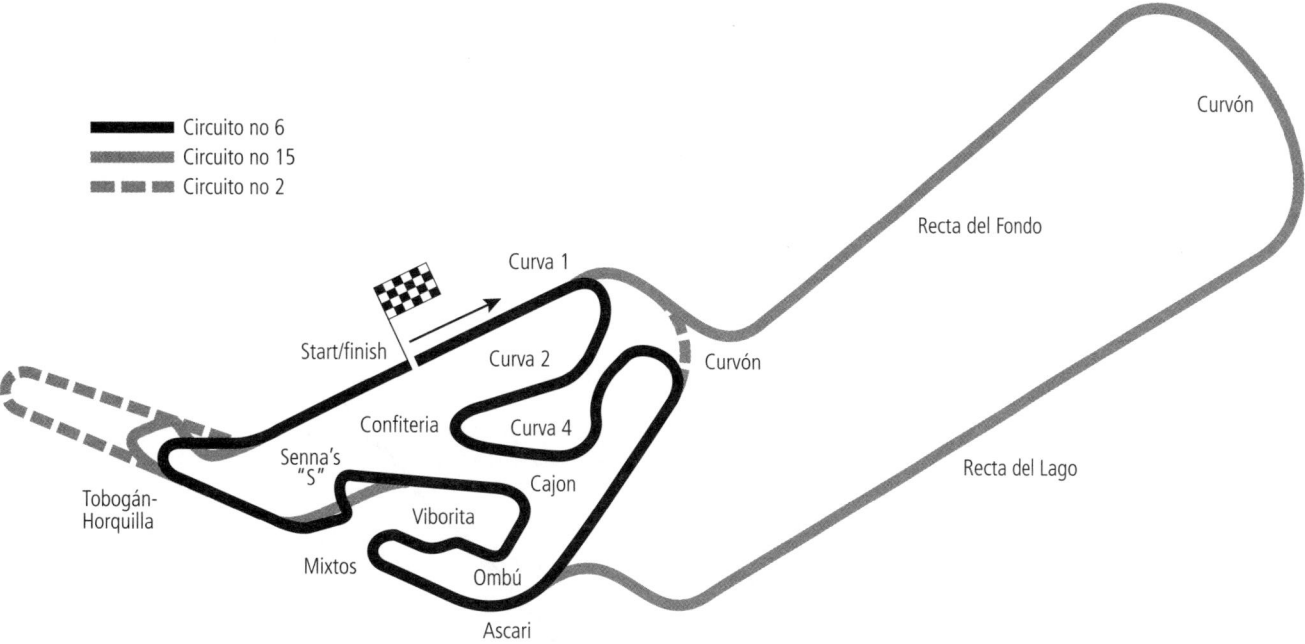

Records:

	Length km	miles	Years (no. of races)	Driver (Car)	Time min:sec	Speed km/h	mph	Year
No. 2								
a)	3.912	2.431	1953-58,60 (7)	Pole: S Moss (Cooper)	1:36.900	145.337	90.309	1960
				F. Lap: S Moss (Cooper)	1:38.900	142.398	88.482	1960
				Winner: B McLaren (Cooper)		136.242	84.657	1960
No. 9 (Tobogán cut back)								
b)	3.345	2.078	1972-73 (2)	Pole: C Regazzoni (BRM)	1:10.540	170.712	106.075	1973
				F. Lap: E Fittipaldi (JPS Lotus)	1:11.220	169.082	105.063	1973
				Winner: E Fittipaldi (JPS Lotus)		165.663	102.938	1973
No. 15 (long circuit)								
c)	5.968	3.708	1974-75,77-81 (7)	Pole: N Piquet (Brabham)	1:42.665	209.271	130.035	1981
				F. Lap: N Piquet (Brabham)	1:45.287	204.059	126.797	1981
				Winner: N Piquet (Brabham)		200.731	124.728	1981
No. 6 (existing infield section added)								
d)	4.259	2.646	1995-98 (4)	Pole: J Villeneuve (Williams)	1:24.473	181.506	112.783	1997
				F. Lap: G Berger (Benetton)	1:27.981	174.269	108.286	1997
				Winner: M Schumacher (Ferrari)		169.304	105.201	1998

ADELAIDE

Location: Adelaide (city centre), South Australia.
First Used: 1985.

One of the best street circuits and a firm favourite with the Grand Prix fraternity. The wide track works its way around the city parkland and even includes part of the Victoria Park racecourse. The main straight is unusually long for a street circuit and is often remembered for the spectacular blow-out suffered by Mansell in the 1986 title decider. There were many sad faces in the Formula 1 world when the venue was switched to Melbourne, although the track is still in use for national racing.

World Championship races: 11

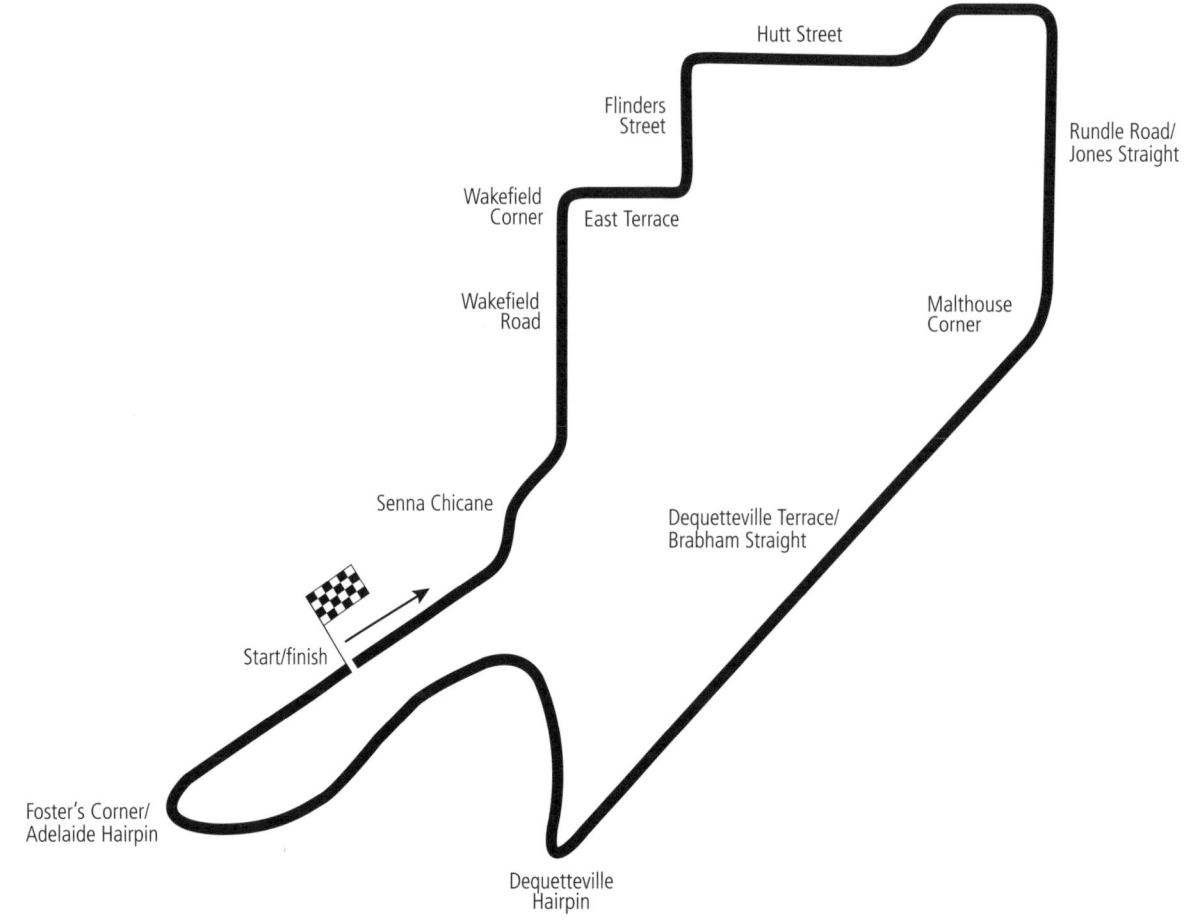

Records:

	Length		Years (no. of races)	Driver (Car)	Time	Speed		Year
	km	miles			min:sec	km/h	mph	
a)	3.778	2.348	1985 (1)					
b)	3.779	2.348	1986 (1)					
c)	3.780	2.349	1987-95 (9)	Pole: A Senna (McLaren)	1:13.371	185.468	115.245	1993
				F. Lap: D Hill (Williams)	1:15.381	180.523	112.172	1993
				Winner: A Senna (McLaren)		173.183	107.611	1993

MELBOURNE

Location: Melbourne (Albert Park, inner southern suburbs), Victoria.
First Used: 1953.

Albert Park was used for the non-championship Australian Grand Prix as early as 1953 and GP racing has now returned to Melbourne, the sporting capital of Australia. Ron Walker brought this popular GP to the area, although it still has its fair share of environmental protesters. The circuit is remarkably unchanged, still weaving around the park lake, although now in a clockwise direction with the old circuit running along the back of the pit area.

World Championship races: 10

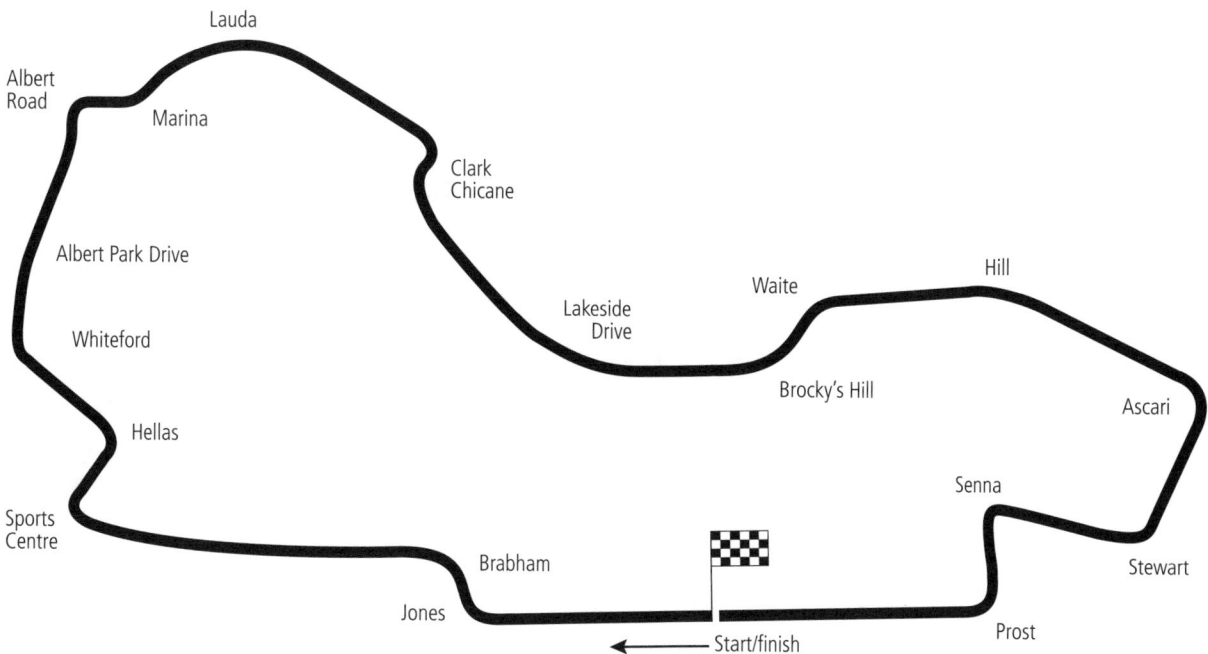

Records:

	Length		Years (no. of races)	Driver (Car)	Time	Speed		Year
	km	miles			min:sec	km/h	mph	
a)	5.302	3.295	1996-97 (2)					
b)	5.303	3.295	1998-05 (8)	Pole: M Schumacher (Ferrari)	1:24.408	226.172	140.537	2004
				F. Lap: M Schumacher (Ferrari)	1:24.125	226.933	141.010	2004
				Winner: M Schumacher (Ferrari)		219.011	136.087	2004

A1-RING (formerly Österreichring)

Location: 6 km (4 miles) west of Knittelfeld.
First Used: 1969.

Built as a replacement for Zeltweg in the wooded Styrian hills, above the airfield circuit. Renowned for its beauty, the track rises and falls in a natural hillside bowl. A chicane was added where Mark Donohue was killed but problems with the narrow start line and deer wandering onto the track, led to its eventual disuse. A shortened and much modified version, now renamed the A1-Ring, returned as a new Grand Prix venue in 1997. In 2004 a programme of redevelopment began but this project has been postponed due to environmental pressure.

World Championship races: 25

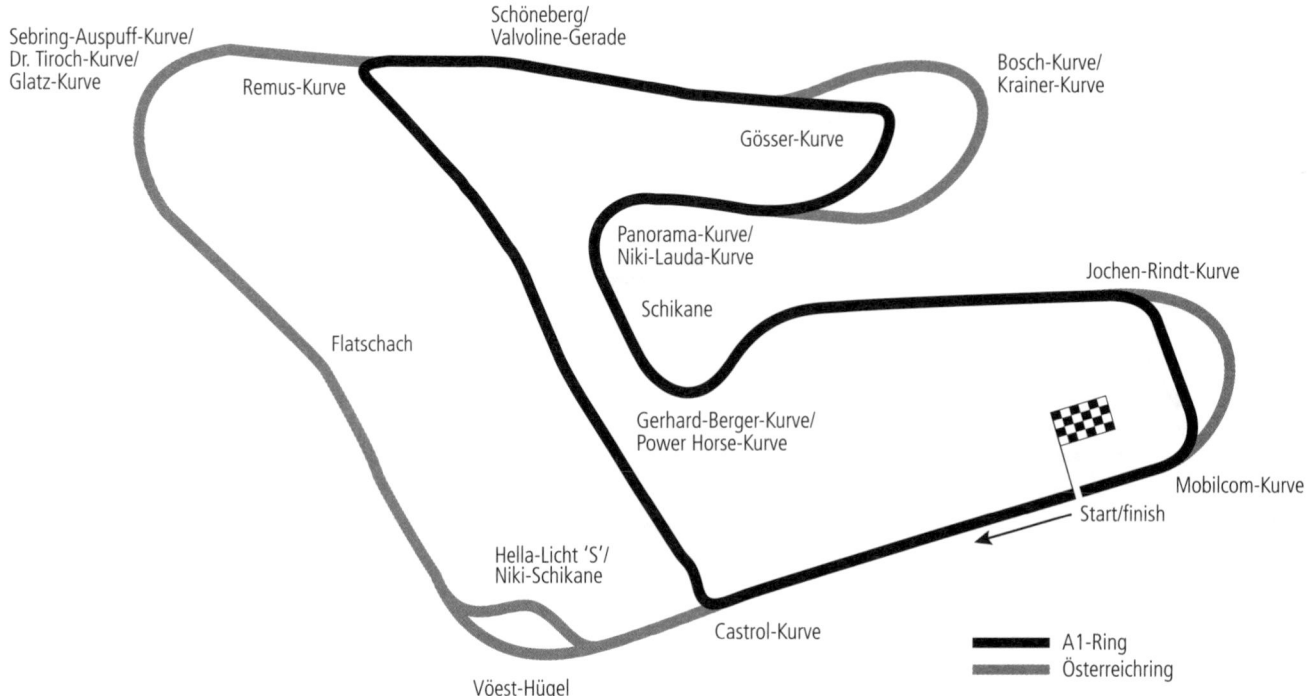

Records:

	Length		Years (no. of races)	Driver (Car)	Time	Speed		Year
	km	miles			min:sec	km/h	mph	
a)	5.911	3.673	1970-75 (6)	Pole: N Lauda (Ferrari)	1:34.850	224.350	139.405	1975
				F. Lap: C Regazzoni (Ferrari)	1:37.220	218.881	136.006	1974
				Winner: C Reutemann (Brabham)		215.804	134.095	1974
First corner eased								
b)	5.910	3.672	1976 (1)	Pole: J Hunt (McLaren)	1:35.020	223.911	139.132	1976
				F. Lap: J Hunt (McLaren)	1:35.910	221.833	137.841	1976
				Winner: J Watson (Penske)		212.451	132.011	1976
Hella-Licht 'S'								
c)	5.942	3.692	1977-87 (11)	Pole: N Piquet (Williams)	1:23.357	256.622	159.457	1987
				F. Lap: N Mansell (Williams)	1:28.318	242.207	150.500	1987
				Winner: N Mansell (Williams)		235.421	146.284	1987
New shortened circuit								
d)	4.323	2.686	1997 (1)					
	4.319	2.684	1998-99 (2)					
	4.326	2.688	2000-03 (4)	Pole: R Barrichello (Ferrari)	1:08.082	228.747	142.137	2002
				F. Lap: M Schumacher (Ferrari)	1:08.337	227.894	141.607	2003
				Winner: M Schumacher (Ferrari)		213.003	132.354	2003

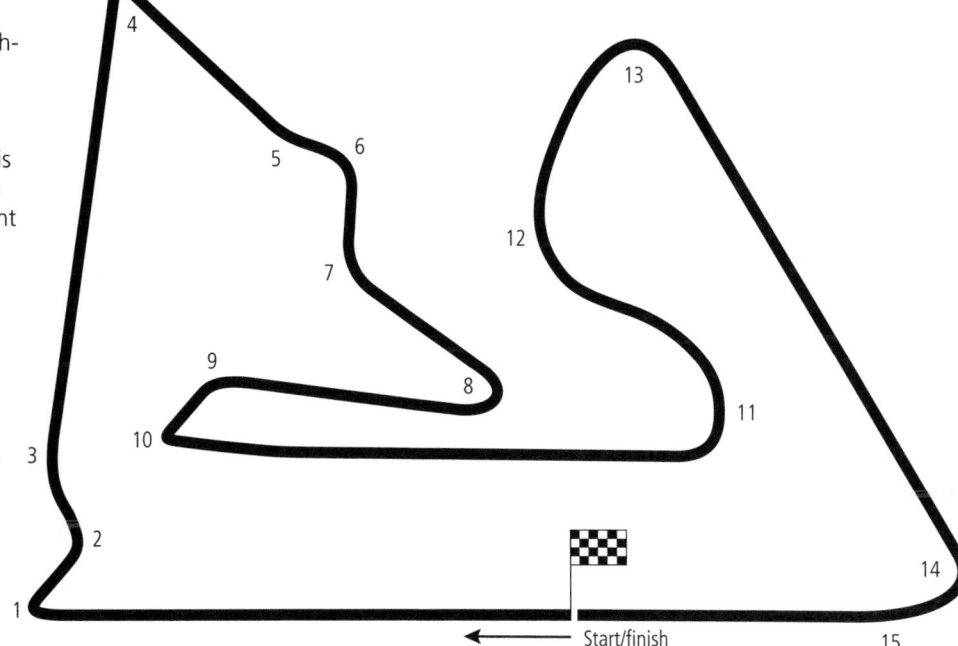

ZELTWEG

Location: 6 km (4 miles) west of Knittelfeld.
First Used: 1958.

A simple circuit, laid out along runways of a NATO fighter base, north of Graz. Situated in the River Mur valley, its bumpy surface meant that the track was redundant as soon as the new 'Zeltweg' appeared.

World Championship races: 1

Records:

	Length		Years (no. of races)	Driver (Car)	Time	Speed		Year
	km	miles			min:sec	km/h	mph	
a)	3.200	1.988	1964 (1)	Pole: G Hill (BRM)	1: 9.840	164.948	102.494	1964
				F. Lap: D Gurney (Brabham)	1:10.560	163.265	101.448	1964
				Winner: L Bandini (Ferrari)		159.615	99.180	1964

Bahrain (BRN)

SAKHIR

Location: 30 km (20 miles) south-west of Manama
First Used: 2004.

Another Hermann Tilke creation this track was built in about 18 months after the inaugural race was brought forward. Built in the desert on a former camel farm it has various permutations including a test oval and a drag strip. Huge investment helped F1 establish a base in the Middle East on a state of the art facility with many new features such as a high-grip asphalt surface.

World Championship races: 2

Records:

	Length		Years (no. of races)	Driver (Car)	Time	Speed		Year
	km	miles			min:sec	km/h	mph	
a)	5.417	3.366	2004 (1)	Pole: M Schumacher (Ferrari)	1:30.139	216.345	134.431	2004
				F. Lap: M Schumacher (Ferrari)	1:30.252	216.074	134.263	2004
				Winner: M Schumacher (Ferrari)		208.976	129.852	2004
Turn 4 eased								
b)	5.412	3.363	2005 (1)	Pole: F Alonso (Renault) *	3:01.902	214.216	133.108	2005
				F. Lap: P de la Rosa (McLaren)	1:31.447	213.054	132.386	2005
				Winner: F Alonso (Renault)		207.082	128.675	2005

Fastest single qualifying lap record was set during 2005 aggregate timing by F Alonso (Renault), 1m 29.848s, 216.846 km/h, 134.742 mph.

NIVELLES-BAULERS

Location: 30 km (20 miles) south of Brussels.

First Used: 1971.

Start/finish

This flat and unpopular purpose-built circuit came into Grand Prix use after the loss of Spa and suffered by comparison. A typical modern facility, it had good safety provisions and was extended to full Grand Prix length in 1972. It held its last race in November 1979 and during 2002 work began to demolish the track to make way for new industrial units.

World Championship races: 2

Records:

	Length		Years (no. of races)	Driver (Car)	Time min:sec	Speed		Year
	km	miles				km/h	mph	
a)	3.724	2.314	1972,74 (2)	Pole: C Regazzoni (Ferrari)	1: 9.820	192.014	119.312	1974
				F. Lap: D Hulme (McLaren)	1:11.310	188.002	116.819	1974
				Winner: E Fittipaldi (JPS Lotus)		182.423	113.353	1972

SPA-FRANCORCHAMPS

Location: 50 km (30 miles) south-east of Liège.

First Used: 1924.

Originated by Jules de Thier on sweeping public roads in the wooded hills of the Ardennes, south of Francorchamps. One of the great circuits, its natural beauty was combined with unpredictable weather patterns that occasionally left isolated parts of the circuit wet. This safety aspect and high speed nature led to the full circuit's disuse, while a new link was built in 1978. The new shorter circuit met with universal acclaim which meant that Eau Rouge, often regarded as motor racing's greatest corner, returned to the World Championship. Tobacco sponsorship disputes led to the race missing its 2003 slot but thankfully this firm favourite with fans and drivers returned the following year.

World Championship races: 39

Records:

	Length		Years (no. of races)	Driver (Car)	Time min:sec	Speed		Year
	km	miles				km/h	mph	
a)	14.120	8.774	1950-56 (7)	Pole: J M Fangio (Lancia Ferrari)	4: 9.800	203.491	126.443	1956
				F. Lap: S Moss (Maserati)	4:14.700	199.576	124.011	1956
				Winner: J M Fangio (Mercedes-Benz)		191.238	118.829	1955
Corners eased								
b)	14.100	8.761	1958,60-68,70 (11)	Pole: J Stewart (March)	3:28.000	244.038	151.638	1970
				F. Lap: C Amon (March)	3:27.400	244.744	152.077	1970
				Winner: P Rodriguez (BRM)		241.308	149.942	1970
Shorter circuit								
c)	6.949	4.318	1983 (1)	Pole: A Prost (Renault)	2: 4.615	200.750	124.740	1983
				F. Lap: A de Cesaris (Alfa Romeo)	2: 7.493	196.218	121.924	1983
				Winner: A Prost (Renault)		191.729	119.135	1983
(circuit length recalculated)								
d)	6.940	4.312	1985-91 (7)	Pole: A Senna (McLaren)	1:47.811	231.739	143.996	1991
				F. Lap: A Prost (Ferrari)	1:55.087	217.088	134.892	1990
				Winner: A Senna (McLaren)		211.729	131.562	1990

Minor revision

e)	6.974	4.333	1992-93,95 (3)	Pole: A Prost (Williams)	1:47.571	233.394	145.024	1993
				F. Lap: A Prost (Williams)	1:51.095	225.990	140.424	1993
				Winner: D Hill (Williams)		217.795	135.331	1993

Chicane at Eau Rouge

f)	7.001	4.350	1994 (1)	Pole: R Barrichello (Jordan)	2:21.163	178.542	110.941	1994
				F. Lap: D Hill (Williams)	1:57.117	215.200	133.719	1994
				Winner: D Hill (Williams)		208.170	129.351	1994

La Source eased

g)	6.968	4.330	1996-01 (6)	Pole: M Häkkinen (McLaren)	1:48.682	230.809	143.418	1998
				F. Lap: M Schumacher (Ferrari)	1:49.758	228.546	142.012	2001
				Winner: M Schumacher (Ferrari)		221.050	137.354	2001

La Source & Bus Stop re-profiled

h)	6.963	4.327	2002 (1)	Pole: M Schumacher (Ferrari)	1:43.726	241.663	150.163	2002
				F. Lap: M Schumacher (Ferrari)	1:47.176	233.884	145.329	2002
				Winner: M Schumacher (Ferrari)		225.970	140.411	2002

Bus Stop re-profiled

i)	6.976	4.335	2004-05 (2)	Pole: J P Montoya (McLaren)	1:46.391	236.050	146.675	2005
				F. Lap: K Räikkönen (McLaren)	1:45.108	238.931	148.465	2004
				Winner: K Räikkönen (McLaren)		204.568	127.113	2005

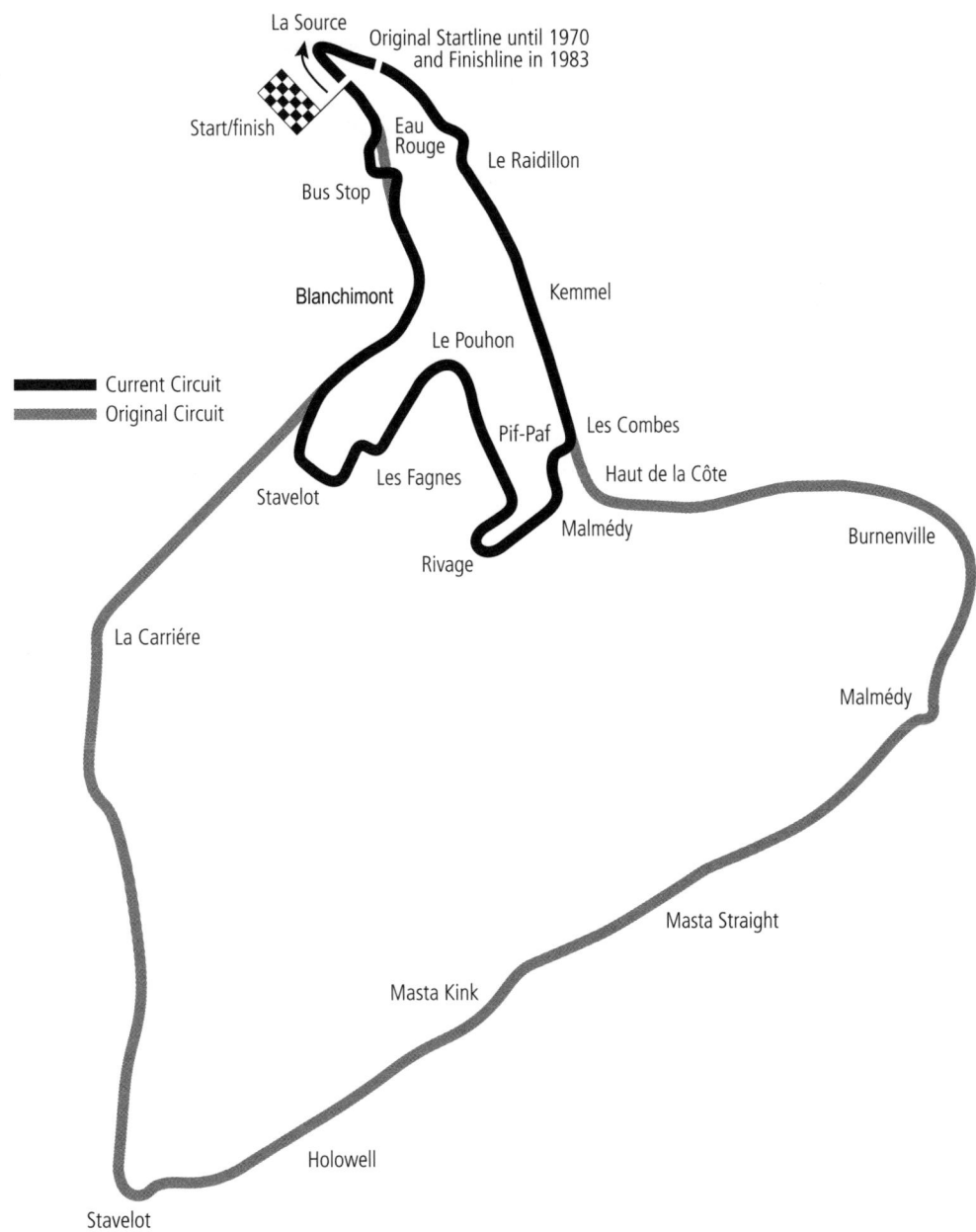

La Source

Original Startline until 1970
and Finishline in 1983

Start/finish

Eau Rouge

Le Raidillon

Bus Stop

Kemmel

Blanchimont

Le Pouhon

Pif-Paf

Les Combes

Haut de la Côte

Les Fagnes

Stavelot

Rivage

Malmédy

Burnenville

La Carriére

Malmédy

Masta Straight

Masta Kink

Holowell

Stavelot

■ Current Circuit
■ Original Circuit

ZOLDER

Location: 10 km (6 miles) north of Hasselt.
First Used: 1965.

Another of the purpose-built circuits of the time, Zolder was situated in sandy woodland hills of Flemish speaking Belgium. As a circuit, it came to be infested with numerous chicanes and in 1981 Osella mechanic Giovanni Amadeo was killed in the narrow pit lane and Dave Luckett of Arrows was injured in a start line accident. The following year saw the fatal accident of Gilles Villeneuve at the approach to Terlamenbocht and a memorial to this popular driver can be found near the pit entrance.

World Championship races: 10

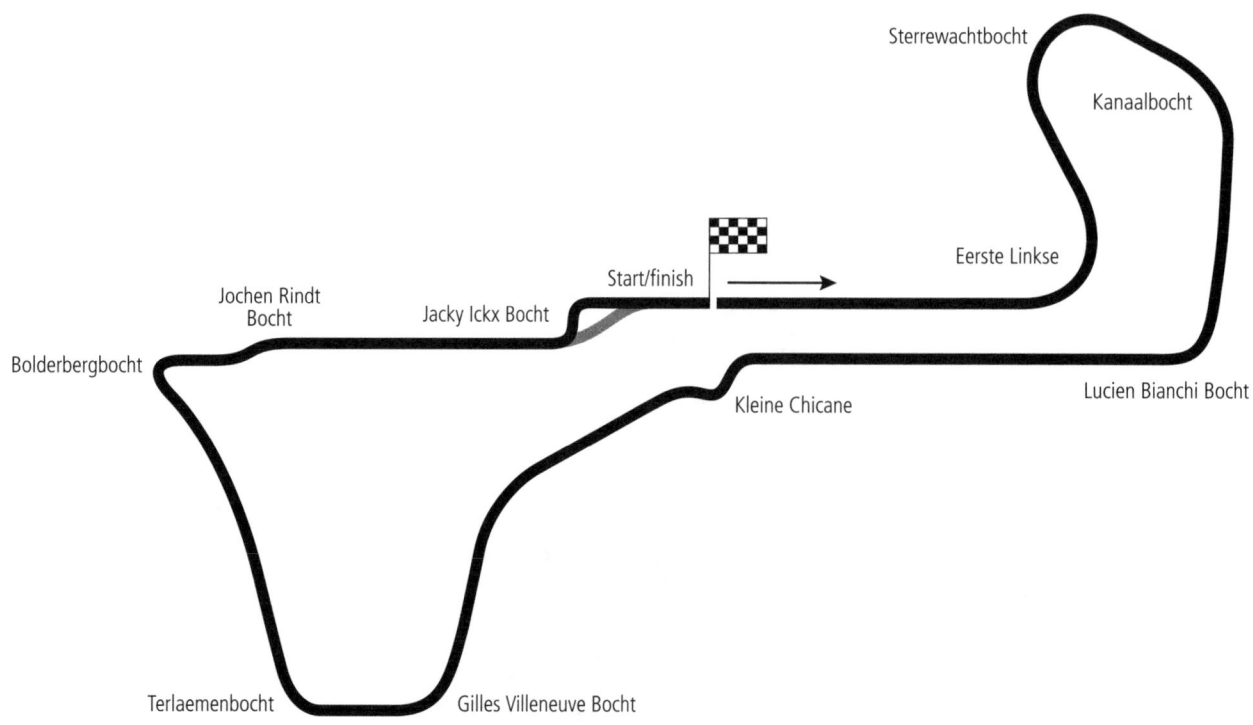

Records:

	Length		Years (no. of races)	Driver (Car)	Time	Speed		Year
	km	miles			min:sec	km/h	mph	
a)	4.220	2.622	1973 (1)	Pole: R Peterson (JPS Lotus)	1:22.460	184.235	114.478	1973
				F. Lap: F Cevert (Tyrrell)	1:25.420	177.851	110.511	1973
				Winner: J Stewart (Tyrrell)		173.384	107.736	1973
New chicane before start/finish								
b)	4.262	2.648	1975-82,84 (9)	Pole: M Alboreto (Ferrari)	1:14.846	204.997	127.379	1984
				F. Lap: R Arnoux (Ferrari)	1:19.294	193.498	120.234	1984
				Winner: J Watson (McLaren)		187.047	116.226	1982

INTERLAGOS

Location: São Paulo suburb, 16 km (10 miles) south of city centre.
First Used: 1940.

The Autodromo José Carlos Pace was built in a natural bowl that has gradually been absorbed by this sprawling city. The original track twisted around itself between two lakes, giving the circuit its name. A new shorter version, missed out much of the old track, but maintained the steep start line straight. This track tends to create interesting races and the event was moved to the end of the season in 2004.

World Championship races: 23

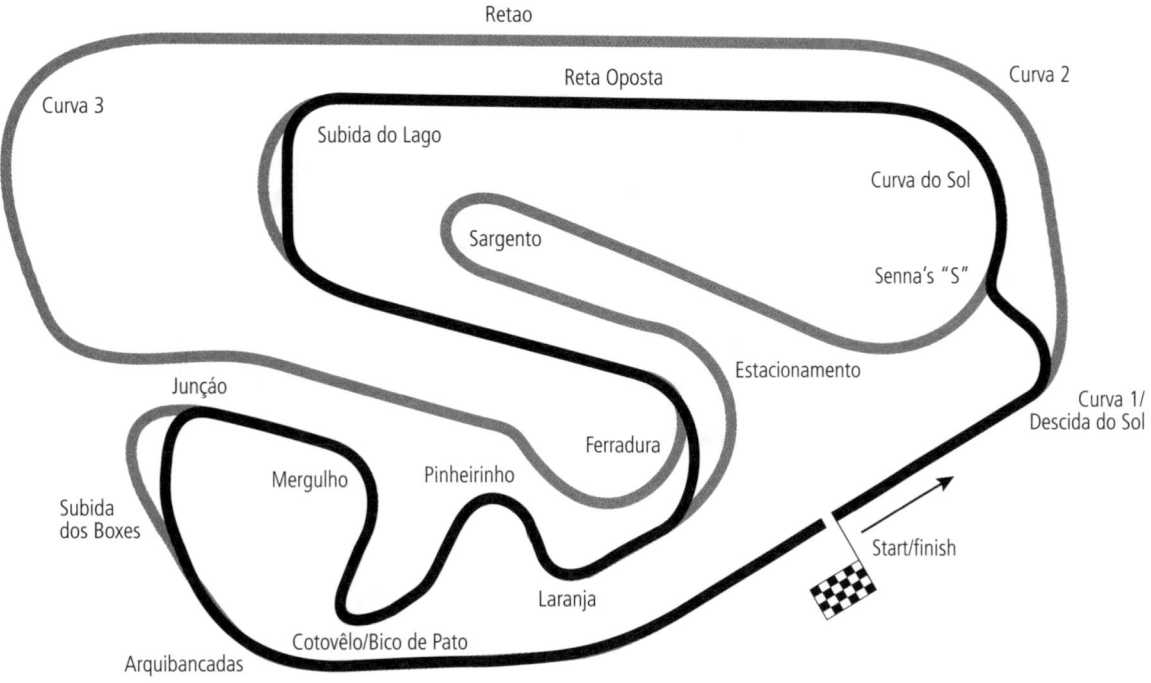

Records:

	Length		Years (no. of races)	Driver (Car)	Time	Speed		Year
	km	miles			min:sec	km/h	mph	
a)	7.960	4.946	1973-77 (5)	Pole: J-P Jarier (Shadow)	2:29.880	191.193	118.802	1975
				F. Lap: J-P Jarier (Shadow)	2:34.160	185.885	115.503	1975
				Winner: E Fittipaldi (JPS Lotus)		183.822	114.222	1973
Corners eased								
b)	7.874	4.893	1979-80 (2)	Pole: J-P Jabouille (Renault)	2:21.400	200.470	124.566	1980
				F. Lap: R Arnoux (Renault)	2:27.310	192.427	119.569	1980
				Winner: R Arnoux (Renault)		188.934	117.398	1980
Shortened circuit								
c)	4.325	2.687	1990-96 (7)	Pole: N Mansell (Williams)	1:15.703	205.672	127.799	1992
				F. Lap: M Schumacher (Benetton)	1:18.455	198.457	123.316	1994
				Winner: M Schumacher (Benetton)		192.632	119.696	1994
Further minor revision								
d)	4.292	2.667	1997-99 (3)	Pole: J Villeneuve (Williams)	1:16.004	203.294	126.321	1997
				F. Lap: J Villeneuve (Williams)	1:18.397	197.089	122.466	1997
				Winner: M Häkkinen (McLaren)		192.994	119.921	1999
Further minor revision								
e)	4.309	2.677	2000-05 (6)	Pole: R Barrichello (Ferrari)	1:10.646	219.579	136.440	2004
				F. Lap: J P Montoya (Williams)	1:11.473	217.038	134.862	2004
				Winner: J P Montoya (Williams)		208.517	129.566	2004

RIO de JANEIRO

Location: 30 km (19 miles) south-west of city centre.
First Used: 1978.

The Jacarepagua circuit was built in the late 1970s, on reclaimed marshland near the sea. The Autodromo International do Rio has a flat, but bumpy surface and rests in a backdrop of impressive mountains. Often used in winter testing, it was renamed in honour of Nelson Piquet in 1988. After losing its place on the F1 calendar the circuit built an oval track before falling into the hands of developers in early 2005.

World Championship races: 10

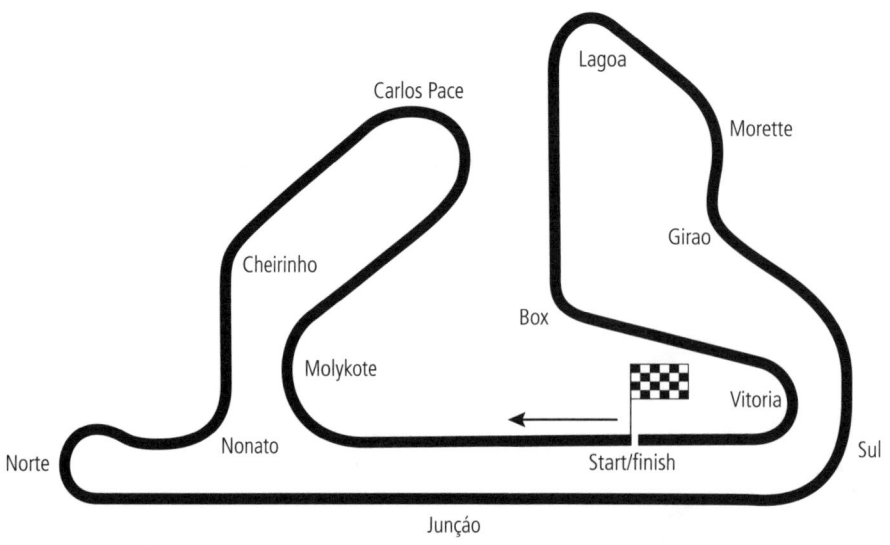

Records:

	Length		Years (no. of races)	Driver (Car)	Time	Speed		Year
	km	miles			min:sec	km/h	mph	
a)	5.031	3.126	1978,81-89 (10)	Pole: A Senna (McLaren)	1:25.302	212.323	131.932	1989
				F. Lap: R Patrese (Williams)	1:32.507	195.786	121.656	1989
				Winner: A Prost (McLaren)		188.438	117.090	1988

MONT-TREMBLANT

Location: 145 km (90 miles) north of Montréal, Québec.
First Used: 1964.

Mont-Tremblant or St.-Jovite as it is sometimes known, is situated in the scenic woodland of the Laurentian Mountains, a well known skiing resort. The original short circuit was lengthened to Grand Prix standards in 1966 but was regarded as too narrow and bumpy for regular use. It still holds regular meetings especially historic and national level events.

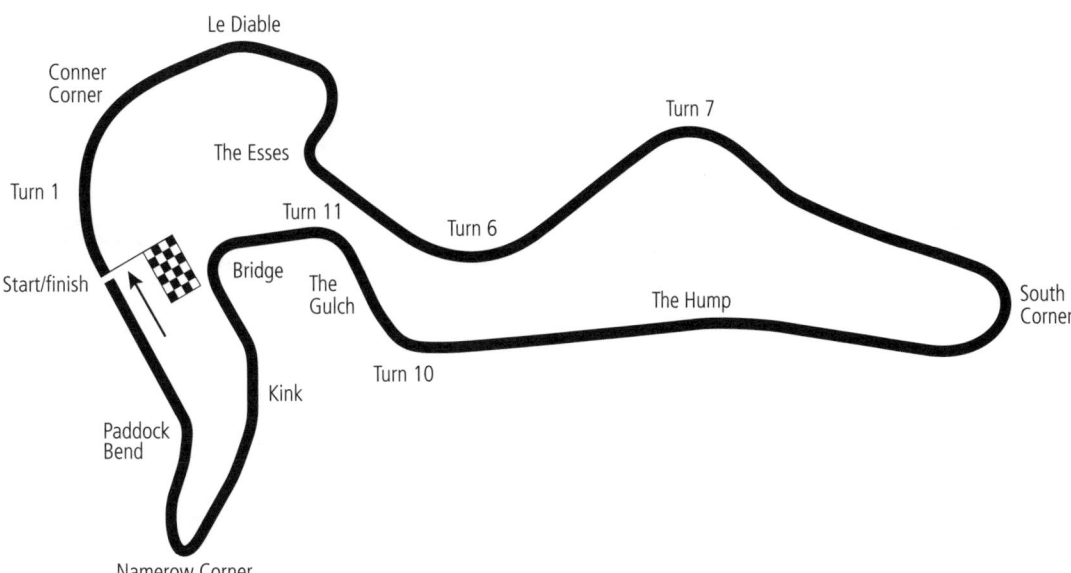

World Championship races: 2

Records:

	Length		Years (no. of races)	Driver (Car)	Time	Speed		Year
	km	miles			min:sec	km/h	mph	
a)	4.265	2.650	1968,70 (2)	Pole: J Stewart (Tyrrell)	1:31.500	167.794	104.262	1970
				F. Lap: C Regazzoni (Ferrari)	1:32.200	166.520	103.471	1970
				Winner: J Ickx (Ferrari)		162.977	101.269	1970

MONTRÉAL

Location: Montréal (east of city centre), Québec.
First Used: 1978.

Now named after the late Gilles Villeneuve, the Ile Notre Dame circuit is built on a man-made island in the St. Lawrence Seaway. Its tight and narrow track is laid out among lakes and parkland pavilions, used in the Expo 67 exhibition. In 1982 GP novice Riccardo Paletti was killed in a fiery start-line accident. The pits were relocated along with other changes, after the race was cancelled in 1987, due to a sponsorship dispute between beer giants Labatt's and Molson.

World Championship races: 27

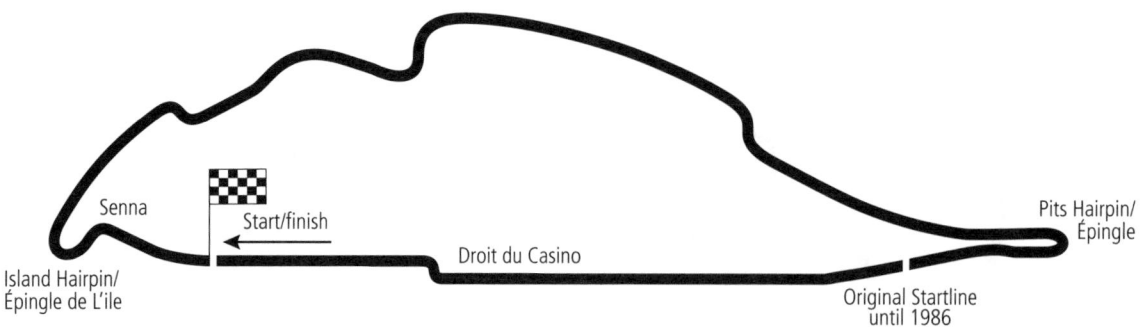

Records:

	Length		Years (no. of races)	Driver (Car)	Time	Speed		Year
	km	miles			min:sec	km/h	mph	
a)	4.500	2.796	1978 (1)	Pole: J-P Jarier (JPS Lotus)	1:38.015	165.281	102.701	1978
				F. Lap: A Jones (Williams)	1:38.072	165.185	102.641	1978
				Winner: G Villeneuve (Ferrari)		160.414	99.677	1978
Corners eased								
b)	4.410	2.740	1979-86 (8)	Pole: N Mansell (Williams)	1:24.118	188.735	117.274	1986
				F. Lap: N Piquet (Williams)	1:25.443	185.808	115.456	1986
				Winner: N Mansell (Williams)		178.225	110.744	1986
Pits/ corner change								
c)	4.390	2.728	1988-90 (3)	Pole: A Senna (McLaren)	1:20.399	196.570	122.143	1990
				F. Lap: G Berger (McLaren)	1:22.077	192.551	119.646	1990
				Winner: A Senna (McLaren)		182.152	113.184	1988
New corner before pits								
d)	4.430	2.753	1991-95 (4)	Pole: A Prost (Williams)	1:18.987	201.907	125.459	1993
				F. Lap: M Schumacher (Benetton)	1:21.500	195.681	121.591	1993
				Winner: A Prost (Williams)		189.667	117.853	1993
Temporary chicane (after old pits)								
e)	4.450	2.765	1994 (1)	Pole: M Schumacher (Benetton)	1:26.178	185.894	115.509	1994
				F. Lap: M Schumacher (Benetton)	1:28.927	180.147	111.939	1994
				Winner: M Schumacher (Benetton)		176.243	109.513	1994
Variation including Chicane								
f)	4.421	2.747	1996-01 (6)	Pole: M Schumacher (Ferrari)	1:15.782	210.018	130.499	2001
				F. Lap: R Schumacher (Williams)	1:17.205	206.147	128.094	2001
				Winner: R Schumacher (Williams)		193.629	120.316	2001
Changes to Hairpin								
h)	4.361	2.710	2002-05 (4)	Pole: R Schumacher (Williams)	1:12.275	217.220	134.974	2004
				F. Lap: R Barrichello (Ferrari)	1:13.622	213.246	132.505	2004
				Winner: M Schumacher (Ferrari)		207.165	128.727	2004

MOSPORT PARK

Location: 100 km (60 miles) north-east of Toronto, Ontario.
First Used: 1961.

Mosport Park is located in wooded hills near Bowmanville, close to Lake Ontario. Characterised by sweeping bends, it is regarded as too dangerous for modern Grand Prix cars. Manfred Winkelhock was killed at turn two in a sports car race and serious accidents have befallen John Surtees (Can-Am) and Ian Ashley (GP practice).

World Championship races: 8

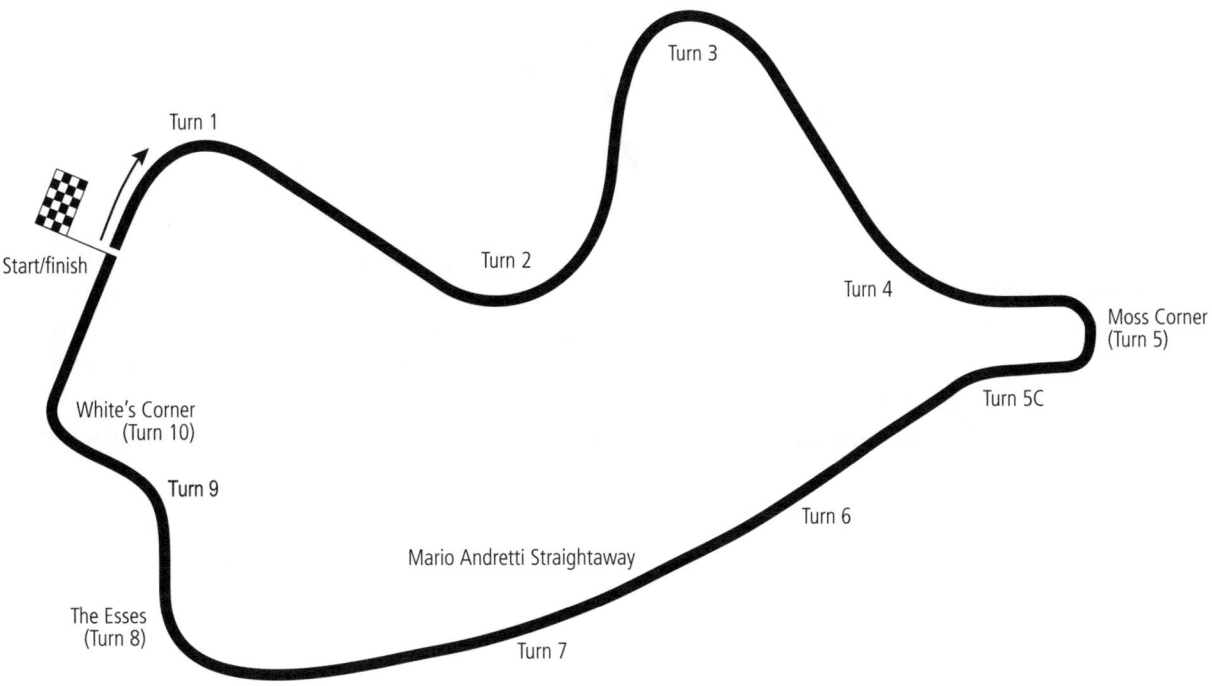

Records:

	Length		Years (no. of races)	Driver (Car)	Time	Speed		Year
	km	miles			min:sec	km/h	mph	
a)	3.957	2.459	1967,69,71-74,76-77 (8)	Pole: M Andretti (JPS Lotus)	1:11.385	199.574	124.009	1977
				F. Lap: M Andretti (JPS Lotus)	1:13.299	194.362	120.771	1977
				Winner: J Scheckter (Wolf)		189.954	118.032	1977

SHANGHAI

Location: 25 km (16 miles) north of Shanghai city
centre.
First Used: 2004.

Designed by the Hermann Tilke team to represent the
Chinese letter for the word 'shang' meaning above
and following the principles of modern computer
designs with a sharp corner following a long
straight. This track represents an important
commercial venture for F1 and was built in 18
months on a foundation of polystyrene blocks
over swampland. This has set new standards in
circuit development and two giant wing
shaped structures dominate either end of
the main straight.

World Championship races: 2

Start/finish

Records:

	Length		Years (no. of races)	Driver (Car)	Time	Speed		Year
	km	miles			min:sec	km/h	mph	
a)	5.451	3.387	2004-05 (2)	Pole: R Barrichello (Ferrari)	1:34.012	208.735	129.702	2004
				F. Lap: M Schumacher (Ferrari)	1:32.238	212.749	132.196	2004
				Winner: R Barrichello (Ferrari)		205.185	127.496	2004

BUGATTI AU MANS

Location: Le Mans.
First Used: 1966.

There has been motor racing around Le Mans since
the first Grand Prix in 1906, and the famous Sarthe
circuit has been used for the 24-hour race since 1923.
The Bugatti track incorporated part of the Le Mans
start-finish straight, before turning infield and
weaving through the car parking area. This twisty
circuit didn't prove to be popular with drivers or
spectators and was used just once in the World
Championship.

World Championship races: 1

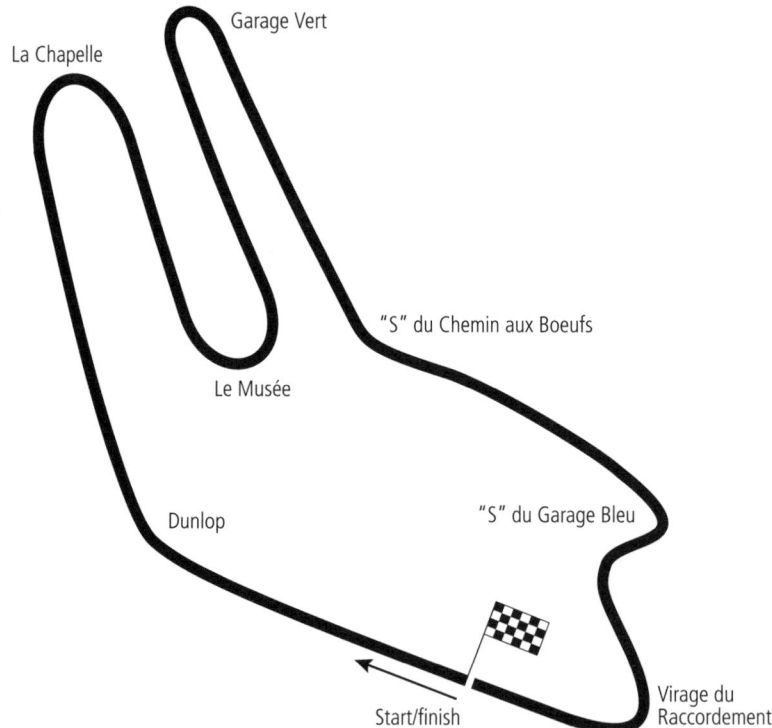

La Chapelle

Garage Vert

"S" du Chemin aux Boeufs

Le Musée

"S" du Garage Bleu

Dunlop

Virage du
Raccordement

Start/finish

	Length		Years (no. of races)	Driver (Car)	Time	Speed		Year
	km	miles			min:sec	km/h	mph	
a)	4.422	2.748	1967 (1)	Pole: G Hill (Lotus)	1:36.200	165.480	102.825	1967
				F. Lap: G Hill (Lotus)	1:36.700	164.625	102.293	1967
				Winner: J Brabham (Brabham)		159.166	98.901	1967

CLERMONT-FERRAND

Location: 10 km (6 miles) south-west of Clermont-Ferrand, Montagne d'Auvergne.
First Used: 1958.

Otherwise known as the Louis Rosier circuit or Charade, this mini Nürburgring was situated south-west of the town itself. In planning for many years and eventually built around volcanic plugs in this mountainous region, it was developed from public roads and was notorious for its up and down layout. The circuit finally closed in 1988.

World Championship races: 4

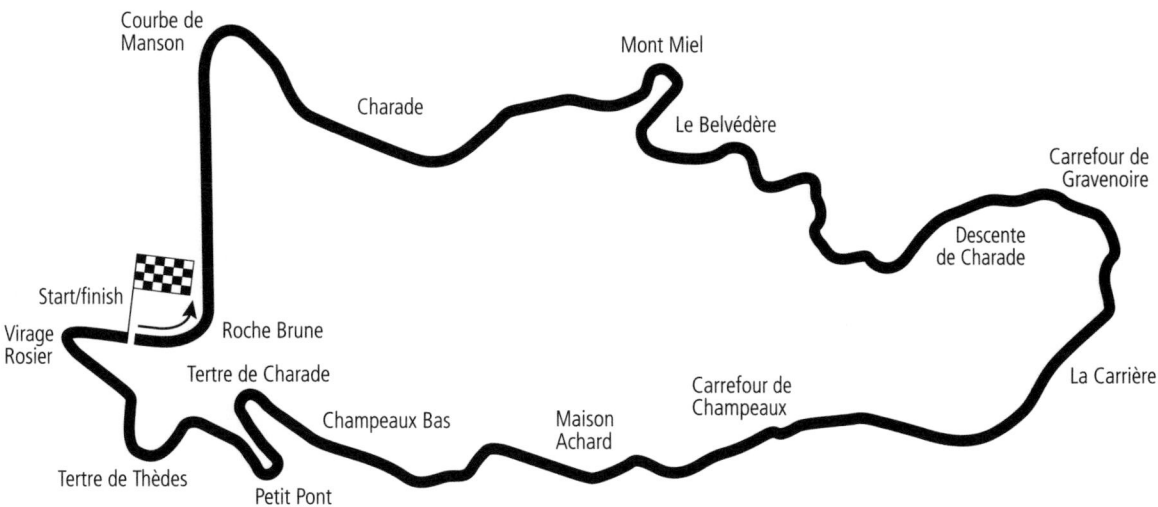

Records:

	Length		Years (no. of races)	Driver (Car)	Time	Speed		Year
	km	miles			min:sec	km/h	mph	
a)	8.055	5.005	1965,69-70,72 (4)	Pole: C Amon (Matra Simca)	2:53.400	167.232	103.913	1972
				F. Lap: C Amon (Matra Simca)	2:53.900	166.751	103.614	1972
				Winner: J Stewart (Tyrrell)		163.454	101.566	1972

DIJON-PRENOIS

Location: 15 km (9 miles) north-west of Dijon.
First Used: 1972.

Situated deep in the Burgundy region and built in the early 70s, it suffered from being too short for F1 purposes. This was overcome with the addition of the Parabolique loop in 1976. This undulating track proved popular with the infield spectators, but never more so than in 1979, when they witnessed the first turbo win and the dramatic Arnoux-Villeneuve fight for second place.

World Championship races: 6 (including Swiss Grand Prix in 1982)

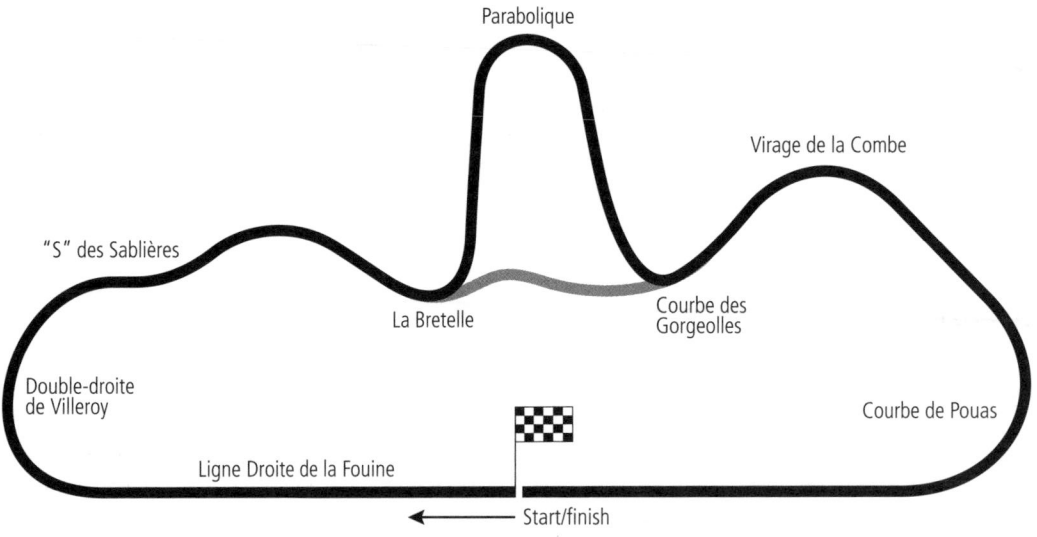

Records:

| | Length | | Years (no. of races) | Driver (Car) | Time | Speed | | Year |
	km	miles			min:sec	km/h	mph	
a)	3.289	2.044	1974 (1)	Pole: N Lauda (Ferrari)	0:58.790	201.402	125.145	1974
				F. Lap: J Scheckter (Tyrrell)	1: 0.000	197.340	122.621	1974
				Winner: R Peterson (JPS Lotus)		192.722	119.752	1974
Parabolique								
b)	3.800	2.361	1977,79,81-82 (4)	Pole: A Prost (Renault)	1: 1.380	222.874	138.487	1982
				F. Lap: A Prost (Renault)	1: 7.477	202.736	125.974	1982
				Winner: K Rosberg (Williams)		196.796	122.283	1982
Minor revision								
c)	3.887	2.415	1984 (1)	Pole: P Tambay (Renault)	1: 2.200	224.971	139.791	1984
				F. Lap: A Prost (McLaren)	1: 5.257	214.432	133.242	1984
				Winner: N Lauda (McLaren)		202.024	125.532	1984

MAGNY-COURS

Location: 12 km (7 miles) south of Nevers.
First Used: 1961.

The circuit de Nevers Magny-Cours was recently redeveloped and has one of the flattest and smoothest surfaces in the business. It is the home of the Knight brothers' Winfield racing school and Ligier later moved its factory to the circuit. Its compact layout makes for good viewing, but access is very poor, being served by only one major road. The circuit was slightly altered in 2004 when the tight final corner was re-profiled.

World Championship races: 15

Records:

| | Length | | Years (no. of races) | Driver (Car) | Time | Speed | | Year |
	km	miles			min:sec	km/h	mph	
a)	4.271	2.654	1991 (1)	Pole: R Patrese (Williams)	1:14.559	206.221	128.140	1991
				F. Lap: N Mansell (Williams)	1:19.168	194.215	120.680	1991
				Winner: N Mansell (Williams)		188.271	116.986	1991
Straightening at "Esse"								
b)	4.250	2.641	1992-99 (8)					
	4.251	2.641	2000-02 (3)	Pole: J P Montoya (Williams)	1:11.985	212.594	132.100	2002
				F. Lap: D Coulthard (McLaren)	1:15.045	203.925	126.714	2002
				Winner: M Schumacher (Ferrari)		199.135	123.737	2002
Reprofile of final corner								
c)	4.411	2.741	2003-05 (3)	Pole: F Alonso (Reanult)	1:13.698	215.468	133.886	2004
				F. Lap: M Schumacher (Ferrari)	1:15.377	210.669	130.904	2004
				Winner: M Schumacher (Ferrari)		205.035	127.403	2004

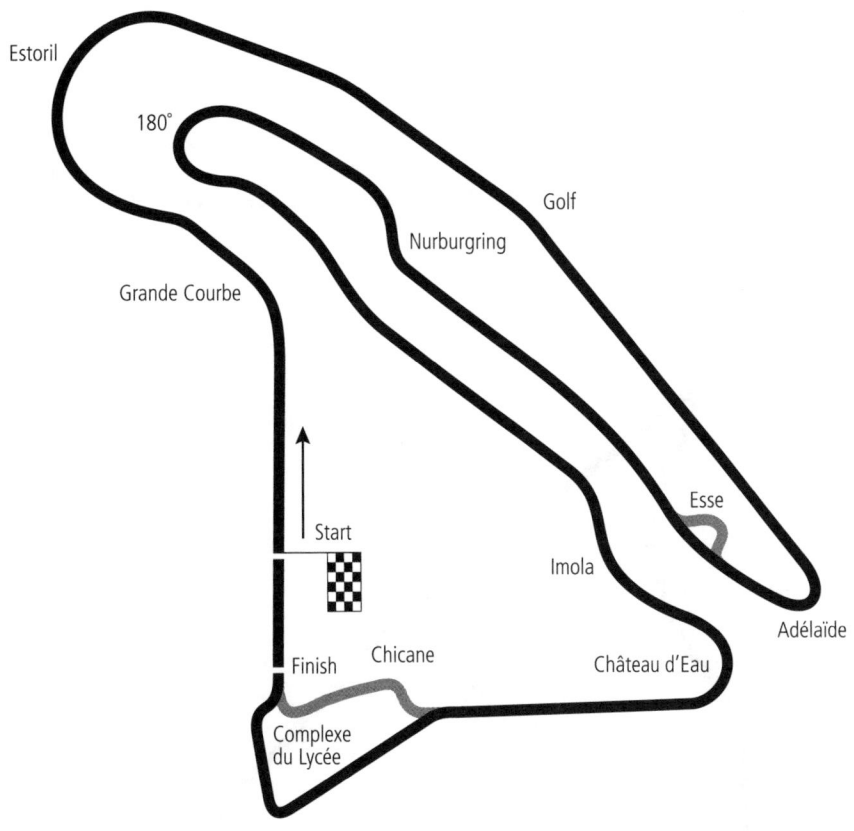

PAUL RICARD

Location: Le Castellet, 34 km (21 miles) east of Marseille.
First Used: 1970.

Inspired and financed by drinks magnate Paul Ricard, this modern complex had a combination of various circuits. Built on a windy plateau and containing the long Mistral Straight, it was radically shortened after Elio de Angelis' testing accident at the 'S' bend after the pits in 1986. Owned since 1999 by Bernie Ecclestone, it is a favourite circuit for testing and may still return to the World Championship at some point.

World Championship races: 14

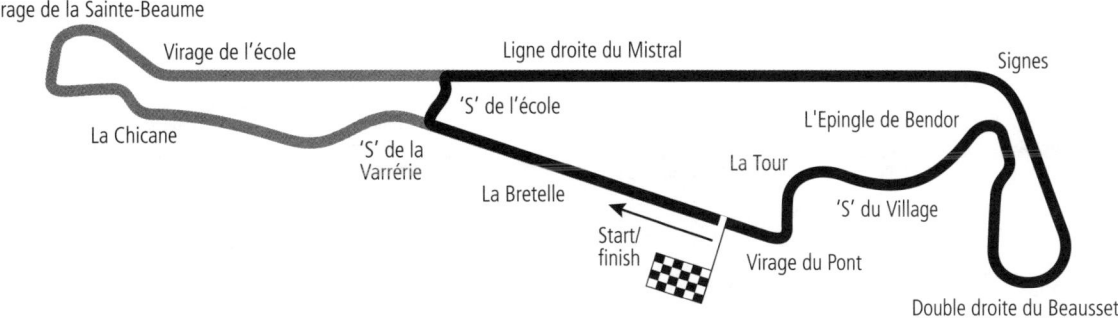

Records:

	Length		Years (no. of races)	Driver (Car)	Time	Speed		Year
	km	miles			min:sec	km/h	mph	
a)	5.810	3.610	1971,73,75-76,78,80,	Pole: K Rosberg (Williams)	1:32.462	226.212	140.562	1985
			82-83,85 (9)	F. Lap: K Rosberg (Williams)	1:39.914	209.340	130.078	1985
				Winner: A Jones (Williams)		203.016	126.148	1980
Shortened circuit								
b)	3.813	2.369	1986-90 (5)	Pole: N Mansell (Ferrari)	1: 4.402	213.142	132.441	1990
				F. Lap: N Mansell (Ferrari)	1: 8.012	201.829	125.411	1990
				Winner: A Prost (Ferrari)		195.761	121.640	1990

REIMS & REIMS-GUEUX

Location: 7 km (4 miles) west of Reims.
First Used: 1925.

A real classic circuit, using public roads around the fields of this Champagne region. Originally called Reims-Gueux, after the village that the cars passed through. This was diverted for safety reasons, but Luigi Musso was killed on the sweeping bend that replaced it. Closed in 1970, but not forgotten, as the old fading pits complex can still been seen at the roadside.

World Championship races: 11

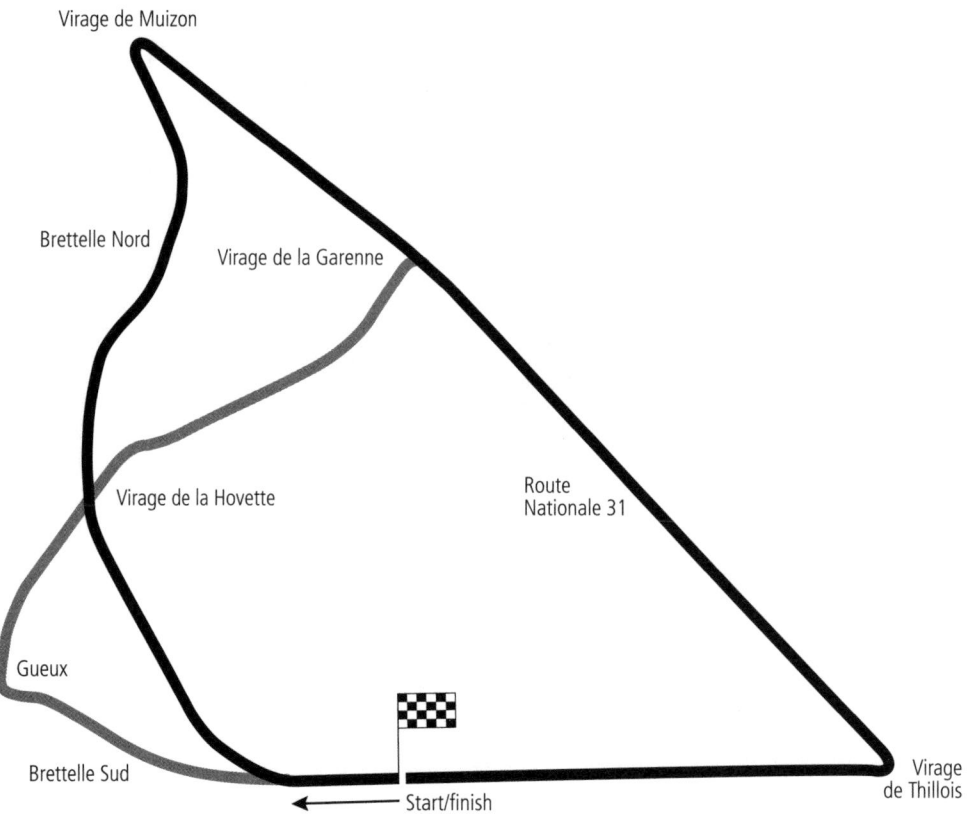

Records:

	Length		Years (no. of races)	Driver (Car)	Time	Speed		Year
	km	miles			min:sec	km/h	mph	
a)	7.816	4.857	1950-51 (2)	Pole: J M Fangio (Alfa Romeo)	2:25.700	193.120	119.999	1951
				F. Lap: J M Fangio (Alfa Romeo)	2:27.800	190.376	118.294	1951
				Winner: L Fagioli/ J M Fangio (Alfa Romeo)		178.600	110.977	1951
Gueux by-pass								
b)	8.347	5.187	1953 (1)	Pole: A Ascari (Ferrari)	2:41.200	186.409	115.829	1953
				F. Lap: J M Fangio (Maserati)/A Ascari (Ferrari)	2:41.100	186.525	115.901	1953
				Winner: M Hawthorn (Ferrari)		182.881	113.637	1953
Thillois eased								
c)	8.302	5.159	1954,56,58-61,63,66 (8)	Pole: L Bandini (Ferrari)	2: 7.800	233.859	145.313	1966
				F. Lap: L Bandini (Ferrari)	2:11.300	227.625	141.440	1966
				Winner: J Brabham (Brabham)		220.322	136.902	1966

ROUEN-les-ESSARTS

Location: 12 km (7 miles) south-west
of Rouen.
First Used: 1950.

Situated in the wooded valley of les-Essarts, it utilises public roads that wind downhill to the cobbled hairpin, a favourite viewing place. The circuit was extended in 1955, but has since been interrupted by a new motorway. No longer in use, it is sadly remembered for Jo Schlesser's fiery crash on the daunting downhill section. In recent years a lot of the original character has been lost in the name of progress including removal of the famous cobblestones.

World Championship races: 5

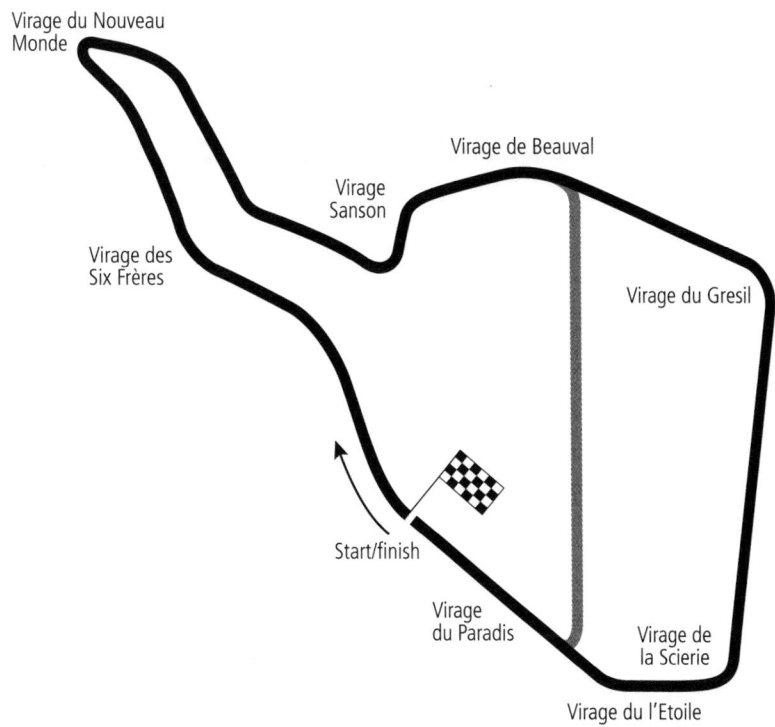

Records:

	Length		Years (no. of races)	Driver (Car)	Time	Speed		Year
	km	miles			min:sec	km/h	mph	
a)	5.100	3.169	1952 (1)	Pole: A Ascari (Ferrari)	2:14.800	136.202	84.632	1952
				F. Lap: A Ascari (Ferrari)	2:17.300	133.722	83.091	1952
				Winner: A Ascari (Ferrari)		128.958	80.131	1952
Extended								
b)	6.542	4.065	1957,62,64,68 (4)	Pole: J Rindt (Brabham)	1:56.100	202.853	126.047	1968
				F. Lap: J Brabham (Brabham)	2:11.400	179.233	111.370	1964
				Winner: D Gurney (Brabham)		175.042	108.766	1964

AVUS

Location: Western Berlin.
First Used: 1921.

The Automobil Verkehrs und Ubungs Strasse was constructed as a dual carriageway in the Grünewald area of the city. Unimaginative in its layout, the addition of a 43 degree banking in 1937 led to extremely fast times. The circuit had to be shortened, with a new south curve in 1954, as the original was in the Soviet sector. Jean Behra perished in his sports car on the banking during the Grand Prix meeting and this was later demolished in 1967. After a period of disuse, a shorter circuit appeared for domestic racing.

World Championship races: 1

Records:

| | Length | | Years (no. of races) | Driver (Car) | Time | Speed | | Year |
	km	miles			min:sec	km/h	mph	
a)	8.300	5.157	1959 (1)	Pole: T Brooks (Ferrari)	2: 5.900	237.331	147.471	1959
				F. Lap: T Brooks (Ferrari)	2: 4.500	240.000	149.129	1959
				Winner: T Brooks (Ferrari)		230.686	143.342	1959

HOCKENHEIM

Location: 25 km (16 miles) south-west of Heidelberg.
First Used: 1939.

Reopened in 1966, after the original oval was cut in two by the construction of an autobahn. This left the circuit in two distinct parts, the winding stadium section and the long blast and return into the thick pine forest. Hockenheim is remembered for the death of Jim Clark on the outward kink of the forest section, a stone cross marking the spot where he sadly perished. After the 2001 GP work began on a substantial remodel by Hermann Tilke which bypassed the forest section resulting in a tree planting project after the tarmac was removed.

World Championship races: 29

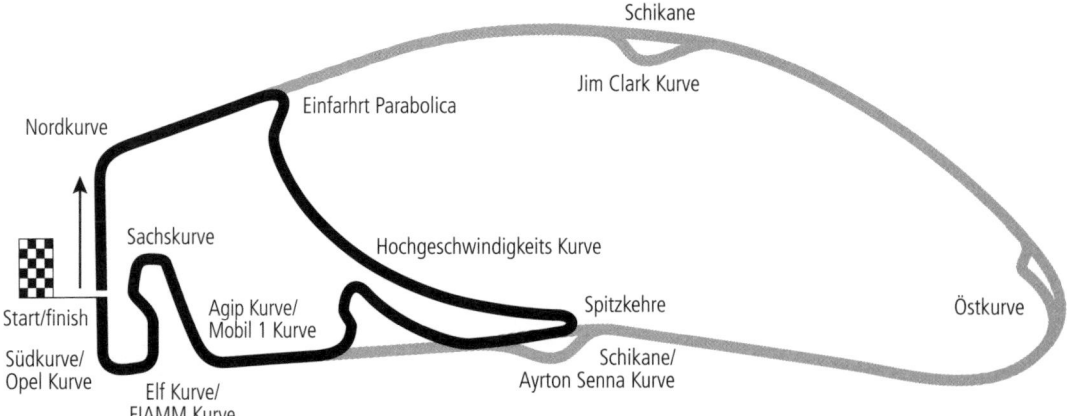

Records:

	Length		Years (no. of races)	Driver (Car)	Time	Speed		Year
	km	miles			min:sec	km/h	mph	
a)	6.789	4.218	1970,77-81 (6)	Pole: A Jones (Williams)	1:45.850	230.897	143.472	1980
				F. Lap: A Jones (Williams)	1:48.490	225.278	139.981	1980
				Winner: J Laffite (Ligier)		220.859	137.235	1980
Östkurve								
b)	6.797	4.223	1982-84,86-89 (7)	Pole: K Rosberg (McLaren)	1:42.013	239.864	149.044	1986
				F. Lap: N Mansell (Williams)	1:45.716	231.462	143.824	1987
				Winner: A Senna (McLaren)		224.566	139.539	1989
Östkurve altered								
c)	6.802	4.227	1990-91 (2)	Pole: N Mansell (Williams)	1:37.087	252.219	156.722	1991
				F. Lap: R Patrese (Williams)	1:43.569	236.434	146.913	1991
				Winner: N Mansell (Williams)		231.028	143.554	1991
Tighter Östkurve								
d)	6.815	4.235	1992-93 (2)	Pole: N Mansell (Williams)	1:37.960	250.449	155.622	1992
				F. Lap: R Patrese (Williams)	1:41.591	241.498	150.060	1992
				Winner: N Mansell (Williams)		234.798	145.897	1992
Ayrton Sennakurve tighter								
e)	6.823	4.240	1994-99 (6)					
	6.825	4.241	2000-01 (2)	Pole: J P Montoya (Williams)	1:38.117	250.415	155.601	2001
				F. Lap: J P Montoya (Williams)	1:41.808	241.336	149.960	2001
				Winner: R Schumacher (Williams)		235.351	146.240	2001
Forest section removed								
f)	4.574	2.842	2002-05 (4)	Pole: M Schumacher (Ferrari)	1:13.306	224.625	139.576	2004
				F. Lap: K Räikkönen (McLaren)	1:13.780	223.182	138.679	2004
				Winner: M Schumacher (Ferrari)		215.852	134.124	2004

NÜRBURGRING

Location: 60 km (37 miles) west of Koblenz.
First Used: 1927.

This giant of a track was built as a government employment programme, around the village of Nürburg, deep in the Eifel mountains. Officially consisting of 174 corners and a shorter separate south circuit, the Nürburgring was a supreme challenge to man and machine. Its length meant that it faded from major international racing on safety grounds. The Nürburgring has caught out more Grand Prix drivers than any other track, amongst them Onofre Marimón, killed at the Wehrseifen bridge, Peter Collins at the Pflanzgarten and Niki Lauda's near fatal accident at Bergwerk which meant the end of this circuit for GP racing. A new shorter and safer circuit was opened in May 1984 that incorporated part of the original start line. It has virtually become a permanent fixture as the European Grand Prix and further modifications have added a new twisty infield section at the first turn.

World Championship races: 35 (including European Grand Prix in 1984, 95, 96, 99-2004 & Luxembourg Grand Prix in 1997 and 98)

Records:

	Length		Years (no. of races)	Driver (Car)	Time	Speed		Year
	km	miles			min:sec	km/h	mph	
a)	22.810	14.173	1951-54,56-58,61-66 (13)	Pole: J Clark (Lotus)	8:16.500	165.390	102.768	1966
				F. Lap: J Clark (Lotus)	8:24.100	162.896	101.219	1965
				Winner: J Clark (Lotus)		160.542	99.756	1965
Bremskurve added								
b)	22.835	14.189	1967-69,71-76 (9)	Pole: N Lauda (Ferrari)	6:58.600	196.383	122.027	1975
				F. Lap: C Regazzoni (Ferrari)	7: 6.400	192.791	119.795	1975
				Winner: C Reutemann (Brabham)		189.474	117.734	1975
New circuit								
c)	4.542	2.822	1984-85 (2)	Pole: T Fabi (Toleman)	1:17.429	211.177	131.219	1985
				F. Lap: N Lauda (McLaren)	1:22.806	197.464	122.698	1985
				Winner: A Prost (McLaren)		191.751	119.149	1984

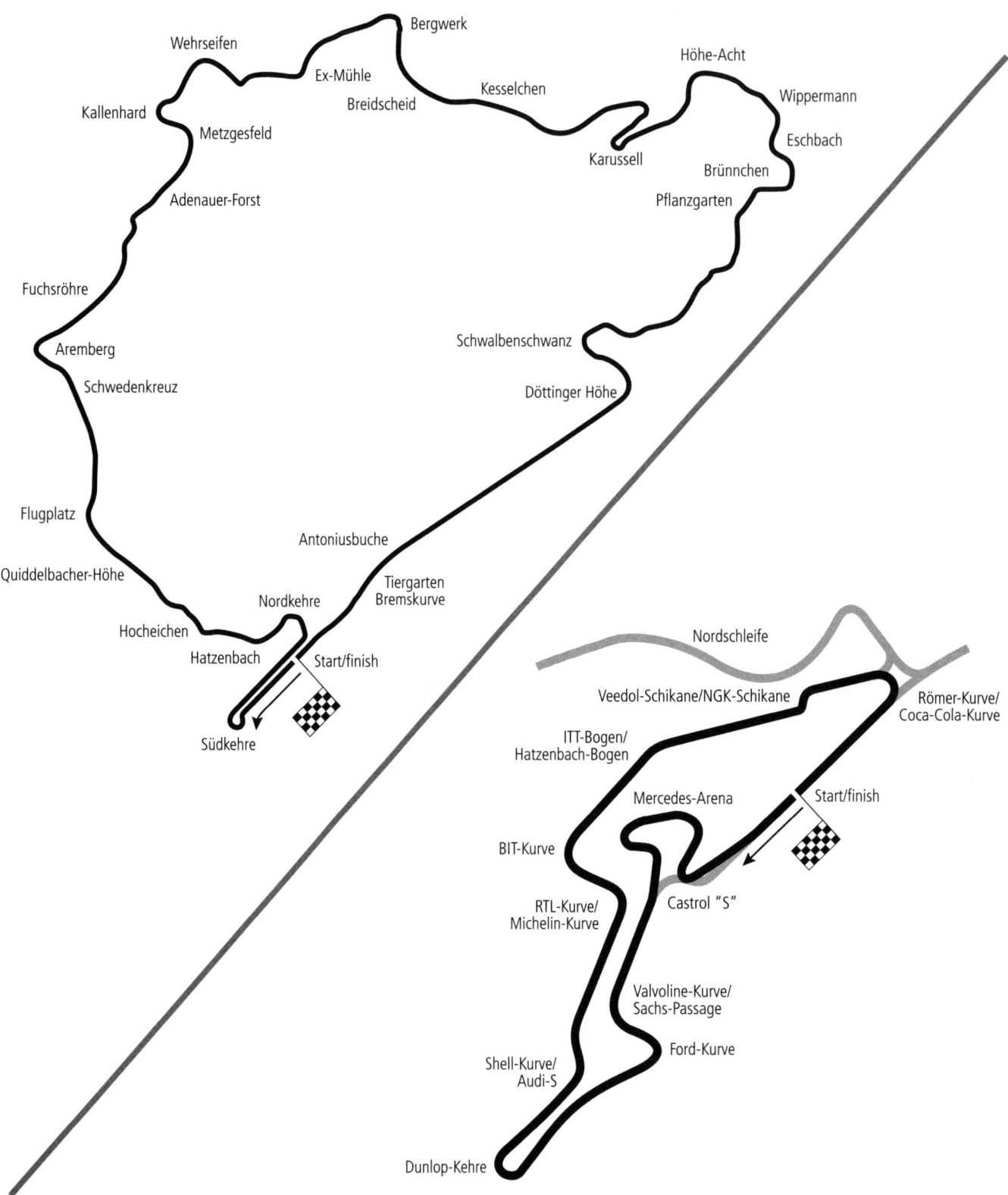

AINTREE

Location: Liverpool, 9 km (6 miles) north-east of city centre, England.
First Used: May 1954.

A flat and featureless track that ran alongside the famous Grand National steeplechase course and shared many of its facilities. It initially ran anti-clockwise, but reverted after the first meeting. With the owner Mirabelle Topham keen to sell the land, it fell out of favour, but the shorter triangular club circuit was revived for local sprint meetings. The last club race was in July 1982 but there have been attempts to use the facility for historic events.

World Championship races: 5

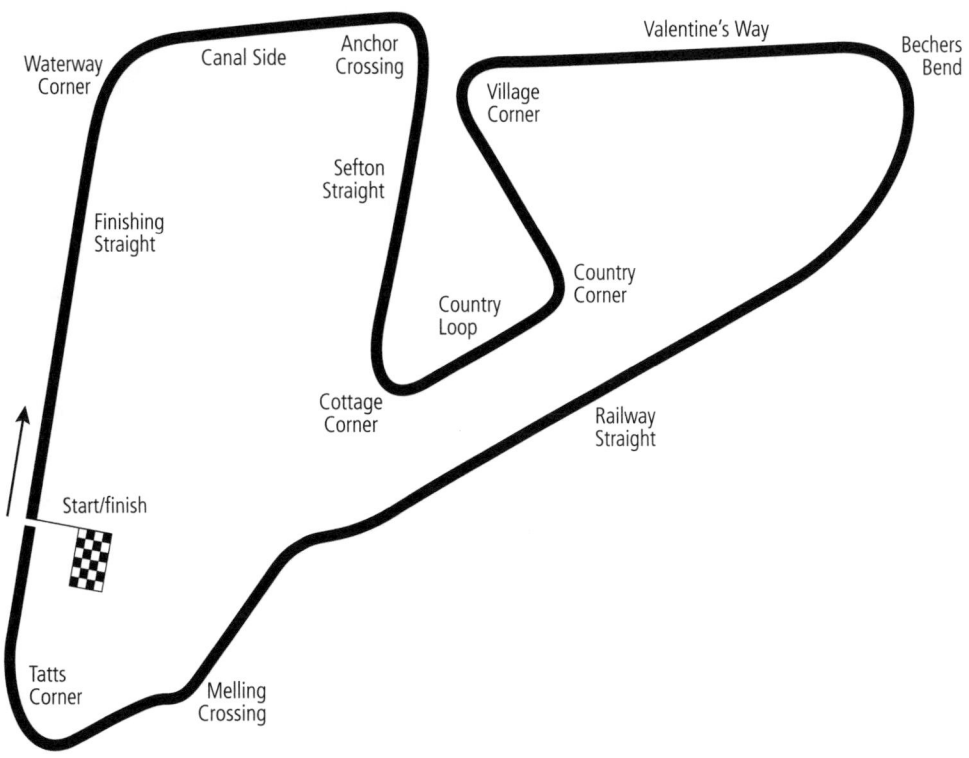

Records:

	Length		Years (no. of races)	Driver (Car)	Time	Speed		Year
	km	miles			min:sec	km/h	mph	
a)	4.828	3.000	1955,57,59,61-62 (5)	Pole: J Clark (Lotus)	1:53.600	153.001	95.070	1962
				F. Lap: J Clark (Lotus)	1:55.000	151.138	93.913	1962
				Winner: J Clark (Lotus)		148.457	92.247	1962

BRANDS HATCH

Location: 12 km (7 miles) south of Dartford, Kent, England.

First Used: April 1950.

Originally a cycle/motorcycle dirt track pre-war, it was surfaced for the first car races which took place anti-clockwise around the natural bowl, later named the Indy circuit. 1954 saw the addition of the Druids section and all racing continued clockwise. John Webb, a major force behind the circuit, instigated a new loop into the woodland to bring it up to Grand Prix length (2.65 miles) in 1960. Alterations to the south bank and pits complex slightly reduced the circuit length in 1976. With Silverstone reaching a deal to stage the British Grand Prix annually, this meant the end of this very popular track as far as the World Championship is concerned. Brands has a revived grand prix connection now that former driver, Jonathan Palmer and his consortium have taken over the circuit.

World Championship races: 14 (including European Grand Prix in 1983 and 1985)

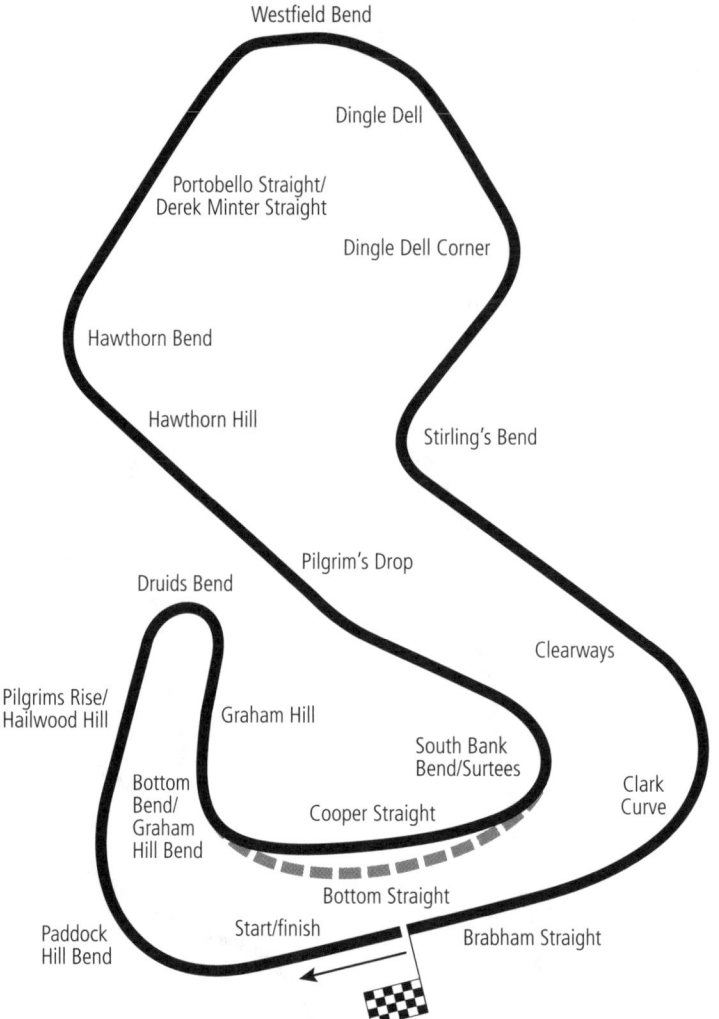

Records:

| | Length | | Years (no. of races) | Driver (Car) | Time | Speed | | Year |
	km	miles			min:sec	km/h	mph	
a)	4.265	2.650	1964,66,68,70,72,74 (6)	Pole: N Lauda (Ferrari)	1:19.700	192.637	119.699	1974
				F. Lap: N Lauda (Ferrari)	1:21.100	189.311	117.633	1974
				Winner: J Scheckter (Tyrrell)		186.258	115.735	1974
South Bank Alterations								
b)	4.207	2.614	1976,78,80,82-86 (8)	Pole: N Piquet (Williams)	1: 6.961	226.170	140.536	1986
				F. Lap: N Mansell (Williams)	1: 9.593	217.616	135.220	1986
				Winner: N Mansell (Williams)		208.853	129.775	1986

DONINGTON PARK

Location: Castle Donington, 13 km (8 miles) south-east of Derby, England.

First Used: March 1933.

Situated in the grounds of 17th century Donington Hall, it became Britain's premier circuit, but fell into disrepair during the war years. Builder Tom Wheatcroft bought the circuit in 1971, adding the magnificent 'Donington Collection' Grand Prix car museum in 1973 and reopening the circuit for racing in 1977. The track followed the lines of the old circuit and even added a new loop in 1985, to mirror the original Melbourne Hairpin, now outside the circuit. After many years of applications, Tom Wheatcroft finally realised his dream of hosting a Grand Prix, with the 1993 European Grand Prix.

World Championship races: 1 (European Grand Prix)

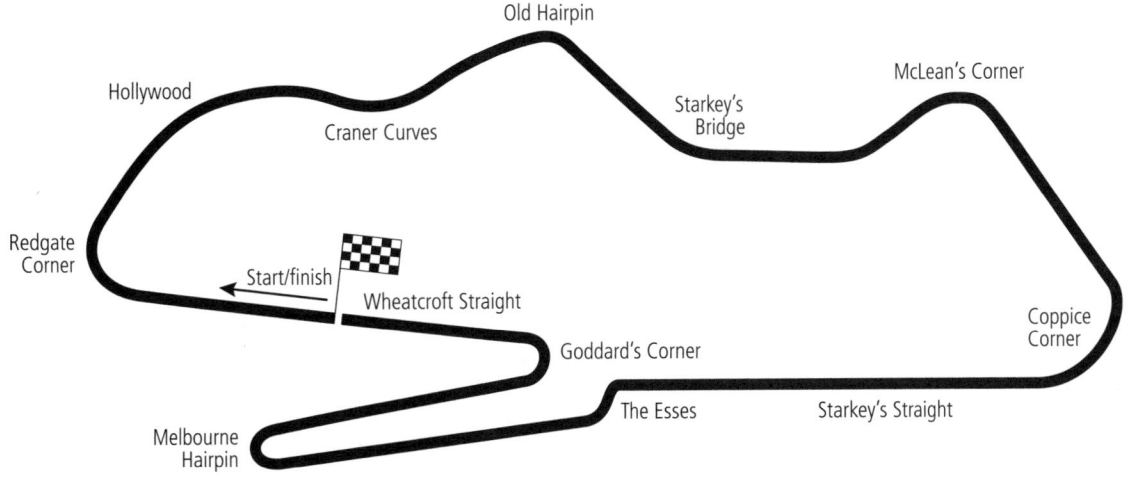

Records:

	Length		Years (no. of races)	Driver (Car)	Time	Speed		Year
	km	miles			min:sec	km/h	mph	
a)	4.023	2.500	1993 (1)	Pole: A Prost (Williams)	1:10.458	205.552	127.724	1993
				F. Lap: A Senna (McLaren)	1:18.029	185.608	115.331	1993
				Winner: A Senna (McLaren)		165.603	102.901	1993

SILVERSTONE

Location: 5 km (3 miles) south of Towcester,
Northamptonshire, England.
First Used: October 1948.

Incorporated from the runways and perimeter roads of a
wartime bomber base, the first permutation formed a
dangerous x shape. The following year, the familiar
perimeter roads were laid out. Jimmy Brown was the first
track manager and the British Racing Drivers' Club (BRDC)
bought the circuit in 1961 and steadily developed it into
Britain's premier circuit. Although not changing its
fundamental shape, Silverstone has undergone many
changes in its years, most notably at Woodcote, the
sweeping right-hander that holds the distinction of being
the first corner faced in the World Championship. The
1991 changes were the most radical but were universally
applauded whereas its facilities are often criticised in its
seemingly annual fight to hold onto its world
championship status.

World Championship races: 39

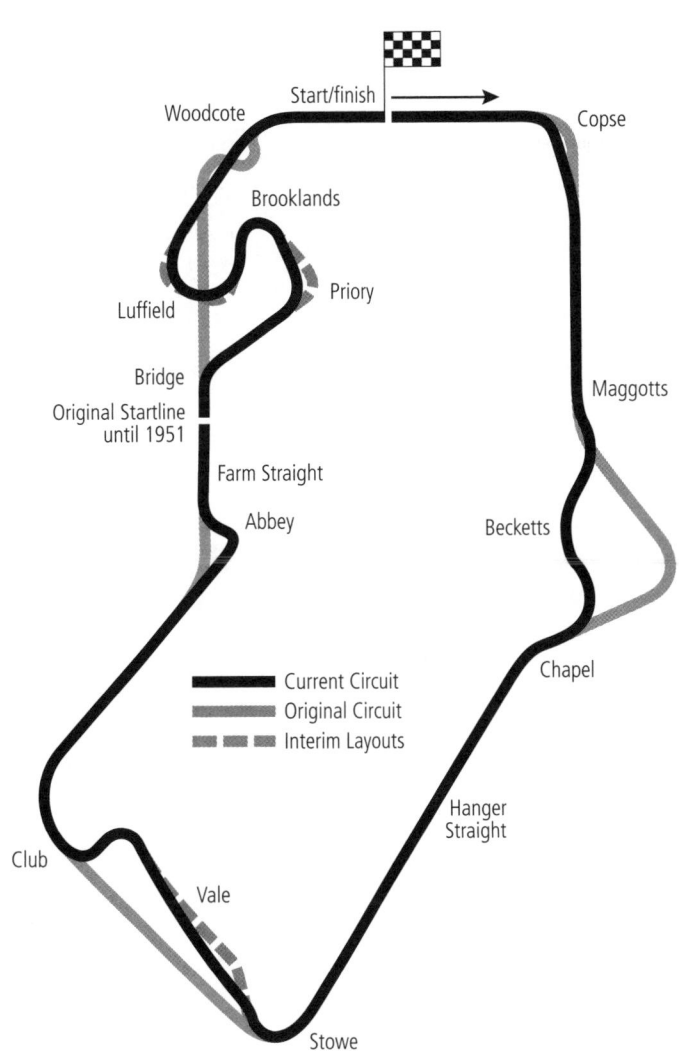

Records:

	Length		Years (no. of races)	Driver (Car)	Time	Speed		Year
	km	miles			min:sec	km/h	mph	
a)	4.649	2.889	1950,51 (2)	Pole: F González (Ferrari)	1:43.400	161.874	100.584	1951
				F. Lap: G Farina (Alfa Romeo)	1:44.000	160.941	100.004	1951
				Winner: F González (Ferrari)		154.690	96.120	1951
New Woodcote/ Pits								
b)	4.711	2.927	1952-54,56,58,60,63,	Pole: R Peterson (Lotus)	1:16.300	222.254	138.102	1973
			65,67,69,71,73 (12)	F. Lap: J Hunt (March)	1:18.600	215.750	134.061	1973
				Winner: P Revson (McLaren)		212.034	131.752	1973
Woodcote Chicane								
c)	4.719	2.932	1975,77,79,81,83,85 (6)	Pole: K Rosberg (Williams)	1: 5.591	258.983	160.925	1985
				F. Lap: A Prost (McLaren)	1: 9.886	243.067	151.035	1985
				Winner: A Prost (McLaren)		235.405	146.274	1985
New Woodcote Corner								
d)	4.778	2.969	1987-88 (2)					
e)	4.780	2.970	1989-90 (2)	Pole: N Piquet (Williams)	1: 7.110	256.315	159.267	1987
				F. Lap: N Mansell (Williams)	1: 9.832	246.324	153.059	1987
				Winner: N Mansell (Williams)		235.298	146.208	1987
New Complex								
f)	5.226	3.247	1991-93 (3)	Pole: N Mansell (Williams)	1:18.965	238.252	148.043	1992
				F. Lap: D Hill (Williams)	1:22.515	228.002	141.674	1993
				Winner: A Prost (Williams)		216.030	134.235	1993
Safety revisions								
g)	5.057	3.142	1994-95 (2)	Pole: D Hill (Williams)	1:24.960	214.279	133.147	1994
				F. Lap: D Hill (Williams)	1:27.100	209.014	129.876	1994
				Winner: D Hill (Williams)		202.143	125.606	1994
Stowe reprofiled								
h)	5.072	3.152	1996 (1)	Pole: D Hill (Williams)	1:26.875	210.177	130.598	1996
				F. Lap: J Villeneuve (Williams)	1:29.288	204.497	127.069	1996
				Winner: J Villeneuve (Williams)		199.576	124.011	1996
Luffield reprofiled								
i)	5.140	3.194	1997-99 (3)					
	5.141	3.194	2000-05 (6)	Pole: K Räikkönen (McLaren)	1:18.233	236.570	146.998	2004
				F. Lap: M Schumacher (Ferrari)	1:18.739	235.049	146.053	2004
				Winner: J P Montoya (McLaren)		218.968	136.060	2005

HUNGARORING

Location: near Mogyoród, 20 km (12 miles) north-east of Budapest.

First Used: 1986.

Hungary has a good racing pedigree; the first Grand Prix in 1906 was won by the Hungarian Ferenc Szisz, and racing in Budapest goes back to 1926. This first Eastern Bloc venue was built with the help of a state loan, and the natural amphitheatre attracted vast crowds to its early races. Initial construction problems with an underground spring meant the track was rather too twisty, but thankfully, this was later overcome. Further modifications were made to aid overtaking in 2003, but it still has a reputation as a tight and twisty track.

World Championship races: 20

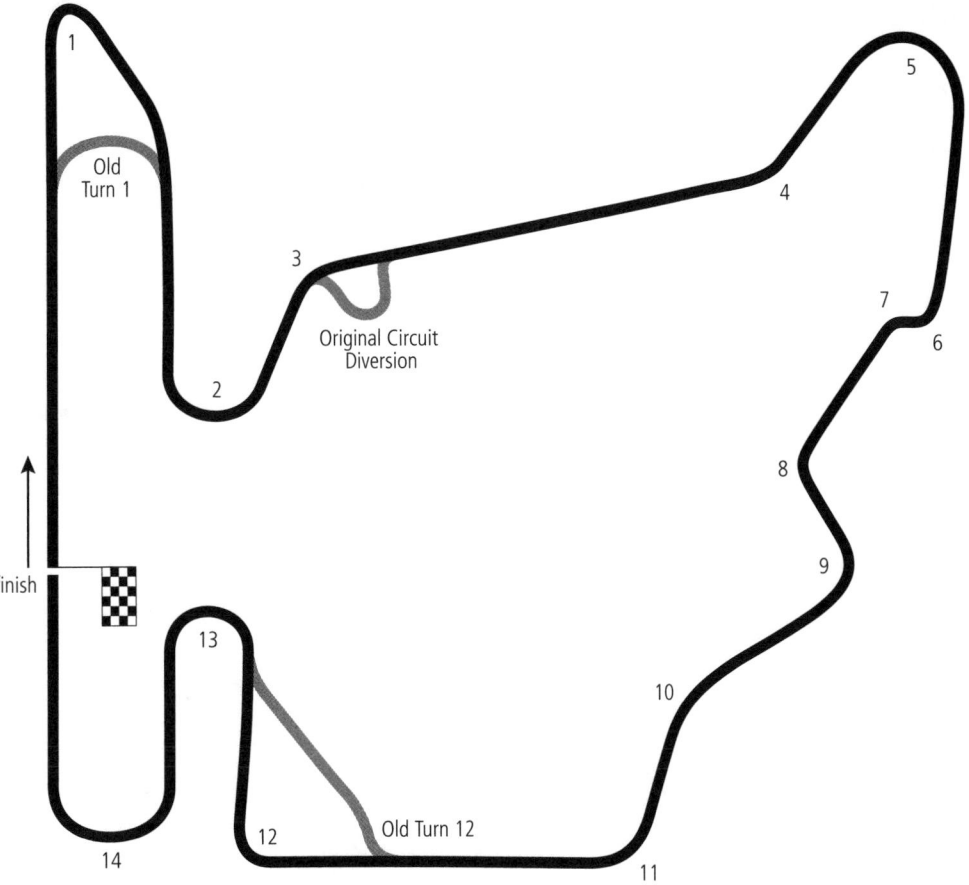

Records:

| | Length | | Years (no. of races) | Driver (Car) | Time | Speed | | Year |
	km	miles			min:sec	km/h	mph	
a)	4.014	2.494	1986-88 (3)	Pole: A Senna (McLaren)	1:27.635	164.893	102.460	1988
				F. Lap: N Piquet (Williams)	1:30.149	160.295	99.602	1987
				Winner: A Senna (McLaren)		155.401	96.562	1988
Spring diverted at "3"								
b)	3.968	2.466	1989-97 (9)					
	3.972	2.468	1998 (1)					
	3.973	2.469	1999 (1)					
	3.975	2.470	2000-02 (3)	Pole: R Barrichello (Ferrari)	1:13.333	195.137	121.253	2002
				F. Lap: M Schumacher (Ferrari)	1:16.207	187.778	116.680	2002
				Winner: R Barrichello (Ferrari)		180.364	112.073	2002
Alterations to turns 1 and 12								
c)	4.381	2.722	2003-05 (3)	Pole: M Schumacher (Ferrari)	1:19.146	199.272	123.822	2004
				F. Lap: M Schumacher (Ferrari)	1:19.071	199.461	123.939	2004
				Winner: M Schumacher (Ferrari)		192.798	119.799	2004

IMOLA

Location: 33 km (20 miles) south-east of Bologna.
First Used: 1950.

The Autodromo Enzo e Dino Ferrari is situated in woodland and runs alongside the Santerno river. A circuit of contrasts with the sweeps of the river side and the twists and gradients of the southern side. Sadly, Imola will always be remembered for the double tragedy during the 1994 San Marino Grand Prix meeting. In the interests of safety, chicanes have been added to the layout taking away many of its former characteristics.

World Championship races: 26 (Italian GP 1980/ San Marino GP from 1981)

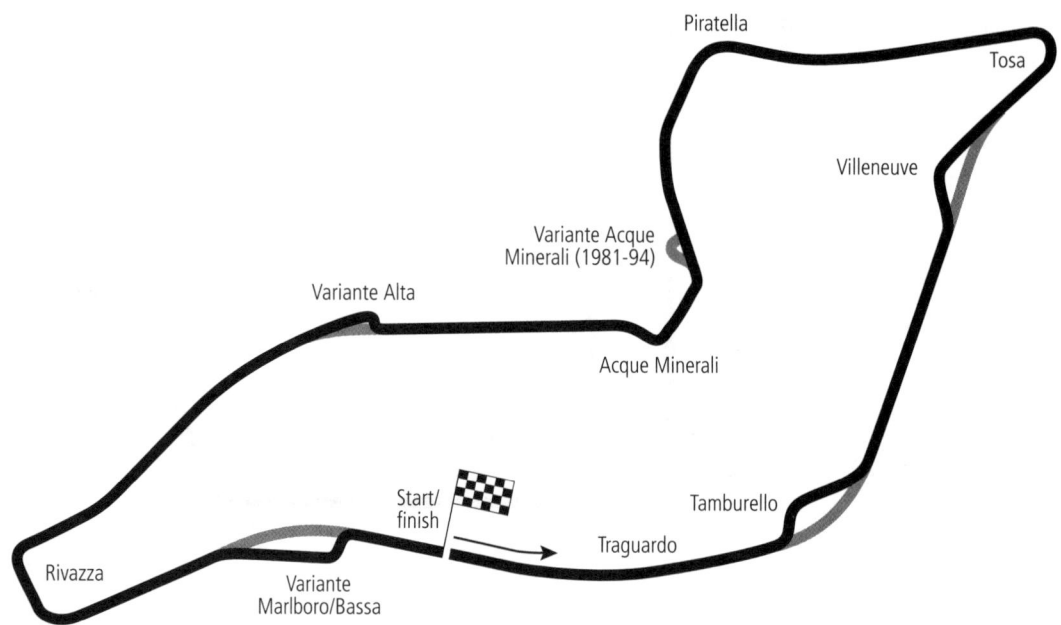

Records:

	Length km	miles	Years (no. of races)	Driver (Car)	Time min:sec	Speed km/h	mph	Year
a)	5.000	3.107	1980 (1)	Pole: R Arnoux (Renault)	1:33.988	191.514	119.001	1980
				F. Lap: A Jones (Williams)	1:36.089	187.326	116.399	1980
				Winner: N Piquet (Brabham)		183.439	113.984	1980
Acque Minerali chicane								
b)	5.040	3.132	1981-94 (14)	Pole: A Senna (Williams)	1:21.548	222.494	138.252	1994
				F. Lap: D Hill (Williams)	1:24.335	215.141	133.683	1994
				Winner: N Mansell (Williams)		204.596	127.130	1992
New chicane and other variations								
c)	4.895	3.042	1995 (1)					
d)	4.892	3.040	1996 (1)	Pole: M Schumacher (Ferrari)	1:26.890	202.683	125.942	1996
				F. Lap: D Hill (Williams)	1:28.931	198.032	123.051	1996
				Winner: D Hill (Williams)		193.760	120.397	1996
Further revision								
e)	4.930	3.063	1997-99 (3)					
	4.933	3.065	2000-05 (6)	Pole: J Button (BAR)	1:19.753	222.672	138.362	2004
				F. Lap: M Schumacher (Ferrari)	1:20.411	220.850	137.230	2004
				Winner: M Schumacher (Ferrari)		212.405	131.983	2004

MONZA

Location: 15 km (9 miles) north-east of Milan.
First Used: 1922.

A circuit steeped in history, built in the grounds of the wooded Monza royal park. The road circuit was rebuilt in 1948 and a new banked speedway section, half sunk in the ground, was constructed in 1955. This section fell into general disuse from 1968, when Monza established itself as the fastest grand prix track, with its slipstreaming battles. The introduction of chicanes in 1972, ensured that the previous GP held the distinction of being the fastest race (as well as the closest ever finish) until the 2003 event.

World Championship races: 55

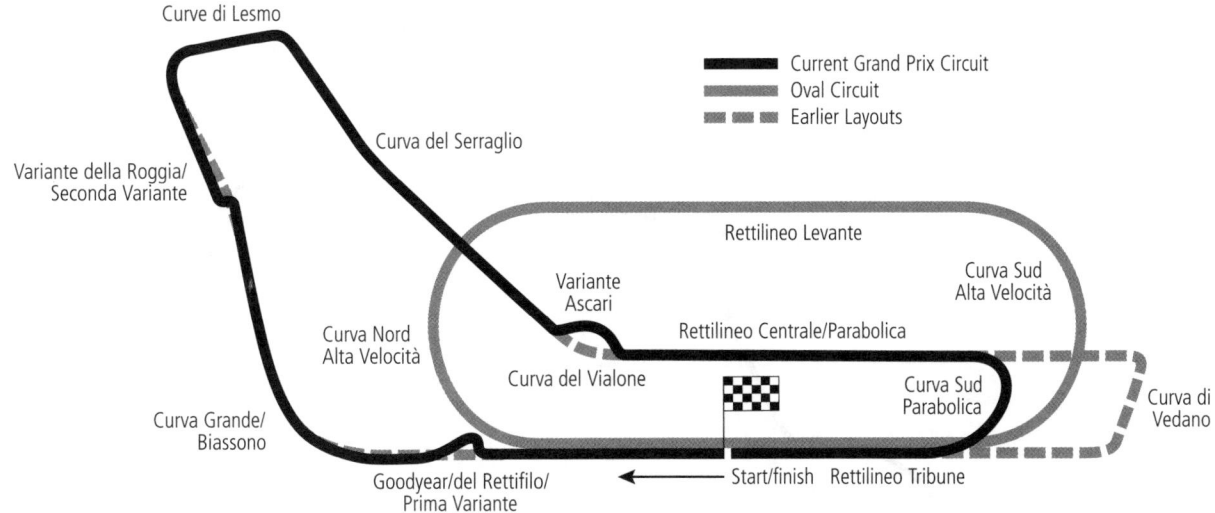

Records:

	Length		Years (no. of races)	Driver (Car)	Time min:sec	Speed		Year
	km	miles				km/h	mph	
a)	6.300	3.915	1950-54 (5)	Pole: J M Fangio (Alfa Romeo)	1:53.200	200.353	124.494	1951
				F. Lap: G Farina (Alfa Romeo)	1:56.500	194.678	120.967	1951
				Winner: A Ascari (Ferrari)		185.915	115.522	1951
Banked oval circuit								
b)	10.000	6.214	1955-56,60-61 (4)	Pole: P Hill (Ferrari)	2:41.400	223.048	138.596	1960
				F. Lap: P Hill (Ferrari)	2:43.600	220.049	136.732	1960
				Winner: P Hill (Ferrari)		212.535	132.063	1960
Parabolica								
c)	5.750	3.573	1957-59,62-71 (13)	Pole: C Amon (Matra Simca)	1:22.400	251.214	156.097	1971
				F. Lap: H Pescarolo (March)	1:23.800	247.017	153.489	1971
				Winner: P Gethin (BRM)		242.616	150.755	1971
Two chicanes								
d)	5.775	3.588	1972-73 (2)	Pole: R Peterson (JPS Lotus)	1:34.800	219.304	136.269	1973
				F. Lap: J Stewart (Tyrrell)	1:35.300	218.153	135.554	1973
				Winner: R Peterson (JPS Lotus)		213.450	132.631	1973
Vialone eased								
e)	5.780	3.592	1974-75 (2)	Pole: N Lauda (Ferrari)	1:32.240	225.585	140.172	1975
				F. Lap: C Regazzoni (Ferrari)	1:33.100	223.502	138.877	1975
				Winner: C Regazzoni (Ferrari)		218.034	135.480	1975
Two more chicanes								
f)	5.800	3.604	1976-79,81-94 (18)	Pole: A Senna (McLaren)	1:21.114	257.415	159.951	1991
				F. Lap: D Hill (Williams)	1:23.575	249.835	155.241	1993
				Winner: D Hill (Williams)		239.144	148.597	1993
Curva Grande and Curve di Lesmo altered								
g)	5.770	3.585	1995-99 (5)	Pole: M Häkkinen (McLaren)	1:22.432	251.989	156.579	1999
				F. Lap: M Häkkinen (McLaren)	1:24.808	244.929	152.192	1997
				Winner: D Coulthard (McLaren)		238.036	147.909	1997
Modification to first two chicanes								
h)	5.793	3.600	2000-05 (6)	Pole: R Barrichello (Ferrari)	1:20.089	260.395	161.802	2004
				F. Lap: R Barrichello (Ferrari)	1:21.046	257.320	159.892	2004
				Winner: M Schumacher (Ferrari)		247.585	153.843	2003

PESCARA

Location: Adriatic Coast (north and west of Pescara).
First Used: 1924.

The longest track in the World Championship consisted of roads linking villages around the coastal town of Pescara. It ran along the edge of the sea, towards the 1934 chicane, before turning inland along the winding Abruzzi mountain track. The inherent dangers meant that after further events for Formula Junior and sports cars, racing around the town stopped in 1961.

World Championship races: 1

Records:

	Length		Years (no. of races)	Driver (Car)	Time	Speed		Year
	km	miles			min:sec	km/h	mph	
a)	25.579	15.894	1957 (1)	Pole: J M Fangio (Maserati)	9:44.600	157.517	97.876	1957
				F. Lap: S Moss (Vanwall)	9:44.600	157.517	97.876	1957
				Winner: S Moss (Vanwall)		154.006	95.695	1957

AIDA

Location: 70 km (44 miles) north-east of Okayama City.
First Used: 1990.

Hajime Tanaka created the Tanaka International Circuit (TI) as a private club racetrack. The inaugural race was for invited English drivers and their historic sports cars, hence the names given to some of the corners. Situated in an isolated, mountainous region, the circuit does have access problems, but coped well with its first big international event.

World Championship races: 2 (Pacific Grand Prix)

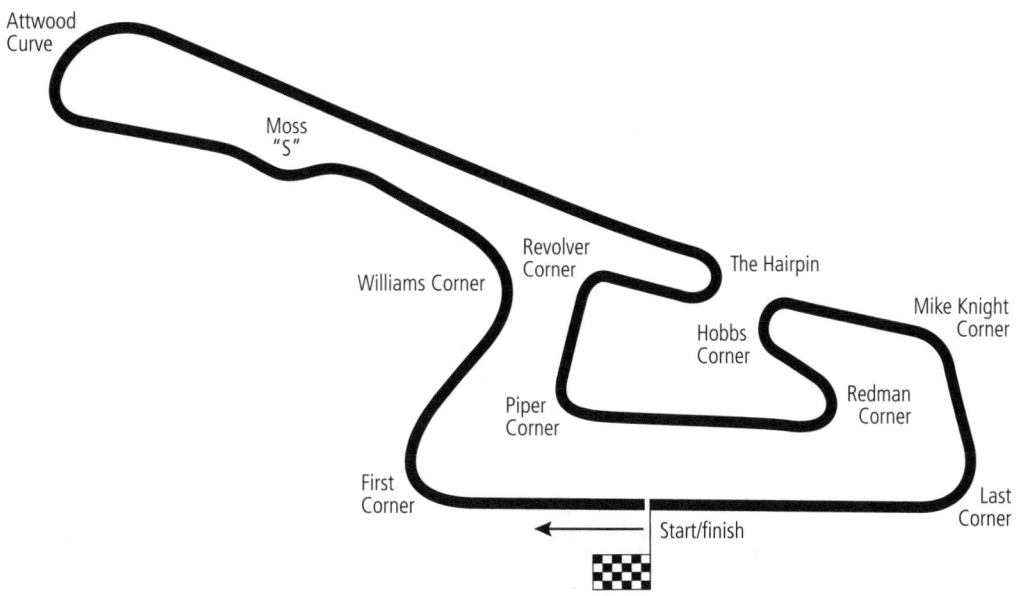

Records:

	Length		Years (no. of races)	Driver (Car)	Time	Speed		Year
	km	miles			min:sec	km/h	mph	
a)	3.703	2.301	1994-95 (2)	Pole: A Senna (Williams)	1:10.218	189.848	117.967	1994
				F. Lap: M Schumacher (Benetton)	1:14.023	180.089	111.903	1994
				Winner: M Schumacher (Benetton)		173.924	108.072	1994

FUJI

Location: 70 km (44 miles) west of Yokohama.
First Used: 1965.

Fuji International Speedway lies in the shadow of the imposing Mount Fuji, a dormant volcano usually hidden in mist. As the name suggests, it was intended as an American style speedway track, but the banked section wasn't used for F1 and was rarely utilised after. Due to its mountainous location, rain is often a factor, as in the 1976 championship decider, when Lauda withdrew due to the appalling conditions. In recent years Toyota purchased the track and have redeveloped it as a potential championship venue.

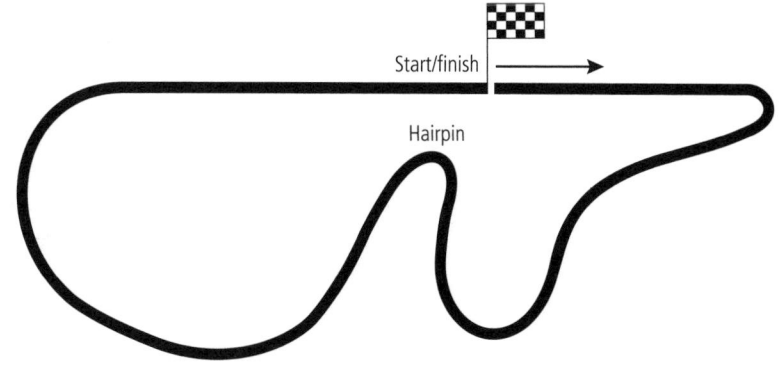

World Championship races: 2

Records:

	Length		Years (no. of races)	Driver (Car)	Time	Speed		Year
	km	miles			min:sec	km/h	mph	
a)	4.359	2.709	1976-77 (2)	Pole: M Andretti (JPS Lotus)	1:12.230	217.256	134.997	1977
				F. Lap: J Scheckter (Wolf)	1:14.300	211.203	131.236	1977
				Winner: J Hunt (McLaren)		207.840	129.146	1977

SUZUKA

Location: 50 km (31 miles) south-west of Nagoya.
First Used: 1961.

Built as a test track for Honda and designed by John Hugenholtz, incorporating a very unusual crossover section. Suzuka is a self contained theme park with a funfair, golf and other facilities, including the Honda racing museum. The track has a variety of corners and cambers, as well as a second fully operational pit area at the other side of the circuit. The rainy conditions of 2004 meant it was the first championship event to have final qualifying on the day of the race.

World Championship races: 19

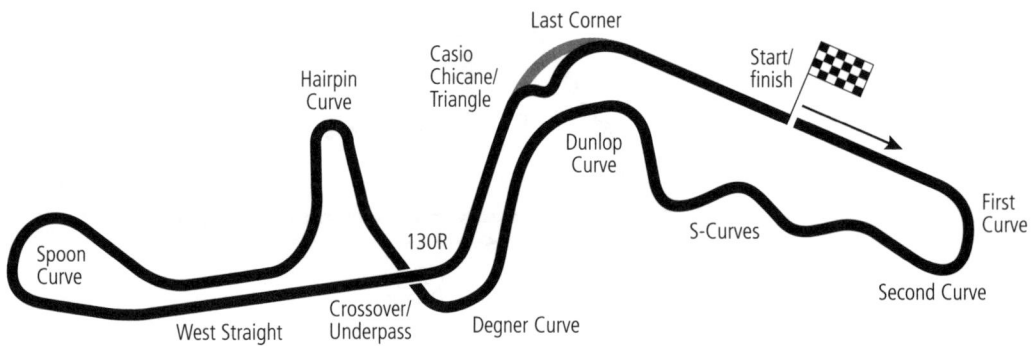

Records:

	Length		Years (no. of races)	Driver (Car)	Time	Speed		Year
	km	miles			min:sec	km/h	mph	
a)	5.859	3.641	1987-90 (4)	Pole: A Senna (McLaren)	1:36.996	217.456	135.121	1990
				F. Lap: A Prost (McLaren)	1:43.506	203.779	126.623	1989
				Winner: N Piquet (Benetton)		196.923	122.362	1990
Chicane moved								
b)	5.864	3.644	1991-00 (10)	Pole: G Berger (McLaren)	1:34.700	222.919	138.515	1991
				F. Lap: H-H Frentzen (Williams)	1:38.942	213.361	132.577	1997
				Winner: M Schumacher (Ferrari)		207.507	128.939	1997
Minor revision								
c)	5.859	3.641	2001 (1)	Pole: M Schumacher (Ferrari)	1:32.484	228.065	141.713	2001
				F. Lap: R Schumacher (Williams)	1:36.944	217.573	135.194	2001
				Winner: M Schumacher (Ferrari)		212.664	132.144	2001
S Curve modification								
d)	5.821	3.617	2002 (1)	Pole: M Schumacher (Ferrari)	1:31.317	229.481	142.593	2002
				F. Lap: M Schumacher (Ferrari)	1:36.125	218.003	135.461	2002
				Winner: M Schumacher (Ferrari)		212.644	132.131	2002
Reprofile of 130R and chicane								
e)	5.807	3.608	2003-05 (3)	Pole: R Barrichello (Ferrari)	1:31.713	227.941	141.636	2003
				F. Lap: K Räikkönen (McLaren)	1:31.540	228.376	141.904	2005
				Winner: R Barrichello (Ferrari)		218.524	135.785	2004

SEPANG

Location: 48 km (30 miles) south of Kuala Lumpur.
First Used: 1999.

This purpose built circuit designed by German Hermann Tilke was met by much praise from enthusiasts and Formula 1 personnel alike. One of its main features is its 30,000-capacity grandstand with the unusual roof in the shape of a banana leaf. The wide track itself has a large variation of corner types as well as an 800 metre pit straight that funnels into a tight first corner.

World Championship races: 7

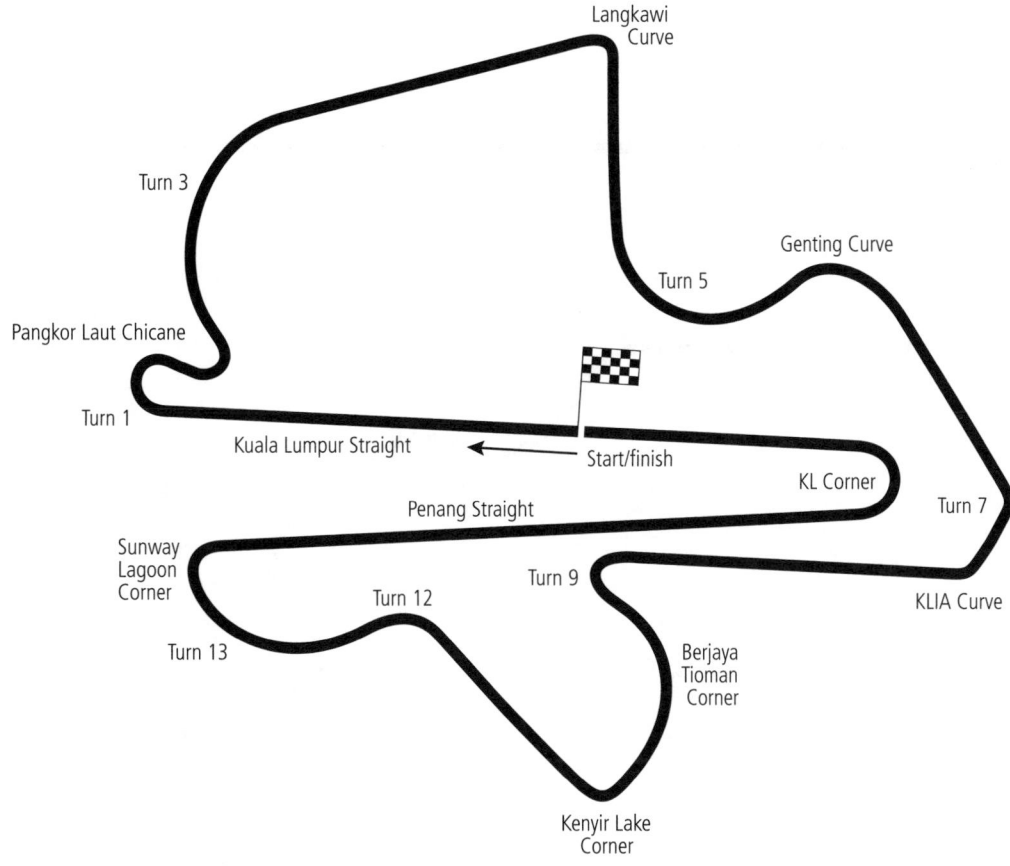

Records:

	Length		Years (no. of races)	Driver (Car)	Time	Speed		Year
	km	miles			min:sec	km/h	mph	
a)	5.542	3.444	1999 (1)					
	5.543	3.444	2000-05 (6)	Pole: M Schumacher (Ferrari) *	1:33.074	214.397	133.220	2004
				F. Lap: J P Montoya (Williams)	1:34.223	211.782	131.596	2004
				Winner: M Schumacher (Ferrari)		204.384	126.998	2004

* Fastest single qualifying lap record was set during 2005 aggregate timing by F Alonso (Renault), 1m 32.582s, 215.536 km/h, 133.928 mph.

MEXICO CITY

Location: Mexico City (eastern suburb).
First Used: 1962.

The Magdalena Mixhuca circuit is situated in a municipal sports park, built on a dried up lake bed and at an altitude of 7,500 feet. In early days, there were always crowd problems and with the very bumpy surface, its days were numbered. The circuit was later renamed Autódromo Hermaños Ricardo y Pedro Rodriguez, in memory of the Rodriguez brothers. After a facelift and revised layout, the track returned, although the magnificent banked Peralta curve was flattened out in 1992. After F1 a baseball stadium was built over the final corner (although the track winds through it) and the circuit continues to feature in the Champ Car calendar.

World Championship races: 15

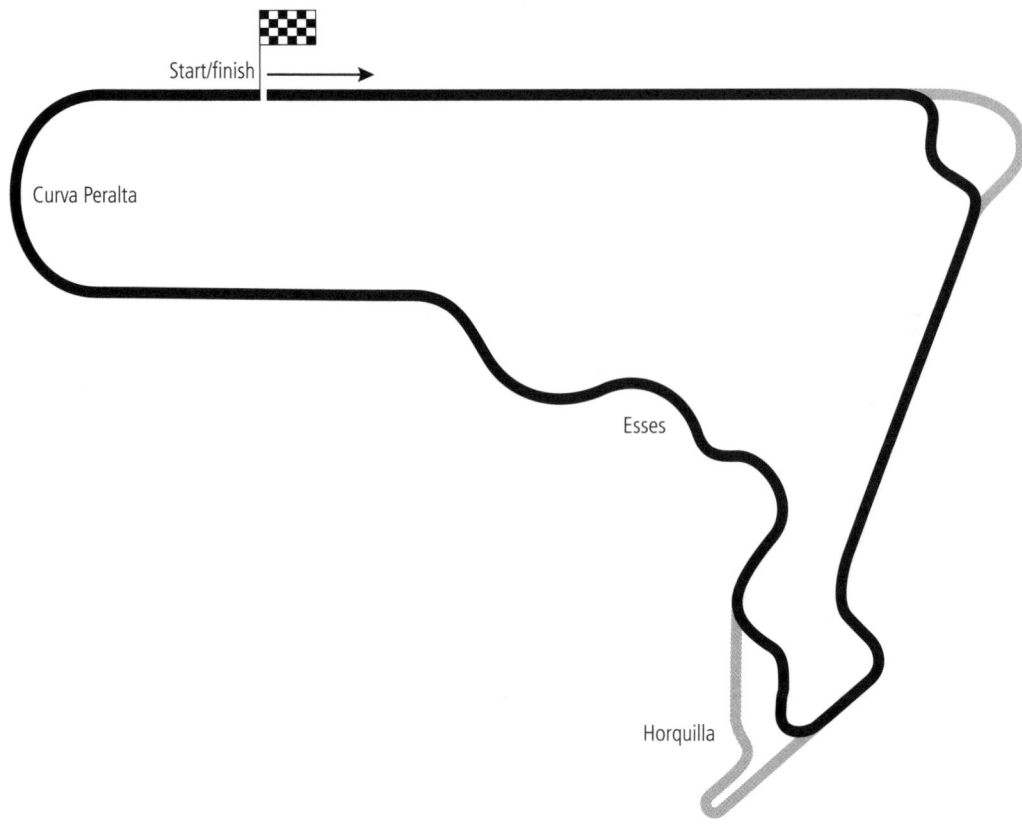

Records:

	Length		Years (no. of races)	Driver (Car)	Time	Speed		Year
	km	miles			min:sec	km/h	mph	
a)	5.000	3.107	1963-70 (8)	Pole: C Regazzoni (Ferrari)	1:41.860	176.713	109.804	1970
				F. Lap: J Ickx (Brabham)	1:43.050	174.672	108.536	1969
				Winner: J Ickx (Ferrari)		171.848	106.781	1970
Revised/ shorter								
b)	4.421	2.747	1986-92 (7)	Pole: N Mansell (Williams)	1:16.346	208.467	129.535	1992
				F. Lap: N Mansell (Williams)	1:16.788	207.267	128.790	1991
				Winner: N Mansell (Williams)		199.176	123.762	1992

Monaco (MC)

MONTE-CARLO

Location: Monte-Carlo (around the harbour of the Principality).
First Used: 1929.

Conceived by Antony Noghès, the Monaco race is the most famous on the Grand Prix calendar. An anachronism for modern machines that gasp and crawl around the tight corners, buildings and harbour front. It is no longer a pure race, given the difficulty in overtaking, but television and the sponsors love it. Its basic layout remained much the same over the years, with the only real change introduced around the waterside swimming pool complex. This race is usually held on the weekend following Ascension Day, a public holiday in France. Major pit redevelopment in 2004 meant that the teams did away with the unpopular temporary facilities.

World Championship races: 52

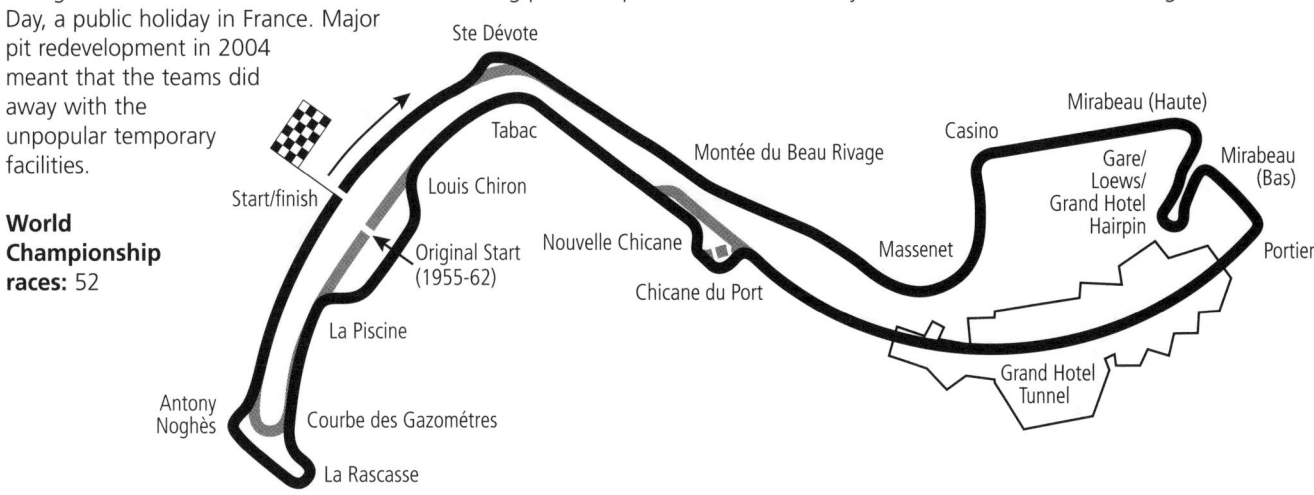

Records:

	Length		Years (no. of races)	Driver (Car)	Time	Speed		Year
	km	miles			min:sec	km/h	mph	
a)	3.180	1.976	1950 (1)	Pole: J M Fangio (Alfa Romeo)	1:50.200	103.884	64.550	1950
				F. Lap: J M Fangio (Alfa Romeo)	1:51.000	103.135	64.085	1950
				Winner: J M Fangio (Alfa Romeo)		98.701	61.330	1950
Chicane repositioned								
b)	3.145	1.954	1955-72 (18)	Pole: E Fittipaldi (JPS Lotus)	1:21.400	139.091	86.427	1972
				F. Lap: J Stewart (Tyrrell)	1:22.200	137.737	85.586	1971
				Winner: J Stewart (Tyrrell)		134.360	83.487	1971
New layout inc. Piscine/La Rascasse								
c)	3.278	2.037	1973-75 (3)	Pole: N Lauda (Ferrari)	1:26.300	136.742	84.967	1974
				F. Lap: R Peterson (JPS Lotus)	1:27.900	134.253	83.421	1974
				Winner: J Stewart (Tyrrell)		130.298	80.963	1973
Tighter Dévote/ Rascasse								
d)	3.312	2.058	1976-85 (10)	Pole: A Senna (Lotus)	1:20.450	148.206	92.091	1985
				F. Lap: M Alboreto (Ferrari)	1:22.637	144.284	89.654	1985
				Winner: A Prost (McLaren)		138.435	86.019	1985
New Chicane								
e)	3.328	2.068	1986-96 (11)	Pole: M Schumacher (Benetton)	1:18.560	152.505	94.762	1994
				F. Lap: M Schumacher (Benetton)	1:21.076	147.772	91.822	1994
				Winner: M Schumacher (Benetton)		141.690	88.042	1994
Swimming Pool complex eased								
f)	3.366	2.092	1997 (1)					
	3.367	2.092	1998-99 (2)					
	3.370	2.094	2000-02 (3)	Pole: J P Montoya (Williams)	1:16.676	158.224	98.316	2002
				F. Lap: R Barrichello (Ferrari)	1:18.023	155.492	96.619	2002
				Winner: D Coulthard (McLaren)		149.280	92.758	2002
Further revision								
g)	3.340	2.075	2003-05 (3)	Pole: J Trulli (Renault) *	1:13.985	162.519	100.985	2004
				F. Lap: M Schumacher (Ferrari)	1:14.439	161.528	100.369	2004
				Winner: J P Montoya (Williams)		152.772	94.928	2003

* Fastest single qualifying lap record was set during 2005 aggregate timing by K Räikkönen (McLaren), 1m 13.644s, 163.271 km/h, 101.452 mph.

ÂIN-DIAB

Location: Western outskirts of Casablanca.
First Used: 1957.

Utilising public roads, by the Atlantic coast on the western outskirts of Casablanca, Âin-Diab was the scene of the 1958 championship decider. Sometimes dusty and covered by sea mist, its fast layout caused high speed accidents and Stuart Lewis-Evans suffered fatal burns at this race.

World Championship races: 1

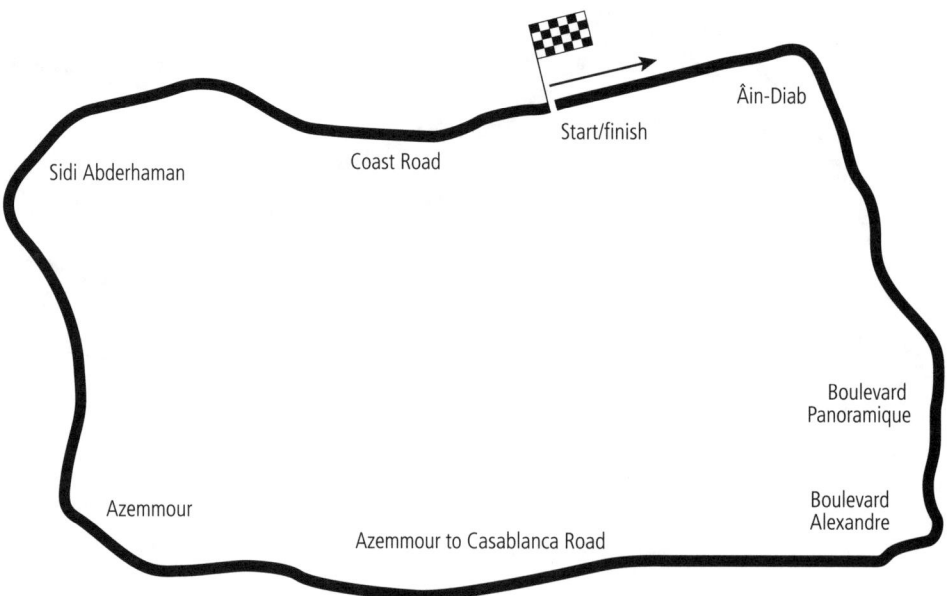

Records:

	Length		Years (no. of races)	Driver (Car)	Time	Speed		Year
	km	miles			min:sec	km/h	mph	
a)	7.618	4.734	1958 (1)	Pole: M Hawthorn (Ferrari)	2:23.100	191.648	119.084	1958
				F. Lap: S Moss (Vanwall)	2:22.500	192.455	119.586	1958
				Winner: S Moss (Vanwall)		187.427	116.462	1958

ZANDVOORT

Location: 9 km (6 miles) west of Haarlem.
First Used: 1948.

Designed by John Hugenholtz, linking new track with existing wartime service roads through the seaside sand dunes. The main straight runs parallel to the North Sea and strong winds often blew sand over the track. The facilities became outdated and with noise pollution problems, the track fell from major use and was drastically remodelled in the late 80s.

World Championship races: 30

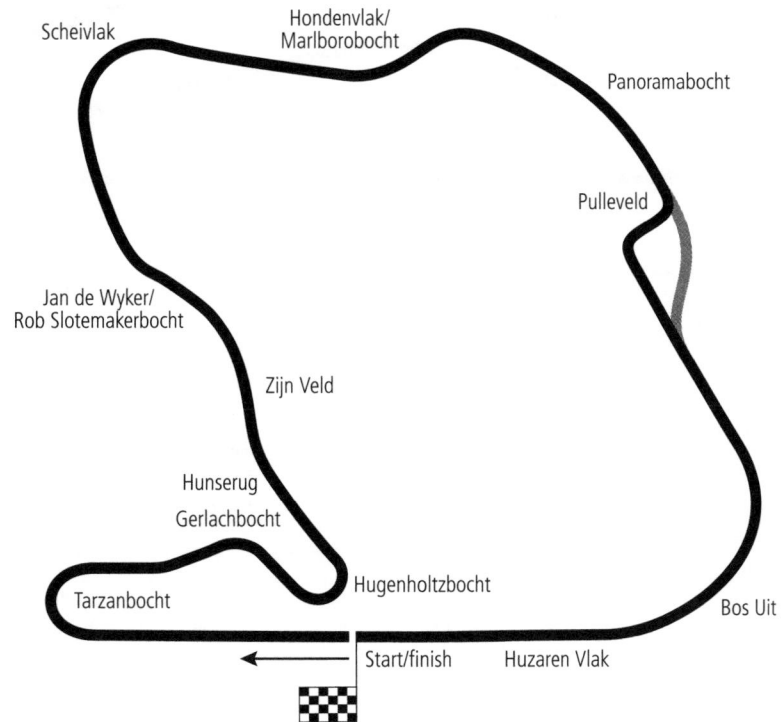

Records:

	Length		Years (no. of races)	Driver (Car)	Time	Speed		Year
	km	miles			min:sec	km/h	mph	
a)	4.193	2.605	1952-53,55,58-71 (17)	Pole: J Ickx (Ferrari)	1:17.420	194.973	121.151	1971
				F. Lap: J Ickx (Ferrari)	1:19.230	190.519	118.383	1970
				Winner: J Rindt (Lotus)		181.772	112.948	1970
New corner at Panoramabocht								
b)	4.226	2.626	1973-79 (7)	Pole: R Arnoux (Renault)	1:15.461	201.609	125.274	1979
				F. Lap: G Villeneuve (Ferrari)	1:19.438	191.515	119.002	1979
				Winner: M Andretti (JPS Lotus)		188.156	116.915	1978
Marlborobocht								
c)	4.252	2.642	1980-85 (6)	Pole: N Piquet (Brabham)	1:11.074	215.370	133.825	1985
				F. Lap: A Prost (McLaren)	1:16.538	199.995	124.271	1985
				Winner: N Lauda (McLaren)		193.089	119.980	1985

ESTORIL

Location: 6.5 km (4 miles) north of Estoril.
First Used: 1972.

Built on a barren, rocky plateau, inland from the popular beach resort. Used for local racing in its early years before falling into disrepair, it was redeveloped in the early 80s ready for a return to international racing. Due to the increase in safety measures, following Imola 1994, a new slower link, called Saca-Rolhas was added before the old turn 8. Pressures from new venues and further safety issues meant that Estoril slipped from the F1 calendar.

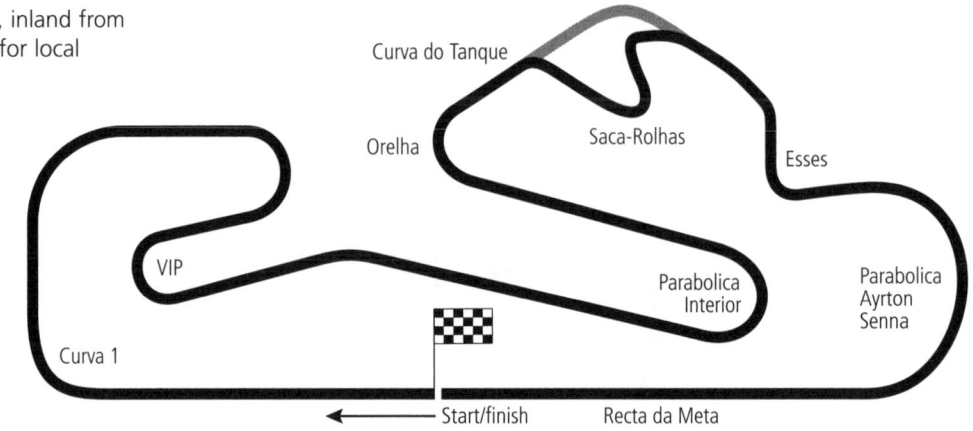

World Championship races: 13

Records:

	Length		Years (no. of races)	Driver (Car)	Time	Speed		Year
	km	miles			min:sec	km/h	mph	
a)	4.350	2.703	1984-93 (10)	Pole: D Hill (Williams)	1:11.494	219.039	136.105	1993
				F. Lap: D Hill (Williams)	1:14.859	209.193	129.987	1993
				Winner: M Schumacher (Benetton)		199.748	124.118	1993
New corner at Saca-Rolhas								
b)	4.360	2.709	1994-96 (3)	Pole: D Hill (Williams)	1:20.330	195.393	121.412	1996
				F. Lap: D Coulthard (Williams)	1:22.446	190.379	118.296	1994
				Winner: D Hill (Williams)		183.589	114.077	1994

MONSANTO PARK

Location: Lisbon, 5 km (3 miles) west of city centre.
First Used: 1953.

A natural circuit, built around the roads of the picturesque Monsanto Park. Its main straight was the dual carriageway of the main Lisbon to Estoril road. Generally used for sports car racing, the circuit quickly faded from international racing, although the shorter national circuit continued until 1971.

World Championship races: 1

Records:

	Length		Years (no. of races)	Driver (Car)	Time	Speed		Year
	km	miles			min:sec	km/h	mph	
a)	5.440	3.380	1959 (1)	Pole: S Moss (Cooper)	2: 2.890	159.362	99.023	1959
				F. Lap: S Moss (Cooper)	2: 5.070	156.584	97.297	1959
				Winner: S Moss (Cooper)		153.398	95.317	1959

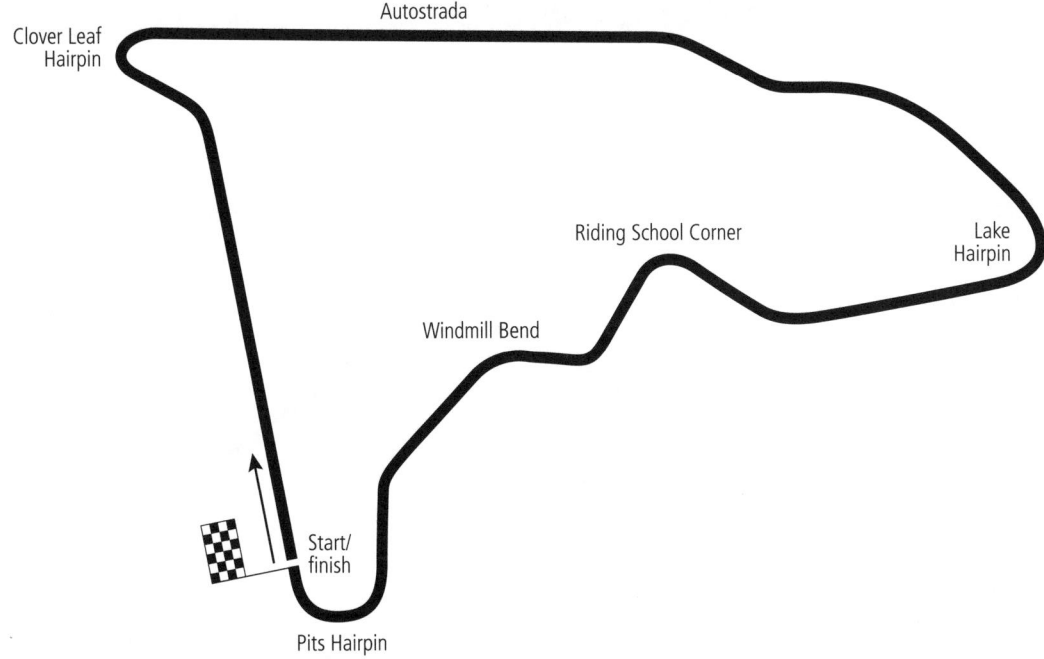

PORTO

Location: Porto (western outskirts of city).
First Used: 1950.

A true street circuit, situated close to the harbour front and incorporating part of a dual carriageway. The Circuito da Boa Vista included all manner of hazards with houses, shops, lamp posts, cobbles and even tram lines. Mainly used for sportscar racing, it was regarded as too dangerous, the last event being staged in 1960.

World Championship races: 2

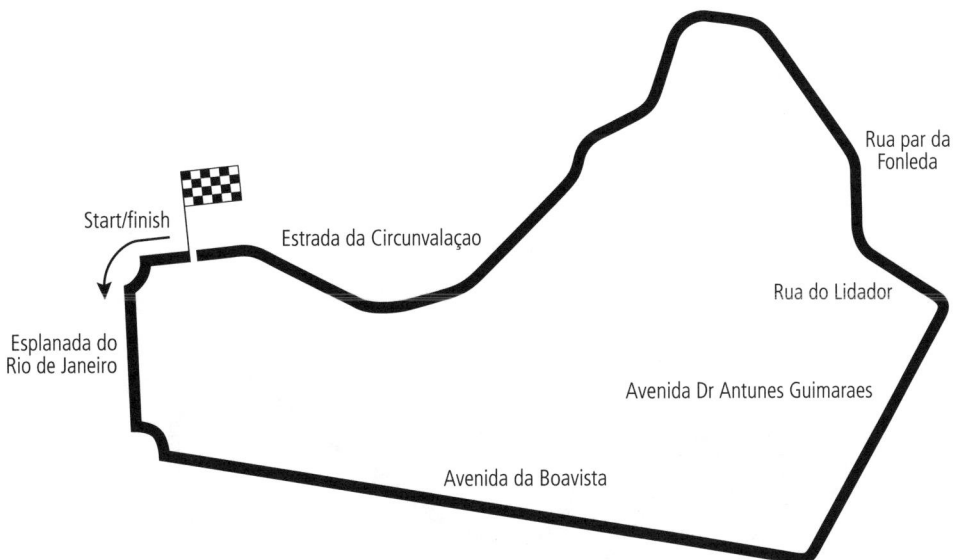

Records:

	Length		Years (no. of races)	Driver (Car)	Time	Speed		Year
	km	miles			min:sec	km/h	mph	
a)	7.407	4.602	1958,60 (2)	Pole: J Surtees (Lotus)	2:25.560	183.190	113.829	1960
				F. Lap: J Surtees (Lotus)	2:27.530	180.744	112.309	1960
				Winner: J Brabham (Cooper)		175.849	109.268	1960

EAST LONDON

Location: Cape Province. South-west outskirts of East London.
First Used: July 1959.

Back in the 1930s, races were run around the public roads of this resort. A new circuit was built into a natural hollow by the coastline, which included a rifle range in part of the complex.

World Championship races: 3

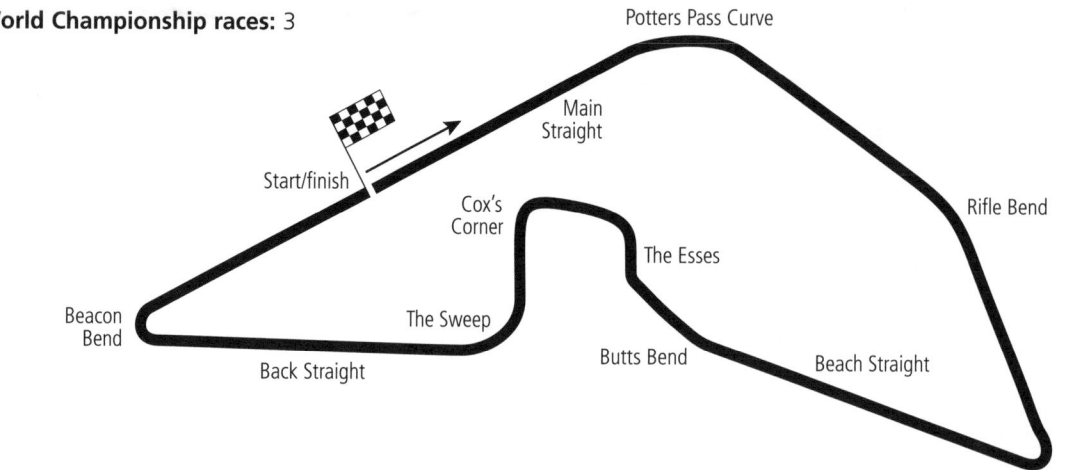

Records:

	Length		Years (no. of races)	Driver (Car)	Time	Speed		Year
	km	miles			min:sec	km/h	mph	
a)	3.920	2.436	1962-63,65 (3)	Pole: J Clark (Lotus)	1:27.200	161.850	100.569	1965
				F. Lap: J Clark (Lotus)	1:27.600	161.111	100.110	1965
				Winner: J Clark (Lotus)		157.722	98.004	1965

KYALAMI

Location: 24 km (15 miles) north of Johannesburg.
First Used: December 1961.

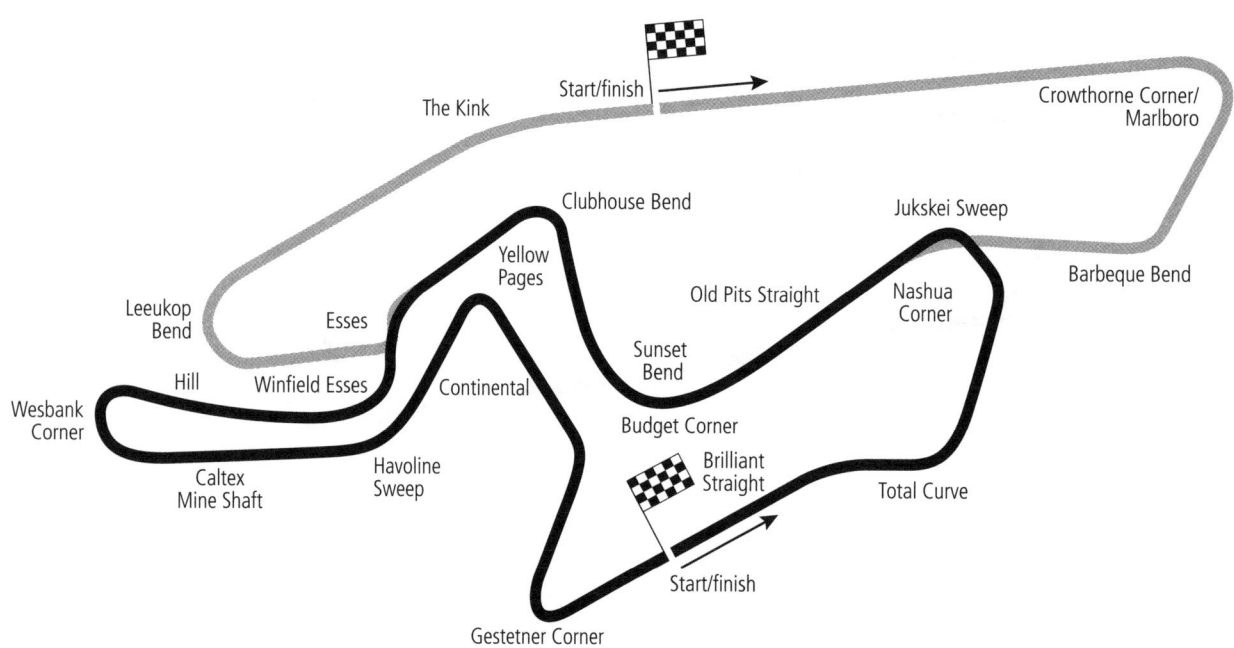

Kyalami, meaning 'my house' in the Sesotho language, is built on a plateau, 5,000 feet above sea level. Its first rate facilities were popular with drivers, however South African politics caused the venue to be dropped from the schedule and part of the circuit was sold to developers. In 1987, work began on a total revamp of the circuit, using part of the old track, although the new tighter version was dropped after just two events.

World Championship races: 20
Records:

	Length		Years (no. of races)	Driver (Car)	Time	Speed		Year
	km	miles			min:sec	km/h	mph	
a)	4.094	2.544	1967 (1)	Pole: J Brabham (Brabham)	1:28.300	166.920	103.719	1967
				F. Lap: D Hulme (Brabham)	1:29.900	163.949	101.873	1967
				Winner: P Rodriguez (Cooper)		156.260	97.095	1967
Widened								
b)	4.104	2.550	1968-80,82-85 (17)	Pole: N Mansell (Williams)	1: 2.366	236.898	147.202	1985
				F. Lap: K Rosberg (Williams)	1: 8.149	216.796	134.711	1985
				Winner: N Mansell (Williams)		208.959	129.841	1985
New circuit								
c)	4.261	2.648	1992-93 (2)	Pole: N Mansell (Williams)	1:15.486	203.211	126.270	1992
				F. Lap: N Mansell (Williams)	1:17.578	197.731	122.865	1992
				Winner: N Mansell (Williams)		190.248	118.215	1992

Spain (E)

JARAMA

Location: 28 km (17 miles) north of Madrid.
First Used: July 1967.

Designed by John Hugenholtz to fit into a small pocket of land in the arid and hilly scrubland north of Madrid. It was considered by many to be too cramped for car racing although the Portago section was extended in 1991. It is still used for motorcycling and other events although there are plans to redevelop the area and build a new circuit nearby.

World Championship races: 9

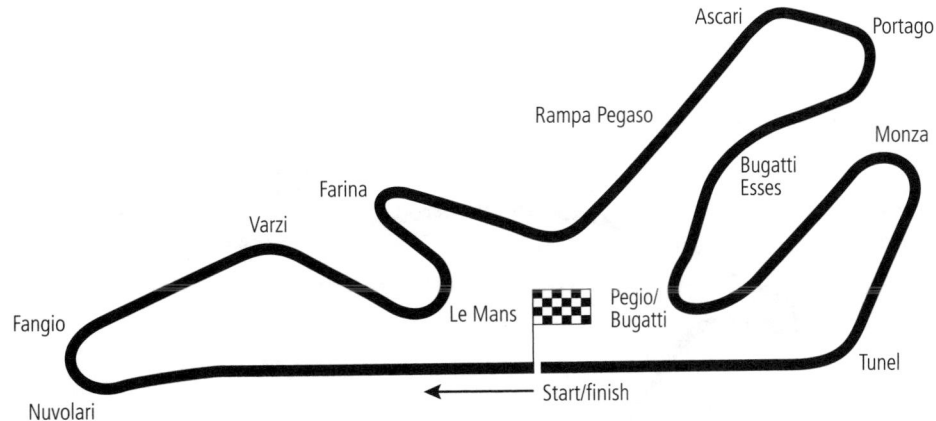

Records:

	Length		Years (no. of races)	Driver (Car)	Time	Speed		Year
	km	miles			min:sec	km/h	mph	
a)	3.404	2.115	1968,70,72,74,76-79 (8)	Pole: J Laffite (Ligier)	1:14.500	164.489	102.208	1979
				F. Lap: G Villeneuve (Ferrari)	1:16.440	160.314	99.614	1979
				Winner: P Depailler (Ligier)		154.419	95.952	1979
Revision								
b)	3.312	2.058	1981 (1)	Pole: J Laffite (Ligier)	1:13.754	161.662	100.452	1981
				F. Lap: A Jones (Williams)	1:17.818	153.219	95.206	1981
				Winner: G Villeneuve (Ferrari)		149.156	92.681	1981

JEREZ de la FRONTERA

Location: North-east of Jerez de la Frontera, 35 km (22 miles) north-east of Cadiz.

First Used: 1986.

Jerez reintroduced F1 to Spain, but due to its isolated location, deep in the sherry producing region of the southern plains, it has never attracted large crowds. It was dropped from the calender after Martin Donnelly's dreadful practice accident in 1990, but returned after a chicane was added prior to that corner, to become a last minute addition to the 1994 calendar. It receives regular visirs from F1 teams during winter testing but was last used in the championship as the final round in 1997 as a parting gesture to Renault in Europe.

World Championship races: 7 (including European Grand Prix in 1994 and 1997)

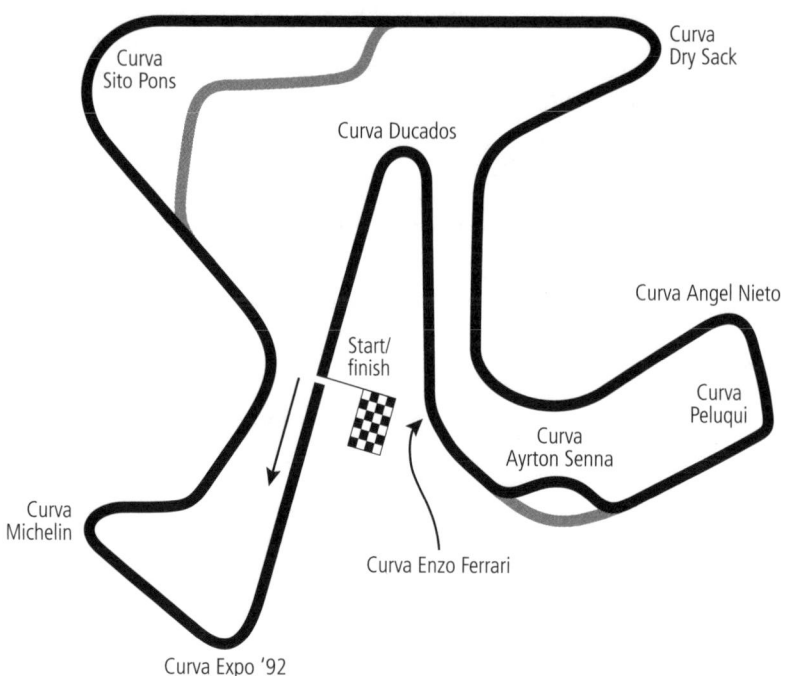

Records:

	Length		Years (no. of races)	Driver (Car)	Time	Speed		Year
	km	miles			min:sec	km/h	mph	
a)	4.218	2.621	1986-90 (5)	Pole: A Senna (McLaren)	1:18.387	193.716	120.369	1990
				F. Lap: R Patrese (Williams)	1:24.513	179.674	111.644	1990
				Winner: A Senna (McLaren)		171.374	106.487	1989
New corner at Sito Pons & chicane								
b)	4.428	2.751	1994-97 (2)	Pole: J Villeneuve (Williams)	1:21.072	196.625	122.177	1997
				F. Lap: H-H Frentzen (Williams)	1:23.135	191.745	119.145	1997
				Winner: M Häkkinen (McLaren)		185.240	115.103	1997

MONTJUÏC

Location: Barcelona (west of city centre).

First Used: 1933.

Situated within the undulating roads of a public park, high on a hill, named the 'Jewish Mountain' after an important cemetery existing there in the Middle Ages and next to Barcelona's Olympic stadium. The circuit was revived in 1966, but saw dreadful accidents in its time. The wings failed on both Lotus cars in 1969 and Rolf Stommelen suffered a similar problem in the same downhill spot in 1975, crashing over the barriers and killing four spectators. Montjuïc was not used again.

World Championship races: 4

Records:

	Length		Years (no. of races)	Driver (Car)	Time	Speed		Year
	km	miles			min:sec	km/h	mph	
a)	3.791	2.356	1969,71,73,75 (4)	Pole: R Peterson (JPS Lotus)	1:21.800	166.841	103.670	1973
				F. Lap: R Peterson (JPS Lotus)	1:23.800	162.859	101.196	1973
				Winner: E Fittipaldi (JPS Lotus)		157.504	97.868	1973

MONTMELÓ

Location: 20 km (12 miles) north of Barcelona.
First Used: 1991.

Built on land purchased by the Real Automóvil Club de Cataluñya, who hoped to bring F1 back to Spain's spiritual home of motorsport on a permanent basis. Completed just in time for the first Grand Prix, it was well laid out for easy access and incorporated good viewing positions. Local drivers Luis Perez Sala and Francisco Godia advised on the layout which follows the principles of many modern day circuits. Drivers are very familiar with the track as it has become a regular venue for winter testing.

World Championship races: 15

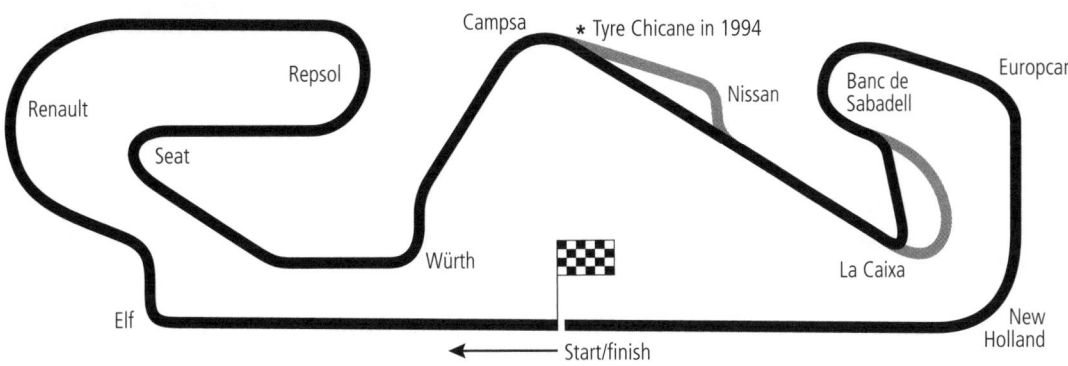

Records:

	Length		Years (no. of races)	Driver (Car)	Time	Speed		Year
	km	miles			min:sec	km/h	mph	
a)	4.747	2.950	1991-94 (4)	Pole: A Prost (Williams)	1:17.809	219.630	136.472	1993
				F. Lap: M Schumacher (Benetton)	1:20.989	211.006	131.113	1993
				Winner: A Prost (Williams)		200.227	124.415	1993
Nissan straightened								
b)	4.727	2.937	1995-96 (2)					
	4.728	2.938	1997-99 (3)					
	4.730	2.939	2000-03 (4)	Pole: M Schumacher (Ferrari)	1:16.364	222.984	138.556	2002
				F. Lap: R Barrichello (Ferrari)	1:20.143	212.470	132.023	2003
				Winner: M Schumacher (Ferrari)		203.753	126.607	2002
Revision at La Caixa								
c)	4.627	2.875	2004-05 (2)	Pole: M Schumacher (Ferrari) *	1:15.022	222.030	137.964	2004
				F. Lap: G Fisichella (Renault)	1:15.641	220.213	136.835	2005
				Winner: K Räikkönen (McLaren)		209.844	130.392	2005

* Fastest single qualifying lap record was set during 2005 aggregate timing by J Trulli (Toyota), 1m 14.795s, 222.704 km/h, 138.382 mph.

PEDRALBES

Location: Barcelona, 7 km (4 miles) north-west of city centre.
First Used: 1946.

The circuit incorporated the wide avenues of the outskirts of the city, in the shadow of the Pedralbes monastery. It was one of the first major venues after the war, when it hosted the Penya Rhin Grand Prix, but soon faded from the international calendar.

World Championship races: 2

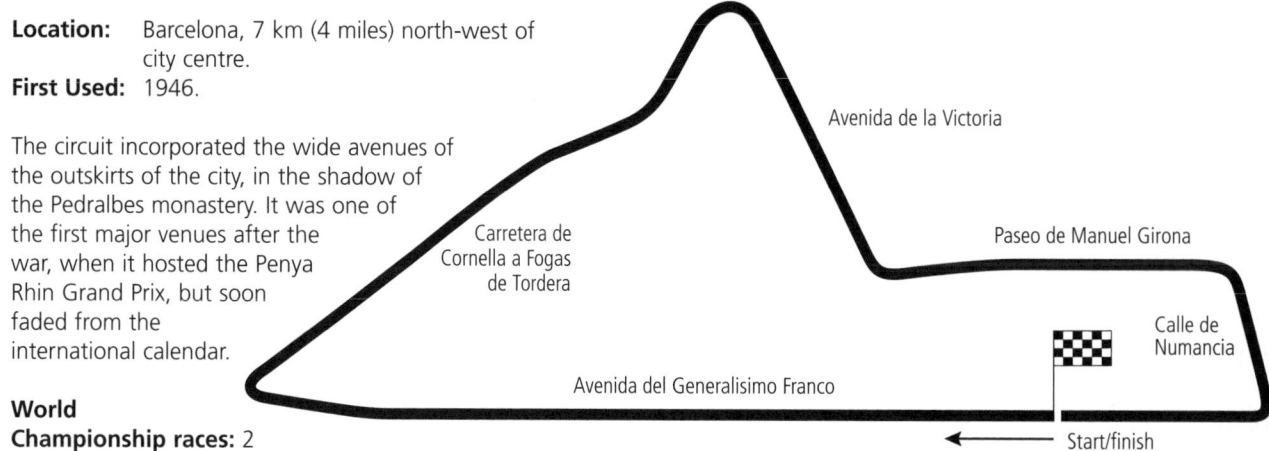

Records:

	Length		Years (no. of races)	Driver (Car)	Time	Speed		Year
	km	miles			min:sec	km/h	mph	
a)	6.316	3.925	1951,54 (2)	Pole: A Ascari (Ferrari)	2:10.590	174.114	108.190	1951
				F. Lap: J M Fangio (Alfa Romeo)	2:16.930	166.053	103.180	1951
				Winner: J M Fangio (Alfa Romeo)		158.939	98.760	1951

Sweden (S)

ANDERSTORP

Location: 80 km (50 miles) south of Jönköping.
First Used: 1968.

Conceived by Sven Asberg and built on flat marshland forest with a runway forming part of the back straight. Also known as the Scandinavian Raceway, Anderstorp was renowned for unpredictable race results such as the Tyrrell six-wheeler 1-2 in 1976 and Ligier's first win the following year.

World Championship races: 6

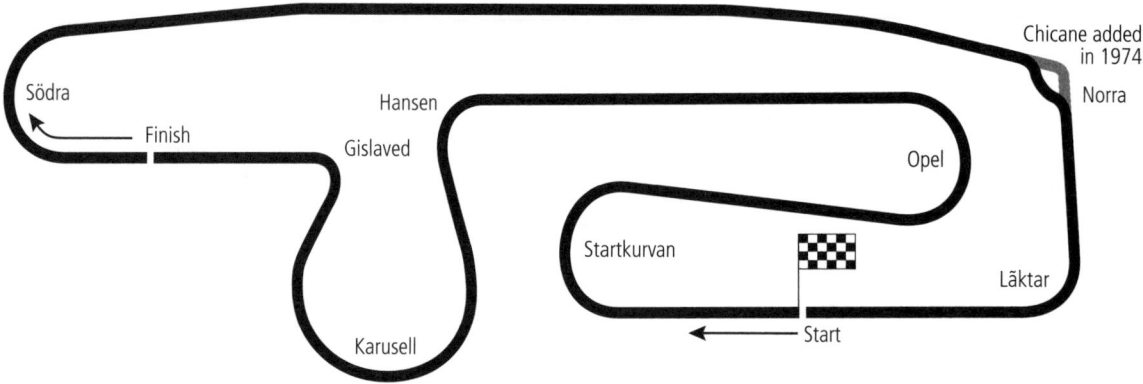

Records:

	Length		Years (no. of races)	Driver (Car)	Time	Speed		Year
	km	miles			min:sec	km/h	mph	
a)	4.018	2.497	1973-77 (5)	Pole: R Peterson (JPS Lotus)	1:23.810	172.590	107.243	1973
				F. Lap: D Hulme (McLaren)	1:26.146	167.910	104.335	1973
				Winner: D Hulme (McLaren)		165.169	102.631	1973
Further revision								
b)	4.031	2.505	1978 (1)	Pole: M Andretti (JPS Lotus)	1:22.058	176.846	109.887	1978
				F. Lap: N Lauda (Brabham)	1:24.836	171.055	106.288	1978
				Winner: N Lauda (Brabham)		167.609	104.147	1978

BREMGARTEN

Location: North-west outskirts of Bern.
First Used: 1931.

Cars first raced in 1934 at this daunting circuit which threads its way through the winding forest roads. There were no straights to speak of and with overhanging trees and cobbled surfaces in places, the circuit took its toll. Racing came to an abrupt end when Switzerland banned motor racing, in the wake of the 1955 Le Mans disaster, which killed over 80 spectators, when Pierre Levegh's Mercedes crashed into the crowd.

World Championship races: 5

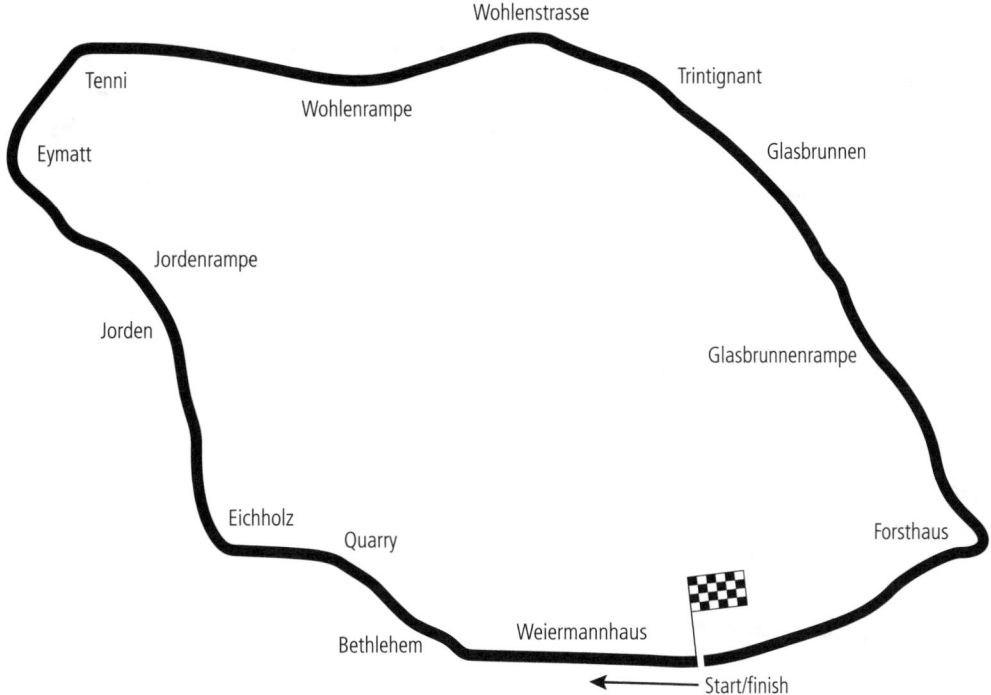

Records:

	Length		Years (no. of races)	Driver (Car)	Time	Speed		Year
	km	miles			min:sec	km/h	mph	
a)	7.280	4.524	1950-54 (5)	Pole: J M Fangio (Alfa Romeo)	2:35.900	168.108	104.457	1951
				F. Lap: J M Fangio (Mercedes-Benz)	2:39.700	164.108	101.972	1954
				Winner: J M Fangio (Mercedes-Benz)		159.650	99.202	1954

ISTANBUL

Location: near Balcik, 48 km (30 miles) east of city centre.
First Used: 2005.

Another Hermann Tilke track design welcomed another new country to the World Championship in 2005. It is unusual in being anti-clockwise and having elevation changes with some sections based on famous corners from other tracks. The Istanbul Otodrom proved very popular with drivers, especially the tricky turn 8.

World Championship races: 1

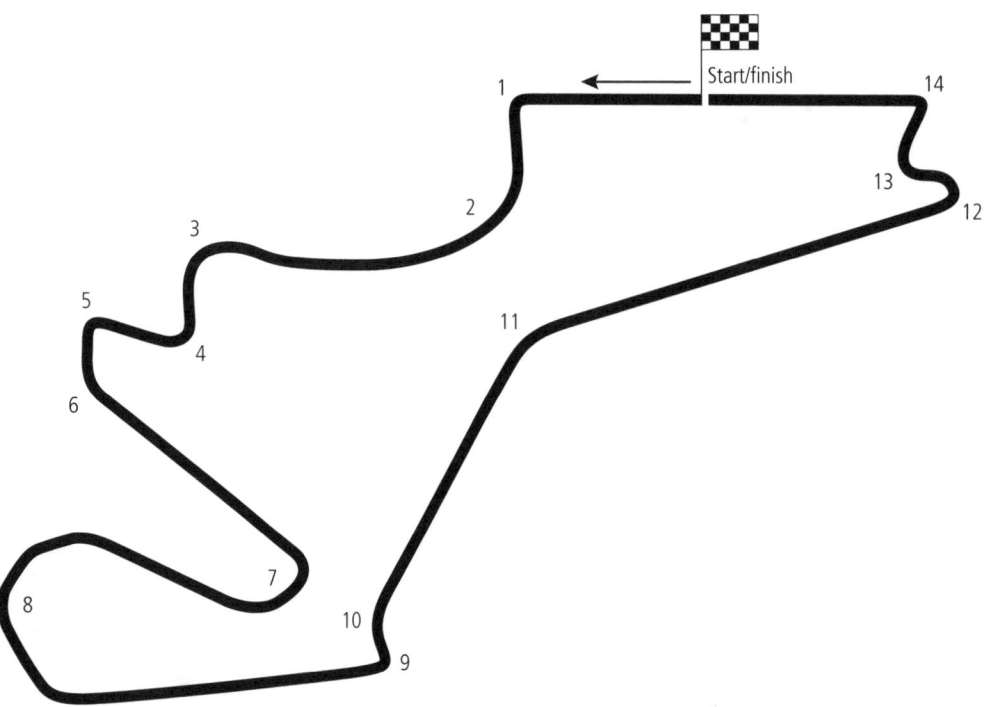

Records:

	Length		Years (no. of races)	Driver (Car)	Time	Speed		Year
	km	miles			min:sec	km/h	mph	
a)	5.338	3.317	2005 (1)	Pole: K Räikkönen (McLaren)	1:26.797	221.399	137.571	2005
				F. Lap: J P Montoya (McLaren)	1:24.770	226.693	140.861	2005
				Winner: K Räikkönen (McLaren)		219.496	136.389	2005

DALLAS

Location: Dallas (city centre), Texas.
First Used: 1984.

Located in the Fair Park area of the city, this was a fairly typical angular street circuit that utilised roads around the famous Cotton Bowl stadium. Used only once, it is best remembered for the poor surface that crumbled during racing, catching out many of the drivers.

World Championship races: 1

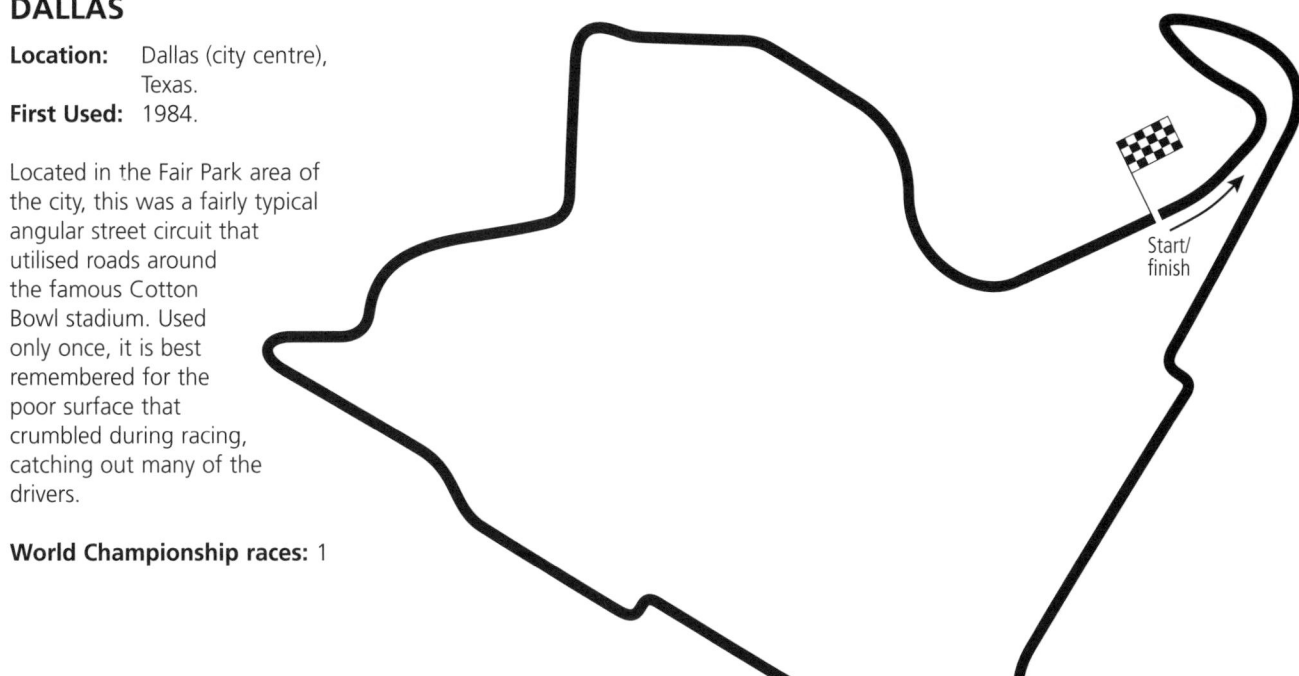

Records:

	Length		Years (no. of races)	Driver (Car)	Time	Speed		Year
	km	miles			min:sec	km/h	mph	
a)	3.901	2.424	1984 (1)	Pole: N Mansell (Lotus)	1:37.041	144.720	89.925	1984
				F. Lap: N Lauda (McLaren)	1:45.353	133.302	82.830	1984
				Winner: K Rosberg (Williams)		129.203	80.283	1984

DETROIT

Location: Detroit (city centre), Michigan.
First Used: 1982.

A street circuit in Motown is a good marketing idea, but the right-angle nature of the course, didn't show F1 cars in their true light. A tunnel and the nearby water, didn't make for another Monaco and the race transferred to the IndyCar series in 1989, before they switched their venue to nearby Belle Isle.

World Championship races: 7

Records:

	Length		Years (no. of races)	Driver (Car)	Time min:sec	Speed		Year
	km	miles				km/h	mph	
a)	4.012	2.493	1982 (1)	Pole: A Prost (Renault)	1:48.537	133.075	82.689	1982
				F. Lap: A Prost (Renault)	1:50.438	130.784	81.266	1982
				Winner: J Watson (McLaren)		125.754	78.140	1982
Corners eased								
b)	4.023	2.500	1983-88 (6)	Pole: A Senna (Lotus)	1:38.301	147.344	91.556	1986
				F. Lap: A Senna (Lotus)	1:40.464	144.172	89.584	1987
				Winner: A Senna (Lotus)		137.915	85.697	1987

INDIANAPOLIS

Location: 10 km (6 miles) west of city centre, Indiana.
First Used: 1909.

The oldest race track in the world. Carl Fisher organised construction of this world famous circuit, perfectly rectangular with corners banked at 9 degrees, eventually paved with over 3 million bricks (these were replaced with asphalt in 1961). The Indianapolis 500 began in 1911 and became the largest attended, one day sports event with over 400,000 spectators. After the war it was purchased by Anton Hulman who redeveloped the grounds to include a museum and a golf course, amongst other attractions. The 500 race was included as part of the World Championship in the early years, to attract American drivers. After a gap of nearly 40 years, the speedway owner, Tony George constructed an infield track to bring Formula 1 back to the United States at this historically significant site.

World Championship races: 17

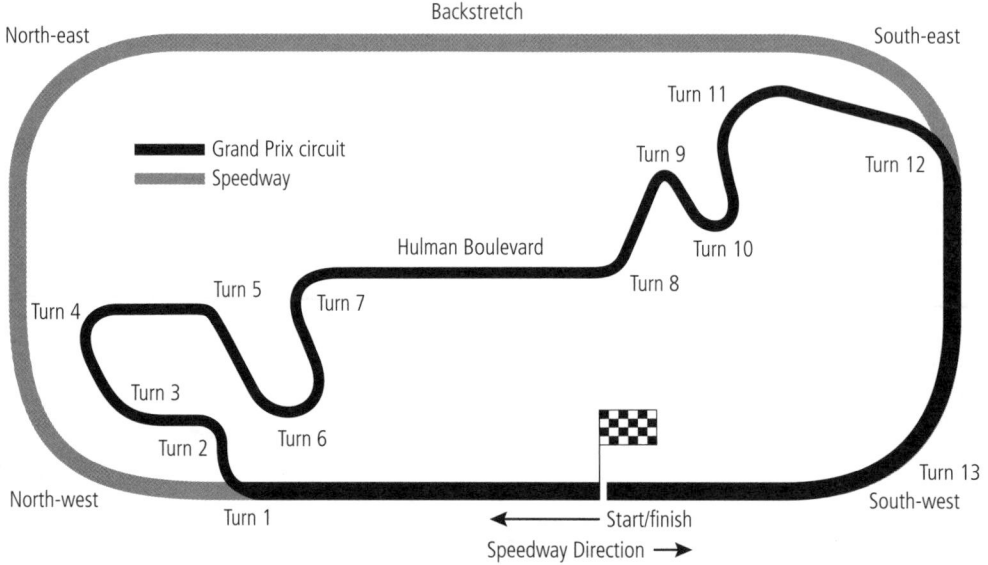

Records:

	Length		Years (no. of races)	Driver (Car)	Time min:sec	Speed		Year
	km	miles				km/h	mph	
a)	4.023	2.500	1950-60 (11)	Pole: E Sachs (Ewing)	1: 1.395	235.917	146.592	1960
				F. Lap: J Rathmann (Watson)	1: 1.590	235.170	146.128	1960
				Winner: J Rathmann (Watson)		223.324	138.767	1960
b) Infield road course								
	4.192	2.605	2000-05 (6)	Pole: R Barrichello (Ferrari)	1:10.223	214.903	133.535	2004
				F. Lap: R Barrichello (Ferrari)	1:10.399	214.366	133.201	2004
				Winner: R Barrichello (Ferrari)		201.475	125.191	2002

LAS VEGAS

Location: West side of 'The Strip', Las Vegas, Nevada.
First Used: 1981.

Built within the confines of Caesars Palace Hotel car park, with the use of interlocking concrete barriers. A true temporary circuit, it ran anti-clockwise and witnessed the championship showdown in both years. Further development in 2003 of this hotel and casino complex meant that this unloved track is now covered by new building work at this popular resort.

World Championship races: 2

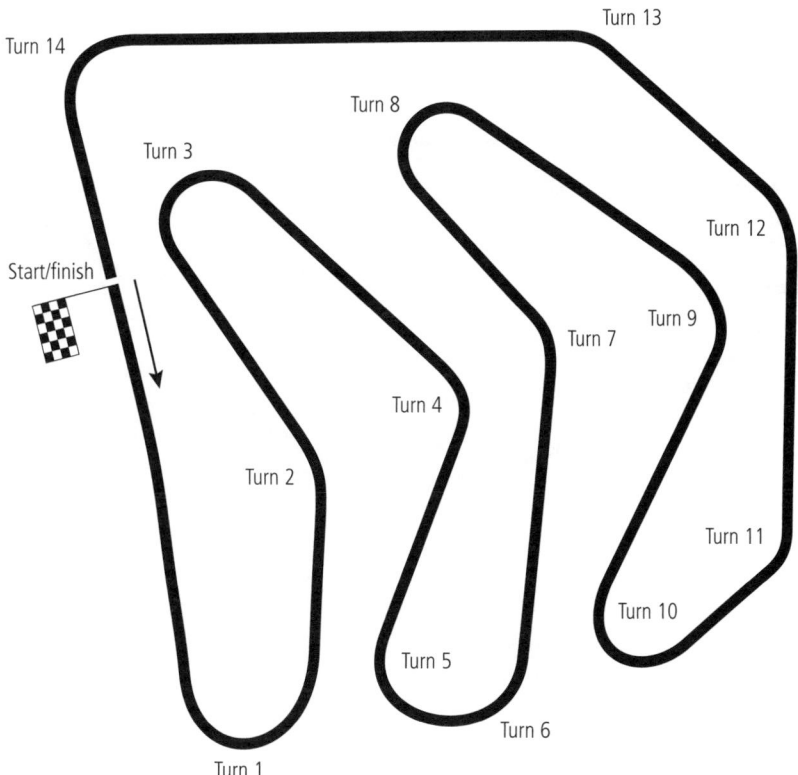

Records:

	Length		Years (no. of races)	Driver (Car)	Time	Speed		Year
	km	miles			min:sec	km/h	mph	
a)	3.650	2.268	1981-82 (2)	Pole: A Prost (Renault)	1:16.356	172.088	106.931	1982
				F. Lap: M Alboreto (Tyrrell)	1:19.639	164.994	102.523	1982
				Winner: M Alboreto (Tyrrell)		161.111	100.110	1982

LONG BEACH

Location: Long Beach (waterfront), southern Los Angeles, California.
First Used: 1975.

Originated by Chris Pook, who arranged for this street race around the sea's edge under the shadow of the Queen Mary ship. The circuit was unusual in having a different start and finish line and was characterised by the long sweeping Shoreline Drive. It achieved its objective of adding glamour to this part of Los Angeles, but after substantial circuit route changes, the race successfully transferred to IndyCars/Champ Cars and continues to this day.

World Championship races: 8

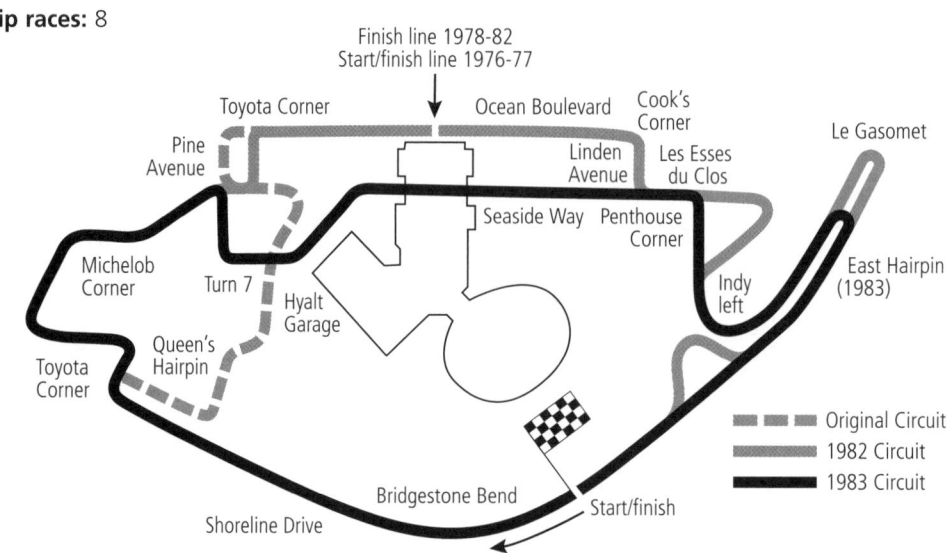

Records:

	Length		Years (no. of races)	Driver (Car)	Time	Speed		Year
	km	miles			min:sec	km/h	mph	
a)	3.251	2.020	1976-81 (6)	Pole: N Piquet (Brabham)	1:17.694	150.637	93.602	1980
				F. Lap: N Piquet (Brabham)	1:19.830	146.607	91.097	1980
				Winner: N Piquet (Brabham)		142.348	88.451	1980
New route (Michelob corner)								
b)	3.428	2.130	1982 (1)	Pole: A de Cesaris (Alfa Romeo)	1:27.316	141.331	87.819	1982
				F. Lap: N Lauda (McLaren)	1:30.831	135.862	84.421	1982
				Winner: N Lauda (McLaren)		131.128	81.479	1982
Shortened (Seaside Way)								
c)	3.275	2.035	1983 (1)	Pole: P Tambay (Ferrari)	1:26.117	136.907	85.070	1983
				F. Lap: N Lauda (McLaren)	1:28.330	133.477	82.939	1983
				Winner: J Watson (McLaren)		129.753	80.625	1983

PHOENIX

Location: Phoenix (west of city centre), Arizona.
First Used: 1989.

Another point and squirt, 90 degree street circuit, laid out amongst concrete barriers. Phoenix never proved to be popular with drivers or spectators, and after an attempt to rearrange the circuit with less right angle bends, it was never used again.

World Championship races: 3

Records:

	Length		Years (no. of races)	Driver (Car)	Time	Speed		Year
	km	miles			min:sec	km/h	mph	
a)	3.798	2.360	1989-90 (2)	Pole: G Berger (McLaren)	1:28.664	154.211	95.822	1990
				F. Lap: G Berger (McLaren)	1:31.050	150.170	93.311	1990
				Winner: A Senna (McLaren)		145.784	90.586	1990

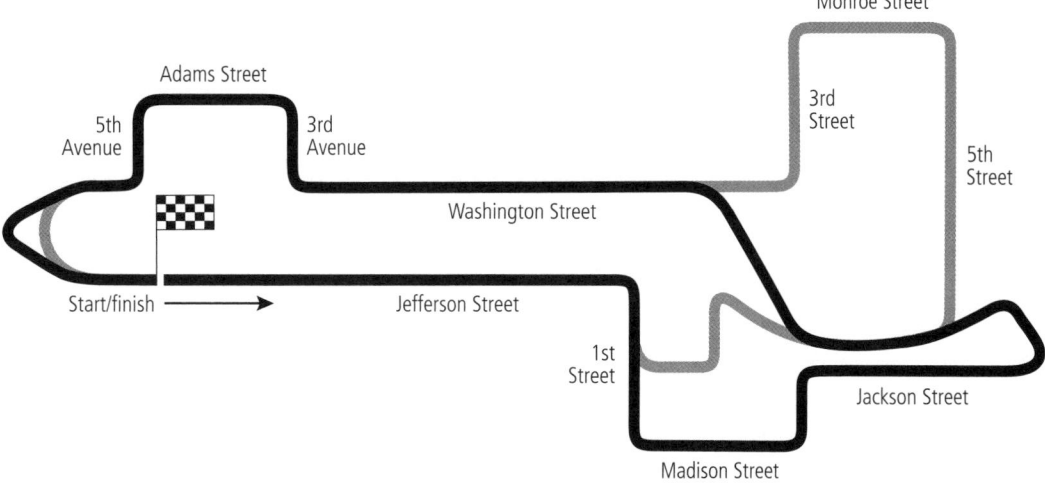

Monroe Street by-pass								
b)	3.721	2.312	1991 (1)	Pole: A Senna (McLaren)	1:21.434	164.488	102.208	1991
				F. Lap: J Alesi (Ferrari)	1:26.758	154.394	95.936	1991
				Winner: A Senna (McLaren)		149.698	93.018	1991

RIVERSIDE

Location: 100 km (60 miles) east of Los Angeles, California.
First Used: 1957.

A purpose-built circuit with various combinations, including a drag strip, in the hilly, dusty desert country south of Highway 60. A popular track it has its dark days such as Rolf Stommelen losing his life in 1983 when he crashed on the approach to turn 9 during an IMSA sports car race. Riverside gradually fell into disrepair and was closed after its last race in June 1989. The Moreno Valley Retail Park was built on the northern part of the circuit and all traces of the track were lost in 2003 after further housing developments.

World Championship races: 1

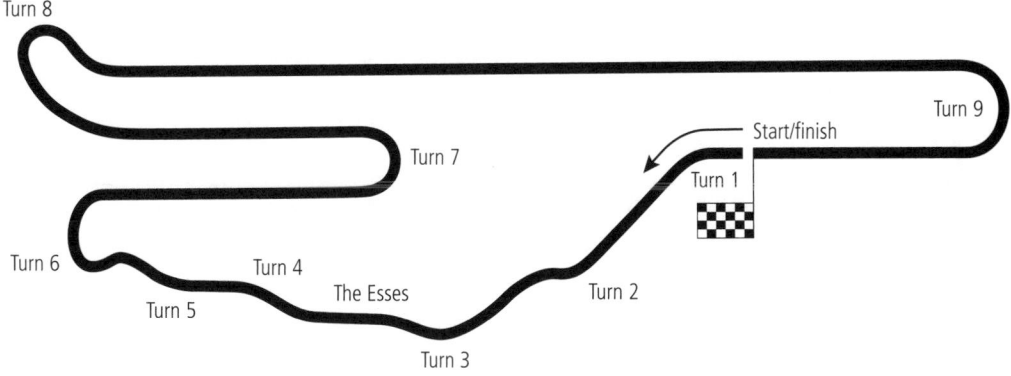

Records:

	Length		Years (no. of races)	Driver (Car)	Time	Speed		Year
	km	miles			min:sec	km/h	mph	
a)	5.271	3.275	1960 (1)	Pole: S Moss (Lotus)	1:54.400	165.858	103.059	1960
				F. Lap: J Brabham (Cooper)	1:56.300	163.148	101.376	1960
				Winner: S Moss (Lotus)		159.318	98.996	1960

SEBRING

Location: Desoto City, 6 km (4 miles) south-east of
Sebring, Florida.
First Used: 1950.

Conceived by Alex Ulmann, who created the circuit from a combination of concrete runway and tarmac roads of the disused wartime Hendrick Field airbase. It has become an important venue for sports car racing with the Sebring 12 hour race each Spring and due to its layout has had various permutations, most notably in 1966 and 1987. American entrepreneur Don Panoz bought the circuit in 1998 and redeveloped the track with a new hotel complex amongst other modifications.

World Championship races: 1

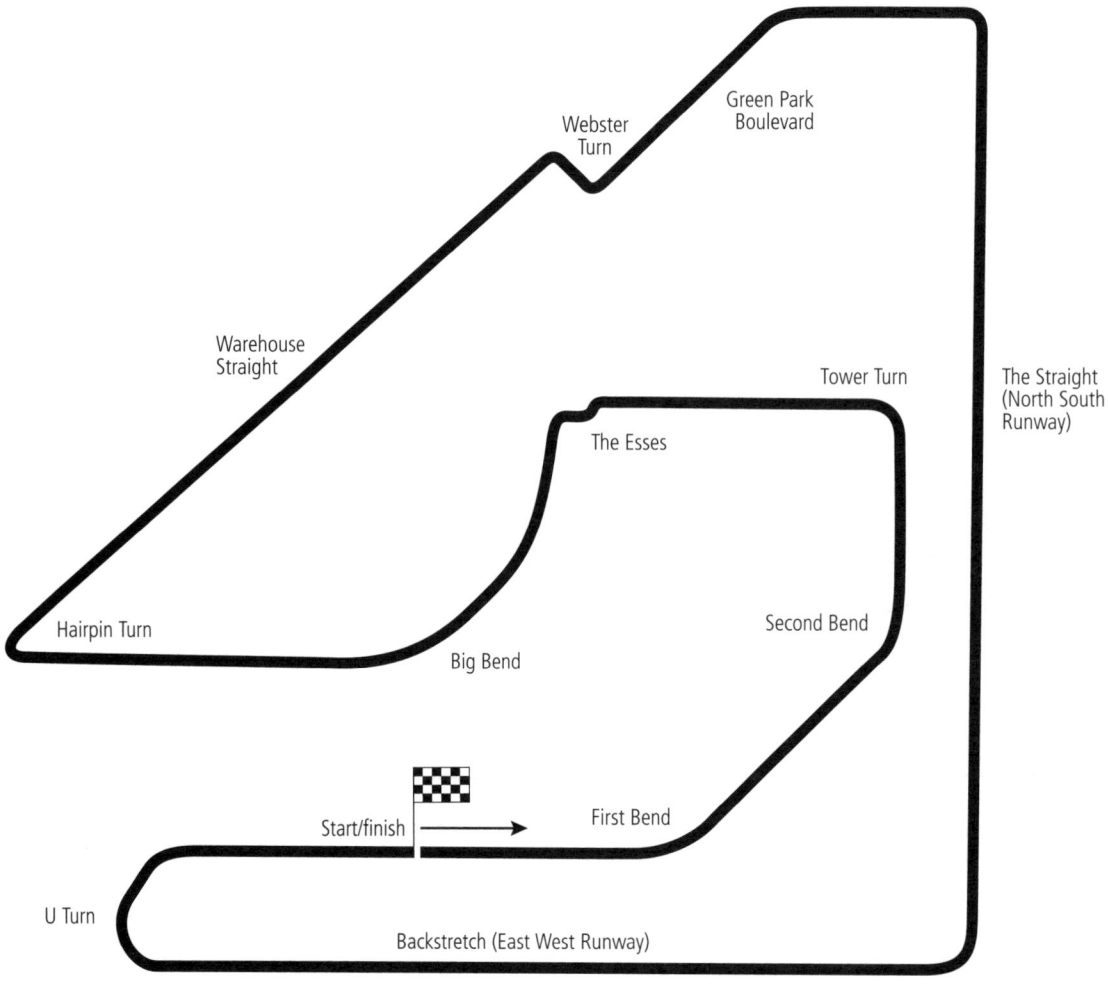

Records:

	Length		Years (no. of races)	Driver (Car)	Time	Speed		Year
	km	miles			min:sec	km/h	mph	
a)	8.369	5.200	1959 (1)	Pole: S Moss (Cooper)	3: 0.000	167.372	104.000	1959
				F. Lap: M Trintignant (Cooper)	3: 5.000	162.848	101.189	1959
				Winner: B McLaren (Cooper)		159.047	98.827	1959

WATKINS GLEN

Location: 30 km (18 miles) north of Elmira, New York State.
First Used: 1956.

After races in the village and on surrounding public roads, a new track, designed by Bill Milliken, was built in the wooded hill tops of the Lake Seneca area. The summer of 1971 saw a radical redesign of the circuit, again with the help of Cornell University. The twisting undulations of the track caught out many drivers including François Cevert, who was killed in practice for what would have been team-mate Jackie Stewart's last race before his retirement. The track fell out of favour with F1 and spent many years on the Stock car program before the IRL series re-introduced major single seater racing back to the revamped track in 2005.

World Championship races: 20

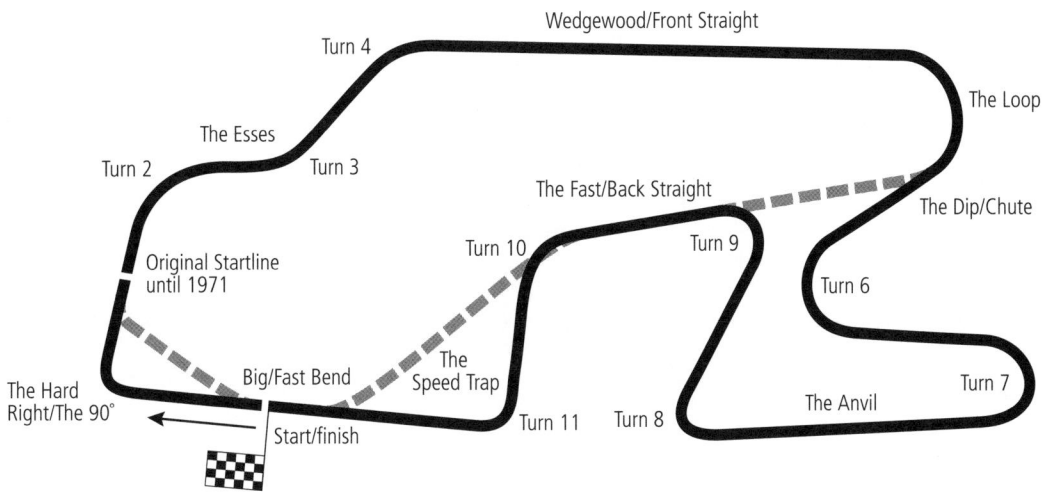

Records:

	Length		Years (no. of races)	Driver (Car)	Time	Speed		Year
	km	miles			min:sec	km/h	mph	
a)	3.701	2.300	1961-70 (10)	Pole: J Ickx (Ferrari)	1: 3.070	211.279	131.283	1970
				F. Lap: J Ickx (Ferrari)	1: 2.740	212.390	131.973	1970
				Winner: E Fittipaldi (Lotus)		204.053	126.792	1970
Revised (including 'The Anvil')								
b)	5.435	3.377	1971-80 (10)	Pole: B Giacomelli (Alfa Romeo)	1:33.291	209.721	130.315	1980
				F. Lap: A Jones (Williams)	1:34.068	207.989	129.238	1980
				Winner: A Jones (Williams)		203.371	126.369	1980

Circuit Summary

Circuit	Country	No. of races	Years
A1-RING/ÖSTERREICHRING, near Knittelfeld	AUSTRIA	25	1970-03
ADELAIDE, South Australia	AUSTRALIA	11	1985-95
AIDA/ TI, near Okayama City	JAPAN	2	1994-95
ÂIN-DIAB, Casablanca	MOROCCO	1	1958
AINTREE, Liverpool	GREAT BRITAIN	5	1955-62
ANDERSTORP/SCANDINAVIAN RACEWAY, near Jönköping	SWEDEN	6	1973-78
AVUS, Berlin	GERMANY	1	1959
BRANDS HATCH, near Dartford, Kent	GREAT BRITAIN	14	1964-86
BREMGARTEN, near Bern	SWITZERLAND	5	1950-54
BUENOS AIRES/ALMIRANTE BROWN no.2,6,9,15	ARGENTINA	20	1953-98
BUGATTI AU MANS, Le Mans	FRANCE	1	1967
CLERMONT-FERRAND, Montagne d'Auvergne	FRANCE	4	1965-72
DALLAS/FAIR PARK, Texas	USA	1	1984
DETROIT, Michigan	USA	7	1982-88
DIJON-PRENOIS, near Dijon	FRANCE	6	1974-84
DONINGTON PARK, near Derby	GREAT BRITAIN	1	1993
EAST LONDON, Cape Province	SOUTH AFRICA	3	1962-65
ESTORIL, near Lisbon	PORTUGAL	13	1984-96
FUJI, near Yokohama/Tokyo	JAPAN	2	1976-77
HOCKENHEIM, near Heidelberg	GERMANY	29	1970-05
HUNGARORING, Mogyorod, Budapest	HUNGARY	20	1986-05
IMOLA/ENZO & DINO-FERRARI, near Bologna	ITALY	26	1980-05
INDIANAPOLIS, Indiana	USA	17	1950-05
INTERLAGOS, São Paulo	BRAZIL	23	1973-05
ISTANBUL	TURKEY	1	2005
JARAMA, near Madrid	SPAIN	9	1968-81
JEREZ de la FRONTERA, near Cadiz	SPAIN	7	1986-97
KYALAMI, near Johannesburg	SOUTH AFRICA	20	1967-93
LAS VEGAS/CAESARS PALACE, Nevada	USA	2	1981-82
LONG BEACH, Los Angeles, California	USA	8	1976-83
MAGNY-COURS, near Nevers	FRANCE	15	1991-05

Circuit	Country	No. of races	Years
MELBOURNE/ALBERT PARK	AUSTRALIA	10	1996-05
MEXICO CITY/HERMANOS R & P RODRIGUEZ/MAGDALENA MIXHUCA	MEXICO	15	1963-92
MONSANTO PARK, Lisbon	PORTUGAL	1	1959
MONT-TREMBLANT/ST.-JOVITE, near Montréal, Québec	CANADA	2	1968-70
MONTE-CARLO	MONACO	52	1950-05
MONTJUÏC, Barcelona	SPAIN	4	1969-75
MONTMELÓ/CATALUNYA, near Barcelona	SPAIN	15	1991-05
MONTRÉAL/GILLES VILLENEUVE/ILE NOTRE DAME, Québec	CANADA	27	1978-05
MONZA, near Milan	ITALY	55	1950-05
MOSPORT PARK, near Bowmanville, Ontario	CANADA	8	1967-77
NIVELLES-BAULERS, near Brussels	BELGIUM	2	1972-74
NÜRBURGRING, near Koblenz	GERMANY	35	1951-05
PAUL RICARD/LE CASTELLET, near Marseille	FRANCE	14	1971-90
PEDRALBES, Barcelona	SPAIN	2	1951-54
PESCARA	ITALY	1	1957
PHOENIX, Arizona	USA	3	1989-91
PORTO	PORTUGAL	2	1958-60
REIMS & REIMS-GUEUX	FRANCE	11	1950-66
RIO de JANEIRO/NELSON PIQUET/JACAREPAGUA	BRAZIL	10	1978-89
RIVERSIDE, near Los Angeles, California	USA	1	1960
ROUEN-les-ESSARTS	FRANCE	5	1952-68
SAKHIR near Manama	BAHRAIN	2	2004-05
SEBRING, Florida	USA	1	1959
SEPANG, Kuala Lumpur	MALAYSIA	7	1999-05
SHANGHAI	CHINA	2	2004-05
SILVERSTONE, near Towcester, Northamptonshire	GREAT BRITAIN	39	1950-05
SPA-FRANCORCHAMPS, near Liège	BELGIUM	39	1950-05
SUZUKA, near Nagoya	JAPAN	19	1987-05
WATKINS GLEN, near Elmira, New York State	USA	20	1961-80
ZANDVOORT, near Haarlem	NETHERLANDS	30	1952-85
ZELTWEG, near Knittelfeld	AUSTRIA	1	1964
ZOLDER, near Hasselt	BELGIUM	10	1973-84

Circuits

6

RECORDS
AND
TRIVIA

Left: *Phil Hill (Ferrari D246) celebrates victory at the 1960 Italian Grand Prix, the last time a front-engined car won a championship race.* (LAT)

Total seasons	56 (to the end of 2005)
Total races	750 (inc. 11 at Indianapolis 500)
Total venues	63
Total countries to host a race	26
Total laps in the World Championship 1950-2005	50,124.6 (inc. 2,138 at Indy 500)
Total distance	246,564.6 km (inc. 8,601.9 km at Indy 500)
Total drivers entrants in the World Championship	858 (inc. 178 only at Indy 500)
Total starting drivers	715 (inc. 103 only at Indy 500) (inc. 4 who started an F1 and Indy 500 race)
Total non-starters	68 plus an additional 75 Indy 500
Total race starters in the World Championship	17,092 (inc. 36 not on grid but who started during races in shared drives)

SEASONS

Season Length

Longest

	months:days
1968	10:2
1965	9:23
1967	9:20
1977	9:14
1960	9:13

Shortest

1952	3:20
1950	3:21
1961	4:24
1951	5:1
1966	5:1

Closed Season

Longest

	months:days
1950/51	8:24
1961/62	7:12
1958/59	6:21
1965/66	6:28
1951/52	6:20

Shortest

1959/60	1:26
1964/65	2:7
1966/67	2:10
1967/68	2:10
1976/77	2:16

Season Opener

Earliest
1 January 1965
1 January 1968
2 January 1967

Latest
27 May 1951
26 May 1963
22 May 1960

Season Closer

Earliest
2 September 1956
3 September 1950
7 September 1952

Latest
29 December 1962
28 December 1963
12 December 1959

The last time that a Grand Prix was run on a Saturday was 3 Nov 1985 in South Africa

Countries staging a Championship race

Italy	82	(a)
Germany	65	(b)
United States	60	(c)
Great Britain	59	(d)
France	56	(e)
Monaco	52	
Belgium	51	
Canada	37	
Spain	37	(f)
Brazil	33	
Netherlands	30	
Austria	26	
Japan	23	(g)
South Africa	23	
Australia	21	
Argentina	20	
Hungary	20	
Portugal	16	
Mexico	15	
Malaysia	7	
Sweden	6	
Switzerland	5	
Bahrain	2	
China	2	
Morocco	1	
Turkey	1	

(a) includes 1 Pescara & 25 San Marino GPs
(b) includes 10 European & 2 Luxembourg GPs
(c) includes 11 Indianapolis 500 races
(d) includes 3 European GPs
(e) includes 1 Swiss GP
(f) includes 2 European GP
(g) includes 2 Pacific GPs
The only countries to produce a race winner and yet never host a Grand Prix are Colombia, Finland and New Zealand.

Circuits used (Most races at)

Monza, I	55	(every year exc. 1980)
Monte-Carlo, MC	52	
Silverstone, GB	39	
Spa-Francorchamps, B	39	
Nürburgring, D	35	
Zandvoort, NL	30	

Opening Venue (Most races at)

Buenos Aires, RA	15	(1953-80)
Melbourne, AUS	10	(1996-05)
Kyalami, ZA	8	(1967-93)
Rio de Janeiro, BR	7	(1983-89)
Monte-Carlo, MC	5	(1959-66)

Closing Venue (Most races at)

Adelaide, AUS	11	(1985-95)
Watkins Glen, USA	8	(1961-80)
Mexico City, MEX	7	(1964-70)
Monza, I	6	(1950-57)
Suzuka, J	6	(1996-03)

Countries Staging Another Country's GP

France (Dijon-Prenois) Swiss GP 1982 (1 race)
Italy (Imola) San Marino GP 1981-2005 (25 races)
Germany (Nürburgring) Luxembourg GP 1997-98 (2 races)

The only country to have staged three races during a season is the USA in 1982 GPs when there were GPs at Long Beach, Detroit & Las Vegas.

USA has also used the greatest number of circuits as Grand Prix venues with 9, two more than France.

Landmarks

100th World Championship race D 61, 200th MC 71, 250th USA 74, 300th ZA 78, 400th A 84, 500th AUS 90, 600th RA 97, 700th BR 03, 750th CHN 05

Races in a Season

Most
19 - 2005
18 - 2004
17 - 1977, 1995, 1997, 2000, 2001 & 2002

Fewest
7 - 1950 & 1955 *
* Includes 1 Indianapolis 500 in each year.

Circuits which have moved their startline

Kyalami	Silverstone
Monaco	Spa-Francorchamps
Montréal	Watkins Glen

Race Length (Time)

Longest
D 54	3h 45m 45.800s
D 56	3h 38m 43.700s
D 57	3h 30m 38.300s
D 51	3h 23m 03.300s
F 51	3h 22m 11.000s
Indy 500	
INDY 51	3h 57m 38.050s

Shortest (all shortened races)
AUS 91	24m 34.899s
E 75	42m 53.700s
A 75	57m 56.690s
MC 84	1h 01m 07.740s
I 78	1h 07m 04.540s

The shortest full distance race was Italy 2003 at 1h 14m 19.838s

Race Length (Distance)

Longest
	km	miles
F 51	601.832	373.961
B 51-56	508.320	315.855
B 60	507.600	315.408
F 54,56	506.422	314.676
Indy 500		
INDY 51-60	804.672	500.000
INDY 50	555.224	345.000

Shortest
	km	miles
AUS 91	52.920	32.883
MC 84	102.672	63.797
E 75	109.939	68.313
A 75	171.419	106.515
B 81	230.148	143.007

Circuit Length

Longest
	km	miles
Pescara 57	25.579	15.894
Nürburgring 67-76	22.835	14.189
" 51-66	22.810	14.173
Spa-Francorchamps 50-56	14.120	8.774
" 58-70	14.100	8.761

Shortest
	km	miles
Monte-Carlo 55-72	3.145	1.954
" 50	3.180	1.976
Zeltweg 64	3.200	1.988
Long Beach 76-81	3.251	2.020
" 83	3.275	2.035

Laps in a Race

Most
USA 63-65	110
USA 66-70	108
MC 57	105
A 64	105
GB 56	101

The Indy 500 ran a full distance of 200 laps from 1951 to 1960.

Fewest
D 71	12
D 68-69,72-76	14
AUS 91	14
D 58,61-67	15

Laps Raced in a Season

Most
2005	1,180
1977	1,132
1995	1,124
2004	1,122
2002	1,090

Fewest
1950	391
1951	415
1952	447 exc Indy

Races in Two Parts, with Times Aggregated

D 59 *	A 78	ZA 79
F 81	DET 82	GB 84
MEX 87	RSM 89	F 92
RSM 94	J 94	

* Intentionally a 2-part race.

Races Stopped and Restarted as a New Race

GB 73	GB 76	D 76	I 78
RA 79	CDN 80	B 81	CDN 82
DET 84	A 84	A 85	GB 86
B 87	A 87 *	P 87	MEX 89
F 89	AUS 89	MC 90	B 90 *
I 90	RA 95	MC 95	I 95
P 95	AUS 96	BR 97	B 98
MC 00	D 01	B 01 *	

* 3 starts

Nationalities in a season

Most
19 - 1974
18 - 1977* & 78*
17 - 1971 & 79
16 - 1976**
16 - 1973*, 80* & 82*

Fewest
10 - 1954, 55, 91* & 99
11 - 1950, 53, 57, 92, 93, 96 & 2000
* plus 1 nq/ns.
** plus 2 nq/ns.
The record for the most entrants in a Grand Prix stands at 39. This occurred for the majority of the races during the 1989 season.

Total driver entrants in a season

Most
76 - 1952	(71 starters)
73 - 1953	(71)
62 - 1974	(56)
61 - 1977	(49)

Fewest
23 - 1998, 2000 & 02
24 - 1996, 99 & 2003
25 - 2004
26 - 2001
27 - 2005
28 - 1997

Gabriele Tarquini became the 500th grand prix driver to start a World Championship event – at San Marino 1987.

Starters per race

Most
D 53	34
I 61	32
GB 52	31
USA 72	31
B 74	31

(exc INDY races which had 33 on each grid)

Fewest
USA 05	6
RA 58	10
B 51	13
B 55	13
RA 56	13
E 68	13
F 69	13
RSM 82	13

Classified Finishers

Most
INDY 50	22
GB 52	22
INDY 52	20
CDN 76	20
I 05	20
INDY 56	19
USAE 77	19
MEX 90	19
AUS 91	19
EUR 94	19
GB 05	19

Fewest
MC 66	4
MC 96	4*
D 56	5
B 66	5
E 68	5
MC 68	5
E 70	5
RSM 82	5
DET 84	5

* Including one driver in the pits at the chequered flag.

Cars on Leading Lap at Finish (Most)

14	- B 99
13	- D 62, D 73, D 74, D 76, AUS 91, GB 99
12	- F 75, GB 03, GB 04, D 04, J 05, CHN 05

Retirements

Most
ZA 93	21
I 61	20
GB 75	20
RSM 86	20 exc Indy

Fewest
NL 61	0
USA 05	0
I 05	0
RA 58	1
GB 05	1

Not only were there no retirements at Netherlands 1961, but there is no record of any pit stops either.

Cars Retired before end of first lap (Most)

D 94	11
GB 73	10
MC 50	9
D 76	9
AUS 02	8
B 66	8

Jackie Oliver was the only driver to be the first retirement in four successive races, from France to Netherlands 1973. He was also the first retirement in three successive races from Spain to Netherlands 1969.

Retirements in a season by driver (Most)

A de Cesaris	16 (1987) (every race)
A Nannini	15 (1987)
I Capelli	15 (1989)

Most Retirements at Home Circuit (Most)

R Barrichello	Brazil	10	1993-03
R Patrese	Italy	10	1977-91
M Alboreto	Italy	9	1981-94
A de Cesaris	Italy	9	1981-94
T Boutsen	Belgium	8	1983-93
G Hill	Britain	8	1958-73

Rubens Barrichello holds the record for the most successive retirements at a home Grand Prix, with 9 from 1995 to 2003.

Retirements before the end of lap 1 by driver (Most)

R Barrichello	11*
J Trulli	11
A de Cesaris	11
P Tambay	10
M Häkkinen	8
J-P Jarier	8
P Martini	8

* Inc B 1998 & B 2001 where he did not take the restart.

STARTS

R Patrese	256	P Tambay	114
M Schumacher	231	D Hulme	112
R Barrichello	215	J Scheckter	112
G Berger	210	J Surtees	111
A de Cesaris	208	M Salo	110
N Piquet	204	P Alliot	109
J Alesi	201	E de Angelis	108
A Prost	199	J Verstappen	107
M Alboreto	194	J Mass	105
D Coulthard	193	J Bonnier	104
N Mansell	187	J Button	100
G Hill	176	B McLaren	100
J Laffite	176	J Stewart	99
N Lauda	171	P Diniz	98
T Boutsen	163	N Heidfeld	97
M Häkkinen	161	C Amon	96
J Herbert	161	J Siffert	96
A Senna	161	P Depailler	95
G Fisichella	159	U Katayama	95
M Brundle	158	I Capelli	93
O Panis	158	J Hunt	92
H-H Frentzen	157	J-P Beltoise	86
J Watson	152	D Gurney	86
J Villeneuve	151	K Räikkönen	86
R Arnoux	149	J P Montoya	84
E Irvine	146	J Palmer	83
C Reutemann	146	M Surer	82
J Trulli	146	M Trintignant	82
D Warwick	146	S Johansson	79
R Schumacher	145	P Ghinzani	76
E Fittipaldi	144	A Nannini	76
J-P Jarier	134	V Brambilla	74
E Cheever	132	M Gugelmin	74
C Regazzoni	132	S Nakajima	74
M Andretti	128	H-J Stuck	74
J Brabham	126	J Clark	72
R Peterson	123	C Pace	72
P Martini	118	S Modena	70
J Ickx	116	D Pironi	70
A Jones	116	F Alonso	69
D Hill	115	B Giacomelli	69
K Rosberg	114		

Active Seasons

G Hill	18	(1958-75)
R Patrese	17	(1977-93)
J Bonnier	16	(1956-71)
J Brabham	16	(1955-70)

Drivers who achieved more than one top six placing by car sharing in the same race were Juan Manuel Fangio in Monaco 1956 and Giuseppe Farina & Maurice Trintignant both in Argentina 1955.

The last time a car was shared in a race was at USA 64 between Mike Spence and Jim Clark.

Starter Age

Youngest

M Thackwell	19y 5m 29d	CDN 80
R Rodriguez	19y 6m 27d	I 61
F Alonso	19y 7m 3d	AUS 01
E Tuero	19y 10m 14d	AUS 98
C Amon	19y 10m 20d	B 63
E Cheever	20y 1m 22d	ZA 78
J Button	20y 1m 22d	AUS 00
T Marques	20y 2m 12d	BR 96

Indy 500

T Ruttman	20y 2m 19d	INDY 50

Oldest

L Chiron	55y 9m 19d	MC 55
P Étançelin	55y 6m 8d	F 52
A Legat	54y 7m 20d	B 53
L Fagioli	53y 0m 22d	F 51
A Brudes	52y 9m 19d	D 52

Successive Starts (Most)

R Patrese	186	B 82-AUS 93
D Coulthard	175	BR 95-CDN 05
A Prost	160	USAW 81-BR 91
A Senna	149	EUR 84-RSM 94
T Boutsen	138	CDN 84-AUS 92
R Barrichello	133	MC 94-RSM 02
G Berger	132	MEX 89-E 97
J Alesi	129	MC 94-J 01
H-H Frentzen	119	E 94-MC 01
M Alboreto	117	A 81-BR 89
J Villeneuve	117	AUS 96-AUS 03
J Herbert	116	J 91-J 98
R Peterson	114	ZA 71-I 78
R Schumacher	113	AUS 97-H 03
J Scheckter	107	CDN 73-I 80
M Schumacher	106	MAL 99-CHN 05
E Irvine	99	D 94-F 00
J Laffite	96	BR 76-USAW 82
G Fisichella	93	AUS 97-GB 02
G Hill	90	USA 60-USA 69

Starts without a Win (Most)

A de Cesaris	208
M Brundle	158
D Warwick	146
J-P Jarier	134
E Cheever	132
P Martini	118
M Salo	110

Starts without a Pole Position (Most)

J Herbert	161
M Brundle	158
O Panis	158
E Irvine	146
D Warwick	146
E Cheever	132
P Martini	118

Starts without a Fastest Lap (Most)

J Herbert	161
M Brundle	158
O Panis	158
J Trulli	146
E Cheever	132
P Martini	118
M Salo	110

Starts without a Point (Most)

L Badoer	49
B Lunger	34
T Takagi	32
E Bernoldi	28
M Beuttler	28
R Rosset	27
R Keegan	25
H Rothengatter	25

Starts without Leading (Most)

M Brundle	158
E Cheever	132
P Alliot	109
J Verstappen	107
P Diniz	98
U Katayama	95
J Palmer	83

German driver Hans Heyer's only Grand Prix start was in Germany 1977, where he started unofficially.

The following drivers only ever started in the F2 section of a Grand Prix: T Bridger, P England, D Gibson, C Goethals, A Guelfi, B Hart, R La Caze, X Perrot, F Picard, P Westbury.

Starts with Same Constructor (Most)

M Schumacher	162	Ferrari
D Coulthard	150	McLaren
J Laffite	132	Ligier
M Häkkinen	131	McLaren
A Prost	107	McLaren
N Piquet	106	Brabham
R Barrichello	102	Ferrari
P Martini	102	Minardi
G Berger	96	Ferrari
A Senna	96	McLaren
N Mansell	95	Williams
R Schumacher	94	Williams
E de Angelis	90	Lotus
D Hulme	86	McLaren
R Patrese	81	Williams
J Villeneuve	81	BAR
M Alboreto	80	Ferrari
M Andretti	80	Lotus
J Brabham	80	Brabham
P Depailler	80	Tyrrell

Jim Clark started the most races exclusively for one constructor, with 72 for Lotus.

Successive Starts with Same Constructor (Most)

D Coulthard	150	(McLaren, 1996-04)
M Schumacher	106	(Ferrari, 1999-05)
J Laffite	96	(Ligier, 1976-82)
A Prost	96	(McLaren, 1984-89)
A Senna	96	(McLaren, 1988-93)
M Häkkinen	91	(McLaren, 1996-01)
R Patrese	81	(Williams, 1987-92)
M Alboreto	80	(Ferrari, 1984-88)
R Schumacher	80	(Williams, 1999-03)
P Depailler	78	(Tyrrell, 1974-78)
M Andretti	72	(Lotus, 1976-80)
J Villeneuve	68	(BAR, 1999-03)
G Fisichella	66	(Benetton, 1998-01)
G Villeneuve	66	(Ferrari, 1977-82)
D Hill	65	(Williams, 1993-96)

Starts with Same Engine Make (Most)

M Schumacher	162	Ferrari
D Coulthard	150	Mercedes-Benz
E Fittipaldi	143	Ford Cosworth
J-P Jarier	129	Ford Cosworth
R Peterson	122	Ford Cosworth
J Watson	115	Ford Cosworth
M Häkkinen	113	Mercedes-Benz
A Jones	111	Ford Cosworth
J Mass	105	Ford Cosworth
R Barrichello	102	Ferrari
M Andretti	101	Ford Cosworth
C Reutemann	100	Ford Cosworth
G Berger	96	Ferrari
A Senna	96	Honda
G Hill	94	Ford Cosworth

Additionally, J Alesi started 123 races with Ferrari including the Petronas and Acer re-badged Ferrari engines.

Starts with Turbocharged Engine (Most)

A Prost	126
R Arnoux	120
N Piquet	106
D Warwick	99
R Patrese	89
M Alboreto	80
E Cheever	79
A Senna	78
A de Cesaris	72

Starts as Team-Mates (Most)

R Barrichello/M Schumacher	102	(2)	2000-05
D Coulthard/M Häkkinen	98	(1)	1996-01
J Alesi/G Berger	77		1993-97
J P Montoya/R Schumacher	61	(1)	2001-04
E de Angelis/N Mansell	59	(2)	1980-84
E Irvine/M Schumacher	58	(1)	1996-99
N Lauda/C Regazzoni	56	(1)	1973-76
I Capelli/M Gugelmin	55	(7)	1988-91
G Fisichella/A Wurz	49		1998-00
G Berger/A Senna	48		1990-92
N Mansell/R Patrese	46		1988-92
E Cheever/D Warwick	45	(2)	1987-89
F Cevert/J Stewart	45	(1)	1970-73
P Depailler/J Scheckter	45		1974-76

The number of races refers to races which both started. Numbers in brackets refer to additional races which one or both did not start.

Drivers who took over in a shared drive and were not on the grid

J Bonnier	I 56
E Chaboud	F 50-
A de Portago	RA 57
R Flockhart	GB 54
P Frère	MC 55
G Gerini	RA 56
O González	RA 56
P Hirt	F 52
U Magliogli	RA 55
L Musso	I 53
A Pilette	MC 56
T Rolt	GB 50
H Schell	RA 53
B Shawe-Taylor	GB 50
O Volonterio	E 54 & I 57
W von Trips	RA 57
P Walker	GB 55

Indy 500

M Ayulo	INDY 51
B Cantrell	INDY 50
J Davies	INDY 54
D Dinsmore	INDY 53
W Faulkner	INDY 54
P Flaherty	INDY 54
G Fonder	INDY 54
J Holmes	INDY 53
B Homeier	INDY 55
J Jackson	INDY 54
E Johnson	INDY 53 & 54
D Kladis	INDY 54
J Mantz	INDY 53
E Russo	INDY 56
P Russo	INDY 55
B Scott	INDY 54
M Teague	INDY 54

Driver Achievements Per Country
(Number of drivers)

	starters	point scorers	winners	world champions
Great Britain	142	57	17	8
Italy	83	47	15	2
France	64	33	12	1
United States	47	16	5	2
Germany	40	16	5	1
Brazil	26	16	5	3
Argentina	22	7	3	1
Switzerland	22	6	2	-
Belgium	19	7	2	-
South Africa	17	3	1	1
Austria	14	8	3	2
Japan	13	5	-	-
Australia	13	4	2	2
Netherlands	13	4	-	-
Canada	11	2	2	1
Spain	10	6	1	1
Sweden	9	6	3	-
New Zealand	8	4	2	1
Finland	6	5	3	2
Mexico	4	3	1	-
Portugal	3	2	-	-
Denmark	3	1	-	-
Ireland	3	1	-	-
South Rhodesia	3	1	-	-
Uruguay	3	-	-	-
Colombia	2	1	1	-
Monaco	2	1	-	-
Morocco	2	-	-	-
Chile	1	1	-	-
Hungary	1	1	-	-
India	1	1	-	-
Thailand	1	1	-	-
Venezuela	1	1	-	-
Czech Republic	1	-	-	-
Liechtenstein	1	-	-	-
Malaysia	1	-	-	-
total	**612**	**266**	**85**	**28**

(eg 142 British drivers have started a Grand Prix, of which 57 have scored points, 17 have won and 8 have gone on to be World Champion.)
Three drivers used dual nationality: Nano da Silva Ramos is regarded as French, Hans Stuck regarded as German and Alfonso Thiele regarded as American in the above table (excludes 103 Indy only drivers).

Successive Finishes in the same Position
(excluding wins) (Most)

4 x 2nd: N Piquet	MC-GB 87
4 x 3rd: H-H Frentzen	B-L 97
4 x 7th: M Alboreto	MC-GB 92
3 x 2nd: R Barrichello	EUR-USA 04
3 x 2nd: D Coulthard	A-H 98
3 x 2nd: L Fagioli	CH-F 50
3 x 2nd: J M Fangio	F-D 53
3 x 2nd: G Farina	CH 53-RA 54
3 x 2nd: M Hawthorn	P-MA 58
3 x 2nd: G Hill	F-D 64
3 x 2nd: J P Montoya	J 01-MAL 02
3 x 2nd: J P Montoya	EUR-GB 03
3 x 2nd: R Patrese	MEX-CDN 89,ZA-BR 92
3 x 2nd: A Prost	D-B 88, BR-MC 89,P-AUS 93
3 x 2nd: C Reutemann	CDN 80-USAW 81
3 x 2nd: J Surtees	USA 64-ZA 65
3 x 3rd: R Barrichello	RSM-A 03
3 x 3rd: J Behra	F-D 56
3 x 3rd: G Berger	RSM-MC 95
3 x 3rd: D Gurney	NL-I 65
3 x 3rd: M Häkkinen	I-EUR 94
3 x 3rd: D Hulme	I-USA 72
3 x 3rd: J Laffite	D-NL 79
3 x 3rd: L Villoresi	B-GB 51
3 x 5th: E de Angelis	CDN-F 85
3 x 5th: G Fisichella	A-CDN 02
3 x 5th: M Häkkinen	E-F 96
3 x 5th: R Schumacher	GB-H 97
3 x 6th: G Berger	AUS 85-E 86
3 x 9th: C Klien	B-J 05
3 x 9th: J J Lehto	MC-F 92
3 x 9th: R Patrese	F-D 80
3 x 10th: R Barrichello	D-TR 05
3 x 10th: A Pizzonia	CDN-F 03
3 x 11th: L Burti	RSM-A 01
3 x 15th: T Glock	CHN-BR 04

Gap Between Starts (longest)

	years:months	
J Lammers	10: 3	F 82-J 92
P Lovely	8:10	USA 60-CDN 69
A Pilette	7:11	F 56-B 64
P Revson	7: 1	I 64-USA 71
E Wietzes	7: 1	CDN 67-CDN 74
M Hailwood	6: 3	MC 65-I 71

Races without a World Champion on the Grid

1950: GB-I
1958: MC-B,GB-MA
1959: MC-USA
1960: I
1975: E
1982: RSM
1994: MC-CDN,GB-P
All of these races were run with drivers who would later become World Champion.

Classified Retirements
(Highest)

2nd	C Pace	GB 75
	D Pironi	MC 82
3rd	J Scheckter	GB 75
	A de Cesaris	MC 82
	E de Angelis	RSM 84
	A de Cesaris	B 87

Dummy Grid Failures

(Did not start Parade Lap)

Y Dalmas	RSM 89
M Donnelly	USA 90
M Gugelmin	GB 90
A Suzuki	BR 91
L Badoer	AUS 95
M Häkkinen	F 01
R Barrichello	E & F 02
J Villeneuve	MAL 03
C Klien	BRN 05

Parade Lap* Failures

(sometimes referred to as Warm-up lap or Formation lap)*

M Fisher	MEX 67
B McLaren	MEX 69
C Amon	RA 72
R Wisell	S 73
L Leoni	BR 78
J-P Jarier	BR 79
D Warwick	RSM 82
M Winkelhock	I 84
J Palmer	RSM 85
A Nannini	E 86
H Rothengatter	USA 86
O Larrauri	BR 88
P Streiff	MC 88
A Prost	RSM 91
O Beretta	E 94
E Irvine	GB 94
P Martini	BR 95
A Montermini	E 95
M Schumacher	F 96
D Hill	AUS 97
J Trulli	RSM 97
J Herbert	AUS 99
J Trulli	MAL 99

Plus the 14 drivers who withdrew at the end of the USA 05 parade lap.
(All above consequently not counted as having started these races as they did not take their place on the race grid.)

WINS

		%
M Schumacher	84	36.36
A Prost	51	25.63
A Senna	41	25.47
N Mansell	31	16.58
J Stewart	27	27.27
J Clark	25	34.72
N Lauda	25	14.62
J M Fangio	24 **	47.06
N Piquet	23	11.27
D Hill	22	19.13
M Häkkinen	20	12.42
S Moss	16*	24.24
J Brabham	14	11.11
E Fittipaldi	14	9.72
G Hill	14	7.95
A Ascari	13	41.94
D Coulthard	13	6.74
A Jones	12	10.34
M Andretti	12	9.38
C Reutemann	12	8.22
J Villeneuve	11	7.28
J Hunt	10	10.87
J Scheckter	10	8.93
R Peterson	10	8.13
G Berger	10	4.76
K Räikkönen	9	10.47
R Barrichello	9	4.19
F Alonso	8	11.59
D Hulme	8	7.14
J Ickx	8	6.90
J P Montoya	7	8.33
R Arnoux	7	4.70
J Rindt	6	10.00
G Villeneuve	6	8.96
J Surtees	6	5.41
R Schumacher	6	4.14
J Laffite	6	3.41
R Patrese	6	2.34
T Brooks	6*	15.79
G Farina	5	15.15
K Rosberg	5	4.39
C Regazzoni	5	3.79
J Watson	5	3.29
M Alboreto	5	2.58
D Gurney	4	4.65
B McLaren	4	4.00
E Irvine	4	2.74
P Collins	3	9.38
M Hawthorn	3	6.67

		%
P Hill	3	6.25
D Pironi	3	4.29
H-H Frentzen	3	1.91
J Herbert	3	1.86
T Boutsen	3	1.84
F González	2	7.69
W von Trips	2	7.41
P Revson	2	6.67
J-P Jabouille	2	4.08
P Rodriguez	2	3.64
M Trintignant	2	2.44
P Depailler	2	2.11
J Siffert	2	2.08
E de Angelis	2	1.85
P Tambay	2	1.75
G Fisichella	2	1.26
L Scarfiotti	1	10.00
P Taruffi	1	5.56
G Baghetti	1	4.76
P Gethin	1	3.33
G Nilsson	1	3.23
L Bandini	1	2.38
F Cevert	1	2.13
I Ireland	1	2.00
R Ginther	1	1.92
C Pace	1	1.39
V Brambilla	1	1.35
A Nannini	1	1.32
J-P Beltoise	1	1.16
J Bonnier	1	0.96
J Mass	1	0.95
J Trulli	1	0.68
O Panis	1	0.63
J Alesi	1	0.50
L Fagioli	1*	14.29
L Musso	1*	4.17
Indy 500		
B Vukovich	2	40.00
L Wallard	1	50.00
B Sweikert	1	20.00
P Flaherty	1	16.67
T Ruttman	1	14.29
S Hanks	1	12.50
J Bryan	1	11.11
J Parsons	1	11.11
J Rathmann	1	10.00
R Ward	1	10.00

* Including shared win(s).

Winning Driver Age

Youngest

F Alonso	22y 0m 26d	H 03
B McLaren	22y 3m 12d	USA 59
K Räikkönen	23y 5m 6d	MAL 03
J Ickx	23y 6m 6d	D 66
M Schumacher	23y 7m 27d	B 91
E Fittipaldi	23y 9m 22d	GB 70

Indy 500

T Ruttman	22y 2m 19d	I 50

Oldest

L Fagioli	53y 0m 22d	F 51
G Farina	46y 9m 3d	B 55
J M Fangio	46y 1m 11d	F 58
P Taruffi	45y 7m 6d	I 56
J Brabham	43y 11m 5d	MEX 70

The greatest number of different winners in successive races, was nine from France 61 to France 62. There were occasions of eight different successive winners during the 1982 and 83 seasons.

Wins in a Season (Most)

M Schumacher	13	2004
M Schumacher	11	2002
M Schumacher	9	1995,2000,01
N Mansell	9	1992
D Hill	8	1996
M Häkkinen	8	1998
A Senna	8	1988
M Schumacher	8	1994
F Alonso	7	2005
J Clark	7	1963
A Prost	7	1984,88,93
K Räikkönen	7	2005
A Senna	7	1991
J Villeneuve	7	1997

The most wins achieved in a season without becoming Champion was 7: A Prost in both 1984 and 88 and K Räikkönen in 2005.

Successive Wins From The Start of a Season (Most)

N Mansell	5	1992
M Schumacher	5	2004
A Senna	4	1991
M Schumacher	4	1994

Successive Seasons of Winning (Most)

M Schumacher	14	1992-05
A Prost	10	1981-90
A Senna	9	1985-93
N Piquet	8	1980-87
J Clark	7	1962-68
D Coulthard	7	1997-03
S Moss	7	1955-61
J Stewart	6	1968-73
J M Fangio	5	1953-57
M Häkkinen	5	1997-01
J Ickx	5	1968-72
N Lauda	5	1974-78

Successive GP Wins (Most)

A Ascari	9	B 52-B 53
M Schumacher	7	EUR-H 04
M Schumacher	6	I 00-MAL 01
J Brabham	5	NL-P 60
J Clark	5	B-D 65
N Mansell	5	ZA-RSM 92
M Schumacher	5	AUS-E 04

Wins at Same Circuit (Most)

M Schumacher	7	Magny-Cours	94-04
	7	Montréal	94-04
M Schumacher	6	Imola	94-04
	6	Montmeló	95-04
	6	Spa-Francorchamps	92-02
	6	Suzuka	95-04
A Senna	6	Monte-Carlo	87-93
G Hill	5	Monte-Carlo	63-69
A Prost	5	Rio de Janeiro	82-88
	5	Silverstone	83-93
M Schumacher	5	Monte-Carlo	94-01
A Senna	5	Spa-Francorchamps	85-91

Wins in Same Grand Prix (Most)

M Schumacher	7	CDN 94-04, F 94-04
A Prost	6	BR 82-90, F 81-93
M Schumacher	6	B 92-02, E 95-04, J 95-04, RSM 94-04
A Senna	6	MC 87-93
J Clark	5	GB 62-67
G Hill	5	MC 63-69
A Prost	5	GB 83-93
M Schumacher	5	EUR 94-04, MC 94-01
A Senna	5	B 85-91, USA 86-91

Successive Wins in Same Grand Prix (Most)

A Senna	5	MC 89-93 (Monte-Carlo)
J Clark	4	B 62-65 (Spa-Francorchamps)
J Clark	4	GB 62-65 (Aintree,Silverstone,Brands Hatch)
J M Fangio	4	RA 54-57 (Buenos Aires No.2)
M Schumacher	4	E 01-04 (Montmeló)
A Senna	4	B 88-91 (Spa-Francorchamps)

Debut Win immediately followed by further Win(s)

3 Wins

D Hill	H-B-I 93
M Häkkinen	EUR 97-AUS-BR 98

2 Wins

A Ascari	D-I 51
P Collins	B-F 56
B McLaren	USA 59-RA 60
R Arnoux	BR-ZA 80
N Mansell	EUR-ZA 85

Races Taken to Achieve First Win

(Fewest)

G Farina	1
G Baghetti	1
J M Fangio	2
T Brooks	3
E Fittipaldi	4
L Scarfiotti	4
J Villeneuve	4
F Gonzalez	5
C Regazzoni	5
L Fagioli	7
P Taruffi	7
J Stewart	8
A Ascari	9
M Hawthorn	9
J Ickx	9
B McLaren	9

(Most)

R Barrichello	124
J Trulli	117
G Fisichella	110
M Häkkinen	96
T Boutsen	95
J Alesi	91
E Irvine	81
N Mansell	72
J Herbert	71
R Patrese	71
R Schumacher	70
P Depailler	69
A Nannini	61
J Siffert	57
E de Angelis	54

Shared Wins

F 51	L Fagioli/J M Fangio
RA 56	L Musso/J M Fangio
GB 57	T Brooks/S Moss

Won Their Final Race

L Fagioli	F 51
J Clark	ZA 68

Winner & Second by Team-Mates (Most)

M Schumacher/R Barrichello	24	AUS 00-USA 05	
A Senna/A Prost	14	RSM 88-B 89	
M Häkkinen/D Coulthard	13	EUR 97-A 00	
N Mansell/R Patrese	8	MEX 91-GB 92	
J Stewart/F Cevert	6	F 71-D 73	
N Mansell/N Piquet	6	GB 86-MEX 87	
D Hill/J Villeneuve	6	AUS-P 96	

Winner of Own National Grand Prix (Most)

A Prost	6	F 81-93
J Clark	5	GB 62-67
J M Fangio	4	RA 54-57
N Mansell	4	GB 86-92

Winner From Lowest Grid Position (Most)

J Watson	22nd	USAW 83
R Barrichello	18th	D 00
K Räikkönen	17th	J 05
J Watson	17th	DET 82
M Schumacher	16th	B 95
J Stewart	16th	ZA 73
J Herbert	14th	EUR 99
A Jones	14th	A 77
B McLaren	13th	RA 60
A Prost	13th	MEX 90
Indy 500		
B Vukovich	19th	INDY 54
B Sweikert	14th	INDY 55

Winning Car Number (Most)

No. 1	135**
No. 5	109*
No. 2	66
No. 3	47
No. 6	43*
No. 8	41
No.11	36
No.12	36

* Including Indy 500 races.

Winning Margin

of 1 lap or more

2 laps: E 69 (J Stewart), AUS 95 (D Hill)
1 lap: MC 50, GB 52, RA 53, I 54, GB 56, P 59, F 62, NL 63, MC 64, NL 66, USA 66, MC 67, CDN 68, GB 69, E 70, GB 75, J 76, MC 82, RSM 85, GB 85, A 86, BR 94

Smallest

0.010s:	I 71 (P Gethin)
0.011s:	USA 02 *
0.014s:	E 86
0.050s:	A 82
0.080s:	I 69
0.100s:	F 54, F 61
0.174s:	CDN 00
0.182s:	A 02 *
0.200s:	GB 55, I 67
0.211s:	E 81
0.215s:	MC 92, RSM 05
0.232s:	NL 85

* Stage managed by Ferrari.

Within 1 Minute of Winning Time (Most drivers)

12:	GB 04
11:	D 98
10:	I 99, F 04, J 05, CHN 05
9:	I 76, ZA 77, I 97, D 00, GB 03, B 04, I 04
8:	I 78, B 95, A 97, L 97, J 97, F 99, AUS 03, BR 03, MC 03, J 03, D 04, J 04, AUS 05, MC 05, D 05
7:	A 76, NL 76, CDN 76, S 77, F 78, E 79, E 81, MEX 90, I 91, AUS 91, BR 97, RA 97, CDN 99, GB 99, D 99, B 99, MAL 99, AUS 00, B 01, A 02, CDN 02, RSM 03, BRN 04, RSM 04, BR 04, EUR 05, I 05

Within 1 Second of Winner (Most drivers)

5:	I 71
4:	D 69
3:	E 81

Win in Debut Season

J Villeneuve	4 in 1996
G Farina	3 in 1950
J M Fangio	3 in 1950
G Baghetti	1 in 1961
J P Montoya	1 in 2001
J Stewart	1 in 1965
C Regazzoni	1 in 1970
E Fittipaldi	1 in 1970

Win in Debut Race

G Farina	GB 50
G Baghetti	F 61

2nd in Debut Race

A Ascari	MC 50
L Fagioli	GB 50
D Serafini	I 50
K Kling	F 54
M Parkes	F 66
J Villeneuve	AUS 96

3rd in Debut Race

J Behra	CH 52
G Perdisa	MC 55
M Gregory	MC 57
P Arundell	MC 64
R Wisell	USA 70
M Donohue	CDN 71

Wins without a World Championship (Most)

S Moss	16
D Coulthard	13
C Reutemann	12
G Berger	10
R Peterson	10
R Barrichello	9
K Räikkönen	9

Stirling Moss finished runner-up in the Championship on four successive occasions (1955-58).

Wins without a Pole Position (Most)

E Irvine	4
B McLaren	4
P Collins	3
J Herbert	3
P Rodriguez	2
M Trintignant	2

Wins without a Fastest Lap (Most)

P Collins	3
J Herbert	3
E de Angelis	2
J-P Jabouille	2
P Revson	2
W von Trips	2

The record for the most different winners in successive grands prix is 9, from France 61 to France 62 and from Monaco 82 to Switzerland 82.

The longest period between wins, belongs to Riccardo Patrese who waited 6 years and 7 months from South Africa 83 to San Marino 90.

Race Winning Speeds

Fastest: M Schumacher (Ferrari)

	km/h	mph
I 03	247.586	153.843
I 05	247.096	153.539
I 04	244.374	151.847
I 71	242.616	150.755
B 70	241.308	149.942
I 02	241.090	149.806
I 93	239.144	148.597
I 01	239.103	148.572

Slowest: J M Fangio (Alfa Romeo)

MC 50	98.701	61.330
MC 84	100.776	62.619
MC 72	102.756	63.849
MC 57	104.165	64.725
MC 56	104.515	64.943
MC 55	105.915	65.813

PODIUMS

		%
M Schumacher	142	61.47
A Prost	106	53.27
A Senna	80	49.69
R Barrichello	61	28.37
D Coulthard	60	31.09
N Piquet	60	29.41
N Mansell	59	31.55
N Lauda	54	31.58
M Häkkinen	51	31.68
G Berger	48	22.86

The most podiums achieved in a season, was Michael Schumacher, with 17 out of 17 in 2002.

Podium Domination – All of Same Nationality

I 50	I	G Farina, D Serafini/ A Ascari, L Fagioli
B 51	I	G Farina, A Ascari, L Villoresi
F 52	I	A Ascari, G Farina, P Taruffi
NL 52	I	A Ascari, G Farina, L Villoresi
B 58	GB	T Brooks, M Hawthorn, S Lewis-Evans
GB 58	GB	P Collins, M Hawthorn, R Salvadori
P 58	GB	S Moss, M Hawthorn, S Lewis-Evans
GB 63	GB	J Clark, J Surtees, G Hill
NL 64	GB	J Clark, J Surtees, P Arundell
GB 64	GB	J Clark, G Hill, J Surtees
ZA 65	GB	J Clark, J Surtees, G Hill
F 65	GB	J Clark, J Stewart, J Surtees
GB 65	GB	J Clark, G Hill, J Surtees
USA 68	GB	J Stewart, G Hill, J Surtees
ZA 80	F	R Arnoux, J Laffite, D Pironi
F 82	F	R Arnoux, A Prost, D Pironi
RSM 83	F	P Tambay, A Prost, R Arnoux

Totals: GB = 10, I = 4, F = 3

Grands Prix with a Debut Pole Driver & a Debut Winner

	Pole	Winner
GB 50	G Farina	G Farina
MC 50	J M Fangio	J M Fangio
GB 51	F González	F González
D 51	A Ascari	A Ascari
GB 55	S Moss	S Moss
NL 59	J Bonnier	J Bonnier
I 60	P Hill	P Hill
B 62	G Hill	J Clark
I 66	M Parkes	L Scarfiotti
F 68	J Rindt	J Ickx
MC 72	E Fittipaldi	J P Beltoise
ZA 74	N Lauda	C Reutemann
S 74	P Depailler	J Scheckter
USAW 80	N Piquet	N Piquet
P 85	A Senna	A Senna
MAL 03	F Alonso	K Räikkönen

POLE POSITIONS

		%
A Senna	65	40.37
M Schumacher	64	27.71
J Clark	33	45.83
A Prost	33	16.58
N Mansell	32	17.11
J M Fangio	29	56.86
M Häkkinen	26	16.15
N Lauda	24	14.04
N Piquet	24	11.76
D Hill	20	17.39
M Andretti	18	14.06
R Arnoux	18	12.08
J Stewart	17	17.17
S Moss	16	24.24
A Ascari	14	45.16
J Hunt	14	15.22
R Peterson	14	11.38
J P Montoya	13	15.48
J Ickx	13	11.21
J Brabham	13	10.32
J Villeneuve	13	8.61
G Hill	13	7.39
R Barrichello	13	6.05
D Coulthard	12	6.22
G Berger	12	5.71
J Rindt	10	16.67
F Alonso	9	13.04
K Räikkönen	8	9.30
J Surtees	8	7.21
R Patrese	8	3.13
J Laffite	7	3.98
P Hill	6	12.50
J-P Jabouille	6	12.24
A Jones	6	5.17
E Fittipaldi	6	4.17
R Schumacher	6	4.14
C Reutemann	6	4.11
G Farina	5	15.15
C Amon	5	5.21
K Rosberg	5	4.39
P Tambay	5	4.39
C Regazzoni	5	3.79
M Hawthorn	4	8.89
D Pironi	4	5.71
F González	3	11.54
T Brooks	3	7.89
T Fabi	3	4.69
D Gurney	3	3.49
E de Angelis	3	2.78
J Scheckter	3	2.68
J-P Jarier	3	2.24
J Trulli	3	2.05
S Lewis-Evans	2	14.29
G Villeneuve	2	2.99
J Siffert	2	2.08
J Button	2	2.00
J Watson	2	1.32
H-H Frentzen	2	1.27
G Fisichella	2	1.26
M Alboreto	2	1.03
J Alesi	2	1.00
M Parkes	1	16.67
E Castellotti	1	7.14
W von Trips	1	3.70
P Revson	1	3.33
L Bandini	1	2.38
T Pryce	1	2.38
B Giacomelli	1	1.45
C Pace	1	1.39
V Brambilla	1	1.35
P Depailler	1	1.05
N Heidfeld	1	1.03
J Bonnier	1	0.96
D Hulme	1	0.89
T Boutsen	1	0.61
A de Cesaris	1	0.48
Indy 500		
D Nalon	1	33.33
J Hoyt	1	25.00
E Sachs	1	25.00
W Faulkner	1	20.00
P O'Connor	1	20.00
D Rathmann	1	20.00
B Vukovich	1	20.00
P Flaherty	1	16.67
J McGrath	1	16.67
F Agabashian	1	12.50
J Thomson	1	12.50

Pole Position Driver Age

Youngest

F Alonso	21y 7m 23d
R Barrichello	22y 3m 5d
A de Cesaris	22y 10m 4d
J Ickx	23y 7m 3d
K Räikkönen	23y 8m 12d

Oldest

G Farina	47y 2m 18d
J M Fangio	46y 6m 26d
J Brabham	44y 0m 17d
M Andretti	42y 6m 15d
N Mansell	41y 3m 5d

The only driver to start his first and last grand prix from pole position was Mario Andretti.

Pole Positions in a Season

(Most)

N Mansell	14	1992
A Senna	13	1988,89
A Prost	13	1993
M Häkkinen	11	1999
M Schumacher	11	2001
A Senna	10	1990
J Villeneuve	10	1997

Successive Pole Positions

(Most)

A Senna	8	E 88-USA 89
A Prost	7	ZA-CDN 93
M Schumacher	7	I 00-BR 01
A Senna	7	E 90-MC 91

Pole Position in Debut race

G Farina	GB 50
M Andretti	USA 68
C Reutemann	RA 72
J Villeneuve	AUS 96

Pole Positions at Same Circuit (Most)

M Schumacher	8	Suzuka	94-04
A Senna	8	Imola	85-94
M Schumacher	7	Hungaroring	94-05
	7	Montmeló	94-04
	6	Montréal	94-01
A Senna	6	Adelaide	85-93
M Schumacher	5	Sepang	99-04
A Senna	5	Monte-Carlo	85-91
	5	Monza	85-91
J M Fangio	5	Monza	50-56

Successive Pole Positions at Same Circuit (Most)

A Senna	7	Imola	85-91
M Schumacher	5	Montmeló	00-04
	5	Suzuka	98-02
J M Fangio	4	Monte-Carlo	50-57
M Schumacher	4	Sepang	99-02
A Senna	4	Adelaide	88-91
	4	Monte-Carlo	88-91
	4	Monza	88-91
	4	Spa-Francorchamps	88-91

Races taken to achieve first Pole

Fewest

M Andretti	1
G Farina	1
C Reutemann	1
J Villeneuve	1
J M Fangio	2
E Castellotti	3
J Surtees	3
M Parkes	4
F González	5
S Lewis-Evans	6
T Brooks	7
C Regazzoni	8
A Ascari	9
P Depailler	9
D Coulthard	10
D Hill	10

Most

J Trulli	117
T Boutsen	115
M Häkkinen	94
N Heidfeld	91
D Hulme	85
J Alesi	81
R Schumacher	76

Pole Position Non-Starters

J-P Jarier	RA 75
D Pironi	D 82
M Schumacher	F 96
J Trulli	USA 05

Pole Position to Retirement Within 1 Lap

D Rathmann	INDY 58
J Brabham	MC 67
N Lauda	D 74 & E 75
J Watson	B 77
A Senna	J 90 & PAC 94
M Schumacher	MC 96
J Villeneuve	AUS 97
M Häkkinen	B 98
R Barrichello	AUS 02

Pole Positions without a Win (Most)

C Amon	5
T Fabi	3
J-P Jarier	3
J Button	2
S Lewis-Evans	2

Pole Positions without a Championship (Most)

R Arnoux	18
S Moss	16
R Peterson	14
R Barrichello	13
J Ickx	13
J P Montoya	13
G Berger	12
D Coulthard	12

Pole Positions without a Fastest Lap (Most)

J-P Jabouille	6
E de Angelis	3
J Trulli	3
J Button	2
S Lewis-Evans	2

Pole Positions without Leading (Most)

T Fabi	3

Pole Position speed

Fastest: R Barrichello (Ferrari)

	km/h	mph
I 04	260.395	161.802
I 02	259.828	161.449
GB 85	258.983	160.925
I 03	257.584	160.055
I 91	257.415	159.951
I 05	257.295	159.876
I 93	257.209	159.822
A 87	256.622	159.457

Slowest: J M Fangio (Alfa Romeo)

MC 50	103.884	64.550
MC 56	108.865	67.646
MC 57	110.243	68.502
MC 55	111.988	69.586
MC 58	113.447	70.493

Pole Position Car Number (Most)

No. 1	122
No. 5	102
No. 2	78*
No.12	59*
No. 6	52*

Including Indy 500 races.

Front Rows (Most)

M Schumacher	105
A Senna	87
A Prost	86
N Mansell	56
J Clark	48
J M Fangio	48
D Hill	47
N Piquet	44
G Hill	42
J Stewart	42

Front Rows without a Pole (Most)

J Behra	10
P Collins	8
R Ginther	8
B McLaren	7
L Musso	6

Front Rows without a Win (Most)

C Amon	19
J Behra	10
J Button	7
E Castellotti	7

FASTEST LAPS

		%				%
M Schumacher	69	29.87	J-P Jarier	3		2.24
A Prost	41	20.60	R Ginther	3 *		5.77
N Mansell	30	16.04	B McLaren	3 *		3.00
J Clark	28	38.89	L Bandini	2		4.76
M Häkkinen	25	15.53	F Cevert	2		4.26
N Lauda	24	14.04	T Fabi	2		3.13
J M Fangio	23 *	45.10	A Nannini	2		2.63
N Piquet	23 *	11.27	J Mass	2		1.90
G Berger	21	10.00	P Tambay	2		1.75
D Hill	19	16.52	D Warwick	2		1.37
A Senna	19	11.80	G Fisichella	2		1.26
S Moss	19 *	28.79	L Scarfiotti	1		10.00
D Coulthard	18	9.32	K Kling	1		9.09
K Räikkönen	16	18.60	D Attwood	1		5.88
J Stewart	15	15.15	R Mières	1		5.88
R Barrichello	15	6.98	H Herrmann	1		5.56
C Regazzoni	15 *	11.36	P Taruffi	1		5.56
J Ickx	14 *	12.07	B Henton	1		5.26
A Jones	13	11.21	G Baghetti	1		4.76
R Patrese	13	5.08	L Musso	1		4.17
A Ascari	13 *	41.94	G Nilsson	1		3.23
J P Montoya	12	14.29	L Villoresi	1		3.23
R Arnoux	12	8.05	R Moreno	1		2.38
J Brabham	12 *	9.52	B Gachot	1		2.13
J Surtees	11 *	9.91	M Hailwood	1		2.00
M Andretti	10	7.81	J Oliver	1		2.00
G Hill	10	5.68	A Wurz	1		1.89
R Peterson	9	7.32	P Rodriguez	1		1.82
J Villeneuve	9	5.96	H Pescarolo	1		1.75
D Hulme	9 *	8.04	P de la Rosa	1		1.56
G Villeneuve	8	11.94	V Brambilla	1		1.35
J Hunt	8	8.70	M Gugelmin	1		1.35
R Schumacher	8	5.52	S Nakajima	1		1.35
J Laffite	7	3.98	M Surer	1		1.22
D Gurney	6	6.98	M Trintignant	1		1.22
C Reutemann	6	4.11	J Palmer	1		1.20
H-H Frentzen	6	3.82	E Irvine	1		0.68
F González	6 *	23.08	T Boutsen	1		0.61
M Hawthorn	6 *	13.33	A de Cesaris	1		0.48
P Hill	6 *	12.50	O Marimón	1 *		9.09
E Fittipaldi	6 *	4.17	I Ireland	1 *		2.00
G Farina	5	15.15	J Behra	1 *		1.92
D Pironi	5	7.14	*Indy 500*			
C Pace	5	6.94	B Vukovich	3		60.00
J Scheckter	5	4.46	J Rathmann	2		20.00
J Watson	5	3.29	L Wallard	1		50.00
M Alboreto	5 *	2.58	J McGrath	1		16.67
J-P Beltoise	4	4.65	P Russo	1		12.50
P Depailler	4	4.21	J Thomson	1		12.50
J Siffert	4	4.17	J Parsons	1		11.11
J Alesi	4	1.99	T Bettenhausen	1		9.09
T Brooks	3	7.89				
J Rindt	3	5.00				
F Alonso	3	4.35				
C Amon	3	3.13				
K Rosberg	3	2.63				

* Includes one or more shared fastest laps.
Fastest Lap times and speeds for the Indianapolis 500 races (1950 to 1960) are based on times recorded on the drivers' fastest leading lap.

Fastest Lap Driver Age

Youngest

F Alonso	21y 10m 17d
B McLaren	21y 10m 18d
K Räikkönen	22y 4m 14d
D Coulthard	23y 4m 4d
M Schumacher	23y 7m 27d
A de Cesaris	23y 11m 21d

Oldest

J M Fangio	46y 6m 26d
P Taruffi	45y 7m 6d
G Farina	44y 10m 17d
J Brabham	44y 3m 16d
L Villoresi	44y 0m 22d

Fastest Laps in a Season
(Most)

K Räikkönen	10	2005
M Schumacher	10	2004
M Häkkinen	9	2000
M Schumacher	8	1994,95
N Mansell	8	1992
N Piquet	7	1986
A Prost	7	1988
M Schumacher	7	2002

Successive Fastest Laps (Most)

A Ascari	7	B 52-RA 53
M Schumacher	5	BRN-EUR 04
J M Fangio	5	F 50-F 51 *
A Ascari	4	F-CH 53
K Räikkönen	4	F-H 05
J Stewart	4	MC-GB 69
G Villeneuve	4	ZA-B 79
N Mansell	4	CDN-GB 91

* Excluding INDY.

Fastest Lap in Debut race

G Farina	GB 50
J Villeneuve	AUS 96

Fastest Laps at Same Circuit (Most)

M Schumacher	7	Montmeló	93-04
N Mansell	6	Silverstone	87-92
A Prost	6	Spa-Francorchamps	85-93
J Clark	5	Zandvoort	61-67
D Coulthard	5	Magny-Cours	98-02
M Schumacher	5	Imola	98-05

Successive Fastest Laps at Same Circuit (Most)

N Mansell	6	Silverstone	87-92
D Coulthard	5	Magny-Cours	98-02
J M Fangio	4	Monte-Carlo	50-57

Races taken to achieve first Fastest Lap (Fewest)

G Farina	1
J Villeneuve	1
J M Fangio	2
H Herrmann	2
G Baghetti	3
P Hill	3
J Hunt	3
K Kling	3
J Surtees	3
D Coulthard	4
R Ginther	4
C Regazzoni	4
L Scarfiotti	4
G Villeneuve	4

(Most)

R Barrichello	114
T Boutsen	114
E Irvine	86
J Palmer	74
R Patrese	71
P de la Rosa	64
P Tambay	63

Fastest Lap on Home Soil

(Most)

N Mansell	8	EUR 83, GB 86-92
M Schumacher	7	D 93-EUR 04
S Moss	5	GB 54-59
A Prost	5	F 81-88, CH 82

Shared Fastest Laps in a Race (Most)

GB 54	7
B 60	3

The last time a fastest lap was shared was at Europe 1984.

Fastest Laps without a Pole

(Most)

J-P Beltoise	4
R Ginther	3
B McLaren	3

Fastest Laps without a Win

(Most)

C Amon	3
J-P Jarier	3
D Coulthard	2
T Fabi	2
D Warwick	2

The only driver to achieve a fastest lap and yet never score a point was Brian Henton in Britain 1982.

Fastest Lap Speed

Fastest: R Barrichello (Ferrari)

	km/h	mph
I 04	257.321	159.892
I 05	255.874	158.993
I 03	254.849	158.356
I 93	249.835	155.241
I 02	249.289	154.901
I 71	247.017	153.489
GB 87	246.324	153.059

Slowest: J M Fangio (Alfa Romeo)

MC 50	103.135	64.085
MC 84	104.284	64.799
MC 57	107.216	66.621
MC 56	108.448	67.387
MC 55	110.566	68.703

The last time that there were 4 cars in a row on a grid was in Germany 1967. The last time that there were 3 cars in a row on a grid was in Netherlands 1973. All grids were 2 x 2 from Germany 1973. The first 2 x 2 grid was however in Italy 1961.

Pole Position/Fastest Lap Doubles (Most)

M Schumacher	25	MC 94-H 04
J Clark	18	MC 62-ZA 68
A Prost	15	BR 82-J 93
J M Fangio	15	MC 50-RA 58
N Mansell	11	D 87-J 92
A Senna	11	P 85-I 91
A Ascari	10	B 52-E 54
M Häkkinen	10	AUS 98-RSM 00

Successive Pole Position/ Fastest Lap Doubles (Most)

J M Fangio	5	F 50-F 51 *
A Ascari	4	D 52-RA 53

* Excluding INDY.

Win/Pole Position Doubles

(Most)

M Schumacher	37	MC 94-J 04
A Senna	29	P 85-AUS 93
A Prost	18	NL 81-D 93
N Mansell	17	ZA 85-AUS 94
J Clark	15	GB 62-ZA 68
J M Fangio	13	MC 50-D 57
M Häkkinen	10	AUS 98-B 00
A Ascari	9	D 51-GB 53
N Lauda	9	E 74-GB 76

Successive Win/Pole Position Doubles (Most)

M Schumacher	6	I 00-MAL 01
A Ascari	5	D 52-NL 53 *
N Mansell	5	ZA-RSM 92
A Senna	4	USA-MC 91

* Excluding INDY.

Win/Pole Position/Fastest Lap Trebles (Most)

M Schumacher	20	MC 94-H 04
J Clark	11	GB 62-ZA 68
J M Fangio	9	MC 50-D 57
A Prost	8	BR 82-RSM 93
A Ascari	7	B 52-GB 53
A Senna	7	P 85-I 90
M Häkkinen	5	AUS 98-BR 99
D Hill	5	GB 94-D 96
N Mansell	5	GB 91-GB 92

Successive Win/Pole Position/Fastest Lap Trebles (Most)

A Ascari	4	D 52-RA 53
A Ascari	2	B-F 52
J Brabham	2	B-F 60
J Clark	2	NL-F 63 &
		MEX 67-ZA 68
M Häkkinen	2	AUS-BR 98 & E-MC 98
J Laffite	2	RA-BR 79
N Mansell	2	F-GB 92

Win/Pole Position/Fastest Lap Trebles and also Led every Lap (Most)

J Clark	8	GB 62-D 65
A Ascari	5	F 52-GB 53
M Schumacher	5	MC 94-H 04
N Mansell	4	GB 91-GB 92
A Senna	4	P 85-I 90
J Stewart	4	F 69-USA 72

Win/Fastest Lap Doubles

(Most)

M Schumacher	44	B 92-USA 05
A Prost	21	F 81-RSM 93
J Clark	18	B 62-ZA 68
J M Fangio	14	MC 50-D 57
N Lauda	12	E 74-I 84
N Mansell	12	F 86-GB 92
J Stewart	12	D 68-USA 72

Successive Win/Fastest Lap Doubles (Most)

A Ascari	7	B 52-RA 53
J Clark	3	B-F 63
M Schumacher	3	EUR-J 95
M Schumacher	3	BRN-E 04
J Stewart	3	NL-GB 69

POINTS

		ratio
M Schumacher	1248.00	5.40
A Prost	798.50	4.01
A Senna	614.00	3.81
D Coulthard	499.00	2.59
R Barrichello	489.00	2.27
N Piquet	485.50	2.38
N Mansell	482.00	2.58
N Lauda	420.50	2.46
M Häkkinen	420.00	2.61
G Berger	386.00	1.84
J Stewart	360.00	3.64
D Hill	360.00	3.13
C Reutemann	310.00	2.12
R Schumacher	304.00	2.10
G Hill	289.00	1.64
J P Montoya	281.00	3.35
K Räikkönen	281.00	3.27
E Fittipaldi	281.00	1.95
R Patrese	281.00	1.10
J M Fangio	277.14	5.43
J Clark	274.00	3.81
J Brabham	261.00	2.07
J Scheckter	255.00	2.28
D Hulme	248.00	2.21
F Alonso	247.00	3.58
J Alesi	241.00	1.20
J Villeneuve	228.00	1.51
J Laffite	228.00	1.30
C Regazzoni	212.00	1.61
A Jones	206.00	1.78
R Peterson	206.00	1.67
B McLaren	196.50	1.97
E Irvine	191.00	1.31
S Moss	186.64	2.83
M Alboreto	186.50	0.96
J Ickx	181.00	1.56
R Arnoux	181.00	1.21
J Surtees	180.00	1.62
M Andretti	180.00	1.41
J Hunt	179.00	1.95
H-H Frentzen	174.00	1.11
G Fisichella	174.00	1.09
J Watson	169.00	1.11

		ratio
J Button	167.00	1.67
J Trulli	160.00	1.10
K Rosberg	159.50	1.40
P Depailler	141.00	1.48
A Ascari	140.64	4.54
D Gurney	133.00	1.55
T Boutsen	132.00	0.81
M Hawthorn	127.64	2.84
G Farina	127.33	3.86
E de Angelis	122.00	1.13
J Rindt	109.00	1.82
R Ginther	107.00	2.06
G Villeneuve	107.00	1.60
P Tambay	103.00	0.90
D Pironi	101.00	1.44
P Hill	98.00	2.04
M Brundle	98.00	0.62
J Herbert	98.00	0.61
F Cevert	89.00	1.89
S Johansson	88.00	1.11
C Amon	83.00	0.86
F González	77.64	2.99
J-P Beltoise	77.00	0.90
O Panis	76.00	0.48
T Brooks	75.00	1.97
M Trintignant	72.33	0.88
P Rodriguez	71.00	1.29
J Mass	71.00	0.68
D Warwick	71.00	0.49
E Cheever	70.00	0.53
J Siffert	68.00	0.71
A Nannini	65.00	0.86
M Webber	62.00	0.91
P Revson	61.00	2.03
A de Cesaris	59.00	0.28
L Bandini	58.00	1.38
C Pace	58.00	0.81
W von Trips	56.00	2.07
N Heidfeld	56.00	0.58
J Behra	53.14	1.02

Yannick Dalmas and Jo Gartner were the only drivers, whose only points did not count towards the Championship (see 1984 & 87)

Point Scorer Age

Youngest
J Button	20y 2m 7d
R Rodriguez	20y 4m 3d
C Amon	20y 10m 4d
F Massa	20y 10m 20d
K Räikkönen	21y 4m 18d
R Barrichello	21y 5m 1d

Oldest
P Étançelin	53y 8m 6d
L Fagioli	53y 0m 22d
L Chiron	50y 9m 18d
L Rosier	50y 9m 0d
F Bonetto	50y 2m 14d

Points in a Season (Most)

M Schumacher	148	2004
M Schumacher	144	2002
F Alonso	133	2005
M Schumacher	123	2001
R Barrichello	114	2004 *
K Räikkönen	112	2005 *
N Mansell	108	1992
M Schumacher	108	2000
A Prost	105	1988 *
M Schumacher	102	1995
M Häkkinen	100	1998

* Not World Champion.

Successive Races in the Points (Most)

M Schumacher	24	H 01-MAL 03
J M Fangio	21	F 53-MC 56 *
M Schumacher	18	RSM 03-E 04
C Reutemann	15	B 80-B 81
A Ascari	13	B 52-CH 53
M Schumacher	13	RSM-J 03
R Barrichello	12	J 03-GB 04
J Clark	12	B 63-B 64
M Häkkinen	12	RSM-I 00
N Lauda	11	D 75-S 76
N Piquet	11	MC-MEX 87

* Includes MC 55 with a single point for fastest lap only.

Points scored in each of a driver's first two (or more) races

	races	points
J Stewart	6	25
R Ginther	6*	20
P Arundell	2	8
C Regazzoni	2*	6
G Follmer	2	5
A Prost	2	3

* Not successive events.

Half Points Awarded (shortened races)

E 75, A 75, MC 84, AUS 91

Points without a Win (Most)

J Button	167
M Brundle	98
S Johansson	88
C Amon	83
D Warwick	71

Points without a World Championship (Most)

D Coulthard	499
R Barrichello	489
G Berger	386
C Reutemann	310
R Schumacher	304

Points without a Pole (Most)

B McLaren	196.5
E Irvine	191
R Ginther	107
M Brundle	98
J Herbert	98

Points without a Fastest Lap (Most)

J Button	167
J Trulli	160
E de Angelis	122
M Brundle	98
J Herbert	98

Top 3 From Lowest Grid Position

	result	grid	
O Marimón	3rd	27th	GB 54
E Fittipaldi	3rd	24th	USAW 80
R Flockhart	3rd	23rd	I 56
N Lauda	2nd	23rd	USAW 83
T Fabi	3rd	23rd	DET 84
J Watson	1st	22nd	USAW 83
W von Trips	3rd	21st	F 58
J Watson	3rd	21st	DET 83
J Laffite	2nd	20th	AUS 85
R Barrichello	3rd	20th	CDN 05
J P Montoya	2nd	20th	D 05
Indy 500			
J Rathmann	2nd	32nd	INDY 57
D Freeland	3rd	26th	INDY 56
P Goldsmith	3rd	26th	INDY 60
G Amick	2nd	25th	INDY 58

6th place but no points

Drivers who never scored points but came 6th prior to points awarded for 6th place

E Barth	1 x 6th
	(F2 section of Grand Prix)
I Burgess	1 x 6th
B Gerard	3 x 6ths
O González	1 x 6th (shared drive)
R Laurent	1 x 6th
L Piotti	1 x 6th
A Simon	2 x 6ths

No top 6th place but scored points

Drivers who scored points under the system established in 2003, but never achieved a position of 6th or above

Z Baumgartner	1 x 8th
R Firman	1 x 8th
T Glock	1 x 7th
V Liuzzi	1 x 8th
A Pizzonia	4 x 7ths
J Wilson	1 x 8th

WORLD CHAMPIONS

year	driver	nat	cars driven	decided
1950	G Farina	I	Alfa Romeo	I, 3 Sep
1951	J M Fangio	RA	Alfa Romeo	E, 28 Oct
1952	A Ascari	I	Ferrari	D, 3 Aug
1953	A Ascari	I	Ferrari	CH, 23 Aug
1954	J M Fangio	RA	Maserati & Mercedes-Benz	CH, 22 Aug
1955	J M Fangio	RA	Mercedes-Benz	I, 11 Sep
1956	J M Fangio	RA	Ferrari	I, 2 Sep
1957	J M Fangio	RA	Maserati	D, 4 Aug
1958	M Hawthorn	GB	Ferrari	MA, 19 Oct
1959	J Brabham	AUS	Cooper-Climax	USA, 12 Dec
1960	J Brabham	AUS	Cooper-Climax	P, 14 Aug
1961	P Hill	USA	Ferrari	I, 10 Sep
1962	G Hill	GB	BRM	ZA, 29 Dec
1963	J Clark	GB	Lotus-Climax	I, 8 Sep
1964	J Surtees	GB	Ferrari	MEX, 25 Oct
1965	J Clark	GB	Lotus-Climax	D, 1 Aug
1966	J Brabham	AUS	Brabham-Repco	I, 4 Sep
1967	D Hulme	NZ	Brabham-Repco	MEX, 22 Oct
1968	G Hill	GB	Lotus-Ford Cosworth	MEX, 3 Nov
1969	J Stewart	GB	Matra-Ford Cosworth	I, 7 Sep
1970	J Rindt	A	Lotus-Ford Cosworth	USA, 4 Oct
1971	J Stewart	GB	Tyrrell-Ford Cosworth	A, 15 Aug
1972	E Fittipaldi	BR	Lotus-Ford Cosworth	I, 10 Sep
1973	J Stewart	GB	Tyrrell-Ford Cosworth	I, 9 Sep
1974	E Fittipaldi	BR	McLaren-Ford Cosworth	USA, 6 Oct
1975	N Lauda	A	Ferrari	I, 7 Sep
1976	J Hunt	GB	McLaren-Ford Cosworth	J, 24 Oct
1977	N Lauda	A	Ferrari	USAE, 2 Oct
1978	M Andretti	USA	Lotus-Ford Cosworth	I, 10 Sep
1979	J Scheckter	ZA	Ferrari	I, 9 Sep
1980	A Jones	AUS	Williams-Ford Cosworth	CDN, 28 Sep
1981	N Piquet	BR	Brabham-Ford Cosworth	LV, 17 Oct
1982	K Rosberg	FIN	Williams-Ford Cosworth	LV, 25 Sep
1983	N Piquet	BR	Brabham-BMW	ZA, 15 Oct
1984	N Lauda	A	McLaren-TAG Porsche	P, 21 Oct
1985	A Prost	F	McLaren-TAG Porsche	EUR, 6 Oct
1986	A Prost	F	McLaren-TAG Porsche	AUS, 26 Oct
1987	N Piquet	BR	Williams-Honda	J, 31 Oct*
1988	A Senna	BR	McLaren-Honda	J, 30 Oct
1989	A Prost	F	McLaren-Honda	J, 22 Oct**
1990	A Senna	BR	McLaren-Honda	J, 21 Oct
1991	A Senna	BR	McLaren-Honda	J, 20 Oct
1992	N Mansell	GB	Williams-Renault	H, 16 Aug
1993	A Prost	F	Williams-Renault	P, 26 Sep
1994	M Schumacher	D	Benetton-Ford Cosworth	AUS, 13 Nov
1995	M Schumacher	D	Benetton-Renault	PAC, 22 Oct
1996	D Hill	GB	Williams-Renault	J, 13 Oct
1997	J Villeneuve	CDN	Williams-Renault	EUR, 26 Oct
1998	M Häkkinen	FIN	McLaren-Mercedes	J, 1 Nov
1999	M Häkkinen	FIN	McLaren-Mercedes	J, 31 Oct
2000	M Schumacher	D	Ferrari	J, 8 Oct
2001	M Schumacher	D	Ferrari	H, 19 Aug
2002	M Schumacher	D	Ferrari	F, 21 Jul
2003	M Schumacher	D	Ferrari	J, 12 Oct
2004	M Schumacher	D	Ferrari	B, 29 Aug
2005	F Alonso	E	Renault	BR, 25 Sep

* The day before the Japanese GP when Mansell flew home.
** Confirmed on day of appeal (31 Oct).

World Championships

M Schumacher	7
J M Fangio	5
A Prost	4
J Brabham	3
N Lauda	3
N Piquet	3
A Senna	3
J Stewart	3
A Ascari	2
J Clark	2
E Fittipaldi	2
M Häkkinen	2
G Hill	2
F Alonso	1
M Andretti	1
G Farina	1
M Hawthorn	1
D Hill	1
P Hill	1
D Hulme	1
J Hunt	1
A Jones	1
N Mansell	1
J Rindt	1
K Rosberg	1
J Scheckter	1
J Surtees	1
J Villeneuve	1

No driver has ever failed to qualify for a GP during his World Championship winning season.

Monaco 1973 was the only race in which the top six finishers were placed in the same order as the eventual Championship table for the year.

World Champion Age

Youngest
F Alonso	24y 1m 27d	(2005)
E Fittipaldi	25y 8m 29d	(1972)
M Schumacher	25y 10m 10d	(1994)
N Lauda	26y 6m 16d	(1975)
J Villeneuve	26y 6m 17d	(1997)
J Clark	27y 6m 4d	(1963)

Oldest
J M Fangio	46y 1m 11d	(1957)
G Farina	43y 10m 3d	(1950)
J Brabham	40y 5m 2d	(1966)
G Hill	39y 8m 19d	(1968)
N Mansell	39y 0m 8d	(1992)

Jochen Rindt who died at age 28, was the only posthumous World Champion.

Country Hosting Championship Decider

Italy	12
Japan	12
United States	6
Germany	3
Mexico	3
Portugal	3

Championship Decided In Final Round

1950 I	1951 E	1956 I	1958 MA
1959 USA	1962 ZA	1964 MEX	1967 MEX
1968 MEX	1974 USA	1976 J	1981 LV
1982 LV	1983 ZA	1984 P	1986 AUS
1994 AUS	1996 J	1997 EUR	1998 J
1999 J	2003 J		

Date Crowned Champion

Earliest
21 Jul 2002	M Schumacher
1 Aug 1965	J Clark
3 Aug 1952	A Ascari
4 Aug 1957	J M Fangio
14 Aug 1960	J Brabham
16 Aug 1992	N Mansell

Latest
29 Dec 1962	G Hill
12 Dec 1959	J Brabham
13 Nov 1994	M Schumacher
3 Nov 1968	G Hill

Races Remaining After Championship Decided (Most)

2002	F	6	(M Schumacher)
1992	H	5	
2001	H	4	
2004	B	4	
1963	I	3	
1965	D	3	
1969	I	3	
1971	A	3	

Seasons where the World Champion was beaten in terms of total wins

1958	M Hawthorn 1	T Brooks 3, S Moss 4
1964	J Surtees 2	J Clark 3
1967	D Hulme 2	J Clark 4
1977	N Lauda 3	M Andretti 4
1979	J Scheckter 3	A Jones 4
1982	K Rosberg 1	R Arnoux 2, N Lauda 2, D Pironi 2, A Prost 2, J Watson 2
1983	N Piquet 3	A Prost 4
1984	N Lauda 5	A Prost 7
1986	A Prost 4	N Mansell 5
1987	N Piquet 3	N Mansell 6
1989	A Prost 4	A Senna 6

GP Starts taken to achieve World Championship

G Farina	6
J M Fangio	13
A Ascari	15
J Brabham	24
E Fittipaldi	25
D Hulme	26
P Hill	27
J Clark	30
J Villeneuve	33
G Hill	41
J Surtees	41
M Hawthorn	45
J Stewart	47
N Piquet	49
K Rosberg	51
J Hunt	52
M Schumacher	52
N Lauda	55
J Rindt	60
F Alonso	67
D Hill	67
A Senna	77
M Andretti	80
A Jones	80
A Prost	87
J Scheckter	97
M Hakkinen	112
N Mansell	176

World Champions not participating in the following Season

M Hawthorn	1958
J Rindt	1970
J Stewart	1973
A Prost	1993
N Mansell	1992 *

* Returned in 1994.

Other World Champions who failed to win the season after being World Champion

A Ascari	1954
J M Fangio	1958
J Brabham	1961
P Hill	1962
J Surtees	1965
M Andretti	1979
J Scheckter	1980
N Piquet	1988
D Hill	1997
J Villeneuve	1998

Reigning World Champion who failed to qualify for at least one race in the following season

N Piquet	DET 82	(1981 Champion)
J Scheckter	CDN 80	(1979 Champion)

Total Career Reign as Champion

Longest

	days
M Schumacher	2,513
J M Fangio	1,799
A Prost	1,532
J Stewart	1,176
N Lauda	1,106
N Piquet	1,080
J Brabham	1,051
A Senna	1,022

Shortest

J Surtees	280
J Rindt	315*
J Hunt	343
M Andretti	364
J Villeneuve	371
D Hill	378
D Hulme	378

* Died before he became World Champion.

Championship Winning Margin

Narrowest (net points)

	Points	Winner
1984	0.5	N Lauda
1958	1	M Hawthorn
1961	1	P Hill
1964	1	J Surtees
1976	1	J Hunt
1981	1	N Piquet
1994	1	M Schumacher

Widest (net points)

2002	67	M Schumacher
2001	58	M Schumacher
1992	52	N Mansell
1997	39	J Villeneuve *
2004	34	M Schumacher
1995	33	M Schumacher
1971	29	J Stewart
1969	26	J Stewart
1993	26	A Prost
1963	25	J Clark
1991	24	A Senna

* Due to M Schumacher's removal from the Championship table.

Continuous Reign as Champion

Longest

	years:	months:	days	winning seasons
M Schumacher	4:	11 :	17	2000-01-02-03-04
J M Fangio	4:	1 :	27	1954-55-56-57
A Prost	2:	0 :	25	1985-86
A Ascari	2:	0 :	19	1952-53
M Häkkinen	1:	11 :	7	1998-99
M Schumacher	1:	11 :	0	1994-95
A Senna	1:	9 :	26	1990-91
J Brabham	1:	8 :	29	1959-60

Shortest

G Hill		8 :	10	1962
J M Fangio		9 :	6	1951
J Surtees		9 :	7	1964

Jackie Stewart, the master of consistent lap times, also carried this over to his Championship seasons – each of his three championships lasted exactly 392 days!

Span Between Championship Deciders

Longest

	days	seasons
P Hill	475	1961-62
M Schumacher	448	2002-03
J M Fangio	441	1957-58
G Farina	420	1950-51
M Hawthorn	419	1958-59

Shortest

J Brabham	246	1959-60
G Hill	253	1962-63
J M Fangio	280	1951-52
J Surtees	280	1964-65

Wins in Championship Season

Fewest

M Hawthorn	1	1958
K Rosberg	1	1982

LAP LEADERS

	laps	races	km	miles
M Schumacher	4,725	130	22,236.4	13,817.0
A Senna	2,931	86	13,430.4	8,345.3
A Prost	2,683	84	12,476.7	7,752.7
N Mansell	2,057	55	9,500.6	5,903.4
J Clark	1,942	43	10,121.1	6,288.9
J Stewart	1,918	51	9,173.4	5,700.1
N Piquet	1,633.5	59	7,757.4	4,820.2
N Lauda	1,591	41	7,062.6	4,388.5
M Häkkinen	1,489	48	7,196.0	4,471.4
D Hill	1,363	45	6,339.2	3,939.0
J M Fangio	1,348	38	9,322.3	5,792.6
S Moss	1,181	31	6,369.0	3,957.5
G Hill	1,105	32	4,763.9	2,960.2
A Ascari	925	21	5,887.0	3,658.0
D Coulthard	895	60	4,201.5	2,610.7
J Brabham	825	28	4,540.1	2,821.1
M Andretti	798	22	3,573.2	2,220.3
G Berger	754	33	3,717.7	2,310.0
R Barrichello	722	44	3,487.2	2,166.8
R Peterson	707	28	3,313.4	2,058.8
J Scheckter	675	23	2,855.0	1,774.0
J Hunt	666	24	3,363.3	2,089.9
C Reutemann	650	19	3,314.2	2,059.4
J Villeneuve	633	20	2,965.1	1,842.5

All distances completed as lap leaders are calculated as complete laps (actual distances in the lead are not recorded for the official results).

Races Led (Most)

M Schumacher	130
A Senna	86
A Prost	84
D Coulthard	60 *
N Piquet	59
N Mansell	55
J Stewart	51

* Most races led without becoming a World Champion.

Distance Led (Most km)

M Schumacher	22,236.4
A Senna	13,430.4
A Prost	12,476.7
J Clark	10,121.1
N Mansell	9,500.6
J M Fangio	9,322.3

Laps Led in Driver's Championship Season

Most (% of total)

A Ascari	348 out of 447	77.9%	1952
A Ascari	415 out of 536	77.4%	1953
J Clark	506 out of 708	71.5%	1963
N Mansell	693 out of 1,036	66.9%	1992
J M Fangio	309 out of 472	65.5%	1955

Fewest (% of total)

K Rosberg	80 out of 1,060.5	7.5%	1982
E Fittipaldi	77 out of 979	7.9%	1974
J Surtees	89 out of 722	12.3%	1964

Laps Led in a Season (Most)

N Mansell	693	1992
M Schumacher	683	2004
M Schumacher	629	1994
M Häkkinen	576	1998
M Schumacher	558	2002
A Senna	553	1988
M Schumacher	548	2000
M Schumacher	533	2001
J Clark	506	1963
A Senna	500	1990
A Senna	487	1989 *

* Not World Champion.

GPs Led in a Season (Most)

M Schumacher	16	2004
A Prost	15	1993
N Mansell	14	1992
M Schumacher	14	1995, 2000
A Senna	14	1990

Led Every GP in a Season

J M Fangio	1951	(6 GPs)
J M Fangio	1955	(6 GPs)
J Stewart	1969	(11 GPs)

Lap Leaders in a GP (Most)

8 -	I 71
7 -	CDN 73, GB 75
6 -	F 61, I 66, I 67, I 70, E 75, F 90 I 95, USA 03, B 04, J 05

Lap Leaders in a Season

Most

15 -	1975
13 -	1968, 77, 82, 03
12 -	1971

Fewest

4 -	1988
5 -	1950, 52, 53, 64, 92, 93

Won without leading a lap

L Fagioli	F 51	(shared drive in which Fangio took over the car)
L Musso	RA 56	(shared drive in which Fangio took over the car)
T Brooks	GB 57	(shared drive in which Moss took over the car)
N Lauda	I 78	(due to Andretti/ Villeneuve penalty)
A Prost	BR 82	(due to Piquet/ Rosberg disqualification)
E de Angelis	RSM 85	(due to Prost disqualification)
D Hill	B 94	(due to Schumacher disqualification)

Luigi Fagioli and Luigi Musso have been credited with a win each although neither actually took the chequered flag in their World Championship careers.

Led Only the Final Lap
(to win the race)

B McLaren	USA 59
J Clark	B 64
J Surtees	I 67
B McLaren	B 68
J Rindt	MC 70
M Andretti	F 77
R Peterson	ZA 78
N Piquet	CDN 91
J Villeneuve	H 97
M Häkkinen	EUR 97

The only driver to lead every lap of a race except the final one was Nigel Mansell in Canada 1991.

Races led without a Championship (Most)

D Coulthard	60
R Barrichello	44
G Berger	33
S Moss	31
J P Montoya	30
R Patrese	29
R Peterson	28
K Räikkönen	28

Led Throughout the GP (Most)

A Senna	19	P 85-AUS 91
J Clark	13	GB 62-D 65
M Schumacher	11	PAC 94-J 04
J Stewart	11	D 68-D 73
N Mansell	9	P 86-P 92
A Ascari	7	F 52-GB 53
A Prost	7	I 81-F 89
N Lauda	6	NL 74-MC 76

Lead Changes in a race (Most)

41 -	I 65
28 -	I 70
27 -	I 64
25 -	I 63
25 -	I 71
22 -	D 59

Races led without a Win (Most)

J Button	9
C Amon	7
J Behra	7

Lead Laps without a Championship (Most)

S Moss	1181	(6,369.0 km)
D Coulthard	895	(4,201.5 km)
G Berger	754	(3,717.7 km)
R Peterson	707	(3,313.4 km)
R Barrichello	722	(3,487.2 km)
C Reutemann	650	(3,314.2 km)
J P Montoya	599	(2,934.9 km)
K Räikkönen	584	(2,793.5 km)
R Patrese	565.5	(2,554.6 km)
G Villeneuve	535	(2,253.9 km)

Lead Laps without a Win (Most)

C Amon	183	(851.5 km)
J Behra	107	(438.7 km)
J Button	79	(406.0 km)
J-P Jarier	79	(452.8 km)
I Capelli	46	(177.4 km)
J Oliver	36	(164.7 km)

Lead Laps without a Pole

(Most)

E Irvine	157	(842.7 km)
F Cevert	129	(560.2 km)
P Collins	127	(945.8 km)
R Ginther	116	(737.0 km)
J Behra	107	(438.7 km)
J-P Beltoise	101	(377.6 km)

Lead Laps without a Fastest Lap (Most)

J-P Jabouille	179	(942.4 km)
W von Trips	156	(787.8 km)
J Trulli	145	(596.1 km)
J Bonnier	139	(546.8 km)
P Collins	127	(945.8 km)
J Button	79	(406.0 km)

One Lap Wonders

(World Championship Career Less Than 1 Lap Duration)

Josef Peters	D 52
Ernst Loof	D 53
Bob Said	USA 59
Arthur Owen	I 60
Massimo Natili	GB 61
Graham McRae	GB 73
Miguel Angel Guerra	RSM 81
Marco Apicella	I 93

Races without even Finishing (Most)

Alex Soler-Roig	6
Clemar Bucci	5
David Murray	4

Female Drivers

Maria-Teresa de Filippis	1958-59
Lella Lombardi *	1974-76
Divina Galica (nq)	1976-78
Desire Wilson (nq)	1980
Giovanna Amati (nq)	1992

* The only female to score World Championship points (at Spain 1975).

Non-English GB Drivers

Northern Ireland

Kenny Acheson, Martin Donnelly, Eddie Irvine, Damien Magee, Desmond Titterington, John Watson

Scotland

Jim Clark, David Coulthard, Jim Crawford, Johnny Dumfries, Ron Flockhart, Innes Ireland Allan McNish, David Murray, Archie Scott Brown, Ian Stewart, Jackie Stewart, Jimmy Stewart, Leslie Thorne

Wales

Jackie Lewis, Tom Pryce, Alan Rees

Relatives in Grands Prix

Father/Son

Mario/Michael Andretti
Jack/David & *Gary* Brabham
Wilson/Christian Fittipaldi
Graham/Damon Hill
Reg/Tim Parnell
André/Teddy Pilette
Hans/Hans-Joachim Stuck
Gilles/Jacques Villeneuve

Brothers

David/*Gary* Brabham
Tino/Vittorio Brambilla
Corrado/Teo Fabi
Emerson/Wilson Fittipaldi
Pedro/Ricardo Rodriguez
Ian/Jody Scheckter
Michael/Ralf Schumacher
Jackie/Jimmy Stewart
Gilles/*Jacques(Sr.)* Villeneuve
Graham/Peter Whitehead (half)
Joachim/Manfred Winkelhock

Uncle/Nephew

Emerson/Christian Fittipaldi
Jo/Jean-Louis Schlesser
Jacques (Sr.)/Jacques Villeneuve

Cousins

José Dolhem/Didier Pironi

Brothers-in-law

Jean-Pierre Beltoise/François Cevert
David Brabham/Mike Thackwell
Jean-Pierre Jabouille/Jacques Laffite
Tony Maggs/Mike Spence

Italicised drivers did not start.

The most drivers with the same surname to enter a Grand Prix, was 4 at Britain 1959. Dennis, Henry, Mike & Trevor Taylor, none of whom were related to each other, all made their debut at this race.

Banned from Entering

For dangerous driving:

M Häkkinen	H 94	(1)
E Irvine	PAC, RSM, MC 94	(3)

For ignoring black flag:

N Mansell	P 89	(1)
M Schumacher	I, P 94	(2)

For running cars under legal weight (team ban):

J Button	MC, E 05	(2)
T Sato	MC, E 05	(2)

Disqualified (Most)

S Bellof	11	BR 84-NL 84 *
M Brundle	8	BR 84-A 87 *
S Johansson	4	GB 84-CDN 89 *

* Includes Tyrrell team disqualifications.

Disqualified from Top 3

J Hunt	1st	GB 76
N Piquet	1st	BR 82
K Rosberg	2nd	BR 82
G Villeneuve	3rd	USAW 82
N Lauda	3rd	B 82
K Rosberg	2nd	BR 83
S Bellof	3rd	MC 84
M Brundle	2nd	DET 84
A Prost	1st	RSM 85
A Senna	2nd	AUS 87
T Boutsen	3rd	B 88
A Senna	1st	J 89
M Schumacher	2nd	GB 94
M Schumacher	1st	B 94
M Häkkinen	3rd	B 97
D Coulthard	2nd	BR 00
R Schumacher	2nd	CDN 04
J Button	3rd	RSM 05

The most disqualifications in one race occurred in CDN 2004 (4), all for brake infringements.

Drivers with Different Constructors in a Season (Most)

S Moss	3	1952	HWM/ERA/Connaught
A Ascari	3	1954	Maserati/Ferrari/Lancia
H Schell	3	1955	Maserati/Ferrari/Vanwall
M Hawthorn	3	1956	Maserati/BRM/Vanwall
R Salvadori	3	1957	BRM (nq)/Vanwall/Cooper
D Gurney	3	1968	Eagle/Brabham/McLaren
J Bonnier	3	1968	Cooper/McLaren/Honda
J Ickx	3	1973	Ferrari/McLaren/Iso Marlboro
J Watson	3	1975	Surtees/Lotus/Penske
J-P Jarier	3	1977	Penske/Shadow/Ligier
N Piquet	3	1978	Ensign/McLaren/Brabham
K Rosberg	3	1978	Theodore/ATS/Wolf
G Lees	3	1980	Shadow/Ensign/Williams (nq)
R Moreno	3	1991	Benetton/Jordan/Minardi
J Herbert	3	1994	Lotus/Ligier/Benetton

Raced in Car of their Surname

C Amon	1974
B Aston	1952
D Brabham	1990
J Brabham	1962,63,64,65,66,67,68, 69,70
E Fittipaldi	(1976,77,78,79)*,80
W Fittipaldi	1975*
A Gordini	1951**
G Hill	1975
B McLaren	1966,67,68,69,70
A Merzario	1978,79
H Rebaque	1979
J Surtees	1970,71,72

* Drove a Copersucar (Fittipaldi).
** Drove a Simca Gordini.

World Champion in Own Car

J Brabham	1966

Race Winner in Own Car

J Brabham	1966,67,70
D Gurney (Eagle)	1967
B McLaren	1968

Different makes of car raced during World Championship career

C Amon	13
A de Cesaris	10
S Johansson	10
S Moss	10
M Trintignant	10
E Cheever	9
J Ickx	9
R Moreno	9

Stirling Moss was the only driver to race two different makes of car in a Grand Prix: a Lotus and a Ferguson in Britain 1961.

Non-qualifications (Most)

G Tarquini	40
B Gachot	37
R Moreno	32
P Ghinzani	31
A Merzario	26
B Schneider	25
Y Dalmas	24
N Larini	23

Aguri Suzuki was the only driver to non pre-qualify in every race during a season (1989).

Unsuccessful qualifying attempts for drivers who never started a race (Most)

C Langes	14
P Chaves	13
V Weidler	10
D Kennedy	7
P McCarthy	7
J Winkelhock	7
E Bertaggia	6
T Trimmer	6

Two drivers have crashed into the harbour at Monte-Carlo: Alberto Ascari in 1955 and Paul Hawkins in 1965. Neither were fatal, although Ascari died 4 days later at Monza on 26 May, and Hawkins died 4 years after his Monaco accident, at Oulton Park, coincidentally also on 26 May.

The only time that car number 13 has been in a Grand Prix, was in Mexico 1963, driven by Moises Solana. Divina Galica did not qualify in car 13 in Britain 1976.

Car number 0 has only been used by two drivers: Jody Scheckter in Canada and USA 1973, and by Damon Hill throughout 1993 and 1994.

The highest car number was 208 (sponsored by Radio Luxembourg) and driven by Lella Lombardi in Britain 1974 (non-qualified).

The highest car number to start a race was 136, driven by Rudolf Krause in Germany 1952.

The lowest number never to be used is 63.

Apart from 13, the lowest number never to win is 29.

SUCCESSES OUTSIDE THE F1 WORLD CHAMPIONSHIP

International Formula 3000
Winners

	F3000 Wins	Best F3000 Championship Season	Best GP Result
N Heidfeld	7	1/1999	2/2005
V Liuzzi	7	1/2004	8 /2005
J P Montoya	7	1/1998	1/2001-05
E Comas	6	1/1990	5/1992
G Pantano	6	2/2002	13/2004
R Moreno	5	1/1988	2/1990
E Naspetti	5	3/1991	11/1992
R Zonta	5	1/1997	6/2000
L Badoer	4	1/1992	7/1993
C Danner	4	1/1985	4/1989
F Lagorce	4	2/1994	11/1994
P Martini	4	2/1986	4/1991
L Sala	4	2/1987	6/1989
M Thackwell	4	2/1985	r/1980-84
M Webber	4	2/2001	3/2005
J Alesi	3	1/1989	1/1995
J Boullion	3	1/1994	5/1995
I Capelli	3	1/1986	2/1990
M Donnelly	3	3/1988	7/1990
T Enge	3	2/2001	12/2001
S Modena	3	1/1987	2/1991
A Montermini	3	2/1992	8/1995
O Panis	3	1/1993	1/1996
E Pirro	3	3/1985-86	5/1989
V Sospiri	3	1/1995	nq/1997
E van de Poele	3	2/1990	9/1991
J Wilson	3	1/2001	8/2003
Y Dalmas	2	5/1987	5/1987
C Fittipaldi	2	1/1991	4/1993-94
P Friesacher	2	5/2003-04	6/2005
J-M Gounon	2	6/1991-92	9/1994
O Grouillard	2	2/1988	6/1989
F Lagorce	2	2/1994	11/1994
A McNish	2	4/1990	7/2002
R Rosset	2	2/1995	8/1996
S Sarrazin	2	4/1999	r/1999
A Zanardi	2	2/1991	6/1993
P Alliot	1	9/1986	5/1993
F Alonso	1	4/2000	1/2003-05
J Bailey	1	7/1987	6/1991
O Beretta	1	6/1993	7/1994
É Bernard	1	3/1989	3/1994
A Chiesa	1	6/1989	r/1992
D Coulthard	1	3/1993	1/1995-03
R Doornbos	1	3/2004	13/2005
P Fabre	1	7/1986	9/1987
G Foitek	1	7/1988	7/1990
M Gugelmin	1	4/1987	3/1989
J Herbert	1	8/1988	1/1995
E Irvine	1	3/1990	1/1999
N Kiesa	1	7/2003	11/2003
P Lamy	1	2/1993	6/1995
T Marques	1	5/1995	10/1997
G Morbidelli	1	5/1990	3/1995
M Papis	1	5/1994	7/1995
A Pizzonia	1	6/2001	7/2004-05

International F3000 Non-Winners who have achieved a top 6 GP placing

	Best F3000 result	F3000 Championship Season	Best GP result
D Hill	2nd	7/1991	1/1993-98
H-H Frentzen	5th	14/1991	1/1997-99
R Barrichello	2nd	3/1992	1/2000-04
M Blundell	2nd	6/1988	3/1993-94
J J Lehto	4th	13/1989	3/1991
T Monteiro	5 th	13/2002	3/2005
P Streiff	3rd	8/1985	3/1985
A Suzuki	11th	-/1988	3/1990
S Nakajima	4th	10/1986	4/1987-89
K Wendlinger	3rd	11/1991	4/1993-94
C Albers	7th	-/2000	5/2005
J Dumfries	6th	16/1985	5/1986
B Gachot	2nd	5/1988	5/1991
M Gené	8th	-/1997	5/2003
U Katayama	18th	-/1989	5/1994
P Diniz	4th	12/1994	5/1997-98
C da Matta	4th	8/1996	6/2003-04
G Tarquini	3rd	6/1985	6/1989

European F2 Champions (1967-84)

R Arnoux	1977
J-P Beltoise	1968
P Depailler	1974
C Fabi	1982
B Giacomelli	1978
M Hailwood	1972
B Henton	1980
J Ickx	1967
J-P Jabouille	1976
J-P Jarier	1973
J Laffite	1975
G Lees	1981
J Palmer	1983
R Peterson	1971
C Regazzoni	1970
J Servoz-Gavin	1969
M Surer	1979
M Thackwell	1984

European F3 Champions (1975-84)

M Alboreto	1980
M Baldi	1981
I Capelli	1984
P Ghinzani	1977
J Lammers	1978
O Larrauri	1982
P Martini	1983
R Patrese	1976
L Perkins	1975
A Prost	1979

All-Japan F2/F3000 (Formula Nippon) Champions

M Apicella	1994
P de la Rosa	1997
M Hasemi	1980
K Hoshino	1978,87,90,93
U Katayama	1991
G Lees	1983
S Nakajima	1981,82,84,85,86
R Schumacher	1996
A Suzuki	1988
T Suzuki	1995
T Takagi	2000
R Firman	2002

Pre-Championship major single-seater Grand Prix Winners

A Ascari	1949
L Chiron	1928-49
E de Graffenried	1949
L Fagioli	1933-35
G Farina	1940-48
H Lang	1937-39
L Rosier	1949
H Stuck	1934-35
L Villoresi	1948
P Whitehead	1949

IndyCar Drivers in the World Championship

Indianapolis 500 Drivers (1950-60) who won the race in other years

A J Foyt	1961,64,67,77
B Holland	1949
M Rose	1941,47,48
R Ward	1962

Indianapolis 500 Winners

Mario Andretti *	1969
E Cheever	1998
J Clark *	1965
M Donohue	1972
E Fittipaldi *	1989,93
G Hill *	1966
J P Montoya	2000
B Rahal	1986
T Ruttman	1952
D Sullivan	1985
B Unser	1968,75,81
J Villeneuve *	1995
R Ward	1959,62

* Also an F1 World Champion.

F1 and IndyCar Race Winners

	F1	IndyCar
Mario Andretti	1971-78	1965-93
J Clark	1962-68	1963-65
E Fittipaldi	1970-75	1985-95
D Gurney	1962-67	1967-70
G Hill	1962-69	1966
N Mansell	1985-94	1993
J P Montoya	2001	1999-00
P Revson	1973	1969
J Villeneuve	1996-97	1994-95

F1 Non-Winners who won an IndyCar/Champ Car race

Michael Andretti	1986-02
M Blundell	1997
R Bucknum	1968
E Cheever	1997-01*
M Donohue	1971-72
T Fabi	1983-89
C Fittipaldi	1999-00
G Follmer	1969
R Guerrero	1987
M Gugelmin	1997
R Moreno	2000-01
D Ongais	1977-78
M Papis	2000-01
B Rahal	1982-92
H Rebaque	1982
L Ruby	1961-70
T Ruttman	1952
E Salazar	1997*
D Sullivan	1984-93
B Unser	1966-81
R Ward	1953-66
J Wilson	2005
A Zanardi	1996-98

* Indy Racing League only.

F1 Drivers who won the IndyCar World Series*

Mario Andretti	1965,66,69,84
Michael Andretti	1991
E Fittipaldi	1989
N Mansell	1993
J P Montoya	1999
B Rahal	1986,87,92
D Sullivan	1988
B Unser	1968,74
J Villeneuve	1995
R Ward	1959,62
A Zanardi	1997,98

* USAC National Championship until 1979, CART IndyCar World Series 1979-91.

F1 and IndyCar World Champions

	F1	IndyCar
M Andretti	1978	1965,66, 69,84
E Fittipaldi	1972,74	1989
N Mansell	1992	1993
J Villeneuve	1997	1995

Nigel Mansell was the only driver to hold the F1 and IndyCar Championships simultaneously.

F1 drivers who started at Indy (1950-60)

A Ascari, L Ruby, T Ruttman, R Ward

Le Mans 24-hours race winners

M Alboreto	1997
C Amon	1966
D Attwood	1970
M Baldi	1994
L Bandini	1963
P Barilla	1985
D Bell	1975,81,82,86,87
L Bianchi	1968
M Blundell	1992
M Brundle	1990
I Bueb	1955,57
E Chaboud	1938
Y Dalmas	1992,94,95,99
J Dumfries	1988
P Étançelin	1934
R Flockhart	1956,57
A J Foyt	1967
P Frère	1960
B Gachot	1991
O Gendebien	1958,60,61,62
F González	1954
M Gregory	1965
D Gurney	1967
D Hamilton	1953
M Hawthorn	1955
J Herbert	1991
H Herrmann	1970
G Hill	1972
P Hill	1958,61,62
J Ickx	1969,75,76,77,81,82
S Johansson	1997
J Lammers	1988
H Lang	1952
G Larrousse	1973,74
J J Lehto	1995,05
H Marko	1971
P Martini	1999
J Mass	1989
B McLaren	1966
A McNish	1998
J Oliver	1969
H Pescarolo	1972,73,74,84
D Pironi	1978
E Pirro	2000,01,02
F Riess	1952
J Rindt	1965
P Rodriguez	1968
T Rolt	1953
L Rosier	1950
R Salvadori	1959
L Scarfiotti	1963
V Schuppan	1983
C Shelby	1959
R Sommer	1932,33
H-J Stuck	1986,87
M Trintignant	1954
N Vaccarella	1964
G Van Lennep	1971,76
P Walker	1951
D Warwick	1992
P Whitehead	1951
J Winkelhock	1999
A Wurz	1996

World Sportscar/GT Champions

J Bailey	2000*
M Baldi	1990*
D Bell	1985*,86
S Bellof	1984
O Beretta	1999*
R Boesel	1987
M Brundle	1988
Y Dalmas	1992*
T Fabi	1991
J Ickx	1982,83
J Lammers	2002,03
J L Schlesser	1989,90*
B Schneider	1997
H-J Stuck	1985*
D Warwick	1992*
K Wendlinger	1999*
R Zonta	1998*

Shared championship.

Can-Am Challenge Champions (1966-86)

M Donohue	1973
G Follmer	1972
D Hulme	1968,70
J Ickx	1979
A Jones	1978
B McLaren	1967,69
J Oliver	1974
P Revson	1971
J Surtees	1966
P Tambay	1977,80

Tasman Cup Champions (1964-75)

C Amon	1969
W Brown	1975
J Clark	1965,67,68
P Gethin	1974
B McLaren	1964
G McRae	1971,72,73
J Stewart	1966

Motorcycle 500cc World Championship Point Scorers

B Anderson	1958-59
J Cecotto *	1976-80
P Driver	1959-65
M Hailwood *	1960-67
N Pagani *	1949-55
J Surtees *	1952-60

Race winners.

John Surtees is the only man to become F1 car and 500cc Motorcycle World Champion.

STARTS

Grands Prix (Most)

Ferrari	722
McLaren	595
Williams	507
Lotus	491
Tyrrell	430
Ligier/Prost	409
Brabham	394
Arrows	382
Minardi	340
Benetton	317
Jordan	250
March	227
Sauber	215
BRM	197
Renault	192
Osella	151
Lola	149
Cooper	129
Surtees	118
BAR	117
Alfa Romeo	110
Fittipaldi	104
Shadow	104

The race that holds the record for the most different constructors starting was Canada 1989, with 18.

Total Race Starts (Most)

(Number of cars to start)

Ferrari	1632
McLaren	1243
Lotus	1237
Williams	976
Brabham	932
Tyrrell	842
Ligier/Prost	742
Arrows	724
Minardi	634
Benetton	613
March	557
BRM	522
Cooper	499
Jordan	491
Sauber	428
Maserati	368
Renault	365
Lola	245
Alfa Romeo	234
BAR	231
Surtees	224
Shadow	211

The last time a constructor had three cars in a Grand Prix was at Germany 1985 (Renault).

Grands Prix without a Win (Most)

Arrows	382
Minardi	340
Sauber	215
Osella	151
Lola	149
Surtees	118

Grands Prix without a Pole Position (Most)

Minardi	340
Sauber	215
Osella	151
Surtees	118
Fittipaldi	104

Grands Prix without a Point (Most)

RAM	31
Forti	23
Spirit	23
Pacific	22
Simtek	21

Constructors' Championships

Ferrari	14
Williams	9
McLaren	8
Lotus	7
Brabham	2
Cooper	2
Benetton	1
BRM	1
Matra	1
Renault	1
Tyrrell	1
Vanwall	1

Drivers' Championships

Ferrari	14
McLaren	11
Williams	7
Lotus	6
Brabham	4
Alfa Romeo	2
Benetton	2
Cooper	2
Maserati	2 *
Mercedes-Benz	2 *
Tyrrell	2
BRM	1
Matra	1
Renault	1

* In 1954, Fangio drove for both Maserati and Mercedes-Benz.

WORLD CHAMPIONS

year		nat
1958	Vanwall	GB
1959	Cooper-Climax	GB
1960	Cooper-Climax	GB
1961	Ferrari	I
1962	BRM	GB
1963	Lotus-Climax	GB
1964	Ferrari	I
1965	Lotus-Climax	GB
1966	Brabham-Repco	GB/AUS
1967	Brabham-Repco	GB/AUS
1968	Lotus-Ford Cosworth	GB
1969	Matra-Ford Cosworth	F/GB
1970	Lotus-Ford Cosworth	GB
1971	Tyrrell-Ford Cosworth	GB
1972	Lotus-Ford Cosworth	GB
1973	Lotus-Ford Cosworth	GB
1974	McLaren-Ford Cosworth	GB
1975	Ferrari	I
1976	Ferrari	I
1977	Ferrari	I
1978	Lotus-Ford Cosworth	GB
1979	Ferrari	I
1980	Williams-Ford Cosworth	GB
1981	Williams-Ford Cosworth	GB
1982	Ferrari	I
1983	Ferrari	I
1984	McLaren-TAG Porsche	GB/D
1985	McLaren-TAG Porsche	GB/D
1986	Williams-Honda	GB/J
1987	Williams-Honda	GB/J
1988	McLaren-Honda	GB/J
1989	McLaren-Honda	GB/J
1990	McLaren-Honda	GB/J
1991	McLaren-Honda	GB/J
1992	Williams-Renault	GB/F
1993	Williams-Renault	GB/F
1994	Williams-Renault	GB/F
1995	Benetton-Renault	GB/F
1996	Williams-Renault	GB/F
1997	Williams-Renault	GB/F
1998	McLaren-Mercedes Benz	GB/D
1999	Ferrari	I
2000	Ferrari	I
2001	Ferrari	I
2002	Ferrari	I
2003	Ferrari	I
2004	Ferrari	I
2005	Renault	F

WINS

Ferrari	183
McLaren	148
Williams	113
Lotus	79
Brabham	35
Benetton	27
Renault	25
Tyrrell	23
BRM	17
Cooper	16
Alfa Romeo	10
Ligier	9
Maserati	9
Matra	9
Mercedes-Benz	9
Vanwall	9
Jordan	4
March	3
Wolf	3
Honda	2
Eagle	1
Hesketh	1
Penske	1
Porsche	1
Shadow	1
Stewart	1

exc Indy

Renault holds the record for the longest gap between wins, 20 years (Austria 83 to Hungary 03). However, Ligier's gap of 15 years (Canada 81 to Monaco 96) was without a break from competing.

Wins in a Season (Most)

Ferrari	15	2002,04
McLaren	15	1988
McLaren	12	1984
Williams	12	1996
Benetton	11	1995
Ferrari	10	2000
McLaren	10	1989,05*
Williams	10	1992,93

* Not Constructors' Champion.

Successive Wins (Most)

Ferrari	14	CH 52-CH 53
McLaren	11	BR-B 88
Ferrari	10	CDN-J 02
Alfa Romeo	9	GB 50-F 51
Ferrari	8	I 03-E 04
McLaren	8	GB 84-BR 85
Ferrari	7	EUR-H 04
Williams	7	CDN-I 93

Successive Seasons of Winning (Most)

McLaren	13	(1981-93)
Ferrari	12	(1994-05)
Lotus	11	(1960-70)
Williams	9	(1979-87 & 1989-97)

Win in Debut Race

Alfa Romeo	GB 50
Mercedes-Benz	F 54
Wolf	RA 77

Top Four Cars Of Same Constructor

D 52	Ferrari
GB 55	Mercedes-Benz
RA 57	Masearati
F 60	Cooper
B 61	Ferrari

(exc Indy)

In Britain 1981, the top 14 cars were of different makes.

First Win For Nationality

Italy	GB 50	Alfa Romeo
Germany	F 54	Mercedes-Benz
Great Britain	GB 57	Vanwall
Japan	MEX 65	Honda
United States	B 67	Eagle
France	NL 68	Matra
Canada	RA 77	Wolf

POLE POSITIONS

Ferrari	179
Williams	125
McLaren	122
Lotus	107
Renault	43
Brabham	39
Benetton	16
Tyrrell	14
Alfa Romeo	12
BRM	11
Cooper	11
Maserati	10
Ligier/Prost	9
Mercedes-Benz	8
Vanwall	7
March	5
Matra	4
Shadow	3
BAR	2
Jordan	2
Lancia	2
Toyota	2
Arrows	1
Honda	1
Lola	1
Porsche	1
Stewart	1
Wolf	1

exc Indy

Pole Positions in a Season (Most)

McLaren	15	1988,89
Williams	15	1992,93
Ferrari	12	2004
Lotus	12	1978
McLaren	12	1990,98
Williams	12	1987,95,96

Successive Pole Positions (Most)

Williams	24	F 92-J 93
McLaren	17	D 88-D 89
McLaren	12	B 89-MEX 90
Ferrari	10	E 51-NL 53
Lotus	10	NL 67-ZA 68

Pole Position in Debut Race

Alfa Romeo	GB 50
Lancia	E 54
Lola	NL 62
March	ZA 70
Mercedes-Benz	F 54
Tyrrell	CDN 70

FASTEST LAPS

Ferrari	185	*
Williams	128	
McLaren	126	*
Lotus	71	*
Brabham	41	*
Benetton	38	
Renault	22	
Tyrrell	20	
BRM	15	*
Maserati	15	*
Alfa Romeo	14	
Cooper	14	*
Matra	12	
Ligier/Prost	10	
Mercedes-Benz	9	*
March	7	
Vanwall	6	
Surtees	3	
Eagle	2	
Honda	2	
Jordan	2	
Shadow	2	
Wolf	2	
Ensign	1	
Hesketh	1	
Lancia	1	
Parnelli	1	
Toyota	1	
Gordini	1	*
exc Indy		

Includes shared fastest laps with another constructor.

Fastest Laps in a Season
(Most)

Ferrari	14	2004
Ferrari	12	2002
McLaren	12	2000,05
Williams	11	1986,92

Successive Fastest Laps
(Most)

Alfa Romeo	13	GB 50-E 51
Ferrari	9	CH 52-NL 53, BRN-GB 04
Ferrari	8	D 70-E 71
Ferrari	6	D-J 02
McLaren	6	RSM-F 88, F-B 99, F-I 05
Williams	6	H-AUS 93

POINTS (Most)

Gross points scored

Ferrari	4349.8
McLaren	3139.5
Williams	2507.5
Lotus	1514
Brabham	983
Benetton	887.5
Renault	719
Tyrrell	711
BRM	537.5
Cooper	484.5
Ligier/Prost	423
Maserati	313.4
Jordan	291
BAR	227
Alfa Romeo	214
Sauber	195
March	193
Matra	184
Arrows	167

Points in a Season (Gross /Most)

Ferrari	262	2004
Ferrari	221	2002
McLaren	199	1988
Renault	191	2005
McLaren	182	2005 *
Ferrari	179	2001
Williams	175	1996
Ferrari	170	2000

Not World Champion constructor.

Points in Debut Race

Alfa Romeo	GB 50
Talbot Lago	GB 50
Ferrari	MC 50
BRM	GB 51
Mercedes-Benz	F 54
March	ZA 70
Shadow	ZA 73
Wolf	RA 77
ATS	USAW 77
Sauber	ZA 93
Toyota	AUS 02
Red Bull	AUS 05

LAP LEADERS

Laps Led (Most)

	laps	km	miles
Ferrari	11,463	60,033.7	37,303.2
McLaren	8,634	40,660.5	25,265.3
Williams	7,468	34,653.8	21,532.9
Lotus	5,498	26,183.4	16,269.6
Brabham	2,722	13,239.8	8,226.8
Renault	1,894	9,197.2	5,714.9
Benetton	1,527	7,248.4	4,503.9
Tyrrell	1,493	6,737.4	4,186.4
BRM	1,347	6,099.4	3,790.0
Cooper	830	4,545.7	2,824.6
Maserati	826	4,723.0	2,934.8
Alfa Romeo	702	4,793.1	2,978.3
Matra	668	3,610.4	2,243.4
Ligier/Prost	602	2,787.7	1,732.2
Mercedes-Benz	589	3,976.4	2,470.8

Led Entire Race (Most races)

Ferrari	57	CH 52-USA 05
McLaren	55	D 76-B 05
Williams	46	GB 79-F 03
Lotus	30	D 61-B 85
Brabham	11	GB 66-DET 84
Tyrrell	8	MC 71-S 74
Mercedes-Benz	7	F 54-I 55

Four-wheel drive entries

first:
Britain 61 Ferguson P99-Climax – J Fairman/ S Moss

last:
Italy 71 Lotus 56B-Pratt & Whitney – E Fittipaldi

From Belgium in 1973, as is common practice today, teams generally held the same numbers throughout the season, with the reigning World Champion holding number 1.

The only time a Constructor had the same name as the Grand Prix, was Pacific in 1994.

The oldest car to race in the Championship was a 1935 ERA type A in Monaco 1950 (chassis number 4A).

MODELS

Grands Prix (Most)

McLaren M23	80
Lotus 72	74
Lotus 25	49

Total Race Starts (Most)

Maserati 250F	248
McLaren M23	166
Lotus 72	149

Wins (Most)

McLaren MP4/2	22
Lotus 72	20
Williams FW11	18

Pole Positions (Most)

McLaren MP4/5	27
Williams FW14	21
Lotus 49	19

Fastest Laps (Most)

Williams FW14	19
Williams FW11	18
McLaren MP4/2	16
Williams FW07	16

Points (Most)

McLaren MP4/2	329.5
McLaren M23	319
Williams FW07	300

TYRES

Wins

Goodyear	368
Bridgestone	95
Michelin	93
Dunlop	83
Firestone	49*
Pirelli	45
Continental	10
Englebert	7

* Includes 11 Firestone at the Indy 500.

Avon was the only other tyre manufacturer to compete in the World Championship, but achieved no wins.

F1 driver Eppie Wietzes drove the first ever Safety car at a Grand Prix, in Canada 1973.

Canada 1999 was the first ever Grand Prix to finish behind the safety car, due to Olivier Panis' accident.

ENGINES

Grands Prix

Ferrari	723
Ford Cosworth @	587
Renault	372
Honda	287
Alfa Romeo	222
Mercedes-Benz	212
BMW	199
BRM	189
Mugen Honda	147
Hart	128*
Matra	124
Yamaha	116*
Peugeot	115*
Maserati	109
Coventry Climax	96

@ Known as Cosworth since 2005.
* Non-winner.

The first race where all the starters were powered by turbo engines was Austria 1984 (the 400th Championship race).

The first race for a rear-engined car was Monaco 1950 (Cooper).

The last race for a front-engined car was Britain 1961 (Ferguson).

Wins

Ferrari	183
Ford Cosworth	176
Renault	105
Honda	71
Mercedes-Benz	53
Coventry Climax	40
TAG Porsche	25
BMW	19
BRM	18
Alfa Romeo	12
Maserati	11
Vanwall	9
Repco	8
Mugen Honda	4
Matra	3
Gurney Weslake	1
Porsche	1
exc Indy

The first win for a rear-engined car was Argentina 1958 (Cooper).

The last win for a front-engined car was Italy 1960 (Ferrari).

Turbo engined cars won 109 Grands Prix, from France 1979 (Renault) to Australia 1988 (McLaren).

Pole Positions

Ferrari	179
Renault	147
Ford Cosworth	139
Honda	76
Mercedes-Benz	51
Coventry Climax	44
BMW	32
Alfa Romeo	15
BRM	11
Maserati	11
Repco	7
TAG Porsche	7
Vanwall	7
Matra	4
Hart	2
Lancia	2
Toyota	2
Mugen Honda	1
Porsche	1
Supertec (Playlife)	1
exc Indy

Fastest Laps

Ferrari	185*
Ford Cosworth	159*
Renault	109
Mercedes-Benz	66
Honda	57
Coventry Climax	44*
BMW	31*
Alfa Romeo	20
TAG Porsche	18
Maserati	17*
BRM	14*
Matra	6
Vanwall	6
Repco	4
Judd	3
Hart	2
Supertec (Playlife)	2
Weslake	2
Lancia	1
Peugeot	1
Toyota	1
Gordini	1*
exc Indy

* Includes shared fastest laps with another constructor.

Drivers who have died from motor racing injuries

It is an overused phrase in journalism, that sportsmen have 'given their all'. It can be said of the drivers listed below, that they have truly given their all, in the name of motor racing, and it is in their memory that the following tables appear.

Grand Prix Drivers

DRIVER	NAT	CAR	RACE FORMULA	EVENT	PLACE
1950					
Joe Fry	GB	Freikaiserwagen	Non F1	Hill-climb	Blandford Camp, Dorset, England
Raymond Sommer	F	Cooper	Non F1	Haute Garonne Grand Prix F3 race	Cadours, nr Toulouse, France
1952					
Luigi Fagioli	I	Lancia	Non F1	Monaco sportscar Grand Prix	Monte-Carlo, Monaco
1953					
Charles de Tornaco	B	Ferrari	Non F1	Modena Grand Prix (F2)	Modena Aerautodrome, Italy
Felice Bonetto	I	Lancia	Non F1	Carrera Panamericana race	Silao, Mexico
1954					
Guy Mairesse	F	Talbot Lago	Non F1	Coupe de Paris practice	Montlhéry, nr Paris, France
Onofré Marimon	RA	Maserati	GP Practice	German Grand Prix	Nürburgring, Germany
1955					
Alberto Ascari	I	Ferrari	Non F1	Sportscar testing	Monza, Italy
Pierre Levegh	F	Mercedes-Benz	Non F1	Le Mans 24 Hours race	Le Mans, France
Don Beauman	GB	Connaught	Non F1	Leinster trophy sportscar race	Rathnew, County Wicklow, Ireland
1956					
Louis Rosier	F	Ferrari	Non F1	Coupe de Salon sportscar race	Montlhéry, nr Paris, France
1957					
Ken Wharton	GB	Ferrari	Non F1	Sportscar race	Ardmore, New Zealand
Eugenio Castellotti	I	Ferrari	GP Testing		Modena Aerautodrome, Italy
Alfonso de Portago	E	Ferrari	Non F1	Mille Miglia sports car race	between Goito and Guidizzolo, Italy
Piero Carini	I	Ferrari	Non F1	Sportscar race	St. Etienne, France
Bill Whitehouse	GB	Cooper	Non F1	Coupe de Vitesse F2 race	Reims, France
Herbert MacKay-Fraser	USA	Lotus	Non F1	Coupe de Vitesse F2 race	Reims, France
1958					
Archie Scott Brown	GB	Lister	Non F1	Sportscar race	Spa-Francorchamps, Belgium
Erwin Bauer	D	Ferrari	Non F1	1,000 km sportscar race	Nürburgring, Germany
Luigi Musso	I	Ferrari	GP Race	French Grand Prix	Reims, France
Peter Collins	GB	Ferrari	GP Race	German Grand Prix	Nürburgring, Germany
Peter Whitehead	GB	Jaguar	Non F1	Tour de France Automobile	Lasalle, nr Nîmes, France
Stuart Lewis-Evans	GB	Vanwall	GP Race	Moroccan Grand Prix	Casablanca, Morocco
1959					
Jean Behra	F	Porsche	Non F1	Berlin sportscar Grand Prix race	AVUS, Berlin, Germany
Ivor Bueb	GB	Cooper	Non F1	Auvergne Trophy F2 race	Clermont-Ferrand, France
1960					
Harry Blanchard	USA	Porsche	Non F1	1,000 km sportscar race	Buenos Aires, Argentina
Ettore Chimeri	I	Ferrari	Non F1	Sportscar practice	Havana, Cuba
Harry Schell	USA	Cooper	Other F1	International trophy practice	Silverstone, England
Chris Bristow	GB	Cooper	GP Race	Belgian Grand Prix	Spa-Francorchamps, Belgium
Alan Stacey	GB	Lotus	GP Race	Belgian Grand Prix	Spa-Francorchamps, Belgium
1961					
Giulio Cabianca	I	Cooper	Non F1	Intercontinental testing	Modena Aerautodrome, Italy
Wolfgang von Trips	D	Ferrari	GP Race	Italian Grand Prix	Monza, Italy
1962					
Peter Ryan	CDN	Lotus	Non F1	Coupe de Vitesse des Juniors race	Reims, France
Ricardo Rodriguez	MEX	Lotus	Other F1	Mexican Grand Prix practice	Mexico City, Mexico
1964					
Timmy Mayer	USA	Cooper	Non F1	Tasman Championship race practice	Longford, Tasmania, Australia
Carol de Beaufort	NL	Porsche	GP Practice	German Grand Prix	Nürburgring, Germany
1966					
Walt Hansgen	USA	Ford	Non F1	Le Mans 24 Hours testing	Le Mans, France
John Taylor	GB	Brabham	GP Race	German Grand Prix	Nürburgring, Germany
1967					
Lorenzo Bandini	I	Ferrari	GP Race	Monaco Grand Prix	Monte-Carlo, Monaco
"Geki"	I	Matra	Non F1	Italian F3 race	Caserta, nr Naples, Italy
Bob Anderson	GB	Brabham	GP Testing		Silverstone, England
Georges Berger	B	Porsche	Non F1	Endurance race	Nürburgring, Germany
Ian Raby	GB	Brabham	Non F1	Formula 2 race	Zandvoort, Netherlands

Grand Prix Drivers (continued)

DRIVER	NAT	CAR	RACE FORMULA	EVENT	PLACE
1968					
Jim Clark	GB	Lotus	Non F1	European Formula 2 race	Hockenheim, Germany
Mike Spence	GB	Lotus	Non F1	Indianapolis 500 practice	Indianapolis, USA
Ludovico Scarfiotti	I	Porsche	Non F1	Mountain climb	Rossfeld, Germany
Jo Schlesser	F	Honda	GP Race	French Grand Prix	Rouen, France
1969					
Lucien Bianchi	B	Alfa Romeo	Non F1	Le Mans 24 Hours testing	Le Mans, France
Paul Hawkins	AUS	Lola	Non F1	Tourist Trophy race	Oulton Park, England
Moises Solana	MEX	McLaren	Non F1	Hill-climb	Valle de Bravo, Mexico
Gerhard Mitter	D	BMW	GP Practice	German Grand Prix	Nürburgring, Germany
1970					
Bruce McLaren	NZ	McLaren	Non F1	Can-Am car testing	Goodwood, England
Piers Courage	GB	de Tomaso	GP Race	Dutch Grand Prix	Zandvoort, Netherlands
Jochen Rindt	A	Lotus	GP Practice	Italian Grand Prix	Monza, Italy
1971					
Ignazio Giunti	I	Ferrari	Non F1	1,000 km sportscar race	Buenos Aires, Argentina
Pedro Rodriguez	MEX	Ferrari	Non F1	Interserie sportscar race	Norisring, Germany
Jo Siffert	CH	BRM	Other F1	Rothmans Victory Race	Brands Hatch, England
1972					
Jo Bonnier	S	Lola	Non F1	Le Mans 24 Hours race	Le Mans, France
1973					
Roger Williamson	GB	March	GP Race	Dutch Grand Prix	Zandvoort, Netherlands
François Cevert	F	Tyrrell	GP Practice	USA Grand Prix	Watkins Glen, USA
Nasif Estéfano	RA	Ford	Non F1	Turismo Carretara	Aimogasta, Argentina
1974					
Peter Revson	USA	Shadow	GP Testing		Kyalami, South Africa
Silvio Moser	CH	Lola	Non F1	Monza 1,000 km sportscar race	Monza, Italy
Helmut Koinigg	A	Surtees	GP Race	USA Grand Prix	Watkins Glen, USA
1975					
Mark Donohue	USA	March	GP Practice	Austrian Grand Prix	Österreichring, Austria
1977					
Tom Pryce	GB	Shadow	GP Race	South African Grand Prix	Kyalami, South Africa
1978					
Ronnie Peterson	S	Lotus	GP Race	Italian Grand Prix	Monza, Italy
1980					
Patrick Depailler	F	Alfa Romeo	GP Testing		Hockenheim, Germany
1982					
Gilles Villeneuve	CDN	Ferrari	GP Practice	Belgian Grand Prix	Zolder, Belgium
Riccardo Paletti	I	Osella	GP Race	Canadian Grand Prix	Montréal, Canada
1983					
Rolf Stommelen	D	Porsche	Non F1	IMSA sportscar race	Riverside, California, USA
1985					
Manfred Winkelhock	D	Porsche	Non F1	Sportscar race (World Endurance)	Mosport, Ontario, Canada
Stefan Bellof	D	Porsche	Non F1	Sportscar race (World Endurance)	Spa-Francorchamps, Belgium
1986					
Elio de Angelis	I	Brabham	GP Testing		Paul Ricard, France
Jo Gartner	A	Porsche	Non F1	Le Mans 24 Hours race	Le Mans, France
1994					
Roland Ratzenberger	A	Simtek	GP Practice	San Marino Grand Prix	Imola, Italy
Ayrton Senna	BR	Williams	GP Race	San Marino Grand Prix	Imola, Italy
2001					
Michele Alboreto	I	Audi	Non F1	Sports car testing	Lausitz, Germany

Additionally the following Grand Prix non-starters died from racing injuries:

Jean Lucienbonnet at Enna, Sicily in 1962 during a Formula Junior race, Brian McGuire at Brands Hatch in 1977 during practice for a Shellsport Championship race and Dennis Taylor at Monte-Carlo in 1962 during the Grand Prix Monaco-Junior race.

Ricardo Rodriguez was the youngest World Championship driver to be killed racing, at the age of 20.

A total of 16 drivers have lost their lives in World Championship Grand Prix races, whilst a further 8 have died during practice sessions.

The Nürburgring has claimed the most lives among Grand Prix drivers with a total of seven, two more than Le Mans and Monza.

16 Grand Prix drivers have died at the wheel of a Ferrari, with Lotus and Porsche resulting in 8 driver fatalities each.

Indianapolis 500 drivers

DRIVER	NAT	EVENT	PLACE
1951			
Walt Brown	USA	Sprint car race	Williams Grove, Pennsylvania
Cecil Green	USA	Sprint car qualifying	Winchester, Indiana
Bill Mackey	USA	Sprint car qualifying	Winchester, Indiana
1952			
Johnny McDowell	USA	Championship car race	Milwaukee, Wisconsin
Jim Rigsby	USA	Sprint car race	Dayton, Ohio
Bill Schindler	USA	Sprint car race	Allentown, Pennsylvania
Joe James	USA	Championship car race	San Jose, California
1953			
Chet Miller	USA	Indianapolis 500 practice	Indianapolis, Indiana
Carl Scarborough	USA	Indianapolis 500 race	Indianapolis, Indiana
1954			
Bobby Ball	USA	Midget car race	Gardena, California
Bob Scott	USA	Championship car race	Darlington, South Carolina
1955			
Larry Crockett	USA	Sprint car race	Langhorne, Pennsylvania
Mike Nazaruk	USA	Sprint car race	Langhorne, Pennsylvania
Manny Ayulo	USA	Indianapolis 500 practice	Indianapolis, Indiana
Bill Vukovich	USA	Indianapolis 500 race	Indianapolis, Indiana
Jerry Hoyt	USA	Sprint car race	Oklahoma City, Oklahoma
Jack McGrath	USA	Championship car race on dirt track	Phoenix, Arizona
1956			
Walt Faulkner	USA	Stock car qualifying	Valleso, California
Bob Sweikert	USA	Sprint car race	Salem, Indiana
1957			
Keith Andrews	USA	Indianapolis 500 practice	Indianapolis, Indiana
1958			
Pat O'Connor	USA	Indianapolis 500 race	Indianapolis, Indiana
George Fonder	USA	Midget car race	Hartfield, Pennsylvania
Art Bisch	USA		Lakewood Speedway, Atlanta, Georgia
Jimmy Reece	USA	Championship car race	Trenton, New Jersey
1959			
Marshall Teague	USA	Championship car testing	Daytona Beach, Florida
George Amick	USA	Championship car race	Daytona Beach, Florida
Jerry Unser	USA	Indianapolis 500 practice	Indianapolis, Indiana
Ed Elisian	USA	Championship car race	Milwaukee, Wisconsin
1960			
Al Herman	USA	Midget car race	West Haven, Connecticut
Jimmy Bryan	USA	Championship car race	Langhorne, Pennsylvania
Johnny Thomson	USA	Sprint car race	Allentown, Pennsylvania
1961			
Tony Bettenhausen	USA	Indianapolis 500 practice	Indianapolis, Indiana
Al Keller	USA	Championship car race	Phoenix, Arizona
1962			
Shorty Templeman	USA	Midget car race	Marion, Ohio
1964			
Eddie Sachs	USA	Indianapolis 500 race	Indianapolis, Indiana
1966			
Jimmy Davies	USA	Midget car race	Santa Fe, Illinois
Jud Larson	USA	Sprint car race	Reading, Pennsylvania
Don Branson	USA	Ascot Park Sprint car race	Gardena, California
1988			
Cal Niday	USA	Antique Car race	Willow Springs, California

Additionally the following Indy 500 non-starter died from racing injuries: Bob Cortner at Indianapolis, USA in 1959 Indianapolis 500 qualifying.

7

ANNIVERSARIES

Left: *Alain Prost (McLaren MP4/5-Honda) winning the 1989 British Grand Prix, on his way to a third world title.* (David Hayhoe)

1 Jan 1909 Marcel Balsa born	13 Jan 1909 Helm Glöckler born	25 Jan 1906 Toni Ulmen born
1 Jan 1928 Hap Sharp born	13 Jan 1925 Ron Tauranac born	25 Jan 1910 Henri Louveau born
1 Jan 1938 Gimax born	13 Jan 1935 Mauro Forghieri born	25 Jan 1930 Heinz Schiller born
1 Jan 1945 Jacky Ickx born	13 Jan 1968 Gianni Morbidelli born	25 Jan 1956 Johnny Cecotto born
1 Jan 1951 Hans-Joachim Stuck born	13 Jan 1974 Denny Hulme last win	25 Jan 1971 Luca Badoer born
1 Jan 1951 Leo Ress born	13 Jan 1980 Alain Prost first start	25 Jan 1976 Ligier first start
1 Jan 1963 Jean-Marc Gounon born		
1 Jan 1965 Jackie Stewart first start	14 Jan 1934 Rodríguez Larreta born	26 Jan 1917 Edgar Barth born
1 Jan 1965 Last GP at East London	14 Jan 1973 Giancarlo Fisichella born	26 Jan 1945 David Purley born
1 Jan 1968 Jim Clark last start & win	14 Jan 1977 Narain Karthikeyan born	26 Jan 1975 Graham Hill last start
1 Jan 1981 Zsolt Baumgartner born	14 Jan 1994 Myron Fohr died	26 Jan 1990 Bob Gerard died
1 Jan 1981 Mauri Rose died	14 Jan 2001 Vic Wilson died	
		27 Jan 1934 George Follmer born
2 Jan 1957 Beppe Gabbiani born	15 Jan 1934 Mário Cabral born	27 Jan 1980 René Arnoux first win
2 Jan 1967 Cooper last win	15 Jan 1953 David Kennedy born	27 Jan 2002 John James died
2 Jan 1967 First GP at Kyalami	15 Jan 1978 Didier Pironi first start	
	15 Jan 1981 Graham Whitehead died	28 Jan 1926 Gene Hartley born
3 Jan 1938 Ove Anderson born		28 Jan 1926 Jimmy Bryan born
3 Jan 1969 Michael Schumacher	16 Jan 1930 Luki Botha born	28 Jan 1934 Juan Manuel Bordeu
born	16 Jan 1930 Alberto Crespo born	born
3 Jan 1988 Joie Chitwood died	16 Jan 1935 A J Foyt born	28 Jan 1977 Takuma Sato born
	16 Jan 1937 Luiz Bueno born	28 Jan 1995 Aldo Gordini died
5 Jan 1920 André Simon born	16 Jan 1952 Piercarlo Ghinzani born	
5 Jan 1938 Keith Greene born		29 Jan 1915 Johnny McDowell born
5 Jan 1978 Franck Montagny born	17 Jan 1924 John Riseley-Prichard born	29 Jan 1915 Brian Shawe-Taylor born
	17 Jan 1983 Gino Bianco died	29 Jan 1929 Jerry Hoyt born
6 Jan 1912 Louis Stanley born	17 Jan 2000 Carl Forberg died	29 Jan 1940 Kunimitsu Takahashi
6 Jan 1924 Pablo Birger born		born
6 Jan 1926 Pat Flaherty born	18 Jan 1940 Pedro Rodríguez born	29 Jan 1950 Jody Scheckter born
6 Jan 1926 Dick Rathmann born	18 Jan 1942 Johnny Servoz-Gavin born	29 Jan 1978 Arrows first start
6 Jan 1989 Jim Hurtubise died	18 Jan 1950 Gianfranco Brancatelli	29 Jan 1978 First GP at Rio de Janeiro
	born	29 Jan 1990 Spider Webb died
7 Jan 1923 Jean Lucienbonnet	18 Jan 1950 Gilles Villeneuve born	
born	18 Jan 1953 First GP at Buenos Aires	30 Jan 1917 Paul Frère born
7 Jan 1939 Brausch Niemann born	18 Jan 1971 Christian Fittipaldi born	30 Jan 1937 Bruce Johnstone born
7 Jan 1946 Mike Wilds born		30 Jan 1939 Bernard Dudot born
7 Jan 1964 Reg Parnell died	19 Jan 1914 Bob Gerard born	
7 Jan 1968 George Constantine	19 Jan 1929 Red Amick born	31 Jan 1908 Bill Cantrell born
died	19 Jan 1958 Climax engine first win	31 Jan 1930 Jo Bonnier born
7 Jan 1991 Henri Louveau died	19 Jan 1958 Cooper first win	31 Jan 1934 Tino Brambilla born
7 Jan 2002 Geoffrey Crossley died	19 Jan 1976 Tarso Marques born	31 Jan 1954 Mauro Baldi born
	19 Jan 1980 Jenson Button born	31 Jan 1960 Harry Blanchard died
8 Jan 2004 Louis Stanley died		31 Jan 1966 J J Lehto born
	20 Jan 1934 Giorgio Bassi born	
9 Jan 1960 Pascal Fabre born	20 Jan 1975 Norberto Fontana born	1 Feb 1932 Xavier Perrot born
9 Jan 1977 Wolf first start & win	20 Jan 1993 Feruccio Lamborghini died	1 Feb 1996 Ray Crawford died
	20 Jan 2004 Alan Brown died	1 Feb 2000 Dick Rathmann died
10 Jan 1918 Harry Merkel born		
10 Jan 1921 Rodger Ward born	21 Jan 1923 Jud Larson born	2 Feb 1937 Tony Shelly born
10 Jan 1944 Rory Byrne born	21 Jan 1930 John Campbell-Jones born	
10 Jan 1953 Bobby Rahal born	21 Jan 1979 Elio de Angelis first start	3 Feb 1920 Tony Gaze born
10 Jan 1958 Eddie Cheever born	21 Jan 1981 Cuth Harrison died	3 Feb 1956 Johnny Claes died
10 Jan 1971 Ignazio Giunti died		3 Feb 1957 Chico Serra born
10 Jan 1992 Roberto Bonomi died	22 Jan 1959 Mike Hawthorn died	3 Feb 1993 Paul Emery died
	22 Jan 1996 Bill Cantrell died	
11 Jan 1923 Carroll Shelby born		4 Feb 1938 Ralph Bellamy born
	23 Jan 1972 Carlos Reutemann first	4 Feb 1949 Roger Williamson born
12 Jan 1924 Olivier Gendebien	start	4 Feb 1979 Giorgio Pantano born
born	23 Jan 1996 Cliff Griffith died	4 Feb 2001 Ernie McCoy died
12 Jan 1928 Lloyd Ruby born		
12 Jan 1938 Alan Rees born	24 Jan 1918 Art Cross born	5 Feb 1922 Alain de Changy born
12 Jan 1957 Ken Wharton died	24 Jan 1925 Owen Maddock born	5 Feb 1956 Hector Rebaque born
12 Jan 1962 Emanuele Pirro born	24 Jan 1943 Tony Trimmer born	
12 Jan 1975 Fittipaldi first start	24 Jan 1954 Jo Gartner born	6 Feb 1916 Cliff Griffith born
12 Jan 1988 Piero Taruffi died	24 Jan 1983 Scott Speed born	6 Feb 1997 Roger Laurent died

Grand Prix Data Book

7 Feb 1983 Christian Klien born
7 Feb 1999 Umberto Maglioli died
7 Feb 2002 Jack Fairman died

8 Feb 1920 Mike Magill born
8 Feb 1932 Cliff Allison born
8 Feb 1969 Kurt Kuhnke died
8 Feb 1978 Hans Stuck died

9 Feb 1937 Tony Maggs born
9 Feb 1951 Ian Phillips born

10 Feb 1917 Danny Kladis born
10 Feb 1919 Eddie Johnson born
10 Feb 1923 Theo Fitzau born
10 Feb 1987 Andy Linden died

11 Feb 1934 John Surtees born
11 Feb 1959 Roberto Moreno born
11 Feb 1959 Marshall Teague died
11 Feb 1973 First GP at Interlagos
11 Feb 1995 Harry Merkel died

12 Feb 1920 Jack Turner born
12 Feb 1952 Patrick Gaillard born
12 Feb 1974 Tora Takagi born
12 Feb 1987 Dennis Poore died

13 Feb 1922 Willi Heeks born
13 Feb 1948 Jim Crawford born
13 Feb 1976 Paul Russo died
13 Feb 2005 Maurice Trintignant died

14 Feb 1913 Bayliss Levrett born
14 Feb 1942 Ricardo Rodríguez born
14 Feb 1944 Ronnie Peterson born
14 Feb 1976 Piero Scotti died
14 Feb 1988 Cal Niday died

15 Feb 1929 Graham Hill born
15 Feb 1937 Vincenzo Lancia died
15 Feb 1974 Alexander Wurz born
15 Feb 1999 Billy Garrett died
15 Feb 2004 Luigi Taramazzo died

16 Feb 1920 Tony Crook born
16 Feb 1920 Walt Faulkner born
16 Feb 1921 Jean Behra born

17 Feb 1959 Mike Coughlan born

18 Feb 1898 Enzo Ferrari born
18 Feb 1958 Giovanni Lavaggi born

19 Feb 1921 Ernie McCoy born
19 Feb 1923 Giulio Cabianca born
19 Feb 1952 Stephen South born
19 Feb 1996 Antonio Creus died

20 Feb 1934 Bobby Unser born
20 Feb 1937 Roger Penske born
20 Feb 1947 Steve Nichols born
20 Feb 1956 Criag Pollock born

21 Feb 1913 Roger Laurent born
21 Feb 1940 Peter Gethin born

22 Feb 1918 George Constantine born
22 Feb 1922 Jesús Iglesias born
22 Feb 1938 Timmy Mayer born
22 Feb 1949 Niki Lauda born

23 Feb 1928 Hans Herrmann born
23 Feb 1946 Alberto Colombo born
23 Feb 1953 Satoru Nakajima born
23 Feb 1960 Arthur Legat died
23 Feb 2001 Sergio Mantovani died

24 Feb 1936 Lance Reventlow born
24 Feb 1955 Clemente Biondetti died
24 Feb 1955 Alain Prost born
24 Feb 1968 Emanuele Naspetti born
24 Feb 1971 Pedro de la Rosa born
24 Feb 1999 Oscar González died

25 Feb 1932 Tony Brooks born
25 Feb 1944 François Cevert born
25 Feb 1946 Jean Todt born

26 Feb 1917 Robert La Caze born
26 Feb 1943 François Mazet born
26 Feb 1955 Rupert Keegan born
26 Feb 2001 Duke Nalon died
26 Feb 2003 Christian Goethals died

27 Feb 1939 Peter Revson born
27 Feb 1954 Bobby Ball died
27 Feb 1960 Ettore Chimeri died
27 Feb 1965 Pedro Chaves born

28 Feb 1908 Albert Scherrer born
28 Feb 1914 Élie Bayol born
28 Feb 1940 Mario Andretti born
28 Feb 1953 Ingo Hoffmann born
28 Feb 1964 Timmy Mayer died
28 Feb 2001 Charles Pozzi died

29 Feb 1932 Masten Gregory born

1 Mar 1969 Repco engine last start
1 Mar 1980 Osella first start
1 Mar 1980 Shadow last start
1 Mar 1984 Peter Walker died
1 Mar 1987 Wolfgang Seidel died
1 Mar 1992 Mugen Honda first start
1 Mar 1995 Jackie Holmes died

2 Mar 1913 Duke Nalon born
2 Mar 1962 Gabriele Tarquini born

3 Mar 1947 Otto Stuppacher born
3 Mar 1956 Ernst Loof died
3 Mar 1961 Perry McCarthy born
3 Mar 1973 Shadow first start
3 Mar 1978 Nicolas Kiesa born
3 Mar 1992 Lella Lombardi died
3 Mar 2002 Toyota first start

4 Mar 1911 Carl Forberg born
4 Mar 1933 Nino Vaccarella born
4 Mar 1936 Jim Clark born
4 Mar 1944 Harvey Postlethwaite born
4 Mar 1971 Satoshi Motoyama born
4 Mar 1972 Jos Verstappen born
4 Mar 1974 Bill Aston died
4 Mar 1978 Eddie Cheever first start
4 Mar 1978 Hesketh last start
4 Mar 1978 Keke Rosberg first start

5 Mar 1940 Graham McRae born
5 Mar 1975 Luciano Burti born
5 Mar 1977 BRM last start
5 Mar 1977 Tom Pryce died

6 Mar 1909 Bill Schindler born
6 Mar 1917 Oswald Karch born
6 Mar 1921 Piero Carini born
6 Mar 1931 Jimmy Stewart born
6 Mar 1940 Willie Ferguson born
6 Mar 1971 Mario Andretti first win
6 Mar 2005 Red Bull first start

7 Mar 1969 Hideki Noda born
7 Mar 1970 Jack Brabham last win
7 Mar 1970 March first start
7 Mar 1978 Rudolf Schoeller died
7 Mar 1999 BAR first start
7 Mar 1999 Eddie Irvine first win

8 Mar 1968 Michael Bartels born
8 Mar 1991 Ludwig Fischer died
8 Mar 1993 Duane Carter died

9 Mar 1937 Brian Redman born
9 Mar 1950 Danny Sullivan born
9 Mar 1951 Gary Anderson born
9 Mar 1955 Teo Fabi born
9 Mar 1963 Jorge Daponte died
9 Mar 1966 Pablo Birger died
9 Mar 1997 Prost first start
9 Mar 1997 Ralf Schumacher first start
9 Mar 1997 Stewart first start
9 Mar 1997 Jarno Tulli first start

10 Mar 1925 Giovanni de Riu born
10 Mar 1946 Hiroshi Fushida born
10 Mar 1955 Toshio Suzuki born
10 Mar 1967 Tony Vandervell died
10 Mar 1991 Mika Häkkinen first start
10 Mar 1991 Ilmor engine first start
10 Mar 1991 Jordan first start
10 Mar 1991 Last GP at Phoenix
10 Mar 1996 Giancarlo Fisichella first start
10 Mar 1996 First GP at Melbourne
10 Mar 1996 Jacques Villeneuve first start
10 Mar 2003 Ottorino Volonterio died

11 Mar 1927 Dempsey Wilson born
11 Mar 1930 Troy Ruttman born
11 Mar 1943 Arturo Merzario born
11 Mar 1953 Derek Daly born
11 Mar 1977 Rodríguez Larreta died
11 Mar 1992 Christian Vanderpleyn died

12 Mar 2000 Jaguar first start

13 Mar 1913 Joe Kelly born
13 Mar 1943 Mike Fisher born
13 Mar 1994 Gene Hartley died
13 Mar 2002 Bayliss Levrett died

14 Mar 1957 Eugenio Castellotti died
14 Mar 1993 Rubens Barrichello first start
14 Mar 1993 Last GP at Kyalami
14 Mar 1993 Sauber first start

15 Mar 1913 Jack Fairman born
15 Mar 1927 Al Herman born

16 Mar 1935 Peter de Klerk born
16 Mar 1942 Gijs van Lennep born
16 Mar 1943 Hans Heyer born

17 Mar 1932 Fred Gamble born
17 Mar 1952 Sergio Rinland born

18 Mar 1937 Mark Donohue born
18 Mar 1946 Michel Leclère born
18 Mar 1950 Larry Perkins born
18 Mar 1962 Volker Weidler born
18 Mar 1964 Alex Caffi born
18 Mar 1977 Carlos Pace died
18 Mar 1982 Theo Fitzau died
18 Mar 1982 Timo Glock born
18 Mar 2003 Karl Kling died

19 Mar 1937 Mike Pilbeam born
19 Mar 1943 Vern Schuppan born
19 Mar 1964 Nicola Larini born
19 Mar 1995 Trevor Blokdyk died

20 Mar 1955 Larry Crockett died
20 Mar 1972 Pedro Lamy born

21 Mar 1913 George Abecassis born
21 Mar 1916 Ken Wharton born
21 Mar 1921 Chico Godia born
21 Mar 1960 Ayrton Senna born
21 Mar 1982 Carlos Reutemann last start

22 Mar 1912 Leslie Johnson born
22 Mar 1974 Peter Revson died
22 Mar 1992 Last GP at Mexico City

23 Mar 1915 Arthur Owen born
23 Mar 1933 John Taylor born
23 Mar 1936 Bruce Kessler born
23 Mar 1939 Robin Herd born
23 Mar 1951 Adrian Reynard born
23 Mar 1976 Ricardo Zonta born
23 Mar 1981 Mike Hailwood died
23 Mar 2003 Kimi Räikkönen first win

24 Mar 1915 Eugène Martin born
24 Mar 1923 Brian Naylor born
24 Mar 1988 Roger Loyer died
24 Mar 2002 Bob Said died

25 Mar 1925 Don Freeland born
25 Mar 1938 Fritz d'Orey born
25 Mar 1984 Philippe Alliot first start
25 Mar 1984 Martin Brundle first start
25 Mar 1995 John Hugenholtz died
25 Mar 1984 Ayrton Senna first start
25 Mar 1984 TAG Porsche engine first win

26 Mar 1941 Lella Lombardi born
26 Mar 1952 Didier Pironi born
26 Mar 1958 Elio de Angelis born
26 Mar 1964 Martin Donnelly born
26 Mar 1966 Nick Wirth born
26 Mar 1989 Johnny Herbert first start
26 Mar 1989 Lamborghini engine first start
26 Mar 1989 Last GP at Rio de Janeiro
26 Mar 1989 Yamaha engine first start

27 Mar 1934 Giampaolo Pavanello born
27 Mar 1965 Gregor Foitek born
27 Mar 1971 David Coulthard born
27 Mar 1983 John Watson last win
27 Mar 1983 Last GP at Long Beach
27 Mar 1994 Heinz-Harald Frentzen first start
27 Mar 1994 Olivier Panis first start
27 Mar 1994 Peugeot engine first start

28 Mar 1911 Consalvo Sanesi born
28 Mar 1929 Paul England born
28 Mar 1935 Hubert Hahne born
28 Mar 1952 Tony Brise born
28 Mar 1976 First GP at Long Beach

29 Mar 1891 Alfred Neubauer born
29 Mar 1900 Bill Aston born
29 Mar 1961 Gary Brabham born
29 Mar 1974 Marc Gené born
29 Mar 1981 David Prophet died
29 Mar 2001 George Connor died

30 Mar 1907 Rudolf Krause born
30 Mar 1910 Peter Hirt born
30 Mar 1941 André De Cortanze born
30 Mar 1948 Eddie Jordan born
30 Mar 1961 Mike Thackwell born
30 Mar 1969 Lucien Bianchi died
30 Mar 1973 Yves Giraud-Cabantous died
30 Mar 1974 Carlos Reutemann first win
30 Mar 1974 Hesketh first start
30 Mar 1980 Nelson Piquet first win
30 Mar 1980 Clay Regazzoni last start

31 Mar 1956 Kevin Cogan born

1 Apr 1909 Bill Whitehouse born
1 Apr 1950 Loris Kessel born
1 Apr 1971 Shinji Nakano born

2 Apr 1926 Jack Brabham born
2 Apr 1928 Gino Munaron born
2 Apr 1940 Mike Hailwood born
2 Apr 1963 Fabrizio Barbazza born
2 Apr 1963 Mike Gascoyne born

3 Apr 1923 Chuck Weyant born
3 Apr 1950 Frank Dernie born
3 Apr 1985 Helmut Niedermayr died
3 Apr 1988 Judd engine first start

4 Apr 1924 Bob Christie born
4 Apr 1928 Bud Tingelstad born
4 Apr 1940 Dickie Attwood born
4 Apr 1958 Christian Danner born
4 Apr 1959 George Amick died
4 Apr 1966 Jimmy Daywalt died
4 Apr 1980 Björn Wirdheim born
4 Apr 2004 First GP at Sakhir, Bahrain

5 Apr 1922 Andy Linden born
5 Apr 1922 Alfonso Thiele born
5 Apr 1936 Ronnie Bucknum born
5 Apr 1973 David Murray died

6 Apr 1909 Hermann Lang born
6 Apr 2003 Giancarlo Fisichella first win

7 Apr 1966 Walt Hansgen died
7 Apr 1968 Jim Clark died
7 Apr 1982 Harald Ertl died
7 Apr 1985 Pierluigi Martini first start
7 Apr 1985 Minardi first start
7 Apr 2005 Cliff Allison died

8 Apr 1966 Mark Blundell born

9 Apr 1921 Jean-Marie Balestre born
9 Apr 1922 Johnny Thomson born
9 Apr 1942 John Judd born
9 Apr 1971 Jacques Villeneuve born
9 Apr 2002 Pat Flaherty died

10 Apr 1913 Duke Dinsmore born
10 Apr 1914 Paul Russo born
10 Apr 1929 Mike Hawthorn born
10 Apr 1934 Carel Godin de Beaufort born

11 Apr 1920 Al Keller born
11 Apr 1926 Pete Lovely born
11 Apr 1987 Rudolf Krause died
11 Apr 1993 GP at Donington Park

12 Apr 1907 Eugène Chaboud born
12 Apr 1917 Robert Manzon born
12 Apr 1942 Carlos Reutemann born
12 Apr 1950 Flavio Briatore born
12 Apr 1961 Corrado Fabi born
12 Apr 1962 Ron Flockhart died
12 Apr 1998 Last GP at Buenos Aires

13 Apr 1926 André Testut born
13 Apr 1931 Dan Gurney born
13 Apr 1940 Mike Beuttler born
13 Apr 1940 Max Mosley born
13 Apr 1949 Ricardo Zunino born
13 Apr 1986 First GP at Jerez
13 Apr 1999 Harvey Postlethwaite
died
13 Apr 2000 Arthur Owen died
13 Apr 2002 Desmond Titterington
died

14 Apr 1912 Joie Chitwood born
14 Apr 1931 Vic Wilson born

15 Apr 1922 Graham Whitehead born
15 Apr 1923 Ernesto Prinoth born
15 Apr 1947 Dave Wass born
15 Apr 1957 Chris Murphy born
15 Apr 1973 Ernst Klodwig died
15 Apr 2001 Ralf Schumacher first win
15 Apr 2005 Art Cross died

16 Apr 1918 Dick Gibson born
16 Apr 1942 Frank Williams born
16 Apr 1979 Christijan Albers born
16 Apr 1988 José Dolhem died

17 Apr 1934 Brian Gubby born
17 Apr 1954 Riccardo Patrese born
17 Apr 1994 First GP at Aida

18 Apr 1942 Jochen Rindt born
18 Apr 1971 Tyrrell first win
18 Apr 1979 Anthony Davidson born
18 Apr 1990 Bob Drake died

19 Apr 1912 Rudi Fischer born
19 Apr 1939 Basil van Rooyen born
19 Apr 1940 Kurt Ahrens born
19 Apr 1944 Jac Nelleman born
19 Apr 1970 March first win
19 Apr 1971 Luigi Piotti died

20 Apr 1927 Phil Hill born
20 Apr 1930 Stuart Lewis-Evans born
20 Apr 1961 Paolo Barilla born
20 Apr 1963 Mauricio Gugelmin born

21 Apr 1985 Ayrton Senna first win

22 Apr 1956 Walt Faulkner died
22 Apr 1978 Esteban Tuero born

23 Apr 1961 Pierluigi Martini born
23 Apr 1963 Paul Belmondo born
23 Apr 1971 Dempsey Wilson died
23 Apr 1992 Ronnie Bucknum died

24 Apr 1933 Billy Garrett born
24 Apr 1934 Mike Taylor born
24 Apr 1941 Silvio Moser born
24 Apr 1954 Guy Mairesse died
24 Apr 1983 Rolf Stommelen died
24 Apr 2001 Josef Peters died

25 Apr 1917 Jean Lucas born
25 Apr 1981 Felipe Massa born
25 Apr 1982 Gilles Villeneuve last start
25 Apr 2001 Michele Alboreto died
25 Apr 2005 John Love died

26 Apr 1921 François Picard born
26 Apr 1937 Jean-Pierre Beltoise born
26 Apr 1937 Gus Hutchison born
26 Apr 1943 Tom Jones born
26 Apr 1944 José Dolhem born
26 Apr 1958 Johnny Dumfries born
26 Apr 1995 Willi Krakau died

27 Apr 1902 Rudolf Schoeller born
27 Apr 1933 Bob Bondurant born
27 Apr 1943 Helmut Marko born
27 Apr 1973 Carlos Menditéguy died
27 Apr 1975 Alan Jones first start
27 Apr 1975 Last GP at Montjuïc
27 Apr 1997 Heinz-Harald Frentzen first
win

28 Apr 1973 Piero Drogo died
28 Apr 1974 Niki Lauda first win
28 Apr 1978 Theo Helfrich died
28 Apr 1996 Jacques Villeneuve first
win

29 Apr 1916 Cal Niday born
29 Apr 1971 Sam Michael born
29 Apr 1984 Last GP at Zolder
29 Apr 1996 François Picard died
29 Apr 2002 Rob Walker died

30 Apr 1910 Kurt Kuhnke born
30 Apr 1920 Duncan Hamilton born
30 Apr 1946 Hughes de Chaunac born
30 Apr 1994 Roland Ratzenberger died

1 May 1928 Desmond Titterington
born
1 May 1951 Geoff Lees born
1 May 1955 Mike Nazaruk died
1 May 1994 Ayrton Senna last start
(died)
1 May 1999 Brian Shawe-Taylor died

2 May 2001 Bill Homeier died

3 May 1924 Ken Tyrrell born
3 May 1949 Boy Hayje born
3 May 1981 Michele Alboreto first start
3 May 2004 Ken Downing died

4 May 1928 Wolfgang von Trips born
4 May 1946 John Barnard born
4 May 1946 John Watson born
4 May 1969 First GP at Montjuïc

5 May 1913 Duane Carter born
5 May 1932 Bob Said born
5 May 1932 Luigi Taramazzo born
5 May 1985 Mot. Moderni engine first
start

6 May 1919 André Guelfi born
6 May 1958 Tommy Byrne born
6 May 1964 Andrea Chiesa born

7 May 1967 Denny Hulme first win
7 May 1968 Mike Spence died

8 May 1975 Gastón Mazzacane born
8 May 1982 Gilles Villeneuve died

9 May 1947 Andy Sutcliffe born

10 May 1914 John James born
10 May 1959 Jack Brabham first win
10 May 1963 Franco Comotti died
10 May 1967 Lorenzo Bandini died
10 May 1970 Bruce McLaren last start
10 May 1970 Ronnie Peterson first start
10 May 1977 Nick Heidfeld born
10 May 1985 Toni Branca died
10 May 1998 Cesare Perdisa died

11 May 1921 Geoffrey Crossley born
11 May 1926 Rob Schroeder born
11 May 1986 Elio de Angelis last start
11 May 1992 Hap Sharp died

12 May 1922 Roy Salvadori born
12 May 1946 Patrick Faure born
12 May 1957 Alfonso de Portago died
12 May 1961 Tony Bettenhausen died
12 May 1963 Stefano Modena born
12 May 1968 First GP at Járama
12 May 1974 Last GP at Nivelles-Baulers

13 May 1913 Theo Helfrich born
13 May 1927 Archie Scott Brown born
13 May 1934 Paddy Driver born
13 May 1950 First World Championship
GP
13 May 1950 Alfa Romeo first start & win
13 May 1950 Alfa Romeo engine first
start & win
13 May 1950 Juan Manuel Fangio first
start
13 May 1950 Giuseppe Farina first start
& win
13 May 1950 Maserati first start
13 May 1960 Harry Schell died
13 May 1994 Duncan Hamilton died

14 May 1972 BRM last win
14 May 1995 Nigel Mansell last start

15 May 1929 Peter Broeker born
15 May 1943 Alan Rollinson born
15 May 1953 Chet Miller died
15 May 1957 Keith Andrews died
15 May 1959 Luis Sala born
15 May 1986 Elio de Angelis died
15 May 1991 Fritz Riess died

16 May 1909 Luigi Villoresi born
16 May 1955 Manny Ayulo died
16 May 1995 Red Amick died

17 May 1948 Mikko Kozarowitsky born
17 May 1959 Jerry Unser died
17 May 1981 Carlos Reutemann last win

18 May 1914 Emmanuel de Graffenried born
18 May 1928 Jo Schlesser born
18 May 1931 Bruce Halford born
18 May 1952 Peter Collins first start
18 May 1958 Graham Hill first start
18 May 1958 Lotus first start
18 May 1967 Heinz-Harald Frentzen born
18 May 1969 Cooper last start
18 May 1969 Graham Hill last win
18 May 2003 Last GP at A1-Ring

19 May 1928 Colin Chapman born
19 May 1931 Bob Anderson born
19 May 1957 Climax engine first start
19 May 1958 Archie Scott Brown died
19 May 1996 Olivier Panis first win
19 May 1996 Ligier last win
19 May 1996 Mugen Honda first win
19 May 1997 Troy Ruttman died

20 May 1921 Aldo Gordini born
20 May 1926 Bob Sweikert born
20 May 1962 Graham Hill first win
20 May 1962 Lola first start
20 May 1965 Edgar Barth died
20 May 1973 First GP at Zolder
20 May 1975 Ralph Firman born
20 May 1984 Bill Holland died
20 May 1984 Last GP at Dijon-Prenois

21 May 1942 Danny Ongais born
21 May 1944 Emilio Zapico born
21 May 1950 Alberto Ascari first start
21 May 1950 Cooper first start
21 May 1950 Juan Manuel Fangio first win
21 May 1950 Ferrari first start
21 May 1978 René Arnoux first start
21 May 2001 Gabriele Rumi died
21 May 2003 Alejandro de Tomaso died

22 May 1921 Marshall Teague born
22 May 1929 Sergio Mantovani born
22 May 1955 Alberto Ascari last start
22 May 1966 McLaren first start
22 May 1966 Repco engine first start
22 May 1970 Pedro Diniz born
22 May 1977 Riccardo Patrese first start
22 May 1983 Thierry Boutsen first start
22 May 1983 First GP at new Spa

23 May 1903 Ernst Klodwig born
23 May 1925 Joe James born
23 May 1940 Gérard Larrousse born
23 May 1958 Tony Purnell born
23 May 1972 Rubens Barrichello born
23 May 1982 Riccardo Patrese first win
23 May 2004 Jarno Trulli first win

24 May 1953 Lamberto Leoni born
24 May 1963 Ivan Capelli born
24 May 1964 Porsche last start
24 May 1990 Dries van der Lof died

25 May 1939 Mike Harris born
25 May 1940 Tony Southgate born
25 May 1995 Élie Bayol died

26 May 1906 Mauri Rose born
26 May 1938 Peter Westbury born
26 May 1939 Cesare Fiorio born
26 May 1944 Sam Posey born
26 May 1955 Alberto Ascari died
26 May 1955 Paul Stoddart born
26 May 1968 Matra engine first start
26 May 1969 Paul Hawkins died
26 May 1974 Silvio Moser died
26 May 2001 Vittorio Brambilla died

27 May 1942 Piers Courage born
27 May 1942 Robin Widdows born
27 May 1951 Stirling Moss first start
27 May 1961 Pierre-Henri Raphanel born
27 May 1979 James Hunt last start

28 May 1927 Eddie Sachs born
28 May 1938 Eppie Wietzes born

29 May 1949 Bob Tyrrell born
29 May 1960 Lotus first win
29 May 1960 John Surtees first start
29 May 1963 Ukyo Katayama born
29 May 1994 David Coulthard first start

30 May 1926 Chuck Arnold born
30 May 1939 Dieter Quester born
30 May 1953 Carl Scarborough died
30 May 1955 Bill Vukovich died
30 May 1957 Piero Carini died
30 May 1958 Pat O'Connor died
30 May 1964 Andrea Montermini born
30 May 1964 Eddie Sachs died
30 May 1965 Denny Hulme first start
30 May 1976 Elmer George died
30 May 1981 Gianmaria Bruni born

31 May 1942 Jo Vonlanthen born
31 May 1959 BRM first win
31 May 1959 Andrea de Cesaris born

1 Jun 1947 Ron Dennis born
1 Jun 1959 Martin Brundle born
1 Jun 1986 Jo Gartner died

2 Jun 1920 Don Branson born
2 Jun 1956 Jan Lammers born
2 Jun 1962 Dennis Taylor died
2 Jun 1970 Bruce McLaren died
2 Jun 1986 Johnnie Tolan died
2 Jun 1991 Nelson Piquet last win

3 Jun 1952 David Richards born
3 Jun 1958 Erwin Bauer died
3 Jun 1973 James Hunt first start

4 Jun 1921 Ettore Chimeri born
4 Jun 1950 First GP at Bremgarten
4 Jun 1967 Ford Cosworth DFV engine first start & win
4 Jun 1972 First GP at Nivelles-Baulers
4 Jun 1989 First GP at Phoenix

5 Jun 1908 Franco Rol born
5 Jun 1923 Jorge Daponte born
5 Jun 1928 Umberto Maglioli born
5 Jun 1946 Patrick Head born
5 Jun 1955 Giuseppe Farina last start
5 Jun 1961 Aldo Costa born
5 Jun 1983 Tyrrell last win

6 Jun 1923 Ivor Bueb born
6 Jun 1923 Jim Rigsby born
6 Jun 1951 Noritake Takahara born
6 Jun 1960 Jim Clark first start
6 Jun 1982 First GP at Detroit
6 Jun 1997 Eitel Cantoni died

7 Jun 1927 Charles de Tornaco born
7 Jun 1970 Last GP at old Spa
7 Jun 1989 Chico Landi died

8 Jun 1952 Johnny McDowell died
8 Jun 1959 Leslie Johnson died
8 Jun 1968 Lodovico Scarfiotti died

9 Jun 1898 Luigi Fagioli born
9 Jun 1903 Felice Bonetto born
9 Jun 1939 David Hobbs born
9 Jun 1968 McLaren first win
9 Jun 1968 Bruce McLaren last win
9 Jun 1974 Jody Scheckter first win

10 Jun 1935 Vic Elford born
10 Jun 1940 Peter Ryan born
10 Jun 1941 Dave Walker born

11 Jun 1939 Jackie Stewart born
11 Jun 1947 Bob Evans born
11 Jun 1949 Tom Pryce born
11 Jun 1953 Pat Symonds born
11 Jun 1955 Pierre Levegh died
11 Jun 1964 Jean Alesi born
11 Jun 1966 Jimmy Davies died
11 Jun 1966 Jud Larson died
11 Jun 1972 Jo Bonnier died
11 Jun 1995 Jean Alesi first win

12 Jun 1916 Phil Cade born
12 Jun 1921 Dennis Taylor born
12 Jun 1927 Bill Cheesbourg born
12 Jun 1930 Innes Ireland born
12 Jun 1948 Hans Binder born
12 Jun 1954 Neil Oatley born
12 Jun 1966 Eagle first start
12 Jun 1994 Ilmor engine last start

13 Jun 1966 Naoki Hattori born
13 Jun 1982 BMW engine first win
13 Jun 1982 Riccardo Paletti died

14 Jun 1913 Henry Banks born
14 Jun 1943 John Miles born
14 Jun 1958 George Fonder died
14 Jun 1995 Bobby Grim died

15 Jun 1916 Gene Force born
15 Jun 1920 Keith Andrews born
15 Jun 1958 Riccardo Paletti born
15 Jun 1961 Giulio Cabianca died
15 Jun 1993 James Hunt died

16 Jun 1923 Ron Flockhart born
16 Jun 1930 Mike Sparken born
16 Jun 1998 Fred Wacker died

17 Jun 1912 Myron Fohr born
17 Jun 1956 Bob Sweikert died
17 Jun 1960 Adrian Campos born
17 Jun 1962 Jim Clark first win
17 Jun 1962 Jo Siffert first start
17 Jun 1973 First GP at Anderstorp
17 Jun 1978 Last GP at Anderstorp

18 Jun 1936 Denny Hulme born
18 Jun 1960 Al Herman died
18 Jun 1967 Eagle first win
18 Jun 1967 Geki died
18 Jun 1967 Dan Gurney last win
18 Jun 1967 Weslake engine win
18 Jun 1977 Franco Rol died

19 Jun 1960 Chris Bristow died
19 Jun 1960 Jimmy Bryan died
19 Jun 1960 Alan Stacey died
19 Jun 1977 Jacques Laffite first win
19 Jun 1977 Ligier first win
19 Jun 1977 Matra engine first win
19 Jun 1988 Last GP at Detroit

20 Jun 1911 Paul Pietsch born
20 Jun 1952 Luigi Fagioli died
20 Jun 1953 Willy Rampf born

21 Jun 1970 Piers Courage died
21 Jun 1970 Clay Regazzoni first start
21 Jun 1981 Last GP at Járama
21 Jun 1981 Gilles Villeneuve last win
21 Jun 1987 Lotus last win

22 Jun 1917 George Fonder born
22 Jun 1952 Mike Hawthorn first start
22 Jun 1975 Hesketh first win
22 Jun 1975 James Hunt first win
22 Jun 1979 Louis Chiron died
22 Jun 1999 Guy Tunmer died

23 Jun 1899 Amédée Gordini born
23 Jun 1915 R Montgomerie-
         Charrington born
23 Jun 1916 Leslie Thorne born
23 Jun 1927 Herbert MacKay-Fraser
         born
23 Jun 1933 John Cannon born
23 Jun 1933 Renato Pirocchi born
23 Jun 1968 Matra car first win

24 Jun 1911 Juan Manuel Fangio born
24 Jun 1934 Tom Bridger born

25 Jun 1932 Tim Parnell born
25 Jun 1949 Patrick Tambay born
25 Jun 1964 Johnny Herbert born

26 Jun 1929 Rodney Nuckey born
26 Jun 1935 Carlo Facetti born
26 Jun 1955 Philippe Streiff born

27 Jun 1942 Chris Irwin born
27 Jun 1965 First GP at Clermont-Ferrand
27 Jun 1985 Nico Rosberg born
27 Jun 1994 Sam Hanks died
27 Jun 1997 Ken Richardson died

28 Jun 1923 Adolfo Schwelm Cruz born
28 Jun 1960 Juan Jover died
28 Jun 1964 Brabham first win
28 Jun 1992 Peter Hirt died

29 Jun 1921 Harry Schell born
29 Jun 1956 Nick Fry born
29 Jun 2000 Rodney Nuckey died

30 Jun 1929 Harry Blanchard born
30 Jun 1966 Giuseppe Farina died
30 Jun 1974 Eddie Johnson died
30 Jun 1975 Ralf Schumacher born

1 Jul 1947 Kazuyoshi Hoshino born
1 Jul 1958 Keith Wiggins born
1 Jul 1973 Ensign first start
1 Jul 1973 Ronnie Peterson first win
1 Jul 1979 Renault first win (first
         turbo win)

2 Jul 1911 Reg Parnell born
2 Jul 1950 First GP at Reims
2 Jul 1952 Beppe Lucchini born
2 Jul 1962 Peter Ryan died
2 Jul 1967 GP at Bugatti au Mans
2 Jul 1972 Last GP at Clermont-Ferrand
2 Jul 1972 Patrick Depailler first start
2 Jul 1978 Matteo Bobbi born
2 Jul 1985 David Purley died

3 Jul 1914 Carl Scarborough born
3 Jul 1960 Vanwall last start
3 Jul 1966 Last GP at Reims
3 Jul 1966 Repco engine first win

4 Jul 1907 Ernst Loof born
4 Jul 1918 Johnnie Parsons born
4 Jul 1926 Wolfgang Seidel born
4 Jul 1927 Jim McWithey born
4 Jul 1938 Ernie Pieterse born
4 Jul 1948 René Arnoux born
4 Jul 1954 Mercedes-Benz first start
         & win
4 Jul 1958 Art Bisch died
4 Jul 1960 Roland Ratzenberger born
4 Jul 1971 First GP at Paul Ricard
4 Jul 1973 Jan Magnussen born

5 Jul 1928 Elmer George born
5 Jul 1953 Mike Hawthorn first win
5 Jul 1954 Bob Scott died
5 Jul 1959 Dan Gurney first start
5 Jul 1981 Alain Prost first win
5 Jul 1986 Albert Scherrer died
5 Jul 2000 Dorino Serafini died
5 Jul 2004 Rodger Ward died

6 Jul 1906 Cuth Harrison born
6 Jul 1930 Ian Burgess born
6 Jul 1952 First GP at Rouen-les-Essarts
6 Jul 1958 Juan Manuel Fangio last
         start
6 Jul 1958 Mike Hawthorn last win
6 Jul 1958 Phil Hill first start
6 Jul 1958 Luigi Musso died

7 Jul 1936 Jo Siffert born
7 Jul 1942 Jean-Claude Rudaz born
7 Jul 1959 Alessandro Nannini born
7 Jul 1968 Jacky Ickx first win
7 Jul 1968 Last GP at Rouen-les-Essarts
7 Jul 1968 Jo Schlesser died
7 Jul 1974 First GP at Dijon-Prenois
7 Jul 1985 Brabham last win
7 Jul 1991 First GP at Magny-Cours

8 Jul 1962 Dan Gurney first win
8 Jul 1962 Porsche first win
8 Jul 1984 GP at Dallas
8 Jul 1990 Last GP at Paul Ricard
8 Jul 1993 John Riseley-Prichard died

9 Jul 1955 Don Beauman died
9 Jul 1982 Sakon Yamamoto born
9 Jul 1989 Jean Alesi first start

10 Jul 1918 Fred Wacker born
10 Jul 1926 Tony Settember born
10 Jul 1928 Alejandro de Tomaso
         born
10 Jul 1940 Guido Forti born
10 Jul 1946 Jean-Pierre Jarier born
10 Jul 1955 Jerry Hoyt died

11 Jul 1922 Fritz Riess born
11 Jul 1924 Alberto Uría born
11 Jul 1941 Clive Puzey born
11 Jul 1943 Rolf Stommelen born
11 Jul 1964 First GP at Brands Hatch
11 Jul 1971 Pedro Rodríguez died
11 Jul 2005 Jesús Iglesias died

12 Jul 1930 Guy Ligier born
12 Jul 1992 Damon Hill first start

13 Jul 1914 Sam Hanks born
13 Jul 1918 Alberto Ascari born
13 Jul 1957 Thierry Boutsen born
13 Jul 1974 Jarno Trulli born
13 Jul 1980 Patrick Depailler last start
13 Jul 1986 Last GP at Brands Hatch
13 Jul 1986 Jacques Laffite last start
13 Jul 1993 Leslie Thorne died

14 Jul	1907	Chico Landi born	
14 Jul	1951	BRM first start	
14 Jul	1951	Ferrari first win	
14 Jul	1956	Tony Brooks first start	
14 Jul	1957	Herbert MacKay-Fraser died	
14 Jul	1957	Bill Whitehouse died	
14 Jul	1973	Jochen Mass first start	
14 Jul	1973	John Watson first start	
14 Jul	1979	Clay Regazzoni last win	
14 Jul	1979	Williams first win	
15 Jul	1914	B Bira born	
15 Jul	1929	Ian Stewart born	
15 Jul	1972	Williams (Politoys) first start	
16 Jul	1928	Jim Rathmann born	
16 Jul	1955	First GP at Aintree	
16 Jul	1955	Jack Brabham first start	
16 Jul	1955	Stirling Moss first win	
16 Jul	1975	Bas Leinders born	
16 Jul	1977	Patrick Tambay first start	
16 Jul	1977	Gilles Villeneuve first start	
16 Jul	1977	Renault first start (first turbo start)	
16 Jul	1995	Johnny Herbert first win	
17 Jul	1912	Erwin Bauer born	
17 Jul	1923	John Cooper born	
17 Jul	1954	Vanwall first start	
17 Jul	1995	Juan Manuel Fangio died	
18 Jul	1920	Eric Brandon born	
18 Jul	1970	Emerson Fittipaldi first start	
18 Jul	1970	Dan Gurney last start	
18 Jul	1970	Surtees first start	
19 Jul	1902	Chet Miller born	
19 Jul	1975	Emerson Fittipaldi last win	
20 Jul	1931	Tony Marsh born	
20 Jul	1943	Chris Amon born	
20 Jul	1957	Tony Brooks first win	
20 Jul	1957	Vanwall first win	
20 Jul	1960	Claudio Langes born	
20 Jul	1962	Giovanna Amati born	
20 Jul	1964	Bernd Schneider born	
20 Jul	1976	Alex Yoong born	
21 Jul	1962	Last GP at Aintree	
21 Jul	2002	Michael Schumacher clinched fifth Championship	
22 Jul	1909	Dorino Serafini born	
22 Jul	1916	Gino Bianco born	
22 Jul	1929	John Barber born	
23 Jul	1935	John Cordts born	
23 Jul	1935	Jim Hall born	
23 Jul	1947	Torsten Palm born	

24 Jul	1906	Franco Comotti born	
24 Jul	1947	Alan Jenkins born	
24 Jul	1972	Lance Reventlow died	
24 Jul	1976	Tiago Monteiro born	
25 Jul	1905	Georges Grignard born	
25 Jul	1910	Jimmy Jackson born	
25 Jul	1911	Len Duncan born	
25 Jul	1936	Gerry Ashmore born	
25 Jul	1982	Jochen Mass last start	
25 Jul	1982	Didier Pironi last start	
25 Jul	1990	Alfredo Pián died	
25 Jul	1993	Alain Prost last win	
26 Jul	1928	Don Beauman born	
26 Jul	1942	Teddy Pilette born	
26 Jul	1946	Emilio de Villota born	
26 Jul	1990	Giorgio Scarlatti died	
27 Jul	1933	Chris Lawrence born	
27 Jul	1943	Max Jean born	
27 Jul	1954	Philippe Alliot born	
27 Jul	1968	Ricardo Rosset born	
27 Jul	1969	Moisés Solana died	
27 Jul	1997	Benetton last win	
27 Jul	1997	Gerhard Berger last win	
28 Jul	1922	Jacques Pollet born	
28 Jul	1924	Luigi Musso born	
28 Jul	1927	Heini Walter born	
28 Jul	1935	Massimo Natili born	
28 Jul	1961	Yannick Dalmas born	
28 Jul	1998	Consalvo Sanesi died	
28 Jul	2002	Arrows last start	
29 Jul	1933	Colin Davis born	
29 Jul	1950	Joe Fry died	
29 Jul	1951	Alberto Ascari first win	
29 Jul	1951	Walt Brown died	
29 Jul	1951	Cecil Green died	
29 Jul	1951	Bill Mackey died	
29 Jul	1963	Chanoch Nissany born	
29 Jul	1973	Roger Williamson died	
29 Jul	1981	Fernando Alonso born	
29 Jul	2002	Renato Pirocchi died	
30 Jul	1940	Giacomo Caliri born	
30 Jul	1972	Jacky Ickx last win	
30 Jul	1978	Nelson Piquet first start	
30 Jul	1981	Bud Tingelstad died	
30 Jul	1991	Tom Bridger died	
30 Jul	1995	Pierluigi Martini last start	
30 Jul	2000	Rubens Barrichello first win	
31 Jul	1954	Onofré Marimón died	
31 Jul	1978	Justin Wilson born	
1 Aug	1899	Raymond Mays born	
1 Aug	1959	Jean Behra died	
1 Aug	1959	Ivor Bueb died	
1 Aug	1961	Allen Berg born	
1 Aug	1965	Jim Clark clinched last Championship	

1 Aug	1965	Climax engine last win	
1 Aug	1969	Gerhard Mitter died	
1 Aug	1976	Last GP at old Nürburgring	
1 Aug	1980	Patrick Depailler died	
1 Aug	1998	Len Duncan died	
1 Aug	2001	Jay Chamberlain died	
2 Aug	1953	Giuseppe Farina last win	
2 Aug	1959	GP at AVUS	
2 Aug	1959	Tony Brooks last win	
2 Aug	1964	Honda first start	
2 Aug	1970	First GP at Hockenheim	
2 Aug	1970	Jochen Rindt last win	
3 Aug	1899	Louis Chiron born	
3 Aug	1952	Alberto Ascari clinched first Championship	
3 Aug	1952	BMW engine first start	
3 Aug	1958	Peter Collins last start (died)	
3 Aug	1958	Bruce McLaren first start	
3 Aug	1964	Carel Godin de Beaufort died	
4 Aug	1917	John Fitch born	
4 Aug	1928	Christian Goethals born	
4 Aug	1957	Juan Manuel Fangio last win (& clinched last Championship)	
4 Aug	1957	Maserati last win	
4 Aug	1957	Porsche first start	
4 Aug	1963	John Surtees first win	
4 Aug	1974	Jacques Laffite first start	
4 Aug	1985	Michele Alboreto last win	
5 Aug	1907	Roger Loyer born	
5 Aug	1930	Richie Ginther born	
5 Aug	1943	Leo Kinnunen born	
5 Aug	1962	Brabham first start	
5 Aug	1973	Jackie Stewart last win	
5 Aug	1991	Soichiro Honda died	
5 Aug	1994	Alain de Changy died	
6 Aug	1941	Michel Têtu born	
6 Aug	1961	Stirling Moss last win	
6 Aug	1980	Vitantonio Liuzzi born	
6 Aug	1996	Emilio Zapico died	
6 Aug	2002	Jim Crawford died	
7 Aug	1944	Dave Morgan born	
7 Aug	1966	Ford Cosworth (F2) engine first start	
7 Aug	1966	Jacky Ickx first start	
7 Aug	1966	Matra car first start	
8 Aug	1926	Piero Drogo born	
8 Aug	1949	Ricardo Londono born	
8 Aug	1953	Nigel Mansell born	
8 Aug	1982	Eric Brandon died	
8 Aug	1989	Brian Naylor died	
9 Aug	1925	Len Sutton born	
9 Aug	1944	Patrick Depailler born	

10 Aug 1910 Guy Mairesse born
10 Aug 1915 Carlos Menditéguy
born
10 Aug 1928 Gerino Gerini born
10 Aug 1986 First GP at
Hungaroring

11 Aug 1916 Johnny Claes born
11 Aug 1984 Marcel Balsa died

12 Aug 1919 Shorty Templeman born
12 Aug 1933 Parnelli Jones born
12 Aug 1985 Manfred Winkelhock died

13 Aug 1944 Divina Galica born
13 Aug 1978 Ronnie Peterson last win
13 Aug 1996 Willi Heeks died
13 Aug 2001 Otto Stuppacher died

14 Aug 1917 Rob Walker born
14 Aug 1922 Leslie Marr born
14 Aug 1942 Jackie Oliver born
14 Aug 1960 Jack Brabham clinched
second Championship
14 Aug 1960 Last GP at Porto
14 Aug 1967 Bob Anderson died
14 Aug 1977 Alan Jones first win
14 Aug 1977 Shadow first win
14 Aug 1988 Enzo Ferrari died
14 Aug 1991 Alberto Crespo died

15 Aug 1948 George Ryton born
15 Aug 1971 Niki Lauda first start
15 Aug 1971 Jackie Stewart clinched
second Championship
15 Aug 1976 Penske first win
15 Aug 1976 John Watson first win
15 Aug 1993 Damon Hill first win

16 Aug 1908 George Connor born
16 Aug 1970 First GP at Österreichring
16 Aug 1970 Jochen Rindt last start
16 Aug 1992 Brabham last start
16 Aug 1992 Judd engine last start
16 Aug 1992 Nigel Mansell clinched
Championship
16 Aug 1997 Jacques Pollet died

17 Aug 1913 Oscar Gálvez born
17 Aug 1952 Nelson Piquet born
17 Aug 1952 First GP at Zandvoort
17 Aug 1980 Nigel Mansell first start

18 Aug 1898 Clemente Biondetti born
18 Aug 1927 John Rhodes born
18 Aug 1929 Jimmy Davies born
18 Aug 1934 Michael May born
18 Aug 1957 GP at Pescara

19 Aug 1916 Dennis Poore born
19 Aug 1926 Johnny Boyd born
19 Aug 1946 Tom Walkinshaw born
19 Aug 1954 Oscar Larrauri born
19 Aug 1962 Jean Lucienbonnet died
19 Aug 1975 Mark Donohue died

19 Aug 1984 Gerhard Berger first start
19 Aug 2001 Michael Schumacher
clinched fourth
Championship

20 Aug 1941 Jo Ramirez born

21 Aug 1911 Ken Richardson born
21 Aug 1913 Freddie Agabashian born
21 Aug 1947 Ettore Bugatti died
21 Aug 1980 Alfred Neubauer died
21 Aug 1983 Gene Force died
21 Aug 1995 Chuck Stevenson died
21 Aug 2005 First GP at Istanbul

22 Aug 1947 Ian Scheckter born
22 Aug 1950 Peter Collins (Lotus) born
22 Aug 1954 Last GP at Bremgarten
22 Aug 1954 Juan Manuel Fangio
clinched second
Championship

23 Aug 1919 Dries van der Lof born
23 Aug 1953 Alberto Ascari last win (&
clinched last Championship)
23 Aug 1959 GP at Monsanto Park
23 Aug 1964 Jochen Rindt first start
23 Aug 1964 GP at Zeltweg
23 Aug 1967 Georges Berger died
23 Aug 1987 Didier Pironi died

24 Aug 1881 Vincenzo Lancia born
24 Aug 1921 Sam Tingle born
24 Aug 1958 First GP at Porto
24 Aug 1962 Shorty Templeman died
24 Aug 1964 Éric Bernard born
24 Aug 1997 Luigi Villoresi died
24 Aug 1999 Roberto Bussinello died
24 Aug 2003 Fernando Alonso first win

25 Aug 1985 Niki Lauda last win
25 Aug 1985 Last GP at Zandvoort
25 Aug 1990 David Hampshire died
25 Aug 1991 Michael Schumacher first
start
25 Aug 2001 Ken Tyrrell died

26 Aug 1925 Bobby Ball born

27 Aug 1909 Charles Pozzi born
27 Aug 1942 Tom Belsø born
27 Aug 1954 Derek Warwick born
27 Aug 1959 Gerhard Berger born
27 Aug 1967 First GP at Mosport Park
27 Aug 1967 Repco engine last win
27 Aug 1976 Mark Webber born
27 Aug 1978 Mario Andretti last win

28 Aug 1924 Jimmy Daywalt born
28 Aug 1977 Mike Parkes died
28 Aug 1983 René Arnoux last win
28 Aug 1983 TAG Porsche engine first
start
28 Aug 1994 Philippe Alliot last start
28 Aug 2001 Phil Cade died

29 Aug 1933 Alan Stacey born
29 Aug 1947 James Hunt born
29 Aug 1977 Brian McGuire died
29 Aug 1982 Keke Rosberg first win
29 Aug 1993 Thierry Boutsen last start
29 Aug 2002 Lance Macklin died
29 Aug 2004 Michael Schumacher
clinched seventh
Championship

30 Aug 1935 Gerhard Mitter born
30 Aug 1937 Bruce McLaren born
30 Aug 1941 Ignazio Giunti born
30 Aug 1959 Ed Elisian died
30 Aug 1992 Michael Schumacher first
win
30 Aug 1998 Damon Hill last win
30 Aug 1998 Jordan first win

31 Aug 1906 Raymond Sommer
born
31 Aug 1918 Bill Homeier born
31 Aug 1942 Sandro Pesenti-Rossi
born
31 Aug 1947 Luca di Montezemolo
born
31 Aug 1948 Harald Ertl born
31 Aug 1952 Jim Rigsby died
31 Aug 1953 Miguel Angel Guerra
born

1 Sep 1968 Franck Lagorce born
1 Sep 1985 Stefan Bellof died

2 Sep 1919 Lance Macklin born
2 Sep 1956 Jo Bonnier first start
2 Sep 1956 Juan Manuel Fangio
clinched fourth
Championship
2 Sep 1958 Olivier Grouillard born
2 Sep 1966 Olivier Panis born
2 Sep 1969 Willy Mairesse died

3 Sep 1950 Giuseppe Farina clinched
Championship

4 Sep 1920 Clemar Bucci born
4 Sep 1920 Jackie Holmes born
4 Sep 1924 Bobby Grim born
4 Sep 1933 Bill Moss born
4 Sep 1939 Gabriele Rumi born
4 Sep 1960 Phil Hill first win
4 Sep 1966 Jack Brabham clinched last
Championship
4 Sep 1966 Weslake engine first start
4 Sep 1997 Chuck Arnold died

5 Sep 1939 Clay Regazzoni born
5 Sep 1963 Taki Inoue born
5 Sep 1965 David Brabham born
5 Sep 1970 Jochen Rindt died
5 Sep 1971 Jean-Pierre Jarier first
start

6 Sep 1970 Clay Regazzoni first win

7 Sep 1936 Brian Hart born
7 Sep 1969 Matra car last win
7 Sep 1969 Jackie Stewart clinched
first Championship
7 Sep 1975 Niki Lauda clinched first
Championship

8 Sep 1898 Tony Vandervell born
8 Sep 1911 Lee Wallard born
8 Sep 1956 Stefan Johansson born
8 Sep 1960 Aguri Suzuki born
8 Sep 1963 Jim Clark clinched first
Championship
8 Sep 1966 John Taylor died
8 Sep 1968 Weslake engine last start
8 Sep 1984 Johnnie Parsons died

9 Sep 1973 Jackie Stewart clinched
last Championship
9 Sep 1979 Jody Scheckter last win (&
clinched Championship)

10 Sep 1950 Raymond Sommer died
10 Sep 1952 Bruno Giacomelli born
10 Sep 1961 Phil Hill last win (&
clinched Championship)
10 Sep 1961 Wolfgang von Trips died
10 Sep 1967 John Surtees last win
10 Sep 1972 Emerson Fittipaldi
clinched first
Championship
10 Sep 1972 John Surtees last start
10 Sep 1978 Alfa Romeo engine last
win
10 Sep 1978 Mario Andretti clinched
Championship
10 Sep 1978 Ronnie Peterson last start

11 Sep 1946 Martin Ogilvie born
11 Sep 1955 Juan Manuel Fangio
clinched third
Championship
11 Sep 1955 Mercedes-Benz last start &
win
11 Sep 1976 Tomás Enge born
11 Sep 1978 Ronnie Peterson died
11 Sep 1980 Antonio Pizzonia born

12 Sep 1916 Tony Bettenhausen born
12 Sep 1944 Eddie Keizan born
12 Sep 1948 Jean-Louis Schlesser born
12 Sep 1950 Gustav Brunner born
12 Sep 1965 Jackie Stewart first win
12 Sep 1976 March last win
12 Sep 1982 Ensign last start
12 Sep 1982 Fittipaldi last start
12 Sep 2004 Jack Turner died

13 Sep 1932 Mike MacDowel born
13 Sep 1953 Maserati first win
13 Sep 1981 Hart engine first start
13 Sep 1981 Toleman (Benetton) first
start
13 Sep 1992 Fondmetal (Osella) last
start

14 Sep 1917 Mack Hellings born
14 Sep 1918 Georges Berger born
14 Sep 1950 Masami Kuwashima born
14 Sep 1980 First GP at Imola

15 Sep 1881 Ettore Bugatti born
15 Sep 1916 Toni Branca born
16 Sep 1910 Karl Kling born
16 Sep 1914 Josef Peters born
16 Sep 2001 Juan Pablo Montoya first
win

17 Sep 1929 Stirling Moss born
17 Sep 1960 Damon Hill born

18 Sep 1918 Johnny Mantz born
18 Sep 1947 Gian Carlo Minardi born
18 Sep 1951 Marc Surer born
18 Sep 1953 Charles de Tornaco died

19 Sep 1946 Brian Henton born
19 Sep 1952 Bernard de Dryver born
19 Sep 1964 Enrico Bertaggia born
19 Sep 1973 Cristiano da Matta born

20 Sep 1921 Horace Gould born
20 Sep 1952 Bill Schindler died
20 Sep 1958 Peter Whitehead died
20 Sep 1969 Climax engine last start
20 Sep 1969 Eagle last start
20 Sep 1970 Last GP at Mont-Tremblant
20 Sep 1970 Tyrrell first start
20 Sep 1975 Juan Pablo Montoya born
20 Sep 1987 TAG Porsche engine last win
20 Sep 1989 Richie Ginther died

21 Sep 1920 Kenneth McAlpine born

22 Sep 1907 P Fotheringham-Parker born
22 Sep 1921 Ian Raby born
22 Sep 1928 Eric Broadley born
22 Sep 1944 Richard Robarts born
22 Sep 1958 Franco Forini born
22 Sep 1958 Jimmy Reece died
22 Sep 1968 First GP at Mont-Tremblant
22 Sep 1974 Penske first start
22 Sep 1996 Last GP at Estoril

23 Sep 1930 Don Edmunds born
23 Sep 1973 Jackie Stewart last start
23 Sep 1981 Robert Doornbos born

24 Sep 1931 Mike Parkes born
24 Sep 1960 Johnny Thomson died
24 Sep 1981 Ryan Briscoe born
24 Sep 1995 David Coulthard first win
24 Sep 2000 First GP at Indianapolis

25 Sep 1938 Neville Lederle born
25 Sep 1942 Henri Pescarolo born
25 Sep 1982 Michele Alboreto first win
25 Sep 1982 Mario Andretti last start
25 Sep 1982 Matra engine last start
25 Sep 1982 Keke Rosberg clinched
Championship

25 Sep 1982 Last GP at Las Vegas
25 Sep 2005 Fernando Alonso clinched
Championship

26 Sep 1943 Tim Schenken born
26 Sep 1980 Patrick Friesacher born
26 Sep 1993 Lola last start
26 Sep 1993 Alain Prost clinched last
Championship
26 Sep 1999 Stewart first win
26 Sep 2004 First GP at Shanghai

27 Sep 1938 Mo Nunn born
27 Sep 1981 Jacques Laffite last win
27 Sep 1981 Matra engine last win
27 Sep 2003 Jean Lucas died

28 Sep 1963 Erik Comas born
28 Sep 1968 Mika Häkkinen born
28 Sep 1980 Andrea de Cesaris first
start
28 Sep 1980 Alan Jones clinched
Championship
28 Sep 1999 Ford Cosworth engine last
win

29 Sep 1969 Rocco Benetton born
29 Sep 1991 First GP at Montmeló

30 Sep 1919 Roberto Bonomi born
30 Sep 1919 Cecil Green born
30 Sep 1941 Reine Wisell born
30 Sep 1946 Jochen Mass born
30 Sep 1961 Eric van de Poele born
30 Sep 2001 Mika Häkkinen last win

1 Oct 1928 Willy Mairesse born
1 Oct 1930 Frank Gardner born
1 Oct 1942 Jean-Pierre Jabouille born
1 Oct 1963 Jean-Denis Deletraz born

2 Oct 1919 Jan Flinterman born
2 Oct 1921 Mike Nazaruk born
2 Oct 1921 Giorgio Scarlatti born
2 Oct 1925 Paul Goldsmith born
2 Oct 1940 Nanni Galli born
2 Oct 1949 Michael Bleekemolen born
2 Oct 1964 Charles Cooper died
2 Oct 1977 Niki Lauda clinched
second Championship
2 Oct 1998 Olivier Gendebien died

3 Oct 1941 Andrea de Adamich born
3 Oct 1969 Max Papis born
3 Oct 1971 Jo Bonnier last start
3 Oct 1971 Jo Siffert last start

4 Oct 1906 Eitel Cantoni born
4 Oct 1927 Roberto Bussinello born
4 Oct 1928 Bob Scott born
4 Oct 1970 Emerson Fittipaldi first win
4 Oct 1970 Jochen Rindt clinched
Championship
4 Oct 1992 Denny Hulme died
4 Oct 1998 Tony Shelly died

5 Oct 1922 Froilán González born
5 Oct 1962 Michael Andretti born
5 Oct 1969 Jochen Rindt first win
5 Oct 1980 Emerson Fittipaldi last start
5 Oct 1980 Jody Scheckter last start

6 Oct 1918 Max de Terra born
6 Oct 1918 André Pilette born
6 Oct 1941 John Nicholson born
6 Oct 1944 Carlos Pace born
6 Oct 1951 Manfred Winkelhock born
6 Oct 1963 Ford engine first start
6 Oct 1968 Mario Andretti first start
6 Oct 1973 François Cevert died
6 Oct 1974 Emerson Fittipaldi clinched last Championship
6 Oct 1974 Denny Hulme last start
6 Oct 1974 Helmut Koinigg died
6 Oct 1985 Nigel Mansell first win
6 Oct 1985 Alain Prost clinched first Championship
6 Oct 1985 John Watson last start

7 Oct 1912 Peter Walker born
7 Oct 1930 Bernard Collomb born
7 Oct 1965 Marco Apicella born
7 Oct 1966 Vincenzo Sospiri born
7 Oct 1979 Jacky Ickx last start
7 Oct 1979 Wolf last start
7 Oct 1984 First GP at new Nürburgring

8 Oct 1904 Yves Giraud-Cabantous born
8 Oct 1910 Spider Webb born
8 Oct 1919 Jack McGrath born
8 Oct 1920 Frank Dochnal born
8 Oct 1954 Huub Rothengatter born
8 Oct 1961 Tony Brooks last start
8 Oct 1961 Stirling Moss last start
8 Oct 1961 First GP at Watkins Glen
8 Oct 1972 Matra last start
8 Oct 1972 Jody Scheckter first start
8 Oct 1978 First GP at Montréal
8 Oct 1978 Surtees last start
8 Oct 1978 Gilles Villeneuve first win
8 Oct 2000 Michael Schumacher clinched third Championship

9 Oct 1928 Pat O'Connor born
9 Oct 1937 David Prophet born
9 Oct 1961 Julian Bailey born
9 Oct 1977 Last GP at Mosport Park
9 Oct 1977 Penske last start
9 Oct 1977 Wolf last win

10 Oct 1930 Eugenio Castellotti born
10 Oct 1952 Siegfried Stohr born
10 Oct 2004 Olivier Panis last start

11 Oct 1911 Nello Pagani born
11 Oct 1928 Alfonso de Portago born

12 Oct 1906 Piero Taruffi born
12 Oct 1918 Frank Armi born
12 Oct 1937 Paul Hawkins born
12 Oct 1943 Bertil Roos born
12 Oct 1985 Duke Dinsmore died
12 Oct 1986 Benetton first win
12 Oct 1986 Gerhard Berger first win
12 Oct 2003 Heinz-Harald Frentzen last start
12 Oct 2003 Michael Schumacher clinched sixth Championship

13 Oct 1899 Piero Dusio born
13 Oct 1943 Peter Sauber born
13 Oct 1949 Patrick Nève born
13 Oct 1981 Philippe Étançelin died
13 Oct 1989 Freddie Agabashian died
13 Oct 1996 Martin Brundle last start
13 Oct 1996 Damon Hill clinched Championship
13 Oct 1996 Ligier last start
13 Oct 2002 Eddie Irvine last start
13 Oct 2005 Wayne Weiler died

14 Oct 1893 Charles Cooper born
14 Oct 1943 Tsutomu Tomita born
14 Oct 1947 Rikky von Opel born
14 Oct 2001 Jean Alesi last start
14 Oct 2001 Benetton last start
14 Oct 2001 Mika Häkkinen last start
14 Oct 2001 Prost last start

15 Oct 1899 Adolf Brudes born
15 Oct 1919 Chuck Stevenson born
15 Oct 1921 Al Pease born
15 Oct 1981 P Fotheringham-Parker died
15 Oct 1983 Jean-Pierre Jarier last start
15 Oct 1983 Nelson Piquet clinched second Championship

16 Oct 1918 Tony Rolt born
16 Oct 1934 Peter Ashdown born
16 Oct 1994 Andrea de Cesaris last start
16 Oct 2005 BAR last start
16 Oct 2005 Jordan last start
16 Oct 2005 Minardi last start
16 Oct 2005 Sauber last start

17 Oct 1926 Roberto Lippi born
17 Oct 1946 Enzo Coloni born
17 Oct 1979 Kimi Räikkönen born
17 Oct 1981 Alan Jones last win
17 Oct 1981 First GP at Las Vegas
17 Oct 1981 Nelson Piquet clinched first Championship
17 Oct 1981 Derek Warwick first start
17 Oct 1999 First GP at Sepang

18 Oct 1933 Lodovico Scarfiotti born
18 Oct 1937 Günther Seifert born
18 Oct 1995 Ted Whiteaway died
18 Oct 1999 John Cannon died

19 Oct 1958 GP at Âin-Diab
19 Oct 1958 Mike Hawthorn last start (& clinched Championship)
19 Oct 1958 Vanwall last win
19 Oct 1978 Enrique Bernoldi born
19 Oct 1987 Hermann Lang died
19 Oct 2003 Nello Pagani died

20 Oct 1921 Manny Ayulo born
20 Oct 1942 Walter Brun born
20 Oct 1978 Gunnar Nilsson died
20 Oct 1991 Ayrton Senna clinched last Championship

21 Oct 1912 Alfredo Pián born
21 Oct 1932 Cesare Perdisa born
21 Oct 1973 Nasif Estéfano died
21 Oct 1984 First GP at Estoril
21 Oct 1984 Niki Lauda clinched last Championship
21 Oct 1990 Ayrton Senna clinched second Championship

22 Oct 1918 Johnnie Tolan born
22 Oct 1967 Denny Hulme clinched Championship
22 Oct 1989 Alain Prost clinched third Championship
22 Oct 1995 Last GP at Aida
22 Oct 1995 Michael Schumacher clinched second Championship
22 Oct 2000 Johnny Herbert last start

23 Oct 1926 Larry Crockett born
23 Oct 1937 Geki born
23 Oct 1941 Gérard Ducarouge born
23 Oct 1966 Alessandro Zanardi born
23 Oct 1977 James Hunt last win
23 Oct 1977 Last GP at Fuji
23 Oct 1993 Innes Ireland died

24 Oct 1924 George Amick born
24 Oct 1954 Last GP at Pedralbes
24 Oct 1960 Joachim Winkelhock born
24 Oct 1965 Honda first win
24 Oct 1971 Jo Siffert died
24 Oct 1976 First GP at Fuji
24 Oct 1976 James Hunt clinched Championship
24 Oct 1993 Eddie Irvine first start
24 Oct 2004 Jaguar last start

25 Oct 1958 Stuart Lewis-Evans died
25 Oct 1964 Phil Hill last start
25 Oct 1964 John Surtees clinched Championship
25 Oct 1970 Jack Brabham last start
25 Oct 1972 Johnny Mantz died
25 Oct 1980 Last GP at Watkins Glen
25 Oct 1992 Riccardo Patrese last win

26 Oct 1915 Ray Crawford born
26 Oct 1915 Joe Fry born
26 Oct 1942 Jonathan Williams born
26 Oct 1947 Ian Ashley born
28 Oct 1951 First GP at Pedralbes
26 Oct 1986 Alan Jones last start
26 Oct 1986 Alain Prost clinched second Championship
26 Oct 1986 Keke Rosberg last start
26 Oct 1986 Patrick Tambay last start
26 Oct 1997 Gerhard Berger last start
26 Oct 1997 Mika Häkkinen first win
26 Oct 1997 Last GP at Jerez
26 Oct 1997 Jacques Villeneuve clinched Championship

27 Oct 1913 Luigi Piotti born
27 Oct 1936 Dave Charlton born
27 Oct 1963 First GP at Mexico City
27 Oct 2003 Johnny Boyd died

28 Oct 1919 Walt Hansgen born
28 Oct 1919 Hans Klenk born
28 Oct 1924 Antonio Creus born
28 Oct 1930 Bernie Ecclestone born
28 Oct 1950 Lord Alexander Hesketh born
28 Oct 1951 Alfa Romeo last win
28 Oct 1951 Juan Manuel Fangio clinched first Championship

29 Oct 1932 Alex Soler-Roig born
29 Oct 1951 Tiff Needell born
29 Oct 1956 Louis Rosier died
29 Oct 1965 Paul Stewart born

30 Oct 1906 Giuseppe Farina born
30 Oct 1917 Maurice Trintignant born
30 Oct 1926 Jacques Swaters born
30 Oct 1988 Alfa Romeo engine last start
30 Oct 1988 Ayrton Senna clinched first Championship

31 Oct 1941 Derek Bell born
31 Oct 1987 Nelson Piquet clinched last Championship
31 Oct 1999 Mika Häkkinen clinched second Championship
31 Oct 1999 Damon Hill last start
31 Oct 1999 Stewart last start

1 Nov 1898 Arthur Legat born
1 Nov 1926 Bob Veith born
1 Nov 1928 Ted Whiteaway born
1 Nov 1936 Jack Lewis born
1 Nov 1962 Ricardo Rodríguez died
1 Nov 1987 First GP at Suzuka
1 Nov 1998 Mika Häkkinen clinched first Championship

2 Nov 1946 Alan Jones born
2 Nov 1974 Stéphane Sarrazin born

3 Nov 1948 Helmut Koinigg born
3 Nov 1968 Graham Hill clinched last Championship
3 Nov 1968 Honda car last start
3 Nov 1985 First GP at Adelaide
3 Nov 1985 Alfa Romeo last start
3 Nov 1985 Niki Lauda last start
3 Nov 1985 Keke Rosberg last win
3 Nov 1991 Nelson Piquet last start

4 Nov 1884 Harry Ferguson born
4 Nov 1919 Eric Thompson born
4 Nov 1953 Jacques Villeneuve Sr. born
4 Nov 1968 Horace Gould died
4 Nov 1976 Toni Ulmen died

5 Nov 1905 Louis Rosier born
5 Nov 1921 Kurt Adolff born
5 Nov 1952 Joe James died
5 Nov 1986 Adolf Brudes died
5 Nov 1989 René Arnoux last start
5 Nov 1989 Eddie Cheever last start

6 Nov 1931 Peter Collins born
6 Nov 1955 Jack McGrath died
6 Nov 1995 Bill Cheesbourg died

7 Nov 1923 Oscar González born
7 Nov 1948 Alex Dias Ribeiro born
7 Nov 1956 Jonathan Palmer born
7 Nov 1967 Ian Raby died
7 Nov 1975 Piero Dusio died
7 Nov 1993 Lamborghini engine last start
7 Nov 1993 Riccardo Patrese last start
7 Nov 1993 Alain Prost last start
7 Nov 1993 Ayrton Senna last win
7 Nov 1993 Derek Warwick last start

8 Nov 1933 Peter Arundell born
8 Nov 1947 Giorgio Francia born
8 Nov 1985 Masten Gregory died
8 Nov 1992 Honda engine last start & win
8 Nov 1992 March last start

10 Nov 1915 Rodney Clarke born
10 Nov 1926 Art Bisch born
10 Nov 1934 Lucien Bianchi born
10 Nov 1965 Eddie Irvine born

11 Nov 1909 Piero Scotti born
11 Nov 1926 Maria Teresa de Filippis born
11 Nov 1937 Vittorio Brambilla born
11 Nov 1951 Mack Hellings died
11 Nov 1967 Gil de Ferran born

12 Nov 1914 Peter Whitehead born
12 Nov 1916 Paul Emery born
12 Nov 1945 George Eaton born
12 Nov 1966 Don Branson died
12 Nov 1995 Last GP at Adelaide

13 Nov 1945 Masahiro Hasemi born
13 Nov 1988 turbo last start & win
13 Nov 1994 Michele Alboreto last start
13 Nov 1994 Lotus last start
13 Nov 1994 Nigel Mansell last win
13 Nov 1994 Michael Schumacher clinched first Championship

14 Nov 1945 Brett Lunger born
14 Nov 1954 Eliseo Salazar born

15 Nov 1932 Jerry Unser born
15 Nov 1987 Mot. Moderni engine last start
15 Nov 1987 TAG Porsche engine last start

16 Nov 1936 Skip Barber born
16 Nov 1936 Gianpaolo Dallara born
16 Nov 1958 Roberto Guerrero born
16 Nov 1973 Christian Horner born

17 Nov 1906 Soichiro Honda born
17 Nov 1929 Jimmy Reece born
17 Nov 1939 Chris Craft born
17 Nov 1945 Damien Magee born
17 Nov 1967 Mimmo Schiattarella born

18 Nov 1932 Nasif Estéfano born

19 Nov 1925 Eddie Russo born
19 Nov 1961 Al Keller died
19 Nov 1969 Philippe Adams born

20 Nov 1919 Alan Brown born
20 Nov 1948 Gunnar Nilsson born
20 Nov 1957 Stefan Bellof born
20 Nov 1960 Maserati last start
20 Nov 1960 GP at Riverside

21 Nov 1943 Jacques Laffite born
21 Nov 1953 Felice Bonetto died

22 Nov 1934 Jackie Pretorius born

23 Nov 1923 Juan Jover born
23 Nov 1954 Ross Brawn born
23 Nov 1969 Olivier Beretta born

24 Nov 1949 John Wickham born
24 Nov 1990 Juan Manuel Bordeu died

25 Nov 1946 Slim Borgudd born
25 Nov 1982 Walt Ader died
25 Nov 1984 Jimmy Jackson died

26 Nov 1953 Desiré Wilson born
26 Nov 1981 Ernesto Prinoth died

27 Nov 1957 Kenny Acheson born
27 Nov 1995 Gincarlo Baghetti died

28 Nov 1963 Lee Wallard died
28 Nov 1990 Chico Godia died
28 Nov 1992 Frank Armi died
28 Nov 1993 Joe Kelly died

29 Nov 1915 Helmut Niedermayr born
29 Nov 1923 Chuck Daigh born
29 Nov 1975 Tony Brise died
29 Nov 1975 Graham Hill died

30 Nov 1935 Trevor Blokdyk born
30 Nov 1966 Mika Salo born

1 Dec 1948 Guy Tunmer born

2 Dec 1930 David Piper born
2 Dec 1937 Chris Bristow born
2 Dec 2001 Bruce Halford died

3 Dec 1924 Roberto Mières born
3 Dec 1932 Gaetano Starrabba born

4 Dec 1911 Willi Krakau born
4 Dec 1944 François Migault born
4 Dec 1957 Raul Boesel born
4 Dec 1988 Alberto Uría died

5 Dec 1917 Ken Downing born
5 Dec 1932 Jim Hurtubise born

6 Dec 1948 Keke Rosberg born

7 Dec 1917 Ottorino Volonterio born
7 Dec 1924 John Love born
7 Dec 1925 Nano da Silva Ramos born
7 Dec 1977 Georges Grignard died

8 Dec 1955 Paul Crooks born

9 Dec 1920 Doug Serrurier born
9 Dec 1926 Ed Elisian born
9 Dec 1928 André Milhoux born
9 Dec 1934 Wayne Weiler born
9 Dec 1936 Ben Pon born

12 Dec 1923 Ken Kavanagh born
12 Dec 1946 Emerson Fittipaldi born
12 Dec 1946 Renzo Zorzi born
12 Dec 1948 Roelof Wunderink born
12 Dec 1959 Jack Brabham clinched
           first Championship
12 Dec 1959 Bruce McLaren first win
12 Dec 1959 GP at Sebring
12 Dec 1978 Enrico Toccacelo born

13 Dec 1918 Bill Vukovich born
13 Dec 1945 Brian McGuire born

14 Dec 1919 Bob Drake born

15 Dec 1913 Walt Ader born
15 Dec 1927 Bill Mackey born

16 Dec 1920 Les Leston born
16 Dec 1932 Henry Taylor born
16 Dec 1982 Colin Chapman died
16 Dec 1989 Oscar Gálvez died

17 Dec 1915 Ludwig Fisher born

18 Dec 1907 Bill Holland born
18 Dec 1991 George Abecassis died
18 Dec 1993 Helm Glöckler died
18 Dec 1994 Henry Banks died

19 Dec 1923 Onofré Marimón born

20 Dec 1968 Karl Wendlinger born

21 Dec 1921 Günther Bechem born
21 Dec 1935 Lorenzo Bandini born

22 Dec 1905 Pierre Levegh born

23 Dec 1956 Michele Alboreto
           born
23 Dec 1959 Geoffrey Willis born
23 Dec 1962 Bertrand Gachot born
23 Dec 1985 B Bira died

24 Dec 1941 Howden Ganley born
24 Dec 1949 Warwick Brown born
24 Dec 2000 John Cooper died

25 Dec 1934 Giancarlo Baghetti
           born
25 Dec 1943 Wilson Fittipaldi born

26 Dec 1922 Asdrúbal Bayardo born
26 Dec 1935 Bill Brack born
26 Dec 1935 Moisés Solana born
26 Dec 1936 Trevor Taylor born
26 Dec 1958 Adrian Newey born
26 Dec 1992 Jan Flinterman died

27 Dec 1900 Hans Stuck born
27 Dec 1969 Jean-Christophe Boullion
           born
27 Dec 1993 André Pilette died

28 Dec 1896 Philippe Étançelin born
28 Dec 1909 David Murray born
28 Dec 1939 Conny Andersson born
28 Dec 1983 Eugène Chaboud died

29 Dec 1917 David Hampshire born
29 Dec 1924 Carlo Chiti born
29 Dec 1925 Jay Chamberlain born
29 Dec 1962 First GP at East London
29 Dec 1962 Graham Hill clinched first
           Championship
29 Dec 1969 Allan McNish born
29 Dec 1982 Max de Terra died
29 Dec 1988 Mike Beuttler died

30 Dec 1911 Walt Brown born
30 Dec 1936 Mike Spence born
30 Dec 1942 Guy Edwards born
30 Dec 1956 François Hesnault born
30 Dec 1976 Rudi Fischer died

(first and last GPs relate to World
Championship Grands Prix)

Bibliography

During compilation of this book, we referred to numerous sources for information, the most useful of which were:

Magazines
Autosport
F1 News
Motoring News
Motorsport

Web Site
http://forix.autosport-atlas.com

Books
33 Anni Di Gran Premio Iridati F.1 (1950-82) • *Autosprint, Italy*
50 Ans de Formule 1 • *various, France*
A Record of Grand Prix and Voiturette Racing (1950-64) • *Sheldon*
Autocourse
Automobile Year
A-Z of Formula Racing Cars • *Hodges*
Benetton-Ford - A Racing Partnership • *Drackett*
Brabham - The Grand Prix Cars • *Henry*
BRM - The Saga of British Racing Motors Vol.1 (1945-60) • *Nye*
Champion Book of World Championship Motor Racing Facts & Figures • *Kettlewell*
Cooper Cars • *Nye*
Directory of Formula One Cars (1966-86) • *Pritchard*
Ferrari - The Grand Prix Cars • *Henry*
FIA Yearbook of Automobile Sport • *FIA, France*
Formula 3000 Yearbook (1987-1992) • *Barbe etc, France*
Formula One Championship Computerised Results & Timing Service (1982-1993) • *Longines, Olivetti & TAG/Heuer*
Grand Prix! (1950-84) • *Lang*
Grand Prix Cars (1945-65) • *Lawrence*
Grand Prix Who's Who • *Small*
Guinness Guide to International Motor Racing • *Higham*
Handbook of Grand Prix Cars - Post-War to Present • *Tanner, USA*
History of the Grand Prix Car (1945-91) • *Nye*
Illustrated History of the Indianapolis 500 (1911-1994) • *Fox, USA*
Kimberley's Team and Driver Guides • *various*
McLaren - The Grand Prix, Can-Am & Indy Cars • *Nye*
Motor Racing and Motor Rally Directory (1957) • *Motor Racing staff*
Palmarès Pilote par Pilote des Grand Prix de Formule 1 • *Naviaux with Piget*
The Complete Book of Formula One • *Arron & Hughes*
The Concise Dictionary of Motorsport • *Bishop*
The Encyclopedia of Motorsport • *Georgano*
The Formula One Record Book (1961-1965) • *Thomson*
The Great Encyclopedia of Formula 1 (1950-2000)) • *Ménard*
The Motor Racing Directory • *Kettlewell*
The Motor Racing Register (1961/62-1966) • *Dempsey*
Theme Lotus - From Chapman To Ducarouge (1956-1986) • *Nye*